Hoover's MasterList of U.S. Companies

2016

MERGENT
BUSINESS PRESS

Hoover's MasterList of U.S. Companies is intended to provide readers with accurate and authoritative information about the enterprises covered in it. The information contained herein is as accurate as we could reasonably make it. In many cases we have relied on third-party material that we believe to be trustworthy but were unable to independently verify. We do not warrant that the book is absolutely accurate or without error. Readers should not rely on any information contained herein in instances where such reliance might cause financial loss.

The publisher, the editors, and their data suppliers specifically disclaim all warranties, including the implied warranties of merchantability and fitness for a specific purpose. This book is sold with the understanding that neither the publisher, the editors, nor any content contributors are engaged in providing investment, financial, accounting, legal, or other professional advice.

Mergent Inc., provided financial data for most public companies in this book. For private companies and historical information on public companies prior to their becoming public, we obtained information directly from the companies or from third-party material that we believe to be trustworthy. Hoover's, Inc., is solely responsible for the presentation of all data.

Many of the names of products and services mentioned in this book are the trademarks or service marks of the companies manufacturing or selling them and are subject to protection under U.S. law. Space has not permitted us to indicate which names are subject to such protection, and readers are advised to consult with the owners of such marks regarding their use. Hoover's is a trademark of Hoover's, Inc.

10 9 8 7 6 5 4 3 2 1

Publishers Cataloging-in-Publication Data

Hoover's MasterList of U.S. Companies 2016, Vol. 2

 Includes indexes.

 ISBN: 978-1-63053-826-2

 ISSN 1549-6457

 1. Business enterprises — Directories. 2. Corporations — Directories.

HF3010 338.7

U.S. AND WORLD BOOK SALES

Mergent Inc.
444 Madison Ave
New York, NY 10022
Phone: 800-342-5647

e-mail: orders@mergent.com
Web: www.mergentbusinesspress.com

Mergent Inc.

CEO: Jonathan Worrall

Executive Managing Director: John Pedernales

Executive Vice President of Sales: Fred Jenkins

Managing Director of Relationship Management: Chris Henry

Managing Director of Print Products: Thomas Wecera

Senior Product Manager: Neel Gandhi

Director of Print Products: Charlot Volny

Director of Data: Mohamed Hanif

Quality Assurance Editor: Wayne Arnold

Production Research Assistant: Wayne Arnold

MERGENT CUSTOMER SERVICE

Support and Fulfillment Manager: Melanie Horvat

ABOUT MERGENT, INC.

Mergent, Inc. is a leading provider of business and financial data on global publicly listed companies. Based in the U.S, the company maintains a strong global presence, with offices in New York, Charlotte, San Diego, London, Tokyo and Melbourne.

Founded in 1900, Mergent operates one of the longest continuously collected databases of: descriptive and fundamental information on domestic and international companies; pricing and terms and conditions data on fixed income and equity securities; and corporate action data.

In addition, Mergent's Indxis subsidiary develops and licenses equity and fixed income investment products based on its proprietary investment methodologies. Our licensed products have over $9 billion in assets under management and are offered by major investment management firms. The Indxis calculation platform is the chosen technology for some of the world's largest index companies. Its index calculation and pricing distribution protocols are used to administer index rules and distribute real-time pricing data.

Abbreviations

AFL-CIO – American Federation of Labor and Congress of Industrial Organizations
AMA – American Medical Association
AMEX – American Stock Exchange
ARM – adjustable-rate mortgage
ASP – application services provider
ATM – asynchronous transfer mode
ATM – automated teller machine
CAD/CAM – computer-aided design/computer-aided manufacturing
CD-ROM – compact disc – read-only memory
CD-R – CD-recordable
CEO – chief executive officer
CFO – chief financial officer
CMOS – complementary metal oxide silicon
COO – chief operating officer
DAT – digital audiotape
DOD – Department of Defense
DOE – Department of Energy
DOS – disk operating system
DOT – Department of Transportation
DRAM – dynamic random-access memory
DSL – digital subscriber line
DVD – digital versatile disc/digital video disc
DVD-R – DVD-recordable
EPA – Environmental Protection Agency
EPROM – erasable programmable read-only memory
EPS – earnings per share
ESOP – employee stock ownership plan
EU – European Union
EVP – executive vice president
FCC – Federal Communications Commission
FDA – Food and Drug Administration
FDIC – Federal Deposit Insurance Corporation
FTC – Federal Trade Commission
FTP – file transfer protocol
GATT – General Agreement on Tariffs and Trade
GDP – gross domestic product
HMO – health maintenance organization
HR – human resources
HTML – hypertext markup language
ICC – Interstate Commerce Commission
IPO – initial public offering
IRS – Internal Revenue Service
ISP – Internet service provider
kWh – kilowatt-hour
LAN – local-area network
LBO – leveraged buyout
LCD – liquid crystal display

LNG – liquefied natural gas
LP – limited partnership
Ltd. – limited
mips – millions of instructions per second
MW – megawatt
NAFTA – North American Free Trade Agreement
NASA – National Aeronautics and Space Administration
NASDAQ – National Association of Securities Dealers Automated Quotations
NATO – North Atlantic Treaty Organization
NYSE – New York Stock Exchange
OCR – optical character recognition
OECD – Organization for Economic Cooperation and Development
OEM – original equipment manufacturer
OPEC – Organization of Petroleum Exporting Countries
OS – operating system
OSHA – Occupational Safety and Health Administration
OTC – over-the-counter
PBX – private branch exchange
PCMCIA – Personal Computer Memory Card International Association
P/E – price to earnings ratio
RAID – redundant array of independent disks
RAM – random-access memory
R&D – research and development
RBOC – regional Bell operating company
RISC – reduced instruction set computer
REIT – real estate investment trust
ROA – return on assets
ROE – return on equity
ROI – return on investment
ROM – read-only memory
S&L – savings and loan
SCSI – Small Computer System Interface
SEC – Securities and Exchange Commission
SEVP – senior executive vice president
SIC – Standard Industrial Classification
SOC – system on a chip
SVP – senior vice president
USB – universal serial bus
VAR – value-added reseller
VAT – value-added tax
VC – venture capitalist
VP – vice president
VoIP – Voice over Internet Protocol
WAN – wide-area network
WWW – World Wide Web

CONTENTS

Volume 1

Volume 2

Hoover's MasterList
of U.S. Companies

Company
Listings

M & F BANCORP INC

NBB: MFBP

2634 Durham Chapel Hill Blvd.
Durham, NC 27707-2800
Phone: 919 687-7800
Fax: –
Web: www.mfbonline.com

CEO: James H Sills III
CFO: Randall C Hall
HR: –
FYE: December 31
Type: Public

M&F Bancorp strives to be the mother and father of lending in the Tar Heel State. It is the holding company for Mechanics and Farmers Bank (M&F Bank) which serves urban markets in central North Carolina from about 10 branch locations. Established in 1907 the bank provides standard products and services including savings and checking accounts IRAs and CDs. M&F Bank is a Community Development Financial Institution a US Treasury-designation signifying organizations that provide services to low-income communities. The bank's loan portfolio is dominated by real estate loans and mortgages much of which are written for faith-based and not-for-profit organizations.

	Annual Growth	12/10	12/11	12/12	12/13	12/14
Assets ($ mil.)	(1.1%)	312.3	304.5	296.1	301.5	298.4
Net income ($ mil.)	6.5%	0.8	0.6	0.3	0.4	1.0
Market value ($ mil.)	12.9%	5.9	4.9	5.2	6.6	9.6
Employees	(3.6%)	81	80	80	73	70

M & F WORLDWIDE CORP.

NYSE: MFW

35 E. 62nd St.
New York NY 10021
Phone: 212-572-8600
Fax: 214-981-0703
Web: www.energytransfer.com

CEO: Barry F Schwartz
CFO: –
HR: –
FYE: December 31
Type: Subsidiary

Check out M & F Worldwide. The holding company's Harland Clarke Corp. business manufactures checks and related products forms treasury supplies and delivery and fraud-prevention services. Its Harland Financial Solutions provides lending and mortgage applications risk management and business intelligence solutions and customer management software for commercial banks and credit unions. M & F's Scantron Corporation offers testing and assessment solutions to schools in North America while its Mafco Worldwide is one of the world's largest makers of licorice extract used primarily for flavoring tobacco and candy products. Diversified holding company MacAndrews & Forbes Holdings owns M & F.

M & H ENTERPRISES INC.

3030 S HIGHLAND DR
LAS VEGAS, NV 891091047
Phone: 702-385-5257
Fax: –
Web: www.martinharris.com

CEO: Frank E Martin
CFO: –
HR: –
FYE: December 31
Type: Private

What M & H Enterprises builds in Vegas stays in Vegas. Also known as Martin-Harris Construction the company provides design/build general construction and construction management services to commercial institutional and industrial projects throughout the Southwest. In addition to its home state Martin-Harris also provides general contracting services in New Mexico Texas Colorado and Utah. Martin-Harris has completed office retail hospitality entertainment high-rise condominium and public works projects for clients such as Neiman Marcus Embassy Suites and US Air Force. The company was founded in 1976 by president and CEO Frank Martin. It has offices in Las Vegas and Phoenix.

	Annual Growth	12/09	12/10*	11/11*	12/12	12/13
Sales ($ mil.)	4.3%	–	168.3	119.3	179.1	191.2
Net income ($ mil.)	6.0%	–	–	1.4	1.6	1.6
Market value ($ mil.)	–	–	–	–	–	–
Employees	–	–	–	–	–	140

*Fiscal year change

M & M MERCHANDISERS INC.

1923 BOMAR AVE
FORT WORTH, TX 761032102
Phone: 817-339-1400
Fax: –
Web: www.mmwholesale.com

CEO: Marty Stenzler
CFO: Kirk Wensel
HR: Amy Odle
FYE: December 31
Type: Private

This M&M is sweet on pawn shops. M&M Merchandisers is a wholesale supplier of electronics musical instruments and accessories primarily to pawn shops in Texas and Georgia. It has expanded to serve several other industries including smaller music retailers and specializes in mobile audio video game accessories music surveillance tools and hardware sporting goods and jewelers supplies. The company distributes monthly newsletters and a semiannual catalog featuring its product offerings. M&M got its start in 1976 as a value added distributor with 150 SKUs; today it offers some 6000 SKUs. The business was founded by CEO Marty Stenzler and his father Mitch (hence the company name M&M).

	Annual Growth	12/04	12/05	12/06	12/07	12/08
Sales ($ mil.)	–	–	–	(49.0)	20.6	21.6
Net income ($ mil.)	612.2%	–	–	0.0	(0.2)	0.8
Market value ($ mil.)	–	–	–	–	–	–
Employees	–	–	–	–	–	78

M & T BANK CORP

NYS: MTB

One M & T Plaza
Buffalo, NY 14203
Phone: 716 635-4000
Fax: –
Web: www.mtb.com

CEO: Robert G. (Bob) Wilmers
CFO: Rene F Jones
HR: Stephen J. Braunscheidel
FYE: December 31
Type: Public

M&T Bank Corporation is making a splash in the mid-Atlantic region. It is the holding company of M&T Bank which offers deposit loan trust investment brokerage and insurance services to more than two million individuals and small- and mid-sized businesses. With about $97 billion in total assets and $74 billion in deposits the bank operates more than 700 branches and 1500 ATMs in New York Pennsylvania and other eastern states and Washington DC in addition to Canada and the Cayman Islands. Its residential mortgage origination unit spans more than a dozen states in the South and West. The firm also manages a proprietary line of mutual funds the Wilmington Funds.

	Annual Growth	12/10	12/11	12/12	12/13	12/14
Assets ($ mil.)	9.2%	68,021.3	77,924.3	83,008.8	85,162.4	96,685.5
Net income ($ mil.)	9.7%	736.2	859.5	1,029.5	1,138.5	1,066.2
Market value ($ mil.)	9.6%	11,517.8	10,100.8	13,028.9	15,403.9	16,621.2
Employees	4.2%	13,365	15,666	14,943	15,893	15,782

M FINANCIAL HOLDINGS INCORPORATED

1125 NW Couch St. Ste. 900
Portland OR 97209
Phone: 503-232-6960
Fax: 503-238-1621
Web: www.mfin.com

CEO: –
CFO: –
HR: –
FYE: December 31
Type: Private

This company wants people who already have money to dial "M" for more. M Financial Holdings which does business as M Financial Group is an association of more than 125 financial services companies. Group members which are spread throughout the US offer a wide range of life insurance and other financial products and services geared toward ultra-wealthy individuals and leading business enterprises. M Financial Group provides product design marketing and securities-related services to its members which deal directly with customers. A subsidiary offers reinsurance (insurance for insurance products). M Financial Group is owned by its members.

M-I L.L.C.

5950 N. Course Dr.
Houston TX 77072
Phone: 713-739-0222
Fax: 310-538-0515

CEO: Paal Kibsgaard
CFO: –
HR: –
FYE: December 31
Type: Subsidiary

M-I known as M-I SWACO supplies drilling and completion fluids and additives to oil and gas companies in more than 75 countries worldwide. Its fluids cool and lubricate drill bits remove rock cuttings and maintain the stability of the wellbore. Through M-I's SWACO division the company provides pressure control rig instrumentation and drilling waste management products and services. It is also a worldwide producer of barite and bentonite used by the oil and gas and industrial markets. Drilling fluids provide the company with more than half of its sales. M-I SWACO is owned by Schlumberger Limited.

M. B. KAHN CONSTRUCTION CO. INC.

101 FLINTLAKE RD
COLUMBIA, SC 29223-7851
Phone: 803-736-2950
Fax: –
Web: www.mbkahn.com

CEO: –
CFO: –
HR: –
FYE: December 31
Type: Private

One of the largest construction companies in the southeastern US M. B. Kahn Construction Co. works on commercial institutional and industrial projects including hospitals airports shopping centers and manufacturing plants. Additionally it is rated as one of the top builders in the nation's education market. The company provides general contracting and design/build delivery services as well as construction management and program management services. Russian immigrant Myron B. Kahn founded the company in 1927. It is now chaired by Alan Kahn his grandson. The group operates through divisions in South Carolina and Georgia.

	Annual Growth	12/08	12/09	12/10	12/11	12/12
Sales ($ mil.)	16.8%	–	–	184.6	248.1	251.6
Net income ($ mil.)	(10.0%)	–	–	8.6	3.9	7.0
Market value ($ mil.)	–	–	–	–	–	–
Employees	–	–	–	–	–	429

M. SHANKEN COMMUNICATIONS INC.

387 Park Ave. South
New York NY 10016
Phone: 212-684-4224
Fax: 212-481-1540
Web: www.mshanken.com

CEO: –
CFO: –
HR: –
FYE: December 31
Type: Private

Wine tasting as spectator sport? Almost. M. Shanken Communications is a magazine publisher best known for its oenophile tome Wine Spectator. The magazine published 15 times a year boasts wine tasting reports and buyers guides as well as upscale dining travel and lifestyle features. M. Shanken Communications also operates Wine Spectator Online an information portal aimed at wine aficionados. In addition the company publishes Cigar Aficionado and Food Arts as well as industry trade titles Impact (beverage distribution and retail) and Market Watch (beverage hospitality). Wine critic Robert Morrisey began publishing Wine Spectator in 1976; it was acquired by publisher Marvin Shanken three years later.

M.D.C. HOLDINGS, INC.

NYS: MDC

4350 South Monaco Street, Suite 500
Denver, CO 80237
Phone: 303 773-1100
Fax: –
Web: www.richmondamerican.com

CEO: Larry A. Mizel
CFO: Robert N. (Bob) Martin
HR: Karen Gard
FYE: December 31
Type: Public

Being king of the mountain isn't enough for M.D.C. Holdings (MDC). Operating through its Richmond American Homes subsidiary and several other units the company is one of the largest homebuilders in Colorado and is active in about a dozen other states in the West and East. The homebuilder targets first-time and move-up buyers and annually builds about 4700 single-family detached homes that sell for an average price of $345000. The company also constructs a limited number of luxury homes. Subsidiary HomeAmerican Mortgage provides loans to buyers of MDC's homes. MDC also has subsidiaries that offer homeowners and title insurance.

	Annual Growth	12/11	12/12	12/13	12/14	12/15
Sales ($ mil.)	22.6%	844.2	1,203.0	1,680.4	1,694.6	1,909.0
Net income ($ mil.)	–	(98.4)	62.7	314.4	63.1	65.8
Market value ($ mil.)	9.7%	861.9	1,797.1	1,576.2	1,294.1	1,248.1
Employees	9.4%	854	920	1,111	1,140	1,225

M/A-COM TECHNOLOGY SOLUTIONS HOLDINGS INC.

NMS: MTSI

100 Chelmsford Street
Lowell, MA 01851
Phone: 978 656-2500
Fax: –
Web: www.macom.com

CEO: John R. Croteau
CFO: Conrad Gagnon
HR: –
FYE: October 02
Type: Public

M/A-COM Technology Solutions (aka MACOM) has many components for all your semiconductor needs. The holding company makes analog semiconductors used in wireless and wireline applications across the radio-frequency (RF) microwave and millimeter wave spectrum. Its portfolio encompasses some 2700 standard and custom integrated circuits modules and subsystems across 37 product lines. MACOM's chips are used in such products as automotive navigation systems point-to-point radios radars CATV set-top boxes MRI systems and unmanned aerial vehicles. Cisco Motorola Solutions Ford Motor Nokia and Samsung are among its top customers. More than half of sales come from customers in the US.

	Annual Growth	09/11	09/12	09/13*	10/14	10/15
Sales ($ mil.)	7.9%	310.3	302.2	318.7	418.7	420.6
Net income ($ mil.)	–	(1.0)	(1.0)	27.3	(15.3)	48.6
Market value ($ mil.)	31.3%	–	672.9	911.0	1,144.9	1,522.9
Employees	13.3%	667	669	675	918	1,100

*Fiscal year change

M/I HOMES INC

NYS: MHO

3 Easton Oval, Suite 500
Columbus, OH 43219
Phone: 614 418-8000
Fax: 614 418-8080
Web: www.mihomes.com

CEO: Robert H. Schottenstein
CFO: Phillip G. Creek
HR: –
FYE: December 31
Type: Public

M/I has its eye on the homebuilding prize in nearly a dozen markets throughout the Midwest Mid-Atlantic and South. M/I Homes sells single-family detached homes to first-time move-up empty-nest and luxury buyers under the M/I Homes Showcase Homes and TriStone Homes names. It delivers more than 2200 homes a year at prices ranging from about $107000 to $1 million (averaging $242000) and sizes ranging from 1200 to 4200 sq. ft. M/I Homes also builds attached townhomes and condominiums in select markets. Its M/I Financial mortgage banking subsidiary provides title and mortgage services. M/I Homes was founded in 1976 by Melvin and Irving Schottenstein.

	Annual Growth	12/10	12/11	12/12	12/13	12/14
Sales ($ mil.)	18.5%	616.4	566.4	761.9	1,036.8	1,215.2
Net income ($ mil.)	–	(26.3)	(33.9)	13.3	151.4	50.8
Market value ($ mil.)	10.5%	377.0	235.3	649.6	623.9	562.8
Employees	14.7%	522	583	651	827	905

MAC BEATH HARDWOOD COMPANY

2150 OAKDALE AVE
SAN FRANCISCO, CA 941241516
Phone: 415-647-0782
Fax: –
Web: www.macbeath.com

CEO: Carter Rothrock
CFO: Jonathan Macbeath
HR: –
FYE: July 31
Type: Private

This MacBeath doesn't want to get the spot out. MacBeath Hardwood Company specializes in spotted and striped specialty hardwoods from the US Mexico Panama India Brazil and several African nations. With wood from its 300000 board feet-capacity drying kiln the company makes furniture squares lumber veneer plywood maple countertops and specialty products like hand rails marine plywood and wood "blanks" to be used for baseball bats. MacBeath has five distribution centers in California Indiana and Utah; it also ships large loads worldwide. It also operates an online store. The company was founded in the early 1950s by K.E. MacBeath.

	Annual Growth	07/04	07/05	07/06	07/07	07/08
Sales ($ mil.)	(0.7%)	–	–	–	26.1	25.9
Net income ($ mil.)	(70.7%)	–	–	–	0.5	0.2
Market value ($ mil.)	–	–	–	–	–	–
Employees	–	–	–	–	–	90

MACALESTER COLLEGE

1600 GRAND AVE
SAINT PAUL, MN 551051899
Phone: 651-696-6000
Fax: –
Web: www.events.macalester.edu

CEO: –
CFO: David Wheaton
HR: –
FYE: May 31
Type: Private

Macalester College provides a private liberal arts education experience in St. Paul Minnesota. The four-year school serves about 2000 students. It offers more than 800 courses in 60 areas of study giving it about 40 major programs in fields including natural science social science fine arts and humanities. Macalester has a student-to-faculty ratio of 10:1 and a staff of about 170 full-time faculty members. It was founded in 1874 by the Rev. Edward Duffield as a Presbyterian-related but non-sectarian college and was named after Charles Macalester a prominent Philadelphia businessman and philanthropist.

	Annual Growth	05/09	05/10	05/11	05/12	05/13
Sales ($ mil.)	(9.4%)	–	131.2	129.4	96.7	97.7
Net income ($ mil.)	–	–	–	(3.1)	(38.2)	75.2
Market value ($ mil.)	–	–	–	–	–	–
Employees	–	–	–	–	–	750

MACATAWA BANK CORP.

NMS: MCBC

10753 Macatawa Drive
Holland, MI 49424
Phone: 616 820-1444
Fax: –
Web: www.macatawabank.com

CEO: Ronald L Haan
CFO: Jon W Swets
HR: –
FYE: December 31
Type: Public

Macatawa Bank Corporation is the holding company for Macatawa Bank. Since its 1997 founding the company has grown into a network of more than 25 branches serving western Michigan's Allegan Kent and Ottawa counties. The bank provides standard services including checking and savings accounts CDs safe deposit boxes and ATM cards. It also offers investment services and products through an agreement with a third-party provider. With deposit funds the bank primarily originates commercial and industrial loans and mortgages which account for nearly 75% of its loan book. Macatawa Bank also originates residential mortgages and consumer loans.

	Annual Growth	12/10	12/11	12/12	12/13	12/14
Assets ($ mil.)	0.1%	1,578.3	1,507.7	1,560.7	1,517.4	1,583.8
Net income ($ mil.)	–	(17.9)	5.8	35.5	9.5	10.5
Market value ($ mil.)	7.2%	139.5	77.2	97.9	169.3	184.2
Employees	(2.0%)	422	432	404	395	389

MACDERMID PRINTING SOLUTIONS

5210 Phillip Lee Dr.
Atlanta GA 30336
Phone: 404-696-4565
Fax: 404-699-3354
Web: www.macdermid.com/printing/index.html

CEO: David Beckerman
CFO: Gerry Miller
HR: –
FYE: December 31
Type: Subsidiary

MacDermid Printing Solutions rolls up its sleeves to provide the printing industry with sleeves and rolls photopolymer plates ColorSpan ink jet printers and other related products. The company's equipment is used to print a wide range of items including aluminum cans books boxes labels magazines newspapers paper cups and pet food bags. MacDermid Printing Solutions also serves the textile and steel industries with its sleeve and roll lineup. It package printing line is sold directly and through partnerships like Kodak. The company operates as a subsidiary of global specialty chemical manufacturer MacDermid.

MACE SECURITY INTERNATIONAL, INC.

NBB: MACE

240 Gibraltar Rd., Suite 220
Horsham, PA 19044
Phone: 267 317-4009
Fax: –
Web: www.mace.com

CEO: John J McCann
CFO: –
HR: Karen Smith
FYE: December 31
Type: Public

Mace Security International (MSI) aims to secure your person and your property. The firm makes a variety of security products including electronic surveillance and access control products cameras monitors alarms and Kindergard brand childproof locks. It also sells Mace brand defense sprays for consumers and law enforcement officers as well as tear gas and animal repellents. While security products account for two-thirds of sales MSI also operates an e-commerce division that sells its own products and those of third parties. MSI is exiting the car wash business which at its peak operated some 60 car and truck washes to focus on its security and e-commerce activities. MSI was founded in 1993.

	Annual Growth	12/10	12/11	12/12	12/13	12/14
Sales ($ mil.)	(19.3%)	18.4	13.9	13.0	8.0	7.8
Net income ($ mil.)	–	(18.1)	(5.1)	(4.0)	(2.0)	(1.7)
Market value ($ mil.)	(0.7%)	23.1	10.9	21.0	23.9	22.5
Employees	(16.8%)	197	164	–	–	–

MACERICH CO. (THE)

NYS: MAC

401 Wilshire Boulevard, Suite 700
Santa Monica, CA 90401
Phone: 310 394-6000
Fax: –
Web: www.macerich.com

CEO: Arthur M. (Art) Coppola
CFO: Thomas E. (Tom) O'Hern
HR: –
FYE: December 31
Type: Public

Mallrats nationwide can get their fix thanks to Macerich. The self-administered real estate investment trust (REIT) acquires develops leases and manages shopping and strip malls. Its portfolio consists of about 50 regional shopping centers and nine community shopping centers totaling more than 55 million sq. ft. of leasable space. The properties are located in about 20 states: Arizona California and the New York metropolitan area are the firm's primary markets. Macerich's tenants include some of the country's leading retailers including L Brands Forever 21 The Gap Dick's Sporting Goods Sears and Best Buy to name a few.

	Annual Growth	12/10	12/11	12/12	12/13	12/14
Sales ($ mil.)	9.9%	758.6	791.3	881.3	1,029.5	1,105.2
Net income ($ mil.)	177.7%	25.2	156.9	337.4	420.1	1,499.0
Market value ($ mil.)	15.2%	7,494.0	8,005.0	9,223.2	9,316.5	13,195.6
Employees	(19.5%)	2,658	1,377	1,368	1,143	1,117

MACH 1 GLOBAL SERVICES INC.

1530 W BROADWAY RD
TEMPE, AZ 852821131
Phone: 480-921-3900
Fax: –
Web: www.mach1global.com

CEO: Jamie Fletcher
CFO: –
HR: –
FYE: December 31
Type: Private

It doesn't ship goods at the speed of sound but Mach1 Global Services does like to think fast. The freight forwarder provides domestic and international air ground ocean and rail shipping services by buying transportation capacity from carriers and reselling it to customers. It also offers a variety of logistics services including project management and supply chain management. Most of Mach1's customers come from the retail automotive high-tech entertainment health care and manufacturing industries. The company has offices in the US Mexico and Asia (mostly China); it operates in other regions via network partners. CEO Michael Entzminger formed Mach1 in 1988.

	Annual Growth	12/03	12/04	12/05	12/06	12/08
Sales ($ mil.)	14.4%	–	57.1	69.7	86.1	97.8
Net income ($ mil.)	(54.9%)	–	–	3.1	1.8	0.3
Market value ($ mil.)	–	–	–	–	–	–
Employees	–	–	–	–	–	210

MACHADO/GARCIA-SERRA PUBLICIDAD INC.

1790 CORAL WAY FL 3
CORAL GABLES, FL 331452785
Phone: 305-444-4647
Fax: –
Web: www.mgscomm.com

CEO: –
CFO: –
HR: –
FYE: December 31
Type: Private

Machado|Garcia-Serra Publicidad provides integrated communications specializing in bridging the cultural gap between US consumer product manufacturers and the Hispanic market. The agency — which does business as Machado Garcia-Serra Communications or MGSCOMM — offers expertise in advertising public relations promotion and event marketing serving clients in the automotive health care and retail industries. The agency maintains three offices in Florida New York and Mexico. It was established in 2003 by public relations and advertising veterans Manual Machado and Al Garcia-Serra.

	Annual Growth	12/03	12/04	12/05	12/06	12/07
Sales ($ mil.)	82.3%	–	–	–	32.2	58.8
Net income ($ mil.)	(20.2%)	–	–	–	0.7	0.6
Market value ($ mil.)	–	–	–	–	–	–
Employees	–	–	–	–	–	22

MACK CALI REALTY CORP

NYS: CLI

343 Thornall Street
Edison, NJ 08837-2206
Phone: 732 590-1000
Fax: 732 205-8237
Web: www.mack-cali.com

CEO: Mitchell E. Hersh
CFO: Barry Lefkowitz
HR: –
FYE: December 31
Type: Public

Mack-Cali Realty is a self-administered real estate investment trust (REIT) that owns develops leases and manages office and industrial buildings primarily in the Northeast. The REIT's portfolio consists primarily of Class A office and office/flex buildings but also includes industrial facilities warehouses stand-alone retail properties and land for development. Its holdings comprise some 280 properties totaling more than 31.5 million sq. ft. concentrated in suburban markets in New Jersey southern New York and eastern Pennsylvania. Recently Mack-Cali has been selling non-core office assets to fund its diversification into residential property.

	Annual Growth	12/10	12/11	12/12	12/13	12/14
Sales ($ mil.)	(5.2%)	787.5	724.3	704.7	667.0	636.8
Net income ($ mil.)	(16.1%)	63.4	81.4	46.3	(19.1)	31.4
Market value ($ mil.)	(12.9%)	2,944.9	2,377.5	2,325.8	1,913.4	1,697.8
Employees	11.4%	390	379	594	635	600

MACK TRUCKS INC.

7825 National Service Rd.
Greensboro NC 27409
Phone: 336-291-9001
Fax: 336-291-9202
Web: www.macktrucks.com

CEO: Paul Vikner
CFO: –
HR: –
FYE: December 31
Type: Subsidiary

Mack Trucks and its "Built like a Mack" bulldog logo are synonymous with heavy duty trucks. A subsidiary of Sweden's AB Volvo the company is one of North America's largest manufacturers of heavy duty trucks used in construction heavy hauling highway and refuse work. They are sold and serviced in more than 45 countries through a global network of some 670 sales parts and repair centers. Mack Trucks also makes powertrains an integrated system that consists of engine transmission and axles and offers truck leasing and financing services. The company was founded in 1900 as Mack Brothers Company.

MACKAY LIFE SCIENCES INC.

OTC: BZEC

1019 W. 9th Ave. Ste. C
King of Prussia PA 19406
Phone: 215-972-1717
Fax: 781-240-0256
Web: www.cubist.com

CEO: Shepard G Bentley
CFO: Steven M Waszak
HR: –
FYE: December 31
Type: Public

MacKay Life Sciences (formerly Biofield) is trying to blaze a trail in the diagnostic equipment market with its Biofield Diagnostic System which employs single-use sensors to detect and examine changes associated with breast cancer. The system is based on the theory that epithelial cancers are characterized by changes in the electrical charge of the affected tissue; the sensors analyze these changes and identify if a lesion is malignant or benign. The process requires less than 20 minutes and has possible applications to cancers of the ovaries skin prostate and colon. Director James MacKay through the MacKay Group owns a majority interest in MacKay Life Sciences.

MACKINAC FINANCIAL CORP

NAS: MFNC

130 South Cedar Street
Manistique, MI 49854
Phone: 888 343-8147
Fax: –
Web: www.bankmbank.com

CEO: Paul D Tobias
CFO: Ernie R Krueger
HR: –
FYE: December 31
Type: Public

Mackinac Financial Corporation is the holding company for mBank which operates about a dozen branches in Michigan's Upper Peninsula and the northern part of the Lower Peninsula as well as suburban Detroit. Serving local consumers and business clients the bank provides traditional deposit products such as checking and savings accounts and CDs. Commercial real estate loans account for about three-quarters of the company's loan portfolio which also consists of agricultural business construction residential and consumer loans. mBank offers treasury management products and services to small and midsized businesses as well. Institutional investors own approximately half of Mackinac Financial's stock.

	Annual Growth	12/10	12/11	12/12	12/13	12/14
Assets ($ mil.)	11.6%	478.7	498.3	546.0	572.8	743.8
Net income ($ mil.)	–	(0.4)	2.2	7.1	5.9	7.4
Market value ($ mil.)	26.8%	28.7	34.0	44.4	62.0	74.3
Employees	10.2%	116	120	127	127	171

MACLEAN-FOGG COMPANY

1000 Allanson Rd.
Mundelein IL 60060-3890
Phone: 847-566-0010
Fax: 847-949-0285
Web: www.maclean-fogg.com

CEO: –
CFO: George H Cook
HR: –
FYE: December 31
Type: Private

The nuts and bolts of MacLean-Fogg's business are nuts bolts and other engineered parts. In 1925 the company launched with just one product: a lock nut made for railroads. Today its MacLean Vehicle Systems unit offers an array of fasteners and components used by auto railroad agricultural and construction industries. The company's operations include extruding forging grinding and machining. MacLean Power Systems sells silicone rubber insulators automatic connectors and other hardware to electric utility and communications customers worldwide. MacLean-Fogg runs 40 plants in North America Asia and Europe. It is owned by president and CEO Barry MacLean grandson of company co-founder John MacLean Sr.

MACOMB OAKLAND REGIONAL CENTER INC

16200 19 MILE RD
CLINTON TOWNSHIP, MI 480381103
Phone: 586-263-8700
Fax: –
Web: www.theamorc.org

CEO: Gerald Provencal
CFO: Richard Stone
HR: –
FYE: September 30
Type: Private

Michigan's disabled citizens have more than a friend in MORC. The Macomb-Oakland Regional Center (MORC) advocates for adults and children with developmental physical or psychiatric disabilities hoping to improve the lives of its clients. In addition to finding homes and jobs and coordinating recreational activities for the disabled the not-for-profit organization helps connect customers with support services including psychology nursing and medical care. It also holds community education seminars and it provides home health visitation and rehabilitation therapy services through its MORC Home Care and MORC Rehab divisions. Founded in 1972 MORC serves over 4000 clients in the state.

	Annual Growth	09/08	09/09	09/10	09/12	09/13
Sales ($ mil.)	2.2%	–	181.5	186.1	193.9	198.3
Net income ($ mil.)	–	–	–	0.4	0.1	(0.2)
Market value ($ mil.)	–	–	–	–	–	–
Employees	–	–	–	–	–	300

MACQUARIE INFRASTRUCTURE CORP

NYS: MIC

125 West 55th Street
New York, NY 10019
Phone: 212 231-1000
Fax: –
Web: www.macquarie.com/mic

CEO: James Hooke
CFO: Todd Weintraub
HR: –
FYE: December 31
Type: Public

If you've flown in a small plane or had a cold drink of water in a building in Chicago you may have done business with Macquarie Infrastructure Company. Its Atlantic Aviation Services unit provides fixed-base operations (FBO) including fueling and aircraft storage services at about 60 US airports. Another unit Hawaii Gas is Hawaii's only government franchised gas company. It also has a stake in District Energy a firm that provides chilled water in Chicago and heating and cooling to a casino complex in Las Vegas. The company holds a 50% stake in International-Matex Tank Terminals. Australia-based Macquarie Bank's Macquarie Infrastructure Management (USA) manages Macquarie Infrastructure Company.

	Annual Growth	12/10	12/11	12/12	12/13	12/14
Sales ($ mil.)	12.6%	840.8	988.8	1,034.0	1,041.0	1,350.9
Net income ($ mil.)	84.1%	90.7	27.3	13.3	31.3	1,042.0
Market value ($ mil.)	35.4%	1,505.0	1,987.0	3,238.8	3,869.4	5,053.8
Employees	0.9%	3,101	3,123	3,070	3,077	3,218

MACROGENICS, INC

NMS: MGNX

9640 Medical Center Drive
Rockville, MD 20850
Phone: 301 251-5172
Fax: –
Web: www.macrogenics.com

CEO: Scott Koenig
CFO: James (Jim) Karrels
HR: –
FYE: December 31
Type: Public

MacroGenics aims its enhanced antibodies at annihilating diseased cells. The clinical-stage biopharmaceutical company is focused on developing monoclonal antibody-based therapeutic treatments for cancer as well as autoimmune disorders and infectious diseases. MacroGenics has a handful of drug candidates in its pipeline and several others in pre-clinical development. Lead candidate margetuximab is being developed as an intravenous drug that would kill tumor cells in breast gastroesophageal and bladder cancer patients. Meanwhile antibody MGA271 is being tested for treating a variety of tumor types.

	Annual Growth	12/10	12/11	12/12	12/13	12/14
Sales ($ mil.)	–	0.0	57.2	63.8	58.0	47.8
Net income ($ mil.)	–	0.0	6.7	8.4	(0.3)	(38.3)
Market value ($ mil.)	–	0.0	–	–	767.9	981.8
Employees	15.2%	–	–	159	166	211

MACY'S INC.

NYSE: M

7 W. 7th St.
Cincinnati OH 45202
Phone: 513-579-7000
Fax: 678-402-3560
Web: www.aaronsinc.com

CEO: Terry J Lundgren
CFO: Karen M Hoguet
HR: –
FYE: January 31
Type: Public

The nation's #1 department store chain has adopted the name of its most famous brand and cash cow: Macy's. Macy's Inc. operates about 840 stores in 45 states the District of Columbia Guam and Puerto Rico under the Macy's and Bloomingdale's banners that ring up some $26 billion in annual sales. The stores sell men's women's and children's apparel and accessories cosmetics and home furnishings among other things. It also operates macys.com and bloomingdales.com. Macy's flagship store in Manhattan's Herald Square is the world's largest. The Macy's Thanksgiving Day Parade started in 1924 is an annual rite. Macy's (formerly Federated Department Stores) began as a dry goods store more than 150 years ago.

MADDEN (STEVEN) LTD.

NMS: SHOO

52-16 Barnett Avenue
Long Island City, NY 11104
Phone: 718 446-1800
Fax: –
Web: www.stevemadden.com

CEO: Edward R. (Ed) Rosenfeld
CFO: Arvind Dharia
HR: Lina Ramirez
FYE: December 31
Type: Public

Steven Madden elevates chunky heels to new heights. It operates through five business segments: wholesale footwear wholesale accessories retail first cost and licensing. Its wholesale business boasts seven divisions such as Madden Girl Steven Steve Madden Men's and Stevies as well as its Daisy Fuentes Betsey Johnson and Olsenboye accessories business through licenses. Its retail operations include about 120 Steve Madden Steven and Report stores along with several websites. Its First Cost segment designs and sources private-label footwear such as Candie's for mass merchants. Steven Madden shoes are sold in the US and Canada through its own shops and such stores as Nordstrom and Dillard's.

	Annual Growth	12/10	12/11	12/12	12/13	12/14
Sales ($ mil.)	20.4%	635.4	968.5	1,227.1	1,314.2	1,335.0
Net income ($ mil.)	10.2%	75.7	97.3	119.6	132.0	111.9
Market value ($ mil.)	(6.5%)	2,654.4	2,195.1	2,689.4	2,328.0	2,025.2
Employees	22.6%	1,440	2,370	2,650	2,864	3,256

MADISON DEARBORN PARTNERS LLC

3 First National Plaza Ste. 4600   CEO: Paul J Finnegan
Chicago IL 60602   CFO: –
Phone: 312-895-1000   HR: –
Fax: 312-895-1001   FYE: December 31
Web: www.mdcp.com   Type: Private

Madison Dearborn Partners is a private equity firm specializing in management buyouts and investments in six sectors: basic industries (natural resources chemicals building products); business and government services (outsourced services IT and education); telecommunications (media and wireless technology); consumer (retail consumer products); financial services (asset management financial outsourcing specialty finance); and health care (acute and ancillary care providers medical equipment). Founded in 1992 Madison Dearborn has raised more than $18 billion from investors such as pension funds endowments and financial institutions.

MADISON ELECTRIC COMPANY

31855 VAN DYKE AVE   CEO: –
WARREN, MI 480931047   CFO: Benjamin Rosenthal
Phone: 586-825-0200   HR: –
Fax: –   FYE: January 31
Web: www.madisonelectric.com   Type: Private

Founded by Morris and Max Blumberg Madison Electric broke ground in a rented room in Detroit in 1914. The company has grown from pushing light bulbs fuses wire and conduit to rival the top 200 electrical and electronics distributors in the US. Joined by affiliate Standard Electric Co. Madison Electric distributes electrical supplies industrial automation commercial lighting and network communication components. Branches dotting Michigan cater to a swath of commercial industrial utility and defense activities. Supply options tout brands by 3M Brady Federal Signal Leviton Panduit Square D/Schneider Electric and Thomas & Betts. The family-owned company is led by the Blumberg's fourth generation.

	Annual Growth	01/09	01/10	01/11	01/12	01/13
Sales ($ mil.)	15.3%	–	53.0	66.1	77.2	81.3
Net income ($ mil.)	–	–	–	(0.4)	1.0	0.6
Market value ($ mil.)	–	–	–	–	–	–
Employees	–	–	–	–	–	200

MADONNA REHABILITATION HOSPITAL

5401 SOUTH ST   CEO: Marsha Lommel
LINCOLN, NE 685062150   CFO: –
Phone: 402-413-3000   HR: –
Fax: –   FYE: June 30
Web: www.madonna.org   Type: Private

Madonna Rehabilitation Hospital finds a rapt audience in recovering patients living in and around Lincoln Nebraska. The hospital has more than 250 beds and provides acute and long-term rehabilitation as well as subacute care. The hospital treats patients with a variety of orthopedic musculoskeletal and neurological conditions such as brain and spinal cord injury stroke cancer cerebral palsy arthritis and multiple sclerosis. Patients have access to a full team of physicians to help integrate and treat all symptoms. Madonna Rehabilitation Hospital was founded as a geriatric hospital by the Benedictine Sisters of Yankton South Dakota in 1958.

	Annual Growth	06/09	06/10	06/11	06/12	06/13
Sales ($ mil.)	3.8%	–	92.1	93.2	96.2	103.2
Net income ($ mil.)	14.7%	–	–	9.1	5.9	12.0
Market value ($ mil.)	–	–	–	–	–	–
Employees	–	–	–	–	–	1,400

MAERSK INC.

2 Giralda Farms Madison Ave.   CEO: Sren Skou
Madison NJ 07940-0880   CFO: Morten K Nicolaisen
Phone: 973-514-5000   HR: –
Fax: 973-514-5410   FYE: December 31
Web: https://www.maerskline.com/link/?page=lhp&path=/north   Type: Subsidiary

A land-based component of a giant water-based business Maersk Inc. is the main US unit of Denmark-based container shipping company Maersk Line which itself is a subsidiary of shipping giant A.P. M?ller - Maersk. Maersk Inc. serves as an agent for its parent handling inland services for Maersk Line's 500 container ships with an overall capacity of approximately 3.4 million TEU (twenty-foot-equivalent units). The unit's network of about 100 offices in the US Canada Central America and the Caribbean also arranges for customs house brokerage storage (demurrage and detention) and electronic tracking and documentation. Its Maersk Line affiliates provide trucking and logistics services in the region.

MAGEE REHABILITATION HOSPITAL

1513 RACE ST   CEO: Jack Carroll
PHILADELPHIA, PA 191021177   CFO: Patricia Underwood
Phone: 215-587-3000   HR: David Brodar
Fax: –   FYE: June 30
Web: www.mageerehab.org   Type: Private

Part of Pennsylvania's Jefferson Health System The Magee Memorial Hospital for Convalescents (operating as Magee Rehabilitation) is a not-for-profit health organization that provides inpatient and outpatient rehabilitative care to patients disabled by stroke arthritis spinal cord and brain injuries or other conditions. With 96 beds it also offers rehabilitation for patients recovering from amputation orthopedic surgery and joint replacements. In addition it provides wellness programs for muscular neurological and neurodegenerative disorders. Outpatient services include physical therapy speech therapy and emotional support.

	Annual Growth	06/02	06/03	06/04	06/06	06/09
Sales ($ mil.)	6.8%	–	36.9	37.5	106.2	54.7
Net income ($ mil.)	–	–	–	3.9	4.0	(7.0)
Market value ($ mil.)	–	–	–	–	–	–
Employees	–	–	–	–	–	600

MAGELLAN HEALTH INC.

      NMS: MGLN

4800 Scottsdale Rd., Suite 4400   CEO: Barry M. Smith
Scottsdale, AZ 85251   CFO: Jonathan N. (Jon) Rubin
Phone: 602 572-6050   HR: –
Fax: –   FYE: December 31
Web: www.magellanhealth.com   Type: Public

Magellan Health has charted its course to become one of the largest managed behavioral health care companies in the nation. The company manages mental health plan employee assistance and work/life programs through its nationwide third-party provider network of some 70000 behavioral health professionals. Magellan also provides radiology benefits management specialty pharmaceutical management and Medicaid management. Overall it serves more than 58 million members through contracts with federal and local government agencies insurance companies and employers. Its services include administration billing claims handling technology programs and coordination of care.

	Annual Growth	12/10	12/11	12/12	12/13	12/14
Sales ($ mil.)	6.1%	2,969.2	2,799.4	3,207.4	3,546.3	3,760.1
Net income ($ mil.)	(13.0%)	138.7	129.6	151.0	125.3	79.4
Market value ($ mil.)	6.2%	1,273.5	1,332.5	1,319.8	1,613.7	1,616.9
Employees	7.7%	4,900	4,800	5,030	5,949	6,600

MAGELLAN MIDSTREAM PARTNERS LP

NYS: MMP

One Williams Center, P.O. Box 22186
Tulsa, OK 74121-2186
Phone: 918 574-7000
Fax: –
Web: www.magellanlp.com

CEO: Michael N. (Mike) Mears
CFO: Aaron L. Milford
HR: Lisa Korner
FYE: December 31
Type: Public

Having circumnavigated the world of midstream energy assets Magellan Midstream Partners is looking to discover even more profits. The energy infrastructure enterprise has ammonia and petroleum products storage transportation and distribution assets. Magellan Midstream Partners' portfolio includes 27 inland terminals and 1100 miles of ammonia pipeline 9600 miles of refined petroleum pipeline and 53 distribution terminals (with a combined usable storage capacity of 4 million barrels) in the US Midwest. The partnership also owns seven marine terminal facilities on the US East and Gulf coasts.

	Annual Growth	12/10	12/11	12/12	12/13	12/14
Sales ($ mil.)	10.3%	1,557.4	1,748.7	1,772.1	1,897.6	2,303.7
Net income ($ mil.)	28.1%	311.6	413.6	435.7	582.2	839.5
Market value ($ mil.)	10.0%	12,829.4	15,640.5	9,807.1	14,366.6	18,769.5
Employees	5.3%	1,271	1,297	1,339	1,459	1,565

MAGELLAN PETROLEUM CORP.

NAS: MPET

1775 Sherman Street, Suite 1950
Denver, CO 80203
Phone: 720 484-2400
Fax: –
Web: www.magellanpetroleum.com

CEO: J Thomas Wilson
CFO: Antoine J Lafargue
HR: –
FYE: June 30
Type: Public

Magellan Petroleum has gone around the world to explore for oil and gas but most of its revenues come from Australia. It operates mainly through Magellan Petroleum Australia Limited (MPAL) a wholly owned Australian subsidiary. MPAL's chief assets are its 35% interest in the Mereenie oil and gas field and its 52% stake in the Palm Valley gas field in the Amadeus Basin in Australia's Northern Territory. MPAL and Magellan Petroleum also own stakes in oil and gas assets in Canada the US and the UK. The company has proved reserves of 3.4 billion cu. ft. of natural gas and 996000 barrels of oil. In 2011 it began developing assets in the Bakken shale in Montana.

	Annual Growth	06/11	06/12	06/13	06/14	06/15
Sales ($ mil.)	(29.6%)	18.2	13.7	7.1	7.6	4.5
Net income ($ mil.)	–	(32.4)	26.5	(19.8)	15.5	(43.0)
Market value ($ mil.)	(29.3%)	9.6	6.3	5.9	12.6	2.4
Employees	(16.9%)	42	35	39	26	20

MAGMA DESIGN AUTOMATION INC.

NASDAQ: LAVA

1650 Technology Dr.
San Jose CA 95110
Phone: 408-565-7500
Fax: 408-565-7501
Web: www.magma-da.com

CEO: Rajeev Madhavan
CFO: Peter S Teshima
HR: –
FYE: April 30
Type: Public

Magma Design Automation has some hot design tips for chip engineers. The company provides electronic design automation (EDA) software used by engineers designing integrated circuits for electronic products such as cell phones Wi-Fi digital video and networking. Its Talus software products combine front- and back-end design processes into a single integrated workflow while its Quartz applications tackle sign-off and verification tasks. Customers have included Texas Instruments NEC Qualcomm and Samsung. The company also offers related services such as consulting training and maintenance. It gets about 60% of sales from North America. In 2012 Magma was acquired by key competitor Synopsys.

MAGNA CARTA COMPANIES

1 Park Ave.
New York NY 10016-5807
Phone: 212-591-9500
Fax: 212-591-9600
Web: www.psmins.com

CEO: A L Furgatch
CFO: –
HR: –
FYE: December 31
Type: Private - Mutual Com

Dividing ownership of the company among all its policyholders Magna Carta Companies sells mutual commercial property and casualty insurance through Public Service Mutual Company and its subsidiaries Paramount Insurance and Western Select Insurance. Offering services in select states the group focuses on property liability and workers' compensation coverage for real estate firms and restaurants. The company also offers coverage to various small-to-medium sized businesses. Established as Public Service Mutual Company in 1925 the New York-based company was founded as a mutual insurance provider for companies in the taxicab business. The company changed its name to Magna Carta Companies in 2000.

MAGNA MIRRORS

49 W 3rd St.
Holland MI 49423
Phone: 616-786-7000
Fax: 616-786-6052
Web: www.magna.com/xchg/vision_systems?rdelocaleatt

CEO: James L Brodie
CFO: –
HR: Becky Jones
FYE: December 31
Type: Subsidiary

As one of the world's largest makers of automotive mirrors Magna Mirrors is not scared of its own competitors' reflections. The Vision Systems unit of Magna International Magna Mirrors produces interior and exterior rearview mirrors with value-added features (e.g. built-in electronic displays and auto-dimming glass) as well as actuators (motors for power mirrors) and electronic vision systems (back-up and blind spot cameras and sensors). The company also makes door handles keyless entry devices and overhead consoles. The company operates worldwide via facilities located in North America Europe Asia and South Africa.

MAGNACHIP SEMICONDUCTOR CORP

NYS: MX

c/o MagnaChip Semiconductor S.A., 1, Allee Scheffer, Grand Duchy of Luxembourg
Luxembourg L-2520
Phone: (352) 45 62 62
Fax: –
Web: www.magnachip.com

CEO: –
CFO: –
HR: –
FYE: December 31
Type: Public

MagnaChip is a pretty big chip off the block. The company was formed to acquire the nonmemory operations of Hynix Semiconductor one of the world's largest producers of memory devices. MagnaChip primarily offers flat-panel display drivers used in high-definition televisions LCD TVs mobile phones notebook PCs and PC monitors. It also does a large business in silicon foundry (contract semiconductor manufacturing) services. Companies of the LG Group primarily LG Display are MagnaChip's biggest customers. Most of the company's sales are in Asia. After going through bankruptcy reorganization in 2009 and an abandoned IPO attempt in 2010 due to a weak market MagnaChip completed a public offering of stock in 2011.

	Annual Growth	12/10	12/11	12/12	12/13	12/14
Sales ($ mil.)	(2.4%)	770.4	772.8	819.6	734.2	698.2
Net income ($ mil.)	–	74.1	21.8	193.3	(64.2)	(117.2)
Market value ($ mil.)	20.2%	–	254.7	542.2	664.1	442.4
Employees	0.5%	3,337	3,342	3,597	3,479	3,399

MAGNECO/METREL INC.

223 W INTERSTATE RD
ADDISON, IL 601014513
Phone: 630-543-6660
Fax: –
Web: www.magneco-metrel.com

CEO: –
CFO: Susan C Malloy
HR: –
FYE: December 31
Type: Private

Magneco/Metrel makes ceramics but you won't find any artistic pieces at this company's plant! Magneco/Metrel uses the world's largest blast furnace to produce high-temperature refractory ceramics. The lineup serves as a lining in pipes and molds carrying molten iron and steel. The heat of molten steel would erode the pipes and molds without the ceramic barrier. Magneco/Metrel also makes a spray-on nano-particulate refractory line that can be used to create a liner for constructing or repairing steel-making molds and pipe. Its ceramics line is sold largely to steel foundries; other applications include iron-making glass and copper. Magneco/Metrel was established in 1979 and is owned by CEO Charles Connors.

	Annual Growth	12/07	12/08	12/10	12/11	12/12
Sales ($ mil.)	1.0%	–	63.4	62.0	66.4	65.9
Net income ($ mil.)	10.8%	–	–	2.3	3.4	2.8
Market value ($ mil.)	–	–	–	–	–	–
Employees	–	–	–	–	–	145

MAGNETEK, INC.

NMS: MAG

N49 W13650 Campbell Drive
Menomonee Falls, WI 53051
Phone: 262 783-3500
Fax: –
Web: www.magnetek.com

CEO: Peter M McCormick
CFO: Marty J Schwenner
HR: Joy Robertson
FYE: December 29
Type: Public

In the world of electrical equipment Magnetek is a power player. Among the largest the company makes digital power and motion-control systems. The systems comprise radio remote controls programmable drives and collision-avoidance devices used in overhead cranes and hoists. Its DC drives and integrated subsystems are used to control high rise high speed elevators. Magnetek also offers power inverters which direct AC power from generator to utility grid for wind turbines and other renewable energy projects. The company sells largely to North American OEMs of industrial cranes and hoists mining equipment and elevators as well as building and renewable energy contractors and systems integrators.

	Annual Growth	06/10*	07/11*	01/12*	12/12	12/13
Sales ($ mil.)	8.6%	80.6	109.8	58.7	114.3	103.3
Net income ($ mil.)	–	(5.1)	3.7	4.3	12.6	3.1
Market value ($ mil.)	175.4%	3.6	5.9	28.1	33.9	75.2
Employees	3.0%	300	311	330	350	328

*Fiscal year change

MAGNOLIA PICTURES INC.

49 W. 27th St. 7th Fl.
New York NY 10001
Phone: 212-924-6701
Fax: 212-924-6742
Web: www.magpictures.com

CEO: –
CFO: –
HR: –
FYE: December 31
Type: Subsidiary

Magnolia Pictures has planted itself in the movie distribution business. The company distributes primarily art house and foreign movies such as the documentary hit films Capturing the Friedmans Control Room and Enron: The Smartest Guys in the Room. Dallas Mavericks' owner Mark Cuban and his business partner Todd Wagner own Magnolia Pictures through their 2929 Entertainment holdings. The company has the ability to operate in tandem with sister firms (Landmark Theatres high definition TV network HDNet and studios 2929 Productions and HDNet Films) to release films simultaneously in the theater on TV and on DVD. Magnolia was founded in 2001 by movie execs Bill Banowsky (CEO) and Eamonn Bowles (president).

MAGNUM HUNTER RESOURCES CORP (DE)

NBB: MHRC Q

909 Lake Carolyn Parkway, Suite 600
Irving, TX 75039
Phone: 832 369-6986
Fax: 832 369-6992
Web: www.magnumhunterresources.com

CEO: Gary C. Evans
CFO: Joseph C. Daches
HR: –
FYE: December 31
Type: Public

The treasure this hunter seeks is gold black gold. Magnum Hunter Resources (MHR) acquires producing oil and natural gas leases conducts exploratory drilling and produces crude oil and natural gas liquids. It has proved reserves of about 75.9 million barrels of oil equivalent about half oil on properties located primarily in Texas Louisiana West Virginia and North Dakota. Most of the company's output comes from West Virginia where it also owns a 182-mile natural gas pipeline through its Triad Hunter subsidiary. Other subsidiaries include an oilfield drilling business and a natural gas wastewater disposal facility. The company filed for Chapter 11 bankruptcy protection in late 2015.

	Annual Growth	12/10	12/11	12/12	12/13	12/14
Sales ($ mil.)	86.0%	32.7	129.2	271.0	280.4	391.5
Net income ($ mil.)	–	(13.8)	(76.7)	(132.7)	(222.2)	(143.5)
Market value ($ mil.)	(18.7%)	1,443.6	1,080.7	800.0	1,465.7	629.6
Employees	27.8%	165	305	420	445	440

MAGYAR BANCORP INC

NMS: MGYR

400 Somerset Street
New Brunswick, NJ 08901
Phone: 732 342-7600
Fax: –
Web: www.magbank.com

CEO: John S Fitzgerald
CFO: Jon R Ansari
HR: –
FYE: September 30
Type: Public

Magyar doesn't mean "bank" in Hungarian it means "Hungarian" in Hungarian. Magyar Bancorp is the holding company for Magyar Bank which serves central New Jersey individuals and businesses through about a half-dozen offices. The bank offers standard deposit products including checking and savings accounts NOW accounts and CDs. It uses these funds to originate loans and invest in securities. Magyar Bank focuses on real estate lending including construction loans residential and commercial mortgages and home equity loans which altogether account for about 90% of its loan portfolio. Mutual holding company Magyar Bancorp MHC owns 56% of Magyar Bancorp.

	Annual Growth	09/11	09/12	09/13	09/14	09/15
Assets ($ mil.)	1.2%	524.0	508.8	537.7	530.4	550.6
Net income ($ mil.)	–	(0.2)	0.5	0.3	0.6	0.9
Market value ($ mil.)	29.6%	20.2	27.3	43.2	49.5	57.0
Employees	0.5%	96	95	95	101	98

MAID-RITE CORPORATION

2951 86th St.
Des Moines IA 50322-4201
Phone: 515-276-5448
Fax: 515-276-5449
Web: www.maid-rite.com

CEO: –
CFO: –
HR:
FYE: December 31
Type: Private

Fans of this restaurant chain might say loose meat is the only way to make a sandwich right. Maid-Rite Corporation operates and franchises about 80 Maid-Rite diners in the Midwest popular for their loose meat sandwiches. The chain and its hallmark sandwiches — made from steamed ground beef flavored with spices and traditionally eaten with mustard as the only condiment — are an institution in Iowa and its bordering states. Maid-Rite was started in the 1920s by butcher Fred Angell who reportedly originated the loose meat sandwich. Company president Brad Burt led an investor group that acquired the company in 2002.

MAIMONIDES MEDICAL CENTER

4802 10th Ave.
Brooklyn NY 11219
Phone: 718-283-6000
Fax: 512-527-2599
Web: www.varsityworld.com

CEO: Pamela Brier
CFO: Robert Naldi
HR: –
FYE: December 31
Type: Private - Not-for-Pr

The name is a mouthful but if you choke while trying to get it out Maimonides Medical Center can help. The not-for-profit hospital offers emergency medicine surgical procedures psychiatric treatment and other traditional hospital services to patients in Brooklyn New York. It has more than 700 beds and a wide variety of specialty treatment programs for a range of conditions including cancer cardiac stroke neurological pediatric and women's health ailments. It also operates outpatient family health and specialty clinics. Maimonides Medical Center is an independent teaching hospital that serves as a training facility for SUNY-Brooklyn St. George's University and other schools.

MAIN STREET AMERICA GROUP INC.

4601 Touchton Rd. E. Ste. 3400
Jacksonville FL 32246
Phone: 904-380-7281
Fax: 904-380-7244
Web: www.msagroup.com

CEO: –
CFO: –
HR: –
FYE: December 31
Type: Private - Mutual Com

Evoking tree- and shop-lined boulevards The Main Street America Group provides personal and commercial property/casualty products including insurance plans for small and midsized businesses and individual auto and homeowners plans through its NGM Insurance subsidiary and its regional subsidiaries and affiliates Grain Dealers Mutual and Spring Valley Mutual Insurance Company. Some 2000 independent agents sell group products in about 25 states. The firm also offers specialized surety bonds (in about 45 states) for contractors executors and public officials and fidelity bonds to protect businesses from employee dishonesty. The company is 99.6%-owned by Main Street America Group Mutual Holdings Incorporated.

MAIN LINE HEALTH INC.

130 S BRYN MAWR AVE
BRYN MAWR, PA 19010-3121
Phone: 484-337-3000
Fax: –
Web: www.mainlinehealth.org

CEO: John J Lynch III
CFO: Mike Buongiorno
HR: Eileen McAnally
FYE: June 30
Type: Private

Part of the Jefferson Health System Main Line Health serves constituents in the Philadelphia area. The health system consists of four acute-care facilities (Bryn Mawr Hospital Lankenau Medical Center Paoli Hospital and Riddle Hospital) with a total of more than 1100 beds. It also operates physician practices a research institute a 150-bed rehabilitation hospital (Bryn Mawr Rehab Hospital) an addiction recovery facility (Mirmont Treatment Center) and various other facilities. Main Line Health provides home health care services and care for the elderly through senior programs. It operates several ambulatory-care centers and provides occupational health as well.

	Annual Growth	06/07	06/08	06/10	06/11	06/12
Sales ($ mil.)	4.8%	–	1,224.6	1,361.3	1,405.2	1,475.3
Net income ($ mil.)	13.1%	–	118.1	111.4	112.6	193.6
Market value ($ mil.)	–	–	–	–	–	–
Employees	–	–	–	–	–	5,840

MAIN STREET CAPITAL CORP

NYS: MAIN

1300 Post Oak Boulevard, 8th floor
Houston, TX 77056
Phone: 713 350-6000
Fax: –
Web: www.mainstcapital.com

CEO: Vincent D Foster
CFO: Brent D Smith
HR: –
FYE: December 31
Type: Public

Main Street Capital doesn't care if its investments are on Main St. Manufacturing Blvd or Professional Services Pkwy. just as long as they are not too big and are (preferably) located in the southwestern US. As an investment firm Main Street provides long-term debt and equity capital to lower middle-market companies with annual revenues between $10 million and $100 million. Its portfolio includes more than 40 active investments in traditional and niche companies in the manufacturing technology restaurant business services and other sectors. Main Street tends to partner with business owners and management and provides capital to support buyouts recapitalizations growth financings and acquisitions.

	Annual Growth	12/10	12/11	12/12	12/13	12/14
Sales ($ mil.)	40.1%	36.5	66.2	90.5	116.5	140.8
Net income ($ mil.)	49.2%	19.3	39.3	59.3	75.4	95.5
Market value ($ mil.)	12.6%	820.0	957.5	1,375.4	1,473.6	1,318.1
Employees	20.5%	18	22	30	37	38

MAIN LINE HOSPITALS INC.

130 S BRYN MAWR AVE
BRYN MAWR, PA 190103121
Phone: 610-526-3000
Fax: –
Web: www.mainlinehealth.org

CEO: Leland I White
CFO: Michael J Buongiorno
HR: –
FYE: June 30
Type: Private

Bryn Mawr Hospital a member of the Main Line Health network is an acute care facility providing a variety of inpatient and outpatient services in the western suburbs of Philadelphia. With some 320 beds Bryn Mawr Hospital is recognized nationally for its orthopedic program. Founded in 1893 by Dr. George Gerhard the teaching hospital also provides cancer cardiac surgical pediatric reproductive health diagnostic imaging psychiatric bariatric and wound care services. Bryn Mawr Hospital and the other Main Line Health facilities are part of community based not-for-profit network Jefferson Health System.

	Annual Growth	06/05	06/06	06/07	06/08	06/10
Sales ($ mil.)	821.0%	–	–	–	11.2	953.7
Net income ($ mil.)	627.4%	–	–	–	2.2	114.4
Market value ($ mil.)	–	–	–	–	–	–
Employees	–	–	–	–	–	3,353

MAINE & MARITIMES CORPORATION

209 State St.
Presque Isle ME 04769
Phone: 207-760-2499
Fax: 207-760-2419
Web: www.maineandmaritimes.com

CEO: Brent M Boyles
CFO: Michael I Williams
HR: Felicia Oclair
FYE: December 31
Type: Subsidiary

Maine & Maritimes (MAM formerly Maine Public Service) is the consumer's main hope for smooth sailing in the waters of regional electricity supply. A holding company formed by electric utility Maine Public Service (MPS) which is now Maine & Maritimes' primary subsidiary it transmits and distributes electricity to customers in a service area that encompasses 73000 people in northern Maine. MAM originally operated a range of energy-related businesses but has since refocused on its utility operations (MAM Utility Services). In 2010 the company was acquired by Canadian energy and services firm Emera.

MAINE EMPLOYERS' MUTUAL INSURANCE COMPANY

261 Commercial St.
Portland ME 04104
Phone: 207-791-3300
Fax: 207-791-3336
Web: www.memic.com

CEO: John T Leonard
CFO: –
HR: –
FYE: December 31
Type: Private - Mutual Com

Maine Employers' Mutual Insurance Company (MEMIC) provides workers' compensation insurance to more than 20000 employers in Maine and elsewhere through subsidiary MEMIC Indemnity. The company is the largest workers' compensation insurer in its home state insuring nearly two-thirds of covered companies. Formed in 2000 MEMIC Indemnity is licensed to write insurance in 45 states. The company also offers safety programs including training workshops and educational materials. Because businesses generally need other insurance products MEMIC has teamed up with one regional property/casualty insurer to offer MEMIC's workers compensation coverage along with other commercial products. MEMIC was established in 1993.

MAINE MEDICAL CENTER

22 BRAMHALL ST
PORTLAND, ME 041023175
Phone: 207-662-0111
Fax: –
Web: www.mmc.org

CEO: Richard W. (Rich) Petersen
CFO: –
HR: –
FYE: September 30
Type: Private

Maine Medical Center (MMC) makes healing happen for the residents of northern New England. Part of MaineHealth the not-for-profit medical center consists of a tertiary care community hospital The Barbara Bush Children's Hospital and outpatient clinics. Specialty services include cancer care geriatrics emergency medicine cardiovascular care rehabilitation neurology orthopedics and women's health. Through its partnership with the Tufts University School of Medicine the 640-bed teaching hospital provides a variety of medical education and training programs. MMC also conducts research through the Maine Medical Center Research Institute. The medical center was founded in 1874 with 40 beds.

	Annual Growth	09/05	09/06	09/07	09/08	09/13
Sales ($ mil.)	5.8%	–	–	–	685.6	908.4
Net income ($ mil.)	18.9%	–	–	–	49.7	118.2
Market value ($ mil.)	–	–	–	–	–	–
Employees	–	–	–	–	–	5,000

MAINEGENERAL HEALTH

35 MEDICAL CENTER PKWY
AUGUSTA, ME 043308160
Phone: 207 626 1000
Fax: –
Web: www.mainegeneral.org

CEO: Charles Hays
CFO: Michael Koziol
HR: –
FYE: June 30
Type: Private

If you're aching or ailing within shouting distance of the Kennebec River in Maine then MaineGeneral Health is the place to head. The comprehensive health care organization features acute care hospitals outpatient clinics and physicians' practices long-term care centers and home health and hospice agencies. Its flagship facilities are the three main campuses (in state capital Augusta and Waterville farther north) of MaineGeneral Medical Center together featuring about 290 inpatient beds. MaineGeneral Health also runs nursing homes with some 270 beds in all as well as senior living apartments lab and imaging centers and inpatient rehabilitation and mental health facilities.

	Annual Growth	06/09	06/10	06/11	06/12	06/13
Sales ($ mil.)	1.8%	–	401.3	421.6	440.3	423.3
Net income ($ mil.)	(11.9%)	–	–	46.1	(2.0)	35.8
Market value ($ mil.)	–	–	–	–	–	–
Employees	–	–	–	–	–	3,800

MAINEHEALTH

110 FREE ST
PORTLAND, ME 041013576
Phone: 207-661-7001
Fax: –
Web: www.mainehealth.org

CEO: –
CFO: –
HR: –
FYE: September 30
Type: Private

MaineHealth provides health care to residents of central southern and western Maine. The health system's facilities include Maine Medical Center Spring Harbor Hospital and Stephens Memorial Hospital (part of Western Maine Health). MaineHealth also operates long-term care facilities a home health care service physician practices medical laboratories and other health care service units. The company's Synernet subsidiary provides administrative and group purchasing services for MaineHealth's members and other health care organizations.

	Annual Growth	09/97	09/98	09/99	09/08	09/13
Sales ($ mil.)	(19.3%)	–	1,489.0	493.8	23.5	59.4
Net income ($ mil.)	(12.0%)	–	–	30.7	(0.1)	5.1
Market value ($ mil.)	–	–	–	–	–	–
Employees	–	–	–	–	–	2,100

MAINSOURCE FINANCIAL GROUP INC

NMS: MSFG

2105 North State Road 3 Bypass
Greensburg, IN 47240
Phone: 812 663-6734
Fax: 812 663-4812
Web: www.mainsourcebank.com

CEO: Archie M. Brown
CFO: James M. (Jamie) Anderson
HR: –
FYE: December 31
Type: Public

MainSource Financial wants to be the main source of financial services for residents and businesses in Indiana and beyond. It is the holding company of MainSource Bank which operates about 80 branches in the Hoosier State as well as neighboring portions of Ohio Illinois and Kentucky. The bank offers standard deposit and lending products in addition to trust and insurance services. Real estate loans account for the majority of MainSource Financial's lending portfolio which also includes other commercial and consumer loans. Through MainSource Insurance the company provides annuities and credit life insurance.

	Annual Growth	12/10	12/11	12/12	12/13	12/14
Assets ($ mil.)	3.0%	2,769.3	2,754.2	2,769.3	2,859.9	3,122.5
Net income ($ mil.)	18.3%	14.8	23.8	27.3	26.3	29.0
Market value ($ mil.)	19.1%	225.8	191.5	274.8	391.0	453.7
Employees	(3.6%)	926	805	808	772	801

MAINSTREET BANKSHARES INC

NBB: MREE

1075 Spruce Street
Martinsville, VA 24112
Phone: 276 632-8054
Fax: –
Web: www.msbsinc.com

CEO: –
CFO: –
HR: –
FYE: December 31
Type: Public

There is no exile on MainStreet BankShares (sorry Mick). The firm is the holding company for Franklin Community Bank which serves southern Virginia from about five offices. Chartered in 2002 Franklin offers such deposit products as checking and savings accounts money markets and CDs. The bank primarily uses funds from deposits to write real estate loans including commercial and residential mortgages construction loans and home equity loans. Franklin Community's market is centered in the rural communities of Virginia's Franklin County.

	Annual Growth	12/08	12/09	12/10	12/11	12/12
Assets ($ mil.)	(5.0%)	224.6	225.2	214.5	203.9	183.1
Net income ($ mil.)	35.4%	0.6	0.1	0.8	(0.1)	2.0
Market value ($ mil.)	(21.7%)	27.4	10.6	6.4	7.3	10.3
Employees	0.0%	53	54	51	50	53

MAJESCO ENTERTAINMENT CO.

NAS: COOL

4041-T Hadley Road
S. Plainfield, NJ 07080
Phone: 732-225-8910
Fax: –
Web: www.majescoentertainment.com

CEO: Jesse Sutton
CFO: Michael Vesey
HR: –
FYE: October 31
Type: Public

Majesco hopes to reign as king of video games over all its subjects not just the gaming nobility. The company develops wider-appeal games primarily for Nintendo (DS Wii) devices as well as for PCs mobile phones and tablets consoles from Sony and Microsoft. Originally known for action titles such as Blood-Rayne and Black & Bruised it now concentrates on mass-appeal games. Its fastest-selling franchise the dance-fueled Zumba Fitness launched in 2010 has shown it has moves selling more than 10 million units worldwide and representing more than 50% of the company's sales. The company's Cooking Mama franchise is still Majesco's crown jewel though at more than nine million units sold.

	Annual Growth	10/11	10/12	10/13	10/14	10/15
Sales ($ mil.)	(51.9%)	125.3	132.3	47.3	34.4	6.7
Net income ($ mil.)	–	6.8	4.6	(12.6)	(16.2)	(3.8)
Market value ($ mil.)	(21.8%)	37.4	11.1	6.7	14.9	14.0
Employees	(50.8%)	85	90	62	23	5

MAJOR LEAGUE BASEBALL PLAYERS ASSOCIATION

12 E 49TH ST FL 24
NEW YORK, NY 100171028
Phone: 212-826-0808
Fax: –
Web: www.mlbpa.org

CEO: –
CFO: –
HR: –
FYE: December 31
Type: Private

The Major League Baseball Players Association (MLBPA) is for big leaguers only. The organization is the collective bargaining representative for Major League Baseball's 1200 players. The union negotiates salaries arbitrates grievances ensures the on-field safety of its players controls the license for MLB and distributes licensing revenues. The MLBPA also certifies player agents. All players coaches managers and trainers who have signed with the league are eligible to pay dues of $50 per day during the 183-day season for membership in the association. MLBPA was organized in 1966 and negotiated the first collective bargaining agreement with team owners in 1968.

	Annual Growth	12/09	12/10	12/11	12/12	12/13
Sales ($ mil.)	(8.5%)	–	42.3	53.3	29.2	32.5
Net income ($ mil.)	(44.6%)	–	–	35.5	12.1	10.9
Market value ($ mil.)	–	–	–	–	–	–
Employees	–	–	–	–	–	36

MAJOR LEAGUE SOCCER L.L.C.

420 5th Ave. 7th Fl.
New York NY 10018
Phone: 212-450-1200
Fax: 212-450-1302
Web: www.mlsnet.com

CEO: –
CFO: Sean Prendergast
HR: –
FYE: December 31
Type: Private - Associatio

Major League Soccer brings the world's most popular sport to the shores of the US. Created in 1993 the 18-team league competes from March to October culminating with the MLS Cup championship. MLS oversees rules and scheduling regulates franchise ownership and negotiates marketing and broadcasting partnerships. Many of the games are broadcast on ABC and ESPN (both owned by Walt Disney); FOX Soccer Channel (part of News Corporation's FOX Sports Net) also telecasts some live MLS matches. The league is part of the U.S. Soccer Federation which oversees the sport in the US as a member of the Federation Internationale de Football Association (FIFA).

MAKE-A-WISH FOUNDATION OF AMERICA

4742 N 24TH ST STE 400
PHOENIX, AZ 850164862
Phone: 602-279-9474
Fax: –

CEO: –
CFO: Paul Melhorne
HR: –
FYE: August 31
Type: Private

The Make-A-Wish Foundation of America's mission is to grant the wishes of children with life-threatening medical conditions. The charitable organization grants wishes to ailing kids between the ages of two-and-a-half and 18 from more than 60 chapters in the US and its territories. Funded through donations in-kind contributions grants chapter fees and corporate donations the not-for-profit foundation boasts a volunteer network of some 25000 people and has granted more than 226000 wishes to children since its creation in 1980. The foundation was originally named the Chris Greicius Make-A-Wish Memorial after the first boy to receive his wish: becoming an honorary Arizona state trooper.

	Annual Growth	08/09	08/10	08/11	08/12	08/13
Sales ($ mil.)	3.4%	–	60.8	64.8	65.1	67.3
Net income ($ mil.)	–	–	–	3.9	(0.0)	(1.7)
Market value ($ mil.)	–	–	–	–	–	–
Employees	–	–	–	–	–	118

MAKITA U.S.A. INC.

14930 Northam St.
La Mirada CA 90638
Phone: 714-522-8088
Fax: 714-522-8133
Web: www.makita.com

CEO: Hiroshi Tsujimura
CFO: –
HR: –
FYE: March 31
Type: Subsidiary

Cutting drilling grinding sanding and demolishing are a little easier thanks to Makita U.S.A. The company makes more than 400 industrial-quality power tools including drills saws wrenches routers sanders blowers vacuums compressors and power generators as well as accessories for those tools. Makita U.S.A. has a manufacturing plant in Georgia four distribution facilities and more than 600 authorized service centers throughout the US. Established in 1970 the company is a subsidiary of global power tool manufacturer Makita Corporation.

MALVERN BANCORP INC.

NASDAQ: MLVF

42 E. Lancaster Ave.
Paoli PA 19301
Phone: 610-644-9400
Fax: 610-644-1943
Web: www.malvernfederal.com

CEO: –
CFO: –
HR: Maureen Wroblewski
FYE: September 30
Type: Public

Malvern Bancorp (formerly Malvern Federal Bancorp) was formed in 2008 to be the holding company for Malvern Federal Savings Bank which has been in business since 1887. The bank operates seven financial centers in Chester County in southeastern Pennsylvania west of Philadelphia. It offers standard deposit services such as checking and savings accounts certificates of deposit and retirement plans. The community-oriented institution has traditionally been a leading originator of residential home loans in Chester County but has been shifting its focus toward issuing more commercial real estate construction and consumer loans.

MAMMATECH CORPORATION

OTC: MAMM

930 NW 8th Ave.
Gainesville FL 32601
Phone: 352-375-0607
Fax: 561-790-4332
Web: www.rangerconstruction.com

CEO: Charles Rimlinger
CFO: Stephen Antol
HR: –
FYE: August 31
Type: Public

Mammatech Corporation wants to help doctors clinicians moms and other women keep an eye on breast cancer. The company manufactures a breast tumor detection training system designed to increase early detection of breast cancer and thus reduce patient deaths from the disease. Using models of a human female breast the MammaCare System trains individuals to perform manual breast exams to detect tumors. The system comes in different interactive training packages targeting medical professionals and individuals including those who are hearing or vision impaired. The company started as a research project in 1974 with support from the National Cancer Institute.

MANAGEMENT AND TRAINING CORPORATION

500 N MARKET PLACE DR # 100
CENTERVILLE, UT 840141708
Phone: 801-693-2600
Fax: –
Web: www.mtctrains.com

CEO: –
CFO: Lyle J Parry
HR: Teresa Aramaki
FYE: December 31
Type: Private

Management & Training Corporation (MTC) prepares prison inmates for re-entry into society. It provides a variety of academic vocational and social-skills training in rehabilitation-oriented private prisons. Its holistic education model offers programs to help inmates avoid substance abuse as they also boost their engagement in community service find work and increase their cognitive skills. As part of its services MTC operates about two dozen correctional facilities in eight states through a contract with the Department of Labor. The company also operates Job Corps centers and provides health care related services to correctional facilities.

	Annual Growth	12/09	12/10	12/11	12/12	12/13
Sales ($ mil.)	3.3%	–	667.4	687.1	704.1	735.4
Net income ($ mil.)	28.9%	–	–	30.5	45.7	50.7
Market value ($ mil.)	–	–	–	–	–	–
Employees	–	–	–	–	–	9,500

MANDALAY SPORTS ENTERTAINMENT LLC

4751 Wilshire Blvd. 3rd Fl.
Los Angeles CA 90010
Phone: 323 549 4300
Fax: 323-549-9821
Web: www.mandalay.com

CEO: Hank Stickney
CFO: Jimmy Bailey
HR: –
FYE: December 31
Type: Private

Mandalay Sports Entertainment plays another game — Hollywood. The company produces finances and distributes movies through its Mandalay Motion Pictures unit. The company has a distribution deal with Universal Pictures and has produced such films as Sleepy Hollow and Enemy at the Gates. Mandalay Entertainment also has a division devoted to baseball Mandalay Baseball Properties which has ownership stakes in Minor League Baseball franchises. Teams include the Hagerstown Suns the Dayton Dragons and the Frisco RoughRiders. Sister company Mandalay Media produces mobile digital content. Mandalay Entertainment was founded in 1995 by former Columbia Pictures head Peter Guber who serves as chairman and CEO.

MANGO CAPITAL INC.

OTC: MGOF-L

108 Village Sq. Ste. 315
Somers NY 10589
Phone: 914-669-5333
Fax: 866-277-3385
Web: www.mangosoft.com

CEO: Dennis M Goett
CFO: Sean M Gavin
HR: –
FYE: December 31
Type: Public

Mango Capital's software products are designed to improve the efficiency of Web-based business applications including online document delivery speed and remote file storage. Customers use the company's applications known as Mangomind to securely manage collaboration and file sharing with remote offices and trading partners. Mango Capital's clients come from a variety of industries and include small and midsized businesses workgroups and large enterprises. Founded in 1995 the company changed its name from MangoSoft to Mango Capital in 2011 to reflect the addition of financial services such as structured settlement to its business plan through its Aspyre Settlement Funding business.

MANHATTAN ASSOCIATES, INC.

NMS: MANH

2300 Windy Ridge Parkway, Tenth Floor
Atlanta, GA 30339
Phone: 770 955-7070
Fax: 770 995-0302
Web: www.manh.com

CEO: Eddie Capel
CFO: Dennis B. Story
HR: –
FYE: December 31
Type: Public

Whether you're in New York or Kansas or points between or beyond Manhattan Associates keeps things moving with its supply chain management software and systems. The Atlanta-based company provides customers in retail distribution transportation and manufacturing with supply chain management software and related services. The company's line of supply chain execution software includes warehouse transportation trading partner distributed order and reverse logistics management applications. Manhattan also offers performance management and radio-frequency identification tools designed to enhance the functionality of its other products and sells third-party hardware such as bar code scanners.

	Annual Growth	12/11	12/12	12/13	12/14	12/15
Sales ($ mil.)	14.0%	329.3	376.2	414.5	492.1	556.4
Net income ($ mil.)	23.2%	44.9	51.9	67.3	82.0	103.5
Market value ($ mil.)	13.1%	2,945.6	4,390.7	8,548.6	2,963.0	4,815.0
Employees	8.2%	2,135	2,400	2,530	2,770	2,930

MANHATTAN BRIDGE CAPITAL, INC.

NAS: LOAN

60 Cutter Mill Road
Great Neck, NY 11021
Phone: 516 444-3400
Fax: 212 779-2974
Web: www.manhattanbridgecapital.com

CEO: Assaf Ran
CFO: Vanessa KAO
HR: –
FYE: December 31
Type: Public

Manhattan Bridge Capital (formerly DAG Media) knew that when it came to a bridge it had to cross it. In 2008 it renamed itself when its DAG Funding Solutions commercial lending subsidiary which the company started in 2007 became its most profitable unit. The company offers short-term secured commercial loans to small businesses. It also offers an online service Nextyellow.com that lets consumers search for a product or service. The consumer's request is matched with appropriate businesses and the matched businesses then call or email the customer. Vendor partners pay the company monthly fees to be featured in the matching process.

	Annual Growth	12/10	12/11	12/12	12/13	12/14
Sales ($ mil.)	24.5%	1.2	1.4	1.8	2.3	2.9
Net income ($ mil.)	46.1%	0.3	0.3	0.4	0.6	1.5
Market value ($ mil.)	33.6%	7.7	6.1	6.6	10.4	24.5
Employees	0.0%	3	2	3	2	3

MANHATTAN COLLEGE CORP

4513 MNHTTAN COLLEGE PKWY
BRONX, NY 104714004
Phone: 718-862-8000
Fax: –
Web: www.engineering.manhattan.edu

CEO: –
CFO: Matthew S McManness
HR: –
FYE: June 30
Type: Private

A trip to Manhattan College doesn't take you to that well-known borough but instead to the Riverdale section of the Bronx. With its campus overlooking Van Cortlandt Park Manhattan College is a private Catholic university with about 3200 undergraduate and graduate students studying a wide range of topics from engineering to the arts to biotechnology. The school grants about 40 undergraduate degrees and graduate degrees in education and engineering. Founded in 1853 by the Brothers of the Christian Schools the college was originally located on Canal Street in Manhattan then later moved to a rural location at 131st Street and Broadway before settling into its present campus in 1922.

	Annual Growth	06/07	06/08	06/09	06/11	06/13
Sales ($ mil.)	11.9%	–	85.9	88.1	124.6	150.7
Net income ($ mil.)	57.7%	–	–	1.3	3.0	7.7
Market value ($ mil.)	–	–	–	–	–	–
Employees	–	–	–	–	–	496

MANHATTANVILLE COLLEGE

2900 PURCHASE ST
PURCHASE, NY 105772132
Phone: 914-694-2200
Fax: –
Web: www.manhattanville.edu

CEO: –
CFO: –
HR: –
FYE: June 30
Type: Private

Manhattanville College is a private liberal arts institution offering undergraduate and masters degree programs in more than 50 fields. Manhattanville is home to about 1700 undergraduate students and 1000 graduate students. In addition to college degree programs the school also offers in-house and on-site corporate training programs in such areas as business writing project management and diversity. Manhattanville was founded in 1841 in New York City by the Religious of the Sacred Heart. It relocated in 1847 to an area just north of New York City on a hill overlooking the village of Manhattanville. The school has been coeducational and non-denominational since 1971.

	Annual Growth	06/09	06/10	06/11	06/12	06/13
Sales ($ mil.)	(14.6%)	–	98.2	98.3	102.7	61.1
Net income ($ mil.)	–	–	–	(0.1)	3.8	1.4
Market value ($ mil.)	–	–	–	–	–	–
Employees	–	–	–	–	–	420

MANITEX INTERNATIONAL INC

NAS: MNTX

9725 Industrial Drive
Bridgeview, IL 60455
Phone: 708 430-7500
Fax: –
Web: www.manitexinternational.com

CEO: David J Langevin
CFO: David H Gransee
HR: –
FYE: December 31
Type: Public

Manitex International makes products that are uplifting — literally. One of the largest manufacturers of lifting equipment in North America Manitex makes and sells boom trucks and sign cranes used in industrial jobs as well as energy exploration construction and commercial building. Through Liftking the company makes rough terrain forklifts heavy handling transports and military specialty vehicles. The Manitex family includes Badger Equipment (cranes and material handling) and Load King (trailers). A Crane & Machinery unit distributes Manitex Terex and Fuchs equipment.

	Annual Growth	12/10	12/11	12/12	12/13	12/14
Sales ($ mil.)	28.8%	95.9	142.3	205.2	245.1	264.1
Net income ($ mil.)	35.5%	2.1	2.8	8.1	10.2	7.1
Market value ($ mil.)	34.8%	57.7	63.6	107.0	238.0	190.5
Employees	30.4%	229	344	386	501	663

MANITOWOC CO INC (THE)

NYS: MTW

2400 South 44th Street
Manitowoc, WI 54221-0066
Phone: 920 684-4410
Fax: –
Web: www.manitowoc.com

CEO: Hubertus M. Muehlhaeuser
CFO: Carl J. Laurino
HR: Ivy Ma
FYE: December 31
Type: Public

Be it hoisting a steel column or a frosty mug The Manitowoc Company (MTW) plays a leading role. MTW's Crane business manufactures lifting equipment such as tower cranes mobile telescopic cranes and boom trucks prevalent in construction and mining operations but also used in petrochemical utilities and energy projects. Its Foodservice segment caters to commercial kitchens in restaurants hotels health care facilities and institutions supplying a slate of ice-making and beverage-dispensing machines as well as food prep and heating equipment. In 2015 it announced plans to spin off its Foodservice business in 2016.

	Annual Growth	12/10	12/11	12/12	12/13	12/14
Sales ($ mil.)	5.5%	3,141.7	3,651.9	3,927.0	4,048.1	3,886.5
Net income ($ mil.)	–	(73.4)	(10.5)	101.7	141.8	144.5
Market value ($ mil.)	13.9%	1,777.0	1,245.6	2,125.3	3,160.9	2,995.5
Employees	(1.9%)	13,300	12,900	13,500	13,400	12,300

MANITOWOC FOODSERVICE COMPANIES INC.

2227 Welbilt Blvd.
New Port Richey FL 34655-5130
Phone: 727-375-7010
Fax: 727-375-0472
Web: www.manitowocfoodservice.com

CEO: –
CFO: –
HR: –
FYE: December 31
Type: Subsidiary

Manitowoc Foodservice (formerly Enodis Corporation) never finds the kitchen too hot to handle. The business is one of the world's largest makers of foodservice kitchen and restaurant equipment. Its cook chill and prep/hold offerings are sold via such brands and subsidiaries as Garland Frymaster Cleveland Range Delfield Kysor/Warren Lincoln Convotherm and Merrychef. The lineup is primarily designed for rapid cooking or to keep hot foods hot and cold foods cold in restaurants convenience stores and other quick-service outlets. Manitowoc Foodservice also supplies ice machines and clean equipment. It expanded into new end markets in late 2008 when parent Enodis plc was acquired by The Manitowoc Company.

MANNATECH INC

NMS: MTEX

600 S. Royal Lane, Suite 200
Coppell, TX 75019
Phone: 972 471-7400
Fax: –
Web: www.mannatech.com

CEO: Alfredo (Al) Bala
CFO: –
HR: –
FYE: December 31
Type: Public

Mannatech's nutritional products provide a sales mantra for independent entrepreneurs. The multi-level marketing company develops and sells nutritional supplements. Many of its proprietary products include Ambrotose a proprietary blend of monosaccharides (simple sugars) that is claimed to promote cell-to-cell communication and support the body's immune system. Its vitamins weight management products and skin care items are distributed through a network of more than 245000 independent salespeople. The company does not maintain its own manufacturing facilities and instead relies upon third-party contract manufacturers.

	Annual Growth	12/10	12/11	12/12	12/13	12/14
Sales ($ mil.)	(4.5%)	228.1	200.7	173.4	177.4	190.1
Net income ($ mil.)	–	(10.6)	(20.7)	(1.4)	3.2	6.5
Market value ($ mil.)	96.3%	4.8	1.2	15.0	45.4	71.3
Employees	(13.8%)	490	387	310	296	270

MANNING & NAPIER INC.

NYS: MN

290 Woodcliff Drive
Fairport, NY 14450
Phone: 585 325-6880
Fax: –
Web: www.manning-napier.com

CEO: Patrick Cunningham
CFO: James Mikolaichik
HR: –
FYE: December 31
Type: Public

Manning & Napier an independent financial services company offers equity fixed income and blended-asset portfolios of collective investment trust funds mutual funds and separately managed accounts (SMAs; individual mutual-fund like accounts managed for specific goals). With more than $53 billion in assets under management the firm serves high-net-worth individuals and large institutions including corporations endowments 401(k) plans pension plans Taft-Hartley plans and foundations. Manning & Napier offers its products through a direct sales force and through financial intermediaries and investment consultants. Formed in 1970 the company went public in 2011.

	Annual Growth	12/10	12/11	12/12	12/13	12/14
Sales ($ mil.)	12.2%	255.5	330.0	339.1	376.1	405.5
Net income ($ mil.)	(35.3%)	53.1	(27.2)	2.5	2.7	9.3
Market value ($ mil.)	3.4%	–	171.3	172.8	242.1	189.5
Employees	3.9%	450	471	502	507	525

MANNKIND CORP

NMS: MNKD

28903 North Avenue Paine
Valencia, CA 91355
Phone: 661 775-5300
Fax: –
Web: www.mannkindcorp.com

CEO: Hakan S Edstrom
CFO: Matthew J Pfeffer
HR: –
FYE: December 31
Type: Public

MannKind seeks to improve the well-being of well mankind. The biopharmaceutical company focuses on developing and commercializing therapeutic products to treat diabetes and cancer. Its lead product candidate AFREZZA uses its Technosphere inhalation system technology to treat type 1 and type 2 diabetes. The system consists of a special inhaler that releases deep into the lungs a formula of dry powder insulin that could raise insulin levels more quickly and with less discomfort than other methods. The company is also developing therapeutic cancer vaccines that could be injected directly into a patient's lymph nodes.

	Annual Growth	12/08	12/09	12/10	12/11	12/12
Sales ($ mil.)	15.0%	0.0	–	0.1	0.1	0.0
Net income ($ mil.)	–	(303.0)	(220.1)	(170.6)	(160.8)	(169.4)
Market value ($ mil.)	(9.4%)	981.1	2,505.7	2,305.4	715.1	660.7
Employees	(19.3%)	580	443	436	250	246

MANPOWERGROUP

NYS: MAN

100 Manpower Place
Milwaukee, WI 53212
Phone: 414 961-1000
Fax: 414 332-0796
Web: www.manpower.com

CEO: Jonas Prising
CFO: John T. (Jack) McGinnis
HR: Lisa Banner
FYE: December 31
Type: Public

Millions of men (and women) have helped power this firm to the upper echelon of the staffing industry. ManpowerGroup is one of the world's largest providers of temporary employees connecting more than 6 million people in office industrial and professional positions every year. It offers services through different brands including ManpowerGroup Solutions Manpower Experis (accounting finance health and engineering positions) Manpower UK and Right Management which provides management consulting services focused on leadership development and assessment. ManpowerGroup has some 3000 owned or franchised offices in 80 countries and territories and assists more than 400000 clients.

	Annual Growth	12/10	12/11	12/12	12/13	12/14
Sales ($ mil.)	2.4%	18,866.5	22,006.0	20,678.0	20,250.5	20,762.8
Net income ($ mil.)	–	(263.6)	251.6	197.6	288.0	427.6
Market value ($ mil.)	2.1%	4,902.4	2,792.6	3,315.2	6,706.9	5,325.0
Employees	(3.5%)	30,000	31,000	28,000	25,000	26,000

MANTECH INTERNATIONAL CORP

NMS: MANT

12015 Lee Jackson Highway
Fairfax, VA 22033
Phone: 703 218-6000
Fax: –

CEO: George J. Pedersen
CFO: Kevin M. Phillips
HR: Tom Painter
FYE: December 31
Type: Public

ManTech International is more than willing to lend a little high-tech manpower to ensure its country's security. ManTech provides security-focused IT services to 50 agencies primarily US government intelligence entities such as the Department of Defense (DoD) Homeland Security the FBI and the military. Its national security offerings include intelligence communications computer forensics and security systems development and support. The contractor also offers network design and installation and system testing and evaluation. ManTech is active in about 40 other countries but makes essentially all of its sales to US customers.

	Annual Growth	12/10	12/11	12/12	12/13	12/14
Sales ($ mil.)	(9.1%)	2,604.0	2,870.0	2,582.3	2,310.1	1,774.0
Net income ($ mil.)	(21.6%)	125.1	133.3	95.0	(6.1)	47.3
Market value ($ mil.)	(7.5%)	1,544.6	1,167.5	969.4	1,118.6	1,129.8
Employees	(8.4%)	10,100	9,300	9,700	7,800	7,100

MANUFACTURED HOUSING ENTERPRISES INC.

9302 US HIGHWAY 6
BRYAN, OH 435069516
Phone: 419-636-4511
Fax: –
Web: www.mheinc.com

CEO: Mary Jane Fitzcharles
CFO: –
HR: –
FYE: December 31
Type: Private

Manufactured Housing Enterprises builds modular sectional and singlewide homes as well as commercial and retail developments for clients in the Midwest. The company is the largest manufactured home builder in Ohio and among the 20 largest in the country. It offers more than 80 floor plans for singlewide homes as well as two-story homes of more than 3000 sq. ft. The company has delivered homes to Illinois Indiana Indiana Kentucky Michigan Missouri Tennessee West Virginia and Wisconsin. Manufactured Housing Enterprises was established in 1965 when being "mod" was fab.

	Annual Growth	12/09	12/10	12/11	12/12	12/13
Sales ($ mil.)	19.1%	–	7.4	8.0	13.1	12.5
Net income ($ mil.)	–	–	–	(0.1)	0.7	0.8
Market value ($ mil.)	–	–	–	–	–	–
Employees	–	–	–	–	–	1

MAPQUEST INC.

1555 Blake St. 3rd Fl.
Denver CO 80202
Phone: 303 406 4000
Fax: +81-75-431-6500
Web: www.screen.co.jp

CEO: –
CFO: –
HR: –
FYE: December 31
Type: Subsidiary

Where are we? MapQuest's products and services are geared for people who are going places. The company supplies maps and proximity information to consumers through its Web site and also offers services to businesses and to travel guides and map publishers. It also publishes road atlases books and laminated street maps. MapQuest's content can be downloaded to wireless devices made by such providers as Sprint Verizon and AT&T. MapQuest reaches more than 40 million visitors per month. MapQuest is a subsidiary of AOL which spun off from media giant Time Warner in 2009. Today it operates as part of AOL's Huffington Post Media Group.

MAR-JAC POULTRY INC.

1020 AVIATION BLVD
GAINESVILLE, GA 305016839
Phone: 770-536-0561
Fax: –
Web: www.marjacpoultry.com

CEO: J Pete Martin
CFO: Mirza M Yaqub
HR: –
FYE: April 26
Type: Private

From farm to table Mar-Jac Poultry's business is "poultry in motion." The company is one of the major processors of chicken sold to the domestic fast-food restaurant and foodservice market. Its operations include a hatchery to raise birds and a feed mill that churns 8500 tons of feed a week for some 200 farmers in Georgia who contract with the company to grow its chicks and broilers. Mar-Jac's plant processes about two million chickens a week which are vacuum-packed in its cold storage facility prior to shipment to mostly local distributors in the US and some international export customers. Mar-Jac was started by brothers Marvin and Jackson McKibbon in 1954 and later acquired by a group of poultry farmers.

	Annual Growth	04/09	04/10	04/11	04/12	04/13
Sales ($ mil.)	6.1%	–	262.9	257.1	284.0	314.3
Net income ($ mil.)	25.4%	–	–	11.2	8.1	17.6
Market value ($ mil.)	–	–	–	–	–	–
Employees	–	–	–	–	–	1,200

MARATHON OIL CORP.

NYS: MRO

5555 San Felipe Street
Houston, TX 77056-2723
Phone: 713 629-6600
Fax: –
Web: www.marathonoil.com

CEO: Lee M. Tillman
CFO: John R. (J.R.) Sult
HR: Deanna Jones
FYE: December 31
Type: Public

In the long-running competition for profits in the oil and gas industry Marathon Oil is keeping up a steady pace. The company explores for oil and gas primarily in Canada Equatorial Guinea Iraq Libya Poland the UK and the US. In 2014 it reported proved reserves of more than 2.2 billion barrels of oil equivalent including 644 million barrels of synthetic oil derived from oil sands mining. Its major areas of production include Europe (the UK); Africa (Equatorial Guinea and Libya); and Canada (the Athabasca Oil Sands Project). In the US the company's core production assets are in Colorado the Gulf of Mexico Louisiana Oklahoma Texas and Wyoming.

	Annual Growth	12/10	12/11	12/12	12/13	12/14
Sales ($ mil.)	(37.5%)	73,621.0	15,282.0	16,221.0	14,959.0	11,258.0
Net income ($ mil.)	4.4%	2,568.0	2,946.0	1,582.0	1,753.0	3,046.0
Market value ($ mil.)	(6.5%)	24,995.3	19,757.3	20,695.5	23,827.5	19,095.8
Employees	(42.1%)	29,677	3,322	3,367	3,359	3,330

MARATHON PETROLEUM CORP.

NYS: MPC

539 South Main Street
Findlay, OH 45840-3229
Phone: 419 422-2121
Fax: –
Web: www.marathonpetroleum.com

CEO: Gary R. Heminger
CFO: Timothy T. Griffith
HR: –
FYE: December 31
Type: Public

Marathon Petroleum has a long running commitment to fuel its customers. The former refining and marketing unit of Marathon Oil Corporation operates seven refineries with the capacity to process about 1.7 million barrels of crude oil a day. Marathon Petroleum sells refined products through a nation-wide network of branded gas stations. It also holds stakes in pipelines and is one of the largest asphalt and light oil product terminal operators in the US. The company distributes petroleum products wholesale to private-brand marketers and to large commercial and industrial consumers as well as to the spot market.

	Annual Growth	12/10	12/11	12/12	12/13	12/14
Sales ($ mil.)	11.9%	62,605.0	78,759.0	82,492.0	100,254.0	98,102.0
Net income ($ mil.)	41.9%	623.0	2,389.0	3,389.0	2,112.0	2,524.0
Market value ($ mil.)	39.4%	–	18,242.9	34,524.0	50,268.0	49,462.5
Employees	15.1%	25,803	24,210	25,985	29,865	45,340

MARC GLASSMAN INC.

5841 W. 130th St.
Cleveland OH 44130
Phone: 216-265-7700
Fax: 408-434-5351
Web: www.intersil.com

CEO: Marc Glassman
CFO: Beth Weiner
HR: Nina Willis
FYE: December 31
Type: Private

Marc Glassman is out to prove that low prices can lead to big things. The regional retailer operates about 60 discount stores most of which are Marc's Deeper Discount Drug Stores in northern and central Ohio but also about five Xpect Discount Drugs stores in Connecticut. The stores range in size from 18000 sq. ft. to 48000 sq. ft. About 50 of the locations have pharmacies and offer a constantly changing mix of closeout and excess merchandise in some 20 categories including clothing cosmetics housewares toys and tools. The company specializes in seasonal products (Christmas Halloween lawn and garden). Owner and chairman Marc Glassman founded the company in Middleburg Heights Ohio in 1979.

MARCH OF DIMES FOUNDATION

1275 MAMARONECK AVE
WHITE PLAINS, NY 106055298
Phone: 914-428-7100
Fax: –
Web: www.marchofdimes.com

CEO: Jennifer L. Howse
CFO: Richard E. Mulligan
HR: –
FYE: December 31
Type: Private

The March of Dimes Foundation has been lending a hand since 1938. Established by President Franklin Roosevelt to fight polio the organization has evolved into an advocate for the prevention of birth defects and infant mortality. Its focus areas include genetic birth defects premature birth parent education and expanding access to health care. The foundation provides information and support services for professionals and the public and supports research efforts. Most of the foundation's revenue comes from contributions to its signature March for Babies event and other fundraisers.

	Annual Growth	12/05	12/06	12/08	12/09	12/13
Sales ($ mil.)	(2.2%)	–	236.7	236.1	214.7	202.8
Net income ($ mil.)	–	–	–	0.0	35.3	(9.7)
Market value ($ mil.)	–	–	–	–	–	–
Employees	–	–	–	–	–	1,200

MARCHEX INC

NMS: MCHX

520 Pike Street, Suite 2000
Seattle, WA 98101
Phone: 206 331-3300
Fax: –
Web: www.marchex.com

CEO: Pete Christothoulou
CFO: Michael A. (Mike) Arends
HR: –
FYE: December 31
Type: Public

This company marches to the beat of the telemarketing drummer. Marchex provides performance-based call advertising services. Advertisers pay Marchex a fee for each call they receive from an ad (online mobile or print) distributed by Marchex. Its Local Advertising Services include call distribution and call analytics services such as phone number and call tracking call mining and keyword tracking. Marchex distributes ads on its Publishing Network which includes more than 200000 owned and -operated websites as well as through search engines such as Google and Yahoo!. Its Publisher Network is focused on local products and services and includes domains such as chicagodoctors.com and bostonmortgage.com.

	Annual Growth	12/10	12/11	12/12	12/13	12/14
Sales ($ mil.)	17.0%	97.6	146.7	138.3	152.6	182.6
Net income ($ mil.)	–	(3.0)	3.0	(35.2)	1.8	(19.1)
Market value ($ mil.)	(16.7%)	401.2	262.8	172.8	363.7	193.0
Employees	0.2%	364	350	331	405	367

MARCHON EYEWEAR INC.

35 Hub Dr.	CEO: Claudio Gottardi
Melville NY 11747	CFO: Phil Hibbert
Phone: 631-755-2020	HR: –
Fax: 631-755-2045	FYE: December 31
Web: www.marchon.com	Type: Subsidiary

Marchon Eyewear believes fashion and glasses go hand in hand. The company designs makes and distributes eyeglasses and sunglasses in more than 100 countries. Marchon sells collections of eyeglasses and sunglasses including Calvin Klein Coach Disney Emilio Pucci Fendi Nautica Michael Kors Sean John and NIKE brands (all under license); the patented Flexon metal memory frames; and its own eponymous frames. Its OfficeMate Software Solutions business makes software under names such as OfficeMate (management) and ExamWRITER (electronic medical records) and offers continuing education courses for eyewear professionals. The company is owned by vision-care provider Vision Service Plan (VSP).

MARCUS & MILLICHAP REAL ESTATE INVESTMENT SERVICES IN

16830 Ventura Blvd. Ste. 100	CEO: –
Encino CA 91436	CFO: –
Phone: 818-907-0600	HR: –
Fax: 818-501-8230	FYE: December 31
Web: www.marcusmillichap.com	Type: Private

If you've got several million burning a hole in your pocket or you're looking to unload that old skyscraper Marcus & Millichap Real Estate Investment Services can help. One of the largest commercial real estate brokers in the US (with about 70 offices) the firm focuses on investment brokerage and provides financing research and advisory services to both buyers and sellers. The company is organized into groups by property type including shopping centers apartments office and industrial buildings and distressed prpoerties. Marcus & Millichap Real Estate Investment Services was one of the earliest brokerages to maintain a centralized database to link potential buyers and sellers.

MARCUS CORP. (THE)

NYS: MCS

100 East Wisconsin Avenue, Suite 1900	CEO: Gregory S. Marcus
Milwaukee, WI 53202-4125	CFO: Douglas A. Neis
Phone: 414 905-1000	HR: –
Fax: 414 905-2879	FYE: May 28
Web: www.marcuscorp.com	Type: Public

With this company it's either showtime or bedtime. The Marcus Corporation operates movie theaters and hotels primarily in the Midwest. It owns or operates more than 55 theaters boastingsome 680 screens in Iowa Illinois Minnesota Nebraska North Dakota Ohio and Wisconsin. Its Marcus Hotels subsidiary owns and operates more than 10 hotels and resorts in Illinois Missouri Oklahoma and Wisconsin; it also manages 10 hotels for third parties in a handful of US states. Other holdings also include Funset Boulevard a family entertainment center adjacent to one of its Wisconsin theatres. Chairman Stephen Marcus and his sister Diane Marcus Gershowitz together control more than 75% of the firm.

	Annual Growth	05/11	05/12	05/13	05/14	05/15
Sales ($ mil.)	6.7%	377.0	413.9	412.8	447.9	488.1
Net income ($ mil.)	15.3%	13.6	22.7	17.5	25.0	24.0
Market value ($ mil.)	17.0%	289.3	367.3	370.6	464.0	541.4
Employees	3.4%	6,200	6,200	6,500	6,900	7,100

MARIAN UNIVERSITY INC.

3200 COLD SPRING RD	CEO: –
INDIANAPOLIS, IN 462221960	CFO: Brian Harris
Phone: 317-955-6000	HR: –
Fax: –	FYE: June 30
Web: www.marian.edu	Type: Private

Marian College is a Franciscan Catholic and liberal arts institution offering undergraduate and graduate programs through academic departments such as business nursing education and sport studies. The school has an enrollment of more than 2000 students and boasts a student-to-teacher ratio of just over 12 to 1. Marian College was founded in 1851 by the Sisters of St. Francis as a teacher training institution for German Catholics in southern Indiana.

	Annual Growth	06/09	06/10	06/11	06/12	06/13
Sales ($ mil.)	(0.5%)	–	70.4	59.8	65.3	69.4
Net income ($ mil.)	(67.6%)	–	–	22.4	(0.6)	2.3
Market value ($ mil.)	–	–	–	–	–	–
Employees	–	–	–	–	–	305

MARIE CALLENDER PIE SHOPS INC.

27101 Puerta Real Ste. 260	CEO: –
Mission Viejo CA 92691	CFO: –
Phone: 949-448-5300	HR: –
Fax: 949-448-5325	FYE: December 31
Web: www.mcpies.com	Type: Subsidiary

Marie Callender Pie Shops founded as a wholesale bakery operates and franchises about 90 restaurants under the name Marie Callender's Restaurant & Bakery. Found mostly in California the eateries feature traditional desserts pot pies and sandwiches as well as salads soups and turkey dishes. About 50 of the restaurants are company owned. Marie Callender also licenses a line of frozen food entrees and pie products to ConAgra. The company is a subsidiary of Perkins & Marie Callender's which is controlled by private equity firm Castle Harlan. Parent company Perkins & Marie Callender's filed Chapter 11 bankruptcy protection in 2011 before emerging late that same year.

MARIN SOFTWARE INC.

NYS: MRIN

123 Mission Street, 27th Floor	CEO: David A. (Dave) Yovanno
San Francisco, CA 94105	CFO: John A. Kaelle
Phone: 415 399-2580	HR: –
Fax: –	FYE: December 31
Web: www.marinsoftware.com	Type: Public

Marin Software helps determine whether you're getting your money's worth from online advertising. The company's cloud-based digital advertising management software which it calls its Revenue Acquisition Management platform lets marketers measure the effectiveness of campaigns execute campaigns across publishers and channels and use analytics to fine tune campaigns in progress. Its software works with ad publishers Baidu Bing Google Facebook and Yahoo! and integrates with enterprise applications. Marin Software sells its software directly to advertisers and through ad agencies; it earns revenue based on the amount of ad spending customers manage. The company formed in 2006 and went public in 2013.

	Annual Growth	12/10	12/11	12/12	12/13	12/14
Sales ($ mil.)	51.2%	19.0	36.1	59.6	77.3	99.4
Net income ($ mil.)	–	(10.9)	(17.4)	(26.5)	(35.9)	(33.2)
Market value ($ mil.)	(17.4%)	–	–	–	360.3	297.6
Employees	16.0%	–	–	424	500	571

MARINA BIOTECH INC

NBB: MRNA

P.O. Box 1559
Bothell, WA 98041
Phone: 425 892-4322
Fax: 425 908-3101
Web: www.marinabio.com

CEO: J Michael French
CFO: –
HR: –
FYE: December 31
Type: Public

While it doesn't technically shoot the messenger Marina Biotech (formerly called MDRNA) certainly works to silence it. The drug discovery company is developing treatments using gene silencing approaches such as RNA interference (RNAi) and messenger RNA (mRNA) blocking. It conducts clinical and preclinical tests on RNAi treatments for a variety of cancers and precancerous conditions. Marina Biotech has built up its holdings by licensing peptides with potential RNAi therapy applications from numerous pharmaceutical companies and universities including the University of Michigan. In 2012 the firm ceased its internal development efforts and placed most of its workforce on leave as it struggled to fund its operations.

	Annual Growth	12/10	12/11	12/12	12/13	12/14
Sales ($ mil.)	(32.9%)	2.5	2.2	4.2	2.1	0.5
Net income ($ mil.)	–	(27.8)	(29.4)	(9.5)	(1.6)	(6.5)
Market value ($ mil.)	(19.4%)	39.5	22.7	11.0	10.2	16.7
Employees	(61.4%)	45	11	1	1	1

MARINE PRODUCTS CORP.

NYS: MPX

2801 Buford Highway, Suite 520
Atlanta, GA 31329
Phone: 404 321-7910
Fax: –
Web: www.marineproductscorp.com

CEO: Richard A. Hubbell
CFO: Ben M. Palmer
HR: Mary Largent
FYE: December 31
Type: Public

A day on the water for you is a day at the office for Marine Products. The company builds recreational powerboats mainly though its Chaparral subsidiary. Its lineup includes fiberglass sterndrive and inboard deckboats cruisers and sport yachts ranging from 18 feet to 42 feet. Marine Products also makes a line of freshwater/saltwater sport fishing boats known for their "unsinkable hull" through subsidiary Robalo. Boats are sold to a network of about 200 independent dealers who then sell the lines to retail customers. The US generates the majority of the company's sales.

	Annual Growth	12/10	12/11	12/12	12/13	12/14
Sales ($ mil.)	14.1%	101.0	106.4	149.0	168.3	171.1
Net income ($ mil.)	23.3%	3.9	6.7	7.0	7.5	8.9
Market value ($ mil.)	6.1%	254.0	189.1	218.1	383.2	321.8
Employees	13.9%	360	450	587	651	605

MARINEMAX INC

NYS: HZO

2600 McCormick Drive, Suite 200
Clearwater, FL 33759
Phone: 727 531-1700
Fax: –
Web: www.marinemax.com

CEO: William H. McGill
CFO: Michael H. (Mike) McLamb
HR: –
FYE: September 30
Type: Public

MarineMax aims to float your boat. The nation's largest recreational boat dealer has about 54 locations in around 19 states. Dealerships sell new and used pleasure boats fishing boats motor yachts ski boats and high-performance boats. Sales of new boats made by Brunswick including Sea Ray and Boston Whaler boats account for around 48% of revenue. The company also sells boat engines trailers parts and accessories; arranges for financing and insurance; provides repair and maintenance; and offers boat brokerage and storage services. MarineMax is the exclusive dealer of Sea Ray in almost all of the areas where it operates. Since its founding in 1998 MarineMax has acquired about 20 boat dealers.

	Annual Growth	09/11	09/12	09/13	09/14	09/15
Sales ($ mil.)	11.8%	480.9	524.5	584.5	624.7	751.4
Net income ($ mil.)	–	(11.5)	1.1	15.0	11.3	48.3
Market value ($ mil.)	21.6%	156.6	200.6	295.2	407.8	341.9
Employees	1.7%	1,203	1,170	1,227	1,228	1,289

MARIST COLLEGE

3399 NORTH RD
POUGHKEEPSIE, NY 126011387
Phone: 845-575-3000
Fax: –
Web: www.clubs.marist.edu

CEO: –
CFO: John Pecchia
HR: Deborah (Deb) Raikes-Colbert
FYE: June 30
Type: Private

Marist College is a gem among small private US colleges. The liberal arts college has a enrollment of more than 6300 students and a student-faculty ratio of 16-to-1. It offers more than 40 bachelor's and a dozen master's programs as well as some 20 certificate programs. It seven schools specialize in communication and the arts computer science and math continuing education liberal arts management science and social and behavioral sciences. In addition to its main 210-acre campus along the shores of the Hudson River the college has several off-campus extension sites that mainly cater to adult students. Marist was founded in 1929 to train new members in the Marist Brothers order of Catholic priests.

	Annual Growth	06/07	06/08	06/09	06/10	06/13
Sales ($ mil.)	–	–	0.0	159.1	211.8	228.9
Net income ($ mil.)	–	–	–	0.0	47.1	33.7
Market value ($ mil.)	–	–	–	–	–	–
Employees	–	–	–	–	–	750

MARITZ HOLDINGS INC.

1375 N HIGHWAY DR
FENTON, MO 630990001
Phone: 636-827-4000
Fax: –
Web: www.maritztravel.com

CEO: W. Stephen (Steve) Maritz
CFO: Rick Ramos
HR: David (Dave) Estes
FYE: March 31
Type: Private

Maritz may not send your employees on business trips but it will motivate them to go. The company's mission is to understand enable and motivate people to unleash their hidden potential enabling people to do things differently by developing their strengths knowledge and confidence. The Steve Maritz-owned company designs employee incentive and reward programs (including incentive travel rewards) and customer loyalty programs. It also plans corporate trade shows and events and offers traditional market research services such as the creation of product launch campaigns. Its programs are designed to help its clients improve workforce quality and customer satisfaction.

	Annual Growth	03/10	03/11	03/12	03/13	03/14
Sales ($ mil.)	1.7%	–	1,158.2	1,155.6	1,256.0	1,218.9
Net income ($ mil.)	54.8%	–	–	47.3	42.1	113.5
Market value ($ mil.)	–	–	–	–	–	–
Employees	–	–	–	–	–	2,955

MARITZ RESEARCH INC.

1355 N. Highway Dr.
Fenton MO 63099
Phone: 877-462-7489
Fax: 636-827-8605
Web: www.maritzresearch.com

CEO: Michael Brereton
CFO: –
HR: –
FYE: March 31
Type: Subsidiary

Maritz Research provides custom market research services primarily for clients in the automotive financial telecommunications and hospitality industries. The company's research areas include customer loyalty and satisfaction employee satisfaction surveys and retail pricing. Its Maritz Poll measures consumer opinions and attitudinal behaviors and is reported on CNN Reuters USA TODAY and other major media outlets. Maritz Research operates through about a dozen offices in the US Canada Germany and the UK and its clients have included Bank of America Pizza Hut Enterprise Rent-A-Car and General Motors. Founded in 1973 Maritz Research is a subsidiary of motivational marketing firm Maritz.

MARK IV LLC

501 John James Audubon Pkwy.
Amherst NY 14226-0810
Phone: 716-689-4972
Fax: 301-987-4438
Web: www.sodexousa.com

CEO: Mark G Barberio
CFO: Joe Greco
HR: James Gramkee
FYE: February 28
Type: Private

Mark IV aims to make its mark in the auto industry through its assortment of components and belts. The company designs and manufactures power transmission components and an array of belts including timing belts poly-rib belts and raw edge belts. Its rigid components division manufacturers dampers idlers pulleys and tensioners. Mark IV sells to OEMs and aftermarket parts suppliers in the Americas Asia and Europe. The company traces its roots back to 1969 when Salvatore Alfiero and Clement Arrison founded Mark IV Homes as a Pennsylvania-based maker of mobile homes.

MARKEL CORP (HOLDING CO)

NYS: MKL

4521 Highwoods Parkway
Glen Allen, VA 23060-6148
Phone: 804 747-0136
Fax: –
Web: www.markelcorp.com

CEO: Alan I. Kirshner
CFO: Anne G. Waleski
HR: –
FYE: December 31
Type: Public

Have you ever thought about who insures the manicurist or an antique motorcycle? Specialty insurer Markel takes on the risks other insurers won't touch from amusement parks to thoroughbred horses to summer camps. Coverage is also available for one-time events such as golf tournaments and auto races. The company provides customized direct and facultative placements in the US and abroad as well as treaty reinsurance. Markel International provides specialty insurance internationally from its base in the UK and Alterra handles specialty insurance and reinsurance in the US and parts of Europe and Latin America. Meanwhile subsidiary Markel Ventures invests in non-insurance companies.

	Annual Growth	12/10	12/11	12/12	12/13	12/14
Assets ($ mil.)	23.5%	10,825.6	11,532.1	12,556.6	23,955.5	25,200.4
Net income ($ mil.)	4.9%	267.7	148.5	258.2	283.8	323.7
Market value ($ mil.)	15.9%	5,279.3	5,789.5	6,051.3	8,102.7	9,533.6
Employees	15.7%	4,800	5,400	6,400	7,200	8,600

MARKET & JOHNSON INC.

2350 GALLOWAY ST
EAU CLAIRE, WI 547033441
Phone: 608-784-9651
Fax: –
Web: www.market-johnson.com

CEO: Dan Market
CFO: –
HR: –
FYE: December 31
Type: Private

Market & Johnson provides commercial construction and general contracting services in western Wisconsin. It offers a full range of services ranging from the planning and preliminary design stages through delivery and maintenance. The company operates in the industrial commercial government health care religion and education markets. Projects range from large buildings to small remodeling jobs. Juel Market and Milt Johnson founded the company as a home builder in 1948. Today Market & Johnson is owned by a group of five principal managers including CEO Dan Market.

	Annual Growth	12/09	12/10	12/11	12/12	12/13
Sales ($ mil.)	(3.7%)	–	116.9	84.6	107.3	104.4
Net income ($ mil.)	80.4%	–	–	1.5	6.2	5.0
Market value ($ mil.)	–	–	–	–	–	–
Employees	–	–	–	–	–	250

MARKET AMERICA INC.

1302 PLEASANT RIDGE RD
GREENSBORO, NC 274099415
Phone: 336-605-0040
Fax: –
Web: www.marketamerica.com

CEO: –
CFO: –
HR: Joe Bolyard
FYE: December 31
Type: Private

Calling itself a cross between Amazon and QVC Market America is an Internet marketer and broker of products and services from a variety of categories including apparel beauty and personal care electronics entertainment nutrition and sports. Market America sells more than 2500 of its own branded products (such as Isotonix Motives and Snap) and spotlights the offerings of more than 3000 other retailers (including Sears Staples and Wal-Mart) on its SHOP.COM web site (acquired in 2010). In addition the company manages UnFranchise a network marketing business with more than 180000 independent shopping consultants. The company was founded in 1992 by president and CEO James "JR" Ridinger.

	Annual Growth	12/05	12/06	12/07	12/08	12/09
Sales ($ mil.)	1.5%	–	–	218.0	229.0	224.5
Net income ($ mil.)	106006.5%	–	–	0.0	3.5	15.8
Market value ($ mil.)	–	–	–	–	–	–
Employees	–	–	–	–	–	650

MARKET STRATEGIES INTERNATIONAL

17430 College Pkwy.
Livonia MI 48152
Phone: 734-542-7600
Fax: 734-542-7620
Web: www.marketstrategies.com

CEO: Rob Stone PHD
CFO: Philip Giroux
HR: –
FYE: December 31
Type: Private

Market Strategies International (MSI) offers full-service custom and syndicated research as well as strategic consulting services to clients in such industries as energy health care financial services information technology and telecommunications. Its research specialties include customer satisfaction measurement market segmentation product and service evaluation and e-commerce assessment. The company also works with customers to better assess develop and position their brands. Founded in 1989 the firm has been steadily growing through acquisitions and operates out of several offices across the US and overseas.

MARKETAXESS HOLDINGS INC.

NMS: MKTX

299 Park Avenue, 10th Floor
New York, NY 10171
Phone: 212 813-6000
Fax: 212 813-6390
Web: www.marketaxess.com

CEO: Richard M. (Rick) McVey
CFO: Antonio L. (Tony) DeLise
HR: Anat Weiss
FYE: December 31
Type: Public

A little creative spelling never got in the way of a good bond trade. MarketAxess offers an electronic multi-dealer platform for institutional traders buying and selling US corporate high-yield and emerging market bonds as well as Eurobonds. Participating broker-dealers include some of the world's largest such as BNP Paribas Citigroup Deutsche Bank Goldman Sachs and Merrill Lynch. In all MarketAxess serves more than 1000 investment firms mutual funds insurance companies pension funds and other institutional investors. The company also provides real-time corporate bond price information through its Corporate BondTicker service.

	Annual Growth	12/10	12/11	12/12	12/13	12/14
Sales ($ mil.)	15.8%	146.2	181.1	198.2	238.7	262.8
Net income ($ mil.)	24.2%	31.4	47.7	60.1	76.0	74.8
Market value ($ mil.)	36.2%	776.6	1,123.7	1,317.4	2,497.7	2,676.1
Employees	7.3%	229	232	240	293	303

MARKETO INC

NMS: MKTO

901 Mariners Island Boulevard, Suite 500
San Mateo, CA 94404
Phone: 650 376-2300
Fax: –
Web: www.marketo.com

CEO: Phillip M. (Phil) Fernandez
CFO: Frederick A. (Fred) Ball
HR: Joan Burke
FYE: December 31
Type: Public

Marketo is making its mark among marketing professionals. The company's marketing automation software comprehensively manages marketing campaigns from email marketing and social media to event planning lead management and analytics to measure each campaign's effectiveness. Its software serves as a database to store current and potential customer data in order to track transactions and facilitate future sales. The software-as-a-service (SaaS) platform can be integrated into customer relationship management (CRM) programs such as salesforce.com Oracle and SAP. Marketo's products are designed to serve both small and large businesses. Founded in 2006 the company went public in 2013.

	Annual Growth	12/10	12/11	12/12	12/13	12/14
Sales ($ mil.)	80.8%	14.0	32.4	58.4	95.9	150.0
Net income ($ mil.)	–	(11.8)	(22.6)	(34.4)	(47.4)	(54.3)
Market value ($ mil.)	(11.7%)	–	–	–	1,537.7	1,357.3
Employees	38.5%	–	–	373	519	715

MARKETTOOLS INC.

150 Spear St.
San Francisco CA 94105-1535
Phone: 415-957-2200
Fax: 415-957-2180
Web: www.markettools.com

CEO: Jan Willem Gerritsen
CFO: –
HR: –
FYE: December 31
Type: Private

MarketTools gives businesses a peek inside their customers' heads. The company provides Web-based online market research services and customer survey technologies helping clients conduct customer satisfaction research develop products and test new concepts in the marketplace. Among the company's offerings are Zoomerang a customizable survey template; and TrueSample a market research sample verification technology. MarketTools has served clients from a range of industries including such corporate giants as Canon Del Monte and Tyco International's fire and security system subsidiary SimplexGrinnell. MarketTools was bought in 2012 by online market research company MetrixLab.

MARKETWATCH INC.

201 California St. 13th Fl.
San Francisco CA 94111
Phone: 415-439-6400
Fax: 415-439-6485
Web: www.marketwatch.com

CEO: Larry S Kramer
CFO: Paul Mattison
HR: –
FYE: December 31
Type: Subsidiary

This company makes business its business. MarketWatch (formerly MarketWatch.com) operates a business news and information website that serves up headline news analysis and stock market data to an audience of more than 10 million people per month. In addition to news and up-to-the-minute market information its MarketWatch.com offers personal finance advice tools for investing and industry research. Its MarketWatch Radio Network broadcasts business-news programming to more than 200 radio stations nation-wide. MarketWatch is owned by news giant and Wall Street Journal publisher Dow Jones & Company itself a subsidiary of News Corporation. It operates as part of The Wall Street Journal Digital Network.

MARKWEST ENERGY PARTNERS L.P.

NYS: MWE

1515 Arapahoe Street, Tower 1, Suite 1600
Denver, CO 80202-2137
Phone: 303 925-9200
Fax: –

CEO: Frank M Semple
CFO: Nancy K Buese
HR: –
FYE: December 31
Type: Public

MarkWest Energy Partners marks its territory as an alpha dog in the US midstream markets. It has oil natural gas natural gas liquids and gathering and processing pipelines as well as storage terminals and fractionation plants. Its Northeast (Appalachia and Michigan) segment includes processing and storing plants and Southwest (Texas and Oklahoma) has port pipeline processing and treating facilities. MarkWest's Liberty segment operates natural gas processing fractionating storage and marketing facilities in the Marcellus Shale play while its Utica segment consists of a joint venture with The Energy & Minerals Group to develop natural gas infrastructure in the Utica Shale play in Ohio.

	Annual Growth	12/09	12/10	12/11	12/12	12/13
Sales ($ mil.)	22.5%	738.3	1,187.6	1,505.4	1,451.8	1,662.4
Net income ($ mil.)	–	(118.7)	0.5	60.7	220.4	38.1
Market value ($ mil.)	22.6%	5,085.1	7,524.2	9,565.6	8,862.0	11,488.8
Employees	21.7%	520	590	683	881	1,139

MARLABS INCORPORATED

1 Corporate Place South
Piscataway NJ 08854
Phone: 732-287-7800
Fax: 732-465-0100
Web: www.marlabs.com

CEO: Vadakekkara Siby A
CFO: Krishnan Ramachandran
HR: –
FYE: March 31
Type: Private

Marlabs will help you mind your claims. The company is an information technology consultant that provides services such as application development maintenance business process outsourcing (BPO) data warehousing enterprise resource planning (ERP) and consulting. Its Web-based MCO Central software suite is used by managed health care organizations to process workers' compensation claims. MCO Central also automates the claims management process from the initial injury report through bill payment. Marlabs has satellite offices in Pennsylvania and Canada as well as three delivery centers India. Customers include The New York Times Tekelec and Toys R Us. Marlabs was founded in 1996 by CEO Siby Vadakekkar.

MARLIN BUSINESS SERVICES CORP

NMS: MRLN

300 Fellowship Road
Mount Laurel, NJ 08054
Phone: 888 479-9111
Fax: –
Web: www.marlincorp.com

CEO: Edward J. (Ed) Siciliano
CFO: W. Taylor Kamp
HR: –
FYE: December 31
Type: Public

Marlin is hooked on equipment leasing. Marlin Business Services leases more than 100 categories of commercial equipment to more than 60000 small and midsized businesses — and it provides the financing for the deals in part through its Marlin Business Bank subsidiary. The market is known in the equipment leasing field as the "small-ticket" segment. Copiers makes up about 30% of Marlin's lease portfolio but its customers also can get products as diverse as computer hardware and software security systems telecom equipment dental implant systems water filtration systems and restaurant equipment. The company primarily operates through its main subsidiary Marlin Leasing.

	Annual Growth	12/10	12/11	12/12	12/13	12/14
Sales ($ mil.)	7.4%	66.6	62.2	70.9	83.7	88.8
Net income ($ mil.)	35.9%	5.7	6.2	11.7	16.2	19.4
Market value ($ mil.)	12.9%	162.4	163.0	257.5	323.5	263.6
Employees	5.1%	234	242	265	285	285

MARQUETTE UNIVERSITY

1250 W WISCONSIN AVE
MILWAUKEE, WI 532332225
Phone: 414-288-7223
Fax: –
Web: www.marquette.edu

CEO: –
CFO: John C Lamb
HR: –
FYE: June 30
Type: Private

A member of the Association of Jesuit Colleges and Universities Marquette University provides undergraduate graduate and professional courses and programs. It specializes in business engineering arts and sciences nursing law dentistry and other fields. The university offers undergraduates some 75 majors and 65 minors and post-graduate students about 50 doctoral and master's degree programs. With an enrollment of more than 11700 students Marquette University boasts a student/faculty ratio of 14:1. Its student population consists of students from all 50 US states and nearly 70 countries. Founded in 1881 the university is named after French missionary explorer Father Jacques Marquette.

	Annual Growth	06/09	06/10	06/11	06/12	06/13
Sales ($ mil.)	(4.5%)	–	449.1	383.1	385.1	391.2
Net income ($ mil.)	(36.0%)	–	–	90.8	9.4	37.2
Market value ($ mil.)	–	–	–	–	–	–
Employees	–	–	–	–	–	3,000

MARRIOTT INTERNATIONAL, INC.

NMS: MAR

10400 Fernwood Road
Bethesda, MD 20817
Phone: 301 380-3000
Fax: –
Web: www.marriott.com

CEO: Arne M. Sorenson
CFO: Leeny K. Oberg
HR: David A. Rodriguez
FYE: December 31
Type: Public

Marriott International signs in at the top of the lodging industry. The company is one of the world's leading hoteliers with some 4300 operated or franchised properties worldwide. Its hotels include such full-service brands as Renaissance Hotels and its flagship Marriott Hotels & Resorts as well as select-service and extended-stay brands Courtyard and Fairfield Inn. It also owns the Ritz-Carlton luxury chain and resort and manages about 45 golf courses. The Marriott family including J. W. Marriott Jr. owns about 30% of Marriott International.

	Annual Growth	12/10	12/11	12/12	12/13	12/14
Sales ($ mil.)	4.2%	11,691.0	12,317.0	11,814.0	12,784.0	13,796.0
Net income ($ mil.)	13.2%	458.0	198.0	571.0	626.0	753.0
Market value ($ mil.)	17.1%	11,627.0	8,164.7	10,210.8	13,813.3	21,840.6
Employees	(1.1%)	129,000	120,000	127,000	123,000	123,500

MARRIOTT VACATIONS WORLDWIDE CORP.

NYS: VAC

6649 Westwood Blvd.
Orlando, FL 32821
Phone: 407 206-6000
Fax: –
Web: www.marriottvacationsworldwide.com

CEO: Stephen P. (Steve) Weisz
CFO: John E. Geller
HR: Michael E. (Mike) Yonker
FYE: January 02
Type: Public

Sometimes it pays to share. Marriott Vacations Worldwide formerly part of hotel giant Marriott International operates more than 50 timeshare resort properties with one- two- and three bedroom villas in prime vacation destinations in the US (such as California Colorado Florida Hawaii and Nevada) and a handful of other countries (Aruba France Spain St. Thomas the West Indies and Thailand). The villas are jointly owned by about 400000 people who have exclusive use of the properties for limited periods of time. Owners can also trade intervals for time at other Marriott Vacation Club resorts or for other rewards programs. Marriott spun off Marriott Vacations as a separately-traded company in 2011.

	Annual Growth	12/10	12/11	12/12*	01/14	01/15
Sales ($ mil.)	1.8%	1,584.0	1,613.0	1,648.0	1,750.0	1,736.0
Net income ($ mil.)	3.9%	67.0	(178.0)	16.0	80.0	81.0
Market value ($ mil.)	44.3%	–	550.7	1,310.3	1,690.0	2,385.5
Employees	0.8%	–	9,700	9,500	10,000	10,000

*Fiscal year change

MARRONE BIO INNOVATIONS INC

NMS: MBII

1540 Drew Avenue
Davis, CA 95618
Phone: 530 750-2800
Fax: –
Web: www.marronebioinnovations.com

CEO: Pamela G Marrone
CFO: James B Boyd
HR: –
FYE: December 31
Type: Public

Marrone Bio Innovations makes pesticide a little less poisonous. The company's biopesticides are made from eco-friendly ingredients such as plant extracts bacterium or fungus. Marrone Bio Innovations has three products on the market and three in development awaiting EPA approval. Its pesticide Grandevo contains bacteria that repels plant-eating insects and kills them if ingested. The company's plant extract-based fungicide Regalia is also used as a seed treatment for corn cotton and soybeans and Zequanox kills mussels found in water pipes. Its products are primarily sold to vegetable growers as alternatives to conventional agricultural chemicals. Marrone Bio Innovations went public in 2013.

	Annual Growth	12/10	12/11	12/12	12/13	12/14
Sales ($ mil.)	–	0.0	5.3	7.1	14.5	9.1
Net income ($ mil.)	–	0.0	(13.2)	(38.8)	(28.5)	(51.7)
Market value ($ mil.)	–	0.0	–	–	435.0	88.3
Employees	(11.2%)	–	–	109	151	86

MARS INCORPORATED

6885 Elm St.
McLean VA 22101-3810
Phone: 703-821-4900
Fax: 703-448-9678
Web: www.mars.com

CEO: –
CFO: Reuben Gamoran
HR: –
FYE: December 31
Type: Private

Mars knows chocolate sales are nothing to snicker at. It makes such worldwide favorites as M&M's Snickers and the Mars bar. Other confections include 3 Musketeers Dove Milky Way Skittles and Twix. Its products portfolio also boasts Seeds of Change organic food the Klix and Flavia beverage systems Combos and Kudos snacks Uncle Ben's rice and pet food made under the Pedigree Sheba and Whiskas labels. Mars owns the world's largest chewing gum maker Wm. Wrigley Jr. Company as well. The Mars family — including siblings and chairman John Franklyn Mars VP Jacqueline Badger Mars and former CEO Forrest Mars Jr. — owns the highly secretive company making the family one of the wealthiest in the US.

MARS PETCARE US INC.

315 Cool Springs Blvd.
Franklin TN 37067
Phone: 615-807-4626
Fax: 214-342-2062
Web: www.bearcom.com

CEO: Douglas J Cahill
CFO: Philip K Woodlief
HR: Catherine Walker
FYE: December 31
Type: Subsidiary

Mars Petcare US has no quibble with kibble. A leading manufacturer of dry pet foods in the US with some 15 production plants nationwide the company makes dry pet foods soft-dry food soft treats and dog biscuits under the Cesar Pedigree Royal Canin and Whiskas brands among others. Mars Petcare also makes products for other pet food companies manufactures store brands for its retail customers and sells its own regional brands. Its customers include mass merchandisers (such as Wal-Mart Meijer) pet supply chains (PETCO PetSmart) supermarkets and farm and feed stores. The company was founded in 1954 as Doane Products and is part of candy and pet food behemoth Mars' pet care division.

MARS SUPER MARKETS INC

9627 PHILADELPHIA RD   CEO: –
BALTIMORE, MD 212374154   CFO: –
Phone: 410-590-0500   HR: Lisa Schautz
Fax: –   FYE: December 26
Web: www.marsfood.com   Type: Private

Whether men and women hail from Mars or Venus Mars Super Markets pays no mind: both sexes eat! The company is a chain of about 15 grocery stores in the Baltimore area. Founded by Joseph D'Anna in 1943 and still owned and run by the D'Anna family Mars Super Markets began in the middle of the Mars Estates military housing community. The regional supermarket chain supplies products to its store locations from its own 300000 sq. ft. distribution center in Baltimore offers a line of its own private label products and sells produce and seafood from local markets.

	Annual Growth	12/03	12/04	12/05	12/06	12/09
Sales ($ mil.)	–	–	0.0	267.5	301.0	280.9
Net income ($ mil.)	(17.5%)	–	–	14.2	11.6	6.6
Market value ($ mil.)	–	–	–	–	–	–
Employees	–	–	–	–	–	1,700

MARSH & MCLENNAN COMPANIES INC.   NYS: MMC

1166 Avenue Of The Americas   CEO: Julio A. Portalatin
New York, NY 10036   CFO: Mark C. McGivney
Phone: 212 345-5000   HR: Sarah Randall
Fax: 212 345-4809   FYE: December 31
Web: www.mmc.com   Type: Public

Marsh & McLennan Companies (MMC) is the ultimate insurance middleman. The company is one of the world's largest insurance brokers. Through core subsidiary Marsh the company provides a broad array of insurance-related brokerage consulting and risk management services to clients in more than 130 countries including large and small companies government entities and not-for-profit organizations. Its global reinsurance brokerage business is handled by subsidiary Guy Carpenter. MMC also owns Mercer which provides human resources and financial consulting services to customers in 40 nations worldwide and Oliver Wyman which provides management consulting services.

	Annual Growth	12/10	12/11	12/12	12/13	12/14
Sales ($ mil.)	5.3%	10,550.0	11,526.0	11,924.0	12,261.0	12,951.0
Net income ($ mil.)	14.4%	855.0	993.0	1,176.0	1,357.0	1,465.0
Market value ($ mil.)	20.3%	14,767.5	17,079.3	18,618.7	26,121.3	30,917.7
Employees	2.8%	51,000	52,400	54,000	55,000	57,000

MARSH SUPERMARKETS INC.

9800 Crosspoint Blvd.   CEO: Frank Lazaran
Indianapolis IN 46256   CFO: Robert J Riesbeck
Phone: 317-594-2100   HR: –
Fax: 715-926-5609   FYE: March 31
Web: www.marten.com   Type: Private

Marsh Supermarkets is no backwater grocery chain. A leading retailer in Indianapolis (behind Kroger and Wal-Mart) Marsh operates about 95 supermarkets under the Marsh Supermarkets O'Malia's Food Markets and Main Street Markets banners in Indiana and Ohio. About 40% of the stores have pharmacy departments. Its floral business — Marsh Floral Fashions — operates floral and gift departments inside Marsh stores. Marsh abandoned self-distribution in 2011 and turned over the supply of all of its stores to C&S Wholesale Grocers. Founded in 1931 by the late Ermal Marsh the regional supermarket operator is owned by private equity firm Sun Capital Partners.

MARSH USA INC.

1166 Avenue of the Americas   CEO: Peter Zaffino
New York NY 10036-2774   CFO: –
Phone: 212-345-6000   HR: –
Fax: 212-345-4808   FYE: December 31
Web: www.marsh.com   Type: Subsidiary

Marsh is the flagship operation of Marsh & McLennan Companies (MMC) one of the world's largest insurance brokerages. The company brokers insurance and provides risk management and consulting services to corporate clients government agencies and other organizations big and small. Marsh has some 25000 agents and hundreds of brokerage locations in more than 100 countries. Marsh also provides risk financing insurance program design and underwriting management as well as claims administration and technological support services. MMC affiliate Guy Carpenter provides similar brokerage and risk management services to reinsurance companies; other MMC companies include consulting firms Mercer and Oliver Wyman.

MARSHALL UNIVERSITY

1 JOHN MARSHALL DR   CEO: Ronald Area
HUNTINGTON, WV 257550003   CFO: Mary E. Heuton
Phone: 304-696-2385   HR: –
Fax: –   FYE: June 30
Web: www.marshall.edu   Type: Private

If "You Are Marshall" you know that Marshall University is a state-supported non-profit educational institution serving about 14000 students including 3500 graduate and medical students. The university offers about 55 baccalaureate and more than 50 graduate programs through more than a dozen colleges and schools. It also offers two Associate Programs two Ed.S four Doctoral Degree Programs and three First Professional programs. Marshall students attend classes either at the university's main campus in Huntington West Virginia; at its regional campuses; or online.

	Annual Growth	06/07	06/08	06/12	06/13	06/14
Sales ($ mil.)	0.2%	–	172.9	175.0	175.8	174.8
Net income ($ mil.)	32.2%	–	–	19.4	26.2	33.8
Market value ($ mil.)	–	–	–	–	–	–
Employees	–	–	–	–	–	1,632

MARSHFIELD CLINIC INC.

1000 N OAK AVE   CEO: –
MARSHFIELD, WI 544495702   CFO: Gary Jankowski
Phone: 715-387-5511   HR: –
Fax: –   FYE: September 30
Web: www.marshfieldclinic.org   Type: Private

Marshfield Clinic is a private group medical practice that operates more than 50 medical locations across Wisconsin. The network provides primary and tertiary care through its more than 700 physicians who represent about 80 medical specialties. Through two hospitals — the 25-bed Flambeau Hospital and the 40-bed Lakeview Medical Center — and dozens of clinics Marshfield annually serves roughly 380000 patients and handles 3.8 million patient encounters. Other parts of the network include Marshfield Laboratories and Security Health Plan of Wisconsin as well as medical education and research organizations.

	Annual Growth	09/06	09/07	09/08	09/09	09/13
Sales ($ mil.)	62.8%	–	–	102.3	1,062.8	1,171.1
Net income ($ mil.)	24.7%	–	–	6.0	78.8	18.2
Market value ($ mil.)	–	–	–	–	–	–
Employees	–	–	–	–	–	6,900

MARTEN TRANSPORT, LTD.

NMS: MRTN

129 Marten Street
Mondovi, WI 54755
Phone: 715 926-4216
Fax: –
Web: www.marten.com

CEO: Randolph L. (Randy) Marten
CFO: James J. (Jim) Hinnendael
HR: –
FYE: December 31
Type: Public

America's Dairyland-based Marten Transport hauls a lot more than cheese. The Wisconsin-based long-haul truckload carrier uses refrigerated and insulated trailers to convey a variety of food products and other temperature-sensitive materials; it also hauls dry freight. Marten Transport operates in 14 terminals throughout the US and also operates in Canada and Mexico; its average haul is about 600 miles. The company's fleet includes about 2420 tractors and 4265 trailers. In addition to freight transportation the company provides logistics services. In 2014 Marten Transport's largest customers were Wal-Mart and supply chain services provider Armada.

	Annual Growth	12/10	12/11	12/12	12/13	12/14
Sales ($ mil.)	6.8%	516.9	603.7	638.5	659.2	672.9
Net income ($ mil.)	10.9%	19.7	24.3	27.3	30.1	29.8
Market value ($ mil.)	0.6%	714.5	601.2	614.6	674.7	730.5
Employees	4.5%	2,764	2,835	2,982	3,094	3,292

MARTHA STEWART LIVING OMNIMEDIA, INC.

NYS: MSO

601 West 26th Street
New York, NY 10001
Phone: 212 827-8000
Fax: –
Web: www.marthastewart.com

CEO: Daniel W Dienst
CFO: Kenneth P West
HR: –
FYE: December 31
Type: Public

Martha Stewart Living Omnimedia (MSLO) seems to prove the old adage that all publicity is good publicity. Legendary lifestyle maven Martha Stewart and her company MSLO have embraced the media spotlight including Stewart's much ballyhooed sentence on federal criminal charges related to insider trading of stock. The domestic guru has her fingers in many revenue-generating pies that center around three business segments: publishing (magazines books websites) broadcasting (TV programs satellite radio) and merchandising. The majority of MSLO's business comes from publishing activities which are driven by its flagship magazine Martha Stewart Living.

	Annual Growth	12/09	12/10	12/11	12/12	12/13
Sales ($ mil.)	(10.0%)	244.8	230.8	221.4	197.6	160.7
Net income ($ mil.)	–	(14.6)	(9.6)	(15.5)	(56.1)	(1.8)
Market value ($ mil.)	(4.0%)	279.8	250.3	249.2	138.7	237.8
Employees	(10.1%)	620	615	582	497	405

MARTIN & BAYLEY INC.

1311A W MAIN ST
CARMI, IL 628211389
Phone: 618-382-2334
Fax: –
Web: www.martinandbayley.com

CEO: –
CFO: –
HR: Audrey L Elwood
FYE: March 29
Type: Private

Martin & Bayley (dba Huck's Food and Fuel) operates 115 Huck's convenience stores and a number travel centers in mostly in Illinois and Indiana but also in Missouri Kentucky and Tennessee. Half of its outlets are in Illinois. The company operates a commissary at its warehouse in Carmi Illinois to supply sandwiches chicken and other food items to its stores. Some stores sell Godfather's Pizza. Family-owned since its inception Martin & Bayley became a 100% employee-owned firm when the Martin and Bayley families sold their stakes in the company.

	Annual Growth	03/07	03/08	03/09	03/10	03/11
Sales ($ mil.)	–	–	–	(1,579.4)	466.2	528.9
Net income ($ mil.)	12031.5%	–	–	0.0	5.3	7.5
Market value ($ mil.)	–	–	–	–	–	–
Employees	–	–	–	–	–	1,500

MARTIN MARIETTA MATERIALS, INC.

NYS: MLM

2710 Wycliff Road
Raleigh, NC 27607-3033
Phone: 919 781-4550
Fax: –
Web: www.martinmarietta.com

CEO: C. Howard (Ward) Nye
CFO: Anne H. Lloyd
HR: Jonathan T (Jon) Stewart
FYE: December 31
Type: Public

Martin Marietta Materials (MMM) is a rock star. The company is the #1 US producer (following its purchase of Texas Industries) of aggregates for highway infrastructure commercial and residential construction. Its Martin Marietta Aggregates unit produces more than 125 million tons of granite gravel limestone and sand annually. Aggregates represents nearly 85% of MMM's sales. The company's Magnesia Specialties unit produces magnesia-based chemicals for industrial environmental and agricultural uses as well as fiber-reinforced composite materials for transportation and military applications. MMM was formed in 1993 from the quarries business of aerospace giant Martin Marietta Corp. (now Lockheed Martin).

	Annual Growth	12/10	12/11	12/12	12/13	12/14
Sales ($ mil.)	13.5%	1,782.9	1,713.8	2,037.7	2,155.6	2,958.0
Net income ($ mil.)	12.5%	97.0	82.4	84.5	121.3	155.6
Market value ($ mil.)	4.6%	6,207.1	5,074.6	6,344.4	6,725.3	7,423.8
Employees	12.4%	4,500	4,993	4,948	5,036	7,193

MARTIN MIDSTREAM PARTNERS LP

NMS: MMLP

4200 Stone Road
Kilgore, TX 75662
Phone: 903 983-6200
Fax: –
Web: www.martinmidstream.com

CEO: Ruben S Martin
CFO: Robert D Bondurant
HR: –
FYE: December 31
Type: Public

Martin Midstream Partners moves petroleum products. The company gets most of its sales from the distribution of natural gas liquids (NGLs). Its NGL customers include retail propane distributors industrial processors and refiners. Martin Midstream owns more than 720 miles of natural gas gathering and transmission pipelines. Martin Midstream also manufactures sulfur and sulfur-based fertilizer products and provides marine transportation (through a fleet of more than 50 inland barges and push boats and four offshore tug barges) and the storage of liquid hydrocarbons (at about 50 terminals). The company an affiliate of Martin Resource Management operates primarily in the Gulf Coast region of the US.

	Annual Growth	12/10	12/11	12/12	12/13	12/14
Sales ($ mil.)	15.8%	912.1	1,237.1	1,490.4	1,633.5	1,642.1
Net income ($ mil.)	–	16.0	24.3	102.0	(13.4)	(11.7)
Market value ($ mil.)	(9.1%)	1,392.4	1,218.2	1,098.5	1,513.7	950.6
Employees	–	–	–	–	–	–

MARTIN'S SUPER MARKETS INC.

760 W. Cotter St.
South Bend IN 46613
Phone: 574-234-5848
Fax: 574-234-9827
Web: www.martins-supermarkets.com

CEO: –
CFO: –
HR: Krista Wendt
FYE: December 31
Type: Private

It's all in the family at Martin's Super Markets. The regional grocery store chain operates about 20 locations mostly in Indiana but also in southwest Michigan. In addition to catering film processing full-service floral departments and traditional supermarket fare Martin's offers ready-made meals for busy shoppers and about a third of its supermarkets have in-store pharmacies. About a third have fuel centers. The company is adding drive-through pharmacies and local delivery service at some of its stores. It's supplied by Spartan Stores. Founded in 1947 by Jane and Martin Tarnow Martin's Super Markets is still family owned and run by CEO Rob Bartels Jr. (third generation).

MARUBENI AMERICA CORPORATION

375 Lexington Ave.
New York NY 10017
Phone: 212-450-0100
Fax: 212-450-0700
Web: www.marubeni-usa.com

CEO: –
CFO: –
HR: –
FYE: December 31
Type: Subsidiary

For Marubeni America Corporation the trick of the trade is the trade. Marubeni America (MAC) is the primary US subsidiary of Japan-based manufacturing and trading company Marubeni; it acts as an independent trader an importer/exporter brokering deals for agricultural goods commodities consumer and energy products and natural resources. The company which was established in 1951 provides related services such as engineering financing insurance leasing marketing logistics and sales. Marubeni America has offices across the US Canada and Mexico. It also distributes crop protection chemicals through subsidiary Helena Chemical and exports wheat and barley through Columbia Grain.

MARVIN ENGINEERING CO. INC.

261 W BEACH AVE
INGLEWOOD, CA 903022904
Phone: 310-674-5030
Fax: –
Web: www.marvingroup.com

CEO: Gerald M Friedman
CFO: Leon Tsimmerman
HR: –
FYE: January 31
Type: Private

Marvin Engineering helps missiles get from Point A to Point B. The company manufactures missile launchers ejector racks test equipment and other hardware for military customers and companies in the aerospace and defense industries. Customers include branches of the US military and major US defense contractors as well as the governments of Australia Canada and Israel. Marvin Engineering is part of the Marvin Group which also includes Aerospace Dynamics International Flyer Defense Marvin Land Systems Geotest-Marvin Test Systems and Clean Water Technologies.

	Annual Growth	01/05	01/06	01/07	01/08	01/09
Sales ($ mil.)	(19.3%)	–	–	205.5	105.7	133.8
Net income ($ mil.)	–	–	–	0.0	0.6	(3.4)
Market value ($ mil.)	–	–	–	–	–	–
Employees	–	–	–	–	–	700

MARY KAY HOLDING CORPORATION

16251 Dallas Pkwy.
Addison TX 75001-6801
Phone: 972-687-6300
Fax: 972-687-1642
Web: www.marykay.com

CEO: David B Holl
CFO: Terry Smith
HR: Carlos Mallen
FYE: December 31
Type: Holding Company

Mary Kay has been measuring its success by being in the pink rather than being in the red. Mary Kay Holding Corporation is a holding company for cosmetics direct-seller Mary Kay which makes and markets cosmetics women's and men's fragrances skin care and personal care products. It sells some 200 items through an independent sales force of more than 2 million consultants in some 35 global markets. The firm's products portfolio spans half a dozen categories such as body care color cosmetics facial skin care fragrance nail care and sun protection. Brand names include TimeWise Velocity Tribute Journey MKMen Stain Lips Indulge and others. The company was founded in Dallas by Mary Kay Ash in 1963.

MARY KAY INC.

16251 Dallas Pkwy.
Addison TX 75001
Phone: 972-687-6300
Fax: 972-687-1611
Web: www.marykay.com

CEO: David Holl
CFO: Terry Smith
HR: –
FYE: December 31
Type: Private

Celebrating more than 40 years in business Mary Kay is in the pink as one of the top direct sellers of beauty products in the US. It offers more than 200 products in six categories: body care color cosmetics facial skin care fragrance nail care and sun protection. Some 2.4 million independent sales consultants demonstrate Mary Kay products in the US and about 35 other countries; the company also sells products through its website. Consultants vie for awards each year that range from jewelry to its trademark pink Cadillac (first awarded in 1969). The Mary Kay Ash Charitable Foundation funds cancer research and domestic violence programs. The family of founder Mary Kay Ash owns most of the company.

MARYLAND AND VIRGINIA MILK PRODUCERS COOPERATIVE ASSOCIATION INC

1985 ISAAC NEWTON SQ W # 200
RESTON, VA 201905031
Phone: 703-742-6800
Fax: –
Web: www.mdvamilk.com

CEO: –
CFO: Jorge Gonzalez
HR: –
FYE: December 31
Type: Private

Milk is "Mar-VA-lous" for the members of the Maryland & Virginia Milk Producers Cooperative Association. Known as Maryland & Virginia the co-op processes and sells milk for nearly 1500 member/farmers with dairy herds in the southeastern US and mid-Atlantic region. Maryland & Virginia produces fluid milk ice cream and cultured dairy products for retail sale under the Marva Maid Maola and Valley Milk brands. Its butter condensed milk and milk-powder products are sold primarily to food manufacturers. As a co-op it also offers agricultural supplies to its members. Maryland & Virginia operates three fluid-milk processing plants a manufacturing plant and an equipment-supply warehouse.

	Annual Growth	12/09	12/10	12/11	12/12	12/13
Sales ($ mil.)	4.0%	–	1,219.2	1,362.5	1,296.4	1,372.8
Net income ($ mil.)	–	–	–	(2.8)	5.5	5.7
Market value ($ mil.)	–	–	–	–	–	–
Employees	–	–	–	–	–	550

MARYLAND SOUTHERN ELECTRIC COOPERATIVE INC

15035 BURNT STORE RD
HUGHESVILLE, MD 206372699
Phone: 301-274-3111
Fax: –
Web: www.smeco.com

CEO: –
CFO: Sonja M Cox
HR: –
FYE: December 31
Type: Private

Historic Southern Maryland gets it power via the South Maryland Electric Cooperative (SMECO) which distributes electricity to about 154000 residential commercial and industrial customers in four counties via about 11360 miles of power line and 54 electric substations. One of the ten largest electric cooperatives in the US the member-owned enterprise gets its wholesale power supply through its membership in wholesale energy trading and risk management service company ACES Power Marketing. Overseen by a board of directors SMECO's single mission is to provide reliable competitively priced energy and related services to its members.

	Annual Growth	12/06	12/07	12/08	12/09	12/10
Sales ($ mil.)	(51.8%)	–	–	2,121.5	462.7	492.7
Net income ($ mil.)	17166.9%	–	–	0.0	3.2	17.1
Market value ($ mil.)	–	–	–	–	–	–
Employees	–	–	–	–	–	375

MARYMOUNT MANHATTAN COLLEGE

221 E 71ST ST   CEO: –
NEW YORK, NY 100214532   CFO: –
Phone: 212-517-0400   HR: –
Fax: –   FYE: June 30
Web: www.mmm.edu   Type: Private

Marymount Manhattan College is a four-year undergraduate liberal arts college in the middle of New York City with an enrollment of more than 2000 students. Marymount Manhattan offers 17 major programs of study in fields including media technology and performing arts. The college has a student-to-teacher ratio of 12:1. It was originally was founded in 1936 by the Religious of the Sacred Heart of Mary in Tarrytown New York; it was independently chartered in 1961 as Marymount Manhattan College.

	Annual Growth	06/07	06/08	06/09	06/10	06/13
Sales ($ mil.)	–	–	0.0	56.4	49.3	60.7
Net income ($ mil.)	(24.6%)	–	–	4.1	0.9	1.3
Market value ($ mil.)	–	–	–	–	–	–
Employees	–	–	–	–	–	630

MASCO CONTRACTOR SERVICES LLC

2339 Beville Rd.   CEO: –
Daytona Beach FL 32119   CFO: –
Phone: 386-304-2222   HR: Kathy Wiggans
Fax: 386-304-2304   FYE: December 31
Web: www.mascocs.com   Type: Subsidiary

Masco Contractor Services (MCS) has all your home installation needs under one roof. Rather than calling upon multiple companies to have bathtubs cabinets fireplaces gutters and insulation installed MCS offers it all as a single-source supplier and service provider to residential construction contractors in North America. One of the larger subsidiaries of Masco Corporation MCS has a network of 180 branches and 70 distribution sites throughout the US. It primarily serves tract and custom home builders and installs products with such brand names as CertainTeed ClosetMaid Kwikset Leviton and Schlage.

MASCO CORP.   NYS: MAS

21001 Van Born Road   CEO: Keith J. Allman
Taylor, MI 48180   CFO: John G. Sznewajs
Phone: 313-274-7400   HR: Cathy Bacha
Fax: –   FYE: December 31
Web: www.masco.com   Type: Public

Masco's ideal customer is a home improvement junkie with a thing for cabinets — and an obsession with hand-washing. It is a leading manufacturer of a variety of home improvement and building products with cabinet and plumbing products accounting for more than half of its sales. Cabinet brands include KraftMaid Quality Cabinets and Merillat in the US and The Moores Group and Tvilum-Scanbirk in Europe. Faucets and bath and shower accessories are sold under the Delta and Peerless brands in the US and as Hansgrohe in Europe. Masco also makes BEHR paints and stains windows doors staple guns locksets and HVAC products. It spun off its installation services business as TopBuild in 2015.

	Annual Growth	12/11	12/12	12/13	12/14	12/15
Sales ($ mil.)	(1.1%)	7,467.0	7,745.0	8,173.0	8,521.0	7,142.0
Net income ($ mil.)	–	(575.0)	(114.0)	272.0	856.0	355.0
Market value ($ mil.)	28.2%	3,463.6	5,506.1	7,525.5	8,328.6	9,353.2
Employees	(5.2%)	31,000	30,000	32,000	32,000	25,000

MASCOMA CORPORATION

67 Etna Rd. Ste. 300   CEO: William J Brady Jr
Lebanon NH 03766   CFO: –
Phone: 603-676-3320   HR: –
Fax: 603-676-3321   FYE: December 31
Web: www.mascoma.com   Type: Private

One man's trash is another man's brilliant idea. Mascoma Corporation's plan is to make a chemical used in cellulosic ethanol a renewable fuel made from the waste products of plants such as wood and agricultural by-products. The company invented genetically-modified yeasts and bacteria that aid in the fermentation of feedstocks and help turn it into biofuel and other chemicals. So far it has only produced test batches of its Mascoma Grain Technology (MGT) but Mascoma plans to begin selling it commercially to corn ethanol producers in 2012 as a less expensive alternative to other enzymes. The company filed a $100 million initial public offering in September 2011.

MASERGY COMMUNICATIONS INC.

2740 N. Dallas Pkwy. Ste. 260   CEO: Chris Macfarland
Plano TX 75093-4834   CFO: Rob Bodnar
Phone: 214-442-5700   HR: –
Fax: 214-442-5756   FYE: June 30
Web: www.masergy.com   Type: Private

Masergy Communications helps businesses manage vital communications. The company offers managed network and cloud communications services for clients in the financial health care entertainment broadcasting and manufacturing industries among others. Providing voice data and video network services and support across the globe its areas of expertise include Ethernet-based virtual private networks (VPNs) and wide area network (WANs). Masergy's cloud services include global cloud communications network and application management and hosted remote access. Its managed services focus on security and disaster recovery. The company is owned by private equity firm ABRY Partners.

MASIMO CORP.   NMS: MASI

52 Discovery   CEO: Joe E. Kiani
Irvine, CA 92618   CFO: Mark P. de Raad
Phone: 949-297-7000   HR: –
Fax: –   FYE: January 03
Web: www.masimo.com   Type: Public

As important as the blood running through your veins is the oxygen it carries. Masimo knows that and makes tools that monitor arterial blood-oxygen saturation levels and pulse rates in patients. The company's product range which is based on Signal Extraction Technology (SET) offers pulse oximeters in both handheld and stand-alone (bedside) form. Product benefits include the provision of real-time information and elimination of signal interference such as patient movements. In addition to general product sales Masimo licenses SET-based products to dozens of medical equipment manufacturers including CareFusion Covidien Medtronic and Welch Allyn.

	Annual Growth	01/11*	12/11	12/12	12/13*	01/15
Sales ($ mil.)	9.7%	405.4	439.0	493.2	547.2	586.6
Net income ($ mil.)	(0.3%)	73.5	63.7	62.3	58.4	72.5
Market value ($ mil.)	(2.9%)	1,528.9	982.7	1,082.4	1,517.9	1,361.1
Employees	10.7%	2,397	2,548	2,866	3,139	3,600
						*Fiscal year end

MASS. ELECTRIC CONSTRUCTION CO.

180 Guest St.
Boston MA 02135
Phone: 617-254-1015
Fax: 617-254-0706
Web: www.masselec.com

CEO: –
CFO: –
HR: –
FYE: December 31
Type: Subsidiary

One of the leading US electrical contractors Mass. Electric Construction Co. (MEC) has worked on projects for the commercial and industrial (Boeing rocket manufacturing facility) power (Northeast Utilities underground transmission project) life sciences (Merck research center) and transportation industries (Amtrak). Services include design construction consulting budgeting procurement testing and start-up and maintenance. It also offers fire alarm security system and telecommunications cabling installation. The company has offices in about a dozen states across the US and in Puerto Rico. Established in 1928 MEC is a wholly-owned subsidiary of Peter Kiewit Sons'.

MASSACHUSETTS HIGHER EDUCATION ASSISTANCE CORPORATION

100 CAMBRIDGE ST STE 1600
BOSTON, MA 021142518
Phone: 617-728-4507
Fax: –
Web: www.asa.org

CEO: Paul Combe
CFO: Michael F Finn
HR: Lauren Rolfe
FYE: June 30
Type: Private

Don't know how you're going to pay for college? You might want to consult ASA ASAP. The Massachusetts Higher Education Assistance Corporation which does business as American Student Assistance or ASA is a federal student loan guarantor one of the first in the country. The not-for-profit company provides Federal Family Education Loan Program (FFELP) guarantee origination fund delivery and default prevention services to students schools and lenders. ASA serves more than 1.6 million college loans borrowers across the US and manages a student loan portfolio worth more than $40 billion.

	Annual Growth	06/07	06/08	06/09	06/10	06/13
Assets ($ mil.)	80.3%	–	19.7	148.5	170.4	375.5
Net income ($ mil.)	–	–	–	0.0	34.1	48.6
Market value ($ mil.)	–	–	–	–	–	–
Employees	–	–	–	–	–	580

MASSACHUSETTS MEDICAL SOCIETY INC

860 WINTER ST
WALTHAM, MA 024511411
Phone: 781-893-4610
Fax: –
Web: www.nejm.org

CEO: –
CFO: –
HR: Melissa Hennessy
FYE: May 31
Type: Private

The Massachusetts Medical Society (MMS) is a professional organization of physicians and medical students with more than 24000 members. The organization an advocate for patients and physicians promotes a code of ethics for medical professions as well as the training research and continuing education of physicians and other health care professionals. It also helps to develop health care policy and publishes the New England Journal of Medicine a leading medical journal. The Massachusetts Medical Society was founded in 1781 and is the oldest continuously operating medical society in the nation.

	Annual Growth	05/08	05/09	05/10	05/11	05/13
Sales ($ mil.)	(0.2%)	–	–	–	118.9	118.5
Net income ($ mil.)	(21.2%)	–	–	–	19.6	12.2
Market value ($ mil.)	–	–	–	–	–	–
Employees	–	–	–	–	–	700

MASSACHUSETTS MUTUAL LIFE INSURANCE COMPANY

1295 State St.
Springfield MA 01111-0001
Phone: 413-744-1000
Fax: 413-744-6005
Web: www.massmutual.com

CEO: Roger W Crandall
CFO: Michael Rollings
HR: –
FYE: December 31
Type: Private - Mutual Com

Massachusetts Mutual Life Insurance known affectionately as MassMutual brings a multitude of financial services to its membership base. A leading US mutual life insurer the firm provides life policies annuities money management and retirement planning to individuals and businesses in the US and abroad. Founded in 1851 MassMutual also offers disability income insurance long-term care insurance structured settlement annuities and trust services. Its subsidiaries include OppenheimerFunds (mutual funds) Baring Asset Management (international investment) and Babson Capital Management (investor services) with its Cornerstone Real Estate Advisors (real estate investment management) subsidiary.

MASSACHUSETTS PORT AUTHORITY

1 HARBORSIDE DR STE 200S
BOSTON, MA 021282905
Phone: 617-561-1600
Fax: –
Web: www.massport.com

CEO: Thomas P. Glynn
CFO: John Pranckevicius
HR: –
FYE: June 30
Type: Private

Massachusetts Port Authority (Massport) operates three airports: Boston Logan International Hanscom Field and Worcester Regional. Logan is home to 50 airlines and is New England's largest airport and the first port of call for many international flights entering the US. (It accounts for the majority of Massport's revenues.) Hanscom Field operates as the region's main aviation airport and offers niche commercial services while Worcester Regional primarily supports commercial flight services. Massport also oversees various waterfront properties of the Port of Boston. The agency was created by the Commonwealth of Massachusetts in 1956. The governor of Massachusetts appoints the agency's board members.

	Annual Growth	06/03	06/04*	12/05*	06/06	06/07
Sales ($ mil.)	8.3%	–	415.0	0.5	497.6	526.8
Net income ($ mil.)	2940.6%	–	–	0.1	74.6	49.0
Market value ($ mil.)	–	–	–	–	–	–
Employees	–	–	–	–	–	1,102

*Fiscal year change

MAST INDUSTRIES INC.

2 Limited Pkwy.
Columbus OH 43230
Phone: 614-337-5600
Fax: 614-337-5080
Web: www.mast.com

CEO: Leslie H Wexner
CFO: –
HR: –
FYE: January 31
Type: Subsidiary

MAST makes clothes so its customers don't have to. MAST Industries (doing business as Mast Global Fashions) is one of the world's largest contract manufacturers importers and distributors of apparel including sportswear for hot brands such as Abercrombie & Fitch. Once a wholly owned subsidiary of Limited Brands a 51% stake in Mast was sold to private equity firm Sycamore Parters in November 2011 to establish it as a standalone company. Limited will continue to own Mast's separate sourcing operation for its Victoria's Secret La Senza and Bath & Body Works brands. Mast has manufacturing operations and joint ventures in more than a dozen countries including China Israel Mexico and Sri Lanka.

MASTEC INC. (FL)

NYS: MTZ

800 S. Douglas Road, 12th Floor
Coral Gables, FL 33134
Phone: 305 599-1800
Fax: –

CEO: Jos © R. Mas
CFO: George L. Pita
HR: Moses Hardie
FYE: December 31
Type: Public

MasTec brings more tech communications and energy to homes offices and other places. The company digs the trenches lays the cable and builds the towers that power communications and providing cell service and high-speed Internet. The contractor provides infrastructure construction to telecom vendors wireless providers cable TV operators and energy and utility companies. Its projects include wireless wireline and satellite communications as well as electrical utility transmission and distribution power generation natural gas and petroleum pipeline infrastructure wind and solar farms industrial infrastructure and water and sewer systems. Chairman Jorge Mas and family own a quarter of the company's stock.

	Annual Growth	12/10	12/11	12/12	12/13	12/14
Sales ($ mil.)	18.9%	2,308.0	3,009.0	3,726.8	4,324.8	4,611.8
Net income ($ mil.)	6.4%	90.5	106.0	107.4	141.0	115.9
Market value ($ mil.)	11.6%	1,236.3	1,471.9	2,112.5	2,772.6	1,915.9
Employees	13.4%	9,400	10,000	12,300	13,450	15,550

MASTECH HOLDINGS INC

ASE: MHH

1305 Cherrington Parkway, Building 210, Suite 400
Moon Township, PA 15108
Phone: 412 787-2100
Fax: –
Web: www.mastech.com

CEO: –
CFO: John J Cronin Jr
HR: Murali Balasubramanyam
FYE: December 31
Type: Public

Mastech provides outsourced staffing services primarily for businesses in need of contract information technology (IT) personnel. The company provides systems integrators and other IT staffing companies with temporary technical staff on a wholesale basis. It also serves companies in other industries directly. The company mainly serves customers in the US but it has international recruiting operations in India. Apart from finance clients come from such industries as consumer products health care retail technology and telecom. Formerly a subsidiary of IGATE Corporation Mastech was spun off to its parent company's shareholders in 2008.

	Annual Growth	12/10	12/11	12/12	12/13	12/14
Sales ($ mil.)	12.1%	71.8	89.4	101.8	106.9	113.5
Net income ($ mil.)	50.7%	0.7	1.1	2.1	3.8	3.4
Market value ($ mil.)	25.9%	18.2	16.1	21.7	60.2	45.7
Employees	14.2%	530	660	850	850	900

MASTER LOCK COMPANY LLC

137 W. Forest Hill Ave.
Oak Creek WI 53154
Phone: 414-444 2800
Fax: 800-308-9245
Web: www.masterlock.com

CEO: –
CFO: –
HR: Carline Hannah
FYE: December 31
Type: Subsidiary

Master Lock's founder figured that if battleships and bank vaults were made of laminated steel why not locks? The world's largest padlock manufacturer invented and patented the laminated steel padlock in 1924. Today it continues to manufacture and market padlocks as well as steering wheel locks cable locks and U-locks window and door locks and alarms and other products for the home and security applications in the automotive consumer goods commercial education and government markets. Master Lock is a wholly-owned subsidiary of Fortune Brands Storage & Security itself a subsidiary of Fortune Brands Home & Security.

MASTERBRAND CABINETS INC.

1 MasterBrand Cabinets Dr.
Jasper IN 47547
Phone: 812-482-2527
Fax: 812-482-9872
Web: www.masterbrandcabinets.com

CEO: –
CFO: –
HR: –
FYE: December 31
Type: Subsidiary

When it comes to cabinets MasterBrand Cabinets is something of a prime minister. The company is one of the leading wall cabinetry manufacturers in the US and beyond after main rival Masco. MasterBrand makes a variety of cabinets for kitchen bath and other parts of the home from custom to semi-custom and stock products used in remodeling and new construction projects. The lineup of wooden cabinetry such as maple and oak as well as laminate-finished products is sold under nine-brands (Aristokraft Decora Diamond Kemper and Schrock to name a few) through home centers lumber outlets and specialty retailers. MasterBrand is a subsidiary Fortune Brands Home & Security formerly a unit of Fortune Brands.

MASTERCARD INC

NYS: MA

2000 Purchase Street
Purchase, NY 10577
Phone: 914 249-2000
Fax: –
Web: www.mastercard.com

CEO: Ajaypal S. (Ajay) Banga
CFO: Martina Hund-Mejean
HR: Meri Wax
FYE: December 31
Type: Public

Surpassing Visa in market share — now that would be priceless. Serving approximately 22000 member financial institutions worldwide MasterCard is the #2 payment system in the US. The company does not issue credit or its namesake cards; rather it markets the MasterCard (credit debit and prepaid cards) and Maestro (debit and prepaid cards mainly in Europe) brands provides a transaction authorization network establishes guidelines for use and collects fees from members. The company provides its services in more than 210 countries and territories and its cards are accepted at more than 35 million locations around the globe. MasterCard also operates the Cirrus ATM network.

	Annual Growth	12/11	12/12	12/13	12/14	12/15
Sales ($ mil.)	9.5%	6,714.0	7,391.0	8,346.0	9,473.0	9,667.0
Net income ($ mil.)	18.9%	1,906.0	2,759.0	3,116.0	3,617.0	3,808.0
Market value ($ mil.)	(28.5%)	416,067.1	548,268.5	932,373.4	96,154.6	108,653.8
Employees	14.0%	6,700	7,500	8,200	10,300	11,300

MASTERPLAN INC.

21540 Plummer St.
Chatsworth CA 91311
Phone: 818-773-2647
Fax: 818-341-9895
Web: www.masterplan-inc.com

CEO: –
CFO: D Perkwell
HR: –
FYE: March 31
Type: Private

Masterplan helps health care providers think long-term when it comes to their medical equipment. The company provides outsourced equipment maintenance consulting and technology management services for hospitals health systems and alternate care sites such as outpatient surgery and diagnostic centers. It operates throughout the US and in select international markets servicing diagnostic imaging equipment (such as CT and MRI machines) and other medical devices including sterilizers monitors and surgical and laboratory equipment. Masterplan was acquired by ARAMARK Healthcare (part of foodservice and uniform provider ARAMARK) in early 2011.

MATADOR RESOURCES COMPANY

NYSE: MTDR

1 Lincoln Centre 5400 LBJ Freeway Ste. 1500
Dallas TX 75240
Phone: 972-371-5200
Fax: 972-371-5201
Web: www.matadorresources.com

CEO: –
CFO: David E Lancaster
HR: –
FYE: December 31
Type: Public

This Matador may be thriving in a bullish oil market but the company itself is more phoenix than bull. Matador Resources was founded by the former executives of Matador Petroleum which was bought by Tom Brown in 2003. Matador Resources focuses on natural gas exploration and production across about 75000 acres in South Texas Northwest Louisiana and East Texas and in the Permian Basin of West Texas and Southeast New Mexico. It reports estimated proved reserves of 154.8 billion cu. ft. of gas and an average daily production of 23.6 million cu. ft. per day. Matador Resources also has rights to another 135000 undeveloped acres in Idaho Utah and Wyoming. In 2011 the company filed an IPO seeking $150 million.

MATANUSKA TELEPHONE ASSOCIATION INCORPORATED

1740 S CHUGACH ST
PALMER, AK 996456796
Phone: 907-745-3211
Fax: –
Web: www.mtasolutions.com

CEO: Greg Berberich
CFO: Wanda Tankersley
HR: –
FYE: December 31
Type: Private

One of the the largest telephone cooperatives in the largest state the Matanuska Telephone Association better known as MTA offers telecommunications services to the residents of south-central Alaska. Established in 1953 the co-op provides local and long-distance voice service and cell phone service (MTA Wireless) Internet access and digital cable television. It also offers telecommunications systems (provided by third-party companies such as Avaya) as well as Internet and wireless plans to businesses.

	Annual Growth	12/09	12/10	12/11	12/12	12/13
Sales ($ mil.)	(3.2%)	–	64.0	98.9	57.6	58.0
Net income ($ mil.)	–	–	–	3.7	5.0	(0.6)
Market value ($ mil.)	–	–	–	–	–	–
Employees	–	–	–	–	–	300

MATERIAL SCIENCES CORP.

NAS: MASC

2200 East Pratt Boulevard
Elk Grove Village, IL 60007
Phone: 847 439-2210
Fax: 847 439-0737
Web: www.matsci.com

CEO: Pat Murley
CFO: James D Pawlak
HR: –
FYE: February 28
Type: Public

Material Sciences Corporation known as MSC makes engineered materials as well as coated steel and electro-galvanized steel products. MSC has two primary product segments: acoustical (anti-noise and vibration products including the trademarked Quiet Steel reduced vibration metal) and coated (decorative and protective metal coatings). The company's products are used by the appliance automotive building systems computer construction furniture HVAC lighting and telecommunications industries. Automobile manufacturers are among the company's largest clients. MSC gets most of its sales in the US.

	Annual Growth	02/09	02/10	02/11	02/12	02/13
Sales ($ mil.)	(10.3%)	187.0	137.8	137.6	136.7	121.0
Net income ($ mil.)	–	(33.1)	(11.6)	12.0	28.5	9.0
Market value ($ mil.)	78.0%	10.3	19.5	74.7	88.3	103.5
Employees	(8.0%)	372	339	264	269	267

MATERION ADVANCED MATERIALS TECHNOLOGIES AND SERVICES INC

2978 Main St.
Buffalo NY 14214
Phone: 716-837-1000
Fax: 858-578-2344
Web: www.tsystemsinternational.com

CEO: –
CFO: –
HR: –
FYE: December 31
Type: Subsidiary

Materion Advanced Materials Technologies and Services (formerly Williams Advanced Materials) is the largest business segment of parent Materion Corp. Materion Advanced Materials also goes by Materion Microelectronics and Services. It makes vapor deposition targets frame lid assemblies clad and precious metal preforms high-temperature braze materials ultra-fine wire advanced chemicals optics performance coatings and microelectronic packages. The company's precious non-precious and specialty metal products are used in the magnetic and optical data storage markets as well as the solar/photovoltaic industry and the hybrid photonic semiconductor and wireless segments of the microelectronics industry.

MATERION CORP

NYS: MTRN

6070 Parkland Blvd.
Mayfield Heights, OH 44124
Phone: 216 486-4200
Fax: 216 383-4091
Web: www.materion.com

CEO: Richard J. (Dick) Hipple
CFO: Joseph P. Kelley
HR: Joe Szafraniec
FYE: December 31
Type: Public

Materion (formerly Brush Engineered Materials) provides advanced engineered materials and services worldwide. It sells products to a number of markets including consumer electronics aerospace and defense industrial components telecommunications infrastructure automotive electronics and medical and appliance. It manufactures a variety of precious and specialty metal products including frame lid assemblies and clad and precious metal pre-forms high temperature braze materials and ultra-fine wire. Other products include precision optics and thin film coatings; inorganic chemicals and powders; specialty coatings; beryllium (which it mines in Utah) beryllium composites and beryllium alloys.

	Annual Growth	12/10	12/11	12/12	12/13	12/14
Sales ($ mil.)	(3.6%)	1,302.3	1,526.7	1,273.1	1,166.9	1,126.9
Net income ($ mil.)	(2.6%)	46.4	40.0	24.7	19.7	41.7
Market value ($ mil.)	(2.3%)	787.1	494.6	525.1	628.4	717.6
Employees	1.8%	2,484	3,015	2,833	2,671	2,671

MATRIX SERVICE CO.

NMS: MTRX

5100 East Skelly Drive, Suite 500
Tulsa, OK 74135
Phone: 918 838-8822
Fax: –
Web: www.matrixservice.com

CEO: John R. Hewitt
CFO: Kevin S. Cavanah
HR: Teresa Colley
FYE: June 30
Type: Public

Matrix Service Company makes sure that oil and water don't mix. The company provides a variety of construction repair and maintenance services mainly to the petroleum and power industries in North America. Its Storage Solutions business which accounts for about 35% of sales specializes in aboveground storage tanks to hold oil gas and specialty materials. It also designs and builds plants refineries and other installations. Through its Oil Gas & Chemical segment Matrix provides preventive routine and emergency repair services focusing on turnarounds outages and shutdowns when time is of the essence. Founded in 1984 the firm has around a dozen locations in the US and Canada.

	Annual Growth	06/11	06/12	06/13	06/14	06/15
Sales ($ mil.)	21.0%	627.1	739.0	892.6	1,263.1	1,343.1
Net income ($ mil.)	(2.5%)	19.0	17.2	24.0	35.8	17.2
Market value ($ mil.)	8.1%	353.8	299.6	411.9	867.0	483.3
Employees	16.5%	2,623	2,692	3,587	4,491	4,826

MATRIX TELECOM INC.

433 E. Las Colinas
Irving TX 75039
Phone: 214-432-1447
Fax: +54-11-4323-7480
Web: www.irsa.com.ar

CEO: Charles G Taylor Jr
CFO: –
HR: –
FYE: December 31
Type: Subsidiary

Matrix Telecom provides telephone Internet and other network service to commercial customers. Operating as Matrix Business Technologies the company offers voice and data services including VoIP (voice-over-Internet protocol) computer telephony local and long distance service virtual private networking audio and Web conferencing and high-capacity broadband Internet connections to commercial clients in a variety of industries. It markets bundled service packages that include voice and data options primarily to small and medium sized businesses. Matrix Telecom has offices in Irving Texas and Atmore Alabama. The company is a subsidiary of information technology investment firm Platinum Equity.

MATRIXX INITIATIVES INC.

4742 N. 24th St. Ste. 455
Phoenix AZ 85016
Phone: 602-385-8888
Fax: 602-387-4112
Web: www.matrixxinc.com

CEO: M'Lou Arnett
CFO: William J Hemelt
HR: –
FYE: March 31
Type: Subsidiary

Matrixx Initiatives offers several ways to get its medicine up your nose without a rubber hose. The company makes oral and nasally delivered over-the-counter cold flu and allergy remedies marketed primarily under the Zicam name. Its Zicam Cold Remedy is a zinc-based product that claims to reduce the duration of cold symptoms. Zicam comes in a variety of delivery methods including nasal swabs cough lozenges chewable tablets and nasal and oral sprays. The company also produces Nasal Comfort a moisturizing nasal spray to treat congestion and Xcid an antacid cream. Major customers include Wal-Mart Walgreens and CVS. Matrixx is owned by an affiliate of investment firm H.I.G. Capital called Wonder Holdings.

MATSON INC

1411 Sand Island Parkway
Honolulu, HI 96819
Phone: 808 848-1211
Fax: –
Web: www.matson.com

NYS: MATX
CEO: Matthew J. (Matt) Cox
CFO: Joel M. Wine
HR: Donna Ota
FYE: December 31
Type: Public

Someone has to get Hawaii's sugar (and other products) out into the world and Matson transports freight between the continental US and ports in Hawaii Guam Micronesia and China. Containerships account for the majority of the company's 18-vessel fleet. Besides containerized freight cargo carried by Matson vessels includes automobiles and building materials. Subsidiary Matson Logistics provides logistics and multimodal transportation services (arrangement of freight transportation by combinations of road rail and air). Matson Terminals specializes in container stevedoring and related services for Matson and other carriers in Honolulu.

	Annual Growth	12/10	12/11	12/12	12/13	12/14
Sales ($ mil.)	1.0%	1,646.0	1,722.0	1,560.0	1,637.2	1,714.2
Net income ($ mil.)	(6.3%)	92.0	34.0	45.9	53.7	70.8
Market value ($ mil.)	(3.6%)	1,729.3	1,763.4	1,067.9	1,128.0	1,491.3
Employees	(17.7%)	2,300	2,100	1,068	1,036	1,056

MATTEL INC

333 Continental Blvd.
El Segundo, CA 90245-5012
Phone: 310 252-2000
Fax: –
Web: www.mattel.com

NMS: MAT
CEO: –
CFO: Kevin M. Farr
HR: Huey Wilson
FYE: December 31
Type: Public

Barbie is the platinum blonde in power at Mattel the #1 toy maker in the world. Its products include Barbie and Polly Pocket dolls Fisher-Price toys Hot Wheels and Matchbox cars American Girl dolls and books and various Barney Ferrari and other licensed items. Mattel also sells action figures and toys based on Walt Disney and Warner Bros. movies. To satisfy techie kids Mattel has accessorized Barbie with interactive games software and a line of MP3 players. The company has even licensed the Barbie name for eyewear. It also sells games (UNO) and puzzles. Mattel is trying to reduce its reliance on its biggest customers — Wal-Mart Toys "R" Us and Target — through its own catalog and Internet sales.

	Annual Growth	12/10	12/11	12/12	12/13	12/14
Sales ($ mil.)	0.7%	5,856.2	6,266.0	6,420.9	6,484.9	6,023.8
Net income ($ mil.)	(7.6%)	684.9	768.5	776.5	903.9	498.9
Market value ($ mil.)	5.0%	8,597.9	9,385.7	12,381.2	16,086.8	10,462.5
Employees	0.0%	31,000	28,000	28,000	29,000	31,000

MATTERSIGHT CORP

200 W. Madison Street, Suite 3100
Chicago, IL 60606
Phone: 877 235-6925
Fax: –
Web: www.mattersight.com

NMS: MATR
CEO: Kelly D. Conway
CFO: Sheau-Ming K. Ross
HR: Tim Hailey
FYE: December 31
Type: Public

Mattersight has an eye for important data. The company (formerly eLoyalty) provides behavioral analytics software used by companies to collect and analyze customer data generated from sources including e-mail call centers as well as field sales and Internet channels. It also offers systems designed to measure financial and operating metrics associated with CRM programs and tools to help insurance companies banks and brokerages to identify instances of identity or financial fraud.

	Annual Growth	01/11*	12/11	12/12	12/13	12/14
Sales ($ mil.)	(29.9%)	88.1	29.1	33.9	34.5	30.3
Net income ($ mil.)	–	(13.3)	18.4	(15.2)	(11.2)	(14.2)
Market value ($ mil.)	(0.8%)	142.9	103.8	111.0	106.9	139.5
Employees	(18.9%)	369	223	230	179	197

*Fiscal year change

MATTESON-RIDOLFI INC.

14450 KING RD
RIVERVIEW MI 481937939
Phone: 734-479-4500
Fax: –
Web: www.mattrid.com

CEO: –
CFO: –
HR: –
FYE: December 31
Type: Private

|Matteson-Ridolfi distributes chemicals such as catalysts pigments resins solvents surfactants and thickening agents to companies in the adhesives and sealants automotive glass and refractory paints and coatings pharmaceuticals pulp and paper and soaps and detergents industries. The company maintains facilities in Cleveland; Detroit; and Louisville Kentucky. Customers include Cabot and other major chemical manufacturers. The family of company president Scot Westerbeek owns Matteson-Ridolfi which was founded in 1932.

	Annual Growth	12/06	12/07	12/08	12/09	12/10
Sales ($ mil.)	–	–	–	(560.6)	28.7	34.4
Net income ($ mil.)	1261.7%	–	–	0.0	1.9	3.0
Market value ($ mil.)	–	–	–	–	–	–
Employees	–	–	–	–	–	18

MATTHEWS INTERNATIONAL CORP

NMS: MATW

Two Northshore Center
Pittsburgh, PA 15212-5851
Phone: 412 442-8200
Fax: –
Web: www.matw.com

CEO: Joseph C. Bartolacci
CFO: Steven F. Nicola
HR: –
FYE: September 30
Type: Public

Matthews International might not bury its competition but it can supply the casket and bronze marker. One of the nation's leading makers of cremation equipment and urns bronze memorials (including Elvis Presley's Graceland marker) metal and wood caskets and commemorative products (Baseball Hall of Fame plaques) Matthews also builds mausoleums. In addition it provides graphic imaging products and services for the consumer packaging and retail industries as well as merchandising services and marking and fulfillment systems. Matthews has operations in Asia Australia Canada and Europe but the US accounts for more than 60% of its sales.

	Annual Growth	09/11	09/12	09/13	09/14	09/15
Sales ($ mil.)	12.2%	898.8	900.3	985.4	1,106.6	1,426.1
Net income ($ mil.)	(3.2%)	72.4	55.8	54.9	43.7	63.4
Market value ($ mil.)	12.4%	1,010.3	980.3	1,251.9	1,442.9	1,609.9
Employees	18.1%	5,300	5,400	5,800	9,400	10,300

MATTINGLY FOODS INC.

302 STATE ST
ZANESVILLE, OH 437013200
Phone: 740-454-0136
Fax: –
Web: www.mattinglycashncarry.com

CEO: Rick Barnes
CFO: Rusty Deaton
HR: –
FYE: December 29
Type: Private

Mattingly Foods is a leading regional foodservice supplier that distributes food products and other goods to chain restaurant operators in more than a dozen states. It delivers a variety of dry goods along with frozen and refrigerated foods. In addition to its distribution business Mattingly Foods operates a cash & carry store where customers can purchase wholesale goods. Robert Mattingly started the family-owned business as Mattingly Seafood with his wife Bette in 1947.

	Annual Growth	12/03	12/04	12/05	12/06	12/07
Sales ($ mil.)	(5.2%)	–	309.2	301.3	290.9	263.4
Net income ($ mil.)	(39.0%)	–	–	3.1	1.0	1.1
Market value ($ mil.)	–	–	–	–	–	–
Employees	–	–	–	–	–	240

MATTRESS FIRM HOLDING CORP

NMS: MFRM

5815 Gulf Freeway
Houston, TX 77023
Phone: 713 923-1090
Fax: –
Web: www.mattressfirm.com

CEO: R. Stephen (Steve) Stagner
CFO: Alexander S. (Alex) Weiss
HR: –
FYE: February 03
Type: Public

Mattress Firm Holding is soft on comfort. The bedding retailer owns and operates or franchises more than 2000 stores primarily under the Mattress Firm name in some 40 states. It sells conventional (Simmons) and specialty (Tempur Sealy) mattresses which together account for most of its sales in addition to other brands. The company also sells bed frames and bedding accessories. From its humble beginnings in 1986 when three friends pooled their resources to purchase a downtrodden spot in a Houston strip center the chain has grown into the top US bedding retailer. Since its 2011 IPO Mattress Firm has made multiple acquisitions to solidify its position as the nation's top mattress seller.

	Annual Growth	02/11*	01/12	01/13	01/14*	02/15
Sales ($ mil.)	38.1%	497.3	708.6	1,012.7	1,222.4	1,810.6
Net income ($ mil.)	235.6%	0.3	34.4	39.9	52.9	44.3
Market value ($ mil.)	20.1%	–	1,159.4	974.1	1,472.5	2,008.2
Employees	35.6%	2,040	2,230	3,340	3,861	6,900
						*Fiscal year change

MATTSON TECHNOLOGY INC

NMS: MTSN

47131 Bayside Parkway
Fremont, CA 94538
Phone: 510 657-5900
Fax: –
Web: www.mattson.com

CEO: Fusen E Chen
CFO: J. Michael Dodson
HR: –
FYE: December 31
Type: Public

Mattson Technology has avoided being taken to the mat by the brutal fluctuations of the microchip industry. The company which has seen its business ebb and flow over the years makes several types of semiconductor manufacturing equipment including systems that deposit materials onto silicon wafers that prepare wafers for photoresist and that etch patterns onto wafers. Top customers TSMC (a contract manufacturer of semiconductors) and Samsung Electronics (an OEM) together account for more than two-thirds of sales.

	Annual Growth	12/10	12/11	12/12	12/13	12/14
Sales ($ mil.)	6.6%	138.3	184.9	126.5	119.4	178.4
Net income ($ mil.)	–	(33.4)	(18.0)	(19.3)	(11.0)	9.9
Market value ($ mil.)	3.2%	222.0	102.1	62.2	202.8	251.6
Employees	(5.9%)	379	382	323	264	297

MAUI LAND & PINEAPPLE CO., INC.

NYS: MLP

200 Village Road, Lahaina
Maui, HI 96761
Phone: 808 877-3351
Fax: –
Web: www.mauiland.com

CEO: Warren H Haruki
CFO: Tim T Esaki
HR: –
FYE: December 31
Type: Public

Aloha! Maui Land & Pineapple (ML&P) invites you to live and play on its Hawaiian island — Maui. Through its Kapalua Land Company subsidiary the company operates the 1650-acre Kapalua Resort on Maui's northwest coast. The resort includes a minority-owned Ritz-Carlton hotel as well as tennis and spa facilities residential homes and condos and shops and restaurants. ML&P also develops residential and commercial property on its 23000 acres surrounding the resort. Its Kapalua Realty Company is a general brokerage real estate firm located within the resort. The company additionally owns forest and nature preserves on the island. Formerly one of Hawaii's largest pineapple producers the company exited that business in 2009.

	Annual Growth	12/10	12/11	12/12	12/13	12/14
Sales ($ mil.)	(5.8%)	42.0	14.5	16.2	15.2	33.0
Net income ($ mil.)	(8.1%)	24.8	5.1	(4.6)	(1.2)	17.6
Market value ($ mil.)	5.0%	93.5	78.3	78.0	114.4	113.6
Employees	(46.0%)	200	29	17	19	17

MAUI WOWI FRANCHISING INC.

5445 DTC Pkwy. Ste. 1050
Greenwood Village CO 80111
Phone: 303-781-7800
Fax: 303-781-2438
Web: www.mauiwowi.com

CEO: Michael Haith
CFO: –
HR: –
FYE: December 31
Type: Private

The smoothie surf is always up at Maui Wowi Franchising. The company operates a leading chain of smoothie stands with more than 600 franchised Maui Wowi Hawaiian locations worldwide. The chain's menu boasts several varieties and flavors of blended fruit smoothies coffee and espresso drinks and other snack beverages. The Maui Wowi chain is made up mostly of retail locations in high-traffic areas but it also includes drive-thru locations and mobile carts. Husband and wife team Jeff and Jill Summerhays started the Maui Wowi concept in 1983; chairman Michael Haith acquired the chain in 1997.

MAURICES INCORPORATED

105 W. Superior St.	CEO: David Gaffe
Duluth MN 55802	CFO: George Goldfarb
Phone: 218-727-8431	HR: –
Fax: 218-720-2102	FYE: July 31
Web: www.maurices.com	Type: Subsidiary

Maurices outfits the young women of small-town America. The chain sells dress work and casual apparel for 17- to 34-year-olds at more than 830 specialty retail and outlet stores in 44 US states Canda and online. It sells clothing under the maurices and Studio Y brands as well as perfume hats gloves and other accessories. The company focuses on small markets with populations of 25000 to 100000 people which offer fewer shopping options than larger cities. Most of its stores are situated around major discount retailers and department stores. Founded in 1931 by Maurice Labovitz as a single shop in Duluth Minnesota the company is owned by apparel retailer Ascena Retail (formerly Dress Barn).

MAVERICK TECHNOLOGIES LLC

265 Admiral Trost Rd.	CEO: Paul J Galeski
Columbia IL 62236	CFO: –
Phone: 618-281-9100	HR: AMI Halloran
Fax: 618-281-9191	FYE: December 31
Web: www.mavtechglobal.com	Type: Private

Standing apart from the information technology (IT) herd MAVERICK Technologies offers systems integration engineering and operational consulting services. Founded in 1999 the company focuses on industrial automation (distribution logistics batch processing) IT (project management system development) and i2i (industrial to information enterprise solutions). MAVERICK provides services to automotive (Enterprise Rent-A-Car) consumer goods (Nestle) chemicals (DuPont) food and beverage (Anheuser-Busch) paper and packaging (International Paper) pharmaceutical (Abbott Labs) and oil and gas (Chevron) industries.

MAVERICK USA INC.

13301 Valentine Rd.	CEO: Steve Williams
North Little Rock AR 72117	CFO: –
Phone: 501-945-6130	HR: –
Fax: 501-955-1500	FYE: December 31
Web: www.maverickusa.com	Type: Private

Maverick USA's freight-hauling herd roams throughout the US. Subsidiary Maverick Transportation uses its fleet of flatbed and specialized trailers to transport steel and building materials; it also operates trailers designed to carry glass and other goods. The company offers long-haul service throughout the US and regional service in the Midwest and Southwest. Collectively it maintains a fleet of more than 1200 tractors. Maverick USA also offers freight brokerage services through its Maverick Logistics unit. A third business Maverick Truck & Trailer Sales sells the company's used equipment. Maverick USA CEO Steve Williams founded the company with a partner in 1980; he took full ownership in 1983.

MAXIM CRANE WORKS L.P.

1225 Washington Pike	CEO: Bryan Carlisle
Bridgeville PA 15017	CFO: –
Phone: 412-504-0200	HR: –
Fax: 412-504-0126	FYE: December 31
Web: www.maximcrane.com	Type: Private - Partnershi

Maxim Crane Works' motto could very well be no strain no gain. The company provides lift equipment rentals used crane sales and services for the North American non-residential construction market. It offers more than 1300 cranes including hydraulic truck cranes rough terrain cranes crawler cranes tower cranes and boom trucks. From some 35 branches in the continental US it serves projects big and small from building refineries to erecting telecommunications towers. It also offers such services as crane training rigging transportation onsite evaluations and project management. Customers include BASF GE Exxon Mobil and Shell. Maxim Crane is a portfolio company of Platinum Equity Partners.

MAXIM HEALTHCARE SERVICES INC.

7227 LEE DEFOREST DR	CEO: W. Bradley (Brad) Bennett
COLUMBIA, MD 210463236	CFO: Raymond (Ray) Carbone
Phone: 410-910-1500	HR: –
Fax: –	FYE: December 31
Web: www.maximhealthcare.com	Type: Private

Good health as the maxim goes is one of life's greatest blessings and Maxim Healthcare Services aims to promote that principle by offering medical staffing and home health care as well as immunizations and other wellness services to clients nationwide. The company provides medical and administrative personnel for hospitals school systems nursing homes and correctional facilities. The company's staffing division offers contract per diem and travel assignments. Maxim Healthcare's consultants are available 24 hours a day seven days a week to provide assistance for clients. The company which operates from more than 360 locations nationwide was established in 1988.

	Annual Growth	12/09	12/10	12/11	12/12	12/13
Sales ($ mil.)	(4.1%)	–	1,390.1	1,341.6	1,241.5	1,226.9
Net income ($ mil.)	–	–	–	(12.5)	(21.9)	(1.4)
Market value ($ mil.)	–	–	–	–	–	–
Employees	–	–	–	–	–	35,000

MAXIM INTEGRATED PRODUCTS, INC.   NMS: MXIM

160 Rio Robles	CEO: Tunc Doluca
San Jose, CA 95134	CFO: Bruce E. Kiddoo
Phone: 408-601-1000	HR: –
Fax: –	FYE: June 27
Web: www.maxim-ic.com	Type: Public

Maxim's maxim has been invent. Maxim Integrated Products makes analog and mixed-signal integrated circuits (ICs); more than 80% of which were invented by the company. Maxim's chips — which include amplifiers data converters transceivers and switching ICs — translate physical data such as temperature pressure and sound into signals for electronic processing. The company serves five major end-markets: automotive industrial communications consumer and computing. Its ICs are used in products such as appliances telecommunications and networking gear automobiles medical devices instruments and utility meters. Some 70% of sales come from customers located in Asia mostly in China.

	Annual Growth	06/11	06/12	06/13	06/14	06/15
Sales ($ mil.)	(1.7%)	2,472.3	2,403.5	2,441.5	2,453.7	2,306.9
Net income ($ mil.)	(19.4%)	489.0	386.7	454.9	354.8	206.0
Market value ($ mil.)	9.6%	6,864.2	7,302.9	7,912.4	9,658.3	9,897.6
Employees	(3.1%)	9,370	9,065	9,019	8,812	8,250

MAXIMUS INC.

NYS: MMS

1891 Metro Center Drive
Reston, VA 20190
Phone: 703 251-8500
Fax: –
Web: www.maximus.com

CEO: Richard A. (Rich) Montoni
CFO: Richard J. Nadeau
HR: –
FYE: September 30
Type: Public

Efforts by government agencies to maximize efficiency mean money for MAXIMUS. The company gets about two-thirds of its sales from its health services segment which offers outsourced program management and administrative services mainly to government agencies responsible for health and human services programs. Its human services segment provides administrative and consulting support to welfare-to-work programs child support enforcement and higher education and K-12 special education schools. MAXIMUS conducts consulting and programs management services for government-sponsored programs such as Medicaid Medicare the Children's Health Insurance Program (CHIP) and Welfare-to-Work.

	Annual Growth	09/11	09/12	09/13	09/14	09/15
Sales ($ mil.)	22.6%	929.6	1,050.1	1,331.3	1,700.9	2,099.8
Net income ($ mil.)	18.1%	81.2	76.1	116.7	145.4	157.8
Market value ($ mil.)	14.3%	2,283.8	3,907.9	2,947.3	2,626.0	3,897.4
Employees	24.4%	7,102	8,657	12,000	13,000	17,000

MAXLINEAR INC

NYS: MXL

5966 La Place Court, Suite 100
Carlsbad, CA 92008
Phone: 760 692-0711
Fax: –
Web: www.maxlinear.com

CEO: Kishore Seendripu
CFO: Adam C. Spice
HR: –
FYE: December 31
Type: Public

MaxLinear provides integrated radio-frequency (RF) and mixed-signal semiconductor receivers used to receive and translate analog or digital radio television and other broadband signals into visual images. Its products which are used in cable TV set-top boxes digital TVs and mobile phones are sold to module makers OEMs and original design manufacturers (ODMs) such as ARRIS Cisco and Toshiba. Nearly all sales are to Asian customers. In 2015 MaxLinear bought Entropic Communications another chip design company for $287 million.

	Annual Growth	12/10	12/11	12/12	12/13	12/14
Sales ($ mil.)	18.0%	68.7	71.9	97.7	119.6	133.1
Net income ($ mil.)	–	10.1	(22.0)	(13.3)	(12.7)	(7.0)
Market value ($ mil.)	(8.9%)	407.9	180.1	190.3	395.4	280.9
Employees	15.8%	210	256	274	336	378

MAXOR NATIONAL PHARMACY SERVICES CORPORATION

320 S POLK ST STE 100
AMARILLO, TX 791011436
Phone: 806-324-5400
Fax: –
Web: www.maxor.com

CEO: John Ward
CFO: Jerry Havard
HR: –
FYE: December 31
Type: Private

Maxor National Pharmacy Services provides health care and pharmacy services including retail and mail order prescriptions (Maxor Pharmacies) pharmacy benefits management (MaxorPlus) pharmacy consulting (Maxor Pharmacy Consulting Services) and infusion and injection services (IVSolutions). The company operates about a dozen Maxor Pharmacy stores mostly in Texas and Washington but also in Colorado and New York. Its correctional division provides services to more than 330000 offenders in more than 250 correctional facilities in 26 states through direct management contracts or via its pharmacy services division. Founded in 1926 as a single pharmacy in Amarillo Maxor put itself up for sale in 2013.

	Annual Growth	12/04	12/05	12/06	12/07	12/09
Sales ($ mil.)	17.2%	–	118.5	0.0	176.3	223.9
Net income ($ mil.)	–	–	–	0.0	0.0	0.0
Market value ($ mil.)	–	–	–	–	–	–
Employees	–	–	–	–	–	481

MAXWELL TECHNOLOGIES, INC.

NMS: MXWL

3888 Calle Fortunada
San Diego, CA 92123
Phone: 858 503-3200
Fax: –
Web: www.maxwell.com

CEO: Franz Fink
CFO: Kevin S Royal
HR: –
FYE: December 31
Type: Public

Maxwell Technologies is more than capable of making products that store energy and deliver power you might even say ultracapable. The company makes ultracapacitors postage stamp-sized cells that are able to provide quick bursts of energy to meet power demands then recharge by capturing excess power that would otherwise be lost. Its ultracapacitors are used to provide additional power for hybrid cars electric trains and semi-trucks as well as in energy grid solid-state memory and other applications that need fast reliable power. Maxwell also makes high-voltage capacitors that protect power grid systems and radiation-shielded microelectronics for satellites and spacecraft.

	Annual Growth	12/10	12/11	12/12	12/13	12/14
Sales ($ mil.)	11.2%	121.9	157.3	159.3	193.5	186.6
Net income ($ mil.)	–	(6.1)	0.8	7.2	6.3	(6.3)
Market value ($ mil.)	(16.6%)	563.8	484.7	247.7	231.9	272.2
Employees	8.5%	368	435	408	448	510

MAYER BROWN LLP

71 S. Wacker Dr.
Chicago IL 60606
Phone: 312-782-0600
Fax: 312-701-7711
Web: www.mayerbrown.com

CEO: –
CFO: –
HR: –
FYE: December 31
Type: Private - Partnershi

One of the world's largest law firms Mayer Brown (formerly Mayer Brown Rowe & Maw) represents many of the companies in the FORTUNE 100 and the FTSE 100 as well as a number of leading banks. Major practice areas include appellate corporate and securities finance litigation real estate and tax. Overall Mayer Brown has about 1800 lawyers in more than 20 offices in the Americas Europe and Asia. It significantly expanded its international reach in 2008 by combining with Hong Kong-based Johnson Stokes & Master (JSM) a 300-lawyer firm. Mayer Brown is made up of three partnerships — Mayer Brown LLP (located in the US) Mayer Brown International LLP (the UK) and JSM.

MAYER ELECTRIC SUPPLY COMPANY INC.

3405 4TH AVE S
BIRMINGHAM, AL 352222300
Phone: 205-583-3500
Fax: –
Web: www.mayerelectric.com

CEO: Nancy Collat Goedecke
CFO: –
HR: –
FYE: December 28
Type: Private

Mayer Electric Supply helps to light up those southern nights. The company is one of the nation's largest distributors of electrical supplies with about 50 branch locations in the southeastern US. It offers some 40000 items made by leading manufacturers such as 3M GE Littelfuse and Schneider Electric. Products include conduit circuit breakers controls and switches fire and safety products LED and low-voltage lighting systems motors power tools transformers and wire and cable. Mayer Electric supplies customers in the construction datacomm government industrial and utility industries. The Collat family including CEO Nancy Collat Goedecke owns Mayer Electric.

	Annual Growth	01/10	01/11*	12/11	12/12	12/13
Sales ($ mil.)	9.1%	–	565.5	623.5	606.8	672.8
Net income ($ mil.)	(6.7%)	–	–	7.6	6.7	6.6
Market value ($ mil.)	–	–	–	–	–	–
Employees	–	–	–	–	–	900

*Fiscal year change

MAYFIELD FUND

2800 Sand Hill Rd. Ste. 250
Menlo Park CA 94025
Phone: 650-854-5560
Fax: 650-854-5712
Web: www.mayfield.com

CEO: –
CFO: –
HR: –
FYE: December 31
Type: Private - Partnershi

Mayfield Fund has a sense of a venture. Since its inception the Silicon Valley venture capital firm has invested in almost 500 companies and has taken more than 100 of them public. The company is an active investor targeting early-stage technology businesses focused on enterprise software consumer services communications cleantech and semiconductors. It has more than $2.4 billion under management. Mayfield Fund which is owned by its partners got its start in 1969 through the efforts of its late founding partner Tommy Davis dubbed "the dean of venture capitalists."

MAYFLOWER BANCORP INC.

NASDAQ: MFLR

30 S. Main St.
Middleboro MA 02346
Phone: 508-947-4343
Fax: 508-923-0864
Web: www.mayflowerbank.com

CEO: Edward M Pratt
CFO: –
HR: –
FYE: April 30
Type: Public

Mayflower Bank (formerly Mayflower Co-operative Bank) has been proudly progressing like a pilgrim since 1889. It is the primary subsidiary of bank holding company Mayflower Bancorp and operates nearly 10 branches in southeastern Massachusetts. Serving individuals and local businesses Mayflower Bank provides standard fare such as checking and savings accounts money market accounts and certificates of deposit. It primarily uses funds from deposits to originate residential mortgages commercial real estate loans and home equity loans and lines of credit. To a far lesser extent Mayflower Bank also originates business consumer and construction loans.

MAYO CLINIC JACKSONVILLE

4500 San Pablo Rd.
Jacksonville FL 32224-1865
Phone: 904-953-2000
Fax: 904-953-0430
Web: www.mayoclinic.org/jacksonville

CEO: William C Rupp
CFO: Mary J Hoffman
HR: –
FYE: December 31
Type: Subsidiary

With more than 370 doctors and scientists on staff Mayo Clinic Jacksonville offers a broad range of medical surgical and research services. The clinic part of the larger Mayo Clinic network offers specialty services including organ transplantation neurology and oncology therapy. Most patients treated at the clinic are treated on an outpatient basis; those who require hospitalization are admitted to the adjacent Mayo Clinic Hospital a 214-bed acute care facility. The Jacksonville campus also includes the Birdsall Medical Research center and the Griffin Cancer Research building.

MAYS (J.W.), INC.

NAS: MAYS

9 Bond Street
Brooklyn, NY 11201-5805
Phone: 718 624-7400
Fax: 718 935-0378
Web: www.jwmays.com

CEO: Lloyd J Shulman
CFO: –
HR: –
FYE: July 31
Type: Public

J. W. Mays can get you space in Brooklyn as long as you're interested in offices and not bridges. The company owns and leases about 10 properties in and around New York City — mostly former MAYS department stores — and a warehouse in central Ohio. It leases its properties to retail restaurant commercial and other tenants. The MAYS department store chain founded in 1924 by Russian immigrant Joe Weinstein closed in 1989 when management realized the New York real estate it occupied was worth more than the struggling discount retail business. Weinstein's descendants including CEO Lloyd Shulman control more than half of the company although relations among the heirs have not always been harmonious.

	Annual Growth	07/11	07/12	07/13	07/14	07/15
Sales ($ mil.)	6.2%	14.8	16.5	15.9	17.1	18.9
Net income ($ mil.)	42.9%	0.5	1.3	0.7	0.7	2.2
Market value ($ mil.)	33.9%	33.3	38.8	53.7	121.1	106.9
Employees	(0.8%)	30	29	29	29	29

MAYVILLE ENGINEERING CO INC

715 SOUTH ST
MAYVILLE, WI 530501823
Phone: 920-387-4500
Fax: –

CEO: –
CFO: Todd Butz
HR: Barry Hoopes
FYE: December 31
Type: Private

Sometimes it's all right to get loaded. Mayville Engineering Company (MEC) manufactures shotshell reloading machinery and equipment used by hunters sport shooting enthusiasts and sporting goods stores. MEC also provides coating welding riveting painting manufacturing prototyping and mechanical assembly services. Its operations are divided across the main divisions of MEC Tube MEC Coatings MEC Fabrication and MEC Shooting Sports. Overall these divisions cater to the agricultural construction military medical and industrial markets.

	Annual Growth	03/08	03/09	03/10*	12/10	12/11
Sales ($ mil.)	–	–	–	(1,003.0)	153.6	177.7
Net income ($ mil.)	5636181.1%	–	–	0.0	15.8	6.9
Market value ($ mil.)	–	–	–	–	–	–
Employees	–	–	–	–	–	1,925

*Fiscal year change

MAZAK CORPORATION

8025 Production Dr.
Florence KY 41042
Phone: 859-342-1700
Fax: 859-342-1710
Web: www.mazakusa.com

CEO: –
CFO: –
HR: –
FYE: March 31
Type: Subsidiary

That's Mazak not Muzak thank you. Mazak builds and sells small and large machine tools and systems for metal-cutting and metal-forming tasks. Its machining centers with vertical horizontal and multi-tasking modes CNC turning centers and turnkey cells are used to make other machines that produce aircraft and construction machinery cars trucks medical devices — tools for daily jobs. The company operates plants in Asia the UK and US. Scattered across North America its technology centers engineer and test new products for improving OEM production. Mazak also offers training services and parts and used machines. It is a subsidiary of Japanese machine tool maker Yamazaki Mazak established in 1919.

MAZZIO'S CORPORATION

4441 S. 72nd East Ave.
Tulsa OK 74145-4692
Phone: 918-663-8880
Fax: 918-641-1236
Web: www.mazzios.com/

CEO: –
CFO: –
HR: –
FYE: December 31
Type: Private

Mazzio's operates and franchises about 170 quick-service restaurants under the Mazzio's Italian Eatery banner that specialize in pizza pasta and sandwiches. Located in Oklahoma and about 10 other states the eateries also feature a variety of appetizers such as spicy chicken wings breadsticks and nachos. In addition the company's Oliveto Italian Bistro restaurant serves specialty pastas and salads along with an extensive wine list. More than 60 of the restaurants are company-owned; the rest are operated by franchisees. Chairman Ken Selby who opened his first pizza parlor in 1961 launched the Mazzio's concept in 1979.

MB FINANCIAL INC

NMS: MBFI

800 West Madison Street
Chicago, IL 60607
Phone: 888 422-6562
Fax: –
Web: www.mbfinancial.com

CEO: Mitchell S. Feiger
CFO: Jill E. York
HR: –
FYE: December 31
Type: Public

The "MB" in MB Financial doesn't stand for "Midsized Businesses" though that's its target market. The holding company owns MB Financial Bank which has about 85 branches in the Chicago area and one in Philadelphia. Commercial-related credits including mortgages operating loans lease financing and construction loans make up nearly 80% of the bank's loan portfolio. In addition to serving small and middle-market businesses MB Financial provides retail banking and lending to consumers. The company also offers wealth management and trust services through its Cedar Hill Associates subsidiary and brokerage through Vision Investment Services. LaSalle Systems leases technology-related equipment to corporations.

	Annual Growth	12/10	12/11	12/12	12/13	12/14
Assets ($ mil.)	9.1%	10,320.4	9,833.1	9,571.8	9,641.4	14,602.1
Net income ($ mil.)	43.1%	20.5	38.7	90.4	98.5	86.1
Market value ($ mil.)	17.4%	1,295.0	1,278.6	1,476.7	2,397.2	2,457.0
Employees	13.6%	1,703	1,684	1,758	1,775	2,839

MBC HOLDINGS INC.

1613 S DEFIANCE ST
ARCHBOLD, OH 435029488
Phone: 419-445-1015
Fax: –
Web: www.mbcholdings.com

CEO: –
CFO: –
HR: –
FYE: December 31
Type: Private

These are brothers heavy in the midwestern construction business. MBC Holdings is the parent company of heavy and civil construction firm Miller Bros. Construction (also known as Team Miller). The firm specializes in highway contracting commercial and industrial construction and paving as well as earthwork and excavation working primarily in Ohio Michigan Indiana and Kentucky. Other subsidiaries include aggregates specialists Cardinal Aggregate; and steel contractors Sawyer Steel Erectors Wymer Steel and DeWitt Rebar. Brothers Dale and Floyd Miller started the family-owned company in 1945.

	Annual Growth	12/03	12/04	12/05	12/06	12/09
Sales ($ mil.)	–	–	–	(563.7)	97.0	89.2
Net income ($ mil.)	–	–	–	0.0	6.0	(1.7)
Market value ($ mil.)	–	–	–	–	–	–
Employees	–	–	–	–	–	721

MBIA INC.

NYS: MBI

1 Manhattanville Road, Suite 301
Purchase, NY 10577
Phone: 914 273-4545
Fax: –
Web: www.mbia.com

CEO: Joseph W. (Jay) Brown
CFO: C. Edward (Chuck) Chaplin
HR: –
FYE: December 31
Type: Public

MBIA will make sure that bonds get paid no matter what. The holding company's independent subsidiary National Public Finance Guarantee Corporation is a leading provider of insurance for municipal bonds and stable corporate bonds (such as utility bonds) in the US. Separately its MBIA Insurance Corporation provides global structured finance products and non-US public financial guarantees. MBIA's Cutwater business manages assets for public-sector clients. Other lines of business include tax compliance and risk management services along with buying and servicing municipal real estate tax liens.

	Annual Growth	12/10	12/11	12/12	12/13	12/14
Assets ($ mil.)	(15.7%)	32,279.0	26,873.0	21,724.0	16,953.0	16,284.0
Net income ($ mil.)	81.4%	52.5	(1,319.0)	1,234.0	250.0	569.0
Market value ($ mil.)	(5.6%)	2,301.4	2,224.6	1,506.8	2,291.8	1,831.1
Employees	(10.5%)	392	382	352	277	252

MBT FINANCIAL CORP.

NMS: MBTF

102 E. Front Street
Monroe, MI 48161
Phone: 734 241-3431
Fax: –
Web: www.mbandt.com

CEO: H Douglas Chaffin
CFO: John L Skibski
HR: –
FYE: December 31
Type: Public

MBT Financial is the holding company for Monroe Bank & Trust which operates some two dozen branches in southeastern Michigan. Serving residents and businesses in Monroe and Wayne counties the bank offers a range of services including checking and savings accounts CDs retirement accounts personal trust services employee benefit plans and investment management. More than 80% of the loans in MBT Financial's portfolio are secured by commercial or residential real estate. The bank also originates business agricultural and personal loans.

	Annual Growth	12/10	12/11	12/12	12/13	12/14
Assets ($ mil.)	0.4%	1,259.4	1,238.0	1,268.6	1,222.7	1,278.7
Net income ($ mil.)	–	(11.9)	(3.8)	8.5	25.5	7.3
Market value ($ mil.)	29.4%	40.4	25.4	53.8	96.8	113.4
Employees	1.7%	348	362	367	381	372

MC DONOUGH COUNTY HOSPITAL DISTRICT

525 E GRANT ST
MACOMB, IL 614553313
Phone: 309-833-4101
Fax: –
Web: www.mdh.org

CEO: Kenny Boyd
CFO: –
HR: –
FYE: June 30
Type: Private

It may be small but that doesn't keep McDonough District Hospital (MDH) from serving the health care needs of patients throughout west-central Illinois. The not-for-profit MDH is an acute care facility with more than 110 beds. The hospital provides general medical emergency and surgical services as well as specialty care including behavioral health cancer cardiopulmonary dialysis nutritional pediatric and women's health services. The hospital also offers home health and hospice programs. It has an active medical staff of more than 35 physicians representing a range of specialties. MDH opened its doors in 1958 with 25 beds.

	Annual Growth	06/05	06/06	06/07	06/08	06/09
Sales ($ mil.)	–	–	–	(282.4)	50.5	54.9
Net income ($ mil.)	52831.1%	–	–	0.0	4.7	6.2
Market value ($ mil.)	–	–	–	–	–	–
Employees	–	–	–	–	–	600

MC NEESE STATE UNIVERSITY

4205 RYAN ST
LAKE CHARLES, LA 706054500
Phone: 337-475-5000
Fax: –
Web: www.mcneese.edu

CEO: –
CFO: –
HR: –
FYE: June 30
Type: Private

Founded in 1938 as Lake Charles Junior College McNeese State is one of eight schools in the University of Louisiana System. Its more than 8000 enrolled students can choose from approximately 75 associate bachelor master and specialist degree programs offered at colleges of business education engineering and technology liberal arts nursing and science the Division of General and Basic Studies and the Dor-© School of Graduate Studies. Its campus includes a 500-plus acre farm and nearly 1600 acres of donated farm property for research farming and ranching. The university is named for Louisiana educator John McNeese.

	Annual Growth	06/10	06/11	06/12	06/13	06/14
Sales ($ mil.)	3.7%	–	47.1	48.7	52.7	52.6
Net income ($ mil.)	–	–	–	0.6	2.2	(3.1)
Market value ($ mil.)	–	–	–	–	–	–
Employees	–	–	–	–	–	894

MCAFEE INC.

2821 Mission College Blvd.
Santa Clara CA 95054
Phone: 972-963-8000
Fax: 408-970-9727
Web: www.mcafee.com

CEO: –
CFO: Jonathan Chadwick
HR: –
FYE: December 31
Type: Subsidiary

McAfee puts a virtual padlock on IT resources. The company sells network security products that protect computers networks and mobile devices. Its software and hardware are used to guard against viruses spam and spyware as well as to manage data loss prevention mobile security host intrusion prevention encryption and e-mail security. McAfee gets a significant portion of its sales from follow-up service support and subscriptions to its software and managed services. The company sells directly and through resellers to corporations and consumers mainly in the US; its largest international market is Europe and it logs sales in Asia and Latin America. McAfee was acquired in 2011 by Intel for $7.68 billion.

MCALISTER'S CORPORATION

731 S. Pear Orchard Rd. Ste. 51
Ridgeland MS 39157
Phone: 601-952-1100
Fax: 601-952-1138
Web: www.mcalistersdeli.com

CEO: Steve Desutter
CFO: Carl Jakaitis
HR:
FYE: December 31
Type: Private

Nothing says "Dixie" like a New York-style deli. McAlister's operates and franchises about 300 deli restaurants in more than 20 states mostly in the Southeast and Midwest. The restaurants operating under the names McAlister's Deli McAlister's Gourmet Deli and the scaled-down McAlister's Select serve club sandwiches hoagies soup and salads as well as secret recipe sweet tea by the gallon. The 100-item menu also includes many vegetarian offerings including meatless chili nachos. Dentist Don Newcomb and his real estate assistant Debra Bryson opened the first McAlister's in a former gas station in 1989 in Oxford Mississippi. The company is owned by private equity firm Roark Capital Group.

MCCANN RELATIONSHIP MARKETING INC.

622 3rd Ave.
New York NY 10017
Phone: 646-865-6230
Fax: 646-865-6264
Web: www.mrmworldwide.com

CEO: Bill Kolb
CFO: Ivan Salazar
HR: –
FYE: December 31
Type: Business Segment

McCann Relationship Marketing doing business as MRM Worldwide is a bit like a matchmaker building relationships between its clients and their customers. The company provides a variety of marketing services and operates an extensive digital network aimed at creating and strengthening customer loyalty. It helps develop and execute marketing and branding campaigns through both traditional and interactive media. It also works with clients to develop effective cost saving and ROI strategies regarding their digital campaigns. Operating through more than 30 offices in 30 countries MRM Worldwide acts primarily as the digital marketing agency of Interpublic's McCann Worldgroup.

MCCARTER & ENGLISH LLP

Four Gateway Center 100 Mulberry St.
Newark NJ 07102
Phone: 973-622-4444
Fax: 973-624-7070
Web: www.mccarter.com

CEO: –
CFO: Michael Leonardi
HR: –
FYE: December 31
Type: Private - Partnershi

McCarter & English wasn't around for the American Revolution but the law firm has been representing clients in the northeastern US since before the Civil War. Today's McCarter & English is made up of more than 400 lawyers who practice from several offices in the region's major business centers from Boston to New York to Philadelphia. The firm's practice areas include business and commercial litigation intellectual property and information technology and labor and employment law. Clients have come from the ranks of the FORTUNE 100 but also have included smaller companies and individuals. McCarter & English traces its roots to the 1840s.

MCCARTHY BUILDING COMPANIES INC.

1341 N ROCK HILL RD
SAINT LOUIS, MO 631241441
Phone: 314-968-3300
Fax: –
Web: www.mccarthy.com

CEO: Michael D. (Mike) Bolen
CFO: Doug Audiffred
HR: –
FYE: December 31
Type: Private

A company that was in construction before Reconstruction McCarthy Building Companies is one of the oldest and largest privately-held builders in the US. The general contractor and construction manager ranks among the top builders of health care education and green building facilities in the country. Contracts include heavy construction projects (bridges and water- and waste-treatment plants) commercial projects (retail and office buildings) and institutional projects (airports schools and prisons). Subsidiary MC Industrial handles energy auto and other manufacturing projects. Founded by Timothy McCarthy in 1864 the company is 100% employee owned and generates $3 billion in annual revenues.

	Annual Growth	12/09	12/10	12/11	12/12	12/13
Sales ($ mil.)	7.9%	–	2,379.1	2,331.3	2,816.1	2,991.9
Net income ($ mil.)	–	–	–	0.0	0.0	0.0
Market value ($ mil.)	–	–	–	–	–	–
Employees	–	–	–	–	–	2,438

MCCLATCHY CO. (THE)

NYS: MNI

2100 "Q" Street
Sacramento, CA 95816
Phone: 916 321-1844
Fax: –
Web: www.mcclatchy.com

CEO: –
CFO: Elaine Lintecum
HR: Billie McConkey
FYE: December 28
Type: Public

The McClatchy Company is the #3 newspaper business in the US (behind USA TODAY publisher Gannett and Tribune Publishing). McClatchy has about 30 daily papers with a combined circulation of about 2 million. Its portfolio includes The Kansas City Star The Miami Herald The Sacramento Bee (California) and the Star-Telegram (Fort Worth Texas). In addition it has a 49.5% stake in The Seattle Times Company publishes more than 40 non-daily newspapers in eight states operates online news sites in conjunction with many of its papers and has stakes in other digital media companies.

	Annual Growth	12/10	12/11	12/12	12/13	12/14
Sales ($ mil.)	(4.4%)	1,375.2	1,269.6	1,230.7	1,242.2	1,146.6
Net income ($ mil.)	79.2%	36.3	54.4	(0.1)	18.8	374.0
Market value ($ mil.)	(7.8%)	417.4	206.5	260.6	290.2	301.5
Employees	(7.5%)	8,473	7,800	7,400	7,080	6,200

MCCORMICK & CO., INC.

NYS: MKC

18 Loveton Circle, P. O. Box 6000
Sparks, MD 21152-6000
Phone: 410 771-7301
Fax: 410 771-7462
Web: www.mccormickcorporation.com

CEO: Lawrence E. Kurzius
CFO: Gordon M Stetz Jr
HR: –
FYE: November 30
Type: Public

McCormick & Company is more than just the flavor of the month. As the world's #1 spice maker the company offers a tasty assortment of herbs spices seasonings flavorings sauces and extracts. McCormick distributes and markets its products under brands including Lawry's Club House and McCormick and ethnic labels Zatarain's Thai Kitchen and Simply Asia as well as regional brands Ducros and Schwartz and private labels. Its products are sold in some 140 countries to customers spanning the entire food industry from food retailers to food service businesses and industrial food manufacturers. McCormick operates in North America and Europe and in South Africa Central America and the Asia/Pacific region.

	Annual Growth	11/11	11/12	11/13	11/14	11/15
Sales ($ mil.)	3.8%	3,697.6	4,014.2	4,123.4	4,243.2	4,296.3
Net income ($ mil.)	1.8%	374.2	407.8	389.0	437.9	401.6
Market value ($ mil.)	15.3%	6,199.5	8,218.5	8,783.7	9,462.2	10,937.6
Employees	2.7%	9,000	9,500	10,000	10,000	10,000

MCCORMICK & SCHMICK'S SEAFOOD RESTAURANTS INC.

NASDAQ: MSSR

1414 NW Northrup St. Ste. 700
Portland OR 97209
Phone: 503-226-3440
Fax: 503-228-5074
Web: www.mccormickandschmicks.com

CEO: William T Freeman
CFO: Michelle M Lantow
HR: –
FYE: December 31
Type: Private

McCormick & Schmick's Seafood Restaurants owns and operates about 80 upscale casual-dining spots that offer fish and other seafood dishes from its approximately 80-dish menu. Located in more than two dozen states the restaurants operate primarily under the McCormick & Schmick's Seafood Restaurant brand while other locations carry such names as M&S Grill McCormick's Fish House & Bar and Jake's Grill. Each restaurant offers a full-service bar. McCormick & Schmick's also owns about a half dozen Boathouse restaurants in Canada. The company was acquired by a subsidiary of Landry's Restaurants in late 2011.

MCCOY-ROCKFORD INC.

6869 OLD KATY RD
HOUSTON, TX 770242105
Phone: 713-862-4600
Fax: –
Web: www.mccoyinc.com

CEO: Stan Bunting
CFO: David Barnett
HR: –
FYE: December 31
Type: Private

McCoy Workplace Solutions is the real McCoy when it comes to business furniture. It will sell it to you — then come help arrange it. The company supplies everything you need to furnish an office — desks chairs tables cubicle systems lighting and even floor coverings. The company sells both new and used furniture from more than 200 manufacturers including Interface NuCraft and Steelcase. McCoy also provides services such as furniture rental installation maintenance project management and repairs. Founded in 1972 the company is currently led by president and CEO Stan Bunting.

	Annual Growth	12/04	12/05	12/06	12/07	12/08
Sales ($ mil.)	(73.3%)	–	–	1,700.5	102.3	121.1
Net income ($ mil.)	35897.2%	–	–	0.0	1.0	3.1
Market value ($ mil.)	–	–	–	–	–	–
Employees	–	–	–	–	–	275

MCDANIEL COLLEGE INC

2 COLLEGE HL
WESTMINSTER, MD 211574303
Phone: 410-848-7000
Fax: –
Web: www.mcdanielathletics.com

CEO: –
CFO: –
HR: –
FYE: June 30
Type: Private

McDaniel College's predecessor school was a true pioneer being the first coeducational institution south of the Mason-Dixon Line and among the first in the nation. McDaniel College is a four-year private university offering undergraduate and graduate studies in liberal arts and sciences. Its 1600 undergraduate students may choose from 23 majors and can even opt to study abroad at its campus in Budapest Hungary. McDaniel College has a faculty of 149 professors; 96% hold the most advanced degrees in their disciplines. Some 90% of undergraduate classes are taught by full-time faculty with Ph.D.s.

	Annual Growth	06/10	06/11	06/12	06/13	06/14
Sales ($ mil.)	1.5%	–	73.4	56.0	71.4	76.7
Net income ($ mil.)	–	–	–	(5.5)	10.3	14.1
Market value ($ mil.)	–	–	–	–	–	–
Employees	–	–	–	–	–	500

MCDERMOTT INTERNATIONAL INC.

NYSE: MDR

757 N. Eldridge Pkwy.
Houston TX 77079
Phone: 281-870-5000
Fax: 630-623-5004
Web: www.mcdonalds.com

CEO: Stephen M. (Steve) Johnson
CFO: Stuart Spence
HR: –
FYE: December 31
Type: Public

Under the sea is the place to be for McDermott International. The global engineering procurement construction and installation firm is focused on designing and building offshore oil and gas projects around the world. Subsidiary J. Ray McDermott builds deepwater and subsea oil and gas production and distribution facilities. McDermott's divides its business into geographic segments: Asia Pacific; Atlantic; and the Middle East. Customers include major energy companies that operate in those areas. McDermott has operations in more than 20 countries around the world. It operates a fleet of marine vessels and has several fabrication facilities in Indonesia Mexico the United Arab Emirates and the US.

MCDONALD'S CORP

NYS: MCD

One McDonald's Plaza
Oak Brook, IL 60523
Phone: 630 623-3000
Fax: –
Web: www.mcdonalds.com

CEO: Stephen J. (Steve) Easterbrook
CFO: Kevin M. Ozan
HR: Richard R Floersch
FYE: December 31
Type: Public

Serving billions of hamburgers has put a shine on these arches. McDonald's has more than 36000 restaurants serving burgers and fries in about 120 countries. (There are more than 14250 Golden Arches locations in the US.) The popular chain is well-known for its Big Macs Quarter Pounders and Chicken McNuggets. Most of the outlets are free-standing units offering dine-in and drive-through service but McDonald's also has many eateries located in airports retail areas and other high-traffic locations. About 80% of the restaurants are run by franchisees or affiliates.

	Annual Growth	12/10	12/11	12/12	12/13	12/14
Sales ($ mil.)	3.3%	24,074.6	27,006.0	27,567.0	28,105.7	27,441.3
Net income ($ mil.)	(1.0%)	4,946.3	5,503.1	5,464.8	5,585.9	4,757.8
Market value ($ mil.)	5.1%	73,912.2	96,607.8	84,937.4	93,430.2	90,223.7
Employees	1.2%	400,000	420,000	440,000	440,000	420,000

MCEWEN MINING INC.

NYS: MUX

150 King Street West, Suite 2800
Toronto, Ontario M5H 1J9
Phone: 886 441-0690
Fax: –
Web: www.mcewenmining.com

CEO: Robert R. (Rob) McEwen
CFO: Andrew Elinesky
HR: –
FYE: December 31
Type: Public

Eureka! Eureka County Nevada that is where McEwen Mining owns the Gold Bar property. The company (formerly US Gold) is evaluating the ongoing development and production of the site which includes an open-pit gold mine a milling facility and support facilities. McEwen Mining took full ownership of the property in 2005 by buying out BacTech Mining. It also has interests in properties in Argentina including one producing both silver and gold. McEwen Mining also owns about 500000 acres of mineral rights in Mexico's Sinaloa state where it is exploring the El Gallo tract. Chairman and CEO Rob McEwen owns a 25% stake in the company.

	Annual Growth	12/10	12/11	12/12	12/13	12/14
Sales ($ mil.)	30.0%	–	–	26.8	46.0	45.3
Net income ($ mil.)	–	(33.1)	(61.9)	(66.7)	(147.7)	(311.9)
Market value ($ mil.)	(39.1%)	2,421.8	1,008.3	1,149.4	588.2	333.1
Employees	10.4%	184	324	335	265	273

MCG CAPITAL CORP

NMS: MCGC

1001 19th Street North, 10th Floor
Arlington, VA 22209
Phone: 703 247-7500
Fax: –
Web: www.mcgcapital.com

CEO: –
CFO: –
HR: –
FYE: December 31
Type: Public

MCG Capital puts its money on the little guy. The closed-end investment firm lends money to and invests in lower middle-market US firms with annual sales of less than $50 million. As a business development company (BDC) MCG is required to invest at least 70% of its assets in private or thinly traded US public companies. It is an active investor working with companies' management teams to set and execute strategy. The company has invested more than $6 billion in more than 600 transactions since its 1999 founding. At the end of 2013 MCG's portfolio included mostly debt and some equity stakes in 34 companies with a combined fair value of about $369 million. MCG is buying back its shares and may liquidate.

	Annual Growth	12/09	12/10	12/11	12/12	12/13
Sales ($ mil.)	(15.7%)	99.8	89.6	85.7	61.0	50.5
Net income ($ mil.)	–	(51.1)	(13.1)	(93.1)	5.0	1.2
Market value ($ mil.)	0.5%	304.6	491.5	281.3	324.3	310.2
Employees	(28.2%)	64	66	37	21	17

MCGLADREY LLP

CEO: –
CFO: –
HR: –

1 S. Wacker Dr. Ste. 800
Chicago IL 60606
Phone: 312-634-3400
Fax: 952-921-7702
Web: mcgladrey.com/

FYE: April 30
Type: Private - Partnershi

McGladrey LLP (formerly McGladrey & Pullen) pulls its weight while offering accounting auditing and consulting services. The certified public accountant serves primarily owner-managed midsized businesses from more than 75 offices across the US. Services include auditing financial statement preparation and public company reporting. Industry specializations include financial institutions not-for-profits and manufacturing concerns. The firm also works globally through its membership in RSM International. The accounting firm which traces its historical roots to 1926 changed its name to McGladrey LLP following the acquisition of RSM McGladrey marking its transition to a single partner-owned CPA firm.

MCGOUGH CONSTRUCTION CO. INC.

2737 Fairview Ave. N.
St. Paul MN 55113-1372
Phone: 651-633-5050
Fax: 651-633-5673
Web: www.mcgough.com

CEO: Thomas McGough Jr
CFO: –
HR: –
FYE: December 31
Type: Private

McGough Construction Company has built its reputation from the North Star State all the way down to the home of the Grand Canyon. The company provides construction services ranging from site acquisition to post-construction facility management. McGough Construction concentrates on commercial residential and civic projects through its four primary units: construction; corporate services (layout planning financial estimates); development (logistics project management zoning); and facility management. Peter McGough and his six sons incorporated the family-owned and operated company in 1956. McGough Construction Company operates from offices in St. Paul and Rochester Minnesota and in Phoenix.

MCGRATH RENTCORP

NMS: MGRC

5700 Las Positas Road
Livermore, CA 94551-7800
Phone: 925 606-9200
Fax: –
Web: www.mgrc.com

CEO: Dennis C. Kakures
CFO: Keith E. Pratt
HR: Kay Dashner
FYE: December 31
Type: Public

McGrath RentCorp helps clients who are short on space. Through subsidiaries the company rents and sells commercial storage and electronic equipment. Its largest subsidiary is Mobile Modular which rents portable buildings used as classrooms field offices health care clinics or rest rooms. Other subsidiaries such as TRS-RenTelco rents and sells electronic test equipment used in the aerospace defense communications and manufacturing industries while Enviroplex makes and sells modular buildings used in California public schools. Adler Tank Rentals provides containers used for storing hazardous and non-hazardous materials. McGrath has most of its operations in California Texas and in Midwestern US states.

	Annual Growth	12/10	12/11	12/12	12/13	12/14
Sales ($ mil.)	8.8%	291.4	342.7	364.1	379.3	408.1
Net income ($ mil.)	5.8%	36.5	49.6	44.8	43.4	45.7
Market value ($ mil.)	8.1%	683.1	755.2	758.0	1,036.8	934.2
Employees	11.0%	655	742	760	911	995

MCGRAW HILL FINANCIAL, INC.

NYS: MHFI

55 Water Street
New York, NY 10041
Phone: 212 438-1000
Fax: –
Web: www.mhfi.com

CEO: Douglas L. (Doug) Peterson
CFO: Jack F. Callahan
HR: France Gingras
FYE: December 31
Type: Public

McGraw-Hill Financial (formerly The McGraw-Hill Companies) is now a provider of credit ratings benchmarks and analytics for the global capital and commodity markets. The company was a leading publisher of textbooks tests and related materials serving the elementary secondary and higher education markets through McGraw-Hill Education (MHE) before it spun that business off in 2013. Other businesses include S&P Ratings (indexes and credit ratings); S&P Capital IQ and S&P Indices (financial and business information); and Commodities and Commercial (Platts J.D. Power and Associates McGraw-Hill Construction and Aviation Week).

	Annual Growth	12/11	12/12	12/13	12/14	12/15
Sales ($ mil.)	(4.0%)	6,246.0	4,450.0	4,875.0	5,051.0	5,313.0
Net income ($ mil.)	6.1%	911.0	437.0	(115.0)	1,376.0	1,156.0
Market value ($ mil.)	21.7%	11,926.0	14,498.5	20,738.6	23,597.5	26,143.4
Employees	(2.6%)	22,660	21,687	17,000	17,000	20,400

MCGUIREWOODS LLP

1 James Center 901 E. Cary St.
Richmond VA 23219-4030
Phone: 804-775-1000
Fax: 804-775-1061
Web: www.mcguirewoods.com

CEO: –
CFO: Elizabeth Burke
HR: –
FYE: December 31
Type: Private - Partnershi

McGuireWoods is a large law firm with about 900 lawyers practicing in more than 15 offices in the US and two European offices. McGuireWoods which has grown through a series of mergers and acquisitions maintains a broad range of practices and specializes in such areas as corporate finance health care labor and employment and litigation. In addition the firm provides lobbying and public relations business advisory and human resources consulting services through McGuireWoods-branded subsidiaries. The firm has represented clients such as CounterPoint Capital MJP Waterjets Park Sterling Corporation (PSTB). McGuireWoods traces its roots to a Virginia practice started in 1834 by Egbert Watson.

MCKEE FOODS CORPORATION

10260 McKee Rd.
Collegedale TN 37315
Phone: 423-238-7111
Fax: 423-238-7127
Web: www.mckeefoods.com

CEO: –
CFO: Barry Patterson
HR: –
FYE: June 30
Type: Private

Little Debbie smiles up from North American lunch bags. McKee Foods' Little Debbie is one of the nation's best-known brands of snack cakes named for and featuring the smiling face of the 4-year-old granddaughter of the company's late founders: O. D. and Ruth McKee. Founded in 1934 McKee also makes ready-to-eat breakfast cereals granola creme-filled cookies crackers and snack bars. It counts more than 160 varieties of Little Debbie-brand products. McKee's baked goods are available in the US Canada and Mexico. The bakery is still owned and operated by the McKee family including CEO Mike McKee and the real Little Debbie Debbie McKee-Fowler who is an EVP.

MCKENNA LONG & ALDRIDGE LLP

1900 K St. NW
Washington DC 20006-1108
Phone: 202-496-7500
Fax: 202-496-7756
Web: www.mckennalong.com

CEO: –
CFO: –
HR: –
FYE: December 31
Type: Private - Partnershi

McKenna Long & Aldridge knows where the concerns of business and government come together. The law firm divides its practices into three broad areas: corporate transactions litigation and government and regulatory services. Its specialties include energy environmental law finance health care intellectual property and technology international law and real estate. McKenna Long has about 475 lawyers and public policy advisers who practice from some 10 offices in the US and one in Belgium. In early 2012 McKenna Long announced it was merging with California-based law firm Luce Forward Hamilton & Scripps LLP in a deal that will create a firm with a combined 600 lawyers and 13 offices.

MCKESSON CORP.

NYS: MCK

One Post Street
San Francisco, CA 94104
Phone: 415 983-8300
Fax: –
Web: www.mckesson.com

CEO: John H. Hammergren
CFO: James A. Beer
HR: Jorge L. Figueredo
FYE: March 31
Type: Public

McKesson moves medicine. As a top pharmaceuticals distributor in North America McKesson delivers prescription and generic drugs as well as health and beauty care products to more than 40000 retail and institutional pharmacies throughout the US. The company is also a major medical supplies wholesaler providing medical and surgical equipment to alternate health care sites such as doctors' offices surgery centers and long-term care facilities. In addition to distribution services McKesson offers software and technical services that help pharmacies health care providers and insurers manage supply chain clinical administrative and financial operations. The company was found in 1883.

	Annual Growth	03/11	03/12	03/13	03/14	03/15
Sales ($ mil.)	12.4%	112,084.0	122,734.0	122,455.0	137,609.0	179,045.0
Net income ($ mil.)	5.3%	1,202.0	1,403.0	1,338.0	1,263.0	1,476.0
Market value ($ mil.)	30.1%	18,339.6	20,362.6	25,046.7	40,964.2	52,478.4
Employees	17.9%	36,400	37,700	43,500	42,800	70,400

MCKESSON MEDICAL-SURGICAL INC.

8741 Landmark Rd.
Richmond VA 23228-2801
Phone: 804-264-7500
Fax: 804-264-7679
Web: www.mckgenmed.com

CEO: –
CFO: James Beer
HR: –
FYE: March 31
Type: Subsidiary

Scalpel suture sponge — McKesson Medical-Surgical wants to be the one handing them over. Long a dominant distributor of medical and surgical supplies to health care sites the company is a subsidiary of top US drug wholesaler McKesson. From a network of more than 35 distribution centers located throughout the US McKesson Medical-Surgical delivers more than 150000 products including its own private-label line of patient exam wound care and laboratory supplies. It serves some 300000 customers including hospitals doctors' offices surgery centers long-term care facilities home care agencies and other health care facilities.

MCKINSTRY CO. LLC

5005 3rd Ave. South
Seattle WA 98134
Phone: 206-762-3311
Fax: 206-762-2624
Web: www.mckinstry.com

CEO: Dean Allen
CFO: Jim Chamberlin
HR: –
FYE: December 31
Type: Private

McKinstry one of the top specialty contractors in the Pacific Northwest provides mechanical electrical and plumbing services in more than 15 US states throughout the West Midwest and Southwest. It designs and maintains complete building systems such as heating ventilation and air conditioning (HVAC) fire protection piping parking and solar panel and rain collection systems. The firm also provides design/build facilities management project management and maintenance services. McKinstry works on new buildings or retrofits existing facilities. It targets the commercial high-tech health care hospitality and industrial markets. The company was founded in 1960 by George Allen and Merrill McKinstry.

MCLAREN HEALTH CARE CORPORATION

G3235 BEECHER RD
FLINT, MI 485323650
Phone: 810-342-1100
Fax: –
Web: www.mclaren.org

CEO: –
CFO: Dennis Kirzemkrski
HR: –
FYE: September 30
Type: Private

McLaren Health Care is where people in The Auto State go for repairs. The health care system includes some 300 facilities including a dozen regional hospitals and a network of cancer dialysis imaging and surgery centers across the state of Michigan. Combined its facilities have about 2900 beds and serve more than 50 counties. Through its subsidiaries McLaren manages a primary care physician network commercial and Medicaid HMOs and assisted living facilities and provides visiting nurse/home health care and hospice services. Its Great Lakes Cancer Institute provides cancer research and treatment with partner Michigan State University.

	Annual Growth	09/02	09/03	09/05	09/06	09/08
Sales ($ mil.)	(37.2%)	–	868.1	1,014.5	883.7	84.5
Net income ($ mil.)	(53.7%)	–	–	40.9	58.0	4.1
Market value ($ mil.)	–	–	–	–	–	–
Employees	–	–	–	–	–	10,003

MCLAREN PERFORMANCE TECHNOLOGIES INC.

32233 W. Eight Mile Rd.
Livonia MI 48152
Phone: 248-477-6240
Fax: 248-477-3349
Web: www.mclarenperformance.com

CEO: Wiley R McCoy
CFO: Chris J Panzl
HR: Kurt Frunbauer
FYE: December 31
Type: Subsidiary

McLaren Performance Technologies (formerly McLaren Automotive Group) always wants more horsepower. Originally established in 1969 to develop engines for Bruce McLaren Motor Racing the company offers engineering services and specializes in the design and development of chassis and automotive powertrain systems (clutch transmission drive shaft and differential) and provides certification of both consumer automotive and racing engines. Boasting prototyping and fabrication facilities with 14 hoist-equipped bays McLaren Performance Technologies has performed work for Ford BMW and General Motors. The company was acquired by Linamar Corp. in 2003 and functions within the transmission/drivetrain division.

MCMASTER-CARR SUPPLY COMPANY

600 N. County Line Rd.
Elmhurst IL 60126-2081
Phone: 630-600-3600
Fax: 630-834-9427
Web: www.mcmaster.com

CEO: Robert Delaney
CFO: –
HR: Monica Holloway
FYE: December 31
Type: Private

McMaster-Carr Supply is ready to fill your pipe pump power transmission and process control needs (and that's only in the P section of its extensive A to Z catalog). The company distributes more than 510000 mechanical electrical and utility products including air conditioners clamps drills exhaust fans generators light bulbs pipes pumps saws switches and valves. Family-owned McMaster-Carr operates through a handful of regional branches in the US that provide customer service sales warehousing and management. Customers order through an online catalog or through its traditional direct mail catalog.

MCNAUGHTON-MCKAY ELECTRIC CO.

1357 E LINCOLN AVE
MADISON HEIGHTS, MI 480714126
Phone: 248-541-2805
Fax: –
Web: www.mc-mc.com

CEO: –
CFO: John D Kuczmanski
HR: John D. Kuczmanski
FYE: December 31
Type: Private

Getting connected at work has a completely different meaning at McNaughton-McKay. Its more than 10000 customers can buy electrical supplies sensors and controls and automation and security software online or through 22 branches in five US states and two offices in Germany. One of the largest employee-owned companies in the US McNaughton-McKay distributes some 300 product lines from manufacturers such as Hubbell GE Brady Belden Coleman Cable Leviton Thomas & Betts Cognex Specter Instruments and Rockwell Automation. It sells to the construction commercial government and industrial automation markets.

	Annual Growth	12/09	12/10	12/11	12/12	12/13
Sales ($ mil.)	10.4%	–	493.6	603.4	641.3	664.0
Net income ($ mil.)	–	–	–	0.0	0.0	0.0
Market value ($ mil.)	–	–	–	–	–	725
Employees	–	–	–	–	–	725

MCNEIL CONSUMER PHARMACEUTICALS CO.

7050 Camp Hill Rd.
Fort Washington PA 19034-2292
Phone: 215-273-7700
Fax: 215-273-4193
Web: www.mylanta.com

CEO: –
CFO: –
HR: –
FYE: December 31
Type: Subsidiary

Got a fire in your belly? McNeil Consumer Pharmaceuticals can help put it out. The company makes and markets OTC Pepcid heartburn relief products as well as medicine cabinet stalwart Mylanta in North America. The Pepcid family includes acid reducer Pepcid AC as well as and Pepcid Complete which adds in the quick relief of an antacid. Its Mylanta products include liquid and chewable tablet formulations for heartburn gas and other tummy ailments. The unit also makes Mylicon an anti-gas OTC product for babies. Formerly known as Johnson & Johnson - Merck Consumer Pharmaceuticals the company was owned equally by major drug companies Johnson & Johnson and Merck until 2011 when J&J acquired full ownership.

MCNEILUS COMPANIES INC.

524 County Rd. 34 East
Dodge Center MN 55927
Phone: 507-374-6321
Fax: 507-374-6394
Web: www.mcneiluscompanies.com

CEO: Charles Szews
CFO: -
HR: -
FYE: September 30
Type: Subsidiary

Talking trash (and transporting it) is big business at McNeilus Companies. The company manufactures garbage trucks (front side and rear loaders) concrete mixers and related heavy duty commercial construction vehicles and components. McNeilus also builds and erects concrete batch plants (machinery used to store and load concrete into concrete trucks) such as conveyors drums dust collectors material storage silos and bins rollers and water systems. The lineup is sold through a network of dealers to waste haulers and ready-mix companies and mining and construction businesses in the US and abroad. McNeilus Companies operates as a subsidiary of truck and vehicle maker Oshkosh.

MCNICHOLS COMPANY

2502 N ROCKY POINT DR # 750
TAMPA, FL 336071421
Phone: 813-282-3828
Fax: -
Web: www.mcnichols.com

CEO: Gene McNichols
CFO: Craig A Stein
HR: -
FYE: December 31
Type: Private

McNichols Company manufactures metal products that are full of holes ... by design. Its products include perforated and expanded metals wire mesh bar and plank gratings fiberglass grating floorings handrail components ladder rungs and mattings. Its perforated metal (aka "hole") products are sold under the brand names Eco-Mesh Grate-Lock Perf-O-Grip Safplate and Vinylmesh among many others. The company also provides custom fabrication services. McNichols operates is business through some 20 service centers nationwide. It was founded in 1952 by the late Robert McNichols grandfather of current president Scott McNichols. The McNichols family runs the firm based on Christian principles.

	Annual Growth	12/05	12/06	12/07	12/08	12/09
Sales ($ mil.)	(38.8%)	-	-	376.2	209.4	140.8
Net income ($ mil.)	-	-	-	0.0	3.7	0.0
Market value ($ mil.)	-	-	-	-	-	-
Employees	-	-	-	-	-	325

MCPHEE ELECTRIC LTD

505 MAIN ST
FARMINGTON, CT 060322912
Phone: 860-677-9797
Fax: -
Web: www.mcpheeusa.com

CEO: Michael Mc Phee
CFO: John Conroy
HR: -
FYE: December 31
Type: Private

McPhee Electric is energized about its work. The company which is a unit of Phalcon provides electrical construction and data and communications installation services (including cellular towers) throughout New England. Services include conceptual planning feasibility studies budgeting design development installation maintenance and service. McPhee Electric's clients come from a wide variety of industries including education financial services government health care manufacturing pharmaceuticals retail and utilities. The company's projects include utility substations Foxwoods Resort Casino a Bristol-Myers Squibb research facility and Cordon Bleu Culinary Institute.

	Annual Growth	12/09	12/10	12/11	12/12	12/13
Sales ($ mil.)	12.0%	-	77.7	87.8	94.5	109.2
Net income ($ mil.)	34.6%	-	-	9.7	11.9	17.5
Market value ($ mil.)	-	-	-	-	-	-
Employees	-	-	-	-	-	500

MCRAE INDUSTRIES, INC.

NBB: MCRA B

400 North Main Street
Mount Gilead, NC 27306
Phone: 910 439-6147
Fax: 910 439-4190
Web: www.mcraeindustries.com

CEO: D Gary Mc Rae
CFO: -
HR: Kay Martin
FYE: August 02
Type: Public

McRae Industries has interests ranging from bar codes to boots. The company's footwear segment consisting of subsidiaries McRae Footwear and Dan Post Boot Co. makes combat boots for the US and foreign militaries Western boots and work boots. Dan Post Boot markets and distributes boot brands Laredo Dingo John Deere and Dan Post. A third subsidiary Compsee makes bar code readers printers and optical data-collection equipment. Compsee also licenses and sells computer software worldwide. McRae Industries makes most of its money from the Western and work boot segment. The McRae family controls more than 50% of the company's voting power.

	Annual Growth	07/10	07/11	07/12*	08/13	08/14
Sales ($ mil.)	13.4%	62.6	74.7	75.7	97.1	103.6
Net income ($ mil.)	26.5%	3.0	3.8	4.8	7.5	7.5
Market value ($ mil.)	22.7%	32.2	33.1	36.0	59.5	72.9
Employees	-	-	-	-	-	-

*Fiscal year change

MCWANE INC.

2900 Hwy. 280 Ste. 300
Birmingham AL 35223
Phone: 205-414-3100
Fax: 205-414-3170
Web: www.mcwane.com

CEO: G Ruffner Page Jr
CFO: Charles F Nowlin
HR: Darrell R Witt
FYE: December 31
Type: Private

As a manufacturer of fire hydrants McWane is a friend to both firefighters and dogs. But fire plugs represent only a fraction of McWane's broad range of products. Orchestrated through five product groups McWane's subsidiaries make a line of water distribution solutions including fire hydrants cast-iron water and sewer pipes fittings and compressed air tanks. Its Amerex subsidiary is one of the world's largest makers of fire extinguishers. Subsidiary Manchester Tank makes pressure vessels from huge propane cylinders to handheld torches. Its M&H Valve Co. a maker of industrial valves for wastewater equipment and fire hydrants has operated since 1854.

MDU RESOURCES GROUP INC.

NYS: MDU

1200 West Century Avenue, P.O. Box 5650
Bismarck, ND 58506-5650
Phone: 701 530-1000
Fax: -
Web: www.mdu.com

CEO: Martin A. Fritz
CFO: Doran N. Schwartz
HR: Anne Jones
FYE: December 31
Type: Public

MDU Resources has branched out from its roots as a regional utility to cover a range of natural resources businesses. Utility subsidiaries Montana-Dakota Utilities Wyoming Utilities Great Plains Natural Gas and Cascade Natural Gas deliver gas to more than 892000 customers and electricity to more than 138000 customers in 177 communities. MDU Resources' energy businesses include natural gas transmission gathering and storage; and oil and gas exploration and production. Its construction materials and contracting division (including Knife River) mines and sells concrete gravel and other materials. MDU Resources' MDU Construction Services unit builds power lines pipelines and telecom systems.

	Annual Growth	12/10	12/11	12/12	12/13	12/14
Sales ($ mil.)	4.5%	3,909.7	4,050.5	4,075.4	4,462.4	4,670.6
Net income ($ mil.)	5.2%	240.7	213.0	(0.8)	278.6	294.3
Market value ($ mil.)	3.8%	3,936.8	4,167.9	4,125.1	5,933.3	4,564.1
Employees	1.7%	7,895	8,021	8,629	9,133	8,451

MEAD JOHNSON NUTRITION CO

NYS: MJN

2701 Patriot Blvd.
Glenview, IL 60026
Phone: 847 832-2420
Fax: –
Web: www.meadjohnson.com

CEO: Peter Kasper Jakobsen
CFO: Michel M.G. Cup
HR: –
FYE: December 31
Type: Public

Mead Johnson Nutrition helps babies grow up healthy. The company specializes in developing and manufacturing nutritional products for infants and children. It distributes its 70-plus products to more than 50 countries. Mead Johnson's Enfamil line of infant formulas is its most visible consumer brand. Other products in its portfolio include Sustagen and Lactum — two fortified beverages for children — and Nutramigen a nutritional supplement for children with dairy allergies. Besides babies the company markets nutritional supplements for use by pregnant and breastfeeding moms. Mead Johnson also produces specialty nutritional products for premature infants and infants with metabolic and digestive disorders.

	Annual Growth	12/10	12/11	12/12	12/13	12/14
Sales ($ mil.)	8.8%	3,141.6	3,677.0	3,901.3	4,200.7	4,409.3
Net income ($ mil.)	12.3%	452.7	508.5	604.5	649.5	719.8
Market value ($ mil.)	12.7%	12,593.2	13,904.1	13,329.5	16,944.6	20,339.2
Employees	4.3%	6,500	6,600	6,800	7,200	7,700

MEADOWBROOK INSURANCE GROUP INC

NYS: MIG

26255 American Drive
Southfield, MI 48034
Phone: 248 358-1100
Fax: –
Web: www.meadowbrook.com

CEO: Robert S Cubbin
CFO: Karen M Spaun
HR: –
FYE: December 31
Type: Public

Meadowbrook Insurance puts its clients' liabilities and risks out to pasture. Through subsidiaries including Star Insurance Savers P&C Williamsburg National Ameritrust ProCentury and Century Surety the company writes a variety of specialty commercial property/casualty insurance policies including workers' compensation commercial auto and multi-peril liability policies. With coverage tailored to fit small to midsized businesses customers include self-insured companies trade groups and associations. Meadowbrook also offers brokering risk management consulting and insurance management services including claims handling and administrative services.

	Annual Growth	12/09	12/10	12/11	12/12	12/13
Assets ($ mil.)	8.5%	1,989.8	2,177.6	2,381.3	2,713.3	2,761.8
Net income ($ mil.)	–	52.7	59.7	43.6	11.7	(112.3)
Market value ($ mil.)	(1.5%)	369.2	511.3	532.8	288.3	347.2
Employees	1.0%	918	967	1,054	1,032	954

MEADWESTVACO CALMAR

11901 Grandview Rd.
Grandview MO 64030
Phone: 816-986-6103
Fax: 816-986-6120
Web: www.calmar.com

CEO: –
CFO: –
HR: –
FYE: December 31
Type: Subsidiary

MeadWestvaco Calmar has a way with spray. The company is a top manufacturer of plastic spray pumps used for everything from cleaning products to perfumes to pharmaceuticals such as nose and throat sprays. Its injection-molded products include trigger sprayers and dispenser pumps as well as dispenser components such as tubes and springs. Calmar which introduced the all-plastic spray pump more than 50 years ago has operations in Asia Europe and North and South America.

MEADWESTVACO CORP.

NYS: MWV

501 South 5th Street
Richmond, VA 23219-0501
Phone: 804 444-1000
Fax: –
Web: www.mwv.com

CEO: John A Luke Jr
CFO: Mark Rajkowski
HR: –
FYE: December 31
Type: Public

MeadWestvaco (MWV) has got your products covered — literally. MWV's packaging business — folding cartons corrugated boxes and printed plastics — serves many of the world's major brands. MWV wraps up health care personal and beauty care food and tobacco as well as home and garden goods. MWV also packages pharmaceuticals and manufactures packaging equipment for dairy and beverage OEMs. It operates through five segments: Food and Beverage; Specialty Chemicals; Home Health and Beauty; Industrial; and Community Development and Land Management.

	Annual Growth	12/09	12/10	12/11	12/12	12/13
Sales ($ mil.)	(2.8%)	6,049.0	5,693.0	6,060.0	5,459.0	5,389.0
Net income ($ mil.)	39.0%	225.0	106.0	246.0	205.0	839.0
Market value ($ mil.)	6.6%	4,994.3	4,563.4	5,224.6	5,559.5	6,442.2
Employees	(5.4%)	20,000	17,500	17,000	16,000	16,000

MEALS ON WHEELS ASSOCIATION OF AMERICA

203 S. Union St.
Alexandria VA 22314
Phone: 703-548-5558
Fax: 703-548-8024
Web: www.mowaa.org

CEO: Ellie Hollander
CFO: –
HR: –
FYE: December 31
Type: Private - Not-for-Pr

Meals on Wheels Association of America (MOWAA) helps to fuel programs throughout the US that deliver meals to people who are elderly homebound disabled or otherwise at risk of going hungry. It provides information via conferences and newsletters and tools including bulk purchasing services to Meals on Wheels programs that are members of the association. MOWAA also works to obtain government grants and distribute money to local meal delivery programs. The Meals on Wheels concept was developed in the UK during WWII and introduced in the US in 1954.

MEASUREMENT SPECIALTIES, INC.

NMS: MEAS

1000 Lucas Way
Hampton, VA 23666
Phone: 757 766-1500
Fax: –
Web: www.meas-spec.com

CEO: Frank D Guidone
CFO: Mark Thomson
HR: –
FYE: March 31
Type: Public

Sensing the pressure? Measurement Specialties would rather do that for you. The company's industrial product line includes sensors that measure such properties as fluid level and properties gas concentration and flow rate humidity torque pressure vibrations and more. Its sensors are used in aerospace consumer appliance environmental water monitoring industrial medical military test and measurement transportation and vehicle applications. The company's biggest customer Sensata Technologies (about 15% of sales) serves the automotive market. US customers account for one-thirds of sales; those in China make up nearly a quarter.

	Annual Growth	03/09	03/10	03/11	03/12	03/13
Sales ($ mil.)	14.2%	203.9	209.6	274.8	313.2	347.0
Net income ($ mil.)	59.5%	5.3	5.9	28.2	27.7	34.2
Market value ($ mil.)	76.6%	63.6	228.8	529.1	524.2	618.6
Employees	9.6%	2,184	2,520	2,923	3,235	3,154

MECHANICAL TECHNOLOGY, INC.　　　　NBB: MKTY

325 Washington Avenue Extension　　　　CEO: Kevin G Lynch
Albany, NY 12205　　　　CFO: Frederick W Jones
Phone: 518 218-2550　　　　HR: Jeuillie Keegan
Fax: –　　　　FYE: December 31
Web: www.mechtech.com　　　　Type: Public

Mechanical Technology Inc. (MTI) is warming up to the alternative energy market. The company's MTI Instruments Inc. subsidiary (MTII) makes computer-based aircraft engine balancing systems capacitance measuring systems and non-contact sensing instrumentation; the US Air Force accounts for about one-quarter of its product sales. MTI is diversifying its offerings by investing and partnering its way into the alternative energy market. The company's MTI MicroFuel Cells subsidiary develops methanol fuel cells for use in portable electronics. The company also has a minority equity interest in Plug Power another developer of fuel cells.

	Annual Growth	12/10	12/11	12/12	12/13	12/14
Sales ($ mil.)	1.1%	8.4	10.3	5.9	8.4	8.8
Net income ($ mil.)	–	(1.8)	2.4	(2.1)	3.7	0.7
Market value ($ mil.)	(3.1%)	4.2	2.6	0.9	5.7	3.7
Employees	(9.0%)	51	43	33	35	35

MECKLERMEDIA CORP　　　　NBB: MECK

50 Washington Street, Suite 902　　　　CEO: Alan M Meckler
Norwalk, CT 06854　　　　CFO: –
Phone: 212 389-2000　　　　HR: Kimberly Guinta
Fax: –　　　　FYE: December 31
　　　　Type: Public

If your brand isn't on the Web WebMediaBrands wants to help. The company provides digital content education job listings events and other resources for media creative and design professionals. Its flagship Mediabistro network of websites targets the media industry including digital and print publishing advertising television and public relations markets. Its AllCreativeWorld reaches creative and design professionals through websites such as Graphics.com and Creativebits. WebMediaBrands also offers community membership and e-commerce offerings such as a freelance listing service and a marketplace for designing and purchasing logos. Chairman and CEO Alan Meckler owns about 40% of WebMediaBrands.

	Annual Growth	12/10	12/11	12/12	12/13	12/14
Sales ($ mil.)	(20.7%)	9.0	12.4	14.0	12.5	3.6
Net income ($ mil.)	–	(3.0)	(11.9)	(8.7)	(5.7)	(3.8)
Market value ($ mil.)	(27.6%)	9.8	2.9	12.2	19.2	2.7
Employees	(28.5%)	69	74	121	94	18

MECO CORPORATION

1500 Industrial Rd.　　　　CEO: –
Greeneville TN 37745　　　　CFO: –
Phone: 423-639-1171　　　　HR: –
Fax: 423-639-2570　　　　FYE: June 30
Web: www.meco.net　　　　Type: Private

Take a seat and then let MECO Corporation meet all of your changing lifestyle needs. The company specializes in manufacturing residential and commercial folding furniture including steel patio chairs heavy-duty banquet tables and covered swing sets. MECO designs and markets its furnishings under the Samsonite Innobella and SuddenComfort brands. It also produces barbecue grills and cooking accessories under the Aussie label. The company's products are available through retail stores nationwide.

MEDA PHARMACEUTICALS INC.

265 Davidson Ave. Ste. 300　　　　CEO: Maria Carell
Somerset NJ 08873-4120　　　　CFO: Jeffrey Hostler
Phone: 732-564-2200　　　　HR: –
Fax: 732-564-2235　　　　FYE: December 31
Web: www.medapharma.us　　　　Type: Subsidiary

You won't turn your nose up at Meda Pharmaceuticals' products especially if you've got a runny one. The specialty drug firm makes a number of prescription remedies for allergies including its flagship product Astelin nasal spray antihistamine. Meda Pharmaceuticals also makes therapies in niche markets such as central nervous system disorders (its Felbatol treats epilepsy) insomnia muscle spasms and women's health products. Its Onsolis is a transdermal version of cancer pain drug fentanyl that dissolves inside the patient's cheek. The company's sales force targets doctors and hospitals; it is the US subsidiary of Swedish drug firm Meda AB.

MEDALLION FINANCIAL CORP.　　　　NMS: TAXI

437 Madison Avenue, 38th Floor　　　　CEO: Alvin Murstein
New York, NY 10022　　　　CFO: Larry D Hall
Phone: 212 328-2100　　　　HR: –
Web: www.medallion.com　　　　FYE: December 31
　　　　Type: Public

Medallion Financial turns taxicab licenses or "medallions" into gold. The specialty finance company makes loans for the purchase of medallions which are usually limited in number per city by law. It targets mainly New York City but also finances medallions in Boston and Cambridge Massachusetts; Chicago; and Newark New Jersey. (A NYC taxi medallion costs more than $1 million.) Subsidiary Medallion Bank funds its taxi and commercial lending activities by issuing certificates of deposit to clients; it also originates loans for boats trailers motorcycles and recreational vehicles. Other subsidiaries including Medallion Capital and Freshstart Venture Capital offer commercial loans ranging from $200000 to $5 million.

	Annual Growth	12/10	12/11	12/12	12/13	12/14
Assets ($ mil.)	3.5%	550.3	537.0	543.5	595.1	632.3
Net income ($ mil.)	11.3%	9.9	10.8	8.8	12.2	15.1
Market value ($ mil.)	5.1%	201.9	280.2	289.0	353.3	246.5
Employees	6.8%	122	127	145	145	159

MEDASSETS INC　　　　NMS: MDAS

100 North Point Center East, Suite 200　　　　CEO: R Halsey Wise
Alpharetta, GA 30022　　　　CFO: Anthony Colaluca
Phone: 678 323-2500　　　　HR: –
Fax: –　　　　FYE: December 31
Web: www.medassets.com　　　　Type: Public

MedAssets helps hospitals widen their profit margins — or at least not lose quite as much. The company's Spend and Clinical Resource Management (SCM) segment is its largest with almost 60% of sales. It operates a group purchasing organization (GPO) that negotiates lower prices on medical supplies and devices for hospitals and health systems. The company's Revenue Cycle Management (RCM) segment provides software and consulting services that help track and analyze a hospital's revenue stream. Such services aim to increase collections and reduce account balances. MedAssets' customers include more than 4200 hospitals and about 122000 non-acute health providers mainly in the US but also in Canada to a lesser extent.

	Annual Growth	12/09	12/10	12/11	12/12	12/13
Sales ($ mil.)	18.8%	341.3	391.3	578.3	640.1	680.4
Net income ($ mil.)	8.3%	19.9	(32.1)	(15.5)	(6.9)	27.4
Market value ($ mil.)	(1.7%)	1,309.5	1,246.5	571.1	1,035.4	1,224.3
Employees	9.8%	2,200	3,100	3,040	3,100	3,200

MEDCATH CORPORATION

NASDAQ: MDTH

10720 Sikes Place Ste. 300
Charlotte NC 28277
Phone: 704-708-6600
Fax: 704-708-5035
Web: www.medcath.com

CEO: –
CFO: Lora Ramsey
HR: Michael D Allen
FYE: September 30
Type: Public

Can heart alone sustain a business? MedCath has learned that despite the best intentions no heart alone is not enough. The company founder of the first stand-alone heart hospital in the US owned and managed a network of medical facilities specializing in cardiology and cardiovascular services mostly in the Southwest. MedCath shared ownership of its hospitals (which are licensed as general acute care) with local physicians. MedCath also provided physician practice management services to heart specialists. However the company has sold off its health care assets and plans to dissolve its remaining operations due to financial difficulties.

MEDECISION INC.

601 Lee Rd. Chesterbrook Corporate Center
Wayne PA 19087
Phone: 610-540-0202
Fax: 610-540-0270
Web: www.medecision.com

CEO: Deborah Gabe
CFO: Kenneth Young
HR: –
FYE: December 31
Type: Subsidiary

MEDecision helps clear the paperwork and leave doctors and other caregivers with only health care to worry about. MEDecision provides a variety of proprietary modular health care management software and data analysis services to physicians and managed care organizations. The company's products enable the health care providers on a patient's care team to share information about a patient's status and history. The company's clients have included Blue Cross and Blue Shield Liberty Mutual and PacifiCare Health Systems. MEDecision was founded in 1988 and acquired by Health Care Service Corp. in 2008.

MEDIA GENERAL INC (NEW)

NYS: MEG

333 E. Franklin St.
Richmond, VA 23219
Phone: 804 887-5000
Fax: 804 649-6898
Web: www.mediageneral.com

CEO: George L. Mahoney
CFO: James F Woodward
HR:
FYE: December 31
Type: Public

With interests in digital publishing and broadcasting this company generally has the media covered. Media General operates about 20 network-affiliated television stations. In addition Media General operates websites for every one of its television stations. Built through a series of acquisitions the company's collection of media properties is organized regionally making Media General a dominant voice in the southeastern US. In 2012 the company sold all of its newspapers and in 2016 Media General agreed to be acquired by Nexstar Broadcasting Group.

	Annual Growth	12/10	12/11	12/12	12/13	12/14
Sales ($ mil.)	(0.1%)	678.1	616.2	359.7	269.9	675.0
Net income ($ mil.)	–	(22.6)	(74.3)	(193.4)	6.1	53.5
Market value ($ mil.)	31.1%	735.4	554.8	558.7	2,936.5	2,173.8
Employees	3.3%	4,650	4,200	1,600	2,600	5,300

MEDIA SCIENCES INTERNATIONAL INC.

PINK SHEETS: MSII

8 Allerman Rd.
Oakland NJ 07463
Phone: 201-677-9311
Fax: 201-677-1440
Web: www.mediasciences.com

CEO: –
CFO: Denise Hawkins
HR: –
FYE: June 30
Type: Public

Media Sciences International supports the art science and business of printing. The company makes printing supplies for color business printers. Its products include solid ink sticks designed for printers from a variety of manufacturers including Brother Dell Konica Minolta Oki Data Ricoh Samsung Seiko Epson and Xerox. Through its INKlusive program Media Sciences supplies customers with color printers for a monthly fee that covers the price of ink supplies; the program requires a multiyear commitment. Media Sciences sells directly and through reseller channels primarily in the US.

MEDIA STORM LLC

99 WASHINGTON ST STE 3
NORWALK, CT 068543080
Phone: 203-852-8001
Fax: –
Web: www.mediastorm.biz

CEO: –
CFO: Frank Connolly
HR: –
FYE: December 31
Type: Private

Media Storm is a rainmaker looking to bring a deluge. The company provides media planning and buying services for television radio print and interactive channels. Media Storm creates showers of customers primarily for clients in the entertainment industry; it specializes in audience acquisition for broadcasters cable networks pay-per-view companies and television program syndicators. Customers have included such big names as HBO NBCUniversal Food Network Twentieth Century Fox and the NFL. The company also drives traffic and memberships for e-commerce client Shopzilla. Managing partners Tim Williams and Craig Woerz created Media Storm in 2001.

	Annual Growth	12/03	12/04	12/05	12/06	12/07
Sales ($ mil.)	50.5%	–	36.5	80.9	114.4	124.3
Net income ($ mil.)	22.2%	–	–	7.1	10.1	10.6
Market value ($ mil.)	–	–	–	–	–	–
Employees	–	–	–	–	–	136

MEDIAMIND TECHNOLOGIES INC.

135 W. 18th St. 5th Fl.
New York NY 10011
Phone: 646-202-1320
Fax: 212-686-9208
Web: www.mediamind.com

CEO: Neil Nguyen
CFO: Sarit Firon
HR: –
FYE: December 31
Type: Subsidiary

MediaMind (formerly Eyeblaster) puts a lot of thought into online advertising. Advertisers and media agencies use the company's campaign management software to create and administer rich media content including online mobile and in-game advertisements. Its portfolio also includes tools for monitoring and measuring such metrics as display time and interaction rate. MediaMind offers services ranging from custom development and testing to data tracking and analysis. Its products have been used in advertisements for NIKE Sony Ford Toyota Vodafone MasterCard and McDonalds among others. The company went public in 2010; it was bought by Digital Generation (formerly DG FastChannel) for $418 million in 2011.

MEDIANET DIGITAL INC.

85 10th Ave. 3rd Fl.
New York NY 10011
Phone: 212-704-0280
Fax: 212-759-9783
Web: www.mndigital.com

CEO: –
CFO: –
HR: –
FYE: December 31
Type: Private

It doesn't write the songs that make the whole world sing but MediaNet Digital can help if the world wants to sell some digital songs. The company formerly MusicNet is a provider of a service that allows its business clients to integrate digital entertainment content into their Web site or other application. All total MediaNet Digital powers more than 100 customers from niche bloggers to global entertainment brands such as Rolling Stone. MediaNet's catalog includes more than 7 million songs and thousands of music videos from the four major music labels and some 80000 independent labels. The company has offices in New York Seattle and London. It was founded in 2001 and is owned by Baker Capital.

MEDICAL MUTUAL OF OHIO

2060 E. 9th St.
Cleveland OH 44115
Phone: 216-687-7000
Fax: 216-687-6044
Web: www.mmoh.com

CEO: Rick A Chiricosta
CFO: –
HR: –
FYE: December 31
Type: Private - Not-for-Pr

Medical Mutual of Ohio is a not-for-profit managed care company that provides health insurance products and related services to some 1.6 million members in a handful of states in the midwestern and southern US. The company's individual and group health plans include HMO PPO POS traditional indemnity and supplemental Medicare. Medical Mutual of Ohio also provides dental vision and prescription drug plans life insurance and third-party administration (TPA) services. Mutual Medical's products are marketed through a network of independent brokers.

MEDICAL ACTION INDUSTRIES, INC.

NMS: MDCI

500 Expressway Drive South
Brentwood, NY 11717
Phone: 631 231-4600
Fax: –
Web: www.medical-action.com

CEO: Paul D Meringolo
CFO: –
HR: Kim Moser
FYE: March 31
Type: Public

Medical Action Industries knows in advance that its products will end up in hospitals' waste bins. The company manufactures markets and distributes a wide range of single-use disposable medical products. Some of its main products include wash basins and bedpans IV start kits containment systems for medical waste sterilization products dressing and surgical sponges and laboratory products (such as Petri dishes and specimen containers). Though it sells primarily to hospitals Medical Action Industries also serves doctors dentists veterinary clinics outpatient centers and nursing homes.

	Annual Growth	03/09	03/10	03/11	03/12	03/13
Sales ($ mil.)	10.5%	296.1	290.1	362.5	437.3	441.6
Net income ($ mil.)	–	5.0	16.8	4.4	0.2	(54.9)
Market value ($ mil.)	(7.8%)	135.9	201.1	137.7	93.8	98.3
Employees	9.1%	854	831	1,289	1,210	1,210

MEDICAL PROPERTIES TRUST INC

NYS: MPW

1000 Urban Center Drive, Suite 501
Birmingham, AL 35242
Phone: 205 969-3755
Fax: 205 969-3756
Web: www.medicalpropertiestrust.com

CEO: Edward K. Aldag
CFO: R. Steven Hamner
HR: –
FYE: December 31
Type: Public

Hospitals trust Medical Properties to provide the leases under which their facilities operate. The self-advised real estate investment trust (REIT) invests in and owns more than 110 health care facilities including acute care hospitals inpatient rehabilitation hospitals and wellness centers in 25 US states and Germany. California and Texas combined account for nearly 50% of the REIT's annual revenue. It leases the facilities to more than 25 hospital operating companies under long-term triple-net leases where the tenant bears most of the operating costs. Prime Healtcare Services and Ernest Health are among the REIT's largest clients. Medical Properties Trust entered the European health care market in 2013.

	Annual Growth	12/10	12/11	12/12	12/13	12/14
Sales ($ mil.)	26.6%	121.8	143.3	201.4	242.5	312.5
Net income ($ mil.)	21.9%	22.9	26.5	89.9	97.0	50.5
Market value ($ mil.)	6.2%	1,870.8	1,705.0	2,066.0	2,110.9	2,380.4
Employees	11.6%	29	29	33	38	45

MEDICAL LIABILITY MUTUAL INSURANCE COMPANY

2 Park Ave. Rm. 2500
New York NY 10016
Phone: 212-576-9800
Fax: 212-725-0916
Web: www.mlmic.com

CEO: –
CFO: –
HR: Regina Kennedy
FYE: December 31
Type: Private - Mutual Com

Medical Liability Mutual Insurance Company (MLMIC) is one of the largest writers of medical malpractice insurance in the US. The New York-based company insures nearly 20000 doctors as well as dentists midwives and other medical professionals and medical facilities in New York New Jersey and surrounding areas. Other offerings include legal services group billing for physicians' groups and free information sessions for medical and dental residents nearing the end of their professional training. MLMIC was established in 1975 and is owned by its policyholders.

MEDICAL STAFFING NETWORK HEALTHCARE LLC

901 Yamato Rd. Ste. 110
Boca Raton FL 33431
Phone: 561-322-1300
Fax: 561-322-1200
Web: www.msnhealth.com

CEO: Brian Poplin
CFO: –
HR: –
FYE: December 31
Type: Private

Is there a nurse or radiology tech in the house? Medical Staffing Network steps in when health care providers need workers. The company places temporary nurses and other medical support staff at health care facilities such as hospitals and nursing homes. Options include per diem staffing (assignments lasting less than two weeks) travel staffing (temporary assignments that require relocation) and allied health assignments (staffing for specialized radiology or other clinical lab technicians). It also offers OneSource a vendor management service for financial and staff utilization rate tracking. Medical Staffing Network owns branch offices throughout the US and serves more than 7000 health care facilities.

MEDICINE SHOPPE INTERNATIONAL INC.

1 Rider Trail Plaza Dr. Ste. 300
Earth City MO 63045
Phone: 314-993-6000
Fax: 314-872-5500
Web: www.medicineshoppe.com

CEO: –
CFO: –
HR: –
FYE: June 30
Type: Subsidiary

With locations spreading like the flu Medicine Shoppe International (MSI) is the nation's largest independent retail pharmacy franchisor. A subsidiary of Cardinal Health since 1995 MSI has more than 700 locations in about 45 US states and the Virgin Islands. Internationally MSI has more than 200 stores in Canada China Indonesia Japan and the Middle East. MSI pharmacies specialize in prescriptions (more than 97% of sales) and offer only health-related inventory including Medicine Shoppe-brand nonprescription products. Many locations offer free services such as immunizations and health screenings. The Medicine Shoppe was founded in 1968 by St. Louis pharmacist Michael Busch.

MEDICINES CO (THE)

NMS: MDCO

8 Sylvan Way
Parsippany, NJ 07054
Phone: 973 290-6000
Fax: –
Web: www.themedicinescompany.com

CEO: Clive A. Meanwell
CFO: William OÂ'Connor
HR: Christian Bovenkamp
FYE: December 31
Type: Public

The Medicines Company will meet you at the hospital. The drug developer focuses on treatments used in acute care settings including the ER the surgical suite and the cardiac catheterization lab. Its marketed products are Angiomax an anticoagulant used during coronary angioplasties and Cleviprex an IV drug used to control blood pressure spikes. It also sells Argatroban and Brilinta. The Medicines Company has other compounds in various stages of development including cangrelor an anti-platelet agent with possible use during cardiac catheterization and antibiotic oritavancin.

	Annual Growth	12/10	12/11	12/12	12/13	12/14
Sales ($ mil.)	13.4%	437.6	484.7	558.6	687.9	724.4
Net income ($ mil.)	–	104.6	127.9	51.3	15.5	(32.2)
Market value ($ mil.)	18.3%	925.2	1,220.4	1,569.4	2,528.6	1,811.7
Employees	14.7%	420	421	538	571	727

MEDICINOVA INC

NMS: MNOV

4275 Executive Drive, Suite 650
La Jolla, CA 92037
Phone: 858 373-1500
Fax: –
Web: www.medicinova.com

CEO: Yuichi Iwaki
CFO: Esther Van Den Boom
HR: –
FYE: December 31
Type: Public

MediciNova has medicine all over the map. The biopharmaceutical company has a diverse pipeline of products in development that aim to treat everything from asthma and cancer to anxiety and insomnia. Two of its core candidates are being clinically tested for use in the treatment of severe asthma and multiple sclerosis. Others are being developed for preterm labor interstitial cystitis (urinary frequency and bladder pain) and urinary incontinence. MediciNova has been building its development portfolio through licensing agreements acquiring product rights primarily from midsized Japanese pharmaceutical companies such as Kissei Pharmaceutical Kyorin Pharmaceutical and Mitsubishi Tanabe Pharma Corporation.

	Annual Growth	12/09	12/10	12/11	12/12	12/13
Sales ($ mil.)	648.0%	–	–	–	0.8	6.0
Net income ($ mil.)	–	(20.4)	(20.2)	(17.7)	(11.0)	(4.0)
Market value ($ mil.)	(25.8%)	158.4	106.0	38.2	36.9	48.1
Employees	(18.6%)	25	18	14	12	11

MEDICIS PHARMACEUTICAL CORPORATION

NYSE: MRX

7720 N. Dobson Rd.
Scottsdale AZ 85256-2740
Phone: 602-808-8800
Fax: 602-808-0822
Web: www.medicis.com

CEO: Jonah Shacknai
CFO: Richard D Peterson
HR: –
FYE: December 31
Type: Public

Medicis Pharmaceutical is a smooth operator when it comes to skin. It is a specialty pharmaceutical company that develops and markets branded prescription products for dermatological and aesthetic conditions. Major products include the Dysport injectable formulation for temporary improvement of frown lines Restalyne injectable gel for smoothing facial wrinkles Solodyn oral tablets for moderate to severe acne and Vanos topical cream for psoriasis and dermatitis. These products are marketed primarily to dermatologists and plastic surgeons in the US. Medicis was acquired for about $2.6 billion by Valeant Pharmaceuticals the largest publicly traded drug maker in Canada in December 2012.

MEDIDATA SOLUTIONS, INC.

NMS: MDSO

350 Hudson Street, 9th Floor
New York, NY 10014
Phone: 212 918-1800
Fax: –
Web: www.mdsol.com

CEO: Tarek A. Sherif
CFO: Cory A. Douglas
HR: Eileen Schloss
FYE: December 31
Type: Public

Medidata Solutions has electronic remedies to help clinical trials run smoothly. Founded in 1999 the company offers cloud-based applications that help biotechnology pharmaceutical and other life sciences companies conduct clinical trials and related research. Its products include hosted software for administering and managing clinical trials electronic data capture applications study management applications and patient diaries. The company also offers a variety of professional services such as consulting implementation integration and maintenance. Medidata operates in more than 115 countries but most of its sales come from the US.

	Annual Growth	12/10	12/11	12/12	12/13	12/14
Sales ($ mil.)	19.1%	166.4	184.5	218.3	276.8	335.1
Net income ($ mil.)	(28.1%)	22.8	39.4	18.0	16.7	6.1
Market value ($ mil.)	18.9%	1,299.4	1,183.5	2,131.9	3,292.1	2,598.2
Employees	15.8%	598	690	796	923	1,077

MEDIFAST INC

NYS: MED

3600 Crondall Lane
Owings Mills, MD 21117
Phone: 410 581-8042
Fax: –
Web: www.medifastnow.com

CEO: Michael C. MacDonald
CFO: Timothy Robinson
HR: Jeanne M. Uphouse
FYE: December 31
Type: Public

Medifast tries to help people slim down and shape up... fast. The company develops and sells Medifast brand health and diet products including food and beverages (meal replacement shakes bars) as well as disease management products for diabetics. Subsidiary Jason Pharmaceuticals makes some of the company's products. Medifast operates through two segments Medifast and MWCC and Wholesale. Medifast includes Direct (customers order Medifast products online) and Take Shape for Life (personal coaching division with independent contractor "health coaches"). MWCC and Wholesale covers Medifast Weight Control Centers' (MWCC) bricks-and-mortar walk-in clinics while Wholesale includes doctor's offices that sell the products.

	Annual Growth	12/10	12/11	12/12	12/13	12/14
Sales ($ mil.)	2.6%	257.6	298.2	356.7	356.9	285.3
Net income ($ mil.)	(9.5%)	19.6	18.5	15.9	24.0	13.2
Market value ($ mil.)	3.8%	348.7	165.7	318.7	315.5	405.1
Employees	3.4%	507	860	947	808	579

MEDIMMUNE L.L.C.

1 MedImmune Way
Gaithersburg MD 20878
Phone: 301-398-0000
Fax: 212-809-9528
Web: www.bnymellon.com

CEO: Tony Zook
CFO: Timothey Pearson
HR: –
FYE: December 31
Type: Subsidiary

MedImmune works to boost the immune systems of babies and grown-ups. Its flagship biotech product Synagis prevents respiratory syncytial virus (RSV) a major cause of pneumonia and other respiratory disease in infants and children. Also on the market are FluMist its nasal spray flu vaccine and Ethyol (amifostine) which treats side effects of chemotherapy and radiation. The company is working on dozens of investigational therapies — including monoclonal antibodies vaccines and small molecule drugs — in the areas of infectious disease cancer inflammation and autoimmune and respiratory conditions. MedImmune is a subsidiary of UK-based pharmaceutical giant AstraZeneca.

MEDIVATION INC

NMS: MDVN

525 Market Street, 36th Floor
San Francisco, CA 94105
Phone: 415 543-3470
Fax: 415 543-3411
Web: www.medivation.com

CEO: David T. Hung
CFO: Rick Bierly
HR: Sandy Cooper
FYE: December 31
Type: Public

Medivation motivates medicine makers. The company acquires develops and sells (or partners with companies working on) biopharmaceuticals. Medivation initiates drug development programs seeking out candidates that address unmet medical needs and have the potential to rapidly enter clinical development and marketing stages. The firm typically develops its drug candidates through early-stage clinical trials and then determines whether to conduct further studies or to seek a partner or buyer to continue later-stage trials. Medivation's lead candidate XTANDI was approved by the FDA to treat certain forms of prostate cancer in 2012; the drug was developed in partnership with Astellas.

	Annual Growth	12/10	12/11	12/12	12/13	12/14
Sales ($ mil.)	83.6%	62.5	60.4	181.7	272.9	710.5
Net income ($ mil.)	–	(34.0)	(38.8)	(41.3)	(42.6)	276.5
Market value ($ mil.)	60.1%	2,370.1	7,204.0	7,993.0	9,970.9	15,562.5
Employees	51.5%	92	121	257	370	485

MEDIWARE INFORMATION SYSTEMS INC.

NASDAQ: MEDW

11711 W. 79th St.
Lenexa KS 66214
Phone: 913-307-1000
Fax: 913-307-1111
Web: www.mediware.com

CEO: Thomas Kelly Mann
CFO: Robert Watkins
HR: –
FYE: June 30
Type: Private

Mediware Information Systems keeps blood banks' computers from becoming a bloody mess. The company offers data management systems for blood banks hospitals and pharmacies. Mediware is known for its clinical information systems which combine third-party and proprietary software to manage hospital departments. Products include the HCLL transfusion management system for tracking blood bank and transfusion facility inventories the WORx drug therapy management software for pharmacies and the InSight performance management software suite. In 2012 Mediware was acquired and taken private by private equity firm Thoma Bravo in a deal valued at about $195 million.

MEDLER ELECTRIC COMPANY

2155 REDMAN DR
ALMA, MI 488019313
Phone: 989-463-1108
Fax: –
Web: www.medlerelectric.com

CEO: –
CFO: –
HR: –
FYE: December 31
Type: Private

|No meddlers here; this company just wants to help customers. Medler Electric Company is a distributor of electrical parts and supplies; it gets the majority of its business from companies in the construction market. Medler Electric carries products (ranging from motors and heaters to lighting and much more) from such manufacturers as 3M Cooper Lighting Daniel Woodhead Ferraz Shawmut Littelfuse and Square D Company. The employee-owned company was established in 1918 by W. W. Medler and operates through 14 branch offices in the state of Michigan.

	Annual Growth	12/09	12/10	12/11	12/12	12/13
Sales ($ mil.)	7.9%	–	34.4	37.6	40.3	43.2
Net income ($ mil.)	29.8%	–	–	0.0	0.0	0.0
Market value ($ mil.)	–	–	–	–	–	–
Employees	–	–	–	–	–	111

MEDLINE INDUSTRIES INC.

1 Medline Place
Mundelein IL 60060
Phone: 847-949-5500
Fax: 800-351-1512
Web: www.medline.com

CEO: Charles N Mills
CFO: Kristofer Howard
HR: –
FYE: December 31
Type: Private

When health care supplies are on the line Medline Industries goes toe-to-toe with the big guys. With more than 125000 products the family-owned company's catalog includes hospital furnishings durable medical equipment housekeeping supplies and exam gloves and garments. The firm manufactures and distributes health care products to such customers as hospitals long-term care facilities physician practices and home health providers. It also acts as a distributor for other manufacturers' products. In addition Medline offers inventory and supply chain solutions for health care providers. Products are marketed by its more than 1100 sales representatives through some 50 distribution centers in 20 countries.

MEDNAX, INC.

NYS: MD

1301 Concord Terrace
Sunrise, FL 33323
Phone: 954 384-0175
Fax: –
Web: www.mednax.com

CEO: Roger J. Medel
CFO: Vivian Lopez-Blanco
HR: –
FYE: December 31
Type: Public

MEDNAX is a multi-specialty medical group with a national focus. Through its Pediatrix Medical Group American Anesthesiology and Mednax Services units the holding company operates a medical network composed of more than 2500 affiliated physicians specialty practitioners and subspecialists who focus on women's and children's health. It provides neonatal obstetric and pediatric care primarily in hospitals; it also operates a growing number of anesthesia practices. In addition MEDNAX conducts clinical research and offers practice administration services to physician members and hospital customers in the areas of billing compliance managed care contracting recruiting risk management and staffing.

	Annual Growth	12/11	12/12	12/13	12/14	12/15
Sales ($ mil.)	15.0%	1,588.2	1,816.6	2,154.0	2,438.9	2,780.0
Net income ($ mil.)	11.4%	218.0	240.9	280.5	317.3	336.3
Market value ($ mil.)	(0.1%)	6,750.1	7,454.1	5,003.8	6,197.1	6,717.3
Employees	14.3%	6,967	7,900	8,800	10,175	11,885

MEDPLUS INC.

4690 Parkway Dr.
Mason OH 45040
Phone: 513-229-5500
Fax: 513-229-5505
Web: www.medplus.com

CEO: –
CFO: –
HR: –
FYE: December 31
Type: Subsidiary

MedPlus is the antidote to administrative headaches for the health care industry. Hospitals clinics and other health care organizations use the company's electronic health records (EHR) software to collect store and manage patient information. Its offerings include ChartMaxx which pools a patient's clinical financial and administrative information into one Internet-accessible record and the Web-based Care360 suite which allows doctors to refill prescriptions order lab tests and send secure messages electronically. It Centergy Data Exchange platform lets hospitals physicians and other parties share patient data. MedPlus is a subsidiary of clinical lab company Quest Diagnostics.

MEDSEEK INC.

3000 RIVERCHASE GALLERIA # 1500
HOOVER, AL 35244-2315
Phone: 205-982-5800
Fax: –
Web: www.medseek.com

CEO: Gale Wilson-Steele
CFO: –
HR: –
FYE: December 31
Type: Private

Hospitals searching for help with website development could find answers from MedSeek. The Web development company designs and manages websites and intranets for more than 1100 hospitals. It offers a propriety content management software called eHealth ecoSystem and also provides custom application design. Its Web portals feature physician directories and job boards and they provide secure access to clinical information and facilitate communication between doctors patients and hospitals. MedSeek was founded in 1996.

	Annual Growth	12/06	12/07	12/08	12/10	12/11
Sales ($ mil.)	21.6%	–	23.0	25.1	34.6	50.2
Net income ($ mil.)	94.6%	–	0.2	1.6	2.4	2.4
Market value ($ mil.)	–	–	–	–	–	–
Employees	–	–	–	–	–	50

MEDSTAR HEALTH INC.

5565 STERRETT PL STE 500
COLUMBIA, MD 21044-2679
Phone: 410-772-6500
Fax: –
Web: www.medstarhealth.org

CEO: Kenneth A Samet
CFO: Michael J Curran
HR: –
FYE: June 30
Type: Private

Whether you're seeing stars or are just plain sickly MedStar Health can cater to you. The not-for-profit organization runs 10 hospitals and about 20 other health-related businesses across Maryland and the Washington DC area including Union Memorial and Georgetown University Hospital. With more than 3000 beds and 5600 affiliated physicians MedStar has a comprehensive service offering including acute and long-term sub-acute care emergency services home health care and rehabilitation. It also operates emergency clinics and assisted living and nursing homes maintains a primary care and specialist physician network (MedStar Physician Partners) and conducts research and medical education activities.

	Annual Growth	06/08	06/09	06/10	06/11	06/12
Sales ($ mil.)	4.3%	–	3,678.0	–	4,011.7	4,175.9
Net income ($ mil.)	–	–	(193.8)	–	271.0	(181.8)
Market value ($ mil.)	–	–	–	–	–	–
Employees	–	–	–	–	–	24,100

MEDSTAR-GEORGETOWN MEDICAL CENTER INC.

3800 RESERVOIR RD NW
WASHINGTON, DC 20007-2113
Phone: 202-444-2000
Fax: –
Web: www.medstargeorgetown.org

CEO: –
CFO: Pipper Williams
HR: –
FYE: June 30
Type: Private

Georgetown University Hospital part of MedStar Health is a 609-bed acute care teaching hospital serving residents of the greater Washington DC area including Maryland and Virginia. The hospital's staff of more than 1100 physicians represents a wide range of medical specializations including cardiology oncology neurology/neurosurgery and surgical transplantation. Georgetown University Hospital (also known as Medstar Georgetown University Hospital) provides a comprehensive array of inpatient outpatient surgical and rehabilitative care services. The hospital is part of a local network of affiliated primary care providers.

	Annual Growth	06/07	06/08	06/09	06/10	06/11
Sales ($ mil.)	3.4%	–	–	–	782.5	809.1
Net income ($ mil.)	(3.7%)	–	–	–	45.4	43.7
Market value ($ mil.)	–	–	–	–	–	–
Employees	–	–	–	–	–	4,000

MEDTEL SERVICES LLC

OTC: TELT

2511 Corporate Way
Palmetto FL 34221
Phone: 941-753-5000
Fax: 941-751-7754
Web: www.medtelservices.com

CEO: Jim Wallace
CFO: –
HR: –
FYE: December 31
Type: Private

MedTel Services (formerly Teltronics) is hooked on communications systems management and switching products. The company's systems and software are used to monitor and manage telecommunication networks (including PBXs and data networks). MedTel's products include digital switching systems for distributing calls customer contact management software and remote maintenance systems for collecting network traffic data and monitoring alarm status. The company also provides contract manufacturing services for companies in industrial control telecom and test and measurement. MedTel gets most of its sales in the US. Teltronics' assets were bought out of bankruptcy in 2012 and renamed MedTel Services LLC.

MEDTOX SCIENTIFIC INC.

NASDAQ: MTOX

402 W. County Rd. D
St. Paul MN 55112
Phone: 651-636-7466
Fax: 651-636-5351
Web: www.medtox.com

CEO: Richard J Braun
CFO: –
HR: Lisa H Starr
FYE: December 31
Type: Public

Doctors depend on MEDTOX Scientific to gather up specimen cups and analyze the contents for any number of substances. Customers can either ship urine samples off to the company's central labs for testing or buy the company's diagnostic and screening tests for use at the point of collection. In addition to testing for drugs of abuse MEDTOX Laboratories specializes in clinical and forensic toxicology including heavy metals analysis and hazardous-materials exposure monitoring. The company's MEDTOX Diagnostics subsidiary develops and manufactures onsite drug testing kits for rapid detection. MEDTOX Scientific was acquired by diagnostics and laboratory services giant LabCorp in 2012.

MEDTRONIC SOFAMOR DANEK USA INC.

2600 Sofamor Danek Dr.
Memphis TN 38132
Phone: 901-396-3133
Fax: 901-344-0843
Web: www.medtronic.com/about-medtronic/business-ove

CEO: –
CFO: Gary Ellis
HR: –
FYE: May 31
Type: Subsidiary

Medtronic Sofamor Danek USA wants to help us all stand up straight and proud. It is the the lead business in Medtronic's Spinal unit and one of the world's biggest maker of spinal implants. It products treat degenerative diseases deformities and spine and cranium trauma. It manufactures both implanted devices and biologic bone graft products. It also develops minimally invasive surgical techniques and computer-assisted surgical instruments. The company's sister business Kyphon develops medical devices to help with spinal fractures caused by osteoporosis and cancer. Medtronic Sofamor Danek USA markets and distributes its products worldwide.

MEDTRONIC, INC.

NYS: MDT

710 Medtronic Parkway
Minneapolis, MN 55432
Phone: 763 514-4000
Fax: 763 514-4879
Web: www.medtronic.com

CEO: Omar Ishrak
CFO: Gary L Ellis
HR: Cox Ashley
FYE: April 26
Type: Public

Sometimes the best medicine is a short sharp shock; that's why Medtronic's products reside in its customers' hearts and minds (among other places). A leading maker of implantable biomedical devices the company makes defibrillators and pacemakers that issue electrical impulses or shocks to keep hearts beating normally. Its Cardiac and Vascular Group also produces catheters stents valves balloons and surgical ablation technologies used to treat vascular and heart disease. The company's Restorative Therapies Group makes nerve and brain stimulation devices implantable drug delivery systems products used to manage diabetes and surgical devices for ear nose and throat (ENT) and spinal conditions.

	Annual Growth	04/09	04/10	04/11	04/12	04/13
Sales ($ mil.)	3.2%	14,599.0	15,817.0	15,933.0	16,184.0	16,590.0
Net income ($ mil.)	12.4%	2,169.0	3,099.0	3,096.0	3,617.0	3,467.0
Market value ($ mil.)	11.9%	30,053.7	44,389.7	42,418.6	38,293.6	47,102.4
Employees	3.3%	41,000	43,000	45,000	44,944	46,659

MEENAN OIL CO. L.P.

3020 Burns Ave.
Wantagh NY 11793-4407
Phone: 516-783-1000
Fax: 516-781-2332
Web: www.meenan.com

CEO: –
CFO: –
HR: David Macagnone
FYE: June 30
Type: Subsidiary

"Me" may be at the beginning of Meenan Oil's name but it's the customer who comes first at the home heating oil company. Meenan Oil offers expert tank analysis heating and cooling services brand-name equipment and home security monitoring services to customers in New Jersey New York and Pennsylvania. The company's headquarters include a garage and repair shop installation equipment warehouses 12 loading and unloading stations and a 1.3 million gallon storage tank. Meenan Oil is a subsidiary of Star Gas Partners which is controlled by investment firm Kestrel Energy Partners LLC.

MEETME INC.

NAS: MEET

100 Union Square Drive
New Hope, PA 18938
Phone: 215 862-1162
Fax: –
Web: www.meetme.com

CEO: Geoffrey Cook
CFO: David D Clark
HR: –
FYE: December 31
Type: Public

MeetMe is all about making new friends. Formerly called Quepasa Corporation the company aims to connect people through social games and apps across iPhone Android Web and mobile Internet platforms. The company took its current shape after merging Quepasa (which targeted a Latin American audience) with Insider Guides (doing business as myYearbook.com) in 2011; it rebranded as MeetMe in 2012. The new name reflects a less regional focus as MeetMe is designed for a global audience. The company earns revenue mainly through display advertising on its site as well as selling virtual currency for its games.

	Annual Growth	12/10	12/11	12/12	12/13	12/14
Sales ($ mil.)	64.9%	6.1	11.9	46.7	40.4	44.8
Net income ($ mil.)	–	(6.7)	(12.8)	(10.3)	(10.9)	(4.0)
Market value ($ mil.)	(39.9%)	525.4	149.1	156.7	82.2	68.7
Employees	12.3%	76	203	162	125	121

MEGAMEX FOODS LLC

4340 Eucalyptus Ave. Unit A
Chino CA 91710-9705
Phone: 909-631-2000
Fax: 909-631-2100
Web: www.megamexfoods.com

CEO: –
CFO: –
HR: –
FYE: December 31
Type: Joint Venture

MegaMex Foods spices up grocery store shelves. The company manufactures Mexican spices and sauces. It distributes them to retailers and food service suppliers throughout the US as well as internationally. Its products include the La Victoria brand of salsas taco and enchilada sauces and chiles as well as the Embasa brand canned salsas and chiles. The company's customers include retail food outlets and food service operators and it makes and distributes private-label products. MegaMex (also known as Authentic Specialty Foods) is a 50-50 joint venture between Herdez Del Fuerte and Hormel Foods.

MEGGITT (NORTH HOLLYWOOD) INC.

12838 Saticoy St.
North Hollywood CA 91605
Phone: 818-765-8160
Fax: 818-759-2190
Web: www.whittakercontrols.com

CEO: James Simpkins
CFO: –
HR: –
FYE: December 31
Type: Subsidiary

Got Meggitt? Meggitt (North Hollywood) has a valve for the situation. Formerly Whittaker Controls the company designs and manufactures valves and controls that regulate the flow of air and fluids under pressure and high temperatures. Its pneumatic and fluid control lines include fuel mixing and starter valves air-oil separators and solenoid valves used in commercial and military aircraft and aero-engines. Industrial offerings provide fuel and bleed-air control valves and ground fuelling products for power generation and mechanical drives. Airbus Boeing GE and Pratt & Whitney are major customers. Meggitt (North Hollywood) a subsidiary of UK-based Meggitt is part of the Meggitt Control Systems division.

MEGGITT AIRCRAFT BRAKING SYSTEMS CORPORATION

1204 Massillon Rd.
Akron OH 44306-4186
Phone: 330-796-4400
Fax: 330-796-1605
Web: www.aircraftbraking.com

CEO: –
CFO: –
HR: Michael Rubino
FYE: December 31
Type: Subsidiary

Meggitt Aircraft Braking Systems (MABS) wants to bring aviation to a screeching halt. MABS makes steel brakes carbon brakes and electric brakes brake control systems landing gear computers brake temperature sensors main and nose wheels and wheel speed transducers. MABS braking systems are used in commercial and business jets military aircraft helicopters regional turboprops and general aviation aircraft. Major customers include Bombardier Embraer Gulfstream Aerospace and Hawker Beechcraft. The company has operations in Africa the Americas Europe the Middle East and Asia/Pacific. It is a subsidiary of Meggitt-USA which is part of UK-based Meggitt PLC. MABS represents 27% of group revenue.

MEGGITT TRAINING SYSTEMS INC.

296 Brogdon Rd.
Suwanee GA 30024
Phone: 678-288-1090
Fax: 678-288-1515
Web: www.meggitttrainingsystems.com

CEO: Ronald Vadas
CFO: Jeff Murphy
HR: –
FYE: March 31
Type: Subsidiary

Meggitt Training Systems (formerly Firearms Training Systems) provides digital technology and laser-emitting weapons for the realistic weapons training of law enforcement military and security personnel in the US and overseas. The training systems integrate video and digitized imagery with laser-emitting firearms that have the look and feel of the real thing — they even recoil. Simulated arms range from semiautomatic pistols to anti-armor rocket launchers and cannons. Meggitt Training Systems (MTS) has locations in Australia Canada the Netherlands Singapore United Arab Emirates the UK and the US. The company is part of Meggitt PLC's Equipment Group.

MEGGITT-USA INC.

1955 N. Surveyor Ave.
Simi Valley CA 93063
Phone: 805-526-5700
Fax: 805-584-4182
Web: www.meggitt.com

CEO: –
CFO: –
HR: –
FYE: December 31
Type: Subsidiary

Meggitt-USA is the bridge between the US and its UK-based mothership Meggitt plc. Meggitt has four divisions: Aircraft Braking Systems (MABS; brakes brake controls) Control Systems (valves pumps fans motors) Polymers & Composites (aircraft seals flexible fuel tanks coatings composite structures) and Sensing Systems (test measurement). Meggitt-USA designs and manufactures original equipment (OE) and aftermarket equipment used in civil aerospace and military defense applications — for air land and sea. Non-military markets include automotive energy transportation industrial and medical. Meggitt's Equipment division makes aircraft fire protection avionics combat systems and training systems.

MEI TECHNOLOGIES INC.

18050 SATURN LN STE 300
HOUSTON, TX 770584502
Phone: 281-283-6200
Fax: –
Web: www.meitechinc.com

CEO: Ed Muniz
CFO: Karen Todd
HR: –
FYE: December 31
Type: Private

MEI Technologies helps companies with high aspirations. The engineering and IT services firm serves government agencies such as NASA and the aerospace industry with cyber services space access test and evaluation and human performance. Other high-tech services include launch vehicle and shuttle payload integration and operations mission safety program management and support and spacecraft systems engineering and design. The company was founded in 1992 as Muñiz Engineering Inc. (MEI) by former CEO Edelmiro Muñiz.

	Annual Growth	12/06	12/07	12/08	12/12	12/13
Sales ($ mil.)	(2.9%)	–	116.1	118.9	137.2	97.5
Net income ($ mil.)	–	–	–	(0.9)	4.8	2.7
Market value ($ mil.)	–	–	–	–	–	–
Employees	–	–	–	–	–	721

MEIJER INC.

2929 Walker Ave. NW
Grand Rapids MI 49544-9424
Phone: 616-453-6711
Fax: 616-791-2572
Web: www.meijer.com

CEO: Hank Meijer
CFO: Dan Webb
HR: –
FYE: January 31
Type: Private

Meijer (pronounced "Meyer") is a giant of retailing in the Midwest. The company's huge combination grocery and general merchandise stores average 200000 to 250000 sq. ft. each (or about the size of four regular grocery stores) and stock about 120000 items including Meijer private-label products. Meijer operates some 200 locations; about half are in Michigan while the rest are in Illinois Indiana Kentucky and Ohio. Customers can choose from 40-plus departments including apparel electronics hardware and toys. Most stores also sell gasoline offer banking services and have multiple in-store restaurants. Founder Hendrik Meijer opened his first store in 1934; the business is still family owned and run.

MEINEKE CAR CARE CENTERS INC.

128 S. Tryon St. Ste. 900
Charlotte NC 28202
Phone: 704-377-8855
Fax: 704-377-1490
Web: www.meineke.com

CEO: Ken Walker
CFO: Miko Carlot
HR: –
FYE: June 30
Type: Private

Careful not to exhaust its options Meineke Car Care Centers (formerly Meineke Discount Mufflers) is thinking outside the muffler. Through 900-plus franchised stores in the US Canada Mexico Saudi Arabia South Korea and China Meineke repairs brakes aligns wheels installs tires and provides factory-scheduled maintenance among other services. From the company website customers can learn about vehicle maintenance and safety print coupons and apply for the Meineke credit card. Sam Meineke founded the company in Houston in 1972. Today it is owned by Driven Brands which also franchises the Maaco and Econo Lube 'N Tune brands among others.

MEMORIAL HEALTH SERVICES CORPORATION

17360 BROOKHURST ST # 160	CEO: James Hobson
FOUNTAIN VALLEY, CA 927088003	CFO: Cheryl Sadro
Phone: 714-377-6748	HR: –
Fax: –	FYE: June 30
Web: www.memorialcare.org	Type: Private

Where do you go after you get sick riding the tea cups at Disneyland? Not-for-profit Memorial Health Services (known as MemorialCare) owns six hospitals in Southern California including Long Beach Memorial Medical Center Miller Children's Hospital Orange Coast Memorial Medical Center and Saddleback Memorial Medical Center. The facilities have a total of more than 1500 beds and offer a full spectrum of medical services including rehabilitation diagnostic/radiology and emergency services. MemorialCare also operates women's health facilities and other specialty and general practice clinics as well as home health and hospice programs. The organization was founded in 1907.

	Annual Growth	06/07	06/08	06/09	06/10	06/13
Sales ($ mil.)	119.3%	–	–	90.6	113.1	2,094.3
Net income ($ mil.)	–	–	–	0.0	6.1	284.5
Market value ($ mil.)	–	–	–	–	–	–
Employees	–	–	–	–	–	2,000

MEMORIAL HEALTH SYSTEM

1400 E. Boulder St.	CEO: Mike Scialdone
Colorado Springs CO 80909	CFO: –
Phone: 719-365-5000	HR: George Soper
Fax: 719-365-5977	FYE: December 31
Web: www.memorialhealthsystem.com	Type: Government-owned

Memorial Health System tries to keep good health more than a memory for the patients in its care. The hospital system's main facility Memorial Hospital Central is a 520-bed general hospital which provides a range of children's and adult health-care services and specialties including cardiac care cancer treatment trauma care women's services pediatric medicine and rehabilitation. Established in 1904 the hospital has about 700 physicians on its medical staff. The Memorial Health System also includes the 100-bed Memorial Hospital North and the Memorial Hospital for Children as well as outpatient clinics throughout the Colorado Springs area.

MEMORIAL HEALTH SYSTEM OF EAST TEXAS

1201 W FRANK AVE	CEO: Bryant H Krenek Jr
LUFKIN, TX 759043357	CFO: Ken Miller
Phone: 936-634-8111	HR: –
Fax: –	FYE: December 31
Web: www.memorialhealth.us	Type: Private

Memorial Health System of East Texas operates deep in the heart of East Texas. The system is anchored by the 270-bed Memorial Medical Center-Lufkin a full-service general acute care hospital offering everything from rehabilitative and diabetes care to specialized centers in heart disease and cancer treatment. The Lufkin hospital also includes Memorial Specialty Hospital a long-term ward for critically ill patients. In addition Memorial Health System of East Texas features two critical access hospitals with limited services including emergency care and diagnostic imaging; it also has a clinic network. It is part of non-profit health care systems operator Catholic Health Initiatives (CHI).

	Annual Growth	12/03	12/04	12/07	12/08	12/09
Sales ($ mil.)	13.5%	–	102.3	–	8.4	192.7
Net income ($ mil.)	–	–	–	–	0.0	22.3
Market value ($ mil.)	–	–	–	–	–	–
Employees	–	–	–	–	–	940

MEMORIAL HEALTH UNIVERSITY MEDICAL CENTER INC.

4700 WATERS AVE	CEO: Magaret Gill
SAVANNAH, GA 314046283	CFO: –
Phone: 912-350-8000	HR: –
Fax: –	FYE: December 31
Web: www.memorialhealth.com	Type: Private

Memorial Health University Medical Center wants to provide memorable health care to residents of Savannah Georgia and surrounding areas. An affiliate of Mercer University School of Medicine the tertiary care facility provides such services as cardiac and trauma care and rehabilitation. Also known as Memorial University Medical Center (MUMC) the hospital has some 620 beds and includes the MUMC Children's Hospital. It also operates specialty cancer care and women's health centers as well as research programs. Founded in 1955 MUMC is the flagship facility in a broader system of entities known as Memorial Health which includes affiliated primary and specialty care clinics in the region.

	Annual Growth	12/00	12/01	12/02*	06/05*	12/08
Sales ($ mil.)	4.7%	–	–	345.0	447.3	453.3
Net income ($ mil.)	–	–	–	0.0	39.4	(29.4)
Market value ($ mil.)	–	–	–	–	–	–
Employees	–	–	–	–	–	5,000
						*Fiscal year change

MEMORIAL HERMANN HEALTHCARE SYSTEM

929 GESSNER RD STE 2600	CEO: Daniel J. Wolterman
HOUSTON, TX 770242593	CFO: Stacey Bevil
Phone: 713-338-5555	HR: –
Fax: –	FYE: June 30
Web: www.memorialhermann.org	Type: Private

Memorial Hermann Healthcare System is a Texas-sized operation. As Houston's largest not-for-profit health care system it includes a dozen hospitals (one is a children's hospital) with more than 3500 beds and dozens of specialty treatment centers. The system also operates three managed acute care hospitals and a retirement community. Through Memorial Hermann Regional Healthcare Services the company is affiliated with more than 20 community hospitals and health centers most serving rural areas within 150 miles of the Houston area. Other services and programs include substance abuse treatment home health services air ambulances medical training and imaging; it also offers health insurance coverage.

	Annual Growth	06/04	06/05	06/06	06/07	06/08
Sales ($ mil.)	13.4%	–	–	–	2,506.6	2,841.3
Net income ($ mil.)	(92.3%)	–	–	–	209.9	16.3
Market value ($ mil.)	–	–	–	–	–	–
Employees	–	–	–	–	–	16,505

MEMORIAL HOSPITAL

1101 MICHIGAN AVE	CEO: –
LOGANSPORT, IN 469471596	CFO: –
Phone: 574-753-7541	HR: Pedro C Vargas
Fax: –	FYE: December 31
Web: www.logansportmemorial.org	Type: Private

If your Eel River boat has been sunk by a Wabash cannonball you're probably a short crawl from a hospital. Logansport Memorial Hospital is a 80-bed acute care regional medical center serving the residents of Cass County and the surrounding communities in north central Indiana. The hospital offers a full range of medical services and programs including primary and emergency care and specialized services in areas such as diabetes cardiac rehabilitation medical imaging respiratory therapy and mammography. Logansport Memorial Hospital has about 40 physicians on its active medical staff. The hospital opened in 1925 as the Cass County Hospital and changed its name to Memorial Hospital in 1947.

	Annual Growth	12/05	12/06	12/07	12/09	12/12
Sales ($ mil.)	(24.0%)	–	319.2	46.8	55.3	61.3
Net income ($ mil.)	–	–	–	(1.6)	1.0	8.7
Market value ($ mil.)	–	–	–	–	–	–
Employees	–	–	–	–	–	507

MEMORIAL PRODUCTION PARTNERS LP

NMS: MEMP

500 Dallas Street, Suite 1800	CEO: John A Weinzierl
Houston, TX 77002	CFO: –
Phone: 713 588-8300	HR: –
Fax: –	FYE: December 31
Web: www.memorialpp.com	Type: Public

Memorial Production Partners was birthed as a limited partnership in April 2011 to own and acquire oil and natural gas properties in North America. With estimated proved reserves of about 325 billion cu. ft. of natural gas equivalent it will own and operate properties in South and East Texas mainly consisting of mature onshore oil and natural gas reservoirs. They were acquired by predecessor entities from the likes of Forest Oil and BP America Production Company. Formed and controlled by Memorial Resource Development LLC Memorial Production Partners is managed by a general partner and conducts operations mainly through one subsidiary. It went public in 2011.

	Annual Growth	12/10	12/11	12/12	12/13	12/14
Sales ($ mil.)	–	0.0	73.4	140.7	343.6	494.1
Net income ($ mil.)	–	0.0	82.3	29.9	20.0	118.0
Market value ($ mil.)	–	0.0	1,552.5	1,531.9	1,884.0	1,252.8
Employees	–	–	–	–	–	–

MEMORIAL SLOAN-KETTERING CANCER CENTER

1275 York Ave.	CEO: Craig B Thompson
New York NY 10065	CFO: –
Phone: 212-639-2000	HR: –
Fax: 212-639-3576	FYE: December 31
Web: www.mskcc.org	Type: Private - Not-for-Pr

Memorial Sloan-Kettering Cancer Center (MSKCC) leads the way in cancer research and treatment. The center includes the 430 bed Memorial Hospital for Cancer and Allied Diseases providing pediatric and adult cancer care and the Sloan-Kettering Institute for cancer research activities. Memorial Hospital specializes in bone-marrow transplants radiation therapy and chemotherapy and it offers programs in cancer prevention diagnosis treatment research and education. The Sloan-Kettering Institute conducts medical and clinical laboratory research on cancer genetics and therapeutics.

MEMORY LANE INC.

333 Elliott Ave. W.	CEO: –
Seattle WA 98119	CFO: –
Phone: 206 301 5700	HR: –
Fax: 262-695-6014	FYE: December 31
Web: www.cibmarine.com	Type: Subsidiary

If you want to take a digital trip down memory lane where else would you turn? Memory Lane operates nostalgia site MemoryLane.com which features 60000 digitized high school yearbooks as well as historical content related to movies music TV headlines sports and other lifestyle topics from the 1940s through 1990s. The site includes photos music and video files. The company also operates Classmates.com a website that reunites classmates friends and family teachers co-workers and military personnel. Memory Lane was founded as Classmates Online in 1995. Today it is a subsidiary of Internet service provider United Online (UOL).

MEMPHIS LIGHT GAS AND WATER DIVISION

220 S. Main St.	CEO: –
Memphis TN 38103	CFO: –
Phone: 901-544-6549	HR: –
Fax: 901-528-4758	FYE: December 31
Web: www.mlgw.com	Type: Government-owned

Memphis Light Gas and Water Division (MLGW) helps lighten up the Memphis blues. The municipally owned utility provides electricity water and natural gas services for all of Shelby County Tennessee including the city of Memphis. It serves primarily residential and commercial customers. MLGW buys electricity from the Tennessee Valley Authority (TVA) and distributes it to almost 430000 customers. The company purchases natural gas on the spot market transmits it through open access pipelines and delivers it to about 320000 customers. Through its artesian water system MLGW supplies water to more than 257000 customers.

MEMRY CORPORATION

3 Berkshire Blvd.	CEO: Dean Tulumaris
Bethel CT 06801	CFO: Richard F Sowerby
Phone: 203-739-1100	HR: –
Fax: 203-798-6606	FYE: June 30
Web: www.memry.com	Type: Subsidiary

Memry's products are designed to have a long memory. The company makes specialized metal and plastic products that are used primarily in medical devices. The company develops manufactures and sells components (wire tubing) and sub-assemblies made from nitinol a nickel-and-titanium-based "shape memory alloy" with more than 10 times the elasticity of normal metals. Nitinol is used in surgical instruments such as peripheral vascular and non-vascular stents guidewires and catheters. Medical applications account for more than 90% of Memry's sales. In 2008 Italian scientific equipment manufacturer SAES Getters bought the company for $78 million making Memry a wholly-owned subsidiary.

MENARD INC.

4777 Menard Dr.	CEO: –
Eau Claire WI 54703-9604	CFO: Pete Liupakka
Phone: 715-876-5911	HR: –
Fax: 715-876-2868	FYE: January 31
Web: www.menards.com	Type: Private

If sticks and stones break bones what can two-by-fours and two-inch nails do? Menard's wondering that now that its biggest rivals (#1 home improvement giant The Home Depot and #2 Lowe's) are busy hammering away at its home turf. One of the Midwest's largest home improvement chains Menard boasts 270 stores in more than a dozen states including Illinois Indiana Iowa Kansas Kentucky Michigan Minnesota Missouri Nebraska North and South Dakota Ohio Wisconsin and Wyoming. Stores sell floor coverings hardware millwork paint and tools. Unlike competitors all the company's stores have full-service lumberyards. Menard is owned by president and CEO John Menard who founded the company in 1972.

MENASHA CORPORATION

1645 Bergstrom Rd.	CEO: –
Neenah WI 54956	CFO: Thomas M Rettler
Phone: 920-751-1000	HR: –
Fax: 920-751-1236	FYE: December 31
Web: www.menasha.com	Type: Private

Packaging giant Menasha definitely has "This End Up." Founded in 1849 as a woodenware business the holding company now manufactures packaging and paperboard returnable materials-handling systems product labels and promotional materials as well as offers logistics and marketing services. Its subsidiaries include Menasha Packaging (corrugated packaging and point-of-purchase displays) ORBIS Corporation (plastic reusable packaging) and LeveragePoint Media (in-store promotional services). Menasha is a family-owned business.

MENASHA PACKAGING COMPANY LLC

1645 Bergstrom Rd.	CEO: James M Kotek
Neenah WI 54956	CFO: –
Phone: 920-751-1000	HR: –
Fax: 920-751-1075	FYE: December 31
Web: www.menashapackaging.com	Type: Subsidiary

Menasha Packaging wants you to have your cake and carry it too. Cake circles and boards and deli boxes are just a few of the products designed and manufactured by this corrugated package maker. The largest of Menasha's three operating units Menasha Packaging produces a slew of specialty packaging as well as point-of-purchase retail aids such as displays paperboard and paperboard substrates protective cartons and commercial printing products. Menasha Packaging also offers consumer goods manufacturers structural and graphical design services. Via sister business Cortegra it provides packaging and services to healthcare markets. The company operates about two dozen corrugated container plants in the US.

MENIL FOUNDATION INC.

1533 SUL ROSS ST	CEO: –
HOUSTON, TX 770064729	CFO: –
Phone: 713-525-9400	HR: –
Fax: –	FYE: June 30
Web: www.menil.org	Type: Private

The Menil Foundation controls the renowned art collection of the late John and Dominique de Menil. The collection was opened to the public in 1987 with the founding of a gallery in Houston. Key elements of the Menils' collection include African and tribal art Byzantine era pieces as well as 20th-century paintings (especially those done by surrealists including Max Ernst and Ren-© Magritte). The war chest for this impressive collection was funded mainly from stock in Schlumberger the oil services firm founded by Dominique's father. (The oil connection explains how the French-born couple found their way to Houston.)

	Annual Growth	06/06	06/07	06/08	06/10	06/13
Sales ($ mil.)	(43.2%)	–	1,782.8	12.2	49.6	59.8
Net income ($ mil.)	–	–	–	(8.0)	35.2	44.6
Market value ($ mil.)	–	–	–	–	–	–
Employees	–	–	–	–	–	70

MENLO COLLEGE

1000 EL CAMINO REAL	CEO: –
ATHERTON, CA 940274300	CFO: –
Phone: 650-543-3753	HR: –
Fax: –	FYE: June 30
Web: www.webmail.menlo.edu	Type: Private

Menlo College is a co-educational baccalaureate institution focused on business management mass communications and liberal arts. The college is located just south of San Francisco in a residential community near the cities of Menlo Park and Palo Alto. Some 700 students are enrolled and tuition costs about $24000 per year. Menlo College was founded in 1927.

	Annual Growth	06/09	06/10	06/11	06/12	06/13
Sales ($ mil.)	(33.7%)	–	–	–	31.9	21.2
Net income ($ mil.)	–	–	–	–	0.5	(1.4)
Market value ($ mil.)	–	–	–	–	–	–
Employees	–	–	–	–	–	125

MENLO WORLDWIDE LLC

2855 Campus Dr. Ste. 300	CEO: –
San Mateo CA 94403-2512	CFO: –
Phone: 650-378-5200	HR: –
Fax: 650-357-9160	FYE: December 31
Web: www.con-way.com/en/logistics	Type: Subsidiary

The world of Menlo Worldwide revolves around logistics. Through flagship Menlo Worldwide Logistics and other subsidiaries the company provides supply chain management services including transportation management and warehousing and distribution and related software. For some customers it provides light assembly or kitting services. Menlo specializes in serving the automotive chemical consumer products government industrial manufacturing and technology sectors. It maintains about 110 warehouses with 17 million sq. ft. of space in nearly 20 countries worldwide; it uses third-party transportation companies. Menlo formed in 1990 is a subsidiary of freight transportation firm Con-way.

MENNO TRAVEL SERVICE INC.

104 LAKE ST	CEO: Michael Bedient
EPHRATA, PA 175222415	CFO: Vickie Unruh
Phone: 717-733-4131	HR: –
Fax: –	FYE: September 30
Web: www.mennotravelservice.com	Type: Private

For travelers with more of a mission than sipping fruit drinks poolside in some tropical locale there's Menno Travel Service which does business as MTS TRAVEL. The company provides travel and tour services to religious and not-for-profit groups through nine offices in the US. MTS focuses on supporting Christian organizations in carrying out their missions worldwide with airfare accommodations and other travel arrangements. It also books religious and pilgrimage tours for groups and individuals; standard vacation tours packages and cruises; and business and meeting travel. MTS was acquired by Raptim Travel a provider of missionary humanitarian and religious travel services in 2009.

	Annual Growth	09/03	09/04	09/05	09/06	09/07
Sales ($ mil.)	8.1%	–	95.2	101.6	111.7	120.2
Net income ($ mil.)	130.9%	–	–	0.0	(0.6)	0.2
Market value ($ mil.)	–	–	–	–	–	–
Employees	–	–	–	–	–	156

MENTOR GRAPHICS CORP

NMS: MENT

8005 S.W. Boeckman Road
Wilsonville, OR 97070-7777
Phone: 503 685-7000
Fax: –
Web: www.mentor.com

CEO: Walden C Rhines
CFO: Gregory K Hinckley
HR: –
FYE: January 31
Type: Public

Mentor Graphics lends a hand to guide engineers who design electronic components. The company is a leading global developer of electronic design automation (EDA) software and systems used by engineers to design simulate and test electronic components such as integrated circuits (IC's) wire harness systems and printed circuit boards (PCBs). Products include PADS (PCB design) Nucleus (operating system) and Calibre (IC design). Its software is used to design components for such products as computers and wireless handsets. Clients come from the aerospace IT telecommunications and increasingly transportation industries. Mentor Graphics gets more than half of its revenues from Europe and the Asia/Pacific region particularly Japan.

	Annual Growth	01/11	01/12	01/13	01/14	01/15
Sales ($ mil.)	8.0%	914.8	1,014.6	1,088.7	1,156.4	1,244.1
Net income ($ mil.)	50.6%	28.6	83.9	138.7	155.3	147.1
Market value ($ mil.)	15.9%	1,474.6	1,606.0	1,983.5	2,408.4	2,664.3
Employees	4.3%	4,700	4,800	5,029	5,220	5,558

MENTOR WORLDWIDE LLC

201 Mentor Dr.
Santa Barbara CA 93111
Phone: 805-879-6000
Fax: 805-964-2712
Web: www.mentorwwllc.com

CEO: –
CFO: –
HR: –
FYE: March 31
Type: Subsidiary

The mentoring that Mentor Worldwide provides is to help cosmetic surgery professionals improve the physical appearance of their patients. A leading supplier of medical products for the global aesthetic medicine market the Johnson & Johnson company produces cosmetic surgery products including Memory Gel breast implants Prevelle Silk tissue expanders and facial implants. Additional products include the Byron line of ultrasonic liposuction systems that remove unwanted fat and a line of post-surgery clothing called Caromed. Its Mentor Solutions software helps busy plastic surgeons manage their practices.

MERA PHARMACEUTICALS INC.

PINK SHEETS: MRPI

73-4460 Queen Ka'ahumanu Hwy. Ste. 110
Kailua-Kona HI 96740
Phone: 808-326-9301
Fax: 808-326-9401
Web: www.merapharma.com

CEO: –
CEO: Charles G Spaniak Sr
HR: –
FYE: October 31
Type: Public

Algae... It's got to be good for something and Mera Pharmaceuticals aims to find out what that might be. The company has developed the technology to cultivate microalgae on a large scale and is working to identify and extract substances it hopes can be used in nutritional supplements vitamins pharmaceuticals and cosmetics. The company's nutritional supplement products AstaFactor and Salmon Essentials contain astaxanthin which acts as an antioxidant and anti-inflammatory agent. Mera Pharmaceuticals also provides private label and bulk astaxanthin sales.

MERCANTILE BANCORP INC.

NYSE AMEX: MBR

200 N. 33rd St.
Quincy IL 62306-3455
Phone: 217-223-7300
Fax: 217-223-8938
Web: www.mercbanx.com

CEO: –
CFO: Michael P McGrath
HR: –
FYE: December 31
Type: Public

If you want to sell the farm Mercantile Bancorp can help. The holding company owns Illinois-based Mercantile Bank (it also has a location in Indiana) Royal Palm Bank in Florida and Kansas' Heartland Bank. Through a total of about a dozen offices the community-oriented banks offer deposit and loan products asset management retail brokerage services and agricultural business management. The majority of the company's loan portfolio is related to real estate including farmland construction and commercial and residential mortgage loans. Mercantile Bancorp sold two Illinois-based banks in 2010 Marine Bank and Trust and Brown County State Bank.

MERCANTILE BANK CORP.

NMS: MBWM

310 Leonard Street N.W.
Grand Rapids, MI 49504
Phone: 616 406-3000
Fax: –

CEO: Michael H. Price
CFO: Charles E. (Chuck) Christmas
HR: Tina Van Valkenburg
FYE: December 31
Type: Public

Mercantile Bank Corporation is the holding company for Mercantile Bank of Michigan (formerly Mercantile Bank of West Michigan) which boasts assets of nearly $3 billion and operates more than 50 branches in central and western Michigan around Grand Rapids Holland and Lansing. The bank targets local consumers and businesses offering standard deposit services such as checking and savings accounts CDs IRAs and health savings accounts. Commercial loans make up more than three-fourths of the bank's loan portfolio. Outside of banking subsidiary Mercantile Insurance Center sells insurance products.

	Annual Growth	12/10	12/11	12/12	12/13	12/14
Assets ($ mil.)	15.4%	1,632.4	1,433.2	1,422.9	1,427.0	2,893.4
Net income ($ mil.)	–	(13.3)	37.5	12.5	17.0	17.3
Market value ($ mil.)	26.5%	139.2	165.5	280.1	366.4	356.9
Employees	27.5%	277	261	264	268	731

MERCEDES-BENZ FINANCIAL SERVICES USA LLC

36455 Corporate Dr.
Farmington Hills MI 48331
Phone: 248-991-6700
Fax: 248-991-6962
Web: www.mbfs.com/corp

CEO: –
CFO: –
HR: Jeremy Gump
FYE: December 31
Type: Subsidiary

Mercedes-Benz Financial Services USA provides financing for dealers and buyers of Daimler-brand cars and trucks in the US Canada Argentina Brazil and Mexico. Doing business as Mercedes-Benz Financial and Daimler Truck Financial the company finances dealer inventories and consumer loans and leases and commercial and municipal truck fleets and equipment. All told the loan portfolio of Mercedes-Benz Financial Services USA weighs in at more than $30 billion. The company also sells auto insurance through an agreement with Liberty Mutual. Mercedes-Benz Financial Services USA is a subsidiary of Daimler Financial Services AG.

MERCEDES-BENZ U.S. INTERNATIONAL INC.

1 Mercedes Dr.
Tuscaloosa AL 35490
Phone: 205-507-3300
Fax: 701-530-1451
Web: www.kniferiver.com

CEO: Herbert Werner
CFO: –
HR: –
FYE: December 31
Type: Subsidiary

Big wheels keep on turning at Mercedes-Benz U.S. International's (MBUSI) sweet home Alabama. Its 3.7 million sq.-ft. factory near Tuscaloosa assembles Mercedes SUVs not only for the Lynyrd Skynynds and Neil Youngs of North America but for customers in 135 markets around the globe. MBUSI builds the Mercedes M-Class sport utility and the full-sized GL-Class luxury SUV. The company also produces the R-Class — a crossover vehicle styled as a touring wagon seating up to six adults. After an expansion of the factory MBUSI can assemble as many as 174000 vehicles a year. MBUSI is a subsidiary of Mercedes-Benz USA which is in turn owned by of Germany's Daimler AG.

MERCER INC.

1166 Avenue of the Americas
New York NY 10036
Phone: 212-345-7000
Fax: 212-345-7414
Web: www.mercer.com

CEO: –
CFO: Helen Shan
HR: –
FYE: December 31
Type: Subsidiary

Mercer offers a wide range of human resources-related consulting investment management and outsourcing services for companies around the world. As a consultant the firm helps its clients design and manage retirement plans and health insurance programs of various types. Mercer's investment management business focuses on retirement plan assets. In addition the firm offers consulting services designed to help clients get the most from their employers. As an outsourcer Mercer administers benefits programs for its customers. The firm operates in more than 180 cities in 40 countries worldwide. Insurance giant Marsh & McLennan wholly owns the company which was established in 1959 as William M. Mercer.

MERCER INSURANCE GROUP INC.

10 N. Hwy. 31
Pennington NJ 08534
Phone: 609-737-0426
Fax: 609-737-8719
Web: https://www.unitedfiregroup.com

CEO: Andrew R Speaker
CFO: David B Merclean
HR: –
FYE: December 31
Type: Subsidiary

Mercer Insurance Group protects small businesses. With roots stretching back to 1844 the firm offers a range of property/casualty insurance policies through subsidiaries Mercer Insurance Company Mercer Insurance Company of New Jersey Franklin Insurance and Financial Pacific Insurance. The company focuses on commercial coverage for small to midsized businesses including multi-peril liability workers' compensation inland marine and commercial automobile as well as personal lines (homeowners auto). The company was acquired by United Fire for some $190 million in 2011.

MERCER INTERNATIONAL INC

NMS: MERC

Suite 1120, 700 West Pender Street
Vancouver, British Columbia V6C 1G8
Phone: 604 684-1099
Fax: –

CEO: –
CFO: –
HR: –
FYE: December 31
Type: Public

Mercer International maintains its health with a high-fiber diet. The company operates primarily in the pulp business producing virgin fiber (wood chips and pulpwood) and recycled fiber. It specializes in manufacturing northern bleached softwood kraft (NBSK) pulp from its mills in Western Canada and Germany. Its three subsidiary mills called Rosenthal Stendal and Celgar have the collective capacity to churn out 1.5 million air-dried metric tons (ADMTs) annually. Pulp is sold mainly to tissue and paper manufacturers. Mercer also produces biochemicals and bio-energy with three mills collectively producing more than 700000 MWh of electric power and more than 20000 tons of biochemicals.

	Annual Growth	12/10	12/11	12/12	12/13	12/14
Sales ($ mil.)	(0.6%)	1,205.3	1,150.4	1,099.4	1,088.4	1,175.1
Net income ($ mil.)	(0.5%)	115.5	64.8	(16.1)	(26.4)	113.2
Market value ($ mil.)	12.2%	498.1	392.1	460.2	640.8	789.9
Employees	(1.0%)	1,491	1,495	1,500	1,460	1,430

MERCHANTS BANCSHARES, INC. (BURLINGTON, VT)

NMS: MBVT

275 Kennedy Drive
South Burlington, VT 05403
Phone: 802 658-3400
Fax: –
Web: www.mbvt.com

CEO: Geoffrey R. (Geoff) Hesslink
CFO: Thomas Meshako
HR: –
FYE: December 31
Type: Public

Merchants Bancshares hopes to provide the missing lynx in your financial chain. With a lynx emblazoned on its logo subsidiary Merchants Bank provides community banking services to the residents of Vermont through about 35 branches across the state. The bank provides standard retail products including checking money market and savings accounts; IRAs; CDs; and debit cards. Commercial real estate business and construction loans account for more than 50% of the company's loan portfolio while agricultural and consumer loans make up the remainder. Its Merchants Trust subsidiary offers trust and investment management services. Organized in 1849 the bank's total assets now exceed $1.7 billion.

	Annual Growth	12/10	12/11	12/12	12/13	12/14
Assets ($ mil.)	3.7%	1,487.6	1,611.9	1,708.6	1,725.5	1,723.5
Net income ($ mil.)	(5.9%)	15.5	14.6	15.2	15.1	12.1
Market value ($ mil.)	2.7%	174.4	184.8	169.4	212.0	193.8
Employees	(1.7%)	336	331	322	329	314

MERCK & CO., INC

NYS: MRK

2000 Galloping Hill Road
Keniworth, NJ 07033
Phone: 908 740-4000
Fax: 908 735-1500
Web: www.merck.com

CEO: Kenneth C. (Ken) Frazier
CFO: Robert M. Davis
HR: Mirian M. Graddick-Weir
FYE: December 31
Type: Public

Merck makes medicines for a number of maladies from stuffy noses and asthma to hypertension and arthritis. The pharmaceutical giant's top prescription drugs include diabetes drugs Januvia and Janumet anti-inflammatory Remicade cholesterol combatants Vytorin and Zetia and hypertension fighters Cozaar and Hyzaar. In addition Merck makes childhood and adult vaccines for such diseases as measles mumps pneumonia and shingles as well as veterinary pharmaceuticals through Merck Animal Health. The company sold its OTC drug and personal care offerings including Claritin allergy pills and Dr. Scholl's foot care products to Bayer AG in 2014.

	Annual Growth	12/10	12/11	12/12	12/13	12/14
Sales ($ mil.)	(2.1%)	45,987.0	48,047.0	47,267.0	44,033.0	42,237.0
Net income ($ mil.)	92.9%	861.0	6,272.0	6,168.0	4,404.0	11,920.0
Market value ($ mil.)	–	0.0	0.0	0.0	0.0	0.0
Employees	(7.1%)	94,000	86,000	83,000	76,000	70,000

MERCURY GENERAL CORP.

NYS: MCY

4484 Wilshire Boulevard
Los Angeles, CA 90010
Phone: 323 937-1060
Fax: 323 857-7116
Web: www.mercuryinsurance.com

CEO: Gabriel Tirador
CFO: Theodore R. Stalick
HR: April Pieger
FYE: December 31
Type: Public

Named after the Roman god of commerce and travel Mercury General hopes to combine the two and become the ultimate auto insurance provider. The company is the parent of a group of insurers including Mercury Casualty Company that write automobile insurance for all risk classifications in more than a dozen states. Plain old private auto insurance accounts for about 80% of premiums written. However Mercury General also sells commercial vehicle insurance and a bit of homeowners mechanical breakdown umbrella and fire insurance. The company is a leader in the California auto market and has significant operations in Florida.

	Annual Growth	12/11	12/12	12/13	12/14	12/15
Assets ($ mil.)	3.3%	4,070.0	4,189.7	4,315.2	4,600.3	4,628.6
Net income ($ mil.)	(21.0%)	191.2	116.9	112.1	177.9	74.5
Market value ($ mil.)	0.5%	2,516.6	2,189.5	2,742.2	3,126.1	2,569.0
Employees	(1.1%)	4,500	4,600	4,500	4,400	4,300

MERCURY MARINE

W6250 W. Pioneer Rd.
Fond Du Lac WI 54935-5636
Phone: 920-929-5000
Fax: 920-929-5893
Web: www.mercurymarine.com

CEO: -
CFO: -
HR: -
FYE: December 31
Type: Subsidiary

Like the mythical messenger Mercury Marine races. It is the world's #1 recreational marine-engine maker and marketer (by sales volume). The company builds sterndrive propulsion systems including inboard and outboard engines under the Mercury MerCruiser Mercury Racing Zeus and other brand names. It also makes a slew of marine parts and accessories under brands like Quicksilver and Kellogg Marine Supply. A remanufacturing arm offers replacement engines and service parts. Mercury Marine operates mainly in North America and the Asia/Pacific region. Its lineup is sold to boat builders domestic and foreign governments and the boat business of its corporate parent Brunswick as well as indirectly to end-users.

MERCURY SYSTEMS INC

NMS: MRCY

201 Riverneck Road
Chelmsford, MA 01824
Phone: 978 256-1300
Fax: -
Web: www.mrcy.com

CEO: Mark Aslett
CFO: Gerald M. (Gerry) Haines
HR: -
FYE: June 30
Type: Public

Mercury Systems (formerly Mercury Computer Systems) delivers digital signals faster than a wing-footed messenger. The company makes real-time digital signal processing (DSP) systems for the homeland security military and aerospace and telecommunications markets. Its military systems process radar sonar and other signals. It also makes specialized electronics used in semiconductor wafer inspection and airport baggage screeners. Mercury Systems acts as a subcontractor to prime contractors such as Northrop Grumman and Raytheon.

	Annual Growth	06/11	06/12	06/13	06/14	06/15
Sales ($ mil.)	0.7%	228.7	244.9	208.8	208.7	234.8
Net income ($ mil.)	(13.4%)	18.4	22.6	(13.2)	(11.4)	10.4
Market value ($ mil.)	(5.9%)	608.4	421.1	300.3	369.4	476.8
Employees	1.1%	602	713	756	632	629

MERCY CHILDREN'S HOSPITAL

2401 GILLHAM RD
KANSAS CITY, MO 64108-4698
Phone: 816-234-3000
Fax: -
Web: www.cmh.edu

CEO: -
CFO: Dwight Hyde
HR: -
FYE: June 30
Type: Private

When you've got sick grumpy kids on your hands beneficence may not be the first word that comes to mind that is unless you're a doctor at The Children's Mercy Hospital. The pediatric hospital offers health care for youngsters in and around Kansas City Missouri. Specialized services include home health endocrinology genetics heart surgery neonatology and rehabilitation. Founded in 1897 the hospital has about 335 beds. The Children's Mercy health care system also includes a small suburban campus outpatient clinics outreach clinics and research facilities.

	Annual Growth	06/07	06/08	06/09	06/10	06/11
Sales ($ mil.)	597.0%	-	2.4	582.4	787.1	816.8
Net income ($ mil.)	-	-	(0.0)	22.8	43.8	13.2
Market value ($ mil.)	-	-	-	-	-	-
Employees	-	-	-	-	-	3,000

MERCY COLLEGE

555 BRDWY
DOBBS FERRY, NY 10522
Phone: 914-693-4500
Fax: -
Web: www.mercy.edu

CEO: -
CFO: Donald B. Aungst
HR: -
FYE: June 30
Type: Private

Mercy College is a private Catholic school founded by the Sisters of Mercy in 1950. The college provides higher education to some 9000 undergraduate and graduate students in the New York City area. Mercy College offers 90 degrees in fields including business accounting civic and cultural studies computer science education health professions literature language communication natural sciences and social sciences. The institution also provides some online courses as well as professional certification programs. Mercy College employs some 200 full-time faculty members.

	Annual Growth	06/06	06/07	06/08	06/09	06/10
Sales ($ mil.)	-	-	-	0.0	128.1	154.1
Net income ($ mil.)	29402.7%	-	-	0.0	0.0	28.2
Market value ($ mil.)	-	-	-	-	-	-
Employees	-	-	-	-	-	500

MERCY CORPS

45 SW ANKENY ST
PORTLAND, OR 972043500
Phone: 503 796 6800
Fax: -
Web: www.mercycorps.org

CEO: -
CFO: -
HR: -
FYE: June 30
Type: Private

Mercy Corps is dedicated to helping the poor and oppressed in developing countries. The not-for-profit organization offers emergency relief and economic support as well as assistance in building sustainable communities. It also develops curriculum guides to introduce students to various topics ranging from Kurdish history and Afghan henna art to the worldwide clean water campaign. Since its founding Mercy Corps programs have provided about $1.5 billion in assistance to people in 106 nations. Originally the organization was named Save the Refugees Fund when it was founded by Dan O'Neill in response to the plight of Cambodian refugees in 1979.

	Annual Growth	06/09	06/10	06/11	06/12	06/13
Sales ($ mil.)	(1.2%)	-	244.9	268.6	233.0	236.3
Net income ($ mil.)	-	-	-	1.5	(7.7)	(4.7)
Market value ($ mil.)	-	-	-	-	-	-
Employees	-	-	-	-	-	450

MERCY HEALTH

14528 S. Outer Forty Dr. Ste. 100	CEO: Lynn Britton
Chesterfield MO 63017	CFO: James Jaacs
Phone: 314-579-6100	HR: –
Fax: 314-628-3723	FYE: June 30
Web: www.mercy.net	Type: Private - Not-for-Pr

Mercy Health formerly known as the Sisters of Mercy Health System provides a range of health care and social services through its network of facilities and service organizations. The organization operates more than 30 acute care hospitals (including two specialty heart hospitals) with almost 3700 licensed beds as well as 200 outpatient facilities in four midwestern states. Its hospital groups include facilities for nursing homes medical practices and outpatient centers. Mercy Health also operates Resource Optimization & Innovation (ROi) its industry-leading health care supply chain organization and health outreach organizations in Louisiana Mississippi and Texas.

MERCY HOSPITAL AND MEDICAL CENTER

2525 S MICHIGAN AVE	CEO: –
CHICAGO, IL 606162332	CFO: Eric Krueger
Phone: 312-567-2201	HR: Nancy Hill-davis
Fax: –	FYE: June 30
Web: www.mercy-chicago.org	Type: Private

Chicagoans in the loop know Mercy Hospital and Medical Center is the place to go for health care. The Catholic hospital located near Chicago's Loop (the historic downtown commercial district) has about 320 beds and operates a network of community clinics and occupational health facilities that provide employment-related services such as drug screening executive physicals and physical therapy. Other services include a cancer treatment center inpatient hospice care unit eye care center heart and vascular center diabetes treatment center stroke center and inpatient and outpatient chemical dependence recovery programs. Chicago's first teaching hospital it is owned by Ohio-based system Trinity Health.

	Annual Growth	06/07	06/08	06/09	06/10	06/13
Sales ($ mil.)		–	(1,500.3)	235.6	250.3	265.7
Net income ($ mil.)	10.9%	–	–	2.7	9.1	4.1
Market value ($ mil.)	–	–	–	–	–	–
Employees	–	–	–	–	–	1,550

MERCY HOSPITAL SPRINGFIELD

1235 E CHEROKEE ST	CEO: Kim Day
SPRINGFIELD, MO 658042203	CFO: –
Phone: 417-820-8620	HR: –
Fax: –	FYE: June 30
Web: www.mercy.net	Type: Private

Mercy Hospital Springfield is an 890-bed acute-care hospital in the Mercy Health system. The facility provides health care to southwestern Missouri and northwestern Arkansas and includes the Mercy Children's Hospital Springfield. Other hospital specialties include cardiology and stroke care as well as women's and seniors' health cancer emergency trauma burn neuroscience rehabilitation and sports medicine. In addition to its hospital in Springfield Mercy Hospital Springfield operates a number of community clinics and specialty care centers in the area.

	Annual Growth	06/09	06/10	06/11	06/12	06/13
Sales ($ mil.)	142.1%	–	68.0	880.7	968.7	965.6
Net income ($ mil.)	1.0%	–	–	86.0	112.4	87.7
Market value ($ mil.)	–	–	–	–	–	–
Employees	–	–	–	–	–	4,400

MERCY MEDICAL CENTER

1000 N VILLAGE AVE	CEO: Dr Alan Guerci
ROCKVILLE CENTRE, NY 115701000	CFO: William Armstrong
Phone: 516-562-6907	HR: –
Fax: –	FYE: December 31
Web: www.chsli.org	Type: Private

Overlooking Long Island's Hempstead Lake State Park Mercy Medical Center offers healthcare services to patients just east of Manhattan. The not-for-profit Catholic hospital has expertise in weight loss and orthopedic surgeries mammograms and breast health and women's health services. It also provides outpatient services such as family and mental health care. With about 380 beds the medical center employs some 700 physicians who deliver about 1300 babies each year. Its acute care facilities include a suburban branch of Memorial Sloan-Kettering Cancer Center. Mercy Medical Center established in 1913 by the Sisters of the Congregation of the Infant Jesus is part of Catholic Health Services of Long Island.

	Annual Growth	12/04	12/05	12/06	12/08	12/09
Sales ($ mil.)	0.8%	–	191.1	206.4	178.2	197.3
Net income ($ mil.)	–	–	–	(3.2)	(8.1)	(8.2)
Market value ($ mil.)	–	–	–	–	–	–
Employees	–	–	–	–	–	1,610

MERCY MEDICAL CENTER INC.

1320 MERCY DR NW	CEO: Thomas E Cecconi
CANTON, OH 447082641	CFO: David K Stewart
Phone: 330-489-1000	HR: –
Fax: –	FYE: December 31
Web: www.cantonmercy.org	Type: Private

Mercy Medical Center keeps patients doing the cancan in Canton. The facility is a 480-bed acute care hospital serving residents of five counties in southeastern Ohio. The Catholic medical center has 700 physicians and provides a comprehensive range of care including inpatient outpatient and rehabilitative services. It operates specialty care centers for cardiac vascular stroke and cancer treatment as well as trauma chest pain and rehabilitation units. Mercy Medical Center also operates outpatient health centers in the communities surrounding Canton Ohio. The facility is part of the Sisters of Charity Health System (SCHS) a not-for-profit ministry of the Sisters of Charity of St. Augustine.

	Annual Growth	12/09	12/10	12/11	12/12	12/13
Sales ($ mil.)	5.1%	–	–	–	269.5	283.2
Net income ($ mil.)	–	–	–	–	(14.2)	10.3
Market value ($ mil.)	–	–	–	–	–	–
Employees	–	–	–	–	–	80

MERCY SHIPS

15862 HIGHWAY 110 N	CEO: Myron E Ullman III
LINDALE, TX 75771	CFO: –
Phone: 903-939-7000	HR: –
Fax: –	FYE: December 31
Web: www.mercyships.org	Type: Private

Mercy Ships brings floating medical care to areas of the world that need it most. The Christian-based not-for-profit serves more than 50 developing nations around the world from its ship Africa Mercy which has six operating rooms and nearly 500 berths and a land-based clinic in Sierra Leone. Staff and volunteers perform cleft lip and cleft palate surgeries cataract and tumor removals and other medical procedures. The organization also distributes water purification kits prescription eyeglasses and prescriptions and offers a variety of training and education programs for local workers. Mercy Ships was founded in 1978 by Don and Deyon Stephens (who still serve as president and company VP respectively).

	Annual Growth	12/05	12/06	12/07	12/08	12/09
Sales ($ mil.)	(82.4%)	–	–	1,707.0	49.1	52.9
Net income ($ mil.)	7942.9%	–	–	0.0	(1.0)	1.1
Market value ($ mil.)	–	–	–	–	–	–
Employees	–	–	–	–	–	650

MEREDITH CORP

NYS: MDP

1716 Locust Street
Des Moines, IA 50309-3023
Phone: 515 284-3000
Fax: –
Web: www.meredith.com

CEO: Stephen M. (Steve) Lacy
CFO: Joseph H. Ceryanec
HR: –
FYE: June 30
Type: Public

Meredith may be the true domestic goddess of media. A home and family media firm Meredith publishes magazines special interest publications and books. Its portfolio of more than 20 subscription magazines includes flagship title Better Homes and Gardens as well as Family Circle Ladies' Home Journal Parents Fitness and More. The company is also active in broadcasting with a dozen network-affiliated TV stations across the US. Meredith additionally operates about 50 websites and some 50 mobile apps offers integrated marketing services and has a large consumer database.

	Annual Growth	06/11	06/12	06/13	06/14	06/15
Sales ($ mil.)	3.3%	1,400.5	1,376.7	1,471.3	1,468.7	1,594.2
Net income ($ mil.)	1.8%	127.4	104.4	123.7	113.5	136.8
Market value ($ mil.)	13.8%	1,389.0	1,425.2	2,128.4	2,157.8	2,326.9
Employees	4.2%	3,250	3,410	3,350	3,600	3,825

MERGE HEALTHCARE INC

NMS: MRGE

350 North Orleans Street, 1st Floor
Chicago, IL 60654
Phone: 312 565-6868
Fax: –
Web: www.merge.com

CEO: –
CFO: –
HR: –
FYE: December 31
Type: Public

Merge Healthcare wants your imaging department to share the health. The company develops image and information exchange management software mainly for cardiology ophthalmology orthopedics radiology and clinical trials. Its products are available as traditional packaged software or hosted in the cloud. Its Merge iConnect suite lets users create information exchanges that enable sharing of diagnostic images and results within a facility and with other entities. The company also serves the business side of health care offering software to manage revenue cycle physician practices imaging centers and billing departments. It has customers in North America Europe and Asia.

	Annual Growth	12/09	12/10	12/11	12/12	12/13
Sales ($ mil.)	36.4%	66.8	140.3	232.4	248.9	231.7
Net income ($ mil.)	–	0.3	(11.5)	(5.5)	(28.8)	(39.0)
Market value ($ mil.)	(8.8%)	325.0	360.7	469.1	238.9	224.4
Employees	20.1%	385	750	925	860	800

MERIAL INC.

3239 Satellite Blvd. Bldg. 500
Duluth GA 30096-4640
Phone: 678-638-3000
Fax: 972-385-9887
Web: www.bb-armr.com

CEO: Carsten Hellman
CFO: Christophe Hirtz
HR: –
FYE: December 31
Type: Subsidiary

Merial keeps animals merry. The company makes a variety of drugs and vaccines that treat and prevent disease in pets livestock and wildlife. Used by veterinarians farmers and pet owners in some 150 countries the company's lead products include Ivomec and Eprinex anti-parasitics for livestock; Frontline flea and tick treatments for cats and dogs; and heartworm prevention drug Heartgard. Merial focuses on four treatment areas: anti-infectious drugs pain medicines parasiticides and vaccines. The company sells its over-the-counter products wherever pet supplies are sold such as pet stores and online retailers and its prescription medications through veterinarians. The company is owned by Sanofi.

MERIDIAN BANCORP INC

NMS: EBSB

67 Prospect Street
Peabody, MA 01960
Phone: 617 567-1500
Fax: –

CEO: Richard J. Gavegnano
CFO: Mark L. Abbate
HR: –
FYE: December 31
Type: Public

Meridian Bancorp is the holding company of East Boston Savings Bank which provides standard deposit and lending services to individuals and businesses in the greater Boston area. The bank writes single-family commercial and multi-family mortgages as well as construction and business loans and consumer loans. East Boston Savings operates about 30 branches in eastern Massachusetts. Mutual holding company Meridian Financial Services owns 59% of Meridian Bancorp.

	Annual Growth	12/10	12/11	12/12	12/13	12/14
Assets ($ mil.)	15.6%	1,835.8	1,974.4	2,278.8	2,682.1	3,278.5
Net income ($ mil.)	13.7%	13.4	12.0	12.4	15.4	22.3
Market value ($ mil.)	–	–	–	–	–	613.8
Employees	6.7%	360	392	433	455	466

MERIDIAN BIOSCIENCE INC.

NMS: VIVO

3471 River Hills Drive
Cincinnati, OH 45244
Phone: 513 271-3700
Fax: –
Web: www.meridianbioscience.com

CEO: John A. Kraeutler
CFO: Melissa A. Lueke
HR: Johnson Marviette
FYE: September 30
Type: Public

Disease detection is the name of Meridian Bioscience's game. The company makes immunodiagnostic test kits and sample transport media for reference laboratories hospitals and doctors' offices. Its products analyze blood urine and other body fluid and tissue samples to diagnose such maladies as respiratory illness (pneumonia influenza) gastrointestinal disease (ulcers diarrhea) viruses (mononucleosis chicken pox) and parasitic diseases. The company's Life Science division makes and sells biological supplies including antigens antibodies and reagents used by research labs and other diagnostics firms; it also provides contract manufacturing of proteins and other biologics for drug developers.

	Annual Growth	09/11	09/12	09/13	09/14	09/15
Sales ($ mil.)	5.1%	159.7	173.5	188.7	188.8	194.8
Net income ($ mil.)	7.3%	26.8	33.4	38.0	34.7	35.5
Market value ($ mil.)	2.1%	658.5	802.5	988.7	740.1	715.4
Employees	2.5%	525	510	550	550	580

MERIDIAN GROUP INTERNATIONAL INC.

9 Parkway North Ste. 500
Deerfield IL 60015
Phone: 847-964-2700
Fax: 847-940-8262
Web: onlinemeridian.com

CEO: Brad Ihlenfeld
CFO: Brad Ihlenfeld
HR: –
FYE: March 31
Type: Private

Meridian Group gets companies the technology they need. Through its group of companies — Concat Meridian Leasing Meridian IT MAC Source Meridian Leasing and Tardis — Meridian provides a range of information technology (IT) services including data center design server configuration maintenance and training. The group also leases and sells computer equipment — storage systems networking hardware workstations and voice and data communication systems — from IBM Sun Microsystems Hewlett-Packard and Fujitsu. Customers have included law firm Bond Schoeneck & King Carrier Holland & Knight and Dupli Envelope & Graphics. The company was founded in 1979.

MERIT MEDICAL SYSTEMS, INC.

NMS: MMSI

1600 West Merit Parkway
South Jordan, UT 84095
Phone: 801 253-1600
Fax: –
Web: www.merit.com

CEO: Fred P. Lampropoulos
CFO: Bernard Birkett
HR: –
FYE: December 31
Type: Public

When it comes to medical devices this company believes its merits speak for themselves. Merit Medical Systems makes disposable medical products used during interventional and diagnostic cardiology radiology gastroenterology and pulmonary procedures. The company's products include catheters guide wires needles and tubing used in heart stent procedures pacemaker placement and angioplasties as well as products for endoscopy dialysis and other procedures. Merit Medical sells its products as stand-alone items or in custom-made kits to hospitals and other health care providers as well as to custom packagers and equipment makers worldwide.

	Annual Growth	12/10	12/11	12/12	12/13	12/14
Sales ($ mil.)	14.5%	296.8	359.4	394.3	449.0	509.7
Net income ($ mil.)	16.5%	12.5	23.0	19.7	16.6	23.0
Market value ($ mil.)	2.3%	690.4	583.6	606.2	686.5	755.8
Employees	9.3%	2,178	2,400	2,760	2,888	3,105

MERITAGE HOMES CORP

NYS: MTH

8800 E. Raintree Drive, Suite 300
Scottsdale, AZ 85260
Phone: 480 515-8100
Fax: –
Web: www.meritagehomes.com

CEO: Steven J. (Steve) Hilton
CFO: Larry W. Seay
HR: Javier Feliciano
FYE: December 31
Type: Public

Meritage Homes sees merit in building houses in high-growth areas of the western and southern US. The company typically constructs single-family homes targeted at first- and second-time homebuyers as well as the luxury and older adult market. Home prices range from about $130000 to $1 million and average about $339000. Meritage Homes controls roughly 15500 lots and most often builds in nearly 190 communities in Arizona California Colorado Florida North Carolina Texas and Tennessee. Homes are sold under the Meritage Homes brand as well as Monterey Homes (in Arizona and Texas) and Phillips Builders (in Tennessee). The company which was founded in 1985 also develops active-adult communities.

	Annual Growth	12/10	12/11	12/12	12/13	12/14
Sales ($ mil.)	23.3%	941.7	861.2	1,193.7	1,820.7	2,179.8
Net income ($ mil.)	111.2%	7.2	(21.1)	105.2	124.5	142.2
Market value ($ mil.)	12.8%	869.1	907.8	1,462.1	1,878.7	1,408.9
Employees	18.9%	650	660	830	1,050	1,300

MERITAGE HOSPITALITY GROUP INC

NBB: MHGU

3310 Eagle Park Drive N.E., Suite 205
Grand Rapids, MI 49525
Phone: 616 776-2600
Fax: 616 776-2776
Web: www.meritagehospitality.com

CEO: –
CFO: Gary A Rose
HR: –
FYE: December 28
Type: Public

This company is really big on the beef in Michigan. Meritage Hospitality Group is a leading franchisee of Wendy's fast food hamburger restaurants with about 70 locations operating mostly in western and southern Michigan. The units franchised from Wendy's/Arby's Group offer a menu of burgers and other sandwiches fries and other items. In addition to its quick-service operations Meritage runs four franchised O'Charley's casual dining restaurants in Michigan near Grand Rapids and Detroit. The company was founded in 1986 as Thomas Edison Inns. The family of chairman Robert Schermer Sr. including CEO Robert Schermer Jr. controls Meritage.

	Annual Growth	01/11	01/12*	12/12	12/13	12/14
Sales ($ mil.)	26.8%	78.6	91.9	99.0	137.8	160.2
Net income ($ mil.)	6.1%	2.3	2.3	2.9	3.1	2.8
Market value ($ mil.)	34.4%	11.5	9.6	14.7	24.1	27.9
Employees	24.0%	2,100	2,500	3,500	3,300	4,000
						*Fiscal year change

MERITER HEALTH SERVICES INC.

202 S PARK ST
MADISON, WI 537151507
Phone: 608-417-5800
Fax: –
Web: www.meriter.com

CEO: James L Woodward
CFO: Beth Erdman
HR: –
FYE: December 31
Type: Private

Meriter Health Services believes that the health concerns of its patients merits its careful attention. A teaching affiliate of the University of Wisconsin the Madison-based system serves residents of southern Wisconsin and northwestern Illinois. Its flagship facility is the 450-bed Meriter Hospital a not-for-profit community hospital providing general medical and surgical care as well as pediatric mental health services through its Child and Adolescent Psychiatric Hospital unit. Meriter Health Services also operates primary care clinics a home health care provider and clinical laboratories. It owns two-thirds of Physicians Plus Insurance a regional HMO.

	Annual Growth	12/09	12/10	12/11	12/12	12/13
Sales ($ mil.)	(0.2%)	–	725.0	773.6	775.0	720.5
Net income ($ mil.)	–	–	–	(16.4)	12.8	38.0
Market value ($ mil.)	–	–	–	–	–	–
Employees	–	–	–	–	–	3,330

MERITOR INC

NYS: MTOR

2135 West Maple Road
Troy, MI 48084-7186
Phone: 248 435-1000
Fax: –
Web: www.meritor.com

CEO: Jeffrey A. (Jay) Craig
CFO: Kevin Nowlan
HR: –
FYE: September 30
Type: Public

Whether it's building axles for big rigs or drum brakes for buses this company's products are meritorious. Meritor makes axles brakes drivelines suspension systems undercarriages and aftermarket transmissions for commercial truck trailer off-highway construction military bus and specialty vehicle manufacturers. It also makes U-joints shafts clutches and ABS and stability control systems. The company divides its operations across two primary segments: Commercial Truck & Industrial and Aftermarket & Trailer. Meritor does business around the globe through operations in roughly 20 countries including Canada China France India Mexico and Sweden.

	Annual Growth	10/11*	09/12	09/13	09/14	09/15
Sales ($ mil.)	(6.7%)	4,622.0	4,418.0	3,701.0	3,766.0	3,505.0
Net income ($ mil.)	0.4%	63.0	52.0	(22.0)	249.0	64.0
Market value ($ mil.)	10.8%	667.9	401.1	743.6	1,026.4	1,005.6
Employees	(5.4%)	10,500	9,300	8,900	9,050	8,400
						*Fiscal year change

MERITUS HEALTH INC.

11116 MEDICAL CAMPUS RD
HAGERSTOWN, MD 217426710
Phone: 301-790-8000
Fax: –
Web: www.meritushealth.com

CEO: Joseph Ross
CFO: –
HR: –
FYE: June 30
Type: Private

Meritus Health provides a wide range of medical services to patients living in western Maryland southern Pennsylvania and adjacent portions of West Virginia. The system's Meritus Medical Center has 250 beds and 40 bassinets and offers acute tertiary and long-term care including inpatient behavioral health services cardiac care obstetrics cancer treatment rehabilitation and trauma care. Meritus Health also operates the for-profit Meritus Enterprises a provider of outpatient health care including diagnostic imaging laboratory services and ambulatory surgery. In addition it provides general practice care at the Robinwood Professional Center.

	Annual Growth	06/09	06/10	06/11	06/12	06/13
Sales ($ mil.)	1112.5%	–	0.2	0.0	380.2	374.5
Net income ($ mil.)	–	–	–	0.0	7.5	17.6
Market value ($ mil.)	–	–	–	–	–	–
Employees	–	–	–	–	–	3,105

MERKLE GROUP INC.

7001 Columbia Gateway Dr.
Columbia MD 21046
Phone: 443-542-4000
Fax: 239-768-0711
Web: www.neogenomics.org

CEO: David S Williams
CFO: Rick Gross
HR: –
FYE: December 31
Type: Private

Has your company's marketing momentum moved from measurable to murky? Meet Merkle a customer relationship marketing agency that has counted enterprises such as Dell GEICO and the American Heart Association among its clients. Merkle helps clients market themselves by providing strategic consulting business intelligence and analytics media targeting and measurement and mail creation and production management services. The agency which manages more than 125 databases serves customers in a wide array of industries. It manages billions of direct mail pieces each year and owns a dozen offices throughout the US. Merkle was founded in 1971.

MERKLEY + PARTNERS INC.

200 Varick St.
New York NY 10014
Phone: 212-805-7500
Fax: 214-350-7624
Web: www.jones-blair.com

CEO: –
CFO: Michael Byrne
HR: –
FYE: December 31
Type: Subsidiary

Some big advertisers hope a partnership with Merkley will bring customers to their business. Merkley + Partners is a leading full-service ad agency offering creative development and brand marketing to such clients as AXA Equitable O'Charley's Ruth's Chris Steak House and Mercedes-Benz. In addition to traditional advertising services the firm provides specialized communications services for health care companies and multimedia services through an interactive marketing division. Founded in 1993 Merkley is a wholly owned subsidiary of global advertising conglomerate Omnicom Group.

MERRILL CORPORATION

1 Merrill Cir.
St. Paul MN 55108
Phone: 651-646-4501
Fax: 651-646-5332
Web: www.merrillcorp.com

CEO: James R Wiley
CFO: Tom Donnelly
HR: –
FYE: January 31
Type: Private

Document services company Merrill is no relation to financial services giant Merrill Lynch but the companies do share an interest in SEC paperwork. Merrill Corporation provides services the help clients gather organize and manage confidential and time-sensitive information for legal and financial transactions. In addition the company provides marketing and communication services such as document composition printing fulfillment and digital delivery as well as technology integration. Subsidiary Merrill Brink International offers translation localization and globalization services. Merrill employees own about 47% of the firm.

MERRILL LYNCH AND CO. INC.

Bank of America Corporate Center 100 N. Tryon St.
Charlotte NC 28255
Phone: 704-386-5681
Fax: 512-479-2553

CEO: –
CFO: –
HR: –
FYE: December 31
Type: Subsidiary

Economic crisis? Merrill Lynch cried bully on that. The Wall Street institution with the iconic bull logo is now the wealth management brokerage and investment banking arm of Bank of America. The retail banking giant acquired the distressed investment bank in 2009 in a move that greatly expanded its wealth management and international operations. Merrill Lynch is among the world's top brokerages with some $2.2 trillion in customer assets. The company also provides corporate finance investment banking and research services to institutional commercial and government clients. Merrill Lynch has offices in some 40 countries around the world.

MERRILL LYNCH CREDIT CORPORATION

4804 Deer Lake Dr. East 5th Fl.
Jacksonville FL 32246-6484
Phone: 904-218-6000
Fax: 503-242-1588
Web: www.stimsonlumber.com

CEO: –
CFO: –
HR: –
FYE: December 31
Type: Subsidiary

Merrill Lynch Credit Corporation works to place more Americans in their dream castles. Doing business as Merrill Lynch Home Loans the company is one of the residential mortgage units of financial giant Bank of America. Its offerings include a variety of adjustable- and fixed-rate mortgages for first and second homes construction loans mortgage refinancing and equity lines of credit. The company also provides loan servicing. Founded in 1981 Merrill Lynch Home Loans serves primarily wealthy customers throughout the US Puerto Rico and the US Virgin Islands. Done in by the global credit crisis direct parent Merrill Lynch was taken over by Bank of America in a $50 billion deal in 2009.

MERRIMACK PHARMACEUTICALS INC.

NMS: MACK

One Kendall Square, Suite B7201
Cambridge, MA 02139
Phone: 617 441-1000
Fax: –
Web: www.merrimackpharma.com

CEO: Robert J. Mulroy
CFO: Yasir Al-Wakeel
HR: –
FYE: December 31
Type: Public

Merrimack Pharmaceuticals takes a technological approach to fighting cancer. A biopharmaceutical company Merrimack develops oncology drugs using its proprietary Network Biology technology which combines biological data and computer-based modeling to discover and develop candidates. The company has six candidates in clinical stage development including a chemotherapy drug to treat pancreatic and gastric cancer and antibody therapies designed to inhibit the growth of cancerous cells. It also has additional candidates in its pipeline in preclinical stages of development. Tracing its roots back to the early 1990s Merrimack became a public company in 2012.

	Annual Growth	12/10	12/11	12/12	12/13	12/14
Sales ($ mil.)	50.0%	20.3	34.2	48.9	47.8	102.8
Net income ($ mil.)	–	(50.1)	(79.2)	(91.3)	(130.9)	(83.3)
Market value ($ mil.)	36.2%	–	–	649.8	568.8	1,205.7
Employees	12.0%	–	218	230	254	306

MERRIMAN HOLDINGS INC.

NBB: MERR

250 Montgomery Street, 16th Floor
San Francisco, CA 94104
Phone: 415 248-5603
Fax: –
Web: www.merrimanco.com

CEO: D Jonathan Merriman
CFO: –
HR: –
FYE: December 31
Type: Public

Merriman Holdings (formerly Merriman Curhan Ford Group) sees funds in its clients' futures. The company provides investment banking venture and corporate services asset management and investment research services with a focus on fast-growth sectors such as clean technology media and consumer services. Offerings include strategic advisory restructuring and private placements of stock warrants and convertibles. The company is also active in the emerging China market. Merriman Holdings has offices in New York City and San Francisco.

	Annual Growth	12/10	12/11	12/12	12/13	12/14
Sales ($ mil.)	(15.1%)	30.7	21.9	12.9	10.0	15.9
Net income ($ mil.)	–	(5.3)	(7.9)	(6.9)	(4.0)	(1.6)
Market value ($ mil.)	0.7%	9.9	1.9	0.3	0.6	10.2
Employees	(20.3%)	77	35	32	29	31

MERRY MAIDS LIMITED PARTNERSHIP

860 Ridge Lake Blvd.
Memphis TN 38120
Phone: 901-537-8100
Fax: 901-597-8140
Web: www.merrymaids.com

CEO: –
CFO: –
HR: –
FYE: December 31
Type: Subsidiary

Merry Maids is happy to scrub straighten and sanitize. Founded in 1979 home cleaning company Merry Maids has more than 600 franchises in the US and Canada and cleans more than 300000 residences a month. The company also has operations in Hong Kong Japan South Korea Malaysia the Philippines and the UK. Cleaning services includes floors and carpets kitchen counters and appliances bathroom fixtures dusting and emptying trash cans. Other services include packing for moves oven and refrigerator cleaning wall washing and upholstery cleaning. Merry Maids is a subsidiary of industry giant ServiceMaster.

MERU NETWORKS INC.

NMS: MERU

894 Ross Drive
Sunnyvale, CA 94089
Phone: 408 215-5300
Fax: –
Web: www.merunetworks.com

CEO: Ken Xie
CFO: Andrew Del Matto
HR: Amanda Mallow
FYE: December 31
Type: Public

Meru Networks believes wireless networking should be a seamless experience for customers who don't want to worry about technology. The company develops networking equipment and software used to build wireless LANs. Its products include access points controllers and network management applications. Meru's products allow for the transmission of video voice and data over Wi-Fi connections. It targets customers in the education healthcare hospitality manufacturing and retail sectors among others. Meru has operations in Australia Canada China Germany India Japan Korea Singapore Sweden the UAE the UK and the US.

	Annual Growth	12/09	12/10	12/11	12/12	12/13
Sales ($ mil.)	11.1%	69.5	85.0	90.5	97.5	105.7
Net income ($ mil.)	–	(17.4)	(36.6)	(26.7)	(31.1)	(12.4)
Market value ($ mil.)	(34.6%)	–	353.7	94.7	60.8	98.9
Employees	14.7%	242	292	403	391	419

MERZ PHARMACEUTICALS INC.

4215 Tudor Ln.
Greensboro NC 27410-8105
Phone: 336-856-2003
Fax: 336-856-0107
Web: www.merzusa.com

CEO: Bill Humphries
CFO: –
HR: –
FYE: June 30
Type: Subsidiary

When the merciless sun has taken its toll on your skin Merz Pharmaceuticals will moisturize and replenish. Merz Pharmaceuticals the US subsidiary of German drugmaker Merz develops and distributes prescription and over-the-counter pharmaceutical treatments for skin and nail care. The company's products include Mederma which is used to reduce the appearance of scarring and Appearex which treats weak and brittle nails. It also makes Naftin a topical antifungal and the Aqua Glycolic line of skin cleansers and moisturizers. In addition Merz Pharmaceuticals distributes a handful of non-dermatology products developed by its parent company.

MESA LABORATORIES, INC.

NMS: MLAB

12100 West Sixth Avenue
Lakewood, CO 80228
Phone: 303 987-8000
Fax: –
Web: www.mesalabs.com

CEO: John J. Sullivan
CFO: John V. Sakys
HR: Steve Peterson
FYE: March 31
Type: Public

Mesa Laboratories measures its progress by the sales of its measurement devices. And so far it hasn't plateaued. The company makes niche-market electronic measurement testing and recording instruments for medical food processing electronics and aerospace applications. Mesa's products include sensors that record temperature humidity and pressure levels; flow meters for water treatment polymerization and chemical processing applications; and sonic concentration analyzers. The company also makes kidney hemodialysis treatment products including metering equipment and machines that clean dialyzers (or filters) for reuse. It also provides repair recalibration and certification services.

	Annual Growth	03/11	03/12	03/13	03/14	03/15
Sales ($ mil.)	21.4%	32.8	39.6	46.4	52.7	71.3
Net income ($ mil.)	11.6%	6.2	7.9	8.5	9.0	9.6
Market value ($ mil.)	25.8%	102.6	175.7	188.0	321.4	257.1
Employees	11.7%	177	186	215	273	276

MESA ROYALTY TRUST

NYS: MTR

The Bank of New York Mellon Trust Company, N.A., Trustee, 601 Travis Street, Floor 17

Houston, TX 77002
Phone: 713 483-6020
Fax: –

CEO: –
CFO: –
HR: –
FYE: December 31
Type: Public

In oil and gas Enduro trusts. Enduro Royalty Trust is a Delaware trust formed in 2011 that owns royalty interests in oil and gas production properties in Texas Louisiana and New Mexico. The trust is entitled to receive 80% of net profits from the sale of oil and natural gas produced by privately held Enduro Sponsor at properties in the Permian Basin and in the East Texas/North Louisiana regions; it then makes monthly distributions to trust unitholders. Enduro Sponsor holds interests in more than 900 net producing wells that are operated by third-party oil and gas companies. Its properties have proved reserves of about 27 million barrels of oil equivalent. Enduro Royalty Trust filed to go public in 2011.

	Annual Growth	12/10	12/11	12/12	12/13	12/14
Sales ($ mil.)	0.0%	6.7	6.7	3.8	3.6	6.7
Net income ($ mil.)	0.0%	6.5	6.5	3.6	3.5	6.5
Market value ($ mil.)	(15.1%)	91.8	74.6	36.0	39.6	47.8
Employees						

MESABI TRUST

NYS: MSB

c/o Deutsche Bank Trust Company Americas, Trust & Agency Services, 60 Wall Street,
16th Floor
New York, NY 10005
Phone: 904 271-2520
Fax: –
Web: www.mesabi-trust.com

CEO: –
CFO: –
HR: –
FYE: January 31
Type: Public

In the Iron Range of Mesabi the stockholders trust. Mesabi Trust collects royalties and bonuses from the sale of minerals that are shipped from Northshore Mining's Silver Bay Minnesota facility. The mining company is a wholly owned subsidiary of Cliffs a supplier of iron ore products to the steel industry. Northshore Mining pays royalties to Mesabi Trust based on production and sales of crude ore pulled from the trust's property; it has curtailed its extraction efforts citing lack of demand. Independent consultants track production and sales for Mesabi Trust. Deutsche Bank Trust Company Americas is the corporate trustee of Mesabi Trust.

	Annual Growth	01/11	01/12	01/13	01/14	01/15
Sales ($ mil.)	(6.0%)	33.3	34.2	31.6	22.0	26.1
Net income ($ mil.)	(6.5%)	32.5	33.2	30.7	21.1	24.8
Market value ($ mil.)	(15.4%)	437.3	420.6	323.7	263.6	224.1
Employees	–	–	–	–	–	–

MESIROW FINANCIAL HOLDINGS INC.

353 N. Clark St.
Chicago IL 60654
Phone: 312-595-6000
Fax: 312-595-4246
Web: www.mesirowfinancial.com

CEO: Richard S Price
CFO: Kristie Paskvan
HR: –
FYE: March 31
Type: Private

Mesirow Financial Holdings is an employee-owned company with nearly $380 million in equity investments and a global reach. Clients which are located in 38 countries include corporations public sector entities brokerages investment advisors and wealthy individuals and families. As part of its business Mesirow Financial manages some $61.7 billion in client assets; more than half ($35.4 billion) of this is invested in currencies and commodities. The company's operations span 18 offices located in metropolitan areas nationwide as well as in London. It was established in 1937 when Norman Mesirow purchased a seat on the New York Stock Exchange.

MESSER CONSTRUCTION CO.

5158 FISHWICK DR
CINCINNATI, OH 452162216
Phone: 513-242-1541
Fax: –
Web: www.messer.com

CEO: –
CFO: E Paul Hitter Jr
HR: –
FYE: September 30
Type: Private

From casinos and courthouses to laboratories and dormitories Messer Construction has built them all. The builder provides commercial construction services (including design/build and project management) for projects in Indiana Kentucky Ohio North Carolina and Tennessee. Messer completes over $830 million worth of projects each year for clients in the life sciences higher education senior living commercial manufacturing/industrial public and health care sectors among others. Its projects have included one of the US's only LEED-certified research buildings (at the University of Louisville) and the Newport Aquarium in Kentucky. Founded in 1932 employee-owned Messer boasts a return-customer rate of 80%.

	Annual Growth	09/10	09/11	09/12	09/13	09/14
Sales ($ mil.)	22.5%	–	560.8	0.0	831.7	1,029.8
Net income ($ mil.)	–	–	–	0.0	0.0	0.0
Market value ($ mil.)	–	–	–	–	–	–
Employees	–	–	–	–	–	900

MESSIAH COLLEGE

1 COLLEGE AVE STE 3000
MECHANICSBURG, PA 170556805
Phone: 717-766-2511
Fax: –
Web: www.storylink.messiah.edu

CEO: –
CFO: David Walker
HR: –
FYE: June 30
Type: Private

As its name implies Messiah College is a private Christian college that offers bachelor's degrees in the liberal and applied arts and sciences. Accredited by the Middle States Association of Colleges and Secondary Schools the institution serves more than 3000 students across more than 80 undergraduate majors. Messiah College with 200 full-time faculty members boasts a student/faculty ratio of 13:1. The institution's main campus located 12 miles southwest of Harrisburg Pennsylvania partners with a satellite campus in Philadelphia associated with Temple University. Previously named the Messiah Bible School and Missionary Training Home Messiah College was founded by the Brethren in Christ Church in 1909.

	Annual Growth	06/09	06/10	06/11	06/12	06/13
Sales ($ mil.)	2.1%	–	83.5	87.9	85.9	88.9
Net income ($ mil.)	(50.2%)	–	–	29.4	(6.6)	7.3
Market value ($ mil.)	–	–	–	–	–	–
Employees	–	–	–	–	–	800

MESTEK INC.

NBB: MCCK

260 North Elm Street
Westfield, MA 01085
Phone: 413 568-9571
Fax: 413 568-2969
Web: www.mestek.com

CEO: John E. Reed
CFO: –
HR: –
FYE: December 31
Type: Public

Keeping the temperature just right is Mestek's main job. Through more than 35 subsidiaries Mestek makes heating ventilating and air-conditioning (HVAC) products such as hydronic heat-distribution units gas-fired heating and ventilating equipment louver and damper equipment boilers and refrigeration equipment. Mestek's Formtek family of companies designs builds and services metal-forming and fabricating systems. Its Embassy Industries arm makes radiant heating and plumbing products sold in North America and Europe. Mestek Technology provides computer software products that allow manufacturers to monitor equipment remotely.

	Annual Growth	12/10	12/11	12/12	12/13	12/14
Sales ($ mil.)	3.8%	297.5	304.6	299.3	331.9	345.5
Net income ($ mil.)	33.6%	5.4	8.7	12.5	16.6	17.4
Market value ($ mil.)	20.7%	68.9	77.7	110.0	129.2	146.1
Employees	–	–	–	–	–	–

META FINANCIAL GROUP INC

NMS: CASH

5501 South Broadband Lane
Sioux Falls, SD 57108
Phone: 605 782-1767
Fax: –
Web: www.metabank.com

CEO: J. Tyler Haahr
CFO: David W Leedom
HR: –
FYE: September 30
Type: Public

Don't worry the money is real. Meta Financial Group is the holding company for MetaBank a thrift with about a dozen branches in Iowa and South Dakota. MetaBank offers standard deposit products and services including checking and savings accounts. Its lending and investment activities are weighted towards real estate and real estate-related assets; commercial and multifamily residential mortgages comprise more than half of the bank's loan portfolio. It also writes single-family residential mortgages and business loans. Meta Financial's bread and butter however is the bank's Meta Payment Systems (MPS) division which provides prepaid cards consumer credit and ATM sponsorship services nationwide.

	Annual Growth	09/11	09/12	09/13	09/14	09/15
Assets ($ mil.)	18.7%	1,275.5	1,648.9	1,692.0	2,054.0	2,529.7
Net income ($ mil.)	40.4%	4.6	17.1	13.4	15.7	18.1
Market value ($ mil.)	22.0%	154.1	198.0	310.2	287.8	341.0
Employees	13.2%	389	410	432	453	638

METABOLEX INC.

3876 Bay Center Place
Hayward CA 94545
Phone: 510-293-8800
Fax: 510-293-9090
Web: www.metabolex.com

CEO: Harold Van Wart
CFO: Sujal Shah
HR: –
FYE: December 31
Type: Private

A high-fat low-exercise lifestyle may be wreaking havoc on the average Joe's metabolism but Metabolex is working to develop new treatments to control metabolic diseases including one of the biggest offenders type 2 diabetes. The private biotech's lead drug candidate MBX-102 is designed to reduce blood glucose levels by making muscle and fat cells more sensitive to insulin. Another candidate in its pipeline is targeted at improving the cholesterol and triglyceride levels in diabetes patients. The firm founded in 1991 is backed by Bay City Capital Biotechnology Turnaround Fund and VantagePoint Ventures among others.

METABOLIX INC

NAS: MBLX

21 Erie Street
Cambridge, MA 02139
Phone: 617 583-1700
Fax: –
Web: www.metabolix.com

CEO: Joseph Shaulson
CFO: Joseph D Hill
HR: –
FYE: December 31
Type: Public

Like a good oxymoron? How about natural plastics? Metabolix is working to make biodegradable plastic products out of corn sugar and other natural products. Metabolix calls its product Mirel (that being easier to say than polyhydroxyalkanoates or PHA). The Mirel natural plastics line is the priority but Metabolix is also developing a process to use switchgrass to co-produce PHA and a biomass feedstock to be used to make biofuels. Metabolix tested switchgrass as a feedstock in commercial trials during 2010. In 2012 agriculture giant Archer-Daniels-Midland (ADM) pulled out of a joint venture with Metabolix called Telles which manufactures Mirel resins.

	Annual Growth	12/10	12/11	12/12	12/13	12/14
Sales ($ mil.)	58.1%	0.4	1.4	42.3	5.4	2.8
Net income ($ mil.)	–	(38.8)	(38.8)	3.6	(30.5)	(29.5)
Market value ($ mil.)	(57.1%)	274.2	102.5	33.3	28.4	9.3
Employees	(1.4%)	72	119	93	98	68

METAL CONTAINER CORPORATION

3636 S. Geyer Rd.
St. Louis MO 63127-1237
Phone: 314-957-9500
Fax: 314-957-0700

CEO: –
CFO: –
HR: Julie Nichols
FYE: December 31
Type: Subsidiary

Connoisseurs of the beer-can chicken recipe owe a toast of gratitude to the Metal Container Corporation (MCC). Part of the Anheuser-Busch (A-B) Packaging Group the subsidiary makes aluminum cans and lids for A-B's domestic beer operations in addition to supplying the US soft drink container market. Hansen Natural's Monster Energy beverages are a major soft drink customer as well as PepsiCo and Coca-Cola. MCC makes more than 25 billion cans and 27 billion lids annually and supplies more than 45% of A-B's domestic cans and 55% of its lids. About 25% of the US aluminum can market is produced by MCC which operates five can and two lid manufacturing plants in the US.

METALICO INC

ASE: MEA

186 North Avenue East
Cranford, NJ 07016
Phone: 908 497-9610
Fax: –
Web: www.metalico.com

CEO: Carlos E Aguero
CFO: Kevin Whalen
HR: –
FYE: December 31
Type: Public

No dude it's not a heavy metal band but Metalico is into metal — specifically scrap metal recycling and lead fabrication. The company collects ferrous and nonferrous metal at about 30 facilities in the eastern midwestern and southern US and recycles it into usable scrap. Recycled ferrous metal (iron and steel) is sold mainly to steelmakers including operators of electric arc furnace minimills and steel mills. Metalico's nonferrous scrap includes aluminum which is sold to makers of aluminum products. Metalico engages in lead fabrication at four US facilities. Its lead products include sheet (for roofing) and shot (for reloading).

	Annual Growth	12/09	12/10	12/11	12/12	12/13
Sales ($ mil.)	16.1%	291.7	553.3	660.9	573.6	530.0
Net income ($ mil.)	–	(3.4)	13.5	17.4	(13.1)	(34.8)
Market value ($ mil.)	(19.5%)	236.9	283.1	158.4	94.4	99.7
Employees	4.1%	658	782	768	766	774

METAVATION LLC

2424 John Daly
Inkster MI 48141
Phone: 313-274-2653
Fax: 313-278-4850

CEO: –
CFO: –
HR: –
FYE: November 30
Type: Private

Metavation (formerly EaglePicher Hillsdale Automotive) makes trips over hill and over dale a little more pleasant. The company once part of EaglePicher Corp. produces machined components and assemblies for the automotive industry. Products include filtration components; noise vibration and harshness dampers; yokes and flanges; automatic-transmission filtration products; chassis corners and knuckle assemblies; and driveline and pump parts. The company also offers services such as rubber mixing and molding as well as heat aging and compression testing. It manufactures in the US and Mexico. Late in 2008 EaglePicher sold Hillsdale to privately held Cerion which changed the company's name to Metavation.

METHES ENERGIES INTERNATIONAL LTD.

NBB: MEIL

3651 Lindell Road, Suite D-272
Las Vegas, NV 89103
Phone: 702 932-9964
Fax: –
Web: www.methes.com

CEO: –
CFO: Edward A Stoltenberg
HR: –
FYE: November 30
Type: Public

Methes Energies International lives and breathes biodiesel. Okay maybe the company doesn't breathe fuel but it resells biodiesel produced by third-party companies sells a line of biodiesel processors under the Denami brand and offers an array of services to biodiesel producers. The company also produces biodiesel through two facilities in Ontario and markets and sells its products throughout Canada and the US. Other offerings include selling feedstock (e.g. vegetable oils and animal fats used in biofuel production) installing and commissioning its Denami processors and licensing related proprietary software used to operate the processors. Founded in 2007 Methes Energies filed to go public in mid-2012.

	Annual Growth	11/10	11/11	11/12	11/13	11/14
Sales ($ mil.)	(1.2%)	5.7	11.8	6.5	8.9	5.5
Net income ($ mil.)	–	(1.0)	(0.8)	(4.0)	(5.7)	(6.3)
Market value ($ mil.)	(53.7%)			49.5	23.8	10.6
Employees	(7.4%)	–	29	33	44	23

METHODE ELECTRONICS, INC.

NYS: MEI

7401 West Wilson Avenue
Harwood Heights, IL 60706-4548
Phone: 708 867-6777
Fax: 708 867-6999
Web: www.methode.com

CEO: Donald W. Duda
CFO: Douglas A. Koman
HR: –
FYE: May 02
Type: Public

When it comes to making gear for manufacturers there's no madness in Methode Electronics' methods. Methode produces a wide variety of components especially electronic connectors and controls that are used by automotive manufacturers (products made for Ford and GM together account for more than half of sales) and in computers communications equipment industrial systems aircraft and spacecraft and consumer electronics. It also makes electrical bus systems and radio remote controls among other products. Methode offers electrical environmental and other industrial testing services through its Trace Laboratories unit.

	Annual Growth	04/11	04/12	04/13*	05/14	05/15
Sales ($ mil.)	19.8%	428.2	465.1	519.8	772.8	881.1
Net income ($ mil.)	50.9%	19.5	8.4	40.7	96.1	101.1
Market value ($ mil.)	37.0%	474.1	331.0	538.9	1,120.0	1,671.9
Employees	11.9%	2,743	3,143	3,960	4,566	4,295

*Fiscal year change

METHODIST HOSPITAL OF SOUTHERN CALIFORNIA

300 W HUNTINGTON DR
ARCADIA, CA 910073402
Phone: 626-898-8000
Fax: –
Web: www.methodisthospital.org

CEO: Dan F Ausman
CFO: William E Grigg
HR: –
FYE: December 31
Type: Private

If you're dehydrated in the Valley Methodist Hospital of Southern California can help. The hospital provides medical care to the residents of California's central San Gabriel Valley. The healthcare facility boasts some 600 beds and is part of Southern California Healthcare Systems. The not-for-profit hospital provides comprehensive acute care including surgical pediatric and intensive care units. It also offers a wide range of specialty services such as cardiology oncology neurology bariatrics and orthopedics. The hospital opened its doors in 1903 with five beds.

	Annual Growth	12/09	12/10	12/11	12/12	12/13
Sales ($ mil.)	1.0%	–	271.0	245.7	281.5	279.4
Net income ($ mil.)	–	–	–	(4.5)	1.0	4.7
Market value ($ mil.)	–	–	–	–	–	–
Employees	–	–	–	–	–	2,200

METHODIST HOSPITALS OF DALLAS INC

1441 N BECKLEY AVE
DALLAS, TX 752031201
Phone: 214-947-8181
Fax: –
Web: www.jobs.methodisthealthsystem.org

CEO: –
CFO: Michael J Schaefer
HR: Cheryl Flynn
FYE: September 30
Type: Private

Methodist Hospitals of Dallas serves the health care needs of North Texas — from Mansfield to McKinney. The church-affiliated organization which does business as Methodist Health System operates more than a dozen hospitals clinics and medical facilities in and around the area deemed by locals as Big D. The original hospital Methodist Dallas Medical Center opened in 1927. The 585-bed teaching and referral hospital boasts a Level II trauma center and an organ transplant program. Other facilities include the 269-bed Methodist Charlton Medical Center the 168-bed Methodist Mansfield Medical Center and the 209-bed Methodist Richardson Medical Center.

	Annual Growth	09/09	09/10	09/11	09/12	09/13
Sales ($ mil.)	5.3%	–	889.5	985.6	969.2	1,038.3
Net income ($ mil.)	60.0%	–	–	51.9	165.3	132.7
Market value ($ mil.)	–	–	–	–	–	–
Employees	–	–	–	–	–	4,804

METHODIST LE BONHEUR HEALTHCARE

1211 UNION AVE STE 700
MEMPHIS, TN 381046600
Phone: 901-516-7000
Fax: –
Web: www.methodisthealth.org

CEO: Gary S Shorb
CFO: Hilder Peake
HR: –
FYE: December 31
Type: Private

Methodist Le Bonheur Healthcare (Methodist Healthcare) is happy to take care of sick people. The not-for-profit health care system serves the Memphis area with seven hospitals; multiple minor medical surgical and diagnostic health centers; and home health agencies. The system has about 1700 beds. In addition to traditional health services Methodist Healthcare offers extended care services sleep disorder centers and physical therapy. It also operates physician practices and a physician referral service. The system's flagship hospital Methodist University Hospital has more than 600 beds and is a teaching hospital affiliated with the University of Tennessee Health Science Center.

	Annual Growth	12/05	12/06	12/08	12/11	12/12
Sales ($ mil.)	(31.3%)	–	1,181.8	1,232.4	136.2	124.7
Net income ($ mil.)	–	–	–	(266.5)	7.1	(3.2)
Market value ($ mil.)	–	–	–	–	–	–
Employees	–	–	–	–	–	11,459

METLIFE INC

NYS: MET

200 Park Avenue
New York, NY 10166-0188
Phone: 212 578-2211
Fax: –
Web: www.metlife.com

CEO: Steven A. (Steve) Kandarian
CFO: John C. R. Hele
HR: Frans Hijkoop
FYE: December 31
Type: Public

While its name evolved from "metropolitan" MetLife's policies are found in villages towns and huge cities around the world. Operating through its Metropolitan Life Insurance subsidiary MetLife is the largest life insurer in the US. Its Insurance Products segment includes all of its group and individual life insurance and non-medical health insurance products (dental disability illness). Its Retirement Products segment includes annuity products. MetLife's Auto & Home segment works through subsidiary Metropolitan Property and Casualty. MetLife is a big player in Japan and growing in more than 50 other countries especially in Latin America. MetLife plans to split off much of its US life business.

	Annual Growth	12/10	12/11	12/12	12/13	12/14
Assets ($ mil.)	5.4%	730,906.0	799,625.0	836,781.0	885,296.0	902,337.0
Net income ($ mil.)	22.6%	2,790.0	6,981.0	1,324.0	3,368.0	6,309.0
Market value ($ mil.)	5.0%	50,302.9	35,293.5	37,285.7	61,033.6	61,226.0
Employees	0.7%	66,000	67,000	64,000	65,000	68,000

METOKOTE CORPORATION

1340 Neubrecht Rd.
Lima OH 45801
Phone: 419-996-7800
Fax: 419-996-7801
Web: www.metokote.com

CEO: Jeffrey J Oravitz
CFO: Patrick Osler
HR: Don Myan
FYE: October 31
Type: Private

MetoKote wants its many customers to say "protective coatings — me too." The manufacturer provides protective coating applications such as electrocoating powder coating and liquid painting. Its equipment division manufactures process lines and support equipment like building racks carriers shipping pallets and part containers. MetoKote services customers primarily in the automotive agricultural and construction equipment and appliance and furniture manufacturing industries. It produces and sells more than 150 coating systems from about 30 manufacturing locations in Brazil Germany Canada Mexico the UK and the US. Other services include labeling specialty packaging and subassembly.

METRICSTREAM INC.

2600 E. Bayshore Rd.	CEO: Shellye Archambeau
Palo Alto CA 94303	CFO: Jeffrey Zellmer
Phone: 650-620-2900	HR: –
Fax: 650-632-1953	FYE: December 31
Web: www.metricstream.com	Type: Private

MetricStream helps companies avoid getting a slap on the wrist — or much worse — for failing to meet regulatory requirements. Founded in 1999 the company provides GRC (governance risk management and compliance) and quality management software that helps firms comply with quality standards (such as Six Sigma) industry-specific regulations (such as FDA requirements) corporate laws (the Sarbanes-Oxley Act) and internal policies. Its software uses e-mail workflow management process dashboard and document management tools to automate compliance and quality assurance processes. Metric-Stream has offices in the US and India.

METRO BANCORP INC PA

NMS: METR

3801 Paxton Street	CEO: Gary L Nalbandian
Harrisburg, PA 17111	CFO: Mark A Zody
Phone: 888 937-0004	HR: –
Fax: –	FYE: December 31
Web: www.mymetrobank.com	Type: Public

Metro Bancorp (formerly Pennsylvania Commerce Bancorp) is the holding company for Metro Bank (formerly Commerce Bank/Harrisburg) which has more than 30 branches in south-central Pennsylvania many of them with extended hours and open seven days a week. The bank provides standard services such as checking savings and money market accounts CDs IRAs and credit cards. Commercial loans including lines of credit and construction land development real estate and operating loans account for the majority of the bank's lending activities. It also originates consumer loans and residential mortgages.

	Annual Growth	12/09	12/10	12/11	12/12	12/13
Assets ($ mil.)	6.7%	2,147.8	2,234.5	2,421.2	2,634.9	2,781.1
Net income ($ mil.)	–	(1.9)	(4.3)	0.3	10.9	17.3
Market value ($ mil.)	14.4%	178.0	155.9	118.6	187.2	304.9
Employees	(1.6%)	1,043	959	957	919	978

METRO PACKAGING & IMAGING INC

5 HAUL RD	CEO: –
WAYNE, NJ 074706624	CFO: Manuel De Torres
Phone: 973-709-9100	HR: –
Fax: –	FYE: December 31
Web: www.metro-pi.com	Type: Private

Metro gives its customers the full printing package. Metro Packaging and Imaging prints product packaging including folding cartons flexible packaging paper bags and curved cups as well as prints directly onto CDs. The company founded as Metro Litho in 1964-, uses gravure flexographic dry offset (letterpress) and silkscreen methods and offers a full range of digital imaging services.-, The company-, expanded its operations and menu of services in 2006 by adding full prepress capabilities. Metro's clients include Kraft Foods Revlon and Hartz. Metro Packaging boasts operations in California Georgia Minnesota New Jersey North Carolina and Ohio.

	Annual Growth	12/04	12/05	12/06	12/09	12/10
Sales ($ mil.)	(60.6%)	–	–	1,312.6	26.6	31.5
Net income ($ mil.)	609.3%	–	–	0.0	0.7	1.2
Market value ($ mil.)	–	–	–	–	–	–
Employees	–	–	–	–	–	120

METRO-GOLDWYN-MAYER INC.

10250 Constellation Blvd.	CEO: Gary Barber
Los Angeles CA 90067-6421	CFO: –
Phone: 310-449-3000	HR: –
Fax: 310-449-8857	FYE: December 31
Web: www.mgm.com	Type: Private

The name is Mayer. Metro-Goldwyn-Mayer (MGM). Home of the venerable James Bond franchise MGM is a Hollywood moviemaker through production units MGM Studios and United Artists (UA). Recent films include 21 Jump Street and The Girl with the Dragon Tattoo. Its MGM Television produces TV shows such as the mini-series Mildred Pierce which aired on HBO while MGM Home Entertainment distributes films on DVD. MGM owns one of the largest film libraries in the world with more than 4000 titles including the Rocky and Pink Panther series as well as some 10000 TV episodes. The firm emerged from Chapter 11 in 2010 under new ownership. The largest shareholder in the rejuvenated MGM is billionaire financier Carl Icahn.

METRO-NORTH COMMUTER RAILROAD COMPANY

347 Madison Ave.	CEO: –
New York NY 10017-3739	CFO: –
Phone: 212-532-4900	HR: –
Fax: 212-878-0186	FYE: December 31
Web: mta.info/mnr/	Type: Subsidiary

Part of New York's Metropolitan Transportation Authority Metro-North Commuter Railroad carries passengers between New York City and its New York and Connecticut suburbs. The company known as MTA Metro-North Railroad or Metro-North covers 775 miles of track and serves a ridership of about 82 million. Three of the company's lines operate from Grand Central Terminal in New York City; the other two operate from Hoboken New Jersey. Metro-North Railroad serves more than 120 stations in seven counties in New York State (Bronx Dutchess New York Orange Putnam Rockland and Westchester) and two in Connecticut (Fairfield and New Haven). Metro-North operates with an annual budget of more than $600 million.

METROCORP HOLDINGS INC.

1818 Market St. 36th Fl.	CEO: –
Philadelphia PA 19103	CFO: –
Phone: 215-564-7700	HR: –
Fax: 215-656-3501	FYE: December 31
Web: www.phillymag.com	Type: Private

Metrocorp Holdings has a thing for Beantown and Philly. The company publishes Boston Magazine and Philadelphia Magazine two glossy monthly publications about about city life and events. The sister titles are best known for their "Best of" lists and regional features. The company also publishes related Web content and ancillary titles such as Pennsylvania Home and Philadelphia Wedding as well as New England Travel Boston Homes and Boston Weddings. Metrocorp Holdings was founded as Philadelphia Magazine: The City of Industry by the Trades League of Philadelphia in 1908.

METROPLEX ADVENTIST HOSPITAL INC.

2201 S CLEAR CREEK RD
KILLEEN, TX 765494110
Phone: 254-526-7523
Fax: –
Web: www.mplex.org

CEO: –
CFO: Robert Brock
HR: –
FYE: December 31
Type: Private

Because the Texas towns of Belton Killeen and Lampasas aren't large they share a large health system between them. Metroplex Health System includes Metroplex Adventist Hospital with 148 beds in Killeen a behavioral health unit with 60 beds and Rollins Brook Community Hospital with 25 beds in Lampasas. The system part of Adventist Health System and served by Scott & White provides all the basics of general medical care including physician office buildings home health services and other outpatient services. Metroplex Adventist Hospital also serves the needs of nearby Ft. Hood making it the largest community healthcare provider to the military in the US.

	Annual Growth	12/0-1	12/00	12/01	12/02	12/09
Sales ($ mil.)	(2.4%)	–	141.0	0.0	64.6	113.3
Net income ($ mil.)	–	–	–	0.0	5.1	8.9
Market value ($ mil.)	–	–	–	–	–	–
Employees	–	–	–	–	–	779

METROPOLITAN EDISON COMPANY

c/o FirstEnergy Corp. 76 S. Main St.
Akron OH 44308
Phone: 800-736-3402
Fax: 330-384-3866
Web: https://www.firstenergycorp.com

CEO: –
CFO: Mark T Clark
HR: –
FYE: December 31
Type: Subsidiary

Metropolitan Edison is an electric company and it knows a thing or two about serving cities and surrounding communities. The company a subsidiary of holding company FirstEnergy provides electric services to a population of 1.3 million in a 3300-sq. ml. service area in south central and eastern Pennsylvania. Metropolitan Edison or Met-Ed as it is sometimes referred to operates almost 16500 miles of power transmission and distribution lines. Although the company's primary source of electricity is derived from oil-and gas-fired units its York Haven Power Company generates hydroelectric power.

METROPOLITAN HEALTH NETWORKS INC.

NYSE AMEX: MDF

777 Yamato Rd. Ste. 510
Boca Raton FL 33431
Phone: 561-805-8500
Fax: 404-236-2626
Web: www.iss.net

CEO: John E Barger III
CFO: Robert J Sabo
HR: S Palmer
FYE: December 31
Type: Public

Metropolitan Health Networks (MetCare) provides a way to keep Florida's senior citizens healthy. Through contracts with Humana and other health insurers the provider service network (PSN) operator provides health benefits to some 70000 members in Florida most of whom are part of Humana's Medicare Advantage and Medicare HMO plans. The company which offers health care services through its network of 30 primary care practices and 250 affiliated practices receives fees for services provided through contracts with insurers. It operates in 18 counties in Central and South Florida. MetCare doubled its network in 2011 by acquiring neighboring Continucare. It is owned by Humana.

METROPOLITAN OPERA ASSOCIATION INC.

Lincoln Center
New York NY 10023
Phone: 212-799-3100
Fax: 914-428-8203
Web: www.modimes.org

CEO: William Morris
CFO: –
HR: Scott Cool
FYE: July 31
Type: Private

Italians and Germans alike desire an American debut at the Met. Well their operas do anyway. The Metropolitan Opera Association manages The Metropolitan Opera company which presents more than 200 performances every year in its residence at the Lincoln Center for the Performing Arts. The Met is known for performing most works in their original languages and for producing regular Saturday radio broadcasts which are aired throughout North America and in South America Europe and the Asia/Pacific region. In association with sponsors the Met makes video and CD recordings of the performances and distributes them worldwide. The Met was founded in 1883.

METROPOLITAN PROPERTY AND CASUALTY INSURANCE COMPANY

700 Quaker Ln.
Warwick RI 02886
Phone: 800-438-6388
Fax: 401-827-2798

CEO: William Moore
CFO: –
HR: –
FYE: December 31
Type: Subsidiary

Because MetLife is practically bigger than life it is able to offer property/casualty insurance for the stuff that fills our lives. Its subsidiary Metropolitan Property and Casualty Insurance (MPC) operates under the MetLife Auto & Home brand and is a leading provider of property/casualty insurance for automobiles boats and homeowners insurance. Its products are sold through workplaces and directly to individuals in the US. Auto insurance accounts for 70% of premiums and includes both standard and non-standard policies. Homeowner's and other coverage including personal excess liability make up the remaining 30% of the company's premiums.

METROPOLITAN SECURITY SERVICES INC.

100 E 10TH ST STE 400
CHATTANOOGA, TN 374024218
Phone: 423-702-8200
Fax: –
Web: www.waldensecurity.com

CEO: Amy S Walden
CFO: –
HR: Deborah Sears
FYE: December 31
Type: Private

Walden Security is something of a right-hand man — or in this case woman — to businesses and government. Majority owned and operated by women (the company is controlled by co-founder chairman and CEO Amy Walden) the security services contractor recruits trains and manages uniformed security professionals to guard such sites as airports auto dealerships manufacturing facilities museums office buildings residences schools and shopping malls. It is also contracted by the US General Services Administration to provide alarm monitors clerks court security officers and police officers. Walden Security has operations in about 15 states.

	Annual Growth	12/06	12/07	12/08	12/09	12/13
Sales ($ mil.)	–	–	(1,277.6)	85.7	95.9	120.8
Net income ($ mil.)	18.9%	–	–	0.2	0.9	0.5
Market value ($ mil.)	–	–	–	–	–	–
Employees	–	–	–	–	–	2,500

METROPOLITAN TRANSIT AUTHORITY OF HARRIS COUNTY TEXAS

1900 Main St.	CEO: –
Houston TX 77002	CFO: Suzzane Bailey
Phone: 713-739-4000	HR: –
Fax: 713-739-4096	FYE: September 30
Web: www.ridemetro.org	Type: Government Agency

The Metropolitan Transit Authority of Harris County Texas (known as METRO in its hometown) provides bus transportation services for passengers in Houston and surrounding Harris County communities. The agency's fleet includes more than 1200 buses (including hybrids). METRO also provides transportation for people with disabilities (METROLift) who are unable to ride buses and oversees high-occupancy vehicle (HOV) lanes transit centers and park-and-ride lots. As an alternative to Houston's car-clogged streets METRORail's 7.5-mile light rail system connects Houston's downtown midtown the museum district and the Texas Medical Center. Metro began operations in 1979.

METROPOLITAN TRANSPORTATION AUTHORITY

347 Madison Ave.	CEO: Thomas F Predergast
New York NY 10017-3739	CFO: –
Phone: 212-878-7000	HR: –
Fax: 212-878-0186	FYE: December 31
Web: www.mta.info	Type: Government-owned

No Sigma Chi or Chi Omega chapter has anything on New York City's Metropolitan Transportation Authority (MTA) — it rushes millions of people every day. The largest public transportation system in the US the government-owned MTA provides about 2.6 billion passenger trips and sees about 300 million vehicles travel its system annually. The MTA's largest agency the New York City Transit Authority operates about 6300 rail and subway cars that provide service across New York's five boroughs; it also runs a fleet of some 5900 buses. Other MTA units offer bus and rail service to Connecticut and Long Island and operate the Triborough system of toll bridges and tunnels.

METROPOLITAN UTILITIES DISTRICT OMAHA NEBRASKA.

1723 HARNEY ST	CEO: –
OMAHA, NE 681021960	CFO: Debra A Schneider
Phone: 402-554-6666	HR: –
Fax: –	FYE: December 31
Web: www.myacount.mudomaha.com	Type: Private

The Metropolitan Utilities District (MUD) distributes natural gas and water in the Omaha Nebraska metropolitan area. The company serves some 220000 natural gas customers and more than 200000 water customers. It also collects sewer and trash fees for municipalities. Customer-owned MUD which claims to be the fifth-largest public gas utility in the nation is a political subdivision of the State of Nebraska. Its board members are elected by residents of its service territory.

	Annual Growth	12/08	12/09	12/11	12/12	12/13
Sales ($ mil.)	2.6%	–	308.4	311.9	292.8	342.0
Net income ($ mil.)	75.4%	–	–	15.3	46.2	47.0
Market value ($ mil.)	–	–	–	–	–	–
Employees	–	–	–	–	–	852

METROPOLITAN WASHINGTON AIRPORTS AUTHORITY

1 Aviation Circle	CEO: –
Washington DC 20001-6000	CFO: Andrew Rountree
Phone: 703-417-8600	HR: –
Fax: 703-549-5796	FYE: December 31
Web: www.metwashairports.com	Type: Government Agency

Politicians might dominate the airwaves in Washington DC but the Metropolitan Washington Airports Authority rules the airways or at least the runways. The Metropolitan Washington Airports Authority operates Washington Dulles International and Ronald Reagan Washington National airports the primary airports serving the nation's capital. The airports generate revenue from aircraft landing fees concessions and space rental. The agency also oversees the Dulles Toll Road. A public agency the Metropolitan Washington Airports Authority was created in 1987 by the District of Columbia and the Commonwealth of Virginia with the consent of the US Congress.

METTLER-TOLEDO INTERNATIONAL, INC.   NYS: MTD

1900 Polaris Parkway	CEO: Olivier A. Filliol
Columbus, OH 43240	CFO: Shawn P Vadala
Phone: 614 438-4511	HR: Mario Sanzo
Fax: 614 438-4646	FYE: December 31
Web: www.mt.com	Type: Public

Mettler-Toledo International bears the weight of the world and does it precisely (say to one ten-millionth of a gram). The company makes precision weighing and analytical instruments for the industrial laboratory and food retail sectors. Products include bench and floor scales transportation and logistics data capture laboratory balances pipettes automated chemistry solutions process analytics software and more. The company also makes products for the retail grocery industry including labeling systems checkout scanner scales receiving scales and data management software. Mettler-Toledo's business is geographically diverse with customers across the Americas Asia and Europe.

	Annual Growth	12/11	12/12	12/13	12/14	12/15
Sales ($ mil.)	0.9%	2,309.3	2,341.5	2,379.0	2,486.0	2,395.4
Net income ($ mil.)	7.0%	269.5	290.8	306.1	338.2	352.8
Market value ($ mil.)	23.1%	4,001.5	5,236.5	6,571.8	8,193.7	9,187.1
Employees	3.0%	12,000	12,400	12,500	13,100	13,500

METWOOD INC   NBB: MTWD

819 Naff Road	CEO: Robert M Callahan
Boones Mill, VA 24065	CFO: Shawn A Callahan
Phone: 540 334-4294	HR: –
Fax: –	FYE: June 30
	Type: Public

Metwood is shaping the future of construction. The company manufactures light-gauge steel building materials usually combined with wood for use in residential and commercial construction in lieu of conventional wood products. The combination increases load strength and structural integrity allowing for durable designs that can't be produced with wood alone. Products include girders and headers; floor joists; roof and floor trusses and rafters; metal framing; structural columns; and garage deck and porch concrete pour-over systems. The company primarily sells to lumber yards and home improvement stores mainly in Virginia. Affiliate Providence Engineering provides civil engineering services.

	Annual Growth	06/11	06/12	06/13	06/14	06/15
Sales ($ mil.)	(6.1%)	2.2	1.9	2.2	1.9	1.7
Net income ($ mil.)	–	(0.1)	(0.4)	(0.3)	(0.2)	(0.0)
Market value ($ mil.)	10.7%	6.6	2.3	6.9	7.6	9.9
Employees	(7.8%)	18	18	14	14	13

MEXCO ENERGY CORP.

ASE: MXC

214 West Texas Avenue, Suite 1101
Midland, TX 79701
Phone: 432 682-1119
Fax: 432 682-1123
Web: www.mexcoenergy.com

CEO: Nicholas C Taylor
CFO: Tamala L McComic
HR: –
FYE: March 31
Type: Public

Mexco Energy gets most of its energy not from Mexico but from its close neighbor — West Texas. The oil and gas exploration and production independent has proved reserves of 7.9 billion cu. ft. of natural gas and 217000 barrels of oil. While the company owns oil and gas properties in other states (including Louisiana New Mexico North Dakota and Oklahoma) the majority of its activities take place in Texas. Chesapeake Operating and ConocoPhillips are Mexco Energy's top customers. Mexco Energy president Nicholas Taylor owns about 48% of the company.

	Annual Growth	03/11	03/12	03/13	03/14	03/15
Sales ($ mil.)	1.8%	3.2	3.2	3.1	4.0	3.4
Net income ($ mil.)	–	0.2	0.3	(0.2)	0.3	(0.3)
Market value ($ mil.)	(19.2%)	26.8	16.2	12.9	15.7	11.4
Employees	4.7%	5	5	6	6	6

MEXICAN RESTAURANTS, INC.

NBB: CASA

12000 Aerospace Ave., Suite 400
Houston, TX 77034-5576
Phone: 832 300-5858
Fax: 832 300-5859
Web: www.mexicanrestaurantsinc.com

CEO: Marcus Jundt
CFO: Andrew J Dennard
HR: –
FYE: December 30
Type: Public

Mexican Restaurants gets the prize for the most straightforward name in the book. The company operates and franchises more than 70 casual-dining Mexican restaurants located primarily in Texas. Its flagship Casa Ole chain serves standard Mexican and Tex-Mex fare including burritos enchiladas and fajitas while its Monterey's Little Mexico and Monterey's Tex-Mex Cafe units offer a mix of more authentic Mexican cuisine. In addition the company operates a chain of half a dozen quick-casual restaurants under the Mission Burritos banner. Other brands include Crazy Jose's and Tortuga Coastal Cantina. More than 50 of the restaurants are company-owned while the rest are franchised.

	Annual Growth	12/08*	01/10	01/11	01/12*	12/12
Sales ($ mil.)	(4.5%)	81.9	72.0	66.2	66.9	68.1
Net income ($ mil.)	–	(4.0)	(0.8)	(5.5)	(0.5)	(0.0)
Market value ($ mil.)	(5.1%)	6.4	7.7	5.2	2.6	5.2
Employees	(9.4%)	2,378	1,950	–	–	–

*Fiscal year change

MEYER & WALLIS INC.

117 N JEFFERSON ST # 204
MILWAUKEE, WI 532026160
Phone: 414-224-0212
Fax: –
Web: www.meyerwallis.com

CEO: Robert L Meyer
CFO: Tod Kinunen
HR: –
FYE: December 31
Type: Private

Meyer & Wallis provides full service advertising and marketing for clients across the US. Services include strategic development advertising design public relations and interactive marketing with a strong background in serving retail clients. The agency also serves companies in health care and consumer products. Its portfolio includes work for such clients as the American Heart Association Quad/Graphics and Vectren Energy. The agency has offices in Indianapolis and Milwaukee. Meyer & Wallis was founded in 1967 by industry veteran CEO Bob Meyer.

	Annual Growth	12/04	12/05	12/06	12/07	12/08
Sales ($ mil.)	19.4%	–	9.8	9.8	17.3	16.7
Net income ($ mil.)	–	–	–	(0.1)	0.7	(0.1)
Market value ($ mil.)	–	–	–	–	–	–
Employees	–	–	–	–	–	27

MFA FINANCIAL, INC.

NYS: MFA

350 Park Avenue, 20th Floor
New York, NY 10022
Phone: 212 207-6400
Fax: 212 207-6420
Web: www.mfa-reit.com

CEO: William S Gorin
CFO: Stephen D Yarad
HR: –
FYE: December 31
Type: Public

MFA Financial (formerly MFA Mortgage Investments) has three good buddies: Fannie Freddie and Ginnie. This self-advised mortgage real estate investment trust (REIT) was incorporated in 1997 to invest in mortgage-backed securities and mortgages such as those guaranteed by government-related entities Fannie Mae Freddie Mac and Ginnie Mae. The REIT's investment portfolio mainly consists of agency mortgage-backed securities AAA-rated mortgage-backed securities corporate and government bonds and cash. MFA Financial buys its securities and loans from the banks savings and loans investment banks and mortgage banking institutions that originate them. Its portfolio weighs in at approximately $8 billion.

	Annual Growth	12/08	12/09	12/10	12/11	12/12
Assets ($ mil.)	6.2%	10,641.4	9,627.2	8,687.4	11,750.6	13,517.6
Net income ($ mil.)	60.9%	45.8	268.2	269.8	316.4	306.8
Market value ($ mil.)	8.3%	2,105.9	2,628.0	2,917.6	2,402.7	2,899.7
Employees	13.9%	22	25	29	35	37

MFA INCORPORATED

201 RAY YOUNG DR
COLUMBIA, MO 652013599
Phone: 573-874-5111
Fax: –
Web: www.californiamfa.com

CEO: Ernie Verslues
CFO: Ernie Verslues
HR: –
FYE: August 31
Type: Private

Agricultural cooperative MFA brings together 45000 farmers in Missouri and adjacent states. One of the US's oldest regional co-ops supplying its member/owners with agronomy distribution financing and purchasing services it runs more than 140 retail farm supply centers and works with independent dealers. MFA supplies animal feeds seed fertilizer and crop protection products. The co-op also provides its members with agronomy services animal-health products and farm supplies. It also offers marketing services and is the publisher of Today's Farmer. Agmo Corporation MFA's finance company provides co-op members longer credit terms for purchases made through MFA's retail outlets.

	Annual Growth	08/10	08/11	08/12	08/13	08/14
Sales ($ mil.)	3.7%	–	1,355.0	1,470.5	1,510.6	1,510.6
Net income ($ mil.)	(8.6%)	–	–	22.3	15.4	18.6
Market value ($ mil.)	–	–	–	–	–	–
Employees	–	–	–	–	–	1,393

MFA OIL COMPANY

1 RAY YOUNG DR
COLUMBIA, MO 652013506
Phone: 573-442-0171
Fax: –
Web: www.mfaoil.com

CEO: Jerry Taylor
CFO: Robert Condron
HR: Lynn Smith
FYE: August 31
Type: Private

Many farmers appreciate MFA Oil. The energy cooperative controlled by its 40000 farmer-members produces fuel and lubrication products and manages bulk petroleum and propane plants in the Central and Western US. Operating 140 propane plants the company sells more propane for farm use and home heating than any other company in Missouri. It also operates nearly 100 oil and lubricant bulk plants and serves customers in Arkansas Iowa Kansas and Oklahoma. Additionally the company operates 76 convenience stores under the Break Time brand (in Arkansas and Missouri) more than 160 Petro-Card 24 fueling locations and owns 10 Jiffy Lube and a dozen Big O Tire franchises.

	Annual Growth	08/10	08/11	08/12	08/13	08/14
Sales ($ mil.)	4.9%	–	1,275.2	1,255.1	1,300.6	1,471.0
Net income ($ mil.)	9.4%	–	–	34.1	55.3	40.8
Market value ($ mil.)	–	–	–	–	–	–
Employees	–	–	–	–	–	1,500

MFRI INC.

NMS: MFRI

7720 N. Lehigh Avenue
Niles, IL 60714
Phone: 847 966-1000
Fax: –
Web: www.mfri.com

CEO: Bradley E. (Brad) Mautner
CFO: Karl J Schmidt
HR: Wayne Bosch
FYE: January 31
Type: Public

MFRI's motto could be: "Pipe down and take a deep breath." The company makes piping systems and air filter elements through subsidiaries Perma-Pipe and Midwesco Filter respectively. It makes pre-insulated specialty piping systems for oil and gas gathering district heating and cooling as well as other applications. The company also makes custom-designed industrial filtration products to remove particulates from air and other gas streams. Perma-Pipe's specialty piping systems are used on college campuses military bases and other large sites. Midwesco provides products and services for industrial air filtration. Its Filtration Products segment supplies filter elements to more than 4000 user locations.

	Annual Growth	01/11	01/12	01/13	01/14	01/15
Sales ($ mil.)	(2.8%)	218.6	233.5	212.0	226.8	194.9
Net income ($ mil.)	–	4.5	(5.0)	(18.5)	21.0	(0.3)
Market value ($ mil.)	(15.4%)	79.4	54.7	43.2	105.9	40.7
Employees	(1.9%)	1,123	1,198	1,212	1,013	1,040

MGA ENTERTAINMENT INC.

16300 Roscoe Blvd. Ste. 150
Van Nuys CA 91406-1257
Phone: 818-894-2525
Fax: 818-894-8094
Web: www.mgae.com

CEO: Isaac Larian
CFO: –
HR: –
FYE: December 31
Type: Private

In a Barbie doll world the Bratz bad girls make good business for MGA Entertainment. The company which in 2011 ended an epic legal battle with archrival Mattel over the Bratz line of multiethnic dolls manufactures children's fashion dolls under the Moxie Girlz Novi Stars and Lalaloopsy names. MGA Entertainment owns Little Tikes (maker of the iconic Cozy Coupe) and produces Rescue Pets brand plush animals as well as lifelike baby dolls through a partnership with Zapf Creation in which MGA holds a 65% stake. Founded in 1982 as ABC Electronics the manufacturer later changed its name to Micro Games of America and then shortened it to MGA when its focus shifted from games to dolls in the late '90s.

MGC DIAGNOSTICS CORP

NAS: MGCD

350 Oak Grove Parkway
Saint Paul, MN 55127-8599
Phone: 651 484-4874
Fax: –
Web: www.mgcdiagnostics.com

CEO: Todd M Austin
CFO: Wesley W Winnekins
HR: –
FYE: October 31
Type: Public

A good diagnosis for disease detection integrated care and wellness is key to the business model of MGC Diagnostics Corporation formerly Angeion. Through subsidiary Medical Graphics Corporation the company designs and sells cardiorespiratory diagnostic systems that analyze lung function and diagnose disease using a patient's breath. It sells systems under the MedGraphics brand to health care providers. The non-invasive MedGraphics devices analyze a patient's inhaled and exhaled breath to help detect emphysema asthma and heart disease among other things. Researchers also use MedGraphics' products in clinical trial studies.

	Annual Growth	10/11	10/12	10/13	10/14	10/15
Sales ($ mil.)	6.6%	29.1	27.2	31.6	30.0	37.5
Net income ($ mil.)	–	(0.2)	(0.0)	1.4	(1.1)	4.0
Market value ($ mil.)	9.4%	19.7	27.6	50.7	28.9	28.2
Employees	7.4%	124	123	121	158	165

MGE ENERGY INC

NMS: MGEE

133 South Blair Street
Madison, WI 53788
Phone: 608 252-7000
Fax: –
Web: www.mgeenergy.com

CEO: Gary J. Wolter
CFO: Jeffrey C. Newman
HR: –
FYE: December 31
Type: Public

MGE Energy warms folks during cold Wisconsin winters. The holding company distributes electricity to 140000 residential commercial and industrial customers in Dane County and natural gas to about 145000 customers in seven southern and western Wisconsin counties through its Madison Gas and Electric subsidiary. The utility has a generating capacity of more than 800 MW; the majority comes from fossil-fueled plants. The company's power-related but unregulated businesses include MGE Power (generating interests) MGE Construct (construction services) Central Wisconsin Development (business support services) and MAGAEL (property development).

	Annual Growth	12/10	12/11	12/12	12/13	12/14
Sales ($ mil.)	3.9%	532.6	546.4	541.3	590.9	619.9
Net income ($ mil.)	8.6%	57.7	60.9	64.4	74.9	80.3
Market value ($ mil.)	1.6%	1,482.4	1,621.4	1,766.3	2,000.8	1,581.2
Employees	(0.1%)	701	712	688	695	699

MGIC INVESTMENT CORP. (WI)

NYS: MTG

250 E. Kilbourn Avenue
Milwaukee, WI 53202
Phone: 414 347-6480
Fax: –
Web: www.mgic.com

CEO: Curt S. Culver
CFO: Timothy Mattke
HR: Kurt Thomas
FYE: December 31
Type: Public

Since a pinkie-promise isn't good enough for most lenders there's MGIC Investment's mortgage insurance to protect lenders from homebuyers who don't hold up their end of the bargain. MGIC owns Mortgage Guaranty Insurance Corporation (MGIC) the largest provider of private mortgage insurance in the US. Such coverage allows otherwise-qualified buyers who aren't able to scrape up the standard 20% down payment to get mortgages. MGIC writes primary insurance on individual loans. The company's customers include banks mortgage brokers credit unions and other residential mortgage lenders. In 2014 MGIC had $159.3 billion primary insurance in force covering 1 million mortgages.

	Annual Growth	12/10	12/11	12/12	12/13	12/14
Assets ($ mil.)	(13.3%)	9,333.6	7,216.2	5,574.3	5,601.4	5,266.4
Net income ($ mil.)	–	(363.7)	(485.9)	(927.1)	(49.8)	251.9
Market value ($ mil.)	(2.2%)	3,449.9	1,262.8	900.6	2,857.4	3,155.4
Employees	(5.7%)	1,010	920	877	819	800

MGM GRAND HOTEL LLC

3799 Las Vegas Blvd.
South Las Vegas NV 89109
Phone: 702-891-1111
Fax: 702-891-3036
Web: www.mgmgrand.com

CEO: –
CFO: –
HR: Christopher Dear
FYE: December 31
Type: Subsidiary

Dubbed The City of Entertainment MGM Grand Hotel operates one of the world's largest casino resorts. Opened in 1993 the MGM Grand Las Vegas includes four towers with more than 6200 guest rooms and narly 160000 sq. ft. of casino space which includes some 2100 slot machines and 165 table games. The casino which takes up an entire city block on the Las Vegas Strip also serves as a venue for concerts sporting events and magic shows. Other attractions include a Cirque du Soleil show restaurants from celebrity chefs such as Wolfgang Puck and Emeril Lagasse shopping outlets a swimming-pool complex a spa a wedding chapel and a lion habitat. MGM Grand is a subsidiary of MGM Resorts International.

MGM RESORTS INTERNATIONAL

NYS: MGM

3600 Las Vegas Boulevard South
Las Vegas, NV 89109
Phone: 702 693-7120
Fax: –
Web: www.mgmresorts.com

CEO: James J. Murren
CFO: Daniel J. D'Arrigo
HR: Michelle Ditondo
FYE: December 31
Type: Public

It's not your imagination — MGM Resorts International (formerly MGM MIRAGE) is one of the world's largest gaming firms. The company's more than 15 partially or wholly owned properties include some of the biggest names on the Las Vegas Strip including MGM Grand The Mirage and the Monte Carlo as well as Luxor Bellagio and Mandalay Bay. MGM Resorts also owns or has a stake in other casinos in Nevada as well as in Michigan (MGM Grand Detroit) and Mississippi (Beau Rivage). Internationally it operates in China and Dubai. The company changed its name from MGM MIRAGE in 2010 to better reflect its family of hotel brands and its expanding global presence.

	Annual Growth	12/10	12/11	12/12	12/13	12/14
Sales ($ mil.)	13.8%	6,019.2	7,849.3	9,160.8	9,809.7	10,082.0
Net income ($ mil.)	–	(1,437.4)	3,114.6	(1,767.7)	(156.6)	(149.9)
Market value ($ mil.)	9.5%	7,295.7	5,124.2	5,718.6	11,555.2	10,503.8
Employees	2.8%	61,000	66,800	66,650	67,800	68,100

MGT CAPITAL INVESTMENTS INC

ASE: MGT

500 Mamaroneck Avenue, Suite 204
Harrison, NY 10528
Phone: 914 630-7431
Fax: –
Web: www.mgtci.com

CEO: Robert Ladd
CFO: Robert Traversa
HR: –
FYE: December 31
Type: Public

MGT Capital Investments is looking for ROI no matter if it's in American dollars or British sterling. The holding company is focused on medical imaging technology. It owns a 55% stake in Medicsight a publicly traded company that develops medical imaging software to help detect cancer. The company narrowed its investments in 2010 when it divested its holdings in Medicexchange XShares HipCricket and Eurindia. The following year it sold its stake in UK financial advisory firm Moneygate. Virtually all of MGT Capital's revenues now stem from Medicsight. Originally listed on the NYSE Amex in 1996 the company began trading on the London Stock Exchange's AIM exchange in 2011.

	Annual Growth	12/10	12/11	12/12	12/13	12/14
Sales ($ mil.)	18.3%	0.5	0.5	0.4	0.4	1.1
Net income ($ mil.)	–	(9.7)	(4.5)	(3.9)	(10.2)	(5.3)
Market value ($ mil.)	23.4%	2.8	1.0	41.4	30.2	6.5
Employees	(22.2%)	30	9	7	15	11

MI WINDOWS AND DOORS INC.

650 W. Market St.
Gratz PA 17030
Phone: 717-365-3300
Fax: 717-365-3844
Web: www.miwd.com

CEO: Peter Desoto
CFO: Sarah W Gutherie
HR: –
FYE: December 31
Type: Private

Mi oh my! MI Windows and Doors has your home's openings covered. The company a subsidiary of J.T. Walker Industries manufactures vinyl aluminum and composite windows and doors. The company's BridgeWood line features composite windows that have the appearance of wood. Other products include single- and double-hung windows sliding windows patio doors awnings and casements used in residential and light commercial applications. MI has plants across the US and distributes its products through such retailers as The Home Depot Stock Building Supply and Lowe's. J.T. Walker and Robert Word established the company making screens in the back of a Florida airplane hangar in 1947.

MIAMI JEWISH HEALTH SYSTEMS INC.

5200 NE 2ND AVE
MIAMI, FL 331372706
Phone: 305-751-8626
Fax: –
Web: www.miamijewishhealthsystems.org

CEO: Jeffrey P Freimark
CFO: –
HR: Natalia I Chaparro
FYE: June 30
Type: Private

With age comes experience and Miami Jewish Health Systems is plenty experienced when it comes to geriatric care. The not-for-profit 460-bed nursing home and 30-bed hospital provides services to southern Florida residents of all ages with a focus on the elderly. It also operates independent and assisted-living centers for seniors as well as an ambulatory health center for general health care services. Its facilities provide a variety of services such as care for Alzheimer's patients assisted and independent living rehabilitation hospice and home health care.

	Annual Growth	06/09	06/10	06/11	06/12	06/13
Sales ($ mil.)	1.4%	–	80.0	98.6	79.8	83.5
Net income ($ mil.)	(7.6%)	–	–	10.6	0.4	9.0
Market value ($ mil.)	–	–	–	–	–	–
Employees	–	–	–	–	–	1,100

MIAMI MARLINS L.P.

2267 Dan Marino Blvd.
Miami FL 33056
Phone: 305-626-7400
Fax: 305-626-7302
Web: miami.marlins.mlb.com

CEO: –
CFO: Michel Bussiere
HR: –
FYE: October 31
Type: Private

These fish can really hustle around a diamond. The Miami Marlines (previously known as the Florida Marlins) professional baseball franchise joined Major League Baseball as an expansion team in 1993 and boasts two World Series titles. Under the deep-pocketed ownership of former Miami Dolphins owner Wayne Huizenga the Marlins quickly rose to success and won its first championship title in 1997. A second Fall Classic victory followed in 2003 two years after the franchise was sold to Jeff Loria who formerly owned the Montreal Expos (now the Washington Nationals). The team plays host at Miami's Marlins Park which opened in 2012.

MIAMI UNIVERSITY

501 E HIGH ST
OXFORD, OH 450561846
Phone: 513-529-1809
Fax: –

CEO: –
CFO: –
HR: –
FYE: June 30
Type: Private

Not that Miami the other one. Named for the Miami Indian Tribe that inhabited the area now known as the Miami Valley Region of Ohio Miami University emphasizes undergraduate study at its main campus in Oxford (35 miles north of Cincinnati) as well as at commuter campuses in Hamilton Middletown and West Chester Ohio and a European Center in Luxembourg. The school offers bachelors masters and doctoral programs in areas including business administration arts and sciences engineering and education. Its student body includes more than 15000 undergraduates on the Oxford campus; 2500 graduate students; and another 5700 students attending satellite campuses. Miami University was established in 1809.

	Annual Growth	06/09	06/10	06/11	06/12	06/13
Sales ($ mil.)	3.1%	–	404.6	418.7	440.5	443.1
Net income ($ mil.)	(12.0%)	–	–	120.8	32.9	93.5
Market value ($ mil.)	–	–	–	–	–	–
Employees	–	–	–	–	–	4,925

MIAMI VALLEY HOSPITAL

1 WYOMING ST	CEO: Bobbie Gerhart
DAYTON, OH 454092711	CFO: Lisa Bishop
Phone: 937-208-8000	HR: –
Fax: –	FYE: December 31
Web: www.miamivalleyhospital.org	Type: Private

Don't go to Florida looking for this hospital! Miami Valley Hospital (MVH) is an acute care facility serving the residents of Dayton Ohio and surrounding areas through two campuses. MVH and MVH South have roughly 950 beds and offer 50 primary and specialty care practices through its Regional Adult Burn Center the MVH Cancer Center MVH Sports Medicine Center and behavioral health units for outpatient and inpatient chemical dependency therapy and other psychiatric services. MVH also offers Level I trauma services Level III-B NICU adult burn center an air ambulance program and blood marrow and kidney transplant services. The hospital is part of the Premier Health Partners network.

	Annual Growth	12/03	12/04	12/05	12/07	12/12
Sales ($ mil.)	6.4%	–	–	502.1	622.1	773.5
Net income ($ mil.)	–	–	–	(0.1)	44.3	77.7
Market value ($ mil.)	–	–	–	–	–	–
Employees	–	–	–	–	–	6,000

MICHAEL FOODS GROUP INC.

301 Carlson Pkwy. Ste. 400	CEO: James E Dwyer Jr
Minnetonka MN 55305	CFO: –
Phone: 952-258-4000	HR: –
Fax: 973-790-3307	FYE: December 31
Web: www3.gehealthcare.com/en/products/categories/c	Type: Private

It's not meat and potatoes but poultry and potatoes and other foods at Michael Foods Group. The group operates through Michael Foods Inc. one of the top US producers and distributors of value-added egg products (frozen liquid precooked and dried). Its Egg Products division comprised of four subsidiaries supplies egg products to foodservice retail grocery and food ingredient customers. The group's business includes Crystal Farms a distributor of cheese butter and other dairy case items to US groceries and Northern Star a supplier of refrigerated potato products to North American foodservice operators and grocery stores. GS Capital Partners and THL own 74% and 21% respectively of Michael Foods.

MICHAELS STORES INC.

8000 Bent Branch Dr.	CEO: Carl S Rubin
Irving TX 75063	CFO: Charles M Sonsteby
Phone: 972-409-1300	HR: –
Fax: 972-409-1556	FYE: January 31
Web: www.michaels.com	Type: Private

Michaels Stores is crafty. The nation's #1 arts and crafts retailer owns and operates about 1075 Michaels Stores across the US and Canada. Michaels sells some 35000 products including art and hobby supplies decor frames needlecraft kits party and seasonal products and silk and dried flowers. It also offers 10 private brands including Artist's Loft Art Minds and Craft Smart. It provides framing and art supplies though some 130 Aaron Brothers stores in California Texas and half a dozen other states. The company's Artistree subsidiary manufactures frames and molding for Michaels and Aaron Brothers stores. Michaels Stores owned by Bain Capital Partners and The Blackstone Group has filed to go public.

MICHELIN NORTH AMERICA INC.

1 Parkway South	CEO: –
Greenville SC 29615	CFO: Thomas Praktish
Phone: 864-458-5000	HR: –
Fax: 864-458-6359	FYE: December 31
Web: www.michelin-us.com	Type: Subsidiary

Planes trains and automobiles rely on Michelin North America's tires to make their rounds. So do airplanes; bicycles; motorcycles; heavy trucks; and agriculture off-road and specialty vehicles (like NASA's lunar rover). With some 18 manufacturing facilities in the US Canada and Mexico Michelin North America makes and sells tires stamped with the Michelin BF Goodrich and Uniroyal brands. Michelin North America (MNA) generates about one-third of parent Compagnie Generale des Etablissements Michelin's annual sales. Its tires are sold to consumers the military OEMs and replacement centers. The company also produces North American road maps and travel guides.

MICHELS CORPORATION

817 W. Main St.	CEO: Patrick D Michels
Brownsville WI 53006-0128	CFO: John Schroeder
Phone: 920-583-3132	HR: –
Fax: 920-583-3429	FYE: January 31
Web: www.michels.us	Type: Private

Michels Corporation is a utility engineering design and construction contractor. The family-owned company links systems for energy transportation distribution and communications customers in North America. It specializes in installing fiber optic networks for telephone broadband and cable providers. Through more than a dozen divisions Michels offers a variety of services including horizontal and directional drilling underground pipe repair tunneling engineering paving and materials production. The company also provides wind farm construction through a wind energy division.

MICHIGAN MILK PRODUCERS ASSOCIATION

41310 BRIDGE ST	CEO: John Dilland
NOVI, MI 483751302	CFO: –
Phone: 248-474-6672	HR: –
Fax: –	FYE: September 30
Web: www.mimilk.com	Type: Private

Ice cream and other dairy products might be missing a major ingredient without Michigan Milk Producers Association (MMPA). The dairy cooperative which serves more than 2100 farmers in Michigan Ohio Indiana and Wisconsin produces some 3.9 billion pounds of milk each year. Milk products include sweetened condensed milk instant nonfat milk and dried buttermilk as well as other items the likes of cream cheese butter and ice-cream mixes. With no consumer brands or products MMPA sells its products as ingredients to food makers who sell baby formulas candy ice cream and yogurt. Founded in 1916 the co-op operates a pair of Michigan plants and a merchandise facility.

	Annual Growth	09/08	09/09	09/10	09/11	09/12
Sales ($ mil.)	15.3%	–	556.7	698.8	870.9	854.1
Net income ($ mil.)	(9.3%)	–	–	6.8	6.4	5.6
Market value ($ mil.)	–	–	–	–	–	–
Employees	–	–	–	–	–	200

MICHIGAN TECHNOLOGICAL UNIVERSITY

1400 TOWNSEND DR
HOUGHTON, MI 499311200
Phone: 906-487-1885
Fax: –
Web: www.mtu.edu

CEO: –
CFO: –
HR: –
FYE: June 30
Type: Private

Michigan Technological University trains techies in the Wolverine State. A premier research university the school affectionately known as Michigan Tech offers a range of programs in computing engineering technology business and technology forest resources and environmental science social work sciences and arts and non-departmental sponsored educational programs. Based in Houghton the school has an enrollment of about 7000 undergraduate and graduate students and a faculty of almost 480 instructors. The company is considered to be a discrete component unit of the State of Michigan because its Board of Control is appointed by the Governor.

	Annual Growth	06/05	06/06	06/07	06/11	06/13
Sales ($ mil.)	5.9%	–	104.3	120.2	147.5	155.4
Net income ($ mil.)	(14.6%)	–	–	7.8	(0.9)	3.0
Market value ($ mil.)	–	–	–	–	–	–
Employees	–	–	–	–	–	1,939

MICREL, INC.

NMS: MCRL

2180 Fortune Drive
San Jose, CA 95131
Phone: 408 944-0800
Fax: 408 944-0970
Web: www.micrel.com

CEO: –
CFO: –
HR: –
FYE: December 31
Type: Public

Micrel's semiconductors make their way into all sorts of electronic gear. The company makes around 3000 kinds of standard integrated circuits (ICs); its lineup includes high-performance analog power radio-frequency (RF) and mixed-signal ICs used in computers networking equipment industrial electronics and wireless phones and other telecom gear. The company also designs and manufactures custom ICs and provides contract wafer manufacturing (foundry) services for commercial and military customers that use Micrel-produced ICs in communications systems and transport aircraft. Customers in Asia account for more than 60% of sales.

	Annual Growth	12/09	12/10	12/11	12/12	12/13
Sales ($ mil.)	2.0%	218.9	297.4	259.0	250.1	237.1
Net income ($ mil.)	2.0%	16.3	50.7	34.0	12.3	17.6
Market value ($ mil.)	4.7%	462.8	733.2	570.6	536.2	557.1
Employees	(0.9%)	755	837	781	796	728

MICRO IMAGING TECHNOLOGY INC.

OTC: MMTC

970 Calle Amanecer Ste. F
San Clemente CA 92673
Phone: 949-485-6000
Fax: 949-485-6005
Web: micro-imaging.com/

CEO: Jeffrey G Nunez
CFO: Victor A Hollander
HR: –
FYE: October 31
Type: Public

Micro Imaging Technology (formerly Electropure) is developing laser-based technology that detects microbes and microorganisms in water. Micro Imaging Technology hopes to commercialize its products for applications such as food inspection and water testing but the company hasn't had enough money to do so. In 2005 the company sold the assets of its Electropure EDI subsidiary a maker of ion-permeable membranes and deionization devices; Electropure then changed its name to Micro Imaging Technology effective 2006. In 2007 the company sold and installed two bacteria identification systems in Tokyo. Former US Postmaster General Anthony Frank owns a 45% stake in Micro Imaging Technology.

MICROCHIP TECHNOLOGY, INC.

NMS: MCHP

2355 West Chandler Boulevard
Chandler, AZ 85224-6199
Phone: 480 792-7200
Fax: 480 792-7790
Web: www.microchip.com

CEO: Steve Sanghi
CFO: J. Eric Bjornholt
HR: –
FYE: March 31
Type: Public

While bigger chip makers fight over your PC and mobile phone Microchip Technology has embedded itself in your car your copier and even your wallet. The semiconductor maker offers a variety of embedded devices including eight-bit microcontrollers (it's one of the top makers of them worldwide); specialty memory products such as electrically erasable programmable read-only memories (EEPROMs); and KEELOQ brand code-hopping devices used in keyless locks garage door openers and smart cards. Its chips are used by tens of thousands of customers in the automotive consumer industrial office automation and telecommunications markets. Microchip gets about 80% of sales from customers outside the US.

	Annual Growth	03/11	03/12	03/13	03/14	03/15
Sales ($ mil.)	9.6%	1,487.2	1,383.2	1,581.6	1,931.2	2,147.0
Net income ($ mil.)	(3.1%)	419.0	336.7	127.4	395.3	369.0
Market value ($ mil.)	6.5%	7,681.1	7,517.4	7,430.5	9,651.4	9,881.7
Employees	(55.2%)	6,970	6,923	8,003	8,604	280

MICROFINANCIAL, INC.

NMS: MFI

16 New England Executive Park, Suite 200
Burlington, MA 01803
Phone: 781 994-4800
Fax: –
Web: www.microfinancial.com

CEO: –
CFO: James R Jackson Jr
HR: –
FYE: December 31
Type: Public

MicroFinancial thinks big when it comes to leasing small-ticket commercial items to small and midsized businesses. Through subsidiary TimePayment MicroFinancial leases items that are generally valued between $500 and $15000. Although the "microticket" leaser provides financing for a variety of office and commercial equipment the majority of the contracts in its portfolio are for point-of-sale authorization systems for debit and credit cards. It doesn't lease and rent equipment directly but through a network of independent dealers across the US. Internet-based TimePaymentDirect processes applications and approves credit; Insta-Lease provides the same services via telephone fax and e-mail.

	Annual Growth	12/08	12/09	12/10	12/11	12/12
Sales ($ mil.)	10.7%	39.5	46.2	50.9	54.7	59.3
Net income ($ mil.)	12.0%	6.0	4.1	5.3	9.0	9.4
Market value ($ mil.)	37.8%	29.2	44.9	58.3	84.2	105.3
Employees	10.2%	103	111	118	135	152

MICROFLUIDICS INTERNATIONAL CORPORATION

30 Ossipee Rd.
Newton MA 02464-9101
Phone: 617-969-5452
Fax: 617-965-1213
Web: microfluidicscorp.com

CEO: Michael C Ferrara
CFO: –
HR: –
FYE: December 31
Type: Subsidiary

Microfluidics International's devotion to fluid-handling equipment is hardly micro in size. The company makes processing equipment namely high shear fluid systems used to produce commercial amounts of processed foods cosmetics inks vaccines and drugs and photographic films. The Microfluidizer lineup is used to formulate products typically resistant to mixing and stabilizing such as emulsions dispersions and liposomes for biotech applications as well as many manufactured consumer and industrial products. It subsidizes R&D of its Microfluidizer processor technology at MIT Purdue University the University of Toronto and other research centers. In spring 2011 IDEX acquired Microfluidics.

MICRON TECHNOLOGY INC.

NMS: MU

8000 S. Federal Way
Boise, ID 83716-9632
Phone: 208 368-4000
Fax: –
Web: www.micron.com

CEO: D. Mark Durcan
CFO: Ernie Maddock
HR: –
FYE: September 03
Type: Public

Micron Technology is one of the largest memory chip makers in the world. It makes DRAM (Dynamic Random Access Memory) NAND Flash and NOR Flash memory and other memory technologies. The company sells to customers in networking and storage consumer electronics solid-state drives and mobile telecommunications but its largest concentration (nearly a third of sales) is the computer market. Micron's products are offered under the Micron Lexar Crucial SpecTek and Elpida brands as well as private labels. The company generates about 84% of sales outside the US.

	Annual Growth	09/11*	08/12	08/13	08/14*	09/15
Sales ($ mil.)	16.5%	8,788.0	8,234.0	9,073.0	16,358.0	16,192.0
Net income ($ mil.)	104.1%	167.0	(1,032.0)	1,190.0	3,045.0	2,899.0
Market value ($ mil.)	30.4%	6,222.2	6,699.1	14,709.9	35,566.0	17,983.6
Employees	5.1%	26,100	27,400	30,900	30,400	31,800

*Fiscal year change

MICRONETICS INC.

NASDAQ: NOIZ

26 Hampshire Dr.
Hudson NH 03051
Phone: 603-883-2900
Fax: 603-882-8987
Web: www.mwireless.com

CEO: –
CFO: –
HR: –
FYE: March 31
Type: Public

Micronetics fights noise with noise. The company designs radio-frequency (RF) components and test equipment that help keep signals clear in cellular wireless cable satellite and radar systems worldwide. Products include RF controls for military radar and communications systems noise source components that test reception and transmission quality and other noise generators and frequency emulators. Micronetics sells primarily to military contractors like Northrop Grumman and Raytheon. ITT's Electronic Warfare Systems unit (22% of sales) is the company's top customer. Micronetics gets most of its sales in North America.

MICROPAC INDUSTRIES, INC.

NBB: MPAD

905 E. Walnut
Garland, TX 75040
Phone: 972 272-3571
Fax: –

CEO: Mark King
CFO: Patrick S Cefalu
HR: –
FYE: November 30
Type: Public

Micropac Industries makes hybrid microelectronic circuits and optoelectronic components/assemblies as well as solid-state relays power controllers and amplifiers Hall-effect sensors light-emitting diodes (LEDs) and displays and high-temperature products. The company also offers contract manufacturing and packaging services with plants in Mexico and the US. Micropac's customers include industrial and medical markets as well as contractors for the US Department of Defense and NASA which account for more 70% of sales. Director Heinz-Werner Hempel owns more than three-quarters of the company. Micropac's products are marketed in the US and Europe.

	Annual Growth	11/10	11/11	11/12	11/13	11/14
Sales ($ mil.)	(4.6%)	23.1	20.2	17.7	19.7	19.1
Net income ($ mil.)	(21.5%)	2.7	1.6	0.5	1.4	1.0
Market value ($ mil.)	7.2%	15.9	12.9	14.9	18.0	21.0
Employees	(3.4%)	133	125	120	119	116

MICROS SYSTEMS, INC.

NMS: MCRS

7031 Columbia Gateway Drive
Columbia, MD 21046-2289
Phone: 443 285-6000
Fax: 443 285-0466
Web: www.micros.com

CEO: Peter A Altabef
CFO: Cynthia A Russo
HR: Carlos Echalar
FYE: June 30
Type: Public

MICROS' systems don't fold sheets bus tables or stock shelves but they do keep hotels restaurants and retail stores in order. MICROS Systems supplies point-of-sale terminals central reservation systems inventory and loss prevention systems and other hardware and software for the hospitality and retail industries. Customers include Hyatt Hotels InterContinental Hotels and Marriott International as well as IHOP Starbucks Wendy's Belk and The Jones Group. Additionally MICROS products are used in related settings such as casinos cruise ships sports arenas airport concourses and theme parks. The company generates more than half of its sales outside the US and Canada.

	Annual Growth	06/09	06/10	06/11	06/12	06/13
Sales ($ mil.)	8.6%	911.8	914.3	1,007.9	1,107.5	1,268.1
Net income ($ mil.)	14.6%	99.3	114.4	144.1	167.0	171.4
Market value ($ mil.)	14.3%	1,942.9	2,445.4	3,814.3	3,928.7	3,311.0
Employees	8.1%	4,757	4,646	4,953	6,383	6,506

MICROSEMI CORP

NMS: MSCC

One Enterprise
Aliso Viejo, CA 92656
Phone: 949 380-6100
Fax: –
Web: www.microsemi.com

CEO: James J Peterson
CFO: John W. Hohener
HR: –
FYE: September 27
Type: Public

Microsemi is on a power trip. The company makes power management semiconductors that regulate and condition electricity to make it more usable by electrical and electronic systems. Its products include discrete components such as diodes and rectifiers along with integrated circuits such as amplifiers and voltage regulators. Microsemi also makes devices for pacemakers GPS products LCD TVs and wireless networks. The company's high-reliability semiconductors go into jet engines missile systems oilfield equipment and satellites. Top customers have included big names like Boeing Dell Honeywell Medtronic Boston Scientific and Lockheed Martin. More than 40% of sales come from outside the US.

	Annual Growth	10/11*	09/12	09/13	09/14	09/15
Sales ($ mil.)	10.5%	835.9	1,012.5	975.9	1,138.3	1,245.6
Net income ($ mil.)	11.6%	54.4	(29.7)	43.7	23.1	84.6
Market value ($ mil.)	19.2%	1,519.7	1,908.7	2,274.8	2,385.1	3,066.0
Employees	8.2%	2,700	2,200	3,100	3,400	3,700

*Fiscal year change

MICROSOFT CORPORATION

NMS: MSFT

One Microsoft Way
Redmond, WA 98052-6399
Phone: 425 882-8080
Fax: –
Web: www.microsoft.com

CEO: Satya Nadella
CFO: Amy E. Hood
HR: Kathleen T. Hogan
FYE: June 30
Type: Public

Microsoft's ambitions to put a computer on every desk have evolved to put a computing device just about anywhere and connect it to the cloud rather than anchor it to a desk. Besides the Windows operating system and Office suite of productivity programs Microsoft makes tablets (Surface) game consoles (Xbox) and smartphones (Lumia). It even introduced its first laptop computer in 2015. Still software — for consumers and businesses — is Microsoft's biggest source of revenue. Much of Microsoft's software is sold through PC makers such as Acer Lenovo Dell Hewlett-Packard and Toshiba who pre-install the software on devices. Microsoft also sells directly online and through resellers. Other products include enterprise applications (Microsoft Dynamics) and server and storage software.

	Annual Growth	06/11	06/12	06/13	06/14	06/15
Sales ($ mil.)	7.5%	69,943.0	73,723.0	77,849.0	86,833.0	93,580.0
Net income ($ mil.)	(14.8%)	23,150.0	16,978.0	21,863.0	22,074.0	12,193.0
Market value ($ mil.)		0.0	0.0	0.0	0.0	0.0
Employees	7.0%	90,000	94,000	99,000	128,000	118,000

MICROSTRATEGY INC.

NMS: MSTR

1850 Towers Crescent Plaza
Tysons Corner, VA 22182
Phone: 703 848-8600
Fax: 703 848-8610
Web: www.microstrategy.com

CEO: Michael J. Saylor
CFO: Phong Le
HR: –
FYE: December 31
Type: Public

MicroStrategy knows you need the details to make a good plan. The company's cloud-based business intelligence software addresses functions such as building reports and dashboards managing mobile applications and capitalizing on social media. Specific analytics modules include human resources management Web traffic analysis and sales and distribution. It sells to many of the world's largest companies such as Aetna and eBay as well as midsized companies and government agencies such as NASA and the US Army. MicroStrategy also offers consulting and support services. Founded in 1989 MicroStrategy has operations in about 25 countries.

	Annual Growth	12/10	12/11	12/12	12/13	12/14
Sales ($ mil.)	6.3%	454.6	562.2	594.6	575.9	579.8
Net income ($ mil.)	(41.8%)	43.8	17.9	20.5	83.3	5.0
Market value ($ mil.)	17.4%	966.7	1,225.1	1,056.1	1,405.2	1,836.7
Employees	(1.2%)	2,597	3,088	3,221	3,158	2,470

MICROTECHNOLOGIES LLC

8330 BOONE BLVD STE 600
VIENNA, VA 221822658
Phone: 703-891-1073
Fax: –
Web: www.microtechnologiesllc.net

CEO: Anthony R Jimenez
CFO: Lynn Wasylina
HR: –
FYE: December 31
Type: Private

MicroTechnologies is a US small business dishing up tech services to some big clients. Also known as MicroTech the Hispanic- and veteran-owned company delivers IT reseller products technical support systems integration and management consulting services to clients ranging from Fortune 500 companies to the federal government. It has added virtualization and cloud computing to its service portfolio. It also serves state city and local agencies. For the US General Services Administration it has provided and set up personal computers Web access data voice and video communications and teleconferencing systems for President Obama's staff.

	Annual Growth	12/06	12/07	12/08	12/10	12/13
Sales ($ mil.)	(40.4%)	–	2,124.0	39.0	93.5	95.2
Net income ($ mil.)	(21.1%)	–	–	2.5	7.4	0.8
Market value ($ mil.)	–	–	–	–	–	–
Employees	–	–	–	–	–	425

MICROVISION INC.

NMS: MVIS

6244 185th Avenue NE, Suite 100
Redmond, WA 98052
Phone: 425 936 6847
Fax: –
Web: www.microvision.com

CEO: Alexander Tokman
CFO: Stephen Holt
HR: –
FYE: December 31
Type: Public

Microvision thinks tiny images have big potential. The company's PicoP display technology can be used to create high-quality video and image displays using an ultra-miniature projector that is embedded into mobile devices such as cell phones DVD players gaming devices and laptops. The projector enables users to display images and data onto a variety of surfaces from mobile products. Microvision's first product — the SHOWWX accessory projector — connects via cable to a video-out connection on a mobile device. It is sold directly and through distributors in Asia and Europe. The company also produces prototypes based on its light scanning technology under government and commercial development contracts.

	Annual Growth	12/10	12/11	12/12	12/13	12/14
Sales ($ mil.)	(7.4%)	4.7	5.6	8.4	5.9	3.5
Net income ($ mil.)	–	(47.5)	(35.8)	(22.7)	(13.2)	(18.1)
Market value ($ mil.)	(1.6%)	83.2	16.1	85.5	59.1	77.9
Employees	(11.6%)	108	103	67	64	66

MICROWAVE FILTER CO., INC.

NBB: MFCO

6743 Kinne Street
East Syracuse, NY 13057
Phone: 315 438-4700
Fax: 315 463-1467
Web: www.microwavefilter.com

CEO: Paul W Mears
CFO: Richard L Jones
HR: –
FYE: September 30
Type: Public

Microwave Filter Company (MFC) can improve your powers of reception. The company's electronic filters process TV radio and other signals and prevent unwanted signals from interfering with transmissions. Its Fastrap filters are used by cable TV operators either to allow or to prevent viewing of pay-per-view broadcasts and premium programming. MFC sells more than 1700 products to the broadcasting cable television defense and mobile radio industries. Subsidiary Niagara Scientific makes material handling equipment for the cosmetics food processing and pharmaceutical industries. Sales are primarily in the US.

	Annual Growth	09/11	09/12	09/13	09/14	09/15
Sales ($ mil.)	(8.5%)	5.0	4.5	2.9	3.6	3.5
Net income ($ mil.)	–	0.2	0.1	(0.6)	0.0	(0.2)
Market value ($ mil.)	(16.8%)	2.3	2.3	1.2	1.2	1.1
Employees	(0.6%)	45	47	42	42	44

MICRUS ENDOVASCULAR CORPORATION

821 Fox Ln.
San Jose CA 95131
Phone: 408-433-1400
Fax: 408-433-1401
Web: www.micruscorp.com

CEO: John T Kilcoyne
CFO: Gordon T Sangster
HR: –
FYE: March 31
Type: Subsidiary

Micrus makes microcoils to help prevent strokes. The company develops implantable and disposable medical devices specifically its microcoils and accessory products such as microcatheters and guidewires used to treat cerebral aneurysms and other cerebral vascular diseases. Physicians can use the microcoils to build scaffolds within an aneurysm to stabilize the blood flow to the brain. The catheterization procedure is less invasive and less expensive than other forms of surgery and aims to give patients a shorter recovery time. Micrus sells its products directly in North America and Europe and through distributors in other countries. The company was acquired by Johnson & Johnson in 2010.

MID AMERICA CLINICAL LABORATORIES LLC

2560 N SHADELAND AVE B
INDIANAPOLIS, IN 462191705
Phone: 317-803-0056
Fax: –
Web: www.choosemacl.com

CEO: Dianne Vanness
CFO: –
HR: Jane A Lloyd
FYE: December 31
Type: Private

Let's hope the Hoosiers at Mid America Clinical Laboratories don't suffer from test anxiety. The company operates more than 30 specimen collection and laboratory sites in Indianapolis and the surrounding central Indiana region. The company processes more than 4.5 million tests every year and its labs are equipped to perform a variety of medical testing including biopsies PAP tests urinalyses and blood tests. Mid America Clinical Laboratories is a joint venture company owned by Ascension Health's St. Vincent Hospital Community Hospital and Quest Diagnostics.

	Annual Growth	12/05	12/06	12/07	12/08	12/09
Sales ($ mil.)	5.8%	–	63.8	67.3	70.9	75.5
Net income ($ mil.)	0.1%	–	–	9.2	8.9	9.2
Market value ($ mil.)	–	–	–	–	–	–
Employees	–	–	–	–	–	525

MID PENN BANCORP, INC.

NMS: MPB

349 Union Street
Millersburg, PA 17061
Phone: 866 642-7736
Fax: –
Web: www.midpennbank.com

CEO: Rory G Ritrievi
CFO: Edward P Williams
HR: Roberta Hoffman
FYE: December 31
Type: Public

Mid Penn Bancorp is the holding company for Mid Penn Bank which operates more than a dozen branches in central Pennsylvania's Cumberland Dauphin Northumberland and Schuylkill counties. The bank offers full-service commercial banking insurance and trust services. Its deposit products include checking savings money market and NOW accounts. Commercial real estate construction and land development loans account for nearly 80% of the company's loan portfolio; the bank also writes residential mortgages and business agricultural and consumer loans. Mid Penn is a descendant of Millersburg Bank founded in 1868. Trust company CEDE & Co. owns about a third of Mid Penn Bancorp.

	Annual Growth	12/10	12/11	12/12	12/13	12/14
Assets ($ mil.)	4.3%	637.5	715.4	705.2	713.1	755.7
Net income ($ mil.)	20.0%	2.7	4.5	5.0	4.9	5.7
Market value ($ mil.)	20.0%	26.2	26.4	39.1	50.2	54.4
Employees	2.5%	184	201	1,904	198	203

MID-AMERICA APARTMENT COMMUNITIES INC

NYS: MAA

6584 Poplar Avenue
Memphis, TN 38138
Phone: 901 682-6600
Fax: 901 682-6667
Web: www.maac.com

CEO: H. Eric Bolton
CFO: Albert M. (Al) Campbell
HR: Cynthia Thompson
FYE: December 31
Type: Public

For Mid-America Apartment Communities the Sunbelt is where it's at. Operating as MAA the firm is a self-administered self-managed real estate investment trust (REIT) that focuses solely on buying multifamily residences. MAA owns or has interests in approximately 79500 apartment units in 15 states primarily located in the West Southeast and south-central US. Its largest markets are California Florida Tennessee and Texas. MAA which has an average property occupancy rate of 95% targets large and midsized markets. MAA bought rival Colonial Properties in 2013 in an $8.6 billion deal.

	Annual Growth	12/10	12/11	12/12	12/13	12/14
Sales ($ mil.)	25.2%	402.2	449.0	497.2	634.7	989.3
Net income ($ mil.)	51.4%	29.8	48.8	105.2	119.3	156.3
Market value ($ mil.)	4.1%	4,778.7	4,708.0	4,873.6	4,571.8	5,621.0
Employees	10.8%	1,389	1,466	1,446	2,241	2,090

MID-CON ENERGY PARTNERS LP

NMS: MCEP

2501 North Harwood Street, Suite 2410
Dallas, TX 75201
Phone: 972 479-5980
Fax: –
Web: www.midconenergypartners.com

CEO: Jeffery R Olmstead
CFO: Michael D Peterson
HR: –
FYE: December 31
Type: Public

Mid-Con Energy Partners is a Delaware limited partnership that owns operates and develops producing oil and natural gas properties in North America. With a focus on the Mid-Continent region of the US in particular Oklahoma and Colorado the company's operations primarily consist of enhancing the development of mature producing oil properties through an oil recovery method called waterflooding. It has total estimated proved reserves of about 8 million barrels of oil equivalent a majority of which is oil. Managed by Mid-Con Energy GP Mid-Con Energy Partners was formed in July 2011 and went public in December 2011.

	Annual Growth	12/10	12/11	12/12	12/13	12/14
Sales ($ mil.)	64.0%	17.5	39.3	67.3	80.1	126.3
Net income ($ mil.)	113.7%	1.1	19.0	29.9	28.2	22.5
Market value ($ mil.)	(29.9%)	–	535.2	545.4	666.4	184.0
Employees	–	–	–	–	–	–

MIDAMERICAN ENERGY HOLDINGS COMPANY

666 Grand Ave. Ste. 500
Des Moines IA 50309-2580
Phone: 515-242-4300
Fax: 515-281-2389
Web: www.midamerican.com

CEO: Gregory E Abel
CFO: Patrick J Goodman
HR: –
FYE: December 31
Type: Subsidiary

MidAmerican Energy Holdings reaches farther than its name implies. The company generates transmits and distributes electricity and natural gas to 7 million customers across the US and the UK primarily through subsidiaries MidAmerican Energy Company and PacifiCorp. UK regional distribution subsidiary Northern Powergrid serves about 3.8 million electricity customers. MidAmerican Energy Holdings also has independent power production operations as well as real estate (HomeServices of America) and gas exploration production and pipeline operations (Kern River Gas Transmission and Northern Natural Gas). It operates 38600 miles of natural gas pipeline.

MIDAS INC.

NYSE: MDS

1300 Arlington Heights Rd.
Itasca IL 60143
Phone: 630-438-3000
Fax: 630-438-3880
Web: www.midas.com

CEO: Alan D Feldman
CFO: William M Guzik
HR: –
FYE: December 31
Type: Subsidiary

Midas hopes to apply a golden touch to the car repair business. In addition to focusing on brake and exhaust system services the company's facilities offer routine maintenance (oil changes fluid replacements) and work on suspensions shocks and struts. The Midas network includes about 1480 franchised and company-owned stores throughout the US and Canada as well as some 775 locations in more than a dozen other countries. (Midas' North American stores account for about 98% of total sales.) In addition to these the company has 160-plus quick-lube and maintenance shops operating under the SpeeDee Oil Change banner in the US and Mexico. Automotive company TBC Corporation owns Midas.

MIDASPLUS INC.

4801 E. Broadway Blvd. Ste. 335
Tucson AZ 85711
Phone: 520-296-7398
Fax: 520-886-4763
Web: www.midasplus.com

CEO: –
CFO: –
HR: –
FYE: June 30
Type: Subsidiary

This Midas turns medical records into gold. MidasPlus is a provider of healthcare management software (known as MIDAS+) that is used to provide HMOs hospitals and health systems with the ability to manage areas such as billing claims documents Medicaid services and patient care. The software can keep track of influenza immunization data or help an emergency room staff act quickly when a patient goes into decline. MidasPlus also provides related services such as consulting support and training. The company is a subsidiary of Xerox.

MIDCOAST ENERGY PARTNERS LP

NYS: MEP

1100 Louisiana Street, Suite 3300	CEO: Mark A Maki
Houston, TX 77002	CFO: –
Phone: 713 821-2000	HR: –
Fax: –	FYE: December 31
Web: www.midcoastpartners.com	Type: Public

Midcoast Energy Partners was formed by Enbridge Energy Partners in 2013 as an investment vehicle to own and grow its natural gas and NGL midstream business. It has minority stakes in Enbridge's network of natural gas and natural gas liquids (NGLs) gathering and transportation systems natural gas processing and treating facilities and NGL fractionation plants in Texas and Oklahoma. Organized as a limited partnership Midcoast Energy Partners is exempt from paying income tax as long as it distributes quarterly dividends to shareholders. It went public in 2013 raising $333 million. All proceeds went to Enbridge Energy Partners.

	Annual Growth	12/10	12/11	12/12	12/13	12/14
Sales ($ mil.)	(3.0%)	6,654.3	7,828.2	5,357.9	5,593.6	5,894.3
Net income ($ mil.)	(2.1%)	157.4	219.2	167.5	53.9	144.3
Market value ($ mil.)	(30.2%)	–	–	–	904.4	631.2
Employees	–	–	–	–	–	–

MIDCONTINENT COMMUNICATIONS INVESTOR LLC

3901 N. Louise Ave.	CEO: –
Sioux Falls SD 57107	CFO: Steven E Grosser
Phone: 800-888-1300	HR: –
Fax: 212-245-1845	FYE: December 31
Web: www.plannedparenthood.org	Type: Subsidiary

Midcontinent Communications provides cable television local and long-distance digital telephone service and high-speed Internet access to more than 200 communities in North and South Dakota and Western Minnesota; subscribers total more than 200000. Internet services are sold under the MidcoNet Broadband brand while its enterprise voice cable data transport and advertising services are sold by its Midcontinent Business Solutions unit. Advertising services include local and national ad sales as well as TV advertisement production services. Midcontinent serves customers from 13 service centers. The company is co-owned by Minneapolis-based Midcontinent Media and cable giant Comcast.

MIDDLE RIVER AIRCRAFT SYSTEMS

103 Chesapeake Park Plaza	CEO: –
Baltimore MD 21220	CFO: William Heskett
Phone: 410 682 1500	HR: –
Fax: 410-682-1230	FYE: December 31
Web: www.mras-usa.com	Type: Subsidiary

Everyone knows that planes can reach great speeds — and that's great when a plane is flying but how in the world do pilots stop large planes on runways? Middle River Aircraft Systems (MRAS) knows that stopping a large aircraft takes more than simple brakes; it takes jet engine thrust reversers. The company which is a subsidiary of General Electric makes thrust reversers — which divert jet thrust backwards thus slowing the plane — for GE and Pratt & Whitney aircraft engines as well as specialized aerostructures such as nacelles and flight control surfaces. MRAS also provides aircraft overhaul and repair services.

MIDDLE TENNESSEE STATE UNIVERSITY

1301 E MAIN ST	CEO: –
MURFREESBORO, TN 371320002	CFO: –
Phone: 615-898-2300	HR: –
Fax: –	FYE: June 30
Web: www.catalog.mtsu.edu	Type: Private

Middle Tennessee State University (MTSU) founded in 1911 as a school for teacher training offers bachelor's and master's degrees through its eight university colleges. The educational institution boasts basic and applied sciences business education and behavioral science honors liberal arts mass communication and graduate studies. The school bestows master's degrees in eight areas including business and education. MTSU also confers a Specialist in Education degree and doctorate degrees. It has an enrollment of more than 25000 students. MTSU is part of the State University and Community College System of Tennessee.

	Annual Growth	06/04	06/05	06/06	06/12	06/13
Sales ($ mil.)	54.9%	–	5.7	5.7	218.3	190.3
Net income ($ mil.)	–	–	–	0.0	18.4	46.8
Market value ($ mil.)	–	–	–	–	–	–
Employees	–	–	–	–	–	2,610

MIDDLEBURG FINANCIAL CORP.

NAS: MBRG

111 West Washington Street	CEO: –
Middleburg, VA 20117	CFO: Rajesh Mehra
Phone: 703 777-6327	HR: Suzanne Withers
Fax: –	FYE: December 31
	Type: Public

Middleburg Financial Corp. (MFC) is the holding company for Middleburg Bank which serves individuals and small to midsized businesses through about a dozen branches in northern Virginia. The bank offers standard deposit products such as checking and savings accounts money market and NOW accounts CDs and IRAs. Middleburg Bank focuses heavily on real estate lending: real estate loans account for about 80% of its loan portfolio. Commercial loans account for about 18%. Consumer installment loans round out the company's loan book. MFC also operates Middleburg Investment Group which offers investment products to the bank's customers. The 90-year-old bank has total assets of more than $1.2 billion.

	Annual Growth	12/10	12/11	12/12	12/13	12/14
Assets ($ mil.)	2.6%	1,104.6	1,192.9	1,236.8	1,227.8	1,222.9
Net income ($ mil.)	–	(2.7)	5.0	6.5	6.2	7.6
Market value ($ mil.)	6.0%	101.7	101.6	125.9	128.7	128.4
Employees	(15.0%)	350	405	410	352	183

MIDDLEBY CORP

NMS: MIDD

1400 Toastmaster Drive	CEO: Selim A. Bassoul
Elgin, IL 60120	CFO: Timothy J. (Tim) Fitzgerald
Phone: 847 741-3300	HR: –
Fax: –	FYE: January 03
Web: www.middleby.com	Type: Public

Founded in 1888 Middleby makes a slew of commercial and institutional foodservice equipment for restaurants retailers and hotels worldwide. Middleby operates through three segments: Commercial Foodservice Equipment Food Processing Equipment and Residential Kitchen Equipment. The largest Foodservice makes machines for most types of cooking and warming activities. Products are sold under some two dozen blue chip brands — Anets Blodgett Southbend and TurboChef among them. Food Processing makes cooking mixing slicing and packaging machines and Residential Kitchen makes ovens refrigerators dishwashers microwaves and other related products.

	Annual Growth	01/11*	12/11	12/12	12/13*	01/15
Sales ($ mil.)	22.8%	719.1	855.9	1,038.2	1,428.7	1,636.5
Net income ($ mil.)	27.6%	72.9	95.5	120.7	153.9	193.3
Market value ($ mil.)	4.1%	4,834.9	5,385.8	7,185.9	13,888.4	5,672.2
Employees	23.9%	2,060	2,150	3,140	4,491	4,860

*Fiscal year change

MIDDLEFIELD BANC CORP.
NAS: MBCN

15985 East High Street
Middlefield, OH 44062-9263
Phone: 440 632-1666
Fax: –
Web: www.middlefieldbank.com

CEO: Thomas G Caldwell
CFO: Donald L Stacy
HR: –
FYE: December 31
Type: Public

Here's your cash stuck in the Middlefield Banc with you. The firm is the holding company for The Middlefield Banking Company (Middlefield Bank) and Emerald Bank (acquired in 2007) which have about 10 offices in northeastern and central Ohio. The community banks offer standard deposit services such as checking and savings accounts CDs and IRAs. Investments insurance and brokerage services are offered through an agreement with UVEST a division of LPL Financial. Residential mortgage loans comprise more than 60% of the company's loan portfolio; commercial and industrial loans make up about 20%. The banks also offer commercial mortgages construction loans and consumer installment loans.

	Annual Growth	12/10	12/11	12/12	12/13	12/14
Assets ($ mil.)	1.7%	632.2	654.6	670.3	647.1	677.5
Net income ($ mil.)	30.0%	2.5	4.1	6.3	7.0	7.2
Market value ($ mil.)	17.3%	36.5	35.4	51.8	53.4	69.0
Employees	6.5%	108	103	120	125	139

MIDDLESEX SAVINGS BANK

6 Main St.
Natick MA 01760
Phone: 508-653-0300
Fax: 508-653-8146
Web: www.middlesexbank.com

CEO: John R Heerwagen
CFO: Paul M Totino
HR: –
FYE: October 31
Type: Private - Mutual Com

About midway between Boston and Worcester in eastern Massachusetts is where you'll find the more than 30 branches of Middlesex Savings Bank. The mutually owned community-oriented financial institution provides such traditional products and services as checking and savings accounts IRAs and certificates of deposit. Its lending activities are focused on residential and commercial mortgages; the bank also has five offices devoted to business lending including Small Business Administration loans. Its Middlesex Financial Group subsidiary provides retail investment services through an agreement with UVEST Financial Services a division of LPL Financial.

MIDDLESEX WATER CO.
NMS: MSEX

1500 Ronson Road
Iselin, NJ 08830
Phone: 732 634-1500
Fax: –
Web: www.middlesexwater.com

CEO: Dennis W. Doll
CFO: A. Bruce O'Connor
HR: –
FYE: December 31
Type: Public

Like all gardens the Garden State needs water to thrive. Middlesex Water provides water and wastewater services to residential business and fire protection customers in New Jersey through its Middlesex Pinelands and Bayview systems. It also distributes water in Delaware through its Tidewater system. All told the utility's subsidiaries have more than 140000 customers and serve a retail population of 450000. The company also is engaged in municipal contract operations and public/private partnerships and provides line maintenance services. Middlesex Water's nonregulated Utility Service Affiliates (Perth Amboy) unit operates the municipal water and wastewater systems in Perth Amboy New Jersey.

	Annual Growth	12/10	12/11	12/12	12/13	12/14
Sales ($ mil.)	3.3%	102.7	102.1	110.4	114.8	117.1
Net income ($ mil.)	6.5%	14.3	13.4	14.4	16.6	18.4
Market value ($ mil.)	5.9%	295.9	300.9	315.4	337.6	371.8
Employees	(0.9%)	292	289	279	279	282

MIDLAND COGENERATION VENTURE LIMITED PARTNERSHIP

100 Progress Place
Midland MI 48640
Phone: 989-839-6000
Fax: 989-633-7935

CEO: Pete Milojevic
CFO: Laurie Valasek
HR: –
FYE: December 31
Type: Private

Midland Cogeneration Venture has the power to go all the way (and the reputation to get away with it). The company formerly Midland Nuclear Power Plant operates one of the largest cogeneration power plants in the US (at one time the largest gas-fired steam recovery power plant in the world). Midland Cogeneration Venture with a generating capacity of more than 1560 MW is responsible for about 10% of the electricity used in Michigan's lower peninsula. It also produces up to 1.35 million pounds per hour of process steam for industrial use. Swedish private equity firm EQT Infrastructure (70%) and US energy investment group Fortistar (30%) bought Midland Cogeneration Venture in 2009.

MIDLAND FINANCIAL CO.

501 NW Grand Blvd.
Oklahoma City OK 73118-6054
Phone: 405-840-7600
Fax: 405-767-5426
Web: www.midfirst.com

CEO: –
CFO: Todd A Dobson
HR: –
FYE: December 31
Type: Private

There's nothing middling about Midland Financial the holding company for MidFirst Bank and other financial services subsidiaries. One of the largest privately held banks in the US MidFirst Bank has more than 50 branches in Oklahoma and Arizona. Serving business and retail customers the bank offers standard services such as checking and savings accounts loans and mortgages CDs IRAs credit cards trust services and private banking. It maintains commercial real estate lending offices in Chicago Houston New York and Southern California. Affiliate Midland Mortgage acquires and services mortgages throughout the US.

MIDLAND PAPER COMPANY

101 E. Palatine Rd.
Wheeling IL 60090
Phone: 847-777-2700
Fax: 847-777-2552
Web: www.midlandpaper.com

CEO: –
CFO: Ralph Deletto
HR: –
FYE: December 31
Type: Private

Midland Paper Company is a middleman for the paper industry. The firm (also known as Midland Paper Packaging Supplies) distributes coated uncoated bond specialty and other types of paper produced by such manufacturers as Boise Neenah Paper Domtar and International Paper. It also sells packaging supplies and equipment as well as janitorial supplies (including mops brooms cleaners and floor-care products). Midland Paper distributes primarily to large companies that print books magazines and catalogs. Founded in 1907 as a paper supplier to Chicago's graphic arts industry the company operates warehouses and sales offices in California Connecticut Illinois Minnesota New York and Wisconsin.

MIDLAND STATES BANCORP INC.

133 W. Jefferson Ave.
Effingham IL 62401
Phone: 217-342-2141
Fax: +86-594-359-8158

CEO: –
CFO: Cindy Kremer
HR: –
FYE: December 31
Type: Private

Born in rural Illinois Midland States Bancorp is now discovering banking life in suburbia. Midland States Bancorp is the holding company for Midland States Bank a community bank that operates 22 branches in central and northern Illinois and seven branches in the St. Louis metropolitan area. The bank offers traditional deposit products like savings checking and money market accounts as well as commercial loans commercial real estate loans residential mortgages and other loan products. The bank also provides wealth management services at select locations. Formed in 1990 Midland States Bancorp filed and withdrew an IPO 2011.

MIDSOUTH BANCORP, INC.

NYS: MSL

102 Versailles Boulevard
Lafayette, LA 70501
Phone: 337 237-8343
Fax: –
Web: www.midsouthbank.com

CEO: C Rusty Cloutier
CFO: James McLemore
HR: –
FYE: December 31
Type: Public

For banking in the Deep South try MidSouth. MidSouth Bancorp is the holding company for MidSouth Bank which boasts roughly $2 billion in assets and around 60 branches across Louisiana and Texas. Targeting individuals and local business customers the bank offers such standard retail services as checking and savings accounts savings bonds investment accounts and credit card services. About 55% of its loan portfolio is made up of real estate mortgages while commercial loans make up more than 35%. Consumer and construction loans round out the rest of its lending activities.

	Annual Growth	12/10	12/11	12/12	12/13	12/14
Assets ($ mil.)	17.9%	1,002.3	1,396.8	1,851.7	1,851.2	1,936.7
Net income ($ mil.)	34.8%	5.8	4.5	9.6	14.2	19.1
Market value ($ mil.)	3.1%	174.2	147.5	185.4	202.5	196.6
Employees	9.0%	389	444	604	604	549

MIDSTATES PETROLEUM CO INC

NBB: MPOY

321 South Boston, Suite 1000
Tulsa, OK 74103
Phone: 918 947-8550
Fax: –
Web: www.midstatespetroleum.com

CEO: Frederic F Brace
CFO: Nelson M Haight
HR: –
FYE: December 31
Type: Public

Midstates Petroleum Company knows there's much more to Louisiana than Creoles crawfish and alligators. An independent oil and gas exploration and production company Midstates operates on some 64700 net acres in the central Louisiana portion of the Upper Gulf Coast Tertiary. The company's assets consist primarily of mature oilfields discovered in the 1940s and '50s that continue to show production potential when developed with modern techniques. The company routinely uses such techniques and technologies to produce oil including hydraulic fracturing and 3D seismic data. In 2013 Midstates reported estimated net proved reserves of 127.8 million barrels of oil equivalent.

	Annual Growth	12/10	12/11	12/12	12/13	12/14
Sales ($ mil.)	88.4%	63.1	–	247.7	469.5	794.2
Net income ($ mil.)	–	(15.6)	–	(156.6)	(344.0)	116.9
Market value ($ mil.)	(53.1%)	–	–	48.2	46.3	10.6
Employees	53.1%	–	51	93	217	183

MIDWEST ENERGY INC.

1330 CANTERBURY DR
HAYS, KS 676012708
Phone: 785-625-3437
Fax: –
Web: www.mwenergy.com

CEO: –
CFO: –
HR: –
FYE: December 31
Type: Private

Some rural residents of the Sunflower State rely on Midwest Energy for their power and gas needs. The multi-utility serves approximately 48000 electricity customers and 42000 natural gas customers in central and western Kansas. It also has some power generation operations; it purchases most of its electric supply from wholesale marketers. The company's Midwest United Energy subsidiary is a competitive natural gas supplier in four states and its WestLand Energy unit sells propane to Kansas consumers. Midwest Energy has seen its power sales grow by 23% since 2006 and its natural gas sales by 17%.

	Annual Growth	12/09	12/10	12/11	12/12	12/13
Sales ($ mil.)	4.7%	–	176.2	197.1	197.1	202.1
Net income ($ mil.)	(1.7%)	–	–	14.9	16.5	14.4
Market value ($ mil.)	–	–	–	–	–	–
Employees	–	–	–	–	–	274

MIDWEST GENERATION LLC

1 Financial Place 440 S. LaSalle St. Ste. 3500
Chicago IL 60605
Phone: 312-583-6000
Fax: 312-583-6111
Web: www.edison.com/ourcompany/emg.asp

CEO: –
CFO: Maria Rigatti
HR: –
FYE: December 31
Type: Subsidiary

As one might expect Midwest Generation sells wholesale electricity to markets in the Midwest. The independent power producer has a generating capacity of almost 5480 MW primarily from its six coal-fired power plants in Illinois (5172 MW); it also oversees the operation of the Fisk and Waukegan on-site generating plants which have 305 MW of capacity. Affiliate Edison Mission Marketing and Trading acts as a conduit for Midwest Generation's wholesale energy activities. Midwest Generation is a subsidiary of Edison International unit Edison Mission Midwest Holdings Co. In 2010 regional transmission organization PJM Interconnection accounted for 79% of the company's revenues.

MIDWESTONE FINANCIAL GROUP, INC.

NMS: MOFG

102 South Clinton Street
Iowa City, IA 52240
Phone: 319 356 5800
Fax: –
Web: www.midwestone.com

CEO: Charles N. Funk
CFO: Gary J Ortale
HR: –
FYE: December 31
Type: Public

This could be the saga of How the MidWest Was One. MidWestOne Financial Group is the holding company for MidwestOne Bank which operates about two dozen branches throughout central and east-central Iowa. The bank offers standard deposit products such as checking and savings accounts CDs and IRAs in addition to trust services credit cards insurance and brokerage and investment services. About two-thirds of MidWestOne Financial's loan portfolio consists of real estate loans including residential and commercial mortgages and farmland and construction loans. Founded in 1983 MidWestOne has total assets of $1.8 billion.

	Annual Growth	12/10	12/11	12/12	12/13	12/14
Assets ($ mil.)	3.3%	1,581.3	1,695.2	1,792.8	1,755.2	1,800.3
Net income ($ mil.)	16.3%	10.1	13.3	16.8	18.6	18.5
Market value ($ mil.)	17.5%	126.3	122.2	171.4	227.3	240.7
Employees	(0.6%)	383	383	390	376	374

MIKART INC.

1750 CHATTAHOOCHEE AVE NW
ATLANTA, GA 303182112
Phone: 404-352-0601
Fax: –
Web: www.mikart.com

CEO: Miguel I Arteche
CFO: R Larry Gunnin
HR: Ellen Wooden
FYE: December 31
Type: Private

In-, the art-, of making pills and capsules Mikart pays attention to the details. The company offers contract pharmaceutical manufacturing services specializing in oral capsule and tablet formulations. Tablets and capsules can be immediate or time-release; the company also makes liquid formulations and provides specialty packaging including laminated foil blister and pouches. Mikart's facilities have the capacity to produce-, everything from small pilot-scale-, batches all the way up to full-scale commercial production. Other services include drug development feasibility studies and product testing. Mikart will also walk customers through all the required regulatory processes.

	Annual Growth	06/04	06/05	06/06*	12/08	12/10
Sales ($ mil.)	(64.6%)	–	–	2,039.0	26.5	32.0
Net income ($ mil.)	862.5%	–	–	0.0	0.5	1.7
Market value ($ mil.)	–	–	–	–	–	–
Employees	–	–	–	–	–	165

*Fiscal year change

MILACRON LLC

3010 Disney St.
Cincinnati OH 45209
Phone: 513-487-5000
Fax: 513-487-5086
Web: www.milacron.com

CEO: Tom Goeke
CFO: Bruce Chalmers
HR: –
FYE: December 31
Type: Private

Milacron people are passionate for plastics. Once a machine toolmaker Milacron retooled in the '90s to focus on plastics processing technologies and industrial fluids. It leads five businesses. The largest a plastics machinery unit makes injection molding and extrusion processing equipment used to produce dashboards decking and other products. Other units include Uniloy (blow molding systems for consumer packaging) DME (parts such as mold bases for plastics machinery) Cimcool (coolants lubricants and cleaners for metal grinding machining and stamping) and Milacron Precision Machining Manufacturing (parts for wind power oil and gas and heavy equipment). North America is Milacron's core market.

MILAEGER"S INC.

4838 DOUGLAS AVE
RACINE, WI 534022447
Phone: 262-639-2040
Fax: –
Web: www.milaegerslandscape.com

CEO: –
CFO: –
HR: Dave Bennett
FYE: December 31
Type: Private

Milaeger's has the difficult task of keeping things green on the banks of Lake Michigan. The company operates two nurseries in Racine and Sturtevant Wisconsin selling seeds soil plants mulch as well as apparel Christmas collectibles figurines folk art outdoor furniture and home decor. It also offers landscape services including lawn tree and shrub care along with design services. Milaeger's regularly hosts shows by collectibles merchants local fashion shows and gardening workshops. The company's Java Garden Cafe onsite at both locations offers hot and cold beverages dessert and light lunch and dinner items. Milaeger's was founded in 1960 by Dan and Joan Milaeger.

	Annual Growth	12/09	12/10	12/11	12/12	12/13
Sales ($ mil.)	3.1%	–	11.5	11.5	12.3	12.6
Net income ($ mil.)	17.5%	–	–	0.1	0.3	0.1
Market value ($ mil.)	–	–	–	–	–	–
Employees	–	–	–	–	–	125

MILBANK TWEED HADLEY & MCCLOY LLP

1 Chase Manhattan Plaza
New York NY 10005-1413
Phone: 212-530-5000
Fax: 212-530-5219
Web: www.milbank.com

CEO: –
CFO: Steven M Gamcsic
HR: Jane Maclennan
FYE: December 31
Type: Private - Partnershi

"Follow the money" could be the motto for the Manhattan law firm of Milbank Tweed Hadley & McCloy. Since 1866 the firm has represented clients such as the Rockefellers the American Cancer Society and JPMorgan Chase. Employing about 570 attorneys the firm's practice areas include intellectual property bankruptcy private equity reinsurance and insurance financial restructuring and compensation and benefits. Milbank's reach extends well beyond the US; it has a strong international presence with eight offices located in Brazil China Germany Singapore Japan and the UK. It caters to a broad spectrum of industries including aviation biotechnology health care pharmaceuticals and technology.

MILBERG LLP

1 Pennsylvania Plaza 49th Fl.
New York NY 10119
Phone: 212-594-5300
Fax: 212-868-1229
Web: www.milberg.com

CEO: –
CFO: –
HR: –
FYE: December 31
Type: Private - Partnershi

Milberg (formerly Milberg Weiss) has made its reputation — and drawn its share of controversy — representing plaintiffs in class-action lawsuits against some leading corporations. It also practices in areas such as antitrust consumer protection and mass torts. The firm has more than 65 lawyers in offices in Los Angeles New York Tampa and Detroit. In June 2008 Milberg agreed to pay a $75 million fine in exchange for the dismissal of a 2006 indictment in which federal prosecutors alleged the firm paid kickbacks to get people to serve as plaintiffs. Earlier in 2008 firm co-founder Melvyn Weiss pleaded guilty to a related conspiracy charge and resigned from the firm which changed its name to Milberg.

MILES HEALTH CARE INC

35 MILES ST
DAMARISCOTTA, ME 045434047
Phone: 207-563-1234
Fax: –
Web: www.mileshealthcare.org

CEO: James Donavan
CFO: –
HR: –
FYE: September 30
Type: Private

Miles Health Care provides acute and specialty health care service to the residents of Maine's Lincoln County. The not-for-profit company operates Miles Memorial Hospital — known as LincolnHealth Miles Campus — a rural medical center with about 40 beds and has emergency intensive care surgery and birthing departments. In addition Miles Health Care operates outpatient and specialty practice clinics physician practice offices and home health rehabilitation and hospice programs. It also provides long-term senior care through its nursing assisted and independent living facilities. Miles Health Care is a member of Lincoln County Healthcare (LincolnHealth) which is part of the MaineHealth network.

	Annual Growth	09/04	09/05	09/06	09/08	09/09
Sales ($ mil.)	111.6%	–	52.0	59.0	14.2	1,043.0
Net income ($ mil.)	54.0%	–	–	3.5	0.6	12.7
Market value ($ mil.)	–	–	–	–	–	–
Employees	–	–	–	–	–	800

MILESTONE SCIENTIFIC INC.

ASE: MLSS

220 South Orange Avenue
Livingston, NJ 07039
Phone: 973 535-2717
Fax: –

CEO: Leonard A Osser
CFO: Joseph D'Agostino
HR: –
FYE: December 31
Type: Public

Trips to the dentist might never be pain-free but they could be less painful if Milestone Scientific has its way. The company develops and markets dental injection devices (based on its CompuFlo technique) that cause less pain than a traditional syringe. Its primary product CompuDent and its accompanying accessory The Wand is a computer-controlled local anesthetic delivery unit that can be used in routine treatments including root canals crowns fillings and cleanings. CompuDent is also marketed as CompuMed to the medical industry for use in dermatology and orthopedics. Milestone sells its products through a global distributor network to dental and medical professionals in more than 25 countries.

	Annual Growth	12/10	12/11	12/12	12/13	12/14
Sales ($ mil.)	1.5%	9.8	8.4	8.6	10.0	10.3
Net income ($ mil.)		(0.6)	(1.5)	(0.9)	1.5	(1.7)
Market value ($ mil.)	0.0%	32.1	32.1	32.1	32.1	32.1
Employees	(1.5%)	17	17	17	10	16

MILFORD REGIONAL MEDICAL CENTER INC.

14 Prospect St.
Milford MA 01757-9971
Phone: 508-473-1190
Fax: 386-325-8178
Web: www.pcmcfl.com

CEO: Francis M Saba
CFO: –
HR: –
FYE: September 30
Type: Private - Not-for-Pr

Medical treatment in south central Massachusetts and northern Rhode Island. is the main affair of Milford Regional Medical Center. The 120-bed hospital provides acute medical services to the residents of Milford Massachusetts and surrounding areas. Specialty services include emergency medicine home health care diagnostic imaging physical therapy obstetrics and cancer treatment. It also has an affiliated physician practice group the Tri-County Medical Associates. The medical center which employs about 200 physicians is a teaching hospital affiliated with the University of Massachusetts.

MILLBROOK DISTRIBUTION SERVICES INC.

88 Huntoon Memorial Hwy.
Leicester MA 01524
Phone: 508-892-8171
Fax: 508-892-4827
Web: www.millbrookds.com

CEO: –
CFO: –
HR: –
FYE: March 31
Type: Subsidiary

Operating as UNFI Specialty Distribution Services Millbrook Distribution Services is a leading wholesale distributor of ethnic natural organic kosher and gourmet foods. The company also specializes in distributing general merchandise such as health and beauty items. The company has distribution centers in Arkansas Florida and Massachusetts that supply about 75000 products to some 7800 retail stores throughout the US. In addition UNFI Specialty offers such support services as logistics merchandising and technology integration. Founded in 1960 as Millbrook Distributors the company is a subsidiary of organic products supplier United Natural Foods.

MILLENNIAL MEDIA INC

NYS: MM

2400 Boston Street, Suite 201
Baltimore, MD 21224
Phone: 410 522-8705
Fax: –
Web: www.millennialmedia.com

CEO: Michael G Barrett
CFO: Andrew Jeanneret
HR: –
FYE: December 31
Type: Public

There's an app for that is music to the ears of Millennial Media. Using a proprietary data and technology platform called MYDAS the independent mobile advertising company connects app developers and major advertisers by buying space in apps to display highly targeted banner and video ads. MYDAS gives developers a way to deliver ads from Warner Bros Patagonia Porsche GM and others to more than 7000 different types of mobile devices. Supported apps come from small developers content providers (New York Times CBS Interactive) and major developers (Zynga Pandora). Millennial Media the nation's second largest mobile advertiser was formed in 2006 and went public in 2012.

	Annual Growth	12/09	12/10	12/11	12/12	12/13
Sales ($ mil.)	99.9%	16.2	47.8	103.7	177.7	259.2
Net income ($ mil.)		(7.6)	(7.1)	(0.3)	(5.4)	(15.1)
Market value ($ mil.)	(42.0%)	–	–	–	1,332.1	772.9
Employees	64.4%	–	–	222	348	600

MILLENNIUM PHARMACEUTICALS INC.

40 Landsdowne St.
Cambridge MA 02139
Phone: 617-679-7000
Fax: 617-374-7788
Web: www.millennium.com

CEO: Deborah Dunsire
CFO: Marsha H Fanucci
HR: Stephen M Gansler
FYE: December 31
Type: Subsidiary

Millennium Pharmaceuticals wants to be "the" drug company for the new millennium. Operating as Millennium: The Takeda Oncology Company it's a subsidiary of Japan's Takeda Pharmaceutical. The company's cancer drug Velcade is approved as a treatment for multiple myeloma (a blood cancer) and mantle cell lymphoma (or MCL an aggressive form of non-Hodgkin's lymphoma). Millennium has more than a dozen other drug candidates in the pipeline most of them cancer-related. Its oncology-focused sales force in partnership with Johnson & Johnson markets the drug with Millennium handling sales in the US and various J&J subsidiaries handling sales in Europe and most other countries where Velcade is approved.

MILLENNIUM PRIME INC

NBB: MLMN

6538 Collins Avenue, Suite 262
Miami Beach, FL 33041
Phone: 786 347-9309
Fax: –
Web: www.millenniumprime.com

CEO: –
CFO: –
HR: –
FYE: September 30
Type: Public

Genio Group has decided that playing cards just isn't in the cards. Until 2005 the company designed and marketed entertainment products including the Genio Cards card collection which consisted of 360 cards spanning 30 different educational categories such as endangered animals man-made landmarks and space travel. The game-playing cards used popular Marvel super heroes to promote learning. Citing lack of sufficient funding Genio Group exited that business. Steven Horowitz succeeded Matthew Cohen as CEO in mid-2006. The firm is currently searching for new operations.

	Annual Growth	09/07	09/08	09/09	09/13	09/14
Sales ($ mil.)	–	–	0.0		0.1	0.1
Net income ($ mil.)	–	(0.3)	(0.3)	(0.8)	(0.2)	(0.3)
Market value ($ mil.)	76.6%	0.3	0.2	0.6	3.9	16.1
Employees	–					

MILLER (HERMAN) INC.

NMS: MLHR

855 East Main Avenue
Zeeland, MI 49464-0302
Phone: 616 654-3000
Fax: –
Web: www.hermanmiller.com

CEO: Brian C. Walker
CFO: Jeffrey M. (Jeff) Stutz
HR: –
FYE: May 30
Type: Public

Desk jockeys can ride Herman Miller's products all the way up the corporate ladder and home again. A top US maker of office furniture it's known for developing designs for corporate government home office leisure and health care environments. Herman Miller's products include ergonomic devices filing and storage systems freestanding furniture seating textiles and wooden casegoods. It makes products in the US UK and China and sells them worldwide through its sales staff and dealer network as well as through independent dealers and online. The US government is Herman Miller's #1 customer. Herman Miller acquired modern furniture maker Design Within Reach in 2014.

	Annual Growth	05/11*	06/12	06/13*	05/14	05/15
Sales ($ mil.)	6.8%	1,649.2	1,724.1	1,774.9	1,882.0	2,142.2
Net income ($ mil.)	8.3%	70.8	75.2	68.2	(22.1)	97.5
Market value ($ mil.)	3.1%	1,466.1	1,066.7	1,678.0	1,866.7	1,653.5
Employees	6.6%	5,805	5,652	5,865	6,792	7,510

*Fiscal year change

MILLER ELECTRIC COMPANY

2251 ROSSELLE ST
JACKSONVILLE, FL 322043125
Phone: 904-388-8000
Fax: –
Web: www.mecojax.com

CEO: Henry K Brown
CFO: Susan A Walden
HR: –
FYE: September 30
Type: Private

Miller Electric Company flips the switch for projects primarily in the Southeast. The Florida-based electrical contractor provides services including construction installation renovation and maintenance of electrical systems. The company serves many industries including the communications construction health care and transportation segments. Outside of Florida the company has offices in Alabama Arkansas Georgia North Carolina Virginia Texas and Washington DC. Clients have included Anheuser Busch Bank of America Blue Cross and Blue Shield and the University of North Florida. Miller Electric was founded by Henry G. Miller in 1928.

	Annual Growth	09/10	09/11	09/12	09/13	09/14
Sales ($ mil.)	5.7%	–	183.1	183.1	204.4	216.2
Net income ($ mil.)	458.2%	–	–	0.2	2.7	6.4
Market value ($ mil.)	–	–	–	–	–	–
Employees	–	–	–	–	–	691

MILLER ELECTRIC CONSTRUCTION INC

4377 WILLIAM FLYNN HWY
ALLISON PARK, PA 151011432
Phone: 412-487-1044
Fax: –
Web: www.millerelectric.com

CEO: Richard R Miller
CFO: –
HR: –
FYE: June 30
Type: Private

If you're looking for an electrical contractor then it could be Miller Electric Construction time for you. Miller Electric Construction specializes in industrial and commercial electrical construction projects in western Pennsylvania and nearby portions of Ohio and West Virginia. The company constructs lighting data communication and power distribution systems for general construction contractors construction managers and area businesses institutions and attractions. Dick Miller founded the company in the early 1960s.

	Annual Growth	06/06	06/07	06/08	06/09	06/10
Sales ($ mil.)	(88.5%)	–	–	1,947.1	34.1	26.0
Net income ($ mil.)	4142.6%	–	–	0.0	0.4	0.2
Market value ($ mil.)	–	–	–	–	–	–
Employees	–	–	–	–	–	150

MILLER ENERGY RESOURCES, INC.

NBB: MILL Q

9721 Cogdill Road, Suite 302
Knoxville, TN 37932
Phone: 865 223-6575
Fax: 865 691-8209
Web: www.millerenergyresources.com

CEO: Carl F Giesler Jr
CFO: Phillip G Elliott
HR: –
FYE: April 30
Type: Public

This Miller's tale is all about oil and gas in the Appalachian region. Miller Energy Resources has been exploring and producing in the southern Appalachian region since 1967. It operates oil and gas wells organizes joint drilling ventures with partners and rebuilds and sells oil field equipment (including compressors oil field trailers and drilling rigs). Active in drilling and production in eastern Tennessee in 2008 Miller had total proved reserves of 1.8 billion cu. ft. of natural gas and 74413 barrels of crude oil. It is developing more than 43490 acres of oil and gas leases. Diversifying in 2009 it acquired Alaskan oil explorer Cook Inlet Energy.

	Annual Growth	04/10	04/11	04/12	04/13	04/14
Sales ($ mil.)	86.2%	5.9	22.8	35.4	34.8	70.6
Net income ($ mil.)	–	249.5	(4.4)	(18.7)	(20.4)	(28.6)
Market value ($ mil.)	(4.4%)	264.5	264.0	248.5	173.9	220.5
Employees	15.6%	47	71	70	79	84

MILLER INDUSTRIES INC. (TN)

NYS: MLR

8503 Hilltop Drive
Ooltewah, TN 37363
Phone: 423 238-4171
Fax: 423 238-5371
Web: www.millerind.com

CEO: Jeffrey I. (Jeff) Badgley
CFO: J. Vincent Mish
HR: –
FYE: December 31
Type: Public

This body builder wants to pump up your chassis. Miller Industries makes bodies for light- and heavy-duty wreckers along with car carriers and multivehicle trailers. It serves as the official recovery team at some of the NASCAR races (including Talladega) as well as the Indy 500 races. Miller makes its recovery and towing vehicles at plants in the US and Europe. Its multi-vehicle transport trailers can carry as many as eight vehicles and loads up to 75 tons. Miller Industries' US brand names include Century Challenger Champion Chevron Eagle Holmes Titan and Vulcan. The company's European brands are Jige (France) and Boniface (UK). Miller and rival Jerr-Dan dominate the US market for wrecker bodies.

	Annual Growth	12/10	12/11	12/12	12/13	12/14
Sales ($ mil.)	12.6%	306.9	412.7	342.7	404.2	492.8
Net income ($ mil.)	6.2%	11.7	23.0	9.1	9.2	14.9
Market value ($ mil.)	10.0%	160.8	177.8	172.4	210.6	235.0
Employees	6.2%	700	760	750	820	890

MILLER PUBLISHING GROUP LLC

1918 Main St. 3rd Fl.
Santa Monica CA 90405
Phone: 310-893-5300
Fax: 305-876-6695
Web: www.arrowcargo.com

CEO: –
CFO: –
HR: –
FYE: December 31
Type: Private

Miller Publishing Group may have lost its vibe but it's moved on to become king of the court. The company formerly owned Vibe Media which published hip hop music and fashion magazine VIBE but it sold that title in 2006. It currently publishes TENNIS magazine. TENNIS published 10 times annually is a leading tennis title with a circulation of more than 600000. Miller Publishing also owns TENNIS.com and the blog Peter Bodo's TennisWorld. The firm has an editorial office in New York with ad sales offices in New York Detroit Los Angeles and Montreal. Company founder Robert L. Miller was previously an executive at Time where along with legendary record producer Quincy Jones he helped launch VIBE.

MILLER TRANSPORTATION SERVICES INC.

5500 HIGHWAY 80 W
JACKSON, MS 392093507
Phone: 601-856-6526
Fax: –
Web: www.millert.com

CEO: –
CFO: –
HR: –
FYE: December 31
Type: Private

No beer here. Tank truck carrier Miller Transporters hauls bulk commodities such as chemicals and petroleum products from a network of more than 20 terminals in the eastern half of the US. The company operates a fleet of some 500 tractors and 1100 trailers and carries cargo domestically as well as between the US and Canada and Mexico. A sister company Miller Intermodal Logistics arranges the transportation of liquid bulk cargo worldwide. The company that became Miller Transporters was founded in 1942 by Harold Dewey Miller. Its founder's family still owns Miller Transporters.

	Annual Growth	12/09	12/10	12/11	12/12	12/13
Sales ($ mil.)	5.6%	–	87.3	96.6	102.9	102.9
Net income ($ mil.)	31.0%	–	–	0.4	1.1	0.7
Market value ($ mil.)	–	–	–	–	–	–
Employees	–	–	–	–	–	1,000

MILLER-VALENTINE PARTNERS LTD.

4000 Miller-Valentine Ct.
Dayton OH 45439
Phone: 937-293-0900
Fax: 937-299-1564
Web: www.mvg.com

CEO: Bill Krul
CFO: –
HR: –
FYE: December 31
Type: Private

Miller-Valentine is sweet on real estate. The company operating as the Miller-Valentine Group is active in such real estate areas as design development construction brokerage leasing financing and property management. The firm which has four offices in Ohio and South Carolina has developed more than 50 million sq. ft. of properties ranging from health care facilities and research centers to industrial processing plants and churches. Its MV Residential division develops multi-family residential properties and senior housing in the Midwest and Southeast. Miller-Valentine was founded in 1963 as a general contractor specializing in highway and bridge construction.

MILLERCOORS LLC

250 S. Wacker Ste.800
Chicago IL 60606
Phone: 312-496-2700
Fax: 203-425-9562
Web: www.mxenergy.com

CEO: Leo Kiely
CFO: Gavin Hattersley
HR: –
FYE: December 31
Type: Joint Venture

MillerCoors is proof that beer can make old foes new friends. Long-time rivals UK-based SABMiller and US-based Molson Coors put aside their differences to merge their operations in the US and Puerto Rico in a joint venture MillerCoors. The #2 brewer in the US operates eight breweries and enjoys some 30% of the domestic beer market. Its flagship brews are sold under the Coors Light and Miller Lite labels and import brews under Peroni and Molson Canadian. A division the Tenth and Blake Beer Company offers craft and import brews such as Blue Moon Foster's and many others. MillerCoors also makes Sparks a line of brand malt-based beverages. The company is 58%-owned by SABMiller with Molson Coors holding 42%.

MILLS-PENINSULA HEALTH SERVICES

1501 TROUSDALE DR
BURLINGAME, CA 94010-4506
Phone: 650-696-5400
Fax: –
Web: www.mills-peninsula.org

CEO: –
CFO: Iftikhar Hussaon
HR: –
FYE: December 31
Type: Private

With health facilities south of San Francisco Mills-Peninsula Health Services provides care to communities in and around Burlingame California. The group includes the 240-bed Mills-Peninsula Medical Center an acute-care hospital in Burlingame; Mills Health Center an outpatient diagnostic surgery and rehabilitation facility in San Mateo; and physician practice offices in surrounding areas. The facilities provide specialty services such as cancer care cardiovascular therapy behavioral health radiology respiratory care and senior services. Mills-Peninsula Health Services is part of the Sutter Health network.

	Annual Growth	12/00	12/01	12/02	12/09	12/11
Sales ($ mil.)	7.9%	–	267.0	274.0	533.8	572.0
Net income ($ mil.)	–	–	20.0	18.0	56.7	(34.0)
Market value ($ mil.)	–	–	–	–	–	–
Employees	–	–	–	–	–	2,200

MILLWARD BROWN INC.

11 Madison Ave. 12th Fl.
New York NY 10010
Phone: 212-548-7200
Fax: 212-548-7201
Web: www.millwardbrown.com

CEO: Mary Ann Packo
CFO: David Sandberg
HR: Cindy Akins
FYE: December 31
Type: Subsidiary

Millward Brown provides market research services specializing in brand performance from more than 75 offices in some 50 countries. Its research data helps customers develop brand strategies select an appropriate media mix choose advertising and evaluate the financial returns. Its DynamicLogic segment offers metrics analysis and other research information on marketing effectiveness. On the qualitative front the company's Firefly Millward Brown operations conduct online focus groups and qualitative interviews. Millward Brown is a subsidiary of The Kantar Group the market research division of UK-based media services conglomerate WPP Group. Millward Brown traces its market research roots back to 1973.

MILWAUKEE ELECTRIC TOOL CORPORATION

13135 W. Lisbon Rd.
Brookfield WI 53005-2550
Phone: 262-781-3600
Fax: 262-781-3611
Web: www.milwaukeetool.com

CEO: –
CFO: –
HR: –
FYE: December 31
Type: Subsidiary

Need a hand? Heavy-duty power tools are never in short supply at Milwaukee Electric Tool. The company manufactures and sells heavy-duty and portable cordless drills impact wrenches chop saws and rotary hammers all branded with a red lightning bolt. Its lineup comprises some 500 tools marketed to professional cabinetmakers carpenters electricians plumbers remodelers and welders. The weekend handyman can also buy Milwaukee products and accessories at home improvement retailers like The Home Depot as well as through the company's e-commerce website. Founded in 1924 by A.F. Siebert Milwaukee Electric Tool operates as a subsidiary of China-based tool maker Techtronic Industries.

MINDEN BANCORP INC.

OTC: MDNB

100 MBL Bank Drive	CEO: Jack E Byrd Jr
Minden, LA 71055	CFO: Becky T Harrell
Phone: 318 371-4156	HR: -
Fax: -	FYE: December 31
Web: www.mblminden.com	Type: Public

You might not mind Minden Bancorp minding your business. The institution is the holding company for MBL Bank (formerly Minden Building and Loan) which has two branches in the northwestern Louisiana town of Minden. Serving local consumers and businesses the bank provides standard deposit services including checking and savings accounts NOW and money market accounts certificates of deposit and individual retirement accounts. MBL Bank's lending activities primarily consist of one-to-four family residential mortgages and consumer loans but it provides business services such as commercial real estate and operating loans as well. Minden Mutual Holding Company owns a majority of Minden Bancorp's stock.

	Annual Growth	12/10	12/11	12/12	12/13	12/14
Assets ($ mil.)	5.7%	247.8	264.6	276.5	288.9	309.4
Net income ($ mil.)	14.9%	2.3	2.6	3.0	3.4	3.9
Market value ($ mil.)	8.7%	-	35.3	37.4	41.6	45.3
Employees	(1.1%)	31	32	31	30	-

MINDSHIFT TECHNOLOGIES INC.

309 Waverley Oaks Rd. Ste. 301	CEO: Paul W Chisholm
Waltham MA 02452	CFO: Lawrence M Ingeneri
Phone: 617-243-2700	HR: -
Fax: 617-243-2799	FYE: December 31
Web: www.mindshift.com	Type: Private

mindSHIFT provides managed information technology and network infrastructure services to small and medium-sized businesses. Services include application development systems maintenance data security oversight and technical support. Through its groupSPARK subsidiary mindSHIFT also offers hosted software for email data backup and customer relationship management (CRM) systems for clients looking to outsource their business processes. The company serves such industries as legal health care and financial services. It has received venture capital funding from Columbia Capital Fidelity Ventures and TDF. mindShift agreed to be acquired by Best Buy for $167 million in 2011.

MINDWIRELESS

6300 Bridgepoint Pkwy. Bldg. 1 Ste. 560	CEO: -
Austin TX 78730	CFO: -
Phone: 512-615-7600	HR: -
Fax: 866-777-1456	FYE: December 31
Web: www.mindwireless.com	Type: Private

mindWireless doens't want your mind occupied with mundane tasks such as trying to manage wireless billing. The company provides services and software that help companies manage their wireless program billing. Looking to reduce the costs and hassles associated with wireless communications programs mindWireless uses its analytical software applications to gather data about corporate wireless expenses calculate and compare costs and manage wireless vendor relationships and billing processes. Founded in 2000 the company offers its wireless billing management services throughout the US.

MINER ENTERPRISES INC.

1200 E. State St. Box 471	CEO: -
Geneva IL 60134	CFO: Gary E Bachman
Phone: 630-232-3000	HR: -
Fax: 630-232-3055	FYE: March 31
Web: www.minerent.com	Type: Private

Miner Enterprises keeps the bump and grind to a minimum. The rail equipment company's draft gears provide cushioning behind railcar couplers — the connectors that link railcars and make a train a train. Miner Enterprises also makes side bearings which help control the ride and curving characteristics of railcars and brake beams. Other products include discharge gates for covered comestibles chemicals and coal; hatch covers; ballast hopper railcars; and branded TecsPak elastomer springs; as well as replacement parts. Customers include freight car builders and private-car and leasing companies. The Withall family owns Miner Enterprises which has its roots in a company that was founded in 1894.

MINERALS TECHNOLOGIES, INC.

NYS: MTX

622 Third Avenue	CEO: Joseph C. (Joe) Muscari
New York, NY 10017-6707	CFO: Douglas T. (Doug) Dietrich
Phone: 212 878-1800	HR: Thomas J. Meek
Fax: -	FYE: December 31
Web: www.mineralstech.com	Type: Public

Minerals Technologies can brighten your day. Its precipitated calcium carbonate (PCC) products brighten and whiten paper polymers and teeth. Paper mills are major users of PCC — many of the company's facilities are adjacent to paper mills — along with food and pharmaceutical companies which use it for calcium and as a buffering agent in tablets. PCC products account for more than half of Minerals Technologies' sales. The company's processed mineral products also include lime (used to make PCC) limestone and talc. Minerals Technologies also sells monolithic and pre-cast refractory products which are used to coat steel cement and glass production surfaces with high-temperature-resistant material.

	Annual Growth	12/10	12/11	12/12	12/13	12/14
Sales ($ mil.)	14.5%	1,002.4	1,044.9	1,005.6	1,018.2	1,725.0
Net income ($ mil.)	8.4%	66.9	67.5	74.1	80.3	92.4
Market value ($ mil.)	1.5%	2,266.4	1,958.8	1,383.2	2,081.4	2,406.4
Employees	20.3%	2,132	2,077	1,992	1,978	4,464

MINERS INCORPORATED

5065 MILLER TRUNK HWY	CEO: James A Miner Sr
HERMANTOWN, MN 558111442	CFO: Greg Borash
Phone: 218-729-5882	HR: -
Fax: -	FYE: June 29
Web: www.superonefoods.com	Type: Private

Miner's is a family-owned chain of about 30 grocery stores in Michigan North Dakota northern Minnesota and Wisconsin. Most of the company's stores fly the Super One Foods banner but there are a few under the U-Save Foods and Marketplace Foods names. Following the acquisition of seven Jubilee and Festival Foods stores in Minnesota from Plaza Holding Co. Miner's converted the stores to its Super One Foods banner most of which are located in Minnesota. Miner's also has a wholesale grocery operation in Duluth. Miner's was founded by Anton and Ida Miner who started out selling groceries out of their tavern in Grand Rapids Michigan in the 1930s. In 1943 they built the family's first store Miner's Market.

	Annual Growth	06/09	06/10	06/11	06/12	06/13
Sales ($ mil.)	4.6%	-	463.6	475.6	501.5	530.6
Net income ($ mil.)	0.1%	-	-	30.2	31.8	30.2
Market value ($ mil.)	-	-	-	-	-	-
Employees	-	-	-	-	-	2,300

MINES MANAGEMENT, INC.

ASE: MGN

905 W. Riverside Avenue, Suite 311
Spokane, WA 99201
Phone: 509-838-6050
Fax: –
Web: www.minesmanagement.com

CEO: Glenn M Dobbs
CFO: Nicole Altenburg
HR: Lynda Fralich
FYE: December 31
Type: Public

Mines Management explores and develops silver and copper properties in the US. The company's primary property is the Montanore project in northwestern Montana which was operated between 1988 and 2002 by Falconbridge. Mines Management would like to further develop the Montanore property and the company is working to complete the required environmental and engineering studies and to determine an economically viable way to conduct mining operations. Its preparation of the property for study was expedited in 2006 and underground testing has taken up most of 2007 through 2009. Silver Wheaton owns an 11% stake in Mines Management while US Global Investors owns just over 7%.

	Annual Growth	12/10	12/11	12/12	12/13	12/14
Sales ($ mil.)	3.8%	0.0	0.0	0.0	0.0	0.0
Net income ($ mil.)	–	(10.7)	(5.6)	(8.2)	(7.4)	(6.5)
Market value ($ mil.)	(42.1%)	124.6	59.6	30.7	17.9	14.0
Employees	(8.9%)	16	15	13	11	11

MINISTRY HEALTH CARE INC.

11925 W LAKE PARK DR # 100
MILWAUKEE, WI 53224-3002
Phone: 414-359-1060
Fax: –
Web: www.hyhc.com

CEO: Nicholas F Desien
CFO: –
HR: Celia Shaughnessy
FYE: September 30
Type: Private

Part of the Marian Health System Ministry Health Care is a network of hospitals clinics and other health facilities serving all of Wisconsin and eastern Minnesota. The network includes 15 acute and tertiary care hospitals (such as the 500-bed Saint Joseph's Hospital of Marshfield) as well as about 50 physician clinics long-term and assisted living facilities home health agencies hospices and other community health programs and services. Ministry Health Care's flagship facility was founded in 1890 by the Sisters of the Sorrowful Mother as a Catholic health care system to contribute to the well-being of the community. Ministry Health Care and Marian Health System merged with Ascension Health in 2013.

	Annual Growth	09/01	09/02	09/03	09/06	09/07
Sales ($ mil.)	–	–	–	(709,296.1)	39.3	58.7
Net income ($ mil.)	122.6%	–	–	0.5	2.7	11.1
Market value ($ mil.)	–	–	–	–	–	–
Employees	–	–	–	–	–	5,000

MINITAB INC.

1829 PINE HALL RD
STATE COLLEGE, PA 168013008
Phone: 814-238-3280
Fax:
Web: www.minitab.com

CEO: Barbara F. Ryan
CFO: William J Vesnesky
HR: –
FYE: December 31
Type: Private

Minitab knows it's no small feat to work in a world of numbers and percentages. The company develops software that enables companies to analyze statistical data for quality improvement training and consulting purposes. It also markets to colleges and universities which use the company's applications in the classroom to instruct statistics students. Clients have included BASF DuPont Toyota Cisco and ExxonMobil. Minitab's original software was created in 1972 by three statistics instructors at Penn State including company CEO Barbara Ryan.

	Annual Growth	12/05	12/06	12/07	12/08	12/09
Sales ($ mil.)	–	–	–	(1,048.8)	63.6	53.7
Net income ($ mil.)	31213.8%	–	–	0.0	3.8	2.8
Market value ($ mil.)	–	–	–	–	–	–
Employees	–	–	–	–	–	321

MINN-DAK FARMERS COOPERATIVE

7525 Red River Rd.
Wahpeton ND 58075
Phone: 701-642-8411
Fax: 701-642-6814
Web: www.mdfarmerscoop.com

CEO: Kurt Wickstrom
CFO: Steven M Caspers
HR: –
FYE: August 31
Type: Private - Cooperativ

Minn-Dak Farmers Cooperative walks the beat for the sugar beet. Minn-Dak serves sugar beet growers in the Red River Valley of Minnesota North Dakota and South Dakota. Located in Wahpeton North Dakota the co-op processes the sugar beets into sugar and products such as molasses and beet pulp pellets (used in animal feed); the products are then marketed through agents worldwide. The co-op's Minn-Dak Yeast segment produces fresh bakers' yeast. Minn-Dak Farmers Cooperative is owned by its farmer/members a group of some 480 sugar beet growers. Founded in 1972 its customers include industrial users such as confectioners breakfast-cereal manufacturers and bakeries.

MINNESOTA TWINS BASEBALL CLUB

1 Twins Way
Minneapolis MN 55403
Phone: 612-659-3400
Fax: 206-346-4100
Web: seattle.mariners.mlb.com

CEO: –
CFO: –
HR: –
FYE: December 31
Type: Private

You might say these former Senators have become a big hit as part of the Midwest sports scene. The Minnesota Twins Baseball Club owns and operates a professional baseball franchise that traces its root to 1901 when Ban Johnson started the Washington Senators. A charter member of the American League the Major League Baseball team moved to Minneapolis in 1960. It boasts six American League pennants and three World Series championships (the last in 1991). The team's roster has featured such Hall of Fame players as Rod Carew Harmon Killebrew and Kirby Puckett. The Twins play host at Target Field in the Twin Cities. The family of CEO James Pohlad has owned the Twins since 1984.

MINNESOTA VIKINGS FOOTBALL CLUB L.L.C.

9520 Viking Dr.
Eden Prairie MN 55344
Phone: 952-828-6500
Fax: 952-828-6540
Web: www.vikings.com

CEO: –
CFO: –
HR: –
FYE: January 31
Type: Private

These Norsemen are looking to plunder their gridiron competition. The Minnesota Vikings Football Club joined the National Football League in 1961 and won its only league championship in 1969; however the team has been unsuccessful in four attempts to win the Super Bowl. Minnesota's roster has included such Hall of Fame players as Warren Moon Alan Page and Fran Tarkenton as well as former head coach Bud Grant. Vikings fans cheer the trumpeting Gjallarhorn at Mall of America Field at the Hubert H. Humphrey Metrodome in Minneapolis. The team has been owned since 2005 by a group headed by New Jersey real estate developer Zygmunt (Zygi) Wilf.

MINNKOTA POWER COOPERATIVE INC.

1822 MILL RD	CEO: Robert McLennan
GRAND FORKS, ND 582031536	CFO: –
Phone: 701-795-4000	HR: –
Fax: –	FYE: December 31
Web: www.minnkotacgf.com	Type: Private

The Minnkota Power Cooperative keeps the juice flowing to power users in northwestern Minnesota and eastern North Dakota. The generation and transmission cooperative supplies electricity to its 11 member-owner distribution cooperatives and as operating agent for the Northern Municipal Power Agency to 12 municipal systems to serve more than 118000 retail customers in a 34500-sq.-mi. region. Minnkota owns and operates the 235 MW lignite coal-fired generation Unit 1 of the Milton R. Young plant in Center North Dakota and 30% of the 400 MW lignite coal-fired Coyote Station near Beulah. The company also has wind power assets.

	Annual Growth	12/07	12/08	12/12	12/13	12/14
Sales ($ mil.)	(5.2%)	–	200.7	137.2	317.8	145.8
Net income ($ mil.)	0.7%	–	–	2.4	7.5	2.4
Market value ($ mil.)	–	–	–	–	–	–
Employees	–	–	–	–	–	355

MINTZ LEVIN COHN FERRIS GLOVSKY AND POPEO P.C.

1 Financial Center	CEO: –
Boston MA 02111	CFO: –
Phone: 617-542-6000	HR: –
Fax: 617-542-2241	FYE: March 31
Web: www.mintz.com	Type: Private - Partnershi

The lawyers of Mintz Levin Cohn Ferris Glovsky and Popeo specialize in such areas as antitrust communications employment and labor and intellectual property law. Overall the firm has about 450 lawyers in more than half a dozen offices in the US and the UK. Clients range from individual entrepreneurs to governmental agencies to FORTUNE 500 companies. Along with its law practices the firm has established affiliated consulting practices (ML Strategies and Mintz Levin Financial Advisors) that counsel clients on project management technology outsourcing financial planning and investment banking and government relations.

MINUTEMAN PRESS INTERNATIONAL INC.

61 EXECUTIVE BLVD	CEO: –
FARMINGDALE, NY 117354710	CFO: Stann Katz
Phone: 631-694-2614	HR: –
Fax: –	FYE: December 31
Web: www.minutemanpress.com	Type: Private

Minuteman Press International wants to be the first in line for your printing business. The company franchises full-service quick printing centers offering graphic design typesetting and printing. It provides franchisees with equipment supplies training marketing services and site selection as well as start-up financing options. Minuteman Press International has more than 950 printing centers worldwide with locations in Australia Canada South Africa the UK and the US. The company was founded by Roy Titus in 1973. His son Bob leads the firm as president.

	Annual Growth	12/04	12/05	12/07	12/12	12/13
Assets ($ mil.)	(0.3%)	–	16.3	16.5	14.0	15.9
Net income ($ mil.)	3.5%	–	–	3.0	1.2	3.6
Market value ($ mil.)	–	–	–	–	–	–
Employees	–	–	–	–	–	120

MIRAMAX FILM CORP.

Watergarden Complex Ste. 2000 1601 Cloverfield Blvd.	CEO: –
Santa Monica CA 90404	CFO: –
Phone: 310-409-4321	HR: –
Fax: 212-466-7888	FYE: September 30
Web: www.sandleroneill.com	Type: Private

Miramax Film Corp. depends on the independent. The company is known for its critically-acclaimed indie films that also perform well at the box office such as and Pulp Fiction and Shakespeare in Love. More recent hits include The Queen and No Country for Old Men. Miramax was formed in 1979 by brothers Bob and Harvey Weinstein. They sold the company to media giant Walt Disney in 1993. After a falling out with the corporate parent in 2005 the Weinsteins left to form their own production business The Weinstein Company. In 2010 Disney closed Miramax. Later that year it sold the label to a group of investors known as Filmyard Holdings who plan to focus on distributing the Miramax library of 700 titles.

MIRAPOINT SOFTWARE INC.

1215 Bordeaux Dr.	CEO: Jeff Witous
Sunnyvale CA 94089	CFO: –
Phone: 408-720-3700	HR: –
Fax: 408-720-3725	FYE: January 31
Web: www.mirapoint.com	Type: Private

Mirapoint wants you to get the message — but not the virus that could come with it. The company makes network appliances designed to route store and process incoming and outgoing e-mail. Its appliances and software also protect against viruses and spam. Combining messaging and server software with hardware the company's messaging tools are designed to work with a variety of mail formats and to integrate with existing e-mail applications wireless devices and Web-based systems. Founded in 1997 Mirapoint has received backing from Amerindo Investment Advisors Goldman Sachs MKS Ventures and Worldview Technology Partners. The company agreed to be acquired by Critical Path in 2010.

MIRATI THERAPEUTICS INC

	NAS: MRTX
9363 Towne Centre Drive, Suite 200	CEO: –
San Diego, CA 92121	CFO: –
Phone: 858 332-3410	HR: –
Fax: 514 337-0550	FYE: December 31
Web: www.methylgene.com	Type: Public

MethylGene's endeavors in the field of medicine may earn it a good look. The company is developing enzyme inhibitors to treat cancer and various infectious diseases. It develops product candidates for treatments for ailments such as solid tumors and hematological malignancies. MethylGene has also researched therapies to battle conditions including fungal infections and antibiotic resistance. The company forms licensing and collaboration agreements with other pharmaceutical firms to further its development programs.

	Annual Growth	12/08	12/09	12/10	12/11	12/12
Sales ($ mil.)	(90.4%)	24.0	2.9	2.4	3.0	0.0
Net income ($ mil.)		(7.3)	(22.5)	(14.7)	(9.5)	(20.4)
Market value ($ mil.)	–	–	–	–	–	–
Employees	(15.9%)	72	–	–	28	36

MIRENCO INC.   OTC: MREOE

206 May St.   CEO: Dwayne L Fosseen
Radcliffe IA 50230   CFO: Glynis M Hendrickson
Phone: 515-899-2164   HR: –
Fax: 515-899-2147   FYE: December 31
Web: www.mirenco.com/   Type: Public

MIRENCO would like to see bus fumes consigned to the scrap heap of history. The company's signature product D-Max is an electronic throttle control for heavy-duty start-and-stop vehicles such as buses and garbage trucks that is designed to improve fuel efficiency and reduce environmental emissions. MIRENCO's HydroFire product adds technology to reduce nitrogen-oxide emissions to the D-Max system. The company's EconoCruise product uses GPS technology to read the road ahead and adjusts the vehicle's cruise control to better manage throttle and emissions . Chairman and CEO Dwayne Fosseen owns about 35% of MIRENCO.

MISONIX, INC.   NMS: MSON

1938 New Highway   CEO: Michael A McManus Jr
Farmingdale, NY 11735   CFO: Richard Zaremba
Phone: 631 694-9555   HR: –
Fax: –   FYE: June 30
Web: www.misonix.com   Type: Public

Did you hear that Misonix is on the cutting edge of ultrasonic medical equipment? The development and manufacturing company makes ultrasonic devices to cut bone remove tumors and clean wounds. Its LySonix system is used to remove soft tissue during liposuction surgery. Subsidiary Hearing Innovations is developing devices to treat deafness and tinnitus. In addition to its therapeutic products Misonix manufactures the Aura line of fume hoods used in scientific and forensic laboratories. The company manufactures its products at its facility in Farmington New York. Misonix markets its products in the US and internationally through a direct sales force and wholesale distributors.

	Annual Growth	06/11	06/12	06/13	06/14	06/15
Sales ($ mil.)	11.4%	14.4	15.7	14.8	17.1	22.2
Net income ($ mil.)	–	(3.5)	0.4	(2.7)	1.4	5.6
Market value ($ mil.)	39.6%	19.4	18.1	39.5	52.4	73.6
Employees	1.0%	77	69	71	68	80

MISSION COMMUNITY BANCORP   NBB: MISN

3380 S. Higuera St.   CEO: –
San Luis Obispo, CA 93401   CFO: –
Phone: 805 782-5000   HR:
Fax: FYE: December 31
Web: www.missioncommunitybank.com   Type: Public

Mission Community Bancorp is on a mission to provide traditional community banking services and foster economic revitalization and community development. Subsidiary Mission Community Bank offers standard checking savings products money market accounts and certificates of deposit. It also focuses on agribusiness commercial construction and consumer loans. The bank has about 10 offices in San Luis Obispo and Santa Barbara counties. In late 2011 Mission Community Bancorp bought Santa Lucia Bancorp in a deal that added four branches in central California. The Carpenter Community BancFund owns about a quarter of Mission Community Bancorp.

	Annual Growth	12/08	12/09	12/10	12/11	12/12
Assets ($ mil.)	19.2%	215.5	193.1	217.8	462.2	435.2
Net income ($ mil.)	–	(3.8)	(6.9)	(6.7)	(3.0)	0.9
Market value ($ mil.)	(23.8%)	82.0	51.0	30.6	27.3	27.7
Employees	16.6%	60	56	64	139	111

MISSION HOSPITAL INC.

509 BILTMORE AVE   CEO: –
ASHEVILLE, NC 288014601   CFO: –
Phone: 828-213-1111   HR: Maria Roloff
Fax: –   FYE: September 30
Web: www.missionhospitals.org   Type: Private

Its mission is clear and bold: Improve the health of all in western North Carolina. Mission Hospital is a 760-bed regional referral center serving the western quarter of North Carolina and portions of adjoining states. A not-for-profit community hospital system Mission is located in Asheville on two adjoining campuses: Memorial and St. Joseph's. It provides tertiary-level services in neurosciences cardiac care trauma care surgery pediatric medicine and women's services and has a medical staff of more than 540. It also includes the Mission Children's Hospital. Mission Hospitals is part of the Mission Health System which is made up of Blue Ridge Regional Hospital McDowell Hospital and other facilities.

	Annual Growth	12/04	12/05*	09/06	09/12	09/13
Sales ($ mil.)	8.2%	–	500.0	0.0	861.0	942.3
Net income ($ mil.)	–	–	–	0.0	86.3	71.9
Market value ($ mil.)	–	–	–	–	–	–
Employees						5,400

*Fiscal year change

MISSION PHARMACAL COMPANY

10999 W IH 10 STE 1000   CEO: Neill B Walsdorf Sr
SAN ANTONIO, TX 782301355   CFO: Tom Dooley
Phone: 210-696-8400   HR: –
Fax: –   FYE: April 30
Web: www.missionpharmacal.com   Type: Private

Mission Pharmacal's purpose objective and undertaking if you will is to make you feel better. The company makes prescription and over-the-counter (OTC) remedies for infection kidney stones and arthritis as well as nutritional supplements. Mission's products include kidney stone preventer Urocit-K dermatitis ointment Texacort bacterial infection fighter Tindamax and CitraNatal prescription prenatal vitamins. The company also offers third-party OTC nutritional and prescription manufacturing packaging and inventory management to pharmaceutical companies. Mission is owned and run by the founding Walsdorf family.

	Annual Growth	04/10	04/11	04/12	04/13	04/14
Sales ($ mil.)	16.9%	–	95.3	118.2	124.1	152.0
Net income ($ mil.)	–	–	–	18.3	7.7	(1.6)
Market value ($ mil.)	–	–	–	–	–	–
Employees	–	–	–	–	–	495

MISSISSIPPI COUNTY ELECTRIC COOPERATIVE INC.

510 N BROADWAY ST   CEO: –
BLYTHEVILLE, AR 723152732   CFO:
Phone: 870-763-4563   HR: –
Fax: –   FYE: December 31
Web: www.mceci.com   Type: Private

Like much of the rest of the state of Arkansas people in Mississippi County get their electricity from a cooperative. Mississippi County Electric Cooperative (MCEC) serves customers in the northeast corner of Arkansas about 60 miles north of Memphis. The area is home to two steel mills owned by Nucor Corporation that are powered by MCEC power; most customers are industrial or agricultural. The coop also offers Internet service via rural satellite broadband provider WildBlue and provides its customers with energy audits and information on saving energy. It is a member of Touchstone Energy a national alliance of electric cooperatives in nearly 40 states. MCEC was formed in 1938.

	Annual Growth	12/06	12/07	12/08	12/09	12/13
Sales ($ mil.)	1.7%	–	141.9	150.5	88.7	157.2
Net income ($ mil.)	(44.3%)	–	–	4.7	2.1	0.2
Market value ($ mil.)	–	–	–	–	–	–
Employees	–	–	–	–	–	16

MISSISSIPPI POWER CO.

NYS: MP PRD

2992 West Beach Boulevard
Gulfport, MS 39501
Phone: 228 864-1211
Fax: –
Web: www.mississippipower.com

CEO: Anthony Wilson
CFO: Moses H Feagin
HR: –
FYE: December 31
Type: Public

Mississippi Power provides electric services to about 186680 residential commercial and industrial customers in the Magnolia State. The utility operates more than 6890 miles of transmission and distribution lines and it generates nearly 3160 MW of capacity from its power plants (of which 1450 MWs are coal-fired). Mississippi Power also sells wholesale electricity to several Florida municipal and cooperative utilities and it offers energy conservation services and sells electrical appliances. Mississippi Power is a subsidiary of utility holding firm Southern Company.

	Annual Growth	12/10	12/11	12/12	12/13	12/14
Sales ($ mil.)	2.1%	1,143.1	1,112.9	1,036.0	1,145.2	1,242.6
Net income ($ mil.)	–	82.0	95.9	149.8	(474.9)	(326.9)
Market value ($ mil.)	0.7%	27.7	29.5	29.3	27.5	28.5
Employees	3.7%	1,280	1,264	1,281	1,344	1,478

MISSOURI STATE UNIVERSITY

901 S NATIONAL AVE
SPRINGFIELD, MO 658970001
Phone: 417-836-5000
Fax: –
Web: www.missouristatebears.com

CEO: –
CFO: –
HR: Tamara Hernandez
FYE: June 30
Type: Private

When Missouri students say "show me" Missouri State University happily obliges. It is the state's second-largest university (after University of Missouri) with an enrollment of 23800 students. The school offers about 85 undergraduate majors 133 undergraduate minors and 50 graduate majors including 14 masters 3 doctoral degrees (audiology physical therapy and nurse practitioner) and one specialist degree. The university' coursework includes accounting biology criminology and physical geography. Missouri State awarded almost 4000 degrees in 2013. It also hosted some 16 NCAA Division One sports teams that year.

	Annual Growth	06/09	06/10	06/11	06/12	06/13
Sales ($ mil.)	1.3%	–	189.3	191.0	201.4	196.7
Net income ($ mil.)	(23.0%)	–	–	33.8	16.9	20.0
Market value ($ mil.)	–	–	–	–	–	–
Employees	–	–	–	–	–	2,066

MISTRAS GROUP, INC.

NYS: MG

195 Clarksville Road
Princeton Junction, NJ 08550
Phone: 609 716-4000
Fax: –
Web: www.mistrasgroup.com

CEO: Sotirios J. Vahaviolos
CFO: Jonathan H. (Jon) Wolk
HR: –
FYE: May 31
Type: Public

Mistras could be all that stands between you and a massive oil refinery explosion nuclear facility meltdown or big bridge collapse. The engineering services company conducts non-destructive testing on critical equipment and processes used by petroleum aerospace infrastructure power generation and chemical manufacturing companies worldwide. It checks plant infrastructure for defects and problems without interrupting production; inspections take place during facility design build maintenance and operation phases. Mistras works from about 75 offices in 15 nations to serve clients that include Alcan Honeywell Bechtel BP Dow Chemical Airbus and federal and state governments.

	Annual Growth	05/11	05/12	05/13	05/14	05/15
Sales ($ mil.)	20.4%	338.6	436.9	529.3	623.4	711.3
Net income ($ mil.)	(0.5%)	16.4	21.4	11.6	22.5	16.1
Market value ($ mil.)	1.5%	499.7	647.0	613.7	653.3	531.3
Employees	20.5%	2,700	3,500	4,400	5,300	5,700

MITCHAM INDUSTRIES, INC.

NMS: MIND

8141 SH 75 South, P.O. Box 1175
Huntsville, TX 77342
Phone: 936 291-2277
Fax: –
Web: www.mitchamindustries.com

CEO: Billy F Mitcham Jr
CFO: Robert P Capps
HR: –
FYE: January 31
Type: Public

Here's a shocker: Mitcham Industries has few rivals that can match 'em when it comes to the leasing and sales of seismic equipment to the global seismic industry. The company's equipment offerings include channel boxes geophones earth vibrators various cables and other peripheral equipment. Through short-term leasing (three to nine months) from Mitcham Industries oil and gas companies - a major customer group — can improve their chances of drilling a productive well and reduce equipment costs. The company also manufactures marine seismic equipment under the Seamap brand.

	Annual Growth	01/11	01/12	01/13	01/14	01/15
Sales ($ mil.)	3.9%	71.4	112.8	104.7	92.1	83.1
Net income ($ mil.)	–	4.7	24.3	17.1	4.8	(9.2)
Market value ($ mil.)	(15.5%)	133.2	265.5	179.1	182.5	67.8
Employees	10.6%	125	169	184	194	187

MITCHELL SILBERBERG & KNUPP LLP

11377 W OLYMPIC BLVD FL 2
LOS ANGELES, CA 900641683
Phone: 310-312-2000
Fax: –
Web: www.msk.com

CEO: –
CFO: –
HR: –
FYE: December 31
Type: Private

Legally representing folks from the entertainment industry may not sound like your cup of tea but somebody's got to do the job — turns out Mitchell Silberberg & Knupp is up for the challenge. Founded in 1908 the law firm provides a variety of business law services with an emphasis on intellectual property and the entertainment industry. Other practice areas include technology; immigration; corporate law and homeland security; tax trust and estates; and international trade. Mitchell Silberberg & Knupp employs about 125 attorneys with three US offices located in Los Angeles New York and Washington D.C.

	Annual Growth	09/07	09/08	09/09	09/10*	12/10
Sales ($ mil.)	–	–	–	0.0	0.2	68.3
Net income ($ mil.)	200518.3%	–	–	0.0	0.0	32.9
Market value ($ mil.)	–	–	–	–	–	–
Employees	–	–	–	–	–	300

*Fiscal year change

MITEK SYSTEMS, INC.

NAS: MITK

8911 Balboa Avenue
San Diego, CA 92123
Phone: 858 309-1700
Fax: –
Web: www.miteksystems.com

CEO: James B Debello
CFO: Russell C Clark
HR: –
FYE: September 30
Type: Public

Mitek Systems is a company with character. Its automated document recognition (ADR) software known as ImageNet uses character recognition technology to digitally convert electronically scanned documents into digital form. While Mitek's products are used primarily to process financial documents the ImageNet suite of products also enables the processing and analysis of digitized still and moving images (Photo & Video) and reading coded print data such as bar codes (DataCapture). The company's FraudProtect group of products is used to detect forgeries and verify the authenticity of checks.

	Annual Growth	09/11	09/12	09/13	09/14	09/15
Sales ($ mil.)	25.4%	10.3	9.1	14.8	19.2	25.4
Net income ($ mil.)	–	(0.1)	(7.8)	(7.3)	(5.3)	2.5
Market value ($ mil.)	(23.4%)	293.4	102.5	163.7	76.4	101.2
Employees	27.7%	32	46	65	49	85

MITEK USA INC.

14515 N. Outer 40 Rd. Ste. 300
Chesterfield MO 63017-5791
Phone: 314-434-1200
Fax: 314-434-5343
Web: www.mitek-us.com/default.aspx

CEO: Thomas Manenti
CFO: –
HR: Kerry Testani
FYE: December 31
Type: Subsidiary

Having learned from the three pigs' example builders now use many more components other than straw and sticks when constructing a building. And MiTek USA makes a lot of those building components. The company manufactures metal connector plates and bracing as well as machinery for making structural trusses wall paneling and related components for the construction industry. Subsidiary Heat Pipe Technology makes energy recovery and dehumidification systems used primarily in research laboratories hospitals and manufacturing facilities. MiTek a subsidiary of Warren Buffett's Berkshire Hathaway also provides design engineering and job summary software.

MITSUBISHI CATERPILLAR FORKLIFT AMERICA INC.

2121 W. Sam Houston Pkwy. North
Houston TX 77043-2305
Phone: 713-365-1000
Fax: 713-365-1441
Web: www.mcfa.com

CEO: –
CFO: –
HR: –
FYE: December 31
Type: Subsidiary

Mitsubishi Caterpillar Forklift America (MCFA) sticks a fork in it to make sure the job's done. Creating one source for three major material handlers MCFA manufactures/distributes forklift trucks under the Mitsubishi and Jungheinrich brands and lift trucks under the Caterpillar brand throughout the Americas. Its affiliate Rapidparts Inc. distributes service parts of material handling equipment. Parts are sold under the Promatch (Caterpillar) and Mastersource (Mitsubishi) brand names. MCFA provides assembly fabrication and supply chain services.

MITSUBISHI POWER SYSTEMS AMERICAS INC.

100 Colonial Center Pkwy.
Lake Mary FL 32746
Phone: 407-688-6100
Fax: 407-688-6990
Web: www.mpshq.com

CEO: Henry E Bartoli
CFO: Arunava Mitra
HR: –
FYE: March 31
Type: Subsidiary

Mitsubishi Power Systems Americas (MPSA) has energy to burn. The US subsidiary of Mitsubishi Heavy Industries manufactures and distributes industrial power generation products such as gas steam hydroelectric wind and geothermal turbines as well as boilers and selective catalytic reduction systems (SCRs) throughout the Americas. The company is developing solar panels and lithium-ion batteries for the renewable energy market. MPSA has two plants in Florida and Georgia that manufacture gas turbines and parts for gas and steam turbines. MPSA is building a $100 million plant in Arkansas to manufacture wind turbines. The company also offers project management for the design and construction of power plants.

MITY ENTERPRISES INC.

1301 W. 400 North
Orem UT 84057
Phone: 801-224-0589
Fax: 801-224-6191
Web: www.mityenterprises.com

CEO: Randall Hales
CFO: –
HR: –
FYE: March 31
Type: Private

Folks on the rubber chicken circuit bingo buffs and church supper aficionados are probably familiar with the MITY Enterprises name. The company through its Mity-Lite unit makes tables (rectangle round specialty) chairs (banquet folding stacking) lecterns and portable panel products. Besides the Mity-Lite brand products are made under the names of DuraMax Host SteelCore Swift-Set and VersiFold. Customers include government agencies religious organizations universities and the hospitality market. MITY serves the health-care industry through its Broda Enterprises subsidiary which makes wheelchairs and adjustable seating for patients in hospitals nursing homes and assisted-living centers.

MKS INSTRUMENTS, INC.

NMS: MKSI

2 Tech Drive, Suite 201
Andover, MA 01810
Phone: 978 645-5500
Fax: –
Web: www.mksinst.com

CEO: Gerald G. Colella
CFO: Seth H. Bagshaw
HR: –
FYE: December 31
Type: Public

In case it's not clear from the name MKS Instruments makes instruments. In particular it makes systems that analyze and control gases during semiconductor manufacturing and other thin film industrial processes such as those used to make flat panel displays LEDs solar cells and data storage media. Top customers include chip equipment heavyweights Applied Materials Lam Research Novellus Systems and Tokyo Electron. Other applications include medical equipment pharmaceutical manufacturing energy generation and environmental monitoring. MKS Instruments generates about half its revenue from the US.

	Annual Growth	12/10	12/11	12/12	12/13	12/14
Sales ($ mil.)	(2.2%)	853.1	822.5	643.5	669.4	780.9
Net income ($ mil.)	(5.1%)	142.6	129.7	48.0	35.8	115.8
Market value ($ mil.)	10.6%	1,302.3	1,478.8	1,370.3	1,590.4	1,945.5
Employees	(3.0%)	2,673	2,429	2,305	2,394	2,371

MKTG, INC.

NBB: CMKG

75 Ninth Avenue
New York, NY 10011
Phone: 212 366 3400
Fax: –
Web: www.mktg.com

CEO: Charles Horsey
CFO: Paul Trager
HR: –
FYE: March 31
Type: Public

Who needs vowels? 'mktg inc.' provides a menu of integrated marketing services primarily for manufacturers of packaged goods and consumer products. Services provided by 'mktg' include strategic consulting direct marketing sales promotion (sampling and sweepstakes) event marketing multicultural marketing and interactive services. Owning main offices in Chicago Cincinnati London Los Angeles New York and San Francisco it designs and coordinates displays artwork and sales campaigns on a local regional and national level. Its U.S. Concepts subsidiary provides experiential marketing campaigns featuring concerts tours and festivals.

	Annual Growth	03/09	03/10	03/11	03/12	03/13
Sales ($ mil.)	8.0%	96.2	78.0	117.9	125.5	130.8
Net income ($ mil.)	–	(2.8)	(0.8)	(0.1)	5.4	1.2
Market value ($ mil.)	10.0%	8.0	3.2	7.2	8.0	11.7
Employees	9.4%	4,750	5,750	6,275	6,900	6,800

MMA CAPITAL MANAGEMENT LLC
NAS: MMAC

621 East Pratt Street, Suite 600
Baltimore, MD 21202
Phone: 443 263-2900
Fax: –
Web: www.mmacapitalmanagement.com

CEO: Michael L Falcone
CFO: Lisa M Roberts
HR: Holly Burkett
FYE: December 31
Type: Public

Municipal Mortgage & Equity (MuniMae) invests in tax-free municipal bonds issued by state and local governments. Those bonds are typically used to build multifamily housing including units for low-income families students and the elderly. The disruption in world credit markets coupled with a deterioration in the tax-exempt bond market hurt MuniMae. The commercial real estate market also tanked driving down the values of the company's assets. The company was forced to drastically reduce the size of its business cut its workforce by 80% and sell off assets at a loss in order to stay afloat. MuniMae continues to look for ways to reduce debt and raise capital.

	Annual Growth	12/10	12/11	12/12	12/13	12/14
Sales ($ mil.)	(21.1%)	107.7	100.1	72.5	42.9	41.6
Net income ($ mil.)	–	(72.5)	(18.8)	(38.7)	99.8	(82.9)
Market value ($ mil.)	193.7%	0.9	1.2	2.9	8.0	67.0
Employees	6.6%	38	55	59	22	49

MMI PRODUCTS INC.

400 N. Sam Houston Pkwy. East Ste. 1200
Houston TX 77060
Phone: 800-254-0080
Fax: 281-448-6302
Web: www.mmiproductsinc.com

CEO: –
CFO: –
HR: Israel F Valenzuela
FYE: December 31
Type: Subsidiary

Fair warning MMI Products insists on concrete results. MMI straddles two business segments: Fence and Concrete Construction Products. The company operates through four divisions. Merchants Metals make galvanized and vinyl coated chain link fence systems while ADC (Anchor Die Cast) Manufacturing makes and distributes aluminum and pressed steel fence fittings for chain link fences. On the construction side Meadow Burke manufactures concrete construction products and Ivy Steel & Wire produces wire mesh that reinforces concrete construction. Customers include barrier wholesalers industrial manufacturers and residential and commercial contractors. MMI is part of the Oldcastle division of parent CRH plc.

MMODAL INC.
NASDAQ: MEDH

9009 Carothers Pkwy.
Franklin TN 37067
Phone: 615-261-1740
Fax: 866-796-5127
Web: mmodal.com

CEO: Scott Mackenzie
CFO: David Woodworth
HR: –
FYE: December 31
Type: Public

MModal Inc. (formerly MedQuist Holdings) helps transcribe and analyze doctors' spoken and written notes. The company is a leading provider of integrated clinical documentation products and outsourced medical transcription services to the US health care industry. Its offerings include mobile voice capture devices speech recognition software web-based workflow platforms and a global network of more than 4000 medical transcriptionists and editors primarily in the US and India. Its customer base consists of more than 2400 hospitals clinics and multifacility health care organizations mostly in the US. MedQuist Holdings adopted the name MModal Inc. in 2012.

MMR GROUP INC.

15961 AIRLINE HWY
BATON ROUGE, LA 708177412
Phone: 225-756-5090
Fax: –
Web: www.mmrgrp.com

CEO: –
CFO: Donald Fairbanks
HR: –
FYE: December 31
Type: Private

That murmur you hear could be the gentle hum of a properly functioning power system. MMG Group provides electrical and instrumentation construction maintenance management and technical services for clients in the oil and gas manufacturing chemical and power generation industries around the world. It also offers services in offshore marine and platform environments. Its Power Solutions division constructs onsite power-generation systems in industrial plants and other facilities. The group primarily operates in the Gulf of New Mexico. Founded in 1990 MMG is 100% management owned and has served such clients as Chevron Shell BP Merck Air Liquide DuPont and 3M.

	Annual Growth	12/09	12/10	12/11	12/12	12/13
Sales ($ mil.)	–	–	0.0	255.0	501.3	681.3
Net income ($ mil.)	70.8%	–	–	11.1	19.5	32.4
Market value ($ mil.)	–	–	–	–	–	–
Employees	–	–	–	–	–	2,500

MMRGLOBAL INC
NBB: MMRF D

4401 Wilshire Blvd., Suite 200
Los Angeles, CA 90010
Phone: 310 476-7002
Fax: –
Web: www.mymedicalrecords.com

CEO: Robert H Lorsch
CFO: Bernard Stolar
HR: –
FYE: December 31
Type: Public

MMRGlobal aims to ride the worldwide digitizing wave as more physicians and consumers switch to digital medical record systems. Its products in development include online professional record storage systems and personal document management systems under the brands MyMedicalRecords Pro and MyEsafeDepositBox. The company's technology allows patient information to be stored securely but be shared with physicians pharmacies or insurance providers through the Internet. Previously operating as a biopharmaceutical development company in early 2009 the company completed a reverse merger with privately held MyMedicalRecords.com eventually changing its name to MMRGlobal in 2010.

	Annual Growth	12/10	12/11	12/12	12/13	12/14
Sales ($ mil.)	27.6%	1.0	1.4	0.8	0.6	2.6
Net income ($ mil.)	–	(17.9)	(8.9)	(5.9)	(7.6)	(2.2)
Market value ($ mil.)	(41.1%)	14.1	6.6	2.9	5.1	1.7
Employees	(23.3%)	49	48	19	19	17

MN AIRLINES LLC

d/b/a Sun Country Airlines 1300 Mendota Heights Rd.
Mendota Heights MN 55120
Phone: 651-681-3900
Fax: 651-681-3970
Web: www.suncountry.com

CEO: –
CFO: –
HR: –
FYE: December 31
Type: Private

Minnesota weather can be gloomy so MN Airlines aims to be a ray of sunshine. The carrier operating as Sun Country Airlines serves nine markets year-round and another 22 destinations seasonally in the US Mexico and the Caribbean from its hub in Minneapolis-St. Paul. US cities served by the carrier include Las Vegas; Los Angeles; New York; Orlando; Phoenix; and San Francisco. Sun Country also offers flights to selected destinations in Mexico and the Dominican Republic. It maintains a fleet of about 10 Boeing 737s. Sun Country in 2011 completed a 28-month trip under Chapter 11 bankruptcy protection forced by former parent Petters Group Worldwide which came under investigation for fraud in 2008.

MNP CORPORATION

44225 UTICA RD	
UTICA, MI 483175464	CEO: Terri Chapman
	CFO: Craig L Stormer
Phone: 586-254-1320	HR: –
Fax: –	FYE: November 30
Web: www.mnp.com	Type: Private

If you are fascinated with fasteners then MNP will galvanize your senses. MNP manufactures a plethora of precision fasteners and cold formed components including screws rivets washers small stampings as well as screw machine parts. Its services range from plating to annealing flat-rolling pickling hot-dip galvanizing and coatings. General Fasteners Cadon Plating & Coatings Marathon Metals and Ohio Pickling & Processing are a few of MNP's affiliated companies that produce a medley of metal parts and jointly operate the GFC/MNP Engineering Center in Michigan. The company serves the automotive heavy truck military and industrial markets.

	Annual Growth	11/09	11/10	11/11	11/12	11/13
Sales ($ mil.)	6.5%	–	150.1	173.6	182.7	181.4
Net income ($ mil.)	27.0%	–	–	8.2	10.9	13.3
Market value ($ mil.)	–	–	–	–	–	–
Employees	–	–	–	–	–	1,000

MOARK LLC

12005 Cabernet Dr.	
Fontana CA 92337	CEO: –
	CFO: Craig Wells
Phone: 951-332-3300	HR: –
Fax: +44-161-829-4475	FYE: December 31
Web: www.co-operativebank.co.uk	Type: Subsidiary

Moark doesn't just lay around; far from taking it easy the Land O'Lakes subsidiary is one of the top egg producers in the US. It owns about 26 million laying hens (layers) in about a dozen facilities nationwide. Moark's hens produce some 520 million dozen eggs a year including specialty shell eggs promoted as higher-value all-natural cage-free Omega-3-enhanced and organic. Fresh eggs are marketed and distributed under private-label and national brand names such as Land O'Lakes and All-Natural Farm Fresh Eggs. Moark is also is a primary franchisee of the Eggland's Best brand of eggs. Most of the company's eggs are sold as shell eggs to retailers and wholesalers for consumer and industrial use in the US.

MOBILE AREA NETWORKS INC

NBB: MANW

2772 Depot Street	
Sanford, FL 32773	CEO: George E Wimbish
	CFO: Jerald R Hoeft
Phone: 407 333-2350	HR: –
Fax: –	FYE: December 31
Web: www.mobilan.com	Type: Public

Mobile enough to move from wireless to plastic Mobile Area Networks provides custom plastic injection molding services. The company originally installed wireless LANs in hotels office buildings and convention centers but in 2002 it moved into plastics manufacturing. Mobile Area Networks focuses on developing proprietary products and custom molding. The company makes air conditioner parts archery bow parts consumer and novelty products hightech military parts irrigation devices non-invasive medical device parts roofing construction items snow ski equipment parts sporting rifle parts and other specialty applications. CEO George Wimbish controls Mobile Area Networks.

	Annual Growth	12/09	12/10	12/11	12/12	12/13
Sales ($ mil.)	(75.7%)	0.3	0.3	0.2	0.0	0.0
Net income ($ mil.)	–	(0.3)	(0.4)	(0.3)	0.3	(0.1)
Market value ($ mil.)	10.7%	0.2	1.0	1.5	0.4	0.3
Employees	(26.9%)	7	6	4	2	2

MOBILE MINI, INC.

NMS: MINI

4646 E. Van Buren Street,, Suite 400	
Phoenix, AZ 85008	CEO: Erik Olsson
	CFO: Mark E. Funk
Phone: 480 894-6311	HR: –
Fax: 480 894-6433	FYE: December 31
Web: www.mobilemini.com	Type: Public

Storing stuff is the stuff of big business for Mobile Mini. The company manufactures leases and sells portable storage containers and mobile buildings. Mobile Mini's lineup features steel and wood containers and residential and office units in various sizes including a selection of 100 different shelving wiring and locking options. Customers are consumer service and retail businesses construction companies and to a lesser degree distributors film producers military and municipal agencies schools and hospitals. Mobile Mini also refurbishes oceangoing containers for storage. The company's leasing arm comprising a fleet of 213500 portable containers and offices represents about 92% of sales.

	Annual Growth	12/11	12/12	12/13	12/14	12/15
Sales ($ mil.)	9.9%	364.4	381.3	406.5	445.5	530.8
Net income ($ mil.)	(35.3%)	31.9	34.2	23.9	44.4	5.6
Market value ($ mil.)	15.6%	778.2	929.7	1,836.4	1,806.5	1,388.2
Employees	5.8%	1,579	1,546	1,538	1,921	1,982

MOBILEPRO CORP.

OTC: MOBL

401 Professional Dr. Ste. 128	
Gaithersburg MD 20879	CEO: Jay O Wright
	CFO: –
Phone: 301-571-3476	HR: –
Fax: 301-315-9027	FYE: March 31
Web: www.mobileprocorp.com	Type: Public

MobilePro has slimmed down divesting its telecommunications and broadband businesses. The company is left with a subsidiary called ProGames Network which is developing online gaming products. In 2007 MobilePro agreed to merge ProGames with Winning Edge International a sports handicapping firm with ProGames owning more than 80% of the combined company. The deal fell apart however due to a lack of financing. MobilePro is considering strategic alternatives in order to maximize shareholder value. The company is vague on what forms those alternatives may take but says its goals are to eliminate debt and to return value to shareholders.

MOBITV INC.

6425 Christie Ave. 5th Fl.	
Emeryville CA 94608	CEO: Charlie Nooney
	CFO: Terri Stevens
Phone: 510 450-5000	HR: –
Fax: 510-450-5001	FYE: December 31
Web: www.mobitv.com	Type: Private

MobiTV turns mobile phones into media centers. The company provides technology that allows television broadcasts and other media content to be delivered to mobile devices. Its subscribers can access content — including on-demand and live television as well as digital music and satellite services — from ABC CBS NBC ESPN and other networks. MobiTV offers its technology as a managed service; it also licenses the server technology to carriers. MobiTV counts the leading US carriers among its partners. Other customers include broadband service providers content providers and handset manufacturers. The company filed an IPO in August 2011 but withdrew it a year later.

MOCON INC.

NMS: MOCO

7500 Mendelssohn Avenue North
Minneapolis, MN 55428
Phone: 763 493-6370
Fax: –
Web: www.mocon.com

CEO: Robert L Demorest
CFO: Elissa Lindsoe
HR: Carol Luo
FYE: December 31
Type: Public

MOCON makes precision instruments that help you look before you leak. Its products include permeation and packaging instruments that measure the rate at which oxygen carbon dioxide and water vapor penetrate packaging. The company also makes materials analyzers that measure the thickness of coatings and thin films. Such products are used by packagers in the food and beverage pharmaceuticals and chemical industries and by paper plastics and coatings manufacturers. MOCON also makes pharmaceutical capsule and tablet weighing and sorting devices automatic sample preparation systems and offers related consulting and development services. More than half of sales come from outside the US.

	Annual Growth	12/10	12/11	12/12	12/13	12/14
Sales ($ mil.)	19.6%	31.5	37.4	49.9	57.1	64.5
Net income ($ mil.)	(23.6%)	4.5	5.5	2.0	3.5	1.5
Market value ($ mil.)	8.5%	74.1	91.7	82.5	90.6	102.6
Employees	17.8%	135	150	250	250	260

MODEL N, INC

NYS: MODN

1600 Seaport Boulevard, Suite 400, Pacific Shores Center a Building 6
Redwood City, CA 94063
Phone: 650 610-4600
Fax: –
Web: www.modeln.com

CEO: Edward F. Sander
CFO: Mark Tisdel
HR: –
FYE: September 30
Type: Public

Model N develops revenue management software primarily for the worldwide life sciences and technology industries. Its product suite which is available on premise and via the cloud supports the entire revenue life cycle including pricing contracting compliance settlements channel management and business intelligence and analytics. Model N counts about 70 customers ranging from multi-national corporations to smaller firms. The company also offers such services as consulting maintenance training and support. It was founded in 1999 and went public in March 2013.

	Annual Growth	09/11	09/12	09/13	09/14	09/15
Sales ($ mil.)	9.5%	65.2	84.3	101.9	81.8	93.8
Net income ($ mil.)	–	1.5	(5.7)	(0.9)	(20.9)	(19.6)
Market value ($ mil.)	0.5%	–	–	264.0	262.9	266.9
Employees	6.3%	–	600	596	589	721

MODERN BUILDERS SUPPLY INC.

3500 Phillips Ave.
Toledo OH 43608
Phone: 419-241-3961
Fax: 419-254-4847
Web: www.modernbuilderssupply.com

CEO: Kevin Leggett
CFO: –
HR: –
FYE: December 31
Type: Private

Despite its name Modern Builders Supply (MBS) is an old hand when it comes to windows and doors. The company founded in 1944 makes and markets window and door systems through its Polaris Technologies division. The company's brands include Polaris Dynatech and Polaris UltraWeld. MBS also distributes products from other leading manufacturers including roofing siding and accessories (Alcoa Certainteed Owens Corning); kitchen components (4B Wood Cabinets Kraftmaid); entry and storm doors (Pease Therma-Tru); and tools and equipment (QualCraft Werner). President and CEO Kevin Leggett runs the company with his brother COO Eric.

MODERN WOODMEN OF AMERICA

1701 1ST AVE
ROCK ISLAND, IL 61201-8779
Phone: 309-793-5537
Fax: –
Web: www.modern-woodmen.org

CEO: –
CFO: –
HR: –
FYE: December 31
Type: Private

No need to pitch a tent to have Modern Woodmen in your camp. One of the largest fraternal benefit societies in the US Modern Woodmen of America provides annuities life insurance and other financial savings products to more than 770000 members through some 1500 agents. The group founded in 1883 is organized into "camps" (or chapters) that provide financial social recreational and service benefits to members. Founder Joseph Cullen Root chose the society's name to compare pioneering woodmen clearing forests to men using life insurance to remove the financial burdens their families could face upon their deaths.

	Annual Growth	12/03	12/04	12/05	12/06	12/07
Assets ($ mil.)	4.9%	–	–	–	7,928.9	8,318.2
Net income ($ mil.)	(2.6%)	–	–	–	99.2	96.6
Market value ($ mil.)	–	–	–	–	–	–
Employees	–	–	–	–	–	2,100

MODINE MANUFACTURING CO

NYS: MOD

1500 DeKoven Avenue
Racine, WI 53403
Phone: 262 636-1200
Fax: 262 636-1424
Web: www.modine.com

CEO: Thomas A. (Tom) Burke
CFO: Michael B. Lucareli
HR: –
FYE: March 31
Type: Public

Modine Manufacturing runs hot and cold but not when it comes to the products it makes for vehicles. Founded in 1916 the company designs and makes highly engineered heating and cooling systems and components for a range of customers worldwide: automotive OEMs agricultural and construction OEMs heating and cooling equipment OEMs construction contractors wholesalers of plumbing and heating equipment and fuel cell manufacturers. Products include heat transfer modules oil coolers radiators and vehicular air conditioning systems. With operations in some 14 countries and technical centers in the US and Germany more than half of Modine's revenues are generated outside of the US.

	Annual Growth	03/11	03/12	03/13	03/14	03/15
Sales ($ mil.)	0.8%	1,448.2	1,577.2	1,376.0	1,477.6	1,496.4
Net income ($ mil.)	37.0%	6.2	38.5	(24.2)	130.4	21.8
Market value ($ mil.)	(4.4%)	773.1	423.0	435.9	701.7	645.2
Employees	1.5%	6,497	6,716	6,500	6,900	6,900

MODIS INC.

10151 Deerwood Park Blvd. Bldg 200 Ste. 400
Jacksonville FL 32256
Phone: 904-360-2000
Fax: 904-360-2110
Web: www.modisit.com

CEO: Theron Ceod Gilliam
CFO: –
HR: –
FYE: December 31
Type: Subsidiary

This company wants to help get your IT staff into readiness mode. Modis is a leading provider of temporary staffing for corporate and government technology support departments with more than 70 offices in North America and Europe. It supplies personnel with skills such as database design programming technical support and Web development. Modis also offers staffing for technology projects and project management services and handles recruiting and hiring for permanent positions. The company which has worked with such clients as the US Department of Defense Military Health System and the Ohio state government started as part of MPS Group which was acquired by global staffing rival Adecco in 2010.

MODUSLINK GLOBAL SOLUTIONS, INC.

NMS: MLNK

1601 Trapelo Road, Suite 170
Waltham, MA 02451
Phone: 781 663-5000
Fax: –
Web: www.moduslink.com

CEO: –
CFO: Joseph B Sherk
HR: Kathleen V Betts
FYE: July 31
Type: Public

ModusLink Global Solutions' modus operandi involves supply chain management services. The company through subsidiaries ModusLink Corporation and ModusLink PTS offers inventory management and distribution services for customers across the consumer electronics and packaged goods retail luxury goods communications computer hardware and software and medical device industries. ModusLink Global Solutions manages more than 470 million product shipments through 25 facilities in 15 countries across the North America Asia/Pacific region and Europe.

	Annual Growth	07/11	07/12	07/13	07/14	07/15
Sales ($ mil.)	(10.5%)	876.5	739.9	754.5	723.4	561.7
Net income ($ mil.)	–	(49.0)	(38.1)	(40.4)	(16.3)	(18.4)
Market value ($ mil.)	–	–	–	–	–	169.8
Employees	(11.1%)	4,000	3,900	3,200	2,900	2,500

MOHAWK INDUSTRIES, INC.

NYS: MHK

160 S. Industrial Blvd.
Calhoun, GA 30701
Phone: 706 629-7721
Fax: –
Web: www.mohawkind.com

CEO: Jeffrey S. Lorberbaum
CFO: Frank H. Boykin
HR: –
FYE: December 31
Type: Public

Mohawk Industries doesn't mind being trampled under foot. The company is one of the largest makers of commercial and residential carpets rugs and other floor coverings in the US (competing with rival Shaw Industries) and one of the largest carpet makers in the world. It produces a range of broadloom carpets and rugs under such names as Mohawk Aladdin Durkan Karastan Lees and Bigelow. Mohawk's Dal-Tile International division is a giant maker of ceramic tile and stone flooring. Unilin's laminate and wood flooring and other wood products round out Mohawk's operations. The company sells its wares to carpet retailers home centers mass merchandisers department stores and dealers.

	Annual Growth	12/10	12/11	12/12	12/13	12/14
Sales ($ mil.)	10.1%	5,319.1	5,642.3	5,788.0	7,348.8	7,803.4
Net income ($ mil.)	30.1%	185.5	173.9	250.3	348.8	532.0
Market value ($ mil.)	28.6%	4,138.5	4,363.8	6,596.4	10,856.7	11,327.8
Employees	4.7%	26,900	26,200	25,100	32,100	32,300

MOHEGAN TRIBAL GAMING AUTHORITY

1 Mohegan Sun Blvd.
Uncasville CT 06382
Phone: 860-862-8000
Fax: 480-596-1384
Web: www.fender.com

CEO: Mitchell Grossinger Etess
CFO: Mario C Kontomerkos
HR: Ann Beinull
FYE: September 30
Type: Private

The sun also rises at Mohegan Sun a gaming and entertainment complex run by the Mohegan Tribal Gaming Authority for the Mohegan Indian tribe of Connecticut. The Native American-themed Mohegan Sun complex includes three casinos (Casino of the Earth Casino of the Sky and Casino of the Wind) that feature slot machines game tables horse race wagering an arena a cabaret stores restaurants and a luxury hotel. The company also owns Pocono Downs a horse racetrack in Pennsylvania. Gambling revenues go to the Mohegan Tribe and are used for cultural and educational programs. The tribe has lived as a community for hundreds of years in what is today southeastern Connecticut and has about 1900 members.

MOLINA HEALTHCARE INC

NYS: MOH

200 Oceangate, Suite 100
Long Beach, CA 90802
Phone: 562 435-3666
Fax: 562 437-1335
Web: www.molinahealthcare.com

CEO: J. Mario Molina
CFO: John C. Molina
HR: –
FYE: December 31
Type: Public

Navigating the murky waters of federal health care plans is no easy feat but Molina Healthcare's mission is to help Medicaid and Medicare members find their way to health care. Its Health Plan segment arranges for the delivery of health services to some 3.5 million people who receive their care through Medicaid Medicare and other government-funded programs in 11 states. Its Medicaid Solutions segment provides business process outsourcing (BPO) solutions to Medicaid agencies in five states for their Medicaid Management Information Systems (MMIS) the tool used to support administration of state health care entitlement programs. The family of founder C. David Molina controls the company through holdings and trusts.

	Annual Growth	12/10	12/11	12/12	12/13	12/14
Sales ($ mil.)	24.0%	4,086.0	4,769.9	6,028.8	6,588.9	9,666.6
Net income ($ mil.)	3.1%	55.0	20.8	9.8	52.9	62.2
Market value ($ mil.)	17.7%	1,384.9	1,110.4	1,345.6	1,728.0	2,661.9
Employees	25.7%	4,200	5,200	5,800	8,200	10,500

MOLLER INTERNATIONAL INC.

OTC: MLER

1222 Research Park Dr.
Davis CA 95616
Phone: 530-756-5086
Fax: 530-756-5179
Web: www.moller.com

CEO: Paul S Moller
CFO: –
HR: David Garside
FYE: June 30
Type: Public

Meet George Jetson...well not quite but Moller International is working on a Vertical Take-off and Landing (VTOL) aircraft that bears more than a passing resemblance to George's daily ride. The company is testing a prototype of its M400 Skycar in preparation for seeking FAA certification. The forecasted specs on the Skycar are intended to make traffic-jam veterans giddy: four passengers (including the pilot) maximum speed of 375 mph cruising speed of 275 mph and a range of 750 miles. No Skycars have been sold though and the resulting lack of revenue has caused Moller International's auditors to question whether the company can stay in business.

MOLLOY COLLEGE

1000 HEMPSTEAD AVE UNIT 1
ROCKVILLE CENTRE, NY 115701135
Phone: 516-678-5733
Fax: –
Web: www.molloy.edu

CEO: –
CFO: –
HR: Lisa Miller
FYE: June 30
Type: Private

Molloy College is a Catholic school on the South Shore of Long Island. In addition to a variety of undergraduate majors the college offers graduate degrees in business criminal justice education nursing and social work. Molloy College has an enrollment of 3500 undergraduate and 1000 graduate students. About 45% of incoming freshmen are first-generation college students. More than 68% of the educational institution's full-time faculty have doctoral degrees. Through its global learning program Molloy College students have studied abroad in a wide variety of locations including Australia Belgium China Italy France India Thailand and the UK.

	Annual Growth	06/07	06/08	06/09	06/10	06/13
Sales ($ mil.)	–	–	0.0	68.0	79.8	108.0
Net income ($ mil.)	–	–	–	0.0	4.8	3.0
Market value ($ mil.)	–	–	–	–	–	–
Employees	–	–	–	–	–	700

MOLSON COORS BREWING COMPANY

NYSE: TAP

1225 17th St. Ste. 3200
Denver CO 80202
Phone: 303-927-2337
Fax: 617-499-3361
Web: www.amagpharma.com

CEO: Mark R Hunter
CFO: –
HR: –
FYE: December 31
Type: Public

Molson Coors Brewing Company (MCBC) drinks with the big boys: the company is one the world's largest beer makers by volume. Operating through its subsidiaries MCBC produces some 19 million hectoliters (502 million US gallons) of beer a year. The beer maker's portfolio of brands led by Molson Canadian and Coors Light dominates the Canadian market accounting for 40% of the beer sold in that country. In the US MCBC does business through Miller-Coors a joint venture 58%-owned by SABMiller. MillerCoors the second-largest US brewer by volume markets Coors Coors Light and Molson brands. In addition to Canada and the US MCBC operates in the UK and as Molson Coors International (MCI) in developing markets.

MOMENTIVE PERFORMANCE MATERIALS INC.

22 Corporate Woods Blvd. 2nd Fl.
Albany NY 12211-2374
Phone: 518-533-4600
Fax: 785-296-0287
Web: www.ksdot.org

CEO: John G Boss
CFO: Brian D Berger
HR: –
FYE: December 31
Type: Private

Gathering momentum on a global scale Momentive Performance Materials is ready to take on the world. The company manufactures silicone quartz and ceramic products for everything from adhesive labels to hair care products to pesticides. Silicone is used in a vast array of products because of its ability to provide resistance to heat UV rays chemical reactions and friction while allowing for different levels of adhesion. Formed in 2006 after General Electric sold its Advanced Materials unit to Apollo Management Momentive became a subsidiary of Momentive Performance Materials Holdings in 2010. It operates 23 production plants around the world and serves customers in more than 100 countries.

MOLYCORP INC. (DE)

NBB: MCPI Q

5619 Denver Tech Center Parkway, Suite 1000
Greenwood Village, CO 80111
Phone: 303 843-8040
Fax: 303 843-8082
Web: www.molycorp.com

CEO: Geoffrey R Bedford
CFO: Michael F. Doolan
HR: –
FYE: December 31
Type: Public

Don't look for any mollycoddling of the earth here. Molycorp is an advanced material manufacturer that both controls a world-class rare earth resource and can produce high-purity custom engineered rare earth products to meet increasingly stringent customer specifications. Molycorp mines and produces lanthanide and molybdenum compounds concentrates and oxides using open-pit mining techniques. Lanthanides (which include cerium lanthanum and yttrium) are used in everything from cell phones and computers to X-ray film and television glass. The company is staking its future on the production of rare earth oxides (REOs). Molycop filed for bankruptcy in 2015.

	Annual Growth	12/10	12/11	12/12	12/13	12/14
Sales ($ mil.)	91.8%	35.2	396.8	528.9	554.4	475.6
Net income ($ mil.)	–	(49.1)	117.5	(449.6)	(374.4)	(604.9)
Market value ($ mil.)	(63.6%)	12,965.6	6,230.8	2,452.8	1,460.3	228.8
Employees	102.1%	150	920	2,700	2,580	2,500

MONARCH CASINO & RESORT, INC.

NMS: MCRI

3800 S. Virginia St.
Reno, NV 89502
Phone: 775 335-4600
Fax: –
Web: www.monarchcasino.com

CEO: John Farahi
CFO: Ron Rowan
HR: –
FYE: December 31
Type: Public

Monarch Casino & Resort hopes high rollers will rediscover Atlantis. The company's tropical-themed Atlantis Casino Resort Spa in Reno Nevada includes nearly 1000 hotel rooms a 51000-sq.-ft. casino nearly ten restaurants a health club a nightclub and a family entertainment center. The company also owns and operates the Monarch Casino Black Hawk in Black Hawk Colorado. Casino operations which account for more than half of revenue include gaming tables slot and video poker machines keno and a race and sports book. The family of founder David Farahi — including John Bob and Ben Farahi — own more than half of the company.

	Annual Growth	12/10	12/11	12/12	12/13	12/14
Sales ($ mil.)	7.2%	142.0	140.6	170.4	188.7	187.8
Net income ($ mil.)	14.6%	8.2	5.7	8.9	18.0	14.2
Market value ($ mil.)	7.3%	210.2	171.3	183.4	337.6	278.9
Employees	3.7%	1,815	1,800	2,100	2,100	2,100

MOMENTA PHARMACEUTICALS INC

NMS: MNTA

675 West Kendall Street
Cambridge, MA 02142
Phone: 617 491-9700
Fax: 617 621-0431
Web: www.momentapharma.com

CEO: Craig A. Wheeler
CFO: Richard P. Shea
HR: Jo-Ann Beltramello
FYE: December 31
Type: Public

Momenta Pharmaceuticals is seizing the moment when it comes to the development of new drugs. The biotech company specializes in unpacking and engineering complex molecules in order to copy existing biologic drugs develop complex generic drugs and discover new drugs. Momenta's primary product is M-Enoxaparin a generic version of Sanofi's heparin drug Lovenox. The drug has received FDA approval in was developed under an agreement with Sandoz. It is used to treat patients with deep-vein thrombosis and acute coronary syndromes. The company is also developing a generic version of biotech multiple sclerosis treatment Copaxone (marketed by Sanofi and Teva).

	Annual Growth	12/10	12/11	12/12	12/13	12/14
Sales ($ mil.)	(18.2%)	116.8	283.1	63.9	35.5	52.3
Net income ($ mil.)	–	37.3	180.4	(58.6)	(108.4)	(98.6)
Market value ($ mil.)	(5.3%)	815.7	947.5	642.4	963.3	656.0
Employees	10.8%	170	197	247	269	256

MONARCH CEMENT CO.

NBB: MCEM

P.O. Box 1000
Humboldt, KS 66748-0900
Phone: 620 473-2222
Fax: 620 473-2447
Web: www.monarchcement.com

CEO: –
CFO: Debra P Roe
HR: –
FYE: December 31
Type: Public

Monarch's chrysalis is made of stone. The Monarch Cement Company quarries clay limestone and gypsum near its Kansas plant to make portland cement ready-mixed concrete and other building materials. It can produce more than 1 million tons of cement annually and serves customers in Kansas Iowa southeast Nebraska western Missouri northwest Arkansas and northern Oklahoma. Its Monarch-brand portland cement is used in the production of ready-mixed concrete for constructing highways bridges and buildings. Chairman and president Walter Wulf Jr. and vice chair Byron Radcliff respectively control about 9% and 10% of the company.

	Annual Growth	12/10	12/11	12/12	12/13	12/14
Sales ($ mil.)	4.9%	121.2	122.1	151.8	127.4	146.9
Net income ($ mil.)	166.6%	0.2	1.6	3.2	5.4	11.3
Market value ($ mil.)	–	–	–	–	–	–
Employees	(5.8%)	610	615	700	510	–

MONARCH COMMUNITY BANCORP INC
NBB: MCBF

375 North Willowbrook Road
Coldwater, MI 49036
Phone: 517 278-4566
Fax: –
Web: www.monarchcb.com

CEO: –
CFO: –
HR: –
FYE: December 31
Type: Public

Monarch Community Bancorp emerged from its chrysalis in 2002 when it was organized to be the holding company for Monarch Community Bank (formerly Branch County Federal Savings and Loan Association). The bank operates more than five branches in southern Michigan's Branch Calhoun and Hillsdale counties. Its lending activities mainly consist of one- to four-family residential mortgages (about half of its loan portfolio) commercial mortgages and home equity loans. To fund its lending the bank offers such deposit products as checking savings and money market accounts CDs and IRAs. It provides insurance mutual funds annuities and financial planning services through an agreement with Prudential Financial.

	Annual Growth	12/09	12/10	12/11	12/12	12/13
Assets ($ mil.)	(11.9%)	283.2	256.9	208.1	190.3	171.0
Net income ($ mil.)	–	(19.4)	(10.9)	(0.4)	(0.4)	(2.2)
Market value ($ mil.)	0.0%	23.4	10.5	9.4	6.7	23.4
Employees	(1.9%)	94	68	79	106	87

MONARCH FINANCIAL HOLDINGS INC
NAS: MNRK

1435 Crossways Blvd.
Chesapeake, VA 23320
Phone: 757 389-5111
Fax: –
Web: www.monarchbank.com

CEO: Brad E Schwartz
CFO: Lynette P Harris
HR: –
FYE: December 31
Type: Public

Money rules at Monarch Financial Holdings. The holding company serves the South Hampton Roads area of southeastern Virginia through Monarch Bank Monarch Mortgage Monarch Capital Monarch Investment and OBXBank. With nearly a dozen branches Monarch Bank offers standard services including savings and checking accounts IRAs and CDS. Bank subsidiary Monarch Mortgage formed in 2007 has about a dozen offices. Other divisions sell insurance title and investment products. Single-family mortgages make up the largest share of the bank's loan portfolio which also includes commercial construction and land development loans. Monarch Bank division OBX Bank operates in North Carolina's Outer Banks area. TowneBank agreed to buy Monarch in late 2015.

	Annual Growth	12/10	12/11	12/12	12/13	12/14
Assets ($ mil.)	6.6%	825.6	908.5	1,215.6	1,016.7	1,066.7
Net income ($ mil.)	17.2%	5.9	7.1	12.8	11.1	11.2
Market value ($ mil.)	15.2%	91.4	90.1	96.3	144.2	161.1
Employees	4.6%	527	579	663	634	631

MONDELEZ INTERNATIONAL INC
NMS: MDLZ

Three Parkway North
Deerfield, IL 60015
Phone: 847 943-4000
Fax: –
Web: www.mondelezinternational.com

CEO: Irene B. Rosenfeld
CFO: Brian T. Gladden
HR: Karen J. May
FYE: December 31
Type: Public

Mondelez International (formerly Kraft Foods Inc.) makes what it takes to survive a global snack attack. The company's pantry of billion-dollar brands includes: Cadbury and Milka chocolates; LU Nabisco and Oreo biscuits; Trident gum; Tang powdered beverages; and Jacobs coffees. Mondelez International comprises the global snacking and food brands of the former Kraft Foods whose North American operations were spun off to form Kraft Foods Group in 2012. Mondelez with about $35 billion in annual sales operations in more than 80 countries and sale in about 165 countries is the larger of the two businesses.

	Annual Growth	12/10	12/11	12/12	12/13	12/14
Sales ($ mil.)	(8.7%)	49,207.0	54,365.0	35,015.0	35,299.0	34,244.0
Net income ($ mil.)	(14.6%)	4,114.0	3,527.0	3,028.0	3,915.0	2,184.0
Market value ($ mil.)	3.6%	52,421.3	62,153.6	42,345.0	58,726.5	60,431.8
Employees	(4.9%)	127,000	126,000	110,000	107,000	104,000

MONEYGRAM INTERNATIONAL INC
NMS: MGI

2828 N. Harwood St., 15th Floor
Dallas, TX 75201
Phone: 214 999-7552
Fax: –
Web: www.moneygram.com

CEO: –
CFO: Lawrence Angelilli
HR: Steven (Steve) Piano
FYE: December 31
Type: Public

MoneyGram International has just the ticket to move money around the world. Operating through primary subsidiary MoneyGram Payment Systems the firm sells MoneyGram-branded cash transfers and money orders at some 335000 locations around the globe and is a leading provider of money orders in the US. Wal-Mart is MoneyGram's largest money-transfer and money order agent accounting for more than 20% of the company's revenues. MoneyGram also offers in-person and electronic bill payment services letting users pay everything from mortgages to utilities and processes official checks for financial institutions. Thomas H. Lee Partners (THL) owns more than half of MoneyGram.

	Annual Growth	12/10	12/11	12/12	12/13	12/14
Sales ($ mil.)	5.7%	1,166.7	1,247.8	1,341.2	1,474.4	1,454.9
Net income ($ mil.)	13.3%	43.8	59.4	(49.3)	52.4	72.1
Market value ($ mil.)	35.3%	143.9	942.3	705.6	1,103.2	482.6
Employees	4.4%	2,292	2,136	2,490	2,590	2,727

MONEYGRAM PAYMENT SYSTEMS INC.

1550 Utica Ave. South
St. Louis Park MN 55416
Phone: 952-591-3000
Fax: 412-544-8368
Web: https://www.highmark.com

CEO: Philip Milne
CFO: –
HR: –
FYE: December 31
Type: Subsidiary

MoneyGram Payment Systems banks on its customers the more than 1800 financial institutions to which it provides payment processing services. The subsidiary of MoneyGram International provides banks thrifts and credit unions with official checks (such as those commonly used in consumer loan closings); it also sells money orders through them and offers them clearinghouse services. MoneyGram Payment Systems charges fees for its services but derives most of its revenue from investing the funds underlying the checks or money orders. Subsidiary Financial Services Management Corporation (FSMC) provides processing services relating to controlled disbursements such as WIC payments and rebate programs.

MONMOUTH MEDICAL CENTER INC.

300 2ND AVE
LONG BRANCH, NJ 077406395
Phone: 732-222-5200
Fax: –
Web: www.barnabashealth.org

CEO: –
CFO: David McClung
HR: –
FYE: December 31
Type: Private

Monmouth Medical Center is a 530-bed tertiary care teaching hospital providing comprehensive health care to residents of central New Jersey. The not-for-profit medical center offers services ranging from orthopedics diagnostics and obstetric care to surgery dentistry and geriatric services. The medical center campus also includes a children's hospital a cancer center a neuroscience institute an outpatient care clinic and hospice and home health facilities. Monmouth Medical Center is a major teaching affiliate of the Drexel University College of Medicine in Philadelphia. The hospital is an affiliate of the Saint Barnabas Healthcare System.

	Annual Growth	12/02	12/03	12/04	12/08	12/09
Sales ($ mil.)	4.4%	–	221.8	228.8	262.4	287.8
Net income ($ mil.)	7.9%	–	–	9.7	(11.8)	14.3
Market value ($ mil.)	–	–	–	–	–	–
Employees	–	–	–	–	–	2,400

MONMOUTH REAL ESTATE INVESTMENT CORP

NYS: MNR

3499 Route 9 North, Suite 3-D
Freehold, NJ 07728
Phone: 732 577-9996
Fax: –
Web: www.mreic.com

CEO: Eugene W. Landy
CFO: Kevin S. Miller
HR: –
FYE: September 30
Type: Public

Monmouth specializes in mammoth industrial properties particularly warehouses and distribution centers. The real estate investment trust (REIT) owns about 80 industrial buildings and a single New Jersey shopping center comprising some 10.7 million sq. ft. in more than 25 states mostly in the East and Midwest. Most are net-leased (in which tenants pay insurance taxes and maintenance costs) under long-term leases. The REIT's two largest tenants FedEx and Milwaukee Electric Tool together account for half of its revenue. The firm also invests in REIT securities. Founded in 1968 Monmouth is one of the oldest public equity REITs in the nation.

	Annual Growth	09/11	09/12	09/13	09/14	09/15
Sales ($ mil.)	12.8%	48.1	53.7	55.3	65.9	78.0
Net income ($ mil.)	13.5%	15.4	18.7	21.4	19.8	25.6
Market value ($ mil.)	5.3%	492.6	695.2	563.5	628.7	605.7
Employees	10.7%	10	11	14	14	15

MONMOUTH UNIVERSITY

400 CEDAR AVE
WEST LONG BRANCH, NJ 077641898
Phone: 732-571-3400
Fax: –
Web: www.outlook.monmouth.edu

CEO: –
CFO: –
HR: –
FYE: June 30
Type: Private

Students looking for a monumental education might want to head to Monmouth University. The private institution offers more than 30 undergraduate and 20 graduate programs through eight schools that include business administration education humanities and social sciences and nursing and health sciences as well as graduate and honors schools. Founded in 1933 as the Monmouth Junior College Monmouth University has an enrollment of roughly an 6500 graduate and undergraduate students. The school's student-teacher ratio is about 14:1.

	Annual Growth	06/06	06/07	06/08	06/10	06/13
Sales ($ mil.)	–	–	–	0.0	166.4	145.2	162.3
Net income ($ mil.)	(0.6%)	–	–	–	14.9	18.3	14.4
Market value ($ mil.)	–	–	–	–	–	–	–
Employees	–	–	–	–	–	–	1,000

MONOGRAM FOOD SOLUTIONS LLC

930 S WHITE STATION RD
MEMPHIS, TN 381175703
Phone: 901-685-7167
Fax: –
Web: www.monogramfoods.com

CEO: –
CFO: Joey Stoner
HR: –
FYE: December 29
Type: Private

Monogram Food Solutions is focused on M E A and T. As a manufacturer of meat and meat snack products the company produces beef jerky sausage hot dogs bacon and other processed food items. Its brands include Circle B King Cotton and Trail's Best Meat Snacks. Through several special licensing agreements Monogram Food Solutions also sells Jeff Foxworthy Jerky Products NASCAR Jerky and Steak Strips and Bass Pro Uncle Buck's Licensed Products. The company which distributes its products nationwide operates facilities in Minnesota Indiana and Virginia. Founded in 2004 Monogram Food Solutions was formed through the merger of assets (King Cotton and Circle B) previously owned by Sara Lee Corp.

	Annual Growth	12/09	12/10	12/11	12/12	12/13
Sales ($ mil.)	17.3%	–	–	173.7	197.6	239.2
Net income ($ mil.)	2.5%	–	–	3.1	1.7	3.2
Market value ($ mil.)	–	–	–	–	–	–
Employees	–	–	–	–	–	790

MONOLITHIC POWER SYSTEMS INC

NMS: MPWR

79 Great Oaks Boulevard
San Jose, CA 95119
Phone: 408 826-0600
Fax: –
Web: www.monolithicpower.com

CEO: Michael R. Hsing
CFO: Meera P. Rao
HR: –
FYE: December 31
Type: Public

Monolithic Power Systems (MPS) sends out mixed signals and that's a good thing. The fabless semiconductor company offers mixed-signal and analog microchips — especially DC-to-DC converters for powering flat-panel TVs wireless communications equipment notebook computers set-top boxes and other consumer electronic devices. MPS outsources production of its chips to three silicon foundries in China. The company's products are incorporated into electronic gear from tech heavyweights such as Dell Hewlett-Packard Samsung Electronics and Sony. The company was founded in 1997.

	Annual Growth	12/10	12/11	12/12	12/13	12/14
Sales ($ mil.)	6.6%	218.8	196.5	213.8	238.1	282.5
Net income ($ mil.)	4.7%	29.6	13.3	15.8	22.9	35.5
Market value ($ mil.)	31.7%	641.5	585.2	865.2	1,345.9	1,931.5
Employees	7.3%	889	922	993	1,105	1,178

MONOTYPE IMAGING HOLDINGS INC

NMS: TYPE

600 Unicorn Park Drive
Woburn, MA 01801
Phone: 781 970-6000
Fax: –
Web: www.monotypeimaging.com

CEO: Douglas J. (Doug) Shaw
CFO: Joseph D. (Joe) Hill
HR: Jennifer (Jen) Peterson
FYE: December 31
Type: Public

Monotype Imaging may be the one to thank if you're reading this whether it's on a portable electronic device or a printed page. With most sales going to device manufacturers (OEMs) the company's text imaging software is integrated into applications and embedded in electronics ranging from mobile phones to laser printers automotive displays and digital cameras. Its applications manage compression scaling color and layout. Providing customers access to thousands of typefaces OEM sales are complemented by about a quarter of revenue coming from licenses to creative professionals mostly commercial clients. Customers have included Nokia Sony and Microsoft.

	Annual Growth	12/10	12/11	12/12	12/13	12/14
Sales ($ mil.)	14.7%	106.7	123.2	149.9	166.6	184.5
Net income ($ mil.)	15.4%	18.4	22.7	29.0	31.1	32.5
Market value ($ mil.)	26.9%	438.1	615.3	630.7	1,257.4	1,137.8
Employees	14.7%	251	272	335	354	435

MONRO MUFFLER BRAKE, INC.

NMS: MNRO

200 Holleder Parkway
Rochester, NY 14615
Phone: 585 647-6400
Fax: 585 647-0945
Web: www.monro.com

CEO: John W. Van Heel
CFO: Catherine D'Amico
HR: Barbara (Barb) Ross
FYE: March 28
Type: Public

If you can't stop point your car toward Monro Muffler Brake and coast on in. The company provides a full range of brake tire exhaust system suspension and steering and alignment services at more than 800 automotive repair shops. Its operations span nearly 20 states in the Northeast and Midwest and include Monro Muffler Brake & Service Mr. Tire Tread Quarters Autotire Car Care Center and Tire Warehouse. Along with under-car work the company offers air conditioning maintenance state inspections and scheduled maintenance services including fleet maintenance. Tire replacements and service account for more than 35% of sales. Monro Muffler Brake services more than 4.4 million vehicles annually.

	Annual Growth	03/11	03/12	03/13	03/14	03/15
Sales ($ mil.)	8.9%	636.7	686.6	732.0	831.4	894.5
Net income ($ mil.)	7.8%	45.8	54.6	42.6	54.5	61.8
Market value ($ mil.)	19.6%	1,011.5	1,320.5	1,263.9	1,798.5	2,067.5
Employees	7.1%	5,005	5,113	5,850	6,139	6,577

MONROVIA NURSERY COMPANY

18331 E. Foothill Blvd.	CEO: Miles R Rosedale
Azusa CA 91702	CFO: –
Phone: 626-334-9321	HR: –
Fax: 626-334-3126	FYE: December 31
Web: www.monrovia.com	Type: Private

A rose of any color keeps Monrovia Nursery in the black. Monrovia grows more than 20 million container-grown plants in 2000 varieties at its five nurseries in California Georgia North Carolina Ohio and Oregon. Among its offerings are camellias conifers ferns perennials rhododendrons and trees. The company has introduced some 300 exclusive varieties holding more than 200 patents and trademarks. Monrovia supplies more than 5000 garden centers with its plants and also crafts topiary forms including some at Disneyland and Walt Disney World. It has additionally developed more than 40 specialized soil mixtures. The company was founded in 1926 by the aptly named Harry Rosedale.

MONSANTO CO.   NYS: MON

800 North Lindbergh Blvd.	CEO: Hugh Grant
St. Louis, MO 63167	CFO: Pierre Courduroux
Phone: 314 694-1000	HR: Steven C. Mizell
Fax: 314 694-1057	FYE: August 31
Web: www.monsanto.com	Type: Public

An ear of corn the size of a Trident missile? Not quite but Monsanto is all about bioengineered crops. The company helps farmers grow more crops like corn cotton oilseeds and vegetables by applying biotechnology and genomics to seeds and herbicides. It produces genetically altered seeds that tolerate Roundup (its flagship product and the world's #1 herbicide) and resist bugs. The company also produces Asgrow DEKALB Deltapine and Seminis seeds. During the past decade Monsanto re-made itself into a seed and biotech company as opposed to one focused on agrochemicals a transition that was sped up with the acquisition of Delta and Pine Land.

	Annual Growth	08/11	08/12	08/13	08/14	08/15
Sales ($ mil.)	6.1%	11,822.0	13,504.0	14,861.0	15,855.0	15,001.0
Net income ($ mil.)	9.5%	1,607.0	2,045.0	2,482.0	2,740.0	2,314.0
Market value ($ mil.)	9.1%	32,252.6	40,759.1	45,803.0	54,113.1	45,690.8
Employees	(0.6%)	26,100	26,000	26,200	27,000	25,500

MONSTER BEVERAGE CORP (NEW)   NMS: MNST

1 Monster Way	CEO: Rodney C. Sacks
Corona, CA 92879	CFO: Hilton H. Schlosberg
Phone: 951 739-6200	HR: –
Fax:	FYE: December 31
Web: www.monsterbevcorp.com	Type: Public

Monster Beverage certainly has the energy to reach beyond the blue sky. Along with its Blue Sky beverages the company serves up a variety of "alternative" sodas juices and teas. Its most popular and now namesake brand Monster is the #2 energy drink behind Red Bull and has spawned the Java Monster coffee drink. Other products include fruit juice smoothies and dry juice mixes. The company sells most of its products in the US and Canada through a distribution network but also directly to retailers such as grocery chains and wholesale clubs. Monster recently formed a long-term strategic partnership with The Coca-Cola Company which acquired a minority stake in the business for $2.1 billion.

	Annual Growth	12/10	12/11	12/12	12/13	12/14
Sales ($ mil.)	17.3%	1,303.9	1,703.2	2,060.7	2,246.4	2,464.9
Net income ($ mil.)	22.9%	212.0	286.2	340.0	338.7	483.2
Market value ($ mil.)	20.0%	8,768.5	15,453.9	8,862.4	11,366.5	18,172.7
Employees	0.7%	1,497	1,900	2,180	2,013	1,538

MONSTER WORLDWIDE INC   NYS: MWW

133 Boston Post Road, Building 15	CEO: Timothy T. (Tim) Yates
Weston, MA 02493	CFO: James M. Langrock
Phone: 978 461-8000	HR: –
Fax: –	FYE: December 31
Web: www.about-monster.com	Type: Public

Finding a new job or a new employee can be a monstrous task but Monster Worldwide aims to help. Its network of online career services is led by Monster.com a job search website operating in local markets globally across 40 countries. Most of Monster's revenue comes from employers who pay to post job listings and search the site's database of resumes. Job seekers can post resumes and search listings free of charge. Monster also generates revenue by selling advertising on its websites which include offerings aimed at students and military personnel.

	Annual Growth	12/11	12/12	12/13	12/14	12/15
Sales ($ mil.)	(10.5%)	1,040.1	890.4	807.6	770.0	666.9
Net income ($ mil.)	8.2%	53.8	(258.7)	(0.5)	(289.3)	73.6
Market value ($ mil.)	(7.8%)	708.1	501.8	636.7	412.6	511.7
Employees	(11.4%)	6,000	5,000	4,000	4,000	3,700

MONTANA STATE UNIVERSITY INC

901 W GARFIELD ST	CEO: –
BOZEMAN, MT 59717	CFO: –
Phone: 406-994-4361	HR: –
Fax: –	FYE: June 30
Web: www.montana.edu	Type: Private

Montana State University helps develop young minds in Big Sky Country. The university located in Bozeman serves more than 14500 students most of whom are undergraduates from Montana. The school offers baccalaureate degrees in 60 fields master's degrees in 45 fields and doctoral degrees in about 20 fields. The school offers primarily a liberal arts education though it is also strong in agriculture and the fine arts. The university provides courses in fields ranging from English to political science to engineering. It has a teaching staff of more than 1150 including 781 full-time and 373 part-time faculty and department heads. Tuition and fees for a resident student is $6705; a non-resident $20062.

	Annual Growth	06/07	06/08	06/11	06/12	06/13
Sales ($ mil.)	2.0%	–	302.9	318.1	334.5	333.7
Net income ($ mil.)	–	–	–	16.9	24.6	(1.2)
Market value ($ mil.)	–	–	–	–	–	–
Employees	–	–	–	–	–	2,500

MONTAVISTA SOFTWARE INC.

2929 Patrick Henry Dr.	CEO: –
Santa Clara CA 95054	CFO: Sanjay Uppal
Phone: 400 572 0000	HR: –
Fax: 408-572-8005	FYE: December 31
Web: www.mvista.com	Type: Subsidiary

MontaVista Software sees a bright future for Linux on the technological horizon. The company develops embedded Linux-based operating systems used to operate a variety of products including automotive electronics communications equipment and television set-top boxes. MontaVista has more than 2000 customers worldwide and partnered with such companies as ACCESS Systems America Freescale Semiconductor and Texas Instruments. Clients such as Emerson NASA and NEC use the company's products to operate devices they built. In 2009 Cavium Networks bought MontaVista Software for $50 million in cash and common stock.

MONTCLAIR STATE UNIVERSITY

1 NORMAL AVE
MONTCLAIR, NJ 070431624
Phone: 973-655-4000
Fax: -
Web: www.montclair.edu

CEO: -
CFO: -
HR: -
FYE: June 30
Type: Private

With its roots as a teaching college it's fitting that today Montclair State University (MSU) is one of a handful of universities in the US offering a doctorate in pedagogy (the art and science of teaching). For more than 100 years MSU has provided a comprehensive curriculum for future educators as well as other students studying a variety of subjects. With an enrollment of some 20000 students MSU operates through six schools and colleges: College of the Arts College of Education and Human Services College of Humanities and Social Sciences College of Science and Mathematics School of Business and the Graduate School.

	Annual Growth	06/06	06/07	06/08	06/12	06/13
Sales ($ mil.)	7.7%	-	179.4	200.6	266.5	280.3
Net income ($ mil.)	(23.5%)	-	-	24.9	29.4	6.5
Market value ($ mil.)	-	-	-	-	-	-
Employees	-	-	-	-	-	2,000

MONUMENTAL SPORTS & ENTERTAINMENT

601 F St. NW
Washington DC 20004
Phone: 202-628-3200
Fax: 202-661-5063
Web: www.verizoncenter.com

CEO: Ted Leonsis
CFO: -
HR: -
FYE: June 30
Type: Private

You might say that professional sports is a big thing with this company. Monumental Sports & Entertainment is a holding company that controls three sports franchises in Washington DC including the Washington Wizards professional basketball team the Washington Capitals hockey club and the Washington Mystics women's basketball franchise. The company also owns and operates the city's Verizon Center an all-purpose venue that serves as home for all three sports teams. In addition Monumental Sports manages the Patriot Center at George Mason University in Fairfax Virginia. Chairman and majority owner Ted Leonsis formed the company when he acquired the Washington Wizards in 2010.

MOODY'S CORP.

NYS: MCO

7 World Trade Center, 250 Greenwich Street
New York, NY 10007
Phone: 212 553-0300
Fax: -
Web: www.moodys.com

CEO: Raymond W. (Ray) McDaniel
CFO: Linda S. Huber
HR: Marianne Fabozzi
FYE: December 31
Type: Public

Moody's provides credit ratings research credit risk management and other services through its two primary segments Moody's Investors Service and Moody's Analytics. Moody's Investors Service publishes credit ratings on more than 108000 commercial and government entities in some 120 countries. Moody's Analytics the cornerstone of which is Moody's KMV sells credit risk management tools and provides portfolio management and training services for financial institutions. The company's famous letter ratings (ranging from "Aaa" to "C") were invented by John Moody in 1909 and are still used today.

	Annual Growth	12/10	12/11	12/12	12/13	12/14
Sales ($ mil.)	13.2%	2,032.0	2,280.7	2,730.3	2,972.5	3,334.3
Net income ($ mil.)	18.1%	507.8	571.4	690.0	804.5	988.7
Market value ($ mil.)	37.8%	5,423.8	6,883.0	10,283.6	16,036.4	19,580.0
Employees	21.8%	4,500	6,100	6,800	8,400	9,900

MOOG, INC.

NYS: MOG A

400 Jamison Road
East Aurora, NY 14052-0018
Phone: 716 652-2000
Fax: -
Web: www.moog.com

CEO: John R. Scannell
CFO: Donald R. Fishback
HR: -
FYE: October 03
Type: Public

Moog (rhymes with "rogue") rules with its precision-control components and systems used in aerospace products industrial machinery and medical equipment. Servoactuators Moog's core product receive electrical signals from computers and then perform specific actions. Using its servoactuators Moog builds flight and control systems for commercial and military aircraft as well as hydraulic and electrical controls for automated industrial machinery wind turbines and control systems for satellites and spacecraft launch vehicles and missiles. It also makes infusion therapy pumps slip rings for CT scanners and motors used in devices for sleep apnea. Customers in the US make up more than half of sales.

	Annual Growth	10/11*	09/12	09/13	09/14*	10/15
Sales ($ mil.)	2.0%	2,330.7	2,469.5	2,610.3	2,648.4	2,525.5
Net income ($ mil.)	(0.8%)	136.0	152.5	120.5	158.2	131.9
Market value ($ mil.)	13.7%	1,197.4	1,390.2	2,139.8	2,518.2	2,001.0
Employees	0.9%	10,320	10,976	11,152	11,031	10,691

*Fiscal year change

MOONEY AEROSPACE GROUP LTD.

165 Al Mooney Rd. North
Kerrville TX 78028
Phone: 830-896-6000
Fax: 830-792-2054
Web: www.mooney.com

CEO: Sol Mayer
CFO: -
HR: -
FYE: December 31
Type: Private

A mooniac for action Mooney Aerospace Group wants to keep flying high. Through operating subsidiary Mooney Airplane the company produces three models of the M20 a high-performance single-engine piston-driven propeller aircraft: the Ovation 2 GX the Ovation 3 and the Acclaim. Mooney also offers financing insurance training aircraft upgrades and retrofit kits. Mooney Airplane was sold by its parent company to Swiss investment firm Allen Holdings & Finance in 2004 and then reacquired later that year as part of Mooney Aerospace Group's reorganization under Chapter 11. Mooney Aerospace Group emerged from bankruptcy protection in December 2004.

MOORE MEDICAL LLC

1690 New Britain Ave.
Farmington CT 06032-4066
Phone: 860-826-3600
Fax: 860-225-4440
Web: www.mooremedical.com

CEO: -
CFO: -
HR: -
FYE: December 31
Type: Subsidiary

Moore Medical is always striving to get more medical products to more medical facilities. The company distributes health care products to some 120000 health care practitioners and facilities in non-hospital settings. Moore Medical markets to physician offices and emergency clinics as well as correctional institutions municipalities and schools. It sells thousands of items including medical surgical and pharmaceutical supplies through the Internet catalogs telemarketing and a small sales force. The company also offers medical office equipment and furniture and handheld blood testing units. Pharmaceutical distributor McKesson owns Moore Medical which is part of the McKesson Medical-Surgical business.

MOOREFIELD CONSTRUCTION INC.

600 N TUSTIN AVE STE 210	CEO: Ann Moorefield
SANTA ANA, CA 927053781	CFO: –
Phone: 714-972-0700	HR: –
Fax: –	FYE: September 30
Web: www.moorefieldconstruction.com	Type: Private

Moorefield Construction wants to be more than just another big-box store builder. The company provides general contracting services for retail projects throughout Arizona California Colorado Idaho Nevada New Mexico Oregon Utah and Washington. Clients have included Lowe's Best Buy and Walgreen. The company operates from offices in Santa Ana and Sacramento. Moorefield Construction was founded in 1957 by the late Harold Moorefield and continues to be owned and operated by his family including his wife Ann (CEO) and their sons Mike (president) Larry (VP) and Hal (VP).

	Annual Growth	09/10	09/11	09/12	09/13	09/14
Sales ($ mil.)	27.7%	–	56.9	93.9	70.0	118.5
Net income ($ mil.)	(27.5%)	–	–	0.2	0.1	0.1
Market value ($ mil.)	–	–	–	–	–	–
Employees	–	–	–	–	–	52

MORAVIAN COLLEGE

1200 MAIN ST	CEO: –
BETHLEHEM, PA 18018-6650	CFO: –
Phone: 610-861-1300	HR: –
Fax: –	FYE: June 30
Web: www.home.moravian.edu	Type: Private

Moravian College America's sixth-oldest college was founded by the Moravian Church in 1742. The private school offers undergraduate coursework in the liberal arts and sciences with programs including chemistry business music and physics. It enrolls about 1500 students. Moravian College also includes the Moravian Theological Seminary an ecumenical graduate school offering master's degrees in divinity pastoral counseling and theological studies. Tuition and fees for the college total about $31000 per year.

	Annual Growth	06/08	06/09	06/10	06/11	06/12
Sales ($ mil.)	(2.6%)	–	57.0	53.6	58.5	52.7
Net income ($ mil.)	–	–	(11.6)	6.1	20.0	(1.9)
Market value ($ mil.)	–	–	–	–	–	–
Employees	–	–	–	–	–	450

MOREDIRECT INC.

1001 Yamato Rd. Ste. 200	CEO: –
Boca Raton FL 33431-4403	CFO: –
Phone: 561-237-3300	HR: –
Fax: 561-237-3390	FYE: December 31
Web: www.moredirect.com	Type: Subsidiary

MoreDirect provides a straightforward approach to technology purchases. The company serves the computer software and hardware procurement needs of corporate and government customers with its proprietary online software which enables them to search many distribution sources compare prices customize and place orders and track shipping in real time. MoreDirect provides its customers with access to information on products from about 2000 distributors and manufacturers including Apple Cisco Systems IBM Dell Hewlett-Packard Microsoft and Samsung Electronics. MoreDirect is a subsidiary of direct marketer PC Connection.

MOREHEAD MEMORIAL HOSPITAL INC

117 E KINGS HWY	CEO: Dana M. Weston
EDEN, NC 272885201	CFO: –
Phone: 336-623-9711	HR: Julie Ross
Fax: –	FYE: September 30
Web: www.morehead.org	Type: Private

Morehead Memorial Hospital is a not-for-profit community hospital that provides health care services to residents of North Carolina's Rockingham County. The hospital has about 110 acute care beds and provides general medical-surgical care including emergency services obstetrical care outpatient surgery and cancer treatment. It also provides home health care services and operates several ancillary facilities such as a freestanding diagnostic imaging facility and a physical rehabilitation center. The hospital's main campus (built in 1960) includes Morehead Nursing Center a long-term care facility with about 120 beds. Morehead Memorial Hospital traces its origin back to 1924.

	Annual Growth	09/10	09/11	09/12	09/13	09/14
Sales ($ mil.)	(7.8%)	–	103.5	112.7	90.7	81.2
Net income ($ mil.)	–	–	–	(2.3)	(1.8)	(7.1)
Market value ($ mil.)	–	–	–	–	–	–
Employees	–	–	–	–	–	850

MOREHOUSE COLLEGE (INC.)

830 WESTVIEW DR SW	CEO: –
ATLANTA, GA 303143776	CFO: Gwendolyn Sykes
Phone: 404-681-2800	HR: Tyra Smith
Fax: –	FYE: June 30
Web: www.giving.morehouse.edu	Type: Private

Morehouse College is the largest private liberal arts college for African-American men. Located three miles from downtown Atlanta the college has an enrollment of more than 2500 students. Facilities include the Leadership Center at Morehouse College Morehouse Research Institute and Andrew Young Center for International Affairs. The school has courses of study in business and economics humanities and social sciences and science and mathematics. It also offers a degree in engineering in conjunction with Georgia Institute of Technology. Notable alumni include civil rights activist Dr. Martin Luther King Jr. filmmaker Shelton "Spike" Lee and actor Samuel L. Jackson.

	Annual Growth	06/06	06/07	06/08*	04/10*	06/10
Sales ($ mil.)	–	–	–	0.0	93.5	99.2
Net income ($ mil.)	30328.3%	–	–	0.0	30.9	16.1
Market value ($ mil.)	–	–	–	–	–	–
Employees	–	–	–	–	–	700

*Fiscal year change

MORGAN KEEGAN & CO. INC.

Morgan Keegan Tower 50 N. Front St.	CEO: –
Memphis TN 38103	CFO: Charles D Maxwell
Phone: 901-524-4100	HR: –
Fax: 901-524-4197	FYE: December 31
Web: www.morgankeegan.com	Type: Subsidiary

Morgan Keegan is keen on more gain for its clients. Acquired by Raymond James from Regions Financial in 2012 the firm offers a range of financial advisory asset management and investment banking services. Working alongside its new parent company its Private Client Group offers individual investors access to stocks bonds mutual funds annuities managed accounts insurance mortgages equity research and financial planning services. Its investment banking practice focuses on financial institutions and tax-exempt entities. Morgan Keegan has more than 300 offices in nearly 20 states.

MORGAN LEWIS & BOCKIUS LLP

1701 Market St.
Philadelphia PA 19103
Phone: 215-963-5000
Fax: 215-963-5001
Web: www.morganlewis.com

CEO: –
CFO: James Diasil
HR: –
FYE: September 30
Type: Private - Partnershi

Long a leading Philadelphia law firm Morgan Lewis & Bockius these days extends its reach well beyond the City of Brotherly Love. The firm is home to some 1400 lawyers in about 25 offices throughout the US Europe and Asia. Morgan Lewis & Bockius also employs about 200 other legal professionals such as patent agents employee benefits advisors regulatory scientists and other specialists. The firm's multiple practice areas include business and finance intellectual property environmental law labor and employment real estate taxes and litigation. It provides services to clients of all sizes. Morgan Lewis & Bockius was founded in 1873 by Charles Morgan Jr. and Francis Lewis.

MORGAN PROPERTIES TRUST

160 Clubhouse Rd.
King of Prussia PA 19406
Phone: 610-265-2800
Fax: 610-265-5889
Web: www.morgan-properties.com

CEO: –
CFO: –
HR: –
FYE: December 31
Type: Private

Morgan Properties Trust wants to hand you the keys to a new apartment. The real estate investment trust (REIT) buys and manages middle-income apartments in the suburbs of Philadelphia New York the Baltimore/Washington DC area and other regions with high barriers to entry due to significant supply constraints. Its 90-plus properties contain more than 21500 apartments; its 30 properties in suburban Philly make up about 40% of revenue. To keep residents happy and living in its apartments Morgan offers newly renovated kitchens and bathrooms and Facebook and Twitter pages for each of its properties. In 2011 CEO Mitchell Morgan formed the company from his real estate business and filed to take it public.

MORGAN STANLEY

NYS: MS

1585 Broadway
New York, NY 10036
Phone: 212 761-4000
Fax: –
Web: www.morganstanley.com

CEO: James P. Gorman
CFO: Jonathan Pruzan
HR: Priya Shah
FYE: December 31
Type: Public

One of the world's top investment banks Morgan Stanley serves up a smorgasbord of financial services. The company operates in three primary business segments: institutional securities (capital raising corporate lending financial advisory services for corporate and institutional investors); wealth management group (brokerage and investment advisory services financial planning for individual investors and businesses); and investment management (services and products including alternative investments equity fixed income; merchant banking; investment activities). Morgan Stanley has a presence in more than 40 nations serving corporate institutional government and individual clients.

	Annual Growth	12/10	12/11	12/12	12/13	12/14
Assets ($ mil.)	(0.2%)	807,698.0	749,898.0	780,960.0	832,702.0	801,510.0
Net income ($ mil.)	(7.3%)	4,703.0	4,110.0	68.0	2,932.0	3,467.0
Market value ($ mil.)	9.3%	53,086.2	29,518.3	37,302.7	61,182.7	75,698.0
Employees	(2.8%)	62,542	61,899	57,061	55,794	55,802

MORGAN STANLEY SMITH BARNEY LLC

2000 Westchester Ave.
Purchase NY 10577
Phone: 914-225-5510
Fax: 914-225-6770
Web: www.morganstanleysmithbarney.com

CEO: James P Gorman
CFO: Ruth Porat
HR: –
FYE: December 31
Type: Joint Venture

Sometimes it takes a complicated family tree to create stellar lineage. Morgan Stanley Smith Barney (doing business as Morgan Stanley Wealth Management or MSWM) formed in 2009 as a joint venture between Morgan Stanley and Citigroup. MSWM is one of the world's largest retail brokerages boasting $1.7 trillion under management and a network of almost 17000 financial advisors. It serves individuals businesses and institutions including brokerage and investment advisory services financial and wealth planning credit and lending cash management annuities and insurance and retirement and trust services. Morgan Stanley upped its stake from 51% to 65% in 2012 as a prelude to acquiring the company outright.

MORGAN'S FOODS, INC.

NBB: MRFD

4829 Galaxy Parkway, Suite S
Cleveland, OH 44128
Phone: 216 359-9000
Fax: –

CEO: –
CFO: Kenneth L Hignett
HR: –
FYE: March 03
Type: Public

Fried chicken rules the roost at this restaurant company. Morgan's Foods is a leading operator of fast food restaurants franchised from YUM! Brands with nearly 100 locations in six states. Most of the company's estate more than 70 restaurants consists of KFC fried chicken outlets. Morgan's Foods also operates Taco Bell units and about 20 co-branded locations that combine two YUM! concepts (KFC Taco Bell Pizza Hut and A&W) in one building. Most of the company's eateries are located in Pennsylvania. Chairman and CEO Leonard Stein-Sapir owns more than 25% of the company.

	Annual Growth	03/09*	02/10	02/11	02/12*	03/13
Sales ($ mil.)	(1.6%)	92.5	90.5	89.9	82.2	86.9
Net income ($ mil.)	–	(1.4)	0.4	(1.0)	(1.7)	(0.1)
Market value ($ mil.)	–	0.0	0.0	0.0	2.6	5.1
Employees	(10.2%)	2,294	1,981	1,722	1,679	1,495

*Fiscal year change

MORGANS HOTEL GROUP CO

NMS: MHGC

475 Tenth Avenue
New York, NY 10018
Phone: 212 277-4100
Fax: –
Web: www.morganshotelgroup.com

CEO: Jason T. Kalisman
CFO: Richard Szymanski
HR: Roger Casalengo
FYE: December 31
Type: Public

Morgans Hotel Group (MHG) is part of a growing trend of staying in boutiques rather than shopping in them. The company owns (wholly or partially) and/or manages more than a dozen luxury boutique hotels in high profile markets. MHG also manages hotels in Isla Verde Puerto Rico and Playa del Carmen Mexico. The design of each location reflects its environs and all feature upscale restaurants and bars. Hotel brands include Delano Clift Hudson Mondrian and Royalton while restaurant and bar brands consist of Asia de Cuba and Skybar among others. The company developed its first property Morgans on Madison Avenue in New York in 1984.

	Annual Growth	12/10	12/11	12/12	12/13	12/14
Sales ($ mil.)	(0.1%)	236.4	207.3	189.9	236.5	235.0
Net income ($ mil.)	–	(81.4)	(85.4)	(55.7)	(44.2)	(50.7)
Market value ($ mil.)	(3.6%)	311.8	202.8	190.5	279.5	269.5
Employees	(13.3%)	4,600	4,500	5,000	4,400	2,600

MORGENTHALER LLP

Terminal Tower 50 Public Sq. Ste. 2700
Cleveland OH 44113
Phone: 216-416-7500
Fax: 216-416-7501
Web: www.morgenthaler.com

CEO: –
CFO: –
HR: –
FYE: December 31
Type: Private

Whether you need early stage financing or you and your colleagues need some help buying out the firm Morgenthaler can help. The firm operates through two divisions. Its venture capital operation provides funding to growth-stage technology and life sciences companies. Its buyout arm focuses on traditional management buyouts and corporate divestitures of manufacturing and business services firms in North America with annual revenues of $25 million to $250 million. Between both divisions Morgenthaler has approximately $3 billion of assets under management. The company has invested in more than 300 companies since it was founded in 1968 by managing partner David Morgenthaler.

MORNINGSTAR INC

NMS: MORN

22 West Washington Street
Chicago, IL 60602
Phone: 312 696-6000
Fax: –
Web: www.morningstar.com

CEO: Joseph (Joe) Mansueto
CFO: St ©phane Biehler
HR: Bevin Desmond
FYE: December 31
Type: Public

Morningstar offers a smorgasbord of financial information to individual professional and institutional investors via Internet software and print-based products. The company provides data on some 375000 investment products including stocks and mutual funds. It also provides real-time global market data on more than 8 million equities indexes futures options and commodities. Its Morningstar Style Box which provides a visual summary of a mutual fund's underlying investment style and Morningstar Ratings which rate past performance based on risk- and cost-adjusted returns have become fixtures on the investment landscape. Company founder Joe Mansueto owns about 50% of Morningstar.

	Annual Growth	12/10	12/11	12/12	12/13	12/14
Sales ($ mil.)	8.2%	555.4	631.4	658.3	698.3	760.1
Net income ($ mil.)	(2.4%)	86.4	98.4	108.1	123.5	78.3
Market value ($ mil.)	5.1%	2,353.9	2,636.4	2,786.2	3,463.0	2,869.6
Employees	3.9%	3,225	3,465	3,495	3,565	3,760

MORO CORPORATION

PINK SHEETS: MRCR

994 Old Eagle School Rd. Ste. 1000
Wayne PA 19087
Phone: 484-367-0300
Fax: 484-367-0305
Web: www.morocorp.com

CEO: –
CFO: –
HR: –
FYE: December 31
Type: Public

More is more for Moro Corporation. The industrial holding company owns a group of businesses that provide a range of materials and services for the commercial construction industry. Its J.M. Ahle J&J Sheet Metal and Whaling City Iron subsidiaries fabricate and distribute sheet metal products and reinforcing and structural steel in addition to other construction accessories. Titchener Iron Works specializes in architectural and ornamental metal. Its Rado Enterprises and Appolo Heating units provide plumbing and HVAC services while Rondout Electric provides electrical contracting services. Chairman and CEO David Menard owns the majority of the company.

MOROSO PERFORMANCE PRODUCTS INC.

80 Carter Dr.
Guilford CT 06437-2116
Phone: 203-453-6571
Fax: 203-453-6906
Web: www.moroso.com

CEO: –
CFO: John Ferretti
HR: –
FYE: September 30
Type: Private

Need more horsepower? Need more chrome bling under the hood? You may need more Moroso. Moroso Performance Products makes a wide range of automotive parts for motorsport racing and street-legal car enthusiasts. The company's lineup includes air cleaners chassis and suspension equipment fuel system equipment ignition wire and ignition components oil pans and oiling systems and valve covers. Moroso sells its products through independent distributors. The company was founded in 1968 by Dick Moroso featured by Hot Rod magazine as one of the 100 most influential people in the history of drag racing. His son Rick Moroso leads the company.

MORPHOTRUST USA INC.

296 Concord Rd.
Billerica MA 01821
Phone: 978-215-2400
Fax: 978-215-2500
Web: www.morphotrust.com

CEO: Robert Eckel
CFO: –
HR: Derek Shoffner
FYE: December 31
Type: Subsidiary

MorphoTrust USA (formerly L-1 Identity Solutions) builds trust with its credentials and biometrics-based recognition systems. MorphoTrust provides driver's licenses passports voter and other government and corporate-issued IDs as well as related data verification systems. Its biometrics products include face finger and iris recognition scanners. The company which operates in all 50 states serves US federal state and local governments and commercial entities; government contracts represent about 95% of revenues. In addition to its contract-based services MorphoTrust operates a network of more than 1200 ID service centers. Paris-based SAFRAN acquired the company for some $1 billion in mid-2011.

MORRIS BUSINESS DEVELOPMENT CO

NBB: MBDE

220 Nice Lane #108
Newport Beach, CA 92663
Phone: 949 444-9090
Fax: –
Web: www.morrisbdc.com

CEO: –
CFO: George Morris
HR: –
FYE: March 31
Type: Public

Morris Business Development hopes to get more out of life as an investment firm. The company formerly Electronic Media Central previously provided CD and DVD replication duplication and packaging services. However in 2007 the firm changed its name to Morris Business Development and became a managed investment company providing early stage capital strategic guidance and operational support to other businesses.

	Annual Growth	03/10	03/11	03/12	03/13	03/14
Sales ($ mil.)	11.5%	0.0	0.0	0.0	0.0	0.0
Net income ($ mil.)	–	(0.0)	(0.0)	(0.0)	(0.0)	(0.0)
Market value ($ mil.)	17.2%	0.9	0.3	0.4	0.9	1.7
Employees			1	1		–

MORRIS COMMUNICATIONS COMPANY LLC

725 Broad St.
Augusta GA 30901
Phone: 706-724-0851
Fax: 419-724-6167
Web: www.blockcommunications.com

CEO: –
CFO: Steve K Stone
HR: –
FYE: December 31
Type: Private

This company has something to say if you are reading or listening. A leading regional media holding company Morris Communications oversees a portfolio of operations that includes publishing and broadcasting. Subsidiary The Globe Pequot Press publishes books focused on leisure and recreation; other publishing operations include regional and special interest magazines (Alaska magazine Western Horseman) and a portfolio of visitor publications (Best Read Guides Where Guestbook). Morris Communications also operates more than 30 radio stations in four states. The family-owned company was started by William Morris Jr. in 1945. The Morris family also owns newspaper publisher Morris Publishing Group.

MORRIS HOSPITAL

150 W HIGH ST
MORRIS, IL 604501497
Phone: 815-942-2932
Fax: –
Web: www.morrishospital.org

CEO: Mark Steadham
CFO: –
HR: –
FYE: December 31
Type: Private

Feeling a little green in Grundy? Morris Hospital & Healthcare Centers will fix you right up! The system operates the 90 bed Morris Hospital as well as a handful of primary care physician practices and eight health care centers (the Braidwood Channahon Dwight Gardner Marseilles Minooka Morris and Newark Healthcare Centers) scattered throughout Grundy and four neighboring counties in northwest Illinois. Specialized services at Morris Hospital include neurology oncology pediatrics rehabilitation pain management and occupational health. It has a level II trauma center and a level II obstetrical unit. Not-for-profit Morris Hospital employs some 200 physicians across most medical specialties.

	Annual Growth	12/07	12/08*	03/09*	12/12	12/13
Sales ($ mil.)	2.7%	–	104.3	28.8	124.2	119.4
Net income ($ mil.)	28.2%	–	–	3.0	7.1	8.0
Market value ($ mil.)	–	–	–	–	–	–
Employees	–	–	–	–	–	525

*Fiscal year change

MORRIS PUBLISHING GROUP LLC

725 Broad St.
Augusta GA 30901
Phone: 706-724-0851
Fax: 816-325-7012
Web: www.ci.independence.mo.us

CEO: William S Morris IV
CFO: Steve K Stone
HR: –
FYE: December 31
Type: Subsidiary

No news would be bad news for Morris Publishing Group. The newspaper company has a portfolio of about a dozen daily newspapers serving small and midsized markets. Papers include The Augusta Chronicle (Georgia) The Florida Times-Union (Jacksonville) and The Topeka Capital-Journal (Kansas). The company also publishes several non-daily papers shoppers and regional interest magazines. Morris Publishing is controlled by the family of chairman William Morris through their Shivers Trading & Operating Company. The Morris family also owns affiliate Morris Communications which has book publishing outdoor advertising and radio broadcasting operations. Morris Publishing emerged from bankruptcy in 2010.

MORRISON & FOERSTER LLP

425 Market St.
San Francisco CA 94105-2482
Phone: 415-268-7000
Fax: 415-268-7522
Web: www.mofo.com

CEO: –
CFO: –
HR: Jill Nefkens
FYE: December 31
Type: Private - Partnershi

The City by the Bay is home to some pretty steep hills but San Francisco law firm Morrison & Foerster knows the legal lay of the land. Morrison & Foerster is known for its expertise in corporate transactions and litigation particularly in matters involving companies in the financial services life sciences and technology industries. Clients have included Apple Medtronic and Wells Fargo. The firm has more than 1000 lawyers in working from about 15 offices not only in California and elsewhere in the US but also in the Asia/Pacific region and in Europe. Today's Morrison & Foerster traces its roots to a firm founded by Alexander Morrison and Thomas O'Brien in 1883.

MORROW-MEADOWS CORPORATION

231 BENTON CT
CITY OF INDUSTRY, CA 91789-5213
Phone: 909-598-7700
Fax: –
Web: www.morrow-meadows.com

CEO: Karen V Price
CFO: Timothy D Langley
HR: –
FYE: October 31
Type: Private

Today and tomorrow Morrow-Meadows Corp. provides electrical contracting services including work on data communications and power distribution systems for commercial and industrial facilities in the western US primarily in California and Oregon. Its divisions include Oregon-based Cherry City Electric and Morrow-Meadows Corp. Northern California. The company provides project development design engineering and construction services on a range of projects such as shopping malls office buildings medical centers hotels parking garages theme parks and water treatment plants. The company counts among its customers Disney Intel Stanford University Hewlett-Packard and Kaiser Permanente.

	Annual Growth	10/0-1	10/00	10/01	10/04	10/11
Sales ($ mil.)	6.4%	–	158.5	201.3	177.5	312.1
Net income ($ mil.)	–	–	4.0	4.9	1.0	0.0
Market value ($ mil.)	–	–	–	–	–	–
Employees	–	–	–	–	–	1,200

MORSE OPERATIONS INC.

2850 S FEDERAL HWY
DELRAY BEACH, FL 334833216
Phone: 561-276-5000
Fax: –
Web: www.edmorse.com

CEO: Edward J Morse Jr
CFO: Dennis Macinnes
HR: Stacey Lebow
FYE: December 31
Type: Private

Morse Operations (dba Ed Morse Automotive Group) has been selling cars and trucks long enough to know the code of the road. It owns about a dozen new car dealerships across Florida most of them operating under the Ed Morse name. Dealerships house more than 15 franchises and 10 domestic and import car brands including Cadillac Fiat Chevrolet Buick GMC Scion Honda Mazda and Toyota. The company's Bayview Cadillac in Fort Lauderdale is one of the world's largest volume sellers of Cadillacs. Morse Operations also sells used cars provides parts and service and operates a fleet sales division. Founder and auto magnate the late Ed Morse entered the automobile business in 1946 with a 20-car rental fleet.

	Annual Growth	12/09	12/10	12/11	12/12	12/13
Sales ($ mil.)	7.9%	–	550.2	513.6	604.0	690.8
Net income ($ mil.)	136.4%	–	–	4.0	(6.1)	22.5
Market value ($ mil.)	–	–	–	–	–	–
Employees	–	–	–	–	–	1,295

MORTON INDUSTRIAL GROUP INC.

1021 W. Birchwood St.
Morton IL 61550
Phone: 309-266-7176
Fax: 309-263-1866
Web: www.mortonmetalcraft.com

CEO: Frank C Lukacs
CFO: –
HR: –
FYE: December 31
Type: Private

No veterinarian Morton Industrial Group helps to produce Cats and Deere. Through its subsidiaries the contract metal fabricator makes metal components and subassemblies for agricultural construction and industrial OEMs. Doing business as Morton Metalcraft it also produces sheet metal products such as engine enclosures and complex weldments for backhoes and tractors. Top customers include Caterpillar Deere Hallmark JLG Industries and Komatsu America. The company operates prototype tooling and related services too. In 2006 Brazos Private Equity Partners picked up Morton taking the company private. Morton filed for Chapter 11 protection from creditors in 2009 citing its debt load and plummeting sales.

MORTON SALT INC.

123 N. Wacker Dr.
Chicago IL 60606-1743
Phone: 312-807-2000
Fax: 312-807-2899
Web: www.mortonsalt.com

CEO: Christian Herrmann
CFO: Andrew J Kotlarz
HR: –
FYE: December 31
Type: Subsidiary

Life without salt would not only be bland but slippery; thankfully Morton Salt produces the grains in bulk and in shaker. It's the #1 consumer salt maker in the US marketed to industrial and retail customers under a big umbrella held by a girl in a yellow dress logo. In addition to household grocery staples (table kosher and canning salt) Morton makes consumer and professional salt for controlling ice on roads conditioning water as well as salt for the foodservice and food-manufacturing industries. The company extends its reach through Canadian Salt Company's Windsor brand. Morton owned by agrichemical giant K+S operates as part of its parent's salt business which generates about a third of all sales.

MORTON'S RESTAURANT GROUP INC.   NYSE: MRT

1510 W. Loop South
Houston TX 77027
Phone: 713-850-1010
Fax: 800-552-6379
Web: www.mortons.com

CEO: –
CFO: –
HR: –
FYE: December 31
Type: Public

Morton's Restaurant Group offers eateries with an aura the Rat Pack would have loved. The company operates about 65 upscale Morton's The Steakhouse locations that serve steak lobster and veal in an upscale setting featuring dark wood interiors and background music by Sinatra. In addition to fine food the chain is well-known for offering an extensive wine list and providing quality service. The restaurants are found in about 25 states and a handful of international markets. Morton's also operates an upscale Italian restaurant concept called Trevi within the Caesars Palace resort complex in Las Vegas. Landry's owner Tilman Fertitta formed Fertitta Morton's Restaurants Inc. to acquire Morton's in early 2012.

MOSAIC

4980 S 118TH ST
OMAHA, NE 68137-2200
Phone: 402-896-3884
Fax: –
Web: www.mosaicinfo.org

CEO: Linda Timmons
CFO: Cindy Schroeder
HR: –
FYE: June 30
Type: Private

Mosaic creates color in the lives of the disadvantaged. The not-for-profit organization provides individualized support and advocacy services living facilities education and employment for people with disabilities. The Christian organization serves some 3500 clients through 40 agencies across the US as well as select international locations. Services include case management foster care vocational training and supervised living arrangements. Mosaic also offers senior independent living services and support at select facilities. The organization is affiliated with the Evangelical Lutheran Church in America.

	Annual Growth	06/09	06/10	06/10	06/12	06/13
Sales ($ mil.)	6.0%	–	197.5	212.1	212.7	235.0
Net income ($ mil.)	–	–	7.9	11.3	4.1	(0.6)
Market value ($ mil.)	–	–	–	–	–	–
Employees	–	–	–	–	–	3,500

MOSAIC CO (THE)   NYS: MOS

3033 Campus Drive, Suite E490
Plymouth, MN 55441
Phone: 800 918-8270
Fax: 763 577-2990
Web: www.mosaicco.com

CEO: James (Joc) O'Rourke
CFO: Richard L. (Rich) Mack
HR: Katherine (Kate) Hoien
FYE: December 31
Type: Public

Lots of little pieces have joined together to form The Mosaic Company's big picture. The company ranks as one of the world's largest makers of phosphate and potash crop nutrients. Mosaic's potash operations position the company at the top of the industry along with Uralkali and PotashCorp. Mosaic ranks as the second-largest potash fertilizer company in North America (behind PotashCorp). Mosaic's potash mines are located in Canada and the US. The company does more than 50% of its business outside North America where India and Brazil are its biggest markets.

	Annual Growth	05/11	05/12	05/13*	12/13	12/14
Sales ($ mil.)	(3.1%)	9,937.8	11,107.8	9,974.1	4,765.9	9,055.8
Net income ($ mil.)	(25.8%)	2,514.6	1,930.2	1,888.7	340.0	1,028.6
Market value ($ mil.)	(13.6%)	26,040.2	17,524.3	22,353.8	17,373.6	16,778.2
Employees	5.7%	7,700	8,000	8,400	8,200	9,100

*Fiscal year change

MOSS ADAMS LLP

999 3rd Ave. Ste. 3300
Seattle WA 98104-4019
Phone: 206-302-6800
Fax: 206-652-2098
Web: www.mossadams.com

CEO: Chris Schmidt
CFO: Tom Bourne
HR: –
FYE: December 31
Type: Private - Partnershi

It may not be one of accounting's Big Four but it's not gathering any moss either. Moss Adams provides assurance tax and consultation services to businesses and organizations primarily in the western US. The company is structured into business groups that specialize in one or two industries ranging from financial services and manufacturing to retail and government. Services include due diligence transaction tax analysis business planning and corporate finance. Affiliate Moss Adams Wealth Advisors offers wealth management while Moss Adams Capital provides investment banking services.

MOSYS INC

NMS: MOSY

3301 Olcott Street
Santa Clara, CA 95054
Phone: 408 418-7500
Fax: –
Web: www.mosys.com

CEO: Leonard C. (Len) Perham
CFO: James W. (Jim) Sullivan
HR: Kristen Myburgh
FYE: December 31
Type: Public

MoSys (formerly Monolithic System Technology) works to keep its licensing mojo workin.' The company knows it can't match the Goliaths of the memory market so rather than spend a lot of time and money on development it focuses on licensing the designs of its embedded memory chips for the high-speed networking communications storage and computing markets. The fabless semiconductor company licenses its 1T-SRAM technology to manufacturers which in turn make the chips and embed them in communications and consumer electronics devices. With a declining number of customers using its 1T-SRAM applications however MoSys is shifting its focus to IC product sales.

	Annual Growth	12/10	12/11	12/12	12/13	12/14
Sales ($ mil.)	(23.3%)	15.6	14.1	6.1	4.4	5.4
Net income ($ mil.)	–	(23.1)	11.3	(27.6)	(24.8)	(32.7)
Market value ($ mil.)	(24.3%)	283.3	209.1	173.3	274.9	93.1
Employees	(8.0%)	162	143	95	104	116

MOTEL 6 OPERATING PARTERSHIP L.P.

4001 International Pkwy.
Carrollton TX 75007
Phone: 972-360-9000
Fax: 847-391-2253
Web: www.uop.com

CEO: Jim Amorosia
CFO: –
HR: –
FYE: December 31
Type: Subsidiary

Here's a motel you can find in the dark. With its homey advertising tag line "We'll leave the light on for you" Motel 6 is the established economy lodging chain with more than 1000 locations in the US and Canada. The brand caters primarily to budget-minded business travelers and families . It offers a limited selection of amenities including cable TV free local calling and complimentary coffee in the morning. It also has an extended-stay offshoot brand Studio 6 which has about 60 locations. Studio 6 provides larger suites equipped with kitchens at a reduced weekly rate. Motel 6 is the flagship budget brand of Accor North America. In 2012 Accor announced plans to sell Motel 6.

MOTHER MURPHY''S LABORATORIES INC.

2826 S ELM EUGENE ST
GREENSBORO, NC 274064435
Phone: 336-273-1737
Fax: –
Web: www.mothermurphys.com

CEO: –
CFO: Timothy Hansen
HR: –
FYE: October 31
Type: Private

This Mother Murphy does her cooking in an industrial-strength kitchen. Mother Murphy's Laboratories develops and manufactures dry and liquid natural and synthetic flavorings and extracts for the bakery beverage dairy tobacco confectionery pharmaceutical tobacco pet product confectionery and snack food industries. The company specializes in vanilla and vanilla variations offering-, a wide array of-, product types of everyone's favorite baking flavoring. Family owned and operated Mother Murphy's Laboratories was founded in 1945 by Kermit Murphy Sr. who named the company after his mother.-, Murphy died in 2008.

	Annual Growth	10/10	10/11	10/12	10/13	10/14
Sales ($ mil.)	(0.7%)	–	43.8	40.6	41.4	42.9
Net income ($ mil.)	(8.3%)	–	–	7.6	7.0	6.3
Market value ($ mil.)	–	–	–	–	–	–
Employees	–	–	–	–	–	92

MOTION INDUSTRIES INC.

1605 Alton Rd.
Birmingham AL 35201
Phone: 205-956-1122
Fax: 713-237-3777
Web: www.iwilson.com

CEO: Timothy P Breen
CFO: –
HR: –
FYE: December 31
Type: Subsidiary

Power transmission products may not be on anyone's Christmas list but Santa's workshop couldn't groove without the parts that Motion Industries sells. A subsidiary of Genuine Parts the company drives Genuine's industrial parts business segment by distributing a slew of bearings hoses material handling and linear motion products. Its short list of offerings includes electrical (motors and drives) and mechanical (belts clutches and chains) as well as fluid (pneumatic and hydraulic) power transmission replacement parts supplied by big brands like Bosch Rexroth Eaton NSK and Timken. Motion Industries sells 4.3 million parts and serves its customers through about 550 locations across North America.

MOTION PICTURE ASSOCIATION OF AMERICA

1600 Eye St. NW
Washington DC 20006
Phone: 202-293-1966
Fax: 202-296-7410
Web: www.mpaa.org

CEO: Christopher J Dodd
CFO: –
HR: –
FYE: December 31
Type: Private - Associatio

The Motion Picture Association of America (MPAA) is rated "E" for entertainment. The trade association represents the interests of major US film TV and home-entertainment companies in the nation's capitol of Washington DC. It is best known as the entity that provides the G PG PG13 R and NC-17 motion-picture ratings. It also leads the fight against piracy and copyright violations and provides TV-show ratings. MPAA's board of directors includes the studio heads of the six major movie companies including Walt Disney Studios Sony Pictures Paramount Pictures Fox Filmed Entertainment Universal Studios and Warner Bros.

MOTIVA ENTERPRISES LLC

700 Milam St.
Houston TX 77002
Phone: 713-277-8000
Fax: +31-31-10-485-0355
Web: www.hunterdouglasgroup.com

CEO: Dan Romasko
CFO: Marcel P Luijten
HR: –
FYE: December 31
Type: Joint Venture

Making money is a major motive behind Motiva Enterprises which operates the eastern and southeastern US downstream businesses of Shell Oil and Saudi Aramco. The company operates three refineries with a total capacity of 740000 barrels a day and it sells fuel at about 8300 Shell-branded gas stations. It also has stakes in about 40 refined product storage terminals (almost 20 billion barrels of storage capacity) in the East and Gulf Coast regions. Motiva and sister company Shell Oil Products US which operates in the West and Midwest together make up the #1 US gasoline retailer. Motiva is a 50-50 joint venture of Shell and Saudi Aramco the national oil company of Saudi Arabia.

MOTIVE INC.

12515 Research Blvd. Bldg. 5
Austin TX 78759-2220
Phone: 512-339-8335
Fax: 512-339-9040
Web: www.motive.com

CEO: Alfred Mockett
CFO: Michael Fitzpatrick
HR: –
FYE: December 31
Type: Subsidiary

Motive is driven to improve communications services management. The company offers software to help service providers manage processes and services in areas such as Internet service mobile broadband home networking and Internet protocol TV and phone. Telecommunications service providers worldwide use Motive's applications to provide their customers with online information diagnostic testing self-help tools Q&A chats mobile and home device management and supplier interconnections. Customers have included AT&T BSkyB and Vodafone. The company is a subsidiary of Alcatel-Lucent.

MOTO FRANCHISE CORPORATION

4444 Lake Center Dr.
Dayton OH 45426
Phone: 937-854-6686
Fax: 937-854-0140
Web: www.motophoto.com

CEO: Harry D Loyle
CFO: –
HR: –
FYE: December 31
Type: Private

You shoot they score. MOTO Franchise (formerly Moto Photo) franchises about 60 photo development stores in about 15 US states and the District of Columbia offering one-hour processing and finishing services such as enlargements digital reproductions and photo and video transfer to DVD. Its stores also sell photo-related items such as frames albums and digital camera accessories as well as offer personalization services for mugs T-shirts and other gift items. In addition some locations feature portrait studios. Moto Photo filed for bankruptcy in 2002 but majority shareholder and now CEO Harry Loyle led a group of franchise developers in buying the company out of bankruptcy the next year.

MOTORCAR PARTS OF AMERICA INC

NMS: MPAA

2929 California Street
Torrance, CA 90503
Phone: 310 212-7910
Fax: –
Web: www.motorcarparts.com

CEO: Selwyn Joffe
CFO: David Lee
HR: –
FYE: March 31
Type: Public

Motorcar Parts of America (MPA) is always ready for a fresh start. The company manufactures remanufactures and distributes alternators and starters for cars and all-weight trucks. MPA sells the remanufactured products to retailers and warehouse distributors which sell to do-it-yourself (DIY) consumers and to repair shops (DIFM or do-it-for-me) primarily in the US and Canada. Some of its top customers include retail chains AutoZone (more than 50% of sales) Advance Genuine Parts Pep Boys and O'Reilly Automotive. Although most of MPA's products are sold under its customers' private labels (about 90%) the company does market alternators and starters with its Quality-Built Reliance and Xtreme brands.

	Annual Growth	03/11	03/12	03/13	03/14	03/15
Sales ($ mil.)	16.9%	161.3	363.7	406.3	258.7	301.7
Net income ($ mil.)	(1.6%)	12.2	(48.5)	(91.5)	107.4	11.5
Market value ($ mil.)	18.7%	251.3	172.9	110.2	477.6	499.5
Employees	8.7%	1,689	3,340	2,756	2,270	2,362

MOTOROLA MOBILITY HOLDINGS INC.

NYSE: MMI

600 N. US Hwy. 45
Libertyville IL 60048
Phone: 847-523-5000
Fax: 515-296-3520
Web: www.linkp.com

CEO: –
CFO: Vanessa Wittman
HR: –
FYE: December 31
Type: Public

Motorola Mobility has a rich wireless heritage thanks to former parent Motorola Solutions (formerly Motorola). An early developer of mobile device technology Motorola Solutions spun off its handset business into the standalone company known as Motorola Mobility in early 2011. Motorola Mobility's products include handsets and smartphones tablets wireless accessories set-top boxes and video distribution products. Top customers include telecom carriers Verizon and Sprint. Though it has operations in some 40 countries more than half of sales comes from the US. Google acquired Motorola Mobility for about $12.5 billion in 2012.

MOTOROLA SOLUTIONS INC.

NYS: MSI

1303 East Algonquin Road
Schaumburg, IL 60196
Phone: 847 576-5000
Fax: 847 576-3477
Web: www.motorolasolutions.com

CEO: Gregory Q. (Greg) Brown
CFO: Gino A. Bonanotte
HR: Marty Rogers
FYE: December 31
Type: Public

Motorola has returned to its roots of providing communications equipment for public safety. The company sold its enterprise unit which provided rugged mobile computers rugged mobile computers tablets and barcode scanners in 2014 and will focus on its public safety and commercial customers. The enterprise sale came three years after Motorola got out of the mobile phone business. Now the company designs and makes two-way radios and wireless broadband products used in private voice and data networks and public safety communications systems. More than half of sales come from customers in the US. The company traces its roots to the 1930s when it made radios for police cars.

	Annual Growth	12/10	12/11	12/12	12/13	12/14
Sales ($ mil.)	(25.7%)	19,282.0	8,203.0	8,698.0	8,696.0	5,881.0
Net income ($ mil.)	19.7%	633.0	1,158.0	881.0	1,099.0	1,299.0
Market value ($ mil.)	64.9%	1,993.6	10,174.5	12,238.5	14,836.5	14,744.2
Employees	(26.4%)	51,000	23,000	22,000	21,000	15,000

MOTORSPORTS AUTHENTICS LLC

6301 Performance Dr.
Concord NC 28027
Phone: 704-454-4000
Fax: 704-454-4006
Web: www.motorsports-authentics.com

CEO: –
CFO: –
HR: –
FYE: September 30
Type: Joint Venture

Motorsports Authentics is in a racy business. The company designs and markets collector-quality die-cast miniature replicas of NASCAR and other racing vehicles. The firm also sells licensed motorsports apparel (T-shirts hats and jackets) and souvenirs and manages race car drivers' fan clubs. Its merchandise is sold in about 45 countries through some 10000 retailers 30 trackside stores and its goracing.com website. Through an exclusive agreement with QVC Motorsports Authentics sells directly to its collectors club. The company changed its name from Action Performance when it was acquired by 50:50 partners International Speedway and Speedway Motorsports for $245 million.

MOTT'S LLP

900 King St.
Rye Brook NY 10573
Phone: 914-612-4000
Fax: 914-612-4100
Web: www.motts.com

CEO: –
CFO: –
HR: –
FYE: December 31
Type: Subsidiary

Mott's would like to put the squeeze on fruit and vegetable juice rivals. The company is the top producer of branded applesauce and apple juice in the US. Mott's products which are available in family-sized and single-serve varieties include Mott's for Tots — single-serving vitamin-C-enhanced reduced-sugar juice drinks that come in a variety of flavors. The company's newer Mott's Medleys juices offer two fruit and veggie servings in each 8-oz. glass. To cater to adult consumers Mott's offers a "plus light" vitamin-fortified apple-juice beverage sweetened with Splenda. Part of the Dr Pepper Snapple Group Mott's sells its products throughout North America.

MOUNT CARMEL HEALTH SYSTEM

6150 E BROAD ST
COLUMBUS, OH 432131574
Phone: 614-234-6000
Fax: –
Web: www.mountcarmelhealth.com

CEO: Claus Von Zychlin
CFO: –
HR: –
FYE: June 30
Type: Private

Mount Carmel Health System cares for the sick in the greater Columbus area and central Ohio. The health care system boasts 1500 physicians at three general hospitals and a specialty surgical hospital offering a comprehensive range of medical and surgical services including cardiovascular care. Mount Carmel Health also operates outpatient centers including primary care and specialty physicians' practices and it offers home health care services. The hospital group is part of Trinity Health one of the largest Catholic health care systems in the US.

	Annual Growth	06/04	06/05	06/09	06/10	06/13
Sales ($ mil.)	1.2%	–	1,088.6	167.6	198.3	1,195.8
Net income ($ mil.)	–	–	–	0.0	2.3	89.4
Market value ($ mil.)	–	–	–	–	–	–
Employees	–	–	–	–	–	8,000

MOUNT CLEMENS REGIONAL MEDICAL CENTER INC.

1000 HARRINGTON ST
MOUNT CLEMENS, MI 480432920
Phone: 586-493-8000
Fax: –

CEO: Tom Brisse
CFO: –
HR: –
FYE: September 30
Type: Private

Mount Clemens Regional Medical Center (doing business as McLaren Medical Center-Macomb) is an general acute care hospital serving the Macomb County area of suburban Detroit. With about 290 beds the hospital offers such specialties as cardiac and cancer care family practice services home and hospice care and emergency care. The McLaren Health Care-controlled company also operates three prompt care centers in nearby townships as well as a wound treatment clinic. Of the more than 420 physicians on staff at the hospital more than 100 are family medicine and internal medicine specialists who provide primary care.

	Annual Growth	05/04	05/05*	09/08	09/09	09/13
Sales ($ mil.)	–	–	0.0	264.4	277.8	303.6
Net income ($ mil.)	4.9%	–	–	14.6	11.7	18.6
Market value ($ mil.)	–	–	–	–	–	–
Employees	–	–	–	–	–	2,249
						*Fiscal year change

MOUNTAIN VALLEY SPRING COMPANY LLC

150 Central Ave.
Hot Springs National Park AR 7
Phone: 501-624-1635
Fax: 501-623-5135
Web: www.mountainvalleyspring.com

CEO: –
CFO: –
HR: –
FYE: December 31
Type: Private

In a world of bottled water hope springs eternal for Mountain Valley Spring. Through its Mountain Valley Spring Water division the company bottles and sells natural spring water collected from three neighboring natural springs via such brands as Mountain Valley Spring Water Mountain Valley Sparkling Water and Diamond Spring Water. The company uses both glass and PET (polyethylene terephthalate resin) bottles. Its Veriplas division makes and sells preforms and finished PET bottles ranging in sizes from 10 ounces to 4 gallons. The company sells its bottled water through grocers such as H-E-B Sprouts Farmers Market and Whole Foods Market. Mountain Valley Spring filed to go public in late 2011.

MOUNTAIRE CORPORATION

204 E 4th St
North Little Rock AR 72114-540
Phone: 501-372-6524
Fax: 501-372-3972
Web: mountaire.com

CEO: –
CFO: Dabbs Cavin
HR: –
FYE: October 31
Type: Private

These birds breathe the mountain air: Mountaire is a leading supplier of private-label chicken and value-added chicken products to supermarkets and foodservice customers worldwide. The company's chicken production business (Mountaire Farms) maintains breeding and chicken-processing facilities in Delaware Maryland and North Carolina. The company sells its products under names such as Black Label (aimed at the foodservice market) Blue Label (wholesale) and Bo-San Roasters (Asian market in the US). Mountaire Grain and Feed produces poultry feeds and operates grain elevators for corn soybeans wheat and barley. Mountaire was founded in 1971 but the company's roots in the feed business date back to 1914.

MOVADO GROUP, INC.

NYS: MOV

650 From Road, Suite 375
Paramus, NJ 07652-3556
Phone: 201 267-8000
Fax: –
Web: www.movadogroup.com

CEO: Efraim Grinberg
CFO: Sallie A. DeMarsilis
HR: –
FYE: January 31
Type: Public

Movado Group knows that time is of the essence. Its watch brands — including namesake Movado Concord and Ebel as well as the licensed Coach Tommy Hilfiger Hugo Boss Lacoste and Juicy Couture lines — are sold worldwide. While its watches range in price from about $75 to $10000 for luxury designs the watch maker is focused on the middle market. Movado sells its watches to major jewelry store and department store chains (including Nordstrom and Macy's) as well as to independent jewelers (such as Zale Corp.). The company operates a growing chain of more than 35 outlet stores across the US. The family of the late Gerry Grinberg who founded Movado controls about 70% of the company's voting power.

	Annual Growth	01/11	01/12	01/13	01/14	01/15
Sales ($ mil.)	11.3%	382.2	468.1	505.5	570.3	587.0
Net income ($ mil.)	–	(44.9)	32.0	57.1	50.9	51.8
Market value ($ mil.)	13.6%	356.0	454.9	903.3	932.7	593.7
Employees	2.6%	1,000	1,000	1,100	1,100	1,110

MOVE INC

NMS: MOVE

10 Almaden Blvd, Suite 800
San Jose, CA 95113
Phone: 408 558-7100
Fax: –
Web: www.move.com

CEO: Steven H Berkowitz
CFO: Rachel C Glaser
HR: –
FYE: December 31
Type: Public

For Move real estate is more about location on the Web. The company provides real estate and move-related information and services through its flagship Move.com REALTOR.com and Moving.com websites. Its REALTOR.com lists some 4 million homes for sale. In addition its Top Producer produce is a customer relationship management application for real estate agents. Revenue primarily comes from advertising (cost-per-click text link and display ads) and software sales. The company attracts visitors via agreements with partners such as the National Association of Realtors (REALTOR.com is the official website of NAR). Move is a portfolio company of private equity firm Elevation Partners.

	Annual Growth	12/08	12/09	12/10	12/11	12/12
Sales ($ mil.)	(4.8%)	242.1	212.0	197.5	191.7	199.2
Net income ($ mil.)	–	(27.6)	(6.9)	(15.5)	7.3	5.6
Market value ($ mil.)	47.5%	63.0	65.3	101.1	248.7	297.9
Employees	(5.5%)	1,181	951	966	889	943

MOZILLA FOUNDATION

650 Castro St. Ste. 300
Mountain View CA 94041-2021
Phone: 650-903-0800
Fax: 650-903-0875
Web: www.mozilla.org

CEO: Mark Surman
CFO: –
HR: –
FYE: December 31
Type: Private - Not-for-Pr

Microsoft's Internet Explorer (IE) may have subdued Netscape in the "browser wars" of the 1990s but Mozilla's Firefox rose from the ashes with renewed vigor. Firefox has clawed market share away from IE over the years (now at about 25%) only to now be harassed itself by the meteoric rise of Google's Chrome being overtaken by the browser in usage share at the end of 2011. The Mozilla Foundation was created in 2003 to carry on the open-source development work of the mozilla.org project (spun off from Netscape in 1998). For-profit subsidiary Mozilla Corporation (spun off in 2005) oversees product development marketing and distribution.

MPHASE TECHNOLOGIES INC.

NBB: XDSL

777 Passaic Avenue, Suite 375
Clifton, NJ 07012
Phone: 973 256-3737
Fax: –
Web: www.mphasetech.com

CEO: Ronald A Durando
CFO: Martin S Smiley
HR: –
FYE: June 30
Type: Public

mPhase Technologies has lots of plans for potential profits. mPhase a development-stage company designed broadband communications equipment that lets telephone companies provide television over DSL lines. It has since shifted its development to middleware that allows telephone companies to deliver voice Internet and television service over Internet protocol (IP). It plans to market its systems to phone companies in areas with relatively little multi-channel television access such as international markets and the rural US. It is also developing power cells that utilize nanotechnology through its AlwaysReady subsidiary.

	Annual Growth	06/11	06/12	06/13	06/14	06/15
Sales ($ mil.)	119.5%	0.0	0.0	0.0	0.6	1.1
Net income ($ mil.)	–	(0.5)	(8.8)	(0.3)	(5.9)	(1.1)
Market value ($ mil.)	–	0.0	0.0	0.0	0.0	0.0
Employees	(4.5%)	6	5	5	6	5

MPI RESEARCH INC.

54943 N. Main St.
Mattawan MI 49071
Phone: 269-668-3336
Fax: 269-668-4151
Web: www.mpiresearch.com

CEO: William U Parfet
CFO: Paul R Sylvester
HR: –
FYE: December 31
Type: Private

MPI Research helps drug developers answer a crucial question: Is it safe? The contract research organization (CRO) specializes in providing preclinical and early clinical research services to pharmaceutical medical device chemical biotechnology and agricultural development companies as well as regulatory and other government agencies. Its toxicology testing services investigate and determine the safety and dosage levels of substances being considered for use in drugs pesticides petrochemicals and food additives. MPI Research which serves clients in more than 30 countries also offers contract bioanalytical pharmacology discovery diagnostic and animal testing services.

MPLX LP

NYS: MPLX

200 E. Hardin Street
Findlay, OH 45840
Phone: 419 672-6500
Fax: –
Web: www.mplx.com

CEO: Gary R Heminger
CFO: –
HR: –
FYE: December 31
Type: Public

MPLX might take more than 30 minutes to deliver crude oil through its pipeline system to the refinery. MPLX was formed by Marathon Petroleum Corporation (MPC) in March 2012 to take over a portion of its midstream operations. MPLX has an indirect 51% stake in about 2800 miles of pipeline across nine states in the Midwest and Gulf Coast as well as a Mississippi River barge dock that can handle 80 million barrels per day of crude oil and tank farms located in Illinois and Indiana. (MPC owns the other 49% of these assets.) MPLX also owns outright a butane cavern in West Virginia with a storage capacity of 1 million barrels. The company began publicly trading in October 2012.

	Annual Growth	08/11	08/12*	12/12	12/13	12/14
Sales ($ mil.)	–	0.0	–	461.9	486.3	548.3
Net income ($ mil.)	–	0.0	–	130.8	77.9	121.3
Market value ($ mil.)	–	0.0	–	2,555.4	3,649.2	6,021.1
Employees	–	–	–	–	–	–

*Fiscal year change

MPW INDUSTRIAL SERVICES GROUP INC.

9711 Lancaster Rd. SE
Hebron OH 43025
Phone: 800-827-8790
Fax: 315-685-3361
Web: www.welchallyn.com

CEO: Monte R Black
CFO: –
HR: –
FYE: June 30
Type: Private

MPW Industrial Services Group knows it takes more than a bar of soap to clean a chemical plant. MPW provides industrial-strength cleaning services for the foul deposits and caustic corrosion created by such processing facilities as well as those in the automotive energy manufacturing and refining industries. The company offers facility maintenance container cleaning and water treatment services; procedures include dry and wet vacuuming power washing water blasting and cryojetic (dry ice) cleaning. Its water unit provides deionization filtration and reverse osmosis for pollution control and chemical cleaning applications. MPW has a network of 40 offices in the US and also serves customers in Canada.

MRC GLOBAL INC

NYS: MRC

2 Houston Center, 909 Fannin Street, Suite 3100
Houston, TX 77010
Phone: 877 294-7574
Fax: –
Web: www.mrcglobal.com

CEO: Andrew R. (Andy) Lane
CFO: James E. (Jim) Braun
HR: Jason Graves
FYE: December 31
Type: Public

MRC Global (formerly McJunkin Red Man) is one the world's largest suppliers of parts and supplies used by energy and industrial customers. Operating from 400-plus locations predominantly in North America the company distributes more than 200000 pipe valves and fittings (PVF) as well as general and specialty products. A major slice of MRC Global's sales comes from maintenance repair and operations (MRO) contracts including procurement warehousing and inventory management. Core customers are oil and gas exploration and production giants as well as transmission and storage oil refining and petrochemical processing companies such as BP Exxon Mobil and Valero.

	Annual Growth	12/10	12/11	12/12	12/13	12/14
Sales ($ mil.)	11.5%	3,845.5	4,832.4	5,570.9	5,230.8	5,933.2
Net income ($ mil.)	–	(51.8)	29.0	118.0	152.1	144.1
Market value ($ mil.)	(26.2%)	–	–	2,836.2	3,293.6	1,546.7
Employees	6.1%	–	4,100	4,780	5,150	4,900

MRI INTERVENTIONS INC

OTC: MRIC

5 Musick
Irvine, CA 92618
Phone: 949 900-6833
Fax: –
Web: www.mriinterventions.com

CEO: Francis P Grillo
CFO: Harold A Hurwitz
HR: –
FYE: December 31
Type: Public

SurgiVision designs products with surgical focus. A medical devices company SurgiVision develops imaging technologies and precision instruments (i.e. needles that deliver radiation) designed for surgeons performing minimally invasive procedures by way of MRI (magnetic resonance imaging) scanners. The company received FDA approval for its first commercial product the ClearPoint system for use in neurological procedures in 2010. It also has candidates in earlier stages of development including its ClearTrace and SafeLead products which are designed for cardiac procedures. SurgiVision was established in 1998; it filed to go public through an IPO in 2009.

	Annual Growth	12/10	12/11	12/12	12/13	12/14
Sales ($ mil.)	7.8%	2.7	3.8	5.1	3.9	3.6
Net income ($ mil.)	–	(9.5)	(8.3)	(5.7)	(7.1)	(4.5)
Market value ($ mil.)	(27.9%)	–	–	119.7	108.5	62.2
Employees	22.8%	–	20	25	35	37

MRIGLOBAL

425 VOLKER BLVD
KANSAS CITY, MO 64110-2241
Phone: 816-753-7600
Fax: –
Web: www.mriglobal.org

CEO: Thomas M Sack
CFO: R Thomas Fleener
HR: –
FYE: June 30
Type: Private

MRIGlobal provides contract research services for government and private-sector clients in fields such as agricultural and food safety analytical chemistry biological sciences energy engineering environment health sciences information technology and national defense. The institute operates laboratories and agricultural research centers in Florida Kansas Maryland Missouri North Carolina and Washington DC. MRIGlobal also manages the US Department of Energy's National Renewable Energy Laboratory in Golden Colorado. Work related to biological and chemical defense accounts for most of MRIGlobal's sales. The not-for-profit organization was founded in 1944.

	Annual Growth	06/09	06/10	06/11	06/12	06/13
Sales ($ mil.)	(3.1%)	–	547.6	625.9	17.2	497.6
Net income ($ mil.)	(22.9%)	–	4.3	6.4	(0.1)	2.0
Market value ($ mil.)	–	–	–	–	–	–
Employees	–	–	–	–	–	2,547

MRV COMMUNICATIONS, INC.

NAS: MRVC

20415 Nordhoff Street
Chatsworth, CA 91311
Phone: 818 773-0900
Fax: –
Web: www.mrv.com

CEO: Mark J Bonney
CFO: Stephen Krulik
HR: Jacqueline Hickey
FYE: December 31
Type: Public

MRV Communications puts the buzz in optical communications. MRV supplies the switching routing Ethernet optical transport and console management equipment used in voice data and video traffic by telecommunications carriers data centers and labs. It also provides network system design services as well as integrated network products and services. It sells to cable operators networking services providers Internet and telecom companies and governments worldwide. About two-thirds of sales are outside the US mostly in Europe.

	Annual Growth	12/10	12/11	12/12	12/13	12/14
Sales ($ mil.)	(10.1%)	263.9	266.8	151.7	166.2	172.1
Net income ($ mil.)	–	48.7	(6.8)	5.7	(6.8)	(12.2)
Market value ($ mil.)	53.5%	13.2	6.4	76.1	79.2	73.3
Employees	(12.0%)	743	678	414	420	445

MSB FINANCIAL CORP

NMS: MSBF

1902 Long Hill Road
Millington, NJ 07946-0417
Phone: 908 647-4000
Fax: –
Web: www.millingtonsb.com

CEO: –
CFO: –
HR: –
FYE: June 30
Type: Public

MSB Financial Corp. is the holding company for Millington Savings Bank a five-branch bank located in north central New Jersey. Millington Savings Bank offers checking savings money market and CD accounts as well as traditional and Roth IRAs to individuals. For small businesses the bank offers checking accounts and courier service. It does not offer credit cards. More than half of its loan portfolio is made up of residential mortgages while home equity loans account for about 20%. Commercial mortgages construction loans and business and consumer loans round out its portfolio. MSB Financial Corp. was founded in 2004; Millington Savings Bank traces it roots back to 1911 when it was founded as Millington Building and Loan.

	Annual Growth	06/10	06/11	06/12	06/13	06/14
Assets ($ mil.)	(1.0%)	358.7	349.5	347.3	352.6	345.2
Net income ($ mil.)	5.2%	0.8	0.7	0.5	(1.4)	1.0
Market value ($ mil.)	0.6%	39.5	27.4	27.6	36.8	40.5
Employees	1.0%	51	52	53	65	53

MSC INDUSTRIAL DIRECT CO., INC.

NYS: MSM

75 Maxess Road
Melville, NY 11747
Phone: 516 812-2000
Fax: 516 349-7096
Web: www.mscdirect.com

CEO: Erik Gershwind
CFO: Rustom F. Jilla
HR: –
FYE: August 29
Type: Public

Many a small thing has been made large by MSC Industrial Direct's business; the company stands as one the largest US direct suppliers of industrial products. It distributes fasteners and measuring instruments cutting tools and plumbing supplies to customers in metalworking and maintenance repair and overhaul (MRO) businesses. MSC Industrial stocks more than 1 million products from 3000 suppliers. The company sells — mainly to small and mid-size firms — through its master catalog (which runs to several thousand pages) promotional mailings and brochures as well as via telemarketing and the Internet.

	Annual Growth	08/11*	09/12*	08/13	08/14	08/15
Sales ($ mil.)	9.5%	2,021.8	2,355.9	2,457.6	2,787.1	2,910.4
Net income ($ mil.)	1.4%	218.8	259.0	238.0	236.1	231.3
Market value ($ mil.)	3.4%	3,637.2	4,272.9	4,686.0	5,557.9	4,158.8
Employees	9.4%	4,644	4,982	6,257	6,576	6,642

*Fiscal year change

MSCI INC

NYS: MSCI

7 World Trade Center, 250 Greenwich Street, 49th Floor
New York, NY 10007
Phone: 212 804-3900
Fax: –
Web: www.msci.com

CEO: Henry A. Fernandez
CFO: Robert Qutub
HR: Michelle (Mitch) Davidson
FYE: December 31
Type: Public

You ask your asset manager how your portfolio is doing but who does he ask? Probably MSCI. The company formerly Morgan Stanley Capital International manages more than 145000 daily equity fixed income and hedge fund indices for use by large asset management firms. MSCI is organized through two business segments. Its Performance and Risk business provides equity indices portfolio risk and performance analytics credit analytics and environmental social and governance (ESG) products under brands such as MSCI RiskMetrics and Barra. Its Governance business provides corporate governance and specialized financial research and analysis. MSCI has about 7500 clients across more than 80 countries.

	Annual Growth	12/10	12/11	12/12	12/13	12/14
Sales ($ mil.)	92.5%	72.5	900.9	950.1	1,035.7	996.7
Net income ($ mil.)	112.9%	13.8	173.5	184.2	222.6	284.1
Market value ($ mil.)	5.0%	4,366.3	3,690.5	3,473.1	4,899.8	5,316.7
Employees	6.4%	–	2,429	2,759	3,261	2,926

MSD CAPITAL L.P.

645 5th Ave. 21st Fl.
New York NY 10022-5910
Phone: 212-303-1650
Fax: 212-303-1634
Web: www.msdcapital.com

CEO: –
CFO: MEI-Ying Tsai
HR: –
FYE: December 31
Type: Private - Partnershi

Poor poor Michael Dell: too much money and nowhere to put it. That's where MSD Capital comes in. Taking its name from Dell's initials the investment firm handles the Dell Inc. founder's personal investments in companies outside his namesake business. Dell bankrolled MSD Capital with approximately $1 billion in seed money in 1998. The firm makes long-term investments in public firms and private equity (typically in the $50 million to $200 million range) including leveraged buyouts and management buyouts. It also invests in real estate and occasionally in other investment firms' limited partnership funds. MSD Capital is part of an investment partnership that is buying failed bank IndyMac for $13.9 billion..

MSG NETWORK INC

NYS: MSGN

11 Pennsylvania Plaza
New York, NY 10001
Phone: 212 465-6400
Fax: –
Web: www.thegarden.com

CEO: Andrea Greenberg
CFO: Sean Creamer
HR: Alan (Al) Gershowitz
FYE: June 30
Type: Public

Like the city it calls home Madison Square Garden (MSG) is the entertainment company that never sleeps. While known for its legendary Madison Square Garden Arena the company owns or operates additional venues including Radio City Music Hall (home of the leggy Rockettes) the Chicago Theatre and the Beacon Theater. MSG also owns sports teams the New York Knicks of the NBA and the NHL's New York Rangers which operate as part of the company's MSG Sports segment. Its MSG Media unit distributes programming through outlets such as cable music network Fuse and MSG Entertainment produces or hosts live shows at the company's various venues. MSG was spun off from Rainbow Media Holdings (now AMC Networks) in 2010.

	Annual Growth	06/11	06/12	06/13	06/14	06/15
Sales ($ mil.)	30.2%	564.3	1,284.0	1,340.8	1,555.6	1,621.6
Net income ($ mil.)	74.3%	27.6	106.5	142.4	115.1	254.7
Market value ($ mil.)	32.0%	2,086.7	2,837.8	4,490.9	4,733.5	6,328.2
Employees	2.0%	8,605	8,518	8,782	9,000	9,300

MSGI TECHNOLOGY SOLUTIONS INC.

OTC: MSGI

NASA Ames Research Center Bldg. 19
Moffett Field CA 94035
Phone: 212-605-0245
Fax: 212-605-0222
Web: msgisecurity.com

CEO: J Jeremy Barbera
CFO: Richard Mitchell
HR: –
FYE: June 30
Type: Public

MSGI Technology Solutions Solutions (formerly Security Solutions) invests in companies that make equipment and software for security safety and surveillance applications. It typically acquires controlling interests in early-stage early growth technology and software development businesses. Majority-owned Innalogic develops software applications that combine biometric sensor text and/or video data for wireless mobile devices to aid in emergency response. The company's Future Developments America subsidiary makes audio and video electronic surveillance equipment. MSGI Technology Solutions has licensing agreements with Hyundai Syscomm and Apro Media through which it aggregates and configures security systems.

MSX INTERNATIONAL INC.

1950 Concept Dr.
Warren MI 48091
Phone: 248-829-6300
Fax: 248-829-6030
Web: www.msxi.com

CEO: Frederick K Minturn
CFO: R Michael Muraske
HR: –
FYE: December 31
Type: Private

MSX International (MSXI) is all revved up to provide outsourced business services. The company provides engineering human resources services and other outsourced business services (including marketing document management and purchasing) to clients primarily from the auto industry. Its offerings also include temporary and permanent staffing executive search career management training product engineering and supply chain management. MSXI has served such major US and European automotive companies as Ford Toyota Mitsubishi Motors and General Motors. Established in 1996 MSXI has a presence in more than 30 countries.

MTM TECHNOLOGIES INC.

PINK SHEETS: MTMC

1200 High Ridge Rd.
Stamford CT 06905
Phone: 203-975-3700
Fax: 203-975-3701
Web: www.mtm.com

CEO: Steven Stringer
CFO: Rosemario Milano
HR: Cheryl Smith
FYE: March 31
Type: Public

When it comes to business technology MTM Technologies has all sorts of technological bases covered. The company provides a variety of IT services and products for Global 2000 and midsized companies. Among MTM Technologies' specialties are virtualization endpoint management unified communications network infrastructure storage and managed services. The company handles products from a variety of suppliers including Cisco Systems Citrix EMC Hewlett-Packard and NetApp. FirstMark Capital which is managed by MTM chairman Gerald Poch owns a majority interest in MTM Technologies.

MTR GAMING GROUP, INC.

NMS: MNTG

State route 2 South, P.O. Box 356	CEO: Gary L Carano
Chester, WV 26034	CFO: Robert M Jones
Phone: 304 387-8000	HR: –
Fax: –	FYE: December 31
Web: www.mtrgaming.com	Type: Public

Gamblers looking beyond casino games can climb the summit of MTR Gaming Group. The company operates three regional casino hotels in the US. Its Mountaineer Racetrack and Gaming Resort in Chester West Virginia includes horse racing and wagering in addition to some 2500 slot machines 25 poker tables and approximatelu 60 additional table games. The Mountaineer resort also boasts a hotel and convention center as well as a fitness center a theater and several restaurants. Its Presque Isle Downs & Casino in Erie Pennsylvania also has horse racing and wagering as well as about 2000 slot machines 50 table games and dining options. MTR also owns Scioto Downs the operator of a harness racetrack in Ohio.

	Annual Growth	12/08	12/09	12/10	12/11	12/12
Sales ($ mil.)	1.0%	470.9	444.2	424.9	428.1	490.0
Net income ($ mil.)	–	(17.7)	(22.5)	(5.1)	(50.4)	(5.7)
Market value ($ mil.)	25.5%	46.5	36.0	56.2	51.8	115.5
Employees	(2.7%)	2,900	2,300	2,500	2,600	2,600

MTS MEDICATION TECHNOLOGIES INC.

2003 Gandy Blvd. North Ste. 800	CEO: Todd E Siegel
St. Petersburg FL 33702	CFO: –
Phone: 727-576-6311	HR: –
Fax: 727-579-8067	FYE: March 31
Web: www.mts-mt.com	Type: Private

MTS Medication Technologies gives pills a safe home until they get to the patient who needs them. Through a pair of subsidiaries — MTS Packaging Systems and MTS Medication Technologies International — the company makes medication punch cards and other medication and vitamin dispensing systems. Institutional pharmacies use them to conveniently and accurately package the drugs they give to patients. The company's custom technology allows caregivers at some 6000 pharmacies located within assisted-living nursing and correctional facilities to administer medicine or vitamins to many people while keeping close tabs on dosages. Rival company Omnicell bought MTS Medication Technologies in 2012.

MTS SYSTEMS CORP.

NMS: MTSC

14000 Technology Drive	CEO: Jeffrey A. (Jeff) Graves
Eden Prairie, MN 55344	CFO: Jeffrey P. Oldenkamp
Phone: 952 937-4000	HR: –
Fax: –	FYE: October 03
Web: www.mts.com	Type: Public

In this world nothing is certain but death and taxes — and those things tested by MTS Systems. The company produces testing systems that simulate repeated or harsh conditions to determine mechanical behavior of materials products and structures. Its systems are used worldwide in infrastructure markets from inspecting steel to locomotive rail testing. MTS caters to auto makers with road simulators. In aerospace MTS tests aircraft fatigue. Services include maintenance and training. MTS also supplies industrial sensors (Temposonics) to increase machine efficiency and safety. About three-quarters of the company's customers operate outside the US.

	Annual Growth	10/11*	09/12	09/13	09/14*	10/15
Sales ($ mil.)	4.8%	467.4	542.3	569.4	564.3	563.9
Net income ($ mil.)	(2.8%)	50.9	51.6	57.8	42.0	45.5
Market value ($ mil.)	17.2%	457.5	799.6	950.4	1,026.4	862.0
Employees	4.6%	2,003	2,147	2,299	2,180	2,400
						*Fiscal year change

MTV NETWORKS COMPANY

1515 Broadway	CEO: Judy McGrath
New York NY 10036	CFO: Jacques Tortoroli
Phone: 212-258-8000	HR: –
Fax: 212-846-1804	FYE: December 31
Web: www.mtv.com	Type: Subsidiary

This company still hopes you want your MTV — and maybe a few other cable channels. MTV Networks operates a leading portfolio of cable TV channels anchored by its music video networks MTV VI11 and CMT (Country Music Television). It operates channels for kids through Nickelodeon the young-male-oriented Spike TV Comedy Central and gay and lesbian channel Logo. Through a total of some 170 branded channels the company reaches 640 million households in more than 160 countries. MTV Networks also produces movies through MTV Films (in association with sister firm Paramount Pictures) and distributes content online. MTV Networks is a unit of media giant Viacom.

MUELLER (PAUL) CO.

NBB: MUEL

1600 West Phelps Street	CEO: David T. Moore
Springfield, MO 65802	CFO: Kenneth E. Jeffries
Phone: 417 575-9000	HR: –
Fax: 417 575-9669	FYE: December 31
Web: www.paulmueller.com	Type: Public

Paul Mueller Company is in the "moo-d" for more than milk. The company manufactures stainless-steel industrial storage tanks and processing equipment and is a world-leading producer of dairy farm equipment such as pasteurizers. Paul Mueller's industrial equipment unit makes processing equipment for brewery food chemical and pharmaceutical applications. Mueller Field Operations the company's field fabrication subsidiary builds storage tanks that are too large to be manufactured and shipped from the factory. Its Mueller Transportation unit delivers the company's products and components. Operating in more than 100 countries Paul Mueller makes about 20% of its sales in international markets.

	Annual Growth	12/10	12/11	12/12	12/13	12/14
Sales ($ mil.)	11.5%	129.6	154.2	179.6	181.3	200.7
Net income ($ mil.)	–	(8.9)	2.0	2.0	18.9	6.9
Market value ($ mil.)	27.8%	22.3	21.7	30.6	39.3	59.4
Employees	7.6%	729	783	869	929	976

MUELLER INDUSTRIES, INC.

NYS: MLI

8285 Tournament Drive, Suite 150	CEO: Gregory L. (Greg) Christopher
Memphis, TN 38125	CFO: Jeffrey A. Martin
Phone: 901 753-3200	HR: James (Jamie) Brown
Fax: –	FYE: December 27
Web: www.muellerindustries.com	Type: Public

Only top brass make it at Mueller Industries — that and copper and aluminum. The company makes materials used to make Mueller tubes and fittings bars and rods forgings extrusions pipes and valves. Mueller also resells a myriad of products from brass and plastic plumbing valves to faucets and malleable iron fittings. Its work is divided between two segments: Plumbing & Refrigeration (a Standard Products Division and European and Mexican Operations) and OEM (Industrial and Engineered Products Divisions and Chinese joint venture Mueller-Xingrong).

	Annual Growth	12/10	12/11	12/12	12/13	12/14
Sales ($ mil.)	3.5%	2,059.8	2,417.8	2,189.9	2,158.5	2,364.2
Net income ($ mil.)	4.2%	86.2	86.3	82.4	172.6	101.6
Market value ($ mil.)	0.9%	1,880.0	2,186.2	2,803.0	3,570.0	1,944.9
Employees	1.7%	3,600	3,750	3,775	3,925	3,850

MUELLER WATER PRODUCTS INC

NYS: MWA

1200 Abernathy Road N.E., Suite 1200
Atlanta, GA 30328
Phone: 770 206-4200
Fax: –
Web: www.muellerwaterproducts.com

CEO: Gregory E. Hyland
CFO: Evan L. Hart
HR: –
FYE: September 30
Type: Public

Mueller Water Products knows how to keep the water flowing. The company is one of the largest manufacturers and marketers of hydrants as well as valves and pipe fittings in North America. Its flow control products are used in new and upgraded municipal infrastructure industrial and residential and non-residential construction projects such as water distribution networks water and wastewater treatment facilities fire protection systems gas distribution and HVAC. Mueller operates through two segments: Mueller Co. and Anvil International. It also is a wholesale distributor of its own products and those made by other companies. The US accounts for most of Mueller's sales.

	Annual Growth	09/11	09/12	09/13	09/14	09/15
Sales ($ mil.)	(3.4%)	1,339.2	1,023.9	1,120.8	1,184.7	1,164.5
Net income ($ mil.)	–	(38.1)	(108.4)	40.8	55.5	30.9
Market value ($ mil.)	32.6%	398.0	786.4	1,282.4	1,328.9	1,229.4
Employees	(3.9%)	4,800	3,900	4,100	4,200	4,100

MULLEN COMMUNICATIONS INC.

40 Broad St.
Boston MA 02109-4308
Phone: 617-226-9000
Fax: 714-549-0557
Web: www.iopinc.com

CEO: Alex Leikikh
CFO: –
HR: –
FYE: December 31
Type: Subsidiary

Brands contemplating an image makeover might consider seeking advice from this firm. Mullen Communications is a leading creative services agency offering campaign development and planning services to both regional and national advertisers. In addition to traditional broadcast and print media work the company provides services for direct response and interactive marketing campaigns along with such services as packaging design and media planning. Mullen also offers corporate communications services through its public relations consultancy. The agency has offices in Boston; Detroit; Pittsburgh; New York; and Winston-Salem North Carolina and is part of global advertising services conglomerate Interpublic Group.

MULLINTBG

100 N. Sepulveda Blvd. Ste. 500
El Segundo CA 90245
Phone: 310 203 0770
Fax: 310-203-9268
Web: www.mullintbg.com

CEO: Michael R Shute
CFO: Michael Glickman
HR: –
FYE: December 31
Type: Subsidiary

MullinTBG helps executives benefit from their benefit plans. Offering more than 600 customized plans MullinTBG helps both large corporations and emerging growth companies retain personnel with executive benefits retirement and compensation packages. It offers such specialty insurance products as company-owned life insurance and customized nonqualified deferred compensation plans. MullinTBG also specializes in plan design enrollment record keeping reporting and communications. Through subsidiary MullinTBG Advisors the firm offers financial planning and investment advice. It has offices throughout the US. Prudential Financial acquired MullinTBG in 2008 and made it part of its Prudential Retirement business.

MULTEK FLEXIBLE CIRCUITS INC.

1150 Sheldahl Rd.
Northfield MN 55057-9444
Phone: 507-663-8000
Fax: 507-663-8545
Web: www.sheldahl.com

CEO: Franck Lize
CFO: Alan Wadleigh
HR: –
FYE: December 31
Type: Private

Multek Flexible Circuits (formerly Sheldahl) is proving its flexibility. Founded in 1955 the company makes flexible circuit boards primarily for automotive and data communications applications. It bases most of its products on its Novaclad patented adhesiveless copper laminate whose properties allow for smaller and more durable electrical circuits. Other products include coated films barrier foils flat cable tapes adhesive specialties membrane switches rigid circuits and splicing tapes. Sheldahl was acquired by Multek a subsidiary of Singapore-based Flextronics (turnkey manufacturing service provider) and its name was changed to Multek Flexible Circuits.

MULTI-COLOR CORP.

NMS: LABL

4053 Clough Woods Dr.
Batavia, OH 45103
Phone: 513 381-1480
Fax: –
Web: www.mcclabel.com

CEO: Nigel A. Vinecombe
CFO: Sharon E. Birkett
HR: –
FYE: March 31
Type: Public

Multi-Color Corporation's labels aren't just black and white and red all over. The company produces printed labels for product makers in markets such as home and personal care wine and spirit food and beverage and specialty consumer goods. Multi-Color serves customers in North and South America Europe the Asia/Pacific region and South Africa. The company prints and affixes heat transfer re-sealable shrink wrap pressure sensitive and other label types to glass and plastic containers. Multi-Color also offers gravure printing and injection in-mold labels. Over the years the company has counted Procter & Gamble and Miller Brewing among its biggest customers. Multi-Color traces its roots to 1916.

	Annual Growth	03/11	03/12	03/13	03/14	03/15
Sales ($ mil.)	24.4%	338.3	510.2	659.8	706.4	810.8
Net income ($ mil.)	25.5%	18.4	19.7	30.3	28.2	45.7
Market value ($ mil.)	36.1%	336.3	374.5	429.1	582.4	1,153.6
Employees	25.5%	1,430	2,749	2,800	3,250	3,550

MULTI-FINELINE ELECTRONIX INC

NMS: MFLX

8659 Research Drive
Irvine, CA 92618
Phone: 949 453-6800
Fax: –
Web: www.mflex.com

CEO: Reza Meshgin
CFO: Thomas D. Kampfer
HR: Choong Pew Lee
FYE: December 31
Type: Public

Multi-Fineline Electronix offers a multitude of fine electronic parts. The WBL Corporation-controlled company which does business as MFLEX manufactures a variety of flexible printed circuit boards (PCBs) and circuit assemblies. These devices are used to connect other components in various kinds of electronics such as mobile phones smartphones laptop computers medical devices and portable bar code scanners. Directly and through subcontractors MFLEX sells to three major customers that combined accounted for 90% of the company's 2013 sales.

	Annual Growth	09/12	09/13	09/14*	12/14	12/15
Sales ($ mil.)	(8.1%)	818.9	787.6	633.2	210.0	636.6
Net income ($ mil.)	15.2%	29.5	(65.5)	(84.5)	16.0	45.1
Market value ($ mil.)	(2.8%)	551.6	396.8	228.7	274.7	505.9
Employees	(32.7%)	23,470	17,310	11,570	9,140	7,170

*Fiscal year change

MULTICARE HEALTH SYSTEM

315 MARTIN LUTHER KING
TACOMA, WA 984054234
Phone: 253-403-1000
Fax: –
Web: www.multicare.org

CEO: William G. (Bill) Robertson
CFO: Anna Loomis
HR: –
FYE: December 31
Type: Private

MultiCare Health System is a not-for-profit health system that serves the residents of four counties in the southern Puget Sound region and southwestern Washington. Altogether the system's five hospitals have more than 1100 beds. The largest facility Tacoma General boasts about 440 beds and provides specialized cancer cardiac orthopedic and trauma care in addition to general medical and surgical care. Other medical centers include Good Samaritan Hospital (with 286 beds) Allenmore Hospital (130 beds) Auburn Regional Medical Center (195 beds) and Mary Bridge Children's Hospital (82 beds).

	Annual Growth	12/08	12/09	12/10	12/11	12/12
Sales ($ mil.)	12.6%	–	1,095.0	1,384.5	1,384.3	1,563.8
Net income ($ mil.)	29.5%	–	–	146.1	27.6	245.0
Market value ($ mil.)	–	–	–	–	–	–
Employees	–	–	–	–	–	6,510

MULTICELL TECHNOLOGIES INC

NBB: MCET

68 Cumberland Street, Suite 301
Woonsocket, RI 02895
Phone: 401 762-0045
Fax: –
Web: www.multicelltech.com

CEO: –
CFO: W Gerald Newmin
HR: –
FYE: November 30
Type: Public

MultiCell Technologies is working on multiple therapeutics but still sells liver cells on the side to help pay the rent. It is developing drug candidates to treat degenerative neurological diseases. Its MCT-125 candidate is being developed as a treatment for the fatigue that comes with multiple sclerosis while MCT-175 is intended to slow the progression of the disease. Two other candidates are targeting breast and cervical cancers. MultiCell also produces liver cells (hepatocytes) and a serum-free culture medium for research. Larger firms including Corning and Pfizer have licensed the company's liver cell lines.

	Annual Growth	11/10	11/11	11/12	11/13	11/14
Sales ($ mil.)	(16.0%)	0.1	0.0	0.0	0.0	0.0
Net income ($ mil.)	–	(1.2)	(1.8)	(1.3)	(1.2)	(0.4)
Market value ($ mil.)	–	0.0	0.0	0.0	0.0	0.0
Employees	0.0%	2	2	2	2	2

MULTIMEDIA GAMES HOLDING COMPANY, INC.

NMS: MGAM

206 Wild Basin Road South, Building B
Austin, TX 78746
Phone: 515 334-7500
Fax: –
Web: www.multimediagames.com

CEO: Ram V Chary
CFO: Adam Chibib
HR: –
FYE: September 30
Type: Public

You might say this company's games help casinos hit the jackpot. Multimedia Games is a leading manufacturer of slot machines and other gaming systems used by both commercial casinos and by establishments in the Native American gaming industry. It makes both video reel and mechanical reel games as well as multi-terminal games that allow gamblers to compete for jackpots. In addition to its proprietary gaming machines Multimedia Games licenses games from third parties such as WMS Industries and Aristocrat Technologies. The company also makes casino management systems that monitor gaming machine performance and tracking player activity as well as video lottery terminals and charitable gaming systems.

	Annual Growth	09/09	09/10	09/11	09/12	09/13
Sales ($ mil.)	10.5%	127.2	117.9	127.9	156.2	189.4
Net income ($ mil.)	–	(44.8)	2.6	5.7	28.2	34.9
Market value ($ mil.)	61.2%	150.5	108.7	118.7	462.3	1,015.3
Employees	6.4%	412	397	410	471	528

MULTIPLAN INC.

115 5th Ave. 7th Fl.
New York NY 10003
Phone: 212-780-2000
Fax: 212-780-0420
Web: www.multiplan.com

CEO: Mark Tabak
CFO: David Redmond
HR: –
FYE: December 31
Type: Private

MultiPlan operates one of the nation's largest preferred provider organization (PPO) healthcare networks with some 900000 doctors serving 57 million consumers. The company offers access to its PPO to health care plan providers; clients can use the PPO either as their primary provider network or as a means of extending or expanding their own networks. MultiPlan also provides other cost management services to payers such as reimbursement management and fee negotiation on specific claims. Customers include HMOs insurance companies third-party administrators union health plans and self-administered employer plans. MultiPlan is owned by private equity investors BC Partners and Silver Lake.

MUNGER TOLLES & OLSON LLP

355 S. Grand Ave. 35th Fl.
Los Angeles CA 90071-1560
Phone: 213-683-9100
Fax: +44-1522-875-530
Web: www.lincat.co.uk

CEO: O'Malley M Miller
CFO: Larry Kleinberg
HR: –
FYE: December 31
Type: Private - Partnershi

This firm toils over the minutiae of law. Founded in 1962 Munger Tolles & Olson (MTO) employs about 175 attorneys and has two offices in California (Los Angeles and San Francisco) but provides legal services nationwide. The firm offers expertise in litigation and transactional law with practice areas that include corporate finance bankruptcy environmental real estate labor and employment law and taxation. The firm caters to clients in the aerospace arts and culture energy financial services gaming education media pharmaceuticals retail and telecommunications industries. MTO has represented clients such as Bank of America Edison International and Transocean.

MUNICH REINSURANCE AMERICA INC.

555 College Rd. East
Princeton NJ 08543
Phone: 609-243-4200
Fax: 609-243-4257
Web: www.munichreamerica.com

CEO: –
CFO: Guy Perinotti
HR: –
FYE: December 31
Type: Subsidiary

Ever wonder who insures insurance companies? Munich Reinsurance America is one of the top providers of property/casualty reinsurance in the US. The company is a subsidiary of German firm Munich Re and it operates as Munich Re in its territories. The firm provides treaty reinsurance (reinsurance for groups or categories of risks) and facultative reinsurance (reinsurance for individually negotiated risks) to both large and small primary insurers. It also offers specialty property/casualty insurance coverage through its American Modern Insurance Group and HSB Group subsidiaries and its Specialty Markets unit provides risk management and niche coverage for self-insured customers and other entities.

MUNICIPAL ELECTRIC AUTHORITY OF GEORGIA

1470 Riveredge Pkwy. NW	CEO: Robert P Johnston
Atlanta GA 30328-4686	CFO: –
Phone: 770-563-0300	HR: –
Fax: 770-563-0004	FYE: December 31
Web: www.meagpower.org	Type: Government-owned

With more juice than a ripe Georgia peach the Municipal Electric Authority of Georgia (MEAG Power) supplies wholesale electric power. The authority has a generating capacity of 2069 MW through its interests in nuclear and fossil-fueled plants. Some 44% of the energy MEAG Power delivered in 2010 came from its nuclear plants. MEAG Power transmits electricity to 48 municipal and one county distribution systems across Georgia that in turn serve some 600000 consumers. It utilizes a transmission network that is co-owned by all the power suppliers in Georgia although it is considering joining a regional transmission organization (RTO) to further defray costs.

MURATA ELECTRONICS NORTH AMERICA INC.

2200 Lake Park Dr.	CEO: David Kirk
Smyrna GA 30080-7604	CFO: –
Phone: 770-436-1300	HR: Debbie Halverson
Fax: 770-436-3030	FYE: March 31
Web: www.murata-northamerica.com	Type: Subsidiary

Murata Electronics North America is the North American sales arm of Murata Manufacturing. Murata designs manufactures and sells power supply modules capacitors sensors and ceramic passive electronic components such as crystal oscillators piezoelectric buzzers inductors and wireless communications filters. The company serves manufacturers of audio visual equipment automotive and wireless communications devices and targets telecommunications and automotive industries. Murata Manufacturing established its North American sales operation in 1965.

MURPHY EXPLORATION & PRODUCTION COMPANY - USA

16290 Katy Frwy. Ste. 600	CEO: –
Houston TX 77094	CFO: –
Phone: 281-675-9000	HR: Colby Smith
Fax: 281-249-1041	FYE: December 31
	Type: Subsidiary

Irish name American focus. Murphy Exploration & Production - USA a subsidiary of integrated oil giant Murphy Oil is engaged in deepwater oil and gas exploration and production primarily in oil and gas fields located in the Gulf of Mexico. It also operates fields onshore in Louisiana. Murphy Exploration & Production - USA operates four major developments in the deepwater Gulf (Medusa Habanero Front Runner and Thunder Hawk). The company also has interests in a number of blocks on the continental shelf of the Gulf of Mexico. In 2007 its largest field (Medusa) reported proved reserves of 9 million barrels of oil and 11 billion cu. ft. of natural hgas.

MURPHY OIL CORP

NYS: MUR

200 Peach Street, P.O. Box 7000	CEO: Roger W. Jenkins
El Dorado, AR 71730-7000	CFO: John W. Eckart
Phone: 870 862-6411	HR: Maria Martinez
Fax: 870 864-3673	FYE: December 31
Web: www.murphyoilcorp.com	Type: Public

Murphy's Law? Turn that oil into money. Newly minted as a pure-play upstream company Murphy Oil explores for and produces oil and gas — primarily in the US but also in Canada Malaysia and the UK. In 2014 the company reported undeveloped proved reserves of 336.2 million barrels of oil 105.6 million barrels of synthetic crude oil and 1.7 trillion cubic feet of natural gas. In 2013 Murphy Oil completed the separation of its US retail marketing operations with the spin-off of Murphy USA Inc. as a stand-alone company. It also began to sell its UK marketing and refining assets in 2014 in order to become an exploration and production player.

	Annual Growth	12/10	12/11	12/12	12/13	12/14
Sales ($ mil.)	(30.4%)	23,345.1	27,745.5	28,626.0	5,390.1	5,476.1
Net income ($ mil.)	3.2%	798.1	872.7	970.9	1,123.5	905.6
Market value ($ mil.)	(9.3%)	13,232.6	9,893.8	10,570.1	11,516.2	8,967.3
Employees	(33.9%)	8,994	8,610	9,185	1,875	1,712

MURPHY OIL USA INC.

200 Peach St.	CEO: R Andrew Clyde
El Dorado AR 71730	CFO: –
Phone: 870-862-6411	HR: Gil Reath
Fax: 870-864-6373	FYE: December 31
Web: www.murphyusa.com	Type: Subsidiary

It may not be the biggest but Murphy Oil USA (MOUSA) is no mouse in the gas station market. A wholly owned subsidiary of Murphy Oil MOUSA markets refined products through its network of branded gasoline stations and convenience stores customers and unbranded wholesale customers in 23 southern and Midwestern US states. The company's 1130 retail gas stations (more than 1000 of which in Wal-Mart Supercenter parking lots) sell gas under the Murphy USA brand. In 2011 the company owned the land underlying about 900 of the more than 1000 gas stations located in Wal-Mart parking lots and rented the rest.

MURPHY USA INC

NYS: MUSA

200 Peach Street	CEO: R. Andrew Clyde
El Dorado, AR 71730-5836	CFO: Mindy K West
Phone: 870 875-7600	HR: –
Fax: –	FYE: December 31
Web: www.murphyusa.com	Type: Public

It may not be the biggest but Murphy USA (ticker symbol MUSA) is no mouse in the gas station market. Murphy USA markets refined products through its network of branded gasoline stations and convenience stores customers and unbranded wholesale customers in 23 southern and midwestern US states. The company's more than 1200 retail gas stations (more than 1000 of which are in Wal-Mart Supercenter parking lots) sell gas under the Murphy USA brand. The company owns the land underlying about 900 of the more than 1000 gas stations located in Wal-Mart lots and rented the rest. Formerly a wholly owned subsidiary of Murphy Oil it was spun off in 2013.

	Annual Growth	12/10	12/11	12/12	12/13	12/14
Sales ($ mil.)	2.5%	15,592.1	19,273.5	19,655.4	18,083.3	17,209.9
Net income ($ mil.)	11.6%	157.4	324.0	83.6	235.0	243.9
Market value ($ mil.)	65.7%	–	–	–	1,899.7	3,147.6
Employees	9.4%	–	–	7,900	8,250	9,450

MURPHY-BROWN LLC

2822 Hwy. 24 West	CEO: –
Warsaw NC 28398	CFO: –
Phone: 910-293-3434	HR: Rina Teel
Fax: 910-289-6400	FYE: April 30
Web: www.murphybrownllc.com	Type: Subsidiary

When it comes to work Murphy-Brown goes 'whole hog.' The livestock production subsidiary of pork-processing giant Smithfield Foods is the world's largest hog producer. Murphy-Brown maintains some 827000 breeding sows (more than 90% of which are genetic lines that produce the leanest hogs possible) and brings to market more than 16 million hogs annually. It operates about 450 company-owned farms in a dozen states. The company extends its hog production through partnerships with more than 1500 independent farmers and contract growers in the US. More than 75% of Murphy-Brown's revenues are attributable to hogs sold to Smithfield Foods' fresh pork and packaged meats subsidiaries including John Morrell.

MUSCULAR DYSTROPHY ASSOCIATION INC.

3300 E SUNRISE DR	CEO: Steven M Derks
TUCSON, AZ 857183299	CFO: Julie Faber
Phone: 520-529-2000	HR: –
Fax: –	FYE: December 31
Web: www.mda.org	Type: Private

The Muscular Dystrophy Association (MDA) is a not-for-profit health agency that supports research into more than 40 neuromuscular diseases including including muscular dystrophy and Lou Gehrig's disease (also known as ALS). MDA believes more than one million Americans have some form of muscular dystrophy. The organization operates more than 200 health care clinics across the US runs summer camps for kids provides funding for research publishes educational materials and engages in national advocacy. It also sponsors more than 200 hospital-affiliated clinics and funds some 330 research projects globally. Founded in 1950 MDA is funded by private contributions.

	Annual Growth	12/09	12/10	12/11	12/12	12/13
Sales ($ mil.)	(4.9%)	–	178.1	159.0	159.0	153.0
Net income ($ mil.)	–	–	–	(53.9)	(11.9)	19.7
Market value ($ mil.)	–	–	–	–	–	–
Employees	–	–	–	–	–	950

MUSEUM OF FINE ARTS

465 HUNTINGTON AVE	CEO: –
BOSTON, MA 021155597	CFO: Mark B Kerwin
Phone: 617-369-3861	HR: –
Fax: –	FYE: June 30
Web: www.smfa.edu	Type: Private

In a city known for its erudite inhabitants the The Museum of Fine Arts (MFA) Boston seeks to entertain and educate. The MFA offers a wide range of collections such as Art of Americas Art of Europe Art of the Ancient World Contemporary Art Textile and Fashion Arts and Musical Instruments. The museum also provides public programs for children and adults including art classes and workshops. With approximately 72000 member households the MFA attracts some 1.2 million visitors annually. Founded in 1870 the museum through a partnership opened the Nagoya/Boston Museum of Fine Arts in 1999.

	Annual Growth	06/07	06/08	06/09	06/10	06/13
Sales ($ mil.)	17.4%	–	–	69.2	122.8	131.5
Net income ($ mil.)	–	–	–	(49.8)	7.2	(8.9)
Market value ($ mil.)	–	–	–	–	–	–
Employees	–	–	–	–	–	1,000

MUSTANG FUEL CORPORATION

9800 N OKLAHOMA AVE	CEO: Carey Joullian IV
OKLAHOMA CITY, OK 731147406	CFO: Scott M Chapline
Phone: 405-884-2092	HR: Stephanie McCarty
Fax: –	FYE: December 31
Web: www.mustangfuel.com	Type: Private

Like a good mustang Mustang Fuel is independent — an independent oil and gas exploration production transportation and marketing company that is. The company owns and operates 200 properties and owns non-operated interests in more than 1300 other properties. It also controls more than 100000 net undeveloped leasehold acres in a four-state service region. Mustang Fuel also owns natural gas gathering and transporting pipelines operates one of the largest gas processing facilities in Oklahoma and has a fleet of trucks that transports petroleum products. It also markets gas. Subsidiaries include Mustang Fuel Marketing Company and Mustang Gas Products LLC.

	Annual Growth	12/03	12/04	12/05	12/08	12/09
Sales ($ mil.)	(5.2%)	–	313.7	441.4	482.2	240.7
Net income ($ mil.)	(13.6%)	–	–	24.6	43.4	13.7
Market value ($ mil.)	–	–	–	–	–	–
Employees	–	–	–	–	–	124

MUSTANG TRACTOR & EQUIPMENT COMPANY

12800 Northwest Fwy.	CEO: Bradford Tucker
Houston TX 77040	CFO: –
Phone: 713-460-2000	HR: Danielle Frost
Fax: 713-329-7747	FYE: November 30
Web: www.mustangcat.com	Type: Private

In need of construction equipment that is as strong as a horse or stronger? Mustang CAT sells and leases new and used Caterpillar brand construction machinery and power systems to its customers in Southeast Texas. Mustang CAT provides Caterpillar construction equipment and a selected group of allied lines and Caterpillar engines as well as the design engineering and fabrication of engine packages in a wide range of power ratings. The Cat Rental Store offers Caterpillar and allied lines of large and small equipment for the building construction industry. Other services include engine repair scheduled oil sampling and performance analysis reports.

MUTUAL OF AMERICA LIFE INSURANCE COMPANY

320 Park Ave.	CEO: Thomas J Moran
New York NY 10022-6839	CFO: Manfred Altstadt
Phone: 212-224-1600	HR: –
Fax: 212-224-2539	FYE: December 31
Web: www.mutualofamerica.com	Type: Private - Mutual Com

Mutual of America Life Insurance provides retirement savings and employee benefit plans to small to midsized companies and to not-for-profit organizations. As part of its business the company typically serves those involved in the health and social services fields. In addition to group pension and insurance plans Mutual of America Life Insurance offers IRAs annuities and life and disability coverage to individual investors and about 35 separate account investment funds that leverage equity fixed-income retirement asset allocation and balanced strategies. Founded in 1945 Mutual of America Life Insurance operates throughout the US through a network of some 35 regional field offices and a pair of satellite offices in Alaska and Hawaii.

MUTUAL OF ENUMCLAW INSURANCE COMPANY

1460 Wells St.
Enumclaw WA 98022
Phone: 360-825-2591
Fax: 360-825-6885
Web: www.mutualofenumclaw.com

CEO: -
CFO: Bradley Gipson
HR: -
FYE: December 31
Type: Private - Mutual Com

Mutual of Enumclaw Insurance Company provides commercial and personal property/casualty insurance in four western states (Idaho Oregon Utah and Washington). Mutual of Enumclaw Insurance Company and Enumclaw Property and Casualty Insurance Company comprise Enumclaw Insurance Group. The group writes a variety of lines including auto homeowners liability and umbrella insurance. Enumclaw also offers specialty package policies for churches farms and business owners. Farmers' Mutual Insurance the group's Washington-based predecessor was founded in 1898.

MUTUAL OF OMAHA INSURANCE CO. (NE)

Mutual Of Omaha Plaza
Omaha, NE 68175
Phone: 402 342-7600
Fax: -
Web: www.mutualofomaha.com

CEO: Daniel P Neary
CFO: David A Diamond
HR: -
FYE: December 31
Type: Public

In the wild kingdom that is today's insurance industry Mutual of Omaha Insurance Company wants to distinguish itself from the pack. The company provides individual group and employee benefits products through a range of affiliated companies. It offers Medicare supplement disability illness and long-term care coverage as well as life insurance and annuities through its United of Omaha Life Insurance unit. Its Mutual of Omaha Investor Services offers brokerage services pension plans and mutual funds while the Mutual of Omaha Bank operates regionally. Mutual of Omaha is owned by its policyholders.

	Annual Growth	12/08	12/09	12/10	12/11	12/12
Assets ($ mil.)	9.9%	21,245.6	23,819.6	26,906.7	29,198.4	30,993.1
Net income ($ mil.)	56.7%	47.0	143.8	247.7	130.1	283.8
Market value ($ mil.)	-	-	-	-	-	-
Employees	-	-	-	-	-	-

MUTUALFIRST FINANCIAL INC

NMS: MFSF

110 E. Charles Street
Muncie, IN 47305-2419
Phone: 765 747-2800
Fax: -
Web: www.bankwithmutual.com

CEO: David W Heeter
CFO: Christopher D Cook
HR: -
FYE: December 31
Type: Public

Before you bank anywhere else this company wants you to head to Mutual-First. MutualFirst Financial is the holding company for MutualFirst Bank which has more than 30 financial centers and trust offices in northern Indiana and a loan production office in southern Michigan. The bank offers standard products and services such as checking and savings accounts CDs IRAs and credit cards. More than 40% of the company's loan portfolio is devoted to residential mortgages. Consumer loans including auto boat RV home equity and home improvement loans account for about 25%. Business loans also make up about a quarter of MutualFirst's loan portfolio.

	Annual Growth	12/10	12/11	12/12	12/13	12/14
Assets ($ mil.)	0.3%	1,406.9	1,427.2	1,422.5	1,391.4	1,424.2
Net income ($ mil.)	13.4%	6.6	3.5	7.2	9.2	10.8
Market value ($ mil.)	23.8%	67.3	51.2	82.7	124.0	158.3
Employees	0.6%	428	415	413	412	438

MUZAK HOLDINGS LLC

3318 Lakemont Blvd.
Fort Mill SC 29708
Phone: 803-396-3000
Fax: 803-396-3095
Web: www.muzak.com

CEO: Stephen P Richards
CFO: R Dodd Haynes
HR: -
FYE: December 31
Type: Private

The hills are alive with the sound of Muzak. Once the king of canned music the company has been busy working to transform its image. Muzak famous for its instrumental versions of pop tunes has turned its focus away from the elevator rider and toward the consumer as it pumps original songs (with lyrics) into retail stores restaurants and bars as well as hotels offices and factories. Its music is heard by some 100 million people daily. The company additionally provides music and marketing for telephone on-hold and in-store messaging. Founded in 1934 Muzak emerged from Chapter 11 bankruptcy protection in 2010 and was acquired by in-store media specialist Mood Media Corporation in May 2011.

MV OIL TRUST

NYS: MVO

The Bank of New York Mellon Trust Company, N.A., Trustee, Global Corporate Trust, 919 Congress Avenue
Austin, TX 78701
Phone: 512 236-6599
Fax: -

CEO: -
CFO: -
HR: -
FYE: December 31
Type: Public

Call it what you will black gold Texas tea or the black blood of the earth MV Oil Trust is wringing out the value from each drop and distributing it to shareholders. MV Oil Trust receives royalty interests from the mature oil and gas properties of MV Partners located in Kansas and Colorado. The properties have proved reserves of 9.5 million barrels of oil from 922 net wells. The trust receives royalties based on the amount of oil (and gas) produced and sold and then distributes virtually all of the proceeds to shareholders on a regular basis. MV Partners a private company engaged in the exploration production gathering aggregation and sale of oil and natural gas has the rights to 80% of net proceeds.

	Annual Growth	12/10	12/11	12/12	12/13	12/14
Sales ($ mil.)	5.3%	32.5	40.6	41.5	37.9	39.9
Net income ($ mil.)	5.4%	31.7	39.7	40.8	37.0	39.0
Market value ($ mil.)	(22.2%)	458.5	455.9	273.2	273.2	167.6
Employees	-	-	-	-	-	-

MV TRANSPORTATION INC.

5910 N CNTRL EXPY # 1145
DALLAS, TX 752065125
Phone: 972-391-4600
Fax: -
Web: www.mvtransit.com

CEO: Brian Kibby
CFO: Bob Pagorek
HR: -
FYE: December 31
Type: Private

Need to supply transportation by bus? MV Transportation will run your bus system so you don't have to. The company operates more than 200 contracts to offer fixed-route and shuttle bus services as well as paratransit (transportation of people with disabilities) and transportation of Medicaid beneficiaries. Its customers consist primarily of transit authorities and other state and local government agencies responsible for public transportation. MV Transportation operates in more than 130 locations spanning 28 US states and in British Columbia Canada and Saudi Arabia; overall the company maintains a fleet of about 7000 vehicles. MV Transportation was founded in 1975.

	Annual Growth	12/06	12/07	12/08	12/09	12/13
Sales ($ mil.)	15.7%	-	422.6	646.0	706.5	1,013.8
Net income ($ mil.)	-	-	-	(3.0)	23.5	32.7
Market value ($ mil.)	-	-	-	-	-	-
Employees	-	-	-	-	-	12,389

MVC CAPITAL INC.

NYSE: MVC

287 Bowman Ave.
Purchase NY 10577
Phone: 914-701-0310
Fax: 914-701-0315
Web: www.mvccapital.com

CEO: Michael Tokarz
CFO: Scott Schuenke
HR: –
FYE: October 31
Type: Public

MVC Capital puts its money where its mouth is. The business development company provides equity and debt investment capital for small and middle-market companies. It generally invests between $3 million and $25 million funding the growth acquisitions and recapitalization plans of companies with sales of between $10 million and $200 million in the US Asia and Europe that have secure market positions but may be underperforming. The company invests in the automotive manufacturing chemical financial services and food service industries through methods including senior and subordinated loans venture capital mezzanine financing and private equity investments.

MVM INC.

1593 Spring Hill Rd. Ste. 700
Vienna VA 22182
Phone: 703-790-3138
Fax: 703-790-9526
Web: www.mvminc.com

CEO: Dario O Marquez
CFO: Joseph D Stanton
HR: –
FYE: December 31
Type: Government Agency

Need a secret agent man? Founded in 1979 by three former US Secret Service agents MVM provides security staffing and consulting services primarily to US government entities. Along with security guards MVM also offers executive protection risk assessment cultural training analytical support program management and technical services. Its language support offerings include transcription translation and summarization services. The company has provided security services in Iraq during reconstruction efforts in that nation. Among MVM's customers are the Department of Justice Internal Revenue Service and the Department of Energy. Chairman and CEO Dario Marquez one of the company's founders controls MVM.

MWH GLOBAL INC.

380 INTERLOCKEN CRES
BROOMFIELD, CO 80021-8022
Phone: 303-533-1900
Fax: –
Web: www.mwhglobal.com

CEO: Alan J Krause
CFO: David G Barnes
HR: –
FYE: December 28
Type: Private

If it's wet MWH Global will make it work. The environmental engineering construction and management firm specializes in water-related projects or "wet infrastructure." Typical projects include building water treatment or desalination plants water transmission systems or storage facilitates. MWH also provides general building services for transportation energy mining ports and waterways and industrial projects. The company is active in some 35 countries and serves governments public utilities and private sector clients. Affiliates of the employee-owned company include software provider Innovyze business and government relations firm mCapitol and MWH Laboratories which conducts research.

	Annual Growth	12/00	12/01*	01/03*	12/05	12/12
Sales ($ mil.)	6.5%	–	774.5	975.9	946.0	1,545.4
Net income ($ mil.)	7.4%	–	19.8	942.3	0.0	43.7
Market value ($ mil.)	–	–	–	–	–	–
Employees	–	–	–	–	–	7,000

*Fiscal year change

MWI VETERINARY SUPPLY INC

NMS: MWIV

3041 W. Pasadena Dr.
Boise, ID 83705
Phone: 208 955-8930
Fax: –
Web: www.mwivet.com

CEO: James F Cleary Jr
CFO: Richard Dubois
HR: –
FYE: September 30
Type: Public

While MWI could stand for Mastiff Weimaraner and Irish Setter MWI Veterinary Supply is actually named after founder and veterinarian Millard Wallace Ickes. The veterinary products distributor supplies drugs diagnostics equipment and other medical supplies for companion animals and livestock. It serves veterinary practices from about a dozen distribution centers across the US and in the UK. The firm offers 41000 products from more than 700 vendors. In addition to medical supplies and equipment MWI distributes pet food and nutritional products. The company in business since 1976 offers customers online ordering tools to manage inventory consultation for equipment and pet cremation services.

	Annual Growth	09/10	09/11	09/12	09/13	09/14
Sales ($ mil.)	24.8%	1,229.3	1,565.3	2,075.1	2,347.5	2,981.0
Net income ($ mil.)	21.1%	33.4	42.6	53.5	62.8	72.0
Market value ($ mil.)	26.6%	745.3	888.6	1,377.5	1,928.5	1,916.1
Employees	15.8%	1,179	1,273	1,629	1,732	2,121

MYERS INDUSTRIES INC.

NYS: MYE

1293 South Main Street
Akron, OH 44301
Phone: 330 253-5592
Fax: 330 761-6156
Web: www.myersindustries.com

CEO: R. David Banyard
CFO: Greggory W. (Gregg) Branning
HR: Ray Cunningham
FYE: December 31
Type: Public

Myers Industries manufactures a host of plastic and rubber products from flower pots to tires through several operating segments. Its largest segment material handling includes plastic and reusable containers and pallets storage bins and wire shelving systems. The lawn and garden segment covers plastic flower pots hanging baskets and planters and the engineered products segment includes tire repair products plastic HVAC components and highway marking tape. The company also distributes products such as hand tools alignment and balancing equipment and tire valves to tire dealers and service centers through Myers Tire Supply.

	Annual Growth	12/10	12/11	12/12	12/13	12/14
Sales ($ mil.)	(4.1%)	737.6	755.7	791.2	825.2	623.6
Net income ($ mil.)	–	(42.8)	24.5	30.0	26.0	(8.7)
Market value ($ mil.)	15.9%	303.5	384.6	472.1	658.2	548.5
Employees	(0.7%)	3,332	3,261	3,378	3,401	3,241

MYLAN INC

NMS: MYL

1000 Mylan Boulevard
Canonsburg, PA 15317
Phone: 724 514-1800
Fax: –
Web: www.mylan.com

CEO: Heather Bresch
CFO: John D. Sheehan
HR: Kristy Terling
FYE: December 31
Type: Public

Mylan knows you probably don't know its name but hopes you'll appreciate the prices of its drugs. Through Mylan Pharmaceuticals and other subsidiaries the company is one of the top global manufacturers of prescription generic drugs. Mylan's medicine cabinet holds generic versions of antibiotics antidepressants anti-inflammatories and respiratory agents in a range of delivery forms. Its specialty division makes branded nebulized and injectable drugs. In addition to finished drugs the Mylan Laboratories unit is a major producer of active pharmaceutical ingredients (APIs) for generic drugs. The company's customers in more than 150 countries include wholesalers distributors retailers and government agencies.

	Annual Growth	12/09	12/10	12/11	12/12	12/13
Sales ($ mil.)	7.9%	5,092.8	5,450.5	6,129.8	6,796.1	6,909.1
Net income ($ mil.)	28.0%	232.6	345.1	536.8	640.9	623.7
Market value ($ mil.)	23.9%	6,848.7	7,852.0	7,974.6	10,200.5	16,127.6
Employees	6.6%	15,500	16,000	18,000	20,000	20,000

MYLAN SPECIALTY L.P.

110 Allen Road
Basking Ridge NJ 07920
Phone: 908-542-1999
Fax: +44-113-306-6001
Web: www.atkinsglobal.com

CEO: –
CFO: –
HR: –
FYE: December 31
Type: Subsidiary

When a peanut or a bee threatens your very existence Mylan Specialty (formerly Dey Pharma) is ready to save the day. Its specialty prescription drugs treat severe allergic reactions respiratory diseases and pschyiatric disorders. It markets EpiPen autoinjectors used by patients to self-administer epinephrine in case of allergic emergencies (anaphylaxis). Its premeasured unit-dose inhalation products include bronchodialators use to treat asthma and chronic obstructive pulmonary disease (COPD). Brands include the EasiVent and Perforomist breathing devices. A subsidiary of generic giant Mylan Mylan Specialty also offers non-branded generic nebulizer treatments and the Emsam transdermal antidepressant patch.

MYMETICS CORP

NBB: MYMX

c/o Mymetics S.A., Biopole, Route de la Corniche, 4
Epalinges 1066
Phone: (41) 21 653 4535
Fax: –
Web: www.mymetics.com

CEO: –
CFO: –
HR: –
FYE: December 31
Type: Public

Mymetics likes to be on the ground floor of vaccine development. The company holds a portfolio of early-stage vaccines being developed to treat HIV malaria herpes and other viruses. Its key technology uses lipid-like virosomes to carry a vaccine's active ingredients. The development-stage biotech has built its portfolio up through acquisitions and hopes it can attract a major pharmaceutical partner once it has advanced a drug candidate through early stage clinical trials. Mymetics conducts its clinical testing in Europe and Africa. Its research and development activities take place at its facilities in Switzerland where it also secures its funding from wealthy individuals.

	Annual Growth	12/10	12/11	12/12	12/13	12/14
Sales ($ mil.)	76.3%	0.3	0.2	0.0	6.0	2.9
Net income ($ mil.)	–	(15.3)	(13.6)	(8.1)	8.3	(4.0)
Market value ($ mil.)	(37.9%)	51.0	7.9	9.8	3.6	7.6
Employees	7.5%	9	9	8	8	12

MYR GROUP INC

NMS: MYRG

1701 Golf Road, Suite 3-1012
Rolling Meadows, IL 60008-4210
Phone: 847 290-1891
Fax: –
Web: www.myrgroup.com

CEO: William A. (Bill) Koertner
CFO: Betty R Johnson
HR: –
FYE: December 31
Type: Public

MYR Group's work can be electrifying. The specialty contractor builds and maintains electric delivery infrastructure systems for utilities and commercial clients. MYR Group constructs transmission and distribution lines for the oil and gas power and telecommunications industries. The company also installs and maintains electrical wiring in commercial and industrial facilities and traffic and rail systems. The group operates nationwide through subsidiaries including The L.E. Myers Co. Harlan Electric Hawkeye Construction Sturgeon Electric MYR Transmission Services and Great Southwestern Construction. MYR's transmission and distribution segment accounts for about three-fourths of the group's revenues.

	Annual Growth	12/10	12/11	12/12	12/13	12/14
Sales ($ mil.)	12.1%	597.1	780.4	999.0	902.7	944.0
Net income ($ mil.)	22.7%	16.1	18.3	34.3	34.8	36.5
Market value ($ mil.)	6.9%	436.6	398.0	462.6	521.5	569.7
Employees	6.9%	2,800	3,000	3,300	3,500	3,650

MYREXIS INC.

NASDAQ: MYRX

305 Chipeta Way
Salt Lake City UT 84108
Phone: 801-214-7800
Fax: 801-214-7992
Web: www.myrexis.com

CEO: –
CFO: –
HR: –
FYE: June 30
Type: Public

Myrexis hoped to convince cancer cells to stop dividing and die with the destabilizing agent drugs in its pipeline. The pharmaceutical development firm's pipeline consisted of oncology compounds in clinical and preclinical R&D stages including drugs aiming to treat solid tumors and relapsed cancers. However the company restructured its operations and slashed its workforce in 2011 after deciding to halt clinical trials on its leading candidate Azixa (a metastatic tumor drug) in order to focus on its more promising early stage development compounds. Then in early 2012 it halted all remaining development activities and began exploring strategic alternatives. In November 2012 Myrexis announced plans to liquidate.

MYRIAD GENETICS, INC.

NMS: MYGN

320 Wakara Way
Salt Lake City, UT 84108
Phone: 801 584-3600
Fax: –
Web: www.myriad.com

CEO: Mark C. Capone
CFO: R. Bryan Riggsbee
HR: Jayne B. Hart
FYE: June 30
Type: Public

There are a myriad of diseases out there and Myriad Genetics is working to detect which ones you might develop based on your genes. The company develops and sells molecular diagnostic tests in three main areas: predictive medicine (to assess a patient's risk for developing disease) personalized medicine (to identify likelihood of drug response to therapies) and prognostic medicine (to assess risk of disease progression or recurrence). Its biggest revenue maker BRACAnalysis helps determine risk for breast or ovarian cancer. Myriad Genetics markets its products in the US through its own sales force and uses collaborations to sell them elsewhere.

	Annual Growth	06/11	06/12	06/13	06/14	06/15
Sales ($ mil.)	15.8%	402.1	496.0	613.2	778.2	723.1
Net income ($ mil.)	(5.5%)	100.7	112.2	147.1	176.2	80.2
Market value ($ mil.)	10.6%	1,564.7	1,637.8	1,851.3	2,681.6	2,341.9
Employees	17.8%	1,057	1,169	1,325	1,649	2,038

MYRIAD RBM INC.

3300 Duval Rd.
Austin TX 78759
Phone: 512-835-8026
Fax: 512-835-4687
Web: www.rulesbasedmedicine.com

CEO: Ralph L McDade
CFO: Bryan Riggsbee
HR: –
FYE: December 31
Type: Subsidiary

A hemato-grapher of sorts Myriad RBM (formerly Rules-Based Medicine) is developing blood tests that it hopes will be used in the diagnosis of mental illnesses. Based on its proprietary multi-analyte profiling (MAP) platform its Psychiatric Diagnostic Panel analyzes protein biomarkers found in blood to help psychiatrists diagnose conditions including schizophrenia bipolar disorder major depressive disorder and to determine how well drugs are working. The Austin Texas-based company was the first to develop blood tests for the diagnosis of mental illnesses. After canceling a planned IPO in 2010 the company was acquired by Myriad Genetics in 2011.

MZINGA INC.

230 3rd Ave.
Waltham MA 02451
Phone: 888-694-6428
Fax: 781-930-5430
Web: www.mzinga.com

CEO: Barry Libert
CFO: Mark Somol
HR: –
FYE: December 31
Type: Private

Mzinga uses social media to help businesses improve their results. The company combines its OmniSocial software and online services to aid customer experience employee productivity and social marketing for more than 40 million users in some 160 countries. OmniSocial promotes customer acquisition engagement and support with collaboration and community-generating tools such as blogs podcasts and user-generated content. The software helps employee productivity with tools for recruiting and then getting new employees up to speed with peer and team learning. The company's social marketing unit focuses on brand awareness and offers social market research and behavior-based analytics.

N-VIRO INTERNATIONAL CORP

NBB: NVIC

2254 Centennial Road
Toledo, OH 43617
Phone: 419 535-6374
Fax: –
Web: www.nviro.com

CEO: –
CFO: James K McHugh
HR: –
FYE: December 31
Type: Public

Wastewater sludge smells like money to N-Viro International. The company's patented process converts sludge and other bio-organic waste into a better-quality soil by treating it with alkaline byproducts. The treated N-Viro Soil is used in agriculture and as a landfill cover material among other applications. N-Viro has licensed its recycling process to more than 25 wastewater treatment plants around the world. Outside the US the company's process is marketed through a network of agents. N-Viro International itself manages two facilities that use the process under a contract with the City of Toledo Ohio and another in Florida.

	Annual Growth	12/10	12/11	12/12	12/13	12/14
Sales ($ mil.)	(29.0%)	5.2	5.6	3.6	3.4	1.3
Net income ($ mil.)	–	(3.0)	(1.6)	(1.6)	(1.6)	(1.8)
Market value ($ mil.)	(4.6%)	25.6	9.1	7.5	10.7	21.2
Employees	(22.9%)	34	28	18	19	12

NABORS COMPLETION AND PRODUCTION SERVICES CO.

515 W. Greens Rd.
Houston TX 77067
Phone: 281-874-0035
Fax: 904-268-5809
Web: www.looppizzagrill.com

CEO: Anthony G Petrello
CFO: Thomas W Stoelk
HR: –
FYE: December 31
Type: Subsidiary

If you're in the oil drilling business Nabors Completion and Production wants to be your neighbor. The oil services company (formerly Superior Well) provides technical pumping services (stimulation nitrogen and cementing) and down-hole surveying services (logging and perforating) that smaller rivals do not provide and at prices competitive to those offered by the big oilfield services companies such as Baker Hughes and Schlumberger. The bulk of Nabors Completion and Production's customers are regional oil and gas companies. The technical pumping services unit operates a fleet of more than 1600 commercial vehicles. The company is part of oil and gas exploration and production firm Nabors Industries.

NACCO INDUSTRIES INC.

NYS: NC

5875 Landerbrook Drive, Suite 220
Cleveland, OH 44124-4069
Phone: 440 229-5151
Fax: –
Web: www.nacco.com

CEO: Robert L. (Bob) Benson
CFO: Elizabeth Loveman
HR: –
FYE: December 31
Type: Public

NACCO Industries has a knack for coal mining housewares and specialty retail. The holding company conducts these businesses through three main independent operating subsidiaries. North American Coal (NACoal) mines and markets coal for power generation and steel production through developed mines located in North Dakota Texas Mississippi Louisiana and Alabama. On the housewares side Hamilton Beach Brands designs small kitchen appliances such as meat grinders blenders and juicers while Kitchen Collection (KC) operates Kitchen Collection and Le Gourmet Chef retail stores in factory outlet and traditional malls across the US.

	Annual Growth	12/10	12/11	12/12	12/13	12/14
Sales ($ mil.)	(24.0%)	2,687.5	3,331.2	873.4	932.7	896.8
Net income ($ mil.)	–	79.5	162.1	108.7	44.5	(38.1)
Market value ($ mil.)	(14.0%)	784.1	645.6	439.1	450.0	429.5
Employees	(21.8%)	8,700	9,300	3,900	3,100	3,250

NACCO MATERIALS HANDLING GROUP INC.

5875 Landerbrook Dr. Ste. 300
Cleveland OH 44124
Phone: 440-449-9600
Fax: 562-926-8955
Web: www.pennlitho.com

CEO: Michael P Brogan
CFO: –
HR: –
FYE: December 31
Type: Subsidiary

NACCO Materials Handling Group (NMHG) reaches great heights with its lift trucks. NMHG designs manufactures and sells warehouse trucks including counterbalanced lifts and large capacity cargo and container handling trucks and aftermarket parts for various lift equipment. Its Hyster Yale and Sumitomo-Yale lines are sold mainly through independent dealers. Wholesale sales of materials handling equipment account for about 75% of NMHG's revenue which all told represents 60% or more of parent NACCO Industries' top line. Customers are warehouses retailers food distributors building materials suppliers and trucking and auto companies. NMHG operates a dozen manufacturing and assembly plants worldwide.

NAKED JUICE COMPANY

935 W. 8th St.
Azusa CA 91702
Phone: 626-812-6022
Fax: 626-334-6439
Web: www.nakedjuice.com

CEO: Monty Sharma
CFO: –
HR: –
FYE: December 31
Type: Subsidiary

Tropicana and Minute Maid may dominate the juice market but Naked Juice makes a splash with its all-natural juices. The company a subsidiary of PepsiCo focuses on preservative-free (thus "naked") no-sugar-added juices smoothies and other beverages. Its Naked Juice line is spiked with combinations of proteins probiotics vitamins and herbs and its divided among seven functional families such as Well Being and Antioxidant. Its products are sold throughout the US at health food stores and neighborhood markets as well as major food retailers and club stores. Naked Juices are also available in Canada and the UK. Customers include Costco Kroger Wal-Mart Target and Whole Foods Market.

NALCO HOLDING COMPANY

NYSE: NLC

1601 W. Diehl Rd.
Naperville IL 60563-1198
Phone: 630-305-1000
Fax: 630-305-2900
Web: www.nalco.com

CEO: J Erik Fyrwald
CFO: Kathryn A Mikells
HR: –
FYE: December 31
Type: Subsidiary

Dirty water? Wastewater? Process-stream water? Nalco treats them all. The company is the world's largest maker of chemicals used in water treatment for industrial processes (ahead of #2 GE Water and Process Technologies). Nalco's Energy Services segment is also #1 worldwide ahead of Baker Petrolite; it provides fuel additives oilfield chemicals and flow assurance services to energy companies. The company's chemicals help clarify water conserve energy prevent pollution separate liquids from solids and prevent corrosion in cooling systems and boilers. In 2011 cleaning products firm Ecolab acquired Nalco in a $5.4 billion cash and stock deal.

NAMASCO CORPORATION

500 Colonial Center Pkwy. Ste. 500
Roswell GA 30076
Phone: 678-259-8800
Fax: 678-259-8873
Web: www.namasco.com

CEO: Bill Partalis
CFO: Kirk Johnson
HR: Debra Knight
FYE: December 31
Type: Subsidiary

Namasco has put the pedal to its metals. The company a subsidiary of German distributor Klockner & Co distributes metals throughout the US. Namasco distributes general steel line products that include bar grating and flooring pipe plate and structural tube. The flat rolled division distributes aluminum and a variety of steel products available coated cold- and hot-rolled prepainted and preplated. Namasco also provides processing services like drilling punching plasma tee splitting and plate rolling. Klockner & Co acquired Macsteel Service Centers USA in 2011 for about $660 million and is combining it with Namasco under the brand Kloeckner Metals.

NANO MASK INC.

PINK SHEETS: NANM

50 W. Liberty St. Ste. 880
Reno NV 89501
Phone: 209-275-9270
Fax: 415-495-8018
Web: www.tealeaf.com

CEO: Edward Suydam
CFO: Michael J Marx
HR: –
FYE: December 31
Type: Public

Nano Mask formerly Emergency Filtration Products aims to mask out germs. The company develops and markets advanced filtration materials and products utilizing its proprietary advanced dual filtration system designed to remove infectious bacteria and viruses from air flow systems. Its products range from enzymatic instrument reprocessing solutions and CPR and environmental masks to replacement filters antimicrobial textiles and other related products. It is working to gain FDA approval for its NanoMask personal environmental mask which is designed to be used by health care providers and emergency response workers. Nano Mask also markets the Viramask a personal face mask made by a third-party manufacturer.

NANOMETRICS, INC.

NMS: NANO

1550 Buckeye Drive
Milpitas, CA 95035
Phone: 408 545-6000
Fax: –
Web: www.nanometrics.com

CEO: Timothy J. Stultz
CFO: Jeffrey (Jeff) Andreson
HR: Dawn Laplante
FYE: December 27
Type: Public

Nanometrics works on a nano scale for electronics manufacturers that need their goods to measure up. The company provides thin-film metrology and inspection systems used by makers of precision electronic gear. These stand-alone integrated and tabletop measurement devices gauge the thickness and consistency of film materials used in making semiconductors LEDs data storage components and power management components. Its systems are used throughout the fabrication process from substrate manufacturing to advanced wafer-scale packaging. Top customers include Samsung Electronics Intel Applied Materials and SK Hynix. Nanometrics generates the majority of its sales in Asia.

	Annual Growth	01/11*	12/11	12/12	12/13	12/14
Sales ($ mil.)	(4.0%)	188.1	230.1	182.9	144.3	166.4
Net income ($ mil.)	–	55.9	28.7	4.5	(14.1)	(31.1)
Market value ($ mil.)	9.0%	305.5	438.6	341.0	443.2	395.1
Employees	4.8%	456	552	536	536	525

*Fiscal year change

NANOPHASE TECHNOLOGIES CORP.

NBB: NANX

1319 Marquette Drive
Romeoville, IL 60446
Phone: 630 771-6708
Fax: –
Web: www.nanophase.com

CEO: Jess Jankowski
CFO: Frank J Cesario
HR: Bob Roseland
FYE: December 31
Type: Public

Nanophase Technologies sweats the small stuff. The company is commercializing its nanocrystalline materials (molecular-size ceramic and metallic materials in powder form) for applications in advanced materials technology such as conductive and antistatic coatings for computer monitors. It also develops abrasion-resistant coatings (with uses from coated vinyl flooring to contact lenses) environmental catalysts health care products (sunscreen) and advanced ceramics (cutting tools and ceramic bearings). Chemicals maker BASF accounts for more than half of Nanophase's sales.

	Annual Growth	12/10	12/11	12/12	12/13	12/14
Sales ($ mil.)	1.2%	9.5	9.7	10.0	9.6	9.9
Net income ($ mil.)	–	(4.1)	(3.4)	(2.4)	(2.5)	(1.7)
Market value ($ mil.)	(24.1%)	34.4	11.7	9.7	15.4	11.4
Employees	(5.5%)	49	49	46	43	39

NANOSPHERE INC

NAS: NSPH

4088 Commercial Avenue
Northbrook, IL 60062
Phone: 847 400-9000
Fax: –
Web: www.nanosphere.us

CEO: Michael K McGarrity
CFO: Ann Wallin
HR: –
FYE: December 31
Type: Public

Nanosphere offers molecular diagnostics for the masses: Its molecular testing system is intended for use in hospital-based laboratories that don't have the money or expertise to maintain the complex genomic testing equipment often reserved for reference labs and research centers. The company's diagnostic Verigene System is a compact and simple workstation designed to perform multiple genomic and protein tests simultaneously on a single sample. Nanosphere also sells Verigene-compatible tests including hematology cystic fibrosis and influenza diagnostic assays and has several other tests including HPV (the virus that causes cervical cancer) in the works.

	Annual Growth	12/10	12/11	12/12	12/13	12/14
Sales ($ mil.)	63.0%	2.0	2.5	5.1	10.0	14.3
Net income ($ mil.)	–	(40.6)	(35.4)	(32.9)	(34.6)	(39.1)
Market value ($ mil.)	(45.3%)	25.6	8.6	16.9	13.4	2.3
Employees	10.1%	115	131	151	165	169

NANOSTRING TECHNOLOGIES INC

NMS: NSTG

530 Fairview Avenue North, Suite 2000
Seattle, WA 98109
Phone: 206 378-6266
Fax: -
Web: www.nanostring.com

CEO: R. Bradley (Brad) Gray
CFO: James A. Johnson
HR: Debbie Krogman
FYE: December 31
Type: Public

NanoString Technologies helps unspool the mystery of the human genome. The company makes a complex genomic analysis device that can be used onsite at clinical laboratories instead of being shipped offsite for study. Called the nCounter Analysis System the device uses tissue extracted from a tumor to analyze up to 800 genes in a single experiment. These tests can help researchers understand the molecular basis of some diseases such as cancer. In addition its Prosigna Breast Cancer Assay a molecular diagnostics test went into wide release in late 2013. Founded in 2003 the company went public in mid-2013.

	Annual Growth	12/10	12/11	12/12	12/13	12/14
Sales ($ mil.)	41.9%	11.7	17.8	23.0	31.4	47.6
Net income ($ mil.)	-	(12.8)	(10.9)	(17.7)	(29.3)	(50.0)
Market value ($ mil.)	(19.2%)	-	-	-	315.0	254.5
Employees	38.4%	-	-	144	174	276

NANOSYS INC.

2625 Hanover St.
Palo Alto CA 94304
Phone: 650-331-2100
Fax: 650-331-2101
Web: www.nanosysinc.com

CEO: Jason Hartlove
CFO: -
HR: -
FYE: December 31
Type: Private

Nanosys develops nanomaterials for use in many different systems. These tiny structures are engineered on a nanometer scale. (To get an idea of how small a nanometer is consider this: If a human hair were the width of the US one nanometer would be as long as three railway locomotives.) The company's patented materials enable enhanced function in a variety of applications including solar cells biological sensors flash memory devices specialized coatings and flexible electronics. The company's customers include Matsushita Electric Works SAIC and agencies of the US government.

NAPCO SECURITY TECHNOLOGIES, INC.

NMS: NSSC

333 Bayview Avenue
Amityville, NY 11701
Phone: 631 842-9400
Fax: -
Web: www.napcosecurity.com

CEO: -
CFO: -
HR: Alison Kanavy
FYE: June 30
Type: Public

Crime pays for Napco Security Technologies. If you're trying to prevent it Napco manufactures a slew of security products used in commercial and residential buildings as well as government and institutional facilities. Products include burglary and fire alarm systems exit alarm-locks and digital-access control locks video surveillance systems such as cameras and monitors and emergency communications systems. Napco also buys and resells security devices made by third-party manufacturers. The company sells its products worldwide mainly through independent distributors dealers and installers of security equipment.

	Annual Growth	06/11	06/12	06/13	06/14	06/15
Sales ($ mil.)	2.2%	71.4	70.9	71.4	74.4	77.8
Net income ($ mil.)	44.2%	1.1	2.3	3.0	3.5	4.8
Market value ($ mil.)	17.9%	56.3	55.8	90.7	103.0	108.7
Employees	(0.7%)	1,042	957	908	994	1,013

NARUS INC.

570 Maude Ct.
Sunnyvale CA 94085
Phone: 408-215-4300
Fax: 408-215-4301
Web: www.narus.com

CEO: -
CFO: -
HR: -
FYE: January 31
Type: Subsidiary

Narus wants to give you insight into the inner workings of your Internet protocol (IP) network. The company provides software used by telecommunications services providers to optimize their IP platforms. Narus' products are used to protect networks against malicious attacks analyze network traffic flow and monitor network activity. The company also offers professional services such as consulting installation training maintenance and support. The company's customers have included Korea Telecom KDDI Telecom Egypt and KPN. Narus was acquired by Boeing in 2010.

NASB FINANCIAL INC

NBB: NASB

12498 South 71 Highway
Grandview, MO 64030
Phone: 816 765-2200
Fax: 816 761-4113
Web: www.nasb.com

CEO: Paul L Thomas
CFO: Rhonda Nyhus
HR: -
FYE: September 30
Type: Public

NASB Financial is the holding company for North American Savings Bank which operates about 15 branches and loan offices in the Kansas City and Springfield Missouri areas. Established in 1927 the bank offers standard deposit products to retail and commercial customers including checking and savings accounts and CDs. Mortgages secured by residential or commercial properties make up most of the bank's lending activities; it also originates business consumer and construction loans. Subsidiary Nor-Am sells annuities mutual funds and credit life and disability insurance. Chairman David Hancock and his wife Linda who is also a member of the company's board of directors own about 45% of NASB Financial.

	Annual Growth	09/10	09/11	09/12	09/13	09/14
Assets ($ mil.)	(5.0%)	1,434.2	1,253.6	1,240.8	1,144.2	1,168.1
Net income ($ mil.)	27.4%	6.3	(16.3)	18.1	27.6	16.7
Market value ($ mil.)	9.4%	124.2	75.2	186.4	205.8	177.9
Employees	3.8%	414	398	436	463	-

NASCAR MEDIA GROUP

2049 Century Park East Ste. 3000
Los Angeles CA 90067
Phone: 310-843-2300
Fax: 304-598-3232
Web: www.mylanpharms.com

CEO: -
CFO: -
HR: -
FYE: December 31
Type: Business Segment

This company brings the need for speed to film and television. A unit of the National Association for Stock Car Auto Racing (NASCAR) NASCAR Media Group is an entertainment production and marketing company that holds exclusive rights to use and license footage from NASCAR racing events. It works with sponsors and other clients to incorporate NASCAR properties into corporate marketing efforts; it also provides post-production and other media services. On the entertainment side NASCAR Media Group works helps create original films and TV programming. Clients have included ESPN FOX Sports TNT and DirecTV.

NASDAQ INC

NMS: NDAQ

One Liberty Plaza	CEO: Robert (Bob) Greifeld
New York, NY 10006	CFO: Lee Shavel
Phone: 212 401-8700	HR: –
Fax: –	FYE: December 31
Web: www.nasdaqomx.com	Type: Public

NASDAQ OMX isn't a place; it's a state of mind. OK that's not exactly true but NASDAQ OMX is the leader in floorless exchanges and has challenged NYSE Euronext as the world's largest stock exchange. The group trades some 3500 companies worth more than $9 trillion in market capital including exchange-traded funds (ETFs) equities options futures derivatives commodities and structured products. In some locations the company provides clearing settlement and depository services. International business accounts for more than 25% of NASDAQ OMX's revenue. The group was formed in 2008 when the NASDAQ Stock Market merged with OMX the owner of Northern Europe's largest securities marketplace.

	Annual Growth	12/10	12/11	12/12	12/13	12/14
Sales ($ mil.)	2.3%	3,197.0	3,438.0	3,119.0	3,211.0	3,500.0
Net income ($ mil.)	1.2%	395.0	387.0	352.0	385.0	414.0
Market value ($ mil.)	19.2%	4,005.5	4,137.2	4,218.2	6,718.1	8,095.4
Employees	11.4%	2,395	2,433	2,506	3,365	3,687

NASSCO HOLDINGS INCORPORATED

2798 Harbor Dr.	CEO: –
San Diego CA 92113	CFO: Eric Murray
Phone: 619-544-8838	HR: –
Fax: 619-544-3540	FYE: December 31
Web: www.nassco.com	Type: Subsidiary

Business is shipshape at NASSCO Holdings dba General Dynamics NASSCO. The General Dynamics subsidiary operates the only major construction shipyard on the US West Coast; it maintains and repairs all facets of large ocean-bound military and commercial surface ships. NASSCO provides new ship construction overhaul and upgrade for the US Navy and less so commercial customers such as TOTE and Shell. Its work includes dry cargo carriers ferries oil tankers and ships for US and NATO combat support. NASSCO serves as a key homeport for the Navy's Pacific Fleet. Formerly National Steel and Ship-building Company it was founded in 1905 as a machine shop. NASSCO is part of General Dynamics' Marine Systems group.

NATHAN'S FAMOUS, INC.

NMS: NATH

One Jericho Plaza, Second Floor - Wing A	CEO: Eric Gatoff
Jericho NY 11753	CFO: Ronald G Devos
Phone: 516 338-8500	HR: –
Fax: –	FYE: March 29
Web: www.nathansfamous.com	Type: Public

Patrons of this restaurateur are in the dog house. Nathan's Famous is a leading franchisor of quick-service restaurants with a chain of about 300 Nathan's outlets known for all-beef frankfurters served with a variety of toppings. The eateries located in about 25 states and a half dozen other countries also serve hamburgers crinkle-cut fries and breakfast sandwiches. More than 50 Nathan's units also feature fish and chips under the Arthur Treacher's brand. In addition to restaurants the company sells Nathan's branded products through vending machines Subway units at Wal-Mart stores and Auntie Anne's pretzel shops. Specialty Foods Group makes Nathan's hot dogs for retail sale under a licensing deal.

	Annual Growth	03/11	03/12	03/13	03/14	03/15
Sales ($ mil.)	14.7%	57.3	66.2	71.5	82.9	99.1
Net income ($ mil.)	51.6%	2.2	6.2	7.5	8.3	11.7
Market value ($ mil.)	44.0%	78.7	96.7	194.5	224.6	338.7
Employees	1.0%	219	219	161	210	228

NATIONAL ACADEMY OF RECORDING ARTS & SCIENCES INC

3030 OLYMPIC BLVD	CEO: Neil Portnow
SANTA MONICA, CA 904045073	CFO: Wayne J Zahner
Phone: 310-392-3777	HR: Gaetano Frizzi
Fax: –	FYE: July 31
Web: www.grammy.com	Type: Private

The National Academy of Recording Arts and Sciences better known as The Recording Academy provides arts advocacy outreach and education and support services to professionals in the recording industry. The membership organization boasts some 18000 members served by a dozen regional chapters throughout the US. The Recording Academy acknowledges outstanding work by musicians producers engineers and recording professionals with its annual GRAMMY Awards ceremonies. Its first international venture The Latin Academy of Recording Arts & Sciences (which produces The Latin GRAMMY Awards) was formed in 1997. The Recording Academy was established in 1957.

	Annual Growth	07/05	07/06	07/07	07/08	07/09
Sales ($ mil.)	(78.2%)	–	–	1,157.5	65.8	55.3
Net income ($ mil.)	–	–	–	0.0	5.1	(4.8)
Market value ($ mil.)	–	–	–	–	–	–
Employees	–	–	–	–	–	110

NATIONAL ALLIANCE TO END HOMELESSNESS INC.

1518 K St. NW Ste. 410	CEO: –
Washington DC 20005	CFO: –
Phone: 202-638-1526	HR: –
Fax: 202-638-4664	FYE: June 30
Web: www.naeh.org	Type: Private - Not-for-Pr

This group wants to put roofs over the heads of the estimated 675000 people who are homeless in America each night. The National Alliance to End Homelessness is dedicated to solving the problem of homelessness in every community. The organization works with around 5000 public private and not-for-profit sectors in its plan to end homelessness in 10 years (or by 2010). The Alliance lobbies government supports local assistance groups and educates the public about the causes effects and solutions to homelessness. It also promotes best practices by sharing the programs that are working in communities. The Alliance was founded in 1983 as homelessness began to be a problem in the US.

NATIONAL AMERICAN UNIVERSITY HOLDINGS INC.

NMS: NAUH

5301 S. Highway 16	CEO: Ronald L Shape
Rapid City, SD 57701	CFO: David K Heflin
Phone: 605 721-5200	HR: –
Fax: –	FYE: May 31
Web: www.national.edu	Type: Public

National American University Holdings believes in the power of continuing education. Through subsidiary Dlorah the for-profit company owns National American University (NAU) which has more than 20 campuses in eight states and offers classes online. Some locations are considered hybrids offering both in-class and online courses. Targeting working adults and other non-traditional students NAU offers associate's bachelor's and master's degrees as well as certification in business criminal justice and health care disciplines. The university was founded in 1941 as the National School of Business; the holding company which was formed in 2007 to acquire an education company purchased Dlorah in 2009.

	Annual Growth	05/11	05/12	05/13	05/14	05/15
Sales ($ mil.)	2.5%	106.8	118.9	129.2	127.8	117.9
Net income ($ mil.)	(10.1%)	10.3	5.0	5.4	3.5	6.7
Market value ($ mil.)	(20.2%)	189.7	98.2	95.2	84.6	77.1
Employees	(11.4%)	1,200	1,716	1,634	1,562	740

NATIONAL AMUSEMENTS INC.

200 Elm St.	CEO: Sumner M Redstone
Dedham MA 02026	CFO: Michael Kszystyniak
Phone: 781-461-1600	HR: –
Fax: 781-407-0052	FYE: December 31
Web: www.national-amusements.com	Type: Private

Media mogul Sumner Redstone puts the business in show business through National Amusements. What began as a humble drive-in theater operation evolved into a powerhouse that controls just under 80% of media giants Viacom and CBS Corporation. Redstone the controlling stockholder of National Amusements is chairman of Viacom and CBS Corporation. True to its roots National Amusements also operates Showcase Cinemas Multiplex Cinemas and Cinema de Lux branded theaters — about 950 screens total — in the US the UK and Latin America. National Amusements additionally operates IMAX theaters in the US and Argentina and is a partner in online ticketing service MovieTickets.com.

NATIONAL ASSOCIATION FOR STOCK CAR AUTO RACING INC.

1801 W. International Speedway Blvd.	CEO: Brian Z France
Daytona Beach FL 32114	CFO: James C France
Phone: 386-253-0611	HR: –
Fax: 386-681-4041	FYE: December 31
Web: www.nascar.com	Type: Private

In the race for riches in the sports world NASCAR is on the right track. The National Association for Stock Car Auto Racing serves as the sanctioning body for stock car racing one of the most popular spectator sports in the US. It runs more than 100 races each year in three circuits: the Nationwide Craftsman Truck and its signature Sprint Cup Series. Featuring popular drivers such as Jeff Gordon and Jimmie Johnson the Sprint Cup draws millions of fans to the tracks each year. In addition to organizing and promoting the races the association negotiates broadcast rights and licenses the NASCAR brand for merchandise. NASCAR was founded in 1948 by Bill France Sr. and is still owned by the France family.

NATIONAL ASSOCIATION OF BROADCASTERS

1771 N ST NW	CEO: –
WASHINGTON, DC 200362800	CFO: Ken Almgrem
Phone: 202-429-5300	HR: –
Fax: –	FYE: March 31
Web: www.nab.org	Type: Private

The National Association of Broadcasters (NAB) represents on-the-air talkers ranging from local radio reporters to TV network news anchors. The trade group serves as its members' eyes ears and of course voice before Congress the courts and federal regulatory agencies in Washington DC. NAB priorities have included spectrum management retransmission consent political advertising rates and limiting content regulation. The NAB predates television and goes back to the early days of radio — the organization was founded in 1923.

	Annual Growth	03/02	03/03	03/12	03/13	03/14
Sales ($ mil.)	0.9%	–	52.2	47.9	57.0	57.9
Net income ($ mil.)	–	–	–	(5.0)	5.8	4.5
Market value ($ mil.)	–	–	–	–	–	–
Employees	–	–	–	–	–	173

NATIONAL AUDUBON SOCIETY INC.

225 VARICK ST FL 7	CEO: David Yarnold
NEW YORK, NY 100144396	CFO: Mary Beth Henson
Phone: 212-979-3000	HR: –
Fax: –	FYE: June 30
Web: www.audubon.org	Type: Private

Audubon has gone to the birds. The National Audubon Society is a not-for-profit organization dedicated to preserving birds and other wildlife and their habitats by conserving and restoring their natural ecosystems. The society operates programs and educational centers in every US state and in several South American and Caribbean countries to encourage grassroots conservation and promote environmental public policy reform. Projects have included saving habitats in the Everglades Arctic Wildlife Refuge Long Island Sound and Mississippi River basin. Audubon also publishes Audubon Magazine. A precursor to the society formed in 1886 but disbanded when it grew too quickly. The current society began in 1905.

	Annual Growth	06/07	06/08	06/09	06/10	06/13
Sales ($ mil.)	(46.6%)	–	2,057.7	74.0	80.1	88.9
Net income ($ mil.)	–	–	–	0.0	(1.8)	0.7
Market value ($ mil.)	–	–	–	–	–	–
Employees	–	–	–	–	–	600

NATIONAL AUTOMOBILE DEALERS ASSOCIATION

8400 WESTPARK DR STE 1	CEO: –
MC LEAN, VA 221023522	CFO: Joseph (Joe) Cowden
Phone: 703-821-7000	HR: –
Fax: –	FYE: December 31
Web: www.nadafrontpage.com	Type: Private

The National Automobile Dealers Association (N.A.D.A.) has been around almost as long as there have been cars. Founded in 1917 N.A.D.A. represents more than 16000 new car and truck dealers in the US and abroad. Through its more than 32500 franchises N.A.D.A. offers a range of services including: government relations (lobbying of Congress education of dealers) legal and public affairs dealership operations and other courses through N.A.D.A University insurance and retirement benefits IT training and convention and exposition support. N.A.D.A. also publishes AutoExec magazine (it sold The N.A.D.A. Official Used Car Guide). Membership is open to any dealer with a new car or truck sales and service franchise.

	Annual Growth	12/01	12/02	12/05	12/09	12/12
Sales ($ mil.)	5.9%	–	59.4	43.0	35.4	105.8
Net income ($ mil.)	24.7%	–	–	4.2	(0.9)	20.0
Market value ($ mil.)	–	–	–	–	–	–
Employees	–	–	–	–	–	500

NATIONAL BANCSHARES CORP. (OHIO)

NBB: NBOH

112 West Market Street, P.O. Box 57	CEO: –
Orrville, OH 44667	CFO: –
Phone: 330 682-1010	HR: –
Fax: –	FYE: December 31
Web: www.discoverfirstnational.com	Type: Public

Bank on the fact that National Bancshares is the holding company for First National Bank which serves northeastern Ohio through about 15 branch locations. Operating in Wayne Medina and Stark counties the bank offers traditional retail products and services such as deposit accounts CDs and credit cards. It mainly uses funds from deposits to originate commercial and consumer loans and mortgages. Real estate loans account for 85% of its loan book. First National Bank also owns 49% of title insurance agency First Kropf Title; National Bancshares chairman John Kropf is a partner of the title company's majority stakeholder law firm Kropf Wagner Hohenberger & Lutz.

	Annual Growth	12/09	12/10	12/11	12/12	12/13
Assets ($ mil.)	6.5%	370.2	374.1	406.1	440.8	476.2
Net income ($ mil.)	26.5%	1.6	1.3	2.6	2.8	4.1
Market value ($ mil.)	11.4%	31.7	28.9	32.5	33.8	48.8
Employees	2.6%	101	113	115	113	112

NATIONAL BANK HOLDINGS CORP

NYS: NBHC

7800 East Orchard Road, Suite 300
Greenwood Village, CO 80111
Phone: 720 529-3336
Fax: –

CEO: G. Timothy (Tim) Laney
CFO: Brian F. Lilly
HR: –
FYE: December 31
Type: Public

As seems only rational National Bank Holdings is the holding company for NBH Bank which has more than 140 branches that operate as Bank Midwest in Kansas and Missouri under the Community Banks of Colorado and Bank of Choice banners in Colorado under the Community Banks of California banner in that state and as Hillcrest Bank in Texas and Colorado. Targeting small to medium-sized businesses and consumers the banks offer traditional checking and savings accounts as well as commercial and residential mortgages agricultural loans and commercial loans.

	Annual Growth	12/10	12/11	12/12	12/13	12/14
Assets ($ mil.)	(8.8%)	–	6,352.0	5,410.8	4,914.1	4,819.6
Net income ($ mil.)	11.0%	6.1	42.0	(0.5)	6.9	9.2
Market value ($ mil.)	1.1%	–	–	738.4	832.1	754.8
Employees	(6.4%)	–	–	1,205	1,108	1,056

NATIONAL BANK OF ARIZONA

6001 N. 24th St.
Phoenix AZ 85016
Phone: 602-235-6000
Fax: 602-955-0612
Web: www.nbarizona.com

CEO: –
CFO: –
HR: –
FYE: December 31
Type: Subsidiary

A subsidiary of Utah-based multibank holding company Zions Bancorporation National Bank of Arizona provides individuals and businesses with a variety of banking and financial services from a network of around 75 branches throughout the state. Services include checking and savings accounts debit and credit cards and the origination of personal commercial real estate and business loans. The bank also provides wealth management and merchant services to area businesses and offers online brokerage and wealth management services through affiliates of its parent company. It added private banking to its menu of services in 2009.

NATIONAL BANKSHARES INC. (VA)

NAS: NKSH

101 Hubbard Street, P.O. Box 90002
Blacksburg, VA 24062-9002
Phone: 540 951-6300
Fax: –
Web: www.nationalbankshares.com

CEO: James G. (Jim) Rakes
CFO: David K. Skeens
HR: Lara Ramsey
FYE: December 31
Type: Public

National Bankshares is the holding company for National Bank of Blacksburg (National Bank for short) which serves consumers and small business in southwest Virginia through some two dozen branches. The community bank's services include deposit accounts credit cards and personal and corporate trust services. Commercial mortgages including loans secured by college housing and professional office buildings account for more than half of National Bankshares' loan portfolio; residential mortgages make up more than a quarter. To a lesser extent the bank also writes business construction and consumer loans. Another subsidiary National Bankshares Financial Services provides investments and insurance.

	Annual Growth	12/10	12/11	12/12	12/13	12/14
Assets ($ mil.)	3.1%	1,022.2	1,067.1	1,104.4	1,110.6	1,154.7
Net income ($ mil.)	2.1%	15.6	17.6	17.7	17.8	16.9
Market value ($ mil.)	(0.9%)	218.9	194.1	225.1	256.4	211.2
Employees	0.0%	18	18	19	20	18

NATIONAL BEVERAGE CORP.

NMS: FIZZ

8100 S.W. Tenth Street, Suite 4000
Fort Lauderdale, FL 33324
Phone: 954 581-0922
Fax: –
Web: www.nationalbeverage.com

CEO: Nick A. Caporella
CFO: –
HR: Heather Haberman
FYE: May 02
Type: Public

National Beverage works to quench America's thirst. The company makes and distributes the Shasta and Faygo brands of flavored soft drinks both of which were launched more than a century ago and come in multiple flavors to appeal to diverse consumer tastes. It also offers spring and flavored waters under the LaCroix and ClearFruit brands Everfresh and Mr. Pure juice and juice-added drinks Rip It energy drinks and Ohana lemonades and teas. Customers include national and regional grocers convenience stores and foodservice distributors. National Beverage operates a dozen facilities located across the US. Company chairman and CEO Nick Caporella owns 74% of the business.

	Annual Growth	04/11	04/12	04/13*	05/14	05/15
Sales ($ mil.)	1.8%	600.2	628.9	662.0	641.1	645.8
Net income ($ mil.)	4.9%	40.8	44.0	46.9	43.6	49.3
Market value ($ mil.)	12.7%	645.7	680.9	675.8	891.1	1,040.0
Employees	0.0%	1,200	1,200	1,200	1,200	1,200

*Fiscal year change

NATIONAL CABLE SATELLITE CORP

400 N CAPITOL ST NW # 650
WASHINGTON, DC 200011511
Phone: 202-737-3220
Fax: –
Web: www.c-span.org

CEO: Robert Kennedy
CFO: –
HR: –
FYE: March 31
Type: Private

National Cable Satellite Corporation is a political junkie. The company (better known as C-SPAN which stands for Cable Satellite Public Affairs Network) is a not-for-profit created in 1979 by the cable industry as a public service to provide live coverage of the US House of Representatives. The corporation's C-SPAN C-SPAN2 and C-SPAN3 air public proceedings such as congressional sessions White House press briefings and speeches British House of Commons sessions and other political and public affairs programs. C-SPAN also runs a radio network with content similar to its TV broadcasts and publishes more than 15 Web sites. The company gets its funds from license fees paid by cable and satellite systems.

	Annual Growth	03/09	03/10	03/11	03/12	03/13
Sales ($ mil.)	6.5%	–	58.4	67.5	70.9	70.6
Net income ($ mil.)	(14.1%)	–	–	16.9	11.0	12.5
Market value ($ mil.)	–	–	–	–	–	–
Employees	–	–	–	–	–	260

NATIONAL CAR RENTAL

6929 N. Lakewood Ave. Ste. 100
Tulsa OK 74117
Phone: 918-401-6000
Fax: 202-513-3329
Web: www.npr.org

CEO: –
CFO: –
HR: –
FYE: December 31
Type: Subsidiary

National Car Rental operates through about 3000 locations in the US Canada Mexico the Caribbean Latin America and Asia. The company markets its services mainly to business travelers but also to leisure travelers. In particular National works to develop corporate accounts and its customers include about one-third of the companies in the FORTUNE 500. Founded in 1947 National and sister company Alamo Rent A Car were acquired by Enterprise Rent-A-Car in 2007 and became part of privately-held Enterprise Holdings in 2009. Together the Alamo Enterprise and National brands form a global network of more than 7600 airport and neighborhood locations.

NATIONAL CINEMEDIA INC

NMS: NCMI

9110 East Nichols Avenue, Suite 200
Centennial, CO 80112-3405
Phone: 303 792-3600
Fax: –
Web: www.ncm.com

CEO: Kurt C. Hall
CFO: David J. Oddo
HR: –
FYE: January 01
Type: Public

National CineMedia (NCM) puts on its show before the real show starts at the movies (and even before the previews of coming attractions). Through its NCM Cinema Network the company distributes in-theater advertising on about 20150 movie screens across the US. NCM also produces and distributes FirstLook a pre-show entertainment program and entertainment industry infomercial. Additionally the company provides advertising to theater lobbies on its Lobby Entertainment Network (LEN). Major NCM shareholders include theater operators Regal Entertainment AMC Entertainment and Cinemark.

	Annual Growth	12/10	12/11	12/12	12/13*	01/15
Sales ($ mil.)	(1.6%)	427.5	435.4	448.8	462.8	394.0
Net income ($ mil.)	(14.4%)	29.2	31.5	13.4	41.2	13.4
Market value ($ mil.)	(6.4%)	1,173.3	706.8	830.2	1,174.4	844.3
Employees	(0.5%)	609	640	641	606	595

*Fiscal year change

NATIONAL COOPERATIVE REFINERY ASSOCIATION

2000 S. Main St.
McPherson KS 67460
Phone: 620-241-2340
Fax: 620-241-5531
Web: www.ncra.coop

CEO: Carl Casale
CFO: Timothy Skidmore
HR: –
FYE: August 31
Type: Private - Cooperativ

Cooperation is a refined art and refining a cooperative art for the National Cooperative Refinery Association (NCRA) which provides three farm supply cooperatives (CHS GROWMARK and MFA Oil) with gasoline and diesel fuel through its oil refinery in McPherson Kansas. The refinery's production rate is 85000 barrels per day. Fuel from the refinery is allocated to member/owners on the basis of ownership percentages. In addition to the refinery NCRA owns Jayhawk Pipeline minority interests in two other pipeline companies and an underground oil storage facility. CHS owns 74% of the cooperative GROWMARK 19% and MFA 7%.

NATIONAL COUNCIL OF YOUNG MEN''S CHRISTIAN ASSOCIATIONS OF THE U

101 N WACKER DR STE 1600
CHICAGO, IL 606067310
Phone: 312-977-0031
Fax: –
Web: www.ymcagreaterprovidence.org

CEO: –
CFO: –
HR: Sharon Berglund
FYE: December 31
Type: Private

A venerable not-for-profit community service organization YMCA of the USA (Y-USA) assists the more than 2700 individual YMCAs across the country and represents them on both national and international levels. Although YMCA stands for Young Men's Christian Association the organization's programs are open to all. Local YMCAs are leading providers of child care in the US. The facilities also offer programs in aquatics arts and humanities education of new immigrants health and fitness and teen leadership. Overall YMCAs serve about 21 million people in some 10000 neighborhoods across the US which includes about 9 million children under the age of 17.

	Annual Growth	06/06	06/07*	09/08*	12/08	12/13
Sales ($ mil.)	–	–	0.0	1.5	0.5	119.0
Net income ($ mil.)	–	–	–	(0.0)	0.0	17.6
Market value ($ mil.)	–	–	–	–	–	–
Employees	–	–	–	–	–	350

*Fiscal year change

NATIONAL COUNCIL ON AGING INC.

1901 L ST NW FL 4
WASHINGTON, DC 20036-3540
Phone: 202-479-1200
Fax: –
Web: www.ncoa.org

CEO: James Firman
CFO: Donna Whitt
HR: –
FYE: June 30
Type: Private

The National Council on the Aging (NCOA) can help us all grow old gracefully. The nonprofit is an advocate for the elderly. Its members include adult day service centers employment services senior housing facilities and faith-based organizations. NCOA monitors public policies business practices and attitudes concerning older Americans. The group operates a Web site called BenefitsCheckUp which allows users to search federal state and private benefit and prescription savings programs for which they might be eligible. Other programs include matching volunteers with at-risk children and families as well as providing training and employment opportunities to those older than 55. NCOA was formed in 1950.

	Annual Growth	06/07	06/08	06/09	06/10	06/11
Sales ($ mil.)	363.7%	–	0.6	0.1	0.1	62.2
Net income ($ mil.)	–	–	(0.0)	(0.0)	(0.0)	(4.4)
Market value ($ mil.)	–	–	–	–	–	–
Employees	–	–	–	–	–	80

NATIONAL DENTEX CORPORATION

2 Vision Dr.
Natick MA 01760
Phone: 508-907-7800
Fax: 508-907-6050
Web: www.nationaldentex.com

CEO: Steven E Casper
CFO: Mark Brockelman
HR: –
FYE: December 31
Type: Private

When your teeth need a little work National Dentex (NDX) has the tools for the job. The company designs and makes dental prosthetic devices. Its products fall into three categories: restorative (crowns and bridges) reconstructive (partial and full dentures) and cosmetic (porcelain veneers and ceramic crowns). They are sold under the brand names NTI-tss Plus Thermo-Guard PMZ and ClearFrame and are made from impressions models and X-rays submitted by dentists. As part of its operations NDX serves some 28000 dentists across more than 40 dental laboratories in the US and Canada. Each lab operates under its own name and boasts a local sales staff.

NATIONAL DISTRIBUTING COMPANY INC.

1 National Dr. SW
Atlanta GA 30336-1631
Phone: 404-696-9440
Fax: 404-505-1013
Web: www.ndcweb.com

CEO: Jay Davis
CFO: –
HR: –
FYE: December 31
Type: Private

Residents of Georgia and New Mexico with a taste for beer or other alcoholic beverage may be fortunate to live in a state that National Distributing Company (NDC) serves. The wholesale wine spirits and beer vendor supplies the Peach Tree State and Land of Enchantment and through NDC affiliate Republic National Distributing Company (RNDC) has a foothold in about 20 other states and Washington DC. Its suppliers include distillers Diageo and Pernod Ricard winemaker E & J Gallo and beer producer United Breweries along with several well-known and specialty alcoholic beverage makers. NDC operates out of four offices one each in Albany Atlanta and Savannah Georgia and one in Albuquerque New Mexico.

NATIONAL EDUCATION ASSOCIATION OF THE UNITED STATES

1201 16TH ST NW
WASHINGTON, DC 200363290
Phone: 202-833-4000
Fax: –
Web: www.nea.org

CEO: –
CFO: Mike McPherson
HR: –
FYE: August 31
Type: Private

The National Education Association (NEA) is dedicated to promoting the cause of public education and the teaching profession. The organization boasts a membership of 3 million elementary and secondary teachers support professionals administrators higher education faculty and student teachers. It operates in all US states through affiliates. The group's key issues include the No Child Left Behind Act professional pay education funding minority community outreach dropout prevention achievement gaps and other matters facing America's schools. Founded in 1857 the NEA also hosts Read Across America a one-day reading event held on Dr. Seuss' birthday.

	Annual Growth	08/06	08/07	08/08*	12/08*	08/10
Sales ($ mil.)	–	–	–	(356.2)	0.6	376.6
Net income ($ mil.)	54061.2%	–	–	0.0	0.0	16.1
Market value ($ mil.)	–	–	–	–	–	–
Employees	–	–	–	–	–	735

*Fiscal year change

NATIONAL FOOTBALL LEAGUE

280 Park Ave. 15th Fl.
New York NY 10017
Phone: 212-450-2000
Fax: 212-681-7573
Web: www.nfl.com

CEO: –
CFO: Anthony Noto
HR: –
FYE: March 31
Type: Private

In the world of professional sports the National Football League blitzes the competition. The organization oversees America's most popular spectator sport acting as a trade association for 32 franchise owners. Among the league's functions the NFL governs and promotes the game of football sets and enforces rules and regulates team ownership. It generates revenue mostly through marketing sponsorships licensing merchandise and by selling national broadcasting rights to the games. The teams operate as separate businesses but share a percentage of the league's overall revenue. Founded in 1920 as the American Professional Football Association the league has been known as the NFL since 1922.

NATIONAL FOOTBALL LEAGUE PLAYERS ASSOCIATION

1133 20TH ST NW FRNT 1
WASHINGTON, DC 200363449
Phone: 202-756-9100
Fax: –
Web: www.nflplayers.com

CEO: –
CFO: –
HR: –
FYE: February 29
Type: Private

The National Football League Players Association (NFLPA) represents the interests of people who go to work in helmets and shoulder pads. The union oversees its members' collective bargaining agreement with the National Football League negotiates and monitors retirement and insurance benefits and works to promote the image of the players through marketing and licensing subsidiary NFL PLAYERS (formerly PLAYERS INC). A member of the AFL-CIO the NFLPA represents both active and retired players. It is governed by a board of player representatives who are chosen by their teammates. The union was established in 1956 more than 35 years after the NFL was organized.

	Annual Growth	02/97	02/98	02/02	02/09	02/12
Sales ($ mil.)	–	–	(1,678.4)	68.7	62.7	81.3
Net income ($ mil.)	–	–	–	4.1	11.5	(36.2)
Market value ($ mil.)	–	–	–	–	–	–
Employees	–	–	–	–	–	89

NATIONAL FROZEN FOODS CORPORATION

1600 FRVIEW AVE E STE 200
SEATTLE, WA 98102
Phone: 541-928-3306
Fax: –
Web: www.nffc.com

CEO: –
CFO: –
HR: Terry Wilson
FYE: August 30
Type: Private

Cool Beans! National Frozen Foods has made a name for itself as one of the nation's largest private-label frozen vegetable producers. The family-owned company's products which include peas sweet corn carrots squash and beans (green Italian lima and wax) as well as vegetable blends organic veggies and pureed items are available in grocery stores worldwide. National Frozen Foods also provides bulk and custom-packaging services. The company operates four processing plants in Washington and Oregon that offer a combined cold storage capacity for nearly 200 million pounds of frozen vegetables.

	Annual Growth	04/10	04/11	04/12*	08/13	08/14
Sales ($ mil.)	4.4%	–	178.1	197.2	18.2	202.6
Net income ($ mil.)	13.5%	–	–	13.6	5.8	17.6
Market value ($ mil.)	–	–	–	–	–	–
Employees	–	–	–	–	–	1,009

*Fiscal year change

NATIONAL FUEL GAS CO. (NJ)

NYS: NFG

6363 Main Street
Williamsville, NY 14221
Phone: 716 857-7000
Fax: –
Web: www.nationalfuelgas.com

CEO: Ronald J. (Ron) Tanski
CFO: David P Bauer
HR: –
FYE: September 30
Type: Public

National Fuel Gas doesn't cover the nation but it does touch all the bases in its industry: The company explores for produces stores transmits and distributes natural gas. The diversified energy concern's public utility National Fuel Gas Distribution (almost half of the company's annual sales) distributes gas to more than 728000 customers in New York and Pennsylvania. National Fuel Gas has gas exploration production storage and transportation units; it also engages in energy marketing timber processing and independent power activities. In 2012 oil and gas subsidiary Seneca Resources reported proved reserves of 988.4 billion cu. ft. of natural gas and 42.9 million barrels of oil.

	Annual Growth	09/11	09/12	09/13	09/14	09/15
Sales ($ mil.)	(0.3%)	1,778.8	1,626.9	1,829.6	2,113.1	1,760.9
Net income ($ mil.)	–	258.4	220.1	260.0	299.4	(379.4)
Market value ($ mil.)	0.7%	4,118.1	4,571.5	5,816.7	5,920.8	4,228.0
Employees	3.8%	1,827	1,874	1,912	2,010	2,125

NATIONAL GRAPE CO-OPERATIVE ASSOCIATION INC.

2 S PORTAGE ST
WESTFIELD, NY 147871400
Phone: 716-326-5200
Fax: –
Web: www.welchs.com

CEO: –
CFO: –
HR: –
FYE: August 31
Type: Private

Well of course grape growers want to hang out in a bunch! The more than 1090 grower/owner-members of the National Grape Cooperative harvest Concord and Niagara grapes from almost 50000 acres of vineyards. The plucked produce supplies the coop's wholly owned subsidiary Welch Foods. Welch Foods makes and sells fruit-based juices jams jellies and spreads under the Welch's and Bama brands in the US and nearly 50 other countries. Offerings include fresh eating grapes distributed by C.H. Robinson Worldwide as well as dried fruit and frozen juice pops. The grape growers own vineyards in Pennsylvania Michigan New York Ohio Washington and Ontario Canada which produce some 300000 tons of grapes annually.

	Annual Growth	08/09	08/10	08/11	08/12	08/13
Sales ($ mil.)	(2.6%)	–	658.7	640.9	649.5	608.5
Net income ($ mil.)	(6.3%)	–	–	74.2	74.4	65.1
Market value ($ mil.)	–	–	–	–	–	–
Employees	–	–	–	–	–	1,325

NATIONAL HEAD START ASSOCIATION

1651 Prince St.	CEO: –
Alexandria VA 22314	CFO: –
Phone: 703-739-0875	HR: –
Fax: 703-739-0878	FYE: June 30
Web: www.nhsa.org	Type: Private - Not-for-Pr

These children aren't cheating they are getting a head start. National Head Start Association (NHSA) is a nonprofit that provides low-income families with education health nutrition and parental support services. The membership organization represents more than 1 million children and 2600 Head Start programs in the US. In addition NHSA provides Head Start's more than 200000 staff with professional development and training. The organization publishes research on early childhood education through the periodicals NHSA Dialog and Children and Families. Formed in the 1970s NHSA was an advocacy group for the Head Start community in Congress. The Head Start program got its start in 1965.

NATIONAL HEALTH INVESTORS, INC.

NYS: NHI

222 Robert Rose Drive	CEO: Justin Hutchens
Murfreesboro, TN 37129	CFO: –
Phone: 615 890-9100	HR: –
Fax: –	FYE: December 31
Web: www.nhireit.com	Type: Public

National Health Investors has a financial investment in the nation's health. The real estate investment trust (REIT) owns or makes mortgage investments in health care properties primarily long-term care facilities. With more than 180 properties in over 30 states its holdings also include residences for people with developmental disabilities assisted-living complexes medical office buildings retirement centers and an acute care hospital. About one-third of National Health Investors' properties are leased to its largest tenant National HealthCare Corporation; half are leased to regional health care providers. A majority of the REIT's facilities are located in Florida Texas and Tennessee.

	Annual Growth	12/10	12/11	12/12	12/13	12/14
Sales ($ mil.)	22.7%	78.4	82.7	97.0	117.8	177.5
Net income ($ mil.)	10.4%	69.4	81.1	90.9	107.2	103.1
Market value ($ mil.)	11.7%	1,687.6	1,648.6	2,119.1	2,103.0	2,622.5
Employees	9.5%	–	–	10	11	12

NATIONAL HEALTHCARE CORP.

ASE: NHC

100 East Vine Street	CEO: Robert G Adams
Murfreesboro, TN 37130	CFO: Donald K Daniel
Phone: 615 890-2020	HR: Donna Miller
Fax: 615 890-0123	FYE: December 31
Web: www.nhccare.com	Type: Public

National HealthCare (NHC) provides long-term care to those who have had long-term lives. Through its subsidiaries NHC manages some 75 skilled nursing homes in 10 states mainly in the southeastern US. Of its facilities the company owns or leases about 55 facilities and manages the other 20 for third-party organizations; together its facilities house about 9400 beds. In addition to its nursing homes NHC manages more than 35 home health programs and about 25 independent and assisted-living facilities. The company provides a number of health services through its facilities including hospice rehabilitation Alzheimer's care and institutional pharmacy services.

	Annual Growth	12/10	12/11	12/12	12/13	12/14
Sales ($ mil.)	5.1%	715.5	773.5	761.3	789.0	871.7
Net income ($ mil.)	0.3%	52.7	64.1	58.0	64.6	53.4
Market value ($ mil.)	8.0%	652.9	591.2	663.5	760.7	886.7
Employees	0.6%	12,760	12,670	12,570	11,500	13,050

NATIONAL HERITAGE ACADEMIES INC.

3850 Broadmoor Ave. SE Ste. 201	CEO: –
Grand Rapids MI 49512	CFO: Stephen Conley
Phone: 616-222-1700	HR: Jenny Delessio
Fax: 616-575-6801	FYE: June 30
Web: www.heritageacademies.com	Type: Private

The traditions at National Heritage Academies (NHA) may not be that old but they are already a part of many families' heritage. The company operates charter schools which are state-funded public schools operated by government-approved independent entities; charter schools are given operational automony while being held accountable to state and local regulations. NHA operates some 57 charter schools that enroll some 35000 students in kindergarten through eighth grades. The schools offer a rigorous curriculum character development and strong parental involvement. NHA was founded in 1995 by J.C. Huizenga a cousin of Wayne Huizenga founder of Waste Management and Blockbuster.

NATIONAL HOLDINGS CORP

NAS: NHLD

410 Park Avenue, 14th Floor	CEO: –
New York, NY 10022	CFO: Alan B Levin
Phone: 212 417-8000	HR: –
Fax: –	FYE: September 30
Web: www.nhldcorp.com	Type: Public

National Holdings helps investors manage their holdings. Through subsidiaries National Securities Corporation vFinance and EquityStation the company provides brokerage services to retail clients wealthy individuals and institutional investors in the US. Products include stocks options bonds mutual funds and annuities. The subsidiaries also provide investment banking services to growth companies. The group employs more than 800 advisors and brokers most of whom are independent contractors responsible for their office expenses. National Holdings provides its representatives with research materials order execution trade processing and compliance support as well as higher-than-average commissions.

	Annual Growth	09/11	09/12	09/13	09/14	09/15
Sales ($ mil.)	6.5%	126.5	118.6	127.6	184.3	163.0
Net income ($ mil.)	–	(4.7)	(1.9)	1.6	18.6	0.3
Market value ($ mil.)	74.5%	3.7	2.4	4.6	5.9	34.3
Employees	3.3%	1,011	948	900	1,187	1,152

NATIONAL INDEMNITY COMPANY

3024 Harney St.	CEO: –
Omaha NE 68131-3580	CFO: –
Phone: 402-536-3000	HR: Beverly Boe
Fax: 402-536-3030	FYE: December 31
Web: www.nationalindemnity.com	Type: Subsidiary

Whether you drive a church bus or a squad car National Indemnity and its affiliates have you covered. National Indemnity (NICO) is part of Berkshire Hathaway's primary insurance group and offers specialized property/casualty insurance. NICO provides coverage for commercial trucks and truckers public auto transportation (such as taxis and buses) and such specialty vehicles as police cars and ambulances. The company also offers prize indemnification for tournaments and charity events (such as hole-in-one prizes and half-court basketball shots); garage liability; and general liability insurance for carpenters electricians and plumbers. NICO also provides reinsurance to other property/casualty insurers.

NATIONAL INFORMATION SOLUTIONS COOPERATIVE INC.

1 Innovation Cir.	CEO: Vern Dosch
Lake St. Louis MO 63367	CFO: Tracy Porter
Phone: 636-755-2300	HR: Joan Ternes
Fax: 701-667-1936	FYE: October 31
Web: www.nisc.coop	Type: Private - Cooperativ

National Information Solutions Cooperative (NISC) is a cooperative company that provides billing software and data processing services for the energy and telecommunications industries in the US and Canada. NISC offers software under the iVUE banner that automates administrative and operational functions related to accounting e-commerce electronic billing customer service and engineering. The cooperative also provides such services as automated mailroom support technical support and meeting facilities rental. NISC is led by an executive committee comprised of representatives from participating electricity and telecommunications organizations from across the US.

NATIONAL INSTRUMENTS CORP.   NMS: NATI

11500 North MoPac Expressway	CEO: James J. Truchard
Austin, TX 78759	CFO: Alexander M. (Alex) Davern
Phone: 512 338-9119	HR: –
Fax: 512 683-9300	FYE: December 31
Web: www.ni.com	Type: Public

National Instruments (NI) makes a measurable difference virtually in the lab. The company's instrumentation hardware and graphical software convert standard PCs into industrial automation and test and measurement systems. These "virtual instruments" can observe measure and control electrical signals and physical attributes such as voltage and pressure. The company also offers programming environments (LabVIEW and Measurement Studio) for creating customizable graphical interfaces controlling instruments and capturing and analyzing data. In addition NI provides test management software for running automated factory test systems. Customers outside the Americas account for around 60% of sales.

	Annual Growth	12/10	12/11	12/12	12/13	12/14
Sales ($ mil.)	9.2%	873.2	1,024.2	1,143.7	1,172.6	1,243.9
Net income ($ mil.)	3.7%	109.1	94.1	90.1	80.5	126.3
Market value ($ mil.)	(4.7%)	4,812.2	3,317.7	3,299.8	4,093.7	3,974.8
Employees	7.6%	5,280	6,235	6,869	7,114	7,084

NATIONAL INTERSTATE CORP   NMS: NATL

3250 Interstate Drive	CEO: David W. Michelson
Richfield, OH 44286-9000	CFO: Julie A. McGraw
Phone: 330 659-8900	HR: –
Fax: 330 659-8909	FYE: December 31
Web: www.natl.com	Type: Public

National Interstate stands behind you when you get on the bus! The specialty property/casualty insurer concentrates on the transportation market. One of the nation's largest insurers of truck and passenger transportation fleets the company also provides insurance to moving companies and personal lines of coverage for recreational vehicles. Additionally National Interstate offers general commercial insurance for small businesses in Alaska and Hawaii. The company distributes its products throughout the US. American Financial Group spun off National Interstate in 2005 but continues to control the company through a 52% stake held by its Great American Insurance Company.

	Annual Growth	12/10	12/11	12/12	12/13	12/14
Assets ($ mil.)	4.2%	1,488.6	1,525.1	1,570.2	1,623.8	1,754.7
Net income ($ mil.)	(27.3%)	39.5	35.6	34.3	17.6	11.0
Market value ($ mil.)	8.6%	423.8	488.3	570.4	455.2	589.8
Employees	6.7%	494	532	546	580	641

NATIONAL LIFE INSURANCE COMPANY

1 National Life Dr.	CEO: Mehran Assadi
Montpelier VT 05604-0001	CFO: Edward Bonach
Phone: 802-229-3333	HR: –
Fax: 802-229-9281	FYE: December 31
Web: https://www.nationallife.com	Type: Private - Mutual Com

One nation under insurance with financial security for all. National Life Group the marketing name for National Life Insurance Company and its affiliated companies is a mutually owned insurer dating back to 1848. Today National Life Group offers a range of insurance and investment products throughout the US through its namesake National Life Insurance Company and other subsidiaries including Equity Services (financial products broker/dealer) Life Insurance Company of the Southwest (insurance and annuities) National Retirement Plan Advisors (a third-party administrator) and Sentinel Investments (mutual funds retirement plans and institutional investment accounts).

NATIONAL MULTIPLE SCLEROSIS SOCIETY

733 3RD AVE FL 3	CEO: –
NEW YORK, NY 100173211	CFO: –
Phone: 212-986-3240	HR: Terry Bell
Fax: –	FYE: September 30
Web: www.nationalmssociety.org	Type: Private

The National Multiple Sclerosis Society funds research intended to find the cause and cure of MS. For people affected by the disease it offers counseling education and equipment assistance. The Society also works to promote public policies and professional education that serve the estimated 500000 people in the US who have MS and more than 2 million worldwide. The Society operates through its national office and a 50-state network of chapters. It generates most of its revenue through fundraising and counts some 16000 federal MS activists. The Society was founded in 1946 after Sylvia Lawry ran a classified ad in The New York Times looking for anyone who had recovered from the disease her brother was battling.

	Annual Growth	09/05	09/06	09/08	09/09	09/13
Sales ($ mil.)	–	–	(143.5)	5.2	2.9	105.7
Net income ($ mil.)	–	–	–	(0.2)	0.0	1.5
Market value ($ mil.)	–	–	–	–	–	–
Employees	–	–	–	–	–	1,200

NATIONAL OILWELL VARCO INC   NYS: NOV

7909 Parkwood Circle Drive	CEO: Clay C. Williams
Houston, TX 77036-6565	CFO: Jose A. Bavardo
Phone: 713 346-7500	HR: –
Fax: –	FYE: December 31
Web: www.natoil.com	Type: Public

National Oilwell Varco has the equipment and skills that big energy companies need. It provides goods and services to exploration and production companies operating in oil patches around the world as well to infrastructure clients. It operating segments are Rig Systems Rig Aftermarket Wellbore Technologies and Completion & Production Solutions. The company makes distributes and services oil and gas drilling equipment for land and offshore drilling rigs. Its mechanical components include drawworks mud pumps cranes jacking systems automated pipehandling tools top drives and traveling equipment. Other products include masts derricks substructures and cranes.

	Annual Growth	12/10	12/11	12/12	12/13	12/14
Sales ($ mil.)	15.2%	12,156.0	14,658.0	20,041.0	22,869.0	21,440.0
Net income ($ mil.)	10.7%	1,667.0	1,994.0	2,491.0	2,327.0	2,502.0
Market value ($ mil.)	(0.6%)	28,176.2	28,486.3	28,637.1	33,321.3	27,455.6
Employees	11.6%	41,027	49,475	60,235	63,779	63,642

NATIONAL PENN BANCSHARES INC.

NASDAQ: NPBC

Philadelphia and Reading Avenues	CEO: Scott V Fainor
Boyertown PA 19512	CFO: Michael J Hughes
Phone: 610-367-6001	HR: –
Fax: 610-369-6118	FYE: December 31
Web: www.natpennbank.com	Type: Public

Pennies or Benjamins it's all good to National Penn Bancshares the holding company for National Penn Bank which operates about 120 branches in eastern and central Pennsylvania and one in Maryland. Originally chartered in 1874 the bank courts small to midsized businesses with annual sales of less than $100 million. Business loans leases and lines of credit make up nearly half of the bank's loan portfolio which also includes commercial real estate loans (around 20%) residential mortgages home equity loans and lines of credit and consumer loans. Other units offer trust investment insurance wealth management retirement plan consulting and health care advisory services.

NATIONAL PRESTO INDUSTRIES, INC.

NYS: NPK

3925 North Hastings Way	CEO: Maryjo Cohen
Eau Claire, WI 54703-3703	CFO: Randy F. Lieble
Phone: 715 839-2121	HR: –
Fax: –	FYE: December 31
	Type: Public

The heat is on at National Presto Industries but it's thermostatically controlled for even-cooking on nonstick surfaces. Under the Presto brand the company makes and distributes small appliances and housewares including pressure cookers fry pans deep fryers griddles coffeemakers can openers electric knives and pizza ovens. The company pours itself into defense work too supplying ammo; cartridge cases; electromechanical assemblies; and Load Assemble and Pack (LAP) setup for regulated goods. Adding to the bottom line its absorbent products unit makes private label and Presto brand diapers and incontinence supplies. The diversified company counts the US government among its largest customers.

	Annual Growth	12/10	12/11	12/12	12/13	12/14
Sales ($ mil.)	(3.7%)	479.0	431.0	472.5	420.2	412.4
Net income ($ mil.)	(19.7%)	63.5	48.0	38.9	41.3	26.5
Market value ($ mil.)	(18.3%)	899.3	647.5	478.0	556.8	401.5
Employees	(0.2%)	1,053	992	1,006	889	1,043

NATIONAL PUBLIC RADIO INC.

1111 N CAPITOL ST NE	CEO: Jarl Mohn
WASHINGTON, DC 200027502	CFO: Debbie Cullen
Phone: 202-513-2000	HR: –
Fax: –	FYE: September 30
Web: www.npr.org	Type: Private

This company helps keep radio listeners informed and entertained without commercial interruptions. National Public Radio (NPR) is a privately supported not-for-profit organization that produces and syndicates radio programming to 900 independently operated noncommercial radio stations including about 750 NPR member stations. Its shows include news programs Morning Edition and All Things Considered as well as cultural programs (Fresh Air) and entertainment shows. Founded in 1970 NPR is funded through private donations member station dues and grants from organizations such as the Corporation for Public Broadcasting and the National Science Foundation.

	Annual Growth	09/05	09/06*	12/07*	09/09	09/13
Sales ($ mil.)	1.6%	–	170.2	170.2	148.7	190.6
Net income ($ mil.)	–	–	–	26.8	(17.5)	(18.7)
Market value ($ mil.)	–	–	–	–	–	–
Employees	–	–	–	–	–	741

*Fiscal year change

NATIONAL RAILROAD PASSENGER CORPORATION

60 Massachusetts Ave. NE	CEO: Joseph H Boardman
Washington DC 20002	CFO: –
Phone: 202-906-3000	HR: Brenda Walls
Fax: 202-906-3306	FYE: September 30
Web: www.amtrak.com	Type: Government-owned

National Railroad Passenger Corporation better known as Amtrak has been riding the rails for more than 40 years. Amtrak is the US' intercity passenger rail provider and its only high-speed rail operator. More than 28 million passengers travel on Amtrak every year on approximately 300 daily trains. It connects 46 states Washington DC and three provinces in Canada. Its network consists of about 21000 route miles of track most of which is owned by freight railroads. Amtrak also operates commuter rail systems on behalf of several states and transit agencies. Owned by the US government through the US Department of Transportation Amtrak depends on subsidies from the federal government to operate.

NATIONAL REALTY & DEVELOPMENT CORP.

3 Manhattanville Rd.	CEO: –
Purchase NY 10577	CFO: John L Scala
Phone: 914-694-4444	HR: –
Fax: 914-694-5448	FYE: December 31
Web: www.nrdc.com	Type: Private

National Realty & Development loves it when you shop 'til you drop. The firm invests in develops manages and operates mostly commercial real estate primarily retail properties in the Northeast. The firm's portfolio spans 20 states and is composed of more than 20 million sq. ft. of retail space. Its 165 projects to-date include shopping centers corporate business centers and residential communities. National Realty & Development's major tenants include The Home Depot Kohl's Lowe's and Wal-Mart. The company currently has about 10 projects under development that will add another 2 million sq. ft. to its portfolio. The family-owned firm was founded by chairman Robert Baker in the 1960s.

NATIONAL RESEARCH CORP

NMS: NRCI A

1245 Q Street	CEO: Michael D Hays
Lincoln, NE 68508	CFO: Kevin Karas
Phone: 402 475-2525	HR: –
Fax: –	FYE: December 31
Web: www.nationalresearch.com	Type: Public

The ultimate father figure National Research Corporation (NRC) is there to let you know when you're not measuring up. Founded in 1981 NRC offers performance measurement and analysis services to clients within the health care industry including hospitals HMOs home care hospice and regulatory groups. The company's performance tracking system uses individualized questionnaires to better determine an organization's satisfaction rating and the NRC Healthcare Market Guide provides industry statistics allowing clients to compare their services to those of competitors. Founder and CEO Michael Hays owns more than 65% of the company.

	Annual Growth	12/10	12/11	12/12	12/13	12/14
Sales ($ mil.)	11.7%	63.4	75.8	86.4	92.6	98.8
Net income ($ mil.)	20.9%	8.5	11.6	15.1	15.5	18.2
Market value ($ mil.)	(25.7%)	–	–	–	459.0	341.2
Employees	6.8%	305	376	383	388	397

NATIONAL RESTAURANTS MANAGEMENT INC.

560 5th Ave.	CEO: Dennis Riese
New York NY 10036	CFO: -
Phone: 212-563-7440	HR: -
Fax: 212-613-1929	FYE: April 30
Web: www.rieserestaurants.com	Type: Private

Without this organization New Yorkers might go hungry. National Restaurants Management which does business as The Riese Organization is among the largest multiple-franchise restaurant operators in New York City. Its portfolio of about 80 eateries includes quick-service outlets (Tim Hortons KFC and Pizza Hut) and chain restaurants (T.G.I. Friday's and Houlihan's); Riese also operates upscale Manhattan night spots such as Charley O's and Times Square Grill. In addition to restaurants the Riese Organization manages several real-estate holdings through a separate division. The company founded by brothers Murray and Irving Riese in 1940 is controlled by CEO Dennis Riese (Murray's son).

NATIONAL RETAIL FEDERATION INC.

1101 NEW YORK AVE NW # 1200	CEO: Matthew Shay
WASHINGTON, DC 200054348	CFO: -
Phone: 202-626-8155	HR: -
Fax: -	FYE: February 28
Web: www.nrf.com	Type: Private

|The National Retail Federation (NRF) wants everyone to shop 'til they drop. The group is a trade association representing the retail industry that works through four divisions addressing technology in retail chain restaurants advertising and marketing and online retail. It functions as both an advocacy group and an informational network for its members lobbying government hosting conferences and seminars and publishing newsletters and books. The NRF magazine Stores is published monthly. NRF includes more than 100 US national state and international retail associations and more than 1.6 million US retailers with about 25 million employees.

	Annual Growth	02/10	02/11	02/12	02/13	02/14
Sales ($ mil.)	13.2%	-	34.8	38.2	44.1	50.5
Net income ($ mil.)	200.7%	-	-	1.1	7.8	9.7
Market value ($ mil.)	-	-	-	-	-	-
Employees	-	-	-	-	-	96

NATIONAL RETAIL PROPERTIES INC   NYS: NNN

450 South Orange Avenue, Suite 900	CEO: Craig Macnab
Orlando, FL 32801	CFO: Kevin B. Habicht
Phone: 407 265-7348	HR: -
Fax: 407 423-2894	FYE: December 31
Web: www.nnnreit.com	Type: Public

For National Retail Properties good things come in big boxes. The self-administered real estate investment trust (REIT) acquires develops and manages freestanding retail properties in heavily traveled commercial and residential areas. Its portfolio includes about 1800 properties totaling more than 20 million sq. ft. of leasable space in nearly all 50 states concentrated in the Southeast the Midwest and Texas. National Retail Properties also invests in mortgages operates the retail businesses on some of its sites and develops properties with the intention of selling them for a profit. Convenience stores make up around 20% of its portfolio.

	Annual Growth	12/10	12/11	12/12	12/13	12/14
Sales ($ mil.)	17.4%	229.1	265.8	331.8	392.3	434.8
Net income ($ mil.)	27.1%	73.0	92.3	142.0	160.1	190.6
Market value ($ mil.)	10.4%	3,498.3	3,482.4	4,118.7	4,003.9	5,197.2
Employees	2.5%	58	59	60	62	64

NATIONAL REVIEW INC.

215 Lexington Ave.	CEO: -
New York NY 10016	CFO: James Kilbridge
Phone: 212-679-7330	HR: -
Fax: 212-849-2835	FYE: December 31
Web: www.nationalreview.com	Type: Private

Folks on the Left might find this review of the nation a bit lacking. National Review is a magazine and book publisher focusing on international and political news and opinion from a conservative Republican viewpoint. In addition to its semimonthly National Review and the online version National Review Online (NRO) the company publishes such book titles as The National Review Treasury of Classic Bedtime Stories and American Conservatism: An Encyclopedia. The National Review was founded in 1955 by conservative commentator William F. Buckley who hosted the weekly PBS TV show Firing Line for more than 20 years. Buckley died in 2008.

NATIONAL RIFLE ASSOCIATION OF AMERICA

11250 WAPLES MILL RD # 1	CEO: -
FAIRFAX, VA 220309400	CFO: Wilson H Phillips
Phone: 703-267-1000	HR: -
Fax: -	FYE: December 31
Web: www.nraila.org	Type: Private

The NRA believes in the right to bear arms. With more than 5 million members The National Rifle Association (NRA) is the staunch defender of Second Amendment rights. It's a major player in the political arena and stands firm in its resolve to protect the right to keep and bear arms. The NRA offers a variety of educational and gun safety programs and publishes magazines (America's 1st Freedom American Hunter Women's Outlook). It also caters to more than one million youth through its shooting sports events and affiliated programs with the likes of 4-H the Boy Scouts of America and others. It also sells NRA merchandise. Union army veterans William Church and George Wingate founded the NRA in 1871.

	Annual Growth	12/05	12/06	12/07	12/09	12/13
Sales ($ mil.)	-	-	(758.7)	363.4	237.5	348.0
Net income ($ mil.)	(14.2%)	-	-	144.0	1.2	57.4
Market value ($ mil.)	-	-	-	-	-	-
Employees	-	-	-	-	-	500

NATIONAL RURAL ELECTRIC COOPERATIVE ASSOCIATION

4301 WILSON BLVD STE 1	CEO: Glenn L English Jr
ARLINGTON, VA 222031867	CFO: -
Phone: 703-907-5500	HR: -
Fax: -	FYE: December 31
Web: www.nreca.coop	Type: Private

Would it shock you to learn that consumer-owned cooperatives provide electricity to more than 42 million people in the US? The National Rural Electric Cooperative Association (NRECA) is the cooperatives' voice in politics and policymaking. It publishes a monthly magazine and a weekly newspaper sponsors conferences and seminars and represents about 900 rural electric co-ops (from 47 states) in the US Congress and state legislatures. As the nation embraces investor-owned utilities NRECA has been lobbying hard for more moderate approaches to deregulation in order to protect consumers from potential monopolies. The association also provides power assistance and technical advice to developing nations.

	Annual Growth	12/04	12/05	12/06	12/08	12/12
Sales ($ mil.)	-	-	(974.7)	139.4	162.7	208.7
Net income ($ mil.)	4.4%	-	-	3.5	0.2	4.5
Market value ($ mil.)	-	-	-	-	-	-
Employees	-	-	-	-	-	885

NATIONAL RURAL UTILITIES COOPERATIVE FINANCE CORP   NL:

20701 Cooperative Way
Dulles, VA 20166
Phone: 703 467-1800
Fax: 703 709-6779
Web: www.nrucfc.coop

CEO: Sheldon C Petersen
CFO: J Andrew Don
HR: –
FYE: May 31
Type: Public

Cooperation may work wonders on Sesame Street but in the real world it takes money to pay the power bill. The National Rural Utilities Cooperative Finance Corporation provides financing and investment services for rural electrical and telephone projects throughout the US. The group is owned by some 1500 member electric utility and telecommunications systems. National Rural supplements the government loans that traditionally have fueled rural electric utilities by selling commercial paper medium-term notes and collateral trust bonds to fund its loan programs. National Rural was formed in 1969 by the National Rural Electric Cooperative Association a lobby representing the nation's electric co-ops.

	Annual Growth	05/11	05/12	05/13	05/14	05/15
Sales ($ mil.)	(9.2%)	990.3	674.6	1,077.9	927.4	672.6
Net income ($ mil.)	–	149.4	(144.7)	353.8	190.1	(19.0)
Market value ($ mil.)	–	0.0	0.0	–	–	–
Employees	1.5%	219	219	231	221	232

NATIONAL SAFETY COUNCIL

1121 SPRING LAKE DR
ITASCA, IL 601433201
Phone: 630-285-1121
Fax: –
Web: www.nsc.org

CEO: Deborah AP Hersman
CFO: Patrick Phelam
HR: –
FYE: June 30
Type: Private

What are the odds of crashing while driving and talking on a cell phone? This is a question the National Safety Council (NSC) can answer. The NSC is a not-for-profit organization dedicated to educating Americans on safety and health to stop as many of the millions of preventable injuries a year as possible. NSC and its about 60 local chapters comprise members from more than 50000 business academic government community and labor organizations as well as individuals. It provides information and training to its members (and members' employees) on injury statistics and prevention. The group also offers consulting services on safety program development incident investigation and hazard recognition.

	Annual Growth	06/10	06/11	06/12	06/13	06/14
Sales ($ mil.)	17.9%	–	35.8	41.4	51.6	58.7
Net income ($ mil.)	68.6%	–	–	3.4	7.4	9.8
Market value ($ mil.)	–	–	–	–	–	–
Employees	–	–	–	–	–	350

NATIONAL SECURITY GROUP, INC   NMS: NSEC

661 East Davis Street
Elba, AL 36323
Phone: 334 897-2273
Fax: –
Web: www.nationalsecuritygroup.com

CEO: William L Brunson Jr
CFO: Brian R McLeod
HR: –
FYE: December 31
Type: Public

This National Security Group is keeping homeowners safe in the South. The company's subsidiaries Omega One Insurance and National Security Fire and Casualty sell property/casualty insurance in about a dozen southern states. Most of National Security Group's revenues are generated by its residential premiums from homeowners and mobile homeowners policies. The unit also offers personal nonstandard automobile insurance. Its life insurance subsidiary National Security Insurance offers basic life health and accident insurance. Alabama and Mississippi together account for about half of the company's sales.

	Annual Growth	12/10	12/11	12/12	12/13	12/14
Assets ($ mil.)	1.4%	136.9	132.5	135.7	134.0	144.9
Net income ($ mil.)	23.6%	3.3	(5.0)	(6.7)	5.7	7.6
Market value ($ mil.)	2.4%	30.7	21.9	21.4	24.9	33.7
Employees	(51.5%)	1,647	1,500	1,512	1,400	91

NATIONAL SPINNING COMPANY INC.

1140 Avenue of the Americas Ste. 1700
New York NY 10036
Phone: 212-382-6400
Fax: 212-382-6450
Web: www.natspin.com

CEO: –
CFO: Linda Fanton
HR: –
FYE: December 31
Type: Private

These days spinning is associated with political doublespeak and exercise bikes. But this company lays claim to the original meaning of the word. National Spinning is a yarn spinner and dyer supplying outerwear home furnishings industrial home crafting and other markets. Its four US plants produce high-value yarns and services for knitters weavers and retailers in the Americas the Caribbean and elsewhere. National Spinning technologies include ring open end and worsted spinning plus package dyeing. Its Caron International and Hampton Art units sell yarn latch kits and other accessories online and through retail stores. In business since 1921 the company has been employee-owned since 1994.

NATIONAL TRUST FOR HISTORIC PRESERVATION IN THE UNITED ST

1785 Massachusetts Ave. NW
Washington DC 20036-2117
Phone: 202-588-6000
Fax: 202-588-6038
Web: www.nationaltrust.org/index.html

CEO: –
CFO: Michael L Forster
HR: –
FYE: September 30
Type: Private - Not-for-Pr

National Trust for Historic Preservation wants to ensure that historic America is protected against destruction and negligence. The not-for-profit organization was founded in 1949 and educates advocates and provides resources for the preservation of historic buildings and land (not to be confused with the National Register of Historical Places which designates buildings and neighborhoods as historic). The group also operates about 30 historic sites across the US. National Trust which boasts about 270000 members operates out of a Washington DC headquarters and nine regional and field offices. It also works with thousands of preservation groups in all 50 states.

NATIONAL UNIVERSITY

11255 N TORREY PINES RD
LA JOLLA, CA 920371011
Phone: 858-642-8000
Fax: –
Web: www.nu.edu

CEO: –
CFO: –
HR: Dana I Montlack
FYE: June 30
Type: Private

National University is the flagship school of the National University System. The institution offers more than 150 undergraduate and graduate degrees and teacher credential and certificate programs. A not-for-profit institution National University programs range across fields including business engineering education media and human services. The university enrolls 23000 students at multiple locations in California and Nevada; it also offers about 70 online degree programs. The school conducts research through the National University Community Research Institute (NUCRI). National University was founded in 1971.

	Annual Growth	06/01	06/02	06/09	06/10	06/11
Sales ($ mil.)	5.4%	–	126.3	165.0	178.6	203.3
Net income ($ mil.)	120.6%	–	–	5.2	18.5	25.2
Market value ($ mil.)	–	–	–	–	–	–
Employees	–	–	–	–	–	1,954

NATIONAL VAN LINES INC.

2800 W ROOSEVELT RD
BROADVIEW, IL 601553771
Phone: 708-450-2900
Fax: –
Web: www.nationalvanlines.com

CEO: Maureen Beal
CFO: –
HR: –
FYE: April 30
Type: Private

National Van Lines provides moving services for households and businesses. The company which operates through a national network of some 400 agents can arrange international as well as domestic moves. Besides consumers and businesses National Van Lines has a dedicated unit National Forwarding Company to serve customers including government agencies such as the US Department of Defense to move military families. CEO Maureen Beal owns National Van Lines which was founded in 1929 by her grandfather F.J. McKee.

	Annual Growth	04/06	04/07	04/08	04/09	04/10
Sales ($ mil.)	–	–	–	(1,696.8)	89.4	80.7
Net income ($ mil.)	27674.5%	–	–	0.0	3.5	2.2
Market value ($ mil.)	–	–	–	–	–	–
Employees	–	–	–	–	–	135

NATIONAL VISION INC.

296 Grayson Hwy.
Lawrenceville GA 30045
Phone: 770-822-3600
Fax: 770-822-3601
Web: www.nationalvision.com

CEO: Reade Fahs
CFO: Paul A Criscills Jr
HR: –
FYE: December 31
Type: Private

Optical retailer National Vision focuses on Wal-Mart but keeps an eye out for other business opportunities too. The company sells low-cost prescription glasses contact lenses and sunglasses at more than 700 locations in 40-plus states about 200 of which are in Wal-Mart stores in the US and Mexico under the Vision Center banner. National Vision also maintains facilities in Fred Meyer stores (Vista Optical) and on military bases (Optical Center) as well as free-standing retail locations (America's Best Contacts & Eyeglasses and Eyeglass World). The company sells contact lenses online through bestcontacts.com. National Vision is owned by investment firm Berkshire Partners.

NATIONAL WESTERN LIFE INSURANCE CO. (AUSTIN, TX) NMS: NWLI

850 East Anderson Lane
Austin, TX 78752-1602
Phone: 512 836-1010
Fax: 512 836-6980
Web: www.nationalwesternlife.com

CEO: Robert L Moody
CFO: Brian M Pribyl
HR: Michelle Simmons
FYE: December 31
Type: Public

National Western Life Insurance sells life insurance and annuity products including individual universal whole and term plans. The company operates throughout the US except in New York and internationally in Central and South America the Caribbean Eastern Europe Asia and the Pacific Rim. Annuities sold by independent agents make up most of its US sales. Some two-thirds of its life insurance premiums come from outside the US where the company targets wealthy individuals. Investments mainly in fixed debt securities account for some 70% of revenues.

	Annual Growth	12/09	12/10	12/11	12/12	12/13
Assets ($ mil.)	9.6%	7,518.7	8,773.9	9,728.0	10,263.9	10,830.4
Net income ($ mil.)	20.6%	45.5	72.9	55.6	92.6	96.2
Market value ($ mil.)	6.5%	631.1	606.0	494.9	573.3	812.6
Employees	(1.3%)	294	292	278	280	279

NATIONAL WILDLIFE FEDERATION INC

11100 WILDLIFE CENTER DR
RESTON, VA 201905362
Phone: 703-438-6000
Fax: –
Web: www.nwf.org

CEO: Collin O'Mara
CFO: –
HR: –
FYE: August 31
Type: Private

The National Wildlife Federation (NWF) works to educate the public about conservation of wildlife and other natural resources. The non-profit organization with some four million members organizes efforts on an educational and political front. Conservation projects include restoring gray wolves to Yellowstone protecting the Everglades preserving wetlands flood plain management and fighting effects of climate change. It also conducts wildlife tours and publishes a number of magazines including National Wildlife Ranger Rick Your Big Backyard and Animal Baby and produces film and television programs on conservation. The NWF was founded in 1936.

	Annual Growth	08/10	08/11	08/12	08/13	08/14
Sales ($ mil.)	(7.0%)	–	107.4	92.7	85.4	86.3
Net income ($ mil.)	–	–	–	(5.6)	3.4	5.6
Market value ($ mil.)	–	–	–	–	–	–
Employees	–	–	–	–	–	350

NATIONSTAR MORTGAGE HOLDINGS INC NYS: NSM

8950 Cypress Waters Blvd
Coppell, TX 75019
Phone: 469 549-2000
Fax: –
Web: www.nationstarholdings.com

CEO: Jay Bray
CFO: Robert D. Stiles
HR: –
FYE: December 31
Type: Public

Nationstar Mortgage helps turn home ownership into more than just a wish upon a star. The company services residential mortgage loans throughout the US. Its servicing portfolio comprises more than 2.3 million loans that total in excess of $425 billion in unpaid principal balances. Nationstar also originates loans primarily government- and agency-backed mortgages which it typically sells or securitizes within one month of origination. The company serves consumers directly through its Texas-based call center; it also offers its products through wholesalers. The firm has seen rapid growth as a result of its expanding servicing portfolio.

	Annual Growth	12/10	12/11	12/12	12/13	12/14
Sales ($ mil.)	65.7%	261.4	377.7	984.3	2,087.0	1,973.1
Net income ($ mil.)	–	(9.9)	20.9	205.3	217.1	220.7
Market value ($ mil.)	(4.6%)	–	–	2,800.5	3,341.1	2,548.3
Employees	28.4%	–	2,599	4,672	6,984	5,500

NATIONSTAR MORTGAGE HOLDINGS INC. NYSE: NSM

350 Highland Dr.
Lewisville TX 75067
Phone: 469-549-2000
Fax: 952-853-1410
Web: www.nathcompanies.com/

CEO: Jay Bray
CFO: David C Hisey
HR: –
FYE: December 31
Type: Public

Nationstar Mortgage helps turn home ownership into more than just a wish upon a star. The company services residential mortgage loans throughout the US. Its servicing portfolio comprises more than 1.8 million loans that total in excess of $300 billion in unpaid principal balances. Nationstar also originates loans primarily government- and agency-backed mortgages which it typically sells or securitizes within one month of origination. The company serves consumers directly through its Texas-based call center; it also offers its products through wholesalers. The firm has seen rapid growth as a result of its expanding servicing portfolio. Nationstar went public in 2012.

NATIONWIDE CHILDREN'S HOSPITAL

700 CHILDRENS DR | CEO: Steve Allen
COLUMBUS, OH 432052639 | CFO: Timothy C. Robinson
Phone: 614-722-3040 | HR: –
Fax: – | FYE: December 31
Web: www.giving.nationwidechildrens.org | Type: Private

Buckeye babies toddlers and teens don't have to travel the country to find pediatric care with Nationwide Children's Hospital at their disposal. The Columbus Ohio health care provider is one of the largest pediatric care centers in the US. The hospital has some 430 licensed beds and offers services in areas such as behavioral health cardiology hospice orthopedics and surgery. It has roughly 1100 health care providers on its medical staff and its emergency department treats more than 83000 patients each year. The hospital also operates outpatient and specialty clinics in the area and a research institute which is investigating gene therapy.

	Annual Growth	12/06	12/07	12/08	12/09	12/13
Sales ($ mil.)	9.4%	–	–	1,059.6	918.7	1,658.2
Net income ($ mil.)	–	–	–	(175.7)	95.6	334.0
Market value ($ mil.)	–	–	–	–	–	–
Employees	–	–	–	–	–	6,000

NATIONWIDE FINANCIAL SERVICES INC.

1 Nationwide Plaza | CEO: –
Columbus OH 43215-2220 | CFO: Timothy G Frommeyer
Phone: 614-249-7111 | HR: Donna A James
Fax: 614-854-5036 | FYE: December 31
Web: www.nationwidefinancial.com | Type: Subsidiary

There's wide there's double-wide and then there's Nationwide. Nationwide Financial Services (NFS) oversees the life insurance and banking services business of insurance giant Nationwide Mutual. Through Nationwide Life Insurance it offers long-term savings and retirement products including individual variable annuity contracts. It also offers group and individual protective life insurance policies. Retirement plans are offered to individuals and through employer-sponsored plans. The company also provides banking services (savings mortgage loan origination) while its Nationwide Better Health offers workplace health management products. Its products are sold through direct sales and brokers.

NATIONWIDE MUTUAL INSURANCE COMPANY

1 Nationwide Plaza | CEO: Steve Rasmussen
Columbus OH 43215-2220 | CFO: Mark R Thresher
Phone: 614-249-7111 | HR: –
Fax: 914-681-6949 | FYE: December 31
Web: www.nypa.gov | Type: Private - Mutual Com

Call it truth in advertising — Nationwide Mutual Insurance Company has offices throughout the US. The company is a leading US property/casualty insurer that also provides life insurance and retirement products through its Nationwide Financial Services subsidiary. Its property/casualty products range from general personal and commercial coverage to such specialty lines as professional liability workers' compensation agricultural insurance and loss-control pet insurance and other coverage. The company sells its products and provides services through Allied Group Harleysville Group Nationwide Agribusiness Insurance GatesMcDonald Scottsdale Insurance and other subsidiaries.

NATIONWIDE RECOVERY SYSTEMS LTD.

2304 Tarpley Rd. Ste. 134 | CEO: –
Carrollton TX 75006 | CFO: –
Phone: 972-798-1000 | HR: –
Fax: 972-798-1020 | FYE: December 31
Web: www.nrs.us | Type: Private

You can run but you can't hide from Nationwide. In fact this debt recovery firm maintains a database of 3.2 million delinquent borrowers. Nationwide Recovery Systems provides commercial consumer and health care collections throughout the US and beyond with services offered in more than 70 countries. Its offerings include diplomatic arbitration pre-litigation intervention asset and liability searches and in-field collections. Since its inception more than 30 years ago Nationwide Recovery Systems has collected more than $1 billion for corporate clients in a variety of industries.

NATIVE ENVIRONMENTAL L.L.C.

3250 S 35TH AVE | CEO: –
PHOENIX, AZ 850096734 | CFO: –
Phone: 602-254-0122 | HR: –
Fax: – | FYE: December 31
Web: www.nativeaz.com | Type: Private

Removal of mold lead and asbestos is not a foreign concept at Native Environmental L.L.C. The Phoenix-based industrial cleaning and environmental contracting company serves Arizona New Mexico and thirty other states. Native Environmental focuses on mold remediation lead-based paint removal and removal of asbestos. The company contracts with customers like hospitals governmental entities and demolition companies and has short and long-term contracts that range in size from small commercial projects to large industrial projects. Founded by CEO Jon W. Riggs Native Environmental has been in business since 2000.

	Annual Growth	12/08	12/09	12/10	12/11	12/12
Sales ($ mil.)	9.9%	–	7.3	9.6	10.2	9.6
Net income ($ mil.)	–	–	–	1.6	1.0	(0.1)
Market value ($ mil.)	–	–	–	–	–	–
Employees	–	–	–	–	–	100

NATURAL ALTERNATIVES INTERNATIONAL, INC.   NMS: NAII

1185 Linda Vista Drive | CEO: Mark A Ledoux
San Marcos, CA 92078 | CFO: Michael E Fortin
Phone: 760 744-7340 | HR: –
Fax: – | FYE: June 30
Web: www.nai-online.com | Type: Public

Natural Alternatives International (NAI) is a natural alternative for nutritional supplement marketers who want to outsource manufacturing. The company provides private-label manufacturing of vitamins minerals herbs and other customized nutritional supplements. Its main customers are direct sellers such as Mannatech and NSA International for whom it makes JuicePlus+ chewables capsules and powdered products. NAI also makes some branded products for sale in the US: the Pathway to Healing brand of nutritional supplements promoted by doctor and evangelist Reginald B. Cherry.

	Annual Growth	06/11	06/12	06/13	06/14	06/15
Sales ($ mil.)	9.2%	55.9	72.8	62.8	73.9	79.5
Net income ($ mil.)	(9.9%)	5.1	4.2	1.6	2.0	3.3
Market value ($ mil.)	4.1%	32.5	51.7	31.1	35.6	38.2
Employees	1.4%	158	175	177	181	167

NATURAL GAS SERVICES GROUP INC

NYS: NGS

508 W. Wall St., Ste 550
Midland, TX 79701
Phone: 432 262-2700
Fax: –

CEO: Stephen C. Taylor
CFO: G. Larry Lawrence
HR: –
FYE: December 31
Type: Public

The pressure is on to enhance oil and gas well production. Natural Gas Services Group (NGS) manufactures and leases natural gas compressors used to boost oil and gas well production primarily in non-conventional plays such as coal bed methane tight gas and oil and gas shales. The company also provides flare tip burners ignition systems and components used to combust waste gases before entering the atmosphere. NGS leases compressors to third parties in Colorado Kansas Louisiana Michigan New Mexico Oklahoma Pennsylvania Texas Utah West Virginia and Wyoming. In 2012 some 1756 units of the company's rental fleet of 2279 compressors were rented out to clients.

	Annual Growth	12/10	12/11	12/12	12/13	12/14
Sales ($ mil.)	15.8%	53.9	65.2	93.7	89.2	97.0
Net income ($ mil.)	19.1%	7.0	9.8	12.7	14.4	14.1
Market value ($ mil.)	5.1%	235.7	180.3	204.7	343.7	287.2
Employees	10.8%	234	277	285	324	353

NATURAL GROCERS BY VITAMIN COTTAGE INC

NYS: NGVC

12612 West Alameda Parkway
Lakewood, CO 80228
Phone: 303 986-4600
Fax: –
Web: www.naturalgrocers.com

CEO: Zephyr Isely
CFO: Sandra M. Buffa
HR: –
FYE: September 30
Type: Public

Natural Grocers by Vitamin Cottage offers the best of both worlds — healthy food and dietary supplements. The fast-growing company operates about 75 stores in more than a dozen states that sell natural and organic food including fresh produce meat frozen food and non-perishable bulk food; vitamins and dietary supplements; personal care products; pet care products; and books. The company uses United Natural Foods as its primary distributor and it also runs a bulk food repackaging facility and distribution center in its home state of Colorado. Founded by Margaret and Philip Isely in 1958 Natural Grocers by Vitamin Cottage is run by members of the Isely family. The chain went public in 2012.

	Annual Growth	09/11	09/12	09/13	09/14	09/15
Sales ($ mil.)	24.0%	264.5	336.4	430.7	520.7	624.7
Net income ($ mil.)	46.6%	3.5	6.6	10.6	13.5	16.2
Market value ($ mil.)	0.5%	–	502.1	893.1	366.2	510.4
Employees	19.6%	–	1,655	2,003	2,346	2,830

NATURAL HEALTH TRENDS CORP.

NAS: NHTC

4514 Cole Avenue, Suite 1400
Dallas, TX 75205
Phone: 972 241-4080
Fax: 972 243-5428
Web: www.naturalhealthtrendscorp.com

CEO: –
CFO: Timothy S. Davidson
HR: Flora Berry
FYE: December 31
Type: Public

When it comes to direct selling Natural Health Trends (NHT) was just born that way. The company through its subsidiaries sells products designed to enhance health happiness as well as beauty to a network of some 16000 independent distributors that use and/or resell the goods direct or through the Internet to consumers. Offerings are produced by third parties under the NHT Global brand (formerly Lexxus International). Core lines include skincare (trademark Skindulgence) sexual enhancement (Alura) and an energizing drink (Premium Noni Juice). NHT also sells herbal and dietary supplements for an array of complaints. Sales are generated primarily outside of North America; Hong Kong is the largest market.

	Annual Growth	12/10	12/11	12/12	12/13	12/14
Sales ($ mil.)	51.6%	23.6	31.2	37.5	52.5	124.6
Net income ($ mil.)	–	(2.4)	2.3	2.6	4.1	20.4
Market value ($ mil.)	0.0%	4.4	4.4	4.4	4.4	4.4
Employees	2.3%	103	90	98	99	113

NATURAL RESOURCES DEFENSE COUNCIL INC.

40 W 20TH ST
NEW YORK, NY 100114211
Phone: 212-727-2700
Fax: –
Web: www.nrdc.org

CEO: Daniel R Tishman
CFO: –
HR: Brian Gourley
FYE: June 30
Type: Private

Natural Resource Defense Council (NRDC) may be Mother Nature's strongest advocate. It is a nonprofit environmental action organization comprising 1.4-million members dedicated to preserving wildlife and the wilderness. To that end the NRDC's mission takes aim at curbing global warming; creating a future fueled by clean energy; restoring the Earth's oceans; saving endangered wildlife and wild places; stemming the tide of pollutants that endanger heath; and accelerating the greening of communities. In addition press releases and blog posts it publishes Nature's Voice a bulletin on environmental campaigns; OnEarth its quarterly magazine; and periodic NRDC Reports on specific issues.

	Annual Growth	06/06	06/07	06/08	06/10	06/13
Sales ($ mil.)	–	–	(1,649.2)	0.0	97.0	116.0
Net income ($ mil.)	–	–	–	0.0	8.0	13.5
Market value ($ mil.)	–	–	–	–	–	–
Employees	–	–	–	–	–	500

NATURAL RESOURCES PARTNERS L.P.

NYS: NRP

601 Jefferson Street, Suite 3600
Houston, TX 77002
Phone: 713 751-7507
Fax: –
Web: www.nrplp.com

CEO: Corbin J Robertson Jr
CFO: –
HR: –
FYE: December 31
Type: Public

Natural Resource Partners (NRP) makes money from coal without getting its hands dirty. Rather than mining the coal itself NRP leases properties to coal producers. The company's properties — mainly in Appalachia but also in the Northern Powder River Basin and the Illinois Basin — contain proved and probable reserves of about 2.4 billion tons of coal. NRP was formed as a partnership between WPP Group (Western Pocahontas Properties New Gauley Coal and Great Northern Properties) and Arch Coal. Arch Coal has sold its stake in NRP but remains one of the company's top lessees along with Alpha Natural Resources. Chairman and CEO Corbin Robertson controls about 35% of NRP primarily through WPP Group.

	Annual Growth	12/10	12/11	12/12	12/13	12/14
Sales ($ mil.)	7.3%	301.4	377.7	379.1	358.1	399.8
Net income ($ mil.)	(8.4%)	154.5	54.0	213.4	172.1	108.8
Market value ($ mil.)	–	–	–	–	–	–
Employees	–	–	–	–	–	–

NATURAL SELECTION FOODS LLC

1721 San Juan Hwy.
San Juan Bautista CA 95045
Phone: 831-623-7880
Fax: 831-623-7614
Web: www.nsfoods.com

CEO: –
CFO: –
HR: –
FYE: December 31
Type: Private

Originally taking root on a three-acre raspberry farm Natural Selection Foods is a leading US supplier of packaged organic salads. The company serves retailers and foodservice operators nationwide. Natural Selection's more than 100 different products also include organic fruits and vegetables juice cookies and granola. Its products are sold in three-fourths of US grocery stores under the Earthbound Farm label as well as under labels such as Bellissima Hy-Vee and Emeril for other companies. Natural Selection Foods sources its produce from company growers who operate more than 40000 certified organic acres in the US Canada Mexico and Chile. The food firm was founded in 1984.

NATURALLY FRESH INC.

1000 Naturally Fresh Blvd.
Atlanta GA 30349
Phone: 404-765-9000
Fax: 404-765-9016
Web: www.naturallyfresh.com

CEO: Edward J Greene
CFO: Pete Rostad
HR: –
FYE: December 31
Type: Subsidiary

Boasting one of the top five refrigerated salad dressings in the US Naturally Fresh sells most of its products in iconic Mason jars. The company's a maker and distributor of Naturally Fresh-branded salad dressings dips sauces marinades and other condiments. It also makes salad toppings and the Jackaroo brand of meat sauce for restaurants. Naturally Fresh produces packages and delivers its products to grocery stores quick-serve operations casual- and fine-dining restaurants and foodservice operators. The company operates some 20 distribution centers throughout the US. Founded in 1966 as Eastern Foods Naturally Fresh was acquired in 2012 by TreeHouse Foods for $25 million in cash.

NATURIPE FARMS LLC

999 Vanderbilt Beach Rd. Ste. 102
Naples FL 34108
Phone: 239-591-1664
Fax: 239-591-8133
Web: www.naturipe.com

CEO: –
CFO: –
HR: Kimberly Samuelson
FYE: October 31
Type: Private

Life has been berry berry good to Naturipe Farms. The company is one of the world's largest suppliers of fresh bushberries. It provides retail food outlets with a year-round selection of conventional organic and premium blackberries blueberries raspberries cranberries and strawberries. It also offers seasonal produce such as Bing cherries gooseberries and red currants. Naturipe's growers are located in Argentina Chili Mexico Canada and the US. The company markets its produce throughout Europe and the US as well as in Asia. Its berries are sold under the Naturipe Farms and Naturipe Farms Gold Label brand names.

NATURE'S SUNSHINE PRODUCTS, INC.

NAS: NATR

2500 West Executive Parkway, Suite 100
Lehi, UT 84043
Phone: 801 341-7900
Fax: –

CEO: Gregory L. (Greg) Probert
CFO: Stephen M. (Steve) Bunker
HR: –
FYE: December 31
Type: Public

If you're in need of some Vitamin D you can do two things: stand in the sunshine or visit Nature's Sunshine Products. The firm is one of the nation's largest manufacturers and marketers of supplementary health care products. It makes more than 700 products including herbal supplements (available in capsule tablet and liquid form) and vitamins. Nature's Sunshine Products also sells essential oils and personal care items. The company has operations and distribution agreements in Asia Europe and North and South America. Its Synergy Worldwide multi-level marketing division sells the company's products in the US and selected Asian and European countries.

	Annual Growth	12/10	12/11	12/12	12/13	12/14
Sales ($ mil.)	1.2%	349.9	367.8	367.5	378.1	366.4
Net income ($ mil.)	–	(1.2)	17.6	25.4	17.6	10.0
Market value ($ mil.)	13.3%	167.6	289.6	270.2	323.2	276.6
Employees	(2.6%)	1,073	1,003	995	1,010	964

NATUS MEDICAL INC.

NMS: BABY

6701 Koll Center Parkway, Suite 120
Pleasanton, CA 94566
Phone: 925 223-6700
Fax: –
Web: www.natus.com

CEO: James B. Hawkins
CFO: Jonathan A. Kennedy
HR: –
FYE: December 31
Type: Public

Natus Medical designs and manufactures audiological and neurological diagnostic and screening products. While the company's focus has historically been on infants (newborn hearing screening neonatal monitoring) it has expanded its product line to include an array of screening and diagnostic systems for use with children and adults. Its systems detect such neurological conditions as epilepsy and balance and sleep disorders. Natus also manufactures newborn and infant care products to diagnose and treat brain injury and jaundice. The company sells its wares worldwide through a direct sales force and distributors.

	Annual Growth	12/10	12/11	12/12	12/13	12/14
Sales ($ mil.)	12.9%	218.7	232.7	292.3	344.1	355.8
Net income ($ mil.)	28.5%	11.9	(11.7)	3.9	22.9	32.5
Market value ($ mil.)	26.3%	463.0	307.9	364.5	734.6	1,176.7
Employees	6.0%	750	835	1,028	943	948

NATUREWORKS LLC

15305 Minnetonka Blvd.
Minnetonka MN 55345
Phone: 952-742-0400
Fax: 952-742-0479
Web: www.natureworksllc.com

CEO: Marc Verbruggen
CFO: Pat Brunner
HR: –
FYE: December 31
Type: Subsidiary

Corn syrup and corn liquor sure. But corn plastic? NatureWorks — a subsidiary of the country's second-largest private company Cargill — makes fibers and packaging materials from corn and other renewable non-polluting resources (as opposed to traditional oil-derived plastics). The company processes natural plant sugars into a proprietary polylactide polymer called Ingeo which is turned into packaging products such as films containers and coated papers or textile fibers in clothing upholstery and carpeting. Among the company's partners are Japanese plastics makers Unitika and Mitsubishi Chemical and a division of Alcoa called Alcoa KAMA.

NAUGATUCK VALLEY FINANCIAL CORPORATION

NASDAQ: NVSL

333 Church St.
Naugatuck CT 06770
Phone: 203-720-5000
Fax: 203-720-5016
Web: www.nvsl.com

CEO: –
CFO: –
HR: –
FYE: December 31
Type: Public

Naugatuck Valley Financial Corporation (NVFC) owns Naugatuck Valley Savings and Loan a community-oriented thrift serving southwestern Connecticut. Operating from more than a half-dozen locations the bank provides traditional retail banking offerings such as checking and savings accounts CDs and IRAs. Naugatuck Valley Savings and Loan concentrates on residential lending. It also writes construction multifamily and commercial real estate loans. NVFC and Southern Connecticut Bancorp called off plans to merge in 2010. Naugatuck Valley Mutual Holding Company owned around 60% of NVFC's stock until the firm converted to a wholly public company in 2011.

NAUTICA APPAREL INC.

40 W. 57th St.
New York NY 10019
Phone: 212-541-5757
Fax: 212-887-8136
Web: www.nautica.com

CEO: Denise Seegal
CFO: –
HR: –
FYE: February 28
Type: Subsidiary

Explorers once sailed the ocean blue unmindful that their legacy would live on in a global apparel brand. Launched under the spinnaker logo in 1983 Nautica designs makes and retails men's sportswear outerwear underwear swimwear and sleepwear. It also licenses the Nautica name in the US for women's and children's clothing and nonapparel (fragrances footwear furniture). Nautica which is owned by brand behemoth V.F. Corporation is marketed to department store and boutique wholesale customers as well as sold through some 80 VF-operated Nautica retail outlets and website. Independent licensees sell the lineup through some 150 Nautica stores mostly in Asia the Middle East and North and South America.

NAUTILUS INC

NYS: NLS

17750 S.E. 6th Way
Vancouver, WA 98683
Phone: 360 859-2900
Fax: –
Web: www.nautilusinc.com

CEO: Bruce M. Cazenave
CFO: Sid Nayar
HR: –
FYE: December 31
Type: Public

Nautilus wants to pump you up. The company makes and markets cardio and strength-building fitness equipment for home use. Its products include home gyms free weights and benches treadmills exercise bikes and elliptical machines that are sold under the popular brand names Bowflex Nautilus Schwinn Fitness and Universal. Nautilus sells its fitness equipment directly to consumers through its variety of brand websites and catalogs as well as through TV commercials. The company also markets its gear through specialty retailers in the US and Canada. Nautilus exited the commercial fitness category in recent years so that it could focus entirely on providing gear that consumers can use at home.

	Annual Growth	12/10	12/11	12/12	12/13	12/14
Sales ($ mil.)	13.0%	168.5	180.4	193.9	218.8	274.4
Net income ($ mil.)	–	(22.8)	1.4	16.9	48.0	18.8
Market value ($ mil.)	70.9%	55.8	54.8	110.0	264.1	475.6
Employees	0.7%	330	320	310	311	340

NAVAJO SHIPPERS INC.

1400 W. 64th Ave.
Denver CO 80221
Phone: 303-287-3800
Fax: 303-286-9661
Web: www.navajo.com

CEO: Don Digby Sr
CFO: –
HR: –
FYE: December 31
Type: Private

Navajo Shippers hopes you'll say hagoonee' (the Navajo word for goodbye) to other refrigerated trucking companies. Through its Navajo Express unit Navajo Shippers provides temperature-controlled freight transportation mainly in the western US. It operates a fleet of about 900 tractors and 1750 trailers from terminals in Arizona California Colorado Tennessee and Washington state and it offers service elsewhere in the 48 contiguous states via partnerships with other carriers. Navajo Shippers also provides logistics services. The company which has grown over the years through acquisitions is owned and run by President Don Digby Sr. and his family.

NAVARRO RESEARCH AND ENGINEERING INC.

669 EMORY VALLEY RD
OAK RIDGE, TN 378307758
Phone: 865-220-9650
Fax: –
Web: www.navarro-inc.com

CEO: Susana Navarro-Valenti PHD
CFO: –
HR: Christa Salyers
FYE: December 31
Type: Private

It's primary mission is about nuclear fission and making sure that it does not happen. Navarro Research and Engineering provides environmental remediation and related services throughout the US. Specialties include nuclear safety and environmental safety and health. Navarro Research and Engineering's offices tend to be located near sites overseen by the US Department of Energy where nuclear materials have been stored. The company had employees in 14 offices and 23 project locations across the country. Navarro Research and Engineering works on projects for the US Department of Energy and the National Nuclear Security Administration and their primary contractors.

	Annual Growth	12/05	12/06	12/07	12/08	12/09
Sales ($ mil.)	(78.2%)	–	–	1,254.8	49.6	59.6
Net income ($ mil.)	199591.0%	–	–	0.0	2.5	4.0
Market value ($ mil.)	–	–	–	–	–	–
Employees	–	–	–	–	–	327

NAVIDEA BIOPHARMACEUTICALS, INC.

ASE: NAVB

5600 Blazer Parkway, Suite 200
Dublin, OH 43017-7550
Phone: 614 793-7500
Fax: 614 793-7520
Web: www.navidea.com

CEO: Ricardo J. (Rick) Gonzalez
CFO: Brent L. Larson
HR: Jayne Skidmore
FYE: December 31
Type: Public

Navidea Biopharmaceuticals is tracking down cancer with targeting agents. The biopharmaceutical company specializes in diagnostics therapeutics and radiopharmaceutical agents. It has several radiopharmaceutical products in development designed to help surgeons detect disease. The firm's targeted products and platforms include Manocept and NAV4694. Its Lymphoseek product part of the Manocept platform gained FDA approval in 2013 (and European approval in 2014) and is marketed in the US to detect cancerous tissues. Other candidates aim to detect cancer and neurological conditions including Parkinson's disease and Alzheimer's disease. Customers include diagnostic laboratories physicians and patients.

	Annual Growth	12/10	12/11	12/12	12/13	12/14
Sales ($ mil.)	(12.5%)	10.7	0.6	0.1	1.1	6.3
Net income ($ mil.)	–	(50.0)	5.6	(29.2)	(42.7)	(35.7)
Market value ($ mil.)	(2.1%)	309.4	393.5	425.1	310.9	283.9
Employees	6.5%	42	41	56	65	54

NAVIGANT CONSULTING, INC.

NYS: NCI

30 South Wacker Drive, Suite 3550
Chicago, IL 60606
Phone: 312 573-5600
Fax: 312 573-5675
Web: www.navigant.com

CEO: Julie M. Howard
CFO: Cindy Baier
HR: –
FYE: December 31
Type: Public

Navigant Consulting aims to help its clients navigate troubled business waters. A significant portion of the firm's practice is devoted to issues related to business disputes litigation and regulatory compliance. Navigant Consulting also offers operational strategic and technical management consulting services. Employing about 1825 consultants it targets customers in regulated industries such as construction energy financial services health care and insurance; in addition the firm works with government agencies and companies involved in product liability cases. Navigant Consulting was formed in 1996 under the name The Metzler Group.

	Annual Growth	12/11	12/12	12/13	12/14	12/15
Sales ($ mil.)	4.0%	784.7	844.6	835.6	859.6	919.5
Net income ($ mil.)	10.1%	41.1	46.2	52.2	(36.4)	60.3
Market value ($ mil.)	8.9%	542.7	530.8	913.2	731.0	763.8
Employees	21.3%	2,542	2,853	2,743	3,559	5,507

NAVIGATORS GROUP, INC. (THE)

NMS: NAVG

400 Atlantic Street
Stamford, CT 06901
Phone: 203 905-6090
Fax: –
Web: www.navg.com

CEO: Stanley A. (Stan) Galanski
CFO: Ciro M. DeFalco
HR: Denise Lowsley
FYE: December 31
Type: Public

The Navigators Group writes specialty lines of insurance and reinsurance to clients whom it hopes are good navigators themselves. The company's various subsidiaries write marine liability and other lines of business primarily in the US and the UK. Its Navigators Insurance and Navigators Underwriting Agency (NUA) units specialize in ocean marine insurance including hull energy and cargo insurance as well as property insurance for inland marine and onshore energy concerns. Navigators Specialty primarily provides excess and surplus (high risk) lines. The firm's subsidiaries are also involved in professional liability especially directors' and officers' coverage as well as general liability for contractors.

	Annual Growth	12/10	12/11	12/12	12/13	12/14
Assets ($ mil.)	6.0%	3,531.5	3,670.0	4,007.7	4,169.5	4,464.2
Net income ($ mil.)	8.2%	69.6	25.6	63.8	63.5	95.3
Market value ($ mil.)	9.9%	719.1	680.9	729.4	902.0	1,047.4
Employees	7.1%	494	522	567	596	651

NAVISITE INC.

400 Minuteman Rd.
Andover MA 01810
Phone: 978-682-8300
Fax: 978-688-8100
Web: www.navisite.com

CEO: –
CFO: –
HR: –
FYE: July 31
Type: Subsidiary

NaviSite helps enterprises manage their IT resources. The company provides managed cloud and software hosting and management services and it specializes in setting up and supporting enterprise applications from such vendors as Microsoft Dynamics and Oracle. NaviSite also provides Web hosting and collocation server management and other outsourced data and network services. The company has about 10 data centers in the US and the UK; as well as operations centers in India Japan and Singapore. Mainly targeting middle-market enterprises in the US NaviSite serves such industries as financial services health care and manufacturing. The company was acquired in 2011 by Time Warner Cable (TWC) for $530 million.

NAVISTAR INTERNATIONAL CORP.

NYS: NAV

2701 Navistar Drive
Lisle, IL 60532
Phone: 331 332-5000
Fax: –
Web: www.navistar.com

CEO: Troy A. Clarke
CFO: Walter G. Borst
HR: –
FYE: October 31
Type: Public

Navistar's gonna roll its truckin' convoy 'cross the USA and beyond. The company makes its products under brand names International (commercial trucks and military/defense vehicles) MaxxForce (diesel engines) and IC Bus (school and commercial buses). It makes diesel engines for the pickup truck van and SUV markets. Navistar's parts group supplies engine parts and its financial sector offers sales and lease financing for dealers and customers. Navistar which operates production plants in Argentina Brazil Canada Mexico and the US derives most of its sales from North America.

	Annual Growth	10/11	10/12	10/13	10/14	10/15
Sales ($ mil.)	(7.7%)	13,958.0	12,948.0	10,775.0	10,806.0	10,140.0
Net income ($ mil.)	–	1,723.0	(3,010.0)	(898.0)	(619.0)	(184.0)
Market value ($ mil.)	(26.5%)	3,428.7	1,528.1	2,947.0	2,882.7	1,002.5
Employees	(8.7%)	19,000	16,900	14,800	14,200	13,200

NAVITAS ENERGY INC.

3001 Broadway St. NE Ste 695
Minneapolis MN 55413-1707
Phone: 612-370-1061
Fax: 612-370-9005
Web: www.windpower.com

CEO: –
CFO: –
HR: –
FYE: December 31
Type: Private

Navitas Energy develops owns and operates wind energy projects in 11 US Midwestern states. The company sells power produced at its facilities to public municipal and cooperative electric utilities looking to provide green energy solutions to consumers. Navitas Energy provides financing engineering product selection construction management and maintenance services. It has wind power facilities with a combined capacity of more than 1040 MW of energy and a further 1500 MW under development. Spanish wind turbine manufacturer Gamesa Corporacion Tecnologica controls Navitas Energy which was founded in 2001 by former CEO Gregory Jaunich.

NAVTEQ CORPORATION

425 W. Randolph St.
Chicago IL 60606
Phone: 312-894-7000
Fax: 312-894-7050
Web: www.navteq.com

CEO: –
CFO: –
HR: –
FYE: December 31
Type: Subsidiary

NAVTEQ helps people get where they're going. Car and navigation system manufacturers incorporate the company's digital mapping database into vehicle navigation and fleet management systems. It also sells to government agencies mobile phone makers software developers and delivery services. The database features such information as street names turn restrictions and the locations of hospitals gas stations and tourist destinations. It includes data for more than 80 countries on six continents. The company counts BMW Garmin MapQuest and Trimble Navigation among its customers. NAVTEQ is a subsidiary of mobile phone maker Nokia.

NAVY FEDERAL CREDIT UNION

820 Follin Ln.
Vienna VA 22180-4907
Phone: 703-255-8000
Fax: 703-255-8741
Web: https://www.navyfederal.org

CEO: Cutler Dawson
CFO: Brady Cole
HR: Louise Foreman
FYE: December 31
Type: Private - Not-for-Pr

"Once a member always a member" promises Navy Federal Credit Union (NFCU). This policy has helped NFCU become one of the nation's largest credit unions claiming more than four million members who can retain their credit union privileges even after discharge from the armed services. Formed in 1933 NFCU provides a variety of financial services to all Department of Defense uniformed personnel reservists National Guard personnel civilian employees and contractors as well as their families. The credit union has more than 220 branch locations in the US and overseas many of them on or near military bases.

NB&T FINANCIAL GROUP, INC.

NAS: NBTF

48 N. South Street	CEO: –
Wilmington, OH 45177	CFO: –
Phone: 937 382-1441	HR: –
Fax: –	FYE: December 31
	Type: Public

NB&T Financial is the holding company for National Bank and Trust which serves southwestern and central Ohio from some two-dozen branches. The bank offers standard deposit products and services including checking and savings accounts CDs and IRAs. Its Really Awesome Dollars (RAD) accounts target the 16-and younger set; a minimum deposit of $1.00 is required. Residential mortgages account for about a third of all loans; commercial loans and mortgages make up another 40%. The bank also offers asset management and retirement planning services. NB&T acquired Community National another Ohio-based community bank in late 2009. The following year it sold subsidiary NB&T Insurance Agency to its management.

	Annual Growth	12/09	12/10	12/11	12/12	12/13
Assets ($ mil.)	(0.4%)	649.3	690.6	675.6	651.1	638.3
Net income ($ mil.)	1.3%	4.0	8.8	3.8	3.9	4.2
Market value ($ mil.)	4.4%	55.9	92.8	67.5	58.4	66.3
Employees	(5.5%)	241	217	211	203	192

NBCUNIVERSAL MEDIA LLC

30 Rockefeller Plaza	CEO: Stephen B Burke
New York NY 10112	CFO: –
Phone: 212-664-4444	HR: Susan Yun
Fax: 212-664-4085	FYE: December 31
Web: www.nbcuni.com	Type: Joint Venture

Television movies and more fill the vastness of this entertainment company. NBCUniversal Media is a leading media conglomerate anchored by its broadcast network NBC with more than 200 affiliate stations (including 10 that are company-owned) and its Universal Studios feature film division. Other broadcasting operations owned by NBCUniversal include Spanish-language network Telemundo and a portfolio of cable TV channels that includes Bravo E! Entertainment Syfy G4 USA Network Oxygen and news channel MSNBC. It also owns online portal iVillage and has a stake in video site Hulu. Comcast the country's #1 cable systems operator owns 51% of NBCUniversal and has agreed to acquire General Electric's 49% stake.

NBHX TRIM USA CORPORATION

1020 7 MILE RD NW	CEO: –
COMSTOCK PARK, MI 493219542	CFO: –
Phone: 616-785-9400	HR: –
Fax: –	FYE: December 31
Web: www.nbhx.com.cn	Type: Private

For those car owners who can't bear to be without the best things in life Behr Industries is there to satisfy those needs. The company manufactures interior wood trim components for OEM automotive heavy-duty truck and marine suppliers across North America. It is the only US-based full-service wood component supplier with a domestic production plant. The Michigan-based facility neighbors the Detroit Big Three production plants. Behr Industries has captured more than 70% of the US market for center consoles instrument panels side door panels and similar wood components. Its fortunes have been closely tied to those of GM's. The company is a subsidiary of Erwin Behr GmbH of Wedlingen Germany.

	Annual Growth	12/09	12/10	12/11	12/12	12/13
Sales ($ mil.)	22.1%	–	–	40.1	49.6	59.9
Net income ($ mil.)	35.4%	–	–	1.1	1.3	2.1
Market value ($ mil.)	–	–	–	–	–	–
Employees	–	–	–	–	–	480

NBT BANCORP. INC.

NMS: NBTB

52 South Broad Street	CEO: Martin A. Dietrich
Norwich, NY 13815	CFO: Michael J. Chewens
Phone: 607 337-2265	HR: Catherine M. Scarlett
Fax: 607 336-7538	FYE: December 31
Web: www.nbtbancorp.com	Type: Public

NBT Bancorp is the holding company for NBT Bank and its Pennstar Bank and Hampshire First Bank divisions which together operate about 155 branches mainly in suburban and rural areas of central and northern New York northeastern Pennsylvania western Massachusetts southern New Hampshire and northwestern Vermont. The banks offer services such as checking and savings accounts CDs and trust services. Its loan portfolio is dominated by business and commercial real estate loans. Its EPIC Advisors unit administers retirement plans while Mang Insurance Agency sells personal and commercial coverage. NBT Capital provides venture funding to growing area businesses. In 2013 the company acquired Alliance Financial.

	Annual Growth	12/10	12/11	12/12	12/13	12/14
Assets ($ mil.)	9.9%	5,338.9	5,598.4	6,042.3	7,652.2	7,797.9
Net income ($ mil.)	6.9%	57.4	57.9	54.6	61.7	75.1
Market value ($ mil.)	2.1%	1,060.1	971.4	889.8	1,136.9	1,153.2
Employees	5.3%	1,499	1,565	1,581	1,742	1,840

NBTY INC.

2100 Smithtown Ave.	CEO: Jeffrey A Nagel
Ronkonkoma NY 11779	CFO: Dipak Golechha
Phone: 631-200-2000	HR: Doris Diaz
Fax: 801-342-4305	FYE: September 30
Web: www.naturessunshine.com	Type: Private

NBTY draws upon nature's bounty to cash in on the market for preventive and alternative health care. As the largest vertically integrated source of nutritional supplements in the US the company manufactures wholesales and retails more than 25000 products including vitamins minerals herbs and sports drinks. Brands include Ester-C Nature's Bounty Solgar and Sundown. NBTY has manufacturing facilities in Canada China the UK and the US and is able to produce and package capsules tablets powders and liquids. The Carlyle Group-owned company sells its goods through pharmacies wholesalers supermarkets and health food stores around the world.

NCH CORPORATION

2727 CHEMSEARCH BLVD	CEO: –
IRVING, TX 750626454	CFO: Christopher T (Chris) Sortwell
Phone: 972-438-0705	HR: –
Fax: –	FYE: April 30
Web: www.us.chemsearch.com	Type: Private

NCH has been cleaning up for years and like everyone else it's been using soaps and detergents to do so. The company makes and sells about 450 chemical maintenance repair and supply products including all kinds of cleaners for customers in more than 50 countries throughout the world. NCH markets its products through a direct sales force to companies in the agricultural home-improvement industrial recreational and utility markets. Other products include fasteners welding supplies pet care supplies plumbing parts lubricants and metal-working fluids.

	Annual Growth	04/09	04/10	04/11	04/12	04/13
Sales ($ mil.)	4.8%	–	885.8	952.5	1,045.1	1,018.3
Net income ($ mil.)	(31.9%)	–	–	6.7	6.8	3.1
Market value ($ mil.)	–	–	–	–	–	–
Employees	–	–	–	–	–	8,500

NCH HEALTHCARE SYSTEM INC.

350 7TH ST N
NAPLES, FL 34102-5754
Phone: 239-436-5000
Fax: –
Web: www.nchmd.org

CEO: Allan Weiss
CFO: –
HR: –
FYE: September 30
Type: Private

NCH Healthcare System provides a comprehensive range of health care services to residents in southwest Florida. The system includes two acute care hospitals (NCH Downtown Naples Hospital and NCH North Naples Hospital) with a combined 715-bed capacity and regional institutes which specialize in orthopedics and the treatment of cancer heart ailments and women's and children's health issues. NCH also operates an area network of outpatient and ambulatory care facilities that provide services ranging from diagnostics to rehabilitative care to surgery and emergency care.

	Annual Growth	09/05	09/06	09/07	09/08	09/11
Sales ($ mil.)	0.3%	–	475.3	524.7	456.4	483.1
Net income ($ mil.)	(27.2%)	–	35.5	49.6	25.4	7.3
Market value ($ mil.)	–	–	–	–	–	–
Employees	–	–	–	–	–	3,500

NCI BUILDING SYSTEMS, INC.

NYS: NCS

10943 North Sam Houston Parkway West
Houston, TX 77064
Phone: 281 897-7788
Fax: –
Web: www.ncilp.com

CEO: Norman C. (Norm) Chambers
CFO: Mark E. Johnson
HR: –
FYE: November 01
Type: Public

NCI's buildings are quite a "steel." NCI Building Systems also known as NCI Group engineers designs manufactures and distributes metal buildings and components (doors roofs walls and trim) for nonresidential construction markets in North America. It sells its products to contractors developers and builders. The group also provides steel coil coating which is used by manufacturers of HVAC systems lighting fixtures and appliances. NCI has about 30 manufacturing facilities in the US and Mexico; it also operates distribution and sales offices in the US and Canada. Investment firm Clayton Dubilier & Rice owns NCI Group.

	Annual Growth	10/11	10/12*	11/13	11/14	11/15
Sales ($ mil.)	13.0%	959.6	1,154.0	1,309.4	1,371.9	1,563.7
Net income ($ mil.)	–	(10.0)	4.9	(12.9)	11.2	17.8
Market value ($ mil.)	2.5%	701.6	832.7	1,070.5	1,472.0	774.9
Employees	10.4%	3,590	4,293	4,484	4,556	5,326

*Fiscal year change

NCI INC

NMS: NCIT

11730 Plaza America Drive
Reston, VA 20190-4764
Phone: 703 707-6900
Fax: 703 707-6901
Web: www.nciinc.com

CEO: –
CFO: Lucas J Narel
HR: John Heim
FYE: December 31
Type: Public

NCI isn't the newest hit show on CBS but an IT services provider primarily for US federal government agencies. Among its services are enterprise systems management and integration health IT cybersecurity and information assurance network design and engineering logistics program management and lifecycle support training and simulation and application development. Defense and intelligence agency clients (which account for about 75% of sales) include the Army Air Force USSOCOM and the National Guard. The company also serves federal civilian agencies such as NASA the Department of Energy and the Senate.

	Annual Growth	12/10	12/11	12/12	12/13	12/14
Sales ($ mil.)	(14.1%)	581.3	558.3	368.4	332.3	317.0
Net income ($ mil.)	(22.8%)	23.9	13.2	(86.8)	7.7	8.5
Market value ($ mil.)	(18.4%)	299.0	151.5	61.0	86.1	132.8
Employees	(8.8%)	2,600	2,600	2,200	1,900	1,800

NCIRCLE NETWORK SECURITY INC.

101 2nd St. Ste. 400
San Francisco CA 94105
Phone: 415-625-5900
Fax: 415-625-5982
Web: www.ncircle.com

CEO: Kelly E Lang
CFO: Mark Elchinoff
HR: –
FYE: December 31
Type: Private

nCircle Network Security helps businesses get their heads around network security threats. To protect against hackers and other nuisances it provides hardware and software systems that assess and monitor enterprise computer network security. nCircle markets its products (including its flagship Suite360 product) to more than 6500 companies in the financial services sector manufacturers insurance companies and government agencies. Related services include risk assessment and training. Its customers have included the US Office of Naval Intelligence Visa and Archer Daniels Midland. Founded in 1998 nCircle has received private equity funding from Alta Partners BV Capital JK&B Capital and Menlo Ventures.

NCR CORP.

NYS: NCR

3097 Satellite Boulevard
Duluth, GA 30096
Phone: 937 445-5000
Fax: –
Web: www.ncr.com

CEO: William R. (Bill) Nuti
CFO: Robert P. (Bob) Fishman
HR: Joyce Hoyle
FYE: December 31
Type: Public

You can still find NCR at the nexus of people and money. Born during the waning days of the Wild West as National Cash Register NCR is a leading maker of ATMs. The company also makes point-of-sale (POS) terminals bar code scanners and related printer consumables. Other retail and financial systems offerings include check image processing systems and self-service kiosks for hospitality retail and travel applications. NCR's services segment provides maintenance and support as well as professional services such as systems integration and managed services. NCR which facilitates more than 550 million transactions daily does business in more than 180 countries. About 60% of its sales are generated outside the US.

	Annual Growth	12/10	12/11	12/12	12/13	12/14
Sales ($ mil.)	8.1%	4,819.0	5,443.0	5,730.0	6,123.0	6,591.0
Net income ($ mil.)	9.3%	134.0	53.0	146.0	443.0	191.0
Market value ($ mil.)	17.3%	2,591.4	2,775.2	4,295.9	5,742.5	4,913.0
Employees	9.5%	21,000	23,500	25,700	29,300	30,200

NCS TECHNOLOGIES INC.

7669 LIMESTONE DR STE 130
GAINESVILLE, VA 201554038
Phone: 703-743-8500
Fax: –
Web: www.ncst.com

CEO: –
CFO: –
HR: –
FYE: December 31
Type: Private

NCS Technologies makes enterprise computing needs personal. The company makes and supplies PC products to clients large and small. NCS Technologies offers personal computers mobile computing thin client computing servers and Internet appliances to clients in the government educational and private sectors. Products include desktops notebooks rugged tablets and servers. In addition to providing built-to-order hardware the company also provides software customizations and installation and technical support services. Founded in 1996 the company's single facility in Washington DC serves clients from across the world.

	Annual Growth	09/04	09/05	09/06*	12/09	12/10
Sales ($ mil.)	–	–	–	(894.5)	80.0	117.5
Net income ($ mil.)	824.7%	–	–	0.0	1.3	0.7
Market value ($ mil.)	–	–	–	–	–	–
Employees	–	–	–	–	–	108

*Fiscal year change

NEACE LUKENS INC.

2305 River Rd.
Louisville KY 40206-1010
Phone: 502-894-2100
Fax: 502-894-8602
Web: www.neacelukens.com

CEO: –
CFO: –
HR: –
FYE: December 31
Type: Private

Neace Lukens is a regional insurance broker in the south-central US with offices in Arizona Georgia Indiana Kentucky Michigan Ohio and Tennessee. The company offers personal and commercial insurance policies such as property/casualty (general and professional liability auto insurance and workers' compensation) employee benefits (health and life insurance) and industry-specific insurance for school districts nursing homes contractors truck drivers manufacturing facilities and lumber yards. Founded in 1991 by chairman John Neace and president Joseph Lukens Neace Lukens was acquired by Florida-based private equity firm AssuredPartners in September 2011.

NEBRASKA BOOK COMPANY INC.

4700 S. 19th St.
Lincoln NE 68501-0529
Phone: 402-421-7300
Fax: 800-869-0399
Web: www.nebook.com

CEO: Benjamin Riggsby
CFO: John Macieo
HR: –
FYE: March 31
Type: Private

If books are engines of change Nebraska Book Company (NBC) is transforming college students across the US. One of the largest textbook distributors in the US NBC sells 6 million-plus books annually. It serves some 2500 booksellers and operates nearly 250 bookstores on or adjacent to college campuses that sell and rent textbooks and other merchandise. NBC also supplies educational materials to private high schools nontraditional colleges and corporate and correspondence classes as well as store management and e-commerce software. Founded in 1915 as a bookstore near The University of Nebraska NBC emerged from Chapter 11 bankruptcy protection in 2012. It is owned by holding company Neebo Inc.

NEBRASKA PUBLIC POWER DISTRICT

1414 15th St.
Columbus NE 68602-0499
Phone: 402-564-8561
Fax: 402-636-3955
Web: www.oppd.com

CEO: Patrick Pope
CFO: Traci Bender
HR: –
FYE: December 31
Type: Government-owned

Nebraska Public Power District (NPPD) electrifies the Cornhusker State. The government-owned electric utility the largest in the state provides power in 91 of the state's 93 counties. The firm has a generating capacity of about 3130 MW and operates more than 5000 miles of transmission lines. NPPD distributes electricity to about 89000 retail customers in 80 cities and towns; it also provides power to about 1 million customers through wholesale power contracts with 52 towns and 25 public power districts. In addition NPPD purchases electricity from the federally owned Western Area Power Administration and operates a surface water irrigation system.

NEENAH FOUNDRY COMPANY

2121 Brooks Ave.
Neenah WI 54956
Phone: 920-725-7000
Fax: 920-729-3661
Web: www.nfco.com

CEO: Thomas J Riordan
CFO: Thomas Adrians
HR: –
FYE: September 30
Type: Private

"Grate" things come from Neenah Foundry. The company makes gray and ductile iron castings (such as iron tree grates and manhole covers) and forged components for the heavy municipal and industrial markets. Its lineup also includes bridge scuppers curb inlets floor drains trenches wheel guards and other castings. Neenah products contain at least 85% recycled material from auto bodies and scrap iron. Founded in 1872 its sales offices and distribution yards dot about a dozen US states. Customers are architects engineers city and state governments heavy duty truck manufacturers HVAC makers and utilities.

NEENAH PAPER INC   NYS: NP

3460 Preston Ridge Road
Alpharetta, GA 30005
Phone: 678 566-6500
Fax: –
Web: www.neenah.com

CEO: John ODonnell
CFO: Bonnie C Lind
HR: Richard Read
FYE: December 31
Type: Public

Neenah Paper regularly attends US Presidential Inaugurations — as the official invitation that is. Neenah's lineup includes technical products (durable saturated coated-base papers and wall coverings) as well as fine paper (premium writing specialty cover digital finish and stationery). The company operates through Neenah Paper and six subsidiaries; each handles select activities such as mills real estate and manufacturing assets and trademarks. Neenah products are sold under several brand names such as CAPITOL BOND NEUTECH and ENVIRONMENT (fine paper) as well as KIMDURA and Soft-Stretch (technical) among others. Customers are global paper distributors converters and specialty companies.

	Annual Growth	12/10	12/11	12/12	12/13	12/14
Sales ($ mil.)	8.2%	657.7	696.0	808.8	844.5	902.7
Net income ($ mil.)	(18.9%)	159.1	29.1	44.3	52.0	68.7
Market value ($ mil.)	32.3%	329.6	373.8	476.8	716.3	1,009.4
Employees	4.8%	1,660	1,635	1,870	1,875	2,000

NEFF RENTAL LLC

3750 NW 87th Ave. Ste. 400
Miami FL 33178
Phone: 305-513-3350
Fax: 305-513-4156
Web: www.neffrental.com

CEO: Graham Hood
CFO: Mark Irion
HR: –
FYE: December 31
Type: Private

Neff neffer says "neffer" to a rental. Equipment rentals account for most of its revenue but it also sells new and used equipment and provides repair and parts services. Earth-moving equipment makes up about 50% of Neff's rental fleet which also includes compressors generators lifts and other equipment for construction and industrial uses. The company has about 60 locations in a dozen or so US states mainly in the South and West. Neff Rental serves a diverse range of customers from golf course developers to oil exploration giants. Neff filed for Chapter 11 bankruptcy in May 2010 emerging in October via a deal that gives control to Wayzata Investment Partners its first-lien lenders.

NEFFS BANCORP INC.

NBB: NEFB

5629 PA Route 873, P.O. Box 10
Neffs, PA 18065-0010
Phone: 610 767-3875
Fax: –
Web: www.neffsnatl.com

CEO: John J Remaley
CFO: –
HR: –
FYE: December 31
Type: Public

Eneff with the megabanks already! Neffs Bancorp is the holding company for The Neffs National Bank an independent bank that has been serving eastern Pennsylvania's Lehigh County since 1923. The bank operates a single office in the village of Neffs north of Allentown. Targeting consumers and local businesses it provides a variety of deposit products including checking and savings accounts CDs and IRAs. The bank is mainly a real estate lender with residential mortgages home equity loans and commercial mortgages comprising some 90% of its portfolio. Business consumer and construction loans round out its lending activities. The Neffs National Bank also offers tax estate and investment planning.

	Annual Growth	12/10	12/11	12/12	12/13	12/14
Assets ($ mil.)	2.7%	278.5	286.5	294.2	303.8	309.9
Net income ($ mil.)	3.9%	3.4	3.7	4.2	4.2	4.0
Market value ($ mil.)	2.2%	40.5	42.4	42.4	43.4	44.1
Employees	–	31	–	–	–	–

NEIGHBORHOOD HEALTH PLAN INC

253 SUMMER ST FL 5
BOSTON, MA 02210-1120
Phone: 617-772-5500
Fax: –
Web: www.nhp.org

CEO: Deborah Enos
CFO: Garrett Parker
HR: –
FYE: December 31
Type: Private

Neighborhood Health Plan (NHP) is a not-for-profit health plan provider that offers health insurance products and related services to more than 200000 members in Massachusetts. The organization is a leading provider of managed health care for members of MassHealth the state's Medicaid program for low-income and disabled residents. But it also provides commercial health plans for small businesses as well as low-cost and no-cost family and individual plans for people who qualify for subsidized health coverage under Massachusetts' 2006 health care reform law. NHP maintains a provider network of more than 2800 primary care physicians 400 specialists and dozens of hospitals. The company was founded in 1986.

	Annual Growth	12/04	12/05	12/06	12/07	12/08
Sales ($ mil.)	(30.7%)	–	–	1,779.2	681.3	855.1
Net income ($ mil.)	64418.0%	–	–	0.0	40.6	27.5
Market value ($ mil.)	–	–	–	–	–	–
Employees	–	–	–	–	–	340

NEIGHBORHOOD REINVESTMENT CORPORATION

999 N CAPITOL ST NE # 900
WASHINGTON, DC 200024684
Phone: 202-220-2300
Fax: –
Web: www.nw.org

CEO: Chuck Wehrwein
CFO: Michael L. Forster
HR: –
FYE: September 30
Type: Private

Neighborhood Reinvestment Corporation (now dba NeighborWorks America) wants to be your neighbor. The not-for-profit organization supports more than 235 independent local organizations in suburban urban and rural communities across the country. Programs include building multi-family dwellings and helping low and middle income families with financing and insurance as well as job creation community facilities and economic development in rural areas. The organization also offers training for community leaders and would-be homeowners on community planning green building and financing among others. Established by Congress in 1978 NeighborWorks is funded by Congress private donations and corporate support.

	Annual Growth	12/07	12/08*	09/09	09/10	09/13
Sales ($ mil.)	197.0%	–	1.1	359.5	312.4	248.0
Net income ($ mil.)	11.5%	–	7.3	2.5	11.3	
Market value ($ mil.)	–	–	–	–	–	–
Employees	–	–	–	–	–	260

*Fiscal year change

NEKTAR THERAPEUTICS

NMS: NKTR

455 Mission Bay Boulevard South
San Francisco, CA 94158
Phone: 415 482-5300
Fax: –
Web: www.nektar.com

CEO: Howard W. Robin
CFO: John Nicholson
HR: Dorian Hirth
FYE: December 31
Type: Public

Nektar Therapeutics has pegged its fortunes to making drugs more effective. The clinical-stage drug development firm uses its PEGylation technology (based upon polyethylene glycol) to improve the delivery and efficacy of existing drugs. Nektar's pipeline includes about 20 drugs focused on anti-infectives and anti-virals immunology oncology and pain treatments. Its lead candidates are NKTR-118 for opioid-induced constipation and NKTR-102 to treat breast cancer. Nektar receives royalties on about a dozen approved products including Neulasta Somavert and Macugen as well as its surgical and imaging technology. The company's development partners include Roche AstraZeneca Amgen and Pfizer.

	Annual Growth	12/10	12/11	12/12	12/13	12/14
Sales ($ mil.)	6.0%	159.0	71.5	81.2	148.9	200.7
Net income ($ mil.)	–	(37.9)	(134.0)	(171.9)	(162.0)	(53.9)
Market value ($ mil.)	4.8%	1,686.1	734.2	972.3	1,489.3	2,033.8
Employees	1.8%	408	423	433	445	438

NELNET INC

NYS: NNI

121 South 13th Street, Suite 100
Lincoln, NE 68508
Phone: 402 458-2370
Fax: –
Web: www.nelnet.com

CEO: Jeffrey R. (Jeff) Noordhoek
CFO: James D. (Jim) Kruger
HR: –
FYE: December 31
Type: Public

Got Ivy League tastes on a community college budget? Nelnet may be able to help. The education planning and financing company helps students and parents plan and pay for college educations. Nelnet is mostly known for servicing federal student loans. The firm manages about $76 billion in student loan assets most of which are government loans. However in light of regulatory changes to the student lending market Nelnet is increasingly expanding its fee-based education services. It serves the K-12 and higher education marketplace providing long-term payment plans college enrollment services and software and technology services. The firm is part of financial holding company Farmers & Merchants Investment.

	Annual Growth	12/10	12/11	12/12	12/13	12/14
Assets ($ mil.)	3.8%	25,893.9	25,852.2	26,607.9	27,770.8	30,098.1
Net income ($ mil.)	12.9%	189.0	204.3	178.0	302.7	307.6
Market value ($ mil.)	18.3%	1,095.5	1,131.6	1,377.6	1,948.7	2,142.5
Employees	9.0%	2,200	2,400	2,500	2,800	3,100

NEMOURS FOUNDATION

10140 CENTURION PKWY N
JACKSONVILLE, FL 322560532
Phone: 904-697-4100
Fax: –
Web: www.nemours.org

CEO: –
CFO: –
HR: –
FYE: December 31
Type: Private

Even if their offspring are fanatical about Finding Nemo parents of sick children may prefer finding Nemours. The Nemours Foundation operates the Nemours/Alfred I. duPont Hospital for Children in Wilmington Delaware; the Nemours Children's Hospital in Orlando Florida; and dozens of pediatric clinics in Delaware Florida New Jersey and Pennsylvania that treat acutely and chronically ill children. Specialties include orthopedics cardiology neurology and oncology. Nemours also has extensive research programs and it operates a clinic in Delaware that serves low-income elderly residents. The not-for-profit foundation was created in 1936 through the will of chemicals pioneer Alfred I. duPont.

	Annual Growth	12/04	12/05	12/06	12/07	12/08
Sales ($ mil.)	(33.5%)	–	546.4	578.7	635.0	160.4
Net income ($ mil.)	–	–	–	29.3	53.9	(81.0)
Market value ($ mil.)	–	–	–	–	–	–
Employees	–	–	–	–	–	4,400

NEOGEN CORP.

NMS: NEOG

620 Lesher Place
Lansing, MI 48912
Phone: 517 372-9200
Fax: 517 372-0108
Web: www.neogen.com

CEO: James L. Herbert
CFO: Steven J. (Steve) Quinlan
HR: –
FYE: May 31
Type: Public

Bacteriophobes have a friend in Neogen a maker of products for the food safety and animal health markets. Its food safety testing products are used by the food industry to make sure our edibles are clean unspoiled and free of toxins pathogens and allergens. In core markets in the Americas and Europe Neogen reaches end users (including dairies meat processors and animal feed producers) through a direct sales force; it uses distributors elsewhere. On the animal health front Neogen produces drugs vaccines diagnostics and instruments for the veterinary market; it also makes rat poisons and disinfectants used in animal production plants and diagnostic products for research laboratories.

	Annual Growth	05/11	05/12	05/13	05/14	05/15
Sales ($ mil.)	13.2%	172.7	184.0	207.5	247.4	283.1
Net income ($ mil.)	10.1%	22.8	22.5	27.2	28.2	33.5
Market value ($ mil.)	1.0%	1,664.8	1,445.8	2,022.4	1,403.1	1,735.4
Employees	12.9%	654	746	781	926	1,062

NEOGENOMICS INC

NAS: NEO

12701 Commonwealth Drive, Suite 9
Fort Myers, FL 33913
Phone: 239 768-0600
Fax: 239 690-4237
Web: www.neogenomics.com

CEO: Douglas M. VanOort
CFO: George A. Cardoza
HR: George Schiano
FYE: December 31
Type: Public

NeoGenomics is a fortune teller of sorts. The company offers genetic and molecular testing in five categories to determine a person's genetic predisposition to certain cancers and other diseases. Testing methods include immunohistochemisty cytogenetics flourescence in-situ hybridization (FISH) flow cytometry and molecular genetic testing. The company serves customers including community-based oncologists pathologists urologists hospitals and other health care facilities through its labs located across the US.

	Annual Growth	12/10	12/11	12/12	12/13	12/14
Sales ($ mil.)	26.2%	34.4	43.5	59.9	66.5	87.1
Net income ($ mil.)	–	(3.3)	(1.2)	0.1	2.0	1.1
Market value ($ mil.)	33.8%	78.3	84.3	149.4	218.1	251.2
Employees	25.2%	185	248	290	339	455

NEOMAGIC CORPORATION

PINK SHEETS: NMGC

3250 Jay St.
Santa Clara CA 95054
Phone: 408-988-7020
Fax: 408-988-7036
Web: www.neomagic.com

CEO: Syed Zaidi
CFO: –
HR: –
FYE: January 31
Type: Public

NeoMagic is trying to deliver chip magic for everything from smart phones to electronic toll collection systems. The company develops and markets semiconductors including a family of system-on-chip (SoC) processors sold under the MiMagic brand and software for audio video imaging graphics and television. It also provides design services on system and software development that help OEMs bring their products to market. NeoMagic sells through distributors and representatives in the US the UK and Asia. Among the company's customers is California-based startup ViV Systems a home theater developer and manufacturer.

NEOMEDIA TECHNOLOGIES, INC.

NBB: NEOM

1515 Walnut Street, Suite 100
Boulder, CO 80302
Phone: 303 546-7946
Fax: –
Web: www.neom.com

CEO: Laura A Marriott
CFO: Barry S Baer
HR: –
FYE: December 31
Type: Public

NeoMedia Technologies has a new approach to mobile marketing. The company develops hardware and software that allows camera-enabled mobile phones to read and transmit data from bar codes embedded in advertisements. Marketers use the technology to link phone users to targeted URLs. It also offers mobile ticketing and coupon systems. The company also generates revenue by licensing its technology and from designing and implementing mobile marketing campaigns. NeoMedia has undergone significant restructuring in recent years including the divestiture of a number of business lines.

	Annual Growth	12/10	12/11	12/12	12/13	12/14
Sales ($ mil.)	23.2%	1.5	2.3	2.3	5.0	3.5
Net income ($ mil.)	–	35.1	(0.8)	(19.4)	(214.1)	(2.5)
Market value ($ mil.)	–	0.0	0.0	0.0	0.0	0.0
Employees	(14.9%)	21	27	14	18	11

NEOPHOTONICS CORP

NYS: NPTN

2911 Zanker Road
San Jose, CA 95134
Phone: 408 232-9200
Fax: –
Web: www.neophotonics.com

CEO: Timothy S. (Tim) Jenks
CFO: Cal R. Hoagland
HR: –
FYE: December 31
Type: Public

NeoPhotonics wants its clients to see communications in a new light. The company develops and manufactures optical network components using laser-reactive deposition. Its products include photonic integrated circuits (PICs) amplifiers glass substrates laser modules passive optical components photodiodes and transceivers. NeoPhotonics' chips and components are used in optical networking equipment for data communications and passive optical networks that enable fiber-to-the-home broadband access among other functions. It has a portfolio of more than 40 product families including ones that enable data transmission at more than 100 gigabits per second.

	Annual Growth	12/10	12/11	12/12	12/13	12/14
Sales ($ mil.)	13.6%	184.1	201.0	245.4	282.2	306.2
Net income ($ mil.)	–	3.2	(14.8)	(17.5)	(34.3)	(19.7)
Market value ($ mil.)	(9.6%)	–	150.0	188.0	231.2	110.7
Employees	(4.9%)	3,112	2,565	2,348	2,094	2,541

NEPHROS INC

OTC: NEPH

41 Grand Avenue
River Edge, NJ 07661
Phone: 201 343-5202
Fax: –
Web: www.nephros.com

CEO: –
CFO: –
HR: –
FYE: December 31
Type: Public

Nephros develops and makes medical devices that are used to treat irreversible loss of kidney function associated with End Stage Renal Disease or ESRD. ESRD is often the result of other health problems such as diabetes and high blood pressure. The company's products are designed to replace a patient's kidney function with the device system. Nephros is positioning its therapeutic devices as an alternative to hemodialysis the most common form of renal replacement therapy. The company's products use a process called "hemodiafiltration" (HDF) combining hemodialysis with hemofiltration to clean the patient's blood.

	Annual Growth	12/10	12/11	12/12	12/13	12/14
Sales ($ mil.)	(12.2%)	2.9	2.2	1.8	1.7	1.7
Net income ($ mil.)	–	(1.9)	(2.4)	(3.3)	(3.7)	(7.4)
Market value ($ mil.)	68.2%	3.0	21.0	36.2	12.9	24.0
Employees	5.7%	8	7	12	10	10

NES RENTALS HOLDINGS INC.

5440 N. Cumberland Ave. Ste. 200	CEO: Andrew P Studdert
Chicago IL 60656	CFO: Michael D Milligan
Phone: 773-695-3999	HR: –
Fax: 602-251-0555	FYE: December 31
Web: www.nesrentals.com	Type: Private

Forklifts and other lifts lift the revenues of NES Rentals formerly National Equipment Services. The company offers industrial and construction customers a range of aerial rental equipment from scissor lifts to boom lifts rough terrain and truck-mounted cranes. It also supplies specialty equipment such as bulldozers trenchers and skid steers as well as scaffolding systems. In addition to equipment rentals and repair and maintenance services for non-residential construction customers NES sells new and used pieces by OEMs including BMC JLG SkyJack Sala Doosan Stow Genie and Terex.

NESS USA INC.

300 Frank W. Burr Blvd. 7th Fl.	CEO: Ofer Segev
Teaneck NJ 07666	CFO: –
Phone: 201-488-7222	HR: –
Fax: 201-488-5040	FYE: December 31
Web: www.ness.com/company/locations/pages/about-nes	Type: Subsidiary

Software developers at Ness USA rock around the clock by coding around the globe. The company provides round-the-clock software development customizing applications from Oracle SAP IBM Microsoft and others. Ness USA also provides product engineering business process outsourcing information management consulting application and systems integration services and Web portal design and development. It targets customers in the financial services health care life sciences media and technology industry sectors. Ness USA is a unit of global information technology services firm Ness Technologies.

NESTLE PROFESSIONAL VITALITY

400 N. Tampa St. Ste. 1500	CEO: Gary Viljoen
Tampa FL 33602	CFO: Kim Johnson
Phone: 813-301-4600	HR: Yvonne Lai
Fax: 813-273-5421	FYE: December 31
Web: www.nestleprofessional.com/united-states/en/be	Type: Subsidiary

This company is energized by beverage distribution. Nestle Professional Vitality (formerly Vitality Foodservice) is a leading supplier of beverages and dispensing equipment to foodservice operators in the US Canada and abroad. It distributes coffee and other hot beverages fruit juices flavored waters and soft drinks to restaurants cruise ships hotels and institutional foodservice operations. In addition to its private-label beverages it supplies Sunkist-branded juices and Tetley tea (owned by Tata Tea Group). Formed in 1999 through the buyout of juice operations from Lykes Bros. Vitality Foodservice was acquired by Nestle Professional the out-of-home food and beverage division of Nestle in 2009.

NESTLE PURINA PETCARE COMPANY

Checkerboard Square	CEO: W Patrick McGinnis
St. Louis MO 63164	CFO: Rock Foster
Phone: 314-982-1000	HR: Karen Peters
Fax: 314-982-2134	FYE: December 31
Web: www.purina.com	Type: Subsidiary

When kitty meows for his chow Nestle Purina PetCare listens. The firm a subsidiary of Swiss food giant Nestle S.A. is the world's largest pet food producer. Its portfolio of some 30 brands includes Alpo Beneful Cat Chow Dog Chow Fancy Feast Friskies Mighty Dog Pro Plan and Purina ONE. It also makes cat and dog litter products under the Tidy Cats Yesterday's News and secondnature names. Purina products are sold internationally by mass merchandisers supermarkets pet supply stores and online retailers including Wal-Mart Target PetSmart Hy-Vee and Amazon.com. Besides pet supplies the firm offers health insurance for dogs and cats through its PurinaCare Insurance Services subsidiary.

NESTLE WATERS NORTH AMERICA INC.

900 Long Ridge Rd. Bldg. 2	CEO: Tim Brown
Stamford CT 06902-1138	CFO: Bill Pearson
Phone: 203-531-4100	HR: –
Fax: 312-926-8283	FYE: December 31
Web: www.nmh.org	Type: Subsidiary

Jack and Jill went up a hill to fetch a pail of water; Nestle Waters North America (NWNA) offers an easier alternative. The company entered the US and Canada by selling Perrier Sparkling Mineral Water in 1976; it has grown to represent about one-third of the bottled water market. Its portfolio boasts national top seller Nestle Pure Life and a dozen or so international and regional water brands: Acqua Panna Deer Park Ozarka Poland Spring and S. Pellegrino to name a few. Non-sparking waters generate some 90% of its sales. NWNA also added tea with the purchase of Sweet Leaf Tea. In addition to selling water via retail outlets the company provides home and office delivery. NWNA is a division of Nestle Waters.

NET MEDICAL XPRESS SOLUTIONS INC   NBB: NMXS

5021 Indian School Road, Suite 100	CEO: Richard F Govatski
Albuquerque, NM 87110	CFO: –
Phone: 505 255-1999	HR: –
Fax: –	FYE: December 31
Web: www.nmxs.com	Type: Public

NMXS.com has a clear image of what good document management looks like. The company provides software and services for archiving and retrieving documents and images primarily to health care and medical providers. Its customers have come from fields including health care government and entertainment as well as not-for-profit organizations. NMSC.com's products are made available under the Software-As-a-Service model.

	Annual Growth	12/10	12/11	12/12	12/13	12/14
Sales ($ mil.)	7.1%	3.5	3.2	3.9	4.8	4.6
Net income ($ mil.)	–	(0.3)	(0.2)	0.0	0.0	(0.5)
Market value ($ mil.)	(19.1%)	7.0	4.2	5.2	14.5	3.0
Employees	8.6%	18	22	121	32	25

NETAPP, INC.

NMS: NTAP

495 East Java Drive
Sunnyvale, CA 94089
Phone: 408 822-6000
Fax: –
Web: www.netapp.com

CEO: George Kurian
CFO: Nicholas R. (Nick) Noviello
HR: Gwendolyn (Gwen) McDonald
FYE: April 24
Type: Public

NetApp knows storage backwards and forwards and on premise and in the cloud. The company makes data storage systems used by businesses for archiving and backup. It's moving much of its hardware and software to cloud-based storage applications. It offers products for hybrid cloud storage extending customers' IT infrastructure to the cloud environments of Amazon Google and Microsoft. NetApp enables customers' use of flash storage another relatively new market for the company. The company's FlexPod product developed with Cisco Systems is designed to helped customers manage applications from Oracle SAP and Citrix. The company mainly sells to the energy financial services government health care and IT sectors through distributors.

	Annual Growth	04/11	04/12	04/13	04/14	04/15
Sales ($ mil.)	4.6%	5,122.6	6,233.2	6,332.4	6,325.1	6,122.7
Net income ($ mil.)	(4.5%)	673.1	605.4	505.3	637.5	559.9
Market value ($ mil.)	(8.8%)	15,950.9	11,947.1	10,673.7	10,713.5	11,056.3
Employees	5.8%	10,212	12,149	13,060	12,490	12,810

NETEZZA CORPORATION

26 Forest St.
Marlborough MA 01752
Phone: 508-382-8200
Fax: 508-382-8300
Web: www.netezza.com

CEO: –
CFO: Patrick J Scannell Jr
HR: –
FYE: January 31
Type: Subsidiary

Netezza understands that there's no point in storing your data if you can't find it again. The company provides data warehouse network appliances used to manage large databases. Tailored for toward government agencies and companies in data-intensive fields such as financial services and health care its network devices integrate database server and storage functions enabling the analysis of huge amounts of data. Netezza's TwinFin appliance is its core product. The Skimmer device is geared for small and midsized clients with less data to manage as well as for testing and development environments. Netezza sells its products directly worldwide. The company was acquired by IBM in 2010 for about $1.8 billion.

NETFLIX INC.

NMS: NFLX

100 Winchester Circle
Los Gatos, CA 95032
Phone: 408 540-3700
Fax: –
Web: www.netflix.com

CEO: Reed Hastings
CFO: David Wells
HR: –
FYE: December 31
Type: Public

Tapping technologies from multiple eras Netflix steers couch potatoes away from the video store to the mailbox or Internet. The company's more than 57 million subscribers in 50 countries can download movies or rent DVDs for a monthly fee through Netflix.com. Movies are delivered via the US Postal Service from distribution centers located in major US cities or streamed to some 1000 devices including PCs and TVs. Netflix ships millions of discs daily in the US and does not charge late fees or have due dates; its service employs user ratings to predict preferences and make recommendations. Netflix is focused on shifting its focus away from DVD rental to its fast-growing steaming service particularly overseas.

	Annual Growth	12/11	12/12	12/13	12/14	12/15
Sales ($ mil.)	20.6%	3,204.6	3,609.3	4,374.6	5,504.7	6,779.5
Net income ($ mil.)	(14.2%)	226.1	17.2	112.4	266.8	122.6
Market value ($ mil.)	13.3%	29,652.0	39,623.0	157,554.8	146,188.7	48,947.8
Employees	6.0%	2,927	2,429	2,327	2,450	3,700

NETGEAR, INC.

NMS: NTGR

350 East Plumeria Drive
San Jose, CA 95134
Phone: 408 907-8000
Fax: –
Web: www.netgear.com

CEO: Patrick C.S. Lo
CFO: Christine M. Gorjanc
HR: Tamesa Rogers
FYE: December 31
Type: Public

NETGEAR keeps consumers and small businesses wired and wireless. The company designs a range of networking equipment — adapters hubs routers switches media servers and interfaces — for connecting PCs in home and small business settings to each other and the Internet. (Manufacturing is outsourced to contractors in Asia.) NETGEAR also supplies network-attached storage (NAS) systems VPN firewalls and digital media receivers. It sells through distributors including Ingram Micro and Tech Data and to retailers such as Best Buy Fry's Electronics and RadioShack. The company generates about half of its sales from international markets.

	Annual Growth	12/10	12/11	12/12	12/13	12/14
Sales ($ mil.)	11.5%	902.1	1,181.0	1,271.9	1,369.6	1,393.5
Net income ($ mil.)	(35.5%)	50.9	91.4	86.5	55.2	8.8
Market value ($ mil.)	1.4%	1,169.0	1,165.2	1,368.6	1,143.3	1,234.9
Employees	12.2%	654	791	850	1,029	1,038

NETIQ CORPORATION

1233 West Loop South Park Towers North Ste. 810
Houston TX 77027
Phone: 713-548-1700
Fax: 713-548-1771
Web: www.netiq.com

CEO: –
CFO: –
HR: –
FYE: June 30
Type: Subsidiary

NetIQ thinks it can help you intelligently manage your IT assets. The company a unit of Attachmate provides enterprise software used to test migrate secure and analyze distributed computer systems. Its products include performance and availability management applications that customers use to diagnose and analyze systems running Windows UNIX and Linux. The unit's security and systems management products encompass a variety of hardware and software including servers databases and VoIP networks. Its products are used by 12000-plus customers — which have included ExxonMobil Ford the Mayo Clinic NASA and Nasdaq — in more than 60 countries and are marketed through resellers worldwide.

NETLIST INC

NAS: NLST

175 Technology Drive, Suite 150
Irvine, CA 92618
Phone: 949 435-0025
Fax: –

CEO: Chun Ki Hong
CFO: Gail Sasaki
HR: –
FYE: December 27
Type: Public

Netlist designs manufactures and markets high-performance memory subsystems for the OEM market. Its line of board-level memory products are used in IT infrastructure equipment such as servers data centers and other high-performance computing and communications markets. Key customers include Dell and IBM which together account for about 60% of sales.

	Annual Growth	01/11*	12/11	12/12	12/13	12/14
Sales ($ mil.)	(20.3%)	37.9	60.7	36.9	23.0	19.2
Net income ($ mil.)	–	(15.1)	(5.6)	(14.0)	(10.8)	(15.4)
Market value ($ mil.)	(34.8%)	106.2	104.2	30.9	30.0	29.5
Employees	(21.1%)	232	276	158	124	114

*Fiscal year change

NETSCOUT SYSTEMS INC

NMS: NTCT

310 Littleton Road
Westford, MA 01886
Phone: 978 614-4000
Fax: -
Web: www.netscout.com

CEO: Anil K. Singhal
CFO: Jean A. Bua
HR: -
FYE: March 31
Type: Public

NetScout Systems helps network administrators stay prepared. The company provides systems that monitor and report on the performance of software applications and the networks on which they run. Its probes — monitoring appliances that can be placed throughout a network — allow administrators to collect information about traffic flow and to optimize application and network performance. Its nGenius Service Assurance Solution monitors systems ranging from VoIP communications to customer relationship management applications. NetScout sells directly and through resellers and distributors to corporate and government customers. Founded in 1984 NetScout's technology is used by more than 90% of FORTUNE 100 companies.

	Annual Growth	03/11	03/12	03/13	03/14	03/15
Sales ($ mil.)	11.8%	290.5	308.7	350.6	396.6	453.7
Net income ($ mil.)	13.2%	37.3	32.4	40.6	49.1	61.2
Market value ($ mil.)	12.6%	1,114.9	830.0	1,002.6	1,533.6	1,789.4
Employees	6.1%	845	887	983	1,021	1,069

NETSMART TECHNOLOGIES INC.

3500 Sunrise Hwy. Ste. D-122
Great River NY 11739
Phone: 631-968-2000
Fax: 631-968-2123
Web: www.ntst.com

CEO: Michael Valentine
CFO: Anthony F Grisanti
HR: -
FYE: December 31
Type: Private

Netsmart Technologies applies its know-how to the behavioral and public health care fields. The company provides practice management billing patient tracking and other software and hardware systems for specialty care providers such as mental health clinics psychiatric hospitals public health agencies managed care organizations and correctional facilities. It also provides related support services such as systems implementation and performs data entry and processing for its customers. Netsmart has served such clients as the Betty Ford Center and the State of Texas. Founded in 1968 the company has satellite offices in California Florida Massachusetts Ohio and South Carolina.

NETSOL TECHNOLOGIES INC

NAS: NTWK

24025 Park Sorrento, Suite 410
Calabasas, CA 91302
Phone: 818 222-9195
Fax: 818 222-9197
Web: www.netsoltech.com

CEO: Najeeb Ghauri
CFO: Roger Almond
HR: Adil Siddiqui
FYE: June 30
Type: Public

NetSol Technologies is sold on the power of IT. The company provides information technology services and software for the banking financial services automotive leasing and financing and healthcare industries. NetSol's Leas-eSoft software for asset-based lending organizations automates such tasks as credit valuation financial comparisons wholesale finance management and services tracking. NetSol also offers a hospital management information product. The company's services include assistance with SAP information security business intelligence project management maintenance and testing. NetSol Technologies was founded in 1997.

	Annual Growth	06/11	06/12	06/13	06/14	06/15
Sales ($ mil.)	8.7%	36.5	39.8	50.8	36.4	51.0
Net income ($ mil.)	-	5.7	2.4	7.9	(11.4)	(5.5)
Market value ($ mil.)	31.1%	17.9	4.5	103.4	39.9	52.9
Employees	16.0%	879	857	1,119	1,389	1,590

NETSUITE INC

NYS: N

2955 Campus Drive, Suite 100
San Mateo, CA 94403-2511
Phone: 650 627-1000
Fax: -
Web: www.netsuite.com

CEO: Zachary A. (Zach) Nelson
CFO: Ronald (Ron) Gill
HR: Harvey North
FYE: December 31
Type: Public

NetSuite is set on helping customers manage their core business processes in a single system. The company's main offering is cloud-based business management software called NetSuite. It automates operations and streamlines processes in accounting customer relationship management (CRM) e-commerce enterprise resource planning (ERP) human resources and inventory. In addition to NetSuite the company offers OneWorld and NetSuite CRM+ designed for use by most types of businesses. OpenAir is designed for professional services businesses. The company serves midsized companies and divisions of large corporations in the consulting distribution manufacturing retail and software industries among others.

	Annual Growth	12/10	12/11	12/12	12/13	12/14
Sales ($ mil.)	30.3%	193.1	236.3	308.8	414.5	556.3
Net income ($ mil.)	-	(27.5)	(32.0)	(35.2)	(70.4)	(100.0)
Market value ($ mil.)	44.6%	1,925.8	3,123.6	5,184.2	7,935.8	8,409.6
Employees	32.7%	1,084	1,265	1,778	2,434	3,357

NETWORK ENGINES INC.

NASDAQ: NEI

25 Dan Rd.
Canton MA 02021-2817
Phone: 781-332-1000
Fax: 781-770-2000
Web: www.nei.com

CEO: Corry Hong
CFO: -
HR: -
FYE: September 30
Type: Public

Network Engines revs up hardware and software integration for many a technology provider. The company doing business as NEI designs and builds server appliances and provides software integration services. Its integration services are used by software vendors and equipment manufacturers who resell and support the finished appliances under their own brands. NEI also offers platform management software and support services. The company targets the communications storage and security sectors. Customers include EMC (60% of sales) Tektronix (10%) ArcSight Juniper Networks and Sophos. In 2012 NEI agreed to be acquired by UNICOM Systems in a deal valued at about $63 million.

NETWORK HARDWARE RESALE LLC

6500 Hollister Ave.
Santa Barbara CA 93117
Phone: 805-964-9975
Fax: 805-964-9405
Web: www.networkhardware.com

CEO: Mike Sheldon
CFO: Andrea Greene
HR: -
FYE: December 31
Type: Private

Network Hardware Resale (NHR) markets used and refurbished computer network components including routers switches access servers and security products. The company specializes in Cisco products but it also offers equipment from Dell Extreme Networks and Juniper Networks. NHR also sells new equipment from Brocade Communications Systems. Its customers include service providers enterprises of all sizes and government agencies. Former IBM employee Charles Sheldon founded NHR in 1986. The Sheldon family still runs and owns the company.

NETWORK MANAGEMENT RESOURCES INC.

15000 CONFERENCE CEN DR
CHANTILLY, VA 201513819
Phone: 703-229-1055
Fax: –
Web: www.nmrconsulting.com

CEO: –
CFO: –
HR: –
FYE: December 31
Type: Private

|Network Management Resources believes there's a lot to be said for a clear descriptive name. The company designs installs and maintains information technology (IT) equipment. Services include help desk support network administration application development software engineering and training. Its customers (which include both public and private sector organizations) come from a range of industries including financial services manufacturing and health care.

	Annual Growth	12/09	12/10	12/11	12/12	12/13
Sales ($ mil.)	7.6%	–	17.2	21.5	11.7	21.4
Net income ($ mil.)	(31.7%)	–	–	3.1	(1.1)	1.5
Market value ($ mil.)	–	–	–	–	–	–
Employees	–	–	–	–	–	131

NETWORK SOLUTIONS LLC

13861 Sunrise Valley Dr. Ste. 300
Herndon VA 20170
Phone: 703-668-4600
Fax: 703-668-5888
Web: www.networksolutions.com

CEO: David L Brown
CFO: –
HR: –
FYE: December 31
Type: Subsidiary

Networksolutionsprovidesdomainnameregistryservicesandmore.com. Network Solutions sells Internet domain names and provides related services such as website hosting and design e-mail online marketing search engine optimization website security and e-commerce development. Primarily targeting small businesses the company manages more than 7 million domains and 350000 websites. It provides business development resources through its Network Solutions Labs site which contains articles forums and webinars designed to grow small businesses. The company was acquired by Web.com from NetSol Technologies in 2011 for $560 million in cash and stock.

NETWORKFLEET INC.

6363 Greenwich Dr. Ste. 200
San Diego CA 92122
Phone: 858-450-3245
Fax: 858-450-3246
Web: www.networkfleet.com

CEO: Keith Schneider
CFO: –
HR: Stephanie Glover
FYE: December 31
Type: Subsidiary

Networkfleet keeps its eyes on the street. A subsidiary of HUGHES Telematics the company provides wireless networking systems that monitor the performance and location of business fleet vehicles. Its products provide Global Positioning System (GPS) tracking confirm driver deliveries and collect preventive maintenance data on engine diagnostics and repairs. Customers include commercial and government fleets including city state and federal agencies. It serves fleets ranging from a few automobiles to thousands of vehicles. Formerly called Networkcar the company changed its name in 2008 to reflect its focus on commercial and government fleets.

NEULION INC.

TORONTO: NLN

1600 Old Country Rd. Ste. 101
Plainview NY 11803
Phone: 516-622-8300
Fax: 516-249-2922
Web: www.neulion.com

CEO: Kanaan Jemili
CFO: Arthur J McCarthy
HR: –
FYE: December 31
Type: Public

|NeuLion is poised to pounce on Internet-delivered television. The company offers hosted services that allow customers to deliver streaming video over Internet-enabled devices. It works mostly with sports content providers (60% of revenues) such as ESPN the NFL and about 150 NCAA schools but also pay-TV networks and operators such as DISH The Independent Film Channel and Univision to distribute live and on-demand programming over the Internet viewed on personal computers laptops cell phones and televisions. NeuLion gets most of its revenues in the US and Canada but also has offices in London and Shanghai. Chairman Charles Wang and CEO Nancy Li who are married together own more than half of the company.

NEUMANN SYSTEMS GROUP INC.

890 ELKTON DR STE 101
COLORADO SPRINGS, CO 809073554
Phone: 719-593-7848
Fax: –
Web: www.neumannsystemsgroup.com

CEO: Todd Tiahrt
CFO: –
HR: –
FYE: December 31
Type: Private

|If you direct a lot of energy to one place you get a beam. At least that's the plan at Neumann Systems Group doing business as Directed Energy Solutions (DES). The company makes lasers and other optical devices used in research remote sensing communication medical and military applications. It also works on chemical and biological decontamination products that could be used to sterilize medical equipment and improve indoor air quality. DES which operates from its 20000-sq.-ft. research production and development facility in Colorado counts various agencies and branches of the US government including the Army and Air Force and Raytheon as customers. CEO David Neumann formed the company in 1999.

	Annual Growth	12/09	12/10	12/11	12/12	12/13
Sales ($ mil.)	0.3%	–	–	22.1	25.7	22.2
Net income ($ mil.)	(5.7%)	–	–	1.9	2.2	1.7
Market value ($ mil.)	–	–	–	–	–	–
Employees	–	–	–	–	–	60

NEURALSTEM INC

NAS: CUR

20271 Goldenrod Lane
Germantown, MD 20876
Phone: 301 366-4841
Fax: –
Web: www.neuralstem.com

CEO: I Richard Garr
CFO: Jonathan B Lloyd Jones
HR: –
FYE: December 31
Type: Public

Neuralstem is using human neural stem cells to find treatments for central nervous disorders. The company uses a proprietary technology to produce commercial quantities of brain and spinal cord stem cells that are used to develop potential treatments for Lou Gehrig's disease (also known as ALS or amyotrophic lateral sclerosis) Huntington's disease spinal cord injury and stroke. Its spinal cord stem cells are part of the first FDA-approved ALS stem cell clinical trial. Neuralstem also has a class of small molecule compounds that it is developing into oral drugs. The first NSI-189 is undergoing trials to treat major depression. These compounds may also be developed for Alzheimer's disease and schizophrenia.

	Annual Growth	12/10	12/11	12/12	12/13	12/14
Sales ($ mil.)	(60.0%)	0.7	0.4	0.4	0.1	0.0
Net income ($ mil.)	–	(18.4)	(12.5)	(10.1)	(19.8)	(22.6)
Market value ($ mil.)	6.4%	186.1	84.7	95.7	255.5	238.8
Employees	7.5%	18	16	17	16	24

NEUROCRINE BIOSCIENCES, INC.   NMS: NBIX

12780 El Camino Real
San Diego, CA 92130
Phone: 858 617-7600
Fax: –
Web: www.neurocrine.com

CEO: Kevin C Gorman
CFO: Timothy P Coughlin
HR: Richard Ranieri
FYE: December 31
Type: Public

For Neurocrine Biosciences drug development is all about body chemistry. The development-stage biotech develops treatments for neurological and endocrine hormone-related diseases such as insomnia depression and menstrual pain. Lead drug candidate Elagolix is designed to treat endometriosis which causes pain and irregular menstrual bleeding in women. Second in line is NBI-98854 a treatment for movement disorders. Neurocrine Biosciences works in additional therapeutic areas including anxiety cancer epilepsy and diabetes. The company has about a dozen drug candidates in various stages of research and clinical development through both internal programs and collaborative agreements with partners.

	Annual Growth	12/09	12/10	12/11	12/12	12/13
Sales ($ mil.)	(0.3%)	3.0	33.5	77.4	53.1	2.9
Net income ($ mil.)	–	(51.0)	(8.0)	37.6	5.0	(46.1)
Market value ($ mil.)	36.1%	183.2	514.6	572.5	503.8	629.1
Employees	5.7%	65	66	71	78	81

NEUROMETRIX INC   NAS: NURO

1000 Winter Street
Waltham, MA 02451
Phone: 781 890-9989
Fax: 781 890-1556
Web: www.neurometrix.com

CEO: Shai N Gozani
CFO: Thomas T Higgins
HR: Jennifer Hayes
FYE: December 31
Type: Public

NeuroMetrix makes medical devices and consumables that detect diagnose and monitor diabetic neuropathies (DPNs) and neurological conditions affecting the peripheral nerves and spine. The company makes two FDA-approved products: a noninvasive NC-stat DPNCheck system designed for endocrinologists podiatrists and primary care doctors and its ADVANCE system used by specialists. Its systems allow doctors to distinguish between pain caused by nerve root compression and pain caused by less-serious factors. NeuroMetrix's pipeline includes the SENSUS device designed to treat painful DPNs and the ADVANCE CTS device for diagnosing and evaluating carpal tunnel syndrome. CEO Shai Gozani founded the company in 1996.

	Annual Growth	12/10	12/11	12/12	12/13	12/14
Sales ($ mil.)	(20.6%)	13.9	10.4	7.6	5.3	5.5
Net income ($ mil.)	–	(16.9)	(10.0)	(10.0)	(8.0)	(7.8)
Market value ($ mil.)	30.0%	1.4	2.5	0.9	6.0	4.0
Employees	(17.5%)	69	55	39	30	32

NEUSTAR, INC.   NYS: NSR

21575 Ridgetop Circle
Sterling, VA 20166
Phone: 571 434-5400
Fax: –
Web: www.neustar.biz

CEO: Lisa A. Hook
CFO: Paul S. Lalljie
HR: –
FYE: December 31
Type: Public

NeuStar shines as a key provider of registry and clearinghouse services used in telecommunications and Internet networks. The company manages the registry of North American area codes and telephone numbers and the database used by telecom carriers (Verizon AT&T) and cable companies (Comcast Cox Communications) to route phone calls. It is also a leading provider of operations support systems (OSS) clearinghouse services that provide ordering service provisioning billing and customer service functions. In addition NeuStar operates an Internet registry supporting domain addresses and provides a host of other registry domain name system and IP services. The company makes most of its sales in North America.

	Annual Growth	12/10	12/11	12/12	12/13	12/14
Sales ($ mil.)	16.3%	526.8	620.5	831.4	902.0	963.6
Net income ($ mil.)	11.4%	106.2	160.8	156.1	162.8	163.7
Market value ($ mil.)	1.6%	1,434.9	1,882.2	2,309.7	2,746.5	1,531.3
Employees	11.4%	1,022	1,488	1,543	1,623	1,576

NEUTRON ENERGY INC.   CEO: –

9000 E. Nichols Ave. Ste. 225
Englewood CO 80112
Phone: 303-531-0470
Fax: +86-10-8456-4234
Web: www.21vianet.com

CEO: –
CFO: –
HR: –
FYE: December 31
Type: Private

Unlike most of mankind Neutron Energy actually wants to dig up lots of radioactive material. The exploration stage company searches for uranium perhaps because one kilogram of uranium can produce as much energy as 3000 metric tons of coal. Neutron energy has more than 63000 acres of land in New Mexico South Dakota and Wyoming. Its primary focus is on confirming uranium at its Cibola and Ambrosia Lake Projects. The company also holds mineral interests in previously owns properties in Arizona and South Dakota. In 2012 the company was acquired by Uranium Resources in a deal valued at $38 million.

NEVADA GOLD & CASINOS, INC.   ASE: UWN

133 E.Warm Springs Road, Suite 102
Las Vegas, NV 89119
Phone: 702 685-1000
Fax: –
Web: www.nevadagold.com

CEO: Michael P Shaunnessy
CFO: James J Kohn
HR: –
FYE: April 30
Type: Public

Nevada Gold & Casinos knows there's gold in them thar casinos. The company owns about 10 small casinos in Washington State. Three of these casinos — the Crazy Moose-Pasco Crazy Moose-Mountlake Terrace and Coyote Bob-Kennewick — are in close proximity to Seattle while the remaining properties are located in western Washington. It also owns AG Trucano Son & Grandsons a slot machine route in Deadwood South Dakota. It acquired AG Trucano which runs the only authorized commercialized gambling location South Dakota in 2012 for about $5.2 million adding some 900 slots and 20 sites to Nevada Gold's portfolio.

	Annual Growth	04/11	04/12	04/13	04/14	04/15
Sales ($ mil.)	7.6%	48.0	55.6	65.9	62.8	64.3
Net income ($ mil.)	–	(0.5)	(7.9)	0.0	0.4	1.8
Market value ($ mil.)	(0.1%)	27.6	21.6	19.5	18.6	27.5
Employees	(4.9%)	1,391	1,458	1,180	1,240	1,140

NEVADA POWER CO.   NL:

6226 West Sahara Avenue
Las Vegas, NV 89146
Phone: 702 402-5000
Fax: –
Web: www.nvenergy.com

CEO: Michael W. Yackira
CFO: Jonathan S. Halkyard
HR: –
FYE: December 31
Type: Public

Those famous bright city lights of gamblers' paradise (Las Vegas) are lit by Nevada Power a subsidiary of NV Energy that also does business as NV Energy. The utility transmits and distributes electricity to 840000 customers in southern Nevada including in "Sin City" North Las Vegas Henderson Searchlight Laughlin and adjoining areas including Nellis Air Force Base and the US Department of Energy's Nevada Test Site in Nye County. Nevada Power's 44 gas and coal generating units produces more than 4340 MW of fossil-fueled capacity; it also buys power from the Hoover Dam and elsewhere and markets excess wholesale power. It is also pursuing the development of renewable energy power sources.

	Annual Growth	12/10	12/11	12/12	12/13	12/14
Sales ($ mil.)	0.9%	2,252.4	2,054.4	2,145.2	2,092.0	2,337.0
Net income ($ mil.)	5.1%	185.9	132.6	257.7	145.0	227.0
Market value ($ mil.)	–	–	–	–	–	–
Employees	(4.7%)	1,694	1,614	1,524	1,500	1,400

NEVADA STATE BANK

750 E. Warm Springs Rd.
Las Vegas NV 89119
Phone: 702-855-4530
Fax: 702-914-4512
Web: www.nsbank.com

CEO: –
CFO: –
HR: –
FYE: December 31
Type: Subsidiary

Believe it or not there's a business in Las Vegas that helps you keep your money. A subsidiary of Zions Bancorporation Nevada State Bank operates more than 50 branches in Sin City and the rest of the state. Serving consumers professionals and small and midsized businesses the bank provides standard services such as checking and savings accounts certificates of deposit and check and credit cards. It also offers financial planning investment management and trust services. Nevada State Bank is mainly a real estate lender with one- to four family residential mortgages commercial real estate loans and construction and land development loans making up most of its portfolio.

NEW AGE ELECTRONICS INC.

21950 Arnold Center Rd.
Carson CA 90810-1646
Phone: 310-549-0000
Fax: 310-549-6931
Web: www.newageinc.com

CEO: –
CFO: –
HR: –
FYE: December 31
Type: Subsidiary

New Age Electronics won't hook you up with an automatic patchouli oil dispenser or crystal polisher but it does provides supply chain management services for leading computer and consumer electronics manufacturers. New Age Electronics offers distribution logistics and remanufacturing services supplying products from such companies as Hewlett-Packard Kodak Panasonic Samsung and Sharp. The company works with retailers including Ritz Camera Staples and Wal-Mart. New Age Electronics is a division of electronics distributor SYNNEX which acquired it for about $54 million in 2008.

NEW BRUNSWICK SCIENTIFIC CO. INC.

44 Talmadge Rd.
Edison NJ 08817-4005
Phone: 732-287-1200
Fax: 732-287-4222
Web: www.nbsc.com

CEO: James T Orcutt
CFO: Thomas Bocchino
HR: –
FYE: December 31
Type: Subsidiary

From rockers and rollers to spinners and shakers New Brunswick Scientific (NBS) designs and manufactures instruments that have the biotech industry all shook up. NBS' equipment and software help scientists create measure and control conditions for growing and detecting microorganisms. NBS makes the INNOVA line of shakers as well as fermentors bioreactors freezers incubators sterilizers and other equipment. The company sells to research institutes universities and pharmaceutical chemical and agricultural firms worldwide. It also provides contract laboratory services when a company is too busy to cook up its own cells. NBS is a wholly owned subsidiary of laboratory equipment maker Eppendorf Group.

NEW CAM COMMERCE SOLUTIONS LLC

17075 Newhope St. Ste. A
Fountain Valley CA 92708
Phone: 714-241-9241
Fax: 714-241-9893
Web: www.camcommerce.com

CEO: –
CFO: –
HR: Andrea Grassi
FYE: September 30
Type: Private

New CAM Commerce Solutions doesn't want you missing a single sale or losing a single inventory item. The company's point-of-sale software automates many functions of a retail business from sales transactions and inventory management to loyalty programs reporting and integrated e-commerce features. The company primarily serves specialty retailers including clothing shoe pet sporting good hardware pharmacy and liquor stores. It offers technical support training and Web store design services. In 2008 CAM Commerce was taken private by Great Hill Partners in a deal valued at $180 million. Great Hill Partners sold the majority of CAM Commerce to Robertson Piper Software Group in 2010.

NEW CONCEPT ENERGY, INC.

ASE: GBR

1603 LBJ Freeway, Suite 300
Dallas, TX 75234
Phone: 972 407-8400
Fax: 972 407-8421
Web: www.newconceptenergy.com

CEO: –
CFO: Gene S Bertcher
HR: –
FYE: December 31
Type: Public

New Concept Energy is exploring possibilities in natural resources while keeping one foot planted in the long-term care industry. The firm owns a residential community for senior citizens in Oregon that provides support services for about 115 independent living units. New Concept Energy also has oil and gas production assets in the midwestern US including about 100 producing wells and 120 non-producing wells with a total proved reserves of some 7.6 million cu. ft. of natural gas. The company has gone through a number of industries over the years; it has divested most of its former assisted living communities and all of its cable and retail shopping assets and it is seeking to grow its energy operations.

	Annual Growth	12/10	12/11	12/12	12/13	12/14
Sales ($ mil.)	0.9%	4.2	3.9	3.9	4.2	4.4
Net income ($ mil.)	–	(0.0)	(11.8)	0.2	0.4	(0.8)
Market value ($ mil.)	(22.2%)	7.9	4.4	2.4	3.5	2.9
Employees	(1.5%)	52	52	50	52	49

NEW EDGE NETWORKS INC.

3000 Columbia House Blvd. Ste. 106
Vancouver WA 98661-2969
Phone: 360-693-9009
Fax: 360-693-9997
Web: www.newedgenetworks.com

CEO: Joseph F Eazor
CFO: Bradley A Ferguson
HR: –
FYE: December 31
Type: Subsidiary

New Edge Networks caters to businesses that want to sharpen their information technology tools. The company builds and manages networks for corporate customers and communications carriers. Areas of specialty include private networks secure public networks and business Internet access. It offers broadband connectivity for customers throughout the US over its own nationwide backbone network. New Edge also installs network equipment and provides engineering services. Customers have included American Express T-Systems North America and First Data. New Edge is a subsidiary of Atlanta-based ISP EarthLink.

NEW ENGLAND BANCSHARES INC.

NASDAQ: NEBS

885 Enfield St.
Enfield CT 06082
Phone: 860-253-5200
Fax: 860-253-5205
Web: www.enfieldfederal.com

CEO: David J O'Connor
CFO: Jeffrey J Levitsky
HR: –
FYE: March 31
Type: Public

New England Bancshares is the holding company for New England Bank a thrift serving central and north-central Connecticut from about 20 branches. It offers standard deposit products and services including checking and savings accounts money market accounts CDs and IRAs. New England Bank primarily originates residential and commercial real estate loans as well as business construction and consumer loans. In 2009 New England Bancshares merged its former Enfield Federal Savings and Valley Banks subsidiaries to create New England Bank. It then acquired the three-branch Apple Valley Bank & Trust.

NEW ENGLAND LIFE INSURANCE COMPANY

501 Boylston St.
Boston MA 02110
Phone: 617-578-2000
Fax: 617-536-2393
Web: www.nefn.com

CEO: –
CFO: Bill Lampley
HR: –
FYE: December 31
Type: Subsidiary

Don't accuse New England Life Insurance of a regional bias. The company which operates as New England Financial provides insurance and financial planning products and services throughout the US. Targeted to small and midsized business owners and wealthy individuals New England's products and services include life long-term care and disability income insurance. Its New England Securities subsidiary offers estate retirement and financial planning products in the form of annuities and mutual funds. New England also provides business planning services and employer-sponsored benefits to its business-owner clients. The company a subsidiary of MetLife since 1996 traces its origins back to 1835.

NEW ENGLAND MOTOR FREIGHT INC.

1-71 North Ave. East
Elizabeth NJ 07201
Phone: 908-965-0100
Fax: 908-965-0795
Web: www.nemf.com

CEO: –
CFO: Craig Eisenberg
HR: –
FYE: December 31
Type: Subsidiary

New England Motor Freight (NEMF) gets the show on the road every day. The company provides less-than-truckload (LTL) transportation services including expedited freight transportation primarily in the northeastern and mid-Atlantic US Canada and Puerto Rico. (LTL carriers combine freight from multiple shippers into a single truckload.) NEMF operates from about 40 terminals. Alliances with carriers such as AAA Cooper Midwest Motor Express and Oak Harbor Freight Lines allow NEMF to extend service to other parts of the US. NEMF is the flagship of several transportation companies controlled by CEO Myron Shevell and his family through Shevell Group.

NEW ENGLAND REALTY ASSOCIATES L.P.

ASE: NEN

39 Brighton Avenue
Allston, MA 02134
Phone: 617 783-0039
Fax: –
Web: www.thehamiltoncompany.com

CEO: –
CFO: Andrew Bloch
HR: –
FYE: December 31
Type: Public

New England Realty Associates invests in develops operates and sells residential and commercial real estate primarily in the Boston area. The company's portfolio includes more than 2300 apartment and condominium units and about 85000 sq. ft. of commercial space that includes a shopping center and mixed-use properties. It also has a 50% stake in a portfolio of about 10 commercial properties. New England Realty Associates is managed by general partner NewReal which in turn is owned by company officers and brothers Ronald and Harold Brown. Harold Brown also owns The Hamilton Company which manages the partnership's properties.

	Annual Growth	12/10	12/11	12/12	12/13	12/14
Sales ($ mil.)	6.5%	33.2	34.0	35.6	38.4	42.6
Net income ($ mil.)	–	(1.4)	9.3	3.6	5.7	1.0
Market value ($ mil.)	(7.3%)	8.4	9.1	3.8	5.7	6.2
Employees	2.1%	63	66	63	67	–

NEW FRONTIER MEDIA INC.

NASDAQ: NOOF

7007 Winchester Cir. Ste. 200
Boulder CO 80301
Phone: 303-444-0900
Fax: 303-444-0734
Web: www.noof.com

CEO: –
CFO: Grant Williams
HR: –
FYE: March 31
Type: Public

This company's erotic wilderness is pleasing to some but others might think New Frontier Media crosses the boundaries of good taste. The firm is an operator of adult entertainment pay-per-view (PPV) and video-on-demand (VOD) channels available to both cable and satellite subscribers. Its PPV and VOD services reach millions of network homes in the US and many more millions of network homes internationally. New Frontier also produces and distributes original films and videos through its Film Production segment. In addition the company generates revenue from its Direct-to-Consumer segment which distributes content through its consumer websites. Hustler magazine founder Larry Flynt is acquiring New Frontier.

NEW GLOBAL TELECOM INC.

600 12th St. Ste. 200
Golden CO 80401
Phone: 303-278-0700
Fax: 303-278-0728
Web: www.ngt.com

CEO: –
CFO: Todd Londa
HR: –
FYE: December 31
Type: Private

The needs of telecommunications providers are at the center of New Global Telecom's world. The company (known as NGT) offers hosted communications network management and operational services to small and midsized companies and telecom carriers in need of Voice over Internet Protocol (VoIP) functionality. Its retail services consist mainly of telephone connectivity and messaging for businesses while it also provides local voice and Internet access for ISPs and other resellers who rebrand the services. The company's wholesale business focuses on local exchange carriers cable operators and ISPs. NGT was acquired by Comcast a key client in 2010.

NEW HAMPSHIRE ELECTRIC COOPERATIVE INC

579 TENNEY MOUNTAIN HWY
PLYMOUTH, NH 032643147
Phone: 603-536-8817
Fax: –
Web: www.nhec.com

CEO: –
CFO: –
HR: –
FYE: December 31
Type: Private

The granite in the Granite State won't keep the folks in New Hampshire warm in winter but New Hampshire Electric Cooperative will. The utility provides electricity to about 80000 residential and business customers (who are also member-owners of the cooperative) in 115 New Hampshire towns and cities. The enterprise operates 5400 miles of distribution lines and is seeking to become a complete energy solutions organization offering energy saving options such as equipment retrofits at local schools and selling energy-efficient compact fluorescent light bulbs. Most of New Hampshire Electric Cooperative's revenues comes from residential customers and the balance form small businesses.

	Annual Growth	12/09	12/10	12/11	12/12	12/13
Sales ($ mil.)	(1.1%)	–	130.0	124.4	115.6	125.7
Net income ($ mil.)	(28.1%)	–	–	12.6	9.9	6.5
Market value ($ mil.)	–	–	–	–	–	–
Employees	–	–	–	–	–	199

NEW HANOVER REGIONAL MEDICAL CENTER AUXILIARY INC.

2131 S 17TH ST
WILMINGTON, NC 284017407
Phone: 910-343-7001
Fax: –
Web: www.nhrmc.org

CEO: Jack Barto
CFO: Ed Ollie
HR: –
FYE: December 31
Type: Private

Those living in the Cape Fear area need not fear when it comes to accessing good medical care. Integrated health system New Hanover Regional Medical Center (NHRMC) serves the Wilmington and Cape Fear area of North Carolina through its flagship 855-bed New Hanover Regional Medical Center the 130-bed Cape Fear Hospital and the 85-bed Pender Memorial Hospital. NHRMC also operates a rehabilitation center a behavioral health facility and a women's and children's hospital as well as home health hospice EMS transport physician practice and outpatient care clinic locations. The not-for-profit health network is affiliated with the UNC-Chapel Hill School of Medicine.

	Annual Growth	12/11	12/12*	09/13	09/14*	12/14
Sales ($ mil.)	(0.9%)	–	204.5	687.7	758.3	200.8
Net income ($ mil.)	(47.8%)	–	–	50.4	63.9	26.3
Market value ($ mil.)	–	–	–	–	–	–
Employees	–	–	–	–	–	3,692

*Fiscal year change

NEW JERSEY INSTITUTE OF TECHNOLOGY (INC)

111 LOCK ST
NEWARK, NJ 071033540
Phone: 973-596-3000
Fax: –
Web: www.njit.edu

CEO: –
CFO: Edward J. Bishof
HR: Theodore (Theo) Johnson
FYE: June 30
Type: Private

A public research university New Jersey Institute of Technology (NJIT) offers about 100 undergraduate and graduate programs including about 20 doctoral programs in fields including architecture engineering computer science and liberal arts. The school also offers continuing education and distance courses. With some 500 full-time faculty members NJIT boasts a student-faulty ratio of 16:1. Its Albert Dorman Honors College provides students with individualized curricula and honors colloquia including travel and featured speakers. About 10000 students attend the NJIT which operates a single campus in Newark. NJIT was founded in 1881 as the Newark Technical School.

	Annual Growth	06/10	06/11	06/12	06/13	06/14
Sales ($ mil.)	6.1%	–	184.6	198.0	210.7	220.5
Net income ($ mil.)	1079.4%	–	–	0.7	17.4	93.6
Market value ($ mil.)	–	–	–	–	–	–
Employees	–	–	–	–	–	1,047

NEW JERSEY MINING CO.

NBB: NJMC

201 N. Third Street
Coeur d'Alene, ID 83814
Phone: 208 503-0153
Fax: –
Web: www.newjerseymining.com

CEO: R Patrick Highsmith
CFO: –
HR: –
FYE: December 31
Type: Public

No product of the Garden State New Jersey Mining seeks out gold silver and base metals in the Coeur d'Alene mining district of northern Idaho and western Montana. The development and exploration company maintains two Idaho-based joint ventures one with Marathon Gold at the Golden Chest gold mine and another with United Mining Group involved in ore processing. The company also holds rights to several mineral properties including the Niagara copper-silver deposit Toboggan gold exploration project (formerly a JV with Newmont Mining) and Silver Strand mine. President Fred Brackebusch controls about a quarter of New Jersey Mining.

	Annual Growth	12/10	12/11	12/12	12/13	12/14
Sales ($ mil.)	(18.0%)	0.2	1.5	0.9	0.1	0.1
Net income ($ mil.)	–	(0.5)	0.1	(0.7)	(0.8)	(1.4)
Market value ($ mil.)	(30.6%)	29.8	18.4	9.2	8.2	6.9
Employees	9.1%	12	18	6	–	17

NEW JERSEY NATURAL GAS COMPANY

1415 Wyckoff Rd.
Wall NJ 07719
Phone: 732-938-7977
Fax: 732-938-2134
Web: www.njng.com

CEO: Lawrence M Downes
CFO: –
HR: –
FYE: September 30
Type: Subsidiary

It's not just the tourists that appreciate the services of New Jersey Natural Gas it's the locals too. The gas utility provides gas distribution service to 500100 residential commercial and industrial customers in New Jersey's vacationland — Monmouth and Ocean counties and parts of Morris and Middlesex counties. The company is the principal subsidiary of publicly traded regional utility New Jersey Resources and operates 6700 miles of distribution pipeline. Sister company NJR Retail Holdings offers appliance installation repair and maintenance service to about 150000 homes and businesses in its service region.

NEW JERSEY RESOURCES CORP

NYS: NJR

1415 Wyckoff Road
Wall, NJ 07719
Phone: 732 938-1480
Fax: –
Web: www.njresources.com

CEO: Laurence M. (Larry) Downes
CFO: Glenn C Lockwood
HR: –
FYE: September 30
Type: Public

Natural gas (a New Jersey resource that predates Bruce Springsteen and the Nets) is the main product of New Jersey Resources (NJR). The company's New Jersey Natural Gas utility unit distributes gas to 512300 residential and business customers in the state. Its 14581 miles of gas mains handle distribution transmission and service and two LNG plants supply peak demand. Nonregulated subsidiary NJR Energy Services which accounts for the bulk of NJR's sales provides wholesale gas supply transportation and storage to customers from the Gulf Coast to New England. It also invests in energy-related ventures (pipelines and storage terminals and other midstream assets) through NJR Energy Holdings.

	Annual Growth	09/11	09/12	09/13	09/14	09/15
Sales ($ mil.)	(2.4%)	3,009.2	2,248.9	3,198.1	3,738.1	2,734.0
Net income ($ mil.)	15.6%	101.3	92.9	114.8	142.0	181.0
Market value ($ mil.)	(8.4%)	3,641.3	3,910.5	3,767.7	4,320.2	2,568.5
Employees	2.7%	891	927	936	968	991

NEW JERSEY TRANSIT CORPORATION

1 Penn Plz East
Newark NJ 07105-2246
Phone: 973-491-7000
Fax: 617-449-4197
Web: www.iprospect.com

CEO: –
CFO: H Charles Wedel
HR: Alma Buczak
FYE: June 30
Type: Government-owned

Government-owned New Jersey Transit (NJ TRANSIT) provides bus rail and light rail passenger transportation services. Its systems connect major points in New Jersey and provide links to the neighboring New York City and Philadelphia metropolitan areas. Overall the NJ TRANSIT service area spans about 5325 sq. miles. One of the largest transportation companies of its kind in the US NJ TRANSIT operates a fleet of more than 2000 buses 710 commuter trains and 45 light rail vehicles. Collectively the agency's passengers make more than 220 million trips a year. NJ TRANSIT oversees public transportation programs for the elderly people with disabilities and people in rural areas.

NEW JERSEY TURNPIKE AUTHORITY

581 Main St.
Woodbridge NJ 07095-5042
Phone: 732-750-5300
Fax: 972-201-2829
Web: www.hillwood.com

CEO: Ronald Gravino
CFO: –
HR: –
FYE: December 31
Type: Government Agency

The New Jersey Turnpike Authority operates two toll-supported highways the New Jersey Turnpike and the Garden State Parkway. The New Jersey Turnpike runs for 148 miles from the Delaware River Bridge at the southern end of the state to the George Washington Bridge that connects New Jersey with New York. The turnpike includes about 10 rest stops or service areas named for former New Jersey residents such as Alexander Hamilton Vince Lombardi and Walt Whitman. The Garden State Parkway runs for 173 miles and spans the length of New Jersey's Atlantic coastline.

NEW MEDIA INVESTMENT GROUP INC

NYS: NEWM

1345 Avenue of the Americas
New York, NY 10105
Phone: 212 479-3160
Fax: –
Web: www.newmediainv.com

CEO: Kirk A. Davis
CFO: Gregory W. (Greg) Freiberg
HR: –
FYE: December 28
Type: Public

New Media Investment Group (formerly GateHouse Media) lets the local news flow freely. The company is a leading community-newspaper publisher with more than 400 publications. Its portfolio includes roughly 80 daily newspapers along with many more weeklies and shoppers that reach about 10 million readers. New Media Investment generates revenue primarily through advertising; its papers serve ads from almost 300000 business advertisers. In conjunction with its print publications the company operates more than 600 websites. New Media Investment also produces a half-dozen yellow page directories and offers commercial printing services.

	Annual Growth	01/12*	12/12*	11/13*	12/13	12/14
Sales ($ mil.)	12.6%	514.7	488.6	413.3	103.2	652.3
Net income ($ mil.)	–	(21.6)	(29.8)	787.4	7.2	(3.2)
Market value ($ mil.)	–	–	–	–	–	902.6
Employees	21.8%	–	4,131	–	5,576	6,133

*Fiscal year change

NEW MILFORD HOSPITAL INC.

21 ELM ST
NEW MILFORD, CT 067762993
Phone: 860-355-2611
Fax: –
Web: www.newmilfordhospital.org

CEO: John M Murphy
CFO: –
HR: Linda Rossi
FYE: September 30
Type: Private

Residents of New Milford Connecticut naturally turn to New Milford Hospital for emergency care. Established in 1921 the acute care hospital has some 85 beds and offers cardiology cancer care pediatric and surgical services. The notfor-profit facility also has family birthing sleep disorder treatment and cancer research facilities. Affiliate New Milford Visiting Nurse Association provides home health services. New Milford Hospital exited its membership in the NewYork-Presbyterian Healthcare System in 2010. It then formed a new affiliation with Danbury Hospital and the two hospitals now operate under the administrative umbrella of Western Connecticut Healthcare (formerly Danbury Health Systems).

	Annual Growth	09/09	09/10	09/11	09/12	09/13
Sales ($ mil.)	(8.8%)	–	91.9	93.4	78.1	69.7
Net income ($ mil.)	–	–	–	(4.3)	(6.5)	(3.2)
Market value ($ mil.)	–	–	–	–	–	–
Employees	–	–	–	–	–	400

NEW MOUNTAIN FINANCE CORP

NYS: NMFC

787 Seventh Avenue, 48th Floor
New York, NY 10019
Phone: 212 720-0300
Fax: 212 582-2277
Web: www.newmountainfinance.com

CEO: Robert A. Hamwee
CFO: Shiraz Y. Kajee
HR: –
FYE: December 31
Type: Public

Investment firm New Mountain Finance Corporation won't make its portfolio companies climb over too many hills for a loan. The affiliate of private equity firm New Mountain Capital makes investments of $10 million-$50 million in middle-market companies (those with annual revenues of less than $200 million). Its portfolio is made up of senior secured first-lien and second-lien term loans and subordinated debt. Organized as a business development company (BDC) New Mountain Finance pays little in income taxes as long as it distributes 90% of its profits back to shareholders. It is externally managed by New Mountain Finance Advisers BDC L.L.C. The company went public in 2011.

	Annual Growth	12/10	12/11	12/12	12/13	12/14
Sales ($ mil.)	34.5%	41.4	13.7	37.5	90.9	135.6
Net income ($ mil.)	20.9%	37.5	8.3	19.8	50.5	80.1
Market value ($ mil.)	3.7%	–	777.8	864.2	872.3	866.5
Employees	–	–	–	–	–	–

NEW PENN MOTOR EXPRESS INC.

625 S. 5th Ave.
Lebanon PA 17042
Phone: 717-274-2521
Fax: 717-274-5593
Web: www.newpenn.com

CEO: Steven D Gast
CFO: –
HR: –
FYE: December 31
Type: Subsidiary

Write it down: This New Penn is a regional less-than-truckload (LTL) freight carrier that operates in the northeastern US. (LTL carriers consolidate freight from multiple shippers into a single truckload.) Next-day deliveries in the New England and mid-Atlantic regions make up the bulk of New Penn Motor Express' shipments; the company also offers service in Canada and in Puerto Rico. It operates a fleet of about 850 tractors and 1700 trailers from a network of nearly 25 terminals. Connections with other carriers including sister companies in the YRC Regional Transportation family enable New Penn to provide coast-to-coast service in the US and Canada.

NEW PRIME INC.

2740 N MAYFAIR AVE
SPRINGFIELD, MO 658035084
Phone: 417-866-0001
Fax: –
Web: www.primeinc.com

CEO: –
CFO: Dean Hoedl
HR: –
FYE: March 29
Type: Private

Check out this Prime number — more than 8200 remotely monitored temperature-controlled trailers. Specialized carrier New Prime (which does business simply as Prime) provides refrigerated flatbed and liquid bulk tanker trucking services throughout North America. The company operates in the US and Canada and serves Mexico through arrangements with other carriers. A subsidiary Prime Floral uses the parent company's refrigerated equipment and facilities to serve the flower industry. In addition to its freight-hauling operations Prime provides logistics services including freight brokerage.

	Annual Growth	03/09	03/10*	04/11*	03/12	03/13
Sales ($ mil.)	11.3%	–	844.2	941.4	1,022.2	1,165.0
Net income ($ mil.)	21.7%	–	–	47.4	61.0	70.2
Market value ($ mil.)	–	–	–	–	–	–
Employees	–	–	–	–	–	5,000

*Fiscal year change

NEW SOURCE ENERGY CORPORATION

914 N. Broadway Suite 230
Oklahoma City OK 73102
Phone: 405-272-3028
Fax: 310-788-1990
Web: www.ilfc.com

CEO: –
CFO: Antranik Armoudian
HR: –
FYE: December 31
Type: Private

New Source Energy is actually looking for the same old energy source - oil and gas - but in a new way. The company formed in July 2011 plans to comb over mature oil and natural gas reservoirs a second time to hunt for leftover deposits. Right away it bought the rights to working interests in about 54000 net acres across the Hunton formation in Oklahoma. The company estimates the properties' net proved reserves to be 19 million barrels of oil equivalent made up of about 60% oil and natural gas liquids and 40% natural gas. New Source Energy filed an IPO in 2011 but withdrew it in 2012.

NEW SOURCE ENERGY PARTNERS LP

914 North Broadway, Suite 230
Oklahoma City, OK 73102
Phone: 405 272-3028
Fax: 405 272-3034
Web: www.newsource.com

NBB: NSLP

CEO: Kristian B Kos
CFO: –
HR: –
FYE: December 31
Type: Public

If at first you don't succeed try try again. That's the ethos behind New Source Energy Partners L.P. a company formed in October 2012 in the hopes of becoming a publicly traded entity. A previous incarnation New Source Energy Corporation formed in July 2011 filed an IPO but withdrew it in May 2012. Should New Source Energy Partners successfully go public it will have working interests across more than 30000 net acres in the Hunton formation in Oklahoma. Those properties produce about 170 barrels of oil per day 6 million cu. ft. of natural gas and almost 2000 barrels per day of natural gas liquids (NGLs). New Source Energy Partners filed an IPO in January 2013 seeking to raise up to $106 million.

	Annual Growth	10/11	10/12*	12/12	12/13	12/14
Sales ($ mil.)	–	0.0	–	–	50.7	165.6
Net income ($ mil.)	–	0.0	–	–	26.6	(42.3)
Market value ($ mil.)	–	0.0	–	–	432.8	133.3
Employees	630.6%	–	8	9	136	427

*Fiscal year change

NEW TANGRAM LLC

9200 SORENSEN AVE
SANTA FE SPRINGS, CA 906702645
Phone: 562-365-5000
Fax: –
Web: www.tangraminteriors.com

CEO: Joseph (Joe) Lozowski
CFO: Nick Greenko
HR: –
FYE: December 31
Type: Private

Tangram Interiors keeps it all on the inside. The company is an office furniture manufacturer and dealer specializing in Steelcase products. Other brands include Brayton Vecta Metro and Lightolier. The company with two showrooms in southern California offers asset management furniture rental network installation remanufacturing and moving and relocation assistance. Tangram sells an "acoustic privacy system" that allows workplace conversations to remain private by broadcasting a signal that scrambles speech patterns into white noise. The company's Tangram Studio provides design services project management and custom architectural elements. Tangram Interiors is part of Steelcase family of companies.

	Annual Growth	12/09	12/10	12/11	12/12	12/13
Sales ($ mil.)	8.3%	–	84.9	92.4	98.5	107.8
Net income ($ mil.)	4.8%	–	–	1.8	0.2	2.0
Market value ($ mil.)	–	–	–	–	–	–
Employees	–	–	–	–	–	50

NEW ULM TELECOM INC

27 North Minnesota Street
New Ulm, MN 56073
Phone: 507 354-4111
Fax: –
Web: www.nutelecom.net

NBB: NULM

CEO: Bill D Otis
CFO: Curtis O Kawlewski
HR: Polly Glaser
FYE: December 31
Type: Public

New Ulm Telecom operates three incumbent local-exchange carriers (ILECs) serving southern Minnesota and northern Iowa: an ILEC serving New Ulm Minnesota and surrounding communities; subsidiary Western Telephone operating in the Springfield Minnesota area; and Peoples Telephone serving portions of Cherokee and Buena Vista counties in Iowa. Operating under the common NU-Telecom brand they make up New Ulm's Telecom Segment and provide traditional phone services such as local exchange access and long-distance as well as cable TV and Internet access. The company's Phonery division provides customer premise equipment (CPE) offers transport services and resells long distance toll services.

	Annual Growth	12/10	12/11	12/12	12/13	12/14
Sales ($ mil.)	5.8%	31.9	33.3	32.5	38.7	40.0
Net income ($ mil.)	7.6%	2.1	2.0	3.2	2.9	2.7
Market value ($ mil.)	7.3%	28.1	35.7	30.6	33.5	37.2
Employees	3.1%	131	131	144	141	148

NEW YORK & COMPANY INC

330 West 34th Street, 9th floor
New York, NY 10001
Phone: 212 884-2000
Fax: –
Web: www.nyandcompany.com

NYS: NWY

CEO: Gregory (Greg) Scott
CFO: Sheamus Toal
HR: Ken Johnson
FYE: January 31
Type: Public

New York & Company has taken a bite out of fashion's big apple. The chain caters to working women ages 25 to 45 looking for moderately priced apparel (jeans dresses and coordinates) and accessories (sunglasses costume jewelry handbags and hosiery) mostly at the mall. It sells its proprietary branded fashions at more than 500 stores including a growing number of New York & Company Outlet shops in 40-plus states and online. Founded in 1918 and operated as a subsidiary of Limited Brands (since renamed L Brands) from 1985 to 2002 the chain was sold for $153 million to an investor team including former CEO Richard Crystal and Irving Place Capital who took New York & Company public in 2004.

	Annual Growth	01/11	01/12*	02/13	02/14*	01/15
Sales ($ mil.)	(2.5%)	1,021.7	956.5	966.4	939.2	923.3
Net income ($ mil.)	–	(76.5)	(38.9)	2.1	2.4	(16.9)
Market value ($ mil.)	(19.2%)	346.9	201.7	251.2	291.0	147.7
Employees	(5.3%)	7,949	7,131	6,624	6,349	6,400

*Fiscal year change

NEW YORK BLOOD CENTER INC.

310 E 67TH ST
NEW YORK, NY 100656273
Phone: 212-570-3010
Fax: –
Web: www.nybloodcenter.org

CEO: –
CFO: Lawrence Hannigan
HR: Doriane Gloria
FYE: March 31
Type: Private

New York Blood Center (NYBC) holds a very literal interpretation of the meaning of life. It is a not-for-profit blood distribution and research organization serving New York City and its environs in New York State and New Jersey as well as parts of Connecticut and Pennsylvania. As one of the largest blood centers in the US NYBC provides nearly 1 million blood components to some 200 hospitals each year. The center's facilities collect blood from more than 2000 donors each day. It also operates the nation's oldest and largest public cord blood bank. In addition its Kimball Research Institute includes more than a dozen research laboratories which study the prevention and treatment of blood-related illnesses.

	Annual Growth	03/07	03/08	03/09	03/10	03/11
Sales ($ mil.)	(7.3%)	–	–	–	375.7	348.3
Net income ($ mil.)	–	–	–	–	20.1	(11.8)
Market value ($ mil.)	–	–	–	–	–	–
Employees	–	–	–	–	–	1,600

NEW YORK CENTRAL MUTUAL FIRE INSURANCE COMPANY

1899 Central Plaza East
Edmeston NY 13335
Phone: 607-965-8321
Fax: 607-965-2712
Web: www.nycm.com

CEO: –
CFO: Albert Pylinski Jr
HR: –
FYE: December 31
Type: Private - Mutual Com

New York Central Mutual Fire Insurance or NYCM to its friends and policyholders sells property/casualty insurance in upstate New York. With offices in Amsterdam Buffalo Edmeston and Sherburne the company specializes in personal auto coverage but also offers homeowners and umbrella coverage and commercial policies for small businesses. More than 1000 independent agents sell the companies' products. Some 524000 policyholders own the mutual firm. NYCM is still managed by the family of VanNess DeMar Robinson who founded the company in 1899.

NEW YORK CITY HEALTH AND HOSPITALS CORPORATION

125 Worth St. Ste. 514
New York NY 10013
Phone: 212-788-3321
Fax: 212-788-0040
Web: www.nyc.gov/html/hhc

CEO: –
CFO: –
HR: –
FYE: June 30
Type: Government-owned

New York City Health and Hospitals Corporation (HHC) takes care of the Big Apple. HHC has facilities in all five boroughs of New York City. As one of the largest municipal health service systems in the US HHC serves 1.4 million New Yorkers and more than 475000 who are uninsured. It operates a network of 11 acute care hospitals (including Bellevue the nation's oldest public hospital) six large diagnostic and treatment centers four skilled nursing centers long-term care facilities and a home health care agency. HHC also operates more than 70 community-based clinics and provides medical services to New York City's correctional facilities. In addition it operates MetroPlus a managed health care plan.

NEW YORK CITY TRANSITIONAL FINANCE AUTHORITY

75 Park Place 6th Fl.
New York NY 10007
Phone: 212-788-5877
Fax: 212-788-9197
Web: www.nyc.gov/html/tfa/home.html

CEO: –
CFO: –
HR: –
FYE: June 30
Type: Government Agency

The New York City Transitional Finance Authority (TFA) won't sell you the Brooklyn Bridge but it will let you invest in repairs. The quasi-independent government agency sells municipal bonds to finance the Big Apple's capital improvement projects — public buildings roads bridges etc. The authority was created in 1997 to circumvent state constitutional limitations on the amount of debt the city could take on. With the authority to issue up to $11.5 billion in bonds the agency proved to be even more useful than anticipated selling $2 billion in bonds for recovery costs following the September 11 attacks that destroyed the World Trade Center. The TFA's bond limit has since been raised to $13.5 billion.

NEW YORK COMMUNITY BANCORP INC.

NYS: NYCB

615 Merrick Avenue
Westbury, NY 11590
Phone: 516 683-4100
Fax: –
Web: www.mynycb.com

CEO: Joseph R. Ficalora
CFO: Thomas R. (Tom) Cangemi
HR: Bernard Terlizzi
FYE: December 31
Type: Public

It's big banking in the Big Apple and beyond. New York Community Bancorp is the holding company for one of the largest thrifts in the US New York Community Bank as well as New York Commercial Bank (also dba Atlantic Bank) and seven other banking divisions. In its home state New York Community Bank operates through Queens County Savings Bank Richmond County Savings Bank Roosevelt Savings Bank and Roslyn Savings Bank. It serves customers in New Jersey through its Garden State Community Bank division. New York Community Bank also does business as AmTrust Bank which operates in Arizona and Florida and Ohio Savings Bank. Altogether New York Community Bancorp has about 275 bank branches in five states.

	Annual Growth	12/10	12/11	12/12	12/13	12/14
Assets ($ mil.)	4.2%	41,190.7	42,024.3	44,145.1	46,688.3	48,559.2
Net income ($ mil.)	(2.7%)	541.0	480.0	501.1	475.5	485.4
Market value ($ mil.)	(4.0%)	8,342.8	5,474.8	5,797.9	7,457.6	7,081.4
Employees	(3.2%)	3,883	3,348	3,458	3,381	3,416

NEW YORK CONVENTION CENTER OPERATING CORPORATION

655 W 34TH ST
NEW YORK, NY 100011114
Phone: 212-216-2000
Fax: –
Web: www.javits.com

CEO: Edward B Macdonald
CFO: Edward B Macdonald
HR: –
FYE: March 31
Type: Private

The New York Convention Center Operating Corporation may be able to claim that it has the whole world in its hand since it's the manager and operator of the "marketplace for the world" (also know as the Jacob K. Javits Convention Center in Manhattan). The center serves as host each year for myriad conventions fashion shows association meetings trade shows and more. The center features such amenities as restaurants and cocktail lounges temporary private office rentals and concierge service. The New York Convention Center Operating Corporation (also known as NYCCOC) was established in 1979 to manage the Javits Center.

	Annual Growth	03/04	03/05	03/06	03/07	03/08
Sales ($ mil.)	8.1%	–	113.4	135.3	133.8	143.1
Net income ($ mil.)	–	–	–	6.8	(8.8)	(8.8)
Market value ($ mil.)	–	–	–	–	–	–
Employees	–	–	–	–	–	350

NEW YORK FOOTBALL GIANTS INC.

Giants Stadium	CEO: Preston R Tisch
East Rutherford NJ 07073	CFO: –
Phone: 201-935-8111	HR: –
Fax: 201-935-8493	FYE: February 28
Web: www.giants.com	Type: Private

It only seems natural that the Big Apple would have a big football team. New York Football Giants owns and operates the New York Giants professional football team one of the oldest and most storied franchises in the National Football League. Started in 1925 the team has played for the league championship a record 19 times winning eight titles including four Super Bowl championships. The Giants roster has included such Hall of Fame players as Frank Gifford Sam Huff Lawrence Taylor and Y.A. Tittle. The team plays host at New Meadowlands Stadium in New Jersey which it shares with the New York Jets. Tim Mara paid $500 to found the franchise; the Mara and Tisch families continue to control the team.

NEW YORK JETS LLC

1 Jets Dr.	CEO: –
Florham Park NJ 07932	CFO: –
Phone: 973-549-4800	HR: –
Fax: 510-864-5160	FYE: February 28
Web: www.raiders.com	Type: Private

These Jets begin boarding at the start of every football season. A storied franchise in the National Football League the New York Jets claim just one Super Bowl title but its victory over the favored Baltimore Colts (now the Indianapolis Colts) in 1969 was one of the more famous matches in the history of championship. The franchise founded by broadcaster Harry Wismer as the Titans was a founding member of the American Football League in 1960 and joined the NFL when the leagues merged in 1970. Robert Johnson IV whose family founded pharmaceutical giant Johnson & Johnson has owned the team since 2000.

NEW YORK LIFE INSURANCE COMPANY

51 Madison Ave.	CEO: Ted Mathas
New York NY 10010	CFO: Michael E Sproule
Phone: 212-576-7000	HR: –
Fax: 914-681-6949	FYE: December 31
Web: www.nypa.gov	Type: Private - Mutual Com

New York Life Insurance has been providing life insurance policies in the Big Apple since it was a tiny seed. While the top mutual life insurer in the US has branched out a bit it retains its core business: life insurance and annuities. Its products include long-term care insurance and special group policies sold through AARP and other affinity groups and professional associations. New York Life Investments' offerings include mutual funds for individuals and investment management services for institutional investors. Through New York Life International the firm provides life policies in overseas markets. Founded in 1841 New York Life is owned by its policyholders.

NEW YORK MEDICAL COLLEGE

40 SUNSHINE COTTAGE RD	CEO: Edward C Halperin
VALHALLA, NY 105951524	CFO: Stephen Piccolo Jr
Phone: 914-594-4100	HR: –
Fax: –	FYE: June 30
Web: www.nymc.edu	Type: Private

It doesn't take a brain surgeon to figure out this school's specialty. New York Medical College (NYMC) confers advanced degrees to those preparing for careers in the medical and health professions. The institution's three divisions — the School of Medicine the School of Public Health and the Graduate School of Basic Medical Sciences — offer programs in more than 20 disciplines. NYMC has an enrollment of more than 1400 students who practice at nearby Westchester Medical Center and the Manhattan location of Saint Vincent Catholic Medical Centers. Founded in 1860 the medical college has been affiliated with the Archdiocese of New York since 1978. NYMC is part of Touro College.

	Annual Growth	06/07	06/08	06/09	06/10	06/13
Sales ($ mil.)	(12.3%)	–	–	–	215.3	145.4
Net income ($ mil.)	–	–	–	–	(1.2)	6.0
Market value ($ mil.)	–	–	–	–	–	–
Employees	–	–	–	–	–	1,300

NEW YORK METHODIST HOSPITAL

506 6TH ST	CEO: Mark J. Mundy
BROOKLYN, NY 112153609	CFO: Edward Zaidberg
Phone: 718-780-3000	HR: –
Fax: –	FYE: December 31
Web: www.nym.org	Type: Private

New York Methodist Hospital is a not-for-profit acute-care teaching hospital serving Brooklyn residents. Established in 1881 as the Methodist Episcopal Hospital the facility has more than 650 licensed beds. It offers a full range of medical services including primary and emergency care as well as specialty services such as women's health cancer cardiovascular pediatric geriatric and behavioral health. The hospital also operates satellite clinics in surrounding areas. A member of New York-Presbyterian Healthcare System New York Methodist is a teaching hospital affiliated with Cornell University's Weill Medical College.

	Annual Growth	12/07	12/08	12/09	12/12	12/13
Sales ($ mil.)	8.4%	–	540.6	516.5	636.7	810.3
Net income ($ mil.)	122.9%	–	–	4.7	44.1	115.4
Market value ($ mil.)	–	–	–	–	–	–
Employees	–	–	–	–	–	3,185

NEW YORK MORTGAGE TRUST INC

NMS: NYMT

275 Madison Avenue	CEO: Steven R. Mumma
New York, NY 10016	CFO: Kristine R. Nario
Phone: 212 792-0107	HR: –
Fax: –	FYE: December 31
Web: www.nymtrust.com	Type: Public

New York Mortgage Trust is a self-advised real estate investment trust (REIT) that invests in mortgage-related real estate assets and some financial assets. It mostly invests in residential mortgage loans including multi-family commercial mortgage-backed securities (CMBS) distressed residential mortgage loans and direct financing to multi-family property owners through mezzanine loans and preferred equity investments. More than 60% of its revenue comes from interest on multi-family loans held in securitization trusts though the REIT's fortunes depend heavily on security gains and losses. New York Mortgage Trust was formed in 2003 and is headquartered in New York City.

	Annual Growth	12/10	12/11	12/12	12/13	12/14
Sales ($ mil.)	109.0%	25.5	22.3	147.2	322.1	486.0
Net income ($ mil.)	111.5%	6.8	4.9	28.2	69.0	136.2
Market value ($ mil.)	2.6%	731.5	757.7	664.2	734.6	810.3
Employees	23.6%	3	3	4	6	7

NEW YORK POWER AUTHORITY

123 MAIN ST STE 1600
WHITE PLAINS, NY 106013132
Phone: 914-681-6200
Fax: –
Web: www.nypa.gov

CEO: Gil C. Quiniones
CFO: Robert F. Lurie
HR: –
FYE: December 31
Type: Private

The hydropower generated by the mighty Niagara Falls is the real authority behind the New York Power Authority (NYPA). More than 70% of the power that NYPA produces is from hydropower resources. The company generates and transmits more than 20% of New York's electricity making it the largest state-owned public power provider in the US. It is also New York's only statewide electricity supplier. NYPA owns hydroelectric and fossil-fueled generating facilities (16 in total) that produce about 5700 MW of electricity and it operates more than 1400 circuit-miles of transmission lines. NYPA is owned by the State of New York.

	Annual Growth	12/09	12/10	12/11	12/12	12/13
Sales ($ mil.)	6.8%	–	–	2,655.0	2,673.0	3,030.0
Net income ($ mil.)	(8.0%)	–	–	294.0	175.0	249.0
Market value ($ mil.)	–	–	–	–	–	–
Employees	–	–	–	–	–	4,450

NEW YORK PUBLIC RADIO

160 VARICK ST FL 7
NEW YORK, NY 100131270
Phone: 212-669-7800
Fax: –
Web: www.wnyc.org

CEO: Laura R Walker
CFO: –
HR: –
FYE: June 30
Type: Private

If you want the NPR in NYC turn your radio dial to WNYC. With more than one million listeners per week WNYC is the most popular public radio station in the country. The stations broadcasts on FM and AM and produces and airs original programming including daily news reports talk shows and music shows including The Brian Lehrer Show Radio Lab and Studio 360. It also features shows from affiliate National Public Radio (NPR) stations (including All Things Considered and Morning Edition) and Public Radio International. Listeners can also access WYNC's Web site to read the news download podcasts and hear recently broadcasted shows. The radio station one of the oldest in the US began broadcasting on AM in 1922.

	Annual Growth	06/01	06/02	06/05	06/08	06/13
Sales ($ mil.)	(3.0%)	–	85.9	0.0	46.7	61.3
Net income ($ mil.)	–	–	–	0.0	11.1	1.0
Market value ($ mil.)	–	–	–	–	–	–
Employees	–	–	–	–	–	120

NEW YORK STATE AND LOCAL RETIREMENT SYSTEM

110 State St.
Albany NY 12244-0001
Phone: 518-474-7736
Fax: 518-402-4433
Web: www.osc.state.ny.us/retire

CEO: –
CFO: –
HR: –
FYE: March 31
Type: Government-owned

When government employees in New York are no longer new what do they do? New York State and Local Retirement System (NYSLRS) provides retirement and pension funds to police firefighters correction officers and other public employees in the Empire State outside of New York City. Administered by the Office of the State Comptroller the system also provides survivor benefits to relatives of state employees. NYSLRS which has more than $110 billion in assets under management has more than a million members about 350000 of whom are retirees and beneficiaries. Some 80% of the retirees continue to reside in New York so their payments eventually go back into the state's economy.

NEW YORK STATE CATHOLIC HEALTH PLAN INC

9525 QUEENS BLVD STE 8
REGO PARK, NY 113744510
Phone: 888-343-3547
Fax: –
Web: www.fideliscare.com

CEO: Mark L. Lane
CFO: Thomas Halloran
HR: –
FYE: December 31
Type: Private

Fidelis Care hopes for always faithful health plan members. The New York State Catholic Health Plan which does business as Fidelis Care serves more than 921000 residents in some 60 counties across the state including the New York City area. The church-sponsored plan's provider network includes more than 63000 physicians hospitals and other health care professionals and facilities. Fidelis Care provides managed Medicaid Medicare and state-sponsored family and children's Health Plus plans as well as long-term care and behavioral health coverage.

	Annual Growth	12/06	12/07	12/08	12/09	12/10
Sales ($ mil.)	33.8%	–	–	–	1,435.2	1,921.0
Net income ($ mil.)	84.2%	–	–	–	27.9	51.4
Market value ($ mil.)	–	–	–	–	–	–
Employees	–	–	–	–	–	1,625

NEW YORK STATE LOTTERY

1 Broadway Center
Schenectady NY 12301-7500
Phone: 518-388-3300
Fax: 518-388-3403
Web: www.nylottery.org

CEO: –
CFO: –
HR: –
FYE: March 31
Type: Government-owned

Winning the New York State Lottery could make you king of the hill top of the heap. The New York State Lottery is one of the largest and oldest state lotteries in the US (only New Hampshire's lottery is older). It runs three jackpot five daily and about a dozen scratch-off games through retailers and online outlets. About a third of the lottery's revenue or some $2 billion a year goes to support New York State education. It also awards Leaders of Tomorrow scholarships to one eligible graduating senior from every public and private school in the state (provided they attend New York universities). The New York Lottery was established by the new state constitution passed in 1966.

NEW YORK STATE TEACHERS' RETIREMENT SYSTEM

10 Corporate Woods Dr.
Albany NY 12211-2395
Phone: 518-447-2900
Fax: 518-447-2875
Web: www.nystrs.org

CEO: George Philip
CFO: Arthur Hewig
HR: –
FYE: June 30
Type: Government Agency

The New York State Teachers' Retirement System known as NYSTRS for short provides retirement death and disability benefits to more than 280000 public school teachers and administrators as well as to some 140000 retirees and beneficiaries. Eligible retirees are guaranteed monthly benefits payments for life. The system which was established by the state in 1921 serves public school educators in the Empire State excluding New York City. Employees of New York State community colleges boards of cooperative educational services The State University of New York system and some charter school employees have the option of participating as well.

NEW YORK TIMES CO.

NYS: NYT

620 Eighth Avenue
New York, NY 10018
Phone: 212 556-1234
Fax: –
Web: www.nytco.com

CEO: Mark Thompson
CFO: James M. Follo
HR: –
FYE: December 28
Type: Public

All the News That's Fit to Print and Post Online would be a more accurate motto for this media titan. The New York Times Company (The Times Co.) publishes The New York Times. The iconic newspaper known to many as The Grey Lady is one of the world's most respected sources of news. The paper boasts a weekday circulation of about 1.3 million. The Times Co. owns The Boston Globe among other big city newspapers and distributes news online through NYTimes.com and other sites. The company sold content portal About Group in late 2012. Chairman Arthur Sulzberger and his family control the firm through a trust.

	Annual Growth	12/10	12/11	12/12	12/13	12/14
Sales ($ mil.)	(9.7%)	2,393.5	2,323.4	1,990.1	1,577.2	1,588.5
Net income ($ mil.)	(25.4%)	107.7	(39.7)	133.2	65.1	33.3
Market value ($ mil.)	8.1%	1,497.4	1,171.1	1,238.8	2,316.7	2,041.6
Employees	(16.6%)	7,414	7,273	5,363	3,529	3,588

NEW YORK YANKEES PARTNERSHIP

Yankee Stadium E. 161st St. and River Ave.
Bronx NY 10451
Phone: 718-293-4300
Fax: 718-293-8431
Web: newyork.yankees.mlb.com

CEO: –
CFO: –
HR: –
FYE: December 31
Type: Private

These Yanks are a big hit with New York baseball fans. New York Yankees Partnership owns and operates the New York Yankees professional baseball team one of the most storied and popular clubs in Major League Baseball. The franchise boasts a record 27 World Series titles and 40 American League pennants making it the most successful professional sports team in history. Along with that success the Yankees organization has been associated with such sports icons as Babe Ruth Lou Gehrig Joe DiMaggio and Mickey Mantle. Once known as the Highlanders the team has represented New York City since 1903. The Steinbrenner family led by Hal Steinbrenner has controlled the Yanks since 1973.

NEWARK BETH ISRAEL MEDICAL CENTER INC.

201 LYONS AVE
NEWARK, NJ 071122027
Phone: 973-926-7000
Fax: –

CEO: –
CFO: Veronica Zichner
HR: Zachary (Zach) Lipner
FYE: December 31
Type: Private

Part of the Saint Barnabas Health Care System Newark Beth Israel Medical Center is a 670-bed acute-care regional referral hospital. The facility serves residents of Newark and surrounding areas in northern New Jersey. The hospital offers services including primary diagnostic emergency surgical and rehabilitative care. It is home to specialized programs such as kidney transplantation cancer care dentistry sleep disorders geriatrics and women's health services. Newark Beth Israel Medical Center also houses the Children's Hospital of New Jersey and the Saint Barnabas Heart Center. The research and teaching hospital has a medical staff of more than 800 physicians.

	Annual Growth	12/01	12/02	12/03*	06/05*	12/08
Sales ($ mil.)	(7.3%)	–	–	641.5	441.6	438.1
Net income ($ mil.)	–	–	–	0.0	0.0	(56.6)
Market value ($ mil.)	–	–	–	–	–	–
Employees	–	–	–	–	–	3,000

*Fiscal year change

NEWAYS INC.

2089 Neways Dr.
Springville UT 84663
Phone: 801-418-2000
Fax: 702-589-7213
Web: www.allegiantair.com

CEO: Robert Conlee
CFO: James Sloan
HR: –
FYE: December 31
Type: Private

Neways helps its consumers find new ways to live clean healthy lives. The company designs and makes products that are free of more than 3000 harmful ingredients for wellness (nutritional supplements weight management) beauty (cosmetics hair treatments) and household care (automotive laundry supplies). The consumer products company distributes its products to about 30 countries worldwide. Neways boasts corporate offices in Australia Israel Japan and the US among other countries. The company was established in 1987 by Tom and Dee Mower veterans of the chemical industry.

NEWBRIDGE BANCORP

NMS: NBBC

1501 Highwoods Boulevard, Suite 400
Greensboro, NC 27410
Phone: 336 369-0900
Fax: –
Web: www.newbridgebank.com

CEO: Pressley A Ridgill
CFO: Ramsey K. Hamadi
HR: –
FYE: December 31
Type: Public

Bridging the gap between its community banks and North Carolinians NewBridge Bancorp is the holding company that owns NewBridge Bank which operates about 40 branches plus a handful of loan production offices located primarily in the state's Piedmont Triad Region. Boasting more than $2.5 billion in total assets the community bank offers personal and business banking products and services including checking and savings accounts and loans as well as wealth management services including investment and asset management and estate planning. Real estate-secured loans make up nearly 90% of the bank's $1.6 billion loan portfolio. Raleigh-based Yadkin Bank agreed to buy NewBridge in late 2015.

	Annual Growth	12/10	12/11	12/12	12/13	12/14
Assets ($ mil.)	8.7%	1,807.2	1,734.6	1,708.7	1,965.2	2,520.2
Net income ($ mil.)	42.6%	3.4	4.7	(25.3)	20.8	14.0
Market value ($ mil.)	16.7%	174.8	143.9	172.2	276.2	324.0
Employees	(0.5%)	497	442	442	449	487

NEWCASTLE INVESTMENT CORP

NYS: NCT

1345 Avenue of the Americas
New York. NY 10105
Phone: 212 798-6100
Fax: –
Web: www.newcastleinv.com

CEO: Kenneth M Riis
CFO: Justine Cheng
HR: –
FYE: December 31
Type: Public

It's not exactly the newest castle on the real estate block but Newcastle Investment is building quite an artillery. A real estate investment trust (REIT) the company underwrites and invests in real estate securities real estate-related loans and residential mortgages. Commercial mortgage-backed securities and similar instruments account for about half of the REIT's portfolio. Newcastle Investment is externally managed by Fortress Investment Group which also owns a minority stake in the company. Newcastle chairman Wesley Edens is also a co-chairman of Fortress.

	Annual Growth	12/10	12/11	12/12	12/13	12/14
Sales ($ mil.)	8.7%	300.3	292.3	330.5	362.7	419.2
Net income ($ mil.)	(52.2%)	621.7	259.4	434.1	152.3	32.4
Market value ($ mil.)	(9.5%)	445.0	308.9	576.6	381.3	298.2
Employees					9,442	4,600

NEWEGG INC.

16839 E. Gale Ave.
City of Industry CA 91745
Phone: 626-271-9700
Fax: 626-271-9403
Web: www.newegg.com

CEO: Danny Lee
CFO: Robert Chang
HR: –
FYE: December 31
Type: Private

Newegg caters to egghead types who build their own computers. The company which prides itself on "fresh" offerings is a leading online-only distributor of consumer electronics and computing products with more than 14 million registered users in the US Canada and China. It sells desktop and laptop computers along with all the related components to build or repair one yourself. Newegg also stocks cell phones digital cameras home appliances networking devices peripherals DVDs accessories and software. Its websites (including its B2B site NeweggBusiness.com) carry products made by vendors including Apple ATi Canon Sony Toshiba and Viewsonic. Founded in 2001 Newegg withdrew an IPO filing in 2011.

NEWELL RUBBERMAID, INC.

NYS: NWL

Three Glenlake Parkway
Atlanta, GA 30328
Phone: 770 418-7000
Fax: –
Web: www.newellrubbermaid.com

CEO: Michael B. (Mike) Polk
CFO: John K. Stipancich
HR: Paula S. Larson
FYE: December 31
Type: Public

Newell Rubbermaid wants to get its products into your drawers your kitchen cabinets and your workbench. The go-to company for men women and children makes housewares (Rubbermaid plastic products Calphalon cookware) home furnishings (Levolor blinds) juvenile products (Graco) hair products (Goody) and office items (DYMO Sanford Sharpie). Newell Rubbermaid sells its items to mass retailers (Target) and home and office supply stores (Staples). Past Gillette executive Michael Cowhig is chairman while Michael Polk took over as president and CEO in 2011. Contrary to popular belief the company's home solutions products are not its largest business; it actually brings in more from its office supply sales.

	Annual Growth	12/10	12/11	12/12	12/13	12/14
Sales ($ mil.)	(0.1%)	5,759.2	5,864.6	5,902.7	5,692.5	5,727.0
Net income ($ mil.)	6.6%	292.8	125.2	401.3	474.6	377.8
Market value ($ mil.)	20.3%	4,894.1	4,347.6	5,995.1	8,724.8	10,253.8
Employees	(2.7%)	19,400	19,900	18,300	18,300	17,400

NEWESCO INC.

1500 ARTHUR AVE STE 200
ELK GROVE VILLAGE, IL 600075744
Phone: 847-437-7050
Fax: –
Web: www.amertranslogistics.com

CEO: John R Westerberg
CFO: Lawrence Cap
HR: –
FYE: December 31
Type: Private

An agent of leading mover Atlas Van Lines (part of Atlas World Group) Nelson Westerberg specializes in handling household moves for employees who are being transferred by their companies. It also offers office and industrial moving services and household moves for individuals. (As an agent the company handles moves within its assigned geographic territory and cooperates with other agents on interstate moves.) Major corporate clients have included Sara Lee and Walgreen. Founded in 1904 by Swedish immigrants Fred Nelson and Oscar Westerberg the company started out in Chicago hauling coal ice and furniture with a horse-drawn wagon. Company chairman and CEO John Westerberg is Oscar's grandson.

	Annual Growth	12/04	12/05	12/06	12/07	12/08
Sales ($ mil.)	–	–	–	(806.2)	61.9	55.8
Net income ($ mil.)	38004.0%	–	–	0.0	5.6	3.6
Market value ($ mil.)	–	–	–	–	–	–
Employees	–	–	–	–	–	400

NEWFIELD EXPLORATION CO.

NYS: NFX

4 Waterway Square Place, Suite 100
The Woodlands, TX 77380
Phone: 281 210-5100
Fax: 281 210-5101
Web: www.newfield.com

CEO: Lee K. Boothby
CFO: Lawrence S. (Larry) Massaro
HR: –
FYE: December 31
Type: Public

Newfield Exploration explores for new fields of oil and natural gas reserves but is happy with old reserves too. The independent oil and gas exploration and production company drills in the Mid-Continent (Anadarko and Arkoma Basins) the Rockies (Uinta and Williston Basins) and the Gulf Coast region of Texas. The company seeks to hedge its exploration and production bets by exploiting assets outside of the US primarily in China and Malaysia. In 2014 Newfield Exploration reported proved reserves In 2014 Newfield Exploration reported proved reserves of 645 million barrels of oil equivalent (47% oil 12% NGLs and 41% natural gas).

	Annual Growth	12/10	12/11	12/12	12/13	12/14
Sales ($ mil.)	5.0%	1,883.0	2,471.0	2,567.0	1,789.0	2,288.0
Net income ($ mil.)	14.5%	523.0	539.0	(1,184.0)	147.0	900.0
Market value ($ mil.)	(21.7%)	9,902.8	5,181.4	3,677.7	3,382.4	3,724.4
Employees	(0.4%)	1,352	1,643	1,760	1,548	1,331

NEWGISTICS INC.

2700 Via Fortuna Ste. 300
Austin TX 78746
Phone: 512-225-6000
Fax: 512-225-6001
Web: www.newgistics.com

CEO: William Razzouk
CFO: Michael Twomey
HR: –
FYE: December 31
Type: Private

Newgistics steps in when that new gizmo you ordered turns out to be not what you wanted. The company provides returns management services for direct retailers manufacturers distributors and other fulfillment businesses; customers have included Victoria's Secret QVC and Neiman Marcus. Shoppers who return purchases attach a label with a bar code provided by Newgistics and mail the package. Postage is deducted from the refund. The Newgistics SmartLabel system is intended to make the return process easier for both customer and company. Newgistics arranges transportation and warehousing for its customers through third-parties. Austin Ventures owns 63% of Newgistics.

NEWLINK GENETICS CORP

NMS: NLNK

2503 South Loop Drive
Ames, IA 50010
Phone: 515 296-5555
Fax: –
Web: www.linkp.com

CEO: Charles J. Link
CFO: John B. (Jack) Henneman
HR: –
FYE: December 31
Type: Public

NewLink Genetics is hoping to give a boost to the immune systems of cancer patients. A biopharmaceutical company focused on discovering cancer treatments NewLink develops and commercializes small-molecule immunotherapy therapies that stimulate patients' immune systems. Its lead candidate HyperAcute Pancreas is designed to treat surgically-resected pancreatic cancer patients undergoing standard chemotherapy treatments. (Surgically-resected patients are those who have had tumors removed.) The candidate is in late-stage clinical development; the company also has similar candidates in earlier-stages of development to treat lung and skin cancer. Founded in 1999 NewLink went public in 2011.

	Annual Growth	12/10	12/11	12/12	12/13	12/14
Sales ($ mil.)	201.9%	2.1	1.9	1.7	1.1	172.6
Net income ($ mil.)	–	(16.2)	(18.1)	(23.3)	(31.2)	102.9
Market value ($ mil.)	78.1%	–	197.0	349.8	615.9	1,112.2
Employees	13.6%	78	77	94	104	130

NEWLY WEDS FOODS INC.

4140 W. Fullerton Ave.
Chicago IL 60639
Phone: 773-489-7000
Fax: 773-292-3809
Web: www.newlywedsfoods.com

CEO: –
CFO: –
HR: Ana Essex
FYE: December 31
Type: Private

Don't let the name fool you Newly Weds Foods doesn't bake wedding cakes. But it might just make that cake tastier. The company makes seasonings marinades glazes sauces batters breadings binders and fillers for the food processing and foodservice industries in some 70 countries throughout the world. Newly Weds uses its proprietary database FlavorTrak to monitor restaurant trends and then develop flavors it hopes will appeal to the most consumers. Newly Weds boasts that it has expertise in providing ingredients for more than 45 cuisines. Based in Chicago the company owns and operates about 25 production plants and 20 laboratories.

NEWMAR CORPORATION

355 N. Delaware St.
Nappanee IN 46550-0030
Phone: 574-773-7791
Fax: 574-773-2895
Web: www.newmarcorp.com

CEO: –
CFO: –
HR: –
FYE: December 31
Type: Private

How can you go on a road trip and still sleep in your own bed every night? Newmar knows. The company manufactures fifth-wheels Class A motor homes (gas- and diesel-powered) and diesel-powered motor coaches. Nameplates include Bay Star Canyon Star Cypress Dutch Star Essex King Aire Mountain Aire Torrey Pine Ventana and X-Aire. Newmar's vehicles feature dual ducting air-conditioning systems dishwashers and refrigerators icemakers ovens full bathrooms with tubs and/or showers and hardwood cabinetry. It provides service support for both Newmar and non-Newmar coaches. Mahlon Miller owns the company which was founded in 1968 by Marvin Miller (no relation to Mahlon) and Marvin Newcomer.

NEWMARKET CORP

NYS: NEU

330 South Fourth Street
Richmond, VA 23219-4350
Phone: 804 788-5000
Fax: –
Web: www.newmarket.com

CEO: Thomas E. (Teddy) Gottwald
CFO: Brian D. Paliotti
HR: Elly Teschke
FYE: December 31
Type: Public

Some people think petroleum is just fine the way it is; NewMarket thinks it needs a little something extra added to it to improve engine performance. The company is a holding entity for two petroleum additive subsidiaries: Afton Chemical and Ethyl Corporation. Afton Chemical manufactures petroleum additives used to improve the performance of gasoline diesel and other fuels and as a lubricant in motor oil fluids and grease. Ethyl's main product is the antiknock additive tetraethyl lead though TEL has lost substantial ground in markets where unleaded gas is preferred.

	Annual Growth	12/11	12/12	12/13	12/14	12/15
Sales ($ mil.)	(0.1%)	2,149.6	2,223.3	2,280.4	2,335.4	2,140.8
Net income ($ mil.)	3.6%	206.9	239.6	264.7	233.3	238.6
Market value ($ mil.)	17.7%	2,367.1	3,132.9	3,992.6	4,821.6	4,549.1
Employees	5.1%	1,625	1,710	1,789	1,866	1,979

NEWMARKET TECHNOLOGY INC.

PINK SHEETS: NWMT

14860 Montfort Dr. Ste. 210
Dallas TX 75254
Phone: 972-386-3372
Fax: 972-386-8165
Web: www.newmarkettechnology.com

CEO: Bruce Noller
CFO: Philip J Rauch
HR: –
FYE: December 31
Type: Public

NewMarket Technology is all about growing into new markets. The holding company invests in development-stage tech firms located in emerging markets outside the US. It has a handful of subsidiaries in its portfolio — China Crescent Enterprises RKM Suministros (Venezuela) and UniOne Consulting (Brazil) — that provide systems integration software development and telecommunications hardware. It also has equity stakes in other companies including mobile payment services company Alternet Systems and wireless broadband operator RedMoon. NewMarket's customers have included international giants such as Siemens ExxonMobil Visa and Bayer; customers in China account for most of the company's sales however.

NEWMONT MINING CORP. (HOLDING CO.)

NYS: NEM

6363 South Fiddler's Green Circle
Greenwood Village, CO 80111
Phone: 303 863-7414
Fax: 303 837-5837
Web: www.newmont.com

CEO: Gary J. Goldberg
CFO: Laurie Brlas
HR: William N. (Bill) MacGowan
FYE: December 31
Type: Public

Newmont Mining goes for the gold. Once the clear #1 gold producing company in the world Newmont now ranks #2 behind Barrick. Newmont produces about 5.6 million ounces of gold annually and has proved and probable reserves of 82.2 million ounces of gold and 7.9 million pounds of copper. It has significant assets in the US mining in Nevada since 1965. It also has assets in Australia Canada Ghana Indonesia Mexico Peru and New Zealand. Newmont mines copper mostly through its Batu Hijau project in Indonesia and Boddington project in Australia. The company produced about 144 million pounds of copper in 2014. Operations in North America and South America account for more than half of Newmont's gold production.

	Annual Growth	12/10	12/11	12/12	12/13	12/14
Sales ($ mil.)	(6.5%)	9,540.0	10,358.0	9,868.0	8,322.0	7,292.0
Net income ($ mil.)	(31.3%)	2,277.0	366.0	1,809.0	(2,462.0)	508.0
Market value ($ mil.)	(25.5%)	30,633.3	29,925.2	23,158.2	11,484.4	9,424.9
Employees	(3.0%)	15,500	17,100	16,400	15,085	13,700

NEWPAGE GROUP INC.

8540 Gander Creek Dr.
Miamisburg OH 45342
Phone: 937-242-9345
Fax: 203-393-1684
Web: www.laticrete.com

CEO: –
CFO: –
HR: –
FYE: December 31
Type: Private

After struggling through several financially challenging years for the coated paper making industry NewPage would like to do jus that turn over a new page. Through subsidiary NewPage Corp. the company is one of the largest makers of coated and specialty paper in North America. From mills in the Eastern and Midwestern US NewPage churns out about 3.5 million tons of paper annually. Its papers are often used to produce annual reports magazines and catalogs. Customers include xpedx Advance Magazine Publishers (dba Conde Nast) McGraw-Hill Time Inc. and Avery Dennison. NewPage Corp. filed for Chapter 11 bankruptcy in late 2011.

NEWPARK RESOURCES, INC.

NYS: NR

9320 Lakeside Boulevard, Suite 100
The Woodlands, TX 77381
Phone: 281 362-6800
Fax: –
Web: www.newpark.com

CEO: Paul L. Howes
CFO: Gregg Piontek
HR: –
FYE: December 31
Type: Public

Oil and gas activity means money for oil field support services company Newpark Resources. The company provides drilling fluid and engineering services to oil and gas drillers. Newpark Resources also supplies prefab work platforms and provides DuraBase brand composite mats used to make temporary access roads and provide related wellsite services and equipment (through its Newpark Mats & Integrated Services unit). In 2014 the industrial services company sold its Environmental Services business which had historically operated as Newpark Resources' third segment.

	Annual Growth	12/10	12/11	12/12	12/13	12/14
Sales ($ mil.)	11.8%	716.0	958.2	1,038.0	1,042.4	1,118.4
Net income ($ mil.)	25.2%	41.6	80.0	60.0	65.3	102.3
Market value ($ mil.)	11.6%	517.4	797.9	659.4	1,032.3	801.3
Employees	25.4%	1,001	2,118	2,248	2,214	2,478

NEWPORT CORP.

NMS: NEWP

1791 Deere Avenue
Irvine, CA 92606
Phone: 949 863-3144
Fax: –
Web: www.newport.com

CEO: Robert J. Phillippy
CFO: Charles F. (Chuck) Cargile
HR: –
FYE: January 03
Type: Public

Newport helps all sorts of customers take a measured approach. The company makes lasers precision components and automated assembly measurement and test equipment. It makes products that are used around the world in such fields as fiber-optic communications health care life sciences military/aerospace scientific research and semiconductor manufacturing. Industrial and scientific components include lenses and other devices for vibration and motion control. Newport also offers automated systems used to make fiber-optic components and photonics. More than half of sales come from outside the US.

	Annual Growth	01/11*	12/11	12/12	12/13*	01/15
Sales ($ mil.)	6.0%	479.8	545.1	595.3	560.1	605.2
Net income ($ mil.)	(3.9%)	41.1	79.7	(89.4)	15.6	35.1
Market value ($ mil.)	1.9%	690.3	539.0	516.8	721.6	743.4
Employees	10.2%	1,745	2,550	2,440	2,400	2,570

*Fiscal year change

NEWS AMERICA MARKETING FSI LLC

1185 Avenue of the Americas 27th Fl.
New York NY 10036
Phone: 212-782-8000
Fax: 212-575-5845
Web: www.newsamerica.com

CEO: –
CFO: –
HR: Jennifer Hayes
FYE: June 30
Type: Business Segment

News America Marketing a subsidiary of global media giant News Corp. provides marketing services primarily through newspaper inserts and in-store coupon displays. The company publishes SmartSource Magazine the largest newspaper insert in the US (it reaches nearly 70 million households in more than 1500 newspapers); its SmartSource Price Pop Guaranteed offers shoppers coupons on the shelf near a product; overall the SmartSource brands reaches more than 150 million consumers each week. News America Marketing's other services include promotional products merchandising database marketing tools and online promotions. It owns 12 offices throughout North America and one in New Zealand.

NEWS CORP (NEW)

NMS: NWSA

1211 Avenue of the Americas
New York, NY 10036
Phone: 212 416-3400
Fax: –
Web: www.newscorp.com

CEO: Joel T. Klein
CFO: Bedi A. Singh
HR: –
FYE: June 30
Type: Public

They say no news is good news but the new News Corp. is making headlines. In mid-2013 media mogul Rupert Murdoch split his print media and broadcast media holdings into separate companies. News Corp. now consists of newspapers (The Wall Street Journal New York Post Australia's Herald Sun and The Sun and The Times in the UK) information services (Dow Jones and Factiva) and book publishing (HarperCollins). It also owns FOX SPORTS Australia a stake in Australian real estate web portal REA Group and a 50% share of Australian pay-TV provider FOXTEL. Murdoch's US-based TV and film holdings are now organized into Twenty-First Century Fox which includes networks FOX and FOX News.

	Annual Growth	06/11	06/12	06/13	06/14	06/15
Sales ($ mil.)	(1.3%)	9,095.0	8,654.0	8,891.0	8,574.0	8,633.0
Net income ($ mil.)	–	678.0	(2,075.0)	506.0	239.0	(147.0)
Market value ($ mil.)	(18.7%)	–	–	–	10,432.9	8,484.7
Employees	1.4%	–	24,000	24,000	22,000	25,000

NEWSTAR FINANCIAL INC

NMS: NEWS

500 Boylston Street, Suite 1250
Boston, MA 02116
Phone: 617 848-2500
Fax: –
Web: www.newstarfin.com

CEO: Timothy J. Conway
CFO: John K. Bray
HR: –
FYE: December 31
Type: Public

No hot air here: NewStar Financial is in the business of providing middle-market companies with the capital they need to create a spark. The commercial financier provides a variety of loans (primarily secured senior debt) for refinancing acquisitions consolidations and commercial real estate and equipment purchases to clients in the retail and consumer health care media and information and energy industries among others. Its loans typically range from $10 million to $50 million. Newstar also offers investment advisory and asset management services to institutional investors through managed credit funds that invest in its originated loans.

	Annual Growth	12/10	12/11	12/12	12/13	12/14
Assets ($ mil.)	9.2%	1,975.0	1,946.4	2,157.1	2,606.9	2,811.0
Net income ($ mil.)	0.9%	10.2	14.1	24.0	24.6	10.6
Market value ($ mil.)	4.9%	492.8	474.1	653.2	828.4	596.7
Employees	4.6%	82	88	104	101	98

NEWTEK BUSINESS SERVICES CORP

NMS: NEWT

212 West 35th Street, 2nd Floor
New York, NY 10001
Phone: 212 356-9500
Fax: –
Web: www.newtekbusinessservices.com

CEO: –
CFO: –
HR: Ted Rallis
FYE: December 31
Type: Public

Newtek Business Services provides a suite of business and financial services to small to midsized businesses including electronic merchant payment processing website hosting Small Business Administration (SBA) loans data storage insurance accounts receivable financing and payroll management. The company serves more than 100000 business accounts throughout the US. Newtek also has investments in certified capital companies (Capcos) which are authorized in eight states and Washington DC. It has stakes in about a dozen Capcos that traditionally have issued debt and equity securities to insurance firms then used the funds to mainly invest in small and midsized financial and business services firms.

	Annual Growth	12/11	12/12	12/13*	11/14*	12/14
Sales ($ mil.)	(74.9%)	125.3	131.1	143.6	131.8	2.0
Net income ($ mil.)	–	3.5	5.6	7.5	3.3	(2.5)
Market value ($ mil.)	134.4%	11.7	19.0	32.0	133.2	150.6
Employees	2.7%	309	310	319	335	335

*Fiscal year change

NEWTON MEMORIAL HOSPITAL INC

175 HIGH ST
NEWTON, NJ 078601099
Phone: 973-383-2121
Fax: –
Web: www.atlantichealth.org

CEO: –
CFO: Robert Ragona
HR: –
FYE: December 31
Type: Private

The folks at Newton Medical Center want to cure what ails you or help you slip into slumber. With about 150 beds and numerous clinical specialties Newton Memorial provides medical care to residents at the crux of northwestern New Jersey southwestern New York and eastern Pennsylvania. Established in 1932 the acute-care hospital offers specialized services such as emergency care pediatrics home health cardiac care respiratory care and aesthetic surgery. The not-for-profit hospital also has a sleep lab and inpatient clinics for orthopedics stroke care cancer treatment and rehabilitation. It is part of Atlantic Health System.

	Annual Growth	12/05	12/06	12/07	12/08	12/09
Sales ($ mil.)	4.4%	–	121.4	122.1	111.3	138.0
Net income ($ mil.)	–	–	–	(0.5)	(5.9)	3.7
Market value ($ mil.)	–	–	–	–	–	–
Employees	–	–	–	–	–	805

NEXSAN CORPORATION

555 St. Charles Dr. Ste. 202
Thousand Oaks CA 91360
Phone: 805-418-2700
Fax: 805-418-2799
Web: www.nexsan.com

CEO: Philip Black
CFO: Gene Spies
HR: –
FYE: June 30
Type: Private

Nexsan makes hoarding so much easier (and cleaner). With space and energy limitations in mind the company provides SAN NAS and unified hybrid storage systems for midsized businesses and mid-level deployments in larger enterprises. Its storage and archiving systems are suitable for a broad range of data including e-mail medical images web content digital video and CAD and other reference materials. Nexsan sells through distributors original equipment manufacturers resellers and systems integrators. The company which has sold more than 28000 systems across 60 countries serves clients in such industries as financial services technology media healthcare and public sector.

NEXSTAR BROADCASTING GROUP INC

NMS: NXST

545 E. John Carpenter Freeway, Suite 700
Irving, TX 75062
Phone: 972 373-8800
Fax: –
Web: www.nexstar.tv

CEO: Perry A. Sook
CFO: Thomas E. (Tom) Carter
HR: –
FYE: December 31
Type: Public

Star light star bright Nexstar Broadcasting wishes for you to tune in tonight. The company is a leading television station operator with more than 70 stations serving 40 small and midsized markets. Nexstar has duopolies (two or more stations) in many of its markets. Its portfolio includes more than a dozen affiliates each of the FOX and NBC networks as well as stations affiliated with ABC CBS The CW and MyNetworkTV. More than 15 of its TV stations are operated through local service agreements with Mission Broadcasting which owns those broadcast licenses. Private investment firm ABRY Partners owns a majority share in the company and controls 88% of the voting power.

	Annual Growth	12/10	12/11	12/12	12/13	12/14
Sales ($ mil.)	19.1%	313.4	306.5	378.6	502.3	631.3
Net income ($ mil.)	–	(1.8)	(11.9)	182.5	(1.8)	64.6
Market value ($ mil.)	71.5%	186.7	244.4	330.1	1,737.2	1,614.4
Employees	13.2%	2,111	2,230	2,411	3,222	3,464

NEXTEC GROUP

1111 North Loop West Ste. 810
Houston TX 77008
Phone: 713-957-8350
Fax: 713-957-4259
Web: www.nextecgroup.com

CEO: –
CFO: –
HR: Janna Y'Barbo
FYE: June 30
Type: Private

NexTec Group is on the lookout for technology products that might improve efficiency for its middle-market business clients. The information technology consulting company evaluates installs and customizes accounting financial and management information software. It also offers training and technical support services. NexTec specializes in enterprise software made by Microsoft and Sage among others. The company serves clients in a variety of industries such as energy financial services manufacturing and health care. It serves clients from satellite offices in California New Jersey New York Ohio and Washington. NexTec was founded in 1994 by president Eric Frank and VP's Russell Harper and Alan Subel.

NEXTERA ENERGY INC

NYS: NEE

700 Universe Boulevard
Juno Beach, FL 33408
Phone: 561 694-4000
Fax: 561 694-4620
Web: www.nexteraenergy.com

CEO: James L. (Jim) Robo
CFO: Moray P. Dewhurst
HR: Deborah H. Caplan
FYE: December 31
Type: Public

For a Florida company without any oranges NextEra Energy produces a lot of juice. Its operations across the US and Canada include an independent power production business but most of its revenues come from utility Florida Power & Light (FPL). The unit distributes electricity to 4.7 million customers. Subsidiary FPL Group Capital owns nonutility businesses including NextEra Energy Resources an independent power producer and energy marketer. Overall NextEra Energy has more than 44900 MW of generating capacity. Subsidiary FPL FiberNet leases wholesale fiber-optic capacity to telephone cable and Internet providers; it operates a 9050 mile network.

	Annual Growth	12/10	12/11	12/12	12/13	12/14
Sales ($ mil.)	2.7%	15,317.0	15,341.0	14,256.0	15,136.0	17,021.0
Net income ($ mil.)	6.0%	1,957.0	1,923.0	1,911.0	1,908.0	2,469.0
Market value ($ mil.)	19.6%	23,031.6	26,969.8	30,651.2	37,929.7	47,086.5
Employees	(2.1%)	15,000	14,800	14,400	13,400	13,800

NEXTRADE HOLDINGS INC.

301 S. Missouri Ave.
Clearwater FL 33756
Phone: 727-446-6660
Fax: 727-441-8880
Web: www.nextrade.com

CEO: –
CFO: –
HR: –
FYE: December 31
Type: Private

What's next for NexTrade Holdings? The company sold the NexTrade electronic communications network (ECN) which provided electronic trading of Nasdaq securities to Citigroup in 2006 and since then has concentrated on becoming a holding company for various subsidiaries. It holds patents on expirationless options (XPOs) which as their name suggests are options on underlying assets such as equities bonds currencies and commodities and have no expiration date. The company also owns broker-dealer Anderen Capital which focuses on securities underwriting and wealth management. In addition NexTrade Holdings is one of the primary owners of Anderen Bank which has about five branches in the Tampa Bay area.

NFI INDUSTRIES INC.

71 W. Park Ave.	CEO: Sidney Brown
Vineland NJ 08360-3508	CFO: –
Phone: 856-691-7000	HR: –
Fax: 973-399-9696	FYE: December 31
Web: www.stuyvesantpress.com	Type: Private

A diversified transportation services company NFI Industries offers a full range of logistics distribution warehousing and related supply chain services to the retail beverage and food and grocery sectors among others across the US and Canada. Overall it maintains a fleet of about 2000 tractors and 7000 trailers. NFI also has more than 20 million sq. ft. of warehouse space and manages some 7 million sq. ft. of real estate. Established in 1932 by Israel Brown NFI is owned and run by members of the founding Brown family. It operates through about a dozen divisions.

NFINANSE INC.

OTC: NFSE

3923 Coconut Palm Dr. Ste. 107	CEO: Jerry R Welch
Tampa FL 33619	CFO: Raymond P Springer
Phone: 813-367-4400	HR: Lynette Kane
Fax: 256-386-0234	FYE: December 31
Web: www.johnsoncont.com	Type: Public

Through nFinanSe Card the company provides stored value cards or SVCs. It offers reloadable Discover-branded spending cards (for consumers without bank cards or credit cards) gift cards payroll cards and corporate reward cards; cards issued by nFinanSe bear a logo in the form of a Discover Financial Services hologram. Customers can purchase load and reload cards at more than 70000 locations that are part of the nFinanSe Network; most load stations are found inside Western Union and MoneyGram locations. Formerly named Morgan Beaumont the company has agreed to be purchased by AccountNow provider of general purpose reloadable prepaid cards in the direct-to-consumer sales channel.

NGAS RESOURCES INC.

120 Prosperous Place Ste. 201	CEO: –
Lexington KY 40509-1844	CFO: Michael P Windisch
Phone: 859-263-3948	HR: Clarence Smith
Fax: 859-263-4228	FYE: December 31
Web: www.ngas.com	Type: Subsidiary

In gas we trust could be the motto of NGAS Resources. The company searches for and produces gas in the Appalachian and Illinois basins. In 2010 NGAS Resources reported proved reserves of 63.1 billion cu. ft. of natural gas equivalent. In the Appalachian basin it holds more than 330000 net acres and stakes in about 1350 gross wells. Through partnerships the company also acts as a contract driller in its core areas. NGAS Resources owns and operates the gas gathering infrastructure for its Illinois Basin acreage and operates the gas gathering system for its Appalachian assets. To boost its Appalachian holdings in 2011 Magnum Hunter Resources acquired debt-laden NGAS Resources in a $98 million deal.

NGL ENERGY PARTNERS LP

NYS: NGL

6120 South Yale Avenue, Suite 805	CEO: H. Michael Krimbill
Tulsa, OK 74136	CFO: Atanas H Atanasov
Phone: 918 481-1119	HR: –
Fax: –	FYE: March 31
Web: www.nglenergypartners.com	Type: Public

NGL Energy Partners' is devoted to natural gas liquids (NGL) logistics crude oil logistics water services and retail propane. Its crude oil logistics segment (its largest) buys crude oil from producers and transports it for resale at pipeline injection points storage terminals barge loading facilities rail facilities refineries and other trade hubs. It also retails wholesales and stores propane and other natural gas liquids. Wholesale operations deliver propane to third-party storage and transportation facilities. Retail operations include leasing propane tanks and other equipment and propane delivery. The retail propane segment has a propane storage capacity of 10.8 million gallons.

	Annual Growth	03/11	03/12	03/13	03/14	03/15
Sales ($ mil.)	128.0%	622.2	1,310.5	4,417.8	9,699.3	16,802.1
Net income ($ mil.)	23.9%	12.7	7.9	48.2	48.8	29.9
Market value ($ mil.)	8.4%	–	2,141.4	2,794.9	3,899.3	2,725.3
Employees	72.1%	353	890	1,970	2,500	3,100

NHL ENTERPRISES INC.

1185 AVE OF THE AMERICAS	CEO: –
NEW YORK, NY 100362601	CFO: –
Phone: 212-789-2000	HR: Allison Winters
Fax: –	FYE: June 30
Web: www.nhl.com	Type: Private

Hockey is more than a cool sport for serious fans. The National Hockey League is one of the four major professional sports associations in North America boasting 30 professional ice hockey franchises in the US and Canada. The NHL governs the game sets and enforces rules regulates team ownership and collects licensing fees for merchandise. It also negotiates fees for national broadcasting rights. (Each team controls the rights to regional broadcasts.) In addition five minor and semi-pro hockey leagues also fly under the NHL banner. The league was organized in Canada in 1917.

	Annual Growth	06/01	06/02	06/05	06/06	06/09
Sales ($ mil.)	(15.9%)	–	249.7	35.2	17.4	74.4
Net income ($ mil.)		–	–	(1.8)	4.9	(1.3)
Market value ($ mil.)	–	–	–	–	–	–
Employees	–	–	–	–	–	200

NHS HUMAN SERVICES INC.

620 GERMANTOWN PIKE	CEO: M Joseph Rocks
LAFAYETTE HILL, PA 19444-1810	CFO: Kevin W McClure
Phone: 610-260-4600	HR: –
Fax: –	FYE: June 30
Web: www.nhsonline.org	Type: Private

Northwestern Human Services (operating as NHS Human Services) exists to lend a helping hand to humans throughout the Northeast. The organization primarily offers a variety of behavioral health care services that include mental health and drug and alcohol rehabilitation mental retardation services juvenile justice autism special education foster care and elder care. The not-for-profit organization provides programs for nearly 40000 adults and children at more than 675 facilities in more than half a dozen eastern US states. NHS' programs are offered through its specialty care facilities mobile clinics and on an independent case management basis.

	Annual Growth	06/06	06/07	06/08	06/10	06/11
Sales ($ mil.)	14.8%	–	288.4	311.5	28.9	501.3
Net income ($ mil.)	6.8%	–	8.7	13.2	0.7	11.4
Market value ($ mil.)	–	–	–	–	–	–
Employees	–	–	–	–	–	6,500

NIAGARA MOHAWK POWER CORPORATION

300 Erie Blvd. West
Syracuse NY 13202
Phone: 315-474-1511
Fax: 315-460-7041
Web: https://www1.nationalgridus.com

CEO: Kenneth Daly
CFO: –
HR: –
FYE: March 31
Type: Subsidiary

Niagara Mohawk Power (which does business as National Grid) distributes electricity to approximately 1.5 million customers and natural gas to 565000 customers in upstate New York. The company owns and operates power transmission and distribution lines; wholesale activities on its transmission grid are managed by the New York ISO. Niagara Mohawk Power is a provider of last resort for customers who do not choose an alternative supplier in New York's deregulated power market. Niagara Mohawk Power is a subsidiary of National Grid USA a unit of UK-based National Grid.

NIC INC.

NMS: EGOV

25501 West Valley Parkway, Suite 300
Olathe, KS 66061
Phone: 877 234-3468
Fax: –
Web: www.egov.com

CEO: –
CFO: Stephen M. (Steve) Kovzan
HR: Jennifer Holden
FYE: December 31
Type: Public

So people can do business with government agencies NIC helps government agencies plug in to the Internet. The company is a leading provider of outsourced Web portal services for federal state and local governments. It designs implements and operates websites under contracts with more than 3500 government agencies. NIC generates much of its revenue from transaction fees for such services as online license renewals and for providing data on motor vehicle titles and business licenses to insurance companies lenders and other authorized organizations.

	Annual Growth	12/10	12/11	12/12	12/13	12/14
Sales ($ mil.)	13.9%	161.5	180.9	211.1	249.3	272.1
Net income ($ mil.)	20.8%	18.4	22.9	26.3	32.0	39.1
Market value ($ mil.)	16.7%	634.1	869.2	1,067.1	1,624.1	1,174.8
Employees	8.2%	596	653	714	773	818

NICE-PAK PRODUCTS INC.

2 Nice-Pak Park
Orangeburg NY 10962-1376
Phone: 845-365-1700
Fax: 845-365-1729
Web: www.nicepak.com

CEO: Robert Julius
CFO: –
HR: –
FYE: June 30
Type: Private

Nice-Pak Products wipes up the competition. The company makes and markets premoistened wipes including baby wipes antibacterial towelettes cloths for cleaning lenses and removing makeup and wipes for surface cleaning and industrial uses. The company's brand names include Grime Boss Hygea Nice'n Clean PDI Sani-Cloth Tar-Off and Wet Nap. The company also offers custom-packaged towelettes for mass marketers and retailers. Arthur Julius founded the family-owned firm in 1957. His son Robert Julius is Nice-Pak's chairman.

NICHOLAS FINANCIAL INC.

NASDAQ: NICK

2454 McMullen Booth Rd. Bldg. C
Clearwater FL 33759
Phone: 727-726-0763
Fax: 727-726-2140
Web: www.nicholasfinancial.com

CEO: Ralph T Finkenbrink
CFO: Katie Macgillivary
HR: –
FYE: March 31
Type: Public

Nickel-less? No problem. Nicholas Financial can still get you behind the wheel of a car. The company buys subprime new and used car loans from some 1500 car dealers in the Southeast and Midwest. It conducts its automobile finance business through approximately 65 offices in about a dozen states. In addition to its indirect lending activities Nicholas Financial also offers and finances extended warranties roadside assistance plans and credit life accident and health insurance to its borrowers. The company also makes some direct consumer loans primarily to customers whose car loans it has bought and serviced.

NICKLOS DRILLING COMPANY

3355 W. Alabama St. Ste. 630
Houston TX 77098
Phone: 713-224-5959
Fax: 713-224-5993
Web: www.nicklosdrilling.com

CEO: James M Nicklos
CFO: –
HR: –
FYE: December 31
Type: Private

It's not by nickel-and-diming but by providing valuable oil field services that Nicklos Drilling makes its money. The company provides land and offshore contract drilling services in the Texas Gulf Coast Southeast Texas and Southwest Louisiana. Nicklos Drilling has four differently configured rigs capable of drilling in a depth range from 6500 feet depth maximum to 17000 feet maximum. The company is owned and managed by Texas oil industry veterans Jim Nicklos (whose previous oil contracting business had gone bankrupt in the mid-1980s) and Jack Blanton (a one-time VP of family-owned Scurlock Oil).

NIELSEN MOBILE INC.

101 Green St.
San Francisco CA 94111
Phone: 415-395-0500
Fax: 415-834-9222
Web: www.telephia.com

CEO: Sid Gorham
CFO: –
HR: –
FYE: December 31
Type: Subsidiary

Nielsen Mobile (formerly Telephia) provides market research and service quality data on the wireless telecommunications industry. It primarily serves more than 100 device makers retailers and service operators in the US Canada and Europe providing insight into the competitive landscape and areas of customer needs. Nielsen Mobile measures such areas as subscriber share network quality device share customer satisfaction and application usage. The company is owned by The Nielsen Company the #1 market research firm in the world.

NIEMANN FOODS INC.

1501 N. 12th St.
Quincy IL 62301
Phone: 217-221-5600
Fax: 217-221-5921
Web: www.discountfoods.com

CEO: Richard H Niemann
CFO: Christopher Niemann
HR: –
FYE: December 31
Type: Private

Niemann knows its midwestern food. Niemann Foods operates more than 80 supermarkets and convenience stores mostly under the Country Market Country Market Express Cub Foods and Save A Lot banners in Illinois Iowa and Missouri. Its Save-A-Lot stores offer a limited assortment of groceries at discount prices while Cub Foods and Country Market are conventional grocery stores. The regional grocery store operator is battling for market share in the Midwest with Hy-Vee and supercenter operator Wal-Mart Stores. The company also runs six pet stores and several hardware stores. The employee-owned family-run firm was founded in 1917 by brothers Ferd and Steve Niemann and is currently run by CEO Rich Niemann.

NIGHTINGALE-CONANT CORPORATION

6245 W. Howard St.
Niles IL 60714
Phone: 847-647-0300
Fax: 847-647-7145
Web: www.nightingale.com

CEO: –
CFO: –
HR: –
FYE: December 31
Type: Private

Long before Deepak Chopra and Tony Robbins showed us how to improve our lives Nightingale-Conant pioneered the publishing of self-development audio-tapes. Its Psychology of Winning produced in 1978 is one of the best selling audio self-improvement programs in history. The company markets its motivational tapes by mail order at business seminars and through resellers. Its recordings offer advice from business authors inspirational speakers and personal skill trainers and are grouped under categories such as personal development business strategy wealth building mind and body spiritual growth and sales training. Nightingale-Conant distributes the work of authors including Dale Carnegie and Zig Ziglar.

NII HOLDINGS INC.

NMS: NIHD

1875 Explorer Street, Suite 800
Reston, VA 20190
Phone: 703 390-5100
Fax: –
Web: www.nii.com

CEO: Steven M. Shindler
CFO: Juan R. Figuereo
HR: –
FYE: December 31
Type: Public

NII Holdings brings the Nextel brand to the two biggest countries in South America Brazil and Argentina. Based on Motorola Mobility's iDEN technology NII's service supports cellular phone numeric and text messaging two-way radio and Internet access. The company also sells mobile handsets most of which it buys from Motorola Mobility. It also offers BlackBerry devices. NII maintains a subscriber base of more than 9 million users targeting small to large business customers and consumers with medium to high usage patterns.

	Annual Growth	12/10	12/11	12/12	12/13	12/14
Sales ($ mil.)	(9.9%)	5,601.3	6,719.3	6,086.5	4,772.6	3,688.7
Net income ($ mil.)	–	341.1	198.8	(765.2)	(1,649.6)	(1,957.7)
Market value ($ mil.)	–	–	–	–	–	–
Employees	(7.7%)	13,500	15,300	16,100	13,600	9,800

NIKE INC

NYS: NKE

One Bowerman Drive
Beaverton, OR 97005-6453
Phone: 503 671-6453
Fax: –
Web: www.nike.com

CEO: Mark G. Parker
CFO: Andrew (Andy) Campion
HR: David J. Ayre
FYE: May 31
Type: Public

Fleet-of-footwear NIKE named for the Greek goddess of victory is the world's #1 shoe and apparel company. NIKE designs develops and sells a variety of products and services to help in playing basketball and soccer (football) as well as in running men's and women's training and other action sports. Under its namesake brand NIKE also markets sports-inspired products for children and various competitive and recreational activities such as golf tennis and walking and sportswear by Converse and Hurley. NIKE sells through more than 930-owned retail stores worldwide an e-commerce site and to thousands of retail accounts independent distributors and licensees.

	Annual Growth	05/11	05/12	05/13	05/14	05/15
Sales ($ mil.)	10.1%	20,862.0	24,128.0	25,313.0	27,799.0	30,601.0
Net income ($ mil.)	11.3%	2,133.0	2,223.0	2,485.0	2,693.0	3,273.0
Market value ($ mil.)	4.7%	144,747.3	185,420.5	105,685.2	131,823.7	174,262.4
Employees	13.3%	38,000	44,000	48,000	56,500	62,600

NIMBLE STORAGE INC

NYS: NMBL

211 River Oaks Parkway
San Jose, CA 95134
Phone: 408 432-9600
Fax: –
Web: www.nimblestorage.com

CEO: Suresh Vasudevan
CFO: Anup V. Singh
HR: Paul Whitney
FYE: January 31
Type: Public

In a mashup of Jack be nimble and Jumpin' Jack Flash Nimble Storage offers data storage systems that are a hybrid between a hard disk drive and a flash memory device. Its CS200 Series is designed for midsize IT organizations while its CS400 Series is geared for larger-scale deployments. The company even offers data analytics through its InfoSight service. Nimble Storage counts more than 2330 customers including cloud-based service providers government agencies and financial services health care manufacturing and technology companies. After launching its first product in 2010 Nimble Storage went public in 2013 and raised $168 million in its IPO. It plans to use the proceeds for general corporate purposes.

	Annual Growth	01/11	01/12	01/13	01/14	01/15
Sales ($ mil.)	241.1%	1.7	14.0	53.8	125.7	227.7
Net income ($ mil.)	–	(6.8)	(16.8)	(27.9)	(43.1)	(98.8)
Market value ($ mil.)	(48.1%)	–	–	–	3,293.7	1,709.0
Employees	26.0%	–	–	528	592	838

NINTENDO OF AMERICA INC.

4600 150th Ave. NE
Redmond WA 98052
Phone: 425-882-2040
Fax: 425-882-3585
Web: www.nintendo.com

CEO: –
CFO: –
HR: –
FYE: March 31
Type: Subsidiary

Good hand/eye coordination serves those who play Nintendo of America games well. Serving as the Western Hemisphere distribution headquarters for Japan's Nintendo the company makes the #1 home game console Wii (pronounced "we") which is motion controlled and able to access Netflix. It also makes the #1 handheld game console Nintendo DS which features two screens and intuitive touch controls. On those consoles users can access and play such classic games as "Mario Bros. Donkey Kong Pokemon" and Zelda. Nintendo of America is also well known for legacy systems NES and Game Boy. Nintendo of America serves the US Canada Mexico and Brazil.

NINYO & MOORE GEOTECHNICAL & ENVIRONMENTAL SCIENCES CONSULTANTS

5710 RUFFIN RD
SAN DIEGO, CA 921231013
Phone: 858-576-1000
Fax: –
Web: www.ninyoandmoore.com

CEO: Avram Ninyo
CFO: David Binns
HR: –
FYE: December 31
Type: Private

Need more engineering services than are immediately at your disposal? Ninyo & Moore provides geological and technical engineering and consulting services for public and private projects throughout the western US. Its offerings include earthquake and fault studies hydrogeologic and geologic hazard evaluations air quality services and environmental consultations for site developments. The company serves a variety of clients including school districts property developers transportation agencies and the military. Past projects include the Las Vegas monorail and the Emporium redevelopment project in San Francisco. Ninyo & Moore was founded in 1986 and today operates about a dozen offices.

	Annual Growth	12/09	12/10	12/11	12/12	12/13
Sales ($ mil.)	(1.1%)	–	52.7	55.0	54.2	50.9
Net income ($ mil.)	(52.1%)	–	–	4.0	3.0	0.9
Market value ($ mil.)	–	–	–	–	–	–
Employees	–	–	–	–	–	350

NIPPON EXPRESS USA INC.

590 Madison Ave. 24th Floor
New York NY 10022
Phone: 212-758-6100
Fax: 212-758-2595
Web: www.nipponexpressusa.com

CEO: Kenji Fujii
CFO: –
HR: –
FYE: March 31
Type: Subsidiary

Nippon Express USA helps its parent company Japan-based transportation giant Nippon Express move customers' cargo around the world. Nippon Express USA provides a variety of freight transportation services including customs brokerage freight forwarding logistics supply chain management and warehousing and distribution. (As a freight forwarder Nippon Express USA buys transportation capacity from carriers and resells it to customers.) Along with its freight transportation offerings Nippon Express USA works with its parent to facilitate international moving of household goods. Operating through about 140 offices the company expanded in 2012 through the acquisition of Associated Global Systems (AGS).

NISKA GAS STORAGE PARTNERS LLC

NYS: NKA

170 Radnor Chester Road, Suite 150
Radnor. PA 19087
Phone: 484 367-7432
Fax: 484 367-7780
Web: www.niskapartners.com

CEO: William H Shea Jr
CFO: Vance E Powers
HR: –
FYE: March 31
Type: Public

Niska Gas Storage Partners provides natural gas storage in North America. The company is a large independent owner and operator of natural gas storage facilities in California Oklahoma and Alberta Canada. It had total gas storage capacity of 204.5 billion cu. ft. in 2011. A small portion of that capacity is contracted from Natural Gas Pipeline Company of America whose pipeline connects the Gulf Coast to certain midwestern US markets. Customers include natural gas producers and marketers pipelines power generators financial institutions and municipalities. Niska's revenues come from multi-year long-term and fixed-fee short-term contracts.

	Annual Growth	03/11	03/12	03/13	03/14	03/15
Sales ($ mil.)	(19.1%)	230.1	268.6	140.7	207.4	98.3
Net income ($ mil.)	–	57.5	(165.8)	(42.7)	(8.8)	(344.3)
Market value ($ mil.)	(46.5%)	830.8	362.4	489.3	551.6	68.0
Employees	(0.6%)	129	130	133	128	126

NISOURCE INC. (HOLDING CO.)

NYS: NI

801 East 86th Avenue
Merrillville, IN 46410
Phone: 877 647-5990
Fax: –
Web: www.nisource.com

CEO: Joseph (Joe) Hamrock
CFO: DOnald Brown
HR: Robert D. (Rob) Campbell
FYE: December 31
Type: Public

NiSource is the main energy source for resourceful Americans living in the Midwest the South and New England. The company's utility subsidiaries distribute natural gas to about 3.8 million customers in seven states. NiSource also generates transmits and distributes power to some 460000 customers in 20 counties in its home state through its largest subsidiary Northern Indiana Public Service Company (NIPSCO). NiSource owned one of the largest natural gas transmission and underground storage systems in the US including a more than 15000-mile interstate pipeline system. However to become a pure play utility group it spun off this business in 2015.

	Annual Growth	12/10	12/11	12/12	12/13	12/14
Sales ($ mil.)	0.2%	6,422.0	6,019.1	5,061.2	5,657.3	6,470.6
Net income ($ mil.)	16.1%	292.0	299.1	416.1	532.1	530.0
Market value ($ mil.)	24.6%	5,568.6	7,524.9	7,866.2	10,391.3	13,406.3
Employees	4.3%	7,604	7,957	8,286	8,477	8,982

NISSAN FORKLIFT CORPORATION NORTH AMERICA

240 N. Prospect St.
Marengo IL 60152-3298
Phone: 815-568-0061
Fax: 815-568-0179
Web: www.nissanforklift.com

CEO: –
CFO: Tom Prusinski
HR: –
FYE: December 31
Type: Subsidiary

Pallets everywhere are given a lift by Nissan Forklift Corporation North America which as the name implies makes forklifts for the North American market. Products include more than 150 models of engine-driven and electric pallet stackers rider trucks tow tractors and other material handling equipment under the Nissan and Barrett brands. Its engine-powered vehicles include cushion and pneumatic lift trucks. The electric motor machinery include stackers tow tractors and pallet trucks. Nissan also has a line of narrow-aisle vehicles. The company is a unit of Nissan's North American operations.

NISSAN NORTH AMERICA INC.

1 Nissan Way
Franklin TN 37067
Phone: 615-725-1000
Fax: 615-725-3343
Web: www.nissanusa.com

CEO: Carlos Ghosn
CFO: –
HR: –
FYE: March 31
Type: Subsidiary

Nissan Motor gets where it's going in North America through Nissan North America. With plants in the US and Mexico Nissan North America designs engineers and produces vehicles under such popular models as Altima Maxima Pathfinder Frontier Murano Sentra Versa and Xterra. It also provides marketing financing distribution and services in Canada Guam Mexico Puerto Rico and the US and it oversees sales of Nissan's luxury Infiniti brand of cars in North America. Through Nissan Forklift the company distributes and sells Nissan's electric and gasoline-powered forklifts. Nissan North America was formed in 1990 to coordinate the company's US Mexican and Canadian operations.

NIXON PEABODY LLP

1300 Clinton Sq.
Rochester NY 14604
Phone: 585-263-1000
Fax: 585-263-1600
Web: www.nixonpeabody.com

CEO: –
CFO: –
HR: –
FYE: January 31
Type: Private - Partnershi

Nixon Peabody no relation to the former US president is a full-service law firm that has about 700 attorneys working in more than 20 major practice areas. Specialties include corporate law intellectual property litigation and representation of parties involved in private equity investments. Nixon Peabody operates from about 20 offices mainly in the northeast US and California. The firm also has four international offices. Nixon Peabody was formed through the 1999 merger of Nixon Hargrave Devans & Doyle and Peabody & Brown. Since then Nixon Peabody has grown by absorbing firms such as Sixbey Friedman Leedom & Ferguson and Hutchins Wheeler & Dittmar.

NL INDUSTRIES, INC.

NYS: NL

5430 LBJ Freeway, Suite 1700
Dallas, TX 75240-2697
Phone: 972 233-1700
Fax: –
Web: www.nl-ind.com

CEO: Robert D. Graham
CFO: Gregory M. (Greg) Swalwell
HR: –
FYE: December 31
Type: Public

NL Industries is looking to paint a bright future. The company owns 30% of Kronos Worldwide one of the world's largest suppliers of titanium dioxide (TiO2) which maximizes the whiteness opacity and brightness of paints plastics paper fibers and ceramics. Kronos produces more than 40 different grades of titanium dioxide. Majority-owned (87%) subsidiary CompX International makes components such as security products (locking systems) ball bearing slides and ergonomic computer support systems. Valhi which is 94%-owned by Contran Corporation in turn owns 83% of NL Industries. Through trusts billionaire Harold C. Simmons controls Contran Valhi and NL Industries.

	Annual Growth	12/10	12/11	12/12	12/13	12/14
Sales ($ mil.)	(6.4%)	135.3	138.8	83.2	92.0	103.8
Net income ($ mil.)	(20.2%)	70.4	81.7	74.5	(55.3)	28.5
Market value ($ mil.)	(6.3%)	543.2	631.3	557.3	544.2	418.6
Employees	(2.0%)	3,268	3,264	3,021	2,956	3,017

NMI HOLDINGS INC

NMS: NMIH

2100 Powell Street
Emeryville, CA 94608
Phone: 855 530-6642
Fax: –
Web: www.nationalmi.com

CEO: Bradley M. (Brad) Shuster
CFO: Glenn Farrell
HR: –
FYE: December 31
Type: Public

Think it's risky to take out a mortgage? Try giving one. NMI Holdings offers insurance to mortgage insurers. Through subsidiary National Mortgage Insurance or National MI the company is one of seven private mortgage insurers licensed to operate in the US. (Many others went out of business following the financial crisis of 2008.) Mortgage insurance protects lenders when borrowers default on their loans. National MI is licensed in 48 states and Washington DC. Led by former executives of the defunct mortgage insurer PMI Group NMI Holdings went public in 2013 raising $27 million. It raised $510 million in a private stock offering in 2012 and plans to use the proceeds to get its business off the ground.

	Annual Growth	12/10	12/11	12/12	12/13	12/14
Assets ($ mil.)	–	0.0	0.2	542.8	481.2	463.3
Net income ($ mil.)	–	0.0	(1.3)	(27.5)	(55.2)	(48.9)
Market value ($ mil.)	–	0.0	–	–	743.8	533.5
Employees	25.5%	–	–	120	141	189

NN, INC

NMS: NNBR

207 Mockingbird Lane
Johnson City, TN 37604
Phone: 423 434-8310
Fax: –
Web: www.nninc.com

CEO: Richard D. Holder
CFO: James H. Dorton
HR: –
FYE: December 31
Type: Public

Hardly an unknown or no name ("NN") supplier NN produces a slew of precision metal components and assemblies for a highly diverse global market. Operating through three manufacturing units NN makes precision steel balls and rollers for bearing makers; carmakers; drilling bit makers whose products extract water oil and gas and minerals; and OEMs of stainless steel valves and pumps. It also churns out precision bearing seals metal and plastic retainers for ball and roller bearings and molded plastic products for automotive electronic instrument and fluid control industries.

	Annual Growth	12/10	12/11	12/12	12/13	12/14
Sales ($ mil.)	7.5%	365.4	424.7	370.1	373.2	488.6
Net income ($ mil.)	6.4%	6.4	20.9	24.3	17.2	8.2
Market value ($ mil.)	13.6%	234.6	113.9	173.9	383.3	390.3
Employees	19.6%	2,065	1,895	1,781	1,861	4,220

NOBEL LEARNING COMMUNITIES INC.

1615 West Chester Pike Ste. 200
West Chester PA 19382-6233
Phone: 484-947-2000
Fax: 484-947-2004
Web: www.nobellearning.com

CEO: George H Bernstein
CFO: Thomas Frank
HR: –
FYE: June 30
Type: Private

This Nobel prizes a strong foundation built on education. Nobel Learning Communities operates more than 180 private schools across 15 states and the District of Columbia. These range from preschools (including six Montessori schools) and elementary schools to middle schools and private high schools. Operating under such brands as Paladin Academy Laurel Springs School and Houston Learning Academy Nobel's schools offer standard curriculum as well as programs for students with mild learning disabilities and online programs. Nobel's Links to Learning pre-K curriculum is designed to prepare children from ages six weeks to five years for school. Founded in 1984 Nobel Learning is owned by Leeds Equity Partners.

NOBILITY HOMES, INC.

NBB: NOBH

3741 S.W. 7th Street
Ocala, FL 34474
Phone: 352 732-5157
Fax: –
Web: www.nobilityhomes.com

CEO: Terry E Trexler
CFO: Thomas W Trexler
HR: –
FYE: October 31
Type: Public

Florida's prince of prefab Nobility Homes is a leading player in the state's competitive manufactured-home market. Nobility has built and sold about 50000 homes through about 20 retail Prestige Home Centers Majestic Homes retail sales centers and on a wholesale basis to independent dealers and residential communities. Nobility offers some 100 models that range in price from about $30000 to more than $100000 and in sizes from about 700 sq. ft. to 2650 sq. ft. The company also provides financing mortgage lending and brokerage and insurance services. Founder and president Terry Trexler and his family control nearly two-thirds of the company.

	Annual Growth	11/11	11/12	11/13	11/14*	10/15
Sales ($ mil.)	20.0%	13.4	15.8	18.5	21.2	27.8
Net income ($ mil.)	–	(5.5)	0.0	0.7	1.3	2.9
Market value ($ mil.)	22.1%	23.3	22.2	37.3	41.3	51.8
Employees	9.1%	91	89	97	110	129

*Fiscal year change

NOBLE ENERGY, INC.

NYS: NBL

1001 Noble Energy Way
Houston, TX 77070
Phone: 281 872-3100
Fax: 281 872-3111
Web: www.nobleenergyinc.com

CEO: David L. Stover
CFO: Kenneth M. (Ken) Fisher
HR: Lee Robison
FYE: December 31
Type: Public

Noble Energy prizes petroleum and has the reserves to prove it. Noble looks for oil and natural gas and produces and markets them in the US and internationally. US operations are focused on the Denver-Julesberg Basin and Marcellus Shale and the Gulf of Mexico. The company's international operations include onshore and offshore activities in the the Asia/Pacific region the Middle East the Mediterranean West Africa and the North Sea. In 2014 Noble reported proved reserves of about 1.4 billion barrels of oil equivalent. The company markets natural gas NGLs and oil.

	Annual Growth	12/10	12/11	12/12	12/13	12/14
Sales ($ mil.)	14.0%	3,022.0	3,763.0	4,223.0	5,015.0	5,101.0
Net income ($ mil.)	13.8%	725.0	453.0	1,027.0	978.0	1,214.0
Market value ($ mil.)	(13.8%)	31,392.8	34,423.4	37,103.9	24,839.3	17,297.4
Employees	11.5%	1,772	1,876	2,190	2,527	2,735

NOBLE ROMAN'S, INC.

NBB: NROM

One Virginia Avenue, Suite 300
Indianapolis, IN 46204
Phone: 317 634-3377
Fax: –
Web: www.nobleromans.com

CEO: A Scott Mobley
CFO: Paul W Mobley
HR: –
FYE: December 31
Type: Public

This patrician gives a thumbs-up to quick-service pizza. Noble Roman's operates a chain of about 820 franchised quick-service restaurants located mostly in high-traffic areas such as shopping malls college campuses and military bases. Operating primarily under the names Noble Roman's Pizza Noble Roman's Express and Noble Roman's Pizza & Subs the eateries offer a limited menu of pizzas pasta and sandwiches. Noble Roman's also has some restaurants operating under the Tuscano's Italian Style Subs brand as well as a self-service concept designed for convenience stores. The company's restaurants operate in about 45 states and in Canada Guam and Italy.

	Annual Growth	12/10	12/11	12/12	12/13	12/14
Sales ($ mil.)	2.1%	7.3	7.4	7.3	7.5	7.9
Net income ($ mil.)	50.5%	0.3	0.8	0.6	0.1	1.6
Market value ($ mil.)	19.9%	21.5	15.7	14.9	39.0	44.4
Employees	0.7%	35	38	32	34	36

NOBLIS INC.

3150 FAIRVIEW PARK DR
FALLS CHURCH, VA 220424504
Phone: 703-610-2000
Fax: –
Web: www.noblis.org

CEO: Amr A. ElSawy
CFO: Mark A. Simione
HR: David Webb
FYE: October 05
Type: Private

Noblis' noble pursuit is through its offering of science-related strategic and technology consulting services. The not-for-profit company which pledges to serve the public interest helps various government entities and other clients evaluate technology options and vendors as well as solve complex technical problems. Noblis provides strategic planning decision analysis and acquisition support services. The company addresses problems in areas such as criminal justice environment and energy health care homeland security public safety and transportation. Noblis has worked with such clients as the US Air Force Army Navy and Departments of Commerce and Defense.

	Annual Growth	10/10	10/11*	09/12	09/13*	10/14
Sales ($ mil.)	18.6%	–	151.1	199.4	200.7	252.1
Net income ($ mil.)	14.3%	–	–	12.8	10.1	16.8
Market value ($ mil.)	–	–	–	–	–	–
Employees	–	–	–	–	–	804

*Fiscal year change

NOCO ENERGY CORP.

2440 Sheridan Dr.
Tonawanda NY 14150
Phone: 716-614-6626
Fax: 716-833-4845
Web: www.noco.com

CEO: James D Newma
CFO: Michael L Bradley
HR: –
FYE: December 31
Type: Private

NOCO is loco for fuel. NOCO Energy distributes residential heating oil industrial lubricants gasoline and diesel fuel to customers located in five states in the Eastern US. Its NOCO Commercial and Industrial Fuels unit is Western New York's largest independent fuel supplier (with a 42-million gallon fuel terminal in Tonawanda). NOCO Lubricants provides lubricant and specialty chemical products. NOCO Express operates more than 30 gasoline and convenience stores primarily in Buffalo and Rochester. Through heating and cooling division NOCO Home Services the company sells installs and services air conditioning equipment and oil natural gas propane and electric heaters.

NOCOPI TECHNOLOGIES, INC.

NBB: NNUP

480 Shoemaker Road, Suite 104
King of Prussia, PA 19406
Phone: 610 834-9600
Fax: 610 834-7777
Web: www.nocopi.com

CEO: –
CFO: Rudolph A Lutterschmidt
HR: –
FYE: December 31
Type: Public

Nocopi Technologies dogs copycats. The company makes anti-counterfeiting and anti-diversion technologies that prevent the unauthorized photocopying of sensitive documents. Offerings include Copimark which allows information to be printed invisibly on certain areas of a document as well as document security products such as its line of printed forms containing areas that can't be copied legibly. Another Nocopi technology Rub-it & Color enables publishers to create children's activity books in which colors appear when a page is rubbed. The company also has a licensing agreement with Elmer's Products which incorporates Nocopi's technologies in its Giddy Up and Color Loco activity book products.

	Annual Growth	12/10	12/11	12/12	12/13	12/14
Sales ($ mil.)	8.8%	0.7	0.7	0.6	0.8	0.9
Net income ($ mil.)	–	(0.2)	(0.0)	(0.1)	0.0	0.0
Market value ($ mil.)	(31.7%)	2.3	3.2	1.1	0.9	0.5
Employees	0.0%	5	5	–	–	5

NON INVASIVE MONITORING SYSTEMS INC.

NBB: NIMU

4400 Biscayne Blvd., Suite 180
Miami, FL 33137
Phone: 305 575-4200
Fax: 305 575-4201
Web: www.nims-inc.com

CEO: Jane H Hsiao
CFO: James J Martin
HR: –
FYE: July 31
Type: Public

Non-Invasive Monitoring Systems (NIMS) believes being rocked in a cradle is good for grown-ups too. The company has developed a moving bed-style device that is intended to improve circulation and joint mobility and possibly to relieve minor aches and pains. Originally tagged as AT-101 the device was sold in Japan and the US until the FDA required the company to get regulatory approval for it. NIMS halted sales and marketing efforts on AT-101 and is seeking FDA approval for a similar but less costly device known as the Exer-Rest intended for home and clinic use.

	Annual Growth	07/10	07/11	07/12	07/13	07/14
Sales ($ mil.)	(61.9%)	0.6	0.7	0.3	0.1	0.0
Net income ($ mil.)	–	(1.6)	(1.4)	(0.6)	(0.5)	(0.4)
Market value ($ mil.)	(17.2%)	26.8	18.2	10.3	14.2	12.6
Employees	(36.1%)	6	2	1	1	1

NONPAREIL CORPORATION

40 N. 400 West
Blackfoot ID 83221-5632
Phone: 208-785-5880
Fax: 208-785-3656
Web: www.nonparl.com

CEO: Chris Abend
CFO: John Fullmer
HR: –
FYE: August 31
Type: Private

One potato two potato — you know how the rest of the ditty goes and so does Nonpareil. The company grows and ships fresh potatoes and manufactures value-added potato products such as hash browns mashed potatoes and potato flakes which it distributes to US foodservice operators. Nonpareil also supplies ingredients including flavor additives made from potatoes to other food manufacturers. The company's potatoes are grown on a 10000 acres in Nebraska and 3000 acres in Idaho. The Nonpareil Corporation was founded in 1946 by Harold and Robert Abend; it continues to be owned and managed by members of the Abend family.

NOODLES & CO.

NMS: NDLS

520 Zang Street, Suite D
Broomfield, CO 80021
Phone: 720 214-1900
Fax: –
Web: www.noodles.com

CEO: Kevin Reddy
CFO: Dave Boennighausen
HR: Erika Meszaros
FYE: December 30
Type: Public

Forty lashes with a wet you-know-what if you don't like what this restaurant company offers. Noodles & Company operates and franchises more than 385 quick-casual restaurants in 30 states that specialize in noodle entrees. Its menu items range in style from American to Asian to Mediterranean and include noodle and vegetable bowls soups and green salads with pasta. Founder Aaron Kennedy a former brand manager at PepsiCo who opened the first Noodles & Company location in Denver in 1995 owns the company with a group of private investors. In 2013 the company went public.

	Annual Growth	12/10*	01/12	01/13*	12/13	12/14
Sales ($ mil.)	16.3%	220.8	256.1	300.4	350.9	403.7
Net income ($ mil.)	48.1%	2.4	3.8	5.2	6.7	11.4
Market value ($ mil.)	(26.6%)	–	–	–	1,068.7	784.9
Employees	35.7%	–	–	7,000	8,200	9,500
						*Fiscal year change

NORANDA ALUMINUM HOLDING CORP

NBB: NORN Q

801 Crescent Centre Drive, Suite 600
Franklin, TN 37067
Phone: 615 771-5700
Fax: –
Web: www.norandaaluminum.com

CEO: Layle K. (Kip) Smith
CFO: Dale Boyles
HR: Edie Thompson
FYE: December 31
Type: Public

Noranda Aluminum succeeds by keeping its operations — and profits — all under the same corporate roof. The company a vertically integrated aluminum producer starts the process by producing bauxite in a Jamaican mining project refining it into alumina in a Louisiana smelter and then using the alumina to make primary aluminum metal products at its processing facility in Missouri and aluminum coils at four flat rolling facilities in the Southeast. Noranda's primary aluminum products include aluminum rods extruded billets and foundry ingots. The downstream business segment manufactures foil and light sheet metal. In 2016 the company filed for Chapter 11 bankruptcy protection.

	Annual Growth	12/10	12/11	12/12	12/13	12/14
Sales ($ mil.)	1.1%	1,294.9	1,559.8	1,394.9	1,343.5	1,355.1
Net income ($ mil.)	–	66.9	140.9	49.5	(47.6)	(26.6)
Market value ($ mil.)	(30.0%)	143.7	81.2	60.1	32.4	34.6
Employees	(9.6%)	2,400	2,500	2,500	2,350	1,600

NORDSON CORP.

NMS: NDSN

28601 Clemens Road
Westlake, OH 44145
Phone: 440 892-1580
Fax: –
Web: www.nordson.com

CEO: Michael F. Hilton
CFO: Gregory A. Thaxton
HR: Shelly M. Peet
FYE: October 31
Type: Public

When it comes to adhesion coating and spraying Nordson dispenses with admirable stick-to-it-ness. Its adhesive dispensing systems are used on a range of packaging paperboard and nonwoven products. A line of sealant systems bond and seal plastic metal and wood products. Nordson's spray systems apply powder paints and coatings to appliances and auto parts. The company also produces inspection systems for high-tech manufacturing. Nordson sells to the appliance automotive medical solar energy and semiconductor markets among others. About 70% of sales come from outside the US.

	Annual Growth	10/11	10/12	10/13	10/14	10/15
Sales ($ mil.)	8.2%	1,233.2	1,409.6	1,542.9	1,704.0	1,688.7
Net income ($ mil.)	(1.3%)	222.4	224.8	221.8	246.8	211.1
Market value ($ mil.)	11.3%	2,659.7	3,385.8	4,134.9	4,390.8	4,086.2
Employees	11.1%	4,094	5,361	5,801	5,966	6,232

NORDSTROM, INC.

NYS: JWN

1617 Sixth Avenue
Seattle, WA 98101
Phone: 206 628-2111
Fax: –
Web: www.nordstrom.com

CEO: Blake W. Nordstrom
CFO: Michael G. Koppel
HR: Chrstine Deputy
FYE: January 31
Type: Public

Service with a smile is a part of Nordstrom's corporate culture. One of the nation's largest upscale apparel and shoe retailers Nordstrom sells clothes shoes and accessories through more than 115 Nordstrom department stores and over 165 off-price outlet stores (Nordstrom Rack) in nearly 40 states and online. It also operates a pair of Jeffrey luxury boutiques a "Last Chance" clearance store online private sale site HauteLook and personalized clothing service Trunk Club. With its easy-return policy and touches such as thank-you notes from employees Nordstrom has earned a reputation for top-notch customer service. Nordstrom family members who own about 25% of the retailer's stock closely supervise the chain.

	Annual Growth	01/11	01/12*	02/13	02/14*	01/15
Sales ($ mil.)	8.6%	9,700.0	10,877.0	12,148.0	12,540.0	13,506.0
Net income ($ mil.)	4.1%	613.0	683.0	735.0	734.0	720.0
Market value ($ mil.)	16.8%	7,777.0	9,229.4	10,478.3	10,921.2	14,485.6
Employees	6.5%	52,000	56,500	61,000	62,500	67,000
						*Fiscal year change

NORFOLK SOUTHERN CORP.

NYS: NSC

Three Commercial Place
Norfolk, VA 23510-2191
Phone: 757 629-2680
Fax: –
Web: www.nscorp.com

CEO: James A. (Jim) Squires
CFO: Marta R. Stewart
HR: –
FYE: December 31
Type: Public

Transportation titan Norfolk Southern is the one big train that could. Its main subsidiary Norfolk Southern Railway transports freight over a network consisting of about 20000 route miles in 20-plus states in the eastern southeastern and Midwestern US and in Ontario and Quebec. The rail system is made up of more than 15000 route miles owned by Norfolk Southern and nearly 5000 route miles of trackage rights which allow the company to use tracks owned by other railroads. Norfolk Southern transports coal and general merchandise including automotive products and chemicals. In late 2015 the company rejected an unsolicited takeover by Canadian Pacific in a deal worth $37.8 billion.

	Annual Growth	12/11	12/12	12/13	12/14	12/15
Sales ($ mil.)	(1.5%)	11,172.0	11,040.0	11,245.0	11,624.0	10,511.0
Net income ($ mil.)	(5.1%)	1,916.0	1,749.0	1,910.0	2,000.0	1,556.0
Market value ($ mil.)	3.8%	21,697.3	18,415.6	27,644.3	32,641.3	25,190.5
Employees	0.1%	30,329	30,943	30,103	29,482	30,456

NORFOLK SOUTHERN RAILWAY COMPANY

3 Commercial Place
Norfolk VA 23510-2191
Phone: 757-629-2600
Fax: 757-664-5069
Web: www.nscorp.com

CEO: Charles W Moorman
CFO: –
HR: –
FYE: December 31
Type: Subsidiary

Norfolk Southern Railway is the main subsidiary of North American transportation provider Norfolk Southern. The rail company operates approximately 20000 route miles in 22 states in the eastern southeastern and midwestern US. It serves every major container port in the eastern US and also transports freight via interchange with other rail carriers to and from the rest of the country. Norfolk Southern Railway primarily carries different types of general merchandise as well as coal and intermodal shipment containers. With key markets in Kentucky Pennsylvania Virginia and West Virginia coal is the single largest commodity group that the railway carries by revenues.

NORFOLK STATE UNIVERSITY

700 PARK AVE STE 310
NORFOLK, VA 235048050
Phone: 757-823-8600
Fax: –
Web: www.nsu.edu

CEO: –
CFO: Marry Weaver
HR: –
FYE: June 30
Type: Private

Founded in 1935 during the Great Depression Norfolk State University (NSU) is one of the nation's largest predominately black institutions of higher education. NSU is a four-year state-supported Virginia university offering undergraduate degrees in about 30 disciplines. The school also offers more than 15 master's and three doctoral degree programs. NSU boasts an enrollment of 7000-plus students at its main campus and at its satellite centers in nearby Virginia cities Portsmouth and Virginia Beach. Some 6400 of students are undergraduates; the remainder are pursuing graduate degrees. Most of the degrees conferred by the school are in liberal arts followed by science and technology and business.

	Annual Growth	06/04	06/05	06/06	06/07	06/08
Sales ($ mil.)	(79.1%)	–	–	1,875.7	80.1	81.8
Net income ($ mil.)	13439.2%	–	–	0.0	25.9	7.4
Market value ($ mil.)	–	–	–	–	–	–
Employees	–	–	–	–	–	1,095

NORKUS ENTERPRISES INC.

505 RICHMOND AVE
POINT PLEASANT BEACH, NJ 087422552
Phone: 732-899-8485
Fax: –

CEO: –
CFO: –
HR: Jeff Lucas
FYE: April 25
Type: Private

They sell pasta shells by the Jersey sea shore. Norkus Enterprises operates grocery stores under the Foodtown and Super Foodtown banners in Monmouth County and Ocean County New Jersey. The regional grocery chain also offers online shopping and home delivery. It was founded when Francis Norkus opened his first grocery store called Table Talk in Freehold New Jersey in 1935. Norkus Enterprises is a member of the Foodtown Supermarket cooperative. The company also owns four Max's Beer Wine & Liquor stores located in New Jersey. In 2011 Norkus sold five of its six Foodtown stores — located in Freehold Township Manalapan Neptune City Point Pleasant Beach and Long Branch — to The Stop & Shop Supermarket Company.

	Annual Growth	04/05	04/06	04/07	04/08	04/09
Sales ($ mil.)	2.0%	–	148.6	153.2	157.7	157.6
Net income ($ mil.)	(17.0%)	–	–	0.9	1.1	0.6
Market value ($ mil.)	–	–	–	–	–	–
Employees	–	–	–	–	–	1,000

NORSE DAIRY SYSTEMS L.P.

1740 Joyce Ave.
Columbus OH 43216
Phone: 614-294-4931
Fax: 614-294-0750
Web: www.norse.com

CEO: –
CFO: –
HR: –
FYE: December 31
Type: Business Segment

Norse Dairy Systems (NDS) leaves its customers cold and that's the way they like it. The company (a division of Interbake Foods) caters to ice cream novelty manufacturers by providing manufacturing equipment that produces sandwiches cups cones and tubes. NDS makes an assortment of ice cream products including sandwich wafers cones crunch and cookie pieces and other baked ingredients. Its research and development team works with customers to create custom products. The company also manufactures packaging for sleeves novelty cups and tube treats. NDS invented the ice cream tube treat in 1960.

NORTECH SYSTEMS INC.

NAS: NSYS

7550 Meridian Circle N
Maple Grove, MN 55369
Phone: 952 345-2244
Fax: –

CEO: Michael J. Degen
CFO: Richard G. (Rich) Wasielewski
HR: Jami Thompson
FYE: December 31
Type: Public

If you design it Nortech will come. The company offers outsourced electronics and cable assembly manufacturing to a variety of industries such as aerospace automotive medical and military contracting. Products include wire harnesses printed circuit boards electronic subassemblies components and more. A bevy of services includes design testing prototyping and supply chain management. Most revenue comes from products following customer design specifications. Combining to account for nearly a quarter of the sales are two GE businesses: GE Healthcare (16%) and GE Transportation (7%); other customers have included Kodak Northrop Grumman Raytheon and SPX.

	Annual Growth	12/10	12/11	12/12	12/13	12/14
Sales ($ mil.)	2.9%	99.8	114.2	106.9	111.1	112.0
Net income ($ mil.)	14.8%	0.5	1.2	0.6	0.8	0.9
Market value ($ mil.)	8.4%	11.3	8.6	8.2	15.1	15.6
Employees	3.5%	709	807	717	777	813

NORTEK INC

NMS: NTK

500 Exchange Street
Providence, RI 02903-2699
Phone: 401 751-1600
Fax: –
Web: www.nortekinc.com

CEO: Michael J. Clarke
CFO: Almon C Hall
HR: –
FYE: December 31
Type: Public

Nortek delivers a breath of fresh air. The company makes and distributes residential and commercial air conditioning and heating systems (HVAC) residential ventilation products and home technology products. In addition to HVAC systems Nortek's wares include range hoods and other ventilation products indoor air-quality systems lighting controls and home entertainment and security system equipment. Products which are sold primarily in North America and Europe bear the Nortek name along with other brands including Broan-NuTone as well as such licensed names as Frigidaire and Maytag. Speaker brands include Niles SpeakerCraft and Xantech.

	Annual Growth	12/10	12/11	12/12	12/13	12/14
Sales ($ mil.)	7.6%	1,899.3	2,140.5	2,201.3	2,287.9	2,546.1
Net income ($ mil.)	–	(13.4)	(55.9)	9.5	(8.3)	(45.6)
Market value ($ mil.)	22.6%	585.1	425.2	1,076.8	1,212.6	1,322.0
Employees	4.2%	9,500	9,300	9,400	9,600	11,200

NORTH CAROLINA ELECTRIC MEMBERSHIP CORPORATION

3400 SUMNER BLVD	CEO: Joe Brannon
RALEIGH, NC 276162950	CFO: Lark James
Phone: 919-872-0800	HR: –
Fax: –	FYE: December 31
Web: www.ncemcs.com	Type: Private

It's a cooperative effort: North Carolina Electric Membership Corporation (NCEMC) generates and transmits electricity to the state's 26 electric cooperatives (more than 2.5 million people) in 93 of 100 North Carolina counties. The co-op owns more than 600 MW of generating capacity through four primarily natural gas peak load generators plus a 61.5% stake in Catawba Nuclear Station Unit 1 and a 31% stake in the Catawba Nuclear Station in South Carolina. It also buys power from Progress Energy American Electric Power and other for-profit utilities. NCEMC's member cooperatives serve more than 950000 metered businesses and homes in North Carolina. The wholesale co-op also operates an energy operations center.

	Annual Growth	12/04	12/05	12/06	12/07	12/08
Sales ($ mil.)	6.8%	–	–	–	942.8	1,006.5
Net income ($ mil.)	106.0%	–	–	–	3.0	6.1
Market value ($ mil.)	–	–	–	–	–	–
Employees	–	–	–	–	–	150

NORTH CAROLINA FARM BUREAU MUTUAL INSURANCE COMPANY INC.

5301 Glenwood Ave.	CEO: –
Raleigh NC 27611	CFO: Ronald Medeiros
Phone: 919-782-1705	HR: –
Fax: 919-783-3593	FYE: December 31
Web: www.ncfbins.com	Type: Private - Associatio

North Carolina Farm Bureau Mutual Insurance offers multiple lines of individual and commercial property/casualty insurance including auto homeowners farm liability and umbrella policies. The company provides insurance to more than 500000 members of the North Carolina Farm Bureau Federation a not-for-profit farm organization offering educational economic and public affairs services to the state's agricultural community. A network of some 900 affiliated agents sells the company's products from about 190 locations throughout the state. North Carolina Farm Bureau Mutual Insurance was founded in 1953. As a mutual company it is owned by its policyholders.

NORTH CASTLE PARTNERS L.L.C.

183 E. Putnam Ave.	CEO: –
Greenwich CT 06830	CFO: –
Phone: 203-862-3200	HR: –
Fax: 203-862-3270	FYE: December 31
Web: www.northcastlepartners.com	Type: Private

North Castle Partners is invested in your health especially if you're a baby boomer. The private equity firm owns interests in consumer-driven health beauty nutrition and fitness companies that provide a variety of products and services particularly for the growing 50-and-over demographic. It targets North American middle-market companies carrying out acquisitions growth capital infusions and leveraged buyouts. The hands-on investor often teams with management to grow its portfolio companies. North Castle's portfolio consists of interests in about a dozen companies including Red Door Spas (operator of the Elizabeth Arden-branded Red Door and Mario Tricoci salons) and Octane Fitness.

NORTH CENTRAL BANCSHARES INC.

NASDAQ: FFFD

825 Central Ave.	CEO: David M Bradley
Fort Dodge IA 50501	CFO: Jane M Funk
Phone: 515-576-7531	HR: –
Fax: 515-576-3398	FYE: December 31
Web: www.firstfederaliowa.com	Type: Public

North Central Bancshares is the holding company for First Federal Savings Bank of Iowa which serves north-central and southeastern portions of the Hawkeye State through about a dozen branches. Offering standard retail deposit products the bank uses funds gathered to write a variety of loans; residential and commercial mortgages account for about three-fourths of the company's loan portfolio. Subsidiaries of the bank offer insurance annuities title services and investment services. The company converted First Federal Savings from a federal thrift to a state-chartered commercial bank in 2011. Great Western Bancorporation is acquiring North Central Bancshares.

NORTH CENTRAL FARMERS ELEVATOR

12 5TH AVE	CEO: –
IPSWICH, SD 57451	CFO: –
Phone: 605-447-5803	HR: –
Fax: –	FYE: December 31
Web: www.ncfe.coop	Type: Private

North Central Farmers Elevator's mission is to give its members a lift. The full-service member-owned agricultural cooperative located in South Dakota offers farm-support goods and services including feed seed and other farm supplies along with agronomy energy and marketing services. In conjunction with LOL Farmland Feeds and South Dakota Wheat Growers North Central Farmers Elevator owns Dakotaland Feeds which makes and markets feed to producers. It also has a marketing alliance with South Dakota Oilseed Processors to sell its member/farmer's soybean crops. The coop's 21 locations serve more than 2500 producer-members in north central South Dakota and south central North Dakota.

	Annual Growth	12/03	12/04	12/05	12/06	12/07
Sales ($ mil.)	(50.3%)	–	–	1,140.7	135.1	281.5
Net income ($ mil.)	15571.1%	–	–	0.0	(1.2)	2.7
Market value ($ mil.)	–	–	–	–	–	–
Employees	–	–	–	–	–	200

NORTH DAKOTA MILL & ELEVATOR ASSOCIATION INC

1823 MILL RD	CEO: –
GRAND FORKS, ND 582031535	CFO: –
Phone: 701-795-7000	HR: –
Fax: –	FYE: June 30
	Type: Private

When bakeries need flour North Dakota Mill & Elevator rises to the occasion. The mill is a producer of wheat flour used specifically in breads and other baked goods like cookies and crackers. It processes more than 78000 bushels of wheat a day and ships most of its flour in bulk to wholesalers. It offers semolina flour as well as specialty products such as wholegrain wheat flour wheat germ and corn flour for tortillas. The mill also sells pancake mixes bread machine mixes and wholewheat all-purpose and bread flours under the Dakota Maid brand to consumers through its online store. Owned by the State of North Dakota it contributes 50% of its profits to the North Dakota State General Fund.

	Annual Growth	06/10	06/11	06/12	06/13	06/14
Sales ($ mil.)	3.9%	–	228.2	262.7	268.1	256.1
Net income ($ mil.)	56.2%	–	–	3.8	5.6	9.2
Market value ($ mil.)	–	–	–	–	–	–
Employees	–	–	–	–	–	120

NORTH DALLAS BANK & TRUST CO.

OTC: NODB

12900 Preston Rd.	CEO: Mike Shipman
Dallas TX 75230	CFO: –
Phone: 972-387-1300	HR: –
Fax: 972-387-2815	FYE: December 31
Web: www.ndbt.com	Type: Public

Like many a native Texan North Dallas Bank & Trust is proud to profess its heritage. The bank operates more than five branches in Dallas and the surrounding communities of Addison Frisco Las Colinas and Plano. Serving local businesses and consumers it offers standard deposit services such as checking and savings accounts CDs and IRAs as well as trust and financial management services. Commercial real estate loans and residential mortgages account for most of the bank's lending activities. It also originates various consumer and business loans. North Dallas Bank has been owned by basically the same group of investors since it was founded in 1961.

NORTH EUROPEAN OIL ROYALTY TRUST

NYS: NRT

Suite 19A, 43 West Front Street	CEO: –
Red Bank, NJ 07701	CFO: –
Phone: 732 741-4008	HR: –
Fax: 732 741-3140	FYE: October 31
Web: www.neort.com	Type: Public

North European Oil Royalty Trust isn't owned by the crowned oil barons of Europe. The passive fixed investment trust receives royalties based on its interests in natural gas (97% of revenues) oil and sulfur producing properties in the former state of Oldenburg and portions of northwest Germany. Royalties are generated by the sale of crude oil natural gas distillate and sulfur mined by Exxon Mobil Royal Dutch Shell and their subsidiaries; the trust then distributes the royalties to shareholders on a quarterly basis. As a grantor trust North European Oil is exempt from paying income taxes; shareholders however are not.

	Annual Growth	10/11	10/12	10/13	10/14	10/15
Sales ($ mil.)	(16.2%)	25.2	23.7	21.6	18.9	12.4
Net income ($ mil.)	(16.8%)	24.2	22.6	20.6	18.0	11.6
Market value ($ mil.)	(26.0%)	304.1	259.5	209.8	168.1	91.0
Employees	0.0%	2	2	2	2	2

NORTH MEMORIAL HEALTH CARE

3300 OAKDALE AVE N	CEO: Andy Cochrane
MINNEAPOLIS, MN 554222900	CFO: Todd Ostendorf
Phone: 763-520-5200	HR: –
Fax: –	FYE: December 31
Web: www.northmemorial.com	Type: Private

North Memorial Health Care seeks victory over illness in the Twin Cities. Established in 1939 as Victory Hospital the healthcare network is home to North Memorial Medical Center a 520-bed hospital that features a Level I trauma center and the Humphrey Cancer Center. The hospital also operates specialty centers for cardiovascular care orthopedics pediatrics and women's health as well as an emergency vehicle fleet of more than 100 ambulances and nearly 10 helicopters. The adjacent outpatient center provides oncology radiation and imaging services. North Memorial Health Care also has a network of primary and specialty care clinics in the Twin Cities region and it provides home health and hospice services.

	Annual Growth	12/05	12/06	12/09	12/12	12/13
Sales ($ mil.)	4.4%	–	544.3	605.5	566.0	735.7
Net income ($ mil.)	–	–	–	(17.4)	(4.6)	51.5
Market value ($ mil.)	–	–	–	–	–	–
Employees	–	–	–	–	–	5,180

NORTH MISSISSIPPI HEALTH SERVICES INC.

830 S GLOSTER ST	CEO: Shane Spees
TUPELO, MS 388014934	CFO: Joe Reppert
Phone: 662-377-3000	HR: –
Fax: –	FYE: September 30
Web: www.nmhs.net	Type: Private

North Mississippi Health Services (NMHS) isn't contained by its name: The health system also provides health care to residents of northwestern Alabama. NMHS includes half a dozen community hospitals including its flagship North Mississippi Medical Center in Tupelo. North Mississippi Medical Clinics a regional network of more than 30 primary and specialty clinics; and nursing homes. Combined the facilities have nearly 1000 beds designated for acute long term and nursing care. Specialty services include home health and long-term care inpatient and outpatient behavioral health and treatment centers for cancer and digestive disorders. NMHS also operates outpatient care and wellness clinics in the region.

	Annual Growth	09/10	09/11	09/12	09/13	09/14
Sales ($ mil.)	(2.3%)	–	834.7	852.5	735.3	779.4
Net income ($ mil.)	–	–	–	(3.1)	83.0	(14.4)
Market value ($ mil.)	–	–	–	–	–	–
Employees	–	–	–	–	–	6,000

NORTH MISSISSIPPI MEDICAL CENTER INC.

830 S GLOSTER ST	CEO: –
TUPELO, MS 388014934	CFO: –
Phone: 662-377-3000	HR: Rodger Brown
Fax: –	FYE: September 30
Web: www.nmhs.net	Type: Private

At North Mississippi Medical Center you might get some Mississippi Mud ice cream after your tonsils are removed. The full-service 650-bed regional referral hospital in Tupelo Mississippi is part of the North Mississippi Health Services system an affiliation of hospitals and clinics serving northern Mississippi northwestern Alabama and parts of Tennessee. It's the largest private not-for-profit hospital in Mississippi and the largest non-metropolitan hospital in America. Specialty services at the medical center include cancer treatment women's health care cardiology and behavioral health care. The hospital also operates a skilled-nursing facility and home health and hospice organizations.

	Annual Growth	09/09	09/10	09/11	09/12	09/13
Sales ($ mil.)	(2.8%)	–	586.0	614.2	620.8	537.6
Net income ($ mil.)	(28.3%)	–	–	4.8	(6.4)	2.5
Market value ($ mil.)	–	–	–	–	–	–
Employees	–	–	–	–	–	6,000

NORTH PACIFIC PAPER CORPORATION

3001 INDL WAY	CEO: –
LONGVIEW, WA 98632	CFO: –
Phone: 360-636-6400	HR: –
Fax: –	FYE: December 31
Web: –	Type: Private

The old adage "all the news fit to print" might not be possible without North Pacific Paper Corporation (NORPAC). The company a joint venture between Weyerhaeuser and Nippon Paper produces newsprint for newspaper publishers and commercial printers. NORPAC manufactures a variety of different paper grades including standard and lightweight newsprint and super- and ultra-lightweight stocks especially for the Japanese market. The company produces more than 250000 tons of newsprint annually at its manufacturing facility in Longview Washington. Its products are sent via truck and train to customers in the western US or are shipped by boat to customers in Japan.

	Annual Growth	12/04	12/05	12/06	12/07	12/08
Sales ($ mil.)	–	–	–	(2,040.0)	474.7	534.4
Net income ($ mil.)	24921.7%	–	–	0.0	(3.8)	22.2
Market value ($ mil.)	–	–	–	–	–	–
Employees	–	–	–	–	–	410

NORTH PARK UNIVERSITY

3225 W FOSTER AVE
CHICAGO, IL 606254895
Phone: 773-244-6200
Fax: –
Web: www.northpark.edu

CEO: –
CFO: –
HR: –
FYE: June 30
Type: Private

North Park University is a Christian university that is located on Chicago's north side and enrolls more than 3100 undergraduate and graduate students. The school specializes in liberal arts business the health sciences and education and also offers seminary degree programs. North Park offers more than 35 majors plus pre-professional programs like engineering law and medicine; more than 40 majors and programs in the liberal arts and sciences. Undergraduate classes average 22 students. Some 87% of North Park full time faculty hold earned PhD's or the highest degree in their field.

	Annual Growth	06/09	06/10	06/11	06/12	06/13
Sales ($ mil.)	(8.4%)	–	69.4	76.5	54.1	53.4
Net income ($ mil.)	(95.7%)	–	–	6.9	0.0	0.0
Market value ($ mil.)	–	–	–	–	–	–
Employees	–	–	–	–	–	375

NORTH SHORE UNIVERSITY HOSPITAL

300 COMMUNITY DR
MANHASSET, NY 11030-3816
Phone: 516-562-0100
Fax: –

CEO: –
CFO: –
HR: –
FYE: December 31
Type: Private

North Shore University Hospital (NSUH) knows you shouldn't have to leave the island for quality health care. The hospital has more than 800 beds devoted to adult and pediatric medicine rehabilitation stroke care women's health orthopedics urology wound healing dentistry and trauma emergency services among other areas. The Long Island hospital is home to specialist institutes for cancer care and cardiology. It also serves as a campus for the New York University School of Medicine the Hofstra North Shore-LIJ School of Medicine and other educational organizations. NSUH is part of the North Shore-Long Island Jewish Health System.

	Annual Growth	12/0-1	12/00	12/01	12/02	12/08
Sales ($ mil.)	5.5%	–	769.3	828.1	930.0	1,184.5
Net income ($ mil.)	–	–	21.9	5.7	42.7	(14.4)
Market value ($ mil.)	–	–	–	–	–	–
Employees	–	–	–	–	–	30,000

NORTH SHORE-LONG ISLAND JEWISH HEALTH SYSTEM

145 Community Dr.
Great Neck NY 11021
Phone: 516-465-8100
Fax: 516-465-8396
Web: www.northshorelij.com

CEO: Michael J Dowling
CFO: Robert Shapiro
HR: –
FYE: December 31
Type: Private - Not-for-Pr

This hospital system has a scope that stretches long beyond Long Island. North Shore-Long Island Jewish Health System (NS-LIJ) operates 16 hospitals in Long Island and New York's outer boroughs; several of these facilities are affiliated with regional medical schools including New York University and the Albert Einstein College of Medicine. The system has a mental health facility (Zucker Hillside Hospital) several long-term care facilities rehabilitation services and outpatient surgery centers. Other operations include home care and hospice services diagnostic laboratory facilities and emergency medical services.

NORTH VALLEY BANCORP (REDDING, CA)

NMS: NOVB

300 Park Marina Circle
Redding, CA 96001
Phone: 530 226-2900
Fax: –
Web: www.novb.com

CEO: –
CFO: –
HR: –
FYE: December 31
Type: Public

NVB wants to be the MVP of banks in Northern California. North Valley Bancorp is the holding company for North Valley Bank (NVB) which operates some two dozen branches in about 10 Northern California counties. The bank offers commercial and retail services such as checking savings money market and NOW accounts and certificates of deposit. Real estate loans dominate the bank's lending portfolio including commercial and residential mortgages and construction loans. NVB has an agreement with Essex National Securities which provides brokerage services and investment advice to the bank's customers.

	Annual Growth	12/08	12/09	12/10	12/11	12/12
Assets ($ mil.)	0.6%	879.6	884.4	884.9	905.0	902.3
Net income ($ mil.)	–	(1.8)	(25.9)	(6.2)	3.0	6.3
Market value ($ mil.)	39.6%	25.6	14.3	61.2	65.7	97.3
Employees	(6.9%)	437	341	346	334	329

NORTH WIND INC.

1425 HIGHAM ST
IDAHO FALLS, ID 834021513
Phone: 505-661-4290
Fax: –
Web: www.northwindinc.com

CEO: –
CFO: –
HR: –
FYE: December 31
Type: Private

The North wind doth blow and we shall have.... clean air and water. North Wind works to keep the air clean the ground fresh and the water clear in North America. The environmental consulting firm's services include site assessment soil and groundwater remediation geographic information system (GIS) data hazardous and nonhazardous waste management and project engineering and construction. North Wind has expanded by buying South Carolina-based Pinnacle Consulting Group which offers engineering environmental and information technology consulting services.

	Annual Growth	12/06	12/07	12/08	12/09	12/10
Sales ($ mil.)	(66.2%)	–	–	750.6	120.2	85.5
Net income ($ mil.)	146601.7%	–	–	0.0	6.3	4.3
Market value ($ mil.)	–	–	–	–	–	–
Employees	–	–	–	–	–	86

NORTHEAST BANCORP (ME)

NMS: NBN

500 Canal Street
Lewiston, ME 04240
Phone: 207 786-3245
Fax: –
Web: www.northeastbank.com

CEO: Richard Wayne
CFO: Brian W Shaughnessy
HR: –
FYE: June 30
Type: Public

Northeast Bancorp is the holding company for Northeast Bank which operates about a dozen branches in western and southern Maine. Founded in 1872 the bank offers standard retail services such as checking and savings accounts NOW and money market accounts CDs and trust services as well as financial planning and brokerage. Residential mortgages account for about a third of all loans; commercial mortgages and consumer loans each make up about 25%. The bank also writes business and construction loans. Newly created investment entity FHB Formation acquired a 60% stake in Northeast Bancorp in 2010. The deal brought in $16 million in capital. The 2011 sale of insurance agency Varney added another $8.4 million.

	Annual Growth	06/11	06/12	06/13	06/14	06/15
Assets ($ mil.)	9.3%	596.4	669.2	670.6	761.9	850.8
Net income ($ mil.)	(13.2%)	12.6	2.2	4.4	2.7	7.1
Market value ($ mil.)	(7.8%)	131.8	81.3	92.7	91.8	95.4
Employees	(6.2%)	247	209	227	195	191

NORTHEAST COMMUNITY BANCORP INC

NBB: NECB

325 Hamilton Avenue
White Plains, NY 10601
Phone: 914 684-2500
Fax: –

CEO: Kenneth A Martinek
CFO: Donald S Hom
HR: Donna Lockwood
FYE: December 31
Type: Public

Northeast Community Bancorp is the holding company for Northeast Community Bank which serves consumers and businesses in the New York metropolitan area and Massachusetts. Through about a half-dozen branches the thrift offers traditional deposit services like checking and savings accounts as well as a variety of lending products such as commercial and multi-family real estate loans home equity construction and secured loans. While its deposit services are confined to New York and Massachusetts it markets its loan products throughout the northeastern US. The bank offers investment and financial planning services through Hayden Wealth Management. Northeast Community Bank's roots date back to 1934.

	Annual Growth	12/10	12/11	12/12	12/13	12/14
Assets ($ mil.)	2.6%	466.0	489.3	444.2	458.2	515.4
Net income ($ mil.)	(2.4%)	1.9	2.4	(2.5)	1.1	1.7
Market value ($ mil.)	6.5%	69.1	69.2	65.0	89.0	89.0
Employees	1.9%	89	104	124	104	96

NORTHEAST HEALTH SYSTEMS INC.

85 HERRICK ST
BEVERLY, MA 019151790
Phone: 978-922-3000
Fax: –
Web: www.beverlyhospital.org

CEO: –
CFO: –
HR: Althea Lyons
FYE: September 30
Type: Private

If a particularly beastly Nor'easter wreaks havoc on your immune system you might want to turn to Northeast Health System (NHS) for a little TLC. The organization provides a continuum of health services to residents of Massachusetts' North Shore communities through its network of hospitals outpatient care facilities and behavioral health and senior care centers. NHS' hospitals include Addison Gilbert Hospital a 60-bed full-service acute care facility; the 60-bed BayRidge Hospital a mental health and drug rehab facility; and Beverly Hospital with more than 220 beds. The company is a part of the Lahey Health System.

	Annual Growth	09/07	09/08	09/09	09/10	09/11
Sales ($ mil.)	(49.9%)	–	–	1,733.6	0.1	434.8
Net income ($ mil.)	–	–	–	0.0	(0.6)	(12.6)
Market value ($ mil.)	–	–	–	–	–	–
Employees	–	–	–	–	–	2,300

NORTHEAST ILLINOIS REGIONAL COMMUTER RAILROAD CORPORATION

547 W. Jackson Blvd.
Chicago IL 60661
Phone: 312-322-6777
Fax: 630-324-3432
Web: www.fprs.com

CEO: –
CFO: Frank Racibozynski
HR: –
FYE: December 31
Type: Government-owned

Every weekday hundreds of thousands of passengers wend their way into and around the Windy City via the Northeast Illinois Regional Commuter Railroad better known as Metra. The company provides rail service in greater Chicago via 11 lines that branch out from the central business district. Portions of the Metra system's 500-plus miles of track are owned by the company; the rest is leased from freight railroads such as Union Pacific and Burlington Northern Santa Fe which also contract to operate some Metra trains. The system includes about 230 stations. Metra's board of directors is appointed by the City of Chicago and surrounding counties. The company is part of Illinois' Regional Transportation Authority.

NORTHEAST INDIANA BANCORP INC.

OTC: NIDB

648 North Jefferson Street
Huntington, IN 46750
Phone: 260 356-3311
Fax: 260 358-0035
Web: www.firstfedindiana.com

CEO: Michael S Zahn
CFO: Randy J Sizemore
HR: Lupka Baloski
FYE: December 31
Type: Public

Northeast Indiana Bancorp is the holding company for First Federal Savings Bank which operates three branches in Huntington and another in Warsaw. First Federal offers checking savings credit cards money market accounts CDs and health savings accounts. Its subsidiary Innovative Financial Services division offers investments financial planning and insurance to individuals and corporate clients can set up retirement plans for employees.

	Annual Growth	12/10	12/11	12/12	12/13	12/14
Assets ($ mil.)	1.9%	256.1	261.5	271.4	268.6	276.2
Net income ($ mil.)	11.7%	2.0	2.0	2.9	2.5	3.1
Market value ($ mil.)	18.9%	15.6	14.6	19.7	25.2	31.2
Employees	–	–	–	–	–	–

NORTHEASTERN SUPPLY INC.

8323 PULASKI HWY
BALTIMORE, MD 212372941
Phone: 410-574-0010
Fax: –
Web: www.northeastern.com

CEO: Stephen D Cook
CFO: –
HR: –
FYE: December 31
Type: Private

Northeastern Supply keeps its little corner of the world cozy. Through more than 30 locations in Delaware Maryland Pennsylvania Virginia and West Virginia the company distributes air conditioning heating plumbing ventilation and water system equipment along with fixtures and hardware to contractors and other building professionals. Major suppliers include American Standard Bradford White Delta Elkay Jacuzzi and Moen. Northeastern also offers online credit applications electronic funds transfers and e-mail invoicing to its customers. Founded in 1945 the company is owned by the family of president Steve Cook.

	Annual Growth	12/07	12/08	12/09	12/11	12/12
Sales ($ mil.)	(0.5%)	–	113.6	100.9	106.5	111.3
Net income ($ mil.)	(3.3%)	–	–	2.6	1.1	2.4
Market value ($ mil.)	–	–	–	–	–	–
Employees	–	–	–	–	–	285

NORTHERN ARIZONA HEALTHCARE CORPORATION

1200 N BEAVER ST
FLAGSTAFF, AZ 860013118
Phone: 928-779-3366
Fax: –
Web: www.flagstaffmedicalcenter.com

CEO: Barbara Dember
CFO: Gregory D Kuzma
HR: –
FYE: June 30
Type: Private

Northern Arizona Healthcare (NAH) is an integrated health care system serving residents of northern and central Arizona. It features two acute care hospitals: Flagstaff Medical Center (FMC) with about 270 beds; and Verde Valley Medical Center in Cottonwood with about 100 beds. NAH also operates several outpatient clinics in the area that provide emergency and primary care services as well as physical therapy cancer treatments and other services. It operates home health hospice and pharmacy divisions as well as a cardiovascular physician practice and a childhood obesity program. NAH serves more than 167000 patients annually and employs some 300 physicians.

	Annual Growth	06/04	06/05	06/09	06/10	06/11
Sales ($ mil.)	(27.6%)	–	372.3	49.4	50.3	53.7
Net income ($ mil.)	–	–	–	(0.6)	(0.6)	(0.8)
Market value ($ mil.)	–	–	–	–	–	–
Employees	–	–	–	–	–	2,500

NORTHERN INDIANA PUBLIC SERVICE COMPANY

801 E. 86th Ave.
Merrillville IN 46410
Phone: 877-647-5990
Fax: 610-366-4851
Web: www.lehighcement.com

CEO: –
CFO: Pete Disser
HR: –
FYE: December 31
Type: Subsidiary

Northern Indiana Public Service Company (NIPSCO) can shine a little light on the topic of Hoosiers. The largest subsidiary of utility holding company NiSource NIPSCO has more than 457000 electricity customers and more than 786000 natural gas customers. The utility has three coal-fired power plants with 2540 MW of generating capacity. On the power side of the business NIPSCO generates transmits and distributes electricity to the northern part of Indiana and engages in electric wholesale and transmission transactions. The company operates approximately 13000 miles of electric transmission and distribution lines and 16000 miles of gas mains.

NORTHERN OIL & GAS INC (NV)

ASE: NOG

315 Manitoba Avenue - Suite 200
Wayzata, MN 55391
Phone: 952 476-9800
Fax: –
Web: www.northernoil.com

CEO: Michael L. Reger
CFO: Thomas Stoelk
HR: –
FYE: December 31
Type: Public

The hydrocarbon-rich shale plays of the northern tier of US states are the main attraction for Northern Oil and Gas which explores for and produces oil and natural gas on properties in the northern US. The company keeps overhead and risk down by purchasing minority or non-operating interests in producing oil and gas projects. With leaseholds on more than 171130 acres in the Williston Basin (the Bakken and Three Forks oil and gas fields in North Dakota and Montana) the company in 2012 reported proved reserves of 67.6 million barrels of oil equivalent.

	Annual Growth	12/10	12/11	12/12	12/13	12/14
Sales ($ mil.)	91.2%	44.6	149.4	311.6	335.8	595.0
Net income ($ mil.)	120.6%	6.9	40.6	72.3	53.1	163.7
Market value ($ mil.)	(32.5%)	1,661.6	1,464.4	1,027.1	920.3	345.0
Employees	20.2%	11	19	19	20	23

NORTHERN STATES FINANCIAL CORP. (WAUKEGAN, IL)

NBB: NSFC

1601 North Lewis Avenue
Waukegan, IL 60085
Phone: 847 244-6000
Fax: 847 244-7853
Web: www.bankofwaukegan.com

CEO: Scott Yelvington
CFO: Steven J Neudecker
HR: –
FYE: December 31
Type: Public

Northern States Financial is the holding company for NorStates Bank which serves individuals and businesses in northeastern Illinois and southeastern Wisconsin through around 10 branches. It provides retail services like savings checking money market accounts CDs and IRAs. The company uses deposits to originate commercial mortgages (accounting for about half of its portfolio) as well as residential mortgages commercial loans construction loans and consumer loans. NorStates Bank was founded in 2005 when Northern States merged its Bank of Waukegan and First State Bank of Round Lake (founded in 1949 and acquired in 2004) subsidiaries.

	Annual Growth	12/08	12/09	12/10	12/11	12/12
Assets ($ mil.)	(10.4%)	640.7	622.3	531.7	463.0	413.3
Net income ($ mil.)	–	(9.3)	(35.6)	(6.4)	(6.7)	(12.6)
Market value ($ mil.)	(37.5%)	17.0	18.9	7.0	3.8	2.6
Employees	(5.8%)	145	137	129	125	114

NORTHERN TECHNOLOGIES INTERNATIONAL CORP.

NMS: NTIC

4201 Woodland Road, P.O. Box 69
Circle Pines, MN 55014
Phone: 763 225-6600
Fax: –
Web: www.ntic.com

CEO: G Patrick Lynch
CFO: David Bonczek
HR: –
FYE: August 31
Type: Public

Ze rust — it must stop! Northern Technologies International (NTI) keeps rust away with its proprietary corrosion-inhibiting packaging. Its ZERUST product line features special packaging that emits corrosion-inhibiting molecules and compounds; the packaging comes in films and bags dunnage trays and bins vapor capsules and pipe strips for residue-free protection of pipes thermal spray coatings and cathodic protection technologies. NTI's customers include automotive electronics power generation and metal processing firms. Northern Technologies International makes about three-quarters of its sales in the US.

	Annual Growth	08/11	08/12	08/13	08/14	08/15
Sales ($ mil.)	11.6%	19.5	22.8	22.5	26.8	30.3
Net income ($ mil.)	(17.7%)	3.9	3.4	3.4	4.1	1.8
Market value ($ mil.)	(1.4%)	74.7	46.5	67.7	94.0	70.7
Employees	15.1%	70	67	70	91	123

NORTHERN TIER ENERGY INC.

NYSE: NTI

38C Grove St. Ste. 100
Ridgefield CT 06877
Phone: 203-244-6550
Fax: 203-431-7672
Web: www.ntenergy.com

CEO: David Lamp
CFO: –
HR: Christine Carnicelli
FYE: December 31
Type: Private

Northern Tier Energy will make your gas and sell it too. The company formed in late 2010 owns one of only two oil refineries in Minnesota and about 230 SuperAmerica gas stations across Minnesota and Wisconsin. Its oil refinery produces 74000 barrels per day of gasoline diesel jet fuel and asphalt. The company also owns storage and transportation assets including terminals storage tanks rail loading and unloading facilities and a dock on the Mississippi River. In addition Northern Tier Energy owns a 17% stake in the 300-mile Minnesota Pipeline (Koch Industries owns the rest) that transports crude oil to its refinery. The company went public with a $200 million IPO in 2012.

NORTHERN TIER ENERGY LP

NYS: NTI

1250 W. Washington Street, Suite 300
Tempe, AZ 85281
Phone: 602 302-5450
Fax: –
Web: www.ntenergy.com

CEO: David L. (Dave) Lamp
CFO: Karen Davis
HR: –
FYE: December 31
Type: Public

Northern Tier Energy makes gasoline and sells it too. The company owns one of only two oil refineries in Minnesota and more than 260 SuperAmerica gas stations across Minnesota and Wisconsin. Its oil refinery produces 97800 barrels per day of gasoline diesel jet fuel and asphalt. The company also owns storage and transportation assets including terminals storage tanks rail loading and unloading facilities and a dock on the Mississippi River. In addition Northern Tier Energy owns a 17% stake in the 300-mile Minnesota Pipeline (Koch Industries owns the rest) that transports crude oil to its refinery.

	Annual Growth	12/10	12/11	12/12	12/13	12/14
Sales ($ mil.)	100.3%	344.9	4,280.8	4,653.9	4,979.2	5,556.0
Net income ($ mil.)	76.7%	24.8	28.3	197.6	231.1	241.6
Market value ($ mil.)	(6.7%)	–	–	2,358.6	2,280.7	2,052.7
Employees	3.4%	–	2,667	2,893	2,896	2,950

NORTHERN TRUST CORP.

NMS: NTRS

50 South LaSalle Street
Chicago, IL 60603
Phone: 312 630-6000
Fax: –
Web: www.northerntrust.com

CEO: Frederick H. (Rick) Waddell
CFO: Stephen B. (Biff) Bowman
HR: S. Gillian Pembleton
FYE: December 31
Type: Public

Northern Trust Corporation works to keep its clients' trust. Founded in 1889 flagship subsidiary The Northern Trust Company and other units bearing the Northern Trust name offer banking and trust services brokerage asset servicing securities lending and proprietary mutual funds (the Northern Funds). The firm provides its services to institutional clients and affluent individuals from more than 90 offices in nearly 20 states and more than 15 countries. Operating through two main segments — Corporate and Institutional Services (C&IS) and Wealth Management — Northern Trust has more than $6 trillion of assets under custody and some $960 billion under management.

	Annual Growth	12/10	12/11	12/12	12/13	12/14
Assets ($ mil.)	7.0%	83,843.9	100,223.7	97,463.8	102,947.3	109,946.5
Net income ($ mil.)	4.9%	669.5	603.6	687.3	731.3	811.8
Market value ($ mil.)	5.0%	12,932.2	9,256.3	11,706.9	14,444.6	15,730.5
Employees	4.7%	12,800	14,100	14,200	14,800	15,400

NORTHERN VIRGINIA ELECTRIC COOPERATIVE

10323 LOMOND DR
MANASSAS, VA 201093113
Phone: 703-335-0500
Fax: –
Web: www.novec.com

CEO: –
CFO: –
HR: –
FYE: December 31
Type: Private

NOVEC is no novice when it comes to electricity distribution. Northern Virginia Electric Cooperative (NOVEC) is a member-owned not-for profit utility that serves more than 150000 residential commercial industrial and government customers in a 651-sq. ml. service area in northern Virginia. NOVEC which has more than 6790 miles of power lines receives its power supply from the PJM Interconnection marketplace. The company also markets natural gas to retail customers in Virginia and Maryland through its NOVEC Energy Solutions unit. Subsidiary NOVEC Solutions sells gas and electric water heaters and other energy appliances and provides optical data networking service for large businesses and government agencies.

	Annual Growth	12/01	12/02	12/08	12/09	12/13
Sales ($ mil.)	4.9%	–	234.3	397.3	419.4	397.0
Net income ($ mil.)	–	–	–	0.0	51.0	23.9
Market value ($ mil.)	–	–	–	–	–	–
Employees	–	–	–	–	–	275

NORTHFIELD BANCORP INC.

NASDAQ: NFBK

581 Main St. Suite 810
Woodbridge NJ 07095
Phone: 732-499-7200
Fax: +86-755-8298-1111
Web: www.visionchina.cn

CEO: John W Alexander
CFO: William R Jacobs
HR: –
FYE: December 31
Type: Public

Northfield Bancorp is the holding company for Northfield Bank which offers checking savings and retirement accounts; CDs; mortgage and home equity loans; life insurance; and credit cards. Its commercial offerings include checking and money market accounts commercial lending and business credit cards. Founded in 1887 Northfield Bank operates some 20 branches in New York and New Jersey. It added a pair of branches in New Jersey through the FDIC-assisted transaction of First State Bank in 2011. And in late 2012 Northfield Bancorp expanded its presence in Brooklyn through its acquisition of Flatbush Federal Bancorp.

NORTHMARQ CAPITAL LLC

3500 American Blvd. W. Ste. 500
Minneapolis MN 55431
Phone: 952-356-0100
Fax: 952-356-0088
Web: www.northmarq.com

CEO: Edward Padilla
CFO: –
HR: –
FYE: December 31
Type: Subsidiary

NorthMarq Capital helps investors make their marq in real estate. The firm provides investment banking brokerage property management construction management and financing services for commercial real estate owners and investors. Operating from more than 30 offices throughout the US NorthMarq offers a variety of transactions including fixed- and variable-rate mortgage bridge loans and mezzanine debt. The company services more than $35 billion worth of loans on behalf of institutional investors. It also manages some 50 million sq. ft. of commercial space. NorthMarq Capital was originally founded in the 1950s as Northland Mortgage. The company is owned by the Pohlad family through Marquette Financial.

NORTHRIM BANCCORP INC

NMS: NRIM

3111 C Street
Anchorage, AK 99503
Phone: 907 562-0062
Fax: –

CEO: Joseph M. Beedle
CFO: Latosha M Frye
HR: –
FYE: December 31
Type: Public

Can you get banking services at the north rim of the world? Of course! Northrim BanCorp formed in 2001 to be the holding company for Northrim Bank provides a full range of commercial and retail banking services and products through some 10 banking offices in Alaska's Anchorage Fairbanks North Star and Matanuska Susitna counties. Division offices that provide short-term capital to customers also are located in Washington and Oregon. The bank offers standard deposit products including checking savings and money market accounts; CDs; and IRAs. It uses funds from deposits to write commercial loans (40% of loan portfolio) and real estate term loans (nearly 35%) as well as construction and consumer loans.

	Annual Growth	12/10	12/11	12/12	12/13	12/14
Assets ($ mil.)	8.3%	1,054.5	1,085.3	1,160.1	1,215.0	1,449.3
Net income ($ mil.)	17.7%	9.1	11.4	12.9	12.3	17.4
Market value ($ mil.)	8.0%	132.4	120.0	155.2	179.9	179.9
Employees	12.3%	268	260	245	269	426

NORTHROP GRUMMAN CORP

NYS: NOC

2980 Fairview Park Drive
Falls Church, VA 22042
Phone: 703 280-2900
Fax: –
Web: www.northropgrumman.com

CEO: Wesley G. (Wes) Bush
CFO: Kenneth L. Beddingfield
HR: Heidi Hendrix
FYE: December 31
Type: Public

Northrop Grumman defends its high place in the defense sector. As one of the world's top military contractors (behind Lockheed Martin and Boeing) the company operates through four business sectors: Aerospace Systems (aircraft spacecraft laser systems electronic subsystems); Electronic Systems (radar sensors chemical detection countermeasure systems); Information Systems (C4ISR or command control communications computers intelligence surveillance reconnaissance); and Technical Services (systems support training and simulation). The US government represents most of Northrop Grumman's sales.

	Annual Growth	12/11	12/12	12/13	12/14	12/15
Sales ($ mil.)	(2.9%)	26,412.0	25,218.0	24,661.0	23,979.0	23,526.0
Net income ($ mil.)	(1.5%)	2,118.0	1,978.0	1,952.0	2,069.0	1,990.0
Market value ($ mil.)	34.0%	10,602.6	12,252.5	20,779.1	26,722.3	34,231.8
Employees	(2.7%)	72,500	68,100	65,300	64,300	65,000

NORTHSHORE UNIVERSITY HEALTHSYSTEM

1301 CENTRAL ST
EVANSTON, IL 602011613
Phone: 847-570-5295
Fax: –
Web: www.northshore.org

CEO: Mark R Neaman
CFO: Gary Weiss
HR: –
FYE: September 30
Type: Private

NorthShore University HealthSystem provides care to residents of Chicago's north side and its suburbs. The health system operates hospitals a home care organization and a Medical Group with hundreds of primary and specialty care physicians. With about 355 beds the organization's flagship Evanston Hospital has teaching and research programs as well as capabilities for trauma cancer cardiology and women's health care. The system also includes Glenbrook Hospital (about 175 beds) while Highland Park Hospital (150 beds) and Skokie Hospital (more than 155 beds). The health care system is affiliated with the University of Chicago Pritzker School of Medicine.

	Annual Growth	09/03	09/04	09/05	09/08	09/09
Sales ($ mil.)	1.3%	–	1,015.7	1,061.0	26.2	1,085.3
Net income ($ mil.)	–	–	–	64.1	0.1	(71.4)
Market value ($ mil.)	–	–	–	–	–	–
Employees	–	–	–	–	–	9,000

NORTHSIDE HOSPITAL INC.

1000 JOHNSON FY RD NE
ATLANTA, GA 303421611
Phone: 404-851-8000
Fax: –
Web: www.northside.com

CEO: Robert T Quattrocchi
CFO: Debbie Mitcham
HR: Renee Ruffin
FYE: September 30
Type: Private

Northside Hospital is no one-trick pony — it actually operates three hospitals serving Atlanta and surrounding areas. Also known as the Northside Healthcare Delivery System the Northside Hospital network includes some 840 licensed beds and more than 2500 physicians on multiple campuses with a host of outpatient health facilities including physician office parks and specialized cancer centers. All of Northside's hospitals are full-service acute-care facilities that provide specialty care including cancer care surgery radiology and women's health. Northside Hospital opened in 1970.

	Annual Growth	09/07	09/08	09/09	09/12	09/13
Sales ($ mil.)	6.0%	–	938.7	1,002.4	829.2	1,253.5
Net income ($ mil.)	91.0%	–	–	8.2	60.7	109.1
Market value ($ mil.)	–	–	–	–	–	–
Employees	–	–	–	–	–	8,000

NORTHSTAR AEROSPACE INC.

TORONTO: NAS

6006 W. 73rd St.
Bedford Park IL 60638
Phone: 708-728-2000
Fax: 708-728-2009
Web: www.nsaero.com

CEO: –
CFO: –
HR: –
FYE: December 31
Type: Private

If you're sighting this Northstar you're probably an aerospace mechanic. Northstar Aerospace manufactures complex machined components for airplanes and helicopters. Primary products include helicopter transmissions helicopter rotor heads and shafts accessory gearboxes and components for auxiliary power units. Northstar also provides machining and fabrication services and maintenance repair and overhaul services (MRO). Clients include Boeing Sikorsky GE Aviation and Rolls-Royce. Northstar Aerospace voluntarily filed for Chapter 11 bankruptcy protection in 2012 and was acquired by affiliates of private equity firm Wynnchurch Capital for $70 million.

NORTHSTAR GROUP SERVICES INC.

150 W 30TH ST FL 8
NEW YORK, NY 100014151
Phone: 212-951-3660
Fax: –
Web: www.lviservices.com

CEO: Scott E. State
CFO: Paul S. Cutrone
HR: –
FYE: December 31
Type: Private

Asbestos lead-based paint nuclear materials and toxic mold don't scare LVI Services one of the top environmental contractors in the US with more than 30 offices across the country. The privately-held company provides integrated facility services such as remediation of hazardous materials decontamination and demolition. It caters to clients in a wide range of business segments from hotels and retail to commercial industrial and institutional. It also serves government and education segments. Customers have included AT&T IBM Marriott Prudential and Raytheon.

	Annual Growth	12/08	12/09	12/10	12/11	12/12
Sales ($ mil.)	(49.5%)	–	–	1,589.1	339.1	404.9
Net income ($ mil.)	11626.6%	–	–	0.0	(6.3)	7.7
Market value ($ mil.)	–	–	–	–	–	–
Employees	–	–	–	–	–	3,500

NORTHSTAR REALTY FINANCE CORP

NYS: NRF

399 Park Avenue, 18th Floor
New York, NY 10022
Phone: 212 547-2600
Fax: –
Web: www.nrfc.com

CEO: –
CFO: Scott A. Berry
HR: –
FYE: December 31
Type: Public

Let NorthStar guide you to higher dividends. A real estate investment trust (REIT) NorthStar Realty manages a portfolio of commercial properties related securities and debt secured by commercial real estate. It largely funds its investments by issuing collateralized debt obligations (CDOs) under its N-Star brand. The REIT also manages and controls a fund it created in 2007 through which it conducts its securities investment activities; assets include mortgage-backed securities and fixed-income securities and equity issued by REITs. NorthStar invests in real estate throughout the US — mostly manufactured housing communities and healthcare properties that together account for more than 70% of its holdings.

	Annual Growth	12/10	12/11	12/12	12/13	12/14
Sales ($ mil.)	21.2%	453.7	527.8	504.7	596.6	978.4
Net income ($ mil.)	–	(389.6)	(242.5)	(273.1)	(87.9)	(321.1)
Market value ($ mil.)	38.7%	716.5	719.5	1,061.9	2,028.8	2,651.8
Employees	(28.3%)	91	107	124	155	24

NORTHWAY FINANCIAL, INC.

NBB: NWYF

9 Main Street
Berlin, NH 03570
Phone: 603 752-1171
Fax: –

CEO: William J Woodward
CFO: Richard P Orsillo
HR: Mark C Bechtold
FYE: December 31
Type: Public

For managing finances way up north try Northway Financial. Northway Financial is the holding company for Northway Bank which operates about 20 branches in New Hampshire. The community-oriented bank serves individuals and local business customers by offering deposit products such as checking and savings accounts NOW and money market accounts CDs and IRAs. Lending activities mainly consist of residential and commercial mortgages which together account for about three-quarters of the company's loan portfolio; other offerings include construction business and consumer loans. The bank offers investments insurance and retirement services through an agreement with a third-party provider Infinex Financial.

	Annual Growth	12/04	12/05	12/06	12/13	12/14
Assets ($ mil.)	3.8%	638.4	632.7	650.9	898.3	925.7
Net income ($ mil.)	8.8%	3.4	2.7	3.2	7.2	7.9
Market value ($ mil.)	(5.0%)	93.9	95.1	92.2	48.2	56.3
Employees	0.6%	246	234	249	–	–

NORTHWEST BANCORPORATION, INC.

NBB: NBCT

421 W. Riverside Ave.
Spokane, WA 99201-0403
Phone: 509 456-8888
Fax: –
Web: www.inb.com

CEO: Randall L Fewel
CFO: Holly A Poquette
HR: Janelle Parenteau
FYE: December 31
Type: Public

Who needs a map? Northwest Bancorporation is the holding company for Inland Northwest Bank which is proud to give directions within its name. The bank has about a dozen locations in eastern Washington and the Idaho panhandle that serve individuals professionals and small to midsized businesses. It offers standard services such as checking and savings accounts money market accounts CDs and credit cards. The bank focuses on commercial lending mainly commercial mortgages construction loans business operating loans and lines of credit. It also writes residential mortgage auto home improvement and land loans.

	Annual Growth	12/10	12/11	12/12	12/13	12/14
Assets ($ mil.)	1.7%	394.6	385.7	398.9	394.2	421.8
Net income ($ mil.)	36.3%	0.9	(0.7)	1.4	3.3	3.3
Market value ($ mil.)	15.3%	20.4	20.8	22.9	31.0	36.0
Employees	(0.8%)	121	125	120	–	117

NORTHWEST BANCSHARES INC.

NASDAQ: NWBI

100 Liberty St.
Warren PA 16365
Phone: 814-726-2140
Fax: 814-728-7716
Web: www.northwestsavingsbank.com

CEO: William J Wagner
CFO: William W Harvey Jr
HR: –
FYE: December 31
Type: Public

Northwest Bancshares is the holding company for Northwest Savings Bank which operates about 170 branches mostly in Pennsylvania but also in northern Maryland western New York and eastern Ohio. Founded in 1896 the bank offers checking and savings accounts CDs credit cards and trust and investment management services. It mainly uses funds from deposits to write a variety of loans and to invest in mortgage-backed securities and municipal bonds. Real estate loans including one- to four-family residential mortgages home equity loans and commercial mortgages make up nearly 90% of the company's loan portfolio.

NORTHWEST BANCSHARES, INC. (MD)

NMS: NWDI

100 Liberty Street
Warren, PA 16365
Phone: 814 726-2140
Fax: –
Web: www.northwestsavingsbank.com

CEO: William J. Wagner
CFO: William W. Harvey
HR: –
FYE: December 31
Type: Public

Northwest Bancshares is the holding company for Northwest Bank which boasts $9 billion in assets and operates about 180 branches in mostly in Pennsylvania but also in northern Maryland western New York and eastern Ohio. Founded in 1896 the bank offers checking and savings accounts CDs credit cards and trust and investment management services. It mainly uses funds from deposits to write a variety of loans and to invest in mortgage-backed securities and municipal bonds. Residential mortgages and home equity loans make up nearly 60% of the company's loan portfolio while commercial real estate loans make up almost 30%. Consumer and business loans make up the remainder.

	Annual Growth	12/10	12/11	12/12	12/13	12/14
Assets ($ mil.)	(1.2%)	8,148.2	7,957.7	7,942.6	7,881.5	7,775.0
Net income ($ mil.)	1.9%	57.5	64.2	63.6	66.7	62.0
Market value ($ mil.)	1.6%	1,115.6	1,178.3	1,149.9	1,400.0	1,186.9
Employees	2.1%	2,040	2,121	2,220	2,231	2,220

NORTHWEST BIOTHERAPEUTICS INC

NAS: NWBO

4800 Montgomery Lane, Suite 800
Bethesda, MD 20814
Phone: 240 497-9024
Fax: –
Web: www.nwbio.com

CEO: Alton L. Boynton
CFO: Linda F Powers
HR: –
FYE: December 31
Type: Public

Northwest Biotherapeutics wants to bring out the killer in you. The development-stage firm's DCVax vaccine platform uses dendritic cells (a type of white blood cells) obtained from a patient's blood to program that patient's own T cells to kill cancer cells. Northwest Biotherapeutics' two DCVax product candidates are being targeted to treat brain and prostate cancer. Both candidates are in late-stage clinical trials. If successful the therapies could work in conjunction with more traditional cancer treatments. Toucan Capital holds over 85% of the company's shares. Toucan's Cognate Therapeutics subsidiary manufactures the DCVax products and provides additional services to Northwest Biotherapeutics.

	Annual Growth	12/10	12/11	12/12	12/13	12/14
Sales ($ mil.)	247.2%	0.0	0.0	0.8	0.8	1.5
Net income ($ mil.)	–	(27.4)	(32.8)	(67.3)	(65.8)	(135.6)
Market value ($ mil.)	61.8%	53.8	25.0	215.1	260.0	368.9
Employees	31.6%	4	10	10	12	12

NORTHWEST DAIRY ASSOCIATION

1130 RAINIER AVE S
SEATTLE, WA 981442842
Phone: 206-284-7220
Fax: –

CEO: Jim Werkhoven
CFO: –
HR: –
FYE: March 31
Type: Private

Northwest Dairy Association (NDA) members milk a lot of cows. The dairy cooperative's 550-plus member/farmers ship 7.2 billion pounds of milk annually which is processed by the co-op's subsidiary Darigold and packaged and sold under the Darigold label. NDA produces fluid and cultured dairy products including milk butter cottage cheese sour cream and yogurt that altogether generate some $2 billion in sales. It also makes bulk butter and cheese milk powder and whey products. The co-op caters to several sectors nationwide. Its customers include food retailers and wholesalers as well as foodservice and food-manufacturing companies. The association's membership spans half a dozen US states.

	Annual Growth	03/02	03/03	03/04	03/07	03/08
Sales ($ mil.)	14.1%	–	1,140.2	1,297.3	1,450.2	2,207.3
Net income ($ mil.)	–	–	–	(6.4)	12.8	87.4
Market value ($ mil.)	–	–	–	–	–	–
Employees	–	–	–	–	–	1,300

NORTHWEST FARM CREDIT SERVICES ACA

1700 S ASSEMBLY ST # 102
SPOKANE, WA 992242116
Phone: 509-838-2429
Fax: –

CEO: –
CFO: Tom Nakano
HR: Andrew Shelton
FYE: December 31
Type: Private

Customer-owned financial cooperative Northwest Farm Credit Services is an agricultural lender that provides financial services to farmers ranchers agribusinesses commercial fishermen timber producers and rural home owners in Alaska Idaho Montana Oregon and Washington. The company has a network of around 45 branches and offers a broad range of flexible loan programs to meet the needs of people in the agriculture business. Northwest Farm Credit also provides leasing services appraisal services and life mortgage disability and crop insurance as well as legal advocacy and assistance to customers in need. It is part of the Farm Credit System a network of lenders serving the US agriculture industry.

	Annual Growth	12/09	12/10	12/11	12/12	12/13
Assets ($ mil.)	3.3%	–	8,705.4	8,696.7	9,471.2	9,604.7
Net income ($ mil.)	22.0%	–	–	159.2	187.3	236.9
Market value ($ mil.)	–	–	–	–	–	–
Employees	–	–	–	–	–	500

NORTHWEST INDIANA BANCORP

OTC: NWIN

9204 Columbia Avenue
Munster, IN 46321
Phone: 219 836-4400
Fax: –
Web: www.ibankpeoples.com

CEO: David A Bochnowski
CFO: Robert T Lowry
HR: –
FYE: December 31
Type: Public

NorthWest Indiana Bancorp is the holding company for Peoples Bank which serves individuals and businesses customers through about 10 branches in northwest Indiana's Lake County. The savings bank offers traditional deposit services such as checking and savings accounts money market accounts and CDs. It primarily uses the funds collected to originate loans secured by single-family residences and commercial real estate; it also makes construction consumer and business loans. The bank's Wealth Management Group provides retirement and estate planning investment accounts land trusts and profit-sharing and 401(k) plans.

	Annual Growth	12/10	12/11	12/12	12/13	12/14
Assets ($ mil.)	5.3%	631.1	651.8	691.8	693.5	775.0
Net income ($ mil.)	9.3%	5.2	5.4	6.9	7.1	7.4
Market value ($ mil.)	15.5%	42.4	41.0	54.3	71.1	75.4
Employees	0.1%	194	201	186	174	195

NORTHWEST NATURAL GAS CO.

NYS: NWN

220 N.W. Second Avenue
Portland, OR 97209
Phone: 503 226-4211
Fax: –
Web: www.nwnatural.com

CEO: Gregg S. Kantor
CFO: Gregory C. Hazelton
HR: Lea Anne Doolittle
FYE: December 31
Type: Public

Warmth in the Pacific Northwest comes naturally for Northwest Natural Gas which does business as NW Natural. The company provides natural gas to 628600 residential 65300 commercial and 1000 industrial customers in western Oregon (including Portland) and southwestern Washington (including Vancouver) through its 14000 miles of transmission and distribution mains and service lines. Responding to increased demand NW Natural is looking to expand its gas transportation and storage services through Gill Ranch Storage and the proposed Palomar Gas Transmission pipeline. It also owns pipeline investment company NNG Financial Corporation.

	Annual Growth	12/10	12/11	12/12	12/13	12/14
Sales ($ mil.)	(1.8%)	812.1	848.8	730.6	758.5	754.0
Net income ($ mil.)	(5.2%)	72.7	63.9	59.9	60.5	58.7
Market value ($ mil.)	1.8%	1,267.9	1,307.7	1,206.0	1,168.3	1,361.5
Employees	1.9%	1,024	1,050	1,092	1,081	1,103

NORTHWEST PIPE CO.

NMS: NWPX

5721 SE Columbia Way, Suite 200
Vancouver, WA 98661
Phone: 360 397-6250
Fax: 360 397-6257
Web: www.nwpipe.com

CEO: Scott J. Montross
CFO: Robin A. Gantt
HR: Shirley Evans
FYE: December 31
Type: Public

Northwest Pipe goes with the flow. It makes welded-steel water transmission lines that form the circulatory systems of water suppliers. Its transmission pipes are made to transport water under pressure and sold primarily to water utilities. Northwest Pipe also makes tubular products from 1.5 inches to 16 inches in diameter for the construction agriculture and energy markets. The Water Transmission Group is a top supplier of high pressure highly engineered steel pipe products. The Tubular Products Group operates three technologically-advanced Electric Resistance Weld (ERW) mill facilities. The Fabricated Products segment fabricates pressure vessels tanks steel pipe and miscellaneous metals products.

	Annual Growth	12/10	12/11	12/12	12/13	12/14
Sales ($ mil.)	1.1%	386.8	511.7	524.5	475.6	403.3
Net income ($ mil.)	–	(1.4)	12.7	16.2	(0.9)	(17.9)
Market value ($ mil.)	5.8%	228.8	217.6	227.1	359.5	286.7
Employees	(5.8%)	1,200	1,200	1,100	1,050	943

NORTHWESTERN CORP.

NYS: NWE

3010 W. 69th Street
Sioux Falls, SD 57108
Phone: 605 978-2900
Fax: –
Web: www.northwesternenergy.com

CEO: Robert C. (Bob) Rowe
CFO: Brian B Bird
HR: –
FYE: December 31
Type: Public

NorthWestern once a holding company for several energy-related businesses is now blowing in one direction only — providing power and gas through regulated utilities. Through its NorthWestern Energy subsidiary the company provides electricity and natural gas to about 678200 customers in Montana Nebraska and South Dakota. In Montana it delivers electricity to approximately 344500 customers in 187 communities and surrounding rural areas 15 rural electric cooperatives and in Wyoming to Yellowstone National Park. NorthWestern delivers gas to 184300 customers in 105 Montana communities. It also distributes natural gas to 86700 customers in 60 Nebraska communities and four South Dakota communities.

	Annual Growth	12/11	12/12	12/13	12/14	12/15
Sales ($ mil.)	2.1%	1,117.3	1,070.3	1,154.5	1,204.9	1,214.3
Net income ($ mil.)	13.1%	92.6	98.4	94.0	120.7	151.2
Market value ($ mil.)	11.0%	1,724.1	1,673.0	2,086.8	2,725.6	2,613.3
Employees	(2.2%)	1,400	1,430	1,493	1,604	1,279

NORTHWESTERN MEMORIAL HEALTHCARE

251 E HURON ST STE 3-708
CHICAGO, IL 60611-2908
Phone: 312-926-2000
Fax: –
Web: www.nmh.org

CEO: Dean Harrison
CFO: –
HR: –
FYE: August 31
Type: Private

If you get blown over in the Windy City Northwestern Memorial HealthCare (NMHC) can get you upright again. Its primary facility Northwestern Memorial Hospital (NMH) is a teaching hospital serving residents of the Chicago area offering virtually every medical specialty. The hospital has more than 890 beds and is affiliated with Northwestern University's Feinberg School of Medicine. NMHC also operates the 200-bed Northwestern Lake Forest Hospital ambulatory surgery centers physicians' practices community clinics a home hospice program and health and wellness centers. Other subsidiaries of the NMHC health system include a philanthropic foundation an insurance company and a managed care contracts provider.

	Annual Growth	08/08	08/09	08/10	08/11	08/12
Assets ($ mil.)	417.7%	–	33.9	37.4	42.5	4,701.7
Net income ($ mil.)	–	–	(0.6)	0.6	1.9	145.5
Market value ($ mil.)	–	–	–	–	–	–
Employees	–	–	–	–	–	6,000

NORTON COMMUNITY HOSPITAL AUXILIARY INC.

100 15TH ST NW
NORTON, VA 242731616
Phone: 276-679-9600
Fax: –
Web: www.nch.org

CEO: Mark Leonard
CFO: –
HR: –
FYE: September 30
Type: Private

Norton Community Hospital provides medical surgical and therapeutic services in southwest Virginia and southeast Kentucky. Established in 1949 as a hospital for miners Norton Community Hospital has grown to an acute care facility with some 130 beds. Specialized services include emergency medicine diagnostics pulmonary health orthopedics obstetrics cardiology psychiatry and oncology. The hospital which is an affiliate of the Mountain States Health Alliance also provides home health services through affiliate Community Home Care and it operates outpatient and family medicine clinics.

	Annual Growth	09/04	09/05*	06/07	06/08*	09/12
Sales ($ mil.)	–	–	(407.2)	–	39.4	53.4
Net income ($ mil.)	38.4%	–	–	–	2.6	9.4
Market value ($ mil.)	–	–	–	–	–	–
Employees	–	–	–	–	–	460

*Fiscal year change

NORTON HEALTHCARE INC.

200 E. Chestnut St.
Louisville KY 40202
Phone: 502-629-8000
Fax: 503-922-6000
Web: www.banfield.net

CEO: Stephen A Williams
CFO: –
HR: –
FYE: December 31
Type: Private - Not-for-Pr

Norton Healthcare takes care of people in the land of horse farms and blue grass. The company owns and operates five hospitals and manages numerous additional health care facilities in Kentucky and southern Indiana. Specialty services include cancer treatment women's health orthopedics and heart care. Its Norton Hospital is a 720-bed facility in Louisville that serves as a teaching facility for the University of Louisville. Other facilities include Norton Audubon Hospital Norton Suburban Hospital and Norton Brownsboro Hospital. One of the largest health care systems in Kentucky Norton Healthcare has a dozen urgent care clinics and more than 90 physician practice locations.

NORWEGIAN CRUISE LINE HOLDINGS LTD.

NASDAQ: NCLH

7665 Corporate Center Dr.
Miami FL 33126
Phone: 305-436-4000
Fax: 503-557-4501
Web: www.nortek-inc.com/cleanpak.html

CEO: Frank J Del Rio
CFO: Wendy Beck
HR: –
FYE: December 31
Type: Private

Norwegian Cruise Line Holdings is always ready to set sail on its next adventure. Incorporated in Bermuda but headquartered in Miami the holding company is a global cruise line operator through its subsidiaries with a fleet of about a dozen vessels and more than 26000 berths. Itineraries originate from 17 ports 10 of which are in North America. The company offers tours to such locales as Alaska the Bahamas Hawaii and South America. Norwegian Cruise Line markets a "freestyle cruising" concept which allows guests to casually roam eat and mingle at their leisure. After several failed attempts the company finally went public in 2013 with an offering worth $447 million.

NORWICH UNIVERSITY

158 HARMON DR
NORTHFIELD, VT 056631035
Phone: 802-485-2000
Fax: –
Web: www.norwich.edu

CEO: –
CFO: Richard E Rebmann
HR: –
FYE: May 31
Type: Private

Whether military man or regular old citizen Norwich University could be the perfect place to learn the ropes. As both a traditional and a military college Norwich accepts military and civilian students. The coeducational school has an undergraduate enrollment of about 2300. It offers 30 on-campus bachelor's programs a teacher lincensure program and four ROTC programs. Its five colleges include the College of Professional Schools and the College of Science and Mathematics. The university is the birthplace of the nation's Reserve Officers' Training Corps (ROTC) program.

	Annual Growth	05/10	05/11	05/12	05/13	05/14
Sales ($ mil.)	2.1%	–	92.4	93.1	96.1	98.4
Net income ($ mil.)	–	–	–	(25.5)	33.2	50.4
Market value ($ mil.)	–	–	–	–	–	–
Employees	–	–	–	–	–	510

NORWOOD FINANCIAL CORP.

NMS: NWFL

717 Main Street
Honesdale, PA 18431
Phone: 570 253-1455
Fax: –
Web: www.waynebank.com

CEO: Lewis J Critelli
CFO: William S Lance
HR: Jamie Padula
FYE: December 31
Type: Public

Norwood Financial not Batman owns Wayne Bank. The bank serves individuals and local businesses through about 15 branches in northeastern Pennsylvania. It offers standard deposit products and services including checking and savings accounts money market savings accounts CDs and IRAs. Residential and commercial mortgages account for about 80% of Wayne Bank's loan portfolio. The bank also runs a trust and wealth management division; subsidiary Norwood Investment provides annuities and mutual funds; Norwood Settlement (70%-owned by the bank) offers title and settlement services. Norwood Financial acquired North Penn Bank in 2011; the deal added five branches to Norwood's network.

	Annual Growth	12/10	12/11	12/12	12/13	12/14
Assets ($ mil.)	7.3%	537.0	668.8	672.3	711.2	711.6
Net income ($ mil.)	1.2%	7.3	7.4	8.4	8.5	7.7
Market value ($ mil.)	1.1%	102.1	101.0	109.4	98.9	106.8
Employees	4.6%	118	149	151	146	141

NORWOOD PROMOTIONAL PRODUCTS LLC

10 W. Market St. Ste. 1400
Indianapolis IN 46204
Phone: 317-275-2500
Fax: 317-275-2570
Web: www.norwood.com

CEO: –
CFO: –
HR: –
FYE: December 31
Type: Subsidiary

Norwood Promotional Products makes its money off schwag. A leading supplier of promotional items in the US Norwood manufactures and imprints (with corporate logos and messages) about 15 product lines featuring more than 5000 items including travel bags golf balls magnets pens and calendars. It is also home to the original Koozie can and bottle holders. The company's wares are sold to thousands of independent promotional product distributors. Norwood was founded in 1989 by Frank Krasovec. It voluntarily filed for Chapter 11 bankruptcy protection in 2009; later that year French consumer products company BIC — maker of the ubiquitous BIC ballpoint pen — acquired the company for $162 million.

NOTIFY TECHNOLOGY CORPORATION

OTC: NTFY

1054 S. De Anza Blvd. Ste. 105
San Jose CA 95129
Phone: 408-777-7920
Fax: 408-996-7405
Web: www.notifycorp.com

CEO: Robert Polychron
CFO: Gerald W Rice
HR: –
FYE: September 30
Type: Public

Notify Technology is betting its future on wireless. Formerly a provider of messaging applications to telecommunications carriers the company has shifted efforts to developing products for the enterprise wireless market. Its NotifyLink application allows mobile employees to connect to their company's email server using wireless handhelds including Blackberry and iPhone devices. The product can be used with Novell GroupWise and Microsoft Exchange e-mail software as well as with offerings from Google Sun and Oracle. Director David Brewer controls about 56% of the company's outstanding shares.

NOVA SOUTHEASTERN UNIVERSITY INC.

3301 COLLEGE AVE
DAVIE, FL 333147796
Phone: 954-262-7300
Fax: –
Web: www.nsunews.nova.edu

CEO: Robert S. Oller
CFO: Alyson Silva
HR: Mark A Jones
FYE: June 30
Type: Private

Nova Southeastern University (NSU) gives a whole new meaning to "school of sharks." NSU whose mascot is the deep sea predator has an enrollment of more than 27000 students and offers a variety of undergraduate graduate and professional academic programs. NSU offers degrees in several medical disciplines (osteopathic medicine pharmacy optometry nursing) marine biology business law education and computer sciences. The not-for-profit independent school operates four campuses in the Miami-Fort Lauderdale area several health centers and an oceanographic center. Founded in 1964 Nova University merged with Southeastern University of the Health Sciences in 1994 to become Nova Southeastern University.

	Annual Growth	06/08	06/09	06/10	06/12	06/13
Sales ($ mil.)	0.9%	–	595.1	612.4	689.2	617.7
Net income ($ mil.)	20.0%	–	–	22.5	48.9	38.8
Market value ($ mil.)	–	–	–	–	–	–
Employees	–	–	–	–	–	2,500

NOVABAY PHARMACEUTICALS INC

ASE: NBY

5980 Horton Street, Suite 550
Emeryville, CA 94608
Phone: 510 899-8800
Fax: 510 225-0371
Web: www.novabaypharma.com

CEO: Mark M. Sieczkarek
CFO: Thomas J. (Tom) Paulson
HR: –
FYE: December 31
Type: Public

NovaBay Pharmaceuticals aims to keep the "bed bugs" away. The clinical-stage biopharmaceutical company develops antimicrobial compounds (known as Aganocide compounds) for the treatment and prevention of infections in hospital and non-hospital environments. Aganocide compounds destroy bacteria by attacking multiple sites and aim to treat and prevent bacterial fungal and viral infections. The compounds are intended to prevent infections resulting from surgical or other hospital procedures such as nasal surgery urinary tract catheterization and wound care as well as for use on patients with infections of the eyes ears sinuses or skin.

	Annual Growth	12/10	12/11	12/12	12/13	12/14
Sales ($ mil.)	(42.7%)	9.8	11.0	6.9	3.5	1.1
Net income ($ mil.)	–	(4.3)	(5.1)	(7.0)	(16.0)	(15.2)
Market value ($ mil.)	–	–	–	–	–	–
Employees	(3.7%)	43	27	30	34	37

NOVARTIS PHARMACEUTICALS CORPORATION

1 Health Plaza
East Hanover NJ 07936-1080
Phone: 862-778-8300
Fax: 973-781-8265
Web: www.pharma.us.novartis.com

CEO: Paulo Costa
CFO: Gary E Rosenthal
HR: –
FYE: December 31
Type: Subsidiary

As the US pharmaceuticals unit of Swiss drug giant Novartis AG Novartis Pharmaceuticals Corporation (NPC) helps with the development manufacturing marketing and sales of its parent company's products in the US. Its product lines address a range of ailments including cardiovascular and respiratory diseases central nervous system disorders cancers bone and skin conditions infectious diseases and organ transplant complications. NPC's key products include tumor growth inhibitor Gleevec high blood pressure drug Diovan and attention deficit disorder therapies Focalin and Ritalin. NPC markets its products through an in-house sales team.

NOVATEL WIRELESS INC.

NMS: MIFI

9645 Scranton Road
San Diego, CA 92121
Phone: 858 812-3400
Fax: –
Web: www.novatelwireless.com

CEO: Sue Swenson
CFO: Michael A. Newman
HR: –
FYE: December 31
Type: Public

Novatel Wireless proves you can take it with you. The company designs wireless modems that let users access the Internet from anywhere. Its MiFi brand of mobile hotspot devices provides wireless connectivity for up to five users at the same time. Novatel also offers a series of wireless PC card modems (Merlin) embedded wireless modules for OEMs (Expedite) and desktop wireless gateway consoles (Ovation). Its MobiLink software bundled with modems and embedded modules connects mobile devices with wireless LANs. Novatel also offers activation provisioning and integration services. The company gets most sales from North America.

	Annual Growth	12/10	12/11	12/12	12/13	12/14
Sales ($ mil.)	(14.0%)	338.9	402.9	344.3	335.1	185.2
Net income ($ mil.)	–	(33.5)	(24.9)	(89.3)	(43.4)	(39.2)
Market value ($ mil.)	(23.8%)	436.8	143.2	60.8	108.4	147.3
Employees	(16.3%)	489	488	459	316	240

NOVATION COMPANIES INC

NBB: NOVC

2114 Central Street, Suite 600
Kansas City, MO 64108
Phone: 816 237-7000
Fax: –
Web: www.novationcompanies.com

CEO: Rodney Schwatken
CFO: Rodney Schwatken
HR: –
FYE: December 31
Type: Public

NovaStar Financial is forging a new life for itself — one with as little to do with subprime mortgages as possible. The firm bought originated serviced and securitized subprime mortgages until that sector experienced its own flame-out. After exiting the lending business NovaStar began investing in other businesses to reinvent itself. In 2008 it acquired a majority of StreetLinks National Appraisal which provides property appraisals to residential mortgage lenders. The next year it bought a majority of Advent Financial Services a startup firm that provides banking services to low- and moderate-income consumers. NovaStar bought 51% of mortgage banking software provider Corvisa in late 2010.

	Annual Growth	12/10	12/11	12/12	12/13	12/14
Sales ($ mil.)	(40.7%)	97.5	137.1	196.1	159.3	12.1
Net income ($ mil.)	(57.9%)	986.7	7.8	59.2	(67.5)	30.9
Market value ($ mil.)	(9.6%)	38.4	40.3	56.7	25.6	25.6
Employees	(12.2%)	284	453	705	522	169

NOVAVAX, INC.

NMS: NVAX

20 Firstfield Road
Gathersburg, MD 20878
Phone: 240 268-2000
Fax: –
Web: www.novavax.com

CEO: Stanley C. Erck
CFO: Barclay A. (Buck) Phillips
HR: –
FYE: December 31
Type: Public

Out to ax the dreaded flu is Novavax a producer of novel next-generation vaccines designed to prevent life-threatening infectious diseases such as the influenza virus. The clinical-stage company uses its own virus-like particle (VLP) technology that unlike traditional vaccines which are grown in chicken eggs use recombinant proteins grown from insect cell lines. Its manufacturing process is also faster and more flexible than traditional manufacturing methods — a fact that might help the vaccines succeed in combating fast-changing strains of pandemic influenza. Candidates in the company's pipeline include vaccines for seasonal and pandemic influenza Respiratory Syncytial virus (RSV) Varicella Zoster (shingles) and HIV.

	Annual Growth	12/10	12/11	12/12	12/13	12/14
Sales ($ mil.)	207.5%	0.3	14.7	22.1	20.9	30.7
Net income ($ mil.)	–	(35.7)	(19.4)	(28.5)	(52.0)	(82.9)
Market value ($ mil.)	25.0%	580.4	300.9	451.4	1,222.8	1,416.3
Employees	36.4%	89	112	137	213	308

NOVELIS INC.

3560 Lenox Rd. Ste. 2000
Atlanta GA 30326
Phone: 404-760-4000
Fax: 512-442-9342
Web: www.artzribhouse.com/

CEO: Steve Fisher
CFO: Steve Pohl
HR: Hr Shashikant
FYE: March 31
Type: Subsidiary

Nothing can foil Novelis because it has the art of rolling aluminum in the can — the aluminum can that is. It is a global leader in aluminum rolled products and can recycling. A 2005 spinoff of what is now Rio Tinto Alcan it manufactures aluminum rolled semi-finished products used by the construction and industrial foil products transportation and beverage and food can industries. The rolled aluminum is made with alloy mixtures in a range of hardnesses thicknesses and widths with various coatings and finishes designed specifically for its end-use segments. The company also recycles more than 35 billion beverage cans annually. India's Hindalco Industries part of the Aditya Birla Group owns Novelis.

NOVO 1 INC.

4301 Cambridge Rd.
Fort Worth TX 76155
Phone: 817-355-8200
Fax: 817-355-8505
Web: www.novo1.com

CEO: Mary Murcott
CFO: John Sykstus
HR: –
FYE: December 31
Type: Private

NOVO 1 wants to be #1 when it comes to providing call center services to its clients. Formed in 1987 and specializing in inbound and outbound customer contact the company's services include direct marketing production custom mail and fulfillment operations answering services lead generation and database management. It operates call centers in Montana Michigan Texas and Wisconsin. The company caters mainly to the financial services health care insurance publishing customer service telecommunications transportation and utilities industries. In late 2009 NOVO 1 was acquired by the Michigan Opportunities Fund belonging to private equity firm Glencoe Capital.

NPC INTERNATIONAL INC.

7300 W. 129th St.
Overland Park KS 66213
Phone: 913-327-5555
Fax: 913-327-5850
Web: www.npcinternational.com

CEO: –
CFO: Troy D Cook
HR: –
FYE: December 31
Type: Private

NPC International is the prince of pepperoni in a pizza empire. The world's largest franchisee of Pizza Hut restaurants NPC owns and operates more than 1230 pizza restaurants and delivery kitchens in about 30 states. The quick-service eateries located mostly in such southern states as Alabama Florida Georgia and Tennessee serve a variety of pizza styles as well as such items as buffalo wings and pasta. The pizza parlors are franchised from YUM! Brands the world's largest fast-food restaurant company. NPC was founded in 1962 by former chairman Gene Bicknell who was one of the first Pizza Hut franchisees. The company was acquired by private equity group NPC International Holdings in late 2011.

NPS PHARMACEUTICALS INC.

NMS: NPSP

550 Hills Drive
Bedminster, NJ 07921
Phone: 908 450-5300
Fax: –
Web: www.npsp.com

CEO: Flemming Ornskov
CFO: –
HR: –
FYE: December 31
Type: Public

Those suffering from intestinal failure are rooting for NPS Pharmaceuticals. The drug development company has a handful of candidates in development for gastrointestinal and endocrine disorders focusing on rare conditions with few available treatment options. Lead candidates Gattex (teduglutide) is a treatment for short bowel syndrome a rare gastrointestinal disorder. Another Natpara is being studied as a treatment for a hormone deficiency disorder known as hyperparathyroidism. The company outsources much of its research; it also often partners with or licenses candidates to larger firms to help fund late-stage development and commercialization efforts. Shire is buying NPS Pharma for $5.2 billion.

	Annual Growth	12/09	12/10	12/11	12/12	12/13
Sales ($ mil.)	16.6%	84.1	89.4	101.6	130.6	155.6
Net income ($ mil.)	–	(17.9)	(31.4)	(36.3)	(18.7)	(13.5)
Market value ($ mil.)	72.9%	348.9	810.6	676.2	933.8	3,115.4
Employees	40.6%	53	63	86	149	207

NRG ENERGY INC

NYS: NRG

211 Carnegie Center
Princeton, NJ 08540
Phone: 609 524-4500
Fax: –
Web: www.nrgenergy.com

CEO: John W. Ragan
CFO: Kirkland B. Andrews
HR: –
FYE: December 31
Type: Public

A company with twice the energy in its name is doubling its efforts to deliver power. NRG Energy a leading power producer with a generating capacity of about 52000 MW (including 1186 MW of solar power assets) is getting greener as it invests in wind and solar power. The vast majority of NRG's power plants are in North America but it also has one in Australia. Its portfolio includes more than 190 generation units at about 100 power plants. It also markets natural gas oil and other commodities NRG's retail units (including Reliant Energy and Green Mountain Energy) distribute power to about 3 million customers across the US. In 2015 it announced plans to spin off its renewables businesses to pay down debt.

	Annual Growth	12/10	12/11	12/12	12/13	12/14
Sales ($ mil.)	15.7%	8,849.0	9,079.0	8,422.0	11,295.0	15,868.0
Net income ($ mil.)	(27.2%)	477.0	197.0	559.0	(386.0)	134.0
Market value ($ mil.)	8.4%	6,578.4	6,100.3	7,739.9	9,669.0	9,073.1
Employees	18.6%	4,964	5,193	8,792	7,786	9,806

NRG YIELD INC

NYS. NYLD

211 Carnegie Center
Princeton, NJ 08540
Phone: 609 524-4500
Fax: –
Web: www.nrgyield.com

CEO: David W. Crane
CFO: Kirkland B. Andrews
HR: –
FYE: December 31
Type: Public

Looking for a current investment opportunity? Try NRG Yield. The company was formed by NRG Energy as an investment vehicle for shareholders to earn quarterly stock dividends. NRG Yield owns a mix of renewable and fossil-fuel powerplants — seven solar power plants three natural gas/oil plants and one wind generation facility. These energy-generation facilities provide power under long-term contracts to customers such as AEP CL&P and PG&E. In addition the company owns eight thermal power systems that provide steam water and electricity. The company went public in 2013 raising $431 million. It plans to use some of the proceeds to complete construction on another solar power plant in California.

	Annual Growth	12/10	12/11	12/12	12/13	12/14
Sales ($ mil.)	–	0.0	0.0	0.0	313.0	583.0
Net income ($ mil.)	–	0.0	0.0	0.0	13.0	16.0
Market value ($ mil.)	–	0.0	0.0	0.0		
Employees	–	–	–	–	–	–

NRT LLC

1 Campus Dr.	CEO: Bruce Zipf
Parsippany NJ 07054	CFO: –
Phone: 973-407-5296	HR: –
Fax: 973-407-7999	FYE: December 31
Web: www.nrtllc.com	Type: Subsidiary

NRT is the #1 residential real estate brokerage company in the US. It holds and operates the company-owned brokerage businesses of parent Realogy Corporation which also owns such brand names as Coldwell Banker Sotheby's International Realty ERA and Corcoran Group. NRT provides commercial and investment property services through Coldwell Banker Commercial; group affiliates offer title warranty mortgage and other support services. The group operates some 750 offices in more than 35 major metropolitan areas throughout the US. Real estate franchisor Cendant (now Avis Budget Group) established the company as National Realty Trust in 1996. In 2012 Realogy parent Domus filed to take itself public.

NSTAR ELECTRIC CO

NBB: NSAR P

800 Boylston Street	CEO: –
Boston, MA 02199	CFO: James J Judge
Phone: 617 424-2000	HR: Christine M Carmody
Fax: –	FYE: December 31
Web: www.nstar.com	Type: Public

NSTAR Electric plays a starring role in bringing electric power to Boston. The NSTAR company's electric transmission and distribution utility serves 1.1 million residential commercial and industrial customers in Beantown and about 80 surrounding communities (including Cambridge New Bedford and Plymouth). NSTAR Electric also sells wholesale power to municipal utilities in the area and it provides standard offer and default supply services to retail customers who choose not to purchase energy from competitive suppliers in the state's deregulated power market. Subsidiary Harbor Electric Energy distributes power to a Massachusetts Water Resources Authority wastewater treatment facility in Boston.

	Annual Growth	12/10	12/11	12/12	12/13	12/14
Sales ($ mil.)	0.6%	2,478.3	2,487.3	2,301.0	2,493.5	2,536.7
Net income ($ mil.)	5.1%	248.6	252.5	190.2	268.5	303.1
Market value ($ mil.)	–	0.0	0.0	0.0	0.0	0.0
Employees	(21.7%)	–	–	–	2,194	1,717

NTELOS HOLDINGS CORP

NMS: NTLS

1154 Shenandoah Village Drive	CEO: Rodney D. (Rod) Dir
Waynesboro, VA 22980	CFO: Stebbins B. Chandor
Phone: 540 946-3500	HR: –
Fax: –	FYE: December 31
Web: www.ntelos.com	Type: Public

NTELOS communicates over the hills and through the woods of the Virginias (and in other US states). The company serves more than 460000 wireless subscribers in Virginia and West Virginia as well as portions of Maryland North Carolina Ohio and Pennsylvania. Wireless operations include its FRAWG and nTelos-branded retail business as well as a wholesale business it operates under a contract with Sprint . In 2013 the company had 1444 cell sites in operation of which 120 sites were company owned. It conducts its business through NTELOS-branded retail operations which sell products and services via direct and indirect distribution channels and provides network access to other telecommunications carriers most notably through an arrangement with Sprint.

	Annual Growth	12/10	12/11	12/12	12/13	12/14
Sales ($ mil.)	(2.8%)	545.7	422.6	454.0	491.9	487.8
Net income ($ mil.)	–	44.8	(23.7)	18.4	24.7	(53.6)
Market value ($ mil.)	(31.5%)	411.8	440.5	283.4	437.3	90.6
Employees	(14.5%)	1,600	975	960	970	854

NTN BUZZTIME INC

ASE: NTN

2231 Rutherford Road, Suite 200	CEO: Jeff Berg
Carlsbad, CA 92008	CFO: –
Phone: 760 438-7400	HR: –
Fax: 760 438-7470	FYE: December 31
Web: www.buzztime.com	Type: Public

NTN Buzztime doesn't see its knowledge contests as mere trivial pursuits. The company distributes interactive trivia and sports games to almost 4000 bars and restaurants in the US and Canada through its Buzztime Network. Players use wireless game controllers or mobile phones to play along with the Buzztime games displayed on television screens. The majority of the company's revenue comes from recurring subscription fees paid by hospitality firms. About 35% of the company's Buzztime Network subscribers are national chains including Hooters and Buffalo Wild Wings. NTN has promotional and marketing partnerships with some of its biggest customers and generates revenue through advertising and marketing services.

	Annual Growth	12/10	12/11	12/12	12/13	12/14
Sales ($ mil.)	0.7%	25.3	23.9	24.1	23.7	26.0
Net income ($ mil.)	–	(0.4)	(3.4)	(1.0)	(1.1)	(5.0)
Market value ($ mil.)	3.7%	34.9	23.0	19.3	57.9	40.4
Employees	29.3%	134	323	331	359	375

NTS INC

ASE: NTS

1220 Broadway	CEO: Brad D Worthington
Lubbock, TX 79401	CFO: –
Phone: 806 771-5212	HR: –
Fax: –	FYE: December 31
Web: www.ntscom.com	Type: Public

Xfone USA offers alternative local and long-distance services to residential and business customers in the south eastern US. The company is certified as a competitive local-exchange carrier in Louisiana Texas and its home state of Mississippi. In addition to traditional phone services Xfone USA offers cable TV and broadband Internet access. Commercial clients include planned communities and apartment buildings. The company also provides such business-oriented services as Web design and hosting as well as data network maintenance and support. Xfone USA is a subsidiary of Texas-based Xfone Inc.

	Annual Growth	12/08	12/09	12/10	12/11	12/12
Sales ($ mil.)	(9.8%)	90.3	85.0	58.9	57.7	59.9
Net income ($ mil.)	–	2.0	(22.2)	(4.6)	(1.2)	(0.5)
Market value ($ mil.)	3.1%	31.3	28.8	50.7	16.5	35.4
Employees	(12.3%)	391	372	294	310	231

NTS REALTY HOLDINGS LTD PARTNERSHIP

ASE: NLP

600 North Hurstbourne Parkway, Suite 300	CEO: Brian F Lavin
Louisville, KY 40222	CFO: Gregory A Wells
Phone: 502 426-4800	HR: –
Fax: 502 426-4994	FYE: December 31
Web: www.ntsdevelopment.com	Type: Public

NTS Realty Holdings invests in develops and manages commercial real estate in the Southeast and Midwest. The company's portfolio includes some 25 properties including about 15 dozen apartment communities about a half-dozen office centers and three retail properties in Kentucky Florida Indiana Tennessee Virginia and Georgia. Chairman J.D. Nichols owns about 60% of NTS Realty Holdings; he and president Brian Lavin control the company's managing general partner NTS Realty Capital. The firm's properties are managed by NTS Development Company an affiliate of NTS Realty Capital. Established in 2004 NTS Realty Holdings is the result of the merger of several property companies and partnerships.

	Annual Growth	12/08	12/09	12/10	12/11	12/12
Sales ($ mil.)	8.3%	41.6	44.5	47.9	54.6	57.3
Net income ($ mil.)	–	7.7	(17.2)	(11.4)	(12.0)	(12.0)
Market value ($ mil.)	19.5%	38.9	49.6	39.7	36.2	79.4
Employees	–	–	–	–	–	–

NTT AMERICA INC.

101 Park Ave. 41st Fl.
New York NY 10178
Phone: 212-661-0810
Fax: 212-661-1078
Web: www.us.ntt.com

CEO: Tetsuro Yamaguchi
CFO: –
HR: –
FYE: March 31
Type: Subsidiary

NTT America offers a combination of managed private network enterprise data hosting Internet access network security and IT services under the Arcstar brand to corporate customers in the US. Top clients have included the US subsidiaries of Mitsui Sumitomo Electric and Nippon Express as well as such domestic companies as Parlance Systems and Neways International. The company also offers private broadband network services linking cities in the US Asia and Europe. NTT America provides bilingual support services to global companies with a presence in Japan. NTT America is a subsidiary and the North American representative of Japanese telecommunications giant Nippon Telegraph and Telephone (NTT).

NU HORIZONS ELECTRONICS CORP.

70 Maxess Rd.
Melville NY 11747
Phone: 631-396-5000
Fax: 631-396-5050
Web: www.nuhorizons.com

CEO: Martin Kent
CFO: Kurt Freudenberg
HR: –
FYE: February 28
Type: Subsidiary

Nu Horizons sees new electronic components on the horizon. The company distributes semiconductors display lighting and power components from manufacturers that include Atmel Connect Tech IXYS Marvell Micron Renesas Silicon Image GE Energy and LG Display. It targets the audio/visual (broadcast consumer surveillance) energy (generation distribution alternative building automation smart metering) and medical (home health imaging patient monitoring instruments) industries. Nu Horizons also value-added services that include device programming materials management packaging tape and reel and display integration. Rival Arrow Electronics bought the company for about $161 million in 2011.

NU SKIN ENTERPRISES, INC.

NYS: NUS

75 West Center Street
Provo, UT 84601
Phone: 801-345-1000
Fax: –
Web: www.nuskinenterprises.com

CEO: M. Truman Hunt
CFO: Ritch N. Wood
HR: –
FYE: December 31
Type: Public

Multi-level marketer Nu Skin Enterprises keeps itself busy exfoliating and polishing. It offers 200-plus personal care products including cleansers toners and anti-aging skin care products through a global network of 950000 independent distributors sales reps and preferred customers. It also sells cosmetics fragrances hair care items and mouthwash. Nu Skin has its foot in the door in 50-plus global markets including cherished China. Its Pharmanex unit sells LifePak nutritional supplements. Its Big Planet subsidiary offers personal and small-business technology and communications products as well as Internet and long-distance services. Nu Skin was founded in 1984 by its former chairman Blake Roney.

	Annual Growth	12/10	12/11	12/12	12/13	12/14
Sales ($ mil.)	13.7%	1,537.3	1,744.0	2,169.7	3,176.7	2,569.5
Net income ($ mil.)	8.6%	136.1	153.3	221.6	364.9	189.2
Market value ($ mil.)	9.6%	1,785.3	2,865.6	2,186.0	8,155.0	2,578.3
Employees	(0.3%)	5,054	5,980	3,733	5,056	5,000

NUANCE COMMUNICATIONS INC

NMS: NUAN

1 Wayside Road
Burlington, MA 01803
Phone: 781-565-5000
Fax: –
Web: www.nuance.com

CEO: Paul A. Ricci
CFO: Daniel D Tempesta
HR: Eric Tinch
FYE: September 30
Type: Public

Nuance Communications can help you see the subtle differences in both speech and images. The company provides speech and digital imaging software. Its speech products include speech recognition systems used to provide customer service embedded systems used in applications ranging from automobiles to consumer electronics and dictation systems. Nuance's digital imaging line includes document creation editing and conversion tools. It serves clients worldwide in a range of industries including financial services government healthcare and telecommunications; the company generates most of its sales in the US.

	Annual Growth	09/11	09/12	09/13	09/14	09/15
Sales ($ mil.)	10.0%	1,318.7	1,651.5	1,855.3	1,923.5	1,931.1
Net income ($ mil.)	–	38.2	207.1	(115.2)	(150.3)	(115.0)
Market value ($ mil.)	(5.3%)	6,300.9	7,710.4	5,786.7	4,775.3	5,071.1
Employees	16.6%	7,300	12,000	12,000	14,000	13,500

NUCLEAR SOLUTIONS INC.

OTC: NSOL

5505 Connecticut Ave. NW Ste. 191
Washington DC 20015
Phone: 202-787-1951
Fax: 202-318-2487
Web: www.nuclearsolutions.com

CEO: –
CFO: –
HR: –
FYE: December 31
Type: Public

Nuclear Solutions is developing technologies related to defense and nuclear remediation. Its projects include a passive system for detecting shielded nuclear weapons and technology for the remediation of tritiated water produced by nuclear power plants. The company is also developing nuclear micro-power sources for low-power microelectronics microelectromechanical systems (MEMS) nanotechnology devices and synthetic ethanol production. In 2007 Inter-Americas Inc. made an unsolicited offer to acquire Nuclear Solutions for $110 million in cash — a bid the company's board of directors initally favored recommending to shareholders — but the companies called off the deal in mid-2008.

NUCO2 INC.

2800 SE Market Place
Stuart FL 34997
Phone: 772-221-1754
Fax: 772-781-3500
Web: www.nuco2.com

CEO: –
CFO: –
HR: –
FYE: June 30
Type: Private

NuCO2 puts tiny bubbles in the soda. The company supplies liquid carbon dioxide (bulk CO_2) for carbonating and dispensing fountain drinks which differs from the traditional method of carbonation that uses high-pressure CO_2. Its more than 130000 customers include restaurants (Pizza Hut) retailers (Costco) convenience stores (7-Eleven) movie theaters (Loews Cineplex) and stadiums and arenas (Madison Square Garden). NuCO2's services include system installation and maintenance product delivery and technical support. Its products are used by 30 million consumers a day. In 2013 Praxair acquired NuCO2 Inc. for $1.1 billion.

NUCOR CORP.

NYS: NUE

1915 Rexford Road
Charlotte, NC 28211
Phone: 704 366-7000
Fax: 704 362-4208
Web: www.nucor.com

CEO: John J. Ferriola
CFO: James D. (Jim) Frias
HR: Leigh Knighton
FYE: December 31
Type: Public

Nucor takes a "minimillist" approach to succeeding in the steel industry. At its minimills Nucor produces hot- and cold-rolled steel steel joists and metal buildings. It has the capacity to produce more than 26 million tons of steel per year. North America's largest recycler of scrap metal it produces steel by melting scrap in electric arc furnaces. Most products are sold to steel service centers manufacturers and fabricators. Subsidiary Harris Steel fabricates rebar for highways and bridges and other construction projects. Its David J. Joseph Company unit processes and brokers metals pig iron hot briquetted iron and direct reduced iron (DRI). In 2014 Nucor recycled 19 million tons of scrap steel.

	Annual Growth	12/10	12/11	12/12	12/13	12/14
Sales ($ mil.)	7.4%	15,844.6	20,023.6	19,429.3	19,052.0	21,105.1
Net income ($ mil.)	51.9%	134.1	778.2	504.6	488.0	713.9
Market value ($ mil.)	2.9%	13,980.0	12,624.1	13,769.5	17,030.0	15,648.6
Employees	3.6%	20,500	20,800	22,200	22,300	23,600

NUCOR STEEL TUSCALOOSA INC.

1700 Holt Rd. NE
Tuscaloosa AL 35404
Phone: 205-556-1310
Fax: 205-556-1476
Web: www.tsteel.com

CEO: –
CFO: –
HR: –
FYE: December 31
Type: Subsidiary

Nucor Steel Tuscaloosa (formerly Corus Tuscaloosa) brings coil to the plate. The company manufactures carbon and pressure vessel steel coil discrete plate and cut-to-length plate products to name a few. Nucor Steel Tuscaloosa was one of the first U.S. steel companies to implement the Steckel mill technology to make value added plate from coil. It produces over 2 million tons annually. Nucor Steel Tuscaloosa operates material handling facilities that are accessible to interstate rail and highway systems from the company's home on Alabama's Black Warrior River. The company is a subsidiary of Nucor after being acquired from Corus in 2004.

NUMOBILE INC.

PINK SHEETS: NUBL

2520 S. 3rd St. Suite 206
Louisiville KY 40208
Phone: 502-636-2807
Fax: 905-670-7869
Web: www.strongco.com

CEO: –
CFO: –
HR: –
FYE: December 31
Type: Public

NuMobile formerly Phoenix Interests is a development stage company that is looking to build a portfolio of software applications and services aimed at the mobile computing and smartphone markets. It plans to use a series of acquisitions targeting technology and infrastructure businesses in order to fulfill its new strategy. The company acquired Stonewall Networks a security software maker for mobile networks and network security specialist Enhance Network Communication in 2009. NuMobile previously focused on gaming and entertainment technologies.

NUO THERAPEUTICS INC

NBB: NUOT Q

207A Perry Parkway, Suite 1
Gaithersburg, MD 20877
Phone: 240 499-2680
Fax: –
Web: www.cytomedix.com

CEO: Martin P. Rosendale
CFO: David E. Jorden
HR: –
FYE: December 31
Type: Public

Here's a concept — using the body's own faculties to heal wounds. Cytomedix has developed and markets an autologous platelet therapy which uses a patient's own blood plasma to promote healing. Its AutoloGel System includes a centrifuge and blood draw kit. The centrifuge is used to separate key blood components including platelets and growth factors which are then combined with reagents to make a topical gel. When applied to a wound the gel spurs the body's own healing process. AutoloGel has received FDA approval to treat chronic exuding wounds such as diabetic ulcers. Other products in Cytomedix' pipeline include an anti-inflammatory peptide that may help treat such diseases as rheumatoid arthritis.

	Annual Growth	12/10	12/11	12/12	12/13	12/14
Sales ($ mil.)	18.7%	3.9	7.2	10.6	11.6	7.8
Net income ($ mil.)	–	(6.8)	(3.5)	(19.8)	(20.2)	(18.9)
Market value ($ mil.)	(46.3%)	527.9	142.0	90.5	59.6	44.0
Employees	23.1%	20	35	50	40	46

NUSTAR ENERGY L.P.

NYS: NS

19003 IH-10 West
San Antonio, TX 78257
Phone: 210 918-2000
Fax: –
Web: www.nustarenergy.com

CEO: Bradley C. (Brad) Barron
CFO: Thomas R. (Tom) Shoaf
HR: Bob Grimes
FYE: December 31
Type: Public

NuStar Energy is following its own star in pursuit of energy profits through terminalling and storing petroleum products transporting petroleum products and anhydrous ammonia and via asphalt marketing. The independent company (operating primarily in the US) manages more than 8650 miles of refined product pipelines 2000 miles of ammonia pipelines 1180 miles of crude oil pipelines 80 refined product terminal facilities and one crude oil storage facility. It has 93 million barrels of storage capacity and operates product terminals around the world. In 2014 NuStar Energy divested its asphalt joint venture.

	Annual Growth	12/10	12/11	12/12	12/13	12/14
Sales ($ mil.)	(8.6%)	4,403.1	6,575.3	5,955.7	3,463.7	3,075.1
Net income ($ mil.)	(3.1%)	239.0	221.5	(226.6)	(273.8)	210.8
Market value ($ mil.)	(4.5%)	5,411.5	4,413.0	3,308.6	3,971.4	4,497.9
Employees	(3.5%)	1,413	1,508	1,478	1,221	1,227

NUSTAR GP HOLDINGS LLC

NYS: NSH

19003 IH-10 West
San Antonio, TX 78257
Phone: 210 918-2000
Fax: –
Web: www.nustargpholdings.com

CEO: Bradley C Barron
CFO: Thomas R Shoaf
HR: –
FYE: December 31
Type: Public

NuStar GP Holdings owns a 2% general-partner interest and a 17% limited-partner interest in NuStar Energy which operates terminals and petroleum-liquids pipeline systems primarily in the US. NuStar Energy has 7480 miles of refined product and ammonia pipelines 940 miles of crude oil pipelines 96 refined product terminal facilities a crude oil storage facility and two asphalt refineries. It also has terminals in Canada Mexico the Netherlands Turkey and the UK. Valero GP Holdings was controlled by Valero Energy. Following Valero GP Holdings' 2006 IPO Valero Energy sold its interest in both Valero L.P. and Valero GP Holdings. In 2007 Valero GP Holdings changed its name to NuStar GP Holdings LLC.

	Annual Growth	12/10	12/11	12/12	12/13	12/14
Sales ($ mil.)	(0.6%)	66.9	65.8	(4.6)	(6.7)	65.4
Net income ($ mil.)	(4.0%)	72.5	69.6	2.1	(11.0)	61.4
Market value ($ mil.)	(1.3%)	1,559.0	1,426.9	1,188.3	1,205.4	1,477.1
Employees	(8.9%)	–	–	1,478	1,221	1,227

NUTRA PHARMA CORP

NBB: NPHC

12502 West Atlantic Blvd.
Coral Springs, FL 33071
Phone: 954 509-0911
Fax: –
Web: www.nutrapharma.com

CEO: Rik J Deitsch
CFO: Rik J Deitsch
HR: –
FYE: December 31
Type: Public

Nutra Pharma is a biotechnology holding company active in several areas. The company's ReceptoPharm subsidiary holds a pipeline of drug candidates that may eventually treat HIV/AIDS rabies and other viral and neurological diseases as well as pain. Another subsidiary NanoLogix develops diagnostic test kits to identify infectious diseases while its Designer Diagnostics subsidiary markets and sells the test kits. One product in development as a possible therapy for MS was based upon cobra venom. That product was then reformulated and launched commercially as an over-the-counter topical analgesic for chronic pain under the brand name Cobroxin.

	Annual Growth	12/10	12/11	12/12	12/13	12/14
Sales ($ mil.)	(19.7%)	1.4	0.2	0.2	0.1	0.6
Net income ($ mil.)	–	(3.1)	(4.4)	(3.6)	(4.3)	(2.5)
Market value ($ mil.)	(48.8%)	2.9	1.0	0.5	0.3	0.2
Employees	(15.9%)	10	3	3	3	5

NUTRACEUTICAL INTERNATIONAL CORP.

NMS: NUTR

1400 Kearns Boulevard, 2nd Floor
Park City, UT 84060
Phone: 435 655-6106
Fax: –
Web: www.nutraceutical.com

CEO: Frank W. Gay
CFO: Cory J. McQueen
HR: –
FYE: September 30
Type: Public

Nutraceutical International is all over the natural foods industry. It manufactures markets and even retails a world of nutritional supplements vitamins minerals body care products and diet and energy products in the US and abroad. Its branded products include such names as KAL Herbs for Kids Nature's Life Solaray Sunny Green and VegLife. Its company-owned US retail stores include Cornucopia Community Market Granola's and The Real Food Company while its Au Naturel unit markets the company's brands in about 55 other countries. Nutraceutical International also publishes natural health books under the Woodland name. The acquisitive company is actively buying up and integrating smaller firms.

	Annual Growth	09/11	09/12	09/13	09/14	09/15
Sales ($ mil.)	3.6%	188.1	200.4	208.4	214.5	216.5
Net income ($ mil.)	(0.7%)	15.7	15.8	17.0	15.9	15.3
Market value ($ mil.)	16.6%	121.3	149.5	225.2	198.4	224.0
Employees	1.3%	803	862	832	913	845

NUTRISYSTEM INC

NMS: NTRI

Fort Washington Executive Center, 600 Office Center Drive
Fort Washington, PA 19034
Phone: 215 706-5300
Fax: –
Web: www.nutrisystem.com

CEO: Dawn M. Zier
CFO: Michael P. (Mike) Monahan
HR: Nancy Adams
FYE: December 31
Type: Public

Nutrisystem helps its customers trim their waistline morning noon and night. It promotes weight loss by selling prepared meals and grocery items that are delivered directly to US consumers. Customers order monthly food packages consisting of 28 days of portion-controlled items such as a breakfast lunch dinner and dessert supplemented with fruits and vegetables. It also offers individualized calorie plans one-on-one diet counseling behavior modification and exercise education and maintenance plans. Nutrisystem also sells its weight-management products through a partnership with TV marketer QVC (3% of revenue) and club retailers the likes of Costco.

	Annual Growth	12/10	12/11	12/12	12/13	12/14
Sales ($ mil.)	(5.7%)	509.5	401.3	396.9	358.1	403.1
Net income ($ mil.)	(13.0%)	33.6	12.3	(2.8)	7.4	19.3
Market value ($ mil.)	(1.8%)	604.4	371.6	234.8	472.5	561.9
Employees	(10.4%)	647	511	398	430	417

NUTRITION 21 LLC

OTC: NXXI

4 Manhattanville Rd.
Purchase NY 10577-2197
Phone: 914-701-4500
Fax: 914-696-0860
Web: www.nutrition21.com

CEO: –
CFO: –
HR: –
FYE: June 30
Type: Private

Nutrition 21 believes in the power of chromium picolinate. The company primarily makes and sells this and other ingredients used in dietary supplement products. It supplies some 80% of the chromium picolinate (sold as Chromax) used in US dietary supplements. Other ingredient products include manganese selenium and zinc all of which are stirred into dietary supplements. In addition to selling ingredients the company supports the health claims for its products with clinical trials. After struggling under a debt burden in mid-2011 Nutrition 21 filed for Chapter 11 bankruptcy protection. In late 2011 the company's assets were purchased by a private investment group.

NUTRITION MANAGEMENT SERVICES COMPANY

PINK SHEETS: NMSCA

725 Kimberton Rd.
Kimberton PA 19442
Phone: 610-935-2050
Fax: 610-935-8287
Web: www.nmsc.com

CEO: Joseph V Roberts
CFO: –
HR: Marie Gaul
FYE: June 30
Type: Public

Nutrition Management Services is a regional foodservices operator that provides retirement communities hospitals and other health care facilities with food management services. It offers supervision of dietary operations through onsite management cost and quality controls and dietary staff training. In addition the company operates a conference center and banquet facility used for training. Chairman and CEO Joseph Roberts controls nearly 75% of Nutrition Management Services.

NUTROGANICS INC

NBB: NUTT

20270 Goldenrod Lane
Germantown, MD 20876-4070
Phone: 301 540-5500
Fax: 301 540-5557
Web: www.mlog.com

CEO: Richard E Meccariella
CFO: –
HR: –
FYE: December 31
Type: Public

Microlog develops software that helps businesses and other organizations keep track of the tiny details involved in providing a good customer service experience. The company's ServiceFirst and Telereminder-branded applications provide a single software environment for managing customer contact via voice email Web and fax. It also offers consulting training and technical support services. Microlog serves such industries as health care and education as well as state and local government agencies. Clients have included the US Department of Homeland Security the University of New Mexico and Walter Reed Army Medical Center.

	Annual Growth	10/02	10/03*	12/12	12/13	12/14
Sales ($ mil.)	2.5%	5.6	5.1	0.9	2.1	7.5
Net income ($ mil.)	–	0.0	(0.4)	(0.5)	(0.2)	(1.1)
Market value ($ mil.)	9.9%	2.0	14.1	7.5	14.4	6.2
Employees	(8.0%)	25	23	–	–	–

*Fiscal year change

NUVASIVE INC

NMS: NUVA

7475 Lusk Boulevard
San Diego, CA 92121
Phone: 858 909-1800
Fax: 858 909-2000
Web: www.nuvasive.com

CEO: Alexis V. Lukianov
CFO: Quentin Blackford
HR: Carol Cox
FYE: December 31
Type: Public

When a back is seriously out of whack NuVasive has some options. The company makes and markets medical devices for the surgical treatment of spinal disorders. NuVasive's products are primarily used in spinal restoration and fusion surgeries. Its minimally disruptive Maximum Access Surgery (MAS) platform enables surgeons to access the spine from the side of the body instead of from the front or back and helps them avoid hitting nerves. NuVasive also features a line of biologic bone grafting materials — both allograft and synthetic — and has a cervical disc replacement system in development. The company sells its FDA-approved products through a network of exclusive sales agents supported by an in-house sales team.

	Annual Growth	12/11	12/12	12/13	12/14	12/15
Sales ($ mil.)	10.7%	540.5	620.3	685.2	762.4	811.1
Net income ($ mil.)	–	(69.8)	3.1	7.9	(16.7)	66.3
Market value ($ mil.)	44.0%	662.4	813.5	1,701.1	2,481.4	2,847.1
Employees	10.0%	1,093	1,173	1,358	1,500	1,600

NUVEEN INVESTMENTS INC.

333 W. Wacker Dr.
Chicago IL 60606
Phone: 312-917-7700
Fax: 312-917-8049
Web: www.nuveen.com

CEO: John P Amboian
CFO: –
HR: –
FYE: December 31
Type: Private

Chicago-based Nuveen Investments once financed the growth of its hometown and other cities by underwriting and trading municipal bonds. Nuveen has since parlayed its investment banking experience into a career as a money manager specializing in municipal bond and stock portfolios for high-net-worth and institutional investors in the US. Offering more than 100 mutual funds about 120 closed-end funds as well as separate accounts and managed accounts the company sells its products through banks brokerages insurance agents and other financial services providers. It has more than $210 billion of assets under management. An investor group led by private equity firm Madison Dearborn Partners owns Nuveen.

NUVERA FUEL CELLS INC.

129 Concord Rd. Bldg. 1
Billerica MA 01821
Phone: 617-245-7500
Fax: 617-245-7511
Web: www.nuvera.com

CEO: Jon Taylor
CFO: –
HR: –
FYE: December 31
Type: Private

Nuvera Fuel Cells hopes to send internal combustion engines and lead acid batteries to the scrap heap of history. The company's clean-burning fuel processors and fuel cell systems were developed for industrial vehicles and original equipment manufacturers. (Fuel cells convert hydrogen into electricity and expel only water.) Its PowerEdge and PowerTap fuel cell systems are used in Deka's hybrid fuel cell/battery packs as an alternative to the lead acid batteries used in forklifts at refrigerated warehouses (lead acid batteries can't withstand extreme temperatures.) Toro is testing Nuvera's PowerFlow system for use in its utility vehicles. Nuvera has operations in Italy and the US and is owned by energy giant Hess.

NUVILEX INC.

PINK SHEETS: NVLX

1971 Old Cuthbert Rd.
Cherry Hill NJ 08034
Phone: 856-354-0707
Fax: 856-354-1077
Web: www.nuvilex.com

CEO: Kenneth L Waggoner
CFO: –
HR: –
FYE: April 30
Type: Public

Nuvilex is out to fill niche markets with its products. The company makes and sells a handful of items that can be classified as a couple of parts nutraceutical a part dermatological and a little bit environmental. Nuvilex's products are sold worldwide and include nutritional supplements Cinnergen and Cinnechol tattoo ink Infinitink and scar cream Talysn. Nuvilex has also developed an environmentally safe germicidal topical spray that kills some of the most frequent bacterial pathogens. The company is also developing a sporicidal to kill anthrax and has formulated Citroxin a product designed to knock out avian flu viruses.

NV5 GLOBAL INC

NAS: NVEE

200 South Park Road, Suite 350
Hollywood, FL 33021
Phone: 954 495-2112
Fax: –
Web: www.nv5.com

CEO: Dickerson Wright
CFO: Michael P. Rama
HR: –
FYE: December 31
Type: Public

NV5 wants the world to envy its engineering services. It offers infrastructure engineering support and consulting services as well as construction quality assurance and asset management. Customers include government agencies along with quasi-public and private firms in education health care and energy. NV5's enviable projects have included the international terminal at Philadelphia International Airport UC Santa Barbara's Marine Center the New Jersey Devils Arena San Diego's Manchester Grand Hyatt and a wind turbine manufacturing plant in Colorado. The company works from about 20 offices in California Colorado Florida New Jersey and Utah. It was formed in 2011 and filed to go public in 2013.

	Annual Growth	12/10	12/11	12/12	12/13	12/14
Sales ($ mil.)	35.6%	32.1	63.4	60.6	68.2	108.4
Net income ($ mil.)	–	(0.2)	1.4	1.3	2.8	4.9
Market value ($ mil.)	59.8%	–	–	–	46.8	74.8
Employees	13.9%	–	439	439	436	649

NVE CORP

NAS: NVEC

11409 Valley View Road
Eden Prairie, MN 55344
Phone: 952 829-9217
Fax: –
Web: www.nve.com

CEO: Daniel A. Baker
CFO: Curt A Reynders
HR: –
FYE: March 31
Type: Public

NVE is definitely a spin zone and one with a certain magnetism. The company develops sensors incorporating spintronic (short for spin-based electronic) materials called giant magnetoresistors (GMR). Spintronics differ from conventional electronics in that they use the spin — rather than the charge — of electrons to store and transmit data. The company's sensors are used in aerospace automotive currency verification and factory automation applications. In addition to analog and digital GMR sensors NVE offers magnetic couplers magnetic random-access memory (MRAM) and custom-designed modules. Customers include the US government Broadcom Limited St. Jude Medical and Digi-Key.

	Annual Growth	03/11	03/12	03/13	03/14	03/15
Sales ($ mil.)	(0.5%)	31.2	28.6	27.0	25.9	30.6
Net income ($ mil.)	1.8%	13.4	11.4	11.8	11.1	14.4
Market value ($ mil.)	5.2%	273.7	257.5	274.1	277.1	334.8
Employees	(4.1%)	58	58	54	54	49

NVIDIA CORP

NMS: NVDA

2701 San Tomas Expressway
Santa Clara, CA 95050
Phone: 408 486-2000
Fax: –
Web: www.nvidia.com

CEO: Jen-Hsun Huang
CFO: Colette M. Kress
HR: –
FYE: January 25
Type: Public

Image-conscious NVIDIA is conscientious about rendering the best images possible. Its products generate images used in many PCs video game consoles mobile devices and super computers. Its high-definition 2D and 3D graphics processing units (GPU) and mobile processors grapple with adversaries such as AMD Apple Intel and QUALCOMM. The fabless semiconductor company's GPU brands are GeForce for games Quadro for designers and digital artists and Tesla for scientists and researchers. The company has 65% share of the market for gaming GPUs. NVIDIA's graphics processors are being used in cloud computing and data centers. Its major mobile processor brand Tegra is designed not only for mobile devices but mobile settings such as automotive systems.

	Annual Growth	01/11	01/12	01/13	01/14	01/15
Sales ($ mil.)	7.2%	3,543.3	3,997.9	4,280.2	4,130.2	4,681.5
Net income ($ mil.)	25.6%	253.1	581.1	562.5	440.0	630.6
Market value ($ mil.)	(3.4%)	12,947.1	8,124.7	6,762.4	8,478.8	11,285.1
Employees	11.2%	6,029	7,133	7,974	8,808	9,228

NVR INC.

NYS: NVR

11700 Plaza America Drive, Suite 500
Reston, VA 20190
Phone: 703 956-4000
Fax: –
Web: www.nvrinc.com

CEO: Paul C. Saville
CFO: Daniel D. Malzahn
HR: –
FYE: December 31
Type: Public

From finished lot to signed mortgage NVR offers homebuyers everything — including the kitchen sink. The company builds single-family detached homes townhomes and condominiums mainly for first-time and move-up buyers primarily in the eastern US. NVR markets its homes as Ryan Homes Fox Ridge Homes Heartland Homes and NVHomes. Its largest markets the Washington DC and Baltimore areas account for nearly half of sales. NVR's housing sizes range from 800 sq. ft. to 7300 sq. ft. with the average price of a home at around $370000. Its subsidiary NVR Mortgage Finance offers mortgage and title services. NVR was founded in 1980 as NVHomes.

	Annual Growth	12/10	12/11	12/12	12/13	12/14
Sales ($ mil.)	9.9%	3,057.4	2,669.6	3,193.2	4,220.9	4,453.1
Net income ($ mil.)	8.1%	206.0	129.4	180.6	266.5	281.6
Market value ($ mil.)	16.6%	2,798.0	2,777.7	3,725.2	4,154.4	5,163.9
Employees	8.7%	2,822	2,765	3,291	3,944	3,942

NXSTAGE MEDICAL INC

NMS. NXTM

350 Merrimack St.
Lawrence, MA 01843
Phone: 978 687-4700
Fax: –
Web: www.nxstage.com

CEO: –
CFO: Robert S. Brown
HR: Darren Scandone
FYE: December 31
Type: Public

Patients suffering from end-stage renal disease can turn to NxStage Medical for help. The medical device company operates through three segments: System One and In-Center. The System One division features NxStage Medical's lead product the System One portable hemodialysis machine which can be used by patients at home or by professionals in a hospital setting. The device is also marketed to hospitals for critical care and to dialysis clinics that want to create or expand their services to home-based patients. The In-Center division sells NxStage Medical's blood tubing sets and needles to dialysis clinics primarily through distributor relationships while Services covers the company's kidney dialysis centers.

	Annual Growth	12/11	12/12	12/13	12/14	12/15
Sales ($ mil.)	11.5%	217.3	242.1	263.4	301.5	336.1
Net income ($ mil.)	–	(21.4)	(15.2)	(18.6)	(23.9)	(15.3)
Market value ($ mil.)	5.4%	1,138.8	720.6	640.5	1,148.4	1,403.4
Employees	9.5%	2,500	2,700	3,200	3,400	3,600

NYACK COLLEGE

1 S BOULEVARD
NYACK, NY 109603698
Phone: 845-675-7498
Fax: –
Web: www.nyack.edu

CEO: –
CFO: David C Jennings
HR: –
FYE: June 30
Type: Private

Nyack College is a Christian liberal arts college of the Christian and Missionary Alliance. The college has more than 3000 undergraduate and graduate students many of whom are enrolled at its main campus in Nyack New York. The university has an additional campus in New York City and it offers theology programs on several campuses of the Alliance Theological Seminary a fellow affiliate of the Christian and Missionary Alliance. Other fields of study include arts sciences counseling music business nursing and adult education. Nyack College was founded in New York City in 1882 as the Missionary Training Institute the first Bible college in America by missionary Dr. A.B. Simpson.

	Annual Growth	06/08	06/09	06/10	06/11	06/13
Sales ($ mil.)	–	–	0.0	59.1	60.9	62.7
Net income ($ mil.)	(60.7%)	–	–	1.8	0.9	0.1
Market value ($ mil.)	–	–	–	–	–	–
Employees	–	–	–	–	–	300

NYPRO INC.

101 UNION ST
CLINTON, MA 01510-2935
Phone: 978-365-9721
Fax: –
Web: www.nypro.com

CEO: –
CFO: Gregory G Adams
HR: –
FYE: June 30
Type: Private

Nypro is a real pro when it comes to injection molding. The company makes plastic parts used in devices that range from cell phones and electric razors to inkjet printer cartridges and personal computers. Nypro's three global units include Consumer & Electronics Packaging and Healthcare (medical devices such as single-use fluid and drug management components). Although custom-precision plastic-injection molding is Nypro's core business the company also offers assembly services to other manufacturers. Major customers include Dell Nokia and Procter & Gamble. Established in 1955 Nypro agreed to be acquired by electronics manufacturing services provider Jabil Circuit in early 2013.

	Annual Growth	06/08	06/09*	07/10	07/11*	06/12
Sales ($ mil.)	1.6%	–	1,089.6	1,234.2	1,169.7	1,144.2
Net income ($ mil.)	–	–	2.6	30.0	9.8	(6.0)
Market value ($ mil.)	–	–	–	–	–	–
Employees	–	–	–	–	–	16,000

*Fiscal year change

O P I PRODUCTS INC.

13034 Saticoy St.
North Hollywood CA 91605
Phone: 818-759-2400
Fax: 661-257-5856
Web: www.starnail.com

CEO: Jules Kaufman
CFO: –
HR: –
FYE: June 30
Type: Subsidiary

OPI Products knows some women like to make a statement with their 20 collective finger and toe nails. The family-owned company is well known for whimsical nail polish names such as Not So Bora-Bora-ing Pink I'm Not Really A Waitress Got A Date To-Knight! and Who the Shrek Are You? The firm offers 200 nail colors among its product portfolio. In addition to nail polish OPI also makes and markets nail care and skin care products. The company peddles its products primarily through salons and specialty beauty stores throughout the US and in about 70 foreign countries. The company's brands include Nail Envy Avoplex Feet Garden Party Avojuice and Nicole. OPI was acquired by fragrance giant Coty.

O'CHARLEY'S INC.

NASDAQ: CHUX

3038 Sidco Dr.
Nashville TN 37204
Phone: 615-256-8500
Fax: 615-782-5044
Web: www.ocharleysinc.com

CEO: –
CFO: R Jeffrey Williams
HR: Jeffrey Campbell
FYE: December 31
Type: Private

O'Charley's is a leading full-service restaurant company with about 360 locations in 25 states. Its flagship casual-dining chain serves mostly traditional American fare including beef chicken and seafood entrees along with burgers sandwiches and a selection of starters. It boasts more than 230 company-owned outposts in the Southeast and Midwest. O'Charley's also owns Ninety Nine Restaurants a pub-style chain with more than 100 locations in Massachusetts and a handful of other New England states. In addition the company operates about a dozen upscale steakhouses under the name Stoney River Legendary Steaks. Fidelity National Financial acquired the company in 2012 and merged it with American Blue Ribbon.

O'MELVENY & MYERS LLP

400 S. Hope St.
Los Angeles CA 90071-2899
Phone: 213-430-6000
Fax: 213-430-6407
Web: www.omm.com

CEO: –
CFO: –
HR: –
FYE: January 31
Type: Private - Partnershi

O'Melveny & Myers has gotten used to playing the role of legal guardian angel. The firm is one of the oldest in Los Angeles and over the years it has developed strong ties to the media and entertainment industries. Among its clients have been such leading players as Walt Disney Sony Pictures Entertainment and Time Warner. Besides entertainment and media law O'Melveny & Myers' practice areas include labor and employment intellectual property and technology and venture capital litigation. The firm has some 900 lawyers located in more than a dozen offices worldwide. O'Melveny & Myers was founded in 1885.

O'REILLY AUTOMOTIVE, INC.

NMS: ORLY

233 South Patterson Avenue
Springfield, MO 65802
Phone: 417 862-6708
Fax: –
Web: www.oreillyauto.com

CEO: Gregory L. (Greg) Henslee
CFO: Thomas G. (Tom) McFall
HR: –
FYE: December 31
Type: Public

No need to jump O'Reilly Automotive's battery. The fast-growing company sells automotive aftermarket parts (both new and remanufactured) maintenance supplies professional service equipment tools and accessories through some 4400 stores in 40-plus states and online. Many O'Reilly Automotive stores also offer customers a range of services including oil and battery recycling battery testing paint mixing and tool rental. The company wheels and deals with automotive professionals as well as do-it-yourself customers. Founded in 1957 by Charles F. O'Reilly and his son "Chub" O'Reilly Automotive is still family run.

	Annual Growth	12/10	12/11	12/12	12/13	12/14
Sales ($ mil.)	7.5%	5,397.5	5,788.8	6,182.2	6,649.2	7,216.1
Net income ($ mil.)	16.7%	419.4	507.7	585.7	670.3	778.2
Market value ($ mil.)	33.6%	6,138.8	8,123.2	9,085.3	13,077.3	19,570.8
Employees	9.6%	47,142	49,148	53,615	62,533	67,926

O'REILLY MEDIA INC.

1005 Gravenstein Hwy. North
Sebastopol CA 95472
Phone: 707-827-7000
Fax: 707-829-0104
Web: www.oreilly.com

CEO: –
CFO: –
HR: –
FYE: December 31
Type: Private

O'Reilly Media aims to be an advocate for computer professionals. The company publishes technology books (including its iconic "animal books" for software developers featuring illustrations of animals on the cover) and produces technical conferences websites and magazines. It also provides research services and software. Topics covered include UNIX Java Windows Apple and Mac and a slew of other operating systems and Internet programming languages. O'Reilly Media also has books devoted to topics in business and culture. Its events include the O'Reilly Open Source Convention and the Maker Faire. Owner Tim O'Reilly founded the company as a technical writing firm in 1978.

O. C. TANNER COMPANY

1930 S STATE ST
SALT LAKE CITY, UT 841152383
Phone: 801-486-2430
Fax: –
Web: www.octanner.com

CEO: David Petersen
CFO: –
HR: –
FYE: December 31
Type: Private

O.C. Tanner recognizes that it's nice to be appreciated. The company designs and helps implement employee recognition programs for customers around the world. Related services intended to help customers take full advantage of their investment in employee recognition include communication consulting research leadership training and social programs. The company which operates from offices in the US Canada and the UK has shipped awards to clients in about 150 countries. Over the years O.C. Tanner has counted numerous Fortune 100 companies among its clients.

	Annual Growth	12/06	12/07	12/08	12/12	12/13
Sales ($ mil.)	–	–	0.0	0.0	316.5	327.7
Net income ($ mil.)	–	–	–	0.0	19.8	28.0
Market value ($ mil.)	–	–	–	–	–	–
Employees	–	–	–	–	–	1,700

O. I. CORPORATION

151 Graham Rd.
College Station TX 77845
Phone: 979-690-1711
Fax: 979-690-0440
Web: www.oico.com

CEO: J Bruce Lancaster
CFO: J Bruce Lancaster
HR: –
FYE: December 31
Type: Subsidiary

O. I. Corporation can tell exactly what's in your air food and water. The company which does business as OI Analytical makes instruments that analyze detect measure monitor and prepare chemical compounds. Its products include instruments that separate organic compounds based on their physical and chemical properties analyzers for measuring acidic levels in water emissions equipment for testing air quality and sample preparation equipment. OI also configures custom gas chromatography systems using instruments purchased from Agilent among others. Customers have included federal state and municipal governments (about one-fifth of sales). The company was acquired by ITT for about $29 million in late 2010.

O.F. MOSSBERG & SONS INC.

7 Grasso Ave.	CEO: A Iver Mossberg Jr
North Haven CT 06473	CFO: –
Phone: 203-230-5300	HR: –
Fax: 203-230-5420	FYE: September 30
Web: www.mossberg.com	Type: Private

Whatever the game whatever the season O.F. Mossberg & Sons is riding shotgun in the small firearms manufacturing industry. The oldest family-owned firearms maker in America and the largest pump-action shotgun maker in the world Mossberg has more than 100 design and utility patents to its name. Shotguns are the company's specialty but it also produces rifles; accessories such as barrels choke tubes and magazines; and hunting apparel. In addition to its guns for hunting home protection and target shooting Mossberg manufactures exclusive firearms for US military and law enforcement agencies. The company is a subsidiary of Mossberg Corporation which also owns shotgun maker Maverick Arms.

OAK MANAGEMENT CORPORATION

901 Main Ave. Ste. 600	CEO: –
Norwalk CT 06851	CFO: Grace A Ames
Phone: 203-226-8346	HR: –
Fax: 203-846-0282	FYE: March 31
Web: www.oakinv.com	Type: Private - Partnershi

You could say mighty acorns from little oaks grow. Oak Management which operates as Oak Investment Partners is a venture capital firm with more than $8 billion in committed capital. It seeks investments in a range of technology firms including those involved in broadband and wireless communications information technology consumer Internet and software services. Other areas of focus include clean energy health care retail and financial services technology. Typical investments range from $25 million to $150 million and secure a minority stake in the target firm. Oak Investment Partners usually takes a seat or two on its portfolio companies' boards of directors to provide strategic guidance.

OAK RIDGE MICRO-ENERGY INC.   OTC. OKME

3046 E. Brighton Place	CEO: Stephen J Barber
Salt Lake City UT 84121	CFO: Tami L Tharp
Phone: 801-201-7635	HR: –
Fax: 801-944-1657	FYE: December 31
Web: www.oakridgemicro.com	Type: Public

Oak Ridge Micro-Energy is hoping to provide macro-power. The development-stage company makes thin-film lithium batteries with consumer industrial and military applications. Oak Ridge Micro-Energy licensed the thin-film battery technology from Oak Ridge National Laboratory (ORNL) on a non-exclusive basis. Mark Meriwether president and CEO owns 20% of Oak Ridge; John Bates (CTO and former CEO) holds about one-quarter of the company. Dr. Bates worked at ORNL for nearly 30 years developing the technology that is being commercialized by Oak Ridge Micro-Energy. The company is moving into the third phase of its strategic plan focusing on commercial licensing and marketing of its technology.

OAK VALLEY BANCORP   NASDAQ: OVLY

125 N. 3rd Ave.	CEO: Ronald C Martin
Oakdale CA 95361	CFO: Rick McCarty
Phone: 209-848-2265	HR: –
Fax: 209-848-1929	FYE: December 31
Web: www.ovcb.com	Type: Public

Oak Valley Bancorp was formed in 2008 to be the holding company for Oak Valley Community Bank which serves individuals and local businesses through about 10 branches in California's Central Valley. Eastern Sierra Community Bank a division of Oak Valley has three locations. The banks provide standard deposit products such as savings checking and retirement accounts and CDs. Their lending activities consist of commercial real estate loans (more than half of their combined loan portfolio) and business real estate construction agricultural residential mortgage and consumer loans. Investment products and services are offered through an agreement with PrimeVest Financial Services.

OAK VALLEY BANCORP (OAKDALE, CA)   NAS: OVLY

125 North Third Avenue	CEO: Christopher M Courtney
Oakdale, CA 95361	CFO: –
Phone: 209 848-2265	HR: –
Fax: –	FYE: December 31
Web: www.ovcb.om	Type: Public

Oak Valley Bancorp was formed in 2008 to be the holding company for Oak Valley Community Bank which serves individuals and local businesses through about 10 branches in California's Central Valley. Eastern Sierra Community Bank a division of Oak Valley has three locations. The banks provide standard deposit products such as savings checking and retirement accounts and CDs. Their lending activities consist of commercial real estate loans (more than half of their combined loan portfolio) and business real estate construction agricultural residential mortgage and consumer loans. Investment products and services are offered through an agreement with PrimeVest Financial Services.

	Annual Growth	12/10	12/11	12/12	12/13	12/14
Assets ($ mil.)	7.9%	552.4	612.2	660.6	671.9	749.7
Net income ($ mil.)	11.4%	4.6	5.9	5.8	5.9	7.1
Market value ($ mil.)	14.6%	47.6	54.5	60.2	67.6	82.0
Employees	6.3%	123	135	139	146	157

OAKLAND UNIVERSITY

2200 N SQUIRREL RD	CEO: –
ROCHESTER, MI 483094401	CFO: –
Phone: 248-370-2100	HR: –
Fax: –	FYE: June 30
Web: www.oakland.edu	Type: Private

Oakland University is the OU of the North. The Michigan public university serves a student body of more than 20000 offering about 130 baccalaureate degree programs and more than 100 graduate degree and certificate programs. It boasts a student-to-faculty ratio of 22-to-1. In addition to academic and specialty programs in areas ranging from business and technology to nursing and athletics its faculty members also coordinate hands-on research projects for graduate students. The main university campus spans some 1400 acres that house seven academic schools and colleges in Rochester Michigan. Oakland University also has satellite campuses in Macomb County and a law school in Auburn Hills.

	Annual Growth	06/09	06/10	06/12	06/13	06/14
Sales ($ mil.)	5.3%	–	172.4	194.0	203.4	212.2
Net income ($ mil.)	2.6%	–	–	37.6	27.0	39.6
Market value ($ mil.)	–	–	–	–	–	–
Employees	–	–	–	–	–	2,650

OAKLEAF WASTE MANAGEMENT LLC

415 Day Hill Rd.
Windsor CT 06095
Phone: 860-290-1250
Fax: 860-290-1251
Web: www.oakleafwastemgmt.com

CEO: Steve Preston
CFO: Tom Nelson
HR: –
FYE: December 31
Type: Subsidiary

OAKLEAF Waste Management is in the garbage business but the firm rarely gets its hands dirty. The company manages waste disposal contracts for customers at more than 90000 locations specializing in industries such as hospitality retail property management construction and health care. To help its customers OAKLEAF installs trash compactors to reduce the volume of waste and arranges for waste collection and recycling services. The company oversees waste disposal services through a network of 2500 OAKLEAF-certified trash haulers at more than 100000 customer locations in the US and Canada. The company was sold by New Mountain Capital to Waste Management in 2011 for $425 million.

OAKLEY INC.

1 Icon
Foothill Ranch CA 92610
Phone: 949-951-0991
Fax: 919-807-5022
Web: www.abb.us

CEO: Colin Baden
CFO: Gianluca Tagliabue
HR: –
FYE: December 31
Type: Subsidiary

Oakley sells so many sunglasses it goggles the mind. The company makes and sells performance sunglasses and ski goggles for sports and fashion enthusiasts. Oakley is known for its lens technologies including 3D and especially for its High-Definition Optics. The brand boasts a retail network of more than 160 Oakley "O" and Vaults stores in malls throughout the US and in Europe Mexico and Asia-Pacific region. It also sells its wares online and at Dillard's Sunglass Hut sporting goods stores and other specialty retail outlets. Oakley also markets a line of apparel and footwear as well as backpacks and accessories for sports enthusiasts. Founded in 1975 Oakley is owned by Italian eyewear giant Luxottica.

OAKRIDGE ENERGY INC.

OTC: OAKR

4613 Jacksboro Hwy.
Wichita Falls TX 76302
Phone: 940-322-4772
Fax: 940-322-9452
Web: oakridgeenergy.com

CEO: –
CFO: –
HR: –
FYE: February 28
Type: Public

Despite the radioactive connotations of this company's name Oakridge Energy is engaged in the exploration and production of more benign natural resources — oil and gas with some gravel thrown into the product mix. The oil and gas independent's assets are primarily in North Texas but Oakridge Energy also receives lease and royalty income from gravel deposits in Colorado and holds real estate assets in that state. Oakridge Energy has proved reserves of 675700 barrels of oil and 234000 million cu. ft. of natural gas. President Sandra Pautsky owns 56% of the company. Due in part to the ill health of its president Oakridge Energy has decided to sell its real estate development project.

OAKRIDGE HOLDINGS, INC.

NBB: OKRG

400 West Ontario Street
Chicago, IL 60654
Phone: 312 505-9267
Fax: –

CEO: Robert C Harvey
CFO: Robert C Harvey
HR: –
FYE: June 30
Type: Public

In a unique arrangement of business services Oakridge Holdings can offer customers support and service whether they are flying high or lying low above the ground or below it. Through two subsidiaries (Oakridge Cemetery and Glen Oak Cemetery) it buries human remains and through another (Stinar Corporation) it makes aviation ground support equipment (lifts truck mounted stairways water and catering trucks). Oakridge provides its customers internment burial plots crypts and cremation as well as stairways for loading aircraft and lavatory water cabin cleaning and catering trucks for servicing airplanes.

	Annual Growth	06/10	06/11	06/12	06/13	06/14
Sales ($ mil.)	(21.8%)	14.1	16.5	13.3	12.8	5.3
Net income ($ mil.)	108.1%	0.1	0.1	(0.5)	(2.0)	2.5
Market value ($ mil.)	(4.5%)	0.6	0.8	0.6	0.6	0.5
Employees	(18.2%)	107	75	124	72	48

OAKTREE CAPITAL GROUP LLC

NYS: OAK

333 South Grand Avenue, 28th Floor
Los Angeles, CA 90071
Phone: 213 830-6300
Fax: –
Web: www.oaktreecapital.com

CEO: Jay S. Wintrob
CFO: David M. Kirchheimer
HR: –
FYE: December 31
Type: Public

Oaktree Capital Group knows money doesn't grow on trees but it often grows on alternative investments. The global investment manager specializes in credit and contrarian value-oriented investments such as distressed debt corporate debt convertible securities real estate private equity (or control investing) and listed equities. Founded in 1995 Oaktree Capital boasts $100 billion of assets under management on behalf of institutional investors such as pension funds corporations government entities universities endowments foundations and private clients. The firm has more than 15 offices in the US Asia and Europe.

	Annual Growth	12/10	12/11	12/12	12/13	12/14
Sales ($ mil.)	(1.5%)	206.2	155.8	145.0	194.9	193.9
Net income ($ mil.)	–	(49.5)	(96.0)	107.8	222.0	126.3
Market value ($ mil.)	6.7%	–	–	6,953.3	8,993.8	7,922.4
Employees	12.4%	–	653	726	809	927

OAKWOOD HEALTHCARE INC.

18101 OAKWOOD BLVD
DEARBORN, MI 48124-4089
Phone: 313-593-7000
Fax: –
Web: www.oakwood.org

CEO: Brain Connolly
CFO: –
HR: –
FYE: December 31
Type: Private

Oakwood Healthcare stands proud as a regional health care provider in southeastern Michigan. It offers a range of health services to residents in more than 35 communities. At the center of the system are four hospitals with a total of more than 1200 beds: Oakwood Hospital & Medical Center a full-service teaching hospital; Oakwood Annapolis Hospital a community hospital; Oakwood Heritage Hospital a tertiary care hospital; and Oakwood Southshore Medical Center a community hospital. Founded in 1953 the system also includes community health and diagnostic facilities retirement and nursing communities rehabilitative care centers and specialty care centers for women children and seniors.

	Annual Growth	12/0-1	12/00	12/01	12/02	12/09
Sales ($ mil.)	4.7%	–	658.3	666.3	744.7	997.0
Net income ($ mil.)	–	–	(9.9)	(4.2)	(4.2)	10.3
Market value ($ mil.)	–	–	–	–	–	–
Employees	–	–	–	–	–	9,200

OASIS PETROLEUM INC.

NYS: OAS

1001 Fannin Street, Suite 1500	CEO: Thomas B. (Tommy) Nusz
Houston, TX 77002	CFO: Michael H Lou
Phone: 281 404-9500	HR: -
Fax: -	FYE: December 31
Web: www.oasispetroleum.com	Type: Public

Oasis Petroleum is combing the northern US for watering holes made of oil. The independent exploration and production company acquires and develops primarily oil and some gas resources in the Williston Basin of Montana and North Dakota specifically in the Bakken and Three Forks formation. In 2013 Oasis reported estimated net proved reserves of 227.9 million barrels of oil equivalent and 515314 net acres of land holdings. The company also reported an average daily production of more than 33904 barrels of oil equivalent from 115 net producing wells. It sells most of its oil to marketing companies and Texon Plains All American Pipeline and Enserco Energy.

	Annual Growth	12/10	12/11	12/12	12/13	12/14
Sales ($ mil.)	81.2%	128.9	330.4	686.7	1,142.0	1,390.2
Net income ($ mil.)	-	(29.7)	79.4	153.4	228.0	506.9
Market value ($ mil.)	(11.6%)	2,748.4	2,948.0	3,222.7	4,760.0	1,676.2
Employees	73.2%	62	146	281	405	558

OBA FINANCIAL SERVICES INC

NAS: OBAF

20300 Seneca Meadows Parkway	CEO: -
Germantown, MD 20876	CFO: -
Phone: 301 916-0742	HR: -
Fax: -	FYE: June 30
Web: www.obabank.com	Type: Public

Don't get OBA Financial Services started on new money vs. old money. OBA Financial Services is the holding company for OBA Bank a community bank that traces its roots back to 1861. OBA Bank serves Montgomery and Howard County Maryland from five branches (it sold its sixth branch in Washington DC to Eagle Bancorp in January 2011). The bank's loan portfolio is made up of residential mortgages (45%) commercial mortgages (30%) home equity loans (15%) and commercial business loans (10%). OBA stands for the Oriental Building Association a 19th century savings and loan that catered to German immigrants. OBA Financial Services went public in January 2010 raising $46.3 million in its initial public offering.

	Annual Growth	06/09	06/10	06/11	06/12	06/13
Assets ($ mil.)	1.3%	362.5	374.1	386.4	392.1	381.6
Net income ($ mil.)	-	(0.6)	(0.7)	0.9	0.3	1.1
Market value ($ mil.)	18.3%	-	45.1	59.9	60.1	74.7
Employees	3.8%	62	62	69	69	72

OBERLIN COLLEGE

173 W LORAIN ST	CEO: -
OBERLIN, OH 440741073	CFO: -
Phone: 440-775-8121	HR: -
Fax: -	FYE: June 30
Web: www.blogs.oberlin.edu	Type: Private

Founded in 1833 Oberlin College was the first college in the US to enroll women on an equal basis with men. The school has a College of Arts and Sciences (about 2300 enrollees) but may be best known for its Conservatory of Music (about 600 enrollees) the oldest such institution in the US. The College of Arts and Sciences offers nearly 50 undergraduate majors the Conservatory about 10. Students can earn bachelor's degrees in either program but can also earn a five-year double-degree in both. In addition Oberlin offers master's degrees in opera theater conducting performance historical performance historical instruments music teaching and education. It has two-year certificate programs as well.

	Annual Growth	06/06	06/07	06/09	06/13	06/14
Sales ($ mil.)	3.2%	-	137.8	147.6	167.5	171.9
Net income ($ mil.)	-	-	-	(224.7)	72.8	119.6
Market value ($ mil.)	-	-	-	-	-	-
Employees	-	-	-	-	-	1,140

OBERTO SAUSAGE COMPANY

7060 S. 238th St.	CEO: -
Kent WA 98032-2914	CFO: -
Phone: 253-437-6100	HR: -
Fax: 877-234-7903	FYE: December 31
Web: www.obertosausagecompany.com	Type: Private

Do you have an oh-so-bad craving for something chewy? Something tasty with a salt kick? Oberto Sausage Company has the answer: Its Oh Boy! meat snacks. The company manufactures more than 400 varieties of dried meat products such as jerky (in beef pork and turkey versions) as well as snack sausages. All these goodies are sold under the brand names Lowrey's Meat Snacks Pacific Gold and of course Oh Boy! Oberto. The company's products are available across the US and Canada in supermarkets and club convenience and mass-merchandising stores.

OCATA THERAPEUTICS INC

NBB: OCAT

33 Locke Drive	CEO: Paul Wotton
Marlborough, MA 01752	CFO: Edward Myles
Phone: 508 756-1212	HR: -
Fax: -	FYE: December 31
Web: www.advancedcell.com/	Type: Public

No need to choose between embryonic and adult stem cells — Advanced Cell Technology (ACT) works with both to develop cellular therapies designed to regenerate human tissue. The company has developed three product platforms based on stem-cell technology. They are retinal pigment epithelial therapy (RPE) for the treatment of degenerative retinal disease; myoblast stem cell therapy to treat chronic heart failure and other heart problems; and the hemangioblast platform (IIG) for the treatment of blood and cardiovascular diseases. Though the company is focused on bringing the clinical-stage technologies to market it is also continuing to conduct research for other regenerative medicine treatments.

	Annual Growth	12/09	12/10	12/11	12/12	12/13
Sales ($ mil.)	(36.9%)	1.4	0.7	0.5	0.5	0.2
Net income ($ mil.)	-	(36.8)	(54.4)	(72.8)	(28.5)	(31.0)
Market value ($ mil.)	(9.6%)	2.4	5.5	2.2	1.5	1.6
Employees	28.4%	14	22	30	36	38

OCCIDENTAL CHEMICAL CORPORATION

5005 LBJ Fwy.	CEO: B Chuck Anderson
Dallas TX 75244-6119	CFO: -
Phone: 972-404-3800	HR: -
Fax: 972-404-3669	FYE: December 31
Web: www.oxy.com/ourbusinesses/chemicals/pages/over	Type: Subsidiary

The chemicals business of Occidental Petroleum Occidental Chemical (OxyChem) manufactures basic chemicals vinyls and performance chemicals. The company is the top US maker of chlorine and caustic soda (used in bleach plastics and pulp and paper) and the top producer of potassium hydroxide or caustic potash (used in fertilizers). Through subsidiary OxyVinyls it's the leading North American maker of vinyl chloride monomer (VCM) which is used to make PVC resins. The company operates some 22 plants throughout the US as well as another three in Brazil Canada and Chile. (OxyChem owns 50% of the Brazilian plant.)

OCCIDENTAL COLLEGE

1600 CAMPUS RD   CEO: –
LOS ANGELES, CA 900413314   CFO: –
Phone: 323-259-2500   HR: –
Fax: –   FYE: June 30
Web: www.oxyathletics.com   Type: Private

It's no accident that Occidental College is a liberal arts school. With more than 2000 students an average class size of 19 and a 10:1 student-to-faculty ratio the school (nicknamed "Oxy") offers a hands-on approach to higher education. Its campus located in Eagle Rock is surrounded by the metropolis of Los Angeles. The college has 180 faculty members and offers about 30 majors including a number of interdisciplinary programs. Occidental students can also take classes at Caltech or the Art Center College of Design and earn joint degrees at Columbia University Keck Graduate Institute and Caltech. Occidental students can also participate in service-learning and study abroad programs.

	Annual Growth	06/08	06/09	06/10	06/11	06/13
Sales ($ mil.)	–	–	0.0	115.6	146.1	109.7
Net income ($ mil.)	–	–	–	(9.0)	10.9	36.1
Market value ($ mil.)	–	–	–	–	–	–
Employees	–	–	–	–	–	610

OCCIDENTAL OIL AND GAS CORPORATION

10889 Wilshire Blvd.   CEO: Armand Hammer
Los Angeles CA 90024-4201   CFO: Stephen I Chazen
Phone: 310-208-8800   HR: –
Fax: 310-443-6690   FYE: December 31
Web: www.oxy.com/our_businesses/oil_and_gas/pages/d   Type: Subsidiary

It is not an accident that Occidental Oil & Gas Corporation is one of the largest independent oil and gas producers in the world. The company a subsidiary of Occidental Petroleum has three-pronged approach to making money from gas and oil — acquisitions exploration and enhanced oil recovery. Occidental Oil & Gas has large long-lived assets concentrated in the US the Middle East and Latin America (Colombia and Argentina). The company is the top oil producer in the Permian Basin (Kansas New Mexico Oklahoma and Texas) the largest natural gas producer in California and a major player in Piceance Basin. It is the largest leaseholder of oil and gas exploration acreage in Libya.

OCCIDENTAL PERMIAN LTD.

10889 Wilshire Blvd.   CEO: –
Los Angeles CA 90024-4201   CFO: –
Phone: 310-208-8800   HR: –
Fax: 601-544-8517   FYE: December 31
    Type: Subsidiary

Occidental Permian is all about oil Texas Tea. The company is the largest oil producer in Texas and has proved reserves in the Permian Basin of 1.2 billion barrels of oil equivalent. Nearly 60% of the oil Occidental Permian obtains comes from CO_2 flooding a procedure that is used when pumping and water injection no longer works. The company is a subsidiary of Occidental Oil and Gas (itself a subsidiary of Occidental Petroleum) and became the major player in the Permian Basin with the parent's acquisition of Altura Energy in 2000 for a reported $3.6 billion.

OCCIDENTAL PETROLEUM CORP   NYS: OXY

5 Greenway Plaza, Suite 110   CEO: Stephen I. (Steve) Chazen
Houston, TX 77046   CFO: Christopher G. (Chris) Stavros
Phone: 713 215-7000   HR: –
Fax: –   FYE: December 31
Web: www.oxy.com   Type: Public

Harnessing its heritage of Western technical know-how Occidental Petroleum engages in oil and gas exploration and production and makes basic chemicals plastics and petrochemicals. In 2014 it reported proved reserves of 2.8 billion barrels of oil equivalent primarily from assets in the US the Middle East North Africa and Latin America. Subsidiary Occidental Chemical (OxyChem) produces acids chlorine and specialty products and owns Oxy Vinyls the #1 maker of polyvinyl chloride (PVC) resin in North America. Occidental Petroleum's midstream and marketing units gather treat process transport store trade and market crude oil natural gas NGLs condensate and CO2 and generate and market power.

	Annual Growth	12/10	12/11	12/12	12/13	12/14
Sales ($ mil.)	3.5%	19,157.0	24,119.0	24,253.0	25,736.0	21,947.0
Net income ($ mil.)	(39.3%)	4,530.0	6,771.0	4,598.0	5,903.0	616.0
Market value ($ mil.)	(4.8%)	87,363.7	83,445.2	68,225.6	84,692.0	71,787.8
Employees	1.6%	11,000	11,300	12,300	12,900	11,700

OCEAN BEAUTY SEAFOODS LLC

1100 W EWING ST   CEO: Mark Palmer
SEATTLE, WA 981191321   CFO: Tony Ross
Phone: 206-285-6800   HR: Donna Keas
Fax: –   FYE: December 28
Web: www.oceanbeauty.com   Type: Private

Prefer your piscatory purchase to be fresh frozen or canned? Ocean Beauty Seafoods has it covered. Doing no fishing of its own the company buys seafood from commercial fishermen and then processes sells and distributes its seafood products in Alaska and across the continental US. Founded in 1910 the company also exports seafood to Mexico Europe Asia Africa and the Middle East. Ocean Beauty's specialty products include smoked salmon smoked salmon spreads pickled and marinated herring shrimp cocktail caviar and lobster pâté. Nonprofit Bristol Bay Economic Development Corporation owns 50% of Ocean Beauty; individual investors own the rest.

	Annual Growth	12/07	12/08	12/11	12/12	12/13
Sales ($ mil.)	0.3%	–	419.0	431.7	409.4	426.0
Net income ($ mil.)	25.4%	–	–	7.1	8.1	11.1
Market value ($ mil.)	–	–	–	–	–	–
Employees	–	–	–	–	–	18,000

OCEAN BIO-CHEM, INC.   NAS: OBCI

4041 SW 47 Avenue   CEO: Peter G Dornau
Fort Lauderdale, FL 33314   CFO: Jeffrey S Barocas
Phone: 954 587-6280   HR: –
Fax: –   FYE: December 31
Web: www.oceanbiochem.com   Type: Public

Ocean Bio-Chem provides everything but the elbow grease to scrub down boats planes RVs and automobiles. The company makes and distributes Star Brite and StarTron brand maintenance and appearance products. Its marine and automotive lines include waxes lubricants and coolants and its recreational vehicle and power sports equipment offerings primarily consist of polishes and cleaners. Ocean Bio-Chem's products are sold by both national retailers and specialty stores including Wal-Mart West Marine and Bass Pro Shops. The company handles its manufacturing in-house through its Alabama-based Kinpak subsidiary which also provides contract services. President and CEO Peter Dornau owns about 70% of the company.

	Annual Growth	12/10	12/11	12/12	12/13	12/14
Sales ($ mil.)	5.5%	27.4	31.7	31.0	32.7	33.9
Net income ($ mil.)	0.4%	2.0	2.4	2.0	1.5	2.0
Market value ($ mil.)	24.6%	16.7	19.2	21.2	22.2	40.3
Employees	4.5%	103	107	117	114	123

OCEAN DUKE CORPORATION

3450 FUJITA ST
TORRANCE, CA 905054019
Phone: 310-326-3198
Fax: –
Web: www.oceanduke.com

CEO: –
CFO: Alice Lin
HR: –
FYE: March 31
Type: Private

Ocean Duke maintains a regal demeanor in a fishy environment. The company is a seafood wholesaler offering a variety of frozen raw fish shrimp mollusks and crustaceans. Ocean Duke also sells breaded fish shrimp and squid. The company imports its products and serves foodservice food processing distribution and wholesale companies throughout the US.

	Annual Growth	03/0-1	03/00	03/01	03/02	03/11
Sales ($ mil.)	–	–	0.0	196.8	191.3	158.3
Net income ($ mil.)	7.4%	–	–	1.1	0.9	2.2
Market value ($ mil.)	–	–	–	–	–	–
Employees	–	–	–	–	–	25

OCEAN POWER TECHNOLOGIES INC

1590 Reed Road
Pennington, NJ 08534
Phone: 609 730-0400
Fax: 609 730-0404
Web: www.oceanpowertechnologies.com

CEO: David L Keller
CFO: Mark A Featherstone
HR: –
FYE: April 30
Type: Public

Harnessing the motion of the ocean is what Ocean Power Technologies (OPT) is all about. The company with offices in the US and UK uses a proprietary system called PowerBouy to generate electricity using the mechanical energy produced when offshore waves move the anchored buoys up and down. OPT offers a buoy system that connects to power grids as well as an autonomous one that can be used in remote locations and for tsunami monitoring oceanographic data collection and offshore aquaculture. Customers include the US Navy Spanish power producer Iberdrola and Spanish energy firm TOTAL. It has a contract with Lockheed Martin to build a large power generation system off the west coast of the US.

	Annual Growth	04/11	04/12	04/13	04/14	04/15
Sales ($ mil.)	(11.5%)	6.7	5.7	3.6	1.5	4.1
Net income ($ mil.)	–	(20.4)	(15.1)	(14.7)	(11.0)	(13.1)
Market value ($ mil.)	(42.1%)	8.9	5.0	2.8	5.0	1.0
Employees	(10.3%)	51	47	34	30	33

OCEAN SHORE HOLDING CO

1001 Asbury Avenue
Ocean City, NJ 08226
Phone: 609 399-0012
Fax: –
Web: www.ochome.com

CEO: Steven E Brady
CFO: Donald F Morgenweck
HR: –
FYE: December 31
Type: Public

That soothing noise you hear in South Jersey isn't waves lapping or gulls flapping it's the sweet sound of money. Ocean Shore Holding owns Ocean City Home Bank a community thrift serving New Jersey's Atlantic and Cape May counties where gaming and tourism thrive. Through about a dozen locations the bank offers individuals businesses and government entities such standard fare as checking and savings accounts CDs and money market accounts. Residential mortgages including loans secured by second homes and rental properties account for more than 80% of the company's loan portfolio. Subsidiary Seashore Financial sells investment and insurance products. Ocean Shore Holding bought rival Select Bank in 2011.

	Annual Growth	12/10	12/11	12/12	12/13	12/14
Assets ($ mil.)	5.1%	839.9	994.7	1,045.5	1,020.0	1,024.8
Net income ($ mil.)	3.7%	5.4	5.1	5.0	5.3	6.3
Market value ($ mil.)	5.8%	73.2	65.6	94.6	87.3	91.6
Employees	2.7%	168	206	196	188	187

OCEANEERING INTERNATIONAL, INC.

NYS: OII

11911 FM 529
Houston, TX 77041
Phone: 713 329-4500
Fax: –
Web: www.oceaneering.com

CEO: M. Kevin McEvoy
CFO: Alan R. Curtis
HR: –
FYE: December 31
Type: Public

Oceaneering International's products are designed to operate in places where most people don't venture from the bottom of the sea to the reaches of space. The company provides offshore oil companies with underwater drilling support construction inspection and repair services. Oceaneering also makes subsea systems to test potential offshore oil fields. The company's advanced technologies unit makes remotely operated diving vessels (ROVs) which are often used in search and recovery operations for the US Navy life-support robotic systems for use in space and robotics for use in the entertainment industry. In 2014 the company owned 336 ROVs the largest fleet in the world.

	Annual Growth	12/10	12/11	12/12	12/13	12/14
Sales ($ mil.)	17.5%	1,917.0	2,192.7	2,782.6	3,287.0	3,659.6
Net income ($ mil.)	20.9%	200.5	235.7	289.0	371.5	428.3
Market value ($ mil.)	(5.5%)	7,334.5	4,595.2	5,358.2	7,857.5	5,858.3
Employees	10.9%	8,200	9,600	10,900	12,200	12,400

OCEANFIRST FINANCIAL CORP

NMS: OCFC

975 Hooper Avenue
Toms River, NJ 08753
Phone: 732 240-4500
Fax: –
Web: www.oceanfirst.com

CEO: Christopher D. Maher
CFO: Michael J. Fitzpatrick
HR: –
FYE: December 31
Type: Public

Ask the folks at OceanFirst Bank for a home loan and they might say "shore." The subsidiary of holding company OceanFirst Financial operates 25 branches in the coastal New Jersey counties of Middlesex Monmouth and Ocean. The community-oriented bank caters to individuals and small to midsized businesses in the Jersey Shore area offering standard products such as checking and savings accounts CDs and IRAs. It uses funds from deposits mainly to invest in mortgages loans and securities. One- to four-family residential mortgages make up more than half of OceanFirst Financial's loan portfolio which also includes commercial real estate (about 30%) business construction and consumer loans.

	Annual Growth	12/10	12/11	12/12	12/13	12/14
Assets ($ mil.)	1.2%	2,251.3	2,302.1	2,269.2	2,249.7	2,356.7
Net income ($ mil.)	(0.6%)	20.4	20.7	20.0	16.3	19.9
Market value ($ mil.)	7.4%	217.5	220.9	232.4	289.5	289.7
Employees	(3.5%)	433	415	401	409	376

OCEANIC EXPLORATION COMPANY

OTC. OCEX.OB

7800 E. Dorado Place Ste. 250
Englewood CO 80111
Phone: 303-220-8330
Fax: 708-687-7466
Web: www.ajsmithbank.com

CEO: James N Blue
CFO: Lori A Brundage
HR: –
FYE: December 31
Type: Public

Exploring the world's oceans for oil and gas opportunities Oceanic Exploration Company's mission is to acquire oil and gas concessions covering large blocks of acreage. With its subsidiaries Oceanic International Properties Corporation (OIPC) and Petrotimor Companhia de Petroleos SA (Petrotimor) the company follows up these acquisitions with oil and gas exploration analysis including geophysical evaluation and drilling. The oil firm also provides management administrative and professional services (its sole source of revenues in 2008). Oceanic Exploration chairman and CEO James Blue through his majority holding in NWO Resources controls 89% of Oceanic Exploration.

OCERA THERAPEUTICS INC

NMS: OCRX

525 University Avenue, Suite 610
Palo Alto, CA 94301
Phone: 650 475-0150
Fax: –
Web: www.ocerainc.com

CEO: Linda S Grais
CFO: Michael Byrnes
HR: –
FYE: December 31
Type: Public

Tranzyme has a gut feeling about its therapies. A drug discovery and development company Tranzyme is developing therapies to treat acute and chronic gastrointestinal (GI) disorders. Its lead candidate ulimorelin is an intravenously-administered treatment for GI motility problems that occur after abdominal surgery. If commercialized the therapy (which is in late clinical stages of development) could be used by hospitals to quickly restore normal intestinal function to patients. The company also has other candidates in earlier stages of development including a mid-stage oral therapy to treat chronic GI motility caused by diabetes. Founded in 1998 Tranzyme went public through a $48 million IPO in 2011.

	Annual Growth	12/10	12/11	12/12	12/13	12/14
Sales ($ mil.)	(55.3%)	8.5	10.2	8.4	0.1	0.3
Net income ($ mil.)	–	(7.3)	(22.2)	(22.8)	(17.5)	(23.4)
Market value ($ mil.)	30.1%	–	57.1	10.7	256.5	125.8
Employees	(20.5%)	40	47	29	14	16

OCH-ZIFF CAPITAL MANAGEMENT GROUP LLC

NYS: OZM

9 West 57th Street
New York, NY 10019
Phone: 212 790-0000
Fax: –
Web: www.ozcap.com

CEO: Daniel S Och
CFO: –
HR: –
FYE: December 31
Type: Public

In the marvelous land of OZ good investments are king. Och-Ziff Capital Management Group provides a variety of alternative asset management services for more than 600 fund investors through offices in New York and overseas in Mumbai Beijing Hong Kong and London. Och-Ziff Capital Management Group's investment strategies include private equity merger arbitrage and equity restructuring among others. With some $46.2 billion in assets under management the majority of its equity holdings are invested in Europe and Asia. The hedge fund firm which boasts about 148 investment professionals including two dozen partners began operations in 1994.

	Annual Growth	12/11	12/12	12/13	12/14	12/15
Sales ($ mil.)	21.0%	616.4	1,211.4	1,895.9	1,542.3	1,323.0
Net income ($ mil.)	–	(419.0)	(315.8)	261.8	142.4	25.7
Market value ($ mil.)	(7.2%)	4,022.9	4,544.3	7,079.5	5,587.1	2,980.1
Employees	11.0%	434	468	546	595	659

OCI PARTNERS LP

NYS: OCIP

5470 N. Twin City Highway
Nederland, TX 77627
Phone: 409 723-1900
Fax: –
Web: www.ocipartnerslp.com

CEO: Frank Bakker
CFO: Fady Kiama
HR: –
FYE: December 31
Type: Public

OCI Partners is bringing methanol production back to the good ol' US of A. The company reopened a methanol and ammonia plant in Beaumont Texas in 2012. (It's actually the largest methanol plant in the US; currently most of the country's methanol is imported from Trinidad.) The plant (shut down by Terra Industries in 2004) has an annual production capacity of 730000 tons of methanol and 265000 tons of ammonia. OCI Partners sells the methanol and ammonia to customers such as Koch Industries Methanex and Transammonia who use it to create other chemicals. OCI Partners is affiliated with Egypt-based Orascom Construction Industries (OCI). It went public in 2013.

	Annual Growth	12/10	12/11	12/12	12/13	12/14
Sales ($ mil.)	–	0.0	–	224.6	428.0	402.8
Net income ($ mil.)	–	0.0	0.3	51.8	154.4	119.4
Market value ($ mil.)	–	0.0	–	–	2,304.5	1,335.9
Employees	–	–	–	–	–	–

OCLARO INC.

NMS: OCLR

225 Charcot Avenue
San Jose, CA 95131
Phone: 408 383-1400
Fax: –

CEO: Greg Dougherty
CFO: Pete J. Mangan
HR: Lisa Paul
FYE: June 27
Type: Public

And you thought splitting hairs was tedious. Oclaro (a combination of the words "optical" and "clarity") integrates the light-processing functions of optical networking components onto silicon chips which it then puts into communications products such as transceivers transponders transmitters receivers and modulators. Typical devices for dividing wavelengths of light combine several components such as tunable lasers lenses and filters. Oclaro sells its optical components to telecommunications and data communications systems and components vendors; other customers come from the laser systems life sciences industrial printing and consumer electronics industries.

	Annual Growth	07/11*	06/12	06/13	06/14	06/15
Sales ($ mil.)	(7.5%)	466.5	385.5	586.0	390.9	341.3
Net income ($ mil.)	–	(46.4)	(66.5)	(122.7)	17.8	(56.7)
Market value ($ mil.)	(23.9%)	740.1	334.1	129.7	236.3	248.3
Employees	(20.5%)	3,085	2,790	2,782	1,294	1,233

*Fiscal year change

OCLC ONLINE COMPUTER LIBRARY CENTER INCORPORATE

6565 KILGOUR PL
DUBLIN, OH 430173395
Phone: 614-764-6000
Fax: –
Web: www.conference-center.oclc.org

CEO: David A Prichard
CFO: –
HR: –
FYE: June 30
Type: Private

Working to reduce the cost of information OCLC Online Computer Library Center is a membership cooperative that provides access to the world's information. The group offers services and tools to some 74000 member libraries in about 170 countries. Services include computer-based cataloging preservation and library management. OCLC additionally facilitates interlibrary loan services administers the Dewey Decimal Classification system and operates the WorldCat database an online resource for finding library materials. OCLC was founded in 1967 by presidents of the colleges and universities in Ohio. OCLC which stands for Ohio College Library Center opened its first location in Ohio State's main library.

	Annual Growth	06/10	06/11	06/12	06/13	06/14
Sales ($ mil.)	1.3%	–	205.6	203.5	206.6	213.6
Net income ($ mil.)	–	–	–	(3.0)	8.3	21.9
Market value ($ mil.)	–	–	–	–	–	–
Employees	–	–	–	–	–	1,227

OCTAGON WORLDWIDE INC.

800 Connecticut Ave. 2nd Fl.
Norwalk CT 06854
Phone: 203-354-7400
Fax: 203-354-7401
Web: www.octagon.com

CEO: Rick Dudley
CFO: Michael Thomas
HR: –
FYE: December 31
Type: Subsidiary

Octagon Worldwide has a game plan for marketing world-class athletes and entertainers. A unit of Interpublic Group the sports marketing firm represents some 800 athletes and "personality clients" including former NFL personalities Bill Cowher and Emmitt Smith and the NBA's Chris Paul. Its services include athlete representation event management TV rights sales and distribution licensing and merchandising TV production and new media. Managing more than 13400 events each year Octagon also owns sporting events and properties (including WTA Tennis Events Beach Volleyball World Tour) which allow it to court corporate sponsors. Octagon was founded in 1997 by Frank Lowe.

OCULUS INNOVATIVE SCIENCES INC

NAS: OCLS

1129 North McDowell Blvd.
Petaluma, CA 94954
Phone: 707 283-0550
Fax: –
Web: www.oculusis.com

CEO: Jim Schutz
CFO: Robert E Miller
HR: –
FYE: March 31
Type: Public

Oculus isn't the name of an all-seeing ancient Latin god or superhero though it does use super-agents in its fight against the evil super-bug MRSA. Oculus Innovative Sciences works with proprietary platform technology Microcyn a super-oxidized water-based solution designed to safely (i.e. without any known side effects) eliminate a wide range of annoying pathogens (including MRSA) attempting to infect patients with open wounds. Aside from use in wound care the solution has potential applications for use in disinfectants and sterilization as well as respiratory dermatology veterinary and dental markets. Oculus' products are primarily sold through partnerships with distributors.

	Annual Growth	03/11	03/12	03/13	03/14	03/15
Sales ($ mil.)	9.2%	9.8	12.7	15.5	13.7	13.9
Net income ($ mil.)	–	(7.9)	(7.3)	(5.4)	3.7	(8.2)
Market value ($ mil.)	(19.6%)	30.2	20.0	6.6	56.7	12.6
Employees	42.5%	32	121	42	102	132

OCWEN FINANCIAL CORPORATION

NYSE: OCN

2002 Summit Blvd. 6th Fl.
Atlanta GA 30319
Phone: 561-682-8000
Fax: 561-682-8177
Web: www.ocwen.com

CEO: Ronald M Faris
CFO: Michael R Bourque Jr
HR: –
FYE: December 31
Type: Public

Oc-what? Oc-who? Ocwen. Ocwen Financial and its subsidiaries service residential and commercial mortgages for third parties. The company also offers special servicing and asset management services. Its main Ocwen Loan Servicing subsidiary is licensed to service loans in all 50 states and two US territories. The company which has offices and call centers in the US South America and India earns fees from the owners of mortgages or foreclosed real estate for which it collects. Clients include banks and other financial institutions including Credit Suisse Deutsche Bank Freddie Mac Goldman Sachs and Morgan Stanley. Ocwen no longer originates subprime loans.

OCZ TECHNOLOGY GROUP INC

NBB: OCZT Q

6373 San Ignacio Avenue
San Jose, CA 95119
Phone: 408 733-8400
Fax: –
Web: www.ocztechnology.com

CEO: Ralph Schmitt
CFO: Rafael Torres
HR: –
FYE: February 28
Type: Public

You down with OCZ? You should be because OCZ Technology's solid-state drives (SSDs) and related products are performing in PCs servers data centers and industrial gear around the world. The company designs manufactures and sells high-performance SSDs which use flash memory chips and are a smaller faster more reliable and more energy-efficient storage device than traditional hard disk drives. OCZ offers some 200 products to more than 400 customers in 60 countries. It sells directly to OEMs and large company and to other end users through systems integrators online retailers such as Amazon and computer distributors that include Memoryworld GmbH (10% of sales).

	Annual Growth	02/09	02/10	02/11	02/12	02/13
Sales ($ mil.)	21.0%	156.0	144.0	190.1	365.8	334.0
Net income ($ mil.)	–	(11.7)	(13.5)	(30.0)	(17.7)	(125.8)
Market value ($ mil.)	(30.9%)	–	357.5	515.5	585.3	117.8
Employees	24.1%	–	312	422	708	597

ODOM CORPORATION

11400 SE 8TH ST STE 300
BELLEVUE, WA 980046409
Phone: 425-456-3535
Fax: –
Web: www.odomcorp.com

CEO: –
CFO: Randy Halter
HR: –
FYE: December 31
Type: Private

The Odom Corporation wants you to drink up if you happen to be in the Pacific Northwest. The company distributes beer wine and spirits as well as sodas energy drinks and bottled waters from more than 500 domestic and foreign suppliers including Coca-Cola Diageo E. & J. Gallo MillerCoors and Pernod Ricard. The company serves retail customers throughout the northwestern US including those in Alaska Idaho Oregon and Washington. It also runs Odom-Southern Holdings a joint venture with Southern Wine and Spirits of America the #1 distributor of alcoholic beverages in the US. Milt Odom founded the company in 1933.

	Annual Growth	12/02	12/03	12/04	12/06	12/07
Sales ($ mil.)	22.1%	–	151.9	211.0	304.6	337.9
Net income ($ mil.)	(8.3%)	–	–	3.8	1.8	2.9
Market value ($ mil.)	–	–	–	–	–	–
Employees	–	–	–	–	–	1,500

ODWALLA INC.

120 Stone Pine Rd.
Half Moon Bay CA 94019-1783
Phone: 650-726-1888
Fax: 301-444-2299
Web: www.optelecom.com

CEO: D Stephen Williamson
CFO: James R Steichen
HR: –
FYE: December 31
Type: Subsidiary

It isn't odd to drink beverages made from fruits and vegetables it's Odwalla (pronounced Oh-DWA-la). The company's juice beverages are known for their colorful packaging and equally colorful names including Mo' Beta Pink Poetry and Wholly Grain! Keenly aware of food trends it periodically introduces beverages that are popular with foodies such as PomaGrand (a trendy tropical fruit) and Protein Monster (for multitaskers who don't have time to sit down for a meal). Odwalla also makes nutritional bars and soy-based drinks including organic soy milk. Its beverages are sold at natural food stores supermarkets and specialty outlets in the US. Odwalla is a unit of Coca-Cola North America.

ODYSSEY HEALTHCARE INC.

717 North Harwood Street Suite 1500
Dallas TX 75201
Phone: 214-922-9711
Fax: 214-922-9752
Web: www.odyssey-healthcare.com

CEO: Tony Strange
CFO: R Dirk Allison
HR: Angie Eidt
FYE: December 31
Type: Subsidiary

Odyssey HealthCare provides comfort for patients in the final stages of life's journey. One of the nation's largest hospice care providers Odyssey HealthCare operates about 100 for-profit hospice programs nationwide. The group offers a full range of hospice care services including pain and symptom management medical social services personal care spiritual support and counseling and daily living assistance. Caregivers consist of registered nurses physicians home healthcare aides social workers and bereavement counselors among others. It serves patients in their homes or in hospitals and nursing facilities; it also operates inpatient hospice facilities. Gentiva Health Services owns Odyssey HealthCare.

ODYSSEY INVESTMENT PARTNERS LLC

280 Park Ave. West Tower 38th Fl.
New York NY 10017
Phone: 212-351-7900
Fax: 212-351-7925
Web: www.odysseyinvestment.com

CEO: –
CFO: –
HR: –
FYE: December 31
Type: Private

The partners of Odyssey Investment are on a quest for companies primed for growth. The firm manages some $2.5 billion in capital via three equity funds that invest mainly in established middle-market companies. An active investor that acquires majority stakes in firms and partners with their management Odyssey Investment Partners seeks out sectors or markets that could benefit from regulatory or economic changes. It focuses on the industrial manufacturing business and financial services aerospace and defense energy equipment rental and logistics industries. Portfolio companies include: SM&A; Wastequip; and Safway.

ODYSSEY MARINE EXPLORATION, INC.

NAS: OMEX

5215 W. Laurel Street
Tampa, FL 33607
Phone: 813 876-1776
Fax: –
Web: www.odysseymarine.com

CEO: Mark D Gordon
CFO: Philip S Devine
HR: Donna Fernandez
FYE: December 31
Type: Public

Gone are the days when one-eyed peg-legged buccaneers counted their steps to where X marked the spot of lost treasure. Odyssey Marine Exploration a new breed of treasure hunter uses sonar magnetometers and remotely operated vehicles (ROVs) to locate and excavate shipwrecks as well as for subsea mineral exploration. The company focuses on deepwater projects where the booty is less susceptible to damage and less likely to have been salvaged. Odyssey Marine Exploration surveys and maps seabeds too; its experience covers more than 10000 sq. mi. The company sells artifacts (coins bullion) salvaged from shipwrecks but also in recent years generates revenue from expedition charter services.

	Annual Growth	12/10	12/11	12/12	12/13	12/14
Sales ($ mil.)	(49.9%)	21.0	15.7	13.2	23.9	1.3
Net income ($ mil.)	–	(23.3)	(16.2)	(18.2)	(10.7)	(26.5)
Market value ($ mil.)	(23.9%)	237.9	234.5	254.2	172.9	79.6
Employees	(2.5%)	42	42	43	43	38

OEC BUSINESS INTERIORS INC.

900 N CHURCH RD
ELMHURST, IL 60126-1014
Phone: 630-589-5500
Fax: –
Web: www.oecbusinessinteriors.com

CEO: –
CFO: –
HR: –
FYE: September 30
Type: Private

Success at OEC Business Interiors is an inside job. The company supplies office equipment in the Chicago area and throughout the Midwest. Products include furniture panel systems floor coverings and textiles from major manufacturers as well as a wide range of services such as remanufacturing rentals brokerage warehouse storage and physical asset management. OEC Business Interiors was founded in 1955 by president Raymond Riha his wife and two partners as Riha Petersen & Vail. In 1961 the company purchased Office Equipment Company which had been in business since 1929.

	Annual Growth	09/08	09/09	09/09	09/11	09/12
Sales ($ mil.)	(0.9%)	–	55.2	47.8	54.7	53.7
Net income ($ mil.)	–	–	(0.1)	(0.4)	0.2	0.0
Market value ($ mil.)	–	–	–	–	–	–
Employees	–	–	–	–	–	135

OFFICE DEPOT, INC.

NMS: ODP

6600 North Military Trail
Boca Raton, FL 33496
Phone: 561 438-4800
Fax: 561 265-4406
Web: www.officedepot.com

CEO: Roland C. Smith
CFO: Stephen E. Hare
HR: –
FYE: December 27
Type: Public

Paper and paper clips add up to big money for Office Depot. The world's #2 office supply chain (behind Staples) Office Depot sells office supplies through some 2000 retail stores in about 60 countries following its merger with OfficeMax. The big-box retail stores sell to both consumers and small and medium-sized businesses. In addition to general office supplies (about two-thirds of sales) its stores offer computer hardware and software furniture art and school supplies and printing and copying services. Office Depot also sells goods through catalogs and call centers the Internet and a contract sales force. Faced with declining organic sales in 2015 the company agreed to be acquired by Staples.

	Annual Growth	12/10	12/11	12/12	12/13	12/14
Sales ($ mil.)	8.5%	11,633.1	11,489.5	10,695.7	11,242.0	16,096.0
Net income ($ mil.)	–	34.9	95.7	(77.1)	(20.0)	(354.0)
Market value ($ mil.)	12.9%	2,971.2	1,172.1	1,782.7	2,829.5	4,819.4
Employees	8.8%	40,000	39,000	38,000	64,000	56,000

OFFICIAL PAYMENTS HOLDINGS INC.

NASDAQ: TIER

10780 Parkridge Blvd. 4th Fl.
Reston VA 20191
Phone: 571-382-1000
Fax: 571-382-1002
Web: www.officialpayments.com

CEO: Alex P Hart
CFO: –
HR: –
FYE: September 30
Type: Public

Official Payments Holdings helps the tax man get what's coming to him. Formerly Tier Technologies the company provides electronic payments services (EPS) services for federal state and local government entities as well as utilities colleges and universities and commercial clients. Through its main subsidiary Official Payments the company processes more than 20 million transactions each year for payment of federal and state income taxes business and property taxes court fees and fines and utility bills among others. It handles more than $8 billion annually. Payments can be made online by phone or mobile device or at the point-of-sale.

OGE ENERGY CORP.

NYS: OGE

321 North Harvey, P.O. Box 321
Oklahoma City, OK 73101-0321
Phone: 405 553-3000
Fax: –
Web: www.oge.com

CEO: R. Sean Trauschke
CFO: Stephen E. (Steve) Merrill
HR: Margaret Walsh
FYE: December 31
Type: Public

OGE Energy is the holding company for the largest electric utility in Oklahoma. It also has a major energy marketing and natural gas transmission unit OGE Energy Resources. OGE Energy owns Oklahoma Gas and Electric (OG&E) a public utility with more than 800000 retail and wholesale customers in Oklahoma (including Oklahoma City) and a slice of western Arkansas. OG&E owns coal- and gas-fired power plants that generate 6845 MW of capacity. Its 27%-owned Enable Midstream Partners affiliate operates 11900 miles of natural gas gathering and transportation pipeline. The company also provides physical asset financial management services through marketing unit OGE Energy Resources.

	Annual Growth	12/10	12/11	12/12	12/13	12/14
Sales ($ mil.)	(9.9%)	3,716.9	3,915.9	3,671.2	2,867.7	2,453.1
Net income ($ mil.)	7.6%	295.3	342.9	355.0	387.6	395.8
Market value ($ mil.)	(6.0%)	9,080.7	11,308.0	11,228.2	6,759.7	7,074.7
Employees	(0.6%)	3,416	3,489	3,377	3,269	3,329

OGILVY & MATHER WORLDWIDE INC.

636 11th Ave.
New York NY 10036
Phone: 212-237-4000
Fax: 212-237-5123
Web: www.ogilvy.com

CEO: Miles Young
CFO: Steven Goldstein
HR: –
FYE: December 31
Type: Subsidiary

Ogilvy & Mather Worldwide does advertising by the book. Founded by ad pioneer David Ogilvy (author of Ogilvy on Advertising) the firm is one of the world's leading creative agency networks providing advertising campaign development and management brand development public relations and strategic planning services to clients such as American Express IBM and Cisco. Ogilvy & Mather offers specialized communications and relationship marketing services through OgilvyOne; its Ogilvy CommonHealth Worldwide unit offers services targeted for global clients in the health care industry. Operating through more than 450 offices around the world it is one of the primary agency subsidiaries of UK-based WPP Group.

OGIO INTERNATIONAL INC.

14926 Pony Express Rd.
Bluffdale UT 84065
Phone: 801-619-4100
Fax: 801-619-4111
Web: www.ogio.com

CEO: Michael Pratt
CFO: –
HR: –
FYE: December 31
Type: Private

Ogio and its products like to be on the go. The company's a bag maker for sports gear; it's unique niche is focusing on bag design for functionality. Ogio manufactures about 400 different types of golf club bags backpacks duffel bags and day packs under the Ogio brand name. The firm makes a line of duffel-type computer bags corporate travel gear gym bags school backpacks motocross bags and other accessories. Ogio's products are sold nationwide through retailers such as Golfsmith Best Buy Dick's Sporting Goods eBags Sport Chalet and Zones. Ogio also manufactures brands for other companies. The company was founded in 1987 by Mike Pratt after he designed the LockerBag gym bag.

OGLETHORPE POWER CORP

2100 East Exchange Place
Tucker, GA 30084-5336
Phone: 770 270-7600
Fax: 770 270-7325
Web: www.opc.com

CEO: Michael L. Smith
CFO: Elizabeth Bush (Betsy) Higgins
HR: –
FYE: December 31
Type: Public

Much ogled for its robust energy supply not-for-profit Oglethorpe Power Corporation is one of the largest electricity cooperatives in the US with contracts to supply wholesale power to 38 member/owners (making up most of Georgia's electric distribution cooperatives) until 2050. Oglethorpe's member/owners which also operate as not-for-profits serve 1.8 million residential commercial and industrial customers (or about 4.1 million people). The company has a generating capacity of about 7080 MW from fossil-fueled nuclear and hydroelectric power plants. Oglethorpe has stakes in 31 generating units. In addition the company purchases power from other suppliers and it markets power on the wholesale market.

	Annual Growth	12/10	12/11	12/12	12/13	12/14
Sales ($ mil.)	2.1%	1,294.0	1,390.3	1,324.1	1,245.4	1,408.2
Net income ($ mil.)	8.4%	33.7	37.7	39.3	41.5	46.6
Market value ($ mil.)	–	–	–	–	–	–
Employees	6.1%	209	216	261	261	265

OHIO EDISON CO

NBB: OECA P

c/o FirstEnergy Corp., 76 South Main Street
Akron, OH 44308
Phone: 800 736-3402
Fax: –

CEO: –
CFO: James F Pearson
HR: –
FYE: December 31
Type: Public

Ohio Edison has taken a shine to the folks in the Buckeye state. The company distributes electricity to a population of about 2.3 million (more than 1 million customers) in a 7000 sq. ml. area of central and northeastern Ohio. Ohio Edison a unit of FirstEnergy also has 5955 MW of generating capacity from interests in primarily fossil-fueled and nuclear generation facilities and it sells excess power to wholesale customers. The utility's power plants are operated by sister companies FirstEnergy Nuclear and FirstEnergy Generation. Subsidiary Pennsylvania Power Company provides electric service to communities in a 1100 sq. ml. area of western Pennsylvania which has a population of approximately 400000.

	Annual Growth	12/08	12/09	12/10	12/11	12/12
Sales ($ mil.)	(11.2%)	2,601.8	2,516.9	1,836.1	1,633.0	1,615.0
Net income ($ mil.)	(16.9%)	211.7	121.9	156.7	128.0	101.0
Market value ($ mil.)						
Employees	(2.6%)	1,551	1,391	1,434	1,426	1,397

OHIO LEGACY CORP

NBB: OLCB

600 South Main Street
North Canton, OH 44720
Phone: 330 499-1900
Fax: –
Web: www.ohiolegacycorp.com

CEO: Rick L Hull
CFO: Jane Marsh
HR: –
FYE: December 31
Type: Public

Ohio Legacy Corp is the holding company for Premier Bank & Trust (formerly Ohio Legacy Bank) which serves northeastern Ohio's Stark and Wayne counties through about five branches. Operating since 2000 the bank offers standard deposit products and services including checking and savings accounts CDs IRAs cash management and safe deposit box facilities. It added trust services in 2010 and changed its name to reflect its new focus. Commercial multifamily and residential mortgages account for some two-thirds of all loans. In exchange for majority ownership of Ohio Legacy Corp a group of local investors provided the company with $15 million to shore up its balance sheet.

	Annual Growth	12/10	12/11	12/12	12/13	12/14
Assets ($ mil.)	11.8%	170.6	146.6	174.7	229.9	266.2
Net income ($ mil.)	–	(3.1)	1.8	0.1	0.9	4.9
Market value ($ mil.)	48.0%	3.9	2.1	12.3	14.8	18.7
Employees	(8.2%)	70	53	59	–	–

OHIO NATIONAL FINANCIAL SERVICES INC.

1 Financial Way
Cincinnati OH 45242
Phone: 513-794-6100
Fax: 513-794-4504
Web: www.ohionatl.com

CEO: Gary T Huffman
CFO: Arthur J Roberts
HR: –
FYE: December 31
Type: Private - Mutual Com

Ohio National Financial Services is the marketing name for Ohio National Life Insurance and Ohio National Life Assurance which sell individual and group life insurance disability insurance pension plans and individual variable and fixed annuities. Other products and services include wholesale and retail brokerage and mutual funds. Ohio National Financial Services sells its products in the US in all states excepti Alaska Hawaii and New York and in the District of Columbia Puerto Rico and through a subsidiary in Santiago Chile. The company distributes its products through independent agents brokers and banks. Mutual holding company Ohio National Mutual Holdings owns a majority of the firm.

OHIO POWER COMPANY NL:

1 Riverside Plaza
Columbus, OH 43215-2373
Phone: 614 716-1000
Fax: -

CEO: Nicholas K Akins
CFO: Brian X Tierney
HR: -
FYE: December 31
Type: Public

To access electricity across the state of Ohio residents and businesses turn to Ohio Power which in tandem with Wheeling Power does business as part of AEP Ohio. AEP Ohio serves 1.5 million retail customers. The company one of American Electric Power's largest utility subsidiaries operates more than 31260 miles of transmission and distribution lines. The utility also generates more than 8500 MW of capacity from primarily hydroelectric and fossil-fueled power plants (the bulk from coal-fired plants) and it sells wholesale electricity to other power companies.

	Annual Growth	12/10	12/11	12/12	12/13	12/14
Sales ($ mil.)	1.2%	3,223.7	5,431.1	4,928.2	4,762.6	3,376.9
Net income ($ mil.)	(8.7%)	311.4	465.0	343.5	410.0	216.4
Market value ($ mil.)		-	-	-	-	-
Employees	(7.8%)	2,100	3,256	3,131	1,524	1,516

OHIO STATE UNIVERSITY RESEARCH FOUNDATION

1960 KENNY RD
COLUMBUS, OH 432101016
Phone: 614-688-8125
Fax: -

CEO: -
CFO: -
HR: -
FYE: June 30
Type: Private

The Ohio State University Research Foundation was established in 1936 to function as a central agency for supporting research and development through grants management and information technology for Ohio State University one of the largest public universities in the US. The not-for-profit corporation provides administrative services for research programs including submitting support requests managing equipment and governmental and university compliance oversight. Ohio State University's total awards reached more than $37 million by July 2007 with some 330 awards.

	Annual Growth	06/09	06/10	06/11	06/12	06/13
Sales ($ mil.)	4.5%	-	437.8	485.6	499.3	499.0
Net income ($ mil.)	10.0%	-	-	0.7	0.3	0.8
Market value ($ mil.)	-	-	-	-	-	-
Employees	-	-	-	-	-	105

OHIO VALLEY BANC CORP NMS: OVBC

420 Third Avenue
Gallipolis, OH 45631
Phone: 740 446-2631
Fax: -
Web: www.ovbc.com

CEO: Thomas E Wiseman
CFO: Scott W Shockey
HR: -
FYE: December 31
Type: Public

Ohio Valley Banc Corp. (OVBC) knows when you go to buy groceries you'll probably need some cabbage. That's why this holding company likes to operate its Ohio Valley Bank branches inside supermarkets. The bank has some 15 branches in Ohio and West Virginia about half of which are in Wal-Marts and other stores. The bank accepts deposits in checking savings time and money market accounts and offers standard banking services such as safe deposit boxes and wire transfers. Commercial and residential real estate loans combine to make up almost three-quarters of the bank's loan portfolio. Business and consumer loans make up the remainder. Also part of OVBC is life insurance agency Ohio Valley Financial Services.

	Annual Growth	12/10	12/11	12/12	12/13	12/14
Assets ($ mil.)	(2.2%)	851.5	804.2	769.2	747.4	778.7
Net income ($ mil.)	12.2%	5.1	5.8	7.1	8.1	8.1
Market value ($ mil.)	5.8%	80.7	76.2	77.4	90.6	101.0
Employees	(1.4%)	279	285	277	273	264

OHIO VALLEY ELECTRIC CORP.

3932 U.S. Route 23, P.O. Box 468
Piketon, OH 45661
Phone: 740 289-7200
Fax: -
Web: www.ovec.com

CEO: -
CFO: -
HR: -
FYE: December 31
Type: Public

Down by the banks of the Ohio Ohio Valley Electric and its subsidiary Indiana-Kentucky Electric generate power for customers across the Ohio River Valley. It operates two coal-fired plants which collectively have about 2290 MW of generating capacity. Ohio Valley Electric's Kyger Creek Plant (Cheshire Ohio) and Indiana-Kentucky Electric's Clifty Creek Plant (Madison Indiana) are linked by 705 miles of transmission lines. Most of Ohio Valley Electric's power goes to its shareholders (a dozen investor-owned utilities utility holding entities led by American Electric Power and units of generation and transmission rural electric cooperatives). It also supplies energy to the Department of Energy.

	Annual Growth	12/09	12/10	12/11	12/12	12/13
Sales ($ mil.)	1.0%	648.6	690.7	716.9	670.8	675.6
Net income ($ mil.)	(6.7%)	2.9	2.2	2.7	2.3	2.2
Market value ($ mil.)	-	-	-	-	-	-
Employees	-	-	-	-	-	-

OHIO VALLEY GENERAL HOSPITAL

25 HECKEL RD
MC KEES ROCKS, PA 151361651
Phone: 412-777-6161
Fax: -
Web: www.ohiovalleyhospital.org

CEO: -
CFO: -
HR: Vicki Mell
FYE: June 30
Type: Private

Ohio Valley General Hospital is a full-service 140-bed medical center serving western Pennsylvania residents. The not-for-profit community hospital's staff of about 250 doctors (representing about 35 medical specialties) provides emergency acute diagnostic and specialty care and a variety of inpatient and outpatient care services. Ohio Valley General Hospital's programs include cardiology occupational medicine pain treatment orthopedics rehabilitation sleep disorder diagnosis geriatric psychiatry and wound care. The hospital also offers assisted living for seniors. Ohio Valley General began serving patients in 1906.

	Annual Growth	06/08	06/09	06/10	06/11	06/13
Sales ($ mil.)	2.8%	-	61.3	64.8	66.9	68.4
Net income ($ mil.)	-	-	-	(0.7)	(0.1)	0.5
Market value ($ mil.)	-	-	-	-	-	-
Employees	-	-	-	-	-	570

OHIO VALLEY MEDICAL CENTER INCORPORATED

2000 EOFF ST
WHEELING, WV 260033823
Phone: 304-234-0123
Fax: -
Web: www.ovmc-eorh.com

CEO: Michael J Caruso
CFO: -
HR: -
FYE: December 31
Type: Private

Ohio Valley Medical Center (OVMC) is a Wheeling West Virginia-based medical provider that administers a variety of acute care primary care and other health services to patients through a 200-bed hospital. The facility established in 1890 as City Hospital specializes in intermediate care physical rehabilitation and skilled nursing. Other services include cardiology cancer care emergency care gynecology neurology oncology and psychiatry as well as home health care. OVMC also operates the Peterson Rehabilitation Center and two-year hospital based education program OVMC School of Radiologic Technology. It partners with nearby East Ohio Regional Hospital to provide 340 total beds.

	Annual Growth	12/04	12/05	12/06	12/07	12/09
Sales ($ mil.)	7.4%	-	79.9	86.1	94.7	106.4
Net income ($ mil.)	-	-	-	(1.9)	6.0	(1.8)
Market value ($ mil.)	-	-	-	-	-	-
Employees	-	-	-	-	-	1,275

OHIOHEALTH CORPORATION

180 E BRD ST	CEO: David P. Blom
COLUMBUS, OH 432153707	CFO: –
Phone: 614-544-4455	HR: –
Fax: –	FYE: June 30
Web: www.ohiohealth.com	Type: Private

Operating throughout the central part of the state OhioHealth aims to keep Buckeyes healthy. The not-for-profit system runs eight acute care hospitals and is affiliated with another 11 community hospitals and area health systems. All told OhioHealth has about 2000 staffed beds in and around Columbus. Additional facilities offer urgent care physical rehabilitation diagnostic imaging and sleep diagnostics services. Subsidiary HomeReach provides home health care and hospice care. Its WorkHealth program offers workers' compensation care management and occupational rehabilitation services. OhioHealth Group OhioHealth's joint venture with The Medical Group of Ohio operates the HealthReach PPO.

	Annual Growth	06/08	06/09	06/10	06/11	06/12
Sales ($ mil.)	3.7%	–	1,794.4	1,967.4	2,328.4	1,999.9
Net income ($ mil.)	17.1%	–	–	221.5	413.0	304.0
Market value ($ mil.)	–	–	–	–	–	–
Employees	–	–	–	–	–	15,000

OIL STATES INTERNATIONAL, INC.

NYS: OIS

Three Allen Center, 333 Clay Street, Suite 4620	CEO: Cindy B. Taylor
Houston, TX 77002	CFO: Lloyd A. Hajdik
Phone: 713 652-0582	HR: Lias J. (Jeff) Steen
Fax: –	FYE: December 31
Web: www.oilstatesintl.com	Type: Public

Oil States International is an oilfield services company with a leading market position as a manufacturer of products for deepwater production facilities and certain drilling equipment as well as a provider of completion services and land drilling services to the oil and gas industry. The company provides well site services including tool rentals and land drilling rig services. It also offers offshore products including flex-element technology and deepwater mooring systems. Oil States International focuses on supporting explorers in major producing regions throughout the world. Anadarko Petroleum and Chevron are among its biggest customers.

	Annual Growth	12/10	12/11	12/12	12/13	12/14
Sales ($ mil.)	(6.8%)	2,412.0	3,479.2	4,413.1	2,670.4	1,819.6
Net income ($ mil.)	1.6%	168.0	322.5	448.6	421.3	179.0
Market value ($ mil.)	(6.5%)	3,397.9	4,048.9	3,792.9	5,392.9	2,592.5
Employees	(6.4%)	6,904	7,949	8,716	9,167	5,290

OIL-DRI CORP. OF AMERICA

NYS: ODC

410 North Michigan Avenue, Suite 400	CEO: Daniel S Jaffee
Chicago, IL 60611-4213	CFO: Daniel T Smith
Phone: 312 321-1515	HR: –
Fax: 312 321-9525	FYE: July 31
Web: www.oildri.com	Type: Public

Oil-Dri Corporation (ODC) of America keeps cat lovers' homes from stinking to high heaven. The company produces sorbent products for the consumer industrial automotive agricultural and fluid-purification markets. It makes and sells traditional coarse and scoopable cat litters under its own Cat's Pride and Jonny Cat brands. ODC manufactures the Fresh Step brand exclusively for Clorox as well as private label cat litters for others. Its litters are sold by mass merchants (Wal-Mart) supermarkets pet stores wholesale clubs and other retailers. ODC also makes sorbents for oil grease and water; bleaching and clarification clays; agricultural and sports fields; and animal health and nutrition products.

	Annual Growth	07/11	07/12	07/13	07/14	07/15
Sales ($ mil.)	3.6%	226.8	240.7	250.6	266.3	261.4
Net income ($ mil.)	5.9%	9.1	6.1	14.6	8.4	11.4
Market value ($ mil.)	6.1%	146.2	155.0	225.2	206.2	185.6
Employees	(0.6%)	815	757	727	793	797

OILTANKING PARTNERS LP

NYS: OILT

333 Clay Street, Suite 2400	CEO: Laurie H Argo
Houston, TX 77002	CFO: Donna Y Hymel
Phone: 281 457-7900	HR: –
Fax: –	FYE: December 31
Web: www.oiltankingpartners.com	Type: Public

What do Germany and Houston have in common? Not much besides Oiltanking Partners. The limited partnership formed in March 2011 by Oiltanking Holding Americas a subsidiary of Oiltanking GmbH the world's second-largest independent storage provider for crude oil liquid chemicals and gases. (Oiltanking GmbH is in turn owned by private German conglomerate Marquard & Bahls). Oiltanking Partners owns and operates pipeline terminals with about 135 tanks in Houston and Beaumont that have a storage capacity of about 18 million barrels. Customers include oil and companies marketers and distributors. Oiltanking Partners raised $215 million in its 2011 initial public offering.

	Annual Growth	12/08	12/09	12/10	12/11	12/12
Sales ($ mil.)	–	0.0	100.8	116.5	117.4	135.5
Net income ($ mil.)	–	0.0	25.1	37.8	62.4	62.6
Market value ($ mil.)	–	0.0	–	–	1,086.1	1,472.7
Employees	–	–	–	–	–	–

OKI DATA AMERICAS INC.

2000 Bishops Gate Blvd.	CEO: Masahiko Morioka
Mt. Laurel NJ 08054-4620	CFO: Akio Samata
Phone: 856-235-2600	HR: Michael Zolty
Fax: 856-222-5320	FYE: March 31
Web: www.okidata.com	Type: Subsidiary

OKI Data Americas makes it easier to produce a hard copy. Operating under the OKI brand the company manufactures peripheral equipment for personal computers. Its products include digital color printers black-and-white printers impact printers facsimile machines and multifunction devices that combine printing copy scan and fax functions. Its newest mulitfunction printer adds wireless capabilities. The company also supplies such items as envelopes paper toner and other supplies. Established in 1972 OKI Data Americas is a subsidiary of Tokyo-based Oki Data.

OLAN MILLS INC.

6060 Shallowford Rd.	CEO: –
Chattanooga TN 37422	CFO: –
Phone: 423-622-5141	HR: –
Fax: 423-629-8128	FYE: December 31
Web: www.olanmills.com	Type: Private

The picture is clear for Olan Mills America's leading producer of family portraits with hundreds of photo studios across the US. The company operates through two divisions: Church Directories (its top revenue generator with about 60% of the national market) and Studio Portrait (featuring several hundred studios in Kmart Belk Macy's and other major retailers in the US and Puerto Rico). The company serves 11000 churches and publishes more than 3 million church directories each year. Founded in 1932 by Olan and Mary Mills the company was owned by their son Olan Mills II until late 2011 when rival Lifetouch acquired the business for an undisclosed amount.

OLD DOMINION ELECTRIC COOPERATIVE

4201 Dominion Boulevard	CEO: –
Glen Allen, VA 23060	CFO: –
Phone: 804 747-0592	HR: Elissa Ecker
Fax: –	FYE: December 31
Web: www.odec.com	Type: Public

Ol' Virginny and neighboring states get power from Old Dominion Electric Cooperative which generates and purchases electricity for its 11 member distribution cooperatives. These in turn serve more than 550000 customer meters in four northeastern states. The member-owned power utility has more than 2000 MW of generating capacity from nuclear hydro and fossil-fueled power plants and diesel generators; it purchases the remainder of its power from neighboring utilities and power marketers. Old Dominion transmits power to its members through the systems of utilities and transmission operators in the region. It also provides power to TEC Trading a wholesale company owned by the distribution cooperatives.

	Annual Growth	12/10	12/11	12/12	12/13	12/14
Sales ($ mil.)	3.0%	844.5	891.5	842.7	842.1	951.6
Net income ($ mil.)	(2.7%)	10.2	10.8	9.9	9.6	9.1
Market value ($ mil.)	–	–	–	–	–	–
Employees	0.9%	107	109	108	111	111

OLD DOMINION FREIGHT LINE, INC.

NMS: ODFL

500 Old Dominion Way	CEO: David S. Congdon
Thomasville, NC 27360	CFO: Adam N. Satterfield
Phone: 336 889-5000	HR: –
Fax: –	FYE: December 31
Web: www.odfl.com	Type: Public

Old Dominion Freight Line still makes its stand in Dixie but the trucking company serves the rest of the US as well. Less-than-truckload (LTL) shipments (freight from multiple shippers consolidated into a single truckload) accounts for the bulk of the company's revenues. Old Dominion operates a fleet of more than 6900 tractors and more than 27000 trailers from more than 220 service centers. In addition to its core LTL services the company offers its customers a broad range of logistics services including ground and air transportation supply chain consulting container delivery and warehousing and household moving.

	Annual Growth	12/10	12/11	12/12	12/13	12/14
Sales ($ mil.)	17.1%	1,481.0	1,882.5	2,110.5	2,337.6	2,787.9
Net income ($ mil.)	37.1%	75.7	139.5	169.5	206.1	267.5
Market value ($ mil.)	24.8%	2,754.2	3,489.4	2,951.3	4,564.7	6,684.4
Employees	10.1%	11,179	12,022	13,016	14,073	16,443

OLD LINE BANCSHARES INC

NAS: OLBK

1525 Pointer Ridge Place	CEO: James W. Cornelsen
Bowie, MD 20716	CFO: Elise M. Hubbard
Phone: 301 430-2500	HR: –
Fax: –	FYE: December 31
Web: www.oldlinebank.com	Type: Public

Old Line Bancshares is the holding company for Old Line Bank serving consumers businesses and wealthy individuals in the Old Line State and in the Washington DC area. With some 20 branch offices and total assets in excess of $1.2 billion the bank offers standard retail products including deposit accounts CDs and credit cards. Commercial and industrial and commercial real estate loans make up 75% of the bank's loan portfolio though it also offers consumer loans and luxury boat financing. The company also owns 50% of real estate firm Pointer Ridge Office Investment.

	Annual Growth	12/10	12/11	12/12	12/13	12/14
Assets ($ mil.)	32.2%	401.9	811.0	861.9	1,167.2	1,227.5
Net income ($ mil.)	47.6%	1.5	5.4	7.5	7.8	7.1
Market value ($ mil.)	18.4%	87.1	87.6	122.1	156.8	171.0
Employees	29.5%	81	177	182	254	228

OLD MUTUAL (US) HOLDINGS INC.

200 Clarendon St. 53rd Fl.	CEO: Peter Bain
Boston MA 02116	CFO: Matthew E Berger
Phone: 617-369-7300	HR: –
Fax: 617-369-7499	FYE: December 31
Web: www.oldmutualus.com	Type: Subsidiary

Old Mutual (US) Holdings is the holding company for a group of about 20 asset management boutiques collectively known as Old Mutual Asset Management (US) or OMAM (US). The firm's multi-manager structure allows it to offer more than 160 different investment strategies across a range of asset classes from domestic and international equities to fixed income and alternative investments to real estate and timber property management. Its offerings include retirement plans mutual funds trust services and separately managed accounts. The company is a subsidiary of UK-based financial services concern Old Mutual.

OLD NATIONAL BANCORP (EVANSVILLE, IN)

NMS: ONB

One Main Street	CEO: Robert G. (Bob) Jones
Evansville, IN 47708	CFO: Christopher A. (Chris) Wolking
Phone: 812 464-1294	HR: Kendra L. Vanzo
Fax: –	FYE: December 31
Web: www.oldnational.com	Type: Public

Old National Bank is old but it's not quite national. Founded in 1834 the main subsidiary of Old National Bancorp operates about 200 bank centers across Indiana Kentucky Michigan and Illinois. The bank serves consumers and business customers offering standard checking and savings accounts credit cards and loans. Its treasury segment manages investments for bank and commercial clients. Business loans commercial and residential mortgages and consumer loans account for most of Old National's lending activity. The company also sells insurance manages wealth for high-net-worth clients and offers investment and retirement services through third-party provider LPL Financial.

	Annual Growth	12/10	12/11	12/12	12/13	12/14
Assets ($ mil.)	12.5%	7,263.9	8,609.7	9,543.6	9,581.7	11,647.6
Net income ($ mil.)	28.3%	38.2	72.5	91.7	100.9	103.7
Market value ($ mil.)	(11.3%)	2,811.3	2,811.3	2,811.3	1,795.9	1,738.7
Employees	4.2%	2,491	2,551	2,684	2,608	2,938

OLD NAVY INC.

2 Folsom St.	CEO: –
San Francisco CA 94105	CFO: John J Lenk
Phone: 650-952-4400	HR: –
Fax: 773-714-4595	FYE: January 31
Web: www.wilson.com	Type: Business Segment

Old Navy commands a fleet of more than 1025 family clothing stores throughout the US and Canada offering items under its own brand name at discounted prices. (The apparel retailer also operates a Web-based store at oldnavy.com.) Products include men's women's and children's (even dogs') apparel and accessories. Founded in 1994 Old Navy is owned by the king of casual apparel Gap Inc. and is known for advertising that plays up the kitsch factor of various celebrities. Old Navy which has suffered from sales declines in recent years appears to be back on track and has extended its brand to include maternity and women's plus-size apparel as well as accessories and personal care products.

OLD POINT FINANCIAL CORP.

NAS: OPOF

1 West Mellen Street
Hampton, VA 23663
Phone: 757 728-1200
Fax: –
Web: www.oldpoint.com

CEO: –
CFO: Laurie D Grabow
HR: –
FYE: December 31
Type: Public

Community banking and wealth management is the point at Old Point Financial. It is the holding company for Old Point National Bank of Phoebus which has more than 20 branches in the Hampton Roads region of southeastern Virginia. Founded in 1923 the bank serves area businesses and consumers offering such services as checking and savings accounts money market accounts and CDs. With these funds the bank mainly originates commercial and residential mortgages which account for a majority of its loans. Subsidiary Old Point Trust & Financial Services provides investment management and tax estate and retirement planning services. Old Point National Bank also owns 49% of Old Point Mortgage.

	Annual Growth	12/10	12/11	12/12	12/13	12/14
Assets ($ mil.)	(0.3%)	886.8	849.5	907.5	864.3	876.3
Net income ($ mil.)	27.7%	1.5	3.3	4.2	3.2	4.1
Market value ($ mil.)	5.6%	59.8	50.1	54.8	63.6	74.4
Employees	(2.4%)	332	334	319	298	301

OLD REPUBLIC INTERNATIONAL CORP.

NYS: ORI

307 North Michigan Avenue
Chicago, IL 60601
Phone: 312 346-8100
Fax: –
Web: www.oldrepublic.com

CEO: Aldo C. (Al) Zucaro
CFO: Karl W. Mueller
HR: Chester Cedars
FYE: December 31
Type: Public

Old Republic International keeps pace with changing financial times. With more than 100 subsidiaries across North America Old Republic International's primary operations are conducted through the Old Republic General Insurance division which offers commercial liability and property/casualty insurance (mostly commercial trucking workers' compensation and general liability policies). In addition the company's Title Insurance group specializes in naturally issuing title insurance to property owners and lenders. Its Old Republic National Title subsidiary is one of the US's oldest and largest title insurance companies with offices throughout the US.

	Annual Growth	12/10	12/11	12/12	12/13	12/14
Assets ($ mil.)	1.7%	15,882.7	16,050.4	16,226.8	16,534.4	16,988.1
Net income ($ mil.)	92.1%	30.1	(140.5)	(68.6)	447.8	409.7
Market value ($ mil.)	1.8%	3,556.7	2,419.0	2,779.1	4,506.6	3,817.7
Employees	0.0%	8,000	7,900	7,800	7,900	8,000

OLD SECOND BANCORP., INC. (AURORA, ILL.)

NMS. OSBC

37 South River Street
Aurora, IL 60507
Phone: 630 892-0202
Fax: –
Web: www.oldsecond.com

CEO: James L. Eccher
CFO: J. Douglas Cheatham
HR: Robert (Bob) Dicosola
FYE: December 31
Type: Public

Old Second isn't a thrift shop but it does cater to the thrifty. Old Second Bancorp is the holding company for Old Second National Bank which serves the Chicago metropolitan area through nearly 30 branches in Kane Kendall DeKalb DuPage LaSalle Will and Cook counties. The bank provides standard services such as checking and savings accounts credit and debit cards CDs mortgages loans and trust services to consumers and business clients. Subsidiary River Street Advisors offers investment management and advisory services. Another unit Old Second Affordable Housing Fund provides home-buying assistance to lower-income customers.

	Annual Growth	12/10	12/11	12/12	12/13	12/14
Assets ($ mil.)	(0.7%)	2,123.9	1,941.4	2,045.8	2,004.0	2,061.8
Net income ($ mil.)	–	(108.6)	(6.5)	(0.1)	82.1	10.1
Market value ($ mil.)	33.3%	50.1	38.3	35.9	136.0	158.1
Employees	(1.8%)	522	492	481	492	485

OLD TIME POTTERY INC.

480 RIVER ROCK BLVD
MURFREESBORO, TN 37128-4804
Phone: 615-890-6060
Fax: –
Web: www.oldtimepotteryindianapolis.com

CEO: Scott Peterson
CFO: Robert Sharp
HR: –
FYE: December 31
Type: Private

You won't find any dusty crocks or cracked pots at Old Time Pottery. The chain markets discounted closeout and overstock housewares silk flowers hanging baskets framed art linens rugs craft supplies seasonal merchandise and more. Its network of more than 30 stores spans some 10 states in the nation's South and Midwest. Old Time Pottery sources its inventory which the retailer displays in a warehouse-type setting from the canceled orders and excess stock of manufacturers. To its benefit the specialty retailer can accommodate lots of inventory as stores average about 2 acres in size. Founded in 1986 Old Time Pottery is controlled by the Peterson family.

	Annual Growth	12/04	12/05	12/06	12/11	12/12
Sales ($ mil.)	(2.8%)	–	188.9	208.5	146.7	154.4
Net income ($ mil.)	9.5%	–	4.1	1.1	6.6	7.8
Market value ($ mil.)	–	–	–	–	–	–
Employees	–	–	–	–	–	3,000

OLD WORLD INDUSTRIES LLC

4065 Commercial Ave.
Northbrook IL 60062
Phone: 847-559-2000
Fax: 847-559-2266
Web: www.oldworldind.com

CEO: Khalid Mahmood
CFO: Mark Rocco
HR: Cathie Barber
FYE: December 31
Type: Private

Old World Industries operates in the relatively new world of automotive chemicals and parts selling its products to the automotive aftermarket. Old World's antifreezes include Peak and Sierra (the latter marketed as a safer alternative to other antifreezes) as well as private-label products. Old World also makes de-icers pickup bed liners (Herculiner) diesel exhaust fluid (BlueDEF) heavy duty coolant (Final Charge) and wiper blades (Blue Mountain Professional). Exiting the chemical production business in 2012 the company sold its US-based ethylene glycol and ethylene glycol oxide plant to Thailand's Indorama Ventures for $795 million.

OLDCASTLE INC.

375 Northridge Rd. Ste. 350
Atlanta GA 30350
Phone: 770-804-3363
Fax: 402-537-9847
Web: www.isecuretrac.com

CEO: Mark S Towe
CFO: Michael G O'Driscoll
HR: –
FYE: December 31
Type: Subsidiary

Oldcastle has the materials to build your modern castle. The North American arm of CRH makes architectural and construction building products in the US and Canada. It operates through six product groups including Oldcastle Materials which produces and sells aggregates asphalt and ready-mix concrete and provides paving services. Masonry products are made by Oldcastle Architectural. Meanwhile Oldcastle Precast provides precast concrete and Oldcastle BuildingEnvelope provides curtain walls and architectural windows and doors. Its distribution arm Allied Building Products delivers to specialty contractors. Oldcastle Construction Accessories sells fencing concrete reinforcements and anchoring systems.

OLDCASTLE MATERIALS INC.

900 Ashwood Pkwy. Ste. 700
Atlanta GA 30338
Phone: 770-522-5600
Fax: 770-522-5602
Web: www.oldcastlematerials.com

CEO: Randy Lake
CFO: Glenn Culpepper
HR: Kathleen Edge
FYE: December 31
Type: Subsidiary

If you need some new materials for your home and castle Oldcastle Materials would be glad to help. A US subsidiary of international building materials group CRH Oldcastle Materials operates more than 640 aggregate production facilities more than 450 asphalt plants and some 280 ready-mix concrete facilities. It produces roughly 120 million tons of aggregates more than 40 million tons of asphalt and some 10 million cu. yd. of ready-mix concrete annually. The company also supplies building materials and architectural glass and performs paving and construction services. Clients include commercial construction companies federal agencies municipalities and residential customers.

OLE' MEXICAN FOODS INC.

6585 CRESCENT DR
NORCROSS, GA 300712901
Phone: 770-582-9200
Fax: –
Web: www.olemexicanfoods.com

CEO: Veronica Moreno
CFO: –
HR: –
FYE: December 31
Type: Private

Its a wrap at Olé Mexican Foods. The company makes Mexican-American foods inducing tortillas and taco shells under brand names La Banderita La Centroamericana Olé and Verolé. The company also produces salsa sour cream Mexican cheeses and sausages tostadas and tortilla chips among other items. Its customers include retail food outlets and food service operations. Headquartered in Norcross Georgia the company has about a dozen distribution centers across the US. It serves customers across the continental US and Alaska as well as in Puerto Rico.

	Annual Growth	12/00	12/01	12/02	12/03	12/13
Sales ($ mil.)	–	–	(988.0)	52.7	65.1	242.7
Net income ($ mil.)	11.9%	–	–	3.6	5.8	12.5
Market value ($ mil.)	–	–	–	–	–	–
Employees	–	–	–	–	–	500

OLIN CORP.

NYS: OLN

190 Carondelet Plaza, Suite 1530
Clayton, MO 63105
Phone: 314 480-1400
Fax: –
Web: www.olin.com

CEO: Joseph D. Rupp
CFO: Todd A. Slater
HR: –
FYE: December 31
Type: Public

The making of bleach and bullets is all in a day's work for Olin Corporation. The company manufactures chemicals used to make bleach water purification and swimming pool chemicals pulp and paper processing agents and PVC plastics. Olin Chlor Alkali Products is one of the top chlor-alkali producers in North America along with Dow and OxyChem. Olin also distributes caustic soda and bleach. In addition in a quite divergent business the company's Winchester Ammunition unit makes branded sporting ammunition reloading components small caliber military ammunition and components and industrial cartridges. BlackRock Inc. owns 15% of Olin.

	Annual Growth	12/10	12/11	12/12	12/13	12/14
Sales ($ mil.)	9.0%	1,585.9	1,961.1	2,184.7	2,515.0	2,241.2
Net income ($ mil.)	13.0%	64.8	241.7	149.6	178.6	105.7
Market value ($ mil.)	2.6%	1,588.2	1,520.9	1,671.1	2,233.0	1,762.4
Employees	1.3%	3,700	3,800	4,100	4,100	3,900

OLMSTED MEDICAL CENTER

210 9TH ST SE STE 1
ROCHESTER, MN 559046400
Phone: 507-288-3443
Fax: –
Web: www.olmmed.org

CEO: –
CFO: –
HR: –
FYE: December 31
Type: Private

Olmsted Medical Center (OMC) provides general medical and surgical care to the Rochester Minnesota area. The not-for-profit hospital also partners with regional schools to provide medical nursing and technical training and it engages in clinical research programs. Specialty services include pediatrics neurology occupational medicine and orthopedics. In addition to its hospital OMC also operates several urgent care specialty and general practice clinics in the region. OMC was formed through the merger of Olmsted Community Hospital and Olmsted Medical Group in 1996.

	Annual Growth	12/01	12/02	12/08	12/09	12/13
Sales ($ mil.)	8.2%	–	79.7	0.3	144.2	189.3
Net income ($ mil.)	–	–	–	0.0	12.3	14.4
Market value ($ mil.)	–	–	–	–	–	–
Employees	–	–	–	–	–	950

OLYMPIC STEEL INC.

NMS: ZEUS

22901 Millcreek Boulevard, Suite 650
Highland Hills, OH 44122
Phone: 216 292-3800
Fax: 216 682-4065
Web: www.olysteel.com

CEO: Michael D. Siegal
CFO: Richard T. Marabito
HR: –
FYE: December 31
Type: Public

Olympic Steel has bypassed gold silver and bronze in favor of carbon coated and stainless steel. A steel service center Olympic Steel provides flat-rolled sheet coil and plate steel products. Its processing services include cutting-to-length slitting and shearing along with blanking laser welding and precision machining. It also makes tubular and pipe products. Olympic Steel operates through subsidiaries including Olympic Steel Lafayette and Chicago Tube and Iron (CTI). It has processing and distribution facilities mainly in the eastern and midwestern US.

	Annual Growth	12/10	12/11	12/12	12/13	12/14
Sales ($ mil.)	15.6%	805.0	1,261.9	1,383.7	1,263.3	1,436.3
Net income ($ mil.)	–	2.1	25.0	2.3	7.6	(19.1)
Market value ($ mil.)	(11.3%)	315.0	256.1	243.2	318.3	195.3
Employees	12.9%	1,113	1,700	1,870	1,790	1,810

OLYMPUS CORPORATION OF THE AMERICAS

3500 Corporate Pkwy.
Center Valley PA 18034-0610
Phone: 484-896-5000
Fax: 484-896-7130
Web: www.olympusamerica.com

CEO: –
CFO: –
HR: –
FYE: March 31
Type: Subsidiary

Olympus Corporation of the Americas (OCA) has turned its focus from pictures of people to pictures of the parts of people. While the company is known to consumers for its digital cameras binoculars and other imaging products its main revenue comes from endoscopes microscopes and other medical and diagnostic devices as well as life science testing and imaging systems. The company also markets audio recording equipment specialty photo lenses and other consumer electronic goods. OCA is sales subsidiary of Tokyo-based parent Olympus Corporation serving North and South America.

OM GROUP, INC.

NYS: OMG

950 Main Avenue, Suite 1300
Cleveland, OH 44113-7210
Phone: 216 781-0083
Fax: –
Web: www.omgi.com

CEO: Joseph Scaminace
CFO: Christopher M Hix
HR: –
FYE: December 31
Type: Public

Mmmmetals is the mantra for OM Group. The company uses unrefined cobalt and other metals to make specialty products and is one of the world's largest refiners of cobalt. It serves markets that include battery materials semiconductors ceramics chemical and defense. It also makes magnetic technologies products for electronic equipment auto and alternative energy markets. Its specialty chemicals segment develops chemicals and products for computer components coating and inks tires and other industries. EaglePicher Technologies makes up its battery technologies segment which serves the defense aerospace and medical markets.

	Annual Growth	12/09	12/10	12/11	12/12	12/13
Sales ($ mil.)	7.3%	871.7	1,196.6	1,514.5	1,637.8	1,157.5
Net income ($ mil.)	–	(17.9)	83.4	37.9	(38.9)	(84.0)
Market value ($ mil.)	3.8%	988.1	1,212.2	704.8	698.8	1,146.1
Employees	30.9%	2,007	2,806	7,067	6,800	5,900

OMAGINE INC.

OTC: AHDS

350 5th Ave. Ste. 1103
New York NY 10118
Phone: 212-563-4141
Fax: 212-563-3355
Web: www.omagine.com

CEO: Frank J Drohan
CFO: Frank J Drohan
HR: –
FYE: December 31
Type: Public

Omagine wants you to imagine investing in beachfront abodes in the Middle East and North Africa (MENA). Formerly Alfa International Omagine repositioned and rebranded itself in 2007 as it exited the apparel business. The company's Journey of Light subsidiary now intends to tap into the high-margin real estate development and luxury travel markets in MENA. In 2008 Journey of Light was granted initial approval to develop the Omagine Project a $1.6 billion government-sponsored entertainment retail commercial residential and hotel real estate development in Oman. Omagine will also provide property management services.

OMAHA STEAKS INTERNATIONAL INC.

11030 O St.
Omaha NE 68137
Phone: 402-597-3000
Fax: 402-597-8125
Web: www.omahasteaks.com

CEO: Alan Simon
CFO: Dave L Hershiser
HR: Dulce Sherman
FYE: December 31
Type: Private

You might say this food company is in a high-protein business. Omaha Steaks International is a leading meat packer and distributor with two manufacturing plants a distribution facility and a freezer warehouse in Nebraska. The company produces boneless sirloin filet mignon and other specialty beef cuts as well as veal lamb poultry and seafood. Omaha Steaks sells its products to customers through 80-plus company-owned retail stores in nearly 30 US states as well as through mail-order catalogs and online. It also distributes beef to food service operators and other retail outlets. The family-owned business was founded as Table Supply Meat Company in 1917 by J. J. Simon and his son.

OMEGA FLEX INC

NMS: OFLX

451 Creamery Way
Exton, PA 19341
Phone: 610 524-7272
Fax: 610 524-7282
Web: www.omegaflex.com

CEO: Kevin R. Hoben
CFO: Paul J. Kane
HR: –
FYE: December 31
Type: Public

Like a reed in a stream Grasshopper sometimes the flexible withstand pressure better than the rigid. That's certainly a concept that Omega Flex can get behind: The company makes corrugated metal and flexible tubular and braided metal (stainless steel bronze) hoses and reinforcements for construction and industrial customers to use in liquid and gas transportation. Its products are designed to deal with high pressure motion extreme temperatures harsh liquids or gases and abrasion. Other applications include cryogenics and propane and natural gas installations. The estate of John Reed and his son chairman Stewart Reed own a majority of Omega Flex which was spun off from Mestek in 2005.

	Annual Growth	12/10	12/11	12/12	12/13	12/14
Sales ($ mil.)	16.1%	46.9	54.2	64.0	77.1	85.2
Net income ($ mil.)	31.0%	4.6	4.6	6.9	10.0	13.5
Market value ($ mil.)	23.0%	166.9	142.6	124.7	206.5	381.6
Employees	7.0%	107	116	129	131	140

OMEGA HEALTHCARE INVESTORS, INC.

NYS: OHI

200 International Circle, Suite 3500
Hunt Valley, MD 21030
Phone: 410 427-1700
Fax: 410 427-8800
Web: www.omegahealthcare.com

CEO: C. Taylor Pickett
CFO: Robert O. Stephenson
HR: –
FYE: December 31
Type: Public

Omega Healthcare Investors can put an end to the burdens of real-estate management. The self-administered real estate investment trust (REIT) invests in health care facilities throughout the US. It owns some 900 properties primarily long-term care facilities in more than 40 states. The REIT specializes in sales/leaseback transactions in which it purchases properties owned by health care providers and leases them back to those companies (thereby freeing the health care companies from the responsibilities of real estate management). The REIT's properties are operated by third-party health care operating companies including Genesis HealthCare System and CommuniCare Health Services.

	Annual Growth	12/10	12/11	12/12	12/13	12/14
Sales ($ mil.)	18.2%	258.3	292.2	350.5	418.7	504.8
Net income ($ mil.)	39.5%	58.4	52.6	120.7	172.5	221.3
Market value ($ mil.)	14.9%	2,863.5	2,469.2	3,043.4	3,802.7	4,985.6
Employees	3.0%	24	24	25	25	27

OMEGA PROTEIN CORP.

NYS: OME

2105 City West Blvd., Suite 500
Houston, TX 77042-2838
Phone: 713 623-0060
Fax: –
Web: www.omegaprotein.com

CEO: Bret Scholtes
CFO: Andrew Johannesen
HR: –
FYE: December 31
Type: Public

Omega Protein is the alpha dog of the fish-meal market. With a handful of US processing plants a fleet of some 40 fishing vessels and 30-plus spotter aircraft the company is the largest US producer of fish meal and fish oil derived from menhaden (an inedible fish found in the Gulf of Mexico and along the East Coast). Animal-feed makers and livestock ranchers use Omega Protein's fish meal for protein additives in feed; the fish oil is used in Europe in margarine and for industrial ends. Rich in Omega-3 fatty acids (linked to health benefits) fish oil is also used as a human food supplement. Through subsidiaries Omega Protein provides nutraceutical ingredients and compounds including Omega-3 fish oils.

	Annual Growth	12/10	12/11	12/12	12/13	12/14
Sales ($ mil.)	16.5%	167.7	235.2	235.6	244.3	308.6
Net income ($ mil.)	0.3%	18.3	34.2	4.1	30.5	18.5
Market value ($ mil.)	6.9%	174.4	153.5	131.7	264.6	227.5
Employees	7.4%	493	495	500	450	657

OMEROS CORP

NMS: OMER

201 Elliott Avenue West
Seattle, WA 98119
Phone: 206 676-5000
Fax: –
Web: www.omeros.com

CEO: Gregory A. Demopulos
CFO: –
HR: –
FYE: December 31
Type: Public

Omeros doesn't claim to soothe the soul but it may be able to tame inflammation caused by surgery. The biopharmaceutical company is developing products based on its PharmacoSurgery platform a combination of low-dose therapeutic agents applied directly to a surgical site to inhibit inflammation. Its first marketed product is Omidria for use in cataract surgery. Omidria was launched in early 2015. Another candidate OMS103HP is in trials for its ability to improve joint function and reduce pain following ACL knee reconstruction surgery and arthroscopic meniscectomy (removal of knee cartilage tears). In addition to inflammation Omeros maintains programs focused on blood clot issues and the central nervous system (CNS).

	Annual Growth	12/10	12/11	12/12	12/13	12/14
Sales ($ mil.)	(28.9%)	2.1	4.5	6.0	1.6	0.5
Net income ($ mil.)	–	(29.3)	(28.5)	(38.4)	(39.8)	(73.7)
Market value ($ mil.)	31.7%	281.7	135.0	177.4	386.0	847.1
Employees	10.1%	70	70	71	75	103

OMNI CABLE CORPORATION

2 HAGERTY BLVD
WEST CHESTER, PA 193827594
Phone: 610-701-0100
Fax: –
Web: www.omnicable.com

CEO: William J Siegfried
CFO: Steve Glinski
HR: –
FYE: December 31
Type: Private

Omni Cable has it down to the wire. The company distributes electrical and electronic cables to wholesale customers in the US through 10 warehouses and distribution centers. Omni Cable also offers custom bundling coloring striping lashing twisting and imprinting of wires and cables. The employee-owned company was founded in 1977. Omni Cable has locations in Atlanta Boston Chicago Denver Houston Los Angeles Philadelphia St. Louis San Francisco and Tampa. It is expanding its facilities within the regions served and has relocated and upgraded its San Francisco branch to serve the Bay Area better.

	Annual Growth	12/07	12/08	12/09	12/10	12/11
Sales ($ mil.)	–	–	–	(2,116.8)	202.9	256.5
Net income ($ mil.)	–	–	–	0.0	12.1	0.0
Market value ($ mil.)	–	–	–	–	–	–
Employees	–	–	–	–	–	216

OMNI ENERGY SERVICES CORP.

4500 NE Evangeline Thruway
Carencro LA 70520
Phone: 337-896-6664
Fax: 337-896-6655
Web: www.omnienergy.com

CEO: Brian J Recatto
CFO: Geoff A Jones
HR: –
FYE: December 31
Type: Private

In the transition-zone oil fields along the US Gulf Coast OMNI Energy Services is omnipresent. OMNI provides oilfield seismic drilling and surveying services for geophysical companies primarily in environmentally sensitive areas such as the shallow waters off the Louisiana and Texas coasts. The company also provides permitting services and leases oil field equipment to geophysical companies. OMNI also has dockside and offshore oil field waste management and environmental cleaning services. In 2010 the company was taken private when it was acquired by Wellspring Capital for $122 million.

OMNI HOTELS CORPORATION

420 Decker Dr. Ste. 200
Irving TX 75062
Phone: 972-730-6664
Fax: 972-871-5669
Web: www.omnihotels.com

CEO: James D Caldwell
CFO: Mike Garcia
HR: –
FYE: December 31
Type: Subsidiary

Not yet omnipresent Omni Hotels has a portfolio of 50 hotel properties in the US Canada and Mexico. The luxury lodgings are targeted to business travelers and upscale tourists. In addition to comfortable room accommodations the properties offer business and fitness centers high-speed and wireless Internet access and gourmet restaurants. Omni Hotels owns most of its hotels but also franchises a small number of properties. The company's Select Guest is a loyalty program that offers more personalized services for returning members. Texas oil billionaire Robert Rowling owns Omni Hotels through his family's holding company TRT Holdings.

OMNIAMERICAN BANCORP, INC.

NMS: OABC

1320 S. University Drive
Fort Worth, TX 76107
Phone: 817 367-4640
Fax: –
Web: www.omniamerican.com

CEO: –
CFO: –
HR: –
FYE: December 31
Type: Public

You might say this institution is omnipresent in the Dallas-Fort Worth metroplex. OmniAmerican Bancorp is the holding company for OmniAmerican Bank which provides deposit and lending services through more than 15 offices. OmniAmerican Bank caters to businesses and individuals. The company also offers wealth management services such as money market and high yield checking accounts and financial planning. OmniAmerican Bank started in 1956 as a small financial institution serving the Carswell Air Force Base military community and converted from a credit union to a thrift in 2006.

	Annual Growth	12/08	12/09	12/10	12/11	12/12
Assets ($ mil.)	4.2%	1,067.9	1,133.9	1,108.4	1,336.7	1,257.3
Net income ($ mil.)	72.5%	0.6	0.7	1.7	4.0	5.7
Market value ($ mil.)	30.6%	–	–	155.1	179.7	264.7
Employees	(2.0%)	372	348	320	334	343

OMNICARE INC.

NYS: OCR

900 Omnicare Center, 201 E. Fourth Street
Cincinnati, OH 45202
Phone: 513 719-2600
Fax: –
Web: www.omnicare.com

CEO: Nitin Sahney
CFO: Robert O Kraft
HR: –
FYE: December 31
Type: Public

Omnicare strives to be omnipresent in US nursing homes. The firm is the country's largest institutional pharmacy services provider dispensing drugs to nursing homes assisted-living centers and other long-term care (LTC) facilities in the US and parts of Canada. In addition it provides clinical and financial software consulting and billing services to LTC facilities as well as infusion respiratory and chronic disease therapy products and services for nursing home residents and hospice patients. It also provides some services to drugmakers. The company has pharmacy and distribution locations across the US and it serves LTC facility customers with a combined capacity of some 1 million patient beds.

	Annual Growth	12/09	12/10	12/11	12/12	12/13
Sales ($ mil.)	(0.6%)	6,166.2	6,146.2	6,182.9	6,160.4	6,013.4
Net income ($ mil.)	–	211.9	(106.1)	86.9	194.9	(43.4)
Market value ($ mil.)	25.7%	2,432.7	2,554.5	3,466.0	3,632.0	6,072.8
Employees	(2.2%)	15,200	15,200	14,600	14,400	13,900

OMNICELL INC

NMS: OMCL

590 East Middlefield Road
Mountain View, CA 94043
Phone: 650 251-6100
Fax: –
Web: www.omnicell.com

CEO: Randall A. Lipps
CFO: Peter Kuipers
HR: Susan (Sue) Moriconi
FYE: December 31
Type: Public

Omnicell dispenses with anything less than full knowledge when it comes to dispensing drugs to patients. A developer of specialized software and hardware products Omnicell makes mobile cabinets and workstations that automatically dispense doses of medication and surgical supplies to help pharmacists and nurses reduce medical errors and increase patient safety. More than 1600 hospitals use its OmniRx medication dispensing cabinets and complementary software such as SinglePointe and AnywhereRN a program that allows nurses to remotely operate the cabinets. Another top seller is WorkflowRx an automated pharmacy management software system that tracks inventory.

	Annual Growth	12/10	12/11	12/12	12/13	12/14
Sales ($ mil.)	18.7%	222.4	245.5	314.0	380.6	440.9
Net income ($ mil.)	58.0%	4.9	10.4	16.2	24.0	30.5
Market value ($ mil.)	23.0%	517.5	591.7	532.6	914.4	1,186.2
Employees	13.2%	753	773	1,089	1,134	1,236

OMNICOM GROUP, INC.

NYS: OMC

437 Madison Avenue
New York, NY 10022
Phone: 212 415-3600
Fax: 212 415-3393
Web: www.omnicomgroup.com

CEO: John D. Wren
CFO: Philip J. Angelastro
HR: Leslie Chiocco
FYE: December 31
Type: Public

It might not be omnipotent but Omnicom Group creates advertising that is omnipresent. The company ranks as the world's #1 corporate media services conglomerate with advertising marketing and public relations operations. It serves global advertising clients through its agency networks BBDO Worldwide DDB Worldwide and TBWA Worldwide while such firms as GSD&M's Idea City Merkley + Partners and Zimmerman Advertising provide services for regional and national clients. Its Diversified Agency Services division including Fleishman-Hillard Integer and Rapp provides public relations and other marketing services.

	Annual Growth	12/11	12/12	12/13	12/14	12/15
Sales ($ mil.)	2.2%	13,872.5	14,219.4	14,584.5	15,317.8	15,134.4
Net income ($ mil.)	3.5%	952.6	998.3	991.1	1,104.0	1,093.9
Market value ($ mil.)	14.1%	10,685.8	11,975.4	17,826.5	18,569.6	18,135.7
Employees	1.5%	70,600	71,000	71,800	74,000	74,900

OMNICOMM SYSTEMS INC

NBB. OMCM

2101 W. Commercial Blvd., Suite 3500
Fort Lauderdale, FL 33309
Phone: 954 473-1254
Fax: –
Web: www.omnicomm.com

CEO: Cornelis F Wit
CFO: Thomas E Vickers
HR: –
FYE: December 31
Type: Public

Computers can't catch the kind of viruses that OmniComm Systems handles. The company's Web-based software helps pharmaceutical and biotechnology companies clinical research organizations and academic research institutions manage data collected during clinical trials. Its TrialMaster software enables researchers to collect validate and analyze data for clinical trials to speed up the process of developing drugs and medical devices. The eClinical Suite combines a clinical data management system (CDMS) and a clinical trial management system (CTMS) to manage all phases of a clinical trial. OmniComm counts almost 100 customers including Boston Scientific and Johnson & Johnson. The majority of its sales are in the US.

	Annual Growth	12/10	12/11	12/12	12/13	12/14
Sales ($ mil.)	7.3%	12.4	13.6	15.6	14.3	16.5
Net income ($ mil.)	–	(3.1)	(3.5)	(7.8)	(3.2)	(4.5)
Market value ($ mil.)	38.2%	7.3	4.1	16.9	15.6	26.6
Employees	3.7%	103	90	100	108	119

OMNISOURCE CORPORATION

7575 W. Jefferson Blvd.
Fort Wayne IN 46804
Phone: 260-422-5541
Fax: 651-649-5894
Web: www.johnsonbrothers.com

CEO: –
CFO: –
HR: –
FYE: December 31
Type: Subsidiary

OmniSource is omnivorous when it comes to scrap metal. One of the largest scrap processors and distributors in North America OmniSource takes unusable metal products and turns them into raw materials for use in mills and foundries that produce steel aluminum and copper. The company operates some 70 scrap processing facilities throughout eastern North America. It recycles more than 7 million tons of ferrous materials and 1 billion pounds of nonferrous scrap annually. Additionally OmniSource engages in brokerage and trading of products such as ferrous and nonferrous scrap scrap alternatives and secondary and primary metals. OmniSource is a subsidiary of Steel Dynamics.

OMNIVISION TECHNOLOGIES INC

NMS: OVTI

4275 Burton Drive
Santa Clara, CA 95054
Phone: 408 567-3000
Fax: –
Web: www.ovt.com

CEO: Shaw Hong
CFO: Anson Chan
HR: –
FYE: April 30
Type: Public

OmniVision Technologies gets the big picture with a single chip. The fabless semiconductor company designs semiconductor image sensors (CameraChips) that capture and convert images for cameras mobile phones notebooks webcams surveillance equipment and medical imaging systems among other applications. Its CameraCubeChip device combines the company's image sensors with wafer-level optics for a complete camera module. OmniVision outsources manufacturing chores to silicon foundries (contract semiconductor manufacturers) primarily Taiwan Semiconductor Manufacturing Company (TSMC). Most sales are from Asia predominantly China.

	Annual Growth	04/10	04/11	04/12	04/13	04/14
Sales ($ mil.)	24.6%	603.0	956.5	897.7	1,407.9	1,453.9
Net income ($ mil.)	93.9%	6.7	124.5	65.8	42.9	95.0
Market value ($ mil.)	2.7%	984.7	1,883.8	1,033.0	752.1	1,095.3
Employees	8.5%	1,450	1,465	1,796	2,057	2,008

OMNOVA SOLUTIONS INC

NYS: OMN

25435 Harvard Road
Beachwood, OH 44122-6201
Phone: 216 682-7000
Fax: –
Web: www.omnova.com

CEO: Kevin M. McMullen
CFO: Paul F. DeSantis
HR: Michael A Quinn
FYE: November 30
Type: Public

OMNOVA Solutions is not quite omnipresent but it does manufacture and sell performance chemicals and engineered decorative surfaces around the world. It is an innovator of emulsion polymers in dry powder and latex forms specialty chemicals and also decorative and functional surfaces for a variety of commercial industrial and residential end uses. The performance chemicals segment produces emulsion polymers and specialty chemicals to makers of paper carpet and textiles. The engineered surfaces segment makes vinyl- and paper-based wall coverings coated fabrics laminates and films.

	Annual Growth	11/11	11/12	11/13	11/14	11/15
Sales ($ mil.)	(8.6%)	1,201.1	1,125.5	1,018.1	987.4	838.0
Net income ($ mil.)	–	(2.8)	27.6	19.6	11.5	(17.8)
Market value ($ mil.)	14.7%	194.9	332.4	392.4	299.3	336.9
Employees	(0.7%)	2,300	2,390	2,300	2,300	2,235

OMRON SCIENTIFIC TECHNOLOGIES INCORPORATED

6550 Dumbarton Circle
Fremont CA 94555
Phone: 510-608-3400
Fax: 510-744-1442
Web: www.sti.com

CEO: Joseph J Lazzara
CFO: –
HR: –
FYE: December 31
Type: Subsidiary

Omron Scientific Technologies Inc. (Omron STI) makes a science of safety. The company supplies safety light guards safety interlocks and relays safety mats and controllers used to protect personnel in hazardous manufacturing environments. Omron STI serves such industries as automotive cosmetics food and beverage pharmaceutical semiconductor and electronic machinery. Former Scientific Technologies Inc. chairman Anthony Lazzara and his family controlled the company until it sold the safety products business to OMRON in 2006. Omron STI's products are supported worldwide by distributors and OMRON offices.

ON ASSIGNMENT, INC.

NYS: ASGN

26745 Malibu Hills Road
Calabasas, CA 91301
Phone: 818 878-7900
Fax: –
Web: www.onassignment.com

CEO: Peter T. Dameris
CFO: Edward L. Pierce
HR: –
FYE: December 31
Type: Public

On Assignment is a specialist staffing agency that places professionals from IT consultants to lab assistants to nurses with clients in need of temporary help. The firm operates through several divisions: Apex (IT and engineering staffing for temporary temp-to-hire and permanent placements); Life Sciences Europe (laboratory and scientific professionals in biotechnology pharmaceutical food and beverage medical device chemical and environmental industries); and Oxford (engineering and specialized high-end IT consultants). On Assignment provides staff to about 7700 clients and was founded in 1985.

	Annual Growth	12/10	12/11	12/12	12/13	12/14
Sales ($ mil.)	43.5%	438.1	597.3	1,239.7	1,632.0	1,859.9
Net income ($ mil.)	–	(9.9)	24.3	42.7	84.5	77.2
Market value ($ mil.)	42.1%	418.8	574.5	1,042.1	1,794.4	1,705.5
Employees	31.5%	12,530	15,511	34,530	33,870	37,500

ON SEMICONDUCTOR CORP

NMS: ON

5005 E. McDowell Road
Phoenix, AZ 85008
Phone: 602 244-6600
Fax: 602 244-6071
Web: www.onsemi.com

CEO: Keith D. Jackson
CFO: Bernard Gutmann
HR: Terri Richway
FYE: December 31
Type: Public

When the power is on ON Semiconductor semiconductors help its customers use less of it. The company designs and manufactures energy efficient low-cost high-volume analog logic and discrete semiconductors with more than 48000 devices in its catalog. These components perform vital power and signal control and interface functions in nearly every sort of electronic gear from networking routers and wireless phones and digital cameras to household appliances and automotive braking systems. It sells directly to OEMs including Cisco GE Honeywell Samsung and Siemens and to distributors such as Avnet and Arrow Electronics. Two-thirds of ON Semiconductor's sales come from the Asia/Pacific region.

	Annual Growth	12/10	12/11	12/12	12/13	12/14
Sales ($ mil.)	8.1%	2,313.4	3,442.3	2,894.9	2,782.7	3,161.8
Net income ($ mil.)	(10.1%)	290.5	11.6	(90.6)	150.8	189.7
Market value ($ mil.)	0.6%	4,288.9	3,351.3	3,060.4	3,577.0	4,397.4
Employees	14.4%	14,307	19,442	20,000	22,000	24,500

ON-SITE FUEL SERVICE INC.

1089 OLD FANNIN RD STE A
BRANDON, MS 390479201
Phone: 601-353-4142
Fax: –
Web: www.onsitefuelservice.com

CEO: Kevin T French
CFO: Margaret Wong
HR: –
FYE: December 31
Type: Private

When it comes down to gassing up the fleet On-Site Fuel Service delivers. The company specializes in dispensing fuel (diesel or regular) to corporate fleets in the most efficient location available. For most customers this means fueling their vehicles once the workday is complete (and eliminating fueling time from the workday). But the company also offers mobile fueling services allowing vehicles to be refueled in the field or at remote job sites. On-Site Fuel Service dispenses the fuel directly into each vehicle and also provides fueling data and reports for each vehicle (to comply with regulatory requirements when necessary). Its operations extend south from North Carolina to Florida and west to Arizona.

	Annual Growth	12/01	12/02	12/06	12/07	12/13
Sales ($ mil.)	–	–	0.0	113.1	119.7	238.0
Net income ($ mil.)	–	–	–	(0.1)	(0.4)	(0.5)
Market value ($ mil.)	–	–	–	–	–	–
Employees	–	–	–	–	–	85

ONCOGENEX PHARMACEUTICALS, INC.

NAS: OGXI

19820 North Creek Parkway
Bothell, WA 98011
Phone: 425 686-1500
Fax: –
Web: www.oncogenex.com

CEO: Scott Cormack
CFO: John Bencich
HR: –
FYE: December 31
Type: Public

OncoGenex Pharmaceuticals is on the hunt for new and better cancer therapies. The company develops novel therapeutics aimed at fighting treatment-resistant tumors. Its lead candidates are custirsen (OGX-011) and apatorsen (OGX-427) — which were gained when the firm then-named Sonus Pharmaceuticals merged with OncoGenex Technologies. Custirsen is a clinical-stage experimental drug which is being tested for the treatment of castration-resistant prostate cancer and non-small cell lung cancer. Apatorsen is being tested for the treatment of bladder cancer. After suffering some setbacks in drug trials the company slashed its workforce by 27% in 2016.

	Annual Growth	12/10	12/11	12/12	12/13	12/14
Sales ($ mil.)	18.8%	13.6	5.5	20.1	29.9	27.1
Net income ($ mil.)	–	(12.6)	(14.7)	(21.1)	(31.8)	(26.2)
Market value ($ mil.)	(39.2%)	379.8	265.6	296.8	188.7	51.8
Employees	6.7%	27	35	44	41	35

ONCOLOGIX TECH INC

NBB: OCLG

1604 W. Pinhook Drive #200
Lafayette, LA 70508
Phone: 616 977-9933
Fax: –

CEO: Roy Wayne Erwin
CFO: Michael A Kramarz
HR: –
FYE: August 31
Type: Public

Oncologix Tech (formerly BestNet Communications) has changed gears. The company which had developed a system using the Internet and text messaging networks to manage voice communications over public phone networks merged with JDA Medical Technologies and sold off most of its telephone business assets to Interactive Media Technologies. Oncologix then became a development-stage medical device firm focused on developing microsphere (particle) technology to treat liver and other soft tissue cancers; however the company licensed out most of its development operations in 2009 to a third party.

	Annual Growth	08/10	08/11	08/12	08/13	08/14
Sales ($ mil.)	1405.6%	–	–	–	0.2	3.7
Net income ($ mil.)	–	(0.7)	(0.2)	(0.3)	(0.7)	(1.3)
Market value ($ mil.)	(28.1%)	3.0	10.8	4.0	1.5	0.8
Employees	212.6%	2	2	2	170	191

ONCOMED PHARMACEUTICALS INC.

NMS: OMED

800 Chesapeake Drive
Redwood City, CA 94063
Phone: 650 995-8200
Fax: –
Web: www.oncomed.com

CEO: Paul J. Hastings
CFO: Sunil Patel
HR: –
FYE: December 31
Type: Public

For OncoMed Pharmaceuticals it's really all there in the name. The development-stage biotech company hopes to produce pharmaceuticals that target cancer cells. Like a growing group of pharma firms its work is focused on cancer stem cells (CSCs) which are believed to be the root cause of cancer tumors. Traditional chemotherapy may kill the tumors but leaves the CSCs to grow more tumors. OncoMed's antibody drugs target both CSCs and the tumors they produce. The company has three candidates in development with four others close behind; it has strategic alliances with major pharma companies GSK and Bayer in conjunction with its product development. OncoMed was formed in 2004 and went public in 2013.

	Annual Growth	12/10	12/11	12/12	12/13	12/14
Sales ($ mil.)	22.2%	17.7	31.4	24.7	37.8	39.6
Net income ($ mil.)	–	(27.0)	(15.0)	(22.2)	(26.1)	(50.0)
Market value ($ mil.)	(26.3%)	–	–	–	881.1	649.5
Employees	14.1%	–	–	83	91	108

ONCONOVA THERAPEUTICS INC

NAS: ONTX

375 Pheasant Run
Newtown, PA 18940
Phone: 267 759-3680
Fax: –

CEO: –
CFO: Ajay Bansal
HR: Sarajane Mackenzie
FYE: December 31
Type: Public

Onconova Therapeutics is taking a novel approach to oncology. The biopharmaceutical company is developing small molecule drug candidates to treat cancer and protect against certain side effects of radiation. Onconova has three clinical-stage product candidates and six preclinical ones. Its leading drug candidate rigosertib is being tested to higher risk myelodysplastic syndromes (MDS) pancreatic cancer and head and neck cancers. Onconova has revenue-generating collaboration agreements with Baxter in Europe and SymBio in Japan and Korea. The company which was formed in 1998 went public in mid-2013 raising $78 million in its IPO. It will use the proceeds to further develop its drug candidates.

	Annual Growth	12/10	12/11	12/12	12/13	12/14
Sales ($ mil.)	–	0.0	1.5	46.2	4.8	0.8
Net income ($ mil.)	–	0.0	(26.3)	(29.9)	(62.5)	(63.7)
Market value ($ mil.)	–	0.0	–	–	249.2	71.4
Employees	(6.3%)	–	–	57	64	50

ONCOR ELECTRIC DELIVERY CO

1616 Woodall Rodgers Fwy.
Dallas, TX 75202
Phone: 214 486-2000
Fax: –
Web: www.oncor.com

CEO: –
CFO: David M Davis
HR: Deborah (Deb) Dennis
FYE: December 31
Type: Public

Oncor Electric Delivery serves miles and miles of Texas' vast energy market. The company operates the regulated power assets of parent Energy Future Holdings which include about 120000 miles of transmission and distribution lines serving more than 400 cities and 91 counties situated in the eastern north-central and western portions of the state. The company provides power to more than 3.2 million meters in homes and businesses. Oncor Electric Delivery maintains streetlights in its service territory. The utility also provides services to competitive retail electric providers.

	Annual Growth	12/10	12/11	12/12	12/13	12/14
Sales ($ mil.)	7.0%	2,914.0	3,118.0	3,328.0	3,552.0	3,822.0
Net income ($ mil.)	6.3%	352.0	367.0	349.0	432.0	450.0
Market value ($ mil.)	–	–	–	–	–	–
Employees	(2.7%)	3,800	3,700	3,500	3,420	3,410

ONCOTHYREON INC.

NASDAQ: ONTY

2601 4th Ave. Ste. 500
Seattle WA 98121
Phone: 206-801-2100
Fax: 206-801-2101
Web: www.oncothyreon.com

CEO: Robert L Kirkman
CFO: Julia M Eastland
HR: –
FYE: December 31
Type: Public

Beating cancer is Oncothyreon's sole goal. The biotechnology company is developing synthetic vaccines and small-molecule (chemical) drugs that aim to battle the dread disease. Oncothyreon's vaccine candidates stimulate cancer-fighting elements in patients' immune systems. Lead candidate Stimuvax is a potential vaccine for non-small cell lung cancer that the company has licensed to Germany's Merck KGaA. Oncothyreon's traditional drug candidates work to inhibit certain cancer-specific proteins; candidates being developed by the company include potential treatments for pancreatic and metastatic cancer.

ONE GAS, INC.

NYS: OGS

15 East Fifth Street
Tulsa, OK 74103
Phone: 918 947-7000
Fax: –
Web: www.onegas.com

CEO: Pierce H. Norton
CFO: Curtis L. Dinan
HR: –
FYE: December 31
Type: Public

ONE Gas consists of former ONEOK natural gas utilities: Kansas Gas Service Oklahoma Natural Gas Company and Texas Gas Service. One of the largest publicly traded natural gas utilities in the US ONE Gas serves more than 2 million customers in three states. Kansas Gas Service has more than 19270 miles of distribution mains and service lines and serves more than 634320 customers; Oklahoma Natural Gas Company has more than 21630 miles of distribution mains and service lines and serves about 847100 customers; while Texas Gas Service has more than 14820 miles of distribution mains and service lines and serves about 634390 customers. ONEOK spun off ONE Gas in early 2014.

	Annual Growth	12/10	12/11	12/12	12/13	12/14
Sales ($ mil.)	–	0.0	1,621.3	1,376.6	1,690.0	1,818.9
Net income ($ mil.)	–	0.0	86.8	96.5	99.2	109.8
Market value ($ mil.)	–	0.0	–	–	–	2,146.9
Employees	6.5%	–	–	–	3,100	3,300

ONE LIBERTY PROPERTIES, INC.

NYS: OLP

60 Cutter Mill Road
Great Neck, NY 11021
Phone: 516 466-3100
Fax: –
Web: www.onelibertyproperties.com

CEO: Patrick J. Callan
CFO: David W. Kalish
HR: –
FYE: December 31
Type: Public

One Liberty Properties may own the space where lovebirds shop for loveseats. Or bird food. The self-managed and self-administered real estate investment trust (REIT) invests in retail industrial and office properties throughout the US. It owns or co-owns some 100 properties totaling some 5.5 million sq. ft. of space; more than half of its portfolio is leased to retailers including Haverty Furniture PetSmart and Giant Food Stores. The REIT also owns warehouses fitness centers and a movie theater. One Liberty Properties targets net-leased properties minimizing its responsibilities for taxes maintenance and other operating costs. The firm is controlled by the family of its chairman.

	Annual Growth	12/10	12/11	12/12	12/13	12/14
Sales ($ mil.)	9.6%	41.9	45.2	44.8	51.0	60.5
Net income ($ mil.)	24.2%	9.3	13.7	32.3	17.9	22.1
Market value ($ mil.)	9.1%	262.7	259.5	319.1	316.6	372.3
Employees	15.8%	5	5	7	7	9

ONE STOP SYSTEMS INC.

2235 ENTP ST STE 110   CEO: Steve Cooper
ESCONDIDO, CA 92029   CFO: –
Phone: 760-737-0122   HR: –
Fax: –   FYE: December 31
Web: www.onestopsystems.com   Type: Private

One Stop Systems designs and manufactures industrial computing systems and components including backplanes enclosures filler panels input/output boards and power supplies. One Stop's catalog includes a number of products built around the CompactPCI industry standard an interconnect technology intended for industrial environments that is also being used for military computers and other rugged electronics. The company also makes single-board computers and a variety of custom CPU and I/O boards enclosures and systems. One Stop Systems was founded in 1998. CEO Steve Cooper is the majority shareholder of the company. With Cooper VP Mark Gunn is a co-founder of One Stop Systems.

	Annual Growth	12/08	12/09	12/10	12/11	12/12
Sales ($ mil.)	4.6%	–	9.9	13.3	13.8	11.4
Net income ($ mil.)	(51.3%)	–	–	0.6	0.2	0.1
Market value ($ mil.)	–	–	–	–	–	–
Employees	–	–	–	–	–	35

ONEBEACON INSURANCE GROUP LTD.

NYSE: OB

601 Carlson Pkwy.   CEO: T Michael Miller
Minnetonka MN 55305   CFO: Paul H McDonough
Phone: 952-852-2431   HR: –
Fax: 888-656-1213   FYE: December 31
Web: www.onebeacon.com   Type: Public

OneBeacon Insurance Group shines its light on several insurance options for its customers across the US. OneBeacon provides specialty property/casualty insurance policies including marine travel professional liability medical malpractice data privacy umbrella property and even tuition coverage for when a student is forced to leave school unexpectedly. Products are sold to businesses and individuals through a network of 2900 independent agents and brokers across the US. Holding company White Mountains Insurance owns a controlling stake in OneBeacon.

ONEIDA LTD.

163-181 Kenwood Ave.   CEO: –
Oneida NY 13421-2899   CFO: Andrew G Church
Phone: 315-361-3000   HR: –
Fax: 315-361-3700   FYE: January 31
Web: www.oneida.com   Type: Private

Oneida knows its place at the table. Once one of the world's largest makers of stainless steel and silver-plated flatware Oneida now designs and supplies flatware dinnerware and crystal for both consumers and the foodservice and institutional markets. Its facilities dot the US Canada Mexico the UK and China. Flatware accounts for more than half of sales. Other tabletop items are cutlery and kitchen utensils and gadgets as well as baby keepsake gifts. Subsidiary Kenwood Silver operates about 15 Oneida outlet stores. Overwhelmed by debt Oneida filed for Chapter 11 bankruptcy protection in 2006 emerging later that year backed by a group of investors. Private equity Monomoy Capital bought Oneida in 2011.

ONEMAIN FINANCIAL INC.

300 St. Paul Place   CEO: –
Baltimore MD 21202   CFO: –
Phone: 410-332-3000   HR: –
Fax: 909-468-2905   FYE: December 31
Web: www.biosensewebster.com   Type: Subsidiary

Whether you're citified or country-fried OneMain Financial wants to help you build that deck or fix your old clunker. The consumer finance company offers secured and unsecured personal loans for debt consolidation home improvements vacations and unexpected expenses such as car repairs and medical bills through some 1300 locations in North America. The company also writes home equity mortgage and refinance loans. Formerly CitiFinancial OneMain is a subsidiary of Citigroup. Founded in 1912 as Commercial Credit it was bought by former Citigroup chairman and CEO Sandy Weill in 1986. Weill who retired in 2006 used the acquisition as a springboard to build what eventually grew into Citigroup.

ONEMAIN HOLDINGS INC

NYS: OMF

601 N.W. Second Street   CEO: Jay N. Levine
Evansville, IN 47708   CFO: Scott T. Parker
Phone: 812 424-8031   HR: –
Fax: –   FYE: December 31
Web: www.springleaffinancial.com   Type: Public

Springleaf Holdings is turning over a new leaf. The company previously serviced subprime mortgage loans until the real estate bust of 2008. Now doing business as Springleaf Financial Services it is a consumer finance company that provides personal loans to high-risk customers who have limited access to credit from banks credit card companies and other lenders. Operating through 830 branches in 26 states it also offers personal loans over the internet through its iLoan division. In addition it provides credit insurance and related products through subsidiaries Merit Life Insurance and Yosemite Insurance. The company traces its roots back to 1920 and went public in 2013.

	Annual Growth	12/10	12/11	12/12	12/13	12/14
Sales ($ mil.)	90.1%	212.7	1,988.0	1,767.9	2,272.0	2,775.0
Net income ($ mil.)	(23.4%)	1,464.3	(224.2)	(218.6)	(19.3)	504.6
Market value ($ mil.)	43.1%	–	–	–	2,903.0	4,153.5
Employees	5.7%	–	–	4,500	4,900	5,030

ONEOK INC.

NYS: OKE

100 West Fifth Street   CEO: Terry K Spencer
Tulsa, OK 74103   CFO: Derek S. Reiners
Phone: 918 588-7000   HR: –
Fax: 918 588-7273   FYE: December 31
Web: www.oneok.com   Type: Public

ONEOK ("one oak") is OK with its singled-minded pursuit of profits from natural gas activities. Through its 37.6%-owned ONEOK Partners (of which it is the general partner) it operates 11300 miles of gas-gathering pipeline and 7400 miles of transportation pipeline as well as gas processing plants and storage facilities. The unit also owns one of the US's top natural gas liquids (NGL) systems. ONEOK's energy services unit focuses on marketing natural gas across the US. To focus on its core pipeline businesses in 2014 ONEOK spun off its regulated utilities (Oklahoma Natural Gas Kansas Gas Service and Texas Gas Service which distribute natural gas to more than 2.1 million customers) as ONE Gas.

	Annual Growth	12/10	12/11	12/12	12/13	12/14
Sales ($ mil.)	(1.6%)	13,030.1	14,805.8	12,632.6	14,602.7	12,195.1
Net income ($ mil.)	(1.6%)	334.6	360.6	360.6	266.5	314.1
Market value ($ mil.)	(2.7%)	11,555.6	18,059.5	8,905.8	12,953.5	10,372.4
Employees	(17.2%)	4,839	4,795	4,859	1,927	2,269

ONEOK PARTNERS LP

NYS: OKS

100 West Fifth Street
Tulsa, OK 74103
Phone: 918 588-7000
Fax: –
Web: www.oneokpartners.com

CEO: Terry K Spencer
CFO: Derek Reiners
HR: –
FYE: December 31
Type: Public

For ONEOK Partners it's OK to have three businesses: natural gas pipelines; gas gathering and processing; and natural gas liquids (NGLs). Its pipelines include Midwestern Gas Transmission Guardian Pipeline Viking Gas Transmission and OkTex Pipeline. The ONEOK affiliate operates 17100 miles of gas-gathering pipeline and 7600 miles of transportation pipeline as well as gas processing plants and storage facilities (with 52 billion cu. ft. of capacity). It also owns one of the US's top natural NGL systems (more than 7200 miles of pipeline).

	Annual Growth	12/10	12/11	12/12	12/13	12/14
Sales ($ mil.)	8.9%	8,675.9	11,322.6	10,182.2	11,869.3	12,191.7
Net income ($ mil.)	17.8%	472.7	830.3	888.0	803.6	910.3
Market value ($ mil.)	(16.0%)	20,178.3	14,655.3	13,703.5	13,363.4	10,058.7
Employees	–	–	–	–	–	–

ONESOURCE INFORMATION SERVICES INC.

300 Baker Ave.
Concord MA 01742
Phone: 978-318-4300
Fax: 978-318-4690
Web: www.onesource.com

CEO: Steve Pogorzelski
CFO: Robert E Bies
HR: –
FYE: December 31
Type: Private

This company brings business information together. OneSource Information Services is a leading provider of business information offering data on millions of companies and executives worldwide. It aggregates company industry and financial information from a variety of sources including news articles websites and regulatory filings. Subscribers access the information through its Web-based OneSource Business Browser or the data can be integrated into a customer's enterprise information system. OneSource has offices in the US the UK Australia Singapore and India. In 2012 former parent Infogroup sold OneSource to private equity firms GTCR and Cannondale Investments.

ONION INC.

212 W. Superior St. Ste. 200
Chicago IL 60654
Phone: 312-751-0503
Fax: 312-751-4137
Web: www.theonion.com

CEO: Steve Hannah
CFO: –
HR: –
FYE: December 31
Type: Private

Tears from this Onion are most likely induced from fits of laughter. Onion Inc. publishes the popular satirical weekly newspaper "The Onion" which is available in both online and print editions. Sister website The Onion A.V. Club features interviews reviews and columns focusing on music and movies. Other operations include book publishing (including the best-seller Our Dumb Century) radio programming (Onion Radio News) online video clips (The Onion News Network) and consumer items such as calendars mugs and T-shirts. The company earns revenue through advertising and subscription fees. The Onion was first published in 1988 by then University of Wisconsin students Tim Keck and Christopher Johnson.

ONLINE VACATION CENTER HOLDINGS CORP

NBB: ONVC

2307 West Broward Blvd., Suite 400
Fort Lauderdale, FL 33312
Phone: 954 377-6407
Fax: 954 377-6399
Web: www.onlinevacationcenter.com

CEO: Edward B Rudner
CFO: –
HR: –
FYE: December 31
Type: Public

Online Vacation Center Holdings has quit the cigar business and is spending its future traveling. Previously called Alec Bradley Cigar Corporation the company was known for importing and selling cigars wholesale. In 2006 the firm completed a reverse merger with Online Vacation Center Holdings. It shuttered its cigar operations and changed its name to reflect its new adventure as an online retailer of vacation packages. The company specializes in cruise deals. Its subsidiaries include Online Vacation Center and Dunhill Vacations. Chairman CEO president and CFO Edward Rudner owns about 60% of Online Vacation Center Holdings.

	Annual Growth	12/10	12/11	12/12	12/13	12/14
Sales ($ mil.)	–	0.0	0.0	0.0	12.6	14.1
Net income ($ mil.)	–	0.0	0.0	0.0	0.6	1.0
Market value ($ mil.)	–	0.0	0.0	0.0	3.0	6.0
Employees	–	–	–	–	–	74

ONSTAR LLC

400 Renaissance Center
Detroit MI 48265
Phone: 248-588-6050
Fax: 313-667-0822
Web: www.onstar.com

CEO: –
CFO: –
HR: –
FYE: December 31
Type: Subsidiary

Lock your keys in your car? Damage to your ego will be minimal if your car has OnStar. A division of General Motors OnStar offers a range of services to motorists that make driving easier and safer. With OnStar's Safe & Sound Plan you can have your doors unlocked get roadside assistance or notify emergency personnel — all with the push of a dash-mounted button (or a phone call if you're locked out). Other basic services include airbag deployment notification and remote diagnostics. Under OnStar's Directions & Connections Plan drivers also enjoy services like turn-by-turn navigation and hotel reservations. The OnStar service is available in most of the US and in parts of Canada as well as China.

ONSTREAM MEDIA CORP

NBB: ONSM

1291 SW 29 Avenue
Pompano Beach, FL 33069
Phone: 954 917-6655
Fax: –
Web: www.onstreammedia.com

CEO: Randy S Selman
CFO: Robert E Tomlinson
HR: –
FYE: September 30
Type: Public

If a picture says a thousand words then Onstream Media Corporation speaks volumes about corporate communication and digital asset management. The company's Digital Media Services Group provides video and audio Webcasting to corporate clients and produces Internet-based multimedia streaming promotional videos for hotels and resorts. The group also includes DMSP (Digital Media Services Platform) and UGC (User Generated Content) divisions which provide encoding storage search retrieval and reuse of photos audio files Web pages and other digital files. Onstream's Audio & Web Conferencing Services Group includes conferencing provider Infinite and audio and video networking services provider EDNet.

	Annual Growth	09/10	09/11	09/12	09/13	09/14
Sales ($ mil.)	0.4%	16.7	17.7	18.2	17.2	16.9
Net income ($ mil.)	–	(9.3)	(5.2)	(2.6)	(7.2)	(1.7)
Market value ($ mil.)	(37.4%)	22.8	16.0	10.5	6.0	3.5
Employees	(3.7%)	100	93	102	88	86

ONVIA INC
NAS: ONVI

509 Olive Way, Suite 400
Seattle, WA 98101
Phone: 206 282-5170
Fax: –

CEO: Henry G. (Hank) Riner
CFO: Cameron S. Way
HR: SoYoung Kwon
FYE: December 31
Type: Public

Onvia aims to help companies win government contracts and government agencies find suppliers by providing a database of business leads. The company identifies purchasing behavior and bid opportunities from some 89000 federal state and local government agencies as well as private-sector enterprises and delivers notices of those opportunities to its 6200 subscribers. Its Onvia database includes data on millions of current and historical contracting opportunities in markets such as construction consulting and information technology. Subscriptions account for about 85% of the company's sales; Onvia also generates revenue by licensing its content to other companies. The company was established in 2000.

	Annual Growth	12/10	12/11	12/12	12/13	12/14
Sales ($ mil.)	(4.3%)	27.0	23.2	22.0	22.0	22.6
Net income ($ mil.)	–	(0.8)	1.6	1.5	(2.7)	(0.7)
Market value ($ mil.)	2.0%	34.3	21.2	27.2	36.7	37.2
Employees	(0.5%)	139	141	132	130	136

OP-TECH ENVIRONMENTAL SERVICES INC.
PINK SHEETS: OPST

6392 Deere Rd.
Syracuse NY 13206
Phone: 315-463-1643
Fax: 315-463-9764
Web: www.op-tech.us

CEO: Charles Morgan
CFO: –
HR: –
FYE: December 31
Type: Public

More than 1000 private industrial and municipal clients opt for OP-TECH Environmental Services which provides spill cleanup remediation and industrial cleaning services including lead abatement. The company also offers transportation and management of hazardous and nonhazardous wastes. OP-TECH Environmental Services provides rapid response to hazardous and non-hazardous spills primarily in New Jersey New York Ohio Pennsylvania and New England. Other services include building demolition and removal and health and safety training classes for clients. Director Richard Messina owns 33% of the company.

OPEN LINK FINANCIAL INC.

1502 RXR PLZ FL 15
UNIONDALE, NY 11556-3810
Phone: 516-227-6600
Fax: –
Web: www.olf.com

CEO: John O'Malley
CFO: David M Obstler
HR: –
FYE: December 31
Type: Private

OpenLink Financial develops risk management trading portfolio management and operations processing software for more than 500 clients in the financial services commodities and energy industries. Its products sold worldwide link and automate front- and back-office applications for banks corporate treasury departments energy marketers and insurance companies. OpenLink also provides professional services (consulting maintenance support and training) as well as complementary niche products through subsidiaries such as dbcS-MARTsoftware (software for agricultural commodities) and iRM (energy trade processing software). Founded in 1992 the company is owned by private equity firm Hellman & Friedman.

	Annual Growth	12/03	12/04	12/05	12/06	12/08
Sales ($ mil.)	(40.7%)	–	–	880.7	83.6	183.6
Net income ($ mil.)	8405.5%	–	–	0.0	0.4	17.2
Market value ($ mil.)	–	–	–	–	–	–
Employees	–	–	–	–	–	750

OPEN SOLUTIONS INC.

455 Winding Brook Dr.
Glastonbury CT 06033
Phone: 860-815-5000
Fax: 510-444-3580
Web: www.scilearn.com

CEO: –
CFO: –
HR: –
FYE: December 31
Type: Private

Open Solutions' software helps run the till for small and midsized banks and credit unions. The company's processing systems manage customer service payroll processing and year-end reporting. It also offers hosted software that enables banks to provide online services such as account information and management electronic bill payment and funds transfer. The firm also offers tools that integrate with its core systems including applications for online procurement business intelligence check imaging financial accounting and interactive voice response. Open Solutions sells directly and via partnerships with distributors and systems integrators. The company is owned by Fiserv which acquired it in 2013.

OPENTABLE INC.
NMS: OPEN

One Montgomery Street, 7th Floor
San Francisco, CA 94104
Phone: 415 344-4200
Fax: –
Web: www.opentable.com

CEO: Christa Quarles
CFO: I Duncan Robertson
HR: –
FYE: December 31
Type: Public

Even if your favorite restaurant is closed for the day you can still try to reserve a table through OpenTable. The firm provides online reservations at about 27000 upscale restaurants around the world. The service is free to diners but OpenTable charges participating restaurants an installation and monthly license fee for its Electronic Reservation Book (ERB) a computerized reservation system. It also provides training and support for ERB and charges a fee for tables booked through Connect a Web-based solution for reservations with less functionality than ERB. Since its founding in 1998 OpenTable has seated more than 200 million diners.

	Annual Growth	12/08	12/09	12/10	12/11	12/12
Sales ($ mil.)	30.4%	55.8	68.6	99.0	139.5	161.6
Net income ($ mil.)	–	(1.0)	5.1	14.1	21.6	24.0
Market value ($ mil.)	24.2%	–	583.0	1,613.9	896.0	1,117.4
Employees	17.5%	304	198	493	558	580

OPENTV CORP.

275 Sacramento St.
San Francisco CA 94111
Phone: 415-962-5000
Fax: 415-962-5300
Web: www.opentv.com

CEO: Ben Bennett
CFO: Shum Mukherjee
HR: –
FYE: December 31
Type: Subsidiary

OpenTV develops software used by cable and satellite television operators to offer their subscribers enhanced interactive content and services. Its applications allow viewers to use the remote control to not only surf TV channels and control camera angles and instant replays during sporting events but also access e-mail download audio and video files from the Internet and complete shopping and banking transactions. The company also develops the middleware used in set-top boxes as well as software used by network operators to manage advertising. OpenTV is a subsidiary of Swiss digital TV systems and digital security provider Kudelski.

OPERATING ENGINEERS FUNDS INC.

100 E. Corson St.	CEO: Mike Roddy
Pasadena CA 91103	CFO: Chuck Killian
Phone: 626-356-1000	HR: –
Fax: 626-356-1065	FYE: June 30
Web: www.oefunds.org	Type: Private - Not-for-Pr

The Operating Engineers Funds are in fact for operating engineers — not the kind who run trains but those who operate other large machinery. The company administers employee benefits including pensions health welfare vacation and holiday benefit for more than 35000 active or retired members of the International Union of Operating Engineers (I.U.O.E.) Local 12 as well as their beneficiaries and dependents. The union consists of individuals in construction-related trades including heavy equipment operators soil testers concrete pumpers inspectors and surveyors.

OPERATION SMILE INC.

3641 FACULTY BLVD	CEO: Magee Jr DDS MD William P
VIRGINIA BEACH, VA 234538000	CFO: –
Phone: 888-677-6453	HR: –
Fax: –	FYE: June 30
Web: www.operationsmile.org	Type: Private

Operation Smile's mission is simple: Make the children of the world grin. The not-for-profit volunteer group provides reconstructive surgery and health-care services to children and young adults suffering from facial deformities such as cleft lips cleft palates burns and tumors. Operation Smile has assisted more than 120000 patients in 25 developing countries and the US. The organization also provides educational fellowship programs in craniofacial surgery and runs a physician training program. Operation Smile was founded in 1982 by Dr. William Magee and his wife Kathleen a nurse and clinical social worker. A plan to merge with Smile Train in 2011 is being called off due to donor opposition.

	Annual Growth	06/07	06/08	06/09	06/10	06/13
Sales ($ mil.)	(35.1%)	–	451.1	33.2	40.6	52.1
Net income ($ mil.)	–	–	–	0.0	2.4	1.2
Market value ($ mil.)	–	–	–	–	–	–
Employees	–	–	–	–	–	128

OPEXA THERAPEUTICS INC   NAS: OPXA

2635 Technology Forest Blvd.	CEO: Neil K Warma
The Woodlands, TX 77381	CFO: Karthik Radhakrishnan
Phone: 281 272-9331	HR: –
Fax: –	FYE: December 31
Web: www.opexatherapeutics.com	Type: Public

Biopharmaceutical company Opexa Therapeutics wants to develop chronic remedies for chronic diseases. Specializing in autologous treatments (those which use the patient's own tissue and cells) Opexa is developing Tovaxin a T-cell vaccine used for the treatment of multiple sclerosis which is caused when the body's immune system (T-cells) attacks the nervous system. Currently in late stages of development Tovaxin works by lowering the levels of harmful T-cells in the body. Opexa was also researching its adult stem cell technology with the goal of developing treatments for diabetes and other chronic diseases but it sold rights to the stem cell technology to Novartis in 2009.

	Annual Growth	12/10	12/11	12/12	12/13	12/14
Sales ($ mil.)	0.4%	–	–	–	1.3	1.3
Net income ($ mil.)	–	(5.5)	(6.0)	(8.9)	(16.7)	(15.1)
Market value ($ mil.)	(16.7%)	5.2	3.3	4.0	6.4	2.5
Employees	37.2%	11	19	26	38	39

OPKO HEALTH INC   NYS: OPK

4400 Biscayne Blvd.	CEO: Phillip Frost
Miami, FL 33137	CFO: Adam Logal
Phone: 305 575-4100	HR: –
Fax: –	FYE: December 31
Web: www.opko.com	Type: Public

Opko Health may have started out in the US developing treatments for eye diseases but it has expanded its geographic and therapeutic reach. In addition to research and development of ophthalmic drug candidates the company is working on biopharmaceuticals for oncology neurology and infectious diseases. It has development programs for vaccines and molecular diagnostic tests and operates clinical laboratories that provide testing services to the medical community. To support its research programs Opko Health sells a number of prescription pharmaceuticals and over-the-counter products in Latin American countries.

	Annual Growth	12/10	12/11	12/12	12/13	12/14
Sales ($ mil.)	25.4%	36.9	28.0	47.0	96.5	91.1
Net income ($ mil.)	–	(18.9)	(1.3)	(29.0)	(114.4)	(171.7)
Market value ($ mil.)	28.4%	1,586.1	2,117.7	2,078.8	3,647.6	4,317.4
Employees	32.3%	220	268	549	625	674

OPLINK COMMUNICATIONS INC.   NMS: OPLK

46335 Landing Parkway	CEO: Joseph Y Liu
Fremont, CA 94538	CFO: Shirley Yin
Phone: 510 933-7200	HR: –
Fax: –	FYE: June 30
Web: www.oplink.com	Type: Public

Oplink Communications has its eye on network connections. The company makes fiber-optic components that increase the capacity of communications networks. Oplink's dense wavelength division multiplexers transmit several light signals simultaneously over a single glass fiber. Other products provide signal functions such as amplification wavelength performance monitoring and preservation redirection connectivity and transmission and reception. Telecommunications equipment makers including Huawei and Tellabs (each more than 10% of sales) incorporate Oplink's components into gear used to build networks both interoffice and international. Customers in Asia primarily in China and Japan account for about a third of sales.

	Annual Growth	06/09	06/10	06/11*	07/12*	06/13
Sales ($ mil.)	6.3%	143.7	138.8	198.8	174.9	183.4
Net income ($ mil.)	–	(13.8)	11.1	48.5	(2.6)	13.4
Market value ($ mil.)	11.1%	218.2	274.3	356.2	259.0	332.5
Employees	13.5%	2,260	3,821	3,570	3,454	3,744

*Fiscal year change

OPNET TECHNOLOGIES INC.   NASDAQ: OPNT

7255 Woodmont Ave.	CEO: Jerry M Kennelly
Bethesda MD 20814	CFO: Ernie Maddock
Phone: 240-497-3000	HR: Lesley Diller
Fax: 240-497-3001	FYE: March 31
Web: www.opnet.com	Type: Public

OPNET Technologies has made its name in network optimization. The company makes network management software for designing building and operating networks. Its products include applications to automate network design provisioning and performance analysis. Its software enables designers to evaluate how networks will perform under simulated conditions analyze collected data and resolve performance problems such as network congestion configuration errors and application bugs. The company also offers such professional services as consulting maintenance and training. OPNET is being acquired by Riverbed Technology for about $1 billion.

OPNEXT INC.

NASDAQ: OPXT

46429 Landing Pkwy.
Fremont CA 94538
Phone: 510-580-8828
Fax: 503-223-0182
Web: www.tripwire.com

CEO: Harry L Bosco
CFO: Robert J Nobile
HR: –
FYE: March 31
Type: Public

Stay tuned: light-speed communication is Opnext. The company makes opto-electronic components used to assemble fiber-optic data and voice communications networks. These laser diode modules transmitter/receiver devices and transceivers are incorporated by other equipment makers into larger multiplexing and digital cross-connect systems used in data communications and telecommunications. Opnext has a limited number of customers. Alcatel-Lucent Cisco Systems and Huawei Technologies together account for about 45% of sales.Other customers include Nokia Siemens Networks and Ciena Corporation. The company gets 40% of sales in North America. In 2012 it was bought by rival Oclaro.

OPPENHEIMER HOLDINGS INC

NYS: OPY

85 Broad Street
New York, NY 10004
Phone: 212 668-8000
Fax: –
Web: www.opco.com

CEO: James P. Carley
CFO: Jeffery J. Alfano
HR: –
FYE: December 31
Type: Public

J. Robert Oppenheimer dealt in mushroom clouds but Oppenheimer Holdings helps mushroom finances. Through subsidiaries Oppenheimer & Co. Oppenheimer Asset Management and Oppenheimer Trust it provides a range of financial services including brokerage investment banking asset management lending and research. Its Private Client segment which offers retail brokerage wealth management and margin lending to affluent and business clients in the US and Latin America makes up the bulk of sales. The group also has operations in the UK Israel and Hong Kong. It has more than $25 billion of client assets under management. The firm is not affiliated with Oppenheimer-Funds a unit of MassMutual Financial Group.

	Annual Growth	12/10	12/11	12/12	12/13	12/14
Sales ($ mil.)	(0.7%)	1,035.1	959.0	952.6	1,019.7	1,004.5
Net income ($ mil.)	(30.7%)	38.3	10.3	(3.6)	25.1	8.8
Market value ($ mil.)	(3.0%)	357.3	219.4	235.4	337.8	316.9
Employees	(1.0%)	3,576	3,576	3,521	3,517	3,434

OPPENHEIMERFUNDS INC.

2 World Financial Center 225 Liberty St.
New York NY 10281-1008
Phone: 212-323-0200
Fax: 212-323-4070
Web: www.oppenheimerfunds.com

CEO: William Glavin Jr
CFO: –
HR: –
FYE: December 31
Type: Subsidiary

Four hands are better than one? OppenheimerFunds (whose logo is four interconnected hands) is a mutual fund manager majority-owned by Massachusetts Mutual Life Insurance better known as MassMutual. Tracing its roots to a mutual fund business launched in 1960 the firm manages more than 65 funds invested in domestic and international equitiesy municipal bonds money markets and alternative investments such as commodities real estate and hedge funds. The company also offers IRAs college savings plans and separate accounts and manages group plans for small and midsized companies. OppenheimerFunds has more than $150 billion in assets under management in some six million shareholder accounts.

OPTICAL CABLE CORP.

NMS: OCC

5290 Concourse Drive
Roanoke, VA 24019
Phone: 540 265-0690
Fax: –
Web: www.occfiber.com

CEO: Neil D Wilkin Jr
CFO: Tracy G Smith
HR: Phil Peters
FYE: October 31
Type: Public

Optical Cable Corporation (OCC) wants to keep you connected with a little help from its products of course. The company makes fiber-optic cable and copper data communications connectivity equipment and systems. Its high-bandwidth cables transmit data video and audio over distances of up to 10 miles. OCC's fiber-optic cables which are suitable for indoor and outdoor use are used in local-area networks (LANs) for schools hospitals manufacturing plants and business facilities. OCC also produces security cables for use with surveillance cameras and specialty fiber-optic cables for military tactical field applications. Customers include electrical contractors OEMs systems resellers and distributors.

	Annual Growth	10/11	10/12	10/13	10/14	10/15
Sales ($ mil.)	0.1%	73.3	83.5	75.3	83.0	73.6
Net income ($ mil.)	–	0.7	2.7	(0.0)	0.7	(4.3)
Market value ($ mil.)	(3.3%)	25.3	29.3	27.1	32.5	22.1
Employees	0.1%	340	367	376	361	342

OPTIMUMBANK HOLDINGS INC

NAS: OPHC

2477 East Commercial Boulevard
Fort Lauderdale, FL 33308
Phone: 954 900-2800
Fax: –
Web: www.optimumbank.com

CEO: Thomas A Procelli
CFO: Thomas A Procelli
HR: Leslie M Legg
FYE: December 31
Type: Public

OptimumBank Holdings is the holding company for OptimumBank which operates three branches in the communities of Plantation Fort Lauderdale and Deerfield Beach in South Florida. The bank is mainly a real estate lender with commercial mortgages representing the largest portion of its loan portfolio followed by residential mortgages land and construction loans and multi-family residential mortgages. It also offers other standard services such as checking and savings accounts CDs credit cards and personal loans. OptimumBank was founded in 2000 by chairman Albert Finch and president Richard Browdy. As a group executive officers and directors of OptimumBank Holdings own more than 40% of the company.

	Annual Growth	12/10	12/11	12/12	12/13	12/14
Assets ($ mil.)	(10.1%)	190.3	154.5	143.7	128.8	124.5
Net income ($ mil.)	–	(8.5)	(3.7)	(4.7)	(7.1)	1.6
Market value ($ mil.)	–	–	–	–	–	–
Employees	(2.7%)	19	17	19	20	17

OPTIONSXPRESS HOLDINGS INC.

311 W. Monroe St. Ste. 1000
Chicago IL 60606
Phone: 312-630-3300
Fax: 312-629-5256
Web: www.optionsxpress.com

CEO: David A Fisher
CFO: Adam J Dewitt
HR: –
FYE: December 31
Type: Subsidiary

In a hurry to do some options trading? optionsXpress is an online brokerage that provides a customized interface for trading options futures stocks and other products. The company is one of the few online brokerages offering futures and options which together account for about 80% of its trading activity. optionsXpress has grown from some 162000 customer accounts to around 400000 accounts since 2005. It averages approximately 45000 trades per day. The company also offers investor education products and services through Optionetics which it acquired in 2009. optionsXpress was acquired by Charles Schwab in 2011.

OPTUMHEALTH INC.

6300 Olson Memorial Hwy.
Golden Valley MN 55427
Phone: 952-936-1300
Fax: 952-936-7430
Web: www.optumhealth.com

CEO: Larry Renfro
CFO: Randall B Odzer
HR: –
FYE: December 31
Type: Subsidiary

OptumHealth's goal is to help members keep their health in tip-top shape. The company provides a variety of wellness services including employee assistance programs (EAPs) and return-to-work solutions. Its three main units Care Solutions Behavioral Solutions and Financial Services provide everything from chronic disease coverage to mental health and financial planning assistance. OptumHealth is a division of UnitedHealth Group; however OptumHealth's programs are available in modular components and aren't dependent on coverage through UnitedHealth though many of OptumHealth's 60 million members are also served by UnitedHealth's traditional health benefit units.

OPTUMINSIGHT

13625 Technology Dr.
Eden Prairie MN 55344
Phone: 952-833-7100
Fax: 952-833-7079
Web: www.optuminsight.com

CEO: Bill Miller
CFO: Gerald Knutson
HR: –
FYE: December 31
Type: Subsidiary

OptumInsight (formerly Ingenix) gives health care insurance and drug discovery companies a fresh look at the hard numbers they require to stay in business. The UnitedHealth Group subsidiary is one of the largest US health care data companies and as such it helps clients make accurate and cost-effective decisions about medical treatments and insurance coding as well as where to focus their marketing strategies and research efforts to meet market needs. Its information services include database management (including electronic health records) analytics and a variety of consulting services to health care providers insurance firms government agencies and life science researchers.

OPTUMRX INC.

2300 Main St.
Irvine CA 92614-9731
Phone: 949-221-9974
Fax: 403-213-3648
Web: www.vereseninc.com

CEO: Mark Thierer
CFO: Jeffrey Grosklags
HR: –
FYE: December 31
Type: Subsidiary

OptumRx (previously Prescription Solutions) has the Rx for insurance providers reeling from high drug costs. The company provides pharmacy benefit management (PBM) services to health insurers managed care organizations employers unions and other clients representing more than 10 million members nationwide. Its services range from formulary management and benefit design to pharmacy network management online reporting and claims processing and tracking. OptumRx also operates mail-order pharmacies and provides specialty pharmacy services for high-cost biotech drugs. Founded in 1993 the business is a subsidiary of UnitedHealth and accounts for about 20% of its parent company's revenues.

ORACLE CORP.

NYS: ORCL

500 Oracle Parkway
Redwood City, CA 94065
Phone: 650 506-7000
Fax: –
Web: www.oracle.com

CEO: Mark V. Hurd
CFO: –
HR: –
FYE: May 31
Type: Public

Oracle can't foretell the future but it helps its customers better manage their way into the future by supporting their business operations. The leader in enterprise software (about 76% of its sales) it also provides hardware and services to help companies improve their processes. Best known for its focus on databases it offers aid in areas such as managing business data collaboration and application development customer relationship management and supply chain management. In recent years the company has aggressively used acquisitions to expand such as its entry into the hardware business with the purchase of Sun Microsystems.

	Annual Growth	05/11	05/12	05/13	05/14	05/15
Sales ($ mil.)	1.8%	35,622.0	37,121.0	37,180.0	38,275.0	38,226.0
Net income ($ mil.)	3.8%	8,547.0	9,981.0	10,925.0	10,955.0	9,938.0
Market value ($ mil.)	–	0.0	0.0	0.0	0.0	0.0
Employees	5.1%	108,000	115,000	120,000	122,000	132,000

ORAGENICS INC

ASE: OGEN

4902 Eisenhower Blvd., Suite 125
Tampa, FL 33634
Phone: 813 286-7900
Fax: 813 286-7904
Web: www.oragenics.com

CEO: Michael Sullivan
CFO: –
HR: –
FYE: December 31
Type: Public

Oragenics wants to get the beneficial microflora in your mouth to bloom. The biotechnology company is developing an oral topical treatment that could provide life-long protection from most forms of tooth decay. It is also researching an antibiotic that could kill harmful bacteria in the mouth such as drug-resistant Staphylococcus. Its ProBiora consumer product launched under the EvoraPlus brand uses beneficial bacteria to promote oral and periodontal health. It is also developing a weight-loss product. Oragenics aims to turn from product development to commercialization through alliances and partnerships.

	Annual Growth	12/10	12/11	12/12	12/13	12/14
Sales ($ mil.)	(7.9%)	1.3	1.4	1.3	1.0	0.9
Net income ($ mil.)	–	(7.8)	(7.7)	(13.1)	(16.1)	(5.8)
Market value ($ mil.)	(26.2%)	108.5	36.5	95.5	101.7	32.2
Employees	(9.1%)	19	15	10	10	13

ORANGE COUNTY TRANSPORTATION AUTHORITY SCHOLARSHIP FOUNDATION IN

550 S MAIN ST
ORANGE, CA 928684506
Phone: 714-636-7433
Fax: –
Web: www.octa.net

CEO: Darrell Johnson
CFO: –
HR: –
FYE: June 30
Type: Private

Public transportation in sunny Orange County California is overseen by the Orange County Transportation Authority (OCTA). The OCTA is the main provider of bus services in its 800-sq.-mi. territory which is home to more than 3 million people. In cooperation with the Southern California Regional Rail Authority the OCTA oversees Metrolink commuter rail service in Orange County. The agency also operates a 10-mile toll road and issues permits to taxi operators. Revenue from a half-cent local sales tax allows the agency to pay for road improvement and mass transit projects.

	Annual Growth	06/09	06/10	06/11	06/12	06/13
Sales ($ mil.)	12.6%	–	421.9	438.1	609.4	602.5
Net income ($ mil.)	(69.6%)	–	–	247.7	23.2	22.9
Market value ($ mil.)	–	–	–	–	–	–
Employees	–	–	–	–	–	1,050

ORASURE TECHNOLOGIES INC.

NMS: OSUR

220 East First Street
Bethlehem, PA 18015
Phone: 610 882-1820
Fax: –
Web: www.orasure.com

CEO: Douglas A. Michels
CFO: Ronald H. Spair
HR: Henry (Hal) Cohen
FYE: December 31
Type: Public

When it comes to diagnostic tests OraSure is certain it can deliver results. The oral specimen kits and other diagnostic tests developed by OraSure Technologies are designed to detect drug use and certain infectious diseases namely HIV and hepatitis C. Its OraSure products use oral specimens rather than traditional blood or urine based methods to test for HIV. The Intercept line uses oral samples to test for marijuana cocaine opiates PCP and amphetamines. OraSure has also developed a rapid HIV blood diagnostic testing method and it has entered the genetic testing market through its DNAG subsidiary. OraSure sells its products in the US and internationally to health care facilities and medical laboratories.

	Annual Growth	12/10	12/11	12/12	12/13	12/14
Sales ($ mil.)	9.1%	75.0	81.9	87.8	98.9	106.5
Net income ($ mil.)	–	(3.5)	(8.8)	(15.1)	(11.2)	(4.6)
Market value ($ mil.)	15.2%	323.1	511.9	403.4	353.4	569.7
Employees	8.5%	231	308	313	293	320

ORBCOMM INC

NMS: ORBC

395 W. Passaic Street
Rochelle Park, NJ 07662
Phone: 703 433-6300
Fax: –

CEO: Marc J. Eisenberg
CFO: Robert G. Costantini
HR: Tom Brennan
FYE: December 31
Type: Public

ORBCOMM uses its fleet of 26 low-Earth-orbit (LEO) satellites to help businesses keep an eye on their earthbound assets. The system's two-way data transmission capabilities enable users to track vehicles and mobile equipment monitor fixed assets such as utility meters and pipelines and communicate with mobile and remote workers around the globe. It also provides machine-to-machine (M2M) communications and telematics services. Key clients include heavy equipment makers Caterpillar (about 20% of sales) Komatsu (10% of sales) and Hitachi (10% of sales). The company also serves government customers with Automatic Identification System (AIS) data services for marine vessel tracking.

	Annual Growth	12/10	12/11	12/12	12/13	12/14
Sales ($ mil.)	27.3%	36.7	46.3	64.5	74.2	96.2
Net income ($ mil.)	–	(5.2)	(0.0)	8.7	4.6	(4.7)
Market value ($ mil.)	26.1%	181.5	209.5	274.7	444.3	458.3
Employees	22.8%	99	136	162	186	225

ORBIT INTERNATIONAL CORP.

NBB: ORBT

80 Cabot Court
Hauppauge, NY 11788
Phone: 631 435-8300
Fax: –
Web: www.orbitintl.com

CEO: Mitchell Binder
CFO: David Goldman
HR: Donna Holzeis
FYE: December 31
Type: Public

Orbit International is at home in the world — on land in the air or at sea. The company's core electronics group is comprised of its instrument division and its Tulip and ICS subsidiaries. It specializes in customized display terminals intercommunication panels and keyboards for military ships and aircraft as well as rugged computing hardware for commercial customers. Orbit's power unit led by subsidiary Behlman Electronics makes electrical AC power supplies and frequency converters; it also reconfigures obsolete military equipment and does repairs for the US Air Force and Navy. Orbit primarily serves the US government and defense contractors such as BAE SYSTEMS.

	Annual Growth	12/10	12/11	12/12	12/13	12/14
Sales ($ mil.)	(8.0%)	26.7	31.0	29.4	24.8	19.2
Net income ($ mil.)	–	(3.0)	3.1	(0.1)	(2.6)	(2.0)
Market value ($ mil.)	(4.6%)	17.0	16.4	14.5	15.2	14.1
Employees	(4.3%)	139	150	141	122	–

ORBIT/FR, INC.

NBB: ORFR

506 Prudential Road
Horsham, PA 19044
Phone: 215 674-5100
Fax: –
Web: www.orbitfr.com

CEO: Per Iversen
CFO: Relland Winand
HR: Lisa Fugelo
FYE: December 31
Type: Public

ORBIT/FR's business revolves around microwave test and measurement. The company manufactures automated hardware and software systems for evaluating microwave signal performance in devices such as cell phones radio transmitters Global Positioning System (GPS) receivers military antennas and guided missiles. Other products include microwave receivers and antennas and anechoic foam (an echo-free microwave-absorbing material). ORBIT/FR designs systems for product manufacturers in the aerospace and defense satellite wireless communications and automotive industries. Customers include BT Group Ford IBM Lufthansa Northrop Grumman Samsung UCLA and the US military.

	Annual Growth	12/10	12/11	12/12	12/13	12/14
Sales ($ mil.)	2.1%	36.2	33.6	34.1	38.2	39.4
Net income ($ mil.)	(23.7%)	2.3	(0.6)	0.7	0.5	0.8
Market value ($ mil.)	(3.4%)	17.0	5.8	4.7	14.5	14.8
Employees	2.2%	138	141	–	–	–

ORBITAL ATK INC

NYS: OA

45101 Warp Drive
Dulles, VA 20166
Phone: 703 406-5000
Fax: –
Web: www.orbitalatk.com

CEO: David W. Thompson
CFO: Garrett E. Pierce
HR: Christine Wolf
FYE: March 31
Type: Public

Space is not the final frontier for Orbital ATK as long as its aerospace/defense offerings are paving new paths. Through several operating segments the company (formerly Alliant Techsystems) is a leading manufacturer of mission-critical products including launch vehicles and related propulsion systems; satellites and associated components and services; composite aerospace structures; tactical missiles subsystems and defense electronics; and precision weapons armament systems and ammunition. It spun off its sporting goods business as Vista Outdoor in 2015 upon its merger with Orbital Sciences.

	Annual Growth	03/11	03/12	03/13	03/14	03/15
Sales ($ mil.)	(10.0%)	4,842.3	4,613.4	4,362.1	4,775.1	3,174.0
Net income ($ mil.)	(10.3%)	313.2	262.6	271.8	340.9	202.5
Market value ($ mil.)	2.0%	4,199.8	2,978.5	4,304.4	8,447.7	4,554.0
Employees	(4.8%)	15,000	17,000	14,000	16,000	12,300

ORBITAL SCIENCES CORP.

NYS: ORB

45101 Warp Drive
Dulles, VA 20166
Phone: 703 406-5000
Fax: –
Web: www.orbital.com

CEO: David W Thompson
CFO: Garrett E Pierce
HR: –
FYE: December 31
Type: Public

Orbital Sciences maintains that what goes up doesn't have to come down — at least not for a long time. The company makes low-Earth-orbit satellites and other spacecraft for communications science and technology research and national security purposes. Orbital Sciences also manufactures satellite launch vehicles as well as interceptors (to stop missile attacks) and target launch vehicles that test missile defense systems. Its advanced space programs division develops and supports human space flight space exploration and launch systems and satellites primarily used for national security programs. The US government and its contractors account for about 71% of the company's sales.

	Annual Growth	12/08	12/09	12/10	12/11	12/12
Sales ($ mil.)	5.3%	1,168.6	1,125.3	1,294.6	1,345.9	1,436.8
Net income ($ mil.)	(0.1%)	61.3	36.6	47.5	67.4	61.0
Market value ($ mil.)	(8.4%)	1,164.3	909.8	1,021.2	866.2	820.9
Employees	0.7%	3,400	3,100	3,400	3,500	3,500

ORBITZ WORLDWIDE INC

NYS: OWW

500 W. Madison Street, Suite 1000
Chicago, IL 60661
Phone: 312 894-5000
Fax: –
Web: www.orbitz.com

CEO: Barney Harford
CFO: Michael Randolfi
HR: Mike Goldwasser
FYE: December 31
Type: Public

Orbiting within the universe among the celestial "big four" giants of online travel (the other three being Expedia Travelocity and Priceline) Orbitz Worldwide offers an assortment of travel products and services to both consumers and professionals. The online travel agency offers plane tickets (from some 400 airlines) lodging (at more than 80000 hotels) rental car services cruises and vacation packages. Its portfolio of brands includes CheapTickets ebookers HotelClub RatesToGo Orbitz for Business and the Away Network. Hotel services are offered through partners such as Hilton Marriott and Hyatt. Orbitz is a division of travel conglomeratge Travelport Limited owned by The Blackstone Group.

	Annual Growth	12/09	12/10	12/11	12/12	12/13
Sales ($ mil.)	3.5%	738.0	757.5	766.8	778.8	847.0
Net income ($ mil.)	–	(337.0)	(58.2)	(37.3)	(301.7)	165.1
Market value ($ mil.)	(0.6%)	795.5	605.8	407.5	294.8	778.1
Employees	(1.8%)	1,400	1,400	1,329	1,328	1,300

ORC INTERNATIONAL INC.

902 Carnegie Center Ste. 220
Princeton NJ 08540-6530
Phone: 609-452-5400
Fax: 609-452-5292
Web: www.orcinternational.com

CEO: Simon Kooyman
CFO: Stace Lee
HR: –
FYE: December 31
Type: Private

Everybody has one and ORC International wants yours. The opinion-seeking company provides survey and market research services for an array of public and private sector customers in the Asia-Pacific Europe and the US. It focuses its research efforts on issues such as customer strategy market development corporate brand strategy employee engagement and competitive intelligence and it has provided traditional market research services for such big names as GM and Johnson & Johnson. In addition ORC International provides poll coverage through a partnership with CNN. Formerly owned by information provider Infogroup the company was acquired by private equity firm Lake Capital in mid-2011.

ORCA BAY SEAFOODS INC.

900 POWELL AVE SW
RENTON, WA 980572907
Phone: 425-204-9100
Fax: –
Web: www.orcabayseafoods.com

CEO: –
CFO: –
HR: –
FYE: February 28
Type: Private

Icy waters produce a lot of frozen fish. Orca Bay Seafoods is a leading supplier of fresh frozen seafood sourcing products from oceans all over the world. The company buys flash-frozen fish from suppliers and keeps it frozen as it cuts individual portions for sale to foodservice companies supermarkets club stores and restaurants across the US. Its products include Ahi tuna Alaskan cod Pacific Ocean pearch sockeye salmon mahi mahi and tilapia as well as Mexican white shrimp. Orca Bay was founded by Mike Samsel in 1985; the giant Japanese seafood company Maruha Nichiro owns a minority interest in the company; Japanese conglomerate Tokusui Corporation owns the controlling interest.

	Annual Growth	02/06	02/07	02/08	02/09	02/10
Sales ($ mil.)	(10.8%)	–	–	–	157.0	140.0
Net income ($ mil.)	(36.6%)	–	–	–	1.4	0.9
Market value ($ mil.)	–	–	–	–	–	–
Employees	–	–	–	–	–	180

ORCHARD SOFTWARE CORPORATION

701 Congressional Blvd. Ste. 360
Carmel IN 46032-5633
Phone: 317-573-6663
Fax: 317-573-2633
Web: www.orchardsoft.com

CEO: Curtis H Johnson
CFO: –
HR: –
FYE: December 31
Type: Private

Orchard Software creates Laboratory Information Systems (LIS) used by health care facilities of all shapes and sizes — from doctor's offices to hospitals. Its Orchard Harvest LIS uses process automation ICD-9 screening and robust instrument billing EMR (electronic medical record) and reference lab interfaces. Orchard Copia is a browser-based system for linking laboratory systems with physicians and Orchard Pathology utilizes a single database to integrate all laboratory departments. The company also offers microbiology and anatomic pathology systems for remote order entry and receiving test results via the Internet. Orchard Software was founded in 1993 and its officers own most of the company.

ORCHID CELLMARK INC.

NASDAQ: ORCH

4390 US Rte. 1
Princeton NJ 08540
Phone: 609-750-2200
Fax: 609-750-6400
Web: www.orchid.com

CEO: Thomas A Bologna
CFO: James F Smith
HR: –
FYE: December 31
Type: Subsidiary

Orchid Cellmark can prove who the baby daddy is and determine if suspects were at the scene of a crime. The company is a leading provider of forensic genetic testing services to criminal justice agencies in the UK and US. It tests DNA found at crime scenes or taken from suspects in custody; it also contributes DNA profiles to law enforcement databases. The company also performs paternity testing (mainly for child support enforcement agencies family-law firms and individuals). Most of its work is through contracts with government agencies. The company was acquired by LabCorp in a deal worth about $84 million.

ORCIIID ISLAND CAPITAL, INC.

NYS: ORC

3305 Flamingo Drive
Vero Beach, FL 32963
Phone: 772 231-1400
Fax: –
Web: www.orchidislandcapital.com

CEO: Robert E. Cauley
CFO: G. Hunter Haas
HR: –
FYE: December 31
Type: Public

No REIT is an island unless your name is Orchid Island Capital. The company which is seeking to become a real estate investment trust invests in residential mortgage-backed securities (RMBS) that are guaranteed by the US government or federally sponsored entities like Fannie Mae Freddie Mac and Ginnie Mae. Its portfolio and principal investment targets consist of pass-through agency RMBS and structured agency RMBS including fixed-rate mortgages adjustable-rate mortgages (ARMs) and hybrid ARMs as well as collateralized mortgage obligations. Formed by mortgage REIT Bimini Capital Management in 2010 Orchid Island Capital filed to go public for the second time in October 2012.

	Annual Growth	12/10	12/11	12/12	12/13	12/14
Sales ($ mil.)	591.2%	0.0	0.5	1.5	2.1	32.0
Net income ($ mil.)	–	(0.0)	(1.2)	0.5	(0.7)	24.5
Market value ($ mil.)	0.4%	–	–	–	217.1	217.9
Employees	–	–	–	–	–	–

ORCHIDS PAPER PRODUCTS CO. (DE)

ASE: TIS

4826 Hunt Street
Pryor, OK 74361
Phone: 918 825-0616
Fax: –
Web: www.orchidspaper.com

CEO: Jeffrey S Schoen
CFO: Keith R. Schroeder
HR: –
FYE: December 31
Type: Public

Orchids Paper Products hopes to leave its end users smelling like a rose. The company makes bulk tissue paper and converts it into bathroom tissue paper napkins and paper towels for the consumer market. Most of the company's products are sold as private-label items by discount retailers; Orchids Paper products also are sold under the company's Colortex and Velvet brands. Dollar General is Orchids Paper's largest customer; other big customers include Family Dollar and Wal-Mart. Orchids Paper sells most of its products within a 500-mile radius of its manufacturing plant in northeastern Oklahoma.

	Annual Growth	12/10	12/11	12/12	12/13	12/14
Sales ($ mil.)	11.5%	92.5	97.8	100.8	116.4	142.7
Net income ($ mil.)	12.5%	5.9	6.2	9.3	13.3	9.5
Market value ($ mil.)	24.2%	107.2	159.4	177.1	287.6	254.9
Employees	1.8%	292	296	290	317	313

OREGON HEALTH & SCIENCE UNIVERSITY MEDICAL GROUP

3181 SW SAM JACKSON PK RD
PORTLAND, OR 972393011
Phone: 503-494-8311
Fax: –
Web: www.ohsu.edu

CEO: –
CFO: Lawrence J Furnstahl
HR: –
FYE: June 30
Type: Private

Oregon Health & Science University (OHSU) builds a bridge to medical education in the Beaver State. OHSU is the state's sole institution providing doctoral degrees in medicine dentistry and nursing. Its other two schools are science and engineering and in partnership with Oregon State University pharmacy. OHSU has about 2800 students. The university is also home to two hospitals (one a children's hospital) as well as specialty and primary care clinics research and interdisciplinary centers and community service programs. OHSU traces its roots to 1867 when members of the medical department at Willamette University began the first formal medical education program in Oregon.

	Annual Growth	06/04	06/05	06/06	06/12	06/13
Sales ($ mil.)	9.1%	–	1,078.8	1,257.8	1,975.6	2,169.5
Net income ($ mil.)	6.7%	–	–	140.7	78.6	221.2
Market value ($ mil.)	–	–	–	–	–	–
Employees	–	–	–	–	–	14,000

OREGON STATE UNIVERSITY

308 KERR ADM BLDG
CORVALLIS, OR 97331
Phone: 541-737-2198
Fax: –
Web: www.coas.oregonstate.edu

CEO: –
CFO: –
HR: –
FYE: June 30
Type: Private

Oregon State University (OSU) offers about 200 undergraduate and more than 80 graduate degree programs at about a dozen colleges and schools including nationally recognized programs in engineering environmental sciences forestry and pharmacy. The university is also home to centers of marine science and gene research and biotechnology a wave research laboratory and the Linus Pauling Institute. It also offers professional certificate non-degree and extension programs as well as precollege programs for elementary and high school students. In addition to its main campus in Corvallis the university operates OSU-Cascades in Bend Oregon. OSU has an annual enrollment of more than 18000 students.

	Annual Growth	06/02	06/03	06/04	06/05	06/12
Sales ($ mil.)	(0.7%)	–	377.4	78.5	78.5	354.8
Net income ($ mil.)	–	–	5.7	33.7	26.9	(22.6)
Market value ($ mil.)	–	–	–	–	–	–
Employees	–	–	–	–	–	8,188

OREXIGEN THERAPEUTICS, INC.

NMS: OREX

3344 North Torrey Pines Court, Suite 200
La Jolla, CA 92037
Phone: 858 875-8600
Fax: –
Web: www.orexigen.com

CEO: Michael A. Narachi
CFO: Jay Hagan
HR: Heather Ace
FYE: December 31
Type: Public

Orexigen Therapeutics thinks it has the skinny on how to stay trim. The company is developing drugs under the names Contrave and Empatic (formerly Excalia) intended for use by obese people who are trying to get a grip on the urge to over-eat. The products are designed to control appetite from the central nervous system; they contain some of the same chemicals used in drugs approved for the treatment of smoking alcoholism and opiate addiction. The development-stage company is conducting late-stage clinical trials on its top two drug candidates. Orexigen was formed in 2002 and went public in 2012.

	Annual Growth	12/10	12/11	12/12	12/13	12/14
Sales ($ mil.)	159.1%	1.2	4.4	3.4	3.4	55.5
Net income ($ mil.)	–	(51.9)	(28.1)	(90.1)	(77.7)	(37.5)
Market value ($ mil.)	(6.9%)	997.6	198.8	648.2	695.1	748.2
Employees	10.1%	34	25	43	51	50

ORGANICALLY GROWN COMPANY

1800 PRAIRIE RD STE B
EUGENE, OR 974029722
Phone: 541-689-5320
Fax: –
Web: www.organicgrown.com

CEO: Josh Hinerfeld
CFO: Robbie Vasilinda
HR: –
FYE: December 31
Type: Private

Started by health-conscious Oregon farmers Organically Grown is exactly what its name says it is. The company grows and sells certified organic fruits vegetables and herbs produced by small to medium family-owned farmers located throughout the US's Pacific Northwest. Its line of more than 100 seasonal produce items are sold under the LADYBUG brand to customers including independent retailers supermarket chains restaurants home-delivery services and wholesalers. Organically Grown which is owned by its employees and growers was founded in 1978.

	Annual Growth	12/09	12/10	12/11	12/12	12/13
Sales ($ mil.)	19.4%	–	85.7	107.1	122.3	145.9
Net income ($ mil.)	27.6%	–	–	1.7	1.1	2.8
Market value ($ mil.)	–	–	–	–	–	–
Employees	–	–	–	–	–	189

ORGANOGENESIS INC.

150 Dan Rd.
Canton MA 02021
Phone: 781-575-0775
Fax: 781-575-1570
Web: www.organogenesis.com

CEO: Gary S Gillheeney Sr
CFO: –
HR: –
FYE: December 31
Type: Private

Organogenesis has the skinny on replacement tissue. Flagship product Apligraf is a human skin substitute approved to treat diabetic foot ulcers and venous leg ulcers caused by poor circulation. Rejection-resistant Apligraf is bio-engineered using living skin cells and has been used to treat chronic open wounds in some 250000 patients; the company is developing a next-generation version of the material (using its VCT technology) using all human components. In addition to Apligraf Organogenesis offers a line of biomaterials used in a range of surgical procedures to seal or reconstruct soft tissue and it also develops regenerative technologies in the area of cosmetic skin rejuvenation.

ORGILL INC.

3742 Tyndale Dr.	CEO: Ron Beal
Memphis TN 38125	CFO: Byrne Whitehead
Phone: 901-754-8850	HR: –
Fax: 901-752-8989	FYE: December 31
Web: www.orgill.com	Type: Private

Orgill is a leading independent distributor of more than 60000 home improvement products ranging from hand and power tools hardware lumber paint and building materials to plumbing and electrical products. Its inventory also includes housewares home furnishings camping gear and garden products. The firm primarily supplies independent retail hardware stores home centers and lumber yards in North America east of the Rocky Mountains; however its customer network extends to more than 60 countries. In addition to an expansive product selection Orgill provides retail services such as electronic business systems and store planning programs. Privately-owned Orgill was founded in 1847.

ORIENTAL FINANCIAL GROUP INC.

NYSE: OFG

997 San Roberto St. Oriental Center 10th Fl.	CEO: Jose R Fernandez
San Juan PR 00926	CFO: Ganesh Kumar
Phone: 787-771-6800	HR: –
Fax: 787-993-4670	FYE: December 31
Web: www.orientalfg.com	Type: Public

Even though Puerto Rico proved not to be home to all those East Indian spices Columbus was seeking you wouldn't know it by Oriental Financial Group. The holding company's main subsidiary Oriental Bank and Trust serves mid- to high-net-worth consumers and entrepreneurs by offering up a mix of banking insurance trust brokerage and financial planning services through about 30 offices around the commonwealth. Residential mortgages make up more than three-quarters of the bank's loan portfolio which also includes commercial mortgages business loans and home equity loans. Florida-based subsidiary Caribbean Pension Consultants administers retirement plans.

ORION ENERGY SYSTEMS INC

NAS. OESX

2210 Woodland Drive	CEO: John H. Scribante
Manitowoc, WI 54220	CFO: William T. Hull
Phone: 920-892-9340	HR: R K Greening
Fax: –	FYE: March 31
Web: www.oesx.com	Type: Public

Orion Energy Systems wants customers to see the light ... high intensity fluorescent (HIF) lighting systems that is. Orion designs manufactures and installs energy management systems that include HIF lighting and intelligent lighting controls. Its Apollo Light Pipe product collects and focuses daylight without consuming electricity. The firm estimates its HIF lineup can help cut customers' lighting-related electricity costs by up to 50% boost quantity and quality of light and reduce related carbon-dioxide emissions. In addition its engineered systems division makes solar photovoltaic products that allow customers to convert sunlight into electricity.

	Annual Growth	03/11	03/12	03/13	03/14	03/15
Sales ($ mil.)	(6.0%)	92.5	100.6	86.1	88.6	72.2
Net income ($ mil.)	–	1.6	0.5	(10.4)	(6.2)	(32.1)
Market value ($ mil.)	(6.1%)	110.6	65.3	68.0	198.8	86.1
Employees	(7.3%)	268	277	233	237	198

ORION HEALTHCORP INC.

1805 Old Alabama Rd. Ste. 350	CEO: Dale Brinkman
Roswell GA 30076	CFO: Stephen H Murdock
Phone: 678-832-1800	HR: –
Fax: 678-832-1888	FYE: December 31
Web: www.orionhealthcorp.com	Type: Private

Orion HealthCorp's constellation of services aims to relieve doctors of the day-to-day headaches of running a practice. Through its subsidiaries the company handles billing and collections and provides practice management services to physicians. Subsidiary Integrated Physician Solutions manages human resources IT and other non-medical operations. Orion's Billing & Collections unit (which comprises several subsidiaries) handles billing collection and other back office operations primarily for hospital-based physician groups (such as anesthesiologists and pathologists). The privately-held company was formed in 2004 through a series of mergers and operates throughout the US.

ORION MARINE GROUP INC

NYS: ORN

12000 Aerospace Dr. Suite 300	CEO: Mark R. Stauffer
Houston, TX 77034	CFO: Christopher J. DeAlmeida
Phone: 713 852-6500	HR: –
Fax: –	FYE: December 31
Web: www.orionmarinegroup.com	Type: Public

As Poseidon's son the Greek god Orion could walk on water. That's about the only thing Orion Marine doesn't do when it comes to water. Through operating subsidiaries the company provides civil construction and maintenance services for marine infrastructure including pipelines bridges waterways and port and other transportation facilities. It also performs dredging surveying inspections excavation and demolition services. Orion Marine serves government commercial and industrial clients; government projects account for some three-fourths of its revenues. The company operates in the Gulf Coast Atlantic Seaboard West Coast Pacific Northwest and Caribbean Basin regions.

	Annual Growth	12/10	12/11	12/12	12/13	12/14
Sales ($ mil.)	2.2%	353.1	259.9	292.0	354.5	385.8
Net income ($ mil.)	(25.1%)	21.9	(13.1)	(11.9)	0.3	6.9
Market value ($ mil.)	(1.2%)	319.3	183.0	201.2	331.1	304.2
Employees	(4.9%)	1,470	990	1,200	1,200	1,200

ORITANI FINANCIAL CORP (DE)

NMS: ORIT

370 Pascack Road	CEO: Kevin J. Lynch
Township of Washington, NJ 07676	CFO: John M. Fields
Phone: 201 664-5400	HR: –
Fax: –	FYE: June 30
Web: www.oritani.com	Type: Public

Oritani Financial could give an oratory on local banking in New Jersey. The holding company owns Oritani Bank which offers retail and commercial deposit and loan banking services from about 25 locations in several Garden State counties. Oritani Financial specializes in multi-family and commercial real estate lending which make up more than half of its loan portfolio. Oritani Financial also writes one- to four-family and second mortgages as well as equity and construction loans. It invests in real property through its Hampshire Financial Oritani LLC and Ormon divisions; Oritani Asset is a real estate investment trust (REIT). Century-old Oritani Bank has more than $2 billion in assets.

	Annual Growth	06/11	06/12	06/13	06/14	06/15
Assets ($ mil.)	6.7%	2,587.2	2,701.0	2,831.9	3,140.2	3,353.1
Net income ($ mil.)	13.3%	28.5	31.7	39.5	41.1	46.9
Market value ($ mil.)	5.8%	562.9	633.3	690.1	677.3	706.4
Employees	3.3%	206	217	212	233	235

ORLANDO HEALTH INC.

1414 KUHL AVE	CEO: David W. Strong
ORLANDO, FL 328062008	CFO: Bernadette Spong
Phone: 321-843-7000	HR: Nancy Dinon
Fax: –	FYE: September 30
Web: www.orlandohealth.com	Type: Private

It's not Disney World but for Floridians needing health care it is a prime destination. Orlando Health is a not-for-profit organization with a network of community and specialty hospitals with nearly 2300 beds in Central Florida. Its flagship facility the Orlando Regional Medical Center features a Level 1 trauma center and provides comprehensive acute care services in a range of specialties. Orlando Health also operates several community hospitals. Its specialty hospitals include the Arnold Palmer Hospital for Children and the Winnie Palmer Hospital for Women and Babies. It also operates the renowned M. D. Anderson Cancer Center Orlando (the first affiliate of Houston-based M. D. Anderson center).

	Annual Growth	09/07	09/08	09/09	09/10	09/13
Sales ($ mil.)	(0.9%)	–	–	1,637.8	1,700.7	1,576.9
Net income ($ mil.)	10.8%	–	–	76.9	91.4	115.9
Market value ($ mil.)	–	–	–	–	–	–
Employees	–	–	–	–	–	10,000

ORLANDO UTILITIES COMMISSION

100 W. Anderson St.	CEO: Kenneth P Ksionek
Orlando FL 32801	CFO: –
Phone: 407-423-9100	HR: –
Fax: 407-236-9616	FYE: September 30
Web: www.ouc.com	Type: Government-owned

Orlando Utilities Commission (OUC) has a simple mission — to provide electricity and water services to customers in and around Orlando Florida. In 2010 the utility was serving 221380 residential and business accounts (51% electric only 33% electric and water customers and 16% water only). In addition it operates fossil-fueled power plants and markets wholesale power. OUC also provides district cooling chilled water and commercial lighting services and advises customers on power and water conservation measures. In 2010 OUC delivered 24.9 billion gallons of water and 7.4 million MW of power.

ORMET CORPORATION

43840 State Rte. 7	CEO: Mike Tanchuk
Hannibal OH 43931	CFO: James Burns Riley
Phone: 740-483-1381	HR: –
Fax: 740-483-2622	FYE: December 31
Web: www.ormet.com	Type: Private

Ormet Corporation is a major producer of primary aluminum in the US and its operations run the gamut of aluminum production. In addition to refining alumina the company through its Primary Aluminum unit manufactures aluminum ingot billet (pressed bars) sheet foil and other products for the fabrication extrusion and conversion markets. Its aluminum smelter in Ohio has the capacity to produce 270000 tons of aluminum per year. Its alumina refinery in Burnside Lousiana can produce up to 540000 tons of smelter-grade alumina per year. The company sells exclusively to traders instead of end-use consumers. Ormet was founded in 1954 as a part of Olin Corporation.

ORRICK HERRINGTON & SUTCLIFFE LLP

405 Howard St.	CEO: –
San Francisco CA 94105-2669	CFO: Linda Havard
Phone: 415-773-5700	HR: Jennifer Santora
Fax: 415-773-5759	FYE: December 31
Web: www.orrick.com	Type: Private - Partnershi

One of California's oldest law firms Orrick Herrington & Sutcliffe was instrumental in developing one of the state's best-known landmarks — the Golden Gate Bridge. Among its practice areas are public finance (a linchpin of the firm's reputation) litigation securities tax and intellectual property. Orrick has some 1100 lawyers in about 25 offices in the US the Asia/Pacific region and Europe. The firm's client list has included such big names as IBM Charles Schwab and Salomon Smith Barney. Orrick was founded in 1863 as Jarboe Harrison & Goodfellow.

ORMAT TECHNOLOGIES INC

NYS: ORA

6225 Neil Road	CEO: Isaac Angel
Reno, NV 89511-1136	CFO: Doron Blachar
Phone: 775 356-9029	HR: –
Fax: –	FYE: December 31
Web: www.ormat.com	Type: Public

Ormat Technologies is on an environmentally safe power trip building geothermal recovered energy and solar power plants. Geothermal technology extracts hot water or steam that is vaporized and used to drive turbines. The fluid is then cooled and recycled back through the process making it a clean and renewable energy source. Recovered energy utilizes heat produced in other industrial processes. The company set up by Israel-based Ormat Industries also sells power units for both types of plants and sells fossil fuel-powered turbo-generators with a capacity of between 400W and 4000W. Ormat operates power plants in Guatemala Kenya Nicaragua and the US.

	Annual Growth	12/10	12/11	12/12	12/13	12/14
Sales ($ mil.)	10.7%	373.2	437.0	514.4	533.2	559.5
Net income ($ mil.)	9.8%	37.3	(43.1)	(206.4)	41.2	54.2
Market value ($ mil.)	(2.1%)	1,347.0	821.0	878.0	1,239.1	1,237.7
Employees	(1.1%)	1,146	1,226	1,252	1,123	1,095

ORRSTOWN FINANCIAL SERVICES, INC.

NAS: ORRF

77 East King Street, P.O. Box 250	CEO: Thomas R Quinn Jr
Shippensburg, PA 17257	CFO: David P Boyle
Phone: 717 532-6114	HR: Barbara E Brobst
Fax: –	FYE: December 31
Web: www.orrstown.com	Type: Public

Orrstown Financial Services keeps both paddles in the money pool. The institution is the holding company for Orrstown Bank which operates some 20 branches in Pennsylvania's Cumberland Perry and Franklin counties as well as in Maryland's Washington County. In addition to traditional retail deposit offerings Orrstown also provides investment management services including retirement planning and investment analysis. Real estate mortgages account for about 40% of the bank's lending portfolio followed by commercial construction and consumer loans. Orrstown is growing its mortgage lending capabilities. It launched an online application system in order to increase mortgage origination sales.

	Annual Growth	12/10	12/11	12/12	12/13	12/14
Assets ($ mil.)	(5.8%)	1,511.7	1,444.1	1,232.7	1,177.8	1,190.4
Net income ($ mil.)	15.1%	16.6	(32.0)	(38.5)	10.0	29.1
Market value ($ mil.)	(11.3%)	226.5	68.2	79.7	135.1	140.5
Employees	0.1%	311	345	352	344	312

ORTHO-CLINICAL DIAGNOSTICS INC.

1001 US Hwy. 202
Raritan NJ 08869
Phone: 908-218-1300
Fax: 908-704-3649
Web: www.orthoclinical.com

CEO: Dr Martin D Madaus
CFO: Joseph Bondi
HR: –
FYE: December 31
Type: Subsidiary

Ortho-Clinical Diagnostics earns an A+ in Chemistry. The Johnson & Johnson subsidiary develops and markets diagnostic tools including VITROS instrumentation systems that use clinical chemistry and immunoassay technologies to diagnose a range of maladies such as cancer heart disease and infectious diseases. It also markets laboratory automation systems under the enGen brand. In addition to making clinical diagnostics products Ortho-Clinical Diagnostics is a leading maker of instruments and reagents used by blood banks and hospitals to screen blood donations for disease and contaminants as well as blood typing systems that guarantee patient-donor compatibility for transfusions.

ORTHOLOGIC CORP.

NASDAQ: CAPS

1275 W. Washington St.
Tempe AZ 85281
Phone: 602-286-5520
Fax: 216-755-1500
Web: www.ddrc.com

CEO: –
CFO: Les M Taeger
HR: –
FYE: December 31
Type: Public

OrthoLogic doing business as Capstone Therapeutics is trying to make sense of scarred skin and damaged hearts with its biopharmaceutical products designed to repair the body's tissues. The biotechnology company is focused on a couple of synthetic peptide technologies that may accelerate healing. Its Chrysalin program has yielded several potential therapies including TP508 which the company is evaluating as a treatment for vascular diseases as well as diabetic foot ulcers. OrthoLogic acquired another candidate AZX100 in 2006 and has begun clinical testing on the drug as a treatment for dermal scarring.

ORTHOSYNETICS INC.

3850 N. Causeway Blvd. Ste. 800
Metairie LA 70002
Phone: 504-834-4392
Fax: 512-476-5680
Web: www.littlefield.com

CEO: Charles W Carroll
CFO: –
HR: –
FYE: December 31
Type: Private

Brace yourself: OrthoSynetics is a dental practice management firm aiming to take a bite out of the nationwide orthodontics market. For a fee the company manages business aspects of orthodontic and dental practices handling advertising payroll processing financial reporting and purchasing as well as real estate construction matters and information technology support. The firm serves about 350 practices mostly across the southern US. OrthoSynetics also helps sell existing practices by providing demographic and market analysis services to potential buyers. Or for the orthodontist who's not quite ready to commit to a full practice the company offers partnership opportunities.

OSAGE BANCSHARES INC.

OTC: OSBK

239 E. Main St.
Pawhuska OK 74056
Phone: 918-287-2919
Fax: 918-287-2974
Web: www.osagefed.com

CEO: Mark S White
CFO: Sue Allen Smith
HR: –
FYE: June 30
Type: Public

Osage Bancshares is the holding company for Osage Federal Bank which provides deposit and lending services to consumers and businesses in Osage and Washington counties in northern Oklahoma. The bank's offerings include checking savings and retirement accounts such as IRAs and CDs as well as consumer commercial construction and real estate loans. One- to four-family real estate loans make up about two-thirds of Osage Federal's total loan portfolio; other real estate loans include multi-family commercial and land. The bank operates a handful of branches in the cities of Pawhuska Bartlesville and Barnsdall. Its roots date back to 1918.

OSBORN & BARR COMMUNICATIONS INC.

914 SPRUCE ST
SAINT LOUIS, MO 631021118
Phone: 314-726-5511
Fax: –
Web: www.osborn-barr.com

CEO: Michael Turley
CFO: –
HR: –
FYE: December 31
Type: Private

You can take the ad agency out of the country but well you know. Osborn & Barr Communications has built its reputation on its work in the agriculture rural-lifestyle and outdoors markets but its portfolio also includes work in government finance and leisure industries. The agency offers advertising public relations brand management creative services social marketing digital marketing media services and strategic marketing for clients across North America. Clients have included Michelin the USDA Intervet and Monsanto. Founded in 1989 Osborn & Barr has offices in St. Louis; Kansas City Missouri; and Des Moines.

	Annual Growth	12/04	12/05	12/06	12/07	12/08
Sales ($ mil.)	2.7%	–	61.2	67.8	56.3	66.3
Net income ($ mil.)	(10.5%)	–	–	1.6	1.5	1.3
Market value ($ mil.)	–	–	–	–	–	–
Employees	–	–	–	–	–	160

OSC SPORTS INC.

5 BRADLEY DR
WESTBROOK, ME 040922013
Phone: 207-854-2794
Fax: –
Web: www.olympiasports.net

CEO: –
CFO: John Lesniak
HR: –
FYE: September 30
Type: Private

Olympia Sports may not make you an Olympian but the company carries the gear to help you go for gold. The sporting goods retailer offers sports equipment fitness gear and apparel athletic shoes casual wear and sports accessories under such brands as Columbia Louisville Slugger Bauer PUMA Reebok and Teva. It sells merchandise through its website and via more than 225 banner stores across the Northeast and Mid-Atlantic states. In addition to its retail business the company oversees the private nonprofit Olympia Sports Foundation which runs a clothing bank and collaborates on projects with local charities and schools within its retail region. Founder and CEO Ed Manganello owns Olympia.

	Annual Growth	09/05	09/06	09/07	09/08	09/09
Sales ($ mil.)	(61.4%)	–	–	1,113.8	191.0	165.8
Net income ($ mil.)	2839.6%	–	–	0.0	4.4	0.3
Market value ($ mil.)	–	–	–	–	–	–
Employees	–	–	–	–	–	2,000

OSF HEALTHCARE SYSTEM

800 NE GLEN OAK AVE
PEORIA, IL 616033200
Phone: 309-655-2850
Fax: –
Web: www.osfhealthcare.org

CEO: Kevin Schoeplein
CFO: –
HR: –
FYE: September 30
Type: Private

OSF Healthcare helps patients who are feeling oh-so-frail in northern Illinois and southwestern Michigan. OSF Healthcare system includes 11 acute care hospitals and one long-term care facility that combined are home to more than 1500 beds and offer a full spectrum of inpatient and outpatient medical and surgical services. The system's primary care physician network consists of about 650 physicians at more than 105 locations throughout its service area. Subsidiary OSF Home Care provides hospice home visit and equipment services and OSF Saint Francis provides ambulance pharmacy and health care management services. The not-for-profit system is a subsidiary of the Sisters of The Third Order of St. Francis.

	Annual Growth	09/04	09/05	09/06	09/08	09/13
Sales ($ mil.)	3.6%	–	–	1,481.7	1,477.4	1,893.0
Net income ($ mil.)	8.7%	–	–	58.9	26.6	105.7
Market value ($ mil.)	–	–	–	–	–	–
Employees	–	–	–	–	–	4,007

OSHKOSH B'GOSH INC.

112 Otter Ave.
Oshkosh WI 54901
Phone: 920-231-8800
Fax: 920-231-8621
Web: www.oshkoshbgosh.com

CEO: Mike Casey
CFO: –
HR: –
FYE: December 31
Type: Subsidiary

OshKosh B'Gosh has panache that's anything but frosh. The company makes and sells colorful apparel for young children in the US and nearly 40 countries worldwide. OshKosh caters specifically to children age 2 to 7 and in general newborn to age 12. It operates about 180 branded stores and peddles its products through major department stores and national retail chains (including J. C. Penney Kohl's and Ross Stores). OshKosh boasts lucrative domestic and international licensing agreements including sub-brand Genuine Kids from OshKosh that is sold exclusively in Target stores. The company is a subsidiary of children's clothing marketer Carter's.

OSHKOSH CORP (NEW)

NYS: OSK

P.O. Box 2566
Oshkosh, WI 54903-2566
Phone: 920 235-9151
Fax: –
Web: www.oshkoshcorporation.com

CEO: Wilson R. Jones
CFO: David M. Sagehorn
HR: Janet L. Hogan
FYE: September 30
Type: Public

Need to plow through Sahara sands or Buffalo snow? Oshkosh has your ride. The company makes and sells heavy-duty vehicles and vehicle bodies for commercial access fire and emergency and defense work. Commercial and access lines include concrete batch plants refuse vehicle bodies (McNeilus brand) tow trucks (Jerr-Dan) and aerial work platforms (JLG). Its emergency offerings range from snow blowers to aircraft rescue and firefighting vehicles (Pierce). More than 30 plants build the lineup. Vehicles are sold via dealers to global airport institutional construction and municipal markets. Oshkosh also makes tactical trucks for the Department of Defense.

	Annual Growth	09/11	09/12	09/13	09/14	09/15
Sales ($ mil.)	(5.3%)	7,584.7	8,180.9	7,665.1	6,808.2	6,098.1
Net income ($ mil.)	(4.3%)	273.4	230.8	318.0	309.3	229.5
Market value ($ mil.)	23.3%	1,187.7	2,069.7	3,695.8	3,331.3	2,741.3
Employees	0.4%	13,100	13,200	11,900	12,000	13,300

OSI GROUP LLC

1225 Corporate Blvd.
Aurora IL 60504
Phone: 630-851-6600
Fax: 630-692-2340
Web: www.osigroup.com

CEO: Sheldon Lavin
CFO: Bill Weimer
HR: Celina Boyle
FYE: December 31
Type: Private

You might say a steady diet of red meat has made this company big and strong. OSI Industries (doing business as OSI Group) is one of the largest suppliers of meat products to US foodservice operators. Through its operating companies OSI boasts a bulging menu that includes a variety of beef pork and poultry products including beef patties hot dogs sausages bacon and chicken nuggets. It has long been a supplier of beef to #1 fast-food chain McDonald's. As part of its business OSI also offers contract manufacturing packaging services and supply chain management for other food processors; it has more than 50 production facilities in 17 countries.

OSI PHARMACEUTICALS LLC

1 Bioscience Park Dr.
Farmingdale NY 11735-1019
Phone: 631-962-2000
Fax: 631-752-3880
Web: www.osip.com

CEO: Colin Goddard PHD
CFO: Pierre Legault
HR: –
FYE: December 31
Type: Subsidiary

Fighting disease in small ways is what OSI Pharmaceuticals is all about. The Astellas Pharma indirect subsidiary focuses on small molecule cures for diseases like cancer allowing for treatment by pill rather than IV infusion. Its top seller Tarceva treats non-small cell lung cancer and pancreatic cancer and is in development for other indications as well. Partner Genentech co-promotes the drug in the US and it is marketed internationally by Roche. OSI also has a pipeline of drug candidates focused on new anti-cancer compounds. UK subsidiary Prosidion manages the company's small-molecule patents for diabetes and obesity treatments.

OSI SYSTEMS, INC. (DE)

NMS: OSIS

12525 Chadron Avenue
Hawthorne, CA 90250
Phone: 310 978-0516
Fax: –
Web: www.osi-systems.com

CEO: Deepak Chopra
CFO: Alan I. Edrick
HR: Rick Merritt
FYE: June 30
Type: Public

OSI Systems is keeping a close scan on transportation security and health care worldwide. The company's security division manufactures specialized inspection equipment under the Rapiscan Systems name used to screen everything from baggage and people to cargo and vehicles at airports ports and borders. Its Spacelabs Healthcare subsidiary makes patient monitoring cardiac monitoring and clinical networking systems primarily for hospitals. A third division makes optoelectronic devices (OSI Optoelectronics) for aerospace/defense electronics industrial automation security medical diagnostics and other applications. That division also offers contract electronics manufacturing services (OSI Electronics).

	Annual Growth	06/11	06/12	06/13	06/14	06/15
Sales ($ mil.)	9.9%	656.1	793.0	802.0	906.7	958.2
Net income ($ mil.)	18.2%	33.4	45.5	44.1	47.9	65.2
Market value ($ mil.)	13.3%	847.8	1,248.8	1,270.1	1,316.1	1,395.7
Employees	11.9%	3,700	3,900	5,200	5,607	5,810

OSIRIS THERAPEUTICS INC

NMS: OSIR

7015 Albert Einstein Drive
Columbia, MD 21046
Phone: 443 545-1800
Fax: –
Web: www.osiris.com

CEO: Dwayne (Bobby) Montgomery
CFO: Gregory I. Law
HR: –
FYE: December 31
Type: Public

Unlike the Eygptian god this Osiris seeks to keep people out of the afterlife. Osiris Therapeutics uses donated bone marrow stem cells to develop its drug candidates. Its lead candidate Prochymal has been approved to treat graft-vs.-host disease in some international markets and is in clinical trials as a treatment for Crohn's disease and graft-vs.-host disease in the US. The drug is also being investigated for use in metabolic cardiology and gastrointestinal conditions. Its second drug candidate Chondrogen is in clinical trials to treat osteoarthritis in the knee. Chairman Peter Friedli owns a controlling stake in the company.

	Annual Growth	12/10	12/11	12/12	12/13	12/14
Sales ($ mil.)	8.5%	43.2	42.4	11.8	24.3	59.9
Net income ($ mil.)	–	13.1	14.9	(11.1)	41.6	(1.8)
Market value ($ mil.)	19.7%	267.6	183.7	308.4	552.3	549.2
Employees	38.5%	59	57	64	75	217

OSISOFT LLC

777 Davis St. Ste. 250
San Leandro CA 94577
Phone: 510-297-5800
Fax: 510-357-8136
Web: www.osisoft.com

CEO: Dr J Patrick Kennedy
CFO: Bob Guilbault
HR: –
FYE: December 31
Type: Private

OSIsoft helps its customers turn process into profit. The company develops software used to collect manage and store data related to manufacturing equipment and processes. Using real-time data from such sources as automated control systems its PI System helps customers monitor and analyze their production processes to find ways to streamline operations. OSIsoft also offers Web-enabled applications to distribute the data across corporate intranets and the Internet and it can integrate the data into other enterprise applications. The company has some 14000 customers in more than 100 countries; it serves the manufacturing energy utilities and life sciences industries among others.

OTELCO INC

NAS: OTEL

505 Third Avenue East
Oneonta, AL 35121
Phone: 205 625-3574
Fax: –
Web: www.otelcoinc.com

CEO: Robert J Souza
CFO: Curtis L Garner Jr
HR: Bill Andrews
FYE: December 31
Type: Public

Otelco makes sure rural areas enjoy all the modern communications conveniences. The company operates six incumbent rural local-exchange carriers (RLECs) that provide local and long-distance phone services. Other services include high-speed and dial-up Internet access as well as cable television. Otelco has four RLECs in north central Alabama one in central Missouri and one adjacent to Bangor Maine. It maintains more than 69000 access lines and has more than 4000 cable-TV customers. Otelco has made a business of acquiring RLECs including assets from Oneonta Telephone that were used to create Otelco Telephone in 1999.

	Annual Growth	12/10	12/11	12/12	12/13	12/14
Sales ($ mil.)	(8.3%)	104.4	101.8	98.4	79.0	73.9
Net income ($ mil.)	64.3%	0.7	2.2	(126.9)	109.1	5.0
Market value ($ mil.)	(13.1%)	–	–	–	17.5	15.2
Employees	(6.5%)	315	330	268	254	241

OTSUKA AMERICA INC

1 EMBARCADERO CTR # 2020
SAN FRANCISCO, CA 94111-3750
Phone: 415-986-5300
Fax: –
Web: www.otsuka-america.com

CEO: Hiromi Yoshikawa
CFO: –
HR: Masami Travis
FYE: December 31
Type: Private

Otsuka America is the holding company for the US operations of Japan's Otsuka Pharmaceutical. Otsuka America oversees pharmaceutical research and development marketing and distribution of both prescription drugs and over-the-counter (OTC) medicines. The company's pharmaceutical subsidiaries include Otsuka America Pharmaceutical (prescription drug marketing) Otsuka Maryland Medicinal Laboratories (research) Cambridge Isotope Laboratories (chemical ingredients) and Pharmavite (nutritionals). To help wash down its pills Otsuka America also holds consumer beverage makers Crystal Geyser (bottled water) Ridge Vineyards (wine) and Soma Beverage Company (specialty bottled water).

	Annual Growth	12/00	12/01	12/02	12/03	12/07
Sales ($ mil.)	30.1%	–	567.7	612.8	1,066.7	2,755.3
Net income ($ mil.)	–	–	(56.1)	153.2	56.3	51.7
Market value ($ mil.)	–	–	–	–	–	–
Employees	–	–	–	–	–	2,065

OTTER PRODUCTS LLC

209 S MELDRUM ST
FORT COLLINS, CO 805212603
Phone: 970-493-8446
Fax: –
Web: www.otterbox.com

CEO: Peter Lindgren
CFO: –
HR: –
FYE: December 31
Type: Private

Otter Products' products keep your precious electronic devices safe and dry. The company which goes by OtterBox makes more than 250 models of protective cases for cell phones smart phones tablet computers and other portable electronics from Apple LG Corp BlackBerry Samsung and other manufacturers. It outsources production and sells its impact and water resistant Defender Reflex Commuter and Impact cases and watertight boxes at Best Buy Target and other retailers. OtterBox was formed in 1998 by CEO Curt Richardson and his wife Nancy who came up with the name after being inspired by otters' water-repellent skin and playful and creative attitudes.

	Annual Growth	12/06	12/07	12/08	12/09	12/10
Sales ($ mil.)	(60.4%)	–	–	1,076.0	48.6	168.9
Net income ($ mil.)	32563.6%	–	–	0.0	15.4	60.4
Market value ($ mil.)	–	–	–	–	–	–
Employees	–	–	–	–	–	320

OTTER TAIL CORP.

NMS. OTTR

215 South Cascade Street, Box 496
Fergus Falls, MN 56538-0496
Phone: 866 410-8780
Fax: –
Web: www.ottertail.com

CEO: Edward J. (Jim) McIntyre
CFO: Kevin G Moug
HR: –
FYE: December 31
Type: Public

Like the broad end of its furry namesake Otter Tail covers a swath of businesses from electric services and construction to manufacturing equipment and plastics. The electric utility (Otter Tail Power Corporation) is the company's core business; it keeps the lights on for more than 129000 residential commercial and industrial customers in Minnesota and the Dakotas. The company also makes PVC pipes (Northern Pipe Products and Vinyltech Corporation) manufactures parts and trays (BTD Manufacturing and T.O. Plastics) and provides construction services (Foley Company and Aevenia).

	Annual Growth	12/10	12/11	12/12	12/13	12/14
Sales ($ mil.)	(8.1%)	1,119.1	1,077.9	859.2	893.3	799.3
Net income ($ mil.)	–	(1.3)	(13.2)	(5.3)	50.9	57.7
Market value ($ mil.)	8.3%	838.9	819.5	930.5	1,089.4	1,152.3
Employees	(16.5%)	3,901	4,623	2,286	2,336	1,893

OUR LADY OF LOURDES MEDICAL CENTER INC

1600 HADDON AVE
CAMDEN, NJ 081033101
Phone: 856-757-3500
Fax: –
Web: www.lourdesnursingschool.org

CEO: Alex Hatala
CFO: Michael Hammond
HR: –
FYE: December 31
Type: Private

Our Lady of Lourdes Medical Center tends to the sick of southern New Jersey. The hospital is a general acute care facility with about 325 inpatient beds. In addition to general medical emergency and surgical care the hospital specializes in organ transplantation joint replacement rehabilitation dialysis treatment cardiac care and birthing care. The hospital also offers nursing and other medical training programs and it operates area clinics and provides community health and outreach services. Our Lady of Lourdes Medical Center part of Catholic Health East's Lourdes Health System is sponsored by the Franciscan Sisters of Allegany New York.

	Annual Growth	12/02	12/03	12/08	12/09	12/12
Sales ($ mil.)	1.2%	–	243.3	296.3	279.9	271.6
Net income ($ mil.)	124.5%	–	–	1.2	(21.4)	30.1
Market value ($ mil.)	–	–	–	–	–	–
Employees	–	–	–	–	–	3,000

OUR LADY OF LOURDES REGIONAL MEDICAL CENTER INC.

4801 AMBSSDOR CFFERY PKWY
LAFAYETTE, LA 705086917
Phone: 337-470-2000
Fax: –

CEO: –
CFO: –
HR: –
FYE: June 30
Type: Private

Established in 1949 as part of the not-for-profit Franciscan Missionaries of Our Lady Health System Our Lady of Lourdes Regional Medical Center is a hospital that provides medical care in southern Louisiana. The facility cares for denizens of the bayou with a medical staff of more than 400 physicians representing some 50 specialties including cardiology neurology and oncology. The medical center also offers oupatient care and urgent care as well as a general family practice and pediatric care. Our Lady of Lourdes extends its reach outside the facility into the Acadiana regional community by offering primary care physicians' offices home health care programs and occupational medicine.

	Annual Growth	06/06	06/07	06/08	06/09	06/10
Sales ($ mil.)	–	–	–	(314.2)	142.7	162.9
Net income ($ mil.)	–	–	–	0.0	(58.3)	(9.2)
Market value ($ mil.)	–	–	–	–	–	–
Employees	–	–	–	–	–	1,700

OUR LADY OF THE LAKE HOSPITAL INC.

5000 HENNESSY BLVD
BATON ROUGE, LA 708084367
Phone: 225-765-7709
Fax: –
Web: www.ololchildrens.com

CEO: K Scott Wester
CFO: –
HR: –
FYE: June 30
Type: Private

Our Lady of the Lake Regional Medical Center reaches out to Baton Rouge residents with a helping hand. Participating in teaching programs for LSU and Tulane medical schools the medical center has some 800 inpatient beds and includes trauma emergency surgery general medical and specialty care centers for conditions including heart disease cancer orthopedics and ENT (ear nose and throat) disorders. Our Lady of the Lake also includes a Children's Hospital two nursing homes and an independent-living facility and it offers outpatient services at its main campus and at satellite facilities throughout the greater Baton Rouge area.

	Annual Growth	12/04	12/05*	06/08	06/10	06/11
Sales ($ mil.)	298.9%	–	0.2	6.3	614.0	826.5
Net income ($ mil.)	470.5%	–	–	1.2	12.4	214.8
Market value ($ mil.)	–	–	–	–	–	–
Employees	–	–	–	–	–	1,800

*Fiscal year change

OURPET'S COMPANY

NBB: OPCO

1300 East Street
Fairport Harbor, OH 44077
Phone: 440 354-6500
Fax: –
Web: www.ourpets.com

CEO: Steven Tsengas
CFO: Scott R Mendes
HR: Jamie McCullough
FYE: December 31
Type: Public

OurPet's is counting on its customers' pets being spoiled rotten. The company makes some 400 pet products (such as feeders toys litter and natural and nutritional pet supplements and treats) for dogs cats and domestic and wild birds. Besides its namesake brands OurPet's makes its items under brand names Flappy Pet Zone SmartScoop Ecopure Naturals Play-N-Squeak Durapet Go! Cat Go and DockDogs. The firm's products are sold through suppliers including PetSmart and Wal-Mart (its two biggest customers accounting for about 43% of sales). Chairman president and CEO Dr. Steven Tsengas and his wife control about 27% of the company's voting shares.

	Annual Growth	12/10	12/11	12/12	12/13	12/14
Sales ($ mil.)	7.4%	17.1	19.7	20.2	21.6	22.8
Net income ($ mil.)	(6.0%)	1.0	0.1	0.2	1.1	0.8
Market value ($ mil.)	(4.1%)	17.6	9.8	6.7	16.0	14.9
Employees	1.4%	53	51	55	59	56

OUTDOOR RESORTS OF AMERICA INC.

79-687 Country Club Dr. Ste. 201
Bermuda Dunes CA 92203
Phone: 760-345-2046
Fax: 760-345-4096
Web: www.outdoor-resorts.com

CEO: –
CFO: –
HR: –
FYE: March 31
Type: Private

Resorting to the outdoors isn't such a bad thing if you know where to go. Outdoor Resorts of America operates about ten high-end RV resorts around the US in locations near vacation areas such as the Ozark Mountains and Hilton Head Island South Carolina. Guests can buy a lot or rent by the night or month. Resorts feature amenities like swimming pools marinas whirlpools and tennis courts. Many locations are restricted to larger Class A motor homes (no pop-ups vans trailers or truck campers) and offer luxuries like on-site massage cable and Internet hookups and private boat slips at each site. The company was founded in 1969.

OUTERWALL INC

NMS: OUTR

1800 114th Avenue SE
Bellevue, WA 98004
Phone: 425 943-8000
Fax: –
Web: www.outerwall.com

CEO: Erik E. Prusch
CFO: Galen Smith
HR: –
FYE: December 31
Type: Public

Outerwall (formerly Coinstar) takes its name from the previously underutilized "fourth wall" area between the cash registers and the front door in retail stores. Once known for its coin-counting Coinstar kiosks the company's Redbox kiosk business which vends DVD and Blu-Ray rentals now generates more than 80% of Outerwall's sales. Redbox operates some 43680 DVD rental kiosks located at supermarkets malls big-box retailers drug and convenience stores and restaurants across North America. The fast-growing company changed its name to Outerwall in 2013 to reflect its evolution from coin counting to an operator of various automated retail businesses.

	Annual Growth	12/11	12/12	12/13	12/14	12/15
Sales ($ mil.)	4.4%	1,845.4	2,202.0	2,306.6	2,303.0	2,193.2
Net income ($ mil.)	(19.2%)	103.9	150.2	174.8	106.6	44.3
Market value ($ mil.)	(5.4%)	758.0	863.8	1,117.2	1,249.2	606.8
Employees	(0.1%)	2,676	2,927	2,900	2,760	2,670

OUTSTART INC.

745 Atlantic Ave. 4th Fl.
Boston MA 02111
Phone: 617-897-6800
Fax: 617-897-6801
Web: www.outstart.com

CEO: –
CFO: –
HR: –
FYE: December 31
Type: Subsidiary

OutStart is a versatile teacher for corporate students. The company develops software that businesses and government entities use to manage the training of employees customers and partners with different needs and learning styles. It offers four software options as well as TrainingEdge.com an integrated suite that combines all four. Individually its Learning Content Management System (LCMS) creates and manages content delivery and publishing. Its Learning Management System (LMS) supports classroom online and mobile education. Participate is its social business software while Hot Lava Mobile delivers content on mobile devices. In 2012 OutStart was acquired by HR software provider Kenexa.

OVERHEAD DOOR CORPORATION

2501 S. State Hwy. 121 Ste. 200
Lewisville TX 75067
Phone: 469-549-7100
Fax: 469-549-7281
Web: www.overheaddoor.com

CEO: Dennis Stone
CFO: Paul A Lehmann
HR: –
FYE: December 31
Type: Subsidiary

This company's business "hinges" on what you need opened. Overhead Door manufactures and sells wood steel and polyurethane garage doors electric door operators security grilles and rolling doors for residential commercial and industrial applications. It operates through four divisions: Access Systems Division (ASD) its largest sells garage doors and openers under the Overhead Door and Wayne-Dalton brands while The Genie Company sells remote-control garage doors under the popular Genie brand name. Horton Automatics makes doors for commercial and industrial use; TODCO sells doors for trucks. Overhead Door was founded in 1921 and is a subsidiary of Japan-based construction products maker Sanwa Shutter.

OVERLAKE HOSPITAL MEDICAL CENTER

1035 116TH AVE NE
BELLEVUE, WA 980044687
Phone: 425-688-5000
Fax: –
Web: www.overlakehospital.org

CEO: Craig Henrickson
CFO: –
HR: Peggy Jung-Simard
FYE: June 30
Type: Private

Over the lake and through the sound to Overlake Hospital Medical Center we go! The not-for-profit hospital provides health care services to residents of Bellevue Washington in the Puget Sound region. The nearly 350-bed facility provides comprehensive inpatient and outpatient services ranging from cancer care and surgery to specialized senior care. Overlake also operates a number of outpatient clinics providing primary care urgent care and specialty care such as weight loss surgery. The organization also provides patients with health and wellness programs addressing issues like women's and children's health.

	Annual Growth	06/10	06/11	06/12	06/13	06/14
Sales ($ mil.)	2.5%	–	417.9	427.1	422.9	450.1
Net income ($ mil.)	78.1%	–	–	18.9	40.1	59.9
Market value ($ mil.)	–	–	–	–	–	–
Employees	–	–	–	–	–	2,450

OVERLAND STORAGE, INC.

NAS: OVRL

9112 Spectrum Center Boulevard
San Diego, CA 92123
Phone: 858 571-5555
Fax: –

CEO: Eric L Kelly
CFO: Kurt L Kalbfleisch
HR: –
FYE: June 30
Type: Public

Overland Storage has your backup. The company sells data storage systems software and related media to businesses of all sizes. Its most popular line the tape-based NEO Series of products protects data with nonstop operation remote library management and other features. SnapServer provides network-attached storage (NAS) and storage-area network (SAN) data management for remote offices and distributed enterprises while the REO family of products offers backup and recovery. With more than 450000 installations the company sells to distributors resellers retailers and manufacturers worldwide. Its distribution partners include Ingram Micro and SYNNEX.

	Annual Growth	06/09	06/10	06/11	06/12	06/13
Sales ($ mil.)	(17.9%)	105.6	77.7	70.2	59.6	48.0
Net income ($ mil.)	–	(18.0)	(13.0)	(14.5)	(16.2)	(19.6)
Market value ($ mil.)	24.8%	14.3	61.4	84.5	57.2	34.7
Employees	(6.1%)	229	190	197	187	178

OVERSEAS SHIPHOLDING GROUP INC (NEW)

ASE: OSGB

1301 Avenue of the Americas
New York, NY 10019
Phone: 212 953-4100
Fax: –
Web: www.osg.com

CEO: Ian T Blackley
CFO: Rick F Oricchio
HR: –
FYE: December 31
Type: Public

Overseas Shipholding Group (OSG) flies the flags of many nations. The marine transportation company's fleet made up mainly of crude oil tankers and product carriers includes vessels registered in the US and in a number of other countries. Through both long-term and spot market contracts the company charters its fleet to commercial shippers and government agencies. Overall the OSG fleet consists of about 110 vessels with a capacity of about 11 million deadweight tons (DWT). Transportation of crude oil and refined petroleum products accounts for the vast majority of the company's business but OSG also transports liquefied natural gas (LNG). In late 2012 OSG voluntarily filed for Chapter 11 bankruptcy.

	Annual Growth	12/10	12/11	12/12	12/13	12/14
Sales ($ mil.)	(2.2%)	1,045.6	1,049.5	1,137.1	1,016.0	957.4
Net income ($ mil.)	–	(134.2)	(192.9)	(480.1)	(638.2)	(152.3)
Market value ($ mil.)	–	–	–	–	–	1,910.4
Employees	(29.0%)	3,500	3,600	3,280	2,860	890

OVERSTOCK.COM INC. (DE)

NMS: OSTK

6350 South 3000 East
Salt Lake City, UT 84121
Phone: 801 947-3100
Fax: –
Web: www.overstock.com

CEO: Patrick M. Byrne
CFO: –
HR: –
FYE: December 31
Type: Public

Overstock.com allows you to shop a Persian bazaar of clothes housewares music books and more. The online discount retailer hawks brand-name merchandise including furniture electronics jewelry travel and insurance. Most of its inventory comes from manufacturers stuck with overproduction older models or some color that wasn't as popular as the designer had envisioned. The company's products portfolio includes such brands as Bissell Hewlett-Packard Movado and Steve Madden among others. Besides its main website Overstock.com manages an online auction site and provides car and real estate listings. The retailer's Club O loyalty program offers discounts to members on selected items and shipping.

	Annual Growth	12/10	12/11	12/12	12/13	12/14
Sales ($ mil.)	8.3%	1,089.9	1,054.3	1,099.3	1,304.2	1,497.1
Net income ($ mil.)	(10.8%)	13.9	(19.4)	14.7	88.5	8.8
Market value ($ mil.)	10.2%	396.1	188.5	344.0	740.1	583.4
Employees	3.2%	1,500	1,300	1,300	1,500	1,700

OVONYX INC.

2956 Waterview Dr.
Rochester Hills MI 48309
Phone: 248-299-6022
Fax: 248-659-1500
Web: www.ovonyx.com

CEO: Tyler Lowrey
CFO: –
HR: –
FYE: December 31
Type: Private

Ovonyx has developed designs for a new type of technology used in nonvolatile memory chips. The technology is known as Ovonic Unified Memory or phase-change memory and it is meant to supplant flash memory devices in consumer electronics. The company has licensing and development agreements with several chip makers including BAE Systems Elpida Memory Hynix Semiconductor Nanochip Samsung Electronics and STMicroelectronics. Ovonyx was founded in 1999 by CEO Tyler Lowrey and Ward Parkinson.

OWENS & MINOR, INC.

NYS: OMI

9120 Lockwood Boulevard
Mechanicsville, VA 23116
Phone: 804 723-7000
Fax: 804 723-7100
Web: www.owens-minor.com

CEO: James L. (Jim) Bierman
CFO: Richard A. (Randy) Meier
HR: –
FYE: December 31
Type: Public

Owens & Minor (O&M) makes sure surgeons aren't left empty handed after shouting "Scalpel stat!" A leading distributor of medical and surgical supplies the company carries more than 220000 products from about 1300 manufacturers. Products distributed by O&M include surgical dressings endoscopic and intravenous products needles syringes sterile procedure trays gowns gloves and sutures. The firm also offers software consulting and other services to help customers manage their supplies. O&M's customers are primarily hospitals and health systems and the purchasing organizations that serve them. It delivers products to roughly 4500 health care providers from about 55 distribution centers across the US.

	Annual Growth	12/10	12/11	12/12	12/13	12/14
Sales ($ mil.)	3.8%	8,123.6	8,627.9	8,908.1	9,071.5	9,440.2
Net income ($ mil.)	(11.9%)	110.6	115.2	109.0	110.9	66.5
Market value ($ mil.)	4.5%	1,856.2	1,752.7	1,798.1	2,305.8	2,214.4
Employees	4.4%	4,800	4,800	4,800	6,700	5,700

OWENS CORNING

NYS: OC

One Owens Corning Parkway
Toledo, OH 43659
Phone: 419 248-8000
Fax: –
Web: www.owenscorning.com

CEO: Michael H. (Mike) Thaman
CFO: Michael C. McMurray
HR: Paula Russell
FYE: December 31
Type: Public

Owens Corning (OC) operates in the PINK. Famous for its Pink Panther mascot and its trademarked PINK glass fiber insulation the company is a top global maker of building and composite material systems. The building materials company makes insulation roofing fiber-based glass reinforcements and other materials for the residential and commercial markets. Its composite products business makes glass fiber reinforcement materials for the transportation industrial infrastructure marine wind energy and consumer markets. Owens Corning traces its historical roots to 1938.

	Annual Growth	12/11	12/12	12/13	12/14	12/15
Sales ($ mil.)	0.1%	5,335.0	5,172.0	5,295.0	5,276.0	5,350.0
Net income ($ mil.)	4.6%	276.0	(19.0)	204.0	226.0	330.0
Market value ($ mil.)	13.1%	3,328.6	4,287.1	4,719.4	4,150.4	5,450.8
Employees	0.0%	15,000	15,000	15,000	14,000	15,000

OWENS-ILLINOIS, INC.

NYS: OI

One Michael Owens Way
Perrysburg, OH 43551
Phone: 567 336-5000
Fax: –
Web: www.o-i.com

CEO: Andres Lopez
CFO: Jan A. Bertsch
HR: Paul Jarrell
FYE: December 31
Type: Public

Owens-Illinois (O-I) is involved in more toasts than party-goers on New Year's Eve. The world's largest maker of glass containers touts a leading market presence with 49000 customers in 85 countries around the world. O-I offers more than 10000 types of glass containers such as bottles in a wide range of shapes sizes and colors used to hold beer wine liquor as well as soft drinks juice and other beverages. It also makes glass containers for foods such as soups salad dressings and dairy products and for pharmaceuticals. Some of its products are made using recycled glass. Major customers have included such heavy hitters as Anheuser-Busch InBev Coca-Cola Diageo H.J. Heinz and Nestle.

	Annual Growth	12/11	12/12	12/13	12/14	12/15
Sales ($ mil.)	(4.4%)	7,358.0	7,000.0	6,967.0	6,784.0	6,156.0
Net income ($ mil.)	–	(510.0)	184.0	184.0	75.0	(74.0)
Market value ($ mil.)	(2.6%)	3,119.4	3,423.7	5,759.2	4,344.4	2,804.0
Employees	3.0%	24,000	22,500	22,500	21,100	27,000

OWENSBORO GRAIN COMPANY LLC

719 E. 2nd St.
Owensboro KY 42303
Phone: 270-926-2032
Fax: 270-686-6509
Web: www.owensborograin.com

CEO: Robert E Hicks Jr
CFO: Jeff Erb
HR: –
FYE: November 30
Type: Private

Owensboro Grain is a contented corporate "bean counter." The company produces a slew of edible products and fuels from soybeans for sale to markets worldwide. Its processed soy offerings include protein meal and hull pellets for animal feeds and vegetable oil and lecithin for recipes for human health. Soy-MAX the company's soybean animal meal was developed in partnership with a private consultant and Tyson Foods Texas A&M and the University of Illinois. Owensboro Grain also operates an alternative-energy facility which produces soy-based biodiesel fuel and its byproduct glycerin used in pharmaceuticals. Founded in 1906 by Henry E. O'Bryan the company is owned by the O'Bryan family's fifth generation.

OWENSBORO MUNICIPAL UTILITIES ELECTRIC LIGHT & POWER SYSTEM

2070 TAMARACK RD
OWENSBORO, KY 423016876
Phone: 270-926-3200
Web: www.omu.org

CEO: –
CFO: –
HR: Michael Moore
FYE: May 31
Type: Private

Owensboro Kentucky (named after Abraham Owen a Shelby County legislator killed in the Battle of Tippecanoe) is served by Owensboro Municipal Utilities which provides power to almost 26000 customers and water to 24500. The city-owned utility operates water treatment facilities and a power plant that uses coal and used tires for fuel. Its operating divisions are Elmer Smith power plant Engineering & Operations Water Production and Customer Service Center. It also offers telecommunications services. Owensboro Municipal Utilities is overseen by the five-member Owensboro Utility Commission which is appointed by the mayor of Owensboro.

	Annual Growth	05/10	05/11	05/12	05/13	05/14
Sales ($ mil.)	(0.2%)	–	138.3	141.5	142.3	137.4
Net income ($ mil.)	13.2%	–	–	0.8	1.0	1.1
Market value ($ mil.)	–	–	–	–	–	–
Employees	–	–	–	–	–	235

OXBO INTERNATIONAL CORPORATION

7275 Batavia Byron Rd.
Byron NY 14422-0100
Phone: 585-548-2665
Fax: 585-548-2599
Web: www.oxbocorp.com

CEO: Gary C Stich
CFO: James Nowicki
HR: –
FYE: November 30
Type: Private

Many years ago bumper crops were produced by oxen joined at the neck by an oxbow; OXBO International has lightened their burden. It manufactures and distributes specialized agricultural equipment. The lineup includes harvesters for citrus to seed corn and wine grapes as well as high clearance sprayers and application tools such as low-pac spreaders. The company also makes hay merging equipment used to upgrade forage quality and harvester productivity. In addition OXBO distributes related equipment by other OEMs replacement parts and offers a slate of job shop services. The company operates three manufacturing plants and six sales and service centers in the US and exports to more than 20 countries.

OXBOW CORPORATION

1601 Forum Pl. Ste. 1400
West Palm Beach FL 33401
Phone: 561-697-4300
Fax: 561-640-8740
Web: www.oxbow.com

CEO: William I Koch
CFO: William D Parmelee
HR: –
FYE: December 31
Type: Private

Oxbow's founder and CEO William Koch is bullish on coke and other energy commodities. The diversified firm's Oxbow Carbon unit markets and distributes coke coal petroleum and carbon products and other commodities to power producers refineries and industrial manufacturers. Oxbow is the world's top marketer of petroleum coke which is used in power generation cement kilns sugar mills and aluminum manufacturing. The company also trades in products that include gypsum anthracite and activated carbon. Oxbow owns a coal mine in Colorado that produces 5 million tons of coal annually.

OXFORD BIOSCIENCE PARTNERS L.P.

222 Berkeley St. Ste. 1650
Boston MA 02116
Phone: 617-357-7474
Fax: 617-357-7476
Web: www.oxbio.com

CEO: –
CFO: Ray Charest
HR: –
FYE: December 31
Type: Private

A British accent is not required at Oxford Bioscience Partners (OBP). The venture capital firm invests in biotech and health care companies at all stages of development but it specializes in seed and early-stage enterprises. OBP typically invests between $1 million to $10 million per transaction and provides assistance to its portfolio companies by taking seats on their boards of directors recruiting executives and facilitating corporate partnerships. The company targets firms that utilize information technology or genomics to discover and develop new drug therapies medical devices research and development equipment and other products.

OXFORD GLOBAL RESOURCES INC.

100 Cummings Center Ste. 206L
Beverly MA 01915
Phone: 978-236-1182
Fax: 978-236-1077
Web: www.oxfordcorp.com

CEO: –
CFO: Jim Brill
HR: –
FYE: December 31
Type: Subsidiary

Need a high-level information technology consultant? Looking for an engineering expert? Oxford Global Resources can fill the void. The company provides IT and engineering consultants for clients in a wide range of industries. It delivers IT consultants and managers in fields such as ERP business intelligence customer relationship management application development and project management; it offers engineers for functions such as software hardware mechanical electrical and regulatory and compliance. The company operates from more than 20 locations across the US plus one in Ireland. Founded in 1984 Oxford Global Resources is a subsidiary of professional staffing specialist On Assignment.

OXFORD HEALTH PLANS LLC

48 Monroe Tpke.
Trumbull CT 06611
Phone: 203-459-6000
Fax: 203-459-6464
Web: www.oxhp.com

CEO: Charles G Berg
CFO: Kurt B Thompson
HR: Bob Consiglio
FYE: December 31
Type: Subsidiary

"Oxford" may conjure images of stuffy learning institutions or stiff-collared shirts but Oxford Health Plans is anything but stuffy or stiff. The managed health care company provides benefit plans to members in Connecticut New Jersey and New York. Oxford Health Plans' products include its Freedom Network and Liberty Network HMOs as well as the Freedom Plan and Liberty Plan point-of-service plans that combine the cost controls of managed care with the flexibility of indemnity coverage. The firm also offers PPOs and Oxford MyPlan a health reserve account. Oxford Health Plans is part of the UnitedHealthcare organization and is a subsidiary of UnitedHealth Group.

OXFORD INDUSTRIES, INC.

NYS: OXM

999 Peachtree Street, N.E., Suite 688
Atlanta, GA 30309
Phone: 404 659-2424
Fax: –

CEO: Thomas C. Chubb
CFO: K. Scott Grassmyer
HR: Joan Wright
FYE: January 31
Type: Public

No longer all buttoned up Oxford has embraced the island life. It's a top US maker of brand name and private-label clothing including golf attire as well as a retailer in the US and UK. Its Tommy Bahama unit makes branded men's and women's casual attire and owns more than 155 stores and restaurants in the US. Lanier Clothes offers men's suits sportcoats and slacks under such brands as Dockers Geoffrey Beene and Kenneth Cole. Oxford's newest lifestyle brand is colorful Lilly Pulitzer. Oxford's customers include national and regional specialty stores direct retailers and department stores. Macy's Nordstrom and Debenhams are some of its biggest customers.

	Annual Growth	01/11	01/12*	02/13	02/14*	01/15
Sales ($ mil.)	13.4%	603.9	758.9	855.5	917.1	997.8
Net income ($ mil.)	(12.7%)	78.7	29.4	31.3	45.3	45.8
Market value ($ mil.)	23.7%	393.2	811.4	817.5	1,243.6	921.8
Employees	7.8%	4,000	4,400	4,800	5,100	5,400

*Fiscal year change

OXFORD LIFE INSURANCE COMPANY

2721 N. Central Ave.
Phoenix AZ 85004
Phone: 602-263-6666
Fax: 602-277-5901
Web: www.oxfordlife.com

CEO: –
CFO: Jason A Berg
HR: –
FYE: December 31
Type: Subsidiary

You don't need a great big dictionary to find out what Oxford Life Insurance does. The company offers individual life insurance annuities and other types of policies targeted to middle-income seniors under its own name and through its subsidiaries. Its Christian Fidelity Life Insurance subsidiary focuses on sales of Medicare supplement and final expense (funeral) insurance to seniors. Subsidiary North American Insurance specializes in third-party administration for Medicare supplement policy holders across the US. Oxford Life Insurance which was founded in 1965 is a subsidiary of AMERCO the owner of U-Haul International.

OXFORD UNIVERSITY PRESS INC.

198 MADISON AVE FL 8
NEW YORK, NY 10016-4308
Phone: 212-726-6000
Fax: –
Web: www.oup.com

CEO: –
CFO: –
HR: Adannette Colon
FYE: March 31
Type: Private

Pick a word any word. Chances are good you'll find it in one of the many books published by the Oxford University Press Inc. The publisher known as OUP USA is affiliated the world's largest university publisher UK-based Oxford University Press (OUP UK) itself a department of the venerable and prestigious University of Oxford. OUP USA publishes some 500 titles a year including scholarly works reference publications Bibles and school texts. Revenues from the not-for-profit Oxford University Press are used to support the University of Oxford.

	Annual Growth	03/02	03/03	03/04*	07/05*	03/09
Sales ($ mil.)	(46.7%)	–	–	2,000.0	1.4	86.3
Net income ($ mil.)	762.8%	–	–	0.0	(0.0)	7.0
Market value ($ mil.)	–	–	–	–	–	–
Employees	–	–	–	–	–	530

*Fiscal year change

OXIGENE, INC.

NAS: OXGN

701 Gateway Boulevard, Suite 210
South San Francisco, CA 94080
Phone: 650 635-7000
Fax: –
Web: www.oxigene.com

CEO: Bill Schwieterman
CFO: Matthew M Loar
HR: –
FYE: December 31
Type: Public

OXiGENE starves cancer to death. The company's drug candidate Zybrestat works by disrupting the functioning of blood vessels that deliver oxygen to tumors. Zybrestat is being investigated as a treatment for patients with ovarian cancer and other forms of cancer. OXiGENE is also working on a second-generation version of its oxygen-starving technology. OXiGene's strategy is to identify and license compounds from academic research centers and then shepherd the compounds through clinical trials. However it has limited its in-house drug development operations instead sponsoring research at academic and other research institutions or using contract research organizations.

	Annual Growth	12/09	12/10	12/11	12/12	12/13
Sales ($ mil.)	(39.1%)	–	–	–	0.2	0.1
Net income ($ mil.)	–	(24.7)	(23.8)	(9.7)	(8.1)	(8.3)
Market value ($ mil.)	21.8%	6.4	1.3	5.5	29.9	14.1
Employees	(31.7%)	46	22	11	10	10

OXIS INTERNATIONAL INC.

NBB: OXIS

4830 W. Kennedy Blvd., Suite 600
Tampa, FL 33609
Phone: 800 304-9888
Fax: –
Web: www.oxis.com

CEO: Anthony J Cataldo
CFO: Steven Weldon
HR: –
FYE: December 31
Type: Public

Don't stress out — call OXIS International. The company specializes in researching and treating conditions related to oxidative stress in which low antioxidant levels throw off metabolic balance at the cellular level. OXIS is focused on the development of nutritional and cosmeceutical products including formulations for use in OTC food supplements and skin products. Its ERGO (L-Ergothioneine) antioxidant product line treats anti-inflammatory ailments and other health conditions. OXIS also licenses out compounds to biotech and pharmaceutical companies.

	Annual Growth	12/10	12/11	12/12	12/13	12/14
Sales ($ mil.)	53.5%	0.0	0.0	0.3	0.4	0.1
Net income ($ mil.)	–	(3.0)	(3.7)	(5.2)	(0.5)	(23.5)
Market value ($ mil.)	(24.0%)	0.3	0.1	0.0	0.0	0.1
Employees	(9.6%)	3	1	2	2	2

OXYGEN MEDIA LLC

75 9th Ave.
New York NY 10011
Phone: 212-651-2000
Fax: 212-651-2099
Web: www.oxygen.com

CEO: Geraldine Laybourne
CFO: –
HR: –
FYE: December 31
Type: Subsidiary

This company wants to be a breath of fresh air for women who watch TV. Oxygen Media operates the Oxygen cable network a channel that targets female viewers with such programs as Bad Girls Club Hair Battle Spectacular and Tori & Dean: Home Sweet Hollywood. It also broadcasts syndicated supermodel-hosted talk show The Tyra Banks Show and past hits like Buffy the Vampire Slayer and Roseanne. In addition Oxygen offers a variety of movies and other programming. The network reaches about 75 million homes in the US. Oxygen Media also publishes content online through several websites. Founded in 1998 the company is part of media and entertainment conglomerate NBCUniversal.

OZARKS ELECTRIC COOPERATIVE CORPORATION

3641 W WEDINGTON DR
FAYETTEVILLE, AR 727045742
Phone: 479-521-2900
Fax: –
Web: www.ozarksecc.com

CEO: Mitchell Johnson
CFO: –
HR: –
FYE: December 31
Type: Private

Even people living up in the Ozark Mountains need power and Ozarks Electric Cooperative aims to deliver. The member-owned not-for-profit cooperative serves more than 62000 customers in about a dozen counties spread across northwest Arkansas and northeast Oklahoma. Its 350 miles of line reach industrial commercial residential and agricultural power users. Ozarks Electric provides its customers with energy audits and information on saving energy as well as energy efficient water heaters and surge protectors. It is a member of Touchstone Energy a national alliance of electric cooperatives in nearly 40 states. The coop was formed in 1938.

	Annual Growth	12/09	12/10	12/11	12/12	12/13
Sales ($ mil.)	0.1%	–	111.1	116.9	111.4	111.4
Net income ($ mil.)	(14.0%)	–	–	13.5	10.0	10.0
Market value ($ mil.)	–	–	–	–	–	–
Employees	–	–	–	–	–	190

O'BRIEN & GERE LIMITED

333 W WASHINGTON ST # 400
SYRACUSE, NY 132025253
Phone: 315-437-6100
Fax: –
Web: www.obg.com

CEO: James A Fox
CFO: Joseph M McNulty
HR: –
FYE: December 28
Type: Private

O'Brien & Gere provides a range of engineering consulting and project management services throughout the US including wastewater management and water resources environmental compliance and remediation civil and facilities engineering and utility services. It also provides contract operations and maintenance. Employee-owned O'Brien & Gere serves municipal environmental manufacturing and federal clients. The company which employs hundreds of scientists engineers construction and other personnel operates nearly 30 offices in about a dozen states.

	Annual Growth	12/0-1	12/00	12/06	12/11	12/13
Sales ($ mil.)	4.5%	–	123.4	125.4	188.0	219.5
Net income ($ mil.)	9.0%	–	–	1.4	2.8	2.5
Market value ($ mil.)	–	–	–	–	–	–
Employees	–	–	–	–	–	800

O'NEIL INDUSTRIES INC.

1245 W WASHINGTON BLVD
CHICAGO, IL 606071929
Phone: 773-244-6003
Fax: –
Web: www.weoneil.com

CEO: Richard J Erickson
CFO: Robert R Dukes
HR: –
FYE: December 31
Type: Private

A family of construction companies O'Neil Industries has also built W.E. O'Neil Construction Company. The employee-owned company operates in Arizona California Colorado and Illinois providing general contracting construction management design/build and structural concrete services for commercial projects in the US and Canada. O'Neil Industries has worked on corporate offices manufacturing and distribution facilities and mixed-use centers for clients in the education gaming health care hospitality and retail industries. The company also serves the residential and senior living sectors. Clients have included Boeing DePaul University and The Nature Conservancy.

	Annual Growth	12/09	12/10	12/11	12/12	12/13
Sales ($ mil.)	–	–	–	0.0	458.3	458.3	458.3
Net income ($ mil.)	0.0%	–	–	2.4	2.4	2.4
Market value ($ mil.)	–	–	–	–	–	–
Employees	–	–	–	–	–	400

P & F INDUSTRIES, INC.

NMS: PFIN

445 Broadhollow Road, Suite 100
Melville, NY 11747
Phone: 631 694-9800
Fax: –
Web: www.pfina.com

CEO: Richard A Horowitz
CFO: Joseph A Molino Jr
HR: –
FYE: December 31
Type: Public

P&F Industries helps craftsmen use less muscle. The company operates through two primary subsidiaries: Continental Tool Group and Countrywide Hardware. Continental Tool Group sells air-powered tools including sanders drills and saws through its Florida Pneumatic Manufacturing and Hy-Tech Machine units. Florida Pneumatic's Berkley Tool division makes pipe-cutting tools and wrenches for machinery for Sears and Home Depot. Countrywide Hardware through its Nationwide Industries unit produces and imports hardware for doors gates fences windows kitchens and bathrooms as well as stair parts. In mid-2010 the company ceased operating through its WM Coffman unit.

	Annual Growth	12/10	12/11	12/12	12/13	12/14
Sales ($ mil.)	10.3%	50.6	54.5	59.9	76.1	75.0
Net income ($ mil.)	32.2%	0.7	2.6	5.4	3.2	2.1
Market value ($ mil.)	21.7%	13.0	12.4	22.4	25.0	28.5
Employees	3.9%	140	142	150	155	163

P & H MINING EQUIPMENT INC.

4400 W. National Ave.
Milwaukee WI 53214
Phone: 414-671-4400
Fax: 414-671-7604
Web: www.phmining.com

CEO: –
CFO: –
HR: –
FYE: October 31
Type: Subsidiary

Like an old hippie but a lot more active P&H Mining Equipment can dig it. The surface mining machinery unit of Joy Global manufactures and services excavating and drilling machines. Its principal product lines include electric mining shovels rotary blasthole drills and walking draglines. P&H also offers field welding machine overhaul equipment maintenance and turnkey equipment erection/relocation services along with more than 250000 P&H parts. Its factory in Milwaukee provides contract manufacturing services as well. The company works in tandem with sister company Joy Mining and has equipment in use at some 90% of the world's surface mines.

P&G-CLAIROL INC.

1 Procter & Gamble Plaza
Cincinnati OH 45202
Phone: 513-983-1100
Fax: 515-643-5350
Web: www.mercyhealthnetwork.com/

CEO: –
CFO: –
HR: –
FYE: June 30
Type: Subsidiary

Clairol is big on hair care — mostly focused on covering up the gray and helping to keep non-blondes blond. A unit of consumer products behemoth Procter & Gamble P&G-Clairol specializes in making and marketing hair-coloring products hair spray shampoo conditioner and hair-styling items. Some of its brands include Nice 'n Easy Hydrience Natural Instincts and Perfect Lights. Besides all-over color the beauty company also sells highlighting products for touches of hair color. Clairol markets its products in the US Australia Canada and the UK. One of P&G's larger acquisitions (behind Gillette) P&G-Clairol is part of its beauty segment which generated 24% of revenue in 2011.

P.A.M. TRANSPORTATION SERVICES, INC.

NMS: PTSI

297 West Henri De Tonti
Tontitown, AR 72770
Phone: 479 361-9111
Fax: –
Web: www.pamtransport.com

CEO: Daniel H. Cushman
CFO: Allen W. West
HR: –
FYE: December 31
Type: Public

Pretty Awesome Mileage that's the goal! Through its subsidiaries truckload carrier P.A.M. Transportation Services moves freight over the road throughout the US and in parts of Canada; the company offers service in Mexico via arrangements with other carriers. It has a fleet of more than 1760 trucks including 4920 trailers. Most of the company's sales come from automakers and suppliers to the auto industry; General Motors represents 20%. For large accounts P.A.M. provides a dedicated fleet in which drivers and equipment are assigned to a particular customer or route long-term. The company also offers brokerage/logistics services such as carrier selection transportation scheduling and routing.

	Annual Growth	12/10	12/11	12/12	12/13	12/14
Sales ($ mil.)	5.5%	332.0	359.2	380.6	402.8	410.9
Net income ($ mil.)	–	(0.7)	(2.9)	2.2	5.9	13.5
Market value ($ mil.)	46.6%	83.3	70.5	75.9	153.8	384.8
Employees	2.3%	2,658	2,764	3,031	3,034	2,911

P.F. CHANG'S CHINA BISTRO INC.

NASDAQ: PFCB

7676 E. Pinnacle Peak Rd.
Scottsdale AZ 85255
Phone: 480-888-3000
Fax: 480-888-3001
Web: www.pfcb.com

CEO: Michael Osanloo
CFO: Mark D Mumford
HR: –
FYE: December 31
Type: Private

The ancient Chinese secret behind P.F. Chang's success is upscale American service. P.F. Chang's China Bistro owns and operates about 200 full-service Asian-style bistro restaurants in about 40 states that offer lunch and dinner menus inspired by five culinary regions of China. The chain's restaurants offer stylish dining areas display kitchens and narrative murals based on ancient Chinese designs. The company also owns and operates 170 quick-casual outlets under the name Pei Wei Asian Diner. The Pei Wei locations offer a limited menu with an emphasis on carry-out service. In 2012 the company was acquired by Centerbridge Partners.

PABST BREWING COMPANY

10635 Santa Monica Blvd. Ste. 305
Los Angeles CA 90025
Phone: 310-470-0962
Fax: 248-299-8514
Web: www.saturnee.com

CEO: Joseph Michel Schulmann
CFO: –
HR: –
FYE: July 31
Type: Private

The Pabst Brewing Company is a 19th-century brewer retooled for the 21st century. The company founded in Milwaukee in 1844 today is something of a "virtual" brewer. Pabst owns no breweries but instead it contracts with Miller-Coors to actually manufacture its beers while Pabst retains the brand ownership of and does the marketing for its stable of blue-collar brands (including Pabst Blue Ribbon Blatz Pearl Lone Star Old Milwaukee Old Style Schlitz and Colt 45). Pabst Brewing was owned by the Kalmanovitz Charitable Foundation until June 2010 when it sold the company to former food executive and billionaire investor C. Dean Metropoulos.

PAC-WEST TELECOMM INC.

555 12th St. Ste. 250
Oakland CA 94607
Phone: 209-926-3300
Fax: 510-380-5955
Web: www.pacwest.com

CEO: Kenneth J Peterson
CFO: –
HR: Mathew Ford
FYE: December 31
Type: Private

Pac-West Telecomm touts itself as a "carrier's carrier." The communications services company sells wholesale voice and data access and managed services to retail carriers Internet service providers VoIP providers cable operators call centers and others. Services include origination (local and toll-free) termination (domestic and international) and transport (broadband private lines and virtual private lines). It also operates colocation facilities in California and Texas allowing customers to house their network systems at Pac-West's switching centers to reduce operational costs. Its growing network footprint covers more than 40 states and about two-thirds of the US population.

PACCAR INC.

NMS: PCAR

777 - 106th Ave. N.E.
Bellevue, WA 98004
Phone: 425 468-7400
Fax: –
Web: www.paccar.com

CEO: Mark C. Pigott
CFO: Robert J. (Bob) Christensen
HR: Jack Levier
FYE: December 31
Type: Public

Old PACCARs never die they just get a new Peterbilt. PACCAR is one of the world's largest designers and manufacturers of big rig diesel trucks. Its lineup of light- medium- and heavy-duty trucks includes the Kenworth Peterbilt and DAF nameplates. The company also manufactures and distributes aftermarket truck parts for these brands. PACCAR's other products include Braden Carco and Gearmatic industrial winches. With the exception of a few company-owned branches PACCAR's trucks and parts are sold through independent dealers. Its PACCAR Financial Services and PacLease subsidiaries offer financing and truck leasing respectively.

	Annual Growth	12/11	12/12	12/13	12/14	12/15
Sales ($ mil.)	4.0%	16,355.2	17,050.5	17,123.8	18,997.0	19,115.1
Net income ($ mil.)	11.4%	1,042.3	1,111.6	1,171.3	1,358.8	1,604.0
Market value ($ mil.)	6.1%	13,163.2	15,882.3	20,786.4	23,891.9	16,651.6
Employees	(0.4%)	23,400	21,800	21,800	23,300	23,000

PACE COMMUNICATIONS INC.

1301 Carolina St.
Greensboro NC 27401
Phone: 336-378-6065
Fax: 336-275-2864
Web: www.pacecommunications.com

CEO: Bonnie McElveen-Hunter
CFO: Leigh Ann Klee
HR: –
FYE: December 31
Type: Private

Short of reading material on a flight and find yourself reading the airline's magazine? If so you've probably read one of Pace Communication's publications. The company publishes more than 20 business-to-business custom publications including magazines for airlines (Delta United Airlines Southwest Airlines) organizations (American Cancer Society) hotels (Four Seasons) and other customers from the travel automotive luxury financial and technology industries. In addition to magazines Pace Communications also provides Web sites catalogs books videos and e-commerce services.

PACE UNIVERSITY

1 PACE PLZ
NEW YORK, NY 100381598
Phone: 212-346-1956
Fax: –
Web: www.pace.edu

CEO: –
CFO: Robert C Almon
HR: –
FYE: June 30
Type: Private

If you want to keep pace with your peers chances are you'll need a higher education. Pace University offers certificate programs as well as undergraduate and doctoral degrees through half a dozen schools: arts and sciences business computer science and information systems education law and nursing. Altogether the school is home to 100 undergraduate majors offering roughly 30 undergraduate and graduate degrees 50 master's programs and four doctoral programs. Nearly 13000 students attend the university's three New York campuses (Lower Manhattan Pleasantville-Briarcliff and White Plains). It has a student-faculty ratio of about 18:1.

	Annual Growth	06/09	06/10	06/11	06/12	06/13
Sales ($ mil.)	6.0%	–	274.0	300.3	310.4	326.4
Net income ($ mil.)	(12.8%)	–	–	26.7	(15.9)	20.3
Market value ($ mil.)	–	–	–	–	–	–
Employees	–	–	–	–	–	1,862

PACER INTERNATIONAL INC

NMS: PACR

6805 Perimeter Drive
Dublin, OH 43016
Phone: 614 923-1400
Fax: –
Web: www.pacer.com

CEO: John T Hickerson
CFO: John J Hardig
HR: –
FYE: December 31
Type: Public

Pacer International wants to move freight at the right pace. The logistics provider's flagship business Pacer Stacktrain arranges intermodal transportation (movement of containerized freight by road and rail). Stacktrain's largely leased fleet includes rail cars that carry containers stacked two high along with the chassis used to transport containers on the road. Sister company Pacer Cartage provides local road transportation of the containers in major markets while Pacer Transportation Solutions arranges door-to-door rail and trucking service. The company's logistics segment provides services such as freight brokerage freight forwarding and supply chain management for shippers.

	Annual Growth	12/08	12/09	12/10	12/11	12/12
Sales ($ mil.)	(9.3%)	2,087.7	1,574.2	1,502.8	1,478.5	1,415.0
Net income ($ mil.)	–	(16.6)	(174.1)	0.9	13.9	4.3
Market value ($ mil.)	(19.3%)	324.2	110.9	240.0	187.7	137.2
Employees	(13.2%)	1,601	1,042	1,060	1,010	908

PACIFIC BIOSCIENCES OF CALIFORNIA INC

NMS: PACB

1380 Willow Road
Menlo Park, CA 94025
Phone: 650 521-8000
Fax: –
Web: www.pacb.com

CEO: Michael Hunkapiller
CFO: Susan K. Barnes
HR: Anjali Jayaprakash
FYE: December 31
Type: Public

In the past it took years to sequence the human and other genomes but Pacific Biosciences of California has introduced a third generation DNA sequencing technology that can map an organism's genome in minutes. The biotechnology company develops proprietary technology known as SMRT (single-molecule real-time) that performs fast and inexpensive DNA sequencing. Pacific Biosciences of California's sequencing machines are designed for use by clinical commercial and institutional research laboratories. The PacBio RS II product is a SMRT DNA sequencing system claims the highest consensus accuracy and longest read lengths of any available sequencing technology.

	Annual Growth	12/10	12/11	12/12	12/13	12/14
Sales ($ mil.)	145.3%	1.7	33.9	26.0	28.2	60.6
Net income ($ mil.)	–	(140.2)	(109.4)	(94.5)	(79.3)	(66.2)
Market value ($ mil.)	(16.2%)	1,176.2	207.0	125.7	386.6	579.6
Employees	(5.5%)	431	326	342	318	344

PACIFIC BUILDING GROUP

9752 ASPEN CREEK CT # 100
SAN DIEGO, CA 921261081
Phone: 858-552-0600
Fax: –
Web: www.pacificbuildinggroup.com

CEO: Gregory A Rogers
CFO: Lisa Hitt
HR: Danielle Weickgenant
FYE: December 31
Type: Private

Pacific Building Group pacifies its clients by taking care of their property construction needs. The general contractor provides services including pre-construction evaluation facility design/build tenant improvements and facilities maintenance. It is known for its work on health care facilities including laboratories and medical office buildings; the company also provides services for corporate hospitality and industrial clients. Pacific Building Group has handled major projects for such customers as IBM Sharp HealthCare Sony and United Airlines. The company operates mainly in Southern California primarily in San Diego County. CEO and owner Greg Rogers founded the group in 1984.

	Annual Growth	12/09	12/10	12/11	12/12	12/13
Sales ($ mil.)	15.0%	–	43.6	51.1	74.9	66.2
Net income ($ mil.)	70.5%	–	–	0.2	1.9	0.6
Market value ($ mil.)	–	–	–	–	–	–
Employees	–	–	–	–	–	190

PACIFIC CITY FINANCIAL CORPORATION

OTC: PFCF

3701 Wilshire Blvd. Ste. 402
Los Angeles CA 90010
Phone: 213-210-2000
Fax: 213-210-2032
Web: https://www.paccitybank.net

CEO: Hae Young Cho
CFO: Andrew Chung
HR: –
FYE: December 31
Type: Public

Pacific City Financial is the holding company for Pacific City Bank. Established in 2003 the bank caters to Korean-Americans from about a half-dozen locations in Southern California. The bank serves consumers professionals and minority-owned small and midsized businesses offering deposit products such as checking and savings accounts money market accounts and CDs. Its lending activities mainly consist of commercial real estate and Small Business Administration (SBA) loans. Additionally the bank offers international trade finance services to small and midsized businesses that have operations overseas. The company called off plans to be acquired by Korean blank-check company North Asia Investment in 2010.

PACIFIC COAST FEATHER CO.

1964 4th Ave. South
Seattle WA 98134
Phone: 206-624-1057
Fax: 206-625-9783
Web: www.pacificcoast.com

CEO: –
CFO: –
HR: –
FYE: March 31
Type: Private

Pacific Coast Feather Co. wants to give its customers the lowdown on down until they're so ducky they'll load up their cars with its products. The company makes and markets basic bedding including pillows comforters sheets and feather beds. It sells its products under a variety of brand names such as Pacific Coast Feather Down Around BestFit! EuroRest and Dockers to major department store chains nationwide. Pacific Coast Feather Co. also peddles its products online through the likes of Amazon.com Costco.com and jcpenney.com. The company has been owned by the Hanauer family since 1924. It's run by president and CEO Eric Moen who is not related to the Hanauers.

PACIFIC COAST PRODUCERS

631 N CLUFF AVE
LODI, CA 952400756
Phone: 209-367-8800
Fax: –
Web: www.canned-fresh.com

CEO: Daniel L Vincent
CFO: Mark Wahlman
HR: –
FYE: May 31
Type: Private

Fruits seafood sauces and organic tomato puree — rather than movies — are the creative output of this particular group of Pacific Coast Producers. The cooperative markets the apricots grapes peaches pears and tomatoes grown by its approximately 160 California-based members. It turns the produce into private-label canned fruit sauces and juices and sells them to the retail and foodservice industries. Pacific Coast Producers typically serves retailers the likes of Albertson's Aldi Kroger Safeway SUPERVALU Whole Foods and Wal-Mart as well as the US Department of Agriculture. The company founded in 1971 operates three production sites and one distribution center in California.

	Annual Growth	05/10	05/11	05/12	05/13	05/14
Sales ($ mil.)	5.6%	–	498.9	500.3	534.6	588.1
Net income ($ mil.)	12.8%	–	–	18.3	18.8	23.3
Market value ($ mil.)	–	–	–	–	–	–
Employees	–	–	–	–	–	1,000

PACIFIC CONTINENTAL CORP

NMS: PCBK

111 West 7th Avenue
Eugene, OR 97401
Phone: 541 686-8685
Fax: –

CEO: Roger S. Busse
CFO: Michael A. (Mick) Reynolds
HR: –
FYE: December 31
Type: Public

Pacific Continental Corporation is the holding company for Pacific Continental Bank which has about 15 branches across the metropolitan areas of Eugene and Portland Oregon and Seattle. It offers standard banking deposit products and specializes in commercial and residential real estate loans. The bank's services for commercial clients also include credit card transaction processing and business credit cards. About 60% of the bank's loan portfolio is secured by commercial and residential real estate while the rest is made up of business construction and consumer loans.

	Annual Growth	12/10	12/11	12/12	12/13	12/14
Assets ($ mil.)	5.6%	1,210.2	1,270.2	1,373.5	1,449.7	1,504.3
Net income ($ mil.)	33.2%	5.1	5.3	12.7	13.8	16.0
Market value ($ mil.)	9.0%	178.2	156.8	172.4	282.4	251.2
Employees	2.6%	263	264	268	290	291

PACIFIC CYCLE INC.

4902 Hammersley Rd.
Madison WI 53711
Phone: 608-268-2468
Fax: 608-268-2466
Web: www.pacific-cycle.com

CEO: –
CFO: Bob Kmoch
HR: –
FYE: December 31
Type: Subsidiary

Don't tread on Pacific Cycle. Founded in 1983 it designs and markets bicycles and scooters under several brands including Schwinn Mongoose DYNO InSTEP Roadmaster Pacific Outdoors and others. It's also a top maker of bicycle helmets in the US. The company's bikes are sold by mass merchandisers (Target Wal-Mart) sporting goods chains (Dick's The Sports Authority) and independent suppliers. Pacific Cycle which outsources its manufacturing to China and Taiwan got its operations in gear by buying Brunswick Bicycles Schwinn/GT Corp. InSTEP and PTI Sports all within a few years. Dorel Industries owns Pacific Cycle alongside its popular Cannondale brand.

PACIFIC DENTAL SERVICES INC.

2860 Michelle Dr. 2nd Fl.
Irvine CA 92606
Phone: 714-508-3600
Fax: 714-508-6400
Web: www.pacificdentalservices.com

CEO: Stephen E Thorne IV
CFO: Brady Ace
HR: –
FYE: December 31
Type: Private

Pacific Dental Services (PDS) brings smiles to dentists' faces. The growing company provides management administration and IT services to affiliated dental practices so that dentists can focus on fixing smiles rather than managing the minutiae of business. Established in 1994 PDS does everything from helping dentists choose practice sites to facilitating the design and staffing of offices. The company also negotiates managed health care contracts and asset management. More than 275 dental practices throughout Arizona California Colorado Nevada New Mexico and Texas make use of PDS' services. The company incorporates close to 4000 team members and affiliated dentists in its business.

PACIFIC ETHANOL INC

NAS: PEIX

400 Capitol Mall, Suite 2060
Sacramento, CA 95814
Phone: 916 403-2123
Fax: 916 446-3937
Web: www.pacificethanol.net

CEO: Neil M. Koehler
CFO: Bryon T. McGregor
HR: –
FYE: December 31
Type: Public

Pacific Ethanol hopes that the fuel alternative it produces will bring some peace of mind to customers worried about the US' fossil fuel dependency. The company is a leading producer of low-carbon renewable fuels in the Western US. Pacific Ethanol buys and sells ethanol to a number of large energy companies that blend it into gasoline. It also sells co-products such as wet distillers grain (WDG) a nutritional animal feed. Serving integrated oil companies and gasoline marketers who blend ethanol into gasoline Pacific Ethanol provides transportation storage and delivery of ethanol through third-party service providers in the Western US. It acquired Aventine Renewable Energy in 2015.

	Annual Growth	12/10	12/11	12/12	12/13	12/14
Sales ($ mil.)	35.5%	328.3	901.2	816.0	908.4	1,107.4
Net income ($ mil.)	(26.7%)	73.9	3.1	(19.1)	(0.8)	21.3
Market value ($ mil.)	94.5%	17.7	26.0	7.7	124.7	253.1
Employees	5.6%	145	155	136	160	180

PACIFIC FINANCIAL CORP.

NBB: PFLC

1101 S. Boone Street
Aberdeen, WA 98520-5244
Phone: 360 533-8870
Fax: –
Web: www.bankofthepacific.com

CEO: Dennis A Long
CFO: Douglas N Biddle
HR: –
FYE: December 31
Type: Public

Pacific Financial Corporation is the holding company for The Bank of the Pacific which has more than 15 branches in southwestern and northwestern portions of Washington as well as neighboring parts of Oregon. Serving small to midsized businesses and professionals the bank offers traditional deposit services including checking and savings accounts NOW and money market accounts CDs and IRAs. Commercial mortgages dominate the bank's loan portfolio which also includes business construction consumer residential farmland and credit card loans. The bank offers investments and financial planning through an agreement with third-party provider Elliott Cove Capital Management.

	Annual Growth	12/10	12/11	12/12	12/13	12/14
Assets ($ mil.)	3.7%	644.4	641.3	643.6	705.0	744.8
Net income ($ mil.)	31.8%	1.6	2.8	4.8	3.7	4.9
Market value ($ mil.)	9.7%	47.2	41.5	49.3	66.4	68.3
Employees	1.3%	222	213	237	234	234

PACIFIC HIDE & FUR DEPOT

5 RIVER DR S
GREAT FALLS, MT 594051872
Phone: 406-771-7222
Fax: –
Web: www.pacific-steel.com

CEO: –
CFO: Tim Culliton
HR: –
FYE: August 28
Type: Private

Pacific Steel & Recycling sells at one end of the steel mill and buys at the other. The company's Pacific Recycling unit supplies steel mills with scrap metal a key raw material. It operates about 35 recycling centers in the northwestern US and Canada that also handle cardboard and scrap paper in addition to metals. The company's Pacific Steel unit buys steel products and resells them from steel service centers and distribution centers in the northwestern US. Pacific Steel's facilities handle items such as bar products and structurals flat-rolled products reinforcing bar and tubing and pipe. The company offers a variety of processing services.

	Annual Growth	08/05	08/06	08/07	08/08	08/10
Sales ($ mil.)	(47.7%)	–	–	2,109.9	241.4	301.6
Net income ($ mil.)	15604.6%	–	–	0.0	2.9	34.9
Market value ($ mil.)	–	–	–	–	–	–
Employees	–	–	–	–	–	780

PACIFIC INVESTMENT MANAGEMENT COMPANY LLC

840 Newport Center Dr. Ste. 100
Newport Beach CA 92660
Phone: 949-720-6000
Fax: 949-720-1376
Web: www.pimco.com

CEO: Douglas M Hodge
CFO: John Maney
HR: –
FYE: December 31
Type: Subsidiary

Pacific Investment Management Company (PIMCO) is fixated on fixed-income products. With more than $1.3 trillion of assets under management the company is one of the world's foremost bond fund managers. PIMCO oversees more than 70 mutual funds invested in such financial instruments as corporate paper emerging markets debt municipal bonds mortgage-backed securities credit default swaps and real estate investment trusts (REITs) as well as stocks. The company also offers managed accounts extrange-traded funds and financial advisory services. Serving both retail and institutional investors PIMCO has about 10 offices worldwide. It is a subsidiary of German insurance giant Allianz.

PACIFIC MERCANTILE BANCORP

NMS: PMBC

949 South Coast Drive, Suite 300
Costa Mesa, CA 92626
Phone: 714 438-2500
Fax: 714 438-1059
Web: www.pmbank.com

CEO: Thomas M. Vertin
CFO: Curt A. Christianssen
HR: Noma J. Bruton
FYE: December 31
Type: Public

Pacific Mercantile is banking on southern California businesses. Pacific Mercantile Bancorp is the holding company for Pacific Mercantile Bank which operates more than a dozen branches in southern California's Los Angeles Orange San Bernardino and San Diego counties. Serving area consumers and businesses the bank provides standard services including checking savings and money market accounts CDs and IRAs as well as online banking and bill payment. It uses deposits primarily to fund business loans including commercial mortgages which account for some 65% of the bank's loan portfolio. The bank also offers residential mortgages construction land development and consumer loans.

	Annual Growth	12/10	12/11	12/12	12/13	12/14
Assets ($ mil.)	2.0%	1,015.9	1,024.6	1,053.9	996.6	1,099.6
Net income ($ mil.)	–	(14.0)	11.6	9.7	(22.2)	0.4
Market value ($ mil.)	17.4%	72.2	63.4	122.4	121.1	137.0
Employees	(6.5%)	220	346	324	245	168

PACIFIC MUTUAL HOLDING CO.

700 Newport Center Drive
Newport Beach, CA 92660-6397
Phone: 949 219-3011
Fax: –
Web: www.pacificmutual.com

CEO: Thomas C Sutton
CFO: –
HR: Anthony J Bonno
FYE: December 31
Type: Public

Life insurance is "alive and whale" at Pacific Mutual Holding. The company's primary operating subsidiary Pacific Life Insurance (whose logo is a breaching whale) is a top California-based life insurer. Lines of business include a variety of life insurance products for individuals and businesses; annuities and mutual funds geared to individuals and small businesses; management of stable value funds fixed income investments and other investments for institutional clients and pension plans; and real estate investing. Additionally its Aviation Capital Group subsidiary provides commercial jet aircraft leasing. The company is owned by its Pacific Life shareholders.

	Annual Growth	12/10	12/11	12/12	12/13	12/14
Assets ($ mil.)	4.3%	115,992.0	116,811.0	123,697.0	129,921.0	137,048.0
Net income ($ mil.)	3.0%	480.0	679.0	460.0	720.0	540.0
Market value ($ mil.)	–	–	–	–	–	–
Employees	–	–	–	–	–	–

PACIFIC NATIONAL GROUP

2392 BATEMAN AVE
IRWINDALE, CA 910103312
Phone: 626-357-4400
Fax: –
Web: www.pacnatgroup.com

CEO: –
CFO: Arden L Boren
HR: –
FYE: December 31
Type: Private

Pacific National Group (PNG) performs general contracting and construction management services in Arizona and Southern California. The company tackles a range of projects including commercial and industrial complexes medical buildings high-tech and aerospace centers and sports and recreation facilities. The company offers pre-construction through post-construction services as well as site supervision. Its Modulex division manufactures aluminum door frames and glazing systems. PNG's client roster includes Northrop Grumman Cedars-Sinai Medical Center Universal Studios and the Jet Propulsion Laboratory in Pasadena California. The company was founded in 1959 as Pacific Luminaire.

	Annual Growth	09/05	09/06	09/07*	12/12	12/13
Sales ($ mil.)	(2.1%)	–	92.9	111.4	110.4	80.0
Net income ($ mil.)	(3.4%)	–	–	1.2	1.7	1.0
Market value ($ mil.)	–	–	–	–	–	–
Employees	–	–	–	–	–	25

*Fiscal year change

PACIFIC NORTHWEST NATIONAL LABORATORY

902 Battelle Blvd.
Richland WA 99352
Phone: 509-375-2121
Fax: 509-375-6550
Web: www.pnl.gov

CEO: –
CFO: –
HR: –
FYE: September 30
Type: Government-owned

Pacific Northwest National Laboratory (PNNL) provides basic and applied scientific research services and facilities to both government agencies and private industries. The laboratory specializes in research about such areas as energy and the environment fundamental and computer sciences and national security. PNNL has about 4900 scientists engineers and staff members. The lab is funded and managed by the US Department of Energy but it is operated by Battelle Memorial Institute. PNNL was established in 1965. Since its inception it has received more than 1600 patents.

PACIFIC OFFICE PROPERTIES TRUST INC

NBB. PCFO

841 Bishop Street, Suite 1700
Honolulu, HI 96813
Phone: 808 521-7444
Fax: –
Web: www.pacificofficeproperties.com

CEO: –
CFO: Lawrence J Taff
HR: –
FYE: December 31
Type: Public

Like the mythical phoenix rising out of the ashes Arizona Land Income gained new life as Pacific Office Properties Trust. The real estate investment trust (REIT) largely languished in inactivity for years but in 2008 joined forces with private commercial property owner Shidler Group. The combined company owns more than 20 commercial properties with some 4.7 million sq. ft. of leasable space in the western US. The REIT is the largest office building owner in Honolulu. Chairman Jay Shidler who founded Shidler Group and has had success with other REITS including Corporate Office Properties Trust and First Industrial Realty Trust owns 94% of Pacific Office Properties Trust.

	Annual Growth	12/10	12/11	12/12	12/13	12/14
Sales ($ mil.)	(11.8%)	73.1	66.7	46.7	45.3	44.1
Net income ($ mil.)	–	(77.9)	(21.8)	(13.9)	(24.1)	(17.4)
Market value ($ mil.)	(55.9%)	26.5	2.0	0.5	1.0	1.0
Employees	–	55	54	–	–	–

PACIFIC SANDS INC

NBB: PFSD

4611 Green Bay Road	CEO: Michael D Michie
Kenosha, WI 53144	CFO: Judson Just
Phone: 262 925-0123	HR: –
Fax: –	FYE: June 30
Web: www.pacificsands.biz	Type: Public

Not a company that caters to resort-goers but one that cares about clean water Pacific Sands makes and markets nontoxic liquid and powder cleaning laundry and water-treatment products under the Natural Choices (cleaning and laundry products) and ecoone (pool and spa water-management systems) brands. The company incorporated in 1994 serves the industrial and consumer products industries. It acquired Natural Choices Home Safe Products in early 2008 to further improve its standing as an environmentally friendly products maker. Natural Choices' best known brand is Oxy-Boost cleaning products. Pacific Sands' products are available online and through dealers in the US and internationally.

	Annual Growth	06/11	06/12	06/13	06/14	06/15
Sales ($ mil.)	8.5%	1.6	1.9	2.0	2.9	2.2
Net income ($ mil.)	–	0.1	(0.0)	(0.1)	(0.3)	(1.3)
Market value ($ mil.)	(28.8%)	11.7	8.7	4.5	3.6	3.0
Employees	8.7%	11	12	13	–	–

PACIFIC SUNWEAR OF CALIFORNIA, INC.

NMS: PSUN

3450 East Miraloma Avenue	CEO: Gary H. Schoenfeld
Anaheim, CA 92806	CFO: Chris Tedford
Phone: 714 414-4000	HR: –
Fax: –	FYE: January 31
Web: www.pacsun.com	Type: Public

Pacific Sunwear of California (PacSun) knows that teens aspire to the "swag" of the board sports world. The company operates more than 600 mall-based apparel stores (down from a peak of 950) in all 50 US states and Puerto Rico under the names Pacific Sunwear and PacSun and an e-commerce site. It courts the young and active consumer by representing brands associated with surfing skateboarding and snowboarding including apparel by Billabong Volcom and Quicksilver as well as footwear by DC Shoes and others. PacSun also sells its own private-label merchandise (Bullhead Black Poppy Kirra and Nollie). Amid a steep decline in sales the teen-focused chain is closing hundreds of stores.

	Annual Growth	01/11	01/12*	02/13	02/14*	01/15
Sales ($ mil.)	(2.9%)	929.5	833.8	803.1	797.8	826.8
Net income ($ mil.)	–	(96.6)	(106.4)	(52.1)	(48.7)	(29.4)
Market value ($ mil.)	(10.4%)	295.8	139.9	139.9	199.5	190.5
Employees	(6.5%)	11,500	9,100	8,200	10,300	8,777

*Fiscal year change

PACIFIC THEATRES CORPORATION

120 N. Robertson Blvd.	CEO: –
Los Angeles CA 90048	CFO: –
Phone: 310-657-8420	HR: –
Fax: 310-657-6813	FYE: June 30
Web: www.pacifictheatres.com	Type: Private

Pacific Theatres Corporation brings a tidal wave of entertainment to moviegoers in California. The company has about 15 theaters housing some 100 movie screens in the Los Angeles area including properties in the ArcLight Cinemas theater chain. Its portfolio consists of theaters such as the Paseo in Pasadena the Culver Stadium in Culver City the Grove in Los Angeles and the ArcLight Cinema in Sherman Oaks. The Forman family founded Pacific Theatres in 1946 and continues to own and operate the company through its Decurion Corp. It has transitioned over the last 50 years from a drive-in theater business to a high-end multi- and megaplex exhibitor.

PACIFIC WEBWORKS, INC.

NBB: PWEB

230 West 400 South, 1st Floor	CEO: –
Salt Lake City, UT 84101	CFO: K Lance Bell
Phone: 801 578-9020	HR: –
Fax: –	FYE: December 31
Web: www.pacificwebworks.com	Type: Public

Pacific WebWorks wants to ensure that you have the power of the Web working for you. Through its subsidiaries the company targets small and midsized businesses with a number of Web page design applications and consulting and training services; it also provides Web site hosting for its customers as well as hosted versions of its products. Customers use the company's products to build Web sites manage e-commerce transactions create online storefronts and track Web site visitor behavior.

	Annual Growth	12/10	12/11	12/12	12/13	12/14
Sales ($ mil.)	(6.4%)	8.6	1.7	1.1	1.7	6.6
Net income ($ mil.)	–	0.0	(1.0)	(0.8)	(3.7)	(0.5)
Market value ($ mil.)	(26.9%)	3.5	2.4	0.3	0.8	1.0
Employees	7.5%	6	8	7	8	8

PACIFICHEALTH LABORATORIES INC.

OTC: PHLI

100 Matawan Rd. Ste. 420	CEO: Fred Duffner
Matawan NJ 07747	CFO: Stephen P Kuchen
Phone: 732-739-2900	HR: –
Fax: 732-739-4360	FYE: December 31
Web: www.pacifichealthlabs.com	Type: Public

PacificHealth Laboratories plans to go the distance with its dietary supplements. The firm develops sports enhancement and weight-loss products as well as treatments for diabetes using its proprietary protein-based technologies. It sells sports drinks Endurox and Accelerade to retail outlets including GNC health clubs and Internet retailers and it launched weight-loss drink Satiatrim in 2007. The company is also working on products for oral rehydration post-surgical muscle recovery and glucose regulation. PacificHealth sold its Endurox and Accelerade lines to Mott's in 2006 but it continues to sell the products under a royalty-free license. The firm sells its products internationally using distributors.

PACIFICORP

NBB: PPWL M

825 N.E. Multnomah Street	CEO: Gregory E. (Greg) Abel
Portland, OR 97232	CFO: Douglas K. (Doug) Stuver
Phone: 503 813-5645	HR: –
Fax: –	FYE: December 31
Web: www.pacificorp.com	Type: Public

PacifiCorp has refocused on its core businesses: regulated utilities Pacific Power and Rocky Mountain Power which together provide electricity to 1.8 million customers in six western states. The subsidiaries operate 16300 miles of transmission lines and 62800 miles of distribution lines. PacifiCorp owns or has stakes in almost 75 thermal hydroelectric and renewable generation facilities that supply its utilities with about 10600 MW of net capacity. Its PacifiCorp Energy unit purchases power from other generators and it sells excess power to wholesale customers in the western US. The company is a unit of Berkshire Hathaway's MidAmerican Energy Holdings.

	Annual Growth	12/10	12/11	12/12	12/13	12/14
Sales ($ mil.)	4.3%	4,432.0	4,586.0	4,882.0	5,147.0	5,252.0
Net income ($ mil.)	5.4%	566.0	555.0	537.0	682.0	698.0
Market value ($ mil.)	(1.9%)	44,625.0	37,485.0	41,412.0	40,980.0	41,412.0
Employees	(1.6%)	6,300	6,400	6,300	6,000	5,900

PACIRA PHARMACEUTICALS INC.

NMS: PCRX

5 Sylvan Way, Suite 300	CEO: David M. (Dave) Stack
Parsippany, NJ 07054	CFO: James S. (Jim) Scibetta
Phone: 973 254-3560	HR: –
Fax: –	FYE: December 31
Web: www.pacira.com	Type: Public

Pacira Pharmaceuticals lets injections last longer with its DepoFoam technology. The company develops sustained-release therapies based on DepoFoam an injectable drug delivery technology that allows both immediate and sustained release. Pacira's newest drug EXPAREL is an injectable local anesthetic. Its two established products are DepoCyt for treating cancer-related neoplastic meningitis and DepoDur for the treatment of post-operative pain. The company is conducting development and licensing programs on other DepoFoam candidates as well.

	Annual Growth	12/10	12/11	12/12	12/13	12/14
Sales ($ mil.)	91.9%	14.6	15.7	39.1	85.6	197.7
Net income ($ mil.)	–	(27.1)	(43.3)	(52.3)	(63.9)	(13.7)
Market value ($ mil.)	117.2%	–	312.7	631.6	2,078.3	3,205.1
Employees	52.3%	83	133	156	310	447

PACKAGING CORP OF AMERICA

NYS: PKG

1955 West Field Court	CEO: Mark W. Kowlzan
Lake Forest, IL 60045	CFO: Robert P. (Bob) Mundy
Phone: 847 482-3000	HR: Harry Well
Fax: –	FYE: December 31
Web: www.packagingcorp.com	Type: Public

Every day is Boxing Day at Packaging Corporation of America (PCA) one of the largest containerboard manufacturers in the US. It produces about 3.5 million tons of containerboard a year most of which is converted into corrugated boxes and ships about 48.2 billion square feet of corrugated products. PCA's mills also churn out about 2.25 million tons of kraft linerboard and about a million tons of semi-chemical corrugating medium. The company sells to a diverse group of industries. Its corrugated packaging includes shipping containers for manufactured goods retail boxes and displays and wax-coated boxes and meat boxes for agricultural use.

	Annual Growth	12/10	12/11	12/12	12/13	12/14
Sales ($ mil.)	24.5%	2,435.6	2,620.1	2,843.9	3,665.3	5,852.6
Net income ($ mil.)	17.6%	205.4	158.0	163.8	436.3	392.6
Market value ($ mil.)	31.8%	2,541.8	2,482.8	3,784.2	6,224.7	7,677.6
Employees	14.7%	8,100	8,300	8,600	13,600	14,000

PACKAGING DYNAMICS CORPORATION

3900 W. 43rd St.	CEO: –
Chicago IL 60632	CFO: Henry Newell
Phone: 773-843-8000	HR: Paul S Christensen
Fax: 773-254-8136	FYE: December 31
Web: www.pkdy.com	Type: Private

Looking for a job with flexibility? Consider flexible packaging and specialty papermaker Packaging Dynamics. It operates through three units: BagcraftPapercon converts paper film and foil into food packaging such as bags and wraps butcher paper pan liners and tissue. International Converter produces adhesive and film extrusion lamination materials used to produce decorative cartons bags cans and other packaging for consumer medical and industrial goods. Thilmany Papers makes specialty lightweight papers for wrapping up an array of pressure sensitive and industrial items (sandwich wraps microwave popcorn bags baggage tags and tapes). Packaging Dynamics is a portfolio company of Kohlberg & Co.

PACTIV LLC

1900 W. Field Ct.	CEO: Richard L Wambold
Lake Forest IL 60045	CFO: –
Phone: 847-482-2000	HR: –
Fax: 408-260-9615	FYE: December 31
Web: www.homedirector.com	Type: Subsidiary

Pactiv is active in containing both food and the people who eat it. The company makes packaging for the foodservice market as well as building products. Pactiv's food packaging products which include plastic cups takeout deli catering containers and tableware are used by the supermarket restaurant packer/processor and institutional industries primarily in North America where most of Pactiv's manufacturing facilities are based. The company's GreenGuard products include insulation board drainage mats and sheathings for residential and commercial buildings. New Zealand's Reynolds Group Holdings an affiliate of billionaire Graeme Hart's Rank Group acquired Pactiv in late 2010.

PACWEST BANCORP

NMS: PACW

10250 Constellation Blvd., Suite 1640	CEO: Matthew P. (Matt) Wagner
Los Angeles, CA 90067	CFO: Patrick J. (Pat) Rusnak
Phone: 310 286-1144	HR: Christopher D. Blake
Fax: –	FYE: December 31
Web: www.pacwestbancorp.com	Type: Public

PacWest Bancorp is the holding company for Pacific Western Bank which operates about 65 branches in Southern California plus three in the San Francisco Bay Area. The bank caters to small and midsized businesses and their owners and employees offering traditional deposit and loan products and services. Commercial real estate mortgages business loans (including Small Business Administration loans) and construction loans account for most of the bank's lending activities. It also originates residential mortgage consumer and other loans. The bank offers investment services and international banking through agreements with correspondent banks.

	Annual Growth	12/10	12/11	12/12	12/13	12/14
Assets ($ mil.)	30.9%	5,529.0	5,528.2	5,463.7	6,533.4	16,234.8
Net income ($ mil.)	–	(62.0)	50.7	56.8	45.1	168.9
Market value ($ mil.)	20.8%	2,202.6	1,952.3	2,551.9	4,349.6	4,683.4
Employees	11.6%	929	982	991	1,110	1,443

PADDOCK POOL CONSTRUCTION COMPANY

6525 E. Thomas Rd.	CEO: Jim Cich
Scottsdale AZ 85251	CFO: –
Phone: 480-947-7261	HR: –
Fax: 480-970-7456	FYE: December 31
Web: www.paddockpoolsandspas.com	Type: Private

Paddock Pool Construction allows Southwestern residents to enjoy the desert backdrop poolside. The company designs builds remodels and maintains luxury swimming pools and spas for homes in Arizona and Nevada. It also runs about half a dozen retail stores and a distribution center in the Phoenix and Las Vegas areas as well as an online retail site which sell barbeque grills fountains hot tubs patio furniture pool equipment and cleaning chemicals tableware and other outdoor products. Paddock Pool's commercial division assists architects and engineers with pool designs for hotel resorts and water parks. Started in 1958 by the late George Ghiz the business is still owned and operated by the Ghiz family.

PAETEC HOLDING CORP.

1 PAETEC Plaza 600 Willowbrook Office Park	CEO: –
Fairport NY 14450	CFO: Anthony W Thomas
Phone: 585-340-2500	HR: –
Fax: 585-340-2801	FYE: December 31
Web: www.paetec.com	Type: Subsidiary

PAETEC gets its paycheck from enterprise users of voice and data communication services. Operating through subsidiary PAETEC Communications the company provides services for local long-distance and Internet-based (VoIP) voice; cloud and data center functions and data access and transport for more than 54000 businesses in about 90 of the largest metropolitan areas of the US. It also provides enterprise telecommunications management software under the PINNACLE brand and it offers premises equipment installation as well as network engineering consulting. Customers include US federal agencies such as the DISA DoD and the FAA. PAETEC was acquired by Windstream in 2011 for about $2.3 billion.

PAGE PARKES CORPORATION

1535 W. Loop S. Ste. 100	CEO: –
Houston TX 77027	CFO: Debbie G Fielding
Phone: 713-807-8200	HR: –
Fax: 713-807-0022	FYE: December 31
Web: www.pageparkes.com	Type: Private

Getting on the pages of available talent in the Page Parkes' portfolio is a good move for aspiring models in the Lone Star state. Page Parkes is one of the largest modeling agencies in the Southwest. With offices in Houston and Dallas the firm represents more than 400 models. Agency talent has been tapped for such clients as Ralph Lauren Abercrombie & Fitch adidas Target and L'Oreal. Page Parkes also operates the Page Parkes Center of Modeling and Acting to help develop potential talent. This unit offers Model Image camps a training and development service for modeling hopefuls and those wanting to update their individual style. Agent Page Parkes started her namesake company in 1981.

PAGE SOUTHERLAND PAGE L.L.P.

1100 LOUISIANA ST STE 1	CEO: James M Wright
HOUSTON, TX 770025246	CFO: –
Phone: 713-871-8484	HR: –
Fax: –	FYE: December 31
	Type: Private

Page Southerland Page performs pre-design planning architectural engineering historic preservation interior design and sustainable design services in Texas and far beyond. Also known as Page since a 2013 rebranding the company boasts a portfolio of projects that includes corporate education healthcare hospitality government sports and science and technology facilities. Page takes on projects in more than 80 countries worldwide including the UK and the Middle East. The construction firm traces its beginnings to a two-person office in Austin Texas established by brothers Charles and Louis Page in 1898; Louis Southerland joined the firm during the 1930s.

	Annual Growth	12/06	12/07	12/08	12/09	12/11
Sales ($ mil.)	127.6%	–	–	5.2	57.2	61.1
Net income ($ mil.)	6824.7%	–	–	0.0	6.7	10.0
Market value ($ mil.)	–	–	–	–	–	–
Employees	–	–	–	–	–	450

PAID INC

NBB: PAYD

200 Friberg Parkway	CEO: W Austin Lewis IV
Westborough, MA 01581	CFO: W Austin Lewis IV
Phone: 617 861-6050	HR: –
Fax: –	FYE: December 31
Web: www.paid-corp.com	Type: Public

Paid Inc. (formerly Sales Online Direct) hopes celebrities and fans will pay it some attention. The company's celebrity services division offers merchandising brand building marketing online ticketing services and it hosts Web-based fan clubs for clients. Its AuctionInc technology processes and calculates transactions for website owners. The company also auctions collectibles sports memorabilia and celebrity-related items through the Internet. Paid Inc. makes its money on collectibles and through related services (such as appraisals and its own auction management software).

	Annual Growth	12/10	12/11	12/12	12/13	12/14
Sales ($ mil.)	(42.3%)	7.2	6.9	14.0	4.4	0.8
Net income ($ mil.)	–	(3.3)	(4.0)	(4.1)	(1.1)	(1.7)
Market value ($ mil.)	(36.1%)	1.8	1.3	0.5	1.2	0.3
Employees	(46.1%)	–	32	11	5	5

PAIN THERAPEUTICS INC

NMS: PTIE

7801 N. Capital of Texas Highway, Suite 260	CEO: Remi Barbier
Austin, TX 78731	CFO: Peter S Roddy
Phone: 512 501-2444	HR: –
Fax: –	FYE: December 31
Web: www.paintrials.com	Type: Public

Pain Therapeutics is providing opiates for the masses. The development-stage pharmaceutical company is working on abuse-resistant painkillers including Remoxy a version of the frequently abused Oxycontin. Pain Therapeutics is developing Remoxy in partnership with Pfizer which holds all of the commercialization rights to the drug except in Australia and New Zealand. In addition to its chronic pain candidates Pain Therapeutics has other development products in early stages. Because many of its drug candidates already contain FDA-approved components the firm hopes for a faster approval process for its lead candidate.

	Annual Growth	12/09	12/10	12/11	12/12	12/13
Sales ($ mil.)	18.9%	20.6	16.8	11.5	10.9	41.1
Net income ($ mil.)	–	(3.5)	(12.0)	(2.6)	(3.4)	31.5
Market value ($ mil.)	(2.4%)	243.9	307.2	172.9	123.3	221.2
Employees	(26.2%)	27	18	10	8	8

PALACE ENTERTAINMENT HOLDINGS LLC

4590 MacArthur Blvd. Ste. 400	CEO: Alexander Weber Jr
Newport Beach CA 92660	CFO: –
Phone: 949-797-9700	HR: Dodie Raley
Fax: 314-429-3137	FYE: December 31
Web: www.claycorp.com	Type: Private

Palace Entertainment Holdings wants to rule the fun realm. The company owns nearly 40 family fun centers theme parks and water parks in some ten states. Its theme park holdings include park operator Kennywood Entertainment while its family locations operate under the Boomers! SpeedZone Malibu and Mountasia names and include such features as go-cart racing video game arcades laser tag and bumper boats. Visitors can also slip and slide at Palace Entertainment's water parks under brands such as Water Country Big Kahuna's Wet 'n Wild and Splish Splash. Palace Entertainment is a subsidiary of European park operator Parques Reunidos.

PALACE SPORTS & ENTERTAINMENT INC.

4 Championship Dr.   CEO: –
Auburn Hills MI 48326   CFO: –
Phone: 248-377-0100   HR: –
Fax: 248-377-3260   FYE: December 31
Web: www.palacenet.com   Type: Private

A veritable sports and entertainment empire is run out of this Palace. Palace Sports & Entertainment is a holding company controlled by Karen Davidson widow of the late billionaire William Davidson through which the family owns The Palace of Auburn Hills. The sports and entertainment arena serves as home of the Detroit Pistons professional basketball team (which is also controlled by Davidson) and it hosts a number of music and entertainment events throughout the year. Other holdings include Michigan's DTE Energy Music Theatre and the Meadow Brook Music Festival.

PALLADIUM EQUITY PARTNERS LLC

Rockefeller Center 1270 Avenue of the Americas Ste. 2200   CEO: –
New York NY 10020   CFO: Kevin Raymond
Phone: 212-218-5150   HR: –
Fax: 212-218-5155   FYE: December 31
Web: www.palladiumequity.com   Type: Private

In the mining world palladium is a rare and precious metal; in the investment world however Palladium is an investment firm known to mine for companies that serve the US Hispanic population. Formed in 1997 Palladium Equity Partners focuses on companies that are in a position to target the Hispanic market which the company deems to be a fast-growing and profitable market segment. It invests in various industries including financial services food retail business services health care manufacturing and media. Palladium has offices in New York and Los Angeles.

PALATIN TECHNOLOGIES INC   ASE: PTN

4B Cedar Brook Drive   CEO: Carl Spana
Cranbury, NJ 08512   CFO: –
Phone: 609 495-2200   HR: –
Fax: –   FYE: June 30
Web: www.palatin.com   Type: Public

Palatin Technologies fights the perils of poor health with protein and peptide-based therapies. The company researches and develops drugs that target melanocortin (MC) receptors and natriuretic receptors in the brain. MC-targeted drugs could be used in the treatment of obesity diabetes and sexual dysfunction. While natriuretic (a type of peptide) focused treatments are being studied for the treatment of heart failure asthma and other cardiovascular diseases. Many of the company's research programs use its MIDAS (Metal Ion-induced Distinctive Array of Structures) technology to design drugs that mimic peptides. The company's lead candidate is bremelanotide to treat sexual dysfunction in men and women.

	Annual Growth	06/09	06/10	06/11	06/12	06/13
Sales ($ mil.)	(82.6%)	11.4	14.2	1.5	0.1	0.0
Net income ($ mil.)	–	(4.8)	(1.8)	(12.8)	(17.3)	(20.9)
Market value ($ mil.)	25.5%	9.8	7.0	50.1	19.6	24.3
Employees	(17.4%)	43	41	19	16	20

PALMETTO BANCSHARES, INC. (SC)   NAS: PLMT

306 East North Street   CEO: –
Greenville, SC 29601   CFO: –
Phone: 800 725-2265   HR: –
Fax: –   FYE: December 31
Web: www.palmettobank.com   Type: Public

Since the palmetto is the official state tree of South Carolina does that make Palmetto Bancshares the state's official bank? Palmetto Bancshares is the holding company for The Palmetto Bank which operates about 40 full- and limited-service branches mostly in upstate South Carolina. Its offerings include checking savings and money market accounts; IRAs; and CDs. Loans secured by commercial real estate account for the largest portion of its loan portfolio with single-family residential mortgages at a distant second. The Palmetto Bank also provides financial planning trust and brokerage services plus bond mutual fund and annuity sales. It's been serving South Carolinians since 1906.

	Annual Growth	12/09	12/10	12/11	12/12	12/13
Assets ($ mil.)	(6.7%)	1,436.0	1,355.2	1,203.2	1,145.5	1,090.2
Net income ($ mil.)	–	(40.1)	(60.2)	(23.4)	(1.9)	27.7
Market value ($ mil.)	12.8%	102.3	38.4	65.3	106.5	165.7
Employees	(7.5%)	413	394	352	323	302

PALL CORP.   NYS: PLL

25 Harbor Park Drive   CEO: Rainer Blair
Port Washington, NY 11050   CFO: Henry Carroll
Phone: 516 484-5400   HR: –
Fax: 516 484-3649   FYE: July 31
Web: www.pall.com   Type: Public

With operations around the globe Pall is not small. The company is a leading supplier of filtration separation and purification technologies. Its products are used to remove solid liquid and gaseous contaminants from a variety of liquids and gases. It operates two businesses globally: Life Sciences and Industrial. The Life Sciences business group is focused on developing manufacturing and selling products to customers in the Medical BioPharmaceuticals and Food & Beverage markets. The Industrial business group is focused on developing manufacturing and selling products to customers in the Process Technologies Aerospace and Microelectronics markets.

	Annual Growth	07/10	07/11	07/12	07/13	07/14
Sales ($ mil.)	3.8%	2,401.9	2,740.9	2,671.7	2,648.1	2,789.1
Net income ($ mil.)	10.8%	241.2	315.5	319.3	574.9	364.0
Market value ($ mil.)	19.3%	4,200.5	5,446.2	5,866.9	7,684.9	8,509.8
Employees	0.0%	10,400	10,900	10,800	9,800	10,400

PALMETTO HEALTH

1301 TAYLOR ST STE 8A   CEO: –
COLUMBIA, SC 292012955   CFO: Paul Duane
Phone: 803-296-2100   HR: Willis Gregory
Fax: –   FYE: September 30
Web: www.palmettohealth.org   Type: Private

Palmetto Health provides health care in the Palmetto State. The not-for-profit organization administers a comprehensive range of medical services to residents of Columbia South Carolina and surrounding areas through a network of hospitals and other medical providers. The 1140-bed system includes a 650-bed teaching hospital Palmetto Health Richland which is affiliated with the University of South Carolina Medical School. Palmetto also operates the 490-bed Palmetto Health Baptist Columbia hospital as well as Baptist Health Easley a 110-bed general acute-care community hospital in the Appalachian highlands which it operates with Greenville Hospital System University Medical Center.

	Annual Growth	09/04	09/05	09/06	09/07	09/08
Sales ($ mil.)	5.0%	–	–	–	1,131.7	1,188.7
Net income ($ mil.)	–	–	–	–	41.2	0.0
Market value ($ mil.)	–	–	–	–	–	–
Employees	–	–	–	–	–	10,200

PALO ALTO MEDICAL FOUNDATION FOR HEALTH CARE RESEARCH AND EDUCAT

795 EL CAMINO REAL AMES B
PALO ALTO, CA 94301
Phone: 650-321-4121
Fax: –
Web: www.pamf.org

CEO: Jeff Gerard
CFO: –
HR: –
FYE: December 31
Type: Private

The Palo Alto Medical Foundation (PAMF) is a not-for-profit multi-specialty physicians group providing medical and outpatient care mostly in the San Francisco Bay Area. It operates through three divisions serving distinct geographical areas: the Palo Alto Medical Clinic and the Camino Medical Group serve Silicon Valley and the East Bay; and the Santa Cruz Medical Foundation operates farther south in and around Santa Cruz. An affiliate of Sutter Health the organization has some 1100 doctors covering dozens of medical specialties; its facilities also provide outpatient surgery diagnostic imaging and women's services. Additionally PAMF houses a Research Institute that performs medical research.

	Annual Growth	08/98	08/99*	12/00	12/01	12/11
Sales ($ mil.)	–	–	0.0	–	322.0	1,434.0
Net income ($ mil.)	–	–	0.0	–	5.0	3.0
Market value ($ mil.)	–	–	–	–	–	–
Employees	–	–	–	–	–	1,168

*Fiscal year change

PALO ALTO NETWORKS, INC

NYS: PANW

4401 Great America Parkway
Santa Clara, CA 95054
Phone: 408 753-4000
Fax: –
Web: www.paloaltonetworks.com

CEO: –
CFO: Steffan C Tomlinson
HR: Wendy Nice-barnes
FYE: July 31
Type: Public

Palo Alto Networks offers enterprise-wide Internet security (including security measures for mobile devices) to protect companies from breaches in their corporate networks. Its hardware and software security products which account for most of company revenue identify network traffic in detail and provide the ability to control access by user. In the past a company could either allow its employees access to applications like Oracle Skype and YouTube or not. But as more work is done online and in the cloud that's not always practical. Palo Alto Networks designs its products to identify and manage threats rather than simply blocking access. It sells products outright as well as through a growing subscription business. Competitors include Juniper Networks and Cisco Systems.

	Annual Growth	07/11	07/12	07/13	07/14	07/15
Sales ($ mil.)	67.3%	118.6	255.1	396.1	598.2	928.1
Net income ($ mil.)	–	(12.5)	0.7	(29.2)	(226.5)	(165.0)
Market value ($ mil.)	48.2%	–	4,844.8	4,149.5	6,856.0	15,756.2
Employees	39.7%	692	755	1,147	1,722	2,637

PALOMAR TECHNOLOGIES INC.

2728 Loker Ave. West
Carlsbad CA 92010
Phone: 760-931-3600
Fax: 760-931-5191
Web: www.palomartechnologies.com

CEO: Gary E Gist
CFO: –
HR: –
FYE: December 31
Type: Private

Palomar Technologies specializes in microelectronic and optoelectronic assembly equipment and packaging as well as gold wire bonding and complex hybrid packaging and die bonding systems. Its systems are employed in producing high-frequency wireless transmitters and receivers hybrid devices for aerospace and military applications and microelectromechanical systems (MEMS) devices. Palomar offers fluid dispensing and component placement systems. Additionally the company provides process development and prototyping services. Established in 1975 as part of Hughes Aircraft's assembly and test operations Palomar became an independent firm in 1995 through a management buyout.

PAMIDA STORES OPERATING COMPANY LLC

8800 F St.
Omaha NE 68127
Phone: 402-339-2400
Fax: 402-596-7330
Web: www.pamida.com

CEO: –
CFO: –
HR: –
FYE: January 31
Type: Private

Pamida Stores Operating Co. offers more small-town values to small town communities. The rural retailer operates some 195 Pamida general merchandise discount stores in more than 15 states mostly in the Midwest. The stores are located in small towns (5500 people on average) most of which are not served by mass merchandisers such as Wal-Mart. Pamida's stores sell brand-name and private-label apparel jewelry health and beauty aids housewares electronics and lawn and garden supplies. Most stores also sell groceries and two-thirds have in-store pharmacies. In 2012 Pamida merged with Shopko; both retailers are portfolio companies of private equity Sun Capital Partners.

PAN AMERICAN GOLDFIELDS LTD.

NBB: MXOM

1000 - 36 Toronto Street
Toronto, Ontario
Phone: 416 848-7744
Fax: –
Web: www.panamgoldfields.com

CEO: Geoffrey A. (Geoff) Burns
CFO: Robert G. Doyle
HR: –
FYE: February 28
Type: Public

Pan American Silver has found a silver lining but it's not in the clouds. The exploration and mining company produces more than 26 million ounces of silver annually and has proved and probable reserves of more than 317 million ounces. Its producing mines all located in the Americas include the Huar- - n silver mine in Peru. It also has mines in Mexico Bolivia and Argentina. Refined silver and gold accounts for nearly 60% of its total sales; lead concentrate 20%. Pan American Silver has development projects in Argentina and Mexico.

	Annual Growth	02/09	02/10	02/11	02/12	02/13
Sales ($ mil.)	110.0%	–	0.5	1.2	2.1	4.9
Net income ($ mil.)	–	(8.0)	(1.2)	(3.2)	(3.4)	(2.3)
Market value ($ mil.)	(15.4%)	35.9	51.0	23.6	18.1	18.4
Employees	(22.7%)	14	11	5	5	5

PANASONIC AVIONICS CORPORATION

26200 Enterprise Way
Lake Forest CA 92630
Phone: 949-672-2000
Fax: 949-462-7100
Web: www.panasonic.aero

CEO: Paul Margis
CFO: –
HR: –
FYE: March 31
Type: Subsidiary

Panasonic Avionics takes entertainment to new heights. The company which is a subsidiary of Panasonic Corporation of North America makes in-flight entertainment and communications systems that allow airborne passengers to get their fix of live TV movies music interactive games and travel guides. Its Global Communications Suite and X Series offer internet access telephone service and broadband connectivity. These systems are usually installed either overhead or in airplane seatbacks. Customers include most commercial airline carriers and aircraft manufacturers such as Airbus and Boeing.

PANATTONI DEVELOPMENT COMPANY INC.

8775 Folsom Blvd. Ste. 200
Sacramento CA 95826-3988
Phone: 916-381-1561
Fax: 916-381-7639
Web: www.panattoni.com

CEO: Adon Panattoni
CFO: Jacklyn Shelby
HR: Tim Iseminger
FYE: December 31
Type: Private

No bread and pasta just commercial real estate at Panattoni Development. The company develops leases and manages industrial office and retail properties in the US Canada and Europe with an emphasis on corporate centers business parks and shopping centers. One of the top firms in the industrial build-to-suit market it averages more than 12 million sq. ft. of development annually. Major projects include overseeing the development of the new headquarters building for CalSTRS which was completed in 2009. In addition to development and property management the firm offers construction financing and asset management services. CEO Carl Panattoni founded Panattoni Development Company in 1986.

PANAVISION INC.

6219 De Soto Ave.
Woodland Hills CA 91367-2602
Phone: 818-316-1000
Fax: 818-316-1111
Web: www.panavision.com

CEO: Kimberly Snyder
CFO: John Suh
HR: –
FYE: June 30
Type: Private

Without Panavision Iron Man and Batman: The Dark Knight wouldn't be much to look at. The company manufactures and rents out cameras lenses and lighting equipment and related accessories to movie and TV production studios. Subsidiary Lee Filters sells lighting color-correction and diffusion filters. Other subsidiaries supply lighting systems and develop digital image sensor chips. Panavision has provided the camera system for every James Bond film ever made. It also supplies camera equipment to popular TV series such as Glee Modern Family and Two and a Half Men. All total it has a global network of about 40 facilities and 20 independent distributors.

PANDA ENERGY INTERNATIONAL INC.

4100 Spring Valley Rd. Ste. 1001
Dallas TX 75244
Phone: 972-361-2000
Fax: 972-361-2001
Web: www.pandaenergy.com

CEO: Robert W Carter
CFO: Michael Trentel
HR: Vinzant Suzanne
FYE: December 31
Type: Private

Pandering to the energy-deprived Panda Energy International develops owns and operates low-cost clean energy power plants. The company has built more than 9000 MW of electric generation capacity in the US. Panda Energy has sold its interests in four gas-fueled power plants in Arkansas Arizona and Texas to TECO Energy and its stakes in projects in China and Nepal. Panda Energy has built the two largest gas-fueled combined-cycle independent electric generation facilities in the US totaling 4400 MW of generating capacity. CEO Bob Carter and his wife EVP Janice Carter own a controlling stake in Panda Energy which they founded in 1982.

PANDA RESTAURANT GROUP INC.

1683 Walnut Grove Ave.
Rosemead CA 91770
Phone: 626-799-9898
Fax: 626-372-8288
Web: www.pandarg.com

CEO: –
CFO: –
HR: –
FYE: December 31
Type: Private

This Panda certainly has food on its mind. Panda Restaurant Group is a leading quick-service restaurant operator with more than 1300 Panda Express locations in more than 40 states Puerto Rico and Mexico. The chain offers Asian-themed food primarily in high-traffic locations including malls airports and sporting arenas. The company also runs almost 30 mall-based Hibachi-San outlets that offer a quick-service Japanese grill menu. For patrons looking for full-service dining Panda Restaurants has a handful of Panda Inn branded units in California. The company is owned by the family of co-chairman Andrew Cherng who opened the first Panda Inn location in 1973.

PANDORA MEDIA INC

NYS: P

2101 Webster Street, Suite 1650
Oakland, CA 94612
Phone: 510 451-4100
Fax: 510 451-4286
Web: www.pandora.com

CEO: Brian P. McAndrews
CFO: Michael S. (Mike) Herring
HR: –
FYE: December 31
Type: Public

This Pandora's box is filled with music. The Internet radio station generates playlists based on a user's favorite artist or song. As part of the company's Music Genome Project songs are analyzed according to musical features — including details of instrumentation harmony lyrics melody rhythm and vocals. Users enter the name of a song and Pandora creates a playlist of songs with similar characteristics. Pandora's service free to its more than 175 million registered users and available only in the US is supported by local and national advertising. Chief strategy officer Tim Westergren founded the company in 2000; Pandora went public in 2011.

	Annual Growth	01/11	01/12	01/13*	12/13	12/14
Sales ($ mil.)	88.4%	137.8	274.3	427.1	600.2	920.8
Net income ($ mil.)	–	(1.8)	(16.1)	(38.1)	(27.0)	(30.4)
Market value ($ mil.)	16.3%	–	2,757.7	2,408.5	5,561.3	3,727.7
Employees	57.9%	359	530	740	1,069	1,414

*Fiscal year change

PANERA BREAD CO.

NMS: PNRA

3630 South Geyer Road, Suite 100
St. Louis, MO 63127
Phone: 314 984-1000
Fax: –
Web: www.panerabread.com

CEO: Ronald M. (Ron) Shaich
CFO: Michael J. Bufano
HR: –
FYE: December 30
Type: Public

Panera Bread Company is ready for an epochal change in American eating habits. The company is a leader in the quick-casual restaurant business with more than 1880 bakery-cafes located throughout the US and Ontario Canada. Its locations which operate under the banners Panera Bread Saint Louis Bread Co. and Paradise Bakery & Café offer made-to-order sandwiches using a variety of artisan breads including Asiago cheese bread focaccia and its classic sourdough bread. The chain's menu also features soups salads and gourmet coffees. In addition Panera sells its bread bagels and pastries to go. About 925 of its locations are company-operated and roughly 955 locations are run by franchisees.

	Annual Growth	12/10	12/11	12/12	12/13	12/14
Sales ($ mil.)	13.2%	1,542.5	1,822.0	2,130.1	2,385.0	2,529.2
Net income ($ mil.)	12.5%	111.9	136.0	173.4	196.2	179.3
Market value ($ mil.)	14.4%	2,739.1	3,782.5	4,247.4	4,739.6	4,691.4
Employees	15.4%	25,600	32,600	36,300	40,100	45,400

PANHANDLE EASTERN PIPE LINE COMPANY LP

5444 Westheimer Rd.
Houston TX 77056
Phone: 713-989-7000
Fax: 713-989-1178
Web: www.panhandleenergy.com/comp_pep.asp

CEO: Kelcy L Warren
CFO: Martin Salinas Jr
HR: –
FYE: December 31
Type: Subsidiary

From the oilfield to the burner under a frying pan Panhandle Eastern Pipe Line can move the gas. The company operates almost 10100 miles of interstate pipelines (Panhandle Eastern — 6000 miles Trunkline — 3700 miles and Sea Robin — 400 miles) that can transport 7.6 billion cu. ft. of natural gas a day primarily to markets in the Midwest and Great Lakes regions of the US. It also provides terminalling services through nearly 50 compressor stations and five gas storage fields capable of holding 68.1 billion cu. ft. of natural gas. The company also has liquefied natural gas (LNG) terminalling assets. Panhandle Eastern Pipe Line operates as part of Southern Union's Panhandle Energy unit.

PANHANDLE OIL & GAS INC

NYS: PHX

Grand Centre, Suite 300, 5400 N. Grand Blvd.
Oklahoma City, OK 73112
Phone: 405 948-1560
Fax: 405 948-2038
Web: www.panhandleoilandgas.com

CEO: Michael C. Coffman
CFO: Lonnie J. Lowry
HR: –
FYE: September 30
Type: Public

You won't find this Panhandle on a street corner but you will find it pocketing the oil and gas royalties from more than 6100 gross producing oil and gas wells. Panhandle Oil and Gas (formerly Panhandle Royalty) owns mineral interests both working and royalty in oil- and gas-producing properties in 10 states. The company does not operate any of its own wells but instead maintains them through partnerships with other oil and gas companies. Its major properties are located primarily in Oklahoma (44% of its net land holdings in fiscal 2013 of 255300 acres). In fiscal 2013 Panhandle Oil and Gas reported proved reserves of 151.8 billion cu. ft. of natural gas equivalent.

	Annual Growth	09/11	09/12	09/13	09/14	09/15
Sales ($ mil.)	12.0%	45.0	48.5	62.9	84.4	70.9
Net income ($ mil.)	2.4%	8.5	7.4	14.0	25.0	9.3
Market value ($ mil.)	(13.1%)	469.8	507.9	468.3	988.7	267.6
Employees	2.5%	19	20	21	22	21

PANINI AMERICA INC.

2300 E. Randol Mill Rd.
Arlington TX 76011
Phone: 817-983-0300
Fax: 817-983-0400
Web: www.paniniamerica.net

CEO: Mark Warsop
CFO: Kelly Munsch
HR: –
FYE: December 31
Type: Private

For football and basketball fans it's all in the cards. Panini America formerly Donruss Playoff publishes sports trading cards under the names Donruss Playoff and Score. The company makes basketball cards as the official licensed trading card publisher for the NBA; it offers NFL cards through shared rights with rival Upper Deck. (It lost its Major League Baseball license in 2006.) The second oldest US card company Donruss was founded in 1954 by brothers Donald and Russel Weiner (the company's name is a combination of their first names — Don and Russ). In 2009 the company was acquired by Italian firm Panini Group a leading publisher of collectibles. Donruss was subsequently renamed Panini America.

PANTHER EXPEDITED SERVICES INC.

4940 Panther Pkwy.
Seville OH 44273
Phone: 330-769-5830
Fax: 330-725-4530
Web: www.pantherexpedite.com

CEO: R Louis Schneeberger
CFO: Bob Businger
HR: –
FYE: December 31
Type: Private

The prospect of moving freight is what makes this Panther pounce. Panther Expedited Services arranges the ground air and ocean transportation of time-sensitive cargo primarily for companies in the automotive and other manufacturing industries but also for government agencies and for other transportation companies. The company transports its 10000+ customers' freight globally through a network of some 1100 owner-operated vehicles 1600 third-party ground-carriers and 500 ocean and air cargo carriers. It also offers warehousing and logistics services. In 2012 Arkansas Best acquired the company from private equity firm Fenway Partners for about $180 million.

PANTRY INC. (THE)

NMS: PTRY

P.O. Box 8019, 305 Gregson Drive
Cary, NC 27511
Phone: 919 774-6700
Fax: –
Web: www.thepantry.com

CEO: –
CFO: –
HR: –
FYE: September 25
Type: Public

If you've ever passed through the Carolinas on business or made the drive to Disney World chances are The Pantry has provided fuel for your car and body. The company is the leading convenience store operator in the southeastern US with some 1500 shops in more than a dozen states. (Florida accounts for about a quarter of all sales.) Most of the company's stores do business under the Kangaroo Express banner; other names include Bean Street Coffee Celeste and Aunt M's. Branded fuel is sold under such names as Marathon BP and ExxonMobil. The stores sell cigarettes beverages candy gasoline magazines among other items. In 2014 the company agreed to be acquired by Alimentation Couche-Tard for $860 million.

	Annual Growth	09/10	09/11	09/12	09/13	09/14
Sales ($ mil.)	1.0%	7,265.3	8,138.5	8,253.2	7,822.0	7,545.7
Net income ($ mil.)	–	(165.6)	9.8	(2.5)	(3.0)	13.2
Market value ($ mil.)	(4.3%)	565.3	300.6	346.3	273.1	474.3
Employees	1.2%	14,419	13,928	13,709	14,903	15,140

PAPA JOHN'S INTERNATIONAL, INC.

NMS: PZZA

2002 Papa Johns Boulevard
Louisville, KY 40299-2367
Phone: 502 261-7272
Fax: –
Web: www.papajohns.com

CEO: John H. Schnatter
CFO: Lance F Tucker
HR: Caroli Miller Oyler
FYE: December 28
Type: Public

Papa John's International makes a lot of dough — pizza dough that is. The company operates the world's #3 pizza chain (behind YUM! Brands' Pizza Hut brand and Domino's) with around 4165 pizzerias across the US and in about 35 international markets. Its restaurants offer several different pizza styles and topping choices as well as a few specialty pies such as The Works and The Meats. Papa John's locations typically offer delivery and carry-out service only. The company owns and operates more than 695 locations while the rest are franchised. Founder and CEO John Schnatter owns more than 20% of the chain.

	Annual Growth	12/10	12/11	12/12	12/13	12/14
Sales ($ mil.)	9.1%	1,126.4	1,217.9	1,342.7	1,439.0	1,598.1
Net income ($ mil.)	9.0%	51.9	55.7	61.7	69.5	73.3
Market value ($ mil.)	19.1%	1,100.4	1,506.9	2,104.1	3,578.4	2,212.7
Employees	7.9%	16,000	16,500	18,800	20,700	21,700

PAPER CONVERTING MACHINE COMPANY

2300 S ASHLAND AVE
GREEN BAY, WI 543045213
Phone: 920-494-5601
Fax: –
Web: www.pcmc.com

CEO: –
CFO: –
HR: –
FYE: September 30
Type: Private

An empire built on paper: The Paper Converting Machine Company (PCMC) does just that — manufactures machinery for the converting packaging printing and laminating of paper. PCMC makes and sells equipment for tissue converting and packaging; wide-web flexo printing coating and laminating; coaters; roll engraving; and non-woven converting. Its equipment is used by manufacturers of flexible packaging non-woven disposable products (wet wipes) and sanitary tissues. PCMC is a division of manufacturing technology supplier Barry-Wehmiller Companies.

	Annual Growth	09/05	09/06	09/10	09/11	09/12
Sales ($ mil.)	4.4%	–	194.1	196.9	215.1	251.6
Net income ($ mil.)	–	–	–	0.0	0.0	0.0
Market value ($ mil.)	–	–	–	–	–	–
Employees	–	–	–	–	–	1,304

PAPERWORKS INDUSTRIES INC.

5000 Flat Rock Rd.
Philadelphia PA 19127
Phone: 215-984-7000
Fax: 215-984-7181
Web: www.paperworksindustries.com

CEO: Richard Leblanc
CFO: Mark Schlei
HR: –
FYE: December 31
Type: Private

PaperWorks Industries is knee deep in paper and that's the way it likes it. With mills in Pennsylvania and Indiana it is a North American producer of coated recycled paperboard (CRB) manufacturing about 300000 tons of it annually. Its MasterWorks product line includes everything from freezer-enhanced CRB to uncoated eco-friendly paperboard. End-use markets for CRB include beverages dry and frozen foods household goods and oral care products. In addition to its CRB offerings PaperWorks produces specialized folding cartons. The current iteration of PaperWorks Industries was formed when it merged with Specialized Packaging Group (SPG) in 2009. It is controlled by investment firm Sun Capital Partners.

PAPPAS RESTAURANTS INC.

642 Yale St.
Houston TX 77006
Phone: 713-869-0161
Fax: 713-869-4932
Web: www.pappas.com

CEO: –
CFO: –
HR: Danielle Geisler
FYE: December 31
Type: Private

Pappas Restaurants has several ways to please the palate. The company owns and operates more than 60 restaurants encompassing more than half a dozen different casual dining concepts including Pappadeaux Seafood Kitchen the Tex-Mex flavored Pappasito's Cantina and Pappas Bar-B-Q. Its casual-dining spots are located primarily in Texas with additional units operating in a half-dozen other states. Pappas Restaurants also has a couple of high-end Pappas Bros. Steakhouses as well as Pappas Burger gourmet hamburger joints. The family-owned company was started by Chris and Harris Pappas in 1976. The brothers also own 10% of Luby's and head the executive team of the Houston-based cafeteria chain.

PAR PACIFIC HOLDINGS INC

ASE: PARR

800 Gessner Road, Suite 875
Houston, TX 77024
Phone: 281 899-4800
Fax: –
Web: www.par-petro.com

CEO: Joseph Israel
CFO: Christopher Micklas
HR: –
FYE: December 31
Type: Public

After some rough years in the oil and gas business Par Petroleum (formerly Delta Petroleum) is looking to at least break even by exploring for oil and gas in the Rocky Mountains. In 2011 it reported reserves of 90.2 billion cu. ft. of natural gas equivalent 99% of which is in the Rocky Mountains. It had oil and gas leasehold properties covering approximately 30384 net undeveloped acres all in Colorado. As Delta Petroleum the company had built up heavy debts over several years and in 2011 it filed for Chapter 11 bankruptcy protection from which it emerged in 2012 as reorganized company with a new name Par Petroleum.

	Annual Growth	12/11*	08/12*	12/12	12/13	12/14
Sales ($ mil.)	265.1%	63.9	23.1	2.1	886.0	3,108.0
Net income ($ mil.)	–	(470.1)	(45.4)	(8.8)	(70.6)	(47.0)
Market value ($ mil.)	267.9%	–	–	44.5	82.7	602.4
Employees	162.2%	32	–	–	536	577

*Fiscal year change

PAR PHARMACEUTICAL COMPANIES INC.

NYSE: PRX

300 Tice Blvd.
Woodcliff Lake NJ 07677
Phone: 201-802-4000
Fax: 201-802-4600
Web: www.parpharm.com

CEO: –
CFO: –
HR: –
FYE: December 31
Type: Private

Generic drugs are par for the course for Par Pharmaceutical Companies. The company markets about 55 generic drugs with a focus on central nervous system cardiovascular and anti-inflammatory medications as well as infectious disease. The generic division manufactures some of its own products but it also distributes drugs manufactured by strategic partners. The company's Strativa division develops updated versions of off-patent branded drugs. Par markets product through its internal sales force mainly to wholesalers retail pharmacy and grocery chains and distributors across the US. Par Pharmaceutical was taken private by investment firm TPG in 2012.

PAR TECHNOLOGY CORP.

NYS: PAR

PAR Technology Park, 8383 Seneca Turnpike
New Hartford, NY 13413-4991
Phone: 315 738-0600
Fax: –
Web: www.partech.com

CEO: Karen E. Sammon
CFO: Michael Bartusek
HR: Denise Milde
FYE: December 31
Type: Public

PAR Technology is par for the course for fast food giants such as McDonald's and Yum! Brands. The company makes point-of-sale (POS) systems that are used to input and display orders by more than 50000 restaurants in some 110 countries. It also offers other software and hardware for restaurants as well as hotels resorts spas retailers entertainment venues and cruise ships. In addition through subsidiaries PAR Government Systems and Rome Research PAR Technology designs data processing systems and develops software for advanced radar and other detection systems used by the US Department of Defense (DOD) and other federal and state agencies. Most sales come from customers in the US.

	Annual Growth	12/10	12/11	12/12	12/13	12/14
Sales ($ mil.)	(0.7%)	239.9	229.4	245.2	241.4	233.6
Net income ($ mil.)	–	3.1	(15.5)	(0.3)	0.4	(3.7)
Market value ($ mil.)	1.9%	88.9	61.3	76.3	84.8	95.7
Employees	(5.6%)	1,538	1,408	1,382	1,301	1,221

PARADE PUBLICATIONS

711 3rd Ave.
New York NY 10017
Phone: 212-450-7000
Fax: 212-450-7284
Web: www.parade.com

CEO: Carlo Vittorini
CFO: –
HR: –
FYE: December 31
Type: Subsidiary

Every week more than 32 million homes see a Parade. Parade Publications publishes "Parade" a newsmagazine insert carried in the Sunday edition of nearly 450 newspapers across the US. Popular features of the publication include Personality Parade Ask Marilyn and In Step With. The first issue of Parade was published in 1941 and the first papers to distribute it were The Nashville Tennessean and The Washington Post. The Post is the magazine's oldest continuous subscriber. Other newspapers distributing Parade include the Boston Globe The Miami Herald and the Los Angeles Times. Publishing giant Advance Publications owns the company.

PARADIGM HOLDINGS INC.

OTC: PDHO

9715 Key West Ave. 3rd Fl.
Rockville MD 20850
Phone: 301-468-1200
Fax: 301-468-1201
Web: www.paradigmsolutions.com

CEO: J P London
CFO: –
HR: Julie Horner
FYE: December 31
Type: Public

Paradigm Holdings serves the big guns of big government. Through subsidiary Paradigm Solutions the company provides IT and database services including consulting systems integration network design project management and technical support. Additionally Paradigm offers custom software and database development and data center and facilities management services. Its key areas of focus are enterprise optimization enterprise solutions mission support and assurance and mission critical infrastructure. Public sector customers have included Homeland Security the State Dept. Defense Dept. Justice Dept. and the Treasury. Paradigm was acquired in 2011 by CACI for $61.5 million.

PARADISE, INC.

NBB: PARF

1200 Dr. Martin Luther King, Jr. Blvd.
Plant City, FL 33563
Phone: 813 752-1155
Fax: –
Web: www.paradisefruitco.com

CEO: Melvin S. Gordon
CFO: Jack M. Laskowitz
HR: –
FYE: December 31
Type: Public

Paradise and fruitcakes are holiday traditions right up there with visiting in-laws. The company is the largest US manufacturer and seller of glac-© fruits a mainstay ingredient in fruitcakes. It sells its dried and candied fruits to home bakers through supermarkets and other retail stores and less so to commercial bakers and foodservice operators under brands Paradise Mor-Fruit and White Swan (licensed) among several. Wal-Mart is the company's biggest customer; most sales are generated during September October and November. The company also makes molded plastic packaging for its products and for third parties through subsidiary Paradise Plastics. Chairman and CEO Melvin Gordon owns 37% of the company.

	Annual Growth	12/10	12/11	12/12	12/13	12/14
Sales ($ mil.)	1.2%	24.0	24.9	25.7	24.1	25.2
Net income ($ mil.)	(8.5%)	0.7	1.2	1.0	0.8	0.5
Market value ($ mil.)	11.8%	7.3	8.6	10.2	14.7	11.4
Employees	0.0%	275	275	275	275	275

PARAGON DEVELOPMENT SYSTEMS INC

1823 EXECUTIVE DR
OCONOMOWOC, WI 530664832
Phone: 262-569-5300
Fax: –

CEO: Craig Schiefelbein
CFO: Thomas Mount
HR: –
FYE: December 31
Type: Private

Paragon Development Systems (PDS) brings Midwestern roots and a nationwide reach to the technology services market. The company offers services ranging from procurement to systems integration reselling and supporting PCs networking equipment printers servers software and storage systems as part of its business. Its supplier list includes Cisco Systems Fujitsu Hewlett-Packard IBM and Microsoft. Paragon also builds and markets its own PCs under the Infinity Vector and Vision brand names. Founded in 1986 PDS partners with US-based medium and large enterprises in a variety of markets such as healthcare corporate government and education.

	Annual Growth	12/04	12/05	12/06	12/07	12/08
Sales ($ mil.)	13.3%	–	94.4	91.1	113.0	137.2
Net income ($ mil.)	–	–	–	(0.3)	2.3	6.9
Market value ($ mil.)	–	–	–	–	–	–
Employees	–	–	–	–	–	260

PARAGON REAL ESTATE EQUITY & INVESTMENT TRUST

NBB: PRLE

10011 Valley Forge Drive
Houston, TX 77042
Phone: 440 283-6319
Fax: –
Web: www.prgreit.com

CEO: James C Mastandrea
CFO: John J Dee
HR: –
FYE: December 31
Type: Public

Ideally Paragon Real Estate Equity and Investment Trust would be the very model of real estate investing but it merely is a corporate shell company. The firm is seeking investment opportunities in land development joint ventures other real estate companies and retail office industrial and hospitality properties. In 2008 it began investing in stock of publicly traded real estate investment trusts (REITs). Entities associated with CEO James Mastandrea control more than three-quarters of Paragon which has expressed doubts about its ability to continue as a going concern and may seek additional investors or sell its corporate shell.

	Annual Growth	12/09	12/10	12/11	12/12	12/13
Sales ($ mil.)	(54.7%)	0.0	0.0	0.0	0.0	0.0
Net income ($ mil.)	–	(0.1)	(0.0)	(0.0)	(0.1)	(0.1)
Market value ($ mil.)	–	0.0	0.0	0.1	0.1	0.3
Employees	0.0%	2	2	2	2	2

PARAGON SOLUTIONS INC.

25 COMMERCE DR STE 100
CRANFORD, NJ 070163615
Phone: 908-709-6767
Fax: –
Web: www.consultparagon.com

CEO: Daniel J. (Dan) Connor
CFO: –
HR: –
FYE: December 31
Type: Private

Paragon Solutions sees itself as a model provider of technical consulting and IT services. The privately-owned company specializes in helping businesses identify enterprise software products that best suit their needs and providing systems integration services to install and support the applications. It also offers such other services as content management document management and data archiving. Paragon focuses on the communications financial services health care insurance and life sciences industries. Customers have included Time Warner Cable Credit Suisse and Merck.

	Annual Growth	12/09	12/10	12/11	12/12	12/13
Sales ($ mil.)	(1.8%)	–	67.8	72.4	76.5	64.1
Net income ($ mil.)	(62.7%)	–	–	1.2	3.5	0.2
Market value ($ mil.)	–	–	–	–	–	–
Employees	–	–	–	–	–	400

PARAGON TECHNOLOGIES INC

NBB: PGNT

101 Larry Holmes Drive, Suite 500
Easton, PA 18042
Phone: 610 252-3205
Fax: 610 252-3102
Web: www.pgntgroup.com

CEO: Hesham M. Gad
CFO: Deborah Mertz
HR: –
FYE: December 31
Type: Public

Paragon Technologies produces automated order picking systems and other order fulfilling products used by manufacturing assembly and order distribution customers. Also known by its major brand name SI Systems the company supplies customers with horizontal transportation and conveyor systems related computer software and other products and services used for improving productivity. Customers are located primarily in the US and have included Caterpillar engine giant Cummins General Motors and contact lense manufacturer Vistakon (a subsidiary of Johnson & Johnson). The company was founded in 1958.

	Annual Growth	12/10	12/11	12/12	12/13	12/14
Sales ($ mil.)	(4.5%)	8.0	8.5	8.9	11.6	6.7
Net income ($ mil.)	–	(1.1)	0.2	(0.3)	(1.8)	(0.4)
Market value ($ mil.)	(24.0%)	4.5	5.0	4.0	4.4	1.5
Employees	3.0%	33	34	–	–	–

PARAMOUNT GOLD & SILVER CORP

ASE: PZG

665 Anderson Street
Winnemucca, NV 89445
Phone: 775 625-3600
Fax: –
Web: www.paramountgold.com

CEO: Christopher Crupi
CFO: Carlo A Buffone
HR: –
FYE: June 30
Type: Public

Paramount Gold and Silver is all about the bling. The development-stage company explores for gold silver and other metals in Mexico and Nevada gold-producing regions. Through subsidiary Paramount Gold de Mexico the company owns 100% of a 450000-acre property in Chihuahua that includes seven advanced stage gold mines. It also owns the Sleeper project in Nevada a 30-square mile site that produced gold and silver from 1986 to 1996. The company is conducting exploration drilling and geological surveys but has no proved reserves. Paramount also holds several earlier stage smaller claims in Nevada and inactive subsidiaries in Mexico and Peru. CEO Christopher Crupi founded the company in 2005.

	Annual Growth	06/10	06/11	06/12	06/13	06/14
Sales ($ mil.)	41.1%	0.0	0.3	0.1	4.5	0.1
Net income ($ mil.)	–	(5.4)	(28.5)	(12.1)	(13.5)	(11.1)
Market value ($ mil.)	(7.3%)	206.9	518.9	382.0	189.4	152.8
Employees	(9.6%)	30	40	40	20	20

PARATEK PHARMACEUTICALS INC

NMS: PRTK

75 Park Plaza
Boston, MA 02116
Phone: 617 807-6600
Fax: 650 228-1088
Web: www.transcept.com

CEO: Michael F. Bigham
CFO: Douglas W. Pagᵛn
HR: –
FYE: December 31
Type: Public

Transcept Pharmaceuticals may not make a bitter pill easier to swallow but it'll make the pill more effective once you swallow it. The company's drug delivery technology enhances absorption rates of active drug agents reducing absorption times as well as the time it takes for the drug to take effect. Transcept targets medications where rapid absorption would significantly benefit treatment including central nervous system and psychiatric disorders. Its first commercial product Intermezzo is a quick-acting low-dosage medication for treating insomnia that occurs in the middle of the night; it launched in 2012. Transcept contracts with third parties for manufacturing and sales.

	Annual Growth	12/10	12/11	12/12	12/13	12/14
Sales ($ mil.)	(23.2%)	12.5	19.7	9.6	(5.1)	4.3
Net income ($ mil.)	–	(9.3)	(3.9)	(12.0)	(27.4)	(17.8)
Market value ($ mil.)	51.1%	106.7	112.9	64.2	48.4	555.8
Employees	(19.5%)	31	17	15	8	13

PARATEK PHARMACEUTICALS INC.

75 Kneeland St.
Boston MA 02111-1901
Phone: 617-275-0040
Fax: 617-275-0039
Web: www.paratekpharm.com

CEO: –
CFO: –
HR: –
FYE: December 31
Type: Private

Paratek Pharmaceuticals wants to teach an old drug new tricks. The development-stage company is working to create new forms of antibiotic compound tetracycline that will be effective against newly resistant strains of bacteria. Its lead antibiotic candidate omadacycline is in clinical trials for the treatment of complicated bacterial skin infections pneumonia and urinary tract infections in the hospital setting. The company also has preclinical and clinical research programs on potential treatments for certain inflammatory and neurodegenerative conditions such as acne rosacea multiple sclerosis and rheumatoid arthritis. Paratek filed to go public in 2012.

PARATURE INC.

13625 Dulles Technology Dr. Ste. B
Herndon VA 20171
Phone: 703-564-7758
Fax: 703-564-7757
Web: www.parature.com

CEO: Ching Ho Fung
CFO: Daniel Yoo
HR: –
FYE: December 31
Type: Private

Parature just wants to help you help your customers. The company develops help desk and customer service support software used to manage internal and external technical support and other customer support functions. Its software includes applications for help desk tracking customer self servicing managing online discussion boards and forums and conducting online surveys. Parature's customers include educational institutions government agencies and businesses; Office Depot Sage Software Florida State University and Blackboard have all been clients of the company. Parature also offers professional services including consulting support implementation and training.

PAREXEL INTERNATIONAL CORP.

NMS: PRXL

195 West Street
Waltham, MA 02451
Phone: 781 487-9900
Fax: –

CEO: Josef H. von Rickenbach
CFO: Ingo Bank
HR: Mark Williams
FYE: June 30
Type: Public

PAREXEL International excels in pharmaceutical development services. A top contract research organization (CRO) the firm counts among its clients some of the world's largest drug biotech and medical device firms. Its Clinical Research Services segment provides clinical trial and data management study design patient recruitment biostatistical analysis clinical pharmacology and industry training and publishing. PAREXEL Consulting Services (PCS) handles the non-clinical aspects of drug development regulatory affairs and new product launches. Its Perceptive Informatics (PI) unit offers information technology systems and services that help manage clinical trials.

	Annual Growth	06/11	06/12	06/13	06/14	06/15
Sales ($ mil.)	13.1%	1,422.4	1,618.2	1,996.0	2,266.3	2,330.3
Net income ($ mil.)	31.9%	48.8	63.2	96.0	129.1	147.8
Market value ($ mil.)	28.5%	1,301.4	1,559.3	2,539.2	2,918.7	3,552.3
Employees	15.2%	10,550	12,695	14,700	15,560	18,600

PARK BANCORP, INC.

NBB: PFED

5400 South Pulaski Road
Chicago, IL 60632
Phone: 773 582-8616
Fax: –
Web: www.parkfed.com

CEO: David A Remijas
CFO: Victor E Caputo
HR: Laura Trujillo
FYE: December 31
Type: Public

Looking for a place to park your money? Try Park Bancorp the holding company for Park Federal Savings Bank. The community-oriented bank serves Chicago and Westmont Illinois through about five offices. It offers deposit products such as checking and savings accounts CDs and IRAs. Its lending activities focus on residential mortgages (one- to two-family residential mortgages account for nearly 60% of its loan portfolio and multifamily mortgages represent more than 15%). Other loan products include commercial real estate mortgages and land construction and consumer loans. Chicago-based Royal Financial Inc. agreed to buy Park Bancorp for $240 thousand in early 2016.

	Annual Growth	12/10	12/11	12/12	12/13	12/14
Assets ($ mil.)	(7.3%)	211.8	198.4	188.6	173.6	156.1
Net income ($ mil.)	–	(5.4)	(3.9)	(4.3)	(2.0)	(2.3)
Market value ($ mil.)	(36.5%)	4.3	2.4	1.6	1.5	0.7
Employees	–	57	–	–	–	–

PARK CITY GROUP INC

NAS: PCYG

299 South Main Street, Suite 2370
Salt Lake City, UT 84111
Phone: 435 645-2000
Fax: –
Web: www.parkcitygroup.com

CEO: Randall K. (Randy) Fields
CFO: Edward L. Clissold
HR: –
FYE: June 30
Type: Public

Park City Group understands that managing complex retail operations is no picnic. The company supplies retailers with operation management software used to optimize supply chains. Park City sells to supermarkets convenience stores and specialty retailers. Its software packages include Fresh Market Manager Supply Chain Profit Link and ActionManager. The company counts Circle K The Home Depot Williams-Sonoma and L Brands among its customers. Park City was founded by chairman and CEO Randy Fields who also co-founded Mrs. Fields Cookies. Fields controls almost half of Park City Group's stock.

	Annual Growth	06/11	06/12	06/13	06/14	06/15
Sales ($ mil.)	6.1%	10.8	10.1	11.3	11.9	13.6
Net income ($ mil.)	–	(0.2)	(0.9)	0.3	(2.5)	(3.8)
Market value ($ mil.)	27.1%	89.7	74.6	143.1	205.6	233.9
Employees	6.4%	53	48	48	57	68

PARK CORPORATION

6200 Riverside Dr.
Cleveland OH 44135
Phone: 216-267-4870
Fax: 216-267-7876
Web: www.parkcorp.com

CEO: –
CFO: Joseph J Adams
HR: Laura Sedor
FYE: December 31
Type: Private

Park Corporation has a division for all seasons. Areas of involvement for the privately held company span the manufacture of machinery and components for the steel and energy industries; the distribution of metalworking and mining equipment; the sale of integrated steel products; and service of oil refining and power generation operations. Other areas include private aircraft services convention and trade show services commercial and industrial real estate development and fixed-income and private equity investments. The company is owned by Cleveland financier Ray Park.

PARK ELECTROCHEMICAL CORP.

NYS: PKE

48 South Service Road
Melville, NY 11747
Phone: 631 465-3600
Fax: –
Web: www.parkelectro.com

CEO: Brian E. Shore
CFO: Matthew Farabaugh
HR: –
FYE: March 01
Type: Public

Printed circuit board manufacturer Park Electrochemical has parked its manufacturing facilities in Asia Europe and North America. The company's Nelco brand of copper-clad laminates and reinforced composite materials are used to make printed circuit boards and other components for laptop computers cellular phones satellite switching systems and other electronics. Park also makes engineered materials include composites for electronics aerospace and industrial markets. About half of Park's sales in fiscal year 2014 came from Asia and Europe.

	Annual Growth	02/11	02/12*	03/13	03/14	03/15
Sales ($ mil.)	(6.5%)	211.7	193.3	176.4	165.8	162.1
Net income ($ mil.)	(11.5%)	32.6	23.4	17.0	(42.3)	20.0
Market value ($ mil.)	(9.2%)	664.3	626.8	524.3	593.5	452.3
Employees	(6.9%)	614	613	535	523	461

*Fiscal year change

PARK NATIONAL CORP. (NEWARK, OH)

ASE: PRK

50 North Third Street
Newark, OH 43055
Phone: 740 349-8451
Fax: –
Web: www.parknationalcorp.com

CEO: David L. Trautman
CFO: Brady T. Burt
HR: –
FYE: December 31
Type: Public

Customers can park their money with Park National. The holding company owns Park National Bank which operates more than 120 branches in Ohio and northern Kentucky through 11 community banking divisions. The banks provide an array of consumer and business banking services including traditional savings and checking accounts and CDs. Business loans including commercial leases and mortgages operating loans and agricultural loans account for about 35% of Park National's loan portfolio. The banks also originate consumer residential real estate and construction loans. Park National's nonbank units include consumer finance outfit Guardian Finance Scope Aircraft Finance and Park Title Agency.

	Annual Growth	12/10	12/11	12/12	12/13	12/14
Assets ($ mil.)	(1.0%)	7,298.4	6,972.2	6,642.8	6,638.3	7,003.3
Net income ($ mil.)	3.2%	74.2	82.1	78.6	77.2	84.1
Market value ($ mil.)	5.0%	1,118.6	1,001.4	994.8	1,309.4	1,361.9
Employees	(2.2%)	1,969	1,920	1,826	1,836	1,801

PARK NICOLLET HEALTH SERVICES

3800 Park Nicollet Blvd.
Minneapolis MN 55416
Phone: 952-993-9900
Fax: 952-993-1392
Web: www.parknicollet.com

CEO: David K Wessner
CFO: David J Cooke
HR: –
FYE: December 31
Type: Private - Not-for-Pr

Park Nicollet Health Services helps Twin Cities medical patients get back on their feet and onto the playground. Park Nicollet operates Methodist Hospital a 425-bed acute care facility that offers a full range of medical and surgical care. It also runs about 30 Park Nicollet Clinic facilities in the Minneapolis/St. Paul metropolitan area that provide primary and specialty care services including cancer treatment and outpatient surgery. Additionally Park Nicollet Health Services operates the Park Nicollet Institute which performs medical research. In 2012 Park Nicollet agreed to merge with HealthPartners a Twin Cities health plan and hospital network operator.

PARK PLACE DEALERSHIPS

6113 Lemmon Ave.
Dallas TX 75209
Phone: 214-526-8701
Fax: 214-443-8270
Web: www.parkplacetexas.com

CEO: Ken Schnitzer
CFO: –
HR: –
FYE: December 31
Type: Private

Park Place Motorcars sells pricey vehicles befitting its high society name. The company operates more than a dozen Texas dealerships in the greater Dallas/Fort Worth area that sell luxury car brands such as Bentley Jaguar Lexus Maserati Maybach Rolls-Royce and Volvo. It also sells smart cars. One Dallas area Park Place dealership sells its Mercedes-Benz and Porsche vehicles in a new 70000 sq. ft. showroom and houses the rest in a 400000 sq. ft. three-story garage. The company's locations also offer used (make that pre-owned) cars service and parts. Park Place Motorcars was founded in 1987. In 2007 the company purchased a Lexus dealership in Mission Viejo California its first outside of Texas.

PARK STERLING CORP

NMS: PSTB

1043 E. Morehead Street, Suite 201
Charlotte, NC 28204
Phone: 704 716-2134
Fax: –
Web: www.parksterlingbank.com

CEO: James C. Cherry
CFO: Donald K. (Don) Truslow
HR: –
FYE: December 31
Type: Public

Park Sterling Corporation owns Park Sterling Bank and CapitalBank community banks with about two dozen branches in North and South Carolina. The banks offer checking and savings accounts to individuals as well as small and midsized businesses such as real estate development and construction firms. With only a few locations the bank emphasizes its customer service. Commercial real estate and construction loans account for more than half of its loan portfolio. Residential mortgages and home equity loans make up another quarter and business loans account for about 10%. The first Park Sterling Bank opened in 2006. In 2012 the company agreed to merge with Citizens South Banking Corporation.

	Annual Growth	12/10	12/11	12/12	12/13	12/14
Assets ($ mil.)	39.9%	616.1	1,113.2	2,032.6	1,960.8	2,359.2
Net income ($ mil.)	–	(7.9)	(8.4)	4.3	15.3	12.9
Market value ($ mil.)	4.4%	277.2	183.0	234.6	320.3	329.7
Employees	69.3%	65	270	482	490	534

PARK-OHIO HOLDINGS CORP.

NMS: PKOH

6065 Parkland Boulevard
Cleveland, OH 44124
Phone: 440 947-2000
Fax: –
Web: www.pkoh.com

CEO: Edward F. Crawford
CFO: Patrick W. Fogarty
HR: –
FYE: December 31
Type: Public

Park-Ohio Holdings troubleshoots industrial supply chain logistics issues and makes a slew of fasteners and other industrial components. The company straddles three business segments: Supply Technologies sources and procures production components for OEMs in industries ranging from automotive to aerospace; Engineered Products produces specialized systems and parts used in such industrial applications as coatings forging oil and gas and rail; and the Assembly Components unit casts and machines metal parts — knuckles oil pans cylinders — used by auto agricultural construction and marine OEMs.

	Annual Growth	12/10	12/11	12/12	12/13	12/14
Sales ($ mil.)	14.1%	813.5	966.6	1,134.0	1,203.2	1,378.7
Net income ($ mil.)	31.6%	15.2	29.4	31.8	43.4	45.6
Market value ($ mil.)	31.8%	261.4	223.0	266.4	655.0	787.8
Employees	98.7%	385	3,200	3,800	5,000	6,000

PARKDALE MILLS INCORPORATED

531 Cotton Blossom Cir.
Gastonia NC 28054-5245
Phone: 704-874-5000
Fax: 704-874-5175
Web: www.parkdalemills.com

CEO: Anderson W Warlick
CFO: Cecelia Meade
HR: Cathy Greene
FYE: September 30
Type: Private

In an industry where margins are thread-thin Parkdale Mills spins cotton into cash. The North Carolina-based company is the largest privately owned yarn spinner in the US. It manufactures cotton and cotton-polyester blend yarns and specializes in spun yarn that winds up in such goods as sheets towels underwear and jeans. Parkdale Mills' global slate of customers include Jockey International Lands' End L.L. Bean and Springmaid. The company operates and owns 66% of Parkdale America a joint venture with polyester and nylon yarn maker Unifi. The company has about two dozen plants in the US Colombia and Mexico and a fiber research center. Its cotton consumption represents 30% of total US cotton demand.

PARKE BANCORP INC

NAS: PKBK

601 Delsea Drive
Washington Township, NJ 08080
Phone: 856 256-2500
Fax: –
Web: www.parkebank.com

CEO: Vito S Pantilione
CFO: John F Hawkins
HR: –
FYE: December 31
Type: Public

Community banking is a walk in the park for Parke Bancorp holding company for Parke Bank which has three branches in the New Jersey communities of Sewell and Northfield as well as two loan production offices in the Philadelphia area. The bank provides such traditional products as checking and savings accounts money market and individual retirement accounts and certificates of deposit. Parke Bank has a strong focus on business lending — including operating loans commercial mortgages and construction loans — which accounts for about 90% of the company's loan portfolio. The bank also writes residential real estate and consumer loans.

	Annual Growth	12/10	12/11	12/12	12/13	12/14
Assets ($ mil.)	2.1%	756.9	790.7	770.5	794.9	821.7
Net income ($ mil.)	9.3%	7.3	7.3	7.3	7.6	10.5
Market value ($ mil.)	3.7%	60.0	32.7	29.8	53.4	69.3
Employees	3.5%	61	58	74	79	70

PARKER DRILLING CO.

NYS: PKD

5 Greenway Plaza, Suite 100
Houston, TX 77046
Phone: 281 406-2000
Fax: 281 406-2001
Web: www.parkerdrilling.com

CEO: Gary G. Rich
CFO: Christopher T. (Chris) Weber
HR: –
FYE: December 31
Type: Public

Parker Drilling parks its oil rigs off the beaten path. Its helicopter-transportable rigs allow drillers to work in otherwise inaccessible desert mountain and remote jungle locations. Its barge rigs allow the company to drill in transition zones (such as bays and marshes). Parker Drilling owns 22 international land rigs and 18 US-based barge drilling rigs in the Gulf of Mexico and two land rigs in Alaska. Subsidiary Quail Tools provides rental tools for oil and gas drilling and workover activities with operations in the Gulf Coast the Rocky Mountains and West Texas regions. Parker Drilling also has project management and drilling rig construction units.

	Annual Growth	12/10	12/11	12/12	12/13	12/14
Sales ($ mil.)	10.1%	659.5	686.6	678.0	874.2	968.7
Net income ($ mil.)	–	(14.5)	(50.5)	37.3	27.0	23.5
Market value ($ mil.)	(9.5%)	557.7	875.1	561.4	992.2	374.7
Employees	14.4%	2,011	2,317	2,085	3,395	3,443

PARKER HANNIFIN CORP.
NYS: PH

6035 Parkland Boulevard
Cleveland, OH 44124-4141
Phone: 216 896-3000
Fax: –
Web: www.parker.com

CEO: Thomas L. (Tom) Williams
CFO: Jon P. Marten
HR: Daniel S. (Dan) Serbin
FYE: June 30
Type: Public

Parker-Hannifin operates on a big scale (its motion control equipment helped sink a replica of the Titanic in the Academy Award-winning film.) Operating through two business segments — Diversified Industrial and Aerospace — Parker-Hannifin is a leading global manufacturer of motion and control technologies including fluid power systems for the manufacturing and processing industries; hydraulic fuel pneumatic and electromechanical systems and components for the aerospace/defense industry; and motion and control systems for the heating ventilation air conditioning and refrigeration (HVACR) and transportation industries. The company traces its historical roots back to 1918.

	Annual Growth	06/11	06/12	06/13	06/14	06/15
Sales ($ mil.)	0.7%	12,345.9	13,145.9	13,015.7	13,216.0	12,711.7
Net income ($ mil.)	(1.1%)	1,057.2	1,155.5	948.8	1,041.4	1,012.6
Market value ($ mil.)	6.7%	12,434.3	10,652.4	13,218.5	17,421.0	16,118.5
Employees	(1.6%)	58,400	59,300	58,150	57,450	54,754

PARKERVISION INC.
NAS: PRKR

7915 Baymeadows Way, Suite 400
Jacksonville, FL 32256
Phone: 904 732-6100
Fax: –
Web: www.parkervision.com

CEO: Jeffrey L Parker
CFO: Cynthia L Poehlman
HR: –
FYE: December 31
Type: Public

Parkervision is more about sound than sight. The company develops radio frequency integrated circuits (RFICs) for use in wireless networking. The company has produced limited numbers of its chips through contract manufacturers but it has not recorded a sale in recent years. If it did the chips could be in mobile handsets tablets data cards femtocells machine-to-machine communications embedded applications even military radios and cable modems. ParkerVision was founded in 1989 by CEO Jeffery Parker. In 2014 it retained advisory firm 3LP Advisors to help execute a licensing strategy and get its business off the ground.

	Annual Growth	12/10	12/11	12/12	12/13	12/14
Sales ($ mil.)	–	0.1	0.0	0.0	0.0	0.0
Net income ($ mil.)	–	(15.0)	(14.6)	(20.3)	(27.9)	(23.6)
Market value ($ mil.)	18.7%	44.6	83.6	197.3	442.2	88.4
Employees	0.5%	48	49	49	50	49

PARKLAND HEALTH & HOSPITAL SYSTEM

5201 Harry Hines Blvd.
Dallas TX 75235
Phone: 214-590-8000
Fax: 214-590-8096
Web: www.parklandhospital.com

CEO: Frederick Cerise
CFO: John Moore
HR: –
FYE: September 30
Type: Private - Not-for-Pr

Many people know Parkland Health and Hospital System (PHHS) as Parkland Memorial Hospital the hospital where JFK died. Parkland Memorial sits at the heart of the health system and is Dallas' only public hospital. PHHS manages a network of 11 community clinics as well as Parkland Community Health Plan a regional HMO for Medicaid and CHIP (Children's Health Insurance Program) members. The system also offers HEALTHplus a medical assistance program for uninsured Dallas County residents. Parkland Memorial Hospital has more than 670 beds and is the primary teaching institution of The University of Texas Southwestern Medical Center.

PARKWAY PROPERTIES INC.
NYS: PKY

Bank of America Center, 390 North Orange Avenue, Suite 2400
Orlando, FL 32801
Phone: 407 650-0593
Fax: –
Web: www.pky.com

CEO: James R. (Jim) Heistand
CFO: David R. O'Reilly
HR: –
FYE: December 31
Type: Public

Parkway Properties knows its way around office spaces. The self-administered real estate investment trust (REIT) acquires owns and operates office properties throughout the Sunbelt region. Parkway owns or has an interest in more than 40 office properties with 10 million sq. ft. of leasable space in 10 states. Nearly a third of its portfolio is held through discretionary funds and joint venture partnerships through which the REIT receives fees for providing asset property and construction management. These services are offered through its subsidiary Parkway Realty Services which manages and leases offices for both its parent and third-parties.

	Annual Growth	12/10	12/11	12/12	12/13	12/14
Sales ($ mil.)	15.5%	256.3	165.9	226.5	291.6	456.7
Net income ($ mil.)	–	(2.6)	(126.9)	(39.4)	(19.7)	42.9
Market value ($ mil.)	1.2%	2,020.8	1,137.3	1,613.6	2,224.9	2,121.1
Employees	5.9%	256	341	286	326	322

PARKWEST MEDICAL CENTER

9352 PARK WEST BLVD
KNOXVILLE, TN 379234387
Phone: 865-373-1000
Fax: –
Web: www.treatedwell.com

CEO: –
CFO: Scott Hamilton
HR: –
FYE: December 31
Type: Private

Parkwest Medical Center is a wholly-owned subsidiary of Covenant Health and the largest medical center in West Knoxville. Parkwest has more than 285 beds and provides health care services to patients of Knox County Tennessee. Its various specialties include cardiology orthopedics neurology and spine care women's services and bariatric surgery. Other services include cardiac rehabilitation diagnostic services outpatient surgery and senior health care. Parkwest's facilities include a 40-bed emergency care center a 30-bed critical care unit and a 20-suite childbirth center. The medical center also has a diabetes center and provides dental care.

	Annual Growth	12/02	12/03	12/04	12/05	12/13
Sales ($ mil.)	(1.3%)	–	384.8	172.8	172.8	337.2
Net income ($ mil.)	20.8%	–	–	5.4	5.4	29.6
Market value ($ mil.)	–	–	–	–	–	–
Employees	–	–	–	–	–	1,300

PARLUX FRAGRANCES LLC
NASDAQ: PARL

5900 N. Andrews Ave. Ste. 500
Fort Lauderdale FL 33309
Phone: 954-316-9008
Fax: 954-316-9152
Web: www.parlux.com

CEO: –
CFO: –
HR: –
FYE: January 31
Type: Subsidiary

If scents could speak Parlux Fragrances (from the French verb parler) might be its lexicon. The fragrance and beauty products designer and manufacturer owns and licenses to third-party manufacturers the perfumes and beauty-related products of a handful of celeb brand names including Paris Hilton Jessica Simpson Marc Ecko Nicole Miller Queen Latifah Rhianna and others. Parlux markets designer and other fragrance blends that are sold primarily through national department stores (Belk Macy's Boscov's) and 340 Perfumania retail stores in the US. Distributors from Canada to the Caribbean cater to retailers mainly perfumeries in 80 countries. Partner fragrance purveyor Perfumania acquired Parlux in 2012.

PARRON-HALL CORPORATION

7700 RONSON RD STE 100	CEO: –
SAN DIEGO, CA 921111553	CFO: –
Phone: 858-268-1212	HR: –
Fax: –	FYE: December 31
Web: www.parronhall.com	Type: Private

This company can outfit your conference room waiting area and hall. Parron-Hall which does business as Parron Hall Office Interiors sells office furniture to customers in the San Diego area. The company's inventory includes products manufactured by such companies as Kimball and Knoll as well as HON Humanscale and izzydesign. Parron Hall also offers space planning installation warehousing and maintenance services. Customers include California Highway Patrol Anheuser-Busch Garden Fresh Restaurant Corp. and Qualcomm. The company was founded in 1947 but grew out of a business founded in the 1880s by the great great grandfather of company president James Herr.

	Annual Growth	12/09	12/10	12/11	12/12	12/13
Sales ($ mil.)	(7.2%)	–	38.8	40.2	29.0	31.0
Net income ($ mil.)	(46.9%)	–	–	1.2	0.3	0.3
Market value ($ mil.)	–	–	–	–	–	–
Employees	–	–	–	–	–	49

PARSONS ENVIRONMENT & INFRASTRUCTURE GROUP INC.

4701 HEDGEMORE DR	CEO: –
CHARLOTTE, NC 282093281	CFO: Leslie Bradley
Phone: 704-529-6246	HR: –
Fax: –	FYE: July 29
Web: www.parsons.com	Type: Private

A unit of Parsons Corporation Parsons Commercial Technology Group (PARCOMM) provides project management engineering construction design maintenance and related services for industrial and commercial projects. The company's clients include firms in the telecommunications health care manufacturing defense petroleum and chemical industries. PARCOMM also completes projects for schools colleges and government entities. Specialized services include industrial environmental remediation factory modernization and developing state vehicle inspection and compliance programs. PARCOMM operates throughout the US and the world.

	Annual Growth	12/09	12/10	12/11	12/12*	07/14
Sales ($ mil.)	7.2%	–	518.5	443.1	684.1	684.1
Net income ($ mil.)	–	–	–	(57.2)	(12.0)	(12.0)
Market value ($ mil.)	–	–	–	–	–	–
Employees	–	–	–	–	–	1,205
						*Fiscal year change

PARSONS INFRASTRUCTURE & TECHNOLOGY GROUP INC.

100 W. Walnut St.	CEO: Charles Harrington
Pasadena CA 91124	CFO: –
Phone: 626-440-2000	HR: James Brookhouser
Fax: 626-440-2630	FYE: December 31
	Type: Business Segment

Parsons Infrastructure & Technology Group is one of the largest members of the Parsons Corporation congregation. The unit provides a range of construction-related services including project planning construction management engineering and start-up and commissioning operations. Parsons Infrastructure & Technology Group is regularly awarded contracts by local and regional government agencies as well as the US Army involving environmental cleanup and chemical neutralization projects across the country. It has also undertaken facilities management work for the US Department of Homeland Security.

PARSONS TRANSPORTATION GROUP INC.

100 M St. SE Ste. 1200	CEO: Charles L Harrington
Washington DC 20003-3520	CFO: Curtis A Bower
Phone: 202-775-3300	HR: –
Fax: 202-775-3422	FYE: December 31
Web: www.parsons.com/about/bus_unit/gbu/transprt/de	Type: Subsidiary

Parsons Transportation Group helps make sure the planes trains and automobiles of the world can get where they need to go. The company provides engineering construction management and maintenance services for infrastructure projects including airports railroads highways and tunnels. In addition to handling large-scale building projects Parsons Transportation Group offers expertise in revenue collection and management systems communication and control systems engineering and transportation planning services. It serves public and private customers around the world. Parsons Transportation Group is a business unit of engineering giant Parsons Corporation.

PARTNERS HEALTHCARE SYSTEM INC.

Prudential Tower 800 Boylston St. 11th Fl.	CEO: –
Boston MA 02199-8001	CFO: –
Phone: 617-278-1000	HR: –
Fax: 617-278-1049	FYE: September 30
Web: www.partners.org	Type: Private - Not-for-Pr

Partners HealthCare System is looking out for the health of the Bay State. Partners HealthCare includes two large acute-care medical centers — Brigham and Women's Hospital and Massachusetts General Hospital — and six community hospitals. The system also provides primary and specialty care through clinics physician offices long-term care facilities and home health and hospice agencies. Its rehabilitation facilities include the Spaulding Rehabilitation Hospital Network. Partners HealthCare also provides medical training and research through an affiliation with Harvard. Other ventures include the Dana-Farber/Partners CancerCare clinic (a collaboration with Harvard and Dana-Farber Cancer Institute).

PASADENA HOSPITAL ASSOCIATION

100 W CALIFORNIA BLVD	CEO: Stephen A Ralph
PASADENA, CA 91105-3010	CFO: Jim Noble
Phone: 626-397-5000	HR: –
Fax: –	FYE: December 31
Web: www.huntingtonhospital.com	Type: Private

No need to hunt for medical care if you're near Huntington Hospital. The not-for-profit Pasadena Hospital Association which does business as Huntington Hospital provides health care to residents of the San Gabriel Valley in Southern California. Founded in 1892 the hospital boasts some 625 beds and offers acute medical and surgical care and community services in a number of specialties including cardiology gastroenterology women's and children's health orthopedics and neurology. It engages in clinical cancer research (as well as diagnosis and treatment) through the Huntington Cancer Center. The hospital is also a teaching facility for the University of Southern California (USC) Keck School of Medicine.

	Annual Growth	12/00	12/01	12/02	12/04	12/09
Sales ($ mil.)	8.4%	–	257.2	309.9	384.5	492.0
Net income ($ mil.)	52.6%	–	3.0	(0.2)	68.3	89.6
Market value ($ mil.)	–	–	–	–	–	–
Employees	–	–	–	–	–	2,800

PASCHALL TRUCK LINES INC.

3443 US Hwy. 641 S.
Murray KY 42071
Phone: 270-753-1717
Fax: 818-909-6070
Web: www.uwink.com

CEO: –
CFO: Charles Wilson
HR: –
FYE: December 31
Type: Private

Truckload carrier Paschall Truck Lines offers freight transportation services throughout the US. It operates a fleet of about 1200 tractors and 3000 trailers from a network of about 60 facilities mainly in the eastern half of the country but also in the Southwest and in California. Major terminals are located in Indiana North Carolina Tennessee and Texas (including four facilities on the US-Mexico border). Paschall Truck Lines hauls a wide range of goods including appliances chemicals foods and home products. The company was founded in 1937.

PATELCO CREDIT UNION

156 2nd St.
San Francisco CA 94105
Phone: 415-442-6200
Fax: 415-442-6245
Web: www.patelco.com

CEO: Erin Mendez
CFO: Sue Gruber
HR: –
FYE: December 31
Type: Private - Not-for-Pr

Just as communication from afar has progressed from smoke signals and carrier pigeons to today's World Wide Web Patelco Credit Union has evolved as well. Founded in 1936 it has grown from a five-member organization with $500 in assets serving employees of Pacific Telephone and Telegraph to a nearly 270000-member credit union serving employees with assets now totaling more than $3.6 billion. A telephone company credit union until 1983 Patelco Credit Union provides deposit lending insurance and investment services as well as credit cards debit cards and online banking. It operates through 40 branches in Northern California.

PASSUR AEROSPACE, INC.

NBB: PSSR

One Landmark Square, Suite 1900
Stamford, CT 06901
Phone: 203 622-4086
Fax: –
Web: www.passur.com

CEO: James T Barry
CFO: Jeffrey P Devaney
HR: –
FYE: October 31
Type: Public

Anxious to arrive at your destination? PASSUR Aerospace's radar network provides arrival and departure information to airline pilots. Such information is displayed through various data management software used by airports and airlines to track landing and weather conditions. The company's FlightNews Live software displays information to passengers while FlightPerform gives pilots accurate estimated time of arrival and graphical flight positioning and OPSnet Airport Communicator incorporates messaging tools. Chairman and former CEO G.S. Beckwith Gilbert owns about 66% of the company.

	Annual Growth	10/11	10/12	10/13	10/14	10/15
Sales ($ mil.)	(2.0%)	13.6	12.5	11.0	11.5	12.5
Net income ($ mil.)	(42.9%)	2.6	2.9	0.3	0.3	0.3
Market value ($ mil.)	(12.0%)	38.3	33.3	23.0	30.6	23.0
Employees	4.4%	37	36	31	37	44

PATHEON INC.

TORONTO: PTI

4721 Emperor Blvd. Ste. 200
Durham NC 27703
Phone: 919-226-3200
Fax: 416-926-5410
Web: www.manulife.com

CEO: James C Mullen
CFO: Stuart Grant
HR: –
FYE: October 31
Type: Public

Patheon makes the production path for pharmaceutical companies a little easier to tread. With facilities in North America and Europe the company provides contract development and manufacturing services to pharmaceutical biotechnology and specialty drug companies worldwide. It develops drug candidates at pre-formulation stage through final stages of launch commercialization and production. On the manufacturing services side it makes mainly prescription drugs in a wide variety of dosage forms — from solids to sprays. Customers include 18 of the top 20 largest pharmaceutical companies in the world.

PATAPSCO BANCORP INC.

OTC: PATD

1301 Merritt Boulevard
Dundalk, MD 21222-2194
Phone: 410 285-1010
Fax: –
Web: www.patapscobank.com

CEO: –
CFO: –
HR: –
FYE: June 30
Type: Public

Patapsco Bancorp deserves a pat on the back for its financial services. It is the holding company for The Patapsco Bank which serves the Baltimore area through about a half dozen branches. The bank provides personal and commercial services and products including checking and savings accounts CDs money market accounts and a variety of loans. Residential mortgages account for about a third of the bank's lending portfolio which also includes construction consumer and commercial real estate loans. Another Baltimore-area bank Bradford Bancorp announced plans to buy Patapsco in 2007 but later called off the deal after it could not secure adequate funding.

	Annual Growth	06/08	06/09	06/10	06/11	06/12
Assets ($ mil.)	(0.7%)	261.3	268.4	269.7	264.6	254.4
Net income ($ mil.)	–	1.4	(5.5)	(2.3)	(2.9)	(1.6)
Market value ($ mil.)	(46.1%)	14.2	6.7	4.9	1.5	1.2
Employees	(7.9%)	86	81	73	70	62

PATHFINDER BANCORP, INC.

NAS: PBHC

214 West First Street
Oswego, NY 13126
Phone: 315 343-0057
Fax: –

CEO: Thomas W Schneider
CFO: James A Dowd
HR: –
FYE: December 31
Type: Public

This bank wants customers beating a path to its door. Pathfinder Bancorp is the holding company for Pathfinder Bank which operates seven branches serving upstate New York's Oswego County and surrounding areas. Founded in 1859 the bank provides standard services such as checking and savings accounts money market accounts IRAs CDs and credit cards. It primarily originates residential real estate loans which account for the majority of the company's loan portfolio. The bank's Pathfinder Investment Services division provides mutual funds insurance brokerage and financial advisory services. Mutual holding company Pathfinder Bancorp M.H.C. owns nearly two-thirds of the company.

	Annual Growth	12/08	12/09	12/10	12/11	12/12
Assets ($ mil.)	7.9%	352.8	371.7	408.5	443.0	477.8
Net income ($ mil.)	63.8%	0.4	1.6	2.5	2.3	2.6
Market value ($ mil.)	13.3%	16.4	14.7	22.3	23.3	27.0
Employees	2.5%	107	109	116	119	118

PATHFINDER CELL THERAPY INC.   NBB: PFND

12 Bow Street
Cambridge, MA 02138
Phone: 617 245-0289
Fax: –

CEO: Richard L Franklin
CFO: John Benson
HR: –
FYE: December 31
Type: Public

Pathfinder Cell Therapy (formerly SyntheMed) keeps surgery patients and disease sufferers off the path towards scarring and organ damage. The company develops polymers aimed at preventing or reducing post-operative adhesions (scar tissue) for a variety of surgical procedures. Its REPEL-CV product used to prevent the formation of scar tissue in open heart surgeries is marketed internationally and is approved for use in pediatric cardiac surgeries in the US. The firm added development-stage tissue regeneration products for diabetics and others at risk of organ damage through its 2011 merger with biotech firm Pathfinder LLC; its name changed from SyntheMed to Pathfinder Cell Therapy following the merger.

	Annual Growth	12/10	12/11	12/12	12/13	12/14
Sales ($ mil.)	–	0.3	0.1	0.1	0.1	0.0
Net income ($ mil.)	–	(2.1)	(11.3)	(2.2)	(1.7)	(1.4)
Market value ($ mil.)	(75.3%)	133.4	33.4	13.3	9.3	0.5
Employees	18.9%	1	2	2	2	2

PATHFINDER INTERNATIONAL

9 GALEN ST STE 217
WATERTOWN, MA 024724523
Phone: 617-924-7200
Fax: –
Web: www.pathfinder.org

CEO: –
CFO: Mike Zeitouny
HR: –
FYE: June 30
Type: Private

Pathfinder International finds a way to provide reproductive health and family planning information and services to people in developing nations. The organization works in some 25 countries in Africa Asia Latin America and the Caribbean. It partners with local governments and other groups to provide access to sexual health and family planning information HIV/AIDS prevention and treatment advocacy for reproductive health policies worldwide abortion support where it's legal and post care where it isn't. Pathfinder also publishes newsletters resource lists guides and training information. Founded in 1957 it gets support from the US and European governments the United Nations and private sources.

	Annual Growth	06/09	06/10	06/11	06/12	06/13
Sales ($ mil.)	0.0%	–	99.9	101.0	101.0	99.9
Net income ($ mil.)	–	–	–	1.3	0.2	(1.1)
Market value ($ mil.)	–	–	–	–	–	–
Employees	–	–	–	–	–	628

PATHMARK STORES INC.

2 Paragon Dr.
Montvale NJ 07645
Phone: 201-573-9700
Fax: 201-505-3054
Web: www.pathmark.com/

CEO: Eric Claus
CFO: Frank Vitrano
HR: –
FYE: February 28
Type: Private

Pathmark Stores hopes it's finally on the upward path. The largest banner belonging to long-struggling grocery operator A&P Pathmark operates about 110 supermarkets under the Pathmark and Pathmark Sav-A-Center banners in densely populated areas in four states: Delaware New Jersey New York and Pennsylvania. Many of its stores are Pathmark Super Centers which offer an expanded selection of general merchandise and foods nearly all have pharmacies and more than half have in-store banks. Pathmark's owner A&P in 2012 emerged after 15 months in Chapter 11 bankruptcy as a private company following a financial restructuring and the closure of many stores including about half a dozen Pathmark locations.

PATHOLOGY ASSOCIATES MEDICAL LABORATORIES

110 W. Cliff Ave.
Spokane WA 99204
Phone: 509-755-8600
Fax: 509-892-2740
Web: www.paml.com

CEO: Francisco R Velzquez
CFO: –
HR: –
FYE: December 31
Type: Subsidiary

Pathology Associates Medical Laboratories (PAML) is heading for the high road as a leading independent laboratory services provider in the Northwest. The company offers a full range of laboratory tests from basic blood tests to specialized esoteric tests including molecular diagnostics. The company serves hospitals and medical clinics in states including California Idaho Montana Oregon Utah and Washington. It operates a full-service reference laboratory in Spokane as well as several ancillary facilities. It also works through joint ventures and on-site lab partnerships with hospitals. Founded in 1957 the company is a subsidiary of Providence Health & Services.

PATIENT SAFETY TECHNOLOGIES INC.   OTC: PSTX

27555 Ynez Rd. Ste. 330
Temecula CA 92591
Phone: 951-587-6201
Fax: 310-895-7751
Web: www.patientsafetytechnologies.com

CEO: Brian E Stewart
CFO: David Dreyer
HR: –
FYE: December 31
Type: Public

Patient Safety Technologies wants to give you one less thing to worry about on your next trip to the operating room. Its SurgiCount Medical subsidiary develops and markets the Safety-Sponge System which uses hand-held barcode scanning technology to help keep track of sponges and towels used during surgeries so that they don't go home inside patients. Hospitals and surgical centers first invest in the system and then must keep ordering the coded products. Cardinal Health is the exclusive distributor of SurgiCount Medical products. China-based A Plus International is the exclusive supplier of its bar-coded surgical dressings.

PATRICK CUDAHY INCORPORATED

1 Sweet Apple-Wood Ln.
Cudahy WI 53110
Phone: 414-744-2000
Fax: 414-744-4213
Web: www.patrickcudahy.com

CEO: –
CFO: –
HR: –
FYE: April 30
Type: Subsidiary

Patrick Cudahy established in 1888 calls itself the "Home of Sweet Apple Wood Smoked Flavor" and that says it all. The company makes sliced ham salami and specialty Italian and deli meats for sandwich shops delicatessens and fast-food operators. Its retail products include sausage bacon boneless hams lean ham and turkey products and sliced luncheon meats. The company has expanded its products to include Hispanic and Latino specialties including such items as chorizo salami higueral salchichon servecero and more. Patrick Cudahy also makes foodservice products and oils for industrial and institutional use. Patrick Cudahy is owned by US pork giant Smithfield Foods which purchased it in 1984.

PATRICK INDUSTRIES, INC.

NMS: PATK

107 West Franklin Street, P.O. Box 638
Elkhart, IN 46515
Phone: 574 294-7511
Fax: –
Web: www.patrickind.com

CEO: Todd M. Cleveland
CFO: Joshua A. Boone
HR: Courtney A. Blosser
FYE: December 31
Type: Public

A recreational vehicle is just an empty motor home until Patrick Industries adds the finishing interior touches. The company makes and distributes a range of building materials and prefinished products primarily for the manufactured home (MH) and RV industries. Patrick Industries manufactures decorative paper and vinyl panels moldings countertops doors and cabinet and slotwall components. In addition to these the firm distributes roofing siding flooring drywall ceiling and wall panels household electronics electrical and plumbing supplies and adhesives. Founded in 1959 the company operates about two dozen production facilities distribution centers and warehouses in a dozen states.

	Annual Growth	12/10	12/11	12/12	12/13	12/14
Sales ($ mil.)	27.5%	278.2	307.8	437.4	594.9	735.7
Net income ($ mil.)	123.7%	1.2	8.5	28.1	24.0	30.7
Market value ($ mil.)	119.4%	29.4	63.6	241.2	448.4	681.7
Employees	43.1%	668	900	1,678	2,387	2,799

PATRIOT COAL CORP

NBB: PATC A

12312 Olive Boulevard, Suite 400
St. Louis, MO 63141
Phone: 314 275-3600
Fax: –
Web: www.patriotcoal.com

CEO: –
CFO: –
HR: –
FYE: December 31
Type: Public

Patriot Coal Corporation is engaged in what many see as a patriotic US tradition — mining for metallurgical and thermal coal. With 11 mining complexes in Appalachia and the Illinois Basin Patriot Coal mines coal used for domestic and international electricity generation (about three-quarters of its production) and steel manufacturing in the eastern US. The company's operations include company-managed mines joint ventures and numerous contractor-operated mines placing about 1.8 billion tons of proved and probable coal reserves in 2013 under Patriot's control.

	Annual Growth	12/09	12/10	12/11	12/12	12/13
Sales ($ mil.)	(8.0%)	2,045.3	2,035.1	2,402.5	1,922.7	1,462.1
Net income ($ mil.)	(9.4%)	127.2	(48.0)	(115.5)	(730.6)	85.8
Market value ($ mil.)	–	–	–	–	–	–
Employees	3.4%	3,500	3,700	4,300	4,100	4,000

PATRIOT NATIONAL BANCORP INC

NMS: PNBK

900 Bedford Street
Stamford, CT 06901
Phone: 203 324-7500
Fax: –
Web: www.pnbdirectonline.com

CEO: Kenneth T. Neilson
CFO: Neil M. McDonnell
HR: –
FYE: December 31
Type: Public

What's red white blue and green? Why Patriot National Bancorp of course. It's the holding company for Patriot National Bank which operates about a dozen branches in affluent southwestern Connecticut and a handful more in neighboring New York. Serving consumers professionals and small to midsized businesses the bank offers checking savings and money market accounts as well as CDs IRAs and health savings accounts. Real estate loans including commercial mortgages residential mortgages and construction loans dominate its lending activities. To a far lesser extent the bank also originates business and consumer loans. PNBK Holdings acquired control of Patriot National Bancorp in 2010.

	Annual Growth	12/10	12/11	12/12	12/13	12/14
Assets ($ mil.)	(5.2%)	784.3	665.8	617.9	541.2	632.6
Net income ($ mil.)	–	(15.4)	(15.5)	(0.5)	(7.3)	15.7
Market value ($ mil.)	(5.9%)	8.3	6.9	4.9	4.1	6.5
Employees	(12.5%)	157	136	118	100	92

PATRIOT SCIENTIFIC CORPORATION

OTC: PTSC

6183 Paseo Del Norte Ste. 180
Carlsbad CA 92011
Phone: 760-547-2700
Fax: 760-547-2705
Web: www.ptsc.com

CEO: Clifford L Flowers
CFO: Clifford L Flowers
HR: –
FYE: May 31
Type: Public

Patriot Scientific proudly designs microprocessors for licensing to other parties. Advanced Micro Devices which has an equity investment in the company licenses Patriot's microprocessor patent portfolio. AMD also has the rights to manufacture and sell Patriot's Ignite 32-bit stack microprocessor. Patriot is in litigation over patented microprocessor technology with other MPU suppliers. CASIO COMPUTER Fujitsu Hewlett-Packard Hoya NEC Nokia Philips Sharp and Sony among others have licensed technology from Patriot. The company also owns part of Scripps Secured Data Inc. (SSDI) and Talis Data Systems both network security software suppliers.

PATTERN ENERGY GROUP INC

NMS: PEGI

Pier 1, Bay 3
San Francisco, CA 94111
Phone: 415 283-4000
Fax: –
Web: www.patternenergy.com

CEO: Michael M. Garland
CFO: Michael J. Lyon
HR: –
FYE: December 31
Type: Public

Pattern Energy wants to be the wind power beneath your energy wings. The company has eight wind power projects (six operating two under construction) in the US Canada and Chile with a generation capacity of more than 1000MW. Nearly all of the company's capacity is contracted to be sold under long-term agreements. Pattern Energy named for the patterns the company says it uses to maximize both production and profits was formed in late 2012 by Pattern Energy Group (PEG) to take over that company's power operations while it focuses on development. Pattern went public in 2013; it intends to use its $352 million in IPO proceeds to repay PEG which still controls it and for general corporate purposes.

	Annual Growth	12/10	12/11	12/12	12/13	12/14
Sales ($ mil.)	52.1%	49.6	135.9	114.5	201.6	265.5
Net income ($ mil.)	–	4.6	8.9	(6.3)	17.0	(31.3)
Market value ($ mil.)	(18.6%)	–	–	–	1,881.1	1,530.5
Employees	29.7%	–	–	41	44	69

PATTERSON COMPANIES INC

NMS: PDCO

1031 Mendota Heights Road
St. Paul, MN 55120
Phone: 651 686-1600
Fax: –
Web: www.pattersoncompanies.com

CEO: Scott P. Anderson
CFO: R Armstrong
HR: Jerome Thygesen
FYE: April 25
Type: Public

Patterson Companies' catalogs are like wish lists for dental veterinary and physical rehabilitation practices. The company's Patterson Dental unit is a leading wholesaler of dental products including X-ray film and machines hand instruments sterilization products dental chairs and lights and diagnostic equipment. Additionally it sells office supplies computer equipment software and other products and services for dental offices and laboratories. Its Patterson Veterinary unit (formerly Webster Veterinary) distributes animal health supplies including equine products in the US and UK. Focusing on its dental and veterinary businesses the firm sold its Patterson Medical unit in 2015.

	Annual Growth	04/11	04/12	04/13	04/14	04/15
Sales ($ mil.)	6.4%	3,415.7	3,535.7	3,637.2	4,063.7	4,375.0
Net income ($ mil.)	(0.2%)	225.4	212.8	210.3	200.6	223.3
Market value ($ mil.)	8.5%	3,584.8	3,510.4	3,869.8	4,225.1	4,977.0
Employees	(0.4%)	7,100	7,059	7,000	7,000	7,000

PATTERSON-UTI ENERGY INC.

NMS: PTEN

450 Gears Road, Suite 500
Houston, TX 77067
Phone: 281 765-7100
Fax: –
Web: www.patenergy.com

CEO: William A. (Andy) Hendricks
CFO: John E. Vollmer
HR: Cheryl Thomas
FYE: December 31
Type: Public

Patterson-UTI Energy's pattern of activity is to drill for oil and gas. The company which provides onshore contract drilling for oil and natural gas producers operates about 286 rigs and a fleet of support vehicles and 332 trailers. It has one of the largest land-based drilling fleets in North America behind that of Nabors Industries. Patterson-UTI complements its contract drilling business in Canada and across the US (Patterson-UTI Drilling) by providing pressure pumping services for oil and natural gas operators primarily in Texas and the Appalachian Basin. Patterson-UTI's marketable drilling rigs have depth capabilities ranging from 10000 ft. to 25000 ft. and a total of 1 million hydraulic horsepower.

	Annual Growth	12/11	12/12	12/13	12/14	12/15
Sales ($ mil.)	(7.3%)	2,565.9	2,723.4	2,716.0	3,182.3	1,891.3
Net income ($ mil.)	–	322.4	299.5	188.0	162.7	(294.5)
Market value ($ mil.)	(6.8%)	2,940.4	2,741.7	3,726.3	2,441.5	2,219.3
Employees	(19.8%)	8,200	7,300	7,800	7,900	3,400

PAUL HASTINGS JANOFSKY & WALKER LLP

515 S. Flower St. 25th Fl.
Los Angeles CA 90071-2371
Phone: 213-683-6000
Fax: 213-627-0705
Web: www.paulhastings.com

CEO: –
CFO: –
HR: –
FYE: January 31
Type: Private - Partnershi

Paul Hastings Janofsky & Walker has built a solid reputation in employment law and over the years companies such as United Parcel Service and Hughes Aircraft have turned to the firm for its expertise in the field. With about 900 attorneys Paul Hastings also practices in such areas as intellectual property litigation mergers and acquisitions and real estate. Paul Hastings operates from about 20 offices not only in the US but also in Europe and the Asia/Pacific region. The firm was founded in 1951; it adopted its current name in 1962.

PAUL WEISS RIFKIND WHARTON & GARRISON LLP

1285 Avenue of the Americas
New York NY 10019-6064
Phone: 212-373-3000
Fax: 212-757-3990
Web: www.paulweiss.com

CEO: –
CFO: Sean McNamara
HR: –
FYE: December 31
Type: Private - Partnershi

Paul Weiss Rifkind Wharton & Garrison doesn't mind the spotlight. The law firm has built a substantial practice related to the entertainment industry to go along with its work on high-profile corporate transactions (including mergers and acquisitions) and litigation. In addition Paul Weiss practices in areas such as bankruptcy and corporate reorganization intellectual property and real estate. Its 700-plus lawyers work from three offices in the US and five in Canada China Japan and the UK. The firm draws clients from the Asia/Pacific region and Europe as well as from the US and Canada. Paul Weiss can trace its roots to 1875; it was established in its modern form in 1946.

PAVILION ENERGY RESOURCES INC.

PINK SHEETS: PVRE

261 S. Robertson Blvd.
Beverly Hills CA 90211
Phone: 310-288-4585
Fax: 713-706-6201
Web: www.americanspectrum.com

CEO: –
CFO: –
HR: –
FYE: June 30
Type: Public

Pavilion Energy Resources (formerly Energetics Holdings and before that formerly Global Business Services) has gone from the mailbox to the oil patch. In 2007 the company acquired Energetics a Texas-based oil and gas development company that holds an oil lease in Louisiana. In conjunction with the deal executives from Energetics took over at Global Business Services which then changed its name to Energetics Holdings. The next year the company again changed its name and the two groups rescinded the 2007 agreement to sell the company. Pavilion Energy Resources also holds oil and gas assets in Tennessee and Kentucky.

PAXTON MEDIA GROUP LLC

201 S 4TH ST
PADUCAH, KY 420031524
Phone: 270-345-3152
Fax: –
Web: www.cadizrecord.com

CEO: –
CFO: Richard Paxton
HR: Eric Rudolph
FYE: December 28
Type: Private

Paxton Media Group owns about 30 daily newspapers in the Midwest and South including its flagship The Paducah Sun (Kentucky) and The Herald-Sun (Durham North Carolina). The company also owns several dozen weekly papers and more than 100 free papers as well as a television station in Paducah Kentucky. W.F. Paxton launched The Paducah Sun in 1896; his family led by CEO David Paxton continues to run the publishing business.

	Annual Growth	12/02	12/03	12/05	12/06	12/08
Sales ($ mil.)	–	–	0.0	0.0	204.5	188.2
Net income ($ mil.)	–	–	–	0.0	0.0	0.0
Market value ($ mil.)	–	–	–	–	–	–
Employees	–	–	–	–	–	2,000

PAYCHEX INC

NMS: PAYX

911 Panorama Trail South
Rochester, NY 14625-2396
Phone: 585 385-6666
Fax: 585 383-3428
Web: www.paychex.com

CEO: Martin Mucci
CFO: Efrain Rivera
HR: Laurie L. Zaucha
FYE: May 31
Type: Public

If Johnny Paycheck had founded Paychex his song might have been "Take This Job and ... Let Us Do Your Payroll." The firm processes the payrolls of about 590000 clients making it the second-largest payroll accounting firm in the US after Automatic Data Processing. Other services include the production of accounting records and management reports; the preparation of payroll tax returns; and the collection and remittance of clients' payroll obligations. Paychex also provides human resources services benefits administration and group insurance management. Paychex focuses on small and midsized businesses (fewer than 100 employees) and owns more than 100 offices worldwide. The company was established in 1971.

	Annual Growth	05/11	05/12	05/13	05/14	05/15
Sales ($ mil.)	7.1%	2,084.3	2,229.8	2,326.2	2,518.9	2,739.6
Net income ($ mil.)	7.0%	515.3	548.0	569.0	627.5	674.9
Market value ($ mil.)	11.2%	11,666.8	10,825.2	13,447.5	14,848.9	17,846.9
Employees	1.2%	12,400	12,400	12,400	12,700	13,000

PAYMENT ALLIANCE INTERNATIONAL INC.

One Paragon Centre 6060 Dutchmans Ln. Ste. 320
Louisville KY 40205-3277
Phone: 502-212-4000
Fax: 502-212-4004
Web: paymentallianceintl.com

CEO: John J Leehy III
CFO: David Kozal
HR: –
FYE: December 31
Type: Private

Who carries cash anymore? Fewer and fewer people these days which is good news for Payment Alliance International (PAI). The company provides electronic payment processing and related services including electronic check authorization services and credit and debt card processing for merchants and banks. The company's ATM Services Group helps merchants outfit their stores with ATMs providing hardware software and maintenance services. It operates the largest ATM network in the US totaling more than 45000 machines. PAI also helps clients create gift card and loyalty programs. CEO John Leehy and COO Greg Sahrmann co-founded PAI in 2005.

PAYMENT DATA SYSTEMS INC

NAS: PYDS

12500 San Pedro, Ste. 120
San Antonio, TX 78216
Phone: 210 249-4100
Fax: 210 249-4130
Web: www.billx.com

CEO: Michael R Long
CFO: Habib Yunus
HR: –
FYE: December 31
Type: Public

Everybody's gotta pay the man and Payment Data Systems wants to be in on the action. The company offers electronic payment processing services including automated clearinghouse (ACH) and credit/debit card transaction processing to merchants and businesses. Payment Data Systems also operates billx.com an online payment processing website that allows consumers to pay anyone anywhere for a flat monthly fee. Additionally the company is developing and marketing prepaid gift cards and debit cards issued by Meta Financial Group. Payment Data Systems operates solely in the US.

	Annual Growth	12/10	12/11	12/12	12/13	12/14
Sales ($ mil.)	50.4%	2.6	4.8	7.3	5.2	13.4
Net income ($ mil.)	–	(0.5)	0.4	1.3	(0.8)	3.8
Market value ($ mil.)	62.7%	0.3	1.2	1.6	1.0	2.1
Employees	17.2%	9	8	11	10	17

PAYMENT PROCESSING INC.

8200 Central Ave.
Newark CA 94560
Phone: 510-795-2290
Fax: 510-795-2299
Web: www.paypros.com

CEO: –
CFO: –
HR: –
FYE: December 31
Type: Private

How's this for alliteration: Payment Processing provides products for processing payments professionally. The company which operates as PayPros does in fact help merchants in the US and Canada process their customers' payments by partnering with various software developers to offer systems that integrate software applications with electronic payment processing functions. PayPros' products support check payments credit cards debit cards and gift cards. Its services include tech and administrative support and risk monitoring. Founded in 1995 the company today works with some 1700 software companies and more than 55000 merchants including restaurants and retailers.

PAYPAL INC.

2211 N. First St.
San Jose CA 95131
Phone: 408-967-1000
Fax: 408-376-7514
Web: www.paypal.com

CEO: Daniel H Schulman
CFO: Patrick Dupuis
HR: –
FYE: December 31
Type: Subsidiary

PayPal wants to be your best bud in the electronic payments industry. The company which is a subsidiary of eBay allows individuals and merchants to transfer money via personal computer or Web-enabled mobile phone with transactions charged to the customer's bank account credit card or PayPal account. The company earns fees mainly from payment transactions foreign exchange and withdrawals from foreign bank accounts as well as on its customer balances and PayPal-branded credit and debit cards. PayPal has about 80 million users in 190 markets and 25 currencies around the world. PayPal revenues account for about 40% of eBay's total sales.

PBF ENERGY INC

NYS: PBF

One Sylvan Way, Second Floor
Parsippany, NJ 07054
Phone: 973 455-7500
Fax: –
Web: www.pbfenergy.com

CEO: Thomas J. Nimbley
CFO: C. Erik Young
HR: –
FYE: December 31
Type: Public

Oil refiners meet the new kid on the block. Less than a decade old PBF Energy's three oil refineries (formerly owned by Valero and Sunoco) and located in Delaware New Jersey and Ohio have a combined production capacity of about 540000 barrels per day. The refineries produce gasoline ultra-low-sulfur diesel heating oil jet fuel lubricants petrochemicals and asphalt for the Midwestern and Northeastern US. The company indirectly owns the general partner and approximately 52.1% of the limited partnership interest of PBF Logistics LP. PBF Energy is majority-owned by investment firms The Blackstone Group and First Reserve.

	Annual Growth	12/10	12/11	12/12	12/13	12/14
Sales ($ mil.)	–	0.0	0.0	20,138.7	19,151.5	19,828.2
Net income ($ mil.)	–	0.0	0.0	2.0	39.5	(38.2)
Market value ($ mil.)	–	0.0	0.0	2,381.6	2,579.1	2,184.0
Employees	3.1%	–	–	1,612	1,735	1,714

PBF ENERGY INC.

NYSE: PBF

1 Sylvan Way
Parsippany NJ 07054
Phone: 973-455-7500
Fax: 605-965-2203
Web: www.poet.com

CEO: Thomas J Nimbley
CFO: Matthew Lucey
HR: –
FYE: December 31
Type: Private

Oil refiners meet the new kid on the block. PBF Energy formed in 2008 and has since spent almost $1 billion buying three oil refineries from Valero and Sunoco. Its refineries located in Delaware New Jersey and Ohio have a combined production capacity of about 540000 barrels per day. The refineries produce gasoline ultra-low-sulfur diesel heating oil jet fuel lubricants petrochemicals and asphalt for the midwestern and northeastern US. PBF Energy which is majority-owned by investment firms The Blackstone Group and First Reserve went public in 2012 with an IPO that raised $429 million.

PC CONNECTION, INC.

NMS: PCCC

730 Milford Road
Merrimack, NH 03054
Phone: 603 683-2000
Fax: –
Web: www.pcconnection.com

CEO: Timothy J. McGrath
CFO: Joseph S. Driscoll
HR: –
FYE: December 31
Type: Public

You won't see a store on every street corner but PC Connection is just a click away. A leading direct marketer of computer products in the US the company sells hardware software networking devices and peripherals. It offers more than 300000 items from manufacturers such as Apple Hewlett-Packard and Microsoft. PC Connection also provides a range of IT services. Through its catalogs websites and direct sales force PC Connection targets small and mid-sized businesses large corporations government agencies and educational institutions as well as individual consumers. PC Connection was founded in 1982 by chairman Patricia Gallup and director David Hall.

	Annual Growth	12/10	12/11	12/12	12/13	12/14
Sales ($ mil.)	5.7%	1,974.2	2,103.3	2,158.9	2,221.6	2,463.3
Net income ($ mil.)	16.8%	23.0	28.8	33.1	35.7	42.7
Market value ($ mil.)	29.0%	233.4	292.1	302.9	654.6	646.7
Employees	7.1%	1,556	1,901	1,938	1,961	2,047

PC GROUP INC.

PINK SHEETS: PCGR

450 Commack Rd.
Deer Park NY 11729-4510
Phone: 631-667-1200
Fax: 631-667-1203
Web: www.pcgrpinc.com

CEO: W Gary Hudkins
CFO: Kathleen P Bloch
HR: Kathy Park
FYE: December 31
Type: Public

PC Group (formerly Langer) wants feet and hands to be soft and comfortable. The firm makes a range of personal care products including soaps lotions and acne creams as well as gel-based therapeutic products. Its Silipos subsidiary makes gel-based foot and hand care products (such as bandages and wraps) for the consumer market as well as orthopedic supports and prosthetic liners for medical devices. PC Group's other main operating unit specialty soap maker Twincraft creates personal care products for mass marketers and specialty retailers including Bath & Body Works.

PC-TEL INC

NMS: PCTI

471 Brighton Drive
Bloomingdale, IL 60108
Phone: 630 372-6800
Fax: –

CEO: Martin H. (Marty) Singer
CFO: John W. Schoen
HR: –
FYE: December 31
Type: Public

PCTEL wants to help its customers find the right connections. The company provides scanning receiver and antenna products to public and private telecom carriers and wireless infrastructure providers. Its products include a broad line of antennas (Bluewave MAXRAD) scanning receivers (SeeGull) and interference management products (CLARIFY). The company also generates a small portion of revenues from licensing intellectual property related to its discontinued modem business. The company sells directly and through resellers distributors and OEM equipment providers. PCTEL serves a variety of markets in addition to telecommunications such as transportation public safety health care energy and agriculture.

	Annual Growth	12/10	12/11	12/12	12/13	12/14
Sales ($ mil.)	11.5%	69.3	76.8	88.8	104.3	107.2
Net income ($ mil.)	–	(3.5)	1.0	(8.6)	3.3	4.6
Market value ($ mil.)	9.6%	111.4	127.0	133.7	177.7	160.8
Employees	7.7%	345	386	467	449	465

PCL CONSTRUCTION ENTERPRISES INC

2000 S COLOR BLVD TOWER T
DENVER, CO 80222
Phone: 303-365-6500
Fax: –
Web: www.enterprises.pcl.com

CEO: –
CFO: –
HR: –
FYE: October 31
Type: Private

PCL Construction Enterprises is the contractor to call on for commercial and civil construction concerns. The company serves as the parent to half a dozen US construction companies: PCL Construction Services PCL Civil Constructors PCL Construction PCL Industrial Services PCL Industrial Construction and Nordic PCL Construction. The companies serve as the operating entities for PCL one of Canada's largest general contracting groups. Having completed projects in nearly every US state PCL Construction Enterprises is active in the commercial institutional multi-family residential heavy industrial and civil construction sectors. PCL first entered the US construction market in 1975.

	Annual Growth	10/06	10/07	10/08	10/09	10/10
Sales ($ mil.)	(25.9%)	–	–	–	2,182.8	1,616.8
Net income ($ mil.)	(55.3%)	–	–	–	52.9	23.6
Market value ($ mil.)	–	–	–	–	–	–
Employees	–	–	–	–	–	3,300

PCM, INC

NMS: PCMI

1940 E. Mariposa Avenue
El Segundo, CA 90245
Phone: 310 354-5600
Fax: –
Web: www.pcm.com

CEO: Frank F. Khulusi
CFO: Brandon H. LaVerne
HR: –
FYE: December 31
Type: Public

Mall rats make way for computer geeks at PCM (formerly PC Mall). The multi-channel retailer sells computers software and other electronics online and through its various catalogs. Titles include PCM MacMall PCMG (formerlyPC Mall Gov) and PCM SARCOM. The firm sells Apple HP Cisco Lenovo and Microsoft products among others through Web sites including its catalog names as well as sarcom.com abreon.com clubmac.com and onsale.com. PCM operates several retail shops in California. Customers include: businesses; federal states and local government agencies; schools; and individual consumers. In 2015 PCM bought California-based IT solutions provider En Pointe Technologies Sales for $15 million.

	Annual Growth	12/10	12/11	12/12	12/13	12/14
Sales ($ mil.)	(0.2%)	1,368.3	1,455.2	1,420.9	1,424.3	1,356.4
Net income ($ mil.)	(7.8%)	7.6	3.1	5.1	8.1	5.5
Market value ($ mil.)	5.9%	92.9	77.0	76.2	126.0	116.8
Employees	0.5%	2,657	3,078	2,892	2,920	2,708

PCRE L.L.C

860 N. Main St.
Wallingford CT 06492
Phone: 860-571-7000
Fax: 860-571-7410
Web: www.prudentialct.com

CEO: –
CFO: –
HR: –
FYE: December 31
Type: Private

Prudential Connecticut Realty helps people buy and sell houses in the Constitution State home to some of the highest-priced homes in the US. The company has more than 60 sales offices throughout the state and some 1800 sales professionals. In addition to residential brokerage services Prudential Connecticut Realty provides relocation services referrals for renters and commercial real estate services. The company also has affiliates that provide financing escrow and insurance services. Chairman CEO and owner Peter G. Helie founded Prudential Connecticut Realty an independent member of Prudential Real Estate Affiliates in 1997.

PCS EDVENTURES!.COM INC

NBB: PCSV

345 Bobwhite Court, Suite 200
Boise, ID 83706
Phone: 208 343-3110
Fax: –

CEO: Robert O Grover
CFO: –
HR: –
FYE: March 31
Type: Public

PCS Edventures!.com provides science and engineering-based educational software for elementary and high school children. The company's software offerings include its Academy of Engineering Lab program which helps students understand simple machines gear systems and power transfer systems; Edventures! Lab which uses Lego materials for online engineering learning; Academy of Robotics Lab which teaches logic engineering and problem-solving skills; and Edventures in Language Arts which offers literacy learning activities for children.

	Annual Growth	03/11	03/12	03/13	03/14	03/15
Sales ($ mil.)	12.1%	1.8	2.3	2.9	1.9	2.9
Net income ($ mil.)	–	(1.9)	(2.0)	(0.7)	(1.0)	(1.4)
Market value ($ mil.)	(37.9%)	14.8	3.7	3.1	4.5	2.2
Employees	(12.3%)	22	19	16	13	13

PDB SPORTS LTD.

13655 Broncos Pkwy.
Englewood CO 80112
Phone: 303-649-9000
Fax: 303-649-0562
Web: www.denverbroncos.com

CEO: –
CFO: –
HR: –
FYE: March 31
Type: Private

This company might just take football fans on a wild ride. PDB Sports owns and operates the Denver Broncos professional football team one of the more successful franchises in the National Football League. The Broncos made four Super Bowl appearances in the 1970s and 1980s before winning back-to-back championships following the 1997 and 1998 seasons. The franchise was founded by local sports entrepreneur Bob Howsam and first took the field in 1960 as part of the American Football League. Denver joined the NFL when the two leagues merged in 1970. The team plays host at Denver's INVESCO Field at Mile High. President and CEO Pat Bowlen and his family have owned the Broncos since 1985.

PDC ENERGY INC

NMS: PDCE

1775 Sherman Street, Suite 3000
Denver, CO 80203
Phone: 303 860-5800
Fax: –
Web: www.pdce.com

CEO: Barton R. (Bart) Brookman
CFO: Gysle R. Shellum
HR: –
FYE: December 31
Type: Public

The hills are alive with opportunity for PDC Energy (formerly Petroleum Development) which explores for and produces natural gas (and some oil) in the Rocky Mountains and the Appalachian Basin; the independent also has operations in the Permian Basin. The company owns interests in more than 5000 wells and in 2013 reported net proved reserves of 740 billion cu. ft. of natural gas equivalent. Subsidiary Riley Natural Gas markets natural gas for the company and others in Appalachia. PDC Energy had drilled and operated wells for its partners but has exited this low-revenue contract drilling business in order to focus on its core exploration and production operations.

	Annual Growth	12/10	12/11	12/12	12/13	12/14
Sales ($ mil.)	25.3%	347.6	396.0	356.1	411.3	856.2
Net income ($ mil.)	123.6%	6.2	13.4	(130.7)	(22.3)	155.4
Market value ($ mil.)	(0.6%)	1,517.0	1,260.7	1,192.4	1,910.9	1,481.9
Employees	1.2%	327	404	421	412	343

PDF SOLUTIONS INC.

NMS: PDFS

333 West San Carlos Street, Suite 1000
San Jose, CA 95110
Phone: 408 280-7900
Fax: 408 280-7915
Web: www.pdf.com

CEO: John K. Kibarian
CFO: Gregory C. Walker
HR: Rebecca Baybrook PHD
FYE: December 31
Type: Public

PDF Solutions can solve chip design and manufacturing inefficiencies. The company provides software and services that help integrated circuit makers get more working chips out of a production batch. PDF's products are used to simulate model and analyze the chip design and manufacturing processes. As part of the Design-to-Silicon-Yield program PDF also receives a portion of customers' cost savings called gain share. Three customers — GLOBALFOUNDRIES IBM and Samsung Electronics — collectively account for about 75% of sales. PDF Solutions generates about 60% of sales outside the US.

	Annual Growth	12/10	12/11	12/12	12/13	12/14
Sales ($ mil.)	12.9%	61.7	66.7	89.5	101.5	100.2
Net income ($ mil.)	200.3%	0.2	1.9	37.2	20.9	18.5
Market value ($ mil.)	32.5%	150.0	216.9	428.8	797.2	462.4
Employees	5.3%	292	319	345	363	359

PDL BIOPHARMA INC

NMS: PDLI

932 Southwood Boulevard
Incline Village, NV 89451
Phone: 775 832-8500
Fax: –

CEO: John P McLaughlin
CFO: Peter S. (Pete) Garcia
HR: –
FYE: December 31
Type: Public

If your body starts fighting you PDL BioPharma hopes to help you fight back. The company's antibody (protein) humanization technology makes it possible to alter mouse monoclonal antibodies (MAbs) for use in human therapies such as preventing and treating autoimmune diseases and cancer. The firm has licensed its technology to such companies as Genentech (a Roche subsidiary) Biogen and Chugai Pharmaceutical. PDL derives nearly all of its revenues from royalties on products including Genentech's cancer medications Herceptin and Avastin and Biogen's multiple sclerosis drug Tysabri.

	Annual Growth	12/10	12/11	12/12	12/13	12/14
Sales ($ mil.)	13.9%	345.0	362.0	374.5	442.9	581.2
Net income ($ mil.)	36.9%	91.9	199.4	211.7	264.5	322.2
Market value ($ mil.)	5.5%	1,010.4	1,005.6	1,141.8	1,368.8	1,250.5
Employees	2.7%	9	10	10	10	10

PDS GAMING CORPORATION

6280 Annie Oakley Dr.
Las Vegas NV 89120
Phone: 702-736-0700
Fax: 702-740-8692
Web: www.pdsgaming.com

CEO: Johan P Finley
CFO: Peter D Cleary
HR: –
FYE: December 31
Type: Private

All companies want to separate people from their money; PDS Gaming provides the machinery to do it one bet at a time. The company is licensed to provide slot machines video games and other gambling devices to casinos in Nevada New Jersey and eight other states. PDS also serves US Native American jurisdictions. Its clients range from small casinos and truck stops to large resort properties and cruise ships. PDS Gaming offers equipment leasing and financing in addition to financial services such as project financing corporate recapitalization and equity buyouts. A management group consisting of husband and wife founders Johan and Lona Finley and president and CFO Peter Cleary own PDS.

PDS TECH INC.

1925 W J CARPENTR FWY 5
IRVING, TX 75063
Phone: 214-647-9600
Fax: –
Web: www.pdstech.com

CEO: Arthur R. (Art) Janes
CFO: Steven Cash Nickerson
HR: Lorri Bloom
FYE: December 29
Type: Private

Need an IT pro to assist with your company's computer needs? PDS Tech wants to help. The company provides temporary technical industrial and general staffing services through more than 30 offices across the US with a concentration in Texas and on the East Coast. PDS Tech's specialties include aviation architecture engineering information technology administration and maritime staffing. Its PDS Engineering division handles engineering placement for the aerospace mechanical and structural engineering industries while the Information Services division offers technical consulting services in the IT and telecommunication industries. The company was founded in 1977 by aerospace engineer Art Janes.

	Annual Growth	12/09	12/10	12/11	12/12	12/13
Sales ($ mil.)	3.3%	–	338.4	397.1	437.0	373.0
Net income ($ mil.)	(53.7%)	–	–	5.1	2.6	1.1
Market value ($ mil.)	–	–	–	–	–	–
Employees	–	–	–	–	–	10,000

PEABODY ENERGY CORP

NYS: BTU

701 Market Street
St. Louis, MO 63101-1826
Phone: 314 342-3400
Fax: –
Web: www.peabodyenergy.com

CEO: Glenn L. Kellow
CFO: Amy B. Schwetz
HR: Andrew P. (Andy) Slentz
FYE: December 31
Type: Public

In a time in which people still get most of their power from coal-fired plants Peabody Energy is king. The world's largest private-sector coal producer Peabody owns stakes in 26 mines (25 majority owned) and processing facilities in the US and Australia. It sells about 249 million tons of coal annually and maintains 7.6 billion tons of proved and probable reserves. US customers primarily power companies account for most of Peabody's sales and its coal fuels almost 50% of US power. Its operations include coal trading and brokering coalbed methane production transportation-related services and development of coal-based generating plants. The company has also begun investing in carbon capture technology.

	Annual Growth	12/10	12/11	12/12	12/13	12/14
Sales ($ mil.)	(0.2%)	6,860.0	7,974.4	8,077.5	7,013.7	6,792.2
Net income ($ mil.)	–	802.2	946.3	(575.1)	(512.6)	(777.3)
Market value ($ mil.)	(41.0%)	1,158.9	599.7	482.0	353.8	140.2
Employees	3.6%	7,200	8,300	8,200	8,300	8,300

PEACEHEALTH

1115 SE 164TH AVE # 334
VANCOUVER, WA 98683-9324
Phone: 425-747-1711
Fax: –
Web: www.peacehealth.org

CEO: Liz Dunne
CFO: Peggy Allen
HR: –
FYE: June 30
Type: Private

PeaceHealth provides patients with a tranquil place to recover. Make that several tranquil places to recover. PeaceHealth serves residents in southeastern Alaska coastal regions of Washington and central portions of Oregon. Its medical centers include PeaceHealth Ketchikan Medical Center PeaceHealth St. Joseph Medical Center PeaceHealth St. John Medical Center Sacred Heart Medical Center (two campuses) Cottage Grove Community Hospital Peace Harbor Hospital PeaceHealth Peace Island Medical Center and PeaceHealth Southwest Medical Center. Other operations include physician practices community clinics hospices chemical dependency rehabilitation clinics and other outpatient facilities and services.

	Annual Growth	06/03	06/04	06/05	06/06	06/09
Sales ($ mil.)	9.2%	–	885.5	978.7	1,048.7	1,372.1
Net income ($ mil.)	–	–	–	41.0	103.2	(88.9)
Market value ($ mil.)	–	–	–	–	–	–
Employees	–	–	–	–	–	6,690

PEAK RESORTS INC

NMS: SKIS

17409 Hidden Valley Drive
Wildwood, MO 63025
Phone: 636 938-7474
Fax: –
Web: www.peakresorts.com

CEO: Timothy Boyd
CFO: Stephen J Mueller
HR: –
FYE: April 30
Type: Public

If you can't fly to Aspen Peak Resorts offers a closer alternative for weekend skiers and snowboarders in the Midwest and Northeast. The company operates a dozen ski resorts in six states - Indiana Missouri New Hampshire Ohio Pennsylvania and Vermont. Its two largest are Mount Snow in Vermont and Attitash in New Hampshire which together account for half of the company's revenues. The Mount Snow resort also has two hotels the Grand Summit and Snow Lake Lodge and Attitash offers a Grand Summit hotel. The company counts about 1.7 million visitors every year to its resorts which are open seasonally generally from December to April. Peak Resorts withdrew its initial public offering in early 2012.

	Annual Growth	04/11	04/12	04/13	04/14	04/15
Sales ($ mil.)	–	0.0	0.0	99.7	105.2	104.9
Net income ($ mil.)	–	0.0	0.0	2.7	(1.5)	(1.9)
Market value ($ mil.)	–	0.0	0.0	–	–	93.5
Employees	–	–	–	–	–	450

PEAK TECHNOLOGIES INC.

10330 Old Columbia Rd.
Columbia MD 21046
Phone: 410-312-6000
Fax: 410-309-6219
Web: www.peaktech.com

CEO: Ross Young
CFO: Michelle Adams
HR: –
FYE: December 31
Type: Private

PEAK Technologies has planted its bar code on a mobile mountain of data. The company distributes bar code scanners and printers radio-frequency identification (RFID) systems handheld computers and related software. PEAK also offers business process consulting and SAP systems integration services for inventory management supply chain management warehousing and distribution operations. Its suppliers include Cisco Printronix and Zebra Technologies. PEAK also provides support and maintenance services and related supplies and consumables such as labels printer ribbons and toner cartridges and spare parts. Founded in 1986 PEAK Technologies is a Platinum Equity portfolio company.

PEAK6 INVESTMENTS L.P.

141 W. Jackson Blvd. Ste. 500
Chicago IL 60604
Phone: 312-362-2401
Fax: +44-20-8732-1510
Web: www.safestore.com

CEO: Matthew Hulsizer
CFO: –
HR: –
FYE: December 31
Type: Private

Six peaks may make a mountain range but PEAK6 is a maker of markets. Through PEAK6 Capital Mangement the company maintains liquidity for some 2000 US- and European-listed equity options and securities matching buyers and sellers of stock at set prices and often selling or purchasing shares for its own account to compensate for steep price changes. It also runs online brokerage OptionsHouse which allows active self-directed retail investors to trade in stocks and options and online community and financial information provider WeSeed. PEAK6 operates on the floor of the Chicago Board Options Exchange.

PEAPACK-GLADSTONE FINANCIAL CORP.

NMS: PGC

500 Hills Drive, Suite 300
Bedminster, NJ 07921-1538
Phone: 908 234-0700
Fax: –
Web: www.pgbank.com

CEO: Douglas L. Kennedy
CFO: Jeffrey J. Carfora
HR: –
FYE: December 31
Type: Public

Peapack-Gladstone Financial hopes its customers are happy as peas in a pod. The company is the parent of Peapack-Gladstone Bank which operates more than 20 branches serving New Jersey's Hunterdon Morris Somerset and Union counties. Founded in 1921 the bank serves area individuals and small businesses by providing such traditional services as checking savings and money market accounts; CDs; IRAs; and credit cards. It offers trust and investment management services through its PGB Trust and Investments unit. Mortgages secured by residential properties represent about half of the company's loan portfolio. The bank also originates commercial real estate construction consumer and business loans

	Annual Growth	12/10	12/11	12/12	12/13	12/14
Assets ($ mil.)	15.8%	1,505.4	1,600.3	1,667.8	1,966.9	2,702.4
Net income ($ mil.)	18.1%	7.7	12.2	9.7	9.3	14.9
Market value ($ mil.)	9.2%	197.8	162.9	213.4	289.5	281.3
Employees	1.9%	284	295	292	326	306

PEARSON EDUCATION INC.

1 Lake St.
Upper Saddle River NJ 07458
Phone: 201-236-7000
Fax: 201-236-3290
Web: www.pearsoned.com

CEO: Will Ethridge
CFO: –
HR: –
FYE: December 31
Type: Subsidiary

Pearson Education dishes out homework to kids and grown-ups alike. As the world's largest educational publisher the company prints textbooks workbooks and other materials for the K-12 higher education and professional markets. Noteworthy academic imprints include Addison-Wesley Longman Allyn & Bacon and Prentice Hall. Pearson Education's professional imprints publish technical books certification materials and courseware. The firm also has electronic testing and assessment and skill development holdings. Pearson Education is the largest part of the UK-based media group Pearson plc which in 2008 expanded significantly when it acquired two of Reed Elsevier's Harcourt Education units for $950 million.

PEAVEY ELECTRONICS CORPORATION

5022 Hartley Peavey Dr.
Meridian MS 39305
Phone: 601-483-5365
Fax: 601-486-1278
Web: www.peavey.com

CEO: Hartley D Peavey
CFO: –
HR: Charlie White
FYE: December 31
Type: Private

The only people who are peeved with Peavey are the ones standing too close to the company's amplifiers and speakers. One of the world's top makers of portable sound gear Peavey Electronics makes amplifiers complete sound systems microphones mixers and recording equipment. It also produces guitars and basses. The company's sound systems are used in more than a quarter of North America's NFL stadiums and in venues from New York's Apollo Theater to the Sydney Opera House. Products are distributed through music stores in the US and Canada and exported to more than 130 countries. Peavey founded in 1965 is owned and managed by Mississippi Music Hall of Famer Hartley Peavey.

PEBBLEBROOK HOTEL TRUST

NYS: PEB

7315 Wisconsin Avenue, 1100 West
Bethesda, MD 20814
Phone: 240 507-1300
Fax: –
Web: www.pebblebrookhotels.com

CEO: Jon E. Bortz
CFO: Raymond D. Martz
HR: –
FYE: December 31
Type: Public

Pebblebrook Hotel Trust wants the term staycation to take a vacation. The self-managed real estate investment trust (REIT) acquires and manages upscale hotels in the US targeting mostly full-service and select-service luxury properties that don't need major renovation in major US gateway cities. The REIT owns more than 30 hotels (with 7400 rooms) across 11 states and has a 49% interest in six more hotels spanning nearly 1800 rooms through its Manhattan Collection joint venture. Nearly 70% of its revenue comes from room fees while the remainder comes from food and beverage services. Pebblebrook Hotel Trust is the brainchild of CEO Jon Bortz who also founded LaSalle Hotel Properties.

	Annual Growth	12/10	12/11	12/12	12/13	12/14
Sales ($ mil.)	79.4%	57.8	288.0	380.7	489.2	598.8
Net income ($ mil.)	–	(6.6)	14.9	26.1	42.9	72.9
Market value ($ mil.)	22.4%	1,454.0	1,372.4	1,652.9	2,201.0	3,265.0
Employees	15.8%	15	20	23	24	27

PECO ENERGY COMPANY

2301 Market St.
Philadelphia PA 19101-8699
Phone: 215-841-4000
Fax: 215-841-5005
Web: www.peco.com

CEO: Craig L Adams
CFO: Phillip S Barnett
HR: –
FYE: December 31
Type: Subsidiary

PECO Energy propels energy currents in the five-county Philadelphia region. The utility a subsidiary of Exelon serves 1.6 million electricity customers and 494000 natural gas customers. PECO Energy owns 29000 circuit miles of regulated power transmission and distribution lines; its transmission assets are controlled by regional operator PJM Interconnection. The company also has more than 6730 miles of underground gas mains. Pennsylvania's largest utility the company operates some 500 electric substations and almost 30 natural gas gate stations. About 90% of PECO Energy's customers are residential with the remainder being commercial and industrial.

PECO II INC.

1376 State Rte. 598
Galion OH 44833
Phone: 419-468-7600
Fax: 419-468-1587
Web: www.peco2.com

CEO: John G Heindel
CFO: John G Heindel
HR: Adela Yang
FYE: December 31
Type: Subsidiary

PECO II caters to the power hungry. The company makes installs and repairs power systems and other power products for telecommunications infrastructure equipment. Its power systems protect the equipment from voltage and frequency fluctuations eliminate electrical "noise" that creeps into transmissions and provide backup power. PECO II also makes power distribution systems for colocated equipment and offers systems integration training maintenance engineering and installation services. Customers include AT&T Mobility Qwest Sprint Nextel and Verizon Wireless. In 2010 Lineage Power Holdings acquired PECO II for about $17 million in cash.

PEDERNALES ELECTRIC COOPERATIVE INC.

201 S. Ave. F	CEO: John Hewa
Johnson City TX 78636	CFO: Frank Skube
Phone: 830-868-7155	HR: –
Fax: 830-868-4993	FYE: December 31
Web: www.pec.coop	Type: Private - Cooperativ

Created by Texas ranchers and business owners Pedernales Electric Cooperative provides electricity services in the Texas Hill Country. The company the largest electric cooperative in the US purchases its electricity from wholesale providers primarily the Lower Colorado River Authority (LCRA) and transmits and distributes it to more than 204770 cooperative members (or about 242000 individual customer meters). Pedernales Electric Cooperative operates more than 17360 miles of power line and maintains 290000 wooden utility poles in its service area.

PEDEVCO CORP

ASE: PED

4125 Blackhawk Plaza Circle, Suite 201	CEO: Frank C Ingriselli
Danville, CA 94506	CFO: Michael L Peterson
Phone: 855 733-2685	HR: –
Fax: –	FYE: December 31
Web: www.pedevco.com	Type: Public

Blast Energy Services (formerly Verdisys) is having a blast helping its customers keep pumping out oil from mature fields. Using specially fabricated mobile drilling rigs the company provides a range of oil and gas services including lateral drilling and well production enhancement. The company which emerged from Chapter 11 bankruptcy protection in 2008 acquired $1.2 million of oil and gas properties in Matagorda County Texas in 2010 as a way to expand its revenue base and to fund the development of its proprietary Applied Fluid Jetting drilling activity. To raise cash in 2011 it sold its oilfield satellite telecommunications services unit to GlobaLogix.

	Annual Growth	12/10	12/11	12/12	12/13	12/14
Sales ($ mil.)	157.5%	0.1	0.4	0.5	0.7	4.8
Net income ($ mil.)	–	(1.5)	(4.1)	(12.0)	(18.1)	(32.6)
Market value ($ mil.)	59.5%	2.3	0.4	67.9	71.2	14.9
Employees	49.5%	3	3	10	9	15

PEDIATRIC SERVICES OF AMERICA INC.

310 Technology Pkwy.	CEO: Daniel J Kohl
Norcross GA 30092-2929	CFO: James M McNeill
Phone: 770-441-1580	HR: –
Fax: 770-263-9340	FYE: September 30
Web: www.psahealthcare.com	Type: Private

Pediatric Services of America (doing business as PSA Healthcare) knows there's no place like home especially when you're a sick kid. The pediatric home health care company provides in-home nursing and related services for infants and children through locations in about 17 states. It also provides limited in-home nursing services for adults with severe conditions. The company offers some outpatient rehabilitation and nursing through pediatric day treatment centers in Florida and Georgia. Additionally PSA Healthcare offers discharge planning services that arrange for the transfer of patients from hospital to home and the supply of medical equipment. The company is owned by private investment firm Portfolio Logic.

PEERLESS INSURANCE COMPANY

62 Maple Ave.	CEO: –
Keene NH 03431	CFO: –
Phone: 603-352-3221	HR: –
Fax: 603-352-6055	FYE: December 31
Web: www.peerless-ins.com	Type: Subsidiary

Peerless Insurance operates in the realm of commercial property/casualty coverage. The company offers a variety of insurance policies for small to midsized businesses schools and religious organizations in eight states in the northeastern US. Its coverage offerings include automobile inland marine and workers' compensation policies as well as package and umbrella coverage. Peerless Insurance is a regional division of the Liberty Mutual Agency Markets unit of Boston-based Liberty Mutual. Through its sister subsidiaries the company provides access to specialty commercial policies (from Liberty Agency Underwriters) and personal property/casualty lines (from Safeco).

PEERLESS SYSTEMS CORP.

NAS: PRLS

1055 Washington Blvd., 8th Floor	CEO: Timothy Brog
Stamford, CT 06901	CFO: Yi Tsai
Phone: 203 350-0040	HR: –
Fax: –	FYE: January 31
Web: www.peerless.com	Type: Public

Peerless Systems lets you peer at digitally produced images more easily. Peerless proffers software-based imaging systems embedded in printers copiers scanners and other digital devices. Its products include designs for application-specific integrated circuits (ASICs) printer drivers and network interfaces that let digital document companies like Adobe and Ricoh incorporate networking support or multifunction features into equipment. Peerless also offers related engineering services. Top customers include Konica Minolta Kyocera Mita Novell and Seiko Epson which together account for more than three-quarters of sales. About 90% of the company's revenues comes from customers in Japan.

	Annual Growth	01/09	01/10	01/11	01/12	01/13
Sales ($ mil.)	(30.0%)	10.4	4.8	6.2	3.7	2.5
Net income ($ mil.)	(43.7%)	17.6	7.2	4.1	1.4	1.8
Market value ($ mil.)	17.1%	5.7	8.0	10.7	12.3	10.7
Employees	(24.0%)	9	5	6	5	3

PEET'S COFFEE & TEA INC.

NASDAQ: PEET

1400 Park Ave.	CEO: David Burwick
Emeryville CA 94608-3520	CFO: –
Phone: 510-594-2100	HR: –
Fax: 510-594-2180	FYE: December 31
Web: www.peets.com	Type: Private

Peet's Coffee & Tea enjoys the daily grind. The company owns and operates about 195 coffee shops in California and half a dozen other states offering java lovers about 25 types of whole bean and fresh ground coffee including about 15 blends. Its teas run the spectrum from India black to herbal blends. The stores also offer freshly brewed coffee biscotti and other pastries along with mugs and brewing equipment. In addition to its retail operation Peet's sells coffee through retail grocery chains such as Safeway and Whole Foods and through its own online mail order operation. The company which also supplies coffee to foodservice operators was acquired in 2012 by privately-held Joh. A. Benckiser.

PEGASUS SOLUTIONS INC.

Three Lincoln Centre 5430 LBJ Fwy. Ste. 1100	CEO: David Millili
Dallas TX 75240	CFO: –
Phone: 214-234-4000	HR: Margaret Pieratt
Fax: 214-234-4040	FYE: December 31
Web: www.pegs.com	Type: Private

Pegasus Solutions has no reservations about providing services to the worldwide hotel industry. Its reservation representation and marketing services operate under the Utell Unirez and PegsTours names in about 200 countries. In addition Pegasus Solutions offers central reservation systems electronic distribution (connecting some 90000 hotel properties to the Internet and the global distribution system) property management and commission processing. Pegasus Solutions which has regional offices in London Singapore and Arizona also powers hotel reservations on travel websites including Expedia Orbitz and Pegasus' affiliate HotelBook.com. Private equity firm Prides Capital Partners owns Pegasus.

PEGASYSTEMS INC.

NMS: PEGA

One Rogers Street	CEO: Alan Trefler
Cambridge, MA 02142-1209	CFO: –
Phone: 617 374-9600	HR: Sanjay Jobanputra
Fax: –	FYE: December 31
Web: www.pega.com	Type: Public

Pegasystems helps companies fly through business changes without being reined in by their old processes. The company provides rules-driven business process management software PegaRules Process Commander designed to help large companies in the financial services insurance and health care industries update their operations and systems to reflect changes in business goals and strategies. Established in 1983 Pegasystems offers tools for analyzing and simulating processes integrating enterprise applications and portals managing content integration and managing processes for customer service claims resolution and transaction processing.

	Annual Growth	12/10	12/11	12/12	12/13	12/14
Sales ($ mil.)	15.1%	336.6	416.7	461.7	509.0	590.0
Net income ($ mil.)	–	(5.9)	10.1	21.9	38.0	33.3
Market value ($ mil.)	(13.2%)	2,797.0	2,244.9	1,731.8	3,755.2	1,585.9
Employees	18.4%	1,509	1,858	2,160	2,627	2,970

PELICAN PRODUCTS INC.

23215 Early Ave.	CEO: Lyndon J Faulkner
Torrance CA 90505	CFO: Richard D Kern
Phone: 310-326-4700	HR: –
Fax: 310-326-3311	FYE: December 31
Web: www.pelican.com	Type: Private

It's tough to make "virtually indestructible" gear but Pelican Products works to do just that. The company designs and makes technically advanced flashlights and high-impact watertight cases. Its plastic- and metal-encased flashlights are sold in the US through specialty retailers such as Grainger and REI. The military is Pelican's top customer however using cases to secure electronics medical supplies and weapons. Pelican operates in about a dozen countries and boasts six manufacturing plants worldwide. Its Peli Products unit does business in Africa Europe and the Middle East. The company founded by husband-and-wife team Dave and Arline Parker in 1976 is owned by private equity firm Behrman Capital.

PEN INC

NBB: PENC D

431 Fairway Drive, Suite 200	CEO: Scott Rickert
Deerfield Beach, FL 33441	CFO: –
Phone: 844 736-6266	HR: –
Fax: –	FYE: December 31
Web: www.appliednanotech.net	Type: Public

Applied Nanotech Holdings hopes to make it big by thinking small. The company conducts research on carbon nanotubes — molecular-sized cylindrical structures that could be used in making electronic displays and other products. Applied Nanotech derives most of its revenues from contracts with agencies of the US government or by doing research on a contract basis with other entities. The company is developing nanomaterials for use in epoxies glass fibers and nylons. Other applications of carbon nanotube technology are in conductive inks (used in communications instrumentation flexible electronics printed circuit boards and radio-frequency identification tags) sensors and thermal management.

	Annual Growth	12/10	12/11	12/12	12/13	12/14
Sales ($ mil.)	5.5%	8.0	6.5	3.6	3.9	10.0
Net income ($ mil.)	–	0.4	(2.6)	(5.1)	(3.1)	(2.4)
Market value ($ mil.)	(45.1%)	1.1	0.8	0.3	0.1	0.1
Employees	5.0%	28	32	25	17	34

PENDLETON GRAIN GROWERS INC.

1000 SW DORION AVE	CEO: Allen Waggoner
PENDLETON, OR 978011938	CFO: –
Phone: 541-276-7611	HR: –
Fax: –	FYE: December 31
Web: www.pggcountry.com	Type: Private

Pendleton Grain Growers (PGG) gets the pendulum swinging faster for farmers wanting to take their harvests to market. The agricultural cooperative provides its member-farmers with a full range of farm products and services. PGG offers its approximately 2400 members crop-processing marketing agronomy and irrigation services along with hardware farm equipment and fuel. It operates about 30 grain-storage facilities and a fleet of nearly 15 storage-to-terminal delivery trucks. PGG was founded in 1930 to create bulk handling transportation and storage services for wheat farmers in the Pendleton Oregon area.

	Annual Growth	12/05	12/06	12/07	12/08	12/09
Sales ($ mil.)	–	–	–	(615.4)	128.9	131.1
Net income ($ mil.)	11257.2%	–	–	0.0	1.2	1.3
Market value ($ mil.)	–	–	–	–	–	–
Employees	–	–	–	–	–	180

PENDLETON WOOLEN MILLS INC.

220 NW Broadway	CEO: Mark Korros
Portland OR 97209	CFO: D M Simmonds
Phone: 503-226-4801	HR: –
Fax: 503-535-5777	FYE: December 31
Web: www.pendleton-usa.com	Type: Private

It doesn't raise the sheep but Pendleton Woolen Mills controls every other step of the production of its men's and women's apparel blankets pillows luggage furniture and other items. It buys raw wool; makes fabric and garments at its Nebraska Oregon and Washington factories; ships finished goods; and even sells the products in about 70 company-owned Pendleton shops. Founded in 1909 as a blanket maker for Native Americans it also sells its products through department stores including Dillard's and Macy's and in specialty shops as well as through catalogs and online. Pendleton's goods are sold in the US Europe Japan and Canada. The sixth generation of the Bishop family owns and operates the firm.

PENDRELL CORP.

NMS: PCO

2300 Carillon Point
Kirkland, WA 98033
Phone: 425 278-7100
Fax: –
Web: www.pendrell.com

CEO: Lee E. Mikles
CFO: Steve Ednie
HR: Mark Fanning
FYE: December 31
Type: Public

Pendrell is an asset management company of the intellectual property (IP) kind. It gathers up patents (it holds about 1200) and licenses them to technology companies thus receiving a cut when a technology is used. Its patent holdings center on technologies for tablets smart phones and other consumer electronics devices. Besides licensing IP Pendrell also develops technologies though none generate revenue yet. Companies that license IP from Pendrell include Casio Hitachi LG Electronics Microsoft Nokia Technicolor and Xerox.

	Annual Growth	12/10	12/11	12/12	12/13	12/14
Sales ($ mil.)	152.7%	–	2.6	33.8	13.1	42.5
Net income ($ mil.)	–	(2.7)	318.9	40.1	(55.1)	(51.0)
Market value ($ mil.)	(2.1%)	400.0	682.6	338.6	535.9	368.0
Employees	13.0%	35	42	51	73	57

PENFORD CORP.

NMS: PENX

7094 South Revere Parkway
Centennial, CO 80112-3932
Phone: 303 649-1900
Fax: –
Web: www.penx.com

CEO: Thomas D Malkoski
CFO: Steven O Cordier
HR: –
FYE: August 31
Type: Public

Penford Corporation doesn't mind its reputation for being stiff and starchy — that's how it makes its money. The company makes carbohydrate-based specialty starches used by the paper packaging and food industries. Paper and packaging manufacturers use the specialty starches and film-forming ingredients from Penford's industrial ingredients segment to improve the strength and quality of containers and magazine and catalog paper. The division also produces and sells ethanol from corn. The company's food ingredients segment makes starches and dextrins that improve the crispness texture and shelf life of various food products (including pet food and treats). Penford generates most of its sales in the US.

	Annual Growth	08/10	08/11	08/12	08/13	08/14
Sales ($ mil.)	14.9%	254.3	315.4	361.4	467.3	443.9
Net income ($ mil.)	3.8%	6.7	(5.1)	(9.6)	4.0	7.8
Market value ($ mil.)	29.1%	62.4	70.0	93.1	172.6	173.5
Employees	7.6%	330	333	396	403	443

PENGUIN COMPUTING INC.

501 2nd St. Ste. 310
San Francisco CA 94107
Phone: 415 954 2800
Fax: 415-954-2899
Web: www.penguincomputing.com

CEO: Tom Coull
CFO: Lisa Cummins
HR: –
FYE: December 31
Type: Private

Penguin Computing hopes to save the world from the cold clutches of monopolistic operating systems. The company builds and customizes Linux-based workstations servers and clustered computing systems. It also offers third-party storage and peripheral equipment. The company's Scyld Software subsidiary which it acquired in 2003 develops clustered computing software including its Scyld Beowulf operating system. Penguin's customers have included Brookhaven National Laboratory CACI International Caterpillar Duke University Genentech the National Institutes of Health Northrop Grumman and Stanford University. Penguin was founded in 1998.

PENN ENGINEERING & MANUFACTURING CORP.

5190 Old Easton Rd.
Danboro PA 18916
Phone: 215-766-8853
Fax: 215-766-7366
Web: www.penn-eng.com

CEO: Mark Petty
CFO: Joseph Coluzzi
HR: –
FYE: December 31
Type: Private

Penn Engineering & Manufacturing is a real clincher! The company's largest division PennEngineering (PEM) is a leading specialty fastener manufacturer. Other subsidiaries include PennEngineering Automotive Fasteners 3V Fasteners Company and QRP. The company's products are used in electronics computer data/telecom medical automotive marine and general manufacturing applications. Penn Engineering & Manufacturing sells through independent distributors and has manufacturing facilities in Asia Europe and North America. It was founded in 1942 by K. A. Swanstrom the former president of WWII war baby Elastic Stop Nut Corporation. A unit of Tinicum Capital Partners acquired the company in 2005.

PENN NATIONAL GAMING, INC.

NMS: PENN

825 Berkshire Blvd., Suite 200
Wyomissing, PA 19610
Phone: 610 373-2400
Fax: 610 376-2842
Web: www.pngaming.com

CEO: Timothy J. (Tim) Wilmott
CFO: Saul V. Reibstein
HR: Gene Clark
FYE: December 31
Type: Public

This gaming company is no one-trick pony. Penn National Gaming owns operates and has ownership interests in about 25 horseracing and casino gaming facilities (including several riverboats) throughout the US and in Ontario Canada. Its casinos operate mainly under the Hollywood and Argosy names. It race track facilities include Raceway Park in Toledo Ohio; Hollywood Casino at Charles Town Races in West Virginia; and Hollywood Casino at Penn National Race Course outside of Harrisburg Pennsylvania. The company also owns the M Resort near the Las Vegas Strip.

	Annual Growth	12/10	12/11	12/12	12/13	12/14
Sales ($ mil.)	1.3%	2,459.1	2,742.3	2,899.5	2,918.8	2,590.5
Net income ($ mil.)	–	(59.5)	242.4	212.0	(794.3)	(233.2)
Market value ($ mil.)	(20.9%)	2,782.5	3,013.7	3,887.6	1,134.4	1,086.9
Employees	1.6%	15,636	16,740	20,003	17,397	16,650

PENN TREATY AMERICAN CORPORATION

PINK SHEETS: PTYA

2500 Legacy Dr. Ste 130
Frisco TX 75034
Phone: 469-287-7044
Fax: 610-687-3688
Web: www.pennvirginia.com

CEO: Eugene Woznicki
CFO: Mark D Cloutier
HR: –
FYE: December 31
Type: Public

Dying takes a lifetime but Penn Treaty offered insurance on just the last few years. The company provided long-term care products including coverage for nursing home and assisted living facilities as well as home health care. It also offered Medicare supplemental policies. The company's products were underwritten by its Penn Treaty Network America American Network Insurance and American Independent Network Insurance Company of New York subsidiaries. Long-term care policies accounted for more than 95% of the company's premiums. While it continues to pay out existing policies the company is no longer writing new business and is operating under rehabilitation.

PENN VIRGINIA CORP

NBB: PVAH

Four Radnor Corporate Center, Suite 200, 100 Matsonford Road
Radnor, PA 19087
Phone: 610 687-8900
Fax: 610 687-3688
Web: www.pennvirginia.com

CEO: H. Baird Whitehead
CFO: Steven A. Hartman
HR: –
FYE: December 31
Type: Public

Incorporated in Virginia and based in Pennsylvania Penn Virginia is an oil and gas exploration and production company operating primarily in South Texas (Eagle Ford Shale). It also has assets in the Mid-Content Mississippi and to a much lesser extent in Appalachia (Marcellus Shale). In 2014 it reported proved reserves of 115 million barrels of oil equivalent of which 77% were oil and natural gas liquids (NGLs) and 40% were proved developed. That year some 83% of the company's proved reserves were located in Texas. Sales of crude oil from the Eagle Ford play accounted for the bulk of Penn Virginia's total revenues in 2014.

	Annual Growth	12/10	12/11	12/12	12/13	12/14
Sales ($ mil.)	25.8%	254.4	306.0	317.1	431.5	636.8
Net income ($ mil.)	–	(8.4)	(132.9)	(104.6)	(143.1)	(409.6)
Market value ($ mil.)	(20.6%)	1,199.4	377.2	314.5	672.4	476.3
Employees	(5.1%)	202	153	130	144	164

PENNANTPARK INVESTMENT CORPORATION

NASDAQ: PNNT

590 Madison Ave. 15th Fl.
New York NY 10022
Phone: 212-905-1000
Fax: 212-905-1075
Web: www.pennantpark.com

CEO: Arthur H Penn
CFO: Aviv Efrat
HR: –
FYE: September 30
Type: Public

PennantPark Investment believes that the higher the leverage the greater the reward. A business development company and closed-end investment firm PennantPark makes debt and equity investments primarily in highly-leveraged (companies with more debt than equity) middle market firms. It invests in senior secured loans mezzanine debt and equity investments and it typically contributes between $10 million and $50 million per transaction. The firm's portfolio comprises 45 companies that operate in a wide range of industries including business services aerospace and defense health care education hospitality and chemicals. Formed in 2007 PennantPark is externally managed by PennantPark Investment Advisers.

PENNEY (J.C.) CO.,INC. (HOLDING CO.)

NYS: JCP

6501 Legacy Drive
Plano, TX 75024-3698
Phone: 972 431-1000
Fax: –
Web: www.jcpenney.com

CEO: Marvin R. Ellison
CFO: Edward J. (Ed) Record
HR: Brynn L. Evanson
FYE: January 31
Type: Public

J. C. Penney Company is a holding company for struggling department store operator J. C. Penney Corp. One of the largest department store and e-commerce retailers in the US J. C. Penney Corp. operates some 1000 JCPenney department stores in 49 states and Puerto Rico. In a bid to revive the aging chain Penney hired — and has since fired — former Apple stores chief Ron Johnson as CEO. Following a disastrous decline in the business ex-CEO Myron Ullman returned to lead the company. He was succeeded by former Home Depot executive Marvin Ellison in mid-2015.

	Annual Growth	01/11	01/12*	02/13	02/14*	01/15
Sales ($ mil.)	(8.9%)	17,759.0	17,260.0	12,985.0	11,859.0	12,257.0
Net income ($ mil.)	–	389.0	(152.0)	(985.0)	(1,388.0)	(771.0)
Market value ($ mil.)	(31.1%)	9,845.2	12,629.0	6,061.4	1,805.0	2,216.6
Employees	(7.5%)	156,000	159,000	116,000	117,000	114,000

*Fiscal year change

PENNICHUCK CORPORATION

NASDAQ: PNNW

25 Manchester St.
Merrimack NH 03054
Phone: 603-882-5191
Fax: 603-882-4125
Web: www.pennichuck.com

CEO: Duane C Montopoli
CFO: Thomas C Leonard
HR: Pam Gorman
FYE: December 31
Type: Government-owned

How much water would Pennichuck pump if Pennichuck could pump water? Well Pennichuck does pump water to about 33200 customers (about 120000 people) in New Hampshire and Massachusetts. Its water utility subsidiaries — Pennichuck Water Works Pennichuck East Utility and Pittsfield Aqueduct — distribute water in more than 30 communities including the city of Nashua. Most of the company's water comes from a system of ponds. Nonregulated subsidiary The Southwood Corporation develops and sells real estate and Pennichuck Water Service offers contract maintenance testing and billing services. In 2012 the company was acquired by the City of Nashua.

PENNONI ASSOCIATES INC.

3001 MARKET ST STE 200
PHILADELPHIA, PA 191042847
Phone: 215-222-3000
Fax: –
Web: www.pennoni.com

CEO: –
CFO: Stacey M McPeak
HR: –
FYE: December 31
Type: Private

Design consulting and engineering firm Pennoni Associates specializes in the creation of civil infrastructure projects. The company offers construction services planning surveys transportation planning lab testing environmental engineering landscape architecture site design and other services. Pennoni serves East Coast clients including government entities and private companies. Affiliate Pennoni Engineering and Surveying of New York specializes in heating ventilation and air conditioning systems electrical plumbing and fire protection engineering. The employee-owned company was established by chairman Celestino "Chuck" Pennoni in 1966.

	Annual Growth	12/09	12/10	12/11	12/12	12/13
Sales ($ mil.)	2.8%	–	117.6	118.8	123.6	127.6
Net income ($ mil.)	(21.4%)	–	–	1.9	0.5	1.2
Market value ($ mil.)	–	–	–	–	–	–
Employees	–	–	–	–	–	900

PENNS WOODS BANCORP, INC. (JERSEY SHORE, PA)

NMS: PWOD

300 Market Street, P.O. Box 967
Williamsport, PA 17703-0967
Phone: 570 322-1111
Fax: –
Web: www.jssb.com

CEO: Richard A. Grafmyre
CFO: Brian L. Knepp
HR: –
FYE: December 31
Type: Public

Penns Woods Bancorp (PWB) is the holding company for Jersey Shore State Bank (named for the Pennsylvania town not the coastal vacation spot) which serves north central Pennsylvania through about a dozen branches. The bank accepts deposits from individuals and local businesses offering checking and savings accounts money market and NOW accounts and CDs. Residential real estate loans and commercial mortgages make up the majority of the bank's loan portfolio. The bank's lending activities are rounded out by agricultural commercial and consumer loans. PWB also owns Luzerne Bank which operates eight branch offices providing financial services in Pennsylvania.

	Annual Growth	12/10	12/11	12/12	12/13	12/14
Assets ($ mil.)	15.8%	691.7	764.0	856.5	1,212.0	1,245.0
Net income ($ mil.)	7.5%	10.9	12.4	13.9	14.1	14.6
Market value ($ mil.)	5.5%	191.2	186.3	179.7	245.0	236.7
Employees	11.8%	182	189	194	291	284

PENNSYLVANIA HIGHER EDUCATION ASSISTANCE AGENCY

1200 N. 7th St.	CEO: James L Preston
Harrisburg PA 17102	CFO: –
Phone: 717-720-2700	HR: Shelly Hauer
Fax: 717-720-3901	FYE: June 30
Web: www.pheaa.org	Type: Private - Not-for-Pr

Understanding how Pennsylvania Higher Education Assistance Agency (PHEAA) is set up may require a higher education. The government-related financial aid agency does business under the name American Education Services. It's one of the nation's top guarantors of the US Department of Education's Federal Family Education Loan Program (FFELP) as well as one of the largest student loan servicers and one of the largest student loan holders. PHEAA uses the funds it generates to improve higher education opportunities lower the cost of financial assistance and streamline the financial aid process.

PENNSYLVANIA REAL ESTATE INVESTMENT TRUST   NYS: PEI

200 South Broad Street	CEO: Joseph F Coradino
Philadelphia, PA 19102	CFO: Robert F. McCadden
Phone: 215 875-0700	HR: –
Fax: –	FYE: December 31
Web: www.preit.com	Type: Public

Pennsylvania Real Estate Investment Trust (PREIT) owns either outright or through partnerships about three dozen enclosed shopping malls and six strip and power centers as well as several retail properties under development. The REIT's portfolio contains more than 30 million sq. ft. of retail space in a dozen states concentrated in the mid-Atlantic region with a focus on Pennsylvania. The company also provides construction management development leasing marketing and property management services. It counts retailers such as Foot Locker J.C. Penney The Gap Macy's and Sears among its largest tenants. Founded in 1960 PREIT was one of the first publicly traded REITs in the US.

	Annual Growth	12/10	12/11	12/12	12/13	12/14
Sales ($ mil.)	(1.3%)	455.6	456.6	427.2	438.7	432.7
Net income ($ mil.)	–	(51.9)	(90.2)	(40.8)	35.9	(13.8)
Market value ($ mil.)	12.7%	999.7	718.3	1,213.6	1,305.8	1,614.1
Employees	(11.7%)	705	649	644	610	429

PENNYMAC FINANCIAL SERVICES INC   NYS: PFSI

6101 Condor Drive	CEO: Stanford L. Kurland
Moorpark, CA 93021	CFO: Anne D. McCallion
Phone: 818 224-7442	HR: –
Fax: –	FYE: December 31
Web: www.pennymacusa.com	Type: Public

If you're thinking residential mortgage this company has more than a penny for your thoughts. The parent of investment management loan services and investment trust companies PennyMac Financial Services (PennyMac) focuses on the US residential mortgage market offering loans and investment management services. Through its Private National Mortgage Acceptance Company the company's PennyMac Loan Services (PLS) originates home loans in 45 states and DC and services loans in 49 states DC and the US Virgin Islands. PLS's counterpart PNMAC Capital Management acts as investment manager and advisor. The companies service and advise PennyMac Mortgage Investment Trust (PMT). PennyMac went public in 2013.

	Annual Growth	12/10	12/11	12/12	12/13	12/14
Sales ($ mil.)	65.4%	69.2	76.7	273.0	386.6	518.3
Net income ($ mil.)	2.8%	33.0	14.7	118.3	14.4	36.8
Market value ($ mil.)	(1.4%)	–	–	–	378.7	373.3
Employees	34.0%	–	–	1,011	1,373	1,816

PENNYMAC MORTGAGE INVESTMENT TRUST   NYS: PMT

6101 Condor Drive	CEO: Stanford L. Kurland
Moorpark, CA 93021	CFO: Anne D. McCallion
Phone: 818 224-7442	HR: –
Fax: –	FYE: December 31
Web: www.pennymac-reit.com	Type: Public

PennyMac Mortgage Investment Trust trusts in its ability to acquire distressed US residential mortgage loans. The company seeks to acquire primarily troubled home mortgage loans and mortgage-backed securities from FDIC liquidations of failed banks US Treasury Legacy Loans Program auctions and direct acquisitions from mortgage and insurance companies and foreign banks. PennyMac is managed by investment adviser PNMAC Capital Management and offers primary and special loan servicing through PennyMac Loan Services. The company is held by Private National Mortgage Acceptance Company (PNMAC).

	Annual Growth	12/10	12/11	12/12	12/13	12/14
Sales ($ mil.)	78.0%	44.1	128.6	335.2	470.7	442.3
Net income ($ mil.)	67.9%	24.5	64.4	138.2	200.2	194.5
Market value ($ mil.)	3.8%	1,352.4	1,238.4	1,884.4	1,710.8	1,571.4
Employees	–	–	–	–	–	–

PENSION BENEFIT GUARANTY CORPORATION

1200 K St. NW	CEO: –
Washington DC 20005-4026	CFO: –
Phone: 202-326-4000	HR: Arrie Etheridge
Fax: 202-326-4042	FYE: September 30
Web: www.pbgc.gov	Type: Government Agency

Underfunded pension plans give PBGC the heebie-jeebies. The Pension Benefit Guaranty Corporation or PBGC — itself operating at a multi-billion-dollar deficit — was set up to promote the growth of defined-benefit pension plans provide payment of retirement benefits and keep pension premiums as low as possible. The government agency protects the pensions of more than 34 million workers and monitors employers to ensure that plans are adequately funded. The agency receives no tax funds; its income is generated by insurance premiums paid by employers investments and assets recovered from terminated plans. The corporation was created by the Employee Retirement Income Security Act of 1974.

PENSKE AUTOMOTIVE GROUP INC   NYS: PAG

2555 Telegraph Road	CEO: Roger S. Penske
Bloomfield Hills, MI 48302-0954	CFO: John D Carlson Jr
Phone: 248 648-2500	HR: Tim Roop
Fax: 248 648-2525	FYE: December 31
Web: www.penskeautomotive.com	Type: Public

Penske Automotive Group (PAG) has lots of lots. The US' #2 publicly traded auto dealer behind AutoNation PAG operates about 180 auto franchises from California to New York and Puerto Rico and another 150 franchises abroad mainly in the UK. It sells more than 40 car brands. Non-US brands including AUDI BMW and Honda generate roughly 70% of sales. PAG also sells used vehicles provides financing and runs about 30 collision repair centers. UK subsidiary Sytner Group operates more than 100 franchises selling 20 brands of mostly high-end models. Additionally PAG holds a 9% stake in Penske Truck Leasing (PTL) known for commercial leasing rental and contract maintenance. Chairman Roger Penske leads PAG.

	Annual Growth	12/10	12/11	12/12	12/13	12/14
Sales ($ mil.)	12.5%	10,713.6	11,556.2	13,163.5	14,705.4	17,177.2
Net income ($ mil.)	27.6%	108.3	176.9	185.5	244.2	286.7
Market value ($ mil.)	29.6%	1,572.1	1,737.2	2,715.5	4,255.9	4,428.3
Employees	10.5%	14,800	15,600	16,700	18,000	22,100

PENSKE MOTOR GROUP

3534 Peck Rd.
El Monte CA 91731
Phone: 626-580-6000
Fax: 626-580-6158
Web: www.penskemotorgroup.com

CEO: –
CFO: David K Jones
HR: –
FYE: December 31
Type: Subsidiary

Race-car legend Roger Penske knows a thing or two about cars: driving them and selling them. He does the latter in California through Penske Motor Group a subsidiary of diversified transportation services firm Penske Corporation. Penske Motor Group operates three dealerships in the Sunshine State two selling Lexus vehicles and another specializing in Toyota and Scion cars. Its 29-acre Longo Toyota dealership in El Monte is the best-selling auto dealership in the country selling some 26000 cars each year. In addition to selling new cars Penske Motor Group dealerships sell used cars of all makes and models and they provide maintenance services and collision repair.

PENSKE TRUCK LEASING CO. L.P.

Rte. 10 Green Hills
Reading PA 19603
Phone: 610-775-6000
Fax: 610-775-2449
Web: www.pensketruckleasing.com

CEO: –
CFO: Frank Cocuzza
HR: –
FYE: December 31
Type: Joint Venture

Penske Truck Leasing is a global player in commercial truck leasing. The company operates about 200000 vehicles from about 1000 locations in the Americas Europe and Asia. The company offers full-service leasing contract maintenance and commercial and consumer truck rental. Penske Logistics provides global transportation management distribution and warehouse management and integrated fleet logistics. Many of the Penske Truck Leasing facilities deliver a full slate of product and service contracts for commercial consumer and government customers. Penske Truck Leasing is a joint venture between General Electric and race-car legend Roger Penske's Penske Corporation and Penske Automotive Group.

PENTAGON FEDERAL CREDIT UNION

2930 Eisenhower Ave.
Alexandria VA 22314
Phone: 703-838-1000
Fax: 800-557-7328
Web: www.penfed.org

CEO: Christopher J Flynn
CFO: Denise McGlone
HR: –
FYE: December 31
Type: Private - Not-for-Pr

Pentagon Federal Credit Union (PenFed) is one of the largest credit unions in the US with about a dozen branches in the Washington DC area and a dozen others on military bases in the US and internationally. The credit union has more than 1 million members primarily employees of the Department of Defense and the Department of Homeland Security; members of the Army Navy Air Force Coast Guard and other uniformed services; employees of defense-related companies; Veterans of Foreign Wars; and their families. PenFed - which provides standard retail financial services such as checking and savings accounts; home mortgages; credit cards; and auto student and personal loans — has more than $15 billion in assets.

PENTAIR LTD.

NYSE: PNR

5500 Wayzata Blvd. Ste. 800
Minneapolis MN 55416-1261
Phone: 763-545-1730
Fax: 763-656-5402
Web: www.pentair.com

CEO: Randall J Hogan
CFO: John L Stauch
HR: –
FYE: December 31
Type: Public

Pentair is pumped about water! Water & Fluid Solutions the company's largest segment manufactures water flow and filtration products for the residential and commercial construction projects and municipal markets. Pentair's Technical Products segment makes custom enclosures (under brands Hoffman and Schroff) that house and protect sensitive electronics as well as thermal management systems used in industrial communications electronics and energy industries. Products are sold to a network of distributors OEMs water treatment facilities retailers and pool and electrical contractors. In 2012 Pentair merged its operations with Tyco Flow Control a unit owned by security products maker Tyco International.

PENTAIR WATER POOL AND SPA INC.

1620 Hawkins Ave.
Sanford NC 27330
Phone: 919-566-8000
Fax: 800-284-4151
Web: www.pentairpool.com

CEO: –
CFO: Robert D Miller
HR: Barb Giarelli
FYE: December 31
Type: Subsidiary

Summertime and the living is well hot and sticky in many places but Pentair Water Pool and Spa can break that heat. The Pentair subsidiary primarily serves the US and manufactures vacuums filters controls and other swimming pool accessories to keep that backyard oasis as well as commercial pools in inviting shape. The company's basic products include filters pumps and standard pool lighting. Additional features include automatic cleaning systems automated controls continuous color changing lights fiber-optic lighting heaters and automatic chemical feeders. Pentair Pool Products Sta-Rite and Rainbow are among the company's brands.

PENTON MEDIA INC.

249 W.17th St.
New York NY 10011
Phone: 212-204-4200
Fax: 914-725-8663

CEO: David Kieselstein
CFO: Nicola Allais
HR: –
FYE: December 31
Type: Private

Penton Media hopes to regain its foothold as a trade magazine publishing powerhouse. The business-to-business information provider produces more than 110 magazines and associated websites and about 60 industry events. It covers nearly 20 markets such as Commercial Aviation Food and Electronics with titles including Air Transport World Electronic Design and Broadcast Engineering. Penton also provides custom media and marketing services and rich data products (how-to manuals valuation guides business lists and technical information). The company was founded by John Penton in 1892. Today it is owned by private equity firm MidOcean Partners and U.S. Equity Partners II an affiliate of Wasserstein & Co.

PEOPLE'S UNITED FINANCIAL, INC.   NMS: PBCT

850 Main Street
Bridgeport, CT 06604
Phone: 203 338-7171
Fax: 203 338-2545
Web: www.peoples.com

CEO: John P. (Jack) Barnes
CFO: R. David Rosato
HR: David K. Norton
FYE: December 31
Type: Public

People's United Financial is the holding company for People's United Bank (formerly People's Bank) which boasts more than 400 traditional branches supermarket branches commercial banking offices investment and brokerage offices and equipment leasing offices across New England and eastern New York. In addition to retail and commercial banking services the bank offers trust wealth management brokerage and insurance services. Its lending activities consist mainly of commercial mortgages (more than a third of its loan portfolio) commercial and industrial loans (more than a quarter) residential mortgages equipment financing and home equity loans. Founded in 1842 the bank has $36 billion in assets.

	Annual Growth	12/10	12/11	12/12	12/13	12/14
Assets ($ mil.)	9.5%	25,037.1	27,567.9	30,324.4	33,213.7	35,997.1
Net income ($ mil.)	30.9%	85.7	198.8	245.3	232.4	251.7
Market value ($ mil.)	2.0%	4,312.3	3,955.2	3,721.3	4,653.9	4,672.4
Employees	0.9%	5,198	5,477	5,442	5,429	5,397

PEOPLECLICK AUTHORIA

300 5th Ave.
Waltham MA 02451
Phone: 781-530-2000
Fax: 781-530-2001
Web: www.peopleclickauthoria.com

CEO: Jeff Carr
CFO: Andrew Keenan
HR: Andy Bennett
FYE: December 31
Type: Private

Peopleclick Authoria has an authoritative view when it comes to human resources. The company provides human capital management software (also known as talent management software) that combines communications compensation and performance management succession planning compliance recruiting and benefits plan administration functions. The global company has some 2400 clients — including many companies in the FORTUNE 100 — in more than 200 countries. Founded in 1997 Authoria was acquired in 2008 by Bedford Funding for about $63 million. In 2010 Bedford Funding acquired Authoria rival Peopleclick for about $100 million; Bedford combined the two companies and renamed the business Peopleclick Authoria.

PEOPLES BANCORP INC (AUBURN, IN)   NBB. PBNI

212 West Seventh Street, P.O. Box 231
Auburn, IN 46706
Phone: 260 925-2500
Fax: 260 925-8303
Web: www.peoplesfed.com/peoples-bancorp.htm

CEO: –
CFO: –
HR: –
FYE: September 30
Type: Public

Peoples Bancorp is the holding company for Peoples Federal Savings Bank of DeKalb County which operates about 15 branches in northeastern Indiana and southern Michigan. Targeting area individuals and small to midsized business customers the bank offers such standard products as checking savings and NOW accounts; CDs; IRAs; and credit cards. One- to four-family residential mortgages make up most of the company's loan portfolio which is rounded out by multifamily real estate commercial real estate land acquisition and development and consumer loans.

	Annual Growth	09/09	09/10	09/11	09/12	09/13
Assets ($ mil.)	(2.0%)	487.8	472.5	480.6	484.3	450.8
Net income ($ mil.)	(4.2%)	3.1	3.3	3.8	3.0	2.6
Market value ($ mil.)	15.7%	30.8	33.0	38.2	46.3	55.2
Employees		–	148	–	–	–

PEOPLES BANCORP OF NORTH CAROLINA INC   NMS: PEBK

518 West C. Street
Newton, NC 28658
Phone: 828 464-5620
Fax: –
Web: www.peoplesbanknc.com

CEO: Lance A Sellers
CFO: A Joseph Lampron Jr
HR: –
FYE: December 31
Type: Public

Peoples Bancorp of North Carolina owns Peoples Bank which serves the Catawba Valley region of North Carolina through about 20 locations. It also runs Banco de la Gente ("Peoples Bank" in Spanish) which serves the area's Latino community. The banks offer standard services such as checking and savings accounts; CDs; mortgage construction development and other real estate loans (combined some 90% of its loan portfolio); and business and consumer loans. Peoples Bank has two subsidiaries: Peoples Investment Services which provides financial planning and investment products through an agreement with Raymond James Financial and Real Estate Advisory Services a real estate brokerage and appraisal services firm.

	Annual Growth	12/10	12/11	12/12	12/13	12/14
Assets ($ mil.)	(0.6%)	1,067.7	1,067.1	1,013.5	1,034.7	1,040.5
Net income ($ mil.)	50.3%	1.8	5.2	5.8	6.7	9.4
Market value ($ mil.)	36.0%	29.5	30.8	51.1	79.6	101.0
Employees	3.8%	273	277	273	291	317

PEOPLES BANCORP, INC. (MARIETTA, OH)   NMS: PEBO

138 Putnam Street, P.O. Box 738
Marietta, OH 45750
Phone: 740 373-3155
Fax: –
Web: www.peoplesbancorp.com

CEO: Charles Sulerzyski
CFO: John C. Rogers
HR: Michael W (Mel) Hager
FYE: December 31
Type: Public

Peoples Bancorp offers banking for the people by the people and of the people. The holding company owns Peoples Bank which has about 50 branches in rural and small urban markets in Ohio Kentucky and West Virginia. The bank offers traditional services such as checking and savings accounts CDs loans and trust services. Commercial and agricultural loans including those secured by commercial real estate account for the majority of the bank's lending activities. Its Peoples Financial Advisors division offers investment management services while Peoples Insurance sells life health and property/casualty coverage.

	Annual Growth	12/10	12/11	12/12	12/13	12/14
Assets ($ mil.)	8.7%	1,838.0	1,794.2	1,918.1	2,059.1	2,567.8
Net income ($ mil.)	31.5%	5.6	12.6	20.4	17.6	16.7
Market value ($ mil.)	13.5%	232.2	219.7	303.1	334.0	384.7
Employees	7.0%	534	513	494	546	699

PEOPLES EDUCATIONAL HOLDINGS, INC.   NBB: PEDH

299 Market Street
Saddle Brook, NJ 07663
Phone: 201 712-0090
Fax: –
Web: www.peopleseducation.com;www.epathknowledge.com

CEO: Brian T Beckwith
CFO: Michael L Demarco
HR: –
FYE: May 31
Type: Public

Peoples Educational Holdings wants to help make sure your student measures up — to state standards. Its subsidiary Peoples Education develops and publishes test preparation and supplementary educational materials for students in grades pre-K through 12 focusing on preparation materials for state-specific standardized tests. Its customized Measuring Up products are available in a dozen states. The company also publishes college preparation materials for high school students. Peoples Educational Holdings distributes its own print and electronic publications as well as titles from other publishers. Subjects covered include language arts mathematics science and social studies.

	Annual Growth	05/08	05/09	05/10	05/11	05/12
Sales ($ mil.)	(10.5%)	40.0	36.9	34.9	31.3	25.6
Net income ($ mil.)		(0.8)	(1.1)	0.3	(0.5)	(9.3)
Market value ($ mil.)	0.0%	31.3	31.3	31.3	31.3	31.3
Employees	(6.2%)	110	82	91	91	85

PEOPLES FEDERAL BANCSHARES, INC.   NAS: PEOP

435 Market Street   CEO: –
Brighton, MA 02135   CFO: –
Phone: 617 254-0707   HR: –
Fax: –   FYE: September 30
Web: www.pfsb.com   Type: Public

Peoples Federal Bancshares is the holding company for Peoples Federal Savings Bank a seven-branch bank in the greater Boston area. Peoples Federal Savings Bank offers traditional checking and NOW accounts; savings accounts include money market and CDs. The bank offers MasterCard debit cards but does not issue credit cards. It originates loans from retail deposits and advances from the Federal Home Loan Bank of Boston; in 2013 66% of its loan portfolio consisted one-to four-family residential mortgages. Peoples Federal Bancshares was incorporated in 2010 to convert from a mutual holding company to a stock company. The bank itself traces its roots bank to 1888.

	Annual Growth	09/10	09/11	09/12	09/13	09/14
Sales ($ mil.)	(1.4%)	23.0	22.3	22.2	21.2	21.7
Net income ($ mil.)	–	(0.2)	3.1	1.7	2.3	1.5
Market value ($ mil.)	16.8%	67.1	80.1	107.8	108.7	124.8
Employees	1.6%	75	82	83	87	80

PEOPLES FINANCIAL CORP. (BILOXI, MS)   NAS: PFBX

Lameuse and Howard Avenues   CEO: Chevis C Swetman
Biloxi, MS 39533   CFO: Lauri A Wood
Phone: 228 435-5511   HR: –
Fax: –   FYE: December 31
Web: www.thepeoples.com   Type: Public

Peoples Financial helps people with their money. The company owns The Peoples Bank which operates more than 15 branches along the Mississippi Gulf Coast. The bank offers traditional checking and savings products. Real estate mortgages make up about nearly 65% of its loan portfolio which also includes business construction and personal loans. Other offerings include fixed-rate mortgages and asset management and trust services. Peoples caters to individuals and middle-market businesses in industries such as seafood retail hospitality gaming and construction. Chairman and CEO Chevis Swetman owns about 16% of the bank; his family has had an interest in the bank since its inception in 1896.

	Annual Growth	12/10	12/11	12/12	12/13	12/14
Assets ($ mil.)	(4.0%)	786.5	804.2	804.9	762.3	668.9
Net income ($ mil.)	–	1.5	1.2	2.6	(0.5)	(10.0)
Market value ($ mil.)	(4.8%)	77.7	52.8	48.4	66.9	63.8
Employees	(2.7%)	196	183	182	180	176

PEOPLES FINANCIAL SERVICES CORP   NMS: PFIS

150 North Washington Avenue   CEO: Alan W. Dakey
Scranton, PA 18503   CFO: Scott Seasock
Phone: 570 346-7741   HR: –
Fax: –   FYE: December 31
Web: www.peoplesnatbank.com   Type: Public

Power to the Peoples Financial Services. The firm is the holding company for Peoples Security Bank and Trust Company (formerly Peoples National Bank) which operates about 25 branches across northeastern Pennsylvania and neighboring Broome County in New York. Established in 1905 the bank offers standard retail products and services including checking and savings accounts CDs and credit cards to local businesses and individuals. Commercial loans including mortgages construction loans and operating loans make up the greatest portion (40%) of the company's loan book followed by residential mortgages (25%) and consumer loans. The company's Peoples Advisors subsidiary provides investment and brokerage services.

	Annual Growth	12/10	12/11	12/12	12/13	12/14
Assets ($ mil.)	32.9%	558.6	621.4	918.0	1,688.2	1,741.7
Net income ($ mil.)	28.4%	6.5	7.8	10.6	5.7	17.6
Market value ($ mil.)	16.9%	200.8	213.2	230.2	286.8	375.0
Employees	30.0%	124	132	–	354	354

PEP BOYS-MANNY, MOE & JACK   NYS: PBY

3111 West Allegheny Avenue   CEO: Scott P Sider
Philadelphia, PA 19132   CFO: David R Stern
Phone: 215 430-9000   HR: –
Fax: –   FYE: February 01
Web: www.pepboys.com   Type: Public

An automotive paradise for do-it-yourselfers The Pep Boys - Manny Moe & Jack hears the cries of "Do it for me!" too. The company sells brand name and private label auto parts and provides select services through some 800 stores in 35 states and Puerto Rico. Pep Boys stock about 25000 car parts and accessories including tires and combined operate more than 7500 service bays for vehicle repairs inspections and parts installations. It also offers credit and parts delivery to commercial customers such as repair shops fleet operators schools and municipalities. The Pep Boys was founded in 1921 by Philadelphians Manny Moe and Jack.

	Annual Growth	01/10	01/11	01/12*	02/13	02/14
Sales ($ mil.)	2.0%	1,910.9	1,988.6	2,063.6	2,090.7	2,066.6
Net income ($ mil.)	(26.1%)	23.0	36.6	28.9	12.8	6.9
Market value ($ mil.)	9.4%	444.2	743.7	642.6	585.7	635.2
Employees	1.6%	17,718	18,279	19,123	19,441	18,914

*Fiscal year change

PEPCO HOLDINGS INC.   NYS: POM

701 Ninth Street, N.W.   CEO: Joseph M. (Joe) Rigby
Washington, DC 20068   CFO: Frederick J. (Fred) Boyle
Phone: 202 872-2000   HR: Robert (Bob) Grasty
Fax: –   FYE: December 31
Web: www.pepcoholdings.com   Type: Public

Pepco Holdings (PHI) arguably has more power in the US capital than most politicians. The holding company distributes electricity and natural gas through its Potomac Electric Power (Pepco) Delmarva Power & Light and Atlantic City Electric utilities to about 2.3 million customers in Delaware Maryland New Jersey and Washington DC. None of the company's three utilities have power generation plants. Nonregulated operations include energy efficiency consultation and renewable energy services for institutional and government clients through the company's Pepco Energy Services unit. In a major industry consolidation move in 2014 PHI agreed to be bought by rival Exelon for $6.8 billion.

	Annual Growth	12/10	12/11	12/12	12/13	12/14
Sales ($ mil.)	(8.8%)	7,039.0	5,920.0	5,081.0	4,666.0	4,878.0
Net income ($ mil.)	65.8%	32.0	257.0	285.0	(212.0)	242.0
Market value ($ mil.)	10.2%	4,612.3	5,130.4	4,956.0	4,834.7	6,806.0
Employees	0.5%	5,014	5,104	5,040	5,025	5,125

PEPPER CONSTRUCTION GROUP LLC

643 N ORLEANS ST   CEO: Bill McCarthy
CHICAGO, IL 606543690   CFO: Joel Thomason
Phone: 312-266-4703   HR: –
Fax: –   FYE: September 30
Web: www.pepperconstruction.com   Type: Private

Pepper Construction Group spices up the construction business with a little of this and a pinch of that. The company provides general contracting and construction management services for commercial office education entertainment health care and institutional clients as well as waterworks projects. (Health care projects account for about 50% of Pepper's revenue.) Its client list includes UBS Northwestern University University of Notre Dame Texas Heart Institute Loyola University Medical Center and NASA. Pepper Construction Group has divisions in Illinois Indiana Ohio and Texas. Stanley F. Pepper founded the company in Chicago in 1927. The group is owned by his family and employees of the firm.

	Annual Growth	09/07	09/08	09/09	09/10	09/11
Sales ($ mil.)	0.0%	–	–	–	911.8	911.8
Net income ($ mil.)	0.0%	–	–	–	15.6	15.6
Market value ($ mil.)	–	–	–	–	–	–
Employees	–	–	–	–	–	1,100

PEPPER HAMILTON LLP

3000 2 Logan Sq. 18th and Arch St.	CEO: Scott Green
Philadelphia PA 19103-2799	CFO: –
Phone: 215-981-4000	HR: –
Fax: 215-981-4750	FYE: December 31
Web: www.pepperlaw.com	Type: Private - Partnershi

Wouldn't you like to be a Pepper too? One of Philadelphia's largest law firms Pepper Hamilton (formerly Pepper Hamilton & Scheetz) provides legal services to national and international clients including large corporations small businesses and individuals. Its more than 500 lawyers counsel clients in commercial litigation intellectual property mergers and securities among other areas. The firm founded in 1890 has more than 10 offices primarily in the northeastern US. Pepper Hamilton also owns consulting company Freeh Group International Solutions. Clients have included private equity firm Advent International Corp. and drugmaker Eli Lilly.

PEPSI BOTTLING VENTURES LLC

4141 ParkLake Ave. Ste. 600	CEO: Paul Finney
Raleigh NC 27612	CFO: Derek Hill
Phone: 919-865-2300	HR: –
Fax: 919-783-6925	FYE: December 31
Web: www.pepsibottlingventures.com	Type: Joint Venture

Pepsi Bottling Ventures (PBV) makes sure East Coasters get their Pepsi fix. One of the largest Pepsi bottlers PBV operates more than 25 bottling distribution and sales facilities in seven states (Delaware Idaho Maryland New York North and South Carolina and Vermont). Its portfolio of beverages includes Pepsi soft-drink brands as well as Aquafina water Starbucks coffees Tropicana juices Gatorade isotonics and Lipton teas. PBV traces its roots to 1943 when the Arundel family began bottling and distributing Pepsi with four trucks on Long Island New York. Today PBV is a joint venture of PepsiCo and Suntory Holdings and is one of Pepsi's anchor bottlers.

PEPSI-COLA BOTTLING CO OF CENTRAL VIRGINIA

1150 PEPSI PL	CEO: –
CHARLOTTESVILLE, VA 22901-2865	CFO: –
Phone: 434-978-2140	HR: Sandra Butler
Fax: –	FYE: December 31
Web: www.pepsicva.com	Type: Private

Pepsi-Cola Bottling Co. of Central Virginia (PCBCCV) operates four soda and water bottling plants and distribution centers throughout the state of Virginia. They are located in Charlottesville Virginia Beach Warrenton and Weyer's Cave. In addition to providing some 18 Virginia counties with Pepsi Gatorade Tropicana and other PepsiCo products the company also distributes Dr Pepper Snapple Group products such as Snapple 7UP and Canada Dry. PCBCCV is the holder of the oldest written franchise (1908) on record with PepsiCo. Founded by Samuel Ambrose Jessup that same year it is still owned and operated by his descendents.

	Annual Growth	12/08	12/09	12/09	12/11	12/12
Sales ($ mil.)	1.4%	–	98.5	100.3	104.3	102.7
Net income ($ mil.)	5.3%	–	4.7	8.9	5.7	5.4
Market value ($ mil.)	–	–	–	–	–	–
Employees	–	–	–	–	–	380

PEPSICO INC.

700 Anderson Hill Road	CEO: Albert P. (Al) Carey
Purchase, NY 10577	CFO: Hugh F. Johnston
Phone: 914 253-2000	HR: Michele Thatcher
Fax: –	FYE: December 26
Web: www.pepsico.com	Type: Public

The PepsiCo challenge (to archrival Coca-Cola) never loses its fizz for the world's #2 carbonated soft drink maker. Its soft drink brands include Pepsi Mountain Dew and their diet alternatives. Cola is not the company's only beverage: Pepsi sells Tropicana orange juice Gatorade sports drink SoBe tea and Aquafina water. The company also owns Frito-Lay the world's #1 snack maker with offerings such as Lay's Ruffles Doritos and Cheetos. The Quaker Foods unit makes breakfast cereals (Life Quaker oatmeal) Rice-A-Roni rice and Near East side dishes. Pepsi products are available in 200-plus countries; the US generates 50% of sales. The company operates its own bottling plants and distribution facilities.

	Annual Growth	12/11	12/12	12/13	12/14	12/15
Sales ($ mil.)	(1.3%)	66,504.0	65,492.0	66,415.0	66,683.0	63,056.0
Net income ($ mil.)	(4.1%)	6,443.0	6,178.0	6,740.0	6,513.0	5,452.0
Market value ($ mil.)	10.9%	96,074.8	98,493.0	119,764.1	140,528.4	145,581.9
Employees	(3.0%)	297,000	278,000	274,000	271,000	263,000

PERCEPTIVE SOFTWARE INC.

22701 W. 68th Terrace	CEO: Scott Coons
Shawnee KS 66226	CFO: –
Phone: 913-422-7525	HR: –
Fax: 913-422-3820	FYE: December 31
Web: www.imagenow.com	Type: Subsidiary

Perceptive hopes your company is receptive to its document management tools. The company provides software and services that companies use to manage documents workflows and other enterprise content. Its ImageNow software suite includes tools for document and content capture integration imaging Web publishing and workflow management. Its customers include Asante Health System Georgia Tech Novant Health and Vulcan Materials. Perceptive has technology alliances with such companies as Canon Hewlett-Packard IBM Microsoft and SAP. It sells products in 30 countries worldwide but gets most of its sales in the US. Perceptive is a subsidiary of Lexmark International.

PERCEPTRON, INC.

47827 Halyard Drive	CEO: W Richard Marz
Plymouth, MI 48170-2461	CFO: David Watza
Phone: 734 414-6100	HR: –
Fax: 734 414-4700	FYE: June 30
Web: www.perceptron.com	Type: Public

Perceptron has a multidimensional view of what constitutes quality assurance for carmakers and building tradesmen. The company's proprietary image-processing systems provide 3-D scanning non-contact measurement and robot guidance systems for the automotive industry. Automakers use Perceptron's products to detect abnormalities and prevent variations — such as metal or paint defects — on formed parts. Perceptron also offers services such as consulting maintenance repair work upgrades and training. General Motors VW BMW and Snap-on are among its top customers. Roughly half of sales come from the Americas primarily the US.

	Annual Growth	06/11	06/12	06/13	06/14	06/15
Sales ($ mil.)	5.8%	59.3	57.4	60.9	59.6	74.4
Net income ($ mil.)	–	1.8	(0.3)	6.2	2.4	(0.5)
Market value ($ mil.)	13.5%	59.5	51.4	73.8	119.2	98.7
Employees	4.6%	289	229	235	245	346

PERDUE INCORPORATED

31149 Old Ocean City Rd.
Salisbury MD 21804
Phone: 410-543-3000
Fax: 410-543-3532
Web: www.perdue.com

CEO: Jim Perdue
CFO: Eileen Burza
HR: –
FYE: March 31
Type: Private

Chickens are always on the menu at this company. Perdue Incorporated is one of the largest poultry (chicken and turkey) producers in the US. The company operates live production and processing facilities in about 15 US states through its some 2200 contracted poultry farmers. The Perdue Farms division processes and packs more than 3 billion pounds of chicken and turkey a year. The company sells poultry in the US and in 100-plus countries through retail food outlets and to foodservice customers most of which are located in the eastern half of the US. Its Perdue AgriBusiness company processes grain for animal feed and pet food ingredients makes vegetable oils and manufactures fertilizer and renewable fuel.

PEREGRINE PHARMACEUTICALS INC.

NAS: PPHM

14282 Franklin Avenue
Tustin, CA 92780
Phone: 714 508-6000
Fax: 714 838-9433
Web: www.peregrineinc.com

CEO: Steven W. (Steve) King
CFO: Paul J. Lytle
HR: –
FYE: April 30
Type: Public

Peregrine Pharmaceuticals is spreading its wings and taking flight to attack and kill its prey: cancer and viral infections. While nearly all its revenue comes from its Avid Bioservices subsidiary which provides contract antibody and protein manufacturing to drug companies Peregrine is focused on shepherding its own candidates through clinical trials. Up first is bavituximab a monoclonal antibody candidate being tested to treat lung pancreatic and liver cancers as well as for other oncology and infectious disease applications. Next is Cotara being tested to treat glioblastoma multiforme a deadly brain cancer. The company also has development programs for potential diagnostic imaging agents.

	Annual Growth	04/11	04/12	04/13	04/14	04/15
Sales ($ mil.)	18.7%	13.5	15.2	21.7	22.4	26.8
Net income ($ mil.)	–	(34.2)	(42.1)	(29.8)	(35.4)	(50.4)
Market value ($ mil.)	(14.7%)	479.5	90.9	268.8	336.4	253.3
Employees	8.3%	156	174	187	184	215

PEREGRINE SEMICONDUCTOR CORPORATION

NASDAQ: PSMI

9380 Carroll Park Dr.
San Diego CA 92121-5201
Phone: 858-731-9400
Fax: 858-731-9499
Web: www.psemi.com

CEO: James S Cable
CFO: Jay C Biskupski
HR: –
FYE: December 31
Type: Private

Peregrine Semiconductor's chips are made to take flight. The fabless company designs radio-frequency integrated circuits (RFICs) used in the wireless infrastructure broadband mobile wireless device aerospace and test and measurement markets. Its UltraCMOS technology combines standard complementary metal oxide semiconductor (CMOS) with a synthetic sapphire substrate that provides enhanced power and performance over silicon substrates. Other products include attenuators mixers and synthesizers. Founded in 1990 Peregrine Semi went public in a 2012 IPO.

PEREZ TRADING COMPANY INC.

3490 NW 125TH ST
MIAMI, FL 331672412
Phone: 305-769-0761
Fax: –
Web: www.pereztrading.com

CEO: –
CFO: –
HR: –
FYE: December 31
Type: Private

No matter how you say it paper or el papel Perez Trading has it. From its Miami warehouse the company distributes more than 15000 tons of paper and paperboard inventory including corrugated box equipment napkin paper printing paper and other printing and shipping equipment and supplies. Customers include commercial printers converters distributors and packaging manufacturers. Perez Trading imports and exports to nearly 30 countries encompassing the Caribbean Islands Central and South America Mexico and the US. Perez Trading has been family owned and operated since 1947.

	Annual Growth	12/09	12/10	12/11	12/12	12/13
Sales ($ mil.)	2.3%	–	492.1	532.0	570.5	527.0
Net income ($ mil.)	(4.7%)	–	–	18.6	20.3	16.9
Market value ($ mil.)	–	–	–	–	–	–
Employees	–	–	–	–	–	148

PERFECTION BAKERIES INC.

350 Pearl St.
Fort Wayne IN 46802
Phone: 260-424-8245
Fax: 260-424-1477
Web: www.auntmillies.com

CEO: John F Popp
CFO: Jay E Miller
HR: –
FYE: September 30
Type: Private

You might say Perfection Bakeries strives for excellence in baking. A leading producer of baked goods the company makes such products as bread hamburger and hotdog buns and English muffins for the retail market under its flagship Aunt Millie's brand. It also supplies baked goods and mixes to the foodservice industry. Perfection Bakeries has operations in Illinois Indiana Kentucky Michigan and Ohio and its products are distributed primarily throughout the Great Lakes region. The family-owned company was founded in 1901 by John Franke as the Wayne Biscuit Company.

PERFICIENT INC.

NMS: PRFT

555 Maryville University Drive, Suite 600
Saint Louis, MO 63141
Phone: 314 529-3600
Fax: –
Web: www.perficient.com

CEO: Jeffrey S. (Jeff) Davis
CFO: Paul E. Martin
HR: –
FYE: December 31
Type: Public

Perficient is proficient in helping its customers use technology to their advantage. The IT consultancy provides software development systems integration and technical support. It specializes in developing middleware applications used to integrate and modernize legacy computer hardware and software. Its expertise also encompasses content management systems ERP and CRM applications business process integration service oriented architectures business intelligence e-commerce and wireless communication. Perficient integrates and supports applications from vendors including IBM EMC Microsoft and Software AG. Customers have included Anheuser-Busch AT&T Mobility and Wachovia.

	Annual Growth	12/10	12/11	12/12	12/13	12/14
Sales ($ mil.)	20.7%	215.0	262.4	327.1	373.3	456.7
Net income ($ mil.)	37.5%	6.5	10.7	16.1	21.4	23.2
Market value ($ mil.)	10.5%	410.7	328.9	387.0	769.5	612.1
Employees	17.5%	1,088	1,484	1,677	1,874	2,074

PERFORMANCE FOOD GROUP COMPANY

12500 W. Creek Pkwy.
Richmond VA 23238
Phone: 804-484-7700
Fax: 804-484-7701
Web: www.pfgc.com

CEO: –
CFO: –
HR: –
FYE: December 31
Type: Private

When it's time to eat out Performance Food Group (PFG) delivers. It's the #3 broadline foodservice distributor in the US (behind SYSCO and U.S. Foodservice). Through its Foodservice division PFG supplies more than 68000 products to independent restaurants hotels other hospitality operators and healthcare facilities through some 20 distribution facilities. The PFG Customized distribution unit serves chain restaurants such as Cracker Barrel and Ruby Tuesday. PFG subsidiary Vistar is a distributor of candy snacks and convenience foods for vending operators retailers and concessions. The company is owned by The Blackstone Group and Wellspring Capital Management which took the business private in 2008.

PERFORMANCE FOOD GROUP INC.

12650 E. Arapahoe Rd. Bldg. D
Centennial CO 80112-3901
Phone: 303-662-7100
Fax: 303-662-7565
Web: www.vistar.com

CEO: Dave Flitman
CFO: Bob Evans
HR: –
FYE: February 28
Type: Subsidiary

Performance Food builds its fortune on snack-food. Doing business as Vistar it distributes more than 3000 snacks quick-serve foods and other impulse items nationwide. In addition to candy savory and sweet bites and beverages it offers equipment including vending machines coffee brewers and hot dog rollers. Vistar also sells its lines through about a dozen Merchant's Mart a vending wholesaler with a handful of cash and carry outlets. Vistar's customers include foodservice vendors office coffee services theater concessions and convenience stores. Formed in 1997 the company operates through some 20 hubs. Vistar is a subsidiary of distribution foodservice giant Performance Food Group Company (PFG).

PERFORMANCE TECHNOLOGIES, INC.   NMS: PTIX

140 Canal View Blvd.
Rochester, NY 14623
Phone: 585 256-0200
Fax: –
Web: www.pt.com

CEO: John M Slusser
CFO: Dorrance W Lamb
HR: –
FYE: December 31
Type: Public

Performance Technologies (PT) contributes to communications convergence. The company makes networking equipment used to integrate traditional telephone and Internet protocol (IP) data networks. Its products include gateways routers and embedded IP switches designed for carrier-grade telecommunication providers. PT also sells related adapters and software. Most of its sales come from equipment manufacturers and systems integrators; it also sells products through distributors. The company's 125-plus customers include Alcatel-Lucent Leap Wireless/Cricket Raytheon and Metaswitch Networks. Recently rebranded as PT the company gets more than half of its sales outside the US.

	Annual Growth	12/08	12/09	12/10	12/11	12/12
Sales ($ mil.)	(12.9%)	40.5	29.5	27.9	36.2	23.3
Net income ($ mil.)	–	1.7	(10.1)	(11.2)	(1.2)	(7.1)
Market value ($ mil.)	(29.6%)	37.1	31.0	18.2	20.1	9.1
Employees	(13.6%)	228	201	172	146	127

PERFORMANT FINANCIAL CORP   NMS: PFMT

333 North Canyons Parkway
Livermore, CA 94551
Phone: 925 960-4800
Fax: –
Web: www.performantcorp.com

CEO: Lisa C Im
CFO: Hakan L Orvell
HR: –
FYE: December 31
Type: Public

For most of us it is best if we have never heard from or about Performant Financial. The company specializes in collecting debts owed mostly to government entities such as the US Department of Education's delinquent student loans improper Medicare payments from the US Department of Health and Human Services and taxes overdue to the US Department of the Treasury and various state governments. The financial firm operates its business nationwide. A relatively small part of Performant Financial's business involves recovering funds for private clients. The company began operations in 1976 but took its present name in 2005. Performant Financial went public in mid-2012.

	Annual Growth	12/10	12/11	12/12	12/13	12/14
Sales ($ mil.)	12.1%	123.5	163.0	210.1	255.3	195.4
Net income ($ mil.)	(1.5%)	10.0	12.4	23.0	36.3	9.4
Market value ($ mil.)	(18.9%)	–	–	498.4	508.3	328.2
Employees	2.0%	–	1,400	1,500	1,479	1,484

PERFUMANIA HOLDINGS INC   NAS: PERF

35 Sawgrass Drive, Suite 2
Bellport, NY 11713
Phone: 631 866-4100
Fax: –
Web: www.perfumaniaholdingsinc.com

CEO: Michael W Katz
CFO: Donna L Dellomo
HR: –
FYE: January 31
Type: Public

Perfumania Holdings makes dollars with scents. The holding company owns scent-seller Perfumania which numbers about 330 stores in 40 states (about a third are located in California Florida and Texas) Puerto Rico and the US Virgin Islands offering some 2000 fragrance products at discounted prices for men and women. Perfumania also sells cosmetics skin care and bath and body products. The company sells perfume online through perfumania.com and operates Scents of Worth which sells fragrances in retail stores (including Kmart) on consignment. Perfumania Holdings which own fragrance manufacturer Parlux is also a wholesale supplier of fragrances to other retailers through its Quality King Fragrance unit.

	Annual Growth	01/11	01/12*	02/13	02/14*	01/15
Sales ($ mil.)	4.8%	484.8	493.5	534.8	575.9	584.0
Net income ($ mil.)	–	(3.7)	4.1	(56.0)	(12.5)	2.6
Market value ($ mil.)	(7.8%)	122.9	152.1	99.0	96.7	89.0
Employees	1.9%	1,996	2,025	2,269	2,287	2,154

*Fiscal year change

PERICOM SEMICONDUCTOR CORP.   NMS: PSEM

1545 Barber Lane
Milpitas, CA 95035
Phone: 408 232-9100
Fax: –
Web: www.pericom.com

CEO: Alex Chiming Hui
CFO: Kevin S Bauer
HR: –
FYE: June 28
Type: Public

Interface chips are hardly peripheral to Pericom Semiconductor's business. The fabless company provides high-performance analog digital mixed-signal interface integrated circuits (ICs) and frequency control products (FCPs) which control the routing and transfer of data among a system's microprocessor memory and peripherals. Targeting the computer networking and telecom markets Pericom offers various chip product lines: interfaces for data transfer switches for digital and analog signals clock management chips and telecommunications switches and component bridges. Most sales come from customers located outside the US primarily in the Asia/Pacific region.

	Annual Growth	07/10	07/11*	06/12	06/13	06/14
Sales ($ mil.)	(3.4%)	146.9	166.3	137.1	129.3	128.1
Net income ($ mil.)	(21.4%)	10.8	13.5	(2.1)	(21.6)	4.1
Market value ($ mil.)	(0.1%)	201.1	195.1	197.8	156.5	200.0
Employees	2.0%	869	991	976	990	940

*Fiscal year change

PERKINELMER, INC.

NYS: PKI

940 Winter Street
Waltham, MA 02451
Phone: 781 663-6900
Fax: 781 663-6052
Web: www.perkinelmer.com

CEO: Robert F. (Rob) Friel
CFO: Frank A. (Andy) Wilson
HR: –
FYE: December 28
Type: Public

PerkinElmer makes tools to find out what's in you and your environment. It develops and sells equipment that researchers use to identify and treat diseases and to analyze food products as well as air water and soil to identify impurities and contaminants. The company which distributes its offerings in more than 150 countries generates most of its sales from lab and other products. Prenatal and newborn testing and screenings in emerging markets such as Brazil and China have been growth areas for the company. China is PerkinElmer's second biggest market behind the US. PerkinElmer traces its roots to 1931.

	Annual Growth	01/11	01/12*	12/12	12/13	12/14
Sales ($ mil.)	9.5%	1,704.3	1,921.3	2,115.2	2,166.2	2,237.2
Net income ($ mil.)	(25.7%)	383.9	7.7	69.9	167.2	157.8
Market value ($ mil.)	19.5%	2,904.3	2,249.6	3,490.3	4,632.0	4,957.0
Employees	7.5%	6,200	7,200	7,500	7,600	7,700

*Fiscal year change

PERKINS & MARIE CALLENDER'S INC.

6075 Poplar Ave. Ste. 800
Memphis TN 38119-4709
Phone: 901-766-6400
Fax: 901-766-6482
Web: www.perkinsrestaurants.com

CEO: Joseph F Trungale
CFO: Fred T Grant Jr
HR: –
FYE: December 31
Type: Private

Perkins & Marie Callender's operates and franchises more than 500 full-service restaurants under the banners Perkins Restaurant & Bakery and Marie Callender's Restaurant & Bakery. Its Perkins chain with about 440 locations offers standard American fare for breakfast lunch and dinner along with fresh muffins pies and cakes. Many locations are open 24 hours a day. Its Marie Callender's chain boasts about 85 locations offering traditional comfort foods and fresh baked desserts. Some 130 of the restaurants are company-owned. Perkins & Marie Callender's filed for Chapter 11 bankruptcy protection in 2011 and emerged late that same year.

PERKINS + WILL INC.

330 N. Wabash Ave. Ste. 3600
Chicago IL 60611
Phone: 312-755-0770
Fax: 312-755-0775
Web: www.perkinswill.com

CEO: Phil Harrison
CFO: Joseph Dailey
HR: –
FYE: December 31
Type: Private

Perkins+Will adds to skylines from Atlanta to Shanghai. The architectural firm designs edifices for corporate and civic clients as well as schools universities and hospitals. Its projects run the gamut from office buildings and high-rise condominiums to hotels and convention centers to laboratories and elementary schools. The company also offers interior design branding planning and urban design. Clients of the firm have included Chicago O'Hare New York University Pfizer and Time Warner. Perkins+Will operates from about two dozen locations worldwide. Lawrence Perkins and Philip Will Jr. founded the firm in 1935.

PERKINS COIE LLP

1201 3rd Ave. Ste. 4900
Seattle WA 98101-3099
Phone: 206-359-8000
Fax: 206-359-9000
Web: www.perkinscoie.com

CEO: –
CFO: –
HR: –
FYE: December 31
Type: Private - Partnershi

Fueled by longtime client Boeing and newer clients from the high-tech arena Perkins Coie is one of the largest law firms in the Northwest. Founded in 1912 the firm has more than 850 lawyers specializing in such areas as antitrust and trade regulation intellectual property and labor and employment. Perkins Coie's clients include individuals government agencies and not-for-profit organizations as well as international companies. The company has about 20 offices across the United States and in China. It has been listed on "FORTUNE"'s "The 100 Best Companies to Work for in America" for nine consecutive years.

PERMA-FIX ENVIRONMENTAL SERVICES, INC.

NAS: PESI

8302 Dunwoody Place, Suite 250
Atlanta, GA 30350
Phone: 770 587-9898
Fax: –
Web: www.perma-fix.com

CEO: Louis F Centofanti
CFO: Ben Naccarato
HR: –
FYE: December 31
Type: Public

Perma-Fix Environmental Services fixes its focus on nuclear waste management and related services. It operates four nuclear waste treatment plants. Its activities include the treatment of radioactive and mixed waste treatment and disposal for customers such as federal agencies nuclear utilities and hospitals and research labs. The company's services segment helps customers address regulatory compliance and other environmental concerns such as permitting and water sampling. Perma-Fix is also involved in researching and developing new ways to process low-level radioactive and mixed waste.

	Annual Growth	12/10	12/11	12/12	12/13	12/14
Sales ($ mil.)	(12.6%)	97.8	118.6	127.5	74.4	57.1
Net income ($ mil.)	–	2.6	14.1	(6.1)	(36.0)	(1.2)
Market value ($ mil.)	27.8%	18.7	17.8	7.8	35.7	49.9
Employees	(19.4%)	667	921	596	300	281

PERMIAN BASIN ROYALTY TRUST

NYS: PBT

Royalty Trust Management, Southwest Bank, 2911 Turtle Creek Boulevard, Suite 850
Dallas, TX 75219
Phone: 855 588-7839
Fax: 214 209-2431
Web: www.pbt-permianbasintrust.com

CEO: –
CFO: –
HR: –
FYE: December 31
Type: Public

Permian Basin Royalty Trust is a tax-deferred pipeline for Texas oil money. Formed in 1980 the trust derives royalties from the sale of certain oil and gas assets produced by ConocoPhillips in mature oil fields in Texas including property that's part of the Waddell Ranch. The trust distributes royalties to shareholders monthly based on the amount of oil and gas produced and sold. The company owns royalty interests on proved reserves of 5.5 million barrels of oil and 18.4 billion cu. ft. of natural gas. It also has interests in 1300 gross wells and more than 76900 gross acres of land. U.S. Trust Bank of America Private Wealth Management acts as Trustee.

	Annual Growth	12/10	12/11	12/12	12/13	12/14
Sales ($ mil.)	(6.9%)	65.3	64.6	55.1	41.7	49.0
Net income ($ mil.)	(7.1%)	64.1	63.4	54.0	40.5	47.7
Market value ($ mil.)	(19.4%)	1,056.2	949.4	571.4	599.4	445.1
Employees		–	–	–	–	–

PERNIX GROUP INC

NBB: PRXG

151 E. 22nd Street
Lombard, IL 60148
Phone: 630 620-4787
Fax: –
Web: www.pernixgroup.com

CEO: Nidal Z. Zayed
CFO: Marco A. Martinez
HR: –
FYE: December 31
Type: Public

Pernix Group (formerly Telesource International) provides engineering and construction services and operates independent power generation projects in the Pacific region and in the US. The group offers project development and management specialized construction and engineering and utility and plant operations. It also brokers goods and services. While its previous focus had been on Fiji and other islands in the Pacific Pernix Group has shifted its business model to emphasize offering construction services and working on power plant projects in North America.

	Annual Growth	12/10	12/11	12/12	12/13	12/14
Sales ($ mil.)	34.4%	26.2	69.8	120.0	73.8	85.3
Net income ($ mil.)	–	(3.9)	1.9	0.5	(4.6)	(1.4)
Market value ($ mil.)	223.6%	0.3	0.5	23.5	25.3	32.9
Employees	(4.8%)	180	175	105	115	148

PERSEON CORP

NBB: PRSN

460 West 50 North
Salt Lake City, UT 84101
Phone: 801 972-5555
Fax: –
Web: www.bsdmedical.com

CEO: Clinton E Carnell Jr
CFO: William S Barth
HR: –
FYE: December 31
Type: Public

BSD Medical has developed equipment to provide hyperthermia treatment specifically for treating cancer (including melanoma breast cancer brain cancer and cervical cancer). Its systems are used in tandem with chemotherapy and radiation therapy or as a stand-alone treatment. BSD Medical was the first to develop an approvable hyperthermia system which uses focused radio frequencies and microwaves to heat cancer cells until they die. The company's devices are designed to target superficial tumors as well as tumors located deep within a patient's body. Its products are sold to clinics hospitals and other cancer-treatment institutions through its sales force and external distributors.

	Annual Growth	08/11	08/12	08/13	08/14*	12/14
Sales ($ mil.)	(28.4%)	3.0	2.1	3.7	5.3	1.1
Net income ($ mil.)	–	(5.3)	(8.0)	(8.3)	(7.1)	(3.8)
Market value ($ mil.)	(50.6%)	11.6	6.9	6.0	2.6	1.4
Employees	6.1%	41	50	48	52	49

*Fiscal year change

PERSHING LLC

1 Pershing Plaza
Jersey City NJ 07399
Phone: 201-413-2000
Fax: 313-578-6377
Web: www.hom.org

CEO: Ronald Decicco
CFO: David Hopkins
HR: –
FYE: December 31
Type: Subsidiary

Pershing marshals its forces in the service of securities clearing execution and settlement for broker/dealers and registered investment advisors. The company deals in domestic and international equities fixed-income products options annuities and foreign exchange. It is a member of more than 65 exchanges around the globe. Additional services include compliance support custody brokerage account reporting and prime brokerage services. Pershing also provides operational support to more than 100000 independent investment advisors that enable them to supply mutual funds retirement planning managed accounts and other investment products and services to their clients.

PERSIAN ARTS SOCIETY INCORPORATED

12021 Wilshire Blvd. #420
Los Angeles CA 90025
Phone: 424-253-4726
Fax: +91-20-4012-2100
Web: www.suzlon.com

CEO: –
CFO: –
HR: –
FYE: December 31
Type: Private - Not-for-Pr

If your idea of Persian art is an intricately woven rug this organization has something to teach you. The not-for-profit group formed in 1993 works to promote and preserve traditional Persian art including music dance cinema and other visual and decorative arts in the US. It hosts lectures performances and exhibitions and offers a variety of classes; it hosts many performers and teachers who are living in Iran and other countries. While covering all the traditional arts Persian Arts Society focuses on music. It formed the first school of Persian music in the US in 2000 and regularly schedules concerts featuring Persian music a combination of vocals instruments and poetry.

PERVASIP CORP

NBB: PVSP

430 North Street
White Plains, NY 10605
Phone: 914 750-9339
Fax: –
Web: www.pervasip.com

CEO: Paul H Riss
CFO: Paul H Riss
HR: –
FYE: November 30
Type: Public

As the popularity of computer telephony spreads Pervasip (formerly eLEC Communications) hopes to cash in on convergence. Through its VoX Communications subsidiary the company provides wholesale Voice-over-Internet Protocol (VoIP) service to cable network operators ISPs competitive local exchange carriers (CLECs) and other resellers. Its customers in turn provide private or co-branded VoIP services to the residential and small business markets. VoX's service packages include such features as call return voicemail caller ID and call waiting.

	Annual Growth	11/10	11/11	11/12	11/13	11/14
Sales ($ mil.)	(23.7%)	1.4	1.3	1.0	0.9	0.5
Net income ($ mil.)	–	(3.4)	(4.4)	3.2	0.1	(0.5)
Market value ($ mil.)	(79.8%)	60.3	14.3	4.3	2.9	0.1
Employees	(13.7%)	9	8	8	4	5

PET SUPERMARKET INC.

1100 INTL PKWY STE 200
SUNRISE, FL 33323
Phone: 954-351-0834
Fax: –
Web: www.petsupermarket.com

CEO: Diane Holtz
CFO: –
HR: –
FYE: December 31
Type: Private

Pet Supermarket has it all for your furry and feathered friends. The company sells more than 10000 pet care products including food toys medicine and clothing through its website and more than 135 stores in a dozen states primarily Florida. Stores also offer vaccinations for dogs cats and ferrets and sell a variety of small animals such as hamsters guinea pigs rabbits and tropical fish. In addition Pet Supermarket works with area organizations to host adoptions and related events for cats and dogs. Like its pet superstore competitors customers can take their pets shopping with them. Founded in 1973 by Chuck West as Pet Circus the family-owned company became Pet Supermarket in 1986.

	Annual Growth	12/08	12/09	12/09	12/11	12/12
Sales ($ mil.)	13.5%	–	168.0	171.1	198.7	245.6
Net income ($ mil.)	–	–	9.4	0.0	0.0	0.0
Market value ($ mil.)	–	–	–	–	–	–
Employees	–	–	–	–	–	1,000

PETCO ANIMAL SUPPLIES INC.

9125 Rehco Rd.
San Diego CA 92121
Phone: 858-453-7845
Fax: 949-255-2605
Web: www.qsii.com

CEO: James M Myers
CFO: Michael E Foss
HR: –
FYE: January 31
Type: Private

PETCO Animal Supplies is a holding company for PETCO Animal Supplies Stores the second-largest US retailer of specialty pet supplies (behind PetSmart). The company boasts about 1150 stores in all 50 states and the District of Columbia making it the only pet store to cover the entire US market. The chain sells more than 10000 pet-related products for dogs cats fish reptiles birds and other small animals. PETCO Animal Supplies holding company was formed to create a foundation for the firm's upcoming growth strategies. Founded in 1965 PETCO Animal Supplies is owned by Texas Pacific Groupand Leonard Green & Partners which took it private in a deal worth $1.8 billion.

PETER KIEWIT SONS' INC.

Kiewit Plaza
Omaha NE 68131
Phone: 402-342-2052
Fax: 402-271-2939
Web: www.kiewit.com

CEO: Bruce E Grewcock
CFO: Michael J Piechoski
HR: –
FYE: December 31
Type: Private

Peter Kiewit Sons' is a heavyweight in the heavy construction industry. The general contractor and its subsidiaries have a breadth of expertise building everything from roads and dams to high-rise office towers and power plants throughout the US and Canada. Its transportation projects which include bridges rail lines airport runways and mass transit systems account for a majority of its sales. Kiewit also serves the oil and gas electrical power and waterworks industries. Affiliate Kiewit Mining owns coal mines in Texas Montana and Wyoming. The company which was founded in 1884 is owned by employees and Kiewit family members.

PETER PAN BUS LINES INC.

1776 MAIN ST STE 1
SPRINGFIELD, MA 011031025
Phone: 413-781-2900
Fax: –
Web: www.peterpanbus.com

CEO: Peter A Picknelly
CFO: –
HR: –
FYE: December 31
Type: Private

The Boy Who Wouldn't Grow Up has given up midnight flights to Neverland for the more mundane bus routes of the northeastern and mid-Atlantic US. Peter Pan Bus Lines provides scheduled service to more than 100 cities in about 10 states along the Boston-to-Washington DC corridor. It transports packages as well as passengers on its scheduled routes; in addition the company offers charter and tour bus services in the US and Canada. Overall the company and its subsidiaries which include Arrow Line and Bonanza Bus Lines operate a fleet of about 300 buses. Peter Pan Bus Lines was founded in 1933 by Peter C. Picknelly grandfather of company president Peter A. Picknelly. The Picknelly family owns the company.

	Annual Growth	12/03	12/04	12/05	12/06	12/08
Sales ($ mil.)	2.9%	–	51.9	52.6	53.9	58.2
Net income ($ mil.)	(12.1%)	–	–	3.2	2.7	2.1
Market value ($ mil.)	–	–	–	–	–	–
Employees	–	–	–	–	–	750

PETERSON AMERICAN CORPORATION

21200 Telegraph Rd.
Southfield MI 48033
Phone: 248-799-5400
Fax: 248-357-5874
Web: www.pspring.com

CEO: Dan Sceli
CFO: Tim Masserant
HR: –
FYE: December 31
Type: Private

So long as its products are under constant tension Peterson American has a spring in its step. The company doing business as Peterson Spring is the top private spring manufacturer in the US. With 10 manufacturing plants in North America and the UK it designs manufactures and supplies an array of springs constant-tension hose clamps snap rings stampings and subassemblies. It also offers a slate of engineering prototyping short run coating and kitting and assembly services. Customers include automotive OEMs Ford and GM engine makers for motorsports such as NASCAR and appliance and agricultural equipment manufacturers. The company is led by its founder's fourth generation chairman Alfred Peterson III.

PETERSON POWER SYSTEMS INC.

2828 Teagarden St.
San Leandro CA 94577
Phone: 510-895-8400
Fax: 510-352-9617
Web: www.petersonpower.com

CEO: Duane Doyle Sr
CFO: Mark Macguidwin
HR: –
FYE: December 31
Type: Private

With a lot more than alliteration going for it Peterson Power Systems has the power to systematically serve Northern California and central and southern Oregon customers by selling Caterpillar diesel and natural gas engines for use in trucks boats and power generation equipment. It also sells air compressors turbines and used equipment and rents generator sets. The company sells parts through its PartStore Web site. G. Howard Peterson founded the company as Peterson Tractor in the mid-1930s; in 1936 it became a regional Caterpillar dealership with six offices. Peterson Power Systems a family-owned business became a separate division in 1977.

PETMED EXPRESS INC

NMS: PETS

1441 S.W. 29th Avenue
Pompano Beach, FL 33069
Phone: 954 979-5995
Fax: –
Web: www.1800petmeds.com

CEO: Menderes Akdag
CFO: Bruce S. Rosenbloom
HR: –
FYE: March 31
Type: Public

Convenience is king to PetMed Express which bills itself as America's largest pet pharmacy. Through 1-800-PetMeds and 1800petmeds.com as well as a catalog with hundreds of items PetMed Express offers prescription and nonprescription medicines and other pet care supplies for your calico collie or colt. Founded in 1996 the company purchases its products at wholesale prices and ships directly to customers. Nonprescription medicines such as flea and tick medications and health and nutritional supplements account for about 55% of PetMed's total sales. The company makes 79% of its sales via its website. It also offers pet health information on a separate site PetHealth101.com which it sponsors.

	Annual Growth	03/11	03/12	03/13	03/14	03/15
Sales ($ mil.)	(0.2%)	231.6	238.3	227.8	233.4	229.4
Net income ($ mil.)	(4.4%)	20.9	16.7	17.2	18.0	17.5
Market value ($ mil.)	1.0%	321.4	250.8	271.8	271.7	334.7
Employees	(2.8%)	204	207	206	190	182

PETRO HOLDINGS INC.

2187 Atlantic St.
Stamford CT 06902
Phone: 203-325-5400
Fax: 203-328-7422
Web: www.petrohp.com

CEO: –
CFO: –
HR: –
FYE: September 30
Type: Subsidiary

When it's chilly in the East residents have warm spots in their hearts for Petro Holdings (formerly Petroleum Heat & Power). The company is a leading retail distributor of home heating oil in the US and sells provides more than 351 million gallons of heating oil a year to approximately 402000 customers and propane to 7000 customers in Connecticut Maryland Massachusetts New Jersey New York Pennsylvania Rhode Island and Virginia. A unit of Star Gas Partners' Star/Petro subsidiary Petro Holdings also sells home heating oil gasoline and diesel to some 28000 customers on a delivery-only basis. Other activities include HVAC equipment repair and home security and plumbing services to 11000 customers.

PETRO STAR INC.

3900 C ST STE 802
ANCHORAGE, AK 995035963
Phone: 907-339-6600
Fax: –
Web: www.petrostar.com

CEO: –
CFO: –
HR: –
FYE: December 31
Type: Private

Petro Star is an oil refining and fuel marketing shining star that brings heating fuel and energy (diesel gasoline and aviation and marine fuel)s to the citizens of the communities in the vast cold and lonely expanses of the US' largest state Alaska. It operates refineries at North Pole and Valdez and distributes fuels and lubricants throughout Interior Alaska Dutch Harbor Kodiak and Valdez. Started in 1984 by a group of petroleum industry veterans the company built its first refinery operations along the Trans-Alaska Pipeline at North Pole Alaska. Petro Star is a subsidiary of Arctic Slope Regional Corp..

	Annual Growth	12/00	12/01	12/02	12/03	12/08
Sales ($ mil.)	19.9%	–	279.2	267.8	291.0	992.1
Net income ($ mil.)	–	–	–	1.9	3.6	0.0
Market value ($ mil.)	–	–	–	–	–	–
Employees	–	–	–	–	–	300

PETROCELLI ELECTRIC CO. INC.

2209 QUEENS PLZ N
LONG ISLAND CITY, NY 11101-4003
Phone: 718-752-2200
Fax: –

CEO: –
CFO: –
HR: –
FYE: March 31
Type: Private

Petrocelli Electric keeps the city that never sleeps wired. Founded in 1933 the contractor installs and maintains electrical communications and lighting systems for commercial institutional and public sector clients in the New York City metropolitan area. Its activities include project management electrical engineering and design-build services such as developing electrical distribution and communications systems installing generators and fiber-optic cables and laying underground feeder cables. In 2009 former owner Santo Petrocelli Sr. pleaded guilty to charges that he made illegal payments to a union official.

	Annual Growth	03/01	03/02	03/03	03/07	03/09
Sales ($ mil.)	(4.2%)	–	159.1	162.1	147.2	118.0
Net income ($ mil.)	(1.1%)	–	0.6	0.1	0.6	0.5
Market value ($ mil.)	–	–	–	–	–	–
Employees	–	–	–	–	–	300

PETROHAWK ENERGY CORPORATION

1000 Louisiana Ste. 5600
Houston TX 77002
Phone: 832-204-2700
Fax: 832-204-2800
Web: www.petrohawk.com

CEO: –
CFO: –
HR: –
FYE: December 31
Type: Subsidiary

Petrohawk Energy (formerly Beta Oil & Gas) is riding rising oil prices to higher profits. The independent company's activities include the exploration development and production of crude oil and natural gas in the Anadarko Arkoma East Texas/North Louisiana Gulf Coast Permian Basin and South Texas regions. Petrohawk Energy has estimated proved reserves of about 2.8 trillion cu. ft. of natural gas equivalent. The company is concentrating its efforts on developing key shale plays including the Haynesville Shale the Lower Bossier Shale and the Eagle Ford Shale. In a move to boost its US shale assets in 2011 BHP Billiton acquired Petrohawk Energy for $12.1 billion.

PETROLEUM MARKETERS INCORPORATED

3000 OGDEN RD
ROANOKE, VA 24018-8857
Phone: 540-772-4900
Fax: –
Web: www.petroleummarketers.com

CEO: Ronald R Hare
CFO: Annette Willis
HR: Donna Farber
FYE: June 30
Type: Private

No fancy name for this company. It is what it says it is. Petroleum Marketers is a full-service petroleum company serving customers in Kentucky Maryland North Carolina Tennessee West Virginia and Virginia. The company's PM Terminals unit supplies gasoline diesel fuel motor oil and antifreeze to customers in its service area from eight bulk fuel storage facilities in Virginia. PMI Lubricants operates a fleet of bulk transport trucks while PM Transport offers for-hire tanker truckers for the transportation of petroleum products. The company also runs a chain of about 70 convenience stores/gas stations in Virginia under the banner Stop In Food Stores.

	Annual Growth	06/09	06/10	06/10	06/12	06/13
Sales ($ mil.)	9.3%	–	797.3	945.1	1,081.4	1,040.6
Net income ($ mil.)	(37.4%)	–	4.6	2.0	2.0	1.1
Market value ($ mil.)	–	–	–	–	–	–
Employees	–	–	–	–	–	1,500

PETROLEUM TRADERS CORPORATION

7120 POINTE INVERNESS WAY
FORT WAYNE, IN 468047928
Phone: 260-432-6622
Fax: –
Web: www.petroleumtraders.com

CEO: Michael Himes
CFO: Linda Stephens
HR: –
FYE: June 30
Type: Private

Petroleum Traders Corporation barters with fuel. The company provides wholesale gasoline diesel fuel and heating oil to fuel distributors government agencies and other large consumers of fuel such as businesses with vehicle fleets. The largest pure wholesale fuel distributor in the country Petroleum Traders operates and trades in 44 US states. It supplies #1 and #2 low sulfur diesel fuels biodiesel high sulfur heating oil and kerosene and conventional ethanol and reformulated blends of gasoline in regular midgrade and premium octane ratings.

	Annual Growth	06/10	06/11	06/12	06/13	06/14
Sales ($ mil.)	2.6%	–	2,470.7	2,796.2	3,066.5	2,670.2
Net income ($ mil.)	3.0%	–	–	13.9	24.2	14.7
Market value ($ mil.)	–	–	–	–	–	–
Employees	–	–	–	–	–	110

PETROLOGISTICS LP

NYSE: PDH

909 Fannin St. Ste. 2630
Houston TX 77010
Phone: 713-255-5990
Fax: 919-872-1645
Web: www.ateb.com

CEO: Nathan Ticatch
CFO: Sharon Spurlin
HR: –
FYE: December 31
Type: Public

PetroLogistics thinks it's perfectly logical to focus on making one petrochemical at a time. The company operates a 67-acre propane dehydrogenation (PDH) plant in Houston that turns propane into propylene a chemical used in the production of polypropylene. PetroLogistics sells its propylene to three major polypropylene manufacturers — Dow INEOS and TOTAL which use it to make petrochemical-based consumer and industrial products such as coatings paints plastic parts reusable containers ropes and textiles. The plant which began production in 2010 has an annual production capacity of 1.2 billion pounds of propylene. The company filed a $600 million IPO in June 2011 and went public in 2012.

PETROQUEST ENERGY INC

NYS: PQ

400 E. Kaliste Saloom Road, Suite 6000
Lafayette, LA 70508
Phone: 337 232-7028
Fax: –
Web: www.petroquest.com

CEO: Charles T Goodson
CFO: J Bond Clement
HR: –
FYE: December 31
Type: Public

Independent oil and gas exploration and production company PetroQuest Energy once focused its quest for petroleum on the hydrocarbon-rich and high margin Gulf Coast Basin but in the last decade in order to diversify its reserve base and allow it more financial flexibility it has looked to grow its assets in long lived lower risk basins onshore. In 2013 PetroQuest had offshore operations in the Gulf of Mexico and onshore operations in Arkansas Louisiana Oklahoma and Texas. That year the company reported proved reserves of 3.1 million barrels of oil 29.1 billion cu. ft. equivalent of natural gas liquids (NGLs) and 254.2 billion cu. ft. of natural gas.

	Annual Growth	12/10	12/11	12/12	12/13	12/14
Sales ($ mil.)	5.8%	179.3	160.7	141.6	182.9	225.0
Net income ($ mil.)	(9.8%)	47.1	10.5	(132.1)	14.1	31.2
Market value ($ mil.)	(16.0%)	487.3	427.2	320.4	279.6	242.1
Employees	9.2%	99	111	116	126	141

PETSMART, INC.

NMS: PETM

19601 North 27th Avenue
Phoenix, AZ 85027
Phone: 623 580-6100
Fax: 623 395-6517
Web: www.petsmart.com

CEO: David K Lenhardt
CFO: Carrie W Teffner
HR: –
FYE: February 02
Type: Public

PetSmart is the top dog and the cat's meow in its industry. The #1 US specialty retailer of pet food and supplies operates about 1350 stores in the US Canada and Puerto Rico. The retailer offers a noteworthy 11000 products which range from scratching posts to iguana harnesses. Products which are also sold through the PetSmart website are marketed under national brands and its own private labels. Unique to PetSmart its stores provide in-store PetsHotel boarding facilities grooming services and obedience training. The company's 20%-owned vet services firm Medical Management International (known as Banfield) offers its services in about 850 stores. Investment company BC Partners is buying PetSmart.

	Annual Growth	01/10	01/11	01/12*	02/13	02/14
Sales ($ mil.)	6.7%	5,336.4	5,693.8	6,113.3	6,758.2	6,916.6
Net income ($ mil.)	20.6%	198.3	239.9	290.2	389.5	419.5
Market value ($ mil.)	25.1%	2,591.9	4,043.4	5,387.2	6,440.1	6,341.5
Employees	4.2%	45,000	47,000	50,000	52,000	53,000

*Fiscal year change

PETTIT OIL COMPANY

820 Myrtle St.
Hoquiam WA 98550
Phone: 360-532-8144
Fax: 360-532-8299
Web: www.pettitoil.com

CEO: –
CFO: –
HR: –
FYE: December 31
Type: Private

Despite its name Pettit Oil Company is not a small French alternative to Big Oil. Rather it represents Big Oil (several of the major oil companies operating in the US including Chevron BP and Shell). The company supplies fuel and lubricant distribution operates convenience stores and cardlock service stations and provides home heating oils to customers in western Washington. Pettit Oil has corporate headquarters in Tacoma and storage and distribution facilities throughout the Olympic Peninsula. It also has offices in Forks Hoquiam Olympia Port Angeles and Tacoma.

PFIZER INC

NYS: PFE

235 East 42nd Street
New York, NY 10017
Phone: 212 733-2323
Fax: –
Web: www.pfizer.com

CEO: Ian C. Read
CFO: Frank A. D'Amelio
HR: Charles H. (Chuck) Hill
FYE: December 31
Type: Public

Pfizer pfabricates pfarmaceuticals pfor quite a pfew inpfirmities. The company is one of the world's largest research-based pharmaceuticals firms producing medicines for ailments in fields including cardiovascular health metabolism oncology immunology and neurology. Its top prescription products include cholesterol-lowering Lipitor pain management drugs Celebrex and Lyrica pneumonia vaccine Prevnar and erectile dysfunction treatment Viagra as well as arthritis drug Enbrel antibiotic Zyvox and high-blood-pressure therapy Norvasc. Consumer health products include such leading brands as Advil Centrum and Robitussin. Pfizer is merging with Allergan in a $160 billion deal — the largest health care merger to date.

	Annual Growth	12/10	12/11	12/12	12/13	12/14
Sales ($ mil.)	(7.5%)	67,809.0	67,425.0	58,986.0	51,584.0	49,605.0
Net income ($ mil.)	2.6%	8,257.0	10,009.0	14,570.0	22,003.0	9,135.0
Market value ($ mil.)	–	0.0	0.0	0.0	0.0	0.0
Employees	(8.3%)	110,600	103,700	91,500	77,700	78,300

PFSWEB INC

NAS: PFSW

505 Millennium Drive
Allen, TX 75013
Phone: 972 881-2900
Fax: –
Web: www.pfsweb.com

CEO: Michael G. (Mike) Willoughby
CFO: Thomas J. Madden
HR: –
FYE: December 31
Type: Public

PFSweb is all in when it comes to outsourcing. The company is an international business process outsourcing (BPO) provider of e-commerce services. Through its End2End eCommerce platform it offers such services as customer care digital marketing financial management logistics and fulfillment and order management. These services support both direct-to-consumer (DTC) and business-to-business (B2B) sales initiatives from developing new products to implementing new business strategies. PFSweb serves major brand name companies across a range of industries including toys (LEGO) consumer goods (Procter & Gamble) cosmetics (L'Oréal) and the US Mint.

	Annual Growth	12/10	12/11	12/12	12/13	12/14
Sales ($ mil.)	(2.6%)	274.5	298.8	281.6	241.6	247.0
Net income ($ mil.)	–	(7.4)	(4.6)	(1.5)	(5.9)	(4.6)
Market value ($ mil.)	33.7%	67.4	56.0	48.5	154.3	215.4
Employees	11.5%	1,100	1,400	1,550	1,300	1,700

PG&E CORP. (HOLDING CO.)   NYS: PCG

77 Beale Street, P.O. Box 770000	CEO: –
San Francisco, CA 94177	CFO: Dinyar B Mistry
Phone: 415 973-1000	HR: –
Fax: 415 267-7265	FYE: December 31
Web: www.pgecorp.com	Type: Public

Pacific Gas and Electric is specific about its services. The utility distributes electricity to almost 5.2 million residential commercial and industrial customers and natural gas to approximately 4.3 million customers in Central and Northern California. Pacific Gas and Electric has interests in power plants with a total of 7414 MW of generating capacity. It is also engaged in electricity procurement and transmission and natural gas procurement transportation and storage. Pacific Gas and Electric is the major subsidiary of holding company PG&E Corporation.

	Annual Growth	12/10	12/11	12/12	12/13	12/14
Sales ($ mil.)	5.4%	13,841.0	14,956.0	15,040.0	15,598.0	17,090.0
Net income ($ mil.)	6.8%	1,113.0	858.0	830.0	828.0	1,450.0
Market value ($ mil.)	2.7%	22,767.7	19,617.2	19,122.2	19,169.8	25,337.6
Employees	3.8%	19,424	19,274	20,593	21,166	22,581

PGT INC   NMS: PGTI

1070 Technology Drive	CEO: Rodney (Rod) Hershberger
North Venice, FL 34275	CFO: Brad West
Phone: 941 480-1600	HR: –
Fax: –	FYE: January 03
Web: www.pgtindustries.com	Type: Public

PGT helps Floridians weather their storms. The company makes and sells WinGuard and PremierVue impact-resistant doors and windows for the residential market. The energy-efficient customizable doors and windows are made of aluminum or vinyl with laminated glass and are designed to withstand hurricane-strength winds. PGT also makes Eze-Breeze porch enclosure panels and garage door screens SpectraGuard vinyl replacement windows and PGT Architectural Systems windows for high-rises. The company has two manufacturing facilities in Florida and North Carolina. PGT sells its products through some 1100 window distributors dealers and contractors in the Southeastern US Canada Central America and the Caribbean.

	Annual Growth	01/11*	12/11	12/12	12/13*	01/15
Sales ($ mil.)	14.9%	175.7	167.3	174.5	239.3	306.4
Net income ($ mil.)	–	(14.5)	(16.9)	9.0	26.8	16.4
Market value ($ mil.)	41.3%	116.9	49.1	217.5	477.5	465.6
Employees	12.2%	1,200	1,020	1,040	1,400	1,900

*Fiscal year change

PH GLATFELTER CO   NYS: GLT

96 South George Street, Suite 520	CEO: Dante C. Parrini
York, PA 17401	CFO: John P. Jacunski
Phone: 717 225-4711	HR: William (Bill) Yanavitch
Fax: 717 846-7208	FYE: December 31
Web: www.glatfelter.com	Type: Public

Turning over a new leaf? P. H. Glatfelter does it every day as a leading global manufacturer of specialty papers and engineered products. The company's largest business unit Specialty Papers produces carbonless paper book publishing paper envelopes and engineered paper for digital imaging postage stamps greeting cards and other niche applications. Its Germany-based Composite Fibers unit makes products like coffee and tea filter paper and self-adhesive labeling paper while the Advanced Airlaid Materials business focuses on nonwoven fabric-like materials used in feminine hygiene products diapers cleaning pads and wipes.

	Annual Growth	12/10	12/11	12/12	12/13	12/14
Sales ($ mil.)	5.4%	1,466.0	1,612.5	1,584.8	1,725.8	1,810.3
Net income ($ mil.)	6.2%	54.4	42.7	59.4	67.2	69.2
Market value ($ mil.)	20.1%	528.3	607.9	752.6	1,190.0	1,100.9
Employees	1.5%	4,337	4,274	4,258	4,403	4,610

PHARMACEUTICAL PRODUCT DEVELOPMENT INC.   NASDAQ: PPDI

929 N. Front St.	CEO: –
Wilmington NC 28401	CFO: Daniel G Darazsdi
Phone: 910-251-0081	HR: –
Fax: 910-762-5820	FYE: December 31
Web: www.ppdi.com	Type: Private

Pharmaceutical Product Development (PPD) is on the hunt for newfangled drugs. One of the world's largest contract research organizations (CROs) PPD provides global research and development services to pharmaceutical biotech and medical device companies seeking regulatory approval for their products. The CRO offers a broad range of services from toxicology testing in the earliest phases of drug research to the management of large multi-site clinical trials in which drug compounds are tested on human subjects. Its customers have included most of the world's top 50 pharma companies. PPD was acquired in 2011 for some $3.9 billion by private investors The Carlyle Group and Hellman & Friedman.

PHARMACISTS MUTUAL COMPANIES

808 Hwy. 18 West	CEO: –
Algona IA 50511-0370	CFO: –
Phone: 515-295-2461	HR: –
Fax: 515-295-9306	FYE: December 31
Web: www.phmic.com	Type: Private - Mutual Com

This company helps to ease the worries of the daily grind for pharmacists across the nation. Pharmacists Mutual focuses on commercial insurance coverage for pharmacists the home health care industry medical equipment suppliers and gift and card shops. The group (which includes Pharmacists Mutual Insurance Pharmacists Life Pharmacists National and Pro Advantage Services) is the largest independent insurer of pharmacists in the US. Offerings include personal property/casualty life and health insurance as well as financial planning services sold through regional sales offices nationwide. Pharmacists Mutual is owned by its policyholders and was founded as Druggists Mutual Insurance Company in 1909.

PHARMACYCLICS, INC.   NMS: PCYC

995 E. Arques Avenue	CEO: –
Sunnyvale, CA 94085-4521	CFO: –
Phone: 408 774-0330	HR: –
Fax: 408 774-0340	FYE: December 31
Web: www.pharmacyclics.com	Type: Public

Pharmacyclics wants to help cancer and other diseases cycle right out of your body. The clinical-stage company develops small-molecule drugs to fight cancer and auto-immune diseases. Its key product Imbruvica is approved in the US to treat mantle cell lymphoma a rare cancer and in testing for three other cancers. Pharmacyclis has two other cancer treatments and an autoimmune disease cure in its pipeline. The company has licensing and development agreements with Janssen Biotech Les Laboratories Servier and Novo Nordisk. It sells its products to specialty pharmacies whose customers are individuals and to specialty distributors whose customers are hospital pharmacies. Pharmacyclics was formed in 1991.

	Annual Growth	06/10	06/11	06/12*	12/12	12/13
Sales ($ mil.)	203.5%	9.3	8.2	82.0	160.7	260.2
Net income ($ mil.)	–	(15.0)	(35.2)	12.0	117.5	67.0
Market value ($ mil.)	151.4%	494.0	774.3	4,050.3	4,285.4	7,845.4
Employees	102.8%	58	77	150	224	484

*Fiscal year change

PHARMANET DEVELOPMENT GROUP INC.

504 Carnegie Center
Princeton NJ 08540
Phone: 609-951-6800
Fax: 609-514-0390
Web: www.pharmanet-i3.com

CEO: –
CFO: Richard Shimota
HR: –
FYE: December 31
Type: Subsidiary

When searching for new drugs drug makers cast their nets wide and PharmaNet Development Group aims to help them pull in a hit. The contract research organization (CRO) which operates as PharmaNet/i3 provides both early stage (Phase I) and late stage (Phase II-IV) clinical trials and bioanalytical laboratory services for biotech and pharmaceutical firms in some 40 countries. Services include recruiting test subjects monitoring trials managing data gathered during the trials and assisting clients with regulatory approval processes. The company serves both branded and generic drug companies as well as medical device makers. PharmaNet/i3 is owned by outsourcing firm inVentiv Health.

PHARMATHENE INC

ASE: PIP

One Park Place, Suite 450
Annapolis, MD 21401
Phone: 410 269-2600
Fax: –
Web: www.pharmathene.com

CEO: Eric I Richman
CFO: Philip Macneill
HR: –
FYE: December 31
Type: Public

Anthrax beware PharmAthene is out to get you and your brethren. The biodefense company in-licenses compounds and develops them into medical products that protect against biological and chemical threats such as bacteria fungi toxins viruses and other infectious or harmful agents. Products in development include SparVax an antigen anthrax vaccine; Valortim a human monoclonal anthrax antibody; Protexia a nerve agent therapy; and RypVax a pneumonic plague vaccine. Also in the works is a new-generation anthrax vaccine candidate that can be stockpiled for a longer period of time. Much of PharmAthene's product development is supported by grant and contract funding from the US government.

	Annual Growth	12/10	12/11	12/12	12/13	12/14
Sales ($ mil.)	(16.5%)	21.0	24.3	25.2	17.9	10.2
Net income ($ mil.)	–	(34.8)	(3.8)	(4.9)	(11.7)	(10.0)
Market value ($ mil.)	(19.1%)	269.0	80.8	71.2	118.3	115.1
Employees	(20.4%)	87	75	57	52	35

PHARMERICA CORP

NYS: PMC

1901 Campus Place
Louisville, KY 40299
Phone: 502 627-7000
Fax: –
Web: www.pharmerica.com

CEO: Gregory S. (Greg) Weishar
CFO: David W. (Dave) Froesel
HR: Todd Haines
FYE: December 31
Type: Public

The only time you'll see PharMerica's products is when a nurse hands you a pill in a paper cup. As the country's second-largest institutional pharmacy operator (behind Omnicare) the firm provides purchasing packaging and dispensing of drugs to hospitals nursing homes assisted living facilities and other long-term care settings. PharMerica operates about 100 institutional pharmacies including 15 focused on infusion therapies and five for oncology medications from which it packages and delivers medications in unit doses (rather than in bulk) to customers in 45 states. It also provides consulting and monitoring services of drug usage to help care facilities comply with government regulations.

	Annual Growth	12/10	12/11	12/12	12/13	12/14
Sales ($ mil.)	0.6%	1,847.3	2,081.1	1,832.6	1,757.9	1,894.5
Net income ($ mil.)	(22.9%)	19.2	23.4	22.9	18.9	6.8
Market value ($ mil.)	16.0%	344.7	457.0	428.7	647.3	623.5
Employees	(5.1%)	7,400	5,900	6,100	5,800	6,000

PHARMOS CORPORATION

PINK SHEETS: PARS

99 Wood Ave. South Ste. 311
Iselin NJ 08830
Phone: 732-452-9556
Fax: 732-452-9557
Web: www.pharmoscorp.com

CEO: –
CFO: S Colin Neill
HR: –
FYE: December 31
Type: Public

Drug developer Pharmos has focused its attention on the central nervous system. Its stable of drug candidates aim to treat conditions such as pain inflammation and autoimmune conditions. It gained its lead candidate dextofisopam when it acquired Vela Pharmaceuticals; the compound is a potential treatment for irritable bowel syndrome a condition associated with the "brain-gut axis" or the connection between the nervous system and the intestines. Pharmos has also discovered several compounds in-house using its expertise in cannabinoid compounds (the kind without psychotropic effects). It is investigating several such compounds as treatments for pain and inflammation.

PHELPS DUNBAR L.L.P.

365 CANAL ST STE 2000
NEW ORLEANS, LA 70130-6534
Phone: 504-566-1311
Fax: –
Web: www.phelpsdunbar.com

CEO: Jeffrey M Baudier
CFO: –
HR: –
FYE: December 31
Type: Private

A leading regional law firm Phelps Dunbar has more than 280 attorneys overall. The firm has represented public and private companies educational institutions governmental agencies health care systems estates and individuals. Clients have included T3 Technologies Louisiana Wholesale Drug Co. and Deutsche Schiffsbank. Among Phelps Dunbar's practice areas are admiralty; bankruptcy; commercial litigation; intellectual property; oil and gas; and product liability. Phelps Dunbar is especially focused on clients operating in the oil gas and energy industries.

	Annual Growth	12/07	12/08	12/09	12/10	12/11
Sales ($ mil.)	3.9%	–	98.0	98.6	109.5	109.8
Net income ($ mil.)	7.3%	–	36.5	36.4	46.4	45.1
Market value ($ mil.)	–	–	–	–	–	–
Employees	–	–	–	–	–	611

PHELPS MEMORIAL HOSPITAL ASSOCIATION

701 N BROADWAY
SLEEPY HOLLOW, NY 105911096
Phone: 914-366-3000
Fax: –
Web: www.phelpshospital.org

CEO: –
CFO: Vincent Desantis
HR: Kevin T Byrne
FYE: December 31
Type: Private

If you happen to spot the headless horseman in Sleepy Hollow it's possible he's on his way to Phelps Memorial Hospital for some medical treatment. The 240-bed hospital provides both physical and mental health care services to residents of Sleepy Hollow and Westchester County New York. Specialized services include cardiology emergency care orthopedics and psychiatry. It also includes a satellite location of the Memorial Sloan-Kettering Cancer Center and it provides geriatric health services through a partnership with Mount Sinai Hospital and operates a senior retirement community with Kendal Corporation. Phelps Memorial is one of four hospitals that make up the Stellaris Health Network.

	Annual Growth	12/03	12/04	12/05	12/06	12/09
Sales ($ mil.)	7.9%	–	124.8	130.0	135.2	182.7
Net income ($ mil.)	0.9%	–	–	5.7	5.4	5.9
Market value ($ mil.)	–	–	–	–	–	–
Employees	–	–	–	–	–	1,200

PHH CORP

NYS: PHH

3000 Leadenhall Road
Mt. Laurel, NJ 08054
Phone: 856 917-1744
Fax: –
Web: www.phh.com

CEO: Glen A. Messina
CFO: Robert B. (Rob) Crowl
HR: Kathryn Ruggieri
FYE: December 31
Type: Public

Through its primary PHH Mortgage segment PHH Corporation offers mortgage-related activities such as originating purchasing selling and servicing mortgage loans. It caters primarily to financial institutions and real estate brokers in the US. PHH Corporation makes nearly 70% of its revenue through mortgage origination service fees and in selling its mortgage loans on the secondary market and another 25% from its mortgage servicing business. The company's former Vehicle Management segment a provider of commercial fleet management services in the US and Canada was sold to Element Financial Corporation in 2014. Its top clients include Fannie Mae Freddie Mac and Ginnie Mae.

	Annual Growth	12/10	12/11	12/12	12/13	12/14
Sales ($ mil.)	(28.4%)	2,438.0	2,214.0	2,743.0	2,842.0	639.0
Net income ($ mil.)	14.0%	48.0	(127.0)	34.0	135.0	81.0
Market value ($ mil.)	0.9%	1,184.0	547.2	1,163.5	1,245.3	1,225.4
Employees	(7.5%)	5,610	5,740	6,700	6,000	4,100

PHH MORTGAGE CORP.

1 Mortgage Way
Mt. Laurel NJ 08054
Phone: 856-917-6000
Fax: 856-917-8037
Web: www.phhmortgage.com

CEO: –
CFO: –
HR: –
FYE: December 31
Type: Subsidiary

Psst.PHH Mortgage provides mortgage financing through a nationwide network of real estate brokers and other financial institutions. A subsidiary of PHH Corporation the company is among the largest originators and servicers of residential mortgages in the US. It provides private-label mortgage origination and servicing to companies such as Merrill Lynch USAA and Charles Schwab; each account for more than 10% of the company's loan volume. Through a joint venture with Realogy PHH Mortgage originates loans for customers of Realogy companies such as Century 21 and Coldwell Banker. The company also works with Realogy's relocation division Cartus.

PHI GROUP INC.

NBB: PHIL

5348 Vegas Drive
Las Vegas, NV 89128
Phone: 702 475-5430
Fax: –
Web: www.phiglobal.com

CEO: –
CFO: Henry D Fahman
HR: –
FYE: June 30
Type: Public

PHI Group rolls a variety of business into one. The holding company focuses its attention on consulting and financial services real estate investment and natural resources and energy. At the center of PHI Group's offerings is PHI Vietnam and PHI Capital which provide assistance to Vietnamese companies that go public in the US. Other PHI Group holdings include PHI Gold Corporation which invests in gold mines around the world. Real estate arm PHI-LAND Ranch develops industrial residential and hospitality properties in southeast Asia.

	Annual Growth	06/11	06/12	06/13	06/14	06/15
Sales ($ mil.)	(25.3%)	0.4	0.6	–	0.1	0.1
Net income ($ mil.)	–	(1.2)	(5.2)	(0.9)	(0.3)	(1.4)
Market value ($ mil.)	–	0.0	3.8	2.7	1.7	0.8
Employees	–	–	–	–	–	–

PHI INC

NMS: PHII K

2001 SE Evangeline Thruway
Lafayette, LA 70508
Phone: 337 235-2452
Fax: 337 235-1357
Web: www.phihelico.com

CEO: Al A. Gonsoulin
CFO: Trudy P. McConnaughhay
HR: –
FYE: December 31
Type: Public

Whirlybird wizard PHI transports people and equipment mainly for oil and gas companies. One of the world's top commercial helicopter operators PHI maintains a fleet of more than 270 aircraft and provides contract transportation services across the US and in Africa primarily for the oil and gas industry. Its fleet is primarily made up of helicopters but also includes fixed-wing aircraft. The company is a leading provider of helicopter transport services in the Gulf of Mexico.In addition to its energy-related operations PHI provides air transportation services to hospitals and other medical facilities and overhauls and maintains airframes engines and components.

	Annual Growth	12/10	12/11	12/12	12/13	12/14
Sales ($ mil.)	12.8%	517.4	540.2	646.7	856.5	836.3
Net income ($ mil.)	46.4%	7.1	4.9	18.1	59.0	32.7
Market value ($ mil.)	18.7%	291.7	384.7	518.5	671.9	579.1
Employees	5.9%	2,265	2,362	2,633	2,791	2,844

PHIBRO ANIMAL HEALTH CORPORATION

Glenpoint Centre East Frank W. Burr Blvd. 3rd Fl 300
Teaneck NJ 07666-6712
Phone: 201-329-7300
Fax: 201-329-7399
Web: www.pahc.com

CEO: Jack C Bendheim
CFO: Richard G Johnson
HR: Adrienne A Mein
FYE: June 30
Type: Private

Phibro Animal Health makes feeding time down on the farm a happy occasion. The company's Animal Health and Nutrition segment produces animal feed additives including trace minerals vitamins and antibiotics for livestock poultry and aquaculture markets worldwide. Phibro's Performance Products segment manufactures specialty chemicals for agricultural and industrial uses including ingredients for the ethanol coatings and adhesives metal and personal care industries. Phibro also supplies antimicrobials used in ethanol production. Chairman and president Jack Bendheim owns a majority stake in Phibro Animal Health.

PHILADELPHIA EAGLES LIMITED PARTNERSHIP

1 NovaCare Way
Philadelphia PA 19145
Phone: 215-463-2500
Fax: 215-339-5464
Web: www.philadelphiaeagles.com

CEO: Jeffrey Lurie
CFO: Don Smolenski
HR: –
FYE: December 31
Type: Private

The spirits of Philly football fans dip and soar with the fortunes of this team. One of the more storied members of the National Football League the Philadelphia Eagles professional football team has represented the City of Brotherly Love since the franchise was awarded to Bert Bell and Lud Wray in 1933. Its roster has featured such Hall of Fame players as Chuck Bednarik Steve Van Buren and Reggie White. Championships though have been few and far between: its last NFL title was won in 1960 and the franchise boasts just two Super Bowl appearances. The team plays host at Philadelphia's Lincoln Financial Field. Jeffrey Lurie a former movie producer has owned the team since 1994.

PHILADELPHIA INSURANCE COMPANIES

1 Bala Plaza Ste. 100
Bala Cynwyd PA 19004
Phone: 610-617-7900
Fax: 610-617-7940
Web: www.phly.com

CEO: Robert D O'Leary
CFO: –
HR: –
FYE: December 31
Type: Subsidiary

Because each industry has its own unique set of risks Philadelphia Insurance Companies and its subsidiaries specialize in designing and underwriting commercial property/casualty insurance. Its niche clients include rental car companies (for that insurance they always want to sell you at the counter) not-for-profits health and fitness centers and day-care facilities. Its specialty lines include loss-control policies and liability coverage for such professionals as lawyers doctors accountants dog groomers and even insurance claims adjusters. The company also sells personal coverage for collectible cars and homeowners flood insurance. Philadelphia Insurance Companies is a subsidiary of Tokio Marine Holdings.

PHILADELPHIA UNIVERSITY

4201 HENRY AVE
PHILADELPHIA, PA 191445409
Phone: 215-951-2700
Fax: –
Web: www.philau.edu

CEO: –
CFO: –
HR: –
FYE: June 30
Type: Private

Located in the heart of The City of Brotherly Love Philadelphia University (PhilaU) offers more than 60 undergraduate and graduate degrees from programs such as architecture business administration design and media engineering and textiles liberal arts and science and health. The private school also offers several accelerated degree programs in disciplines such as business and the health sciences aimed primarily at adult learners. It has an enrollment of about 3200 students. Founded in 1884 as the Philadelphia Textile School the school changed its name several times before receiving university status in 1999. PhilaU announced plans to merge with Thomas Jefferson University in late 2015.

	Annual Growth	06/06	06/07	06/08	06/09	06/10
Sales ($ mil.)	–	–	–	0.0	106.5	113.6
Net income ($ mil.)	131856.1%	–	–	0.0	0.0	7.0
Market value ($ mil.)	–	–	–	–	–	–
Employees	–	–	–	–	–	625

PHILADELPHIA WORKFORCE DEVELOPMENT CORPORATION

1617 JFK BLVD STE 1300
PHILADELPHIA, PA 191031813
Phone: 215-963-2100
Fax: –
Web: www.philaworks.org

CEO: Mark Edwards
CFO: Dale Porter
HR: –
FYE: June 30
Type: Private

The Philadelphia Workforce Development Corporation (PWDC) wants Philadelphians-, to get a job. A tax-exempt not-for-profit PWDC has served the city's workforce-, since 1982. For-, businesses it offers employee-, recruitment development and retention-, services; assessment and testing;-, job fair coordination;-, wage subsidies; and tax credits. It trains-, job seekers (including ex-offenders the homeless workers with disabilities-, and unemployed adults) in-, areas such as-, skills development resume writing interviewing and salary negotiations. The agency also-, funnels state and federal dollars to-, agencies that provide workforce training. Philadelphia area employers-, that have partnered with PWDC include-, ARAMARK-, and-, -, IKEA.

	Annual Growth	06/08	06/09	06/10	06/11	06/12
Sales ($ mil.)	(24.3%)	–	110.5	112.8	120.3	47.9
Net income ($ mil.)	–	–	–	0.0	(0.2)	(0.2)
Market value ($ mil.)	–	–	–	–	–	–
Employees	–	–	–	–	–	100

PHILIP MORRIS INTERNATIONAL INC

NYS: PM

120 Park Avenue
New York, NY 10017
Phone: 917 663-2000
Fax: 917 663-5372
Web: www.pmi.com

CEO: Andr © Calantzopoulos
CFO: Jacek Olczak
HR: Mike Haywood
FYE: December 31
Type: Public

Philip Morris International (PMI) knows how to light up a room. The company makes seven of the world's top 15 tobacco brands laying claim to at least 15% of the international cigarette market outside the US. The company's brands by sales volume are Marlboro (the world's #1-selling cigarette) L&M Bond Street Philip Morris Chesterfield and Parliament. (Marlboro accounts for about a third of PMI's total shipment volume.) Top local brands include Fortune Morven Gold and Dji Sam Soe. PMI's portfolio spans the price spectrum with premium mid-priced and value-priced products. Formerly part of Altria PMI has grown through acquisitions and alliances with cigarette and smokeless tobacco makers.

	Annual Growth	12/10	12/11	12/12	12/13	12/14
Sales ($ mil.)	4.3%	67,713.0	76,346.0	77,393.0	80,029.0	80,106.0
Net income ($ mil.)	0.8%	7,259.0	8,591.0	8,800.0	8,576.0	7,493.0
Market value ($ mil.)	8.6%	90,540.0	121,400.7	129,382.7	134,781.4	125,995.0
Employees	1.3%	78,300	78,100	87,100	91,100	82,500

PHILIPS ELECTRONICS NORTH AMERICA CORPORATION

3000 Minuteman Rd.
Andover MA 01810
Phone: 800-223-1828
Fax: 310-952-2199
Web: www.pioneerelectronics.com

CEO: Brent Shafer
CFO: –
HR: –
FYE: December 31
Type: Subsidiary

Whether you need an early morning shave or a late night TV fix Philips Electronics North America has got the goods. The US arm of Dutch company Royal Philips Electronics the company oversees Philips operations in the US Canada and Mexico. Its divisions include Philips Healthcare (imaging patient information systems home healthcare products clinical management and equipment financing) Consumer Lifestyle (consumer electronics home appliances personal care) and Lighting (home industrial and municipal light bulbs fixtures and systems). Philips Electronics North America's Corporate Technologies group conducts R&D and partners with outside groups to feed the development pipeline for the other units.

PHILIPS LUMILEDS LIGHTING COMPANY LLC

370 W. Trimble Rd.
San Jose CA 95131
Phone: 408-964-2900
Fax: 408-435-6855
Web: www.philipslumileds.com

CEO: Pierre Yves Lesaicherre
CFO: –
HR: –
FYE: December 31
Type: Subsidiary

Philips Lumileds Lighting hopes the world will take more of a shine to LEDs. A subsidiary of Philips Lighting the company designs and produces LED core materials and packaging that are integrated into general lighting products. Its red amber blue green and white light-emitting diodes (LEDs) including its high-brightness LUXEON line are used in indoor and outdoor lighting LCD displays traffic signals automotive lighting and camera flashes. LUXEON LEDs are designed to match the brightness of other light sources such as incandescent halogen and fluorescent bulbs but are smaller last longer and draw less power. Philips Lumileds has international operations in China Malaysia and Singapore.

PHILIPS ORAL HEALTHCARE INC.

35301 SE Center St.
Snoqualmie WA 98065
Phone: 425-396-2000
Fax: 425-396-4838
Web: www.sonicare.com

CEO: –
CFO: –
HR: Holli Marley
FYE: December 31
Type: Subsidiary

Philips Oral Healthcare (POH) deserves a plaque for fighting uh plaque. The company makes Sonicare a high-tech toothbrush line that uses patented sonic technology fluid dynamics and electromechanical design to aid in removing plaque bacteria from between teeth and at the gumline. POH sells its products in the US through warehouse clubs (Costco) mass merchandisers (Target and Wal-Mart) department stores (Sears) and other outlets. It also distributes its products in Canada Europe and Japan. Founded in 1988 the company was initially funded by a grant from the National Institutes of Health. It is now a part of Royal Philips Electronics.

PHILIPS SOLID-STATE LIGHTING SOLUTIONS INC.

3 Burlington Woods Dr. 4th Fl.
Burlington MA 01803
Phone: 617-423-9999
Fax: 617-423-9998
Web: www.colorkinetics.com

CEO: Jeffrey Cassis
CFO: Eugene De Lannoy
HR: –
FYE: December 31
Type: Subsidiary

Philips Solid-State Lighting Solutions (formerly Color Kinetics) can give a chameleon a run for its money. Operating as Philips Color Kinetics the company makes digital lighting products for a variety of commercial and consumer applications. Its Chromacore products generate millions of colors and a variety of dynamic lighting effects using microprocessor-controlled light emitting diodes (LEDs). The company also makes power supplies and controllers used in conjunction with its lighting products. Customers come from the aerospace architectural entertainment and vending and gaming industries. Philips Color Kinetics is part of Royal Philips Electronics.

PHILLIPS 66

NYS: PSX

3010 Briarpark Drive
Houston, TX 77042
Phone: 281-293-6600
Fax: –
Web: www.phillips66.com

CEO: Greg C. Garland
CFO: Greg G. Maxwell
HR: Deborah Hill
FYE: December 31
Type: Public

Phillips 66 is one of the largest independent refiners in the US and the world by sales (though rival Valero Energy leads it by capacity). The company has global refining and marketing midstream and chemical operations. It has a crude processing capacity of more than 3.6 million barrels per day and it sells fuel at about 8600 retail outlets in the US and Europe under such brands as 76 Conoco JET and Phillips 66. Its midstream business handles natural gas gathering and processing partly through DCP Midstream a joint venture with Spectra Energy. Phillips 66's chemicals business is conducted through CPChem a joint venture with Chevron.

	Annual Growth	12/10	12/11	12/12	12/13	12/14
Sales ($ mil.)	2.5%	148,656.0	200,614.0	182,922.0	174,809.0	164,093.0
Net income ($ mil.)	59.5%	735.0	4,775.0	4,124.0	3,726.0	4,762.0
Market value ($ mil.)	16.2%	–	–	29,012.9	42,142.4	39,175.6
Employees	4.1%	–	12,400	13,500	13,500	14,000

PHILLIPS 66 COMPANY

NYSE: PSX

600 N. Dairy Ashford
Houston TX 77079
Phone: 281-293-6600
Fax: 775-284-4426
Web: argonautgoldinc.com

CEO: Greg Garland
CFO: –
HR: –
FYE: December 31
Type: Public

Phillips 66 is one of the largest independent refiners in the US and the world by sales (though rival Valero Energy leads it by capacity). The company has global refining and marketing midstream and chemical operations. It has a crude processing capacity of more than 2.2 million barrels per day and it sells fuel at about 10000 retail outlets in the US and Europe under such brands as 76 Conoco JET and Phillips 66. Its midstream business handles natural gas gathering and processing partly through DCP Midstream a joint venture with Spectra Energy. Phillips 66's chemicals business is conducted through CPChem a joint venture with Chevron. Phillips 66 was spun off by ConocoPhillips in 2012.

PHILLIPS 66 PARTNERS LP

NYS: PSXP

3010 Briarpark Drive
Houston, TX 77042
Phone: 855 283-9237
Fax: –
Web: www.phillips66partners.com

CEO: Greg C Garland
CFO: –
HR: –
FYE: December 31
Type: Public

How many ways can you break up an oil and gas company? The ConocoPhillips and Phillips 66 family of companies may be trying to find out. Phillips 66 Partners is the mid-stream component owning and acquiring crude oil refined petroleum and natural gas liquids pipelines terminals and storage facilities in the US. The company has capacity for about 650 million barrels a day and its assets include 135 miles of pipeline terminals and docks connected to Phillips 66 refineries in Texas Louisiana and Illinois. Phillips 66 Partners earns revenue from fees it charges for transportation and storage of petroleum. The company was formed by Phillips 66 and went public in 2013.

	Annual Growth	12/11	12/12	12/13	12/14	12/15
Sales ($ mil.)	46.3%	76.0	80.1	106.8	229.1	348.1
Net income ($ mil.)	49.9%	38.5	41.1	60.7	124.4	194.2
Market value ($ mil.)	27.2%	–	–	3,192.6	5,801.9	5,168.1
Employees	–	–	–	–	–	–

PHILLIPS AND JORDAN INCORPORATED

10201 PARKSIDE DR STE 300
KNOXVILLE, TN 379221983
Phone: 865-688-8342
Fax: –
Web: www.pandj.com

CEO: –
CFO: –
HR: Jolana Carpenter
FYE: December 31
Type: Private

While some like to clear the air Phillips and Jordan (P&J) prefers to clear the land. Founded in 1952 as a small land clearing firm P&J is a general and specialty contractor that still provides land clearing services in addition to industrial commercial and residential site development and heavy civil construction on dams highways bridges railroads and waterways. P&J also performs reclamation landfill and disaster recovery services. The latter includes handling some of the nation's worst disaster cleanups including hurricanes floods toxic spills and land and rock slides. P&J operates about a dozen offices in eight states. The Phillips family owns and runs the company.

	Annual Growth	12/09	12/10	12/11	12/12	12/13
Sales ($ mil.)	(6.3%)	–	261.8	356.4	284.5	215.2
Net income ($ mil.)	(39.0%)	–	–	12.2	11.3	4.5
Market value ($ mil.)	–	–	–	–	–	–
Employees	–	–	–	–	–	650

PHILLIPS DE PURY & COMPANY LLC

450 W. 15th St.
New York NY 10011
Phone: 212-940-1200
Fax: 212-924-3306
Web: www.phillips-dpl.com

CEO: Edward Dolman
CFO: Annette Schwaer
HR: Sheri Frumer
FYE: December 31
Type: Private

If creating a masterpiece is hard enough ask Phillips de Pury & Company how difficult it can be to sell one. Finding it hard to compete with auction giants Sotheby's and Christie's the auction house has scaled back its operations. It has exited the impressionist and modern art market (traditionally the most lucrative area of art sales) almost entirely — limiting its sales to American and contemporary art design jewelry and photography. Until late 2008 the company was owned by Simon de Pury (co-owner Daniella Luxembourg left the company years ago prompting the name change from Phillips de Pury & Luxembourg). Mercury Group bought a majority interest in the firm in October 2008.

PHILLIPS-MEDISIZE CORPORATION

1201 Hanley Rd.
Hudson WI 54555-5401
Phone: 715-386-4320
Fax: 715-381-3291
Web: www.phillipsmedisize.com

CEO: Matthew J Jennings
CFO: E Gary Willenbrecht
HR: –
FYE: June 30
Type: Private

Phillips-Medisize Corporation injects itself into the competitive world of molded products. The manufacturing company is a custom injection molder of plastic and metal creating end products that range from calculators to fishing reels to radios. It even makes molded parts for firearms. The company's tooling department offers market-entry design production and prototype tooling services. Phillips-Medisize serves customers primarily in the automotive consumer electronics defense and medical markets. The company has 14 locations throughout China Europe and the US in addition to design centers in California and Wisconsin. It is owned by private equity firm Kohlberg & Co.

PHOENIX CHILDREN'S HOSPITAL INC.

1919 E THOMAS RD
PHOENIX, AZ 850167710
Phone: 602-546-1000
Fax: –
Web: www.surgery4children.com

CEO: Robert L. Meyer
CFO: Craig L. McKnight
HR: –
FYE: December 31
Type: Private

Phoenix Children's Hospital (PCH) invests in the health of the next generation. Founded in 1983 the hospital provides a comprehensive range of medical services specifically for children and adolescents in the greater Phoenix area. The hospital has about 360 beds and provides care in a number of pediatric sub-specialties including childhood cancers hematology neuroscience heart disease trauma and orthopedics. In addition to a newborn intensive care unit (NICU) at its main campus PCH operates a second NICU on the campus of Banner Good Samaritan Regional Medical Center (a member of Banner Health).

	Annual Growth	12/07	12/08	12/09	12/11	12/13
Sales ($ mil.)	9.1%	–	424.6	408.2	498.7	655.2
Net income ($ mil.)	(26.0%)	–	–	106.4	(5.1)	31.9
Market value ($ mil.)	–	–	–	–	–	–
Employees	–	–	–	–	–	3,000

PHOENIX COMPANIES, INC. (THE)

NYS: PNX

One American Row
Hartford, CT 06102-5056
Phone: 860 403-5000
Fax: –
Web: www.phoenixwm.com

CEO: James D Wehr
CFO: Bonnie J Malley
HR: –
FYE: December 31
Type: Public

Fiscal firestorms might reduce assets to ashes but The Phoenix Companies gives its customers a chance to rise again. The holding company's primary subsidiary Phoenix Life Insurance offers life insurance annuities and a hybrid of the two it calls "alternative retirement solutions." Historically the company targeted wealthy individuals and institutions but it is newly focused on the merely secure. The Phoenix Companies' distribution arm Saybrus Partners wholesales its products which are sold through third-party agents brokers and financial planning firms. Phoenix has about $5.5 billion in funds under management.

	Annual Growth	12/10	12/11	12/12	12/13	12/14
Assets ($ mil.)	0.8%	21,076.9	21,439.9	21,629.8	21,624.6	21,745.9
Net income ($ mil.)	–	(12.6)	8.1	(168.5)	5.1	(213.2)
Market value ($ mil.)	128.3%	14.7	9.7	143.4	356.1	399.4
Employees	0.6%	625	600	600	620	640

PHOENIX FOOTWEAR GROUP, INC.

NBB: PXFG

5937 Darwin Court, Suite 109
Carlsbad, CA 92008
Phone: 760 602-9688
Fax: 760 602-9619
Web: www.phoenixfootwear.com

CEO: James R Riedman
CFO: Dennis Nelson
HR: –
FYE: January 03
Type: Public

Phoenix Footwear is a well-shod bird. The company manufactures comfort footwear under the Trotters and SoftWalk names for women and H.S. Trask for men. Trotters products include sandals boots and dress and casual footwear. Focused on comfort the SoftWalk brand boasts clogs slings and casual styles. Its Western-inspired footwear H.S. Trask comprises boots oxfords moccasins and slippers. Phoenix Footwear's products are manufactured overseas — primarily in Brazil and China — and are sold through some 1155 US retailers including mass merchants major department stores mail order companies and specialty shoe retailers. Founded in 1882 as Daniel Green Company the shoemaker changed its name in 2001.

	Annual Growth	01/10	01/11*	12/12	12/13*	01/15
Sales ($ mil.)	2.0%	19.9	17.3	16.7	19.2	22.0
Net income ($ mil.)	–	(7.0)	(1.7)	(0.5)	0.1	0.3
Market value ($ mil.)	12.9%	4.2	3.0	1.3	3.3	7.7
Employees	(19.2%)	52	42	–	–	–

*Fiscal year change

PHOENIX TECHNOLOGIES LTD.

915 Murphy Ranch Rd.
Milpitas CA 95035
Phone: 408-570-1000
Fax: 408-570-1001
Web: www.phoenix.com

CEO: Rich Geruson
CFO: Brian Stein
HR: –
FYE: September 30
Type: Private

Phoenix Technologies' fortunes rise every time a computer maker decides to employ its software to fire up their PCs. The company develops basic input/output systems (BIOS) — the software that loads a computer's operating system (OS) each time it is turned on. BIOS software also manages the settings and connections between the OS and basic hardware such as the keyboard and monitor. Core system software (CSS) is the modern form of BIOS software that the company provides primarily through its Phoenix SecureCore SecureCore Tiano and Embedded BIOS products. Phoenix Technologies also makes similar software for manufacturers of other computer peripherals and electronics.

PHOSPHATE HOLDINGS INC.
OTC: PHOS

100 Webster Circle Ste. 4
Madison MS 39110
Phone: 601-898-9004
Fax: 601-898-9915
Web: www.missphosphates.com

CEO: James L Sherbert
CFO: –
HR: –
FYE: December 31
Type: Public

Phosphate Holdings wades through the crooked letters and over the hump-backs to bring the world its fertilizers. The company which operates through subsidiary Mississippi Phosphates Corporation (MPC) manufactures diammonium phosphate (DAP) the world's most used phosphate fertilizer product. It sells most of its products in the US though international sales primarily to Latin America account for more than a quarter of its total sales. Agrochem distributor Transammonia sells a majority of MPC's products; it is the company's lone exporter and also handles some domestic business. Mississippi Phosphates emerged from the bankrupt Mississippi Chemical in 2004 and has operated as a stand-alone entity since then.

PHOTOMEDEX, INC.
NMS: PHMD

100 Lakeside Drive, Suite 100
Horsham, PA 19044
Phone: 215 619-3600
Fax: –
Web: www.photomedex.com

CEO: Dolev Rafaeli
CFO: Dennis M McGrath
HR: –
FYE: December 31
Type: Public

For PhotoMedex beauty is skin deep. The company manufactures and markets dermatological treatments for skin disorders such as acne psoriasis and vitiligo (loss of skin pigmentation). Other products include gels and creams intended to promote skin rejuvenation and hair growth. PhotoMedex also develops lasers and fiber-optic equipment for dermatological and surgical applications. Its FDA-approved XTRAC Excimer laser system is used for the treatment of psoriasis and eczema and its VTRAC lamp system is sold outside the US to treat the same ailments. Customers in the US and overseas include consumers dermatologists cosmetic surgeons and spas.

	Annual Growth	12/10	12/11	12/12	12/13	12/14
Sales ($ mil.)	47.2%	34.8	132.1	220.7	224.7	163.5
Net income ($ mil.)	–	(8.7)	(0.7)	22.5	18.4	(121.5)
Market value ($ mil.)	(28.7%)	121.0	262.9	296.1	263.9	31.2
Employees	5.6%	144	183	177	168	179

PHOTRONICS, INC.
NMS: PLAB

15 Secor Road
Brookfield, CT 06804
Phone: 203 775-9000
Fax: –
Web: www.photronics.com

CEO: Peter S. Kirlin
CFO: Sean T Smith
HR: –
FYE: November 01
Type: Public

Photronics is a company behind the photomasks. The company makes high-precision quartz photomasks a key tool in the construction of integrated circuits (ICs) and flat-panel displays (FPDs). Photomasks carry microscopic images of electronic circuits and are used as stencils to transfer circuit patterns onto semiconductor wafers during the manufacture of integrated circuits and FPDs. Photronics also provides maintenance for etching systems as well as research and consulting in techniques for wafer cleaning and etching. The company gets more than half of sales from customers in Asia.

	Annual Growth	10/11	10/12*	11/13	11/14	11/15
Sales ($ mil.)	0.6%	512.0	450.4	422.2	455.5	524.2
Net income ($ mil.)	28.8%	16.2	27.9	18.0	26.0	44.6
Market value ($ mil.)	10.3%	432.2	321.7	551.5	598.8	638.7
Employees	3.5%	1,350	1,300	1,300	1,500	1,550
						*Fiscal year change

PHYSICAL PROPERTY HOLDINGS, INC.
NBB: PPYH

23/F AIA Tower, No. 183 Electric Road, North Point

Phone: (852) 2917 0000
Fax: –

CEO: –
CFO: –
HR: –
FYE: December 31
Type: Public

Physical Property Holdings formerly Physical Spa & Fitness preferred real estate over exercise. Previously an operator of nearly 20 US-styled fitness and spa facilities throughout Hong Kong and China the company now deals in the business of buying investing in renovating renting and selling real estate in Hong Kong. It owns and operates five residential apartments. Physical Property Holdings made the switch (including a name change) in 2007.

	Annual Growth	12/10	12/11	12/12	12/13	12/14
Sales ($ mil.)	8.3%	0.1	0.1	0.1	0.1	0.1
Net income ($ mil.)	–	(0.1)	(0.1)	(0.1)	(0.1)	(0.1)
Market value ($ mil.)	–	0.1	0.0	0.0	0.0	0.0
Employees	31.6%	1	1	1	1	3

PHYSICIANS FORMULA HOLDINGS INC.
NASDAQ: FACE

1055 W. 8th St.
Azusa CA 91702
Phone: 626-334-3395
Fax: 626-812-9462
Web: www.physiciansformula.com

CEO: Ingrid Jackel
CFO: –
HR: –
FYE: December 31
Type: Private

Physicians Formula Holdings (PFH) boasts the professional formula for skin imperfections. It develops and makes prestige cosmetics products focusing on face and eye makeup. Physicians Formula label includes facial powders bronzers concealers blushes foundations eye shadows eye liners brow makeup and mascaras. It sells its products through 25000 stores including mass merchandisers (Wal-Mart and Target) drugstores (CVS and Rite Aid) and specialty cosmetics shops (Ulta). PFH caters to the US but also sells its beauty aids in Canada Australia and beyond. Founded in 2003 PFH is owned by Markwins International.

PHYSICIANS MUTUAL INSURANCE COMPANY

2600 Dodge St.
Omaha NE 68131
Phone: 402-633-1000
Fax: 402-633-1096
Web: www.physiciansmutual.com

CEO: Robert A Reed
CFO: Roger J Hermsen
HR: –
FYE: December 31
Type: Private - Mutual Com

Although the name seems narrow Physicians Mutual Insurance Company offers insurance to a wide range of customers. Established in 1902 to insure doctors and dentists Physicians Mutual now provides general and supplemental health insurance products such as cancer dental long-term care and Medicare supplements to members nationwide. It offers packaged insurance products for consumers and small business employees. The company's Physicians Life Insurance subsidiary provides individual life insurance and annuity products. Physicians Mutual has some 1 000 agents distributing its products nationwide.

PHYSICIANS REALTY TRUST

NYS: DOC

309 N. Water Street,, Suite 500
Milwaukee, WI 53202
Phone: 414 367-5600
Fax: –

CEO: John T. Thomas
CFO: Jeff Theiler
HR: –
FYE: December 31
Type: Public

Physicians Realty Trust doesn't make house calls. The real estate investment trust (REIT) owns and invests in doctor's offices and other health care properties that are leased to hospitals and medical groups. A self-managed REIT its portfolio consists of more than 25 medical office buildings in about a dozen states. Tenants include Fresenius Dialysis Hackley Hospital and Piedmont Hospital. Physicians Realty Trust was formed in 2013 with properties owned by investment bank B.C. Ziegler & Company. As a REIT it is exempt from paying federal income tax as long as it distributes 90% of profits back to shareholders. Physicians Realty Trust went public in 2013 raising $120 million.

	Annual Growth	04/11	04/12	04/13*	12/13	12/14
Sales ($ mil.)	–	0.0	0.0	–	16.8	53.3
Net income ($ mil.)	–	0.0	0.0	–	(1.7)	(4.0)
Market value ($ mil.)	–	0.0	0.0	–	645.2	840.6
Employees	180.0%	–	–	–	5	14

*Fiscal year change

PICERNE INVESTMENT CORPORATION

75 Lambert Lind Hwy.
Warwick RI 02886
Phone: 401-732-3700
Fax: 401-738-6452
Web: www.picerne.com

CEO: –
CFO: Ken Richard
HR: –
FYE: December 31
Type: Private

Picerne Investment (through its Picerne Real Estate Group) develops builds invests in and manages residential properties including affordable and upscale apartments military housing and single-family homes. The company also manages office buildings shopping centers and industrial properties. Picerne is active throughout the US and in Puerto Rico but has a stronghold in its home state of Rhode Island. The company has built more than 10000 houses and owns some 32000 apartment units in that state alone. The Picerne family established the company in 1925. The family continues to own the business which has offices in Arizona Nevada Florida and Rhode Island.

PICIS INC.

100 Quannapowitt Pkwy. Ste. 405
Wakefield MA 01880
Phone: 781-557-3000
Fax: 781-557-3140
Web: www.picis.com

CEO: Jeff Bender
CFO: Todd Richardson
HR: –
FYE: December 31
Type: Private

Picis wants ER and OR docs thinking about their patients' health not about how to manage all the data they generate. The company provides software for automating the most costly and resource-intensive hospital departments: the operating room the intensive care unit and the emergency room. Its Care-Suite software includes tools for managing preoperative operating room and postoperative functions as well as documenting anesthesia use tracking surgical patients and managing critical care charts and clinical documentation. The company sells internationally through offices in Europe and partners in Asia. InPicis was acquired in 2010 by health care information provider Ingenix a subsidiary of UnitedHealth.

PICO HOLDINGS INC.

NMS: PICO

7979 Ivanhoe Avenue, Suite 300
La Jolla, CA 92037
Phone: 858 456-6022
Fax: –
Web: www.picoholdings.com

CEO: John R. Hart
CFO: Maxim C. W. Webb
HR: Adriana Wendland
FYE: December 31
Type: Public

For PICO Holdings the pick o' the litter might look like a diamond in the rough. The holding company invests in what it believes to be undervalued businesses involved in agribusiness real estate and other industries. PICO owns Vidler Water Company a firm that acquires and develops water resources and water storage operations in the American Southwest. Its majority-owned UCP business acquires and develops finished and unfinished residential lots in select California and Washington markets. Another unit Northstar Agri Industries is active in the production of canola oil and canola meal.

	Annual Growth	12/10	12/11	12/12	12/13	12/14
Sales ($ mil.)	82.2%	32.2	85.2	150.1	344.8	354.9
Net income ($ mil.)	–	(11.2)	(54.5)	(29.1)	(22.3)	(52.4)
Market value ($ mil.)	(12.3%)	731.6	473.4	466.3	531.6	433.6
Employees	49.0%	57	70	150	189	281

PIEDMONT NATURAL GAS CO INC

NYS: PNY

4720 Piedmont Row Drive
Charlotte, NC 28210
Phone: 704 364-3120
Fax: –
Web: www.piedmontng.com

CEO: Thomas E. (Tom) Skains
CFO: Karl W. Newlin
HR: –
FYE: October 31
Type: Public

Piedmont Natural Gas seeks to fulfill the burning desires of natural gas users in a wide part of the Southeast. The utility distributes natural gas to more than 1 million residential commercial and industrial customers (including 53000 wholesale customers) in the Carolinas and Tennessee. It also has gas transportation and storage operations and sells residential and commercial gas appliances in Tennessee. Piedmont Natural Gas is involved in unregulated energy supply through its 15% stake in SouthStar Energy Services which serves gas customers in Georgia and through other joint ventures.

	Annual Growth	10/11	10/12	10/13	10/14	10/15
Sales ($ mil.)	(1.1%)	1,433.9	1,122.8	1,278.2	1,470.0	1,371.7
Net income ($ mil.)	4.8%	113.6	119.8	134.4	143.8	137.0
Market value ($ mil.)	15.1%	2,644.1	2,577.7	2,761.3	3,074.4	4,635.4
Employees	2.2%	1,782	1,752	1,795	1,879	1,943

PIEDMONT OFFICE REALTY TRUST INC

NYS: PDM

11695 Johns Creek Parkway, Ste. 350
Johns Creek, GA 30097
Phone: 770 418-8800
Fax: –
Web: www.piedmontreit.com

CEO: Donald A Miller
CFO: Robert E Bowers
HR: –
FYE: December 31
Type: Public

Piedmont Office Realty Trust provides office space for life in the big city. A self-managed and self-administered real estate investment trust (REIT) the company invests in develops and manages primarily Class A office buildings in major US markets. One of the nation's largest office REITs Piedmont owns or partially owns about 75 office and industrial properties comprising some 21 million sq. ft. of leasable space. Many of its properties are located in Chicago the New York Metro area and Washington DC. Piedmont's holdings include Chicago's Aon Center and the headquarters buildings for US Bancorp and Nestlé USA.

	Annual Growth	12/10	12/11	12/12	12/13	12/14
Sales ($ mil.)	(1.0%)	588.8	541.6	536.4	554.5	566.3
Net income ($ mil.)	(22.5%)	120.4	225.0	93.2	98.7	43.3
Market value ($ mil.)	(1.7%)	3,108.1	2,629.7	2,785.5	2,549.4	2,907.5
Employees	4.3%	110	116	116	121	130

PIER 1 IMPORTS INC.

NYS: PIR

100 Pier 1 Place	CEO: Alexander W. (Alex) Smith
Fort Worth, TX 76102	CFO: Jeff Boyer
Phone: 817 252-8000	HR: Gregory S. (Greg) Humenesky
Fax: 817 252-8174	FYE: February 28
Web: www.pier1.com	Type: Public

When shoppers fish for home decor Pier 1 wants to be sure they catch something. The company sells more than 6000 items (imported from more than 50 countries) through more than 1070 Pier 1 Imports stores across North America. Its stores offer a wide selection of indoor and outdoor furniture lamps vases baskets ceramics dinnerware candles and other decorative accessories. Pier 1 To-Go allows shoppers to order and reserve items online for pick up and payment in its stores. In addition the company supplies merchandise to more than 55 stores in Mexico owned by Grupo Sanborns. After a rough patch in the 2000s Pier 1 appears to have gotten its house in order.

	Annual Growth	02/11	02/12*	03/13	03/14*	02/15
Sales ($ mil.)	7.5%	1,396.5	1,533.6	1,704.9	1,771.7	1,865.8
Net income ($ mil.)	(6.9%)	100.1	168.9	129.4	107.5	75.2
Market value ($ mil.)	5.4%	879.3	1,478.2	2,027.5	1,701.1	1,084.3
Employees	9.0%	17,000	19,700	21,400	22,200	24,000

*Fiscal year change

PIERCE MANUFACTURING INC.

2600 American Dr.	CEO: Wilson Jone
Appleton WI 54912	CFO: David Sagehorn
Phone: 920-832-3000	HR: –
Fax: 920-832-3084	FYE: September 30
Web: www.piercemfg.com	Type: Subsidiary

If you were to call "Jim Dandy to the Rescue" odds are the R&B music hero would wheel up in a vehicle made by Pierce Manufacturing. The company is a subsidiary of Oshkosh Corporation's Fire & Emergency business and the top North American maker of custom fire apparatus. Its lineup includes aerials commercial pumpers elliptical tankers and rescue trucks. The company also builds homeland security apparatus designed to help police and emergency crews better respond to terrorist events. Many vehicle bodies are assembled on major commercial chassis brands to meet customer needs such as the US Army's. Its innovations include the industry's first side roll protection and frontal airbag systems for fire apparatus.

PIGGLY WIGGLY MIDWEST LLC

2215 Union Ave.	CEO: –
Sheboygan WI 53081	CFO: Elwood F Winn
Phone: 920-457-4433	HR: –
Fax: 205-942-6601	FYE: December 31
Web: www.booksamillioninc.com	Type: Private

If they're so inclined shoppers can squeal down the aisle at these supermarkets. Piggly Wiggly Midwest operates a leading grocery store chain with about 110 locations in Wisconsin and northern Illinois under the Piggly Wiggly and Butera banners. About 20 stores are company-owned and -operated while the rest are franchised; Piggly Wiggly Midwest supplies all of its stores from two distribution centers. The corporate stores account for about 16% of total sales. The grocery wholesaler and retailer has been converting its corporate-owned stores into franchise operations. Piggly Wiggly Midwest traces its roots back to the early 1900s; it is owned by CEO Paul Butera.

PIKE CORP

NYS: PIKE

100 Pike Way	CEO: J Eric Pike
Mount Airy, NC 27030	CFO: Richard Wimmer
Phone: 336 789-2171	HR: Zack Blackmon
Fax: –	FYE: June 30
Web: www.pike.com	Type: Public

Pike Electric helps its customers stay current. The electrical services contractor (also known as Pike Energy Solutions) provides services for more than 200 public municipal and cooperative utility companies primarily in the eastern and southern US. Activities include the planning design engineering construction maintenance and repair of electric substations and transmission lines including renewable energy systems. Pike Electric owns a fleet of more than 4700 pieces of motorized equipment including trucks trailers cranes backhoes and generators. The company is active in some 40 states.

	Annual Growth	06/09	06/10	06/11	06/12	06/13
Sales ($ mil.)	10.6%	613.5	504.1	593.9	685.2	918.7
Net income ($ mil.)	3.5%	31.6	(13.5)	1.4	10.9	36.2
Market value ($ mil.)	0.5%	382.2	298.8	280.4	244.9	390.1
Employees	6.1%	4,500	4,500	4,600	5,400	5,700

PIKEVILLE MEDICAL CENTER INC.

911 BYPASS RD	CEO: Walter E May
PIKEVILLE, KY 415011689	CFO: Michelle Hagey
Phone: 606-218-3500	HR: –
Fax: –	FYE: September 30
Web: www.pikevillehospital.org	Type: Private

Taking a nasty fall while hiking the rugged Appalachians will likely land you at Pikeville Medical Center (PMC). Serving patients in eastern Kentucky the hospital boasts more than 260 beds and provides a full range of inpatient outpatient and surgical services. PMC's centers and departments handle a number of specialties such as diagnostic imaging echocardiogram neurosurgery cancer care and bariatric surgery. Employing some 350 physicians PMC also operates a rehabilitation hospital a home health agency and outpatient family practice and specialty clinics as well as a physician residency program. PMC first opened on Christmas Day in 1924.

	Annual Growth	09/01	09/02	09/03	09/09	09/13
Sales ($ mil.)	10.8%	–	127.6	132.1	267.3	394.7
Net income ($ mil.)	(13.9%)	–	–	12.3	27.2	2.8
Market value ($ mil.)		–	–	–	–	–
Employees		–	–	–	–	1,025

PILGRIMS PRIDE CORP.

NMS: PPC

1770 Promontory Circle	CEO: Don Jackson
Greeley, CO 80634-9038	CFO: Fabio Sandri
Phone: 970 506-8000	HR: Doug Schult
Fax: –	FYE: December 28
Web: www.pilgrims.com	Type: Public

Pilgrim's Pride couldn't be blamed if it spread its tail feathers and did a barnyard strut. As one of the world's top chicken processors it boasts operations in the US Mexico and Puerto Rico in breeding hatching raising processing and distributing chicken. The company sells prepared poultry products under the Pilgrim's Pride and EatWellStayHealthy labels to retail food outlets distributors and food service operators. It sells fresh frozen value-added prepared chicken and deli products. In addition to producing 10.2 billion pounds of live chicken annually Pilgrim's Pride also produces table eggs and chicken by-products for use as animal feed. The company is majority owned by Brazil's JBS.

	Annual Growth	12/10	12/11	12/12	12/13	12/14
Sales ($ mil.)	5.7%	6,881.6	7,535.7	8,121.4	8,411.1	8,583.4
Net income ($ mil.)	69.0%	87.1	(496.8)	174.2	549.6	711.6
Market value ($ mil.)	47.9%	1,844.3	1,551.6	1,862.4	4,266.2	8,825.1
Employees	(20.8%)	89,100	39,500	33,000	36,700	35,000

PILKINGTON NORTH AMERICA INC.

811 Madison Ave.
Toledo OH 43604-5684
Phone: 419-247-3731
Fax: 419-247-3821
Web: www.pilkington.com/the+americas/usa/english/de

CEO: –
CFO: –
HR: –
FYE: March 31
Type: Subsidiary

Pilkington North America has a clear view of the US glass market. The company manufactures and markets glass and glazing products primarily for the automotive and building industries. Benefits of its glass include fire protection noise control solar heat control and thermal insulation. A majority of its sales come from automotive glass sold to the original equipment and replacement markets. More than a quarter of sales are made from building glass geared at homeowners and architects. A small but growing part of its business focuses on specialty glass used in solar energy conversion. Pilkington North America is a subsidiary of UK-based Pilkington plc which operates as part of Japanese glass giant Nippon Sheet Glass.

PILLAR DATA SYSTEMS INC.

2840 Junction Ave.
San Jose CA 95134
Phone: 408-503-4000
Fax: 408-503-4050
Web: www.pillardata.com

CEO: Michael L Workman
CFO: Edward Hayes
HR: –
FYE: December 31
Type: Subsidiary

What do you get if you give Larry Ellison's wallet to a bunch of IBM alums with data storage expertise? A maker of network data storage systems Pillar Data Systems was heavily backed by Oracle's billionaire CEO Larry Ellison's via his Tako Ventures investment firm before Oracle acquired the entire company in 2011. The Pillar Axiom enterprise storage system incorporates both network-attached storage (NAS) and storage area network (SAN) functionality. Pillar Data Systems also offers software including applications for file replication volume replication and thin provisioning. The company also provides related services for SAN and NAS implementation data protection data migration and backup and recovery.

PILLSBURY WINTHROP SHAW PITTMAN LLP

1540 Broadway
New York NY 10036-4039
Phone: 212-858-1000
Fax: 212-858-1500
Web: www.pillsburylaw.com

CEO: –
CFO: Sean Whelan
HR: Kacy Zuchowski
FYE: December 31
Type: Private - Partnershi

With a geographic reach that connects San Francisco with Shanghai and London with Los Angeles law firm Pillsbury Winthrop Shaw Pittman represents the interests of its clients around the world. It has more than 1000 attorneys in about 15 offices in the US Asia and Europe. The firm identifies corporate and securities environment and land use finance global sourcing intellectual property litigation public policy real estate and regulatory law as key practice areas. The firm was founded in 1848 and it has grown through a series of mergers. The former Pillsbury Winthrop was combined in 2005 with Washington DC-based law firm Shaw Pittman.

PILOT CORPORATION

5508 LONAS DR
KNOXVILLE, TN 37909-3221
Phone: 865-588-7488
Fax: –
Web: www.pilotflyingj.com

CEO: John Compton
CFO: James P Pardue
HR: Dave Parmly
FYE: December 31
Type: Private

Pilot offers a salve to those suffering from white-line fever. Its Pilot Flying J a joint venture between Pilot and CVC Capital Partners runs more than 650 travel centers that sell fuel and food across North America. Its truck stops feature restaurant chains such as Subway Pizza Hut and Taco Bell and offer hot showers. Pilot has fuel islands large enough to service several 18-wheelers. Pilot Truck Care Centers provide TLC (tender loving care) for big rigs while some 45 Pilot Food Marts (all in Tennessee) keep drivers fed. James Haslam II got Pilot off the ground in 1958 as a gas station that sold cigarettes and soft drinks; now his son CEO James Haslam III runs the firm. The Haslam family owns the company.

	Annual Growth	12/07	12/08	12/09	12/10	12/11
Sales ($ mil.)	(3.2%)	–	–	–	415.1	402.0
Net income ($ mil.)	(2.0%)	–	–	–	373.2	365.7
Market value ($ mil.)	–	–	–	–	–	–
Employees	–	–	–	–	–	13,000

PILOT FLYING J

5508 Lonas Dr.
Knoxville TN 37909
Phone: 865-588-7488
Fax: 865-450-2800
Web: www.pilotflyingj.com

CEO: John Compton
CFO: –
HR: –
FYE: December 31
Type: Joint Venture

Pilot Flying J (PFJ) formerly Pilot Travel Centers steers truckers and other motorists to more than 550 company-owned and -operated Travel Centers in 43 states and six Canadian provinces. In addition to selling fuel the travel plazas house Arby's Subway Wendy's and Taco Bell. PFJ is expanding through licensing agreements with local travel centers including Montana's Town Pump. As a leading supplier of diesel fuel to the trucking industry the company provides about 10% of the on-road truck diesel consumed in the US. PFJ acquired and merged with is rival Flying J in July 2010 to form Pilot Flying J.

PINE GROVE MANUFACTURED HOMES INC.

2 PLEASANT VALLEY RD
PINE GROVE, PA 179639563
Phone: 570-345-2011
Fax: –
Web: www.pinegrovehomes.com

CEO: Wayne A Fanelli
CFO: Joseph Gallagher
HR: Joy Motley
FYE: October 28
Type: Private

Pine Grove Manufactured Homes designs and builds manufactured homes in the mid-Atlantic and northeastern regions of the US. Its single-section homes range in width from 12 ft. to 16 ft.; its multi-section homes range from 20 ft. to 32 ft. in width and can be built up to 76 ft. in length. Special features offered include gourmet kitchens and spa baths. Sister company Pleasant Valley Modular Homes manufactures ranch split-level and two-story residences as well as log-sided homes and duplexes in a variety of styles ranging in size from around 1000 sq. ft. to 3000 sq. ft. Pine Grove markets its homes through independent retailers and developers. Privately held Pine Grove was established in 1982.

	Annual Growth	10/03	10/04	10/05	10/06	10/07
Sales ($ mil.)	–	–	–	(1,460.1)	42.5	31.9
Net income ($ mil.)	1281.9%	–	–	0.0	5.5	3.1
Market value ($ mil.)	–	–	–	–	–	–
Employees	–	–	–	–	–	100

PINEBRIDGE INVESTMENTS

399 Park Ave. 4th Fl.
New York NY 10022
Phone: 646-857-8000
Fax: 847-948-8610
Web: www.beamglobal.com

CEO: David T Jiang
CFO: David Kolker
HR: –
FYE: December 31
Type: Private

PineBridge Investments hopes to build a bridge toward economic recovery. Previously part of the asset management arm of embattled insurance giant AIG the company was spun off to Pacific Century Group for some $500 million in 2010. PineBridge manages investments in equities fixed-income securities and alternative assets including hedge funds and real estate. Effective mid-2012 it has some $68 billion in assets under management for its institutional and individual customers. Pacific Century Group is an investment vehicle of Hong Kong businessman Richard Li chairman of PCCW and Pacific Century Premium Developments.

PINNACLE DATA SYSTEMS INC.

NYSE AMEX: PNS

6600 Port Rd.
Groveport OH 43125
Phone: 614-748-1150
Fax: 614-409-1269
Web: www.pinnacle.com

CEO: John D Bair
CFO: Nicholas Tomashot
HR: –
FYE: December 31
Type: Subsidiary

Pinnacle Data Systems Inc. (PDSi) has a custom approach to computing. The company builds and services made-to-order UNIX-based servers and other application-specific computer systems used in the medical telecommunications and process control industries as well as in government markets. PDSi combines third-party equipment — including processors from AMD Intel and Oracle — with its own custom parts to create its systems. The company provides its build and repair services to manufacturers that include Hewlett-Packard and Silicon Graphics International. PDSi gets most of its revenues in the US. The company was acquired by electronic components distributor Avnet in early 2012.

PINNACLE BANCSHARES, INC.

NBB: PCLB

1811 Second Avenue
Jasper, AL 35501
Phone: 205 221-4111
Fax: –

CEO: Robert B Nolen Jr
CFO: –
HR: –
FYE: December 31
Type: Public

Pinnacle is on top of Alabama's banking needs. Pinnacle Bancshares is the holding company for Pinnacle Bank which serves central and northwestern Alabama through more than a half-dozen offices. The bank provides consumer and business banking services including checking and money market accounts as well as a variety of consumer and commercial loans. Real estate lending dominates the loan portfolio with one- to four-family residential mortgages making up the largest percentage followed by commercial mortgages business loans and construction and land development loans. The bank also makes consumer and farm loans.

	Annual Growth	12/10	12/11	12/12	12/13	12/14
Assets ($ mil.)	2.2%	200.9	199.2	208.4	220.4	219.0
Net income ($ mil.)	32.6%	0.7	1.2	2.0	1.9	2.0
Market value ($ mil.)	15.3%	11.5	11.9	14.0	17.1	20.3
Employees	–	–	–	–	–	–

PINNACLE ENTERTAINMENT INC

NMS: PNK

3980 Howard Hughes Parkway
Las Vegas, NV 89169
Phone: 702 541-7777
Fax: –
Web: www.pnkinc.com

CEO: Anthony M. Sanfilippo
CFO: Carlos Ruisanchez
HR: Christine Rury
FYE: December 31
Type: Public

Pinnacle Entertainment realizes most gamblers don't know when they've reached their peak. The Las Vegas-based gaming company actually has no casinos in Vegas; instead the regional casino operator owns 15 casinos in other locations. Pinnacle also owns the Retama Park Horse Racetrack located near San Antonio Texas. Three of Pinnacle's casinos operate under the Boomtown banner. Its L'Auberge du Lac Hotel & Casino property in Lake Charles Louisiana is the company's largest casino resort. In St. Louis the company owns Lumière Place (including the Lumière Place Casino the Pinnacle-owned Four Seasons Hotel St. Louis and HoteLumière) and the River City Casino.

	Annual Growth	12/10	12/11	12/12	12/13	12/14
Sales ($ mil.)	19.1%	1,098.4	1,141.2	1,197.1	1,487.8	2,210.5
Net income ($ mil.)	–	(23.4)	(2.5)	(31.8)	(255.9)	43.8
Market value ($ mil.)	12.2%	840.9	609.4	949.5	1,558.9	1,334.6
Employees	18.3%	7,533	7,463	8,479	14,569	14,738

PINNACLE BANKSHARES CORP

NBB: PPBN

622 Broad Street
Altavista, VA 24517-1830
Phone: 434 369-3000
Fax: –
Web: www.1stnatbk.com

CEO: Aubrey H Hall III
CFO: Bryan M Lemley
HR: –
FYE: December 31
Type: Public

Pinnacle Bankshares is always looking for the high point. The firm is the holding company for the First National Bank which operates about 10 branches and loan production centers in central Virginia. Serving individuals and businesses in the area the bank offers standard products and services including checking and savings accounts IRAs and merchant bankcard processing. The company uses funds from deposit accounts to originate real estate loans consumer loans and business loans. The company which traces its roots to 1908 also has two real estate subsidiaries First Properties and FNB Property Corp.

	Annual Growth	12/10	12/11	12/12	12/13	12/14
Assets ($ mil.)	1.8%	337.1	342.5	348.7	359.0	362.2
Net income ($ mil.)	33.0%	0.7	1.1	1.3	3.0	2.1
Market value ($ mil.)	19.3%	13.3	12.3	12.6	22.8	26.9
Employees	0.0%	110	105	105	107	110

PINNACLE FINANCIAL PARTNERS INC.

NMS: PNFP

150 Third Avenue South, Suite 900
Nashville, TN 37201
Phone: 615 744-3700
Fax: –
Web: www.pnfp.com

CEO: M. Terry Turner
CFO: Harold R. Carpenter
HR: –
FYE: December 31
Type: Public

Pinnacle Financial Partners works to be at the top of the community banking mountain in central Tennessee. It's the holding company for Tennessee-based Pinnacle Bank which has grown to nearly 35 branches in the Nashville and Knoxville areas since its founding in 2000. Serving consumers and small- to mid-sized business the $6 billion financial institution provides standard services such as checking and savings accounts CDs credit cards and loans and mortgages. The company also offers investment and trust services through Pinnacle Asset Management while its insurance brokerage subsidiary Miller Loughry Beach specializes in property/casualty policies.

	Annual Growth	12/10	12/11	12/12	12/13	12/14
Assets ($ mil.)	5.2%	4,909.0	4,864.0	5,040.5	5,563.8	6,018.2
Net income ($ mil.)	–	(24.3)	43.7	41.9	57.7	70.5
Market value ($ mil.)	30.6%	485.2	577.1	673.2	1,162.4	1,412.9
Employees	0.1%	764	743	726	748	767

PINNACLE FOODS FINANCE LLC

1 Bloomfield Ave.
Mountain Lakes NJ 07046
Phone: 973-541-6620
Fax: 901-345-8511
Web: www.elvis.com

CEO: Robert J Gamgort
CFO: Craig Steeneck
HR: –
FYE: December 31
Type: Subsidiary

Pinnacle Foods holds a mouthful of big-name brands. The company makes markets and distributes such North American grocery store staples as Duncan Hines baking mix and frosting Armour canned meat Vlasic pickles and Comstock pie and pastry filling. It owns Birds Eye Foods' lineup acquired in 2009 of frozen breakfast (Aunt Jemima) vegetable (Birds Eye) dinner (Hungry Man) seafood (Mrs. Paul's) and pizza (Celeste) brand products. A specialty foods unit supplies snacks as well as distributes frozen products to foodservice operators and makes private label food products. Pinnacle has grown by buying and expanding upon the lines of name brands. The company is owned by private equity The Blackstone Group.

PINNACLE FOODS INC.

NYS: PF

399 Jefferson Road
Parsippany, NJ 07054
Phone: 973 541-6620
Fax: –
Web: www.pinnaclefoods.com

CEO: Robert J. Gamgort
CFO: Craig D. Steeneck
HR: Mary Beth DeNooyer
FYE: December 28
Type: Public

Pinnacle Foods' grocery products enjoy a bird's-eye view from store shelves across North America. Pinnacle Foods is the holding company of Pinnacle Foods Finance which manufactures markets and distributes the Birds Eye frozen food line Duncan Hines line of baking mixes and frostings Snyder of Berlin snack foods and other grocery brands. The company also offers food service and private-label services. Its product lines sold predominantly through major US retailers like Wal-Mart and top grocery-store chains hold top market-share positions across several food product categories. In 2013 Pinnacle Foods became a publicly traded company.

	Annual Growth	12/10	12/11	12/12	12/13	12/14
Sales ($ mil.)	1.5%	2,436.7	2,469.6	2,478.5	2,463.8	2,591.2
Net income ($ mil.)	83.2%	22.0	(46.9)	52.5	89.3	248.4
Market value ($ mil.)	30.7%	–	–	–	3,167.8	4,140.1
Employees	4.0%	–	–	3,700	3,700	4,000

PINNACLE FRAMES AND ACCENTS INC.

12201 Technology Blvd. Ste. 1200
Austin TX 78727
Phone: 512-506-3900
Fax: 512-506-3933
Web: www.pinnacleframe.com

CEO: –
CFO: –
HR: –
FYE: June 30
Type: Private

Pinnacle Frames and Accents has plenty of frames but what it needs is a prettier picture. Once home to nearly 20 retailing and manufacturing companies the company now makes and markets photo frames and albums under its own brand name and private labels in addition to other decor. The firm's Gallery Solutions brand features matted wall frames in mix-and-match styles while its Snap collection targeted to cost-conscious digital photographers consists of clear and magnetic frames key chains and coasters. Pinnacle's products are available at major retail stores in the US and Canada including Wal-Mart and Target. The company formerly named Tandycrafts is owned by investment firm Newcastle Partners.

PINNACLE GAS RESOURCES INC.

1 E. Alger St.
Sheridan WY 82801
Phone: 307-673-9710
Fax: 307-673-9711
Web: www.pinnaclegas.com

CEO: Pete Schoonmaker
CFO: Ronald T Barnes
HR: –
FYE: December 31
Type: Private

Pinnacle Gas Resources' mission culminates in the development of US natural gas reserves. The company focuses on acquiring and developing coalbed methane (CBM) properties in the Rocky Mountain region. It owns natural gas and oil leasehold interests in 477000 gross (332000 net) acres primarily in the Powder River Basin and Green River Basin in Wyoming and Montana. Pinnacle Gas Resources owns interests in 663 gross wells on its properties. In 2008 the company had proved reserves of 27.7 billion cu. ft. of natural gas equivalent; that year Pinnacle Gas Resources drilled 117 gross (82 net) wells. In 2011 the company was acquired in a leveraged buy out by company managers supported by Scotia Waterous (USA).

PINNACLE HEALTH SYSTEM

409 S 2ND ST STE 2B
HARRISBURG, PA 17104-1612
Phone: 717-231-8245
Fax: –
Web: www.pinnaclehealth.org

CEO: Michael A Young
CFO: –
HR: –
FYE: June 30
Type: Private

PinnacleHealth helps central Pennsylvanians reach the peaks of wellness. PinnacleHealth System provides a continuum of care through its four hospitals that have a combined total of about 600 beds. Together Community General Hospital Harrisburg Hospital Polyclinic Hospital and the Helen M. Simpson Rehab Hospital provide general and specialty services in areas such as oncology cardiovascular medicine neurology mental health physical therapy women's health and orthopedics. PinnacleHealth is also home to a network of community health diagnostic ambulatory surgery and outpatient centers. Additionally the system administers home care and hospice care programs.

	Annual Growth	06/06	06/07	06/08	06/09	06/11
Sales ($ mil.)	5.9%	–	486.9	578.6	0.0	612.8
Net income ($ mil.)	3.8%	–	32.9	(23.5)	(2.6)	38.2
Market value ($ mil.)	–	–	–	–	–	–
Employees	–	–	–	–	–	4,837

PINNACLE WEST CAPITAL CORP.

NYS: PNW

400 North Fifth Street, P.O. Box 53999
Phoenix, AZ 85072-3999
Phone: 602 250-1000
Fax: 602 379-2625
Web: www.pinnaclewest.com

CEO: Donald E. (Don) Brandt
CFO: James R. (Jim) Hatfield
HR: –
FYE: December 31
Type: Public

Pinnacle West Capital is at the peak of the energy pyramid in Arizona. It is the holding company for the state's largest electric utility Arizona Public Service which transmits and distributes electricity to more than 1.1 million residential commercial and industrial customers throughout most of the state. The power distribution utility also has 6300 MW of regulated generating capacity and has a mix of both long-term and short-term purchased power agreements for additional capacity including a range of agreements for the purchase of energy from renewable sources.

	Annual Growth	12/10	12/11	12/12	12/13	12/14
Sales ($ mil.)	1.7%	3,263.6	3,241.4	3,301.8	3,454.6	3,491.6
Net income ($ mil.)	3.2%	350.1	339.5	381.5	406.1	397.6
Market value ($ mil.)	13.3%	4,583.2	5,327.3	5,636.9	5,851.4	7,553.1
Employees	(1.4%)	6,740	6,663	6,613	6,433	6,366

PINNACOL ASSURANCE

7501 E. Lowry Blvd.	CEO: Phil Kalin
Denver CO 80230	CFO: –
Phone: 303-361-4000	HR: –
Fax: 303-361-5000	FYE: December 31
Web: www.pinnacol.com	Type: Government-owned

Pinnacol Assurance aspires to be the tops in workers' compensation insurance. The not-for-profit company is the insurer of last resort in Colorado and by law it must provide coverage to employers in that state regardless of risk. And cover it does: the quasi-governmental entity provides coverage to some 55000 employers and their employees — more than half of all Colorado workers — making it the state's largest workers' compensation insurer. It also provides short-term disability insurance. In addition Pinnacle Assurance provides loss prevention services such as claims management fraud investigation and return-to-work programs as well as safety program development and OSHA compliance assistance.

PIONEER BANKSHARES INC.

OTC: PNBI

263 E. Main St.	CEO: Thomas R Rosazza
Stanley VA 22851	CFO: Lori G Hassett
Phone: 540-778-2294	HR: –
Fax: 540-778-5140	FYE: December 31
Web: www.pioneerbks.com	Type: Public

Although you don't get a coonskin cap when you open an account Pioneer Bankshares likes to maintain that pioneer spirit. The financial institution is the holding company for Pioneer Bank which serves northeastern Virginia through about a half dozen branches. It provides standard retail products and services to individuals and small to midsized businesses. Lending activities are focused on real estate loans and mortgages: Loans secured by real estate account for some 80% of its total loan book. The company also offers business and consumer loans. The bank has two subsidiaries Pioneer Financial Services (insurance and investment products) and Pioneer Special Assets (foreclosures with added liabilities).

PIONEER ENERGY SERVICES CORP

NYS: PES

1250 N.E. Loop 410, Suite 1000	CEO: William S. (Stacy) Locke
San Antonio, TX 78209	CFO: Lorne E. Phillips
Phone: 855 884-0575	HR: Scott Keenen
Fax: –	FYE: December 31
Web: www.pioneeres.com	Type: Public

Pioneer Energy Services (formerly Pioneer Drilling) digs down deep to make money from beneath the land where Texas pioneers used to roam as well as in other locations. The company provides contract drilling services primarily to oil and gas companies in Texas and to a lesser degree in the Rockies and in Colombia. Pioneer Energy Services owns 64 land drilling rigs that can reach depths of 8000-18000 feet. In addition the company's Pioneer Production Services Division provides workover rig services wireline services and fishing and rental services to US-based oil and gas producers.

	Annual Growth	12/10	12/11	12/12	12/13	12/14
Sales ($ mil.)	21.3%	487.2	715.9	919.4	960.2	1,055.2
Net income ($ mil.)	–	(33.3)	11.2	30.0	(35.9)	(38.0)
Market value ($ mil.)	(10.9%)	562.3	617.8	463.3	511.2	353.6
Employees	7.5%	2,550	3,330	3,750	3,650	3,400

PIONEER HI-BRED INTERNATIONAL INC.

7100 NW 62nd Ave.	CEO: –
Johnston IA 50131	CFO: –
Phone: 515-270-3200	HR: –
Fax: 515-334-4515	FYE: December 31
Web: www.pioneer.com	Type: Subsidiary

Forget T-bills and mutual funds. Pioneer Hi-Bred International a subsidiary of chemical giant DuPont boasts the best yields. One of the world's largest commercial seed producers Pioneer uses genetic research to develop hybrid seeds designed to increase the quantity quality and sustainability of crop yields for farmers. The company produces Pioneer brand corn hybrid and soybean varieties sunflower canola rice sorghum and wheat as well as forage and grain additives. It offers ag services including crop management and agronomy. Since its acquisition in 1999 Pioneer has grown through new products and services aided by DuPont's deep research capabilities and cash. Pioneer has customers in 90 countries.

PIONEER INVESTMENT MANAGEMENT USA INC.

60 State St.	CEO: Daniel K Kingsbury
Boston MA 02109	CFO: Tony Koenig
Phone: 617-742-7825	HR: –
Fax: 800-225-4240	FYE: December 31
Web: us.pioneerinvestments.com	Type: Subsidiary

A subsidiary of Italian banking giant Unicredit Pioneer Investment Management USA offers investment management services to individual and institutional investors. Also known as Pioneer Investments the firm and its subsidiaries act as an investment manager and distributor for about 50 mutual funds invested in domestic and international equities fixed-income products and asset allocation strategies. Other products include closed-end funds variable annuities individual retirement plans and 401(k) plans for small businesses. The company's flagship Pioneer Fund established in 1928 is one of the oldest in the US.

PIONEER NATURAL RESOURCES CO

NYS: PXD

5205 N. O'Connor Blvd., Suite 200	CEO: Scott D. Sheffield
Irving, TX 75039	CFO: Richard P. (Rich) Dealy
Phone: 972 444-9001	HR: David Williams
Fax: 972 969-3587	FYE: December 31
Web: www.pxd.com	Type: Public

Oil and gas explorer Pioneer Natural Resources' frontier is not in the Western prairies but below them and below the Rocky Mountains the Midcontinent West Texas South Texas and elsewhere. The large independent exploration and production company reported proved reserves of about 799.5 million barrels of oil equivalent in 2014. The vast majority of the company's reserves are found within the US (including in Alaska where the company was the first independent explorer to produce from a North Slope oilfield). Its main assets are in Texas. It has stakes in more than 10710 net producing wells.

	Annual Growth	12/10	12/11	12/12	12/13	12/14
Sales ($ mil.)	19.6%	2,471.6	2,786.6	3,228.3	3,719.5	5,055.0
Net income ($ mil.)	11.3%	605.2	834.5	192.3	(838.4)	930.0
Market value ($ mil.)	14.4%	12,936.2	13,332.5	15,881.9	27,426.4	22,178.7
Employees	16.0%	2,248	3,304	3,667	4,203	4,075

PIONEER RAILCORP

NBB: PRRR

1318 S. Johanson Road
Peoria, IL 61607
Phone: 309 697-1400
Fax: 309 697-5387
Web: www.pioneer-railcorp.com

CEO: J Michael Carr
CFO: –
HR: –
FYE: December 31
Type: Public

Although Pioneer Railcorp doesn't often chart new territory the company's multiple railroad subsidiaries cover a lot of ground. Pioneer's short-line freight railroads travel 600-plus miles of track in about a dozen states neighboring Indiana Illinois and Michigan. More than half operate as interline carriers with major railroads. They haul such freight as lumber pulpboard fertilizer grain and plastic. Subsidiary Pioneer Railroad Equipment owns a fleet of some 600 railcars that are used by the company's railroads and leased to other rail carriers. Illinois businessman Guy Brenkman founded Pioneer Railcorp in 1986. Shortly after his retirement in 2006 the company switched from the NASDAQ to OTC markets.

	Annual Growth	12/10	12/11	12/12	12/13	12/14
Sales ($ mil.)	2.4%	18.9	19.5	20.4	21.6	20.8
Net income ($ mil.)	(11.2%)	3.3	3.5	0.9	4.5	2.0
Market value ($ mil.)	32.1%	12.3	12.7	19.3	39.5	37.5
Employees	–	–	–	–	–	–

PIPER JAFFRAY COMPANIES

NYS: PJC

800 Nicollet Mall, Suite 1000
Minneapolis, MN 55402
Phone: 612 303-6000
Fax: –
Web: www.piperjaffray.com

CEO: Andrew S. Duff
CFO: Debbra L. Schoneman
HR: Esete Bekele
FYE: December 31
Type: Public

Investment bank Piper Jaffray specializes in supplying clients with mergers and acquisitions advice financing and industry research. The bank's Institutional Brokerage business also offers equity and debt underwriting sales and trading services; while its Asset Management division boasts some $11.5 billion in assets under management. Piper Jaffray serves a variety of clients from corporations to government entities and not-for-profits targeting middle-market companies across the consumer financial services health care technology and industrial sectors among others. Founded in 1895 Piper Jaffray serves clients globally with offices across the US and in two European cities.

	Annual Growth	12/10	12/11	12/12	12/13	12/14
Sales ($ mil.)	5.2%	530.1	458.1	489.0	525.2	648.1
Net income ($ mil.)	26.9%	24.4	(102.0)	41.3	45.1	63.2
Market value ($ mil.)	13.5%	534.4	308.4	490.5	603.7	886.8
Employees	0.0%	1,053	1,014	966	1,053	1,055

PISMO COAST VILLAGE, INC.

165 South Dolliver Street
Pismo Beach, CA 93449
Phone: 805 773-5649
Fax: –
Web: www.pismocoastvillage.com

CEO: –
CFO: Wayne Hardesty
HR: –
FYE: September 30
Type: Public

Pismo Coast Village will prove that half the fun of owning an RV is parking it. The company runs a full-service recreational vehicle (RV) resort on more than 25 acres in Pismo Beach California that accommodates up to 400 RVs. Vacationers have access to an onsite general store heated swimming pool laundry facilities mini-golf course recreation hall video arcade wireless Internet and several playgrounds. Pismo Coast's recreation department aims to keep kids and families busy by renting out sports equipment and planning activities such as arts and crafts mini-golf tournaments pet costume contests and scavenger hunts. The resort also offers an RV repair shop.

	Annual Growth	09/10	09/11	09/12	09/13	09/14
Sales ($ mil.)	5.4%	5.8	5.9	6.2	6.6	7.1
Net income ($ mil.)	9.9%	0.5	0.5	0.5	0.7	0.7
Market value ($ mil.)	–	–	–	–	–	–
Employees	2.6%	56	58	58	60	62

PISTON AUTOMOTIVE L.L.C.

12723 TELEGRAPH RD STE 1
REDFORD, MI 48239-1489
Phone: 313-541-8689
Fax: –
Web: www.pistongroup.com

CEO: –
CFO: –
HR: Angela Harvey
FYE: December 31
Type: Private

Surprisingly there are no pistons on the workbenches and pallets of Piston Automotive. Less surprisingly a former Detroit Pistons player Vinnie "the Microwave" Johnson leads it as chairman. Piston Automotive specializes in the supply of powertrain systems front-end and powertrain cooling systems chassis systems and interior systems for the automotive industry. The company was formed in 1995 by Johnson to serve major automotive makers and related OEM suppliers in the greater Detroit area. A year later Piston Automotive began suspension module assembly and sequencing operations.

	Annual Growth	12/07	12/08	12/09	12/10	12/11
Sales ($ mil.)	42.9%	–	162.3	0.0	326.4	473.8
Net income ($ mil.)	424.6%	–	0.1	0.0	9.7	10.2
Market value ($ mil.)	–	–	–	–	–	–
Employees	–	–	–	–	–	380

PITCO FOODS

567 Cinnabar St.
San Jose CA 95110
Phone: 408-727-4826
Fax: 408-282-9711
Web: www.pitcofoods.com

CEO: Peri Navab
CFO: –
HR: –
FYE: December 31
Type: Private

PITCO Foods formed by the merger of Pacific Groservice and Pittsburg Wholesale Grocers operates a handful of members-only warehouse stores under the PITCO banner name across California in San Francisco Sacramento San Jose and Oakland. The outlets stock more than 9000 items including Hispanic and Asian products and cater to some 10000 independently-owned retailers and food service operators throughout the Central Valley and Northern California. Customers include supermarkets and convenience stores drug stores vending operations restaurants and caterers. In addition to various food items the wholesaler stocks tobacco janitorial supplies housewares health and beauty aids and auto supplies.

PITNEY BOWES INC

NYS: PBI

3001 Summer Street
Stamford, CT 06926
Phone: 203 356-5000
Fax: 203 351-7336
Web: www.pb.com

CEO: Marc B. Lautenbach
CFO: Michael Monahan
HR: Johnna G. Torsone
FYE: December 31
Type: Public

As the world's largest producer of postage meters Pitney Bowes puts it stamp on managing mail. The company nearly a century old makes other mailing equipment and provides shipping and weighing systems and it offers online postage services and financing for office equipment purchases. PB also develops software to create mailers and manage shipping transportation and logistics for government agencies and corporations. The company exited the document management services business in 2013 with the sale of Pitney Bowes Management Services. The company gets the majority of its revenue from small and medium-sized businesses (SMB). The company counts 1.5 million customers in 100 countries but as mail volumes fall so have PB's sales.

	Annual Growth	12/10	12/11	12/12	12/13	12/14
Sales ($ mil.)	(8.4%)	5,425.3	5,278.0	4,904.0	3,869.4	3,821.5
Net income ($ mil.)	3.4%	292.4	617.5	445.2	142.8	333.8
Market value ($ mil.)	0.2%	4,860.9	3,727.1	2,138.9	4,684.0	4,899.1
Employees	(16.1%)	30,700	28,700	27,400	16,100	15,200

PITNEY BOWES SOFTWARE INC.

1 Global View	CEO: –
Troy NY 12180-8371	CFO: –
Phone: 518-285-6000	HR: –
Fax: 518-285-6070	FYE: December 31
Web: www.pbinsight.com	Type: Subsidiary

Pitney Bowes Software can help you map it and mail it. Formed from the combination of Group 1 Software and MapInfo (acquired in 2007 for $408 million) the company's software and database products enable firms to integrate geographical data (including street addresses and ZIP codes) into business intelligence functions including analysis and forecasting. The company also offers mailstream applications used for address cleansing data integration document composition and managing mailing efficiency. In addition to its customer interaction optimization products the company also offers consulting business process outsourcing and predictive analytics services.

PITT COUNTY MEMORIAL HOSPITAL INCORPORATED

2100 STANTONSBURG RD	CEO: Dave McRae
GREENVILLE, NC 278342832	CFO: –
Phone: 252-847-4100	HR: –
Fax: –	FYE: September 30
Web: - www.vidanthealth.com	Type: Private

Vidant Medical Center is an acute health services facility that serves the vibrant community of Greenville North Carolina and surrounding areas. The 909-bed regional referral hospital's specialty divisions include Vidant Children's Hospital East Carolina Heart Institute a rehabilitation center and the outpatient Vidant SurgiCenter. Other services include oncology transplant women's health orthopedic behavioral care and home health and hospice care units. The center also serves as a teaching facility for East Carolina University's Brody School of Medicine. Vidant Medical Center (formerly Pitt County Memorial Hospital) is a member of University Health Systems of Eastern Carolina (dba Vidant Health).

	Annual Growth	09/07	09/08	09/09*	12/12*	09/13
Sales ($ mil.)	5.3%	–	796.7	- 878.2	395.8	1,031.7
Net income ($ mil.)	36.5%	–	–	26.5	19.1	91.9
Market value ($ mil.)	–	–	–	–	–	–
Employees	–	–	–	–	–	8,373

*Fiscal year change

PITT-OHIO EXPRESS LLC

15 27TH ST	CEO: –
PITTSBURGH, PA 152224729	CFO: Scott R. Sullivan
Phone: 412-232-3015	HR: Penny Pilatas
Fax: –	FYE: December 31
Web: www.pittohio.com	Type: Private

Primarily a regional less-than-truckload (LTL) freight carrier Pitt Ohio operates a fleet of about 1000 tractors and 3100 trailers. (LTL carriers consolidate freight from multiple shippers into a single truckload.) It maintains straight trucks and vans in its fleet. Pitt Ohio additionally provides truckload (TL) transportation through ECM Transport. It operates a network of about 20 terminals primarily in the Midwest and Mid-Atlantic US. Beyond freight hauling Pitt Ohio provides specialized logistics services for shippers. The family of Charles Hammel III owns Pitt Ohio which has grown from a business established by Hammel's grandfather in 1919.

	Annual Growth	12/01	12/02	12/04	12/06	12/07
Sales ($ mil.)	5.0%	–	205.6	221.4	243.7	261.8
Net income ($ mil.)	(5.4%)	–	–	22.2	24.7	18.8
Market value ($ mil.)	–	–	–	–	–	–
Employees	–	–	–	–	–	3,000

PITTSBURGH STEELERS SPORTS INC.

3400 S. Water St.	CEO: –
Pittsburgh PA 15203-2349	CFO: –
Phone: 412-432-7800	HR: –
Fax: 412-432-7878	FYE: March 31
Web: www.steelers.com	Type: Private

Pittsburgh Steelers Sports has forged a championship tradition in Steel Town. The company owns and operates the Pittsburgh Steelers professional football franchise which has won a record six Super Bowl titles. The team joined the National Football League in 1933 as the Pirates (renamed in 1940) but claimed only eight winning seasons during its first 40 years. However the Steelers dominated the 1970s when the team won four championships under head coach Chuck Noll with the help of such stars as Terry Bradshaw and Lynn Swann. Pittsburgh won its latest Super Bowl following the 2008 season. Dan Rooney son of late team founder Art Rooney and his son Art Rooney II lead a group that owns the Steelers.

PIXAR ANIMATION STUDIOS INC.

1200 Park Ave.	CEO: James W Morris
Emeryville CA 94608	CFO: –
Phone: 510-922-3000	HR: –
Fax: 510-922-3151	FYE: December 31
Web: www.pixar.com	Type: Subsidiary

Pixar Animation Studios keeps computer-generating hits. The company has produced about a dozen full-length animated movies including the first fully computer-animated feature "Toy Story" (1995) as well as the more recent Brave (2012) Cars 2 (2011) and Toy Story 3 (2010). Its proprietary software — Marionette (modeling animating lighting) Ringmaster (production management) and RenderMan (image rendering) — makes 3D-style animation. RenderMan was used to create some of the dinosaurs in Jurassic Park and space creatures in the Star Wars films. Pixar has accounted for a large chunk of the animation box office in recent years. Its films are released by Disney which in 2006 bought Pixar for $7.4 billion.

PIXELWORKS INC

NMS. PXLW

224 Airport Parkway, Suite 400	CEO: Stephen Domenik
San Jose, CA 95110	CFO: Steven L. Moore
Phone: 408 200-9200	HR: –
Fax: –	FYE: December 31
Web: www.pixelworks.com	Type: Public

Pixelworks' chips put the sizzle in digital displays. The company's display controller integrated circuits (ICs) power visual displays in PCs TVs and other electronic devices. Its ImageProcessor system-on-chip ICs combine microprocessor memory software and digital signal processor components onto a single device. Distributor Tokyo Electron Device (TED) accounts for about 44% of sales; distributors are behind more than 60% of Pixelworks' sales. Other customers include SANYO Electric Seiko Epson and Hitachi which each account for 10% of sales. About 90% of the company's sales come from customers in Asia primarily Japan.

	Annual Growth	12/10	12/11	12/12	12/13	12/14
Sales ($ mil.)	(3.2%)	69.5	64.6	59.7	48.1	60.9
Net income ($ mil.)	–	0.4	(6.6)	(5.7)	(8.9)	(10.0)
Market value ($ mil.)	7.0%	80.8	56.2	52.0	111.9	105.9
Employees	(2.5%)	243	242	233	223	220

PIZZA HUT INC.

14841 Dallas Pkwy.
Dallas TX 75254
Phone: 972-338-7700
Fax: 972-338-6869
Web: www.pizzahut.com

CEO: Scott Bergren
CFO: –
HR: –
FYE: December 31
Type: Subsidiary

When it comes to tossing around dough no one does it more often than Pizza Hut. The unit of YUM! Brands operates the world's #1 pizza chain with more than 13000 outlets in about 90 countries worldwide. The chain serves a variety of pizza styles including its flagship Pan Pizza as well as Thin n' Crispy Stuffed Crust Hand Tossed and Sicilian. Other menu items include pasta salads and sandwiches. Pizza Hut offers dine-in service at its characteristic red-roofed restaurants as well as carry-out and delivery service. About 15% of the restaurants are company-operated while the rest are franchised. The world's largest fast food company YUM! Brands runs KFC and Taco Bell in addition to Pizza Hut.

PJ UNITED INC.

2300 Resource Dr.
Birmingham AL 35242
Phone: 205-981-2800
Fax: 205-981-2881
Web: www.pjunited.com

CEO: Doug Stephens
CFO: –
HR: –
FYE: December 31
Type: Private

PJ United's pizza comes from Papa. The company is the largest franchisee of Papa John's International with about 115 pizza delivery locations in six states including Alabama Louisiana and Texas. In addition to its original crust and thin crust pizzas available with a variety of toppings the company's pizza outlets serve cheese sticks breadsticks chicken strips and dipping sauces. PJ United procures its pizza dough food products and paper products from the commissary system of Papa John's the #3 pizza chain behind Pizza Hut (part of YUM! Brands) and Domino's. Private equity firm The Halifax Group led a management buyout of the company in 2008.

PJM INTERCONNECTION LLC

955 JEFFERSON AVE
NORRISTOWN, PA 194032410
Phone: 610-666-8980
Fax: –
Web: www.pjmsettlement.com

CEO: W. Terry Boston
CFO: Suzanne Daugherty
HR: –
FYE: December 31
Type: Private

Interdependence is a given at PJM Interconnection which oversees a 62555-mile section of the North American power transmission grid that spans 13 northeastern and midwestern states and the District of Columbia. The regional transmission organization monitors and coordinates the movement of wholesale electricity in its service territory; its 850 members have a combined generating capacity of 185600 MW. Sanctioned by the Federal Energy Regulatory Commission PJM is charged with ensuring fair competition among power purchasers sellers and traders; it also is responsible for the reliable delivery of distributed electricity to 61 million consumers in its territory.

	Annual Growth	12/04	12/05	12/06	12/08	12/12
Sales ($ mil.)	2.8%	–	–	274.9	241.3	324.3
Net income ($ mil.)	9.4%	–	–	0.5	0.7	0.8
Market value ($ mil.)	–	–	–	–	–	–
Employees	–	–	–	–	–	600

PLACID REFINING COMPANY LLC

1601 ELM ST STE 3400
DALLAS, TX 752017201
Phone: 214-880-8479
Fax: –
Web: www.placidrefining.com

CEO: –
CFO: –
HR: –
FYE: December 31
Type: Private

A calm presence in the volatile oil and gas industry Placid Refining owns and operates the Port Allen refinery in Louisiana which converts crude oil into a number of petroleum products including diesel ethanol gasoline liquid petroleum gas jet fuel and fuel oils. Placid Refining's refinery has the capacity to process 80000 barrels of crude oil per day. The company is one of the largest employers and taxpayers in West Baton Rouge Parish. Placid Refining which is controlled by Petro-Hunt distribute fuels across a dozen states in the southeastern US from Texas to Virginia and is a major supplier of jet fuel to the US military.

	Annual Growth	12/05	12/06	12/10	12/11	12/13
Sales ($ mil.)	7.7%	–	2,925.7	3,686.1	4,699.6	4,929.2
Net income ($ mil.)	6.8%	–	–	39.3	4.2	47.9
Market value ($ mil.)	–	–	–	–	–	–
Employees	–	–	–	–	–	200

PLAINS ALL AMERICAN PIPELINE, L.P.

NYS: PAA

333 Clay Street, Suite 1600
Houston, TX 77002
Phone: 713 646-4100
Fax: –
Web: www.plainsallamerican.com

CEO: Greg L. Armstrong
CFO: Al Swanson
HR: –
FYE: December 31
Type: Public

The term "All American" includes Canada for Plains All American Pipeline which has pipeline operations in the US and north of the border. The limited partnership is engaged in the transportation storage terminalling and marketing of crude oil refined products natural gas liquids (NGL) and liquefied petroleum gas (LPG) and owns extensive gathering terminal and storage facilities in across the US and in Canada. At the end of 2014 Plains All American Pipeline owned 17800 miles of gathering crude oil NGL and refined product pipelines throughout the US and Canada operated a fleet of 800 trailers 150 barges and 72 transport tugs and owned 29 million barrels of storage capacity.

	Annual Growth	12/10	12/11	12/12	12/13	12/14
Sales ($ mil.)	13.8%	25,893.0	34,275.0	37,797.0	42,249.0	43,464.0
Net income ($ mil.)	28.7%	505.0	966.0	1,094.0	1,361.0	1,384.0
Market value ($ mil.)	(4.9%)	23,553.0	27,551.7	16,969.9	19,419.3	19,250.5
Employees	10.9%	3,500	3,800	4,700	4,900	5,300

PLAINS COTTON COOPERATIVE ASSOCIATION

3301 E 50TH ST
LUBBOCK, TX 794044331
Phone: 806-763-8011
Fax: –
Web: www.pcca.com

CEO: Kevin Brinkley
CFO: Billy Morton
HR: –
FYE: June 30
Type: Private

Plainly speaking most of the US cotton used by textile mills worldwide starts with the Plains Cotton Cooperative Association (PCCA). The farmer-owned co-op markets millions of bales annually for members in Oklahoma Kansas and Texas. To obtain a competitive price for their cotton PCCA takes advantage of Telmark LP's access to The Seam an online cotton marketplace that continually updates cotton prices buyer data and more. The co-op operates cotton warehouses in Texas Oklahoma and Kansas. PCCA sold its textile and apparel operations in 2014 to focus exclusively on cotton marketing and warehousing. Formed in 1953 PCCA's customers include Replay Urban Outfitters and Abercrombie & Fitch.

	Annual Growth	06/10	06/11	06/12	06/13	06/14
Sales ($ mil.)	(19.8%)	–	1,835.8	793.7	1,080.1	947.5
Net income ($ mil.)	–	–	–	8.4	10.4	(37.0)
Market value ($ mil.)	–	–	–	–	–	–
Employees	–	–	–	–	–	800

PLANAR SYSTEMS INC.

NMS: PLNR

1195 NW Compton Drive
Beaverton, OR 97006
Phone: 503 748-1100
Fax: –
Web: www.planar.com

CEO: Gerald Perkel
CFO: Ryan Gray
HR: –
FYE: September 26
Type: Public

Planar Systems has no qualms about making a public display. The company makes custom embedded and video wall displays used in such applications as vehicle dashboards instrumentation security monitoring and retail systems. Planar also sells desktop monitors and home theater systems. Its products — marketed under the Planar Clarity and Runco brands — include matrix and mosaic LCD systems flat-panel displays rear-project cube displays touch monitors and theater front-projection systems. The company serves consumers as well as clients in the retail industrial transportation and education industries among others. It generates most of its sales in the US.

	Annual Growth	09/10	09/11	09/12	09/13	09/14
Sales ($ mil.)	0.5%	175.7	186.5	171.4	166.8	179.0
Net income ($ mil.)	–	(5.1)	(4.7)	(16.2)	(6.5)	3.8
Market value ($ mil.)	14.4%	47.0	43.1	29.3	39.5	80.4
Employees	(8.0%)	429	471	422	298	308

PLANET HOLLYWOOD INTERNATIONAL INC.

6052 Turkey Lake Rd. Ste. 201
Orlando FL 32819
Phone: 407-903-5500
Fax: 617-679-5592
Web: www.iderapharma.com

CEO: Robert I Earl
CFO: Bruce Hawkins
HR: Jerilyn Gregory
FYE: December 31
Type: Private

This Planet serves a little glitz and glamour with its burgers and fries. Planet Hollywood International operates and franchises a chain of about 15 showbiz-themed restaurants offering casual-dining fare (burgers steaks seafood) along with a collection of movie memorabilia and celebrity merchandise. The eateries are found mostly in tourist hotspots such as Las Vegas London and New York City's Times Square. The Planet Hollywood name also graces a Las Vegas resort casino (operated by Caesars Entertainment) and the company owns the Buca di Beppo chain through subsidiary BUCA. Chairman Robert Earl who founded Planet Hollywood in 1991 controls the company in partnership with Bay Harbour Management.

PLANET PAYMENT, INC.

NAS: PLPM

670 Long Beach Boulevard
Long Beach, NY 11561
Phone. 516 670-3200
Fax: 516 670-3520
Web: www.planetpayment.com

CEO: Carl J Williams
CFO: Raymond D' Aponte
HR: –
FYE: December 31
Type: Public

Planet Payment may not be able to break language barriers but its systems can break currency barriers. Through its Pay in Your Currency and other services Planet Payment provides point-of-sale and e-commerce payment processing services that allow merchants to accept Visa MasterCard and American Express credit and debit card payments in multiple currencies. The company's services also help merchants set up pricing in different currencies. It operates at more than 60000 merchant locations in 20-plus counties in the Asia Pacific region and North America. Customers include hotels restaurants and retailers operating in international business and tourist centers. Chairman Philip Beck founded Planet Payment in 1999.

	Annual Growth	12/10	12/11	12/12	12/13	12/14
Sales ($ mil.)	(7.5%)	64.7	41.9	43.6	46.6	47.4
Net income ($ mil.)	–	(3.3)	2.4	(4.5)	0.0	3.2
Market value ($ mil.)	–	–	–	–	–	–
Employees	(8.8%)	–	–	201	205	167

PLANET SMOOTHIE FRANCHISES LLC

1425 Ellsworth Industrial Blvd. NW Ste. 38
Atlanta GA 30318
Phone: 404-856-4320
Fax: 703-790-6360
Web: www.exelisinc.com

CEO: Bryan O'Rourke
CFO: –
HR: –
FYE: December 31
Type: Private

You might say this company orbits the blended fruit drink market. Planet Smoothie Franchises operates a chain of more than 125 franchised smoothie stands in about 20 states. The outlets offer about 30 types of blended fruit drinks with such names as Frozen Goat Mr. Mongo and Spazz. Enthusiasts can customize the beverages by adding blends of supplements and vitamins (Blasts) designed to increase energy help burn fat or aid immune systems. The company also has a small number of Planet Smoothie Cafes featuring salads sandwiches and wraps. Entrepreneur Martin Sprock opened the first Planet Smoothie in 1995. The company is owned by Petrus Brands a holding company backed by private-equity firm Edmonds Capital.

PLANGRAPHICS INC.

OTC: PGRA

112 E. Main St.
Frankfort KY 40601
Phone: 502-223-1501
Fax: 502-223-1235
Web: www.plangraphics.com

CEO: John C Antenucci
CFO: –
HR: –
FYE: September 30
Type: Public

PlanGraphics can do more than read a map. The company provides IT services for geographic information systems (GIS) computer-based mapping applications used with database management software to analyze customer demographics mineral exploration military surveillance crop forecasting and other data. PlanGraphics' customers include government entities utilities and corporations such as Entergy and the US Army Corps of Engineers. In 2009 Integrated Freight Corp. a Florida-based transportation company acquired a majority stake in PlanGraphics which then acquired Integrated Freight. The merged company then sold PlanGraphics' operating subsidiary to CEO John Antenucci.

PLANNED PARENTHOOD FEDERATION OF AMERICA INC.

434 W 33RD ST FL 12
NEW YORK, NY 100012600
Phone: 212-541-7800
Fax: –
Web: www.plannedparenthoodaction.org

CEO: –
CFO: Julia Nelson
HR: –
FYE: June 30
Type: Private

He who fails to plan plans to fail could refer to parenting. No fear the Planned Parenthood Federation Of America provides sexual health information as well as reproductive healthcare through 800 affiliated health centers to more than 5 million people each year. PPFA also lobbies for reproductive rights and reproductive health issues and works to extend access to family planning services for all. The not-for-profit organization is supported by private and corporate donations and patient fees as well as government grants. Founded in 1916 by Margaret Sanger PPFA has grown to 84 affiliates in all 50 US states and the District of Columbia and is part of the International Planned Parenthood Federation.

	Annual Growth	06/09	06/10	06/11	06/12	06/13
Sales ($ mil.)	17.6%	–	85.6	184.7	159.5	139.4
Net income ($ mil.)	(86.8%)	–	–	87.9	34.0	1.5
Market value ($ mil.)	–	–	–	–	–	–
Employees	–	–	–	–	–	210

PLANTE & MORAN PLLC

27400 Northwestern Hwy.
Southfield MI 48034
Phone: 248-352-2500
Fax: 248-352-0018
Web: www.plantemoran.com

CEO: –
CFO: Jerry Smith
HR: –
FYE: May 31
Type: Private

Plante & Moran is planted firmly in the upper Midwest. With some 20 offices in Michigan Ohio and Illinois the firm provides a variety of accounting and management consulting services. Its offerings include tax preparation employee benefits consulting technology assessment and planning and wealth management. The firm has expertise in several industries ranging from retail and dealerships to health care financial services and manufacturing. It also serves the not-for-profit and public sectors. Plante & Moran which is affiliated with international accounting alliance Praxity also has offices in Mexico India and China. The company was founded by Elorion Plante in 1924.

PLANTRONICS, INC.

NYS: PLT

345 Encinal Street
Santa Cruz, CA 95060
Phone: 831 426-5858
Fax: 831 426-6098
Web: www.plantronics.com

CEO: S. Kenneth (Ken) Kannappan
CFO: Pamela (Pam) Strayer
HR: Pat Wadors
FYE: March 31
Type: Public

Plantronics' customers appreciate its hands-off approach. The company makes lightweight communications headsets that can be worn over the head behind the ear or in the ear freeing hands for other tasks. Its other products include the Clarity brand of amplified telephone handsets for hearing-impaired users text telephones emergency response systems and mobile phone headsets. Serving the consumer and business markets worldwide Plantronics sells its products through distributors manufacturers and communications service providers. The company gets about 60% of its sales in the US.

	Annual Growth	03/11	03/12	03/13	03/14	03/15
Sales ($ mil.)	6.1%	683.6	713.4	762.2	818.6	865.0
Net income ($ mil.)	0.7%	109.2	109.0	106.4	112.4	112.3
Market value ($ mil.)	9.7%	1,523.4	1,674.9	1,838.3	1,849.2	2,202.8
Employees	1.5%	3,200	3,100	3,400	3,400	3,397

PLANVIEW INC.

8300 N MO PAC EXPY # 300
AUSTIN, TX 78759-8330
Phone: 512-346-8600
Fax: –
Web: www.planview.com

CEO: Gregory Gilmore
CFO: Randy Jonkers
HR: –
FYE: December 31
Type: Private

This company's plan is to stay on the lookout for clients in need of a good IT strategy. PlanView develops enterprise software that helps large and midsized companies make the most of their information technology processes and related assets (including software computers printers and servers). Its applications combine tools for business process management (Process Builder) and resource project and portfolio management (Enterprise). The company offers a comprehensive portfolio management solutions in the industry to enable better decision making and business accountability.

	Annual Growth	12/04	12/05	12/06	12/07	12/08
Sales ($ mil.)	(81.6%)	–	–	1,988.8	70.0	67.1
Net income ($ mil.)	70246.3%	–	–	0.0	1.8	2.0
Market value ($ mil.)	–	–	–	–	–	–
Employees	–	–	–	–	–	262

PLASKOLITE INC.

1770 Joyce Ave.
Columbus OH 43219
Phone: 614-294-3281
Fax: 614-297-7287
Web: www.plaskolite.com

CEO: –
CFO: Mark Grindley
HR: Paul Washington
FYE: December 31
Type: Private

Plaskolite knows that not all sheets go on a bed. The plastics company manufactures its trademarked OPTIX and DURAPLEX (impact resistant) extruded acrylic sheet used in products such as lighting panels picture frames and signs. Other offerings include acrylic resin polystyrene sheet FABBACK mirror sheet and protective coatings and backings (UV & thermal). Plaskolite which was founded in 1950 also offers a Run-to-Size program that enables customers to buy the exact sheet specifications they need for their applications. The company operates US manufacturing and distribution facilities in California Mississippi Ohio and Texas and international sites in Canada Mexico and the Netherlands.

PLASTIPAK PACKAGING INC.

41605 Ann Arbor Rd.
Plymouth MI 48170
Phone: 734-455-3600
Fax: 734-354-7391
Web: www.plastipak.com

CEO: –
CFO: Michael Plotzke
HR: –
FYE: October 31
Type: Private

Plastipak likes to keep things bottled up. Plastipak Packaging produces more than 8 billion plastic containers a year for consumer products' manufacturers. Containers are used to hold beverages (soft drinks water juice beer) cleansers (laundry soap household cleaners) processed foods (coffee creamer salad dressing) hygiene (mouthwash perfume) and industrial and automotive goods (motor oil windshield washer fluid). The company has served established companies such as Kraft Foods Kroger Procter & Gamble Reckitt Benckiser and Pepsico. Plastipak operates in the US Europe and South America. Founded in 1967 it is owned and led by the Young family.

PLATINUM ENERGY SOLUTIONS INC.

2100 West Loop South Ste. 1601
Houston TX 77027
Phone: 713-622-7731
Fax: 832-553-7431
Web: www.platinumenergysolutions.com

CEO: –
CFO: –
HR: –
FYE: December 31
Type: Private

Platinum Energy Solutions (PES) is a regular frack of all trades. The oilfield services company provides hydraulic fracturing (fracking) coiled tubing and other onshore pressure pumping services to three customers Petrohawk Energy Encana Oil & Gas and El Paso E&P Company. (Fracking is a somewhat controversial method to extract oil and natural gas by pumping pressurized chemicals into the ground to break it up). PES formed in 2010 and began fracking services the next year. PES also filed a $300 million initial public offering in September 2011 but withdrew it in January 2013 citing unfavorable market conditions.

PLATINUM EQUITY LLC

360 N. Crescent Dr.
Beverly Hills CA 90210
Phone: 310-712-1850
Fax: 310-712-1848
Web: www.platinumequity.com

CEO: –
CFO: Mary Ann Sigler
HR: –
FYE: December 31
Type: Private

Platinum Equity thinks its portfolio companies are just precious. The investment firm typically seeks to acquire private companies public firms that want to become private and units that large corporations are looking to divest; these enterprises usually have established brands and customer bases and most importantly recurring revenues. Platinum Equity also looks for acquisitions as strategic add-ons to its portfolio companies which have operations worldwide. Founder and CEO Tom Gores who started Platinum Equity in 1995 is the brother of Alec Gores who founded another investment firm Gore Technology Group (now The Gores Group).

PLATO LEARNING INC.

5600 W. 83rd St. Ste. 300 8200 Tower
Bloomington MN 55437
Phone: 952-832-1000
Fax: 952-832-1200
Web: www.plato.com

CEO: Vin Riera
CFO: Robert J Rueckl
HR: –
FYE: October 31
Type: Private

Whether you want the Socratic method or a more modern approach to education PLATO Learning has the tools for teaching. The company's PLATO Learning System is an interactive instructional and testing system that provides teachers with curriculum and instructional management and assessment tools. The company offers courseware tutorials (covering topics such as reading and writing mathematics science social studies and job skills) as well as consulting curriculum planning and other services. PLATO markets its products to K-12 schools colleges job training programs military education programs and corporations. Thoma Bravo took the company private in 2010 when it acquired PLATO for nearly $145 million.

PLAYERS NETWORK (THE)

NDD: PNTV

1771 E. Flamingo Road, #201-A
Las Vegas, NV 89119
Phone: 702-734-3457
Fax: –
Web: www.playersnetworkcom

CEO: Mark Bradley
CFO: Mark Bradley
HR: –
FYE: December 31
Type: Public

Players Network acquires produces and distributes video content focused on Las Vegas gaming and nightlife. It has a library of more than 1000 videos including instructional programs on gambling and features on Las Vegas casinos and nightspots as well as videos featuring Vegas entertainers and other personalities. Players Network distributes its programming primarily through cable and satellite video-on-demand (VOD) services and through content partnerships with online video sites including Google. CEO Mark Bradley and president Michael Berk (who helped create the TV series Baywatch) together own about 30% of the company.

	Annual Growth	12/10	12/11	12/12	12/13	12/14
Sales ($ mil.)	(38.1%)	0.1	0.1	0.1	0.0	0.0
Net income ($ mil.)	–	(1.7)	(1.2)	(1.1)	(1.7)	(3.3)
Market value ($ mil.)	(39.4%)	26.7	16.5	6.9	5.6	3.6
Employees	(20.6%)	–	4	4	2	2

PLAYNETWORK INC.

8727 148th Ave. NE
Redmond WA 98052
Phone: 425-497-8100
Fax: 425-497-8181
Web: www.playnetwork.com

CEO: Craig Hubbell
CFO: Sue Hoover
HR: –
FYE: December 31
Type: Private

PlayNetwork provides audio and video branding services for retail hospitality health and fitness and retail banking businesses. Its offerings include branded video (digital signage) audio (music and messaging) promotional media and the design and installation of audio/video systems. PlayNetwork has contracts with clients such as such as Starbucks Chili's Grill & Bar The Timberland Company Rubio's Restaurants Jockey International and dELiA*s. The company was founded in 1996 and is backed by private investors Chartwell Capital Edgewater Private Equity Fund Talon Opportunity Fund Velocity Capital and WHP Partners.

PLEXUS CORP.

NMS: PLXS

One Plexus Way
Neenah, WI 54957
Phone: 920 969-6000
Fax: 920 751-5395
Web: www.plexus.com

CEO: Dean A. Foate
CFO: Patrick J. (Pat) Jermain
HR: Joseph E Mauthe
FYE: October 03
Type: Public

Plexus flexes its manufacturing muscles in doing contract work for customers in a wide range of businesses. The company develops and manufactures electronic products for companies in the telecommunications medical industrial and defense markets. Plexus does product design assembly and testing of printed circuit boards (PCBs) test equipment and other electronic components. The company also offers prototyping materials procurement warehousing and distribution and other support services. Customers include Arris Group (12% of sales) and General Electric (about 10% of sales). Plexus gets most of its sales from customers in the US and Malaysia.

	Annual Growth	10/11*	09/12	09/13	09/14*	10/15
Sales ($ mil.)	4.4%	2,231.2	2,306.7	2,228.0	2,378.2	2,654.3
Net income ($ mil.)	1.4%	89.3	62.1	82.3	87.2	94.3
Market value ($ mil.)	13.8%	757.8	1,014.7	1,236.2	1,266.0	1,273.0
Employees	11.7%	9,000	9,600	9,200	12,000	14,000

*Fiscal year change

PLUG POWER INC

NAS: PLUG

968 Albany Shaker Road
Latham, NY 12110
Phone: 518 782-7700
Fax: 518 782-9060
Web: www.plugpower.com

CEO: Andrew J. (Andy) Marsh
CFO: Paul B. Middleton
HR: Joseph Millington
FYE: December 31
Type: Public

Plug Power wants to give alternative power sources a lift. The company develops on-site power generation systems used in forklifts and material handling equipment and in remote power applications. Plug Power uses proton exchange membrane (PEM) fuel cells to generate electricity from hydrogen gas without combustion. The company's GenDrive product is sold to large distribution centers as a replacement for lead-acid batteries in lift trucks including pallet trucks and narrow-aisle reach trucks. Plug Power caters primarily to the US market; customers have included SYSCO Wal-Mart Central Grocers Whole Foods and FedEx Freight.

	Annual Growth	12/10	12/11	12/12	12/13	12/14
Sales ($ mil.)	34.8%	19.5	27.6	26.1	26.6	64.2
Net income ($ mil.)	–	(47.0)	(27.5)	(31.9)	(62.7)	(88.5)
Market value ($ mil.)	68.6%	64.3	353.5	86.6	268.6	519.8
Employees	21.6%	149	195	156	214	326

PLUM CREEK TIMBER CO., INC.

NYS: PCL

601 Union Street, Suite 3100
Seattle, WA 98101-1374
Phone: 206 467-3600
Fax: 206 467-3795
Web: www.plumcreek.com

CEO: Rick R. Holley
CFO: David W. Lambert
HR: Barbara (Barb) Crowe
FYE: December 31
Type: Public

Plum Creek Timber is not only one of the largest timber companies in the US it is also one of the country's largest private landowners. The real estate investment trust (REIT) which owns and manages some 6.8 million acres of timberlands in 19 states harvests old- and new-growth timber and sells logs to sawmills and pulp and paper mills around the country. Plum Creek's manufacturing operations include two softwood lumber mills two medium-density fiberboard (MDF) plants two plywood plants and two lumber manufacturing facilities in Idaho and Montana. Major customers include Evergreen Packaging Georgia-Pacific Graphic Packaging and West Fraser. Forest products company Weyerhaeuser agreed to purchase Plum Creek for $8.4 billion in late 2015.

	Annual Growth	12/10	12/11	12/12	12/13	12/14
Sales ($ mil.)	5.5%	1,190.0	1,167.0	1,339.0	1,340.0	1,476.0
Net income ($ mil.)	0.1%	213.0	193.0	203.0	214.0	214.0
Market value ($ mil.)	3.4%	6,587.5	6,430.9	7,804.7	8,181.1	7,526.8
Employees	2.5%	1,202	1,192	1,223	1,308	1,325

PLUMAS BANCORP INC

NAS: PLBC

35 S. Lindan Avenue
Quincy, CA 95971
Phone: 530 283-7305
Fax: –
Web: www.plumasbank.com

CEO: Andrew J Ryback
CFO: Richard L Belstock
HR: –
FYE: December 31
Type: Public

Plumas Bancorp is the holding company for Plumas Bank which serves individuals and businesses in the northeastern corner of California from Lake Tahoe to the Oregon border. Through more than a dozen branches the bank offers deposit products such as checking savings and retirement accounts and certificates of deposit. Loans secured by real estate account for more than half of Plumas Bank's loan portfolio; combined commercial and agricultural loans make up about a quarter. The bank writes consumer loans as well. It also provides access to investment products and services such as financial planning mutual funds and annuities.

	Annual Growth	12/10	12/11	12/12	12/13	12/14
Assets ($ mil.)	2.7%	484.5	455.3	477.8	515.7	538.9
Net income ($ mil.)	48.6%	1.0	0.9	2.0	3.4	4.7
Market value ($ mil.)	36.0%	11.2	11.4	15.6	29.9	38.3
Employees	(0.3%)	157	156	151	159	155

PLUMB SUPPLY COMPANY

1622 NE 51ST AVE
DES MOINES, IA 503132194
Phone: 515-262-9511
Fax: –
Web: www.plumbsupply.com

CEO: –
CFO: –
HR: –
FYE: December 31
Type: Private

Plumb Supply is plum tickled with the plumbing and HVAC business. Through about 20 locations in Iowa Plumb Supply distributes plumbing heating cooling and bathroom products to builders and contractors. In addition to air conditioners and heaters the company sells pipes valves fittings and about 200 other product lines from Bemis Manufacturing Honeywell Kohler Mueller Industries and Whirlpool. About 10 stores feature Water Concepts Galleries which showcase kitchen and bathroom fixtures from major brands. The company was founded in 1946 and purchased by Templeton Coal in 1965.

	Annual Growth	12/09	12/10	12/11	12/12	12/13
Sales ($ mil.)	–	–	0.0	0.0	97.9	97.9
Net income ($ mil.)	–	–	–	0.0	3.3	3.3
Market value ($ mil.)	–	–	–	–	–	–
Employees	–	–	–	–	–	215

PLURISTEM THERAPEUTICS INC

NAS: PSTI

MATAM Advanced Technology Park, Building No.5
Haifa 31905
Phone: (972) 74 7108607
Fax: –
Web: www.pluristem.com

CEO: –
CFO: –
HR: –
FYE: June 30
Type: Public

This company does its navel-gazing on the clock. Pluristem Therapeutics (formerly Pluristem Life Systems) employs a patented technology to artificially grow stromal stem cells and T-cells from umbilical cord blood generating quantities sufficient to be used in cell therapies and bone marrow transplants. The company's PluriX Bioreactor system a technological stem cell expansion platform that employs this stem cell growth is being developed with the hope of producing and selling cell therapy products for ailments including degenerative cardiovascular and immune system disorders.

	Annual Growth	06/11	06/12	06/13	06/14	06/15
Sales ($ mil.)	(19.1%)	–	0.7	0.7	0.4	0.4
Net income ($ mil.)	–	(10.8)	(14.8)	(21.2)	(26.9)	(24.7)
Market value ($ mil.)	(3.4%)	228.4	189.1	241.0	245.8	198.5
Employees	24.7%	70	99	148	169	169

PLX TECHNOLOGY INC

NMS: PLXT

870 W. Maude Avenue
Sunnyvale, CA 94085
Phone: 408 774-9060
Fax: –
Web: www.plxtech.com

CEO: David K Raun
CFO: Arthur O Whipple
HR: –
FYE: December 31
Type: Public

PLX Technology's devices handle complex traffic inside electronic gear. PLX makes input/output accelerators and other chips used to manage data transfer between the microprocessor memory and peripheral chips within an embedded system. It also sells hardware and software development kits used to design subsystems that employ its chips. Its chips are compatible with communications processors made by industry leaders such as Broadcom. OEMs use the company's industry-standard PCI interconnect chips in products such as digital TVs media servers cable modems printers and video surveillance equipment.

	Annual Growth	12/08	12/09	12/10	12/11	12/12
Sales ($ mil.)	5.5%	81.1	82.8	116.6	115.8	100.2
Net income ($ mil.)	–	(56.5)	(18.8)	(3.3)	(24.8)	(32.6)
Market value ($ mil.)	20.5%	77.6	145.7	162.8	129.4	163.7
Employees	(0.3%)	158	197	260	205	156

PLY GEM HOLDINGS INC

NYS: PGEM

5020 Weston Parkway, Suite 400
Cary, NC 27513
Phone: 919 677-3900
Fax: –
Web: www.plygem.com

CEO: –
CFO: Shawn K Poe
HR: David (Dave) Schmoll
FYE: December 31
Type: Public

Ply Gem brings out a new side of homes. The company makes and supplies exterior building materials used in home construction and renovation. Its products — vinyl siding aluminum windows and doors stone veneer and fencing — are supplied to home-center retailers distributors construction companies and contractors in North America. Subsidiaries include Variform (vinyl siding) Napco (vinyl and metal exterior siding and trim) Kroy Building Products (vinyl fencing) and Great Lakes Window (energy-efficient vinyl windows and patio doors). Ply Gem Holdings was founded in 2004 to acquire the Ply Gem brand and related assets from building materials manufacturer Nortek. The company went public in 2013.

	Annual Growth	12/10	12/11	12/12	12/13	12/14
Sales ($ mil.)	12.0%	995.9	1,034.9	1,121.3	1,365.6	1,566.6
Net income ($ mil.)	–	27.7	(84.5)	(39.1)	(79.5)	(31.3)
Market value ($ mil.)	(22.5%)	–	–	–	1,223.8	948.9
Employees	28.8%	–	–	4,992	6,390	8,277

PM REALTY GROUP L.P.

1000 Main St. Ste. 2400
Houston TX 77002
Phone: 713-209-5800
Fax: 713-209-5784
Web: www.pmrg.com

CEO: –
CFO: Roger Gregory
HR: –
FYE: December 31
Type: Private

PM Realty Group (PMRG) keeps its properties running day and night. The privately held company manages a $30 billion client portfolio (some 180 million sq. ft. of office retail residential health care and industrial space) of real estate throughout the US. It provides services including property management marketing and leasing development construction management engineering and investment sales. PMRG serves corporations government agencies and investors through 20 regional and divisional offices. Clients include Chevron JPMorgan Chase and TIAA-CREF.

PMA COMPANIES INC.

380 Sentry Pkwy.
Blue Bell PA 19422-0754
Phone: 610-397-5298
Fax: 610-397-5422
Web: www.pmacompanies.com

CEO: Vincent T Donnelly
CFO: John M Cochrane
HR: –
FYE: December 31
Type: Subsidiary

PMA Companies (formerly PMA Capital) has been insuring Pennsylvania and the mid-Atlantic states since 1915. Through companies operating under the PMA Companies and PMA Insurance Group trade names PMA underwrites workers' compensation and commercial insurance (including commercial automobile and multi-peril). Customers include businesses ranging from industrial manufacturers to nursing homes. The company targets middle-market and large accounts; most of its policies are sold through independent brokers and agents. Licensed to do business throughout the country and in Puerto Rico PMA Companies operates primarily in the eastern US. The company was acquired by insurance group Old Republic International in 2010.

PMC-SIERRA INC.

NMS: PMCS

1380 Bordeaux Drive
Sunnyvale, CA 94089
Phone: 408 239-8000
Fax: –
Web: www.pmcs.com

CEO: Gregory S Lang
CFO: Steven J Geiser
HR: –
FYE: December 28
Type: Public

For PMC-Sierra success is all about networking. The company develops and markets some 700 semiconductor products designed to support the Internet infrastructures of corporations and enterprise clients as well as the communications networking equipment industry. Its controllers mappers multiplexers processors switches and transceivers are used in laser and multifunction printers servers and storage devices communications infrastructure equipment and fiber-to-the-home equipment. OEM customers include Alcatel-Lucent Cisco EMC HP Huawei Nokia Siemens and ZTE. PMC-Sierra sells products directly and through distributors. It gets more than three-quarters of its sales in the Asia/Pacific region.

	Annual Growth	12/09	12/10	12/11	12/12	12/13
Sales ($ mil.)	0.6%	496.1	635.1	654.3	531.0	508.0
Net income ($ mil.)	–	46.9	83.2	84.7	(336.2)	(32.3)
Market value ($ mil.)	(7.0%)	1,666.1	1,650.6	1,071.2	995.4	1,244.3
Employees	7.6%	1,079	1,449	1,564	1,546	1,448

PMFG, INC.

NMS: PMFG

14651 North Dallas Parkway, Suite 500
Dallas, TX 75254
Phone: 214 357-6181
Fax: 214 351-0194
Web: www.peerlessmfg.com

CEO: –
CFO: –
HR: –
FYE: June 28
Type: Public

Even though its name has changed PMFG (formerly Peerless Mfg.) is still without peer when it comes to making products that remove contaminants. It operates through two segments: environmental systems and process products. Its process products include separation filtration systems that remove solid and liquid contaminants from natural gas and saltwater aerosols from the air intakes of marine gas turbine and diesel engines. The segment also makes industrial noise control and heat transfer products. PMFG's environmental systems unit makes air pollution abatement products primarily catalytic reduction systems used to convert nitrogen oxide produced by the burning of fossil fuels into nitrogen and water vapor.

	Annual Growth	06/10*	07/11*	06/12	06/13	06/14
Sales ($ mil.)	2.8%	116.8	121.8	135.3	133.9	130.7
Net income ($ mil.)	–	(4.2)	5.7	(1.0)	(2.1)	(38.4)
Market value ($ mil.)	(24.3%)	319.1	421.7	164.5	145.8	104.7
Employees	5.7%	400	400	500	450	500

*Fiscal year change

PNC FINANCIAL SERVICES GROUP (THE)

NYS: PNC

One PNC Plaza, 249 Fifth Avenue
Pittsburgh, PA 15222-2707
Phone: 412 762-2000
Fax: 412 762-5798
Web: www.pnc.com

CEO: Joseph C. (Joe) Guyaux
CFO: Robert Q. (Rob) Reilly
HR: –
FYE: December 31
Type: Public

PNC Financial Services has returned to its traditional banking roots but it also offers a wide range of other financial services. Its flagship PNC Bank subsidiary operates nearly 2700 branches in more than a dozen states in the mid-Atlantic the Midwest and Florida. In addition to retail and corporate banking the company offers insurance investments personal and institutional asset management and capital markets products and services. Boasting total assets of roughly $345 billion and total deposits exceeding $230 billion the firm also owns boutique investment bank Harris Williams and about a quarter of money management giant BlackRock.

	Annual Growth	12/10	12/11	12/12	12/13	12/14
Assets ($ mil.)	6.9%	264,284.0	271,205.0	305,107.0	320,296.0	345,072.0
Net income ($ mil.)	5.5%	3,397.0	3,071.0	3,001.0	4,227.0	4,207.0
Market value ($ mil.)	10.7%	31,756.6	30,161.4	30,496.1	40,574.3	47,713.3
Employees	1.4%	50,769	51,891	56,285	54,433	53,587

PNC REAL ESTATE FINANCE COMPANY

26901 Agoura Rd. Ste. 200
Calabasas Hills CA 91301-5109
Phone: 818-880-3300
Fax: 818-880-3333
Web: www.askarcs.com

CEO: Timothy White
CFO: –
HR: –
FYE: December 31
Type: Subsidiary

In a pinch PNC Real Estate Finance will fund your property. Formerly ARCS Commercial Mortgage and doing business as PNC ARCS the mortgage banking company provides funding for multifamily and co-op buildings affordable housing and investment properties specifically hotels industrial parks office buildings and shopping centers. It operates through five divisions: multifamily and co-op buildings affordable housing small properties FHA and capital markets. PNC ARCS is consistently among the top five of Fannie Mae's #1 Delegated Underwriting and Servicing (DUS) multifamily loan originators and one of its top three affordable housing lenders. PNC Financial Services Group bought ARCS in 2007.

PNM RESOURCES INC

NYS: PNM

414 Silver Ave. S.W.
Albuquerque, NM 87102-3289
Phone: 505 241-2700
Fax: –
Web: www.pnmresources.com

CEO: Patricia K. (Pat) Vincent-Collawn
CFO: Charles N. (Chuck) Eldred
HR: –
FYE: December 31
Type: Public

Most glowing lights in New Mexico are lit by PNM Resources. The company's primary utility Public Service Company of New Mexico (PNM Electric) distributes power to residential commercial and industrial customers in the state. PNM Resources has (or purchases power from) plants with 2707 MW of generating capacity and markets energy to wholesale customers in the western US. Its Texas-New Mexico Power Company (TNMP) unit provides transmission and distribution services at regulated rates to retail electricity providers. PNM Resources' two regulated utilities serve 753000 residential commercial and industrial customers and end-users of electricity in New Mexico and Texas.

	Annual Growth	12/10	12/11	12/12	12/13	12/14
Sales ($ mil.)	(3.8%)	1,673.5	1,700.6	1,342.4	1,387.9	1,435.9
Net income ($ mil.)	–	(31.1)	190.9	120.1	115.6	130.9
Market value ($ mil.)	22.8%	1,037.1	1,452.1	1,633.7	1,921.2	2,360.1
Employees	(3.1%)	2,134	1,951	1,909	1,924	1,881

PNY TECHNOLOGIES INC.

299 Webro Rd.
Parsippany NJ 07054-0218
Phone: 973-515-9700
Fax: 973-560-5590
Web: www3.pny.com

CEO: Gadi Cohen
CFO: –
HR: –
FYE: December 31
Type: Private

PNY Technologies is hardly puny when it comes to memory. The company makes high-speed flash memory cards USB flash drives solid-state drives and computer memory upgrade modules. It also offers HDMI cables as well as PC graphics cards that combine NVIDIA's graphics chips with its own memory devices. PNY focuses on selling to the business photography gaming and wireless sectors. The company sells its products directly and through retail stores like Best Buy Staples and Wal-Mart. It also sells through online distributors including Newegg Amazon.com and TigerDirect.com. PNY sells products in more than 50 countries. It has international offices in China France Germany Taiwan and the UK.

POAGE BANKSHARES INC

NAS: PBSK

1500 Carter Avenue
Ashland, KY 41101
Phone: 606 324-7196
Fax: –
Web: www.hfsl.com

CEO: Ralph E Coffman Jr
CFO: Jane Gilkerson
HR: –
FYE: December 31
Type: Public

Poage Bankshares is the holding company for Home Federal Savings and Loan Association a small bank with six branches in northeast Kentucky located along the Ohio and West Virginia state line. Home Federal caters to area individuals and small businesses offering checking and savings accounts; NOW COD and money market accounts; retirement accounts; and Visa debit and credit cards. Its loan portfolio primarily consists of fixed-rate residential mortgages followed by nonresidential real estate loans home equity loans and lines of credit auto and personal loans and commercial business loans. Home Federal traces its history back to 1889 when it was founded as Home and Saving Fund Association.

	Annual Growth	09/11	09/12	09/13*	12/13	12/14
Assets ($ mil.)	8.1%	328.0	317.2	291.0	289.2	414.7
Net income ($ mil.)	3.0%	1.7	1.6	2.2	(0.2)	1.8
Market value ($ mil.)	10.5%	42.7	47.8	56.0	54.3	57.6
Employees	25.3%	61	73	79	82	120

*Fiscal year change

POCONO HEALTH SYSTEM

206 E. Brown St.
East Stroudsburg PA 18301
Phone: 570-421-4000
Fax: 570-476-3469
Web: www.poconohealthsystem.org

CEO: Charles Garris
CFO: –
HR: –
FYE: June 30
Type: Private - Not-for-Pr

The Poconos may be a popular destination among honeymooners but they probably don't have the Pocono Health System on their lists of must-sees. Nevertheless the health care provider can treat whatever ails visitors and residents of eastern Pennsylvania. The system's Pocono Medical Center is an acute care community hospital with some 200 beds. The system also operates a community health center for children a surgical center and specialty care centers for cancer and heart disease. Its medical staff includes more than 200 physicians and it has more than 1800 staff members. Subsidiaries include Pocono Medical Center Pocono Healthcare Management Pocono Healthcare Partners Pocono Ambulatory Services and Pocono Health Foundation

POINT LOMA NAZARENE UNIVERSITY

3900 LOMALAND DR
SAN DIEGO, CA 921062899
Phone: 619-221-2200
Fax: –
Web: www.pointloma.edu

CEO: –
CFO: –
HR: Joyce Falk
FYE: June 30
Type: Private

Point Loma Nazarene University (PLNU) intends to provide a rounded education for Christian students. PLNU offers liberal arts and professional programs in 60 areas of study on its main campus in San Diego and select graduate and professional programs at regional centers in the California towns of Bakersfield Inland Empire (Corona) and Mission Valley (San Diego). Areas of study include art science business administration teaching medicine and ministry. Some 2700 undergraduate and graduate students are enrolled at the school which boasts a 14-to-1 faculty-student ratio. PLNU dates back to 1902 when it was established by Dr. Phineas F. Bresee one of the founders of the Church of the Nazarene.

	Annual Growth	06/10	06/11	06/12	06/13	06/14
Sales ($ mil.)	3.4%	–	83.4	84.0	87.9	92.3
Net income ($ mil.)	352.9%	–	–	0.3	11.4	5.5
Market value ($ mil.)	–	–	–	–	–	–
Employees	–	–	–	–	–	688

POINT.360

NBB: PTSX

2701 Media Center Drive
Los Angeles, CA 90065
Phone: 818 565-1400
Fax: –
Web: www.point360.com

CEO: Haig S. Bagerdjian
CFO: Alan R. Steel
HR: –
FYE: June 30
Type: Public

Just how do the latest movie trailers make it to a theater near you? The answer is simple: Point.360. The company provides audio video and film management and post-production services (including color correction editing and animation) for TV programming feature films and movie trailers. Clients include film studios ad agencies TV networks and production firms. Point.360 also offers editing mastering reformatting archiving and electronic distribution services for commercials press kits and corporate training. In addition the company rents and sells DVDs and video games directly to consumers through its Movie>Q retail stores. Chairman and CEO Haig Bagerdjian owns more than 50% of Point.360.

	Annual Growth	06/11	06/12	06/13	06/14	06/15
Sales ($ mil.)	(11.5%)	35.2	35.0	30.9	25.7	21.6
Net income ($ mil.)	–	(2.8)	0.4	(1.2)	(2.7)	(2.9)
Market value ($ mil.)	(18.0%)	6.2	6.3	10.7	3.8	2.8
Employees	(8.0%)	250	240	231	201	179

POKERTEK INC

NAS: PTEK

1150 Crews Road, Suite F
Matthews, NC 28105
Phone: 704 849-0860
Fax: –
Web: www.pokertek.com

CEO: –
CFO: –
HR: –
FYE: December 31
Type: Public

PokerTek is bringing technology to the poker table. The company's electronic poker table automatically tracks bets and the outcome of hands as players pit their poker skills against each other. The PokerTek technology — currently available at casinos in the US Canada Macau Panama Germany Australia South Africa and several major cruise lines — can increase revenue for casino operators because PokerTek says more hands can be played with an automated dealer; casinos earn money from poker tables by taking a percentage of all bets made — also known as the rake.

	Annual Growth	12/08	12/09	12/10	12/11	12/12
Sales ($ mil.)	(22.6%)	14.4	6.7	5.9	6.5	5.2
Net income ($ mil.)	–	(7.6)	(5.7)	(4.0)	(1.8)	(0.8)
Market value ($ mil.)	0.2%	11.2	6.0	6.1	8.2	11.3
Employees	(18.6%)	57	35	32	30	25

POLARIS INDUSTRIES INC.

NYS: PII

2100 Highway 55
Medina, MN 55340
Phone: 763 542-0500
Fax: –
Web: www.polaris.com

CEO: Scott W. Wine
CFO: Michael (Mike) Speetzen
HR: –
FYE: December 31
Type: Public

A bump in the road is big business for Polaris Industries. The company is one of the world's top makers of off-road vehicles comprising all-terrain vehicles (ATVs) and side-by-side recreational and utility RANGER-brand vehicles. It also manufactures snowmobiles on-road vehicles such as the Victory brand motorcycle and small electric vehicles (SEVs). Offerings include replacement parts accessories (covers windshields backrests) and riding gear (bags and helmets). Polaris' lineup is sold through dealers and distributors in North America and Europe.

	Annual Growth	12/10	12/11	12/12	12/13	12/14
Sales ($ mil.)	22.5%	1,991.1	2,656.9	3,209.8	3,777.1	4,479.6
Net income ($ mil.)	32.5%	147.1	227.6	312.3	377.3	454.0
Market value ($ mil.)	18.0%	5,173.3	3,711.9	5,579.7	9,657.0	10,028.3
Employees	23.6%	3,000	3,900	4,500	5,400	7,000

POLARIS VENTURE MANAGEMENT CO. L.L.C.

1000 Winter St. Ste. 3350
Waltham MA 02451
Phone: 781-290-0770
Fax: 781-290-0880
Web: www.polarisventures.com

CEO: –
CFO: –
HR: –
FYE: December 31
Type: Private

Polaris Venture Partners provides venture capital to start-up and early-stage information technology and life sciences companies. Taking a diverse approach the firm also seeks to invest in high-growth middle-market companies in the e-commerce consumer products and business services sectors. Most of its portfolio companies are based in the US but Polaris Venture Partners is not averse to investing in Europe and Asia. The company has more than $3 billion in assets under management and investments in some 90 companies including Akamai Technologies and Centra Software. Founded in 1996 it has offices in Boston and Seattle.

POLK AUDIO INC.

5601 Metro Dr.
Baltimore MD 21215
Phone: 410-358-3600
Fax: 410-764-5470
Web: www.polkaudio.com

CEO: James E Minarik
CFO: Kevin P Duffy
HR: –
FYE: March 31
Type: Subsidiary

Audiophiles beware — Polk Audio is letting the masses in on its speaker secret. The company makes and markets home and car loudspeakers under the Polk Audio brand ranging from elaborate home theater systems to small bookshelf speakers to satellite radio home component tuners. Polk Audio sells its products through audio specialty and mass retailers in North America distributors in more than 75 other countries and online. The company was founded in 1972 by Johns Hopkins classmates Matthew Polk George Klopfer and Sandy Gross. Today it is a subsidiary of DEI Holdings (formerly Directed Electronics).

POLLO OPERATIONS INC.

7300 N. Kendall Dr. 8th Fl.
Miami FL 33156
Phone: 305-670-7696
Fax: 305-670-6403
Web: www.pollotropical.com

CEO: Alan Vituli
CFO: Lynn Schweinfurth
HR: –
FYE: December 31
Type: Subsidiary

These cluckers have soaked in the flavor of the islands. Pollo Operations a subsidiary of quick-service restaurateur Fiesta Restaurant Group operates more than 90 Pollo Tropical grilled chicken outlets located primarily in south Florida. Its restaurants serve grilled chicken that is marinated with tropical spices and fruit juices along with such Caribbean side dishes as fried bananas yucca and black beans and rice. It also offers salads and dessert items. In addition to its company-owned locations Pollo Tropical has about 30 franchised outlets in Puerto Rico and Ecuador. Parent company Fiesta Restaurant Group also owns and operates sister chain Taco Cabana.

POLYCOM INC.

NMS: PLCM

6001 America Center Drive
San Jose, CA 95002
Phone: 408 586-6000
Fax: –
Web: www.polycom.com

CEO: Peter A. Leav
CFO: Laura J. Durr
HR: –
FYE: December 31
Type: Public

Polycom's vision is a world united by video. The company makes video-conferencing and immersive telepresence (which combines digital audio video and content sharing) systems that let users collaborate as if they were in the same room. Its products combine camera microphone network connection and external audio and video devices. The company also offers PC-based phones that transmit both voice and video. Polycom's software enables users to manage conferencing locations and connect with them using ISDN and Internet protocol connections. It partners with the likes of Microsoft and IBM to develop open standards-based products. Polycom gets more than half of its sales from outside the US.

	Annual Growth	12/10	12/11	12/12	12/13	12/14
Sales ($ mil.)	2.5%	1,218.5	1,495.8	1,392.6	1,368.4	1,345.2
Net income ($ mil.)	(11.5%)	68.4	135.8	9.8	(18.1)	42.1
Market value ($ mil.)	(23.3%)	5,270.3	2,203.8	1,414.2	1,518.4	1,825.3
Employees	2.2%	3,230	3,839	3,747	3,774	3,525

POLYMER GROUP INC.

9335 Harris Corners Pkwy. Ste. 300
Charlotte NC 28269
Phone: 704-697-5100
Fax: 704-697-5116
Web: www.polymergroupinc.com

CEO: J Joel Hackney Jr
CFO: Dennis Norman
HR: Lola Alvarez
FYE: December 31
Type: Private

Polymer Group Inc.'s (PGI) business is interwoven with nonwovens. Rivaling Ahlstrom and E.I. du Pont de Nemours the company is a leading developer and maker of nonwoven textiles and other engineered materials used by consumer and industrial product manufacturers. Its absorbent and disposable fabrics go into baby wipes diapers and other hygiene and medical products. On the industrial side they are incorporated into filtration insulation and automotive acoustics products. PGI operates more than a dozen manufacturing and converting facilities worldwide. In 2011 the company was acquired by Scorpio Acquisition an affiliate of private equity group Blackstone Capital Partners.

POLYONE CORP.

NYS: POL

33587 Walker Road
Avon Lake, OH 44012
Phone: 440 930-1000
Fax: –
Web: www.polyone.com

CEO: –
CFO: Bradley C. Richardson
HR: Kenneth M. Smith
FYE: December 31
Type: Public

PolyOne Corporation (a top North American plastics compounders and resins distributor) has one focus — providing specialized polymer products and services through a handful of business segments. The company's Performance Products and Solutions unit produces custom-made compounded plastics and custom-formulated colorants for plastics manufacturers throughout North America and Europe. Other units include Global Color Additives and Inks; Global Specialty Engineered Materials; PolyOne Distribution which distributes more than 3500 thermoplastic resins and compounds from 25 major material suppliers: and Designed Structures and Solutions (plastic sheet color and engineered materials).

	Annual Growth	12/11	12/12	12/13	12/14	12/15
Sales ($ mil.)	4.2%	2,863.5	2,992.6	3,771.2	3,835.5	3,377.6
Net income ($ mil.)	(4.3%)	172.6	71.8	243.8	79.2	144.6
Market value ($ mil.)	28.8%	985.2	1,741.8	3,015.4	3,233.7	2,709.1
Employees	10.1%	4,700	5,000	7,000	6,900	6,900

POLYPORE INTERNATIONAL INC

NYS: PPO

11430 North Community House Road, Suite 350
Charlotte, NC 28277
Phone: 704 587-8409
Fax: –
Web: www.polypore.net

CEO: Shgeki Takayama
CFO: Lynn Amos
HR: John O'Malley
FYE: December 28
Type: Public

Polypore International believes in separation of states — mainly liquid from materials such as ions gases and particles. The company develops and manufactures polymer-based membranes containing millions of pores per square inch that are used in separation and filtration processes. Through its Energy Storage segment Polypore sells membrane separators that help the performance of lead-acid batteries used in electronic drive vehicles (EDVs) and lithium batteries used in a variety of consumer electronics from laptops to mobile phones. Its Separations Media segment makes membranes for health care applications (hemodialysis and blood oxygenation) and specialty applications (ultra-pure water filtration and degasification).

	Annual Growth	01/10	01/11*	12/11	12/12	12/13
Sales ($ mil.)	7.2%	516.9	616.6	763.1	717.4	636.3
Net income ($ mil.)		(117.3)	63.6	105.2	71.0	81.6
Market value ($ mil.)	47.3%	534.5	1,829.5	1,975.9	2,072.0	1,707.3
Employees	8.1%	1,900	2,200	2,500	2,700	2,400

*Fiscal year change

POLYVISION CORPORATION

3970 Johns Creek Ct. Ste. 325
Suwanee GA 30024
Phone: 678-542-3100
Fax: 678-542-3200
Web: www.polyvision.com

CEO: Robert L Crain
CFO: Peter Lewchanin
HR: –
FYE: February 28
Type: Subsidiary

No presentation is complete without visual displays so PolyVision wants all eyes on its boards. The company makes static and electronic whiteboards writing slates and other visual communication products for schools offices and public places. Its brands include eno and the TS Series. The firm also markets educational software and projectors from such makers as 3M and Hitachi that operate in conjunction with its products. Polyvision runs manufacturing facilities in Oklahoma and Oregon and its lines are sold by audiovisual equipment dealers throughout the US as well as Europe. Founded in 1954 the company has been owned by office furniture maker Steelcase since 2002.

POMONA COLLEGE

550 N COLLEGE AVE
CLAREMONT, CA 917114434
Phone: 909-621-8135
Fax: –
Web: www.pomona.edu

CEO: David Oxtoby
CFO: –
HR: –
FYE: June 30
Type: Private

Looking to get an education in sunny California? You might want to consider Pomona College. The school offers about 50 academic programs in areas such as art humanities biology psychology computer science and English. It also has research and interdisciplinary study opportunities. The liberal arts college enrolls about 1600 students. Formed in 1887 Pomona College is the founding member of The Claremont Colleges an affiliated group of seven independent colleges located on adjoining campuses in Claremont California. The affiliated campuses are coordinated by one of the member institutions the Claremont University Consortium.

	Annual Growth	06/09	06/10	06/11	06/12	06/13
Sales ($ mil.)	(1.9%)	–	152.7	197.2	139.5	144.0
Net income ($ mil.)	101.7%	–	–	37.9	(21.0)	154.2
Market value ($ mil.)	–	–	–	–	–	–
Employees	–	–	–	–	–	500

POMP'S TIRE SERVICE INC..

1123 CEDAR ST
GREEN BAY, WI 543014703
Phone: 920-435-8301
Fax: –
Web: www.pompstire.com

CEO: –
CFO: –
HR: Donna Gustafson
FYE: December 31
Type: Private

If by circumstance you have a flat tire in the Midwest limp on over to Pomp's Tire Service. The company sells tires for agricultural commercial and industrial vehicles as well as everyday cars and trucks from more than 75 locations in eight Midwestern states. (More than half are located in Wisconsin and Illinois.) Brands include Bridgestone Goodrich Goodyear and Michelin. Pomp's Tire Service also offers roadside assistance and retread services and it has extensive contracts with the US Army for vehicle parts. Originally called Pomprowitz Tire Co. the company was founded in 1939 by Andrew "Sparky" Pomprowitz. It is owned by the family of Roger Wochinske who bought the firm in 1964.

	Annual Growth	12/08	12/09	12/10	12/11	12/12
Sales ($ mil.)	14.5%	–	284.8	342.4	398.2	427.6
Net income ($ mil.)	16.3%	–	–	11.1	12.7	15.0
Market value ($ mil.)	–	–	–	–	–	–
Employees	–	–	–	–	–	1,200

POOL CORP

NMS: POOL

109 Northpark Boulevard
Covington, LA 70433-5001
Phone: 985 892-5521
Fax: 985 892-2438
Web: www.poolcorp.com

CEO: Manuel J. Perez de la Mesa
CFO: Mark W. Joslin
HR: –
FYE: December 31
Type: Public

Pool Corp. swims laps around its competitors. The world's largest wholesale distributor of swimming pool supplies it operates about 330 service centers throughout North America South America Europe and Australia serving more than 80000 wholesale customers such as pool builders and remodelers retail pool stores and pool repair and service companies. Pool Corp.'s more than 160000 products include private-label and name-brand pool maintenance items (chemicals cleaners) equipment (pumps filters) accessories (heaters lights) and packaged pool kits. Founded in 1993 as SCP Holding Corp. Pool Corp's. business is picking up after taking a dive during the downturn in new home (and pool) construction.

	Annual Growth	12/10	12/11	12/12	12/13	12/14
Sales ($ mil.)	8.6%	1,613.7	1,793.3	1,954.0	2,079.7	2,246.6
Net income ($ mil.)	17.7%	57.6	72.0	82.0	97.3	110.7
Market value ($ mil.)	29.5%	980.7	1,309.7	1,841.4	2,529.7	2,760.3
Employees	3.7%	3,200	3,300	3,400	3,600	3,700

POPE RESOURCES LP

NAS: POPE

19950 7th Avenue NE, Suite 200
Poulsbo, WA 98370
Phone: 360 697-6626
Fax: 360 697-1156
Web: www.poperesources.com

CEO: Thomas M. (Tom) Ringo
CFO: John D. Lamb
HR: –
FYE: December 31
Type: Public

More earthly than divine Pope Resources owns or manages more than 150000 acres of timberland and development property in Washington. Its holdings include the 70000-acre Hood Canal and 44000-acre Columbia tree farms in Washington. It sells its Douglas fir and other timber products mainly in the US Japan China and Korea; Weyerhaeuser and Simpson Investment Company are major customers. Pope Resources also invests in and manages two timberland investment funds and provides investment management and consulting services to third-party timberland owners and managers in Washington Oregon and California. Its real estate unit acquires develops resells and rents residential and commercial real estate.

	Annual Growth	12/10	12/11	12/12	12/13	12/14
Sales ($ mil.)	29.4%	31.2	57.3	54.0	70.7	87.5
Net income ($ mil.)	57.1%	2.0	8.8	(4.7)	13.1	12.4
Market value ($ mil.)	14.7%	157.7	184.2	238.5	287.0	272.6
Employees	7.5%	45	48	55	58	60

POPEYES LOUISIANA KITCHEN INC

NMS: PLKI

400 Perimeter Center Terrace, Suite 1000
Atlanta, GA 30346
Phone: 404 459-4450
Fax: –

CEO: Cheryl A. Bachelder
CFO: William P. (Will) Matt
HR: –
FYE: December 28
Type: Public

This company's recipe for success features fried chicken and biscuits. A leading fast-food company Popeyes Louisiana Kitchen (formerly AFC Enterprises) operates the Popeyes restaurant chain the #2 quick-service chain specializing in chicken behind YUM! Brands' KFC. The chain boasts more than 2300 locations in the US and in more than 25 other countries. The restaurants feature Cajun-style fried chicken and seafood that is typically served with buttermilk biscuits and a variety of sides including Cajun rice coleslaw mashed potatoes or french fries. Only 40 Popeyes locations are company-owned.

	Annual Growth	12/10	12/11	12/12	12/13	12/14
Sales ($ mil.)	12.6%	146.4	153.8	178.8	206.0	235.6
Net income ($ mil.)	13.5%	22.9	24.2	30.4	34.1	38.0
Market value ($ mil.)	39.6%	341.6	344.4	594.1	878.8	1,296.7
Employees	14.7%	1,245	1,275	1,530	2,006	2,158

POPULAR INC.

NMS: BPOP

Popular Center Building, 209 Munoz Rivera Avenue, Hato Rey
San Juan 00918
Phone: (787) 765 9800
Fax: –
Web: www.popular.com

CEO: Richard L. Carri In
CFO: Carlos J. V ´zquez
HR: –
FYE: December 31
Type: Public

Popular is popular and not just in Puerto Rico. Founded in 1893 Popular is the holding company for Banco Popular de Puerto Rico (BPPR) the largest bank on the island with approximately 175 branches. In addition to offering commercial and retail banking BPPR owns subsidiaries that specialize in vehicle financing and leasing (Popular Auto) insurance (Popular Insurance) financial advisory and brokerage services (Popular Securities) and mortgages (Popular Mortgage). Popular also owns Banco Popular North America (BPNA) which targets the US Hispanic population from about 100 branches across five major US states.

	Annual Growth	12/10	12/11	12/12	12/13	12/14
Assets ($ mil.)	(3.8%)	38,723.0	37,348.4	36,507.5	35,749.3	33,096.7
Net income ($ mil.)	–	137.4	151.3	245.3	599.3	(313.5)
Market value ($ mil.)	81.5%	324.9	143.8	2,151.3	2,972.9	3,523.4
Employees	(1.6%)	8,277	8,329	8,072	8,059	7,752

POPULATION SERVICES INTERNATIONAL

1120 19TH ST NW STE 600
WASHINGTON, DC 200363605
Phone: 202-785-0072
Fax: –
Web: www.psi.org

CEO: Tommy Thompson
CFO: –
HR: –
FYE: December 31
Type: Private

Population Services International (PSI) goes far beyond the scope of its name. Founded in 1970 to promote global family planning PSI has established social programs that use local networks in low-income regions to distribute such lifelines as insecticide-treated mosquito nets iodized salt snake boots and insect repellent along with condoms contraceptives and pregnancy test kits. The group prides itself on using business principals to confront health issues in more than 65 countries worldwide. It reportedly has averted 4.2 million unintended pregnancies some 29 million malaria cases and provided 1.8-plus million clients with of HIV testing and counseling. PSI is also active ensuring safe water supplies.

	Annual Growth	12/0-2	12/0-1	12/00	12/01	12/13
Sales ($ mil.)	14.8%	–	–	96.8	121.7	584.0
Net income ($ mil.)	2.9%	–	–	3.2	(0.8)	4.7
Market value ($ mil.)	–	–	–	–	–	–
Employees		–	–	–	–	250

POPULOUS INC.

300 Wyandotte Ste. 200
Kansas City MO 64105
Phone: 816-221-1500
Fax: 816-221-1578
Web: www.populous.com

CEO: –
CFO: –
HR: –
FYE: December 31
Type: Private

If Populous builds it they will come. Formerly known as HOK Sport Venue Event the global architecture firm specializes in sports and entertainment facility design and also offers graphic design interior design and facility assessment services which are intended to help facility owners make operational changes and improvements. Clients include the Major League Baseball and National Football League franchises colleges and universities and soccer and rugby teams. Outside of the US Populous has completed projects in Asia Australia and Europe. The company was spun off from HOK Group in a management buyout in early 2009.

PORT OF HOUSTON AUTHORITY

111 EAST LOOP N	CEO: –
HOUSTON, TX 770294326	CFO: Tim Finley
Phone: 713-670-2400	HR: –
Fax: –	FYE: December 31
Web: www.portofhouston.com	Type: Private

Houston is too far inland to be a port city by the strictest of definitions but don't try to tell that to the Port of Houston Authority. The agency manages the Port of Houston complex including the Barbours Cut Container Terminal one of the busiest in the US. Port of Houston facilities are arrayed along the Houston Ship Channel which connects Houston with Galveston Bay and the Gulf of Mexico and with intracoastal waterways. The Port of Houston Authority itself operates more than 40 cargo wharves; however most of the terminal facilities along the ship channel are managed by private companies. The ship channel was opened in 1914; the Port of Houston Authority was created by the Texas Legislature in 1927.

	Annual Growth	12/09	12/10	12/11	12/12	12/13
Sales ($ mil.)	7.8%	–	186.7	206.8	225.4	233.7
Net income ($ mil.)	43.2%	–	–	33.0	54.4	67.7
Market value ($ mil.)	–	–	–	–	–	–
Employees	–	–	–	–	–	595

PORT OF LOS ANGELES

425 S. Palos Verdes St.	CEO: –
San Pedro CA 90731	CFO: –
Phone: 310-732-7678	HR: –
Fax: 310-521-8344	FYE: June 30
Web: www.portoflosangeles.org	Type: Government-owned

The Port of Los Angeles one of the busiest US trade gateways encompasses about 7500 acres and includes about 45 miles of waterfront property at San Pedro Bay. Operating as a landlord port it leases property to tenants that manage terminals and other port facilities. The Port of Los Angeles consists of more than 25 major cargo terminals which include liquid bulk container automobile breakbulk (cargo not in a container) and dry bulk terminals as well as facilities used by cruise lines. Containers account for most of the port's traffic. A department of the City of Los Angeles the Port of Los Angeles was established in 1907.

PORT OF SEATTLE

2711 Alaskan Way	CEO: Ted J Fick
Seattle WA 98121	CFO: –
Phone: 206-787-3000	HR: –
Fax: 206-787-3004	FYE: December 31
Web: www.portseattle.org	Type: Government Agency

The Port of Seattle oversees both an airport (Seattle-Tacoma International also known as Sea-Tac) and a seaport. The agency's aviation division sees more than 30 million passengers a year. The seaport division serves more than 20 container carriers that import and export containerized and bulk cargo. It also handles calls from some 220 cruise ships. In addition the seaport division oversees commercial fishing marinas and portside commercial properties. Most of the agency's revenue comes from airport operations. The Port of Seattle is run by a five-member commission elected by King County voters. In 2011 the Port marked its centennial year for moving people and cargo in and out of the Pacific Northwest.

PORTAGE INC.

1075 S UTAH AVE STE 200	CEO: Nick Stanisich
IDAHO FALLS, ID 83402-3320	CFO: –
Phone: 208-528-6608	HR: –
Fax: –	FYE: December 31
Web: www.portageinc.com	Type: Private

Portage Environmental helps carry the load for customers needing environmental engineering services. The firm's offerings include environmental remediation process and project engineering and decontamination and decommissioning services. Portage Environmental counts US government agencies (such as the Department of Defense and the Department of Energy) and Native American tribes among its clients and has conducted projects in 20 US states as well as in Afghanistan Guam Iraq Japan Kuwait Qatar and South Korea. The firm operates from some two dozen offices throughout the US. President and CEO Michael Spry helped found Portage Environmental in 1992.

	Annual Growth	12/03	12/04	12/05	12/06	12/10
Sales ($ mil.)	46.4%	–	24.9	29.9	33.4	245.3
Net income ($ mil.)	68.4%	–	0.3	1.9	1.9	6.4
Market value ($ mil.)	–	–	–	–	–	–
Employees	–	–	–	–	–	300

PORTEC RAIL PRODUCTS INC.

900 Old Freeport Rd.	CEO: –
Pittsburgh PA 15238-8250	CFO: David Russo
Phone: 412-782-6000	HR: –
Fax: 412-782-1037	FYE: December 31
Web: www.portecrail.com	Type: Subsidiary

Portec Rail Products has kept railroads on track since 1906. The company manufactures and distributes a slew of rail products. Friction Management its largest line specializes in products and services that control friction between the wheel and rail a key problem for customers. The Wayside Data Collection and Data Management Systems unit provides measurement and detection products services and support for improved equipment usage. Securement Systems help secure freight onto cars and Track Components make rail anchors and track spikes. Norfolk Southern and Canadian National Railway are the company's top customers. Rival L. B. Foster acquired Portec Rail for $113 million in late 2010.

PORTER BANCORP INC
NAS: PBIB

2500 Eastpoint Parkway	CEO: John T Taylor
Louisville, KY 40223	CFO: Phillip W Barnhouse
Phone: 502 499-4800	HR: –
Fax: –	FYE: December 31
Web: www.pbibank.com	Type: Public

Porter Bancorp could be a stout evaluator of what "ales" your finances. It is the holding company for PBI Bank which serves local residents and businesses through about 20 offices in Louisville and other portions of central Kentucky. The company also operates Ascencia a nationwide online banking platform. PBI Bank offers standard financial services such as checking savings and money market accounts certificates of deposit and trust services. Loans collateralized by real estate such as commercial mortgages (more than 35% of the company's loan portfolio) residential mortgages (more than 25%) and construction loans (approximately 20%) comprise the lion's share of the company's loan portfolio.

	Annual Growth	12/10	12/11	12/12	12/13	12/14
Assets ($ mil.)	(12.3%)	1,724.0	1,455.4	1,162.6	1,076.1	1,018.0
Net income ($ mil.)	–	(4.4)	(107.3)	(32.9)	(1.6)	(11.2)
Market value ($ mil.)	(53.6%)	153.5	43.2	10.4	15.0	7.1
Employees	(2.0%)	286	291	278	260	264

PORTER NOVELLI INC.

7 World Trade Center 250 Greenwich St. 36th Flr.	CEO: Gary Stockman
New York NY 10007	CFO: Michael Gehb
Phone: 212-601-8000	HR: –
Fax: 212-601-8101	FYE: December 31
Web: www.porternovelli.com	Type: Subsidiary

International public relations firm Porter Novelli provides advertising event management investor and media relations and other services through some 90 offices in about 60 countries. The firm specializes in several major areas: consumer marketing corporate and public affairs health care marketing digital and social media and strategy for technology companies. Clients have included such heavy hitters as Procter & Gamble Hewlett-Packard and McDonald's. The company was founded in 1972 by John Porter and Bill Novelli. Porter Novelli is a business segment of advertising and media conglomerate Omnicom.

PORTER-CABLE

4825 Hwy. 45 N.	CEO: Randall J Hohan
Jackson TN 38305	CFO: –
Phone: 731-668-8600	HR: Abu Noaman
Fax: 731-660-9535	FYE: December 31
Web: www.porter-cable.com	Type: Subsidiary

Looking for real power? Let's talk circular saws model 100 routers and orbit finishing sanders. Thanks in part to the home makeover movement Porter-Cable tools are picked up by handymen and women professional woodworkers and construction workers as well as electricians and plumbers. The company makes electric tools (tabletop saws bench top planers and radial drill presses) cordless tools (drills and drivers) air tools (hammers nailers and spray guns) and related accessories. Its lines are sold primarily through retailers such as home centers mass merchants hardware stores and lumber yards including Home Depot and Lowe's and online dealers. Porter-Cable is owned by Stanley Black & Decker.

PORTION PAC INC.

7325 Snider Rd.	CEO: –
Mason OH 45040	CFO: –
Phone: 513-398-0400	HR: –
Fax: 513-459-5300	FYE: April 30
Web: www.portionpac.com	Type: Subsidiary

Who actually makes those little white cups that hold the honey you drizzle on your morning bagel? Or the foil-topped grape jelly containers the waitperson brings you at the local breakfast joint? Portion Pac that's who. A subsidiary of Heinz Foodservice Portion Pac manufactures and markets shelf-stable portion-control food products for the catering fast-food restaurant and vending-machine industries. Its national licensed products include cream cheese jams jellies ketchup mustard salad dressings steak sauce salsa syrup and more. They're marketed under popular name brands such as Welch's Log Cabin Musselman's Mrs. Butterworths and ReaLemon.

PORTLAND GENERAL ELECTRIC CO.

NYS: POR

121 S.W. Salmon Street	CEO: James J. (Jim) Piro
Portland, OR 97204	CFO: Maria M. Pope
Phone: 503 464-8000	HR: –
Fax: 503 464-2676	FYE: December 31
Web: www.portlandgeneral.com	Type: Public

Portland General Electric (PGE) keeps many Birkenstock-shod feet warm. The company formerly a subsidiary of Enron generates purchases and distributes electricity to about 842270 customers in Oregon including more than 105230 commercial customers. PGE's service territory covers 52 cities including Portland and Salem. Its 15 hydroelectric coal-fired and gas-fired plants had a generating capacity of 3414 MW in 2014. PGE also markets wholesale electricity and natural gas to other utilities and marketers in the western US. In keeping with the "green" image of Portland residents PGE leads the nation in residential customers who purchase power from renewable sources.

	Annual Growth	12/11	12/12	12/13	12/14	12/15
Sales ($ mil.)	1.2%	1,813.0	1,805.0	1,810.0	1,900.0	1,898.0
Net income ($ mil.)	4.0%	147.0	141.0	105.0	175.0	172.0
Market value ($ mil.)	9.5%	2,245.6	2,429.4	2,681.5	3,359.0	3,229.4
Employees	0.1%	2,634	2,603	2,596	2,600	2,646

PORTOLA PHARMACEUTICALS, INC.

NMS: PTLA

270 E. Grand Avenue	CEO: William Lis
South San Francisco, CA 94080	CFO: Mardi C. Dier
Phone: 650 246-7000	HR: –
Fax: –	FYE: December 31
Web: www.portola.com	Type: Public

Portola Pharmaceuticals is putting blood sweat and tears into developing new medications for blood disorders. The company has three drug candidates in the works that if approved will treat thrombosis (blood clots). Its lead candidate Betrixaban is an oral medication that would prevent certain types of blood clots in seriously ill patients. Betrixaban is currently in Phase 3 study. Another medication in development PRT4445 would help with uncontrolled bleeding episodes after surgery and PRT2070 is being developed for hematologic or blood cancers and inflammatory disorders. Another version of PRT2070 is being developed with Biogen. Founded in 2003 Portola Pharmaceuticals went public in 2013.

	Annual Growth	12/10	12/11	12/12	12/13	12/14
Sales ($ mil.)	(27.7%)	35.3	78.0	72.0	10.5	9.6
Net income ($ mil.)	–	(20.3)	20.0	11.4	(83.4)	(137.1)
Market value ($ mil.)	10.0%	–	–	–	1,255.7	1,381.1
Employees	31.8%	–	–	57	70	99

PORTSMOUTH SQUARE, INC.

NBB: PRSI

10940 Wilshire Blvd., Suite 2150	CEO: John V Winfield
Los Angeles, CA 90024	CFO: David T Nguyen
Phone: 310 889-2500	HR: –
Fax: 310 899-2525	FYE: June 30
Web: www.intgla.com	Type: Public

Investments are a square deal for Portsmouth Square which owns a 50% partnership interest in Justice Investors a property investment firm based in San Francisco. Justice Investors owns and operates the Hilton San Francisco Financial District a hotel property that includes more than 500 individual units a health and beauty spa a Chinese cultural center and an underground parking garage. Portsmouth Square has an investment portfolio valued at some $3 million that includes consumer financial material and communications equities. Through Santa Fe Financial and other entities CEO John Winfield controls more than 80% of Portsmouth Square.

	Annual Growth	06/11	06/12	06/13	06/14	06/15
Sales ($ mil.)	11.9%	36.3	42.5	46.6	51.0	56.8
Net income ($ mil.)	–	2.9	0.2	0.5	(6.9)	(1.8)
Market value ($ mil.)	21.4%	16.9	18.4	22.0	25.7	36.7
Employees	(9.6%)	3	3	3	2	2

POSITIVEID CORPORATION

NASDAQ: PSID

1690 S. Congress Ave. Ste. 200
Delray Beach FL 33445
Phone: 561-805-8008
Fax: 561-805-8001
Web: www.positiveidcorp.com

CEO: –
CFO: William J Caragol
HR: –
FYE: December 31
Type: Public

Who knew something the size of a grain of rice could protect so much? PositiveID formerly VeriChip knows it well. The firm provides implantable radio frequency identification (RFID) microchips for humans and animals. The chip is inserted under the skin and has a unique verification number used to access a subscriber-supplied database providing information when scanned. While its implantable technology has made headlines most of its business comes from wearable and attachable ID tags as well as vibration monitoring systems used to monitor and protect people and assets. In 2009 the company changed its name from VeriChip to PositiveID to reflect a new focus on electronic health records.

POSITRON CORP

NBB: POSC

530 Oakmont Lane
Westmont, IL 60559
Phone: 317 576-0183
Fax: –
Web: www.positron.com

CEO: –
CFO: Corey N Conn
HR: –
FYE: December 31
Type: Public

Positron is positive that its imaging systems can figure out what's wrong with you. The company makes positron emission tomography (PET) scanners under the POSICAM and mPower trade names. The scanners are primarily used to detect coronary artery disease but also have applications in neurology and oncology. Medical centers such as the University of Texas Health Science Center at Houston and the Heart Center of Niagara use the system; the company has an installed base of about 30 systems in the US and abroad. Subsidiary IS2 Medical Systems (acquired in 2006) makes nuclear imaging devices including the PulseCDC cardiac gamma camera.

	Annual Growth	12/10	12/11	12/12	12/13	12/14
Sales ($ mil.)	(25.0%)	4.6	6.7	2.8	1.6	1.5
Net income ($ mil.)	–	(10.9)	(6.1)	(8.0)	(7.1)	(2.6)
Market value ($ mil.)	–	0.7	0.1	0.1	0.1	0.0
Employees	(8.4%)	27	32	26	22	19

POST HOLDINGS INC

NYS: POST

2503 S. Hanley Road
St. Louis, MO 63144
Phone: 314 644-7600
Fax: –
Web: www.postholdings.com

CEO: James L. (Jim) Holbrook
CFO: Jeff A. Zadoks
HR: –
FYE: September 30
Type: Public

The cereals that have filled millions of breakfast bowls worldwide since the 1890s found themselves boxed up in new company Post Holdings when private-label-cereal-giant Ralcorp Holdings spun it off in 2012. The maker of Grape-Nuts Toasties Honey Bunches of Oats Raisin Bran Shredded Wheat Bran Flakes Pebbles and Alpha-Bits is the third-best-selling breakfast cereal brand in the US (after Kellogg and General Mills). Post's manufacturing facilities are located in the US and Canada. Since its separation from Ralcorp Post Holdings has moved beyond the breakfast table adding snacks active nutrition products and pasta through acquisitions. However breakfast cereal still accounts for about 95% of sales.

	Annual Growth	09/11	09/12	09/13	09/14	09/15
Sales ($ mil.)	48.0%	968.2	958.9	1,034.1	2,411.1	4,648.2
Net income ($ mil.)	–	(361.3)	49.9	15.2	(343.2)	(115.3)
Market value ($ mil.)	25.3%	–	1,812.6	2,434.3	2,000.8	3,563.7
Employees	59.9%	1,300	1,400	1,600	7,950	8,500

POST PROPERTIES, INC.

NYS: PPS

4401 Northside Parkway, Suite 800
Atlanta, GA 30327
Phone: 404 846-5000
Fax: –

CEO: David P. (Dave) Stockert
CFO: Christopher J. Papa
HR: Linda Ricklef
FYE: December 31
Type: Public

Post Properties offers Southerners a place to hang their hats but has also started showing Yankees some down-home hospitality. A self-administered and self-managed real estate investment trust (REIT) Post Properties owns develops and manages primarily upscale multi-family apartment communities. Operating through Post Apartment Homes it owns some 60 properties with about 22500 apartment units. Its primary markets are Atlanta Dallas Tampa and Washington DC with additional holdings in New York North Carolina and other markets in Florida and Texas. Post Properties also acts as a property manager and provides furnished short-term corporate apartments in several markets.

	Annual Growth	12/10	12/11	12/12	12/13	12/14
Sales ($ mil.)	7.3%	285.1	305.3	334.9	362.7	377.8
Net income ($ mil.)	–	(7.0)	25.5	83.9	110.5	215.1
Market value ($ mil.)	12.8%	1,978.7	2,383.1	2,722.7	2,465.4	3,203.5
Employees	(0.1%)	597	609	625	635	594

POSTROCK ENERGY CORP

NBB: PSTR

210 Park Avenue
Oklahoma City, OK 73102
Phone: 405 600-7704
Fax: –
Web: www.pstr.com

CEO: Clark Edwards
CFO: –
HR: Kyle Essmiller
FYE: December 31
Type: Public

PostRock Energy (formerly Quest Resource) is looking to create a rock solid energy company specializing in oil and gas exploration and production and the transportation of natural gas. Its exploration and drilling efforts are focused in the Cherokee Basin of southeastern Kansas and northeastern Oklahoma and the Appalachian Basin where it is accumulating leasehold acreage. PostRock Energy has net proved reserves of 192.2 billion cu. ft. of net proved reserves (the bulk of which is coal bed methane gas) and operates more than 2200 miles of gas gathering pipeline in Kansas and Oklahoma. It also operates more than 1100 miles of interstate natural gas transmission pipelines in the region.

	Annual Growth	12/10	12/11	12/12	12/13	12/14
Sales ($ mil.)	0.3%	82.4	96.3	55.0	72.3	83.5
Net income ($ mil.)	(46.0%)	45.2	20.0	(47.6)	(9.0)	3.9
Market value ($ mil.)	(44.2%)	23.8	17.7	9.1	7.4	2.3
Employees	(9.8%)	300	233	216	209	199

POTBELLY CORP

NMS: PBPB

111 N. Canal Street, Suite 850
Chicago, IL 60606
Phone: 312 951-0600
Fax: –
Web: www.potbelly.com

CEO: Aylwin B. Lewis
CFO: Michael W. (Mike) Coyne
HR: –
FYE: December 28
Type: Public

Eating too many of this chain's sandwiches might give you a potbelly. Maybe try a salad next time? Potbelly owns 280 quick-service restaurants that specialize in fresh-made sandwiches in 18 states and Washington DC (mostly in the Midwest and East Coast although Texas has more than 40 locations). Six more US locations are franchised along with a dozen more franchised shops in the Middle East. The chain's menu features a variety of sandwich styles including such specialty items as its four-meat stacker called A Wreck. The eateries also serve salads soup and chili as well as homemade cookies ice cream and smoothies. In 2013 the company went public raising $105 million.

	Annual Growth	12/10	12/11	12/12	12/13	12/14
Sales ($ mil.)	10.3%	220.6	238.0	274.9	299.7	327.0
Net income ($ mil.)	–	(0.5)	7.2	24.0	1.3	4.4
Market value ($ mil.)	(51.6%)	–	–	–	730.3	353.3
Employees	18.3%	–	–	5,000	5,200	7,000

POTLATCH CORP

NMS: PCH

601 West First Avenue, Suite 1600
Spokane, WA 99201
Phone: 509 835-1500
Fax: –
Web: www.potlatch.com

CEO: Michael J. Covey
CFO: Jerald W. (Jerry) Richards
HR: –
FYE: December 31
Type: Public

Potlatch is Chinook for giving but you'll have to pay for Potlatch's wood products. The real estate investment trust (REIT) harvests timber from some 1.4 million acres of hardwood and softwood forestland in Arkansas Idaho and Minnesota; it claims to be the largest private landowner in Idaho. The company sells real estate that it believes has more value for development or recreation than as timberland; more than 15% of its land potentially falls under this category. Potlatch also operates sawmills in four states that produce logs and fiber and lumber and panels. Additionally it generates revenue from its land by selling hunting leases recreation permits or mineral rights leases.

	Annual Growth	12/11	12/12	12/13	12/14	12/15
Sales ($ mil.)	3.7%	497.4	525.1	570.3	607.0	575.3
Net income ($ mil.)	(5.8%)	40.3	42.6	70.6	89.9	31.7
Market value ($ mil.)	(0.7%)	1,265.6	1,592.6	1,698.0	1,703.3	1,230.2
Employees	1.2%	885	875	880	887	927

POWELL ELECTRONICS INC.

200 COMMODORE DR
SWEDESBORO, NJ 080851270
Phone: 856-241-8000
Fax: –
Web: www.powell.com

CEO: Ernest Schilling Jr
CFO: Schawn E Beatty
HR: –
FYE: December 31
Type: Private

Powell Electronics distributes switches sensors connectors relays and other electronic components. The company stocks more than 100000 parts from such manufacturers as 3M Amphenol AVX Emerson Network Power EnerSys Honeywell ITT RF Industries Winchester Electronics and TE Connectivity. It also manufactures custom assemblies and offers several services including bar coding special packaging materials management and wire cutting. Powell Electronics was founded in 1946 by the late Harold Powell who started selling components from his garage after World War II. His family continues to own the company.

	Annual Growth	03/09	03/10*	12/10	12/11	12/12
Sales ($ mil.)	120.1%	–	22.4	98.8	109.8	108.5
Net income ($ mil.)	2.3%	–	–	3.7	3.7	3.8
Market value ($ mil.)	–	–	–	–	–	–
Employees	–	–	–	–	–	205

*Fiscal year change

POWELL INDUSTRIES, INC.

NMS: POWL

8550 Mosley Road
Houston, TX 77075-1180
Phone: 713 944-6900
Fax: –
Web: www.powellind.com

CEO: Michael Lucas
CFO: Don R Madison
HR: –
FYE: September 30
Type: Public

Powell Industries gets a charge out of making equipment and computer systems that monitor and control the flow of electricity in industrial commercial and government facilities. Products include switchgears (units that manage the flow of electricity to motors transformers and other equipment); bus ducts (insulated power conductors housed in a metal enclosure); process control systems for instrumentation computer control and communications; and data management systems. Powell sells to oil and gas producers and pipelines refineries utilities paper mills petrochemical plants and transportation companies among other customers.

	Annual Growth	09/11	09/12	09/13	09/14	09/15
Sales ($ mil.)	4.2%	562.4	717.2	674.8	647.8	661.9
Net income ($ mil.)	–	(2.7)	29.7	42.1	29.2	9.4
Market value ($ mil.)	(0.7%)	354.0	442.0	700.6	467.0	344.1
Employees	0.7%	2,722	2,812	3,122	2,940	2,803

POWELL'S BOOKS INC.

7 NW 9th Ave.
Portland OR 97209
Phone: 503-228-0540
Fax: 503-228-1142
Web: www.powells.com

CEO: Emily Powell
CFO: Miriam Sontz
HR: –
FYE: June 30
Type: Private

Powell's may not be the big dog when it comes to books but its dog-eared volumes keep it near the front of the pack. The book retailer maintains more than a handful of stores in the Portland Oregon area including its flagship City of Books store which covers a city block and contains more than 1 million volumes. It sells new used out-of-print and rare books; it even sells books that are returned to online bookseller Amazon.com. The company operates specialty stores for cookbooks and gardening technical books and travel books; it also features author readings and book discussion groups and sells books online. President Michael Powell whose father Walter opened City of Books in 1971 owns the firm.

POWER CONSTRUCTION COMPANY LLC

2360 PALMER DR
SCHAUMBURG, IL 60173-3824
Phone: 847-925-1300
Fax: –
Web: www.powerconstruction.net

CEO: –
CFO: –
HR: –
FYE: December 31
Type: Private

The Midwest is the best for Power Construction Company a general contractor operating in the Chicago area for nearly 90 years. The company provides customers with preconstruction planning construction management and design/build services. It serves several markets such as health care education hotel and corporate projects. Power Construction is engaged in new building construction as well as buildouts expansions and renovations. More than 90% of the firm's business comes from repeat customers which have included Astellas Pharma US Federal Express and Walgreen. Jerome Goldstein founded the company which is still owned by management in 1926.

	Annual Growth	12/07	12/08	12/09	12/10	12/11
Sales ($ mil.)	106.6%	–	29.4	0.0	259.5	259.5
Net income ($ mil.)	–	–	0.0	0.0	9.9	9.9
Market value ($ mil.)	–	–	–	–	–	–
Employees	–	–	–	–	–	185

POWER INTEGRATIONS INC.

NMS: POWI

5245 Hellyer Avenue
San Jose, CA 95138
Phone: 408 414-9200
Fax: 408 414-9201
Web: www.power.com

CEO: Balu Balakrishnan
CFO: Sandeep Nayyar
HR: Ana Ordonez
FYE: December 31
Type: Public

Power Integrations develops high-voltage analog integrated circuits (ICs) that convert alternating current (AC) to lower-voltage direct current (DC). The fabless company's high-voltage analog semiconductors which account for virtually all of its sales are used in PCs cell phones cable boxes and other consumer and industrial electronics. The TOPSwitch line features products made with its environmentally friendly EcoSmart technology which reduces energy waste. Power Integrations sells its chips to electronics manufacturers and distributors such as ATM Electronic and Burnon. It makes nearly all of its sales overseas.

	Annual Growth	12/11	12/12	12/13	12/14	12/15
Sales ($ mil.)	3.6%	298.7	305.4	347.1	348.8	344.0
Net income ($ mil.)	3.4%	34.3	(34.4)	57.3	59.5	39.1
Market value ($ mil.)	10.0%	950.1	963.0	1,599.4	1,482.5	1,393.4
Employees	7.7%	443	526	562	590	595

POWERBAR INC.

800 N. Brand Blvd.	CEO: Brian Maxwell
Glendale CA 91203	CFO: –
Phone: 800-587-6937	HR: –
Fax: 818-549-5646	FYE: December 31
Web: www.powerbar.com	Type: Subsidiary

Bellying up to a PowerBar won't slake your thirst but it might boost your energy. A leader in the world of high-carbohydrate snacks PowerBar originally designed its energy bars for athletes. However the company's products are now available in a variety of flavors and are just as likely to be pulled out of purses and desk drawers and eaten as meal replacements. PowerBar also markets sport drinks called Endurance and Ironman a protein powder drink mix under the ProteinPlus name and a carbohydrate gel that comes in a variety of flavors. The company a unit of Nestle's performance nutrition segment sells its products in supermarkets and at health-food and sports retailers worldwide in more than 30 markets.

POWERSECURE INTERNATIONAL, INC.

NYS: POWR

1609 Heritage Commerce Court	CEO: Sidney Hinton
Wake Forest, NC 27587	CFO: Eric Dupont
Phone: 919 556-3056	HR: –
Fax: 919 556-3596	FYE: December 31
Web: www.powersecure.com	Type: Public

PowerSecure International helps its utility energy and water customers stay on top of what is going on with their gas electricity and water. Its Energy & Smart Grid Solutions segment offers distributed generation electricity systems to industrial and commercial users which help to monitor and more efficiently dispatch the flow of electricity. It also provides management consulting and utility engineering planning design and construction services as well energy efficiency products (such as LED lighting). In order to focus on its core smart grid segment in mid-2011 the company sold its WaterSecure subsidiary which operated water processing facilities in northeastern Colorado.

	Annual Growth	12/10	12/11	12/12	12/13	12/14
Sales ($ mil.)	27.4%	97.5	130.0	162.0	270.2	256.7
Net income ($ mil.)	–	3.5	24.1	3.1	4.4	(7.0)
Market value ($ mil.)	10.6%	174.0	110.7	174.7	384.1	260.6
Employees	18.8%	415	516	654	753	827

POWERSOUTH ENERGY COOPERATIVE

2027 E THREE NOTCH ST	CEO: Gary Smith
ANDALUSIA, AL 364212427	CFO: Rick Kyle
Phone: 334-222-2571	HR: –
Fax: –	FYE: December 31
Web: www.powersouth.com	Type: Private

Several hundred thousand Alabamans and Floridians get their electric power courtesy of the work of PowerSouth Energy Cooperative which provides wholesale power to its member-owners (16 electric cooperatives and four municipal distribution utilities). Its distribution members provide electric services to almost 417200 customer meters in central and southern Alabama and western Florida. PowerSouth operates a more than 2200-mile power transmission system and has more than 2000 MW of generating capacity from interests in six fossil-fueled and hydroelectric power plants.

	Annual Growth	12/09	12/10	12/11	12/12	12/13
Sales ($ mil.)	(3.3%)	–	673.7	640.2	591.7	609.7
Net income ($ mil.)	(6.0%)	–	–	28.3	26.6	25.0
Market value ($ mil.)	–	–	–	–	–	–
Employees	–	–	–	–	–	600

POWERSTEERING SOFTWARE INC.

25 First St.	CEO: Stephen Sharp
Cambridge MA 02141	CFO: Jon Choate
Phone: 617-492-0707	HR: –
Fax: 617-492-9444	FYE: December 31
Web: www.powersteeringsoftware.com	Type: Private

PowerSteering Software helps its clients drive their companies in the right direction. Founded in 1998 the company develops Web-based software applications that help corporations manage enterprise-wide strategic projects and initiatives. PowerSteering's products include project management applications that enable organizations to implement Six Sigma operational processes; portfolio management tools for managing numerous complex projects simultaneously; and program management applications that help companies manage corporate mergers and streamline the task of integrating another company's people products and processes. In 2012 it was bought by SilverBack Enterprise Group and merged with Tenrox.

POWERTECH URANIUM CORP.

TORONTO: PWE

5575 DTC Parkway Ste. 140	CEO: –
Greenwood Village CO 80111	CFO: –
Phone: 303-790-7528	HR: –
Fax: 303-790-3885	FYE: March 31
Web: www.powertechuranium.com	Type: Public

Powertech Uranium has traded stainless steel and boilers for something a little more radioactive. The company formerly called Powertech Industries sold off subsidiary Gasmaster Industries — a maker of stainless steel products condensing boilers and water heaters — in 2005. In 2006 the company acquired Denver Uranium Company a uranium-exploration firm focused exclusively on the Dewey Burdock deposit in South Dakota. In 2007 Powertech Uranium's uranium holdings covered more than 59000 acres in the western US.

POWERVERDE INC

NBB: PWVI

420 S. Dixie Highway, Suite 4-B	CEO: Richard H Davis
Coral Gables, FL 33146	CFO: John Hofmann
Phone: 305 666-0024	HR: –
Fax: –	FYE: December 31
Web: www.powerverdeenergy.com	Type: Public

PowerVerde (formerly known as Vyrex) has abandoned its quest for a molecular fountain of youth. These days it's only interested in power. The development-stage biotech company had been researching antioxidants to develop cures for respiratory cardiovascular and neurodegenerative diseases and other conditions related to aging. Unable to continue funding its activities however Vyrex executed a reverse merger with PowerVerde which has designed a power system that generates electricity with zero emissions. The system created by the company's founders George Konrad and Fred Barker uses solar-heated water to power an environmentally friendly motor.

	Annual Growth	12/10	12/11	12/12	12/13	12/14
Sales ($ mil.)	88.7%	0.0	0.2	0.2	0.4	0.4
Net income ($ mil.)	–	(0.3)	(2.6)	(4.8)	(1.1)	(0.6)
Market value ($ mil.)	(22.2%)	17.5	40.3	12.4	5.4	6.4
Employees	10.7%	2	3	3	3	3

POZEN INC.

NMS: POZN

1414 Raleigh Road, Suite 400
Chapel Hill, NC 27517
Phone: 919 913-1030
Fax: –
Web: www.pozen.com

CEO: Adrian Adams
CFO: William L Hodges
HR: –
FYE: December 31
Type: Public

POZEN is no poseur when it comes to its single-minded focus on pain management. The drug development company is creating what it hopes will be better treatments for pain and pain-related conditions. In 2008 it won FDA approval for adult migraine treatment Treximet which it developed in partnership with GlaxoSmithKline; GlaxoSmithKline has commercialization rights to the drug. The company is also working on a combination drug with AstraZeneca that may treat the pain and inflammation of osteoarthritis with fewer gastrointestinal side effects than existing treatments. It has licensed US rights to another pain treatment called lornoxicam from Nycomed.

	Annual Growth	12/09	12/10	12/11	12/12	12/13
Sales ($ mil.)	(24.7%)	32.2	68.5	87.0	5.3	10.3
Net income ($ mil.)	–	(6.9)	23.1	42.3	(25.3)	(16.7)
Market value ($ mil.)	7.7%	183.5	204.0	121.2	153.7	246.6
Employees	(15.2%)	31	29	32	29	16

PPG INDUSTRIES, INC.

NYS: PPG

One PPG Place
Pittsburgh, PA 15272
Phone: 412 434-3131
Fax: –
Web: www.ppg.com

CEO: Charles E. Bunch
CFO: Frank S. Sklarsky
HR: –
FYE: December 31
Type: Public

Thanks to its range of product offerings you won't catch PPG Industries painting itself into a corner. Performance and industrial coatings — such as paints (Pittsburgh Paints Lucite and Monarch) stains (Olympic) and sealants — account for most of its sales; the remainder comes from glass materials. PPG's glass offerings include flat glass for buildings fabricated glass and continuous-strand fiberglass used in aircraft and buildings. The company has sold its chemical commodities and optical products businesses in order to focus on its core coating and glass segments.

	Annual Growth	12/10	12/11	12/12	12/13	12/14
Sales ($ mil.)	3.4%	13,423.0	14,885.0	15,200.0	15,108.0	15,360.0
Net income ($ mil.)	28.6%	769.0	1,095.0	941.0	3,231.0	2,102.0
Market value ($ mil.)	28.8%	22,864.1	22,706.3	36,810.4	51,580.8	62,864.6
Employees	3.8%	38,300	38,400	39,200	41,400	44,400

PPL CORP

NYS: PPL

Two North Ninth Street
Allentown, PA 18101-1179
Phone: 610 774-5151
Fax: 610 774-5106
Web: www.pplweb.com

CEO: Victor A. Staffieri
CFO: Vincent (Vince) Sorgi
HR: –
FYE: December 31
Type: Public

PPL packs a powerful punch in Kentucky Pennsylvania Tennessee Virginia and the UK. It distributes electricity to 10 million customers through regulated subsidiaries PPL Electric Utilities two utilities in Kentucky and Western Power Distribution Holdings in the UK. The company has 19000 MW of generating capacity and also sells energy wholesale in key US markets. Western Power Distribution operates four of the 15 distribution networks providing electricity service in the UK though WPD (South West) and WPD (South Wales). In 2015 PPL sold its competitive energy operations in order to focus on its regulated utility businesses.

	Annual Growth	12/10	12/11	12/12	12/13	12/14
Sales ($ mil.)	7.8%	8,521.0	12,737.0	12,286.0	11,860.0	11,499.0
Net income ($ mil.)	16.7%	938.0	1,495.0	1,526.0	1,130.0	1,737.0
Market value ($ mil.)	8.4%	17,525.1	19,589.3	19,063.3	20,035.4	24,190.3
Employees	5.6%	14,000	17,722	17,729	18,108	17,391

PPL ELECTRIC UTILITIES CORP

NL:

Two North Ninth Street
Allentown, PA 18101-1179
Phone: 610 774-5151
Fax: 610 774-4198
Web: www.pplelectric.com

CEO: –
CFO: –
HR: –
FYE: December 31
Type: Public

PPL Electric Utilities pulls its weight in Pennsylvania's power market. The company which transmits and distributes electricity to 1.4 million customers in 29 counties in eastern and central portions of the state is a subsidiary of PPL Corporation. The regulated utility operates more than 48000 miles of overhead and underground power distribution lines and it is a member of the PJM Interconnection regional transmission organization (RTO). Under the state's Customer Choice Act PPL Electric also acts as the Provider of Last Resort for customers who don't choose an alternative supplier.

	Annual Growth	12/10	12/11	12/12	12/13	12/14
Sales ($ mil.)	(4.5%)	2,455.0	1,892.0	1,763.0	1,870.0	2,044.0
Net income ($ mil.)	18.1%	135.0	189.0	136.0	209.0	263.0
Market value ($ mil.)	–	–	–	–	–	–
Employees	(1.9%)	2,293	2,304	2,311	2,239	2,122

PQ CORPORATION

300 Lindenwood Dr. Valleybrooke Corporate Center
Malvern PA 19355-1740
Phone: 610-651-4200
Fax: 610-651-4504
Web: www.pqcorp.com

CEO: George J Blitz
CFO: –
HR: –
FYE: December 31
Type: Private

PQ Corporation minds its Ps and Qs when producing industrial chemicals. It is one of the world's largest producers of sodium silicates (a glass product made from sand). Glass-bead products from its Potters Industries affiliate are used in highway striping to reflect headlights. PQ's glass beads are also used to grind and process pigments for paints inks and cosmetics. Its potassium silicates are used in welding rods soaps and detergents. PQ's magnesium sulfate is used in animal feed packaging and pharmaceuticals. Zeolytst International (a partnership with a Royal Dutch Shell unit) makes zeolite-based catalysts and adsorbents for a range of chemical and petrochemical applications.

PR NEWSWIRE ASSOCIATION LLC

350 Hudson St. Ste. 300
New York NY 10014-5827
Phone: 888-776-0942
Fax: 360-694-7755
Web: www.nautilusinc.com/nautilus_incorporated/ourb

CEO: Robert Gray
CFO: Dave Wein
HR: –
FYE: December 31
Type: Subsidiary

Corporate communication is the language this company speaks. PR Newswire Association is a leading distributor of corporate news and public relations materials to outlets in 170 countries serving customers through its offices in more than a dozen countries. The company broadcasts press releases photos and multimedia presentations in 40 languages to thousands of news organizations and more than 5500 websites online databases and other information outlets. In addition PR Newswire provides tools that allow its customers to target their communications to specific audiences and to monitor how effectively their messages are getting out. PR Newswire is a subsidiary of UK-based media firm UBM.

PRA GROUP INC

NMS: PRAA

120 Corporate Boulevard
Norfolk, VA 23502
Phone: 888 772-7326
Fax: –
Web: www.portfoliorecovery.com

CEO: Steven D. (Steve) Fredrickson
CFO: Kevin P. Stevenson
HR: –
FYE: December 31
Type: Public

When times are tough businesses find the going a little easier with PRA Group (formerly Portfolio Recovery Associates). The company specializes in consumer debt collection on behalf of clients (including banks credit unions consumer and auto finance companies and retail merchants) in the US and Scotland. PRA also buys charged-off and bankrupt consumer debt portfolios and then collects the debts on its own behalf. The company operates through its subsidiaries which specialize in location and skip tracing (PRA Location Services) class action claims monitoring (Claims Compensation Bureau or CCB) and government accounts receivable management (PRA Government Services).

	Annual Growth	12/10	12/11	12/12	12/13	12/14
Sales ($ mil.)	24.0%	372.7	458.9	592.8	735.1	881.0
Net income ($ mil.)	24.5%	73.5	100.8	126.6	175.3	176.5
Market value ($ mil.)	(6.3%)	3,728.2	3,347.4	5,297.8	2,619.6	2,872.0
Employees	12.1%	2,473	2,641	3,200	3,500	3,900

PRA INTERNATIONAL

4130 ParkLake Ave. Ste. 400
Raleigh NC 27612
Phone: 919-786-8200
Fax: 919-786-8201
Web: www.prainternational.com

CEO: Colin Shannon
CFO: Linda Baddour
HR: Stacy Dickinson
FYE: December 31
Type: Private

PRA International knows it takes more than laboratory research to get drugs approved. The company is a clinical research organization (CRO) that provides an array of drug development services to pharmaceutical and biotechnology companies around the world. Services it offers include clinical trials management drug safety and risk management database development and regulatory filing preparation. PRA's clients are engaged in most major therapeutic areas but the company's particular strengths lie in cardiovascular disease infectious diseases neurology oncology and respiratory and allergy disorders.

PRAIRIE FARMS DAIRY INC.

1100 BROADWAY
CARLINVILLE, IL 626261183
Phone: 217-854-2547
Fax: –
Web: www.prairiefarms.com

CEO: –
CFO: Tom Weber
HR: Ray Silvey
FYE: September 30
Type: Private

Prairie Farms Dairy is very cooperative. With some 700 dairy farmer/members the cooperative offers a full line of retail and food service dairy products. It turns raw milk into fresh fluid cultured and frozen dairy products under the Prairie Farms label. It also makes juices and ice cream novelties. The company's customers include food drug and convenience stores mass merchandisers schools restaurants and other food service operators. Located in Carlinville Illinois it is the managing partner for joint ventures with smaller regional dairies. It makes its products at 24 Prairie Farms-owned plants and 13 joint-venture plants which are located throughout the midwestern and southern areas of the US.

	Annual Growth	09/10	09/11	09/12	09/13	09/14
Sales ($ mil.)	5.3%	–	1,607.2	1,649.9	1,721.3	1,878.5
Net income ($ mil.)	–	–	–	38.8	14.2	(5.2)
Market value ($ mil.)	–	–	–	–	–	–
Employees	–	–	–	–	–	1,965

PRAIRIE VIEW A & M UNIVERSITY

UNIVERSITY DRV AT FM 1098
PRAIRIE VIEW, TX 77446
Phone: 936-261-3311
Fax: –
Web: www.pvamu.edu

CEO: –
CFO: –
HR: –
FYE: August 31
Type: Private

A historically African American institution of higher learning Prairie View A&M University offers its 8400 students baccalaureate degrees in about 50 academic majors nearly 40 graduate degree programs and four doctoral programs through nine colleges and schools. Its main campus in southeast Texas home to the university's nine colleges and schools is about 40 miles outside of Houston; its nursing college maintains a branch in that city's Texas Medical Center. Part of The Texas A&M University System Prairie View A&M was founded in 1876 and was originally known as Alta Vista Agricultural and Mechanical College of Texas for Colored Youth.

	Annual Growth	08/10	08/11	08/12	08/13	08/14
Sales ($ mil.)	3.7%	–	74.5	80.5	76.9	83.1
Net income ($ mil.)	35.8%	–	–	20.7	24.0	38.1
Market value ($ mil.)	–	–	–	–	–	–
Employees	–	–	–	–	–	–

PRATT INDUSTRIES (USA)

1800 C Sarasota Pkwy.
Conyers GA 30013
Phone: 770-918-5678
Fax: 770-918-5679
Web: www.prattindustries.com

CEO: Brian McPheely
CFO: David Wiser
HR: Debbie McCall
FYE: December 31
Type: Private

Pratt Industries (USA) doesn't mill around when it comes to recycling and caring for the environment. The company rivals the world's largest manufacturers of recycled paper and packaging and claims to be the 5th largest box manufacturer in the US and the world's largest privately-held 100% recycled paper and packaging company. Pratt has seven divisions: recycling mills corrugating converting displays packaging systems and national accounts. Its products which include container board and corrugated sheets are sold to clients such as Rubbermaid and Pringles. Pratt operates some 50 plants in about 20 states in the US and Mexico.

PRAXAIR, INC.

NYS: PX

39 Old Ridgebury Road
Danbury, CT 06810-5113
Phone: 203 837-2000
Fax: –
Web: www.praxair.com

CEO: Stephen F. (Steve) Angel
CFO: Matthew J. (Matt) White
HR: –
FYE: December 31
Type: Public

Praxair makes lighter than air and heavier than air gases available for practical applications. The largest North American industrial gas supplier it produces and sells atmospheric gases (oxygen nitrogen argon and rare gases) as well as process and specialty gases (CO_2 helium and hydrogen) for the chemicals food and beverage semiconductor and healthcare industries worldwide. It serves 25 diverse industries across more than 50 countries. Its Praxair Surface Technologies unit supplies high-temperature and corrosion-resistant metallic ceramic and powder coatings mainly to the aircraft plastics and primary metals markets. Praxair builds on-site gas plants and also provides gases by the cylinder.

	Annual Growth	12/10	12/11	12/12	12/13	12/14
Sales ($ mil.)	5.0%	10,116.0	11,252.0	11,224.0	11,925.0	12,273.0
Net income ($ mil.)	9.1%	1,195.0	1,672.0	1,692.0	1,755.0	1,694.0
Market value ($ mil.)	7.9%	27,615.8	30,922.1	31,659.7	37,612.7	37,476.7
Employees	1.4%	26,261	26,184	26,539	27,560	27,780

PRECISION AUTO CARE, INC.
NBB: PACI

748 Miller Drive, S.E.
Leesburg, VA 20175
Phone: 703 777-9095
Fax: 703 771-7108
Web: www.precisiontune.com

CEO: Robert R Falconi
CFO: Mark P Francis
HR: –
FYE: June 30
Type: Public

If it's in a car Precision Auto Care can lube flush or grease it. The company franchises about 380 Precision Tune Auto Care centers in the US and half a dozen other countries. The centers provide general maintenance and repair services including brake service engine tune-ups oil and fluid changes tire rotation and wheel alignments. Precision Auto Care was founded in 1976 by Bill Childs in Beaumont Texas. Former director Arthur Kellar owns about 40% of the company; chairman Louis Brown owns about 15%.

	Annual Growth	06/10	06/11	06/12	06/13	06/14
Sales ($ mil.)	14.0%	15.1	21.0	26.7	26.0	25.4
Net income ($ mil.)	5.3%	0.8	0.6	0.4	0.6	1.0
Market value ($ mil.)	22.0%	3.3	7.9	5.2	5.8	7.3
Employees	39.4%	88	138	171	–	–

PRECISION CASTPARTS CORP.
NYS: PCP

4650 S.W. Macadam Avenue, Suite 400
Portland, OR 97239-4262
Phone: 503 946-4800
Fax: –

CEO: Mark Donegan
CFO: Shawn R Hagel
HR: Kym Dressel
FYE: March 30
Type: Public

Though it has expertise in casting you won't find Precision Castparts Corp. (PCC) offering Hollywood stars any movie roles. The company is a maker of investment castings used in jet aircraft satellite launches aerostructures armaments and medical applications (prostheses). Its Investment Cast products segment makes jet engine parts fluid management valves and deep-hole boring tools. Forged Products and Airframe Products round out PCC's three segments and cover the power generation and paper and pulp industries as well as general industry. The cyclical aerospace sector accounts for more than half of PCC's sales and customers have included noteworthy names like General Electric and Pratt & Whitney.

	Annual Growth	03/10*	04/11	04/12*	03/13	03/14
Sales ($ mil.)	15.1%	5,486.6	6,220.1	7,214.6	8,377.8	9,616.0
Net income ($ mil.)	17.8%	921.8	1,013.5	1,224.1	1,426.6	1,777.0
Market value ($ mil.)	18.9%	17,964.4	21,706.1	25,085.2	27,511.0	35,920.1
Employees	12.6%	18,064	18,308	21,500	28,510	29,085

*Fiscal year change

PRECISION OPTICS CORP INC (MA)
NBB: PEYE

22 East Broadway
Gardner, MA 01440-3338
Phone: 978 630-1800
Fax: –
Web: www.poci.com

CEO: Joseph N Forkey
CFO: Jack P Dreimiller
HR: –
FYE: June 30
Type: Public

Precision Optics plays it up close and personal. The company makes specialized video cameras and stereo endoscopes for use in minimally invasive surgery. Its other products include laparoscopes (for abdominal surgery) and arthroscopes (for joint surgery) as well as sterilizable image couplers and beamsplitters that connect endoscopes to video cameras. The US is Precision Optics' biggest market accounting for almost all sales although the company has received regulatory approval to sell its products in Europe. In 2008 the company sold it custom optical thin film coatings business to privately held Optometrics a subsidiary of Dynasil.

	Annual Growth	06/11	06/12	06/13	06/14	06/15
Sales ($ mil.)	14.9%	2.2	2.2	2.5	3.7	3.9
Net income ($ mil.)	–	(1.1)	1.0	(1.8)	(1.2)	(1.2)
Market value ($ mil.)	29.6%	1.7	9.6	4.5	4.6	4.8
Employees	11.0%	25	28	32	39	38

PRECYSE SOLUTIONS LLC

1275 Drummers Ln. Ste. 200
Wayne PA 19087
Phone: 610-688-2464
Fax: 610-688-1798
Web: www.precyse.com

CEO: Christopher A Powell
CFO: –
HR: Karen Heisler
FYE: December 31
Type: Private

Precyse Solutions pays attention to the details so health care organizations can focus on helping patients get well. The company provides a wide range of health information management (HIM) and medical transcription services and software to hospitals health networks and physician practices throughout the US. Precyse Solutions offers consulting business process outsourcing medical coding software electronic health record (EHR) platforms oncology data management customized projects and compliance and regulatory services. Founded in 1999 as Capital MT the firm has since grown through acquisitions. Private equity firms Altaris Capital Partners and NewSpring Capital own Precyse Solutions.

PREFERRED APARTMENT COMMUNITIES INC.
NYS: APTS

3284 Northside Parkway NW, Suite 150
Atlanta, GA 30327
Phone: 770 818-4100
Fax: –
Web: www.pacapts.com

CEO: John A Williams
CFO: –
HR: –
FYE: December 31
Type: Public

Preferred Apartment Communities prefers to own a good mix of multifamily real estate. The company was formed in 2009 to acquire both newer and older multifamily apartment complexes near major metropolitan cities throughout the US. It oversees the operations of more than 31000 multifamily units in more than 20 national markets including Boston Dallas Denver Los Angeles New York Philadelphia and Washington DC. Other target assets it seeks to acquire are senior mortgage loans or mezzanine debt and membership or partnership interests in multifamily properties. Preferred Apartment Communities went public in 2011.

	Annual Growth	12/10	12/11	12/12	12/13	12/14
Sales ($ mil.)	99.2%	–	7.2	12.5	28.5	56.5
Net income ($ mil.)	–	(0.8)	(8.5)	(0.1)	(4.0)	2.1
Market value ($ mil.)	14.6%	–	129.5	166.7	172.1	194.8
Employees	–	–	–	–	–	–

PREFERRED BANK (LOS ANGELES, CA)
NMS: PFBC

601 S. Figueroa Street, 29th Floor
Los Angeles, CA 90017
Phone: 213 891-1188
Fax: –
Web: www.preferredbank.com

CEO: Li Yu
CFO: Edward J. Czajka
HR: Karen Cangey
FYE: December 31
Type: Public

Preferred Bank wants to be the bank of choice of Chinese-Americans in Southern California. Employing a multilingual staff the bank provides international banking services to companies doing business in the Asia/Pacific region. It targets middle-market businesses typically manufacturing service distribution and real estate firms as well as entrepreneurs professionals and high-net-worth individuals through about a dozen branches in Los Angeles Orange and San Francisco Counties. Preferred Bank offers standard deposit products such as checking accounts savings money market and NOW accounts. Specialized services include private banking and international trade finance.

	Annual Growth	12/10	12/11	12/12	12/13	12/14
Assets ($ mil.)	13.1%	1,255.9	1,309.8	1,554.9	1,769.0	2,054.2
Net income ($ mil.)	–	(16.8)	12.2	23.9	19.2	24.6
Market value ($ mil.)	99.4%	23.8	100.6	191.7	270.7	376.6
Employees	8.0%	120	130	133	148	163

PREFERRED CARE PARTNERS INC.

One Datran Center 9100 S. Dadeland Blvd. Ste. 1250
Miami FL 33156
Phone: 305-670-8440
Fax: 909-869-6310
Web: www.acni.net

CEO: Joseph Caruncho
CFO: –
HR: –
FYE: December 31
Type: Private

Preferred Care Partners manages senior health policies in sunny Florida. The insurance company offers Medicare Advantage plans as well as prescription drug vision and dental coverage. With more than 50000 members Preferred Care Partners serves 15 counties in southern and central Florida as well as the Tampa area. In addition Preferred Care Partners' CareFlorida unit provides Medicaid services to some 5000 customers. The company founded by CEO Joseph Caruncho in 1996. In 2012 the company was acquired by US health insurance giant UnitedHealth.

PREFORMED LINE PRODUCTS CO.

NMS: PLPC

660 Beta Drive
Mayfield Village, OH 44143
Phone: 440 461-5200
Fax: 440 442-8816
Web: www.preformed.com

CEO: Robert G. Ruhlman
CFO: Eric R. Graef
HR: –
FYE: December 31
Type: Public

Masterful "preformances" are expected from Preformed Line Products (PLP) by its audience in the energy and communications industries. The company designs and manufactures components and systems used by utility crews and others to construct repair and maintain overhead and underground networks for energy communications and broadband network companies. It provides formed wire products (for maintenance and repair of aging plant infrastructures) protective fiber-optic closures and splice cases solar hardware and data communication interconnect devices and enclosures for data communications networks.

	Annual Growth	12/10	12/11	12/12	12/13	12/14
Sales ($ mil.)	3.5%	338.3	424.4	439.2	409.8	388.2
Net income ($ mil.)	(13.6%)	23.1	31.0	29.3	20.6	12.9
Market value ($ mil.)	(1.7%)	315.9	322.0	320.7	394.9	294.8
Employees	1.2%	2,617	2,854	2,901	2,794	2,744

PREMERA BLUE CROSS

7001 220th SW Bldg. 1
Mountlake Terrace WA 98043
Phone: 425-918-4000
Fax: 425-918-4791
Web: https://www.premera.com

CEO: –
CFO: Kent S Marquardt
HR: –
FYE: December 31
Type: Private - Not-for-Pr

It's no mistake that Premera sounds an awful lot like premier. Premera Blue Cross is a leading health care coverage provider to 1.5 million residents of Washington State and Alaska. A licensee of the Blue Cross and Blue Shield Association (BCBSA) Premera offers Blue-branded health care coverage including group and individual PPO HMO and consumer-directed plans as well as Medicare supplemental dental vision and prescription drug coverage. Its health care networks encompass some 27000 health care providers and 100 hospitals. The not-for-profit Premera also operates several for-profit subsidiaries offering non-Blue health life and disability insurance in the Western US.

PREMIER AG CO-OP INC.

785 S MARR RD
COLUMBUS, IN 472017490
Phone: 812-379-9501
Fax: –
Web: www.premierag.com

CEO: Harold Cooper
CFO: –
HR: –
FYE: July 31
Type: Private

Premier AG Co-Op provides the agricultural communities in Bartholomew Decatur and Johnson counties of south-central Indiana with farming supplies services and marketing assistance. It operates four grain elevators that handle corn soybeans and wheat. The co-op operates CountryMark gas stations as well as one Countrymart store in Greensburg Indiana. The store sells seed fertilizer and chemical treatments lawn and garden products hardware apparel pet food and supplies animal feed and plants (in season). Premier also owns Premier Energy and Heyob Energy suppliers of propane and home heating oil.

	Annual Growth	07/10	07/11	07/12	07/13	07/14
Sales ($ mil.)	(0.7%)	–	142.9	159.3	141.7	139.8
Net income ($ mil.)	16.7%	–	–	3.5	4.5	4.8
Market value ($ mil.)	–	–	–	–	–	–
Employees	–	–	–	–	–	100

PREMIER EXHIBITIONS INC

NBB: PRXI

3340 Peachtree Road, N.E., Suite 900
Atlanta, GA 30326
Phone: 404 842-2600
Fax: –
Web: www.prxi.com

CEO: Daoping Bao
CFO: Michael J Little
HR: –
FYE: February 28
Type: Public

The Titanic was on her maiden trip when an iceberg hit the ship and Premier Exhibitions is here to tell the tale. The company owns RMS Titanic which salvages and displays artifacts from the doomed Titanic ocean liner runs a touring Titanic exhibit and sells Titanic merchandise. It is considered the salvor-in-possession or owner of the wrecked ship. Premier's other exhibits include "Bodies...The Exhibition" and "Bodies Revealed" (preserved bodies and organs) and "Dialog in the Dark" (exploring a world without sight). Premier was created as a holding company in 2004 when it spun off RMS Titanic. The company has announced plans to sell its Titanic holdings to focus on other touring exhibits.

	Annual Growth	02/11	02/12	02/13	02/14	02/15
Sales ($ mil.)	(10.0%)	44.8	31.7	39.5	29.3	29.4
Net income ($ mil.)	–	(12.5)	(5.8)	2.0	(0.7)	(10.5)
Market value ($ mil.)	(32.4%)	8.6	12.0	11.3	4.3	1.8
Employees	(5.9%)	222	201	191	196	174

PREMIER FINANCIAL BANCORP, INC.

NMS: PFBI

2883 Fifth Avenue
Huntington, WV 25702
Phone: 304 525-1600
Fax: –

CEO: Robert W Walker
CFO: Brien M Chase
HR: –
FYE: December 31
Type: Public

Premier Financial Bancorp is the holding company for Citizens Deposit Bank and Premier Bank rural and small-town banks with locations across Kentucky Virginia Ohio Maryland West Virginia and the District of Columbia. Altogether the banks have about 40 branches that offer standard deposit trust and lending services. Premier bought the $245-milion First National Bankshares along with its six First National Bank branch locations in early 2016 boosting Premier's total assets by nearly 20% to $1.5 billion while expanding its presence in Greenbrier Valley in West Virgnia and into Covington Virginia. The firm entered the DC area with the 2009 purchase of Adams National Bank for some $11 million.

	Annual Growth	12/10	12/11	12/12	12/13	12/14
Assets ($ mil.)	1.4%	1,183.3	1,124.1	1,120.8	1,100.2	1,252.8
Net income ($ mil.)	9.4%	9.2	7.2	10.3	13.2	13.2
Market value ($ mil.)	24.9%	52.1	35.8	88.2	115.2	126.9
Employees	0.8%	354	364	327	328	366

PREMIERE GLOBAL SERVICES INC

NYS: PGI

3280 Peachtree Road N.E., The Terminus Building, Suite 1000
Atlanta, GA 30305
Phone: 404 262-8400
Fax: –
Web: www.pgi.com

CEO: Boland T Jones
CFO: David E Trine
HR: –
FYE: December 31
Type: Public

Premiere Global Services (PGi) knows you don't actually have to meet to have a meeting. The company provides cloud-based software services that enable small and midsized businesses as well as larger corporate clients to collaborate virtually using audio video and Web-based communications. Its conferencing services — provided primary through iMeet and GlobalMeet - include audio and video conferencing operator-assisted event conferencing social networking and file sharing. PGi serves some 45000 clients in about 25 countries but does about two-thirds of its business in North America.

	Annual Growth	12/09	12/10	12/11	12/12	12/13
Sales ($ mil.)	(3.3%)	601.5	441.8	473.8	505.3	526.9
Net income ($ mil.)	7.7%	13.6	4.8	21.4	27.6	18.3
Market value ($ mil.)	8.9%	398.8	328.7	409.4	472.7	560.2
Employees	(2.2%)	2,250	1,700	1,700	1,830	2,060

PREMIO INC.

918 RADECKI CT
CITY OF INDUSTRY, CA 917481132
Phone: 626-839-3100
Fax: –
Web: www.premioinc.com

CEO: –
CFO: –
HR: –
FYE: December 31
Type: Private

Premio can sell you one of its computers or build one of your own design. The company provides contract manufacturing services including the design and assembly testing and support of products ranging from computer servers and displays to medical equipment. The company markets its own line of built-to-order desktop and notebooks PCs servers workstations along with third-party peripherals. It sells to customers in the education medical government security and surveillance markets. Customers have included Sourcefire and Rapiscan Systems. Founded in 1989 by CEO Crystal Wu and Tom Tsao Premio is owned by its officers.

	Annual Growth	12/09	12/10	12/11	12/12	12/13
Sales ($ mil.)	1.2%	–	61.3	58.9	64.5	63.5
Net income ($ mil.)	(21.5%)	–	–	0.5	0.4	0.3
Market value ($ mil.)	–	–	–	–	–	–
Employees	–	–	–	–	–	140

PREMIUM BEERS OF OKLAHOMA L.L.C.

9537 N KELLEY AVE STE A
OKLAHOMA CITY, OK 731312444
Phone: 405-608-6881
Fax: –

CEO: –
CFO: –
HR: –
FYE: December 31
Type: Private

Premium Beers of Oklahoma is the leading beer distributor in the Sooner State and one of the top Anheuser-Busch distributorships in the country. The company supplies such brands as Budweiser Michelob and Busch from distribution facilities in Ardmore Clinton and Lawton. It also distributes Mexican beers from Grupo Modelo such as Corona Corona Light and Modelo Especial as well as BACARDI Silver branded malt beverages Rolling Rock and Stella Artois beers non-alcoholic O'Doul's beverages and Monster energy drinks. Premium Beers serves customers primarily in central and south-central Oklahoma. Denny Cresap started the company in 1968 as a one-person one-route delivery service.

	Annual Growth	12/03	12/04	12/05	12/06	12/07
Sales ($ mil.)	5.5%	–	114.8	114.5	121.7	134.7
Net income ($ mil.)	(31.4%)	–	–	5.6	4.6	2.6
Market value ($ mil.)	–	–	–	–	–	–
Employees	–	–	–	–	–	300

PRESIDENT & TRUSTEES OF BATES COLLEGE

2 ANDREWS RD
LEWISTON, ME 042406020
Phone: 207-786-6255
Fax: –
Web: www.bates.edu

CEO: –
CFO: –
HR: –
FYE: June 30
Type: Private

Bates College is a selective private co-educational liberal arts college granting bachelor of arts and bachelor of science degrees. The institute of higher learning's more than 1750 students can choose from 30 majors the most popular of which include history environmental studies political science English biology economics and psychology. Students enjoy a 10-to-1 student to faculty ratio. Bates' endowment is an estimated $150 million. With tuition and fees hitting almost $59000 most students receive financial aid. The college has about 220 faculty members.

	Annual Growth	06/10	06/11	06/12	06/13	06/14
Sales ($ mil.)	2.7%	–	93.6	97.3	98.8	101.3
Net income ($ mil.)	–	–	–	(15.3)	19.4	38.9
Market value ($ mil.)	–	–	–	–	–	–
Employees	–	–	–	–	–	720

PRESIDENT & TRUSTEES OF WILLIAMS COLLEGE

880 MN ST HOPKS HL FL 1
WILLIAMSTOWN, MA 01267
Phone: 413-597-4412
Fax: –
Web: www.williams.edu

CEO: –
CFO: –
HR: –
FYE: June 30
Type: Private

Liberals need apply. Liberal arts majors that is! Williams College is a private liberal arts school with an enrollment of more than 2000 students at its main campus in the Berkshires of northwestern Massachusetts. It also offers programs in England (Williams-Exeter Programme at Oxford) Connecticut (Williams-Mystic Program) and Williams in New York. The majority of its students come from New York followed by Massachusetts and California. Williams College offers more than 30 undergraduate majors in three academic divisions: humanities sciences and social sciences. Founded in 1793 by Colonel Ephraim Williams the school also confers master's degrees in the history of art and in policy economics.

	Annual Growth	06/07	06/08	06/09	06/10	06/11
Sales ($ mil.)	2.1%	–	–	–	146.9	150.0
Net income ($ mil.)	165.3%	–	–	–	92.4	245.3
Market value ($ mil.)	–	–	–	–	–	–
Employees	–	–	–	–	–	950

PRESIDENT AND BOARD OF TRUSTEES OF SANTA CLARA COLLEGE

500 EL CAMINO REAL
SANTA CLARA, CA 95050-4345
Phone: 408-554-4000
Fax: –
Web: www.scu.edu

CEO: –
CFO: –
HR: –
FYE: June 30
Type: Private

Santa Clara University wants its students to achieve clarity. The Jesuit Catholic school offers degrees in more than 40 disciplines. Its variety of graduate programs include business engineering law pastoral ministries counseling psychology and education. With more than 8800 students Santa Clara University boasts a student/faculty ratio of 12:1 and support from a $688 million endowment. Notable alumni include Oakland mayor and former governor of California Jerry Brown soccer player Brandi Chastain Cirrus Logic chairman Michael Hackworth and winemaker Sam Sebastiani. Santa Clara University was founded in 1851 making it California's oldest higher-education institution.

	Annual Growth	06/04	06/05	06/05	06/11	06/12
Sales ($ mil.)	–	–	0.0	341.3	351.5	312.1
Net income ($ mil.)	–	–	0.0	33.0	24.3	(38.4)
Market value ($ mil.)	–	–	–	–	–	–
Employees	–	–	–	–	–	1,431

PRESIDENT AND FELLOWS OF MIDDLEBURY COLLEGE

38 COLLEGE ST   CEO: –
MIDDLEBURY, VT 05753   CFO: –
Phone: 802-443-5000   HR: Drew Macan
Fax: –   FYE: June 30
Web: www.middlebury.edu   Type: Private

President and Fellows of Middlebury College operates Middlebury College a private liberal arts school in Vermont that offers courses of study in the arts humanities literature foreign languages social sciences and natural sciences. About 2450 undergraduates are enrolled at the educational institution. Founded in 1800 it is home to the Bread Loaf School of English known for its summer graduate courses in literature as well as instruction in creative writing and theatre. Bread Loaf is located in the Green Mountains a dozen miles east of Middlebury. Every summer Middlebury College also opens the Language Schools from which the college provides instruction in 10 languages to more than 2000 students.

	Annual Growth	06/05	06/06	06/08	06/12	06/13
Sales ($ mil.)	5.3%	–	182.0	278.5	233.4	260.7
Net income ($ mil.)	17.3%	–	–	50.9	(24.7)	113.1
Market value ($ mil.)	–	–	–	–	–	–
Employees	–	–	–	–	–	1,000

PRESIDENTIAL LIFE CORPORATION   NASDAQ: PLFE

69 Lydecker St.   CEO: Donald L Barnes
Nyack NY 10960   CFO: Paul B Pheffer
Phone: 845-358-2300   HR: –
Fax: 845-353-0273   FYE: December 31
Web: www.presidentiallife.com   Type: Public

Do you need a new annuity? Presidential Life Corporation is the parent of Presidential Life Insurance which focuses on individual annuities. The company sells single-premium and flexible-premium annuity products. It also offers short-term disability contracts in New York and medical stop loss coverage to employers. Most of its life insurance business was placed in run-off in 2004 so although the company still services its existing policies it does not write new business. The firm does offer some more limited graded-benefit and simplified-issue life policies. Presidential Life distributes its products through independent agents and brokers. The company agreed to be acquired by Athene Annuity & Life in 2012.

PRESIDENTIAL REALTY CORP.   NBB: PDNL B

1430 Broadway, Suite 503   CEO: Nickolas W Jekogian III
New York, NY 10018   CFO: –
Phone: 914 948-1300   HR: –
Fax: 914 948-1327   FYE: December 31
Web: www.presrealty.com   Type: Public

This president may have been elected for a second term. Presidential Realty is a real estate investment trust (REIT) that invests in commercial real estate loans secured by real estate and other property-related assets. Its portfolio includes stakes in a handful of properties in Massachusetts and Puerto Rico including office and industrial properties. Faced with ongoing revenue declines in the turbulent economy the REIT began liquidating itself in 2011. Later that year it terminated the liquidation instead coming to an investment agreement with new CEO Nickolas Jekogian through Signature Community Investment Group.

	Annual Growth	12/10	12/11	12/12	12/13	12/14
Sales ($ mil.)	(34.3%)	4.7	4.7	0.8	0.8	0.9
Net income ($ mil.)	–	(2.2)	(5.4)	(1.8)	1.0	(0.9)
Market value ($ mil.)	(65.4%)	7.0	4.4	0.7	0.9	0.1
Employees	(20.5%)	15	6	7	7	6

PRESIDIO INC.

7601 Ora Glen Dr. Ste. 100   CEO: Bob Cagnazzi
Greenbelt MD 20770   CFO: Paul Fletcher
Phone: 301-313-2000   HR: –
Fax: 301-313-2400   FYE: December 31
Web: www.presidioincorporated.com   Type: Private

Presidio can help you preside over your technology infrastructure. The company provides a variety of IT services such as network management and implementation virtual private networks leasing and project management. Customers come from industries including financial services health care manufacturing and telecommunications. Presidio counts Cisco EMC IBM HP and NetApp among its vendor partners. The company operates through three subsidiaries: Atlantix Global Systems (equipment reseller) Presidio Networked Solutions (IT services) and Presidio Technology Capital (leasing). Presidio was founded in 2003 by CEO Joel Schleicher.

PRESONUS AUDIO ELECTRONICS INC.

7257 FLORIDA BLVD   CEO: –
BATON ROUGE, LA 70806-4634   CFO: Allan Smith
Phone: 225-216-7887   HR: –
Fax: –   FYE: December 31
Web: www.presonus.com   Type: Private

PreSonus Audio Electronics makes digital audio equipment for amateur musicians and professionals alike. Its product lineup (designed for the purposes of broadcasting live sound reinforcement live streaming of audio and recording) includes items such as preamplifiers processors and equalizers. PreSonus sells through more than 800 specialty music retailers (Guitar Center Hermes) in the US as well as internationally. The company was founded in 1995.

	Annual Growth	12/01	12/02	12/10	12/11	12/12
Sales ($ mil.)	–	–	0.0	28.1	43.4	50.3
Net income ($ mil.)	–	–	0.0	1.1	4.5	3.6
Market value ($ mil.)	–	–	–	–	–	–
Employees	–	–	–	–	–	115

PRESSTEK INC.   NASDAQ: PRST

55 Executive Dr.   CEO: Jeffrey Beck
Hudson NH 03051   CFO: Sean Downey
Phone: 603-595-7000   HR: –
Fax: 800-447-1231   FYE: December 31
Web: www.presstek.com   Type: Public

Image is everything at Presstek which combines printing press and computer technologies in its PEARL direct imaging (DI) systems. These systems produce color printing plates and non-photosensitive films and also transfer images from computer to press. The PEARLdry process results in high-resolution plates without chemical processing or hazardous byproducts. Presstek markets its products through 30 graphic arts dealers worldwide. Heidelberger Druckmaschinen AG Harold M. Pitman and Eastman Kodak are Presstek's leading customers as well as competitors. Presstek is being acquired by MAI Holdings an affiliate of American Industrial Partners Capital Fund IV.

PRESSURE BIOSCIENCES INC
NBB: PBIO

14 Norfolk Avenue
South Easton, MA 02375
Phone: 508 230-1828
Fax: –
Web: www.pressurebiosciences.com

CEO: Richard T Schumacher
CFO: Richard P Thomley
HR: –
FYE: December 31
Type: Public

Pressure BioSciences knows how to strong-arm at the molecular level. Using its pressure cycling technology (PCT) which uses cycles of hydrostatic pressure to control molecular interactions the company has developed the PCT Sample Preparation System for life science research. The system which consists of the Barocycler instrument and related consumables helps researchers extract DNA or other molecules from plant and animal tissues for further study. Pressure BioSciences is working on other applications for PCT such as protein purification diagnostics DNA sequencing and enzyme reaction control.

	Annual Growth	12/10	12/11	12/12	12/13	12/14
Sales ($ mil.)	0.6%	1.3	1.0	1.2	1.5	1.4
Net income ($ mil.)	–	(3.1)	(3.0)	(3.5)	(4.1)	(4.6)
Market value ($ mil.)	(34.9%)	26.1	11.2	3.7	4.8	4.7
Employees	1.7%	14	16	15	12	15

PRESTIGE BRANDS HOLDINGS INC
NYS: PBH

660 White Plains Road
Tarrytown, NY 10591
Phone: 914 524-6800
Fax: –
Web: www.prestigebrands.com

CEO: Matthew M. (Matt) Mannelly
CFO: David S. (Dave) Marberger
HR: –
FYE: March 31
Type: Public

Prestige Brands is a lifesaver in the business of resuscitating offloaded consumer brands. The company acquires develops and markets over-the-counter (OTC) drugs and household cleaning products. Its portfolio includes Chloraseptic Clear Eyes Comet Compound W Dermoplast Doctor's Nightguard Little Remedies Pedia-Care Murine Monistat New-Skin and many other big-name brands. Prestige Brands contracts out manufacturing of its products which are sold through mass merchandisers and retail stores primarily in North America. The company was formed in 1996 to acquire and revitalize leading but neglected consumer brands divested by major consumer companies such as Procter & Gamble.

	Annual Growth	03/11	03/12	03/13	03/14	03/15
Sales ($ mil.)	20.7%	336.5	441.1	623.6	601.9	714.6
Net income ($ mil.)	27.9%	29.2	37.2	65.5	72.6	78.3
Market value ($ mil.)	39.0%	601.4	914.1	1,343.5	1,425.1	2,243.0
Employees	16.9%	100	105	117	155	187

PRESTIGE TRAVEL INC

6175 SPRING MOUNTAIN RD 2C
LAS VEGAS, NV 891468845
Phone: 702-248-1300
Fax: –
Web: www.prestigecruises.com

CEO: –
CFO: –
HR: Christine Hagan
FYE: December 31
Type: Private

What happens in Vegas may stay in Vegas but if you don't want to stay in Vegas Prestige Travel can help you out. The company provides leisure and corporate travel services — serving the US Southwest — through about 15 Las Vegas-area locations. Prestige Travel's TripRes.com subsidiary allows visitors to book airfare hotel car cruise and package arrangements as well as Vegas shows. However the company's specialty is low-roller rates in high-roller Vegas hotels and casinos. Prestige Travel an affiliate of American Express was founded in 1980 by president and CEO Kathy Falkensammer.

	Annual Growth	09/00	09/01	09/02	09/03*	12/09
Sales ($ mil.)	(19.1%)	–	–	342.7	82.3	77.9
Net income ($ mil.)	–	–	–	0.0	(0.1)	(0.5)
Market value ($ mil.)	–	–	–	–	–	–
Employees	–	–	–	–	–	170

*Fiscal year change

PRETIUM PACKAGING LLC

15450 S Outer 40 Ste 120
Chesterfield MO 63017-2062
Phone: 314-727-8200
Fax: 314-727-0249
Web: www.pvcc.com

CEO: George Abd
CFO: Robert A Robison
HR: –
FYE: June 30
Type: Private

Content with containment Pretium Packaging (formerly NOVAPAK) makes blow-molded plastic bottles and containers using polyvinyl chloride (PVC) compounds high-density polyethylene (HDPE) and polyethylene terephthalate (PET) resins. It caters to a high-margin niche comprised of small to medium orders for custom containers. Pretium is joined by sister companies Airopak and Marpac in turning out an array of specialty designed plastics. Its industrial and consumer customers include General Mills Colgate-Palmolive Proctor & Gamble and Spectrum Brands. In 2010 Pretium in partnership with Castle Harlan merged with the former NOVAPAK and its parent PVC Container Corp. as part of a double-barrel transaction.

PRGX GLOBAL, INC.
NMS: PRGX

600 Galleria Parkway, Suite 100
Atlanta, GA 30339-5986
Phone: 770 779-3900
Fax: –

CEO: Ronald E Stewart
CFO: Peter Limeri
HR: –
FYE: December 31
Type: Public

PRGX helps clients get every bit of bang from their buck. The firm provides recovery audit services to organizations with high volumes of payment transactions including retail and wholesale businesses manufacturers health care providers and government agencies. It uses proprietary tools to mine clients' books and identify erroneous overpayments which over time can represent a significant loss of money (sometimes to the annual aggregate tune of more than $1 billion). PRGX charges a percentage of the savings realized. The company does business in more than 30 countries around the world: the US accounts for about 60% of its revenue.

	Annual Growth	12/10	12/11	12/12	12/13	12/14
Sales ($ mil.)	(2.8%)	184.1	203.1	208.5	195.2	164.2
Net income ($ mil.)	–	3.3	2.8	5.4	(0.2)	(7.5)
Market value ($ mil.)	(2.5%)	169.4	159.2	172.6	179.8	153.1
Employees	0.0%	1,500	1,600	1,700	1,650	1,500

PRICELINE GROUP INC. (THE)
NMS: PCLN

800 Connecticut Avenue
Norwalk, CT 06854
Phone: 203 299-8000
Fax: 203 595-0160
Web: www.pricelinegroup.com

CEO: Matthew (Matt) Roberts
CFO: Daniel J Finnegan
HR: –
FYE: December 31
Type: Public

The Priceline Group (formerly priceline.com) would like to name itself the king of online travel. At website priceline.com buyers can choose set-price options or "name their own price" for airline tickets hotel rooms rental cars cruises and vacation packages. With its patented business model Priceline generates most of its sales from travel-related services. In the case of airline tickets and hotel reservations it generates sales on the margin keeping the difference between the price paid by the individual and what it shelled out for the ticket or hotel room. Founded in 1997 Priceline operates six brands: Booking.com Priceline.com Agoda.com KAYAK and Rentalcars.com and OpenTable.

	Annual Growth	12/11	12/12	12/13	12/14	12/15
Sales ($ mil.)	20.6%	4,355.6	5,261.0	6,793.3	8,442.0	9,224.0
Net income ($ mil.)	24.6%	1,059.1	1,424.0	1,892.8	2,421.8	2,551.4
Market value ($ mil.)	28.5%	23,203.8	30,778.5	57,668.5	56,567.6	63,252.3
Employees	32.7%	5,000	7,000	9,500	12,700	15,500

PRICESMART INC

NMS: PSMT

9740 Scranton Road
San Diego, CA 92121
Phone: 858 404-8800
Fax: –
Web: www.pricesmart.com

CEO: Jose L. Laparte
CFO: John M. Heffner
HR: Fabiola Burbano
FYE: August 31
Type: Public

PriceSmart is wise in the ways of members-only club retailing. The retailer runs some 35 membership stores under the PriceSmart name in about a dozen countries and one US territory in Latin America and the Caribbean. It sells low-cost food pharmacy and basic consumer items. In each store nearly half of the merchandise comes from the US and the other half is sourced locally. In-store services include auto/tire centers banking and photo developing. PriceSmart stores are typically smaller than wholesale clubs in the US averaging about 48000-100000 sq. ft. and the membership fees average about $35. Chairman and former CEO Robert Price (individually and through The Price Group) owns 30% of PriceSmart.

	Annual Growth	08/11	08/12	08/13	08/14	08/15
Sales ($ mil.)	13.1%	1,714.2	2,050.7	2,299.8	2,517.6	2,802.6
Net income ($ mil.)	9.6%	61.8	67.6	84.3	92.9	89.1
Market value ($ mil.)	6.8%	1,975.9	2,207.7	2,595.0	2,705.1	2,566.0
Employees	8.6%	5,455	5,752	6,371	6,772	7,592

PRICEWATERHOUSECOOPERS LLP

300 Madison Ave. 24th Fl.
New York NY 10017
Phone: 646-471-4000
Fax: 925-355-1591
Web: www.pixion.com

CEO: –
CFO: –
HR: –
FYE: June 30
Type: Private - Partnershi

What price accounting? Perhaps the better question is what Pricewaterhouse-Coopers accounting? PricewaterhouseCoopers LLP is the US arm of Big Four accounting firm PricewaterhouseCoopers International (which formally rebranded itself PwC in 2010). The accountancy's offerings include auditing and human resources tax-related and other advisory services. Focus industries include consumer products and services; industrial products and services; financial services; entertainment; utilities; and technology. PricewaterhouseCoopers also has a practice area geared specifically to private companies. It has about 80 offices in more than 30 states and accounts for 35% of its parent company's revenue.

PRIDGEON & CLAY INC.

50 COTTAGE GROVE ST SW
GRAND RAPIDS, MI 495071685
Phone: 616-241-5675
Fax: –
Web: www.pridgeonandclay.com

CEO: –
CFO: –
HR: Jenna Geisler
FYE: December 31
Type: Private

A moving target not a sitting duck Pridgeon & Clay (P&C) takes on all rivals within the metal forming industry. An independent manufacturer and supplier of stamped and fine blanked components the family-owned company designs and produces an array of parts for auto assembly plants across the US. Its lineup includes steering column lock nuts brackets for headlights to engines control arms flanges exhaust parts and muffler shields. Stamping equipment runs from fine blanking presses to high tonnage and progressive presses. P&C also makes blanks for equipment in other industries. The company touts hand assembly spot welding and tapping services along with a global sales force.

	Annual Growth	12/09	12/10	12/11	12/12	12/13
Sales ($ mil.)	9.3%	–	220.5	267.6	294.8	287.7
Net income ($ mil.)	19.8%	–	–	5.0	1.1	7.2
Market value ($ mil.)	–	–	–	–	–	–
Employees	–	–	–	–	–	600

PRIMEENERGY CORP.

NAS: PNRG

9821 Katy Freeway
Houston, TX 77024
Phone: 713 735-0000
Fax: –
Web: www.primeenergy.com

CEO: –
CFO: Beverly A Cummings
HR: –
FYE: December 31
Type: Public

PrimeEnergy hopes to keep the pump primed with its oil and gas exploration and production activities which take place primarily in Colorado Louisiana New Mexico Oklahoma Texas West Virginia and the Gulf of Mexico. The company has proved reserves of 87 billion cu. ft. of natural gas equivalent. It operates 1500 wells and owns interests in 850 non-operating wells. Its PrimeEnergy Management unit is the managing general partner of 18 oil and gas limited partnerships and two trusts. Subsidiary Southwest Oilfield Construction provides site preparation and construction services for PrimeEnergy and third parties. CEO Charles Drimal owns 32% of the firm.

	Annual Growth	12/10	12/11	12/12	12/13	12/14
Sales ($ mil.)	5.2%	118.2	127.1	121.0	125.1	144.6
Net income ($ mil.)	77.0%	2.8	4.8	15.1	12.3	27.0
Market value ($ mil.)	39.3%	45.1	52.7	53.7	117.8	169.7
Employees	3.0%	240	244	233	244	270

PRIMEVEST FINANCIAL SERVICES INC.

400 1st St. S. Ste. 300
St. Cloud MN 56301
Phone: 320-656-4300
Fax: 320-656-4002
Web: www.primevest.com

CEO: Catherine Bonneau
CFO: Mark Shelson
HR: –
FYE: December 31
Type: Subsidiary

PrimeVest Financial Services is sort of a big-box store of investment products for community banks credit unions and other financial institutions. One of the largest third-party marketers of financial services in the US the firm allows its clients to expand their range of services by affording access to a menu of stocks bonds annuities mutual funds retirement plans insurance and other products from third-party financial services firms. It also provides broker-dealer trust and clearing services. PrimeVest serves approximately 600 financial institutions throughout the US and in Guam. Investment firm Lightyear Capital purchased the company from ING in 2010.

PRIMEX INTERNATIONAL TRADING CORP

5777 W CENTURY BLVD # 1485
LOS ANGELES, CA 90045-5600
Phone: 310-568-8855
Fax: –
Web: www.primex-usa.com

CEO: Ali Amin
CFO: –
HR: –
FYE: December 31
Type: Private

Primex International Trading is a leading exporter and international trader that specializes in dried fruits and nuts. Through affiliate offices located around the world the company ships such products as almonds hazelnuts and pecans as well as apricots figs and raisins. Primex also has its own pistachio orchards and a processing plant in California. The company was founded in 1989 by Ali Amin whose family has been involved in producing pistachios for four generations. It first started planting pistachio orchards in 1990. In 2008 the company shipped about 30 million pounds of pistachios and more than 40 million pounds of almonds.

	Annual Growth	12/98	12/99	12/00	12/01	12/11
Sales ($ mil.)	–	–	(836.8)	47.8	57.2	262.9
Net income ($ mil.)	153.4%	–	0.0	0.2	0.2	2.0
Market value ($ mil.)	–	–	–	–	–	–
Employees	–	–	–	–	–	31

PRIMO WATER CORP

NMS: PRMW

104 Cambridge Plaza Drive
Winston-Salem, NC 27104
Phone: 336 331-4000
Fax: –
Web: www.primowater.com

CEO: Billy D Prim
CFO: Mark Castaneda
HR: –
FYE: December 31
Type: Public

Among the amenities of today's home a water dispenser appears near indispensable. Serving the growing trend of household purified water dispensers Primo Water provides water dispensers along with three- and five-gallon purified bottled water and carbonating beverage appliances. The company's products are sold through US and Canadian retailers such as Lowe's Wal-Mart Kroger HEB Grocery and Walgreen. Empty bottles are exchanged at retail locations with Primo Water recycling centers (where consumers receive a discount toward buying a new Primo bottle) or refilled at a self-serve filtered drinking water display. Started in 2005 Primo expanded quickly and went public in both 2010 and 2011.

	Annual Growth	12/10	12/11	12/12	12/13	12/14
Sales ($ mil.)	24.3%	44.6	84.0	91.5	91.2	106.3
Net income ($ mil.)	–	(12.9)	(14.4)	(111.0)	(10.7)	(13.5)
Market value ($ mil.)	(25.8%)	350.2	74.9	29.3	64.8	106.2
Employees	(1.8%)	126	122	77	95	117

PRIMORIS SERVICES CORP

NMS: PRIM

2100 McKinney Avenue, Suite 1500
Dallas, TX 75201
Phone: 214 740-5600
Fax: –
Web: www.prim.com

CEO: Randy Kessler
CFO: Peter J. Moerbeek
HR: –
FYE: December 31
Type: Public

Since the beginning of time or at least since the 20th century Primoris has played a part in the evolution of the utility and infrastructure landscape. Through subsidiaries the firm provides construction engineering and maintenance services such as replacing and repairing underground pipelines upgrading and maintaining industrial plants designing and building concrete structures and managing the construction of water and wastewater facilities. It also engineers industrial machinery used in oil refineries petrochemical plants and other facilities. The firm primarily operates in the US. Primoris' clients have included Duke Energy Chevron Sempra and Kinder Morgan as well as public sector entities.

	Annual Growth	12/10	12/11	12/12	12/13	12/14
Sales ($ mil.)	22.0%	941.8	1,460.2	1,541.7	1,944.2	2,086.2
Net income ($ mil.)	17.1%	33.6	58.6	56.8	69.7	63.2
Market value ($ mil.)	24.9%	491.9	769.8	775.5	1,605.1	1,198.3
Employees	13.8%	4,034	4,058	6,911	7,079	6,757

PRIMUS BUILDERS INC.

8294 HIGHWAY 92 STE 210
WOODSTOCK, GA 301893672
Phone: 770-928-7120
Fax: –
Web: www.primusbuilders.com

CEO: Richard A O'Connell
CFO: –
HR: –
FYE: December 31
Type: Private

Primus Builders is proud of leaving its customers in the cold. The design/build firm makes refrigerated frozen and ambient storage processing and distribution facilities and other industrial buildings. It offers turnkey services as well as planning and design construction and construction management a la carte. Primus Builders specializes in restaurants condominiums health clubs office buildings and retail centers. The company's Primus Properties leases office park space to businesses. Primus Builders shares work and officers with SubZero Constructors but the two do not share any corporate linkage.

	Annual Growth	12/01	12/02	12/05	12/06	12/07
Sales ($ mil.)	–	–	0.0	16.2	85.3	66.3
Net income ($ mil.)	112.4%	–	–	0.4	2.5	1.7
Market value ($ mil.)	–	–	–	–	–	–
Employees	–	–	–	–	–	88

PRINCIPAL FINANCIAL GROUP, INC.

NYS: PFG

711 High Street
Des Moines, IA 50392
Phone: 515 247-5111
Fax: –
Web: www.principal.com

CEO: Daniel J. (Dan) Houston
CFO: Terrance J. (Terry) Lillis
HR: Mindy Moss
FYE: December 31
Type: Public

For a child in elementary school avoiding the principal is paramount. But for folks looking toward retirement seeking The Principal may be wise. Founded in 1879 Principal Financial Group (or The Principal) is a top administrator of employer-sponsored retirement plans offering pension products and services as well as mutual funds annuities asset management trust services and investment advice. Its insurance segment provides group and individual life and disability insurance and group dental and vision coverage. To compete with banks encroaching on the company's territory and to maximize customer asset retention subsidiary Principal Bank offers online banking.

	Annual Growth	12/11	12/12	12/13	12/14	12/15
Assets ($ mil.)	10.2%	148,298.0	161,926.5	208,191.4	219,087.0	218,685.9
Net income ($ mil.)	14.6%	715.0	805.9	912.7	1,144.1	1,234.0
Market value ($ mil.)	16.3%	7,168.4	8,310.7	14,368.9	15,135.3	13,107.2
Employees	2.4%	13,527	13,373	14,792	14,873	14,895

PRINCIPAL GLOBAL INVESTORS LLC

801 Grand Ave.
Des Moines IA 50392-0490
Phone: 515-247-6582
Fax: 866-850-4024
Web: www.principalglobal.com

CEO: James P McCaughan
CFO: Gerald Hipner
HR: –
FYE: December 31
Type: Subsidiary

Principal Global Investors is the institutional asset management division of Principal Financial Group (aka The Principal). The firm manages approximately $230 billion of assets mainly for retirement plans and other institutional clients such as foundations endowments insurance companies investment banks and government entities. A majority of assets under management are invested in fixed income securities but the company also focuses on equities real estate and alternative investments. Principal Global Investors and its affiliates have more than a dozen offices in the US Brazil Europe Asia and Australia.

PRINTINGFORLESS.COM INC.

211 E. Geyser St.
Livingston MT 59047
Phone: 406-222-2689
Fax: 406-222-4990
Web: www.printingforless.com

CEO: Andrew S Field
CFO: –
HR: –
FYE: December 31
Type: Private

They love the smell of ink in the morning. PrintingForLess.com provides color printing services through an online ordering system. The company prints brochures business cards magnets newsletters posters presentation folders and stationery. It targets small and home businesses offering customers online quotes orders and proofing. The company offers black-and-white and four-color printing on conventional and digital presses. Prepress services are also offered. Headquartered in Montana the online commercial printing company was established in 1996.

PRINTRONIX INC.

15345 Barranca Pkwy.
Irvine CA 92618
Phone: 714-368-2300
Fax: 714-368-2600
Web: www.printronix.com

CEO: Werner Heid
CFO: Rhonda Longmore-Grund
HR: Carol Anderson
FYE: March 31
Type: Private

Printronix produces a plethora of practical printing products. A leading maker of high-speed industrial printers Printronix develops line matrix printers for heavy-duty jobs such as invoicing continuous form printing and bar code label printing. Its laser and thermal printers are used for business and industrial applications. Other products include radio-frequency identification (RFID) printers and printer management systems that let users monitor and configure networked printers from standard Web browsers. The company has offices throughout Europe and Asia in addition to the US. Printronix was acquired by private equity firm Vector Capital for $108 million in 2008.

PRIORITY HEALTH MANAGED BENEFITS INC.

1231 E. Beltline NE
Grand Rapids MI 49525-4501
Phone: 616-942-0954
Fax: 616-942-5651
Web: www.priority-health.com

CEO: Joan Budden
CFO: Greg Hawkins
HR: –
FYE: June 30
Type: Private - Not-for-Pr

Priority Health Managed Benefits' chief concern is its members' wellbeing. A subsidiary of Spectrum Health the health insurance provider serves some 600000 members throughout the state of Michigan. The company offers managed care plans to about 12000 employer groups; it also provides individual coverage. It contracts with a network of some 100 acute care hospitals and more than 16000 health care providers including primary care doctors and specialists. Health plan offerings include HMO POS PPO Medicaid and Medicare plans. Priority Health also offers health savings accounts (HSAs) and provides administrative services for companies with self-funded plans.

PRISON REHABILITATIVE INDUSTRIES AND DIVERSIFIED ENTERPRISES INC

223 MORRISON RD
BRANDON, FL 335114835
Phone: 813-324-8700
Fax: –
Web: www.pride-enterprises.org

CEO: –
CFO: Pete Radanovich
HR: –
FYE: December 31
Type: Private

Even convicted felons can take PRIDE in their work. Prison Rehabilitative Industries and Diversified Enterprises (PRIDE Enterprises) a not-for-profit corporation enables inmates in some 20 Florida prisons to learn job skills. PRIDE operates in about 40 industries employing inmates in activities such as furniture making license plate embossing meat processing and eyewear production. Customers such as schools local governments and nonprofits buy the products made by the inmates. PRIDE also offers labor outsourcing to private businesses. The group's revenue is dedicated to inmate room and board inmate wages and transition services and victim restitution. PRIDE was founded in 1981.

	Annual Growth	12/09	12/10	12/11	12/12	12/13
Sales ($ mil.)	(0.1%)	–	64.4	63.1	64.4	64.1
Net income ($ mil.)	531.5%	–	–	0.0	4.1	1.0
Market value ($ mil.)	–	–	–	–	–	–
Employees	–	–	–	–	–	287

PRIVATEBANCORP, INC.

NMS: PVTB

120 South LaSalle Street
Chicago, IL 60603
Phone: 312 564-2000
Fax: –
Web: www.pvtb.com

CEO: Larry D. Richman
CFO: Kevin M. Killips
HR: –
FYE: December 31
Type: Public

It's your private banker a banker for money and any old teller won't do. PrivateBancorp is the holding company for The PrivateBank and Trust Co which provides commercial and community banking real estate lending investments and money management services to middle-market companies commercial real estate professionals small business owners executives and wealthy individuals and their families. The bank boasts over $15.6 billion in assets around 25 branches in the Chicago area and 10 branches across Atlanta Cleveland Denver Des Moines Detroit Milwaukee Minneapolis Kansas City and St. Louis. Specializing in mid-market business lending commercial loans make up 66% of its loan portfolio.

	Annual Growth	12/10	12/11	12/12	12/13	12/14
Assets ($ mil.)	5.8%	12,465.6	12,416.9	14,057.5	14,085.7	15,603.4
Net income ($ mil.)	216.9%	1.5	44.4	77.9	122.9	153.1
Market value ($ mil.)	23.5%	1,124.2	858.4	1,197.7	2,261.7	2,611.1
Employees	2.5%	1,060	1,045	1,105	1,116	1,168

PRO UNLIMITED INC.

301 Yamato Rd. Ste. 3199
Boca Raton FL 33431
Phone: 561-995-5160
Fax: 888-693-1099
Web: www.prounlimited.com

CEO: Andrew Schultz
CFO: –
HR: –
FYE: December 31
Type: Subsidiary

PRO Unlimited wants to give your company unlimited access to the pros it needs. The company provides services to help clients locate and manage temporary employees. It offers managed services programs (MSP) in areas such as billing payroll tracking training and benefits while its vendor management software and contractor vetting processes keep everything running smoothly. PRO Unlimited's staff consists of professionals with backgrounds in procurement of labor services human resources IT legal and taxes. PRO Unlimited established in 1991 has six offices located in Hong Kong Japan the UK and the US.

PRO-DEX INC. (CO)

NAS: PDEX

2361 McGaw Avenue
Irvine, CA 92614
Phone: 949 769-3200
Fax: –
Web: www.pro-dex.com

CEO: Richard L. (Rick) Van Kirk
CFO: Alisha Charlton
HR: –
FYE: June 30
Type: Public

Pro-Dex is responsible for that high-pitched whirring sound at the dentist's office. The company designs and manufactures rotary drive systems used in the dental and medical instrument industries. Its motors are used in instruments for arthroscopic cranial dental orthopedic and spinal surgery. It also markets its own line of dental handpieces under the Micro Motors brand. Pro-Dex also develops motion control systems for industrial manufacturing and scientific research industries under the Oregon Micro Systems brand. In addition to manufacturing Pro-Dex also offers repair services on its products.

	Annual Growth	06/11	06/12	06/13	06/14	06/15
Sales ($ mil.)	(16.2%)	27.1	17.3	12.2	10.8	13.4
Net income ($ mil.)	–	2.6	(0.9)	(1.8)	(0.5)	(0.4)
Market value ($ mil.)	3.1%	8.6	8.4	7.9	8.7	9.7
Employees	(13.0%)	115	74	67	62	66

PROASSURANCE CORP.   NYS: PRA

100 Brookwood Place	CEO: W. Stancil (Stan) Starnes
Birmingham, AL 35209	CFO: Edward L. (Ned) Rand
Phone: 205 877-4400	HR: –
Fax: 205 802-4799	FYE: December 31
Web: www.proassurance.com	Type: Public

ProAssurance protects professional health associates — the doctors dentists and nurses of the US. One of the largest medical liability insurance providers in the nation ProAssurance is the holding company for ProAssurance Indemnity ProAssurance Casualty and other subsidiaries that sell liability coverage for health care providers primarily in the South and Midwest. Its customers include individual doctors in private practice as well as large physician groups clinics and hospitals. Its ProAssurance Specialty Insurance subsidiary writes excess and surplus (higher risk) lines of medical professional liability insurance. ProAssurance Casualty also provides some coverage for legal professionals.

	Annual Growth	12/10	12/11	12/12	12/13	12/14
Assets ($ mil.)	1.5%	4,875.1	4,998.9	4,876.6	5,150.9	5,169.2
Net income ($ mil.)	(4.0%)	231.6	287.1	275.5	297.5	196.6
Market value ($ mil.)	(7.1%)	3,425.9	4,512.5	2,385.2	2,740.8	2,552.5
Employees	7.0%	739	652	690	962	967

PROBUILD HOLDINGS INC.

7595 Technology Way 5th Fl.	CEO: Robert Marchbank
Denver CO 80237	CFO: Jeff Pinkerman
Phone: 303-262-8500	HR: John O' Loughlin
Fax: +55-11-2162-0630	FYE: December 31
Web: www.vcimentos.com.br	Type: Private

ProBuild Holdings is where the pros go for building supplies. The company is one of the nation's largest suppliers of building materials to professional builders contractors and project-oriented consumers serving customers through 10 regional brands. ProBuild boasts more than 470 locations where it operates lumber and building product manufacturing sites and distribution centers. It supplies lumber millwork windows doors roofing insulation engineered wood siding and trim and gypsum. Its specialty building products business line provides hardware fasteners tools for residential and light commercial construction. Dixieline ProBuild and Stober Building Supply are among ProBuild's regional holdings.

PROCERA NETWORKS INC   NMS: PKT

47448 Fremont Boulevard	CEO: Lyndon Cantor
Fremont, CA 94538	CFO: Charles Constanti
Phone: 510 230-2777	HR: –
Fax: –	FYE: December 31
Web: www.proceranetworks.com	Type: Public

Procera Networks makes it easier for broadband and mobile service providers to run a tight ship. The company's deep packet inspection (DPI) devices are sold under the brand name PacketLogic. As network management equipment it monitors network traffic optimizes bandwidth identifies security threats and manages application usage. Customers also use PacketLogic to differentiate service levels. Procera sells directly and through resellers distributors and systems integrators worldwide. Its customers include cable phone and Internet service providers as well as businesses and schools that manage their own networks. The company was established in 2003.

	Annual Growth	12/09	12/10	12/11	12/12	12/13
Sales ($ mil.)	38.8%	20.1	20.3	44.4	59.6	74.7
Net income ($ mil.)	–	(7.4)	(2.9)	3.8	5.3	(16.3)
Market value ($ mil.)	141.6%	9.1	12.8	321.8	383.1	310.2
Employees	44.4%	52	70	96	151	226

PROCTER & GAMBLE CO.   NYS: PG

One Procter & Gamble Plaza	CEO: David S. Taylor
Cincinnati, OH 45202	CFO: Jon R. Moeller
Phone: 513 983-1100	HR: –
Fax: –	FYE: June 30
Web: www.pg.com	Type: Public

The Procter & Gamble Company (P&G) boasts dozens of billion-dollar brands for home hair and health. The world's largest maker of consumer packaged goods divides its business into five global segments. The company also makes pet food water filters and over-the-counter acid-reflux medication. About two dozen of P&G's brands are billion-dollar sellers including Always Braun Crest Fusion Gillette Head & Shoulders Mach3 Olay Oral-B Pantene and Wella in the beauty and grooming segment as well as Bounty Charmin Dawn Downy Duracell Gain Pampers and Tide in the household care segment. P&G's hundreds of brands are available in more than 180 countries.

	Annual Growth	06/11	06/12	06/13	06/14	06/15
Sales ($ mil.)	(2.0%)	82,559.0	83,680.0	84,167.0	83,062.0	76,279.0
Net income ($ mil.)	(12.1%)	11,797.0	10,756.0	11,312.0	11,643.0	7,036.0
Market value ($ mil.)	–	0.0	0.0	0.0	0.0	0.0
Employees	(3.9%)	129,000	126,000	121,000	118,000	110,000

PROCURESTAFF LTD.

560 Lexington Ave. 15th Fl.	CEO: –
New York NY 10022	CFO: –
Phone: 212-520-2100	HR: –
Fax: 212-719-7821	FYE: October 31
Web: www.procurestaff.com	Type: Subsidiary

If a virtual purchasing department for a contingent workforce sounds better to you than the real thing ProcureStaff can produce one for you. The company which does business as ProcureStaff Technologies is a subsidiary of Volt Information Sciences. Its electronic procurement software is designed to help clients manage bids billing and supplier relationships. ProcureStaff's time and expense applications allow clients to develop metrics using basic labor data in order to improve workforce productivity and to determine pricing of employee resources. The company's procurement services include accounting business process consulting implementation on-site management supplier management and training.

PROCURIAN INC.

211 South Gulph Rd. Ste. 500	CEO: Carl Guarino
King of Prussia PA 19406	CFO: Joseph Waterman
Phone: 484-690-5000	HR: –
Fax: 484-690-5292	FYE: December 31
Web: www.procurian.com	Type: Private

Procurian formerly ICG Commerce wants to eliminate the extensive paperwork and never-ending phone calls that some people associate with traditional corporate buying. The company oversees the purchasing process for its customers by identifying suppliers managing lists of preferred providers and ensuring that items are properly shipped and paid for. Procurian's customers have included oil and gas equipment manufacturer Cameron educational materials publisher Houghton Mifflin Harcourt aircraft component manufacturer Vought and home appliance manufacturer Whirlpool. Investment firm ICG Group owns a controlling stake in Procurian which was founded in 1992.

PROCYON CORPORATION

OTC: PCYN

1300 S. Highland Ave.	CEO: Regina W Anderson
Clearwater FL 33756	CFO: James B Anderson
Phone: 727-443-0530	HR: –
Fax: 727-447-5617	FYE: June 30
Web: www.amerigel.com	Type: Public

Procyon sees past people's scars — though it tries to rid the world of scarring altogether. Through subsidiary Amerx Health Care Procyon Corporation makes medical products used to treat pressure ulcers inflammation dermatitis and other wounds and skin problems. Amerx makes the AmeriGel wound dressing used by many podiatrists. The company's skin treatment products are sold primarily to distributors doctors pharmacies and end-users. Procyon's Sirius Medical Supply division is a mail-order diabetic medical supply distributor selling mostly to Medicare customers. The founding Anderson family including CEO Regina Anderson owns about 40% of the company.

PRODUCERS RICE MILL INC.

518 E HARRISON ST	CEO: –
STUTTGART, AR 721603700	CFO: –
Phone: 870-672-4420	HR: –
Fax: –	FYE: July 31
Web: www.producersrice.com	Type: Private

These producers aren't just milling about they're about milling. Producers Rice Mill dries mills and markets more than 50 million bushels of rice each year which it sells both domestically and overseas. The growers' cooperative is one of the largest private-label producers of rice in the US packaging more than 100 brands for the foodservice retail private label export and industrial industries. Its brands include ParExcellence LeGourment Golden Harvest Classic Grains Granada Mandalay Bamboo 103 Calrose and Thai Orchard. It also processes rice for animal feeds such as Buck Grub deer feed and Equi-Jewel horse feed.

	Annual Growth	07/10	07/11	07/12	07/13	07/14
Sales ($ mil.)	3.0%	–	500.0	478.6	568.5	546.9
Net income ($ mil.)	4.0%	–	–	302.9	368.1	327.4
Market value ($ mil.)	–	–	–	–	–	–
Employees	–	–	–	–	–	730

PRODUCTION RESOURCE GROUP LLC

200 Business Park Dr.	CEO: Jeremiah Harris
Armonk NY 10504	CFO: Ryan Schroeter
Phone: 212-589-5400	HR: –
Fax: 212-589-5425	FYE: December 31
Web: www.prg.com	Type: Private

You can't produce without the proper resources. And Production Resource Group (PRG) is a proper provider. The company offers lighting audio scenery video and labor services for entertainment entities in markets such as corporate and special events tradeshow theater concert touring television and film production retail and themed attraction. PRG has more than 30 offices located in North America Europe Africa and Asia. The company's clients and past projects include Aerosmith Pearl Jam and Celebrity Poker Showdown. PRG was founded in 1982 by chairman and CEO Jere Harris who was formerly active in Broadway production management.

PRODUCTION TOOL SUPPLY COMPANY LLC

8655 E 8 MILE RD	CEO: –
WARREN, MI 480894030	CFO: Michael D Brenner
Phone: 586-755-2200	HR: –
Fax: –	FYE: December 31
Web: www.pts-tools.com	Type: Private

Production Tool Supply totes the tools of the trade — and it distributes them to customers worldwide. With nine showrooms in Michigan and Ohio the company (PTS) distributes brand-name discount industrial tools and machinery. It markets approximately 235000 products through a 1700-page catalog on the Internet and through independent distributors. Products include cutting tools carbide tools abrasives measuring tools clamps and vises power tools tool safety products and power machinery by blue chip OEMs such as Bosch Porter-Cable and Sandvik. D. Dan Kahn founded PTS in 1951 to serve small factories and shops in the Detroit area. The Kahn family still controls the company.

	Annual Growth	10/07	10/08	10/09	10/10*	12/13
Sales ($ mil.)	–	–	(1,519.3)	117.2	129.1	228.5
Net income ($ mil.)	21.7%	–	–	10.7	15.0	23.5
Market value ($ mil.)	–	–	–	–	–	–
Employees	–	–	–	–	–	357

*Fiscal year change

PROFESSIONAL DIVERSITY NETWORK, INC.

NAS: IPDN

801 W. Adams Street, Sixth Floor	CEO: James Kirsch
Chicago, IL 60607	CFO: David Mecklenburger
Phone: 312 614-0950	HR: –
Fax: –	FYE: December 31
Web: www.prodivnet.com	Type: Public

Birds of a feather can build careers together at Professional Diversity Network (PDN). An online professional networking company PDN operates minority-focused websites that facilitate professional networking within ethnic and social communities. Its websites include iHispano.com which serves Hispanic-American professionals and AMightyRiver.com which caters to African-Americans. The company also operates sites that serve other societal subsets including women Asian-Americans gays and lesbians and enlisted and veteran military personnel. Together its websites have 1.8 million members and provide access to job listings a social network professional groups and mentoring. PDN went public in 2013.

	Annual Growth	12/10	12/11	12/12	12/13	12/14
Sales ($ mil.)	27.7%	4.4	5.6	6.2	4.0	11.6
Net income ($ mil.)	–	1.9	2.7	2.4	(1.4)	(3.7)
Market value ($ mil.)	5.6%	–	–	–	58.6	61.9
Employees	181.9%	–	23	23	49	515

PROFESSIONAL GOLFERS ASSOCIATION OF AMERICA INC

100 AVENUE OF CHAMPIONS	CEO: Jim L Awtrey
PALM BEACH GARDENS, FL 334183653	CFO: –
Phone: 561-624-8400	HR: –
Fax: –	FYE: June 30
Web: www.georgiapga.com	Type: Private

You have to be a real swinger to get into this organization. The Professional Golfers' Association of America (PGA) is the world's largest professional sports organization with more than 28000 members. PGA members are primarily club pros but most touring professionals are also members in addition to holding membership in the separate PGA TOUR organization. The PGA conducts some 40 tournaments and runs four major golf competitions: the Ryder Cup the PGA Championship the Senior PGA Championship and the PGA Grand Slam of Golf. It also operates the PGA Learning Center a golf instruction school in Port St. Lucie Florida. Rodman Wanamaker a Philadelphia department store tycoon organized the PGA in 1916.

	Annual Growth	12/07	12/08*	06/09	06/10	06/13
Sales ($ mil.)	–	–	0.0	72.7	56.4	91.1
Net income ($ mil.)	167.0%	–	–	0.2	(10.6)	12.4
Market value ($ mil.)	–	–	–	–	–	–
Employees	–	–	–	–	–	178

*Fiscal year change

PROFESSIONAL PROJECT SERVICES INC.

1100 BETHEL VALLEY RD
OAK RIDGE, TN 378308073
Phone: 865-220-4300
Fax: –
Web: www.p2s.trademarkads.org

CEO: Dr L Barry Goss
CFO: Mike Webster
HR: –
FYE: December 31
Type: Private

Pro2Serve Professional Project Services lives to serve. The contractor provides technical and engineering services that support the security of infrastructures in the US defense energy and environmental markets. Pro2Serve designs high-level security systems to protect national laboratories government facilities and US nuclear weapons. Its work with the US Department of Energy's National Nuclear Security Administration aims to secure nuclear sites and dangerous radiological materials around the world. The company also offers environmental services which include facility planning compliance consulting remediation and waste management. Founded by president Barry Goss Pro2Serve is privately held.

	Annual Growth	12/06	12/07	12/08	12/09	12/10
Sales ($ mil.)	–	–	–	(983.8)	50.5	58.0
Net income ($ mil.)	8575.1%	–	–	0.0	1.7	2.8
Market value ($ mil.)	–	–	–	–	–	–
Employees	–	–	–	–	–	340

PROFESSIONAL SYSTEMS CORPORATION

105 Montgomery Ave.
Oaks PA 19456
Phone: 610-650-3900
Fax: 610-666-9700
Web: www.pscinfogroup.com

CEO: Joseph J Greco
CFO: –
HR: –
FYE: December 31
Type: Private

Professional Systems (which does business as PSC Info Group) can help you collect all sorts of debts and manage all sorts of documents. The company provides outsourced billing and collection services to medical offices as well as document management software for the accounting collections financial services and health care industries. In addition the company also offers direct mail graphic design and printing services as well as consulting support training and implementation.. The company's strategic partners and dealers include SearchAmerica IPR International DigitalMailer and Comtech Systems.

PROGENICS PHARMACEUTICALS, INC.

NMS: PGNX

777 Old Saw Mill River Road
Tarrytown, NY 10591
Phone: 914-789-2800
Fax: –

CEO: Mark R. Baker
CFO: Patrick Fabbio
HR: –
FYE: December 31
Type: Public

Progenics Pharmaceuticals is taking a proactive approach to fighting cancer. The company develops biotech drugs with oncology applications as well as therapeutics used in clinical care settings. Its oncology pipeline includes prostate cancer treatments; it also has potential drugs targeting viral and infectious diseases. Progenics' sole commercial product Relistor blocks the side effects of opioids without lessening their pain-killing power and is approved as an injectable treatment for opioid-induced constipation (OIC) in seriously ill patients. The company has licensed out marketing rights for Relistor to third parties in order to focus on its R&D activities.

	Annual Growth	12/10	12/11	12/12	12/13	12/14
Sales ($ mil.)	53.7%	8.0	84.8	14.0	7.9	44.4
Net income ($ mil.)	–	(69.7)	10.4	(35.4)	(42.6)	4.4
Market value ($ mil.)	8.5%	380.2	594.7	207.5	371.1	526.4
Employees	(22.6%)	159	105	76	69	57

PROGINET CORPORATION

200 Garden City Plaza Ste. 220
Garden City NY 11530
Phone: 516-535-3600
Fax: 516-535-3601
Web: www.proginet.com

CEO: Sandison E Weil
CFO: Joe Christel
HR: –
FYE: July 31
Type: Subsidiary

Proginet had a secure grasp on enterprise data. The company provided software that businesses use to create encrypted documents — including text graphics and executable files — so that they can safely be sent over public networks. The company also offers identity management process automation software as well as password management tools that eliminate the need for users to remember multiple access codes. Its service portfolio ranges from installation and support to project management requirements analysis and security assessments. Proginet was acquired in 2010 by TIBCO Software in an all-cash deal valued at about $20 million.

PROGRESS ENERGY INC.

NYSE: PGN

410 S. Wilmington St.
Raleigh NC 27601-1748
Phone: 919-546-6111
Fax: 919-546-2920
Web: www.progress-energy.com

CEO: Lynn J Good
CFO: Steven K Young
HR: April Legnosky
FYE: December 31
Type: Public

Without progress millions of people would be without energy. Progress Energy provided electricity to 3.1 million customers. It serves customers in North and South Carolina through utility Carolina Power & Light (dba Progress Energy Carolinas) and in Florida through Florida Power (or Progress Energy Florida). The company generated most of its energy from nuclear and fossil-fueled plants and has a total capacity of about 23000 MW. Progress Energy had been seeking to improve its operational efficiency while expanding its alternative energy power sources in order to reduce its greenhouse gas emissions. In 2012 the debt-laden company was acquired by Duke Energy in a $32 billion transaction.

PROGRESS SOFTWARE CORP.

NMS: PRGS

14 Oak Park
Bedford, MA 01730
Phone: 781-280-4000
Fax: 781-280-4095
Web: www.progress.com

CEO: Philip M. (Phil) Pead
CFO: Chris E. Perkins
HR: –
FYE: November 30
Type: Public

Progress Software can help you make significant headway when managing and deploying business applications. The company's platform-as-a-service PaaS software is used for tasks such as business process management application integration data management and analysis and application development and deployment. Progress' products encompass desktops servers mainframes and data centers and can be implemented in a variety of computing environments such as Linux Unix and Windows. Progress serves about 140000 organizations in more than 180 countries with clients coming from industries such as financial services health care manufacturing and technology.

	Annual Growth	11/11	11/12	11/13	11/14	11/15
Sales ($ mil.)	(8.3%)	533.6	335.2	334.0	332.5	377.6
Net income ($ mil.)	–	58.8	47.4	74.9	49.5	(8.8)
Market value ($ mil.)	4.2%	1,030.3	1,017.2	1,332.3	1,304.4	1,213.4
Employees	0.3%	1,744	1,395	942	1,075	1,766

PROGRESSIVE CORP. (OH)

NYS: PGR

6300 Wilson Mills Road
Mayfield Village, OH 44143
Phone: 440 461-5000
Fax: 440 446-7168
Web: www.progressive.com

CEO: Glenn M. Renwick
CFO: John P. Sauerland
HR: Patricia (Pat) Bemer
FYE: December 31
Type: Public

It's risky business and Progressive loves it. Long a leader in nonstandard high-risk personal auto insurance Progressive has motored beyond its traditional business into standard-risk and preferred auto insurance as well as other personal-use vehicle coverage (motorcycles RVs and snowmobiles) through carriers including majority-owned American Strategic Insurance. Progressive also offers commercial policies for heavy trucks vans and lighter trucks. It writes a bit of professional liability insurance for directors and officers as well. The company markets directly to consumers online and by phone and through more than 35000 independent agents who account for the majority of its business.

	Annual Growth	12/10	12/11	12/12	12/13	12/14
Assets ($ mil.)	5.1%	21,150.3	21,844.8	22,694.7	24,408.2	25,787.6
Net income ($ mil.)	4.6%	1,068.3	1,015.5	902.3	1,165.4	1,281.0
Market value ($ mil.)	8.0%	11,679.6	11,468.0	12,402.6	16,029.3	15,864.7
Employees	1.8%	24,638	25,007	25,889	26,145	26,501

PROHEALTH CARE INC

N57W 24950 N CORP CIR N 57 W
SUSSEX, WI 53089
Phone: 262-544-2011
Fax: –
Web: www.prohealthcare.org

CEO: Donald W Fundingsland
CFO: –
HR: –
FYE: December 31
Type: Private

That cheddar-and-beer diet take a toll on your health? Might be time to turn your health over to the pros. ProHealth Care provides health care services to southeastern Wisconsin through a network of three hospitals (Waukesha Memorial Oconomowoc Memorial and the Rehabilitation Hospital of Wisconsin) about two dozen clinics assisted living facilities (Regency Senior Communities) a rehabilitation partnership home health care services and a hospice facility. The community-based organization's specialized services include advanced cancer care cardiology orthopedic and obstetrical and neonatal intensive care.

	Annual Growth	09/11	09/12	09/13	09/14*	12/14
Sales ($ mil.)	(48.5%)	–	702.6	687.9	710.9	186.4
Net income ($ mil.)	(84.6%)	–	–	97.2	58.1	14.9
Market value ($ mil.)	–	–	–	–	–	–
Employees	–	–	–	–	–	3,000

*Fiscal year change

PROJECT ENHANCEMENT CORP

20300 CENTURY BLVD # 175
GERMANTOWN, MD 208741132
Phone: 240-686-3059
Fax: –
Web: www.projectenhancement.com

CEO: Ricardo Martinez
CFO: –
HR: –
FYE: May 31
Type: Private

Project Enhancement offers a variety of environmental services including hazardous waste management nuclear plant decommissioning and stabilization and disposition of nuclear materials. The company serves customers throughout the US from offices in Maryland Tennessee and Washington state. Clients have included several US Department of Energy nuclear sites as well a range of industrial manufacturing companies and utilties including Bechtel British Nuclear Fuels Commonwealth Edison Fluor Lockheed Martin Morrison Knudsen and Science Applications International.

	Annual Growth	05/10	05/11	05/12	05/13	05/14
Sales ($ mil.)	(18.0%)	–	19.7	14.5	12.4	10.9
Net income ($ mil.)	58.0%	–	–	0.2	0.3	0.4
Market value ($ mil.)	–	–	–	–	–	–
Employees	–	–	–	–	–	45

PROJECT LEADERSHIP ASSOCIATES INC.

120 S. LaSalle St. Ste. 1200
Chicago IL 60603
Phone: 312-441-0077
Fax: 312-441-0088
Web: www.projectleadership.net

CEO: Daniel Porcaro
CFO: –
HR: –
FYE: December 31
Type: Private

Project Leadership Associates (PLA) may not be leading the market but it is fast rising among the pantheon of business consulting firms. The employee-owned company has been profitable every year since its founding in 1998 advising small middle-market and large US companies on strategy performance and merger and acquisition integration. It also advises on complementary IT matters helping clients assess which software applications and infrastructures are best suited for their operations. Industries it serves include financial services health care insurance legal manufacturing and utilities. The company works with partners such as Citrix Microsoft and Symantec to deliver its services.

PROLIANCE ENERGY LLC

111 Monument Circle Ste. 2200
Indianapolis IN 46204-5178
Phone: 317-231-6800
Fax: 317-231-6900
Web: www.proliance.com

CEO: –
CFO: –
HR: –
FYE: December 31
Type: Joint Venture

Energy professionals rely on ProLiance Energy. In fact more than 2200 industrial commercial municipal and utility customers rely on ProLiance Energy for their natural gas supply. The energy marketer operates in 8 US states offering procurement supply storage transportation management and consulting services. ProLiance Energy is a subsidiary of ProLiance Holdings a joint-venture owned by Vectren and Public Utilities of the City of Indianapolis (which does business as Citizens Energy). Subsidiary Signature Energy Management offers energy management services across the US and Canada.

PROLOGIS INC

NYS: PLD

Pier 1, Bay 1
San Francisco, CA 94111
Phone: 415 394-9000
Fax: 415 394-9001
Web: www.prologis.com

CEO: Eugene F. (Gene) Reilly
CFO: Thomas S. (Tom) Olinger
HR: –
FYE: December 31
Type: Public

Prologis is a pro when it comes to logistics. The industrial real estate investment trust (REIT) acquires and develops warehouses and distribution facilities for some 4700 clients including retailers and manufacturers such as The Home Depot Amazon.com and Hitachi. The company owns more than 1600 properties in North America Europe and Asia. Altogether Prologis owns has stakes in or is developing some 590 million sq. ft. of space. The company is selective about development and usually only develops pre-leased properties. Its fund management operations oversee long-term property investments. Prologis became the world's largest warehouse REIT when it joined forces with smaller rival AMB Property in 2011.

	Annual Growth	12/10	12/11	12/12	12/13	12/14
Sales ($ mil.)	29.1%	633.5	1,533.3	2,006.0	1,750.5	1,760.8
Net income ($ mil.)	120.1%	27.1	(153.4)	(39.7)	342.9	636.2
Market value ($ mil.)	7.9%	16,156.2	14,566.5	18,591.6	18,826.0	21,923.7
Employees	1.1%	–	1,457	1,445	1,468	1,505

PROMEGA CORPORATION

2800 Woods Hollow Rd.
Madison WI 53711
Phone: 608-274-4330
Fax: 608-277-2516
Web: www.promega.com

CEO: William A Linton
CFO: –
HR: –
FYE: December 31
Type: Private

Promega helps researchers plumb the depths of the life sciences. The company sells more than 2000 products that allow scientists to conduct various experiments in gene protein and cellular research. Its offerings fall into more than two dozen categories including DNA and RNA purification genotype analysis protein expression and analysis and DNA sequencing. Promega has branches in 15 countries around the world. The firm sells its products directly and through about 50 distributors. Customers include academic pharmaceutical and clinical labs as well as government agencies and energy and chemical companies.

PROMETHEUS LABORATORIES INC.

9410 Carroll Park Dr.
San Diego CA 92121
Phone: 858-824-0895
Fax: 858-824-0896
Web: www.prometheuslabs.com

CEO: Lisa A Miller
CFO: Mark Spring
HR: –
FYE: December 31
Type: Private

If you've got fire in your belly Prometheus Laboratories can help put it out. The pharmaceutical company markets several drugs that treat gastrointestinal disorders such as irritable bowel syndrome gout and kidney stones as well as certain cancers and other medical conditions. Prometheus Laboratories markets its products mainly to US gastroenterologists and oncologists. It also pairs its drug offerings with a diagnostic testing products and services that helps doctors diagnose and treat gastrointestinal and oncology conditions. The company was acquired by Nestle in mid-2011.

PROMETRIC INC.

1501 S. Clinton St.
Baltimore MD 21224
Phone: 443-455-8000
Fax: 253-475-1906
Web: www.romanmeal.com

CEO: Michael Brannick
CFO: Chris Derr
HR: –
FYE: December 31
Type: Subsidiary

Sharpen your No. 2 pencils it's test time. Prometric a subsidiary of Educational Testing Service: (A) Provides technology-enabled testing services including test design and development testing sites and administration scoring and results through centers in some 160 countries. (B) Offers pre-employment assessments employee post-training tests professional certification and licensing tests and academic assessments such as the GRE and Test of English as a Foreign Language (TOEFL). (C) Has clients including academic institutions corporations and organizations such as the National Board of Medical Examiners. (D) All of the above. If you answered (D) All of the above you're correct. Pencils down.

PROMISE TECHNOLOGY INC.

TAIWAN: 3057

580 Cottonwood Dr.
Milpitas CA 95035
Phone: 408-228-1400
Fax: 408-228-0730
Web: www.promise.com

CEO: Jiang-Tseun Ju
CFO: –
HR: –
FYE: December 31
Type: Public

Promise Technology keeps data storage under control. The company makes storage controller cards and other products supporting cloud storage A/V postproduction virtual tape libraries and surveillance storage. Its products are powered by RAID (redundant array of independent disks) technology interfacing through the Parallel Advanced Technology Attachment standard as well as the newer Serial ATA. Promise Technology serves the enterprise small and medium business small office/home office and consumer markets worldwide. The company partners with hard-disk drive makers such as Seagate and Western Digital as well as Dell Gateway Fujitsu and other computer makers.

PROMMIS SOLUTIONS LLC

400 Northridge Rd.
Atlanta GA 30350
Phone: 877-685-3453
Fax: 615-370-9539
Web: www.regionalcare.net

CEO: Charles T Piper
CFO: Daniel Weinblatt
HR: –
FYE: December 31
Type: Private

Prommis Solutions found a way to make lemonade out of lemons with the lemons being the US foreclosure market. The company's software helps mortgage lenders process defaulted loans with foreclosure bankruptcy loss mitigation and loan settlement processing services; it also offers tax examination title search and other document management services. Prommis Solutions provides outsourced foreclosure processing services in 19 states and bankruptcy processing services in all 50 states. Customers include mortgage services law firms and mortgage insurance companies such as Radian Group. Prommis Solutions filed to go public in April 2010 but withdrew the IPO in May 2010.

PROOFPOINT INC

NMS: PFPT

892 Ross Drive
Sunnyvale, CA 94089
Phone: 408 517-4710
Fax: –
Web: www.proofpoint.com

CEO: Gary L. Steele
CFO: Paul R. Auvil
HR: Julie Currie
FYE: December 31
Type: Public

Proofpoint is like a bouncer for your computer – it needs to see some proof of ID. The company provides security for e-mails instant messages and other communications. Its Proofpoint Protection Server and Messaging Security Gateway defend against computer viruses hacker attacks on networks and spam. Clients come from the health care financial services government education retail and technology sectors; customers include HCA Bank of America the Dept. of Agriculture the University of North Carolina at Charlotte PETCO and T-Mobile. It has offices across the US Europe Asia/Pacific and Latin America. Founded in 2002 by chairman Eric Hahn Proofpoint went public in 2012.

	Annual Growth	12/10	12/11	12/12	12/13	12/14
Sales ($ mil.)	31.8%	64.8	81.8	106.3	137.9	195.6
Net income ($ mil.)	–	(20.9)	(20.1)	(20.4)	(27.5)	(64.2)
Market value ($ mil.)	97.9%	–	–	476.0	1,282.5	1,864.8
Employees	31.7%	–	376	449	680	859

PROPHASE LABS INC

NMS: PRPH

621 N. Shady Retreat Road
Doylestown, PA 18901
Phone: 215 345-0919
Fax: 215 345-5920
Web: www.prophaselabs.com

CEO: Ted Karkus
CFO: Robert V Cuddihy Jr
HR: –
FYE: December 31
Type: Public

ProPhase Labs wants cold sufferers to put away their tissues and tonics and take Cold-EEZE lozenges instead. The firm contends that its Cold-EEZE remedy (a zinc-based nutritional formula available in lozenge tablet liquid and gum forms) lessens the length and severity of the common cold. ProPhase markets its products primarily in the US market. The company's Pharmaloz Manufacturing subsidiary makes Cold-EEZE lozenges and provides contract manufacturing of lozenges for other firms. ProPhase is also conducting research and development programs into potential new OTC medicines.

	Annual Growth	12/10	12/11	12/12	12/13	12/14
Sales ($ mil.)	11.1%	14.5	17.5	22.4	25.0	22.1
Net income ($ mil.)	–	(3.5)	(2.7)	(1.1)	0.4	(7.8)
Market value ($ mil.)	5.0%	19.1	18.3	21.6	25.6	23.2
Employees	5.1%	45	49	50	50	55

PROPHOTONIX LTD.

NBB: STKR

32 Hampshire Road
Salem, NH 03079
Phone: 603 893-8778
Fax: 603 893-5604
Web: www.stockeryale.com

CEO: Mark W Blodgett
CFO: Timothy P Losik
HR: –
FYE: December 31
Type: Public

ProPhotonix (formerly StockerYale) lights the way with lasers and LEDs. The company makes light-emitting diode (LED) modules used in semiconductor manufacturing machine vision biomedical and other applications. It also makes custom LED modules for OEMs systems integrators and end users with unique lighting needs. Its Photonic Products Ltd. (PPL) subsidiary makes custom laser modules and other electro-optical subassemblies and optoelectronic components based on semiconductor laser diode technology. It also distributes precision optical lenses from Panasonic to OEMs in the industrial medical scientific and defense markets. ProPhotonix has operations in Ireland the UK and the US.

	Annual Growth	12/10	12/11	12/12	12/13	12/14
Sales ($ mil.)	2.0%	15.2	17.0	13.9	15.6	16.4
Net income ($ mil.)	–	(2.6)	(1.4)	(2.9)	(1.2)	(1.3)
Market value ($ mil.)	(35.9%)	14.2	8.5	1.7	3.3	2.4
Employees	–	–	–	–	–	–

PROS HOLDINGS INC

NYS: PRO

3100 Main Street, Suite 900
Houston, TX 77002
Phone: 713 335-5151
Fax: –
Web: www.pros.com

CEO: Andres D. Reiner
CFO: Stefan B. Schulz
HR: –
FYE: December 31
Type: Public

PROS Holdings can help you squeeze the most out of every single penny. The company provides price and revenue optimization software that customers use for tasks such as forecasting demand optimizing inventory allocation modeling price elasticity and monitoring transaction profitability. PROS' customers come from the distribution manufacturing services and travel industries. Some 800 companies such as airline Deutsche Lufthansa paper mill NewPage and industrial conglomerate Honeywell. It also offers professional services such as consulting support maintenance and implementation. PROS was founded in 1985.

	Annual Growth	12/10	12/11	12/12	12/13	12/14
Sales ($ mil.)	27.2%	71.0	96.6	117.8	144.8	185.8
Net income ($ mil.)	–	(1.9)	6.4	5.0	3.4	(36.6)
Market value ($ mil.)	24.6%	331.0	432.4	531.5	1,159.5	798.6
Employees	24.9%	415	541	709	848	1,011

PROSEK PARTNERS

1552 Post Rd.
Fairfield CT 06824
Phone: 203-254-1300
Fax: 203-254-1330
Web: www.prosek.com

CEO: –
CFO: Russel Polin
HR: –
FYE: December 31
Type: Private

Public relations firm Prosek Partners is positively pleased to provide financial communications and investor relations. It also offers traditional and digital media relations corporate advisory editorial public affairs and graphic and Web design services. Customers include energy professional services financial services insurance and technology companies. Prosek Partners serves regional national and international clients through offices in London; New York; and Fairfield Connecticut. Formerly Cubitt Jacobs & Prosek Communications the public relations agency is a minority- and women-owned business; it changed its name to Prosek Partners in 2012.

PROSIGHT SPECIALTY INSURANCE GROUP INC.

919 3rd Ave. 10th Fl.
New York NY 10022
Phone: 212-551-0600
Fax: 212-986-1310
Web: www.prosightspecialty.com

CEO: George R Trumbull
CFO: Thomas J Iacopelli
HR: –
FYE: December 31
Type: Private

Need hull insurance or cargo war risk insurance? Want to make sure your offshore drilling rig is covered? ProSight Specialty Insurance Group might be your best bet. The company writes niche specialty insurance coverage throughout the US through subsidiaries including New York Marine and General Insurance Gotham Insurance and Southwest Marine and General Insurance which provide hull cargo shoreline and other marine and liability policies. Its non-marine products include professional liability excess workers' compensation and truck fleet insurance. ProSight operates in the UK through a Lloyd's of London syndicate. The company is a subsidiary of private equity-backed ProSight Specialty Insurance Holdings.

PROSKAUER ROSE LLP

11 Times Sq.
New York NY 10036
Phone: 212-969-3000
Fax: 212-969-2900
Web: www.proskauer.com

CEO: –
CFO: –
HR: –
FYE: October 31
Type: Private - Partnershi

Proskauer Rose understands both law and home runs. Founded in 1875 the law firm is one of the largest in the US and among the nation's leading practitioners of sports law. Its clients include Major League Baseball the National Hockey League and the National Basketball Association (former partner David Stern is commissioner of the NBA). Although its sports practice is dominant the law firm also supports more than 50 industry and practice groups. It has garnered attention for its strength in labor and employment; other practice areas include banking copyright First Amendment and real estate. Proskauer Rose employs more than 750 lawyers in 12 offices.

PROSPECT CAPITAL CORPORATION
NMS: PSEC

10 East 40th Street, 42nd Floor
New York, NY 10016
Phone: 212 448-0702
Fax: –
Web: www.prospectstreet.com

CEO: John F Barry III
CFO: Brian H Oswald
HR: –
FYE: June 30
Type: Public

Prospect Capital is a closed-end investment fund with holdings in the consumer food health care and manufacturing sectors among others. The company targets privately held middle-market firms with annual revenues of less than $750 million; it also considers thinly traded public companies or turn-around situations. Prospect's portfolio includes interests in more than 100 companies mainly through senior loans and mezzanine debt. The company also makes equity and secured debt investments. Typically investing from $5 million to $250 million per transaction Prospect is a long-term investor that maintains regular contact with its portfolio company's management and participates in their board meetings.

	Annual Growth	06/11	06/12	06/13	06/14	06/15
Assets ($ mil.)	44.7%	1,549.3	2,255.3	4,448.2	6,477.3	6,798.1
Net income ($ mil.)	40.1%	94.2	186.7	324.9	357.2	362.7
Market value ($ mil.)	(7.6%)	3,630.4	4,090.0	3,878.2	3,815.3	2,646.5
Employees	–	–	–	–	–	–

PROSPECT MEDICAL HOLDINGS INC.

10780 Santa Monica Blvd. Ste. 400
Los Angeles CA 90025
Phone: 310-943-4500
Fax: 310-943-4501
Web: www.prospectmedicalholdings.com

CEO: Samuel S Lee
CFO: Mike Heather
HR: –
FYE: September 30
Type: Private

Prospect Medical Holdings sees synergies between hospitals and managed health care. The company owns and manages seven hospitals and about a dozen independent physicians associations (IPAs) in Southern California and Texas. Its hospital segment which includes the majority owned Brotman Medical Center has a total of about 1050 beds and provide acute care and specialty medical services. The firm's medical group segment provides administrative management services to about 7000 IPA member physicians which in turn provide health care to 181000 HMO enrollees for fixed monthly fees paid by the managed care organization to which they belong. Prospect is owned by private equity firm Leonard Green & Partners.

PROSPERITY BANCSHARES INC.
NYS: PB

Prosperity Bank Plaza, 4295 San Felipe
Houston, TX 77027
Phone: 713 693-9300
Fax: –
Web: www.prosperitybankusa.com

CEO: David Zalman
CFO: David Hollaway
HR: –
FYE: December 31
Type: Public

Prosperity Bancshares reaches banking customers across the Lone Star State. The holding company for Prosperity Bank operates about 230 branches across Texas and about 15 more in Oklahoma. Serving consumers and small to mid-sized businesses the bank offers traditional deposit and loan services in addition to wealth management retail brokerage and mortgage banking investment services. Prosperity Bank focuses on real estate lending: Commercial mortgages make up the largest segment of the company's loan portfolio (33%) followed by residential mortgages (24%). Credit cards business auto consumer home equity loans round out its lending activities.

	Annual Growth	12/10	12/11	12/12	12/13	12/14
Assets ($ mil.)	22.7%	9,476.6	9,822.7	14,583.6	18,642.0	21,507.7
Net income ($ mil.)	23.5%	127.7	141.7	167.9	221.4	297.4
Market value ($ mil.)	9.0%	2,740.9	2,815.6	2,930.7	4,423.3	3,863.0
Employees	16.0%	1,708	1,664	2,266	2,995	3,096

PROSYS INFORMATION SYSTEMS INC.

4900 Avalon Ridge Pkwy.
Norcross GA 30071
Phone: 678-268-1300
Fax: 770-300-0486
Web: www.prosysis.com

CEO: Ted Glahn
CFO: –
HR: –
FYE: December 31
Type: Subsidiary

ProSys Information Systems provides a variety of IT services such as consulting network design application development supply chain planning project management training implementation and support. The company's customers come from fields including financial services manufacturing health care and technology. It primarily serves small and midsized companies as well as educational institutions and other public sector clients. ProSys operates from more than 20 offices in the southeastern and mid-Atlantic US. Parent company Bell Microproducts was acquired by rival Avnet in 2010.

PROTALEX INC
NBB: PRTX

131 Columbia Turnpike, Suite 1
Florham Park, NJ 07932
Phone: 215 862-9720
Fax: –
Web: www.protalex.com

CEO: –
CFO: Kirk M Warshaw
HR: –
FYE: May 31
Type: Public

Protalex is developing a technique called bioregulation to make drugs that control a disease instead of treating the symptoms after the disease has wreaked havoc on the body. The company's development programs target autoimmune diseases and inflammatory ailments. Lead drug candidate PRTX-100 is in early stage trials to target rheumatoid arthritis and idiopathic thrombocytopenic purpura (ITP) an autoimmune disorder characterized by excessive bleeding. Other potential disease targets include skin diseases psoriasis and pemphigus inflammatory bowel condition Crohn's disease and autoimmune disorders multiple sclerosis and lupus.

	Annual Growth	05/11	05/12	05/13	05/14	05/15
Sales ($ mil.)	–	0.0	0.0	0.0	0.0	0.0
Net income ($ mil.)	–	(3.4)	(4.4)	(6.3)	(11.9)	(11.6)
Market value ($ mil.)	33.2%	50.3	28.8	69.0	236.5	158.2
Employees	0.0%	3	3	3	3	3

PROTECTION ONE INC.

1035 N. 3rd St. Ste. 101
Lawrence KS 66044
Phone: 785-856-5500
Fax: 213-687-8792
Web: www.rsac.com

CEO: Timothy J Whall
CFO: Dan Bresingham
HR: –
FYE: December 31
Type: Private

Safety is the #1 priority for Protection One (P-One). The company provides security alarm monitoring services to about 1.5 million US customers. Its alarm systems are designed to detect intrusions smoke and fire. P-One offers access and remote entry systems in addition to its traditional security offerings. The company provides constant monitoring services from two facilities located in the US; it also serves customers through some 60 field offices. P-One's business is conducted through three segments: retail (homes and businesses) wholesale (independent alarm companies) and multifamily (apartments and condos). Chicago-based private equity firm GTCR Golder Rauner acquired P-One in mid-2010.

PROTECTIVE LIFE CORP.

NYS: PL

2801 Highway 280 South
Birmingham, AL 35223
Phone: 205 268-1000
Fax: –
Web: www.protective.com

CEO: John D Johns
CFO: Richard J Bielen
HR: –
FYE: December 31
Type: Public

Protective Life wants to cushion its customers from the nasty blows of life and death. The company primarily sells life insurance products through its Life Marketing business segment including universal term and bank-owned life insurance coverage; Protective Life also brings in and manages blocks of life insurance policies sold elsewhere through its Acquisitions segment. The firm's Asset Protection unit sells extended service contracts and credit life insurance while its Annuities division offers fixed and variable annuities. The Stable Value Products unit sells guaranteed funding agreements for financial instruments such as municipal bonds and the ProEquities brokerage serves independent financial advisors.

	Annual Growth	12/08	12/09	12/10	12/11	12/12
Assets ($ mil.)	9.7%	39,572.4	42,311.6	47,562.8	52,932.1	57,384.7
Net income ($ mil.)	–	(41.9)	271.5	260.2	339.1	302.5
Market value ($ mil.)	18.8%	1,121.3	1,293.2	2,081.6	1,762.8	2,233.2
Employees	(0.9%)	2,372	2,317	2,315	2,332	2,284

PROTECTIVE LIFE INSURANCE CO

2801 Highway 280 South
Birmingham, AL 35223
Phone: 205 268-1000
Fax: –
Web: www.protective.com

CEO: John D. Johns
CFO: Richard Bielen
HR: –
FYE: December 31
Type: Public

Need protection in New York? Hire a body guard. Need to protect your assets? Protective Life & Annuity Insurance would like to help. Protective Life and Annuity Insurance markets and sells financial security in the form of term and universal life insurance policies and fixed and variable annuity products. Although the company is based in Alabama and licensed to sell insurance throughout the US it exclusively serves clients in New York. Protective Life and Annuity Insurance is a subsidiary of Protective Life Insurance Company which is part of Protective Life Corporation.

	Annual Growth	12/10	12/11	12/12	12/13	12/14
Assets ($ mil.)	10.2%	47,476.3	52,791.9	57,157.6	68,296.5	69,992.1
Net income ($ mil.)	17.5%	258.2	347.4	308.5	291.6	492.0
Market value ($ mil.)	–	–	–	–	–	–
Employees	7.5%	1,840	2,058	2,284	2,415	2,457

PROTESTANT MEMORIAL MEDICAL CENTER INC.

4500 MEMORIAL DR
BELLEVILLE, IL 622265360
Phone: 618-233-7750
Fax: –
Web: www.memhosp.com

CEO: Mark J Turner
CFO: –
HR: –
FYE: December 31
Type: Private

With more than 315 beds Memorial Hospital has plenty of space to take care of Prairie Staters. The Bellevue Illinois-based hospital is owned and operated by Protestant Memorial Medical Center a community-based not-for-profit organization. Memorial Hospital provides general medical surgical and emergency care as well as pediatric home health and cardiovascular care. Specialty services include treatment for sleep disorders and women's health. The hospital also operates Memorial Convalescent Center a nearly 110-bed skilled nursing facility and the Belleville Health and Sports Center which provides fitness facilities to promote community health.

	Annual Growth	12/08	12/09	12/11	12/12	12/13
Sales ($ mil.)	0.8%	–	248.9	259.4	263.3	256.6
Net income ($ mil.)	–	–	–	9.5	15.9	(36.1)
Market value ($ mil.)	–	–	–	–	–	–
Employees	–	–	–	–	–	2,344

PROTEXT MOBILITY INC

NBB: TXTM

22 S.E. 2nd Avenue
Delray Beach, FL 33444
Phone: 800 215-4212
Fax: –
Web: www.protextmobility.net

CEO: Steve Berman
CFO: –
HR: –
FYE: December 31
Type: Public

Echo Metrix (formerly SearchHelp) makes sure children are always under a watchful eye. The company provides parental control software designed to monitor the activity of children while they surf the Web send instant messages or chat online. Its Sentry At Home software alerts parents via e-mail or mobile phone when established usage guidelines are violated. The company's Sentry Remote software allows parents to monitor their children's online activities in real-time and remotely shut down their computers. Echo Metrix also developed an application for tracking registered sex offenders but it decided to discontinue that line in 2008.

	Annual Growth	12/09	12/10	12/11	12/12	12/13
Sales ($ mil.)	(62.2%)	0.0	0.0	0.0	0.0	0.0
Net income ($ mil.)	–	(4.5)	(5.7)	(3.6)	(2.2)	(1.4)
Market value ($ mil.)	–	0.1	0.3	0.0	0.0	0.0
Employees	(38.5%)	7	5	4	1	1

PROTO LABS INC

NYS: PRLB

5540 Pioneer Creek Drive
Maple Plain, MN 55359
Phone: 763 479-3680
Fax: –
Web: www.protolabs.com

CEO: Victoria M. (Vicki) Holt
CFO: John R. Judd
HR: –
FYE: December 31
Type: Public

Need a prototype pronto? Proto Labs can help with that. The industrial manufacturer creates custom parts in quick turnaround for prototype and short-run production. The company uses 3D CAD software to upload new parts designs and then its computer numerical control (CNC) process analyzes the design quotes a price and makes the parts. Proto Labs creates machined metal (Firstcut) and injection-molded plastic (Protomold) parts and can ship them the next business day. Its medical device electronics consumer products appliance and automotive manufacturing customers use the parts for prototyping market evaluation and functional testing. The company was established in 1999 and went public in 2012.

	Annual Growth	12/10	12/11	12/12	12/13	12/14
Sales ($ mil.)	34.0%	64.9	98.9	126.0	163.1	209.6
Net income ($ mil.)	39.6%	11.0	18.0	24.0	35.3	41.6
Market value ($ mil.)	30.5%	–	–	1,018.5	1,839.2	1,735.3
Employees	28.2%	–	511	622	749	1,077

PROVECTUS PHARMACEUTICALS INC.

OTC: PVCT

7327 Oak Ridge Hwy. Ste. A
Knoxville TN 37931
Phone: 865-769-4011
Fax: 865-769-4013
Web: www.pvct.com

CEO: H Craig Dees
CFO: Peter R Culpepper
HR: –
FYE: December 31
Type: Public

Provectus prospects the death of cancer. Provectus Pharmaceuticals designs pharmaceuticals for the treatment of cancer and various skin problems. Its Provectus Pharmatech division is developing prescription drugs for the treatment of eczema psoriasis and acne as well as therapeutics targeting breast liver and prostate cancers and melanoma. In addition the company develops laser-based medical devices and anti-cancer vaccines through its Provectus Devicetech and Provectus Biotech divisions respectively. Provectus also has over-the-counter drug assets through its Pure-ific division. Together CEO Craig Dees president Timothy Scott and EVP Eric Wachter control about 16% of the company's shares.

PROVIDE COMMERCE INC.

5005 Wateridge Vista Dr.	CEO: Chris Shimojima
San Diego CA 92121	CFO: Adam Fischer
Phone: 858-638-4900	HR: –
Fax: 858-638-4708	FYE: June 30
Web: www.providecommerce.com	Type: Subsidiary

Provide Commerce keeps the perishable goods and gift markets fresh. The majority of the e-tailer's sales are generated by ProFlowers.com and ProPlants.com which ship flowers plants and wreaths directly from growers to residential and corporate clients. The Internet florist also offers chocolate popcorn and fruit and cheese baskets. Provide Commerce's Cherry Moon Farms and Sharis Berries virtual shops offer hand-picked fruits hand-dipped sweets and wine. In addition to gourmet perishables the company operates RedEnvelope (acquired in 2008) and Personal Creations (acquired in 2010) which sell upscale and personalized gifts and jewelry. Founded in 1998 Provide Commerce is owned Liberty Interactive.

PROVIDENCE & WORCESTER RAILROAD CO.　　NMS: PWX

75 Hammond Street	CEO: Robert H Eder
Worcester, MA 01610	CFO: Daniel T Noreck
Phone: 508 755-4000	HR: –
Fax: –	FYE: December 31
Web: www.pwrr.com	Type: Public

Giving an island its link Providence and Worcester Railroad (P&W) stands as Rhode Island's sole interstate freight carrier. The regional freight railroad operates over a network of about 545 miles of track in Connecticut Massachusetts New York and Rhode Island. It hauls such goods as chemicals and plastics construction aggregate food and forest and paper products for more than 160 customers. Major customers include Cargill Dow Chemical Frito-Lay International Paper and GDF SUEZ Energy. P&W interchanges freight traffic with CSX the New England Central Railroad the New York and Atlantic Railroad and Pan Am Railways (formerly Springfield Terminal Railway).

	Annual Growth	12/10	12/11	12/12	12/13	12/14
Sales ($ mil.)	3.5%	29.9	33.7	30.0	33.3	34.3
Net income ($ mil.)	–	(0.3)	0.9	3.5	1.4	3.2
Market value ($ mil.)	1.9%	81.4	55.4	67.8	95.0	87.9
Employees	0.2%	137	147	147	141	138

PROVIDENCE COLLEGE

1 CUNNINGHAM SQ	CEO: –
PROVIDENCE, RI 029180001	CFO: –
Phone: 401-865-1000	HR: James Feeney
Fax: –	FYE: June 30
Web: www.support.providence.edu	Type: Private

Students don't need divine intervention to get into Providence College they just need good grades and an interest in liberal arts. The Catholic institution of higher education offers undergraduate and graduate degrees at its four schools: Arts and Sciences Business Continuing Education and Professional Studies. It offers degrees in about 50 academic disciplines including biology business education marketing politics and psychology. It has a student-to-faculty ratio of 12:1 with students primarily coming from New England and the Midwest and Mid-Atlantic regions. Providence College was founded in 1917 by the Dominican Friars of the Province of St. Joseph and the Diocese of Providence.

	Annual Growth	06/08	06/09	06/10	06/11	06/13
Sales ($ mil.)	13.6%	–	142.4	145.6	216.9	237.6
Net income ($ mil.)	(2.3%)	–	–	24.0	24.3	22.4
Market value ($ mil.)	–	–	–	–	–	–
Employees	–	–	–	–	–	800

PROVIDENCE HOSPITAL

16001 W 9 MILE RD	CEO: –
SOUTHFIELD, MI 480754803	CFO: Dave Mast
Phone: 248-849-3000	HR: –
Fax: –	FYE: June 30
Web: www.promedica.org	Type: Private

Providence Hospital and Medical Centers provides health care in the Motor City and surrounding areas. The main Providence Hospital is a 408-bed teaching facility that has been recognized for its cardiology program and clinical expertise in behavioral medicine. It offers a variety of other services ranging from cancer treatment and neurosurgery to orthopedics and women's health. The network also includes dozens of affiliated general practice and specialty health clinics. The not-for-profit medical center founded in 1845 as St. Vincent's Hospital in Detroit by the Daughters of Charity is part of Catholic health ministry St. John Health (itself a subsidiary of Ascension Health).

	Annual Growth	12/07	12/08*	06/09	06/10	06/11
Sales ($ mil.)	9994.4%	–	0.0	532.0	593.5	706.6
Net income ($ mil.)	–	–	–	(53.4)	2.0	27.8
Market value ($ mil.)	–	–	–	–	–	–
Employees	–	–	–	–	–	4,700

*Fiscal year change

PROVIDENCE HOSPITAL

1150 VARNUM ST NE	CEO: Amy Freeman
WASHINGTON, DC 200172104	CFO: –
Phone: 202-269-7000	HR: Yomi Fabiyi
Fax: –	FYE: June 30
Web: www.provhosp.org	Type: Private

Providence Hospital is a pillar in the health care community of Washington DC. The oldest continuously operating hospital in our nation's capitol the 410-bed facility provides a full spectrum of services from behavioral health to women's services. It also administers programs for sleep disorders geriatric care and palliative care in addition to its comprehensive medical and surgical services. Providence Hospital's affiliates include the adjacent Carroll Manor Nursing and Rehabilitation Center a 250-bed facility for long-term and rehabilitative care as well as several outpatient family behavioral and occupational health clinics in the region. Providence Hospital is part of the Ascension Health network.

	Annual Growth	06/07	06/08	06/09	06/10	06/13
Sales ($ mil.)	–	–	0.0	230.6	235.1	198.6
Net income ($ mil.)	–	–	–	(13.5)	8.1	(8.4)
Market value ($ mil.)	–	–	–	–	–	–
Employees	–	–	–	–	–	2,517

PROVIDENCE RESOURCES INC.　　OTC: PVRS

5300 Bee Caves Rd. Bldg. 1 Ste. 240	CEO: Nora Coccaro
Austin TX 78746	CFO: Nora Coccaro
Phone: 512-970-2888	HR: –
Fax: 501-666-4741	FYE: December 31
Web: www.cdicon.com	Type: Public

Guided perhaps by Providence Providence Resources (formerly Healthbridge a development-stage company that had plans to market medical waste sterilization and disposal systems) changed course in 2006 and acquired Providence Exploration a company that drills for oil and natural gas and provides drilling services in Texas. It has interests in approximately 6272 acres of oil and gas leases in Comanche and Hamilton Counties and holds 12832 acres of oil and gas leases in Val Verde County. Providence Resources also provides drilling services through its PDX Drilling I LLC subsidiary. Company director Markus Mueller owns 14% of Providence Resources.

PROVIDENCE SERVICE CORP
NMS: PRSC

64 East Broadway Blvd.
Tucson, AZ 85701
Phone: 520 747-6600
Fax: 520 747-6605
Web: www.provcorp.com

CEO: Herman M. Schwarz
CFO: David Shackelton
HR: –
FYE: December 31
Type: Public

When it comes to social services there's not much that isn't in this company's providence. Providence Service Corporation operates through two divisions: Social Services and Non-Emergency Transportation Services (NET) to provide behavioral health and counseling services as well as non-emergency transportation to people in home and community-based settings. Providence manages foster care systems provides correctional support such as probation supervision offers job training and provides substance abuse treatment. Its NET services are provided to people with disabilities hospital patients and Medicare and Medicaid members among others. Providence operates in about 40 states and British Columbia.

	Annual Growth	12/10	12/11	12/12	12/13	12/14
Sales ($ mil.)	13.9%	879.7	943.0	1,105.9	1,122.7	1,481.2
Net income ($ mil.)	(3.8%)	23.6	16.9	8.5	19.4	20.3
Market value ($ mil.)	22.7%	254.8	218.2	269.4	407.8	577.8
Employees	18.3%	7,000	7,600	8,400	8,500	13,700

PROVIDENT COMMUNITY BANCSHARES, INC.
NBB: PCBS

2700 Celanese Road
Rock Hill, SC 29732
Phone: 803 325-9400
Fax: –
Web: www.providentonline.com

CEO: –
CFO: –
HR: –
FYE: December 31
Type: Public

Provident Community Bancshares (formerly Union Financial Bancshares) is the holding company for Provident Community Bank which operates about 10 branches in Laurens Union Fairfield Greenville and York counties in northern South Carolina. The bank attracts deposits from local consumers and businesses by offering checking and savings accounts money market and NOW accounts CDs and IRAs. Its lending activities mainly consist of business loans commercial mortgages and consumer and installment loans. The bank also offers investments brokerage services retirement planning and credit cards.

	Annual Growth	12/08	12/09	12/10	12/11	12/12
Assets ($ mil.)	(5.3%)	434.2	457.0	408.7	376.6	349.9
Net income ($ mil.)	–	(0.4)	(7.4)	(13.8)	(0.2)	(0.1)
Market value ($ mil.)	(59.1%)	17.9	4.2	1.2	0.2	0.5
Employees	(3.8%)	84	79	77	74	72

PROVIDENT FINANCIAL HOLDINGS, INC.
NMS: PROV

3756 Central Avenue
Riverside, CA 92506
Phone: 951 686-6060
Fax: –
Web: www.myprovident.com

CEO: Craig G Blunden
CFO: Donavon P Ternes
HR: –
FYE: June 30
Type: Public

Provident Financial Holdings is the holding company for Provident Savings Bank which operates more than a dozen branches in Southern California's Riverside and San Bernardino counties. Catering to individuals and small to midsized businesses the bank offers such standard retail products as checking and savings accounts money market accounts and CDs as well as retirement planning services. Real estate loans including single-family multifamily and commercial mortgages and construction loans make up essentially all of the company's loan portfolio. Single-family residential mortgages make up more than half of all loans.

	Annual Growth	06/11	06/12	06/13	06/14	06/15
Assets ($ mil.)	(2.8%)	1,314.5	1,260.9	1,211.0	1,105.6	1,174.6
Net income ($ mil.)	(7.2%)	13.2	10.8	25.8	6.6	9.8
Market value ($ mil.)	20.2%	69.2	99.6	137.1	125.5	144.5
Employees	4.9%	436	543	595	521	528

PROVIDENT FINANCIAL SERVICES INC
NYS: PFS

239 Washington Street
Jersey City, NJ 07302
Phone: 732 590-9200
Fax: –
Web: www.providentnj.com

CEO: Christopher P. Martin
CFO: Thomas M. Lyons
HR: Janet D. Krasowski
FYE: December 31
Type: Public

Provident wants to be a prominent force in the New Jersey banking scene. Provident Financial Services owns The Provident Bank which serves individuals businesses and families from 85 branches across more than 10 northern and central New Jersey counties. Founded in 1839 the $8.5 billion-bank offers traditional deposit and lending products as well as wealth management and trust services. About 50% of its revenue comes from real estate loan interest while another 25% comes from interest on commercial and consumer loans. Construction loans round out its lending activities. The company's Provident Investment Services subsidiary sells life and health insurance and investment products.

	Annual Growth	12/10	12/11	12/12	12/13	12/14
Assets ($ mil.)	5.7%	6,824.5	7,097.4	7,283.7	7,487.3	8,523.4
Net income ($ mil.)	10.3%	49.7	57.3	67.3	70.5	73.6
Market value ($ mil.)	4.5%	982.0	869.1	968.4	1,254.0	1,172.2
Employees	1.6%	957	963	941	942	1,021

PROXIM WIRELESS CORPORATION
PINK SHEETS: PRXM

1561 Buckeye Dr.
Milpitas CA 95035
Phone: 408-383-7600
Fax: 408-383-7680
Web: www.proxim.com

CEO: –
CFO: Steve Button
HR: –
FYE: December 31
Type: Public

Proxim Wireless works without a wire when it builds nets. The company provides broadband wireless network equipment including radios bridges and access gear. Communication carriers and service providers enterprises government agencies schools and health care providers use its products to offer network access build video surveillance and public safety systems and provide telecom backhaul connections. Proxim sells its products worldwide through distributors resellers systems integrators and OEMs. Its engineering team works with channel partners and end users.

PRUDENTIAL ANNUITIES LIFE ASSURANCE CORP
NL:

One Corporate Drive
Shelton, CT 06484
Phone: 203 926-1888
Fax: –
Web: www.investor.prudential.com

CEO: Robert F O'Donnell
CFO: Yanela C Frias
HR: –
FYE: December 31
Type: Public

Prudential Annuities Life Assurance has a name that fits — the company is the annuities business unit of life insurance giant Prudential Financial. It offers variable and fixed annuities and other retirement and long-term investment products and services. Prudential Annuities Life Assurance's products are distributed through independent financial planners brokers and banks. It holds the lead position in the US variable annuities market; its variable annuities are distributed by Prudential Annuities Distributors. The company which is part of Prudential Financial's US Retirement Solutions and Investment Management Division targets US residents with a household income level of above $100000.

	Annual Growth	12/10	12/11	12/12	12/13	12/14
Assets ($ mil.)	(2.2%)	57,266.9	52,313.0	52,855.5	53,521.3	52,472.8
Net income ($ mil.)	(12.2%)	421.6	(212.3)	634.1	848.1	250.8
Market value ($ mil.)	–	–	–	–	–	–
Employees	–	–	–	–	–	–

PRUDENTIAL FINANCIAL, INC.   NYS: PRU

751 Broad Street
Newark, NJ 07102
Phone: 973 802-6000
Fax: –
Web: www.investor.prudential.com

CEO: John R. Strangfeld
CFO: Robert M. Falzon
HR: Dawn Gammon
FYE: December 31
Type: Public

Prudential Financial wants to make sure its position near the top of the life insurance summit is set in stone. Prudential known for its Rock of Gibraltar logo is one of the top US life insurers and also one of the largest life insurance companies worldwide. The firm is perhaps best known for its individual life insurance though it also sells group life and disability insurance as well as annuities. Prudential also offers investment products and services including asset management services mutual funds and retirement planning. In Asia the company operates through its Gibraltar Life Insurance unit. Prudential has some $1.2 trillion in assets under management.

	Annual Growth	12/10	12/11	12/12	12/13	12/14
Assets ($ mil.)	9.2%	539,854.0	624,521.0	709,298.0	731,781.0	766,655.0
Net income ($ mil.)	(18.9%)	3,195.0	3,666.0	469.0	(667.0)	1,381.0
Market value ($ mil.)	11.4%	26,703.3	22,796.3	24,256.3	41,944.7	41,144.2
Employees	4.2%	41,044	50,104	48,498	47,355	48,331

PRUDENTIAL INVESTMENT MANAGEMENT INC.

3 Gateway Center 15th Flr.
Newark NJ 07102-4064
Phone: 973-802-6000
Fax: 208-338-1830
Web: www.westair.com

CEO: David Hunt
CFO: –
HR: –
FYE: December 31
Type: Subsidiary

Prudential Investment Management tries to exercise prudent judgment when it comes to investing its clients' money. The company a subsidiary of Prudential Financial is one of the nation's largest institutional asset managers. It serves more than 3000 clients including corporations endowments foundations insurance companies and pension funds. It also serves high-net-worth retail customers. Prudential Investment Management possesses expertise in equities public and private fixed income private fixed income real estate and commercial mortgage investments. The company has some $470 billion in assets under management approximately half of it invested in public fixed-income securities.

PRUDENTIAL OVERALL SUPPLY INC.

16901 ASTON
IRVINE, CA 926064829
Phone: 949-250-4855
Fax: –
Web: www.prudentialuniforms.com

CEO: Dan Clark
CFO: John Thompson
HR: –
FYE: December 31
Type: Private

Prudential works to outfit every member of your organization. From uniforms to career apparel Prudential Overall Supply rents sells and leases workwear to those in food service health care manufacturing and the government. The company also rents and sells industrial-grade products (entrance and logo mats) and janitorial supplies (dust mops paper towels and cleansers). In addition to its products Prudential offers industrial cleaning and laundering services. The company operates about 30 branches in the US more than half of which are located in California and sells its products online and through catalogs. Prudential has been family-owned and -operated since its founding in 1932.

	Annual Growth	12/07	12/08	12/10	12/11	12/12
Sales ($ mil.)	–	–	0.0	139.9	141.0	145.6
Net income ($ mil.)	93.4%	–	–	1.3	4.3	5.0
Market value ($ mil.)	–	–	–	–	–	–
Employees	–	–	–	–	–	1,457

PRWT SERVICES INC.

1835 MARKET ST STE 800
PHILADELPHIA, PA 191032919
Phone: 215-563-7698
Fax: –

CEO: –
CFO: Don Peloso
HR: Malik Majeed
FYE: December 31
Type: Private

Vowels are overrated. PRWT Services provides outsourced customer support services to a variety of industries. Services include payment processing call center services document processing claims administration mailroom operations and other technical support services. PRWT also provides toll operations services for Delaware River Authority and fulfillment of stationary forms envelopes business cards and other business supplies. PRWT's subsidiaries include U.S. Facilities (facilities maintenance and management) and Cherokee Pharmaceuticals (pharmaceutical ingredients manufacturer). PRWT considered forming a subsidiary and merging with KBL Healthcare Acquisition Corp. but the deal fell through in July 2009.

	Annual Growth	12/03	12/04	12/05	12/06	12/10
Sales ($ mil.)	–	–	–	(563.3)	66.5	89.8
Net income ($ mil.)	869.8%	–	–	0.0	0.2	7.7
Market value ($ mil.)	–	–	–	–	–	–
Employees	–	–	–	–	–	1,312

PS BUSINESS PARKS, INC   NYS: PSB

701 Western Avenue
Glendale, CA 91201-2397
Phone: 818 244-8080
Fax: 818 242-0566
Web: www.psbusinessparks.com

CEO: Joseph D. Russell
CFO: Edward A. Stokx
HR: –
FYE: December 31
Type: Public

Pssst! Know where a fella can find some spare flex space? PS Business Parks does. The company is a self-managed real estate investment trust (REIT) that owns develops and operates industrial office and flex (combined industrial and office) properties. The REIT owns assets in eight states with concentrations in California Virginia Florida and Texas. Its portfolio includes some 27 million sq. ft. of multi-tenant industrial and office space including light manufacturing plants warehouses distribution centers and research and development facilities. The company also manages more than 1 million sq. ft. of properties owned by self-storage giant Public Storage which owns some 23% of PS Business Parks.

	Annual Growth	12/10	12/11	12/12	12/13	12/14
Sales ($ mil.)	7.8%	279.1	298.5	347.2	359.9	376.9
Net income ($ mil.)	19.5%	85.3	94.1	89.1	103.2	174.0
Market value ($ mil.)	9.3%	1,499.9	1,492.1	1,749.2	2,057.2	2,141.2
Employees	4.3%	142	145	161	176	168

PS ENERGY GROUP INC.

2987 Clairmont Rd. Ste. 500
Atlanta GA 30329
Phone: 404-321-5711
Fax: 404-321-3938
Web: www.psenergy.com

CEO: Livia Whisenhunt
CFO: –
HR: –
FYE: December 31
Type: Private

Once you've completed your company charter add a postscript to hire PS Energy Group. The company provides transportation fuel (including alternative fuels) fleet management and risk management services to small and midsize service-based businesses Fortune 500 companies utilities and government agencies. Other services include emergency fueling for utilities disaster relief efforts and telematics-based wireless tracking services (known as etrac) to help customers monitor and track vehicles in their fleets. PS Energy was founded in 1985 and is owned by CEO Livia Whisenhunt.

PSB HOLDINGS INC

NAS: PSBH

40 Main Street
Putnam, CT 06260
Phone: 860 928-6501
Fax: 860 928-2147
Web: www.putnambank.com

CEO: –
CFO: –
HR: –
FYE: June 30
Type: Public

PSB Holdings thinks it offers Pretty Smart Banking for the businesses and individuals of Connecticut's Windham and New London counties. The holding company owns Putnam Savings Bank a thrift with about 10 bank branches and lending offices. Putnam Savings Bank offers standard deposit products and services including checking and savings accounts merchant and check cards CDs and IRAs. It largely uses funds from deposits to write real estate loans: Residential and commercial mortgages together account for about 95% of the bank's loan portfolio. Mutual holding company Putnam Bancorp owns a majority stake in PSB Holdings.

	Annual Growth	06/10	06/11	06/12	06/13	06/14
Assets ($ mil.)	(1.5%)	489.4	472.5	452.3	454.4	461.0
Net income ($ mil.)	(5.6%)	1.3	1.1	1.1	1.3	1.0
Market value ($ mil.)	8.6%	31.6	34.0	27.3	36.7	44.0
Employees	0.0%	121	120	122	118	121

PSCU INCORPORATED

560 CARILLON PKWY
SAINT PETERSBURG, FL 337161294
Phone: 727-572-8822
Fax: –
Web: www.pscu.com

CEO: Michael J. (Mike) Kelly
CFO: Brian Caldarelli
HR: Lynn Heckler
FYE: September 30
Type: Private

Credit unions turn to PSCU to provide key card services. Ass one of the nation's largest credit union service organizations PSCU (short for Payment Systems for Credit Unions) provides credit debit ATM and prepaid card servicing as well as electronic banking bill payment risk management specialized marketing and contact center services to credit unions across the US. The not-for-profit cooperative serves more than 1300 institutions nationwide which combined represent more than 18 million cardholder accounts and one million online bill payment subscribers. PSCU is owned by about 800 member credit unions.

	Annual Growth	12/09	12/10	12/11	12/12*	09/13
Sales ($ mil.)	(16.3%)	–	662.0	425.2	377.0	388.1
Net income ($ mil.)	18.6%	–	–	29.3	38.6	41.2
Market value ($ mil.)	–	–	–	–	–	–
Employees	–	–	–	–	–	1,400

*Fiscal year change

PSEG GLOBAL L.L.C.

80 Park Plaza- T20
Newark NJ 07102
Phone: 973-430-7000
Fax: 918-495-4511
Web: www.citgo.com

CEO: –
CFO: –
HR: –
FYE: December 31
Type: Subsidiary

PSEG Global keeps the global interests of Public Service Enterprise Group (PSEG) close to its heart. A subsidiary of PSEG Energy Holdings it owns stakes in power plants and electric and gas distribution utilities primarily in the US (in California Hawaii New Hampshire and Texas. It also has small investments power assets in India Italy and Venezuela. PSEG Global owns stakes in Energy Storage and Power LLC (compressed air energy storage) and Garden State Offshore Energy which is exploring the development of a 350MW wind farm off the coast of New Jersey. In the mid-2000s the company had more than 30 distribution and transmission projects across the globe but pulled back as PSEG refocused on the US.

PSEG POWER LLC

NYS: PEG 31

80 Park PlazaaT25
Newark, NJ 07102-4194
Phone: 973 430-7000
Fax: –
Web: www.pseg.com

CEO: Ralph Izzo
CFO: Daniel J Cregg
HR: –
FYE: December 31
Type: Public

Power player PSEG Power does not play with power it markets it for profit. The company is the independent power production and energy marketing subsidiary of Public Service Enterprise Group (PSEG). The unit owns and/or manages about 25 power stations in Connecticut New Jersey New York and Pennsylvania. It oversees PSEG Nuclear LLC (which operates the Salem and Hope Creek generating stations in New Jersey and owns 50% of the Peach Bottom plant in Pennsylvania) and PSEG Fossil LLC (which has gas oil coal and natural gas power plants). PSEG Power has installed capacity of more than 13466 MW. Its PSEG Energy Resources and Trade unit buys and sells wholesale power natural gas and other energy commodities.

	Annual Growth	12/10	12/11	12/12	12/13	12/14
Sales ($ mil.)	(4.6%)	6,558.0	6,143.0	4,865.0	5,063.0	5,434.0
Net income ($ mil.)	(9.7%)	1,143.0	1,098.0	647.0	644.0	760.0
Market value ($ mil.)	–	–	–	–	–	–
Employees	1.5%	2,803	2,699	2,614	2,633	2,973

PSYCHEMEDICS CORP.

NAS: PMD

125 Nagog Park
Acton, MA 01720
Phone: 978 206-8220
Fax: –
Web: www.psychemedics.com

CEO: Raymond C Kubacki
CFO: –
HR: Tom Hardy
FYE: December 31
Type: Public

Beware of giving a lock of hair as a keepsake — it could end up at Psychemedics which provides drug testing services through the analysis of hair samples. Its tests which it markets under the brand name RIAH (or Radioimmunoassay of Hair) not only reveal that a substance has been consumed but also detect patterns of use over time; the tests look for cocaine marijuana PCP Ecstasy and opiates. The company's primary market is employers who use the service for pre-employment screening as well as random testing of current employees. Psychemedics also sells its service to hundreds of schools nationwide (and in some foreign countries) and offers a service to parents worried that their kids might be on drugs.

	Annual Growth	12/10	12/11	12/12	12/13	12/14
Sales ($ mil.)	9.8%	20.1	24.1	25.2	26.9	29.2
Net income ($ mil.)	5.2%	2.6	3.5	3.0	3.8	3.2
Market value ($ mil.)	16.6%	44.1	48.9	57.8	79.0	81.4
Employees	14.4%	91	119	132	151	156

PTC INC

NMS: PTC

140 Kendrick Street
Needham, MA 02494
Phone: 781 370-5000
Fax: –
Web: www.ptc.com

CEO: James E. (Jim) Heppelmann
CFO: Andrew D. Miller
HR: –
FYE: September 30
Type: Public

PTC (formerly Parametric Technology Corporation) helps its customers TCB with CAD PLM and the IoT. The company takes care of business by developing software used in computer-aided design manufacturing and mechanical engineering (CAD/CAM/CAE) applications. Its Creo product is used to create 3D computer models for aircraft engines car bodies mobile phones and toys. PTC also offers the Windchill software suite for product lifecycle management which enables collaborative content and process management — from design to supplier sourcing and production — over the Internet. With ThingWorx PTC provide a platform for developing applications for the Internet of Things (IoT).

	Annual Growth	09/11	09/12	09/13	09/14	09/15
Sales ($ mil.)	1.8%	1,166.9	1,255.7	1,293.5	1,357.0	1,255.2
Net income ($ mil.)	(13.6%)	85.4	(35.4)	143.8	160.2	47.6
Market value ($ mil.)	19.9%	1,749.4	2,476.2	3,237.2	4,197.2	3,610.3
Employees	(0.6%)	6,122	5,897	6,000	6,444	5,982

PTC THERAPEUTICS INC

NMS: PTCT

100 Corporate Court
South Plainfield, NJ 07080
Phone: 908 222-7000
Fax: –
Web: www.ptcbio.com

CEO: –
CFO: Shane Kovacs
HR: Martin (Marti) Rexroad
FYE: December 31
Type: Public

PTC Therapeutics has some real GEMS in its pipeline. The company uses a proprietary technology called GEMS to screen for small molecules that modulate post-transcriptional control mechanisms which regulate protein synthesis and thereby offer potential control over certain diseases. PTC is targeting these mechanisms to develop oral drugs designed to treat various genetic disorders infectious diseases and cancers. Lead drug candidate ataluren is in later-stage clinical trials for Duchenne muscular dystrophy and cystic fibrosis. Candidates in earlier stages of development address spinal muscular atrophy chemo-resistant cancers HIV and Duchenne muscular dystrophy. In 2013 went public.

	Annual Growth	12/10	12/11	12/12	12/13	12/14
Sales ($ mil.)	–	0.0	105.4	33.9	34.7	25.2
Net income ($ mil.)	–	0.0	30.9	(26.2)	(51.6)	(93.8)
Market value ($ mil.)	–	0.0	–	–	558.3	1,703.1
Employees	23.3%	–	–	127	137	193

PUBLIC BROADCASTING SERVICE

2100 CRYSTAL DR STE 100
ARLINGTON, VA 222023784
Phone: 703-739-5000
Fax: –
Web: www.pbs.org

CEO: Paula A. Kerger
CFO: Barbara L. Landes
HR: Carole Dickert-scherr
FYE: June 30
Type: Private

You might say these shows get a lot of public support. Public Broadcasting Service (PBS) is a non-profit organization that provides educational and public interest programming to more than 350 member public TV stations in the US. In addition to such programs as NOVA This Old House and Downton Abbey it provides related services such as distribution fundraising support and technology development. PBS gets its revenue from underwriting membership dues federal funding (including grants from the not-for-profit Corporation for Public Broadcasting) royalties license fees and product sales. The organization was founded in 1969 to provide cultural and educational programming.

	Annual Growth	06/06	06/07	06/08	06/09	06/10
Sales ($ mil.)	–	–	–	0.0	502.6	505.6
Net income ($ mil.)	4045.9%	–	–	0.0	(80.6)	28.2
Market value ($ mil.)	–	–	–	–	–	–
Employees	–	–	–	–	–	507

PUBLIC COMMUNICATIONS SERVICES INC.

11859 WILSHIRE BLVD # 600
LOS ANGELES, CA 90025-6621
Phone: 310-231-1000
Fax: –
Web: www.teampcs.com

CEO: –
CFO: –
HR: –
FYE: December 31
Type: Private

Public Communications Services (PCS) designs and installs inmate telephone systems for state federal and county correctional facilities across the US. Its systems feature collect pre-paid and debit calling as well as automated call processing and security features like blocking of certain phone numbers. Clients can also use the company's proprietary systems management software called SOPHIA to run reports on inmate usage and to monitor and record conversations. Customers include the Ventura County California Sheriff's Department and the Federal Bureau of Prisons.

	Annual Growth	12/02	12/03	12/04	12/07	12/08
Sales ($ mil.)	10.1%	–	49.2	34.7	80.5	79.7
Net income ($ mil.)	21.2%	–	1.8	2.8	3.8	4.8
Market value ($ mil.)	–	–	–	–	–	–
Employees	–	–	–	–	–	150

PUBLIC HEALTH SOLUTIONS

40 WORTH ST FL 5
NEW YORK, NY 100132955
Phone: 646-619-6400
Fax: –
Web: www.healthsolutions.org

CEO: Ellen Rautenberg
CFO: –
HR: –
FYE: December 31
Type: Private

Public Heath Solutions (formerly Medical and Health Research Association of New York City) is here to help. Public Health Solutions (PHS) is a not-for-profit organization that works with the NYC Department of Health to create and administer projects aimed at providing better healthcare to the city's low-income at-risk population. It helps about 200000 people a year with studies like the Human Papillomavirus Screening Project and others looking at disease awareness and prevention in minority groups. Services include women's and children's health HIV/AIDS health care smoking cessation counseling and access to health care. The organization was founded in 1957 to conduct health research projects.

	Annual Growth	12/03	12/04	12/05	12/06	12/07
Sales ($ mil.)	(55.3%)	–	–	1,130.8	214.2	225.6
Net income ($ mil.)	2019.1%	–	–	0.0	(2.1)	7.4
Market value ($ mil.)	–	–	–	–	–	–
Employees	–	–	–	–	–	650

PUBLIC SERVICE COMPANY OF NEW HAMPSHIRE

780 N. Commercial St.
Manchester NH 03101-1134
Phone: 603-669-4000
Fax: 603-634-2597
Web: www.psnh.com

CEO: Leon J Olivier
CFO: James J Judge
HR: Bonnie Kurylo
FYE: December 31
Type: Subsidiary

The public service that Public Service Company of New Hampshire (PSNH) provides is supplying electricity across the Granite State. The company provides electric utility services to about 500000 homes and businesses in a 5630-sq.-mi. area that encompasses more than 210 New Hampshire communities. Although the Northeast Utilities subsidiary owns three fossil-fueled and nine hydroelectric power plants that generate more than 1110 MW of capacity for transition and default energy services it also has contracts to purchase power and buy it in the open market.

PUBLIC SERVICE COMPANY OF OKLAHOMA

NBB: PSOK

1 Riverside Plaza
Columbus, OH 43215-2373
Phone: 614 716-1000
Fax: –
Web: www.aep.com

CEO: Nicholas K Akins
CFO: Brian X Tierney
HR: –
FYE: December 31
Type: Public

Where the wavin' wheat can sure smell sweet Public Service Company of Oklahoma helps its customers to beat the heat. The utility serves approximately 540000 homes and businesses in eastern and southwestern Oklahoma. The American Electric Power (AEP) subsidiary operates more than 22080 miles of electric transmission and distribution lines in eastern and southwestern Oklahoma. The utility also has about 4230 MW of capacity from interests in fossil-fueled power plants and it markets wholesale electricity to other utilities and energy companies in the region. it also has wind energy assets.

	Annual Growth	12/10	12/11	12/12	12/13	12/14
Sales ($ mil.)	1.5%	1,273.7	1,363.4	1,232.9	1,295.5	1,351.6
Net income ($ mil.)	4.5%	72.8	124.6	114.1	97.8	86.9
Market value ($ mil.)	–	–	–	–	–	–
Employees	(50.4%)	18,712	1,131	1,127	1,148	1,133

PUBLIC SERVICE ELECTRIC AND GAS COMPANY

80 Park Plaza	CEO: Ralph Izzo
Newark NJ 07101-0570	CFO: Caroline Dorsa
Phone: 973-430-7000	HR: –
Fax: 973-623-5389	FYE: December 31
Web: www.pseg.com	Type: Subsidiary

Public Service Electric and Gas (PSE&G) serves up gas and electricity in the Garden State. PSE&G is New Jersey's largest utility serving the majority of the state's population. The company provides regulated electricity and natural gas transmission and distribution services to residential commercial and industrial customers in New Jersey's deregulated energy market. PSE&G a subsidiary of Public Service Enterprise Group also acts as a supplier of last resort for retail customers who don't choose an alternate supplier. The company has 2.2 million electric customers and 1.8 million gas customers in more than 300 cities towns and suburbs.

PUBLIC SERVICE ENTERPRISE GROUP INC.   NYS: PEG

80 Park Plaza, P.O. Box 1171	CEO: Ralph Izzo
Newark, NJ 07101-1171	CFO: Caroline Dorsa
Phone: 973 430-7000	HR: –
Fax: –	FYE: December 31
Web: www.pseg.com	Type: Public

In the Garden State Public Service Enterprise Group's (PSEG) diversified business model has it smelling like a rose. Regulated subsidiary Public Service Electric and Gas (PSE&G) transmits and distributes electricity to 2.2 million customers and natural gas to 1.8 million customers in New Jersey. Nonregulated subsidiary PSEG Power operates PSEG's generating plants. PSEG Power's 13146-MW generating capacity comes mostly from nuclear and fossil-fueled plants in the US Northeast and Mid-Atlantic regions. The company's total generating output in 2014 was 54000 GWh. Other operations (under PSEG Energy Holdings) include energy infrastructure investments solar and other renewable plant development.

	Annual Growth	12/10	12/11	12/12	12/13	12/14
Sales ($ mil.)	(2.0%)	11,793.0	11,079.0	9,781.0	9,968.0	10,886.0
Net income ($ mil.)	(0.7%)	1,564.0	1,503.0	1,275.0	1,243.0	1,518.0
Market value ($ mil.)	6.8%	16,090.7	16,697.7	15,478.6	16,207.0	20,946.7
Employees	6.2%	9,965	9,784	9,798	9,887	12,689

PUBLIC STORAGE   NYS: PSA

701 Western Avenue	CEO: Ronald L. Havner
Glendale, CA 91201-2349	CFO: John Reyes
Phone: 818 244-8080	HR: Candice N. Krol
Fax: 818 244-0581	FYE: December 31
Web: www.publicstorage.com	Type: Public

If the attic or garage are packed Public Storage can help. The real estate investment trust (REIT) is one of the largest self-storage companies in the US. It operates more than 2250 storage facilities comprising some 146 million sq. ft. of storage space in the US and more than 190 facilities in Europe (through its Shurgard Europe affiliate). The firm's self-storage properties located in densely populated areas generate more than 90% of the company's sales. Public Storage which was founded in 1980 also rents trucks and sells moving supplies such as locks boxes and packing supplies. It also owns about 42% of publicly traded PS Business Parks an office building REIT.

	Annual Growth	12/10	12/11	12/12	12/13	12/14
Sales ($ mil.)	7.5%	1,646.7	1,752.1	1,826.7	1,981.7	2,195.4
Net income ($ mil.)	14.2%	672.0	823.8	939.3	1,052.5	1,144.2
Market value ($ mil.)	16.2%	17,489.4	23,187.0	24,997.7	25,956.5	31,876.6
Employees	2.0%	4,900	5,000	5,000	5,200	5,300

PUBLIC UTILITIES BOARD

1425 ROBINHOOD ST	CEO: John C Bruciak
BROWNSVILLE, TX 785214230	CFO: Leandro G Garcia
Phone: 956-350-8819	HR: –
Fax: –	FYE: September 30
Web: www.brownsville-pub.com	Type: Private

This PUB has no beer. Brownsville Public Utilities Board (Brownsville PUB) is a municipally-owned utility company providing electric water and wastewater services to residential and commercial customers in Brownsville Texas. Brownsville PUB serves 46000 with electric service and 47000 with water and wastewater service. The utility's two water treatment plants have the capacity to provide 40 million gallons of treated water per day. It gets its water supply from the Rio Grande. The utility's wastewater system has 174 lift stations and two treatment plants.

	Annual Growth	09/04	09/05	09/06	09/08	09/09
Sales ($ mil.)	–	–	–	(421.0)	209.0	164.0
Net income ($ mil.)	2707.7%	–	–	0.0	34.7	10.3
Market value ($ mil.)	–	–	–	–	–	–
Employees	–	–	–	–	–	482

PUBLIC UTILITY DISTRICT NO. 1 OF CHELAN COUNTY WASHINGTON

327 N. Wenatchee Ave.	CEO: –
Wenatchee WA 98801	CFO: –
Phone: 509-663-8121	HR: Beverly Freeman
Fax: 509-661-8126	FYE: December 31
Web: www.chelanpud.org	Type: Government-owned

It's Number One! Public Utility District No. 1 of Chelan County Washington (Chelan County PUD) provides power and water to residents of the county located in the middle of the Evergreen State. The utility operates three hydroelectric generation facilities on or near the Columbia River that have a combined capacity of almost 2000 MW. About 30% of the district's electricity goes to its more than 48000 residential commercial and industrial customers; the rest is sold wholesale to other utilities operating in the northwestern US. Chelan County PUD also provides water and wastewater services to about 5900 customers. The company's major power purchasers serve 7 million homes and businesses in the Northwest.

PUBLIC UTILITY DISTRICT NO. 1 OF CLARK COUNTY

1200 Fort Vancouver Way	CEO: Wayne Nelson
Vancouver WA 98663	CFO: –
Phone: 360-992-3000	HR: –
Fax: 360-992-3204	FYE: December 31
Web: www.clarkpublicutilities.com	Type: Government-owned

There are no "we're No 1" signs waving at this publicly minded company's head office. Public Utility District No. 1 of Clark County (Clark Public Utilities) provides utility services to residents and businesses in Clark County Washington. Clark Public Utilities transmits and distributes electricity to more than 184100 customers; the company operates a 250-MW gas-fired power plant but purchases the bulk of its power from the Bonneville Power Administration. Clark Public Utilities also distributes water to more than 30640 customers and collects and treats wastewater for the City of La Center Washington.

PUBLIC UTILITY DISTRICT NO. 1 OF SNOHOMISH COUNTY WASHING

2320 California St.	CEO: –
Everett WA 98201	CFO: –
Phone: 425-783-1000	HR: –
Fax: 425-783-8675	FYE: December 31
Web: www.snopud.com	Type: Government-owned

Keeping its customers satisfied is priority No. 1 at Public Utility District No. 1 of Snohomish County Washington (Snohomish County PUD) which distributes electricity to about 320230 commercial industrial and residential customers in Washington State. The utility the largest PUD in the state with a 2200 sq. ml. service area purchases most of its power supply from third parties (Bonneville Power Administration and other producers. It operates hydroelectric and fossil-fueled power plants and participates in wholesale power transactions to balance its supply load. Snohomish County PUD also serves about 20100 water utility customers in a 205 sq. ml. service territory via more than 380 miles of pipe.

PUBLIC UTILITY DISTRICT NO. 2 OF GRANT COUNTY WASHINGTON

30 C St. SW	CEO: –
Ephrata WA 98823	CFO: –
Phone: 509-754-0500	HR: –
Fax: 509-754-5013	FYE: December 31
Web: www.gcpud.org	Type: Government-owned

Utilitarian sounding Public Utility District No. 2 of Grant County Washington probably used up its initial budget before it could hire a team of branding and identity consultants. But its dour name does not stop the power provider (commonly referred to as Grant County PUD) from operating two hydroelectric power plants on the Columbia River (the Priest Rapids and Wanapum dams with 2000 MW of generating capacity) and distributing electricity to the 46000 retail customers in Washington's Grant County. The district also sells excess power to twelve Pacific Northwest utilities and is developing a residential fiber-optic data network (with 6000 end-users at the end of 2010).

PUBLICIS & HAL RINEY

2001 The Embarcadero	CEO: Kristi Vandenbosch
San Francisco CA 94133	CFO: Lyn Mueqqe
Phone: 415-293-2001	HR: –
Fax: 415-293-2619	FYE: December 31
Web: www.hrp.com	Type: Subsidiary

This Bay Area firm brings together Hollywood style and Madison Avenue savvy. Publicis & Hal Riney is a leading creative advertising agencies in the US known for its visually stunning and sometimes edgy campaigns. It has provided creative development and campaign planning services for such clients as 24 Hour Fitness Jamba Juice SanDisk and Sprint. Established by celebrated ad man Hal Riney in 1977 it was acquired by Paris-based advertising and media services conglomerate Publicis Groupe in 1998. It operates today as the flagship San Francisco outpost of Publicis Worldwide.

PUBLICIS MODEM

85 Tenth Ave. 3rd Floor	CEO: –
New York NY 10011	CFO: –
Phone: 212-336-3300	HR: –
Fax: +44-1754-494-201	FYE: December 31
Web: www.viatel.com	Type: Subsidiary

This modem can connect your business to more than just the Internet. Previously known as Modem Media Publicis Modem is a leading digital and direct marketing agency that provides Web site and intranet development creative development for online advertising campaigns and management of e-mail marketing strategies. It offers consulting and planning services aimed at improving customer services and brand loyalty. Publicis Modem has served such clients as General Motors IBM and Sprint. It operates through 40 offices worldwide. The company is a unit of Digitas which itself is owned by French advertising conglomerate Publicis. Publicis changed the company's name to Publicis Modem in mid-2007.

PUBLISHERS CLEARING HOUSE LLC

382 Channel Dr.	CEO: Andrew C Goldberg
Port Washington NY 11050	CFO: –
Phone: 516-883-5432	HR: –
Fax: 516-883-5769	FYE: December 31
Web: www.pch.com	Type: Private

If your doorbell rings unexpectedly it's probably just your neighbor stopping by for a chat. But it could be the Publishers Clearing House (PCH) Prize Patrol letting you know that you've won $10 million. PCH is one of the world's largest direct marketing organizations. Once known primarily for its magazines (and PCH giveaways) the company now makes most of its money from direct mail offerings for household items personal care products entertainment collectibles and food items. More than 40% of the company's profits go to charities. PCH was founded in 1953 by Harold and LuEsther Mertz and their daughter Joyce Mertz-Gilmore. It is still owned largely by foundations established by the Mertz family.

PUBLIX SUPER MARKETS, INC.

NBB: PUSH

3300 Publix Corporate Parkway	CEO: Charles H. (Charlie) Jenkins
Lakeland, FL 33811	CFO: David P. Phillips
Phone: 863 688-1188	HR: –
Fax: –	FYE: December 27
Web: www.publix.com	Type: Public

Publix Super Markets tops the list of privately owned grocery operators in the US. By emphasizing service and a family-friendly image over price Publix has outgrown and outperformed its regional rivals. More than two-thirds of its 1095 stores are in Florida but it also operates in Alabama Georgia South Carolina Tennessee and North Carolina (a new market for the company). Publix makes some of its own bakery deli dairy goods and fresh prepared foods at its own manufacturing plants in Florida and Georgia. Also many stores house pharmacies and banks. Founder George Jenkins began offering stock to Publix employees in 1930. Employees own about 31% of Publix which is still run by the Jenkins family.

	Annual Growth	12/10	12/11	12/12	12/13	12/14
Sales ($ mil.)	5.0%	25,328.1	27,178.8	27,706.8	29,147.5	30,802.5
Net income ($ mil.)	6.7%	1,338.1	1,492.0	1,552.3	1,654.0	1,735.3
Market value ($ mil.)	(1.2%)	12,004.3	12,004.3	12,004.3	12,004.3	11,423.5
Employees	4.3%	148,000	152,000	158,000	166,000	175,000

PUERTO RICO ELECTRIC POWER AUTHORITY

Avenida Ponce de Leon 17 1/2
Santurce PR 00909
Phone: 787-289-3434
Fax: 787-289-4120
Web: www.prepa.com

CEO: –
CFO: –
HR: –
FYE: June 30
Type: Government-owned

Puerto Rico Electric Power Authority (PREPA) is prepared to serve an entire island nation. The government-owned utility is the sole electricity distributor for Puerto Rico where it serves more than 1.4 million residential and business customers. PREPA owns five primarily fossil-fueled power plants that with private cogenerators and purchased power give it nearly 5840 MW of generating capacity and it has about 33900 miles of transmission and distribution lines. In order to provide cheaper options for power production the Puerto Rican government has allowed independent power producers to build cogeneration plants on the island to sell power to PREPA.

PUGET ENERGY INC.

10885 NE 4th St. Ste. 1200
Bellevue WA 98004-5591
Phone: 425-454-6363
Fax: 425-424-6537
Web: www.pugetenergy.com

CEO: Kimberly J Harris
CFO: Daniel A Doyle
HR: –
FYE: December 31
Type: Private

A sound investment Puget Energy is the holding company for one of Washington State's largest utilities Puget Sound Energy. The utility provides electricity to almost 1.1 million customers and natural gas to almost 760900 customers in 11 counties in western Washington. Puget Sound Energy owns fossil-fueled and hydroelectric plants as well as wind farms with a cumulative total of 4707 MW of capacity. It is one of the largest wind energy producers in the US with 430 MW of capacity. The utility has more than 2600 miles of power transmission lines and 20500 miles of distribution lines. Puget Sound Energy also has about 12000 miles of gas mains and about 13000 miles of gas service lines.

PUGET SOUND BLOOD CENTER & PROGRAM

921 TERRY AVE
SEATTLE, WA 981041239
Phone: 206-292-6500
Fax: –
Web: www.psbc.org

CEO: James P Aubuchon
CFO: Bob Gleason
HR: –
FYE: June 30
Type: Private

Residents of the Emerald City can go here to give red. Bloodworks Northwest (formerly Puget Sound Blood Center) is a not-for-profit blood and tissue bank serving nearly 90 hospitals and clinics in the Pacific Northwest. The blood center collects and processes donated blood through about a dozen donation centers and several mobile units; it also registers bone marrow donors provides testing and training services to patients with hemophilia and collects cord blood for use in stem cell transplantation. Bloodworks Northwest Research Institute conducts research on improving transfusion and transplantation medicine. The organization was formed in 1944.

	Annual Growth	06/09	06/10	06/11	06/12	06/13
Sales ($ mil.)	0.5%	–	150.0	164.6	150.1	152.4
Net income ($ mil.)	–	–	–	9.9	(1.6)	(2.4)
Market value ($ mil.)	–	–	–	–	–	–
Employees	–	–	–	–	–	750

PULASKI FINANCIAL CORP

NMS: PULB

12300 Olive Boulevard
St. Louis, MO 63141-6434
Phone: 314 878-2210
Fax: –
Web: www.pulaskibank.com

CEO: Gary W Douglass
CFO: Paul J Milano
HR: –
FYE: September 30
Type: Public

Community-oriented banking is the push at Pulaski. Pulaski Financial is the holding company for Pulaski Bank which provides financial services to residents and businesses from about a dozen branches throughout the St. Louis and Kansas City metropolitan areas. The bank offers standard deposit products including checking and savings accounts NOW accounts and money market accounts. Pulaski's loan portfolio includes primarily commercial and residential mortgages as well as home equity and construction loans. Through subsidiaries the bank offers title insurance annuities and insurance and fixed-income investment and trading. Illinois-based First Busey Corporation holder of Busey Bank agreed to buy Pulaski for nearly $211 million in late 2015.

	Annual Growth	09/11	09/12	09/13	09/14	09/15
Assets ($ mil.)	3.8%	1,309.2	1,347.5	1,275.9	1,380.1	1,521.7
Net income ($ mil.)	15.0%	8.1	9.8	9.8	11.0	14.1
Market value ($ mil.)	19.9%	77.4	97.5	121.9	136.0	160.2
Employees	5.6%	410	416	454	441	509

PULSE ELECTRONICS CORP

NBB: PULS

12220 World Trade Drive
San Diego, CA 92128
Phone: 858 674-8100
Fax: –
Web: www.pulseelectronics.com

CEO: Mark C J Twaalfhoven
CFO: Michael C Bond
HR: –
FYE: December 27
Type: Public

Pulse Electronics (formerly Technitrol) pulses with the desire to control electronic impulses. The company makes a variety of electronic components used in network power and wireless devices. Network products include passive magnetic components including chokes filters transformers and splitters. Power components include current and voltage sensors ignition coils power transformers and magnetic devices. Its wireless devices are primarily antennas and mounting devices for handsets. Pulse Electronics has manufacturing facilities in China and the US. The company gets around 85% of its sales from outside the US.

	Annual Growth	12/09	12/10	12/11	12/12	12/13
Sales ($ mil.)	(2.8%)	398.8	432.5	369.3	373.2	355.7
Net income ($ mil.)	–	(193.2)	(38.4)	(53.4)	(32.0)	(27.1)
Market value ($ mil.)	(9.9%)	34.0	42.3	22.3	2.2	22.4
Employees	(15.3%)	19,400	16,100	14,000	12,000	10,000

PULSE NETWORK LLC

1301 McKinney Ste. 2500
Houston TX 77010
Phone: 832-214-0100
Fax: 425-519-5999
Web: www.bsquare.com

CEO: Stan Paur
CFO: –
HR: –
FYE: November 30
Type: Subsidiary

If money is the lifeblood of the US economy are ATMs the pulse? PULSE thinks so. The company operates a network of more than 265000 PULSE-branded ATMs and millions point-of-sale (POS) terminals in all 50 states. PULSE manages the network's electronic switching but the terminals are installed and managed by the more than 4500 banks thrifts and credit unions that participate in the network. The company also invests heavily in electronic funds transfer (EFT) research. PULSE is a business unit of Discover Financial Services which acquired the company in early 2005.

PULTEGROUP, INC.

NYS: PHM

3350 Peachtree Road NE, Suite 150
Atlanta, GA 30326
Phone: 404 978-6400
Fax: –
Web: www.pultegroupinc.com

CEO: Richard J. Dugas
CFO: Robert T. (Bob) O'Shaughnessy
HR: James R. (Jim) Ellinghausen
FYE: December 31
Type: Public

PulteGroup pulls its weight in providing homes for American families. Pulte-Group targets a cross-section of home buyers nationwide by buying land to build single-family houses duplexes townhouses and condominiums. Its Centex brand is marketed to entry-level buyers while Pulte Homes aims to capture customers looking to trade up. PulteGroup also builds Del Webb retiree communities mostly in Sun Belt locales for the growing number of buyers in the 55-plus age range. The company sells its homes in some 50 markets across more than 25 states. In 2014 its homes sold for an average price of $329000. The company became one of the top homebuilders in the US when it merged with rival Centex Homes in 2009.

	Annual Growth	12/11	12/12	12/13	12/14	12/15
Sales ($ mil.)	9.7%	4,136.7	4,820.0	5,679.6	5,822.4	5,982.0
Net income ($ mil.)	–	(210.4)	206.1	2,620.1	474.3	494.1
Market value ($ mil.)	29.6%	2,203.1	6,340.5	7,112.2	7,492.7	6,221.8
Employees	6.1%	3,579	3,634	3,843	4,149	4,542

PURADYN FILTER TECHNOLOGIES INC

NBB: PFTI

2017 High Ridge Road
Boynton Beach, FL 33426
Phone: 561 547-9499
Fax: –
Web: www.puradyn.com

CEO: Joseph V Vittoria
CFO: –
HR: –
FYE: December 31
Type: Public

Check your oil? Puradyn Filter Technologies would like to. The company has developed a bypass oil filtration system that can be used in internal combustion engines and pieces of hydraulic equipment that rely on lubricating oil. The Puradyn system works in conjunction with a standard oil filter to remove solids as small as a micron (1/39 millionth of an inch) along with liquid and gaseous contaminants. Puradyn markets its filtration systems worldwide; target customers include OEMs commercial trucking fleets and operators of construction machinery. Puradyn has not been profitable however and the company's auditors have questioned whether it can stay in business.

	Annual Growth	12/10	12/11	12/12	12/13	12/14
Sales ($ mil.)	0.0%	3.1	2.7	2.6	2.5	3.1
Net income ($ mil.)	–	(1.6)	(1.6)	(2.2)	(1.3)	(1.2)
Market value ($ mil.)	(2.2%)	11.7	7.3	6.7	6.9	10.7
Employees	(2.2%)	23	22	21	22	21

PURDUE PHARMA L.P.

1 Stamford Forum 201 Tresser Blvd.
Stamford CT 06901-3431
Phone: 203-588-8000
Fax: 203-588-8850
Web: www.purduepharma.com

CEO: Mark Timney
CFO: Edward B Mahony
HR: –
FYE: December 31
Type: Private

Purdue Pharma helps bring patients relief from pain. The company specializes in developing manufacturing and marketing prescription and over-the-counter medicines and healthcare products which include sustained-release and long-acting treatments for chronic and severe pain. Purdue has an exclusive US licensing and co-promotion agreement with Labopharm Inc. of Laval Canada for Ryzolt (tramadol HCl extended-release tablets) an extended release formulation of tramadol. Its other opioid drugs for pain relief include controlled-release analgesic OxyContin (a version of oxycodone) and morphine drug MS Contin.

PURE BIOSCIENCE INC

NBB: PURE

1725 Gillespie Way
El Cajon, CA 92020
Phone: 619 596-8600
Fax: 619 596-8790
Web: www.purebio.com

CEO: Henry R Lambert
CFO: Mark Elliott
HR: –
FYE: July 31
Type: Public

PURE Bioscience is all about killing what's on the surface. The company makes and markets a patented low-toxicity disinfectant (Axenohl in its concentrated form Axen Axen30 or Axen50 in diluted form) approved for use in hospitals restaurants and schools among other commercial and industrial locations. PURE's consumer sanitation products for home use are sold under the PureGreen 24 label. The company is also working to develop consumer products and drug treatments using the disinfectant's base compound silver dihydrogen citrate which it also sells as a product ingredient to other manufacturers. PURE Bioscience's products are marketed in countries around the globe.

	Annual Growth	07/11	07/12	07/13	07/14	07/15
Sales ($ mil.)	11.9%	0.5	0.8	0.8	0.6	0.7
Net income ($ mil.)	–	(8.3)	(8.9)	(7.7)	(11.1)	(7.6)
Market value ($ mil.)	(8.9%)	38.1	15.9	18.8	41.9	26.2
Employees	(18.6%)	25	23	13	12	11

PURE CYCLE CORP.

NAS: PCYO

34501 E. Quincy Avenue, Bldg. 34, Box 10
Watkins, CO 80137
Phone: 303 292-3456
Fax: –
Web: www.purecyclewater.com

CEO: Mark W Harding
CFO: Mark W Harding
HR: –
FYE: August 31
Type: Public

Struggling to survive in the barren waste without a trace of water is no longer the fate of inhabitants of the Lowry Range thanks to Pure Cycle. The water utility has the exclusive right to provide water and wastewater services to about 24000 acres of the Lowry Range near Denver. Pure Cycle generates revenues from three sources: water and wastewater fees; construction fees; and monthly service fees. In 2009 it served 247 single-family water connections and 157 wastewater connections in the southeastern Denver area. It also has 60000 acre-feet of water rights in the Arkansas River basin in Southern Colorado. In 2010 Pure Cycle acquired the 931-acre Sky Ranch Property near Denver for $7 million.

	Annual Growth	08/11	08/12	08/13	08/14	08/15
Sales ($ mil.)	69.4%	0.3	0.3	1.9	3.1	2.3
Net income ($ mil.)	–	(6.0)	(17.4)	(4.2)	(0.3)	(23.1)
Market value ($ mil.)	14.0%	71.2	48.1	125.1	156.8	120.3
Employees	8.8%	5	4	5	7	7

PURPLE COMMUNICATIONS INC.

PINK SHEETS: PRPL

773 San Marin Dr. Ste. 2210
Novato CA 94945
Phone: 415-408-2300
Fax: 415-408-2301
Web: www.purple.us

CEO: –
CFO: –
HR: Cindy Dobrinsky
FYE: December 31
Type: Public

Purple Communications (formerly GoAmerica) provides a colorful alternative to traditional phone services for the hearing impaired. It offers telecommunications relay services such as text relay video relay and Internet Protocol text relay whereby hard of hearing subscribers can video chat send and receive text telephone messages faxes and e-mail over computers or wireless devices. Purple Communications maintains 15 call centers in the US to facilitate the calls. The company also offers on-site live interpreting services in a dozen US cities and via video across the country. Clearlake Capital Group owns nearly all of the company's stock.

PUTNAM INVESTMENTS LLC

1 Post Office Sq.
Boston MA 02109
Phone: 617-292-1000
Fax: 408-436-4699
Web: www.onetouch.com

CEO: –
CFO: Clare Richer
HR: –
FYE: December 31
Type: Subsidiary

One of the world's largest mutual fund administrators Putnam (aka Putnam Investments) provides investment management for institutional and individual customers offering around 80 mutual funds as well as 401(k) plans and IRAs. It has agreements with Allstate and The Hartford to sell variable annuities. Putnam offers its products through independent brokers dealers financial planners banks and retirement plans. Founded in 1937 Putnam has more than $110 billion of assets under management in some 5 million shareholder accounts. Putnam is a subsidiary of insurer Great-West Lifeco (itself a subsidiary of Power Corporation of Canada) which bought Putnam from Marsh & McLennan for nearly $1 billion in 2007.

PVH CORP

NYS: PVH

200 Madison Avenue
New York, NY 10016
Phone: 212 381-3500
Fax: –
Web: www.pvh.com

CEO: Emanuel (Manny) Chirico
CFO: Michael A Shaffer
HR: David F. (Dave) Kozel
FYE: February 01
Type: Public

PVH has the buttoned-up look covered. A top global apparel player it is the world's largest dress shirt and neckwear company. PVH owns and globally markets lifestyle brands Calvin Klein and Tommy Hilfiger. Its closet also overflows with clothing accessories and footwear for men women and children. PVH owns Heritage Brands which include Van Heusen IZOD ARROW and Bass. Private-label and licensed brands such as DKNY Kenneth Cole New York and MICHAEL Michael Kors round out its wardrobe. PVH generates sales from multiple channels: more than 1900 company-operated retail stores retailers licensees franchisees distributors who resell and royalty and advertising fees.

	Annual Growth	01/11	01/12*	02/13	02/14	02/15
Sales ($ mil.)	15.5%	4,636.8	5,890.6	6,043.0	8,186.4	8,241.2
Net income ($ mil.)	69.0%	53.8	317.9	433.8	143.5	439.0
Market value ($ mil.)	17.4%	4,789.9	6,328.7	9,592.9	9,973.3	9,097.8
Employees	10.7%	22,700	25,700	28,700	33,200	34,100

*Fiscal year change

PVR PARTNERS LP

NYS: PVR

Three Radnor Corporate Center, Suite 301, 100 Matsonford Road
Radnor, PA 19087
Phone: 610 975-8200
Fax: –

CEO: –
CFO: –
HR: –
FYE: December 31
Type: Public

Penn Virginia Resource Partners (PVR) owns and manages a variety of natural resources including coal reserves and natural gas midstream pipelines and processing plants. It leases mining rights on its properties to third-party mine operators collecting royalties based on the amount of coal produced and the price at which it is sold. Its land contains nearly 900 million tons of proven or probable reserves (mostly low-sulfur bituminous coal). However most of PVR's revenue comes from natural gas processing and collection. The company operates seven processing facilities and more than 4400 miles of pipeline in Oklahoma Pennsylvania and Texas.

	Annual Growth	12/08	12/09	12/10	12/11	12/12
Sales ($ mil.)	3.4%	881.6	656.7	864.1	1,160.0	1,007.8
Net income ($ mil.)	–	104.5	65.2	68.5	97.0	(70.6)
Market value ($ mil.)	22.9%	1,458.6	2,765.8	3,633.0	3,275.1	3,332.9
Employees	18.1%	157	167	210	250	305

PVS TECHNOLOGIES INC.

10900 HARPER AVE
DETROIT, MI 482133364
Phone: 313-571-1100
Fax: –
Web: www.pvschemicals.com

CEO: James B. (Jim) Nicholson
CFO: Candee Saferian
HR: –
FYE: December 31
Type: Private

When it comes to making chemicals for wastewater treatment and manufacturing PVS Chemicals is in its element. The company's product list includes sulfuric and hydrochloric acids liquid caustic soda ferric chloride and ammonium thiosulfate. These chemicals are used in applications such as water treatment (wastewater process and municipal) electronics manufacture (including semiconductor etching) gold and copper mining and food and aluminum production. PVS Chemicals' subsidiaries include PVS Technologies (water treatment) Dynecol (transportation analysis treatment and recycling of chemicals) and PVS Nolwood (chemical distribution).

	Annual Growth	12/09	12/10	12/11	12/12	12/13
Sales ($ mil.)	14.8%	–	35.2	45.0	48.3	53.3
Net income ($ mil.)	(17.2%)	–	–	4.1	2.7	2.8
Market value ($ mil.)	–	–	–	–	–	–
Employees	–	–	–	–	–	60

PYCO INDUSTRIES INC.

2901 AVENUE A
LUBBOCK, TX 794042231
Phone: 806-747-3434
Fax: –
Web: www.pycoindustriesinc.com

CEO: Gail Kring
CFO: Anthony Morton
HR: Jake Bentley
FYE: September 30
Type: Private

Ginning up business is the secret to this vegetable oil producer's success. PYCO Industries is said to be the largest cotton seed co-op to serve the southern US. The Texas-based cooperative comprising more than 60-member gins processes cottonseed for a broad market through two cottonseed oil mills. Its cottonseed oil is shipped to food manufacturers and other foodservice customers across the country. The co-op also markets whole cottonseed as well as the by-products of crushing cottonseed such as cottonseed hulls and cottonseed meal for beef and dairy cattle feed. Cottonseed linters another byproduct are used by manufacturers of mattresses and upholstery padding paper and plastics and other products.

	Annual Growth	09/05	09/06	09/12	09/13	09/14
Sales ($ mil.)	(2.9%)	–	234.6	196.3	176.0	184.7
Net income ($ mil.)	41.2%	–	–	11.4	18.7	22.8
Market value ($ mil.)	–	–	–	–	–	–
Employees	–	–	–	–	–	160

PZENA INVESTMENT MANAGEMENT INC

NYS: PZN

320 Park Avenue
New York, NY 10022
Phone: 212 355-1600
Fax: –
Web: www.pzena.com

CEO: Richard S. Pzena
CFO: Gary J. Bachman
HR: –
FYE: December 31
Type: Public

It takes money to make money and Pzena Investment Management has made plenty. The firm serves corporate institutional and high-net-worth individual clients in the US and abroad and has about $21 billion in assets under management. Through a dozen funds Pzena makes long-term investments in domestic and international companies — particularly financial services firms. Pzena also acts as a sub-investment adviser for about two dozen mutual funds and offshore funds. The firm is the sole managing member of its operating company Pzena Investment Management LLC. The employee-owned firm was founded by chairman and CEO Richard Pzena in 1995.

	Annual Growth	12/10	12/11	12/12	12/13	12/14
Sales ($ mil.)	9.8%	77.5	83.0	76.3	95.8	112.5
Net income ($ mil.)	20.7%	3.8	3.4	3.8	6.7	8.1
Market value ($ mil.)	6.5%	484.6	285.5	356.1	775.4	623.8
Employees	3.7%	70	67	70	76	81

Q.E.P. CO., INC.

NBB: QEPC

1001 Broken Sound Parkway N.W., Suite A	CEO: Lewis Gould
Boca Raton, FL 33487	CFO: Mark S Walter
Phone: 561 994-5550	HR: –
Fax: 561 241-2830	FYE: February 28
Web: www.qepcorporate.com	Type: Public

Q.E.P. keeps getting underfoot. The company makes and distributes hardwood flooring and flooring installation tools (including adhesives trowels wet saws and carpet trimmers) for professionals and do-it-yourselfers. It sells more than 7000 flooring and flooring-related products mainly for installing marble carpet ceramic tile and drywall under the QEP Capitol ROBERTS Elastiment and RhinoGrip brands among others. Q.E.P. makes about 25% of its products and acquires the rest from about 200 suppliers. Its customers include retailers and distributors to the home improvement hardware and construction trades primarily in the US. The family-run company was founded by chairman and CEO Lewis Gould in 1979.

	Annual Growth	02/11	02/12	02/13	02/14	02/15
Sales ($ mil.)	5.8%	237.9	261.4	283.7	302.7	297.7
Net income ($ mil.)	(33.4%)	9.4	10.2	8.1	16.1	1.9
Market value ($ mil.)	5.4%	45.8	65.9	50.9	61.1	56.6
Employees	–	–	–	–	–	–

QAD, INC.

NMS: QADA

100 Innovation Place	CEO: Karl F. Lopker
Santa Barbara, CA 93108	CFO: Daniel Lender
Phone: 805 566-6000	HR: Ray Harding
Fax: –	FYE: January 31
Web: www.qad.com	Type: Public

QAD tries to boost manufacturing prowess. The company provides enterprise resource planning and supply chain software used by some 2500 manufacturers in the automotive food and beverage life sciences and high-tech industries among others to streamline their production processes. Its applications automate the management of manufacturing distribution customer relationships and financial applications. QAD is placing increasing emphasis on it cloud-based subscription service. It maintains a large base of customers that deploy QAD software on their own servers. The company which also offers related maintenance and consulting services generates nearly 60% of sales outside North America.

	Annual Growth	01/11	01/12	01/13	01/14	01/15
Sales ($ mil.)	7.6%	220.0	247.3	252.2	266.3	295.1
Net income ($ mil.)	47.8%	2.7	10.8	6.6	6.4	12.9
Market value ($ mil.)	22.5%	155.1	233.8	251.1	328.9	349.7
Employees	5.1%	1,350	1,460	1,540	1,570	1,650

QC HOLDINGS INC

NBB: QCCO

9401 Indian Creek Parkway, Suite 1500	CEO: Darrin J. Andersen
Overland Park, KS 66210	CFO: Douglas E. Nickerson
Phone: 913 234-5000	HR: –
Fax: –	FYE: December 31
Web: www.qcholdings.com	Type: Public

Need cash PDQ? Cue QC. QC Holdings runs about 500 payday loan stores operating mostly as Quik Cash or National Quik Cash but also under about a half-dozen other brands including California Budget Finance Express Check Advance of South Carolina First Payday Loans Nationwide Budget Finance and QC Financial Services. Targeting working-class individuals its stores provide short-term loans ranging from $100 to $500 for a fee typically between 15% to 20% per each $100 of the loan. The company also offers check cashing services title loans and Western Union money orders and transfers. It is active in nearly two dozen states; Missouri California Illinois and Kansas are its largest markets.

	Annual Growth	12/10	12/11	12/12	12/13	12/14
Sales ($ mil.)	(5.0%)	188.1	187.5	180.6	152.0	153.1
Net income ($ mil.)	(18.2%)	11.9	10.2	5.4	(14.0)	5.3
Market value ($ mil.)	(18.6%)	64.8	69.6	56.1	31.0	28.4
Employees	(7.3%)	1,681	1,593	1,563	1,347	1,244

QCR HOLDINGS INC

NMS: QCRH

3551 7th Street	CEO: Larry J. Helling
Moline, IL 61265	CFO: Darrell Rains
Phone: 309 743-7724	HR: –
Fax: –	FYE: December 31
Web: www.qcbt.com	Type: Public

Quad City is muscling in on the community banking scene in the Midwest. QCR Holdings is the holding company for Quad City Bank and Trust Cedar Rapids Bank and Trust Rockford Bank and Trust and First Wisconsin Bank and Trust. Together the banks have about 10 offices serving the Quad City area of Illinois and Iowa as well as the communities of Cedar Rapids Iowa; Rockford Illinois; and Milwaukee. The banks offer traditional deposit products and services and concentrate their lending activities on local businesses: Commercial real estate loans make up nearly half of the loan portfolio; commercial loans and leases make up another third.

	Annual Growth	12/10	12/11	12/12	12/13	12/14
Assets ($ mil.)	8.3%	1,836.6	1,966.6	2,093.7	2,395.0	2,525.0
Net income ($ mil.)	22.7%	6.6	9.7	12.6	14.9	15.0
Market value ($ mil.)	25.7%	56.8	72.4	105.2	135.5	142.0
Employees	4.0%	350	355	356	400	409

QEP RESOURCES INC

NYS: QEP

1050 17th Street, Suite 800	CEO: Charles B. (Chuck) Stanley
Denver, CO 80265	CFO: Richard J. Doleshek
Phone: 303 672-6900	HR: Margo Fiala
Fax: –	FYE: December 31
Web: www.qepres.com	Type: Public

QEP Resources has the resources to conducts exploration and production gas gathering processing and storage and energy trading operations in the Rockies Midcontinent and Southeast regions of the US. Its QEP Energy unit acquires and develops gas and oil properties generates and drills prospects and develops gas reserves (71% in the Northern Region). In 2014 it reported proved reserves of 3.9 trillion cu. ft. of natural gas equivalent. QEP Marketing markets equity and third-party gas and oil owns and operates an underground gas storage reservoir and provides risk-management services.

	Annual Growth	12/10	12/11	12/12	12/13	12/14
Sales ($ mil.)	11.0%	2,246.4	3,159.2	2,349.8	2,935.8	3,414.3
Net income ($ mil.)	24.5%	326.2	267.2	128.3	159.4	784.4
Market value ($ mil.)	(13.6%)	6,368.8	5,139.2	5,309.4	5,376.0	3,546.6
Employees	(1.8%)	823	876	936	1,001	765

QLIK TECHNOLOGIES INC.

NMS: QLIK

150 N. Radnor Chester Road, Suite E220	CEO: Lars Bjork
Radnor, PA 19087	CFO: Tim MacCarrick
Phone: 888 828-9768	HR: –
Fax: –	FYE: December 31
Web: www.qlikview.com	Type: Public

Qlik Technologies (QlikTech) puts important business data just a click away. The company provides its QlikView business intelligence (BI) software that gives clients the tools to search and query business data in a variety of ways; reports are displayed in a visual format that can be explored and analyzed further. QlikTech serves midsized and large enterprises throughout the world; its approximately 34000 customers have included Campbell Soup Company Colonial Life Hertz Kraft Foods the UK National Health Service and QUALCOMM. The company was founded in Sweden in 1993.

	Annual Growth	12/10	12/11	12/12	12/13	12/14
Sales ($ mil.)	25.2%	226.5	320.6	388.5	470.5	556.8
Net income ($ mil.)	–	13.5	9.0	3.8	(10.0)	(24.6)
Market value ($ mil.)	4.5%	2,350.4	2,198.6	1,973.3	2,419.4	2,806.4
Employees	27.1%	780	1,054	1,425	1,721	2,038

QLOGIC CORP.

NMS: QLGC

26650 Aliso Viejo Parkway
Aliso Viejo, CA 92656
Phone: 949 389-6000
Fax: −
Web: www.qlogic.com

CEO: Jean Hu
CFO: Jean Hu
HR: Vina Leite
FYE: March 29
Type: Public

QLogic keeps its customers on a steady diet of Fibre...Channel. The company designs server and storage system networking products including switches adapters and storage routers. QLogic's products are primarily Fibre Channel and Ethernet-based but can also operate as Internet Small Computer System Interface (iSCSI) products or as a combination of technologies. The company also provides controllers for embedded applications. QLogic uses contract manufacturers to build its products which are sold directly to server and workstation manufacturers and through distributors. Customers include Hewlett-Packard (more than a quarter of sales) Dell (17%) and IBM (15%).

	Annual Growth	04/11	04/12*	03/13	03/14	03/15
Sales ($ mil.)	(3.4%)	597.2	558.6	484.5	460.9	520.2
Net income ($ mil.)	(22.3%)	139.1	229.4	73.1	(18.3)	50.6
Market value ($ mil.)	(5.7%)	1,583.9	1,549.0	1,011.8	1,089.4	1,250.3
Employees	(5.2%)	1,147	1,121	1,229	1,044	927

*Fiscal year change

QNB CORP.

NBB: QNBC

15 North Third Street, P.O. Box 9005
Quakertown, PA 18951-9005
Phone: 215 538-5600
Fax: −
Web: www.qnbbank.com

CEO: David W Freeman
CFO: Janice S McCracken Erkes
HR: −
FYE: December 31
Type: Public

QNB Corp. is the holding company for QNB Bank which provides commercial banking services through about 10 branches serving Bucks Lehigh and Montgomery counties in southeastern Pennsylvania. QNB offers standard banking services including checking savings and money market acccounts; IRAs; and CDs. It uses funds from deposits to originate business loans residential mortgages and consumer loans. Commercial loans and mortgages account for more than half of its lending portfolio. Unlike many of its peers QNB Bank does not directly offer trust services or full-service insurance. Through a partnership with Raymond James Financial though it offers wealth management services.

	Annual Growth	12/10	12/11	12/12	12/13	12/14
Assets ($ mil.)	4.8%	809.3	868.8	919.9	932.9	977.1
Net income ($ mil.)	5.7%	7.2	8.9	9.2	8.4	9.0
Market value ($ mil.)	9.3%	66.3	74.0	77.8	83.9	94.5
Employees	1.8%	172	174	182	183	185

QORVO INC

NMS: QRVO

7628 Thorndike Road
Greensboro, NC 27409-9421
Phone: 336 664-1233
Fax: −
Web: www.qorvo.com

CEO: Robert A. (Bob) Bruggeworth
CFO: Steven J. (Steve) Buhaly
HR: −
FYE: March 28
Type: Public

Qorvo thinks it can meet its customers needs in radio frequency (RF) devices with increasing frequency. The result of the early 2015 combination of RF Micro Devices and TriQuint Qorvo develops makes and sells a wide range of RF technologies that enable devices big and small to communicate with each other. Its products are made for mobile devices (from phones to cell towers) infrastructure applications (smart meters and Wi-Fi base stations) and aerospace and defense systems (radar and satellites). Customers include Foxconn and Samsung. Unlike many other chip companies Qorvo operates its own foundry where RF devices can be made to specifications. It has operations in the US Costa Rica Singapore China and Germany.

	Annual Growth	03/11	03/12	03/13	03/14	03/15
Sales ($ mil.)	−	0.0	0.0	964.1	1,148.2	1,711.0
Net income ($ mil.)	−	0.0	0.0	(53.0)	12.6	196.3
Market value ($ mil.)	−	0.0	0.0	−	−	11,817.4
Employees	−	−	−	−	−	6,700

QR ENERGY LP

NYS: QRE

5 Houston Center, 1401 McKinney Street, Suite 2400
Houston, TX 77010
Phone: 713 452-2200
Fax: 713 452-2202
Web: www.qrenergylp.com

CEO: Halbert S Washburn
CFO: −
HR: −
FYE: December 31
Type: Public

QR Energy has the power to make quick profits for its shareholders. The company owns mature land-based oil and natural gas reservoirs in the south central US. Its holdings include total proved reserves of 30 million barrels of oil equivalent about 70% of which is oil and natural gas liquids with options on other similar properties. QR Energy's properties are located in the oil producing regions of Permian Basin (Texas) Ark-La-Tex Mid-Continent (Kansas to Texas including Arkansas and Louisiana) and along the Gulf Coast. Quantum Resource Funds formed the limited partnership in 2010; it receives administrative and operational services from Quantum Resources Management. QR Energy went public in 2010.

	Annual Growth	12/08	12/09	12/10	12/11	12/12
Sales ($ mil.)	−	0.0	0.0	3.0	259.9	372.0
Net income ($ mil.)	−	0.0	0.0	(7.1)	61.1	79.8
Market value ($ mil.)	−	0.0	0.0	1,176.9	1,179.3	969.9
Employees	17.8%	−	−	211	250	293

QST INDUSTRIES INC.

550 W. Adams St. Ste. 200
Chicago IL 60661
Phone: 312-930-9400
Fax: 312-648-0312
Web: www.qst.com

CEO: −
CFO: Jeffrey A Carlevato
HR: Charee Sontep
FYE: December 31
Type: Private

Pockets mean more than pocket change to QST Industries. QST supplies clothing construction components — including pocketing materials elastics linings and interlinings insulations and waistbands — to the apparel industry in about 30 countries worldwide. Its brands include Q-Loop belt loop tape (guards against belt loop fray on blue jeans) Quick-Stretch clear elastics and Ban-Rol waistband fabric. The US Army is a customer. QST also supplies home furnishing fabrics and offers custom printing and die and table cutting. Sam Haber founded QST in 1880 when he began selling trimmings to Chicago tailors and sewers. Haber's descendants including nonagenarian chairman Ely Lionheart still own the company.

QTS REALTY TRUST INC

NYS: QTS

12851 Foster Street
Overland Park, KS 66213
Phone: 913 312-5503
Fax: −
Web: www.qtsdatacenters.com

CEO: Chad L. Williams
CFO: William H. Schafer
HR: −
FYE: December 31
Type: Public

In the world of server farms QTS Realty sows a lot of concrete. The company owns secure office buildings that house data centers — where companies keep their computer equipment. QTS (which stands for Quality Technology Services) owns and operates 10 data centers across seven states totaling 3.8 million sq. ft. It counts almost 900 corporations and government agencies as customers. Organized as a real estate investment trust (REIT) QTS is exempt from paying federal income tax as long as it makes quarterly distributions to shareholders. It went public in 2013 raising $257 million which it will use to pay down debt as well as buy and renovate more data centers.

	Annual Growth	12/10	12/11	12/12	12/13	12/14
Sales ($ mil.)	16.0%	120.2	130.4	145.8	40.5	217.8
Net income ($ mil.)	1.2%	14.4	(0.9)	(9.8)	3.2	15.1
Market value ($ mil.)	36.6%	−	−	−	728.7	995.2
Employees	15.0%	−	−	−	400	460

QUAD/GRAPHICS, INC.   NYS: QUAD

N6I W23044 Harry's Way   CEO: J. Joel Quadracci
Sussex, WI 53089-3995   CFO: John C. Fowler
Phone: 414 566-6000   HR: –
Fax: –   FYE: December 31
Web: www.qg.com   Type: Public

Your mailbox might be filled with Quad/Graphics' handiwork. A leading US printing company Quad/Graphics produces catalogs magazines books direct mail and other commercial materials. The company's services include production design photography binding wrapping and distribution. Quad/Graphics has produced catalogs for Bloomingdale's books for National Geographic and magazines such as Time Inc.'s People. The company operates facilities in about a dozen countries around the world. Quad/Graphics was founded in 1971 by the late Harry Quadracci.

	Annual Growth	12/10	12/11	12/12	12/13	12/14
Sales ($ mil.)	9.4%	3,391.7	4,324.6	4,094.0	4,795.9	4,862.4
Net income ($ mil.)	–	(250.1)	(46.9)	87.4	32.5	18.6
Market value ($ mil.)	(13.6%)	2,017.6	701.2	997.1	1,331.5	1,122.7
Employees	(0.9%)	25,000	24,300	21,400	25,600	24,100

QUAKER CHEMICAL CORPORATION   NYSE: KWR

1 Quaker Park 901 E. Hector St.   CEO: Michael F Barry
Conshohocken PA 19428-2380   CFO: Margaret M Loebl
Phone: 610-832-4000   HR: –
Fax: 610-832-8682   FYE: December 31
Web: www.quakerchem.com   Type: Public

Rolling lubricants like rolled oats have a Quaker as a maker. This Quaker — Quaker Chemical — rolls out specialty chemicals for industrial and manufacturing processes. Its rolling lubricants are used in making rolled aluminum products and hot- and cold-rolled steel products. Quaker Chemical also makes corrosion preventives metal finishing compounds hydraulic fluids and machining grinding and forming compounds. Other products and services include aerospace milling compounds metal and concrete coatings and chemical management services. Quaker Chemical's subsidiaries and joint ventures operate worldwide although it sells primarily to the steel auto and appliance industries in the US and Europe.

QUAKER VALLEY FOODS INC.

2701 RED LION RD   CEO: –
PHILADELPHIA, PA 191141019   CFO: Pat Veasey
Phone: 215-992-0900   HR: Judy Harris
Fax: –   FYE: December 31
Web: www.quakervalleyfoods.com   Type: Private

Quaker Valley Foods (QVF) is known by friends high and low for its take-out fresh and frozen staples. The food distributor makes daily deliveries of meat and other provisions to foodservice customers across the Northeast US. QVF a member of the UNIPRO Foodservice coop offers beef pork poultry frozen seafood imported meats (mutton and goat) cheeses salads and other items from its Philadelphia warehouse. Customers range from wholesalers and jobbers to independent retail and wholesale groceries and major supermarket chains. Its vendors include Hormel Swift Packerland Carolina Turkey Tyson Alpine Lace and Land O' Lakes. QVF was started by two brothers-in-law in 1975 and is led by its founders' sons.

	Annual Growth	01/08	01/09	01/10	01/11*	12/11
Sales ($ mil.)	(87.4%)	–	–	1,546.5	177.3	195.5
Net income ($ mil.)	108686.2%	–	–	0.0	0.4	0.4
Market value ($ mil.)	–	–	–	–	–	–
Employees	–	–	–	–	–	145

*Fiscal year change

QUALCOMM ATHEROS INC.

1700 Technology Dr.   CEO: –
San Jose CA 95110   CFO: –
Phone: 408-773-5200   HR: –
Fax: 408-773-9940   FYE: December 31
Web: www.qca.qualcomm.com   Type: Subsidiary

Qualcomm Atheros (formerly Atheros Communications) builds high-speed connections right through the ether. Its radio-frequency (RF) transceiver chipsets combine features such as a radio power amplifier low-noise amplifier and a media access control processor onto just two or three chips eliminating the need for bulkier components in wireless networking gear. Customers have included Apple Dell Fujitsu HP Hon Hai Microsoft Nintendo and Sony. The fabless chip company was started by faculty members from Stanford and Berkeley. Most of its sales are to customers in Asia principally in Taiwan and China. In 2011 QUALCOMM bought Atheros Communications in a deal valued at around $3 billion and changed its name.

QUALCOMM FLARION TECHNOLOGIES

Bedminster One 135 Route 202/206 South   CEO: Raymond Dolan
Bedminster NJ 07921-2608   CFO: –
Phone: 908-947-7000   HR: –
Fax: 908-947-7090   FYE: December 31
Web: www.qualcomm.com/qft   Type: Subsidiary

QUALCOMM Flarion Technologies (QFT) has a talent for transmission. The makes radio-frequency base stations (RadioRouter) that enable mobile wireless carriers to offer high-speed data services to subscribers. The transmission technology it uses (called Flash-OFDM — orthogonal frequency division multiplexing) was developed by Bell Labs. QFT also designs chipsets for wireless gear as well as wireless network cards that connect PDAs and other devices to broadband networks. Additionally the company licenses its technology to other equipment makers. Flarion was founded in 2000 with initial investment from Bell Labs. The company was acquired by QUALCOMM in 2006.

QUALCOMM, INC.   NMS: QCOM

5775 Morehouse Dr.   CEO: Steven M. (Steve) Mollenkopf
San Diego, CA 92121-1714   CFO: George S. Davis
Phone: 858 587-1121   HR: Daniel L (Dan) Sullivan
Fax: –   FYE: September 27
Web: www.qualcomm.com   Type: Public

Cell phone makers wireless carriers and governments worldwide call on QUALCOMM to engineer a quality conversation. The company pioneered the commercialization of the code-division multiple access (CDMA) technology used in digital wireless communications equipment and satellite ground stations mainly in North America. It generates most of its sales through the development and marketing of semiconductor chips and system software based on CDMA and other technologies. QUALCOMM also licenses technology rights from its large intellectual property portfolio (patents copyrights trade secrets). Smaller segments are focused on wireless communications products and strategic investments in start-ups and other firms.

	Annual Growth	09/11	09/12	09/13	09/14	09/15
Sales ($ mil.)	14.0%	14,957.0	19,121.0	24,866.0	26,487.0	25,281.0
Net income ($ mil.)	5.5%	4,260.0	6,109.0	6,853.0	7,967.0	5,271.0
Market value ($ mil.)	1.4%	76,642.0	95,204.3	102,687.1	114,391.4	81,107.3
Employees	11.7%	21,200	26,600	31,000	31,300	33,000

QUALITY DINING INC.

4220 Edison Lakes Pkwy.
Mishawaka IN 46545
Phone: 574-271-4600
Fax: 574-271-4612
Web: www.qdi.com

CEO: Daniel B Fitzpatrick
CFO: -
HR: -
FYE: October 31
Type: Private

You might say this company sets a high standard for eating out. Quality Dining is a leading multi-concept restaurant operator with about 175 locations in a half dozen states. It is one of the largest franchisees of fast-food giant Burger King operating some 120 quick-service outlets in Indiana and Michigan. The company also taps into the casual dining market with about 50 Chili's Grill & Bar locations franchised from Brinker International. In addition it runs a handful of restaurants under the banners blue20 seafood grill + bar Papa Vino's Italian Kitchen and Spageddies Italian Kitchen. Started in 1981 the company is owned by a management group led by chairman Daniel Fitzpatrick.

QUALITY OIL COMPANY LLC

1540 SILAS CREEK PKWY
WINSTON SALEM, NC 271273705
Phone: 336-722-3441
Fax: -
Web: www.qualityoilnc.com

CEO: -
CFO: -
HR: Christopher Arceneaux
FYE: December 31
Type: Private

With more services than your average oil company Quality Oil helps its customers get fueled up cooled off and well rested. And they can smoke if they want to. The company distributes fuel oil and propane to customers in the Winston-Salem area of North Carolina. Quality Oil provides air conditioning and heating equipment service operates 47 convenience stores (Quality Marts) and about 20 service stations and owns hotels in five southern states. In addition the company operates 60 Quality Plus locations at which drivers can buy cigarettes at discount prices. The company also provides Right-a-Way oil change services at many of its gas stations.

	Annual Growth	12/05	12/06	12/07	12/08	12/09
Sales ($ mil.)	5.4%	-	542.2	619.7	806.4	634.8
Net income ($ mil.)	4.0%	-	-	10.9	27.6	11.8
Market value ($ mil.)	-	-	-	-	-	-
Employees	-	-	-	-	-	1,000

QUALITY DISTRIBUTION INC (FL)

NMS: QLTY

4041 Park Oaks Boulevard, Suite 200
Tampa, FL 33610
Phone: 813 630-5826
Fax: -
Web: www.qualitydistribution.com

CEO: Gary Enzor
CFO: Joseph Troy
HR: -
FYE: December 31
Type: Public

As far as North American bulk chemicals carriers go Quality Distribution is the bulkiest. Through subsidiary Quality Carriers Inc. (QCI) the company operates the largest chemical bulk tank truck network running through the US Canada and Mexico. It transports both liquid and dry bulk chemicals (including plastics) and provides logistics services through about 30 independent affiliates with 90 trucking terminals and three company-operated trucking terminals. Quality Distribution is also the largest provider of intermodal tank container and depot services in North America through subsidiary Boasso America. Key customers include BASF Dow DuPont Exxon Mobil Procter & Gamble and PPG Industries.

	Annual Growth	12/09	12/10	12/11	12/12	12/13
Sales ($ mil.)	10.9%	613.6	686.6	746.0	842.1	929.8
Net income ($ mil.)	-	(180.5)	(7.4)	23.4	50.1	(42.0)
Market value ($ mil.)	34.1%	108.0	247.3	306.0	163.2	349.0
Employees	(1.4%)	810	752	2,741	2,001	765

QUALITY SYSTEMS, INC.

NMS: QSII

18111 Von Karman Avenue, Suite 700
Irvine, CA 92612
Phone: 949 255-2600
Fax: -
Web: www.qsii.com

CEO: Rusty Frantz
CFO: John Stumpf
HR: -
FYE: March 31
Type: Public

Quality Systems can't help doctors' with the legibility of their signatures but it knows how to insure the integrity of their digital records. The company develops data management software for medical and dental practices and a variety of other health care businesses. Its NextGen subsidiary (more than 75% of sales) makes electronic records and practice management software tailored for patient data scheduling billing and claims handling. Its RCM unit focuses on electronic claims submission remittance and payments services. The company's QSI Dental division makes practice management software for dentists. Its Hospital Solutions unit focuses on clinical and financial software for rural hospitals.

	Annual Growth	03/11	03/12	03/13	03/14	03/15
Sales ($ mil.)	8.5%	353.4	429.8	460.2	444.7	490.2
Net income ($ mil.)	(18.4%)	61.6	75.7	42.7	15.7	27.3
Market value ($ mil.)	(33.8%)	5,025.7	2,637.1	1,101.7	1,017.9	963.6
Employees	16.8%	1,579	1,938	2,333	2,697	2,939

QUALITY FOOD CENTERS INC.

10116 NE 8th St.
Bellevue WA 98004
Phone: 425-455-3761
Fax: 425-462-2146
Web: www.qfconline.com

CEO: -
CFO: Paul Lammert
HR: -
FYE: January 31
Type: Subsidiary

If you're sleepless — and hungry — in Seattle consider Quality Food Centers (QFC). The grocery chain operates about 70 stores (most open 24 hours) primarily in the Puget Sound region of Washington (including Seattle) but also including about a half a dozen supermarkets in Portland Oregon. QFC stores offer more than just groceries: Seattle's Best Coffee and Cinnabon serve up goodies at some locations and many stores offer services such as catering video rental in-store banking pharmacies floral departments and film developing. Founded more than 60 years ago QFC is a division of grocery giant Kroger.

QUALSERV CORPORATION

7400 S 28TH ST
FORT SMITH, AR 72908-7800
Phone: 479-646-8386
Fax: -
Web: www.qualservcorp.com

CEO: Larry D Hughes
CFO: Peter Duff
HR: -
FYE: December 31
Type: Private

QualServ serves up quality by providing everything to turn an empty building into a functioning restaurant. The turnkey company brings together everything — from design and construction to millwork equipment furniture and fixtures — for opening a restaurant or a wide variety of other businesses and institutions. QualServ also serves up installation maintenance and repair services. Don't need a complete restaurant? Customers may also order a la carte from QualServ's menu of products and services. QualServ's clientele has included the likes of Chipotle Mexican Grill Extended Stay America Papa John's and Red Robin Gourmet Burgers. QualServ partners with Direct Capital Corporation to offer financing.

	Annual Growth	12/07	12/08	12/09	12/10	12/11
Sales ($ mil.)	(1.0%)	-	-	69.8	68.4	68.4
Net income ($ mil.)	-	-	-	(1.0)	(0.3)	(0.3)
Market value ($ mil.)	-	-	-	-	-	-
Employees	-	-	-	-	-	192

QUALSTAR CORP

NAS: QBAK

31248 Oak Crest Drive Suite #120
Westlake Village, CA 91361
Phone: 805 583-7744
Fax: –
Web: www.qualstar.com; www.n2power.com

CEO: Steven N Bronson
CFO: Louann L Negrete
HR: –
FYE: June 30
Type: Public

People often refer to “tape” when speaking about digital video. But Qualstar means it when it talks about tape especially when storing archival information on tape library systems. The company's products — tape drives and tape library data storage systems — house retrieve and manage large amounts of data in computer networks. Its other business is power supplies that convert AC voltage to DC. Qualstar's systems are compatible with a variety of operating systems and with storage management software from companies such as Symantec. The company which incorporates tape drives and media from Quantum and Sony into its libraries sells mainly to manufacturers and resellers. Two customers account for a combined quarter of revenues.

	Annual Growth	06/11	06/12	06/13	06/14	06/15
Sales ($ mil.)	(8.4%)	18.3	17.1	12.6	10.9	12.9
Net income ($ mil.)	–	(0.7)	(4.1)	(10.4)	(5.6)	(1.3)
Market value ($ mil.)	(10.6%)	22.2	23.3	17.2	16.2	14.2
Employees	(14.2%)	70	68	57	43	38

QUALYS, INC.

NMS: QLYS

1600 Bridge Parkway
Redwood City, CA 94065
Phone: 650 801-6100
Fax: –
Web: www.qualys.com

CEO: Philippe F. Courtot
CFO: Donald C. (Don) McCauley
HR: –
FYE: December 31
Type: Public

Qualys puts a premium on high-grade IT security. Its QualysGuard Cloud Platform is a cloud security and compliance management software suite that automates security weakness detection and network security asset auditing. Qualys also remotely manages the integrity of networks for clients looking to outsource their data security endeavors. QualysGuard is geared toward small midsized and large businesses across a range of industries. The company counts some 7700 customers in more than 100 countries by partnerships with managed service providers and consultants including Accuvant Cognizant Technology Solutions Dell SecureWorks and Wipro. Founded in 1999 it went public in 2012.

	Annual Growth	12/10	12/11	12/12	12/13	12/14
Sales ($ mil.)	19.5%	65.4	76.2	91.4	108.0	133.6
Net income ($ mil.)	144.4%	0.8	2.0	2.3	1.6	30.2
Market value ($ mil.)	59.8%	–	–	496.9	776.4	1,268.2
Employees	8.9%	–	334	359	406	431

QUANEX BUILDING PRODUCTS CORP

NYS: NX

1800 West Loop South, Suite 1500
Houston, TX 77027
Phone: 713 961-4600
Fax: –
Web: www.quanex.com

CEO: William C. (Bill) Griffiths
CFO: Brent L. Korb
HR: Kevin Farrell
FYE: October 31
Type: Public

Quanex Building Products (QBP) makes engineered materials and components for naturally enough OEMs of building products. Its Engineered Products and Aluminum Sheet Products operations serve the new home building and remodeling markets in North America and lesser so in Asia and Europe. QBP produces aluminum flat-rolled products used in exterior home trims screens and gutters. It also churns out window and door components insulating glass spacers solar panel sealants and extruded vinyl and composite framing material for fenestration OEMs. QBP generates around 80% of its total sales in the US.

	Annual Growth	10/11	10/12	10/13	10/14	10/15
Sales ($ mil.)	(6.6%)	848.3	829.0	952.6	595.4	645.5
Net income ($ mil.)	15.4%	9.1	(16.5)	(11.7)	29.2	16.1
Market value ($ mil.)	6.4%	500.9	671.4	603.9	679.9	640.9
Employees	3.6%	2,340	2,228	2,565	2,206	2,693

QUANTA SERVICES, INC.

NYS: PWR

2800 Post Oak Boulevard, Suite 2600
Houston, TX 77056
Phone: 713 629-7600
Fax: –
Web: www.quantaservices.com

CEO: James F. O'Neil
CFO: Derrick A. Jensen
HR: –
FYE: December 31
Type: Public

To quickly quantify Quanta's services: This specialty contractor designs installs repairs and maintains network infrastructure across North America and abroad. The company serves the electric power and the oil and natural gas pipeline industries mainly in the US Canada and Australia. Quanta's other services include outsource management and other specialty work such as installing traffic and light rail control systems directional drilling and constructing wind and solar power facilities. Founded in 1997 more than two-thirds of the company's revenues now come from its Electric Power Infrastructure segment.

	Annual Growth	12/10	12/11	12/12	12/13	12/14
Sales ($ mil.)	18.9%	3,931.2	4,623.8	5,920.3	6,522.8	7,851.3
Net income ($ mil.)	18.0%	153.2	132.5	306.6	401.9	296.7
Market value ($ mil.)	9.3%	4,345.5	4,698.9	5,953.2	6,884.7	6,193.2
Employees	15.7%	13,751	17,500	17,800	20,900	24,600

QUANTUM CORP.

NYS: QTM

224 Airport Parkway, Suite 300
San Jose, CA 95110
Phone: 408 944-4000
Fax: –
Web: www.quantum.com

CEO: Jon W. Gacek
CFO: Linda M Breard
HR: Linda M. Breard
FYE: March 31
Type: Public

Quantum is a storage facility for your data. The company provides hardware and software used for data archiving backup and recovery. Its products include tape- and disk-based storage devices automated tape library (ATL) systems and related media. It also provides data management software and offers services in configuration installation technical support and training. Quantum sells its products through resellers and distributors and to computing equipment makers such as Dell EMC HP IBM and Oracle. The company makes two-thirds of its sales in the Americas; its top five customers account for about 30% of sales.

	Annual Growth	03/11	03/12	03/13	03/14	03/15
Sales ($ mil.)	(4.8%)	672.3	652.4	587.6	553.2	553.1
Net income ($ mil.)	38.6%	4.5	(8.8)	(52.4)	(21.5)	16.8
Market value ($ mil.)	(10.7%)	650.7	676.5	330.5	315.0	413.1
Employees	(9.1%)	1,830	1,820	1,660	1,290	1,250

QUANTUM FUEL SYSTEMS TECHNOLOGIES WORLDWIDE INC.

NAS: QTWW

25242 Arctic Ocean Drive
Lake Forest, CA 92630
Phone: 949 399-4500
Fax: 949 399-4600
Web: www.qtww.com

CEO: W Brian Olson
CFO: Bradley J Timon
HR: –
FYE: December 31
Type: Public

If you're ready to make a quantum leap to a new fuel source then Quantum Fuel Systems Technologies Worldwide is the place to land. Quantum makes fuel storage delivery devices and electronic control systems for alternative-fueled vehicles. It serves the military with its branded HyHauler Plus a transportable hydrogen refueling station that powers battlefield vehicles. Fisker Automotive a joint venture between Quantum and Fisker Coachbuild is developing the Karma an environmentally friendly luxury sports sedan using Quantum's plug-in-hybrid engine technology. Its customer base also includes aerospace and government entities.

	Annual Growth	04/11*	12/11	12/12	12/13	12/14
Sales ($ mil.)	18.9%	20.3	24.5	22.7	31.9	34.1
Net income ($ mil.)	–	(11.0)	(38.5)	(30.9)	(23.0)	(14.9)
Market value ($ mil.)	(6.8%)	60.1	17.0	15.9	181.6	48.6
Employees	15.4%	112	123	122	147	172

*Fiscal year change

QUARK PHARMACEUTICALS INC.

6501 Dumbarton Cr.
Fremont CA 94555
Phone: 510-402-4020
Fax: 510-402-4021
Web: www.quarkbiotech.com

CEO: Daniel Zurr
CFO: –
HR: –
FYE: December 31
Type: Private

Quarks may be the basic building blocks of matter but it's a fundamental unit of biology — genes — that Quark Pharmaceuticals is interested in. The drug development company is using cutting-edge RNA interference (RNAi) technology to develop small-interfering RNA (siRNA) molecules or drugs that inhibit targeted genes from producing proteins associated with certain diseases. Its lead product RTP801i-14 which it has licensed to Pfizer aims to treat wet age-related macular degeneration (a cause of blindness in the elderly). Quark Pharmaceuticals is developing other candidates for ailments such as acute renal (kidney) failure hearing loss and dyslipidemia (a metabolic syndrome).

QUEEN OF THE VALLEY MEDICAL CENTER

1000 TRANCAS ST
NAPA, CA 945582906
Phone: 707-251-1761
Fax: –
Web: www.thequeen.org

CEO: Walt Mickens
CFO: Don Miller
HR: –
FYE: June 30
Type: Private

The Queen of the Valley Medical Center reigns over the whole of Napa Valley. The 190-bed hospital provides acute and tertiary care to the residents of California's Napa County. It operates a level III trauma center and provides emergency surgery and wound care services as well as specialty family work health nutritional and rehabilitation services. "The Queen" as it is known colloquially operates regional cancer orthopedic women's and heart centers as well as the Napa Valley Imaging Center and the Napa Valley Women's Healthcare Center. Queen of the Valley Medical Center is part of St. Joseph Health.

	Annual Growth	06/07	06/08	06/09	06/10	06/13
Sales ($ mil.)	(3.0%)	–	333.1	242.4	277.0	285.3
Net income ($ mil.)	–	–	–	(5.2)	25.1	23.0
Market value ($ mil.)	–	–	–	–	–	–
Employees	–	–	–	–	–	1,070

QUEENS-LONG ISLAND MEDICAL GROUP P.C.

1000 Zeckendorf Blvd.
Garden City NY 11530
Phone: 516-542-5500
Fax: 516-282-2738
Web: www.qlimg.com

CEO: –
CFO: Peter Wolf
HR: Annette Dente
FYE: December 31
Type: Private

Queens-Long Island Medical Group (QLIMG) cures medical ailments in the Queens-Long Island area. A physician-owned practice group boasting some 350 primary and specialty care doctors QLIMG was established in 1991. The group operates more than 20 medical clinics as well as urgent care centers serving residents in New York's Queens Nassau and Suffolk counties. It is also affiliated with the North Shore-Long Island Jewish Health System network of acute care and specialty hospitals. QLIMG's physician's specialties include pediatrics women's health immunology cardiology radiology rehabilitation and neurology; the group also has disease management programs for chronically ill patients.

QUEST DIAGNOSTICS, INC.

NYS: DGX

Three Giralda Farms
Madison, NJ 07940
Phone: 973 520-2700
Fax: –
Web: www.questdiagnostics.com

CEO: Stephen H. (Steve) Rusckowski
CFO: Mark J. Guinan
HR: –
FYE: December 31
Type: Public

Quest Diagnostics is testing its ability to be the world's leading clinical lab. The company performs diagnostics on some 156 million specimens each year including routine clinical tests such as cholesterol checks Pap smears and HIV screenings. Quest Diagnostics also performs esoteric testing (such as genetic screening) and anatomic pathology testing (such as tissue biopsies for cancer testing). In all the company serves half of the physicians and hospitals in the US as well as government agencies and other clinical labs. Quest Diagnostics has more than 2200 patient service centers where samples are collected and the Quest Diagnostic Nichols Institute where new diagnostics are developed.

	Annual Growth	12/10	12/11	12/12	12/13	12/14
Sales ($ mil.)	0.2%	7,368.9	7,510.5	7,382.6	7,146.0	7,435.0
Net income ($ mil.)	(6.3%)	720.9	470.6	555.7	849.0	556.0
Market value ($ mil.)	5.6%	7,771.7	8,360.6	8,390.9	7,709.8	9,656.6
Employees	1.7%	42,000	42,000	41,000	41,000	45,000

QUEST MEDIA & SUPPLIES INC.

5822 ROSEVILLE RD
SACRAMENTO, CA 958423071
Phone: 916-338-7070
Fax: –
Web: www.questsys.com

CEO: Timothy Burke
CFO: Francine Walrath
HR: Laurie Handelman
FYE: December 31
Type: Private

Quest wants to help guide clients in their technology journeys. Quest Media & Supplies provides a wide range of IT consulting and management services to Fortune 5000 firms as well as educational institutions government agencies and small and midsized companies across the US. Its offerings include cloud hosting application development networking security and disaster recovery data storage telecommunications and transport services and technology staffing. Quest is Gold Certified in the US for Cisco Systems and also supplies products from Blue Coat Dell Hitachi IBM Microsoft Polycom VMware and Xerox among other vendors. The company was founded in 1982 by CEO Tim Burke with his wife Cindy.

	Annual Growth	12/09	12/10	12/11	12/12	12/13
Sales ($ mil.)	13.0%	–	82.0	81.2	118.4	118.3
Net income ($ mil.)	113.6%	–	–	0.8	2.1	3.9
Market value ($ mil.)	–	–	–	–	–	–
Employees	–	–	–	–	–	130

QUEST SOFTWARE INC.

NASDAQ: QSFT

5 Polaris Way
Aliso Viejo CA 92656
Phone: 949-754-8000
Fax: 949-754-8999
Web: www.quest.com

CEO: Michael Dell
CFO: Brian T Gladden
HR: –
FYE: December 31
Type: Public

Quest Software has made enterprise systems management its personal mission. The company's software is designed to improve application performance manage transitions to new software platforms and monitor the delivery of data over corporate networks and the Internet. Its applications which are compatible with Oracle Microsoft and IBM database systems are used for diagnostics network monitoring application deployment and data replication in the event of system failures. Quest also offers virtualization software and provides a range of application database and other IT services. Customers come from the telecom manufacturing energy and public sectors. In 2012 Quest was acquired by Dell for $2.4 billion.

QUESTAR CAPITAL CORPORATION

5701 Golden Hills Dr.	CEO: Sherri Dumond
Minneapolis MN 55416	CFO: –
Phone: 888-446-5872	HR: –
Fax: 818-992-8970	FYE: December 31
Web: www.keyisit.com	Type: Subsidiary

Questar Capital wants to be a shining example of a financial services provider. The brokerage offers a full range of investment products — including stocks bonds mutual funds annuities and insurance — via a network of more than 500 representatives throughout the country. Customers of Questar Capital can choose products from about 90 mutual fund companies some 70 variable life and annuity companies and 15 fee-based money managers. Insurance provider Allianz Life acquired Questar Capital in 2005 combined it with USAllianz Securities and gave the combined entity the Questar Capital name.

QUESTAR CORP.

NYS: STR

333 South State Street, P.O. Box 45433	CEO: Ronald W. (Ron) Jibson
Salt Lake City, UT 84145-0433	CFO: Kevin W. Hadlock
Phone: 801 324-5900	HR: –
Fax: –	FYE: December 31
Web: www.questar.com	Type: Public

Questar is on a quest for natural gas — finding it producing it and transporting storing and distributing it. The integrated energy company operates through three major units. Public utility Questar Gas its largest unit distributes natural gas to more than 900000 customers in Utah southwestern Wyoming and southeastern Idaho. Questar Pipeline operates a 2640-mile natural gas transportation system and gas storage facilities in Colorado Utah and Wyoming. Its exploration activities are led by its Wexpro business. In 2014 the company reported proved reserves of 566.1 billion cu. ft. of natural gas equivalent.

	Annual Growth	12/10	12/11	12/12	12/13	12/14
Sales ($ mil.)	1.4%	1,123.6	1,194.4	1,098.9	1,220.0	1,189.3
Net income ($ mil.)	(9.6%)	339.2	207.9	212.0	161.2	226.5
Market value ($ mil.)	9.8%	3,053.7	3,483.4	3,465.9	4,032.4	4,434.1
Employees	0.6%	1,705	1,730	1,738	1,725	1,745

QUESTAR GAS CO.

333 South State Street, P.O. Box 45433	CEO: Ronald W Jibson
Salt Lake City, UT 84145-0433	CFO: Kevin W Hadlock
Phone: 801 324-5900	HR: –
Fax: –	FYE: December 31
Web: www.questar.com	Type: Public

Questar Gas's quest is to distribute natural gas to almost 919230 customers throughout Utah and in southeastern Idaho and southwestern Wyoming. The regulated utility which a subsidiary of integrated energy concern Questar Corporation operates more than 27000 miles of gas distribution mains and service lines. The company is regulated by the Public Service Commission of Utah and the Wyoming Public Service Commission. With an efficient and low-cost gas supply and a low ratio of customers to employees rates paid by Questar Gas customers are among the lowest in the US.

	Annual Growth	12/10	12/11	12/12	12/13	12/14
Sales ($ mil.)	1.6%	902.9	968.8	862.2	985.8	960.9
Net income ($ mil.)	5.9%	43.9	46.1	47.1	52.8	55.2
Market value ($ mil.)	–	–	–	–	–	–
Employees	17.4%	920	928	888	917	1,745

QUESTCOR PHARMACEUTICALS INC

NMS: QCOR

1300 North Kellogg Drive, Suite D	CEO: Don M Bailey
Anaheim, CA 92807	CFO: Juergen Hermann
Phone: 714 786-4200	HR: –
Fax: –	FYE: December 31
Web: www.questcor.com	Type: Public

Questcor Pharmaceuticals is on a journey for better health for patients and some good profitability for itself to boot. The company makes and develops drugs for neurological conditions and kidney treatments. Most of its revenue comes from the sale of II.P. Acthar Gel (or Acthar). Acthar is approved for the treatment of nearly 20 indications but the company receives the majority of its income from sales related to three of those: multiple sclerosis nephrotic syndrome and infantile spasms (a rare form of pediatric epilepsy). Questcor also sells insomnia treatment Doral. The company's BioVectra subsidiary provides contract manufacturing to other pharma firms.

	Annual Growth	12/08	12/09	12/10	12/11	12/12
Sales ($ mil.)	52.1%	95.2	88.3	115.1	218.2	509.3
Net income ($ mil.)	48.6%	40.5	26.6	35.1	79.6	197.7
Market value ($ mil.)	30.2%	545.0	278.1	862.4	2,434.3	1,564.3
Employees	86.5%	46	77	152	206	557

QUICK-MED TECHNOLOGIES INC.

OTC: QMDT

902 NW 4th St.	CEO: –
Gainesville FL 32601	CFO: Paul H Jenssen
Phone: 888-835-2211	HR: –
Fax: 616-392-2438	FYE: June 30
Web: www.russells-tech.com	Type: Public

Quick-Med Technologies hopes to be floating on a cloud — but not a cloud of mustard gas. The life sciences development company is working with the US Army to develop a therapy to treat people exposed to mustard gas. The underlying technology for the potential therapy MultiStat is also the basis for wound care products and cosmetic ingredient applications. A second technology NIMBUS (Novel Intrinsically Micro-Bonded Utility Substrate) uses bioengineered antimicrobial polymers to protect wounds from infection and industrial and consumer goods from harmful microscopic pests.

QUICKEN LOANS INC.

1 Campus Martius Compuware Bldg. 1050 Woodward Ave.	CEO: Bill Emerson
Detroit MI 48226	CFO: Julie Booth
Phone: 313-373-3000	HR: –
Fax: 734-947-7931	FYE: July 31
Web: www.unitedroad.com	Type: Private

People searching for a loan quick click on Quicken Loans. A leading online mortgage lender Quicken Loans offers residential mortgages in all 50 states and provides such financing options as fixed- and adjustable-rate mortgages reverse mortgages and refinancing through its interactive website. The company also has loan centers in Michigan Ohio and Arizona. Affiliate Title Source offers title insurance property valuations and closing services. Its San Diego-based One Reverse Mortgage unit handles FHA-backed reverse mortgage programs. Another division In-House Realty includes a network of 4000 real estate agents. Rock Holdings which is led by founder and chairman Dan Gilbert owns Quicken Loans.

QUICKLOGIC CORP   NMS: QUIK

1277 Orleans Drive
Sunnyvale, CA 94089
Phone: 408 990-4000
Fax: 408 990-4040
Web: www.quicklogic.com

CEO: –
CFO: Ralph S Marimon
HR: Catherine Rousteau
FYE: December 28
Type: Public

QuickLogic is quick to get embed. The company designs and sells logic chips that can be programmed by OEMs as well as low-power customizable chips used to add features to and extend the battery life of mobile consumer and business electronics. It also offers related hardware and software plus custom programming services. The fabless company — it uses contract manufacturers to produce its chips — targets smartphone tablet and access card manufacturers. Customers for its logic chips come from the aerospace instrumentation and military industries among others. Honeywell (15% of sales) is a top customer.

	Annual Growth	01/11	01/12*	12/12	12/13	12/14
Sales ($ mil.)	2.1%	26.2	21.0	14.9	26.1	27.8
Net income ($ mil.)	–	0.1	(7.6)	(12.3)	(12.3)	(13.1)
Market value ($ mil.)	(20.6%)	359.6	146.1	126.4	216.9	179.8
Employees	7.9%	78	81	86	89	98

*Fiscal year change

QUICKSILVER PRODUCTION PARTNERS LP

801 Cherry St. Ste. 3700 Unit 19
Fort Worth TX 76102
Phone: 817-665-5000
Fax: 214-302-5980
Web: www.redmangousa.com

CEO: –
CFO: –
HR: –
FYE: December 31
Type: Private

Silver is nowhere to be found on Quicksilver Production Partners' production radar. An oil and gas exploration and development company Quicksilver Production owns and operates mature properties in the Barnett Shale in north Texas. Its assets which produce primarily natural gas and natural gas liquids (NGLs) have total proved reserves of some 430 billion of cubic feet equivalent. The company uses hydraulic fracturing to extract gas and NGLs from its wells which are found in terrain that makes extracting resources difficult or impossible to do using conventional methods. Quicksilver Production Partners was formed in late 2011 by Quicksilver Resources; it filed to go public in early 2012.

QUICKSILVER RESOURCES, INC.   NBB: KWKA Q

801 Cherry Street, Suite 3700, Unit 19
Fort Worth, TX 76102
Phone: 817 665-5000
Fax: 817 665-5008
Web: www.qrinc.com

CEO: –
CFO: Vanessa Gomez Lagatta
HR: Anne Self
FYE: December 31
Type: Public

With mercurial speed Quicksilver Resources seeks to turn oil and gas finds into profits. The independent oil and gas company acquires explores for develops and produces onshore oil and gas in North America. Its US and Canadian producing properties are primarily located in Colorado Montana Texas and Wyoming as well as Alberta with a focus on the Barnett Shale Horn River and Horseshoe Canyon basins. The company also has oil exploration opportunities in the Midland and Delaware basins in West Texas and Sand Wash basin in northwestern Colorado. In 2012 Quicksilver Resources had total proved reserves of 1.5 trillion cubic feet of natural gas equivalent.

	Annual Growth	12/10	12/11	12/12	12/13	12/14
Sales ($ mil.)	(11.5%)	928.3	943.6	709.0	561.6	569.4
Net income ($ mil.)	–	435.1	90.0	(2,352.6)	161.6	(103.1)
Market value ($ mil.)	(66.0%)	2,658.5	1,210.2	515.8	553.7	35.7
Employees	(10.3%)	452	477	417	338	293

QUIDEL CORP.   NMS: QDEL

12544 High Bluff Drive, Suite 200
San Diego, CA 92130
Phone: 858 552-1100
Fax: –
Web: www.quidel.com

CEO: Douglas C. (Doug) Bryant
CFO: Randall J. (Randy) Steward
HR: –
FYE: December 31
Type: Public

Is it the flu or are you pregnant? Quidel can tell you quickly enough. The company makes rapid diagnostic in vitro test products used at the point-of-care (POC) usually at a doctor's office or other outpatient setting. Unlike tests sent off to a lab POC tests can be read on the spot. Quidel's leading products are diagnostics for infectious diseases (such as influenza and strep throat) and reproductive health sold under the QuickVue D3 Direct Detection and Thyretain brands. The company also makes diagnostics for streptococci chlamydia and the ulcer-causing H. pylori bacterium as well as Sofia a next generation rapid immunofluorescence-based point-of-care diagnostic test system.

	Annual Growth	12/10	12/11	12/12	12/13	12/14
Sales ($ mil.)	12.7%	113.3	158.6	155.7	175.4	182.6
Net income ($ mil.)	–	(11.3)	7.6	5.0	7.4	(7.1)
Market value ($ mil.)	18.9%	497.6	521.0	642.9	1,063.6	995.8
Employees	3.5%	532	488	514	572	610

QUIKSILVER, INC.   NYS: ZQK

15202 Graham Street
Huntington Beach, CA 92649
Phone: 714 889-2200
Fax: 714 645-0313
Web: www.quiksilverinc.com

CEO: Pierre Agnes
CFO: Thomas Chambolle
HR: –
FYE: October 31
Type: Public

Quiksilver rides the wave of youth appeal. It caters to the young and athletic with surfwear snowboardwear sportswear and swimwear sold under the Quiksilver Roxy Hawk Lib Technologies and Gnu names. Quiksilver owns the DC Shoes brand of footwear and apparel for young men and juniors. It sells its apparel footwear and accessories in specialty and department stores worldwide including Zumiez Nordstrom Dick's Sporting Goods El Corte Ingles Galeries Lafayette and Macy's. The retailer boasts about 940 owned and licensed stores under the Quiksilver DC Roxy (young women's apparel) and Quiksilver Youth banners. Quiksilver has expanded its products to include eyewear watches and personal care items.

	Annual Growth	10/10	10/11	10/12	10/13	10/14
Sales ($ mil.)	(3.9%)	1,837.6	1,953.1	2,013.2	1,810.6	1,570.4
Net income ($ mil.)	–	(9.7)	(21.3)	(10.8)	(232.6)	(309.4)
Market value ($ mil.)	(19.5%)	713.8	573.4	547.8	1,424.2	299.6
Employees	(0.4%)	6,200	6,600	7,000	6,300	6,100

QUIKTRIP CORPORATION

4705 S. 129th East Ave.
Tulsa OK 74134
Phone: 918-615-7700
Fax: 918-615-7377
Web: www.quiktrip.com

CEO: Chet Cadieux
CFO: Sandra J Westbrook
HR: –
FYE: April 30
Type: Private

QuikTrip provides a quick fix for those on the go. QuikTrip (QT) owns and operates more than 615 gasoline/convenience stores in nearly a dozen states mostly in the central US. QT stores which average 4600 sq. ft. feature the company's own QT brand of gas and diesel fuel as well as brand-name beverages candy and tobacco and QT's Quik 'n Tasty and HOTZI lines of sandwiches. QT's 15-plus travel centers offer scales food fuel showers and other services for truckers. The firm's FleetMaster program offers commercial trucking companies detailed reports showing drivers' product purchases amounts spent and odometer readings. QT was co-founded in 1958 by chairman Chester Cadieux. His son Chet runs the firm.

QUILL CORPORATION

100 Schelter Rd.
Lincolnshire IL 60069-3621
Phone: 847-634-6690
Fax: 847-821-2347
Web: www.quill.com

CEO: –
CFO: –
HR: –
FYE: January 31
Type: Subsidiary

Not quite as old-fashioned as its name suggests Quill distributes office products to about 1 million small and midsized US businesses. To compete with office supply superstores Quill markets some 50000 products under the Quill brand as well as under the Bic Hewlett-Packard Mead Papermate and Xerox names. It sells office supplies and furniture including technology products (cameras monitors) through a catalog and the company's website. Quill also equips medical professionals with workplace goods through its Medical Arts Press business. Jack Miller founded Quill in 1956. It was acquired in 1998 by office retailer Staples which counts Quill among its North American delivery segment.

QUINN EMANUEL URQUHART & SULLIVAN LLP

865 S. Figueroa St. 10th Fl.
Los Angeles CA 90017
Phone: 213-443-3000
Fax: 213-443-3100
Web: www.quinnemanuel.com

CEO: –
CFO: –
HR: Deb Klaeger
FYE: December 31
Type: Private - Partnershi

Business litigation specialist Quinn Emanuel Urquhart & Sullivan has about 600 lawyers working out of a dozen offices. The firm organizes its trial practices into areas such as antitrust and trade regulation class actions construction health care intellectual property real estate and white-collar crime. Quinn Emanuel was founded in 1986. In March 2010 it added Kathleen Sullivan as a partner and as the head of its appellate practice; the firm updated its name from Quinn Emanuel Urquhart Oliver & Hedges to Quinn Emanuel Urquhart & Sullivan at that time.

QUINNIPIAC UNIVERSITY

275 MOUNT CARMEL AVE
HAMDEN, CT 065181908
Phone: 203-582-8200
Fax: –
Web: www.quinnipiac.edu

CEO: –
CFO: –
HR: –
FYE: June 30
Type: Private

At Quinnipiac University the first thing you may have to learn is how to pronounce it (for the record it's KWIN-uh-pe-ack). The private university offers a variety of liberal arts undergraduate programs as well as graduate programs in selected professional fields (business education health sciences communications arts and sciences nursing and law) to some 9000 students with a student-to-faculty ration of 16 to 1. It often appears on lists of top colleges including those published by U.S. News & World Report. The university known to political junkies and others for its polling operation includes eight schools and colleges across three Connecticut campuses (Mount Carmel York Hill and North Haven).

	Annual Growth	06/07	06/08	06/09	06/10	06/13
Sales ($ mil.)	12.4%	–	–	235.6	290.8	376.5
Net income ($ mil.)	–	–	–	(0.3)	45.3	46.0
Market value ($ mil.)	–	–	–	–	–	–
Employees	–	–	–	–	–	900

QUINSTREET, INC.

NMS: QNST

950 Tower Lane, 6th Floor
Foster City, CA 94404
Phone: 650 578-7700
Fax: –
Web: www.quinstreet.com

CEO: Douglas (Doug) Valenti
CFO: Gregory Wong
HR: –
FYE: June 30
Type: Public

QuinStreet connects companies with potential customers through the information superhighway. The online direct marketing company uses proprietary technologies to provide leads to companies. Clients use the leads as the targets of their direct marketing campaigns. As a sign of its confidence in its quality QuinStreet has adopted a pay-for-performance model of pricing in which customers are charged based on lead performance. Catering mainly to the education and financial services sectors its customers have included big organizations such as DeVry and ADT. QuinStreet has offices in the US Brazil and India. The company was founded in 1999 and went public in 2010.

	Annual Growth	06/11	06/12	06/13	06/14	06/15
Sales ($ mil.)	(8.5%)	403.0	370.5	305.1	282.5	282.1
Net income ($ mil.)	–	27.2	13.0	(67.4)	(146.4)	(20.0)
Market value ($ mil.)	(16.0%)	579.1	413.2	385.1	245.8	287.8
Employees	(1.4%)	675	673	599	667	638

QUINTILES TRANSNATIONAL HOLDINGS INC

NYS: Q

4820 Emperor Blvd.
Durham, NC 27703
Phone: 919 998-2000
Fax: –
Web: www.quintiles.com

CEO: Thomas H. (Tom) Pike
CFO: Kevin K. Gordon
HR: –
FYE: December 31
Type: Public

Quintiles Transnational has plenty to CRO about. One of the world's largest contract research organizations (CROs) it helps pharmaceutical biotechnology and medical device companies develop and sell their products. The firm provides a comprehensive range of clinical trials management services including patient recruitment data analysis laboratory testing and regulatory filing assistance. Its consulting unit offers strategic advice at every stage of drug discovery and development and its capital and commercial divisions assist with project funding and sales and marketing efforts. Quintiles which had been a private company since 2003 went public again in 2013.

	Annual Growth	12/11	12/12	12/13	12/14	12/15
Sales ($ mil.)	7.3%	4,327.7	4,865.5	5,099.5	5,460.0	5,737.6
Net income ($ mil.)	12.5%	241.8	177.5	226.6	356.4	387.2
Market value ($ mil.)	21.7%	–	–	5,532.0	7,027.8	8,196.5
Employees	13.1%	–	–	28,200	32,600	36,100

QUMU CORP

NMS: QUMU

510 1st Avenue North, Suite 305
Minneapolis, MN 55403
Phone: 612 638-9100
Fax: –
Web: www.qumu.com

CEO: Vern Hanzlik
CFO: Peter J. Goepfrich
HR: Lottie Bischoff
FYE: December 31
Type: Public

Qumu constructs the technology that creates your computer discs. The company (formerly known as Rimage) makes CD recordable (CD-R) DVD recordable (DVD-R) and Blu-ray Disc production and duplication equipment. Products include systems for premastering recording and labeling discs as well as thermal printers for labeling and decorating recorded media. Qumu offers separate product lines for high-volume production environments (Producer) front office production (Professional) and smaller office applications (Desktop). Customers include professional photography medical imaging and law enforcement organizations. The company changed its name from Rimage Corporation to Qumu Corporation in late 2013.

	Annual Growth	12/10	12/11	12/12	12/13	12/14
Sales ($ mil.)	(26.1%)	88.7	83.6	79.4	82.5	26.5
Net income ($ mil.)	–	7.7	2.8	(48.3)	(9.7)	(8.5)
Market value ($ mil.)	(2.1%)	136.1	102.7	61.0	116.8	124.8
Employees	4.1%	189	246	268	259	222

QUOVA INC.

707 California St.
Mountain View CA 94041
Phone: 650-528-3700
Fax: 650-625-9809
Web: www.quova.com

CEO: Marie Alexander
CFO: Jean-Louis Casabonne
HR: –
FYE: December 31
Type: Private

Quova provides software and services that facilitate the process of gathering information about Internet users and their whereabouts. The company's geolocation technology can pinpoint the physical location of an Internet user's IP address information that can then be used to assess levels of Internet traffic monitor browsing activities enhance network security minimize the risk of online fraud and provide regionally relevant marketing information. The company's customers come from industries including gaming financial services e-commerce and media distribution as well as government agencies and organizations.

QVC INC.

1200 Wilson Dr.
West Chester PA 19380
Phone: 484-701-1000
Fax: 415-200-4422
Web: www.mypoints.com

CEO: Michael A George
CFO: Thaddeus J Jastrzebski
HR: Anthony Dolferno
FYE: December 31
Type: Subsidiary

The phones are ringing off the hook at television home shopping company QVC. QVC (its name stands for "quality value and convenience") offers about 1150 items each week to TV-tied consumer shoppers. Merchandise includes apparel cosmetics electronics housewares jewelry and toys. It broadcasts 24 hours a day; viewers call in their orders to one of its three US call centers. If you can't find what you're shopping for on the tube it also sells online through mobile apps and some half dozen outlet stores in four states. The company has shopping channels in Germany Japan Italy and the UK. QVC is a subsidiary of shopping and travel site operator Liberty Interactive (formerly Liberty Media).

QVIDIAN CORPORATION

175 Cabot St. Ste. 210
Lowell MA 01854
Phone: 513-631-1155
Fax: 978-703-7631
Web: www.qvidian.com

CEO: Lewis Miller
CFO: D Tyler Drolet
HR: –
FYE: December 31
Type: Private

Qvidian (formerly Kadient) helps you close the deal in the clouds. The company offers cloud-based sales effectiveness software. Its Sales Playbooks and Analytics module provides best practices content and reporting functions designed to get sales reps up to speed quickly. Its Proposal Automation module assists in creating client proposals including setting queries for requests for proposals (RFPs) assembling presentations and ensuring consistent content across documents. A Content Library tool gives sales teams access to relevant and personalized sales content expertise and feedback. Qvidian was formed in 2011 after Kadient and The Sant Corporation merged in mid-2010.

R&R PRODUCTS INC.

3334 E. Milber St.
Tucson AZ 85714
Phone: 520-889-3593
Fax: 520-294-1045
Web: www.rrproducts.com

CEO: –
CFO: Brian Larson
HR: Debi Gillmore
FYE: December 31
Type: Private

If a round or two of golf is your idea of R&R then you may well have R&R Products to thank. The family-owned and operated company manufactures commercial golf course accessories including ball washers sand trap rakes and golf club cleaners. R&R also sells a line of turf products (spray applicators irrigation gauges and submersible pumps) and power equipment (generators mowers chainsaws power washers and leaf blowers) made by other manufacturers including Briggs & Stratton Kubota and Husqvarna. Safety equipment such as chemical distribution cans storage cabinets and personnel safety wear is included in R&R's lineup.

R. B. PAMPLIN CORPORATION

805 SW Broadway Ste. 2400
Portland OR 97205
Phone: 503-248-1133
Fax: 503-248-1175
Web: www.pamplin.org

CEO: Robert B Pamplin Jr
CFO: –
HR: –
FYE: December 31
Type: Private

Founded by a man of the cloth R. B. Pamplin casts a wide net. The family-owned conglomerate started in 1957 by ordained minister and company chairman and CEO Robert Pamplin Jr. has operations ranging from entertainment to retail stores to manufacturing interests (asphalt concrete and textiles). The company's Mount Vernon Mills is one of the top denim producers in the US. Pamplin's entertainment concerns include radio broadcasting newspapers and record labels in the northwestern US. Other units are as diverse as retail stores offering Christian products to Columbia Empire Farms which grows berries and grapes used in jams and wine that are then sold through its Your NorthWest stores.

R. E. MICHEL COMPANY

1 RE MICHEL DR
GLEN BURNIE, MD 210606408
Phone: 410-760-4000
Fax: –
Web: www.remichel.com

CEO: –
CFO: –
HR: Holly Porter
FYE: December 31
Type: Private

Blowing hot and cold is good for R.E. Michel. The company is one of the nation's largest wholesale distributors of heating air-conditioning and refrigeration (HVAC-R) equipment parts and supplies. The family-owned and operated firm offers more than 16000 items through about 2 sales offices located across the Southern Mid-Atlantic and Northeastern regions of the country. R.E. Michel ships more than 20000 items each day from its 900000-sq.-ft. distribution center in Maryland. Its Exclusive Supplier Partnership (ESP) program offers customers inventory control advertising and marketing support. R.E. Michel was founded in 1935 as a supplier to the home heating oil burner industry.

	Annual Growth	12/09	12/10	12/11	12/12	12/13
Sales ($ mil.)	4.9%	–	593.1	607.0	611.7	685.1
Net income ($ mil.)	93.4%	–	–	8.4	3.9	31.5
Market value ($ mil.)	–	–	–	–	–	–
Employees	–	–	–	–	–	1,674

R. L. JORDAN OIL COMPANY OF NORTH CAROLINA INC.

1451 FERNWOOD GLENDALE RD
SPARTANBURG, SC 293073044
Phone: 864-585-2784
Fax: –
Web: www.rljoc.com

CEO: Wilton Jordan
CFO: –
HR: Elizabeth Gladson
FYE: September 30
Type: Private

R. L. Jordan Oil Company takes gas from hot spots and sells it — and lots more — at Hot Spots. The company operates a chain of more than 50 convenience stores and gas stations under the Hot Spots banner as well as about 10 fast food restaurants under the Hardee's and Subway names. It operates in the Carolinas. About 75% of the company's stores are located in South Carolina. The family-owned and -operated company was founded by its namesake and former chairman in 1950 the late R. L. Jordan. As part of its operations the Jordan family also owns a real estate business Jordan Properties which operates several hotels and properties in North Carolina.

	Annual Growth	09/03	09/04	09/05	09/06	09/07
Sales ($ mil.)	–	–	–	(1,428.8)	271.0	278.6
Net income ($ mil.)	–	–	–	0.0	(1.7)	(0.3)
Market value ($ mil.)	–	–	–	–	–	–
Employees	–	–	–	–	–	900

R.J. O'BRIEN & ASSOCIATES INC.

222 S. Riverside Plaza Ste. 900
Chicago IL 60606
Phone: 312-373-5000
Fax: 312-373-5238
Web: www.rjobrien.com

CEO: Gerald F Corcoran
CFO: Jason Manumaleuna
HR: –
FYE: December 31
Type: Private

Founded in 1914 R.J. O'Brien (RJO) is one of the oldest independent futures brokerage firms in the US and a founding member of the CME's Chicago Mercantile Exchange. RJO provides electronic execution and clearing services for more than 80000 clients on futures exchanges worldwide. Serving a network of some 300 introducing brokers as well as corporations and individual traders the company deals in commodities such as grains currencies metals energy livestock and energy. It oversees some $2 billion in client assets. The O'Brien family owns a majority of RJO.

R.S. HUGHES COMPANY INC.

1162 SONORA CT
SUNNYVALE, CA 940865378
Phone: 408-739-3211
Fax: –
Web: www.rshughes.com

CEO: Robert McCollum
CFO: Gail Zimmerman
HR: –
FYE: September 28
Type: Private

R.S. Hughes distributes the stuff that holds the world together — duct tape that is — plus a lot more. Established in 1954 the employee-owned company maintains some 45 warehouse locations in the US and Mexico. It supplies adhesives (epoxies aerosols hot glues silicones) electrical specialties (tubing terminals films tape and barriers) safety products (glasses ear plugs masks) tapes (masking foam vinyl cloth foil duct joining) and abrasives (roll disc brush wheel belt and air tools). R.S. Hughes also distributes labels and signs (printable labels and tags safety signs) and aerosols and coatings (WD-40 paints lubricants oils cleaners).

	Annual Growth	10/10	10/11*	09/12	09/13	09/14
Sales ($ mil.)	9.2%	–	231.9	253.5	281.1	302.3
Net income ($ mil.)	(1.0%)	–	–	15.7	15.4	15.4
Market value ($ mil.)	–	–	–	–	–	–
Employees	–	–	–	–	–	460

*Fiscal year change

RABOBANK N.A.

1448 Main St.
El Centro CA 92243
Phone: 760-337-3200
Fax: 508-634-3394
Web: www.seracare.com

CEO: Ronald Blok
CFO: Charles Caswell
HR: –
FYE: December 31
Type: Subsidiary

Rabobank N.A. is the primary US subsidiary of Netherlands-based Rabobank Group. It operates about 120 bank branches agricultural field offices and financial service centers in Central and Southern California that offer commercial and consumer loans; checking savings and time deposits; trust and investment services; Visa credit cards; and more. Rabobank Group entered the US in 2005 when it bought Valley Independent Bank which was founded more than twenty years earlier by local farmers and business owners to serve agricultural concerns. The strategy mirrors that of Rabobank Group which was founded by Dutch farmers in the 1890s.

RACETRAC PETROLEUM INC.

3225 Cumberland Blvd. Ste. 100
Atlanta GA 30339
Phone: 770-431-7600
Fax: 713-268-3812
Web: www.randalls.com

CEO: Carl E Bolch Jr
CFO: Robert J Dumbacher
HR: –
FYE: December 31
Type: Private

RaceTrac Petroleum hopes it's a popular pit stop for gasoline and snacks in the Southeast. The company operates more than 630 gas stations and convenience stores in a dozen southeastern states under the RaceTrac and RaceWay names. (RaceWay stores are operated by independent contractors.) The chain plans to grow by expanding its store count by about 10% a year. Carl Bolch founded RaceTrac in Missouri in 1934. His son chairman and CEO Carl Bolch Jr. moved the company into high-volume gas stations with long self-service islands that can serve as many as two dozen vehicles at one time. RaceTrac's convenience stores sell fresh deli food and offer some fast-food fare. The Bolch family owns the company.

RACKSPACE HOSTING INC   NYS: RAX

1 Fanatical Place, City of Windcrest
San Antonio, TX 78218
Phone: 210 312-4000
Fax: –
Web: www.rackspace.com

CEO: William T. (Taylor) Rhodes
CFO: Karl Pichler
HR: Wayne Roberts
FYE: December 31
Type: Public

Looking for server rack space to host your company's data network needs? Well look no further than Rackspace Hosting. The company provides a range of web hosting and managed network services for businesses. It offers traditional hosting services with dedicated servers but is expanding into cloud hosting which lets customers use pooled server resources on an on-demand basis. Its cloud computing services include public private and hybrid cloud hosting which provides a combination of dedicated hosting and cloud computing. Founded in 1998 Rackspace has more than 200000 business customers in 120 countries.

	Annual Growth	12/10	12/11	12/12	12/13	12/14
Sales ($ mil.)	23.1%	780.6	1,025.1	1,309.2	1,534.8	1,794.4
Net income ($ mil.)	24.3%	46.4	76.4	105.4	86.7	110.6
Market value ($ mil.)	10.5%	4,427.1	6,062.1	10,468.0	5,515.2	6,597.6
Employees	16.1%	3,262	4,040	4,852	5,651	5,936

RADIAN GROUP, INC.

NYS: RDN

1601 Market Street	CEO: Sanford A. Ibrahim
Philadelphia, PA 19103	CFO: J. Franklin (Frank) Hall
Phone: 215 231-1000	HR: Robert E Croner
Fax: –	FYE: December 31
Web: www.radian.biz	Type: Public

Radian Group is glowing from a conflagration of private mortgage insurance claims. Through subsidiaries Radian Guaranty Radian Mortgage Assurance and Radian Insurance Radian Group provides traditional private mortgage insurance coverage to protect lenders from defaults by borrowers who put down a deposit of less than 20% when buying a home. Such coverage provides protection on individual loans and covers unpaid loan principal and delinquent interest. Its pool insurance covers limited exposure on groups of loans. Radian still insures municipal bonds written before 2008 through its financial guaranty business. Radian Group's customers include mortgage bankers commercial banks and savings institutions.

	Annual Growth	12/10	12/11	12/12	12/13	12/14
Assets ($ mil.)	(2.6%)	7,620.9	6,656.8	5,903.2	5,621.7	6,860.0
Net income ($ mil.)	–	(1,805.9)	302.2	(451.5)	(197.0)	959.5
Market value ($ mil.)	20.0%	1,541.8	447.1	1,167.3	2,697.7	3,194.4
Employees	22.1%	767	650	696	782	1,702

RADIANT LOGISTICS, INC.

ASE: RLGT

405 114th Avenue S.E., Third Floor	CEO: Kevin Kyles
Bellevue, WA 98004	CFO: Glenn Moore
Phone: 425 943-4599	HR: –
Fax: 425 462-0768	FYE: June 30
Web: www.radiantdelivers.com	Type: Public

When companies need someone to transport their freight Radiant Logistics delivers. Operating through its Airgroup and Adcom Worldwide subsidiaries the company offers logistics services such as domestic and international air ocean and ground freight forwarding (Radiant purchases transportation capacity from carriers and resells to its customers). In addition Radiant provides supply chain management services such as warehousing order fulfillment and inventory management. Government and automotive sectors (e.g. US Transportation Command Ford and General Motors) make up the company's customer base. Radiant operates through more than 100 offices located throughout North America.

	Annual Growth	06/11	06/12	06/13	06/14	06/15
Sales ($ mil.)	25.3%	203.8	297.0	310.8	349.1	502.7
Net income ($ mil.)	19.8%	2.9	1.9	3.7	5.1	5.9
Market value ($ mil.)	32.1%	102.2	74.5	83.0	131.5	311.1
Employees	49.8%	151	181	206	300	760

RADIANT SYSTEMS INC.

3925 Brookside Pkwy.	CEO: John Bruno
Alpharetta GA 30022	CFO: Mark E Haidet
Phone: 770-576-6000	HR: –
Fax: 770-754-7790	FYE: December 31
Web: www.radiantsystems.com	Type: Subsidiary

Radiant Systems helps businesses provide shining service. The company's point-of-sale (POS) systems combine hardware and software to manage centralized merchandising functions like ordering and scheduling customer access and visibility across an enterprise. Its touchscreen-based POS systems are used largely in the US hospitality industry; other clients include retail businesses like gas stations and cinemas. Radiant has historically gotten about half of its revenues from sales of maintenance subscription transaction and other services. The company markets directly and through resellers. Clients have included 7-Eleven Exxon Mobil and The Home Depot. Radiant was acquired by NCR for $1.2 billion in 2011.

RADIATION THERAPY SERVICES INC.

2270 Colonial Blvd.	CEO: Daniel E Dosertz
Fort Myers FL 33907	CFO: David N Watson
Phone: 239-931-7333	HR: –
Fax: 239-931-7380	FYE: December 31
Web: www.rtsx.com/index.asp	Type: Private

Radiation Therapy Services (RTSI) operates almost 120 radiation treatment centers in several countries including seven that involve hospital-based treatment centers and other groups. Operating primarily as 21st Century Oncology the company provides a wide variety of radiation therapy services including image-guided radiation therapy tomotherapy for treatment directly into affected areas seed implantation for prostate cancer and stereotactic radiosurgery for treating brain tumors. Its centers also participate in clinical research trials for cancer treatment.

RADIO FLYER INC.

6515 W. Grand Ave.	CEO: –
Chicago IL 60707	CFO: –
Phone: 773-637-7100	HR: Amy Bastuga
Fax: 773-637-8874	FYE: December 31
Web: www.radioflyer.com	Type: Private

Radio Flyer makes those wittle wed wagons adults adore and kids covet. An icon of childhood play the #18 Classic Red Wagon has rolled out of the plant for more than 70 years — an American toy industry record and the reason Radio Flyer owns a sizable stake in the US toy market. The company makes plastic wagons and models with oversized terrain-friendly tires and wooden rails as well as bikes and trikes for little tikes and scooters and pedal-powered cars. Radio Flyer sells its items in retail outlets in the US and Canada and online through the likes of Amazon.com. Italian immigrant Antonio Pasin chose the name "Radio Flyer" in 1933 because it sounded futuristic. His grandchildren own and operate the firm.

RADIO FREQUENCY SYSTEMS INC.

200 Pondview Dr.	CEO: –
Meriden CT 06450-7195	CFO: –
Phone: 203-630-3311	HR: –
Fax: 203-634-2272	FYE: December 31
Web: www.rfsworld.com	Type: Private

Radio Frequency Systems has radio antennas and related products to enable everything from the rush hour traffic report to battlefield communications. The company which does business as RFS designs and manufactures a wide range of wireless and radio network infrastructure equipment used by broadcasters telecommunications service providers network equipment manufacturers and government agencies. Products include radio-frequency (RF) systems antennas filters and combiners cables connectors accessories and related software. The company operates globally from 32 sales and support offices and nine manufacturing facilities located in Asia Australia Europe and the Americas.

RADIO ONE INC

NAS: ROIA K

1010 Wayne Avenue, 14th Floor
Silver Spring, MD 20910
Phone: 301 429-3200
Fax: –

CEO: –
CFO: Peter D Thompson
HR: –
FYE: December 31
Type: Public

Radio One ranks #1 among African-American audiences. The largest radio broadcaster serving black listeners the company owns about 55 stations in 15 mostly urban markets. Its radio stations which mostly operate in market clusters offer a variety of music formats as well as news and talk shows. In addition to broadcasting Radio One has a 80% stake in Reach Media. Radio One operates several websites and the company also owns more than 50% of TV One a cable television venture with Comcast. Founder and chairperson Catherine Hughes and her son president and CEO Alfred Liggins together control more than 90% of the company.

	Annual Growth	12/10	12/11	12/12	12/13	12/14
Sales ($ mil.)	12.1%	279.9	364.6	424.6	448.7	441.4
Net income ($ mil.)	–	(28.6)	2.9	(54.1)	(43.5)	(42.7)
Market value ($ mil.)	10.5%	56.2	50.1	38.1	190.0	83.7
Employees	2.1%	1,252	1,278	1,219	1,472	1,359

RADISSON HOTELS & RESORTS

11340 Blondo St.
Omaha NE 68164
Phone: 973-430-7000
Fax: 973-623-5389
Web: www.pseg.com/companies/energy_res/overview.jsp

CEO: Thorsten Kirschke
CFO: Trudy Rautio
HR: –
FYE: December 31
Type: Subsidiary

This hotel caters to explorers traveling in style. Radisson Hotels & Resorts is a leading upscale hotel brand with about 420 franchised locations in some 70 countries. The chain offers a full complement of amenities for both business and leisure travelers including fine dining fitness centers and meeting rooms. Its resort locations typically boast such niceties as beachfront locations golf courses or skiing. Radisson Hotels takes its name from the French explorer Pierre Esprit Radisson who visited many parts of the Upper Midwest and Canada during the 17th century. The company is the flagship luxury brand of Carlson Hotels Worldwide part of the hospitality and business services giant Carlson Companies.

RADISYS CORP.

NMS: RSYS

5435 N.E. Dawson Creek Drive
Hillsboro, OR 97124
Phone: 503 615-1100
Fax: –
Web: www.radisys.com

CEO: Brian Bronson
CFO: Jonathan (Jon) Wilson
HR: Cheryl Spencer
FYE: December 31
Type: Public

RadiSys makes hardware and software that help its customers run their networks more efficiently. Its products help route video and audio traffic to systems that will process it most effectively in terms of quality and cost. Radisys' offerings include application-specific systems board-level modules and chip-level components. The company also offers system integration software training and repair services. RadiSys sells its products to companies that make telecommunications products automated manufacturing devices gaming machines cars medical instruments and test and measurement tools. Customers range from Aastra and AT&T to Verint Systems and West Corp.

	Annual Growth	12/10	12/11	12/12	12/13	12/14
Sales ($ mil.)	(9.3%)	284.3	330.9	286.1	237.9	192.7
Net income ($ mil.)	–	(0.4)	(4.2)	(43.5)	(49.4)	(27.6)
Market value ($ mil.)	(28.4%)	325.1	184.9	108.9	83.7	85.5
Employees	8.5%	619	1,024	976	984	859

RADIUS HEALTH INC.

201 Broadway 6th Fl.
Cambridge MA 02139
Phone: 617-551-4700
Fax: 617-551-4701
Web: www.radiuspharm.com

CEO: Robert E Ward
CFO: B Nicholas Harvey
HR: –
FYE: December 31
Type: Private

Radius Health would like to banish the fear of Grandma falling and breaking a hip. The biopharmaceutical company targets osteoporosis and other women's health concerns through the development of new drugs. Its leading candidate is a synthetic version of a naturally occurring human bone-building protein. Administered via injection or transdermal patch the drug could be used to promote new bone growth and restore bone density in patients with osteoporosis. The company's pipeline also contains a treatment for hot flashes and one for age-related weigh loss frailty and muscle loss; 3M Lonza and Vetter Pharma make its drugs. Radius Health which formed in 2008 filed and withdrew an IPO in 2012.

RADNET INC

NMS: RDNT

1510 Cotner Avenue
Los Angeles, CA 90025
Phone: 310 478-7808
Fax: –
Web: www.radnet.com

CEO: Howard G. Berger
CFO: Mark D. Stolper
HR: Ruth Wilson
FYE: December 31
Type: Public

Image is everything at RadNet. The company owns and manages about 250 centers that offer a variety of diagnostic imaging services including magnetic resonance imaging (MRI) computed tomography (CT) PET scanning X-ray ultrasound and mammography. Its facilities are typically organized in regional clusters around urban hubs. RadNet contracts with groups of radiologists and other third-parties to provide the actual medical services while it runs the administration of the facilities and takes a cut of the revenues plus a management fee. It also develops radiology software and provides teleradiology interpretation services.

	Annual Growth	12/10	12/11	12/12	12/13	12/14
Sales ($ mil.)	6.9%	548.5	619.8	647.2	703.0	717.6
Net income ($ mil.)	–	(12.9)	7.2	64.5	2.1	1.4
Market value ($ mil.)	31.9%	120.8	91.2	108.3	71.5	365.7
Employees	8.6%	4,581	6,321	5,946	5,931	6,361

RADY CHILDREN'S HOSPITAL-SAN DIEGO

3020 CHILDRENS WAY
SAN DIEGO, CA 921234223
Phone: 858-309-7701
Fax: –
Web: www.rchsd.org

CEO: Stephen Kingsmore
CFO: –
HR: Mamoon Syed
FYE: June 30
Type: Private

Rady Children's Hospital-San Diego handles the big injuries of pint-sized patients. Serving as the region's only pediatric trauma center the nonprofit hospital boasts more than 520 beds. As part of its services Rady Children's Hospital-San Diego offers comprehensive pediatric care including surgical services convalescent care a neonatal intensive care unit and orthopedic services. Across its service area the hospital also operates about 25 satellite centers that provide such primary and specialized care services as physical therapy and hearing diagnostics. Rady Children's Hospital a teaching hospital affiliated with the University of California San Diego Medical School was founded in 1954.

	Annual Growth	06/07	06/08	06/09	06/10	06/13
Sales ($ mil.)	13.6%	–	–	490.9	619.9	818.6
Net income ($ mil.)	–	–	–	(56.5)	42.6	117.8
Market value ($ mil.)	–	–	–	–	–	–
Employees	–	–	–	–	–	2,313

RAE SYSTEMS INC.

3775 N. 1st St.
San Jose CA 95134
Phone: 408-952-8200
Fax: 408-952-8480
Web: www.raesystems.com

CEO: –
CFO: Michael Hansen
HR: Cathi Hinshaw
FYE: December 31
Type: Private

You may not learn who dealt it but the detection and monitoring instruments of RAE Systems will confirm the presence of gas and detail its chemical composition. The company went from being a supplier of stand-alone analytical instruments to providing networked instrumentation that can be used in many locales from factories to spills of hazardous materials and even to find those pesky missing weapons of mass destruction. RAE Systems counts the US Departments of Homeland Security Justice and State among its customers along with many sports facilities in the US. Customers in Asia account for about 40% of sales. In 2011 Vector Capital took RAE Systems private in a deal valued at about $138 million.

RAILAMERICA INC.

NYSE: RA

7411 Fullerton St. Ste. 300
Jacksonville FL 32256
Phone: 904-999-5000
Fax: 716-854-8480
Web: www.randcapital.com

CEO: John E Giles
CFO: Clyde Preslar
HR: –
FYE: December 31
Type: Public

Piece by piece RailAmerica has assembled an extensive rail transportation network. The company operates short-line railroads (generally less than 350 miles long) and regional freight lines in the US and Canada. RailAmerica owns interests in more than 40 railroads that operate over a network of about 7500 miles of track. RailAmerica has about 1500 customers and transports such items as coal lumber and forest products chemicals and agricultural products. RailAmerica's real estate division handles track and land leases and handles road and other access requests. In late 2012 the company was acquired by rival Genesee & Wyoming.

RAINMAKER SYSTEMS INC.

NBB: RMKR

900 East Hamilton Avenue, Suite 400
Campbell, CA 95008
Phone: 408 626-3800
Fax: 408 369-0910
Web: www.rainmakersystems.com

CEO: Terry Lydon
CFO: Bryant Tolles
HR: –
FYE: December 31
Type: Public

Rainmaker Systems is tapping into the power of the cloud. The company is a global provider of cloud-based business-to-business (B2B) selling services designed to help companies boost buying activity among their customers online. Its Rainmaker Revenue Delivery Platform provides a hosted technology portal for clients to sell and renew product and service contracts. It allows Rainmaker to resell subscriptions software licenses and warranties on behalf of its clients. Additionally it aids in sales lead development and in selling training services. Operating from offices in the US Europe and Asia Rainmaker primarily serves clients in computer hardware and software telecommunications and financial services.

	Annual Growth	12/09	12/10	12/11	12/12	12/13
Sales ($ mil.)	(22.0%)	47.8	42.8	37.0	25.4	17.7
Net income ($ mil.)	–	(8.3)	(10.0)	(11.0)	(10.3)	(21.0)
Market value ($ mil.)	(36.6%)	61.8	58.8	33.9	30.3	10.0
Employees	(37.0%)	950	1,450	1,050	130	150

RAIT FINANCIAL TRUST

NYS: RAS

2929 Arch Street, 17th Floor
Philadelphia, PA 19104
Phone: 215 243-9000
Fax: –

CEO: Scott F. Schaeffer
CFO: James J. Sebra
HR: –
FYE: December 31
Type: Public

RAIT Financial Trust is a real estate investment trust (REIT) that specializes in originating commercial real estate loans and acquiring and managing commercial real estate properties. Its loan portfolio is made up of mezzanine and short-term bridge financing mainly secured by multifamily office and retail properties. RAIT also provides loan servicing commercial property and asset management and asset repositioning and sales services for other real estate firms. Subsidiary Taberna Realty Finance provides long-term real estate capital while Independence Realty Trust (IRT) owns apartment properties in opportunistic US markets. Altogether RAIT boasts some $4.5 billion in assets under management.

	Annual Growth	12/10	12/11	12/12	12/13	12/14
Sales ($ mil.)	17.2%	153.4	234.2	200.8	246.9	289.7
Net income ($ mil.)	–	110.9	(37.7)	(168.3)	(285.4)	(290.0)
Market value ($ mil.)	36.8%	180.7	391.9	466.2	740.1	632.8
Employees	18.3%	405	366	376	394	794

RALCORP FROZEN BAKERY PRODUCTS INC.

3250 Lacey Rd. Ste. 600
Downers Grove IL 60515
Phone: 630-455-5200
Fax: 630-455-5202
Web: www.ralcorpfrozen.com

CEO: –
CFO: –
HR: –
FYE: September 30
Type: Subsidiary

Go ahead bask in the applause; Ralcorp Frozen Bakery Products makes you the chef. The company manufactures frozen food products from ready-to-eat and thaw-and-sell to toastable and microwaveable baked goods. Products are sold under private- and global name brands such as Bakery Chef (biscuits) Krusteaz (pancakes) and Lofthouse (cookies). It also makes breakfast items for McDonald's. Ralcorp Frozen a division of private-brand food giant Ralcorp accounts for some 20% of its parent's revenues selling to in-store bakeries but also retail groceries and industrial and institutional food service operators. To puff up its frozen offerings Ralcorp acquired Sara Lee's refrigerated dough business in 2011.

RALEY'S

500 W CAPITOL AVE
WEST SACRAMENTO, CA 956052696
Phone: 916-373-3333
Fax: –
Web: www.raleys.com

CEO: Michael J. (Mike) Teel
CFO: Ken Mueller
HR: –
FYE: June 29
Type: Private

Raley's has to stock plenty of fresh fruit and great wines — it sells to the people that produce them. The company operates about 130 supermarkets and superstores in California and Nevada. In addition to about 80 flagship Raley's Superstores the company operates about 20 Bel Air Markets (in the Sacramento area) Nob Hill Foods (an upscale Bay Area chain with more than 20 locations) and nearly 10 discount warehouse stores under the Food Source banner in Northern California and Nevada. Raley's stores typically offer groceries natural foods and liquor as well as in-store pharmacies. Founded during the Depression by Thomas Porter Raley the company is owned by Tom's daughter Joyce Raley Teel.

	Annual Growth	06/08	06/09	06/10	06/12	06/13
Sales ($ mil.)	–	–	0.0	3,064.4	3,162.3	3,054.4
Net income ($ mil.)	–	–	–	0.0	(1.3)	(8.1)
Market value ($ mil.)	–	–	–	–	–	–
Employees	–	–	–	–	–	14,000

RALLY SOFTWARE DEVELOPMENT CORP.

3333 Walnut St.	CEO: Timothy Miller
Boulder CO 80301	CFO: James M Lejeal
Phone: 303-565-2800	HR: Laura Durfey
Fax: 303-226-1179	FYE: January 31
Web: www.rallydev.com	Type: Private

Rally Software Development helps software makers mobilize toward a common goal. Its flagship products Rally Enterprise and Rally Community focus on Agile application lifecycle management practices and help developers streamline the collaborative creation of new software. The company sells subscriptions to its products and it provides services such as training software developers on how to apply Agile practices to their organizations. Rally Software counts Cisco Moody's and Sony Ericsson among its customers. The company was founded in 2002 by CTO and serial entrepreneur Ryan Martens. In 2013 the company filed to go public.

RALPH LAUREN CORP

NYS: RL

650 Madison Avenue	CEO: Stefan Larsson
New York, NY 10022	CFO: Robert L Madore
Phone: 212 318-7000	HR: Helene Pliner
Fax: –	FYE: March 28
Web: www.ralphlauren.com	Type: Public

Ralph Lauren Corporation is galloping at a faster clip than when its namesake founder first entered the arena over 45 years ago. With golden mallet brands such as Polo by Ralph Lauren Chaps RRL Club Monaco and RLX Ralph Lauren the company designs and markets apparel and accessories home furnishings and fragrances. Its collections are available at nearly 13000 retail locations worldwide including many upscale and mid-tier department stores (Macy's contributes 12% of RL's wholesale revenue). It operates 460-plus Ralph Lauren and Club Monaco retail stores worldwide as well as 540 concession-based shops-within-shops and 10 e-commerce sites. American style icon and founder Lauren is stepping down as CEO.

	Annual Growth	04/11*	03/12	03/13	03/14	03/15
Sales ($ mil.)	7.7%	5,660.3	6,859.5	6,944.8	7,450.0	7,620.0
Net income ($ mil.)	5.5%	567.6	681.0	750.0	776.0	702.0
Market value ($ mil.)	0.9%	10,928.2	15,044.7	14,611.5	13,656.1	11,324.3
Employees	1.0%	24,000	25,000	23,000	23,000	25,000
						*Fiscal year change

RAMBUS INC. (DE)

NMS: RMBS

1050 Enterprise Way, Suite 700	CEO: Ronald D. (Ron) Black
Sunnyvale, CA 94089	CFO: Satish Rishi
Phone: 408 462-8000	HR: –
Fax: –	FYE: December 31
Web: www.rambus.com	Type: Public

While Rambus sits around and thinks of new semiconductor technologies other companies put its designs to work. Rambus licenses its intellectual property designs for computer memory — called Rambus DRAM or RDRAM — that speeds the exchange of signals between a computer's memory and logic chips. RDRAM chips are used in PCs video game consoles and other electronic systems. Rambus' leading licensees include AMD Fujitsu NEC Panasonic and Toshiba. It also licenses LCD lighting product designs. The company holds more than 1700 patents and has more than 1100 patent applications pending.

	Annual Growth	12/10	12/11	12/12	12/13	12/14
Sales ($ mil.)	(2.1%)	323.4	312.4	234.1	271.5	296.6
Net income ($ mil.)	(35.5%)	150.9	(43.1)	(134.3)	(33.7)	26.2
Market value ($ mil.)	(14.2%)	2,358.5	869.5	560.8	1,090.6	1,277.1
Employees	6.7%	390	456	455	447	505

RAMCO-GERSHENSON PROPERTIES TRUST (MD)

NYS: RPT

31500 Northwestern Highway, Suite 300	CEO: Dennis E. Gershenson
Farmington Hills, MI 48334	CFO: Geoffrey Bedrosian
Phone: 248 350-9900	HR: Karen Childress-newberger
Fax: 248 350-9925	FYE: December 31
Web: www.rgpt.com	Type: Public

Ramco-Gershenson Properties Trust makes no bones about horning in on the retail world. A self-administered real estate investment trust (REIT) it owns develops and manages a property portfolio of about 90 shopping centers in about a dozen states east of the Mississippi River. The REIT's properties contain approximately 20 million sq. ft. of leasable space in the Midwest mid-Atlantic and Southeast. Nearly all of its assets are community shopping centers in metropolitan areas anchored by grocery or big-box stores. The REIT also owns one enclosed regional mall and one single-tenant property and has a handful of projects under development.

	Annual Growth	12/10	12/11	12/12	12/13	12/14
Sales ($ mil.)	16.2%	119.8	121.3	128.7	170.1	218.4
Net income ($ mil.)	–	(20.1)	(26.8)	7.2	11.0	(2.4)
Market value ($ mil.)	10.8%	965.8	762.5	1,032.5	1,221.0	1,453.7
Employees	(2.0%)	126	106	109	108	116

RAMTRON INTERNATIONAL CORPORATION

NASDAQ: RMTR

1850 Ramtron Dr.	CEO: Eric A Balzer
Colorado Springs CO 80921	CFO: Gery E Richards
Phone: 719-481-7000	HR: –
Fax: 719-481-9294	FYE: December 31
Web: www.ramtron.com	Type: Public

Ramtron International provides the F-RAM needed to watch Tron in the palm of your hand. Ramtron designs ferroelectric random-access memories (F-RAMs) which it touts as providing better performance than other kinds of memory chips and which are used in products such as power meters laser printers and handheld devices. It partners with Fujitsu Infineon and Toshiba among others. The company sells directly and through distributors including Future Electronics Mouser (a subsidiary of TTI) and Tokyo Electron Device. Most of Ramtron's sales come from outside the US. In 2012 the company agreed to be acquired by Cypress Semiconductor in a $3.10 per share deal with a total value of around $110 million.

RANBAXY PHARMACEUTICALS INC.

600 College Rd. E. Ste. 2100	CEO: Venkat Krishnan
Princeton NJ 08540	CFO: –
Phone: 609-720-9200	HR: –
Fax: 609-720-1155	FYE: December 31
Web: www.ranbaxyusa.com	Type: Subsidiary

Ranbaxy Pharmaceuticals (RPI) is in a real no-name business. The company the US arm of Indian generic pharmaceuticals giant Ranbaxy Laboratories Limited makes and markets dozens of generic and over-the-counter (OTC) drugs. RPI's generic offerings produced by manufacturing subsidiary Ohm Laboratories include anti-infectives and treatments for cardiovascular gastrointestinal and central nervous system disorders. Its OTC products include analgesics antihistamines and decongestants. Sister subsidiary Ranbaxy Laboratories Inc. (RLI) develops branded pharmaceuticals.

RAND LOGISTICS INC

NAS: RLOG

500 Fifth Avenue, 50th Floor
New York, NY 10110
Phone: 212 644-3450
Fax: –
Web: www.randlogisticsinc.com

CEO: Edward Levy
CFO: Mark S Hiltwein
HR: –
FYE: March 31
Type: Public

Rand Logistics plies its trade from port to port in the boundary waters. The company hauls dry bulk cargo across the Great Lakes calling on ports in the US and Canada. Through subsidiaries Lower Lakes Towing (Canadian ports) Lower Lakes Transportation (US ports) and Grand River Navigation the company operates a fleet of more than a dozen vessels consisting mainly of self-unloading bulk carriers. (Self-unloading vessels don't require land-based assistance so they can arrive at a dock and unload any time.) Conventional bulk carriers and an integrated tug/barge unit make up the rest of Rand Logistics' fleet. Cargo carried by the company includes construction aggregates coal grain iron ore and salt.

	Annual Growth	03/11	03/12	03/13	03/14	03/15
Sales ($ mil.)	6.7%	118.0	147.8	156.6	155.8	153.0
Net income ($ mil.)	–	0.1	8.1	(3.8)	(4.5)	(9.4)
Market value ($ mil.)	(18.3%)	131.8	151.9	110.5	124.4	58.6
Employees	6.7%	397	482	543	504	515

RANDA LEATHER GOODS

2009 W. Hastings St.
Chicago IL 60608
Phone: 312-997-2358
Fax: 312-997-2147
Web: www.randa.net

CEO: Jeffrey O Spiegel
CFO: –
HR: –
FYE: December 31
Type: Subsidiary

Thank Randa for helping you keep your pants on and your neck dressed up. Randa Leather Goods makes men's and boys' belts and other personal leather goods as part of Randa Accessories which is known for its neckwear expertise. The division also makes and distributes lines of suspenders packaged gifts and boys' neckwear. Parent Randa Accessories boasts more than 10 licensing agreements to make accessories under the Levi's Dockers Dickies Columbia Izod and Arrow brand names among others. The company also markets products under its own handful of proprietary labels such as Bill Adler Studio Reward and Dante. Randa Leather Goods sells its products through retail and specialty stores and catalogs.

RANDOLPH-BROOKS FEDERAL CREDIT UNION

Creswell Center 1 Randolph Brooks Pkwy.
Live Oak TX 78233-2416
Phone: 210-945-3333
Fax: 210-945-3764
Web: www.rbfcu.org

CEO: Randy M Smith
CFO: –
HR: –
FYE: December 31
Type: Private - Not-for-Pr

Randolph-Brooks Federal Credit Union (RBFCU) provides deposit and lending services including checking and savings accounts and loans for homes cars education and consumer goods. Serving some 410000 members RBFCU operates more than 40 locations primarily in San Antonio and Austin as well as other Central Texas communities. Products offered by the credit union include business loans MasterCard credit cards and term certificates. Its assets exceed $5 billion. Through its Randolph Brooks Services Group subsidiary the credit union offers investment and insurance products such as mutual funds IRAs annuities dental benefits home warranties roadside assistance programs and financial planning services.

RANDOM HOUSE INC.

1745 Broadway
New York NY 10019
Phone: 212-782-9000
Fax: 919-554-4361
Web: www.thebodyshop.com

CEO: –
CFO: –
HR: –
FYE: December 31
Type: Subsidiary

Its not-so-random acts of publishing have transformed Random House into the world's largest trade book publisher. The book publishing subsidiary of media giant Bertelsmann Random House operates its eponymous imprint and some 200 others such as Alfred A. Knopf Ballantine Bantam Dell and Doubleday. Its top-sellers include Dan Brown's The Da Vinci Code and its stable of authors includes Elmore Leonard Toni Morrison and Dr. Seuss. In addition the company publishes Fodor's popular travel books audio products and electronic books. Outside the US Random House oversees publishers such as McClelland & Stewart (Canada) and Plaza & Janes (Spain). In 2012 it announced plans to combine with The Penguin Group.

RANDSTAD US L.P.

2015 S. Park Place SE
Atlanta GA 30339
Phone: 770-937-7000
Fax: 305-593-2393
Web: www.goldcoastbeverage.com

CEO: –
CFO: Ron Fucillo
HR: –
FYE: December 31
Type: Subsidiary

Randstad US provides office industrial technical creative and professional staffing services through more than 500 branches across the US and Canada. The company also provides skills assessments career counseling health coverage vacation and 401(k) benefits and training to its eligible internal and external employees. It places about 45000 people in job positions each week in the US. Headquartered in Atlanta the company is a subsidiary of Netherlands-based staffing powerhouse Randstad Holding nv which began operations in the US in 1993. Randstad US works in tandem with Randstad Professionals US another unit owned by its parent.

RANGE RESOURCES CORP

NYS: RRC

100 Throckmorton Street, Suite 1200
Fort Worth, TX 76102
Phone: 817 870-2601
Fax: –
Web: www.rangeresources.com

CEO: Jeffrey L. (Jeff) Ventura
CFO: Roger S. Manny
HR: Carol Culpepper
FYE: December 31
Type: Public

Range Resources is riding the range as an independent acquirer and developer of US oil and gas resources. The company's long-term strategy involves acquiring long-lived established properties and it has major development areas in the Appalachian and Southwest (West Texas western Oklahoma and Texas Panhandle) regions. Natural gas accounted for 67% of Range Resources' proved reserves of 10.3 trillion cu. ft. of natural gas equivalent in 2014. The company holds more than 2 million net acres of leasehold properties and an inventory of more than 9000 net drilling locations.

	Annual Growth	12/10	12/11	12/12	12/13	12/14
Sales ($ mil.)	27.1%	1,039.0	1,218.7	1,457.7	1,862.7	2,711.7
Net income ($ mil.)	–	(239.3)	58.0	13.0	115.7	634.4
Market value ($ mil.)	4.4%	7,584.9	10,444.8	10,594.9	14,217.0	9,013.2
Employees	8.6%	713	756	841	867	990

RAPID CITY REGIONAL HOSPITAL INC.

353 FAIRMONT BLVD	CEO: Charles Hart
RAPID CITY, SD 57701-7393	CFO: –
Phone: 605-719-1000	HR: –
Fax: –	FYE: June 30
Web: www.regionalhealth.com	Type: Private

Mt. Rushmore sightseers bikers and locals alike can seek medical care at Rapid City Regional Hospital. The medical facility is a general and psychiatric hospital with some 330 acute care beds and 50 psychiatric beds located in the Black Hills region of western South Dakota. In addition to emergency and acute care the not-for-profit hospital also offers a behavioral health center a rehabilitation facility a cancer care institute and women's and children's departments. Rapid City Regional Hospital which was established in 1973 is part of Regional Health a network of regional hospitals medical clinics and senior care centers.

	Annual Growth	06/08	06/09	06/10	06/11	06/12
Sales ($ mil.)	5.1%	–	381.2	409.4	142.8	443.1
Net income ($ mil.)	3.7%	–	42.0	65.5	39.4	46.9
Market value ($ mil.)	–	–	–	–	–	–
Employees	–	–	–	–	–	4,200

RAPP WORLDWIDE INC.

437 Madison Ave. 3rd Fl.	CEO: Alexei Orlov
New York NY 10022	CFO: Matt Hafkin
Phone: 212-817-6800	HR: –
Fax: +44-1953-608-300	FYE: December 31
Web: www.lotuscars.co.uk	Type: Subsidiary

You might say this firm has the marketing rap down pat. Rapp Worldwide is one of the world's leading direct marketing and customer relationship management agencies with about 50 offices in 30 countries. Rapp offers services for planning and implementing integrated marketing campaigns involving direct mail television telemarketing and interactive media including creative development data analysis and production and fulfillment. Units include Rapp UK and The Kern Organization (TKO) which specializes in customer acquisition and demand generation services. Rapp is part of the Diversified Agency Services division of Omnicom Group one of the largest media services conglomerates in the world.

RAPPAHANNOCK ELECTRIC COOPERATIVE

247 INDUSTRIAL CT	CEO: Kent D Farmer
FREDERICKSBURG, VA 224082443	CFO: –
Phone: 540-898-8500	HR: –
Fax: –	FYE: December 31
Web: www.myrec.coop	Type: Private

Like the river it's named after the Rappahannock Electric Cooperative (REC) keeps the power running smoothly. The consumer-owned cooperative provides electricity to homes businesses and industries in parts of 22 counties from the Blue Ridge Mountains to the mouth of the Rappahannock River in eastern Virginia. REC supplies power to more than 157000 members over more than 16000 miles of power line. REC offers surge protection internet services and home security plans to entice customers as competition from other suppliers arrives. Once rural in nature the cooperative's territory has seen large pockets of suburban growth.

	Annual Growth	12/09	12/10	12/11	12/12	12/13
Sales ($ mil.)	4.3%	–	353.0	410.5	4.8	400.8
Net income ($ mil.)	(6.7%)	–	–	17.3	16.9	15.1
Market value ($ mil.)	–	–	–	–	–	–
Employees	–	–	–	–	–	423

RAPTOR NETWORKS TECHNOLOGY INC.   OTC: RPTN

1508 S. Grand Ave.	CEO: Dmitriy Nikitin
Santa Ana CA 92705	CFO: –
Phone: 949-623-9300	HR: –
Fax: 949-623-9400	FYE: December 31
Web: www.raptor-networks.com	Type: Public

Raptor Networks Technology preys on network latency. The company develops switching hardware and software for enterprise networks. Its core and edge switching products are designed specifically for high-bandwidth applications such as Internet Protocol television (IPTV) and Voice over Internet Protocol (VoIP). The company also offers network interface cards (NICs) for PCs and servers. It targets the education financial services government health care and telecommunications markets. Raptor sells directly and through resellers; the company is also pursuing an OEM channel strategy. The company has a systems integration partnership with government IT contractor CACI.

RAPTOR PHARMACEUTICALS CORP.   NMS: RPTP

7 Hamilton Landing, Suite 100	CEO: Julie Anne Smith
Novato, CA 94949	CFO: Kim R. Tsuchimoto
Phone: 415 408-6200	HR: Justin Ford
Fax: –	FYE: December 31
Web: www.raptorpharma.com	Type: Public

Raptor Pharmaceuticals (formerly TorreyPines Therapeutics) can help you calm your nerves. The drug company is developing small molecule therapies to treat central nervous system disorders specifically migraines and chronic pain. Its lead candidate tezampanel is undergoing clinical testing as a treatment for migraines and muscle spasms; the compound was licensed from Eli Lilly. Other discovery and development programs target neuropathic pain (pain caused by nerve damage) dry mouth Alzheimer's disease and cognitive impairment associated with schizophrenia. In mid-2009 the former TorreyPines was acquired by Raptor Pharmaceuticals.

	Annual Growth	08/11	08/12*	12/12	12/13	12/14
Sales ($ mil.)	–	–	0.0	0.0	16.9	69.5
Net income ($ mil.)	–	(37.2)	(38.6)	(19.3)	(69.4)	(52.5)
Market value ($ mil.)	30.5%	325.7	342.2	402.8	896.6	724.4
Employees	106.3%	14	38	42	72	123

*Fiscal year change

RARITAN AMERICAS INC.

400 Cottontail Ln.	CEO: Ching-I Hsu
Somerset NJ 08873	CFO: Bob Dennerlein
Phone: 732-764-8886	HR: –
Fax: 732-764-8887	FYE: December 31
Web: www.raritan.com	Type: Private

Raritan Americas makes specialized computing products used in data centers and other corporate environments that engage in intensive IT activities. The company's products include PC keyboard video and mouse (KVM) switches which enable multiple PC servers and networking equipment to be controlled from a single set of devices and related connectivity devices including serial console and remote management systems. Raritan sells directly and through resellers and distributors to computer hardware vendors and enterprise customers. The company's global customer base has included Cisco Dell Earth-Link Merrill Lynch NASA and Oklahoma State University. Raritan was founded in 1985 by chairman and CEO Ching-I Hsu.

RARITAN BAY MEDICAL CENTER.

530 NEW BRUNSWICK AVE
PERTH AMBOY, NJ 088613685
Phone: 732-442-3700
Fax: –
Web: www.rbmc.org

CEO: –
CFO: Thomas Shanahan
HR: Vincent Constantino
FYE: December 31
Type: Private

Health care is not rare at Raritan Bay Medical Center (RBMC). The not-for-profit center operates two hospitals in central New Jersey: Its Perth Amboy campus has about 390 beds and its Old Bridge campus has more than 110 beds. RBMC provides acute care and emergency services as well as ambulatory care through its outpatient clinics. Its Perth Amboy location provides specialized care in fields including women's and children's health. RBMC is affiliated with the University of Medicine and Dentistry of New Jersey - Robert Wood Johnson Medical School as well as the Cancer Institute of New Jersey.

	Annual Growth	12/03	12/04	12/05	12/06	12/08
Sales ($ mil.)	(1.3%)	–	240.8	230.9	232.3	228.6
Net income ($ mil.)	–	–	–	(2.5)	3.5	(6.9)
Market value ($ mil.)	–	–	–	–	–	–
Employees	–	–	–	–	–	1,970

RARITAN VALLEY COMMUNITY COLLEGE

118 LAMINGTON RD
BRANCHBURG, NJ 088763315
Phone: 908-526-1200
Fax: –
Web: www.rvccathletics.com

CEO: –
CFO: –
HR: –
FYE: June 30
Type: Private

Raritan Valley Community College offers more than 90 associate degree and certification programs to residents in central New Jersey's Somerset and Hunterdon counties. The school offers nine academic departments including Business and Public Service; Communication & Languages; Computer Science; English; Health Science Education; Humanities; Social Science & Education; Mathematics; Science & Engineering; and Visual and Performing Arts. The college which boasts some 1400 courses also provides customized training programs and non-credit courses as well as job and career counseling services. More than 8400 students take classes at Raritan Valley Community College which was founded in 1965.

	Annual Growth	06/05	06/06	06/08	06/10	06/13
Sales ($ mil.)	–	–	(1,421.9)	56.5	61.4	62.6
Net income ($ mil.)	–	–	–	3.6	0.7	(0.6)
Market value ($ mil.)	–	–	–	–	–	–
Employees	–	–	–	–	–	550

RAVE RESTAURANT GROUP INC

NAS: RAVE

3551 Plano Parkway
The Colony, TX 75056
Phone: 469 384-5000
Fax: –
Web: www.pizzainn.com

CEO: Randy E Gier
CFO: Timothy E Mullany
HR: –
FYE: June 28
Type: Public

Pizza is the in thing for this company. Pizza Inn operates a chain of franchised quick-service pizza restaurants with more than 300 locations in the US and the Middle East. The eateries feature a menu of pizzas pastas and sandwiches along with salads and desserts. Most locations offer buffet-style and table service while other units are strictly delivery and carryout units. The chain also has limited-menu express carryout units in convenience stores and airport terminals and on college campuses. Pizza Inn's domestic locations are concentrated in more than 15 southern states with about half located in Texas and North Carolina. Chairman Mark Schwarz owns more than 35% of the company.

	Annual Growth	06/11	06/12	06/13	06/14	06/15
Sales ($ mil.)	2.9%	43.0	43.0	41.9	42.2	48.2
Net income ($ mil.)	–	1.4	0.3	(1.3)	(1.6)	(1.8)
Market value ($ mil.)	49.6%	27.4	32.3	58.8	63.6	137.4
Employees	31.2%	188	268	287	304	557

RAVEN INDUSTRIES, INC.

NMS: RAVN

205 East 6th Street, P.O. Box 5107
Sioux Falls, SD 57117-5107
Phone: 605 336-2750
Fax: –
Web: www.ravenind.com

CEO: Daniel A Rykhus
CFO: Steven (Steve) Brazones
HR: –
FYE: January 31
Type: Public

Quoth the Raven "Balloons (and more) evermore!" Raven Industries is a diversified technology company that caters to the industrial agricultural energy construction military and aerospace sectors. The company's Aerostar division sells high-altitude research balloons as well as parachutes and protective wear used by US agencies while its Engineered Films Division makes reinforced plastic sheeting for various applications. The Applied Technology Division manufactures high-tech agricultural aids from global positioning system (GPS)-based steering devices and chemical spray equipment to field computers.

	Annual Growth	01/11	01/12	01/13	01/14	01/15
Sales ($ mil.)	4.7%	314.7	381.5	406.2	394.7	378.2
Net income ($ mil.)	(5.9%)	40.5	50.6	52.5	42.9	31.7
Market value ($ mil.)	(17.9%)	1,797.5	2,469.1	1,024.7	1,425.0	815.8
Employees	1.9%	1,112	1,405	1,379	1,286	1,200

RAWLINGS SPORTING GOODS COMPANY INC.

510 Maryville University Dr. Ste. 110
St. Louis MO 63141
Phone: 314-819-2800
Fax: 314-819-2988
Web: www.rawlings.com

CEO: Michael Zlaket
CFO: –
HR: –
FYE: December 31
Type: Subsidiary

In a league of its own Rawlings Sporting Goods is known for its ties to Major League Baseball (MLB); the company is the MLB's exclusive supplier of baseball helmets. Rawlings makes and distributes a variety of equipment and protective gear for playing baseball football and basketball. Its equipment is also used by the National Collegiate Athletic Association (NCAA) as well as amateur organizations and in interscholastic athletics. Rawlings sells through mass merchandisers sporting goods retailers and its namesake website. It licenses its brand for an array of merchandise including apparel toys and shoes. Rawlings is a subsidiary of consumer products maker Jarden which acquired the business in 2007.

RAYBURN COUNTRY ELECTRIC COOPERATIVE INC

980 SIDS RD
ROCKWALL, TX 750326512
Phone: 972-771-1336
Fax: –
Web: www.rayburnelectric.com

CEO: –
CFO: Loretto Martin
HR: –
FYE: December 31
Type: Private

This is indeed Sam Rayburn country. Rayburn Country Electric Cooperative (Rayburn Electric) operates in the old stomping grounds of the legendary Texas politician and former speaker of the US House of Representatives. Rayburn Electric is a power generation and transmission organization that supplies wholesale power to five rural distribution cooperatives operating in 16 counties in north central and northeastern Texas. Five distribution cooperatives (Fannin County Electric Coop Farmers Electric Coop Grayson-Collin Electric Coop Lamar Electric Coop and Trinity Valley Electric Coop) collectively own the company.

	Annual Growth	12/08	12/09	12/10	12/11	12/13
Sales ($ mil.)	6.0%	–	238.3	238.6	316.0	301.3
Net income ($ mil.)	(91.2%)	–	–	1.6	0.0	0.0
Market value ($ mil.)	–	–	–	–	–	–
Employees	–	–	–	–	–	8

RAYCOM MEDIA INC.

RSA Tower 201 Monroe St. 20th Fl.
Montgomery AL 36104
Phone: 334-206-1400
Fax: 334-206-1555
Web: www.raycommedia.com

CEO: Paul McTear
CFO: –
HR: –
FYE: December 31
Type: Private

Raycom Media's TV stations will electrify you with entertainment or satiate you with sports. The company is a leading television station group with more than 45 stations serving some 35 markets in about 20 states. It has local stations affiliated with all four major networks as well as smaller networks The CW and MyNetworkTV. In addition to its TV stations Raycom is involved in sports programming and promotion through its Raycom Sports subsidiary which holds the broadcasting rights to Atlantic Coast Conference (ACC) college basketball games as well as syndication rights to ACC football games. Raycom also has post production and advertising sales operations. The employee-owned company was formed in 1996.

RAYMOND JAMES FINANCIAL, INC.

NYS: RJF

880 Carillon Parkway
St. Petersburg, FL 33716
Phone: 727 567-1000
Fax: –
Web: www.raymondjames.com

CEO: Dennis W. Zank
CFO: Jeffrey P. Julien
HR: Andrea Grayson
FYE: September 30
Type: Public

Call it Ray or Ray Jay. Raymond James Financial doesn't mind as long as it's getting calls from customers. The diversified financial services company offers investment and financial planning services primarily through subsidiary Raymond James & Associates (RJA) which provides securities brokerage investment banking and financial advisory services in North America and Europe. Its Raymond James Financial Services offers financial planning and brokerage services via independent financial advisors as well as through alliances with community banks. Other units provide asset management trust and banking services. The firm has more than 2500 branches offices and independent contractor branches.

	Annual Growth	09/11	09/12	09/13	09/14	09/15
Sales ($ mil.)	11.8%	3,399.9	3,897.9	4,595.8	4,965.5	5,308.2
Net income ($ mil.)	15.9%	278.4	295.9	367.2	480.2	502.1
Market value ($ mil.)	17.6%	3,710.2	5,238.0	5,955.4	7,657.6	7,093.1
Employees	7.1%	11,300	13,900	13,650	13,900	14,850

RAYMOURS FURNITURE COMPANY INC.

7248 MORGAN RD
LIVERPOOL, NY 130904535
Phone: 315-453-2500
Fax: –
Web: www.raymourflanigan.com

CEO: –
CFO: James Poole
HR: –
FYE: December 29
Type: Private

Raymours Furniture is heating up the oft-chilly Northeast doing business as Raymour & Flanigan. The company operates in several states through 94 retail stores including nearly a dozen clearance centers. It sells furniture for just about every room in the house (bedroom dining room home office living room) offering such pieces as bookcases entertainment centers headboards mattresses nightstands recliners sofas and tables. Brands such as Broyhill La-Z-Boy Natuzzi and Tempur Sealy are represented. Raymours is run by founding Goldberg family.

	Annual Growth	12/03	12/04	12/05	12/06	12/07
Sales ($ mil.)	–	–	–	(46.6)	780.6	881.8
Net income ($ mil.)	46328.7%	–	–	0.0	23.4	30.4
Market value ($ mil.)	–	–	–	–	–	–
Employees	–	–	–	–	–	4,400

RAYONIER INC.

NYS: RYN

225 Water Street, Suite 1400
Jacksonville, FL 32202
Phone: 904 357-9100
Fax: –
Web: www.rayonier.com

CEO: David L. (Dave) Nunes
CFO: Mark McHugh
HR: –
FYE: December 31
Type: Public

Timber is at the root of Rayonier's business. The real estate investment trust (REIT) owns and manages timberlands grows and sells timber and manufactures Southern pine lumber specialty cellulose fibers and fluff pulp used in absorbent consumer products. The company owns leases or manages about 2.4 million acres of timberland and real estate in the US in addition to some 300000 acres in New Zealand through a joint venture. Rayonier operates two cellulose fiber mills and lumber sawmills in Georgia and Florida. The firm also ships wood pulp to China and Japan. Founded in 1926 as a pulp and paper manufacturer the name Rayonier is derived from rayon (a manufactured cellulose fiber) and Mount Rainier.

	Annual Growth	12/10	12/11	12/12	12/13	12/14
Sales ($ mil.)	(17.7%)	1,315.2	1,488.6	1,571.0	1,707.8	603.5
Net income ($ mil.)	(17.8%)	217.6	276.0	278.7	371.9	99.3
Market value ($ mil.)	(14.6%)	6,658.1	5,657.9	6,570.6	5,337.1	3,542.0
Employees	(35.1%)	1,800	1,900	1,900	1,600	320

RAYTHEON APPLIED SIGNAL TECHNOLOGY INC.

460 W. California Ave.
Sunnyvale CA 94086
Phone: 408-749-1888
Fax: 408-522-2800
Web: www.appsig.com

CEO: John R Treichler
CFO: James E Doyle
HR: –
FYE: October 31
Type: Subsidiary

Eavesdropping is big business at Raytheon Applied Signal Technology (AST). The company makes reconnaissance systems — including receivers processors and software — used by the US government and its contractors to collect and process electronic communications. Its products are used to scan and filter cell phone ship-to-shore microwave and military transmissions and evaluate them for relevant information. Others are designed to collect and process radar signals for weapons systems. The company sells mostly to intelligence and military agencies but it has some commercial clients. Formerly known simply as Applied Signal Technology the company was acquired by top military contractor Raytheon in 2011 for $490 million.

RAYTHEON CO.

NYS: RTN

870 Winter Street
Waltham, MA 02451
Phone: 781 522-3000
Fax: –
Web: www.raytheon.com

CEO: John D. Harris
CFO: Anthony F. O'Brien
HR: Randall Fort
FYE: December 31
Type: Public

Raytheon ("light of the gods") shines in the upper pantheon of US military contractors; the company regularly places among the Pentagon's top 10 prime contractors. Its air/land/sea/space/cyber defense offerings include reconnaissance targeting and navigation systems as well as missile systems (Patriot Sidewinder and Tomahawk) unmanned ground and aerial systems sensing technologies and radars. Additionally Raytheon makes systems for communications (satellite) and intelligence radios cybersecurity and air traffic control. It also offers commercial electronics products and services as well as food safety processing technologies. The US government accounts for a large portion of sales.

	Annual Growth	12/11	12/12	12/13	12/14	12/15
Sales ($ mil.)	(1.7%)	24,857.0	24,414.0	23,706.0	22,826.0	23,247.0
Net income ($ mil.)	2.7%	1,866.0	1,888.0	1,996.0	2,244.0	2,074.0
Market value ($ mil.)	26.7%	14,465.6	17,210.4	27,119.3	32,342.8	37,234.5
Employees	(3.7%)	71,000	67,800	63,000	61,000	61,000

RAYTHEON TECHNICAL SERVICES COMPANY LLC

22265 Pacific Blvd.
Dulles VA 20166
Phone: 571-250-3000
Fax: 903-457-4413
Web: www.l-3com.com/is

CEO: –
CFO: –
HR: –
FYE: December 31
Type: Subsidiary

Some people talk about supporting the troops but this company really does. Raytheon Technical Services Company (RTSC) is a leading provider of logistical operational engineering and technical support services for the US Department of Defense (DoD) and other agencies of the federal government. It offers project and program management services in support of equipment and installations as well as base operations support and maintenance services. RTSC also provides engineering services for design and development of avionics communications systems and surveillance equipment as well as such IT services as systems integration and software development. RTSC is a business segment of defense contractor Raytheon.

RB RUBBER PRODUCTS INC.

904 NE 10th Ave.
McMinnville OR 97128
Phone: 503-472-4691
Fax: 503-434-4455
Web: www.rbrubber.com

CEO: –
CFO: –
HR: –
FYE: April 30
Type: Subsidiary

When tires are too tired to be functional RB Rubber Products recycles them. The company produces rubber matting which can be found in horse and livestock trailers as well as gym weight rooms. Secondary product lines include truck bed liners roof pads anti-fatigue mats and drain tiles. RB Rubber's Waste Recovery subsidiary operates a tire collection and processing facility that shreds tires to form tire chips used to make the company's products. RB Rubber sells its products to distributors retailers and OEMs and directly to consumers. Dash Multi-Corp — whose president Marvin Wool was RB Rubber's chairman — acquired the company in early 2003.

RBC BEARINGS INC

NMS: ROLL

One Tribology Center
Oxford, CT 06478
Phone: 203 267-7001
Fax: –
Web: www.rbcbearings.com

CEO: Michael J. Hartnett
CFO: Daniel A. (Dan) Bergeron
HR: –
FYE: March 28
Type: Public

RBC Bearings keeps businesses on a roll. The company makes an array of plain roller and ball bearing products. It specializes in regulated bearings used by OEMs and their aftermarkets of commercial/military aircraft automobiles and commercial trucks industrial/agricultural machinery as well as air turbines. Targeting high-end markets its precision lineup satisfies thousands of applications from engine controls to radar systems mining tools and gear pumps. RBC's top customers include Boeing GE Lockheed Martin and the US Department of Defense. RBC Bearings has grown since 1919 to some 35 manufacturing facilities in Europe and North America.

	Annual Growth	04/11*	03/12	03/13	03/14	03/15
Sales ($ mil.)	7.3%	335.6	397.5	403.1	418.9	445.3
Net income ($ mil.)	13.7%	34.9	50.0	56.3	60.2	58.2
Market value ($ mil.)	18.1%	909.1	1,079.1	1,182.8	1,473.1	1,768.1
Employees	6.3%	1,950	2,137	2,145	2,361	2,490

*Fiscal year change

RBC CAPITAL MARKETS LLC

1 Liberty Plaza 165 Broadway
New York NY 10006-1404
Phone: 212-858-7000
Fax: 212-428-6200
Web: www.rbccm.com

CEO: –
CFO: Troy Maxwell
HR: –
FYE: October 31
Type: Subsidiary

RBC Capital Markets is the corporate and investment banking arm of the Royal Bank of Canada and the leading debt and equity underwriter in the Great White North. As the only Canadian bank designated as a primary dealer in the US RBC Capital Markets offers mergers and acquisitions support securities trading and research foreign exchange infrastructure finance and advisory services. It serves a number of industries including aerospace media mining energy healthcare forest products transportation and the public sector. The US accounts for nearly half of the company's business. The firm runs 70 offices spanning 15 countries such as North America Australasia Europe South America and Africa.

RBC LIFE SCIENCES INC

NBB: RBCL

2301 Crown Court
Irving, TX 75038
Phone: 972 893-4000
Fax: 972 893-4111
Web: www.rbclifesciences.com

CEO: Clinton H Howard
CFO: Steven E Brown
HR: Leanne Tsirigotis
FYE: December 31
Type: Public

RBC Life Sciences offers really big changes to its clients' bodies. RBC markets and distributes more than 75 nutritional weight loss and personal care products under the RBC Life brand. The company's leading product Microhydrin is touted to increase energy and slow the effects of aging. The company relies on a multi-level marketing network of some 10000 independent distributors in the US and Canada. It also markets and distributes wound care pain management and cancer care products used in clinical settings and sold under the MPM Medical brand.

	Annual Growth	12/10	12/11	12/12	12/13	12/14
Sales ($ mil.)	0.1%	28.2	28.4	25.2	25.5	28.3
Net income ($ mil.)	–	0.6	(0.1)	(0.4)	(0.5)	(0.6)
Market value ($ mil.)	48.3%	0.6	0.4	0.2	3.4	2.9
Employees	5.4%	72	77	76	76	89

RBS GLOBAL INC.

4701 W. Greenfield Ave.
Milwaukee WI 53214
Phone: 414-643-3000
Fax: 414-643-3078
Web: www.rexnord.com

CEO: Todd A Adams
CFO: Mark W Peterson
HR: –
FYE: March 31
Type: Private

RBS Global is the parent company of Rexnord LLC whose subsidiaries serve the company's two main segments. Process Motion Control (formerly Power Transmission) makes gear drives couplings bearings and chains and conveying equipment for use in the aerospace construction energy mining marine and petrochemical industries. Its Water Management segment is supported by three primary companies: Zurn Industries GA Industries and Rodney Hunt. It designs and makes water-related products for conservation quality drainage safety and flow control. The US accounts for about three-quarters of the company's sales. RBS Global is owned by Rexnord Corporation which began trading in 2012 after filing an IPO in 2011.

RC2 CORPORATION

1111 W. 22nd St. Ste. 320
Oak Brook IL 60523
Phone: 630-573-7200
Fax: 630-573-7575
Web: www.rc2corp.com

CEO: Harold Meij
CFO: –
HR: Karen Knepper
FYE: March 31
Type: Subsidiary

RC2 is tackling the Learning Curve of selling playthings. The company designs child care products and toys for infants toddlers and preschool-aged children and markets them through its Learning Curve unit whose brand portfolio includes The First Years Lamaze and JJ Cole. For bigger kids it offers plastic and die-cast collectibles such as Ertl agricultural vehicle replicas and Johnny Lightning vintage cars and trucks. The firm also holds licensing agreements to make products under such names as Thomas & Friends Bob the Builder and John Deere. Its goods are sold at toy and discount stores in the US and more than 60 other countries. In early 2011 RC2 was acquired by TOMY for about $640 million in cash.

RCI HOSPITALITY HOLDINGS INC

NMS: RICK

10959 Cutten Road
Houston, TX 77066
Phone: 281 397-6730
Fax: –
Web: www.rcihospitality.com

CEO: Eric S Langan
CFO: Phillip Marshall
HR: –
FYE: September 30
Type: Public

Far from Casablanca these night clubs offer topless entertainment as part of the floor show. Rick's Cabaret International operates more than 30 adult night clubs in Arizona Florida Minnesota New York North Carolina and Texas. Most of the gentlemen's clubs are run under the Rick's Cabaret name while others operate under such banners as Club Onyx and XTC. Rick's caters to highbrow patrons with dough to blow: It offers VIP memberships for individual and corporate clients that can cost hundreds of dollars annually. In addition to its night clubs Rick's operates adult websites and an auction site for adult entertainment products.

	Annual Growth	09/11	09/12	09/13	09/14	09/15
Sales ($ mil.)	14.7%	83.5	95.2	112.2	129.2	144.7
Net income ($ mil.)	4.4%	7.8	7.6	9.2	11.2	9.3
Market value ($ mil.)	11.9%	68.4	85.2	121.3	113.3	107.2
Employees	15.7%	1,200	1,400	1,750	1,750	2,150

RCM TECHNOLOGIES, INC.

NMS. RCMT

2500 McClellan Avenue, Suite 350
Pennsauken, NJ 08109-4613
Phone: 856 356-4500
Fax: –
Web: www.rcmt.com

CEO: Rocco Campanelli
CFO: Kevin D Miller
HR: –
FYE: January 03
Type: Public

Whether you need brains in people form or of the digital persuasion RCM Technologies has it covered. The company is an IT services and engineering firm that performs design and implementation of technology and software systems project management and engineering analysis services. Recently it has become more of an engineering services firm primarily to the energy industry. It also provides specialty health care staffing for therapists nurses and caregivers. The company mainly targets midsized firms and federal government agencies; clients have included the Treasury Department and its largest client United Technologies.

	Annual Growth	01/11*	12/11	12/12	12/13*	01/15
Sales ($ mil.)	4.6%	162.0	143.8	145.8	170.8	193.8
Net income ($ mil.)	4.1%	5.8	4.3	3.2	2.0	6.8
Market value ($ mil.)	10.4%	58.7	65.6	67.4	88.1	87.3
Employees	6.7%	1,590	1,520	1,460	1,755	2,059

*Fiscal year change

RCN TELECOM SERVICES LLC

650 College Rd. East
Princeton NJ 08540
Phone: 609-452-8197
Fax: 212-893-9575
Web: www.welshcarson.com

CEO: Jim Hollanda
CFO: –
HR: –
FYE: December 31
Type: Private

You could say RCN is at home in the big city. The company operates cable-based broadband networks that serve the Boston Chicago and New York City areas as well as eastern Pennsylvania and Washington DC. A facilities-based competitive carrier (its fiber network spans 10000 miles) it offers cable television Internet local and long-distance phone and VoIP services to about 400000 residential and small business customers. In addition to providing basic and digital cable TV services RCN offers video on demand and HDTV. The company also provides wholesale data transport services to large enterprises and communications carriers through its Sidera Networks division. ABRY Partners took RCN private in 2010.

RCS CAPITAL CORP

NBB: RCAP Q

405 Park Avenue, 14th Floor
New York, NY 10022
Phone: 866 904-2988
Fax: –
Web: www.rcscapital.com

CEO: R. Lawrence (Larry) Roth
CFO: David Orlofsky
HR: –
FYE: December 31
Type: Public

RCS Capital is a holding company with its fingers in a variety of financial services businesses namely securities brokering investment banking and securities record-keeping services. Its Realty Capital Securities is a wholesale broker and dealer specializing in REIT investments. RCS Advisory Services is a company that provides financing and consulting to clients served by the brokerage. Finally American National Stock Transfer among other services registers the securities with the SEC. RCS Capital is affiliated with American Realty Capital which has accumulated $7 billion of real estate in the US. RCS Capital filed for Chapter 11 bankruptcy protection in January 2016 to reduce its debt.

	Annual Growth	12/10	12/11	12/12	12/13	12/14
Sales ($ mil.)	107.2%	114.1	174.7	287.5	886.5	2,102.2
Net income ($ mil.)	–	(2.4)	3.7	7.4	98.4	(119.6)
Market value ($ mil.)	(33.3%)	–	–	–	1,295.0	863.8
Employees	215.2%	–	–	198	183	1,967

RDO EQUIPMENT CO

700 7TH ST S
FARGO, ND 581032704
Phone: 701-239-8700
Fax: –
Web: www.rdoequipment.com

CEO: Christi J. Offutt
CFO: David Frear
HR: Megan Wahl
FYE: January 31
Type: Private

RDO Equipment has built a business herding Deere in a big way. The company sells and rents new and used trucks and heavy equipment to customers in the agriculture and construction industries. As the largest independent dealer of John Deere equipment RDO Equipment operates 70 locations in nearly 10 states. Of these 10 locations are dedicated Vermeer dealerships while its RDO Truck Centers offer heavy-duty Volvo GMC Isuzu and Mack trucks. RDO Integrated Controls is the company's acquisitive positioning division. RDO also supplies lawn and garden equipment and provides maintenance and repair services and replacement parts. Ronald Offutt founded the family owned and operated company in 1968.

	Annual Growth	01/10	01/11	01/12	01/13	01/14
Sales ($ mil.)	19.3%	–	1,000.0	1,251.3	1,650.3	1,698.4
Net income ($ mil.)	14.5%	–	–	63.2	82.2	82.9
Market value ($ mil.)	–	–	–	–	–	–
Employees	–	–	–	–	–	1,500

RE/MAX INTERNATIONAL INC.

5075 S. Syracuse St.
Denver CO 80237-2712
Phone: 303-770-5531
Fax: 303-796-3599
Web: www.remax.com

CEO: Margaret Kelly
CFO: David M K Metzger
HR: Sandy Matchen-Day
FYE: December 31
Type: Private

RE/MAX International knows there's no place like home and it will help you get there. With some 90000 real estate agents in a franchise network of independently owned offices in more than 75 nations the real estate behemoth sells homes from Albania to Zimbabwe. Residential sales make up most of the company's business but RE/MAX sells commercial property too. RE/MAX also conducts real estate auctions and provides advisory and relocation services. The RE/MAX corporate logo a red white and blue hot-air balloon is more than symbolic: The company boasts one of the largest balloon fleets in the world. The company's colorful chairman Dave Liniger and vice chairman Gail Liniger co-founded RE/MAX in 1973.

REACHLOCAL INC.

NMS: RLOC

21700 Oxnard Street, Suite 1600
Woodland Hills, CA 91367
Phone: 818 274-0260
Fax: –
Web: www.reachlocal.com

CEO: Sharon T. Rowlands
CFO: Ross G. Landsbaum
HR: –
FYE: December 31
Type: Public

When looking to broaden their online presence local business owners can get a hand from ReachLocal. Targeting small to midsized businesses ReachLocal offers Internet-based advertising and marketing services including search engine marketing (for preferred placement of a company's listing on Yahoo! or Google's search results pages) marketing analytics and display advertising. The company serves mostly US businesses through a network of locally based marketing consultants that use among other tools the company's proprietary technology platform to create advertising and marketing campaigns. ReachLocal was founded in 2003; it launched an initial public offering in mid-2010.

	Annual Growth	12/10	12/11	12/12	12/13	12/14
Sales ($ mil.)	13.0%	291.7	375.2	455.4	514.1	474.9
Net income ($ mil.)	–	(11.1)	(10.2)	(0.2)	(2.5)	(45.0)
Market value ($ mil.)	(35.5%)	582.7	180.9	377.9	372.0	100.7
Employees	8.3%	1,381	1,668	1,900	2,100	1,900

READING HOSPITAL

6TH AND SPRUCE ST
READING, PA 196111428
Phone: 484-628-8000
Fax: –
Web: www.readinghealth.org

CEO: David Clint Matthews
CFO: –
HR: –
FYE: June 30
Type: Private

No it's not a square on the game of Monopoly but The Reading Hospital and Medical Center does treat patients in Berks County Pennsylvania and the surrounding area. Operating as Reading Health System the not-for-profit 735-bed medical center provides acute care and rehabilitation programs as well as behavioral and occupational health services. Specialty units include cancer cardiovascular weight management diabetes orthopedic trauma (level II) and women's health centers. In addition to the main hospital the Reading Health System includes Reading Health Rehabilitation Hospital and medical centers in nearby communities as well as laboratory imaging and outpatient centers throughout its region.

	Annual Growth	06/04	06/05	06/06	06/08	06/09
Sales ($ mil.)	–	–	–	0.0	640.6	675.7
Net income ($ mil.)	–	–	–	0.0	50.1	42.0
Market value ($ mil.)	–	–	–	–	–	–
Employees	–	–	–	–	–	5,500

READING INTERNATIONAL, INC.

NAS: RDI

6100 Center Drive, Suite 900
Los Angeles, CA 90045
Phone: 213 235-2240
Fax: –
Web: www.readingrdi.com

CEO: Ellen M. Cotter
CFO: Devasis (Dev) Ghose
HR: –
FYE: December 31
Type: Public

Reading International is all about the show not the book. The company owns about 60 movie theaters in Australia New Zealand and the US. Cinemas operate under brands such as Reading and Rialto. Its Angelika Film Center & Caf-© in New York (50%) and Dallas show art house films. Reading also has real estate operations that develop and rent entertainment commercial retail space. Holdings include three live theaters in New York (the Union Square Orpheum and Minetta Lane) and one in Chicago (the Royal George) as well as the Australia Newmarket shopping center. Chairman and CEO James Cotter owns about 70% of the voting stock of the firm which is descended from Reading Railroad of Monopoly fame.

	Annual Growth	12/10	12/11	12/12	12/13	12/14
Sales ($ mil.)	2.6%	229.8	245.8	254.4	258.2	254.7
Net income ($ mil.)	–	(12.7)	10.0	(0.9)	9.0	25.7
Market value ($ mil.)	27.3%	117.3	98.5	139.7	174.0	308.1
Employees	4.5%	2,056	2,188	2,330	2,385	2,453

READY PAC FOODS INC.

4401 Foxdale Ave.
Irwindale CA 91706
Phone: 626-856-8686
Fax: 626-856-0088
Web: www.readypac.com

CEO: Tony Sarsam
CFO: Craig Delaney
HR: –
FYE: December 31
Type: Private

Attention shoppers this company hopes you'll pack your shopping cart with its fresh ready-to-eat fruit and salads. A leading producer of fresh-cut produce Ready Pac Foods offers packaged salads sliced fruits and mixed vegetables. The company's customers include supermarkets and other food retailers including club stores the likes of Costco and mass-market retailers. In addition Ready Pac Foods makes private-label salad products for retailers including natural food store Trader Joe's. It also supplies fresh-cut produce and salad blends to restaurant operators and other foodservice businesses. Ready Pac Foods' products are available throughout the US and Canada.

REAL GOODS SOLAR INC

NAS: RGSE

833 West South Boulder Road
Louisville, CO 80027-2452
Phone: 303 222-8300
Fax: –
Web: www.realgoodssolar.com

CEO: Dennis Lacey
CFO: –
HR: –
FYE: December 31
Type: Public

Real Goods Solar enjoys its time in the sun. The company which got its start as a small seller of solar panels in 1978 designs and installs solar power systems for homes and small businesses across the US. In addition to design and installation Real Goods Solar also provides permitting grid connection financing referrals and warranty services. The company does not manufacture its own solar panels or equipment but procures supplies from other companies such as Sharp SunPower Sanyo and Kyocera Solar.

	Annual Growth	12/10	12/11	12/12	12/13	12/14
Sales ($ mil.)	(2.2%)	77.3	109.3	92.9	101.3	70.8
Net income ($ mil.)	–	1.2	(1.9)	(47.2)	(11.3)	(57.1)
Market value ($ mil.)	(33.4%)	6.6	3.7	2.0	7.9	1.3
Employees	(2.3%)	270	394	343	499	246

REAL MEX RESTAURANTS INC.

5660 Katella Ave. Ste. 100
Cypress CA 90630
Phone: 562-346-1200
Fax: 562-346-1469
Web: www.realmexrestaurants.com

CEO: Bryan Lockwood
CFO: Richard P Dutkiewicz
HR: –
FYE: December 31
Type: Private

This company is a real combinacion grande. Real Mex Restaurants operates and franchises more than 100 Mexican restaurants in California and more than 15 other states. Its flagship El Torito chain has about 68 locations that offer full-service Mexican dining while its chain of about 65 Chevys Fresh Mex (operated through Chevys Restaurants) provides a more laid-back cantina atmosphere. Real Mex also operates more than 20 full-service Acapulco restaurants featuring California-Mexican cuisine. Emerging from bankruptcy in early 2012 Real Mex is owned by an investment group that includes Tennenbaum Capital Z Capital Partners and J.P. Morgan Investment Management.

REALD INC.

NYS: RLD

100 North Crescent Drive, Suite 200
Beverly Hills, CA 90210
Phone: 310 385-4000
Fax: 310 385-4001
Web: www.reald.com

CEO: Michael V. Lewis
CFO: Andrew A. (Drew) Skarupa
HR: –
FYE: March 31
Type: Public

Thanks to RealD a new era of 3-D movies is upon us. The new crop of feature films projected by RealD's three-dimensional digital projection equipment is dispelling the schlocky image of such 1950s fare as It Came from Outer Space. Recent films that have used RealD's 3-D technology include Kung Fu Panda 2 Toy Story 3 and Despicable Me. The firm has outfitted more than 15000 movie screens in some 60 countries with its 3-D systems. Its products are also used by engineers industrial designers and scientific researchers for applications such as consumer electronics education aerospace defense and health care. (RealD has even helped pilot the Mars Rover.) The company filed an IPO in 2010.

	Annual Growth	03/11	03/12	03/13	03/14	03/15
Sales ($ mil.)	(9.7%)	246.1	246.6	215.6	199.2	163.5
Net income ($ mil.)	–	(6.8)	37.0	(9.9)	(11.2)	(23.7)
Market value ($ mil.)	(14.2%)	1,192.8	659.7	655.6	563.3	645.0
Employees	9.2%	114	129	163	148	162

REALNETWORKS, INC.

NMS: RNWK

1501 First Avenue South, Suite 600
Seattle, WA 98134
Phone: 206 674-2700
Fax: –
Web: www.realnetworks.com

CEO: Robert (Rob) Glaser
CFO: Marjorie Thomas
HR: Jennifer Armstrong
FYE: December 31
Type: Public

Best known for its RealPlayer media playback software RealNetworks' primary revenue now comes from Software-as-a-Service (SaaS) used by mobile phone carriers for ringback tones (RBT) music and video on-demand and text messaging. RealNetworks' other core products are the licensing of its Helix streaming software used to broadcast live and on-demand media and content subscription service SuperPass which offers access to video games and music. It also creates and publishes downloadable and online games (GameHouse). The company makes about 40% of its sales in the US.

	Annual Growth	12/10	12/11	12/12	12/13	12/14
Sales ($ mil.)	(21.0%)	401.7	335.7	258.8	206.2	156.2
Net income ($ mil.)	–	5.0	(27.1)	44.8	(59.0)	(71.8)
Market value ($ mil.)	13.8%	151.6	270.7	272.9	272.5	254.1
Employees	(15.8%)	1,528	1,224	991	946	769

REALOGY HOLDINGS CORP

NYS: RLGY

175 Park Avenue
Madison, NJ 07940
Phone: 973 407-2000
Fax: –
Web: www.realogy.com

CEO: Richard A. Smith
CFO: Anthony E. (Tony) Hull
HR: Sunita Holzer
FYE: December 31
Type: Public

Realogy Holdings (formerly Domus Holdings) has the goods for domestic bliss for a lot of people. It is the largest franchisor of residential real estate offices in the world with about 13500 offices in more than 100 countries. Its brands include Century 21 Coldwell Banker ERA Better Homes and Gardens Real Estate and Sotheby's. In addition to franchising the company owns and operates about 700 offices under the already mentioned brands along with the Corcoran Group and Citi Habitats labels. It also provides relocation title and settlement services and mortgages. The residential real estate giant changed its name and went public in late 2012.

	Annual Growth	12/10	12/11	12/12	12/13	12/14
Sales ($ mil.)	6.8%	4,090.0	4,093.0	4,672.0	5,289.0	5,328.0
Net income ($ mil.)	–	(99.0)	(441.0)	(543.0)	438.0	143.0
Market value ($ mil.)	3.0%	–	–	6,142.2	7,241.6	6,512.6
Employees	(5.6%)	13,500	10,400	10,800	10,800	10,700

REALPAGE INC

NMS: RP

4000 International Parkway
Carrollton, TX 75007-1951
Phone: 972 820-3000
Fax: –
Web: www.realpage.com

CEO: Stephen T. (Steve) Winn
CFO: W. Bryan Hill
HR: –
FYE: December 31
Type: Public

RealPage's keeps real estate operations on the same page for property managers. The company's on-demand software platform is designed to make the property management process more efficient enabling owners and managers of single- and multifamily rental properties to oversee their accounting leasing marketing pricing and screening operations from a single shared database. The centralized system helps with managing incoming and outgoing residents and overseeing property functions from hiring plumbers to training staff. Its customers include all of the top 10 largest multifamily property management companies in the US.

	Annual Growth	12/10	12/11	12/12	12/13	12/14
Sales ($ mil.)	21.1%	188.3	258.0	322.2	377.0	404.6
Net income ($ mil.)	–	0.1	(1.2)	5.2	20.7	(10.3)
Market value ($ mil.)	(8.2%)	2,444.6	1,997.3	1,704.8	1,847.9	1,735.7
Employees	21.8%	1,759	2,273	2,893	3,337	3,875

REALTY INCOME CORP.

NYS: O

11995 El Camino Real
San Diego. CA 92130
Phone: 858 284-5000
Fax: –
Web: www.realtyincome.com

CEO: John P. Case
CFO: Paul M. Meurer
HR: –
FYE: December 31
Type: Public

Retail real estate is a reality for Realty Income Corporation. The self-administered real estate investment trust (REIT) acquires owns and manages primarily free-standing highly-occupied single-tenant properties which it leases to regional and national consumer retail and service chains. Realty Income owns more than 4320 (mostly retail) properties spanning some 71 mil. sq. ft. of leasable space across every US state except Hawaii though nearly half of the REIT's rental revenue comes from its properties in Texas California Florida Minnesota Georgia Illinois and Virginia. Realty Income's top five tenants include Walgreens FedEx Dollar General LA Fitness and Family Dollar.

	Annual Growth	12/11	12/12	12/13	12/14	12/15
Sales ($ mil.)	24.9%	421.1	475.5	778.4	933.5	1,023.3
Net income ($ mil.)	15.9%	157.0	159.2	245.6	270.6	283.8
Market value ($ mil.)	10.2%	8,754.6	10,069.3	9,348.1	11,947.4	12,929.0
Employees	12.3%	83	97	116	125	132

RECALL CORPORATION

1 Recall Center 180 Technology Pkwy.
Norcross GA 30092
Phone: 770-776-1000
Fax: 770-776-1001
Web: www.recall.com

CEO: Doug Pertz
CFO: Allison Aden
HR: –
FYE: June 30
Type: Subsidiary

It's not necessary to memorize your documents: this company can Recall them for you. Recall Corporation is one of the world's largest information management companies helping some 80000 customers store and protect (and sometimes destroy) important documents and data. Recall's services include physical and electronic document storage and retrieval protection of computer backup data and destruction of sensitive documents. The company operates about 300 facilities in more than 20 countries on five continents. Recall was established in 1977. Today it is a subsidiary of Australian industrial conglomerate Brambles Group.

RECKITT BENCKISER INC.

399 Interpace Pkwy.
Parsippany NJ 07054
Phone: 973-404-2600
Fax: 973-404-5700
Web: www.reckittprofessional.com

CEO: Rakesh Kapoor
CFO: –
HR: –
FYE: December 31
Type: Subsidiary

If it doesn't clean or taste good it doesn't cut the mustard with Reckitt Benckiser. A subsidiary of UK-based Reckitt Benckiser plc the company makes and markets household cleaning and food products for sale in North America. The firm holds a vast brand portfolio that includes French's Foods (Cattlemen's Barbecue Sauce French's Mustard Frank's RedHot GourMayo Worcestershire). Some of Reckitt Benckiser's household and cleaning products include Air Wick air fresheners Electrasol dish detergent Jet-Dry rinse agent Lysol cleaners and disinfectants Resolve cleaners and Spray 'n Wash laundry stain removers. It expanded into skin care in 2011. Its parent bought Adams Respiratory Therapeutics in 2008.

RECOLOGY INC.

50 California St. 24th Fl.
San Francisco CA 94111
Phone: 415-875-1000
Fax: 415-875-1124
Web: www.recology.com

CEO: Michael J Sangiacomo
CFO: Mark R Lomele
HR: –
FYE: September 30
Type: Private

San Francisco's trash collector since 1921 Recology (formerly Norcal Waste Systems) cleans up in California Nevada Oregon and Washington. Through its subsidiaries Recology handles garbage collection recycling and other waste management services for more than 670000 residential customers and 95000 commercial customers. The employee-owned company operates landfills transfer stations and hundreds of recycling programs. Recology's recycling operations include materials-recovery facilities recycling of construction and demolition debris and composting of food and other organic waste.

RECYCLENET CORPORATION

OTC: GARM

175 E. 400 South Ste. 900
Salt Lake City UT 84111
Phone: 801-531-0404
Fax: 801-531-0707
Web: www.recyclenet.com

CEO: –
CFO: –
HR: –
FYE: December 31
Type: Public

You can even use the Internet to reduce re-use and recycle. RecycleNet Corporation owns a network of Web sites that acts as an online trading system for scrap. Buyers and sellers of recyclable materials (glass metal rubber paper wood and plastic) are brought together at the company's electronic exchange system which uses a buy/sell/trade and bid/ask order matching system. RecycleNet earns money by charging a subscription fee for access to its service. Google pay-per-click advertising accounts for about 20% of revenue.

RED BLOSSOM SALES INC.

162 MONTGOMERY AVE
OXNARD, CA 930361075
Phone: 805-981-1839
Fax: –
Web: www.redblossom.com

CEO: Craig A Casca
CFO: –
HR: –
FYE: December 31
Type: Private

Red Blossom Sales is berry enthusiastic about its market. The company is one of California's leading strawberry producers with more than 1200 acres across the cities of Baja Irvine Oxnard Santa Maria and Salinas/Watsonville. It contracts a hefty chunk of its production to growers in California and Mexico and ships a total of about 8 million cartons of field-packed strawberries throughout the US every year. Red Blossom's products are sold in large retail grocery stores nationwide including Costco Safeway and Vons; it also exports some to Canada and Hong Kong. Established in 2004 the company took on its current moniker when Red Blossom Farms merged with ASG Produce in 2008.

	Annual Growth	12/09	12/10	12/11	12/12	12/13
Sales ($ mil.)	0.6%	–	–	–	105.2	105.8
Net income ($ mil.)	28.3%	–	–	–	0.9	1.2
Market value ($ mil.)	–	–	–	–	–	–
Employees	–	–	–	–	–	1,046

RED GOLD INC.

120 E. Oak St.
Orestes IN 46063
Phone: 765-754-7527
Fax: 765-754-3230
Web: www.redgold.com

CEO: Brian Reichart
CFO: –
HR: –
FYE: December 31
Type: Private

Red Gold uses a vegetable-patch-colored pallet to produce the perfect mix of red and gold in its tomato sauces. It makes its own brand and private-label canned and bottled tomato products including ketchup tomato juice diced and crushed tomatoes salsa and pasta sauces under the Red Gold Redpack Sacramento and Tuttorosso labels. It operates three manufacturing sites in Indiana where it makes products for retail food service and private-label distribution. Products are available nationwide and in more than 15 countries. In its third-generation of family ownership Red Gold was founded in 1942 by Grover Hutcherson. The Reicharts now own and operate Red Gold and employ more than a dozen family members.

RED HAT INC

NYS: RHT

100 East Davie Street
Raleigh, NC 27601
Phone: 919 754-3700
Fax: –
Web: www.redhat.com

CEO: James M. (Jim) Whitehurst
CFO: Frank A. Calderoni
HR: –
FYE: February 28
Type: Public

Red Hat doffs its cap to businesses that embrace open-source computing tools. The company dominates the market for Linux the open-source computer operating system (OS) that is the chief rival to Microsoft's Windows operating system. In addition to its Red Hat Enterprise Linux OS the company's product line includes database content and collaboration management applications; server and embedded operating systems; and software development tools. Red Hat also provides consulting custom application development support and training services. The company's business model is a mix of providing free open-source software paired with subscription-based support training and integration services.

	Annual Growth	02/11	02/12	02/13	02/14	02/15
Sales ($ mil.)	18.4%	909.3	1,133.1	1,328.8	1,534.6	1,789.5
Net income ($ mil.)	13.8%	107.3	146.6	150.2	178.3	180.2
Market value ($ mil.)	13.8%	7,577.0	9,078.4	9,326.2	10,827.7	12,687.1
Employees	18.5%	3,700	4,500	5,600	6,300	7,300

RED LIONS HOTELS CORP

NYS: RLH

201 W. North River Drive, Suite 100
Spokane, WA 99201
Phone: 509 459-6100
Fax: 509 325-7324
Web: www.redlion.com

CEO: Greg Mount
CFO: James A. (Jim) Bell
HR: Karla Gehlen
FYE: December 31
Type: Public

Red Lion Hotels (formerly WestCoast Hospitality) wants to be the leader of the pack when it comes to running hotels. The company has 55 hotels under the Red Lion brand in ten US states and one Canadian province. Red Lion owns and leases about 35 of its hotels and franchises the rest. Hotels account for the majority of the company's business. Choosing not to live by beds alone Red Lion operates an entertainment segment that promotes and presents entertainment options such as Broadway-style shows and includes TicketsWest.com a ticketing service for hotel guests. In addition it owns a retail mall in Montana which is attached to one of its hotels and has other miscellaneous real estate investments.

	Annual Growth	12/10	12/11	12/12	12/13	12/14
Sales ($ mil.)	(2.9%)	163.5	156.1	150.7	120.1	145.4
Net income ($ mil.)	–	(8.6)	(7.1)	(14.7)	(17.0)	2.3
Market value ($ mil.)	(5.6%)	158.4	137.5	156.6	120.1	125.8
Employees	(9.9%)	2,463	2,225	2,054	1,847	1,622

RED RIVER COMPUTER CO. INC.

21 Water St. Ste. 500
Claremont NH 03743
Phone: 603-448-8880
Fax: 603-448-8844
Web: www.redriver.com

CEO: –
CFO: Edmund I Mangini III
HR: –
FYE: December 31
Type: Private

Red River Computer helps its customers get data flowing. The company is a computer and communications hardware software and peripherals reseller that provides related support services such as installation network design and network engineering. Other areas of specialty include data storage and network security. Red River primarily serves government agencies (GSA NASA and NIH) and acts as a subcontractor for major defense contractors. It also counts other commercial enterprises such as health care companies and universities among its clients. Founded in 1995 the company is owned by its management team. FusionStorm Global offered to buy Red River for $12.5 million in 2011.

RED ROBIN GOURMET BURGERS INC

NMS: RRGB

6312 S. Fiddler's Green Circle, Suite 200 N
Greenwood Village, CO 80111
Phone: 303 846-6000
Fax: –
Web: www.redrobin.com

CEO: Stephen E. (Steve) Carley
CFO: Stuart B. Brown
HR: Bill Streitberger
FYE: December 28
Type: Public

Hamburger fans are chirping about Red Robin Gourmet Burgers. The company operates a chain of about 475 casual-dining restaurants that specialize in high-end hamburgers. Its menu features more than 20 different twists on the American classic including the Banzai Burger (marinated in teriyaki) Bleu Ribbon Burger and the jalapeño-charged Burnin' Love Burger. The signature Royal Red Robin Burger features bacon and a fried egg on top of the beef. Red Robin also serves chicken seafood and turkey burgers as well as vegetarian alternatives. Non-burger entrées include salads pasta seafood and fajitas.

	Annual Growth	12/10	12/11	12/12	12/13	12/14
Sales ($ mil.)	7.3%	864.3	914.9	977.1	1,017.2	1,146.1
Net income ($ mil.)	45.3%	7.3	20.6	28.3	32.2	32.6
Market value ($ mil.)	37.0%	304.6	406.5	472.7	1,056.2	1,073.2
Employees	4.4%	23,198	22,302	22,342	24,336	27,543

RED ROOF INN

121 E. Nationwide Blvd.
Columbus OH 43215
Phone: 614-744-2600
Fax: 512-391-3901
Web: www.arthrocare.com

CEO: Andrew Alexander
CFO: Brendan P Foley
HR: –
FYE: December 31
Type: Private

This business believes a night's lodging shouldn't put you in the red. Red Roof Inn is a leading budget motel chain with nearly 350 locations in some 35 US states. Its hotels are primarily located in the Midwest the East and the South. While popular with families the brand also caters to business travelers with such amenities as continental breakfast meeting rooms photocopy services and wireless Internet access. It also offers larger suites and deluxe rooms with executive-style desks and microwave ovens. Red Roof Inn was founded by James Trueman in 1973.

REDNER'S MARKETS INC.

3 QUARRY RD
READING, PA 196059787
Phone: 610-926-3700
Fax: –
Web: www.rednersmarkets.com

CEO: –
CFO: –
HR: Robert McDonough
FYE: September 27
Type: Private

Redner's Markets operates about 45 warehouse club-style supermarkets under the Redner's Warehouse Markets banner and more than a dozen Quick Shoppe convenience stores. Most of the company's stores are located in eastern Pennsylvania while the regional grocer also operates several locations in Maryland and Delaware having closed its one New York supermarket. Redner's Warehouse Markets house bakery deli meat produce and seafood departments as well as in-store banks. The employee-owned company was founded by namesake Earl Redner in 1970. It is still operated by the Redner family including chairman and CEO Richard and COO Ryan Redner.

	Annual Growth	10/09	10/10*	12/12*	09/13	09/14
Sales ($ mil.)	2.1%	–	831.7	0.1	892.5	902.6
Net income ($ mil.)	974.5%	–	–	0.0	4.6	1.6
Market value ($ mil.)	–	–	–	–	–	–
Employees	–	–	–	–	–	4,800

*Fiscal year change

REDPOINT BIO CORPORATION

OTC: RPBC

7 Graphics Dr.
Ewing NJ 08628
Phone: 609-637-9700
Fax: 609-637-0126
Web: www.redpointbio.com

CEO: –
CFO: Scott M Horvitz
HR: –
FYE: December 31
Type: Public

Redpoint Bio believes a spoonful of sugar helps the medicine go down. So the development stage biotechnology company is developing compounds that make foul medicines foods and drinks a thing of the bitter past. The company is working on developing bitter blockers compounds that will prevent taste buds from sensing bitter flavors in pharmaceutical products. It is also developing flavor enhancers which will amplify sweet savory and salty taste sensations in foods and beverages and possibly make processed foods and drinks healthier. Redpoint Bio was founded in 1995 by Robert Margolskee to capitalize on a taste-specific protein he discovered four years earlier.

REDPRAIRIE CORPORATION

3905 Brookside Pkwy.
Alpharetta GA 30022-4429
Phone: 678-639-5000
Fax: 678-623-3116
Web: www.redprairie.com

CEO: Michael R Mayoras
CFO: –
HR: –
FYE: December 31
Type: Private

RedPrairie today is not the RedPrairie of yesterday. The company — a provider of retail workforce warehouse inventory and transportation management software systems — does business under the JDA Software brand name after acquiring JDA Software Group in December 2012 in a $1.9 billion deal that created a new industry leader in global supply chain management. RedPrairie is currently a wholly owned subsidiary of RP Crown Parent LLC which is owned by private equity firm New Mountain Capital. New Mountain Capital acquired RedPrairie in 2010 after RedPrairie called off its IPO in 2009.

REDWOOD TRUST INC.

NYSE: RWT

1 Belvedere Place Ste. 300
Mill Valley CA 94941
Phone: 415-389-7373
Fax: 415-381-1773
Web: www.redwoodtrust.com

CEO: Martin S Hughes
CFO: Christopher J Abate
HR: –
FYE: December 31
Type: Public

Redwood Trust a real estate investment trust (REIT) is cultivating a forest of real estate mortgage assets. The REIT finances manages and invests in residential real estate mortgages and securities backed by such loans. It also invests in commercial real estate loans and securities. Redwood acquires assets throughout the US but has a concentration of credit risk in California Florida and Georgia three of the markets hardest hit by the housing bust. Redwood Trust slowed loan origination acquisition and securitization during the recent recession but has picked up those activities as the economy has recovered.

REEBOK INTERNATIONAL LTD.

1895 J. W. Foster Blvd.
Canton MA 02021
Phone: 781-401-5000
Fax: 781-401-7402
Web: www.reebok.com

CEO: Ulrich Becker
CFO: John Warren
HR: –
FYE: December 31
Type: Subsidiary

Reebok International feels comfortable stepping out onto any surface. The company a subsidiary of Germany's adidas AG has long been at home in sporting arenas as a top US maker of athletic shoes. In addition to its namesake sportswear and accessories Reebok caters to hockey aficionados through its Canadian Reebok-CCM Hockey division and its Sports Licensed Division. It operates more than 220 retail stores. Reebok which has been credited with igniting the aerobics craze of the early 1980s has fallen out of step since then. Under adidas the company is trying to regain traction in the athletic shoe and apparel market.

REED & BARTON CORPORATION

144 W. Britannia St.
Taunton MA 02780
Phone: 508-824-6611
Fax: 508-822-7269
Web: www.reedandbarton.com

CEO: –
CFO: Charles Daly
HR: –
FYE: January 31
Type: Private

Reed & Barton has built a business out of setting an exquisite table. Founded in 1824 Reed & Barton is one of the nation's oldest privately-held silversmiths that designs and manufactures high-quality flatware gifts and household collectibles. The company's brands include Reed & Barton Miller Rogaska Crystal by Reed & Barton The Sheffield Collection R&B EveryDay Belleek Fine Parian China and Aynsley Fine English Bone China. Reed & Barton sells its products in regional specialty shops jewelry stores and department stores including Belk Dillard's Macy's and Neiman Marcus. The company also operates about 10 retail stores located primarily in outlet centers.

REED'S INC

ASE: REED

13000 South Spring St.
Los Angeles, CA 90061
Phone: 310 217-9400
Fax: –
Web: www.reedsgingerbrew.com

CEO: Christopher J Reed
CFO: Daniel Miles
HR: Sheri Ross
FYE: December 31
Type: Public

Everybody needs a Reed's. The company makes two dozen all-natural soft drinks such as Original Ginger Brew and Virgil's Root Beer as well as ginger candy and three ginger-flavored ice creams. Reed's brews its drinks from roots herbs spices and fruits in a manner similar to how beer is brewed from malt and hops (without alcohol though — carbonation is added to Reed's drinks separately). The company also owns the China Cola brand which contains an herbal mixture designed to help digestion. Reed's products are sold in some 10500 natural food and traditional supermarkets as well as specialty stores and restaurants throughout North America. It also makes private-label products for retailers.

	Annual Growth	12/10	12/11	12/12	12/13	12/14
Sales ($ mil.)	20.8%	20.4	25.0	30.0	37.3	43.4
Net income ($ mil.)	–	(1.3)	(0.9)	(0.5)	(1.5)	(0.8)
Market value ($ mil.)	30.9%	26.3	14.5	74.2	104.3	77.2
Employees	9.5%	57	55	61	61	82

REFAC OPTICAL GROUP

1 Bridge Plaza Ste. 550	CEO: –
Fort Lee NJ 07024-7102	CFO: –
Phone: 856-228-0077	HR: –
Fax: 856-228-5577	FYE: January 31
Web: www.refacopticalgroup.com	Type: Private

Refac Optical Group keeps its eye on the business of vision care. The company manages more than 700 U.S. Vision and OptiCare retail optical stores in the US and Canada. Shops carry designer and private-label frames sunglasses contact lenses and accessories as well as offer optometric services. Brands have included Armani Exchange Calvin Klein Revlon and Vera Wang. In addition to its retail operations Refac operates two surgical centers and two manufacturing laboratories. Founded in 1952 Refac Optical Group is owned by private equity firm ACON Investments.

REGAL BELOIT CORP

NYS: RBC

200 State Street	CEO: Mark J. Gliebe
Beloit, WI 53511	CFO: Charles A. (Chuck) Hinrichs
Phone: 608 364-8800	HR: Terry R Colvin
Fax: –	FYE: January 03
Web: www.regal-beloit.com	Type: Public

Regal Beloit might not be able to move mountains but it does make a range of electric motors mechanical motion control and power generation products that moves mechanical equipment around the world. The company's commercial and industrial systems group makes AC and DC electric motors (LEESON Electric Lincoln Motors and Marathon Electric brands) used for heating and air conditioning as well as generators for prime and standby power. Its power transmissions group makes aftermarket auto and marine transmissions gear reducers and gear drives used in conveyors waste treatment facilities and street pavers.

	Annual Growth	01/11*	12/11	12/12	12/13*	01/15
Sales ($ mil.)	9.8%	2,238.0	2,808.3	3,166.9	3,095.7	3,257.1
Net income ($ mil.)	(32.5%)	149.4	152.3	195.6	120.0	31.0
Market value ($ mil.)	3.1%	2,984.2	2,278.4	3,071.8	3,290.8	3,369.0
Employees	6.8%	18,500	24,400	23,800	22,900	24,100

*Fiscal year change

REGAL ENTERTAINMENT GROUP

NYS: RGC

7132 Regal Lane	CEO: Amy E. Miles
Knoxville, TN 37918	CFO: David H. Ownby
Phone: 865 922-1123	HR: Jackie McClure
Fax: –	FYE: January 01
Web: www.regmovies.com	Type: Public

Regal Entertainment Group hopes to create loyal subjects out of fickle moviegoers. The largest theater owner and exhibitor in the US has more than 565 theaters with nearly 7325 screens in 40-plus states through its Regal Cinemas Edwards Theatres United Artists Theatre Company and Hoyts Cinemas brands. Its theaters house an average of 12.8 screens and more than 75% of its screens are in theaters with stadium seating. It also claims to be one of the most modern theater circuits in the country. Regal Entertainment co-owns National CineMedia a joint venture that sells in-theater ads and operates a video network that distributes digital content to theaters. Regal Entertainment Group was formed in 2002.

	Annual Growth	12/10	12/11	12/12	12/13*	01/15
Sales ($ mil.)	1.3%	2,807.9	2,681.7	2,824.2	3,038.1	2,990.1
Net income ($ mil.)	6.4%	77.6	40.3	144.8	157.7	105.6
Market value ($ mil.)	12.6%	1,846.0	1,889.7	2,166.1	3,068.8	3,335.9
Employees	1.0%	22,061	20,728	22,056	24,201	23,168

*Fiscal year change

REGAL WARE INC.

1675 Reigle Dr.	CEO: Jeffrey A Reigle
Kewaskum WI 53040	CFO: –
Phone: 262-626-2121	HR: –
Fax: 262-626-8504	FYE: December 31
Web: www.regalware.com	Type: Private

Regal Ware provides the wares for the party fare. The company a manufacturer of cookware and appliances sells its products through home parties nationwide. About 90% of its sales are generated from its stainless-steel and ceramic cookware. The company's brand names include Royal Queen Lifetime and Marcus among others. Regal Ware also supplies foodservice operators with commercial coffeemaker urns drinking water systems and other beverage accessories. Regal Ware maintains a presence on retail shelves through agreements with the likes of Euromarket Designs' Crate & Barrel and Williams-Sonoma. Regal Ware is owned and run by the Reigle family.

REGENCE BLUECROSS BLUESHIELD OF OREGON

100 SW Market St.	CEO: Mark B Ganz
Portland OR 97201-5766	CFO: Vince Price
Phone: 503-225-5336	HR: –
Fax: 503-225-5274	FYE: December 31
Web: www.or.regence.com	Type: Subsidiary

Regence BlueCross BlueShield of Oregon provides health insurance products and other managed care services to some 1 million members in Oregon and Washington's Clark county. A subsidiary of Cambia Health Solutions (formerly Regence Group) and Oregon's largest health plan provider the company offers both group and individual health policies including PPO plans and high-deductible plans paired with health savings accounts. It also provides dental and prescription coverage as well as Medicare Advantage and Medicare supplement plans for seniors. Life policies are offered through affiliate Regence Life. Regence BlueCross BlueShield of Oregon was founded in 1941. It is an independent licensee of the Blue Cross and Blue Shield Association.

REGENCY CENTERS CORP.

NYS: REG

One Independent Drive, Suite 114	CEO: Martin E. (Hap) Stein
Jacksonville, FL 32202	CFO: Lisa Palmer
Phone: 904 598-7000	HR: –
Fax: –	FYE: December 31
Web: www.regencycenters.com	Type: Public

Regency Centers' bread and butter comes from grocery stores. A real estate investment trust (REIT) the firm owns manages and develops neighborhood shopping centers in about two dozen states and Washington DC many of them anchored by a Kroger Publix or Safeway supermarket. Other tenants include retailers restaurants and professional services firms. The REIT wholly owns or has interests in about 330 properties measuring more than 44 million sq. ft. of leaseable space. The REIT focuses on high-growth areas in states including California Florida Texas Georgia and Colorado home to the majority of its wholly-owned holdings.

	Annual Growth	12/10	12/11	12/12	12/13	12/14
Sales ($ mil.)	2.5%	486.8	500.4	496.9	489.0	537.9
Net income ($ mil.)	98.7%	12.0	51.4	25.9	149.8	187.4
Market value ($ mil.)	10.9%	3,957.2	3,524.3	4,414.3	4,337.5	5,975.1
Employees	(1.4%)	392	369	368	363	370

REGENCY ENERGY PARTNERS LP

NYS: RGP

2001 Bryan Street, Suite 3700
Dallas, TX 75201
Phone: 214 750-1771
Fax: 214 750-1749
Web: www.regencygasservices.com

CEO: Michael J Bradley
CFO: Thomas E Long
HR: –
FYE: December 31
Type: Public

Midstream is the decisive choice of Regency Energy Partners. The independent energy partnership focuses on the gathering processing marketing and transportation of natural gas and natural gas liquids (NGLs) in Arkansas Kansas Louisiana and Texas. Its gathering and processing unit moves natural gas from the wellhead through gathering systems primarily for producers. Regency's gathering and processing assets include 8 gas treating/processing plants and 5260 miles of related gathering and pipeline infrastructure. Its transportation segment ships natural gas across Louisiana. The company also offers natural gas compression services and provides treating services to gas producers and pipeline companies.

	Annual Growth	05/10*	12/10	12/11	12/12	12/13
Sales ($ mil.)	70.9%	505.1	716.6	1,433.9	1,339.0	2,521.0
Net income ($ mil.)	–	(5.4)	(6.1)	72.4	46.0	19.0
Market value ($ mil.)	6.7%	4,751.1	5,996.1	5,468.2	4,768.7	5,776.1
Employees	14.4%	–	793	729	781	1,187

*Fiscal year change

REGENCY ENTERPRISES

10201 W. Pico Blvd. Bldg. 12
Los Angeles CA 90035
Phone: 310-369-8300
Fax: 310-969-0470
Web: www.newregency.com

CEO: Brad Weston
CFO: Mimi Mtseng
HR: –
FYE: December 31
Type: Private

Regency Enterprises lords over a kingdom of Hollywood movies. The company's New Regency Production unit produces and distributes movies such as Mr. & Mrs. Smith Fight Club and JFK. News Corp.'s Fox Entertainment owns 20% of Regency and distributes the company's movies worldwide. Fox also co-finances many of Regency's films. The company's Regency Television unit had produced TV shows such as Malcolm in the Middle and The Bernie Mac Show; however the company had failed to find another hit after those two shows series ran their course and in 2008 Regency closed the TV unit.

REGENERON PHARMACEUTICALS, INC.

NMS: REGN

777 Old Saw Mill River Road
Tarrytown, NY 10591-6707
Phone: 914 847-7000
Fax: –
Web: www.regeneron.com

CEO: Leonard S. Schleifer
CFO: Robert E. Landry
HR: –
FYE: December 31
Type: Public

Regeneron is fighting some serious enemies. Regeneron Pharmaceuticals develops protein-based drugs used to battle a variety of diseases and conditions including cancer inflammatory ailments and eye diseases. The biotechnology company's first commercialized product is ARCALYST a treatment for rare inflammatory diseases including Muckle-Wells Syndrome. Regeneron collaborates with Sanofi to develop candidate aflibercept (VEGF Trap) as a possible treatment for cancerous tumors. It is also developing aflibercept with Bayer HealthCare to treat eye diseases using intraocular delivery with EYLEA approved in the US and Australia as a treatment of neovascular age-related macular degeneration (wet AMD).

	Annual Growth	12/11	12/12	12/13	12/14	12/15
Sales ($ mil.)	74.2%	445.8	1,378.5	2,104.7	2,819.6	4,103.7
Net income ($ mil.)	–	(221.8)	750.3	424.4	348.1	636.1
Market value ($ mil.)	76.9%	5,800.7	17,902.3	28,803.6	42,932.2	56,810.8
Employees	26.0%	1,704	1,950	2,340	2,925	4,300

REGENERX BIOPHARMACEUTICALS INC

NBB: RGRX

15245 Shady Grove Road, Suite 470
Rockville, MD 20850
Phone: 301 208-9191
Fax: –
Web: www.regenerx.com

CEO: J J Finkelstein
CFO: –
HR: –
FYE: December 31
Type: Public

RegeneRx Biopharmaceuticals may not care about the state of your soul but it does want to help damaged bodily tissue be born again. The firm's main drug candidate called Thymosin beta 4 ("T- -4") is undergoing clinical trials for use in accelerating wound healing and for treating other medical problems such as certain kinds of ulcers and ophthalmic conditions. The company operates using an outsourcing business model contracting most of its research and manufacturing operations to third-parties. It has research and licensing agreements with the National Institutes of Health and George Washington University.

	Annual Growth	12/09	12/10	12/11	12/12	12/13
Sales ($ mil.)	(67.4%)	–	0.8	1.5	1.3	0.0
Net income ($ mil.)	–	(6.5)	(5.0)	(6.0)	(0.8)	(0.7)
Market value ($ mil.)	(63.1%)	237.0	18.0	11.4	7.3	4.4
Employees	(15.9%)	10	10	8	8	5

REGINA MEDICAL CENTER

1175 NININGER RD
HASTINGS, MN 55033-1098
Phone: 651-480-4100
Fax: –
Web: www.reginamedical.org

CEO: Ty W Erickson
CFO: Greg Kopp
HR: –
FYE: September 30
Type: Private

Regina Medical Center provides acute and long-term health care services to the Dakota County Minnesota area. Services include cardiology obstetrics pediatrics and neurology. Regina Medical also operates the Hastings Surgery Center jointly with Allina Health System; the Hastings Surgery Center serves the Hastings area and specializes in same-day surgery.

	Annual Growth	09/05	09/06	09/07	09/08	09/09
Sales ($ mil.)	18.3%	–	50.9	52.9	81.9	84.4
Net income ($ mil.)	(34.3%)	–	3.2	(1.1)	(1.6)	0.9
Market value ($ mil.)	–	–	–	–	–	–
Employees	–	–	–	–	–	520

REGIONAL MANAGEMENT CORP

NYS: RM

509 West Butler Road
Greenville, SC 29607
Phone: 864 422-8011
Fax: –
Web: www.regionalmanagement.com

CEO: Michael R. Dunn
CFO: Donald E. (Don) Thomas
HR: –
FYE: December 31
Type: Public

Regional Management is looking to give credit where credit is due. Consumer finance company Regional Management provides secured personal loans (up to $27500) auto loans and furniture and appliance loans to consumers who may otherwise have limited access to credit through banks and other traditional lenders. The company which operates under the Regional Finance RMC Financial Services Anchor Finance and Sun Finance banners among others has some 265 branch locations in eight states in the south and southwest. It also provides loans through pre-screened live check mailings auto dealerships and its e-commerce site. Founded in 1987 Regional Management went public via an IPO in 2012.

	Annual Growth	12/10	12/11	12/12	12/13	12/14
Sales ($ mil.)	23.9%	86.8	105.2	136.0	170.6	204.7
Net income ($ mil.)	(2.6%)	16.4	21.2	25.4	28.8	14.8
Market value ($ mil.)	(2.3%)	–	–	211.0	432.5	201.5
Employees	29.1%	–	670	912	1,117	1,443

REGIONS FINANCIAL CORP

NYS: RF

1900 Fifth Avenue North
Birmingham, AL 35203
Phone: 205 581-7890
Fax: –
Web: www.regions.com

CEO: O. B. Grayson Hall
CFO: David J. Turner
HR: David R. (Dave) Keenan
FYE: December 31
Type: Public

Regions Financial ain't just whistling Dixie anymore. The holding company for Regions Bank which sprouted in the US South has grown by acquiring other financial services firms over the years. Boasting nearly $120 billion in total assets the bank has more than 1600 branches and 2000 ATMs across 16 states stretching from the Southeast and Texas northward through the Mississippi River Valley. In addition to providing standard banking services such as deposit accounts loans and mortgages and credit cards to retail customers and small businesses Regions Financial also serves larger corporations and boasts wealth management division for affluent individuals.

	Annual Growth	12/11	12/12	12/13	12/14	12/15
Assets ($ mil.)	(0.2%)	127,050.0	121,347.0	117,396.0	119,679.0	126,050.0
Net income ($ mil.)	–	(215.0)	1,120.0	1,122.0	1,155.0	1,062.0
Market value ($ mil.)	22.2%	5,578.5	9,250.0	12,830.6	13,699.8	12,454.4
Employees	(2.8%)	26,813	23,427	24,255	23,723	23,916

REGIONS HOSPITAL FOUNDATION

640 JACKSON ST
SAINT PAUL, MN 551012595
Phone: 651-254-3456
Fax: –
Web: www.regionshospital.com

CEO: –
CFO: Greg Klugherz
HR: –
FYE: December 31
Type: Private

If you live around the Twin Cities Regions Hospital can help with your medical needs. The not-for-profit hospital has more than 450 beds and provides acute medical and emergency care services as well as specialty programs in areas including behavioral health rehabilitation burn care cancer cardiovascular orthopedic pediatrics and women's care. Regions Hospital is one of a handful of level I trauma centers in Minnesota and is also a teaching and residency center for the University of Minnesota Medical School. Regions Hospital is part of HealthPartners which operates a network of medical centers and a health plan in the Twin Cities area.

	Annual Growth	12/03	12/04	12/05	12/06	12/12
Sales ($ mil.)	71.3%	–	7.9	430.7	413.9	582.0
Net income ($ mil.)	17.1%	–	–	12.1	4.0	36.6
Market value ($ mil.)	–	–	–	–	–	–
Employees	–	–	–	–	–	3,000

REGIS CORP.

NYS: RGS

7201 Metro Boulevard
Edina, MN 55439
Phone: 952 947-7777
Fax: –
Web: www.regiscorp.com

CEO: Daniel J. (Dan) Hanrahan
CFO: Steven M. (Steve) Spiegel
HR: Carmen D. Thiede
FYE: June 30
Type: Public

Regis is hair there and everywhere. The hair care giant is a global leader in beauty salons and cosmetology education. It owns franchises or holds ownership interests in nearly 9650 locations worldwide most of which operate in North America. Salons are its main business from which Regis derives revenues from hair care services and products sold to franchisees. Its company-owned and franchised locations operate under the banners Regis Salons SmartStyle Supercuts MasterCuts Promenade Sassoon Style America and Cost Cutters among several others. Regis maintains additional ownership stakes in Empire Education Group in the US and MY Style concepts in Japan.

	Annual Growth	06/11	06/12	06/13	06/14	06/15
Sales ($ mil.)	(5.7%)	2,325.9	2,273.8	2,018.7	1,892.4	1,837.3
Net income ($ mil.)	–	(8.9)	(114.1)	29.2	(135.7)	(33.8)
Market value ($ mil.)	0.7%	822.1	963.8	881.2	755.6	845.8
Employees	(3.9%)	55,000	52,000	50,000	49,000	47,000

REGULUS THERAPEUTICS INC

NMS: RGLS

3545 John Hopkins Ct., Suite 210
San Diego, CA 92121
Phone: 858 202-6300
Fax: –
Web: www.regulusrx.com

CEO: Paul C. Grint
CFO: –
HR: –
FYE: December 31
Type: Public

At the heart of it Regulus Therapeutics hopes to fight disease with leonine ferocity. It targets recently discovered microRNA (ribonucleic acid; miRNA) which is important in regulating cellular and biological functions. The company is developing anti-miRNAs that it believes will have the same sort of impact on drug discovery that monoclonal antibodies and biologics have. Through strategic alliances with GlaxoSmithKline AstraZeneca and Sanofi Regulus has five products in development. The candidates target cancer (liver and brain) kidney fibrosis Hepatitis C and atherosclerosis (vascular disease). Formed in 2007 by Alnylam Pharmaceuticals and Isis Pharmaceuticals the company went public in 2012.

	Annual Growth	12/10	12/11	12/12	12/13	12/14
Sales ($ mil.)	(2.8%)	8.6	13.8	12.7	19.6	7.7
Net income ($ mil.)	–	(15.6)	(7.6)	(17.4)	(18.7)	(56.7)
Market value ($ mil.)	59.6%	–	–	308.4	361.7	785.1
Employees	14.9%	–	56	72	76	85

REI SYSTEMS INC.

45335 VINTAGE PARK PLZ
STERLING, VA 201666721
Phone: 703-937-9100
Fax: –

CEO: Veer Bhartiya
CFO: –
HR: –
FYE: December 31
Type: Private

No they don't sell hiking boots or kayaks. REI Systems provides information technology services and develops custom Web-based software used to automate the management of internal business communications contracts customer relationships and grants. Its Electronic Handbooks application is used to manage a variety of data collection and reporting functions; Maintenance-Max is an organizational tool for equipment maintenance providers. The company's IT services include database design software integration and network security. REI Systems' clientele is made up largely of US government agencies such as the Department of Energy and the Department of Defense; commercial clients have included Raytheon.

	Annual Growth	12/09	12/10	12/11	12/12	12/13
Sales ($ mil.)	6.7%	–	56.9	66.6	73.3	69.1
Net income ($ mil.)	(61.3%)	–	–	4.3	2.0	0.6
Market value ($ mil.)	–	–	–	–	–	–
Employees	–	–	–	–	–	311

REICHHOLD INC.

2400 Ellis Rd.
Durham NC 27703
Phone: 919-990-7500
Fax: 919-990-7749
Web: www.reichhold.com

CEO: –
CFO: –
HR: –
FYE: December 31
Type: Private

Reichhold's products have clearly taken hold. It is one of the world's top suppliers of unsaturated polyester resins for composites and a leading supplier of resins used in coatings. Its makes gel coats and bonding agents for the composites industry (to make tubs and showers in marine applications and to provide corrosion-resistance). It provides coating resins (powder coating epoxy and radiation-cured resins) for the automotive aerospace industrial maintenance and other markets. It also provides latex rosin and other resins for the graphic arts market. Reichhold operates in the Americas Asia Europe and the Middle East and has 20 manufacturing plants and five technology centers in 13 countries.

REINSURANCE GROUP OF AMERICA, INC.

NYS: RGA

16600 Swingley Ridge Road
Chesterfield, MO 63017
Phone: 636 736-7000
Fax: –
Web: www.rgare.com

CEO: A. Greig Woodring
CFO: Jack B. Lay
HR: Gay Burns
FYE: December 31
Type: Public

Just what is reinsurance? Here hold this pile of insurance risk while we explain that holding company Reinsurance Group of America (RGA) is one of the largest life reinsurers in the US. RGA provides insurance companies with reinsurance on the risks they've taken on allowing them to reduce their liability and increase their business volume. Its operations are organized into three large groups: Global Mortality which covers individual life insurance policies; Global Group Health and Long-Term Care including critical illness coverage; and Global Financial Markets for annuities and financial coverage. RGA operates in about 30 countries in North America the Asia/Pacific Europe and South Africa.

	Annual Growth	12/10	12/11	12/12	12/13	12/14
Assets ($ mil.)	11.3%	29,081.9	32,104.0	40,360.4	39,674.5	44,679.6
Net income ($ mil.)	4.5%	574.4	599.6	631.9	418.8	684.0
Market value ($ mil.)	13.0%	3,693.8	3,593.4	3,680.7	5,323.7	6,025.9
Employees	7.8%	1,535	1,655	1,766	1,890	2,070

REIS, INC

NMS: REIS

530 Fifth Avenue
New York, NY 10036
Phone: 212 921-1122
Fax: 212 921-2533
Web: www.reis.com

CEO: Lloyd Lynford
CFO: Mark P. Cantaluppi
HR: –
FYE: December 31
Type: Public

Reis knows how to get below the surface of real estate. The company provides commercial real estate market information through online databases containing information on apartment retail office and industrial properties in several US metropolitan markets. Its flagship product Reis SE offers trend and forecast analysis as well as information on rent vacancy rates lease terms sale prices and new construction listings. Reis also furnishes data to small businesses through its ReisReports product. Its databases are used by real estate investors lenders and brokers to make buying selling and financing decisions. Customers access Reis' data through subscription or by purchasing reports individually.

	Annual Growth	12/10	12/11	12/12	12/13	12/14
Sales ($ mil.)	10.6%	27.6	27.2	31.2	34.7	41.3
Net income ($ mil.)	56.9%	0.7	1.9	(4.3)	17.6	4.0
Market value ($ mil.)	38.9%	78.4	101.7	145.4	214.5	292.0
Employees	9.6%	142	160	190	208	205

RELAX THE BACK CORPORATION

6 Centerpointe Dr. Ste. 350
La Palma CA 90623
Phone: 714-523-2870
Fax: 714-523-2980
Web: www.relaxtheback.com

CEO: –
CFO: –
HR: –
FYE: January 31
Type: Private

Relax the Back tries to take the "ERRRGG!" out of ergonomic injuries and chronic back pain. The firm offers muscle-soothing products for the office home and gym including back and neck supports custom and Tempur-Pedic mattresses desk chairs educational books and DVDs exercise and therapy equipment massage loungers and recliners. Doctors and therapists advise the company on decisions about products many of which are supplied by manufacturing unit BackSaver Products. Relax the Back sells through catalogs and the Internet as well as through more than 100 stores in 30 states in the US and Canada that it owns or franchises. Dominion Ventures owns Relax the Back; it was founded in 1986 by an osteopath.

RELIABILITY INCORPORATED

OTC: REAL

410 Park Ave. 15th Fl.
New York NY 91362
Phone: 212-231-8359
Fax: 503-331-2734
Web: www.rentrak.com

CEO: –
CFO: –
HR: –
FYE: December 31
Type: Public

Reliability wanted integrated circuit (IC) manufacturers to rely on its testing systems but after a number of moves it is looking for a new line of business. The company designed manufactured and supported testing and conditioning equipment that helped detect defects in ICs. Running low on cash and needing to repay debt in 2006 Reliability sold its headquarters closed its Singapore burn-in and testing services operations and sold the assets of its Power Sources division (which made DC-to-DC converters) to Reliability Power an unaffiliated firm. The company in 2007 acquired Medallion Electric a Florida-based electrical contractor but sold it back six months later.

RELIANCE STEEL & ALUMINUM CO.

NYS: RS

350 South Grand Avenue, Suite 5100
Los Angeles, CA 90071
Phone: 213 687-7700
Fax: –
Web: www.rsac.com

CEO: Gregg J. Mollins
CFO: Karla R. Lewis
HR: –
FYE: December 31
Type: Public

Reliance Steel & Aluminum shows its mettle as North America's largest metals service center company. Through a network of 300-plus service and distribution centers (many dealing only in specialty metals) in 39 US states it processes and distributes more than 100000 metal products worldwide to more than 125000 customers in a broad range of industries. Reliance markets carbon alloy stainless steel and specialty steel products as well as aluminum brass copper and titanium products. Markets include the aerospace construction manufacturing semiconductor and electronics and transportation industries.

	Annual Growth	12/10	12/11	12/12	12/13	12/14
Sales ($ mil.)	13.4%	6,312.8	8,134.7	8,442.3	9,223.8	10,451.6
Net income ($ mil.)	17.6%	194.4	343.8	403.5	321.6	371.5
Market value ($ mil.)	4.6%	3,951.9	3,765.6	4,802.6	5,865.3	4,738.5
Employees	11.6%	9,610	10,650	11,600	14,000	14,900

RELIV' INTERNATIONAL, INC.

NMS: RELV

136 Chesterfield Industrial Boulevard
Chesterfield, MO 63005
Phone: 636 537-9715
Fax: 636 537-9753
Web: www.reliv.com

CEO: Robert L Montgomery
CFO: Steven D Albright
HR: –
FYE: December 31
Type: Public

Reliv' International is offering its customers more than a beverage it's offering a way of life. Reliv' develops manufactures and sells powdered nutritional supplements weight-management products sports nutrition drinks and skin care products. Top seller Reliv' Classic and Reliv NOW are vegetarian beverage powders that contains vitamins minerals and soy protein. Other products include Innergize! sports drink and high-fiber supplement FibRestore. The company uses a multi-level marketing system selling its products through more than 57000 independent distributors primarily in the US but also in Canada Mexico Europe and the Pacific Rim.

	Annual Growth	12/10	12/11	12/12	12/13	12/14
Sales ($ mil.)	(7.6%)	78.7	73.9	68.7	68.2	57.3
Net income ($ mil.)	(19.0%)	1.7	1.0	1.4	0.8	0.7
Market value ($ mil.)	(11.9%)	24.9	15.8	16.8	36.0	15.0
Employees	(5.6%)	246	205	214	208	195

RELM WIRELESS CORP.

ASE: RWC

7100 Technology Drive
West Melbourne, FL 32904
Phone: 321-984-1414
Fax: –
Web: www.relm.com

CEO: David P Storey
CFO: William P Kelly
HR: –
FYE: December 31
Type: Public

RELM Wireless spreads communications across the land. The company makes portable land mobile radio (LMR) products used for mobile handheld and vehicle communications. In addition to radios its products include base stations repeaters and related subsystems. The US government and public safety agencies account for the vast majority of RELM's sales but the company also markets to hotels construction firms schools and transportation service providers. RELM Wireless sells its radio communications systems under the BK Radio RELM and RELM/BK brands.

	Annual Growth	12/10	12/11	12/12	12/13	12/14
Sales ($ mil.)	4.5%	26.0	24.1	27.6	27.0	31.0
Net income ($ mil.)	–	(0.7)	(0.5)	2.1	1.1	1.6
Market value ($ mil.)	27.8%	24.6	15.0	23.0	46.1	65.6
Employees	1.3%	96	89	91	87	101

REMY COINTREAU USA INC.

1290 Avenue of the Americas
New York NY 10019
Phone: 212-424-2244
Fax: 212-424-2259
Web: www.remyusa.com

CEO: Tom Jensen
CFO: Dennis Floam
HR: Maren Boot
FYE: March 31
Type: Subsidiary

Brands across the water. They're made in France — distributed and enjoyed in the US. Remy Cointreau USA makes sure les Americains have ample opportunity to enjoy all of parent company Remy Cointreau's libations. Remy Cointreau USA (formerly known as Remy Amerique) distributes its parent's the champagnes liqueurs and distilled spirits such as cognacs brandy rum and scotch in the US and Caribbean. The company's brands include Remy Martin cognacs; The Famous Grouse scotch; orange-flavored Cointreau and passion fruit-flavored Passoa liqueurs; Mount Gay rum; and Piper-Heidsieck and Charles Heidsieck champagnes. In late 2010 the company's French parent said it will sell its champagne business.

REMY INTERNATIONAL INC.

PINK SHEETS: REMYI

600 Corporation Dr.
Pendleton IN 46064
Phone: 765-778-6499
Fax: 561-241-4628
Web: www.pwg-inc.com

CEO: John J Pittas
CFO: Albert F Vanderbergh
HR: –
FYE: December 31
Type: Private

Remy International (formerly Delco Remy International) revs up cars and light- and heavy-duty trucks. The manufacturer and distributor offers starter motors alternators hybrid electric motors and transmission components. Most parts are sold under the Delco Remy brand which debuted in 1918. The company holds the top spot for remanufacturing starters and alternators for the automotive aftermarket in North America. Its roster of customers includes OEMs (General Motors is largest customer generating almost 25% of annual sales) and aftermarket businesses such as Advance Auto Parts and AutoZone. Fidelity National a title insurance company owns 49% of Remy which filed to go public in 2011.

RENAISSANCE LEARNING INC.

2911 Peach St.
Wisconsin Rapids WI 54495
Phone: 715-424-3636
Fax: 715-424-4242
Web: www.renlearn.com

CEO: John J Lynch Jr
CFO: Mary T Minch
HR: –
FYE: December 31
Type: Private

Renaissance Learning offers a technical approach to education. The company's educational software designed for grades pre-K through 12 is used by schools in North America. Offered on CD-ROMs and on a hosted basis its software includes its flagship Accelerated Reader program as well as applications for writing math language acquisition and early literacy. Renaissance also markets portable computing devices pre-loaded with software to improve writing skills. Husband and wife Terrance Paul (chairman) and Judith Paul (vice chairman) who founded the company in 1986 together owned 54% of Renaissance before it was acquired in 2011 by London-based private equity firm Permira Funds for about $440 million.

RENASANT CORP

NMS: RNST

209 Troy Street
Tupelo, MS 38804-4827
Phone: 662-680-1001
Fax: –
Web: www.renasant.com

CEO: E. Robinson (Robin) McGraw
CFO: Kevin D. Chapman
HR: –
FYE: December 31
Type: Public

Those who are cognizant of their finances may want to do business with Renasant Corporation. The holding company owns Renasant Bank which serves consumers and local business through about 80 locations in Alabama Georgia Mississippi and Tennessee. The bank offers standard products such as checking and savings accounts CDs credit cards and loans and mortgages as well as trust retail brokerage and retirement plan services. Its loan portfolio is dominated by residential and commercial real estate loans. The bank also offers agricultural business construction and consumer loans and lease financing. Subsidiary Renasant Insurance sells personal and business coverage.

	Annual Growth	12/10	12/11	12/12	12/13	12/14
Assets ($ mil.)	7.8%	4,297.3	4,202.0	4,178.6	5,746.3	5,805.1
Net income ($ mil.)	17.1%	31.7	25.6	26.6	33.5	59.6
Market value ($ mil.)	14.4%	533.4	473.2	603.8	992.4	912.6
Employees	10.2%	996	1,030	1,096	1,483	1,471

RENEWABLE ENERGY GROUP INC.

NASDAQ: REGI

416 S. Bell Ave.
Ames IA 50010
Phone: 515-239-8000
Fax: 515-239-8009
Web: www.regfuel.com

CEO: Daniel J OH
CFO: –
HR: –
FYE: December 31
Type: Public

Renewable Energy Group or REG wants alternative fuel to become a regular thing for its customers. The company sells SoyPOWER brand biodiesel throughout the US controlling about 40% of US sales. Biodiesel is a clean burning fuel made from waste including vegetable oil corn grain and soybeans. REG owns four and manages five plants that make more than 300 million gallons of biofuel per year; that fuel is sold to fleet operators the military and mining agriculture and home-heating companies. In addition to its production and distribution activities REG also builds biodiesel production plants for other firms. The company was formed in 2003 by West Central Cooperative. REG went public in 2011 with an IPO.

RENEWABLE ENERGY GROUP, INC.
NMS: REGI

416 South Bell Avenue
Ames, IA 50010
Phone: 515 239-8000
Fax: –
Web: www.regi.com

CEO: Jeffrey (Jeff) Stroburg
CFO: Chad Stone
HR: –
FYE: December 31
Type: Public

Renewable Energy Group or REG wants alternative fuel to become a regular thing for its customers. The company sells SoyPOWER brand biodiesel throughout the US controlling about 40% of US sales. Biodiesel is a clean burning fuel made from waste including vegetable oil corn grain and soybeans. REG owns four and manages five plants that make about 260 million gallons of biofuel per year; that fuel is sold to fleet operators the military and mining agriculture and home-heating companies. In addition to its production and distribution activities REG also builds biodiesel production plants for other firms.

	Annual Growth	12/10	12/11	12/12	12/13	12/14
Sales ($ mil.)	55.8%	216.5	824.0	1,015.0	1,498.1	1,273.8
Net income ($ mil.)	–	(21.6)	88.9	22.3	186.4	82.6
Market value ($ mil.)	28.7%	–	–	260.3	509.1	431.3
Employees	21.0%	234	245	279	368	502

RENFRO CORPORATION

661 LINVILLE RD
MOUNT AIRY, NC 270303101
Phone: 336-719-8000
Fax: –
Web: www.renfro.com

CEO: Andrew L Kilby Jr
CFO: Andrew L. Kilby
HR: –
FYE: January 29
Type: Private

For those who tend to misplace their socks Renfro can foot the bill. The company designs and manufacturers hundreds of styles of socks and legwear products and markets them in North America through department stores specialty stores and e-commerce sites. Renfro's products are sold under several brands including Carhartt Fruit of the Loom Dr. Scholl's Copper Sole Polo Work King and Wrangler among others. The company also sells its owns brands K. Bell and Hot Sox. The clothing company's customers include well-known retailers such as Costco Kmart J.C. Penney Target and Wal-Mart.

	Annual Growth	01/06	01/07	01/08	01/10	01/11
Sales ($ mil.)	(13.1%)	–	–	593.5	375.6	390.1
Net income ($ mil.)	2454.2%	–	–	0.0	11.7	9.7
Market value ($ mil.)	–	–	–	–	–	–
Employees	–	–	–	–	–	5,000

RENNOVA HEALTH INC
NAS: RNVA

44 Montgomery Street, Suite 800
San Francisco, CA 94104
Phone: 415 248-5350
Fax: –
Web: www.collabrx.com

CEO: Seamus Lagan
CFO: Jason P Adams
HR: –
FYE: March 31
Type: Public

CollabRx (formerly Tegal Corporation) is collaborating between data and health care. The company provides data analytics through its product a web-based application named Therapy Finder which allows physicians and their patients to learn about appropriate cancer tests. Customers include Life Technologies Inc. and Everyday Health Inc.

	Annual Growth	03/11	03/12	03/13	03/14	03/15
Sales ($ mil.)	136.2%	0.0	0.1	0.4	0.7	0.5
Net income ($ mil.)	–	(3.1)	(1.4)	(3.9)	(3.3)	(5.2)
Market value ($ mil.)	16.0%	6.3	36.3	32.6	33.6	11.4
Employees	16.7%	7	5	11	17	13

RENO CONTRACTING INC.

1450 FRAZEE RD STE 100
SAN DIEGO, CA 921084341
Phone: 619-220-0224
Fax: –
Web: www.renocon.com

CEO: Matthew J Reno
CFO: Linda Melemed
HR: –
FYE: October 31
Type: Private

Reno Contracting is building on its commercial state of mind in the southern part of the Golden State. The general contractor specializes in commercial construction projects primarily in its home region of San Diego County California. Projects include office retail and hospitality construction biotech and industrial facilities and hospitals. Reno develops properties from the ground up and also performs interior tenant improvements. Clients have included Diversa Corporation Biosite and Bridgepoint Education. Reno's green building division Reno ESP utilizes energy efficient products and technology in the construction process. The company was founded in 1993 by CEO Matt Reno.

	Annual Growth	10/05	10/06	10/07	10/08	10/10
Sales ($ mil.)	(59.1%)	–	–	884.1	213.7	60.5
Net income ($ mil.)	5313.5%	–	–	0.0	1.4	1.0
Market value ($ mil.)	–	–	–	–	–	–
Employees	–	–	–	–	–	32

RENT-A-CENTER INC.
NMS: RCII

5501 Headquarters Drive
Plano, TX 75024
Phone: 972 801-1100
Fax: 972 701-0360
Web: www.rentacenter.com

CEO: Robert D. Davis
CFO: Guy J. Constant
HR: –
FYE: December 31
Type: Public

Rent-A-Center (RAC) wants its customers to rent while it buys. The #1 rent-to-own chain nationwide owns and operates some 2946 stores (down from 3400 in 2006) throughout the US Canada Mexico and Puerto Rico under the Rent-A-Center Get It Now and Home Choice names; and franchises 187 stores through subsidiary Rent-A-Center Franchising International (formerly ColorTyme). The stores rent name-brand home electronics furniture accessories appliances and computers. While customers have the option to eventually own their rented items only about 25% ever do. The company's Acceptance Now business operates from kiosks on the premises of other retailers.

	Annual Growth	12/10	12/11	12/12	12/13	12/14
Sales ($ mil.)	3.7%	2,731.6	2,882.2	3,082.6	3,104.2	3,157.8
Net income ($ mil.)	(13.4%)	171.6	164.6	183.5	128.2	96.4
Market value ($ mil.)	3.0%	1,710.3	1,960.4	1,820.5	1,766.5	1,924.4
Employees	4.9%	18,300	19,700	20,200	22,200	22,200

RENTECH, INC.
NAS: RTK

10877 Wilshire Boulevard, 10th Floor
Los Angeles, CA 90024
Phone: 310 571-9800
Fax: –

CEO: Keith B. Forman
CFO: Jeffrey R. Spain
HR: –
FYE: December 31
Type: Public

Rentech owns and operates wood fiber processing and nitrogen fertilizer manufacturing businesses. It also owns the intellectual property including patents pilot and demonstration data and engineering designs for a number of clean energy technologies designed to produce certified synthetic fuels and renewable power when integrated with third-party technologies. Originally a clean energy business that rented (licensed) its alternative energy technology (hence "rent-tech") the company now gets most of its revenues from its fertilizers and wood fiber processing operations.

	Annual Growth	09/11*	12/11	12/12	12/13	12/14
Sales ($ mil.)	37.9%	180.1	63.1	261.9	374.9	472.7
Net income ($ mil.)	–	(64.3)	(8.5)	(14.0)	(1.5)	(32.5)
Market value ($ mil.)	17.3%	17.9	30.0	60.3	40.1	28.9
Employees	49.6%	266	265	347	760	891

*Fiscal year change

RENTRAK CORP.

NMS: RENT

7700 NE Ambassador Place
Portland, OR 97220
Phone: 503 284-7581
Fax: –
Web: www.rentrak.com

CEO: William P Livek
CFO: David I Chemerow
HR: –
FYE: March 31
Type: Public

What a bargain movie matinee is to parents Rentrak strives to be to mom-and-pop video rental stores: a lower-priced necessity. Rentrak provides content to regional and independent video entertainment rental outlets in the US and Canada via its Pay-Per-Transaction (PPT) system. This system enables retailers to lease content such as movies TV and games at lower distribution costs in return for a cut of the rental revenue. Rentrak also provides nearly real-time viewer transaction measurement services to the entertainment and advertising industries reporting consumer viewing behavior for on-demand TV Internet and theatrical release content. Customers include Starcom MediaVest and Fisher Communications.

	Annual Growth	03/10	03/11	03/12	03/13	03/14
Sales ($ mil.)	(4.5%)	91.1	97.1	91.1	99.2	75.6
Net income ($ mil.)	–	0.6	(0.8)	(6.4)	(22.6)	(4.3)
Market value ($ mil.)	29.3%	263.2	328.8	277.2	268.4	736.2
Employees	8.2%	382	423	448	471	524

REPAIRCLINIC.COM INC.

48600 Michigan Ave.
Canton MI 48188-2240
Phone: 734-495-3079
Fax: 734-495-3150
Web: www.repairclinic.com

CEO: Larry Beach
CFO: –
HR: –
FYE: December 31
Type: Private

The Maytag repairman just got a little lonelier thanks to RepairClinic.com. The company is an online source for appliance parts and repair advice. In addition to Maytag RepairClinic also carries parts for about 80 brands including Kenmore Haier Samsung Frigidaire GE Sears and Whirlpool for such items as air conditioners dishwashers dryer washing machines and microwaves. RepairClinic.com helps do-it-yourselfers with maintenance tips parts identification special parts ordering and diagnostic assistance through its ApplianceRepair.com Web site. The company was founded in 1999 partly to help protect the environment by promoting repair and maintenance rather than replacement of used appliances.

REPLACEMENT PARTS INC.

1901 E ROOSEVELT RD
LITTLE ROCK, AR 722062533
Phone: 501-375-1215
Fax: –
Web: www.replacementparts.com

CEO: William (Bill) Schlatterer
CFO: –
HR: Martha Harper
FYE: December 31
Type: Private

Replacement Parts works Bumper to Bumper. The company's subsidiary Crow-Burlingame operates about 160 stores under the Bumper To Bumper banner in Arkansas Louisiana Mississippi Missouri Oklahoma and Texas. Replacement Parts also distributes auto parts through three Parts Warehouses in Arkansas Louisiana and Oklahoma. The company was founded in 1919 by grocer J.G. Burlingame and candy salesman William Robert Crow grandfather of president Fletcher Lord Jr. The duo first entered the auto business by purchasing new cars in St. Louis and driving them around Little Rock to attract buyers. Employees own about 15% of the company through its stock ownership program.

	Annual Growth	12/02	12/03	12/04	12/06	12/07
Sales ($ mil.)	8.0%	–	137.9	149.4	179.0	187.3
Net income ($ mil.)	3.8%	–	–	2.8	5.1	3.1
Market value ($ mil.)	–	–	–	–	–	–
Employees	–	–	–	–	–	1,115

REPLACEMENTS LTD.

1089 KNOX RD
MC LEANSVILLE, NC 27301-9228
Phone: 336-697-3000
Fax: –
Web: www.replacements.com

CEO: Robert L Page
CFO: –
HR: –
FYE: September 30
Type: Private

Face it the good china is going to get chipped. While throwing it all out is always an option Replacements offers a cheaper solution. The company offers new and previously-owned china crystal flatware and collectibles from its facilities spanning some 500000 sq. ft. Its inventory consists of nearly14 million pieces in more than 340000 patterns. In addition to its bridal and gift registry Replacements' website features a dinnerware knowledge base place-setting guides pattern identification tools and showroom tour. Customers can place their orders by mail phone fax e-mail or in person at the company's store in Greensboro North Carolina. Replacements was founded by CEO Bob Page in 1981.

	Annual Growth	09/08	09/09	09/10	09/11	09/12
Sales ($ mil.)	0.1%	–	79.0	80.7	80.1	79.3
Net income ($ mil.)	58.6%	–	2.8	9.7	15.3	11.1
Market value ($ mil.)	–	–	–	–	–	–
Employees	–	–	–	–	–	450

REPLIGEN CORP.

NMS: RGEN

41 Seyon Street, Bldg.1, Suite 100
Waltham, MA 02453
Phone: 781 250-0111
Fax: 781 250-0115
Web: www.repligen.com

CEO: Walter C. Herlihy
CFO: Jon K. Snodgres
HR: Kelly Capra
FYE: December 31
Type: Public

Repligen replies to the needs of the pharmaceutical industry by supplying bio-engineered drug ingredients. Repligen's bioprocessing business develops and commercializes proteins and other agents used in the production of biopharmaceuticals. The firm also conducts drug research activities include development of a pancreatic imaging agent and potential therapies for bipolar disorder Friedreich's ataxia (a debilitating early adulthood disease) and spinal muscular atrophy. While all of Repligen's own drugs are in the clinical development stage it does receive royalty payments from Bristol-Myers Squibb (BMS) on sales of BMS' Orencia rheumatoid arthritis drug as well as by licensing out its technologies.

	Annual Growth	03/11*	12/11	12/12	12/13	12/14
Sales ($ mil.)	32.5%	27.3	23.5	62.3	68.2	63.5
Net income ($ mil.)	–	(0.0)	(1.6)	14.2	16.1	8.2
Market value ($ mil.)	74.3%	122.6	113.7	205.8	447.0	648.9
Employees	27.3%	66	137	120	116	136

*Fiscal year change

REPRO-MED SYSTEMS, INC.

NBB: REPR

24 Carpenter Road
Chester, NY 10918
Phone: 845 469-2042
Fax: 845 469-5518
Web: www.rmsmedicalproducts.com

CEO: Andrew I Sealfon
CFO: Karen Fisher
HR: –
FYE: February 28
Type: Public

Repro-Med Systems (aka RMS Medical Products) doesn't want to repo your medical devices it wants to supply you with them! The company manufactures portable medical devices for respiratory and infusion therapy. Most of RMS' products are designed for simplicity and do not require batteries or electricity. The company's biggest seller is a hand-powered airway suction device (RES-Q-VAC) used in emergency situations in hospitals and ambulances. Its other key product is a portable self-powered infusion system (FREEDOM60) for ambulatory home and hospital use. The company also has a line of gynecological instruments. Founder CEO Andrew Sealfon owns 20% of the company he established in 1980.

	Annual Growth	02/11	02/12	02/13	02/14	02/15
Sales ($ mil.)	23.0%	4.9	6.4	7.8	8.7	11.2
Net income ($ mil.)	1.7%	0.7	0.8	0.7	0.7	0.8
Market value ($ mil.)	22.3%	6.8	9.5	8.0	8.0	15.2
Employees	14.3%	44	55	60	63	75

REPROS THERAPEUTICS INC

NAS: RPRX

2408 Timberloch Place, Suite B-7
The Woodlands, TX 77380
Phone: 281 719-3400
Fax: 281 363-8796
Web: www.reprosrx.com

CEO: Joseph S Podolski
CFO: Katherine A Anderson
HR: –
FYE: December 31
Type: Public

Repros Therapeutics focuses on reproductive health. The pharmaceutical firm develops small-molecule drugs to treat hormonal and reproductive system disorders. Its lead candidate Proellex is a possible therapy for uterine fibroids endometriosis and associated anemia. The company is developing an orally delivered version as well as a vaginally delivered one. Repros' second candidate Androxal may treat testosterone deficiencies in men particularly when the deficiency is caused by obesity. The company was formed in 1987 and went public in mid-2013.

	Annual Growth	12/10	12/11	12/12	12/13	12/14
Sales ($ mil.)	(61.8%)	0.4	0.0	0.0	0.0	0.0
Net income ($ mil.)	–	(4.8)	(12.5)	(18.2)	(27.7)	(32.5)
Market value ($ mil.)	34.6%	73.8	117.0	382.3	444.3	242.0
Employees	47.0%	6	13	21	25	28

REPUBLIC AIRWAYS HOLDINGS INC

NMS: RJET

8909 Purdue Road, Suite 300
Indianapolis, IN 46268
Phone: 317 484-6000
Fax: –
Web: www.rjet.com

CEO: Bryan K. Bedford
CFO: Joe Allman
HR: –
FYE: December 31
Type: Public

Many US airlines pledge allegiance to Republic Airways. The airline holding company's subsidiaries Chautauqua Airlines Republic Airlines and Shuttle America offer passenger flight service to major airports and smaller markets as well as regional service under code-sharing agreements with American Continental Delta United and US Airways. (Code-sharing allows airlines to sell tickets on one another's flights and extend their network.) The company maintains a fleet of about 240 aircraft and offer scheduled passenger service with more than 1250 flights daily to 100 cities. Republic made headlines in late 2015 as it engaged in heated talks with its pilots union to settle contract disputes.

	Annual Growth	12/10	12/11	12/12	12/13	12/14
Sales ($ mil.)	(15.2%)	2,653.7	2,864.5	2,810.9	1,346.5	1,375.4
Net income ($ mil.)	–	(13.8)	(151.8)	51.3	26.7	64.3
Market value ($ mil.)	18.8%	366.2	171.6	284.1	534.8	729.9
Employees	(11.9%)	9,850	9,420	9,140	5,821	5,935

REPUBLIC BANCORP, INC. (KY)

NMS: RBCA A

601 West Market Street
Louisville, KY 40202
Phone: 502 584-3600
Fax: –
Web: www.republicbank.com

CEO: Steven E. (Steve) Trager
CFO: Kevin Sipes
HR: –
FYE: December 31
Type: Public

The second-largest bank holding company based in Kentucky Republic Bancorp is the parent of Republic Bank & Trust which has about 40 branches in central Kentucky and southern Indiana. It also owns Republic Bank a thrift with a handful of branches in metropolitan Tampa and a single location in the Cincinnati area. In 2012 Republic Bancorp entered the Nashville and Minneapolis market through the FDIC-assisted acquisitions of the failed Tennessee Commerce Bank and First Commercial Bank respectively. The company's banks offer deposit accounts loans and mortgages credit cards private banking and trust services.

	Annual Growth	12/10	12/11	12/12	12/13	12/14
Assets ($ mil.)	0.8%	3,622.7	3,420.0	3,394.4	3,371.9	3,747.0
Net income ($ mil.)	(18.3%)	64.8	94.1	119.3	25.4	28.8
Market value ($ mil.)	1.0%	495.2	477.4	440.5	511.6	515.4
Employees	(1.0%)	766	728	820	750	735

REPUBLIC FIRST BANCORP, INC.

NMS: FRBK

50 South 16th Street
Philadelphia, PA 19102
Phone: 215 735-4422
Fax: –
Web: www.myrepublicbank.com

CEO: Harry D Madonna
CFO: Frank A Cavallaro
HR: –
FYE: December 31
Type: Public

Republic First Bancorp is the holding company for Republic Bank which serves the Greater Philadelphia area and southern New Jersey from more than 15 branches. Boasting over $1 billion in assets the bank targets individuals and small to midsized businesses offering standard deposit products including checking and savings accounts money market accounts IRAs and CDs. Commercial mortgages account for more than 70% of the company's loan portfolio which also includes consumer loans business loans and residential mortgages. Republic has been transitioning from a commercial bank into a major regional retail and commercial bank.

	Annual Growth	12/10	12/11	12/12	12/13	12/14
Assets ($ mil.)	8.5%	876.1	1,047.4	988.7	961.7	1,214.6
Net income ($ mil.)	–	(10.7)	(24.7)	3.6	(3.5)	2.4
Market value ($ mil.)	11.4%	92.3	54.9	78.3	112.8	141.9
Employees	2.9%	210	212	205	226	235

REPUBLIC MORTGAGE INSURANCE COMPANY

101 N. Cherry St.
Winston-Salem NC 27105
Phone: 336-661-0015
Fax: 336-661-3275
Web: www.rmic.com

CEO: –
CFO: David Cash
HR: –
FYE: December 31
Type: Subsidiary

Republic Mortgage Insurance Company (RMIC) aimed to protect lenders but was ultimately unable to recover from its own losses following the real estate crisis. RMIC is operating in runoff mode meaning it services existing mortgage insurance policies (which protect lenders from losses on first mortgage defaults for single-family residential properties) but no longer writes new mortgage insurance policies. RMIC is a subsidiary of diversified insurance company Old Republic International. The company is operating under the supervision of the North Carolina Department of Insurance.

REPUBLIC SERVICES, INC.

NYS: RSG

18500 North Allied Way
Phoenix, AZ 85054
Phone: 480 627-2700
Fax: –
Web: www.republicservices.com

CEO: Donald W. (Don) Slager
CFO: Charles F. (Chuck) Serianni
HR: Jeffrey A. (Jeff) Hughes
FYE: December 31
Type: Public

Homeowners and businesses across the US and in Puerto Rico pledge allegiance to Republic Services and the trash collection for which it stands. The company is the second-largest nonhazardous waste management provider in the US behind leader Waste Management in terms of revenues and geographic coverage. Republic provides waste disposal services for commercial industrial municipal and residential customers through its network of 340 collection companies. The company owns or operates 189 solid waste landfills 198 transfer stations and 60 recycling centers. It also has 72 landfill-to-gas and a handful of other renewable energy projects.

	Annual Growth	12/11	12/12	12/13	12/14	12/15
Sales ($ mil.)	2.7%	8,192.9	8,118.3	8,417.2	8,788.3	9,115.0
Net income ($ mil.)	6.2%	589.2	571.8	588.9	547.6	749.9
Market value ($ mil.)	12.4%	9,521.3	10,136.4	11,473.9	13,910.4	15,202.9
Employees	2.4%	30,000	30,000	31,000	31,000	33,000

REPUBLIC WESTERN INSURANCE COMPANY

2721 N. Central Ave.
Phoenix AZ 85004
Phone: 602-263-6755
Fax: 602-277-5203
Web: www.repwest.com

CEO: –
CFO: Kristin N Korinek
HR: –
FYE: March 31
Type: Subsidiary

Republic Western Insurance (aka RepWest) insures the stuff we can't live without and the stuff we have no room for. A subsidiary of AMERCO the parent of DIY moving company U-Haul International RepWest handles the property/casualty insurance needs of U-Haul as well as its customers and dealers. The company administers and underwrites parts of the insurance products U-Haul offers to its customers. Its policies protect against damage to rented vehicles and the cargo inside them and they provide medical and life coverage to drivers as well. Other products cover damage to property stored in U-Haul storage facilities (Safestor) and business insurance for storage facility owners.

RES-CARE INC.

9901 Linn Station Rd.
Louisville KY 40223
Phone: 502-394-2100
Fax: 502-394-2206
Web: www.rescare.com

CEO: Ralph G Gronefeld Jr
CFO: David W Miles
HR: –
FYE: December 31
Type: Private

Through its residential training and support services ResCare offers RESpect and CARE to people with physical and mental disabilities. ResCare has residential and nonresidential facilities in more than 40 states and some international locations. The company operates through four primary segments: ResCare HomeCare Services ResCare Residential Services ResCare Workforce Services and ResCare Youth Services. The segments provide in-home personal care and training in social vocational and functional skills as well as counseling and therapy programs. Additionally Res-Care runs correctional and care programs for at-risk youth and assistance for adults. The company is owned by investment firm Onex.

RESEARCH CORPORATION TECHNOLOGIES INC.

5210 E. Williams Cir. Ste. 240
Tucson AZ 85711-4410
Phone: 520-748-4400
Fax: 520-748-0025
Web: www.rctech.com

CEO: Gary Munsinger
CFO: Christopher Martin
HR: –
FYE: December 31
Type: Private

Research Corporation Technologies (RCT) specializes in early-stage funding for biotechnology companies and technologies originating at universities and research institutions. Through investments partnerships and licensing programs the venture capital and management firm helps to develop therapeutics medical devices and medical technology. A UK affiliate Cambridge Research Bioventures and an alliance with Start-Up Australia pursue biotechnology opportunities in those countries. RCT also invests in new materials optics technologies and geophysics instruments. Founded in 1987 the company has more than $300 million in assets under management.

RESEARCH FRONTIERS INC.

NAS: REFR

240 Crossways Park Drive
Woodbury, NY 11797
Phone: 516 364-1902
Fax: –

CEO: Joseph M Harary
CFO: Seth L Van Voorhees
HR: –
FYE: December 31
Type: Public

Research Frontiers is exploring smart light frontiers. The company's suspended-particle device (SPD) technology controls the flow of light. When microscopic particles in a liquid suspension or film are electrically excited they align. By varying voltage the amount of light transmitted can be controlled. Applications include "smart windows" that control light transmission eyewear auto sunroofs and mirrors and flat-panel displays for computers and other electronic devices. Research Frontiers licenses its technologies to such manufacturers as Asahi Glass Dainippon Ink and Chemicals General Electric Hitachi Chemical and Polaroid.

	Annual Growth	12/10	12/11	12/12	12/13	12/14
Sales ($ mil.)	20.1%	0.8	0.8	2.0	2.2	1.6
Net income ($ mil.)	–	(3.9)	(4.1)	(3.1)	(5.8)	(4.4)
Market value ($ mil.)	(0.8%)	126.6	81.1	89.5	138.3	122.5
Employees	2.0%	12	13	13	13	13

RESEARCH INCORPORATED

7128 Shady Oak Rd.
Eden Prairie MN 55344-3517
Phone: 952-949-9009
Fax: 952-949-9559
Web: www.researchinc.com

CEO: –
CFO: –
HR: –
FYE: September 30
Type: Private

Research Inc. keeps the heat on its customers. The company makes reflow ovens drying systems and heating devices used in the graphic arts semiconductor and plastics industries. Its ink-drying products provide precise heat control in printing processes (such as ink-jet printing). The company's reflow ovens are used in surface-mount applications such as semiconductor production and printed circuit board assembly and its heating devices produce items such as silicone tubing and plastic bottles. Research Inc. markets its integrated heating systems to the graphic arts and print media markets under the Speed-Dri Roll-Dri and Web-Dri brands. In 2007 the company was acquired by Precison Control Systems Inc.

RESEARCH TRIANGLE INSTITUTE INC

3040 CORNWALLIS RD
DURHAM, NC 277090128
Phone: 919-541-6000
Fax: –
Web: www.rti.org

CEO: E. Wayne Holden
CFO: Michael H. (Mike) Kaelin
HR: –
FYE: September 30
Type: Private

The scientists at Research Triangle Institute address the problems of a sphere (the planet). Operating mainly under its trade name RTI International (RTI) the not-for-profit enterprise conducts research in such areas as advanced technologies environmental resources and medicine. It provides such services as certification and materials testing as well as software used in laboratories and research projects. Serving the US federal government other governments nonprofits and for-profit companies RTI offers analytical perspectives on public policy and has more than 3740 researchers working in offices around the world.

	Annual Growth	09/09	09/10	09/11	09/12	09/13
Sales ($ mil.)	1.0%	–	758.7	777.1	733.5	782.7
Net income ($ mil.)	23.7%	–	–	24.5	11.8	37.5
Market value ($ mil.)	–	–	–	–	–	–
Employees	–	–	–	–	–	2,680

RESERVE PETROLEUM CO.

NBB: RSRV

6801 Broadway Ext., Suite 300
Oklahoma City, OK 73116-9037
Phone: 405 848-7551
Fax: –
Web: www.reserve-petro.com

CEO: Cameron R McLain
CFO: –
HR: –
FYE: December 31
Type: Public

The Reserve Petroleum Company has petroleum reserves of about 266870 barrels of oil. It also has 1.6 billion cu. ft. of natural gas reserves. In 2008 the oil and gas exploration and production company owned non-producing properties of more than 262000 gross acres (90330 net acres) located in nine states. About 64800 net acres of this land asset are in Oklahoma South Dakota and Texas. About 53% of Reserve Petroleum's oil production in 2008 was derived from royalty interests. The company has royalty interests in 33 gross (1.1 net) wells that were drilled and completed as producing wells. President Mason McLain owns about 10% of Reserve Petroleum.

	Annual Growth	12/10	12/11	12/12	12/13	12/14
Sales ($ mil.)	11.2%	13.8	13.0	15.1	18.8	21.2
Net income ($ mil.)	6.5%	5.3	5.3	4.6	6.1	6.8
Market value ($ mil.)	2.7%	50.9	47.9	46.2	67.4	56.6
Employees	3.0%	8	8	8	8	9

RESMED INC.

NYS: RMD

9001 Spectrum Center Blvd.
San Diego, CA 92123
Phone: 858 836-5000
Fax: –
Web: www.resmed.com

CEO: Michael Farrell
CFO: Brett Sandercock
HR: –
FYE: June 30
Type: Public

Breathe easy because you won't lose any sleep while using ResMed's products. ResMed develops makes and distributes medical equipment used to diagnose and treat respiratory disorders that occur during sleep such as sleep apnea. Most of its products treat obstructive sleep apnea (OSA) a condition in which a patient's air flow is periodically obstructed causing multiple disruptions during sleep that can lead to daytime sleepiness and other conditions such as high blood pressure. Its products include air-flow generators face masks diagnostic products and accessories. ResMed sells directly and through distributors worldwide to home health equipment dealers sleep clinics and hospitals.

	Annual Growth	06/11	06/12	06/13	06/14	06/15
Sales ($ mil.)	7.8%	1,243.1	1,368.5	1,514.5	1,555.0	1,678.9
Net income ($ mil.)	11.7%	227.0	254.9	307.1	345.3	352.9
Market value ($ mil.)	16.2%	4,347.7	4,382.8	6,339.6	7,112.2	7,918.6
Employees	5.9%	3,450	3,700	3,900	4,100	4,340

RESOLUTE FOREST PRODUCTS INC

NYS: RFP

111 Duke Street, Suite 5000
Montreal, Quebec H3C 2M1
Phone: 514 875-2515
Fax: –

CEO: –
CFO: –
HR: –
FYE: December 31
Type: Public

Resolute Forest Products makes newsprint commercial printing paper mechanical paper pulp and wood products. It relies on 20 pulp and paper mills and 20 wood products plants in Canada South Korea and the US to distribute its products to about 80 countries; it is one of the world's largest recyclers of newspapers and magazines. Resolute owns or has cutting rights to more than 40 million acres of forestland in North America and has power generation assets in Canada. The US account for more than 65% of the company's sales. Canada is its second largest market with about 15% of sales. Other markets for Resolute's products include Brazil Mexico Italy and South Korea.

	Annual Growth	12/10	12/11	12/12	12/13	12/14
Sales ($ mil.)	(2.7%)	4,746.0	4,756.0	4,503.0	4,461.0	4,258.0
Net income ($ mil.)	–	2,614.0	41.0	(2.0)	(639.0)	(277.0)
Market value ($ mil.)	(7.1%)	2,243.9	1,379.3	1,255.2	1,518.7	1,669.4
Employees	(7.5%)	10,500	10,400	9,300	8,400	7,700

RESORTQUEST INTERNATIONAL INC.

546 Mary Esther Cut-Off NW Ste. 3
Fort Walton Beach FL 32548
Phone: 850-837-4774
Fax: 850-837-5390
Web: www.resortquest.com

CEO: –
CFO: –
HR: –
FYE: December 31
Type: Subsidiary

Your search for the perfect vacation spot could involve a resort quest; if so ResortQuest International would like to help. The company provides rental management services at more than 6000 vacation properties which are primarily located in the southeast and western US. Its portfolio includes condominiums and houses that ResortQuest markets and maintains on behalf of the individual owners. The company reaches out to prospective clients using the Internet direct-mail marketing and referrals. In addition ResortQuest offers real estate brokerage services for vacation properties. Investment holding company Leucadia National sold the company in late 2010 to Wyndham Worldwide.

RESOURCE AMERICA, INC.

NMS: REXI

One Crescent Drive, Suite 203, Navy Yard Corporate Center
Philadelphia, PA 19112
Phone: 215 546-5005
Fax: –
Web: www.resourceamerica.com

CEO: Crit S. DeMent
CFO: Thomas C. Elliott
HR: –
FYE: December 31
Type: Public

Resource America's resource of choice is real estate investment. The company manages a series of funds that invest in real estate-related debt commercial mortgages and other real estate assets as well as trust-preferred securities and asset-backed securities. Its financial fund management operations finance structure and manage investments in bank loans securities bonds and other instruments. Through its Trapeza Capital Management and Ischus Capital Management divisions and other ventures the company focuses on financial funds for collateralized debt and loan obligations. Resource America and its affiliates manage some $17.8 billion in assets.

	Annual Growth	09/10	09/11	09/12*	12/13	12/14
Sales ($ mil.)	17.5%	88.7	86.0	64.4	153.7	169.3
Net income ($ mil.)	–	(16.7)	(7.4)	26.2	52.0	68.4
Market value ($ mil.)	12.3%	129.1	102.5	155.4	212.7	205.4
Employees	3.0%	656	737	602	655	737

*Fiscal year change

RESOURCE CAPITAL CORP

NYS: RSO

712 5th Avenue, 12th Floor
New York, NY 10019
Phone: 212 506-3870
Fax: –
Web: www.resourcecapitalcorp.com

CEO: Jonathan Z. Cohen
CFO: David J. (Dave) Bryant
HR: –
FYE: December 31
Type: Public

Resource Capital is looking to pump some capital into real estate resources. The real estate investment trust (REIT) was launched in 2005 and invests in commercial real estate debt and other real estate-related assets including first mortgage loans mezzanine debt and commercial and residential mortgage-backed securities. To a lesser extent the REIT invests in commercial finance assets such as syndicated bank loans and equipment leases. Bank loans account for about half of the REIT's portfolio after it disposed of its risky residential mortgage backed securities (RMBS) investments. The firm's investments are managed by Resource Capital Manager a subsidiary of Resource America.

	Annual Growth	12/10	12/11	12/12	12/13	12/14
Sales ($ mil.)	8.7%	103.9	124.6	166.5	152.0	144.9
Net income ($ mil.)	33.7%	19.4	37.7	64.4	46.5	62.2
Market value ($ mil.)	(9.1%)	245.3	186.5	186.2	197.1	167.5
Employees	–	–	–	–	–	–

RESOURCES CONNECTION INC

NMS: RECN

17101 Armstrong Avenue
Irvine, CA 92614
Phone: 714 430-6400
Fax: –
Web: www.rgp.com

CEO: Anthony (Tony) Cherbak
CFO: Nathan W. (Nate) Franke
HR: –
FYE: May 30
Type: Public

Resources Connection is there when a pocket calculator just won't do. The company which operates through its principal subsidiary Resources Global Professionals generates the majority of its sales by providing accounting and finance professionals to clients on a project-by-project basis for services that include financial analyses audits and preparation of public filings. Resources Global Professionals also supplies professionals in the fields of human resources risk management legal services supply chain management and information technology. Founded in 1996 the company serves clients from 80 offices in the US and abroad.

	Annual Growth	05/11	05/12	05/13	05/14	05/15
Sales ($ mil.)	2.0%	545.5	571.8	556.3	567.2	590.6
Net income ($ mil.)	2.6%	24.9	41.1	20.5	19.9	27.5
Market value ($ mil.)	3.3%	513.2	450.3	409.3	462.2	584.8
Employees	2.2%	2,984	3,017	2,915	3,113	3,258

RESTAURANT TECHNOLOGIES INC.

2250 Pilot Knob Rd. Ste. 100
Mendota Heights MN 55120
Phone: 651-796-1600
Fax: 651-379-4082
Web: www.rti-inc.com

CEO: Jeffrey R Kiesel
CFO: Robert E Weil
HR: Richard Copeland
FYE: December 31
Type: Private

Restaurant Technologies Inc. (RTI) regularly strikes oil. It provides oil-management equipment and supplies to restaurants and other foodservice operations specializing in its MaxLife system for handling and disposing of used cooking oil. It also offers oil-disposal services to cart away used frying oil. RTI's Global Tier division markets equipment for monitoring restaurant kitchen equipment such as walk-in coolers and fryers. The company distributes clean cooking oil and other supplies to more than 17000 customers from facilities in about 35 metropolitan areas. In mid-2011 Swedish investor EQT Infrastructure acquired the company from Parthenon Capital Partners and ABS Capital Partners.

RESTORATION HARDWARE HOLDINGS INC.

NYSE: RH

15 Koch Rd. Ste. J
Corte Madera CA 94925
Phone: 415-924-1005
Fax: 415-927-9133
Web: www.restorationhardware.com

CEO: Gary Friedman
CFO: –
HR: –
FYE: January 31
Type: Private

Restoration Hardware puts vintage American fixtures and fittings into homes old and new. The company sells upscale home and outdoor furnishings garden products hardware bathware lighting textiles baby and child products and more through about 85 retail and outlet stores in 30 states the District of Columbia and Canada. It also markets products through its catalogs and e-commerce sites (more than 40% of overall sales). Founded in 1980 Restoration Hardware was taken private in 2008 by Catterton Partners and Tower Three Partners in a deal valued at about $175 million. In 2012 the high-end home accessories retailer went public.

RESTORATION HARDWARE HOLDINGS, INC.

NYS: RH

15 Koch Road, Suite K
Corte Madera, CA 94925
Phone: 415 924-1005
Fax: –
Web: www.restorationhardware.com

CEO: Gary G. Friedman
CFO: Karen Boone
HR: –
FYE: January 31
Type: Public

Restoration Hardware puts vintage American fixtures and fittings into homes old and new. The company sells upscale home and outdoor furnishings garden products hardware bathware lighting textiles baby and child products and more through about 85 retail and outlet stores in 30 states the District of Columbia and Canada. It also markets products through its catalogs and e-commerce sites (more than 40% of overall sales). Founded in 1980 Restoration Hardware was taken private in 2008 by Catterton Partners and Tower Three Partners in a deal valued at about $175 million. In 2012 the high-end home accessories retailer went public.

	Annual Growth	01/11	01/12*	02/13	02/14*	01/15
Sales ($ mil.)	24.7%	772.8	958.1	1,193.0	1,551.0	1,867.4
Net income ($ mil.)	–	(7.1)	20.6	(12.8)	18.2	91.0
Market value ($ mil.)	55.4%	–	–	1,445.3	2,263.5	3,491.8
Employees	13.6%	–	–	3,100	3,600	4,000

*Fiscal year change

RESTORGENEX CORP

NBB: RESX

1800 Century Park East, 6th Floor
Los Angeles, CA 90067
Phone: 805 229-1829
Fax: 313 995-6337
Web: www.stratusmediagroup.com

CEO: Stephen M Simes
CFO: Phillip B Donenberg
HR: Nina Bass
FYE: December 31
Type: Public

This company wants you to get your head out of the clouds and into the bleachers. Stratus Media Group provides marketing and management services for live entertainment and sporting events including action sports automotive shows and trade shows and expositions. The company makes money through corporate sponsorships TV and broadcast fees tickets event merchandise concessions and consulting services. Specific events have included the Core Tour (action sports) the Freedom Bowl (college football) the Napa Jazz Festival and the Long Beach Marathon. Stratus Media also offers talent representation services to athletes and is buying motor sports promoter Hot Import Nights.

	Annual Growth	12/09	12/10	12/11	12/12	12/13
Sales ($ mil.)	21.3%	–	0.0	0.6	0.4	0.1
Net income ($ mil.)	–	(3.4)	(8.4)	(15.8)	(6.8)	(2.5)
Market value ($ mil.)	(64.8%)	13.1	3.7	2.9	1.1	0.2
Employees	–	–	–	–	13	–

RETAIL OPPORTUNITY INVESTMENTS CORP

NMS: ROIC

8905 Towne Centre Drive, Suite 108
San Diego, CA 92122
Phone: 858 677-0900
Fax: –
Web: www.roireit.net

CEO: Stuart A. Tanz
CFO: Michael B. (Mike) Haines
HR: –
FYE: December 31
Type: Public

For this company opportunity knocking sounds a lot like a neighborhood shopping center. Retail Opportunity Investments (ROIC) true to its name invests in owns leases and manages shopping centers. It targets densely populated middle and upper class markets and looks for centers anchored by large grocery or drug stores. The self-managed real estate investment trust (REIT) owns more than 50 shopping centers comprising 5.5 million sq. ft. in Oregon Washington and California. It makes money from rent management expenses and mortgage interest. ROIC was formed in 2007 as an acquisition company. It purchased NRDC Capital Management in 2009 and took its current name in 2010.

	Annual Growth	12/10	12/11	12/12	12/13	12/14
Sales ($ mil.)	75.8%	16.3	51.7	75.1	111.2	155.9
Net income ($ mil.)	–	(0.4)	9.7	7.9	33.8	20.3
Market value ($ mil.)	14.1%	921.5	1,101.0	1,195.1	1,368.8	1,561.3
Employees	46.8%	14	21	22	61	65

RETAIL PROPERTIES OF AMERICA, INC
NYS: RPAI

2021 Spring Road, Suite 200
Oak Brook, IL 60523
Phone: 630 634-4200
Fax: –
Web: www.rpai.com

CEO: Steven P Grimes
CFO: Angela M Aman
HR: –
FYE: December 31
Type: Public

You could say Retail Properties of America (formerly Inland Western Retail Real Estate Trust) is a bit of a shopaholic. The self-managed real estate investment trust (REIT) buys owns and operates one of the largest retail shopping center portfolios in the US with more than 225 wholly or partially owned properties that include power centers community centers and lifestyle centers. Among its tenants are big-box stores such as Best Buy Ross Stores and TJX Cos. It also has about 20 property management offices to serve its diverse client base with leasing asset management and property management services. The company went public in 2012. It was formerly sponsored by an affiliate of The Inland Group.

	Annual Growth	12/10	12/11	12/12	12/13	12/14
Sales ($ mil.)	(1.3%)	632.4	605.7	567.0	551.2	600.6
Net income ($ mil.)	–	(95.8)	(72.6)	(0.4)	13.6	43.3
Market value ($ mil.)	18.1%	–	–	2,832.1	3,009.6	3,948.9
Employees	(1.4%)	–	265	250	255	254

RETAILMENOT, INC.
NMS: SALE

301 Congress Avenue, Suite 700
Austin, TX 78701
Phone: 512 777-2970
Fax: –
Web: www.retailmenot.com

CEO: G. Cotter Cunningham
CFO: J. Scott Di Valerio
HR: –
FYE: December 31
Type: Public

Do an Internet search for "coupon code" and you've got this company's formula for success. RetailMeNot is a leading provider of digital coupons that allow consumers to obtain discounts on retailers' websites and in-store purchases. E-tail is big business and promo codes are incentives that appeal to both retailers and consumers. RetailMeNot has its flagship US website retailmenot.com as well as deals2buy.com which features sale items from selected retailers. Its international brand portfolio includes VoucherCodes.co.uk in the UK Web.Bons-de-Reduction.com and Poulpeo.com in France Actiepagina.nl in the Netherlands and Deals.com in Germany. RetailMeNot became a public company in 2013.

	Annual Growth	12/10	12/11	12/12	12/13	12/14
Sales ($ mil.)	99.0%	16.9	80.4	144.7	209.8	264.7
Net income ($ mil.)	84.2%	2.3	17.0	26.0	31.5	27.0
Market value ($ mil.)	(49.2%)	–	–	–	1,562.0	793.2
Employees	26.2%	–	–	331	444	527

RETIREMENT HOUSING FOUNDATION

911 N. Studebaker Rd.
Long Beach CA 90815-4900
Phone: 562-257-5100
Fax: 562-257-5200
Web: www.rhf.org

CEO: Laverne R Joseph
CFO: John Von Rusten
HR: –
FYE: November 30
Type: Private - Not-for-Pr

The Retirement Housing Foundation (RHF) has been giving old folks homes since the mid-1960s. Affiliated with the United Church of Christ the not-for-profit RHF manages nearly 160 communities — ranging from a 12-unit home to an apartment complex for more than 1000 — in 24 states Puerto Rico and the Virgin Islands. RHF's facilities also include skilled nursing homes respite care and assisted living homes. Its memory care facilities provide specialized care for people suffering from memory loss. Over its 47 years in operation RHF has expanded its service line to include people with disabilities and disadvantaged families; today nearly 17000 people live in RHF housing.

RETRACTABLE TECHNOLOGIES INC
ASE: RVP

511 Lobo Lane
Little Elm, TX 75068-5295
Phone: 972 294-1010
Fax: –
Web: www.vanishpoint.com

CEO: Thomas J Shaw
CFO: Douglas W Cowan
HR: –
FYE: December 31
Type: Public

Retractable Technologies knows you can't be too safe when you work around needles all day. The company develops makes and markets safety syringes and other injection technologies for the health care industry. Its flagship VanishPoint syringe retracts after injection reducing the risk of both syringe reuse and accidental needlesticks (both are means of transmitting HIV and other infectious diseases). Retractable also makes blood collection needles and IV catheters using the VanishPoint technology which was invented by Thomas Shaw the company's founder CEO and majority owner. The firm sells to hospitals and other care providers in the US and abroad both directly and through distributors.

	Annual Growth	12/10	12/11	12/12	12/13	12/14
Sales ($ mil.)	(1.2%)	36.2	32.1	33.6	30.8	34.5
Net income ($ mil.)	–	2.4	1.4	(4.1)	(6.2)	(2.4)
Market value ($ mil.)	30.0%	48.3	32.6	24.0	85.0	138.1
Employees	(4.5%)	159	148	158	156	132

REVAL HOLDINGS INC.

420 Fifth Ave. 5th Fl.
New York NY 10018
Phone: 212-393-1313
Fax: 212-901-9797
Web: www.reval.com

CEO: Jiro Okochi
CFO: Dino Ewing
HR: –
FYE: December 31
Type: Private

Reval wants you to revel in their products and revile all rivals. The company makes cloud-based software used by CFOs finance managers and treasurers for treasury and risk management. Its products let customers examine and analyze cash liquidity and risk across an enterprise and incorporate hedging accounting and compliance. Reval's software-as-a-service (SaaS) is deployed so that the company can seamlessly and automatically push out updates every six months to reflect changing financial regulations. Reval has more than 550 clients including Tiffany & Co Microsoft Starbucks Ford and Visa in 20 countries and claims a 90% customer retention rate. Formed in 1999 Reval filed to go public in 2012.

REVANCE THERAPEUTICS INC
NMS: RVNC

7555 Gateway Boulevard
Newark, CA 94560
Phone: 510 742-3400
Fax: –
Web: www.revance.com

CEO: L Daniel Browne
CFO: Lauren P. Silvernail
HR: –
FYE: December 31
Type: Public

Revance Therapeutics wants to rev up the revenue engine with poison. The company's candidates include a topical application of botulinum toxin the deadly toxin that causes botulism and a longer-acting injectable form. Though Botox has made aesthetic uses well known Revance also wants it for medical reasons including as a cure for excessive sweating (hyperhidrosis) and migraines. Current treatment requires up to 30 shots compared to Revance's single-application gel. Once its candidates are approved the company will do its own manufacturing and sales. Revance was formed in 1999 and went public in 2014. It raised $96 million which it plans to use to fund R&D and clinical trials and to pay debt.

	Annual Growth	12/10	12/11	12/12	12/13	12/14
Sales ($ mil.)	–	0.0	0.6	0.7	0.6	0.4
Net income ($ mil.)	–	0.0	(44.9)	(58.3)	(52.4)	(62.9)
Market value ($ mil.)	–	0.0	–	–	–	402.7
Employees	3.8%	–	–	77	75	83

REVETT MINING CO INC

ASE: RVM

11115 East Montgomery, Suite G
Spokane Valley, WA 99206
Phone: 509 921-2294
Fax: 509 891-8901
Web: www.revettminerals.com

CEO: John G Shanahan
CFO: Ken Eickerman
HR: –
FYE: December 31
Type: Public

Revett gets revved up over minerals in Montana. The mining company produces copper and silver at the state's Troy Mine. Its holdings there include proved and probable reserves of 10.5 tons of minerals. Troy has produced 6.4 million ounces of silver and 44 million pounds of copper with estimated future annual production of 1.3 million ounces of silver and 11 million pounds of copper. Revett also owns the Rock Creek Project an exploratory property in northwestern Montana with inferred resources of about 230 million ounces of silver and 2 billion pounds of copper. Revett Silver the company's operating subsidiary was formed in 1999 to buy the Troy and Rock Creek mines. Revett Minerals was created in 2004.

	Annual Growth	12/09	12/10	12/11	12/12	12/13
Sales ($ mil.)	(77.7%)	29.5	47.0	70.1	59.2	0.1
Net income ($ mil.)	–	(5.0)	4.4	13.5	4.1	(11.6)
Market value ($ mil.)	22.1%	11.4	169.1	163.3	97.6	25.3
Employees	(23.4%)	186	198	194	209	64

REVLON INC

NYS: REV

One New York Plaza
New York, NY 10004
Phone: 212 527-4000
Fax: –
Web: www.revloninc.com

CEO: –
CFO: Roberto Simon
HR: Jim Morrissey
FYE: December 31
Type: Public

Revlon has the look of a leader in the US mass-market cosmetics business alongside L'Oréal's Maybelline and Procter & Gamble's Cover Girl. Aside from its Almay and Revlon brands of makeup and beauty tools the company makes Revlon ColorSilk hair color Mitchum antiperspirants and deodorants Charlie and Jean Naté fragrances and Ultima II and Gatineau skincare products. Its beauty aids are distributed in more than 150 countries though the US is its largest market generating more than half of sales. Revlon products are primarily sold by mass merchandisers and drugstores such as CVS Target Shoppers Drug Mart A.S. Watson Boots and Wal-Mart. Charles Revson founded Revlon in 1931.

	Annual Growth	12/10	12/11	12/12	12/13	12/14
Sales ($ mil.)	10.1%	1,321.4	1,381.4	1,426.1	1,494.7	1,941.0
Net income ($ mil.)	(40.5%)	327.3	53.4	51.1	(5.8)	40.9
Market value ($ mil.)	36.5%	523.0	790.3	770.6	1,326.6	1,815.5
Employees	3.4%	4,900	5,200	5,100	6,900	5,600

REVOLUTION LIGHTING TECHNOLOGIES INC

NAS. RVLT

177 Broad Street, 12th Floor
Stamford, CT 06901
Phone: 203 504-1111
Fax: –
Web: www.rvlti.com

CEO: Robert V Lapenta
CFO: James A Depalma
HR: –
FYE: December 31
Type: Public

Because you can't have a revolution without light. Revolution Lighting Technologies (formerly Nexxus Lighting) designs produces and sells light-emitting diode (LED) replacement light bulbs. Its products which include multiple-color temperatures and optic/lens options are marketed for their energy savings improved lighting and reliability as well as eco-friendly benefits. It also makes Hyperion R-Lite and Lumeon 360 LED-based signage systems for decorative lighting strips through subsidiary Lumificient Corp. In late 2012 Nexxus Lighting changed its name to Revolution Lighting Technologies to reflect what it believes is the new change taking place — LED technology — in the lighting industry.

	Annual Growth	12/10	12/11	12/12	12/13	12/14
Sales ($ mil.)	94.0%	5.4	9.0	4.5	26.1	76.8
Net income ($ mil.)	–	(8.0)	(5.5)	(8.6)	(16.8)	(5.2)
Market value ($ mil.)	(9.9%)	265.9	141.4	81.9	444.3	175.1
Employees	57.5%	34	30	48	103	209

REWARDS NETWORK INC.

2 N. Riverside Plaza Ste. 950
Chicago IL 60606
Phone: 312-521-6767
Fax: 312-521-6769
Web: www.rewardsnetwork.com

CEO: Dan Kazan
CFO: Christopher J Locke
HR: Vaiva Vaisnys
FYE: December 31
Type: Private

Rewards Network helps out restaurants by rewarding its customers. The company powers a leading North American dining rewards program that reaches more than 3 million members. Rewards Network contracts with some 10000 restaurants and other merchants to provide services at a discounted price. Membership consisting of frequent diners receive loyalty rewards such as rebates frequent flier miles and other discounts on food lodging travel gifts and entertainment. Rewards Network was founded in 1984 as Transmedia Network by Mel Chasen a former president of Caesar's Palace (now part of Caesar's Entertainment). Private equity firm EGI Acquisition owns Rewards Network.

REX AMERICAN RESOURCES CORP

NYS: REX

7720 Paragon Road
Dayton, OH 45459
Phone: 937 276-3931
Fax: 937 276-8643
Web: www.rexamerican.com

CEO: Stuart A. Rose
CFO: Douglas L. Bruggeman
HR: –
FYE: January 31
Type: Public

REX American Resources Corporation has gone from retail to renewables. The company formerly REX Stores closed its chain of retail appliance and electronics stores to move in a major way into the alternative energy — mainly ethanol — business. In 2013 the company has about $71 million investments in ethanol producers Big River Resources LLC and Patriot Holdings LLC; and invested about $105 million in its four ethanol entities. REX American's consolidated ethanol entities owned a combined 408 acres of land and two facilities had an annual nameplate capacity of 100 million gallons of ethanol each.

	Annual Growth	01/11	01/12	01/13	01/14	01/15
Sales ($ mil.)	17.4%	301.7	410.0	657.7	666.1	572.2
Net income ($ mil.)	103.7%	5.1	28.3	(2.3)	35.1	87.3
Market value ($ mil.)	38.5%	119.0	203.0	172.5	323.5	438.5
Employees	16.3%	58	105	102	105	106

REX ENERGY CORP

NMS: REXX

366 Walker Drive
State College, PA 16801
Phone: 814 278-7267
Fax: –
Web: www.rexenergy.com

CEO: Thomas C. Stabley
CFO: Thomas Rajan
HR: –
FYE: December 31
Type: Public

Though it isn't exactly the T. Rex of the oil and gas industry Rex Energy is taking a bite out of available hydrocarbon assets. The exploration and production company has estimated proved reserves of In fiscal 2012 the company reported estimated proved reserves of 618.1 billion cu. ft. of natural gas equivalent (42% proved developed) primarily from two regions: the Illinois Basin (in Illinois and Indiana) and the Appalachian Basin (Pennsylvania and West Virginia). The company's Lawrence Field ASP (alkaline-surfactant-polymer) Flood Project uses ASP technology which washes residual oil from reservoir rock improving the existing waterflow's ability to sweep the residual oil and increasing oil recoveries.

	Annual Growth	12/10	12/11	12/12	12/13	12/14
Sales ($ mil.)	44.3%	68.8	114.6	148.1	237.9	298.0
Net income ($ mil.)	–	6.0	(15.4)	45.5	(2.1)	(46.7)
Market value ($ mil.)	(21.8%)	739.5	799.6	705.4	1,067.8	276.3
Employees	13.8%	191	204	230	298	320

REX HEALTHCARE INC.

4420 LAKE BOONE TRL
RALEIGH, NC 276077505
Phone: 919-784-3100
Fax: –
Web: www.rexhealth.com

CEO: Gary Park
CFO: Bernadette Spong
HR: –
FYE: June 30
Type: Private

Rex is a king of health care in Raleigh. Part of the UNC HealthCare System Rex Healthcare is a not-for-profit health care provider that serves residents of Raleigh and the rest of Wake County North Carolina. Founded in 1894 Rex Healthcare includes the more than 430-bed acute-care Rex Hospital and two nursing homes with nearly 230 beds as well as primary and specialty care clinics throughout the area. Specialty centers and clinics provide services such as birthing cancer treatment same-day surgery heart and vascular care pain management and sleep disorder therapy. Rex also provides home health and mobile emergency medical services. UNC HealthCare also includes affiliate UNC Hospitals.

	Annual Growth	06/09	06/10	06/11	06/12	06/13
Sales ($ mil.)	8.6%	–	571.0	628.6	719.9	731.4
Net income ($ mil.)	(64.1%)	–	–	69.1	34.7	8.9
Market value ($ mil.)	–	–	–	–	–	–
Employees	–	–	–	–	–	5,500

REXAHN PHARMACEUTICALS INC.

NYSE AMEX: RNN

15245 Shady Grove Rd. Ste. 455
Rockville MD 20850
Phone: 240-268-5300
Fax: 240-268-5310
Web: www.rexahn.com

CEO: Peter D Suzdak
CFO: Tae Heum Jeong
HR: –
FYE: December 31
Type: Public

Rexahn Pharmaceuticals has its R&D sights set on difficult-to-treat cancers and central nervous system (CNS) disorders. A biopharmaceutical company Rexahn has three drug candidates in clinical stages of development including its lead candidate and pancreatic cancer treatment Archexin (designed to inhibit a protein involved in cancer cell proliferation); Serdaxin a depression and Parkinson's disease drug; and Zoraxel a treatment for erectile dysfunction. The company also has seven cancer drugs in preclinical development. It develops its candidates through its own R&D arm and through partnerships with pharmaceutical and biopharmaceutical companies like Teva Pharmaceutical and TheraTarget.

REXAM BEVERAGE CAN COMPANY

8770 W. Bryn Mawr Ave.
Chicago IL 60631
Phone: 773-399-3000
Fax: 773-399-8088

CEO: William R Barker
CFO: Thomas Holz
HR: Jennifer Mackie
FYE: December 31
Type: Subsidiary

Can you think of a better way to preserve protect and promote beverages? Rexam Beverage Can! Rexam Beverage Can is one of the biggest consumer beverage can manufacturers in the world. It has manufacturing plants in the North and South America Europe and Asia that produce roughly 60 billion cans annually. The company's lineup includes a slew of gee-whiz offerings such as screw-top closures and slim and sleek versions. The can-maker can also boost product differentiation and brand awareness for customers through print options from thermo to glow-in-the-dark and wet-look inks to tactile-finishes. Rexam Beverage Can is a subsidiary of Rexam and accounts for about 80% of the UK packaging giant's revenues.

REXEL INC.

14951 Dallas Pkwy.
Dallas TX 75254
Phone: 972-387-3600
Fax: 972-308-9831
Web: www.rexelusa.com

CEO: –
CFO: –
HR: –
FYE: December 31
Type: Subsidiary

When it comes to electrical distribution Rexel excels. The company is one of the largest distributors of datacom and electrical parts and supplies in the US. Its products include home electrical equipment; networking communications and security products; solar energy systems; and heating and lighting materials. Rexel's customers are primarily contractors utilities government institutions and industrial manufacturers. The company operates distribution locations in some 30 states and the Bahamas. Rexel also provides consulting leasing logistics and technical support services. Rexel Inc. is a division of International Electric Supply Corp. a holding company for Rexel S.A.'s US operations.

REXFORD INDUSTRIAL REALTY INC

NYS: REXR

11620 Wilshire Boulevard, Suite 1000
Los Angeles, CA 90025
Phone: 310 966-1680
Fax: –
Web: www.rexfordindustrial.com

CEO: Howard Schwimmer
CFO: Adeel Khan
HR: –
FYE: December 31
Type: Public

Rexford Industrial Realty knows that there's more to business in Southern California than moviemaking and fashion. A real estate investment trust or REIT Rexford Industrial owns and manages a portfolio of nearly 70 industrial properties in Los Angeles County and surrounding areas. Its portfolio comprises about 7.6 million sq. ft. of warehouse distribution and light manufacturing space that's leased to small and midsized businesses. It manages 20 more properties — altogether comprising 1.2 million sq. ft. of rentable space. A self-administered and self-managed REIT Rexford Industrial was formed in 2013 from the assets of its predecessor. In mid-2013 the company went public.

	Annual Growth	03/11	03/12	03/13*	12/13	12/14
Sales ($ mil.)	–	0.0	0.0	–	21.6	66.6
Net income ($ mil.)	–	0.0	0.0	–	(0.6)	0.9
Market value ($ mil.)	–	0.0	0.0	–	576.9	686.6
Employees	54.8%	–	–	31	40	48

*Fiscal year change

REXNORD CORP (NEW)

NYS: RXN

247 Freshwater Way, Suite 300
Milwaukee, WI 53204
Phone: 414 643-3739
Fax: –
Web: www.rexnord.com

CEO: Todd A. Adams
CFO: Mark W. Peterson
HR: Amanda Hanks
FYE: March 31
Type: Public

Rexnord's products help to give machines motion and manage the flow of water. The company does business through two divisions: process and motion control (PMC; 60% of sales) and water management (40%). PMC makes gears couplings bearings industrial chains and other highly engineered mechanical components with brand names such as Rex Falk FlatTop and Link-Belt. Water management makes products used in commercial plumbing water control and treatment and wastewater markets with names such as Fontaine Rodney Hunt Wilkins VAG GA and Zurn.

	Annual Growth	03/11	03/12	03/13	03/14	03/15
Sales ($ mil.)	4.8%	1,699.6	1,969.6	2,005.1	2,082.0	2,050.2
Net income ($ mil.)	–	(51.3)	29.9	50.1	30.2	83.8
Market value ($ mil.)	8.1%	–	2,147.6	2,160.8	2,949.6	2,716.5
Employees	2.0%	7,400	7,400	7,300	7,400	8,000

REYNOLDS AMERICAN INC   NYS: RAI

401 North Main Street | CEO: Susan M. Cameron
Winston-Salem, NC 27101 | CFO: Andrew D. Gilchrist
Phone: 336 741-2000 | HR: Lisa J. Caldwell
Fax: 336 728-8888 | FYE: December 31
Web: www.reynoldsamerican.com | Type: Public

Hot does not begin to describe Reynolds American Inc. (RAI). The holding company holds the #2 spot among US makers of cigarettes and smokeless tobacco through RJR Tobacco (smokeless) and American Snuff. RJR Tobacco produces many of the top-selling cigarette brands: Camel Doral Kool Pall Mall Newport Salem and Winston. It also makes and markets smoke-free Camel tobacco products. American Snuff offers moist snuff under the value-priced Grizzly and premium Kodiak brands. RAI businesses include cigarette makers Santa Fe Natural Tobacco and Lorillard and nicotine gum maker Niconovum. RAI is the result of a merger of R.J. Reynolds Tobacco and Brown & Williamson a subsidiary of British American Tobacco that owns 42% of RAI.

	Annual Growth	12/11	12/12	12/13	12/14	12/15
Sales ($ mil.)	5.7%	8,541.0	8,304.0	8,236.0	8,471.0	10,675.0
Net income ($ mil.)	23.3%	1,406.0	1,272.0	1,718.0	1,470.0	3,253.0
Market value ($ mil.)	2.7%	59,120.5	59,134.8	71,352.8	91,735.2	65,871.8
Employees	1.1%	5,450	5,050	5,290	5,400	5,700

REYNOLDS FOOD PACKAGING

6641 W. Broad St. | CEO: –
Richmond VA 23230 | CFO: –
Phone: 301-610-4300 | HR: –
Fax: 301-610-4301 | FYE: December 31
Web: www.startec.com | Type: Subsidiary

Reynolds Food Packaging has food wrapped sealed served and stored. The company offers a comprehensive array of packaging products for the restaurant agricultural supermarket and food processor markets. Products are made from aluminum foil plastic film and molded plastic; they include containers platters lids wraps bags and baking cups and liners. Custom-made products are also available to its customers which include bakeries caterers delis and fast food joints. Reynolds Food Packaging's has operations in the US Canada Mexico Spain and the UK. The company's parent Reynolds Group Holdings is part of Rank Group Ltd. an investment firm controlled by New Zealand billionaire Graeme Hart.

RF INDUSTRIES LTD.   NMS: RFIL

7610 Miramar Road, Building 6000 | CEO: Johnny Walker
San Diego, CA 92126-4202 | CFO: Mark Turfler
Phone: 858 549-6340 | HR: –
Fax: – | FYE: October 31
Web: www.rfindustries.com | Type: Public

RF Industries (RFI) helps keep the world connected. The company's core business is conducted by its RF Connector division which makes coaxial connectors used in radio-frequency (RF) communications and computer networking equipment. Its Neulink Division makes wireless digital transmission devices such as modems and antennas used to link wide-area computer networks and global positioning systems. Through its Bioconnect division RF Industries also makes cable assemblies including electric cabling and interconnect products used in medical monitoring applications. RF Industries operates from locations in California and Nevada; customers in the US account for more than 80% of sales.

	Annual Growth	10/11	10/12	10/13	10/14	10/15
Sales ($ mil.)	14.0%	19.4	30.2	36.6	23.1	32.8
Net income ($ mil.)	6.4%	0.8	2.6	3.8	1.4	1.0
Market value ($ mil.)	9.3%	27.5	38.4	80.1	39.5	39.3
Employees	8.0%	166	178	143	143	226

RF MICRO DEVICES, INC.   NMS: RFMD

7628 Thorndike Road | CEO: Robert A Bruggeworth
Greensboro, NC 27409-9421 | CFO: Steve Buhaly
Phone: 336 664-1233 | HR: –
Fax: – | FYE: March 30
Web: www.rfmd.com | Type: Public

RF Micro Devices was raised on radio — high-performance radio-frequency (RF) components that is. RFMD makes a variety of RF devices and compound semiconductor technologies for markets that include cellular handsets wireless infrastructure wireless local area networks (WLAN or WiFi) cable television broadband and advanced metering for Smart Energy. Many of the company's chips are made from gallium arsenide (GaAs) — a material valued for wireless applications because of its speed and efficiency. RFMD's top customer is Nokia which accounts for nearly 40% of the company's sales. Customers in Asia represent more than 75% of sales.

	Annual Growth	03/09*	04/10	04/11*	03/12	03/13
Sales ($ mil.)	2.1%	886.5	978.4	1,051.8	871.4	964.1
Net income ($ mil.)	–	(898.6)	71.0	124.6	0.9	(53.0)
Market value ($ mil.)	40.4%	383.8	1,406.4	1,790.2	1,395.2	1,490.5
Employees	0.6%	4,095	3,687	3,726	3,986	4,191

*Fiscal year change

RF MONOLITHICS INC.   NASDAQ: RFMI

4441 Sigma Rd. | CEO: Farlin A Halsey
Dallas TX 75244-4589 | CFO: Harley E Barnes III
Phone: 972-233-2903 | HR: –
Fax: 972-387-8148 | FYE: August 31
Web: www.rfm.com | Type: Public

RF Monolithics (RFM) says welcome to the machine. The company designs and sells wireless connectivity products for machine-to-machine communications. Its wireless solutions group provides surface acoustic wave (SAW) and radio-frequency (RF) integrated circuit short-range radios RF modules and stand-alone radio systems. Its wireless components unit covers communications products that include frequency control filters oscillators and optical timing products. RFM markets its wares to distributors and OEMs worldwide. Customers include Delphi Flextronics GE and Avnet. RFM gets two-thirds of its sales outside North America. In 2012 the company was acquired by Murata Electronics North America.

RGC RESOURCES, INC.   NMS: RGCO

519 Kimball Ave. N.E. | CEO: John S. D'Orazio
Roanoke, VA 24016 | CFO: Paul W. Nester
Phone: 540 777-4427 | HR: –
Fax: 540 777-2636 | FYE: September 30
Web: www.rgcresources.com | Type: Public

RGC Resources is not only sticking to its knitting (the regulated distribution of natural gas) it is also staying close to home (Roanoke Virginia). RGC's Roanoke Gas unit distributes natural gas to 56000 customers in Roanoke. The holding company's Application Resources provides information system services for the utility industry. RGC Resources has taken the proceeds from the sale of its noncore operation to reinvest in its core gas distribution business. In 2008 it installed nine miles of plastic mains and replaced 684 steel main-to-meter service lines with modern plastic service lines (a 40% increase over 2007).

	Annual Growth	09/11	09/12	09/13	09/14	09/15
Sales ($ mil.)	(0.9%)	70.8	58.8	63.2	75.0	68.2
Net income ($ mil.)	2.3%	4.7	4.3	4.3	4.7	5.1
Market value ($ mil.)	2.2%	87.9	85.6	91.5	94.4	95.8
Employees	1.8%	124	120	127	138	133

RGIS LLC

2000 E. Taylor Rd.
Auburn Hills MI 48326
Phone: 248-651-2511
Fax: 248-656-6628
Web: www.rgisinv.com

CEO: Brian McDonald
CFO: –
HR: –
FYE: December 31
Type: Private

At RGIS (formerly RGIS Inventory Specialists) you can count on a lot of counting. Rivaling WIS International the company is among the top third-party inventory takers in the US. RGIS employees count inventory for customers primarily large retailers but also manufacturers using scanners that send information to a computer system at RGIS headquarters. It also provides data collection and store optimization services. The company operates from facilities throughout the US Canada and Mexico as well as in the Asia/Pacific region Europe the Middle East and South America; it has more than 400 offices worldwide. Investment firm The Blackstone Group owns a controlling stake in RGIS which was founded in 1958.

RHE HATCO INC.

601 Marion Dr.
Garland TX 75042
Phone: 972-494-0511
Fax: 972-494-2369
Web: www.stetsonhat.com

CEO: –
CFO: Paul Corbett
HR: –
FYE: June 30
Type: Private

RHE Hatco has built a business topping off Western wear for dress or work and doing it with style to boot. The company makes and markets western hats for men and women under iconic names such as Stetson Resistol and Charlie 1 Horse; it makes dress hats under the Dobbs label. In August 2009 the hat manufacturer was acquired by an affiliate of Pro Equine Group whose expertise lies in other cowboy accoutrements such as saddles ropes and protective legwear for horses. Previous owner Arena Brands had been shedding its stable of products such as Imperial Headwear and Montana Silversmiths when Pro Equine picked up the longtime hat makers.

RHI ENTERTAINMENT LLC

PINK SHEETS: RHIE

1325 Avenue of the Americas 21st Fl.
New York NY 10019
Phone: 212-977-9001
Fax: 602-926-3429
Web: www.azsenate.gov

CEO: Stewart Till
CFO: William J Aliber
HR: –
FYE: December 31
Type: Private

You might say this company takes its time telling stories on television. RHI Entertainment is a producer and distributor of long-form television content including made-for-TV movies and miniseries programming. Its original productions have included The Summit for ION and Tin Man on Syfy. The company also boasts a library of more than 1000 titles that include Alice in Wonderland Call of the Wild Merlin The Lion in Winter The Odyssey and Lonesome Dove. In addition to supplying programming to broadcast and cable networks RHI Entertainment distributes its shows on video and DVD and online through digital outlets such as Apple's iTunes store. RHI emerged from Chapter 11 bankruptcy protection in 2011.

RHINO RESOURCE PARTNERS LP

NBB: RHNO

424 Lewis Hargett Circle, Suite 250
Lexington, KY 40503
Phone: 859 389-6500
Fax: –
Web: www.rhinolp.com

CEO: Joseph E Funk
CFO: Richard A Boone
HR: Bill May
FYE: December 31
Type: Public

Rhino Resource Partners is looking to take the coal industry by the horn. The company operates both surface and underground mines in Colorado Kentucky Ohio West Virginia and Utah. Rhino Energy controls more than 309 million tons of proved and probable coal reserves of which about three-quarters is used for electricity generation by utilities and industrial customers. It produces approximately 4 million tons annually. Subsidiary Rhino Trucking hauls much of that production to preparation plants. The company operated as CAM Holdings until 2006. Hoping the third time is a charm Rhino went public in 2010 with an initial public offering (IPO).

	Annual Growth	12/10	12/11	12/12	12/13	12/14
Sales ($ mil.)	(6.0%)	305.6	367.2	352.0	277.9	239.1
Net income ($ mil.)	4.5%	41.1	38.1	40.2	9.4	49.0
Market value ($ mil.)	(44.3%)	678.8	561.3	397.3	331.0	65.4
Employees	(5.5%)	897	1,033	750	686	715

RHODE ISLAND SCHOOL OF DESIGN INC

2 COLLEGE ST
PROVIDENCE, RI 029032784
Phone: 401-454-6141
Fax: –
Web: www.library.risd.edu

CEO: –
CFO: –
HR: Candace Baer
FYE: June 30
Type: Private

The Rhode Island School of Design (RISD pronounced RIZ-dee) is among the highest-rated fine arts colleges in the US. The private school enrolls about 2400 undergraduate and graduate students. It offers about 20 fine arts and design programs including art history apparel design architecture jewelry industrial design film printmaking textiles and painting. The college also offers continuing education through classes lectures workshops gallery talks and a six-week pre-college program designed for high schoolers. Notable alumni include David Byrne Tina Weymouth and Chris Frantz of the Talking Heads. RISD was founded in 1877.

	Annual Growth	06/07	06/08	06/09	06/10	06/13
Sales ($ mil.)	–	–	0.0	101.6	150.8	142.8
Net income ($ mil.)	–	–	–	(27.7)	27.6	1.7
Market value ($ mil.)	–	–	–	–	–	–
Employees	–	–	–	–	–	948

RHODES COLLEGE

2000 N PARKWAY
MEMPHIS, TN 381121690
Phone: 901-843-3000
Fax: –
Web: www.rhodes.edu

CEO: –
CFO: –
HR: Leigh Powell
FYE: June 30
Type: Private

Rhodes College helps its students get further down the road to edification. A private liberal arts school in historic downtown Memphis Rhodes College enrolls about 1700 students in academic majors including biology English international studies and business administration. Rhodes College's students come from about 45 states and 15 countries. It additionally offers a Master's degree in accounting. In total Rhodes College offers more than 30 majors and 35 minors. The school also provides continuing education courses to the community. Founded in 1848 the college is supported by an endowment of more than $230 million. The student-to-faculty ratio is about 10:1 and the average class size is just 13.

	Annual Growth	06/10	06/11	06/12	06/13	06/14
Sales ($ mil.)	6.0%	–	64.6	66.3	70.7	76.9
Net income ($ mil.)	–	–	–	(12.4)	26.4	51.2
Market value ($ mil.)	–	–	–	–	–	–
Employees	–	–	–	–	–	400

RHYTHM & HUES STUDIOS INC.

5404 Jandy Pl.
Los Angeles CA 90066
Phone: 310-448-7500
Fax: 310-448-7600
Web: www.rhythm.com

CEO: –
CFO: –
HR: –
FYE: December 31
Type: Private

Rhythm & Hues Studios dances to the pulse of the movie industry. A leading post-production and special effects firm the company's services include film advertisement and production design as well as live action visual effects used in commercials. Rhythm & Hues has put its digital stamp on such features as Happy Feet Superman Returns and X-Men 2. Its work on the movies Babe and The Golden Compass earned the company Academy Awards for Best Visual Effects. Notable ad campaigns have includes the Coca-Cola Polar Bears and GEICO's Gecko.

RIB-X PHARMACEUTICALS INC.

300 George St. Ste. 301
New Haven CT 06511-6663
Phone: 203-624-5606
Fax: 203-624-5627
Web: www.rib-x.com

CEO: Mary T Szela
CFO: Paul Estrem
HR: –
FYE: December 31
Type: Private

Rib-X Pharmaceuticals has found a weak spot in bacteria's ribosomes. The biopharmaceutical drug discovery and development company is working to create new antibiotics to treat drug-resistant infections. Rib-X's leading drug candidates are delafloxacin for the treatment of methicillin-resistant Staphylococcus aureus (MRSA) and radezolid to treat community acquired bacterial pneumonia (CABP). Its research targets binding sites on bacterial ribosomes to interrupt cell reproduction. The company was founded by Susan Froshauer Peter Moore and Thomas Steitz who received the Nobel Prize in Chemistry for the ribosome science that is the basis for the company's research. Rib-X withdrew its IPO in 2012.

RICE ENERGY INC

NYS: RICE

400 Woodcliff Drive
Canonsburg, PA 15317
Phone: 724-746-6720
Fax: –
Web: www.riceenergy.com

CEO: Daniel J Rice IV
CFO: Grayson T Lisenby
HR: –
FYE: December 31
Type: Public

Rice Energy is engaged in the purchasing of and exploration and development of natural gas and oil properties in the Appalachian Basin. It has holdings in the Marcellus Shale in southwestern Pennsylvania and the Utica Shale in southeastern Ohio. The company holds more than 43350 net acres in the southwestern core of the Marcellus Shale primarily in Washington County. In 2012 it bought 33500 of its 48660 net acres in the southeastern core of the Utica Shale primarily in Belmont County. Rice Energy operates a majority of its acreage. In fiscal 2013 the company's pro forma estimated proved reserves stood at 552 billion cu. ft. of natural gas equivalent all of which were in southwestern Pennsylvania. Rice Energy completed an IPO in early 2014.

	Annual Growth	12/10	12/11	12/12	12/13	12/14
Sales ($ mil.)	–	0.0	14.0	27.2	88.6	390.9
Net income ($ mil.)	–	0.0	(0.9)	(19.3)	(35.8)	218.5
Market value ($ mil.)	–	0.0	–	–	–	2,857.8
Employees	108.6%	–	–	–	139	290

RICEBRAN TECHNOLOGIES

NAS: RIBT

6720 North Scottsdale Road, Suite 390
Scottsdale, AZ 85253
Phone: 602 522-3000
Fax: –
Web: www.ricebrantech.com

CEO: W John Short
CFO: Jerry Dale Belt
HR: –
FYE: December 31
Type: Public

RiceBran Technologies (formerly NutraCea) hopes that one person's trash really can be another person's treasure. The company uses one of the world's largest wasted food resources rice bran — a rice by-product containing oil protein carbohydrates vitamins minerals fibers and antioxidants — to make and enhance the nutritional value of consumer products such as dietary and food supplements and animal feed. Its products are used by food manufacturers nutraceutical makers and petfood and feed manufacturers. Following a strategic change in focus from a multidivisional company to one focused solely on rice bran bio-refining the company in 2012 changed its name to RiceBran Technologies.

	Annual Growth	12/10	12/11	12/12	12/13	12/14
Sales ($ mil.)	6.1%	31.6	37.0	37.7	35.1	40.1
Net income ($ mil.)	–	(15.7)	(10.9)	(11.1)	(17.6)	(26.6)
Market value ($ mil.)	122.2%	1.6	1.0	0.5	46.8	39.0
Employees	0.7%	287	273	288	260	295

RICELAND FOODS INC.

2120 S PARK AVE
STUTTGART, AR 721606822
Phone: 870-673-5500
Fax: –
Web: www.riceland.com

CEO: Daniel Kennedy
CFO: Harry E Loftis
HR: –
FYE: July 31
Type: Private

Handling more than 125 million bushels of grain a year Riceland Foods is ingrained in its business. The agricultural cooperative processes and markets the rice soybeans and wheat grown by its 9000 member/owners who farm in Arkansas Louisiana Mississippi Missouri and Texas. One of the world's largest rice millers it sells white and brown rice plus flavored rices and meal kits under the Riceland and private-label brands. The co-op sells to food retailers and food service and food manufacturing companies worldwide. Riceland also makes cooking oils and processes soybeans bran and lecithin and offers rice bran and hulls to pet food makers and livestock farmers as feed and bedding.

	Annual Growth	07/10	07/11	07/12	07/13	07/14
Sales ($ mil.)	1.2%	–	1,107.8	1,159.2	1,314.7	1,148.1
Net income ($ mil.)	33.2%	–	–	1.5	58.3	2.6
Market value ($ mil.)	–	–	–	–	–	–
Employees	–	–	–	–	–	1,646

RICH PRODUCTS CORPORATION

1 ROBERT RICH WAY
BUFFALO, NY 142131701
Phone: 716-878-8422
Fax: –
Web: www.richs.com

CEO: William G. (Bill) Gisel
CFO: James R. (Jim) Deuschle
HR: –
FYE: December 31
Type: Private

Starting in 1945 with "the miracle cream from the soya bean" Rich Products has grown from a niche maker of soy-based whipped toppings and frozen desserts to a global US frozen foods maker. The family-owned business has developed other products such as toppings and icings and Coffee Rich (nondairy coffee creamer). It has expanded its product line to include frozen bakery and pizza doughs and ingredients for the food service and in-store bakery markets plus appetizers baked goods seafood meatballs and barbecue meat. Rich Products markets more than 2000 frozen food items that are sold in more than 110 countries; it has kitchens and bakeries around the world including about 50 locations on six continents.

	Annual Growth	12/08	12/09	12/10	12/11	12/12
Sales ($ mil.)	7.7%	–	–	2,465.0	2,736.3	2,858.5
Net income ($ mil.)	–	–	–	0.0	0.0	0.0
Market value ($ mil.)	–	–	–	–	–	–
Employees	–	–	–	–	–	8,400

RICHARD J. CARON FOUNDATION

243 N GALEN HALL RD
WERNERSVILLE, PA 195659331
Phone: 610-678-2332
Fax: –
Web: www.caron.org

CEO: Brian J Boon
CFO: –
HR: –
FYE: June 30
Type: Private

Caron cares — about addiction to drinking and drugs. The Richard J. Caron Foundation is a not-for-profit organization that runs clinical treatment centers for substance abuse in Pennsylvania New York Florida and Bermuda. It tailors its services gender specifically (under the idea that men and women respond to treatment differently) and serves adolescents adults seniors and families. The foundation offers addiction assessment as well as residential treatment extended care and outpatient counseling. To complement its medical and psychological programs Caron offers self-development workshops and pastoral services for those wanting to participate in meditation journal writing and other exercises.

	Annual Growth	06/09	06/10	06/11	06/12	06/13
Sales ($ mil.)	18.5%	–	62.1	71.8	81.8	103.3
Net income ($ mil.)	34.3%	–	–	11.6	1.6	21.0
Market value ($ mil.)	–	–	–	–	–	–
Employees	–	–	–	–	–	500

RICHARDSON ELECTRONICS LTD

NMS: RELL

40W267 Keslinger Road, P.O. Box 393
LaFox, IL 60147-0393
Phone: 630 208-2200
Fax: 630 208-2550
Web: www.rell.com

CEO: Edward J. Richardson
CFO: Robert J Ben
HR: –
FYE: May 30
Type: Public

Richardson Electronics runs the kind of superstore that isn't open to the public. The company distributes electronics products including electron devices semiconductor manufacturing equipment and video display equipment from suppliers that include GE Thales TE Connectivity and Vishay. Richardson also sells its own products under such the National Electronics brand and provides components customized to its customers' specifications. The company primarily sells to the alternative energy avionics broadcast and communication marine medical and semiconductor markets. Chairman and CEO Edward Richardson has about 64% voting control of the company.

	Annual Growth	05/11*	06/12	06/13*	05/14	05/15
Sales ($ mil.)	(3.6%)	158.9	157.8	141.1	138.0	137.0
Net income ($ mil.)	–	90.1	8.5	1.2	(0.5)	(5.6)
Market value ($ mil.)	(10.4%)	183.7	157.6	163.5	139.2	118.4
Employees	2.4%	307	324	314	308	338

*Fiscal year change

RICOH USA INC.

70 Valley Stream Pkwy.
Malvern PA 19355-0989
Phone: 610-296-8000
Fax: 610-408-7025
Web: www.ikon.com

CEO: Zenji Miura
CFO: Gary Crowe
HR: –
FYE: March 31
Type: Subsidiary

In the battle for business equipment Ricoh USA wants to be your right hand man. Formerly known as IKON Office Solutions the company sells and services office equipment made by its parent Ricoh Americas. Ricoh USA's office offerings include copiers printers scanners and fax machines which are distributed through about 400 locations in North Central and South America as well as Europe. The company also provides managed document support commercial and production printing and other IT services. Customers are primarily large and small professional offices (such as law and financial services firms) and government agencies. Parent Ricoh Americas is a subsidiary of office equipment giant Ricoh.

RIDGE TOOL COMPANY

400 Clark St.
Elyria OH 44035-2023
Phone: 440-323-5581
Fax: 440-329-4551
Web: www.ridgid.com

CEO: –
CFO: –
HR: –
FYE: September 30
Type: Subsidiary

Business for Ridge Tool customers is wrenching and draining. The company manufactures the RIDGID brand of tools which includes 300 types of professional products in more than 4000 models and sizes for a variety of industries. The usual run of hand tools including more than 60 kinds of wrenches bear the RIDGID name in addition to such power tools as band saws drill presses lathes planers and sanders. Plumbing tools and equipment made under the RIDGID brand include drain cleaners pipe cutters sump pumps and tube wrenches. The brand also includes tools for workers in mechanical pipe fitting construction HVAC and facility maintenance. Ridge Tool is a subsidiary of Emerson Electric.

RIDGEWOOD SAVINGS BANK

71-02 Forest Ave.
Ridgewood NY 11385
Phone: 718-240-4800
Fax: 860-638-2969
Web: www.liberty-bank.com

CEO: –
CFO: Leonard Sekol
HR: –
FYE: December 31
Type: Private

Serving the New York City metropolitan area and Long Island Ridgewood Savings Bank is New York State's largest mutually owned bank with $4.8 billion in assets. The financial institution operates about 40 branches and loan centers in Brooklyn the Bronx Manhattan and Queens as well as in Nassau Suffolk and Westchester counties. It provides standard retail and commercial deposits including checking and savings accounts CDs and IRAs. It services loans for residential real estate — mainly for one- to four-family homes — but also multifamily housing. Loans comprise nearly 90% of the bank's portfolio. Ridgewood Savings Bank was founded in 1921.

RIGEL PHARMACEUTICALS INC

NMS: RIGL

1180 Veterans Blvd.
South San Francisco, CA 94080
Phone: 650 624-1100
Fax: 650 624-1101
Web: www.rigel.com

CEO: Raul R. Rodriguez
CFO: Ryan D. Maynard
HR: –
FYE: December 31
Type: Public

When immune systems attack Rigel Pharmaceuticals wants to be there. The drug discovery and development firm focuses its research and development efforts on inflammatory/autoimmune muscle and immuno-oncology-related diseases. Drugs in development include candidates for treating rheumatoid arthritis psoriasis muscle wasting multiple sclerosis and transplant rejection. Rigel Pharmaceuticals prefers to collaborate with larger pharmaceutical companies in the development of its drug candidates. The company has more than 90 pending patent applications and more than 230 issued patents in the US as well as corresponding pending foreign patent applications and issued foreign patents.

	Annual Growth	12/10	12/11	12/12	12/13	12/14
Sales ($ mil.)	(49.3%)	125.0	4.8	2.3	7.2	8.3
Net income ($ mil.)	–	37.9	(86.0)	(98.8)	(89.0)	(90.9)
Market value ($ mil.)	(25.9%)	663.0	694.6	572.3	250.9	199.9
Employees	(3.3%)	145	153	157	129	127

RIGHT MANAGEMENT INC.

1818 Market St. 33rd Fl.	CEO: Owen J Sullivan
Philadelphia PA 19103-3614	CFO: –
Phone: 215-988-1588	HR: –
Fax: 215-988-0150	FYE: December 31
Web: www.right.com	Type: Subsidiary

Right Management is there for employees who find themselves right out of a job. The outplacement firm a subsidiary of staffing powerhouse Manpower-Group offers consulting in career transition and human resources management to thousands of corporate clients including the majority of "FORTUNE" 500 companies. It advises on termination interviews and benefits and offers career planning and counseling services to individual employees. The company's organizational consulting services include leadership development organizational performance and employee management. Established in 1980 Right Management has more than 300 offices across 50 countries.

RIGNET INC

	NMS: RNET
1880 S. Dairy Ashford, Suite 300	CEO: Mark B. Slaughter
Houston, TX 77077-4760	CFO: Charles E. (Chip) Schneider
Phone: 281 674-0100	HR: Greg Burns
Fax: –	FYE: December 31
Web: www.rig.net	Type: Public

Because no one wants to be stranded on a desert island much less an offshore oil rig there's RigNet. A telecommunications company that caters mainly to the oil and gas drilling industry it provides Cisco-powered Internet protocol-based voice fax video and high-speed Internet to remote offshore and land-based locations. It serves drilling rigs and production platforms in the Gulf of Mexico South America West Africa the Middle East the North Sea and Asia. RigNet's 500 customers such as Noble Corporation (12% of sales) span 1200 remote sites in more than 50 countries. Customers outside the US make up the majority of sales.

	Annual Growth	12/10	12/11	12/12	12/13	12/14
Sales ($ mil.)	37.3%	92.9	109.4	161.7	220.7	330.2
Net income ($ mil.)	–	(15.6)	9.5	11.9	16.3	15.6
Market value ($ mil.)	31.7%	240.3	295.1	360.2	845.0	723.4
Employees	36.0%	204	243	375	481	698

RINGCENTRAL INC

	NYS: RNG
20 Davis Drive	CEO: Vladimir (Vlad) Shmunis
Belmont, CA 94002	CFO: Clyde R. Hosein
Phone: 650 472-4100	HR: –
Fax: –	FYE: December 31
Web: www.ringcentral.com	Type: Public

RingCentral runs a one-line platform that supports multiple users for business communications. With its hosted platform workers no longer need settle for simply having their office lines forwarded to a mobile device. Small and midsized businesses use RingCentral to connect smartphones tablets PCs and desk phones from various locations and allow for communication across multiple channels including voice text and fax. The company rings up more than 300000 businesses across a wide range of industries including advertising finance and legal and technology. Founded in 1999 RingCentral went public in 2013 raising $97 million.

	Annual Growth	12/10	12/11	12/12	12/13	12/14
Sales ($ mil.)	44.7%	50.2	78.9	114.5	160.5	219.9
Net income ($ mil.)	–	(7.3)	(13.9)	(35.4)	(46.1)	(48.3)
Market value ($ mil.)	(18.8%)	–	–	–	1,259.4	1,022.9
Employees	109.5%	–	–	399	1,551	1,751

RIP GRIFFIN TRUCK SERVICE CENTER INC.

4710 4TH ST	CEO: Mark Griffin
LUBBOCK, TX 794164900	CFO: –
Phone: 806-795-8785	HR: Darci Aaron
Fax: –	FYE: December 31
Web: www.ripgriffin.com	Type: Private

Rip Griffin Truck Service Center tries to make sure you never go hungry again (in Scarlett O'Hara's words) at least when you're driving on the highways of North Texas. Rip Griffin's network of about 10 travel centers offers truckers tour buses and other travelers a smorgasbord of features such as convenience stores fuel game rooms laundry facilities restaurants and showers. Locations also offer truck maintenance and repair services. In addition to its travel center business Rip Griffin sells Freightliner trucks through two Texas dealerships and provides fuel transportation services. In 2004 CEO Rip Griffin sold the company to Ohio-based TravelCenters of America.

	Annual Growth	12/09	12/10	12/11	12/12	12/13
Assets ($ mil.)	3.4%	–	114.4	119.9	122.2	126.5
Net income ($ mil.)	2.3%	–	–	3.1	4.1	3.2
Market value ($ mil.)	–	–	–	–	–	–
Employees	–	–	–	–	–	88

RIPLEY ENTERTAINMENT INC.

7576 Kingspointe Pkwy. #188	CEO: –
Orlando FL 32819	CFO: Darren Loblaw
Phone: 407-345-8010	HR: Anne M Malleau
Fax: 407-345-0801	FYE: December 31
Web: www.ripleys.com	Type: Subsidiary

Ripley Entertainment believes in weirdness. The company a subsidiary of Canadian conglomerate Jim Pattison publishes the "Ripley's Believe It or Not!" oddities comic strip that appears in about 200 newspapers in more than 40 countries and licenses its name for toys and games as well as a Paramount Pictures-produced movie based on the life of the company's founder. It also owns about 60 other entertainment attractions — including Ripley's Believe It or Not! museums (called odditoriums) Louis Tussaud's Wax Museum aquariums 3-D simulation theaters haunted house adventure parks miniature golf courses and sightseeing trains. The brand was created by cartoonist Robert L. Ripley in 1918.

RIPPLEWOOD HOLDINGS L.L.C.

1 Rockefeller Plaza 32nd. Fl.	CEO: Timothy C Collins
New York NY 10020	CFO: –
Phone: 212-582-6700	HR: –
Fax: 212-582-4110	FYE: December 31
	Type: Private

Ripplewood Holdings tries to make waves in the private equity pond. The firm participates in leveraged buyouts management buyouts growth capital investments and other transactions. Ripplewood has a variety of interests but primarily focuses on the automotive consumer products financial manufacturing and communications and media sectors. Over the years the firm has made investments in such companies as Direct Holdings Worldwide (parent of direct marketer Time Life) Shinsei Bank and The Reader's Digest Association (RDA). Current holdings include Hostess Brands RSC and 3W Power Holdings. It manages about $10 billion in capital. CEO Tim Collins founded Ripplewood in 1995.

RISK (GEORGE) INDUSTRIES INC

NBB: RSKI A

802 South Elm St.
Kimball, NE 69145
Phone: 308 235-4645
Fax: –
Web: www.grisk.com

CEO: –
CFO: Stephanie Risk-Mcelroy
HR: –
FYE: April 30
Type: Public

George Risk Industries (GRI) wants customers to be able to manage risks. The company makes burglar alarm components and systems including panic buttons (for direct access to alarm monitoring centers). In addition to security products GRI manufactures pool alarms which are designed to sound alerts when a pool or spa area has been entered. The company also makes thermostats specialty computer keyboards and keypads custom-engraved key caps and push-button switches. Chairman and president Ken Risk a son of founder George Risk owns more than half of the company.

	Annual Growth	04/11	04/12	04/13	04/14	04/15
Sales ($ mil.)	7.7%	8.9	10.3	10.5	11.0	11.9
Net income ($ mil.)	11.7%	2.0	2.6	3.8	3.1	3.2
Market value ($ mil.)	6.6%	32.3	29.4	36.4	37.7	41.7
Employees	0.8%	160	150	160	165	165

RITE AID CORP.

NYS: RAD

30 Hunter Lane
Camp Hill, PA 17011
Phone: 717 761-2633
Fax: 717 975-5905
Web: www.riteaid.com

CEO: John T. Standley
CFO: Darren W. Karst
HR: Dedra N. Castle
FYE: February 28
Type: Public

Rite Aid ranks a distant third (behind Walgreen and CVS) in the US retail drugstore business with nearly 4600 drugstores in some 30 states and the District of Columbia. Rite Aid stores generate roughly 70% of their sales from filling prescriptions while the rest comes from selling health and beauty aids convenience foods greeting cards and more including some 3500 Rite Aid brand private-label products. More than 60% of all Rite Aid stores are free-standing and over half have drive-through pharmacies. The company was founded in 1962 and is being purchased by pharmacy leader Walgreens Boots Alliance.

	Annual Growth	02/11*	03/12	03/13	03/14*	02/15
Sales ($ mil.)	1.3%	25,214.9	26,121.2	25,392.3	25,526.4	26,528.4
Net income ($ mil.)	–	(555.4)	(368.6)	118.1	249.4	2,109.2
Market value ($ mil.)	58.0%	1,265.4	1,650.9	1,660.8	6,514.6	7,888.7
Employees	(0.8%)	91,800	90,000	89,000	89,000	89,000

*Fiscal year change

RIVER VALLEY BANCORP

NAS: RIVR

430 Clifty Drive
Madison, IN 47250
Phone: 812 273-4949
Fax: 812 273-4944
Web: www.rvfbank.com

CEO: Matthew P Forrester
CFO: –
HR: –
FYE: December 31
Type: Public

This River wants to help manage your revenue stream. River Valley Bancorp is the holding company for River Valley Financial Bank a thrift serving southeast Indiana and neighboring communities in Kentucky from about 10 branches. The bank offers standard deposit products including checking and savings accounts CDs NOW accounts and IRAs. It uses funds from deposits to write a variety of commercial and consumer loans; single-family mortgages make up about half of its loan portfolio. River Valley Financial also invests in government bonds municipal securities and mortgage-backed securities. The bank's wealth management arm offers brokerage trust and advisory services. German American Bancorp agreed to buy the bank in 2015 for $83.5 million.

	Annual Growth	12/10	12/11	12/12	12/13	12/14
Assets ($ mil.)	7.1%	386.6	406.6	472.9	482.8	509.5
Net income ($ mil.)	19.9%	2.3	1.8	4.0	4.4	4.8
Market value ($ mil.)	7.3%	40.2	39.0	44.4	65.4	53.2
Employees	8.4%	92	96	125	128	127

RIVERBED TECHNOLOGY INC

NMS: RVBD

680 Folsom Street
San Francisco, CA 94107
Phone: 415 247-8800
Fax: 415 247-8801
Web: www.riverbed.com

CEO: Jerry M Kennelly
CFO: Ernest E Maddock
HR: –
FYE: December 31
Type: Public

Riverbed Technology keeps data flowing. The company develops hardware and software that improves the performance of software shared over wide area networks (WANs) and reduce network traffic. Its Steelhead network appliances and software tools are designed for small businesses and global enterprises. Riverbed's other products enable mobile access to business software and data facilitate online data storage (Whitewater) and manage network performance (Cascade). Customers have included Carhartt OMV and Tatts Group. The company makes most of its sales through resellers distributors and systems integrators. Riverbed sells worldwide but it does more than half of its business in the US.

	Annual Growth	12/09	12/10	12/11	12/12	12/13
Sales ($ mil.)	27.5%	394.1	551.9	726.5	836.9	1,041.0
Net income ($ mil.)	–	7.1	34.2	63.8	54.6	(12.4)
Market value ($ mil.)	(5.8%)	3,671.6	5,621.7	3,756.4	3,152.1	2,890.0
Employees	26.0%	1,013	1,244	1,610	2,566	2,556

RIVERSIDE HEALTHCARE ASSOCIATION INC.

701 TOWN CENTER DR # 1000
NEWPORT NEWS, VA 236064286
Phone: 757-534-7000
Fax: –

CEO: –
CFO: Bill Douglas
HR: –
FYE: December 31
Type: Private

Extra! Extra! Read all about it! Residents of Newport News (and about a dozen other cities in Eastern Virginia) Turn to Riverside Health for Medical Care. The not-for-profit health care provider administers general emergency and specialty medical services from five hospitals Riverside Regional Medical Center Riverside Walter Reed Hospital Riverside Tappahannock Hospital and Riverside Shore Memorial Hospital and Riverside Doctors Hospital as well as a psychiatric hospital a physical rehabilitation facility and retirement communities. Riverside also operates physician offices and medical training facilities. Specialty centers provide home and hospice care cancer treatment and dialysis.

	Annual Growth	12/09	12/10	12/11	12/12	12/13
Sales ($ mil.)	5.3%	–	872.3	952.4	948.0	1,017.5
Net income ($ mil.)	–	–	–	(26.0)	41.7	102.0
Market value ($ mil.)	–	–	–	–	–	–
Employees	–	–	–	–	–	8,000

RIVERSIDE HOSPITAL INC.

500 J CLYDE MORRIS BLVD
NEWPORT NEWS, VA 236011929
Phone: 757-594-2000
Fax: –
Web: www.riversideonline.com

CEO: William B Downey
CFO: –
HR: –
FYE: December 31
Type: Private

Riverside Hospital operates as Riverside Regional Medical Center a 450-bed acute-care facility that serves the residents of Newport News Virginia. Founded in 1916 the hospital moved to its current 72-acre campus in 1963 providing more than 30 medical specialties including cancer treatment cardiology birthing and diagnostic imaging. It specializes in cardiovascular and neurological surgeries and provides radiosurgery (radiation surgery) through a partnership with the University of Virginia Health System. Its emergency department is a 42-room Level II Trauma Center that treats more than 57000 patients each year. Riverside Hospital is part of the Riverside Health System.

	Annual Growth	12/08	12/09	12/10	12/11	12/12
Sales ($ mil.)	5.0%	–	413.6	429.7	466.1	479.4
Net income ($ mil.)	84.0%	–	–	20.8	36.2	70.6
Market value ($ mil.)	–	–	–	–	–	–
Employees	–	–	–	–	–	8,000

RIVERVIEW BANCORP, INC.

NMS: RVSB

900 Washington Street, Suite 900
Vancouver, WA 98660
Phone: 360 693-6650
Fax: –
Web: www.riverviewbank.com

CEO: Patrick Sheaffer
CFO: Kevin J Lycklama
HR: –
FYE: March 31
Type: Public

Riverview Bancorp is the holding company for Riverview Community Bank which operates about 20 branches located primarily in the Columbia River Gorge area of Washington State and Oregon. Serving consumers and local businesses the bank offers such standard retail banking services as checking and savings accounts money market accounts NOW accounts and CDs. Commercial construction and commercial real estate loans account for nearly 90% of its lending portfolio which also includes residential mortgages residential construction loans and other consumer loans. Trust and investment services are provided through the company's Riverview Asset Management Corp. Riverview Community Bank was founded in 1923.

	Annual Growth	03/11	03/12	03/13	03/14	03/15
Assets ($ mil.)	(0.0%)	859.3	856.0	777.0	824.5	858.8
Net income ($ mil.)	1.0%	4.3	(31.7)	2.6	19.4	4.5
Market value ($ mil.)	10.3%	68.4	50.8	59.4	77.0	101.2
Employees	(0.7%)	238	224	238	219	231

RIVERVIEW HOSPITAL

395 WESTFIELD RD
NOBLESVILLE, IN 460601434
Phone: 317-773-0760
Fax: –
Web: www.riverview.org

CEO: –
CFO: –
HR: –
FYE: December 31
Type: Private

Riverview Hospital (which changed its operating name to Riverside Health in 2014) provides general medical and surgical care to residents in central Indiana. With about 155 beds and 300 physicians representing more than 35 medical specialties the hospital is a full-service facility that offers specialty care in a number of areas including heart disease cancer women's health and orthopedics. Besides its main campus Riverview operates several outpatient facilities including an occupational health center a community health clinic and several rehab and fitness centers.

	Annual Growth	12/04	12/05	12/06	12/08	12/12
Sales ($ mil.)	3.4%	–	118.0	136.8	133.5	149.4
Net income ($ mil.)	25.1%	–	–	4.4	(0.5)	16.9
Market value ($ mil.)	–	–	–	–	–	–
Employees	–	–	–	–	–	949

RIVIERA HOLDINGS CORPORATION

2901 Las Vegas Blvd. South
Las Vegas NV 89109
Phone: 702-734-5110
Fax: 702-794-9442
Web: www.rivierahotel.com

CEO: –
CFO: –
HR: –
FYE: December 31
Type: Private

It may not be the south of France but gamblers at the more than 50-year-old Riviera Holdings' Riviera Hotel & Casino probably don't care. The casino located on the Las Vegas Strip has about 900 slot machines 35 gaming tables a keno lounge poker room a sports-betting club and bingo. The Riviera also has a 2100-room hotel with bars restaurants a convention center and entertainment such as An Evening at La Cage (a female impersonation show). The Riviera opened in 1955. The company filed for Chapter 11 in 2010 and exited bankruptcy in 2011.

RJF INTERNATIONAL CORPORATION

3875 Embassy Pkwy.
Fairlawn OH 44333
Phone: 330-668-7600
Fax: 330-668-7701
Web: www.rjfinternational.com

CEO: John L Baechle
CFO: Tony Cox
HR: –
FYE: December 31
Type: Private

At one time the idea of using polymers in everyday settings was Pollyannaish. Now it is an accepted part of the world we all live in. RJF International makes specialty engineered polymer products used by decorative industrial transit and office products industries. Its range of offerings turn to wall coverings protective coatings flexible bonded magnetic strips flooring and guard rails. The company also makes PVC strip and sheet for transparent and opaque strip doors and industrial barriers. Their applications include loading docks interior plant passageways even freezer doors. RJF International is the former fabricated polymers division of Goodrich.

RKA PETROLEUM COMPANIES INC.

28340 Wick Rd.
Romulus MI 48174
Phone: 734-946-2199
Fax: 734-946-4772
Web: www.rkapetroleum.com

CEO: –
CFO: –
HR: –
FYE: December 31
Type: Private

Arcane name widely available products. RKA Petroleum (named after former president Roger K. Albertie who died in 2004) is a regional wholesale distributor of petroleum products to commercial and retail fueling locations in the US. Led by the RKA Petroleum Terminal in Romulus Michigan the company has storage capacity of more than 13 million gallons of product including an additional storage capacity of more than 60000 gallons for alternative fuels. The family-owned company also operates a fleet dispatching service a heating and cooling company and a work clothing retailer.

RLI CORP.

NYS: RLI

9025 North Lindbergh Drive
Peoria, IL 61615
Phone: 309 692-1000
Fax: 309 692-1068
Web: www.rlicorp.com

CEO: Jonathan E. Michael
CFO: Thomas L. Brown
HR: Jeffrey (Jeff) Fick
FYE: December 31
Type: Public

You might wonder what folks in Illinois know about earthquake insurance but as a specialty property/casualty insurer Peoria-based RLI knows how to write such policies. Through its subsidiaries the company mainly offers coverage for US niche markets — risks that are hard to place in the standard market and are otherwise underserved. It focuses on public and private companies as well as non-profit organizations. RLI's commercial property/casualty lines include products liability property damage marine cargo directors and officers liability medical malpractice and general liability. It also writes commercial surety bonds and a smattering of specialty personal insurance.

	Annual Growth	12/10	12/11	12/12	12/13	12/14
Assets ($ mil.)	2.5%	2,514.6	2,695.2	2,644.6	2,740.3	2,775.5
Net income ($ mil.)	1.5%	127.4	130.6	103.3	126.3	135.4
Market value ($ mil.)	(1.5%)	2,265.9	3,140.5	2,787.0	4,197.3	2,129.3
Employees	4.7%	734	862	897	870	882

ROADRUNNER TRANSPORTATION SERVICES HOLDINGS INC. NYSE: RRTS

4900 S. Pennsylvania Ave.
Cudahy WI 53110-8903
Phone: 414-615-1500
Fax: 414-615-1513
Web: www.rrts.com

CEO: –
CFO: –
HR: –
FYE: December 31
Type: Public

Running your cargo down the road is Roadrunner Transportation Services' (RRTS) business. The company offers less-than-truckload (LTL) freight transportation which combines freight from multiple shippers into a single truckload. In addition it arranges the transportation of truckload freight as well as provides logistics services. RRTS caters to small and mid-size shippers and some large national accounts throughout the US via a network of 15-plus service centers. Rather than owning trucks and trailers the company relies on a network of independent contractors and on purchased transportation capacity. Investment firm Thayer Hidden Creek owns a majority of RRTS.

ROADRUNNER TRANSPORTATION SYSTEMS INC NYS: RRTS

4900 S. Pennsylvania Ave.
Cudahy, WI 53110
Phone: 414 615-1500
Fax: –

CEO: Mark A. DiBlasi
CFO: Peter R. Armbruster
HR: Paul Hoff
FYE: December 31
Type: Public

Running your cargo down the road is Roadrunner Transportation Systems (RRTS) business. The company offers less-than-truckload (LTL) freight transportation which combines freight from multiple shippers into a single truckload. In addition it arranges the transportation of truckload freight as well as provides logistics services. RRTS caters to small and mid-size shippers and some large national accounts throughout the US via a network of service centers. Rather than owning trucks and trailers the company relies on a network of independent contractors and on purchased transportation capacity.

	Annual Growth	12/10	12/11	12/12	12/13	12/14
Sales ($ mil.)	31.2%	632.0	843.6	1,073.4	1,361.4	1,872.8
Net income ($ mil.)	95.0%	3.6	25.9	37.5	49.0	52.0
Market value ($ mil.)	12.7%	548.4	535.9	688.0	1,022.1	885.5
Employees	40.0%	1,054	1,848	2,395	2,756	4,045

ROAMWARE INC.

3031 Tisch Way Ste. 1000
San Jose CA 95128
Phone: 408-861-9300
Fax: 408-861-9301
Web: www.roamware.com

CEO: Ori Sasson
CFO: Neil Laird
HR: –
FYE: December 31
Type: Private

Roamware makes sure mobile phone subscribers have a full range of services wherever they may roam. The company provides software and services that wireless network operators use to improve their roaming voice and data services. Used by service providers in more than 160 countries its Roamware Service Delivery System improves traffic management user experience quality control and functionality. Roamware also provides digital media applications that enhance ring tone and messaging capabilities. The company counts AT&T Vodafone and Optimus among its customers.

ROBERT BOSCH LLC

38000 Hills Tech Dr.
Farmington Hills MI 48331
Phone: 248-876-1000
Fax: 703-709-6086
Web: www.rolls-royce.com/northamerica

CEO: –
CFO: Maximiliane Straub
HR: –
FYE: December 31
Type: Subsidiary

Robert Bosch LLC is your one-stop shop for German-engineered auto parts appliances and power tools. The North American subsidiary of German giant Robert Bosch GmbH Bosch LLC divides its operations among three divisions. Automotive Technology produces gasoline/diesel systems (and electrical drives); chassis and steering systems; and auto electronics for OEMs and the aftermarket. The Consumer Goods and Building Technology division builds various power tools security systems home appliances and HVAC equipment. Automation drive controls solar/wind power and packaging systems are the focus of its Industrial Technology division. Operating since 1906 Bosch LLC has grown to more than 100 North American locations.

ROBERT BOSCH TOOL CORPORATION

1800 W. Central Rd.
Mt. Prospect IL 60056
Phone: 224-232-2000
Fax: 224-232-2645
Web: www.boschtools.com

CEO: Heiko Fischer
CFO: Katina Xouria
HR: Ellen Reese
FYE: December 31
Type: Subsidiary

Bosch likes DIYers to tool around the home with Skil. Robert Bosch Tool Corporation makes power tools and accessories for do-it-yourselfers (DIYers) and professionals. The manufacturer boasts a vast portfolio of brand name products including Bosch Dremel RotoZip Skil and Vermont American. Its better-known lines are the Dremel rotary tool and the RotoZip spiral saw. Robert Bosch Tool also makes lawn and garden tools under the Gilmour brand. The company is a US subsidiary of Germany-based Robert Bosch. Robert Bosch Tool originally created through the merger of S-B Power Tool Company and Vermont American combined with its parent's North American power tool accessory and lawn and garden divisions in 2003.

ROBERT HALF INTERNATIONAL INC. NYS: RHI

2884 Sand Hill Road, Suite 200
Menlo Park, CA 94025
Phone: 650 234-6000
Fax: –
Web: www.rhi.com

CEO: Harold M. Messmer
CFO: M. Keith Waddell
HR: Kelly Cline
FYE: December 31
Type: Public

Robert Half International carries the full load of personnel services. The company places temporary and permanent staff through eight divisions: Accountemps Robert Half Finance and Accounting Robert Half Legal OfficeTeam (general administrative) Robert Half Technology (information technology) Robert Half Management Resources (senior level professionals) and The Creative Group (advertising marketing and Web design). The firm also publishes job reports and surveys on the latest employment trends and annual salary guides to track pay trends and has an internal audit and risk consulting division in Protiviti.

	Annual Growth	12/10	12/11	12/12	12/13	12/14
Sales ($ mil.)	10.3%	3,175.1	3,777.0	4,111.2	4,245.9	4,695.0
Net income ($ mil.)	46.7%	66.1	149.9	209.9	252.2	305.9
Market value ($ mil.)	17.5%	4,135.1	3,845.9	4,300.0	5,674.3	7,889.1
Employees	4.8%	186,400	199,300	203,000	210,000	225,000

ROBERT MORRIS UNIVERSITY

6001 UNIVERSITY BLVD
CORAOPOLIS, PA 151081189
Phone: 412-262-8324
Fax: –
Web: www.rmu.edu

CEO: –
CFO: –
HR: Patricia A Thompson
FYE: May 31
Type: Private

Robert Morris University is a private four-year institution located in suburban Pittsburgh. It offers more than 30 undergraduate degree programs and nearly 20 master's and doctoral degree programs as well as adult and continuing education programs. The school has an enrollment of more than 5000 students. Named for a Pennsylvanian patriot who helped finance the Revolutionary War and signed the Declaration of Independence Robert Morris University was founded in 1921. Formerly Robert Morris College the institution gained university status in 2002.

	Annual Growth	05/03	05/04	05/05	05/09	05/10
Sales ($ mil.)	–	–	0.0	69.4	105.1	112.6
Net income ($ mil.)	(8.4%)	–	–	4.3	0.0	2.8
Market value ($ mil.)	–	–	–	–	–	–
Employees	–	–	–	–	–	500

ROBERT WOOD JOHNSON UNIVERSITY HOSPITAL

1 ROBERT WOOD JOHNSON PL
NEW BRUNSWICK, NJ 089011928
Phone: 732-828-3000
Fax: –
Web: www.rwjuh.edu

CEO: –
CFO: John Gantner
HR: Martin Everhart
FYE: December 31
Type: Private

Robert Wood Johnson University Hospital (RWJUH) is the flagship facility of the Robert Wood Johnson Health System and Network. The medical center offers patients acute and tertiary care including cardiovascular services organ and tissue transplantation pediatric care (at The Bristol-Myers Squibb Children's Hospital) Level I trauma care cancer treatment (at the Cancer Hospital of New Jersey) women's health and emergency medicine. Founded in 1884 the 600-bed facility serves as a teaching center for the Robert Wood Johnson Medical School (RWJMS). The Robert Wood Johnson Health System plans to merge with fellow New Jersey hospital system Barnabas Health.

	Annual Growth	09/11	09/12*	12/12	12/13	12/14
Sales ($ mil.)	29.4%	–	622.5	823.0	833.6	1,043.0
Net income ($ mil.)	(0.1%)	–	–	83.7	108.2	83.5
Market value ($ mil.)	–	–	–	–	–	–
Employees	–	–	–	–	–	4,674

*Fiscal year change

ROBERT WOOD JOHNSON UNIVERSITY HOSPITAL AT RAHWAY

865 STONE ST
RAHWAY, NJ 07065-2742
Phone: 732-381-4200
Fax: –
Web: www.rwjuhr.com

CEO: –
CFO: –
HR: –
FYE: December 31
Type: Private

Robert Wood Johnson University Hospital at Rahway (RWJUHR) has the people of Rahway cheering for it. Providing health care services for Rahway and 15 other communities of eastern New Jersey the hospital has 265 beds. Founded in 1915 RWJUHR offers patients ambulatory cardiac geriatric psychiatric pulmonary rehabilitation and surgical services. The hospital also has a community outreach program particularly focused on geriatric care. Part of the Robert Wood Johnson Health System and Network since 2003 RWJUH is also affiliated with The University of Medicine and Dentistry of New Jersey.

	Annual Growth	12/01	12/02	12/03	12/04	12/12
Sales ($ mil.)	–	–	0.0	0.2	0.2	114.4
Net income ($ mil.)	–	–	0.0	0.0	(0.0)	8.8
Market value ($ mil.)	–	–	–	–	–	–
Employees	–	–	–	–	–	50

ROBERTS DAIRY COMPANY LLC

2901 CUMING ST
OMAHA, NE 681312108
Phone: 402-344-4321
Fax: –
Web: www.robertsdairyefcu.org

CEO: –
CFO: –
HR: Tim Nelson
FYE: September 30
Type: Private

Holy cow! Roberts Dairy Foods is a leading producer of fluid cultured and frozen dairy products. It offers milk yogurt sour cream cottage cheese and other dairy products. A division of Hiland Dairy the firm operates production plants in Omaha and Kansas City and 10 distribution centers located in the Midwest. The company markets its products under the Roberts and Hiland-Dairy brands; it also provides private-label services and school milk. Through a joint venture named Hiland-Roberts the company makes ice cream products from a facility in Norfolk Nebraska. Founded as a milk route by J.R. Roberts in 1906 Roberts Dairy Foods serves retail food and food service customers throughout the Midwest.

	Annual Growth	09/04	09/05	09/06	09/07	09/08
Sales ($ mil.)	–	–	–	(591.9)	319.7	359.7
Net income ($ mil.)	8220.6%	–	–	0.0	2.2	0.9
Market value ($ mil.)	–	–	–	–	–	–
Employees	–	–	–	–	–	320

ROBINSON (C.H.) WORLDWIDE, INC.

NMS: CHRW

14701 Charlson Road
Eden Prairie, MN 55347-5088
Phone: 952 937-8500
Fax: 952 937-6714
Web: www.chrobinson.com

CEO: John P. Wiehoff
CFO: Andrew C. Clarke
HR: –
FYE: December 31
Type: Public

C.H. Robinson Worldwide (CHRW) keeps merchandise moving. A third-party logistics (3PL) provider the company arranges freight transportation using trucks trains ships and airplanes belonging to other companies. It contracts with some 66000 carriers. CHRW handles about 14.3 million shipments per year for its 46000-plus customers that include companies in the food and beverage manufacturing and retail industries. Besides transportation the company also offers logistics for supply chain management services through some 280 offices. In addition CHRW buys sells and transports fresh produce throughout the US.

	Annual Growth	12/10	12/11	12/12	12/13	12/14
Sales ($ mil.)	9.8%	9,274.3	10,336.3	11,359.1	12,752.1	13,470.1
Net income ($ mil.)	3.8%	387.0	431.6	593.8	415.9	449.7
Market value ($ mil.)	(1.7%)	11,744.5	10,219.8	9,259.1	8,545.8	10,968.2
Employees	10.9%	7,628	8,353	10,929	11,676	11,521

ROBINSON MEMORIAL HOSPITAL

6847 N CHESTNUT ST
RAVENNA, OH 442663999
Phone: 330-297-0811
Fax: –
Web: www.robinsonmemorial.org

CEO: –
CFO: –
HR: –
FYE: December 31
Type: Private

Robinson Memorial Hospital is a 117-bed medical facility serving communities in northeast Ohio. In addition to a Level II trauma center the hospital offers programs in pediatrics women's health home health care and oncology. It also engages in community outreach programs and operates outpatient facilities including urgent care clinics a freestanding surgery center an occupational health center and several physician practices. Robinson Memorial Hospital has nearly 400 physicians representing more than 40 medical specialties. It is overseen by the Portage County Board of Hospital Trustees.

	Annual Growth	12/06	12/07	12/08	12/09	12/12
Sales ($ mil.)	(0.6%)	–	141.4	146.8	6.9	137.2
Net income ($ mil.)	–	–	–	10.1	(0.1)	(7.0)
Market value ($ mil.)	–	–	–	–	–	–
Employees	–	–	–	–	–	974

ROBINSON OIL CORPORATION

955 MARTIN AVE
SANTA CLARA, CA 950502608
Phone: 408-327-4300
Fax: –
Web: www.robinsonoilcorp.com

CEO: –
CFO: Stephen F White
HR: –
FYE: December 31
Type: Private

Like Hamlet's Denmark something's rotten in the state of Robinson Oil. The company owns and operates Rotten Robbie a regional brand of independent gas stations that caters to consumer and commercial motorists. The chain consists of some 35 stops in Northern California mainly around the San Francisco Bay Area. Some stops are kiosks; about half are larger with Mrs. Robbie's Markets a food store and several offer commercial fleet fueling services affiliated with Pacific Pride and other cardlock networks. Diesel is available at all locations and at certain stores kerosene propane and biodiesel. Founded in the 1930s as a private-label fuel retailer Robinson Oil is a fourth-generation family-owned business.

	Annual Growth	12/07	12/08	12/09	12/12	12/13
Sales ($ mil.)	2.7%	–	409.9	292.4	464.2	468.7
Net income ($ mil.)	2.2%	–	–	8.2	10.7	8.9
Market value ($ mil.)	–	–	–	–	–	–
Employees	–	–	–	–	–	250

ROCHE BROS. SUPERMARKETS INC.

70 Hastings St.
Wellesley MA 02481
Phone: 781-235-9400
Fax: 781-235-3153
Web: www.rochebros.com

CEO: Patrick E Roche Sr
CFO: Dale Shores
HR: –
FYE: December 31
Type: Private

Roche Bros. has been stocking Massachusetts pantries for more than 50 years. The regional grocery chain operates about 15 Roche Brothers Supermarkets and several Sudbury Farms stores in eastern Massachusetts as well as online and call-in shopping and delivery services. Besides traditional supermarket fare Roche Bros. Supermarkets have in-store chefs to prepare ready-to-serve meals as well as specialty bakery floral meat and seafood departments. The stores also house self-serve chicken wing bars and at some stores foodservice departments account for as much as 10% of sales. Founded in 1952 as a meat and produce store by Pat and Bud Roche the business is still owned and operated by the Roche family.

ROCHESTER INSTITUTE OF TECHNOLOGY (INC)

1 LOMB MEMORIAL DR
ROCHESTER, NY 146235698
Phone: 585-475-2411
Fax: –
Web: www.rit.edu

CEO: –
CFO: –
HR: Judy Bender
FYE: June 30
Type: Private

The Rochester Institute of Technology (RIT) is a privately-endowed university with nine colleges focused on providing career-oriented education to about 18000 students. The school which has a student-faculty ratio of about 14:1 offers more than 90 bachelor's degree programs in art and design business engineering science and hotel management. RIT also confers master's and doctorate degrees. The university's National Technical Institute for the Deaf is the first and largest technological college for learners who suffer from hearing loss. RIT which traces its roots back to 1829 counts among its alumni the CEOs of Kodak and The Associated Press.

	Annual Growth	06/04	06/05	06/06	06/12	06/13
Sales ($ mil.)	4.6%	–	350.8	370.7	490.3	504.1
Net income ($ mil.)	2.2%	–	–	45.1	16.8	52.4
Market value ($ mil.)	–	–	–	–	–	–
Employees	–	–	–	–	–	2,400

ROCK CREEK PHARMACEUTICALS INC

NMS: RCPI

2040 Whitfield Ave., Suite 300
Sarasota, FL 34243
Phone: 844 727-0727
Fax: –

CEO: Michael John Mullan
CFO: William L McMahon
HR: –
FYE: December 31
Type: Public

Rock Creek Pharmaceuticals (formerly Star Scientific) has a new name and business strategy focused on the development of drugs to treat chronic inflammatory conditions and neurological disorders. The company has adopted the name of its Rock Creek Pharmaceuticals subsidiary (founded in 2007) which makes nutraceuticals using alkaloids found in tobacco and other plants. Its core products are Anatabloc to reduce inflammation and CigRx a tobacco alternative. (Both products are the subject of warning letters from the US Food and Drug Administration.) Formerly a seller of discount cigarettes the emerging drug development company has since exited the cigarette and dissolvable tobacco businesses.

	Annual Growth	12/09	12/10	12/11	12/12	12/13
Sales ($ mil.)	89.6%	0.7	0.8	1.7	6.2	9.1
Net income ($ mil.)	–	(22.8)	(28.3)	(38.0)	(22.9)	(32.8)
Market value ($ mil.)	13.5%	120.7	336.1	375.8	462.0	200.0
Employees	(5.2%)	31	31	39	23	25

ROCK ENERGY RESOURCES INC.

OTC: RCKE.PK

10375 Richmond Ste. 2100
Houston TX 77042
Phone: 713-954-3600
Fax: 916-649-3594
Web: www.casepower.com

CEO: –
CFO: –
HR: –
FYE: December 31
Type: Public

Rock Energy Resources is pushing to release oil and gas energy from the rocks in which they are trapped. The former Hanover Gold Company is in the business of natural gas and crude oil production in Texas and California. In 2008 not long after changing its name and its business focus Rock Energy Resources doubled its ownership interest in the Orcutt project in California. It plans to continue drilling more wells and increase its overall reserve base. In 2010 after a hiatus during which the company sought to obtain more capital it recommenced work on its Garwood Wilcox properties in Colorado County Texas.

ROCK OF AGES CORPORATION

772 Graniteville Rd.
Graniteville VT 05654
Phone: 802-476-3121
Fax: 802-476-3110
Web: www.rockofages.com

CEO: Robert Pope
CFO: Laura A Plude
HR: Dan Ginsberg
FYE: December 31
Type: Private

Rock of Ages (ROA) is into hard rock — as long as it's granite. The company which is known for its personalized cemetery memorials (including a full-size replica of a Mercedes-Benz) quarries its own granite and makes finished granite memorials. ROA operates about 10 quarries and a handful of manufacturing and sawing facilities mostly in Vermont and Quebec. ROA sells its memorials through more than 100 independent retailers in the US and another 100 retailers in Canada. Chairman Kurt Swensen and his brother Kevin own ROA through Swenson Granite which completed the purchase of the 30% of ROA's stock it did not already own in 2011.

ROCK-TENN CO.

NYS: RKT

504 Thrasher Street
Norcross, GA 30071
Phone: 770 448-2193
Fax: –
Web: www.rocktenn.com

CEO: Steven C Voorhees
CFO: Ward H Dickson
HR: –
FYE: September 30
Type: Public

A rock-solid reputation? You betcha. One of North America's containerboard giants Rock-Tenn produces packaging for food hardware apparel and other consumer goods. With approximately 9.4 million tons of mill capacity the company's lineup includes recycled and bleached paperboard containerboard consumer and corrugated packaging and point-of-purchase displays. Specialty paperboard is also converted into book cover and laminated paperboard and sold to other manufacturers for such applications as furniture storage and automotive components. Rock-Tenn traces its roots back to 1936 and operates through 240 locations worldwide.

	Annual Growth	09/10	09/11	09/12	09/13	09/14
Sales ($ mil.)	34.7%	3,001.4	5,399.6	9,207.6	9,545.4	9,895.1
Net income ($ mil.)	20.8%	225.6	141.1	249.1	727.3	479.7
Market value ($ mil.)	(1.1%)	6,973.4	6,815.2	10,105.2	14,177.8	6,661.2
Employees	26.5%	10,400	26,600	26,300	25,800	26,600

ROCKEFELLER GROUP INTERNATIONAL INC.

1221 Avenue of the Americas
New York NY 10020-1001
Phone: 212-282-2000
Fax: 212-282-2179
Web: www.rockefellergroup.com

CEO: Atsushi Nakajima
CFO: –
HR: –
FYE: March 31
Type: Subsidiary

This Rock Group's anthem could be "We Built This City." Rockefeller Group International founded as John D. Rockefeller Jr.'s Metropolitan Square Corporation spearheaded the development of Manhattan's Rockefeller Center during the Great Depression. (Radio City Music Hall and 30 Rockefeller Plaza are among its notable attractions.) Now a subsidiary of Japan's Mitsubishi Estate Rockefeller Group controls the industrial conglomerate's US-based real estate interests including ownership or management of most of Rockefeller Center's office space. Subsidiaries include entities devoted to commercial property development rental of serviced office suites and telecommunications services to office towers.

ROCKET FUEL INC

NMS: FUEL

1900 Seaport Boulevard, Pacific Shores Center
Redwood City, CA 94063
Phone: 650 595-1300
Fax: –
Web: www.rocketfuel.com

CEO: George H. John
CFO: David (Dave) Sankaran
HR: –
FYE: December 31
Type: Public

Rocket Fuel employs data science not rocket science to help its customers keep pace with the escape velocity of digital advertising. The company's proprietary software uses big data and artificial intelligence to simultaneously run more than 1000 online ad campaigns for customers ranging from UCLA and Kraft Foods to Choice Hotels and Johns Manville with 130% revenue retention. Its program learns from customers' behavior and adjusts individual campaigns on the fly to follow the clicks faster than human analysis would allow. Rocket Fuel was formed in 2008 and went public in 2013 raising $116 million for general corporate purposes.

	Annual Growth	12/10	12/11	12/12	12/13	12/14
Sales ($ mil.)	–	0.0	44.7	106.6	240.6	408.6
Net income ($ mil.)	–	0.0	(4.3)	(10.3)	(20.9)	(64.3)
Market value ($ mil.)	–	0.0	–	–	2,582.7	677.1
Employees	55.4%	–	–	465	619	1,123

ROCKET SOFTWARE INC.

275 Grove St.
Newton MA 02466-2272
Phone: 617-614-4321
Fax: 617-630-7100
Web: www.rocketsoftware.com

CEO: Andy Youniss
CFO: Kevin Thimble
HR: –
FYE: December 31
Type: Private

Rocket Software develops enterprise infrastructure software for companies looking for a boost in the power of their back office systems. Its products address such needs as data network application and storage management as well as business intelligence and security; brand names include Mainstar Seagull Software Servergraph and BlueZone. The company partners with information technology product vendors including IBM HP and Microsoft. It serves a global client base from about 20 offices in nine countries in Outside of North America where Rocket has 12 offices it serves clients from offices in Europe China and Australia. Rocket was established in 1990 by CEO Andy Youniss and director Johan Magnusson Gedda.

ROCKHURST UNIVERSITY

1100 ROCKHURST RD
KANSAS CITY, MO 641102508
Phone: 816-501-4000
Fax: –
Web: www.rockhurst.edu

CEO: –
CFO: Guy Swanson
HR: –
FYE: June 30
Type: Private

Rockhurst University provides education and leadership training in a Catholic Jesuit institutional environment. The university serves approximately 3000 students from two campuses in Kansas City Missouri. The university offers more than 50 undergraduate and graduate programs. Its undergraduate arts and science degrees include business nursing information and engineering programs. On the graduate level the university offers the Helzberg Executive Fellows MBA program as well as programs in occupational therapy physical therapy speech pathology and education. Rockhurst was founded by the Jesuits in 1910.

	Annual Growth	06/10	06/11	06/12	06/13	06/14
Sales ($ mil.)	(0.8%)	–	89.6	86.7	91.0	87.4
Net income ($ mil.)	–	–	–	(8.1)	6.7	3.6
Market value ($ mil.)	–	–	–	–	–	–
Employees	–	–	–	–	–	250

ROCKVIEW DAIRIES INC.

7011 STEWART AND GRAY RD
DOWNEY, CA 902414347
Phone: 562-927-5511
Fax: –
Web: www.rockviewfarms.com

CEO: Egbert De Groot
CFO: Joe Valadez
HR: –
FYE: March 31
Type: Private

Got organic milk? Rockview Dairies does. Doing business as Rockview Farms the company produces milk and other dairy products under brand names Rockview Farms and Good Heart Organic Milk. Bucking modern trends the dairy owns its own farms and cows which have not been treated with bovine growth hormones. Rockview Dairies processes packages and distributes its own milk. It also offers eggs dressings fruit drinks and desserts. The company wholesales its products to food retailers and foodservice operators and as a bonus offers home-delivery service. Established in 1927 by Bob Hops Rockview Dairies serves Southern California. It has been owned and operated by the DeGroot family since 1965.

	Annual Growth	03/04	03/05	03/06	03/07	03/08
Sales ($ mil.)	–	–	–	(2,112.3)	265.2	333.7
Net income ($ mil.)	13235.1%	–	–	0.0	4.0	8.1
Market value ($ mil.)	–	–	–	–	–	–
Employees	–	–	–	–	–	250

ROCKWELL AUTOMATION, INC.

NYS: ROK

1201 South Second Street
Milwaukee, WI 53204
Phone: 414 382-2000
Fax: –
Web: www.rockwellautomation.com

CEO: Keith D. Nosbusch
CFO: Theodore D. (Ted) Crandall
HR: –
FYE: September 30
Type: Public

Rockwell Automation only rocks to the scintillating sounds of its control products. The company is one of the world's largest industrial automation companies serving automotive food and beverage (including dairy) personal care life sciences oil and gas mining and paper and pulp markets. Rockwell's control products & solutions unit makes industrial automation products such as motor starters and contractors relays timers signaling devices and variable-speed drives. To complement its automation product offerings its architecture & software unit offers factory management software and motion control sensors and machine safety components.

	Annual Growth	09/11	09/12	09/13	09/14	09/15
Sales ($ mil.)	1.3%	6,000.4	6,259.4	6,351.9	6,623.5	6,307.9
Net income ($ mil.)	4.4%	697.8	737.0	756.3	826.8	827.6
Market value ($ mil.)	16.0%	7,414.4	9,208.4	14,158.9	14,548.1	13,434.6
Employees	1.7%	21,000	22,000	22,000	22,500	22,500

ROCKWELL COLLINS, INC.

NYS: COL

400 Collins Road N.E.
Cedar Rapids, IA 52498
Phone: 319 295-1000
Fax: –
Web: www.rockwellcollins.com

CEO: Robert` K. (Kelly) Ortberg
CFO: Patrick E. Allen
HR: Martha L. May
FYE: September 30
Type: Public

Rockwell Collins a spin-off of Rockwell Automation makes aviation electronics and communication equipment for commercial and military aircraft. The company boasts that nearly every commercial cockpit contains something made by Rockwell Collins. It also provides flight simulation and training MRO services navigation and surveillance systems. The company has three primary segments: commercial systems (avionics and in-flight entertainment systems for commercial aircraft); government systems (airborne/ground/shipboard communication systems with military applications and overhaul services); and information management services business (communications systems integration and security solutions).

	Annual Growth	09/11	09/12	09/13	09/14	09/15
Sales ($ mil.)	2.2%	4,806.0	4,726.0	4,610.0	4,979.0	5,244.0
Net income ($ mil.)	2.0%	634.0	609.0	632.0	604.0	686.0
Market value ($ mil.)	11.6%	6,959.0	7,075.1	8,950.7	10,354.2	10,794.7
Employees	(1.2%)	20,500	19,000	18,300	20,000	19,500

ROCKWELL MEDICAL, INC

NMS: RMTI

30142 Wixom Road
Wixom, MI 48393
Phone: 248 960-9009
Fax: –

CEO: Robert L Chioini
CFO: Thomas E. Klema
HR: –
FYE: December 31
Type: Public

Rockwell Medical (formerly Rockwell Medical Technologies) keeps on trucking with its hemodialysis products. The company makes hemodialysis concentrates (in liquid and dry powder form) dialysis kits and other related products for treatment of end-stage renal disease (chronic kidney failure). Its lead Triferic drug is the only FDA-approved iron product for dialysate delivery for the treatment of anemia in the hemodialysis patient population. The company markets and distributes its products directly to hemodialysis providers across the US as well as through independent distributors abroad. To expand its product range Rockwell Medical is also developing new renal drug therapies.

	Annual Growth	12/10	12/11	12/12	12/13	12/14
Sales ($ mil.)	(2.3%)	59.6	49.0	49.8	52.4	54.2
Net income ($ mil.)	–	(2.7)	(21.4)	(54.0)	(48.8)	(21.3)
Market value ($ mil.)	6.8%	397.2	425.9	404.8	525.0	516.9
Employees	(1.4%)	300	240	287	286	283

ROCKWOOD HOLDINGS INC

NYS: ROC

100 Overlook Center
Princeton, NJ 08540
Phone: 609 514-0300
Fax: –
Web: www.rockwoodspecialties.com

CEO: Seifi Ghasemi
CFO: Robert J Zatta
HR: –
FYE: December 31
Type: Public

Rockwood Holdings which operates as Rockwood Specialties manages a portfolio of world-class specialty chemicals and advanced materials businesses. Its specialty chemicals operations (which the company restructured in 2012) include lithium compounds metal treatments and performance additives such as wood preservation chemicals and iron oxide pigments. Other products include titanium dioxide advanced ceramics an performance additives. A leader in most of its niches Rockwood serves the construction paper and water treatment industries. Sales to Germany outpace those to any other region including the US.

	Annual Growth	12/08	12/09	12/10	12/11	12/12
Sales ($ mil.)	0.9%	3,380.1	2,962.9	3,191.6	3,669.3	3,506.9
Net income ($ mil.)	–	(588.4)	21.1	239.4	411.3	383.5
Market value ($ mil.)	46.3%	847.4	1,848.7	3,069.6	3,089.2	3,880.9
Employees	0.0%	10,200	9,500	9,600	9,700	10,200

ROCKY BRANDS INC

NMS: RCKY

39 E. Canal Street
Nelsonville, OH 45764
Phone: 740 753-1951
Fax: 740 753-4024
Web: www.rockybrands.com

CEO: –
CFO: James E McDonald
HR: Mark Dean
FYE: December 31
Type: Public

Rocky is a sole survivor. Rocky Brands makes and sells men's and women's footwear and apparel. Its footwear brands include Rocky Georgia Boot Creative Recreation Durango Lehigh and licensed brand Michelin. The company targets six markets: outdoor duty work military lifestyle and western. (Its Rocky brand is sold to the US military.) A wholesaler and retailer the company's products are sold in the US and Canada through more than 10000 retail stores such as sporting goods and outdoor stores (Bass Pro Shops Cabela's) mass merchandisers and farm store chains. It also sells Lehigh-brand footwear online and through mobile and outlet stores. Brothers William and F. M. Brooks founded Rocky in 1932.

	Annual Growth	12/10	12/11	12/12	12/13	12/14
Sales ($ mil.)	3.2%	252.8	239.6	228.3	244.9	286.2
Net income ($ mil.)	6.4%	7.7	8.3	8.9	7.4	9.8
Market value ($ mil.)	7.6%	75.7	68.1	98.4	110.0	101.3
Employees	2.6%	2,450	2,225	2,225	2,546	2,714

ROCKY MOUNTAIN CHOCOLATE FACTORY INC (DE)

NMS: RMCF

265 Turner Drive
Durango, CO 81303
Phone: 970 259-0554
Fax: –
Web: www.rmcf.com

CEO: Franklin E Crail
CFO: Bryan J Merryman
HR: –
FYE: February 28
Type: Public

Rocky Mountain Chocolate Factory knows that tourists often leave their diets at home. That's why many of its candy stores are intentionally placed in factory outlet malls regional malls and tourist areas. The company and its franchisees operate about 300 chocolate stores and another 55 co-branded stores in in 40 US states Canada Japan and the United Arab Emirates. Its majority-owned subsidiary U-Swirl operates more than 65 self-serve frozen yogurt stores. The chocolate maker's products are also wholesaled and sold through fundraising programs and a company website. Most of the retailer's sales come from its 300 factory-made premium chocolates and confections; the remainder comes from franchise fees.

	Annual Growth	02/11	02/12	02/13	02/14	02/15
Sales ($ mil.)	7.5%	31.1	34.6	36.3	39.2	41.5
Net income ($ mil.)	0.2%	3.9	3.9	1.5	4.4	3.9
Market value ($ mil.)	10.4%	61.9	56.5	73.8	71.4	91.8
Employees	3.6%	260	300	200	350	300

RODALE INC.

400 S. 10th St.	CEO: –
Emmaus PA 18098	CFO: –
Phone: 610-967-5171	HR: –
Fax: 610-967-8963	FYE: December 31
Web: www.rodaleinc.com	Type: Private

Rodale helps readers keep their gardens green and their bodies lean. Its portfolio of seven magazines focusing on health and wellness includes "Men's Health" Organic Gardening (published since 1942) and Runner's World. Its book unit publishes titles on subjects such as cooking health and nature that it markets through retail and direct marketing channels. The company has a database of more than 26 million customers. Rodale also has an international book publishing division based in London and its Rodale Magazines International division distributes more than 80 editions of its titles in some 50 countries. In addition Rodale operates about 40 websites. J.I. Rodale founded the family-owned company in 1930.

ROEHL TRANSPORT INC.

1916 E. 29th St.	CEO: Richard Roehl
Marshfield WI 54449	CFO: –
Phone: 715-591-3795	HR: –
Fax: 800-626-8752	FYE: December 31
Web: www.roehl.net	Type: Private

The Roehl in Roehl Transport is pronounced "rail" but Roehl rolls down roads not train tracks. Roehl Transport hauls a variety of freight with a fleet of some 1800 trucks and 4900 trailers. Its equipment includes flatbeds standard dry vans dry bulk carriers and trailers designed to carry extra-heavy loads. Roehl also offers refrigerated transportation and logistics services. The company operates throughout the continental US and Canada; however it does most of its business east of the Rocky Mountains particularly in midwestern states. Everett Roehl founded Roehl Transport in 1962 with a single truck.

ROFIN SINAR TECHNOLOGIES INC.

NMS: RSTI

40984 Concept Drive	CEO: Gunther Braun
Plymouth, MI 48170	CFO: Ingrid Mittelstaedt
Phone: 734-455-5400	HR: –
Fax: –	FYE: September 30
Web: www.rofin.com	Type: Public

Any way you slice it ROFIN-SINAR Technologies is one of the world's leading makers of industrial lasers. The company designs manufactures and markets lasers primarily used for cutting welding and marking a wide range of materials. Its macro (cutting and welding) line is targeted at the machine tool and automotive markets while its laser marking and micro (fine cutting and welding) product lines are principally geared toward the semiconductor electronics and photovoltaic markets. ROFIN sells directly to OEMs systems integrators and industrial end users that integrate its lasers into their own systems. Europe (mainly Germany) is its largest market followed by Asia and North America.

	Annual Growth	09/11	09/12	09/13	09/14	09/15
Sales ($ mil.)	(3.4%)	597.8	540.1	560.1	530.1	519.6
Net income ($ mil.)	(8.9%)	60.0	34.5	34.8	25.2	41.3
Market value ($ mil.)	7.8%	541.1	556.0	682.3	649.9	730.8
Employees	1.4%	2,108	2,213	2,265	2,270	2,231

ROGER CLEVELAND GOLF COMPANY INC.

5601 Skylab Rd.	CEO: Greg Hopkins
Huntington Beach CA 92647	CFO: William Bird
Phone: 714-889-1300	HR: –
Fax: 714-889-5890	FYE: March 31
Web: clevelandgolf.com	Type: Private

Roger Cleveland Golf Company is in the swing of things. A maker of woods irons and putters it sells its golf clubs as well as apparel and accessories online and through pro shops and sporting goods stores in about 25 countries. The company also offers custom club fitting at golf courses and retailers across the US. Roger Cleveland who got his start making replicas of classic golf clubs from the 1940s and 1950s established his namesake firm in 1979. Today the company designs and forges its clubs from sturdy lightweight materials such as steel graphite and titanium. It is owned by Japan's SRI Sports a unit of Sumitomo Rubber Industries.

ROGERS CORP.

NYS: ROG

P.O. Box 188, One Technology Drive	CEO: Bruce D. Hoechner
Rogers, CT 06263-0188	CFO: Janice E. Stipp
Phone: 860 774-9605	HR: –
Fax: –	FYE: December 31
Web: www.rogerscorp.com	Type: Public

Rogers lives in a material world and it is a materials company. The company's specialty materials are used in a variety of electronic and consumer products. Its products include printed circuit board laminates and polyester-based industrial laminates which are used in wireless communications systems including hand-held devices GPS and direct broadcast TV. Rogers' high-performance foams include urethane and silicone foams used for making vehicle gaskets and seals communication devices computers and footwear insoles. It also makes high-performance elastomer components sold to OEMs in various markets including ground transportation office equipment and consumer industries.

	Annual Growth	12/10	12/11	12/12	12/13	12/14
Sales ($ mil.)	12.7%	379.2	553.2	498.8	537.5	610.9
Net income ($ mil.)	11.2%	34.6	37.1	68.7	37.8	52.9
Market value ($ mil.)	20.8%	703.9	678.3	913.9	1,131.8	1,498.7
Employees	9.6%	1,940	2,600	2,400	2,500	2,800

ROGUE WAVE SOFTWARE INC.

5500 Flatiron Pkwy. Ste 200	CEO: Bryan Pierce
Boulder CO 80301	CFO: Kevin Naughton
Phone: 303-473-9118	HR: Deanna Bonnell
Fax: 303-473-9137	FYE: December 31
Web: www.roguewave.com	Type: Private

Need to quickly develop software to simulate a tsunami striking Sheboygan Wisconsin? Rogue Wave Software can help. The company provides application development software for building client/server and Web-based applications in a variety of programming languages. Programmers can cut development time by using Rogue's software which provides "objects" or building blocks of pre-written code. Quovadx acquired Rogue Wave in late 2003 for about $71 million; in 2007 Qvovadx was purchased by Battery Ventures which has operated Quovadx and Rogue Wave as independent companies.

ROLLINS COLLEGE

1000 HOLT AVE 2715
WINTER PARK, FL 327894409
Phone: 407-646-2000
Fax: –
Web: www.rollins.edu

CEO: –
CFO: –
HR: –
FYE: May 31
Type: Private

Students get rolling at Rollins College. The school is a liberal arts college with an enrollment of some 3200 undergraduate students seeking associate bachelor and master's degrees. Rollins' core arts and sciences and professional studies programs offer about 30 majors. In addition its Crummer Graduate School of Business offers an MBA program and its Hamilton Holt School provides undergraduate and graduate evening degree and outreach programs in 10 major fields. The college has 200 faculty members and a student-to-teacher ratio of 10:1. Rollins was founded in 1885 by New England Congregationalists and is the oldest college in Florida. It is named for Chicago businessman and philanthropist Alonzo Rollins.

	Annual Growth	05/10	05/11	05/12	05/13	05/14
Sales ($ mil.)	7.3%	–	99.5	105.1	154.5	123.0
Net income ($ mil.)	–	–	–	(27.3)	2.2	17.6
Market value ($ mil.)	–	–	–	–	–	–
Employees	–	–	–	–	–	645

ROLLINS, INC.

NYS: ROL

2170 Piedmont Road, N.E.
Atlanta, GA 30324
Phone: 404 888-2000
Fax: –
Web: www.rollins.com

CEO: Gary W Rollins
CFO: Eddie Northen
HR: –
FYE: December 31
Type: Public

If Rollins Inc. has anything to do with it you'll sleep tight and the bed bugs won't bite. Rollins' subsidiaries led by famous bug killer Orkin serve more than 2 million customers mainly in the Americas but also in Asia and in the Middle East. The founding family-controlled company provides residential and commercial pest control and termite control services. With more than 500 company-owned and franchised locations operating under various brands Rollins offers inspections baits traps and crack and crevice treatments. Other major brands include and HomeTeam Pest Defense and IFC (serving the food market).

	Annual Growth	12/10	12/11	12/12	12/13	12/14
Sales ($ mil.)	5.6%	1,136.9	1,205.1	1,270.9	1,337.4	1,411.6
Net income ($ mil.)	11.2%	90.0	100.7	111.3	123.3	137.7
Market value ($ mil.)	13.8%	4,311.1	4,850.2	4,811.0	6,611.8	7,225.2
Employees	1.4%	10,330	10,100	10,470	10,650	10,936

ROMACORP INC.

9304 Forest Ln. Ste. 200
Dallas TX 75243
Phone: 214-343-7800
Fax: 214-343-2680
Web: www.tonyromas.com

CEO: Stephen K Judge
CFO: –
HR: –
FYE: March 31
Type: Private

You might say this restaurant company wants to put a little meat on your ribs. Romacorp operates and franchises about 200 Tony Roma's casual dining locations in more than 15 states and more than 30 other countries. The restaurants are popular for their baby back ribs and other beef and barbeque entrees. The eateries also serve chicken and seafood dishes as well as burgers sandwiches and salads and a hearty menu of appetizers. Most of Romacorp's restaurants are located outside the US; about 20 locations are company-owned. The late Tony Roma opened his first barbecue restaurant in North Miami in 1972.

RONCO ACQUISITION CORPORATION

110 Wall St. 21st Fl. Ste. C
New York NY 10005
Phone: 646-378-4044
Fax: 646-378-4090
Web: www.ronco.com

CEO: Larry Nusbaum
CFO: –
HR: –
FYE: June 30
Type: Private

Operators are standing by so have your credit card ready. Ronco's former head huckster (and inventor) Ron Popeil is by his 1995 autobiographical account "The Salesman of the Century". Ronco uses TV infomercials (and the Internet) to sell food dehydrators rotisseries cutlery flavor injectors inside-the-shell egg scramblers pasta makers and GLH (great looking hair) a hair-in-a-can remedy for baldness. The company went public in mid-2005 through a $50-million reverse merger with Fi-Tek. Popeil divested his interest that year. Ronco filed for Chapter 11 bankruptcy protection in mid-2007. By August it emerged from bankruptcy headed by industry veteran Larry Nusbaum and Marlin Equity Partners.

RONILE INC.

701 ORCHARD AVE
ROCKY MOUNT, VA 241511848
Phone: 540-483-0261
Fax: –
Web: www.ronile.com

CEO: Phillip C Essig
CFO: –
HR: –
FYE: June 30
Type: Private

Ronile can spin a yarn — a textile one that is. The company manufactures custom-dyed accent yarns including twisted space-dyed air-ply and heatset yarns. Ronile's slew of finished yarn goods include nylon polyester acrylic and other wool fibers which are marketed to carpet rug home furnishings craft and automotive markets. Ronile also operates through subsidiary Bacova Guild Ltd. a manufacturer and supplier of printed accent rugs room-size rugs and bath ensembles to US retail chains and Gulistan a division supplying broadloom carpet. Employee-owned the company is led by its founder's son Phillip Essig.

	Annual Growth	07/03	07/04	07/05	07/06*	06/07
Sales ($ mil.)	(37.6%)	–	–	597.2	245.5	232.4
Net income ($ mil.)	–	–	–	0.0	0.0	0.0
Market value ($ mil.)	–	–	–	–	–	–
Employees	–	–	–	–	–	1,383

*Fiscal year change

ROOFING WHOLESALE CO. INC.

1918 W GRANT ST
PHOENIX, AZ 850095991
Phone: 602-258-3794
Fax: –
Web: www.rwc.org

CEO: –
CFO: Stephen K Rold
HR: Mike Nelson
FYE: December 31
Type: Private

Business at Roofing Wholesale doesn't have to be complicated but it should be over your head. Roofing Wholesale Company (RWC) distributes residential and commercial roofing stone flooring and stucco to contractors builders and do-it-yourself home owners through ten locations in Arizona California Nevada and New Mexico. It also operates an online store. Products include asphalt shingles cedar shakes and shingles clay tiles fasteners marble floors and slate roofs. John Lisherness father of current president Harley Lisherness founded the family-owned company in 1958.

	Annual Growth	12/09	12/10	12/11	12/12	12/13
Sales ($ mil.)	3.9%	–	95.2	128.1	105.6	106.9
Net income ($ mil.)	(36.6%)	–	–	11.9	7.4	4.8
Market value ($ mil.)	–	–	–	–	–	–
Employees	–	–	–	–	–	225

ROOMLINX INC
NBB: RMLX

433 Hackensack Avenue 6th Floor, Continental Place
Hackensack, NJ 07601
Phone: 201 968-9797
Fax: –
Web: www.roomlinx.com

CEO: Aaron Dobrinsky
CFO: Steven Vella
HR: –
FYE: December 31
Type: Public

Roomlinx believes high-speed networking should be a standard hotel amenity. The company provides wireless and wired Internet installation and support services primarily to customers in the hospitality industry. Roomlinx's services are used to provide access in hotel rooms convention centers corporate apartments and for special events. The company has serviced more than 140 hotels equipping more than 24000 rooms. The company is also moving into the in-room entertainment market offering a system that includes a flat-panel display and a media console for distributing movies advertising and other content.

	Annual Growth	12/10	12/11	12/12	12/13	12/14
Sales ($ mil.)	13.2%	4.5	6.2	13.6	9.4	7.4
Net income ($ mil.)	–	(1.3)	(2.7)	(7.4)	(4.1)	(2.7)
Market value ($ mil.)	(60.8%)	38.1	36.8	26.0	1.4	0.9
Employees	6.8%	33	51	59	39	43

ROOMS TO GO

11540 Hwy. 92 East
Seffner FL 33584
Phone: 813-623-5400
Fax: 813-620-1717
Web: www.roomstogo.com

CEO: Jeffrey Seaman
CFO: Lewis Stein
HR: –
FYE: December 31
Type: Private

Need that sofa recliner table and lamp in a hurry? Rooms To Go — with more than 150 stores in 10 southern states and Puerto Rico — has transformed itself into one of the top-selling furniture retailers in the US by taking the package approach to retailing. Rooms To Go (RTG) markets its limited selection of furniture to brand-conscious time-pressed customers. It packages low- to moderately-priced furniture and accessories and offers discounts for those willing to buy a roomful. The chain also operates the Rooms to Go Kids chain that sells furniture for kids and teens from more than 45 stores. CEO and owner Jeffrey Seaman and his father Morty founded RTG in 1990 after selling Seaman Furniture Company.

ROOT LEARNING INC.

5470 Main St.
Sylvania OH 43560
Phone: 419-874-0077
Fax: 419-874-4801
Web: www.rootinc.com

CEO: Jim Haudan
CFO: –
HR: –
FYE: December 31
Type: Private

Root Learning wants to ensure your employees aren't just learning by rote. The company provides teaching tools facilitator training and consultative services including leadership alignment and strategy clarification for businesses. Services help clients create training content implement learning programs and measure results. Root also offers software for learning visualization game-based education and knowledge management as well as off-the-shelf courseware that addresses subjects such as workplace diversity emotional literacy branding and business process mapping. Major clients have included Delta and Pepsi. The company was founded in 1993 by former president Randall Root.

ROOT9B TECHNOLOGIES INC
NBB: RTNB

4521 Sharon Road, Suite 300
Charlotte, NC 28211
Phone: 704 521-8077
Fax: –
Web: www.premieralliance.com

CEO: Joseph J Grano Jr
CFO: Ken Smith
HR: –
FYE: December 31
Type: Public

First and foremost Premier Alliance Group looks to be a business and technology ally to its customers. Premier Alliance provides technology consulting and professional services to organizations in the education financial health care utility and other sectors. Core consulting services include systems implementation and architecture information management business intelligence and analysis. It also offers expertise in key professional areas such as risk management compliance and finance. Founded in 1995 Premier Alliance has counted Duke Energy Bank of America and a handful of other large companies as among its key customers. In 2012 it acquired environmental consulting firm GreenHouse Holdings.

	Annual Growth	12/10	12/11	12/12	12/13	12/14
Sales ($ mil.)	4.2%	17.1	17.9	19.5	26.4	20.2
Net income ($ mil.)	–	0.1	0.2	(9.5)	(6.1)	(24.4)
Market value ($ mil.)	12.7%	46.7	26.8	37.0	28.2	75.4
Employees	12.0%	–	153	160	151	215

ROPER TECHNOLOGIES INC
NYS: ROP

6901 Professional Parkway East, Suite 200
Sarasota, FL 34240
Phone: 941 556-2601
Fax: –
Web: www.roperind.com

CEO: Brian D. Jellison
CFO: John Humphrey
HR: –
FYE: December 31
Type: Public

Roper Technologies (formerly Roper Industries) is an industrial manufacturer with products that control pump scan authorize and analyze. Its business segments include medical and scientific imaging (digital imaging products and software) energy systems and controls (controls and sensors testing/inspection equipment) industrial technology (pumps leak testing flow measurement) and RF technology (toll/traffic systems card systems and software). Roper's lines are used in niche markets engaged in RF (radio frequency) water energy research and medical education transportation and security applications. The company aims for end-markets seeking value-added engineered products.

	Annual Growth	12/10	12/11	12/12	12/13	12/14
Sales ($ mil.)	10.4%	2,386.1	2,797.1	2,993.5	3,238.1	3,549.5
Net income ($ mil.)	19.0%	322.6	427.2	483.4	538.3	646.0
Market value ($ mil.)	19.6%	7,652.6	8,697.9	11,162.0	13,885.5	15,654.7
Employees	5.9%	8,050	8,570	9,475	9,913	10,137

ROPES & GRAY LLP

Prudential Tower 800 Boylston St.
Boston MA 02199-3600
Phone: 617-951-7000
Fax: 617-951-7050
Web: www.ropesgray.com

CEO: –
CFO: –
HR: –
FYE: December 31
Type: Private - Partnershi

Ropes & Gray answers the questions "What was the preferred means of dispensing justice in the 19th century?" and "What color suits were the trial lawyers wearing?" Actually Ropes & Gray one of Boston's largest law firms is named after Harvard Law School graduates John Ropes and John Gray who founded it in 1865. The firm which has more than 1000 attorneys at more than 10 offices is a leader in areas such as leveraged buyouts trusts and estates and health care. Other practices include creditors' rights labor and employment litigation and tax.

ROSE ACRE FARMS INC.

Rural Rte. 5
Seymour IN 47274
Phone: 812-497-2557
Fax: 812-497-3311
Web: www.roseacre.com

CEO: –
CFO: Greg Marshall
HR: –
FYE: July 31
Type: Private

Pity the poor rooster; Rose Acre Farms relies instead on millions of hens to produce its profits. Among the largest egg suppliers in the US the business farms and sells fresh chicken eggs under the Rose Acre Farm and Eggland's Best brand. It offers eggs from pen-kept hens and free-roaming cage-free hens both of which peck on a natural hormone-free feed made in the farm's own feed mill. Rose Acre also makes dried egg products such as egg white protein used in animal feed and nutritional supplements for athletes. The company's operations are supported by a fleet of refrigerated Rose Acre semi-trailers that deliver the eggs to retailers or distributors. The founding Rust family owns and operates the farm.

ROSE INTERNATIONAL INC.

16401 SWINGLEY RIDGE RD
CHESTERFIELD, MO 630170757
Phone: 636-532-3126
Fax: –
Web: www.roseint.com

CEO: Himanshu Bhatia
CFO: –
HR: A Haydar
FYE: December 31
Type: Private

Rose International keep its customers' tech gardens in bloom. The company provides outsourced IT services including database performance optimization application development and project management to businesses and government agencies in the US. Other services include vendor management payroll processing training and staffing and call center operations. Rose — its name is an acronym for "reliable open systems engineering" — serves customers in the financial services energy technology telecommunications and health care industries. Its software development activities in Missouri and India are overseen by subsidiary Rose I.T. Solutions.

	Annual Growth	12/08	12/09	12/10	12/11	12/12
Sales ($ mil.)	30.5%	–	161.1	228.7	357.4	358.0
Net income ($ mil.)	12.9%	–	–	9.1	13.6	11.6
Market value ($ mil.)	–	–	–	–	–	–
Employees	–	–	–	–	–	6,000

ROSE PAVING CO.

7300 W 100TH PL
BRIDGEVIEW, IL 604552414
Phone: 708-430-1100
Fax: –
Web: www.rosepaving.com

CEO: Alan Rose
CFO: Jim Muckerheide
HR: –
FYE: December 31
Type: Private

A rose by this name smells of hot tar and asphalt. Rose Paving a pavement maintenance contractor provides site evaluation installation management and maintenance of asphalt and concrete parking lots throughout the US. Its activities include pavement removal resurfacing repair and installation lot marking seal coating crack sealing storm sewer repair and installation and installation and repair of concrete curbs walks and pads. The company tailors its services for specific regional situations and circumstances. Clients include commercial and industrial customers in the retail real estate hospitality health care industries as well as homeowner associations schools and religious institutions.

	Annual Growth	12/03	12/04	12/05	12/07	12/08
Sales ($ mil.)	–	–	0.0	25.0	18.3	30.4
Net income ($ mil.)	–	–	–	0.0	0.2	1.5
Market value ($ mil.)	–	–	–	–	–	–
Employees	–	–	–	–	–	120

ROSE ROCK MIDSTREAM L P

NYS: RRMS

Two Warren Place, 6120 South Yale Avenue, Suite 700
Tulsa, OK 74136-4216
Phone: 918 524-7700
Fax: –
Web: www.rrmidstream.com

CEO: Carlin G Conner
CFO: –
HR: –
FYE: December 31
Type: Public

A rose by any other name would smell as sweet or so says Rose Rock Midstream the new name for SemCrude L.P. Rose Rock Midstream was established in 2011 to take over the assets of SemCrude the storage and pipeline division of SemGroup. Rose Rock Midstream's new assets include SemCrude's crude oil storage terminal in Cushing Oklahoma; its gathering and transportation system in Kansas and Oklahoma; its Bakken Shale operations and its Platteville Colorado crude oil unloading facility. The only midstream operation Rose Rock won't handle is the White Cliffs Pipeline which will continue to be 51%-owned by SemCrude Pipeline L.L.C. In 2014 Rose Rock Midstream acquired trucking assets from a unit of Chesapeake Energy.

	Annual Growth	12/10	12/11	12/12	12/13	12/14
Sales ($ mil.)	57.8%	208.1	431.3	620.4	766.5	1,290.6
Net income ($ mil.)	23.6%	23.5	23.2	24.0	36.7	54.8
Market value ($ mil.)	30.2%	–	673.4	1,029.7	1,266.3	1,487.1
Employees	65.1%	–	80	80	230	360

ROSE"S SOUTHWEST PAPERS INC.

1701 2ND ST SW
ALBUQUERQUE, NM 871024505
Phone: 505-842-0134
Fax: –
Web: www.rosessouthwest.com

CEO: Roberto E Espat
CFO: –
HR: –
FYE: December 31
Type: Private

Roses Southwest Papers has bloomed in the desert Southwest by manufacturing napkins tissue paper and paper bags used in fast food restaurants and other places of business. The company's tissue products include bathroom tissue center pull towels facial tissue fold towels kitchen roll towels jumbo roll tissue and roll towels. Roses Southwest Papers also provides custom converting and private labeling services. The company counts McDonald's and Burger King among its major clients. Roses Southwest Papers is owned and operated by CEO Roberto Espat and other members of the Espat family.

	Annual Growth	12/03	12/04	12/05	12/06	12/07
Sales ($ mil.)	12.0%	–	66.9	76.7	79.9	94.0
Net income ($ mil.)	40.1%	–	–	1.2	1.2	2.3
Market value ($ mil.)	–	–	–	–	–	–
Employees	–	–	–	–	–	225

ROSEN HOTELS AND RESORTS INC.

8990 INTL DR STE 200
ORLANDO, FL 328199321
Phone: 407-996-1706
Fax: –
Web: www.rosenhotels.com

CEO: –
CFO: Frank A. Santos
HR: –
FYE: January 31
Type: Private

Want to make your Florida stay a little rosy? Rosen Hotels & Resorts owns and operates seven hotels in Orlando collectively totaling more than 6300 rooms and suites. Its properties are located near major area attractions such as Disney World (from Walt Disney Parks) and Universal Studios Orlando (from Universal Parks & Resorts). Its portfolio consists of hotels such as the Rosen Plaza Hotel and Rosen Inn. Three of its hotels are home to major Orlando convention centers: Rosen Plaza Rosen Centre and Rosen Shingle Creek. In addition subsidiary Millennium Technology Group manages computer systems for its hotels. The family-owned Rosen Hotels & Resorts was founded by president Harris Rosen in 1974.

	Annual Growth	01/10	01/11	01/12	01/13	01/14
Sales ($ mil.)	216.0%	–	8.5	8.5	268.8	268.8
Net income ($ mil.)	–	–	–	0.0	76.6	76.6
Market value ($ mil.)	–	–	–	–	–	–
Employees	–	–	–	–	–	3,420

ROSEN'S DIVERSIFIED INC.

1120 Lake Ave.	CEO: Thomas J Rosen
Fairmont MN 56031	CFO: Robert A Hovde
Phone: 507-238-6001	HR: Rita Willett
Fax: 507-238-6086	FYE: September 30
Web: rosensdiversifiedinc.com	Type: Private

Rosen's Diversified (RDI) has the goods to make the grass greener for its cash cows. The agricultural holding company's subsidiaries cover agricultural chemicals pet food and treats (Performance Pet) beef processing trucking and marketing (Light Inc.). The slaughtering operations of American Foods Group consist of nine meatpacking plants with the capacity to handle 4 million pounds of beef a day. America's Service Line delivers the meat to restaurants and food manufacturers in the US; RDI also ships to nearly 40 countries worldwide. Rosen's Inc. distributes agricultural chemicals and fertilizer. RDI was founded in 1946 by brothers Elmer and Ludwig Rosen and is still controlled by the Rosen family.

ROSENDIN ELECTRIC INC.

880 Mabury Rd.	CEO: Tom Sorley
San Jose CA 95133	CFO: Lorne Rundquist
Phone: 408-286-2800	HR: –
Fax: 559-591-6462	FYE: December 31
Web: www.elmonterey.com	Type: Private

Things are looking rosy for Rosendin Electric. The company has risen to the top ranks of US electrical contractors since it was founded in 1919 by Moses Rosendin. The employee-owned firm provides a range of services including estimating and engineering/design and installation of communications networks; traffic signals; gas water and electrical utility lines; and airport lighting. It also designs and constructs wind energy and solar power plants including grids and collection systems. Rosendin Electric has officers in California and five other mostly western states. Rosendin Electric does business in Texas through its wholly-owned subsidiary KST Electric.

ROSETTA MARKETING GROUP LLC

100 American Metro Blvd.	CEO: Eric Healy
Hamilton NJ 08619	CFO: Richard Demilt
Phone: 609-689-6100	HR: –
Fax: 410-540-7556	FYE: December 31
Web: www.allegisgroup.com	Type: Subsidiary

This group wants to be the proverbial Rosetta Stone for all your online marketing needs. Rosetta Marketing Group provides personality-based marketing services (analyzing the different brand choices consumers make across a wide spectrum of marketing channels) and offers digital marketing telemarketing sales training media planning and buying services. Founded in 1998 it targets a wide array of industries such as financial services health care telecommunications media and retail among others. Clients have included such big names as AstraZeneca Bank of America Procter & Gamble and Pfizer. In mid-2011 Rosetta was acquired by France-based media conglomerate Publicis Groupe.

ROSETTA RESOURCES, INC.

NMS: ROSE

1111 Bagby Street, Suite 1600	CEO: –
Houston, TX 77002	CFO: –
Phone: 713 335-4000	HR: –
Fax: –	FYE: December 31
Web: www.rosettaresources.com	Type: Public

Rosetta Resources is hoping that its hard work translates into oil and natural gas discoveries. The company which was built onCalpine Corporation's former domestic oil and natural gas exploration assets primarily focuses on developing acreage and production and Texas. In 2012 the company reported estimated proved reserves of 201 million barrels of which 37% was proved developed. Calpine (which spun off its US oil and gas business in 2005) accounted for 12% of Rosetta Resources' revenues in 2012. The company's management is largely made up of former Calpine employees.

	Annual Growth	12/09	12/10	12/11	12/12	12/13
Sales ($ mil.)	29.0%	294.0	308.4	446.2	613.5	814.0
Net income ($ mil.)	–	(219.2)	19.0	100.5	159.3	199.4
Market value ($ mil.)	24.6%	1,221.2	2,307.6	2,666.9	2,778.5	2,945.2
Employees	5.6%	203	168	165	183	252

ROSETTA STONE, INC.

NYS: RST

1919 North Lynn St., 7th Fl.	CEO: A John Hass
Arlington, VA 22209	CFO: Thomas M Pierno
Phone: 703 387-5800	HR: –
Fax: –	FYE: December 31
Web: www.rosettastone.com	Type: Public

Rosetta Stone holds itself out as the key to common language — at least to understanding another language. The provides language-learning software via digital download online subscriptions and CD-ROM. It's Rosetta Stone Language Library combines images text and audio without the traditional translation or grammar explanations to mimic the way children learn their native languages. With consumer and institutional customers in more than 150 countries Rosetta Stone offers software for about 30 languages. Its products are available through direct sales channels and at selected retailers such as Amazon.com Barnes & Noble and Staples.

	Annual Growth	12/10	12/11	12/12	12/13	12/14
Sales ($ mil.)	0.3%	258.9	268.4	273.2	264.6	261.9
Net income ($ mil.)	–	13.3	(20.0)	(35.8)	(16.1)	(73.7)
Market value ($ mil.)	(17.6%)	465.5	167.4	270.7	268.1	214.1
Employees	(9.3%)	1,910	1,888	1,550	1,313	1,292

ROSS STORES, INC.

NMS: ROST

5130 Hacienda Drive	CEO: Barbara Rentler
Dublin, CA 94568-7579	CFO: Michael J Hartshorn
Phone: 925 965-4400	HR: Ken Caruana
Fax: –	FYE: January 31
Web: www.rossstores.com	Type: Public

Ross wants to let you dress (and lots more) for less. A leading off-price apparel retailer (behind TJX Cos. and Kohl's) Ross operates more than 1300 Ross Dress for Less and dd's DISCOUNTS stores that sell closeout merchandise including men's women's and children's clothing at prices well below those of department and specialty stores. While apparel accounts for more than half of sales it also sells small furnishings toys and games luggage and jewelry. Featuring the Ross "Dress for Less" trademark the chain targets 18- to 54-year-old white-collar shoppers from primarily middle-income households. Ross and dd's stores are located in strip malls in more than 30 states mostly in the western US and Guam.

	Annual Growth	01/11	01/12*	02/13	02/14*	01/15
Sales ($ mil.)	8.8%	7,866.1	8,608.3	9,721.1	10,230.4	11,041.7
Net income ($ mil.)	13.6%	554.8	657.2	786.8	837.3	924.7
Market value ($ mil.)	8.8%	27,162.0	21,199.3	24,659.9	28,178.6	38,054.1
Employees	9.6%	49,500	53,900	57,500	66,300	71,400

*Fiscal year change

ROSS-SIMONS OF WARWICK INC.

9 Ross-Simons Dr.
Cranston RI 02920
Phone: 401-463-3100
Fax: 401-463-8599
Web: www.ross-simons.com

CEO: Darrell Ross
CFO: Robert Pulciani
HR: –
FYE: January 31
Type: Private

Look no further than Ross-Simons of Warwick for the perfect wedding gift. Bringing a little taste of luxury to the masses the multi-channel retailer sells jewelry (estate jewelry diamond pieces) tableware (fine china sterling silver flatware) collectibles (Lladro figurines Swarovski crystal) and home decor at discounted prices. It also markets supermodel Christie Brinkley's signature jewelry collection. Ross-Simons mails at least 20 million catalogs annually and operates about 15 retail and outlet stores in seven East Coast states. The company also sells jewelry through QVC. Ross-Simons opened its first retail store in 1952 added catalog sales in the early '80s and has a thriving Internet business.

ROTARY INTERNATIONAL

1560 SHERMAN AVE STE LL1
EVANSTON, IL 602013698
Phone: 847-866-3000
Fax: –
Web: www.rotary.org

CEO: John Hewko
CFO: Lori O. Carlson
HR: –
FYE: June 30
Type: Private

The rotary phone may be a thing of the past but Rotary International (founded in 1905 and now with more than 1.2 million members) is still going strong. The service organization with a motto of Service Above Self comprises 34000-plus clubs in more than 200 countries and territories. Rotary service projects are intended to alleviate problems such as hunger illiteracy poverty and violence. Grants from the Rotary Foundation support its efforts. Along with its service projects Rotary aims to promote high ethical standards in the workplace. Membership in Rotary clubs is by invitation. Each club strives to include representatives from major businesses professions and institutions in its community.

	Annual Growth	06/09	06/10	06/11	06/12	06/13
Sales ($ mil.)	688.0%	–	0.2	433.5	90.6	93.0
Net income ($ mil.)	–	–	–	168.4	(1.0)	(5.7)
Market value ($ mil.)	–	–	–	–	–	–
Employees	–	–	–	–	–	800

ROTH CAPITAL PARTNERS LLC

24 Corporate Plaza
Newport Beach CA 92660
Phone: 949-720-5700
Fax: 949-720-7215
Web: www.rothcp.com

CEO: Byron Roth
CFO: –
HR: –
FYE: June 30
Type: Private

ROTH Capital Partners is an investment banking firm with a focus on small-cap companies. The employee-owned company offers its clients a full spectrum of investment banking services including capital raising research coverage trading and market making merger and acquisition advisory services and investor conferences. Activities include IPO underwriting and strategic advice. ROTH which operates in the US and China has investment banking teams devoted to the business services energy industrial consumer financial services gaming health care media technology and consumer sectors.

ROTH PRODUCE CO.

3882 AGLER RD
COLUMBUS, OH 432193607
Phone: 614-337-2825
Fax: –

CEO: Benson I Roth
CFO: –
HR: –
FYE: December 31
Type: Private

|Roth Produce provides fresh produce herbs exotic vegetables dairy products and frozen breads to foodservice customers in the greater Columbus Ohio area. The company distributes to caterers country clubs hotels and other fine dining establishments as well as to local eateries pizza parlors and schools. Roth Produce's gift basket division Bensoni's Baskets makes custom gift baskets and fruit baskets.

	Annual Growth	09/07	09/08	09/09	09/10*	12/11
Sales ($ mil.)	–	–	–	0.0	17.6	20.6
Net income ($ mil.)	–	–	–	0.0	(0.0)	0.0
Market value ($ mil.)	–	–	–	–	–	–
Employees	–	–	–	–	–	45

*Fiscal year change

ROTH STAFFING COMPANIES L.P.

333 CITY BLVD W STE 100
ORANGE, CA 928682952
Phone: 714-939-8600
Fax: –
Web: www.adamsmartingroup.com

CEO: Ben Roth
CFO: –
HR: –
FYE: December 31
Type: Private

Roth Staffing Companies L.P. offers temporary and temp-to-hire staffing and permanent placement services through its specialized business lines. Ultimate Staffing Services specializes in administrative customer service clerical manufacturing & production positions. Ledgent Finance & Accounting focuses on accounting and finance professionals while Ledgent Technology & Engineering concentrates on professionals in those fields. Adams & Martin Group recruits legal professionals. The company serves clients in 21 US states and Washington DC through more than 100 branches and a number of on-premise locations.

	Annual Growth	12/09	12/10	12/11	12/12	12/13
Sales ($ mil.)	8.6%	–	202.1	244.4	244.4	258.6
Net income ($ mil.)	–	–	–	0.0	0.0	0.0
Market value ($ mil.)	–	–	–	–	–	–
Employees	–	–	–	–	–	500

ROTHSCHILD NORTH AMERICA INC.

1251 Avenue of the Americas 51st Fl.
New York NY 10020
Phone: 212-403-3500
Fax: 212-403-3501
Web: www.us.rothschild.com

CEO: –
CFO: –
HR: –
FYE: March 31
Type: Subsidiary

Rothschild North America is the US-based asset management and investment banking arm of venerable UK financial services provider N M Rothschild & Sons. Investment banking services include debt and equity advising; mergers and acquisition consulting; and restructuring consultations for businesses in the Americas. Rothschild North America's Asset Management unit offers equity and fixed-income investments to customers that include corporations endowments foundations and other institutional clients. The company has operations in Montreal New York Toronto and Washington D.C.

ROTHSTEIN KASS & COMPANY P.C.

4 Becker Farm Rd.
Roseland NJ 07068
Phone: 973-994-6666
Fax: 973-994-0337
Web: www.rkco.com

CEO: –
CFO: –
HR: –
FYE: December 31
Type: Private - Partnershi

Rothstein Kass firm provides publicly traded and private businesses and individuals with accounting auditing staffing and computer consulting services. Target industries include sports and entertainment transportation alternative energy and manufacturing. The firm also provides retirement planning and lifestyle management for families as well as accounting services for entrepreneurs. Through its affiliated operations Rothstein Kass offers business consulting and coaching executive search services family wealth planning and risk management.

ROUND TABLE PIZZA INC.

1320 Willow Pass Rd. Ste. 600
Concord CA 94520
Phone: 925-969-3900
Fax: 925-969-3978
Web: www.roundtablepizza.com

CEO: Robert McCourt
CFO: Keith Davis
HR: Janet Olsen
FYE: December 31
Type: Private

If King Arthur's knights had sat at this Round Table they would have been eating pizza. Round Table Pizza operates a chain of about 450 family-oriented pizza parlors located primarily in the western US. The pizzerias are known for the colorful names given to menu items including Guinevere's Garden Delight and Montague's All Meat Marvel. Round Table also serves sandwiches salads and appetizers. The eateries offer dine-in seating along with carry-out and delivery services. William Larson opened the first Round Table Pizza in 1959 and began franchising the restaurant concept three years later. The company filed for Chapter 11 bankruptcy protection in 2011 before emerging late that same year.

ROUNDY'S INC.

NYSE: RNDY

875 E. Wisconsin Ave.
Milwaukee WI 53202
Phone: 414-231-5000
Fax: 414-231-7939
Web: www.roundys.com

CEO: –
CFO: –
HR: –
FYE: December 31
Type: Public

If you live in Wisconsin you can probably find one of these grocery stores right 'round the corner. Roundy's owns and operates about 160 grocery stores in Milwaukee the Twin Cities area of Minnesota and now greater Chicago under five banners: Pick 'n Save Copps Food Centers Rainbow Foods Metro Market and its newest format Mariano's Fresh Market (launched in 2010). About 100 of the supermarkets have in-store pharmacies. Once a major food distributor to independent grocery stores in the Midwest Roundy's shed its wholesale operations to concentrate on its growing retail businesses. Founded in Milwaukee in 1872 Roundy's went public in 2012 in a offering worth $163 million.

ROUSE PROPERTIES, INC.

NYS: RSE

1114 Avenue of the Americas, Suite 2800
New York, NY 10036
Phone: 212 608-5108
Fax: –
Web: www.rouseproperties.com

CEO: Andrew P. Silberfein
CFO: John Wain
HR: Bobbie Lyons
FYE: December 31
Type: Public

Rouse Properties wants to keep the shopping mall a part of life in small town America. The real estate investment trust (REIT) owns and manages about 35 regional malls in more than 20 states across the country. Rouse Properties' malls are located in secondary and tertiary markets where they are often the only mall in the area. With more than 23 million sq. ft. of space the company's malls house big retail names such as American Eagle Footlocker Old Navy Target and Victoria's Secret as well as sit-down restaurants (Buffalo Wild Wings Red Robin) and food court standbys (Panda Express and Starbucks). Rouse Properties was spun off from General Growth Properties in 2012.

	Annual Growth	12/10	12/11	12/12	12/13	12/14
Sales ($ mil.)	69.3%	35.5	234.8	234.0	243.5	292.1
Net income ($ mil.)	–	(2.9)	(27.0)	(68.7)	(54.7)	(51.8)
Market value ($ mil.)	4.6%	–	–	977.0	1,281.3	1,069.4
Employees	13.7%	–	225	284	269	331

ROVI CORP.

NMS: ROVI

2830 De La Cruz Boulevard
Santa Clara, CA 95050
Phone: 408 562-8400
Fax: –
Web: www.rovicorp.com

CEO: Thomas (Tom) Carson
CFO: Peter C. Halt
HR: Dustin K. Finer
FYE: December 31
Type: Public

Rovi wants to help roving media junkies find their fix. The company develops and licenses technology to enable and enhance video content discovery distribution and advertising. Products include interactive programming guides media recognition technology and e-commerce platforms. Clients include consumer electronics (CE) makers (Dell Samsung Panasonic) and service providers (Cox Sky plc Verizon) which together account for nearly 90% of sales; others include online retailers and portals (Best Buy Ticketmaster Sony's PlayStation) and content providers (Universal Studios Disney PBS). Geographically sales are about evenly split between US and international customers.

	Annual Growth	12/10	12/11	12/12	12/13	12/14
Sales ($ mil.)	0.0%	541.5	690.8	650.6	538.1	542.3
Net income ($ mil.)	–	212.9	(41.3)	(34.3)	(172.1)	(69.7)
Market value ($ mil.)	(22.3%)	5,688.1	2,254.7	1,415.4	1,806.1	2,072.2
Employees	0.0%	1,200	2,024	1,500	1,220	1,200

ROWAN COMPANIES INC.

NYSE: RDC

2800 Post Oak Blvd. Ste. 5450
Houston TX 77056-6189
Phone: 713-621-7800
Fax: 713-960-7660
Web: www.rowancompanies.com

CEO: –
CFO: William Well
HR: –
FYE: December 31
Type: Public

Where does a gorilla drill for oil? Anywhere it wants if it is one of Rowan Companies' Gorilla-class heavy-duty offshore drilling rigs. Rowan performs contract drilling of oil and gas wells. Its fleet consists of more than 30 jack-up rigs. The company performs contract drilling primarily in the US (which accounts for more than one-quarter of revenues) as well as the Middle East Mexico and the North Sea. Rowan seeks to maintain its competitive edge by beefing up its current fleet of drilling rigs. It has rigs with a drilling capacity of 35000 feet in water of 550 feet depth although the new ultra-deepwater rigs will drill down to 40000 feet in water depths of 12000 feet.

ROWE FINE FURNITURE INC.

8484 Westpark Dr. Ste. 710	CEO: Stefanie J Lucas
McLean VA 22102	CFO: Mark Freitas
Phone: 703-847-8670	HR: –
Fax: 703-847-8686	FYE: November 30
Web: www.rowefurniture.com	Type: Private

Rowe Rowe Rowe yourself toward a house full of furniture. Rowe Fine Furniture makes upholstered sofas love seats and chairs in traditional contemporary and transitional styles under the Rowe Robin Bruce and Clayton Marcus brands. The company operates manufacturing centers in Virginia and a showroom in the furniture Mecca of High Point North Carolina. Its offerings are sold through major and independent home furnishings retailers across the US and overseas in such countries as Ireland the Netherlands and Taiwan. The company was founded in 1946 by Ronald Rowe Sr. Ralph E. Bentz and Donald Jordan under the name Rowe-Jordan Furniture. An affiliate of Sun Capital Partners owns Rowe.

ROWLAND COFFEE ROASTERS INC.

5605 NW 82nd Ave.	CEO: Jose Enrique Souto
Miami FL 33166	CFO: –
Phone: 305-594-9062	HR: –
Fax: 305-594-7603	FYE: April 30
Web: www.rowlandcoffee.com	Type: Subsidiary

There's a rich aroma coming from Florida home of Rowland Coffee Roasters. One of North America's largest producers of coffee products the company is known for espresso. Rowland roasts some 80% of all espresso sold in the US and owns the top two Hispanic brands: Cafe Bustelo and Pilon. The company also markets European and Cabana blends (such as Cafe Estrella El Pico and Medaglia D'Oro) specialty mixes and canned coffee drinks. In addition to wholesale operations the company sells coffee online through its Java Cabana website. Established in Cuba in 1865 the previously family-run company is part of the Folgers and Kava coffee brand empire owned by J. M. Smucker which acquired the business in 2011.

ROYAL APPLIANCE MFG. CO.

7005 Cochran Rd.	CEO: –
Glenwillow OH 44139	CFO: Matthew Shene
Phone: 440-996-2000	HR: –
Fax: 440-996-2027	FYE: December 31
Web: www.royalvacuums.com	Type: Subsidiary

Royal Appliance wants you to make a deal with the Devil. The company makes the popular Dirt Devil canister hand stick and upright vacuums. It also markets flooring shampooers accessories and replacement parts under the Dirt Devil name and manufactures vacuum cleaners under the brands Regina and Royal (which offers both household and commercial products). Royal Appliance's floor care products are sold through mass merchandisers (such as Kmart and Wal-Mart) and independent dealers. In addition the company's Privacy Technologies subsidiary makes TeleZapper a phone attachment that blocks telemarketing calls. Royal Appliance itself is a subsidiary of Hong Kong-based power tool maker Techtronic Industries.

ROYAL BANCSHARES OF PENNSYLVANIA, INC   NMS: RBPA A

One Bala Plaza, Suite 522, 231 St. Asaph's Road, Bala	CEO: F Kevin Tylus
Cynwyd, PA 19004	CFO: Michael S Thompson
Phone: 610 668-4700	HR: –
Fax: –	FYE: December 31
Web: www.royalbankamerica.com	Type: Public

Frederick the Great never did business with this bank even though it serves a town named after him. Royal Bancshares of Pennsylvania is the holding company of Royal Bank America which operates about 15 branches in southeastern Pennsylvania (including Philadelphia and its King of Prussia suburb) and another in New Jersey. It offers products such as checking and savings accounts CDs loans and credit cards. Royal Bancshares has other units devoted to equipment leasing (Royal Leasing) commercial finance (Royal Investments America) and lender financing (RAB Capital).

	Annual Growth	12/10	12/11	12/12	12/13	12/14
Assets ($ mil.)	(7.0%)	980.6	848.4	773.7	732.3	732.6
Net income ($ mil.)	–	(24.1)	(8.6)	(15.6)	2.1	5.1
Market value ($ mil.)	3.6%	41.6	37.2	35.7	41.0	47.9
Employees	(6.8%)	155	152	152	115	117

ROYAL CARIBBEAN CRUISES LTD.   NYSE: RCL

1050 Caribbean Way	CEO: Richard D. Fain
Miami FL 33132-2096	CFO: Jason Liberty
Phone: 305-539-6000	HR: –
Fax: 801-265-9882	FYE: December 31
Web: www.securitynational.com	Type: Public

Royal Caribbean Cruises takes to the waves and drops anchor to see the sights. The world's second-largest cruise line (behind the combined Carnival Corporation and Carnival plc behemoth) the company operates about 40 ships with about 95850 berths overall. Its three main cruise brands — Royal Caribbean International Celebrity Cruises and Pullmantur Cruises — carry about 4 million passengers a year to about 420 ports including ones in Alaska Asia Australia Canada the Caribbean Europe and Latin America. Its other brands include Azamara Club Cruises and CDF Croisieres de France. In addition Royal Caribbean operates land-based tours and expeditions through Royal Celebrity Tours.

ROYAL GOLD, INC.   NMS: RGLD

1660 Wynkoop Street, Suite 1000	CEO: Tony Jensen
Denver, CO 80202	CFO: Stefan L. Wenger
Phone: 303 573-1660	HR: David Odell
Fax: –	FYE: June 30
Web: www.royalgold.com	Type: Public

Royal Gold deals only with royalty. Rather than operating gold mines the company buys the right to collect royalties from mine operators. This strategy allows Royal Gold to minimize its exposure to the costs of mineral exploration and development. The company also owns interests in exploration- and development-stage projects. Its operations in Chile accounted for 29% of the company's 2013 revenues; operations in Canada 24%. Royal Gold holds royalty stakes in other producing properties elsewhere in the Americas as well as in Africa and Australia.

	Annual Growth	06/11	06/12	06/13	06/14	06/15
Sales ($ mil.)	6.5%	216.5	263.1	289.2	237.2	278.0
Net income ($ mil.)	(9.1%)	77.3	98.3	73.4	63.5	52.7
Market value ($ mil.)	1.3%	3,809.0	5,098.6	2,736.6	4,951.0	4,005.4
Employees	(1.2%)	21	19	21	20	20

ROYAL HAWAIIAN ORCHARDS LP

NBB: NNUT U

688 Kinoole Street, Suite 121
Hilo, HI 96720
Phone: 808 747-8471
Fax: –
Web: www.royalhawaiianorchards.com

CEO: Scott C Wallace
CFO: –
HR: –
FYE: December 31
Type: Public

Business is nuts (and that's a good thing) at ML Macadamia Orchards. As the world's largest macadamia nut grower the company owns or leases some 4200 acres of macadamia orchards located on the southeastern portion of the island of Hawaii where it produces a yearly average of 21 million pounds of nuts. ML Macadamia is strictly a nut grower; it sells its crop to Hawaiian nut processors including the Mauna Loa Macadamia Nut Corporation MacFarms of Hawaii and others under various contract agreements. The company decided to become vertically integrated in 2008 and is looking to acquire processing operations in order to insulate itself from low commodity prices.

	Annual Growth	12/10	12/11	12/12	12/13	12/14
Sales ($ mil.)	1.2%	15.3	18.0	20.1	13.9	16.0
Net income ($ mil.)	–	(1.5)	0.7	(0.5)	(3.7)	(6.2)
Market value ($ mil.)	4.1%	28.9	28.5	40.0	27.9	33.9
Employees	(0.1%)	270	290	284	279	269

ROYALE ENERGY, INC.

NBB: ROYL

3777 Willow Glen Drive
El Cajon, CA 92019
Phone: 619 383-6600
Fax: –
Web: www.royl.com

CEO: Jonathan Gregory
CFO: Stephen M Hosmer
HR: –
FYE: December 31
Type: Public

The geological basins of Northern California are getting the Royale treatment. Using modern computer-aided exploration technologies Royale Energy concentrates its exploration and production efforts in the Sacramento and San Joaquin basins. The company pursues a strategy of acquiring stakes in oil and gas reserves via private joint ventures. It also owns leasehold interests in Louisana Texas and Utah. Royale Energy has estimated proved reserves of 4 billion cu. ft. of natural gas equivalent. CEO Donald Hosmer CFO Stephen Hosmer and their father and company chairman Harry Hosmer together own approximately 36% of Royale Energy.

	Annual Growth	12/10	12/11	12/12	12/13	12/14
Sales ($ mil.)	(27.4%)	11.6	11.7	4.4	2.6	3.2
Net income ($ mil.)	–	1.3	(4.1)	(12.0)	1.1	(2.2)
Market value ($ mil.)	(1.5%)	33.5	68.5	38.6	38.7	31.5
Employees	(2.4%)	22	23	20	19	20

RPC, INC.

NYS: RES

2801 Buford Highway, Suite 520
Atlanta, GA 30329
Phone: 404 321-2140
Fax: –
Web: www.rpc.net

CEO: Richard A. Hubbell
CFO: Ben M. Palmer
HR: –
FYE: December 31
Type: Public

RPC helps to grease the wheels of oil and gas production through a number of business units. Through its Cudd Energy Services division the company provides oil industry consulting and technical services including snubbing coiled tubing nitrogen services and well control. Another unit Patterson Services rents specialized tools and equipment such as drill pipe tubing and blowout preventers. RPC also provides maintenance emergency services and storage and inspection services for offshore and inland vessels. The company operates in most of the world's major oil producing regions.

	Annual Growth	12/10	12/11	12/12	12/13	12/14
Sales ($ mil.)	20.8%	1,096.4	1,809.8	1,945.0	1,861.5	2,337.4
Net income ($ mil.)	13.7%	146.7	296.4	274.4	166.9	245.2
Market value ($ mil.)	(7.9%)	3,923.7	3,951.8	2,650.4	3,865.2	2,823.7
Employees	15.8%	2,500	3,400	3,600	3,900	4,500

RPM INTERNATIONAL INC (DE)

NYS: RPM

P.O. Box 777, 2628 Pearl Road
Medina, OH 44258
Phone: 330 273-5090
Fax: 330 225-8743
Web: www.rpminc.com

CEO: Frank C. Sullivan
CFO: Russell L. Gordon
HR: –
FYE: May 31
Type: Public

If you've ever done any sort of home improvement there's a good chance you've used RPM International's products. Maker of home repair favorites like Rust-Oleum Zinsser and DAP RPM is divided into two units: industrial and consumer products. Industrial offerings (which account for almost two-thirds of total sales) include products for waterproofing corrosion resistance floor maintenance and wall finishing. RPM's consumer do-it-yourself items include caulks and sealants rust preventatives and general-purpose paints repair products personal care items and hobby paints.

	Annual Growth	05/11	05/12	05/13	05/14	05/15
Sales ($ mil.)	8.0%	3,381.8	3,777.4	4,078.7	4,376.4	4,594.6
Net income ($ mil.)	6.1%	189.1	215.9	98.6	291.7	239.5
Market value ($ mil.)	20.8%	3,130.3	3,511.2	4,413.0	5,737.1	6,664.1
Employees	9.3%	9,025	9,713	10,553	10,848	12,864

RPX CORP

NMS: RPXC

One Market Plaza, Suite 800
San Francisco, CA 94105
Phone: 866 779-7641
Fax: –
Web: www.rpxcorp.com

CEO: John A. Amster
CFO: Robert Heath
HR: –
FYE: December 31
Type: Public

In our litigious society RPX Corporation helps keep technology companies out of the courtroom. RPX owns a portfolio of more than 1500 intellectual property patents that it licenses to customers in order to prevent patent infringement lawsuits. (So one company can't sue another over a patent since it's RPX that owns the patent). Its patent portfolio spans six industries — consumer electronics software media content mobile communications and devices networking and semiconductors. RPX counts more than 70 customers including Cisco Google Nokia Sharp Sony and Verizon and earns one-third of its revenues from Asian firms. Founded in 2008 RPX launched an IPO in 2011.

	Annual Growth	12/10	12/11	12/12	12/13	12/14
Sales ($ mil.)	28.6%	94.9	154.0	197.7	237.5	259.3
Net income ($ mil.)	29.8%	13.9	29.1	39.0	40.8	39.3
Market value ($ mil.)	2.9%	–	683.9	488.7	913.6	745.0
Employees	18.9%	76	110	125	137	152

RSA SECURITY LLC

NMS: RPXC

174 Middlesex Tpke.
Bedford MA 01730
Phone: 781-515-5000
Fax: 781-515-5010
Web: www.rsasecurity.com

CEO: Joseph M Tucci
CFO: –
HR: –
FYE: December 31
Type: Subsidiary

RSA Security wants everyone to show ID. The company provides software and hardware used to protect monitor and manage access to computer networks and enterprise software. A subsidiary of data storage systems maker EMC it offers Web access and digital certificate management software as well as development tools for creating encryption tools. The company's growing services segment offers data security consulting systems design and integration maintenance and training. RSA sells directly and through resellers distributors and manufacturers. Customers come from a variety of industries including telecommunications health care and financial services.

RSM MCGLADREY INC.

3600 American Blvd. West 3rd Fl.
Bloomington MN 55431
Phone: 952-921-7700
Fax: 952-921-7702
Web: www.rsmmcgladrey.com

CEO: Joseph Adams
CFO: Doug Opheim
HR: –
FYE: April 30
Type: Subsidiary

RSM McGladrey will gladly service your business if you happen to be a mid-sized company. The firm created in 1999 when H&R Block acquired it from McGladrey & Pullen has some 90 offices in about 25 states. The RSM McGladrey group of companies offer such services as tax consulting investment banking retirement planning wealth management and international business services to clients in industries including construction health care and manufacturing. In December 2011 RSM McGladrey was reunited with McGladrey & Pullen when its former parent bought back RSM McGladrey to reorganize itself into a more robust partnership structure capable of offering a wide array of consulting services.

RTI INTERNATIONAL METALS, INC.

NYS: RTI

Westpointe Corporate Center One, 5th Floor, 1550 Coraopolis Heights Road
Pittsburgh, PA 15108-2973
Phone: 412 893-0026
Fax: 330 544-7876
Web: www.rtiintl.com

CEO: Klaus Kleinfield
CFO: Glenn Miller
HR: –
FYE: December 31
Type: Public

RTI International Metals has titanium on the cranium. Through its Titanium Group the company produces ingots bars plates sheets strips pipes wire and welded tubing used primarily by the aerospace industry to make bulkheads tail sections engine components and wing supports. Fabrication and Distribution groups operate through subsidiary RTI Energy Systems making pipe and tubing for offshore oil and gas exploration and production as well as geothermal energy production. RTI caters to commercial aerospace and defense industries which represent almost 80% of sales and a growing number of industrial and consumer customers.

	Annual Growth	12/09	12/10	12/11	12/12	12/13
Sales ($ mil.)	17.7%	408.0	431.8	529.7	738.6	783.3
Net income ($ mil.)	–	(67.2)	3.4	6.6	23.5	14.1
Market value ($ mil.)	8.0%	770.0	825.4	710.1	843.2	1,046.6
Employees	13.3%	1,478	1,534	1,729	2,362	2,437

RTI SURGICAL, INC.

NAS: RTIX

11621 Research Circle
Alachua, FL 32615
Phone: 386 418-8888
Fax: –
Web: www.rtix.com

CEO: Brian K. Hutchison
CFO: Robert P. (Rob) Jordheim
HR: –
FYE: December 31
Type: Public

When it comes to surgical implants RTI Surgical (formerly RTI Biologics) recommends the natural alternative. The firm develops products made from human and animal tissue that are used in orthopedic dental and other surgeries to repair fractures spinal disorders sports injuries breast reconstruction and other procedures. Using its BioCleanse Cancelle SP and Tutoplast processes the company sterilizes tissue — including bone tendons and skin — that is then used in surgeries. RTI Surgical sells its allografts (made from human tissue) and xenografts (made from animals) in the US and more than 50 countries around the globe. Its direct sales force targets the sports medicine and general orthopedic markets.

	Annual Growth	12/10	12/11	12/12	12/13	12/14
Sales ($ mil.)	12.1%	166.2	169.3	178.1	198.0	262.8
Net income ($ mil.)	–	(129.4)	8.4	8.4	(17.8)	2.7
Market value ($ mil.)	18.1%	151.5	251.9	242.3	200.8	295.0
Employees	11.6%	711	706	756	1,100	1,102

RTW INC.

8500 Normandale Lake Blvd. Ste. 1400
Bloomington MN 55437
Phone: 952-893-0403
Fax: 952-893-3700
Web: www.rtwi.com

CEO: Jeffrey B Murphy
CFO: Alfred L Latendresse
HR: –
FYE: December 31
Type: Subsidiary

RTW helps employees to Return To Work with its disability and absence management services. Its subsidiaries American Compensation Insurance Company (ACIC) and Bloomington Compensation Insurance Company (BCIC) sell workers' compensation coverage while its Absentia division is a third-party administrator to self-insured employers. It services help cut the cost of workers' compensation claims through pre-hire screening accident prevention programs and a proprietary system to identify and manage potentially high-cost injuries. The firm targets small employers that have had high workers' comp losses; clients include businesses in manufacturing retail health care and hospitality. Rockhill Holdings owns RTW.

RUAN TRANSPORTATION MANAGEMENT SYSTEMS INC.

3200 Ruan Center 666 Grand Ave.
Des Moines IA 50309
Phone: 515-245-2688
Fax: 515-245-2684
Web: www.ruan.com

CEO: John Ruan III
CFO: Tracey Ball
HR: –
FYE: December 31
Type: Private

When it comes to trucking sometimes you have to walk before you can Ruan. Ruan (pronounced RUE-on) Transportation Management Systems provides a variety of trucking-related services including dedicated contract carriage transportation of liquid and dry bulk cargo and logistics such as warehouse management and freight brokerage. For dedicated contract carriage customers Ruan assigns drivers and equipment to an account long-term. In total the company operates a fleet of 3380 tractors 25 trucks and 5600 trailers across 160-plus locations. John Ruan father of chairman John Ruan III founded what is now Ruan Transportation Management Systems in 1932 with a used Ford Model AA truck and a load of gravel.

RUBICON TECHNOLOGY INC

NMS: RBCN

900 East Green Street
Bensenville, IL 60106
Phone: 847 295-7000
Fax: –
Web: www.rubicon-es2.com

CEO: William F Weissman
CFO: Mardel A Graffy
HR: –
FYE: December 31
Type: Public

Sapphires are the jewel in Rubicon Technology's crown. Using proprietary crystal growth technology Rubicon makes sapphire materials wafers and components for a variety of products. In the field of optoelectronics the vertically integrated company makes sapphire components for light-emitting diodes (LEDs) used in cell phones video screens and other items. Rubicon's sapphire materials also are used for compound semiconductor manufacturing and laser imaging. In the telecom sector the company's silicon materials are in demand for the silicon-on-sapphire (SOS) components of cellular and fiber-optics products. The majority of its sales are to customers in Asia.

	Annual Growth	12/10	12/11	12/12	12/13	12/14
Sales ($ mil.)	(12.3%)	77.4	134.0	67.2	41.5	45.7
Net income ($ mil.)	–	29.1	38.1	(5.5)	(30.4)	(44.0)
Market value ($ mil.)	(31.8%)	551.0	245.4	159.7	260.1	119.5
Employees	3.1%	250	376	322	292	283

RUBY TUESDAY, INC.   NYS: RT

150 West Church Avenue   CEO: James J. (J. J.) Buettgen
Maryville, TN 37801   CFO: Jill M. Golder
Phone: 865 379-5700   HR: Lois Collins
Fax: –   FYE: June 02
Web: www.rubytuesday.com   Type: Public

The patrons of this restaurant chain are hopefully well fed when it's time to say good bye. Ruby Tuesday (RTI) which takes its name from the song by the Rolling Stones operates a chain of casual-dining restaurants. There are about 665 company-owned Ruby Tuesday locations in the US. The company also has about 20 franchised locations in the US and roughly 50 franchised international outposts. The full-service eateries offer a menu of American and ethnic foods including burgers fajitas pasta ribs seafood steak and a variety of appetizers.

	Annual Growth	05/11*	06/12	06/13	06/14	06/15
Sales ($ mil.)	(2.9%)	1,265.2	1,325.8	1,251.5	1,168.7	1,126.6
Net income ($ mil.)	–	46.9	(0.2)	(39.4)	(64.3)	(3.2)
Market value ($ mil.)	(12.7%)	658.2	422.3	589.9	477.5	382.5
Employees	(5.6%)	40,500	36,300	34,100	33,000	32,100
						*Fiscal year change

RUCKUS WIRELESS INC   NYS: RKUS

350 West Java Drive   CEO: Selina Y. Lo
Sunnyvale, CA 94089   CFO: Seamus Hennessy
Phone: 650 265-4200   HR: Kathleen Swift
Fax: –   FYE: December 31
Web: www.ruckuswireless.com   Type: Public

When a crowd of Internet users generates a ruckus of signals Ruckus Wireless aims to smooth the commotion and get everyone connected. Ruckus makes network gateways controllers and access points used to provide and manage large-scale Wi-Fi access in office buildings hospitals stadiums and the Internet of Things. Its Smart-branded products help Internet and telecom providers extend range and reliability and offer scalability for rapidly growing companies. Ruckus sells worldwide through a network of more than 5300 resellers and distributors to about 48000 customers in a variety of industries. Its customers have included Bright House Networks Time Warner Cable Sky plc and KDDI. The company formed in 2002 as Sceos Technologies and went public in late 2012.

	Annual Growth	12/10	12/11	12/12	12/13	12/14
Sales ($ mil.)	44.3%	75.5	120.0	214.7	263.1	326.9
Net income ($ mil.)	–	(4.4)	4.2	31.7	1.8	8.2
Market value ($ mil.)	(27.0%)	–	–	1,917.5	1,208.6	1,023.0
Employees	15.8%	–	606	669	824	940

RUDOLPH AND SLETTEN INC.

1600 Seaport Blvd. Ste. 350   CEO: Martin B Sisemore
Redwood City CA 94063-5575   CFO: Norma Swinger
Phone: 650-216-3600   HR: –
Fax: 650-599-9030   FYE: June 30
Web: www.rsconstruction.com   Type: Subsidiary

Rudolph and Sletten ... the little-known tenth reindeer? More like the elves who built Santa's workshop. The firm is a mainstay of the California construction scene especially Silicon Valley. It has built corporate campuses for Apple Microsoft and AAA as well as Lucasfilm's Skywalker Ranch production facility. Rudolph and Sletten is one of the US' largest general building contractors with site selection design/build and construction management capabilities. Key projects also include biotech labs hospitals and schools. Onslow "Rudy" Rudolph founded the company in 1959 and was joined by partner Kenneth Sletten in 1962. Rudolph and Sletten is a subsidiary of Tutor Perini Corporation.

RUDOLPH FOODS COMPANY INC.

6575 Bellefontaine Rd.   CEO: James Rudolph
Lima OH 45804   CFO: –
Phone: 419-648-3611   HR: –
Fax: 419-648-4087   FYE: December 31
Web: www.rudolphfoods.com   Type: Private

Whatever you want to call them — pork rinds pork skins cracklins chicharrones bacon rinds — this company has got your fix. Rudolph Foods is the world's largest producer of pork rinds and related snacks producing more than 100 million pounds per year from plants in the US (Ohio Georgia Texas and California) and Brazil. The company sells the pork treats under such brands as Rudolph's Pepe's Rudy's Lee's Pig Skins Smithfield Farms Southern Recipe and Grandpa John's. John and Mary Rudolph started the business in 1955 as a peanut roaster. After selling the business to Beatrice Foods in 1966 the Rudolph family re-acquired control of the company in 1987.

RUDOLPH TECHNOLOGIES, INC.   NYS: RTEC

One Rudolph Road, P.O. Box 1000   CEO: Michael P. Plisinski
Flanders, NJ 07836   CFO: Steven R. Roth
Phone: 973 691-1300   HR: –
Fax: 973 691-4863   FYE: December 31
Web: www.rudolphtech.com   Type: Public

Rudolph Technologies' inspection and metrology systems lead the way to better yields for chip makers. To create semiconductors manufacturers deposit precise layers of conducting and insulating materials on silicon wafers. Rudolph's process control metrology equipment monitors these layers to ensure that the material doesn't get too thick or too thin. Its inspection equipment (around half of sales) looks for defects not obvious to the human eye such as tiny scratches or gouges in the surface of a silicon wafer. The company also makes a range of data analysis and process control software. Rudolph gets about two-thirds of sales from customers outside the US.

	Annual Growth	12/10	12/11	12/12	12/13	12/14
Sales ($ mil.)	(1.9%)	195.3	187.2	218.5	176.2	181.2
Net income ($ mil.)	–	27.0	25.2	43.9	3.5	(4.6)
Market value ($ mil.)	5.6%	264.1	297.2	431.3	376.8	328.3
Employees	1.6%	550	564	651	615	586

RUMSEY ELECTRIC COMPANY

15 COLWELL LN   CEO: Gerald M. (Jerry) Lihota
CONSHOHOCKEN, PA 194281878   CFO: Scott M. Cutler
Phone: 610-832-9000   HR: –
Fax: –   FYE: December 31
Web: www.rumsey.com   Type: Private

This company delivers the juice and it's not O.J. Rumsey Electric distributes electrical construction equipment utility products and services and systems for relay and power and lighting for retailers. Operating through one central distribution facility and a dozen branches the company caters to construction and industrial businesses and utilities as well as OEMs institutions and commercial Mid-Atlantic markets. It is the authorized distributor of Rockwell Automation a large industrial automation firm. Employee-owned Rumsey Electric has been in business for over 110 years.

	Annual Growth	12/09	12/10	12/11	12/12	12/13
Sales ($ mil.)	6.4%	–	187.4	196.3	197.5	225.9
Net income ($ mil.)	112.9%	–	–	2.0	10.7	9.2
Market value ($ mil.)	–	–	–	–	–	–
Employees	–	–	–	–	–	284

RUSH ENTERPRISES INC.

NMS: RUSH A

555 I.H. 35 South, Suite 500
New Braunfels, TX 78130
Phone: 830 626-5200
Fax: –
Web: www.rushenterprises.com

CEO: –
CFO: Steven L. (Steve) Keller
HR: Kimberly Suarez
FYE: December 31
Type: Public

Rush Enterprises has been truckin' along as a heavy-duty commercial vehicle dealer since 1965. The company operates a growing network of more than 100 commercial vehicle and service dealerships under the name Rush Truck Centers in some 20 states. It is one of the largest Peterbilt truck dealers in the US but it also sells trucks manufactured by Blue Bird Ford Isuzu Hino Mitsubishi Fuso and UD. Additionally Rush offers aftermarket parts and services such as body shop repairs insurance and third-party financing and rentals and leasing. Founded in 1965 Rush's reach has spread as far as California and Florida. Retired chairman W. Marvin Rush and his family control the rapidly growing company.

	Annual Growth	12/10	12/11	12/12	12/13	12/14
Sales ($ mil.)	33.3%	1,497.9	2,580.6	3,090.6	3,384.7	4,727.4
Net income ($ mil.)	26.4%	31.3	55.2	62.5	49.2	80.0
Market value ($ mil.)	11.9%	815.3	834.5	824.5	1,182.7	1,278.4
Employees	20.3%	3,010	3,865	4,372	5,295	6,297

RUSH-COPLEY MEDICAL CENTER INC.

2000 OGDEN AVE
AURORA, IL 605045893
Phone: 630-978-6200
Fax: –
Web: www.rushcopley.com

CEO: –
CFO: Brenda Van Wyhe
HR: –
FYE: June 30
Type: Private

People in a rush to get healthy can find help at Rush-Copley Medical Center. A member of the Rush System for Health family the medical center serves Illinois' Fox Valley area. The hospital has about 210 beds and provides acute and tertiary medical services including cardiac care cancer treatment neurology women's services neonatal care and health education programs. Its Rush-Copley Surgery Center performs both day surgeries and inpatient procedures while its nearby Rush-Copley Healthcare Center houses doctors' offices and offers outpatient diagnostic imaging services. Other programs include a neuroscience center a home health care agency and its Healthplex fitness center.

	Annual Growth	06/09	06/10	06/11	06/12	06/13
Sales ($ mil.)	–	–	0.0	0.0	296.8	319.9
Net income ($ mil.)	–	–	–	0.0	17.7	41.3
Market value ($ mil.)	–	–	–	–	–	–
Employees	–	–	–	–	–	2,000

RUSS DARROW GROUP INC.

W133 N8569 Executive Pkwy.
Menomonee Falls WI 53051
Phone: 262-250-9600
Fax: 262-253-7530
Web: www.russdarrow.com

CEO: Russell M Darrow Jr
CFO: Phillip Harrington
HR: –
FYE: December 31
Type: Private

Russ Darrow Group packs Packer fans into new and used cars. The company's 15 dealerships in Wisconsin sell new cars minivans sport utility vehicles and trucks made by Chrysler GM Honda Isuzu Kia Mazda Nissan Suzuki and Toyota. The autodealer's Chrysler-Jeep dealership in Madison has won a reprieve from the mass closings of Chrysler dealerships. (It can remain open if it reorganizes its product offerings.) The company also performs service and repair work sells spare parts and operates a leasing company. Russ Darrow Jr. was just 25 when he started his company in 1965 using a $50000 loan from his parents to purchase a Chrysler-Plymouth dealership and become the youngest car lot owner in the US.

RUSSELL INVESTMENTS

1301 2nd Ave. 18th Fl.
Seattle WA 98101
Phone: 206-505-7877
Fax: +47-66-77-65-71
Web: www.telecomputing.no

CEO: –
CFO: Francis Sean Ryan
HR: Philip Young
FYE: December 31
Type: Subsidiary

No longer Frank Russell's company (it's a subsidiary of Northwestern Mutual) Russell Investments provides investment services to institutional clients in more than 35 countries. Previously known as Frank Russell Company the firm is perhaps best known for lending its name to equity indices such as the Russell 2000 and others in the US the UK (the FTSE indices) and Japan. Founded in 1936 Russell manages more than $160 billion in assets on behalf of millions of individual investors and some 2300 institutional clients such as pension plans endowments foundations and corporations including AT&T Boeing and Caterpillar.

RUSSELL REYNOLDS ASSOCIATES INC.

200 Park Ave. Ste. 2300
New York NY 10166-0002
Phone: 212-351-2000
Fax: 212-370-0896
Web: www.russellreynolds.com

CEO: Clarke Murphy
CFO: Albert H Morris
HR: –
FYE: December 31
Type: Private

Need a top gun? Russell Reynolds Associates a leading executive search firm has filled executive positions for clients ranging from Aetna to Hewlett-Packard to the National Football League. The firm maintains several practice areas organized by job function and industry including consumer markets financial services not-for-profit and technology. Other areas include private equity health care and natural resources. Russell Reynolds Associates operates from about 40 offices mainly in the US Europe and Asia/Pacific region but also in South America. The company was founded in 1969 by its namesake.

RUSSELL SIGLER INC.

9702 W TONTO ST
TOLLESON, AZ 853539703
Phone: 623-388-5100
Fax: –
Web: www.siglers.com

CEO: –
CFO: Robert D Osborne
HR: Pat Crocker
FYE: December 31
Type: Private

Russell Sigler has built a business providing a rather cool service in a hot region. Through about 30 offices located primarily in California and Arizona (but also in Idaho Nevada New Mexico and Texas) the company provides commercial and residential air conditioning contractors with equipment parts supplies and technical support. Its brands include Carrier Bryant and Payne. Russell Sigler has distributed Carrier products for more than 60 years. As part of its business the company also operates a residential and commercial distribution joint venture with industry giant Carrier. Russell Sigler owns a 60% stake while Carrier holds 40%.

	Annual Growth	12/05	12/06	12/08	12/09	12/13
Sales ($ mil.)	(19.0%)	–	2,141.1	176.9	140.2	488.7
Net income ($ mil.)	35.3%	–	–	1.5	(0.5)	6.6
Market value ($ mil.)	–	–	–	–	–	–
Employees	–	–	–	–	–	550

RUTH'S HOSPITALITY GROUP INC

NMS: RUTH

1030 W. Canton Avenue, Suite 100
Winter Park, FL 32789
Phone: 407 333-7440
Fax: –
Web: www.rhgi.com

CEO: Michael ODonnell
CFO: Arne Haak
HR: Laura Kimbrough
FYE: December 28
Type: Public

High end and "chain restaurant" are not mutually exclusive terms for this company. Ruth's Hospitality Group is one of the largest upscale dining operators in the country with some 160 restaurants anchored by the Ruth's Chris Steak House chain. Boasting about 140 restaurants in 30 states and some international markets Ruth's Chris is the largest high-end steak house chain in terms of number of locations. Its menu features a variety of steak cuts along with lamb veal and fresh seafood. About 65 of the restaurants are company-owned and 95 are franchised. In 2014 Ruth's Hospitality agreed to sell its Mitchell's Fish Market restaurants to Landry's.

	Annual Growth	12/10	12/11	12/12	12/13	12/14
Sales ($ mil.)	(0.8%)	357.6	369.6	398.6	406.6	346.1
Net income ($ mil.)	0.8%	16.0	19.5	16.4	22.5	16.5
Market value ($ mil.)	30.3%	170.8	188.1	248.1	514.3	493.0
Employees	(6.9%)	5,768	5,658	5,669	5,571	4,342

RUTHERFORD ELECTRIC MEMBERSHIP CORPORATION

186 HUDLOW RD
FOREST CITY, NC 280432575
Phone: 704-245-1621
Fax: –
Web: www.carolinaenergies.com

CEO: –
CFO: –
HR: –
FYE: December 31
Type: Private

Through a kind of power sharing "brotherhood" Rutherford Electric Membership Corporation provides power to more than 67000 members located in 10 counties (Burke Catawba Caldwell Cleveland Gaston Lincoln McDowell Mitchell Polk and Rutherford) in the Southwestern Piedmont region of North Carolina. The cooperative (which had a membership of only 394 in 1938 but grew rapidly after WWII) owns and maintains about 7000 miles of power line. Rutherford Electric has total assets of more than $300 million. The cooperative is a member of the Touchstone Energy Cooperatives network.

	Annual Growth	12/00	12/01	12/04	12/05	12/09
Sales ($ mil.)	5.3%	–	78.3	94.3	110.6	118.4
Net income ($ mil.)	101.8%	–	–	0.3	7.0	10.4
Market value ($ mil.)	–	–	–	–	–	–
Employees	–	–	–	–	–	178

RUTLAND HOSPITAL INC.

160 ALLEN ST
RUTLAND, VT 057014595
Phone: 802-775-7111
Fax: –
Web: www.rrmc.org

CEO: –
CFO: Edward Ogorzalek
HR: Allison Wollen
FYE: September 30
Type: Private

For those seeking health care in the New England region Rutland Regional Medical Center (RRMC) just might be the destination for you. Part of Rutland Regional Health Services it runs a hospital that boasts more than 120 beds and serves patients in Vermont and eastern New York. RRMC offers about 40 medical specialties including cancer care diabetes treatment and total joint replacement. The acute-care facility also has centers dedicated to cardiac rehabilitation and women's health. To meet growing community medical needs RRMC also operates a prostate care unit and a 30-bed psychiatric unit. Along with a range of specialty care options RRMC administers primary care and emergency medical transport.

	Annual Growth	09/07	09/08	09/09	09/10	09/13
Sales ($ mil.)	(30.0%)	–	1,267.3	173.0	181.0	213.0
Net income ($ mil.)	–	–	–	(18.9)	(1.2)	8.5
Market value ($ mil.)	–	–	–	–	–	–
Employees	–	–	–	–	–	1,350

RVUE HOLDINGS INC

NBB: RVUE

17W220 22nd Street, Suite 200
Oak Brook Terrace, IL 60181
Phone: 855 261-8370
Fax: –
Web: www.rvue.com

CEO: –
CFO: –
HR: –
FYE: December 31
Type: Public

rYou ready to reach your target audience? rVue brings advertisers and consumers together. Through its flagship rVue platform the company helps agencies and advertisers plan media campaigns by delivering proprietary advertising content directly to retail outlets (where people are ready to buy) and other venues for its advertising clients. rVue partners with companies that provide digital signage networks installed across the US playing ads infotainment and other programming aimed at increasing sales. Content is tweaked based on performance reports and sales figures reported by stores.

	Annual Growth	12/10	12/11	12/12	12/13	12/14
Sales ($ mil.)	19.5%	0.6	0.6	0.6	0.7	1.3
Net income ($ mil.)	–	(2.1)	(3.6)	(3.8)	(2.1)	(0.9)
Market value ($ mil.)	(45.6%)	169.0	35.2	9.9	12.7	14.8
Employees	(18.1%)	20	14	7	9	9

RW STEARNS INC.

201 Mission St. Ste. 2030
San Francisco CA 94105
Phone: 415-593-1000
Fax: 415-593-1001
Web: www.rwstearns.com

CEO: Jay M Stearns
CFO: –
HR: –
FYE: December 31
Type: Private

RW Stearns puts the "hunt" in executive head-hunting — researching information for corporate recruiting sales leads or comparisons with competitors. Utilizing its proprietary database of more than 1 million names titles and organizational structures the company furnishes custom research reports and offers profiling services to businesses ranging from startups to the FORTUNE 1000. Over the years the company has increased its competitive intelligence services offering benchmarking strategic recruiting and mapping competitors' organizational and employment structures. RW Stearns serves all industries but has roots in the high-tech biotech and pharmaceutical sectors. The company was founded in 1984.

RYAN BUILDING GROUP INC.

2700 PATRIOT BLVD STE 430
GLENVIEW, IL 600268078
Phone: 847-995-8700
Fax: –
Web: www.williamryanhomes.com

CEO: –
CFO: John Rushin
HR: –
FYE: December 31
Type: Private

Ryan Building Group understands that there's no place like home there's no place like home there's no place like home. Doing business as William Ryan Homes the company builds and sells single-family homes townhouses and duplexes in Arizona Florida Illinois Texas and Wisconsin. Its homes have from two to five bedrooms and range in size from 1400 sq. ft. to about 3500 sq. ft. The company also offers mortgages and insurance through affiliates. CEO William Ryan (part of the building family that also spawned the Ryland Group) founded Ryan Building Group in 1992.

	Annual Growth	12/04	12/05	12/06	12/07	12/08
Sales ($ mil.)	(78.7%)	–	–	1,831.8	214.2	83.4
Net income ($ mil.)	–	–	–	0.0	(0.5)	(19.3)
Market value ($ mil.)	–	–	–	–	–	–
Employees	–	–	–	–	–	85

RYAN LLC

13155 NOEL RD STE 100
DALLAS, TX 752405050
Phone: 972-934-0022
Fax: –
Web: www.ryan.com

CEO: G. Brint Ryan
CFO: David English
HR: Adrianne Court
FYE: December 31
Type: Private

The professionals at Ryan aren't too concerned when clients notice their SALT-y language. One of the US's largest state and local tax (SALT) consulting firms Ryan provides tax advice preparation and planning for major corporations and other businesses. It also offers advice on federal and international tax issues. The firm specializes in consulting services such as audit defense dispute resolution strategic planning tax process efficiencies and tax recovery. Ryan serves customers through some 65 offices in more than 20 US states and 40 countries including Canada and Europe.

	Annual Growth	12/09	12/10	12/11	12/12	12/13
Sales ($ mil.)	21.7%	–	212.5	225.3	242.0	382.6
Net income ($ mil.)	25.5%	–	–	25.2	9.9	39.6
Market value ($ mil.)	–	–	–	–	–	–
Employees	–	–	–	–	–	1,595

RYDER SYSTEM, INC.

NYS: R

11690 N.W. 105th Street
Miami, FL 33178
Phone: 305 500-3726
Fax: –
Web: www.ryder.com

CEO: Robert E. Sanchez
CFO: Art A. Garcia
HR: Greg Greene
FYE: December 31
Type: Public

When it comes to commercial vehicles and distribution Ryder System wants to be the designated driver. The company's Fleet Management Solutions (FMS) segment acquires manages maintains and disposes of fleet vehicles for commercial customers. Similarly the Supply Chain Solutions (SCS) segment provides logistics and supply chain services from industrial start (raw material supply) to finish (product distribution). SCS also offers dedicated contract carriage service by supplying trucks drivers and management and administrative services to customers on a contract basis. Ryder's worldwide fleet of more than 207000 vehicles ranges from tractor-trailers to light-duty trucks.

	Annual Growth	12/11	12/12	12/13	12/14	12/15
Sales ($ mil.)	2.1%	6,050.5	6,257.0	6,419.3	6,638.8	6,571.9
Net income ($ mil.)	15.8%	169.8	210.0	237.8	218.6	304.8
Market value ($ mil.)	1.7%	2,842.5	2,670.8	3,946.5	4,966.6	3,039.9
Employees	4.7%	27,500	27,700	28,900	30,600	33,100

RYERSON HOLDING CORP

NYS: RYI

227 W. Monroe, 27th Floor
Chicago, IL 60606
Phone: 312 292-5000
Fax: –
Web: www.ryerson.com

CEO: Edward J. Lehner
CFO: Erich S. Schnaufer
HR: Roger W. Lindsay
FYE: December 31
Type: Public

Ryerson has a heart of steel. A distributor and processor of metals the company offers its customers more than 70000 products made of steel (carbon stainless and alloy) and aluminum brass copper and nickel alloys. It buys bulk metal products (in sheets bars and other forms) from metal producers and processes them to meet the specifications of its customers — machine shops fabricators and machinery makers. The company also offers pipes valves and fittings; metal roofing flooring and grating products; and fabrication services. Most of Ryerson's almost 100 facilities are in the US. Ryerson went public in late 2014.

	Annual Growth	12/10	12/11	12/12	12/13	12/14
Sales ($ mil.)	(1.8%)	3,895.5	4,729.8	4,024.7	3,460.3	3,622.2
Net income ($ mil.)	–	(104.0)	(8.1)	47.1	127.3	(25.7)
Market value ($ mil.)	–	–	–	–	–	318.1
Employees	(3.4%)	4,200	4,000	–	–	3,650

RYLAND GROUP, INC.

NYS: RYL

3011 Townsgate Road, Suite 200
Westlake Village, CA 91361-3027
Phone: 805 367-3800
Fax: –
Web: www.ryland.com

CEO: –
CFO: –
HR: –
FYE: December 31
Type: Public

Building the American dream is home sweet home for The Ryland Group. The homebuilder founded by James Ryan and Bob Gaw in 1967 constructs single-family detached homes as well as attached condominiums for entry-level first- and second-time move-up and retired buyers. Ryland has constructed more than 300000 homes in hundreds of communities around the US. The average price for a Ryland Home is around $260000. The company offers services that span the homeownership process. Homebuyers can select custom home finishes at a My Style Design Center. The group also provides mortgage financing title and escrow and insurance services.

	Annual Growth	12/09	12/10	12/11	12/12	12/13
Sales ($ mil.)	13.6%	1,283.6	1,063.9	890.7	1,308.5	2,140.8
Net income ($ mil.)	–	(162.5)	(85.1)	(50.8)	40.4	379.2
Market value ($ mil.)	21.8%	910.8	787.4	728.7	1,687.6	2,007.1
Employees	8.2%	1,019	991	922	1,100	1,395

RYMAN HOSPITALITY PROPERTIES INC

NYS: RHP

One Gaylord Drive
Nashville, TN 37214
Phone: 615 316-6000
Fax: –
Web: www.rymanhp.com

CEO: Colin V. Reed
CFO: Mark Fioravanti
HR: Shawn Smith
FYE: December 31
Type: Public

Ryman Hospitality Properties (formerly Gaylord Entertainment) may be hollerin' for attention in the hospitality game but it's no corporate hayseed. Its properties consist of resort hotels tethered closely to attractions that appeal to the meetings and conventions market. They include the Gaylord Opryland Resort & Convention Center in Nashville the Gaylord Palms Resort in Florida (close to Disney World) the Gaylord Texan Resort near Dallas and the Gaylord National Resort and Convention Center in the Washington DC area. Ryman's hotels are managed by hotel giant Marriott. In 2012 the company changed its name convered to a REIT and sold its hotel brand and management business to Marriott.

	Annual Growth	12/10	12/11	12/12	12/13	12/14
Sales ($ mil.)	7.8%	770.0	952.1	986.6	954.6	1,041.0
Net income ($ mil.)	–	(89.1)	10.2	(26.6)	118.4	126.5
Market value ($ mil.)	10.1%	1,834.5	1,232.2	1,963.2	2,132.6	2,692.1
Employees	(48.5%)	9,717	10,363	646	641	682

S & T BANCORP INC (INDIANA, PA)

NMS: STBA

800 Philadelphia Street
Indiana, PA 15701
Phone: 800 325-2265
Fax: –
Web: www.stbancorp.com

CEO: Todd D. Brice
CFO: Mark Kochvar
HR: –
FYE: December 31
Type: Public

S&T Bancorp is the bank holding company for S&T Bank which boasts nearly $5 billion in assets and serves customers from some 60 branch offices in western Pennsylvania. Targeting individuals and local businesses the bank offers such standard retail products as checking savings and money market accounts CDs and credit cards. Business loans including commercial mortgages make up more than 80% of the company's loan portfolio. The bank also originates residential mortgages construction loans and consumer loans. Through subsidiaries S&T Bank sells life disability and commercial property/casualty insurance provides investment management services and advises the Stewart Capital Mid Cap Fund.

	Annual Growth	12/10	12/11	12/12	12/13	12/14
Assets ($ mil.)	4.8%	4,114.3	4,120.0	4,526.7	4,533.2	4,964.7
Net income ($ mil.)	7.4%	43.5	47.3	34.2	50.5	57.9
Market value ($ mil.)	7.2%	673.1	582.5	538.4	754.1	888.2
Employees	0.2%	936	909	1,027	948	945

S&ME INC

3201 SPRING FOREST RD
RALEIGH, NC 276162821
Phone: 919-872-2660
Fax: –
Web: www.smeinc.com

CEO: –
CFO: Bruce L Altstaetter
HR: –
FYE: December 31
Type: Private

This is not your S&ME old engineering company. S&ME which services both public and private entities focuses on environmental and engineering services. The company's main areas of expertise are: geotechnical engineering; environmental engineering; natural and cultural resource preservation; occupational health and safety; constructional materials engineering and testing; and water resources and solid waste engineering. The employee-owned company which mainly serves clients in the Southeast operates from more than 26 offices in nine US states.

	Annual Growth	12/09	12/10	12/11	12/12	12/13
Sales ($ mil.)	3.2%	–	110.7	128.7	116.9	121.8
Net income ($ mil.)	7.8%	–	–	1.4	0.8	1.6
Market value ($ mil.)	–	–	–	–	–	–
Employees	–	–	–	–	–	950

S&W SEED CO.

7108 North Fresno Street, Suite 380
Fresno, CA 93720
Phone: 559 884-2535
Fax: –
Web: www.swseedco.com

NAS: SANW

CEO: Mark S Grewal
CFO: Mathew Szot
HR: –
FYE: June 30
Type: Public

S&W Seed breeds seeds of the alfalfa variety. The agricultural company contracts locally grown alfalfa seeds from farmers in California's San Joaquin Valley processes them at its production facility and sells them to agribusinesses and farmers worldwide for use in growing animal feed — particularly alfalfa hay — for dairy and beef cattle horses and other livestock. About 50% of its certified seeds are sold to customers in the Middle East and Latin America since the varieties it produces are better suited for warmer climates. S&W Seed also produces wheat on occasion and supplies PureCircle with stevia a natural no-calorie sweetener. The company went public in May 2010.

	Annual Growth	06/11	06/12	06/13	06/14	06/15
Sales ($ mil.)	117.3%	3.6	14.1	37.3	51.5	81.2
Net income ($ mil.)	–	(0.8)	0.4	(2.5)	0.4	(3.2)
Market value ($ mil.)	3.2%	58.0	71.2	112.7	87.3	65.7
Employees	33.0%	23	29	29	36	72

S. D. WARREN COMPANY

255 State St.
Boston MA 02109
Phone: 617-423-7300
Fax: +82-2-3777-3428
Web: www.lge.com

CEO: –
CFO: Annette Luchene
HR: –
FYE: September 30
Type: Subsidiary

There's nothing sticky about Sappi. Sappi Fine Paper North America (SFPNA) the dba for S.D. Warren Company produces fine paper for use in annual reports magazines and high-end advertising. SFPNA's high-end paper includes coated specialty and uncoated fine papers marketed under multiple brands including the mill-branded LOE (Lustro Offset Environmental) paper the first premium sheet to use 30% post-consumer waste content. It also produces graphic and packaging paper and bleached chemical pulp. Since 1995 SFPNA has operated as a subsidiary of South Africa-based Sappi Limited. It touts a production capacity of 1.3 million tons a year.

S.C. JOHNSON & SON INC.

1525 Howe St.
Racine WI 53403-5011
Phone: 262-260-2000
Fax: 262-260-6004
Web: www.scjohnson.com

CEO: H Fisk Johnson
CFO: –
HR: –
FYE: June 30
Type: Private

S.C. Johnson & Son has helped to make the flyswatter a thing of the past with its pest control in a can. It's one of the world's largest makers of consumer chemical products boasting big brands such as Raid OFF! Glade Mr. Muscle Pledge Drano fantastik Scrubbing Bubbles Shout Vanish Windex and Ziploc among others. S.C. Johnson founded in 1886 sells its products in more than 70 countries. The founder's great-grandson and once one of the richest men in the US Samuel Johnson died in 2004. His immediate family owns about 60% of the company; descendants of the founder's daughter own about 40%. Chairman Dr. Fisk Johnson assumed the title of CEO when president and CEO Bill Perez left for NIKE in 2004.

S.P. RICHARDS COMPANY

6300 Highlands Pkwy.
Smyrna GA 30082
Phone: 770-436-6881
Fax: 770-433-3586
Web: www.sprichards.com

CEO: Wayne Beacham
CFO: J Philip Welch
HR: –
FYE: December 31
Type: Subsidiary

S.P. Richards has plenty of parts to play as a genuine office supplier. The subsidiary of Genuine Parts is a leading distributor of office supplies and other business products including furniture computer accessories office machines (such as printers and faxes) cleaning supplies and break room necessities. It also offers products for health care providers and classrooms. S.P. Richards has more than 40 distribution centers throughout the US and Canada and delivers some 50000 products — including proprietary brands such as SPARCO Elite Image and Lorell — to almost 4000 resellers. The company generates about 15% of its parent's revenue. It was founded in 1848 by Samuel P. Richards.

SA INTERNATIONAL INC.

1490 N. 2200 West Ste. 120
Salt Lake City UT 84116
Phone: 801-478-1900
Fax: 801-401-7234
Web: www.saintl.biz

CEO: Mark Blundell
CFO: –
HR: –
FYE: December 31
Type: Private

SA International (SAi) wants the sign-making process to be easy going with no snags or difficulties. The company formerly Scanvec Amiable develops CAD software for sign-making digital printing machining and screen-printing applications. Its software translated into more than 25 languages enables users to manipulate graphics and reproduce them through a variety of output devices including engraving and woodworking machines. The company's large-format printing and graphics software includes plug-ins for programs like Adobe Photoshop and Illustrator. SAi uses a global network of resellers to move its product to more than 100000 customers in 50-plus countries. SAi has offices in Belgium Puerto Rico China and Brazil.

SAATCHI & SAATCHI NORTH AMERICA INC.

375 Hudson St.
New York NY 10014-3620
Phone: 212-463-2000
Fax: 212-463-9855
Web: www.saatchi.com

CEO: Kevin Roberts
CFO: –
HR: –
FYE: December 31
Type: Business Segment

This advertising firm is so nice they named it twice. Saatchi & Saatchi is one of the world's top advertising agency networks with more than 140 offices in about 80 countries. It provides creative advertising services and plans marketing campaigns for some of the largest advertisers and top global brands. Its Saatchi & Saatchi X agency acts primarily as a shopper's marketing services network in the US while Saatchi & Saatchi S is a consulting firm with expertise in assisting clients with sustainability citizenship and social good initiatives. Founded in the UK by Maurice and Charles Saatchi in 1970 Saatchi & Saatchi is part of Paris-based advertising conglomerate Publicis.

SABRE INDUSTRIES INC.

1120 Welsh Rd. Ste. 210
North Wales PA 19454
Phone: 267-263-1300
Fax: 267-263-1301
Web: www.sabreindustriesinc.com

CEO: Peter Sandore
CFO: Timothy Rossetti
HR: –
FYE: April 30
Type: Private

Sabre Industries designs and builds steel towers poles shelters and other utility structures for the wireless communications and electric transmission and distribution (T&D) industries. It also offers tower parts and accessories and provides a full range of services such as pole and structure testing turnkey construction site development interior integration and field maintenance. Customers include wireless service providers tower management companies utilities and government agencies. The company which is owned by private equity firm Kohlberg & Co operates primarily in the US.

SABINE ROYALTY TRUST

NYS: SBR

Southwest Bank, Park Place, 2911 Turtle Creek Blvd, Suite 850
Dallas, TX 75219
Phone: 855 588-7839
Fax: 214 508-2431
Web: www.sbr-sabineroyalty.com

CEO: –
CFO: –
HR: –
FYE: December 31
Type: Public

Sabine Royalty Trust owns royalty interests in oil and gas properties located on about 2.1 million gross acres (216551 net) in Florida Louisiana Mississippi New Mexico Oklahoma and Texas. The trust which was formed in 1983 receives royalties based on the amount of oil and gas produced and sold and distributes them on a monthly basis to shareholders. Although royalty trusts distribute essentially all royalties received to shareholders (at substantial tax advantage) their profitability depends on the price of oil and gas and the continued productivity of the properties. Sabine Royalty Trust's properties have proved reserves of about 5.3 million barrels of oil and 35.6 billion cu. ft. of natural gas.

	Annual Growth	12/10	12/11	12/12	12/13	12/14
Sales ($ mil.)	2.2%	56.1	60.7	54.7	60.8	61.1
Net income ($ mil.)	2.1%	54.0	58.6	52.3	58.7	58.7
Market value ($ mil.)	(12.0%)	868.2	919.2	580.1	737.1	521.6
Employees	–	–	–	–	–	–

SACRAMENTO MUNICIPAL UTILITY DISTRICT

6201 S St.
Sacramento CA 95817-1889
Phone: 916-452-3211
Fax: 916-732-5835
Web: www.smud.org

CEO: Ross Hartman
CFO: Jim Tracy
HR: –
FYE: December 31
Type: Government-owned

The Sacramento Municipal Utility District (SMUD) doesn't want its name to be mud. One of the largest locally owned electric utilities in the US SMUD serves about 600000 residential and commercial customer meters (a service area population of 1.4 million) in California's Sacramento and Placer counties. The utility generates about 70% of its electricity (its 1300-MW capacity is derived primarily from hydroelectric and cogeneration power plants) and buys the rest. SMUD also sells power to wholesale customers and has one of the largest solar energy distribution systems in the US.

SABRA HEALTH CARE REIT INC

NMS: SBRA

18500 Von Karman Avenue, Suite 550
Irvine, CA 92612
Phone: 888 393-8248
Fax: –
Web: www.sabrahealth.com

CEO: Richard K. Matros
CFO: Harold W. Andrews
HR: –
FYE: December 31
Type: Public

Sabra Health Care REIT doesn't mind a little healthy competition in the real estate sector. The company invests in income-producing health care facilities in the US. The REIT's investment portfolio includes about 120 properties most of which are skilled nursing/post-acute centers. It also invests in assisted living and independent living facilities and hospitals. Sabra's facilities house more than 12300 beds and are located in more than 25 states. Substantially all of the properties are leased to and operated by subsidiaries of Sun Healthcare Group which spun off its real estate assets to form Sabra Health Care REIT in 2010.

	Annual Growth	12/10	12/11	12/12	12/13	12/14
Sales ($ mil.)	113.7%	8.8	84.2	103.2	134.8	183.5
Net income ($ mil.)	805.0%	0.0	12.8	19.5	33.7	47.0
Market value ($ mil.)	13.3%	1,086.5	713.9	1,282.5	1,543.5	1,793.3
Employees	16.4%	6	7	8	9	11

SACRED HEART HOSPITAL INC.

900 W CLAIREMONT AVE
EAU CLAIRE, WI 547015105
Phone: 715-839-4121
Fax: –

CEO: Julie Manas
CFO: –
HR: –
FYE: June 30
Type: Private

Sacred Heart Hospital not only cares for hearts that are holey but also for the rest of what ails residents of western Wisconsin. The more than 300-bed medical center provides specialized services that include cardiology cancer care pediatrics and emergency medicine. The hospital provides community-wide care through affiliations with the Marshfield Clinic (a provider network with more than 700 physicians) Oakleaf Medical Network (an organization of providers and clinics) and Infinity Healthcare and Pathology Services (supplies the hospital with medical x-ray professionals). Founded in 1889 by the Hospital Sisters of the Third Order of St. Francis the center is part of the Hospital Sisters Health System.

	Annual Growth	06/02	06/03	06/05	06/08	06/13
Sales ($ mil.)	–	–	(1,258.3)	144.9	174.2	234.6
Net income ($ mil.)	9.8%	–	–	19.4	22.1	41.1
Market value ($ mil.)	–	–	–	–	–	–
Employees	–	–	–	–	–	1,000

SACRED HEART HOSPITAL OF ALLENTOWN

421 CHEW ST
ALLENTOWN, PA 181023406
Phone: 610-776-4500
Fax: –
Web: www.shh.org

CEO: –
CFO: Thomas Regner
HR: –
FYE: June 30
Type: Private

Hearts (and all other parts of the body) are sacred to Sacred Heart Hospital of Allentown. The acute care facility has some 230 beds and serves the residents of Pennsylvania's Lehigh Valley. Specialty services include pediatrics cardiology obstetrics weight-loss surgery orthopedics behavioral health and cancer treatment. Sacred Heart Hospital is part of the Sacred Heart Health System which also operates more than a dozen family practice clinics as well as specialty clinics long-term care facilities and imaging and rehabilitation centers. The hospital was founded by the Missionary Sisters of the Most Sacred Heart (a Catholic religious order) in 1912.

	Annual Growth	06/06	06/07	06/08	06/09	06/10
Sales ($ mil.)	–	–	–	(1,546.0)	107.1	106.8
Net income ($ mil.)	28013.7%	–	–	0.0	0.0	0.8
Market value ($ mil.)	–	–	–	–	–	–
Employees	–	–	–	–	–	1,058

SADDLEBACK MEMORIAL MEDICAL CENTER

24451 HEALTH CENTER DR
LAGUNA HILLS, CA 926533689
Phone: 949-837-4500
Fax: –
Web: www.memorialcare.org

CEO: Steve Geidt
CFO: Adolfo Chanez
HR: –
FYE: June 30
Type: Private

Saddleback Memorial Medical Center part of Memorial Health Services (MHS) serves the residents of southern Orange County in California. With some 325 beds the not-for-profit medical center provides general medical and surgical services as well as specialty care in areas such as cancer heart disease and physical rehabilitation. It operates two campuses one in Laguna Hills and one in San Clemente. The medical center also features several facilities for women's health including the Saddleback Women's Hospital and the MemorialCare Breast Center. In addition Saddleback Memorial provides home health care and hospice services.

	Annual Growth	06/97	06/98	06/99	06/01	06/08
Sales ($ mil.)	(17.9%)	–	–	2,141.2	170.3	364.1
Net income ($ mil.)	261.8%	–	–	0.0	4.3	32.2
Market value ($ mil.)	–	–	–	–	–	–
Employees	–	–	–	–	–	1,209

SAEHAN BANCORP

3580 Wilshire Blvd. Ste. 1500
Los Angeles CA 90010
Phone: 213-388-5550
Fax: 213-637-9899
Web: www.saehanbank.com

OTC: SAEB
CEO: Dong IL Kim
CFO: –
HR: –
FYE: December 31
Type: Public

Saehan Bancorp is the holding company for Saehan Bank which serves the Korean-American community in Southern California's Los Angeles and Orange counties through seven branches. Serving both individuals and businesses the bank offers standard deposit products such as checking savings and money market accounts and certificates of deposit. Its lending activities mainly consist of commercial mortgages and business loans with residential mortgage construction and land development and consumer loans rounding out its portfolio. Ancillary services include online banking wire transfers and debit cards.

SAFE RIDE SERVICES INC.

2001 W. Camelback Rd.
Phoenix AZ 85015
Phone: 602-627-6705
Fax: 602-627-6751
Web: www.saferideservices.com

CEO: –
CFO: –
HR: Monique Jordan
FYE: August 31
Type: Subsidiary

Safe Ride Services provides non-emergency medical transportation services in Arizona Colorado Florida Illinois Kansas Missouri New Mexico New York Oklahoma Texas Utah and Washington. The company offers its services through a fleet of vans configured to carry people in wheelchairs or on stretchers as well as those who are ambulatory. Safe Ride clients include Medicaid beneficiaries; the company also contracts with other health insurance programs. The company is part of the First Transit unit of FirstGroup America which itself is a subsidiary of UK-based bus and train operator FirstGroup. Safe Ride Services was founded in 1989.

SAFECO INSURANCE COMPANY OF AMERICA

Safeco Plaza 1001 4th Ave.
Seattle WA 98154
Phone: 206-545-5000
Fax: 425-376-6533
Web: www.safeco.com

CEO: –
CFO: –
HR: –
FYE: December 31
Type: Subsidiary

While the name doesn't tell you much about the business Safeco does sound secure and with insurance that counts for a lot. As Safeco Insurance Co. the company offers personal property/casualty insurance including auto homeowners and fire coverage. In addition to its bread and butter standard products it also offers specialty products including classic car insurance rental property insurance and personal umbrella coverage. Its 4.8 million policies are sold and maintained nationally through a network of independent agents and brokers. Liberty Mutual acquired Safeco in a 2008 deal valued at $6.2 billion.

SAFEGUARD SCIENTIFICS INC.

435 Devon Park Dr. Building 800
Wayne PA 19087-1945
Phone: 610-293-0600
Fax: 610-293-0601
Web: www.safeguard.com

NYSE: SFE
CEO: Stephen T Zarrilli
CFO: Jeffrey B McGroarty
HR: –
FYE: December 31
Type: Public

Safeguard Scientifics' goal is to nurture investments not protect Poindexters in a lab. The firm invests in early-stage high-tech and life sciences ventures with prospects for growth. It focuses on companies involved in the development of diagnostics medical devices regenerative medicine specialty pharmaceuticals new media and financial services and health care information technology. Safeguard Scientifics has significant minority stakes in about a dozen companies; holdings include specialty pharmaceutical maker NuPathe biotechnology firm Tengion and Swap.com a web site that enables users to swap books and other media.

SAFELITE GROUP INC.

2400 Farmers Dr. 5th Fl.	CEO: Thomas Feeney
Columbus OH 43235	CFO: Douglas Herron
Phone: 614-210-9000	HR: –
Fax: 614-210-9451	FYE: March 31
Web: www.belronus.com	Type: Subsidiary

Safelite Group (formerly Belron US) has the answer to what blew into your windshield. The company an operating segment of global auto glass repair giant Belron is one of the largest auto glass repair providers in the US. It fixes and replaces windshields through a network of facilities in all 50 states operating under the names of Safelite AutoGlass AutoGlass Specialists and Elite Auto Glass among others. In addition Safelite Group makes its own replacement windshields distributes materials and tools to other auto glass repair companies and operates Safelite Solutions (which handles fleet and insurance claims processing). Founded in 1947 the company was acquired by D'Ieteren Belron's parent in 2007.

SAFENET INC.

4690 Millennium Dr.	CEO: Prakash Panjwani
Belcamp MD 21017	CFO: Jon McCabe
Phone: 410-931-7500	HR: –
Fax: 410-931-7524	FYE: December 31
Web: www.safenet-inc.com	Type: Private

SafeNet makes the digital world a safer place. The company provides security products that protect networks intellectual property software and personal identity. Its software and hardware systems employ encryption technology in USB identity tokens and smart cards virtual private networks (VPNs) and security appliances and software antipiracy and digital rights management products. Clients include financial institutions corporations and government agencies. SafeNet counts Citigroup Dell Starbucks Netflix Cisco and the US Defense Department among its blue-chip customers. Private equity firm Vector Capital took SafeNet private in 2007; the company filed for an IPO in 2010 but withdrew it in 2012.

SAFETY INSURANCE GROUP, INC.   NMS: SAFT

20 Custom House Street	CEO: David F. Brussard
Boston, MA 02110	CFO: William J. Begley
Phone: 617 951-0600	HR: –
Fax: 617 603-4837	FYE: December 31
Web: www.safetyinsurance.com	Type: Public

Buckle up Bostonians car safety first! Safety Insurance Group through its subsidiaries (Safety Insurance Safety Indemnity Insurance and Safety Property and Casualty) sells property/casualty insurance exclusively in Massachusetts and New Hampshire. The company is one of the top private passenger automobile and commercial automobile insurers in the state controlling more than 11% of each market. Safety Insurance Group also provides homeowners dwelling fire personal umbrella and business-owner policies; it cross-sells its non-auto property/casualty products to increase its share of the market. The company sells its products through more than 850 independent agents and about 990 offices.

	Annual Growth	12/10	12/11	12/12	12/13	12/14
Assets ($ mil.)	3.9%	1,439.5	1,472.6	1,574.3	1,625.5	1,675.7
Net income ($ mil.)	1.3%	56.3	13.7	58.1	61.4	59.4
Market value ($ mil.)	7.6%	716.2	607.6	693.0	845.0	960.7
Employees	1.2%	581	590	599	605	610

SAFETY-KLEEN INC.

2600 N. Central Expressway Ste. 400	CEO: –
Richardson TX 75080	CFO: Jeff Richard
Phone: 972-265-2000	HR: Jean Lee
Fax: 972-265-2990	FYE: December 31
Web: www.safety-kleen.com	Type: Private

Safety-Kleen is a North American leader in oil re-refining and parts cleaning services. It provides these services to commercial industrial and automotive customers to meet their environmental needs. The company's Oil Re-refining segment processes about 160 million gallons of used oil annually to produce base and blended lubricating oils which are sold to distributors fleets government agencies railroads and retailers. Its Environmental Services segment collects about 200 million gallons of used oil; other services offered include containerized waste collection and parts cleaning. Safety-Kleen filed for a $400 million IPO in mid-2012. That year Clean Harbors offered to buy the company for $1.25 billion.

SAFEWAY INC.   NYS: SWY

5918 Stoneridge Mall Road	CEO: Robert L Edwards
Pleasanton, CA 94588-3229	CFO: –
Phone: 925 467-3000	HR: –
Fax: 925 467-3323	FYE: December 29
Web: www.safeway.com	Type: Public

For many Americans "going to Safeway" is synonymous with "going to the grocery store." Safeway is one of the nation's largest food retailers with some 1400 stores located mostly in the western Midwestern and mid-Atlantic regions of the US. It also operates regional supermarket companies including The Vons Companies (primarily in Southern California) Dominick's Finer Foods (Chicago) Carr-Gottstein Foods (Alaska's largest retailer) and Randall's Food Markets (Texas). Safeway owns grocery e-retailer GroceryWorks.com. Outside the US Safeway owns 49% of Casa Ley which operates about 195 food and variety stores in western Mexico. It exited the Canadian market in 2013.

	Annual Growth	01/09	01/10	01/11*	12/11	12/12
Sales ($ mil.)	0.1%	44,104.0	40,850.7	41,050.0	43,630.2	44,206.5
Net income ($ mil.)	(14.8%)	965.3	(1,097.5)	589.8	516.7	596.5
Market value ($ mil.)	(9.7%)	5,760.0	5,099.0	5,386.4	5,039.1	4,239.2
Employees	(4.6%)	197,000	186,000	180,000	178,000	171,000
						*Fiscal year change

SAFEWAY INSURANCE GROUP

790 Pasquinelli Dr.	CEO: William J Parrillo
Westmont IL 60559-1254	CFO: –
Phone: 630-887-8300	HR: Mary Hels
Fax: 630-887-9101	FYE: December 31
Web: www.safewayinsurance.com	Type: Private

Safeway Insurance wants to keep things safe whether you're driving on the highway or the byway. Through about a half dozen subsidiaries the group provides automobile insurance coverage primarily in the southern US. The company specializes in nonstandard policies (insurance written for drivers that are considered higher claims risks). Through some 450 in-house representatives and a network of more than 3000 independent agents Safeway insures more than 250000 policyholders in about a dozen states. Chairman William Parrillo founded the family owned company in 1959.

SAFRA NATIONAL BANK OF NEW YORK

546 5th Ave.	CEO: Simone Morato
New York NY 10036	CFO: Carlos Bertaco
Phone: 212-704-5500	HR: Madeline Holmes
Fax: 212-704-5527	FYE: December 31
Web: www.safra.com	Type: Private

Rich folks are wild about Safra and Safra's wild about them. Private bank Safra National Bank of New York serves high-net-worth individuals local businesses and international corporations through branches in New York and Miami. It offers certificates of deposit investment funds money market instruments alternative investments and gold bullion. In addition to wealth management the bank also performs equity brokerage services bond trading and correspondent banking. Established in 1987 Safra National Bank is owned by the Safra family benefactors of hospitals synagogues and universities in the US and abroad.

SAGA COMMUNICATIONS, INC.

ASE: SGA

73 Kercheval Avenue	CEO: Edward K. (Ed) Christian
Grosse Pointe Farms, MI 48236	CFO: Samuel D. (Sam) Bush
Phone: 313 886-7070	HR: –
Fax: 313 886-7150	FYE: December 31
Web: www.sagacom.com	Type: Public

This company could spin a good tale about the radio and television industries. Saga Communications is a leading radio broadcaster with more than 90 stations serving about 25 markets in 15 states offering a variety of formats including sports talk and news as well as several music formats. Most of the stations serve small and midsized markets; the company typically has clusters of stations in each market allowing it to combine certain business functions. Saga also operates five regional radio networks. In addition the company owns a portfolio of five full-power and four low-power TV stations in Mississippi Missouri and Texas. Chairman and CEO Edward Christian has about two-thirds control of Saga.

	Annual Growth	12/10	12/11	12/12	12/13	12/14
Sales ($ mil.)	1.2%	127.8	127.3	130.3	129.5	134.0
Net income ($ mil.)	(0.4%)	15.1	12.6	17.9	15.3	14.9
Market value ($ mil.)	13.7%	150.8	216.8	269.7	291.7	252.2
Employees	(1.7%)	1,161	1,168	1,118	1,140	1,086

SAGARSOFT INC.

78 EASTERN BLVD STE 8	CEO: –
GLASTONBURY, CT 060334325	CFO: –
Phone: 860-633-2880	HR: –
Fax: –	FYE: March 31
Web: www.sagarsoft.com	Type: Private

|Sagarsoft hopes to take all of the hard work out of information technology. The company provides information technology (IT) services such as software development data warehousing and enterprise application integration. Additional offerings include project management network design systems architecture and support. Sagarsoft's clients have included Pfizer General Electric Sprint and CA. It has partnered with technology products providers including Microsoft Oracle Cisco and others. The company was founded in 1995

	Annual Growth	03/10	03/11	03/12	03/13	03/14
Sales ($ mil.)	(5.7%)	–	18.7	18.3	15.7	15.6
Net income ($ mil.)	(7.7%)	–	–	0.2	0.2	0.2
Market value ($ mil.)	–	–	–	–	–	–
Employees	–	–	–	–	–	95

SAGE INSTRUMENTS INC.

240 Airport Blvd.	CEO: Dave McIntosh
Freedom CA 95019	CFO: Ray Levasseur
Phone: 831-761-1000	HR: –
Fax: 831-761-1008	FYE: December 31
Web: www.sageinst.com	Type: Private

Sage Instruments makes field test sets automated wireless test systems and various other test components and systems for the telecommunications and wireless test industry. The company specializes in VoIP (Voice over Internet Protocol) testing a burgeoning area in communications test as more telecommunications occur over Internet protocol networks rather than the copper-wiring infrastructure of AT&T Deutsche Telekom France Telecom NTT Verizon Communications and other telecom giants. NASA is one of the company's customers. Sage Instruments was established in 1984 by CEO Brett Mackinnon who is the majority shareholder in the company.

SAGE SOFTWARE INC.

6561 Irvine Center Dr.	CEO: –
Irvine CA 92618-2301	CFO: Marc Scheipe
Phone: 949-753-1222	HR: –
Fax: 949-753-0374	FYE: September 30
Web: www.na.sage.com	Type: Subsidiary

Sage Software caters to businesses that appreciate the wisdom of planning. The company (which does business as Sage North America) is the North American subsidiary of UK-based software developer The Sage Group plc. Sage North America provides small and midsized companies with a variety of business management applications focused on such functions as accounting customer relationship management not-for-profit and government management human resources and fixed asset management and contact management. The company also provides industry-specific applications for customers in fields that include construction real estate and health care.

SAGENT PHARMACEUTICALS INC

NMS: SGNT

1901 North Roselle Road, Suite 700	CEO: Allan Oberman
Schaumburg, IL 60195	CFO: Jonathon Singer
Phone: 847 908-1600	HR: –
Fax: –	FYE: December 31
Web: www.sagentpharma.com	Type: Public

Sagent Pharmaceuticals is imbued with a restorative spirit. Through its subsidiaries Sagent develops markets and sells a range of generic injectable products used by US hospitals and other health care organizations. Its products — which include anti-infection drugs chemotherapy drugs and critical care treatments used for anesthesia or to stabilize cardiac conditions like blood clotting and arrhythmia — consist of more than 30 ready-to-use pre-filled syringes single and multiple-dose vials and pre-mixed bags. Sagent develops its products using active pharmaceutical ingredients (APIs) and finished drugs supplied by partner pharmaceutical companies.

	Annual Growth	12/10	12/11	12/12	12/13	12/14
Sales ($ mil.)	40.5%	74.1	152.4	183.6	244.8	289.0
Net income ($ mil.)	–	(24.5)	(26.4)	(16.8)	29.6	39.9
Market value ($ mil.)	6.1%	–	671.5	514.5	811.6	802.9
Employees	53.0%	85	99	98	269	466

SAIA INC

NMS: SAIA

11465 Johns Creek Parkway, Suite 400
Johns Creek, GA 30097
Phone: 770 232-5067
Fax: –
Web: www.saia.com

CEO: Richard D. (Rick) O'Dell
CFO: Frederick J. Holzgrefe
HR: –
FYE: December 31
Type: Public

Saia — you say it "sigh-ah" — is a holding company for less-than-truckload (LTL) carrier Saia Motor Freight Line. (LTL carriers consolidate freight from multiple shippers into a single truckload.) Saia Motor Freight specializes in regional and interregional services including time-definite and expedited transportation; it also offers truckload freight hauling. The carrier operates a fleet of some 3600 tractors and 11160 trailers from a network of about 150 terminals. Saia's service territory spans about 35 states in the South Southwest Midwest as well as Pacific Northwest and West US. It offers coverage elsewhere in North America through partnerships with other carriers.

	Annual Growth	12/10	12/11	12/12	12/13	12/14
Sales ($ mil.)	9.0%	902.7	1,030.2	1,098.7	1,139.1	1,272.3
Net income ($ mil.)	127.0%	2.0	11.4	32.0	43.6	52.0
Market value ($ mil.)	35.2%	412.6	310.4	575.0	797.1	1,376.9
Employees	4.4%	7,500	7,900	7,900	8,400	8,900

SAINT AGNES MEDICAL CENTER

1303 E HERNDON AVE
FRESNO, CA 937203309
Phone: 559-450-3000
Fax: –
Web: www.samc.com

CEO: –
CFO: Derek Miller
HR: Cecelia Rocha
FYE: June 30
Type: Private

Protecting and caring for the vulnerable Saint Agnes continues to ward off death for the patients at Saint Agnes Medical Center. The medical center provides healthcare to Valley residents of Fresno California through a 436-bed acute care hospital. Along with general surgery the hospital offers a variety of services including asthma management bariatric surgery (for which it has scored state-wide accolades) cardiac rehabilitation hospice care and home care. The facility also has centers dedicated to cancer child development and women's health. The hospital is part of Trinity Health one of the largest Catholic health care systems in the US.

	Annual Growth	06/07	06/08	06/09	06/10	06/13
Sales ($ mil.)	17.6%	–	223.5	394.9	438.9	503.7
Net income ($ mil.)	–	–	–	(52.4)	8.1	19.0
Market value ($ mil.)	–	–	–	–	–	–
Employees	–	–	–	–	–	2,400

SAINT ALPHONSUS REGIONAL MEDICAL CENTER INC.

1055 N CURTIS RD
BOISE, ID 837061309
Phone: 208-367-2121
Fax: –
Web: www.saintalphonsus.org

CEO: –
CFO: Kenneth Fry
HR: –
FYE: June 30
Type: Private

Saint Alphonsus Regional Medical Center makes medical care its primary mission. The 384-bed hospital provides Boise Idaho and the surrounding region (including eastern Oregon and northern Nevada) with general acute and specialized health care services. Its facilities and operations include a level II trauma center an orthopedic spinal care unit an air transport service and a home health and hospice division. Saint Alphonsus Regional Medical Center is part of Trinity Health's four-hospital Saint Alphonsus Health System which serves Boise and Nampa in Idaho and Ontario and Baker City in Oregon. The Sisters of the Holy Cross founded the hospital in 1894.

	Annual Growth	06/07	06/08	06/09	06/10	06/13
Sales ($ mil.)	–	–	–	0.0	428.7	450.0	545.1
Net income ($ mil.)	–	–	–	–	(8.7)	13.8	43.1
Market value ($ mil.)	–	–	–	–	–	–
Employees	–	–	–	–	–	3,500

SAINT ANSELM COLLEGE

100 SAINT ANSELM DR
MANCHESTER, NH 031021310
Phone: 603-641-7000
Fax: –
Web: www.anselm.edu

CEO: –
CFO: –
HR: –
FYE: June 30
Type: Private

It may be named after a philosopher and theologian but students of all types are welcome at Saint Anselm College. The Benedictine Catholic liberal arts college offers degrees in more than 40 majors as well as over 20 certificate programs. With an enrollment of some 2000 and a full-time faculty of around 150 (90% of which hold a doctorate or other terminal degree) the school's student-teacher enrollment is 11:1 with an average class size of 18. Saint Anselm College's core curriculum includes classes in English humanities philosophy foreign language science and theology. Located on a hill overlooking Manchester New Hampshire Saint Anselm College was founded in 1889 by monks of the Benedictine order.

	Annual Growth	06/09	06/10	06/11	06/12	06/13
Sales ($ mil.)	(8.8%)	–	86.5	65.9	66.5	65.7
Net income ($ mil.)	(2.0%)	–	–	20.8	(12.0)	20.0
Market value ($ mil.)	–	–	–	–	–	–
Employees	–	–	–	–	–	700

SAINT BARNABAS CORPORATION

95 Old Short Hills Rd.
West Orange NJ 07052
Phone: 570-622-4141
Fax: 570-622-4011
Web: www.yuengling.com

CEO: –
CFO: Pat Ahearn
HR: –
FYE: December 31
Type: Private

Garden Staters who overdo it during the feast of St. Barnabas can always head to his namesake medical center for a little relief. Saint Barnabas Corporation (dba Barnabas Health) is the state's largest private hospital network with some 3300 acute-care beds in its network. The system has dozens of facilities including six acute-care hospitals a number of specialty medical centers as well as nursing and assisted-living facilities rehabilitation centers and outpatient and ambulatory care clinics. Barnabas Health also offers behavioral health home health and hospice programs and it specializes in the areas of pediatrics women's health oncology cardiology stroke care diabetes and transplants.

SAINT EDWARD''S UNIVERSITY INC.

3001 S CONGRESS AVE
AUSTIN, TX 787046489
Phone: 512-448-8400
Fax: –
Web: www.stedwards.edu

CEO: –
CFO: Rhonda Cartwright
HR: –
FYE: June 30
Type: Private

St. Edward's University is a private Catholic liberal arts university in Austin Texas. With an enrollment of more than 5000 students and a student-to-faculty ratio of 14:1 the university offers undergraduate degrees in more than 60 areas of study at schools of behavioral and social sciences management and business the humanities education and natural sciences. St. Edward's also has about ten master's degree programs in fields including accounting business administration information systems and counseling. It offers numerous study abroad programs in Europe Latin America and Asia as well as continuing education programs through its New College.

	Annual Growth	06/09	06/10	06/11	06/12	06/13
Sales ($ mil.)	5.3%	–	95.9	105.7	109.7	112.1
Net income ($ mil.)	34.9%	–	–	18.2	18.6	33.1
Market value ($ mil.)	–	–	–	–	–	–
Employees	–	–	–	–	–	964

SAINT ELIZABETH MEDICAL CENTER INC.

1 MEDICAL VILLAGE DR	CEO: Garren Colvin
EDGEWOOD, KY 410173403	CFO: Marc Hoffman
Phone: 859-301-2000	HR: Linda D
Fax: –	FYE: December 31
Web: www.sainte.pps-inc.com	Type: Private

It doesn't have much to do with the Holy Trinity except for the fact that St. Elizabeth Medical Center (operating as St. Elizabeth Healthcare) does business in a trinity of states. The system provides health care services to residents in Kentucky Ohio and West Virginia. St. Elizabeth Healthcare's programs include stroke and cardiac care hospice services and neurosurgery. The system is home to six hospitals with about 1200 beds and dozens of primary care offices. St. Elizabeth Healthcare was formed through a merger between St. Elizabeth Medical and nearby St. Luke Hospitals. The organization has one board of directors and one management structure and is sponsored by the Catholic Diocese of Covington.

	Annual Growth	12/03	12/04	12/05	12/06	12/08
Sales ($ mil.)	6.2%	–	–	520.6	484.0	623.7
Net income ($ mil.)	–	–	–	0.0	49.2	(32.4)
Market value ($ mil.)	–	–	–	–	–	–
Employees	–	–	–	–	–	6,227

SAINT ELIZABETH REGIONAL MEDICAL CENTER

555 S 70TH ST	CEO: –
LINCOLN, NE 685102462	CFO: –
Phone: 402-219-5200	HR: –
Fax: –	FYE: June 30
Web: www.saintelizabethonline.org	Type: Private

Saint Elizabeth Regional Medical Center a Catholic Health Initiatives (CHI) affiliate is a 260-bed acute care hospital that serves the Lincoln Nebraska area. The not-for-profit hospital also known as CHI Health St. Elizabeth provides a variety of services such as obstetrics bariatrics cancer care burn and wound care and cardiac and pulmonary care. Some 430 physicians are affiliated with the facility. The hospital also operates community health clinics urgent care centers and physical therapy clinics as well as home health and hospice organizations. CHI Health St. Elizabeth was originally founded as a simple frontier hospital in 1889 by the Sisters of St. Francis of Perpetual Adoration.

	Annual Growth	06/07	06/08	06/09	06/10	06/13
Sales ($ mil.)	(24.2%)	–	1,071.4	251.1	1.1	268.1
Net income ($ mil.)	–	–	–	(5.5)	0.4	27.6
Market value ($ mil.)	–	–	–	–	–	–
Employees	–	–	–	–	–	1,825

SAINT FRANCIS HOSPITAL AND MEDICAL CENTER FOUNDATION INC.

114 WOODLAND ST	CEO: Christopher M. (Chris) Dadlez
HARTFORD, CT 061051208	CFO: John N. Giamalis
Phone: 860-714-4006	HR: Dawn L Bryant
Fax: –	FYE: September 30
Web: www.saintfranciscare.com	Type: Private

Saint Francis takes care of the hearts of Hartford Connecticut. The Saint Francis Hospital and Medical Center also known as Saint Francis Care is a regional medical center with some 620 beds. The hospital specializes in cardiology oncology neurology orthopedics and women's and children's health services. It also offers behavioral health weight management trauma care and injury rehabilitation programs. Saint Francis serves as a teaching hospital affiliated with the University of Connecticut Schools of Medicine and Dentistry. It also operates the nearby Mount Sinai Rehabilitation Hospital a 60-bed facility that provides brain trauma sports medicine and orthopedic care.

	Annual Growth	09/06	09/07	09/08	09/09	09/10
Sales ($ mil.)	(19.9%)	–	–	1,017.0	638.9	651.9
Net income ($ mil.)	–	–	–	0.0	(16.8)	(10.8)
Market value ($ mil.)	–	–	–	–	–	–
Employees	–	–	–	–	–	3,270

SAINT FRANCIS UNIVERSITY

117 EVERGREEN DR	CEO: –
LORETTO, PA 159409704	CFO: –
Phone: 814-472-3000	HR: –
Fax: –	FYE: June 30
Web: www.francis.edu	Type: Private

Saint Francis University is a Catholic liberal arts college with more than 2500 full- and part-time students. The university offers undergraduate and graduate degree programs in areas such as business administration education medical science nursing and computer science. It also has doctorate programs in fields such as education and physical therapy. Its four schools cover arts and letters health sciences business and sciences. Saint Francis University was established when six Franciscan Friars from Ireland founded a boys' academy in the mountain hamlet of Loretto Pennsylvania in 1847. Now more than 60% of the student body is made up of women. The former St. Francis College gained university status in 2001.

	Annual Growth	06/07	06/08	06/10	06/12	06/13
Sales ($ mil.)	5.5%	–	69.4	59.8	84.5	90.8
Net income ($ mil.)	13.5%	–	–	6.5	5.2	9.4
Market value ($ mil.)	–	–	–	–	–	–
Employees	–	–	–	–	–	420

SAINT JOSEPH'S UNIVERSITY

5600 CITY AVE	CEO: –
PHILADELPHIA, PA 191311376	CFO: Edward W Moneypenny
Phone: 610-660-1000	HR: –
Fax: –	FYE: May 31
Web: www.sju.edu	Type: Private

Saint Joseph's University (SJU) has been educating Joes and Janes for more than 150 years. The Catholic Jesuit university provides higher education for about 8000 students a year from its campus on the outskirts of Philadelphia. It has more than 300 full-time faculty members and offers 50 undergraduate majors and 40 graduate and professional study areas including an Ed.D. in Educational Leadership. About 650 undergraduates attend its College of Professional and Liberal Studies; the remainder attend the College of Arts and Sciences and the Haub School of Business. SJU also conducts study abroad honors service and faith learning and other special study programs. It was founded in 1851 by the Society of Jesus.

	Annual Growth	05/07	05/08	05/09	05/10	05/11
Sales ($ mil.)	–	–	–	0.0	246.6	267.5
Net income ($ mil.)	2331.4%	–	–	0.0	18.4	9.7
Market value ($ mil.)	–	–	–	–	–	–
Employees	–	–	–	–	–	1,138

SAINT LOUIS UNIVERSITY

1 N GRAND BLVD	CEO: –
SAINT LOUIS, MO 631032006	CFO: Robert Woodruff
Phone: 314-977-2500	HR: Michael Luna
Fax: –	FYE: June 30
Web: www.concentra.com	Type: Private

This university gives students a SLU of opportunities. Saint Louis University (SLU) is a Jesuit Catholic school offering about 100 undergraduate 70 graduate and a host of professional degree programs through about a dozen schools and colleges including a school of medicine and a campus in Madrid Spain. Most programs require core classes in philosophy and theology. SLU has an enrollment of about 9000 undergraduate and 5000 graduate and professional students. Its student-teacher ratio is 12:1. Saint Louis University was founded in 1818 by Reverend Louis William Du Bourg Catholic Bishop of Louisiana.

	Annual Growth	06/06	06/07	06/08	06/09	06/10
Sales ($ mil.)	7.6%	–	–	–	697.5	750.7
Net income ($ mil.)	–	–	–	–	0.0	28.5
Market value ($ mil.)	–	–	–	–	–	–
Employees	–	–	–	–	–	7,500

SAINT MARY''S UNIVERSITY OF MINNESOTA

700 TERRACE HTS
WINONA, MN 559871321
Phone: 507-457-1436
Fax: –
Web: www.roch.edu

CEO: –
CFO: –
HR: Genellegroh Beck
FYE: May 31
Type: Private

Saint Mary's University of Minnesota is a private Roman Catholic institution that enrolls about 6000 students. About 20% of students are traditional undergraduates while the majority are adult learners in the Schools of Graduate and Professional Programs. The school which was founded in 1912 by Bishop Patrick R. Heffron has been administered by the Christian Brothers organization (under the De La Salle order) since 1933. It offers instruction in about 55 major minor and professional fields including arts science education and psychology.

	Annual Growth	05/09	05/10	05/11	05/12	05/14
Sales ($ mil.)	5.5%	–	65.7	68.9	66.3	81.3
Net income ($ mil.)	14.6%	–	–	8.4	3.3	12.6
Market value ($ mil.)	–	–	–	–	–	–
Employees	–	–	–	–	–	1,000

SAINT TAMMANY PARISH HOSPITAL SERVICE DISTRICT 1

1202 S TYLER ST
COVINGTON, LA 704332330
Phone: 985-898-4000
Fax: –
Web: www.stph.org

CEO: Patti Ellish
CFO: David Mabe
HR: –
FYE: December 31
Type: Private

St. Tammany Parish Hospital serves communities in St. Tammany Parish and Washington Parish along the northern shores of Lake Ponchartrain in eastern Louisiana. The not-for-profit hospital has about 240 beds and offers acute care diagnostic rehabilitation and community wellness services. It also includes centers and clinics specializing in surgery breast care cardiology and sleep disorders. In addition St. Tammany Parish Hospital operates a home health and hospice agency an outpatient services center and a primary care physicians' office. The company's facilities are served by doctors in St. Tammany Physicians Network.

	Annual Growth	12/07	12/08	12/09	12/11	12/12
Sales ($ mil.)	270.6%	–	1.2	200.2	223.1	225.3
Net income ($ mil.)	17.9%	–	–	8.3	16.9	13.6
Market value ($ mil.)	–	–	–	–	–	–
Employees	–	–	–	–	–	1,520

SAINT-GOBAIN ABRASIVES INC.

1 New Bond St.
Worcester MA 01606-2614
Phone: 508-795-5000
Fax: 508-795-5741
Web: www.sgabrasives.com

CEO: Patrick Millot
CFO: George B Amoss
HR: Mark Stacey
FYE: December 31
Type: Subsidiary

Keep your nose to the grindstone and you'll surely succeed at Saint-Gobain Abrasives. The company makes and distributes bonded coated and superabrasive products to cut shape and polish materials such as ceramics metals plastics and glass. Expanding its refining mix the company reaches all types of industrial construction homebuilding automotive and do-it-yourself markets. The lineup of grinding wheels (more than 250000) from sandpaper on up to diamond-based sharpeners is sold under brand names Norton Carborundum Merit and Winter. Saint-Gobain Abrasives is one of eight subsidiaries comprising the High Performance Materials sector of French manufacturing giant Compagnie de Saint-Gobain.

SAINT-GOBAIN CONTAINERS INC.

1509 S. Macedonia Ave.
Muncie IN 47302-3664
Phone: 765-741-7000
Fax: 765-741-7012
Web: www.sgcontainers.com

CEO: Niall Wall
CFO: –
HR: –
FYE: December 31
Type: Subsidiary

Saint-Gobain Containers is a glass act. The company is the #2 producer of glass containers in the US behind Owens-Illinois. Its glassmaking process includes melting glass conditioning forming and annealing and coating. Its products mainly serve the food and beverage industry. Everything from apple juice and beer to pickles and barbecue sauce are sold in Saint-Gobain Containers' jars and bottles. The company is also a major consumer of recycled glass. Saint-Gobain Containers operates under the umbrella of holding company Saint-Gobain Corporation which oversees the North American operations of French building materials giant Compagnie de Saint-Gobain.

SAJAN INC.

NAS: SAJA

625 Whitetail Blvd.
River Falls, WI 54022
Phone: 715 426-9505
Fax: –
Web: www.sajan.com

CEO: –
CFO: Shannon Zimmerman
HR: –
FYE: December 31
Type: Public

Sajan wants to make sure nothing is lost in translation. Formerly known as MathStar Sajan offers global language services and software for document and translation management Web site localization and multilingual desktop publishing. The company's offerings which are supported by its Global Communication Management Systems (GCMS) Web-based platform allow companies to expand into untapped international markets by making their Web sites accessible and culturally suitable for target audiences. Sajan also adapts Web pages for images e-learning and search engine optimization. The company's Ireland-based subsidiary Sajan Software covers markets in Europe Africa and the Middle East.

	Annual Growth	12/10	12/11	12/12	12/13	12/14
Sales ($ mil.)	15.4%	16.0	20.9	20.5	24.0	28.3
Net income ($ mil.)	–	(3.0)	0.1	(1.1)	0.0	0.2
Market value ($ mil.)	55.7%	4.6	4.6	2.1	6.9	27.0
Employees	3.2%	112	114	99	112	127

SAKS FIFTH AVENUE INC.

12 E. 49th St.
New York NY 10017
Phone: 212-753-4000
Fax: 703-684-3478
Web: www.salvationarmyusa.org

CEO: –
CFO: –
HR: –
FYE: January 31
Type: Business Segment

Saks Fifth Avenue is Saks Inc.'s most expensive accessory. A subsidiary of Saks Saks Fifth Avenue (SFA) operates about 45 upscale department stores in 20-plus states. The retailer is near the top of the line in fashion selling apparel cosmetics jewelry and shoes from top designers such as Burberry Chanel and Prada as well as Saks' own private label merchandise. SFA's fast-growing off-price sister chain Off 5th caters to thriftier customers and has overtaken SFA with more than 60 locations across the US. SFA also operates a catalog and an online store and runs smaller shops in chic vacation spots. The flagship store at 611 Fifth Ave. opened in 1924 rings up about 20% of SFA's total sales.

SALARY.COM INC.

160 Gould St.
Needham MA 02494
Phone: 781-464-7300
Fax: 781-726-7880
Web: www.salary.com

CEO: –
CFO: –
HR: –
FYE: March 31
Type: Subsidiary

Think you're grossly underpaid? Check out Salary.com to find out for sure. (Just refrain from doing so while you're at work.) The company's website provides the Salary Wizard which offers employee compensation data and analysis geared toward individuals managers and businesses. Other tools include a Cost of Living Wizard Benefits Wizard Performance Self Test and Job Assessor. The firm provides employer-reported data on more than 4000 job titles. Salary.com also operates Salary.com for Business (at http://business.salary.com) a separate site that offers articles tips and tools for companies. Most revenue comes from advertising. Salary.com is a division of human resources firm Kenexa Corporation.

SALEM HOSPITAL

890 OAK ST SE
SALEM, OR 973013905
Phone: 503-561-5200
Fax: –
Web: www.salemhealth.org

CEO: –
CFO: Aaron Crane
HR: Laurie Barr
FYE: September 30
Type: Private

Salem Hospital serves the healthcare needs of residents in and around Oregon's Willamette Valley. The acute care hospital boasts about 455 beds and a medical staff of 440-plus physicians that represents some 45 specialty areas such as oncology joint replacement obstetrics diabetes weight loss and mental health among others. The not-for-profit hospital offers a range of services from emergency and critical care to rehabilitation and community wellness programs. Its Center for Outpatient Medicine provides cancer care outpatient surgery and imaging services and has a sleep disorders center. Salem Hospital is part of Salem Health which also includes West Valley Hospital and Willamette Health Partners.

	Annual Growth	09/03	09/04	09/08	09/09	09/13
Sales ($ mil.)	5.7%	–	321.9	2.9	493.8	531.1
Net income ($ mil.)	–	–	–	(1.2)	20.7	61.4
Market value ($ mil.)	–	–	–	–	–	–
Employees	–	–	–	–	–	3,400

SALEM MEDIA GROUP, INC.

NMS: SALM

4880 Santa Rosa Road
Camarillo, CA 93012
Phone: 805 987-0400
Fax: –
Web: www.salem.cc

CEO: Edward G Atsinger III
CFO: Evan D Masyr
HR: –
FYE: December 31
Type: Public

His eye may be on the sparrow but Salem Media Group (formerly Salem Communications) hopes His ear is tuned to the radio. The leading Christian radio company operates about 100 stations serving more than 35 markets. Its stations offer Christian-themed talk shows Christian music country music and traditional talk radio. The company also produces and syndicates religious programming through the Salem Radio Network which boasts about 2000 affiliates. In addition Salem Media publishes books and magazines operates a radio advertising sales firm and operates the Salem Web Network a provider of online Christian content. Chairman Stuart Epperson CEO Edward Atsinger and other family members control about 85% of the company.

	Annual Growth	12/10	12/11	12/12	12/13	12/14
Sales ($ mil.)	6.5%	206.9	218.2	229.2	236.9	266.5
Net income ($ mil.)	29.7%	1.9	5.6	4.4	(2.7)	5.5
Market value ($ mil.)	25.3%	80.3	65.1	138.2	220.3	198.0
Employees	2.3%	1,465	1,457	1,459	1,555	1,605

SALESFORCE.COM INC

NYS: CRM

The Landmark @ One Market, Suite 300
San Francisco, CA 94105
Phone: 415 901-7000
Fax: –
Web: www.salesforce.com

CEO: Marc Benioff
CFO: Mark J. Hawkins
HR: –
FYE: January 31
Type: Public

Salesforce.com champions the power of the social enterprise. The company offers Internet-based applications that manage employee collaboration as well as customer information for sales (Salesforce Sales Cloud) marketing (Salesforce Marketing Cloud) and customer support (Salesforce Service Cloud) providing clients with a rapidly deployable alternative to traditional more time-consuming and user-maintained software installations. Salesforce counts more than 100000 users of its customer relationship management (CRM) software and its customers come from a variety of industries including financial services telecommunications manufacturing and entertainment. It generates most of its revenues from the US.

	Annual Growth	01/11	01/12	01/13	01/14	01/15
Sales ($ mil.)	34.2%	1,657.1	2,266.5	3,050.2	4,071.0	5,373.6
Net income ($ mil.)	–	64.5	(11.6)	(270.4)	(232.2)	(262.7)
Market value ($ mil.)	(18.7%)	84,018.0	75,989.6	111,987.1	39,380.6	36,726.1
Employees	31.8%	5,306	7,785	9,800	13,300	16,000

SALINE MEMORIAL HOSPITAL AUXILIARY

1 MEDICAL PARK DR
BENTON, AR 720153353
Phone: 501-922-2619
Fax: –
Web: www.salinememorial.org

CEO: Bob Trautman
CFO: Carla Robertson
HR: –
FYE: June 30
Type: Private

Saline Memorial Hospital (SMH) is a not-for-profit medical facility serving the western region of Arkansas. The full-service hospital has about 167 beds and provides inpatient and outpatient care in the areas of cardiology neurology otolaryngology (ear nose and throat) ophthalmology pediatrics psychiatry and wound care among others. The hospital's campus also includes a sleep disorder laboratory two separate medical office buildings and a home health and hospice services center. In addition SMH operates two primary care clinics in nearby Bryant.

	Annual Growth	06/06	06/07	06/08	06/09	06/12
Sales ($ mil.)	(16.9%)	–	–	198.3	0.0	94.8
Net income ($ mil.)	–	–	–	(1.4)	0.0	2.4
Market value ($ mil.)	–	–	–	–	–	–
Employees	–	–	–	–	–	950

SALISBURY BANCORP, INC.

NAS: SAL

5 Bissell Street
Lakeville, CT 06039
Phone: 860 435-9801
Fax: –
Web: www.salisburybank.com

CEO: Richard J. Cantele
CFO: Donald E. White
HR: –
FYE: December 31
Type: Public

Salisbury Bancorp has a stake in New England's financial market. The holding company owns the Salisbury Bank and Trust Company which operates seven branches in northwestern Connecticut southwestern Massachusetts and southeastern New York. With roots dating to 1848 the bank offers a variety of financial products and services including checking savings and money market accounts CDs credit cards and trust services. Residential real estate mortgages make up the largest portion of the bank's loan portfolio by far; commercial real estate construction land development business financial agricultural and consumer loans round out its lending activities.

	Annual Growth	12/10	12/11	12/12	12/13	12/14
Assets ($ mil.)	10.4%	575.5	609.3	600.8	587.1	855.4
Net income ($ mil.)	(8.9%)	3.7	4.1	4.1	4.1	2.5
Market value ($ mil.)	2.0%	68.6	63.5	63.5	73.2	74.4
Employees	5.5%	147	137	147	147	182

SALIX PHARMACEUTICALS LTD

NMS: SLXP

8510 Colonnade Center Drive
Raleigh, NC 27615
Phone: 919-862-1000
Fax: –
Web: www.salix.com

CEO: Carolyn J Logan
CFO: –
HR: –
FYE: December 31
Type: Public

Salix Pharmaceuticals is a finishing school for drugs. With a focus on treating gastrointestinal ailments the company prefers to acquire drug candidates nearing commercial viability. It then takes them through the final development stages and brings them to market. The company's marketed products include Xifaxan (an antibiotic for gastrointestinal troubles) Pepcid (gastric ulcers and acid reflux) and Apriso and Colazal (for ulcerative colitis). Other products include colonoscopy preparatory bowel purgatives MoviPrep Osmo-Prep and Visicol. Its late-stage candidates include both new drugs and new uses for existing drugs.

	Annual Growth	12/09	12/10	12/11	12/12	12/13
Sales ($ mil.)	41.5%	232.9	337.0	540.5	735.4	933.8
Net income ($ mil.)	–	(43.6)	(27.1)	87.4	64.2	143.0
Market value ($ mil.)	37.2%	1,598.0	2,955.6	3,011.6	2,547.2	5,660.6
Employees	8.7%	395	390	490	525	552

SALLY BEAUTY HOLDINGS INC

NYS: SBH

3001 Colorado Boulevard
Denton, TX 76210
Phone: 940-898-7500
Fax: –
Web: www.sallybeauty.com

CEO: Christian A. (Chris) Brickman
CFO: Mark J. Flaherty
HR: Jim Biggerstaff
FYE: September 30
Type: Public

Sally Beauty Holdings (SBH) has untangled itself from former parent Alberto-Culver. Formerly Sally Beauty Co. the firm is one of the US's largest retailers and distributors of professional beauty supplies. While the US accounts for most of its sales the company also has stores in Canada Europe and South America. Some 3560 Sally Beauty Supply stores sell more than 8000 hair skin and nail products. Sally Beauty also sells its products online. SBH's Beauty Systems Group (BSG) employs more than 980 sales consultants and operates more than 1000 CosmoProf and Armstrong McCall stores that sell products only to salons and beauty professionals.

	Annual Growth	09/11	09/12	09/13	09/14	09/15
Sales ($ mil.)	4.1%	3,269.1	3,523.6	3,622.2	3,753.5	3,834.3
Net income ($ mil.)	2.4%	213.7	233.1	261.2	246.0	235.1
Market value ($ mil.)	9.4%	2,514.1	3,799.9	3,962.0	4,145.2	3,597.0
Employees	3.6%	24,615	25,525	26,450	27,470	28,330

SALON MEDIA GROUP INC.

NBB: SLNM

870 Market Street
San Francisco, CA 94102
Phone: 415-275-3911
Fax: –
Web: www.salon.com

CEO: Cynthia Jeffers
CFO: Elizabeth Hambrecht
HR: –
FYE: March 31
Type: Public

Salon Media Group (formerly Salon.com) hopes to satisfy sophisticated Web surfers weary of run-of-the-mill Internet schlock. The company that garnered attention for essays by the likes of Camille Paglia and Allen Barra has expanded from its original online magazine format. Salon.com's content includes news features interviews columns and blogs covering topics such as politics business technology books sports and arts and entertainment. Revenues come from advertising and subscription fees. Salon.com and its online communities (Table Talk and The Well) attract more than six million unique visitors a month.

	Annual Growth	03/11	03/12	03/13	03/14	03/15
Sales ($ mil.)	2.0%	4.6	3.8	3.6	6.0	4.9
Net income ($ mil.)	–	(2.6)	(4.1)	(3.9)	(2.2)	(3.9)
Market value ($ mil.)	(24.8%)	38.1	38.1	19.1	13.0	12.2
Employees	4.6%	41	45	48	44	49

SALT LAKE COMMUNITY COLLEGE

4600 S REDWOOD RD
SALT LAKE CITY, UT 841233145
Phone: 801-957-4111
Fax: –
Web: www.slcc.edu

CEO: –
CFO: –
HR: –
FYE: June 30
Type: Private

Salt Lake Community College (SLCC) provides day night and weekend courses for early risers and night owls alike. SLCC serves more than 60000 students and has a student-to-teacher ratio of 23:1. The two-year school has more than a dozen campuses and outreach centers in Salt Lake City Utah as well as online courses available to reach both traditional and non-traditional students. In addition to being a top US source of associate degrees in arts science applied science and pre-engineering the community college also has career and technical programs. SLCC was founded in 1948 to provide skilled workforce training for Utah residents.

	Annual Growth	06/09	06/10	06/11	06/12	06/13
Sales ($ mil.)	2.2%	–	88.1	90.7	87.7	94.1
Net income ($ mil.)	10.3%	–	–	3.2	3.9	3.9
Market value ($ mil.)	–	–	–	–	–	–
Employees	–	–	–	–	–	3,200

SALVE REGINA UNIVERSITY

100 OCHRE POINT AVE
NEWPORT, RI 028404149
Phone: 401-847-6650
Fax: –
Web: www.salve.edu

CEO: –
CFO: –
HR: –
FYE: June 30
Type: Private

Salve Regina isn't just an anthem that Catholics sing near Christmas. It's also a college they attend in Rhode Island. Salve Regina (meaning Hail Holy Queen) is a Catholic university serving more than 2500 undergraduate and graduate students. The university offers degrees in more than 45 disciplines including accounting anthropology biology economics education and religious studies. Salve Regina offers associate baccalaureate and master's degrees a Certificate of Advanced Graduate Study and a Ph.D. in humanities. Salve Regina was founded by the Sisters of Mercy in 1934; it opened its doors in 1947.

	Annual Growth	06/09	06/10	06/11	06/13	06/14
Sales ($ mil.)	1.3%	–	59.9	82.3	64.0	63.1
Net income ($ mil.)	34.8%	–	–	3.4	7.6	8.2
Market value ($ mil.)	–	–	–	–	–	–
Employees	–	–	–	–	–	450

SAM ASH MUSIC CORPORATION

278 Duffy Ave.
Hicksville NY 11801
Phone: 516-932-6400
Fax: 201-825-3524
Web: www.okonite.com

CEO: Richard Ash
CFO: Stuart Leibowitz
HR: –
FYE: August 31
Type: Private

Sam Ash Music (SAM) has been instrumental in selling the tools that make tunes. The nation's #2 musical instrument retailer (behind Guitar Center) SAM operates 45 stores in more than 15 states mostly in California New York and Florida. Besides instruments the company sells sheet music recording equipment lighting computers and music software. It also sells online. In addition SAM sells vintage guitars offers custom-built instruments and music clinics and buys used musical instruments. It runs a pro services and parts division Sam Ash Professional and an Educational Division serving schools. The company was founded in 1924 by Sam and Rose Ashkynase whose descendants still own and run the company.

SAM LEVIN INC.

301 FITZ HENRY RD
SMITHTON, PA 154798715
Phone: 724-872-2055
Fax: –
Web: www.levinfurniture.com

CEO: –
CFO: –
HR: Irene Fostyk
FYE: December 31
Type: Private

Founded in 1920 as a furniture and hardware store by the husband-and-wife team Sam and Jessie Levin Sam Levin (dba Levin Furniture) sells a wide variety of dining room bedroom living room and office furniture as well as mattresses at about a dozen retail locations in northeastern Ohio and southwestern Pennsylvania. It also operates a Sleep Center bedding store in Pennsylvania and a clearance outlet in Ohio. The family-owned-and run-company offers self-service kiosks in its showrooms and creative exhibits that include sports- and Wizard of Oz-themed displays. Robert Levin Sam and Jessie's grandson is president of the company.

	Annual Growth	12/09	12/10	12/11	12/12	12/13
Sales ($ mil.)	8.8%	–	145.9	170.0	187.9	188.0
Net income ($ mil.)	(21.3%)	–	–	11.6	7.7	7.2
Market value ($ mil.)	–	–	–	–	–	–
Employees	–	–	–	–	–	400

SAM SWOPE AUTO GROUP LLC

10 SWOPE AUTOCENTER DR
LOUISVILLE, KY 402991806
Phone: 812-282-8285
Fax: –
Web: www.samswopeautogroup.wisebuyingmall.com

CEO: –
CFO: –
HR: –
FYE: December 31
Type: Private

Sam Swope Auto Group has plenty of new cars for old Kentucky. The company owns about two dozen automobile dealerships in the Blue Grass State. Located in Louisville Lexington Radcliff and Elizabethtown Swope dealerships sell General Motors cars including Buicks Cadillacs GMC trucks and Saturns. Other company dealerships sell BMW Honda Lexus Toyota and Volvo models. Sam Swope Auto Group also sells used cars and offers parts and service. In 1952 founder Sam Swope parlayed his love of cars into his first dealership which sold Plymouth and Dodge cars in Elizabethtown Kentucky. The company is still owned and managed by the Swope family.

	Annual Growth	12/03	12/04	12/05	12/06	12/07
Sales ($ mil.)	(47.2%)	–	–	1,598.4	434.3	444.9
Net income ($ mil.)	66206.2%	–	–	0.0	57.2	59.8
Market value ($ mil.)	–	–	–	–	–	–
Employees	–	–	–	–	–	900

SAM'S WEST INC.

702 SW 8th St.
Bentonville AR 72716-8611
Phone: 479-277-7000
Fax: 281-870-6661
Web: www.exxonmobilchemical.com

CEO: –
CFO: –
HR: –
FYE: January 31
Type: Subsidiary

Even folks over 21 get carded at Sam's Club the #2 US warehouse club chain (behind Costco). A division of Wal-Mart Stores since 1983 Sam's Club accounts for 12% of Wal-Mart's sales. It runs about 610 locations in 47 US states plus another 165-plus stores in Brazil China Mexico and Puerto Rico. Sam's Club charges its small business and individual members in the US annual fees that range from $35 to $100. The warehouse club stores average 134000 square feet and offer more than 4000 discounted items including bulk office supplies and food electronic goods jewelry clothes insurance and travel services and Member's Mark store-brand products. Samsclub.com is the company's online incarnation.

SAMARITAN REGIONAL HEALTH SYSTEM

1025 CENTER ST
ASHLAND, OH 44805-4097
Phone: 419-289-0491
Fax: –
Web: www.samaritanhospital.org

CEO: Danny L Boggs
CFO: Mary Griest
HR: –
FYE: December 31
Type: Private

Samaritan Regional Health System (SRHS) provides a wide range of inpatient and outpatient services to the residents of north central Ohio. Among its specialty services are emergency medicine orthopedics obstetrics rehabilitation cardiology gastrointestinal disease pediatrics and home health care. Its flagship facility Samaritan Hospital has about 110 licensed beds and is located in Ashland Ohio which is located between the Cleveland and Columbus metropolitan areas. The not-for-profit health system also includes outpatient general care diagnostic and specialty clinics. SRHS was founded in 1912 by philanthropists J.L. and Mary Clark.

	Annual Growth	12/07	12/08	12/08	12/10	12/12
Sales ($ mil.)	1.7%	–	72.1	76.0	80.6	77.1
Net income ($ mil.)	–	–	(11.1)	4.3	6.3	2.0
Market value ($ mil.)	–	–	–	–	–	–
Employees	–	–	–	–	–	650

SAMMONS ENTERPRISES INC.

5949 Sherry Ln. Ste. 1900
Dallas TX 75225
Phone: 214-210-5000
Fax: 214-210-5099
Web: www.sammonsenterprises.com

CEO: Heather Kreager
CFO: Pam Doeppe
HR: –
FYE: December 31
Type: Private

Sammons Enterprises summons its revenues from several sources. The diversified holding company's operations include the Sammons Financial Group (life insurance and financial services) and Briggs Equipment (heavy equipment sales and rentals). Its insurance and financial group includes Midland National Life Insurance North American Company for Life and Health Insurance and Sammons Annuity Group. The company's list of partially owned holdings runs the range from real estate investments to oilfield suppliers. It is owned by its employees and prefers to invest in companies with strong employee-ownership programs.

SAMSON INVESTMENT COMPANY

Samson Plaza 2 W. 2nd St.
Tulsa OK 74103-3103
Phone: 918-591-1791
Fax: 918-591-1796
Web: www.samson.com

CEO: Randy Limbacher
CFO: Philip Cook
HR: –
FYE: December 31
Type: Private

A strong presence among privately owned energy companies Samson Investment is an independent oil and gas entity with exploration development and production activities in a number of producing areas in the US. Key regions include East Texas Texas Gulf Coast the Gulf of Mexico and the Anadarko Permian San Juan Green River and Williston basins. Samson Investment's assets include 1 million acres across 12 plays and stakes in more than 10000 wells. To gain access to capital to fund further expansion in 2011 the company was acquired by a consortium led by KKR and including ITOCHU for $7.2 billion.

SAMSUNG ELECTRONICS AMERICA INC.

85 Challenger Rd.	CEO: Yangkyu Kim
Ridgefield Park NJ 07660	CFO: –
Phone: 201-229-4000	HR: –
Fax: 864-752-1632	FYE: December 31
Web: www.samsung.com/us	Type: Subsidiary

Samsung Electronics America (SEA) sells everything Samsung from sea to shining sea. A subsidiary of electronics giant Samsung Electronics the company's Consumer Business division markets consumer electronics and household appliances including TVs Blu-ray disc players portable audio players home theater systems hard drives cameras and camcorders refrigerators and washers and dryers. It also sells printers monitors laptops digital signage and projectors through its Enterprise Business division. Formed in 1977 SEA also manages the North American operations of Samsung Semiconductor Inc. (a leading global chip maker) and Samsung Telecommunications America (mobile phones and telephony equipment).

SAMSUNG SEMICONDUCTOR INC.

3655 N. 1st St.	CEO: Young Chang Bae
San Jose CA 95134	CFO: Damian Huh
Phone: 408-544-4000	HR: –
Fax: 408-544-4980	FYE: December 31
Web: www.samsung.com/us/business/oem-solutions/inde	Type: Subsidiary

Samsung Semiconductor Inc. is the North American subsidiary of silicon powerhouse Samsung Electronics. The company markets Samsung's many semiconductor product lines including its DRAM SRAM and flash memory chips; solid-state drives; liquid-crystal display panels and screens; LED backlight technology; and system LSI products (application-specific integrated circuits image sensors display drivers and logic chips). Samsung Semiconductor's components are used in a wide range of applications including computers consumer electronics mobile devices and industrial equipment.

SAMSUNG TELECOMMUNICATIONS AMERICA L.L.C.

1301 E. Lookout Dr.	CEO: –
Richardson TX 75082	CFO: –
Phone: 972-761-7000	HR: –
Fax: 972-761-7001	FYE: December 31
Web: www.samsungwireless.com	Type: Subsidiary

Samsung Telecommunications America which is also known as Samsung Mobile and Samsung Wireless provides a variety of personal and business communications products — including mobile phones and tablets wireless infrastructure equipment fiber optics and enterprise communications systems — to customers throughout North America. The company's phones are compatible with the networks of leading wireless service providers including AT&T Sprint Nextel T-Mobile USA and Verizon Communications. Founded in 1996 Samsung Telecommunications America is a subsidiary of Samsung Electronics the flagship of South Korea's Samsung Group.

SAMUELS JEWELERS

2914 Montopolis Dr. Ste. 200	CEO: –
Austin TX 78741	CFO: Robert J Herman
Phone: 512-369-1400	HR: –
Fax: 512-369-1527	FYE: May 31
Web: www.samuelsjewelers.com	Type: Subsidiary

In addition to diamonds and gemstones Samuels Jewelers knows something about millstones — the bankruptcy kind (it has been thrice drawn into bankruptcy court since the early 1990s). Samuels sells fine jewelry items through about 85 jewelry stores in California Texas and about 15 other states; stores are primarily located in regional shopping malls power centers and strip centers. Samuels also operates some stand-alone stores and sells jewelry online at SamuelsJewelers.com. Its stores operate under the Samuels Diamonds and Samuels Jewelers banners. Founded in 1891 Texas-based Samuels Jewelers was acquired by India's Gitanjali Gems Ltd. a jewelry maker and retailer in late 2006.

SAN DIEGO COUNTY WATER AUTHORITY

4677 Overland Ave.	CEO: –
San Diego CA 92123	CFO: Eric Sandler
Phone: 858-522-6600	HR: –
Fax: 858-522-6568	FYE: June 30
Web: www.sdcwa.org	Type: Government-owned

When you are a big urban area located between the salty sea and a blazing hot desert and with scant local water resources making sure that all your 3.1 million citizens have access to safe reliable drinking water is no easy task. But that is the job of the San Diego County Water Authority (SDCWA) which is in charge of supplying about 95% of San Diego County's potable water supply (80% of which comes directly and indirectly from the Colorado River). The authority provides water to its 24 member agencies (primarily cities and municipal districts) which in turn distribute the water to residents and businesses in the county. SDCWA also has hydroelectric power generation operations.

SAN DIEGO PADRES BASEBALL CLUB LIMITED PARTNERSHIP

9449 Friars Rd.	CEO: –
San Diego CA 92108	CFO: –
Phone: 619-881-6500	HR: Sara Greenspan
Fax: 619-497-5339	FYE: October 31
Web: www.padres.com	Type: Private

These padres offer their sermon from the plate instead of the pulpit. The San Diego Padres Baseball Club joined Major League Baseball as an expansion team in 1969 the same year as the Kansas City Royals Montreal Expos (now the Washington Nationals) and the Seattle Pilots (later the Milwaukee Brewers). The franchise boasts two National League pennants its first in 1984 and its last in 1998. San Diego fans attend baseball services at PETCO Park. A group led by CEO Jeff Moorad controls more that third of the team; BMC Software co-founder John Moores owns the rest.

SAN DIEGO UNIFIED PORT DISTRICT

3165 PACIFIC HWY
SAN DIEGO, CA 921011128
Phone: 619-686-6200
Fax: –
Web: www.portofsandiego.org

CEO: John Bolduc
CFO: Robert Deangelis
HR: Anna L Acedo
FYE: June 30
Type: Private

The San Diego Unified Port District (better known as the Port of San Diego) brings in cash from land and sea. The agency manages two marine cargo facilities as well as a terminal used by cruise ships. Its real estate operations include leasing and managing land around the port including almost 20 bayfront parks and commercial property. In addition the Port of San Diego is charged with protecting San Diego Bay and adjoining tidelands from pollution. The agency which was created in 1962 is governed by a seven-member board appointed by the city councils of San Diego and four neighboring cities.

	Annual Growth	06/10	06/11	06/12	06/13	06/14
Assets ($ mil.)	0.4%	–	683.3	683.0	677.5	692.3
Net income ($ mil.)	–	–	–	(8.9)	(4.1)	8.3
Market value ($ mil.)	–	–	–	–	–	–
Employees	–	–	–	–	–	604

SAN FRANCISCO BAY AREA RAPID TRANSIT DISTRICT

300 Lakeside Dr.
Oakland CA 94612
Phone: 510-464-6000
Fax: 510-464-6255
Web: www.bart.gov

CEO: –
CFO: –
HR: Elaine Curts
FYE: June 30
Type: Government Agency

If you're going to San Francisco — from Oakland Berkeley or another Bay Area community — San Francisco Bay Area Rapid Transit District (BART) can take you there. BART's trains carry about 365000 daily weekday riders from more than 40 stations over more than 100 miles of track including the 3.6 mile Transbay Tube under the San Francisco Bay that links the City by the Bay with Oakland and other East Bay communities. Directors elected from nine districts in Alameda Contra Costa and San Francisco counties oversee BART which operates with an annual budget of about $672 million. Construction on the rail system began in 1964 and BART carried its first passengers in 1972.

SAN FRANCISCO FORTY NINERS LTD.

4949 Centennial Blvd.
Santa Clara CA 95054
Phone: 408-562-4949
Fax: 408-727-4937
Web: www.49ers.com

CEO: Peter Harris
CFO: Larry Macneil
HR: –
FYE: December 31
Type: Subsidiary

It took some digging but these 49ers finally struck the motherload of championship gold. San Francisco Forty Niners owns and operates the San Francisco 49ers professional football team which boasts five Super Bowl championships (a mark it shares with the Dallas Cowboys). The franchise was started in 1946 as part of the All-American Football Conference (AAFC) and joined the National Football League in 1950. Its burst of championship glory came in the 1980s and 1990s with the help of such stars as Joe Montana and Steve Young. The team was started by brothers Anthony and Victor Morabito; it is owned by Denise DeBartolo York through her family's DeBartolo Corporation.

SAN FRANCISCO OPERA ASSOCIATION

301 VAN NESS AVE
SAN FRANCISCO, CA 941024509
Phone: 415-861-4008
Fax: –
Web: www.sfopera.com

CEO: –
CFO: Michael Simpson
HR: –
FYE: July 31
Type: Private

The San Francisco Opera has mighty big lungs. The company is the nation's second largest and its Western Opera Theater is the only national opera touring group. In addition to presenting new and classic works at War Memorial Opera House it offers the annual free Opera in the Park as well as education and apprenticeship programs for children and young professionals. Considered an innovator the company pioneered the US use of "supertitles" (an English translation projected over the stage) and has commissioned operas based on plays (A Streetcar Named Desire) people (slain San Francisco city supervisor Harvey Milk) and books (Dead Man Walking Dangerous Liaisons). It was founded in 1923 by Gaetano Merola.

	Annual Growth	07/08	07/09	07/10	07/12	07/13
Sales ($ mil.)	(2.5%)	–	34.0	27.1	68.8	30.8
Net income ($ mil.)	(20.1%)	–	–	18.1	(1.2)	9.2
Market value ($ mil.)	–	–	–	–	–	–
Employees	–	–	–	–	–	1,050

SAN JOAQUIN REFINING CO. INC.

3129 STANDARD ST
BAKERSFIELD, CA 93308-6242
Phone: 661-327-4257
Fax: –
Web: www.sjr.com

CEO: –
CFO: –
HR: –
FYE: December 31
Type: Private

The late Buck Owens is not the only natural resource to come from Bakersfield. California's San Joaquin Valley serves as the backdrop for Bakersfield-based independent refiner San Joaquin Refining which refines locally produced heavy crude oil. The majority of its crude oil is derived from Kern County. San Joaquin Refining's refined products are used in the development of adhesives asphalt electrical insulation lubricants paints plastics printing inks rubber roofing materials and other items. The company also owns more than 90 storage tanks capable of storing 800000 barrels of crude oil.

	Annual Growth	12/03	12/04	12/05	12/06	12/11
Sales ($ mil.)	14.9%	–	215.4	288.8	371.9	567.8
Net income ($ mil.)	33.5%	–	3.4	16.5	26.3	25.4
Market value ($ mil.)	–	–	–	–	–	–
Employees	–	–	–	–	–	20

SAN JUAN BASIN ROYALTY TRUST

NYS: SJT

Compass Bank, 300 West 7th Street, Suite B
Fort Worth, TX 76102
Phone: 866 809-4553
Fax: –
Web: www.sjbrt.com

CEO: –
CFO: –
HR: –
FYE: December 31
Type: Public

Trusting in the power of rising oil prices to keep investors happy has been a good strategy for San Juan Basin Royalty Trust. The trust owns working and royalty interests in oil and gas properties in the San Juan Basin of northwestern New Mexico. Carved from interests owned by Southland Royalty (now controlled by ConocoPhillips) San Juan Basin Royalty Trust's holdings consist of a 75% stake in about 151900 gross (119000 net) productive acres in San Juan Rio Arriba and Sandoval counties. The property contains 3823 gross producing wells with estimated proved reserves of 249000 barrels of oil and more than 156.3 billion cu. ft. of natural gas.

	Annual Growth	12/10	12/11	12/12	12/13	12/14
Sales ($ mil.)	(6.4%)	80.3	68.7	35.1	38.0	61.6
Net income ($ mil.)	(6.5%)	78.4	67.2	33.5	36.5	59.9
Market value ($ mil.)	(11.8%)	1,096.8	1,060.8	625.0	780.2	664.2
Employees	–					

SANCHEZ ENERGY CORP.

NYS: SN

1000 Main Street, Suite 3000
Houston, TX 77002
Phone: 713 783-8000
Fax: −
Web: www.sanchezenergycorp.com

CEO: Antonio R. (Tony) Sanchez
CFO: Michael G. (Mike) Long
HR: Alicia Gutierrez
FYE: December 31
Type: Public

The Sanchez family has been around South Texas almost as long as the oil found in the Eagle Ford Shale. Sanchez Energy is a spin off from Sanchez Oil & Gas Corporation (SOG) a private firm owned by the Sanchez family who trace their family history back to the founding of Laredo in 1755. Sanchez Energy was formed in 2011 to take over almost 39000 acres (about 60 sq. mi.) of land in the oil-rich Eagle Ford Shale in South Texas. In 2013 it had 140000 net acres in the Eagle Ford play and 40000 net acres in the Tuscaloosa Marine Shale in Louisiana. It also has undeveloped acreage in Montana. The company reported estimated proved reserves of in 21.2 million barrels of oil equivalent in 2012.

	Annual Growth	12/10	12/11	12/12	12/13	12/14
Sales ($ mil.)	247.8%	4.6	14.5	43.2	314.4	666.1
Net income ($ mil.)	−	(2.8)	2.0	(16.3)	26.9	(21.8)
Market value ($ mil.)	(18.7%)	−	1,011.1	1,054.5	1,435.8	544.2
Employees	−	70	−	−	−	−

SANCHEZ PRODUCTION PARTNERS LP

ASE: SPP

1000 Main Street, Suite 3000
Houston, TX 77002
Phone: 832 783-8000
Fax: −
Web: www.constellationenergypartners.com

CEO: Gerald F Willinger
CFO: Charles C Ward
HR: −
FYE: December 31
Type: Public

Constellation Energy Partners' domain is decidedly more terrestrial than stellar. A spin off from Constellation Energy the company is a coalbed methane exploration and production company that operates in Alabama's Black Warrior Basin (one of the oldest and most lucrative coalbed methane basins in the US) the Cherokee Basin in Kansas and Oklahoma and the Woodford Shale in the Arkoma Basin in Oklahoma. In 2010 Constellation Energy Partners reported proved reserves of 221 billion cu. ft. of natural gas equivalent. That year the company operated 87% of the more than 2780 wells in which it held an interest.

	Annual Growth	12/10	12/11	12/12	12/13	12/14
Sales ($ mil.)	(15.4%)	150.8	105.2	59.3	44.1	77.3
Net income ($ mil.)	−	(276.9)	19.6	(86.5)	(28.5)	9.5
Market value ($ mil.)	(15.7%)	8.1	5.7	3.5	7.0	4.1
Employees	(20.0%)	127	117	84	79	52

SANDERS/WINGO

221 N. Kansas 9th Fl.
El Paso TX 79901
Phone: 915-533-9583
Fax: 915-533-3601
Web: www.sanderswingo.com

CEO: Robert V Wingo
CFO: Daphne Restovick
HR: −
FYE: December 31
Type: Private

Sanders/Wingo provides multicultural advertising and public relations services through two Texas offices in El Paso and Austin. The agency's portfolio includes print broadcast and interactive work in fashion healthcare and energy industries. Founded in 1958 it targets the Hispanic and African American demographic with its creative work. Sanders/Wingo has worked with such clients as AT&T the American Heart Association and Shell. Sanders/Wingo has two Texas offices: El Paso and Austin. The agency was known as Sanders Wingo Galvin & Morton Advertising (SWG&M) until late 2005 when it changed its name.

SANDERSON FARMS, INC.

NMS: SAFM

127 Flynt Road
Laurel, MS 39443
Phone: 601 649-4030
Fax: 601 426-1461
Web: www.sandersonfarms.com

CEO: Joseph F. (Joe) Sanderson
CFO: D. Michael (Mike) Cockrell
HR: −
FYE: October 31
Type: Public

Sanderson Farms has steadily scratched its way up the pecking order. As the third-largest poultry processor in the US it produces processes sells and distributes fresh chill-pack and frozen chicken (whole and cut-up) under the Sanderson Farms label. In addition to buying chicks from some 190 breeders the company contracts with 800-plus independent chicken farmers who raise the breeder flocks for Sanderson. Its prepared-foods business processes sells and distributes partially cooked or marinated chicken including frozen entrées. Customers are food retailers distributors and restaurants and foodservice operators. The company processed more than 476 million chickens in 2015.

	Annual Growth	10/11	10/12	10/13	10/14	10/15
Sales ($ mil.)	9.1%	1,978.1	2,386.1	2,683.0	2,774.8	2,803.5
Net income ($ mil.)	−	(127.1)	53.9	130.6	249.0	216.0
Market value ($ mil.)	8.9%	1,114.8	1,020.2	1,423.5	1,891.3	1,565.4
Employees	2.0%	11,333	11,313	11,271	11,461	12,264

SANDIA NATIONAL LABORATORIES

1515 Eubank Blvd. SE
Albuquerque NM 87123
Phone: 505-845-0011
Fax: 505-844-1120
Web: www.sandia.gov

CEO: −
CFO: −
HR: −
FYE: September 30
Type: Government-owned

Sandia stands for national security. Established in 1949 as part of the Manhattan Project Sandia National Laboratories performs research and development related to national security and defense. Its focus is nuclear weapons systems research but the lab also performs nonproliferation assessments infrastructure assurance and research and development in such areas as energy and environmental security. Sandia's duties have expanded in recent years to combat terrorism aid homeland security and support the US military in Afghanistan and Iraq. Sandia which operates with a $2.5 billion annual budget is managed by Lockheed Martin for the US Department of Energy's National Nuclear Security Administration.

SANDISK CORP.

NMS: SNDK

951 SanDisk Drive
Milpitas, CA 95035
Phone: 408 801-1000
Fax: 408 542-0503
Web: www.sandisk.com

CEO: Sanjay Mehrotra
CFO: Judy Bruner
HR: −
FYE: January 03
Type: Public

SanDisk is a top producer of data storage products based on flash memory which retains data even when power is interrupted. Its products — which are sold to four primary end-markets (mobile consumer electronics computing and enterprise and hyperscale data centers) — include removable and embedded memory cards used in digital cameras mobile phones digital audio/video players GPS devices tablets and other electronic gear. It also licenses technologies from its portfolio of some 4700 US and international patents. SanDisk serves consumers and enterprises worldwide with most of its sales coming from outside the US. In 3Q 2015 SanDisk agreed to be bought by Western Digital the leading maker of disk drives. The value of the cash-and-stock transaction was set at $19 billion.

	Annual Growth	01/12*	12/12	12/13	12/14*	01/16
Sales ($ mil.)	(0.4%)	5,662.1	5,052.5	6,170.0	6,627.7	5,564.9
Net income ($ mil.)	(20.8%)	987.0	417.4	1,042.7	1,007.4	388.5
Market value ($ mil.)	11.5%	9,889.9	8,577.5	14,116.4	20,360.6	15,272.0
Employees	22.2%	3,939	4,636	5,459	8,696	8,790

*Fiscal year change

SANDOZ INC.

506 Carnegie Center Ste. 400
Princeton NJ 08540
Phone: 609-627-8500
Fax: 609-627-8659
Web: www.us.sandoz.com

CEO: –
CFO: Eric Evans
HR: Lori Escobedo
FYE: December 31
Type: Subsidiary

Sandoz Inc. makes it easier to swallow the cost of prescription medicines. As the US arm of Swiss giant Novartis' generic Sandoz International division the firm is one of the largest generic drugmakers in the US manufacturing and selling more than 200 generic oral-dosage drugs. The company's product portfolio includes drugs to fight infections cancers respiratory ailments cardiovascular and gastrointestinal disorders and central nervous system (CNS) diseases. The Sandoz organization markets its products to wholesalers and retailers as well as directly to consumers physicians and hospitals. Sandoz Inc. operates two manufacturing facilities in the US.

SANDRIDGE ENERGY INC

NBB: SDOC

123 Robert S. Kerr Avenue
Oklahoma City, OK 73102
Phone: 405 429-5500
Fax: –
Web: www.sandridgeenergy.com

CEO: James D. Bennett
CFO: Julian M. Bott
HR: –
FYE: December 31
Type: Public

This sand ridge reveals not a desert but a vista of future profits. SandRidge Energy explores for and produces oil and natural gas in the Mississippian Oil Play in the Mid-Continent and in West Texas. In 2014 SandRidge Energy reported estimated proved reserves of 515.9 million barrels of oil equivalent. The company a has 35 drilling rigs (25 operational) a related oilfield services business and gas gathering marketing and processing subsidiaries. Through subsidiaries SandRidge Energy also operates treating and transportation facilities and has tertiary oil recovery operations.

	Annual Growth	12/10	12/11	12/12	12/13	12/14
Sales ($ mil.)	13.7%	931.7	1,415.2	2,731.0	1,983.4	1,558.8
Net income ($ mil.)	7.4%	190.6	108.1	141.6	(553.9)	253.3
Market value ($ mil.)	(29.4%)	3,548.9	3,956.1	3,078.6	2,942.9	882.4
Employees	(3.8%)	2,192	2,432	2,510	1,911	1,878

SANDSTON CORPORATION

OTC: SDON

40950 Woodward Ave. Ste. 304
Bloomfield Hills MI 48304
Phone: 248-723-3007
Fax: 212-622-7301
Web: www.aljregionalholdings.com

CEO: Daniel J Dorman
CFO: –
HR: –
FYE: December 31
Type: Public

Sandston had control issues. The company formerly known as Nematron is a public shell that is pursuing investment opportunities. In 2004 it sold the assets of its control systems business to a group of private investors and changed its name to Sandston. (The private investors continue to provide industrial workstations used to control factory equipment under the Nematron name.) Dorman Industries a company controlled by CEO Daniel Dorman owns about 49% of Sandston; Patricia Dorman his wife owns another 5%.

SANDVIK COROMANT COMPANY

1702 Nevins Rd.
Fair Lawn NJ 07410-0428
Phone: 201-794-5000
Fax: 201-794-5165
Web: www.coromant.sandvik.com

CEO: –
CFO: –
HR: –
FYE: December 31
Type: Subsidiary

Sandvik Coromant Company's tools are run of the mill — that is they help the mill run. One of three core businesses of Sweden-based engineering group Sandvik Sandvik Coromant is part of its parent's Tooling division. It manufactures metal cutting and machine tools used in milling turning boring and drilling. The tools are made from cemented carbide and other extremely hard materials like synthetic diamond and cubic boron nitride ceramics and high speed steel. Sandvik Coromant offers more than 25000 products to customers in the aerospace automotive general engineering medical and die and mold industries. It has operations in some 60 countries worldwide.

SANDY SPRING BANCORP INC

NMS: SASR

17801 Georgia Avenue
Olney, MD 20832
Phone: 301 774-6400
Fax: –
Web: www.sandyspringbank.com

CEO: Daniel J. (Dan) Schrider
CFO: Philip J. Mantua
HR: –
FYE: December 31
Type: Public

Sandy Spring Bancorp is the holding company for Sandy Spring Bank which operates around 50 branches in the Baltimore and Washington DC metropolitan areas. Founded in 1868 the bank is one of the largest and oldest headquartered in Maryland. It provides standard deposit services including checking and savings accounts money market accounts and CDs. Commercial and residential real estate loans account for nearly three-quarters of the company's loan portfolio; the remainder is a mix of consumer loans business loans and equipment leases. The company also offers personal investing services wealth management trust services insurance and retirement planning.

	Annual Growth	12/10	12/11	12/12	12/13	12/14
Assets ($ mil.)	5.7%	3,519.4	3,711.4	3,955.2	4,106.1	4,397.1
Net income ($ mil.)	12.9%	23.5	34.1	36.6	44.4	38.2
Market value ($ mil.)	9.1%	461.6	439.5	486.4	706.0	653.2
Employees	0.6%	711	713	707	725	727

SANFILIPPO (JOHN B.) & SON, INC.

NMS: JBSS

1703 North Randall Road
Elgin, IL 60123-7820
Phone: 847 289-1800
Fax: –
Web: www.jbssinc.com

CEO: Jeffrey T. Sanfilippo
CFO: Michael J. Valentine
HR: Tom Fordonski
FYE: June 25
Type: Public

John B. Sanfilippo & Son (JBSS) has built an empire out of working for peanuts. One of the largest processors of peanuts almonds pecans walnuts cashews and other nuts in the US JBSS markets the nuts as a snack and a baking ingredient under a number of private labels as well as its own name brands including Fisher Orchard Valley Harvest and Sunshine Country. It also produces and distributes other foods and snacks such as peanut butter dried fruit and trail mixes corn snacks sesame sticks and candy. Its products are sold worldwide to consumers (via retailers) and less so commercial ingredient channels (food service and industrial markets) contract packagers and export distributors.

	Annual Growth	06/11	06/12	06/13	06/14	06/15
Sales ($ mil.)	7.1%	674.2	700.6	734.3	778.6	887.2
Net income ($ mil.)	79.3%	2.8	17.1	21.8	26.3	29.3
Market value ($ mil.)	59.2%	94.3	188.0	221.3	293.7	606.2
Employees	0.9%	1,400	1,300	1,300	1,300	1,450

SANFORD C. BERNSTEIN & CO. LLC

1345 Avenue of the Americas
New York NY 10105
Phone: 212-969-1000
Fax: 212-969-6189
Web: www.bernsteinresearch.com

CEO: Robert P Van Brugge
CFO: –
HR: –
FYE: December 31
Type: Subsidiary

Heed this firm's advice and you may wind up with your toes in the sand and money to burn. Sanford C. Bernstein a unit of AllianceBernstein (formerly Alliance Capital Management) was founded by the late Sanford Bernstein in 1967 to manage the discretionary accounts of the wealthy; it has approximately $80 billion of assets under management for affluent families as well as pension funds and corporate investors. Sanford Bernstein's hallmark however is the fundamental company and industry research and securities valuation services it performs for institutional clients. The company also offers customized qualitative research services and publishes Blackbooks which contain its company and industry forecasts.

SANFORD HEALTH OF NORTHERN MINNESOTA

1300 Anne St. NW
Bemidji MN 56601
Phone: 218-751-5430
Fax: 218-333-5880
Web: www.nchs.com

CEO: –
CFO: –
HR: –
FYE: September 30
Type: Subsidiary

If ya have a run-in with a snowmobile up Bemidji then ya may need Sanford Health of Northern Minnesota doncha know. Formerly named North Country Health Services the system serves residents of the town of Bemidji and other parts of Beltrami County in northern Minnesota. Its flagship facility is Sanford Bemidji Medical Center (formerly North Country Regional Hospital) a 120-bed acute care hospital founded in 1898 providing general surgical psychiatric cardiac and other specialty services. The system also has home health and hospice agencies community clinics and assisted living facilities. It added the Sanford Bemidji Clinic when it joined the Sanford Health-Meritcare network in 2011.

SANFORD-BURNHAM MEDICAL RESEARCH INSTITUTE

10901 N TORREY PINES RD
LA JOLLA, CA 920371005
Phone: 858-795-5000
Fax: –
Web: www.sanfordburnham.org

CEO: Perry Nisen
CFO: Gary F. Raisl
HR: –
FYE: June 30
Type: Private

Founded in 1976 as the La Jolla Cancer Research Foundation the Sanford-Burnham Medical Research Institute is a nonprofit organization that performs biomedical research in areas such as cellular biology cancer genetics degenerative diseases and developmental neurobiology. Known for its stem cell research and drug discovery technologies Sanford-Burnham boasts a handful of research centers including its Cancer Center which has been supported by National Cancer Institute (part of the NIH) since 1981. Sanford-Burnham's other centers include the Sanford Children's Health Research Center and the Del E. Webb Neuroscience Aging and Stem Cell Research Center.

	Annual Growth	06/10	06/11	06/12	06/13	06/14
Sales ($ mil.)	(1.9%)	–	163.2	162.7	152.9	154.0
Net income ($ mil.)	376.5%	–	–	0.7	7.8	16.7
Market value ($ mil.)	–	–	–	–	–	–
Employees	–	–	–	–	–	1,157

SANGAMO BIOSCIENCES INC

NMS: SGMO

501 Canal Blvd.
Richmond, CA 94804
Phone: 510 970-6000
Fax: –

CEO: Edward O. Lanphier
CFO: H. Ward Wolff
HR: –
FYE: December 31
Type: Public

Sangamo BioSciences hopes zinc fingers have the Midas touch when it comes to regulating gene expression. The company's zinc finger DNA-binding proteins (ZFPs) control gene expression (activation) and cell function; the firm aims to develop gene-correcting therapeutics for a variety of indications including human genetic disorders as well as genetic modifications in plants and animals. Sangamo BioSciences has candidates in clinical trials and research stages for conditions such as hemophilia HIV/AIDS sickle cell disease blood disorders and Alzheimer's disease. Other ZFP development programs include research in the areas of lysosomal storage disorders.

	Annual Growth	12/10	12/11	12/12	12/13	12/14
Sales ($ mil.)	21.9%	20.8	10.3	21.7	24.1	45.9
Net income ($ mil.)	–	(24.9)	(35.8)	(22.3)	(26.6)	(26.4)
Market value ($ mil.)	23.0%	458.6	196.1	415.1	959.3	1,050.4
Employees	5.9%	81	83	84	85	102

SANMINA CORP

NMS: SANM

2700 N. First St.
San Jose, CA 95134
Phone: 408 964-3500
Fax: –
Web: www.sanmina.com

CEO: Jure Sola
CFO: Robert K. (Bob) Eulau
HR: Alan M. Reid
FYE: October 03
Type: Public

Sanmina means to be a top contract manufacturer of sophisticated electronic components. It designs and makes printed circuit boards and board assemblies backplanes and backplane assemblies enclosures cable assemblies optical components and modules and memory modules. In addition the company provides services such as design and engineering materials management order fulfillment and in-circuit testing. It serves OEMs in the health care defense medical aerospace telecommunications and technology industries among others. Because its customers have production facilities in lower-cost regions some 84% of sales come from outside the US.

	Annual Growth	10/11*	09/12	09/13	09/14*	10/15
Sales ($ mil.)	(0.9%)	6,602.4	6,093.3	5,917.1	6,215.1	6,374.5
Net income ($ mil.)	53.0%	68.9	180.2	79.4	197.2	377.3
Market value ($ mil.)	33.7%	521.4	664.3	1,369.1	1,686.1	1,668.1
Employees	(0.9%)	45,505	44,879	40,909	43,101	43,854

*Fiscal year change

SANOFI PASTEUR INC.

Discovery Dr.
Swiftwater PA 18370
Phone: 570-839-7187
Fax: 570-839-0955
Web: www.sanofipasteur.us

CEO: –
CFO: –
HR: –
FYE: December 31
Type: Subsidiary

Sanofi Pasteur helps you guard against getting sick in the first place. The company is the US unit of Sanofi Pasteur SA the vaccines division of French drugmaker Sanofi. It researches makes and markets about 20 vaccines that protect against such bacterial and viral diseases as diphtheria hepatitis polio and meningitis. Some of Sanofi Pasteur's top sellers are Fluzone influenza vaccines childhood combination vaccines and adult booster shots. It also makes travelers' vaccines that keep globetrotters safe from typhoid cholera yellow fever and the like.

SANOFI-AVENTIS U.S. LLC

55 Corporate Dr.
Bridgewater NJ 08807
Phone: 908-231-4000
Fax: 415-466-2300
Web: www.intermune.com

CEO: Christopher A Viehbacher
CFO: –
HR: Laura Bruno
FYE: December 31
Type: Subsidiary

Yes Sanofi-Aventis US is "just" a subsidiary but it's still one of the largest pharmaceutical companies in the country. As the US operations of global drug-maker Sanofi the company develops manufactures and markets pharmaceutical products for a range of ailments. Its principal therapeutic areas include cardiovascular disease central nervous system ailments internal medicine metabolic disorders oncology and ophthalmology. Some of its key products include injectable insulin Lantus cancer drug Taxotere thrombosis treatment Lovenox and blood thinner Plavix. Also known as simply Sanofi US the firm markets its parent's products in the US through its thousands of field sales professionals.

SANTA CRUZ SEASIDE COMPANY INC

400 BEACH ST
SANTA CRUZ, CA 950605416
Phone: 831-423-5590
Fax: –
Web: www.beachboardwalk.com

CEO: –
CFO: –
HR: Derek Wolf
FYE: December 31
Type: Private

Santa Cruz Seaside Company has been making people scream laugh and spend money for more than a century. The company operates the Santa Cruz Boardwalk amusement park in California which has been touted the "Coney Island of the West". The park features about 35 rides 30 restaurants 15 retail shops arcades miniature golf bowling and conference and banquet facilities. The property is a State Historic Landmark while its Looff Carousel (1911) and Giant Dipper roller coaster (1924) are both National Historic Landmarks. In addition some arcade games date back to 1910. The Canfield family including chairman and president Charles own the company. The Boardwalk celebrated its 100th anniversary in 2007.

	Annual Growth	12/09	12/10	12/11	12/12	12/13
Sales ($ mil.)	6.9%	–	45.2	47.5	51.9	55.2
Net income ($ mil.)	38.7%	–	–	3.8	6.1	7.3
Market value ($ mil.)	–	–	–	–	–	–
Employees	–	–	–	–	–	1,000

SANTA FE FINANCIAL CORP.

NBB: SFEF

10940 Wilshire Blvd., Suite 2150
Los Angeles, CA 90024
Phone: 310 889-2500
Fax: 310 889-2525
Web: www.intgla.com

CEO: John V Winfield
CFO: David T Nguyen
HR: –
FYE: June 30
Type: Public

No Santa Fe Financial doesn't invest in the City Different but it does know its way around city living. Santa Fe Financial invests in residential and commercial real estate mostly in California. Its majority-owned Portsmouth Square jointly owns the land improvements and leaseholds for a Hilton hotel in San Francisco. It also owns a majority stake in a Los Angeles apartment complex and owns a smaller residential building through its Acanto Properties subsidiary. Portsmouth also invested in a residential development in Hawaii. Investments derived from Portsmouth along with rental income make up most of Santa Fe Financial's revenue. CEO John Winfield also serves as CEO of InterGroup and Portsmouth Square.

	Annual Growth	06/11	06/12	06/13	06/14	06/15
Sales ($ mil.)	11.7%	36.8	43.0	47.1	51.6	57.4
Net income ($ mil.)	–	4.0	(1.2)	(0.4)	(5.1)	(2.5)
Market value ($ mil.)	7.1%	23.6	19.2	24.2	23.6	31.0
Employees	(9.6%)	3	3	3	2	2

SANTA FE GOLD CORP

NBB: SFEG Q

1219 Banner Mine Road
Lordsburg, NM 88405
Phone: 505 255-4852
Fax: –
Web: www.santafegoldcorp.com

CEO: Catalin Chiloflishi
CFO: Frank Mueller
HR: –
FYE: June 30
Type: Public

Santa Fe Gold hopes it has the Midas touch. The company controls the Summit silver and gold mining project and the Lordsburg mill in southwestern New Mexico. It has also been developing the Ortiz gold property in north-central New Mexico and holds the Black Canyon mica deposit and processing equipment near Phoenix. With an increased emphasis on those projects Santa Fe Gold has transformed itself into a precious metals miner. The company focuses on acquiring and developing gold silver copper and industrial mineral assets. Although it dropped its bid to acquire Columbus Silver in 2012 the company plans to buy some of that company's mineral properties.

	Annual Growth	06/10	06/11	06/12	06/13	06/14
Sales ($ mil.)	60.0%	0.3	6.4	11.5	14.6	2.1
Net income ($ mil.)	–	(1.2)	(4.6)	(4.2)	(10.4)	(11.6)
Market value ($ mil.)	(49.2%)	114.0	121.8	42.9	17.7	7.6
Employees	(39.0%)	36	53	71	65	5

SANTANDER CONSUMER USA HOLDINGS INC

NYS: SC

1601 Elm Street, Suite 800
Dallas, TX 75201
Phone: 214 634-1110
Fax: –
Web: www.santanderconsumerusa.com

CEO: Jason A Kulas
CFO: Jennifer Popp
HR: –
FYE: December 31
Type: Public

This auto finance company aims to put credit-impaired car buyers in the driver's seat. Santander Consumer USA (SCUSA) makes subprime new and used vehicle loans to buyers at more than 14000 Chrysler Ford GM and Toyota dealerships throughout the US. The technology-driven company also originates loans through independent dealers such as CarMax banks and its direct-to-consumer website Roadloans.com. SCUSA also provides refinancing and cash-back refinancing services. While subprime loans make up more than 80% of its loan portfolio the company is looking to increase its prime loan business. Founded in 1995 SCUSA is owned by Spanish banking giant Banco Santander SA. The company went public in 2014.

	Annual Growth	12/10	12/11	12/12	12/13	12/14
Sales ($ mil.)	27.4%	2,325.6	3,047.0	3,244.2	4,245.6	6,127.3
Net income ($ mil.)	15.0%	438.1	768.2	715.0	697.5	766.3
Market value ($ mil.)	–	–	–	–	–	6,843.5
Employees	6.2%	–	–	3,900	4,100	4,400

SANTANDER HOLDINGS USA INC.

NYS: SOV PRC

75 State Street
Boston, MA 02109
Phone: 617 346-7200
Fax: –
Web: www.sovereignbank.com

CEO: Scott Powell
CFO: Gerald Plush
HR: –
FYE: December 31
Type: Public

Santander Holdings USA is the parent company of Sovereign Bank which reigns in the Northeast with more than 700 branch locations. The bank caters to individuals and small to midsized businesses offering deposits credit cards insurance and investments as well as commercial loans and mortgages (which together account for nearly half of its total portfolio) and residential mortgages and home equity loans (more than a quarter). Santander Holdings also owns a majority of Santander Consumer USA which purchases and services subprime car loans made by auto dealerships and other companies. Spain-based banking giant Banco Santander acquired the rest of Sovereign Bancorp it didn't already own in 2009.

	Annual Growth	12/10	12/11	12/12	12/13	12/14
Sales ($ mil.)	19.7%	5,814.0	7,249.7	3,687.5	3,384.0	11,919.2
Net income ($ mil.)	22.9%	1,022.1	1,172.6	561.2	628.1	2,335.2
Market value ($ mil.)	0.4%	13,339.3	13,259.8	13,349.9	13,467.7	13,540.9
Employees	4.6%	11,714	8,557	8,920	9,100	14,000

SAP AMERICA INC.

3999 West Chester Pike
Newtown Square PA 19073
Phone: 610-661-1000
Fax: 919-832-8322
Web: fwv-us.com

CEO: William McDermott
CFO: Mark R White
HR: –
FYE: December 31
Type: Subsidiary

SAP America represents its German parent SAP in the US providing enterprise software and services for managing accounting distribution human resources and manufacturing functions. The company's products include business intelligence enterprise resource planning customer relationship management and supply chain management software. SAP America offers industry-specific applications for markets ranging from aerospace and defense to wholesale distribution. Its services include consulting and support as well as custom development and application hosting. SAP America accounts for more about one-quarter of SAP's sales and three-quarters of all the Americas.

SAPIENT CORP.

NMS: SAPE

131 Dartmouth St.
Boston, MA 02116
Phone: 617 621-0200
Fax: 617 621-1300
Web: www.sapient.com

CEO: Alan J Herrick
CFO: Joseph S Tibbetts Jr
HR: –
FYE: December 31
Type: Public

Sapient is no sap when it comes to helping businesses make the jump to the digital age. The company offers consulting software development digital marketing and other services that help clients transform their businesses to compete for a global digital audience. Its customers have included AT&T Mobility Unilever and the US government. Sapient has expertise in providing services for financial and commodity markets though it also targets global blue-chip customers in the consumer travel and automotive industries among others. It has more than 30 offices worldwide; about half of those are in North America.

	Annual Growth	12/08	12/09	12/10	12/11	12/12
Sales ($ mil.)	14.0%	687.5	666.7	863.5	1,062.2	1,161.5
Net income ($ mil.)	1.1%	62.5	88.1	43.8	73.6	65.2
Market value ($ mil.)	24.2%	612.8	1,141.4	1,670.0	1,739.0	1,457.5
Employees	13.9%	6,360	7,052	9,015	9,950	10,700

SAPP BROS. INC.

9915 S 148TH ST
OMAHA, NE 681383876
Phone: 402-895-7038
Fax: –
Web: www.sappbrostruckstops.com

CEO: William Sapp
CFO: Allen J Marsh
HR: –
FYE: September 30
Type: Private

Need air in those 18 wheels? Sapp Bros Travel Centers (formerly Sapp Bros Truck Stops) has the usual air gas food but also offers human conveniences such such as laundry rooms mailbox rentals private showers and TV lounges. The company operates a chain of some 15 truck stops — readily identifiable by the giant red-and-white coffeepot logo — along interstate highways from Utah to Pennsylvania; with a concentration in Nebraska. Half of the locations also operate service centers offering oil changes new tires and safety checks. Its sister company Sapp Bros Petroleum distributes fuels and lubricants to more than 200 retailers. The firm is run by CEO Bill Sapp one of the four founding Sapp brothers.

	Annual Growth	09/10	09/11	09/12	09/13	09/14
Sales ($ mil.)	7.2%	–	1,271.2	1,677.7	1,483.0	1,566.7
Net income ($ mil.)	(3.8%)	–	–	13.8	14.8	12.8
Market value ($ mil.)	–	–	–	–	–	–
Employees	–	–	–	–	–	1,115

SAPP BROS. PETROLEUM INC.

9915 S 148TH ST STE 2
OMAHA, NE 681383876
Phone: 402-895-2202
Fax: –
Web: www.sappbrospetro.com

CEO: Bill Sapp
CFO: Allen Marsh
HR: –
FYE: October 31
Type: Private

There have been few poor saps in this family since the Sapp brothers made a go of their petroleum products business. Sapp Bros Petroleum distributes petroleum products such as fuels lubricants propane antifreeze absorbents additives and equipment through more than 10 locations in Nebraska and western Iowa. It has a sideline selling used computer parts such as modems processors and keyboards. The regional fuel distributor was founded by the four Sapp brothers in 1980 and is run by CEO Bill Sapp who also runs sister company Sapp Bros Truck Stops.

	Annual Growth	10/05	10/06	10/07	10/08	10/09
Sales ($ mil.)	–	–	–	(1,566.9)	922.3	564.0
Net income ($ mil.)	19890.6%	–	–	0.0	3.2	5.6
Market value ($ mil.)	–	–	–	–	–	–
Employees	–	–	–	–	–	285

SARAH BUSH LINCOLN HEALTH CENTER

1000 HEALTH CENTER DR
MATTOON, IL 619389261
Phone: 217-258-2525
Fax: –
Web: www.sarahbush.org

CEO: Timothy A Ols
CFO: –
HR: Lori Springman
FYE: June 30
Type: Private

With the moniker of the Illinois' favorite son's stepmother (Sarah Bush Lincoln) who wouldn't want to go to this health center? And apparently the locals agree since Sarah Bush Lincoln Health Center (SBLHC) has a market share of about 44% in its seven-county service area in east-central Illinois and an inpatient market share for Coles County of nearly 80%. SBLHC has 128 beds and provides a wide range of health care services including emergency medicine behavioral health care surgical services and cancer treatment. Its network also includes about 30 clinics doctors' offices and hospice centers. The hospital also offers support groups and continuing education classes.

	Annual Growth	06/06	06/07	06/08	06/09	06/11
Sales ($ mil.)	(34.6%)	–	–	699.1	132.6	195.7
Net income ($ mil.)	849.5%	–	–	0.0	(6.7)	14.0
Market value ($ mil.)	–	–	–	–	–	–
Employees	–	–	–	–	–	1,543

SARAH LAWRENCE COLLEGE

1 MEAD WAY
BRONXVILLE, NY 107085999
Phone: 914-337-0700
Fax: –
Web: www.library.slc.edu

CEO: –
CFO: –
HR: –
FYE: May 31
Type: Private

Sarah Lawrence College (SLC) was founded in 1926 as an institution of higher education for young women. The private liberal arts school located on a 44-acre campus in suburban New York has been coeducational since 1968 and has an annual enrollment of some 1300 undergraduate and about 350 graduate students. Most of its courses are seminars limited to 14 students; the school has a student-to-faculty ratio of approximately 10-to-1 one of the lowest at any US university. SLC offers a wide range of academic concentrations including performing arts natural science history teaching and literature. It was founded by William Lawrence who named the school after his wife Sarah a supporter of women's suffrage.

	Annual Growth	05/10	05/11	05/12	05/13	05/14
Sales ($ mil.)	0.6%	–	71.1	68.7	70.7	72.4
Net income ($ mil.)	–	–	–	(16.4)	15.4	4.3
Market value ($ mil.)	–	–	–	–	–	–
Employees	–	–	–	–	–	450

SARATOGA RESOURCES INC

NBB: SARA Q

9225 Katy Freeway, Suite 100
Houston, TX 77024
Phone: 713 458-1560
Fax: –
Web: www.saratogaresources.com

CEO: Thomas F Cooke
CFO: –
HR: –
FYE: December 31
Type: Public

Saratoga Resources (SRI) hopes to find more than springs underground. The independent oil and gas company explores for and produces oil and natural gas along the coast of Louisiana. The company's 13 oil fields are spread across more than 52000 acres with about 90 wells and have proved and probable reserves of about 342 million barrels of oil equivalent 46% of which is natural gas. SRI produces about 803400 barrels of oil equivalent per year about 75% of it oil. The company owns associated infrastructure assets on its oilfields including 100 miles of pipeline about 90 wellbores and 10 saltwater disposal wells which it uses and provides to third parties for a fee.

	Annual Growth	12/10	12/11	12/12	12/13	12/14
Sales ($ mil.)	(0.3%)	55.0	80.9	84.0	67.4	54.4
Net income ($ mil.)	–	(19.4)	20.8	(3.7)	(26.4)	(143.9)
Market value ($ mil.)	28.2%	69.7	188.4	188.4	188.4	188.4
Employees	1.6%	30	40	31	34	32

SAREPTA THERAPEUTICS INC

NMS: SRPT

215 First Street, Suite 415
Cambridge, MA 02142
Phone: 617 274-4000
Fax: –
Web: www.sarepta.com

CEO: Ed Kaye
CFO: Sandy Mahatme
HR: Joan Wood
FYE: December 31
Type: Public

Sarepta Therapeutics has a sixth sense about antisense. A developer of bio-pharmaceutical compounds the company's investigational therapies are based on its RNA-based antisense drug technology which can halt disease processes at the genetic level. The drug developer is working on drugs that could potentially be used in the treatment of a wide range of conditions including genetic and infectious diseases. Sarepta has research and development programs for targets including muscular dystrophy the Ebola and Marburg viruses dengue fever anthrax and pandemic influenza.

	Annual Growth	12/10	12/11	12/12	12/13	12/14
Sales ($ mil.)	(24.1%)	29.4	47.0	37.3	14.2	9.8
Net income ($ mil.)	–	(32.2)	(2.3)	(121.3)	(112.0)	(135.8)
Market value ($ mil.)	61.6%	87.6	30.8	1,065.8	841.5	597.8
Employees	20.1%	98	98	103	146	204

SARGENT ELECTRIC COMPANY

2767 LIBERTY AVE
PITTSBURGH, PA 152224703
Phone: 412-338-8480
Fax: –
Web: www.sargent.com

CEO: Stephan H Dake
CFO: Elizabeth Lawrence
HR: –
FYE: December 31
Type: Private

Sargent Electric Company has earned its stripes providing electrical services for its customers. Founded in 1907 to serve Pittsburgh's steel industry the electrical contractor performs construction work for utilities foundries oil refineries chemical processing firms and steelmakers. Clients have included Allegheny Energy Duquesne Light General Electric and United States Steel. The company also provides electric service and maintenance services to residential commercial and government customers. Its service area encompasses about 20 states in the eastern half of the US. Sargent Electric is owned and managed by the Sargent family.

	Annual Growth	12/08	12/09	12/10	12/11	12/13
Sales ($ mil.)	14.9%	–	107.7	79.4	89.1	187.7
Net income ($ mil.)	152.9%	–	–	0.6	0.3	10.2
Market value ($ mil.)	–	–	–	–	–	–
Employees	–	–	–	–	–	400

SAS INSTITUTE INC.

100 SAS Campus Dr.
Cary NC 27513-2414
Phone: 919-677-8000
Fax: 919-677-4444
Web: www.sas.com

CEO: James H Goodnight
CFO: Don Parker
HR: –
FYE: December 31
Type: Private

Don't talk back to this company about business intelligence. SAS (pronounced "sass") specializes in software used for business analytics data warehousing and data mining activities employed by corporations to gather manage and analyze enormous amounts of data. Clients mainly financial services firms government agencies and telecom carriers use its applications to find patterns in customer data manage resources and target new business. SAS also offers software and support packages for other segments such as leisure manufacturing and retail. It has more than 400 offices in over 50 countries. Founder and CEO James Goodnight owns about two-thirds of the company; co-founder and EVP John Sall owns the rest.

SASCO

2750 Moore Ave.
Fullerton CA 92833
Phone: 714-870-0217
Fax: 714-738-3571
Web: www.sasco.com

CEO: –
CFO: –
HR: –
FYE: December 31
Type: Private

SASCO helps companies get wired to the Net and to the power grid. The electrical contractor is one of the largest privately-held electrical and data contractors in the US. It offers preconstruction consulting design/build services multimedia infrastructure planning and other services for clients around the world. SASCO also specializes in data systems installation and the servicing of data voice and video networks. SASCO works from a network of offices in California Washington and Texas. The company has worked on electrical systems for small office buildings hotels and larger projects such as Dodger Stadium Los Angeles International Airport and Kodak Theater in Hollywood.

SATMETRIX SYSTEMS INC.

1100 Park Place
San Mateo CA 94403
Phone: 650-227-8300
Fax: 650-227-8301
Web: www.satmetrix.com

CEO: Richard Owen
CFO: Robert Promm
HR: –
FYE: June 30
Type: Private

Survey says Satmetrix Systems can help you know if your customers are satisfied. The company's software uses customer surveys to provide feedback on sales products training and support services. Survey results can be displayed in standard charts and graphs or in customized reports in a real-time Web-based environment. Satmetrix software can also integrate data from existing call tracking or customer relationship management systems. Customers come from a wide range of industries and have included firms such as AT&T eBay and Hewlett-Packard.

SATTERFIELD AND PONTIKES CONSTRUCTION INC.

11000 EQUITY DR STE 100
HOUSTON, TX 770418235
Phone: 210-637-5250
Fax: –
Web: www.satpon.com

CEO: George A Pontikes Jr
CFO: Angelina Salinas
HR: –
FYE: December 31
Type: Private

Satterfield & Pontikes Construction (S&P) provides general contracting consultation and construction management services primarily in the Gulf Coast region of Texas and Louisiana. The company often works on buildings for the commercial retail industrial educational entertainment and recreational sectors. High profile projects include the Texas A&M University Health Science Center and the expansion of the World War II Museum in New Orleans. S&P specializes in concrete work and early-stage site work as well as 3-D modeling and virtual design. The company was founded in 1989 and is headed by majority owner and CEO George Pontikes.

	Annual Growth	12/09	12/10	12/11	12/12	12/13
Sales ($ mil.)	(5.7%)	–	445.1	388.8	377.3	373.6
Net income ($ mil.)	–	–	–	0.3	(8.9)	(7.8)
Market value ($ mil.)	–	–	–	–	–	–
Employees	–	–	–	–	–	300

SAUL CENTERS, INC.

NYS: BFS PRC

7501 Wisconsin Avenue, Suite 1500
Bethesda, MD 20814-6522
Phone: 301 986-6200
Fax: –
Web: www.saulcenters.com

CEO: B. Francis Saul
CFO: Scott V. Schneider
HR: –
FYE: December 31
Type: Public

This company might say that with shopping properties it's "Saul" good. A self-managed and self-administered real estate investment trust (REIT) Saul Centers acquires develops and manages commercial real estate primarily in the Washington DC metropolitan area. The REIT owns about 50 strip malls and shopping centers anchored by big-box retailers and supermarkets along with half a dozen mixed-use properties. Altogether its properties comprise some 9.3 million sq. ft. of leasable space. Outside of its core market the company has properties in the Southeast and Midwest. Its major tenants include the likes of Giant Food Safeway Capital One Bank and the US government.

	Annual Growth	12/10	12/11	12/12	12/13	12/14
Sales ($ mil.)	6.1%	163.5	174.4	190.1	197.9	207.1
Net income ($ mil.)	6.3%	36.8	26.7	33.4	30.9	46.9
Market value ($ mil.)	20.1%	–	–	–	465.7	559.1
Employees	0.0%	65	63	60	65	65

SAVAGE COMPANIES

6340 S. 3000 East Ste. 600
Salt Lake City UT 84121
Phone: 801-944-6600
Fax: +852-2498-5382
Web: www.peakf.com

CEO: Allen B Alexander
CFO: –
HR: –
FYE: December 31
Type: Private

Through a collection of subsidiaries led by Savage Services Corporation Savage Companies arranges transportation of bulk cargo and provides materials handling services from facilities throughout the US and in parts of Canada. Freight handled by the company includes chemicals construction materials food-grade products mineral products (including coal petroleum coke and sulfur) plastics and waste products. Savage arranges for bulk cargo to be transported over the water (by barge or tanker) over the road and over the rails. Its materials management services include transferring cargo between carriers; it also contracts to handle bulk materials at customers' plants. Savage began operations in 1946.

SAVE THE CHILDREN FEDERATION INC.

501 KINGS HWY E STE 400
FAIRFIELD, CT 068254861
Phone: 203-221-4000
Fax: –
Web: www.savethechildren.org

CEO: Carolyn Miles
CFO: –
HR: Maria Nolan
FYE: December 31
Type: Private

Save the Children helps poor and malnourished children in some 15 US states and nearly 120 countries focusing on such areas as health and nutrition economic development education child protection and HIV/AIDS. The humanitarian organization also participates in international disaster relief efforts focusing on children and their families. Save the Children spends about 90% of its budget on program services with the rest allocated to administration and fundraising. The group was founded in 1932 inspired by the international children's rights movement begun in the UK in 1919 by Eglantyne Jebb founder of the British Save the Children Fund. It is a member of the International Save the Children Alliance.

	Annual Growth	09/04	09/05	09/06	09/07*	12/13
Sales ($ mil.)	(11.3%)	–	1,710.9	332.4	356.2	657.8
Net income ($ mil.)	(21.0%)	–	–	20.9	9.9	4.0
Market value ($ mil.)	–	–	–	–	–	–
Employees	–	–	–	–	–	3,000

*Fiscal year change

SAVI TECHNOLOGY INC.

351 E. Evelyn Ave.
Mountain View CA 94041-1530
Phone: 650-316-4700
Fax: 650-316-4750
Web: www.savi.com

CEO: –
CFO: –
HR: –
FYE: December 31
Type: Subsidiary

Savi brings practical know-how to supply chains. The company's systems combine supply chain asset management security and collaborative software with radio-frequency identification (RFID) tracking devices to enable the monitoring of supplies equipment and other cargo through a global supply chain. Partners who have integrated Savi's products with their own supply chain management products include 3M CheckPoint and Sensormatic. Its products are also used in airport security and are certified in the US by the FAA. Savi also offers logistics optimization services to federal agencies including the Department of Defense. The company is a subsidiary of Lockheed Martin.

SAVIENT PHARMACEUTICALS INC

NBB: SVNT Q

400 Crossing Boulevard, 3rd Floor
Bridgewater, NJ 08807
Phone: 732 418-9300
Fax: –
Web: www.savient.com

CEO: Louis Ferrari
CFO: John P Hamill
HR: –
FYE: December 31
Type: Public

Savient Pharmaceuticals is a savant of gout management weight gain encouragement and joint pain relief commercializing niche drug products that address these conditions which it then sells to medical specialists. The biopharmaceutical company gets most of its revenues from KRYSTEXXA a treatment for chronic gout which it launched commercially in 2011. Savient's other marketed products are Oxandrin a synthetic derivative of testosterone used to treat involuntary weight loss caused by trauma surgery or disease (mainly HIV) and the the generic form of that drug known as Oxandrolone.

	Annual Growth	12/08	12/09	12/10	12/11	12/12
Sales ($ mil.)	54.3%	3.2	3.0	4.0	9.6	18.0
Net income ($ mil.)	–	(84.2)	(90.9)	(73.1)	(102.0)	(118.3)
Market value ($ mil.)	(34.8%)	423.2	994.7	814.1	163.0	76.7
Employees	13.7%	73	43	129	173	122

SAVVIS INC.

1 Savvis Pkwy.	CEO: James E Ousley
Chesterfield MO 63017	CFO: Gregory W Freiberg
Phone: 314-628-7000	HR: –
Fax: 845-695-2699	FYE: December 31
Web: www.mediacomcc.com	Type: Subsidiary

SAVVIS serves up a wide array of network services. The company primarily provides hosting services including data colocation and hosted software for businesses from its 32 data centers. It also provides managed network services such as network security and utility computing and it sells network bandwidth on a wholesale basis. SAVVIS markets directly to customers mainly in the Americas region but it also has clients and operations in Europe and Asia. The company targets large and midsized businesses and federal government entities. Customers have included Procter & Gamble Reuters and Virgin Entertainment. SAVVIS was acquired in 2011 by CenturyLink a leading US phone company for $2.5 billion.

SAWNEE ELECTRIC MEMBERSHIP CORPORATION

543 ATLANTA RD	CEO: Michael A Goodroe
CUMMING, GA 300402701	CFO: Sandra Fraro
Phone: 770-887-2363	HR: –
Fax: –	FYE: December 31
Web: www.sawnee.com	Type: Private

Sawnee Electric Membership Corporation (Sawnee EMC) wasn't around on the night the lights went out in Georgia but it plans to make sure they stay on. The electric distribution cooperative serves about 152000 residential commercial and industrial meters in a seven-county area of northern Georgia comprised of Cherokee Dawson Forsyth Fulton Gwinnett Hall and Lumpkin counties. Residential customers in the area (which includes the sprawling Atlanta suburbs) account for two-thirds of electricity usage. While small and medium users must get their electricity from Sawnee potential customers with loads exceeding 900 kilowatts can shop around. Sawnee EMC distributes electricity over 9970 miles of power line.

	Annual Growth	12/02	12/03	12/08	12/12	12/13
Sales ($ mil.)	5.2%	–	201.9	0.2	326.0	335.6
Net income ($ mil.)	–	–	–	(0.0)	0.0	0.0
Market value ($ mil.)	–	–	–	–	–	–
Employees	–	–	–	–	–	300

SAYERS40 INC.

825 Corporate Woods Pkwy.	CEO: –
Vernon Hills IL 60061	CFO: John Altergott
Phone: 847-391-4040	HR: –
Fax: 847-294-0750	FYE: December 31
Web: www.sayers.com	Type: Private

The game has changed from football to technology products but NFL Hall of Famer Gale Sayers is still trying to leave his competition in the dust. The former Chicago Bear's eponymous company Sayers sells computer hardware and software. It offers services ranging from computer installation to consulting services such as operating system migration and network design. Other services include technical training voice and data cabling and financing. The company offers products from leading manufacturers such as Cisco Systems Hewlett-Packard and Sun Microsystems. Chairman and CEO Sayers is the majority owner of the company which he founded in 1982.

SB FINANCIAL GROUP INC

NAS: SBFG

401 Clinton Street	CEO: Mark A Klein
Defiance, OH 43512	CFO: Anthony V Cosentino
Phone: 419 783-8950	HR: –
Fax: –	FYE: December 31
Web: www.yoursbfinancial.com	Type: Public

SB Financial Group (formerly Rurban Financial) is the holding company The State Bank and Trust Company (dba State Bank) which has more than 20 branches in northwestern Ohio and another in northeastern Indiana. The banks offer products including checking and savings accounts money market accounts credit cards IRAs and CDs. Commercial and agricultural loans account for approximately two-thirds of the company's loan portfolio; the bank also writes mortgage and consumer loans. State Bank Wealth Management (formerly Reliance Financial Services) a unit of State Bank offers trust and investment management services as well as brokerage services through an alliance with Raymond James.

	Annual Growth	12/10	12/11	12/12	12/13	12/14
Assets ($ mil.)	0.9%	660.3	628.7	638.2	631.8	684.2
Net income ($ mil.)	–	(15.6)	1.7	4.8	5.2	5.3
Market value ($ mil.)	–	–	–	–	–	–
Employees	(5.6%)	239	208	184	200	190

SBA COMMUNICATIONS CORP.

NMS: SBAC

8051 Congress Avenue	CEO: Jeffrey A. (Jeff) Stoops
Boca Raton, FL 33487	CFO: Brendan T Cavanagh
Phone: 561 995-7670	HR: Jo Carol
Fax: –	FYE: December 31
Web: www.sbasite.com	Type: Public

SBA Communications wants to tower over the wireless communications industry. The company is a top independent owner and operator of wireless communications towers in the US. It leases antenna space to wireless service carriers and provides site development services including network design zoning and permit assistance and tower construction. SBA owns and operates more than 20000 towers in North and Latin America. It built most of the towers it operates often through build-to-suit arrangements with carriers. AT&T Mobility Sprint Nextel Verizon Wireless and T-Mobile are its four largest customers.

	Annual Growth	12/10	12/11	12/12	12/13	12/14
Sales ($ mil.)	24.9%	626.6	698.2	954.1	1,304.9	1,527.0
Net income ($ mil.)	–	(194.7)	(126.5)	(181.0)	(55.9)	(24.3)
Market value ($ mil.)	28.3%	5,286.7	5,547.6	9,165.9	11,601.4	14,302.9
Employees	15.0%	720	814	1,022	1,117	1,259

SC FUELS

1800 W. Katella Ste. 400	CEO: Frank P Greinke
Orange CA 92863-4159	CFO: Mimi Taylor
Phone: 714-744-7140	HR: –
Fax: 714-922-7200	FYE: September 30
Web: www.scfuels.com	Type: Private

Southern name Western beat. SC Fuels (formerly Southern Counties Oil) is the oldest and largest wholesale distributor of gasoline diesel fuel and lubricants to more than 35000 customers in the western US. SC Fuels delivers fuel and lubricants to commercial accounts in varied industries in Northern and Southern California. Clients include Costco and Albertsons. Through its Pacific Northwest Energy subsidiary SC Fuels provides heating oils propane delivery and heating and air conditioning repair services to residential construction industrial and fleet operating customers in Washington state.

SCA TISSUE NORTH AMERICA LLC

Cira Centre Ste. 2600 2929 Arch St.
Philadelphia PA 19104
Phone: 610-499-3700
Fax: 610-499-3455
Web: www.scanorthamerica.com/

CEO: –
CFO: Joseph Fahley
HR: –
FYE: December 31
Type: Subsidiary

SCA Tissue North America aims to wipe out the competition. The company produces paper products for washroom tabletop tissue personal care and health care facility applications. It also makes wiper and soap dispensers for industrial use. It is reportedly one of the largest producers of AFH (away-from home) tissue products in North America supplying restaurants schools convenience stores even Giants Stadium. Its foodservice products include napkins paper towels and dispensers. Other products stem from its packaging and forest products divisions. SCA Tissue is a unit of Sweden-based Svenska Cellulosa Aktiebolaget (SCA) one of Europe's leading tissue products providers.

SCANA CORP

NYS: SCG

100 SCANA Parkway
Cayce, SC 29033
Phone: 803 217-9000
Fax: –
Web: www.scana.com

CEO: Kevin B. Marsh
CFO: James E. (Jimmy) Addison
HR: –
FYE: December 31
Type: Public

SCANA (from "South CAroliNA") is cooking with natural gas and electricity in South Carolina North Carolina and Georgia. The holding company serves 692000 electricity customers and 342000 gas customers through utilities South Carolina Electric & Gas (SCE&G) Public Service Company of North Carolina and SCANA Energy (in Georgia). SCANA has an electric generating capacity of about 5240 MW derived from fossil-fueled power plants and hydro-electric and nuclear generation facilities. Unregulated operations include retail and wholesale energy marketing and trading gas transportation power plant management and appliance and HVAC maintenance.

	Annual Growth	12/10	12/11	12/12	12/13	12/14
Sales ($ mil.)	1.8%	4,601.0	4,409.0	4,176.0	4,495.0	4,951.0
Net income ($ mil.)	9.4%	376.0	387.0	420.0	471.0	538.0
Market value ($ mil.)	10.4%	5,793.6	6,430.1	6,512.8	6,696.9	8,619.1
Employees	0.0%	5,877	5,889	5,842	5,989	5,886

SCANSOURCE, INC.

NMS: SCSC

6 Logue Court
Greenville, SC 29615
Phone: 864 288-2432
Fax: –
Web: www.scansourceinc.com

CEO: Michael L. (Mike) Baur
CFO: Charles A. Mathis
HR: –
FYE: June 30
Type: Public

There are more than a few fine lines between ScanSource and its competitors. The company is a leading distributor of automatic identification and data capture (AIDC) products such as bar code scanners label printers and portable data collection terminals. It also provides point-of-sale (POS) products including PC-based alternatives to cash registers. In addition ScanSource distributes voice data and converged communications products as well as video surveillance and wireless networking equipment. It sells more than 100000 products from vendors such as Avaya Cisco Intermec and Zebra Technologies to resellers and systems integrators. Founded in 1992 ScanSource operates in the Americas and Europe.

	Annual Growth	06/11	06/12	06/13	06/14	06/15
Sales ($ mil.)	4.8%	2,666.5	3,015.3	2,877.0	2,913.6	3,218.6
Net income ($ mil.)	(2.9%)	73.5	74.3	34.7	81.8	65.4
Market value ($ mil.)	0.4%	1,057.5	864.5	902.9	1,074.4	1,073.8
Employees	9.9%	1,370	1,500	1,400	1,500	2,000

SCANTRON CORPORATION

1313 Lone Oak Rd.
Eagan MN 55121-1334
Phone: 651-683-6000
Fax: 512-899-1900
Web: www.leetilford.com

CEO: Kevin Brueggeman
CFO: –
HR: –
FYE: December 31
Type: Subsidiary

Scantron's computerized assessment products make students testy. They might query which of the following statements are true. a) The company makes prepackaged educational software and offers software services and systems for the collection management and interpretation of data. b) Scantron manufactures peripheral hardware equipment specializing in optical scanning devices and magnetic ink readers sorters and inscribers. c) Its clients include educational institutions financial corporations health care providers and government agencies. d) Michael Sokolski William Sanders and Richard Stewart started the business in 1972. e) All of the above.

SCHAWK, INC.

NYS: SGK

1695 South River Road
Des Plaines, IL 60018
Phone: 847 827-9494
Fax: –
Web: www.schawk.com

CEO: David Schawk
CFO: Timothy J Cunningham
HR: –
FYE: December 31
Type: Public

Schawk has designs on consumers' products. The company provides digital prepress and other graphic services primarily for consumer product packaging advertising and point-of-sale marketing. It offers digital imaging color separations electronic retouching and platemaking services for lithography gravure and flexography. Ultimately the company is responsible for manipulating images used to entice consumers to buy a product. The family of founder and chairman Clarence Schawk owns a controlling stake (more than 50%) in the company. It has been in operation since 1953.

	Annual Growth	12/08	12/09	12/10	12/11	12/12
Sales ($ mil.)	(1.7%)	494.2	452.4	460.6	455.3	460.7
Net income ($ mil.)	–	(60.0)	19.5	32.4	20.6	(23.4)
Market value ($ mil.)	3.5%	299.3	355.1	537.4	292.7	343.7
Employees	3.8%	3,100	3,100	3,200	3,600	3,600

SCHEIN (HENRY), INC.

NMS: HSIC

135 Duryea Road
Melville, NY 11747
Phone: 631 843-5500
Fax: –
Web: www.henryschein.com

CEO: James P. Breslawski
CFO: Steven Paladino
HR: –
FYE: December 26
Type: Public

From Poughkeepsie to Prague Henry Schein outfits dental offices around the world with everything they need. The company is a leading global distributor of dental supplies equipment and pharmaceuticals. Henry Schein provides everything from the delicate hand held tools up to the X-ray equipment and patient chairs as well as office supplies and anesthetics. But the company isn't only interested in teeth: It also supplies doctors' offices veterinarians and other office-based health care providers with diagnostic kits surgical tools drugs vaccines and animal health products. Other offerings include practice management software repair services and financing.

	Annual Growth	12/11	12/12	12/13	12/14	12/15
Sales ($ mil.)	5.7%	8,530.2	8,940.0	9,560.6	10,371.4	10,629.7
Net income ($ mil.)	6.8%	367.7	388.1	431.6	466.1	479.1
Market value ($ mil.)	25.0%	5,310.0	6,589.9	9,430.8	11,322.6	12,946.6
Employees	6.1%	15,000	15,000	16,000	17,500	19,000

SCHEWEL FURNITURE COMPANY INCORPORATED

1031 MAIN ST	CEO: Marc A Schewel
LYNCHBURG, VA 245041800	CFO: -
Phone: 434-845-2326	HR: -
Fax: -	FYE: March 31
Web: www.schewels.com	Type: Private

Schewel Furniture Company operates about 50 retail furniture and bedding stores in Virginia West Virginia and North Carolina. In addition to home furnishings the chain sells appliances electronics carpeting and related accessories. Typical store units average 18000 sq. ft. and primarily target the lower- and middle-income markets. Newer stores are larger in the 40000-55000 square foot range. Customers can also browse furniture collections and other items available at Schewel stores through the company's Web site. The family-run company now in its fourth generation of management got its start in 1897 when Elias Schewel began selling small furniture pieces out of his horse-drawn wagon.

	Annual Growth	03/10	03/11	03/12	03/13	03/14
Sales ($ mil.)	3.0%	-	111.6	118.0	121.6	122.0
Net income ($ mil.)	7.3%	-	-	3.9	6.4	4.5
Market value ($ mil.)	-	-	-	-	-	-
Employees	-	-	-	-	-	850

SCHIFF HARDIN LLP

233 South Wacker Dr. Ste. 6600	CEO: -
Chicago IL 60606-6473	CFO: -
Phone: 312-258-5500	HR: -
Fax: 312-258-5600	FYE: December 31
Web: www.schiffhardin.com	Type: Private - Partnershi

Law firm Schiff Hardin has represented corporate clients in Chicago since the middle of the 19th century. The firm maintains a wide range of practices which it groups into four main areas: corporate and securities; estate planning and administration; litigation; and real estate. Besides its Chicago headquarters Schiff Hardin has eight additional offices spread throughout major metropiltan areas in the country. Hardin's hundreds of attorneys have represented such clients as Newell Rubbermaid the Chicago Bears and NiSource. The firm traces its historical roots all the way back to 1864 through the formation of law firm Hitchcock & Dupee.

SCHIFF NUTRITION INTERNATIONAL INC.
NYSE: WNI

2002 S. 5070 West	CEO: Tarang P Amin
Salt Lake City UT 84104-4726	CFO: Joseph W Baty
Phone: 801-975-5000	HR: Philip H Cooper
Fax: 801-972-2223	FYE: December 31
Web: www.schiffnutrition.com	Type: Public

Schiff Nutrition International believes in better living through better nutrition. The company makes vitamins nutritional supplements and snack bars under the Schiff Fi-Bar MegaRed Move Free Tiger's Milk Sustenex Digestive Advantage and Airborne brands. It also makes private-label products for retailers. Most of Schiff Nutrition's goods are made at its manufacturing center in Salt Lake City. Products are sold nationwide at supermarkets drugstores health food shops and mass merchandisers as well as to private label manufacturers. Weider Health and Fitness and private investment firm TPG Growth each own a 35% stake in the company; however Schiff Nutrition has agreed to be acquired Reckitt Benckiser.

SCHINDLER ELEVATOR CORPORATION

20 Whippany Rd. Ste. 225	CEO: -
Morristown NJ 07960-4524	CFO: -
Phone: 973-397-3700	HR: -
Fax: 973-397-3710	FYE: December 31
Web: www.us.schindler.com	Type: Subsidiary

You'll never have to take the stairs if you work at Schindler Elevator. The company is the North American operation of Switzerland-based Schindler Holding the world's largest escalator maker and second largest in elevators after Otis Elevator. Schindler Elevator designs manufactures installs and services passenger and freight elevators (low- mid- and high-rise) escalators and moving walkways for almost every type of building. Its products have been installed in such notable places as The White House The Pentagon and New York City's Rockefeller Center. Founded in 1979 the company operates from about 230 locations in the US and Canada.

SCHLOTZSKY'S LTD.

301 Congress Ave. Ste. 1100	CEO: Russ Umphenour
Austin TX 78701	CFO: Ronny Jordan
Phone: 512-236-3600	HR: -
Fax: 512-236-3601	FYE: December 31
Web: www.schlotzskys.com	Type: Subsidiary

This chain makes its bread selling sandwiches. Schlotzsky's operates a chain of more than 350 deli sandwich shops worldwide (in Texas 34 other US states and in four other countries). The eateries offer a selection of toasted sandwiches wrap-style sandwiches and paninis along with gourmet pizzas salads and dessert items. Most locations are franchised; some include bakeries coffee bars and computers with free Internet access. The Schlotzsky's chain was founded in 1971 by Don Dissman. It is owned by private-equity firm Roark Capital Group through that firm's FOCUS Brands affiliate.

SCHLUMBERGER LIMITED
NYSE: SLB

5599 San Felipe 17th Fl.	CEO: Paal Kibsgaard
Houston TX 77056	CFO: Simon Ayat
Phone: 713-513-2000	HR: Siukumar Nadarajah
Fax: 201-703-4205	FYE: December 31
Web: www.sealedair.com	Type: Public

Schlumberger has the know-how to get oil and gas drillers out of a slump. One of the world's largest oilfield services companies it provides a full range of services including seismic surveys formation evaluation drilling technologies and equipment cementing well construction and completion and project management. Schlumberger also provides reservoir evaluation development and management services and is developing new technologies for reservoir optimization. Through its WesternGeco business the company provides seismic and other surveying services to customers worldwide. In a blockbuster deal valued at $11 billion Schlumberger acquired drilling services giant Smith International in 2010.

SCHMITT INDUSTRIES INC (OR)
NAS: SMIT

2765 N.W. Nicolai Street
Portland, OR 97210-1818
Phone: 503 227-7908
Fax: 503 223-1258
Web: www.schmitt-ind.com

CEO: James A Fitzhenry
CFO: Ann M Ferguson
HR: –
FYE: May 31
Type: Public

What can we tell you about Schmitt? Schmitt Industries takes a balanced approach; most of its sales comes from its computerized balancing equipment which machine tool builders and grinding machine operators use to improve the efficiency of rotating devices. Customers incorporate the company's flagship Schmitt Dynamic Balance System into grinding machines. Subsidiary Schmitt Measurement Systems makes laser-based precision-measurement instruments for computer disk drive manufacturing and for military and industrial applications. Schmitt Industries has operations in the UK and the US. Customers in North America account for more than half of the company's sales.

	Annual Growth	05/11	05/12	05/13	05/14	05/15
Sales ($ mil.)	3.3%	11.5	14.4	12.5	12.1	13.1
Net income ($ mil.)	–	(0.2)	0.1	(0.5)	(0.5)	(0.1)
Market value ($ mil.)	(6.9%)	10.9	10.9	9.0	8.5	8.2
Employees	3.9%	49	55	54	46	57

SCHMITT MUSIC COMPANY

100 N. Sixth St. Ste. 850B
Minneapolis MN 55403-1505
Phone: 612-339-4811
Fax: 612-339-3574
Web: www.schmittmusic.com

CEO: Thomas M Schmitt
CFO: Robert Baker
HR: –
FYE: May 31
Type: Private

Schmitt Music is all for marching to the beat of a different drummer. Or any drummer really. The company operates about 15 retail music stores in Minnesota and about a half a dozen other midwestern states under the Schmitt Music Organ Center and Wells Music (keyboard) names. The stores offer musical instruments (guitars pianos organs band instruments) accessories and lessons. They also sell music books sheet music for piano competitions and guides to planning the music for church services. School band and orchestra members are Schmitt's biggest customer group. Fourth generation Schmitt family members Tom (president) and Doug (VP) run and own the company their grandfather founded in 1896.

SCHNEIDER NATIONAL INC.

3101 S. Packerland Dr.
Green Bay WI 54306
Phone: 920-592-2000
Fax: 920-592-3063
Web: www.schneider.com

CEO: Christopher B Lofgren
CFO: Lori Lutey
HR: –
FYE: December 31
Type: Private

If you think that's the Great Pumpkin behind you on the highway look again. With its signature bright-orange fleet of 10000 trucks and 31500 trailers Schneider National is one of the largest truckload carriers in the US. Its Schneider National Carriers unit provides truckload service throughout North America including long-haul regional dedicated expedited one-way van and bulk freight transportation. The company also offers transborder freight intermodal service (transportation of freight by multiple methods such as road and rail) warehousing and brokerage services while subsidiary Schneider Logistics offers supply chain management services. The company was founded in 1935.

SCHNITZER STEEL INDUSTRIES, INC.
NMS: SCHN

299 S.W. Clay St., Suite 350
Portland, OR 97201
Phone: 503 224-9900
Fax: –
Web: www.schnitzersteel.com

CEO: Tamara L. Lundgren
CFO: Richard D. Peach
HR: Belinda G. Hyde
FYE: August 31
Type: Public

Your old car could end up as part of a Malaysian office building if Schnitzer Steel Industries gets its steel jaws on it. The company processes scrap steel and iron which it obtains from sources such as auto salvage yards industrial manufacturers and metals brokers. The company sells more of that scrap to steelmakers in Asia than anywhere else; much of the rest goes to Schnitzer's own steelmaking business including Cascade Steel Rolling Mills which produces merchant bar steel reinforcing bar and other products at its mini-mill in Oregon. Schnitzer's Pick-N-Pull Auto Dismantlers unit operates auto salvage yards.

	Annual Growth	08/11	08/12	08/13	08/14	08/15
Sales ($ mil.)	(13.7%)	3,459.2	3,340.9	2,621.9	2,543.6	1,915.4
Net income ($ mil.)	–	118.4	27.4	(281.4)	5.9	(197.0)
Market value ($ mil.)	(21.5%)	1,219.6	739.7	676.2	741.5	463.6
Employees	(7.8%)	4,090	3,626	3,643	3,371	2,955

SCHNUCK MARKETS INC.

11420 Lackland Rd.
St. Louis MO 63146-6928
Phone: 314-994-9900
Fax: 614-449-0403

CEO: Scott C Schnuck
CFO: David Bell
HR: –
FYE: September 30
Type: Private

If you'll meet me in St. Louis chances are there'll be a Schnucks in sight. The region's largest food chain Schnuck Markets operates about 100 stores two-thirds of which are in the St. Louis area. The other stores are in Missouri Illinois Indiana Iowa and Wisconsin. All stores offer a full line of groceries and 95% have pharmacies. Other services include Redbox video rentals in-store banking and florist shops. Although most stores operate under the Schnucks banner the company also runs about half a dozen Logli supermarkets in Illinois and Wisconsin and a specialty pharmacy. Founded in 1939 the company is owned by the Schnuck family and run by CEO Scott Schnuck and president and COO Todd Schnuck.

SCHOLASTIC CORP.
NMS: SCHL

557 Broadway
New York, NY 10012
Phone: 212 343-6100
Fax: –
Web: www.scholastic.com

CEO: Richard (Dick) Robinson
CFO: Maureen O'Connell
HR: –
FYE: May 31
Type: Public

Once upon a time a company grew up to become one of the world's leading children's book publishers. Scholastic Corporation sells books to children in more than 150 countries. It operates through three divisions: Children's Book Publishing and Distribution; Education; and International. Scholastic owns the rights to properties such as Goosebumps and The Baby-Sitters Club and is the US distributor of the Harry Potter books the best-selling children's series of all time. Known for its school book fairs Scholastic also publishes magazines textbooks and software for students and teachers and produces children's TV shows.

	Annual Growth	05/11	05/12	05/13	05/14	05/15
Sales ($ mil.)	(3.8%)	1,906.1	2,148.8	1,792.4	1,822.3	1,635.8
Net income ($ mil.)	65.4%	39.4	102.4	31.1	44.4	294.6
Market value ($ mil.)	13.0%	902.6	892.9	1,002.0	1,056.3	1,472.8
Employees	(1.4%)	9,400	9,200	9,600	9,700	8,900

SCHOOL EMPLOYEES RETIREMENT SYSTEM OF OHIO

300 E. Broad St. Ste. 100	CEO: –
Columbus OH 43215-3746	CFO: Virginia Briszendine
Phone: 614-222-5853	HR: –
Fax: 614-340-1295	FYE: June 30
Web: www.ohsers.org	Type: Government Agency

In retirement there's no free lunch - even for the lunch lady. That's where the School Employees Retirement System of Ohio comes in. The system also known as SERS manages pension health care retirement and other benefits for about 190000 non-teaching public school employees and retirees in the Buckeye State. More than half its portfolio consists of US and international stocks with the rest invested in bonds real estate private equity and short-term securities. The School Employees Retirement System of Ohio was established in 1937 and now manages more than $7 billion in plan assets. It pays out approximately $900 billion in benefits annually.

SCHOOLSFIRST FCU

2115 N. Broadway	CEO: –
Santa Ana CA 92706	CFO: –
Phone: 714-258-4000	HR: –
Fax: 847-426-4630	FYE: December 31
Web: www.revcor.com	Type: Private - Not-for-Pr

SchoolsFirst FCU formerly Orange County Teachers Federal Credit Union (OCTFCU) serves more than 500000 members through nearly 30 branches and seven express centers located in Southern California. Founded in 1934 the credit union changed its name to better reflect its membership which is open to all school employees and their family members across 10 Southern California counties. As part of its business SchoolsFirst FCU offers traditional financial products such as checking and savings accounts and credit cards. It also provides members with financial advice insurance and retirement and college savings plans. Lending activities at SchoolsFirst FCU consist of home auto and personal loans.

SCHOTTENSTEIN REALTY TRUST INC.

4300 E. 5th Ave.	CEO: –
Columbus OH 43219	CFO: –
Phone: 614-445-8461	HR: –
Fax: 214-303-4901	FYE: December 31
Web: www.isnetworld.com	Type: Private

As long as US consumers are shopping Schottenstein Realty will do a little shopping of its own. A self-administered and self-managed real estate company Schottenstein Realty acquires and re-develops retail properties and shopping centers anchored by big-box stores. It prefers to acquire distressed or bankrupt properties in major metropolitan areas invest in expansion and redevelopment and then bring in large retailers like Wal-Mart Bed Bath & Beyond and T.J. Maxx as tenants. Upon its 2010 formation the company filed to go public and sought to qualify as a REIT (real estate investment trust). If all goes according to plan Schottenstein Realty will own interests in some 156 properties in 27 states.

SCHREIBER FOODS INC.

425 Pine St.	CEO: Michael J Haddad
Green Bay WI 54301	CFO: Matt P Mueller
Phone: 920-437-7601	HR: –
Fax: 920-437-1617	FYE: September 30
Web: www.schreiberfoods.com	Type: Private

Want cheese with that? That's Schreiber Foods. The company is a major supplier of cheese used in hamburgers and other dishes served by US fastfood chains and restaurants schools and universities hospitals and other foodservice operators. Schreiber produces some 575 private-label processed and natural cheeses as well as dairy ingredients for grocers club stores and wholesalers and food manufacturers. It offers a few of its own brands for retail sale including American Heritage and Cooper. The company has expanded its presence to more than 20 countries by acquiring or forming joint ventures with smaller cheese makers. Schreiber Foods is arguably the largest employee-owned dairy company in the world.

SCHULMAN (A.), INC.

NMS: SHLM

3637 Ridgewood Road	CEO: Bernard Rzepka
Fairlawn, OH 44333	CFO: Joseph J. (Joe) Levanduski
Phone: 330 666-3751	HR: –
Fax: 330 668-7204	FYE: August 31
Web: www.aschulman.com	Type: Public

A. Schulman might consider itself the master of all masterbatches. The company is a global leader in masterbatches color and additive concentrates that are combined with polymer resins by its customers to provide color to plastic products or enhance their performance in some way. A. Schulman also produces engineered plastics (compounded products used in making durable goods appliances and toys) and specialty powders (compounded resin powders used in rotationally molded products ranging from kayaks to gas tanks). It also serves as a distributor for polymer producers worldwide. Its high-performance plastic compounds and resins are used in packaging consumer products and automotive and industrial products.

	Annual Growth	08/11	08/12	08/13	08/14	08/15
Sales ($ mil.)	2.2%	2,193.0	2,106.8	2,133.4	2,447.0	2,392.2
Net income ($ mil.)	(10.2%)	41.0	50.9	26.1	56.2	26.6
Market value ($ mil.)	17.1%	534.3	711.5	789.7	1,137.4	1,005.6
Employees	13.6%	3,000	3,100	3,200	3,900	5,000

SCHULTE ROTH & ZABEL LLP

919 3rd Ave.	CEO: –
New York NY 10022	CFO: –
Phone: 212-756-2000	HR: –
Fax: 212-593-5955	FYE: December 31
Web: www.srz.com	Type: Private - Partnershi

Law firm Schulte Roth & Zabel is known for its investment management practice and for its work forming and operating domestic and foreign hedge funds. The firm made its initial splash in hedge funds before branching into individual trust and estate planning which gained the firm such clients as the Rockefeller family Charles Lazarus (founder of Toys "R" Us) and billionaire investor George Soros. Schulte Roth also has a large practice specializing in business reorganization. The firm has about 400 attorneys who practice in areas such as employee benefits litigation intellectual property real estate and tax.

SCHULZE AND BURCH BISCUIT CO.

1133 W. 35th St.
Chicago IL 60609
Phone: 773-927-6622
Fax: 773-376-4528
Web: www.schulzeburch.com

CEO: –
CFO: –
HR: –
FYE: December 31
Type: Private

Pick a toaster pastry any toaster pastry. Odds are that it was made by Schulze and Burch Biscuit Company. The company makes and markets toaster pastries under its Toast'em Pop-ups brand as well as for private- and branded-label customers. It also makes Snackin' Fruits pastry bars and it offers contract manufacturing for such food items as cereal bars granola bars breakfast cereal crackers and fruit snacks for other food companies. The privately-held company which invented the saltine cracker in 1949 was founded by German immigrant Paul Schulze Sr. in 1896.

SCHUMACHER ELECTRIC CORPORATION

801 E BUSINESS CENTER DR
MOUNT PROSPECT, IL 600562179
Phone: 847-385-1600
Fax: –
Web: www.batterychargers.com

CEO: Donald A. (Don) Schumacher
CFO: Daniel Frano
HR: Dorothy Tow
FYE: December 31
Type: Private

Schumacher Electric gets a charge out of starting things up. The company makes and sells its own brand of battery starters and chargers including automatic manual wheel and bench battery chargers. The chargers rev up cars boats light trucks commercial trucks snowmobiles motorcycles recreational vehicles and farm vehicles and equipment. Schumacher Electric also makes power inverters and testers as well as welding machines and accessories and custom-built transformers. The specialty manufacturing company is run by veteran drag car racer Don Schumacher.

	Annual Growth	12/00	12/01	12/02	12/03	12/13
Sales ($ mil.)	–	–	0.0	0.0	85.3	142.6
Net income ($ mil.)	–	–	–	0.0	0.0	3.0
Market value ($ mil.)	–	–	–	–	–	–
Employees	–	–	–	–	–	125

SCHWAB (CHARLES) CORP.

NYS: SCHW

211 Main Street
San Francisco, CA 94105
Phone: 415 667-7000
Fax: 415 627-8894
Web: www.aboutschwab.com

CEO: Walter W. (Walt) Bettinger
CFO: Joseph R. Martinetto
HR: Martha Tuma
FYE: December 31
Type: Public

The once-rebellious Charles Schwab is all grown up as the discount broker now offers the same traditional brokerage services it shunned some three decades ago. Schwab manages about $2.5 trillion in assets for nearly 11 million individual investors and institutional clients. Traders can access its services via telephone wireless device the Internet and through more than 325 offices in some 45 states plus London and Hong Kong. Besides discount brokerage the firm offers financial research advice and planning; investment management; retirement and employee compensation plans; and about 70 proprietary Schwab and Laudus mutual funds. Chairman Charles Schwab owns more than 13% of his namesake firm.

	Annual Growth	12/10	12/11	12/12	12/13	12/14
Sales ($ mil.)	9.3%	4,248.0	4,691.0	4,883.0	5,435.0	6,058.0
Net income ($ mil.)	30.6%	454.0	864.0	928.0	1,071.0	1,321.0
Market value ($ mil.)	15.3%	22,426,5	14,758.7	18,822.0	34,078.8	39,570.7
Employees	3.3%	12,800	14,100	13,800	13,800	14,600

SCHWEITZER-MAUDUIT INTERNATIONAL, INC.

NYS: SWM

100 North Point Center East, Suite 600
Alpharetta, GA 30022
Phone: 800 514-0186
Fax: –
Web: www.swmintl.com

CEO: Fr ©d ©ric P. Villoutreix
CFO: Jeffrey A. Cook
HR: –
FYE: December 31
Type: Public

Business is smokin' at Schweitzer-Mauduit International (SWM) one of the world's leading suppliers of fine papers to the tobacco industry. About 90% of its sales come from tobacco-related products including cigarette wraps plug wraps (used to wrap filters) and tipping paper (used to join the filter to the rest of the cigarette) low ignition propensity (fire-safe) cigarettes as well as reconstituted tobacco leaf (RTL) — virgin tobacco blended by cigarette manufacturers. Non-tobacco lines comprise a mix of products from drinking-straw wrappers to lightweight printing paper and business forms. SWM markets its lineup in Europe the Americas and Asia garnering about 70% of its sales outside the US.

	Annual Growth	12/10	12/11	12/12	12/13	12/14
Sales ($ mil.)	1.8%	740.2	816.2	788.1	772.8	794.3
Net income ($ mil.)	8.3%	65.3	92.6	79.8	76.1	89.7
Market value ($ mil.)	(9.5%)	1,916.9	2,024.7	1,189.1	1,568.1	1,288.7
Employees	1.7%	2,800	2,800	2,800	3,000	3,000

SCICLONE PHARMACEUTICALS, INC.

NMS: SCLN

950 Tower Lane, Suite 900
Foster City, CA 94404
Phone: 650 358-3456
Fax: –
Web: www.sciclone.com

CEO: Friedhelm Blobel
CFO: Wilson W. Cheung
HR: –
FYE: December 31
Type: Public

SciClone hopes its drug sales create a whirlwind in China. The drug firm's flagship product Zadaxin is approved for use in some 30 countries including China its primary market. Zadaxin treats hepatitis B as a vaccine adjuvant (to boost a vaccine's effectiveness) as well as certain cancers. The company also partners with other drug makers including Baxter International and Pfizer to market those companies' products in China. SciClone also maintains a pipeline of products that it is shepherding through the approval process in China. The company filed for bankruptcy in 2014

	Annual Growth	12/10	12/11	12/12	12/13	12/14
Sales ($ mil.)	12.2%	85.1	133.6	156.3	127.1	134.8
Net income ($ mil.)	4.6%	21.1	28.5	9.6	11.0	25.2
Market value ($ mil.)	20.3%	208.8	214.3	215.3	251.7	437.6
Employees	21.6%	261	875	870	570	570

SCIENCE APPLICATIONS INTERNATIONAL CORP (NEW)

NYS: SAIC

1710 SAIC Drive
McLean, VA 22102
Phone: 703 676-6942
Fax: –
Web: www.saic.com

CEO: Anthony J. (Tony) Moraco
CFO: John R. Hartley
HR: Kimberly S. Admire
FYE: January 30
Type: Public

This SAIC may be something of a shadow of the former SAIC but it's still a pretty big operation. Science Applications International Corporation was spun off in 2013 when the old SAIC took its main business of providing services for the national security engineering and health care markets and changed its name to Leidos. The new SAIC kept the relatively smaller business of furnishing government technical and enterprise IT services. Nearly 75% of SAIC's revenues derive from the US Defense Department mainly due to its capacity for systems integration of large complex government projects. The reorg also eliminates some internal conflicts of interest present in the former company's business.

	Annual Growth	01/11	01/12	01/13	01/14	01/15
Sales ($ mil.)	(5.5%)	4,863.0	4,733.0	4,781.0	4,121.0	3,885.0
Net income ($ mil.)	(9.3%)	208.0	182.0	182.0	113.0	141.0
Market value ($ mil.)	31.8%	–	–	–	1,702.5	2,243.9
Employees	0.0%	–	–	–	13,000	13,000

SCIENTIFIC INDUSTRIES, INC.

NBB: SCND

80 Orville Drive, Suite 102
Bohemia, NY 11716
Phone: 631 567-4700
Fax: –
Web: www.scientificindustries.com

CEO: Helena R Santos
CFO: –
HR: Marie Schindlar
FYE: June 30
Type: Public

There's a whole lotta shakin' goin' on at Scientific Industries. The company manufactures research laboratory equipment featuring the Genie line of mixers particularly the Vortex-Genie mixer as well as orbital magnetic and microplate mixers and refrigerated and shaking incubators. The company's products are generally used by clinics hospitals and universities among other customers. In business for more than five decades Scientific Industries has distributors worldwide. The company also carries spinner flasks made by Bellco Biotechnology. Scientific Industries gets more than half of its sales outside the US.

	Annual Growth	06/11	06/12	06/13	06/14	06/15
Sales ($ mil.)	7.5%	5.9	6.2	7.1	6.8	7.8
Net income ($ mil.)	(55.8%)	0.2	0.1	0.4	(0.1)	0.0
Market value ($ mil.)	(3.4%)	4.7	3.0	4.5	5.2	4.1
Employees	3.3%	29	28	26	31	33

SCIENTIFIC LEARNING CORP.

NBB: SCIL

300 Frank H. Ogawa Plaza, Suite 600
Oakland, CA 94612-0212
Phone: 888 665-9707
Fax: –
Web: www.scilearn.com

CEO: Robert C. Bowen
CFO: Jane (Ginny) Freeman
HR: Becca Pease
FYE: December 31
Type: Public

Scientific Learning uses computers to help teach language reading and reading comprehension skills in public and private schools in the US and about 45 countries. Its flagship Fast ForWord software offers products to build language skills (elementary students) literacy skills (for students in middle and high school) and reading skills (all levels). The software is used in computer labs and the classroom in before and after school programs and during summer school. About 90% of sales come from some 117000 US schools; international sales are mostly to tutoring and learning centers professionals working with language-impaired children and ESL programs. The company also sells directly to parents.

	Annual Growth	12/10	12/11	12/12	12/13	12/14
Sales ($ mil.)	(18.5%)	43.4	41.1	28.1	21.1	19.2
Net income ($ mil.)	–	(9.7)	(6.5)	(9.7)	(6.2)	1.4
Market value ($ mil.)	(58.0%)	73.9	60.4	15.2	5.7	2.3
Employees	(17.1%)	212	240	140	121	–

SCIENTIFIC RESEARCH CORP

2300 WINDY RIDGE PKWY SE 400S
ATLANTA, GA 303395665
Phone: 770-859-9161
Fax: –
Web: www.scires.com

CEO: –
CFO: –
HR: Sandra Holtzclaw
FYE: December 31
Type: Private

Scientific Research Corporation (SRC) doesn't limit its services to the laboratory. The government contractor provides a wide variety of engineering and research services including consulting systems engineering project management network design hardware and software development prototyping testing and evaluation systems integration and training. Its expertise encompasses communications and intelligence systems electronic warfare simulation and instrumentation systems. In some cases SRC works as a subcontractor for larger companies such as Booz Allen. SRC's clients include the US government and military state agencies and private sector businesses.

	Annual Growth	12/09	12/10	12/11	12/12	12/13
Sales ($ mil.)	4.9%	–	322.7	326.2	360.0	372.8
Net income ($ mil.)	6.9%	–	–	21.8	26.2	25.0
Market value ($ mil.)	–	–	–	–	–	–
Employees	–	–	–	–	–	1,006

SCIOS INC.

1 Johnson & Johnson Plaza
New Brunswick NJ 08933
Phone: 732-524-0400
Fax: 408-367-8430
Web: www.calwatergroup.com

CEO: –
CFO: –
HR: –
FYE: December 31
Type: Subsidiary

Scios goes straight to the heart of the matter. The company a subsidiary of health care giant Johnson & Johnson develops treatments targeting cardiovascular disease. Its flagship product Natrecor is an intravenously administered drug approved by the FDA for treating patients with acute heart failure who also experience shortness of breath with minimal activity. When the drug was introduced in 2001 it was the first new treatment for heart failure in more than 14 years. The drug is not without controversy about both its long-term health effects and the company's marketing of it. Scios maintains the drug is safe and has launched a large clinical trial.

SCIQUEST INC

NMS: SQI

3020 Carrington Mill Blvd., Suite 100
Morrisville, NC 27560
Phone: 919 659-2100
Fax: –
Web: www.sciquest.com

CEO: Stephen J. Wiehe
CFO: Jennifer G. Kaelin
HR: Ann Thomas
FYE: December 31
Type: Public

SciQuest is on a mission to help organizations take better control of their supplies. The company's on-demand procurement automation software helps customers manage costs by integrating with their suppliers. Its SciQuest Supplier Network enables clients to tap into a marketplace of more than 30000 different suppliers and includes tools for negotiating discounts automating orders and managing contracts. The SciQuest Supplier Network is available in tailored versions for specific industries: higher education life sciences health care and government. It can also be integrated with other existing enterprise software so that data can easily be shared when procurement accounting and settlement functions are managed.

	Annual Growth	12/10	12/11	12/12	12/13	12/14
Sales ($ mil.)	24.5%	42.5	53.4	66.5	90.2	101.9
Net income ($ mil.)	–	1.7	2.8	(1.2)	(4.7)	(0.1)
Market value ($ mil.)	2.7%	358.7	393.5	437.3	785.3	398.4
Employees	30.8%	192	265	479	538	562

SCL HEALTH - FRONT RANGE INC.

2420 W 26TH AVE STE 100D
DENVER, CO 802115302
Phone: 303-813-5000
Fax: –

CEO: –
CFO: Lydia W Jumonville
HR: Scott Day
FYE: December 31
Type: Private

Exempla aims to provide exemplary health care to residents in the Denver area. The Exempla medical network operating as Exempla Healthcare includes three hospitals: Exempla Saint Joseph Hospital (570 beds) Exempla Lutheran Medical Center (400 beds) and Good Samaritan Medical Center (more than 230 beds). It also operates the Exempla Physician Network a chain of primary care clinics. The company employs more than 2100 physicians. Among its specialties are cardiovascular services and surgeries rehabilitation cancer care orthopedics and women's and children's services. Exempla Healthcare is sponsored by the Catholic faith-based Sisters of Charity of Leavenworth Health System (SCL Health System).

	Annual Growth	12/01	12/02	12/04	12/05	12/09
Sales ($ mil.)	12.2%	–	267.6	335.0	472.4	597.8
Net income ($ mil.)	(26.9%)	–	–	37.5	30.5	7.8
Market value ($ mil.)	–	–	–	–	–	–
Employees	–	–	–	–	–	5,300

SCOTT & WHITE HEALTH PLAN

1206 WEST CAMPUS DR
TEMPLE, TX 765027124
Phone: 254-298-3000
Fax: –
Web: www.sw.org

CEO: –
CFO: –
HR: –
FYE: December 31
Type: Private

The Scott & White Health Plan (SWHP) works to keep its members Safe & Well. The not-for-profit company provides health insurance plans and related services to more than 200000 members across some 50 counties in and around Central Texas. Owned by the Scott & White network of hospitals and clinics SWHP has employer-sponsored plans (including HMO PPO and consumer choice options) as well as several choices for individuals and families. It also offers COBRA state-administered continuation plans the Young Texan Health Plan for children Medicare and dental and vision benefits. The company began offering its services in 1982. Owner Scott & White is exploring a merger with Baylor Health Care System.

	Annual Growth	12/05	12/06	12/07	12/08	12/09
Sales ($ mil.)	5.8%	–	557.5	586.3	621.2	660.1
Net income ($ mil.)	27.0%	–	–	8.2	(4.0)	13.3
Market value ($ mil.)	–	–	–	–	–	–
Employees	–	–	–	–	–	426

SCOTT & WHITE MEMORIAL HOSPITAL

2401 S 31ST ST
TEMPLE, TX 76508-0001
Phone: 254-724-2111
Fax: –
Web: www.careers.sw.org

CEO: Robert Pryor
CFO: Ken Johnson
HR: –
FYE: August 31
Type: Private

Scott & White Healthcare serves the health care needs of Central Texas. The not-for-profit health care organization is a multi-specialty physician-led system with a dozen hospital sites and more than 60 regional clinics; it also has affiliate entities throughout the area. The network has more than 1700 licensed beds and 900 associated doctors. Scott & White's flagship campus in Temple with about 640 beds includes a children's hospital a long-term acute care hospital and a mental health clinic. It also owns health maintenance organization Scott & White Health Plan and is a teaching affiliate of Texas A&M University. Founded in the 1890s Scott & White has agreed to merge with Baylor Health Care System.

	Annual Growth	08/05	08/06	08/09	08/10	08/11
Sales ($ mil.)	12.5%	–	804.0	814.9	902.6	1,446.5
Net income ($ mil.)	–	–	0.0	0.1	41.9	91.3
Market value ($ mil.)	–	–	–	–	–	–
Employees	–	–	–	–	–	8,000

SCOTT EQUIPMENT COMPANY L.L.C.

1000 MARTIN LUTHER KING J
MONROE, LA 712035543
Phone: 318-387-4160
Fax: –
Web: www.scottcompanies.com

CEO: George J Bershen Sr
CFO: –
HR: –
FYE: December 31
Type: Private

Scott Equipment Company sells and rents construction and farm equipment through some 25 locations located in the South and Midwest. The company also offers parts and service financing and insurance. Scott Equipment is part of the Scott family of companies which also includes Scott Toyota Lift (material handling) Scott Irrigation (pivot irrigation systems) and Scott Truck (sales leasing and service). The company's beginnings date back to 1939 when Tom Scott founded Scott Truck & Tractor. It is operated by descendants of the founder. Scott Equipment has shut down several agricultural stores (Scott Tractor) to focus on its Construction Equipment division.

	Annual Growth	12/04	12/05	12/06	12/07	12/08
Sales ($ mil.)	6.1%	–	266.0	299.3	323.4	317.6
Net income ($ mil.)	43.5%	–	–	6.2	17.7	12.9
Market value ($ mil.)	–	–	–	–	–	–
Employees	–	–	–	–	–	525

SCOTT'S LIQUID GOLD, INC.

NBB: SLGD

4880 Havana Street, Suite 400
Denver, CO 80239
Phone: 303 373-4860
Fax: –

CEO: Mark E Goldstein
CFO: Barry J Levine
HR: –
FYE: December 31
Type: Public

Known for its wood furniture cleaner Scott's Liquid Gold is banking on striking gold in skin care and cosmetics products. While the company generates 46% of its sales from its namesake cleaning product a growing portion of its business is from its Neoteric Cosmetics subsidiary which sells skin care products under the Alpha Hydrox and Diabetic Skin Care brand names. Scott's Liquid Gold also makes household items such as Touch of Scent air fresheners. The company sells its products through retailers in the US Canada and abroad; it also distributes Montagne Jeunesse sachets. The children of the late founder Jerome Goldstein (including president and CEO Mark Goldstein) own about a quarter of the company.

	Annual Growth	12/10	12/11	12/12	12/13	12/14
Sales ($ mil.)	14.0%	14.4	15.6	16.0	19.3	24.3
Net income ($ mil.)	–	(0.5)	(0.6)	(1.4)	0.6	2.1
Market value ($ mil.)	47.5%	2.3	2.0	3.1	7.4	10.9
Employees	0.4%	64	64	67	60	65

SCOTTS MIRACLE-GRO CO (THE)

NYS: SMG

14111 Scottslawn Road
Marysville, OH 43041
Phone: 937 644-0011
Fax: 937 644-7614
Web: www.scotts.com

CEO: James (Jim) Hagedorn
CFO: Thomas R. (Randy) Coleman
HR: Denise S. Stump
FYE: September 30
Type: Public

The grass certainly seems greener at Scotts Miracle-Gro one of the world's largest makers and marketers of horticultural and turf products. Its Global Consumer segment serves lawn and garden and pest control markets. Its garden and indoor plant care items include grass seeds fertilizers herbicides potting soils and tools. Some of Scotts Miracle-Gro's brands (Ortho Miracle-Gro Scotts and Turf Builder) are household names and it also markets Monsanto's Roundup herbicide. The company's Scotts LawnService segment offers lawn tree and shrub care.

	Annual Growth	09/11	09/12	09/13	09/14	09/15
Sales ($ mil.)	1.6%	2,835.7	2,826.1	2,816.5	2,841.3	3,016.5
Net income ($ mil.)	(1.2%)	167.9	106.5	161.1	166.5	159.8
Market value ($ mil.)	8.1%	2,738.4	2,669.1	3,378.8	3,377.0	3,734.3
Employees	5.8%	6,300	6,100	6,200	6,700	7,900

SCOTTSDALE HEALTHCARE CORP.

8125 N HAYDEN RD
SCOTTSDALE, AZ 852582463
Phone: 480-882-4000
Fax: –
Web: www.shc.org

CEO: Thomas J Sadvary
CFO: Todd Laporte
HR: –
FYE: September 30
Type: Private

Scottsdale Healthcare a not-for-profit organization serves the health care needs of central Arizona residents. Its operations include three acute care hospitals that combined boast some 900 beds. Scottsdale Healthcare also operates other campuses that offer physician offices a cancer center home health and other health care services. It conducts clinical research through the Scottsdale Healthcare Research Institute. The group's Essential Touch Wellness Center and Boutique provides spa-like stress-reduction therapies. With nearly 2000 medical and surgical staff members the company offers some 35 medical specialties. Scottsdale Healthcare is an affiliate of Scottsdale Lincoln Health Network along with John C. Lincoln Health Network.

	Annual Growth	09/05	09/06	09/07	09/09	09/13
Sales ($ mil.)	2.4%	–	–	748.8	808.1	862.4
Net income ($ mil.)	(10.9%)	–	–	67.4	12.0	33.6
Market value ($ mil.)	–	–	–	–	–	–
Employees	–	–	–	–	–	6,500

SCOTTSDALE INSURANCE COMPANY

8877 N. Gainey Center Dr.
Scottsdale AZ 85258
Phone: 480-365-4000
Fax: 480-483-6752
Web: www.scottsdaleins.com

CEO: Michael D Miller
CFO: –
HR: –
FYE: December 31
Type: Subsidiary

Scottsdale Insurance Company insures the riskier parts of life the universe and everything. The property/casualty insurer specializes in excess and surplus insurance lines (E&S) — insurance coverage for higher-risk individuals and businesses including alarm contractors bars exterminators and tree trimmers. The company also offers such niche products as pet insurance professional liability and products for public entities (cities and counties). E&S providers are not allowed to advertise directly to consumers so Scottsdale Insurance relies upon wholesale general agents brokers and managers to sell its products through local agents. The company is a subsidiary of Nationwide Mutual Insurance.

SCRIPPS (E.W.) CO (THE)

NYS: SSP

312 Walnut Street
Cincinnati, OH 45202
Phone: 513 977-3000
Fax: –
Web: www.scripps.com

CEO: Richard A. (Rich) Boehne
CFO: Timothy M. Wesolowski
HR: Lisa Knutson
FYE: December 31
Type: Public

You might say this media company tries to be appealing to both newspaper readers and television viewers. The E. W. Scripps Company is a venerable newspaper publisher with a portfolio of more than 15 dailies including The Commercial Appeal (Memphis Tennessee) the Knoxville News Sentinel (Tennessee) and the Ventura County Star (California). Scripps also owns about 20 local TV stations most of which are affiliated with ABC and NBC. In addition subsidiaries Scripps Howard News Service and United Media distribute syndicated news and other content including columnists editorial cartoons and such comic strips as Dilbert and Peanuts. The Scripps family controls the company through various trusts.

	Annual Growth	12/10	12/11	12/12	12/13	12/14
Sales ($ mil.)	2.8%	776.9	728.7	903.5	816.9	869.1
Net income ($ mil.)	(46.7%)	130.5	(15.5)	40.2	(0.5)	10.5
Market value ($ mil.)	21.8%	578.5	456.5	616.1	1,237.9	1,273.8
Employees	1.1%	4,600	4,800	4,700	4,800	4,800

SCRIPPS COLLEGE

1030 COLUMBIA AVE
CLAREMONT, CA 917113948
Phone: 909-621-8000
Fax: –
Web: www.media.scrippscollege.edu

CEO: –
CFO: –
HR: Julie B Elliott
FYE: June 30
Type: Private

Scripps helps empower women through academic knowledge. Part of the Claremont University Consortium the all-women liberal arts college maintains an enrollment of fewer than 1000 students to encourage active participation in academic and campus life. Students participate in the Core Curriculum for their first three semesters at Scripps; the Core consists of lectures team teaching and seminar classes. The college also offers a wide range of courses from art to mathematics to psychology. Notable alumni include late best-selling author Molly Ivins and former White House chief counsel Beth Nolan. The college was founded in 1926 by Ellen Browning Scripps a newspaper publisher and philanthropist.

	Annual Growth	08/08	08/09*	06/10	06/11	06/13
Sales ($ mil.)	–	–	0.0	52.4	55.9	97.6
Net income ($ mil.)	96.3%	–	–	3.1	8.3	23.5
Market value ($ mil.)	–	–	–	–	–	–
Employees	–	–	–	–	–	180

*Fiscal year change

SCRIPPS HEALTH

4275 CAMPUS POINT CT
SAN DIEGO, CA 921211513
Phone: 858-678-7000
Fax: –
Web: www.scripps.org

CEO: Christopher D. Van Gorder
CFO: Richard K. Rothberger
HR: Vic Buzachero
FYE: September 30
Type: Private

Scripps Health houses many a script-writing physician in its hospitals. The not-for-profit health system serves the San Diego area through four acute-care hospitals on five campuses. Altogether the health system is home to 1400 inpatient beds and a network of outpatient clinics. The system also offers home health care and operates community outreach programs. Its hospitals along with more than 20 outpatient Scripps Clinic and Scripps Coastal Medical Center locations employ more than 2600 affiliated general practice and specialty physicians. The Scripps Health Foundation raises philanthropic funds for Scripps Health is affiliated with biomedical research center The Scripps Research Institute.

	Annual Growth	09/05	09/06	09/07	09/08	09/13
Sales ($ mil.)	6.9%	–	–	1,781.1	1,953.8	2,654.8
Net income ($ mil.)	5.7%	–	–	223.9	18.6	311.7
Market value ($ mil.)	–	–	–	–	–	–
Employees	–	–	–	–	–	13,445

SCRIPPS NETWORKS INTERACTIVE INC

NYS: SNI

9721 Sherrill Boulevard
Knoxville, TN 37932
Phone: 865 694-2700
Fax: –
Web: www.scrippsnetworksinteractive.com

CEO: Kenneth W. (Ken) Lowe
CFO: Lori A Hickok
HR: –
FYE: December 31
Type: Public

Lifestyle TV is a livelihood for this company. Scripps Networks Interactive operates six lifestyle cable networks including Home & Garden Television (home building and decoration) the Food Network (culinary programs) DIY - Do It Yourself Network (home repair and improvement) the Cooking Channel (culinary how-to programming) and the Travel Channel (travel and tourism). The company additionally owns music channel Great American Country and has minority interests in Asian Food Channel and regional sports network FOX Sports Net South. It also owns a 50% stake in UKTV. Trusts for the Scripps family own majority control of the company.

	Annual Growth	12/10	12/11	12/12	12/13	12/14
Sales ($ mil.)	6.6%	2,067.2	2,072.0	2,307.2	2,530.8	2,665.5
Net income ($ mil.)	7.3%	411.0	411.6	681.5	505.1	545.3
Market value ($ mil.)	9.8%	6,836.5	5,604.0	7,651.6	11,415.4	9,943.7
Employees	1.2%	2,000	1,800	2,100	2,200	2,100

SCULPTZ INC.

1150 Northbrook Dr. Ste. 200
Trevose PA 19053-8443
Phone: 877-745-5437
Fax: 218-751-0355
Web: www.riverwoodbank.com

CEO: –
CFO: Deidra Mistri
HR: –
FYE: December 31
Type: Private

Bursting at the seams? Sculptz is likely to have the right fit. The company makes and sells hosiery under the Silkies brand in more than a dozen styles and nearly as many colors. It also manufactures and sells knee-highs socks and tights under the Sculptz Shapewear and Legwear labels Silkies Enriche anti-aging skincare products and PainVanish a pain-relieving cream. Founded in 1974 Sculptz claims to be the largest direct marketer of pantyhose counting 1.5 million-plus member customers (mainly women) worldwide. Made in the US the hosiery is sold through a direct mail and online continuity program whereby additional pairs continue to be sent. Formerly HCI Direct the company changed its name in 2010.

SDB TRADE INTERNATIONAL L.P.

817 SOUTHMORE AVE STE 301
PASADENA, TX 775021130
Phone: 713-475-0048
Fax: –
Web: www.thesdbgroup.com

CEO: Dilip Bhargava
CFO: –
HR: –
FYE: December 31
Type: Private

For SDB Trade International the product pipeline more than a buzzword. An international metals trading company SDB Trade International deals in steel pipe ferrous and non-ferrous scrap coils and beams. SBD Trade provide import and export services for its products sourcing its materials primarily from mills in India and China. Specializing in metal pipes for the Oil and Gas delivery and transmission industry — the company products include seamless tubing and casing electric resistance welded steel pipes seamless steel pipes and large diameter pipes. SDB Trade serves clients located around the world and provides shipping trucking storage repair and inspection services upon request.

	Annual Growth	12/05	12/06	12/09	12/11	12/12
Sales ($ mil.)	0.4%	–	50.4	29.2	4.0	51.5
Net income ($ mil.)	(13.9%)	–	–	1.7	2.0	1.1
Market value ($ mil.)	–	–	–	–	–	–
Employees	–	–	–	–	–	–

SDI HEALTH LLC

1 SDI Dr.
Plymouth Meeting PA 19462
Phone: 610-834-0800
Fax: 610-834-8817
Web: www.sdihealth.com

CEO: –
CFO: –
HR: –
FYE: December 31
Type: Private

SDI Health isn't connected to the vice squad but it does keep a close eye on the drug trade. The company provides market research and sales data on prescription drugs to pharmaceutical makers biotechnology companies consumer packaged goods manufacturers and other firms in the health care industry. Its database and online tools are used to target sales operations manage marketing campaigns and measure the experience of the customer. It also performs survey and opinion research used to help pharmaceutical companies communicate more effectively with patients and physicians and it monitors regulatory affairs affecting the health care industry. In early 2011 SDI agreed to be acquired by rival IMS Health.

SDI TECHNOLOGIES INC.

1299 Main St.
Rahway NJ 07065-5024
Phone: 732-574-9000
Fax: 732-574-1486
Web: www.sdidirect.com

CEO: Ezra S Ashkenazi
CFO: Isaac Ashkenazi
HR: –
FYE: December 31
Type: Private

SDI Technologies has been waking up the world for more than half a century. The company founded in 1956 as Realtone Electronics is licensed to make alarm clocks clock radios iPod accessories and home and portable speaker systems under several well known brands including iHome and Timex. Soundesign its cornerstone brand featured the industry's first telephone clock radio and its iHome division manufactures audio accessories for Apple electronics. Affiliate KIDdesigns sells Barbie Fisher-Price and Matchbox electronic toys. The company has facilities throughout the US and Asia and sells its products in more than 45 countries via retailers such as Wal-Mart Best Buy and Toys R Us.

SEABOARD CORP.

ASE: SEB

9000 W. 67th Street
Shawnee Mission, KS 66202
Phone: 913 676-8800
Fax: –
Web: www.seaboardcorp.com

CEO: Steven J. Bresky
CFO: Robert L. Steer
HR: Kay Stinson
FYE: December 31
Type: Public

With pork and turkey from the US flour from Haiti and sugar from Argentina Seaboard has a lot on its plate. The diversified agribusiness and transportation firm has operations in some 45 countries in the Americas the Caribbean and Africa. Seaboard sells its pork and poultry in the US and abroad. Overseas it trades grain (wheat soya) operates power plants and feed and flour mills and grows and refines sugar cane. Seaboard owns a shipping service for containerized cargo between the US the Caribbean and South America; it has shipping terminals in Miami and Houston and a fleet of about 20 vessels (two owned the rest chartered) and ships to ports worldwide. Seaboard is run by descendants of founder Otto Bresky.

	Annual Growth	12/10	12/11	12/12	12/13	12/14
Sales ($ mil.)	10.2%	4,385.7	5,746.9	6,189.1	6,670.4	6,473.1
Net income ($ mil.)	6.5%	283.6	345.8	282.3	205.2	365.3
Market value ($ mil.)	20.5%	2,330.6	2,383.2	2,961.4	3,271.7	4,913.9
Employees	(0.2%)	10,865	10,573	11,295	11,397	10,778

SEABROOK BROTHERS & SONS INC

85 FINLEY RD
BRIDGETON, NJ 083026078
Phone: 856-455-8080
Fax: –
Web: www.seabrookfarms.com

CEO: –
CFO: –
HR: R Scott Elliott
FYE: May 31
Type: Private

Seabrook Brothers and Sons almost has an alphabet of products. From asparagus to water chestnuts the company grows processes and freezes a harvest of vegetables. In addition to producing items for retail sale under its Seabrook Farms label the company supplies vegetables to customers in the industrial ingredients foodservice and private-label retail sectors. It serves customers throughout the US as well as in internationally in Canada Chile Israel Puerto Rico Mexico and Saudi Arabia. Seabrook also makes such value-added products as frozen skillet meals creamed spinach and butter and cheese sauces. In business since 1978 the company is still run by the founding Seabrook family.

	Annual Growth	05/10	05/11	05/12*	06/13*	05/14
Sales ($ mil.)	5.6%	–	89.3	102.3	110.6	105.1
Net income ($ mil.)	–	–	–	4.1	2.3	(0.3)
Market value ($ mil.)	–	–	–	–	–	–
Employees	–	–	–	–	–	200

*Fiscal year change

SEACHANGE INTERNATIONAL INC.

NMS: SEAC

50 Nagog Park
Acton, MA 01720
Phone: 978 897-0100
Fax: –
Web: www.schange.com

CEO: Jay Samit
CFO: Anthony Dias
HR: –
FYE: January 31
Type: Public

SeaChange International sees a change coming in how we watch television. The company provides software and services used by TV stations and cable system operators to manage and distribute digital video. The company's back office software products allow operators to offer video-on-demand (VOD) and other interactive services to their subscribers while its set-top box middleware allows cable subscribers to access a variety of interactive features. Its VividLogic software acts as a hub for video distribution to devices located throughout the home. SeaChange's media services business provides content aggregation and distribution. Nearly half of sales come from customers in the US.

	Annual Growth	01/11	01/12	01/13	01/14	01/15
Sales ($ mil.)	(14.6%)	216.7	197.7	157.2	146.3	115.4
Net income ($ mil.)	–	29.5	(4.0)	(17.3)	(3.0)	(27.5)
Market value ($ mil.)	(3.9%)	270.7	234.7	364.5	391.0	230.8
Employees	(12.5%)	1,202	983	722	723	703

SEACOAST BANKING CORP. OF FLORIDA

NMS: SBCF

815 Colorado Avenue
Stuart, FL 34994
Phone: 772 287-4000
Fax: –
Web: www.seacoastbanking.com

CEO: Dennis S. (Denny) Hudson
CFO: William R. Hahl
HR: –
FYE: December 31
Type: Public

Seacoast Banking Corporation is the holding company for Seacoast National Bank which has about 35 branches in Florida with a concentration on the state's southeastern coast. Serving individuals and areas businesses the bank offers a range of financial products and services including deposit accounts credit cards trust services and private banking. Commercial and residential real estate loans account for most of the bank's lending activities; to a lesser extent it also originates business and consumer loans. The bank also provides financial planning services as well as mutual funds and other investments.

	Annual Growth	12/10	12/11	12/12	12/13	12/14
Assets ($ mil.)	11.3%	2,016.4	2,137.4	2,173.9	2,268.9	3,093.3
Net income ($ mil.)	–	(33.2)	6.7	(0.7)	52.0	5.7
Market value ($ mil.)	75.2%	48.4	50.4	53.3	404.3	455.6
Employees	9.8%	398	420	508	519	579

SEACOR HOLDINGS INC

NYS: CKH

2200 Eller Drive, P.O. Box 13038
Fort Lauderdale, FL 33316
Phone: 954 523-2200
Fax: –
Web: www.seacorholdings.com

CEO: ivind Lorentzen
CFO: Matthew R. Cenac
HR: –
FYE: December 31
Type: Public

SEACOR Holdings' diverse operations are anchored in offshore oil and gas and marine transportation. SEACOR's offerings include offshore marine inland river storage and handling distribution of petroleum chemical and agricultural commodities and shipping. The company operates one of the world's largest fleets of marine support vessels serving the offshore oil and gas industry delivering cargo and crew to offshore platforms. Its marine operations include US coastal tanker transportation of fuel and chemicals and inland river barge transportation of chemicals and bulk agricultural products.

	Annual Growth	12/10	12/11	12/12	12/13	12/14
Sales ($ mil.)	(16.0%)	2,649.4	2,141.9	1,581.2	1,247.3	1,319.4
Net income ($ mil.)	(20.0%)	244.7	41.1	61.2	37.0	100.1
Market value ($ mil.)	(7.6%)	1,833.8	1,613.7	1,520.1	1,654.4	1,338.9
Employees	(2.0%)	5,311	6,043	5,316	4,653	4,901

SEALASKA CORPORATION

1 SEALASKA PLZ STE 400
JUNEAU, AK 998011276
Phone: 907-586-1512
Fax: –

CEO: Chris E. McNeil
CFO: Doug Morris
HR: –
FYE: December 31
Type: Private

Sealaska Corporation is a native-owned investment firm active in natural resources manufacturing services and gaming. The holding company owns land in southeastern Alaska home to the Tlingit Haida and Tsimshian peoples. Sealaska core holdings include Sealaska Timber Corporation Alaska Coastal Aggregates Sealaska Constructors Sealaska Environmental Services and Colorado-based information technology services provider Managed Business Solutions. Subsidary End-to-End Enterprises manages the company's gaming business. Sealaska's subsidiaries operate throughout North America and around the world. Its companies often win government contracts for construction environmental and engineering projects.

	Annual Growth	12/09	12/10	12/11	12/12	12/13
Sales ($ mil.)	(9.7%)	–	223.8	259.5	311.6	165.0
Net income ($ mil.)	–	–	–	8.2	13.4	(33.3)
Market value ($ mil.)	–	–	–	–	–	–
Employees	–	–	–	–	–	1,400

SEALED AIR CORP.

NYS: SEE

8215 Forest Point Boulevard
Charlotte, NC 28273
Phone: 201 791-7600
Fax: 201 703-4205
Web: www.sealedair.com

CEO: Jerome A. Peribere
CFO: Carol P. Lowe
HR: –
FYE: December 31
Type: Public

Pop-Pop-Pop sounds like cha-ching for Sealed Air. Best known as the company that created Bubble Wrap Sealed Air also makes Instapak foam Jiffy mailers and Fill-Air inflatable packaging systems through its Product Care segment. Its largest segment Food Care makes Cryovac bags trays and absorbent pads for use by food processors and supermarkets to protect meat and poultry. Other products include shrink packaging for consumer goods such as toys and CDs; medical packaging for pacemakers and IV fluid; and specialty packaging for fabricators and the manufacturing industry. Sealed Air serves customers in 175 countries and operates through three major subsidiaries: Sealed Air Cryovac and Diversey.

	Annual Growth	12/10	12/11	12/12	12/13	12/14
Sales ($ mil.)	14.6%	4,490.1	5,640.9	7,648.1	7,690.8	7,750.5
Net income ($ mil.)	0.2%	255.9	149.1	(1,410.3)	124.2	258.1
Market value ($ mil.)	13.6%	5,358.0	3,623.3	3,686.4	7,168.6	8,932.9
Employees	10.5%	16,100	26,300	25,000	25,000	24,000

SEARS HOLDINGS CORP

NMS: SHLD

3333 Beverly Road
Hoffman Estates, IL 60179
Phone: 847 286-2500
Fax: –
Web: www.sears.com

CEO: Edward S. (Eddie) Lampert
CFO: Robert A. (Rob) Schriesheim
HR: Phillip (Phil) Etter
FYE: January 31
Type: Public

In the world of retail Sears Holdings is an appliance giant. In addition to home appliances the company is a leading retailer of tools as well as lawn and garden fitness and automotive repair equipment. With roughly 1700 retail stores across the US Sears Holdings operates through subsidiaries Sears Roebuck and Co. and Kmart offering proprietary Sears brands including Kenmore Craftsman and DieHard. Beyond retail Sears Holdings is the largest provider of home installation and product repair services in the US. In 2014 Sears Holdings spun off Lands' End and reduced its once majority stake in Sears Canada to just 12% as it sought to raise cash to overcome struggling store sales.

	Annual Growth	01/11	01/12*	02/13	02/14*	01/15
Sales ($ mil.)	(7.9%)	43,326.0	41,567.0	39,854.0	36,188.0	31,198.0
Net income ($ mil.)	–	133.0	(3,140.0)	(930.0)	(1,365.0)	(1,682.0)
Market value ($ mil.)	(19.6%)	8,140.6	4,714.4	5,087.9	3,891.6	3,406.9
Employees	(8.5%)	280,000	293,000	246,000	249,000	196,000

*Fiscal year change

SEARS HOMETOWN & OUTLET STORES INC

NAS: SHOS

5500 Trillium Boulevard, Suite 501
Hoffman Estates, IL 60192
Phone: 847 286-7000
Fax: –
Web: www.shos.com

CEO: William A. (Will) Powell
CFO: Ryan D. Robinson
HR: Becky Iliff
FYE: January 31
Type: Public

With more than 1200 stores across 50 US states there's a good chance Sears Hometown and Outlet Stores has a store in your hometown. A spinoff of Sears Holdings Corp. the newly-formed company sells hardware tools home appliances and lawn and garden equipment at about 945 small Sears Hometown stores 95 Sears Hardware stores and 75 Home Appliance Showrooms. More than 120 Sears Outlet stores offer discounted new used discontinued damaged and overstock merchandise. The stores carry Sears' proprietary Craftsman Kenmore and DieHard brands. In late 2012 Sears Holdings separated its hardware and outlet stores from its ailing Sears Roebuck and Kmart businesses.

	Annual Growth	01/11	01/12*	02/13	02/14*	01/15
Sales ($ mil.)	0.1%	2,347.4	2,344.2	2,453.6	2,421.6	2,356.0
Net income ($ mil.)	–	49.8	33.1	60.1	35.6	(168.8)
Market value ($ mil.)	(47.0%)	–	–	918.3	477.2	258.1
Employees	(11.8%)	–	5,300	4,935	4,485	3,634

*Fiscal year change

SEARS ROEBUCK AND CO.

3333 Beverly Rd.
Hoffman Estates IL 60179
Phone: 847-286-2500
Fax: 262-703-6143
Web: www.kohlscorporation.com

CEO: Edward S Lampert
CFO: Glenn R Richter
HR: -
FYE: January 31
Type: Subsidiary

Sears Roebuck and Co. hasn't outgrown the mall scene but it's spending more time in other places. Beyond its 840 US mall-based stores Sears has more than 1400 other locations nationwide. These include more than 900 independently owned Sears Hometown Stores (formerly known as dealer stores) in small towns 105 Sears hardware stores and about 30 free-standing Sears Auto Centers. Sears' stores sell apparel tools and appliances (Kenmore) and provide home services (remodeling appliance repairs) under the Sears Parts & Repair Services and A&E Factory brands. It also operates a growing online business. Sears was acquired by Kmart Holding Corp. in 2005. The deal formed Sears Holdings which owns both chains.

SEATTLE CHILDREN'S HOSPITAL

4800 SAND POINT WAY NE
SEATTLE, WA 981053901
Phone: 206-987-2000
Fax: -
Web: www.uwmedicine.org

CEO: Thomas N. Hansen
CFO: Kelly Wallace
HR: -
FYE: September 30
Type: Private

Children's Hospital and Regional Medical Center was a big name for little kids so they changed it to what everyone already used: Seattle Children's Hospital. The hospital which has some 325 beds serves children and infants of all ages. Its specialty units include psychiatric care neonatal intensive care and rehabilitation for children disabled by injuries illness or congenital complications. In addition to its primary campus Seattle Children's Hospital operates numerous outpatient clinics in the Puget Sound area. It also provides outreach services throughout the Pacific Northwest as well as in Alaska and Montana. Seattle Children's Hospital provides telemedicine services in Idaho.

	Annual Growth	09/09	09/10	09/11	09/12	09/13
Sales ($ mil.)	25.1%	-	-	-	814.0	1,018.0
Net income ($ mil.)	27.9%	-	-	-	150.4	192.3
Market value ($ mil.)	-	-	-	-	-	-
Employees	-	-	-	-	-	2,800

SEATTLE GENETICS INC

NMS: SGEN

21823 30th Drive SE
Bothell, WA 98021
Phone: 425 527-4000
Fax: -
Web: www.seattlegenetics.com

CEO: -
CFO: Todd E Simpson
HR: Christopher (Chris) Pawlowicz
FYE: December 31
Type: Public

To heck with verbs Seattle Genetics is conjugating antibodies and drugs to fight cancer. The company's technologies use genetically engineered monoclonal antibodies (MAbs or single source proteins) to trigger cell death in some cancers but when they can't do it alone Seattle Genetics pairs them up with drugs using its Antibody-Drug Conjugate (ADC) technology for a one-two punch. Its first product Adcetris gained FDA approval in 2011 for the treatment of lymphoma in specific patient categories. With partner Millennium Pharmaceuticals the company is working to expand Adcetris' indications. Seattle Genetics also licenses its ADC technology to larger drugmakers to develop their own new cancer therapies.

	Annual Growth	12/10	12/11	12/12	12/13	12/14
Sales ($ mil.)	27.8%	107.5	94.8	210.8	269.3	286.8
Net income ($ mil.)	-	(66.3)	(152.0)	(53.8)	(62.5)	(76.1)
Market value ($ mil.)	21.1%	1,853.4	2,072.2	2,872.5	4,945.3	3,983.3
Employees	17.2%	348	483	538	582	657

SEATTLE UNIVERSITY

901 12TH AVE
SEATTLE, WA 981224411
Phone: 206-296-6150
Fax: -
Web: www.law.seattleu.edu

CEO: -
CFO: -
HR: -
FYE: June 30
Type: Private

Seattle University isn't very big but as one of 28 Jesuit universities in the US it is part of a Roman Catholic teaching legacy that spans the country and the world. With an enrollment of about 7500 students the school offers 64 undergraduate more than 35 graduate degree programs and 28 certificate programs through its eight schools (College of Arts and Sciences Albers School of Business and Economics College of Education School of Law Matteo Ricci College College of Nursing College of Science and Engineering and School of Theology and Ministry).

	Annual Growth	06/07	06/08	06/09	06/10	06/13
Sales ($ mil.)	-	-	0.0	236.4	236.7	277.5
Net income ($ mil.)	-	-	-	0.0	11.5	1.4
Market value ($ mil.)	-	-	-	-	-	-
Employees	-	-	-	-	-	1,100

SEAWORLD ENTERTAINMENT INC.

NYS: SEAS

9205 South Park Center Loop, Suite 400
Orlando, FL 32819
Phone: 407 226-5011
Fax: -
Web: www.seaworldentertainment.com

CEO: Joel Manby
CFO: Peter J. Crage
HR: -
FYE: December 31
Type: Public

Swimming with the fishes takes on a whole new meaning at these parks. Sea-World Entertainment is one of the US's largest theme park operators. The company markets its parks as family-friendly offering learning opportunities (SeaWorld and Discovery Cove where visitors can swim with dolphins and other marine life) all-ages entertainment (the Sesame Street-themed park Sesame Place) and traditional amusement parks (Busch Gardens). Previously a subsidiary of brewer Anheuser-Busch the company was sold to Blackstone for about $2.3 billion in late 2009 and became a public company in 2013.

	Annual Growth	12/10	12/11	12/12	12/13	12/14
Sales ($ mil.)	3.6%	1,196.1	1,330.8	1,423.8	1,460.3	1,377.8
Net income ($ mil.)	-	(45.5)	19.1	77.4	50.5	49.9
Market value ($ mil.)	(37.8%)	-	-	-	2,476.7	1,540.9
Employees	(29.1%)	-	-	22,100	11,800	11,100

SECURA INSURANCE HOLDINGS INC.

2401 S. Memorial Dr.
Appleton WI 54915
Phone: 920-739-3161
Fax: 920-739-7363
Web: www.secura.net

CEO: John A Bykowski
CFO: Kathryn J Sieman
HR: -
FYE: December 31
Type: Private - Mutual Com

SECURA Insurance keeps the homestead secure. The company offers a range of personal and commercial property/casualty insurance throughout the Midwest including auto homeowners and farm-owners lines. Commercial lines include property liability workers' compensation and risk management as well as specialty coverage for niche markets such as the manufacturing restaurant and service industries. The mutual firm does business in about a dozen midwestern states and its products are marketed by independent agencies. SECURA was founded in 1900 as The Farmers Home Mutual Hail Tornado and Cyclone Insurance Company.

SECUREWORKS INC.

1 Concourse Pkwy. Ste. 500
Atlanta GA 30328
Phone: 404-327-6339
Fax: 404-728-0144
Web: www.secureworks.com

CEO: Michael R Cote
CFO: Michael R Vandiver
HR: –
FYE: December 31
Type: Subsidiary

SecureWorks endeavors to keep corporate networks free from instrusion and harm. The company offers a suite of data security services as well as 24x7 monitoring and management by IT analysts in its operations centers designed to protect its clients' computer networks from hackers viruses and other digital threats. Its services include intrusion prevention systems Internet firewalls and e-mail filtering and encryption. SecureWorks also provides services such as consulting and testing related to threat assessment and regulatory compliance. Customers are typically mid-sized businesses from a variety of industries including financial services government health care and retail. Dell bought the company in 2011.

SECURIAN FINANCIAL GROUP INC.

400 Robert St. North
St. Paul MN 55101-2098
Phone: 651-665-3500
Fax: 651-665-4488
Web: www.securian.com

CEO: Christopher M Hilger
CFO: Warren Zaccaro
HR: –
FYE: December 31
Type: Private

After 125 years of being in business Minnesota Mutual felt secure enough to change its name to Securian Financial Group and serve the entire US. The company still operates through its subsidiary Minnesota Life which offers individual and group life and disability insurance and annuities as well as retirement services. Other subsidiaries include its brokerage network Securian Financial Services and its Allied Solutions business which distributes Securian products. Its Advantus Capital Management provides institutional asset management. It also offers a small amount of property/casualty surety coverage nationwide. The company was founded in 1880 and restructured as a mutual holding company in 2005.

SECURITIES INVESTOR PROTECTION CORPORATION

805 15TH ST NW STE 800
WASHINGTON, DC 200052207
Phone: 202-371-8300
Fax: –
Web: www.sipc.org

CEO: Stephen P Harbeck
CFO: –
HR: –
FYE: December 31
Type: Private

Securities Investor Protection Corporation (SIPC) is an industry-financed insurance plan that protects clients of most broker-dealers registered with the US Securities and Exchange Commission (SEC). SIPC insures customers' securities (up to $500000 per account) against losses due to the financial failure of brokerage firms. Losses caused by fluctuations in market value are not protected. The not-for-profit membership corporation was mandated by the Securities Investor Protection Act and has more than 6000 members. Its board is appointed by the US president the treasury secretary and the Federal Reserve Board. Assessments from members and investments in government securities provide money for the SIPC Fund.

	Annual Growth	12/08	12/09	12/10	12/11	12/12
Assets ($ mil.)	13.5%	–	1,307.5	1,382.9	1,606.1	1,913.0
Net income ($ mil.)	–	–	–	(271.7)	131.6	512.3
Market value ($ mil.)	–	–	–	–	–	–
Employees	–	–	–	–	–	35

SECURITY BENEFIT CORPORATION

1 Security Benefit Place
Topeka KS 66636-0001
Phone: 785-438-3000
Fax: 785-438-5177
Web: www.securitybenefit.com

CEO: Howard Fricke
CFO: –
HR: –
FYE: December 31
Type: Private

Security Benefit Corporation might be talking more about investments but it got its start in life insurance. Operating through subsidiaries the company provides investment products to individual and institutional clients in all 50 states with a focus on employees in the education banking health care government and corporate sectors. Subsidiary Security Financial Resources provides retirement plan services for some 135000 accounts mainly in the education market. Its Rydex SGI affiliate manages and distributes more than 140 mutual funds and exchange-traded funds; the unit has some $22 billion of assets under management. Investment advisory firm Guggenheim Partners acquired Security Benefit in 2010.

SECURITY FEDERAL CORP (SC)

NBB: SFDL

238 Richland Avenue Northwest
Aiken, SC 29801
Phone: 803 641-3000
Fax: –
Web: www.securityfederalbank.com

CEO: J Chris Verenes
CFO: Jessica T Cummins
HR: Sandra M Bartlett
FYE: December 31
Type: Public

Security Federal is the holding company for Security Federal Bank which has about a dozen offices in southwestern South Carolina's Aiken and Lexington counties. It expanded into Columbia South Carolina and eastern Georgia in 2007. The bank offers checking and savings accounts credit cards CDs IRAs and other retail products and services. Commercial business and mortgage loans make up more than 60% of the company's lending portfolio which also includes residential mortgages (about 25%) and consumer loans. Security Federal also offers trust services investments and life home and auto insurance.

	Annual Growth	03/11	03/12*	12/12	12/13	12/14
Assets ($ mil.)	(4.0%)	933.5	924.6	890.4	849.2	825.4
Net income ($ mil.)	46.6%	1.8	1.8	2.0	3.8	5.8
Market value ($ mil.)	17.1%	32.1	26.5	23.8	34.6	51.5
Employees	(3.8%)	230	218	216	203	205

*Fiscal year change

SECURITY FINANCE CORPORATION OF SPARTANBURG

181 SECURITY PL
SPARTANBURG, SC 293075450
Phone: 864-582-8193
Fax: –
Web: www.security-finance.com

CEO: –
CFO: A Greg Williams
HR: –
FYE: December 31
Type: Private

Folks looking for a little financial security just might turn to Security Finance Corporation of Spartanburg. Founded in 1955 the consumer loan company provides personal loans typically ranging from $100 to $600 (some states however allow loan amounts as high as $3000). Customers can also turn to Security Finance for credit reports and tax preparation services. The company operates approximately 900 offices in more than 15 states that are marketed under the Security Finance Sunbelt Credit and PFS banner names. A subsidiary of Security Group the financial institution also has locations operating as Security Financial Services in North Carolina and Longhorn Finance in Texas.

	Annual Growth	12/09	12/10	12/11	12/12	12/13
Assets ($ mil.)	7.6%	–	495.6	322.9	461.1	616.7
Net income ($ mil.)	21.8%	–	–	42.3	53.4	62.7
Market value ($ mil.)	–	–	–	–	–	–
Employees	–	–	–	–	–	2,500

SECURITY HEALTH PLAN OF WISCONSIN INC.

1515 N SAINT JOSEPH AVE
MARSHFIELD, WI 544491343
Phone: 715-387-5621
Fax: –
Web: www.securityhealth.org

CEO: Julie Brussow
CFO: –
HR: –
FYE: December 31
Type: Private

Security Health Plan of Wisconsin provides health insurance coverage and related services to some 200000 members in more than 35 Wisconsin counties. Its managed network of providers includes more than 4000 physicians 40 hospitals and health care facilities as well as 55000 pharmacies across the US. Security Health Plan provides policies for groups and individuals. Its products include HMO coverage plans and supplemental Medicare plans as well as prescription drug and equipment coverage disease management programs and administration services for self-funded plans. Established in 1986 the company is the managed healthcare arm of Marshfield Clinic which operates medical practices across the state.

	Annual Growth	12/01	12/02	12/04	12/05	12/09
Sales ($ mil.)	16.1%	–	285.8	369.8	385.6	814.8
Net income ($ mil.)	9.7%	–	–	17.5	0.0	27.7
Market value ($ mil.)	–	–	–	–	–	–
Employees	–	–	–	–	–	1,006

SECURITY LAND & DEVELOPMENT CORP.

NBB: SLDV

2816 Washington Road, #103
Augusta, GA 30909
Phone: 706 736-6334
Fax: –

CEO: –
CFO: –
HR: –
FYE: September 30
Type: Public

The management of Security Land and Development could very well equate security with real estate. Security Land and Development invests in and develops land and property for sale or lease. Its primary asset is National Plaza a 69000-sq. ft. strip shopping center anchored by a Publix Super Markets grocery store in Augusta Georgia; it also owns a smattering of additional properties in the area (land office space and a single-family residence). Chairman Stewart Flanagin CEO Greenlee Flanagin and other members of their family own 44% of Security Land and Development.

	Annual Growth	09/11	09/12	09/13	09/14	09/15
Sales ($ mil.)	1.6%	1.4	1.4	1.4	1.5	1.5
Net income ($ mil.)	53.4%	0.3	0.3	0.4	0.3	1.5
Market value ($ mil.)	–	–	–	–	–	–
Employees	0.0%	4	4	4	4	4

SECURITY NATIONAL FINANCIAL CORP.

NMS: SNFC A

5300 South 360 West, Suite 250
Salt Lake City, UT 84123
Phone: 801 264-1060
Fax: 801 265-9882
Web: www.securitynational.com

CEO: Scott M Quist
CFO: Garrett S Sill
HR: –
FYE: December 31
Type: Public

There are three certainties — life death and mortgage payments — and Security National Financial has you covered on all fronts. Its largest unit SecurityNational Mortgage makes residential and commercial mortgage loans through some 70 offices in more than a dozen states. Its Security National Life Memorial Insurance Company and Southern Security Life subsidiaries sell life and diving or related sports accident insurance annuities and funeral plans in about 40 states. Security National Financial also owns about 15 mortuaries and cemeteries in Utah Arizona and California. The family of chairman and CEO George Quist controls more than half of Security National Financial.

	Annual Growth	12/10	12/11	12/12	12/13	12/14
Assets ($ mil.)	9.6%	465.6	521.1	597.2	618.8	671.1
Net income ($ mil.)	–	(0.4)	1.3	16.7	7.6	7.8
Market value ($ mil.)	30.3%	27.0	22.0	118.6	65.1	77.8
Employees	15.2%	840	940	1,232	1,287	1,480

SECURITY SERVICE FEDERAL CREDIT UNION

16211 La Cantera Pkwy.
San Antonio TX 78256-2419
Phone: 210-476-4000
Fax: 210-444-3000
Web: www.ssfcu.org

CEO: –
CFO: –
HR: –
FYE: December 31
Type: Private - Not-for-Pr

Security Service Federal Credit Union (SSFCU) works to keep its members' cash secure. It boasts nearly 40 branches in the San Antonio area and across South Texas plus more than 30 more in Colorado and Utah that provide such financial services as checking and savings accounts CDs credit cards insurance and investment products residential mortgages and business and consumer loans. The not-for-profit member-owned credit union was founded in 1956 to serve the US Air Force Security Service Command and today has more than 900000 members. One of the largest credit unions in the US SSFCU also has its own political action committee to participate in legislative activities related to the credit union industry.

SED INTERNATIONAL HOLDINGS, INC.

NBB: SEDN

2150 Cedars Road, Suite 200
Lawrenceville, GA 30043
Phone: 770 243-1200
Fax: –
Web: www.sedonline.com

CEO: Hesham M Gad
CFO: Juan Orlando Bravo
HR: –
FYE: June 30
Type: Public

SED International keeps North and South America computing. The company distributes PCs tablet and notebook computers components televisions small appliances and more to resellers and retailers throughout the US and Latin America. Its computer hardware products traditionally the company's primary business line include components storage devices networking equipment peripherals and systems from about 170 vendors such as Acer Dell Lenovo and Microsoft. SED also offers customized supply chain management services to its e-commerce business-to-business and business-to-consumer clients. Founded in 1980 as Southern Electronics Distributors SED International is restructuring its operations in the US.

	Annual Growth	06/10	06/11	06/12	06/13	06/14
Sales ($ mil.)	(19.1%)	541.7	607.0	577.3	517.4	232.5
Net income ($ mil.)	–	0.3	3.1	1.4	(15.7)	(18.4)
Market value ($ mil.)	(50.7%)	13.5	27.3	27.3	27.3	0.8
Employees	(5.5%)	388	402	425	327	–

SEDANO'S MANAGEMENT INC.

3140 W. 76th St.
Hialeah FL 33018
Phone: 305-824-1034
Fax: 305-556-6981
Web: www.sedanos.com

CEO: Agustin Herran
CFO: –
HR: Javier Herranz
FYE: December 31
Type: Private

The story behind Sedano's Management strikes a chord with many of its South Florida customers. Armando Guerra Sr. a Cuban banker and grocer came to the US in 1961 and bought a small grocery store called Sedano's. He kept the name and grew it into a chain of about 35 supermarkets in southern and central Florida. The stores play salsa music on the speakers and the clerks greet customers in Spanish. Packaged Hispanic foods and Latin American fruits and vegetables sit on the shelves next to typical American fare. The company is the largest member of Associated Grocers of Florida. The Guerra and Herran families (CEO Manuel Herran married the founder's niece) own most of Sedano's.

SEDGWICK CLAIMS MANAGEMENT SERVICES INC.

1100 Ridgeway Loop Rd.	CEO: David North
Memphis TN 38120	CFO: W Jay Potter
Phone: 901-415-7400	HR: –
Fax: 901-415-7406	FYE: December 31
Web: www.sedgwickcms.com	Type: Private

Unlike Kyra this Sedgwick probably can't play the "Six Degrees of Kevin Bacon" game but it can help employers save a little bacon playing today's insurance game. Sedgwick Claims Management Services (Sedgwick CMS) offers insurance claims administration services to major employers focusing on workers' compensation; short- and long-term disability; and general auto and professional liability coverage. Other activities include risk management analytics worker care and absence management and Medicare compliance services. The firm serves clients in such industries as financial services health care utilities education manufacturing and retail.

SEDGWICK LLP

333 Bush St. 30th Fl.	CEO: –
San Francisco CA 94104-2806	CFO: Carrie Knudsen
Phone: 415-781-7900	HR: –
Fax: 415-781-2635	FYE: December 31
Web: www.sedgwicklaw.com	Type: Private - Partnershi

Sedgwick LLP (formerly Sedgwick Detert Moran & Arnold LLP) concentrates on corporate America. Working mainly on commercial and complex litigation matters the firm specializes in areas such as product and professional liability employment and labor antitrust intellectual property media entertainment and sports health care reinsurance and bankruptcy. Sedgwick employs more than 370 attorneys in about a dozen US offices as well as international offices in Bermuda London and Paris. Sedgwick LLP was founded in 1933 as Keith & Creede.

SEDONA CORPORATION

OTC: SDNA

1003 W. 9th Ave. 2nd Fl.	CEO: David R Vey
King of Prussia PA 19406	CFO: –
Phone: 610-337-8400	HR: –
Fax: 610-337-8490	FYE: December 31
Web: www.sedonacorp.com	Type: Public

SEDONA's software bridges the canyon between financial institutions and their customers. The company provides Web-based customer relationship management software that analyzes customer data manages marketing campaigns and generates leads for small and midsized financial institutions. Its Intarsia software also generates customer profiles that include demographic behavioral and preference information provided by third parties. Customers include community banks credit unions brokerage firms and insurance agencies.

SEE'S CANDIES INC.

210 El Camino Real	CEO: Brad Kinstler
South San Francisco CA 94080	CFO: –
Phone: 650-583-7307	HR: Liz Hartel
Fax: 650-225-9430	FYE: December 31
Web: www.sees.com	Type: Subsidiary

One suspects that investment guru and billionaire Warren Buffett has a sweet tooth. If we're correct he knows that See's Candies has what it takes to satisfy it. Owned by Buffett's firm Berkshire Hathaway See's Candies makes about 100 varieties of premium chocolate truffles caramels toffee and other confections including boxed assortments lollipops peppermints and licorice treats. The company sells its sweets at some 210 franchised black-and-white-decorated shops in the US primarily in California and other western states. Its products also are sold for fundraisers through its website and by mail order. A highly seasonal operation some 50% of its revenue is generated in November and December.

SEFTON RESOURCES INC.

LONDON: SER

2050 S. Oneida St. Ste. 102	CEO: –
Denver CO 80224	CFO: –
Phone: 303-759-2700	HR: –
Fax: 303-759-2701	FYE: December 31
Web: www.seftonresources.com	Type: Public

Looking to strike it rich by sifting through a number of hydrocarbon resource assets Sefton Resources explores for and produces oil and gas primarily in California and Kansas. Its core area of exploration and production is the East Ventura Basin in California where Sefton Resources owns two oil fields (Tapia Canyon and Eureka Canyon). In addition the company owns more than 40000 acres in the Forest City Basin of Eastern Kansas which has coalbed methane and conventional oil and gas deposits. The company has proved reserves of 7.6 million barrels of oil equivalent. Its operating subsidiaries are TEG Oil & Gas USA and TEG Oil & Gas MidContinent.

SEGA OF AMERICA INC.

350 Rhode Island St. Ste. 400	CEO: Mike Hayes
San Francisco CA 94103	CFO: John Cheng
Phone: 415-701-6000	HR: –
Fax: 604-412-5224	FYE: March 31
Web: www.bestbuycanadaltd.ca	Type: Subsidiary

To get SEGA of America to smile for a photo try "Say 'Games!'" The subsidiary of Japan-based SEGA Corporation makes video games for PCs handheld devices and home consoles from Sony Nintendo and Microsoft. Its better-known titles include releases in the Sonic the Hedgehog series Virtua Fighter and Crazy Taxi as well as games based on comic book characters such as Iron Man Thor and Captain America movie-related titles such as a number of games based on the film Aliens and franchise team-ups such as Mario & Sonic at the Olympic Games.

SEGWAY INC.

14 Technology Dr.
Bedford NH 03110
Phone: 603-222-6000
Fax: 603-222-6001
Web: www.segway.com

CEO: –
CFO: –
HR: –
FYE: December 31
Type: Private

Thanks to Segway's Personal Transporter or PT (formerly called the Human Transporter) being a highly advanced bipedal primate has gotten a lot easier! Similar in appearance to an old-fashioned lawnmower the battery-powered PT is anything but old-fashioned. Using computer processors that mimic human equilibrium the PT moves forward when the standing rider leans forward; a backward lean sends the PT in reverse. The PT has a range of 24 miles on a single charge. It is designed for congested urban areas and various commercial uses as well as policing. Segway's Robotic Mobility Platform (RMP) is used for tasks requiring robotic applications. Inventor Dean Kamen founded the company in 1999.

SEI INVESTMENTS CO.

NMS: SEIC

1 Freedom Valley Drive
Oaks, PA 19456-1100
Phone: 610 676-1000
Fax: –
Web: www.seic.com

CEO: Alfred P. West
CFO: Dennis J. McGonigle
HR: Richard Frederick
FYE: December 31
Type: Public

SEI Investments provides outsourced investment and fund processing for about 7000 private banks trust companies investment advisors and managers and institutional investors. Services include securities and trust processing and accounting portfolio analysis treasury and cash management and performance measurement reporting. Its fund processing segment serves managers and distributors of mutual funds hedge funds and alternative investments. The company administers more than $625 billion in mutual fund separate account and pooled assets. It also provides customized investment programs and manages some $53 billion for retirement plans not-for-profits and affluent individuals and families.

	Annual Growth	12/10	12/11	12/12	12/13	12/14
Sales ($ mil.)	8.9%	900.8	929.7	992.5	1,126.1	1,266.0
Net income ($ mil.)	8.3%	231.7	205.0	206.8	288.1	318.7
Market value ($ mil.)	13.9%	3,965.5	2,892.0	3,890.5	5,789.1	6,674.2
Employees	5.4%	2,290	2,430	2,579	2,749	2,824

SELECT BANCORP INC (NEW)

NMS: SLCT

700 W. Cumberland Street
Dunn, NC 28334
Phone: 910 892-7080
Fax: –

CEO: William L Hedgepeth II
CFO: Mark A Jeffries
HR: –
FYE: December 31
Type: Public

Select Bancorp (formerly New Century Bancorp) is the holding company for the aptly named Select Bank & Trust (formerly New Century Bank). The bank has about a dozen branches across North Carolina. Targeting individuals and small to midsized businesses Select Bank & Trust offers such services as checking and savings accounts CDs IRAs and loans. Its loan book largely comprises real estate loans; the remaining portfolio includes business and consumer loans. New Century Bancorp acquired Select Bancorp in 2014 and took its name.

	Annual Growth	12/10	12/11	12/12	12/13	12/14
Assets ($ mil.)	5.1%	626.9	589.7	585.5	525.6	766.1
Net income ($ mil.)		(5.0)	(0.2)	4.6	2.9	2.4
Market value ($ mil.)	10.3%	56.7	22.8	63.7	75.9	83.9
Employees	3.3%	135	113	111	97	154

SELECT COMFORT CORP.

NMS: SCSS

9800 59th Avenue North
Minneapolis, MN 55442
Phone: 763 551-7000
Fax: –
Web: www.sleepnumber.com

CEO: Shelly R. Ibach
CFO: David R. Callen
HR: –
FYE: January 03
Type: Public

Select Comfort has got your number. The firm's line of Sleep Number beds which can carry hefty price tags use air-chamber technology to allow sleepers to adjust the firmness on each side of the mattress providing better sleep quality and addressing sleep-related problems such as lower back pain. Select Comfort also offers foundations frames pillows and a sofa bed. A leading bedding retailer in the US Select Comfort operates more than 425 company-owned stores. The air-bed maker also sells through a company-operated call center its own website and on the QVC shopping channel. Select Comfort was founded in 1987 has grown to become one of the nation's leading bed makers and retailers.

	Annual Growth	01/11*	12/11	12/12	12/13*	01/15
Sales ($ mil.)	17.6%	605.7	743.2	935.0	960.2	1,156.8
Net income ($ mil.)	21.1%	31.6	60.5	78.1	60.1	68.0
Market value ($ mil.)	31.0%	482.0	1,145.2	1,294.1	1,120.4	1,418.7
Employees	9.8%	2,165	2,328	2,791	2,858	3,149

*Fiscal year change

SELECT INCOME REAL ESTATE INVESTMENT TRUST

NYS: SIR

Two Newton Place, 255 Washington Street, Suite 300
Newton, MA 02458-1634
Phone: 617 796-8303
Fax: –
Web: www.sirreit.com

CEO: –
CFO: John C. Popeo
HR: –
FYE: December 31
Type: Public

When it comes to real estate it doesn't get any more selective than Hawaii. And Select Income REIT (SIR) has amassed quite a land portfolio in the Aloha State. The externally-managed real estate investment trust owns 11 properties measuring nearly 18 million sq. ft. of single-tenant commercial and industrial properties on the island of Oahu. Tenants include an oil refinery for Tesoro and a Coca-Cola bottling plant and distribution center. On the mainland SIR owns another 37 office and warehouse properties totaling more than 8 million sq. ft. in about 20 states. The company was formed in December 2011 as a subsidiary of CommonWealth REIT. It went public in 2012.

	Annual Growth	12/11	12/12	12/13	12/14	12/15
Sales ($ mil.)	40.9%	108.6	122.8	188.3	222.7	428.4
Net income ($ mil.)	2.0%	68.9	65.9	93.1	105.9	74.7
Market value ($ mil.)	(7.2%)	–	2,213.8	2,389.9	2,181.6	1,771.4
Employees	–	–	–	–	–	–

SELECT MEDICAL HOLDINGS CORP

NYS: SEM

4714 Gettysburg Road, P.O. Box 2034
Mechanicsburg, PA 17055
Phone: 717 972-1100
Fax: –
Web: www.selectmedicalholdings.com

CEO: David S. Chernow
CFO: Martin F. Jackson
HR: John A. Saich
FYE: December 31
Type: Public

Learning to walk or talk again is hard enough so Select Medical wants to make selecting a medical rehabilitation facility easier. The firm provides inpatient rehabilitation at more than 110 long-term acute care hospitals (LTCH) and 17 inpatient rehabilitation facilities in 28 states. These centers usually located in leased space within general hospitals specialize in treating complex medical conditions such as respiratory failure or spinal cord injury that require long term care. Most patients are admitted as transfers from general hospitals. It operates more than 1000 outpatient rehab clinics in 31 US states and Washington DC. Select Medical also offers contract rehab services at nursing homes and other locations.

	Annual Growth	12/10	12/11	12/12	12/13	12/14
Sales ($ mil.)	6.4%	2,390.3	2,804.5	2,949.0	2,975.6	3,065.0
Net income ($ mil.)	11.6%	77.6	107.8	148.2	114.4	120.6
Market value ($ mil.)	18.5%	959.3	1,112.9	1,237.5	1,523.6	1,889.8
Employees	4.9%	25,900	28,800	29,900	31,200	31,400

SELECT PORTFOLIO SERVICING INC.

3815 SW Temple
Salt Lake City UT 84115
Phone: 800-258-8602
Fax: 801-293-2555
Web: www.spservicing.com

CEO: Timothy O'Brien
CFO: –
HR: –
FYE: December 31
Type: Subsidiary

Pssst: Select Portfolio Servicing (SPS) services mostly subprime single-family residential mortgage loans. The company collects on impaired-credit loans and non-performing loans for clients such as mortgage companies banks and bond insurers. It also also performs loss recovery and contingency collections and offers valuation services through its Residential Real Estate Review affiliate. SPS's servicing portfolio is worth some $30 billion. Founded in 1999 SPS operates offices in Jacksonville Florida and Salt Lake City. Credit Suisse bought SPS and its parent SPS Holding from mortgage insurer PMI Group in 2005 for more than $140 million.

SELECTIVE INSURANCE GROUP INC

NMS: SIGI

40 Wantage Avenue
Branchville, NJ 07890
Phone: 973 948-3000
Fax: 973 948-0282
Web: www.selective.com

CEO: Gregory E. Murphy
CFO: Dale A. Thatcher
HR: Kimberly Burnett
FYE: December 31
Type: Public

Selective Insurance Group is trying to be more accepting — without becoming indiscriminate. Since the early 1990s the property/casualty insurance holding company has been expanding its service area beyond its native New Jersey to reach the entire eastern US seaboard and much of the Midwest. Commercial policies sold by its nine subsidiaries include workers' compensation and commercial automobile property and liability insurance. Personal lines include homeowners and automobile insurance. The company also offers federal flood insurance administration services and some excess and surplus (E&S nonstandard) insurance.

	Annual Growth	12/10	12/11	12/12	12/13	12/14
Assets ($ mil.)	5.9%	5,231.8	5,736.4	6,794.2	6,270.2	6,581.6
Net income ($ mil.)	21.3%	65.5	19.9	38.0	106.4	141.8
Market value ($ mil.)	10.6%	1,027.2	1,003.4	1,090.6	1,531.5	1,537.7
Employees	3.7%	1,900	2,000	2,100	2,100	2,200

SEMCO ENERGY INC.

1411 3rd St. Ste. A
Port Huron MI 48060
Phone: 810-987-2200
Fax: 909-394-1382
Web: www.aswater.com/

CEO: David M Harris
CFO: Mark Moses
HR: –
FYE: December 31
Type: Private

Alaska and Michigan have more in common than a cold climate. SEMCO ENERGY serves approximately 409000 natural gas consumers in both states. The company's main subsidiary is utility SEMCO ENERGY Gas which distributes gas to more than 280500 customers in 24 Michigan counties. SEMCO's ENSTAR Natural Gas unit distributes gas to more than 126000 customers in and around Anchorage Alaska. The company's unregulated operations include propane distribution in Michigan and Wisconsin; pipeline and storage facility operation; and information technology outsourcing. In 2012 SEMCO ENERGY was acquired by AltaGas.

SEMGROUP CORP

NYS: SEMG

Two Warren Place, 6120 S. Yale Avenue, Suite 700
Tulsa, OK 74136-4216
Phone: 918 524-8100
Fax: –
Web: www.semgroupcorp.com

CEO: Carlin G. Conner
CFO: Robert N. (Bob) Fitzgerald
HR: –
FYE: December 31
Type: Public

Midstream energy player SemGroup moves oil and gas from the wellhead to the marketplace. Through its Crude unit it owns about 55% of Rose Rock Midstream which has a 5 million-barrel storage terminal in Cushing Oklahoma and operates 570 miles of crude oil pipeline in Oklahoma and Kansas. Rose Rock Midstream owns 51% of the nearly 530-mile White Cliffs Pipeline which links Midcontinent oil producers to the Cushing terminal. SemGas operates 1400 miles of natural gas and NGL transportation gathering and distribution pipelines. SemMexico makes asphalt products. The company also operates SemCAMS (Canadian natural gas) and SemLogistics (UK oil terminal).

	Annual Growth	12/10	12/11	12/12	12/13	12/14
Sales ($ mil.)	6.8%	1,630.3	1,479.5	1,237.5	1,427.0	2,122.6
Net income ($ mil.)	–	(132.3)	2.4	22.1	48.1	29.2
Market value ($ mil.)	26.0%	1,190.8	1,142.1	1,712.8	2,858.8	2,997.3
Employees	7.8%	800	710	690	890	1,080

SEMINOLE ELECTRIC COOPERATIVE INC.

16313 N DALE MABRY HWY
TAMPA, FL 336181427
Phone: 386-328-9255
Fax: –
Web: www.seminole-electric.com

CEO: Lisa Johnson
CFO: John W Geeraerts
HR: –
FYE: June 30
Type: Private

This Seminole is not only a native Floridian but it has also provided electricity in the state since 1948. Seminole Electric Cooperative generates and transmits electricity for 10 member distribution cooperatives that serve 1.4 million residential and business customers in 42 Florida counties. Seminole Electric has more than 3350 MW of primarily coal-fired generating capacity. The cooperative also buys electricity from other utilities and independent power producers and it owns 350 miles of transmission lines. Some 90% of its power load uses the transmission systems of other utilities through long-term contracts.

	Annual Growth	09/12	09/13*	12/13*	03/14*	06/14
Sales ($ mil.)	23.2%	–	957.6	1,213.2	1,199.7	1,179.5
Net income ($ mil.)	62.6%	–	–	17.7	6.7	28.8
Market value ($ mil.)	–	–	–	–	–	–
Employees	–	–	–	–	–	528

*Fiscal year change

SEMLER SCIENTIFIC INC

NAS: SMLR

2330 N.W. Everett St.
Portland, OR 97210
Phone: 877 774-4211
Fax: –
Web: www.semlerscientific.com

CEO: Douglas Murphy-Chutorian
CFO: James M Walker
HR: –
FYE: December 31
Type: Public

Semler Scientific is an emerging medical device maker with a single product. The company markets the FloChec a medical device that measures arterial blood flow to the extremities (fingers and toes) quickly and easily in the doctor's office to diagnose peripheral artery disease. FloChec received FDA clearance in early 2010 and the company began commercially leasing the product in 2011. Founded in 2007 by Dr. Herbert Semler who invented the technology used in FloChec the Portland-based company went public in 2014 with an offering valued at $10 million.

	Annual Growth	12/10	12/11	12/12	12/13	12/14
Sales ($ mil.)	–	0.0	0.0	1.2	2.3	3.6
Net income ($ mil.)	–	0.0	0.0	(2.7)	(2.2)	(4.5)
Market value ($ mil.)	–	0.0	0.0	–	–	9.2
Employees	100.0%	–	–	–	12	24

SEMPRA ENERGY

NYS: SRE

488 8th Avenue
San Diego, CA 92101
Phone: 619 696-2000
Fax: –
Web: www.sempra.com

CEO: Debra L. (Debbie) Reed
CFO: Joseph A. (Joe) Householder
HR: –
FYE: December 31
Type: Public

Sempra Energy's takes a pragmatic approach to make money in utility and other energy markets in the US and around the world. In the US Sempra distributes natural gas to more than 7.2 million customer meters and electricity to 3.4 million customer meters through its Southern California Gas (SoCalGas) and San Diego Gas & Electric (SDG&E) utilities. Other reporting segments include Sempra US Gas & Power (natural gas and renewables) and Sempra International (Sempra Mexico and Sempra South American Utilities) which were formerly known as Sempra Global. Sempra Energy companies serve more than 31 million consumers worldwide.

	Annual Growth	12/10	12/11	12/12	12/13	12/14
Sales ($ mil.)	5.2%	9,003.0	10,036.0	9,647.0	10,557.0	11,035.0
Net income ($ mil.)	14.5%	733.0	1,407.0	920.0	1,088.0	1,262.0
Market value ($ mil.)	20.7%	12,927.4	13,548.2	17,474.7	22,110.7	27,431.4
Employees	6.0%	13,504	17,483	16,893	17,122	17,046

SEMTECH CORP.

NMS: SMTC

200 Flynn Road
Camarillo, CA 93012-8790
Phone: 805 498-2111
Fax: 805 498-3804
Web: www.semtech.com

CEO: Mohan R. Maheswaran
CFO: Emeka Chukwu
HR: Michelle Hook
FYE: January 25
Type: Public

If Semtech's products seem highly technical it's because they are. Not to be confused with semiconductor research consortium SEMATECH Semtech makes analog and mixed-signal semiconductors used by manufacturers of computer communications consumer and industrial electronics. The company's chips are used for power management circuit protection transmission and other functions in a variety of devices including cellular phones and base stations notebook and desktop PCs network transmission equipment and automated test equipment. It counts Samsung Electronics (nearly 15% of sales) Huawei (10%) and Frontek Technology among its customers. Semtech generates more than 70% of its sales in Asia/Pacific.

	Annual Growth	01/11	01/12	01/13	01/14	01/15
Sales ($ mil.)	5.3%	454.5	480.6	578.8	595.0	557.9
Net income ($ mil.)	(21.2%)	72.6	89.1	41.9	(164.5)	27.9
Market value ($ mil.)	5.6%	1,452.5	1,935.6	1,993.7	1,551.4	1,808.6
Employees	10.3%	982	929	1,433	1,455	1,456

SENECA COMPANIES INC.

4140 E. 14th St.
Des Moines IA 50313
Phone: 515-262-5000
Fax: 515-264-4360
Web: www.senecaco.com

CEO: –
CFO: Phyllis Jones
HR: Matthew Puller
FYE: December 31
Type: Private

Seneca keeps cars clean in control and ready to go. The company designs and installs automobile wash systems fueling systems and other vehicle service equipment including lifts lubrication equipment and compressor systems. Seneca's data digital security camera systems and offered primarily to help secure auto dealerships. It also provides petroleum services and equipment environmental consulting remediation and waste removal general construction electrical contracting and industrial coating equipment. Seneca Companies operates from offices in Iowa Illinois and Nebraska.

SENECA FOODS CORP.

NMS: SENE A

3736 South Main Street
Marion, NY 14505
Phone: 315 926-8100
Fax: –
Web: www.senecafoods.com

CEO: Kraig H. Kayser
CFO: Timothy Benjamin
HR: Walter Iruegas
FYE: March 31
Type: Public

Seneca Foods has a can-do attitude. The company is one of the world's largest manufacturers and suppliers of canned vegetables. Its canned (as well as frozen and bottled) produce lineup is sold under numerous private labels and national and regional brands such as Aunt Nellie's Farm Kitchen Libby's Seneca and Stokely that the company owns or licenses. Customers are primarily big grocery chains and some export markets and food service operators and food processors including General Mills (GMOL). Seneca also supplies frozen fruit and vegetables to primarily private-label retail and food service customers and GMOL. A short list of fruit and snack chip products are sold to retailers and food processors.

	Annual Growth	03/11	03/12	03/13	03/14	03/15
Sales ($ mil.)	1.9%	1,194.6	1,261.8	1,276.3	1,340.2	1,286.4
Net income ($ mil.)	(13.5%)	17.7	11.3	41.4	13.8	9.9
Market value ($ mil.)	(0.1%)	295.5	260.6	326.7	311.5	294.9
Employees	0.0%	3,400	3,400	3,500	3,500	3,400

SENIOR HOUSING PROPERTIES TRUST

NYS: SNH

Two Newton Place, 255 Washington Street, Suite 300
Newton, MA 02458-1634
Phone: 617 796-8350
Fax: 617 796-8349
Web: www.snhreit.com

CEO: –
CFO: Richard W. Siede
HR: –
FYE: December 31
Type: Public

Senior Housing Properties Trust (SHPT) offers those in their golden years a place to rest their weary bones. The real estate investment trust (REIT) owns some 375 health care-related properties in about 40 states and Washington DC. Its portfolio includes senior apartments independent and assisted living facilities nursing homes medical office buildings biotechnology laboratories rehabilitation hospitals and gymnasiums. Tenants such as Sunrise Senior Living and Brookdale Senior Living sign triple-net leases which require them not only to pay rent but to also pay operating expenses remove hazardous waste and carry insurance on their properties.

	Annual Growth	12/10	12/11	12/12	12/13	12/14
Sales ($ mil.)	25.6%	339.0	450.0	644.8	761.4	844.9
Net income ($ mil.)	8.0%	116.5	151.4	135.9	151.2	158.6
Market value ($ mil.)	0.2%	4,473.8	4,575.7	4,820.4	4,532.9	4,508.5
Employees	–	–	–	–	–	–

SENIOR WHOLE HEALTH LLC

58 Charles St. 2nd Fl.
Cambridge MA 02141
Phone: 617-494-5353
Fax: 617-494-5599
Web: www.seniorwholehealth.com/

CEO: –
CFO: –
HR: –
FYE: December 31
Type: Private

Seniors hate living in nursing homes; states hate paying for them. Enter Senior Whole Health (SWH) a health services plan that aims to keep more low-income seniors living independently at home. SWH consolidates the benefits of Medicare and Medicaid into one easy-to-join plan that pays claims handles customer service issues and contracts with primary care providers. It also offers around-the-clock access to nurses exercise programs prescription drug coverage transportation and multilingual translators. SWH serves more than 6000 members in the states of Connecticut Massachusetts and New York. It is at the top of the heap as one of the country's 500 fastest-growing private companies according to Inc.

SENOMYX INC

NMS: SNMX

4767 Nexus Centre Drive
San Diego, CA 92121
Phone: 858 646-8300
Fax: –

CEO: Kent Snyder
CFO: Antony E. (Tony) Rogers
HR: –
FYE: December 31
Type: Public

Senomyx nose a good thing when it smells it. The company has identified human receptor genes related to the detection of smells and tastes and using this genetic research the company is developing sweet salty and savory flavor enhancers and bitter taste modulators. Potential products include agents that can block bitter tastes in coffee and make low-sodium snacks taste salty. Senomyx collaborates with the likes of PepsiCo Nestlé and Firmenich. The company also works with Japan's largest flavors company Ajinomoto which has opened up the Asian market for Senomyx.

	Annual Growth	12/10	12/11	12/12	12/13	12/14
Sales ($ mil.)	(0.9%)	28.7	31.3	31.3	29.3	27.7
Net income ($ mil.)	–	(10.7)	(8.7)	(9.2)	(11.9)	(12.2)
Market value ($ mil.)	(4.2%)	309.2	150.9	72.9	219.5	260.7
Employees	(0.7%)	113	112	111	113	110

SENSE TECHNOLOGIES INC.

OTC: SNSG

2535 N. Carleton Ave.
Grand Island NE 68803
Phone: 308-381-1355
Fax: 308-381-6557
Web: www.sensetech.com

CEO: Bruce E Schreiner
CFO: Bruce E Schreiner
HR: Monty L Bishop
FYE: February 28
Type: Public

Objects in your rearview mirror may be LOUDER than they appear with Sense Technologies' Guardian Alert backup warning system. The Guardian Alert uses microwave radar technology to alert drivers of obstacles behind their vehicles. The systems can be attached to car bumpers or license plates. When an obstacle is detected the system emits an audio and visual warning inside the vehicle. Sense Technologies outsources both the manufacturing and distribution of its Guardian Alert products. The company also markets ScopeOut a mirror system designed to expand drivers' side and rear views. Sense Technologies' target customers include car dealers fleet operators and automotive aftermarket retailers.

SENSIENT TECHNOLOGIES CORP.

NYS: SXT

777 East Wisconsin Avenue
Milwaukee, WI 53202-5304
Phone: 414 271-6755
Fax: 414 347-4795
Web: www.sensient.com

CEO: Paul Manning
CFO: Stephen J Rolfs
HR: –
FYE: December 31
Type: Public

Sensient Technologies is a purveyor of good taste. The company which has two main segments the Flavors & Fragrances Group and the Color Group makes flavors aromas and colors that are added to food beverages pharmaceuticals cosmetics and household products. Sensient also manufactures inks for inkjet printers and specialty chemicals such as industrial dyes for the manufacture of writing instruments tinted motor-vehicle windshields and household cleaners. The company operates some 75 sites in about 35 countries and counts customers in more than 150 countries worldwide. Its customers include food processors pharmaceutical companies and personal-care and household-product manufacturers.

	Annual Growth	12/10	12/11	12/12	12/13	12/14
Sales ($ mil.)	2.2%	1,328.2	1,430.8	1,459.1	1,467.6	1,447.8
Net income ($ mil.)	(8.9%)	107.1	120.5	123.9	113.3	73.6
Market value ($ mil.)	13.2%	1,741.9	1,797.4	1,686.4	2,301.1	2,861.6
Employees	2.9%	3,618	3,887	3,983	4,130	4,053

SENTARA HEALTHCARE

6015 POPLAR HALL DR
NORFOLK, VA 235023819
Phone: 757-455-7000
Fax: –
Web: www.sentara.com

CEO: David L. Bernd
CFO: Robert A. (Rob) Broerman
HR: Michael (Mel) Taylor
FYE: December 31
Type: Private

Sentara Healthcare is not-for-profit organization that operates a network of hospitals and other health facilities primarily in the coastal Hampton Roads area of southeastern Virginia. The system includes a dozen acute care hospitals housing a total of more than 2000 beds. One of its hospitals Sentara Norfolk includes a dedicated cardiac hospital with more than 100 beds. In addition to its acute care facilities Sentara Healthcare operates several outpatient care facilities as well as nursing homes rehab centers medical practices imaging centers and home health agencies. Its Optima Health unit provides HMO PPO and other health insurance products to about 450000 Virginians.

	Annual Growth	12/09	12/10	12/11	12/12	12/13
Sales ($ mil.)	8.3%	–	3,385.5	3,930.4	4,068.2	4,298.7
Net income ($ mil.)	187.9%	–	–	103.9	307.7	861.6
Market value ($ mil.)	–	–	–	–	–	–
Employees	–	–	–	–	–	22,000

SENTARA RMH MEDICAL CENTER

2010 HEALTH CAMPUS DR
HARRISONBURG, VA 228018679
Phone: 540-433-4100
Fax: –
Web: www.rmhonline.com

CEO: –
CFO: –
HR: Mark Zimmerman
FYE: December 31
Type: Private

Sentara RMH Medical Center (RMH) formerly known as Rockingham Memorial Hospital serves residents in Virginia's Shenandoah Valley offering some 240 beds. In addition to emergency services and general surgeries and care procedures RMH offers specialized services including cardiovascular care cancer treatment sleep disorder diagnosis behavioral health care medical imaging orthopedic procedures obstetrics and rehabilitation as well as home health hospice and wellness services. Founded in 1912 RMH is part of the Sentara Healthcare system.

	Annual Growth	12/03	12/04	12/05	12/06	12/08
Sales ($ mil.)	8.9%	–	188.3	214.4	229.5	264.8
Net income ($ mil.)	24.2%	–	–	5.3	18.0	10.1
Market value ($ mil.)	–	–	–	–	–	–
Employees	–	–	–	–	–	1,892

SENTIENT FLIGHT GROUP LLC

97 Libbey Pkwy. Ste. 400
Weymouth MA 02189
Phone: 866-789-5661
Fax: 770-232-1242
Web: www.phillipblount.com

CEO: Andrew Collins
CFO: –
HR: –
FYE: December 31
Type: Private

To be sentient is to be aware and to be Sentient is to be aware of a market niche in private jet transportation. Unlike charter jet users Sentient Flight Group customers pay a membership fee in advance for guaranteed access to aircraft. With fractional jet ownership customers buy a portion of a jet and then pay for flight expenses; Sentient member-customers pay for flight time only. Customers choose types of jets (light midsize super-mid heavy) rather than individual aircraft. The jets are flown by independent operators. Once a part of Sentient Jet Holdings the company was purchased in August 2008 by Macquarie Global Opportunities Partners a fund managed by global investment firm Macquarie Group.

SENTRY TECHNOLOGY CORPORATION

OTC: SKVY

1881 Lakeland Ave.	CEO: Peter L Murdoch
Ronkonkoma NY 11779	CFO: Joan E Miller
Phone: 800-645-4224	HR: –
Fax: 631-739-2117	FYE: December 31
Web: www.sentrytechnology.com	Type: Public

Always on guard against pilferage Sentry Technology's surveillance products keep watch over stores and distribution centers. The company manufactures and installs electronic article surveillance (EAS) radio frequency (RF) and closed-circuit television (CCTV) systems. Its traveling SentryVision Smart-Track CCTV system is designed to pan tilt and zoom in order to provide unobstructed views. Clients include retailers wanting to deter theft and institutions wanting to protect assets and people. In addition Sentry Technology's electromagnetic (EM) and RF identification (RFID) based Library Management systems are used by libraries to secure inventory and improve operating efficiency.

SEPATON INC.

400 Nickerson Rd.	CEO: Michael R Thompson
Marlborough MA 01752-4658	CFO: Paul McDermott
Phone: 508-490-7900	HR: –
Fax: 508-490-7908	FYE: December 31
Web: www.sepaton.com	Type: Private

SEPATON develops backup and data migration appliances for use in medium and large-scale data centers. The company's virtual tape library (VTL) systems can contain up to 2 petabytes of data. SEPATON also offers data protection recovery and deduplication software applications. The company's customers include Coach Colgate-Palmolive Golub and Hyundai. SEPATON was established in 1999 as SANgate Systems. The SEPATON name is the phrase "no tapes" backwards in reference to the company's virtual tape technology. The company has international offices in China Germany and the UK.

SEPHORA USA INC.

First Market Tower 525 Market St. 11th Fl.	CEO: Calvin McDonald
San Francisco CA 94105-2708	CFO: Alexis Rollier
Phone: 415-284-3300	HR: –
Fax: 415-284-3434	FYE: December 31
Web: www.sephora.com	Type: Subsidiary

Shopping for cosmetics at Sephora is meant to be a hands-on experience. Through more than 280 stand-alone stores in North America and 300-plus locations in J. C. Penney department stores Sephora USA takes a self-service approach to buying makeup fragrances and skin care products. It offers more than 200 brands of prestige products including its own-brand products all of which customers are encouraged to sample. The company also sells via catalog and online at Sephora.com. Part of luxury brand giant LVMH Sephora USA is the North American retail arm of France-based Sephora which was founded in 1969 and has a global network of about 1200 stores. Sephora USA's first shop opened in New York in 1998.

SEQUA CORPORATION

200 Park Ave.	CEO: Armand F Lauzon Jr
New York NY 10166	CFO: Donna Costello
Phone: 212-986-5500	HR: –
Fax: 212-370-1969	FYE: December 31
Web: www.sequa.com	Type: Private

Sequa serves the aerospace and metal coatings sectors through its two primary operating segments. Chromalloy Gas Turbine its largest unit makes and repairs jet engine parts such as major rotating parts cases frames and combustors for airlines industrial customers and other aftermarket customers. A North American industry leader Precoat Metals coats coiled steel for construction residential and industrial projects. In late 2012 its Sequa Automotive Group — which made airbag inflators for many OEMs and featured CASCO Products as a tier one automotive supplier — was sold to investment firm The Jordan Company. Sequa is owned by global private investment powerhouse The Carlyle Group.

SEQUACHEE VALLEY ELECTRIC CO-OPERATIVE INC

512 S CEDAR AVE	CEO: Robert W Matheny
SOUTH PITTSBURG, TN 373801310	CFO: Floyd Hatfield
Phone: 423-837-8605	HR: –
Fax: –	FYE: June 30
Web: www.svalleyec.com	Type: Private

Sequachee Valley Electric Cooperative squeezes the most efficiency out of the power distribution cooperative it manages. One of 23 rural electric cooperatives in Tennessee Sequachee Valley Electric Cooperative distributes power to more than 33000 residential commercial and industrial members in part or all of Bledsoe Coffee Grundy Hamilton Marion Rhea Sequatchie and Van Buren counties. It buys wholesale power from the Tennessee Valley Authority. Sequachee Valley Electric is governed by an 11-person board of directors directly elected by its membership.

	Annual Growth	06/09	06/10	06/11	06/12	06/13
Sales ($ mil.)	3.4%	–	73.8	81.7	78.6	81.5
Net income ($ mil.)	11.4%	–	–	2.3	3.0	2.8
Market value ($ mil.)	–	–	–	–	–	–
Employees	–	–	–	–	–	74

SEQUENOM INC

NMS: SQNM

3595 John Hopkins Court	CEO: Dirk van den Boom
San Diego, CA 92121	CFO: Carolyn D. Beaver
Phone: 858 202-9000	HR: –
Fax: –	FYE: December 31
Web: www.sequenom.com	Type: Public

Sequenom develops and manufactures tests for the molecular diagnostics market. Its laboratory developed tests are primarily focused on prenatal and ophthalmological diseases and conditions. Tests include MaterniT21 Plus (screen for fetal chromosomal abnormalities) HerediT CF (screen for cystic fibrosis genetic mutations) and SensiGene RHD (screen for fetal Rhesus D factor) as well as RetnaGene AMD (predictive test for age-related macular degeneration). The company formerly offered technology and tools (principally based on its MassARRAY sequencing system) used by researchers but sold that business in 2014. Sequenom generates about a quarter of sales outside the US.

	Annual Growth	12/10	12/11	12/12	12/13	12/14
Sales ($ mil.)	33.7%	47.5	55.9	89.7	162.4	151.6
Net income ($ mil.)	–	(120.8)	(74.2)	(117.0)	(107.4)	1.0
Market value ($ mil.)	(17.6%)	943.0	522.6	553.1	274.8	434.5
Employees	17.3%	237	382	594	570	448

SERCO INC.

1818 Library St. Ste. 1000
Reston VA 20190
Phone: 703-939-6000
Fax: 866-987-3726
Web: www.serco-na.com

CEO: Daniel D Allen
CFO: Gary A Shankman
HR: –
FYE: December 31
Type: Subsidiary

Serco Inc. serves the US government by land sea and air. The US arm of UK outsourcer Serco Group plc is one of the top private contractors to the US military the federal government state agencies and corporations. Primarily an information technology (IT) services provider Serco Inc. operates in four divisions: national security and intelligence IT and professional services staffing and engineering and logistics. It has more than 200 contracts to provide program management and administrative support to the military help with border and port security and assist the Navy with hazardous waste removal. The company also manages about 65 air traffic control towers for the FAA in the US and its territories.

SERENA SOFTWARE INC.

1850 Gateway Dr. 4th Fl.
San Mateo CA 94404
Phone: 650-481-3400
Fax: 650-481-3700
Web: www.serena.com

CEO: Greg Hughes
CFO: Robert I Pender Jr
HR: –
FYE: January 31
Type: Private

SERENA Software isn't afraid of capitalizing on change. The company's change management software controls potentially disruptive changes during software installation migration and upgrades across multiple platforms including mainframe client/server and Web-based environments. Its applications are designed to help information technology staff manage upgrades improve productivity and reduce development costs. Customers have included American Express General Electric and IBM. The company which does much of its business in North America operates from 29 offices in 14 countries. SERENA is controlled by investment firm Silver Lake Partners which acquired the company in 2006.

SERRA AUTOMOTIVE INC.

3118 E. Hill Rd.
Grand Blanc MI 48439
Phone: 810-694-1720
Fax: 810-694-6405
Web: www.serrausa.com

CEO: –
CFO: Matthew S Daugherty
HR: –
FYE: June 30
Type: Private

Whatever will be will be and Serra Automotive will be too. The company owns more than 20 auto dealerships in California Colorado Michigan New Jersey Ohio and Tennessee where it sells BMW Buick Cadillac Honda Volkswagen Ford and other vehicle makes. All Serra Automotive locations offer parts and service and some locations including Team Chevrolet in Colorado Springs also operate body shops. Chairman president and CEO Joseph Serra owns the company. Serra's father Albert established Serra Automotive in 1973.

SERTA INC.

2600 Forbs Ave.
Hoffman Estates IL 60192
Phone: 847-645-0200
Fax: 561-640-5580
Web: www.embroidme.com

CEO: Gary T Fazio
CFO: –
HR: Jennifer Cristino
FYE: December 31
Type: Private

The #1 mattress maker in the US Serta asserts that it's also one of the world's top mattress producers (behind rival Sealy). The company is a top mattress supplier to hotels and motels such as Hilton and Waldorf. Its Perfect Sleeper line is the nation's best-selling premium mattress; its top-of-the-line collection sells under the Perfect Day name. Founded in 1931 Serta boasts nearly 30 manufacturing facilities in North America. Serta has been majority owned by Simmons Bedding owner Advent International since late 2012 when AOT Bedding Super Holdings a holding company formed in 2010 by Ares Management and the Ontario Teachers' Pension Plan reduced its ownership to a significant equity stake.

SERVCO PACIFIC INC.

2850 PUKOLOA ST STE 300
HONOLULU, HI 968194475
Phone: 808-564-1300
Fax: –
Web: www.servco.com

CEO: Mark H Fukunaga
CFO: Jeffery A Bell
HR: –
FYE: June 30
Type: Private

Servco Pacific's business flows through an ocean's worth of enterprises. The company sells passenger vehicles (including Toyota Subaru Suzuki and Chevrolet models) and commercial trucks through dealerships in Hawaii and Australia. In addition Servco Home & Appliance wholesales kitchen and bath products to building professionals throughout the South Pacific; Servco Raynor Overhead Doors installs residential and commercial garage doors; Servco Insurance Services offers insurance coverage for businesses and individuals; and Servco School & Office Furniture outfits educational institutions and government agencies with desks seating and other furnishings. Servco Pacific was founded by Peter Fukunaga in 1919.

	Annual Growth	06/10	06/11*	12/11	12/12*	06/13
Sales ($ mil.)	17.6%	–	791.5	–	923.0	1,094.3
Net income ($ mil.)	30.4%	–	–	–	15.9	20.7
Market value ($ mil.)	–	–	–	–	–	–
Employees	–	–	–	–	–	925
						*Fiscal year change

SERVICE CORP. INTERNATIONAL

NYS: SCI

1929 Allen Parkway
Houston, TX 77019
Phone: 713 522-5141
Fax: –
Web: www.sci-corp.com

CEO: Thomas L. Ryan
CFO: Eric D, Tanzberger
HR: Dania Schoolfield
FYE: December 31
Type: Public

Service Corporation International (SCI) is to death what H&R Block is to taxes. SCI the largest funeral and cemetery services company in North America operates about 1560 funeral homes and about 465 cemeteries in 45 US states eight Canadian provinces the District of Columbia and Puerto Rico. The company's primary services include embalming burial and cremation. As part of its business SCI also sells traditional funeral necessities including prearranged funeral services caskets burial vaults cremation receptacles flowers and burial garments. The company has expanded significantly in recent years through acquisitions and is aggressively pursuing the cremation market.

	Annual Growth	12/10	12/11	12/12	12/13	12/14
Sales ($ mil.)	8.1%	2,190.6	2,316.0	2,410.5	2,556.4	2,994.0
Net income ($ mil.)	8.1%	126.4	144.9	152.5	143.8	172.5
Market value ($ mil.)	28.8%	1,690.2	2,181.8	2,829.2	3,714.2	4,650.5
Employees	3.4%	20,725	20,891	20,567	25,719	23,662

SERVICEMAGIC INC.

14023 Denver West Pkwy. Bldg. 64 Ste. 200
Golden CO 80401
Phone: 303-963-7200
Fax: 303-980-3003
Web: www.servicemagic.com

CEO: Chris Terrill
CFO: –
HR: –
FYE: December 31
Type: Subsidiary

Need advice on how to fix your home? HomeAdvisor (formerly ServiceMagic) helps you hire residential contractors with the click of a mouse. The company operates an online marketplace where homeowners can find information about qualified contractors and service professionals in their area and post projects and service requests for contractors to bid on. HomeAdvisor fields requests for services in more than 700 categories including bathroom remodeling locksmiths and handymen. It has more than 80000 pre-screened businesses that pay fees for leads received as a result of the service. Michael Beaudoin and Rodney Rice started the firm as ServiceMagic in 1998. Today it is a part of IAC/InterActiveCorp (IAC).

SERVICENOW INC

NYS: NOW

3260 Jay Street
Santa Clara, CA 95054
Phone: 408 501-8550
Fax: –
Web: www.servicenow.com

CEO: Frank Slootman
CFO: Michael P. Scarpelli
HR: Shelly Begun
FYE: December 31
Type: Public

ServiceNow believes in self help. A provider of cloud-based services to IT departments the company serves the financial services IT services and health care industries among others. ServiceNow offers software and services that help IT organizations automate and integrate various enterprise technologies. Its cloud-based software works across operating systems servers networking equipment PCs mobile devices and other technologies to facilitate workflow automation data consolidation and administration of organizations' business processes. Customers also use its platform to create custom applications for automating processes unique to their organizations.

	Annual Growth	06/11*	12/11	12/12	12/13	12/14
Sales ($ mil.)	94.6%	92.6	73.4	243.7	424.7	682.6
Net income ($ mil.)	–	9.8	(6.7)	(37.3)	(73.7)	(179.4)
Market value ($ mil.)	50.3%	–	–	4,489.8	8,374.0	10,144.2
Employees	57.2%	–	728	1,077	1,830	2,826

*Fiscal year change

SERVICES GROUP OF AMERICA INC.

16100 N. 71st St. Ste. 500
Scottsdale AZ 85254
Phone: 480-927-4000
Fax: 312-460-7000
Web: www.seyfarth.com

CEO: Peter Smitth
CFO: Jim Keller
HR: –
FYE: December 31
Type: Private

Supplying American restaurants with food is the primary service of this company. Services Group of America (SGA) is one of the leading foodservice suppliers in the country. Subsidiary Food Services of America distributes a wide range of food and nonfood items to foodservice operators in 15 mostly western states through nine distribution facilities. It also has specialist subsidiaries such as Amerifresh (fresh produce) Ameristar Meats and Systems Services of America (chain restaurants). In addition SGA offers event planning services through Event Services of America while its Development Services of America manages the company's commercial real estate. SGA was formed in 1989 by the late Thomas Stewart.

SERVICESOURCE INTERNATIONAL, INC.

NMS: SREV

760 Market Street, 4th floor
San Francisco, CA 94102
Phone: 415 901-6030
Fax: –
Web: www.servicesource.com

CEO: Christopher Carrington
CFO: Robert Pinkerton
HR: –
FYE: December 31
Type: Public

ServiceSource is hoping to bring a sense of renewal to its clients. Part sales professional staffer part software developer ServiceSource offers sales staff outsourcing and proprietary customer management software geared toward increasing sales contract renewals. Its software which includes data management platforms and cloud applications aggregates customer data from its clients' different enterprise systems (e.g. CRM billing order management) to facilitate customer management and analysis from a single online location. Serving clients primarily in the technology sector ServiceSource often markets its sales professionals in tandem with its software offerings.

	Annual Growth	12/10	12/11	12/12	12/13	12/14
Sales ($ mil.)	15.5%	152.9	205.5	243.7	272.5	272.2
Net income ($ mil.)	–	(2.6)	15.1	(42.8)	(22.9)	(95.2)
Market value ($ mil.)	(33.2%)	–	1,314.9	490.3	702.3	392.2
Employees	18.4%	1,536	2,110	2,609	2,914	3,017

SERVIGISTICS INC.

2300 Windy Ridge Pkwy. 450 North Tower
Atlanta GA 30339
Phone: 770-565-2340
Fax: 770-565-8767
Web: www.servigistics.com

CEO: Eric Hinkle
CFO: Peter Vlerick
HR: –
FYE: December 31
Type: Private

Servigistics makes sure companies aren't waiting on wading in or wrongly pricing parts. The company provides service lifecycle management (SLM) software and services including Web-based software that helps companies optimize parts inventory levels for their customer service operations price parts and manage field organizations (including workforce scheduling and routing). Its offerings help companies manage inventory levels and insure parts availability with the aim of improving revenue profitability and customer loyalty. Customers have included American Airlines BMW Cisco Cummins Kodak Philips Southern Company and Toshiba. In 2012 Servigistics was acquired by Parametric Technology.

SERVISFIRST BANCSHARES, INC.

NMS: SFBS

850 Shades Creek Parkway
Birmingham, AL 35209
Phone: 205 949-0302
Fax: –
Web: www.servisfirstbank.com

CEO: Thomas A. (Tom) Broughton
CFO: William M. Foshee
HR: –
FYE: December 31
Type: Public

ServisFirst Bancshares is a bank holding company for ServisFirst Bank a regional commercial bank with about a dozen branches located in Alabama and the Florida panhandle. The bank also has a loan office in Nashville. ServisFirst Bank targets privately-held businesses with $2 million to $250 million in annual sales as well as professionals and affluent customers. The bank focuses on traditional commercial banking services including loan origination deposits and electronic banking services such as online and mobile banking. Founded in 2005 by its chairman and CEO Thomas Broughton III the bank went public in 2014 with an offering valued at nearly $57 million.

	Annual Growth	12/10	12/11	12/12	12/13	12/14
Assets ($ mil.)	–	0.0	–	2,906.3	3,520.7	4,098.7
Net income ($ mil.)	–	0.0	23.4	34.4	41.6	52.4
Market value ($ mil.)	–	0.0	–	–	–	817.2
Employees	13.7%	–	–	–	262	298

SERVOTRONICS, INC.

ASE: SVT

1110 Maple Street
Elma, NY 14059
Phone: 716 655-5990
Fax: –
Web: www.servotronics.com

CEO: Nicholas D. Trbovich
CFO: Cari L. Jaroslawsky
HR: Susan Scuz
FYE: December 31
Type: Public

Servotronics knows how to get things moving and cut to the chase. The company makes devices that convert electricity into mechanical movement and cutlery products. Its advanced technology products include servo-control components (torque motors electromagnetic actuators and hydraulic and pneumatic valves) which it sells mainly to clients in the aerospace industry. These include Honeywell United Technologies and the US government. Servotronics' cutlery unit makes a broad range of products from machetes and bayonets to kitchen knives and putty knives. Customers include retailers restaurants and agencies of the US government.

	Annual Growth	12/10	12/11	12/12	12/13	12/14
Sales ($ mil.)	(0.0%)	31.7	34.2	30.5	30.3	31.6
Net income ($ mil.)	–	2.1	2.6	0.3	1.0	(3.1)
Market value ($ mil.)	(6.2%)	19.1	20.5	17.8	18.5	14.8
Employees	(1.3%)	286	285	244	247	271

SERVPRO INTELLECTUAL PROPERTY INC.

801 INDUSTRIAL BLVD
GALLATIN, TN 370663742
Phone: 615-451-0200
Fax: –
Web: www.servpro.com

CEO: Sue Isaacson Steen
CFO: Rick Forster
HR: –
FYE: December 31
Type: Private

If you're dealing with fire or water damage Servpro hopes you'll let the pros come to your rescue. Servpro Industries provides emergency mitigation services for water- fire- and smoke-damaged properties as well as mold and mildew situations. It operates through more than 1500 franchised locations throughout the US. Mitigation services include cleaning of carpets upholstery air ducts drapes ceilings and walls. The company also offers instruction and training on water- and fire-damage restoration. Originally established as a painting business the family-owned Servpro Industries was founded in 1967 by Ted and Doris Isaacson.

	Annual Growth	12/01	12/02	12/03	12/09	12/10
Sales ($ mil.)	–	–	0.0	58.5	122.5	136.1
Net income ($ mil.)	18.8%	–	–	8.7	24.8	29.1
Market value ($ mil.)	–	–	–	–	–	–
Employees	–	–	–	–	–	111

SETON HALL UNIVERSITY

400 S ORANGE AVE
SOUTH ORANGE, NJ 070792697
Phone: 973-761-9000
Fax: –

CEO: –
CFO: Stephen A. Graham
HR: –
FYE: June 30
Type: Private

Seton Hall University is a Catholic institution with an enrollment of almost 10000 students (5500 undergraduates and 4300 graduates) who hail from 70 countries. The university offers more than 90 undergraduate and graduate degree programs as well as more than a dozen doctoral programs at eight colleges and schools including the Whitehead School of Diplomacy and International Relations Stillman School of Business and Immaculate Conception Seminary School of Theology. Seton Hall also offers degree and certificate programs online. Seton Hall is the US' oldest diocesan university and is under purview of the Archdiocese of Newark.

	Annual Growth	06/10	06/11	06/12	06/13	06/14
Sales ($ mil.)	1.9%	–	256.2	256.1	269.1	270.8
Net income ($ mil.)	–	–	–	(0.2)	38.9	52.5
Market value ($ mil.)	–	–	–	–	–	–
Employees	–	–	–	–	–	2,700

SETON HEALTHCARE NETWORK

1201 W. 38th St.
Austin TX 78705
Phone: 512-324-1100
Fax: 512-324-1924
Web: www.seton.net

CEO: Jesus Garza
CFO: Doug Waite
HR: –
FYE: June 30
Type: Subsidiary

For those who overdo it at the Austin City Limits music festival it's a good thing Seton Healthcare Network operates within Austin's city limits. The not-for-profit health care provider operates 11 urban and rural acute-care hospitals in Central Texas as well as psychiatric and children's hospitals and a network of community clinics. With a capacity of some 1700 beds Seton's facilities (known as the Seton Family of Hospitals) offer a range of services including trauma heart transplant neurological and neonatal intensive care as well as primary and specialty care services. Seton in Austin was formed in 1902 by the Daughters of Charity of St. Vincent de Paul. Today it is part of Ascension Health.

SEVCON INC

NAS: SEV

155 Northboro Road
Southborough, MA 01772
Phone: 508 281-5510
Fax: –
Web: www.techopssevcon.com

CEO: Matthew Boyle
CFO: Paul N Farquhar
HR: –
FYE: September 30
Type: Public

You might say that Tech/Ops Sevcon prevents electric vehicles from becoming speed demons. The company makes Sevcon solid-state controllers which regulate motor speed and acceleration in battery-powered vehicles such as forklifts and coal mining equipment. Through a UK-based subsidiary Tech/Ops Sevcon also makes metalized film capacitors for power electronics signaling and audio equipment applications. Targeting manufacturers of aerial lifts forklift trucks and underground mining vehicles Tech/Ops sells directly and through a network of independent dealers in Asia Europe and the US. About 60% of sales are to customers outside the US.

	Annual Growth	09/11	09/12	09/13	09/14	09/15
Sales ($ mil.)	6.2%	32.3	35.5	32.2	37.9	41.1
Net income ($ mil.)	22.0%	0.7	1.2	(1.1)	0.9	1.6
Market value ($ mil.)	10.4%	23.4	17.6	17.9	30.1	34.8
Employees	7.7%	113	125	119	136	152

SEVEN SEAS TECHNOLOGIES INC.

720 SPIRIT 40 PARK DR
CHESTERFIELD, MO 630051122
Phone: 636-778-0705
Fax: –
Web: www.s2tech.com

CEO: –
CFO: –
HR: David Godwin
FYE: December 31
Type: Private

Seven Seas Technologies which does business as S2 Tech provides IT services such as custom software development database administration and networking. Founded in 1997 the company specializes in managing Medicaid systems and HIPAA compliance with clients that have included CACI MasterCard and Sallie Mae. S2 Tech has locations in the US and India.

	Annual Growth	12/09	12/10	12/11	12/12	12/13
Sales ($ mil.)	27.5%	–	9.5	11.3	14.2	19.7
Net income ($ mil.)	5.0%	–	–	0.4	0.4	0.4
Market value ($ mil.)	–	–	–	–	–	–
Employees	–	–	–	–	–	120

SEVENTH GENERATION INC.

60 Lake St.	CEO: Chuck Maniscalco
Burlington VT 05401-5218	CFO: –
Phone: 802-658-3773	HR: John Lebourveau
Fax: 802-658-1771	FYE: December 31
Web: www.seventhgeneration.com	Type: Private

To Seventh Generation green is good. The term means environmentally friendly and nontoxic. For the conscientious company it also means money in the bank. It makes cleaning and laundry supplies paper products personal care items and diapers and wipes under the Seventh Generation name which is derived from the Iroquois practice of considering how decisions may affect the next seven generations. Suppliers make its products which are sold in the US and Canada through such retailers as Target Whole Foods Wal-Mart and Amazon.com from recycled or renewable materials using nontoxic ingredients. In business since 1988 the company is owned by its founder Jeffrey Hollender and a group of investors.

SEVIN ROSEN FUNDS

2 Galleria Tower 13455 Noel Rd. Ste. 1670	CEO: –
Dallas TX 75240	CFO: Jan Gaulding
Phone: 972-702-1100	HR: –
Fax: 972-702-1103	FYE: December 31
Web: www.srfunds.com	Type: Private

Founded in 1981 by former electrical engineers L. J. Sevin and Benjamin Rosen (the former chairman of Compaq Computer) Sevin Rosen Funds invests in early-stage companies. It targets Internet media software technology and communications infrastructure energy and materials and technology-related health care industries. The firm which has offices in Texas and the Silicon Valley typically provides up to $15 million in start-up capital. The company has helped build tech powerhouses such as Compaq Cisco Systems Intel Hewlett-Packard Lotus and National Semiconductor. Current portfolio holdings include InfoNow Cytokinetics and Ceterus Networks. It sold Wi-Fi service provider Wayport to AT&T in 2008.

SEVERN BANCORP INC (ANNAPOLIS MD)

NAS: SVBI

200 Westgate Circle, Suite 200	CEO: Alan J Hyatt
Annapolis, MD 21401	CFO: Thomas G Bevivino
Phone: 410 260-2000	HR: –
Fax: –	FYE: December 31
Web: www.severnbank.com	Type: Public

Severn Bancorp is the holding company for Severn Savings Bank which operates about five bank branches in Anne Arundel County Maryland. The thrift provides traditional retail products including checking and savings accounts CDs and IRAs. Severn uses funds from deposits to originate loans and mortgages primarily residential and commercial mortgages construction loans and business loans. The holding company also owns SBI Mortgage which originates riskier loans than Severn Savings Bank does; it also invests in real estate on its own behalf. Severn is working towards recovery after suffering real estate- and mortgage-related losses in the economic recession.

	Annual Growth	12/10	12/11	12/12	12/13	12/14
Assets ($ mil.)	(5.2%)	962.5	900.6	852.1	799.6	776.3
Net income ($ mil.)	25.9%	1.2	1.2	3.7	(25.2)	2.9
Market value ($ mil.)	7.1%	34.7	24.8	31.6	47.7	45.7
Employees	6.6%	116	127	142	160	150

SEVION THERAPEUTICS INC

OTC: SVON

4045 Sorrento Valley Boulevard	CEO: David Rector
San Diego, CA 92121	CFO: James Schmidt
Phone: 858 909-0749	HR: –
Fax: –	FYE: June 30
Web: www.senesco.com	Type: Public

Senesco Technologies wants to find the fountain of youth for melons tomatoes bananas and lettuce. The company does research surrounding new plant gene technologies for use in combating senescence or cell aging in fruits vegetables and flowers. Its research activities are geared toward developing plants whose crops will have longer shelf-lives and higher yields. Senesco Technologies' research work is performed by third parties primarily researchers at the University of Waterloo in Ontario Canada. The company is also investigating some of its technologies for use as treatments for inflammatory diseases and/or to delay or inhibit apoptosis i.e. cell aging in humans (for possible use in cancer treatment).

	Annual Growth	06/11	06/12	06/13	06/14	06/15
Sales ($ mil.)	(27.9%)	–	0.2	–	0.1	0.1
Net income ($ mil.)		(7.3)	(5.1)	(6.1)	(9.2)	(18.1)
Market value ($ mil.)	(24.8%)	56.3	56.3	0.5	52.5	18.0
Employees	(6.1%)	18	7	9	21	14

SEVERSTAL NORTH AMERICA INC.

14661 Rotunda Dr.	CEO: –
Dearborn MI 48120-1699	CFO: –
Phone: 313-317-8900	HR: –
Fax: 313-337-9377	FYE: December 31
Web: www.severstalna.com	Type: Subsidiary

Severstal North America makes crude steel as well as flat-rolled carbon steel products (hot-rolled cold-rolled electrogalvanized and hot-dip galvanized). Steel converters are the company's largest customers accounting for about a third of its business though the auto industry is also a major segment at a quarter of sales. Severstal North America operates a couple of large steel plants that had been run by other larger companies until parent company Severstal swooped in. Russian steel producer Severstal has steadily built up its North American operations since it formed this unit in 2004.

SEYFARTH SHAW LLP

131 S DEARBORN ST # 2400	CEO: Robert Saccone
CHICAGO, IL 606035863	CFO: –
Phone: 312-460-5000	HR: –
Fax: –	FYE: December 31
Web: www.seyfarth.com	Type: Private

Every day is labor day at law firm Seyfarth Shaw which specializes in handling employment-related matters for its clients. The firm divides its numerous practices into four main areas: business services employee benefits labor and employment and litigation. Overall Seyfarth Shaw has about 800 attorneys in 14 offices — ten spread throughout the US plus four international outposts. Seyfarth Shaw draws clients from industries such as financial services life sciences and telecommunications. Henry Seyfarth Lee Shaw and Owen Fairweather founded the firm in 1945.

	Annual Growth	12/04	12/05	12/06	12/07	12/08
Sales ($ mil.)	11.7%	–	332.2	385.6	431.8	463.0
Net income ($ mil.)	3.9%	–	–	136.3	141.9	147.0
Market value ($ mil.)	–	–	–	–	–	–
Employees	–	–	–	–	–	1,608

SFN GROUP INC.

2050 Spectrum Blvd.
Fort Lauderdale FL 33309
Phone: 954-308-7600
Fax: 954-308-7666
Web: www.sfngroup.com

CEO: Roy G Krause
CFO: Mark W Smith
HR: Deborah Stowers
FYE: December 31
Type: Subsidiary

This group seeks to circumvent your personnel problems. SFN Group (formerly Spherion) provides traditional temporary staffing along with services such as professional and executive recruitment and employee consulting and assessment. Through several subsidiaries and specialized staffing units SFN Group offers staffing and technology services in such areas as project management quality assurance and data center and network operations. It operates through a network of some 550 locations in the US and Canada serving more than 8000 clients ranging from small businesses to FORTUNE 500 companies. In September 2011 SFN Group was acquired by staffing powerhouse rival Randstad.

SFX ENTERTAINMENT, INC.

NBB: SFXE Q

902 Broadway, Fifteenth Floor
New York, NY 10010
Phone: 646 561-6400
Fax: –
Web: www.sfxii.com

CEO: Robert F. X. Sillerman
CFO: Richard Rosenstein
HR: –
FYE: December 31
Type: Public

SFX Entertainment makes flashing strobe lights hot musical acts big crowds and a driving dance beat its business. The company founded in 2011 produces music festivals in North America and Europe that attract fans of “electronic music culture” or EDM (electronic dance music). As much as a fifth of the company's sales come from digital music sales between and around its musical events which earn revenue through sales of tickets concessions sponsorships promotion fees and advertising. In 2013 SFX went public in a $260 million IPO. In 2016 the company filed for bankruptcy.

	Annual Growth	12/10	12/11	12/12	12/13	12/14
Sales ($ mil.)	–	0.0	–	24.8	170.5	354.4
Net income ($ mil.)	–	0.0	(0.1)	(16.2)	(111.9)	(131.0)
Market value ($ mil.)	–	0.0	–	–	1,111.2	419.5
Employees	87.4%	–	–	178	450	625

SGS NORTH AMERICA INC.

201 Rte. 17 North
Rutherford NJ 07070
Phone: 201-508-3000
Fax: 201-508-3193
Web: www.us.sgs.com

CEO: Christopher Kirk
CFO: Geraldine Matchett
HR: Andrea Daz
FYE: December 31
Type: Subsidiary

You know those little stickers that say "Inspected by 2438"? Meet 2438. SGS North America a division of global testing and verification giant SGS offers technical services such as product testing conformity assessment quality inspection product safety inspections design reviews statutory certification quality assurance environmental impact and consultancy. SGS North America tests everything under the sun and targets such industries as power generation and transmission oil and gas refineries and pipelines metals and minerals agriculture transportation construction aerospace pharmaceuticals and industrial manufacturing.

SGT INC.

7701 GREENBELT RD STE 400
GREENBELT, MD 207706521
Phone: 301-614-8600
Fax: –
Web: www.sgt-inc.com

CEO: Kam Ghaffarian
CFO: Joe Morway
HR: –
FYE: September 30
Type: Private

Like its acronym name suggests SGT (aka Stinger Ghaffarian Technologies) is used to taking military orders; in this case very specific technical ones. An engineering services firm SGT provides aerospace engineering project management IT systems development and related services to NASA the US Navy the US Air Force and other primarily military-related government entities through contracts. The company also offers science-related services such as earth climate and planetary modeling and analysis. SGT's facilities are located near airfields and other military facilities.

	Annual Growth	09/07	09/08	09/12	09/13	09/14
Sales ($ mil.)	7.5%	–	293.0	374.7	416.5	453.1
Net income ($ mil.)	40.0%	–	–	9.0	15.5	17.7
Market value ($ mil.)	–	–	–	–	–	–
Employees	–	–	–	–	–	1,500

SHAKEY'S USA INC.

2200 W. Valley Blvd.
Alhambra CA 91803
Phone: 626-576-0616
Fax: 626-458-9224
Web: www.shakeys.com

CEO: –
CFO: David Reid
HR: Julie Bosworth
FYE: December 31
Type: Subsidiary

Fans of the old time pizza parlor can still shake their groove thang at these restaurants. Shakey's USA operates and franchises a chain of about 60 restaurants in half a dozen states that serve a variety of pizzas along with other quick-serve menu favorites including fried chicken and Mojo potatoes (fried potato skins). Many of the eateries also feature a buffet-style all-you-can-eat menu along with a salad and dessert bar. Found primarily in Southern California most of the restaurants are operated by franchisees. The chain was founded in 1954 by Sherwood "Shakey" Johnson. Shakey's is owned by holding company The Jacmar Companies.

SHAKLEE CORPORATION

4747 Willow Rd.
Pleasanton CA 94588
Phone: 925-924-2000
Fax: 925-924-2862
Web: www.shaklee.com

CEO: Roger Barnett
CFO: Mike Batesole
HR: –
FYE: March 31
Type: Private

Shaklee works to keep its customers healthy clean beautiful and green. The company manufactures and sells directly to customers its vitamins cosmetics personal care items nutrition products and environmentally friendly household cleaners. Its products are marketed under the Cinch Enfuselle Get Clean Shaklee and Vita-Lea brands among others and it holds 50-plus patents and patents pending worldwide. Products are sold through Shaklee's website and by more than 750000 members and distributors in the US Canada Mexico China Japan Malaysia and Taiwan. Founded in 1956 by Dr. Forrest C. Shaklee Sr. the company is controlled by private equity firms Ripplewood Holdings and Activated Holdings.

SHAMROCK FOODS COMPANY

3900 E CAMELBACK RD # 300
PHOENIX, AZ 850182614
Phone: 602-477-2500
Fax: –
Web: www.shamrockfarms.net

CEO: Norman P McClelland
CFO: F. Phillips (Phil) Giltner
HR: –
FYE: September 30
Type: Private

You might say Shamrock Foods is milking the food service business for all it's worth. Distribution business Shamrock Foods ranks in the top 10 US food services companies while its Shamrock Farms unit represents one of the largest dairy operators in the southwestern US. The company's distribution operations supply food and related products to food service operators in 10 states in the Intermountain region through a handful of distribution centers. Shamrock Farms home to more than 10000 cows produces and offers a full line of dairy products including fluid milk half and half and ice cream. Founded in 1922 as a mom-and-pop dairy Shamrock Foods is still owned and operated by the founding McClelland family.

	Annual Growth	09/10	09/11	09/12	09/13	09/14
Sales ($ mil.)	21.6%	–	1,353.7	1,353.7	1,353.7	2,433.8
Net income ($ mil.)	–	–	–	0.0	0.0	0.0
Market value ($ mil.)	–	–	–	–	–	–
Employees	–	–	–	–	–	2,600

SHANDS JACKSONVILLE MEDICAL CENTER INC.

655 W 8TH ST
JACKSONVILLE, FL 322096511
Phone: 904-244-5576
Fax: –
Web: www.rainbow.jax.ufl.edu

CEO: –
CFO: William J Ryan
HR: Lesli Ward
FYE: June 30
Type: Private

Close to the shifting sands of the northern Florida coast Shands Jacksonville Medical Center (doing business as UF Health Jacksonville) offers a range of services to the 19 counties it serves in Florida and southern Georgia. The 695-bed hospital includes a cardiovascular center Level III neonatal intensive care unit and a Level I trauma center. It also operates primary and specialty clinics in the Jacksonville area. The medical center is affiliated with the University of Florida and is the largest of seven hospitals in the Shands HealthCare family.

	Annual Growth	06/06	06/07	06/08	06/09	06/10
Sales ($ mil.)	–	–	–	(1,174.4)	591.6	593.0
Net income ($ mil.)	23854.6%	–	–	0.0	7.1	19.2
Market value ($ mil.)	–	–	–	–	–	–
Employees	–	–	–	–	–	3,000

SHANDS TEACHING HOSPITAL AND CLINICS INC.

1600 SW Archer Rd.
Gainesville FL 32608
Phone: 352-265-7962
Fax: 937-276-8337
Web: www.goodsamdayton.org

CEO: Marvin Dewar
CFO: Michael E Gleason
HR: –
FYE: June 30
Type: Private - Not-for-Pr

While its full name is Shands Teaching Hospital and Clinics most folks call it UF&Shands. The network affiliated with the University of Florida Health Science Center provides health care services to patients in north-central and northeast Florida. The company is made up of seven not-for-profit acute care community and specialty hospitals as well as more than 80 physician practices and outpatient rehabilitation centers. It also operates a home health care agency. The Shands network has some 2000 licensed beds and about 1000 affiliated University of Florida doctors. Specialty services include oncology pediatrics cardiovascular transplants and neurological care.

SHANER HOTEL GROUP LIMITED PARTNERSHIP

1965 Waddle Rd.
State College PA 16803
Phone: 814-234-4460
Fax: 814-278-7295
Web: www.shanerhotels.com

CEO: Lance T Shaner
CFO: Amanda Droll
HR: Brenda Loving
FYE: December 31
Type: Private

Shaner makes hotels shine. The Shaner Hotel Group buys renovates repositions re-brands and builds hotels. The company owns and manages more than 20 hotels containing around 3500 rooms in 15 states mainly in the East and the South. Shaner's hotels are affiliated with several major brands including Hampton Inn Holiday Inn Marriott and Radisson. In addition to maintaining its existing portfolio of hotels the company also is working together with investors and colleges and universities to develop new hotels on or near campuses. Shaner is affiliated with business services outsourcing firm Shaner Solutions.

SHAPELL INDUSTRIES INC.

8383 Wilshire Blvd. Ste. 700
Beverly Hills CA 90211
Phone: 323-655-7330
Fax: 323-651-4349
Web: www.shapell.com

CEO: Nathan Shapell
CFO: Margaret F Leong
HR: –
FYE: December 31
Type: Private

Want to live in style? Let Shapell show you how. Real estate developer Shapell Industries builds single-family detached homes and develops residential communities in Northern and Southern California. It specializes in customizable luxury homes and estates ranging in price from about $600000 to the millions of dollars. Among its most notable developments is the Porter Ranch master-planned community in the San Fernando Valley. The company also builds multifamily residential properties as well as commercial properties (office buildings shopping centers) near its homes. Shapell Industries provides home financing through Westminster Mortgage. The company was founded as S&S Construction Company in 1955.

SHARI'S MANAGEMENT CORPORATION

9400 SW GEMINI DR
BEAVERTON, OR 970087105
Phone: 503-605-4299
Fax: –
Web: www.sharis.com

CEO: Bruce Macdiarmid
CFO: –
HR: –
FYE: January 02
Type: Private

This Shari keeps the kitchen open all day and all night. Shari's Management Corporation owns and operates more than 100 Shari's family restaurants in six states (primarily in the Northwest) that serve breakfast lunch and dinner 24 hours a day. The chain of eateries offers standard American fare such as pancakes and eggs sandwiches and burgers and beef chicken and pasta dishes as well as a selection of appetizers and desserts through a menu of about 120 items. The company is owned by a group of private investors led by Circle Peak Management. Ron and Sharon (Shari) Berquist opened the first Shari's in Hermiston Oregon in 1978.

	Annual Growth	01/04	01/05	01/06	01/07	01/08
Sales ($ mil.)	3.0%	–	–	–	165.3	170.3
Net income ($ mil.)	(96.2%)	–	–	–	40.2	1.5
Market value ($ mil.)	–	–	–	–	–	–
Employees	–	–	–	–	–	4,000

SHARON REGIONAL HEALTH SYSTEM INC.

740 E STATE ST	CEO: John R Jack Janoso Jr
SHARON, PA 16146-3328	CFO: Jeffrey Chrobak
Phone: 724-983-5864	HR: –
Fax: –	FYE: June 30
Web: www.sharonregional.com	Type: Private

Ready to show some mercy to the ill in Mercer County is Sharon Regional Health System (SRHS) serving residents throughout northwestern Pennsylvania and northeastern Ohio. The not-for-profit hospital has some 240 beds and operates a network of nearly 20 outpatient clinics. Specialty services include behavioral health care cancer treatment home health and hospice care women's health services rehabilitation and speech and occupational therapy. As one of the region's primary health care providers SRHS has had to work to keep up with patient demand by opening a new $2 million diagnostic and imaging clinic expanding existing facilities and adding new care programs such as its Cancer Genetics Program.

	Annual Growth	06/08	06/09	06/10	06/11	06/12
Sales ($ mil.)	(1.5%)	–	172.5	174.6	184.5	165.1
Net income ($ mil.)	–	–	(5.5)	(6.4)	8.4	0.3
Market value ($ mil.)	–	–	–	–	–	–
Employees	–	–	–	–	–	1,850

SHARP ELECTRONICS CORPORATION

Sharp Plaza	CEO: Toshiyki Osawa
Mahwah NJ 07495-1163	CFO: Mamoru Kondo
Phone: 201-529-8200	HR: –
Fax: 201-529-8425	FYE: March 31
Web: www.sharpusa.com	Type: Subsidiary

Sharp Electronics positions itself as a purveyor of cutting-edge products for both consumers and corporate clients. The company is the US sales and marketing arm of Osaka Japan-based appliance and electronic components maker Sharp Corporation. Sharp Electronics is known as a leading seller of LCDs which are used in everything from airplane cockpits to pinball machines and computers to HDTV sets. The company also markets solar energy products (modules inverters) home appliances (air conditioners microwave ovens) entertainment products (TVs Blu-ray Disc players) and business electronics (cash registers PCs calculators copiers). Sharp Electronics sells through retailers and resellers.

SHARP HEALTHCARE

8695 SPECTRUM CENTER BLVD	CEO: Michael W. (Mike) Murphy
SAN DIEGO, CA 921231489	CFO: Ann Pumpian
Phone: 858-499-4000	HR: Ky Lewis
Fax: –	FYE: September 30
Web: www.myecare.sharp.com	Type: Private

Sharp HealthCare stands on the cutting edge of health care delivery in Southern California. The system of not-for-profit hospitals and health care facilities is the largest in the San Diego area. The network includes four acute-care hospitals (Sharp Chula Vista Sharp Coronado Sharp Grossmont and Sharp Memorial) as well as three specialty hospitals for women's care psychiatry and chemical dependence. It also operates two physician medical groups and a number of urgent care and outpatient facilities and clinics. With some 2100 beds and about 2600 physicians Sharp HealthCare offers cancer and cardiac care fertility and maternity services surgical procedures and hospice care.

	Annual Growth	09/04	09/05	09/06	09/09	09/13
Sales ($ mil.)	(4.4%)	–	1,663.4	1,790.7	897.6	1,158.6
Net income ($ mil.)	–	–	–	43.0	(0.6)	(11.4)
Market value ($ mil.)	–	–	–	–	–	–
Employees	–	–	–	–	–	13,000

SHARP MEMORIAL HOSPITAL

7901 FROST ST	CEO: Tim Smith
SAN DIEGO, CA 921232701	CFO: –
Phone: 858-939-3636	HR: –
Fax: –	FYE: September 30
Web: www.sharp.com	Type: Private

The docs and the scalpels are sharp at Sharp Memorial Hospital. The flagship facility of Sharp HealthCare the not-for-profit hospital has roughly 675 beds and is a designated trauma center for San Diego County. Specialties include cardiac care women's health multi-organ transplantation and cancer treatment. It also provides skilled nursing home health and hospice services. Sharp Memorial Hospital first opened in 1955. Sharp HealthCare completed reconstruction efforts on the Sharp Memorial facility in 2009; the new hospital has improved inpatient surgery emergency trauma and intensive care facilities.

	Annual Growth	09/07	09/08	09/09	09/12	09/13
Sales ($ mil.)	8.2%	–	670.7	735.0	965.8	992.9
Net income ($ mil.)	38.8%	–	–	49.5	194.7	183.5
Market value ($ mil.)	–	–	–	–	–	–
Employees	–	–	–	–	–	3,500

SHARPE RESOURCES CORPORATION

OTC: SHGP

3258 Mob Neck Rd.	CEO: –
Heathsville VA 22473	CFO: –
Phone: 804-580-8107	HR: –
Fax: 804-580-4132	FYE: December 31
Web: www.sharperesourcescorporation.com	Type: Public

Sharpe Resources keeps a sharp eye out for natural resource opportunities in the US. Through subsidiary Standard Energy Company it focuses on developing coal bed methane (CBM) coal and shale projects in West Virginia. Coal bed methane is natural gas trapped in coal beds; the CBM is more easily drilled and utilized than other sources of natural gas. Sharpe leases and holds options on about 17000 acres in West Virginia that it hopes to tap for CBM and coal. It is also exploring the option of creating relatively clean coal energy from underground coal gasification which allows for the coal to be used in the generation of electricity without the coal having to be mined first.

SHARPS COMPLIANCE CORP.

NAS: SMED

9220 Kirby Drive, Suite 500	CEO: David P Tusa
Houston, TX 77054	CFO: Diana P Diaz
Phone: 713 432-0300	HR: –
Fax: –	FYE: June 30
Web: www.sharpsinc.com	Type: Public

Sharps Compliance is on the cutting edge of the medical waste disposal business — and wants to make sure people don't get hurt. The company offers services to health care providers to make the disposal of medical waste safer and more efficient. It also serves customers in the pharmaceutical agricultural hospitality industrial and retail industries. Products include medical sharps (needles and other sharp objects) disposal systems disposable IV poles waste and equipment return boxes linen recovery systems and biohazardous spill clean-up kits. Sharps Compliance also provides regulatory compliant waste tracking incineration and disposal verification services as well as consulting services.

	Annual Growth	06/11	06/12	06/13	06/14	06/15
Sales ($ mil.)	12.4%	19.4	21.8	21.5	26.6	30.9
Net income ($ mil.)	–	(3.0)	(3.6)	(2.7)	1.0	1.2
Market value ($ mil.)	13.4%	64.6	52.0	40.3	67.7	106.9
Employees	7.1%	57	56	62	62	75

SHAWMUT WOODWORKING & SUPPLY INC.

560 HARRISON AVE STE 200
BOSTON, MA 021182632
Phone: 617-338-6200
Fax: –
Web: www.shawmut.com

CEO: Les Hiscoe
CFO: Roger C. Tougas
HR: –
FYE: November 30
Type: Private

Shawmut Woodworking & Supply which does business as Shawmut Design and Construction provides beginning-to-end construction services from pre-construction planning to post-construction quality assurance checks. The $860 million national construction management firm has experience building retail hotel gaming spa sports restaurant education banking healthcare and life science facilities. It also handles corporate interiors and high-end residential construction and boasts expertise in cultural and historical preservation projects. Founded in 1982 by Jim Ansara the employee-owned company serves clients nationwide from offices in a handful of US states.

	Annual Growth	12/04	12/05*	11/09	11/11	11/12
Sales ($ mil.)	6.4%	–	440.7	618.3	662.8	680.3
Net income ($ mil.)	–	–	–	(21.6)	3.7	4.1
Market value ($ mil.)	–	–	–	–	–	–
Employees	–	–	–	–	–	711

*Fiscal year change

SHAWNEE MISSION MEDICAL CENTER INC.

9100 W 74TH ST
SHAWNEE MISSION, KS 662044004
Phone: 913-676-2000
Fax: –
Web: www.shawneemission.org

CEO: –
CFO: Jack Wagnar
HR: Brad Hoffman
FYE: December 31
Type: Private

Shawnee Mission Medical Center (SMMC) cares for Kansas City residents primarily on the Kansas-side. The health care facility located in the city's southwest suburbs has some 500 inpatient beds. It also offers outpatient surgery and other health services in areas such as pediatrics rehabilitation oncology and radiology. The medical center's emergency department receives some 50000 visits each year. SMMC also operates satellite facilities including the Shawnee Mission Outpatient Pavilion in nearby Lenexa which offers emergency and outpatient diagnostic general practice and surgical care. SMMC is part of Adventist Health System.

	Annual Growth	12/06	12/07	12/08	12/09	12/12
Sales ($ mil.)	3.0%	–	–	304.7	358.7	343.4
Net income ($ mil.)	12.1%	–	–	19.5	24.1	30.8
Market value ($ mil.)	–	–	–	–	–	–
Employees	–	–	–	–	–	1,850

SHEA HOMES LIMITED PARTNERSHIP

655 Brea Canyon Rd.
Walnut CA 91789
Phone: 909-594-9500
Fax: 909-869-0897
Web: www.sheahomes.com

CEO: –
CFO: –
HR: –
FYE: December 31
Type: Private

Building communities comes naturally for Shea Homes. The company designs builds and markets single-family homes in Arizona California Colorado the Carolinas Florida Nevada and Washington. The home builder specializes in detached and attached residences including condominiums townhomes and luxury estates Its Trilogy brand builds active adult housing. The company's SPACES brand targets younger buyers. Shea Homes touts its master-planned communities and serves entry-level move-up and luxury buyers. The average price of a Shea home is $423000. Affiliated Shea Mortgage provides mortgage financing services. Shea Homes is a member of the J.F. Shea group.

SHEARER'S FOODS INC.

692 Wabash Ave. North
Brewster OH 44613-1056
Phone: 330-767-3426
Fax: 330-767-3393
Web: www.shearers.com

CEO: Christopher Fraleigh
CFO: Fritz Kohmann
HR: Dianne Ford
FYE: September 30
Type: Private

Shearer's Foods' potato chips are Shearer perfection. Using Grandma Shearer's "hand-cooked" kettle recipe the snacks company produces more than 30 million pounds of potato chips each year. Shearer's also makes and markets tortilla chips cheese curls corn puffs pretzels and pork rinds as well as dips and salsa. The food maker's products are sold around the country and in the Shearer's Marketplace Factory Outlet store across the street from its headquarters in Brewster Ohio. In addition to the Shearer brand the firm makes a variety of snacks for private-label customers. Shearer's produces kettle-cooked potato chips for snack-food giant Frito-Lay.

SHELCO INC.

5016 Parkway Plaza Blvd. Ste. 100
Charlotte NC 28217
Phone: 704-367-5600
Fax: 704-364-0120
Web: www.shelcoinc.com

CEO: –
CFO: J Scott Bengel
HR: –
FYE: December 31
Type: Private

Shelco is trying to see that the South will rise again — the southeast that is. One of the largest contractors in the southeastern US Shelco specializes in the construction of warehouse and distribution facilities; educational manufacturing retail and health care facilities; and office buildings. Repeat customers account for nearly three-quarters of Shelco's business. Not content to stay in its home state of North Carolina the company is also active in South Carolina Georgia and Virgina. The company was founded in 1978 in Winston-Salem North Carolina by Charles and Edwin Shelton. The Sheltons owned the company until 2003 when they sold Shelco to six senior managers.

SHELL OIL COMPANY

910 Louisiana St.
Houston TX 77002
Phone: 713-241-6161
Fax: 713-241-4044
Web: www.shell.us

CEO: –
CFO: –
HR: –
FYE: December 31
Type: Subsidiary

Shell Oil doesn't shilly-shally around as it explores for produces and markets oil and natural gas and produces and markets chemicals. The company's Shell Exploration & Production unit focuses its exploration on the deepwater plays in the Gulf of Mexico. Shell partners with Saudi Aramco in a US refining and marketing venture (Motiva) and owns Motiva's sister company Shell Oil Products US. Shell also produces petrochemicals (Shell Chemical) and liquefied natural gas (Shell US Gas & Power) and markets natural gas and electricity. Shell's parent Royal Dutch Shell vies with Exxon Mobil) to be the world's #1 integrated oil company.

SHELL OIL PRODUCTS US

910 Louisiana St.
Houston TX 77210
Phone: 713-241-6161
Fax: 713-241-4044
Web: www.shell.us/home/content/usa/aboutshell/shell

CEO: –
CFO: K M Fisher
HR: –
FYE: December 31
Type: Subsidiary

Oil refiner and marketer Shell Oil Products US and its sister company Motiva have the US covered. The Royal Dutch Shell unit operates refineries and crude oil pipelines in the western US and markets petroleum products via Shell-branded outlets in the West and Midwest. Motiva does the same in the eastern US. Together Motiva (8300 gas stations) and Shell Oil Products US (6000 gas stations) form the #1 US gasoline retailing business. Motiva is a 50-50 joint venture between Shell Oil and Saudi Arabia's national oil company Saudi Aramco. Shell operates four refineries throughout the country; Motiva has three of its own.

SHENANDOAH TELECOMMUNICATIONS CO.

NMS: SHEN

500 Shentel Way
Edinburg, VA 22824
Phone: 540 984-4141
Fax: –
Web: www.shentel.com

CEO: Christopher E. (Chris) French
CFO: Adele M. Skolits
HR: Becky Nucilli
FYE: December 31
Type: Public

If Virginia is for lovers Shenandoah Telecommunications must carry some interesting conversations. Through subsidiaries the company (which does business as Shentel) provides telecom services in the Shenandoah Valley and beyond. Shenandoah Telephone has more than 22000 access lines in service; (the population of Shenandoah County is 41000). As a Sprint Nextel affiliate subsidiary Shenandoah Personal Communications offers wireless services to more than 262000 customers. The company's cable TV unit serves about 115000 customers while about 13000 households subscribe to its dial-up and broadband Internet access.

	Annual Growth	12/10	12/11	12/12	12/13	12/14
Sales ($ mil.)	13.8%	194.9	251.1	288.1	308.9	326.9
Net income ($ mil.)	17.0%	18.1	13.0	16.3	29.6	33.9
Market value ($ mil.)	13.7%	904.0	505.8	738.9	1,239.0	1,508.3
Employees	2.7%	636	669	693	682	708

SHEPHERD CENTER INC.

2020 PEACHTREE RD NW
ATLANTA, GA 303091465
Phone: 404-352-2020
Fax: –
Web: www.shepherd.org

CEO: Gary R Ulicny
CFO: Stephen B Holleman
HR: –
FYE: March 31
Type: Private

Here to shepherd those with catastrophic injuries back to good health is Shepherd Center. The not-for-profit hospital specializes in medical treatment research and rehabilitation for people with spinal cord and brain injuries as well as patients with neuromuscular disorders (such as spina bifida) and chronic pain. Shepherd Center boasts more than 150 beds and a 10-bed intensive care unit. Of its patients who have suffered injuries about 60% have been in car accidents. The hospital conducts neurological and neuromuscular research through its Virginia C. Crawford Research Institute.

	Annual Growth	03/10	03/11	03/12	03/13	03/14
Sales ($ mil.)	8.1%	–	135.0	159.4	168.6	170.6
Net income ($ mil.)	7.5%	–	–	23.5	23.4	27.2
Market value ($ mil.)	–	–	–	–	–	–
Employees	–	–	–	–	–	800

SHEPHERD ELECTRIC COMPANY INCORPORATED

7401 PULASKI HWY
BALTIMORE, MD 212372542
Phone: 410-866-6000
Fax: –
Web: www.shepherdelec.com

CEO: Charles C Vogel III
CFO: –
HR: –
FYE: December 31
Type: Private

For well over a hundred years Shepherd Electric has steered customers through a range of electrical needs. The company supplies a variety of electrical products to wholesale and retail customers primarily to the commercial construction market but it also serves government entities industrial firms and OEMs. Shepherd Electric carries products from major manufacturers such as 3M Brady Eaton Hadco Fluke General Electric and Thomas & Betts among many others. The company was founded in 1892 by Ernest Fluharty and Henry Shepherd. Shepherd Electric is owned by the Vogel family which has had a controlling interest in the company since 1931.

	Annual Growth	12/09	12/10	12/11	12/12	12/13
Sales ($ mil.)	7.5%	–	151.6	163.2	183.9	188.4
Net income ($ mil.)	3.5%	–	–	2.9	5.5	3.1
Market value ($ mil.)	–	–	–	–	–	–
Employees	–	–	–	–	–	185

SHEPPARD MULLIN RICHTER & HAMPTON LLP

333 S. Hope St. 43th Fl.
Los Angeles CA 90071
Phone: 213-620-1780
Fax: 213-620-1398
Web: www.sheppardmullin.com

CEO: –
CFO: –
HR: –
FYE: December 31
Type: Private - Partnershi

A leading regional law firm Sheppard Mullin Richter & Hampton has expanded over the years beyond its California roots to serve clients with national and international business interests such as DHL Nordstrom and Samsung. The firm maintains a wide range of practice areas; it has been recognized for work related to corporate transactions entertainment labor and employment and real estate. It has about 550 lawyers overall. In addition to several offices in California the firm has outposts in New York Washington DC and Shanghai. Sheppard Mullin was founded in Los Angeles in 1927.

SHERIDAN COMMUNITY HOSPITAL (OSTEOPATHIC)

301 N MAIN ST
SHERIDAN, MI 488849235
Phone: 989-291-3261
Fax: –
Web: www.sheridanhospital.com

CEO: –
CFO: Mindy Buffman
HR: –
FYE: March 31
Type: Private

Sheridan Community Hospital certainly lives up to its "community" moniker. Local volunteers are considered a mainstay of the hospital logging more than 4000 hours of service every year. The facility offers residents of Montcalm Michigan and surrounding counties emergency services occupational health cardiology orthopedics and general surgery. The hospital has begun testing the waters of 21st century technology by investing in digital imaging and high-tech scanning systems. Sheridan Community Hospital has also opened Edmore Care-West its second family practice location in Edmore.

	Annual Growth	03/09	03/10	03/11	03/12	03/13
Sales ($ mil.)	1.1%	–	14.3	13.9	16.2	14.7
Net income ($ mil.)	–	–	–	0.3	0.6	(0.3)
Market value ($ mil.)	–	–	–	–	–	–
Employees	–	–	–	–	–	153

SHERIDAN HEALTHCARE INC.

1613 N. Harrison Pkwy. Ste. 200
Sunrise FL 33323
Phone: 954-838-2371
Fax: 631-234-1460
Web: www.discgraphics.com

CEO: –
CFO: Thomas Kiraly
HR: –
FYE: December 31
Type: Private

Sheridan Healthcare shoulders office responsibilties for busy doctors and hospital administrators. The firm is a physician practice management company that serves anesthesiologists neonatologists pediatricians radiologists emergency room and other general and specialty care physicians. The firm also provides outsourced staffing recruitment billing compliance and administration services to hospitals group practices ambulatory surgery centers and other health care facilities. The company provides services to more than 1600 doctors and 100 facilities in about 20 states. Sheridan Healthcare is controlled by private equity firm Hellman & Friedman.

SHERWIN-WILLIAMS CO.

NYS: SHW

101 West Prospect Avenue
Cleveland, OH 44115-1075
Phone: 216 566-2000
Fax: 216 566-3310
Web: www.sherwin.com

CEO: John G. Morikis
CFO: Sean P. Hennessy
HR: Thomas Hopkins
FYE: December 31
Type: Public

No matter how you coat it Sherwin-Williams is one of the top paint manufacturers in the US and worldwide (along with Akzo-Nobel PPG Industries and Henkel). Sherwin-Williams' products include a variety of paints finishes coatings applicators and varnishes sold under brands such as Dutch Boy Krylon Sherwin-Williams Thompson's WaterSeal Ronseal Sayerlack and Minwax. The company operates more than 4000 paint stores worldwide. It sells automotive finishing and refinishing products through wholesale branches worldwide. Other outlets include mass merchandisers home centers independent dealers and automotive retailers. Employees own 13% of the company via an Employee Stock Purchase and Savings Plan.

	Annual Growth	12/10	12/11	12/12	12/13	12/14
Sales ($ mil.)	9.4%	7,776.4	8,765.7	9,534.5	10,185.5	11,129.5
Net income ($ mil.)	17.0%	462.5	441.9	631.0	752.6	865.9
Market value ($ mil.)	33.1%	7,931.5	8,454.2	14,567.4	17,378.2	24,911.0
Employees	5.3%	32,228	32,988	34,154	37,633	39,674

SHI INTERNATIONAL CORP.

290 DAVIDSON AVE
SOMERSET, NJ 088734145
Phone: 732-764-8888
Fax: –
Web: www.shi.com

CEO: Thai Lee
CFO: Paul Ng
HR: –
FYE: December 31
Type: Private

Businesses that need more than boxes of hardware and software can call SHI International. The company distributes scores of computer hardware and software products from suppliers such as Adobe Cisco HP Microsoft and McAfee. It resells PCs networking products data storage systems printers software and keyboards among other items. SHI offers a range of professional services including software licensing asset management managed desktop services systems integration and vocational training. The company serves corporate government and health care customers from more than 30 offices across the US Canada the UK Germany France and Hong Kong. SHI was founded in 1989 by Chairman Koguan Leo.

	Annual Growth	12/07	12/08	12/11	12/12	12/13
Sales ($ mil.)	–	–	0.0	3,757.6	4,389.9	5,003.1
Net income ($ mil.)	44.4%	–	–	35.9	61.3	74.8
Market value ($ mil.)	–	–	–	–	–	–
Employees	–	–	–	–	–	2,500

SHILOH INDUSTRIES, INC.

NMS: SHLO

880 Steel Drive
Valley City, OH 44280
Phone: 330 558-2600
Fax: 330 558-2666
Web: www.shiloh.com

CEO: Ramzi Hermiz
CFO: W. Jay Potter
HR: –
FYE: October 31
Type: Public

When Shiloh Industries draws a blank it's a good thing. The company produces stampings modular assemblies and steel and welded blanks for the automotive heating and air-conditioning and lawn and garden equipment industries. It also makes tools and assembly equipment for its own use and to sell to OEMs and other suppliers. Shiloh's largest customer is General Motors accounting for about 20% of sales. Other customers include Ford Chrysler (15% of sales) and Toyota as well as home appliance manufacturers construction companies and steel producers. The company traces its roots back to 1950 when it was founded as Shiloh Tool & Die Manufacturing.

	Annual Growth	10/11	10/12	10/13	10/14	10/15
Sales ($ mil.)	21.0%	517.7	586.1	700.2	878.7	1,109.2
Net income ($ mil.)	1.3%	7.8	13.5	21.6	22.4	8.3
Market value ($ mil.)	(1.2%)	136.7	197.0	284.2	295.0	130.5
Employees	27.9%	1,270	1,430	1,824	3,200	3,400

SHIMADZU SCIENTIFIC INSTRUMENTS INC.

7102 Riverwood Dr.
Columbia MD 21046
Phone: 410-381-1227
Fax: 410-381-1222
Web: www.ssi.shimadzu.com

CEO: –
CFO: –
HR: –
FYE: March 31
Type: Subsidiary

Shimadzu Scientific Instruments helps researchers work magic in the lab. The company develops and manufactures analytical and monitoring equipment for scientific and medical laboratories. Products include diagnostic imaging systems such as ultrasound systems and mobile X-ray systems environmental testing and inspection machinery and mass spectrometers for the biotechnology sector. Its equipment is also available for lease. The company has more than 50 offices that offer sales service and support to clients. Founded in 1975 Shimadzu Scientific Instruments is the American arm of analytical instruments manufacturer Shimadzu Corporation.

SHINER INTERNATIONAL INC

NBB: BEST

19th Floor, Didu Building, Pearl River Plaza, No. 2 North Longkun Road
Haikou, Hainan Province 570125
Phone: (86) 898 68581104
Fax: –
Web: www.shinerinc.com

CEO: Jian Fu
CFO: –
HR: –
FYE: December 31
Type: Public

Shiner International knows how to put a shiny finish on its customers' products. Through its operating subsidiaries the company manufactures plastic-based packaging such as coating film shrink-wrap anti-counterfeiting laser holographic film and tobacco film. These film products are used as packaging for food products pharmaceuticals cosmetics CDs cigarettes and other consumer goods. In addition the company also offers color printing services for packaged products. Most of Shiner International's customers are located in China; its other customers are located in Europe North America and Southeast Asia. The company was established in 2003.

	Annual Growth	12/10	12/11	12/12	12/13	12/14
Sales ($ mil.)	14.8%	58.2	75.3	72.0	85.6	101.1
Net income ($ mil.)	(0.6%)	4.2	1.7	(9.1)	(1.7)	4.1
Market value ($ mil.)	(36.5%)	37.5	11.0	4.1	9.4	6.1
Employees	(6.1%)	510	470	420	384	397

SHINTECH INC.

#3 Greenway Plaza Ste. 1150
Houston TX 77046
Phone: 713-965-0713
Fax: 713-965-0629
Web: www.shintechinc.com

CEO: Chihiro Kanagawa
CFO: –
HR: –
FYE: March 31
Type: Subsidiary

Shintech is the largest producer of polyvinyl chloride (PVC) in the US. PVC is a plastic resin used in a wide range of consumer goods and industrial materials. Known for its durability it is often used as a substitute for wood. Through manufacturing plants in Texas and Louisiana Shintech serves customers primarily in North America but it also exports its resin products worldwide. The only other product the company makes is caustic soda used by the chemical industry and also found in consumer products such as paper soap synthetic textiles and food. Established in 1973 Shintech is the US subsidiary of Japanese diversified chemical giant Shin-Etsu Chemical Co.

SHOE CARNIVAL, INC.

NMS: SCVL

7500 East Columbia Street
Evansville, IN 47715
Phone: 812 867-6471
Fax: –
Web: www.shoecarnival.com

CEO: Clifton E. (Cliff) Sifford
CFO: W. Kerry Jackson
HR: Sean Georges
FYE: January 31
Type: Public

Shoe Carnival works hard to make shoe shopping a toe-tappin' good time. The company operates more than 350 family footwear stores across 30-plus US states including Puerto Rico that feature bright lights and neon signs. It also sells shoes online. In line with its name in-store "barkers" bellow out specials and organize games soliciting customer participation to promote the "carnival-like" atmosphere the retailer hopes will edge out rivals. Shoe Carnival sells brand-name and private-label men's and children's footwear as well as its primary women's and athletic shoes which together generate 64% of sales. The family of Chairman J. Wayne Weaver owns 25% of Shoe Carnival's shares.

	Annual Growth	01/11	01/12*	02/13	02/14*	01/15
Sales ($ mil.)	6.2%	739.2	762.5	855.0	884.8	940.2
Net income ($ mil.)	(1.2%)	26.8	26.4	29.3	26.9	25.5
Market value ($ mil.)	(1.4%)	499.2	522.7	416.0	501.2	471.2
Employees	8.2%	4,300	4,500	5,000	5,300	5,900

*Fiscal year change

SHONEY'S NORTH AMERICA CORP.

1717 Elm Hill Pike Ste. B-1
Nashville TN 37210
Phone: 615-391-5395
Fax: 615-231-2604
Web: www.shoneys.com

CEO: David Davoudpour
CFO: Steve Neuroth
HR: –
FYE: October 31
Type: Private

This company adds a touch of Southern hospitality to the family dining scene. Shoney's North America operates and franchises about 250 family-style restaurants in about 20 states mostly in Tennessee and states to the southeast. Popular for breakfast the chain offers such morning fare as bacon and eggs biscuits and gravy and pancakes while it lunch and dinner menu includes burgers chicken seafood and steak. Many Shoney's locations also offer an all-you-can-eat buffet. Most of the eateries are operated by franchisees. The Shoney's chain was founded by Alex Schoenbaum in the 1940s. It is part of Royal Hospitality Corp. an Atlanta-based foodservice operator controlled by Shoney's CEO David Davoudpour.

SHOOK HARDY & BACON L.L.P.

2555 Grand Blvd.
Kansas City MO 64108
Phone: 816-474-6550
Fax: 816-421-5547
Web: www.shb.com

CEO: –
CFO: –
HR: –
FYE: December 31
Type: Private - Partnershi

Shook Hardy & Bacon (SHB) likes to shake things up when it comes to practicing complex litigation. The law firm practices in a wide range of areas including corporate environmental intellectual property product liability and toxic tort. Many of its cases involve complex scientific or technical issues and SHB employs more than 200 researchers and analysts to go along with its stable of more than 470 lawyers. Clients have included tobacco companies such as Brown & Williamson and Philip Morris pharmaceutical companies Eli Lilly and Merck and mobile phone maker Motorola Mobility. SHB operates from about 10 offices in the US and Europe. The firm traces its roots to a law partnership established in 1889.

SHOP 'N SAVE ST. LOUIS INC.

10461 Manchester Rd.
St. Louis MO 63122
Phone: 314-984-0900
Fax: 314-984-1350
Web: www.shopnsave.com/

CEO: –
CFO: –
HR: –
FYE: February 28
Type: Subsidiary

Shop 'N Save St. Louis operates about 40 discount supermarkets in the St. Louis metro area and several in Springfield Illinois. The regional chain is owned by SUPERVALU and is part of that company's growing retail organization which also includes Shop 'N Save Warehouse Foods and about 20 Shop 'n Save markets in Pittsburgh where along with rival Giant Eagle it is one of the city's two biggest grocery chains. Shop 'N Save supermarkets offer savings of up to 20% and bakery deli pharmacy seafood and video departments among other amenities. The stores also feature dollar sections with merchandise sourced by sister company Save-A-Lot. Shop 'N Save was founded in 1979 as a single store in Illinois.

SHOPPING.COM LTD.

8000 Marina Blvd. 5th Fl.
Brisbane CA 94005
Phone: 650-616-6500
Fax: 650-616-6510
Web: www.shopping.com

CEO: Gautam Thakar
CFO: Robert J Krolik
HR: –
FYE: December 31
Type: Subsidiary

Whether you are a shopper in Peoria Illinois or Paris France Shopping.com wants you to compare before you buy. The subsidiary of online auction giant eBay operates a leading comparison shopping website where users can check prices on millions of retail items and read consumer product reviews from sister site Epinions.com. The site aggregates product and pricing information from thousands of online merchants and redirects interested buyers to the merchant's website to make their purchase. It features products from domestic and foreign merchants and is searchable by thousands of attributes. The company operates as part of eBay's Marketplaces segment which also includes the main eBay site.

SHOPZILLA INC.

12200 W. Olympic Blvd. Ste. 300
Los Angeles CA 90064
Phone: 310-571-1235
Fax: 310-903-4452
Web: www.shopzilla.com

CEO: Bill Glass
CFO: Brad Kates
HR: –
FYE: December 31
Type: Private

No need to fear Shopzilla. It's not a monster but a shopping search engine that lists more than 100 million products from several thousand retailers. Shopzilla offers clothes electronics and other consumer items to more than 40 million shoppers through several websites and brands including bizrate Shopzilla and beso in the US; Shopzilla.co.uk and bizrate.co.uk in the UK; Shopzilla.fr in France; and Shopzilla.de in Germany among other sites. Shopzilla has was founded in 1996 by entrepreneurs Farhad Mohit and Henri Asseily and David Reibstein former vice dean of The Wharton School of The University of Pennsylvania. Private equity firm Symphony Technology Group acquired Shopzilla in 2011.

SHORE BANCSHARES INC.

NMS: SHBI

28969 Information Lane
Easton, MD 21601
Phone: 410 763-7800
Fax: –
Web: www.shorebancshares.com

CEO: Lloyd L Beatty Jr
CFO: George S Rapp
HR: –
FYE: December 31
Type: Public

Shore Bancshares sits on the edge of the banking ocean. The institution is the holding company for three bank subsidiaries: The Centreville National Bank of Maryland; The Talbot Bank of Easton Maryland; and The Felton Bank. Combined the banks operate about 20 branches serving individuals and businesses in the Maryland counties of Caroline Dorchester Kent Queen Anne and Talbot as well as in Kent County Delaware. The company sells insurance through subsidiaries The Avon-Dixon Agency and Elliott Wilson Insurance. Jack Martin & Associates acquired in 2007 offers marine insurance products.

	Annual Growth	12/10	12/11	12/12	12/13	12/14
Assets ($ mil.)	(0.7%)	1,130.3	1,158.2	1,185.8	1,054.1	1,100.4
Net income ($ mil.)	–	(1.7)	(0.9)	(9.6)	(9.6)	5.1
Market value ($ mil.)	(3.0%)	133.0	65.0	68.0	116.3	117.9
Employees	(2.7%)	345	340	328	332	309

SHORE MEMORIAL HOSPITAL

100 MEDICAL CENTER WAY
SOMERS POINT, NJ 082442389
Phone: 609-653-3800
Fax: –
Web: www.shoremedicalcenter.org

CEO: –
CFO: David Hughes
HR: –
FYE: December 31
Type: Private

You might be able to get a room with a view of the ocean at Shore Memorial Hospital. Operating as Shore Medical Center the facility is a not-for-profit community hospital with some 300 beds. It offers acute care services and more than 35 specialized care programs including oncology cardiology neurology obstetrics and orthopedic care. Shore Medical Center is affiliated with The University of Pennsylvania Health System and The Children's Hospital of Philadelphia. In addition to the hospital Shore Medical Center operates community-based health and fitness centers.

	Annual Growth	12/06	12/07	12/08	12/09	12/12
Sales ($ mil.)	2.0%	–	183.5	180.1	202.1	202.7
Net income ($ mil.)	–	–	–	(8.0)	5.2	(3.5)
Market value ($ mil.)	–	–	–	–	–	–
Employees	–	–	–	–	–	1,600

SHORETEL INC

NMS: SHOR

960 Stewart Drive
Sunnyvale, CA 94085-3913
Phone: 408 331-3300
Fax: 408 331-3333
Web: www.shoretel.com

CEO: Donald (Don) Joos
CFO: Michael E. (Mike) Healy
HR: Joan Burke
FYE: June 30
Type: Public

ShoreTel's Internet protocol-based telephony hardware and software offers small and midsized businesses government agencies and schools a less expensive alternative to standard phone service. It provides voice video data and mobile communications; products include phones and switches as well as messaging and systems management software. The company licenses its software for use in customers' own data centers and offers a cloud-based subscription service. ShoreTel which outsources its manufacturing operations generates most of its sales in the US. It has sold systems to about 35000 customers in the financial services health care manufacturing and technology industries among others.

	Annual Growth	06/11	06/12	06/13	06/14	06/15
Sales ($ mil.)	15.9%	200.1	246.6	313.5	339.8	360.7
Net income ($ mil.)	–	(11.5)	(20.7)	(25.7)	(1.0)	(4.3)
Market value ($ mil.)	(9.7%)	663.6	284.9	262.2	424.2	441.1
Employees	13.8%	634	933	965	954	1,063

SHOREWOOD PACKAGING CORPORATION

400 Atlantic St. 14th Fl.
Stamford CT 06921
Phone: 203-541-8100
Fax: 203-541-8195
Web: www.internationalpaper.com/us/en/business/shor

CEO: –
CFO: –
HR: –
FYE: December 31
Type: Subsidiary

How many cartons would a company cut if a company could cut cartons? A lot if it's Shorewood Packaging. The company makes paperboard packaging for cosmetics drugs tobacco and other consumer products in North America Europe and Asia. It provides conversion and finishing processes such as hot foil stamping die cutting and folding as well as sheet-fed and Web printing. The company specializes in entertainment and multimedia packaging including products for computer software and music. It also offers graphic design and art direction in conjunction with its packaging services. In 2012 parent International Paper merged Shorewood Packaging with Atlas Holdings' AGI World to create AGI-Shorewood.

SHPS INC.

9200 Shelbyville Rd. Ste. 700
Louisville KY 40222
Phone: 502-426-4888
Fax: 502-420-5590
Web: www.shps.com

CEO: –
CFO: –
HR: –
FYE: December 31
Type: Private

SHPS works to bring out the best in an employer's health plan and its employees. The company's primary subsidiary Carewise Health offers employers ways to control healthcare costs through disease management programs medical bill review and personal wellness perks that encourage employees to stay healthy and use benefits responsibly. SHPS' clients include midsized and large employer groups. The company divested its human resource and information technology operations in 2012 to focus on Carewise. Investment firm Welsh Carson Anderson & Stowe owns SHPS.

SHRINERS HOSPITALS FOR CHILDREN

2900 N ROCKY POINT DR
TAMPA, FL 33607-1460
Phone: 813-281-0300
Fax: –
Web: www.support.shrinershospitals.org

CEO: –
CFO: –
HR: –
FYE: December 31
Type: Private

The Shriners' red fez and mini-scooter parades are the goofy side to their very serious support of the Shriners Hospitals For Children. The system operates nearly two dozen hospitals throughout North America. The majority of its hospitals specialize in orthopedic conditions; others specialize in treating serious burn injuries spinal cord injuries and cleft lips and palates. Founded by the fellowship Shriners International the hospitals are supported by a multitude of fundraising events arranged by the organization's 340000 members. As a result Shriners Hospitals is able to treat children regardless of their families' ability to pay.

	Annual Growth	12/04	12/05	12/06	12/08	12/09
Sales ($ mil.)	(16.4%)	–	583.7	616.2	0.2	285.1
Net income ($ mil.)	–	–	278.7	636.3	0.2	(300.9)
Market value ($ mil.)	–	–	–	–	–	–
Employees	–	–	–	–	–	6,100

SHUTTERFLY INC

2800 Bridge Parkway
Redwood City, CA 94065
Phone: 650 610-5200
Fax: –
Web: www.shutterflyinc.com

CEO: Jeffrey T. (Jeff) Housenbold
CFO: Michael W. (Mike) Pope
HR: Gautam Srivastava
FYE: December 31
Type: Public

Whether or not you are the consummate shutterbug you can rely on Shutterfly for digital prints. An e-commerce company specializing in digital photo products and services for the consumer and professional photography markets the company offers customers the ability to upload share store and edit digital photos through its website. In addition to traditional 4-inch by 6-inch prints Shutterfly provides prints ranging from wallet-sized to jumbo enlargements. The company also offers personalized items including mugs photo books and calendars through its personalized products and services business segment. In 2012 Shutterfly acquired Kodak Imaging Network (doing business as KODAK Gallery).

	Annual Growth	12/10	12/11	12/12	12/13	12/14
Sales ($ mil.)	31.6%	307.7	473.3	640.6	783.6	921.6
Net income ($ mil.)	–	17.1	14.0	23.0	9.3	(7.9)
Market value ($ mil.)	4.6%	1,322.5	862.7	1,132.3	1,930.6	1,580.5
Employees	31.2%	611	956	1,107	1,573	1,812

SHUTTERSTOCK INC

350 Fifth Avenue, 21st Floor
New York, NY 10118
Phone: 646 419-4452
Fax: –
Web: www.shutterstock.com

CEO: Jonathan (Jon) Oringer
CFO: Steven Berns
HR: –
FYE: December 31
Type: Public

Shutterstock brings the online marketplace mentality to the world of digital images illustrations and videos. Its 35000+ contributors have uploaded more than 19 millions bits of content perused by 550000 subscribers. The company's primary customers include marketing agencies media organizations and communications departments of businesses that subscribe to single downloads a set number of images or unlimited downloads for a month or a year; average cost per image is $3. Shutterstock's marketplace is available in 10 languages and 150 countries where its images are used for corporate communications websites ads and books and other published materials. Formed in 2007 the company went public in 2012.

	Annual Growth	12/10	12/11	12/12	12/13	12/14
Sales ($ mil.)	41.0%	83.0	120.3	169.6	235.5	328.0
Net income ($ mil.)	3.9%	18.9	21.9	47.5	26.5	22.1
Market value ($ mil.)	63.0%	–	–	925.7	2,977.4	2,460.1
Employees	31.7%	–	224	237	345	512

SI FINANCIAL GROUP INC (MD)

803 Main Street
Willimantic, CT 06226
Phone: 860 423-4581
Fax: –
Web: www.mysifi.com

NMS: SIFI

CEO: Rheo A Brouillard
CFO: Lauren L Murphy
HR: –
FYE: December 31
Type: Public

Sigh. You mean you still don't know SI? SI Financial Group is the holding company for Savings Institute Bank and Trust Company a community savings bank serving eastern Connecticut and southern Rhode Island from 20-plus locations including branches within retail stores. In addition to traditional deposit services like checking and savings accounts and CDs the bank and its subsidiaries offer financial services such as trust services investment management retirement planning and life insurance. Residential and commercial mortgages dominate Savings Institute's lending portfolio which also includes commercial business and consumer loans. SI Financial Group acquired Rhode Island's Newport Bancorp. in 2013.

	Annual Growth	12/10	12/11	12/12	12/13	12/14
Assets ($ mil.)	9.9%	926.4	955.0	953.3	1,346.4	1,350.5
Net income ($ mil.)	10.1%	3.0	2.4	1.1	(0.9)	4.4
Market value ($ mil.)	4.8%	–	125.8	146.9	154.0	144.8
Employees	2.1%	275	276	265	315	299

SIDLEY AUSTIN LLP

1 S. Dearborn St.
Chicago IL 60603
Phone: 312-853-7000
Fax: 312-853-7036
Web: www.sidley.com

CEO: –
CFO: –
HR: –
FYE: December 31
Type: Private - Partnershi

Sidley Austin aims to be a one-stop shop for large and small businesses government agencies and individuals needing legal help. The firm's 1600-plus lawyers practice in a wide range of areas from about 15 offices in the US Europe and the Asia/Pacific region. Sidley focuses on business transactions and litigation and the firm's geographic diversity enables it to handle multinational matters. Sidley took its modern form in 2001 when Chicago-based Sidley & Austin (founded by Norman Williams and John Thompson in 1866) merged with New York-based Brown & Wood (established 1914). The combined firm was known as Sidley Austin Brown & Wood until 2006 when it changed to Sidley Austin.

SIEBERT FINANCIAL CORP.

885 Third Avenue
New York, NY 10022
Phone: 212 644-2400
Fax: –
Web: www.siebertnet.com

NAS: SIEB

CEO: Joseph M Ramos
CFO: –
HR: –
FYE: December 31
Type: Public

Siebert Financial through subsidiary Muriel Siebert & Co. provides discount securities brokerage and institutional financial services. Its retail division offers equity trading mutual fund access and retirement accounts to self-directed individual investors. Customers can access their accounts and trade by phone Internet wireless device or in person at seven retail branches in California Florida New Jersey and New York. Siebert Financial provides securities trading and underwriting and other services to corporations and government entities. Founder and president Muriel "Mickie" Siebert the first woman member of the New York Stock Exchange owns about 90% of the company.

	Annual Growth	12/10	12/11	12/12	12/13	12/14
Sales ($ mil.)	(6.6%)	20.8	20.2	21.0	16.4	15.8
Net income ($ mil.)	–	(2.6)	(5.4)	(0.2)	(5.9)	(6.6)
Market value ($ mil.)	6.3%	38.0	31.6	36.9	35.6	48.6
Employees	(9.0%)	70	62	55	54	48

SIEMENS INDUSTRY INC.

1000 Deerfield Pkwy.	CEO: Joe Kaeser
Buffalo Grove IL 60089	CFO: –
Phone: 847-215-1000	HR: –
Fax: 847-215-1093	FYE: September 30
Web: www.siemens.com/industry	Type: Subsidiary

Siemens Industry caters to the needs of industrial customers. Its divisions provide specialty engineering services and equipment for customers in the automotive cement chemical food and beverage mining metals and waste water industries. Siemens Industry provides automation technology and products and services for drive train systems. Its services arm provides maintenance and repair functions as well as planning and technical consulting and engineering support. Siemens Industry is part of Siemens Corporation the US holding company of German electrics and engineering giant Siemens AG.

SIERRA BANCORP

NMS: BSRR

86 North Main Street	CEO: Kevin J. McPhaill
Porterville, CA 93257	CFO: Kenneth R. (Ken) Taylor
Phone: 559 782-4900	HR: –
Fax: –	FYE: December 31
Web: www.bankofthesierra.com	Type: Public

Sierra Bancorp is the holding company for Bank of the Sierra which operates about two dozen branches in Central California's San Joaquin Valley between (and including) Bakersfield and Fresno. Founded in 1977 the bank gathers funds from individuals and small and midsized business customers by offering traditional deposit products including savings and checking accounts money market accounts CDs and IRAs. Its lending activities consist largely of loans secured by real estate (some three-fourths of the company's loan portfolio. The bank also issues commercial and industrial loans (including Small Business Administration loans) consumer loans agricultural loans and equipment leasing.

	Annual Growth	12/10	12/11	12/12	12/13	12/14
Assets ($ mil.)	6.2%	1,286.6	1,335.4	1,437.9	1,410.2	1,637.3
Net income ($ mil.)	19.9%	7.4	7.8	8.2	13.4	15.2
Market value ($ mil.)	13.1%	146.9	120.5	156.5	220.3	240.4
Employees	1.7%	408	402	418	406	437

SIERRA CLUB

85 2ND ST FL 2	CEO: –
SAN FRANCISCO, CA 941053456	CFO: –
Phone: 415-977-5500	HR: –
Fax: –	FYE: December 31
Web: www.sierraclub.org	Type: Private

Wanna take a hike with the Sierra Club? The growing grassroots organization promotes outdoor activities and environmental activism on both the local and national levels through political lobbies education outings litigation and publications. The club's more than 2.4 million members are organized into state and regional chapters throughout the US and Canada. Founded in 1892 by naturalist John Muir Sierra Club publishes books calendars SIERRA magazine and activist newsletter Currents. Some of Sierra Club's current issues include smart energy solutions clean water stopping commercial logging in national forests ending sprawl and protecting wetlands.

	Annual Growth	12/04	12/05	12/06	12/08	12/09
Sales ($ mil.)	–	–	–	0.0	87.4	97.3
Net income ($ mil.)	–	–	–	0.0	(14.4)	6.0
Market value ($ mil.)	–	–	–	–	–	–
Employees	–	–	–	–	–	600

SIERRA MONITOR CORP

NBB: SRMC

1991 Tarob Court	CEO: Varun Nagaraj
Milpitas, CA 95035	CFO: Tamara S Allen
Phone: 408 262-6611	HR: –
Fax: –	FYE: December 31
Web: www.investor.sierramonitor.com	Type: Public

If there's hazardous gas in the air Sierra Monitor wants its customers to know — fast. Sierra Monitor manufactures distributes and services gas and flame detection devices for oil and gas petrochemical transportation and wastewater treatment industries. Sierra Monitor also makes environmental and security monitoring equipment for remote telecommunications facilities along with communications bridging equipment and software (FieldServer and ProtoCessor) that allow building automation systems and gas detection systems that use different communications protocols to exchange data. Directors Richard Kramlich and Jay Last own 21% and 18% of Sierra Monitor respectively. CEO Gordon Arnold owns 11%.

	Annual Growth	12/10	12/11	12/12	12/13	12/14
Sales ($ mil.)	7.7%	14.4	15.5	18.8	18.3	19.3
Net income ($ mil.)	(17.6%)	0.7	0.9	1.2	1.4	0.3
Market value ($ mil.)	2.6%	13.7	11.6	16.7	20.3	15.2
Employees	10.0%	54	60	58	59	79

SIERRA NEVADA CORPORATION

444 Salomon Cir.	CEO: Fatih Ozmen
Sparks NV 89434	CFO: –
Phone: 775-331-0222	HR: –
Fax: 775-331-0370	FYE: December 31
Web: www.sncorp.com	Type: Private

Sierra Nevada Corporation (SNC) believes that military agility isn't just about how fast a soldier completes the obstacle course in basic training. It's also about employing technology to support the soldier. The company provides defense electronics engineering manufacturing and integration services. Its operations include seven primary business units: Command Control Computers Communications and Networks (C4N); Communications Navigation Surveillance and Air Traffic Management (CNS/ATM); Integrated Mission Systems (IMS); Intelligence Surveillance and Reconnaissance (ISR); Electronic Warfare/Range Instrumentation (EWR); Sensors Systems and Technologies (SST); and Space Systems (SS).

SIERRA PACIFIC INDUSTRIES

19794 Riverside Ave.	CEO: George Emmerson
Anderson CA 96007	CFO: –
Phone: 530-378-8000	HR: Jim Blunt
Fax: 530-378-8109	FYE: December 31
Web: www.spi-ind.com	Type: Private

Trees are in Sierra Pacific Industries' blood. The third-generation family-owned firm owns and manages nearly 1.9 million acres of timberland in California and Washington. With a network of sawmills it's among the top lumber producers in the US. SPI's manufacturing plants also make mouldings and millwork windows and doors fencing and wood fiber by-products such as chips and shavings. Several of its sawmills also house co-generation facilities that recycle wood waste into power for its plants; excess electricity is sold to local public utilities. Additionally SPI is involved in residential and commercial real estate. The company traces its roots to the 1920s when it was founded by R. H. "Curly" Emmerson.

SIERRA PACIFIC POWER CO.

NL:

6100 Neil Road
Reno, NV 89511
Phone: 775 834-4011
Fax: −
Web: www.sierrapacific.com

CEO: −
CFO: E Kevin Bethel
HR: Alice Cobb
FYE: December 31
Type: Public

Sierra Pacific Power mitigates the effects of hot Sierra winds and moist Pacific breezes. The company is a natural gas and electricity distribution utility serving customers in towns and cities across Nevada. Sierra Pacific Power a subsidiary of NV Energy Inc does business as NV Energy. The company serves about 323000 power customers and 153000 natural gas customers. Sierra Pacific Power also owns more than 15 fossil-fueled and hydroelectric power plants with about 1510 MW of generating capacity and it sells excess energy to wholesale customers.

	Annual Growth	12/10	12/11	12/12	12/13	12/14
Sales ($ mil.)	(3.2%)	1,027.8	888.9	833.9	853.0	904.0
Net income ($ mil.)	4.7%	72.4	59.9	84.4	55.0	87.0
Market value ($ mil.)	−					
Employees	(2.6%)	1,113	1,092	1,075	1,000	1,000

SIFCO INDUSTRIES INC.

ASE: SIF

970 East 64th Street
Cleveland, OH 44103
Phone: 216 881-8600
Fax: −
Web: www.sifco.com

CEO: Michael S Lipscomb
CFO: Salvatore Incanno
HR: −
FYE: September 30
Type: Public

Airplanes need parts and SIFCO coats machines and produces jet engine and aerospace components. It forges parts and offers forging heat-treating and precision component machining services. Products include components for aircraft and industrial gas turbine engines structural airframe components aircraft landing gear components brakes and wheels. Aerospace components for both fixed wing aircraft and rotorcraft account for nearly 80% of its total sales. SIFCO caters to original equipment manufacturers (OEMs) for both commercial and defense aerospace applications. It also serves the energy market.

	Annual Growth	09/11	09/12	09/13	09/14	09/15
Sales ($ mil.)	0.4%	107.4	125.1	116.0	119.7	109.3
Net income ($ mil.)	−	7.4	6.5	10.2	5.0	(2.9)
Market value ($ mil.)	(11.4%)	100.3	99.5	100.6	164.6	61.7
Employees	13.3%	360	565	538	465	593

SIGA TECHNOLOGIES INC

NDD: SIGA Q

660 Madison Avenue, Suite 1700
New York, NY 10065
Phone: 212 672-9100
Fax: −
Web: www.siga.com

CEO: Eric A Rose
CFO: Daniel J Luckshire
HR: −
FYE: December 31
Type: Public

SIGA Technologies is trying to put itself on the front lines of US biodefense efforts. The drug company has a number of development programs for vaccines antivirals and antibiotics for drug resistant infections; however its main focus is on vaccines for bio-defense. Its smallpox vaccine Arestvyr (aka Tecovirimat or ST-246) which is intended to both prevent and treat the disease has received Fast Track and Orphan Drug designations from the FDA. SIGA is also developing vaccines for use against hemorrhagic fevers and other infectious diseases and biothreats. Much of its work is done through funding from the NIH and the HHS. SIGA filed for Chapter 11 bankruptcy protection in 2014.

	Annual Growth	12/10	12/11	12/12	12/13	12/14
Sales ($ mil.)	(36.4%)	19.2	12.7	9.0	5.5	3.1
Net income ($ mil.)	−	(28.2)	13.6	(14.5)	(17.2)	(265.5)
Market value ($ mil.)	(43.4%)	749.1	134.8	140.2	175.0	77.0
Employees	(15.0%)	65	68	71	34	34

SIGE SEMICONDUCTOR INC.

200 Brickstone Sq. Ste. 203
Andover MA 01810
Phone: 978-327-6850
Fax: 978-475-0859
Web: www.sige.com

CEO: Sohail Khan
CFO: −
HR: −
FYE: December 31
Type: Subsidiary

SiGe Semiconductor sized up the wireless semiconductor market and made its move. The fabless chip company designs radio-frequency (RF) semiconductors used in wireless communications gear. Its WiMAX and Bluetooth power amplifiers RF front-end devices GPS receiver chips and other chip products are used to link laptops printers phones and cameras; enable wireless gaming and streaming video; and provide GPS location and mapping services. Its chips are made from silicon germanium (SiGe) which offers better performance than chips made from silicon alone. Most of its sales come from Asia. SiGe Semi filed for an IPO in 2010; it was acquired by Skyworks Solutions the following year for about $275 million.

SIGMA DESIGNS, INC.

NMS: SIGM

47467 Fremont Boulevard
Fremont, CA 94538
Phone: 510 897-0200
Fax: 408 957-9740
Web: www.sigmadesigns.com

CEO: Thinh Q. Tran
CFO: Elias Nader
HR: −
FYE: January 31
Type: Public

Everyone loves to watch videos these days and that's just fine with Sigma Designs which designs semiconductors used in home entertainment systems. The company's system-on-chip (SoC) devices go into set-top boxes and gateways for Internet protocol TVs (IPTVs) HDTVs Blu-ray players media communication devices and professional audio/visual devices. Sigma Designs which outsources the fabrication of its chips to Taiwan Semiconductor Manufacturing also offers services such as custom development of MPEG decoding chips and software support. Customers include Flextronics Gemtek and Motorola Mobility. The majority of Sigma Designs' sales come from Asia; China is its largest market.

	Annual Growth	01/11	01/12*	02/13	02/14*	01/15
Sales ($ mil.)	(10.0%)	286.9	182.6	216.6	199.2	188.3
Net income ($ mil.)	−	9.1	(168.0)	(101.8)	(11.0)	(21.7)
Market value ($ mil.)	(17.8%)	491.9	209.1	186.1	165.6	224.6
Employees	3.9%	592	691	945	716	691

*Fiscal year change

SIGMA-ALDRICH CORP.

NMS: SIAL

3050 Spruce Street
St. Louis, MO 63103
Phone: 314 771-5765
Fax: 314 286-7874
Web: www.sigma-aldrich.com

CEO: Rakesh Sachdev
CFO: Jan A Bertsch
HR: −
FYE: December 31
Type: Public

Check the shelves of any research (or mad) scientist and you'll likely find Sigma-Aldrich's chemical products. The company is a leading supplier of chemicals to research laboratories. It has more than 100000 accounts including 230000 labs involved in government and commercial research for 230000 chemical and biochemical and 45000 equipment products it offers in its Sigma Aldrich Fluka and Supelco catalogs. It makes about 110000 of the products it sells. The business derives revenues from two major areas: Research Chemicals (essentials specialties and biotech) and Fine Chemicals (commercial applications). In 2014 the company agreed to be acquired by Germany-based pharmaceutical giant Merck for $17 billion.

	Annual Growth	12/10	12/11	12/12	12/13	12/14
Sales ($ mil.)	5.2%	2,271.0	2,505.0	2,623.0	2,704.0	2,785.0
Net income ($ mil.)	6.8%	384.0	457.0	460.0	491.0	500.0
Market value ($ mil.)	19.8%	7,920.6	7,432.7	8,756.0	11,187.2	16,335.1
Employees	4.2%	7,890	8,300	9,000	9,000	9,300

SIGMATRON INTERNATIONAL INC.

NAS: SGMA

2201 Landmeier Road
Elk Grove Village, IL 60007
Phone: 847 956-8000
Fax: 847 956-9801
Web: www.sigmatronintl.com

CEO: Gary R Fairhead
CFO: Linda K Frauendorfer
HR: –
FYE: April 30
Type: Public

An assembly at SigmaTron International doesn't mean fraternizing over a keg. The company produces electronic components printed circuit board assemblies and box-build (completely assembled) electronic products on a contract basis for customers in the appliance automotive consumer electronics fitness equipment industrial electronics and telecommunications industries. SigmaTron also offers design testing shipping and storage services. Major customers include electronic controls manufacturer Spitfire Controls and fitness equipment maker Life Fitness together accounting for nearly half of sales. Besides its US manufacturing facilities the company boasts plants in China Mexico and Taiwan.

	Annual Growth	04/11	04/12	04/13	04/14	04/15
Sales ($ mil.)	11.0%	151.7	156.6	198.4	222.5	230.2
Net income ($ mil.)	(17.8%)	2.0	1.1	0.5	2.9	0.9
Market value ($ mil.)	11.0%	21.6	15.4	16.8	42.1	32.8
Employees	11.1%	1,780	1,700	2,700	2,800	2,710

SIGNATURE BANK (NEW YORK, NY)

NMS: SBNY

565 Fifth Avenue
New York, NY 10017
Phone: 646 822-1500
Fax: –
Web: www.signatureny.com

CEO: Joseph J. DePaolo
CFO: Vito Susca
HR: –
FYE: December 31
Type: Public

Signature Bank marks the spot where some professional New Yorkers bank. The institution provides customized banking and financial services to smaller private businesses their owners and their top executives through 30 branches across the New York metropolitan area including all five boroughs Long Island and affluent Westchester County. The bank's lending activities mainly entail real estate and business loans. Subsidiary Signature Securities offers wealth management financial planning brokerage services asset management and insurance while its Signature Financial subsidiary offers equipment financing and leasing. Founded in 2001 the bank now boasts assets of roughly $29 billion.

	Annual Growth	12/10	12/11	12/12	12/13	12/14
Assets ($ mil.)	23.7%	11,673.1	14,666.1	17,456.1	22,376.7	27,318.6
Net income ($ mil.)	30.6%	102.1	149.5	185.5	228.7	296.7
Market value ($ mil.)	25.9%	2,518.9	3,018.6	3,589.7	5,405.1	6,338.0
Employees	11.2%	660	720	844	945	1,010

SIGNATURE CONSULTANTS LLC

2101 W COML BLVD STE 3000
FORT LAUDERDALE, FL 33309
Phone: 954-677-1020
Fax: –
Web: www.sigconsult.com

CEO: Jay Cohen
CFO: Philip Monti
HR: Candace Whitaker
FYE: December 31
Type: Private

Signature Consultants wants your John Hancock when it comes to signing up for its staffing services. The company provides information technology staffing services to clients from a variety of industries. Signature places IT professionals with expertise in areas like project management Web application development database administration storage and network security. The firm has experience placing IT professionals across such industries as aerospace automotive banking and financial services education electronics government technology pharmaceutical and manufacturing.

	Annual Growth	12/07	12/08	12/09	12/12	12/13
Sales ($ mil.)	9.7%	–	127.4	106.9	153.0	202.2
Net income ($ mil.)	3.4%	–	–	3.3	(1.3)	3.7
Market value ($ mil.)	–	–	–	–	–	–
Employees	–	–	–	–	–	1,450

SIGNATURE EYEWEAR INC.

OTC: SEYE

498 N. Oak St.
Inglewood CA 90302
Phone: 310-330-2700
Fax: 310-330-2765
Web: www.signatureeyewear.com

CEO: Michael Prince
CFO: Michael Prince
HR: –
FYE: October 31
Type: Public

Signature Eyewear views prescription eyeglasses and sunglasses as the ultimate fashion statement and an integral part of its business. Laura Ashley Nicole Miller and bebe licensed eyewear accounts for about three-fourths of the firm's sales. Signature Eyewear also licenses frames by Michael Stars Dakota Smith and Hart Schaffner Marx. Its own Signature line of frames is produced by contract manufacturers in Hong Kong China Japan and Italy and markets them to optical retailers in more than 20 countries. The company markets footwear and accessories through its Signature Fashion Group division which was formed in 2010.

SIGNATURE FLIGHT SUPPORT CORPORATION

201 S. Orange Ave. Ste. 1100-S
Orlando FL 32801
Phone: 407-648-7200
Fax: 407-206-8428
Web: www.signatureflight.com

CEO: –
CFO: –
HR: Connie Alden
FYE: December 31
Type: Subsidiary

Signature Flight Support does not write checks but its services and facilities do help to underwrite the business and general aviation communities' ability to take to the skies. The company one of the world's largest providers of fixed-base operations (FBO) services offers a full-slate of support from fueling and ground handling to hangar and office rentals and maintenance. Signature Flight Support's network consists of more than 100 FBO facilities at airports around the world. The company is a unit of UK-based BBA Aviation a world leader in flight support and aftermarket services and systems for business aviation regional airline military and commercial aviation operators.

SIKA CORPORATION

201 Polito Ave.
Lyndhurst NJ 07071-3601
Phone: 201-933-8800
Fax: 201-804-1076
Web: www.sikacorp.com

CEO: Christoph Ganz
CFO: Stephen Lysik
HR: –
FYE: December 31
Type: Subsidiary

When plain old mortar won't do Sika Corporation offers its construction customers specialty mortars. Sika also manufactures adhesives coatings epoxies acrylics silicones and polyurethane. Its products are used to seal bond dampen sounds reinforce and protect load-bearing structures. It markets to the construction and manufacturing industries including transportation marine and automotive. Sika's Construction Products division is based along with its headquarters in New Jersey and its Industry and Automotive divisions are based in Michigan. Sika is the US unit as well as the largest manufacturing segment of global chemicals company Sika AG. Sika Corporation was founded in 1937.

SIKORSKY AIRCRAFT CORPORATION

6900 Main St.
Stratford CT 06615
Phone: 203-386-4000
Fax: +46-8-728-00-28
Web: www.bonnier.se

CEO: –
CFO: Mary Gallagher
HR: –
FYE: December 31
Type: Subsidiary

Russian-born helicopter pioneer Igor Sikorsky is long dead but helicopters bearing his name still soar the skies. A subsidiary of United Technologies Sikorsky Aircraft designs manufactures and services such military helicopters as the Black Hawk (combat support border security medevac); Seahawk (anti-submarine/surface warfare search/rescue); and Superhawk (military operations). Sikorsky's CH-53K helicopter is used by the US Marines for heavy lift operations. Civil aircraft include the S-76 and S-92 which are used for rescue offshore oil medical and corporate use. Sikorsky also offers fixed-wing aircraft aftermarket spare parts and MRO services for helicopters used by US and foreign governments.

SILGAN CONTAINERS LLC

21800 Oxnard St. Ste. 600
Woodland Hills CA 91367
Phone: 818-348-3700
Fax: 818-593-2255
Web: www.silgancontainers.com

CEO: –
CFO: Ron Ford
HR: –
FYE: December 31
Type: Subsidiary

Do most of your meals come straight out of can? If so Silgan Containers would like to thank you for not going out to eat. The company a subsidiary of Silgan Holdings is North America's largest manufacturer of metal food containers carving off for itself about half of the US market. Its steel and aluminum containers and traditional and convenience ends are used by food processors to package fruit vegetables meat coffee soups sauces and other products such as pet food. Customers include Campbell Soup Nestle ConAgra and General Mills. Silgan Containers which operates some 30 manufacturing plants in the US accounts for roughly 60% of Silgan Holdings' sales and more than 75% of its operating income.

SILGAN HOLDINGS INC.

NMS: SLGN

4 Landmark Square
Stamford, CT 06901
Phone: 203 975-7110
Fax: 203 975-7902
Web: www.silganholdings.com

CEO: Anthony J. (Tony) Allott
CFO: Robert B. (Bob) Lewis
HR: –
FYE: December 31
Type: Public

Success comes in cans; failure in can'ts; who would know better than Silgan Holdings? Silgan Holdings — through subsidiary Silgan Containers — is the leading maker of metal food containers in North America. Its containers are used by customers such as Campbell Soup Del Monte and Nestlé to package soups vegetables meat seafood and pet food. Through Silgan Plastics Silgan also makes plastic containers used by personal care pharmaceutical and other companies. Silgan applies its "can-do" attitude to producing metal composite and plastic vacuum closures as well for the food and beverage industries.

	Annual Growth	12/10	12/11	12/12	12/13	12/14
Sales ($ mil.)	6.2%	3,071.5	3,509.2	3,588.3	3,708.5	3,911.8
Net income ($ mil.)	6.0%	144.6	193.2	151.3	185.4	182.4
Market value ($ mil.)	10.6%	2,263.3	2,442.2	2,625.5	3,035.0	3,387.7
Employees	5.6%	7,400	8,700	9,000	9,500	9,200

SILGAN PLASTICS LLC

14515 N. Outer Forty Ste. 210
Chesterfield MO 63017
Phone: 314-542-9223
Fax: 314-469-5387
Web: www.silganplastics.com

CEO: –
CFO: –
HR: –
FYE: December 31
Type: Subsidiary

Most companies don't make the plastic containers used to package their products; rather they turn to companies like Silgan Plastics to design and manufacture whatever packaging they desire. A subsidiary of Silgan Holdings Silgan Plastics serves customers from the food and beverage health and pharmaceutical cosmetics and toiletry household automotive marine agricultural and industrial products markets. To suit its diverse group of customers Silgan offers more than 1200 different bottles jars tubes food containers and closures which it manufactures at some two dozen US and Canadian facilities. It also provides engineering and creative design services through its commercial development center.

SILICON GRAPHICS INTERNATIONAL CORP

NMS: SGI

900 North McCarthy Blvd.
Milpitas, CA 95035
Phone: 669 900-8000
Fax: –
Web: www.sgi.com

CEO: Jorge L. Titinger
CFO: Mack Asrat
HR: Nancy Hanna
FYE: June 26
Type: Public

Silicon Graphics International (SGI) handles computing on a large scale. The company provides high-performance computer servers that are based on the Linux operating system and designed for large-scale data center deployments. SGI also offers data storage servers as well as modular data center systems sold under the ICE brand. Its equipment is tailored to quickly access analyze process manage visualize and store large amounts of data. SGI targets the IT Internet financial services government and electronics sectors as well as scientific community. Clients have included Amazon.com (18% of sales in 2014) Microsoft Yahoo! and Deutsche Bank; the US federal government is also a top client.

	Annual Growth	06/11	06/12	06/13	06/14	06/15
Sales ($ mil.)	(4.6%)	629.6	753.0	767.2	529.9	521.3
Net income ($ mil.)	–	(21.2)	(24.5)	(2.8)	(52.8)	(39.1)
Market value ($ mil.)	(19.1%)	537.3	224.1	467.1	330.2	230.1
Employees	(7.5%)	1,500	1,500	1,400	1,150	1,100

SILICON IMAGE INC

NMS: SIMG

1140 East Arques Avenue
Sunnyvale, CA 94085
Phone: 408 616-4000
Fax: –
Web: www.siliconimage.com

CEO: Darin G Billerbeck
CFO: Joe Bedewi
HR: –
FYE: December 31
Type: Public

It would be silly to imagine that Silicon Image's chips only produce pretty pictures. Silicon Image designs and sells a variety of integrated circuits including digital video controllers receivers transmitters and processors that are built into mobile devices digital TVs camera personal computers and DVD and Blu-ray players. The company helped create HDMI and DVI industry standards as well as MHL the standard for mobile devices and the 60GHz wireless HID video standard WirelessHD. Through subsidiary Simplay Labs it offers HDMI licensing and compliance testing services. Customers located outside the US account for about 60% of the company's sales.

	Annual Growth	12/09	12/10	12/11	12/12	12/13
Sales ($ mil.)	16.4%	150.6	191.3	221.0	252.4	276.4
Net income ($ mil.)	–	(129.1)	8.2	(11.6)	(11.2)	11.5
Market value ($ mil.)	24.3%	199.7	569.0	363.9	384.0	476.1
Employees	5.0%	526	432	521	623	640

SILICON LABORATORIES INC   NMS: SLAB

400 West Cesar Chavez   CEO: G. Tyson Tuttle
Austin, TX 78701   CFO: John C. Hollister
Phone: 512 416-8500   HR: –
Fax: –   FYE: January 02
Web: www.silabs.com   Type: Public

Silicon Laboratories makes little translation machines. The company develops mixed-signal integrated circuits (ICs) which translate real-world analog signals (such as sound) into digital signals that can be processed by electronic products. Silicon Labs provides ICs used in set-top boxes game consoles portable electronics industrial monitoring and control devices and wireless handsets. Products include microcontrollers clocks and oscillators sensors and broadcast communications chips. Top customers include Cisco Huawei LG Electronics Pace Samsung Technicolor Varian Medical Systems and ZTE. About 85% of the company's sales come from customers outside the US.

	Annual Growth	12/11	12/12	12/13*	01/15	01/16
Sales ($ mil.)	5.6%	491.6	563.3	580.1	620.7	644.8
Net income ($ mil.)	(3.6%)	35.5	63.5	49.8	38.0	29.6
Market value ($ mil.)	2.3%	1,811.8	1,731.3	1,767.1	1,982.4	2,025.4
Employees	5.7%	908	997	1,060	1,107	1,199

*Fiscal year change

SILVER BAY REALTY TRUST CORP   NYS: SBY

3300 Fernbrook Lane North, Suite 210   CEO: Thomas Brock
Plymouth, MN 55447   CFO: Christine Battist
Phone: 952 358-4400   HR: –
Fax: –   FYE: December 31
Web: www.silverbayrealtytrustcorp.com   Type: Public

Silver Bay makes green on rentals in sunny locales. The real estate investment trust (REIT) is externally managed by PRCM Real Estate Advisers. It focuses on buying single-family homes in urban markets with an oversupply of housing. Silver Bay acquires properties via foreclosures auctions sales listings and bulk purchases and uses its manager's rental property experience to achieve economies of scale for property management and maintenance. The company has a portfolio of about 2250 income-generating single-family homes that it leases in Arizona California Florida Georgia Nevada North Carolina and Texas. Real estate investor Two Harbors formed Silver Bay in 2012 and it went public later that year.

	Annual Growth	12/10	12/11	12/12	12/13	12/14
Sales ($ mil.)	–	0.0	0.0	3.6	49.6	77.9
Net income ($ mil.)	–	0.0	0.0	(5.5)	(24.5)	(56.6)
Market value ($ mil.)	–	0.0	0.0	691.3	587.0	607.9
Employees	–	–	–	–	–	106

SILVER CROSS HOSPITAL AND MEDICAL CENTERS

1900 SILVER CROSS BLVD   CEO: Paul Pawlak
NEW LENOX, IL 604519509   CFO: William Brownlow
Phone: 815-740-1234   HR: –
Fax: –   FYE: September 30
Web: www.silvercross.org   Type: Private

Silver Cross Hospital and Medical Centers serve the Illinois counties of Will Grundy and Cook through its 290-bed main hospital campus and nine satellite facilities throughout the area. Services provided by the medical facility include cardiovascular care women's health rehabilitation and behavioral health care. Its outpatient facilities provide primary and specialty care services such as medical imaging and dialysis. The Silver Cross Hospital and Medical Centers name comes from the emblem (the Maltese Cross) of the Christian organization that founded the not-for-profit hospital the International Order of The King's Daughters and Sons.

	Annual Growth	12/04	12/05*	09/06	09/08	09/13
Sales ($ mil.)	(8.1%)	–	601.2	187.3	244.3	306.7
Net income ($ mil.)	(10.5%)	–	–	13.7	21.1	6.3
Market value ($ mil.)	–	–	–	–	–	–
Employees	–	–	–	–	–	1,700

*Fiscal year change

SILVER EAGLE DISTRIBUTORS L.P.

7777 Washington Ave.   CEO: John L Nau III
Houston TX 77007   CFO: Robert Boblitt
Phone: 713-869-4361   HR: –
Fax: 713-867-8112   FYE: December 31
Web: www.wideworldofbud.com   Type: Private

John Nau III president and CEO of Silver Eagle Distributors probably doesn't lose sleep if there's a bear market on Wall Street — just as long as there's a "beer" market in Houston. Silver Eagle one of the nation's leading beer wholesalers and the top beer distributor in Houston handles mostly Anheuser-Busch products but it also offers Michelob and Modelo products such as Corona Negra Modelo and Pacifico. The beer peddler also handles a number of other imported brews including Kirin Harbin St. Pauli Girl and Tiger. As part of its business the company serves some 11000 customers in 16 Texas counties including the metro areas of Houston and San Antonio.

SILVER LAKE TECHNOLOGY MANAGEMENT L.L.C.

2775 Sand Hill Rd. Ste. 100   CEO: –
Menlo Park CA 94025   CFO: –
Phone: 650-233-8120   HR: –
Fax: 650-233-8125   FYE: December 31
Web: www.silverlake.com   Type: Private

Silver Lake likes its companies big and technological. Founded in 1999 the private investment firm focuses its sights on leveraged buyouts (LBO) of large technology companies and provides technological and management expertise to its portfolio companies to help them develop and grow. Silver Lake has more than $14 billion in assets under management in funds such as its flagship large-cap Silver Lake Partners fund; middle-market technology fund Silver Lake Sumeru; Silver Lake Financial which invests in undervalued and distressed debt; and Silver Lake Kraftwerk a provider of growth capital to companies focused on renewable energy and energy efficiency. In 2013 it joined other investors in a planned LBO of Dell.

SILVER SPRING NETWORKS INC   NYS: SSNI

555 Broadway Street   CEO: Michael (Mike) Bell
Redwood City, CA 94063   CFO: James (Jim) Burns
Phone: 650 839-4000   HR: –
Fax: –   FYE: December 31
                                         Type: Public

Silver Spring Networks helps utility companies plug into the 21st century. Its Smart Energy Platform modernizes a utility's existing power grid infrastructure into the "smart" grid i.e. one that is connected to a digital network and more energy efficient. The Smart Energy Platform is a secure Internet-based network made up of hardware such as access points communications modules bridges and relays; its UtilOS-brand network operating system; and software. It also offers managed services to maintain and regulate the network. Silver Spring sells its platform to electric gas and water utilities — FPL PG&E and OG&E account for almost 80% of service revenue. The company went public in 2013.

	Annual Growth	12/10	12/11	12/12	12/13	12/14
Sales ($ mil.)	28.5%	70.2	237.1	196.7	326.9	191.3
Net income ($ mil.)	–	(148.4)	(92.4)	(89.7)	(66.8)	(89.2)
Market value ($ mil.)	(59.9%)	–	–	–	1,030.3	413.6
Employees	0.9%	–	–	566	602	576

SILVERLEAF RESORTS INC.

1221 River Bend Dr. Ste. 120	CEO: Thomas J Morris
Dallas TX 75247	CFO: Robert M Sinnott
Phone: 214-631-1166	HR: –
Fax: 214-637-0585	FYE: December 31
Web: www.silverleafresorts.com	Type: Private

Silverleaf Resorts helps vacationers get away without going far away. The company owns and operates more than a dozen time-share resorts in six states (Florida Georgia Illinois Massachusetts Missouri and Texas). Its resorts feature amenities such as golf clubhouses and indoor water parks. Silverleaf's portfolio of properties include six "destination resorts" located near national tourist areas and seven affordable "getaway resorts" located near major metropolitan markets. The company also owns and operates a hotel near the Winter Park recreational area in Colorado. Previously a public company in 2011 SL Resort Holdings an affiliate of Cerberus Capital Management purchased Silverleaf for $94 million.

SILVERSTEIN PROPERTIES INC.

7 World Trade Center 250 Greenwich St. 38th Fl.	CEO: Marty Burger
New York NY 10007	CFO: Thomas Dowd
Phone: 212-490-0666	HR: –
Fax: 212-302-6847	FYE: December 31
Web: www.silversteinproperties.com	Type: Private

September 11 staggered a nation but Silverstein Properties stands steady in its plans to rebuild the landmark property that fell in the terrorist attacks. The major New York City landlord — with more than 7 million sq. ft. of office and residential space in Manhattan - intends to redevelop all of the commercial space from the World Trade Center. One building Seven World Trade Center is already open. The centerpiece of the planned project Freedom Tower is to be open by 2011. The family-owned company controlled by Larry Silverstein won a 99-year lease to the World Trade Center's office space from The Port Authority of New York and New Jersey in summer 2001 just weeks before the towers' destruction.

SIMMONS FIRST NATIONAL CORP.   NMS: SFNC

501 Main Street	CEO: George A. Makris
Pine Bluff, AR 71601	CFO: Robert A. Fehlman
Phone: 870 541-1000	HR: Susan Robinson
Fax: –	FYE: December 31
Web: www.simmonsfirst.com	Type: Public

Simmons First National thinks it's only natural it should be one of the largest financial institutions in The Natural State. The holding company owns Simmons First National Bank and seven other community banks that bear the Simmons First Bank name and maintain local identities; together they operate around 90 branches throughout Arkansas and in Kansas and Missouri. Serving consumers and area businesses the banks offer standard deposit products like checking and savings accounts IRAs and CDs. Lending activities mainly consist of commercial real estate loans single-family mortgages and consumer loans such as credit card and student loans.

	Annual Growth	12/10	12/11	12/12	12/13	12/14
Assets ($ mil.)	8.8%	3,316.4	3,320.1	3,527.5	4,383.1	4,643.4
Net income ($ mil.)	(1.0%)	37.1	25.4	27.7	23.2	35.7
Market value ($ mil.)	9.3%	514.5	490.8	457.8	670.6	733.8
Employees	4.7%	1,108	1,075	1,052	1,306	1,331

SIMON PROPERTY GROUP, INC.   NYS: SPG

225 West Washington Street	CEO: David Simon
Indianapolis, IN 46204	CFO: Andrew A. (Andy) Juster
Phone: 317 636-1600	HR: –
Fax: 317 685-7336	FYE: December 31
Web: www.simon.com	Type: Public

Simon says: "Shop!" And millions do. Simon Property Group is the nation's largest shopping mall and retail center owner with a portfolio of more than 225 retail properties totaling approximately 189 million sq. ft. of leasable space across more than 35 states and Puerto Rico. The self-managed self-administered real estate investment trust (REIT) owns develops and manages regional shopping malls outlet malls (under the Premium Outlet Prime Outlet and The Mills brands) boutique malls and shopping centers. Its portfolio is concentrated in the US's Southeast Midwest and Northeast. The REIT also has stakes in outlet centers in Canada Japan Malaysia Mexico and South Korea.

	Annual Growth	12/10	12/11	12/12	12/13	12/14
Sales ($ mil.)	5.3%	3,957.6	4,306.4	4,880.1	5,170.1	4,870.8
Net income ($ mil.)	21.7%	753.5	1,245.9	1,719.6	1,551.6	1,651.5
Market value ($ mil.)	16.3%	30,920.3	40,073.0	49,132.5	47,289.5	56,597.6
Employees	(2.9%)	5,900	5,500	5,500	5,700	5,250

SIMON WORLDWIDE INC.   PINK SHEETS: SWWI

5200 W. Century Blvd.	CEO: Greg Mays
Los Angeles CA 90045	CFO: Anthony Espiritu
Phone: 310-417-4660	HR: –
Fax: 858-513-1870	FYE: December 31
Web: www.aldila.com	Type: Public

Here is a true business tragedy a successful company brought low by the machinations of a lone employee. Simon Worldwide once offered an array of promotional marketing services but the firm was dealt a severe blow in 2001 when a Simon employee rigged McDonald's "Monopoly" game promotion by hoarding winning game pieces. (The employee pleaded guilty to embezzlement.) McDonald's a 25-year client that accounted for the bulk of Simon's sales stopped doing business with the company as did Simon's second-largest client Philip Morris. The company then shut down its promotional marketing business to focus on resolving legal issues arising from the scandal; it has no operations.

SIMPLEX HEALTHCARE INC.

6840 Carothers Pkwy. Ste. 600	CEO: Michael Iskra
Franklin TN 37067	CFO: –
Phone: 615-771-6683	HR: Amy Carter
Fax: 615-226-8088	FYE: December 31
Web: www.simplexhealthcare.com	Type: Private

Simplex Healthcare wants to be simply the best — and the biggest — among US diabetic testing suppliers. The company founded in 2007 as Simplex Diabetic Supply provides direct-to-consumer home delivery of medical supplies to diabetes patients through subsidiary Diabetes Care Club (DCC) a free membership club for those who qualify. DCC is one of the top three mail-order distributors of diabetes testing supplies in the country. Products include batteries glucose meters test strips and lancet devices to check blood sugar levels. It serves mainly senior citizens covered by Medicare Medicaid and private insurance. Product delivery covers all 50 states as well as Puerto Rico and the Virgin Islands.

SIMPLEXGRINNELL LP

1501 Yamato Rd.	CEO: George R Oliver
Boca Raton FL 33431	CFO: –
Phone: 561-988-3600	HR: Rick Klotz
Fax: 617-772-5510	FYE: September 30
Web: www.nhp.org	Type: Subsidiary

This company does more than simply grin at the thought of fire and security risks it does something about it. SimplexGrinnell a part of Tyco International's Fire Protection Services segment provides integrated security alarm fire suppression healthcare communications and emergency lighting systems. It reaches some 1 million customers in the US and Canada through more than 150 district offices located in the Americas Europe Asia and other regions. Clients include members of local state and federal government agencies corporations oil and gas companies hospitals and educational facilities.

SIMPLICITY BANCORP, INC   NMS: SMPL

1359 N. Grand Avenue	CEO: –
Covina, CA 91724	CFO: –
Phone: 800 524-2274	HR: –
Fax: –	FYE: June 30
Web: www.simplicitybancorp.com	Type: Public

Simplicity Bancorp (formerly Kaiser Federal Financial) is the holding company of Simplicity Bank (formerly Kaiser Federal Bank) a community thrift operating in Southern California and the San Francisco Bay area. With about 10 full-service branches and financial services offices Simplicity Bank offers such traditional retail deposit products as checking accounts savings accounts and CDs. The company uses deposit funds to originate or purchase a variety of loans; real estate loans make up the bulk of a lending portfolio that also includes automobile home equity and other consumer loans. Simplicity Bancorp converted to a stock holding structure in 2010.

	Annual Growth	06/10	06/11	06/12	06/13	06/14
Sales ($ mil.)	(5.8%)	49.7	48.1	45.1	43.2	39.1
Net income ($ mil.)	12.3%	3.3	8.8	7.2	6.2	5.3
Market value ($ mil.)	12.3%	–	90.8	108.9	106.8	128.6
Employees	3.1%	107	117	132	130	121

SIMPSON HOUSING LLLP

8110 E. Union Ave. Ste. 200	CEO: J Robert Love
Denver CO 80237	CFO: –
Phone: 303-283-4100	HR: –
Fax: 303-283-4262	FYE: December 31
Web: www.simpsonhousing.com	Type: Private

Simpson Housing doesn't build apartments in the mythical metropolis of Springfield (d'oh) but it is a major force behind multifamily housing in the US. The holding company invests in develops constructs acquires and manages residential properties primarily luxury apartment communities around the country. Its Simpson Property Group subsidiary established in 1948 oversees a $3 billion portfolio of about 100 apartment and senior communities in about a dozen states. Great West Contractors provides construction management services. The Michigan State Employees' Retirement System owns about 45% of the company; the Alaska Permanent Fund owns another 45%.

SIMPSON INVESTMENT COMPANY

917 E. 11th St.	CEO: –
Tacoma WA 98421	CFO: –
Phone: 253-779-6400	HR: –
Fax: 253-280-9000	FYE: December 31
Web: www.simpson.com	Type: Private

Holding company Simpson Investment Company is one of the oldest privately owned forest products companies in the northwestern US. Through Simpson Lumber Company it operates two facilities in Washington that convert Douglas fir and hemlock logs into dimension lumber for the home construction market; its facilities in Georgia and South Carolina utilize yellow pine. The company also produces wood chips bark sawdust and shavings for use in paper manufacturing construction products and landscaping. Simpson Investment Company also owns Simpson Door Company which manufactures interior and exterior wood doors.

SIMPSON MANUFACTURING CO., INC. (DE)   NYS: SSD

5956 W. Las Positas Blvd.	CEO: Karen W. Colonias
Pleasanton, CA 94588	CFO: Brian J. Magstadt
Phone: 925 560-9000	HR: –
Fax: 925 833-1496	FYE: December 31
Web: www.simpsonmfg.com	Type: Public

Through its subsidiaries Simpson Manufacturing makes connectors and venting systems for the building remodeling and do-it-yourself industries. Subsidiary Simpson Strong-Tie (SST) makes more than 15000 types of standard and custom products that are used to connect and reinforce joints between wood concrete and masonry building components which the company markets globally and distributes through home centers and a network of contractor and dealer distributors. The company's products are sold primarily in Canada Europe Asia the US and the South Pacific.

	Annual Growth	12/10	12/11	12/12	12/13	12/14
Sales ($ mil.)	7.9%	555.5	603.4	657.2	706.3	752.1
Net income ($ mil.)	22.1%	28.6	50.9	41.9	51.0	63.5
Market value ($ mil.)	2.9%	1,513.5	1,648.2	1,605.6	1,798.5	1,694.2
Employees	7.1%	1,851	1,975	2,188	2,295	2,434

SIMPSON STRONG-TIE COMPANY INC.

5956 W. Las Positas Blvd.	CEO: Karen Colonias
Pleasanton CA 94588	CFO: –
Phone: 925-560-9000	HR: –
Fax: 925-847-1597	FYE: December 31
Web: www.strongtie.com	Type: Subsidiary

Blessed be the ties that bind a building together. Simpson Strong-Tie (SST) manufactures steel connectors for wood concrete and masonry that support buildings. The company's reinforcement products include anchors angles bases caps connectors fasteners and hangers; it also offers prefabricated shearwalls powder-actuated tools and adhesives. The Home Depot is its largest customer. SST is the operating subsidiary of Simpson Manufacturing. It serves customers in the commercial and residential construction furniture and do-it-yourself (DIY) markets. The company has manufacturing and warehouse operations in North America Europe and the Asia/Pacific region; it markets its products through distributors.

SIMPSON THACHER & BARTLETT LLP

425 Lexington Ave.
New York NY 10017-3954
Phone: 212-455-2000
Fax: 212-455-2502
Web: www.simpsonthacher.com

CEO: –
CFO: –
HR: –
FYE: December 31
Type: Private - Partnershi

When the urge to merge strikes corporate America Simpson Thacher & Bartlett is ready to serve. The firm's specialties include transactional work and litigation and it has built a substantial mergers and acquisitions practice over the years. Other practice areas include capital markets government investigations intellectual property real estate and tax. Simpson Thacher's 850 lawyers practice from five offices in the US (Los Angeles; Houston New York; Palo Alto California; and Washington DC) as well as in Beijing Hong Kong London Tokyo and S?o Paulo. The firm was founded in 1884 by three former Columbia Law School graduates: John Woodruff Simpson Thomas Thacher and William Milo Barnum.

SIMULATIONS PLUS INC.

NAS: SLP

42505 10th Street West
Lancaster, CA 93534-7059
Phone: 661 723-7723
Fax: 661 723-5524
Web: www.simulations-plus.com

CEO: Walter S Woltosz
CFO: John R Kneisel
HR: –
FYE: August 31
Type: Public

Molecular modeling software plus applications to help individuals with disabilities equals Simulations Plus. The company is a leading provider of applications used by pharmaceutical researchers to model absorption rates for orally dosed drug compounds. Its Words+ subsidiary provides augmentative communication software and input devices that help people with disabilities use computers. Simulations Plus also provides educational software targeted to high school and college students through its FutureLab unit. Pharmaceutical giants GlaxoSmithKline and Roche are among its clients. CEO Walter Woltosz and his wife Virginia (a director) together own about 40% of the company.

	Annual Growth	08/11	08/12	08/13	08/14	08/15
Sales ($ mil.)	11.8%	11.7	9.4	10.1	11.5	18.3
Net income ($ mil.)	9.1%	2.7	3.0	2.9	3.0	3.8
Market value ($ mil.)	20.3%	54.7	75.6	81.0	113.9	114.4
Employees	11.4%	39	25	27	66	60

SINAI HOSPITAL OF BALTIMORE INC

2401 W BELVEDERE AVE
BALTIMORE, MD 212155270
Phone: 410-601-5678
Fax: –
Web: www.lifebridgehealth.org

CEO: Neil Meltzer
CFO: –
HR: –
FYE: June 30
Type: Private

Sinai Hospital of Baltimore part of the LifeBridge Health network provides medical care in northwestern Baltimore. The 470-bed hospital is a not-for-profit medical center that includes such facilities as a heart center a children's hospital a cancer institute and a rehab center. Other specialties include orthopedics neurology and women's care. Medical students from Johns Hopkins University and the University of Maryland do some of their training at the hospital. Sinai Hospital of Baltimore was founded in 1866 as the Hebrew Hospital and Asylum and became a subsidiary of LifeBridge when it merged with other area providers in 1998.

	Annual Growth	06/08	06/09	06/10	06/11	06/13
Sales ($ mil.)	–	–	(1,237.8)	665.0	691.6	742.7
Net income ($ mil.)	31.3%	–	–	14.3	36.5	32.2
Market value ($ mil.)	–	–	–	–	–	–
Employees	–	–	–	–	–	1,403

SINCLAIR BROADCAST GROUP, INC.

NMS: SBGI

10706 Beaver Dam Road
Hunt Valley, MD 21030
Phone: 410 568-1500
Fax: 410 568-1533
Web: www.sbgi.net

CEO: David D. Smith
CFO: Christopher S. Ripley
HR: Donald H Thompson
FYE: December 31
Type: Public

To find out what's happening at Sinclair Broadcast Group (SBG) you could consult the TV Guide. The company is a leading television operator with more than 160 stations serving about 80 midsized markets. Its portfolio reaches 26% of US households and includes affiliates of all four major broadcast networks as well as several affiliates of The CW Network and MyNetworkTV. (Most of the stations are affiliated with FOX.) About half of SBG's stations are owned and operated while the rest are operated under local market agreements; the company has duopolies (more than one station) in about 20 of markets. The family of founder Julian Sinclair Smith led by CEO David Smith controls the company.

	Annual Growth	12/10	12/11	12/12	12/13	12/14
Sales ($ mil.)	26.7%	767.2	765.3	1,061.7	1,363.1	1,976.6
Net income ($ mil.)	29.2%	76.1	75.8	144.7	73.5	212.3
Market value ($ mil.)	35.2%	781.2	1,082.1	1,205.3	3,412.5	2,613.1
Employees	34.5%	2,350	3,130	4,000	6,400	7,700

SINCLAIR OIL CORPORATION

550 E. South Temple
Salt Lake City UT 84102
Phone: 801-524-2700
Fax: 801-524-2880
Web: www.sinclairoil.com

CEO: –
CFO: Charles Barlow
HR: Wendell White
FYE: December 31
Type: Private

Way out west where fossils are found brontosaur signs appear all 'round — and they belong to Sinclair Oil. The iconic brontosaur logo appears at more than 2700 Sinclair-branded service stations owned by independent operators in 22 western and midwestern US states. The company also operates two oil refineries more than 1000 miles of pipelines exploration operations and a trucking fleet. It owns a 60000-barrels-per-day refinery in Sinclair near Rawlins Wyoming and a 20000-barrels-per-day unit in Casper Wyoming. Sinclair Oil is owned and led by R. Earl Holding. Holding also owns the Grand America Hotel the Little America hotel chain and two ski resorts (Sun Valley in Idaho and Snowbasin in Utah).

SINGING MACHINE CO., INC.

NBB: SMDM

6301 NW 5th Way, Suite 2900
Fort Lauderdale, FL 33309
Phone: 954 596-1000
Fax: 954 596-2000
Web: www.singingmachine.com

CEO: Gary Atkinson
CFO: Lionel Marquis
HR: –
FYE: March 31
Type: Public

The Singing Machine Company strives to give everyone their 15 minutes of fame. It sells more than 50 different models of karaoke audio equipment from basic players to semi-professional machines. The karaoke machines primarily made in China are sold through electronics retailers and mass merchants such as Best Buy Costco and RadioShack. About a third of its sales come from outside the US. The Singing Machine Company also produces CDs and audio tapes for use in its karaoke equipment and offers a catalog of more than 2500 songs. To clear its books of liabilities The Singing Machine Company sold its Hong Kong unit in late 2006 and consolidated its Hong Kong office into Starlight International Holdings Ltd.

	Annual Growth	03/11	03/12	03/13	03/14	03/15
Sales ($ mil.)	19.7%	19.2	25.9	34.4	31.4	39.3
Net income ($ mil.)	–	(0.6)	0.5	3.1	1.0	0.2
Market value ($ mil.)	44.3%	1.5	4.2	9.5	6.5	6.5
Employees	1.0%	25	27	23	26	26

SINO-GLOBAL SHIPPING AMERICA, LTD.

NAS: SINO

1044 Northern Boulevard, Suite 305
Roslyn, NY 11576-1514
Phone: 718 888-1814
Fax: –
Web: www.sino-global.com

CEO: Lei Cao
CFO: Tuo Pan
HR: –
FYE: June 30
Type: Public

Sino-Global Shipping America assists foreign companies in navigating the murky regulatory waters of China's marine shipping industry. Through subsidiaries Trans Pacific and Sino-China the company is a shipping agent for US Australian and Hong Kong companies transporting iron ore to China. (Currently freight forwarding company Beijing Shou Rong is Sino-Global's largest customer representing more than half of the company's revenues.) Trans Pacific has operations at six ports in China; however each of the country's 76 ports have different rules. CEO Cao Lei owns more than 70% of Sino-Global Shipping America and Sino-China. Sino-Global Shipping America was founded in 2001.

	Annual Growth	06/11	06/12	06/13	06/14	06/15
Sales ($ mil.)	(23.4%)	32.9	33.9	17.3	11.6	11.3
Net income ($ mil.)	–	(0.9)	(1.8)	(1.8)	1.6	0.7
Market value ($ mil.)	1.3%	11.4	21.0	11.1	15.8	12.0
Employees	(20.9%)	51	52	33	16	20

SIPI METALS CORP.

1720 N. Elston Ave.
Chicago IL 60622-1579
Phone: 773-276-0070
Fax: 773-276-7014
Web: www.sipimetals.com

CEO: –
CFO: –
HR: –
FYE: October 30
Type: Private

Sipi Metals recovers precious metals (including gold silver and platinum group metals) from scrap generated by the aerospace chemical electronics and photographic industries. An old hand at metal recycling — the company was founded in 1905 — Sipi specializes in recovering metals that are often covered in and enmeshed with substances such as fiberglass and plastic. The company also produces brass bronze and other copper alloys. It operates processing facilities in Asia Europe and the Americas. Sipi employees own a majority of the company through an employee stock ownership plan.

SIRCHIE ACQUISITION COMPANY LLC

100 Hunter Place
Youngsville NC 27596-9447
Phone: 919-554-2244
Fax: 800-899-8181
Web: www.sirchie.com

CEO: –
CFO: Jennifer Walton
HR: –
FYE: September 30
Type: Private

Sirchie Acquisition Company leaves old fingerprinting methods in the dust. The company develops manufactures and sells crime-scene investigation equipment including fingerprint gathering and recording materials forensic analysis equipment DNA kits narcotic and blood alcohol test kits and software that assists in creating composite images of crime suspects. Sirchie also has a vehicle division in New Jersey that makes surveillance vehicles for law enforcement agencies. Its corporate headquarters in North Carolina includes manufacturing facilities. The company was founded in 1927 by Francis Sirchie originally specializing in fingerprint recording. It is a portfolio company of Raymond James Financial.

SIRIUS AMERICA INSURANCE COMPANY

1 Liberty Plaza 19th Fl.
New York NY 10006
Phone: 212-312-2500
Fax: 212-385-2279
Web: www.siriusamerica.com

CEO: Daniel Wilson
CFO: Michael E Tyburski
HR: –
FYE: December 31
Type: Subsidiary

Sirius America Insurance (formerly White Mountains Reinsurance Company of America) helps insurers throughout North America Latin America and the Caribbean to manage risk effectively. The firm which is owned by White Mountains Insurance Group and is part of that company's Sirius Group global reinsurance business underwrites treaty and facultative reinsurance for multi-line property/casualty insurers. It also provides reinsurance to health insurers and writes some international non-marine business. Sirius America Insurance operates offices in Miami New York and Toronto.

SIRIUS XM HOLDINGS INC

NMS: SIRI

1221 Avenue of the Americas, 36th Floor
New York, NY 10020
Phone: 212 584-5100
Fax: –
Web: www.siriusxm.com

CEO: James E Meyer
CFO: David J Frear
HR: –
FYE: December 31
Type: Public

You might say radio programming from this company comes from a higher plane. SIRIUS XM Holdings operating through SIRIUS XM Radio manages satellite radio systems under the SIRIUS and XM brands that together boast more than 25 million subscribers. Each service offers more than 150 channels of CD-quality music news and talk shows. Programming includes National Football League Major League Baseball and college games as well as talk shows featuring hosts Howard Stern Martha Stewart and Oprah Winfrey. The company has equipment alliances with several automakers; it also sells satellite radio equipment through its website and through such retail outlets as Best Buy and Wal-Mart.

	Annual Growth	12/11	12/12	12/13	12/14	12/15
Sales ($ mil.)	11.0%	3,014.5	3,402.0	3,799.1	4,181.1	4,570.1
Net income ($ mil.)	4.5%	427.0	3,472.7	377.2	493.2	509.7
Market value ($ mil.)	–	0.0	0.0	0.0	0.0	0.0
Employees	11.1%	1,526	1,596	2,195	2,327	2,323

SIRONA DENTAL SYSTEMS INC

NMS: SIRO

30-30 47th Avenue, Suite 500
Long Island City, NY 11101
Phone: 718 482-2011
Fax: –
Web: www.sirona.com

CEO: Jeffrey T. Slovin
CFO: Ulrich Michel
HR: Heloise Matias
FYE: September 30
Type: Public

Factoid for the day: The first electric dental drill was invented in 1882 and the company that made it is now known as Sirona Dental Systems. The firm still makes handheld dental instruments as well as imaging systems dental CAD/CAM systems used in restorations and a full line of other products used by dentists and dental laboratories worldwide. Its CEREC system is a 3-D computer-aided contraption for making ceramic restorations (such as crowns and bridges) in the dentist's office rather than a lab. Its imaging systems include traditional X-ray equipment and digital radiography systems. Other products include dental chairs and instrument cleaning systems. DENTSPLY is buying Sirona for $5.5 billion.

	Annual Growth	09/11	09/12	09/13	09/14	09/15
Sales ($ mil.)	6.2%	913.9	979.4	1,101.5	1,171.1	1,161.3
Net income ($ mil.)	11.2%	121.8	133.8	146.7	175.7	186.2
Market value ($ mil.)	21.8%	2,370.5	3,183.8	3,741.1	4,286.1	5,217.3
Employees	6.3%	2,705	2,979	3,216	3,327	3,458

SIRVA INC.

700 Oakmont Ln.
Westmont IL 60559
Phone: 630-570-3047
Fax: 415-442-4803
Web: www.frogdesign.com

CEO: Wes W Lucas
CFO: Douglas V Gathany
HR: –
FYE: December 31
Type: Private

Whether you're moving across the street across town or across the ocean SIRVA is serious about the business of packing. One of the world's largest relocation and moving services companies SIRVA operates in more than 150 countries. Its North American brands include Allied Van Lines Global Van Lines and northAmerican Van Lines. It uses brands such as Allied Pickfords and Concept Mobility Services in other regions. The company boasts 300000-plus relocations a year; outsourced moves delivered under contract with corporate employers and government and military customers to transfer personnel account for the majority of SIRVA's sales.

SITESTAR CORPORATION

7109 Timberlake Road
Lynchburg, VA 24502
Phone: 434 239-4272
Fax: –
Web: - www.sitestar.com

OTC: SYTE

CEO: Steven L. Kiel
CFO: Daniel A. (Dan) Judd
HR: –
FYE: December 31
Type: Public

Sitestar wants to sparkle in the Internet firmament. The Internet service provider (ISP) primarily serves markets in the mid-Atlantic and Northwest states offering dial-up and DSL Internet access as well as Web hosting and design within its regional service area. Sitestar's retail division sells and makes computer systems and recharges toner and ink cartridges. The company sold its programming and consulting division and has acquired the dial-up customer base of IDACOMM a subsidiary of IDACORP.

	Annual Growth	12/10	12/11	12/12	12/13	12/14
Sales ($ mil.)	(17.1%)	5.1	4.6	3.6	2.6	2.4
Net income ($ mil.)	–	(0.8)	0.8	0.4	0.1	0.4
Market value ($ mil.)	36.8%	1.0	1.4	1.9	3.3	3.5
Employees	(21.0%)	18	15	11	10	7

SIX FLAGS ENTERTAINMENT CORP

924 Avenue J East
Grand Prairie, TX 75050
Phone: 972 595-5000
Fax: –
Web: www.sixflags.com

NYS: SIX

CEO: James Reid-Anderson
CFO: John M Duffey
HR: –
FYE: December 31
Type: Public

For millions of people Six Flags is the standard-bearer for theme park thrills. The company is the #2 amusement park operator in the world (behind Walt Disney) drawing about 25 million visitors to its nearly 20 parks in North America. Fancying itself a regional entertainment destination most of its parks operate under the Six Flags banner (including Six Flags Fiesta Texas and Six Flags Magic Mountain) offering roller coasters and other thrill rides water slides and additional family entertainment. Revenues come from gate receipts food and merchandise. Six Flags licenses characters from Warner Bros. and DC Entertainment such as Looney Tunes and Batman.

	Annual Growth	12/10	12/11	12/12	12/13	12/14
Sales ($ mil.)	8.5%	847.8	1,013.2	1,070.3	1,109.9	1,175.8
Net income ($ mil.)	11.0%	50.1	(22.7)	354.0	118.6	76.0
Market value ($ mil.)	(5.6%)	5,055.8	3,832.7	5,687.8	3,422.0	4,010.3
Employees	8.1%	29,900	4,600	40,900	40,900	40,900

SJW CORP.

110 West Taylor Street
San Jose, CA 95110
Phone: 408 279-7800
Fax: –
Web: www.sjwcorp.com

NYS: SJW

CEO: W. Richard (Rich) Roth
CFO: James P. Lynch
HR: –
FYE: December 31
Type: Public

SJW slakes thirst in Silicon Valley and elsewhere. Its main subsidiary regulated utility San Jose Water distributes water to 228000 customer connections (or about 1 million people) in San Jose and other cities in California's Santa Clara County. San Jose Water taps wells and surface sources and buys water from the Santa Clara Valley Water District. Besides its utility operations San Jose Water contracts to operate municipal water systems. Its SJWTX subsidiary (which does business as Canyon Lake Water Service) serves about 11000 water connections (about 36000 people) in Central Texas. The company's Texas Water Alliance unit is developing a water supply project in Texas.

	Annual Growth	12/10	12/11	12/12	12/13	12/14
Sales ($ mil.)	10.3%	215.6	239.0	261.5	276.9	319.7
Net income ($ mil.)	20.7%	24.4	20.9	22.3	22.4	51.8
Market value ($ mil.)	5.0%	537.0	479.6	539.6	604.3	651.6
Employees	1.3%	375	385	385	379	395

SKADDEN ARPS SLATE MEAGHER & FLOM LLP

4 Times Sq.
New York NY 10036
Phone: 212-735-3000
Fax: 212-735-2000
Web: www.skadden.com

CEO: –
CFO: Noah Puntus
HR: –
FYE: December 31
Type: Private - Partnershi

More than just a series of interesting surnames Skadden Arps Slate Meagher & Flom is a firm that knows a thing or two about corporate law. A major US law firm and one of the largest in the world Skadden Arps Slate Meagher & Flom employs some 1800 attorneys in about 40 different practice areas. It operates approximately 25 offices around the globe from Boston to Beijing and from London to Los Angeles. The firm is best known for its work in mergers and acquisitions corporate restructuring and corporate finance. Skadden Arps Slate Meagher & Flom was founded in 1948.

SKANSKA USA BUILDING INC.

1633 Littleton Rd.
Parsippany NJ 07054
Phone: 973-753-3500
Fax: 973-753-3499
Web: www.skanskausa.com

CEO: Michael McNally
CFO: Leo Sinicin
HR: Thomas B Crane
FYE: December 31
Type: Subsidiary

As you might expect Skanska USA Building continues building in the good old US of A. One of a handful of US-based units of the Swedish construction giant Skanska AB the company is one of the nation's top general contractors and construction groups. Offerings include pre-construction consultation design-build and construction management. It serves sectors ranging from infrastructure sports and entertainment education and health care. The company also provides specialist validation services for pharmaceutical and biotech customers. Skanska's other US companies include Skanska USA Civil and Skanska Commercial Development USA.

SKANSKA USA CIVIL

16-16 Whitestone Expwy.
Whitestone NY 11357
Phone: 718-747-3454
Fax: 718-747-3458
Web: www.usa.skanska.com/our-organization/skanska-u

CEO: Salvatore Mancini
CFO: Hans Andersson
HR: –
FYE: December 31
Type: Subsidiary

Skanska USA Civil builds some of the world's largest cable-stayed bridges. Part of the US operations of Swedish engineering and construction giant Skanska Skanska USA Civil focuses on infrastructure projects throughout the country. Along with sister firm Skanska USA Building it is a market leader in the New York area where it has worked on the Brooklyn Bridge the AirTrain light-rail system and Roosevelt Island Bridge. It builds roads tunnels and rail systems in addition to bridges and industrial and marine facilities such as power and water filtration plants gas-treatment plants and dry docks. Projects have included the Meadowlands Football Stadium and Boston's Central Artery.

SKECHERS U S A, INC.

NYS: SKX

228 Manhattan Beach Blvd.
Manhattan Beach, CA 90266
Phone: 310 318-3100
Fax: –
Web: www.skechers.com

CEO: Robert Greenberg
CFO: David Weinberg
HR: –
FYE: December 31
Type: Public

Skechers' top executive Robert Greenberg knows how to land on his feet. The founder of 1980s icon L.A. Gear heads Skechers USA which designs and sells more than 3000 styles of lifestyle and athletic footwear including oxfords boots sandals sneakers training shoes and semi-dressy shoes. It caters to men women and children. In addition to its namesake products the company offers fashion and street-focused footwear under the Marc Ecko Zoo York and Mark Nason brands. Its shoes are sold through department and specialty stores in more than 160 countries as well as some 360 company-owned concept and outlet stores and its website. Sketchers footwear is manufactured primarily by Chinese contractors.

	Annual Growth	12/10	12/11	12/12	12/13	12/14
Sales ($ mil.)	4.4%	2,011.4	1,613.6	1,567.4	1,854.1	2,386.7
Net income ($ mil.)	0.5%	136.1	(67.5)	9.5	54.8	138.8
Market value ($ mil.)	28.9%	3,045.4	1,845.5	2,817.0	5,044.7	8,413.0
Employees	9.3%	5,440	5,636	5,666	6,868	7,772

SKIDMORE COLLEGE

815 N BROADWAY
SARATOGA SPRINGS, NY 128661698
Phone: 518-580-5000
Fax: –
Web: www.skidmore.edu

CEO: –
CFO: –
HR: –
FYE: May 31
Type: Private

Skidmore College offers more than 40 degree programs including majors in both traditional liberal arts disciplines and pre-professional areas. The private college grants bachelor's and master's degrees in the sciences humanities social sciences business education social work and the arts. Skidmore enrolls about 2400 students from the US and some 40 other countries and boasts a student-faculty ratio of about 9 to 1. It was founded by Lucy Skidmore Scribner in 1903 as the Young Women's Industrial Club of Saratoga.

	Annual Growth	05/09	05/10	05/11	05/12	05/13
Sales ($ mil.)	1.4%	–	134.7	135.2	137.2	140.2
Net income ($ mil.)	(0.6%)	–	–	33.2	(23.4)	32.8
Market value ($ mil.)	–	–	–	–	–	–
Employees	–	–	–	–	–	720

SKINVISIBLE INC

NBB: SKVI

6320 South Sandhill Road, Suite 10
Las Vegas, NV 89120
Phone: 702 433-7154
Fax: –

CEO: Terry H Howlett
CFO: Terry H Howlett
HR: –
FYE: December 31
Type: Public

Skinvisible keeps invisible substances like lotion and sunscreen from washing off your skin. The company develops topical drug delivery systems for dermatology and healthcare products including products to treat acne eczema fungal infections and inflammation as well as sunscreens anti-aging products pre-surgical preparations and various other medical treatments using its Invisicare technology. Licensing its delivery technology is the goal of the firm; its clients include dermatological and other drugmakers cosmetics companies and manufacturers of personal care items in Asia Europe and the US. Licensees include DRJ Group J.D. Nelson & Associates and Embil Pharmaceutical.

	Annual Growth	12/10	12/11	12/12	12/13	12/14
Sales ($ mil.)	–	0.0	0.0	0.3	0.1	0.1
Net income ($ mil.)	–	0.0	0.0	(1.5)	(1.3)	(1.9)
Market value ($ mil.)	–	0.0	0.0	3.9	2.2	5.1
Employees	66.7%	–	–	–	3	5

SKULLCANDY INC

NMS: SKUL

1441 West Ute Boulevard, Suite 250
Park City, UT 84098
Phone: 435 940-1545
Fax: –
Web: www.skullcandy.com

CEO: Hoby Darling
CFO: Jason Hodell
HR: –
FYE: December 31
Type: Public

If your head craves sweet tunes Skullcandy has a treat for you. The youth-oriented firm designs and sells edgy stylish headphones ear buds docking speakers and other audio goodies as well as apparel and accessories under the Skullcandy Astro Gaming and 2XL brands. Featuring an aesthetic that appeals to its target audience of action sports enthusiasts the gear was originally sold at specialty shops but can also be found nationwide at Target and Best Buy through the company's website and in more than 80 countries where youth culture thrives. Skullcandy retains its street cred by sponsoring boarders surfers and BMX bikers. Founded in 2003 Skullcandy went public in 2011.

	Annual Growth	12/10	12/11	12/12	12/13	12/14
Sales ($ mil.)	11.5%	160.6	232.5	297.7	210.1	247.8
Net income ($ mil.)	–	(9.7)	18.6	25.8	(3.0)	7.6
Market value ($ mil.)	(9.8%)	–	353.6	220.0	203.6	259.5
Employees	10.7%	200	290	335	295	300

SKYLINE CORP.

ASE: SKY

P.O. Box 743, 2520 By-Pass Road
Elkhart, IN 46515
Phone: 574 294-6521
Fax: 574 295-7061
Web: www.skylinecorp.com

CEO: Richard W. (Rich) Florea
CFO: Jon S. Pilarski
HR: –
FYE: May 31
Type: Public

Skyline's idea of a beautiful skyline would probably include several rows of double-wides. The company and its subsidiaries design and make manufactured homes. It distributes them to independent dealers and manufactured housing communities throughout the US and Canada. About half of Skyline's revenues come from selling HUD-code manufactured homes (products built according to US Housing and Urban Development standards); the rest of its typically two- to four-bedroom homes are modular in design.

	Annual Growth	05/11	05/12	05/13	05/14	05/15
Sales ($ mil.)	3.6%	162.3	182.8	177.6	191.7	187.0
Net income ($ mil.)	–	(26.6)	(19.4)	(10.5)	(11.9)	(10.4)
Market value ($ mil.)	(34.8%)	153.1	38.1	34.2	40.4	27.7
Employees	(2.0%)	1,300	1,100	1,100	1,300	1,200

SKYMALL INC.

1520 E. Pima St.
Phoenix AZ 85034
Phone: 602-254-9777
Fax: 602-254-6075
Web: www.skymall.com

CEO: Kevin Weiss
CFO: –
HR: Jutta Garner
FYE: December 31
Type: Private

While some shop 'til they drop SkyMall customers shop 'til they come to a complete stop. The company is the nation's #1 distributor of in-flight catalogs that feature about 2000 products provided by big-name retailers including Hammacher Schlemmer Lillian Vernon and The Wine Enthusiast. Formerly a subsidiary of Gemstar-TV Guide International SkyMall catalogs are found in the seat pockets of about 88% of US flights reaching about 650 million passengers annually. Its catalogs are also found in hotel rooms airport lounges and on some international flights. Founded in 1990 the firm also sells through skymall.com. Gemstar sold SkyMall to private equity firm Spire Capital Partners and ZelnickMedia in 2005.

SKYY SPIRITS LLC

1 Beach St. Ste. 300
San Francisco CA 94133
Phone: 415-315-8000
Fax: 415-315-8001
Web: www.skyyspirits.com

CEO: Jackques Jean Dubau
CFO: –
HR: –
FYE: December 31
Type: Subsidiary

Don't fault Skyy Spirits if it's up bright and early to raise the American flag. The company touts its SKYY Vodka as the #1 domestically made US premium vodka. Founded in 1992 by an inventor tired of hangovers Skyy claims that its distilling process eliminates toxins which results in a cleaner vodka that makes the morning after less er shall we say painful. Skyy is the exclusive US importer for Campari Cutty Sark Scotch Whiskey and other liqueurs and spirits. The company has won many awards for its innovative marketing of its premium SKYY Vodka and its SKYY flavored vodkas in their distinctive blue bottles. Skyy Spirits is a subsidiary of Davide Campari-Milano and manages its brands in the US.

SKYWEST INC.

NMS: SKYW

444 South River Road
St. George, UT 84790
Phone: 435 634-3000
Fax: –
Web: www.skywest.com

CEO: Jerry C. Atkin
CFO: Robert J. (Rob) Simmons
HR: –
FYE: December 31
Type: Public

SkyWest traverses the skies in every direction — not just west. The airline operates through two main segments: SkyWest Airlines and ExpressJet. SkyWest has destinations to about 275 cities in the US Canada Mexico and the Caribbean supporting 3500 daily departures. Combined SkyWest's carriers operate a fleet of about 700 aircraft consisting of Canadair regional jets (CRJs made by Bombardier) and turboprops. SkyWest also has a code-sharing agreement with Delta Air Lines and United Continental's United Airlines. (Code-sharing allows airlines to sell tickets on one another's flights.)

	Annual Growth	12/10	12/11	12/12	12/13	12/14
Sales ($ mil.)	4.0%	2,765.1	3,654.9	3,534.4	3,297.7	3,237.4
Net income ($ mil.)	–	96.4	(27.3)	51.2	59.0	(24.2)
Market value ($ mil.)	(4.0%)	799.5	644.4	637.8	759.1	679.8
Employees	0.2%	18,378	18,418	18,145	18,358	18,500

SL GREEN REALTY CORP.

NYS: SLG

420 Lexington Avenue
New York, NY 10170
Phone: 212 594-2700
Fax: –
Web: www.slgreen.com

CEO: Marc Holliday
CFO: Matthew DiLiberto
HR: Shea Taylor
FYE: December 31
Type: Public

SL Green is a very big fish in a very large pond. A self-managed real estate investment trust (REIT) SL Green acquires develops renovates manages and leases commercial properties primarily office buildings in Manhattan (the US's largest office market by far). The firm has interests some some 95 properties Manhattan buildings totaling 44.1 million square feet. SL Green specializes in Class B assets — buildings older than 25 years but in desirable locations and in generally good condition. SL Green's largest tenants include Citigroup Credit Suisse and Viacom. The REIT also provides real estate financing via structured finance originations and preferred equity investments.

	Annual Growth	12/10	12/11	12/12	12/13	12/14
Sales ($ mil.)	8.4%	1,101.2	1,263.4	1,400.3	1,469.1	1,520.0
Net income ($ mil.)	14.6%	300.6	647.4	196.4	135.4	518.1
Market value ($ mil.)	15.2%	6,570.4	6,485.7	7,460.0	8,990.9	11,583.6
Employees	0.8%	1,027	1,047	1,092	1,076	1,060

SKYWORKS SOLUTIONS, INC.

NMS: SWKS

20 Sylvan Road
Woburn, MA 01801
Phone: 781 376-3000
Fax: –
Web: www.skyworksinc.com

CEO: David J. Aldrich
CFO: Donald W. (Don) Palette
HR: –
FYE: October 02
Type: Public

Skyworks Solutions makes integrated circuits (ICs) for wireless phones networks and other applications. Its flagship handset products include power amplifiers and front-end modules used by OEMs like Bose Cisco Systems HTC Nest Sonos and ZTE in their mobile phones and communications infrastructure gear. Other analog devices include attenuators diodes couplers phase shifters receivers and switches used in a broad array of industries. Skyworks uses gallium arsenide (GaAs) a material that is faster and uses less energy than industry-standard silicon in many of its devices. The company gets more than 90% of its sales from customers in the Asia and Asia/Pacific regions.

	Annual Growth	09/11	09/12	09/13*	10/14	10/15
Sales ($ mil.)	23.1%	1,418.9	1,568.6	1,792.0	2,291.5	3,258.4
Net income ($ mil.)	37.0%	226.6	202.1	278.1	457.7	798.3
Market value ($ mil.)	47.1%	3,417.8	4,483.5	4,713.7	10,514.1	15,996.6
Employees	11.1%	4,400	4,700	4,750	5,550	6,700

*Fiscal year change

SL INDUSTRIES INC.

ASE: SLI

520 Fellowship Road, Suite A114
Mt. Laurel, NJ 08054
Phone: 856 727-1500
Fax: –
Web: www.slindustries.com

CEO: William T Fejes
CFO: Louis J Belardi
HR: Mary Henderson
FYE: December 31
Type: Public

SL Industries has the power to protect. Operating through four business segments SL Industries makes and markets custom and standard AC/DC and DC/DC power supplies surge suppressors conditioning and distribution units motion-control systems and power protection equipment. Products are typically married to larger systems to improve their operating performance and safety. SL sells its power electronics and systems and related products to OEMs in the aerospace computer medical wireless and wireline communications infrastructure and transportation industries as well as to US military contractors and municipal utilities.

	Annual Growth	12/10	12/11	12/12	12/13	12/14
Sales ($ mil.)	1.9%	189.8	212.3	200.6	204.7	204.4
Net income ($ mil.)	64.9%	2.6	8.2	7.8	8.2	18.9
Market value ($ mil.)	22.2%	72.5	67.1	74.6	112.3	161.6
Employees	(3.3%)	1,600	1,600	1,400	1,400	1,400

SLALOM LLC

821 2nd Ave. Ste. 1900
Seattle WA 98104
Phone: 206-438-5700
Fax: 206-438-5686
Web: www.slalom.com

CEO: –
CFO: –
HR: –
FYE: December 31
Type: Private

Slalom has both feet on the ground when it comes to helping businesses succeed. Operating as Slalom Consulting the company provides consulting services in the areas of information technology management and development (application development system analysis and design project and program management); business management (business intelligence and improving corporate processes strategies and operations); and financial (enterprise resource planning compliance and reporting). Slalom Consulting maintains a dozen offices in Atlanta Chicago Dallas Denver Los Angeles New York San Francisco Portland Oregon and other major cities. The company was founded in 2001.

SLEEPMED INCORPORATED

200 CORPORATE PL STE 5B
PEABODY, MA 019603840
Phone: 978-536-7400
Fax: –
Web: www.sleepmedinc.com

CEO: Sean Heyniger
CFO: Jack Fiedor
HR: –
FYE: December 31
Type: Private

SleepMed tracks your vital signs while you count sheep. The company provides diagnostic tests and treatments for patients with sleep disorders through more than 160 sleep centers located in hospitals medical clinics and free-standing clinics nationwide. SleepMed also partners with epilepsy centers to provide brain monitoring services to patients suffering from seizures or unexplained neurologic episodes. Patients who don't want to travel for treatment can make use of SleepMed's in-home diagnostic services. The company designs and produces neurological testing equipment under the DigiTrace brand. SleepMed was formed by the 1999 merger of DigiTrace Care Services and Sleep Disorder Centers of America.

	Annual Growth	12/06	12/07	12/08	12/09	12/10
Sales ($ mil.)	(54.2%)	–	–	437.3	96.0	91.9
Net income ($ mil.)	5680.4%	–	–	0.0	2.3	1.7
Market value ($ mil.)	–	–	–	–	–	–
Employees	–	–	–	–	–	945

SLEEPY'S INC.

1000 S. Oyster Bay Rd.
Hicksville NY 11801
Phone: 516-861-8800
Fax: 516-861-8847
Web: www.sleepys.com

CEO: Harold Acker
CFO: Joseph Graci
HR: –
FYE: December 31
Type: Private

Sleepy's — a leading mattress and bedding retailer — isn't napping it's expanding. The company operates more than 700 stores mostly in New York and New Jersey but also in about 10 other eastern states. Some of the stores have Sleepy's Kids concessions inside. Sleepy's outlets sell the mattresses and box springs of more than a dozen major manufacturers including Simmons Sealy and Serta as well as brass iron and motorized beds. The firm offers low-price guarantees delivery and other services and it sells products throughout the US by phone. Sleepy's also owns 1800Mattress.com along with its 1-800-Mattress telephone network. Chairman Harry Acker who founded the firm in 1957 owns Sleepy's.

SLM CORP.

NMS: SLM

300 Continental Drive
Newark, DE 19713
Phone: 302 451-0200
Fax: –
Web: www.salliemae.com

CEO: Raymond J. Quinlan
CFO: Steven J. McGarry
HR: –
FYE: December 31
Type: Public

Those who graduated magna cum payments may not be familiar with SLM but they probably know its more common moniker Sallie Mae. Holding more than $8 billion in student loans SLM's main subsidiary Sallie Mae Bank is one of the nation's largest education loan providers and specializes in originating acquiring financing and servicing private student loans which are not guaranteed by the government. The company also earns fees for its processing and administrative offerings through various subsidiaries. SLM spun off its education loan management servicing and asset recovery business to form Navient Corporation in 2014.

	Annual Growth	12/10	12/11	12/12	12/13	12/14
Assets ($ mil.)	(49.9%)	205,307.0	193,345.0	181,260.0	159,543.0	12,972.2
Net income ($ mil.)	(22.2%)	530.4	633.0	939.0	1,418.0	194.2
Market value ($ mil.)	(5.2%)	5,331.1	5,674.1	7,253.5	11,128.0	4,314.8
Employees	(39.8%)	7,600	6,600	6,800	7,200	1,000

SLOAN IMPLEMENT COMPANY INC.

120 N BUSINESS 51
ASSUMPTION, IL 625101120
Phone: 217-226-4411
Fax: –
Web: www.sloans.com

CEO: –
CFO: –
HR: –
FYE: December 31
Type: Private

There's no slowin' down at Sloan Implement. The company provides the tools of trade for farmers in Illinois. Headquartered in Assumption Illinois Sloan is an authorized dealer of John Deere equipment and new and used parts. Founded in 1931 the company sells and services new and used Deere equipment including combines tractors manure spreaders tillers earth moving and lawn machinery and grain-handling equipment at five locations in Wisconsin and at 11 locations in Illinois; it also ships products nationwide and to international customers.

	Annual Growth	12/03	12/04	12/05	12/06	12/07
Sales ($ mil.)	10.8%	–	159.4	150.5	146.2	217.2
Net income ($ mil.)	34.8%	–	–	5.2	4.3	9.4
Market value ($ mil.)	–	–	–	–	–	–
Employees	–	–	–	–	–	350

SM ENERGY CO.

NYS: SM

1775 Sherman Street, Suite 1200
Denver, CO 80203
Phone: 303 861-8140
Fax: 303 861-0934
Web: www.sm-energy.com

CEO: Javan D. (Jay) Ottoson
CFO: A. Wade Pursell
HR: –
FYE: December 31
Type: Public

SM Energy looks for energy (mainly natural gas) across the continental US. While the oil and gas exploration and production company spreads its operations across the US (the Midcontinent the Gulf Coast the Williston Basin in North Dakota and Montana and the Permian Basin in West Texas and New Mexico the Eagle Ford shale in South Texas and the Haynesville Shale play in East Texas) it gets most of its revenues from South Texas and the Gulf Coast. In 2014 the company posted estimated proved reserves of 547.7 million barrels of oil equivalent 28% up from 2013 reflecting increased activity in its shale plays.

	Annual Growth	12/10	12/11	12/12	12/13	12/14
Sales ($ mil.)	23.3%	1,092.8	1,603.3	1,505.1	2,293.4	2,522.3
Net income ($ mil.)	35.6%	196.8	215.4	(54.2)	170.9	666.1
Market value ($ mil.)	(10.0%)	3,975.6	4,931.5	3,522.2	5,606.9	2,602.7
Employees	12.0%	569	639	725	793	896

SMALLBIZPROS INC.

160 Hawthorne Park   CEO: Steven Rafsky
Athens GA 30606   CFO: –
Phone: 706-548-1040   HR: –
Fax: 800-548-1040   FYE: May 31
Web: www.smallbizpros.com   Type: Private

SmallBizPros knows the pros and cons of small businesses. Through Padgett Business Services the company and its franchisees provide business advice tax consulting and preparation government compliance and financial reporting and payroll services to small businesses throughout the US and Canada. As suggested by its name SmallBizPros targets owner-operated companies with fewer than 20 employees. There are more than 400 owner-operated offices in the company's network. SmallBizPros was founded as an accounting firm in 1965 and began franchising in 1975.

SMART & FINAL INC.

600 Citadel Dr.   CEO: George Golleher
Commerce CA 90040   CFO: –
Phone: 323-869-7500   HR: –
Fax: 323-869-7865   FYE: December 31
Web: www.smartandfinal.com   Type: Private

Smart & Final caters to caterers — as well as small businesses restaurants and households in the western US. Its 235 non-membership warehouse stores stock groceries party supplies paper products cleaning supplies and more in bulk sizes and quantities. The stores operate under the Smart & Final Smart & Final Extra! and Cash & Carry banners in urban and suburban areas in Arizona California Idaho Nevada Oregon and Washington as well as northern Mexico. Founded in 1871 in Los Angeles it later took the names of owners J. S. Smart and H. D. Final. The chain's owner Apollo Management has agreed to sell a majority stake in Smart & Final to private equity firm Ares Management for about $975 million.

SMART MODULAR TECHNOLOGIES INC.

39870 Eureka Dr.   CEO: Iain Mackenzie
Newark CA 94560   CFO: Jack Pacheco
Phone: 510-623-1231   HR: –
Fax: 510-623-1434   FYE: August 31
Web: www.smartm.com   Type: Private

SMART is smart because of its memory. The company is a top global designer and manufacturer of memory products such as flash memory cards solid-state drives (SSDs) and DRAM modules. Original equipment makers in the computer defense gaming networking telecom and other sectors use its products and supply chain services. SMART has counted HP Cisco and Dell among its largest customers. In 2011 the company was taken private by equity investors Silver Lake Partners and Silver Lake Sumeru in a deal valued at around $645 million. The move allowed it shed the regulatory and market burdens of a public company to better navigate the notoriously cyclical DRAM industry.

SMARTFINANCIAL INC

NAS: SMBK

5401 Kingston Pike, Suite 600   CEO: Nathaniel F Hughes
Knoxville, TN 37919   CFO: Gary W Petty Jr
Phone: 865 453-2650   HR: –
Fax: –   FYE: December 31
Web: www.cscbank.com   Type: Public

Cornerstone Bancshares is the holding company for Cornerstone Community Bank which operates about five locations in Chattanooga Tennessee and surrounding communities in addition to two loan production offices in Knoxville Tennessee and Dalton Georgia. The bank offers standard retail and commercial services including checking and savings accounts money market accounts and CDs. Its lending activities primarily consist of commercial real estate loans residential mortgages real estate construction loans and business and agricultural loans. Another subsidiary of Cornerstone Bancshares Eagle Financial purchases accounts receivable and acts as a conduit lender.

	Annual Growth	12/10	12/11	12/12	12/13	12/14
Assets ($ mil.)	(1.5%)	441.5	422.7	443.4	432.2	415.7
Net income ($ mil.)	–	(4.7)	1.0	1.4	1.7	1.6
Market value ($ mil.)	15.4%	3.1	2.5	3.8	3.9	5.5
Employees	(1.8%)	112	109	105	107	104

SMARTPROS LTD

NAS: SPRO

12 Skyline Drive   CEO: Allen S Greene
Hawthorne, NY 10532   CFO: Stanley P Wirtheim
Phone: 914 345-2620   HR: –
Fax: –   FYE: December 31
Web: www.smartpros.com   Type: Public

SmartPros counts on accountants and engineers to keep its numbers shipshape. SmartPros offers professional development courses in online DVD and CD-ROM formats. Its classes are used by accounting finance engineering legal and business professionals to build skills keep certifications current and prepare for certification testing. The company also offers executive workshops consulting and e-learning training program development. Among its offerings are courses in auditing design compliance ethics financial reporting project management and safety. CPE (continuing professional education) credits can be earned immediately by passing tests offered at the end of accredited courses.

	Annual Growth	12/09	12/10	12/11	12/12	12/13
Sales ($ mil.)	(3.3%)	19.3	17.6	17.0	15.9	16.8
Net income ($ mil.)	(22.6%)	0.4	(0.1)	0.2	(1.9)	0.1
Market value ($ mil.)	(8.0%)	16.3	11.2	8.8	6.9	11.7
Employees	(8.2%)	100	89	82	76	71

SMARTRONIX INC.

44150 SMARTRONIX WAY   CEO: –
HOLLYWOOD, MD 206363172   CFO: Joseph Gerczak
Phone: 301-373-6000   HR: –
Fax: –   FYE: December 31
Web: www.smartronix.com   Type: Private

Smartronix works an intelligent approach to electronics. Serving the US Department of Defense and other federal agencies its IT products and services include cyber security cloud computing enterprise software health IT network operations and mission-focused engineering. The company specializes in application development business management network management and systems engineering. Founded in 1995 Smartronix offers ruggedized computing and communications equipment and network diagnostic tools. The company counts the US Air Force Marine Corps and Navy among its regular clients as well as the Department of Homeland Security and the Transportation Security Administration.

	Annual Growth	10/03	10/04	10/05	10/06*	12/07
Sales ($ mil.)	0.0%	–	–	–	78.5	78.5
Net income ($ mil.)	0.0%	–	–	–	4.1	4.1
Market value ($ mil.)	–	–	–	–	–	–
Employees	–	–	–	–	–	566

*Fiscal year change

SMC NETWORKS INC.

20 Mason
Irvine CA 92618
Phone: 949-679-8000
Fax: 949-502-3400
Web: www.smc.com

CEO: Alex Kim
CFO: Lane Ruoff
HR: –
FYE: December 31
Type: Subsidiary

SMC Networks serves up networking equipment with or without wires. The company makes wireless local area network (LAN) devices designed for use in homes and businesses. Its key products are modems network gateways and wireless routers. SMC also sells a line of Ethernet products including adapters and switches for small and midsized businesses. Other products include Voice-over-Internet Protocol (VoIP) network gateways and physical security system components such as wireless cameras keypads motion sensors and sensors for detecting broken glass. The company sells though resellers distributors and retailers. It has partnerships with electronics vendors including Intel Texas Instruments and Vitesse.

SMEAD MANUFACTURING COMPANY

600 Smead Blvd.
Hastings MN 55033
Phone: 651-437-4111
Fax: 800-959-9134
Web: www.smead.com

CEO: Sharon L Avent
CFO: –
HR: Sherry McCleery
FYE: April 30
Type: Private

Smead Manufacturing has kept its customers' offices organized for more than a century. The company manufactures and distributes more than 1500 paper filing products in the US that are sold in office supply stores nationwide (including Office Depot) and authorized resellers (such as Amazon.com). Smead's product assortment includes folders (hanging tabbed and expandable) labels fasteners and binder and report covers. The company also provides open and secure shelving systems. The company was founded in 1906 by Charles Smead; following his death Smead Manufacturing was purchased by P. A. Hoffman an employee whose granddaughter Sharon Hoffman Avent is president and CEO.

SMG INDIUM RESOURCES LTD

NBB: SMGI W

176 LaGuardia Ave.
Staten Island, NY 10314
Phone: 347 286-0712
Fax: –
Web: www.smg-indium.com

CEO: Ailon Z Grushkin
CFO: Mary E Paetzold
HR: –
FYE: December 31
Type: Public

SMG Indium Resources has a simple plan. The company has amassed a stockpile of indium (42.5 metric tons) in a vault and plans to sit on it for a few years and ride the appreciation all the way to the bank. The group may lease lend or sell portions (or even all) of its stockpile based on market conditions but does not have any plans to actively speculate on the short-term fluctuations in the price of the metal. Number 49 on the Periodic Table indium has a number of industrial applications and its use in the manufacture of flat panel displays has created significant demand for the metal. Indium is also used in solar energy technology. SMG Indium filed an IPO in 2011 and made its first sale in 2012.

	Annual Growth	12/10	12/11	12/12	12/13	12/14
Sales ($ mil.)	121.8%	–	–	–	9.5	21.1
Net income ($ mil.)	–	(0.1)	(4.8)	(3.9)	1.0	4.8
Market value ($ mil.)	(19.4%)	–	6.5	4.5	3.1	3.4
Employees	(15.7%)	–	5	5	5	3

SMG MANAGEMENT INC

300 Conshohocken State Rd. Ste. 770
West Conshohocken PA 19428
Phone: 610-729-7900
Fax: 610-729-1590
Web: www.smgworld.com

CEO: Wes Westley
CFO: John Burns
HR: –
FYE: December 31
Type: Private

SMG Management wants to take you out to a ball game or a concert or a convention. SMG is one of the world's largest entertainment facility management companies. The firm manages arenas stadiums performing arts centers and convention centers throughout North America and Europe as well as one in Dubai United Arab Emirates. Its services include event booking and management cash management maintenance and risk management and security. Facilities managed by SMG annually host more than 10000 events and include more than 1.5 million seats. SMG was founded in 1977 with the management of its first facility New Orleans' Louisiana Superdome which is owned by the state.

SMILE BRANDS GROUP INC.

201 E. Sandpointe Ste. 800
Santa Ana CA 92707
Phone: 714-668-1300
Fax: 714-428-1300
Web: www.smilebrands.com

CEO: Daniel M Wechsler
CFO: –
HR: –
FYE: December 31
Type: Private

Smile Brands Group is smiling all the way to the bank. The company provides dental practice management services to more than 350 dental offices across the nation through three primary brands: Bright Now! Dental Castle Dental and Monarch Dental. Its affiliated practices are typically found in high-traffic retail areas and offer general specialty and cosmetic dentistry. It also offers managed care plans through Newport Dental. The company supports its dental practices with administrative and technical services such as accounting and information technology. Investment firm Welsh Carson Anderson & Stowe controls the majority of the company.

SMITH & WESSON HOLDING CORP

NMS: SWHC

2100 Roosevelt Avenue
Springfield, MA 01104
Phone: 800 331-0852
Fax: –
Web: www.smith-wesson.com

CEO: P. James Debney
CFO: Jeffrey D Buchanan
HR: –
FYE: April 30
Type: Public

Smith & Wesson has built a successful business shooting for the stars. Operating through subsidiary Smith & Wesson Corp. Smith & Wesson Holding Corporation makes and markets pistols revolvers tactical rifles and police accessories as well as gun-safety devices under the M&P Series name. The company founded in 1852 also sells handcuffs and hunting rifles and car boat and home alarm system packages. Smith & Wesson is the exclusive importer of Walther pistols with US production rights for the Walther PPK model. To diversify and add breadth to its brand the company licenses its name to makers of apparel watches sunglasses gift sets and more.

	Annual Growth	04/11	04/12	04/13	04/14	04/15
Sales ($ mil.)	8.9%	392.3	412.0	587.5	626.6	551.9
Net income ($ mil.)	–	(82.8)	16.1	78.7	89.3	49.6
Market value ($ mil.)	42.6%	194.6	446.0	474.7	829.9	803.6
Employees	3.6%	1,520	1,346	1,475	1,758	1,749

SMITH (A.O.) CORP

NYS: AOS

11270 West Park Place
Milwaukee, WI 53224-9508
Phone: 414 359-4000
Fax: 414 359-4115
Web: www.aosmith.com

CEO: Ajita G. Rajendra
CFO: John J. Kita
HR: –
FYE: December 31
Type: Public

A.O. Smith has water on the brain. Controlled by the founding Smith family the company makes water heating equipment for residential and commercial users. Its products include home gas and electric water heaters and large-scale commercial water heating systems. Its Lochinvar subsidiary specializes in high efficiency water heaters boilers pool heaters and storage tanks. A.O. Smith sells its products in North America and China through a network of more than 1000 wholesale distributors as well as retailers such as Lowe's and Sears. A.O. Smith has operations in the U.S. Canada Mexico China India the UK and the Netherlands.

	Annual Growth	12/10	12/11	12/12	12/13	12/14
Sales ($ mil.)	12.1%	1,489.3	1,710.5	1,939.3	2,153.8	2,356.0
Net income ($ mil.)	16.8%	111.7	305.7	158.7	169.7	207.8
Market value ($ mil.)	10.3%	3,404.3	3,586.7	5,638.4	4,822.2	5,043.0
Employees	4.5%	10,400	10,600	10,900	11,400	12,400

SMITH MICRO SOFTWARE, INC.

NMS: SMSI

51 Columbia
Aliso Viejo, CA 92656
Phone: 949 362-5800
Fax: –
Web: www.smithmicro.com

CEO: William W. Smith
CFO: Steven (Ziggy) Yasbek
HR: –
FYE: December 31
Type: Public

Smith Micro Software provides wireless connectivity software designed to enhance the mobile experience for users and optimize network operations for enterprises and wireless service providers. Its primary product families include QuickLink (mobile internet connection) NetWise (data traffic management) and CommSuite (voice messaging and video). The company which operates primarily in the Americas counts wireless carriers such as Sprint and Verizon Wireless among its leading customers. In addition to wireless connectivity software Smith Micro develops productivity and graphics software for artists educators and other consumers.

	Annual Growth	12/10	12/11	12/12	12/13	12/14
Sales ($ mil.)	(27.0%)	130.5	57.8	43.3	42.7	37.0
Net income ($ mil.)	–	12.3	(159.6)	(25.5)	(28.0)	(11.8)
Market value ($ mil.)	(50.2%)	708.3	50.9	67.5	66.6	43.7
Employees	(24.0%)	549	410	337	241	183

SMITH'S FOOD & DRUG CENTERS INC.

1550 S. Redwood Rd.
Salt Lake City UT 84104
Phone: 801-974-1400
Fax: 801-974-1676
Web: www.smithsfoodanddrug.com

CEO: –
CFO: –
HR: –
FYE: January 31
Type: Subsidiary

From a small grocery store founded by Ren Smith in Brigham City Utah Smith's Food & Drug has grown into a regional powerhouse with supermarkets in Nevada New Mexico and Utah. Major markets include Las Vegas Salt Lake City and Albuquerque. Most of its 130-plus stores are conventional supermarkets with in-store pharmacy departments and many offering bakeries one-hour photo labs and other services. The regional chain also operates about a half a dozen larger Smith's Marketplace stores (154000 sq. ft. on average) in Utah that combine full-service grocery pharmacy and general merchandise departments. Smith's joined the Kroger family when Kroger the #1 US grocer bought its parent Fred Meyer in 1999.

SMITH-MIDLAND CORP.

NBB: SMID

5119 Catlett Road, P.O. Box 300
Midland, VA 22728
Phone: 540 439-3266
Fax: 540 439-1232
Web: www.smithmidland.com

CEO: Rodney I Smith
CFO: William A Kenter
HR: –
FYE: December 31
Type: Public

Smith-Midland has cemented its reputation with stone and concrete products. The company sells its patented precast concrete products to contractors and federal state and local transportation authorities in the mid-Atlantic midwestern and northeastern US. Products include lightweight concrete and steel exterior wall systems (Slenderwall) precast concrete safety and sound barriers (J-J Hooks) roadside sound barriers (Sierra Wall) portable concrete buildings and farm products primarily cattleguards and water and feed troughs. Smith-Midland licenses its products to precast concrete makers in Australia Belgium New Zealand North America and Spain.

	Annual Growth	12/10	12/11	12/12	12/13	12/14
Sales ($ mil.)	(8.3%)	31.7	26.7	24.9	27.7	22.5
Net income ($ mil.)	–	2.4	(0.4)	0.4	0.7	(0.8)
Market value ($ mil.)	5.7%	8.5	6.8	9.5	10.4	10.6
Employees	(2.6%)	173	149	155	146	156

SMOKIN JOES CIGARS LLC

2293 Saunders Settlement Rd.
Sanborn NY 14132-9336
Phone: 716-215-2000
Fax: 716-754-4184
Web: www.smokinjoes.com

CEO: –
CFO: –
HR: –
FYE: December 31
Type: Private

Nervous newlyweds headed to Niagara Falls can take a pit stop down the road at Smokin Joes Cigars. The retail outlet on the Tuscarora Indian Nation in New York started off as a place to buy low-priced tobacco and tax-free gasoline but now offers a range of other products from groceries and housewares to jewelry and apparel items including casual clothing from major labels (such as Burton and Calvin Klein) Western wear footwear and accessories. In addition to selling name-brand tobacco products Smokin Joes manufactures its own line of cigars cigarettes and pipe tobacco at a factory on the Tuscarora Indian Reservation. It also sells products online.

SMTC CORP.

NMS: SMTX

2302 Trade Zone Boulevard
San Jose, CA 95131
Phone: 408 347-100
Fax: –
Web: www.smtc.com

CEO: Sushil Dhiman
CFO: Jim Currie
HR: –
FYE: December 28
Type: Public

SMTC stays ahead by working behind the scenes. The company provides contract electronics manufacturing services such as surface-mount and through-hole circuit board assembly product design and prototyping testing inspection packaging and supply chain management. Manufacturers use products built or assembled by SMTC in their manufacturing and test equipment computer servers and communications gear. The company also makes enclosures for electronic systems as well as power and telecom cable interconnection assemblies. Leading customers have included Harris Ingenico and MEI. Customers in North America account for more than 85% of sales.

	Annual Growth	01/11	01/12*	12/12	12/13	12/14
Sales ($ mil.)	(4.5%)	262.6	220.4	296.3	270.7	228.6
Net income ($ mil.)	–	12.4	1.2	7.5	(11.9)	(3.9)
Market value ($ mil.)	(18.0%)	52.5	46.3	39.2	38.4	28.9
Employees	(3.0%)	1,500	1,875	2,300	1,800	1,370

*Fiscal year change

SMUCKER (J.M.) CO.

NYS: SJM

One Strawberry Lane
Orrville, OH 44667-0280
Phone: 330 682-3000
Fax: –
Web: www.jmsmucker.com

CEO: Richard K. Smucker
CFO: Mark R. Belgya
HR: –
FYE: April 30
Type: Public

The J. M. Smucker Company gets its bread and butter from more than just making and marketing jelly. The company known for manufacturing its namesake Smucker's fruit spread and for selling the Jif peanut butter brand has expanded its product portfolio to include Folgers the #1-coffee brand in the US as well as market leaders in espresso (Café Bustelo) and premium java (Dunkin' Donuts licensed). Other top-shelf lines are Hungry Jack and Pillsbury baking mixes and frostings Eagle canned milk and Crisco shortening and oils among others. Smucker's brands are sold to consumers through retail outlets in the US and Canada with some products exported.

	Annual Growth	04/11	04/12	04/13	04/14	04/15
Sales ($ mil.)	4.2%	4,825.7	5,525.8	5,897.7	5,610.6	5,692.7
Net income ($ mil.)	(7.9%)	479.5	459.7	544.2	565.2	344.9
Market value ($ mil.)	11.5%	8,976.7	9,521.9	12,344.0	11,560.7	13,861.4
Employees	13.1%	4,500	4,850	4,875	4,775	7,370

SNAP-ON, INC.

NYS: SNA

2801 80th Street
Kenosha, WI 53143
Phone: 262 656-5200
Fax: 262 656-5577
Web: www.snapon.com

CEO: Nicholas T. Pinchuk
CFO: Aldo J. Pagliari
HR: Jim McKibbin
FYE: January 02
Type: Public

Snap-on understands the mechanics of the automotive repair business. The company is a leading manufacturer and distributor of high-quality hand tools as well as auto diagnostic equipment and "under-car" shop implements such as hydraulic lifts and tire changers. Snap-on has built a business serving mechanics car makers and government and industrial organizations. Other products — with brand names such as Snap-on Blackhawk Lindström ShopKey and Sun — include collision repair equipment management software roll cabinets tool chests wheel balancers and wrenches. Founded in 1920 Snap-on originated the mobile-van tool distribution channel in the automotive repair market.

	Annual Growth	12/11	12/12	12/13*	01/15	01/16
Sales ($ mil.)	3.7%	2,996.5	3,099.2	3,237.5	3,492.6	3,593.1
Net income ($ mil.)	11.6%	276.3	306.1	350.3	421.9	478.7
Market value ($ mil.)	27.6%	2,940.3	4,492.4	6,289.0	7,916.5	9,957.7
Employees	0.0%	11,500	11,200	11,300	11,400	11,500
						*Fiscal year change

SNAPPING SHOALS ELECTRIC TRUST INC.

14750 BROWN BRIDGE RD
COVINGTON, GA 300164113
Phone: 770-786-3484
Fax: –
Web: www.co.henry.ga.us

CEO: Bradley Kent Thomas
CFO: Carl Smith
HR: Claire Chapman
FYE: December 31
Type: Private

Named after a geographic area that sounds like an angler's dream Snapping Shoals Electric Membership Corporation (Snapping Shoals EMC) distributes electricity to 95000 residential commercial and industrial customers in an 8-county region in the southeastern portion of the Atlanta metropolitan area. The member-owned cooperative also provides competitive retail natural gas supply services to customers through Snapping Shoals Energy Management Company a partnership with SCANA. Snapping Shoals EMC also offers security systems surge protection services and security lighting options.

	Annual Growth	12/08	12/09	12/10	12/11	12/12
Sales ($ mil.)	(1.8%)	–	179.3	186.3	176.5	170.0
Net income ($ mil.)	(31.3%)	–	–	4.4	2.8	2.1
Market value ($ mil.)	–	–	–	–	–	–
Employees	–	–	–	–	–	270

SNELL & WILMER L.L.P.

One Arizona Center 400 E. Van Buren St.
Phoenix AZ 85004-2202
Phone: 602-382-6000
Fax: 602-382-6070
Web: www.swlaw.com

CEO: –
CFO: David Boden
HR: –
FYE: December 31
Type: Private - Partnershi

Snell & Wilmer employs some 420 attorneys and is one of the largest full-service law firms in the western US. Its legal expertise covers such practice areas as antitrust and trade regulation bankruptcy health care litigation immigration and employment law. Snell & Wilmer also offers practices that are important to the region it serves such as gaming water law and American Indian law. Clients have included such notable names as Bank of America Ford Motor Company General Motors and Prudential. The firm was founded in Phoenix in 1938 and has grown to nine offices in about half a dozen US states and Mexico.

SNYDER'S-LANCE INC.

NMS: LNCE

13515 Ballantyne Corporate Place
Charlotte, NC 28277
Phone: 704 554-1421
Fax: –
Web: www.snyderslance.com

CEO: Carl E. Lee
CFO: Richard D. (Rick) Puckett
HR: Emily Berwager
FYE: January 03
Type: Public

If you're familiar with the munchies named Toastchee Nipchee and Captain's Wafers Snyder's-Lance (formerly Lance) has undoubtedly helped you satisfy a snack attack. The company produces single-serve multi-pack and family-sized packages of bakery products and sweet and savory snack foods including cookies crackers nuts potato chips and pretzels. Its snacks are sold under the Lance Cape Cod Tom's Archway and Snyder's brands at food retailers mass merchants and convenience and club stores in the US. The company also makes private-label and branded snacks for food makers. The company is buying fellow snack maker Diamond Foods.

	Annual Growth	01/11*	12/11	12/12	12/13*	01/15
Sales ($ mil.)	13.4%	979.8	1,635.0	1,618.6	1,761.0	1,620.9
Net income ($ mil.)	195.9%	2.5	38.3	59.1	78.7	192.6
Market value ($ mil.)	6.3%	1,650.3	1,584.1	1,667.2	2,031.2	2,110.1
Employees	(8.1%)	7,000	6,100	5,900	5,700	5,000
						*Fiscal year change

SOA SOFTWARE INC.

12100 Wilshire Blvd. Ste. 1800
Los Angeles CA 90025
Phone: 310-826-1317
Fax: 310-820-8601
Web: www.soa.com

CEO: Paul Gigg
CFO: Janine Bushman
HR: –
FYE: December 31
Type: Private

SOA Software provides software used to deploy and manage secure Web-based applications. It also provides a number of services including custom software development strategic planning and systems implementation. The "SOA" in the corporate moniker comes from service-oriented architecture a standardized way of offering Web services which tie together the applications of customers suppliers and other collaborators using the XML programming language. Customers have included Hewlett-Packard JetBlue Mercury Insurance Staples and Verizon. The company was established in 1998.

SOCIETY OF MANUFACTURING ENGINEERS

1 SME DR	CEO: Jeffrey M. Krause
DEARBORN, MI 481282408	CFO: –
Phone: 313-425-3000	HR: –
Fax: –	FYE: December 31
Web: www.sme.org	Type: Private

The Society of Manufacturing Engineer (SME) has members in more than 70 countries. The society provides manufacturing engineers and executives with ongoing information on new and improved technologies as well as professional-development resources. It also organizes expositions and other industry-related events and publishes the monthly magazine Manufacturing Engineering along with a number of peer-reviewed journals and research publications. SME was founded by 33 original members in 1932 as The Society of Tool Engineers. It adopted its current name in 1969. Along with its headquarters in Dearborn Michigan SME also has an office in Toronto.

	Annual Growth	12/00	12/01	12/09	12/10	12/13
Sales ($ mil.)	(25.9%)	–	1,994.3	0.4	26.9	55.1
Net income ($ mil.)	–	–	–	(0.2)	1.8	3.2
Market value ($ mil.)	–	–	–	–	–	–
Employees	–	–	–	–	–	200

SOCKET MOBILE, INC.

NBB: SCKT

39700 Eureka Drive	CEO: Kevin J Mills
Newark, CA 94560	CFO: David W Dunlap
Phone: 510 933-3000	HR: –
Fax: –	FYE: December 31
Web: www.socketmobile.com	Type: Public

Socket Mobile plugs expansion devices. The company provides PC and CompactFlash cards for handheld and notebook computers. Its products include peripheral connection and Ethernet cards. It also offers handheld computers bar code scanners and scanner cards and cards for digital phones as well as embedded products including Bluetooth modules and interface chips. Socket Mobile's largest sales segment mobile peripheral products accounts for about half of its revenues. The segment encompasses bar code scanners data collection plug-in cards and serial interface products.The company sells worldwide through original equipment manufacturers (OEMs) resellers and distributors including Ingram Micro and Tech Data.

	Annual Growth	12/10	12/11	12/12	12/13	12/14
Sales ($ mil.)	6.0%	13.5	17.5	13.6	15.7	17.0
Net income ($ mil.)	–	(4.0)	(2.4)	(3.3)	(0.6)	0.4
Market value ($ mil.)	4.3%	10.8	10.1	5.9	4.1	12.8
Employees	(6.0%)	64	66	50	48	50

SODEXO REMOTE SITES PARTNERSHIP

5749 Susitna Dr.	CEO: –
Harahan LA 70123	CFO: –
Phone: 504-733-5761	HR: –
Fax: 504-733-2017	FYE: August 31
Web: www.sodexousa.com	Type: Subsidiary

Start building it and they will come — to feed you. Sodexo Remote Sites (formerly Universal Sodexho) provides foodservices and catering for employees working at remote locations such as construction sites mining operations and off-shore oil rigs. It also offers facilities maintenance services including janitorial and grounds-keeping services procurement and logistics and vehicle maintenance. In addition the company serves some military bases primarily those in Korea. Sodexo Remote Sites is a unit of Paris-based contract foodservices provider Sodexo.

SOFT COMPUTER CONSULTANTS INC.

5400 TECH DATA DR	CEO: Gilbert Hakim
CLEARWATER, FL 337603116	CFO: –
Phone: 727-789-0100	HR: –
Fax: –	FYE: August 31
Web: www.softcomputer.com	Type: Private

Soft Computer Consultants makes sure medical labs don't have a hard time managing their information. The company (which does business as SCC Soft Computer) develops laboratory information systems (LIS) and clinical information systems for medical laboratories radiology departments genetics laboratories pharmacies and blood banks. Its software links labs to other departments in order to enable quick distribution of data and test results. The company also offers clinical accounts receivable and billing software for finance departments and consulting services to help customers improve their workflow processes. SCC was founded in 1979 by the Hakim brothers Gilbert (CEO) and Jean (President).

	Annual Growth	08/06	08/07	08/08	08/09	08/10
Sales ($ mil.)	–	–	–	(1,521.7)	97.7	107.8
Net income ($ mil.)	3678.0%	–	–	0.0	13.7	23.4
Market value ($ mil.)	–	–	–	–	–	–
Employees	–	–	–	–	–	900

SOFTECH, INC

NBB: SOFT

650 Suffolk Street, Suite 415	CEO: Joseph P Mullaney
Lowell, MA 01854	CFO: Amy E McGuire
Phone: 978 513-2700	HR: –
Fax: 978 458-4096	FYE: May 31
Web: www.softech.com	Type: Public

SofTech has designs on product manufacturers with its product lifecycle management (PLM) products. SofTech's ProductCenter suite allows users to consolidate product information automate processes such as review cycles and change orders facilitate collaboration and ensure regulatory compliance. The company also provides consulting maintenance and training services. Clients include GE Honeywell Sikorsky Aircraft Siemens and the US Army.

	Annual Growth	05/11	05/12	05/13	05/14	05/15
Sales ($ mil.)	(13.0%)	6.9	6.4	6.4	5.0	3.9
Net income ($ mil.)	–	(0.2)	0.4	0.4	(0.7)	(1.3)
Market value ($ mil.)	86.1%	0.1	1.4	1.9	1.8	1.2
Employees	(9.9%)	41	41	40	31	27

SOFTSHEEN/CARSON PRODUCTS

575 5th Ave. 19th Fl.	CEO: –
New York NY 10017	CFO: –
Phone: 212-818-1500	HR: Robert Keller
Fax: 212-984-4999	FYE: December 31
Web: www.softsheen-carson.com	Type: Business Segment

SoftSheen/Carson Products is keeping the shine on its ethnic beauty. The company is one of the world's leading makers of ethnic hair care and beauty products including shampoos conditioners gels hair straighteners relaxers shaving products. Its brands include Let's Jam Baby Love Optimum Care Dark and Lovely Magic Shave and Weave Care. Founded in 1964 by Edward and Bettiann Gardner SoftSheen was the largest African-American-owned beauty products company in the country until its acquisition in 1998 by L'Oreal USA a division of French cosmetics giant L'Oreal. Carson was a subsidiary of L'Oreal USA before being merged with SoftSheen in 2000.

SOFTWARE & INFORMATION INDUSTRY ASSOCIATION

1090 Vermont Ave. NW
Washington DC 20005-4095
Phone: 202-289-7442
Fax: 202-289-7097
Web: www.siia.net

CEO: –
CFO: –
HR: –
FYE: June 30
Type: Private - Associatio

The SIIA keeps tabs on Congressional representatives and pirates alike. The Software & Information Industry Association (SIIA) is an international trade organization for the software and digital content industries. Its more than 500 corporate members include Bank of America Bloomberg Dow Jones and Sun Microsystems. SIIA offers market research access to industry information lobbying awards and conferences. It also investigates and prosecutes companies accused of using software or content illegally. SIIA was formed in 1999 by the merger of the Software Publishers Association and the Information Industry Association. The Specialized Information Publishers Association is becoming a division of SIIA.

SOLAR TURBINES INCORPORATED

2200 Pacific Hwy.
San Diego CA 92186
Phone: 619-544-5000
Fax: 619-544-5825
Web: esolar.cat.com

CEO: –
CFO: C K Scott-Stanfel
HR: Bridget Denihan
FYE: December 31
Type: Subsidiary

In spite of its name products from Solar Turbines are not powered by the sun. The Caterpillar subsidiary designs manufactures and services industrial gas turbines. Its products are used in oil and gas production natural gas transmission and crude oil pumping systems as well as for electrical and thermal power generation. In addition to gas turbine engines gas compressors and gas turbine-powered compressor sets Solar Turbines offers mechanical-drive packages and generator sets. Services include financing installation and aftermarket parts support. The company which sells and services its products from some 30 locations worldwide exports 75% of its products from the US.

SOLARCITY CORP

NMS: SCTY

3055 Clearview Way
San Mateo, CA 94402
Phone: 650 638-1028
Fax: –
Web: www.solarcity.com

CEO: Lyndon R. Rive
CFO: Tanguy Serra
HR: Raj Nanda
FYE: December 31
Type: Public

Ready to get off the grid? SolarCity can help. The company sells installs finances and monitors turnkey solar energy systems that convert sunlight into electricity. Its systems either mounted on a building's roof or the ground are used by residential commercial and government customers such as eBay Intel Wal-Mart and Homeland Security. SolarCity doesn't manufacture its systems but uses solar panels from Trina Solar Yingli Green Energy and Kyocera Solar and inverters from Power-One SMA Solar Technology and Schneider Electric. It is a licensed contractor in more than a dozen states including Arizona California and Texas.

	Annual Growth	12/11	12/12	12/13	12/14	12/15
Sales ($ mil.)	60.9%	59.6	128.7	163.8	255.0	399.6
Net income ($ mil.)	–	43.5	(64.2)	(55.8)	(56.0)	(58.3)
Market value ($ mil.)	62.3%	–	1,167.5	5,560.6	5,233.8	4,993.0
Employees	60.5%	2,300	2,510	4,312	9,051	15,273

SOLARWINDS INC

NYS: SWI

7171 Southwest Parkway, Building 400
Austin, TX 78735
Phone: 512 682-9300
Fax: –
Web: www.solarwinds.com

CEO: Kevin B Thompson
CFO: Jason Ream
HR: –
FYE: December 31
Type: Public

SolarWinds helps IT professionals improve IT infrastructure management without burning holes in their wallets. The company provides fault and performance management configuration management and compliance and troubleshooting applications. Designed to work on single devices or networks with as many as 100000 machines its downloadable software can be installed and configured without professional implementation services. The company's customers range from small businesses to large enterprises and government agencies. Its clients have included Booz Allen Hamilton FedEx Lockheed Martin Microsoft Chevron and NASA. SolarWinds gets 70% of sales from customers in the US.

	Annual Growth	12/09	12/10	12/11	12/12	12/13
Sales ($ mil.)	30.3%	116.4	152.4	198.4	269.0	335.4
Net income ($ mil.)	32.1%	29.5	44.7	62.4	81.3	89.8
Market value ($ mil.)	13.2%	1,726.0	1,443.9	2,096.5	3,934.3	2,837.6
Employees	38.7%	354	458	628	865	1,312

SOLAZYME INC.

NMS: SZYM

225 Gateway Boulevard
South San Francisco, CA 94080
Phone: 650 780-4777
Fax: –
Web: www.solazyme.com

CEO: Jonathan S. Wolfson
CFO: Tyler W. Painter
HR: –
FYE: December 31
Type: Public

We make oil may seem like a strange statement but in the case of Solazyme it's true. The company manufactures a variety of oils by feeding plant sugars to microalgae. Its "tailored oils" can be created to replace fuel and chemical edible or personal skin care oil traditionally derived from petroleum or animal fats. The microbial-based oils work with existing production refining and distribution infrastructure systems. Solazyme feeds its microalgae sugarcane corn and biomass-derived sugars; its oils cost half to a third as much to produce as traditional oils. The company also sells protein fiber and other system by-products.

	Annual Growth	12/10	12/11	12/12	12/13	12/14
Sales ($ mil.)	12.3%	38.0	39.0	44.1	39.8	60.4
Net income ($ mil.)	–	(16.3)	(53.9)	(83.1)	(116.4)	(162.1)
Market value ($ mil.)	(39.9%)	–	944.7	624.0	864.5	204.8
Employees	23.1%	116	168	229	271	266

SOLE TECHNOLOGY INC.

20161 Windrow Dr.
Lake Forest CA 92630
Phone: 949-460-2020
Fax: 949-460-2010
Web: www.soletechnology.com

CEO: Pierre Senizergues
CFO: –
HR: –
FYE: December 31
Type: Private

Sole Technology aims to put soul into its sportswear. The company makes and markets action sport footwear and gear including apparel backpacks hats wallets and other accessories for men and women. Its brands include etnies etnies Plus eS Altamont Emerica and ThirtyTwo. Etnies is not only eco-friendly the brand is working to become completely carbon neutral by 2020. Targeting skateboarders and BMXers Sole Technology distributes its products through specialty retailers in the US and internationally in 70-plus countries. The company operates a large distribution facility in California and a New York City showroom. Formed in 1996 Sole Technology is owned by founder and CEO Pierre Senizergues.

SOLERA CAPITAL LLC

625 Madison Ave. 3rd Fl.
New York NY 10022
Phone: 212-833-1440
Fax: 212-833-1460
Web: www.soleracapital.com

CEO: –
CFO: –
HR: –
FYE: December 31
Type: Private

Solera Capital is a private equity investment firm that typically invests between $10 million and $40 million in its target companies. Its portfolio includes natural and organic food company Annie's consumer health care provider The Little Clinic and publisher Latina Media Ventures. Solera Capital was founded in 1999 with an all-female staff led by CEO Molly Ashby. The firm emphsizes its diversity with 14 of its 17 professionals being women from backgrounds as diverse as Singapore and Ethiopia.

SOLERA HOLDINGS INC

NYS: SLH

1301 Solana Blvd. Building #2, Suite 2100
Westlake, TX 76262
Phone: 817 961-2100
Fax: –
Web: www.solerainc.com

CEO: Tony Aquila
CFO: Renato Giger
HR: –
FYE: June 30
Type: Public

The next time you report a fender bender your adjuster might be using technology from Solera to process the claim. Solera Holdings develops software for the auto insurance industry. Its Audatex software automates such processes as auditing claims management and damage estimation. Solera serves insurance companies worldwide; other customers include auto repair shops and independent assessors. Its Hollander subsidiary provides the Hollander Interchange parts catalog in print or electronic form to car recyclers as an inventory management supplement. In Brazil and Mexico it operates an online marketplace for salvage vehicle sales. Vista Equity Partners acquired Solera in 2015.

	Annual Growth	06/11	06/12	06/13	06/14	06/15
Sales ($ mil.)	13.6%	684.7	790.2	838.1	987.3	1,140.8
Net income ($ mil.)	–	157.4	107.0	93.9	(8.7)	(100.8)
Market value ($ mil.)	(6.8%)	3,962.8	2,799.3	3,727.7	4,498.0	2,984.9
Employees	24.7%	2,247	2,483	2,767	3,638	5,442

SOLIGENIX INC

OTC: SNGX

29 Emmons Drive, Suite C-10
Princeton, NJ 08540
Phone: 609 538-8200
Fax: 609 452-6467
Web: www.soligenix.com

CEO: –
CFO: Joseph (Jo) Warusz
HR: –
FYE: December 31
Type: Public

Soligenix (formerly DOR BioPharma) is opening the door to more effective biodefense. The company's BioDefense unit is focusing on the development of nasally administered vaccines for such bioterror threats as ricin and botulinum toxins. Ricin vaccine candidate RiVax is in early-stage clinical trials. Through its BioTherapeutics division Soligenix is developing lead candidate orBec an orally administered drug using the same active ingredient as GlaxoSmithKline's allergy and asthma drug Beconase; orBec is a potential therapy for intestinal graft-versus-host disease a life-threatening complication of bone marrow transplantation.

	Annual Growth	12/10	12/11	12/12	12/13	12/14
Sales ($ mil.)	37.9%	1.9	7.7	3.1	3.2	7.0
Net income ($ mil.)	–	(7.4)	(2.4)	(4.2)	(10.1)	(6.7)
Market value ($ mil.)	51.0%	4.5	0.7	14.4	43.1	23.4
Employees	3.2%	15	13	10	17	17

SOLITARIO EXPLORATION & ROYALTY CORP

ASE: XPL

4251 Kipling St., Suite 390
Wheat Ridge, CO 80033
Phone: 303 534-1030
Fax: –
Web: www.solitarioresources.com

CEO: Christopher E Herald
CFO: James R Maronick
HR: –
FYE: December 31
Type: Public

Solitude can be a precious resource but Solitario Exploration & Royalty is more interested in finding precious minerals. The company explores and develops gold silver platinum and zinc properties in Brazil Mexico and Peru. Solitario has formed alliances to help finance its exploration work with industry giants like Newmont Mining and Anglo Platinum. None of its properties are in development. The company changed its name from Solitario Resources in 2008. The following year it agreed to buy Metallic Ventures Gold which has properties in Nevada. Not long after International Minerals came in with its own offer for Metallic Ventures.

	Annual Growth	12/10	12/11	12/12	12/13	12/14
Sales ($ mil.)	0.0%	0.2	0.2	0.3	0.3	0.2
Net income ($ mil.)	–	(4.1)	(3.4)	(3.3)	(2.1)	(1.8)
Market value ($ mil.)	(29.1%)	142.5	56.1	65.9	33.4	36.1
Employees	(32.0%)	28	28	18	7	6

SOLITRON DEVICES, INC.

NBB: SODI

3301 Electronics Way
West Palm Beach, FL 33407
Phone: 561 848-4311
Fax: 561 863-5946
Web: www.solitrondevices.com

CEO: Shevach Saraf
CFO: Shevach Saraf
HR: –
FYE: February 28
Type: Public

Solitron Devices' tiny devices have taken some big trips — to Jupiter on the Galileo spacecraft and to Mars on the Sojourner. Used primarily in military and aerospace applications the company's solid-state semiconductor components include thin-film resistors field-effect and power transistors and hybrid circuits. Nearly all of Solitron's sales come from US government contractors including Raytheon (about 39% of sales) and Lockheed Martin. The US government itself accounts for 10% of sales. Solitron has faced ongoing financial challenges (plus attention from the EPA in relation to some of the company's former manufacturing sites) since it emerged from Chapter 11 bankruptcy in 1996.

	Annual Growth	02/11	02/12	02/13	02/14	02/15
Sales ($ mil.)	2.2%	8.9	8.3	8.4	8.7	9.8
Net income ($ mil.)	(7.4%)	1.3	0.7	0.8	0.9	0.9
Market value ($ mil.)	7.3%	7.1	6.9	8.2	8.9	9.4
Employees	(1.5%)	85	84	84	82	80

SOLO CUP COMPANY

150 S. Saunders Rd. Ste. 150
Lake Forest IL 60045
Phone: 847-444-5000
Fax: 847-236-6049
Web: www.solocup.com

CEO: Robert M Korzenski
CFO: Robert D Koney Jr
HR: –
FYE: December 31
Type: Private

Solo Cup is not just the maker of the iconic red solo cup it's a major player in the disposable consumer products industry. The company makes single-use cups plates cutlery take-out containers and other similar products under the Solo Sweetheart Creative Carryouts and Bare brand names. Solo's plastic paper and foam items are sold through retailers and foodservice distributors around the world. In addition Solo makes specialty party supplies upscale disposable products and plastic and paper packaging for manufacturers of snack foods and dairy products. In mid-2012 Solo was acquired by rival Dart Container in a deal valued at $1 billion.

SOLSTAS LAB PARTNERS LLC

4380 Federal Dr. Ste. 100
Greensboro NC 27410
Phone: 336-664-6100
Fax: 336-852-0003
Web: www.solstas.com

CEO: David C Weavil
CFO: –
HR: –
FYE: December 31
Type: Private

Solstas Lab Partners will be your lab partner through the longest day or night. The company provides an array of routine and esoteric clinical laboratory testing services to High Point Regional Health System Moses Cone Health System Carilion Clinic and Wellmont Health System as well as doctors home health agencies clinics and hospitals in more than half a dozen states in the eastern US. Solstas Lab Partners provides online ordering and result retrieval services and courier services for blood and urine sample collection. Investment firm Welsh Carson Anderson & Stowe owns a majority stake in Solstas Lab Partners.

SOLUTIA INC.

NYSE: SOA

575 Maryville Centre Dr.
St. Louis MO 63141
Phone: 314-674-1000
Fax: 314-674-1585
Web: www.solutia.com

CEO: Jeffry N Quinn
CFO: James M Sullivan
HR: –
FYE: December 31
Type: Public

Solutia looks to provide industrial solutions by manufacturing plastics films and chemicals for the construction automotive and rubber manufacturing industries. The company operates through three segments. Its Technical Specialties unit manufactures specialty chemicals for rubber and transmission fluids customers through its Flexsys Terminol and Skydrol businesses. Its Advanced Interlayers unit produces polyvinyl butyral (PVB) sheet which is used in the manufacture of glass. Performance Films makes various plastic films for use in glass tapes and packaging products. Solutia has operations in 50 locations worldwide. In 2012 the company was acquired by Eastman Chemical in a $4.7 billion deal.

SOMERSET MEDICAL CENTER

110 REHILL AVE
SOMERVILLE, NJ 08876-2598
Phone: 908-685-2200
Fax: –
Web: www.smcfoundation.com

CEO: –
CFO: –
HR: –
FYE: December 31
Type: Private

Serving central New Jersey Somerset Medical Center provides a variety of health care services including cancer care women's health cardiology and surgical and rehabilitative services. Founded in 1899 the hospital has 355 beds as well as a medical and dental staff of approximately 650 members. The medical center is affiliated with the University of Medicine and Dentistry of New Jersey - Robert Wood Johnson Medical School campus. It also provides clinical research services in affiliation with The Cancer Institute of New Jersey. Somerset Medical Center agreed to merge with Robert Wood Johnson University Hospital in 2013.

	Annual Growth	12/07	12/08	12/08	12/11	12/12
Sales ($ mil.)	0.5%	–	240.3	260.5	260.4	245.3
Net income ($ mil.)	–	–	1.0	(1.2)	(4.5)	(1.3)
Market value ($ mil.)	–	–	–	–	–	–
Employees	–	–	–	–	–	1,743

SOMERSET TIRE SERVICE INC.

1 STS DR BLDG STE 1
BRIDGEWATER, NJ 08807
Phone: 732-356-8500
Fax: –
Web: www.ststire.com

CEO: William Caulin
CFO: Anthony Losardo
HR: –
FYE: December 31
Type: Private

Somerset Tire Service (STS) operates about 145 tire and auto centers throughout New Jersey New York and Pennsylvania. The company primarily sells tires auto parts batteries and accessories under such top brand names as Bridgestone Firestone Michelin Toyo Pirelli Goodyear Yokohama and Continental. Operating under the banner STS Tire & Auto Centers the company's locations feature a window between the store and service bays so customers can watch the work being done on their cars. STS has grown by acquiring other regional tire and service centers with hopes of saturating the Northeast before moving outside its home region. Founded in 1958 the company is employee-owned.

	Annual Growth	12/09	12/10	12/11	12/12	12/13
Sales ($ mil.)	4.4%	–	189.2	201.4	203.6	214.9
Net income ($ mil.)	6.8%	–	–	8.7	7.7	9.9
Market value ($ mil.)	–	–	–	–	–	–
Employees	–	–	–	–	–	800

SONEPAR MANAGEMENT US INC.

510 Walnut St. Ste. 400
Philadelphia PA 19106
Phone: 215-399-5900
Fax: 215-399-5950
Web: www.sonepar-us.com

CEO: –
CFO: Kathleen Rusko
HR: –
FYE: December 31
Type: Subsidiary

Sonepar Management US operating as Sonepar USA is a subsidiary of French distribution giant Sonepar. The US company distributes electrical products and industrial supplies ranging from power cables and light fixtures to security systems and switchgear. Sonepar USA manages a network of a dozen-plus regional distributors across the US and the Caribbean with individual firms varying in size — many with vast networks of their own. For example Hagemeyer North America operates some 500 branches throughout the US and in Canada and Mexico. On the other hand Cooper Electric Supply serves New Jersey New York and Pennsylvania through 25 locations and Brook Electric Distribution has three offices in northern Illinois.

SONESTA INTERNATIONAL HOTELS CORPORATION

NASDAQ: SNSTA

116 Huntington Ave.
Boston MA 02116
Phone: 617-421-5400
Fax: 617-421-5402
Web: www.sonesta.com

CEO: Carlos Flores
CFO: –
HR: –
FYE: December 31
Type: Public

Siesta whenever you want at Sonesta International Hotels. The company operates several hotels in the US (Boston Miami New Orleans and Orlando) and Egypt while its name is licensed to additional hotels in Chile Columbia Egypt St. Maarten Brazil and Peru. The nearly 30 luxury properties cater to upscale business and leisure travelers and are designed to showcase the history and culture of their locales. Sonesta also operates six cruise ships on the Nile. The firm was founded by "Sonny" Sonnabend in the 1940s. Members of the Sonnabend family (including executive chairman Peter and CEO Stephanie) continue to run the business. "Sonesta" is a combination of the names of Sonny and his wife Esther.

SONIC AUTOMOTIVE, INC.

NYS: SAH

4401 Colwick Road
Charlotte, NC 28211
Phone: 704 566-2400
Fax: 704 536-5116
Web: www.sonicautomotive.com

CEO: B. Scott Smith
CFO: Heath R. Byrd
HR: –
FYE: December 31
Type: Public

No stranger to speed O. Bruton Smith has raced Sonic Automotive to the front of the pack of US auto dealers behind larger rivals such as AutoNation and Penske Automotive. Founded with five dealerships in 1997 Sonic today owns more than 120 new- and used-vehicle dealerships and about 20 collision repair centers in major markets in more than a dozen states including Texas the Carolinas Alabama and Tennessee. The company sells some 25 brands of cars and light trucks and offers vehicle financing. Chairman Smith who runs Sonic Automotive with his son Scott is also the majority owner of Speedway Motorsports which operates more than half a dozen NASCAR auto racetracks.

	Annual Growth	12/10	12/11	12/12	12/13	12/14
Sales ($ mil.)	7.5%	6,880.8	7,871.3	8,365.5	8,843.2	9,197.1
Net income ($ mil.)	2.0%	89.9	76.3	89.1	81.6	97.2
Market value ($ mil.)	19.5%	674.2	754.1	1,063.7	1,246.5	1,376.9
Employees	0.3%	9,200	9,200	9,300	9,100	9,300

SONIC CORP.

NMS: SONC

300 Johnny Bench Drive
Oklahoma City, OK 73104
Phone: 405 225-5000
Fax: –
Web: www.sonicdrivein.com

CEO: J. Clifford (Cliff) Hudson
CFO: Claudia S. San Pedro
HR: –
FYE: August 31
Type: Public

Keeping the drive-in burger joint alive sounds like a good idea to this company. Sonic Corp. operates the largest chain of quick-service drive-ins in the US with more than 3500 locations throughout the country. The chain has a significant presence in the South namely in Texas. The eateries offer a menu of hamburgers hot dogs (Coneys) onion rings tater tots and breakfast items along with specialty drinks such as cherry limeade and frozen desserts. Most locations offer drive-thru service with skating carhops and some have indoor seating. The company operates and has a majority interest in about 410 of the restaurants while the rest are operated by franchisees.

	Annual Growth	08/11	08/12	08/13	08/14	08/15
Sales ($ mil.)	2.6%	546.0	543.7	542.6	552.3	606.1
Net income ($ mil.)	35.3%	19.2	36.1	36.7	47.9	64.5
Market value ($ mil.)	30.6%	473.3	478.4	814.9	1,077.9	1,378.6
Employees	142.1%	316	314	333	10,743	10,863

SONIC FOUNDRY, INC.

NAS: SOFO

222 W. Washington Ave
Madison, WI 53703
Phone: 608 443-1600
Fax: –
Web: www.sonicfoundry.com

CEO: Gary R Weis
CFO: Kenneth A Minor
HR: –
FYE: September 30
Type: Public

It's about more than just sound at Sonic Foundry. The company's Mediasite recorders and software enable educational institutions (more than half of sales) corporations and government agencies to capture stream and archive online multimedia presentations. Its products are used for corporate meetings media analysis distance learning and content publishing. Sonic Foundry also provides webcasting services and it offers managed communications services — including content hosting and delivery. It markets through resellers its own sales team and system integrator partnerships. The company's customers have included Thermo Fisher Scientific BAE Systems and Georgetown University.

	Annual Growth	09/11	09/12	09/13	09/14	09/15
Sales ($ mil.)	9.6%	25.2	26.1	27.8	35.8	36.5
Net income ($ mil.)	–	(0.2)	0.2	(0.8)	(2.8)	(4.5)
Market value ($ mil.)	(0.8%)	37.9	34.9	40.2	41.3	36.7
Employees	21.1%	94	109	116	183	202

SONICS & MATERIALS INC.

CEO: Robert Soloff

53 Church Hill Rd.
Newtown CT 06470
Phone: 203-270-4600
Fax: 203-270-4610
Web: www.sonicsandmaterials.com

CEO: Robert Soloff
CFO: –
HR: –
FYE: June 30
Type: Private

Acoustic sounds abound — and they're not all coming from MTV's Unplugged. Sonics & Materials makes standard and customized equipment that uses sound to bond thermoplastic components textiles and other synthetic materials. The ultrasonic process creates clean welding of metal and materials that are difficult to bond by other means; it also offers liquid processing (dispersing blending cleaning) and food cutting. The company serves a broad range of customers including appliance automotive chemical consumer products industrial medical packaging synthetic textile and toy manufacturers. President and CEO Robert Soloff founded Sonics & Materials in 1969; the company was delisted in 2002.

SONICWALL INC.

2001 Logic Dr.
San Jose CA 95124-3452
Phone: 408-745-9600
Fax: 408-745-9300
Web: www.sonicwall.com

CEO: Matt Medeiros
CFO: Robert D Selvi
HR: –
FYE: December 31
Type: Subsidiary

SonicWALL offers more substantial safeguards than sound barriers. The company provides network security devices and software designed to protect digital communications between headquarters and branch offices secure broadband Internet access and filter content. Other products include data backup devices and related software. SonicWALL also offers services such as content filtering and intrusion prevention on a subscription basis. The company sells largely through distributors including Tech Data Arrow and Ingram Micro. End-users include retailers restaurants and public schools among others. SonicWALL was acquired by PC maker Dell in 2012.

SONO-TEK CORP.

NBB: SOTK

2012 Route 9W
Milton, NY 12547
Phone: 845 795-2020
Fax: –
Web: www.sono-tek.com

CEO: Christopher L Coccio
CFO: Stephen J Bagley
HR: –
FYE: February 28
Type: Public

Sono-Tek wants to spray it not say it. The company makes ultrasonic liquid atomizing nozzles that can apply fluids such as flux (used with solder on electronic circuit boards) molten metals and polymeric coatings. Its SonoFlux 2000F spray fluxer product is designed for high-volume operations. SonoFlux XL applies solder flux to electronic printed circuit boards that vary from two inches up to 24 inches in width. Sono-Tek's MediCoat product is used for stent coating applying thin layers of expensive polymer and drug coating to arterial stents.

	Annual Growth	02/11	02/12	02/13	02/14	02/15
Sales ($ mil.)	2.3%	9.9	12.1	9.5	10.3	10.8
Net income ($ mil.)	0.5%	0.6	1.4	0.1	0.5	0.6
Market value ($ mil.)	3.1%	15.5	14.2	8.9	15.4	17.5
Employees	0.9%	55	63	50	57	57

SONOCO PRODUCTS CO.

NYS: SON

1 North Second Street	CEO: M. Jack Sanders
Hartsville, SC 29550	CFO: Barry L. Saunders
Phone: 843 383-7000	HR: –
Fax: 843 383-7008	FYE: December 31
Web: www.sonoco.com	Type: Public

Sonoco Products believes you can judge a container by its packaging. The company is one of the world's largest makers of industrial and consumer packaging used by the food consumer goods construction and automotive industries. Its consumer packaging segment produces round and shaped composite cans for snack foods powdered beverages pet food and more. Sonoco makes flexible and rigid packaging (paper and plastic) for food personal care items and chemicals and it produces paperboard tubes and cores too for industrial protective packaging. The company's end-to-end packaging services include co-packing and fulfillment supply chain management and point-of-purchase display design/assembly.

	Annual Growth	12/10	12/11	12/12	12/13	12/14
Sales ($ mil.)	5.0%	4,124.1	4,498.9	4,786.1	4,848.1	5,014.5
Net income ($ mil.)	4.4%	201.1	217.5	196.0	219.1	239.2
Market value ($ mil.)	6.7%	3,387.3	3,315.9	2,990.9	4,197.2	4,396.4
Employees	4.7%	17,300	19,600	19,900	19,900	20,800

SONOMAWEST HOLDINGS INC.

PINK SHEETS: SWHI

2064 Hwy. 116 North	CEO: Craig R Stapleton
Sebastopol CA 95472	CFO: Craig R Stapleton
Phone: 707-824-2534	HR: –
Fax: 707-829-4630	FYE: June 30
Web: www.sonomawestholdings.com	Type: Public

Formerly Vacu-dry SonomaWest sold its dehydrated fruit business in 2000 and 2001 in search of a candy apple future in real estate. The company now owns two former agricultural production properties (totaling some 90 acres) left over from its fruity past. The properties are located in Northern California's Sonoma County and are leased to multiple tenants for commercial use; Benziger Family Winery is one of its largest tenants. SonomaWest also holds an investment in telecommunications firm MetroPCS Communications. The Stapleton family including CEO Craig Stapleton acquired SonomaWest and took it private in 2011.

SONOSITE INC.

NASDAQ: SONO

21919 30th Dr. SE	CEO: Naohiro Fujitani
Bothell WA 98021-3904	CFO: Marcus Y Smith
Phone: 425-951-1200	HR: –
Fax: 425-951-1201	FYE: December 31
Web: www.sonosite.com	Type: Public

Size is everything for SonoSite. The firm makes handheld ultrasonic imaging devices that health care providers can use outside traditional imaging facilities for instance in the ER at a patient's bedside or in the doctor's office. Its fourth- and fifth-generation systems include the handheld NanoMaxx tool and the M-Turbo and Edge portable consoles that produce imaging quality comparable to larger cart-based systems. Its S Series of products feature customized interfaces for different clinical applications including the ER or the ICU. SonoSite also sells some earlier-generation products and accessories used with its products. Diversified imaging company FUJIFILM Holdings acquired SonoSite in 2012.

SONUS NETWORKS, INC.

NMS: SONS

4 Technology Park Drive	CEO: Raymond P. (Ray) Dolan
Westford, MA 01886	CFO: Mark T. Greenquist
Phone: 978 614-8100	HR: Kathy Harris
Fax: –	FYE: December 31
Web: www.sonus.net	Type: Public

Sonus Networks has found a sound place in the voice infrastructure market. The company makes hardware and software that public network providers — including long-distance carriers ISPs and cable operators — use to provide voice and data communications services to their subscribers. Service providers use Sonus' switches session border control (SBC) products and related network software partly to transition from older circuit-based equipment to VoIP-based systems. The company also provides installation support and training services. Customers include AT&T BT Group Verizon and Deutsche Telekom; Sonus operates worldwide but generates most of its sales in the US.

	Annual Growth	12/10	12/11	12/12	12/13	12/14
Sales ($ mil.)	4.4%	249.3	259.7	254.1	276.7	296.3
Net income ($ mil.)	–	(10.7)	(12.7)	(50.2)	(22.1)	(16.9)
Market value ($ mil.)	10.4%	131.8	118.5	83.9	155.5	195.9
Employees	5.4%	968	1,095	1,093	1,059	1,193

SONY CORPORATION OF AMERICA

550 Madison Ave.	CEO: Howard Stringer
New York NY 10022	CFO: Rob Weisenthal
Phone: 212-833-6722	HR: –
Fax: 212-833-6938	FYE: March 31
Web: www.sony.com/sca/	Type: Subsidiary

Sony Corporation of America (SCA) is a wholly owned subsidiary and the US headquarters of Japan's mighty Sony Corporation. Based in New York SCA is made up of a number of global businesses that also have headquarters in the US including Sony Electronics and Sony Mobile Communications (electronics and mobile); Sony Pictures Entertainment (film and TV); Sony Music Entertainment and Sony/ATV Music Publishing (music); Sony Computer Entertainment America and Sony Online Entertainment (games); Sony Network Entertainment and Sony DADC (digital services); and other business like Illinois-based Sony Biotechnology which supplies flow cytometry analysis and sorting technology for life science research.

SONY PICTURES DIGITAL PRODUCTION INC.

10202 W. Washington Blvd.	CEO: –
Culver City CA 90232	CFO: Mark Henderson
Phone: 310-840-8676	HR: –
Fax: 310-840-8390	FYE: March 31
Web: www.sonypictures.com	Type: Subsidiary

There's nothing analog about this division of Sony Pictures Entertainment. Sony Digital Production (formerly Sony Pictures Digital) is responsible for the studio's digital content creation and includes subsidiaries Sony Pictures Imageworks and Sony Pictures Animation. Imageworks produces Academy Award-winning movie visual effects while Sony Pictures Animation is active in CGI feature film production. The first two titles for Sony Pictures Animation were Open Season (2006) and the Academy Award-nominated Surf's Up! (2007). The studio also has a deal to produce animated films for Aardman Animation.

SONY PICTURES ENTERTAINMENT INC.

10202 W. Washington Blvd.
Culver City CA 90232-3195
Phone: 310-244-4000
Fax: 310-244-2626
Web: www.sonypictures.com

CEO: Michael Lynton
CFO: –
HR: –
FYE: March 31
Type: Subsidiary

Sony Pictures Entertainment (SPE) is a movie-making monster. The producer of Godzilla is a unit of Sony Corporation of America the US arm of Japanese electronics giant Sony. It operates Columbia TriStar Motion Picture Group which includes Columbia Pictures (big budget films); Screen Gems (midsized budget); Sony Pictures Classics (small budget); and marketing and acquisitions unit TriStar Pictures. Its film library contains more than 3500 titles including classics such as Bridge on the River Kwai and Lawrence of Arabia. Other holdings include operations devoted to TV (Sony Pictures Television) DVDs (Sony Pictures Home Entertainment) digital production (Sony Digital Production) and online video (Crackle).

SONY PICTURES HOME ENTERTAINMENT

10202 W. Washington Blvd.
Culver City CA 90232
Phone: 310-244-4000
Fax: 310-244-2626
Web: www.sonypictures.com/homevideo

CEO: David Bishop
CFO: –
HR: –
FYE: March 31
Type: Business Segment

The home video collection of Sony Pictures Home Entertainment (SPHE) is the envy of film buffs worldwide. The firm distributes movies on DVD and videocassette to the home entertainment market. Among the more than 3500 titles in its library are films produced by its parent company Sony Pictures Entertainment. Popular DVD titles include Paul Blart: Mall Cop Superbad and Spider-Man 3. SPHE also distributes television programming on DVD including all nine seasons of the hit show Seinfeld. SPHE is responsible for the launch of the next-generation of DVD hardware and software technology Blu-ray.

SONY PICTURES TELEVISION

10202 W. Washington Blvd.
Culver City CA 90232
Phone: 310-244-4000
Fax: 310-244-2626
Web: https://www.sonypicturestelevision.com

CEO: Steve Mosko
CFO: Drew Shearer
HR: Simon Baker
FYE: March 31
Type: Business Segment

Sony makes the TVs so why shouldn't it make the TV shows as well? Sony Pictures Television (SPT) part of the entertainment arm of the consumer electronics giant is one of the leading producers of television content. It creates series programming such as Breaking Bad (which airs on AMC) Damages (FX Networks) and Rules of Engagement (CBS). SPT also produces and distributes such syndicated shows as Jeopardy! and Wheel of Fortune as well as daytime dramas Days of Our Lives and The Young and the Restless. In addition it oversees a 35% stake in the Game Show Network (GSN) cable channel. SPT is a unit of Sony Pictures Entertainment (SPE).

SONY/ATV MUSIC PUBLISHING LLC

550 Madison Ave. 5th Fl.
New York NY 10022
Phone: 212-833-7730
Fax: 212-833-5552
Web: www.sonyatv.com

CEO: Martin N Bandier
CFO: –
HR: –
FYE: December 31
Type: Private

The King of Pop was no "Fool on the Hill" when he invested in the music publishing business. Sony/ATV Music Publishing jointly owned by the estate of singer Michael Jackson and Sony Corporation of America is one of the world's top publishing firms with rights to more than 750000 songs including some 250 recordings from the Beatles. Sony/ATV licenses its songs for use in movies TV and advertising and collects royalties for its songwriters. Jackson avoided having to sell his half to pay off debts when Sony loaned him money in 2006. The pop star died in 2009 at the age of 50. In 2012 the Sony/ATV catalog expanded by about 1.3 million songs through the addition of EMI Music Publishing to its holdings.

SOROS FUND MANAGEMENT LLC

888 7th Ave. 33rd Fl.
New York NY 10106
Phone: 212-262-6300
Fax: 212-245-5154

CEO: –
CFO: Abbas Eddy Zuaiter
HR: Eddy Zuaiter
FYE: December 31
Type: Private

George Soros makes headlines but not nearly as well as he makes money. His Soros Fund Management's generally successful hedge funds including its flagship Quantum Fund often invest according to macroeconomic trends. The company oversees some $25 billion which it uses to buy large stakes in the energy transportation financial retail and other industries. It owns stakes in oil exploration firm Hess Corporation and Ford Motor Company. Other investments include containership owner Global Ship Lease retail site Bluefly and Lattice Semiconductor. In 2011 Soros Fund Management announced that it would close itself to outside investors and focus solely on managing the money of Soros and his family.

SOTERA DEFENSE SOLUTIONS INC.

2121 Cooperative Way Ste. 400
Herndon VA 20171-5393
Phone: 703-738-2840
Fax: 703-883-4037
Web: www.soteradefense.com

CEO: Deb Alderson
CFO: John C Pitsenberger
HR: –
FYE: December 31
Type: Private

Military intelligence is no joking matter at Sotera Defense Solutions. The company formerly Global Defense Technology & Systems operates through an array of subsidiaries. It provides software system engineering and technology development to help the Department of Defense CIA Homeland Security and other government agencies fight terrorism and enforce national security. Sotera's services include design of mobile computers (called Force Mobility and Modernization Systems) for military clients. Its Intelligence business focuses on counter-terrorism and communications systems; a Cyber operation collects and analyzes information in cyberspace. The company was acquired by an Ares Management affiliate in 2011.

SOTHEBY'S

NYS: BID

1334 York Avenue
New York, NY 10021
Phone: 212 606-7000
Fax: –
Web: www.sothebys.com

CEO: Kevin S. H. Ching
CFO: Patrick S. McClymont
HR: –
FYE: December 31
Type: Public

Sotheby's believes that one man's collection is another man's treasure — especially when that collection is a rare antique a unique collectible or a distinctive work of art. Along with rival Christie's International Sotheby's dominates the world's auction house market. It orchestrates hundreds of sales each year at its auction centers dealing mainly in fine art antiques and collectibles. Sotheby's receives commissions and fees from both the buyer and the seller on each sale. It also provides loans (secured against works of art) to clients as part of its finance services and acts as an art dealer through its Noortman Master Paintings business which specializes in Dutch Flemish and French paintings.

	Annual Growth	12/10	12/11	12/12	12/13	12/14
Sales ($ mil.)	4.9%	774.3	831.8	768.5	853.7	938.1
Net income ($ mil.)	(7.5%)	161.0	171.4	108.3	130.0	117.8
Market value ($ mil.)	(1.0%)	3,104.6	1,968.3	2,319.5	3,670.4	2,979.1
Employees	2.9%	1,380	1,446	1,501	1,577	1,550

SOTHERLY HOTELS INC

NMS: SOHO

410 West Francis Street
Williamsburg, VA 23185
Phone: 757 229-5648
Fax: –
Web: www.mhihospitality.com

CEO: Andrew M Sims
CFO: Anthony E Domalski
HR: –
FYE: December 31
Type: Public

MHI Hospitality owns seven full-service hotels operating under the Hilton Holiday Inn Sheraton and Crowne Plaza brands in the mid-Atlantic and southeastern US. The company also holds a minority stake in another hotel has two under development and owns leasehold interests in common areas of the Shell Island Resort in Wilmington North Carolina. MHI Hotel Services which spun off MHI Hospitality in 2004 manages the REIT's properties. Executive officers and board members of MHI Hospitality collectively own more than a quarter of the company.

	Annual Growth	12/10	12/11	12/12	12/13	12/14
Sales ($ mil.)	12.3%	77.4	81.2	87.3	89.4	122.9
Net income ($ mil.)	–	(2.4)	(4.8)	(4.1)	(3.5)	(0.6)
Market value ($ mil.)	37.3%	22.3	25.2	35.1	62.8	79.3
Employees	6.8%	10	9	7	9	13

SOUND FINANCIAL INC.

OTC: SNFL

2005 5th Ave. Ste. 200
Seattle WA 98121
Phone: 206-448-1884
Fax: 403-538-7033
Web: www.swenergy.ca

CEO: Laurie Stewart
CFO: Matthew Deines
HR: –
FYE: December 31
Type: Public

Sounds heard by Sound Financial's banks could include that of crisp $100 bills and the foghorns of passing ships. Located in the Puget Sound region surrounding Seattle Sound Financial is a bank holding company operating principally through Sound Community Bank and its five area locations. The bank offers traditional savings and checking accounts to retail and business customers as well as residential mortgages home equity loans and various secured and unsecured consumer loans. It also provides construction land commercial business and multifamily housing loans but to a lesser extent. Sound Community Bank traces it roots back to 1953 when it was founded as a credit union.

SOUPER SALAD INC.

140 Heimer Ste. 400
San Antonio TX 78232
Phone: 210-495-9644
Fax: 210-495-9655
Web: www.soupersalad.com/

CEO: Ward T Olgreen
CFO: –
HR: Lynn Brazee
FYE: December 31
Type: Private

Despite its name Souper Salad isn't only interested in leafy greens. Souper Salad is a leading multi-concept restaurant company with about 145 company-owned and franchised locations mostly in Texas and Oklahoma. The company's eponymous flagship chain with more than 70 units in more than a dozen states features an all-you-can-eat soup and salad bar along with a menu of sandwiches pizzas and desserts. Souper Salad also owns the Grandy's chain of family-style eateries serving hungry customers in about 10 states. About half the company's restaurants are owned and operated by franchisees. Private equity firm Sun Capital Partners owns Souper Salad.

SOURCEONE HEALTHCARE TECHNOLOGIES INC.

8020 Tyler Blvd.
Mentor OH 44060
Phone: 440-701-1200
Fax: 440-701-1248
Web: estore.sourceonehealth.com

CEO: Leo Zuckerman
CFO: –
HR: –
FYE: December 31
Type: Private

SourceOne Healthcare Technologies is a leading distributor of medical imaging equipment accessories and supplies. In addition to portable X-ray units ultrasound machines and other imaging systems the company offers related supplies and accessories such as film contrast media furniture aprons and leaded eyewear. Through its distribution center network and vehicle fleet SourceOne delivers products to some 50000 clients in the US including hospitals doctors' offices and imaging centers. The company also provides installation repair and maintenance services.

SOUTH BEND MEDICAL FOUNDATION INC

530 N LAFAYETTE BLVD
SOUTH BEND, IN 466011004
Phone: 574-234-4176
Fax: –
Web: www.sbmf.org

CEO: –
CFO: –
HR: –
FYE: December 31
Type: Private

South Bend Medical Foundation provides clinical testing and blood bank services for communities in Illinois Indiana Kentucky Michigan and Ohio. The foundation works together with local hospitals clinics and doctors' offices to provide diagnostic laboratory services for patients. It operates about a dozen lab facilities at medical facilities and independent locations. The company's forensic toxicology department conducts employee and athletic drug testing. South Bend Medical Foundation also provides public health screenings for diseases such as sickle cell anemia and prostrate cancer. The foundation was formed in 1912 by a group of physicians.

	Annual Growth	12/98	12/99	12/00	12/01	12/11
Sales ($ mil.)	4.7%	–	56.2	61.4	70.4	97.7
Net income ($ mil.)	28.5%	–	–	0.1	(0.9)	2.3
Market value ($ mil.)	–	–	–	–	–	–
Employees	–	–	–	–	–	800

SOUTH BROWARD HOSPITAL DISTRICT

3501 Johnson St.	CEO: Frank V Sacco
Hollywood FL 33021-5421	CFO: Matthew Muhart
Phone: 954-987-2000	HR: –
Fax: 863-965-1079	FYE: April 30
Web: www.driveccc.com	Type: Government-owned

South Broward Hospital District (dba Memorial Healthcare System) is a community-owned health services network that provides health service to residents of Florida's Broward Dade and Palm Beach counties. The system's major hospitals include Memorial Regional Hospital Memorial Hospital Pembroke Memorial Hospital West and Memorial Hospital Miramar. The hospitals have a combined capacity of roughly 1800 beds and provide services including diagnostic emergency surgical and rehabilitative care. Memorial also operates a pediatric hospital cardiac and vascular medicine institute a cancer treatment center and a center for women's health as well as nursing home facilities and community clinics.

SOUTH CAROLINA ELECTRIC & GAS COMPANY

1426 Main St.	CEO: Kevin B Marsh
Columbia SC 29201	CFO: Jimmy E Addison
Phone: 803-217-9000	HR: –
Fax: 803-217-8825	FYE: December 31
Web: www.sceg.com	Type: Subsidiary

South Carolina Electric & Gas (SCE&G) is a regulated utility with 669000 electricity and 317000 natural gas customers in the Palmetto State. The utility a subsidiary of SCANA owns more than 24900 miles of power distribution lines and almost 16200 miles of gas transmission mains; it also operates 17 fossil-fueled nuclear and hydroelectric power generation facilities with about 5270 MW of capacity. Its power service area covers 17000 sq. mls. gas 22600 sq. mls. SCE&G purchases additional power from other independent generators and utility companies including SCANA-owned affiliate South Carolina Generating and it sells wholesale power to other utilities and marketers.

SOUTH CAROLINA PUBLIC SERVICE AUTHORITY

1 Riverwood Dr.	CEO: Lonnie N Carter
Moncks Corner SC 29461-2901	CFO: Elaine Peterson
Phone: 843-761-8000	HR: –
Fax: 843-761-4122	FYE: December 31
Web: www.santeecooper.com	Type: Government-owned

Someone's got to turn on those bright lights in the big city — and in the small cities too. South Carolina Public Service Authority known as Santee Cooper (after two interconnected river systems) provides wholesale electricity to 20 cooperatives and two municipalities that serve more than 700000 customers in South Carolina. It directly retails electricity to more than 164680 customers. One of the largest US state-owned utilities Santee Cooper operates in all 46 counties in South Carolina and has stakes in power plants (fossil-fueled nuclear hydro and renewable) that give it more than 5660 MW of generating capacity. The Santee Cooper Regional Water System distributes water to 137000 consumers.

SOUTH CAROLINA STATE PORTS AUTHORITY

176 CONCORD ST	CEO: James I. (Jim) Newsome
CHARLESTON, SC 294012642	CFO: Peter N. Hughes
Phone: 843-723-8651	HR: –
Fax: –	FYE: June 30
Web: www.scspa.com	Type: Private

Offering gateways for trade in the Palmetto State The South Carolina State Ports Authority (SCSPA) operates marine terminals at the ports in Charleston and Georgetown. The agency maintains its own container terminals at each port and provides container handling services; in addition space at the ports is leased to other terminal operators. The Port of Charleston provides services for cruise ships as well as for freight-carrying vessels including freight rail service. SCSPA is overseen by a nine-member board appointed by the governor along with the Secretaries of Transportation and Commerce. The agency which was founded in 1942 does not receive state money and is funded primarily by its operations.

	Annual Growth	06/04	06/05	06/06	06/11	06/12
Sales ($ mil.)	(0.7%)	–	138.0	154.0	124.6	130.9
Net income ($ mil.)	(18.5%)	–	–	60.1	21.2	17.6
Market value ($ mil.)	–	–	–	–	–	–
Employees	–	–	–	–	–	493

SOUTH CENTRAL COMMUNICATIONS CORPORATION

20 NW 3RD ST FL 14	CEO: John P Engelbrecht
EVANSVILLE, IN 477081200	CFO: Randy Champion
Phone: 812-463-7950	HR: –
Fax: –	FYE: December 31
Web: www.southcentralcommunications.net	Type: Private

South Central Communications-, enjoys making waves in the-, central US radio market. The company owns and operates more than a dozen radio stations serving midsized and large markets in Tennessee and Indiana with a range of mostly music programming. In addition the company operates-, Muzak-, franchises (subscriber-based radio and voice services targeted to businesses) in seven states. Other operations include Dish Network installation services restaurant drive-thru intercoms and office paging systems. Its also owns Knoxville independent digital television station WMAK-, The family-owned company was started in 1946 by John A. Engelbrecht.

	Annual Growth	12/08	12/09	12/10	12/11	12/12
Sales ($ mil.)	3.5%	–	–	38.6	40.8	41.3
Net income ($ mil.)	37.2%	–	–	3.2	4.1	6.0
Market value ($ mil.)	–	–	–	–	–	–
Employees	–	–	–	–	–	298

SOUTH DAKOTA STATE UNIVERSITY

2201 ADMINISTRATION LANE	CEO: –
BROOKINGS, SD 570070001	CFO: –
Phone: 605-688-6101	HR: –
Fax: –	FYE: June 30
Web: www.sdbor.edu	Type: Private

South Dakota State University (SDSU) is big on education in the Mount Rushmore State. The college offers undergraduate graduate and pre-professional programs to some 13000 students. Academic offerings include agriculture engineering and pharmacy courses. Its SDSU Sioux Falls Program targets non-traditional students (such as students with jobs and families) by providing evening and weekend classes. Notable SDSU alumni include former US Senator Tom Daschle and professional football players Adam Timmerman and Adam Vinatieri. SDSU a public school governed by the South Dakota Board of Regents was founded as a land grant college in 1881.

	Annual Growth	06/07	06/08	06/11	06/12	06/13
Sales ($ mil.)	7.7%	–	134.9	190.9	198.9	195.4
Net income ($ mil.)	(25.8%)	–	–	31.6	17.7	17.4
Market value ($ mil.)	–	–	–	–	–	–
Employees	–	–	–	–	–	2,000

SOUTH DAKOTA WHEAT GROWERS ASSOCIATION

908 LAMONT ST S
ABERDEEN, SD 574015515
Phone: 605-225-5500
Fax: –
Web: www.wheatgrowers.com

CEO: –
CFO: Robert Porter
HR: –
FYE: July 31
Type: Private

Who loves you a bushel and a peck? South Dakota Wheat Growers may; it is an agricultural co-op comprising some 5400 member-farmers. It provides a grain warehouse along with grain marketing services intended to compete with big food and ag companies. In addition to storage and drying Wheat Growers offers agronomy spreading and spraying and transportation. It supplies feed fertilizer chemicals and other farm-related provisions for members in and around counties in North and South Dakota. Wheat Growers generates more than half of its revenues through marketing some 160 million bushels of grain (corn wheat and soybeans) each year. Remaining revenues are made through agronomy and retail sales and services.

	Annual Growth	07/09	07/10	07/12	07/13	07/14
Sales ($ mil.)	10.1%	–	1,020.4	1,667.3	1,847.6	1,498.8
Net income ($ mil.)	12.0%	–	–	16.3	20.9	20.4
Market value ($ mil.)	–	–	–	–	–	–
Employees	–	–	–	–	–	638

SOUTH JERSEY GAS CO.

NL:

1 South Jersey Plaza
Folsom, NJ 08037
Phone: 609 561-9000
Fax: –
Web: www.sjindustries.com

CEO: Jeffrey E Dubois
CFO: Stephen H Clark
HR: –
FYE: December 31
Type: Public

Atlantic City gamblers don't have to gamble on getting hot showers thanks to South Jersey Gas which transmits and distributes natural gas to more than 343560 customers in its regulated service territory in seven southern New Jersey counties. The utility a subsidiary of South Jersey Industries also provides gas transportation services and sells wholesale gas to power plant operators and other energy marketing companies. South Jersey Gas's service territory of 2500 sq. miles includes 112 towns and cities throughout Atlantic Cape May Cumberland and Salem Counties and in portions of Burlington Camden and Gloucester Counties with an estimated total population of 1.2 million.

	Annual Growth	12/10	12/11	12/12	12/13	12/14
Sales ($ mil.)	1.3%	476.0	412.4	421.9	446.5	501.9
Net income ($ mil.)	10.9%	43.9	52.9	58.2	62.2	66.5
Market value ($ mil.)	–	–	–	–	–	–
Employees	4.3%	407	443	457	475	481

SOUTH JERSEY INDUSTRIES, INC.

NYS: SJI

1 South Jersey Plaza
Folsom, NJ 08037
Phone: 609 561-9000
Fax: –
Web: www.sjiindustries.com

CEO: –
CFO: Stephen H. Clark
HR: Kathleen McEndy
FYE: December 31
Type: Public

South Jersey Industries (SJI) is Atlantic City's answer to cold casino nights. In 2014 its main subsidiary South Jersey Gas (SJG) provided natural gas to 342155 residents 24253 commercial customers and 446 industrial customers in southern New Jersey including Atlantic City. The utility has more than 6000 miles of transmission and distribution mains; it also sells and transports wholesale gas. SJI's deregulated retail supplier South Jersey Energy (SJE) provides retail gas electricity and energy management services. Its South Jersey Resources (SJR) unit is a wholesale gas marketer and services provider in the Southeast US. Subsidiary Marina Energy develops and operates on-site energy projects.

	Annual Growth	12/10	12/11	12/12	12/13	12/14
Sales ($ mil.)	(1.0%)	925.1	828.6	706.3	731.4	887.0
Net income ($ mil.)	9.8%	66.7	89.3	91.6	81.6	97.0
Market value ($ mil.)	2.8%	3,609.4	3,882.1	3,439.3	3,824.0	4,027.0
Employees	1.9%	650	675	700	700	700

SOUTH MIAMI HOSPITAL INC.

6200 SW 73RD ST
SOUTH MIAMI, FL 331434679
Phone: 786-662-4000
Fax: –
Web: www.baptisthealth.net

CEO: –
CFO: –
HR: Melissa (Mel) Lupisella
FYE: September 30
Type: Private

South Miami Hospital offers primary and tertiary health care services to the residents living near the University of Miami. The hospital has about 470 beds and is one of the largest members of Baptist Health South Florida a top regional health system. Specialty services include emergency care cardiovascular services oncology neurology women's health metabolic care and rehabilitation. It operates an addiction treatment residential facility provides home health care and provides child development diagnostic and early intervention services. South Miami Hospital was founded in 1960.

	Annual Growth	09/09	09/10	09/11	09/12	09/13
Sales ($ mil.)	(0.0%)	–	–	–	484.7	484.7
Net income ($ mil.)	63.1%	–	–	–	36.7	59.8
Market value ($ mil.)	–	–	–	–	–	–
Employees	–	–	–	–	–	2,205

SOUTH PENINSULA HOSPITALS INC.

4300 BARTLETT ST
HOMER, AK 996037005
Phone: 907-235-0369
Fax: –
Web: www.sphosp.com

CEO: Robert Letson
CFO: Lori Meyer
HR: –
FYE: June 30
Type: Private

South Peninsula Hospital provides a variety of medical services including home health care emergency medicine surgery orthopedics and ophthalmology for the residents of the Kenai Peninsula and surrounding areas in Alaska. The hospital also provides a 25-bed long-term facility that offers physical and occupational therapy services. In addition South Peninsula Hospital provides community and staff education classes.

	Annual Growth	06/09	06/10	06/11	06/12	06/13
Sales ($ mil.)	7.3%	–	41.1	34.4	39.3	50.8
Net income ($ mil.)	–	–	–	(0.2)	2.2	1.4
Market value ($ mil.)	–	–	–	–	–	–
Employees	–	–	–	–	–	350

SOUTH STATE CORP

NMS: SSB

520 Gervais Street
Columbia, SC 29201
Phone: 800 277-2175
Fax: –
Web: www.southstatebank.com

CEO: Robert R. Hill
CFO: John C. Pollok
HR: –
FYE: December 31
Type: Public

South State Corporation (formerly First Financial Holdings) is the holding company for South State Bank (formerly South Carolina Bank and Trust and South Carolina Bank and Trust of the Piedmont both known as SCBT). The bank operates branches throughout the Palmetto state as well as in select counties in Georgia and North Carolina. Serving retail and business customers the banks provide deposit accounts loans and mortgages as well as trust and investment planning services. More than half of the company's loan portfolio is devoted to commercial mortgages while consumer real estate loans make up more than a quarter. South State has assets of nearly $8 billion.

	Annual Growth	12/10	12/11	12/12	12/13	12/14
Assets ($ mil.)	21.5%	3,594.8	3,896.6	5,136.4	7,931.5	7,826.2
Net income ($ mil.)	9.8%	51.9	22.6	30.0	49.2	75.4
Market value ($ mil.)	19.6%	790.9	700.6	970.4	1,606.3	1,620.0
Employees	19.7%	1,015	1,071	1,324	2,106	2,081

SOUTHCO DISTRIBUTING COMPANY

2201 S JOHN ST
GOLDSBORO, NC 275307163
Phone: 919-735-8012
Fax: –
Web: www.southcodistributing.com

CEO: Sherwin Herring
CFO: Chris Wise
HR: –
FYE: December 28
Type: Private

This company makes sure you can get subs on the go from the convenience store. Southco Distributing is a leading convenience food supplier that distributes prepackaged sandwiches and other products to retail stores in seven states in the Southeast and Midwest. In addition to prepackaged foods Southco provides branded quick-service kiosks and equipment that allow convenience stores and other retailers to offer food on the go. Its foodservice programs are branded under the names AutoFry Pizza Primo Sub Express and Squawkers.

	Annual Growth	12/0-1	12/00	12/05	12/06	12/12
Sales ($ mil.)	5.7%	–	203.8	0.0	253.9	397.2
Net income ($ mil.)	–	–	–	0.0	1.1	2.6
Market value ($ mil.)	–	–	–	–	–	–
Employees	–	–	–	–	–	225

SOUTHCOAST FINANCIAL CORP

NMS: SOCB

530 Johnnie Dodds Boulevard
Mt. Pleasant, SC 29464
Phone: 843 884-0504
Fax: –
Web: www.southcoastbank.com

CEO: L Wayne Pearson
CFO: William C Heslop
HR: –
FYE: December 31
Type: Public

Southcoast Financial Corporation pays a great deal of interest to the Palmetto State. The institution is the holding company for Southcoast Community Bank which was established in 1998. It serves South Carolina's Berkeley Charleston and Dorchester counties through about 10 branches. Catering to individuals and local small businesses the bank offers savings checking money market and individual retirement accounts as well as certificates of deposit. Its lending activities consist of real estate mortgages (around 45% of the company's loan portfolio) commercial loans (more than one-third) and to a lesser extent consumer construction and land development loans. BNC Bancorp acquired Southcoast in 2015.

	Annual Growth	12/10	12/11	12/12	12/13	12/14
Assets ($ mil.)	(0.1%)	478.3	427.5	438.2	447.4	476.8
Net income ($ mil.)	171.4%	0.1	(16.5)	3.5	9.1	3.7
Market value ($ mil.)	23.1%	21.8	10.1	36.2	41.2	50.0
Employees	(2.4%)	98	93	92	92	89

SOUTHCOAST HOSPITALS GROUP INC.

363 HIGHLAND AVE
FALL RIVER, MA 027203703
Phone: 508-679-3131
Fax: –
Web: www.southcoast.org

CEO: –
CFO: –
HR: Patricia (Pat) Roberts
FYE: September 30
Type: Private

When you feel more than a little physically washed up get to one of the Southcoast Hospitals Group facilities. The not-for-profit company provides medical services in the southeastern corner of Massachusetts and in Rhode Island. Its primary facilities in Massachusetts are the Charlton Memorial Hospital (with about 330 beds) in Fall River St. Luke's Hospital (420 beds) in New Bedford and Tobey Hospital (65 beds) in Wareham which provide acute medical care and specialty services including cardiology neurology orthopedics and women's care. Southcoast Hospitals Group also operates about 20 ancillary facilities including nursing and assisted-living facilities and home health and hospice agencies.

	Annual Growth	09/03	09/04	09/06	09/12	09/13
Sales ($ mil.)	4.9%	–	445.7	506.5	704.4	687.7
Net income ($ mil.)	6.9%	–	–	14.0	49.3	22.4
Market value ($ mil.)	–	–	–	–	–	–
Employees	–	–	–	–	–	3,853

SOUTHCROSS ENERGY PARTNERS LP

NYS: SXE

1717 Main Street, Suite 5200
Dallas, TX 75201
Phone: 214 979-3720
Fax: –
Web: www.southcrossenergy.com

CEO: John E Bonn
CFO: –
HR: David Lawrence
FYE: December 31
Type: Public

Southcross Energy Partners transports natural gas and natural gas liquids (NGLs) across the southern US. The company operates about 2500 miles of intrastate pipeline in Alabama Mississippi and South Texas. More than half of its pipeline mileage is located in Texas where it also has two gas processing plants that can process 185 million cu. ft. per day two treating plants and one fractionator. Top customers Formosa Hydrocarbons (a subsidiary of Formosa Plastics) and Sherwin Alumina together account for about 35% of sales. Southcross Energy formed in 2009 after it bought the Alabama Mississippi and Texas pipeline from Crosstex for $220 million. It went public in late 2012 raising about $170 million.

	Annual Growth	12/10	12/11	12/12	12/13	12/14
Sales ($ mil.)	14.0%	498.7	523.1	496.1	634.7	842.7
Net income ($ mil.)	–	9.7	7.5	(4.5)	(16.0)	(31.3)
Market value ($ mil.)	(18.2%)	–	–	1,235.2	936.5	825.9
Employees	–	–	–	156	–	–

SOUTHEAST TEXAS INDUSTRIES INC.

35911 US HIGHWAY 96 S
BUNA, TX 776124031
Phone: 409-994-3570
Fax: –
Web: www.setxind.com

CEO: –
CFO: James Parsley
HR: –
FYE: December 31
Type: Private

Southeast Texas Industries is a down home manufacturer that likes staying local but it also keeps an eye open for international opportunities. The company specializes in the fabrication of pipe plate pressure vessel sheet metal heavy structural steel and drilling rig products. Southeast Texas Industries also provides project management construction and maintenance services. Customers include companies in the oil and gas power generation pulp and paper and petrochemical industries along with engineering firms that work on industrial projects. Southeast Texas Industries was founded in 1977.

	Annual Growth	12/01	12/02	12/03	12/04	12/07
Sales ($ mil.)	25.9%	–	40.1	36.8	36.8	126.7
Net income ($ mil.)	123.9%	–	–	0.2	0.2	5.3
Market value ($ mil.)	–	–	–	–	–	–
Employees	–	–	–	–	–	850

SOUTHEASTERN BANK FINANCIAL CORP

NBB: SBFC

3530 Wheeler Road
Augusta, GA 30909
Phone: 706 738-6990
Fax: –
Web: www.georgiabankandtrust.com

CEO: R Daniel Blanton
CFO: Darrell R Rains
HR: Lindsey Strong
FYE: December 31
Type: Public

Southeastern Bank Financial has Georgia (and its neighbors) on its mind. It is the holding company for Georgia Bank & Trust of Augusta and Southern Bank & Trust which serve the Augusta-Richmond County metropolitan area of Georgia and South Carolina from about a dozen branches. The company also has mortgage operations in Augusta and Savannah. The banks offer standard deposit products including checking and savings accounts. Funds from deposits are primarily used to originate real estate loans which make up about 85% of its loan book. The company also offers commercial and consumer loans in addition to wealth mangement and trust services.

	Annual Growth	12/10	12/11	12/12	12/13	12/14
Assets ($ mil.)	1.9%	1,607.1	1,614.8	1,662.5	1,689.3	1,732.8
Net income ($ mil.)	24.8%	6.9	11.0	14.4	16.3	16.6
Market value ($ mil.)	27.1%	67.1	72.8	112.0	137.2	175.3
Employees	(0.7%)	349	345	344	340	340

SOUTHEASTERN FREIGHT LINES INC.

420 Davega Rd.
Lexington SC 29073
Phone: 803-794-7300
Fax: 803-794-8131
Web: www.sefl.com

CEO: –
CFO: –
HR: Peggy Lyons
FYE: December 31
Type: Private

Less-than-truckload (LTL) carrier Southeastern Freight Lines hauls freight throughout the southern US with a fleet of about 3700 tractors and 11400 trailers. (LTL carriers consolidate freight from multiple shippers into a single truckload.) Southeastern Freight Lines operates from a network of about 75 terminals in a dozen states and Puerto Rico. Clients have included Lowe's and Masco. Through partnerships with carriers including Quik X Transportation A. Duie Pyle Dayton Freight and Oak Harbor Freight Lines Southeastern Freight Lines provides service throughout the US Mexico and Canada.

SOUTHEASTERN PENNSYLVANIA TRANSPORTATION AUTHORITY

1234 Market St.
Philadelphia PA 19107-3780
Phone: 215-580-7800
Fax: 713-952-5637
Web: www.mcguyerhomebuilders.com

CEO: –
CFO: Richard Burnfield
HR: –
FYE: June 30
Type: Government Agency

The Southeastern Pennsylvania Transportation Authority known as SEPTA provides passenger transportation services in the Philadelphia area. The agency's operations include buses subways and elevated trains trolleys and light rail and commuter rail lines. All together SEPTA maintains more than 300 stations and bus terminals chiefly in five Pennsylvania counties (Bucks Chester Delaware Montgomery and Philadelphia) and in the neighboring states of Delaware and New Jersey. Its territory spans some 2200 sq. mi. The Pennsylvania legislature established SEPTA in 1964 and over the years the agency has acquired the assets of several for-profit transportation companies that operated in the region.

SOUTHERN BANC CO., INC.

NBB: SRNN

221 South 6th Street
Gadsden, AL 35901-4102
Phone: 256 543-3860
Fax: 256 543-3864

CEO: Gates Little
CFO: –
HR: –
FYE: June 30
Type: Public

The Southern Banc Company is the holding company for The Southern Bank which operates about five branches in Etowah Cherokee and Marshall counties in northeastern Alabama. Serving both local businesses and consumers the bank offers standard deposit products including checking and savings accounts certificates of deposit and individual retirement accounts. Its loan portfolio is dominated by one-to-four family residential mortgages business loans and consumer loans but Southern Bank also writes nonresidential real estate mortgages and loans secured by savings accounts. The bank also offers "factoring" services for its business-to-business clients which conducts account receivables management.

	Annual Growth	06/06	06/11	06/12	06/13	06/14
Assets ($ mil.)	(1.1%)	102.6	95.4	111.3	95.6	94.3
Net income ($ mil.)	–	0.2	(0.1)	0.0	(0.3)	(0.3)
Market value ($ mil.)	(6.6%)	13.0	5.7	4.4	8.2	7.5
Employees	–	31	–	–	–	–

SOUTHERN CALIFORNIA EDISON CO.

NBB: SCED P

2244 Walnut Grove Avenue, P.O. Box 800
Rosemead, CA 91770
Phone: 626 302-1212
Fax: –

CEO: Ted Craver
CFO: Maria Rigatti
HR: Patricia (Pat) Miller
FYE: December 31
Type: Public

One of the Golden State's largest utilities Southern California Edison (SCE) distributes power to a population of more than 14 million people (5 million customer accounts) in central coastal and southern California (excluding Los Angeles and some other cities). SCE has 6310 MW of net generating capacity from stakes in nuclear hydroelectric and fossil-fueled power plants (although it has sold a number of its fossil-fueled facilities in response to the state's deregulation legislation). The utility sells excess power to wholesale customers. SCE is a unit of utility and competitive power holding company Edison International.

	Annual Growth	12/10	12/11	12/12	12/13	12/14
Sales ($ mil.)	7.6%	9,983.0	10,577.0	11,851.0	12,562.0	13,380.0
Net income ($ mil.)	9.4%	1,092.0	1,144.0	1,660.0	1,000.0	1,565.0
Market value ($ mil.)	4.0%	8,349.9	9,828.5	9,654.5	8,950.0	9,785.0
Employees	(7.1%)	18,230	18,069	16,515	13,599	13,600

SOUTHERN CALIFORNIA GAS CO.

NBB: SOCG P

555 West Fifth Street
Los Angeles, CA 90013
Phone: 213 244-1200
Fax: –
Web: www.socalgas.com

CEO: Dennis V. Arriola
CFO: Robert M. Schlax
HR: –
FYE: December 31
Type: Public

Southern California Gas (SoCalGas) figures being the largest gas utility in the US gives it the right to call itself "The Gas Company." The utility an indirect subsidiary of Sempra Energy distributes natural gas to 5.8 million residential commercial and industrial meters (20.9 million customers) in more than 500 communities throughout the southern half of California. SoCalGas owns and operates about 97000 miles of gas distribution mains and service lines as well as about 4000 miles of transmission and storage pipeline. The utility also owns gas transmission compressor stations and underground storage facilities.

	Annual Growth	12/10	12/11	12/12	12/13	12/14
Sales ($ mil.)	0.2%	3,822.0	3,816.0	3,282.0	3,736.0	3,855.0
Net income ($ mil.)	3.8%	287.0	288.0	290.0	365.0	333.0
Market value ($ mil.)	6.1%	2,229.5	2,411.5	2,475.2	2,329.6	2,821.0
Employees	4.2%	7,067	7,370	7,788	8,196	8,324

SOUTHERN CALIFORNIA PERMANENTE MEDICAL GROUP INC.

393 E. Walnut St.
Pasadena CA 91188
Phone: 626-405-5000
Fax: 626-405-3176
Web: www.kaiserpermanente.org

CEO: Irwin Goldstein
CFO: –
HR: –
FYE: December 31
Type: Subsidiary

Southern California Permanente Medical Group (SCPMG) is a for-profit organization of doctors who serve the 3.3 million members of Kaiser Permanente's Southern California region health care network. The Southern California Kaiser Permanente regional organization is made up of a not-for-profit company that administers the company's health plan a group of about a dozen community hospitals and the for-profit SCPMG. The physician group practice organization provides general practice and specialist care services. Its Southern California service territory encompasses Metropolitan Los Angeles San Diego County the Inland Empire Orange County and western Ventura County.

SOUTHERN CALIFORNIA PUBLIC POWER AUTHORITY

225 S. Lake Ave. Ste. 1250
Pasadena CA 91101
Phone: 626-793-9364
Fax: 626-793-9461
Web: www.scppa.org

CEO: -
CFO: Ron Davis
HR: -
FYE: June 30
Type: Government-owned

Southern Californians soak up the sun and the energy. The latter is where Southern California Public Power Authority comes in. The power authority generates and transmits electricity for 10 municipal distribution utilities and one irrigation district in southwestern California. Members include the municipal utilities of the cities Anaheim Burbank Colton Glendale Los Angeles Pasadena and Riverside. The authority has interests in three power plants and three transmission projects in the western US. It is constructing a fourth generation project. Southern California Public Power Authority also provides legislative representation and cost efficiency services to its members.

SOUTHERN CALIFORNIA REGIONAL RAIL AUTHORITY

1 GATEWAY PLZ FL 12
LOS ANGELES, CA 900123747
Phone: 213-452-0200
Fax: -
Web: www.mobile.metrolinktrains.com

CEO: Michael De Pallo
CFO: Sam Joumblat
HR: -
FYE: June 30
Type: Private

Is there a place for a passenger railroad operator in a land of legendary freeways (and legendary traffic jams)? Yes says the Southern California Regional Rail Authority (SCRRA). The SCRRA operates Metrolink a regional rail system that offers transportation for commuters and other passengers. Metrolink trains serve more than 55 stations in the greater Los Angeles area on several regional lines including Antelope Valley Orange County Riverside San Bernardino and Ventura County. Overall Metrolink operates over a network of about 510 miles of track including lines controlled by other entities. The SCRRA was established in 1991; operations began the next year.

	Annual Growth	06/06	06/07	06/08	06/09	06/10
Sales ($ mil.)	5.7%	-	96.9	108.9	113.4	114.3
Net income ($ mil.)	61.8%	-	-	46.0	71.6	120.4
Market value ($ mil.)	-	-	-	-	-	-
Employees	-	-	-	-	-	207

SOUTHERN COMMUNITY FINANCIAL CORPORATION

NASDAQ: SCMF

4605 Country Club Rd.
Winston-Salem NC 27104
Phone: 336-768-8500
Fax: 336-768-2437
Web: www.smallenoughtocare.com

CEO: F Scott Bauer
CFO: James Hastings
HR: -
FYE: December 31
Type: Public

Southern Community Financial is the holding company for Southern Community Bank and Trust which operates more than 20 branches in the Piedmont Triad region and other parts of North Carolina. Serving area individuals small and midsized businesses and homebuilders the bank offers such retail services as checking and savings accounts money market accounts and credit cards. The bulk of Southern Community Financial's loan portfolio is made up of commercial mortgages residential mortgages construction loans and commercial and industrial loans. The bank also offers insurance products through an agreement with The Phoenix Companies. Capital Bank Financial Corporation is buying Southern Community Financial.

SOUTHERN COMPANY (THE)

NYS: SO

30 Ivan Allen Jr. Boulevard, N.W.
Atlanta, GA 30308
Phone: 404 506-5000
Fax: 404 506-0455
Web: www.southerncompany.com

CEO: Thomas A. Fanning
CFO: William C. (Bill) Grantham
HR: Marsha Johnson
FYE: December 31
Type: Public

Southern Power is responding to the power of the burgeoning population growth in the South. The company owns builds acquires and markets energy in the competitive wholesale supply business. It develops and operates independent power plants in the southeastern US. The company which is part of Southern Company's generation and energy marketing operations has more than 8800 MW of primarily fossil-fueled facilities generating capacity operating or under construction in Alabama California Florida Georgia Nevada North Carolina Texas and New Mexico. Southern Power's electricity output is marketed to wholesale customers in the region. It is also developing solar power facilities.

	Annual Growth	12/10	12/11	12/12	12/13	12/14
Sales ($ mil.)	1.4%	17,456.0	17,657.0	16,537.0	17,087.0	18,467.0
Net income ($ mil.)	(0.1%)	2,040.0	2,268.0	2,415.0	1,710.0	2,031.0
Market value ($ mil.)	6.5%	34,704.3	42,021.0	38,861.9	37,318.7	44,580.9
Employees	0.4%	25,940	26,377	26,439	26,300	26,369

SOUTHERN CONNECTICUT BANCORP INC.

NYSE AMEX: SSE

215 Church St.
New Haven CT 06510
Phone: 203-782-1100
Fax: 203-787-5056
Web: www.scbancorp.com

CEO: Joseph J Greco
CFO: Stephen V Ciancarelli
HR: -
FYE: December 31
Type: Public

Southern Connecticut Bancorp is the holding company for The Bank of Southern Connecticut which serves greater New Haven from about five locations. The bank offers standard deposit products such as checking and savings accounts CDs and IRAs. It is mainly a business lender with operating loans and commercial loans secured by real estate comprising about 90% of the company's loan portfolio. Construction consumer installment and home equity loans round out its lending activities. Southern Connecticut Bancorp and Naugatuck Valley Financial called off plans to merge in 2010.

SOUTHERN ENERGY HOMES INC.

144 Corporate Way
Addison AL 35540
Phone: 256-747-8589
Fax: 256-747-8586
Web: www.soenergyhomes.com

CEO: Keith O Holdbrooks
CFO: -
HR: -
FYE: December 31
Type: Subsidiary

Southern Energy Home is all about Southern comfort. A subsidiary of Clayton Homes (itself a subsidiary of Warren Buffett's Berkshire Hathaway) the company builds manufactured homes in single or double sections. Its homes range range from less than 1000 sq. ft. to more than 2500 sq. ft. The company operates under brands including Southern Estates SE Texas Southern Homes and Giles Industries. It sells its homes primarily through dealers in the southern and southeastern US. Southern Energy Homes bought fellow manufactured home company Cavalier Homes for nearly $50 million in 2009.

SOUTHERN FIRST BANCSHARES, INC.

NMS: SFST

100 Verdae Boulevard, Suite 100
Greenville, SC 29606
Phone: 864 679-9000
Fax: –

CEO: R Arthur Seaver
CFO: Michael D Dowling
HR: –
FYE: December 31
Type: Public

Southern First Bancshares operates in two markets: Greenville South Carolina where it operates under the Greenville First Bank moniker and in Columbia South Carolina as Southern First Bank. Selling itself as a local alternative to larger institutions the company which has more than five bank branches targets individuals and small to midsized businesses. It offers traditional deposit services and products including checking accounts savings accounts and CDs. The banks use funds from deposits mainly to write commercial mortgages residential mortgages and commercial business loans.

	Annual Growth	12/10	12/11	12/12	12/13	12/14
Assets ($ mil.)	8.7%	736.5	767.7	798.0	890.8	1,029.9
Net income ($ mil.)	65.2%	0.9	2.1	3.9	5.1	6.6
Market value ($ mil.)	22.9%	46.4	44.5	57.8	82.6	105.8
Employees	10.5%	104	113	125	138	155

SOUTHERN ILLINOIS HEALTHCARE ENTERPRISES INC

1239 E MAIN ST
CARBONDALE, IL 62901-3114
Phone: 618-457-5200
Fax: –
Web: www.sih.net

CEO: Rex Budde
CFO: Mike Kasser
HR: –
FYE: March 31
Type: Private

Southern Illinois Healthcare a nonprofit health care system operates the flagship 140-bed tertiary-care Memorial Hospital of Carbondale as well as Herrin Hospital (with 114 beds) and St. Joseph Memorial Hospital (with 25 beds). The hospitals serve residents of a 16-county region across southern Illinois. The nearly 280-bed system provides services such as birthing cardiac cancer and emergency care as well as surgery and rehabilitation. Its cardiac care is offered through an affiliation with the Prairie Heart Institute at St. John's Hospital in Springfield Illinois. The medical school at Southern Illinois University conducts its Family Practice Residency Program at Memorial Hospital of Carbondale.

	Annual Growth	03/09	03/10	03/11	03/12	03/13
Sales ($ mil.)	5.6%	–	–	394.6	385.7	440.3
Net income ($ mil.)	(4.9%)	–	–	52.3	6.5	47.3
Market value ($ mil.)	–	–	–	–	–	–
Employees	–	–	–	–	–	1,600

SOUTHERN MAINE HEALTH CARE

1 MEDICAL CENTER DR
BIDDEFORD, ME 040059422
Phone: 207-283-7000
Fax: –

CEO: –
CFO: Norm Belair
HR: –
FYE: September 30
Type: Private

Southern Maine Medical Center (SMMC) provides health care services to the residents of York County Maine. The central facility of the not-for-profit medical organization is its 150-bed full-service hospital. Founded in 1906 the medical center also operates a home health care service and outpatient diagnostic and therapy centers. Specialty services include pediatrics cardiology oncology and emergency care. The medical center has a staff of about 200 physicians. SMMC is a member of MaineHealth a network of area hospitals and health clinics.

	Annual Growth	04/06	04/07*	03/09*	04/09*	09/13
Sales ($ mil.)	–	–	(95.0)	0.1	3.4	171.8
Net income ($ mil.)	–	–	–	(0.1)	0.0	5.2
Market value ($ mil.)	–	–	–	–	–	–
Employees	–	–	–	–	–	1,000

*Fiscal year change

SOUTHERN METHODIST UNIVERSITY INC

6425 BOAZ LN
DALLAS, TX 75205
Phone: 214-768-2000
Fax: –
Web: www.smu.edu

CEO: –
CFO: –
HR: –
FYE: May 31
Type: Private

What do former first lady Laura Bush actress Kathy Bates and NFL Hall-of-Famer Doak Walker have in common? They're all graduates of Southern Methodist University (SMU). Founded in 1911 by what is now The United Methodist Church SMU is a nonsectarian private institution offering undergraduate graduate and professional degrees in arts business engineering humanities law science and theology through seven schools. It's one of a handful of schools nationwide to offer an academic major in human rights. Some 11000 students attend the university which has a student-faculty ratio of 11:1. About 85% of the 700-member full-time faculty hold the doctorate or highest degree in their fields.

	Annual Growth	05/07	05/08	05/09	05/11	05/13
Sales ($ mil.)	24.3%	–	–	236.3	602.6	563.3
Net income ($ mil.)	–	–	–	(171.9)	58.1	115.6
Market value ($ mil.)	–	–	–	–	–	–
Employees	–	–	–	–	–	2,200

SOUTHERN MICHIGAN BANCORP INC (UNITED STATES)

NBB: SOMC

51 West Pearl Street
Coldwater, MI 49036
Phone: 517 279-5500
Fax: 517 279-5578
Web: www.smb-t.com

CEO: John H Castle
CFO: Danice L Chartrand
HR: –
FYE: December 31
Type: Public

Southern Michigan Bancorp is the holding company for Southern Michigan Bank & Trust which operates about 20 branches in a primarily rural area near Michigan's border with Indiana and Ohio. The bank provides standard deposit services such as checking and savings accounts money market and heath savings accounts CDs and IRAs. It originates commercial financial agricultural consumer and mortgage loans. The banks also offers trust and investment services. Southern Michigan Bank & Trust got its start in the room of a hotel named Southern Michigan Hotel in 1872.

	Annual Growth	12/10	12/11	12/12	12/13	12/14
Assets ($ mil.)	2.4%	493.9	509.2	528.9	539.5	543.3
Net income ($ mil.)	11.5%	3.1	3.4	4.4	4.5	4.8
Market value ($ mil.)	12.8%	29.5	25.6	37.5	40.2	47.8
Employees	(6.8%)	204	179	187	165	–

SOUTHERN MINNESOTA BEET SUGAR COOPERATIVE

83550 COUNTY ROAD 21
RENVILLE, MN 56284
Phone: 320-329-8305
Fax: –
Web: www.smbsc.com

CEO: Kelvin Thompsen
CFO: –
HR: –
FYE: August 31
Type: Private

Southern Minnesota Beet Sugar Cooperative (SMBSC) offers a sweet deal to its approximately 585 member/farmers. The co-op slices about 3 million tons of Minnesota-grown sugar beets annually. Converted products include baker's sugar and fruit sugar as well as molasses beet pulp pellets and shreds and raffinate (liquid from desugaring molasses). The co-op also provides member services such as seed agronomy research farm support products and workers' compensation insurance. SMBSC's refined and liquid sugars are marketed through Cargill Sweeteners; the by-products (dried beet pulp and beet molasses for use in cattle feed) are marketed by Midwest Agri-Commodities in North American and Europe.

	Annual Growth	08/07	08/08	08/10	08/11	08/12
Sales ($ mil.)	5.7%	–	380.3	439.5	509.0	474.6
Net income ($ mil.)	12.9%	–	120.6	154.9	214.8	196.1
Market value ($ mil.)	–	–	–	–	–	–
Employees	–	–	–	–	–	610

SOUTHERN MISSOURI BANCORP, INC.
NMS: SMBC

531 Vine Street
Poplar Bluff, MO 63901
Phone: 573 778-1800
Fax: –
Web: www.bankwithsouthern.com

CEO: Greg A Steffens
CFO: Matthew T Funke
HR: –
FYE: June 30
Type: Public

Southern Missouri Bancorp is the holding company for Southern Bank (formerly Southern Missouri Bank and Trust) which serves local residents and businesses in southeastern Missouri and northeastern Arkansas through more than 10 branches. Residential mortgages account for the largest percentage of the bank's loan portfolio followed by commercial mortgages and business loans. Construction and consumer loans round out its lending activities. Deposit products include checking savings and money market accounts CDs and IRAs. The bank also offers financial planning and investment services. Originally chartered in 1887 Southern Bank acquired Arkansas-based Southern Bank of Commerce in 2009.

	Annual Growth	06/11	06/12	06/13	06/14	06/15
Assets ($ mil.)	17.2%	688.2	739.2	796.4	1,021.4	1,300.1
Net income ($ mil.)	4.5%	11.5	10.1	10.1	10.1	13.7
Market value ($ mil.)	(2.4%)	154.2	159.5	190.5	264.8	139.9
Employees	17.1%	174	179	181	247	327

SOUTHERN NATIONAL BANCORP OF VIRGINIA INC
NMS: SONA

6830 Old Dominion Drive
McLean, VA 22101
Phone: 703 893-7400
Fax: –

CEO: Georgia S Derrico
CFO: William H Lagos
HR: –
FYE: December 31
Type: Public

Southern National Bancorp of Virginia is the holding company for Sonabank which has some 20 locations in central and northern Virginia and southern Maryland. Founded in 2005 the bank serves small and midsized businesses their owners and retail consumers. It offers standard deposit products including checking savings and money market accounts and CDs. The bank's lending is focused on commercial real estate single-family residential construction and single-family homes as well as other types of consumer and commercial loans. In 2009 Southern National Bancorp acquired the failed Greater Atlantic Bank in an FDIC-assisted transaction; in 2012 it acquired the loans and deposits of HarVest Bank of Maryland.

	Annual Growth	12/10	12/11	12/12	12/13	12/14
Assets ($ mil.)	11.6%	590.8	611.4	723.8	716.2	916.6
Net income ($ mil.)	42.8%	1.8	4.4	6.6	6.3	7.5
Market value ($ mil.)	10.5%	92.8	74.5	99.4	122.3	138.5
Employees	12.8%	107	112	134	140	173

SOUTHERN NEW HAMPSHIRE MEDICAL CENTER

8 PROSPECT ST
NASHUA, NH 030603925
Phone: 603-577-2000
Fax: –
Web: www.snhhs.org

CEO: Thomas E. (Tom) Wilhelmsen
CFO: Michael S. Rose
HR: Horace Porras
FYE: September 30
Type: Private

Southern New Hampshire Medical Center (SNHMC) provides medical care for the residents of the Nashua New Hampshire area and surrounding region through Southern New Hampshire Medical Center and Foundation Medical Partners. The two-campus hospital which has about 190 beds and is part of the Southern New Hampshire Health System offers centers for cancer treatment diabetes education fertility and childbirth obesity sleep disorders trauma and other programs. Outpatient and rehabilitation services are offered through several clinic locations. SNHMC is also affiliated with physician practice organization Foundation Medical Partners and it is a teaching facility for the Dartmouth Medical School.

	Annual Growth	09/09	09/10	09/11	09/12	09/13
Sales ($ mil.)	10.0%	–	214.6	274.2	194.9	285.8
Net income ($ mil.)	–	–	–	(4.9)	16.2	32.6
Market value ($ mil.)	–	–	–	–	–	–
Employees	–	–	–	–	–	1,200

SOUTHERN NUCLEAR OPERATING COMPANY INC.

40 Inverness Center Pkwy.
Birmingham AL 35242-4809
Phone: 205-992-5000
Fax: 619-275-6367
Web: www.allstarglass.net

CEO: Thomas A Fanning
CFO: –
HR: –
FYE: December 31
Type: Subsidiary

The night the lights went out in Georgia they should have called Southern Nuclear Operating Company. The company a subsidiary of Southern Company since 1990 operates six nuclear power units at three plant locations which combined provide about 20% of the electricity used in Alabama and Georgia. Southern Nuclear's Joseph M. Farley Nuclear Plant began commercial operation in 1977. The Edwin I. Hatch Nuclear Plant and the Alvin W. Vogtle Electric Generating Plant are jointly owned by Southern Company's Georgia Power (50%) Oglethorpe Power (30%) the Municipal Electrical Authority of Georgia (18%) and the city of Dalton.

SOUTHERN PIPE & SUPPLY COMPANY INC.

4330 HIGHWAY 39 N
MERIDIAN, MS 393011082
Phone: 601-693-2911
Fax: –
Web: www.southernpipe.com

CEO: –
CFO: Marc Ransier
HR: –
FYE: December 31
Type: Private

Southern Pipe and Supply Co. sells pipes and anything that connects to them. Serving everyone from contractors and homeowners to commercial real estate property owners Southern Pipe sells plumbing heating and air-conditioning supplies through more than 90 stores located throughout seven southeastern states. The company operates a central distribution center and a handful of Southern Bath & Kitchen showrooms that feature various products for homeowners. Southern Pipe's vendors include dozens of supply companies and manufacturers such as MOEN Kohler and Amana Heating and Air Conditioning. Southern Pipe and Supply Co. was founded in 1938.

	Annual Growth	12/0-2	12/0-1	12/00	12/09	12/10
Sales ($ mil.)	–	–	–	(1,879.3)	261.2	284.2
Net income ($ mil.)	231.4%	–	–	0.0	3.4	6.1
Market value ($ mil.)	–	–	–	–	–	–
Employees	–	–	–	–	–	767

SOUTHERN RESEARCH INSTITUTE INC

2000 9TH AVE S
BIRMINGHAM, AL 352052708
Phone: 205-581-2000
Fax: –
Web: www.southernresearch.org

CEO: Arthur J. (Art) Tipton
CFO: David A. Rutledge
HR: –
FYE: January 03
Type: Private

Southern Research Institute performs contract research in areas such as drug development and discovery engineering and environmental and energy issues. The not-for-profit organization launched a life science R&D consulting firm BioSafety Solutions in 2008. The institute's clients have included large government agencies such as the National Institutes of Health the US Department of Defense and NASA as well as corporate clients Mercedes-Benz and Southern Company. The organization tests anti-influenza and anti-HIV drugs for NanoViricides Inc.

	Annual Growth	12/09	12/10	12/11	12/12*	01/14
Sales ($ mil.)	(5.2%)	–	89.9	89.8	79.6	72.6
Net income ($ mil.)	–	–	–	3.5	(3.2)	(5.6)
Market value ($ mil.)	–	–	–	–	–	–
Employees	–	–	–	–	–	535

*Fiscal year change

SOUTHERN UNION COMPANY
NYSE: SUG

5444 Westheimer Rd.	CEO: George L. Lindemann
Houston TX 77056-5306	CFO: Richard N Marshall
Phone: 713-989-2000	HR: –
Fax: 713-989-1121	FYE: December 31
Web: www.southernunionco.com	Type: Subsidiary

Diversified natural gas player Southern Union (a subsidiary of Energy Transfer Equity) is looking to form a more perfect union of natural gas transportation storage gathering processing and distribution assets. Its major utilities Missouri Gas Energy and New England Gas distribute natural gas to more than 550000 customers. Southern Union has gas storage facilities and more than 15000 miles of interstate natural gas pipeline across the US (primarily through Panhandle Energy and its 50% ownership of Florida Gas). It also operates 5500 miles of gathering pipelines and one of North America's largest liquefied natural gas import terminals. In 2012 the company was acquired by Energy Transfer Equity.

SOUTHFIRST BANCSHARES INC.
OTC: SZBI

126 N. Norton Ave.	CEO: Sandra H Stephens
Sylacauga AL 35150	CFO: –
Phone: 256-245-4365	HR: –
Fax: 256-245-6341	FYE: September 30
Web: www.southfirst.com	Type: Public

SouthFirst Bancshares is the holding company for SouthFirst Bank which has three branches in Alabama. Deposit products include checking and savings accounts NOW and money market accounts CDs and IRAs. One- to four-family residential mortgages account for more than half of the company's loan portfolio; SouthFirst Bank also writes commercial mortgages business loans and consumer loans. Residential and commercial construction loans are offered through subsidiary SouthFirst Mortgage. SouthFirst Bancshares agreed to be acquired by Palm Financial in 2009 but Palm terminated the deal later that year and SouthFirst sued the company for breach of agreement. The case is pending in Alabama state court.

SOUTHLAND INDUSTRIES

7390 LINCOLN WAY	CEO: Andrew A. Fimiano
GARDEN GROVE, CA 928411427	CFO: Jon Spallino
Phone: 714-901-5800	HR: Gregory Michaud
Fax: –	FYE: September 30
Web: www.southlandind.com	Type: Private

Southland Industries designs builds and maintains a variety of mechanical systems for facilities around North America. The employee-owned mechanical engineering firm provides design construction fabrication and maintenance of plumbing process piping fire protection HVAC and controls and automation systems. Southland Industries' clients are in the health care life sciences hospitality industrial education government and telecommunication sectors. Projects include the renovation of the Pentagon following the terrorist attacks of September 11 and the M Resort in Las Vegas. Founded in 1949 Southland Industries has offices in the Northern California Southern California Mid-Atlantic and Southwest regions.

	Annual Growth	09/06	09/07	09/08	09/11	09/13
Sales ($ mil.)	(0.1%)	–	363.8	471.6	407.3	362.6
Net income ($ mil.)	(25.4%)	–	–	44.4	61.1	10.2
Market value ($ mil.)	–	–	–	–	–	–
Employees	–	–	–	–	–	1,900

SOUTHSIDE BANCSHARES, INC.
NMS: SBSI

1201 S. Beckham Avenue	CEO: Sam Dawson
Tyler, TX 75701	CFO: Lee R. Gibson
Phone: 903 531-7111	HR: –
Fax: –	FYE: December 31
Web: www.southside.com	Type: Public

Southside Bancshares is the holding company for Southside Bank which boasts nearly 65 branches across East North and Central Texas with many around the cities of Tyler and Longview. About one-third of its branches are located in supermarkets (including Albertsons and Brookshire stores) and 40% are motor bank facilities. The bank provides traditional services such as savings money market and checking accounts CDs and other deposit products as well as trust and wealth management services. Real estate loans primarily residential mortgages make up about half of the company's loan portfolio which also includes business consumer and municipal loans. The bank has total assets exceeding $4.8 billion.

	Annual Growth	12/10	12/11	12/12	12/13	12/14
Assets ($ mil.)	12.5%	2,999.6	3,303.8	3,237.4	3,445.7	4,807.3
Net income ($ mil.)	(14.8%)	39.5	39.1	34.7	41.2	20.8
Market value ($ mil.)	8.2%	533.4	548.3	533.1	692.1	731.8
Employees	8.9%	578	557	574	640	813

SOUTHWALL TECHNOLOGIES INC.
OTC: SWTX

3788 Fabian Way	CEO: B Travis Smith
Palo Alto CA 94303	CFO: –
Phone: 650-798-1200	HR: Dave Cragg
Fax: 650-798-1403	FYE: December 31
Web: www.southwall.com	Type: Subsidiary

Southwall Technologies has developed a thin skin. The company makes thin-film coatings for auto glass electronic displays and architectural uses. The films absorb reflect and transmit energy such as UV light rays. Customers include glass makers like Saint Gobain and Pilkington. Southwall also makes films that reduce glare on computer screens LCDs phones and ATMs. Its architectural films are used on glass to insulate and to protect interiors from UV light. Investment firms with stakes in Southwall include Needham Capital Management (50%) and Dolphin Direct Equity Partners (21%). In 2011 Solutia acquired Southwall for an estimated $113 million.

SOUTHWEST AIRLINES CO
NYS: LUV

P.O. Box 36611	CEO: Gary C. Kelly
Dallas, TX 75235-1611	CFO: Tammy Romo
Phone: 214 792-4000	HR: –
Fax: 214 792-5015	FYE: December 31
Web: www.southwest.com	Type: Public

Southwest Airlines will fly any plane (as long as it's a Boeing) and let passengers sit anywhere they like (as long as they get there first). Sticking with what has worked Southwest has expanded its low-cost no-frills no-reserved-seats approach to air travel throughout the US to serve nearly 90 destinations across North America. Now the largest carrier of US domestic passengers Southwest still stands as an inspiration for scrappy low-fare upstarts the world over. The carrier has enjoyed 41 straight profitable years amid the airline industry's ups and downs. Southwest's fleet numbers about 700 aircraft including 665 Boeing 737s.

	Annual Growth	12/11	12/12	12/13	12/14	12/15
Sales ($ mil.)	6.1%	15,658.0	17,088.0	17,699.0	18,605.0	19,820.0
Net income ($ mil.)	87.1%	178.0	421.0	754.0	1,136.0	2,181.0
Market value ($ mil.)	49.8%	5,543.5	6,631.4	12,200.8	27,406.5	27,885.7
Employees	2.2%	45,392	45,861	44,831	46,278	49,583

SOUTHWEST BANCORP, INC. (OK)

NMS: OKSB

608 South Main Street	CEO: Mark W. Funke
Stillwater, OK 74074	CFO: Joe T Shockley
Phone: 405 742-1800	HR: –
Fax: –	FYE: December 31
Web: www.oksb.com	Type: Public

Southwest does what it can to make its earnings charts point northeast. Southwest Bancorp is the holding company for Bank SNB (formerly Stillwater National Bank and Trust Company) which has more than 20 branches across the states of Oklahoma Texas and Kansas. The bank primarily uses the funds it collects from deposits such as CDs and checking savings and money market accounts to originate commercial mortgages construction loans and commercial loans. Southwest Bancorp specializes in serving the health care industry offering such niche services as financing to launch physicians' practices and document imaging.

	Annual Growth	12/10	12/11	12/12	12/13	12/14
Assets ($ mil.)	(8.9%)	2,820.5	2,382.9	2,122.3	1,981.4	1,942.0
Net income ($ mil.)	5.5%	17.0	(68.3)	16.2	17.4	21.0
Market value ($ mil.)	8.8%	238.0	114.4	215.0	305.6	333.2
Employees	(4.5%)	432	435	422	402	359

SOUTHWEST CATHOLIC HEALTH NETWORK CORPORATION

4350 E COTTON CENTER BLVD	CEO: Mark Fisher
PHOENIX, AZ 850408852	CFO: –
Phone: 602-230-9921	HR: –
Fax: –	FYE: June 30
Web: www.mercycareplan.com	Type: Private

Southwest Catholic Health Network (SCHN) which does business as Mercy Care Plan is a not-for-profit provider of managed health care services in Arizona. The Mercy Care Plan provides these services under a contract with the Arizona Health Care Cost Containment System the state of Arizona's Medicaid program. The plan provides health coverage and prescription drug benefits to some 300000 members. The company founded in 1985 is affiliated with St. Joseph's Hospital & Medical Center (which is part of Catholic Healthcare West) Dignity Health and Carondelet Health Network. The plan is administered by health care management firm Schaller Anderson.

	Annual Growth	06/08	06/09	06/10	06/11	06/12
Sales ($ mil.)	(1.3%)	–	1,814.8	1,904.2	1,939.8	1,747.6
Net income ($ mil.)	(24.0%)	–	–	49.0	58.3	28.3
Market value ($ mil.)	–	–	–	–	–	–
Employees	–	–	–	–	–	500

SOUTHWEST GAS CORPORATION

NYS: SWX

5241 Spring Mountain Road, P.O. Box 98510	CEO: John P. Hester
Las Vegas, NV 89193-8510	CFO: Roy R. Centrella
Phone: 702 876-7237	HR: –
Fax: 702 873-3820	FYE: December 31
Web: www.swgas.com	Type: Public

The sunny southwestern US is smiling on Southwest Gas. The largest gas supplier in Arizona and Nevada it provides natural gas to 1.93 million customers in the two states as well as in portions of California. Southwest Gas acquires its natural gas from 46 suppliers and pumps it through distribution mains. It also owns a transmission pipeline that supplies the Las Vegas area and affiliate Paiute Pipeline transports gas from the Idaho-Nevada border to Reno and Lake Tahoe. Another Southwest Gas unit NPL Construction is an underground piping contractor that serves gas distributors. During 2014 its construction holding company Centuri led by NPL Construction served more than 100 major customers.

	Annual Growth	12/10	12/11	12/12	12/13	12/14
Sales ($ mil.)	3.8%	1,830.4	1,887.2	1,927.8	1,950.8	2,121.7
Net income ($ mil.)	8.0%	103.9	112.3	133.3	145.3	141.1
Market value ($ mil.)	13.9%	1,706.0	1,976.8	1,973.0	2,601.1	2,875.6
Employees	6.7%	4,802	5,754	6,015	5,980	6,232

SOUTHWEST GEORGIA FINANCIAL CORP.

ASE: SGB

201 First Street, S.E.	CEO: Dewitt Drew
Moultrie, GA 31768	CFO: George R Kirkland
Phone: 229 985-1120	HR: –
Fax: 229 985-0251	FYE: December 31
Web: www.sgfc.com	Type: Public

Southwest Georgia Financial is the holding company for Southwest Georgia Bank which also operates as Baker County Bank Bank of Pavo and Sylvester Banking Company. With about 10 locations the bank provides such retail services as checking and savings accounts NOW accounts CDs and credit cards as well as property/casualty life and disability insurance and trust and investment services. Bank subsidiary Empire Financial Services provides commercial mortgage banking services. Real estate loans account for some three-fourths of the company's lending portfolio. Southwest Georgia Bank was founded as Moultrie National Bank in 1928.

	Annual Growth	12/10	12/11	12/12	12/13	12/14
Assets ($ mil.)	6.0%	296.4	305.7	347.2	373.9	374.3
Net income ($ mil.)	11.8%	1.9	1.5	1.9	2.8	2.9
Market value ($ mil.)	7.1%	27.8	21.5	24.8	29.5	36.6
Employees	(2.2%)	127	127	125	117	116

SOUTHWEST LOUISIANA ELECTRIC MEMBERSHIP CORPORATION

3420 NE EVANGELINE TRWY	CEO: J U Gajan
LAFAYETTE, LA 705072554	CFO: Katherine Domingue
Phone: 337-896-5384	HR: –
Fax: –	FYE: December 31
Web: www.slemco.com	Type: Private

Southwest Louisiana Electric Membership Corporation (SLEMCO) is no slow-poke when it comes to serving more than 93400 power customers in eight Louisiana parishes. SLEMCO provides regulated power transmission and distribution services via 9000 miles of power lines to its residential commercial and industrial members. It also provides energy conservation and street and security lighting services. SLEMCO extended assistance to help repair the badly damaged infrastructure in parishes from New Orleans to the Mississippi border following the devastation caused by Hurricane Katrina.

	Annual Growth	12/05	12/06	12/07	12/08	12/13
Sales ($ mil.)	–	–	(1,743.5)	152.7	161.8	198.5
Net income ($ mil.)	–	–	–	10.5	9.2	(0.1)
Market value ($ mil.)	–	–	–	–	–	–
Employees	–	–	–	–	–	270

SOUTHWEST RESEARCH INSTITUTE INC

6220 CULEBRA RD	CEO: –
SAN ANTONIO, TX 782385100	CFO: –
Phone: 210-684-5111	HR: –
Fax: –	FYE: September 26
Web: www.swri.org.cn	Type: Private

If you're looking for research at an institute in the Southwest look no further. Founded in 1947 by oilman and rancher Thomas Slick Jr. Southwest Research Institute (SwRI) is an independent not-for-profit research and development institution that contracts to explore subjects in areas including automation and data systems applied physics space science and engineering and chemistry. SwRI has about 2700 scientists engineers and support staff at some 40 laboratories and offices in the US China and the UK. Customers include the private sector and government agencies. SwRI's Signature Science subsidiary researches national security environmental management and biotechnology.

	Annual Growth	09/10	09/11	09/12	09/13	09/14
Sales ($ mil.)	(1.9%)	–	581.4	584.2	569.6	548.8
Net income ($ mil.)	(53.3%)	–	–	36.1	29.9	7.9
Market value ($ mil.)	–	–	–	–	–	–
Employees	–	–	–	–	–	2,973

SOUTHWEST WATER COMPANY

1325 N. Grand Ave. Ste. 100	CEO: Robert Carroll
Covina CA 91724	CFO: Ben Smith
Phone: 626-543-2500	HR: –
Fax: 404-846-6282	FYE: December 31
Web: www.postproperties.com	Type: Private

As any resident of the Southwest can tell you you need water to survive and thrive in this arid region of the US. SouthWest Water Company provides water and wastewater services to more than 1 million customers and utility-related contract services to 400 clients in five states. Its Utility Group owns and operates more than 130 regulated water and wastewater systems in Alabama California Mississippi Oklahoma and Texas. The company's non-regulated segment contracts with cities public agencies and private companies to provide them with water and wastewater services.

SOUTHWESTERN ELECTRIC POWER CO.   NL:

1 Riverside Plaza	CEO: Nicholas K Akins
Columbus, OH 43215-2373	CFO: Brian X Tierney
Phone: 614 716-1000	HR: –
Fax: –	FYE: December 31
	Type: Public

Southwestern Electric Power cuts a wide welcome swath through the southwestern US to help beat the sweltering heat. The utility founded in 1912 serves some 520400 electricity customers in portions of Arkansas Louisiana and Texas. Southwestern Electric Power operates 20450 miles of transmission and distribution lines. Southwestern Electric Power also has interests in fossil-fueled power plants (including 73% of the $1.7 billion Turk plant in Arkansas) that give it a generating capacity of 4850 MW and it sells power to wholesale customers. The utility is a subsidiary of American Electric Power Company (AEP).

	Annual Growth	12/10	12/11	12/12	12/13	12/14
Sales ($ mil.)	4.9%	1,523.5	1,653.8	1,577.8	1,795.8	1,846.4
Net income ($ mil.)	(0.4%)	142.6	161.3	198.9	149.8	140.4
Market value ($ mil.)	–	–	–	–	–	–
Employees	1.5%	1,382	1,462	1,472	1,449	1,468

SOUTHWESTERN ENERGY COMPANY   NYS: SWN

10000 Energy Drive	CEO: William J. (Bill) Way
Spring, TX 77389	CFO: R. Craig Owen
Phone: 832 796-1000	HR: Jennifer Perkins
Fax: –	FYE: December 31
Web: www.swn.com	Type: Public

Southwestern Energy is putting a lot of energy into gas and oil exploration and production and midstream activities — natural gas gathering transportation and marketing — primarily in the Southwest of the US. The company operates in Arkansas Oklahoma and Texas but also in Pennsylvania and New Brunswick Canada. In 2014 the oil and gas company reported estimated proved reserves of more than 10 trillion cu. ft. of natural gas equivalent all of which was natural gas. Southwestern's core properties include assets in the Fayetteville Shale play and the Marcellus Shale. SEECO Inc. and Southwestern Energy Production Company (SEPCO) are the company's primary exploration and production units.

	Annual Growth	12/10	12/11	12/12	12/13	12/14
Sales ($ mil.)	11.5%	2,610.7	2,952.9	2,715.0	3,371.1	4,038.0
Net income ($ mil.)	11.2%	604.1	637.8	(707.1)	703.5	924.0
Market value ($ mil.)	(7.6%)	13,268.1	11,322.0	11,843.1	13,941.6	9,673.7
Employees	7.4%	2,088	2,287	2,427	2,621	2,781

SOUTHWESTERN UNIVERSITY

1001 E UNIVERSITY AVE	CEO: –
GEORGETOWN, TX 786266107	CFO: –
Phone: 512-863-1435	HR: Elma Benavides
Fax: –	FYE: June 30
Web: www.southwestern.edu	Type: Private

The first institution of higher learning in Texas Southwestern University was chartered by the Republic of Texas in 1840. The liberal arts university consists of The Brown College of Arts and Sciences and The Sarofim School of Fine Arts. It offers more than two-dozen undergraduate majors as well as pre-professional and certification programs and confers bachelor's degrees in arts music fine arts and science. Affiliated with The United Methodist Church Southwestern University has an enrollment of more than 1500 students. More than 80% of students live in residence halls on campus which is located on the edge of the Texas Hill Country in Georgetown Texas just north of Austin.

	Annual Growth	06/09	06/10	06/12	06/13	06/14
Sales ($ mil.)	(1.8%)	–	62.7	46.1	69.0	58.2
Net income ($ mil.)	–	–	–	(25.2)	43.3	24.4
Market value ($ mil.)	–	–	–	–	–	–
Employees	–	–	–	–	–	357

SOVRAN SELF STORAGE, INC.   NYS: SSS

6467 Main Street	CEO: David L. Rogers
Williamsville, NY 14221	CFO: Andrew J. Gregoire
Phone: 716 633-1850	HR: –
Fax: 716 633-1860	FYE: December 31
Web: www.unclebobs.com	Type: Public

Sovran Self Storage may not be the ruler of all storage companies but it does have the power to store your goods. A self-administered real estate investment trust (REIT) the company operates self-storage facilities under the Uncle Bob's Self Storage brand name. The REIT owns and manages more than 470 facilities totaling more than 31 million sq. ft. of storage space. Its properties usually offer features such as humidity-controlled spaces; outdoor storage for cars boats and RVs; and the use of a free truck to help clients haul their stuff. Serving both individual and business customers the company owns properties in about two dozen states.

	Annual Growth	12/10	12/11	12/12	12/13	12/14
Sales ($ mil.)	14.1%	192.1	211.2	236.0	273.5	326.1
Net income ($ mil.)	21.5%	40.6	30.6	55.1	74.1	88.5
Market value ($ mil.)	24.1%	1,255.4	1,455.3	2,118.0	2,222.7	2,974.7
Employees	7.6%	1,027	1,164	1,228	1,268	1,378

SP PLUS CORP   NMS: SP

200 E. Randolph Street, Suite 7700	CEO: G. Marc Baumann
Chicago, IL 60601-7702	CFO: Vance C. Johnston
Phone: 312 274-2000	HR: –
Fax: –	FYE: December 31
Web: www.spplus.com	Type: Public

SP Plus (formerly Standard Parking) wants to be the driving force in the parking industry — and it likely is. The parking behemoth manages about 4200 surface and multilevel parking facilities for airports hospitals hotels local governments office buildings retail centers sports venues and universities in more than 400 cities throughout the US and Canada. Its airport facilities consist of parking and shuttle bus operations at more than 75 airports including Chicago O'Hare and Dallas/Fort Worth International. Overall SP Plus provides more than 2.1 million parking spaces. In a sweeping move for the parking industry it acquired Central Parking Corporation one of its biggest rivals in 2012.

	Annual Growth	12/10	12/11	12/12	12/13	12/14
Sales ($ mil.)	20.4%	721.1	729.7	953.9	1,466.8	1,514.7
Net income ($ mil.)	8.2%	16.8	17.9	3.1	12.1	23.1
Market value ($ mil.)	7.4%	420.0	395.4	486.6	576.2	558.3
Employees	19.0%	11,971	11,914	25,011	23,937	24,030

SPACE SYSTEMS/LORAL INC.

3825 Fabian Way
Palo Alto CA 94303-4604
Phone: 650-852-4000
Fax: 610-926-6327
Web: www.rednersmarkets.com

CEO: –
CFO: Ron Haley
HR: –
FYE: December 31
Type: Subsidiary

For Space Systems/Loral (SS/L) business is up in the air. The company makes satellites and related accessories for commercial and government customers. Its fixed satellite services supplies satellites that beam TV radio and other communications information from orbit to a fixed location on the ground. Its direct broadcast satellites send TV to DISH and DIRECTV subscribers' homes while broadband services facilitate Internet connections across North America. The mobile broadcast services and mobile satellite services groups send audio video and communications signals to cars and cell phones. SS/L is a subsidiary of Loral Space & Communications which has agreed to sell SS/L to a rival.

SPACELABS HEALTHCARE INC.

5150 220th Ave. SE
Issaquah WA 98029
Phone: 425-657-7200
Fax: 425-657-7212
Web: www.spacelabshealthcare.com

CEO: Deepak Chopra
CFO: Alan Edrick
HR: –
FYE: June 30
Type: Subsidiary

Spacelabs Healthcare launched monitoring the health of NASA astronauts; now it designs makes sells and services diagnostic and therapeutic equipment for Earth-bound patients. The company operates through four divisions: Patient Monitoring & Connectivity Anesthesia Delivery & Ventilation Diagnostic Cardiology and Clinician Education. Its Ultraview bedside patient monitor and telemetry systems monitor patient data and transmit it to caregivers through a wireless network. Its Blease anesthesia delivery systems and ventilators are used in operative and perioperative settings. Spacelabs Healthcare is owned by OSI Systems and accounts for about 30% of its parent company's sales.

SPACENET INC.

1750 Old Meadow Rd.
McLean VA 22102
Phone: 703 040 1000
Fax: 703-848-1012
Web: www.spacenet.com

CEO: Daryl Woodward
CFO: Rodney Kramer
HR: –
FYE: December 31
Type: Subsidiary

Spacenet comes from Israel not outer space. The US arm of Israeli satellite network provider Gilat provides high-speed broadband Internet access via satellite to corporate customers across the US Puerto Rico and the US Virgin Islands. (Corporations use satellite Internet to speed up retail transactions and reduce network downtime). Spacenet also offers on-demand satellite connectivity rural telephone voice and videoconferencing services. Residential customers are served through its StarBand brand which is also offered in several Caribbean and Central American countries. Subsidiary Spacenet Integrated Government Solutions (SIGS) caters to federal agencies such as the Depts. of Defense and Homeland Security.

SPAN-AMERICA MEDICAL SYSTEMS, INC.

NMS: SPAN

70 Commerce Center
Greenville, SC 29615
Phone: 864 288-8877
Fax: –
Web: www.spanamerica.com

CEO: James D Ferguson
CFO: Richard C Coggins
HR: –
FYE: October 03
Type: Public

With its mattresses and cushioning products Span-America Medical Systems offers more comfort to the sick and wounded than Grandma's chicken soup. The company's medical products division makes therapeutic mattresses and mattress overlays (under the Geo-Matt and PressureGuard brand names) as well as Span-Aid patient positioners (used to elevate and support body parts) and Isch-Dish pressure-relief seat cushions to aid wound healing. Span-America also markets skin care creams for wound management and consumer bedding and industrial foam products. It sells its wares through sales staff and distributors to hospitals home health care dealers and extended-care facilities in the US and Canada.

	Annual Growth	10/11*	09/12	09/13	09/14*	10/15
Sales ($ mil.)	5.2%	52.6	76.1	73.8	55.9	64.3
Net income ($ mil.)	1.9%	3.7	5.2	5.1	2.6	4.0
Market value ($ mil.)	6.5%	37.4	45.9	58.6	52.1	48.2
Employees	0.6%	255	344	275	253	261

*Fiscal year change

SPANISH BROADCASTING SYSTEM, INC.

NMS: SBSA

7007 NW 77th Avenue
Miami, FL 33166
Phone: 305 441-6901
Fax: –
Web: www.spanishbroadcasting.com

CEO: Raul Alarcon Jr
CFO: Joseph A Garcia
HR: –
FYE: December 31
Type: Public

You might say this company is turning up the volume on Spanish radio. Spanish Broadcasting System (SBS) is one of the largest Spanish-language radio broadcasters in the US (along with Univision Radio and Entravision) with 20 stations in the US and Puerto Rico. Its radio stations serve such large markets as Chicago Los Angeles New York City and Miami reaching about half the US Hispanic population with music formats ranging from regional Mexican to Spanish tropical. In addition the company operates website LaMusica.com and several TV stations that offer original and syndicated Spanish-language programming under the Mega TV brand. Chairman and CEO Raúl Alarcón Jr. controls about 80% of SBS.

	Annual Growth	12/10	12/11	12/12	12/13	12/14
Sales ($ mil.)	1.8%	136.1	141.0	139.5	153.8	146.3
Net income ($ mil.)	–	15.0	23.7	(1.3)	(88.6)	(20.0)
Market value ($ mil.)	41.6%	4.7	19.5	16.3	21.5	18.9
Employees	2.9%	497	525	561	603	557

SPANSION INC

NYS: CODE

915 DeGuigne Drive
Sunnyvale, CA 94088
Phone: 408 962-2500
Fax: –
Web: www.spansion.com

CEO: John H Kispert
CFO: Randy W Furr
HR: –
FYE: December 29
Type: Public

Spansion favors flash expansion. The company originally formed as a joint venture between Advanced Micro Devices and Fujitsu makes and markets flash memory devices. Flash memory is used in a wide variety of electronic devices including wireless phones networking equipment and automotive subsystems. Although the flash memory market is dominated by NAND flash memory (used in MP3 players digital cameras USB flash drives) Spansion primarily sells NOR flash memory (used mainly in wireless phones). To address the NAND market the company is developing new NAND products based on its MirrorBit technology. Spansion also provides hardware development tools and production manufacturing support.

	Annual Growth	05/10*	12/10	12/11	12/12	12/13
Sales ($ mil.)	34.0%	403.6	764.7	1,069.9	915.9	971.7
Net income ($ mil.)	–	363.6	(96.7)	(55.9)	24.9	(78.3)
Market value ($ mil.)	(12.5%)	–	1,185.9	457.5	803.8	794.9
Employees	2.7%	–	3,400	3,375	2,838	3,685

*Fiscal year change

SPAR GROUP, INC.

NAS: SGRP

333 Westchester Avenue, South Building, Suite 204
White Plains, NY 10604
Phone: 914 332-4100
Fax: –
Web: www.sparinc.com

CEO: Jill M. Blanchard
CFO: James R. Segreto
HR: –
FYE: December 31
Type: Public

SPAR Group knows how to fight for shelf space. Founded in 1967 the company provides an array of marketing and merchandising services to manufacturers and retailers. Clients include drugstore chains grocery stores and convenience stores. SPAR Group offers services such as in-store product demonstration and sampling shelf maintenance mystery shopping database marketing teleservices and market research. The company has an international presence through operations and joint ventures located in about 10 countries including Australia Canada India Japan New Zealand Romania South Africa and China.

	Annual Growth	12/10	12/11	12/12	12/13	12/14
Sales ($ mil.)	17.9%	63.2	73.5	102.8	112.0	122.0
Net income ($ mil.)	10.8%	2.2	2.2	2.9	3.4	3.3
Market value ($ mil.)	13.9%	17.1	20.6	35.8	40.7	28.8
Employees	(34.9%)	10,000	12,000	18,300	19,000	1,800

SPARK NETWORKS INC

ASE: LOV

11150 Santa Monica Boulevard, Suite 600
Los Angeles, CA 90025
Phone: 310 893-0550
Fax: –
Web: www.spark.net

CEO: Michael S. Egan
CFO: Robert W. O'Hare
HR: –
FYE: December 31
Type: Public

Find yourself humming "Matchmaker Matchmaker make me a match" just a little too often? Spark Networks (formerly MatchNet) can help. The company owns and operates a variety of online personal sites including dating sites JDate.com (for Jewish singles) BlackSingles.com and ChristianMingle.com. Spark Networks also operates websites in English Hebrew and French. Most revenue comes from subscriptions — members pay a monthly fee to communicate with other users. (Customers are offered discounts for longer-term subscriptions.) In addition the company offers offline events and opportunities for travel (such as cruises dinners speed dating and mixers) designed to encourage live social interaction.

	Annual Growth	12/10	12/11	12/12	12/13	12/14
Sales ($ mil.)	10.8%	40.9	48.5	61.7	69.4	61.6
Net income ($ mil.)	–	3.7	(1.6)	(15.0)	(12.4)	(1.1)
Market value ($ mil.)	4.9%	72.9	93.3	191.5	151.3	88.2
Employees	11.4%	144	161	182	200	222

SPARKS MARKETING GROUP INC.

2828 Charter Rd.
Philadelphia PA 19154
Phone: 215-676-1100
Fax: 215-676-1991
Web: www.sparksonline.com

CEO: Scott Tarte
CFO: –
HR: –
FYE: December 31
Type: Private

Remember those junior high classmates whose great science fair project backdrops made yours look like a monkey put it together? Well they now work for Sparks Marketing Group making exhibits displays and fixtures for trade shows theme parks museums and retailers. The company operates primarily through subsidiaries Sparks Exhibits & Environments and Sparks Custom Retail and manages projects from start to finish including event coordination and marketing refurbishing and storage. Customers include "FORTUNE" 1000 companies which typically spend more than $200000 on exhibits. Sparks serves hundreds of clients worldwide through almost 10 facilities across the US and China.

SPARTA INC.

25531 Commercentre Dr. Ste. 120
Lake Forest CA 92630-8874
Phone: 949-768-8161
Fax: 949-583-9113
Web: www.sparta.com

CEO: Charles L Harrington
CFO: –
HR: Eloise Carnell
FYE: December 31
Type: Subsidiary

SPARTA (doing business as Cobham Analytic Solutions) equips modern soldiers with something more than a spear and shield. The company provides technical products and services to the US military the Department of Defense and the Department of Homeland Security. As a prime contractor and subcontractor it contributes to the design and development of tactical and strategic weapons and defense systems including ballistic missile defense systems. The company also fabricates prototype hardware and makes composite parts for aircraft and missile systems. Parent Cobham plc sold SPARTA to Parsons Corporation in November 2011 for $350 million in cash.

SPARTAN MOTORS, INC.

NMS: SPAR

1541 Reynolds Road
Charlotte, MI 48813
Phone: 517 543-6400
Fax: –
Web: www.spartanmotors.com

CEO: Daryl M. Adams
CFO: Frederick (Rick) Sohm
HR: Thomas (Thom) Schultz
FYE: December 31
Type: Public

Spartan Motors has built itself on the foundation of its chassis. Founded in 1975 Spartan Motors (through its core Spartan Chassis unit) makes custom chassis for fire trucks motor homes and other specialty vehicles including mine resistant and light armored vehicles for the US military. The company also manufactures emergency vehicles through three subsidiaries that make up its Emergency Vehicle Team (EVTeam) segment. Its Crimson Fire subsidiary builds fire truck bodies while its Crimson Fire Aerials business makes ladder units for fire trucks. Other operations include subsidiary Utilimaster which makes custom walk-in and hi-cube service and delivery vans truck bodies and other commercial vehicles.

	Annual Growth	12/10	12/11	12/12	12/13	12/14
Sales ($ mil.)	1.3%	480.7	426.0	470.6	469.5	506.8
Net income ($ mil.)	(27.0%)	4.1	0.8	(2.5)	(6.0)	1.2
Market value ($ mil.)	(3.6%)	207.6	164.0	167.7	228.4	179.3
Employees	0.9%	1,541	1,635	554	1,900	1,600

SPARTANNASH CO.

NMS: SPTN

850 76th Street S.W., P.O. Box 8700
Grand Rapids, MI 49518
Phone: 616 878-2000
Fax: –

CEO: Dennis Eidson
CFO: David M. (Dave) Staples
HR: –
FYE: January 03
Type: Public

In the grocery and distribution wars SpartanNash (formerly Spartan Stores) is up for the fight. The grocery retailer and wholesaler operates 100 Michigan supermarkets under the Family Fare Supermarkets No Frills D&W Fresh Market VG's Food and Pharmacy Sun Mart and more than a dozen other banners. Besides selling national brand-goods stores offer private-label items under the Spartan TopCare Valu Time and Full Circle names. SpartanNash is also a leading grocery wholesaler distributing more than 55000 food and merchandise items to 2100 independent supermarkets in Michigan Indiana and Ohio. Founded in 1917 as a cooperative grocery distributor Spartan Stores acquired Nash-Finch in 2013.

	Annual Growth	03/11	03/12	03/13*	12/13*	01/15
Sales ($ mil.)	33.0%	2,533.1	2,634.2	2,608.2	2,597.2	7,916.1
Net income ($ mil.)	16.0%	32.3	31.8	27.4	0.7	58.6
Market value ($ mil.)	14.4%	565.9	679.9	658.5	890.4	968.9
Employees	17.0%	8,600	8,400	8,650	15,900	16,100

*Fiscal year change

SPARTON CORP.

NYS: SPA

425 N. Martingale Road, Suite 1000
Schaumburg, IL 60173-2213
Phone: 847 762-5800
Fax: –
Web: www.sparton.com

CEO: Joseph J. Hartnett
CFO: Joseph G. McCormack
HR: Melanie Farrell
FYE: June 30
Type: Public

As its name implies Sparton is big on defense. Working for aerospace defense and medical companies the company provides contract electronics manufacturing services primarily the design and production of electronic and electromechanical devices. Its products include printed circuit boards sensors and electromechanical components as well as fully built systems and devices. The company also manufactures an anti-submarine warfare device called a sonobuoy for the US Navy and foreign governments. Sparton which tracks its roots to 1900 generates most of its sales in the US.

	Annual Growth	06/11	06/12	06/13	06/14	06/15
Sales ($ mil.)	17.1%	203.4	223.6	266.0	336.1	382.1
Net income ($ mil.)	10.2%	7.5	9.5	13.6	13.0	11.0
Market value ($ mil.)	27.9%	101.0	97.9	170.4	274.3	270.1
Employees	18.4%	1,013	950	1,375	1,483	1,990

SPAW GLASS CONSTRUCTION CORPORATION

13800 WEST RD
HOUSTON, TX 77041-1114
Phone: 281-970-5300
Fax: –
Web: www.spawglass.com

CEO: Joel Stone
CFO: –
HR: –
FYE: December 31
Type: Private

You don't need a spyglass to notice general contractor SpawGlass Construction Corp.'s projects. The buildings include the Cynthia Woods Mitchell Pavillion the Cockrell Butterfly Center and Wortham IMAX Theatre. SpawGlass provides design/build and preconstruction services to its clients for projects that range from office buildings special events facilities and dormitories to retail institutional and health care facilities. The company founded in 1953 is an employee-owned subsidiary of SpawGlass Holding LP which also owns general builder SpawGlass Contractors.

	Annual Growth	12/02	12/03	12/04	12/05	12/10
Sales ($ mil.)	(5.6%)	–	226.4	259.3	241.4	150.7
Net income ($ mil.)	33.9%	–	1.4	2.5	2.7	10.5
Market value ($ mil.)	–	–	–	–	–	–
Employees	–	–	–	–	–	220

SPAW GLASS HOLDING L.P.

9331 CORPORATE DR
SELMA, TX 781541250
Phone: 210-651-9000
Fax: –
Web: www.spawglass.com

CEO: Joel Stone
CFO: Robert Friedel
HR: –
FYE: December 31
Type: Private

Deep in the heart of Texas SpawGlass Holding is busy providing general building and construction management services for commercial and institutional projects through its SpawGlass Construction and SpawGlass Contractors subsidiaries. The group also offers design/build delivery and tenant finish-out services. Among its landmark projects is the interior restoration of the Texas State Capitol. It also worked on the NASA Shuttle Flight Training Facility near Houston and the University of Texas Health Science Center at San Antonio. Louis Spaw and Frank Glass formed SpawGlass in 1953. The company now employee-owned has offices in Austin Houston San Antonio and the Rio Grande Valley in Texas.

	Annual Growth	12/05	12/06	12/07	12/09	12/13
Sales ($ mil.)	–	–	(1,121.7)	336.5	461.0	442.6
Net income ($ mil.)	(7.2%)	–	–	5.9	8.7	3.8
Market value ($ mil.)	–	–	–	–	–	–
Employees	–	–	–	–	–	450

SPEAKEASY INC.

1201 Western Ave.
Seattle WA 98101
Phone: 206-728-9770
Fax: 206-728-1500
Web: www.speakeasy.net

CEO: Bruce Chatterley
CFO: John Higgie
HR: –
FYE: December 31
Type: Subsidiary

You need a modem — not a secret knock — to get into this Speakeasy. Speakeasy offers broadband voice and data services such as DSL access and Voice over Internet Protocol (VoIP) primarily to consumers and small businesses. Speakeasy's services for businesses include private wide-area networks for companies with multiple locations as well as such managed services as Web and e-mail hosting. It also offers dial-up connections and personal Web page hosting for consumers. Speakeasy serves 120 cities across the US through points of presence (POPs) in Atlanta Chicago Dallas Los Angeles New York Seattle San Francisco and Washington DC. The company was sold by electronics retailer Best Buy to MegaPath in 2010.

SPECIAL DEVICES INCORPORATED

14370 White Sage Rd.
Moorpark CA 93021
Phone: 805-553-1200
Fax: 805-553-1211
Web: www.specialdevices.com

CEO: –
CFO: Harry Rector
HR: –
FYE: October 31
Type: Private

For now Special Devices is facing delays in blasting off. The company aims to take its place among the leading US makers of initiators (pyrotechnic devices) — used primarily in automotive airbag systems. The airbag initiators activate inflators that enable the airbag to be deployed. The company also makes micro gas generators that remove seatbelt slack in the event of a collision. Special Devices sells its products primarily to airbag manufacturers including Autoliv and TRW Automotive. Special Devices filed for Chapter 11 protection from creditors in late 2008. The company's initiators have since exited their application in aerospace/military and mining blasting operations.

SPECIAL DIVERSIFIED OPPORTUNITIES INC

NBB: SDOI

1521 Concord Pike, Suite 301
Wilmington DE 19803
Phone: 302 824-7062
Fax: 302 456-6770
Web: www.sdix.com

CEO: Philip T Blazek
CFO: Kevin J Bratton
HR: Beth Knight
FYE: December 31
Type: Public

Strategic Diagnostics dba SDIX provides life sciences test design and development products and services. Offerings include antibodies reagents bio-processing and custom assay design and development. Its products are used by and embedded in the products of pharmaceutical biotech diagnostic and biomedical research customers around the world. The company also offers detection kits for tasks such as food pathogen testing to the food and beverage manufacturing and agricultural and agro-science industries. Companies that SDIX has forged research partnerships with have included BD Diagnostics McDonald's Monsanto and Johnson & Johnson. Sales to non-domestic customers account for less than 15% of sales.

	Annual Growth	12/08	12/09	12/10	12/11	12/12
Sales ($ mil.)	(14.1%)	27.7	27.2	28.3	24.2	15.1
Net income ($ mil.)	–	(15.8)	(1.7)	(1.0)	(0.3)	4.3
Market value ($ mil.)	4.7%	18.7	28.6	37.1	38.8	22.5
Employees	(9.2%)	169	154	155	148	115

SPECIAL METALS CORPORATION

3200 Riverside Dr.
Huntington WV 25705-1771
Phone: 304-526-5100
Fax: 304-526-5643
Web: www.specialmetals.com

CEO: Joseph Snowden
CFO: Douglas D Watts
HR: –
FYE: December 31
Type: Subsidiary

Special Metals makes nickel- and cobalt-based alloys and superalloys for aircraft engine rotating components and other high-performance systems. The company's products are designed to withstand extreme heat stress and corrosion. They are available as billet plate and tube; extruded shapes; and wire and welding consumables. Special Metals also makes wrought superalloys and superalloy powders. Customers include companies in the aerospace automotive chemical petroleum and power generation industries. The company is owned by Precision Castparts which makes investment castings used in aerospace and power generation applications.

SPECIAL OLYMPICS INC.

1133 19TH ST NW STE 1200
WASHINGTON, DC 200363645
Phone: 202-628-3630
Fax: –
Web: www.kms.specialolympics.org

CEO: Timothy P. (Tim) Shriver
CFO: –
HR: –
FYE: December 31
Type: Private

Special Olympics gives special attention to the differently abled. The organization offers year-round athletic training and competition in about 30 team and individual sports for adults and children with intellectual disabilities. More than 4 million athletes in about 170 countries take part in the group's programs. Special Olympics believes participation in its activities helps athletes improve physical fitness and motor skills while developing self-confidence. The group's support comes mainly from contributions made in response to direct-mail campaigns and from individual and corporate sponsorships and donations. The late Eunice Kennedy Shriver organized the First International Special Olympic Games in 1968.

	Annual Growth	12/07	12/08	12/09	12/10	12/13
Sales ($ mil.)	6.4%	–	70.1	101.5	90.7	95.5
Net income ($ mil.)	–	–	–	9.2	0.1	(3.4)
Market value ($ mil.)	–	–	–	–	–	–
Employees	–	–	–	–	–	160

SPECIALTY COMMERCE CORP.

400 Manley St.
West Bridgewater MA 02379
Phone: 508-638-7000
Fax: 207-729-7280
Web: www.ocvtechnicalfabrics.com

CEO: Christian Feuer
CFO: –
HR: –
FYE: December 31
Type: Private

You just might flip your wig for Specialty Commerce. The leading direct marketer of hairpieces in the US its Specialty Commerce Direct division sells women's wigs wiglets and extensions mostly through catalogs such as Paula Young but also through the website Wig.com. A similar catalog Especially Yours sells wigs apparel and accessories for African-American women. Its Daxbourne International unit sells similar products in the UK through catalogs and websites. A third division Specialty Commerce Publishing (which is unrelated to hair) offers continuing education for health care professionals via study-at-home courses. Specialty Commerce is owned by Canadian private equity firm EdgeStone Capital Partners.

SPECIALTY PRODUCTS & INSULATION CO.

1097 Commercial Ave.
East Petersburg PA 17520-0576
Phone: 717-569-3900
Fax: 717-519-4046
Web: www.spi-co.com

CEO: –
CFO: –
HR: –
FYE: December 31
Type: Business Segment

Cold outside? Specialty Products & Insulation (SPI) can help warm things up. SPI distributes insulation for the commercial industrial HVAC and building industries through about 70 operation centers and a dozen fabrication facilities. Other products include architectural and acoustic wall panels and ceilings and fire-protection products. SPI also offers customized fabrication (pipe and tank wrap) and such services as recycling and disposal assistance warehousing and product training seminars. Its Paragon Plus operation distributes tools stepladders and scaffolding. In 2009 SPI was acquired by Superior Plus Canada's largest propane dealer and supplier of construction products for about $132 million.

SPECIALTY VEHICLE ACQUISITION CORP.

6115 Thirteen Mile Rd.
Warren MI 48092
Phone: 586-446-4701
Fax: 586-446-3401
Web: www.ascglobal.com

CEO: Joe Bione
CFO: –
HR: –
FYE: December 31
Type: Private

Are you brave enough to go topless? Specialty Vehicle Acquisition Corp. (dba ASC) thinks you are. Formerly a simple sunroof maker ASC works with carmakers to provide full-service design and development of specialty vehicles — roof and body systems — through its Creative Services and Open Air Systems divisions. ASC has brought many car models to life including the Chevy SSR Toyota Camry Solara and the Dodge Viper coupe. Other customers include BMW Ford and Honda. With its unique approach ASC can help a car company reinvigorate a tired brand. The company filed for Chapter 11 bankruptcy protection in 2007 and was sold the following year to private equity firm Hancock Park Associates.

SPECTRA ENERGY CORP

NYS: SE

5400 Westheimer Court
Houston, TX 77056
Phone: 713 627-5400
Fax: –
Web: www.spectraenergy.com

CEO: Gregory Rizzo
CFO: John Patrick (Pat) Reddy
HR: –
FYE: December 31
Type: Public

Spectra Energy covers the spectrum of natural gas activities — gathering processing transmission storage and distribution. Spectra Energy operates more than 22000 miles of transmission pipeline and has 305 billion cu. ft. of storage capacity in the US and Canada. Units include U.S. Gas Transmission Texas Eastern Transmission Algonquin Gas Transmission BC Pipeline Division Natural Gas Liquids Division and Market Hub Partners. It also has stakes in DCP Midstream (a gas gathering and NGL joint venture) Maritimes & Northeast Pipeline Gulfstream Natural Gas System Spectra Energy Income Fund and 61% of Spectra Energy Partners. Its Union Gas unit distributes gas to 1.4 million Ontario customers.

	Annual Growth	12/10	12/11	12/12	12/13	12/14
Sales ($ mil.)	4.5%	4,945.0	5,351.0	5,075.0	5,518.0	5,903.0
Net income ($ mil.)	0.8%	1,049.0	1,184.0	940.0	1,038.0	1,082.0
Market value ($ mil.)	9.8%	16,768.3	20,633.3	18,372.0	23,901.0	24,357.3
Employees	81.0%	550	5,700	5,600	5,800	5,900

SPECTRA ENERGY PARTNERS LP

NYS: SEP

5400 Westheimer Court
Houston, TX 77056
Phone: 713 627-5400
Fax: –
Web: www.spectraenergypartners.com

CEO: Gregory L Ebel
CFO: J Patrick Reddy
HR: –
FYE: December 31
Type: Public

When you take one company's energy holdings and splinter them you get Spectra Energy Partners. Formed by Spectra Energy out of the former natural gas holdings of Duke Energy the company is a natural gas pipeline and storage facility operator. Its assets include a liquefied natural gas storage location in Tennessee 50% of Market Hub (two natural gas storage facilities in Texas and Louisiana) and 49% of Gulfstream Natural Gas System. All told Spectra Energy Partners has 3200 miles of natural gas transmission and gathering pipelines capable of moving about 3.6 billion cu. ft. per day. It also has 57 billion cu. ft. of gas storage capacity.

	Annual Growth	12/10	12/11	12/12	12/13	12/14
Sales ($ mil.)	84.1%	197.7	205.0	236.8	1,965.0	2,269.0
Net income ($ mil.)	61.4%	147.9	172.0	193.5	1,070.0	1,004.0
Market value ($ mil.)	14.8%	9,878.0	9,610.4	9,390.9	13,636.7	17,130.9
Employees		–	–	–	–	–

SPECTRANETICS CORP. (THE)

NMS: SPNC

9965 Federal Drive
Colorado Springs, CO 80921
Phone: 719 633-8333
Fax: –
Web: www.spnc.com

CEO: Scott Drake
CFO: Stacy McMahan
HR: Robert (Bob) Fuchs
FYE: December 31
Type: Public

Spectranetics takes its mission to heart: The company develops markets and distributes an excimer laser system that uses ultraviolet radiation rays to conduct minimally invasive treatment of various coronary and vascular conditions. Its CVX-300 laser unit and disposable delivery devices (fiber-optic catheters and sheaths) remove partial or total arterial blockages caused by plaque buildup; the laser system can also be used to remove lead wires from pacemakers and implantable defibrillators. The company's customers include major cardiac catheterization labs and hospitals in the US. Although its products are sold in some 65 countries Spectranetics generates nearly 85% of its sales in the US and Canada.

	Annual Growth	12/10	12/11	12/12	12/13	12/14
Sales ($ mil.)	14.8%	117.9	127.3	140.3	158.8	204.9
Net income ($ mil.)	–	(13.1)	0.9	2.2	(0.4)	(40.9)
Market value ($ mil.)	60.9%	217.0	303.7	621.2	1,051.5	1,454.5
Employees	12.5%	470	504	548	575	753

SPECTRUM BRANDS HOLDINGS INC

NYS: SPB

3001 Deming Way
Middleton, WI 53562
Phone: 608 275-3340
Fax: –
Web: www.spectrumbrands.com

CEO: Andreas Rouv ©
CFO: Douglas L. (Doug) Martin
HR: –
FYE: September 30
Type: Public

And you will know them by their trail of brands. Spectrum Brands makes and markets products sold under some of the most recognizable names in the world. They include batteries (Rayovac and VARTA) pet foods and supplies (Tetra Marineland Dingo) personal care (Remington) and garden care (Spectracide Cutter Hot Shot). Its small appliances unit includes such notable brands as Stanley Black & Decker George Foreman Toastmaster and Farberware. A leader in the sale of rechargeable batteries and hearing aid batteries to manufacturers Spectrum Brands markets its products in more than 1 million stores spanning 140 countries.

	Annual Growth	09/11	09/12	09/13	09/14	09/15
Sales ($ mil.)	10.1%	3,186.9	3,252.4	4,085.6	4,429.1	4,690.4
Net income ($ mil.)	–	(75.2)	48.6	(55.2)	214.1	148.9
Market value ($ mil.)	40.3%	1,403.0	2,376.6	3,910.9	5,377.5	5,435.7
Employees	27.3%	5,900	5,850	13,500	13,400	15,500

SPECTRUM CONTROL INC.

CEO: –
CFO: Phil Rehkemper
HR: –
FYE: November 30
Type: Subsidiary

8031 Avonia Rd.
Fairview PA 16415
Phone: 814-474-2207
Fax: 814-474-2208
Web: www.spectrumcontrol.com

Custom electronic components and systems are within the scope of Spectrum Control's product offerings. The company designs and manufactures components for many industry applications its largest being military/defense and communications equipment. It operates in four segments: advanced specialty products (antennas connectors ceramics and electromagnetic interference filters); microwave components and systems (amplifiers filters oscillators and synthesizers); power management systems (power distribution units and power strips); and sensors and controls (temperature sensors). Most of its sales are made in the US. Spectrum Control was acquired in 2011 by API Technologies for about $270 million in cash.

SPECTRUM GROUP INTERNATIONAL INC

NBB: SPGZ

1063 McGaw, Suite 250
Irvine, CA 92614
Phone: 949 748-4800
Fax: –
Web: www.spectrumgi.com

CEO: Gregory N Roberts
CFO: Paul Soth
HR: –
FYE: June 30
Type: Public

From gold bullion to fine wine and baseball memorabilia one auction house spans the spectrum of global collectibles. Spectrum Group International serves both collectors and dealers operating in two primary areas: trading (the majority of its business) and collectibles (handled through both auctions and direct sales). Its trading business operates through A-Mark Precious Metals which sells coins and other precious metals on a wholesale basis. Spectrum Group has auction houses in North America Europe and Asia. The company was founded by Greg Manning who started collecting stamps at age 7 and opened an office to market stamps in 1971 at the age of 25.

	Annual Growth	06/09	06/10	06/11	06/12	06/13
Sales ($ mil.)	14.6%	4,293.3	6,012.4	7,202.2	7,974.8	7,406.0
Net income ($ mil.)	(17.1%)	7.1	(1.1)	3.8	4.1	3.4
Market value ($ mil.)	0.0%	0.1	0.1	0.1	0.1	0.1
Employees	1.2%	142	143	177	190	149

SPECTRUM HEALTH SYSTEM

100 MICHIGAN ST NE
GRAND RAPIDS, MI 495032560
Phone: 616-391-1774
Fax: –
Web: www.spectrumhealth.org

CEO: Richard C. (Rick) Breon
CFO: Michael P (Mike) Freed
HR: David Beach
FYE: June 30
Type: Private

Offering more health services than colors in the rainbow Spectrum Health is a regional health system serving western Michigan. The not-for-profit network operates 12 hospitals that boast more than 1900 beds. Its health system provides a variety of services from general surgery to specialized cancer care. Besides its Spectrum Health Medical Group and West Michigan Heart Spectrum Health also operates Priority Health a health plan with 648000 members and Helen Devos Children's Hospital. The group runs more than 170 service sites including urgent care centers primary care physician offices community clinics rehabilitation and other outpatient facilities and continuing care residences for the elderly.

	Annual Growth	06/06	06/07	06/08	06/09	06/10
Sales ($ mil.)	14.2%	–	–	–	1,266.2	1,446.2
Net income ($ mil.)	–	–	–	–	0.0	142.7
Market value ($ mil.)	–	–	–	–	–	–
Employees	–	–	–	–	–	16,996

SPECTRUM PHARMACEUTICALS INC

NMS: SPPI

11500 South Eastern Avenue, Suite 240
Henderson, NV 89052
Phone: 702 835-6300
Fax: –
Web: www.spectrumpharm.com

CEO: Rajesh C. Shrotriya
CFO: Kurt A. Gustafson
HR: –
FYE: December 31
Type: Public

Spectrum Pharmaceuticals sees a rainbow of opportunities in its drug development pipeline. The biotechnology firm which focuses on anti-cancer therapies markets injectable Fusilev (levoleucovorin) for use by osteosarcoma (a type of bone cancer) and colorectal cancer patients; the drug reduces the toxic effects of a certain type of chemotherapy. Spectrum also sells Zevalin (ibritumomab) a treatment for non-Hodgkin's lymphoma; Marqibo for leukemia; and Beleodaq and Folotyn for peripheral T-cell lymphoma. In addition the company has other oncology and urology therapeutic drug candidates in research and development stages partially through licensing agreements or collaborative partnerships with other drugmakers.

	Annual Growth	12/10	12/11	12/12	12/13	12/14
Sales ($ mil.)	26.0%	74.1	193.0	267.7	155.9	186.8
Net income ($ mil.)	–	(48.8)	48.5	94.5	(62.1)	(45.7)
Market value ($ mil.)	0.2%	453.2	965.1	737.9	583.8	457.2
Employees	14.7%	139	176	193	226	241

SPEED COMMERCE, INC.

NBB: SPDC

1303 E. Arapaho Road, Suite 200
Richardson, TX 75081
Phone: 866 377-3331
Fax: –
Web: www.speedcommerce.com

CEO: Dalton Edgecomb
CFO: Bruce Meier
HR: –
FYE: March 31
Type: Public

Before there was streaming there was Speed Commerce. Speed Commerce (formerly Navarre Corporation) distributes home entertainment and multimedia software products and provides logistics for major retail chains (Best Buy Wal-Mart) and Internet-based retail channels (Amazon iTunes) throughout North America. Its smaller publishing segment is run through its Encore Software subsidiary which provides print education and family entertainment under such titles as The Print Shop Mavis Beacon Teaches Typing Hoyle PC Gaming and Punch Home Design. Founded in 1983 as an entertainment distributor Speed Commerce has diversified into a licenser and publisher of entertainment.

	Annual Growth	03/11	03/12	03/13	03/14	03/15
Sales ($ mil.)	(29.7%)	490.9	480.8	485.3	107.1	120.0
Net income ($ mil.)	–	11.2	(34.3)	(11.8)	(26.6)	(56.0)
Market value ($ mil.)	(23.8%)	125.4	117.5	149.8	240.3	42.2
Employees	40.5%	413	279	819	1,123	1,609

SPEEDUS CORP.

PINK SHEETS: SPDE

1 Dag Hammarskjold Blvd.
Freehold NJ 07728
Phone: 214-740-6500
Fax: 214-740-6556
Web: www.sourcecorp.com

CEO: Shant S Hovnanian
CFO: John A Kallassy
HR: –
FYE: December 31
Type: Public

Speedus is a holding company with investments in two technology companies: medical software firm Zargis Medical Corp. and data storage maker Density Dynamics Inc. Zargis makes Cardioscan a software application that can help diagnose heart problems which is marketed with 3M's Littman brand products. (Speedus owns 90% of Zargis; Siemens holds the remainder of the joint venture.) In 2009 the FDA cleared Zargis to market its Signal X6 device which records heart and lung sounds through adhesive acoustic sensors. Zargis holds several contracts with the US Army to develop prototype telemedicine systems for use in cardiology. Density Dynamics 75%-owned develops solid-state storage devices used in data centers.

SPEEDWAY LLC

500 Speedway Dr.
Enon OH 45323
Phone: 937-864-3000
Fax: 937-863-6722
Web: www.speedway.com

CEO: –
CFO: –
HR: Corey Perkins
FYE: December 31
Type: Subsidiary

If filling the tank with gas and picking up some snacks is something you want to do in hurry Speedway supports that. A subsidiary of Marathon Petroleum the company (formerly Speedway SuperAmerica) operates more than 1350 combination gas station/convenience stores primarily under the Speedway banner in seven midwestern states. The stores offer Marathon brand gas naturally as well as fresh coffee fountain drinks hot dogs pastry sandwiches and other grab-and-go food. Frequent Speedway customers can participate in Speedy Rewards program which allows them to earn points for fuel and merchandise purchases. Points are redeemed in-store for gift cards or free merchandise. Speedway was formed in 1997.

SPEEDWAY MOTORSPORTS, INC.

NYS: TRK

5555 Concord Parkway South
Concord, NC 28027
Phone: 704 455-3239
Fax: –
Web: www.speedwaymotorsports.com

CEO: Marcus G. Smith
CFO: William R. (Bill) Brooks
HR: –
FYE: December 31
Type: Public

Here's one sports company that lives life in the fast lane. Speedway Motorsports is the #2 operator of auto racing facilities in the US behind International Speedway Corporation (ISC) with eight motorsports facilities. Its tracks including Atlanta Motor Speedway Las Vegas Motor Speedway and Texas Motor Speedway (Fort Worth) host a number of events sanctioned by such US racing bodies as the Indy Racing League the National Hot Rod Association and the World of Outlaws; however more than 80% of the company's revenue comes from NASCAR events. Chairman and CEO Bruton Smith head of auto dealership empire Sonic Automotive owns about 70% of Speedway Motorsports.

	Annual Growth	12/10	12/11	12/12	12/13	12/14
Sales ($ mil.)	(0.9%)	502.2	505.8	490.2	480.6	484.3
Net income ($ mil.)	(8.5%)	44.5	(6.4)	42.1	(6.5)	31.1
Market value ($ mil.)	9.3%	633.3	633.7	737.5	820.6	904.1
Employees	(1.1%)	1,118	1,038	1,074	1,077	1,070

SPELMAN COLLEGE

350 SPELMAN LN SW 589
ATLANTA, GA 303144399
Phone: 404-681-3643
Fax: –
Web: www.spelman.edu

CEO: –
CFO: Robert D Flanigan
HR: –
FYE: June 30
Type: Private

Spelman College is a private historically African American college for women. The college enrolls more than 2100 students from more than 40 states in the US and 15 countries. It offers majors in areas such as English economics mathematics music psychology art and religion. Tuition (for 12-20 credit hours) costs about $10650 and the student-faculty ratio is 12-to-1. Its alumnae include Sam's Club CEO Rosalind Brewer; former acting Surgeon General and Spelman's first alumna President Audrey Forbes Manley; author Pearl Cleage; and actress LaTanya Richardson Jackson. Spelman boasts a graduation rate of more than 80%.

	Annual Growth	06/10	06/11	06/12	06/13	06/14
Sales ($ mil.)	(4.0%)	–	103.2	87.0	88.6	91.3
Net income ($ mil.)	–	–	–	(6.3)	23.1	50.9
Market value ($ mil.)	–	–	–	–	–	–
Employees	–	–	–	–	–	550

SPF ENERGY INC.

100 27TH ST NE
MINOT, ND 587035164
Phone: 701-852-1194
Fax: –
Web: www.spfenergy.com

CEO: Jeffrey Farstad
CFO: Bruce Hest
HR: Savannah Arnott
FYE: December 31
Type: Private

Super-jobber SPF Energy is also a super-pumper of petroleum. The company's Superpumper subsidiary runs a chain of about 15 convenience stores and gas stations in Minnesota Montana and North Dakota under the Cenex Conoco Exxon SinclairTesoro and Shell banners. Its Farstad Oil subsidiary offers bulk transportation of petroleum products including the annual distribution of about 250 million gallons of gas 20 million gallons of propane and 2.5 million gallons of lubricants. The Farstad fleet serves businesses and government agencies from Montana to eastern Minnesota and from northern Wyoming to the Canadian border. SPF Energy is owned by North American fuel wholesaler Parkland Fuel Corporation.

	Annual Growth	12/10	12/11	12/12	12/13	12/14
Sales ($ mil.)	(1.6%)	–	1,078.8	1,062.7	1,012.9	1,026.9
Net income ($ mil.)	76.1%	–	–	5.3	8.9	16.4
Market value ($ mil.)	–	–	–	–	–	–
Employees	–	–	–	–	–	300

SPHERIX INC.

NMS: SPEX

6430 Rockledge Drive, Suite 503
Bethesda, MD 20817
Phone: 703 992-9260
Fax: –
Web: www.spherix.com

CEO: Anthony Hayes
CFO: Richard Cohen
HR: –
FYE: December 31
Type: Public

Spherix is sweet on health. The company's BioSpherix division is developing products from tagatose a low-calorie sweetener with possible applications for improving health. Approved for use in foods the company sold the food-use rights for tagatose to Arla Foods but hung onto the non-food rights which it then branded Naturlose. The product is in clinical trials as a possible treatment for Type 2 diabetes although patient recruitment has been slower than expected. Spherix reported it will likely need a development partner to see the product through to market. To supplement its income Spherix launched a Health Sciences division to provide regulatory and technical consulting services to other biotech firms.

	Annual Growth	12/10	12/11	12/12	12/13	12/14
Sales ($ mil.)	(71.1%)	1.4	0.8	0.0	0.0	0.0
Net income ($ mil.)	–	(7.7)	(3.5)	(3.9)	(18.0)	(30.5)
Market value ($ mil.)	11.1%	20.3	33.5	195.3	230.6	30.9
Employees	(13.7%)	9	10	3	3	5

SPIEGEL BRANDS INC.

711 3rd Ave.
New York NY 10017
Phone: 212 906 2505
Fax: 212-916-8281
Web: www.spiegel.com

CEO: Geralynn Madonna
CFO: –
HR: Susan Koste
FYE: December 31
Type: Private

Spiegel Brands comforts the fashionable and dresses up the comfortable. The direct marketer's Spiegel Newport News Carabella Shape fx and AB Lambdin catalogs and websites feature private-label women's clothing footwear and accessories designed to create what the company describes as easy style. Apparel (dresses jackets coordinates swimwear lingerie and denim) comprises most of its sales. The first Spiegel catalog was mailed in 1905. After several ownership changes Spiegel Brands was acquired by Patriarch Partners a private equity firm led by turnaround investor Lynn Tilton through a newly-formed company — Signature Styles LLC — in 2009.

SPINDLETOP OIL & GAS CO (TEX)

NBB: SPND

12850 Spurling Rd., Suite 200
Dallas, TX 75230
Phone: 972 644-2581
Fax: –
Web: www.spindletopoil.com

CEO: –
CFO: –
HR: –
FYE: December 31
Type: Public

In 1901 the discovery of oil at Spindletop marked the beginning of the modern petroleum industry. Today Spindletop Oil & Gas is keeping that tradition alive in its exploration for and production of oil and natural gas. The company has major operations throughout Texas as well as interests in oil and gas properties in more than a dozen other states. Spindletop Oil & Gas has proved reserves of more than 323000 barrels of oil and 12.5 billion cu. ft. of natural gas. The company also operates more than 26 miles of gas pipelines and an oilfield equipment rental business. It manages subsidiaries Prairie Pipeline and Spindletop Drilling. Chairman and president Chris Mazzini and his wife own 77% of the company.

	Annual Growth	12/10	12/11	12/12	12/13	12/14
Sales ($ mil.)	14.6%	7.7	9.3	12.1	13.5	13.2
Net income ($ mil.)	63.6%	0.4	1.8	3.7	3.5	3.2
Market value ($ mil.)	23.3%	15.6	11.8	18.0	22.3	36.1
Employees	3.1%	62	62	62	70	70

SPIRE CORP.

NBB: SPIR

One Patriots Park
Bedford, MA 01730-2396
Phone: 781 275-6000
Fax: –
Web: www.spirecorp.com

CEO: Roger G Little
CFO: Robert S Lieberman
HR: –
FYE: December 31
Type: Public

Success in solar is more than an aspiration for Spire. Factories worldwide use Spire's photovoltaic solar cell manufacturing equipment including cell testers and assemblers to produce modules that convert sunlight into electricity. Its solar systems unit also uses the equipment to make solar energy modules for buildings and homes. Though Spire's roots are in solar energy the company also has a biomedical unit that provides coating services to orthopedic and other medical device makers. Its products are manufactured at its US headquarters and Spire gets almost half of its sales domestic customers. Key customers include First Solar and Stryker Orthopedics.

	Annual Growth	12/09	12/10	12/11	12/12	12/13
Sales ($ mil.)	(32.4%)	69.9	79.8	61.6	22.1	14.6
Net income ($ mil.)	–	(5.3)	(0.4)	(1.5)	(1.9)	(8.5)
Market value ($ mil.)	(43.6%)	49.4	48.0	5.8	4.6	5.0
Employees	(20.1%)	211	194	173	118	86

SPIRIT AEROSYSTEMS HOLDINGS INC

NYS: SPR

3801 South Oliver
Wichita, KS 67210
Phone: 316 526-9000
Fax: –
Web: www.spiritaero.com

CEO: Larry Lawson
CFO: Sanjay Kapoor
HR: –
FYE: December 31
Type: Public

Unlike the Wright Brothers modern aerospace designers and manufacturers like Spirit AeroSystems Holdings operate with more resources than a wing and a prayer. The company makes commercial and military airplane components such as fuselages propulsion systems wings and underwing parts. It designs and builds aerostructures for every Boeing aircraft currently in production and provides components to Boeing's chief rival Airbus. Spirit AeroSystems claims to be the largest supplier of wing parts for Airbus' A320 aircraft and produces the majority of aerostructures for Boeing's 737. Spirit AeroSystems maintains operations in the US the UK and Asia.

	Annual Growth	12/11	12/12	12/13	12/14	12/15
Sales ($ mil.)	8.1%	4,863.8	5,397.7	5,961.0	6,799.2	6,643.9
Net income ($ mil.)	42.3%	192.4	34.8	(621.4)	358.8	788.7
Market value ($ mil.)	24.6%	2,616.7	2,137.0	4,291.6	5,419.8	6,305.1
Employees	2.2%	13,932	14,623	14,177	15,402	15,200

SPIRIT AIRLINES INC

NMS: SAVE

2800 Executive Way
Miramar, FL 33025
Phone: 954 447-7920
Fax: –
Web: www.spirit.com

CEO: Robert L. (Bob) Fornaro
CFO: Ted Christie
HR: –
FYE: December 31
Type: Public

Spirit Airlines can lift the spirits of people seeking sunshine. The ultra low-cost carrier (ULCC) operates more than 280 daily flights between major US cities and popular vacation spots in South Florida the Caribbean and Latin America serving nearly 50 destinations. It operates an all Airbus fleet of nearly 55 single-aisle aircraft including A319s A320s and A321s. Spirit capitalizes on an ancillary service model charging separately for baggage advance seat selection and other travel-related upgrades. In addition to scheduled service the company partners with third-party vendors to offer a slate of vacation packages via its website.

	Annual Growth	12/10	12/11	12/12	12/13	12/14
Sales ($ mil.)	25.4%	781.3	1,071.2	1,318.4	1,654.4	1,931.6
Net income ($ mil.)	32.8%	72.5	76.4	108.5	176.9	225.5
Market value ($ mil.)	69.2%	–	1,135.3	1,290.3	3,304.7	5,500.4
Employees	15.3%	2,385	2,580	3,033	3,619	4,219

SPLUNK INC

NMS: SPLK

250 Brannan Street
San Francisco, CA 94107
Phone: 415 848-8400
Fax: –
Web: www.splunk.com

CEO: Doug Merritt
CFO: David F. Conte
HR: –
FYE: January 31
Type: Public

Splunk loves diving for data. The company's software collects and indexes machine-generated data - an automated log produced by nearly every piece of hardware and software that contains a time-stamped record of its activities such as transactions user activities and security threats. IT professionals use Splunk to analyze monitor and report on machine-generated data for operational intelligence application management security and compliance and web analytics. Splunk counts about 5200 corporate and government customers including Bank of America Comcast the Department of Defense salesforce.com and Zynga. The company went public in 2012.

	Annual Growth	01/11	01/12	01/13	01/14	01/15
Sales ($ mil.)	61.5%	66.2	121.0	198.9	302.6	450.9
Net income ($ mil.)	–	(3.8)	(11.0)	(36.7)	(79.0)	(217.1)
Market value ($ mil.)	25.2%	–	–	4,071.8	9,516.2	6,380.8
Employees	44.6%	–	463	736	1,000	1,400

SPOK HOLDINGS INC

NMS: SPOK

6850 Versar Center, Suite 420
Springfield, VA 22151-4148
Phone: 800 611-8488
Fax: –
Web: www.spok.com

CEO: Vincent D. (Vince) Kelly
CFO: Shawn E. Endsley
HR: –
FYE: December 31
Type: Public

Paging Dr. Spok? Actually it's Spok Holdings (formerly USA Mobility) doing the paging as a leading US provider of paging and other wireless services primarily for health care and large enterprises and government agencies. It offers one-way and two-way paging services nationwide over its own network while also marketing and reselling wireless voice and data services through an agreement with Sprint Nextel. Spok also provides customized wireless connectivity systems for health care government and education clients as well as telemetry systems used for asset tracking utility meter reading and other remote monitoring applications. It serves also has customers in Europe and Australia.

	Annual Growth	12/10	12/11	12/12	12/13	12/14
Sales ($ mil.)	(3.7%)	233.3	242.9	219.7	209.8	200.3
Net income ($ mil.)	(28.2%)	77.9	88.6	27.0	27.5	20.7
Market value ($ mil.)	(0.6%)	390.6	304.8	256.7	313.9	381.6
Employees	3.1%	519	692	667	631	587

SPORT CHALET, INC.

NMS: SPCH A

One Sport Chalet Drive
La Canada, CA 91011
Phone: 818 949-5300
Fax: –
Web: www.sportchalet.com

CEO: Craig L Levra
CFO: Howard K Kaminsky
HR: –
FYE: March 31
Type: Public

For those who play there's Sport Chalet. The sporting goods retailer operates 50-plus stores mostly in California but also in Arizona Nevada and Utah. It also sells its goods through its online shopping site. The stores which average about 41000 sq. ft. are known for carrying specialty products such as mountain climbing and SCUBA gear. Sport Chalet has traditionally specialized in gear for cold-weather sports such as skiing and snowboarding but its stores sell brand-name footwear apparel and equipment for many other activities too. Shoppers at Sport Chalet can sign up for SCUBA training and join dive clubs associated with the stores. Sport Chalet was founded in 1959 by the late Norbert Olberz.

	Annual Growth	03/09	03/10*	04/11	04/12*	03/13
Sales ($ mil.)	(0.8%)	372.7	353.7	362.5	349.9	360.6
Net income ($ mil.)	–	(52.2)	(8.3)	(3.0)	(5.1)	(3.3)
Market value ($ mil.)	67.7%	2.4	37.6	28.7	18.2	19.0
Employees	(1.6%)	3,200	3,000	3,100	2,900	3,000

*Fiscal year change

SPORTVISION INC.

4410 N. Ravenswood
Chicago IL 60640
Phone: 773-293-4300
Fax: 773-293-2155
Web: www.sportvision.com

CEO: Hank Adams
CFO: –
HR: –
FYE: December 31
Type: Private

This company adds digital bells and whistles to TV sports events. Sportvision is a leading media effects company that specializes in broadcast TV enhancements such as the virtual first down line in football games (1st and Ten) a virtual strike zone for baseball (KZone) and a system for illustrating course details in golf (Virtual Caddy). It also creates in-game graphics for network teases and marketing as well as provides services for interactive digital media. Sportvision was founded in 1998 by former News Corporation executives who helped develop the glowing hockey puck for FOX Sports broadcasts.

SPR INC.

233 S. Wacker Dr. Ste. 3330
Chicago IL 60606
Phone: 312-756-1760
Fax: 312-756-1751
Web: www.sprinc.com

CEO: –
CFO: –
HR: –
FYE: December 31
Type: Private

SPR is an IT services firm that helps corporate and government clients manage their IT systems with a portfolio of services ranging from application integration to technology staffing. It specializes in developing and implementing such systems as information portals and intranets content management systems and business intelligence tools. Its clients include FORTUNE 100 companies and state government agencies. SPR has offices in Illinois and Wisconsin. Business computing pioneer Gene Figliulo started the company in 1972; his family continues to own the firm led by son Robert (now company president).

SPRAGUE RESOURCES LP

NYS: SRLP

185 International Drive
Portsmouth, NH 03801
Phone: 800 225-1560
Fax: –
Web: www.spragueenergy.com

CEO: David C. (Dave) Glendon
CFO: Gary A. Rinaldi
HR: –
FYE: December 31
Type: Public

Venerable but spry Sprague Resources delivers when it comes energy delivery. The company founded in 1870 as a coal and oil supplier has grown into one of the largest fuel suppliers in the northeast. Sprague Resources' products include diesel gasoline home heating oil jet fuel and residual fuels. The company distributes about 50 billion cu. ft. of natural gas 1.3 billion gallons of petroleum products and 2.5 million tons of bulk materials each year. It also owns or operates 15 storage terminals that can hold more than 9 million barrels of refined products. In 2013 the company went public raising $153 million which it will use for working capital and to pay down debt.

	Annual Growth	12/10	12/11	12/12	12/13	12/14
Sales ($ mil.)	15.8%	2,817.2	3,797.4	4,043.9	4,600.7	5,069.8
Net income ($ mil.)	67.2%	15.7	29.6	(12.8)	(27.5)	122.8
Market value ($ mil.)	28.6%	–	–	–	380.9	489.7
Employees	20.4%	–	–	400	–	580

SPRAYLAT CORPORATION

143 Sparks Ave.
Pelham NY 10803
Phone: 914-738-1600
Fax: 914-712-2838
Web: www.spraylat.com

CEO: Michael E Borner
CFO: John Ragazzini
HR: Ileana Flesher
FYE: December 31
Type: Private

Spraylat makes more than 100 coatings used to protect a variety of surfaces from dust heat and even environmental hazards. The company makes liquid and powder coatings as well as coatings for signs wheels and electronics. Its Hilemn business segment makes coatings for mirrors. Customers include the aerospace automotive electronics and general manufacturing industries — primarily in the US but also in Asia and Europe. Spraylat expanded its global reach in 2008 when it formed the Automotive Coatings World Alliance with two paint companies Japan's Ohashi Chemical and France's Mader Group. Spraylat was founded in 1936 and is controlled by the family of CEO Michael Borner.

SPRING ARBOR UNIVERSITY

106 E MAIN ST
SPRING ARBOR, MI 492839701
Phone: 517 750 1200
Fax: –
Web: www.arbor.edu

CEO: –
CFO: Jerry White
HR: –
FYE: May 31
Type: Private

Spring Arbor University is an evangelical Christian university affiliated with the Free Methodist Church. The liberal arts institution offers more than 70 undergraduate and 10 graduate degrees as well as professional programs. It has an enrollment of more than 4000 students most of which hail from Michigan. The school's main 100-acre campus in Spring Arbor Michigan is supplemented by about 20 satellite locations in Michigan and Ohio. Academic fields include business nursing and spiritual leadership. Spring Arbor University was founded as an elementary and secondary school in 1873.

	Annual Growth	05/06	05/07	05/09	05/12	05/13
Sales ($ mil.)	8.1%	–	42.2	58.2	68.9	67.4
Net income ($ mil.)	–	–	–	0.0	1.7	3.6
Market value ($ mil.)	–	–	–	–	–	–
Employees	–	–	–	–	–	340

SPRINGFIELD HOSPITAL

25 RIDGEWOOD RD
SPRINGFIELD, VT 05156-3057
Phone: 802-885-2151
Fax: –
Web: www.springfieldhospital.org

CEO: Timothy Ford
CFO: Andrew J Majka
HR: William Grass
FYE: September 30
Type: Private

Bart Simpson might wind up in Springfield Hospital after cruising down the town's hilly roads on his skateboard. The 70-bed facility located in Springfield Vermont (also known as the Home of the Simpsons) serves 16 communities in southeastern Vermont and southwestern New Hampshire. Specialized services include adult day care emergency medicine physical therapy rehabilitation and surgery. Founded in 1913 the hospital also offers a childbirth center breast care center and inpatient and outpatient units for psychiatry neurology oncology and cardiac care. Springfield Hospital is part of the Springfield Medical Care Systems.

	Annual Growth	09/03	09/04	09/05	09/06	09/07
Sales ($ mil.)	–	–	–	(1,482.4)	49.5	52.1
Net income ($ mil.)	9607.2%	–	–	0.0	1.2	2.7
Market value ($ mil.)	–	–	–	–	–	–
Employees	–	–	–	–	–	337

SPROUTS FARMERS MARKET INC

NMS: SFM

5455 East High Street, Suite 111
Phoenix, AZ 85054
Phone: 480 814-8016
Fax: –
Web: www.sprouts.com

CEO: Amin N. Maredia
CFO: Susannah Livingston
HR: James Reynolds
FYE: December 28
Type: Public

This company is sprouting up all over the place. A fast-growing natural foods retailer Sprouts Farmers Market operates more than 200 stores in over a dozen US states including Arizona California Colorado Nevada New Mexico Oklahoma Texas and Utah. The stores (ranging from 28000 to 30000 sq. ft.) sell organic and local produce baked goods all-natural meats and seafood imported cheeses bulk foods and vitamins and supplements. Stores also boast more than 300 bins of bulk rice spices nuts and grains. Sprouts merged with Sunflower Farmers Market in 2012 giving Sprouts the #2 spot in the natural organic retail market behind Whole Foods Market. It went public in 2013.

	Annual Growth	01/11	01/12*	12/12	12/13	12/14
Sales ($ mil.)	79.1%	516.8	1,105.9	1,794.8	2,437.9	2,967.4
Net income ($ mil.)	180.9%	4.9	(27.4)	19.5	51.3	107.7
Market value ($ mil.)	(14.3%)	–	–	–	5,798.5	4,969.5
Employees	11.8%	–	–	13,600	14,000	17,000

*Fiscal year change

SPS COMMERCE, INC.

NMS: SPSC

333 South Seventh Street, Suite 1000
Minneapolis, MN 55402
Phone: 612 435-9400
Fax: –
Web: www.spscommerce.com

CEO: Archie C. Black
CFO: Kimberly K. (Kim) Nelson
HR: –
FYE: December 31
Type: Public

SPS Commerce answers the supply chain SOS. Founded in 1987 as St. Paul Software the company offers an Internet-based suite of supply chain management software to consumer goods suppliers retailers distributors and logistics companies in North America. Its software which is maintained and delivered as a service via the cloud is used by customers to manage place and fill orders and track the shipments of goods. Customers can electronically send invoices shipping notices and purchase orders automate shipment functions and evaluate the performance of their vendors or suppliers. Best Buy Costco and Callaway Golf are among SPS's thousands of customers.

	Annual Growth	12/10	12/11	12/12	12/13	12/14
Sales ($ mil.)	30.1%	44.6	58.0	77.1	104.4	127.9
Net income ($ mil.)	(1.6%)	2.9	13.7	1.2	1.1	2.7
Market value ($ mil.)	37.6%	258.3	424.3	609.3	1,067.6	925.8
Employees	27.8%	353	474	631	771	943

SPX CORP.

NYS: SPXC

13320-A Ballantyne Corporate Place
Charlotte, NC 28277
Phone: 980 474-3700
Fax: 704 752-4505
Web: www.spx.com

CEO: Gene Lowe
CFO: Scott Sproule
HR: –
FYE: December 31
Type: Public

SPX Corp. controls the ebb and flow of multiple industries. The company operates in a couple of areas: thermal equipment and services (cooling heating ventilation) and industrial products and services (compactors power systems broadcast antenna systems aerospace components). SPX serves core markets which include infrastructure processing equipment and diagnostic tools. In turn these markets support electricity processed foods and beverages and vehicle services. It operates in 35-plus countries with a sales presence in 150 countries. In mid-2015 SPX spun off its flow technology operations (pumps valves other fluid handling devices).

	Annual Growth	12/10	12/11	12/12	12/13	12/14
Sales ($ mil.)	(0.9%)	4,886.8	5,461.9	5,100.2	4,717.2	4,721.1
Net income ($ mil.)	17.9%	205.6	180.6	259.2	210.2	397.9
Market value ($ mil.)	4.7%	2,920.9	2,462.5	2,866.2	4,069.9	3,510.5
Employees	(2.5%)	15,500	18,000	15,000	14,000	14,000

SPX FLOW INC

NYS: FLOW

13320 Ballantyne Corporate Place
Charlotte, NC 28277
Phone: 704 752-4400
Fax: –
Web: www.spxflow.com

CEO: Christopher J. Kearney
CFO: Jeremy W. Smeltzer
HR: –
FYE: December 31
Type: Public

At SPX Flow cash flow isn't the only flow that matters. A former unit of SPX Corporation SPX Flow manufactures products such as pumps valves heat exchangers fluid mixers agitators metering systems filters and dehydration equipment. The company's products serve a wide range of end markets including food and beverage oil and gas power generation chemical mining and general industrial. A short list of its brands include Bran + Luebbe Lightnin Waukesha Cherry-Burrell and WCB-Flow Products. SPX Flow was spun off from its former parent in mid-2015.

	Annual Growth	12/11	12/12	12/13	12/14	12/15
Sales ($ mil.)	–	0.0	2,846.3	2,804.8	2,769.6	2,388.5
Net income ($ mil.)	–	0.0	126.9	131.0	134.5	87.5
Market value ($ mil.)	–	0.0	–	–	–	1,155.1
Employees	0.0%	–	–	–	8,000	8,000

SPY INC

NBB: XSPY

2070 Las Palmas Drive
Carlsbad, CA 92011
Phone: 760 804-8420
Fax: –
Web: www.spyoptic.com

CEO: Seth Hamot
CFO: James McGinty
HR: –
FYE: December 31
Type: Public

SPY Inc. formerly known as Orange 21 has its sights set on the colorful Gen Y. The company designs and distributes high-end sunglasses and goggles under the Spy Spy Optic Margaritaville and O'Neill brands. SPY markets its upscale eyewear to the club kid scene for use in surfing skateboarding snowboarding and other extreme action sports. The line is available at about 3000 outlets in the US and Canada including Sunglass Hut Sport Chalet and Zumiez and internationally through around 3000 retailers. SPY also markets some apparel and accessories. In late 2010 the company refocused and sold its LEM subsidiary which made up most of SPY's eyewear and provided manufacturing services for other companies.

	Annual Growth	12/10	12/11	12/12	12/13	12/14
Sales ($ mil.)	2.2%	35.0	33.4	35.6	37.8	38.1
Net income ($ mil.)	–	(4.6)	(10.9)	(7.2)	(2.9)	(1.9)
Market value ($ mil.)	(12.3%)	18.1	24.1	20.1	19.4	10.7
Employees	0.8%	91	108	86	85	94

SPYR INC

NBB: SPYR

4643 S. Ulster St., Suite 1510
Denver, CO 80237
Phone: 303 991-8000
Fax: –
Web: www.eatatjoesltd.com

CEO: –
CFO: Barry D Loveless
HR: –
FYE: December 31
Type: Public

Eat At Joe's operates a themed casual-dining restaurant at the Philadelphia airport that offers breakfast lunch and dinner. The concept features such interior appointments as 1950s-era Harley-Davidsons booths resembling 1957 Chevy interiors and tabletop jukeboxes. Patrons can choose from such menu items as hot dogs burgers and meatloaf. CEO Joseph Fiore owns more than 60% of Eat at Joe's.

	Annual Growth	12/10	12/11	12/12	12/13	12/14
Sales ($ mil.)	4.0%	1.2	1.1	1.1	1.3	1.5
Net income ($ mil.)	–	(0.6)	(0.2)	1.9	(1.4)	2.2
Market value ($ mil.)	121.7%	1.4	0.7	0.8	4.4	33.8
Employees	2.7%	9	11	10	10	10

SRAM INTERNATIONAL CORPORATION

1333 N. Kingsbury St. 4th Fl.
Chicago IL 60642
Phone: 312-664-8800
Fax: 312-664-8826
Web: www.sram.com

CEO: Stanley R Day Jr
CFO: Mike Herr
HR: –
FYE: December 31
Type: Private

SRAM International keeps the wheels of commerce spinning as it makes and sells bicycle shifters derailleurs brakes chains pedals power meters and other cycling parts. Its components are used by bicycle manufacturers (some 65% of sales) and sold in the aftermarket to distributors or directly to high-end US bicycle retailers. Products are marketed under the SRAM (drivetrain systems) RockShox (suspension) Avid (brakes) Truvativ (cranks) and Zipp (wheelsets) brand names. The firm's products are sold worldwide (the US accounts for only 15%). SRAM International was founded in 1987 by president and CEO Stanley Day Jr.

SRI INTERNATIONAL

333 RAVENSWOOD AVE
MENLO PARK, CA 940253493
Phone: 650-859-2000
Fax: –
Web: www.sri.com

CEO: William Jeffrey
CFO: Luther Lau
HR: Jeanie Tooker
FYE: December 28
Type: Private

SRI International sometimes called "Silicon Valley's soul" is a not-for-profit think tank pondering advances in biotechnology chemicals and energy computer science electronics and public policy — and ways to commercialize those advances. It focuses on technology research and development business strategies and analysis. The organization has patents and patent applications in IT communications robotics and pharmaceuticals. SRI's clients have included Samsung General Motors and AT&T. The artificial intelligence it designed for the Department of Defense became Apple's Siri. Originally founded in 1946 as Stanford Research Institute SRI became fully independent in 1970.

	Annual Growth	12/09	12/10	12/11	12/12	12/13
Sales ($ mil.)	2.9%	–	502.8	585.2	560.5	547.4
Net income ($ mil.)	–	–	–	14.8	(5.6)	(5.6)
Market value ($ mil.)	–	–	–	–	–	–
Employees	–	–	–	–	–	2,437

SRI/SURGICAL EXPRESS INC.

NASDAQ: STRC

12425 Race Track Rd.
Tampa FL 33626
Phone: 813-891-9550
Fax: 813-818-9076
Web: www.srisurgical.com

CEO: Richard Steeves
CFO: Mark R Faris
HR: –
FYE: December 31
Type: Public

SRI/Surgical Express has doctors and patients covered even when the gown opens to the back. The company which conducts business under the name SRI Surgical provides hospital and surgical centers with such reusable surgical products as gowns and towels. It also provides reprocessed surgical instruments basins and surgical accessories that it sorts sterilizes and packages at about a dozen regional facilities in the US. The company offers pick-up and delivery service as an alternative to in-house recovery programs. SRI Surgical forms multi-year or short-term agreements with such customers as Kaiser Permanenteand Novation. SRI/Surgical Express was acquired by Synergy Health in 2012.

SRT COMMUNICATIONS INC.

3615 N BROADWAY
MINOT, ND 587030408
Phone: 701-858-1200
Fax: –
Web: www.srt.com

CEO: Steve D Lysne
CFO: Perry G Erdmann
HR: –
FYE: December 31
Type: Private

SRT Communications provides local-exchange access and long-distance telephone service to residents of north central North Dakota and Montana. The cooperative serves about 48000 access lines and operates 25 telephone exchanges including those in the towns of Minot Burlington and Surrey as well as the Minot Air Force Base. In addition to voice service the company sells Internet services (including broadband access and Web hosting) as well as PCS wireless service. SRT Communications also distributes business phone systems made by Avaya Mitel and 3Com and offers cable television to subscribers in nearly 20 cities and towns.

	Annual Growth	12/09	12/10	12/11	12/12	12/13
Sales ($ mil.)	(8.9%)	–	47.2	47.9	50.7	35.7
Net income ($ mil.)	–	–	–	3.2	5.7	(9.7)
Market value ($ mil.)	–	–	–	–	–	–
Employees	–	–	–	–	–	221

SS&C TECHNOLOGIES HOLDINGS, INC.

NMS: SSNC

80 Lamberton Road
Windsor, CT 06095
Phone: 860-298-4500
Fax: –
Web: www.ssctech.com

CEO: William C. (Bill) Stone
CFO: Patrick J. Pedonti
HR: –
FYE: December 31
Type: Public

SS&C Technologies helps its clients buy low and sell high and do some of it automatically. The company develops software for managing financial portfolios loans real estate equity back-office processing and securities trading and it provides consulting and outsourcing services. Its applications automate investment portfolio management asset and liability management for actuaries property and casualty insurance risk management trade ordering and financial modeling. SS&C serves asset managers insurance companies banks corporate treasuries hedge funds and government agencies among others. Clients have included Middlebury College and Monro Muffler Brake. It has offices in North America Europe and Asia. SS&C bought one of its competitors Advent Software for more than $2.5 billion in 2015.

	Annual Growth	12/10	12/11	12/12	12/13	12/14
Sales ($ mil.)	23.6%	328.9	370.8	551.8	712.7	767.9
Net income ($ mil.)	41.8%	32.4	51.0	45.8	117.9	131.1
Market value ($ mil.)	29.9%	1,726.7	1,520.4	1,943.9	3,726.1	4,924.0
Employees	35.2%	1,399	1,484	4,086	4,194	4,674

SSAB ENTERPRISES LLC

650 Warrenville Rd. Ste. 500
Lisle IL 60532
Phone: 630-810-4800
Fax: 630-810-4600
Web: www.ssab.com/en/about-ssab1/the-ssab-group/ssa

CEO: –
CFO: Phillip Marusarz
HR: –
FYE: December 31
Type: Business Segment

SSAB Enterprises really deals the steel. The steelmaker produces steel mill products (coil and discrete plate) and fabricated products that include cut-to-length products (hollow structural hot-rolled coil sheet and slab steel). The company operates two steel mills and three cut-to-length facilities in Canada and the US. The division stays adaptable by using Steckel mill technology which permits the company to alternate between coil and discrete plate production in response to market demand. Its markets include the manufacturing agricultural and transportation industries. The North American business unit of Swedish steel company SSAB Svenskt St?l produces around 2.5 million tons of steel annually.

SSI (U.S.) INC.

353 N. Clarke St. Ste. 2400
Chicago IL 60654
Phone: 312-822-0088
Fax: 312-822-0116
Web: www.spencerstuart.com

CEO: Kevin Connelly
CFO: Richard Kurkowski
HR: –
FYE: September 30
Type: Private

When the board of directors ousts your CEO for running the company into the ground it might look to SSI (U.S.) — more commonly known as Spencer Stuart Management Consultants — for a replacement. Founded in 1956 the firm offers leadership consulting and executive search services specializing in searches for top-level executives and board directors. Clients hire Spencer Stuart to recruit the best chief executives and functional leaders in such areas as finance human resources information technology legal and marketing. The firm operates from 50 offices worldwide. Citing the desire to protect client confidentiality the firm's partners have declined to follow rivals into the public marketplace.

SSM HEALTH CARE CORPORATION

477 N. Lindbergh Blvd.
St. Louis MO 63141
Phone: 314-994-7800
Fax: 314-994-7900
Web: www.ssmhc.com

CEO: Bill Thompson
CFO:
HR: –
FYE: December 31
Type: Private - Not-for-Pr

The mission of SSM Health Care System began with five nuns who fled religious persecution in Germany in 1872 only to arrive in St. Louis in the midst of a smallpox epidemic. They formed their first hospital there in 1877. Today the not-for-profit system sponsored by the Franciscan Sisters of Mary owns some 15 acute care hospitals with about 4000 licensed beds; it also has management or affiliation agreements with a number of other area hospitals. The company also operates physicians' practices and two nursing homes and it offers rehabilitation home health care hospice and skilled nursing services. Its facilities are located in Illinois Missouri Oklahoma and Wisconsin.

SSP AMERICA INC.

19465 Deerfield Ave. Ste. 105
Lansdowne VA 20176
Phone: 703-729-2333
Fax: 703-858-7091
Web: www.foodtravelexperts.com/america

CEO: Les Cappetta
CFO: Roger Worrell
HR: –
FYE: September 30
Type: Subsidiary

SSP America encourages travelers to get to the airport early and to show up hungry. The company is a leading contract foodservices provider that operates food courts and concession facilities at more than 40 airports in the US Canada and the Caribbean. Most of its eateries operate under national chain brands licensed from such fast-food companies as Arby's Chick-fil-a and Quiznos. It also partners with some independent and local restaurant operators and it has proprietary brands such as bakery cafe Upper Crust. SSP America is a regional operating unit of global foodservice contractor SSP Group.

ST BARNABAS MEDICAL CENTER INC

94 OLD SHORT HILLS RD # 1
LIVINGSTON, NJ 070395668
Phone: 973-322-5000
Fax: –
Web: www.njburncenter.com

CEO: Ronald J Del Mauro
CFO: Patrick Aheran
HR: –
FYE: December 31
Type: Private

Part of the Saint Barnabas Health Care System Saint Barnabas Medical Center is a 600-bed acute-care hospital that provides a full range of health services to residents of Livingston New Jersey and surrounding areas. The not-for-profit medical center provides general inpatient and outpatient care programs as well as burn and perinatal care. It also houses units specializing in organ transplant stroke care cardiac surgery and comprehensive cancer treatment. Its Institute for Reproductive Medicine and Science provides assisted reproductive technology services. Saint Barnabas Medical Center treats some 35000 inpatients and more than 85000 emergency-room patients each year.

	Annual Growth	12/02	12/03	12/05	12/08	12/12
Sales ($ mil.)	(9.2%)	–	1,550.8	438.5	510.9	652.7
Net income ($ mil.)	34.7%	–	–	9.3	(5.0)	75.0
Market value ($ mil.)	–	–	–	–	–	–
Employees	–	–	–	–	–	479

ST BONAVENTURE UNIVERSITY

3261 W STATE RD
SAINT BONAVENTURE, NY 147789800
Phone: 716-375-2000
Fax: –
Web: www.sbu.edu

CEO: –
CFO: –
HR: –
FYE: May 31
Type: Private

St. Bonaventure University is a private Catholic liberal arts institution in southwestern New York. With some 2700 students the liberal arts school offers both undergraduate majors and graduate programs in areas including education psychology and journalism. A group of Franciscan friars live on the campus and the university is the home of the School of Franciscan Studies and the Franciscan Institute which conduct research and education on the history spirituality and intellectual life of the Franciscan movement. St. Bonaventure University was founded in 1858 by the Franciscan Friars of the Holy Name Province.

	Annual Growth	05/10	05/11	05/12	05/13	05/14
Sales ($ mil.)	0.5%	–	53.7	54.0	54.6	54.6
Net income ($ mil.)	5.0%	–	–	4.9	9.5	5.4
Market value ($ mil.)	–	–	–	–	–	–
Employees	–	–	–	–	–	540

ST DAVID ROUND ROCK MEDICAL CENTER

2400 ROUND ROCK AVE
ROUND ROCK, TX 786814004
Phone: 512-341-1000
Fax: –
Web: www.stdavidsfoundation.org

CEO: Deborah Ryl
CFO: –
HR: AMI Noak
FYE: February 28
Type: Private

St. David's Round Rock Medical Center serves the growing Williamson County community located in Central Texas. The facility includes an acute care hospital with approximately 175 beds a heart center a women's center and an outpatient surgery center. Other services include respiratory therapy vascular lab work orthopedics and intermediate care. The medical center is part of St. David's HealthCare Partnership a joint venture between St. David's Health Care System and HCA. The hospital's size was almost doubled through expansion construction in 2006.

	Annual Growth	12/02	12/03	12/04	12/05*	02/13
Sales ($ mil.)	16.0%	–	–	–	40.0	131.3
Net income ($ mil.)	(7.1%)	–	–	–	36.1	20.0
Market value ($ mil.)	–	–	–	–	–	–
Employees	–	–	–	–	–	610

*Fiscal year change

ST FRANCIS HOSPITAL

100 PORT WASHINGTON BLVD
ROSLYN, NY 115761353
Phone: 516-627-3813
Fax: –
Web: www.stfrancisheartcenter.com

CEO: Alan Guerci
CFO: William C Arms
HR: Betty Anson
FYE: December 31
Type: Private

Sure St. Francis Hospital can handle your gall bladder and sinus difficulties but it's really on top of your heart problems. The hospital's Heart Center — New York State's only specially designated cardiac center — provides surgical diagnostic and treatment services. The 365-bed St. Francis Hospital also has centers for ENT (ear nose and throat) orthopedic vascular prostate cancer gastrointestinal and general surgery services. As part of Catholic Health Services of Long Island St. Francis opened its doors in 1954 to children and adults. It was originally established as St. Francis Hospital and Sanatorium for Cardiac Children in 1936.

	Annual Growth	12/00	12/01	12/02	12/04	12/08
Sales ($ mil.)	–	–	–	(828.9)	366.7	385.1
Net income ($ mil.)	606.6%	–	–	0.0	47.4	28.5
Market value ($ mil.)	–	–	–	–	–	–
Employees	–	–	–	–	–	2,184

ST JOHN FISHER COLLEGE

3690 EAST AVE OFC
ROCHESTER, NY 146183597
Phone: 585-385-8000
Fax: –
Web: www.webmail.sjfc.edu

CEO: –
CFO: –
HR: –
FYE: May 31
Type: Private

St. John Fisher College is a Catholic liberal arts institution. The independent school offers more than 30 academic majors in the business education humanities natural sciences and nursing as well as about a dozen pre-professional programs 10 master's programs and three doctoral programs. Its enrollment includes more than 2700 full-time undergraduate students as well as 200 part time students. The student-faculty ratio is 13:1. The college is guided by the educational philosophy of the Congregation of St. Basil.

	Annual Growth	05/08	05/09	05/10	05/11	05/13
Sales ($ mil.)	–	–	0.0	105.0	111.8	122.6
Net income ($ mil.)	9.0%	–	–	8.4	9.2	10.8
Market value ($ mil.)	–	–	–	–	–	–
Employees	–	–	–	–	–	574

ST JOHNS HOSPITAL SISTERS OF THE THIRD ORDER OF ST FRANCIS

800 E CARPENTER ST	CEO: Dr Charles Lucore
SPRINGFIELD, IL 627690002	CFO: Larry Ragel
Phone: 217-544-6464	HR: –
Fax: –	FYE: June 30
Web: www.stjohnscollegespringfield.edu	Type: Private

Truck-struck Homer Simpson might use his last gasp trying to blurt out "St. John's Hospital of the Hospital Sisters of the Third Order of St. Francis-Springfield" to his ambulance driver but he might be better off using the hospital's more common name St. John's. D'oh! The 440-bed St. John's Hospital serves residents of central and southern Illinois with general and specialized health care services. The teaching hospital affiliated with Southern Illinois University's School of Medicine has centers devoted to women and children's health trauma cardiac care cancer orthopedics and neurology. It also operates area health clinics. Founded in 1875 St. John's is part of the Hospital Sisters Health System.

	Annual Growth	06/02	06/03	06/04	06/05	06/08
Sales ($ mil.)	–	–	–	(1,737.9)	387.5	393.2
Net income ($ mil.)	–	–	–	0.0	50.8	(8.7)
Market value ($ mil.)	–	–	–	–	–	–
Employees	–	–	–	–	–	3,000

ST JOHN'S UNIVERSITY NEW YORK

8000 UTOPIA PKWY	CEO: –
JAMAICA, NY 114399000	CFO: –
Phone: 718-990-6161	HR: –
Fax: –	FYE: May 31
Web: www.stjohns.edu	Type: Private

No university is an island but one of St. John's campuses is on Manhattan Island. A private co-educational Roman Catholic school St. John's University offers undergraduate and graduate programs in more than 100 majors through five colleges a law school and a distance learning program. St. John's has more than 20000 students at five campuses (Queens Staten Island and Manhattan in New York City one in Oakdale New York and one graduate center in Rome). The school has a 17-to-1 student-faculty ratio. More than 80% of its graduates reside in the New York region including notable alumni such as former New York governors Hugh Carey and Mario Cuomo. The school was founded in 1870 by the Vincentian Community.

	Annual Growth	05/09	05/10	05/11	05/12	05/13
Sales ($ mil.)	2.4%	–	440.8	450.1	471.5	473.8
Net income ($ mil.)	(11.9%)	–	–	82.7	2.9	64.2
Market value ($ mil.)	–	–	–	–	–	–
Employees	–	–	–	–	–	3,310

ST JOSEPH''S COLLEGE NEW YORK

245 CLINTON AVE	CEO: Sister Elizabeth Hill
BROOKLYN, NY 112053688	CFO: John Roth
Phone: 718-940-5300	HR: –
Fax: –	FYE: June 30
Web: www.sjcny.edu	Type: Private

St. Joseph's College is a liberal arts college with two locations in the metropolitan New York City area — one in Brooklyn and one in Long Island. St. Joseph's offers more than 20 undergraduate majors pre-professional and certificate programs and graduate degrees in management business and infant/toddler early childhood special education to over 5000 students. Its School of Adult and Professional Education provides adult students with certificate and degree programs in fields such as management computer information systems and health. Its Brooklyn campus also houses the Dillon Child Study Center a working preschool where child-study majors gain hands-on experience. St. Joseph's was founded in 1916.

	Annual Growth	06/02	06/03	06/04	06/05	06/13
Sales ($ mil.)	(25.0%)	–	1,417.0	50.1	56.0	80.0
Net income ($ mil.)	–	–	–	1.0	1.2	(4.6)
Market value ($ mil.)	–	–	–	–	–	–
Employees	–	–	–	–	–	800

ST JOSEPH''S HOSPITAL

9515 HOLY CROSS LN	CEO: Mark Kloserman
BREESE, IL 622303618	CFO: –
Phone: 618-526-4511	HR: –
Fax: –	FYE: June 30
Web: www.stjoebreese.com	Type: Private

St. Joseph's Hospital of the Hospital Sisters of the Third Order of St. Francis (Breese)is an 85-bed hospital sponsored by the Hospital Sisters of the Third Order of St. Francis. Founded in 1918 this acute-care institution provides a wide range of health care services such as emergency medicine pediatrics physical therapy and surgery. The hospital also operates a women and children's cneter as well as provides community education. Its full-time medical staff includes about 20 primary physicians.

	Annual Growth	05/08	05/09*	06/09*	05/10*	06/13
Sales ($ mil.)	–	–	0.0	40.4	0.1	53.3
Net income ($ mil.)	–	–	–	0.0	0.0	10.0
Market value ($ mil.)	–	–	–	–	–	–
Employees	–	–	–	–	–	300
						*Fiscal year change

ST JOSEPHS WAYNE HOSPITAL INC

224 HAMBURG TPKE STE 1	CEO: –
WAYNE, NJ 074702124	CFO: –
Phone: 973-942-6900	HR: John Bruno
Fax: –	FYE: December 31
Web: www.stjosephshealth.org	Type: Private

St. Joseph's Wayne Hospital (SJWH) helps its patients get back into a healthy realm. The acute care facility serves the residents of northern New Jersey. With some 230 beds and more than 400 physicians on staff SJWH offers services including cancer care neurology radiology surgery rehabilitation and senior care. It also includes an ambulatory center that offers minor surgery infusions and other outpatient procedures as well as a sleep diagnostics center and affiliated home health and hospice agencies. Established in 1871 the Catholic hospital is part of the St. Joseph's Healthcare System which is sponsored by the Sisters of Charity of Saint Elizabeth.

	Annual Growth	12/01	12/02	12/03*	06/05*	12/08
Sales ($ mil.)	3.3%	–	66.3	73.3	73.3	80.7
Net income ($ mil.)	–	–	–	(7.9)	0.0	3.3
Market value ($ mil.)	–	–	–	–	–	–
Employees	–	–	–	–	–	925
						*Fiscal year change

ST JUDE MEDICAL INC

NYS: STJ

One St. Jude Medical Drive	CEO: Michael T. Rousseau
St. Paul, MN 55117	CFO: Donald J. Zurbay
Phone: 651 756-2000	HR: –
Fax: 651 756-3301	FYE: January 03
Web: www.sjm.com	Type: Public

If your heart has trouble catching the beat St. Jude Medical's got rhythm to spare. The company is a global medical device manufacturer focused on improving the treatment of some of the world's most expensive epidemic diseases. St. Jude Medical operates in one segment producing six principal product categories: ICD (implantable cardiac defibrillator) Systems (the largest category representing 35% of total earnings) Pacemaker Systems Atrial Fibrillation Products Vascular Products Structural Heart Products and Neuromodulation Products. The company sells its products in more than 100 countries; the US is its largest market. St. Jude Medical was formed in 1976.

	Annual Growth	01/11*	12/11	12/12	12/13*	01/15
Sales ($ mil.)	2.1%	5,164.8	5,611.7	5,503.0	5,501.0	5,622.0
Net income ($ mil.)	2.5%	907.4	825.8	752.0	723.0	1,002.0
Market value ($ mil.)	11.0%	12,254.7	9,832.4	10,167.8	17,844.6	18,615.7
Employees	1.6%	15,000	16,000	15,000	16,000	16,000
						*Fiscal year change

ST LAWRENCE UNIVERSITY

23 ROMODA DR
CANTON, NY 136171501
Phone: 315-229-5011
Fax: –
Web: www.alumni.stlawu.edu

CEO: –
CFO: –
HR: –
FYE: June 30
Type: Private

St. Lawrence University is a four-year liberal arts college that also offers graduate degrees in education. The university has an enrollment of more than 2500 students as well as 200 faculty members and a student-to-teacher ratio of 12:1. Major fields of study include biology computer science economics history psychology foreign language and religious studies. Actors Kirk Douglas and Viggo Mortensen and US Senator Susan Collins are among the school's alumni. Founded in 1856 by members of the Universalist Church (now Unitarian Universalist) St. Lawrence is the oldest continuously coeducational institution of higher learning in New York State.

	Annual Growth	06/10	06/11	06/12	06/13	06/14
Sales ($ mil.)	1.9%	–	110.9	112.0	112.3	117.2
Net income ($ mil.)	–	–	–	(13.5)	19.5	36.9
Market value ($ mil.)	–	–	–	–	–	–
Employees	–	–	–	–	–	650

ST MARY''S REGIONAL HEALTH CENTER

1027 WASHINGTON AVE
DETROIT LAKES, MN 565013409
Phone: 218-847-5611
Fax: –

CEO: –
CFO: Ryan Hill
HR: Lori Bakken
FYE: June 30
Type: Private

St. Mary's Innovis Health (formerly St. Mary's Regional Health Center) provides acute and long-term health care services to central Minnesota including general medical and surgical care cardiac rehabilitation and skilled nursing services for the elderly. The health care company's hospital has nearly 90 beds and its nursing center has about 100 beds. The organization also includes two senior housing facilities community clinics surgery centers home health providers and an affiliated physician network. St. Mary's is an affiliate of Innovis Health which operates a network of health care facilities in North Dakota and Minnesota.

	Annual Growth	06/08	06/09	06/10	06/11	06/13
Sales ($ mil.)	–	–	(1,581.2)	65.0	71.9	78.6
Net income ($ mil.)	59.6%	–	–	0.3	2.3	1.2
Market value ($ mil.)	–	–	–	–	–	–
Employees	–	–	–	–	–	400

ST PATRICK HOSPITAL CORPORATION

500 W BROADWAY ST
MISSOULA, MT 598024008
Phone: 406-543-7271
Fax: –
Web: www.saintpatrick.org

CEO: –
CFO: Loren Jacobson
HR: Kerry Schultz
FYE: December 31
Type: Private

Feeling a little green? St. Patrick Hospital and Health Sciences Center is there to help. The not-for-profit hospital boasts some 250 beds (acute-care and transitional) and serves nearly 20 counties in and around Missoula Montana. Its specialty services include cancer treatment surgery and occupational health. The center also provides Life Flight air transport to critically ill or injured patients. The hospital provides outpatient primary and specialty care through a host of affiliated physician practices and clinics throughout the area. St. Patrick Hospital and Health Sciences Center is part of Providence Health & Services which has two hospitals and more than 40 clinics across Montana.

	Annual Growth	12/01	12/02	12/04	12/05	12/12
Sales ($ mil.)	(16.4%)	–	1,361.6	163.3	191.8	227.7
Net income ($ mil.)	25.3%	–	–	6.2	8.2	37.7
Market value ($ mil.)	–	–	–	–	–	–
Employees	–	–	–	–	–	1,460

ST PETER'S MEDICAL CENTER

254 EASTON AVE
NEW BRUNSWICK, NJ 089011766
Phone: 732-745-8600
Fax: –
Web: www.saintpetershcs.com

CEO: Ronald Rak
CFO: Garrick Stoldt
HR: –
FYE: December 31
Type: Private

Serving the central portions of the Garden State Saint Peter's University Hospital has about 480 beds. The facility is sponsored by the Roman Catholic Diocese of Metuchen New Jersey and provides patients with a staff of more than 900 physicians and dentists. Saint Peter's also offers one of the country's largest Neonatal Intensive Care Units minimally invasive surgical (MIS) procedures and specialized cancer diabetes and geriatric care. In affiliation with the Children's Hospital of Philadelphia Saint Peter's provides cardiac care for infants and children. The teaching hospital is also affiliated with the Drexel University College of Medicine.

	Annual Growth	12/03	12/04	12/05	12/06	12/08
Sales ($ mil.)	2.7%	–	351.8	373.8	392.6	391.0
Net income ($ mil.)	–	–	–	4.1	4.0	(34.4)
Market value ($ mil.)	–	–	–	–	–	–
Employees	–	–	–	–	–	2,475

ST. ALEXIUS MEDICAL CENTER

900 E BROADWAY AVE
BISMARCK, ND 585014520
Phone: 701-530-7000
Fax: –
Web: www.st.alexius.org

CEO: Gary P Miller
CFO: –
HR: –
FYE: June 30
Type: Private

Established in 1885 CHI St. Alexius Health (formerly St. Alexius Medical Center) has been serving the health care needs of those who reside in the Dakotas and Montana longer than any other area hospital. The medical facility with more than 300 beds caters to central and western North Dakota and parts of South Dakota and Montana. Specialty services include cancer care trauma care geriatrics orthopedics and rehabilitation. As part of its operations the longtime hospital also owns and manages a handful of smaller regional hospitals and community clinics. In 2014 St. Alexius joined the Catholic Health Initiatives health care system.

	Annual Growth	06/09	06/10	06/11	06/12	06/13
Sales ($ mil.)	6.2%	–	243.3	275.0	294.9	291.4
Net income ($ mil.)	–	–	–	12.8	11.0	(2.0)
Market value ($ mil.)	–	–	–	–	–	–
Employees	–	–	–	–	–	1,947

ST. ANTHONY'S HOSPITAL INC.

1200 7TH AVE N
SAINT PETERSBURG, FL 33705-1388
Phone: 727-825-1100
Fax: –
Web: www.stanthonysfoundation.org

CEO: –
CFO: Carl Tremonti
HR: –
FYE: December 31
Type: Private

Saint or not if you need medical care in St. Petersburg Florida St. Anthony's Hospital has you covered. The facility offers a full array of health care services including emergency medicine surgery cancer treatment and heart care as well as services in fields including neurology orthopedics and metabolic care. The 400-bed hospital also provides outpatient services through several ambulatory surgery rehabilitation and imaging centers. St. Anthony's Hospital is a member of the BayCare Health System and as such provides home health and occupational health services through agencies affiliated with that system.

	Annual Growth	12/02	12/03	12/06	12/08	12/09
Sales ($ mil.)	8.5%	–	111.5	150.8	159.3	181.5
Net income ($ mil.)	24.2%	–	1.9	(4.3)	(12.6)	7.0
Market value ($ mil.)	–	–	–	–	–	–
Employees	–	–	–	–	–	1,076

ST. ANTHONY'S MEDICAL CENTER

10010 KENNERLY RD
SAINT LOUIS, MO 631282106
Phone: 314-525-1000
Fax: –
Web: www.stanthonysmedcenter.com

CEO: –
CFO: –
HR: –
FYE: June 30
Type: Private

St. Anthony's Medical Center applies its skills to medical cases in the Midwest. The hospital serves residents in the areas surrounding St. Louis Missouri as well as portions of southwestern Illinois. With about 770 beds and some 800 affiliated physicians the hospital provides a comprehensive offering including inpatient and outpatient medical surgical diagnostic and behavioral health care. The hospital operates a level II trauma center cancer and chest pain units and a pediatric emergency center as well as several urgent care facilities. It also offers home health hospice laboratory and pharmacy services. St. Anthony's Medical Center was founded in 1900 by the Franciscan Sisters of Germany.

	Annual Growth	06/09	06/10	06/11	06/12	06/13
Sales ($ mil.)	0.3%	–	439.3	473.5	467.2	443.8
Net income ($ mil.)	(15.0%)	–	–	53.5	(29.7)	38.6
Market value ($ mil.)	–	–	–	–	–	–
Employees	–	–	–	–	–	3,900

ST. BERNARD HOSPITAL

326 W 64TH ST
CHICAGO, IL 60621-3146
Phone: 773-962-3900
Fax: –
Web: www.stbh.org

CEO: –
CFO: –
HR: –
FYE: December 31
Type: Private

Like a giant dog trudging through blinding snow to rescue a traveler in need St. Bernard Hospital is a powerhouse of betterment for the people it serves. St. Bernard Hospital and Health Care Center serves the residents of Chicago's south side neighborhood of Englewood. The facility has about 200 beds and its specialties include pediatrics psychiatry neurology orthopedics and cardiology services. The hospital also offers inpatient detoxification services for patients dependent on opiates or alcohol. St. Bernard has a separate nonprofit unit that takes care of south side residents' residences: Bernard Place Housing Development is a 90-unit affordable homes initiative in the Englewood neighborhood.

	Annual Growth	12/05	12/06	12/08	12/09	12/11
Sales ($ mil.)	2.8%	–	78.7	85.1	94.7	90.3
Net income ($ mil.)	10.8%	–	3.4	4.2	11.8	5.7
Market value ($ mil.)	–	–	–	–	–	–
Employees	–	–	–	–	–	875

ST. FRANCIS" HOSPITAL POUGHKEEPSIE NEW YORK

241 NORTH RD
POUGHKEEPSIE, NY 12601-1154
Phone: 845-471-2000
Fax: –
Web: www.sfhospital.org

CEO: –
CFO: –
HR: –
FYE: December 31
Type: Private

When leaf-peepers sprain their ankles or landscape painters fall on their brushes they turn to Saint Francis for help. Saint Francis Hospital provides primary and specialty health care services to residents throughout New York's Hudson Valley area. The Poughkeepsie-based organization includes centers specializing in behavioral health home care orthopedics plastic surgery and trauma care. The hospital also operates a chemical dependency treatment program. It is licensed for 33 beds and provides medical care for more than 10000 inpatients every year.

	Annual Growth	12/01	12/02*	06/05*	12/08	12/09
Sales ($ mil.)	1.3%	–	132.7	709.0	124.7	145.5
Net income ($ mil.)	–	–	3.5	48.0	(7.5)	(4.5)
Market value ($ mil.)	–	–	–	–	–	–
Employees	–	–	–	–	–	1,490

*Fiscal year change

ST. JOE CO. (THE)

NYS: JOE

133 South WaterSound Parkway
WaterSound, FL 32413
Phone: 850 231-6400
Fax: –
Web: www.joe.com

CEO: Jorge Gonzalez
CFO: Marek Bakun
HR: –
FYE: December 31
Type: Public

Wanna buy some swampland in Florida? Perhaps something a bit more upscale? St. Joe has it along with timberland and beaches. Formerly operating in paper sugar timber telephone systems and railroads St. Joe is a Florida real estate developer and one of the state's largest private landowners. It holds some 573000 acres of land located mostly in northwest Florida. Some 70% of its land holdings are within 15 miles of the Gulf of Mexico including beach frontage and other waterfront properties. The company is primarily engaged in developing residential resorts and towns commerce parks and rural property sales. St. Joe also operates a forestry segment which grows harvests and sells timber and wood fiber.

	Annual Growth	12/10	12/11	12/12	12/13	12/14
Sales ($ mil.)	63.0%	99.5	145.3	139.4	131.3	701.9
Net income ($ mil.)	–	(35.9)	(330.3)	6.0	5.0	406.5
Market value ($ mil.)	(4.2%)	2,016.8	1,353.2	2,130.3	1,771.3	1,697.4
Employees	(15.2%)	118	75	74	67	61

ST. JOHN HEALTH SYSTEM INC.

1923 S UTICA AVE
TULSA, OK 741046520
Phone: 918-744-2180
Fax: –
Web: www.stjohnprovidence.org

CEO: –
CFO: Lex Anderson
HR: Page Bachman
FYE: June 30
Type: Private

St. John Health System aims to bring health into the lives of the ill. The not-for-profit system provides health care services to residents of Tulsa and surrounding areas in northeastern Oklahoma and southern Kansas. In addition to flagship facility St. John Medical Center it owns or manages eight other community hospitals as well as urgent care and long-term care facilities. St. John Health System provides primary and specialty medical care through OMNI Medical Group and offers health insurance through CommunityCare health plan. Established in 1926 by the Sisters of the Sorrowful Mother the health system is part of Marian Health.

	Annual Growth	09/09	09/10	09/11	09/12*	06/14
Sales ($ mil.)	3.5%	–	919.7	895.5	977.4	1,057.0
Net income ($ mil.)	64.9%	–	–	17.7	74.8	79.3
Market value ($ mil.)	–	–	–	–	–	–
Employees	–	–	–	–	–	4,011

*Fiscal year change

ST. JOHN KNITS INTERNATIONAL INCORPORATED

17622 Armstrong Ave.
Irvine CA 92614
Phone: 949-863-1171
Fax: 949-223-3396
Web: www.stjohnknits.com

CEO: Geoffroy Van Raemdonck
CFO: Tammy Storino
HR: –
FYE: October 31
Type: Private

The patron saint of tailored attire St. John (formerly St. John Knits) has clothed some of the nation's most couture-worthy women including Hillary Rodham Clinton and Diane Sawyer. The company designs colorful classically styled sportswear career separates and evening wear under the St. John name as well as jewelry shoes handbags and belts. St. John Knits sells its apparel and accessories through more than 25 company-operated boutiques in the US and Canada and via its e-commerce site. The St. John brand is also sold in high-end department stores in more than 25 countries. Vestar/Gray Investors a partnership between the founding Gray family and Vestar Capital Partners owns a majority of the company.

ST. JOHN''S COLLEGE

60 COLLEGE AVE
ANNAPOLIS, MD 214011655
Phone: 410-263-2371
Fax: –
Web: www.stjohnscollege.edu

CEO: –
CFO: Bronte Jones
HR: Gotz-Ulrich Luttenberger
FYE: June 30
Type: Private

St. John's College believes in the "Great Books" even as the canon is under attack elsewhere in academia. Students at the college study the classics in literature math philosophy and science. The curriculum starts with Aeschylus Aristotle Euclid and Plato taught freshman year; students work their way through the millennia of higher learning finishing with the works of contemporary thinkers and writers which are taught to seniors. St. John's (not to be confused with the university in New York City) is the third-oldest institution of higher learning in the US (after Harvard and William & Mary); it was founded in Maryland in 1696 and opened a Santa Fe campus in 1964. Each campus has about 450 students.

	Annual Growth	06/08	06/09	06/10	06/11	06/13
Sales ($ mil.)	35.6%	–	–	29.1	34.1	72.6
Net income ($ mil.)	19.5%	–	–	2.0	6.9	3.4
Market value ($ mil.)	–	–	–	–	–	–
Employees	–	–	–	–	–	250

ST. JOSEPH HEALTH SYSTEM

3345 MICHELSON DR STE 100
IRVINE, CA 926120693
Phone: 949-381-4000
Fax: –
Web: www.stjhs.org

CEO: Joe Mark
CFO: Jo Escasa-Haigh
HR: Ryan Faulkner
FYE: June 30
Type: Private

St. Joseph Health System has earned a medal for decades by caring for patients on the West Coast and more recently the South Plains. The health care network includes 16 acute care hospitals home health agencies hospice care outpatient services skilled nursing facilities community clinics and physician organizations throughout California and in eastern New Mexico and West Texas. In its primary market of California the health system has some 2900 beds at 10 hospitals. Its Covenant Health System unit operates in Texas and New Mexico with about 1200 beds in its network of some 50 primary care facilities. St. Joseph is merging with fellow not-for-profit Providence Health & Services.

	Annual Growth	06/07	06/08	06/10	06/13	06/14
Sales ($ mil.)	6.1%	–	3,943.8	4,268.6	4,955.7	5,631.7
Net income ($ mil.)	7.1%	–	–	268.0	2,082.8	353.3
Market value ($ mil.)	–	–	–	–	–	–
Employees	–	–	–	–	–	21,500

ST. JOSEPH HOSPITAL OF ORANGE

1100 W STEWART DR
ORANGE, CA 928683891
Phone: 714-633-9111
Fax: –
Web: www.sjo.org

CEO: Larry K Ainsworth
CFO: Tina Nycroft
HR: –
FYE: June 30
Type: Private

If you're feeling green or blue in Orange County St. Joseph Hospital of Orange is there to help get back to feeling pink and rosy. The California hospital provides general medical and surgical services as well as specialty care such as women's health mental health services oncology cardiology and physical rehabilitation. Part of the St. Joseph Health System the hospital provides primary care and specialty outpatient services through a network of affiliated physician practices. It also operates low-income and mobile clinics. The hospital has about 468 beds and a medical staff of some 1000.

	Annual Growth	06/09	06/10	06/11	06/12	06/13
Sales ($ mil.)	1.6%	–	638.2	661.3	646.0	668.9
Net income ($ mil.)	21.1%	–	–	32.7	23.0	47.9
Market value ($ mil.)	–	–	–	–	–	–
Employees	–	–	–	–	–	3,300

ST. JOSEPH'S HOSPITAL HEALTH CENTER

301 PROSPECT AVE
SYRACUSE, NY 132031899
Phone: 315-448-5111
Fax: –
Web: www.sjhsyr.org

CEO: –
CFO: –
HR: –
FYE: December 31
Type: Private

With about 430 inpatient beds St. Joseph's Hospital Health Center serves the residents of 16 central New York counties. The not-for-profit hospital system provides general emergency and surgical care as well as specialty services in areas such as obstetrics cardiology dialysis and wound care. In addition to its inpatient facilities the organization operates a home health agency a nursing school medical and dental residency programs and several outpatient care centers. Its Franciscan Companies affiliate offers some ancillary services including the provision of medical supplies home health equipment and senior services. St. Joseph's Hospital Health Center was founded in 1869.

	Annual Growth	12/97	12/98	12/05	12/08	12/09
Sales ($ mil.)	6.4%	–	221.3	363.7	399.1	436.3
Net income ($ mil.)	(17.7%)	–	–	11.7	6.3	5.4
Market value ($ mil.)	–	–	–	–	–	–
Employees	–	–	–	–	–	3,300

ST. JUDE CHILDREN'S RESEARCH HOSPITAL INC.

262 DANNY THOMAS PL
MEMPHIS, TN 381053678
Phone: 901-595-3300
Fax: –
Web: www.stjude.org

CEO: James Downing
CFO: Pat Keel
HR: –
FYE: June 30
Type: Private

St. Jude Children's Research Hospital studies and treats catastrophic diseases in children especially pediatric cancers. The hospital which only has about 80 beds annually treats more than 7800 children most of whom are treated on an outpatient basis as part of its research efforts into finding cures and more effective treatments. The hospital not only helps children with their health it also helps their parents: It pays all expenses that are not covered by insurance and doesn't require payment from patients without insurance. St. Jude Children's Research Hospital was founded in 1962.

	Annual Growth	06/07	06/08	06/09	06/10	06/11
Sales ($ mil.)	(2.7%)	–	–	–	589.9	573.7
Net income ($ mil.)	–	–	–	–	(5.0)	(26.3)
Market value ($ mil.)	–	–	–	–	–	–
Employees	–	–	–	–	–	2,500

ST. JUDE HOSPITAL

101 E VALENCIA MESA DR
FULLERTON, CA 928353875
Phone: 714-871-3280
Fax: –
Web: www.stjudemedicalcenter.org

CEO: Robert Fraschetti
CFO: Ed Salvador
HR: –
FYE: June 30
Type: Private

St. Jude Medical Center gets sickly Southern Californians on their feet again. The faith-based not-for-profit acute care facility with some 385 beds serves the residents of Orange County. The medical center provides an onsite cancer center (the Virginia K. Crosson Cancer Center) and a heart institute that offers cardiac surgeries and rehabilitation programs. It also provides inpatient and outpatient physical rehabilitation services and a variety of community outreach programs. Established by the Sisters of St. Joseph of Orange religious order in the 1950s St. Jude Medical Center is part of the St. Joseph Health System.

	Annual Growth	06/07	06/08	06/09	06/10	06/13
Sales ($ mil.)	–	–	(21.9)	412.7	492.2	476.5
Net income ($ mil.)	–	–	–	0.0	61.3	62.8
Market value ($ mil.)	–	–	–	–	–	–
Employees	–	–	–	–	–	2,600

ST. LOUIS CARDINALS L.P.

250 Stadium Plaza	CEO: –
St. Louis MO 63102-1722	CFO: –
Phone: 314-345-9600	HR: Kim Buchannon
Fax: 314-345-9523	FYE: October 31
Web: stlouis.cardinals.mlb.com	Type: Private

Fans of these Cardinals take flight to the stadium every season. The St. Louis Cardinals is one of the oldest teams in Major League Baseball joining the National League as the St. Louis Browns in 1892. Renamed the Cardinals in 1900 the team has gone on to win 18 league pennants and 11 World Series championships (second only to the New York Yankees) its last in 2011. The team's roster has included such stars as Albert Pujols Bob Gibson Stan Musial and Ozzie Smith. An investment group led by St. Louis attorney Fred Hanser Andrew Baur and William DeWitt Jr. owns the Cardinals.

ST. LUKE'S HEALTH NETWORK INC.

801 OSTRUM ST	CEO: –
BETHLEHEM, PA 18015-1000	CFO: –
Phone: 610-954-4000	HR: Brian Spillers
Fax: –	FYE: June 30
Web: www.bethlehem.slhn.org	Type: Private

St. Luke's University Hospital (formerly St. Luke's Hospital - Bethlehem Campus) serves residents of Pennsylvania's Lehigh Valley with primary specialty and emergency care services. The not-for-profit teaching hospital has about 480 acute-care beds. Its medical specialties include trauma oncology cardiology orthopedics neurology open-heart surgery radiology and robotic surgery. The medical center also operates outpatient surgery centers and general physician care clinics and it operates home health and community wellness programs. St. Luke's University Hospital was founded in 1872 and is part of the St. Luke's University Health Network.

	Annual Growth	06/07	06/08	06/09	06/10	06/11
Sales ($ mil.)	1.9%	–	–	–	670.3	682.9
Net income ($ mil.)	67.2%	–	–	–	23.1	38.6
Market value ($ mil.)	–	–	–	–	–	–
Employees	–	–	–	–	–	2,958

ST. LUKE'S HEALTH SYSTEM LTD.

190 E. Bannock St.	CEO: Chris Roth
Boise ID 83712-9987	CFO: –
Phone: 208-381-2222	HR: Maureen Okeefe
Fax: 317-216-9346	FYE: September 30
Web: www.syscoindy.com	Type: Private - Not-for-Pr

To Catholics St. Luke is also known as the "beloved physician" and St. Luke's Health System strives to live up to its namesake. The regional not-for-profit health system provides a range of health services to residents of Idaho eastern Oregon and northern Nevada. St. Luke's is home to five general acute care hospitals with a total of about 800 beds. Its flagship facility is the 400-bed St. Luke's Boise Medical Center which also includes a full-service children's hospital. St. Luke's also runs a network of cancer care sites under the name Mountain States Tumor Institute (MSTI) as well as a number of family practice and specialty health centers under the St. Luke's Clinics banner.

ST. LUKE'S EPISCOPAL-PRESBYTERIAN HOSPITALS

232 S WOODS MILL RD	CEO: Gary Olson
CHESTERFIELD, MO 630173417	CFO: –
Phone: 314-434-1500	HR: –
Fax: –	FYE: June 30
Web: www.stlukes-stl.com	Type: Private

St. Luke's Episcopal-Presbyterian Hospital doing business as St. Luke's Hospital provides health care services to St. Louis residents and surrounding areas of eastern Missouri. The medical center houses more than 490 beds and offers general medical and surgical care as well as specialty services in areas such as heart disease cancer neuroscience orthopedics pediatrics and women's health. St. Luke's also operates half a dozen urgent care clinics in St. Louis and St. Charles counties providing treatment for minor emergencies such as cuts and animal bites as well as a skilled-nursing facility rehabilitation hospital and several diagnostic imaging centers. The not-for-profit hospital was founded in 1866.

	Annual Growth	06/01	06/02	06/03	06/04	06/13
Sales ($ mil.)	–	–	(1,170.2)	263.5	274.1	415.8
Net income ($ mil.)	10.4%	–	–	9.3	11.2	25.2
Market value ($ mil.)	–	–	–	–	–	–
Employees	–	–	–	–	–	3,000

ST. LUKE'S HOSPITAL OF DULUTH

915 E 1ST ST	CEO: John Strange
DULUTH, MN 558052193	CFO: James Wuellner
Phone: 218-726-5555	HR: –
Fax: –	FYE: December 31
Web: www.slhduluth.com	Type: Private

St. Luke's cares for colds cancers and other conditions in the chilly northern US. St. Luke's Hospital provides a variety of health care services to patients in northeastern Minnesota northwestern Wisconsin and parts of Michigan. The medical center has some 270 beds and a staff of about 370 physicians. Services include cardiology emergency medicine pediatrics oncology rehabilitation and vascular surgery. In addition to acute care services the organization offers primary and specialty health care services through a network of outpatient clinics.

	Annual Growth	12/05	12/06	12/08	12/09	12/13
Sales ($ mil.)	5.2%	–	264.9	276.2	307.1	377.9
Net income ($ mil.)	13.2%	–	–	1.6	8.0	3.0
Market value ($ mil.)	–	–	–	–	–	–
Employees	–	–	–	–	–	2,200

ST. MARY'S HEALTH CARE SYSTEM INC.

1230 BAXTER ST	CEO: Don McKenna
ATHENS, GA 30606-3712	CFO: –
Phone: 706-389-3000	HR: –
Fax: –	FYE: December 31
Web: www.stmarysathens.com	Type: Private

St. Mary's Health Care System cares for the residents of northeast Georgia. Its primary facility St. Mary's Hospital has almost 200 acute-care beds. From health and wellness programs to women's and children's services the hospital also has centers dedicated to outpatient rehabilitation home health and long-term care. Specialty services include neurology cardiovascular care orthopedics and gastroenterology. It also operates the 25-bed St. Mary's Good Samaritan Hospital and a retirement village. The organization is sponsored by the Sisters of Mercy of the Americas St. Mary's Health Care System is a member of the Catholic Health East family of hospitals.

	Annual Growth	12/06	12/07	12/08	12/09	12/12
Sales ($ mil.)	(2.3%)	–	–	–	173.2	161.7
Net income ($ mil.)	37.7%	–	–	–	11.4	29.9
Market value ($ mil.)	–	–	–	–	–	–
Employees	–	–	–	–	–	1,350

ST. MARY'S MEDICAL CENTER

2900 1ST AVE
HUNTINGTON, WV 257021241
Phone: 304-526-1234
Fax: –
Web: www.stmarys.org

CEO: Michael G. Sellards
CFO: Angie Swearingen
HR: Susan (Sue) Robinson
FYE: September 30
Type: Private

Nobody wants to get sick but if you're ailing in West Virginia St. Mary's Medical Center wants you to know you are in good hands. The not-for-profit 395-bed medical facility serves patients in areas such as cardiac emergency neuroscience and cancer treatment. The largest health care facility in the tri-state region St. Mary's Medical Center is also a teaching facility affiliated with Joan C. Edwards Marshall University School of Medicine. St. Mary's Home Health Services administers care for patients in a six county area in Ohio and West Virginia. Services include IV therapy and occupational and physical therapies. St. Mary's Medical Center was founded in 1924.

	Annual Growth	09/06	09/07	09/09	09/13	09/14
Sales ($ mil.)	4.8%	–	289.2	341.8	366.8	401.2
Net income ($ mil.)	45.8%	–	–	1.7	31.9	10.9
Market value ($ mil.)	–	–	–	–	–	–
Employees	–	–	–	–	–	2,000

ST. NORBERT COLLEGE INC.

100 GRANT ST
DE PERE, WI 541152099
Phone: 920-337-3181
Fax: –
Web: www.snc.edu

CEO: Thomas Kunkel
CFO: –
HR: –
FYE: May 31
Type: Private

St. Norbert College is a private Catholic liberal arts institution offering undergraduate and graduate programs to approximately 2200 students. The school offers more than 40 undergraduate programs of study in the natural sciences social sciences and humanities and fine arts. It also confers Master's degrees in Science in Education and Theological Studies. The college is one of only a handful of institutions in the US that offer a Peace Corps Preparatory Program. St. Norbert College was founded in 1898 by Abbot Bernard Pennings a Dutch immigrant priest as a school to ready men for the priesthood. It became coeducational in 1952.

	Annual Growth	05/10	05/11	05/12	05/13	05/14
Sales ($ mil.)	3.3%	–	57.0	58.7	61.2	62.8
Net income ($ mil.)	84.7%	–	–	6.8	34.3	23.1
Market value ($ mil.)	–	–	–	–	–	–
Employees	–	–	–	–	–	490

ST. OLAF COLLEGE

1520 SAINT OLAF AVE
NORTHFIELD, MN 550571574
Phone: 507-786-2222
Fax: –
Web: www.stolaftelephone.com

CEO: –
CFO: –
HR: –
FYE: May 31
Type: Private

The hills of Northfield Minnesota are alive with the sounds of St. Olaf College. The private liberal arts university offers undergraduate and pre-professional education to more than 3000 students offering degrees in about 45 academic focus areas. The school has a faculty of more than 250 teachers and is recognized for its choral and orchestral music programs as well as its mathematics department. Other popular majors include English psychology biology economics social services theology language medical science and chemistry. St. Olaf College was founded in 1874 by Norwegian immigrants and is affiliated with the Evangelical Lutheran Church of America.

	Annual Growth	05/09	05/10	05/11	05/12	05/13
Sales ($ mil.)	18.4%	–	116.2	121.3	124.6	193.0
Net income ($ mil.)	(39.4%)	–	–	60.3	(10.7)	22.2
Market value ($ mil.)	–	–	–	–	–	–
Employees	–	–	–	–	–	800

ST. PETER'S HEALTH PARTNERS

315 S MANNING BLVD
ALBANY, NY 122081707
Phone: 518-525-1111
Fax: –
Web: www.che.org

CEO: –
CFO: Thomas Schuhle
HR: Barbara (Barb) Mccandless
FYE: June 30
Type: Private

St. Peter's Health Partners (formerly St. Peter's Health Care Services) is a not-for-profit health care system that serves northeastern New York. It includes health networks Seton Health and Northeast Health. Its primary facility St. Peter's Hospital has more than 440 acute-care beds and a medical staff of more than 600 physicians. Specialty services include emergency medicine cancer and cardiovascular care and women's health. St. Peter's also operates community health clinics long-term care facilities mental health centers and home health and hospice agencies. Founded by the Religious Sisters of Mercy in 1869 St. Peter's operates from more than 125 locations and is a subsidiary of Catholic Health East.

	Annual Growth	12/10	12/11	12/12*	06/13	06/14
Sales ($ mil.)	5.3%	–	–	1,069.6	571.4	1,185.2
Net income ($ mil.)	(11.0%)	–	–	61.1	23.9	48.4
Market value ($ mil.)	–	–	–	–	–	–
Employees	–	–	–	–	–	12,000

*Fiscal year change

STAAR SURGICAL CO.

NMS: STAA

1911 Walker Avenue
Monrovia, CA 91016
Phone: 626 303-7902
Fax: –
Web: www.staar.com

CEO: Caren L. Mason
CFO: Stephen P. Brown
HR: –
FYE: January 02
Type: Public

STAAR Surgical can't put stars in your eyes but it will help you to see more clearly. The company makes products for minimally invasive ophthalmic surgical procedures. Its primary products include Visian-branded implantable lenses (ICLs) for correcting such refractive conditions as near- and far-sightedness and astigmatism. More than 500000 of its ICLs have been implanted to date with more than 75000 being Visian Toric ICLs (approved in major global markets except the US). STAAR also makes foldable intraocular lenses (IOLs) to replace natural lenses removed in cataract surgery. Its other products include AquaFlow implantable devices used to treat glaucoma. The company sells its products in about 60 countries.

	Annual Growth	12/10	12/11	12/12*	01/14	01/15
Sales ($ mil.)	6.4%	55.0	62.8	63.8	72.2	75.0
Net income ($ mil.)	–	0.1	1.3	(1.8)	0.4	(8.4)
Market value ($ mil.)	8.2%	234.4	403.1	223.7	618.7	347.0
Employees	1.5%	279	297	301	335	300

*Fiscal year change

STAFF FORCE INC.

15915 KATY FWY STE 160
HOUSTON, TX 770941707
Phone: 281-492-6044
Fax: –
Web: www.staff-force.com

CEO: –
CFO: Glenn T Van Dusen
HR: –
FYE: December 31
Type: Private

Companies in need of interviewing hiring or payroll expertise trust in this Force. Staff Force — which does business as Staff Force Personnel Services — provides temporary temp-to-hire and direct hire staffing and payroll services in areas such as technology light industrial and hospitality. The company also provides employee handbooks (available in both English and Spanish) employee benefits and criminal background and reference checks. Customers come from industries such as health care manufacturing transportation and consumer goods. Founded in 1989 the company has locations throughout Texas.

	Annual Growth	12/07	12/08	12/10	12/12	12/13
Sales ($ mil.)	8.0%	–	64.1	72.4	91.6	94.2
Net income ($ mil.)	0.6%	–	–	0.7	0.7	0.7
Market value ($ mil.)	–	–	–	–	–	–
Employees	–	–	–	–	–	20,000

STAFFMARK HOLDINGS INC.

435 Elm St. Ste. 300	CEO: Lesa J Francis
Cincinnati OH 45202-2644	CFO: William E Aglinsky
Phone: 513-651-1111	HR: Suzanne M Perry
Fax: 650-230-0625	FYE: December 31
Web: www.castironsys.com	Type: Private

Staffmark Holdings (formerly CBS Personnel Services) wants to ensure your business gets its fill of people. Providing temporary and permanent staffing to about 6000 clients across the US the company fills positions in such areas as light industrial financial health care legal scientific IT and clerical. Staffmark's geographical reach extends across more than 30 states primarily concentrated in the northern US through about 200 branch offices and 90 client onsite locations. Formerly owned by middle-market investor Compass Diversified Holdings Staffmark was sold to Japan-based Recruit Co. Ltd in late 2011.

STAG INDUSTRIAL INC.

NYS: STAG

One Federal Street, 23rd Floor	CEO: Benjamin S. Butcher
Boston, MA 02110	CFO: William R. Crooker
Phone: 617 574-4777	HR: –
Fax: 617 574-0052	FYE: December 31
Web: www.stagindustrial.com	Type: Public

If STAG Industrial were to show up alone at a party it would likely be on the hunt for single tenants looking to lease industrial space. The self-managed and self-administered real estate investment trust (REIT) has built a business acquiring and managing single-tenant industrial properties located across more than 35 states. The company's portfolio consists primarily of 50 million sq. ft. of leasable warehouse distribution manufacturing and office space located in secondary markets. STAG conducts most of its business through its operating partner STAG Industrial Operating Partnership. The Massachusetts-based REIT went public in 2011.

	Annual Growth	04/11*	12/11	12/12	12/13	12/14
Sales ($ mil.)	176.2%	8.2	44.9	85.5	133.9	173.8
Net income ($ mil.)	–	(0.2)	(9.2)	(6.5)	5.5	(4.0)
Market value ($ mil.)	26.2%	784.8	739.1	1,157.9	1,313.8	1,578.7
Employees	24.5%	–	28	36	44	54

*Fiscal year change

STAGE STORES INC.

NYS: SSI

10201 Main Street	CEO: Michael L. Glazer
Houston, TX 77025	CFO: Oded Shein
Phone: 800 579-2302	HR: Ron D. Lucas
Fax: –	FYE: January 31
Web: www.stagestoresinc.com	Type: Public

If the world is a stage Stage Stores wants to dress the actors. The company operates about 885 department stores mainly in rural towns in some 40 US states. (More than a quarter of the stores are in Texas.) Through its Peebles Bealls Stage Palais Royal and Goody's Family Clothing chains the retailer offers small-town America moderately priced apparel and accessories cosmetics and footwear. Nationally recognized brands such as Tommy Hilfiger Carter's Levi Strauss Chaps and Polo account for about 85% of sales and are sold alongside Stage Stores' private-label merchandise. Stage Stores is rapidly expanding its Goody's chain and sold its off-price 35-store Steele's chain (launched in 2011) in 2014.

	Annual Growth	01/11	01/12*	02/13	02/14*	01/15
Sales ($ mil.)	2.7%	1,470.6	1,511.9	1,645.8	1,633.6	1,638.6
Net income ($ mil.)	(4.9%)	37.6	31.0	38.2	16.6	30.9
Market value ($ mil.)	6.2%	497.3	499.8	726.3	620.0	632.6
Employees	1.4%	13,500	14,000	14,500	14,700	14,300

*Fiscal year change

STAMFORD HEALTH SYSTEM INC.

30 Shelburne Rd.	CEO: –
Stamford CT 06902	CFO: Dean Swindle
Phone: 203-276-1000	HR: Jose G Melecio
Fax: 203-276-7905	FYE: September 30
Web: www.stamfordhospital.org	Type: Private

It sounds like one of the most famous universities in the country but it's actually a comprehensive medical center located on the opposite coast. Stamford Health System provides health services to residents of Stamford Connecticut and surrounding areas through a not-for-profit 300-bed community medical center called Stamford Hospital. The hospital administers acute and specialty services that include oncology cardiology orthopedics and women's health services. It is a teaching facility for the Columbia University College of Physicians and Surgeons and a member of the New York Presbyterian Health System.

STAMPS.COM INC.

NMS: STMP

1990 E. Grand Avenue	CEO: Kenneth (Ken) McBride
El Segundo, CA 90245	CFO: Kyle Huebner
Phone: 310 482-5800	HR: –
Fax: –	FYE: December 31
Web: www.stamps.com	Type: Public

Stamps.com hopes its customers keep putting letters in the mail. Its PC Postage Service lets registered users who have downloaded Stamps.com software buy stamps online and print the postage directly onto envelopes and labels. Customers can order US Postal Service options such as registered mail certified mail and delivery confirmation as well as print custom stamps using virtually any image through its PhotoStamps.com website. Stamps.com charges a monthly fee for its service which is aimed at consumers home offices and small businesses. In addition customers can buy mailing labels scales and dedicated postage printers from Stamps.com. Postage fees are sent directly to the US Postal Service.

	Annual Growth	12/10	12/11	12/12	12/13	12/14
Sales ($ mil.)	14.5%	85.5	101.6	115.7	127.8	147.3
Net income ($ mil.)	60.7%	5.5	26.3	38.6	44.2	36.9
Market value ($ mil.)	37.9%	212.0	418.0	403.1	673.5	767.7
Employees	11.7%	220	226	233	250	343

STANADYNE CORPORATION

92 Deerfield Rd.	CEO: David P Galuska
Windsor CT 06095-4209	CFO: Stephen S Langin
Phone: 860-525-0821	HR: –
Fax: 860-683-4500	FYE: December 31
Web: www.stanadyne.com	Type: Private

Stanadyne's products give engines their growl. The Kohlberg Management-portfolio company manufactures fuel pumps for gas and diesel engines and injectors and filters for diesel engines. The line focuses on diesel engine components used by OEMs of agricultural and industrial off-highway equipment. The company also makes fuel filters fuel heaters and oil pumps for diesel engines and related parts distributed by diesel engine aftermarkets. On an exclusive contract basis its services are tapped by businesses for precision manufacturing assembly and testing.

STANCORP FINANCIAL GROUP INC

NYS: SFG

1100 SW Sixth Avenue
Portland, OR 97204
Phone: 971 321-7000
Fax: –
Web: www.stancorpfinancial.com

CEO: J. Greg Ness
CFO: Floyd F. Chadee
HR: Dennis Hopwood
FYE: December 31
Type: Public

Providing insurance and related financial services is standard operating procedure at StanCorp Financial Group. Through Standard Insurance (aka The Standard) and other divisions the company offers a range of financial products nationwide including group and individual disability coverage life and accident insurance retirement plans and supplemental group benefit plans. The insurance services segment holds approximately 42000 group policies covering 6.1 million employees throughout the US. The company's asset management segment provides investment advisory retirement planning mortgage lending and other financial services. Meiji Yasuda Life Insurance is buying StanCorp for approximately $5 billion.

	Annual Growth	12/10	12/11	12/12	12/13	12/14
Assets ($ mil.)	6.2%	17,843.3	18,433.8	19,791.3	21,393.3	22,729.9
Net income ($ mil.)	3.8%	189.0	139.3	138.5	228.5	219.3
Market value ($ mil.)	11.5%	1,899.4	1,546.4	1,543.0	2,787.7	2,939.6
Employees	(2.4%)	3,091	2,974	2,875	2,702	2,803

STAND ENERGY CORPORATION

1077 CELESTIAL ST STE 110
CINCINNATI, OH 45202-1629
Phone: 513-621-1113
Fax: –
Web: www.stand-energy.com

CEO: Judith Phillips
CFO: Robert Embry
HR: –
FYE: December 31
Type: Private

Stand Energy Corporation (SEC) took a stand in the 1980s when the US government deregulated the natural gas industry. The company markets natural gas to large commercial and industrial customers in nine states (Illinois Indiana Kentucky Maryland New York Ohio Pennsylvania Virginia and West Virginia) and the District of Columbia. SEC also constructs bypass pipelines for its customers (allowing companies to bypass the local utility) and designs and builds propane backup systems to take advantage of reduced gas rates. SEC was founded in 1984 by Chairman Matth Toebben and CEO Judith Phillips. Customers include Coors and the Ohio Hospital Association.

	Annual Growth	12/08	12/09	12/09	12/11	12/12
Sales ($ mil.)	(14.1%)	–	149.3	12.7	117.4	94.6
Net income ($ mil.)	–	–	0.0	0.0	0.0	0.0
Market value ($ mil.)	–	–	–	–	–	–
Employees	–	–	–	–	–	32

STANDARD ELECTRIC COMPANY

2650 TRAUTNER DR
SAGINAW, MI 486049599
Phone: 989-497-2100
Fax: –
Web: www.standardelectricco.com

CEO: –
CFO: –
HR: –
FYE: February 28
Type: Private

Standard Electric and its affiliates distribute electrical and electronic products and supplies to customers through about 30 locations in Michigan. The company was founded in 1929 by Samuel Cohen and brothers Morris and Max Blumberg. The Blumberg brothers earlier established another Michigan-based electrical distributor Madison Electric an affiliate of Standard Electric with 10 Michigan locations. Another affiliated firm U.P. Electric/Wittock Supply Co. is a distributor of electrical and mechanical products with four locations on the upper Michigan peninsula. The company is owned by its directors and their families.

	Annual Growth	02/10	02/11	02/12	02/13	02/14
Sales ($ mil.)	6.5%	–	132.6	155.4	152.2	160.0
Net income ($ mil.)	0.8%	–	–	1.8	1.6	1.8
Market value ($ mil.)	–	–	–	–	–	–
Employees	–	–	–	–	–	250

STANDARD ENERGY CORPORATION

OTC: STDE

447 Bearcat Dr.
Salt Lake City UT 84115-2517
Phone: 801-364-9000
Fax: 450-680-4501
Web: www.bellushealth.com

CEO: –
CFO: Dean W Rowell
HR: –
FYE: March 31
Type: Public

The standard energy sources that Standard Energy taps into are oil and natural gas. The company acquires unproven oil and gas leaseholds (often owned by the US government) and resells them to third parties. The company holds 2698 net acres of oil and gas leaseholds in Utah and 1243 net acres of leasehold properties in Wyoming. Through its subsidiary Petroleum Investment Company Standard Energy also provides a range of geologic lease evaluation services. The company is also working in the biofuels technology field to commercially recover inorganic materials from the recycling of municipal waste. CEO Dean Rowell owns 65% of the oil and gas independent.

STANDARD FINANCIAL CORP (MD)

NBB: STND

2640 Monroeville Boulevard
Monroeville, PA 15146
Phone: 412 856-0363
Fax: –
Web: www.standardbankpa.com

CEO: –
CFO: Colleen Brown
HR: –
FYE: September 30
Type: Public

Standard Financial provides standard banking services and a little bit more. Standard Financial is the holding company of Standard Bank which offers traditional personal and business checking and savings accounts as well as loan products. It operates 10 branches that serve communities throughout southwestern Pennsylvania and northern Maryland. Standard Bank's lending activities includes issuing loans for one-to-four-family residential mortgages commercial real estate home equity and commercial businesses; to a lesser extent it provides consumer and construction loans as well. The bank also offers brokerage services retirement planning and other investment services through PrimeVest Financial Services.

	Annual Growth	09/11	09/12	09/13	09/14	09/15
Assets ($ mil.)	1.9%	434.6	443.4	436.9	445.5	468.3
Net income ($ mil.)	9.9%	2.4	3.0	2.9	3.2	3.5
Market value ($ mil.)	12.5%	40.3	46.3	50.2	56.5	64.6
Employees	(1.0%)	96	92	94	–	–

STANDARD FORWARDING LLC

2925 MORTON DR
EAST MOLINE, IL 61244-1960
Phone: 309-755-4504
Fax: –

CEO: Al Toliver
CFO: Ross Resetich
HR: –
FYE: December 31
Type: Private

Standard Forwarding specializes in less-than-truckload (LTL) freight transportation services. (LTL carriers consolidate freight from multiple shippers into a single trailer.) The company operates a fleet of about 300 tractors and 790 trailers from a network of more than a dozen terminals in Illinois Indiana Iowa Minnesota and Wisconsin. The company also offers freight transportation in Canada through partnerships. Farm equipment manufacturer Deere is a major customer as it has been since Standard Forwarding was founded in 1934. As a result of experiencing higher-than-market operating costs in the midst of the recession the company voluntarily filed for Chapter 11 bankruptcy protection in November 2009.

	Annual Growth	12/04	12/05	12/06	12/07	12/08
Sales ($ mil.)	9.4%	–	60.6	66.2	73.9	79.3
Net income ($ mil.)	(47.6%)	–	2.0	64.0	(0.7)	0.3
Market value ($ mil.)	–	–	–	–	–	–
Employees	–	–	–	–	–	510

STANDARD MICROSYSTEMS CORPORATION

NASDAQ: SMSC

80 Arkay Dr.	CEO: Christine King
Hauppauge NY 11788-3728	CFO: Kris Sennesael
Phone: 631-435-6000	HR: –
Fax: 937-221-1855	FYE: February 28
Web: www.standardregister.com	Type: Public

Standard Microsystems (SMSC) knows the ins and outs of chips. The fabless company (it farms out production to contract manufacturers) develops input/output (I/O) chips which perform basic control and interface functions inside of or between PCs and peripherals such as keyboards and disk drives. Its I/O chips are used by PC makers including Dell and HP. SMSC also makes Universal Serial Bus (USB) and Ethernet networking devices as well as products for portable electronics and automotive applications. Other customers include AUDI Toyota Samsung Electronics and Sony. Most of SMSC's sales come from Asia. In 2012 the company was acquired by Microchip Technology in a deal valued at about $939 million.

STANDARD MOTOR PRODUCTS, INC.

NYS: SMP

37-18 Northern Blvd.	CEO: Lawrence I. Sills
Long Island City, NY 11101	CFO: James J. Burke
Phone: 718 392-0200	HR: Thomas (Thom) Tesoro
Fax: 718 472-0122	FYE: December 31
Web: www.smpcorp.com	Type: Public

Standard Motor Products (SMP) is a manufacturer and distributor of replacement parts for the automotive industry. The company is organized into two major operating segments. Its largest segment Engine Management makes ignition and emission parts ignition wires battery cables and fuel system parts. Its Temperature Control segment manufactures and remanufactures air conditioning compressors heating parts engine cooling system parts power window accessories and windshield washer parts. Customers include warehouse distributors CARQUEST and NAPA Auto Parts and retail chains Advance Auto Parts and AutoZone. North America is SMP's core market but a small portion of sales comes from Europe.

	Annual Growth	12/10	12/11	12/12	12/13	12/14
Sales ($ mil.)	4.9%	810.9	874.6	948.9	983.7	980.4
Net income ($ mil.)	18.3%	22.0	62.4	41.4	51.5	43.0
Market value ($ mil.)	29.2%	313.6	459.0	508.7	842.5	872.7
Employees	1.5%	3,200	3,400	3,500	3,400	3,400

STANDARD REGISTER CO.

NYS: SR

600 Albany Street	CEO: Kevin M Carmody
Dayton, OH 45417	CFO: Benjamin T Cutting
Phone: 937 221-1940	HR: –
Fax: 937 221-3431	FYE: December 29
Web: www.standardregister.com	Type: Public

When it comes to managing communication The Standard Register Company (SRC) helps businesses maintain a certain set of standards. SRC primarily provides print services (both digital and traditional) for healthcare manufacturing financial services and other commercial businesses helping manage their communications so that they align with corporate standards and priorities. Formerly a provider of traditional document services the company is now focused on providing market-driven communication services that help companies in specific industries build and enhance their brands and reputations reduce risk and operate more efficiently. The 100-year-old firm was founded by John Q. Sherman in 1912.

	Annual Growth	01/10	01/11	01/12*	12/12	12/13
Sales ($ mil.)	1.2%	694.0	668.4	648.1	602.0	719.8
Net income ($ mil.)	–	(12.4)	2.6	(87.7)	(9.1)	(7.4)
Market value ($ mil.)	10.6%	43.7	29.2	20.0	5.2	59.1
Employees	8.5%	2,900	2,600	2,700	2,200	3,700
						*Fiscal year change

STANDARD STEEL LLC

1200 Reedsdale St.	CEO: Daniel J Condon
Pittsburgh PA 15233	CFO: –
Phone: 412-237-2260	HR: Jeff Norman
Fax: 816-713-8810	FYE: December 31
Web: www.uspremiumbeef.com	Type: Private

Much has changed over the past 200 years but Standard Steel products have stayed much the same. The company makes wheels and axles for the railway industry. Its products are used on freight railcars locomotives and passenger railcars. Customers include Class I railroads freight car manufacturers and railroad maintenance providers as well as Amtrak. Standard Steel was founded in 1795 as Freedom Forge to make iron bars and rods; its name was changed to Standard Steel in 1875. In 1895 the company introduced the first bolted and steel-tired railroad wheel. In mid-2011 Sumitomo Metal Industries announced its plans to pay $340 million to acquire Standard Steel before the end of the year.

STANDARD TEXTILE CO. INC.

1 Knollcrest Dr.	CEO: Gary Heiman
Cincinnati OH 45237	CFO: Chris Bopp
Phone: 513-761-9255	HR: –
Fax: 513-761-0467	FYE: December 31
Web: www.standardtextile.com	Type: Private

Meeting industry standards is not enough for Standard Textile. The company designs manufactures and distributes decorative and workwear textiles for healthcare hospitality and institutional use. Healthcare products include bedding surgical gowns and incontinence care. Its Hospitality goods include custom towels blankets and woven sheeting. Standard Textile's Workwear line offers coveralls to sport jackets. Bedspreads flame-resistant drapery and window treatments are part of its Decorative Products mix. The company manages its own R&D manufacturing distribution and technical services. The privately held company is led by its founder's grandson Gary Heiman.

STANDEX INTERNATIONAL CORP.

NYS: SXI

11 Keewaydin Drive	CEO: –
Salem, NH 03079	CFO: Thomas D. DeByle
Phone: 603 893-9701	HR: Michael A (Mel) Pattison
Fax: –	FYE: June 30
Web: www.standex.com	Type: Public

Be it a rotisserie or a rocket part Standex stands and delivers. The company is a manufacturer and service provider for various industrial markets. It has five main reportable segments: Food Service Equipment a manufacturer of commercial food service equipment; Engraving a maker of molds used to produce plastic components; Engineering Technologies a provider of custom fabrication and machining services for engineered components; and Electronics and Hydraulics which consists of the Custom Hoists and Standex Electronics businesses. Standex traces its historical roots back to the 1950s.

	Annual Growth	06/11	06/12	06/13	06/14	06/15
Sales ($ mil.)	5.1%	633.8	634.6	701.3	716.2	772.1
Net income ($ mil.)	11.5%	35.4	30.9	44.8	42.9	54.7
Market value ($ mil.)	27.1%	388.0	538.6	667.4	942.3	1,011.2
Employees	6.3%	4,000	3,900	4,400	4,200	5,100

STANFORD HOSPITAL AND CLINICS

300 Pasteur Dr.
Stanford CA 94305
Phone: 650-723-4000
Fax: 650-723-0074
Web: stanfordhospital.org

CEO: Amir Dan Rubin
CFO: –
HR: –
FYE: August 31
Type: Private

Doctors patients medical students and researchers gather at Stanford Hospital and Clinics. As Stanford University's primary medical teaching facility the 600-bed Stanford Hospital specializes in such areas as cardiac care cancer treatment neurology surgery and organ transplant. The affiliated Stanford Clinics is a physician group practice organization that represents more than 100 specialized fields of medicine. Stanford Hospital and Clinics is part of the Stanford Medicine organization which also includes the nearby Stanford University School of Medicine and the 270-bed Lucile Packard Children's Hospital (named for the wife of Hewlett-Packard co-founder David Packard).

STANION WHOLESALE ELECTRIC CO. INC.

812 S MAIN ST
PRATT, KS 671242600
Phone: 620-672-6939
Fax: –
Web: www.stanion.com

CEO: –
CFO: –
HR: –
FYE: December 31
Type: Private

Stanion Wholesale Electric distributes electrical products and supplies to customers through nearly 20 branch locations in Kansas and Missouri. The company specializes in products for factory automation lighting telecommunications and utilities carrying items from such manufacturers as Cooper Industries General Electric Rockwell Automation and Thomas & Betts. Stanion Wholesale Electric makes all of its product catalog available over its corporate Web site along with other e-commerce functions. The family-owned company was founded in 1961 by chairman Jud Stanion and his wife Bobbe. Stanion Wholesale Electric is owned by Bill Keller (president and CEO) and his wife Cindy Stanion Keller.

	Annual Growth	12/08	12/09	12/11	12/12	12/13
Sales ($ mil.)	2.9%	–	77.0	86.2	87.4	86.2
Net income ($ mil.)	12.5%	–	–	2.7	3.5	3.4
Market value ($ mil.)	–	–	–	–	–	–
Employees	–	–	–	–	–	197

STANLEY BLACK & DECKER INC

NYS: SWK

1000 Stanley Drive
New Britain, CT 06053
Phone: 860 225-5111
Fax: 860 827-3895
Web: www.stanleyblackanddecker.com

CEO: John F. Lundgren
CFO: Donald (Don) Allan
HR: Stephen (Steve) Subasic
FYE: January 03
Type: Public

Stanley Black & Decker has the tools that neighbors envy. As a top US toolmaker it markets hand tools mechanics' tools power tools pneumatic tools and hydraulic tools. The company's tool shed is bulging with additional items such as garden tools plumbing products (Pfister) and cleaning items (Dustbuster) as well as security hardware (Kwikset) and door products. Besides the Stanley and Black & Decker brands it sells such brands as Bostitch Mac Tools and DEWALT. Stanley Black & Decker peddles its products through home centers and mass-merchant distributors as well as through third-party distributors. Founded in 1843 Stanley changed its name after merging with Black & Decker in 2010.

	Annual Growth	01/11*	12/11	12/12	12/13*	01/15
Sales ($ mil.)	7.8%	8,409.6	10,376.4	10,190.5	11,001.2	11,338.6
Net income ($ mil.)	40.0%	198.2	674.6	883.8	490.3	760.9
Market value ($ mil.)	9.5%	10,507.0	10,621.7	11,322.5	12,728.7	15,087.2
Employees	8.3%	36,700	44,700	45,327	50,700	50,400

*Fiscal year change

STANLEY ELECTRIC SALES OF AMERICA INC.

2660 Barranca Pkwy.
Irvine CA 92606-5029
Phone: 949-222-0777
Fax: 949-222-0555
Web: www.stanley-electric.com

CEO: –
CFO: AMI Ken
HR: –
FYE: March 31
Type: Private

Dr. Livingstone presumably had no idea that one day Stanley Electric Sales of America a subsidiary of the Japan-based Stanley Electric Company would be making and selling a myriad of semiconductors subminiature lamps and related electronic components. The parent company was named after 19th-century explorer Sir Henry Morton Stanley known exploring the Dark Continent hoping that some of that aptitude would be reflected in the business activities of Stanley Electric. Similarly Stanley Electric Sales of America reaches to supply North America's demand in electronics automotive computer and communications. Since 2007 the company's growth however has been heavily curtailed by the global economic downturn.

STANLEY FURNITURE CO., INC.

NMS: STLY

200 North Hamilton Street, No. 200
High Point, NC 27260
Phone: 336 884-7700
Fax: 276 629-5114
Web: www.stanleyfurniture.com

CEO: Glenn Prillaman
CFO: Anita W Wimmer
HR: Robert Sitler
FYE: December 31
Type: Public

Stanley Furniture needs lots of rooms to spread out. The company established in 1924 primarily makes wood furniture that retails in the upper-medium price range. Its products include furniture for adult bedrooms dining rooms youth bedrooms home offices and living rooms as well as for home entertainment centers. Youth furniture is made under the Young America brand. Stanley Furniture makes and markets furniture styles such as European and American traditional lines as well as contemporary/transitional and country/casual. With a manufacturing facility in North Carolina the company sells its products through furniture and department stores. International customers account for about 10% of sales.

	Annual Growth	12/10	12/11	12/12	12/13	12/14
Sales ($ mil.)	(18.4%)	137.0	104.6	98.6	96.9	60.6
Net income ($ mil.)	–	(43.8)	(5.0)	30.4	(12.6)	(29.9)
Market value ($ mil.)	(3.1%)	46.0	44.2	66.5	56.8	40.5
Employees	(32.5%)	650	595	490	544	135

STANLEY SECURITY SOLUTIONS INC.

6161 E. 75th St.
Indianapolis IN 46250-2701
Phone: 317-849-2250
Fax: 317-806-3276
Web: www.stanleysecuritysolutions.com

CEO: –
CFO: –
HR: –
FYE: December 31
Type: Subsidiary

Stanley Security Solutions (SSS) a subsidiary of Stanley Black & Decker has got your back and your front. The company provides a swath of security entry products and services to residences institutions and governments. Its lineup includes mechanical access products entry locking mechanisms as well as electronic security systems and software. (SSS software products are combined with existing security systems or custom designed.) Other offerings range from automatic doors to patient/resident safety products and services such as wireless nurse calling magnetic door locks and key entry systems. Products are sold under brand names Best Senior Technologies Safemasters Sargent and Greenleaf and Sonitrol.

STANLEY STEEMER INTERNATIONAL INC.

5800 INNOVATION DR
DUBLIN, OH 430163271
Phone: 614-764-2007
Fax: –
Web: www.stanleysteemer.com

CEO: Wesley C. Bates
CFO: Mark Bunner
HR: Patricia Newton
FYE: December 31
Type: Private

Carpet stains don't startle this Stanley. Stanley Steemer International provides residential and commercial carpet and upholstery cleaning through more than 300 franchise and corporate locations in 48 states. In addition to cleaning carpets the company provides cleaning services for tile and grout and air ducts as well as cars boats and RVs. The company which is known for its fleet of yellow vans sells its own brand of cleaning products through an online store. Founded by Jack Bates in 1947 when he established his own one-man carpet cleaning business Stanley Steemer is owned by his descendants including CEO Wesley Bates and President Justin Bates.

	Annual Growth	12/09	12/10	12/11	12/12	12/13
Sales ($ mil.)	2.3%	–	186.7	191.0	192.2	199.8
Net income ($ mil.)	23.9%	–	–	12.0	10.5	18.4
Market value ($ mil.)	–	–	–	–	–	–
Employees	–	–	–	–	–	2,000

STANT MANUFACTURING INC.

1620 Columbia Ave.
Connersville IN 47331-1696
Phone: 765-825-3121
Fax: 419-782-5145
Web: www.fdef.com

CEO: Ron Cervelli
CFO: Phillip Fitzpatrick
HR: –
FYE: April 30
Type: Subsidiary

Gentlemen "Stant" your engines. Formerly a subsidiary of Tomkins PLC Stant manufactures a broad line of automotive parts and tools. The company produces fuel radiator and oil filler caps as well as gaskets and seals. Other products include thermal products such as thermostats and thermostat housings. The company also makes testers used to measure radiator cap pressure fuel cap leakage compliance and engine vacuum pressure. Stant sells to automakers and aftermarket retailers. Tomkins sold Stant to Miami-based private equity firm H.I.G. Capital in 2008. The company filed Chapter 11 bankruptcy and emerged in 2009.

STAPLE COTTON CO-OPERATIVE ASSOCIATION

214 W MARKET ST
GREENWOOD, MS 389304329
Phone: 662 746 4941
Fax: –
Web: www.staplcotn.com

CEO: Meredith Allen
CFO: Charles Robertson
HR: Russell Robersto
FYE: August 31
Type: Private

Referred to as Staplcotn the Staple Cotton Cooperative has been a staple of its member-producers' business lives since 1921. One of the oldest and largest cotton marketing co-ops in the US it provides domestic and export marketing cotton warehousing and agricultural financing to some 9730 members in 47 states. As of 2011 the co-op handles nearly 14000 farm accounts in 10 states. Staplcotn's inventory is consigned by member-producers and averages from 2.5 million to 3 million bales of cotton a year. The co-op operates though 15 warehouses serving the mid-south and southeastern US to supply more than 25% of the cotton consumed by the US textile industry as well as the needs of textile mills overseas.

	Annual Growth	08/10	08/11	08/12	08/13	08/14
Sales ($ mil.)	(3.5%)	–	963.4	1,236.4	1,138.3	865.4
Net income ($ mil.)	894.3%	–	–	8.2	6.0	807.0
Market value ($ mil.)	–	–	–	–	–	–
Employees	–	–	–	–	–	187

STAPLES INC

NMS: SPLS

Five Hundred Staples Drive
Framingham, MA 01702
Phone: 508 253-5000
Fax: 508 370-8955
Web: www.staples.com

CEO: Ronald L. (Ron) Sargent
CFO: Christine T. Komola
HR: Susan S Hoyt
FYE: January 31
Type: Public

Staples is clipping along as the #1 office supply superstore operator in the US and as a worldwide leader in the office category. It sells office products furniture computers and other supplies through more than 1900 Staples stores in the Americas Europe and Australia. In addition to its retail outlets Staples sells office products via the Internet and through its catalog and direct sales operations including subsidiary Quill Corp. The company also provides document management and copying services at its stores. Facing increasing competition from the merged Office Depot and OfficeMax Staples agreed to acquire the combined company in early 2015.

	Annual Growth	01/11	01/12*	02/13	02/14*	01/15
Sales ($ mil.)	(2.2%)	24,545.1	25,022.2	24,380.5	23,114.3	22,492.4
Net income ($ mil.)	(37.5%)	881.9	984.7	(210.7)	620.1	134.5
Market value ($ mil.)	(6.5%)	14,292.0	10,251.5	8,650.7	8,426.6	10,917.5
Employees	(2.9%)	89,019	87,782	85,087	83,008	79,075

*Fiscal year change

STAR BUFFET INC.

NASDAQ: STRZ

1312 N. Scottsdale Rd.
Scottsdale AZ 85257
Phone: 480-425-0397
Fax: 203-334-5114
Web: www.bigelowtea.com

CEO: Robert E Wheaton
CFO: –
HR: –
FYE: January 31
Type: Public

Star Buffet is a leading operator of buffet-style restaurants with more than 40 dining locations in about 15 states. The eateries located primarily in the southeastern and western US offer a wide array of menu items for breakfast lunch and dinner. In addition to its buffet-style units Star Buffet operates a small number of family-style restaurants under the 4B's banner as well as a couple of WesterN SizzliN steak-buffet restaurants (franchised from Western Sizzlin). CEO Robert Wheaton owns more than 40% of the company. Star Buffet filed for bankruptcy in late 2011.

STAR GAS PARTNERS L.P.

NYS: SGU

9 West Broad Street, Suite 310
Stamford, CT 06902
Phone: 203 328-7310
Fax: –
Web: www.star-gas.com

CEO: Steven J Goldman
CFO: Richard F Ambury
HR: –
FYE: September 30
Type: Public

Those who wish for heat and power can wish upon a star — Star Gas Partners. The company is the nation's largest retail distributor of home heating oil. Its Petro Holdings subsidiary provides heating oil and propane to 416000 customers in the US Northeast and Mid-Atlantic. The company sells home heating oil gasoline and diesel fuel to 48000 customers on a delivery only basis and provides HVAC and ancillary home services including home security and plumbing to 11500 customers. Investment firm Kestrel Energy Partners controls the general partner of Star Gas Partners.

	Annual Growth	09/11	09/12	09/13	09/14	09/15
Sales ($ mil.)	1.3%	1,591.3	1,497.6	1,741.8	1,961.7	1,674.3
Net income ($ mil.)	11.4%	24.3	26.0	29.9	36.1	37.6
Market value ($ mil.)	14.7%	282.3	248.9	283.4	328.9	489.1
Employees	3.7%	2,677	2,582	2,577	2,958	3,101

STAR MULTI CARE SERVICES INC.

115 Broad Hollow Road Suite 275
Melville NY 11747
Phone: 631-423-6689
Fax: 631-427-5466
Web: www.starmulticare.com/

CEO: –
CFO: David Schoenberg
HR: –
FYE: May 31
Type: Private

When you wish upon this Star a nurse will come to where you are. Star Multi Care Services along with its two subsidiary companies provides home health care to the elderly infirm and disabled 24 hours a day seven days a week. The company's Extended Family Care subsidiary provides services in Pennsylvania; Central Star Home Health covers Ohio; and Star Multi Care provides services in Florida and New York. In addition to its in-home health care the company offers occupational physical respiratory and speech therapies as well as medical social services. The privately-held firm was founded in 1938 and is led by CEO Stephen Sternbach.

STAR OF THE WEST MILLING COMPANY

121 E TUSCOLA ST
FRANKENMUTH, MI 487341731
Phone: 330-673-2941
Fax: –
Web: www.starofthewest.com

CEO: –
CFO: –
HR: –
FYE: December 31
Type: Private

All hands are on the mill floor at Star of the West Milling. The company operates five flour mills in four US states an about 10 storage elevators. The mills and elevators store and process wheat corn and soybeans. Its flour milling capacity is about 20000 lbs. per day. North Star Bean a division of Star of the West processes beans such as navy pinto kidney and black beans into dry commodity products. The company also owns Eastern Michigan Grain an elevator that offers grain handling and marketing services. Star of the West Milling sells its flour and beans worldwide to canning and packaging customers the likes of Kellogg General Mills Nabisco and Pepperidge Farm.

	Annual Growth	12/09	12/10	12/11	12/12	12/13
Sales ($ mil.)	12.3%	–	294.1	394.6	445.0	416.9
Net income ($ mil.)	(0.9%)	–	–	15.8	17.1	15.6
Market value ($ mil.)	–	–	–	–	–	–
Employees	–	–	–	–	–	239

STAR TRIBUNE MEDIA COMPANY LLC

425 Portland Ave.
Minneapolis MN 55488
Phone: 612-673-4000
Fax: 612-673-4359
Web: www.startribunecompany.com

CEO: Michael J Klingensmith
CFO: –
HR: –
FYE: December 31
Type: Private

This company shines a light on current events for Minnesotans. Star Tribune Media Company is a leading newspaper publisher serving the Minneapolis-St. Paul area and readers around the state of Minnesota. Its Star Tribune newspaper boasts a weekday circulation of about 300000 and is one of the nation's top 20 daily metropolitan papers. The company also publishes news on its website. In addition to its news operations Star Tribune Media provides direct marketing services and produces such specialty publications as Lakeshore Living Minnesota Explorer and Senior Living Showcase. The company was formed in 2009 by a group of investors led by private equity firm Angelo Gordon.

STARBUCKS CORP.

NMS: SBUX

2401 Utah Avenue South
Seattle, WA 98134
Phone: 206 447-1575
Fax: –
Web: www.starbucks.com

CEO: Howard D. Schultz
CFO: Scott H. Maw
HR: Adrienne Gemperle
FYE: September 27
Type: Public

Wake up and smell the coffee — Starbucks is everywhere. The world's #1 specialty coffee retailer Starbucks has more than 21000 coffee shops in about 60 countries. The outlets offer coffee drinks and food items as well as roasted beans coffee accessories and teas. Starbucks operates more than 10700 of its own shops which are located mostly in the US while licensees and franchisees operate roughly 10600 units worldwide (including many locations in shopping centers and airports). In addition Starbucks markets its coffee through grocery stores food service customers and licenses its brand for other food and beverage products.

	Annual Growth	10/11*	09/12	09/13	09/14	09/15
Sales ($ mil.)	13.1%	11,700.4	13,299.5	14,892.2	16,447.8	19,162.7
Net income ($ mil.)	22.0%	1,245.7	1,383.8	8.3	2,068.1	2,757.4
Market value ($ mil.)	11.7%	55,379.4	75,309.4	114,842.8	111,635.0	86,120.9
Employees	12.4%	149,000	160,000	182,000	191,000	238,000

*Fiscal year change

STARCOM MEDIAVEST GROUP INC.

35 W. Wacker Dr.
Chicago IL 60601
Phone: 312-220-3535
Fax: 312-220-6530
Web: www.smvgroup.com

CEO: Jack Klues
CFO: –
HR: –
FYE: December 31
Type: Subsidiary

This business helps advertisers reach out to the consumer universe. Starcom MediaVest Group is a leading media planning and buying agency (along with rivals OMD Worldwide and Mindshare) with 110 offices in almost 70 countries. The media group helps advertisers determine the correct mix of media to get their message out and buys air time and space in print publications for the ads. In addition it offers specialized media services through such units as SMG Search (search marketing expertise) and Forty-Two Degrees at MediaVest (multicultural media). Starcom MediaVest is part of VivaKi an advertising and marketing communications division of Paris-based advertising conglomerate Publicis.

STARKEY LABORATORIES INC.

6700 Washington Ave. South
Eden Prairie MN 55344
Phone: 952-941-6401
Fax: 952-927-0976
Web: www.starkey.com

CEO: William F Austin
CFO: –
HR: –
FYE: December 31
Type: Private

Having trouble hearing your old Beatles records? Never fear aging boomer Starkey Laboratories wants to be your key to better hearing. The company doing business as Starkey Hearing Technologies makes digital wireless and invisible hearing aids and other hearing devices for adults and children. Its hearing aids lines offer improved filtering and response technology (including BluWave signal processing) to eliminate whistling and background noise interference problems. Starkey also makes hearing protection devices for industrial workers swimmers hunters and musicians; hands-free communication and mobile headsets; and audio monitors and music headphones. CEO William "Bill" Austin started the company in 1967.

STARRETT (L.S.) CO.
NYS: SCX

121 Crescent Street
Athol, MA 01331-1915
Phone: 978 249-3551
Fax: –
Web: www.starrett.com

CEO: Douglas A. Starrett
CFO: Francis J O'Brien
HR: –
FYE: June 30
Type: Public

L.S. Starrett has forged its business inch by inch. It makes more than 5000 products including hand measuring tools (Evans Rule tape measures steel rules combination squares micrometers) and precision instruments (vernier calipers and height and depth gauges). Starrett sells its products in more than 100 countries boasting major subsidiaries in Brazil Scotland and China. The company also makes levels vises lubricants saw blades and vocational and educational materials. Starrett caters to machinists in the metalworking industry but also serves the DIY automotive aviation construction marine and farm equipment industries. The company was founded in 1880 in Massachusetts by Laroy S. Starrett.

	Annual Growth	06/11	06/12	06/13	06/14	06/15
Sales ($ mil.)	(0.3%)	244.8	260.1	243.8	247.1	241.6
Net income ($ mil.)	(6.4%)	6.8	0.9	(0.2)	6.7	5.2
Market value ($ mil.)	10.0%	71.9	81.1	71.7	107.9	105.2
Employees	(1.9%)	1,951	1,928	1,814	1,811	1,804

STARTEK, INC.
NYS: SRT

8200 E. Maplewood Ave., Suite 100
Greenwood Village, CO 80111
Phone: 303 262-4500
Fax: –
Web: www.startek.com

CEO: Chad A. Carlson
CFO: Don Norsworthy
HR: Jay Kirksey
FYE: December 31
Type: Public

This company wants to be your proverbial star when it comes to optimizing your business process. StarTek provides process management outsourcing offering expertise in a variety of services such as customer care and technical support e-commerce fulfillment and provisioning management (across various platforms such as Web voice video fax and e-mail). Most of its top clients including AT&T Mobility (which contributed about more than 30% of sales in fiscal 2012) reside in high-tech industries. Founded in 1987. Former chairman Emmet Stephenson Jr. and his family still own about 19% of StarTek. In 2015 StarTek bought ACCENT Marketing Services from MDC Partners.

	Annual Growth	12/10	12/11	12/12	12/13	12/14
Sales ($ mil.)	(1.5%)	265.4	219.5	198.1	231.3	250.1
Net income ($ mil.)	–	(19.4)	(26.5)	(10.5)	(6.4)	(5.5)
Market value ($ mil.)	17.7%	78.2	29.6	62.1	100.0	150.3
Employees	7.3%	8,900	9,100	10,200	11,600	11,800

STARWOOD HOTELS & RESORTS WORLDWIDE INC
NYS: HOT

One StarPoint
Stamford, CT 06902
Phone: 203 964-6000
Fax: –
Web: www.starwoodhotels.com

CEO: Thomas B. (Tom) Mangas
CFO: Alan M. Schnaid
HR: Jeffrey M. (Jeff) Cava
FYE: December 31
Type: Public

Starwood Hotels & Resorts Worldwide knows how to shine a light on hospitality. One of the world's largest hotel companies it has about 1125 properties in about 100 countries. Starwood's hotel empire consists of upscale brands such as Sheraton and Westin. It operates about 100 luxury resorts and hotels through its St. Regis and Luxury Collection units while its 40 W Hotels offer ultra-modern style. Other brands include Four Points (value-oriented) Le Méridien (European-inspired) Aloft (select-service) and Element (extended stay). Starwood Vacation Ownership operates about 15 time-share resorts. In 2015 Marriott agreed to acquire Starwood for about $12.2 billion.

	Annual Growth	12/10	12/11	12/12	12/13	12/14
Sales ($ mil.)	4.2%	5,071.0	5,624.0	6,321.0	6,115.0	5,983.0
Net income ($ mil.)	7.3%	477.0	489.0	562.0	635.0	633.0
Market value ($ mil.)	7.5%	10,496.4	8,284.1	9,905.7	13,720.6	14,000.3
Employees	5.6%	145,000	154,000	171,000	181,400	180,400

STARWOOD PROPERTY TRUST INC.
NYS: STWD

591 West Putnam Avenue
Greenwich, CT 06830
Phone: 203 422-8100
Fax: –
Web: www.starwoodpropertytrust.com

CEO: Barry S Sternlicht
CFO: Rina Paniry
HR: –
FYE: December 31
Type: Public

Starwood Property Trust hopes to shine brightly in the world of mortgages. A real estate investment trust (REIT) the company originates finances and manages US commercial and residential mortgage loans commercial mortgage-backed securities and other commercial real estate debt investments. It acquires discounted loans from failed banks and financial institutions some through the FDIC which typically auctions off large pools of loan portfolios. Starwood Property Trust is externally managed by SPT Management LLC an affiliate of Starwood Capital Group. As a REIT the trust is exempt from paying federal income tax so long as it distributes quarterly dividends to shareholders.

	Annual Growth	12/10	12/11	12/12	12/13	12/14
Sales ($ mil.)	65.6%	93.5	205.0	307.0	565.7	702.9
Net income ($ mil.)	71.6%	57.0	119.4	201.2	305.0	495.0
Market value ($ mil.)	2.0%	4,801.6	4,137.7	5,132.4	6,192.0	5,195.0
Employees	365.1%	1	2	2	2	468

STARZ
NMS: STRZ A

8900 Liberty Circle
Englewood, CO 80112
Phone: 720 852-7700
Fax: –
Web: www.starz.com

CEO: Christopher P Albrecht
CFO: Scott D Macdonald
HR: –
FYE: December 31
Type: Public

Starz (formerly Liberty Media Corporation) has a galaxy of premium cable properties including the Starz Encore and MoviePlex networks. The company's 17 channels across those three networks — Starz Comedy Encore Black Encore Espanol Indieplex and Retroplex among them — serve nearly 60 million subscribers. Starz also distributes content digitally and through DVDs in the US and internationally through its Anchor Bay Entertainment subsidiary and produces animated content via Film Roman. In 2013 the company spun off its other operations (the Atlanta Braves a majority stake in SIRIUS XM and other holdings) into the new Liberty Media Corporation; it then took the Starz name.

	Annual Growth	12/10	12/11	12/12	12/13	12/14
Sales ($ mil.)	(5.1%)	2,050.0	3,024.0	1,630.7	1,777.5	1,663.9
Net income ($ mil.)	(28.2%)	1,021.0	812.0	254.5	247.3	271.3
Market value ($ mil.)	(17.0%)	6,365.3	7,941.3	11,803.6	2,975.1	3,021.9
Employees	131.5%	–	77	926	959	955

STARZ LLC
CEO: Chris Albrecht

8900 Liberty Circle
Englewood CO 80112
Phone: 720-852-7700
Fax: 720-852-8555
Web: www.starz.com

CEO: Chris Albrecht
CFO: Scott D Macdonald
HR: David Laughlin
FYE: December 31
Type: Subsidiary

This cable TV company hopes you'll want an Encore from its movie Starz. Starz LLC operates a portfolio of 16 cable movie channels under the brands Encore and Starz offering about 1000 movie titles every month. Its Encore channels reach about 33 million US homes while its Starz channels (including Starz Comedy Starz Edge and Starz Kids & Family) reach more than 18 million subscribers. Starz also offers high definition and video on demand (VOD) channels. John Sie launched the Encore movie channel in 1991 followed by the Starz channel in 1994. The company is a subsidiary of John Malone's Liberty Media holding company.

STATE AUTO FINANCIAL CORP.
NMS: STFC

518 East Broad Street
Columbus, OH 43215-3976
Phone: 614 464-5000
Fax: –

CEO: Michael E. (Mike) LaRocco
CFO: Steven E. English
HR: –
FYE: December 31
Type: Public

Thanks to State Auto Financial the state of auto insurance is healthy in the Midwest. The company sells property/casualty policies through several subsidiaries writing personal commercial and specialty coverage including automobile homeowners multi-peril and workers' compensation insurance. It also participates in an insurance pool through its parent company State Auto Mutual Insurance which owns more than 60% of State Auto Financial and provides the offices for its headquarters. Subsidiary Stateco Financial Services manages the company's invested assets. State Auto Financial is the only part of State Auto Mutual that is publicly traded.

	Annual Growth	12/10	12/11	12/12	12/13	12/14
Assets ($ mil.)	0.4%	2,722.0	2,790.8	2,477.8	2,496.4	2,766.9
Net income ($ mil.)	44.7%	24.5	(146.8)	10.7	60.8	107.4
Market value ($ mil.)	6.3%	712.5	555.8	611.0	868.7	908.8
Employees	(2.2%)	2,483	2,451	2,423	2,384	2,274

STATE BANK FINANCIAL CORP
NAS: STBZ

3399 Peachtree Road N.E., Suite 1900
Atlanta, GA 30326
Phone: 404 475-6599
Fax: –

CEO: Joseph W. (Joe) Evans
CFO: Sheila E. Ray
HR: –
FYE: December 31
Type: Public

State Bank Financial Corp. aspires to one day live in the center of central Georgia's banking world. A holding company State Bank Financial operates through subsidiary State Bank and Trust Company a state-charted commercial bank that serves individuals and businesses throughout central Georgia and in the Atlanta metropolitan area. Through some two dozen branches the bank offers traditional checking and savings accounts as well as commercial and residential real estate mortgages construction and commercial loans and consumer loans. Formed in 2010 State Bank Financial holds more than $2.8 billion in assets.

	Annual Growth	12/10	12/11	12/12	12/13	12/14
Assets ($ mil.)	0.5%	2,828.6	2,746.9	2,663.0	2,600.7	2,882.2
Net income ($ mil.)	(9.2%)	45.5	43.0	22.7	12.7	30.9
Market value ($ mil.)	8.3%	467.9	487.6	512.4	587.0	644.7
Employees	3.4%	495	605	605	577	566

STATE COMPENSATION INSURANCE FUND

333 Bush St. 8th Fl.
San Francisco CA 94104
Phone: 415-565-1234
Fax: +33-1-53-63-38-58
Web: www.atics.fr

CEO: –
CFO: Jay Stewart
HR: –
FYE: December 31
Type: Government-owned

From San Diego in the south to Eureka up north State Compensation Insurance Fund (State Fund) keeps workers in the Golden State covered. Run like a mutual company State Fund is a not-for-profit public enterprise fund. Its primary product is workers' compensation insurance but the company also offers claims management coordinated care plans and loss control services to policyholders. Employers can purchase coverage directly from the insurer or through independent brokers. It boasts some 180000 policy holders. As the insurer of last resort State Fund has prospered as other insurers have withdrawn from the workers' compensation market in California. The company was established in 1914.

STATE FARM MUTUAL AUTOMOBILE INSURANCE COMPANY

1 State Farm Plaza
Bloomington IL 61710-0001
Phone: 309-766-2311
Fax: 309-766-3621
Web: www.statefarm.com

CEO: Edward B Rust Jr
CFO: Michael L Tipsord
HR: –
FYE: December 31
Type: Private - Mutual Com

Like an enormous corporation State Farm is everywhere. The leading US personal lines property/casualty company (by premiums) State Farm Mutual Automobile Insurance Company is the #1 provider of private auto insurance. It also is the leading home insurer and offers nonmedical health and life insurance through its subsidiary companies. Its products are marketed via more than 18000 agents in the US and Canada. State Farm's efforts to diversify include a federal savings bank charter (State Farm Bank) that offers consumer and business loans through its agents and by phone mail and the Internet.

STATE OF NEW YORK MORTGAGE AGENCY

641 Lexington Ave. 4th Fl.
New York NY 10022
Phone: 212-688-4000
Fax: 212-872-0789
Web: www.nyshcr.org/agencies/sonyma/

CEO: Steve Hunt
CFO: –
HR: –
FYE: October 31
Type: Government Agency

The State of New York Mortgage Agency (SONYMA pronounced "Sony Mae") is a public benefit corporation of the State of New York that makes homebuying more affordable for low- and moderate-income residents of the state. SONYMA has two program divisions: Its single-family programs and financing division provides low-interest rate mortgages to first-time homebuyers with low and moderate incomes through the issuance of mortgage revenue bonds while its mortgage insurance fund provides mortgage insurance and credit support for multi-family affordable residential projects and special care facilities throughout the state.

STATE STREET CORP.
NYS: STT

One Lincoln Street
Boston, MA 02111
Phone: 617 786-3000
Fax: –
Web: www.statestreet.com

CEO: Ronald P. (Ron) O'Hanley
CFO: Michael W. Bell
HR: Alison A. Quirk
FYE: December 31
Type: Public

Ol' Blue Eyes sang about the State Street in Chicago but investors may find Boston's State Street more melodious. Through its flagship State Street Bank and other subsidiaries the company provides investment management and servicing trading and research services. Its activities include trust and custody fund accounting foreign exchange shareholder services and other administrative services for institutional clients such as mutual and other investment funds pension plans insurance companies foundations endowments and investment managers. Founded in 1792 State Street has more than $28 trillion of assets under custody and administration in addition to more than $2.4 trillion under management.

	Annual Growth	12/10	12/11	12/12	12/13	12/14
Assets ($ mil.)	14.3%	160,505.0	216,827.0	222,582.0	243,291.0	274,119.0
Net income ($ mil.)	7.0%	1,556.0	1,920.0	2,061.0	2,136.0	2,037.0
Market value ($ mil.)	14.1%	19,240.1	16,736.5	19,518.3	30,471.2	32,592.8
Employees	1.1%	28,670	29,740	29,660	29,430	29,970

STATE UNIVERSITY OF IOWA FOUNDATION

1 W PARK RD
IOWA CITY, IA 522422000
Phone: 319-335-3305
Fax: –
Web: www.uifoundation.org

CEO: –
CFO: –
HR: –
FYE: June 30
Type: Private

If you ever find yourself shouting "Fight! Fight! Fight! for IOWA" most likely you're a current former or honorary Hawkeye. Since 1956 The University of Iowa Foundation has been organizing University of Iowa fund-raising campaigns to get private contributions for equipment facilities fellowships professorships research and scholarships. Its endowment which is almost entirely restricted to donor-specified uses is valued at more than $690 million. Though independent of the school the not-for-profit organization is the university's preferred channel for contributions.

	Annual Growth	06/08	06/09	06/11	06/12	06/13
Sales ($ mil.)	(1.9%)	–	114.1	96.0	79.3	105.6
Net income ($ mil.)	–	–	–	6.5	(34.6)	(2.5)
Market value ($ mil.)	–	–	–	–	–	–
Employees	–	–	–	–	–	180

STATER BROS. HOLDINGS INC.

ASE: HGN A

301 S. Tippecanoe Avenue
San Bernardino, CA 92408
Phone: 909 733-5000
Fax: –
Web: www.staterbros.com

CEO: Jack H Brown
CFO: David J Harris
HR: Jennifer Guidubaldi
FYE: September 29
Type: Public

Stater Bros. has no shortage of major-league rivals operating in the same crowded Southern California markets as Kroger-owned Ralphs and Safeway-owned Vons. Stater Bros. Holdings operates more than 165 full-service Stater Bros. Markets in six counties primarily in the Riverside and San Bernardino areas. Most of the grocery chain's stores have deli department about 45% house bakeries while another 25 host Super Rx Pharmacies. The Southern California grocery operator builds and remodels its own stores through its Stater Bros. Development subsidiary. Founded in 1936 by twin brothers Leo and Cleo Stater Stater Bros. is owned by chairman and CEO Jack Brown through La Cadena Investments.

	Annual Growth	09/09	09/10	09/11	09/12	09/13
Sales ($ mil.)	0.6%	3,766.0	3,606.8	3,693.3	3,873.2	3,859.8
Net income ($ mil.)	(3.3%)	34.8	24.6	26.3	37.7	30.4
Market value ($ mil.)	–	–	–	–	–	–
Employees	(2.1%)	17,500	16,300	16,500	16,500	16,100

STATIC CONTROL COMPONENTS INC.

3010 LEE AVE
SANFORD, NC 27332-6210
Phone: 919-774-3808
Fax: –
Web: www.scc-inc.com

CEO: –
CFO: –
HR: –
FYE: December 31
Type: Private

Static Control Components (SCC) isn't stuck on static cling. The company that made a name for itself by selling anti-static products has made an even greater impression by selling parts for rebuilt toner cartridges. Its Imaging Division which sells parts to recycle used printer cartridges has captured more than half of the world market. SCC also makes electrical testing tools. In 2006 Static Control Components sold its SCC Products affiliate to 3M. President and CEO Ed Swartz founded Static Control Components in 1987; the company is owned and operated by his family.

	Annual Growth	12/01	12/02	12/03	12/04	12/11
Sales ($ mil.)	(2.4%)	–	238.9	245.8	264.1	191.2
Net income ($ mil.)	8.8%	–	3.7	5.3	0.0	7.9
Market value ($ mil.)	–	–	–	–	–	–
Employees	–	–	–	–	–	1,200

STATION CASINOS LLC

1505 S. Pavilion Center Dr.
Las Vegas NV 89135
Phone: 702-495-3000
Fax: 702-495-3530
Web: www.stationcasinos.com

CEO: –
CFO: –
HR: –
FYE: December 31
Type: Private

When the train pulls out of this station you might find you've left some money behind. Station Casinos owns and operates nearly 20 casinos and hotel casinos that cater primarily to local Las Vegas area residents. Most operate under the Station and Fiesta brand names and feature gaming restaurants and entertainment options. Included in its holdings are Green Valley Ranch Resort Red Rock Resort and Palace Station. Frank Fertitta III (chairman and CEO) and his brother Lorenzo (vice chairman) sons of Station Casinos founder Frank Fertitta Jr. own the biggest share of the company. Station Casinos filed for Chapter 11 in 2009. It exited bankruptcy in 2011 in a reorganization that slashed its massive debt.

STATOIL MARKETING & TRADING (US) INC.

1055 Washington Blvd. 7th Fl.
Stamford CT 06901
Phone: 203-978-6900
Fax: 203-978-6952
Web: www.statoil.com/en/ouroperations/tradingproduc

CEO: –
CFO: –
HR: Scott Steiger
FYE: December 31
Type: Subsidiary

Check the stats. Oil. Hundreds of thousands of barrels of oil gasoline and more. Statoil Marketing & Trading is a wholesaler of oil and petroleum products. The company is the US trading arm of Statoil the leading Scandinavian oil and gas enterprise. Statoil Marketing & Trading delivers about 600000 barrels a day in the form of crude oil gasoline liquefied petroleum gas (LPG) propane and butane to the North American market. In addition to supplying Norwegian crude the company trades crude oil from Africa South America and North America. Statoil Marketing & Trading sells it oil products primarily to customers in Northeastern Canada the US East Coast and Gulf Coast.

STATS LLC

2775 Shermer Rd.
Northbrook IL 60062
Phone: 847-583-2100
Fax: 847-470-9140
Web: www.stats.com

CEO: Kenneth Fuchs
CFO: –
HR: –
FYE: June 30
Type: Joint Venture

This company takes sports fans beyond the win-loss column. STATS LLC (formerly STATS Inc.) is the world's leading provider of sports information and statistics offering up-to-the-minute data on more than 230 sports (50000 events) a year through a network of reporters. It sells the data to news organizations magazines television sports networks and other media outlets including Yahoo! The Wall Street Journal Online and CBS. STATS also licenses its data for use in fantasy sports games trading cards and video games as well as for use on the Web sites of many professional sports teams. STATS is a 50-50 joint venture between News Corporation and The Associated Press.

STAYINFRONT INC.

107 Little Falls Rd.	CEO: Thomas R Buckley
Fairfield NJ 07004-2105	CFO: –
Phone: 973-461-4800	HR: –
Fax: 973-461-4801	FYE: December 31
Web: www.stayinfront.com	Type: Subsidiary

When it comes to customer relationship management (CRM) StayinFront doesn't want you falling behind. The company provides CRM software and services that customers use for tasks such as field force automation call center management telemarketing and customer data synchronization. StayinFront also offers applications for analyzing customer data and decision support. The company primarily targets midsized clients in the pharmaceutical consumer goods and manufacturing industries and has expanded its product lines to include software for mobile devices.

STC MICROWAVE SYSTEMS

340 N. Roosevelt Ave.	CEO: George E Lombard
Chandler AZ 85226	CFO: –
Phone: 480-940-1655	HR: –
Fax: 480-961-6297	FYE: December 31
Web: www.sigtech.com	Type: Subsidiary

STC Microwave Systems gets attention with waves. Its components and subsystems generate and control radio and microwave frequencies and electrical currents for military space and wireless communications equipment. Applications for STC Microwave's aerospace and military products include precision missile guidance radar satellite communications and surveillance. The company's products include oscillators power amplifiers switches transmitters and signal combiners. STC Microwave Systems is a subsidiary of industrial manufacturer Crane and is a part of that company's aerospace and electronics operations.

STEEL DYNAMICS INC.

NMS: STLD

7575 West Jefferson Blvd	CEO: Mark D. Millett
Fort Wayne, IN 46804	CFO: Theresa E. Wagler
Phone: 260 969-3500	HR: Benjamin Eisbart
Fax: –	FYE: December 31
Web: www.steeldynamics.com	Type: Public

Steel Dynamics may operate mini-mills but it produces big steel. Steel Dynamics operates electric arc furnace mini-mills steel scrap processing and metals recycling centers and steel fabrication facilities. The company sells to companies in the automotive construction and manufacturing industries as well as to steel processors and service centers primarily in the Midwestern and eastern US. Among its mini-mill output are beams rails and other products used in the construction industrial machinery and transportation industries. Steel Dynamics' annual steel shipping capacity is 11 million tons.

	Annual Growth	12/10	12/11	12/12	12/13	12/14
Sales ($ mil.)	8.6%	6,300.9	7,997.5	7,290.2	7,372.9	8,756.0
Net income ($ mil.)	2.8%	140.7	278.1	163.6	189.3	157.0
Market value ($ mil.)	1.9%	4,418.5	3,175.1	3,315.1	4,717.9	4,766.2
Employees	5.9%	6,180	6,530	6,670	6,870	7,780

STEEL OF WEST VIRGINIA INC.

17th St. and 2nd Ave.	CEO: Timothy R Duke
Huntington WV 25703	CFO: –
Phone: 304-696-8200	HR: –
Fax: 304-529-1479	FYE: October 31
Web: www.swvainc.com	Type: Subsidiary

Steel of West Virginia (SWV) a subsidiary of Steel Dynamics owns and operates a steel minimill and steel fabrication facilities in West Virginia and Tennessee. The company custom-designs and manufactures finished steel products including structural beams channels and special shape sections using electric furnace steel. SWV's products are used as structural elements of trucks trailers heavy machinery and manufactured housing as well as in guardrail posts mining applications and light-rail systems. SWV's custom-finished products are intended to go directly into its customers' assembly lines. Its Tennessee-based subsidiary Marshall Steel fabricates steel cross members. SWV got its start in 1909.

STEEL PARTNERS HOLDINGS LP

NYS: SPLP

590 Madison Avenue, 32nd Floor	CEO: –
New York, NY 10022	CFO: James F McCabe Jr
Phone: 212 520-2300	HR: Pete Marciniak
Fax: –	FYE: December 31
	Type: Public

Steel Partners Holdings is a hedge fund that rules with an iron fist. The activist fund invests in a variety of businesses from banks to hot dog restaurants. It often takes positions on those companies' boards and is not bashful about making sweeping changes within those enterprises. The firm also likes to hold on to its portfolio assets for the long term. Among its holdings is Utah-based WebBank which offers commercial consumer and mortgage loans as well as federally guaranteed USDA and SBA loans. With some $4 billion in assets under management Steel Partners also owns portions of Unisys Aerojet Rocketdyne Selectica SL Industries and Nathan's Famous. Activist investor Warren Lichtenstein heads the firm.

	Annual Growth	12/10	12/11	12/12	12/13	12/14
Sales ($ mil.)	–	0.0	624.2	711.6	805.2	849.5
Net income ($ mil.)	–	0.0	35.5	41.0	19.5	(7.6)
Market value ($ mil.)	–	0.0	332.2	325.0	478.3	486.8
Employees	10.3%	–	–	–	2,745	3,028

STEEL TECHNOLOGIES LLC

15415 Shelbyville Rd.	CEO: Michael J Carroll
Louisville KY 40245-4137	CFO: –
Phone: 502-245-2110	HR: –
Fax: 502-244-0182	FYE: September 30
Web: www.steeltechnologies.com	Type: Joint Venture

If you need sheets for a bed try a white sale; if you need sheets to make a car try Steel Technologies. Founded in 1971 Steel Technologies' lineup includes close-tolerance cold- and hot-rolled strip and sheet high-carbon hot-rolled pickle strip and sheet and alloy strip and sheet metal. The company purchases steel coils from steel mills and produces flat-rolled steel used by the agricultural appliance automotive HVAC lawn and garden machinery and office equipment industries. Automotive customers represent about half of Steel Technologies' sales. In 2010 the company's ownership changed to a 50/50 joint venture between Nucor and former parent Mitsui & Co. (U.S.A.) a subsidiary of Japan's Mitsui.

STEELCASE, INC.

NYS: SCS

901 44th Street S.E.
Grand Rapids, MI 49508
Phone: 616 247-2710
Fax: –
Web: www.steelcase.com

CEO: James P. (Jim) Keane
CFO: David C. (Dave) Sylvester
HR: Larry Lewis
FYE: February 27
Type: Public

For those really tough office meetings there's Steelcase — a top office furniture maker that serves customers worldwide. Through its Systems and Storage business the company manufactures and sells panel-based and freestanding furniture such as storage systems tables and ergonomic work tools. It Seating business makes casual and shared seating and specialty chairs for the health care and education markets. Steelcase also provides a variety of services including workspace planning interior construction and project management. The company's major brands include Coalesse Designtex Details PolyVision Steelcase and Turnstone. Founded in 1912 Steelcase has operations in North America Europe and Asia.

	Annual Growth	02/11	02/12	02/13	02/14	02/15
Sales ($ mil.)	5.9%	2,437.1	2,749.5	2,868.7	2,988.9	3,059.7
Net income ($ mil.)	43.3%	20.4	56.7	38.8	87.7	86.1
Market value ($ mil.)	17.7%	1,184.3	1,119.9	1,675.1	1,806.2	2,273.9
Employees	5.5%	10,000	10,000	12,100	12,300	12,400

STEELCLOUD INC.

PINK SHEETS: SCLD

14040 Park Center Rd. Ste. 210
Herndon VA 20171
Phone: 703-674-5500
Fax: 703-674-5506
Web: www.steelcloud.com

CEO: Brian H Hajost
CFO: Steven Snyder
HR: –
FYE: October 31
Type: Public

Federal agencies defense contractors and businesses looking for custom systems may have a SteelCloud on their horizon. The company builds network appliances and servers including ruggedized hardware that customers sell under their own brand names. SteelCloud integrates the customers' software or software from third-party providers. The company primarily targets systems integrators serving the federal government and independent software vendors (ISVs). SteelCloud also offers an appliance specifically designed to run Research In Motion's Blackberry Enterprise Server in commercial and defense agency settings.

STEFANINI TECHTEAM

27335 W. 11 Mile Rd.
Southfield MI 48033-2231
Phone: 248 357-2866
Fax: 248-357-2570
Web: www.techteam.com

CEO: Antonio Moreira
CFO: Sally A Brandtneris
HR: –
FYE: December 31
Type: Private

When your help desk needs a few more players Stefanini TechTeam is ready to get in the game. The company's business process outsourcing (BPO) and IT services include consulting help desk support systems integration technical staffing and training. TechTeam serves corporations in a range of industries and other organizations in the US. Its customers have included Ford Motor Company Exxon Mobil GE and Heinz. The company is a subsidiary of Brazil-based Stefanini IT Solutions a unit of leading Latin American IT services provider Stefanini International Holdings. The Stefanini family of businesses was established in 1987 by president Marco Stefanini.

STEIN MART, INC.

NMS: SMRT

1200 Riverplace Blvd.
Jacksonville, FL 32207
Phone: 904 346-1500
Fax: –
Web: www.steinmart.com

CEO: –
CFO: Gregory W. (Greg) Kleffner
HR: Jennifer (Jen) Wellington
FYE: January 31
Type: Public

Stein Mart's style is to operate department-like stores that feature discount prices. With more than 260 shops in some 30 states it sells off-price women's men's and children's brand-name clothing. Fashions range from casual to formal. Stein Mart also sells jewelry handbags linens home decor and gifts. Independent firms lease Stein Mart's shoe and fragrance departments. Its upscale women's boutiques are sometimes staffed by socialites who work part-time to receive employee discounts. Russian immigrant Sam Stein founded Stein Mart in the early 1900s. The company had one store in Greenville Mississippi until 1977 when it began growing rapidly. Chairman Jay Stein the founder's grandson controls Stein Mart.

	Annual Growth	01/11	01/12*	02/13	02/14*	01/15
Sales ($ mil.)	2.8%	1,181.5	1,160.4	1,232.4	1,263.6	1,317.7
Net income ($ mil.)	(13.8%)	48.8	19.8	25.0	25.6	26.9
Market value ($ mil.)	14.9%	354.4	330.2	397.1	556.1	618.1
Employees	(0.4%)	11,500	11,400	10,900	11,000	11,300

*Fiscal year change

STEINER ELECTRIC COMPANY

1250 TOUHY AVE
ELK GROVE VILLAGE, IL 60007-4985
Phone: 847-228-0400
Fax: –
Web: www.steiner-electric.com

CEO: –
CFO: Edward Carroll
HR: –
FYE: December 31
Type: Private

Steiner Electric electrifies Chicago by distributing electrical products and providing related supplies and services through locations in northern Illinois and northwest Indiana. Besides such standard electrical supplies as ballasts and fasteners the company's products include industrial supplies automation products motors and drives lighting products generators and bar code devices. Services include energy audits turnkey project management motor repair and electric vehicle charging. Customers purchase Steiner Electric's products for commercial construction residential and industrial applications. The founding Steiner family owns the firm.

	Annual Growth	12/08	12/09	12/09	12/11	12/12
Sales ($ mil.)	–	–	0.0	181.0	181.0	230.0
Net income ($ mil.)	–	–	0.0	0.0	0.0	0.0
Market value ($ mil.)	–	–	–	–	–	–
Employees	–	–	–	–	–	500

STEMCELLS INC

NAS: STEM

7707 Gateway Blvd.
Newark, CA 94560
Phone: 510 456-4000
Fax: –
Web: www.stemcellsinc.com

CEO: Ian Massey
CFO: Greg Schiffman
HR: –
FYE: December 31
Type: Public

StemCells hopes a small focus will mean big business. The company discovers cell-based therapies to treat diseases of the central nervous system (CNS) such as cerebral palsy and macular degeneration as well as spinal cord injury. It is researching stem cells and progenitor cell (cells that have developed from stem cells) therapies to repair neural tissue damaged by disease and injury and has discovered markers for CNS stem cells and a way to reproduce them for transplant. Its lead therapy candidate may treat Batten disease a fatal genetic enzyme deficiency. In addition to its CNS research StemCells is also studying liver cells hoping to find treatments for diseases such as hepatitis and liver cancer.

	Annual Growth	12/10	12/11	12/12	12/13	12/14
Sales ($ mil.)	(8.2%)	1.4	1.2	1.4	1.2	1.0
Net income ($ mil.)	–	(25.2)	(21.3)	(28.5)	(26.4)	(32.7)
Market value ($ mil.)	(3.4%)	74.2	56.6	112.0	84.5	64.5
Employees	(1.7%)	74	50	49	58	69

STEMLINE THERAPEUTICS INC

NAS: STML

750 Lexington Avenue, Eleventh Floor
New York, NY 10022
Phone: 646 502-2311
Fax: –
Web: www.stemline.com

CEO: Ivan Bergstein
CFO: –
HR: –
FYE: December 31
Type: Public

Stemline Therapeutics believes it has a direct line to eradicating cancer stem cells (CSC) and tumors. The development-stage biopharmaceutical company's pipeline includes two lead clinical-stage candidates for leukemia and brain cancer in children and adults. Its drugs work by targeting CSCs which are believed to be the seeds of tumors that often survive traditional cancer treatment. Stemline is part of the biopharma race to be the first to successfully kill CSCs and usher in a new era of cancer drugs. Once its candidates are approved the company intends to create an in-house sales and marketing team for North America and Europe. Stemline went public in early 2013 with an offering worth $33.2 million.

	Annual Growth	12/10	12/11	12/12	12/13	12/14
Sales ($ mil.)	372.2%	–	–	–	0.1	0.3
Net income ($ mil.)	–	(1.8)	(2.8)	(6.3)	(24.2)	(28.8)
Market value ($ mil.)	(13.0%)	–	–	–	260.4	226.6
Employees	40.1%	–	8	8	17	22

STEPAN CO.

NYS: SCL

Edens & Winnetka Road
Northfield, IL 60093
Phone: 847 446-7500
Fax: –
Web: www.stepan.com

CEO: F. Quinn Stepan
CFO: Scott D. Beamer
HR: Greg Servatius
FYE: December 31
Type: Public

Company secrets aside makers of laundry detergents shampoos toothpaste and other personal care products can come clean with Stepan Company. Surfactants the company's largest sector by far are chemicals most commonly used as cleaning agents used in consumer products like detergents toothpastes and cosmetics. Stepan's surfactants are also used in commercial and industrial applications ranging from emulsifiers for agricultural insecticides to agents used in oil recovery. The company also makes phthalic anhydride (an acid used in making polyester resins) and other polymers as well as specialty chemicals for food and pharmaceutical uses.

	Annual Growth	12/10	12/11	12/12	12/13	12/14
Sales ($ mil.)	7.7%	1,431.1	1,843.1	1,803.7	1,880.8	1,927.2
Net income ($ mil.)	(3.3%)	65.4	72.0	79.4	72.8	57.1
Market value ($ mil.)	(14.9%)	1,697.4	1,784.0	1,236.1	1,460.6	892.0
Employees	3.4%	1,768	1,848	1,920	2,015	2,024

STEPHAN CO. (THE)

NBB: SPCO

1500 E. Lancaster Avenue, Suite 205
Paoli, PA 19301
Phone: 800 637-1996
Fax: –
Web: www.thestephanco.com

CEO: Frank F Ferola
CFO: Robert C Spindler
HR: –
FYE: December 31
Type: Public

From hair cream to stretch mark cream The Stephan Company manages a vast portfolio of products as a maker of branded and private-label personal care items. The company's brands include Cashmere Bouquet Quinsana Medicated Balm Barr Stretch Mark Cr-¨me Protein 29 Stiff Stuff Wildroot and Frances Denney. It sells them worldwide by mail order and in retail stores and salons through its subsidiaries including Morris Flamingo-Stephan Old 97 American Manicure Lee Stafford Beauty Group Williamsport Barber and Beauty Corp. and Scientific Research Products among others. Chairman president and CEO Frank Ferola owns about 21% of the firm which bought Bowman Beauty and Barber Supply Company in August 2008.

	Annual Growth	12/10	12/11	12/12	12/13	12/14
Sales ($ mil.)	(18.0%)	19.6	17.2	15.7	12.8	8.8
Net income ($ mil.)	–	0.9	0.4	(14.4)	(3.4)	(2.7)
Market value ($ mil.)	(9.8%)	9.5	9.1	6.6	4.8	6.3
Employees	(30.4%)	–	–	95	75	46

STEPHEN F AUSTIN STATE UNIVERSITY

1936 NORTH ST
NACOGDOCHES, TX 75965-3940
Phone: 936-468-2304
Fax: –
Web: www.sfanew.sfasu.edu

CEO: –
CFO: –
HR: –
FYE: August 31
Type: Private

Stephen F. Austin State University (SFA) is a public university located in the Pineywoods of East Texas. Its campus in the heart of Nacogdoches was part of the original homestead of Thomas J. Rusk an early Texas patriot and US senator. The school's 13000-plus enrolled students may choose from about 85 majors in study areas including business and nursing. The student-to-faculty ratio is 20:1. Stephen F. Austin also offers a number of undergraduate graduate and certification programs online or partially online. Notable alumni include former NFL coach Bum Phillips and Don Henley of the Eagles. Named for the founding father of Texas the university was created in 1923 as a teacher's college.

	Annual Growth	08/01	08/02	08/03	08/04	08/11
Sales ($ mil.)	6.0%	–	71.3	78.2	71.3	120.6
Net income ($ mil.)	(15.7%)	–	8.4	3.2	5.6	1.8
Market value ($ mil.)	–	–	–	–	–	–
Employees	–	–	–	–	–	2,914

STEPHEN GOULD CORPORATION

35 S JEFFERSON RD
WHIPPANY, NJ 079811043
Phone: 973-428-1510
Fax: –
Web: www.stephengould.com

CEO: –
CFO: Anthony Lupo
HR: Tammy Pombo
FYE: December 31
Type: Private

Others can worry about what's inside — Stephen Gould Corporation concentrates on the package. The company provides a full range of packaging-related design and printing services for customers worldwide. Its products include gift packaging point-of-purchase displays product merchandising and retail and industrial packaging. Stephen Gould Corporation also provides graphic design and package-engineering services as well as assembly and fulfillment. The company was originally founded in 1939 by Stephen Gould David Golden and Leonard Beckerman.

	Annual Growth	12/09	12/10	12/11	12/12	12/13
Sales ($ mil.)	1.7%	–	500.0	519.1	526.7	526.7
Net income ($ mil.)	(1.9%)	–	–	4.1	3.9	3.9
Market value ($ mil.)	–	–	–	–	–	–
Employees	–	–	–	–	–	325

STEPHENSON WHOLESALE COMPANY INC.

230 S 22ND AVE
DURANT, OK 747015646
Phone: 580-920-0125
Fax: –
Web: www.inwsupply.com

CEO: Tammy Cross
CFO: –
HR: –
FYE: December 31
Type: Private

Buying a candy bar and a box of nails is made easier thanks to Stephenson Wholesale. Operating through subsidiaries Indian National Wholesale Company and GLC Marketing the company is a leading supplier of food and nonfood goods to convenience stores and other retail outlets in Oklahoma and Texas. It also distributes goods to snack bars concessions operators and tribal smoke shops. The family-owned company was founded in 1953 by Ralphen Cross.

	Annual Growth	12/09	12/10	12/11	12/12	12/13
Sales ($ mil.)	(2.7%)	–	401.4	404.4	395.2	369.8
Net income ($ mil.)	(8.6%)	–	–	3.5	3.0	3.0
Market value ($ mil.)	–	–	–	–	–	–
Employees	–	–	–	–	–	305

STEREOTAXIS INC

NAS: STXS

4320 Forest Park Avenue, Suite 100
St. Louis, MO 63108
Phone: 314 678-6100
Fax: –
Web: www.stereotaxis.com

CEO: William C. Mills
CFO: Martin C. Stammer
HR: David A. Giffin
FYE: December 31
Type: Public

Stereotaxis can drive in the fast lane through your veins because it has the road map to your heart. The company's systems are used to treat abnormal heart rhythms known as arrhythmias as well as coronary artery disease. Via digital remote control doctors steer catheters guidewires and stent delivery devices through blood vessels all the way to the chambers of the heart (and all the way back out if necessary) in a procedure that is less invasive than traditional heart surgeries. Stereotaxis markets the cardiology instrument control system to interventional surgery labs (or "cath labs") research hospitals and large commercial medical centers worldwide.

	Annual Growth	12/10	12/11	12/12	12/13	12/14
Sales ($ mil.)	(10.3%)	54.1	42.0	46.6	38.0	35.0
Net income ($ mil.)	–	(19.9)	(32.0)	(9.2)	(68.8)	(5.2)
Market value ($ mil.)	(21.2%)	78.4	16.9	52.2	74.1	30.3
Employees	(10.1%)	204	171	134	123	133

STERICYCLE INC.

NMS: SRCL

28161 North Keith Drive
Lake Forest, IL 60045
Phone: 847 367-5910
Fax: –
Web: www.stericycle.com

CEO: Charles A. (Charlie) Alutto
CFO: Daniel V. Ginnetti
HR: –
FYE: December 31
Type: Public

A leading medical and pharmaceutical waste management company Stericycle serves more than 600000 clients worldwide: 16500 large waste generators (pharmaceutical manufacturers hospitals and blood banks) and 524500 small waste generators (dental and medical offices veterinary offices pharmacies and municipalities). Services include disposing of used needles and expired drugs. Through 181 processing and collection sites and 214 transfer sites and 97 recall and returns or communication services facilities Stericycle treats waste through incineration autoclaving (using high temperature and pressure to kill pathogens) and electro-thermal-deactivation (using low-frequency radio waves to kill pathogens).

	Annual Growth	12/10	12/11	12/12	12/13	12/14
Sales ($ mil.)	15.4%	1,439.4	1,676.0	1,913.1	2,142.8	2,555.6
Net income ($ mil.)	11.9%	207.9	234.8	268.0	311.4	326.5
Market value ($ mil.)	12.8%	6,868.8	6,614.1	7,917.9	9,860.9	11,126.5
Employees	17.7%	9,715	11,122	13,245	14,924	18,656

STERIS CORP.

NYS: STE

5960 Heisley Road
Mentor, OH 44060-1834
Phone: 440 354-2600
Fax: –
Web: www.steris.com

CEO: Walter M. (Walt) Rosebrough
CFO: Michael J. Tokich
HR: –
FYE: March 31
Type: Public

STERIS has hygiene hysteria. The company makes sterilization systems for health care pharmaceutical research and industrial markets. In addition to the company's sanitizing lotions and soaps health care professionals use the firm's steam and chemical sterilization systems to sterilize surgical and diagnostic devices. STERIS also makes disinfection systems and infection prevention consumables. The company sells such surgical support products as exam lights surgical tables and scrub sinks. STERIS sells its equipment and consumables in more than 60 countries. In North America its Isomedix unit offers contract sterilization for more than a dozen health care industrial and consumer products makers.

	Annual Growth	03/10	03/11	03/12	03/13	03/14
Sales ($ mil.)	6.6%	1,257.7	1,207.4	1,406.8	1,501.9	1,622.3
Net income ($ mil.)	0.2%	128.5	51.3	136.1	160.0	129.4
Market value ($ mil.)	9.1%	1,984.9	2,036.8	1,864.6	2,453.7	2,815.7
Employees	4.7%	5,000	5,000	5,000	6,000	6,000

STERLING BANCORP (DE)

NYS: STL

400 Rella Boulevard
Montebello, NY 10901
Phone: 845 369-8040
Fax: –
Web: www.sterlingbancorp.com

CEO: Jack L Kopnisky
CFO: Luis Massiani
HR: –
FYE: December 31
Type: Public

Sterling Bancorp is the holding company for Sterling National Bank a community-based thrift operating dozens of offices in New York's Hudson Valley region and Greater New York City area. Founded in 1888 the bank attracts consumers and business clients by offering traditional deposit products such as checking and savings accounts and CDs. It uses funds from deposits to originate primarily real estate loans and mortgages. Sterling Bancorp which has assets of more than $7 billion was formerly Provident New York Bancorp; Provident acquired the former Sterling Bancorp in late 2013 and changed its name as well as the name of its banking subsidiary to Sterling.

	Annual Growth	09/11	09/12	09/13	09/14*	12/14
Assets ($ mil.)	33.3%	3,137.4	4,023.0	4,049.2	7,337.4	7,424.8
Net income ($ mil.)	13.1%	11.7	19.9	25.3	27.7	17.0
Market value ($ mil.)	35.2%	488.5	789.8	914.0	1,073.4	1,206.9
Employees	14.7%	550	522	543	836	829

*Fiscal year change

STERLING CHEMICALS INC.

333 Clay St. Ste. 3600
Houston TX 77002-4109
Phone: 713-650-3700
Fax: 713-654-9551
Web: www.sterlingchemicals.com

CEO: John V Genova
CFO: Carla E Stucky
HR: –
FYE: December 31
Type: Subsidiary

Sterling Chemicals focuses on producing a small number of products and selling those products to a small number of customers. Its core product is acetic acid (used to make vinyl acetate monomer which is an ingredient in adhesives coatings and fibers). It is also used to make purified terephthalic acid an ingredient in the production of plastic bottle resins. Sterling Chemicals supplies all of its acetic acid to BP. Although the loss of a contract forced the company to close its plasticizers facility (used to make flexible plastics such as automotive parts and shower curtains) in early 2011 it plans to manufacture non-phthalate plasticizers. Sterling Chemicals is owned by Eastman Chemical.

STERLING CONSTRUCTION INC

NMS: STRL

1800 Hughes Landing Blvd.
The Woodlands, TX 77380
Phone: 281 214-0800
Fax: –

CEO: –
CFO: Ronald A Ballschmiede
HR: Craig Allen
FYE: December 31
Type: Public

Sterling Construction company specializes in the building reconstruction and repair of transportation and water infrastructure. It also works on specialty projects such as excavation shoring and drilling. The heavy civil construction company and its subsidiaries (Texas Sterling Construction Ralph L. Wadsworth Contractors RDI Foundation Drilling Myers and Sons Banicki Construction and Road and Highway Builders) primarily serve public sector clients throughout the Southwest and West. Transportation projects include excavation and asphalt paving as well as construction of bridges and rail systems. Water projects include work on sewers and storm drainage systems.

	Annual Growth	12/10	12/11	12/12	12/13	12/14
Sales ($ mil.)	10.0%	459.9	501.2	630.5	556.2	672.2
Net income ($ mil.)	–	19.1	(35.9)	(0.3)	(73.9)	(9.8)
Market value ($ mil.)	(16.3%)	245.2	202.5	186.9	220.6	120.1
Employees	8.5%	1,300	1,606	1,685	1,655	1,799

STERLING FINANCIAL CORP. (WA)

NAS: STSA

111 North Wall Street
Spokane, WA 99201
Phone: 509 358-8097
Fax: 509 458-2391
Web: www.sterlingfinancialcorporation-spokane.com

CEO: –
CFO: –
HR: –
FYE: December 31
Type: Public

Sterling Financial Corporation is the holding company for Sterling Bank (formerly Sterling Savings Bank) one of the largest regional community banks in the Pacific Northwest. The bank operates about 190 branch locations in northern California Idaho Oregon and Washington and lends throughout the West from more than 30 loan origination offices. In California it does business under the name Sonoma Bank. Real estate and construction loans account for the majority of the bank's portfolio. Its wealth management division markets stocks bonds mutual funds annuities and other investments to bank customers. Sterling Financial is regaining its luster after being hard hit by the downturn in the housing market.

	Annual Growth	12/08	12/09	12/10	12/11	12/12
Assets ($ mil.)	(7.8%)	12,790.7	10,877.4	9,493.2	9,193.2	9,236.9
Net income ($ mil.)	–	(335.5)	(838.1)	(224.3)	39.1	385.7
Market value ($ mil.)	24.1%	547.4	38.6	1,180.1	1,038.9	1,300.1
Employees	0.5%	2,481	2,641	2,498	2,496	2,532

STERLING JEWELERS INC.

375 Ghent Rd.
Fairlawn OH 44333
Phone: 330-668-5000
Fax: 330-668-5052
Web: www.sterlingjewelers.com

CEO: Mark Light
CFO: –
HR: –
FYE: January 31
Type: Subsidiary

There's more in store at Sterling Jewelers than sterling silver. The jewelry firm sells gold silver diamond and gemstone jewelry watches and gifts from more than 1300 stores in all 50 US states. Sterling Jewelers operates Kay Jewelers which has about 910 stores in shopping centers and malls nationwide as well as the off-mall format Jared the Galleria of Jewelry and some 230 regional jewelry stores under other names (Belden JB Robinson Marks & Morgan). Some 180 Jared stores sell diamond jewelry and loose diamonds as well as luxury watches such as Rolex Tag Heuer and Raymond Weil. Sterling Jewelers is the US subsidiary of London-based Signet Jewelers the world's largest jewelry retailer.

STERLING METS LP

123-01 Roosevelt Ave.
Flushing NY 11368-1699
Phone: 718-507-8499
Fax: 718-507-6395
Web: www.mets.com

CEO: Fred Wilpon
CFO: –
HR: –
FYE: September 30
Type: Private

This team from Queens has twice been crowned king of baseball. Sterling Mets owns and operates the New York Mets professional baseball franchise which joined Major League Baseball as an expansion club in 1962. After losing a record 120 games in its first season the team earned the nickname "the Miracle Mets" when it toppled the Baltimore Orioles for the franchise's first World Series title in 1969. A second championship came in 1986 over the Boston Red Sox. The Mets faced the New York Yankees in the 2000 "Subway Series" but lost to the Bronx Bombers. CEO Fred Wilpon has controlled the Mets since 2002.

STETSON UNIVERSITY INC.

421 N WOODLAND BLVD
DELAND, FL 327238300
Phone: 386-822-7000
Fax: –
Web: www.stetson.edu

CEO: –
CFO: –
HR: –
FYE: June 30
Type: Private

Not everyone at Stetson University wears a cowboy hat but there is a connection (it was named after hat maker and benefactor John B. Stetson). The school offers Stetson offers 73 academic programs with undergraduate and graduate studies offered through its College of Arts and Sciences School of Business Administration School of Music and College of Law. The university enrolls about 2200 undergraduate students. Stetson has four campuses located in DeLand (main) Celebration (graduate degrees and continuing education) Tampa (law) and St. Petersburg/Gulfport (law). The university enrolls about 3900 students a year of which 2500 are undergraduate students and about 1400 graduate students from 43 states the District of Columbia and 47 other nations.

	Annual Growth	06/09	06/10	06/12	06/13	06/14
Sales ($ mil.)	(4.8%)	–	146.9	110.0	109.8	120.6
Net income ($ mil.)	199.9%	–	–	3.6	33.4	32.1
Market value ($ mil.)	–	–	–	–	–	–
Employees	–	–	–	–	–	1,033

STEVENS INDUSTRIES INC

704 W MAIN ST
TEUTOPOLIS, IL 62467-1212
Phone: 217-540-3100
Fax: –
Web: www.stevensadvantage.com

CEO: –
CFO: –
HR: –
FYE: December 31
Type: Private

What do children playing at school nurses at work in hospitals and receptionists typing away at their computers have in common? Chances are they've all used products from Stevens Industries. The company manufactures cabinets countertops workstations and other furniture for schools hospitals and medical clinics. It also produces hardware (pulls hooks) and laminated paneling for use by office furniture and shelving manufacturers. Stevens' products offer an array of decorative inlays and color finishes. The company was founded in 1956 by Chuck Stevens.

	Annual Growth	12/03	12/04	12/05	12/06	12/07
Sales ($ mil.)	(72.7%)	–	–	1,090.1	81.0	81.4
Net income ($ mil.)	13663.4%	–	–	0.0	3.5	1.4
Market value ($ mil.)	–	–	–	–	–	–
Employees	–	–	–	–	–	500

STEVENS INSTITUTE OF TECHNOLOGY (INC)

1 CASTLE POINT TER
HOBOKEN, NJ 070305906
Phone: 201-216-5000
Fax: –
Web: www.dc.stevens.edu

CEO: –
CFO: Randy L. Greene
HR: Taylor Race
FYE: June 30
Type: Private

Even before the advent of the internal combustion engine Stevens Institute of Technology was educating students in science technology and engineering. Founded in 1870 through an endowment from engineer Edwin Stevens the university offers undergraduate master's and doctoral degrees in engineering science humanities computer science and technology management. The school enrolls roughly 3000 undergraduates and some 3500 graduate students. Stevens Institute teams up with corporate and military institutions to provide students with hands-on research experience; Stevens Technologies a for-profit subsidiary of the school licenses and sells the technological fruits of these partnerships.

	Annual Growth	06/06	06/07	06/08	06/10	06/13
Sales ($ mil.)	–	–	0.0	168.2	211.5	259.3
Net income ($ mil.)	–	–	–	(1.8)	8.5	29.2
Market value ($ mil.)	–	–	–	–	–	–
Employees	–	–	–	–	–	500

STEVENS TRANSPORT INC.

9757 MILITARY PKWY
DALLAS, TX 752274805
Phone: 972-216-9000
Fax: –
Web: www.stevenstransporttl.com

CEO: –
CFO: –
HR: –
FYE: December 31
Type: Private

Staying cool is a must for Stevens Transport. An irregular-route refrigerated truckload carrier (or reefer) Stevens hauls temperature-controlled cargo throughout the US covering the 48 contiguous states. Through alliances Stevens also covers every province in Canada and every state in Mexico. The company operates a fleet of about 2000 Kenworth and Peterbuilt tractors and 3500 Thermo King refrigerated trailers from a network of more than a dozen service centers. Partnerships with railroads allow Stevens to arrange intermodal transport of temperature-controlled cargo. The company also provides third-party logistics services. Stevens Transport was founded in 1980.

	Annual Growth	12/07	12/08	12/11	12/12	12/13
Sales ($ mil.)	–	–	0.0	566.9	607.4	636.1
Net income ($ mil.)	5.1%	–	–	76.5	85.3	84.6
Market value ($ mil.)	–	–	–	–	–	–
Employees	–	–	–	–	–	2,100

STEVENSON UNIVERSITY INC.

1525 GREENSPRING VLY RD
STEVENSON, MD 211530641
Phone: 410-486-7000
Fax: –
Web: www.stevenson.edu

CEO: –
CFO: Tim Campbell
HR: Brenda Balzer
FYE: June 30
Type: Private

Stevenson University is a career-focused liberal arts college with about 4300 undergraduate and graduate students. It has more than 500 faculty members and a student-to-teacher ratio of 15:1. The school has two locations in Stevenson and Owings Mills Maryland near Baltimore. Stevenson University offers more than 20 bachelor's degree programs as well as a handful of master's degree programs at six schools in areas including business and leadership education design humanities information technologies and forensic studies. About 83% of the student body are Maryland residents.

	Annual Growth	06/09	06/10	06/11	06/12	06/13
Sales ($ mil.)	12.5%	–	87.6	84.8	120.0	125.0
Net income ($ mil.)	(55.1%)	–	–	13.4	6.9	2.7
Market value ($ mil.)	–	–	–	–	–	–
Employees	–	–	–	–	–	550

STEW LEONARD'S LLC

100 Westport Ave.
Norwalk CT 06851
Phone: 203 047 7214
Fax: 203-846-3472
Web: www.stewleonards.com

CEO: –
CFO: –
HR: –
FYE: December 31
Type: Private

Shoppers don't stew at Stew Leonard's where the customer is always right. While singing milk cartons and farm animals amuse the kids four locations operating under the Stew Leonard's banner in Connecticut and New York sell a selection of dairy products juice wine and meats to some 300000 people each week. Stew Leonard's also offers catering services and sells products online. The company produces its own milk and is thought to sell more orange juice than any other store in the world. Years after Charles Leonard began bottling milk in 1924 his son Stew built the first retail store in 1969. Stew Leonard and his family including CEO Stew Jr. own and run Stew Leonard's.

STEWARD HEALTH CARE SYSTEM LLC

500 BOYLSTON ST
BOSTON, MA 021163740
Phone: 617-419-4700
Fax: –
Web: www.steward.org

CEO: –
CFO: –
HR: Melinda Braithwaite
FYE: September 30
Type: Private

Steward Health Care System is a steward of its patients' good health. With a total of 2100 beds Steward Health operates 10 hospitals including Carney Hospital Good Samaritan Medical Center Holy Family Hospital Norwood Hospital St. Elizabeth's Medical Center and Saint Anne's Hospital. Several of the hospitals are affiliated with Boston-area medical schools. The company is a top health care provider in New England; its territory ranges from Rhode Island to eastern Massachusetts and southern New Hampshire. In addition to hospitals Steward Health also includes a physician practice organization an outpatient clinic network and a home care and hospice agency. Steward is owned by Cerberus Capital Management.

	Annual Growth	09/03	09/04	09/05	09/06	09/07
Sales ($ mil.)	1.7%	–	–	–	1,220.5	1,240.7
Net income ($ mil.)	(35.9%)	–	–	–	47.6	30.5
Market value ($ mil.)	–	–	–	–	–	–
Employees	–	–	–	–	–	12,000

STEWARDSHIP FINANCIAL CORP.

NAS: SSFN

630 Godwin Avenue
Midland Park, NJ 07432
Phone: 201 444-7100
Fax: –
Web: www.asbnow.com

CEO: Paul Van Ostenbridge
CFO: Claire M Chadwick
HR: –
FYE: December 31
Type: Public

Like any good steward this company likes to give back to the community it lives in. Stewardship Financial is the holding company for Atlantic Stewardship Bank which serves northeastern New Jersey's Bergen Morris and Passaic counties from about a dozen branches. Catering to area consumers professionals and small to midsized businesses the bank offers standard products and services including checking and savings accounts certificates of deposit loans and credit cards. Stewardship Financial donates 10% of its pre-tax profits to Christian and civic organizations in its market area.

	Annual Growth	12/10	12/11	12/12	12/13	12/14
Assets ($ mil.)	0.2%	688.1	708.8	688.4	673.5	693.6
Net income ($ mil.)	25.8%	1.2	0.7	0.5	2.5	3.1
Market value ($ mil.)	(4.1%)	34.8	32.0	24.0	29.3	29.4
Employees	0.3%	149	160	159	155	151

STEWART & STEVENSON INC.

1000 Louisiana St., Suite 5900
Houston, TX 77002
Phone: 713 751-2700
Fax: –

CEO: John B Simmons
CFO: –
HR: –
FYE: January 31
Type: Public

Houstonian Stewart & Stevenson helps its customers quench their thirst for Texas Tea. The company is a leading supplier of equipment used in oilfield services. Stewart & Stevenson operates three divisions: Equipment (oil well stimulation coil tubing engines and material handling equipment) Aftermarket Parts and Service (parts and service for customers in oil and gas marine power generation mining and construction industries) and Rental (rental of generators material handling equipment and air compressors). While the company primarily sells and markets its products directly through its own sales and service centers it also uses authorized dealers and independent overseas sales representatives.

	Annual Growth	01/08	01/09	01/10	01/11	01/12
Sales ($ mil.)	(0.2%)	1,335.4	1,217.1	688.7	861.2	1,324.0
Net income ($ mil.)	1.6%	91.8	50.6	(23.9)	(10.0)	97.9
Market value ($ mil.)	–	–	–	–	–	–
Employees	(3.7%)	3,374	2,852	2,276	2,300	2,900

STEWART BUILDERS INC.

16575 VILLAGE DR
JERSEY VILLAGE, TX 770401124
Phone: 713-983-8002
Fax: –
Web: www.keystoneconcrete.com

CEO: –
CFO: –
HR: –
FYE: December 31
Type: Private

Concrete is the key to Stewart Builders' success in the construction industry. Stewart Builders through main subsidiaries Keystone Concrete Placement and Keystone Structural Concrete provides concrete construction services for commercial industrial and institutional facilities as well as for residential markets primarily serving working on projects in the Lone Star State. Other subsidiaries do site work and construct basements. President Don Stewart and his sons founded the firm in 1993. The company has operations in Austin Georgetown Houston and San Antonio Texas.

	Annual Growth	12/08	12/09	12/10	12/12	12/13
Sales ($ mil.)	8.7%	–	169.5	144.0	206.6	237.0
Net income ($ mil.)	–	–	–	0.0	5.1	10.2
Market value ($ mil.)	–	–	–	–	–	–
Employees	–	–	–	–	–	1,400

STEWART INFORMATION SERVICES CORP.

NYS: STC

1980 Post Oak Blvd.
Houston, TX 77056
Phone: 713 625-8100
Fax: 713 629-2244
Web: www.stewart.com

CEO: Matthew W. (Matt) Morris
CFO: J. Allen Berryman
HR: Kelly Buice
FYE: December 31
Type: Public

Stewart Information Services is happy to have a place in that mountain of papers to sign whenever real estate changes hands. The company writes title insurance through its top-ranking Stewart Title National Title and other units and distributes policies through more than 8500 offices and independent agencies in the US and abroad. Unlike most insurance that covers future events or losses title insurance protects lenders and buyers against past problems with titles. Stewart Title offers real estate information services through PropertyInfo and a variety of mortgage origination process services through Stewart Lender Services. Stewart also provides services to US and international government clients.

	Annual Growth	12/10	12/11	12/12	12/13	12/14
Assets ($ mil.)	5.1%	1,141.2	1,156.1	1,291.2	1,326.1	1,392.5
Net income ($ mil.)	–	(12.6)	2.3	109.2	63.0	29.8
Market value ($ mil.)	33.9%	276.8	277.3	624.1	774.7	889.2
Employees	6.7%	5,700	5,600	6,300	6,600	7,400

STEWART'S SHOPS CORP.

2907 ROUTE 9
BALLSTON SPA, NY 12020
Phone: 518-581-1201
Fax: –
Web: www.stewartsshops.com

CEO: –
CFO: –
HR: –
FYE: December 29
Type: Private

I scream you scream we all scream for Stewart's ice cream — especially if we live in upstate New York or Vermont home to some 330 Stewart's Shops. The chain of convenience stores sells more than 3000 products across 30-plus counties. They include dairy items groceries food to go (soup sandwiches hot entrees) beer coffee gasoline and of course ice cream. In addition to its retail business the company owns about 100 rental properties including banks hair salons and apartments near its stores. Stewart's Shops formerly known as Stewart's Ice Cream Company was established in 1945. The founding Dake family owns about two-thirds of the company; employee compensation plans own the rest.

	Annual Growth	01/09	01/10	01/11*	12/12	12/13
Sales ($ mil.)	9.9%	–	1,187.9	1,296.2	1,528.2	1,577.1
Net income ($ mil.)	17.1%	–	–	53.9	64.5	73.9
Market value ($ mil.)	–	–	–	–	–	–
Employees	–	–	–	–	–	3,800

*Fiscal year change

STG INC.

12011 SUNSET HILLS RD
RESTON, VA 201905918
Phone: 703-691-2480
Fax: –
Web: www.stg-inc.com

CEO: Simon S. Lee
CFO: Patrick G. Attilio
HR: –
FYE: December 31
Type: Private

STG provides technical TLC to government agencies. Serving the US Defense Department and about 50 other federal agencies the company provides information technology services such as project management application development network implementation security systems support and IT systems integration. It also offers data security assessment and compliance reporting services as well as foreign language translation and transcription. In addition to the DOD STG counts the US departments of State and Agriculture among its clients as well as Fortune 100 companies. Internationally the company has worked with NATO the Korea Airports Authority and other agencies.

	Annual Growth	12/10	12/11	12/12	12/13	12/14
Sales ($ mil.)	(7.0%)	–	261.1	212.8	248.9	209.7
Net income ($ mil.)	(14.3%)	–	–	5.9	3.8	4.3
Market value ($ mil.)	–	–	–	–	–	–
Employees	–	–	–	–	–	1,250

STIFEL FINANCIAL CORP.

NYS: SF

501 N. Broadway
St. Louis, MO 63102-2188
Phone: 314 342-2000
Fax: –
Web: www.stifel.com

CEO: Ronald J. (Ron) Kruszewski
CFO: James M. Zemlyak
HR: –
FYE: December 31
Type: Public

Stifel Financial doesn't repress investors. Through subsidiaries Stifel Nicolaus (founded 1890) Thomas Weisel Century Securities Associates Stifel Bank & Trust and others the financial services holding company provides asset management financial advice and banking services for private individuals corporations municipal and institutional clients in the US. Stifel also offers brokerage and mergers and acquisitions advisory services for corporate clients underwrites debt and equity and provides research on more than 1000 US and European equities. The firm boasts nearly 370 US offices with a concentration in the Midwest and mid-Atlantic regions and additional offices in Canada and Europe.

	Annual Growth	12/10	12/11	12/12	12/13	12/14
Assets ($ mil.)	22.6%	4,213.1	4,951.9	6,966.1	9,008.9	9,518.2
Net income ($ mil.)	210.0%	1.9	84.1	138.6	162.0	176.1
Market value ($ mil.)	(4.8%)	4,115.5	2,126.1	2,120.8	3,178.8	3,384.5
Employees	6.0%	4,906	5,097	5,343	5,862	6,200

STILES CORPORATION

301 E LAS OLAS BLVD
FORT LAUDERDALE, FL 333012295
Phone: 954-627-9150
Fax: –
Web: www.stiles.com

CEO: –
CFO: –
HR: George Bou
FYE: December 31
Type: Private

Stiles Corporation is a full-service commercial real estate development and investment firm. It provides architectural design and construction realty services and property management. The firm operates primarily throughout the southeastern US with a special interest in Florida. The company's Capital Group unit offers asset management and arranges financing for development projects. Since 1951 when the company was founded Stiles has built more than 37 million sq. ft. of office industrial retail and mixed use properties. The firm's completed projects include Fort Lauderdale's Las Olas City Centre and Trump International Tower as well as the PGA Financial Plaza at MacArthur Center in Palm Beach Gardens.

	Annual Growth	12/09	12/10	12/11	12/12	12/13
Sales ($ mil.)	19.1%	–	84.9	89.8	170.2	143.4
Net income ($ mil.)	–	–	–	(3.3)	3.3	0.8
Market value ($ mil.)	–	–	–	–	–	–
Employees	–	–	–	–	–	284

STILLWATER MINING CO. NYS: SWC

26 West Dry Creek Circle, Suite 400	CEO: Michael J. (Mick) McMullen
Littleton, CO 80120	CFO: Christopher M. (Chris) Bateman
Phone: 406 373-8700	HR: Kristen K. (Kris) Koss
Fax: –	FYE: December 31
Web: www.stillwatermining.com	Type: Public

Stillwater Mining has staked a claim to one of the few significant sources of platinum and palladium outside South Africa and Russia. The company extracts processes and refines platinum group metals (PGMs) — platinum palladium and associated minerals — at mines and a smelter in Montana. PGMs are used in catalytic converters for automobiles as well as in jewelry and other applications. Stillwater Mining also owns exploratory properties of PGM and copper in Canada and copper and gold in Argentina. It produces about 404000 ounces of palladium and 120000 ounces of platinum annually. By-products include copper gold nickel and silver. The company has 22 million ounces of proved and probable PGM reserves.

	Annual Growth	12/10	12/11	12/12	12/13	12/14
Sales ($ mil.)	14.1%	555.9	906.0	800.2	1,039.5	943.6
Net income ($ mil.)	8.7%	50.4	144.3	55.0	(270.2)	70.3
Market value ($ mil.)	(8.8%)	2,570.2	1,259.2	1,538.5	1,485.5	1,774.4
Employees	4.6%	1,354	1,567	1,664	1,773	1,619

STOCK BUILDING SUPPLY LLC

8020 Arco Corporate Dr.	CEO: Jeff REA
Raleigh NC 27617	CFO: James F Major Jr
Phone: 919-431-1000	HR: –
Fax: 919-431-1700	FYE: July 31
Web: www.stockbuildingsupply.com	Type: Joint Venture

Stock Building Supply (SBS) has crafted itself into a leading supplier of lumber and building materials to home builders and contractors. SBS operates about 100 building supply stores (down from 200 prior to a stint in bankruptcy) in about a dozen states and Washington DC. Products include lumber plywood sheetrock tools and trusses. It also operates commercial flooring and roofing services. Founded in 1922 by B.B. Benson to sell boards and plaster base it is owned by Los Angeles-based private equity firm The Gores Group. The building supplies retailer emerged from Chapter 11 bankruptcy protection in mid-2009 and is anxiously awaiting the rebound of the US housing market.

STOCK YARDS BANCORP INC NMS: SYBT

1040 East Main Street	CEO: David P. Heintzman
Louisville, KY 40206	CFO: Nancy B. Davis
Phone: 502 582-2571	HR: –
Fax: –	FYE: December 31
	Type: Public

Stock Yards Bancorp is the holding company of Stock Yards Bank & Trust which operates about 35 branches primarily in and around Louisville Kentucky but also in Indianapolis and Cincinnati. Founded in 1904 the bank targets individuals and regional business customers offering standard retail services such as checking and savings accounts credit cards certificates of deposit and IRAs. Trust services are also available; brokerage and credit card services are offered through agreements with other banks. Real estate mortgages account for about 60% of the bank's loan portfolio which also includes commercial (27%) construction and consumer loans.

	Annual Growth	12/10	12/11	12/12	12/13	12/14
Assets ($ mil.)	7.7%	1,902.9	2,053.1	2,148.3	2,389.3	2,563.9
Net income ($ mil.)	11.0%	23.0	23.6	25.8	27.2	34.8
Market value ($ mil.)	8.0%	362.0	302.7	330.6	470.7	491.6
Employees	2.5%	475	480	495	519	524

STONE ENERGY CORP. NYS: SGY

625 E. Kaliste Saloom Road	CEO: David H. Welch
Lafayette, LA 70508	CFO: Kenneth H. Beer
Phone: 337 237-0410	HR: –
Fax: 337 521-9880	FYE: December 31
Web: www.stoneenergy.com	Type: Public

You can't squeeze blood from a stone but as Stone Energy knows you can squeeze energy. Stone Energy acquires and exploits mature oil and natural gas properties that have high potential. The company which for 2011 reported estimated proved reserves of 602 billion cu. ft. of natural gas equivalent has about 50 producing properties in the Gulf of Mexico. It has sold the bulk of its Rocky Mountain oil and gas properties in order to focus its energy on targeting reserves and production in the deep shelf and deep water areas of the Gulf of Mexico the Gulf Coast and in Appalachia. In 2012 the company had 1.2 million gross acres of undeveloped properties of which about 90000 are in the Marcellus Shale play in Appalachia.

	Annual Growth	12/10	12/11	12/12	12/13	12/14
Sales ($ mil.)	5.0%	654.3	864.6	951.5	974.2	795.5
Net income ($ mil.)	–	96.4	194.3	149.4	117.6	(189.5)
Market value ($ mil.)	(6.7%)	1,223.0	1,447.4	1,125.9	1,897.9	926.2
Employees	3.8%	331	352	386	409	384

STONEGATE MORTGAGE CORP NYS: SGM

9190 Priority Way West Drive, Suite 300	CEO: Richard A. Kraemer
Indianapolis, IN 46240	CFO: Robert B. Eastep
Phone: 317 663-5100	HR: –
Fax: –	FYE: December 31
Web: www.stonegatemtg.com	Type: Public

Stonegate Mortgage is opening doors for homeowners to finance their dream homes. The mortgage company originates acquires sells and services residential mortgage loans. It also owns a warehouse lender mortgage financing company NattyMac. Stonegate Mortgage's servicing portfolio contains more than 40000 million loans that total $7.5 billion in unpaid principal balances. The company is licensed in 45 states (excluding the West) and Washington DC. It serves customers from more than 25 retail branches in a dozen states and works with more than 950 mortgage brokers. The company went public in 2013 raising $115 million which it will use to make investments and spend on general corporate purposes.

	Annual Growth	12/10	12/11	12/12	12/13	12/14
Sales ($ mil.)	–	0.0	26.0	95.5	157.9	185.6
Net income ($ mil.)	–	0.0	2.3	17.1	22.6	(30.7)
Market value ($ mil.)	–	0.0	–	–	426.2	308.3
Employees	40.9%	–	–	652	1,219	1,294

STONEMOR PARTNERS L P NYS: STON

311 Veterans Highway, Suite B	CEO: Lawrence Miller
Levittown, PA 19056	CFO: Sean P McGrath
Phone: 215 826-2800	HR: –
Fax: –	FYE: December 31
Web: www.stonemor.com	Type: Public

StoneMor Partners can show you some of the best locations for an extended stay locations where you may even want to reside permanently. The company operates more than 275 cemeteries and about 90 funeral homes in more than 25 states primarily along the East Coast but also in Puerto Rico. It also owns most of its properties. StoneMor sells burial lots lawn and mausoleum crypts cremation niches and perpetual care. It offers burial vaults caskets grave markers and bases and memorials. The company has grown since its formation in 2004 when it took over more than 120 properties previously owned by CFSI (then named Cornerstone Family Services) a significant shareholder.

	Annual Growth	12/10	12/11	12/12	12/13	12/14
Sales ($ mil.)	9.9%	197.3	228.4	242.6	246.6	288.1
Net income ($ mil.)	–	(1.4)	(9.7)	(3.0)	(19.0)	(10.8)
Market value ($ mil.)	(3.8%)	877.6	684.8	608.3	745.3	752.6
Employees	(20.9%)	2,571	2,958	3,027	3,017	1,009

STONERIDGE INC.

NYS: SRI

9400 East Market Street
Warren, OH 44484
Phone: 330 856-2443
Fax: –
Web: www.stoneridge.com

CEO: John C. Corey
CFO: George E. Strickler
HR: Alisa A Nagle
FYE: December 31
Type: Public

Stoneridge makes sure your vehicle's electrical system can send power to all the places where it needs to go — whether it's an automobile medium- or heavy-duty truck or agricultural/off-highway vehicle. The company's electronics unit makes electronic control units instrumentation displays and driver information and electrical distribution systems. Its control devices segment products monitor and measure specific functions of a vehicle using switches control actuation devices and sensors. Stonebridge also has a PST segment that makes vehicle security alarms and tracking devices.

	Annual Growth	12/10	12/11	12/12	12/13	12/14
Sales ($ mil.)	1.0%	635.2	765.4	938.5	947.8	660.6
Net income ($ mil.)	–	10.8	49.4	5.4	15.1	(47.1)
Market value ($ mil.)	(5.0%)	445.6	237.9	144.5	359.8	362.9
Employees	(11.3%)	6,800	10,800	8,700	9,300	4,200

STORR OFFICE ENVIRONMENTS INC

10800 WORLD TRADE BLVD
RALEIGH, NC 276174200
Phone: 919 313-3700
Fax: –
Web: www.storr.com

CEO: –
CFO: Terry McGuire
HR: –
FYE: December 31
Type: Private

Change the way you store your employees with the help of Storr Office Environments. The firm is an office furniture supplier to companies in the southeastern US carrying more than 200 products under brands such as Peter Pepper and Steelcase. It offers the usual desks and seating as well as interior architecture floor coverings and office technology. Storr also provides professional space planning facility management and installation services for its clients. The company operates a warehouse showroom and distribution center in North Carolina and has offices in Florida. Storr was founded in 1914.

	Annual Growth	12/03	12/04	12/05	12/06	12/07
Sales ($ mil.)	19.6%	–	29.7	34.9	42.5	50.9
Net income ($ mil.)	36.5%	–	–	1.5	2.1	2.8
Market value ($ mil.)	–	–	–	–	–	–
Employees	–	–	–	–	–	200

STR HOLDINGS INC.

NBB: STRI

10 Water Street
Enfield, CT 06082
Phone: 860 272-4235
Fax: –
Web: www.strsolar.com

CEO: Robert S. Yorgensen
CFO: Thomas D. Vitro
HR: Carol Dyjak
FYE: December 31
Type: Public

Think of it as plastic wrap for solar cells. STR Holdings operates primarily through subsidiary Specialized Technology Resources which manufactures solar encapsulants — polymer films that hold solar modules (panels) together and protect semiconductors from exposure to the elements. The company pioneered the development of ethylene vinyl acetate- (EVA-) based encapsulants for the US Department of Energy in the 1970s. Its PhotoCap-brand encapsulants are sold worldwide to photovoltaic (PV) module makers.The company has production plants in Malaysia and Spain each with an annual production capacity of 3000 MW.

	Annual Growth	12/10	12/11	12/12	12/13	12/14
Sales ($ mil.)	(43.0%)	371.8	232.4	95.3	31.9	39.3
Net income ($ mil.)	–	49.3	(1.3)	(207.3)	(18.3)	(23.6)
Market value ($ mil.)	(48.8%)	361.5	148.7	45.5	28.4	24.8
Employees	(43.8%)	2,200	500	375	200	220

STRACK AND VAN TIL SUPER MARKET INC

9632 CLINE AVE
HIGHLAND, IN 463223094
Phone: 219-924-7588
Fax: –
Web: www.strackandvantil.com

CEO: –
CFO: Keith Bruxvoort
HR: –
FYE: August 01
Type: Private

One of Chicagoland's leading grocery chains Strack & Van Til operates more than 35 supermarkets in and around Chicago and northern Indiana. Stores operate under the banners of Strack & Van Til Town & Country Food Market and Ultra Foods. The regional grocery chain offers fresh and packaged foods and has delicatessen and bakery divisions in each of its stores. Its websites offer weekly circulars and coupons as well as feature recipes cooking videos meal planners and food-related articles. The company is owned by Chicago-based grocery distributor Central Grocers which also operates supermarkets under the Berkot's and Key Market banners.

	Annual Growth	08/06	08/07	08/08	08/09	08/10
Sales ($ mil.)	(3.4%)	–	–	–	995.1	961.6
Net income ($ mil.)	16.1%	–	–	–	13.8	16.0
Market value ($ mil.)	–	–	–	–	–	–
Employees	–	–	–	–	–	2,300

STRATA SKIN SCIENCES INC

NAS: SSKN

100 Lakeside Drive, Suite 100
Horsham, PA 19044
Phone: 215 619-3200
Fax: –

CEO: Michael R. (Mike) Stewart
CFO: Christina L. Allgeier
HR: –
FYE: December 31
Type: Public

Strata Skin Sciences (formerly MELA Sciences) can detect whether that mole is a sign of a more serious medical condition — melanoma. The company's lead product is a hand-held imaging device called MelaFind which captures images of suspicious skin lesions compares them to other malignant and benign lesions stored in a database and provides information about whether they should be biopsied. Strata Skin Sciences markets the point-of-care product to primary care physicians dermatologists and plastic surgeons in the US. Pipeline products include XTRAC (which produces ultraviolet light to treat psoriasis and vitiligo) and VTRAC (a system utilizing a precise wavelength excimer lamp to treat vitiligo patches).

	Annual Growth	12/10	12/11	12/12	12/13	12/14
Sales ($ mil.)	81.3%	–	–	0.3	0.5	0.9
Net income ($ mil.)	–	(19.9)	(20.4)	(22.7)	(25.9)	(14.1)
Market value ($ mil.)	(22.7%)	20.2	22.3	10.8	3.9	7.2
Employees	(7.8%)	47	51	74	50	34

STRATEGIC HOTELS & RESORTS, INC.

NYS: BEE

200 West Madison Street, Suite 1700
Chicago, IL 60606-3415
Phone: 312 658-5000
Fax: 312 658-5799
Web: www.strategichotels.com

CEO: –
CFO: –
HR: –
FYE: December 31
Type: Public

Hotels & Resorts (SHR) is a busy BEE when it comes to hospitality. The self-administered and self-managed real estate investment trust (REIT) which is traded under the symbol BEE owns or has interests in more than 15 upscale and luxury hotels (some 8200 rooms) in the US. It also has interests in two Marriott hotels in Europe and owns the Four Seasons Punta Mita resort in Mexico. In addition SHR owns land for development which is adjacent to existing hotel resorts. Affiliated brands include Four Seasons Hyatt InterContinental and Marriott. Focused on the asset management aspect of its properties SHR does not manage its hotels directly. It relies on third-party management companies to handle day-to-day operations.

	Annual Growth	12/09	12/10	12/11	12/12	12/13
Sales ($ mil.)	5.6%	723.8	686.3	763.8	808.3	900.0
Net income ($ mil.)	–	(243.9)	(231.1)	(5.2)	(55.3)	11.0
Market value ($ mil.)	50.1%	382.4	1,087.5	1,104.0	1,315.7	1,942.8
Employees	(3.0%)	43	43	42	39	38

STRATOSPHERE CORPORATION

2000 Las Vegas Blvd. South
Las Vegas NV 89104
Phone: 702-380-7777
Fax: 702-383-4734
Web: www.stratospherehotel.com

CEO: –
CFO: –
HR: –
FYE: December 31
Type: Private

Even if you crap out in its casino Stratosphere Corporation hopes you'll still enjoy the view. The company's Stratosphere Tower Casino & Hotel in Las Vegas is the tallest free-standing observation tower in the US at 1149 ft. It features a revolving restaurant observation decks and a roller coaster that wraps around the top. More grounded is the firm's hotel with some 2400 rooms an 80000-sq.-ft. casino a Broadway showroom and a retail center with shops and fast-food outlets. Located slightly off the beaten path the hotel offers a nightly evening shuttle service to the center of the Las Vegas Strip. Whitehall Street Real Estate Fund an affiliate of The Goldman Sachs Group owns the Stratosphere.

STRATTEC SECURITY CORP.

NMS: STRT

3333 West Good Hope Road
Milwaukee, WI 53209
Phone: 414 247-3333
Fax: 414 247-3329
Web: www.strattec.com

CEO: Frank J Krejci
CFO: Patrick J Hansen
HR: –
FYE: June 28
Type: Public

STRATTEC SECURITY has your car under lock and key. The company designs and makes mechanical security locks electro-mechanical locks and keys and ignition lock housings primarily for global automakers. It also makes access control products including door handles latches power sliding doors and power lift gates. Chrysler Ford and General Motors account for the majority of STRATTEC's sales. In addition to cars and light trucks its products are used in the heavy truck and recreational vehicle markets as well as in precision die castings. With facilities in the US and Mexico STRATTEC delivers products mainly in North America but also abroad in Asia Europe and South America.

	Annual Growth	07/11	07/12*	06/13	06/14	06/15
Sales ($ mil.)	12.1%	260.9	279.2	298.2	348.4	411.5
Net income ($ mil.)	39.7%	5.4	8.8	9.4	16.4	20.7
Market value ($ mil.)	35.0%	74.5	74.2	131.8	233.0	247.8
Employees	7.6%	2,556	2,507	2,670	3,276	3,420

*Fiscal year change

STRATUS PROPERTIES INC.

NMS: STRS

212 Lavaca Street, Suite 300
Austin, TX 78701
Phone: 512 478-5788
Fax: –
Web: www.stratusproperties.com

CEO: William H Armstrong III
CFO: Erin D Pickens
HR: –
FYE: December 31
Type: Public

Stratus Properties is on cloud nine over real estate investments. The company develops owns and manages commercial residential and mixed-use properties primarily in Texas primarily in the Austin area where it has some 2500 acres of developed and undeveloped land. The firm's principal developments include Austin's Barton Creek subdivision and portions of the metro area's Circle C Ranch. In partnership with other developers Stratus is developing two high-profile mixed-use projects in the city. It also owns a couple of undeveloped acres in San Antonio and has completed the development and sale of a project in Plano.

	Annual Growth	12/10	12/11	12/12	12/13	12/14
Sales ($ mil.)	79.2%	9.1	137.0	115.7	127.7	94.1
Net income ($ mil.)	–	(15.3)	(10.4)	(1.6)	2.6	13.4
Market value ($ mil.)	11.0%	73.1	62.8	68.4	137.6	110.9
Employees	34.0%	35	110	102	110	113

STRATUS TECHNOLOGIES INTERNATIONAL INC.

111 Powdermill Rd.
Maynard MA 01754-3409
Phone: 978-461-7000
Fax: 978-461-3670
Web: www.stratus.com

CEO: David C Laurello
CFO: Robert C Laufer
HR: –
FYE: December 31
Type: Private

There's nothing cloudy about this company's goal: continuous availability. Stratus Technologies makes fault-tolerant servers that can be configured with its proprietary Avance High Availability software. Its systems are sold under the ftServer V Series and Continuum brands. Stratus offers product support and managed service programs covering continuous availability and recovery. The company's products are used by banks and other financial services providers; it also serves the government health care and manufacturing markets among others. Customers have included Pitney Bowes KapStone Paper and Packaging and Isuzu Motors. More than half of Stratus' sales come from outside the US.

STRAYER EDUCATION, INC.

NMS: STRA

2303 Dulles Station Boulevard
Herndon, VA 20171
Phone: 703 561-1600
Fax: –
Web: www.strayereducation.com

CEO: Karl McDonnell
CFO: Daniel W. Jackson
HR: Lily Garcia
FYE: December 31
Type: Public

Students who wander from traditional learning paths can turn to Strayer Education. The company's Strayer University offers some 90 different degree diploma and certificate programs from about 80 campuses in about 15 states and Washington DC. The university which was founded in 1892 serves some 43000 students most of whom are working adults seeking degrees in such fields as business administration computer networking and information systems. Strayer Education offers internet-based classes in synchronous (real-time) and asynchronous formats through Strayer University Online. Strayer Education also offers an executive MBA online through its Jack Welsh Management Institute (acquired in 2011).

	Annual Growth	12/10	12/11	12/12	12/13	12/14
Sales ($ mil.)	(8.5%)	636.7	627.4	562.0	503.6	446.0
Net income ($ mil.)	(22.9%)	131.3	106.0	65.9	16.4	46.4
Market value ($ mil.)	(16.4%)	1,659.7	1,059.7	612.4	375.8	809.9
Employees	(9.5%)	2,291	2,282	2,152	1,602	1,534

STREAM GLOBAL SERVICES INC.

NYSE AMEX: SGS

Wellesley Office Park 20 William St. Ste. 310
Wellesley MA 02481
Phone: 781-304-1800
Fax: 781-304-1701
Web: www.stream.com

CEO: Kathryn V Marinello
CFO: Michael Henricks
HR: –
FYE: December 31
Type: Private

This company can handle a torrent of customer service calls. Stream Global Services is a leading provider of business process outsourcing (BPO) services such as customer care and technical support. The company maintains about 50 call centers in more than 20 countries from which it works with its customers' customers over the telephone via e-mail and through online chat sessions in 35 different languages. In addition to customer service Stream offers sales support and order processing. After several years as a public company Stream Global Services went private in 2012.

STREAMLINE HEALTH SOLUTIONS INC

NAS: STRM

1230 Peachtree Street, N.E., Suite 600
Atlanta, GA 30309
Phone: 404 920-2396
Fax: –
Web: www.streamlinehealth.net

CEO: Robert E Watson
CFO: Nicholas A Meeks
HR: –
FYE: January 31
Type: Public

Streamline Health Solutions (formerly LanVision Systems) helps health care providers streamline business processes. The software developer and service provider offers medical records workflow and document management software that consolidates information from existing media (paper disk X-ray film photographs video and audio) into a single database. Products include accesANYware which captures and manages medical documents; a multimedia system for accessing patient records; and hosted medical records management tools. The company also offers application hosting project management and disaster recovery services.

	Annual Growth	01/11	01/12	01/13	01/14	01/15
Sales ($ mil.)	11.9%	17.6	17.1	23.8	28.5	27.6
Net income ($ mil.)	–	(3.0)	0.0	(5.4)	(11.7)	(12.0)
Market value ($ mil.)	21.3%	34.5	30.6	100.7	112.1	74.6
Employees	7.5%	92	76	117	108	123

STREAMSERVE INC.

3 Van de Graaff Dr.
Burlington MA 01803-5188
Phone: 781-863-1510
Fax: 781-229-6622
Web: www.streamserve.com

CEO: Dennis Ladd
CFO: –
HR: –
FYE: December 31
Type: Subsidiary

StreamServe makes software to manage the flow of business communications. Its enterprise document presentment (EDP) software is used by companies to manage documents for customers partners and suppliers. The software automates the creation and presentment of documents in any format and channel. Customers can present a range of interactive electronic and print documents generated by enterprise applications. The company has alliances with major application vendors systems integrators and strategic application providers including IBM SAP and Oracle. In 2010 Open Text acquired StreamServe in a transaction valued at about $71 million.

STRIKE LLC

5170 WESTWAY PARK BLVD
HOUSTON, TX 77041
Phone: 281-362-9708
Fax: –
Web: www.strikeconstruction.com

CEO: –
CFO: –
HR: –
FYE: December 31
Type: Private

Strike Construction aims to strike it rich by constructing installing and testing pipelines for the oil and gas industry. The family-owned contracting firm builds and repairs onshore pipelines and meter stations for customers the likes of Kinder Morgan SandRidge Energy and TransCanada. It also performs state-mandated integrity tests to ensure pipeline safety and offers remediation services in case a pipe should require repairs. Subsidiary Pickett Systems designs and installs flow measurement systems for onshore and offshore use; it also offers fabrication services. Strike Construction is licensed to work in about 30 states but the bulk of its business is concentrated in oil-rich Texas and along the Gulf Coast.

	Annual Growth	12/06	12/07	12/08	12/10	12/12
Sales ($ mil.)	56.5%	–	58.1	114.2	192.4	545.2
Net income ($ mil.)	57.1%	–	–	7.7	7.9	47.1
Market value ($ mil.)	–	–	–	–	–	–
Employees	–	–	–	–	–	1,000

STRIKEFORCE TECHNOLOGIES INC

NBB: SFOR

1090 King Georges Post Road, Suite 603
Edison, NJ 08837
Phone: 732 661-9641
Fax: –
Web: www.strikeforcetech.com

CEO: Mark L Kay
CFO: Phillip E Blocker
HR: –
FYE: December 31
Type: Public

StrikeForce Technologies doesn't want your identity getting away from you. The company develops software that guards consumers and businesses against identity theft encompassing areas such as identity management remote access and biometric layering. StrikeForce's products guard against phishing attempts keylogging malware and spyware. StrikeForce also offers professional services such as consulting implementation maintenance and support. Its customers come from a range of industries including financial services health care and manufacturing.

	Annual Growth	12/10	12/11	12/12	12/13	12/14
Sales ($ mil.)	5.1%	0.3	0.4	0.8	0.4	0.3
Net income ($ mil.)	–	(2.9)	(5.5)	(1.2)	(2.4)	(3.4)
Market value ($ mil.)	–	0.0	0.0	0.0	0.0	0.0
Employees	(3.8%)	7	7	7	7	6

STRONGWELL CORPORATION

400 COMMONWEALTH AVE
BRISTOL, VA 242013800
Phone: 276-645-8000
Fax: –
Web: www.strongwell.com

CEO: G David Oakley Jr
CFO: –
HR: –
FYE: December 31
Type: Private

Strong wells and a myriad of other products can be made by Strongwell a top pultruder of fiber-reinforced polymer composites. The company's primary division is its pultrusion manufacturing operation (comprised of 65 pultrusion machines) which makes structural shapes fabricates fiberglass structures and systems and builds pultrusion equipment and tooling. It primarily has expertise in making grating panels fencing products and stair treads. It serves such markets as energy automotive construction marine and leisure. Strongwell has three pultrusion manufacturing facilities in Virginia and Minnesota. Through these locations the company maintains about 647000 sq. ft. of total manufacturing space.

	Annual Growth	12/07	12/08	12/09	12/10	12/11
Sales ($ mil.)	–	–	–	(205.0)	70.5	96.4
Net income ($ mil.)	15365.5%	–	–	0.0	1.0	2.6
Market value ($ mil.)	–	–	–	–	–	–
Employees	–	–	–	–	–	500

STRUCTURAL GROUP INC.

7455 New Ridge Rd. Ste. T
Hanover MD 21076
Phone: 410-850-7000
Fax: 410-850-4111
Web: www.structural.net

CEO: Peter Emmons
CFO: Dan Fangio
HR: –
FYE: December 31
Type: Private

Structural Group (STRUCTURAL) has overseen more facelifts than a plastic surgeon. It consists of five companies that serve industrial commercial and public sectors. Specialty contractors Structural Preservation Systems and SPS Infrastructure offer structural repair strengthening waterproofing and geotechnical construction on everything from bridges to historic buildings. VSL provides heavy lifting and post-tensioning services (a method of reinforcing concrete with high-strength steel bars). STRUCTURAL's Pullman Power arm repairs chimneys stacks and silos. UK-based Electro Tech provides corrosion control and water intrusion services worldwide. The group was founded in 1976 by owner and CEO Peter Emmons.

STRYKER CORP.

NYS: SYK

2825 Airview Boulevard
Kalamazoo, MI 49002
Phone: 269-385-2600
Fax: 269-385-1062
Web: www.stryker.com

CEO: Kevin A. Lobo
CFO: William R. Jellison
HR: –
FYE: December 31
Type: Public

Is this an operating room or Dad's workshop? Stryker's surgical products include such instruments as drills saws and even cement mixers. The company's Orthepaedic segment makes artificial hip and knee joints trauma implants bone cement and other orthopedic supplies. The MedSurg equipment segment houses microsurgery instruments endoscopy equipment and communications and patient handling tools. Stryker's neurotechnology and spine unit provides rods screws and artificial discs for spinal surgeries as well as coils and stents for cerebral vascular procedures. The firm's products are marketed globally to hospitals doctors and other health care facilities via direct sales personnel and distributors.

	Annual Growth	12/11	12/12	12/13	12/14	12/15
Sales ($ mil.)	4.6%	8,307.0	8,657.0	9,021.0	9,675.0	9,946.0
Net income ($ mil.)	1.7%	1,345.0	1,298.0	1,006.0	515.0	1,439.0
Market value ($ mil.)	16.9%	18,541.8	20,447.9	28,027.2	35,185.1	34,666.6
Employees	6.2%	21,241	22,010	25,000	26,000	27,000

STUART C. IRBY COMPANY

815 S. State St.
Jackson MS 39201-5908
Phone: 601-960-7304
Fax: 601-960-7575
Web: www.irby.com

CEO: Michael Wigton
CFO: John Honigfort
HR: –
FYE: October 30
Type: Subsidiary

Stuart C. Irby has dished up electrical products Southern style since 1926. The company distributes some 45000 electrical products to electrical utilities industrial customers and commercial builders from locations in about 20 states throughout the US. It has around 56 branches and serves 650 electric utilities. Utility products include grounding equipment meters transformers anchors conductors and safety equipment; commercial and industrial products include drives conduits controllers transformers I IVAC equipment lighting products and wiring; residential products include lighting ceiling fans intercom systems and door chimes. Sonepar USA acquired the company in 2005 from the Irby family.

STUART-DEAN CO. INC.

450 FASHION AVE STE 3800
NEW YORK, NY 101233801
Phone: 212-273-6900
Fax: –
Web: www.stuartdean.com

CEO: –
CFO: Robert T. (Bob) Cook
HR: Karishma Israni
FYE: December 31
Type: Private

The Stuart Dean Company provides restoration refinishing conservation and maintenance services for architectural metal stone and woodwork in residential institutional and commercial buildings. Projects include curtain wall restorations bronze statue preservation church pew refinishing and marble restorations. The company serves a variety of customers including homeowners corporations and building industry professionals such as property managers and maintenance engineers. Its diverse group of clients have included AT&T Hyatt Hotels and Resorts The Kennedy Center and Stanford University.

	Annual Growth	12/09	12/10	12/11	12/12	12/13
Sales ($ mil.)	5.1%	–	54.3	55.7	58.2	63.0
Net income ($ mil.)	(31.3%)	–	–	0.7	1.0	0.3
Market value ($ mil.)	–	–	–	–	–	–
Employees	–	–	–	–	–	450

STUDLEY INC.

399 Park Ave. 11th Fl.
New York NY 10022
Phone: 212-326-1000
Fax: 212-326-1034
Web: www.studley.com

CEO: Mitchel S Steir
CFO: –
HR: –
FYE: December 31
Type: Private

Ready to settle down with someone who has only your interests in mind? Studley is a commercial real estate brokerage firm focusing solely on tenant representation. Its services include strategic planning financial analysis and transaction management. Studley clients typically lease office industrial and retail properties; the firm also has divisions that specialize in legal and higher-education tenants. Clients have included law firm Baker Botts American Trucking Associations and the American Red Cross. The company boasts about 20 offices throughout the US. International services are offered through a London office and European subsidiary AOS Studley. Julien Studley founded the company in 1954.

STULLER INC.

302 Rue Louis XIV
Lafayette LA 70508
Phone: 337-262-7700
Fax: 337-981-1655
Web: www.stuller.com

CEO: Matthew G Stuller
CFO: Linus J Cortez III
HR: –
FYE: December 31
Type: Private

Stuller makes and distributes fine jewelry including diamonds and bridal jewelry charms colored stones fabricated precious metals jewelry supplies and watch bands. The company serves more than 40000 accounts (mainly professional jewelers) throughout North America and abroad with some 200000 different items. The jewelry wholesaler offers just-in-time delivery service to its clients. Stuller's manufacturing and administrative facilities (located in Louisiana) measure almost 600000 sq. ft. Chairman Matthew Stuller founded the company in 1970.

STURDY MEMORIAL HOSPITAL INC.

211 PARK ST
ATTLEBORO, MA 027033137
Phone: 508-222-5200
Fax: –
Web: www.sturdymemorial.org

CEO: –
CFO: –
HR: Sue Darling
FYE: September 30
Type: Private

Sturdy Memorial Hospital has been a stalwart provider of health care to southeast Massachusetts and Rhode Island since 1913. In addition to comprehensive medical surgical and emergency care the hospital offers cardiac and pulmonary rehabilitation women's health services diagnostic imaging and a center devoted to treating multiple sclerosis patients. It also operates pain management cancer and wound care centers. In 2014 Sturdy Memorial admitted some 7000 patients facilitated around 700 births and had some 51000 emergency department visits. The not-for-profit hospital employs more than 150 physicians.

	Annual Growth	09/10	09/11	09/12	09/13	09/14
Sales ($ mil.)	1.2%	–	155.8	164.1	158.8	161.3
Net income ($ mil.)	(14.2%)	–	–	30.3	74.3	22.3
Market value ($ mil.)	–	–	–	–	–	–
Employees	–	–	–	–	–	1,300

STURGIS BANCORP INC

NBB: STBI

113-125 E. Chicago Road
Sturgis, MI 49091
Phone: 269 651-9345
Fax: –
Web: www.sturgisbank.com

CEO: –
CFO: Brian Hoggatt
HR: Emily Frohriep
FYE: December 31
Type: Public

Sturgis Bancorp is the holding company for Sturgis Bank & Trust which has about 10 branches in south-central Michigan. Founded in 1905 the bank offers checking and savings accounts CDs trust services and other standard banking fare. Real estate loans comprise the bulk of its lending activities: one-to four-family residential mortgages make up more than half of the company's loan portfolio. Subsidiary Oak Leaf Financial Services provides insurance and investment products and services from third-party provider Linsco/Private Ledger.

	Annual Growth	12/10	12/11	12/12	12/13	12/14
Assets ($ mil.)	(4.1%)	370.0	314.3	317.0	305.0	312.5
Net income ($ mil.)	–	(0.7)	0.5	1.9	1.6	1.9
Market value ($ mil.)	6.1%	14.5	12.4	13.7	16.8	18.4
Employees	–	–	–	–	–	–

STURM, RUGER & CO., INC.

NYS: RGR

Lacey Place
Southport, CT 06890
Phone: 203 259-7843
Fax: 203 256-3367
Web: www.ruger.com

CEO: Michael O. Fifer
CFO: Thomas A. Dineen
HR: –
FYE: December 31
Type: Public

Whether you like to shoot birdies or bogeys Sturm Ruger & Company can accommodate you. The company also called Ruger is one of the nation's biggest gun makers and produces all four categories of firearms: pistols revolvers rifles and shotguns. Models include hunting and target rifles single- and double-action revolvers muzzleloading guns and double-barreled shotguns. Its guns are sold by independent wholesale distributors to independent firearms retailers and chains including Academy Sports and Cabelas. Ruger also makes metal products — known as castings — for the commercial and military markets. Sturm Ruger & Company was founded in 1949 by William Ruger and Alexander Sturm.

	Annual Growth	12/10	12/11	12/12	12/13	12/14
Sales ($ mil.)	20.9%	255.2	328.8	491.8	688.3	544.5
Net income ($ mil.)	8.1%	28.3	40.0	70.6	111.3	38.6
Market value ($ mil.)	22.7%	286.5	626.9	850.7	1,369.5	648.9
Employees	15.6%	1,160	1,540	2,040	2,380	2,073

STV GROUP INCORPORATED

205 W. Welsh Dr.
Douglassville PA 19518-8713
Phone: 610-385-8200
Fax: 610-385-8500
Web: www.stvinc.com

CEO: Milo E Riverso
CFO: Thomas Butcher
HR: –
FYE: September 30
Type: Private

STV Group helps create the systems through which SUVs LRVs and 747s can travel. Its subsidiaries and partnerships provide architectural engineering environmental construction management interior design and planning services for infrastructure projects that include airports light-rail systems ports and railroads. STV Group's security division conducts threat assessments and mitigates safety strategies for facilities. Its STV Canada Consulting joint venture is developing the Ottawa Light Rail Transit Project. The group serves public and private clients worldwide but primarily in the US. The employee-owned STV Group was founded in 1912 and taken private in 2001.

SUB-ZERO INC.

4717 Hammersley Rd.
Madison WI 53711-2798
Phone: 608-271-2233
Fax: 608-270-3339
Web: www.subzero.com

CEO: Jim Bakke
CFO: Edward Murphy
HR: –
FYE: December 31
Type: Private

Sub-Zero has cornered the market on hot and cold. The company's purchase of Wolf Gourmet married Sub-Zero's built-in customized refrigerators freezers and wine storage systems with Wolf's ovens cooktops and ranges. The deal has enabled Sub-Zero to compete head-to-head with rival Viking Range. The company hides bulky refrigerators and freezers behind cabinetry with complementary hardware. The manufacturer's units are available in several configurations including over-and-under side-by-side and undercounter. Sub-Zero's US-made products are sold nationwide and internationally through a network of distributors. Founded by Westye Bakke in 1945 the company is still owned by the Bakke family.

SUBJEX CORPORATION

OTC: SBJX

3245 Hennepin Ave. South Ste. 1
Minneapolis MN 55408
Phone: 612-827-2203
Fax: 866-468-4988
Web: www.subjex.com

CEO: Andrew D Hyder
CFO: Sharon Rae Hyder
HR: –
FYE: December 31
Type: Public

Subjex is more than happy to change the subject even when it comes to business. The company was originally formed in 1999 as PageLab Network to develop Internet search engine technology but changed direction when it came up with an artificial intelligence-based program that can function as a virtual customer service representative "talking" with customers through a website interface. Subjex has since focused its efforts on developing software for individual investors that forecasts a variety of financial indexes such as the Dow Jones Industrial Average.

SUBURBAN HOSPITAL INC

8600 OLD GEORGETOWN RD
BETHESDA, MD 20814-1497
Phone: 301-896-3100
Fax: –
Web: www.suburbanhospital.org

CEO: Brian A Gragnolati
CFO: –
HR: Dale Fulton
FYE: June 30
Type: Private

Don't let the name fool you this hospital isn't just for big city expatriates. Suburban Hospital a member of the Johns Hopkins Medicine network is an acute-care medical-surgical hospital with about 235 beds that provides all major medical services except obstetrics to the residents of Montgomery County in Maryland. Specialized services include behavioral health cardiology cancer care home care and pediatrics. Founded in 1943 Suburban Hospital serves as the regional trauma center for the county and is equipped with a helipad. Other services include a center for sleep disorders 24-hour stroke team diagnostic pathology and radiology departments and a range of inpatient and outpatient programs.

	Annual Growth	06/08	06/09	06/10	06/11	06/12
Sales ($ mil.)	2.7%	–	243.9	240.8	256.4	263.9
Net income ($ mil.)	–	–	(5.9)	15.4	32.8	(2.5)
Market value ($ mil.)	–	–	–	–	–	–
Employees	–	–	–	–	–	1,550

SUBURBAN PROPANE PARTNERS L.P.
NYS: SPH

240 Route 10 West
Whippany, NJ 07981
Phone: 973 887-5300
Fax: –
Web: www.suburbanpropane.com

CEO: Michael A. Stivala
CFO: Michael A. Kuglin
HR: Barry Trowbridge
FYE: September 26
Type: Public

Ranch-style homes are heated and backyard barbecues fueled by Suburban Propane Partners a leading US retail propane marketer which competes with Energy Transfer Partners AmeriGas Ferrellgas and other propane providers. With more than 300 service centers in 30 states Suburban Propane serves some 608000 retail customers. It annually sells about 300 million gallons of propane and more than 37 million gallons of fuel oil and refined petroleum products to wholesale and large end-users. It also sells natural gas and electricity and installs HVAC systems. In a major expansion in 2012 the company acquired Inergy's propane assets for $1.8 billion.

	Annual Growth	09/11	09/12	09/13	09/14	09/15
Sales ($ mil.)	4.4%	1,190.6	1,063.5	1,703.6	1,938.3	1,417.0
Net income ($ mil.)	(7.4%)	115.0	1.9	78.8	94.5	84.4
Market value ($ mil.)	(7.8%)	2,809.2	2,503.6	2,804.4	2,706.9	2,034.4
Employees	11.2%	2,385	4,144	3,933	3,796	3,646

SUCAMPO PHARMACEUTICALS INC
NMS: SCMP

805 King Farm Boulevard, Suite 550
Rockville, MD 20850
Phone: 301 961-3400
Fax: –
Web: www.sucampo.com

CEO: Peter S. Greenleaf
CFO: Andrew Smith
HR: Max Donley
FYE: December 31
Type: Public

Sucampo Pharmaceuticals works to alleviate some of life's more ahem uncomfortable conditions. Sucampo works with a group of compounds derived from fatty acids called prostones; it uses prostones in the development of therapies for the treatment of age-related gastrointestinal respiratory vascular and central nervous system disorders. It has two FDA-approved products: AMITIZA which treats chronic constipation in adults and irritable bowel syndrome in adult women and Rescula for the treatment of glaucoma and ocular hypertension. Sucampo's pipeline has other candidates in pre-clinical and early stage clinical development to treat a range of conditions.

	Annual Growth	12/10	12/11	12/12	12/13	12/14
Sales ($ mil.)	16.9%	61.9	54.8	81.5	89.6	115.5
Net income ($ mil.)	–	(2.8)	(17.3)	4.8	6.4	13.1
Market value ($ mil.)	38.9%	171.3	197.6	218.6	419.3	636.9
Employees	(3.7%)	93	108	128	77	80

SUCCESSFACTORS INC.
NASDAQ: SFSF

1500 Fashion Island Blvd. Ste. 300
San Mateo CA 94404
Phone: 650-645-2000
Fax: 650-645-2099
Web: www.successfactors.com

CEO: –
CFO: Klein Christian
HR: –
FYE: December 31
Type: Public

SuccessFactors has a recipe for business success. The SAP subsidiary provides software designed to help align business strategies boost employee productivity and manage development and performance. Its Business Execution Software provides everyone from FORTUNE 500 companies to small businesses with a Software-as-a-Service (SaaS) platform that automates goal planning progress tracking and performance reviews. The company targets customers in markets ranging from financial services (Wells Fargo) and health care (Baylor Health Care System) to education (Kaplan) retail (LensCrafters) and technology (EMC). About 80% of sales comes from customers in the US. SAP acquired the company in 2012.

SUCCESSORIES LLC

2520 Diehl Rd.
Aurora IL 60502
Phone: 630-820-7200
Fax: 630-820-3599
Web: www.successories.com

CEO: –
CFO: Neil Eisenband
HR: –
FYE: January 31
Type: Private

At a time when workplace cynicism is in vogue Successories is the anti-Dilbert. The company makes personal motivation and self-improvement items including awards books coffee mugs computer and desk accessories framed desk and wall decor greeting cards and pens. Products produced by Successories are sold through the millions of catalogs it mails each year its Web site and a handful of retail stores in Florida Indiana North Carolina and Texas. Successories was founded in 1985 by Arnold (Mac) Anderson. It published its first catalog in 1988 went public in 1990 and was taken private in 2003. TWS Partnership acquired the company in June 2009.

SUFFOLK BANCORP
NYS: SCNB

4 West Second Street, P.O.Box 9000
Riverhead, NY 11901
Phone: 631 208-2400
Fax: 631 727-3214
Web: www.scnb.com

CEO: Howard C. Bluver
CFO: Brian K. Finneran
HR: –
FYE: December 31
Type: Public

Suffice it to say that Suffolk Bancorp serves the banking needs of folks on Long Island. The holding company owns Suffolk County National Bank which serves Suffolk County New York through about 30 branches. Targeting individuals and small to midsized businesses the bank offers standard services such as checking savings and money market accounts and trust and asset management. It also provides insurance and investment products including IRAs mutual funds annuities bonds and brokerage services. Commercial mortgages account for nearly half of the company's loan portfolio; business loans make up another 20%.

	Annual Growth	12/10	12/11	12/12	12/13	12/14
Assets ($ mil.)	4.0%	1,618.2	1,484.2	1,622.5	1,699.8	1,895.3
Net income ($ mil.)	0.5%	15.0	(0.1)	(1.7)	12.7	15.3
Market value ($ mil.)	(2.1%)	288.0	125.9	152.9	242.8	265.0
Employees	(5.3%)	414	414	373	350	333

SUFFOLK CONSTRUCTION COMPANY INC.

65 ALLERTON ST
BOSTON, MA 021192923
Phone: 617-445-3500
Fax: –
Web: www.suffolkconstruction.com

CEO: John F. Fish
CFO: Michael (Mike) Azarela
HR: –
FYE: August 31
Type: Private

Suffolk Construction Company provides construction services from top to bottom. The company kicks off the building process with pre-construction services and follows through with design/build general contracting and construction management. Suffolk Construction builds for both the public and private organizations in the science and technology health care education government and commercial sectors operating in the Northeast Mid-Atlantic Southeast and West Coast regions of the US. Founded in 1982 the privately-held firm is owned by president and CEO John Fish whose family has been in construction for four generations.

	Annual Growth	08/10	08/11	08/12	08/13	08/14
Sales ($ mil.)	10.9%	–	1,290.1	1,349.9	1,825.0	1,761.1
Net income ($ mil.)	–	–	–	0.0	0.0	0.0
Market value ($ mil.)	–	–	–	–	–	–
Employees	–	–	–	–	–	1,150

SUFFOLK COUNTY WATER AUTHORITY INC

4060 SUNRISE HWY
OAKDALE, NY 117691005
Phone: 631-563-0255
Fax: –
Web: www.scwa.com

CEO: Jeffrey W Szabo
CFO: Larry B Kulick
HR: –
FYE: May 31
Type: Private

Sufficient to say Suffolk County Water Authority makes sure that there is potable water across Long Island in addition to the seawater that surrounds it. The utility provides water services to about 1.2 million people in New York's Suffolk County on the eastern end of Long Island. The water authority's system (the largest water system in the nation operating entirely with groundwater) includes more than 5500 miles of mains. The authority also runs the largest groundwater testing facility in the US. Suffolk County Water Authority is a public benefit corporation of the state of New York.

	Annual Growth	05/04	05/05	05/06	05/07	05/08
Sales ($ mil.)	7.5%	–	–	–	130.2	140.0
Net income ($ mil.)	55.6%	–	–	–	9.7	15.2
Market value ($ mil.)	–	–	–	–	–	–
Employees	–	–	–	–	–	570

SUFFOLK UNIVERSITY

8 ASHBURTON PL
BOSTON, MA 021082770
Phone: 617-573-8000
Fax: –
Web: www.law.suffolk.edu

CEO: –
CFO: –
HR: Carol Powers
FYE: June 30
Type: Private

Suffolk University provides a well-rounded education around the Athens of America and abroad. From its main campus in Boston and its satellite and branch campuses across Massachusetts as well as through study abroad programs the university provides undergraduate and graduate degrees in more than 70 areas of study through the College of Arts and Sciences Sawyer Business School and Suffolk Law School. It also runs about 25 institutes and research centers. More than 9000 students attend the private university which has a 12:1 student-to-faculty ratio and offers courses taught by about 900 faculty members. The university was founded in 1906 as the Suffolk School of Law.

	Annual Growth	06/09	06/10	06/11	06/13	06/14
Sales ($ mil.)	(4.5%)	–	282.7	298.3	236.8	235.1
Net income ($ mil.)	87.0%	–	–	5.4	28.6	35.4
Market value ($ mil.)	–	–	–	–	–	–
Employees	–	–	–	–	–	800

SUGAR CANE GROWERS COOPERATIVE OF FLORIDA

1500 W. Sugar House Rd.
Belle Glade FL 33430
Phone: 561-996-5556
Fax: 561-996-4780
Web: www.scgc.org

CEO: –
CFO: Brian R Lohmann
HR: –
FYE: December 31
Type: Private - Cooperativ

How sweet it is. The Sugar Cane Growers Cooperative of Florida (SCGC) is a 54-member sugar farmers' cooperative that offers its members help with farms administration and provides agricultural and planting advice as well as harvesting processing and marketing operations for their more than 70000 acres of sugar cane. The cooperative's member/growers produce more than 350000 tons of raw cane sugar every year. SCGC is a joint-owner of American Sugar Refining (along with Florida Crystals) a top New York refiner that owns Domino Foods producer of Domino branded sugar products. The joint venture grew exponentially in late 2010 following the purchase of Tate & Lyle's European sugar-refining business.

SUGAR FOODS CORPORATION

950 3rd Ave.
New York NY 10022
Phone: 212-753-6900
Fax: 212-753-6988
Web: www.sugarfoods.com

CEO: Marty Wilson
CFO: Jack Vivinetto
HR: –
FYE: December 31
Type: Private

The sweet spot for this company is at your favorite restaurant. Sugar Foods owns the marketing and foodservice distribution rights to Cumberland Packing's products which include Sweet 'n Low Sugar in the Raw and Stevia in the Raw. The company also carries Blue Diamond Almonds N'Joy non-dairy creamer and a line of snack foods croutons breadcrumbs stuffing mixes and dried salad dressing mixes in its product portfolio. Sugar Foods' products are available mainly to hotels restaurants and institutional foodservice operators throughout the country. The company also offers custom private-label and contract packaging services.

SULLIVAN & CROMWELL LLP

125 Broad St.
New York NY 10004-2498
Phone: 212-558-4000
Fax: 212-558-3588
Web: www.sullcrom.com

CEO: –
CFO: Robert Howard
HR: –
FYE: December 31
Type: Private - Partnershi

Sullivan & Cromwell is a law firm with a long and storied history. Founded in 1879 by Algernon Sullivan and William Cromwell the firm was on hand for the foundation of both General Electric in 1882 and United States Steel in 1901. Today Sullivan & Cromwell has about 800 lawyers in four US and eight international offices. It focuses on advising companies on mergers and acquisitions and on corporate law for industrial commercial and financial clients more than half of which are located abroad. Sullivan & Cromwell's clients include industrial and commercial companies financial services firms private funds governments educational and charitable institutions and individuals estates and trusts.

SUMMA HEALTH SYSTEM

95 ARCH ST STE G50
AKRON, OH 443041477
Phone: 330-375-3000
Fax: –
Web: www.summahealth.org

CEO: Thomas Malone
CFO: Brian Derrick
HR: –
FYE: December 31
Type: Private

Acute care hospitals plus a network of outpatient and primary care clinics plus a health care plan yields the sum of Summa Health System. The not-for-profit system serves the residents of the greater Akron Ohio area through five acute care hospitals and a whole slew of other health care sites. It also has an affiliation and management agreement with the nearby Robinson Memorial Hospital. Together its hospitals are home to more than 2000 beds. In addition to general medical and surgical care Summa's key services include cardiac stroke behavioral health cancer care emergency services and women's health.

	Annual Growth	12/05	12/06	12/07	12/08	12/09
Sales ($ mil.)	(40.4%)	–	797.1	940.8	1,264.1	168.6
Net income ($ mil.)	(69.9%)	–	–	71.1	(75.1)	6.5
Market value ($ mil.)	–	–	–	–	–	–
Employees	–	–	–	–	–	7,406

SUMMER INFANT INC
NAS: SUMR

1275 Park East Drive
Woonsocket, RI 02895
Phone: 401 671-6550
Fax: –
Web: www.summerinfant.com

CEO: Robert Stebenne
CFO: William E Mote Jr
HR: –
FYE: January 03
Type: Public

Summer Infant makes products for infants and children that can be used in any season. Through its operating subsidiaries Summer Infant develops and markets health and safety and wellness products for children from birth to 3 years old mostly under the Summer Infant and Born Free brand names. Some of its products include booster seats audio and video monitors bed rails safety gates bedding and durable bath items. Most of its products are manufactured in Asia (primarily China) and Israel. The company earns the majority of its revenue from the North American market selling through retailers such as Toys "R" Us Target Wal-Mart and Amazon.com. In Europe customers include Tesco Argos and Mothercare.

	Annual Growth	12/10	12/11	12/12	12/13*	01/15
Sales ($ mil.)	1.1%	194.5	238.2	247.2	208.2	205.4
Net income ($ mil.)	–	6.6	3.8	(65.7)	(2.8)	(0.2)
Market value ($ mil.)	(15.1%)	137.5	127.7	31.6	32.8	60.6
Employees	(1.4%)	218	247	237	211	203

*Fiscal year change

SUMMIT BANCSHARES INC.
OTC: SMAL

2969 Broadway
Oakland CA 94611
Phone: 510-839-8800
Fax: 510-839-8853
Web: www.summitbanking.com

CEO: Shirley Nelson
CFO: Kikuo Nakahara
HR: –
FYE: December 31
Type: Public

Summit Bancshares wants your business to operate at peak performance. Holding company Summit Bancshares does business through its primary subsidiary Summit Bank which operates four branch offices in the East Bay communities of Emeryville Oakland and Walnut Creek California. The bank targets professionals entrepreneurs and executives and their businesses offering them standard business and personal checking and savings accounts as well as commercial loans and online banking. It also offers courier service for its busy business-owner customers. Summit Bancshares was formed in 1981.

SUMMIT CORPORATION OF AMERICA

1430 Waterbury Rd.
Thomaston CT 06787
Phone: 860-283-4391
Fax: 860-283-4010
Web: www.scact.com

CEO: –
CFO: –
HR: Leeza Day
FYE: September 30
Type: Private

Summit Corporation of America is at the peak of its game. The electroplating company offers a number of services including continuous coil stock plating wire plating and continuous stampings plating. Summit Corporation also electroplates metal ribbon tape wire and individual manufactured metal parts such as pins springs washers cans and chemically etched materials. Its major customers include component manufacturers and other companies in the aerospace automotive battery computer defense marine metal distribution semiconductor and telecommunications industries. Summit Corporation offers prototypes and contract manufacturing as well as research and development and testing services.

SUMMIT ELECTRIC SUPPLY CO. INC

2900 STANFORD DR NE
ALBUQUERQUE, NM 871071814
Phone: 505-346-2900
Fax: –
Web: www.summit.com

CEO: Victor R. Jury
CFO: Thomas Klemp
HR: –
FYE: December 31
Type: Private

SUMMIT continues its ascent within the electronics distribution sector. SUMMIT Electric Supply distributes goods from manufacturers such as Dialight Eaton Fluke and Thomas & Betts. Products include cable conduits switches fuses lamps light fixtures instruments and safety equipment. The company offers in-house marine cable braiding for offshore oil and gas customers. SUMMIT also sells to electrical contractors government agencies construction firms and public utilities. It has nearly 25 branches located in New Mexico Arizona Louisiana Oklahoma and Texas and a service center in Dubai.

	Annual Growth	12/09	12/10	12/11	12/12	12/13
Sales ($ mil.)	10.4%	–	301.6	358.5	384.7	406.0
Net income ($ mil.)	29.8%	–	–	7.5	10.1	12.7
Market value ($ mil.)	–	–	–	–	–	–
Employees	–	–	–	–	–	497

SUMMIT ENERGY SERVICES INC.

10350 Ormsby Park Place Ste. 400
Louisville KY 40223
Phone: 502-429-3800
Fax: 502-753-2248
Web: www.summitenergy.com

CEO: James B Headlee
CFO: –
HR: –
FYE: December 31
Type: Private

To sum it up: Summit Energy Services is a major provider of energy management and procurement services for industrial and commercial companies and operates in 56 countries. A consolidator in a fragmented industry the company's offerings include market intelligence reporting need and competitive supply analysis contract negotiation utility bill auditing risk advisory planning and energy efficiency projects. Summit Energy Services has more than 650 industrial institutional and governmental clients. In 2011 the company agreed to be acquired by Schneider Electric for $268 million.

SUMMIT FINANCIAL GROUP INC
NAS: SMMF

300 North Main Street
Moorefield, WV 26836
Phone: 304 530-1000
Fax: –
Web: www.summitfgi.com

CEO: H Charles Maddy III
CFO: Robert S Tissue
HR: –
FYE: December 31
Type: Public

Summit Financial Group is at the peak of community banking in West Virginia and northern Virginia. The company owns Summit Community Bank which operates about 15 branches that offer standard retail banking fare such as deposit accounts loans and cash management services. Commercial real estate loans including land development and construction loans account for about 40% of Summit Financial Group's loan portfolio which also includes residential mortgages and a smaller percentage of business and consumer loans. The bank's Summit Insurance Services unit sells both commercial and personal coverage.

	Annual Growth	12/10	12/11	12/12	12/13	12/14
Assets ($ mil.)	(0.6%)	1,478.5	1,450.1	1,387.1	1,386.2	1,443.6
Net income ($ mil.)	–	(2.0)	4.1	5.7	8.1	11.4
Market value ($ mil.)	30.9%	33.6	22.7	40.2	82.3	98.8
Employees	(1.3%)	234	230	229	224	222

SUMMIT HOTEL PROPERTIES INC
NYS: INN

12600 Hill Country Boulevard, Suite R-100
Austin, TX 78738
Phone: 512 538-2300
Fax: –
Web: www.shpreit.com

CEO: Daniel P. Hansen
CFO: Greg A. Dowell
HR: –
FYE: December 31
Type: Public

From the southern states to the Mountain States Summit Hotel Properties has plenty of room for US travelers. Operating through its subsidiaries Summit Hotel is a self-advised real estate investment trust (REIT) that holds a portfolio of more than 80 midscale and upscale hotels in about 21 states including major markets in western and southern states like Arizona Colorado Idaho and Texas. Its hotels which comprise more than 7500 rooms operate primarily under brands owned by Marriott International as well as Hilton Hyatt and ICH. Formed in 2010 Summit Hotel went public via a 2011 IPO.

	Annual Growth	02/11*	12/11	12/12	12/13	12/14
Sales ($ mil.)	202.3%	14.6	134.3	189.5	299.0	403.5
Net income ($ mil.)	–	(6.2)	(2.9)	(1.1)	5.9	20.9
Market value ($ mil.)	8.3%	844.3	813.3	818.4	775.3	1,071.7
Employees	29.4%	–	18	25	33	39

*Fiscal year change

SUMMIT PARTNERS L.P.

222 Berkeley St 18th Fl.
Boston MA 02116
Phone: 617-824-1000
Fax: 617-824-1100
Web: www.summitpartners.com

CEO: –
CFO: –
HR: –
FYE: December 31
Type: Private

Summit Partners' dough rises a little later rather than earlier. The firm funds later-stage companies preferring those that are profitable and growing. It invests in a range of industries including business and financial services energy education health care communications media industrial and consumer products software and semiconductors. Summit Partners' private equity investments range from $30 million to more than $500 million per transaction; venture capital investments usually are between $5 million to $30 million. The company also provides mezzanine debt financing of up to $125 million. Its current portfolio includes stakes in more than 70 firms in North America Europe and Asia.

SUMMIT STATE BANK
NMS: SSBI

500 Bicentennial Way
Santa Rosa, CA 95403
Phone: 707 568-6000
Fax: –
Web: www.summitstatebank.com

CEO: Thomas Duryea
CFO: Dennis Kelly
HR: –
FYE: December 31
Type: Public

Contrary to its name Summit State Bank does business in both the hills and the valleys of Sonoma County in western California. Serving consumers and small to midsized businesses the bank offers standard deposit services like checking savings and retirement accounts as well as lending services such as real estate and commercial loans. Commercial real estate loans account for about 40% of the bank's loan portfolio while commercial and agriculture loans make up about 20%. Its other lending products include single-family and multifamily mortgages construction loans and consumer loans. Summit State Bank operates about half a dozen branches in Petaluma Rohnert Park Santa Rosa and Windsor.

	Annual Growth	12/10	12/11	12/12	12/13	12/14
Assets ($ mil.)	7.2%	347.9	387.6	444.9	454.1	459.7
Net income ($ mil.)	32.0%	1.8	2.2	3.4	4.3	5.5
Market value ($ mil.)	18.7%	33.4	24.8	32.3	50.2	66.3
Employees	(0.4%)	62	60	61	64	61

SUN BANCORP INC. (NJ)
NMS: SNBC

350 Fellowship Road, Suite 101
Mount Laurel, NJ 08054
Phone: 856 691-7700
Fax: –
Web: www.sunnb.com

CEO: Sidney R. (Sid) Brown
CFO: Thomas R. Brugger
HR: –
FYE: December 31
Type: Public

Sun Bancorp revolves around New Jersey. Boasting nearly $3 billion in total assets the holding company for Sun National Bank targets individuals and local businesses in central and southern New Jersey through some 60 branch locations. Sun National Bank offers standard retail services including savings accounts CDs and IRAs. The company's primary lending focus is originating industrial and commercial loans (including Small Business Administration (SBA) loans and lines of credit) which account for some 75% of its portfolio. Sun National Bank stopped providing residential mortgage and home equity loans in the second half of 2014. It offers investment services through Prosperis Financial Solutions.

	Annual Growth	12/10	12/11	12/12	12/13	12/14
Assets ($ mil.)	(5.6%)	3,417.5	3,183.9	3,224.0	3,087.6	2,715.3
Net income ($ mil.)	–	(185.4)	(67.5)	(50.5)	(9.9)	(29.8)
Market value ($ mil.)	43.0%	86.4	45.1	65.9	65.5	361.1
Employees	(7.5%)	696	713	750	690	509

SUN CAPITAL PARTNERS INC.

5200 Town Center Cir. Ste. 600
Boca Raton FL 33486
Phone: 561-394-0550
Fax: 561-394-0540
Web: www.suncappart.com

CEO: Marc Leder
CFO: –
HR: –
FYE: December 31
Type: Private

Sun Capital Partners can be a ray of sunshine for flourishing (or struggling) companies. The private investment firm specializes in leveraged buyouts and equity and debt investments. It also acquires interests in bankrupt or under-performing firms. After acquisition Sun Capital provides operating advice and additional capital to its portfolio companies. It targets firms with $50 million to $5 billion in annual sales. It does not rule out any industry when considering investments but is partial to specialty manufacturers retailers restaurants and apparel technology telecommunications and home furnishing companies. Sun Capital has some $8 billion of capital under management.

SUN CHEMICAL CORPORATION

35 Waterview Blvd.
Parsippany NJ 07054-1285
Phone: 973-404-6000
Fax: 973-404-6001
Web: www.sunchemical.com

CEO: Rudi Lenz
CFO: Gerry Brady
HR: –
FYE: December 31
Type: Subsidiary

Sun Chemical shines as the largest inks maker on the planet; it also makes all manner of coatings. In addition to inks and coatings for paper packaging metal and other products Sun Chemical manufactures printing plates for corrugated packaging. Its inks and coatings products are sold under the Sun Chemical Kohl & Madden US Ink and Coates brands. A part of Japan's DIC the US-based company operates more than 300 manufacturing sales and service locations in Europe Asia and the Americas.

SUN COAST RESOURCES INC.

6405 CAVALCADE ST BLDG 1
HOUSTON, TX 770264315
Phone: 713-844-9600
Fax: –
Web: www.suncoastresources.com

CEO: Kathy Lehne
CFO: Sheila Kahanek
HR: –
FYE: December 31
Type: Private

Breaking the glass ceiling with large containers of Texas tea woman-owned Sun Coast Resources buys refined oil and sells it to more than 10000 third-party customers such airlines and construction educational energy industrial and retail companies in about 40 states. The company has an extensive truck fleet (more than 1000 vehicles) and delivers gasoline and diesel fuels marine and aviation fuels and lubricants. It also provides oilfield transportation and services onsite and fleet fueling petroleum tanks and generator fueling services. In 2013 the Houston Chronicle ranked Sun Coast as the 8th largest private company based in Houston.

	Annual Growth	12/03	12/04	12/05	12/06	12/07
Sales ($ mil.)	15.1%	–	697.8	867.9	864.2	1,064.1
Net income ($ mil.)	(55.1%)	–	–	13.9	7.2	2.8
Market value ($ mil.)	–	–	–	–	–	–
Employees	–	–	–	–	–	1,649

SUN COMMUNITIES, INC.
NYS: SUI

27777 Franklin Rd., Suite 200
Southfield, MI 48034
Phone: 248 208-2500
Fax: –
Web: www.suncommunities.com

CEO: Gary A. Shiffman
CFO: Karen J Dearing
HR: –
FYE: December 31
Type: Public

Sun Communities helps residents in the Sunshine State and around the US. The self-managed real estate investment trust (REIT) owns develops and operates manufactured housing communities (trailer and recreation vehicle parks) in nearly 30 states. Its portfolio includes more than 200 properties with nearly 80000 developed manufactured home and RV sites. Its Sun Home Services unit sells new and used homes for placement on its properties the majority of which are in Michigan Florida Indiana Texas and Ohio. Sun Communities also acquires at a discount and resells mobile homes that have been repossessed by lenders in its communities.

	Annual Growth	12/10	12/11	12/12	12/13	12/14
Sales ($ mil.)	15.7%	263.1	289.2	339.6	415.2	471.7
Net income ($ mil.)	–	(3.5)	(0.5)	8.0	16.7	28.5
Market value ($ mil.)	16.1%	1,618.0	1,774.4	1,937.6	2,071.2	2,936.7
Employees	19.5%	747	775	915	1,236	1,525

SUN HYDRAULICS CORP.
NMS: SNHY

1500 West University Parkway
Sarasota, FL 34243
Phone: 941 362-1200
Fax: –
Web: www.sunhydraulics.com

CEO: Allen J. Carlson
CFO: Tricia L. Fulton
HR: –
FYE: December 27
Type: Public

It's not solar power that Sun Hydraulics delivers but fluid power. The company makes screw-in hydraulic cartridge valves and custom manifolds used to control speed force and motion in fluid power systems. Cartridge valves offer a general purpose floating design that is unique in pressure capacity reliability reduced size and installation. Sun Hydraulics' valves and manifolds are used in myriad industrial and mobile products including construction agricultural and utility equipment and to a lesser extent in machine tools and material handling equipment. The company operates through subsidiaries and distributors in the US UK Germany Korea China and India. The Americas represents 45% of sales.

	Annual Growth	01/11*	12/11	12/12	12/13	12/14
Sales ($ mil.)	14.7%	150.7	204.2	204.4	205.3	227.7
Net income ($ mil.)	26.9%	21.4	37.7	37.4	38.0	43.8
Market value ($ mil.)	1.6%	1,004.5	622.6	663.5	1,091.1	1,053.3
Employees	5.2%	618	717	903	684	719

*Fiscal year change

SUN ORCHARD FRUIT COMPANY INC.

2087 TRANSIT RD
BURT, NY 140289797
Phone: 716-778-8544
Fax: –
Web: www.sunorchardapples.com

CEO: –
CFO: –
HR: –
FYE: August 31
Type: Private

Sun Orchard Fruit-, doesn't grow any fruit. Instead it gets fruit where it needs to go. The company stores packages and delivers apples grown by New York farmers. It fresh-packs some 500000 cartons of apples harvested by 60 growers in central and western New York and ships them to food wholesalers and retailers around the globe. The company handles-, 17 of the the most popular Eastern varieties of eating apples including Gala Honeycrisp Jonagold and Empire. Founded in 1952 Sun Orchard Fruit is owned and operated by the Riessen family.

	Annual Growth	08/10	08/11	08/12	08/13	08/14
Sales ($ mil.)	10.8%	–	12.3	14.0	10.9	16.8
Net income ($ mil.)	330.3%	–	–	0.0	0.0	0.8
Market value ($ mil.)	–	–	–	–	–	–
Employees	–	–	–	–	–	54

SUN-MAID GROWERS OF CALIFORNIA

13525 S BETHEL AVE
KINGSBURG, CA 936319212
Phone: 559-897-6235
Fax: –
Web: www.sunmaid.com

CEO: Barry F Kriebel
CFO: Braden Bender
HR: –
FYE: July 31
Type: Private

The Sun-Maid's basket runneth over. Sun-Maid Growers is the producer of Sun-Maid Raisins. Packaged in the familiar red boxes with the smiling red-sunbonneted maid Lorraine Collett Petersen offering her basket laden with grapes the brand is seen in just about every food store in the US. In addition to offering every toddler's (and moms of toddlers) favorite little-red-boxed snack the grower-owned cooperative manufactures industrial and food service products and exports to more than 50 countries. The company's other dried fruits include pitted prunes currants apricots cranberries figs dates apples fruit bits and tropical fruit mixtures. Founded in 1912 the coop is owned by 750 family farmers.

	Annual Growth	07/10	07/11	07/12	07/13	07/14
Sales ($ mil.)	3.4%	–	352.4	360.9	360.7	389.2
Net income ($ mil.)	19.2%	–	–	8.3	15.6	11.9
Market value ($ mil.)	–	–	–	–	–	–
Employees	–	–	–	–	–	800

SUNAMERICA ANNUITY AND LIFE ASSURANCE COMPANY

21650 Oxnard St.
Woodland Hills CA 91367
Phone: 800-445-7862
Fax: 310-772-6000
Web: www.sunamerica.com/home.asp

CEO: Jay Wintrob
CFO: N Scott Gillis
HR: –
FYE: December 31
Type: Subsidiary

SunAmerica Annuity and Life Assurance will assure you that when you retire it won't. The company is one of insurance giant AIG's domestic life insurance and retirement products businesses. Along with its sister company VALIC it is one of the US's top issuers of variable annuities which are distributed through independent financial advisors brokerages and financial institutions. It also offers 401(k) products for small to medium-sized businesses. The company operates throughout the US; policies in New York are issued by affiliate First SunAmerica Life Insurance.

SUNAMERICA FINANCIAL GROUP INC.

1 SunAmerica Center Century City	CEO: Jay Wintrob
Los Angeles CA 90067-6022	CFO: –
Phone: 310-772-6000	HR: –
Fax: 310-772-6574	FYE: December 31
Web: www.safg.com	Type: Subsidiary

SunAmerica Financial Group represents the life and retirement services segment of insurance giant American International Group (AIG). Operating as AIG Life and Retirement its subsidiaries sell a variety of investment products including life policies (American General Life); fixed annuities (Western National Life Insurance); group retirement services for education health care and not-for-profit organizations (VALIC); and variable annuities (SunAmerica Annuity and Life Assurance). SagePoint Financial provides broker/dealer services. Other units include SunAmerica Asset Management (retail mutual funds) and AIG SunAmerica Retirement Markets.

SUNBELT BEVERAGE COMPANY LLC

60 E. 42nd St.	CEO: Charles Merinoff
New York NY 10165	CFO: Gene D Luciana
Phone: 212-699-7000	HR: –
Fax: 212-699-7099	FYE: December 31
Web: www.charmer-sunbelt.com	Type: Private

Sunbelt Beverage (doing business as The Charmer Sunbelt Group) is one of the biggest swigs in its industry. A leading US distributor of fine wines beer and spirits the company serves more than a dozen states (mostly along the East Coast) and the District of Columbia. It operates through 10 subsidiaries and eight joint ventures including Florida subsidiary Premier Beverage and Maryland subsidiary Bacchus Importers as well as joint ventures R & R Marketing (New Jersey) and Associated Distributors (Virginia). These entities link up suppliers with retailers in more than a dozen major markets. Aside from alcoholic beverages Charmer Sunbelt also offers non-alcoholic drinks such as bottled water.

SUNCOAST SCHOOLS FEDERAL CREDIT UNION

6801 E. Hillsborough Ave.	CEO: Tom R Dorety
Tampa FL 33680	CFO: –
Phone: 813-621-7511	HR: –
Fax: 813-621-8693	FYE: December 31
Web: www.suncoastfcu.org	Type: Private - Cooperativ

Suncoast Schools Federal Credit Union is Florida's largest credit union and one of the largest in the US based on assets. It serves public and private school employees municipal workers students and those working for a select group of more than 1000 employers (and their families) in about 15 western Florida counties. The credit union offers standard services such as checking and savings accounts residential mortgages credit cards and consumer loans in addition to insurance investment trust and real estate services. Founded in 1934 as Hillsborough County Teachers Credit Union the not-for-profit member-owned cooperative has about 50 locations (including a mobile branch) and some 500000 members.

SUNCOKE ENERGY INC

NYS: SXC

1011 Warrenville Road, Suite 600	CEO: Frederick A. (Fritz) Henderson
Lisle, IL 60532	CFO: Fay West
Phone: 630 824-1000	HR: Gary Yeaw
Fax: 630 824-1001	FYE: December 31
Web: www.suncoke.com	Type: Public

If you're looking for a new soda product look elsewhere; if you're looking to produce steel SunCoke Energy's products may be right up your alley. One of North America's largest coke producers SunCoke produces metallurgical coke (a coal-derived fuel used in steel production) for steel companies. Its owned and operated plants — located in Virginia Indiana Ohio Illinois in the US Vitória Brazil (operated only) and India— operate about 1240 coke ovens and can produce an aggregate 4.2 million tons of coke per year. Major customers include ArcelorMittal US Steel and AK Steel.

	Annual Growth	12/10	12/11	12/12	12/13	12/14
Sales ($ mil.)	2.6%	1,326.5	1,538.9	1,914.1	1,647.7	1,472.7
Net income ($ mil.)	–	139.2	60.6	98.8	25.0	(126.1)
Market value ($ mil.)	20.0%	–	742.3	1,033.2	1,511.7	1,281.7
Employees	8.5%	–	1,160	1,214	1,577	1,480

SUNCOKE ENERGY PARTNERS LP

NYS: SXCP

1011 Warrenville Road, Suite 600	CEO: Frederick A Henderson
Lisle, IL 60532	CFO: Fay West
Phone: 630 824-1000	HR: –
Fax: –	FYE: December 31
Web: www.sxcpartners.com	Type: Public

SunCoke Energy Partners is a master limited partnership formed by its parent and one of the largest coke producers in the Americas SunCoke Energy Inc. SunCoke Energy Partners was formed in 2012 for the purpose of owning a majority interest in SunCoke Energy's Ohio-based Haverhill and Middletown cokemaking facilities. Today the partnership owns a 65% interest in each of those facilities which make metallurgical coke a raw material used in steelmaking. Together they have 300 cokemaking ovens with a capacity of 1.7 million tons per year. The company's two main customers are AK Steel and ArcelorMittal USA. SunCoke Energy Partners went public in early 2013 with an offering worth $256.5 million.

	Annual Growth	12/10	12/11	12/12	12/13	12/14
Sales ($ mil.)	–	0.0	0.0		687.3	648.4
Net income ($ mil.)	–	0.0	0.0	(0.0)	62.1	56.0
Market value ($ mil.)	–	0.0	0.0	–	1,013.6	1,014.8
Employees	30.4%	–	–	–	431	562

SUNEDISON INC

NYS: SUNE

13736 Riverport Drive, Suite 180	CEO: Ahmad R. Chatila
Maryland Heights, MO 63043	CFO: Brian Wuebbels
Phone: 314 770-7300	HR: –
Fax: –	FYE: December 31
Web: www.sunedison.com	Type: Public

SunEdison (formerly MEMC Electronic Materials) turns sun into power. The company not only makes solar modules polysilicon and silicon wafers used in solar panels it also designs makes installs and maintains solar installations for individuals and corporate customers. The company has 2.4 gigawatts of electricity-producing panels installed and a pipeline of 5.1 ggawatts. It has also begun generating electricity from solar power and selling that electricity to utility customers. The sale of silicon wafers and solar panels are becoming less of the company's business as it focuses on solar power. SunEdison spun off 20% of its silicon wafer fabrication business and part of its solar business.

	Annual Growth	12/10	12/11	12/12	12/13	12/14
Sales ($ mil.)	2.6%	2,239.2	2,715.5	2,529.9	2,007.6	2,484.4
Net income ($ mil.)	–	34.4	(1,536.0)	(150.6)	(586.7)	(1,180.4)
Market value ($ mil.)	14.7%	3,063.8	1,072.1	873.4	3,550.9	5,308.7
Employees	2.9%	6,480	6,840	56,680	6,358	7,260

SUNESIS PHARMACEUTICALS INC

NAS: SNSS

395 Oyster Point Boulevard, Suite 400
South San Francisco, CA 94080
Phone: 650 266-3500
Fax: –
Web: www.sunesis.com

CEO: Daniel N Swisher
CFO: –
HR: Christine Day
FYE: December 31
Type: Public

Sunesis builds drugs in miniature first before it builds them in full scale. The biotech firm's method involves building small drug fragments then examining their protein-binding ability and potential for development. Once a fragment shows potential Sunesis then builds a larger therapeutic compound based upon its model. Its drug candidates target various forms of cancer. Its lead candidate Vosaroxin (SNS-595) is in clinical trials to evaluate its effect on ovarian cancer and acute myeloid leukemia. Other candidates are being studied for treatment of solid tumors and other forms of cancer both independently and through partnerships. Milestone payments from those partnerships are Sunesis' only revenue to date.

	Annual Growth	12/10	12/11	12/12	12/13	12/14
Sales ($ mil.)	262.8%	0.0	5.0	3.8	8.0	5.7
Net income ($ mil.)	–	(24.6)	(20.1)	(44.0)	(34.6)	(43.0)
Market value ($ mil.)	48.8%	34.4	77.3	277.6	313.3	168.6
Employees	9.6%	27	31	25	32	39

SUNFLOWER ELECTRIC POWER CORPORATION

301 W 13TH ST
HAYS, KS 676013087
Phone: 785-628-2845
Fax: –
Web: www.sunflower.net

CEO: –
CFO: H Davis Rooney
HR: –
FYE: December 31
Type: Private

Rural Kansans bloom under the light provided by Sunflower Electric Power an electricity generation and transmission cooperative. The utility has interests in six fossil-fueled generation facilities (600 MW of capacity) and operates a more-than-1150-mile transmission system with 76 substations. Sunflower Electric Power provides electricity to its owners six member distribution cooperatives which collectively have more than 51000 customers in western Kansas; it also indirectly serves a further 10000 meters as wholesale power suppliers to regional cities and towns.

	Annual Growth	12/06	12/07	12/08	12/09	12/10
Sales ($ mil.)	(61.5%)	–	–	1,440.7	195.2	213.8
Net income ($ mil.)	15493.7%	–	–	0.0	16.0	21.8
Market value ($ mil.)	–	–	–	–	–	–
Employees	–	–	–	–	–	215

SUNGARD AVAILABILITY SERVICES LP

680 E. Swedesford Rd.
Wayne PA 19087
Phone: 610-878-2644
Fax: 610-225-1132
Web: www.sungardas.com

CEO: Andrew A Stern
CFO: Bob Singer
HR: –
FYE: December 31
Type: Subsidiary

SunGard Availability Services wants to be every big company's virtual IT department. The company provides managed network hosting business continuity and related consulting services via data centers located throughout the US and Europe (primarily in the UK). Areas of specialty include online backup data co-location managed hosting and disaster recovery. SunGard Availability Services serves more than 9000 clients in a wide range of industries including energy financial services healthcare and manufacturing. Its customers include Reply! Inc. and First Citizens Bank. The company is a subsidiary of software and IT services provider SunGard Data Systems.

SUNGARD DATA SYSTEMS INC.

680 E. Swedesford Rd.
Wayne PA 19087-1586
Phone: 484-582-2000
Fax: 610-225-1120
Web: www.sungard.com

CEO: Russell P Fradin
CFO: Charles J Neral
HR: –
FYE: December 31
Type: Private

Nearly every top financial services company under the sun relies on this company's data systems. A majority of Nasdaq trades pass through SunGard's investment support systems which banks stock exchanges mutual funds insurance companies governments and others use for transaction processing asset management securities and commodities trading and investment accounting. This business is part of SunGard's Financial Systems business segment which serves the 25 largest global financial services firms. Its other primary segments Public Sector and Availability Services provide software and business continuity managed IT and professional services to datacentric businesses worldwide.

SUNGARD PUBLIC SECTOR INC.

1000 Business Center Dr.
Lake Mary FL 32746
Phone: 407-304-3235
Fax: 407-304-1005
Web: www.sungardps.com

CEO: –
CFO: Bruce E Langston
HR: –
FYE: December 31
Type: Subsidiary

Whether it's in your school your town your state or your favorite charity SunGard Public Sector thrives on bureaucracy. The company provides enterprise resource planning (ERP) and administrative software for public-sector organizations ranging from utility companies and schools to public safety departments and government agencies. Its applications include tools for state and local governments law enforcement agencies and utility companies. The company also offers consulting and other IT services. SunGard Public Sector a unit of financial services software maker SunGard Data Systems does business primarily in the US.

SUNKIST GROWERS INC.

14130 RIVERSIDE DR
SHERMAN OAKS, CA 914232392
Phone: 818-986-4800
Fax: –
Web: www.sunkist.com

CEO: Russell Hanlin II
CFO: Richard G French
HR: –
FYE: October 31
Type: Private

Sunkist Growers is one business that is least susceptible to an outbreak of scurvy among its employees. America's oldest continually operating citrus cooperative the company is owned by California and Arizona citrus growers who farm some 300000 acres of citrus trees. Sunkist offers traditional and organic fresh oranges lemons limes grapefruit and tangerines worldwide. The co-op which operates some 20 packing facilities also makes juice and cut fruit packaged in jars. Fruit that doesn't meet fresh market standards is turned into oils and peels for use in food products made by other manufacturers. Sunkist's customers include food retailers and manufacturers and foodservice providers worldwide.

	Annual Growth	12/08	12/09*	10/12	10/13	10/14
Sales ($ mil.)	–	–	0.0	1,003.9	1,046.8	1,234.4
Net income ($ mil.)	6.2%	–	–	6.0	33.5	6.8
Market value ($ mil.)	–	–	–	–	–	–
Employees	–	–	–	–	–	500

*Fiscal year change

SUNLINK HEALTH SYSTEMS INC

ASE: SSY

900 Circle 75 Parkway, Suite 1120
Atlanta, GA 30339
Phone: 770 933-7000
Fax: –
Web: www.sunlinkhealth.com

CEO: –
CFO: Mark J Stockslager
HR: Barbara Patrick
FYE: June 30
Type: Public

SunLink Health Systems is hoping to shine brightly in the health care business through the management of community hospitals. Through its subsidiaries the firm operates five community hospitals with a total of more than 280 beds in Alabama Georgia Mississippi and Missouri. Each hospital is the only acute care facility in its service area. The company also operates two nursing facilities that have a collective bed count of about 170 beds to serve the geographical areas surrounding the hospitals. SunLink also operates a home health agency and SunLink ScriptsRx a specialty pharmacy business.

	Annual Growth	06/11	06/12	06/13	06/14	06/15
Sales ($ mil.)	(15.6%)	181.2	146.7	108.2	105.4	91.8
Net income ($ mil.)	–	(10.7)	1.1	4.5	(0.5)	0.2
Market value ($ mil.)	(5.5%)	17.9	11.3	7.8	11.5	14.3
Employees	–	–	–	–	–	–

SUNOCO LOGISTICS PARTNERS L.P.

NYS: SXL

3807 West Chester Pike
Newtown Square, PA 19073
Phone: 866 248-4344
Fax: –
Web: www.sunocologistics.com

CEO: Michael J Hennigan
CFO: Peter J Gvazdauskas
HR: –
FYE: December 31
Type: Public

Sunoco Logistics Partners acquires owns and operates a large swath of midstream and downstream assets primarily in tandem with former parent and current affiliate Sunoco. This includes ownership of more than 7900 miles of crude oil refined product and oil gathering pipelines and minority interests in four refined product pipelines (Explorer Pipeline Wolverine Pipe Line West Shore Pipe Line and Yellowstone Pipe Line) as well as more than 40 terminals and other storage assets related to Sunoco's refining and marketing operations in the Midwest Gulf Coast and Eastern states. Sunoco Logistics Partners also purchases domestic crude and resells it to Sunoco's refining and marketing unit.

	Annual Growth	12/11*	10/12*	12/12	12/13	12/14
Sales ($ mil.)	18.3%	10,918.0	9,950.0	3,194.0	16,639.0	18,088.0
Net income ($ mil.)	(2.4%)	313.0	381.0	139.0	463.0	291.0
Market value ($ mil.)	2.0%	8,907.3	11,188.3	11,242.6	17,064.0	9,445.3
Employees	14.5%	1,500	–	1,700	2,000	2,250
						*Fiscal year change

SUNOCO LP

NYS: SUN

555 East Airtex Drive
Houston, TX 77073
Phone: 832 234-3600
Fax: –
Web: www.sunocolp.com

CEO: Rocky B Dewbre
CFO: Clare P McGrory
HR: Juan Flores
FYE: December 31
Type: Public

Sunoco LP (formerly Susser Petroleum Partners) pairs with its parent to proffer petroleum. It distributes gasoline and other petroleum products to its parent Susser Holdings Corp. (SHC) for use at SHC's more than 540 Stripes brand convenience stores across Texas. It also provides fuel to third parties in Texas Oklahoma New Mexico and Louisiana; total annual fuel deliveries total about 1.3 billion gallons. Sunoco LP's clients include convenience stores government entities corporate fleets and school districts. It also earns money by leasing real estate to retailers mostly its parent. SHC formed the company in 2012 to operate its wholesale fuel distribution business. Sunoco LP went public in September.

	Annual Growth	12/11	12/12	12/13*	08/14*	12/14
Sales ($ mil.)	(20.9%)	3,820.4	4,277.3	4,492.6	3,492.2	1,889.8
Net income ($ mil.)	49.3%	10.6	17.6	37.0	22.5	35.3
Market value ($ mil.)	40.6%	–	881.6	1,159.8	2,000.0	1,743.9
Employees	–	–	–	–	–	–
						*Fiscal year change

SUNOVION PHARMACEUTICALS INC.

84 Waterford Dr.
Marlborough MA 01752
Phone: 508-481-6700
Fax: 508-357-7499
Web: www.sunovion.com

CEO: Hiroshi Nomura
CFO: –
HR: –
FYE: December 31
Type: Subsidiary

Helping people breathe easy and sleep properly are the core of Sunovion. The company focuses its drug development efforts in two main therapeutic categories: respiratory and central nervous system (CNS) disorders. Among its marketed products are asthma drug Xopenex insomnia therapy Lunesta schizophrenia treatment Latuda and chronic obstructive pulmonary disease (COPD) treatment Brovana. Sunovion markets its products to primary care physicians and some specialists in the US. Sunovion is a subsidiary of Japanese firm Dainippon Sumitomo Pharma (DSP).

SUNPOWER CORP

NMS: SPWR

77 Rio Robles
San Jose, CA 95134
Phone: 408 240-5500
Fax: –
Web: www.sunpowercorp.com

CEO: Thomas H. (Tom) Werner
CFO: Charles D. (Chuck) Boynton
HR: –
FYE: December 28
Type: Public

SunPower is all about being a stellar provider of solar. The company makes solar panels and systems under the SunPower SunTile and PowerGuard brands among others. It sells these products to dealers distributors and system integrators for use by residential commercial government and utility customers around the world. SunPower generates more than 50% its sales from large-scale solar projects (solar farms for utility companies to offer alternative energy) and a third from solar products and projects for residential and small commercial customers. The company has offices across the globe; the Americas account for the majority of the company's sales. SunPower is majority owned by France's TOTAL SA.

	Annual Growth	01/11	01/12*	12/12	12/13	12/14
Sales ($ mil.)	10.9%	2,219.2	2,312.5	2,417.5	2,507.2	3,027.3
Net income ($ mil.)	11.2%	178.7	(603.9)	(352.0)	95.6	245.9
Market value ($ mil.)	27.1%	1,686.7	819.0	721.8	3,800.7	3,460.2
Employees	11.8%	5,150	5,220	5,020	6,320	7,188
						*Fiscal year change

SUNQUEST INFORMATION SYSTEMS INC.

250 S. Williams Blvd.
Tucson AZ 85711
Phone: 520-570-2000
Fax: 520-901-9449
Web: www.sunquestinfo.com

CEO: Richard Atkin
CFO: Kathy Jehle
HR: –
FYE: December 31
Type: Private

Sunquest Information Systems keeps lab work from getting lost in the paperwork shuffle. Founded in 1979 the company provides LIS (laboratory information system) software to more than 1700 hospitals and laboratories. Sunquest's systems integrate various applications containing medical records billing and financial information laboratory data and other lab-related information into a unified system. The company also offers systems for radiology and pharmacy departments. Many of the company's customers are US hospitals; however the company also serves customers in Europe and the Middle East. Sunquest was acquired by Roper Industries for about $1.4 billion in 2012.

SUNRISE MEDICAL INC.

7477 E. Dry Creek Pkwy.	CEO: Thomas Julius Rossnagel
Longmont CO 80503	CFO: –
Phone: 303-218-4600	HR: –
Fax: 303-218-4590	FYE: June 30
Web: www.sunrisemedical.com	Type: Private

Sunrise Medical wants its customers to greet the day on a roll. The company manufactures and supplies wheelchairs and wheelchair accessories and replacement parts. Its Quickie wheelchairs range from manual to motorized adult to child-sized and from everyday use to sports models for athletes. Its products are targeted for use in both institutional and home use. Sunrise Medical also makes Jay brand cushions and wheelchair backs. The company's A.R.T. division designs and manufactures custom configured seating and positioning equipment. Sunrise Medical markets its products in about 100 countries around the globe through an inside sales force and through distributors.

SUNSHINE SILVER MINES CORPORATION

370 17th Street Ste. 3800	CEO: Stephen Orr
Denver CO 80202	CFO: Roger Johnson
Phone: 303-784-5350	HR: –
Fax: 310-214-0075	FYE: December 31
Web: www.emmausmedical.com	Type: Private

Mining is a tight race and Sunshine Silver Mines intends to take home the silver metal. The precious metals exploration and development company is trying to become a major silver producer initially through two main projects: the Sunshine Mine in Idaho (a previously prolific producing mine) and Los Gatos in Mexico (a relatively new prospecting area). In total it owns or controls about 20 exploration properties in the US and Mexico. Formed in early 2011 after its predecessor converted from a limited liability company to a Delaware corporation Sunshine Silver Mines filed to go public mid-year in an IPO worth about $250 million.

SUNRISE SENIOR LIVING INC.

NYSE: SRZ

7900 Westpark Drive	CEO: Mark S Ordan
McLean VA 22102	CFO: Marc Richards
Phone: 703-273-7500	HR: –
Fax: 703-744-1601	FYE: December 31
Web: www.sunriseseniorliving.com/	Type: Public

From sunrise to sunset Sunrise Senior Living helps the elderly make the most of life. A top senior living services provider Sunrise operates some 300 assisted living communities with some 30000 units across the US and into Canada and the UK. Sunrise owns outright or has an interest in half of the facilities and manages the rest for third parties under long-term contracts. The company's communities offer a range of care for their residents; some provide opportunities for independent living while others offer special care for Alzheimer's patients or skilled nursing care. Sunrise is being acquired by Health Care REIT.

SUNSTONE HOTEL INVESTORS INC.

NYSE: SHO

120 Vantis Ste. 350	CEO: Ken Cruse
Aliso Viejo CA 92656	CFO: Jon D Kline
Phone: 949-330-4000	HR: –
Fax: 424-288-2900	FYE: December 31
Web: www.caa.com	Type: Public

Sunstone Hotel Investors shines brightly in the hospitality investment sector. The real estate investment trust (REIT) invests in develops and renovates mostly upscale and upper-upscale hotels in major markets around the US. The company owns more than 30 hotels with some 13000 rooms in more than a dozen states. Most of Sunstone Hotel Investors' properties are located in Southern California and have affiliations with such franchises as Hilton Worldwide Hyatt Marriott and Starwood. Sunstone's hotels are managed by third parties; a division of Interstate Hotels & Resorts operates about half of the properties.

SUNRUN INSTALLATION SERVICES INC.

775 FIERO LN STE 200	CEO: Paul J. Detering
SAN LUIS OBISPO, CA 934017904	CFO: Betsy Wallace
Phone: 805-528-9705	HR: –
Fax: –	FYE: December 31
Web: www.recsolar.com	Type: Private

REC Solar is helping its customers to say "So long!" to fossil fuel-buring power dependence. The company designs and installs solar electric systems for residential small commercial government and utilty customers in six states — Arizona California Colorado Hawaii New Jersey and Oregon. Its systems range from simple rooftop panel displays for residential customers to industrial solar electric systems for Costco. REC Solar uses solar panels manufactured by Kyocera Mitsubishi Sanyo and Sharp and components by Satcon SMA Solar Technology and Xantrex.

SUNSWEET GROWERS INC.

901 N WALTON AVE	CEO: Dane Lance
YUBA CITY, CA 959939370	CFO: –
Phone: 530-674-5010	HR: –
Fax: –	FYE: July 31
Web: www.sunsweet.com	Type: Private

Being all dried up is a good thing at Sunsweet Growers. The more than 400 member/grower-owned cooperative processes and markets dried fruit. Sunsweet produces one-third of the world's prunes (it processes more than 50000 tons of prunes each year). Its other fruit products include prune and other juices as well as dried apples apricots dates cranberries blueberries mangoes peaches pears pineapples and more. Sunsweet which has gotten into dietary supplement beverages supplies its products to retail food and foodservice outlets worldwide. Sunsweet produces some 40000 cases of dried fruit products every day. The co-op was founded in 1917 as the California Prune and Apricot Growers Association.

	Annual Growth	04/03	04/04	04/05	04/06*	12/08
Sales ($ mil.)	420.8%	–	–	–	5.7	155.8
Net income ($ mil.)	–	–	–	–	1.4	(3.4)
Market value ($ mil.)	–	–	–	–	–	–
Employees	–	–	–	–	–	350

*Fiscal year change

	Annual Growth	07/10	07/11	07/12	07/13	07/14
Sales ($ mil.)	2.1%	–	245.8	281.3	266.2	261.8
Net income ($ mil.)	12.9%	–	–	64.2	71.2	81.9
Market value ($ mil.)	–	–	–	–	–	–
Employees	–	–	–	–	–	700

SUNTRON CORPORATION

2401 W. Grandview Rd.
Phoenix AZ 85023
Phone: 602-789-6600
Fax: 602-789-6200
Web: www.suntroncorp.com

CEO: –
CFO: –
HR: –
FYE: December 31
Type: Private

Suntron offers a constellation of manufacturing services. The electronics manufacturing services provider assembles printed circuit boards cables harnesses and other products. Its services include design engineering testing and prototype creation. Suntron focuses on the aerospace and defense semiconductor capital equipment industrial instrumentation medical networking and telecommunications equipment markets. Customers have included Hart InterCivic ZeeVee and Northrop Grumman. The privately held company sells primarily to customers in the US.

SUPER 8 MOTELS INC.

1 Sylvan Way
Parsippany NJ 07054
Phone: 800-800-8000
Fax: 973-753-8137
Web: www.travelodge.com

CEO: Franz S Hanning
CFO: –
HR: –
FYE: December 31
Type: Subsidiary

This chain wants to make your night's stay super comfortable and inexpensive. Super 8 Motels is a leading franchiser of budget and economy hotels with more than 2000 locations throughout the US Canada and China. Its properties typically offer affordable lodging with limited amenities for families and frugal business travelers. Many locations have cable television and swimming pools while some of its motels offer complimentary breakfast service. Super 8 was founded in 1974 by South Dakota natives Dennis Brown and Ronald Rivett. The company began with one motel in Aberdeen South Dakota offering rooms for $8.88 per night. Super 8 is a subsidiary of Wyndham Worldwide Corporation.

SUNTRUST BANKS, INC.

NYS: STI

303 Peachtree Street, N.E.
Atlanta, GA 30308
Phone: 800 786-8787
Fax: –
Web: www.suntrust.com

CEO: William H. (Bill) Rogers
CFO: Aleem Gillani
HR: Kenneth J. (Ken) Carrig
FYE: December 31
Type: Public

Coca-Cola fast cars and SunTrust Banks — this Sun Belt company is southern to its core. Its flagship SunTrust Bank subsidiary operates about 1450 branches in about a dozen southeastern and mid-Atlantic states. With total assets of about $190 billion and total deposits of about $140 billion the bank offers standard retail and commercial services such as credit deposit and investment services. SunTrust also operates subsidiaries that offer mortgage wealth and investment management insurance investment banking equipment leasing and brokerage services. The official bank of Grand American Road Racing it was an underwriter for the IPO of icon Coca-Cola and was one of its largest shareholders.

	Annual Growth	12/10	12/11	12/12	12/13	12/14
Assets ($ mil.)	2.4%	172,874.0	176,859.0	173,442.0	175,335.0	190,328.0
Net income ($ mil.)	75.0%	189.0	647.0	1,958.0	1,344.0	1,774.0
Market value ($ mil.)	9.2%	15,479.2	9,284.4	14,870.7	19,308.3	21,978.2
Employees	(4.0%)	29,056	29,182	26,778	26,281	24,638

SUPER CENTER CONCEPTS INC.

15510 Carmenita Rd.
Santa Fe Springs CA 90670
Phone: 562-345-9000
Fax: +49-9342-806-150
Web: www.k-m.de

CEO: Mimi R Song
CFO: William Cote
HR: –
FYE: December 31
Type: Private

Super Center Concepts is big on superlatives as well as groceries. One of the largest independently-owned grocery supercenter chains in the Los Angeles metropolitan area the company operates about 40 outlets under the Superior Grocers banner. The regional grocery chain has continued to expand in spite of operating in the super competitive supercenter market where it competes with national chains including Wal-Mart and Costco Wholesale. The stores sell name brand and private label merchandise in the traditional grocery departments (produce meat bakery) and offer services such as check cashing and money orders. The first Superior Super Warehouse opened in Los Angeles in 1981.

SUNVALLEY SOLAR INC (NV)

NBB: SSOL

398 Lemon Creek Drive, Suite A
Walnut, CA 91789
Phone: 909 598-0618
Fax: –

CEO: Zhijian James Zhang
CFO: Mandy Chung
HR: –
FYE: December 31
Type: Public

Homes and businesses looking to go eco turn to companies like Sunvalley Solar. Sunvalley Solar offers solar power system design installation and maintenance services to owners builders and architecture firms in the residential commercial and government sectors primarily in California. The company also distributes solar equipment including solar panels inverters and related goods from such manufacturers as Canadian Solar and China Electric Equipment Group (CEEG). A portion of Sunvalley Solar's resources are spent on solar technology research and development. Founded in 2007 Sunvalley Solar was the first Chinese-American owned solar installation company in Southern California.

	Annual Growth	12/10	12/11	12/12	12/13	12/14
Sales ($ mil.)	(8.0%)	4.6	5.8	3.7	4.1	3.3
Net income ($ mil.)	–	(0.4)	(0.4)	(1.8)	0.8	(1.3)
Market value ($ mil.)	–	0.0	0.0	0.0	0.1	0.1
Employees	(13.9%)	20	20	20	11	11

SUPER MICRO COMPUTER INC

NMS: SMCI

980 Rock Avenue
San Jose, CA 95131
Phone: 408 503-8000
Fax: –
Web: www.supermicro.com

CEO: Charles Liang
CFO: Howard Hideshima
HR: Sara Liu
FYE: June 30
Type: Public

Super Micro Computer manufactures high-performance server products based on open standard components (including Intel AMD and NVIDIA processors). Its nearly 7000 offerings include motherboards and serverboards blade servers rackmounts GPU systems chassis and Ethernet switches and network adaptors. The company also sells a host of subsystems and accessories. Super Micro markets its products — primarily through distributors and resellers such as Ingram Micro and Arrow Electronics — to customers in some 100 countries; about 40% of its sales are generated outside the US.

	Annual Growth	06/11	06/12	06/13	06/14	06/15
Sales ($ mil.)	20.6%	942.6	1,013.9	1,162.6	1,467.2	1,991.2
Net income ($ mil.)	26.2%	40.2	29.9	21.3	54.2	101.9
Market value ($ mil.)	16.4%	763.1	752.2	504.6	1,198.5	1,402.9
Employees	46.3%	499	1,503	1,595	1,869	2,285

SUPERCONDUCTOR TECHNOLOGIES INC

NAS: SCON

9101 Wall Street, Suite 1300
Austin, TX 78754
Phone: 512 334-8900
Fax: –
Web: www.suptech.com

CEO: Jeffrey A Quiram
CFO: William J Buchanan
HR: –
FYE: December 31
Type: Public

Superconductor Technologies Inc. (STI) can cool even the most heated conversation. The company uses high-temperature superconducting (HTS) technology in its line of communications products which combine low-noise amplifiers and filters are designed to improve the quality of radio-frequency (RF) transmissions between cellular base stations and mobile devices in wireless networks. It also makes cryogenic cooling devices used to cool HTS materials. STI relies on government contracts to fund its R&D operations; on the commercial side the company serves such top wireless network operators as AT&T Verizon Wireless Sprint Nextel and T-Mobile.

	Annual Growth	12/10	12/11	12/12	12/13	12/14
Sales ($ mil.)	(47.9%)	8.5	3.5	3.5	1.7	0.6
Net income ($ mil.)	–	(12.0)	(13.4)	(10.9)	(12.2)	(8.3)
Market value ($ mil.)	16.2%	21.7	17.5	4.2	30.7	39.5
Employees	(13.1%)	79	38	36	36	45

SUPERIOR BULK LOGISTICS INC.

711 JORIE BLVD STE 101N
OAK BROOK, IL 605232285
Phone: 630-573-2555
Fax: –
Web: www.superiorbulklogistics.com

CEO: Len Fletcher
CFO: –
HR: –
FYE: December 31
Type: Private

Superior Bulk Logistics through subsidiaries Superior Carriers and Carry Transit hauls liquid and dry bulk cargo including both chemical and food-grade products. Overall the trucking units of Superior Bulk Logistics operate a fleet of some 875 tractors and 2000 trailers. The company's SuperFlo unit provides transloading services — the transfer of cargo between railcars and trucks. Superior Bulk Logistics' Sanicare Wash Systems unit cleans tank truck trailers and other bulk containers used for food products. Superior Bulk Logistics offers service between Mexico and the US and Canada through a partnership with Transpormex a division of Grupo Dexel.

	Annual Growth	12/04	12/05	12/06	12/07	12/09
Sales ($ mil.)	(25.6%)	–	–	457.7	235.0	188.2
Net income ($ mil.)	1546.7%	–	–	0.0	7.2	2.0
Market value ($ mil.)	–	–	–	–	–	–
Employees	–	–	–	–	–	1,160

SUPERIOR ENERGY SERVICES, INC.

NYS: SPN

1001 Louisiana Street, Suite 2900
Houston, TX 77002
Phone: 713 654-2200
Fax: –
Web: www.superiorenergy.com

CEO: David D. Dunlap
CFO: Robert S. Taylor
HR: –
FYE: December 31
Type: Public

Priding itself on its superior operations Superior Energy Services provides specialized oil field services services (including drilling completion and production-related activities) to oil and gas companies operating in the Gulf of Mexico the US mainland and further afield. It sells and rents oil and gas well drilling equipment and offers tools and services worldwide including in Canada the Middle East Trinidad and Tobago the UK Venezuela and West Africa. The company furnishes well access services to acquire data and perform remedial activities. It also makes rents and sells specialized drilling and spill containment gear.

	Annual Growth	12/10	12/11	12/12	12/13	12/14
Sales ($ mil.)	28.3%	1,681.6	2,070.2	4,568.1	4,611.8	4,556.6
Net income ($ mil.)	33.2%	81.8	142.6	365.9	(111.4)	257.8
Market value ($ mil.)	(12.9%)	5,238.3	4,257.7	3,102.0	3,983.8	3,016.6
Employees	25.9%	5,700	6,500	14,500	14,500	14,300

SUPERIOR GROUP INC.

One Tower Bridge 100 Front St. Ste. 525
West Conshohocken PA 19428
Phone: 610-397-2040
Fax: 610-397-2041
Web: www.superior-group.com

CEO: –
CFO: –
HR: –
FYE: December 31
Type: Private

Metal-centric holding company Superior Group makes and sells tubing products through its subsidiaries Fine Tubes (precision tubing) and Superior Tube (small metal tubing). Its Sharp unit provides contract packaging services for pharmaceutical manufacturers. Superior Group companies operate from facilities in the US and the UK where Fine Tubes is based. The company dates back to the mid-1930s when it was established to meet the growing need for industrial tubing. Superior later performed a critical role in supplying metal tubing for Allied aircraft in WWII. Superior Group is owned by the Warden family heirs of one of its founders.

SUPERIOR INDUSTRIES INTERNATIONAL, INC.

NYS: SUP

24800 Denso Drive, Suite 225
Southfield, MI 48033
Phone: 248 352-7300
Fax: 818 780-3500
Web: www.supind.com

CEO: Donald J. (Don) Stebbins
CFO: Kerry A. Shiba
HR: –
FYE: December 31
Type: Public

Superior Industries International is one of the world's largest makers of aluminum road wheels for passenger cars and light trucks. It sells roughly 80% of its wheels to OEMs General Motors Ford Motor and Chrysler for factory installation or as optional or standard items on some models. Other customers include BMW Nissan and Toyota. North America is its core market; sales to international OEMs supply assembly plants mainly in the US. Superior Industries operates five manufacturing facilities; nearly 65% of Superior Industries' wheels are made in Mexico. Remaining production is primarily in the US and to a small extent through an investment in India.

	Annual Growth	12/10	12/11	12/12	12/13	12/14
Sales ($ mil.)	0.9%	719.5	822.2	821.5	789.6	745.4
Net income ($ mil.)	(35.7%)	51.6	67.2	30.9	22.8	8.8
Market value ($ mil.)	(1.7%)	567.2	442.1	545.3	550.6	529.0
Employees	(3.8%)	3,500	3,800	3,900	3,700	3,000

SUPERIOR OIL COMPANY INC

1402 N CAPITOL AVE # 100
INDIANAPOLIS, IN 462022375
Phone: 574-264-0161
Fax: –
Web: www.superiorsolvents.com

CEO: Robert W Andersen
CFO: –
HR: Jay Baker
FYE: December 31
Type: Private

Despite the name Superior Oil actually distributes industrial products and provides chemical and waste services. Superior's solvents and chemicals division supplies manufacturers of paints and coatings pharmaceuticals fabricated metal products and adhesives. The fiberglass and resins unit sells to clients that make products ranging from parts for recreational vehicles to bathtubs and showers. Superior Oil also provides blending solvent reclamation and hazardous waste removal services. The company has nine stocking facilities and a fleet of trucks trailers and tankers. The company is owned by members of its management team.

	Annual Growth	12/09	12/10	12/11	12/12	12/13
Sales ($ mil.)	8.2%	–	167.5	191.7	202.6	212.0
Net income ($ mil.)	–	–	–	0.0	0.0	0.0
Market value ($ mil.)	–	–	–	–	–	–
Employees	–	–	–	–	–	250

SUPERIOR UNIFORM GROUP, INC.
NMS: SGC

10055 Seminole Boulevard
Seminole, FL 33772-2539
Phone: 727 397-9611
Fax: –
Web: www.superioruniform.com

CEO: Michael Benstock
CFO: Andrew D. Demott
HR: –
FYE: December 31
Type: Public

Superior Uniform Group works to keep its business all sewn up. The company makes work clothing and accessories for US employees in several industries. The apparel firm designs makes and markets uniforms for employees in the medical and health fields as well as those who work in hotels fast food joints and other restaurants and public safety industrial and commercial markets. About half of its products are sold under the Fashion Seal brand. The company also makes and distributes specialty labels such as Martin's Worklon Blade and UniVogue. Chairman Gerald Benstock and his son CEO Michael run company which began as Superior Surgical Mfg. Co. in 1920.

	Annual Growth	12/10	12/11	12/12	12/13	12/14
Sales ($ mil.)	16.7%	105.9	112.4	119.5	151.5	196.2
Net income ($ mil.)	31.4%	3.8	4.1	3.0	5.9	11.3
Market value ($ mil.)	27.8%	148.7	165.8	154.7	209.2	396.9
Employees	13.8%	630	647	690	973	1,055

SUPERNUS PHARMACEUTICALS INC
NMS: SUPN

1550 East Gude Drive
Rockville, MD 20850
Phone: 301 838-2500
Fax: –
Web: www.supernus.com

CEO: Jack Khattar
CFO: Gregory S. Patrick
HR: –
FYE: December 31
Type: Public

Supernus Pharmaceuticals wouldn't mind being a drug-maker superhero of sorts to epileptics. As a specialty pharmaceutical company Supernus develops treatments for epilepsy and other central nervous system disorders. Its lead candidate is a once-daily extended-release oral epilepsy drug developed from topiramate an existing immediate-release drug that is administered multiple times daily. Another candidate Epliga is a similar epilepsy treatment developed from another immediate-release drug oxcarbazepine. Both candidates are in late-stage development; other pipeline products include treatments for attention deficit hyperactivity disorder (ADHD). Supernus launched its initial public offering in 2012.

	Annual Growth	12/10	12/11	12/12	12/13	12/14
Sales ($ mil.)	482.5%	0.1	0.8	1.5	12.0	122.0
Net income ($ mil.)	–	(38.5)	53.8	(46.3)	(92.3)	19.9
Market value ($ mil.)	7.6%	–	–	308.1	324.0	356.7
Employees	63.3%	–	71	193	235	309

SUPERTEX, INC.
NMS: SUPX

1235 Bordeaux Drive
Sunnyvale, CA 94089
Phone: 408 222-8888
Fax: –
Web: www.supertex.com

CEO: –
CFO: –
HR: –
FYE: March 30
Type: Public

In many ways Supertex is a superhero for manufacturers needing integrated circuits (ICs). The company designs and manufactures high-voltage analog and mixed-signal integrated circuits (ICs) and transistors. Its ICs are used in a variety of applications including automated test equipment industrial electronics flat-panel TV displays medical ultrasound imaging equipment printers and telecommunications gear. Supertex touts its proprietary technologies as enabling it to combine low power consumption with high-voltage output on a single chip. About two-thirds of Supertex's sales come from customers outside the US more than half from Asia/Pacific.

	Annual Growth	03/09*	04/10	04/11*	03/12	03/13
Sales ($ mil.)	(6.2%)	78.8	66.7	83.2	65.5	61.0
Net income ($ mil.)	(23.7%)	12.5	5.1	12.3	4.7	4.2
Market value ($ mil.)	(2.4%)	281.6	319.2	254.1	208.3	256.0
Employees	(1.6%)	352	350	373	361	330

*Fiscal year change

SUPERVALU INC.
NYS: SVU

11840 Valley View Road
Eden Prairie, MN 55344
Phone: 952 828-4000
Fax: –
Web: www.supervalu.com

CEO: Mark Gross
CFO: Susan Grafton
HR: Michele A. Murphy
FYE: February 28
Type: Public

SUPERVALU understands the lure of a good deal. The company offers wholesale grocery distribution and logistics services to more than 2000 independent retailers and about 185 military commissaries in the US and overseas. It supplies brand-name and private-label goods in every price range. It also has more than 1330 owned and licensed Save-A-Lot grocery stores which hold the #1 spot (by revenue) in the extreme-value grocery category. SUPERVALU's retail operations include nearly 200 regional grocery stores under the Cub Foods Shoppers Food & Pharmacy Shop 'n Save Farm Fresh Hornbachers and Rainbow banners. All told the company covers about 40 states through nearly 20 distribution centers.

	Annual Growth	02/11	02/12	02/13	02/14	02/15
Sales ($ mil.)	(17.0%)	37,534.0	36,100.0	17,097.0	17,155.0	17,820.0
Net income ($ mil.)	–	(1,510.0)	(1,040.0)	(1,466.0)	182.0	192.0
Market value ($ mil.)	3.7%	2,223.0	1,729.0	1,001.0	1,586.0	2,568.8
Employees	(27.8%)	142,000	130,000	35,000	35,800	38,500

SUPPORT.COM, INC.
NMS: SPRT

900 Chesapeake Drive, 2nd Floor
Redwood City, CA 94063
Phone: 650 556-9440
Fax: –
Web: www.support.com

CEO: Elizabeth Cholawsky
CFO: Roop Lakkaraju
HR: –
FYE: December 31
Type: Public

Support.com wants to be a pillar of tech support. The company's cloud-based Nexus platform proactively identifies and repairs hardware and software problems reducing the need for technical support staffing. It also specializes in phone and Web support for a wide variety of technology issues related to computer security data recovery networking file management and software installation. Support.com serves consumers and small businesses with its offerings available through its website and through partners such as retailers broadband providers and anti-virus software providers. Nearly all sales come from customers in the Americas.

	Annual Growth	12/10	12/11	12/12	12/13	12/14
Sales ($ mil.)	17.1%	44.2	53.8	72.0	88.2	83.0
Net income ($ mil.)	–	(18.1)	(18.6)	(5.4)	10.4	(3.5)
Market value ($ mil.)	(24.5%)	351.6	122.1	226.3	205.7	114.5
Employees	27.7%	761	1,137	877	1,344	2,023

SUPREME INDUSTRIES, INC.
ASE: STS

2581 E. Kercher Road
Goshen, IN 46528
Phone: 574 642-3070
Fax: 574 642-3208
Web: www.supremeind.com

CEO: Mark D Weber
CFO: Matthew W Long
HR: –
FYE: December 27
Type: Public

Supreme Industries keeps businesses rolling on the road. The company builds and distributes specialized commercial truck bodies and buses such as armored trucks dry-freight and insulated cargo vans service vans shuttle buses and trolleys. Its custom-made options include cargo-handling devices lift gates refrigeration equipment and special doors and bumpers. Supreme Industries sells its lineup under the Kold King Iner-City Spartan StarTrans and other brand names. In addition to vehicle bodies which represent most sales the company makes Fuel Shark branded fiberglass wind deflectors. Supreme Industries' customers are truck distributors commercial dealers and end-users mainly in the US.

	Annual Growth	12/10	12/11	12/12	12/13	12/14
Sales ($ mil.)	1.7%	220.9	300.8	286.1	282.3	236.3
Net income ($ mil.)	–	(11.5)	0.7	11.8	6.4	6.9
Market value ($ mil.)	29.2%	45.1	41.1	56.3	91.7	125.7
Employees	(6.5%)	1,700	1,700	1,500	1,700	1,300

SUREWEST COMMUNICATIONS

NASDAQ: SURW

8150 Industrial Ave. Bldg. A
Roseville CA 95678
Phone: 916-786-6141
Fax: 916-786-7170
Web: www.surewest.com

CEO: Steven C Oldham
CFO: Steven L Childers
HR: Maria Helmericks
FYE: December 31
Type: Public

SureWest Communications wants to be a sure bet for communications in Northern California and beyond. The company's broadband unit provides Internet access TV data and voice service to about 110000 residential customers and about 8000 business clients in the Sacramento California and Kansas City area as well as network access and exchange services to other carriers. SureWest's telecommunications segment (which includes subsidiary SureWest Telephone) is the company's incumbent local and long-distance business. In 2012 the company was acquired by Consolidated Communications Holdings in a cash and stock transaction valued at around $324 million excluding debt.

SURGE COMPONENTS, INC.

NBB: SPRS

95 East Jefryn Boulevard
Deer Park, NY 11729
Phone: 631 595-1818
Fax: 631 595-1283
Web: www.surgecomponents.com

CEO: –
CFO: Steven Lubman
HR: –
FYE: November 30
Type: Public

Surge Components offers a wave of components for use in all sorts of electrical and electronic gear. The company distributes capacitors and other electronic components such as diodes semiconductor rectifiers and transistors. Most of its clients are manufacturers. The company's Challenge/Surge subsidiary (also known as Challenge Electronics) deals in electronic components as a broker and distributor. Surge represents Lelon Electronics a Taiwanese manufacturer of aluminum electrolytic capacitors in North America. Surge Components was established in 1981.

	Annual Growth	11/10	11/11	11/12	11/13	11/14
Sales ($ mil.)	5.9%	21.6	23.2	22.3	25.3	27.2
Net income ($ mil.)	(26.4%)	1.5	2.9	1.5	1.2	0.4
Market value ($ mil.)	6.4%	6.4	6.7	3.9	7.4	8.2
Employees	4.8%	24	24	27	33	29

SURGE GLOBAL ENERGY INC

NBB: SRGG

75-153 Merle Drive, Suite B
Palm Desert, CA 92211
Phone: 800 284-3898
Fax: 786 923-0963
Web: www.surgeglobalenergy.com

CEO: Clark Morton
CFO: E Jamie Schloss
HR: –
FYE: December 31
Type: Public

Surge Global Energy has the urge to acquire crude oil and natural gas properties in the US and Canada. The company's portfolio includes a well in Wyoming which it is drilling for commercial production of oil and gas and the Green Springs Prospect in Nevada which it plans to tap. Surge also invests in businesses engaged in alternative fuel technologies such as biodiesel developer 11 Good Energy. Other investments include minority stakes in two Alberta-based companies Andora Energy and North Peace Energy. Surge divested its interest in an Argentina project in 2008 to focus on its core North American operations and investments. Officers and board members as a group own about one-third of the company.

	Annual Growth	12/10	12/11	12/12	12/13	12/14
Sales ($ mil.)	–	0.0	0.0	–	0.0	0.0
Net income ($ mil.)	–	0.0	0.0	(1.7)	(0.9)	(0.9)
Market value ($ mil.)	–	0.0	0.0	0.1	1.2	1.5
Employees	(20.0%)	–	–	–	5	4

SURGICAL CARE AFFILIATES INC

NMS: SCAI

520 Lake Cook Road, Suite 250
Deerfield, IL 60015
Phone: 847 236-0921
Fax: –
Web: www.scasurgery.com

CEO: Andrew P. Hayek
CFO: Peter Clemens
HR: –
FYE: December 31
Type: Public

Surgical Care Affiliates can stitch 'em up and move 'em out. The company operates one of the largest networks of outpatient surgery centers in the US. (Also known as ambulatory surgical centers or ASCs these facilities charge less than hospitals to perform routine surgeries.) Surgical Care Affiliates operates about 195 surgery centers six surgical hospitals and one sleep center with about a dozen locations. Its facilities are located in about 35 states and offer non-emergency day surgeries in orthopedics ophthalmology gastroenterology pain management otolaryngology (ear nose and throat) urology and gynecology. The company went public in 2013.

	Annual Growth	12/10	12/11	12/12	12/13	12/14
Sales ($ mil.)	5.3%	730.3	741.6	766.9	825.4	897.3
Net income ($ mil.)	–	(14.9)	(9.7)	(20.0)	(51.3)	32.0
Market value ($ mil.)	(3.4%)	–	–	–	1,346.5	1,300.5
Employees	9.8%	–	–	4,150	5,000	5,000

SURGLINE INTERNATIONAL INC.

OTC: CNUV

319 Clematis St. Ste. 703
West Palm Beach FL 33401
Phone: 561-514-9042
Fax: 770-751-0543
Web: www.kidsii.com

CEO: Thomas G Toland
CFO: –
HR: –
FYE: July 31
Type: Public

Holding company SurgLine International owns SurgLine and Nuvo Solar Energy. SurgLine distributes medical and surgical products at a discount. It recently expanded that business with the 2012 acquisition of Eden Surgical Technologies which distributes trauma products and the creation of subsidiary SurgLine MDC Holdings which has been tasked with forming joint ventures with orthopedic surgeons to lower the costs of surgical implants. The company's other holding Nuvo Solar Energy is a development-stage company with patent pending solar and photovoltaic related technology. The company changed its name from China Nuvo Solar Energy to SurgLine International in 2012.

SURMODICS, INC.

NMS: SRDX

9924 West 74th Street
Eden Prairie, MN 55344
Phone: 952 500-7000
Fax: –
Web: www.surmodics.com

CEO: Gary R. Maharaj
CFO: Andrew D C (Andy) LaFrence
HR: –
FYE: September 30
Type: Public

SurModics doesn't want to scratch the surface of the medical device market — it just wants to coat it with its own special agent. The company's medical device unit makes special coatings that make the devices easier to use less traumatic to the body and even useful in delivering drugs to patients. The company's Bravo polymer coating is used on Cordis' drug-coated coronary stent (among other products) and delivers drugs that prevent re-narrowing of the artery. SurModics' in vitro diagnostics (IVD) unit handles diagnostic test and research kits and products. Three scientists formed the company in 1979.

	Annual Growth	09/11	09/12	09/13	09/14	09/15
Sales ($ mil.)	(2.2%)	67.8	51.9	56.1	57.4	61.9
Net income ($ mil.)	–	(12.8)	10.2	15.2	12.0	11.9
Market value ($ mil.)	24.5%	117.8	261.8	307.8	235.1	282.7
Employees	10.4%	113	120	114	120	168

SURREY BANCORP (NC)

NBB: SRYB

145 North Renfro Street, P.O. Box 1227
Mount Airy, NC 27030
Phone: 336 783-3900
Fax: –

CEO: Edward C Ashby III
CFO: –
HR: –
FYE: December 31
Type: Public

This surrey doesn't have fringe on top but it does have funds inside. Surrey Bancorp is the holding company for Surrey Bank & Trust which serves northwestern North Carolina's Surry County and neighboring portions of Virginia through about five offices and a lending center. The bank offers standard retail services including checking and savings accounts CDs IRAs and credit and debit cards. Surrey Bank & Trust writes mostly commercial and industrial loans (more than two-thirds of its portfolio) followed by residential mortgages (about 20%). Subsidiary SB&T Insurance sells property/casualty coverage. The bank offers investment services through a third-party provider UVEST which is part of LPL Financial.

	Annual Growth	12/10	12/11	12/12	12/13	12/14
Assets ($ mil.)	4.3%	213.7	224.7	229.9	240.9	253.2
Net income ($ mil.)	29.1%	1.2	2.2	2.8	2.9	3.4
Market value ($ mil.)	24.8%	20.8	32.8	31.1	41.7	50.5
Employees	2.4%	71	72	82	72	78

SURVEY SAMPLING INTERNATIONAL LLC

6 Research Dr.
Shelton CT 06484
Phone: 203-567-7200
Fax: 203-567-7367
Web: www.surveysampling.com

CEO: Chris Fanning
CFO: Rick Essex
HR: –
FYE: December 31
Type: Private

Survey Sampling International (SSI) makes sure marketing research firms are talking to all the right people. The company's sample services help clients minimize research risk reduce costs and improve research quality by identifying the best subjects for a survey. SSI can screen potential respondents by age sex ethnic background income and other demographic criteria as well as interests and lifestyle. It also provides highly defined samples for business surveys. SSI has more than 1800 clients worldwide that use its services for Internet telephone and mail polls and surveys (although 85% of SSI's business derives from the Internet). SSI has more than 15 offices around the globe and was founded in 1977.

SUSQUEHANNA BANCSHARES, INC

NMS: SUSQ

26 North Cedar St.
Lititz, PA 17543
Phone: 717 626-4721
Fax: –
Web: www.susquehanna.net

CEO: –
CFO: –
HR: –
FYE: December 31
Type: Public

Susquehanna Bancshares which bears the name of the river that flows through the heart of its market area is the holding company for Susquehanna Bank. The bank serves individuals and regional businesses through more than 245 branches in south-central and southeastern Pennsylvania Maryland New Jersey and West Virginia. It offers standard services such as deposits loans and credit cards. Non-banking subsidiaries provide wealth management insurance brokerage and employee benefits and vehicle leasing. Loans secured by commercial and residential real estate account for more nearly 60% of the bank's portfolio. Susquehanna Bancshares boasts assets of some $18.5 billion.

	Annual Growth	12/09	12/10	12/11	12/12	12/13
Assets ($ mil.)	7.8%	13,689.3	13,954.1	14,974.8	18,037.7	18,473.5
Net income ($ mil.)	92.4%	12.7	31.8	54.9	141.2	173.7
Market value ($ mil.)	21.5%	1,103.6	1,813.7	1,570.1	1,963.6	2,405.7
Employees	2.7%	3,055	3,039	3,122	3,464	3,395

SUSSER HOLDINGS CORP

NYS: SUSS

4525 Ayers Street
Corpus Christi, TX 78415
Phone: 361 884-2463
Fax: 361 884-2494
Web: www.susser.com

CEO: Sam L Susser
CFO: Mary E Sullivan
HR: –
FYE: December 30
Type: Public

Stripes are in Circles are out at Susser Holdings. The company operates about 560 Stripes convenience stores in Texas New Mexico and Oklahoma. (The company's Circle K stores were converted to the Stripes name several years ago.) The chain offers restaurant service in about 360 of its stores primarily under its proprietary Laredo Taco Company (LTC) brand. LTC serves up breakfast and lunch tacos rotisserie chicken and other hot foods. Susser Holdings is the largest independent c-store operator and non-refining motor fuel distributor through Susser Petroleum in Texas. (Fuel accounts for more than 80% of total sales.) Founded by Sam J. Susser in 1938 the company is now run by his son.

	Annual Growth	12/08*	01/10	01/11	01/12*	12/12
Sales ($ mil.)	8.2%	4,239.9	3,307.3	3,930.6	5,194.2	5,818.1
Net income ($ mil.)	29.8%	16.5	2.1	0.8	47.5	46.7
Market value ($ mil.)	26.7%	281.1	182.4	294.0	480.2	724.6
Employees	7.3%	6,567	7,211	7,165	7,584	8,697

*Fiscal year change

SUSSEX BANCORP

NMS: SBBX

100 Enterprise Drive, Suite 700
Rockaway, NJ 07866
Phone: 844 256-7328
Fax: –
Web: www.sussexbank.com

CEO: Anthony Labozzetta
CFO: Steven M Fusco
HR: –
FYE: December 31
Type: Public

Sussex Bancorp is the holding company for Sussex Bank which operates about 10 branches in Sussex County New Jersey and two others in Orange County New York. Targeting individuals and local businesses the bank offers such standard retail products as checking and savings accounts NOW and money market accounts and certificates of deposit. It also provides trust and financial advisory and insurance services. Lending activities consist primarily of commercial mortgages (more than half of the company's loan portfolio) and residential mortgages (more than 20%). To a lesser extent the bank also writes construction land development business and consumer loans. Anthony Labozzetta was named CEO in 2010.

	Annual Growth	12/10	12/11	12/12	12/13	12/14
Assets ($ mil.)	5.9%	474.0	507.0	514.7	533.9	595.9
Net income ($ mil.)	4.6%	2.2	2.5	0.7	1.4	2.6
Market value ($ mil.)	14.5%	27.7	20.1	25.1	36.4	47.6
Employees	2.5%	123	137	114	134	136

SUTHERLAND GLOBAL SERVICES INC.

1160 Pittsford-Victor Rd.
Pittsford NY 14534
Phone: 585-586-5757
Fax: 585-784-2154
Web: www.sutherlandglobal.com

CEO: Dilip R Vellodi
CFO: Micheal Bartusek
HR: –
FYE: June 30
Type: Private

Sutherland Global Services is willing to do all the legwork when it comes to helping your business close a sale or complete a transaction. The company offers business-process outsourcing (BPO) services primarily for clients in the airline technology retail banking and finance and telecommunications industries. It provides outsourced customer acquisition and retention technical assistance sales support functions and back-office services from more than 30 centers in Bulgaria Canada Egypt India the Philippines Mexico Nicaragua the United Arab Emirates the UK and the US. Established in 1986 Sutherland also acts as a consultant to companies looking to improve their call center operations.

SUTRON CORP.

NAS: STRN

22400 Davis Drive
Sterling, VA 20164
Phone: 703 406-2800
Fax: –
Web: www.sutron.com

CEO: Raul S McQuivey
CFO: Glen E Goold
HR: –
FYE: December 31
Type: Public

Through its Hydromet unit and other segments Sutron makes equipment that collects and transmits water and weather data. The company also provides related hydrological services. Customers use Sutron products to manage water resources obtain early warning of potentially disastrous floods or storms and help hydropower plants operate as efficiently as possible. The company's largest customer is the US government. Other customers include state and local governments engineering companies and power companies. In 2012 it acquired meterological firm IPS Meteostar for $4.2 million. Sutron sells its products globally; customers outside the US account for about 40% of sales. CEO Raul McQuivey owns 19% of the company.

	Annual Growth	12/09	12/10	12/11	12/12	12/13
Sales ($ mil.)	6.9%	20.9	23.0	20.2	25.2	27.2
Net income ($ mil.)	(22.7%)	2.2	3.0	1.5	1.1	0.8
Market value ($ mil.)	(8.1%)	36.4	33.5	25.8	25.6	26.0
Employees	8.1%	90	92	89	127	123

SUTTER WEST BAY HOSPITALS

633 FOLSOM ST FL 7
SAN FRANCISCO, CA 94107-3618
Phone: 415-563-4321
Fax: –
Web: www.cpmc.org

CEO: Martin Brotman
CFO: –
HR: –
FYE: December 31
Type: Private

Sutter West Bay Hospitals (doing business as California Pacific Medical Center or CPMC) is a health care complex located in the heart of hospital-heavy San Francisco. The private not-for-profit center's four area campuses (California Davies Pacific and St. Luke's) offer acute and specialty care including obstetrics and gynecology cardiovascular services pediatrics neurosciences orthopedics and organ transplantation. With more than 1300 beds between its campuses the center also conducts professional education and biomedical clinical and behavioral research. CPMC is part of the West Bay Region division of the Sutter Health hospital system.

	Annual Growth	12/03	12/04	12/08	12/09	12/11
Sales ($ mil.)	10.5%	–	801.7	830.0	1,245.9	1,616.0
Net income ($ mil.)	(9.9%)	–	139.0	168.9	159.1	67.0
Market value ($ mil.)	–	–	–	–	–	–
Employees	–	–	–	–	–	3,597

SVB FINANCIAL GROUP

NMS: SIVB

3003 Tasman Drive
Santa Clara, CA 95054-1191
Phone: 408 654-7400
Fax: –
Web: www.svb.com

CEO: Gregory W. (Greg) Becker
CFO: Michael (Mike) Descheneaux
HR: –
FYE: December 31
Type: Public

SVB Financial Group is the holding company for Silicon Valley Bank which serves emerging and established companies involved in technology life sciences and private equity and provides customized financing to entrepreneurs executives and investors in such industries. It also offers deposit accounts loans and international banking and plays matchmaker for young firms and private investors. SVB Financial also provides investment advisory brokerage and asset management services; and provides credit and banking services to wealthy individuals.

	Annual Growth	12/10	12/11	12/12	12/13	12/14
Assets ($ mil.)	22.4%	17,527.8	19,968.9	22,766.1	26,417.2	39,344.6
Net income ($ mil.)	49.8%	95.0	171.9	175.1	546.1	478.7
Market value ($ mil.)	21.6%	2,701.6	2,428.6	2,850.3	5,340.0	5,910.9
Employees	9.0%	1,357	1,526	1,615	1,704	1,914

SWAGELOK COMPANY

29500 Solon Rd.
Solon OH 44139
Phone: 440-248-4600
Fax: 440-349-5970
Web: www.swagelok.com

CEO: Arthur F Anton
CFO: Frank Roddy
HR: –
FYE: December 31
Type: Private

With sales partners worldwide Swagelok has to speak many languages "fluidly". The company makes fluid system components which include plug pinch and radial diaphragm valves regulators filters flexible tubing and welding systems. Its products are used in the instrumentation oil and gas power petrochemical alternative fuels and semiconductor industries as well as biopharmaceutical research companies. Swagelok also offers technical support custom kitting made-to-order products and third-party sourcing services. It has more than 200 sales and service locations in almost 60 countries. Founded in 1947 by Fred Lennon in his kitchen Swagelok is still controlled by the Lennon family.

SWANK INC.

PINK SHEETS: SNKI

90 Park Ave. 13th Fl.
New York NY 10016
Phone: 212-867-2600
Fax: 212-370-1039
Web: www.swankinc.com

CEO: –
CFO: –
HR: –
FYE: December 31
Type: Public

No guy's outfit would be complete without some swank. Swank makes and distributes men's fashion accessories including leather goods (belts wallets) and jewelry (cuff links chains). The items are sold under brand names such as its namesake Swank Claiborne Kenneth Cole Tommy Hilfiger Guess? Nautica and Donald Trump. Swank also distributes products under the Pierre Cardin name as well as under its clients' private labels. Its clients are mainly US national department stores specialty stores mass merchandisers catalog retailers and some US military retail exchanges. Swank was acquired in 2012 by Randa Accessories a maker and marketer of consumer fashion must-haves for some $57 million.

SWARTHMORE COLLEGE

500 COLLEGE AVE STE 2
SWARTHMORE, PA 190811390
Phone: 610-328-8000
Fax: –
Web: www.swarthmore.edu

CEO: –
CFO: –
HR: Pamela Caesar
FYE: June 30
Type: Private

The Borough of Swarthmore southwest of Philadelphia was founded in 1893 and literally evolved around the College on the Hill aka Swarthmore College which had been founded nearly three decades earlier by the Religious Society of Friends more commonly known as the Quakers. With a student-teacher ratio of 8:1 the private co-educational liberal arts and engineering college offers more than 50 academic programs and bachelor's degrees in the arts and sciences. Swarthmore enrolls about 1550 students or nearly 25% of the town's population. Notable alumni include Pulitzer Prize-winning author James Michener and former governor of Massachusetts Michael Dukakis.

	Annual Growth	06/10	06/11	06/12	06/13	06/14
Sales ($ mil.)	5.7%	–	117.8	122.3	245.4	139.2
Net income ($ mil.)	–	–	–	(13.0)	84.6	253.5
Market value ($ mil.)	–	–	–	–	–	–
Employees	–	–	–	–	–	700

SWEDISH HEALTH SERVICES

747 BROADWAY
SEATTLE, WA 981224379
Phone: 206-386-6000
Fax: –

CEO: Anthony A. (Tony) Armada
CFO: Dan Harris
HR: –
FYE: December 31
Type: Private

Swedish Health Services doing business as Swedish Medical Center hopes that the Swedish reputation for good health is transferred to its patients in the Pacific Northwest. The largest not-for-profit health provider in the greater Seattle area Swedish Health operates five acute care hospitals. It also runs two ambulatory care centers and the Swedish Medical Group physician practice organization which has more than 100 primary and specialty care offices in the greater Puget Sound region. Swedish Health is affiliated with Providence Health & Services a Catholic not-for-profit organization with about 30 hospitals in five states.

	Annual Growth	12/03	12/04	12/05	12/06	12/07
Sales ($ mil.)	6.1%	–	–	–	1,087.3	1,153.3
Net income ($ mil.)	40.5%	–	–	–	56.1	78.8
Market value ($ mil.)	–	–	–	–	–	–
Employees	–	–	–	–	–	6,916

SWEDISH MATCH NORTH AMERICA INC.

2 James Center 1021 E. Cary St. Ste. 1600
Richmond VA 23219
Phone: 804-787-5100
Fax: 804-225-7000
Web: www.swedishmatch.com

CEO: Lars Dahlgren
CFO: Thomas Hayes
HR: –
FYE: December 31
Type: Business Segment

Business is up to snuff at Swedish Match North America — that's snuff tobacco. A subsidiary of Stockholm-based Swedish Match AB the company (SMNA) primarily makes and sells moist snuff and increasingly General-brand snus (a spit-free smokeless pouch) in the US. SMNA also ranks as the largest manufacturer of US chewing tobacco; Red Man is the country's #1 selling label. Snuff brands include Longhorn and Timber Wolf. Among other offerings SMNA makes mass market cigars sold under the ubiquitous White Owl and Garcia y Vega brands and matches and Cricket brand disposable lighters. The company expanded its presence in the tobacco space when Swedish Match acquired premium cigar maker General Cigar (2005).

SWEETBAY SUPERMARKET

3801 Sugar Palm Dr.
Tampa FL 33619
Phone: 813-620-1139
Fax: 813-626-9550
Web: www.sweetbaysupermarket.com

CEO: –
CFO: –
HR: –
FYE: December 31
Type: Subsidiary

Sweetbay Supermarket is searching for the sweet spot in the Florida grocery market. Number three in the market (behind market leader Publix and Winn-Dixie) Sweetbay operates about 105 supermarkets along Florida's west coast. Squeezed between Publix at the high end and discounters including Wal-Mart Stores and ALDI at the low end of the market Sweetbay emphasizes value and caters to the Sunshine State's large Hispanic population with expanded produce sections (featuring exotic produce) as well as more organic foods and nutraceuticals. Formerly known as Kash n' Karry Food Stores Sweetbay is owned by Brussels-based Delhaize Group.

SWH CORPORATION

18872 MacArthur Blvd Ste 400
Irvine CA 92612
Phone: 949-825-7000
Fax: 513-754-8778
Web: www.harrisproductsgroup.com

CEO: Daniel R Dillon
CFO: Edward T Bartholemy
HR: –
FYE: April 30
Type: Subsidiary

This company pairs the bistro life with home-style cooking. SWH Corporation owns and operates about 145 casual dining spots operating under the Mimi's Cafe banner. The New Orleans bistro-themed restaurants serve a variety of American classic dishes for breakfast lunch and dinner including chicken pot pie pancakes and eggs and pot roast as well as seafood pasta and sandwiches. The company has locations in more than 20 states mostly in California. Founded by Tom Simms and his family in 1978 SWH is owned by family-restaurant operator Bob Evans Farms.

SWIFT ENERGY COMPANY

NBB: SFYW Q

17001 Northchase Drive, Suite 100
Houston, TX 77060
Phone: 281 874-2700
Fax: –
Web: www.swiftenergy.com

CEO: Terry E Swift
CFO: Alton D Heckaman Jr
HR: –
FYE: December 31
Type: Public

No laggard oil and gas exploration and production company Swift Energy is hoping to be a industry high flyer by developing its interests in a handful of oil and gas fields in Louisiana and Texas. The company's core exploration areas are the Lake Washington Field and Bay de Chene fields in Louisiana and the AWP Olmos Field and Eagle Ford Play in Texas. Swift Energy aims to increase reserves and production by adjusting the balance between drilling and acquisition activities in response to market conditions. Facing a slumping oil market in late 2015 the company filed for Chapter 11 bankruptcy protection.

	Annual Growth	12/10	12/11	12/12	12/13	12/14
Sales ($ mil.)	5.8%	438.4	599.1	557.3	587.7	549.5
Net income ($ mil.)	–	46.3	98.8	20.9	(19.0)	(283.4)
Market value ($ mil.)	(43.3%)	1,719.4	1,305.2	675.9	592.9	177.9
Employees	0.2%	292	309	332	313	294

SWIFT TRANSPORTATION CO

NYS: SWFT

2200 South 75th Avenue
Phoenix, AZ 85043
Phone: 602 269-9700
Fax: –

CEO: Jerry C. Moyes
CFO: Virginia (Ginnie) Henkels
HR: Rachel Monti
FYE: December 31
Type: Public

Swift but within the speed limit: Truckload carrier Swift Transportation hauls freight such as building materials food paper products and retail merchandise throughout the North America. The company operates a fleet of more than 20600 tractors (about 75% are company-owned) and 63000 trailers via a network of more than 40 terminals. Its services include dedicated contract carriage (drivers and equipment assigned to a customer long-term). Besides standard dry vans Swift's fleet includes refrigerated flatbed and specialized trailers and about 9150 intermodal containers.

	Annual Growth	12/10	12/11	12/12	12/13	12/14
Sales ($ mil.)	10.1%	2,929.7	3,333.9	3,493.2	4,118.2	4,298.7
Net income ($ mil.)	–	(125.4)	90.6	114.6	155.4	161.2
Market value ($ mil.)	23.0%	1,777.6	1,170.9	1,295.9	3,155.9	4,068.2
Employees	4.3%	18,000	17,400	17,600	19,600	21,274

SWIMWEAR ANYWHERE INC.

85 SHERWOOD AVE	CEO: –
FARMINGDALE, NY 117351717	CFO: Joseph Roehrig
Phone: 631-420-1400	HR: –
Fax: –	FYE: December 31
Web: www.swimwearanywhere.com	Type: Private

Life would certainly be more interesting if consumers took heed and sported their swimwear anywhere and everywhere. Swimwear Anywhere is a major North American swimwear manufacturer that makes and markets swimwear and beachwear lines under its own private labels and through licensing agreements for brands including DKNY Juicy Couture and Carmen Marc Valvo. The company's subsidiary TYR Sport (named after mythical Norse god of warriors and athletes) makes swimwear and gear designed primarily for professional athletes. Spokespeople have included Olympic swimming medalist Amanda Weir. Swimwear Anywhere was founded in 1993 by its owners Joseph and Rosemarie DiLorenzo.

	Annual Growth	06/0-1	06/00	06/03	06/04*	12/12
Sales ($ mil.)	0.0%	–	53.7	47.1	46.0	53.8
Net income ($ mil.)	(30.5%)	–	–	17.2	0.9	0.7
Market value ($ mil.)	–	–	–	–	–	–
Employees	–	–	–	–	–	150

*Fiscal year change

SWINERTON BUILDERS

260 TOWNSEND ST	CEO: –
SAN FRANCISCO, CA 941071719	CFO: Linda G Schowalter
Phone: 415-421-2980	HR: –
Fax: –	FYE: December 31
Web: www.swinerton.com	Type: Private

Swinerton Builders a subsidiary of Swinerton focuses on commercial and sustainable construction and renovation projects. Operating primarily in the western US its interiors group offers interior tenant finishes and remodeling working on such projects as high-tech and lab renovations hospitals retail facilities and seismic upgrades. The employee-owned company's building group focuses on new construction and retrofitting for such projects as the San Francisco Museum of Modern Art a Lockheed Martin launch vehicle assembly plant in Colorado and the Bay Bridge toll operations building in San Francisco. Swinerton Builders operates from offices in California Colorado Hawaii Texas New Mexico and Washington.

	Annual Growth	12/09	12/10	12/11	12/12	12/13
Sales ($ mil.)	28.1%	–	797.0	948.1	1,429.4	1,674.6
Net income ($ mil.)	–	–	–	0.0	6.2	4.4
Market value ($ mil.)	–	–	–	–	–	–
Employees	–	–	–	–	–	900

SWINERTON INCORPORATED

260 TOWNSEND ST	CEO: Jeffrey C Hoopes
SAN FRANCISCO, CA 941071719	CFO: Linda G Showalter
Phone: 415-421-2980	HR: –
Fax: –	FYE: December 31
Web: www.swinerton.com	Type: Private

Swinerton is building up the West just as it helped rebuild San Francisco after the 1906 earthquake. One of the largest contractors in California the construction group builds commercial industrial and government facilities including resorts subsidized housing public schools soundstages hospitals and airport terminals. Through its subsidiaries (including Swinerton Builders) Swinerton offers general contracting and design/build services as well as construction and program management. The firm also provides property management for conventional subsidized and assisted living residences and is active in the renewable energy sector. The 100% employee-owned company traces its roots to 1888.

	Annual Growth	12/09	12/10	12/11	12/12	12/13
Sales ($ mil.)	19.7%	–	981.5	1,080.2	1,506.1	1,681.7
Net income ($ mil.)	–	–	–	0.0	0.0	6.0
Market value ($ mil.)	–	–	–	–	–	–
Employees	–	–	–	–	–	900

SWISHER HYGIENE INC

NBB: SWSH

c/o Akerman LLP, Las Olas Centre II, Suite 1600, 350 East Las Olas Boulevard	CEO: William M Pierce
Fort Lauderdale, FL 33301-2999	CFO: William T Nanovsky
Phone: 203 682-8331	HR: Kimberly Dziuk
Fax: –	FYE: December 31
Web: www.swsh.com	Type: Public

Swisher Hygiene sweeps away the competition in the corporate world. The company provides commercial cleaning services equipment and supplies to more than 50000 businesses in North America and abroad. Recognized for its restroom cleaning and disinfection services Swisher also sells soap cleaning chemicals and paper products and it rents facility service items (such as floor mats and mops). The company sells rents and maintains commercial dishwashers and other cleaning equipment. Swisher has expertise in serving customers in the foodservice hospitality health care industrial and retail industries. It boasts a global network of about 80 company-owned operations 10 franchises and 10 master licensees.

	Annual Growth	12/10	12/11	12/12	12/13	12/14
Sales ($ mil.)	32.1%	63.7	220.0	230.5	213.7	193.8
Net income ($ mil.)	–	(17.6)	(25.3)	(73.2)	(153.0)	(46.8)
Market value ($ mil.)	(20.8%)	83.7	65.9	30.8	9.1	32.9
Employees	2.7%	1,077	2,105	1,641	1,375	1,200

SWISS VALLEY FARMS COOPERATIVE

247 Research Pkwy.	CEO: Don Boelens
Davenport IA 52808	CFO: Don Boelens
Phone: 563-468-6600	HR: –
Fax: 563-468-6616	FYE: September 30
Web: www.swissvalley.com	Type: Private - Cooperativ

You don't need to be a mountain climber to view a Swiss valley. Just go to Iowa where Swiss Valley Farms operates a rather large and expanding dairy cooperative. The cooperative which represents more than 1000 member/farmers in the upper Midwest offers milk cheese butter yogurt dips and soft-serve and shake mixes. The organization also sells orange juice lemonade fruit drinks and bottled water. Swiss Valley's customers include retail food outlets and school lunch programs as well as other foodservice providers. As part of its operations the co-op manages several manufacturing and packaging plants in Iowa Wisconsin and Minnesota.

SWS GROUP, INC.

NYS: SWS

1201 Elm Street, Suite 3500	CEO: –
Dallas, TX 75270	CFO: –
Phone: 214 859-1800	HR: –
Fax: 214 749-0810	FYE: June 30
Web: www.swsgroupinc.com	Type: Public

Southwest Securities hopes stock prices go northeast. The primary subsidiary of SWS Group provides securities clearing and brokerage services to retail and institutional clients in the US and Canada. Accounting for some three-fourths of revenues Southwest Securities counts some 150 financial services organizations among its clients. It also serves individual investors through its private client brokerages located in California Texas Nevada and Oklahoma. Southwest Securities performs securities underwriting securities lending and public finance activities for institutional customers. Thrift subsidiary Southwest Securities FSB specializes in commercial lending and mortgage banking in Texas and New Mexico.

	Annual Growth	06/09	06/10	06/11	06/12	06/13
Assets ($ mil.)	(2.6%)	4,199.0	4,530.7	3,802.2	3,546.8	3,780.4
Net income ($ mil.)	–	–	23.6	(2.9)	(23.2)	(4.7)	(33.4)
Market value ($ mil.)	(20.3%)	441.5	331.8	184.0	173.9	177.8
Employees	(2.6%)	1,170	1,142	1,073	1,065	1,055

SYBASE INC.

1 Sybase Dr.
Dublin CA 94568
Phone: 925-236-5000
Fax: 925-236-4321
Web: www.sybase.com

CEO: John S Chen
CFO: Jeffrey G Ross
HR: –
FYE: December 31
Type: Subsidiary

Sybase has your databases covered. Long known for its relational database products the company develops enterprise software used to store and distribute content throughout businesses. Its extensive product suite encompasses database servers data warehousing and business analytics; it also includes data encryption and device management tools. Other applications enable the delivery of information and messaging to mobile devices. Sybase markets its products worldwide with historically about half of its revenues coming from outside North America. The financial services industry is one of its largest markets but it also serves government health care and telecom clients. Sybase is a subsidiary of SAP.

SYBRON DENTAL SPECIALTIES INC.

1717 W. Collins Ave.
Orange CA 92867-5422
Phone: 714-516-7400
Fax: +44-20-7306-8697
Web: www.channel4.com

CEO: Dan Even
CFO: –
HR: –
FYE: September 30
Type: Subsidiary

Crooked teeth may have met their match in Sybron Dental Specialties. The company makes and distributes dental and orthodontic appliances and tools through subsidiaries including Axis Dental Kerr SybronEndo and Ormco. Its product lines include braces dental implant systems cleaning tools and impression and restorative materials. The company also makes endodontic (dental surgery) supplies including hand pieces disinfectants curatives and other tools. Outside of dentistry the company has a smaller line of products for physicians. Sybron markets its products both directly through its subsidiaries and through dealers around the world. The company is a subsidiary of tools and technology giant Danaher.

SYCAMORE ENTERTAINMENT GROUP INC.

NBB: SEGI

Lexington Avenue, Suite 120
Hollywood, CA 90038
Phone: 323 790-1717
Fax: –
Web: www.imarx.com

CEO: –
CFO: –
HR: –
FYE: December 31
Type: Public

Sycamore Entertainment Group intends to grow fast and get its products up on screens across North America. The newly sprouted film marketing and distribution company went public in 2010 by acquiring the shell of a former pharmaceutical development company. Hopeful that public investors will make it rain the company is seeking to pick up market and distribute feature-length films. Sycamore Entertainment hopes to occupy a niche in the industry left vacant by the departure or demise of larger distribution companies — namely the distribution of art films independent films and foreign films.

	Annual Growth	12/10	12/11	12/12	12/13	12/14
Sales ($ mil.)	(83.4%)	–	–	0.2	0.2	0.0
Net income ($ mil.)	–	(3.5)	(1.0)	(1.8)	(0.3)	(0.6)
Market value ($ mil.)	(57.0%)	14.6	11.6	0.8	0.5	0.5
Employees	–	–	–	–	–	–

SYKES ENTERPRISES, INC.

NMS: SYKE

400 North Ashley Drive, Suite 2800
Tampa, FL 33602
Phone: 813 274-1000
Fax: 813 273-0148
Web: www.sykes.com

CEO: Charles E. (Chuck) Sykes
CFO: W. Michael Kipphut
HR: Jenna R. Nelson
FYE: December 31
Type: Public

When that software won't install Sykes can take your call. Sykes Enterprises operates about 70 technical help and customer support centers in 20 countries across Africa the Americas Asia and Europe that use phone e-mail and chat to serve those in need of help. Sykes specializes in customer service and inbound technical support and also provides large corporations with technical staffing and consulting relating to customer relationship management. Sykes predominantly serves the communications consumer financial services and technology industries.

	Annual Growth	12/10	12/11	12/12	12/13	12/14
Sales ($ mil.)	3.5%	1,158.7	1,169.3	1,127.7	1,263.5	1,327.5
Net income ($ mil.)	–	(10.3)	48.3	28.4	37.3	57.8
Market value ($ mil.)	3.7%	874.4	675.9	656.9	941.3	1,012.9
Employees	3.8%	43,400	41,000	46,200	47,900	50,450

SYLVAN INC.

90 Glade Dr.
Kittanning PA 16201
Phone: 724-543-3900
Fax: 724-543-7583
Web: www.sylvaninc.com

CEO: –
CFO: Donald A Smith
HR: –
FYE: December 31
Type: Private

When Sylvan says business is mushrooming it quite literally is. The company is one of the leading producers of mushroom spawn ("seeds") for growers in more than 60 countries. The company itself is also a major grower of fresh mushrooms in the US. In addition to producing and distributing spawn the company sells casing inoculum (mushroom-growth accelerator) and supplements for growing mushrooms including pesticides fungicides and disinfectants. The mushrooms are grown at Quincy Farms Sylvan's Tallahassee Florida facility. The company went private in 2004 when it was purchased by Snyder Associated Companies which operates nearly 10 different companies.

SYMANTEC CORP.

NMS: SYMC

350 Ellis Street
Mountain View, CA 94043
Phone: 650 527-8000
Fax: –
Web: www.symantec.com

CEO: Michael A. Brown
CFO: Thomas J. Seifert
HR: –
FYE: April 03
Type: Public

Digital security isn't just a matter of semantics for Symantec. The company provides security storage and systems management software for businesses and consumers. Symantec's applications handle such functions as virus protection PC maintenance data backup and recovery intrusion detection data loss prevention spam control content filtering and remote server management. The company also provides managed services and training. Symantec is probably best known for its popular Norton consumer security software which the company markets to PC users worldwide. But with declining revenue the company agreed to sell its data storage business Veritas for $8 billion. This deal forestalls a move to break off Veritas into an independent public company.

	Annual Growth	04/11*	03/12	03/13	03/14*	04/15
Sales ($ mil.)	1.3%	6,190.0	6,730.0	6,906.0	6,676.0	6,508.0
Net income ($ mil.)	10.1%	597.0	1,172.0	765.0	898.0	878.0
Market value ($ mil.)	6.3%	12,626.6	12,790.8	16,881.1	13,536.4	16,108.2
Employees	0.5%	18,600	20,500	21,500	20,800	19,000
						*Fiscal year change

SYMBION INC.

40 Burton Hills Blvd. Ste. 500
Nashville TN 37215
Phone: 615-234-5900
Fax: 615-234-5998
Web: www.symbion.com

CEO: Richard E Francis Jr
CFO: Teresa F Sparks
HR: –
FYE: December 31
Type: Private

The speedier the surgery the better says Symbion. The company owns and manages about 60 outpatient surgery centers in more than two dozen states mainly in the eastern midwestern and southern regions of the US. Physicians at the centers perform a variety of non-emergency procedures in such fields as gastrointestinal medicine orthopedics pain management ophthalmology and plastic surgery. Symbion operates the centers through partnerships with local doctors or hospitals; it owns a majority interest in most of its practices. The company provides services to its clinics including staff training accounting information systems and quality assurance. Private equity firm Crestview Partners controls Symbion.

SYMETRA FINANCIAL CORP

NYS: SYA

777 108th Avenue NE, Suite 1200
Bellevue, WA 98004
Phone: 425 256-8000
Fax: –
Web: www.symetra.com

CEO: Thomas M Marra
CFO: Margaret A Meister
HR: –
FYE: December 31
Type: Public

Symetra Financial seeks a symmetrical balance of work retirement and life insurance products. The holding company's subsidiaries offer life insurance annuities retirement plans health insurance and employee benefit plans to some 1.7 million customers throughout the US. Its workplace products include such goodies as medical stop-loss insurance disability insurance and group annuities. These products are distributed by brokers independent agents consultants financial institutions and third-party administrators. For individual consumers Symetra offers annuities individual retirement accounts and life insurance sold through banks.

	Annual Growth	12/09	12/10	12/11	12/12	12/13
Assets ($ mil.)	7.6%	22,437.5	25,636.9	28,212.7	29,460.9	30,129.5
Net income ($ mil.)	14.5%	128.3	200.9	199.6	205.4	220.7
Market value ($ mil.)	11.4%	–	1,612.9	1,067.8	1,528.1	2,232.2
Employees	2.8%	1,100	1,100	1,100	1,250	1,230

SYMMETRY MEDICAL INC.

NYS: SMA

3724 North State Road 15
Warsaw, IN 46582
Phone: 574 260 2252
Fax: –
Web: www.symmetrymedical.com

CEO: William Dow
CFO: John Connollyn
HR: –
FYE: December 29
Type: Public

Symmetry Medical covers both sides of any orthopedic implant procedure. The company makes orthopedic implants for hips and knees and the surgical instruments used to insert such devices. In addition to its numerous products for the orthopedic implant market Symmetry sells its wares to physicians who deal with spinal injuries and general trauma dental work cardiovascular care and ophthalmology. Symmetry also makes plastic and metal cases to organize hold and transport medical devices. For a few aerospace customers the company makes aerofoils and aircraft engine parts. Symmetry's sales and marketing team promote its products to global orthopedic device makers and others.

	Annual Growth	01/09	01/10	01/11*	12/11	12/12
Sales ($ mil.)	(1.0%)	423.4	365.9	360.8	359.0	410.5
Net income ($ mil.)	(27.6%)	24.0	21.8	14.0	2.9	9.1
Market value ($ mil.)	7.9%	305.0	296.6	340.4	294.0	383.0
Employees	(2.1%)	2,688	2,357	2,797	2,520	2,520
					*Fiscal year change	

SYMPHONYIRI GROUP INC.

150 N. Clinton St.
Chicago IL 60661-1416
Phone: 312-726-1221
Fax: 936-639-3673
Web: www.treeconresources.com

CEO: Andrew Appel
CFO: Mike Duffey
HR: –
FYE: December 31
Type: Private

When products fly off the shelves this company is watching — and counting. SymphonyIRI Group is a market research and shopper intelligence firm providing sales data for consumer packaged goods gathered from checkout scanners at more than 95000 retail locations (excluding Wal-Mart which doesn't release data) in the US and Europe. In addition to checkout scanner data it gathers information via consumer panels and offers test marketing services. It also offers business intelligence software and tools and it advises customers on key strategies such as strategic pricing growth and innovation shopper marketing and customer and channel management. SymphonyIRI was founded in 1979 as Information Resources.

SYNACOR, INC.

NMS: SYNC

40 La Riviere Drive, Suite 300
Buffalo, NY 14202
Phone: 716 853-1362
Fax: –
Web: www.synacor.com

CEO: Himesh Bhise
CFO: William J Stuart
HR: Melissa Vollmer
FYE: December 31
Type: Public

When it comes to digital entertainment Synacor is at your service. The firm provides a technology platform to broadband service providers cable TV operators and other telecom companies that lets end-users receive digital entertainment services and apps. It builds the private label portals customers see when they log onto their telecom provider's website and makes money by selling ads on these sites. Synacor also offers premium online content e-mail and security services. It has relationships with content and service providers including CinemaNow CNN and MediaNet Digital. Synacor went public in 2011.

	Annual Growth	12/10	12/11	12/12	12/13	12/14
Sales ($ mil.)	12.6%	66.2	91.1	122.0	111.8	106.6
Net income ($ mil.)	–	(3.6)	9.9	3.8	(1.4)	(12.9)
Market value ($ mil.)	(39.5%)	–	–	149.8	67.1	54.8
Employees	(0.3%)	261	261	328	373	258

SYNAGEVA BIOPHARMA CORP.

NASDAQ: GEVA

128 Spring St. Ste. 520
Lexington MA 02421
Phone: 781-357-9900
Fax: 781-357-9901
Web: www.synageva.com

CEO: –
CFO: –
HR: –
FYE: December 31
Type: Public

Synageva BioPharma wants to sync up rare diseases with effective therapies. The company is focused on conducting research and development efforts into drug candidates that target rare conditions including enzyme deficiencies. Synageva also receives royalties on its sole commercial product HIV drug Fuzeon which is approved in the US and the European Union; development partner Roche markets Fuzeon worldwide. The company formerly Trimeris changed its name following a 2011 reverse-merger with the predecessor Synageva BioPharma.

SYNALLOY CORP.

NMS: SYNL

775 Spartan Blvd., Suite 102	CEO: Craig C. Bram
Spartanburg, SC 29304	CFO: Dennis M. Loughran
Phone: 864 585-3605	HR: –
Fax: –	FYE: January 03
Web: www.synalloy.com	Type: Public

Synalloy brings stainless steel and specialty chemicals together under one company. Operating through Bristol Metals and Ram-Fab the company manufactures welded pipe and fabricates piping systems from stainless steel and other alloys or carbon and chrome alloy. Its customers who require corrosion resistance or high purity are chiefly engaged in the chemical petrochemical water and waste water treatment and paper industries. Steel pipe branded Brismet is sold to distributors and directly to end-users. Synalloy's chemicals business Manufacturers Chemicals produces specialty chemicals and dyes (defoamers surfactants softening agents) for the textile chemical paper mining and metals industries.

	Annual Growth	01/11*	12/11	12/12	12/13*	01/15
Sales ($ mil.)	7.2%	151.1	170.6	197.7	220.7	199.5
Net income ($ mil.)	7.9%	4.0	5.8	4.2	1.8	5.5
Market value ($ mil.)	9.9%	105.6	89.5	117.5	135.3	153.9
Employees	1.3%	441	441	597	670	464

*Fiscal year change

SYNAPSE GROUP INC.

225 High Ridge Rd. East Building	CEO: Sebastien Bilodeau
Stamford CT 06905	CFO: –
Phone: 203-595-8255	HR: –
Fax: +33-1-42-44-22-89	FYE: December 31
Web: www.kelkoo.com	Type: Subsidiary

Want to subscribe to a magazine? Synapse Group can help. The group markets more than 1000 magazine titles through direct mail credit card bill inserts relationships with catalog marketers and the Internet. The company typically sells subscriptions by credit card then bills renewals automatically. Synapse also markets subscriptions through frequent flier programs allowing customers to redeem miles for magazines. Clients have included Hearst Magazines American Express and Delta Air Lines. Former CEO Michael Loeb and priceline.com founder Jay Walker began the company in 1991. Publisher Time holds a majority stake in Synapse.

SYNAPTICS INC

NMS: SYNA

1251 McKay Drive	CEO: Richard A. (Rick) Bergman
San Jose, CA 95131	CFO: Wajid Ali
Phone: 408 904-1100	HR: Karen Gaydon
Fax: –	FYE: June 27
Web: www.synaptics.com	Type: Public

Synaptics keeps you in touch with your electronics. The company's human interface products are sold to contract manufacturers for use in mobile phones (more than half of sales) notebook and handheld computers and other mobile electronic devices. Its TouchPad product can be used in peripherals such as monitors and remote controls; ClickPad replaces a mouse for notebook PCs and netbooks; and ClearPad provides touchscreen control for various mobile devices. Synaptics also relies on contract manufacturers to make its products. Most sales go to manufacturers in Asia more than two thirds in China. US customers provide 10% of sales.

	Annual Growth	06/11	06/12	06/13	06/14	06/15
Sales ($ mil.)	29.9%	598.5	548.2	663.6	947.5	1,703.0
Net income ($ mil.)	14.7%	63.8	54.1	98.9	46.7	110.4
Market value ($ mil.)	36.3%	939.0	1,074.5	1,447.1	3,354.4	3,239.6
Employees	27.5%	676	697	852	1,230	1,789

SYNARC INC.

7707 GATEWAY BLVD FL 3	CEO: Claus Christiansen
NEWARK, CA 94560-1160	CFO: –
Phone: 415-817-8900	HR: –
Fax: –	FYE: December 31
Web: www.synarc-ccbr.com	Type: Private

You put up the compounds Synarc puts up the trials. The biomedical testing and contract research organization provides medical imaging patient recruitment and biomechanical marker services for clinical trials conducted by drug development companies around the globe. Synarc operates clinical research centers in North America Europe and Asia. The company has a main focus on neurological research including Alzheimer's disease studies; other clinical areas include oncology cardiovascular disease orthopedics infectious disease arthritis and osteoporosis. Synarc also conducts studies on medical devices.

	Annual Growth	09/0-2	09/0-1	09/00	09/00*	12/07
Sales ($ mil.)	–	–	–	(1,600.1)	12.2	102.2
Net income ($ mil.)	–	–	–	0.0	(3.0)	(3.1)
Market value ($ mil.)	–	–	–	–	–	–
Employees	–	–	–	–	–	400

*Fiscal year change

SYNCHRONOSS TECHNOLOGIES INC

NMS: SNCR

200 Crossing Boulevard, 8th Floor	CEO: Stephen G. Waldis
Bridgewater, NJ 08807	CFO: Karen L. Rosenberger
Phone: 866 620-3940	HR: –
Fax: –	FYE: December 31
Web: www.synchronoss.com	Type: Public

Synchronoss Technologies helps telephone companies synch up a variety of customer service efforts. The company provides hosted software and services that communications service providers use to manage tasks such as phone service activation account changes and customer transactions including credit card billing inventory management and trouble ticketing. Customers include service providers such as AT&T Mobility Level 3 Time Warner Cable Verizon and Vodafone as well as equipment manufacturers such as Apple Dell and Sony. Synchronoss was founded in 2001.

	Annual Growth	12/10	12/11	12/12	12/13	12/14
Sales ($ mil.)	28.8%	166.0	229.1	273.7	349.0	457.3
Net income ($ mil.)	78.0%	3.9	15.1	27.1	23.4	38.9
Market value ($ mil.)	11.9%	1,140.8	1,290.3	900.8	1,327.0	1,787.9
Employees	24.2%	758	970	1,340	1,401	1,804

SYNERGETICS USA INC

NAS: SURG

3845 Corporate Centre Drive	CEO: J Michael Pearson
O'Fallon, MO 63368	CFO: Robert L Rosiello
Phone: 636 939-5100	HR: –
Fax: 636 939-6885	FYE: July 31
Web: www.synergeticsusa.com	Type: Public

Synergetics USA is in sync with surgeons' needs. The firm makes microsurgical instruments and electrosurgery systems used in minimally invasive surgeries primarily in the fields of ophthalmology and neurology. Among its products are forceps retractors scissors and illuminators used in vitreoretinal surgeries as well as precision neurosurgery instruments. It also makes bipolar electrosurgical generators which use electrical currents to cut tissue and seal blood vessels. Synergetics USA sells its products to hospitals physicians and clinics directly and through distributors in the US and abroad; it also sells certain items through partnerships with original equipment manufacturers (OEMs).

	Annual Growth	07/10	07/11	07/12	07/13	07/14
Sales ($ mil.)	5.6%	52.1	55.8	60.0	62.8	64.8
Net income ($ mil.)	(14.5%)	5.7	5.6	5.6	2.6	3.1
Market value ($ mil.)	4.2%	67.0	133.4	126.6	110.8	79.1
Employees	3.2%	348	344	349	336	395

SYNERGX SYSTEMS INC.

209 Lafayette Dr.
Syosset NY 11791
Phone: 516-433-4700
Fax: 516-433-1131
Web: www.synergxsystems.com

CEO: Paul Mendez
CFO: John A Poserina
HR: Robert Lin
FYE: September 30
Type: Subsidiary

Before a situation gets too hot to handle Synergx Systems sounds the alarm. The diversified technology and systems integration company formerly called Firetector makes sells and services fire alarm life safety and audio/visual communication systems. Synergx also markets security and intercom systems used in apartments hospitals schools and subways. The company conducts business through its Casey Systems subsidiary which services New York City and Long Island New York. Synergx Systems operates as a subsidiary of security monitoring equipment manufacturer Firecom.

SYNERGY PHARMACEUTICALS INC.

NASDAQ: SGYP

420 Lexington Ave. Ste. 1609
New York NY 10170
Phone: 212-297-0020
Fax: 212-297-0019
Web: www.synergypharma.com

CEO: Gary S Jacob
CFO: Gary L Sender
HR: –
FYE: December 31
Type: Public

Synergy Pharmaceuticals is working to sooth inflamed irritable and sluggish bowels. The development stage drug company's lead candidate plecanatide is in clinical trials as a treatment for chronic idiopathic constipation. It also has another candidate in pre-clinical development as a treatment for inflammatory bowel disease. Synergy has conducted the development of these drugs on behalf of Callisto Pharmaceuticals. Callisto which has held 40% of Synergy has agreed to let its subsidiary acquire it and take full control of its drug pipeline. Synergy raised the necessary money with additional public offerings in 2012.

SYNERGY RESOURCES CORP

ASE: SYRC

1625 Broadway, Suite 300
Denver, CO 80202
Phone: 720 616-4300
Fax: 970 737-1045
Web: www.syrginfo.com

CEO: Lynn A. Peterson
CFO: James P. (Jimmy) Henderson
HR: –
FYE: August 31
Type: Public

Synergy Resources is on a quest to "synergize" the natural resources found in the Denver-Julesburg Basin (D-J Basin) which spans Colorado Kansas Nebraska and Wyoming. The company is exploring the Wattenberg Field a 50-mile area north of Denver rich with oil and gas deposits. Synergy Resources reports proved reserves of about 41 billion cu. ft. of natural gas and 7 million barrels of oil and condensate. It has about 245000 net acres under lease with 290 producing wells. The company was founded in 2005 and began operations three years later.

	Annual Growth	08/11	08/12	08/13	08/14	08/15
Sales ($ mil.)	88.0%	10.0	25.0	46.2	104.2	124.8
Net income ($ mil.)	–	(11.6)	12.1	9.6	28.9	18.0
Market value ($ mil.)	36.3%	326.9	294.3	983.7	1,414.6	1,128.8
Employees	34.5%	11	11	16	29	36

SYNIVERSE HOLDINGS INC.

8125 Highwoods Palm Way
Tampa FL 33647-1776
Phone: 813-637-5000
Fax: 309-344-3522
Web: www.jjdog.com

CEO: Stephen C Gray
CFO: David W Hitchcock
HR: –
FYE: December 31
Type: Subsidiary

Syniverse Holdings opens up new worlds of communication for its clients. The company which operates as Syniverse Technologies provides business and network engineering services and software for managing and interconnecting voice and data network systems. It also offers clearing and settlement services voice and data roaming facilitation fraud management software and customer data analysis services to mobile operators fixed-line carriers and other telecommunications service providers worldwide. Customers have included Verizon Wireless and Vodafone Group. Syniverse is owned by private equity asset management firm The Carlyle Group.

SYNNEX CORP

NYS: SNX

44201 Nobel Drive
Fremont, CA 94538
Phone: 510 656-3333
Fax: –
Web: www.synnex.com

CEO: Kevin M. Murai
CFO: Marshall Witt
HR: Debra Torette
FYE: November 30
Type: Public

SYNNEX connects technology sellers with buyers and helps with customer service after the sale. The company distributes PCs peripherals software and consumer electronics from manufacturers that include Dell Hewlett-Packard Panasonic Lenovo Seagate and Microsoft. SYNNEX also provides design and support services. Its Concentrix segment offers customer support services using phone chat Web e-mail and digital print. The company's online services include parts catalogs configuration and ordering. In addition the company offers contract design and assembly build-to-order and configure-to-order services for manufacturers and systems integrators.

	Annual Growth	11/11	11/12	11/13	11/14	11/15
Sales ($ mil.)	6.4%	10,409.8	10,285.5	10,845.2	13,839.6	13,338.4
Net income ($ mil.)	8.5%	150.3	151.4	152.2	180.0	208.5
Market value ($ mil.)	33.9%	1,150.2	1,294.0	2,592.7	2,799.7	3,694.3
Employees	60.4%	10,948	11,615	14,500	64,000	72,500

SYNOPSYS INC

NMS: SNPS

690 East Middlefield Road
Mountain View, CA 94043
Phone: 650 584-5000
Fax: –
Web: www.synopsys.com

CEO: Chi-Foon Chan
CFO: Trac Pham
HR: –
FYE: October 31
Type: Public

To sum up Synopsys is a leading provider of electronic design automation (EDA) software and services. Its products are used by designers of integrated circuits (ICs) to develop simulate and test the physical design of ICs before production and then to test finished products. The company also provides semiconductor intellectual property (SIP) pre-designed circuits used as part of larger chips. Customers come from a variety of markets but particularly the semiconductor and electronics manufacturing industries. (Intel is its top customer.) Synopsys offers time-based software licenses where customers make yearly payments for use and support. It generates about half its sales outside the US.

	Annual Growth	10/11	10/12	10/13	10/14	10/15
Sales ($ mil.)	9.9%	1,535.6	1,756.0	1,962.2	2,057.5	2,242.2
Net income ($ mil.)	0.5%	221.4	182.4	247.8	259.1	225.9
Market value ($ mil.)	16.8%	4,159.8	4,996.1	5,650.8	6,358.3	7,754.7
Employees	10.9%	6,803	8,138	8,573	9,436	10,284

SYNOVIS LIFE TECHNOLOGIES INC.

NASDAQ: SYNO

2575 University Ave. West
St. Paul MN 55114-1024
Phone: 651-796-7300
Fax: 651-642-9018
Web: www.synovislife.com

CEO: –
CFO: Brett A Reynolds
HR: –
FYE: October 31
Type: Subsidiary

Duct tape can patch a lot of life's leaks and holes but when it comes to reconstructive surgery Synovis Life Technologies has some better options. The company makes instruments and biomaterials used to patch up soft tissue to prevent leaks of air blood or other fluids. Its products include the Peri-Strip buttress used to reinforce surgical staple lines in gastric bypass procedures. Other implant tissue lines are used to repair and replace soft tissue during reconstructive surgeries including abdominal wall breast and chest wall operations. It also makes orthopedic tissues chronic wound aids and microsurgical devices to connect vessels or nerves. Synovis was acquired by Baxter International in 2012.

SYNOVUS FINANCIAL CORP.

NYS: SNV

1111 Bay Avenue, Suite 500
Columbus, GA 31901
Phone: 706 649-2311
Fax: –
Web: www.synovus.com

CEO: Kessel D. Stelling
CFO: Thomas J. Prescott
HR: Amy Goins
FYE: December 31
Type: Public

Synovus Financial has a nose for community banking. The holding company owns flagship subsidiary Synovus Bank and more than 25 locally-branded banking divisions that offer deposit accounts and consumer and business loans in Alabama Florida Georgia South Carolina and Tennessee. Through more than 280 branches the bank provides checking and savings accounts loans and mortgages and credit cards. Other divisions offer insurance private banking wealth and asset management and other financial services. Nonbank subsidiaries include Synovus Mortgage Synovus Trust investment bank and brokerage Synovus Securities and GLOBALT which provides asset management and financial planning services.

	Annual Growth	12/10	12/11	12/12	12/13	12/14
Assets ($ mil.)	(2.6%)	30,093.1	27,162.8	26,760.0	26,201.6	27,051.2
Net income ($ mil.)	–	(790.7)	(60.6)	830.2	159.4	195.2
Market value ($ mil.)	79.0%	359.4	191.9	333.5	490.0	3,687.6
Employees	(7.3%)	6,109	5,224	4,963	4,696	4,511

SYNOVUS MORTGAGE CORP.

2204 Lakeshore Dr. Ste. 325
Birmingham AL 35209
Phone: 205-874-1459
Fax: 205-874-1516
Web: www.synovus.com/index.cfm?catid=1&subject=8

CEO: Michael L Padalino
CFO: Mary Beth Balzli
HR: –
FYE: December 31
Type: Subsidiary

Synovus Mortgage is synonymous with home lending. The subsidiary of holding company Synovus Financial originates and services residential mortgage loans in the Southeast. It offers a wide range of products including fixed- and adjustable-rate mortgages home renovation and construction loans refinancing and loans backed by the Federal Housing Administration (FHA) and Veterans Administration (VA). Synovus Mortgage targets traditional home buyers as well as those with low to moderate incomes second home buyers veterans and investors. The company operates more than 80 offices in its target markets of Alabama Florida Georgia Mississippi South Carolina and Tennessee.

SYNTA PHARMACEUTICALS CORP

NMS: SNTA

45 Hartwell Avenue
Lexington, MA 02421
Phone: 781 274-8200
Fax: 781 274-8228
Web: www.syntapharma.com

CEO: Chen Schor
CFO: Marc Schneebaum
HR: –
FYE: December 31
Type: Public

Synta Pharmaceuticals doesn't fill stockings but it might eventually fill the medical need of treating cancer. The drug development company has a handful of candidates in clinical and pre-clinical development stages. Its ganetespib and elesclomol compounds are in clinical trials as possible treatments for several types of cancer including non-small cell lung cancer (NSCLC) acute myeloid leukemia melanoma and rectal pancreatic ovarian prostate and breast cancers. Synta's preclinical research efforts include potential therapies for autoimmune diseases transplant acceptance respiratory conditions and cancerous tumors.

	Annual Growth	12/08	12/09	12/10	12/11	12/12
Sales ($ mil.)	(51.3%)	2.6	144.2	14.8	7.6	0.1
Net income ($ mil.)	–	(92.6)	79.1	(37.5)	(47.4)	(62.8)
Market value ($ mil.)	10.2%	421.9	348.8	421.9	321.9	621.7
Employees	(1.0%)	129	127	112	122	124

SYNTEL INC.

NMS: SYNT

525 E. Big Beaver Road, Suite 300
Troy, MI 48083
Phone: 248 619-2800
Fax: 248 619-2888
Web: www.syntelinc.com

CEO: Nitin Rakesh
CFO: Arvind S Godbole
HR: –
FYE: December 31
Type: Public

Syntel is in the know about information technology. The IT services provider offers outsourced applications development knowledge process outsourcing (KPO) and IT consulting and staffing for global corporate client list. Its largest segment applications outsourcing focuses on the development management and maintenance of business software. Syntel offers KPO services for middle and back-office functions such as transaction processing and loan servicing to financial services health care and insurance companies. Its top clients include American Express and State Street. Co-founding spouses Bharat Desai and Neerja Sethi are the company's biggest shareholders.

	Annual Growth	12/10	12/11	12/12	12/13	12/14
Sales ($ mil.)	14.4%	532.1	642.4	723.9	824.8	911.4
Net income ($ mil.)	21.8%	113.6	122.9	185.5	219.7	249.7
Market value ($ mil.)	(1.5%)	4,002.9	3,916.6	4,490.9	7,616.3	3,766.7
Employees	9.0%	17,383	19,484	21,407	23,652	24,553

SYNTELLECT INC.

2095 W. Pinnacle Peak Rd. Ste. 110
Phoenix AZ 85027
Phone: 602-789-2800
Fax: 602-789-2768
Web: www.syntellect.com

CEO: Stephen Sadler
CFO: Douglas Bryson
HR: –
FYE: December 31
Type: Subsidiary

Syntellect helps clients customize their customer service. The company's software platform is used by businesses to manage customer interactions by blending telephone interactive voice response voicemail email Web chat fax and agent functions to centralize interactions with customers. Its customer interaction applications also enable reporting and analytics quality monitoring and call recording. Syntellect's contact center software and services are used in the information technology financial services utilities government and consumer products industries. It has partnerships with enterprise software makers including Oracle. Founded in 1984 Syntellect was acquired by Enghouse Systems in 2002.

SYNTHESIS ENERGY SYSTEMS, INC.

NMS: SYMX

Three Riverway, Suite 300
Houston, TX 77056
Phone: 713 579-0600
Fax: 713 579-0610
Web: www.synthesisenergy.com

CEO: Robert W. Rigdon
CFO: Roger L. Ondreko
HR: –
FYE: June 30
Type: Public

Synthesis Energy Systems (SES) prefers it when a little waste is produced posthaste. The company owns a coal gasification plant in China that began production in 2008. (Coal gasification converts low-rank coal and coal waste into fuels such as synthetic natural gas methanol ammonia and dimethyl ether which are used to make gasoline). SES leases the technology behind the plant from the Gas Technology Institute. The company has four more coal gasification plants under development — two in China with AEI and two in the US with North American Coal Corporation and CONSOL Energy.

	Annual Growth	06/11	06/12	06/13	06/14	06/15
Sales ($ mil.)	11.2%	10.2	3.1	0.6	17.5	15.5
Net income ($ mil.)	–	(15.5)	(19.9)	(19.9)	(14.2)	(37.9)
Market value ($ mil.)	(6.5%)	159.8	104.3	66.4	160.7	122.2
Employees	(6.9%)	189	130	91	213	142

SYNTROLEUM CORP

NAS: SYNM

5416 S. Yale Suite 400
Tulsa, OK 74135
Phone: 918 592-7900
Fax: –
Web: www.syntroleum.com

CEO: –
CFO: –
HR: –
FYE: December 31
Type: Public

Syntroleum is looking for business synergies with energy companies. The company licenses its patented gas-to-liquids (GTL) process (also known as the Fischer-Tropsch process) which converts natural gas into synthetic crude oil by using air instead of pure oxygen. The liquids produced can be refined into fuels such as diesel and kerosene as well as specialty products such as synthetic lubricants waxes and chemical feed stocks. In 2007 Syntroleum formed a joint venture called Dynamic Fuels with chicken giant Tyson Foods. The JV will uses Syntroleum's biorefining technologies to process Tyson's animal fat greases and vegetable oils into synthetic fuel used for jet diesel and military applications.

	Annual Growth	12/08	12/09	12/10	12/11	12/12
Sales ($ mil.)	37.6%	4.9	27.4	8.4	4.2	17.5
Net income ($ mil.)	–	(4.1)	5.0	(9.5)	(16.9)	(1.1)
Market value ($ mil.)	(7.4%)	5.3	26.1	18.2	9.4	3.9
Employees	(3.6%)	22	19	19	21	19

SYNUTRA INTERNATIONAL INC

NMS: SYUT

2275 Research Blvd., Suite 500
Rockville, MD 20850
Phone: 301 840-3888
Fax: –
Web: www.synutra.com

CEO: Liang Zhang
CFO: Ning (Clare) Cai
HR: –
FYE: March 31
Type: Public

Chinese dairy products manufacturer Synutra International knows how to pack a nutritional punch — and put it into a can. The company develops manufactures and sells enriched milk- and rice-powder products for infants and children under the Super U-Smart My Angel and Dutch Cow brands. The company also makes powdered nutritional products including chondroitin and glucosamine for joint health for adults; however most of the company's business comes from the sale of its infants' and children's powders. Synutra products are sold in some 24000 retail outlets throughout mainland China. Chairman and CEO Liang Zhang owns the majority of the Synutra's shares.

	Annual Growth	03/11	03/12	03/13	03/14	03/15
Sales ($ mil.)	13.6%	248.5	342.5	265.8	370.5	413.9
Net income ($ mil.)	–	(40.1)	16.7	(63.9)	30.9	69.5
Market value ($ mil.)	(13.6%)	659.0	336.9	269.3	383.3	366.7
Employees	(15.1%)	5,200	4,250	3,400	3,200	2,700

SYNYGY INC.

CEO: –

2501 Seaport Dr. Ste. 100
Chester PA 19013-1889
Phone: 610-494-3300
Fax: 610-494-3301
Web: www.synygy.com

CFO: Robert Mooney
HR: –
FYE: December 31
Type: Private

In addition to its fondness for the letter Y Synygy likes for employee salaries to provide workers with incentive. The company develops sales performance management software used by such clients as GE Pfizer Deutsche Bank and AMD. Its incentive management applications are designed to help organizations align measure analyze and report sales employee compensation in order to better manage employee performance. Synygy offers its software as an on-demand service or installed on-site. The company also designs and manages compensation plans and provides reporting sales communication and training services. Founded in 1991 Synygy is owned by CEO Mark Stiffler and other members of the management team.

SYPRIS SOLUTIONS, INC.

NMS: SYPR

101 Bullitt Lane, Suite 450
Louisville, KY 40222
Phone: 502 329-2000
Fax: –
Web: www.sypris.com

CEO: Jeffrey T Gill
CFO: Anthony C Allen
HR: –
FYE: December 31
Type: Public

Sypris Solutions provides its customers with simple solutions for their manufacturing chores. The company's Industrial Group makes heavy-duty truck components including axle shafts gear sets differential cases trailer axle beams and other components. Its Electronics Group provides circuit board and box build manufacturing services primarily for the aerospace and defense industries as well as secure communications and data storage products for government clients. Sypris' top customers have traditionally included Dana Holding ArvinMeritor Raytheon Honeywell Lockheed Martin and the US Defense Department.

	Annual Growth	12/10	12/11	12/12	12/13	12/14
Sales ($ mil.)	7.4%	266.7	335.6	341.6	310.7	354.8
Net income ($ mil.)	–	(10.2)	7.9	3.0	(9.9)	(1.2)
Market value ($ mil.)	(11.1%)	87.1	80.3	81.1	62.7	54.5
Employees	4.1%	1,133	1,360	1,277	1,181	1,332

SYRACUSE UNIVERSITY

900 S CROUSE AVE STE 620
SYRACUSE, NY 132440001
Phone: 315-443-1870
Fax: –
Web: www.syr.edu

CEO: –
CFO: –
HR: –
FYE: June 30
Type: Private

Syracuse University is a serious school with a silly mascot. While it wasn't until 1995 that Otto the Orange was officially adopted as the school's mascot Syracuse's tradition of quality higher education dates back to 1870. The school enrolls more than 21000 undergraduate and graduate students and has some 1000 full-time faculty members on its campus in central New York State. It offers about 500 degree programs in areas such as communications computer science engineering psychology art mathematics music and information. Notable alumni include Dick Clark Ted Koppel Joyce Carol Oats Joe Biden and Aaron Sorkin.

	Annual Growth	06/09	06/10	06/11	06/12	06/13
Sales ($ mil.)	(3.9%)	–	979.0	839.7	818.7	869.6
Net income ($ mil.)	(3.0%)	–	–	145.4	(73.1)	136.9
Market value ($ mil.)	–	–	–	–	–	–
Employees	–	–	–	–	–	4,350

SYSCO CORP.

NYS: SYY

1390 Enclave Parkway
Houston, TX 77077-2099
Phone: 281 584-1390
Fax: 281 584-2880
Web: www.sysco.com

CEO: William J. (Bill) DeLaney
CFO: Robert C. (Chris) Kreidler
HR: Susan (Sue) Billiot
FYE: June 27
Type: Public

This company has the menu that people depend on. Sysco is the #1 food service supplier in North America serving more than 425000 customers with a fleet of 9400 delivery vehicles and 190 distribution centers in the US Bahamas Canada and Ireland. Its core broadline distribution business supplies food and non-food products to restaurants schools hotels health care institutions and other customers while its SYGMA Network focuses on supplying chain restaurants. Sysco distributes both nationally-branded products and its own private-label goods. In addition Sysco supplies customers with specialty produce and meat products and it distributes kitchen equipment and supplies for the hospitality industry.

	Annual Growth	07/11*	06/12	06/13	06/14	06/15
Sales ($ mil.)	5.5%	39,323.5	42,380.9	44,411.2	46,516.7	48,680.8
Net income ($ mil.)	(12.1%)	1,152.0	1,121.6	992.4	931.5	686.8
Market value ($ mil.)	5.1%	18,655.6	17,716.6	20,301.9	22,494.9	22,804.0
Employees	3.0%	46,000	47,800	48,100	50,300	51,700

*Fiscal year change

SYSCO GUEST SUPPLY LLC

4301 US Hwy. One
Monmouth Junction NJ 08852-090
Phone: 609-514-9696
Fax: 609-514-2692
Web: www.guestsupply.com

CEO: Paul Xenis
CFO: Mike Louro
HR: –
FYE: June 30
Type: Subsidiary

You know those hotel goodies we've all come to know and pack for home? Thank Sysco Guest Supply. A subsidiary of food distributing giant Sysco Corporation the company makes more than 7000 guest-room accessories and operating supplies for the hospitality industry. Its products include personal care items (mini soaps shampoos) housekeeping and laundry supplies room accessories paper products and bed bath and table linens. It offers brand-name products such as Bath & Body Works Dial and Neutrogena as well as custom and generic items and distributes them from its more than 15 facilities. Sysco Guest Supply also offers hotel furniture fixtures and equipment coffee appliances and kitchenware.

SYSKA HENNESSY GROUP INC.

1515 Broadway
New York NY 10036
Phone: 212-921-2300
Fax: 212-556-3333
Web: www.syska.com

CEO: Gary Brennen
CFO: Robert Discone
HR: –
FYE: December 31
Type: Private

Syska Hennessy Group is a smooth operator in world of engineering and consulting. With offices in the US and China the firm tackles some of the world's most technically sophisticated buildings including part of the Pentagon after the 9/11 terrorist attacks and high-tech data centers for the likes of Oracle SAS and Verizon. Services consist of sustainable design consulting architectural lighting design security consulting audio/visual design facilities management and commissioning (which ensures that a facility's performance complies with its design intent). The group serves a wide range of markets including corporations government facilities hospitals colleges aquariums and sports venues.

SYSTEMAX, INC.

NYS: SYX

11 Harbor Park Drive
Port Washington, NY 11050
Phone: 516 608-7000
Fax: –
Web: www.systemax.com

CEO: Robert Leeds
CFO: Lawrence P. (Larry) Reinhold
HR: –
FYE: December 31
Type: Public

Systemax's system involves being direct. The company is primarily a direct marketer of computers electronics and technology products in North America and Europe (where it operates under the Misco brand). Through catalogs websites and retail stores Systemax markets thousands of brand-name and private-label computer networking camera GPS cell phone video game and other electronic products. Systemax also sells material-handling equipment shelving storage items furniture and other industrial products. Its customers include businesses government agencies and schools as well as individual consumers.

	Annual Growth	12/10	12/11	12/12	12/13	12/14
Sales ($ mil.)	(1.0%)	3,590.0	3,682.0	3,544.6	3,352.3	3,442.8
Net income ($ mil.)	–	42.6	54.4	(8.3)	(43.8)	(37.5)
Market value ($ mil.)	(1.1%)	519.0	604.0	355.2	414.1	496.9
Employees	(1.4%)	5,600	5,500	5,300	5,100	5,300

T ROWE PRICE GROUP INC.

NMS: TROW

100 East Pratt Street
Baltimore, MD 21202
Phone: 410 345-2000
Fax: 410 752-3477
Web: www.troweprice.com

CEO: James A. C. Kennedy
CFO: Kenneth V. Moreland
HR: Jason Phr
FYE: December 31
Type: Public

T. Rowe Price Group administers an eponymous family of about 100 mutual funds in a variety of investment styles. Traditionally oriented toward growth investing the funds offer products in many risk and taxation profiles including small- mid- and large-cap stock funds; money market funds; and bond funds both taxable and nontaxable. Other services include asset management advisory services (including retirement plan advice for individuals) corporate retirement plan management separately managed accounts variable annuity life insurance plans discount brokerage and transfer agency and shareholder services. Founded in 1937 T. Rowe Price has nearly $747 billion in assets under management.

	Annual Growth	12/11	12/12	12/13	12/14	12/15
Sales ($ mil.)	11.2%	2,747.1	3,022.5	3,484.2	3,982.1	4,200.6
Net income ($ mil.)	12.1%	773.2	883.6	1,047.7	1,229.6	1,223.0
Market value ($ mil.)	5.8%	14,264.2	16,309.8	20,981.8	21,505.3	17,906.0
Employees	3.4%	5,255	5,372	5,668	5,870	5,999

T-3 ENERGY SERVICES INC.

7135 Ardmore St.
Houston TX 77054
Phone: 713-996-4110
Fax: 713-996-4123

CEO: –
CFO: –
HR: Pete Skertich
FYE: December 31
Type: Subsidiary

T-3 Energy Services (T-3) would like to get a chokehold on the oil and gas industry. The Robbins & Myers company manufactures and repairs high-pressure oilfield equipment including valves chokes actuators blow-out preventers and wellhead equipment. T-3 refurbishes and repairs pumps electric motors and generators; manufactures specialty bolts and fasteners; and fabricates equipment used for oil and gas operations. It also distributes pipes valves gaskets and other products. The company serves oil and gas customers in the US and Canada as well as in Australia Belgium Indonesia and Venezuela.

T-MOBILE US INC

NMS: TMUS

12920 S.E. 38th Street
Bellevue, WA 98006-1350
Phone: 425 378-4000
Fax: –
Web: www.t-mobile.com

CEO: John J. Legere
CFO: J. Braxton Carter
HR: Molly Luna
FYE: December 31
Type: Public

T-Mobile US is one of the largest providers of wireless voice and data communications services in the US. The company's 61 million T-Mobile and MetroPCS contract and prepaid consumer customers use its networks domestically and are able to connect to the compatible network of Deutsche Telekom when in Europe. It also offers low-cost no-contract mobile services through the GoSmart brand. In addition T-Mobile sells phones tablets PDAs and accessories from such vendors as Apple Nokia and Samsung. It has about 8000 T-Mobile and MetroPCS branded retail sites. In 2013 Deutsche Telekom acquired smaller rival MetroPCS via a reverse merger and combined it with T-Mobile; Deutsche Telekom owns about two-thirds of the combined company.

	Annual Growth	12/10	12/11	12/12	12/13	12/14
Sales ($ mil.)	–	0.0	20,618.0	19,719.0	24,420.0	29,564.0
Net income ($ mil.)	–	0.0	(4,718.0)	(7,336.0)	35.0	247.0
Market value ($ mil.)	–	0.0	7,008.8	8,026.2	27,163.2	21,753.2
Employees	12.5%	–	–	–	40,000	45,000

T. D. WILLIAMSON INC.

6120 S. Yale Ave. Ste. 1700
Tulsa OK 74136
Phone: 918-447-5100
Fax: 918-446-6327
Web: www.tdwilliamson.com

CEO: Robert D McGrew
CFO: –
HR: David R Miller
FYE: December 31
Type: Private

Keeping onshore and offshore pipelines operating safely flowing freely is what T. D. Williamson is all about. The world's leading pipeline equipment and services provider it designs manufactures and maintains oil field machinery and systems including pipeline pigging (scraping) gas leak detection pipeline inspection plugging tapping valve and clamp and cathodic protection equipment. The company also offers general pipeline training turnkey and repair services. T. D. Williamson operates a global network of sales offices and representatives.

T. MARZETTI COMPANY

37 W. Broad St.
Columbus OH 43215
Phone: 614-846-2232
Fax: 614-848-8330
Web: www.marzetti.com

CEO: –
CFO: –
HR: Angela Logsdon
FYE: June 30
Type: Subsidiary

Specialty food is the specialty of the house at this company. T. Marzetti is a leading maker of specialty food products including salad dressings condiments dips and other food toppings mostly sold under the Marzetti brand name. Its other product include croutons (Chatham Village) dry and frozen egg noodles (Inn Maid Amish Kitchen and Reames) and frozen baked goods (Marshall's Mamma Bella and Sister Schubert's). The food manufacturer sells its items nationwide primarily through retail grocers; however it also supplies foodservice operators. Begun by Teresa Marzetti in 1896 as a small restaurant in Columbus Ohio the company represents the specialty foods division of Lancaster Colony.

T.J.T., INC.

NBB: AXLE

843 North Washington Avenue
Emmett, ID 83617
Phone: 208 472-2500
Fax: 208 472-2525
Web: www.tjtusa.com

CEO: Larry E Kling
CFO: Nicole L Glisson
HR: Stephen Robbins
FYE: September 30
Type: Public

The next time you pass a house being carted down the road bet that it will be riding on some of T.J.T.'s tires. T.J.T. buys used axles and tires from manufactured housing dealers inspects and reconditions them and then sells them to manufactured home builders. The company also distributes vinyl siding and skirting to manufactured housing dealers and sells vinyl siding to the site-built and manufactured housing markets. It has expanded its line of products and aftermarket accessories for these markets to include skylights adhesives and sealants foundation and other set-up materials. T.J.T. operates primarily in the western US. CEO Terrence Sheldon controls a 30% stake in the company.

	Annual Growth	09/11	09/12	09/13	09/14	09/15
Sales ($ mil.)	1.0%	6.0	4.0	4.0	6.2	6.3
Net income ($ mil.)	–	(1.1)	(1.1)	(0.3)	0.8	0.2
Market value ($ mil.)	(10.1%)	2.3	0.7	1.5	1.9	1.5
Employees	(8.3%)	35	23	24	27	–

T.R. WORLD GYM LLC

113 Crosby Rd. Ste. 15
Dover NH 03820-4370
Phone: 603-742-4443
Fax: 781-229-8030
Web: www.openlinksw.com

CEO: Christopher Rondeau
CFO: –
HR: –
FYE: December 31
Type: Private

They're here to pump (clap) you up! Previously endorsed by former Mr. Universe and Mr. Olympia (aka the governor of California) Arnold Schwarzenegger T. R. World Gym operates World Gym International which runs and franchises health and fitness centers. The company doing business as World Gym International also earns revenue by selling workout gear including apparel water bottles sports bags and related accessories as well as nutrition products. World Gym has more than 200 franchisees worldwide in regions such as North America (including 36 US states) South America Asia/Pacific and the Middle East. Joe Gold formed World Gym in 1977; today it is owned by the family of managing director Guy Cammilleri.

TA ASSOCIATES INC.

John Hancock Tower 56th Fl. 200 Clarendon St.
Boston MA 02116
Phone: 617-574-6700
Fax: 617-574-6728
Web: www.ta.com

CEO: Elizabeth De Saint-Aignan
CFO: –
HR: –
FYE: December 31
Type: Private

If your private company has a lot of growth potential but is getting a little long in the tooth TA Associates won't discriminate. Managing some $16 billion raised from university endowments municipal and corporate pension funds and other investors the private equity firm primarily targets later-stage companies funding growth acquisitions share repurchases or leveraged buyouts. The company has offices in the US UK and India. It invests between $60 million and $500 million in business financial and health care services; consumer products and services; and technology companies. Since its founding in 1968 TA has invested in nearly 400 companies including Federal Express Jenny Craig and Tempur-Pedic.

TAB PRODUCTS CO LLC

605 4th St.
Mayville WI 53050
Phone: 888-466-8228
Fax: 800-304-4947
Web: www.tab.com

CEO: Thaddeus Jaroszewicz
CFO: John Palmer
HR: Dana Noel
FYE: May 31
Type: Private

TAB Products help offices get organized. A provider of record management systems the company makes products for paper-based and automated file-tracking systems. In addition to color-coded files ranging from individual folders to complete systems TAB develops tracking and labeling computer software filing cabinets and shelving. It also provides file conversion and other records management consulting services. Customers include the legal medical pharmaceutical banking and energy industries in the US as well as in Australia Canada and Europe. TAB Products was founded in 1950 by two ex-IBM salesmen Harry LeClaire and Si Foote. Today it is owned by HS Morgan Limited Partnership.

TABLE TRAC INC.

OTC: TBTC

15612 Hwy. 7 Ste. 250
Minnetonka MN 55345
Phone: 952-548-8877
Fax: 952-938-5629
Web: www.tabletrac.com

CEO: Brian Hinchley
CFO: Brian Hinchley
HR: –
FYE: December 31
Type: Public

You might say this company doesn't fold under pressure when it comes to tracking money at casino tables. Table Trac markets information management systems designed to help casino operators monitor their gaming operations. Its Table Trac system records and analyzes win-loss percentages dealer performance and cash movements. It also makes self-service kiosks for customer service and administering players club promotional programs. The company's customers are located mostly in the US; it also sells to markets in Central and South America. Chairman and CEO Chad Hoehne owns nearly 30% of Table Trac.

TABLEAU SOFTWARE, INC.

NYS: DATA

837 North 34th Street, Suite 200
Seattle, WA 98103
Phone: 206 633-3400
Fax: –
Web: www.tableausoftware.com

CEO: Christian Chabot
CFO: Thomas (Tom) Walker
HR: Brett Thompson
FYE: December 31
Type: Public

Tableau Software wants businesses to be able to better see and understand their data. The company develops business intelligence software designed to retrieve large volumes of data and quickly generate interactive dashboards reports and other data visualization tools with products like Tableau Desktop Tableau Public and Tableau Server. It serves more than 26000 businesses across various industries including Du Pont Sears and Deere & Company. Tableau was founded in 1996 by CEO Christian Chabot and chief development officer Chris Stolte. It started as a research project at Stanford University funded by the US Department of Defense. In mid-2013 Tableau became a public company.

	Annual Growth	12/10	12/11	12/12	12/13	12/14
Sales ($ mil.)	86.4%	34.2	62.4	127.7	232.4	412.6
Net income ($ mil.)	21.0%	2.7	3.4	1.4	7.1	5.9
Market value ($ mil.)	23.0%	–	–	–	4,816.0	5,922.0
Employees	52.8%	–	–	834	1,212	1,947

TACHYON NETWORKS INC.

9339 Carroll Park Dr. #150
San Diego CA 92121
Phone: 858-882-8100
Fax: 858-882-8122
Web: www.tachyon.net

CEO: Peter A Carides
CFO: Laurence A Hinz
HR: –
FYE: April 30
Type: Private

Tachyon Networks sells speed. No. Not that kind of speed. The company takes its name from a term from physics that describes a particle that is able to travel faster than the speed of light. Tachyon provides broadband satellite services — including remote Internet access virtual private networks (VPNs) and emergency network backup — to business and government clients. Large enterprises in such industries as energy construction and real estate use its service to connect to employees customers and suppliers who are beyond the reach of traditional wired networks. The company also serves US military agencies including the Naval Criminal Investigative Service and the US Army.

TACO BELL CORP.

1 Glen Bell Way
Irvine CA 92618
Phone: 949-863-4500
Fax: 949-863-2252
Web: www.tacobell.com

CEO: Brian Niccol
CFO: –
HR: –
FYE: December 31
Type: Subsidiary

Don't ask for whom the Taco Bell tolls; it tolls for millions of diners seeking a tortilla-wrapped meal. A unit of fast-food behemoth YUM! Brands Taco Bell is the #1 Mexican fast-food chain in the US with more than 5600 locations. The restaurants feature a wide range of Mexican-style menu items including tacos burritos gorditas quesadillas and nachos. Taco Bell units can be found operating as free-standing units and as quick-service kiosks in such places as shopping malls and airports. Taco Bell also has more than 250 international locations in 20 countries. More than 20% of the restaurants are company-operated. Parent YUM! Brands the world's #1 fast-food company also operates KFC and Pizza Hut.

TACO CABANA INC

8918 Tesoro Dr. Ste. 200
San Antonio TX 78217
Phone: 210-804-0990
Fax: 210-804-1970
Web: www.tacocabana.com

CEO: –
CFO: David Lloyd
HR: –
FYE: December 31
Type: Subsidiary

This company knows salsa is not just a dance. A division of quick-service restaurant operator Fiesta Restaurant Group Taco Cabana operates more than 150 Mexican patio cafes located in Texas Oklahoma and New Mexico. The restaurants are highlighted by Southwestern design accents and courtyards and serve Tex-Mex and traditional Mexican fare including fajitas enchiladas tacos and breakfast foods. Patrons can also take advantage of its salsa and seasoning bar. Most units are open 24 hours a day. In addition to its corporate-run locations Taco Cabana has a handful of franchised units.

TACOMA POWER

3628 S. 35th St. CEO: –
Tacoma WA 98409 CFO: –
Phone: 253-502-8600 HR: –
Fax: 203-485-4300 FYE: December 31
Web: www.partnerre.com Type: Business Segment

It is the destiny of the citizens of the City of Destiny to get their power from Tacoma Power which provides electric power services to more than 162580 customers in Tacoma Washington and surrounding areas. The utility a division of Tacoma Public Utilities one of the oldest and largest municipally owned utilities in the US operates four hydroelectric power plants and approximately 2275 miles of transmission and distribution lines. In addition Tacoma Power offers energy efficiency products and services manages fish hatcheries and recreational facilities and operates the Click! Network a high-speed telecommunications network (855 miles of cable).

TACONIC FARMS INC.

1 HUDSON CITY CTR CEO: Robert J Rosenthal
HUDSON, NY 125342354 CFO: –
Phone: 518-697-3900 HR: –
Fax: – FYE: December 31
Web: www.taconic.com Type: Private

Yes they are cute but Taconic Farms prefers that you don't pet their animals. The family-owned company provides research rodents and related products and services to pharmaceutical and biomedical companies government agencies and academic institutions in Asia Europe and North America through its facilities in Denmark Germany and the US. Taconic specially breeds rats and mice the workhorses of the biomedical industry to be disease-free or genetically modified to exhibit certain traits to help researchers develop new therapies for human disease. Other company units offer drug- and animal-safety testing and monoclonal antibody production.

	Annual Growth	12/08	12/09	12/10	12/11	12/12
Sales ($ mil.)	(1.7%)	–	142.6	151.7	144.9	135.5
Net income ($ mil.)	81.4%	–	–	1.2	(23.0)	4.1
Market value ($ mil.)	–	–	–	–	–	–
Employees	–	–	–	–	–	720

TAHOE RESOURCES INC.

5190 Neil Rd. Ste. 460 CEO: –
Reno NV 89502 CFO: Mark Sadler
Phone: 775-825-8574 HR: –
Fax: 775-562-2628 FYE: December 31
Web: www.tahoeresourcesinc.com Type: Public

Tahoe Resources is looking for silver a little farther south than the lake that straddles California and Nevada. The company was founded as CKM Resources in 2009 by Kevin McArthur the former CEO of Goldcorp. It changed its name to Tahoe Resources two months later when it bought a mining property in Guatemala from two affiliates of Goldcorp. The company is developing the property known as Escobal into a silver mine. Construction on the mine is expected to begin in 2012 with production beginning in 2014. Tahoe Resources went public in June 2010 raising C$383 ($372 million) in its IPO. Goldcorp is the company's largest shareholder owning 41% of its stock.

TAILORED BRANDS INC

NYS: TLRD

6380 Rogerdale Road CEO: Douglas S. (Doug) Ewert
Houston, TX 77072-1624 CFO: Jon W. Kimmins
Phone: 281 776-7000 HR: Beverly Bullock
Fax: – FYE: January 31
Web: www.menswearhouse.com Type: Public

With a business strategy tailored for growth The Men's Wearhouse has made alterations even a haberdasher would be hard-pressed to follow. It's one of the largest specialty retailers of men's business and formal attire with more than 1760 stores throughout North America and the UK. Its primary operations are Men's Wearhouse with about 700 stores and some 210 Men's Wearhouse and Tux stores that sell and rent tuxedos. It also has about 120 stores in Canada under the Moores name. Its 90-store K&G unit caters to thriftier shoppers and sells women's careerwear. Newly-acquired Jos. A Bank Clothiers operates about 330 locations. The company also supplies uniforms through its corporate apparel division.

	Annual Growth	01/11	01/12*	02/13	02/14*	01/15
Sales ($ mil.)	11.5%	2,102.7	2,382.7	2,488.3	2,473.2	3,252.5
Net income ($ mil.)	–	67.7	120.5	132.1	84.2	(0.1)
Market value ($ mil.)	15.7%	1,250.1	1,662.6	1,405.1	2,312.5	2,236.9
Employees	12.0%	16,600	17,200	17,500	18,200	26,100

*Fiscal year change

TAITRON COMPONENTS INC.

NAS: TAIT

28040 West Harrison Parkway CEO: Stewart Wang
Valencia, CA 91355-4162 CFO: David H. Vanderhorst
Phone: 661 257-6060 HR: –
Fax: – FYE: December 31
Web: www.taitroncomponents.com Type: Public

With more than a billion components in stock Taitron Components is a superstore for a small subset of the electronic component market: discrete semiconductors. Taitron also distributes optoelectronic devices and passive components such as capacitors and resistors. Discrete semiconductors are the forefathers of complex integrated circuits and are used in most consumer industrial and military electronic devices from appliances to airplanes. Taitron distributes more than 14000 different products from about 40 suppliers including Everlight Electronics Princeton Technology Samsung Electro-Mechanics and Vishay. The company gets the bulk of its sales in the US.

	Annual Growth	12/10	12/11	12/12	12/13	12/14
Sales ($ mil.)	(5.1%)	7.2	6.8	7.2	6.3	5.8
Net income ($ mil.)	–	(0.3)	(0.6)	(0.7)	(0.9)	(1.1)
Market value ($ mil.)	(11.1%)	8.8	6.3	5.7	5.8	5.5
Employees	(14.3%)	37	27	27	20	20

TAKE TWO INTERACTIVE SOFTWARE, INC.

NMS: TTWO

622 Broadway CEO: Strauss Zelnick
New York, NY 10012 CFO: Lainie J. Goldstein
Phone: 646 536-2842 HR: David Messenger
Fax: – FYE: March 31
Web: www.take2games.com Type: Public

Crime might not pay in the real world but in the gaming universe it means big money for Take-Two. The company's popular mature-rated Grand Theft Auto series and other games are developed by subsidiary Rockstar Games. Its 2K Games subsidiary publishes franchises such as BioShock Borderlands and Sid Meier's Civilization; the 2K Sports unit carries titles such as Major League Baseball 2K and NBA 2K. Take-Two's games are played on Microsoft Sony and Nintendo game consoles but also on PCs and handheld devices. Its products are sold through outlets including retail chains such as GameStop (20% of sales) Wal-Mart Best Buy and Amazon and as digital downloads. About half of its sales comes from the US.

	Annual Growth	03/11	03/12	03/13	03/14	03/15
Sales ($ mil.)	(1.2%)	1,136.9	825.8	1,214.5	2,350.6	1,082.9
Net income ($ mil.)	–	48.5	(108.8)	(29.5)	361.6	(279.5)
Market value ($ mil.)	13.5%	1,357.6	1,359.4	1,426.9	1,937.6	2,249.1
Employees	7.6%	2,118	2,235	2,440	2,530	2,840

TAKEDA SAN DIEGO INC.

10410 Science Center Dr. Ste. 100
San Diego CA 92121
Phone: 858-622-8528
Fax: 858-550-0526
Web: www.takedasd.com

CEO: –
CFO: –
HR: –
FYE: December 31
Type: Subsidiary

Takeda San Diego develops high-throughput protein crystallography systems used to speed up the drug discovery process. The company's technology can detect the three-dimensional shape of proteins an important step in determining how a drug can be attached to a protein to produce a therapeutic effect. The US biotech developer is one of Japanese drug maker Takeda's main research and development facilities. The subsidiary's drug discovery know-how is being used to develop new therapies for metabolic diseases such as diabetes cancer and inflammatory conditions. It

TALLAN INC.

175 Capital Blvd. Ste. 401
Glastonbury CT 06033
Phone: 860-633-3693
Fax: 860-513-4870
Web: www.tallan.com

CEO: Craig Branning
CFO: Michelle Hall
HR: –
FYE: December 31
Type: Private

Tallan helps companies wrap their claws around cutting-edge technologies. Specializing in e-business data warehousing supply chain management and customer relationship management applications the company provides information technology services for global corporations and Internet companies. Tallan's primary service offerings are custom software development creative design and infrastructure architecture. The company's software development expertise ranges from corporate Web portals to mobile and wireless applications; its creative design services include branding and streaming media customization; and its infrastructure architecture services include data center development and security planning.

TAL INTERNATIONAL GROUP INC   NYS: TAL

100 Manhattanville Road
Purchase, NY 10577-2135
Phone: 914 251-9000
Fax: 914 697-2549
Web: www.talinternational.com

CEO: Brian M. Sondey
CFO: John Burns
HR: Michael (Mel) Limoncelli
FYE: December 31
Type: Public

If your freight is going by truck train or ship tall odds are it might be going in a container owned by TAL International Group. The company is a leading lessor of intermodal freight containers — steel boxes that come in standard sizes and can be used to move goods over the road over the rails or over the water. Marine shipping lines are among the company's top customers. TAL maintains a fleet of more than 1250000 containers or about 2.1 million 20-foot equivalent units (TEUs) of capacity. Besides its leasing operations TAL International sells used containers. Investment firm Jordan Company through its Resolute Fund affiliate and other entities controls about a 40% stake in TAL.

	Annual Growth	12/10	12/11	12/12	12/13	12/14
Sales ($ mil.)	15.4%	366.8	516.7	589.2	642.9	650.4
Net income ($ mil.)	21.1%	57.7	109.7	130.1	143.2	124.0
Market value ($ mil.)	9.0%	1,024.2	955.1	1,207.0	1,902.7	1,445.5
Employees	(0.3%)	172	174	173	172	170

TALLGRASS ENERGY PARTNERS, LP   NYS: TEP

4200 W. 115th Street, Suite 350
Leawood, KS 66211
Phone: 913 928-6060
Fax: –
Web: www.tallgrassenergy.com

CEO: David G Dehaemers Jr
CFO: Gary J Brauchle
HR: –
FYE: December 31
Type: Public

This company hopes there's plenty of green out there in the tall grass. Tallgrass Energy Partners (TEP) provides transportation and storage of natural gas in the Rocky Mountains and Midwest. It also provides natural gas processing and treating at its three facilities in Wyoming. TEP's transportation capacity is about 978 million cu. ft. per day; its storage capacity is about 15 billion cu. ft. Both systems have contracts for about 73% of capacity. The company's treatment facilities process about 138 million cu. ft. per day or 100% of capacity. TEP was formed in early 2013 to hold the midstream assets of its parent Tallgrass Development. It became a public company a few months later.

	Annual Growth	11/11	11/12*	12/12	12/13	12/14
Sales ($ mil.)	–	0.0	220.3	38.6	267.7	371.6
Net income ($ mil.)	–	0.0	51.5	(2.4)	14.2	70.7
Market value ($ mil.)	–	0.0	–	–	1,296.6	2,229.1
Employees	–	–	–	–	–	–

*Fiscal year change

TALLAHASSEE MEMORIAL HEALTHCARE INC.

1300 MICCOSUKEE RD
TALLAHASSEE, FL 323085054
Phone: 850-431-1155
Fax: –
Web: www.tmh.org

CEO: –
CFO: William Giudice
HR: –
FYE: September 30
Type: Private

Tallahassee Memorial HealthCare (TMH) aims to take the hassle out of health care. The community health system serves residents of Florida's state capital and its surrounding communities. The system is anchored by Tallahassee Memorial Hospital a not-for-profit facility with more than 770 beds and about 560 physicians on staff who represent some 50 different specialties. TMH provides general medical and surgical care as well as specialty care in areas such as oncology rehabilitation women's and children's health obesity and diabetes. TMH also has a trauma center offers a family practice residency program and provides primary medical care through a handful of regional clinics.

	Annual Growth	09/07	09/08	09/09	09/12	09/13
Sales ($ mil.)	6.6%	–	411.5	435.9	480.0	566.2
Net income ($ mil.)	6.3%	–	–	24.7	40.2	31.5
Market value ($ mil.)	–	–	–	–	–	–
Employees	–	–	–	–	–	6,430

TALMER BANCORP INC   NAS: TLMR

2301 West Big Beaver Rd., Suite 525
Troy, MI 48084
Phone: 248 498-2802
Fax: –
Web: www.talmerbank.com

CEO: Gary S. Collins
CFO: Dennis L. Klaeser
HR: –
FYE: December 31
Type: Public

Talmer Bancorp is a bank holding company primarily serving states in the Midwest. It offers online banking and bill payment services online cash management safe deposit box rentals debit card and ATM card services. It supplies a variety of loans including loans for small and medium-sized businesses residential mortgages commercial real estate and a variety of commercial and consumer demand savings and time deposit products. The company owns three subsidiary banks: Talmer Bank and Trust a Michigan state-chartered bank; First Place Bank a federal savings association; and Talmer West Bank a Michigan state-chartered bank. Chemical Bank agreed to buy Talmer Bancorp for $1.1 billion in January 2016.

	Annual Growth	12/10	12/11	12/12	12/13	12/14
Assets ($ mil.)	40.3%	–	2,123.6	2,347.5	4,547.4	5,870.8
Net income ($ mil.)	19.4%	44.7	33.4	21.7	98.6	90.9
Market value ($ mil.)	–	–	–	–	–	990.3
Employees	(4.7%)	–	–	1,550	1,446	1,408

TALON INTERNATIONAL, INC.
NBB: TALN

21900 Burbank Boulevard, Suite 270
Woodland Hills, CA 91367
Phone: 818 444-4100
Fax: –
Web: www.talonzippers.com

CEO: Larry Dyne
CFO: Nancy Agger-Nielsen
HR: –
FYE: December 31
Type: Public

Talon has clawed its way to the top with some thread trim and hang tags. Formerly Tag It Pacific it develops brand-identity programs for manufacturers of fashion apparel and accessories and for specialty retailers and mass merchants. Talon's "trim packages" include items such as thread zippers labels buttons and hangers as well as printed marketing materials (hang tags barcoded tags pocket flashers size stickers) designed to promote and sell the items. It also distributes its Talon-brand metal and synthetic zippers and other apparel components such as waistbands under its TEKFIT name. Its more than 800 customers include Abercrombie & Fitch Express PVH and Victoria's Secret.

	Annual Growth	12/10	12/11	12/12	12/13	12/14
Sales ($ mil.)	4.4%	41.5	41.7	44.6	52.4	49.3
Net income ($ mil.)	–	(1.5)	0.7	0.7	9.7	0.6
Market value ($ mil.)	(16.5%)	34.1	10.1	4.5	23.1	16.6
Employees	6.0%	168	171	188	215	212

TALON THERAPEUTICS INC.
OTC: TLON

7000 Shoreline Ct. Ste. 370
South San Francisco CA 94080
Phone: 650-588-6404
Fax: 650-588-2787
Web: www.talontx.com/

CEO: Joseph W Turgeon
CFO: –
HR: –
FYE: December 31
Type: Public

Talon Therapeutics (formerly Hana Biosciences) has its claws sunk deeply into the fight against cancer. The development stage pharmaceutical company acquires and develops new drugs with a focus on cancer treatments. Specifically the company seeks to find treatments that kill tumors without damaging surrounding healthy tissue. Talon's lead product candidates include Marqibo a unique formulation of an existing cancer drug targeting forms of leukemia and melanoma and Menadione a topical lotion meant to treat rashes caused by some cancer treatments. The company has other oncology pharmaceuticals in its pipeline including therapies to treat solid tumor cancers (including lung and ovarian).

TAMIR BIOTECHNOLOGY INC.
PINK SHEETS: ACEL

300 Atrium Dr.
Somerset NJ 08873
Phone: 732 652 4525
Fax: 732-652-4575
Web: www.alfacell.com

CEO: Jamie Sulley
CFO: Joanne M Barsa
HR: –
FYE: July 31
Type: Public

Development-stage Tamir Biotechnology (formerly Alfacell) is willing to kiss a few frogs in hopes one will transform into a princely product. The biotechnology firm has isolated proteins from Northern Leopard frog eggs and embryos as possible therapies for cancerous tumors that have become resistant to chemotherapy. The company's lead drug candidate Onconase is being studied as a possible treatment for a variety of cancers including non-small cell lung cancer. Tamir Biotechnology is researching applications for Onconase and other amphibian proteins for applications in other areas of oncology as well as infectious diseases.

TAMPA ELECTRIC COMPANY

TECO Plaza 702 N. Franklin St.
Tampa FL 33602
Phone: 813-228-4111
Fax: 813-228-1670
Web: www.tampaelectric.com

CEO: John B Ramil
CFO: Sandra W Callahan
HR: Clinton E Childress
FYE: December 31
Type: Subsidiary

Tampa Electric Company (TECO) helps to illuminate the sunshine state when the sun is not shining. The company transmits and distributes electricity in a 2000-square mile service territory in West Central Florida (including Tampa). Its Tampa Electric division provides electric service to more than 678000 customers and has a generating capacity of about 4700 MW. The TECO Energy subsidiary also operates four fossil-fueled power plants and distributes natural gas to 340000 customers through its Peoples Gas unit. Other services include residential surge protection and the trimming of trees interfering with power lines.

TANDEM DIABETES CARE INC
NMS: TNDM

11045 Roselle Street
San Diego, CA 92121
Phone: 858 366-6900
Fax: –
Web: www.tandemdiabetes.com

CEO: Kim D. Blickenstaff
CFO: John Cajigas
HR: –
FYE: December 31
Type: Public

Tandem Diabetes Care is taking insulin pumps into the 21st century. The company's t:slim pump has the look of a smartphone not a pager and differs from traditional syringe-and-plunger insulin pumps in that it uses a miniature pump to draw insulin from a flexible bag within the cartridge rather than a mechanical syringe. The FDA approved t:slim in 2011 and the company sold more than 5000 pumps its first year. (It was one of the first products approved under the FDA's Infusion Pump Improvement Initiative.) Tandem Diabetes Care manufactures the t:slim and its accessories at a plant in California and sells them through distributors. The company went public in 2013 and raised $120 million which it will use to expand its business.

	Annual Growth	12/10	12/11	12/12	12/13	12/14
Sales ($ mil.)	–	0.0	–	2.5	29.0	49.7
Net income ($ mil.)	–	0.0	(25.5)	(33.0)	(63.1)	(79.5)
Market value ($ mil.)	–	0.0	–	–	609.6	300.4
Employees	19.3%	–	–	307	324	437

TANDY BRANDS ACCESSORIES, INC.
NBB: TBAC Q

3631 West Davis, Suite A
Dallas, TX 75211
Phone: 214 519-5200
Fax: –
Web: www.tandybrands.com

CEO: –
CFO: Chuck Talley
HR: –
FYE: June 30
Type: Public

When it comes to waist management Tandy Brands Accessories knows how to buckle down. It designs and markets leather goods including belts and wallets and other accessories such as scarves and neckties. Although the company has licenses to make products for national brands (including Dockers Totes and Dr. Martens Airwair) most of its products are proprietary brands and private-label items made for companies such as Wal-Mart Target and J. C. Penney. Some of these proprietary brands include Amity Rolfs Canterbury and Princess Gardner. Most of Tandy Brands' finished goods are manufactured in China and the Dominican Republic. Amid declining sales Tandy Brands is restructuring.

	Annual Growth	06/09	06/10	06/11	06/12	06/13
Sales ($ mil.)	(3.0%)	129.0	141.9	123.8	117.6	114.0
Net income ($ mil.)	–	(15.1)	1.2	(13.5)	(3.7)	(19.2)
Market value ($ mil.)	(28.4%)	16.4	25.7	14.0	10.3	4.3
Employees	(11.7%)	655	570	583	539	399

TANDY LEATHER FACTORY INC

NMS: TLF

1900 Southeast Loop 820
Fort Worth, TX 76140
Phone: 817 872-3200
Fax: –
Web: www.tandyleatherfactory.com

CEO: Shannon L. Greene
CFO: Shannon L Greene
HR: –
FYE: December 31
Type: Public

Tandy Leather Factory (aka TLF) has built a business turning hides into a cash cow. The company makes distributes and sells leather goods and related products such as leatherworking tools buckles and belt supplies leather dyes saddle and tack hardware do-it-yourself craft kits suede lace and fringe. Its Retail Leathercraft unit which generates more than 50% of sales operates about 75 retail leathercraft stores under the Tandy Leather banner that cater to leatherworking hobbyists in the US and Canada. It also sells merchandise online. The company also operates some 30 wholesale stores across in North America. Tandy Leather Factory was founded in 1980 as Midas Leathercraft Tool Co.

	Annual Growth	12/10	12/11	12/12	12/13	12/14
Sales ($ mil.)	8.6%	59.9	66.1	72.7	78.3	83.4
Net income ($ mil.)	16.7%	4.2	4.8	5.6	7.3	7.7
Market value ($ mil.)	17.5%	48.4	50.0	56.6	100.0	92.2
Employees	6.7%	466	534	566	571	603

TANGER FACTORY OUTLET CENTERS, INC.

NYS: SKT

3200 Northline Avenue, Suite 360
Greensboro, NC 27408
Phone: 336 292-3010
Fax: 336 297-0931
Web: www.tangeroutlet.com

CEO: Steven B. Tanger
CFO: Frank C. Marchisello
HR: –
FYE: December 31
Type: Public

Brand name bargains are on shoppers' lists when they visit Tanger Factory Outlet Centers. One of the top outlet mall developers (along with retail giant Simon Property and its Chelsea Property Group subsidiary) Tanger is a real estate investment trust (REIT) that develops owns and manages about 45 retail outlet centers in 25 states and Canada. A typical center has 75 stores and totals at least 300000 sq. ft. housing shops from more than 400 brand name companies including The Gap Ralph Lauren Ann Taylor Phillips-Van Heusen and Nike. Tanger's outlet centers which maintain about 99% occupancy are built away from malls and shopping districts so tenants don't compete with their full-price stores.

	Annual Growth	12/10	12/11	12/12	12/13	12/14
Sales ($ mil.)	10.9%	276.3	315.2	357.0	385.0	418.6
Net income ($ mil.)	21.2%	34.2	44.6	53.2	107.6	74.0
Market value ($ mil.)	(7.8%)	4,889.1	2,800.3	3,266.4	3,058.2	3,530.0
Employees	9.7%	432	476	542	614	625

TANGOE, INC.

NMS: TNGO

35 Executive Boulevard
Orange, CT 06477
Phone: 203 859-9300
Fax: –
Web: www.tangoe.com

CEO: Albert R. (Al) Subbloie
CFO: Gary R. Martino
HR: –
FYE: December 31
Type: Public

Tangoe dances to a telecom tempo. The company provides communications lifecycle management (CLM) software and services enabling large and mid-sized businesses and other organizations to manage their fixed and mobile assets and services. Its flagship hosted software suite the Communications Management Platform includes an inventory of industry reference metrics and tools to support lifecycle functions such as service provisioning inventory contracts management billing auditing reporting and analysis. Tangoe also offers such services as consulting contract negotiation bill auditing and carrier migration. The company was founded in 2000 as TelecomRFQ by CEO Albert Subbloie and went public in 2011.

	Annual Growth	12/10	12/11	12/12	12/13	12/14
Sales ($ mil.)	32.7%	68.5	104.9	154.5	188.9	212.5
Net income ($ mil.)	–	(1.8)	(3.0)	3.0	5.0	2.9
Market value ($ mil.)	(5.4%)	–	594.8	458.4	695.6	503.2
Employees	32.6%	757	1,004	1,383	2,056	2,339

TANIMURA & ANTLE FRESH FOODS INC.

1 Harris Rd.
Salinas CA 93908
Phone: 831-455-2255
Fax: 760-804-1331
Web: www.nexprise.com

CEO: Rick Antle
CFO: Vic Feuerstein
HR: Carmen Ponce
FYE: December 31
Type: Private

Tanimura & Antle Fresh Foods is a leading producer of fresh vegetables that serves food producers and suppliers as well as retail markets. With more than 30000 acres of farmland located in the US Mexico and South America the company grows and packages asparagus cabbage celery lettuce onions and other vegetables. Tanimura & Antle ships its produce throughout the US as well as to customers in Asia and Europe. Founded in 1982 the company is still owned and operated by the Tanimura and Antle families. The families decided to go into business together after becoming involved in the California produce industry in the early 1900s.

TANNER INDUSTRIES INC.

735 DAVISVILLE RD STE 3
SOUTHAMPTON, PA 189663277
Phone: 215-322-1238
Fax: –
Web: www.tannerind.com

CEO: Stephen B. Tanner
CFO: –
HR: –
FYE: December 31
Type: Private

Tanner plies the trade of chemical shipping and warehousing. The company distributes anhydrous ammonia and ammonium hydroxide by tank truck railcar drum and cylinder to US customers from approximately 20 facilities. It makes more than 20000 deliveries per year and operates 200 trucks and 150 rail cars. The company also provides custom blending contract packaging and safety training services. Tanner's products are sold to companies in the refrigeration metal treatment agriculture personal care product pulp and paper and water treatment industries. The company which was founded in 1954 by Lawrence Tanner is run by a third generation of Tanner family members.

	Annual Growth	12/03	12/04	12/05	12/06	12/07
Sales ($ mil.)	15.5%	–	52.1	64.7	74.1	80.2
Net income ($ mil.)	8.2%	–	–	3.5	6.8	4.1
Market value ($ mil.)	–	–	–	–	–	–
Employees	–	–	–	–	–	130

TAOS HEALTH SYSTEMS INC.

1397 WEIMER RD
TAOS, NM 875716253
Phone: 575-758-8883
Fax: –
Web: www.taoswomenshealth.org

CEO: Bill Patten
CFO: Ken Verdon
HR: –
FYE: May 31
Type: Private

Whether you're skiing in the winter or hiking in the summer Taos visitors and residents can turn to Holy Cross Hospital for medical care. The medical center provides inpatient and outpatient health care services for Taos and surrounding counties in northern New Mexico. The hospital opened its doors in 1937 and has expanded its facilities to include about 50 licensed beds. Among its specialty services are emergency medicine general surgery obstetrics orthopedics cardiology urology and women's health care. Holy Cross Hospital is part of the Taos Health Systems network which includes area general care rehabilitation surgical and specialist clinics.

	Annual Growth	05/09	05/10	05/11	05/12	05/13
Sales ($ mil.)	(4.2%)	–	59.2	57.9	64.5	52.1
Net income ($ mil.)	–	–	–	(3.9)	(0.2)	(5.1)
Market value ($ mil.)	–	–	–	–	–	–
Employees	–	–	–	–	–	412

TAPIMMUNE INC.

OTC: TPIV

2815 Eastlake Ave. East Ste. 300
Seattle WA 98102
Phone: 866-359-7541
Fax: 323-436-7755
Web: www.lamodels.com

CEO: –
CFO: –
HR: –
FYE: December 31
Type: Public

TapImmune taps into the immune system to take out autoimmune disorders. Its research is primarily focused on the biological TAP system which triggers an immune system response in cells. The TAP system shuts down in many cancer tumor cells but the company is developing a vaccine to restore the immune function. TapImmune is also researching a vaccine adjuvant product designed to enhance the effectiveness of existing and new infectious disease vaccines. The company also has technologies that could be used to identify or screen drugs for potential effectiveness in treating cancers and viral and infectious diseases.

TARGA RESOURCES CORP

NYS: TRGP

1000 Louisiana St., Suite 4300
Houston, TX 77002
Phone: 713 584-1000
Fax: 713 584-1100
Web: www.targaresources.com

CEO: Joe Bob Perkins
CFO: Mattthew J. (Matt) Meloy
HR: –
FYE: December 31
Type: Public

Targa Resources Corp. (formerly Targa Resources Investments) has targeted natural gas profits. It indirectly owns Targa Resources GP the general partner and 2% owner of Targa Resources Partners. Targa Resources Partners is a midstream natural gas and natural gas liquids (NGLs) company that gathers processes transports and sells natural gas and NGLs in the US. It owns or operates about 11400 miles of natural gas gathering pipelines moving gas from wells in Texas and the Louisiana coast and other Gulf of Mexico locations. The partnership also operates scores of processing plants and storage facilities primarily in the southwestern US.

	Annual Growth	12/10	12/11	12/12	12/13	12/14
Sales ($ mil.)	12.0%	5,469.2	6,994.5	5,885.7	6,556.0	8,616.5
Net income ($ mil.)	–	(15.0)	30.7	38.1	65.1	423.0
Market value ($ mil.)	41.0%	1,129.9	1,714.8	2,226.9	3,715.8	4,469.3
Employees	7.3%	1,020	1,096	1,192	1,277	1,350

TARGA RESOURCES PARTNERS LP

NYS: NGLS

1000 Louisiana St, Suite 4300
Houston, TX 77002
Phone: 713 584-1000
Fax: –
Web: www.targaresources.com

CEO: Joe Bob Perkins
CFO: –
HR: Bonnie Neely
FYE: December 31
Type: Public

Targa Resources Partners fuels its business by producing and processing natural gas. The midstream energy company owns or operates 11300 miles of natural gas gathering pipeline (and ten processing plants) with access to gas reserves in the New Mexico West and North Texas and the Gulf Coast. Targa Resources Partners also operates natural gas liquids (NGLs) storage and transportation facilities located primarily in the southern and southwestern US. Customers include oil and gas companies and utilities. Targa Resources Corp. holds a minority limited partner stake and a 2% general partner stake in Targa Resources Partners.

	Annual Growth	12/09	12/10	12/11	12/12	12/13
Sales ($ mil.)	12.5%	4,095.6	5,460.2	6,987.1	5,883.6	6,556.2
Net income ($ mil.)	45.6%	52.0	109.1	204.5	174.6	233.5
Market value ($ mil.)	21.1%	2,760.0	3,855.6	4,232.5	4,243.9	5,937.8
Employees	–	–	–	–	–	–

TARGET CORP

NYS: TGT

1000 Nicollet Mall
Minneapolis, MN 55403
Phone: 612 304-6073
Fax: –
Web: www.target.com

CEO: Brian C. Cornell
CFO: Cathy R. Smith
HR: Jodeen A. Kozlak
FYE: January 31
Type: Public

Purveyor of all that is cheap yet chic Target is the US's #2 discount chain (behind Wal-Mart). The fashion-forward discounter operates some 1795 Target and SuperTarget stores across North America as well as an online business at Target.com. Target and its larger grocery-carrying incarnation SuperTarget have carved out a niche by offering more upscale trend-driven merchandise than rivals Wal-Mart and Kmart. Target also issues its proprietary Target credit card good only at Target. The company is growing its grocery business and aggressively expanding stores. It entered the Canadian market in 2013 with 124 stores but pulled out in early 2015 after failing to win over Canadian shoppers.

	Annual Growth	01/11	01/12*	02/13	02/14*	01/15
Sales ($ mil.)	1.9%	67,390.0	69,865.0	73,301.0	72,596.0	72,618.0
Net income ($ mil.)	–	2,920.0	2,929.0	2,999.0	1,971.0	(1,636.0)
Market value ($ mil.)	7.9%	34,795.6	32,042.7	39,149.1	36,261.7	47,126.2
Employees	(0.6%)	355,000	365,000	361,000	366,000	347,000

*Fiscal year change

TASER INTERNATIONAL INC.

NMS: TASR

17800 North 85th Street
Scottsdale, AZ 85255
Phone: 480 991-0797
Fax: –
Web: www.taser.com

CEO: Patrick W. (Rick) Smith
CFO: Daniel M. (Dan) Behrendt
HR: –
FYE: December 31
Type: Public

TASER International's weapons aim to take perps down but not out. The company is well known for designing and manufacturing various non-lethal TASER lines of stun guns including its best-selling TASER X26. These electronic control devices (ECDs) are geared at the law enforcement corrections military and private security markets as well as consumers. The company also offers AXON wearable video cameras for officers and a hosted product called Evidence.com that allows digital evidence to be viewed shared and managed from a Web browser. Products are sold worldwide through a direct sales force distribution partners and online store and third-party resellers.

	Annual Growth	12/10	12/11	12/12	12/13	12/14
Sales ($ mil.)	17.3%	86.9	90.0	114.8	137.8	164.5
Net income ($ mil.)	–	(4.4)	(7.0)	14.7	18.2	19.9
Market value ($ mil.)	54.1%	249.1	271.4	473.8	841.7	1,403.5
Employees	11.6%	365	394	433	485	567

TATUNG COMPANY OF AMERICA INC.

2850 E EL PRESIDIO ST
LONG BEACH, CA 908101119
Phone: 310-637-2105
Fax: –
Web: www.tatungusa.com

CEO: Huei-Jihn Jih
CFO: Michael Lai
HR: –
FYE: December 31
Type: Private

Tongue tied by the alphabet soup of electronics? Tatung Company of America untangles the LCDs (liquid crystal displays) from the LEDs (light-emitting diodes). It offers an array of high-tech goods and manufacturing services for PC and electronics OEMs. Its digital line ranges from signage and security surveillance tools like cameras and monitors to computer monitors for PCs point-of-sale terminals and touch screens. The company also sells home appliances such as air purifiers and rice cookers as well as hospitality conveniences like microwaves and coffee makers. The company is the US arm of Taiwan's Tatung Company.

	Annual Growth	12/03	12/04	12/05	12/07	12/08
Sales ($ mil.)	(15.1%)	–	246.9	265.4	138.3	128.5
Net income ($ mil.)	(41.2%)	–	–	3.0	1.3	0.6
Market value ($ mil.)	–	–	–	–	–	–
Employees	–	–	–	–	–	300

TAUBER OIL COMPANY

55 WAUGH DR STE 700
HOUSTON, TX 770075837
Phone: 713-869-8700
Fax: –
Web: www.tauberoil.com

CEO: –
CFO: –
HR: –
FYE: December 31
Type: Private

No liquid petrochemical product is taboo for oil refiner and marketer Tauber Oil. The family owned company markets refined petroleum products carbon black feedstocks liquefied petroleum gases chemicals and petrochemicals (including benzene styrene monomer and methanol). Tauber Oil is one of the US's leading suppliers of feedstocks for reforming and olefin cracking. It also has oil and gas exploration and production operations. Subsidiary Tauber Petrochemical was created in 1997 to beef up the company's international petrochemical business. Tauber Oil which is owned by David and Richard Tauber maintains a fleet of more than 500 rail cars to supply its customers.

	Annual Growth	12/09	12/10	12/11	12/12	12/13
Sales ($ mil.)	14.8%	–	3,155.0	4,427.8	5,088.2	4,769.4
Net income ($ mil.)	43.1%	–	–	8.0	21.2	16.3
Market value ($ mil.)	–	–	–	–	–	–
Employees	–	–	–	–	–	135

TAUBMAN CENTERS, INC.

NYS: TCO

200 East Long Lake Road, Suite 300
Bloomfield Hills, MI 48304-2324
Phone: 248 258-6800
Fax: –
Web: www.taubman.com

CEO: Robert S. Taubman
CFO: Lisa A. Payne
HR: –
FYE: December 31
Type: Public

Taubman's favorite seasonal activity is most likely holiday shopping. The real estate investment trust (REIT) through its majority-owned operating partnership acquires owns and develops shopping malls primarily in the US. Taubman owns nearly 20 properties (mostly super-regional malls with more than 800000 sq. ft. each) in urban and suburban shopping centers in 10 states. Its largest tenants have included L Brands The Gap and Forever 21. Its Taubman Asia subsidiary in Hong Kong develops malls in China and South Korea. Taubman was founded in 1950 by former chairman A. Alfred Taubman who with his family controls about one-quarter of the REIT.

	Annual Growth	12/10	12/11	12/12	12/13	12/14
Sales ($ mil.)	0.9%	654.6	644.9	748.0	767.2	679.1
Net income ($ mil.)	93.4%	63.9	192.9	106.2	132.6	893.0
Market value ($ mil.)	10.9%	3,196.6	3,932.4	4,984.9	4,047.7	4,839.3
Employees	0.7%	582	821	665	708	598

TAWA SUPERMARKET INC.

6281 Regio Ave.
Buena Park CA 90620
Phone: 714-521-8899
Fax: 714-521-3366
Web: www.99ranch.com

CEO: Chang Hua K Chen
CFO: –
HR: –
FYE: December 31
Type: Private

TAWA Supermarket brings ethnic food mainstream with more than 25 Asian-American grocery stores. Operated under the 99 Ranch Market banner the chain is primarily found in California but it also has locations in Georgia Nevada and Washington. In addition to groceries fresh seafood and produce 99 Ranch Market stores sell everything from Chinese DVDs to ginseng. Founded in 1984 by a Taiwanese expatriate Roger Chen to serve immigrants who craved the food products of their homeland 99 Ranch Market has grown to become the biggest Asian supermarket retailer in California.

TAXUS CARDIUM PHARMACEUTICALS GROUP INC

NBB: CRXM

11750 Sorrento Valley Rd, Suite 250
San Diego, CA 92121
Phone: 858 436-1000
Fax: –
Web: www.cardiumthx.com

CEO: –
CFO: Dennis M Mulroy
HR: –
FYE: December 31
Type: Public

At the heart of Cardium Therapeutics is a hope to hit it big with one of its assorted holdings. Its Cardium Biologics unit includes lead candidate Generx which is in development as a treatment for candidates ischemic heart disease (such as angina) and restoring heart functioning after a heart attack. Meanwhile its Tissue Repair Company business received FDA approval for Excellagen a topical gel intended to promote healing diabetic foot ulcers and other wounds in 2012. A third business To Go Brands develops and sells nutritional supplements and skin care products.

	Annual Growth	12/09	12/10	12/11	12/12	12/13
Sales ($ mil.)	(29.6%)	0.4	0.2	0.0	0.8	0.1
Net income ($ mil.)	–	(11.7)	(4.7)	(7.1)	(8.3)	(8.9)
Market value ($ mil.)	5.0%	6.0	3.5	2.6	1.7	7.3
Employees	(5.9%)	14	15	15	24	11

TAYLOR (CALVIN B.) BANKSHARES, INC. (MD)

NBB: TYCB

24 North Main Street
Berlin, MD 21811
Phone: 410 641-1700
Fax: –
Web: www.taylorbank.com

CEO: Raymond M Thompson
CFO: William H Mitchell
HR: –
FYE: December 31
Type: Public

Calvin B. Taylor Bankshares be the holding company for Calvin B. Taylor Banking Company (aka Taylor Bank) which has about 10 branches in southeastern Maryland and another in Delaware. The bank offers standard commercial and retail services including checking and savings accounts money market accounts and credit cards. It also offers discount securities brokerage through an affiliation with correspondent bank M&T Securities. Real estate loans account for some 90% of the bank's lending portfolio including residential and commercial mortgages. The bank is named after its founder who opened a predecessor to Calvin B. Taylor Banking Company in 1890.

	Annual Growth	12/10	12/11	12/12	12/13	12/14
Assets ($ mil.)	2.7%	406.1	416.2	442.9	447.3	451.0
Net income ($ mil.)	(3.5%)	5.2	4.6	4.4	4.1	4.5
Market value ($ mil.)	(1.4%)	78.8	64.9	75.8	72.9	74.5
Employees	1.7%	89	88	92	–	–

TAYLOR CAPITAL GROUP, INC

NMS: TAYC

9550 West Higgins Road
Rosemont, IL 60018
Phone: 847 653-7978
Fax: –
Web: www.coletaylor.com

CEO: –
CFO: –
HR: –
FYE: December 31
Type: Public

This company is tailor-made for small and midsized business owners. Taylor Capital Group is the holding company for Cole Taylor Bank which specializes in commercial banking real estate lending and wealth management services aimed primarily at closely-held and family-run businesses in the construction manufacturing distribution transportation and professional services industries. Business loans including working capital owner-occupied real estate financing and letters and lines of credit account for approximately 90% of the bank's loan portfolio. With about 10 branches in the Chicago metropolitan area the bank also offers traditional banking services to consumers.

	Annual Growth	12/08	12/09	12/10	12/11	12/12
Assets ($ mil.)	7.2%	4,388.9	4,403.5	4,483.9	4,685.8	5,802.4
Net income ($ mil.)	–	(124.5)	(31.6)	(53.8)	91.1	61.9
Market value ($ mil.)	32.5%	168.4	327.9	378.6	279.9	519.7
Employees	20.1%	451	434	591	638	938

TAYLOR DEVICES INC.

NAS: TAYD

90 Taylor Drive
North Tonawanda, NY 14120-0748
Phone: 716-694-0800
Fax: 716-695-6015
Web: www.taylordevices.com

CEO: Douglas P Taylor
CFO: Mark V McDonough
HR: –
FYE: May 31
Type: Public

Taylor Devices helps buffer buildings and other structures from the forces of earthquakes high winds and even roaring crowds. The company makes seismic dampers and other equipment used to absorb shock control vibration and store energy. Along with giant dampers used in multi-story buildings — including Safeco Field home of the Seattle Mariners baseball team — Taylor Devices produces a variety of shock absorbers liquid die springs and vibration dampers used in equipment and machinery. Taylor Devices primarily sells its products in the US and Canada.

	Annual Growth	05/11	05/12	05/13	05/14	05/15
Sales ($ mil.)	10.0%	20.9	29.0	24.7	20.0	30.6
Net income ($ mil.)	11.3%	1.4	2.2	2.5	1.1	2.2
Market value ($ mil.)	21.8%	19.7	32.1	27.1	29.7	43.3
Employees	7.2%	90	106	102	104	119

TAYLOR MORRISON HOME CORP

NYS: TMHC

4900 N. Scottsdale Road, Suite 2000
Scottsdale, AZ 85251
Phone: 480-840-8100
Fax: –
Web: www.taylormorrison.com

CEO: Sheryl Palmer
CFO: C. David (Dave) Cone
HR: –
FYE: December 31
Type: Public

Building the American dream suits Taylor Morrison. Through its subsidiaries the company designs builds and sells mid- to high-end homes and condominiums in the US under the Taylor Morrison and Darling Homes brands. Its home sale prices range from $170000 to nearly $2 million with an average sale price of about $415000 in the Eastern US and $540000 in the West. The builder has more than 425 communities under construction in Arizona California Colorado Florida and Texas. The company also offers financing through its Taylor Morrison Home Funding subsidiary.

	Annual Growth	12/10	12/11	12/12	12/13	12/14
Sales ($ mil.)	–	0.0	0.0	–	2,323.2	2,708.4
Net income ($ mil.)	–	0.0	0.0	–	45.4	71.5
Market value ($ mil.)	–	0.0	0.0	–	2,745.4	2,310.0
Employees	20.0%	–	–	1,041	1,259	1,498

TAYLOR OIL CO. INC.

77 2nd St.
Somerville NJ 08876
Phone: 900-725-7737
Fax: 908-725-7746
Web: www.tayloroilco.com

CEO: George F Taylor III
CFO: –
HR: –
FYE: December 31
Type: Private

Taylor Oil keeps on trucking to make sure that it provides petroleum distribution and on-site fueling services to construction crews contractors marinas and trucking fleets along the East Coast. The company's trucks visit job sites on a predetermined schedule and time to custom-deliver and fill all of a client's equipment tanks and vehicles. Many of Taylor Oil's trucks carry both on- and off-road diesel so that it can fuel all types of equipment not just construction machinery. It delivers loads to meet the needs of 10000-gallons-per-day users as well as clients needing as little as 50 gallons per day.

TAYLOR PRECISION PRODUCTS INC.

2311 W. 22nd St. Ste. 103
Oak Brook IL 60523
Phone: 630-954-1250
Fax: 630-954-1275
Web: www.taylorusa.com

CEO: –
CFO: Donald Robinson
HR: –
FYE: December 31
Type: Private

Measure for measure Taylor Precision Products knows what it takes to build a scalable business. The company makes precision thermometers scales hygrometers and other measuring equipment. From connoisseur thermometers designed to ensure that Thanksgiving turkeys are cooked to perfection to altimeters used in fighter planes the company is committed to dependability and accuracy in its measuring equipment. Its product lines include bathroom scales body fat analyzers scales food scales indoor and outdoor thermometers kitchen timers and thermometers and rain gauges. Established in 1851 Taylor Precision Products was sold by HoMedics to private equity firm Centre Partners in 2012.

TAYLOR-LISTUG INC.

1980 Gillespie Way
El Cajon CA 92020-1096
Phone: 619-258-1207
Fax: 619-258-1623
Web: www.taylorguitars.com

CEO: Kurt Listug
CFO: Barbara Wight
HR: –
FYE: December 31
Type: Private

You might say these guitars are Taylor-made to exacting specifications. Taylor-Listug which does business as Taylor Guitars is one of the premier acoustic guitar manufacturers in the US. It markets more than 130 models and styles of six- and twelve-string guitars known for their quality workmanship. Played by such artists as Dave Matthews Jason Mraz and Prince the guitars range in price from moderate to thousands of dollars (for a Brazilian rosewood 12-string model). Taylor also sells acoustic basses guitar accessories and apparel through more than 800 dealers in the US and 25 other countries. The company is owned by president Bob Taylor and CEO Kurt Listug who started the business in 1974.

TAYLORMADE ADIDAS GOLF

5545 Fermi Ct.
Carlsbad CA 92008-7324
Phone: 760-918-6000
Fax: 760-918-6014
Web: www.tmag.com

CEO: –
CFO: –
HR: –
FYE: December 31
Type: Subsidiary

TaylorMade-adidas Golf has the drive to be the best in the golf equipment industry. The top golf club maker makes metal drivers and irons (R11 Burner R500 Series) putters (Spider Rossa) and balls (Distance Plus TP Tour) that are sold worldwide. Other products include bags apparel and accessories as well as items for women and kids. It sponsors players on the PGA (Mike Weir) Senior PGA (Gary McCord) European PGA and LPGA (Se Ri Pak) tours. Gary Adams founded TaylorMade in 1979 after discovering that balls struck by metal drivers travel farther than those struck by traditional woods. TaylorMade is part of sporting behemoth adidas also owner of Reebok.

TB WOOD'S CORPORATION

440 N. 5th Ave.
Chambersburg PA 17201
Phone: 717-264-7161
Fax: 717-264-6420
Web: www.tbwoods.com

CEO: –
CFO: Christian Storch
HR: –
FYE: December 31
Type: Subsidiary

The only thing TB Wood's and Tiger Woods have in common is that both make drives. TB Wood's makes power transmission devices that transfer power from motors or engines to industrial machinery. Its mechanical products include synchronous and variable speed drives couplings clutches brakes and gearboxes for the construction oil field and pulp and paper industries. Customers include distributors Motion Industries and Kaman Industrial Technologies. The company was founded in 1857 as a foundry for wood-burning stoves. It shifted its manufacturing emphasis to electrical products as the 19th century ended. Altra Holdings acquired TB Wood's in 2007 for around $92 million in cash.

TBA GLOBAL LLC

220 W. 42nd St. 10th Fl.
New York NY 10036
Phone: 646-445-7000
Fax: 646-445-7001
Web: www.tbaglobal.com

CEO: Paula Balzerm
CFO: Joseph Lugo
HR: –
FYE: December 31
Type: Private

TBA Global may have found its niche producing corporate events. The company generates most of its sales by producing corporate meetings and events (award presentations product launches road shows business meetings sales conferences) for a variety of corporate clients that have included such notable names as Bank of America IBM Nike Monster Worldwide Wal-Mart and McDonald's. TBA — which stands for Think Believe Act — has a half dozen offices in the US and two international offices in Canada. Founded in 1994 the company was acquired by investment firm Post Capital Partners along with its management in 2013.

TBC CORPORATION

7111 Fairway Dr. Ste. 201
Palm Beach Gardens FL 33418
Phone: 561-227-0955
Fax: 901-541-3625
Web: www.tbccorp.com

CEO: Lawrence C Day
CFO: Timothy J Miller
HR: –
FYE: December 31
Type: Subsidiary

TBC is a big wheel in tire distribution and the Big O in tire retailing. A unit of Sumitomo Corporation of America (SCOA) it's one of the largest private-brand tire marketers in North America. Its TBC Private Brands and Treadways units distribute about 10 proprietary brands (including Multi-Mile Cordovan and Sigma) to wholesalers and retailers in the US Canada and Mexico. TBC also sells tires and offers automotive services through 500-plus Big O Tires stores in 20 US states and Canada. TBC also operates more than 730 retail locations under the Tire Kingdom Merchant's Tire and Auto Centers and National Tire & Battery banners. It added a hefty 2250 Midas shops to its retail network in 2012.

TBWA WORLDWIDE INC.

488 Madison Ave. 5th Fl.
New York NY 10022-5702
Phone: 212-804-1300
Fax: 212-804-1333
Web: www.tbwa.com

CEO: Troy Ruhanen
CFO: James Fenton
HR: Andy McCown
FYE: December 31
Type: Subsidiary

This firm has some big ideas about how to market a brand. One of the world's leading advertising agencies TBWA Worldwide is known for executing highly creative work for such clients as Apple Energizer and Nissan. In addition to creative advertising TBWA provides relationship marketing promotional marketing and branding services through its TEQUILA subsidiary and Integer Group agency. Overall the TBWA has about 275 offices in 100 countries; in the US it operates through TBWAChiatDay with offices in Los Angeles New York San Francisco and Toronto. TBWAManchester acts as another UK unit under the TBWA umbrella as well. TBWA is a unit of Omnicom Group the world's #1 media services conglomerate.

TCF FINANCIAL CORP

NYS: TCB

200 Lake Street East, Mail Code EXO-03-A
Wayzata, MN 55391-1693
Phone: 952 745-2760
Fax: –
Web: www.tcfbank.com

CEO: Craig R. Dahl
CFO: Thomas F. (Tom) Jasper
HR: Barbara (Barb) Shaw
FYE: December 31
Type: Public

TCF Financial is the holding company for TCF National Bank which offers retail and small-business services through more than 430 locations. TCF provides standard services such as checking and savings accounts CDs consumer and business loans mortgages and insurance and is a leading issuer of Visa debit cards. Residential mortgages account for nearly half of the company's loan and lease portfolio. TCF also offers specialized lending services such as commercial leasing equipment finance inventory finance and indirect auto loans across the US.

	Annual Growth	12/10	12/11	12/12	12/13	12/14
Assets ($ mil.)	1.2%	18,465.0	18,979.4	18,225.9	18,379.8	19,394.6
Net income ($ mil.)	4.4%	146.6	109.4	(212.9)	151.7	174.2
Market value ($ mil.)	1.8%	2,480.1	1,728.2	2,034.7	2,721.2	2,661.0
Employees	(1.2%)	7,363	7,143	7,328	7,449	7,023

TCI INTERNATIONAL INC.

47300 Kato Rd.
Fremont CA 94538
Phone: 510-687-6100
Fax: 510-687-6101
Web: www.tcibr.com

CEO: –
CFO: Mary A Alcon
HR: –
FYE: December 31
Type: Subsidiary

TCI International finds loose lips before they sink the wrong ships. The company is a developer of broadband products for broadcasting communications intelligence collection specialized radio communications and spectrum management. Its Broadcast and Communications Group provides high-power broadcasting antennas for a variety of military and civilian use. The TCI Signal Processing Group designs and manufactures spectrum monitoring equipment direction finding and signal collection products for military and intelligence uses as well as for use by regulatory authorities. The company also provides engineering installation and integration services. TCI International is a subsidiary of SPX Corporation.

TD AMERITRADE HOLDING CORP

NMS: AMTD

200 South 108th Avenue
Omaha, NE 68154
Phone: 402 331-7856
Fax: 402 597-7789
Web: www.amtd.com

CEO: Fredric J. (Fred) Tomczyk
CFO: Stephen J. (Steve) Boyle
HR: Karen Ganzlin
FYE: September 30
Type: Public

If your stock makes a big move while you're stuck in traffic don't worry — TD Ameritrade lets you buy low and sell high even when you're on the go. Through several subsidiaries it provides electronic discount brokerage and related financial services that enable retail investors to trade common and preferred stocks of US companies exchange-traded funds (ETFs) mutual funds bonds options futures and foreign currencies. TD Ameritrade also runs the Investools investor education program. In addition to its online offerings the company provides services through a retail network of more than 100 branches nationwide. TD Ameritrade holds some $670 billion in client assets across 6.6 million funded client accounts.

	Annual Growth	09/11	09/12	09/13	09/14	09/15
Sales ($ mil.)	4.1%	2,767.5	2,647.0	2,771.0	3,129.0	3,247.0
Net income ($ mil.)	6.3%	637.8	586.0	675.0	787.0	813.0
Market value ($ mil.)	5.7%	7,896.6	9,870.1	9,870.1	9,870.1	9,870.1
Employees	1.1%	5,451	5,312	5,429	5,771	5,690

TEACHERS INSURANCE AND ANNUITY ASSOCIATION - COLLEGE RETI

730 3rd Ave.
New York NY 10017
Phone: 212-490-9000
Fax: 212-913-2803
Web: www.tiaa-cref.org

CEO: Roger W Ferguson Jr
CFO: –
HR: –
FYE: December 31
Type: Private

With a name that could almost teach literacy by itself Teachers Insurance and Annuity Association - College Retirement Equities Fund (TIAA-CREF) is one of the largest if not longest-named private retirement systems in the US. It provides for more than 3.5 million members of the academic cultural medical and research communities and for investors outside of academia's ivied confines. It also serves institutional investors. TIAA-CREF's core offerings include financial advice investment information retirement plans and accounts annuities life insurance brokerage and trust services (through TIAA-CREF Trust). The system a not-for-profit organization also manages a line of mutual funds.

TEAM HEALTH HOLDINGS INC

NYS: TMH

265 Brookview Centre Way, Suite 400
Knoxville, TN 37919
Phone: 865 693-1000
Fax: –

CEO: Michael D. (Mike) Snow
CFO: David P. Jones
HR: Eric Norman
FYE: December 31
Type: Public

Team Health keeps its cool in an emergency room and it runs a smooth back office. The company is a leading provider of clinical outsourcing services across the US. It provides physician staffing and administrative services to hospital emergency rooms and handles everything from doctor recruitment to billing payroll and claims management. The company provides similar services for anesthesiology inpatient care (hospitalist) and pediatric programs. Team Health contracts with civilian and military hospitals clinics and physician groups across the US.

	Annual Growth	12/10	12/11	12/12	12/13	12/14
Sales ($ mil.)	16.7%	1,519.3	1,745.3	2,069.0	2,383.6	2,819.6
Net income ($ mil.)	64.5%	13.3	65.5	63.8	87.4	97.7
Market value ($ mil.)	38.7%	1,107.7	1,573.2	2,050.8	3,246.9	4,100.9
Employees	18.9%	8,600	9,800	11,500	12,400	17,200

TEAM INDUSTRIES INC.

105 PARK AVE NW
BAGLEY, MN 566219558
Phone: 218-694-3550
Fax: –
Web: www.team-ind.com

CEO: David Ricke
CFO: Steve Kast
HR: –
FYE: September 28
Type: Private

It takes a team TEAM Industries to make the drivetrains that and other vehicles parts. The Ricke family owned company designs tests manufacturers and assembles powertrain transmissions drivetrains gear sets and chassis components for snowmobile all-terrain vehicle lawn mowers and other vehicles through partnerships with CNH Ford Honda Ingersoll-Rand Kawasaki Textron Yamaha and other OEMs. TEAM maintains half a dozen facilities throughout Minnesota and North Carolina; its manufacturing capabilities run from ductile iron and shaft machining to aluminum die-casting and gear/spline making. The company also offers engineering R&D and testing services.

	Annual Growth	09/09	09/10	09/11	09/12	09/13
Sales ($ mil.)	14.8%	–	193.0	251.2	288.4	291.9
Net income ($ mil.)	(3.0%)	–	–	22.8	25.4	21.4
Market value ($ mil.)	–	–	–	–	–	–
Employees	–	–	–	–	–	1,100

TEAM, INC.

NYS: TISI

13131 Dairy Ashford, Suite 600
Sugar Land, TX 77478
Phone: 281 331-6154
Fax: –
Web: www.teamindustrialservices.com

CEO: Ted W. Owen
CFO: Greg L. Boane
HR: Mark Hinderliter
FYE: May 31
Type: Public

Consider it the A-Team for high-pressure situations. Team provides specialized maintenance services for piping systems including repairing leaks hot tapping (adding new connections to pressurized pipelines) and detecting escaping emissions. It also offers field heat treatment and testing and inspection services. The firm makes custom equipment clamps and enclosures to augment its standard materials and sealant products. Mainly serving companies in heavy industries such as the petrochemical refining power pulp and paper pipeline and steel industries. The firm operates from more than 150 locations worldwide but its largest markets are the US and Canada.

	Annual Growth	05/11	05/12	05/13	05/14	05/15
Sales ($ mil.)	13.5%	508.0	623.7	714.3	749.5	842.0
Net income ($ mil.)	10.8%	26.6	32.9	32.4	29.9	40.1
Market value ($ mil.)	14.7%	468.3	543.3	734.5	853.6	810.4
Employees	8.2%	3,500	3,800	4,200	4,300	4,800

TEARLAB CORP.

NAS: TEAR

9980 Huennekens Street, Suite 100
San Diego, CA 92121
Phone: 858 455-6006
Fax: –
Web: www.tearlab.com

CEO: Elias Vamvakas
CFO: Wes Brazell
HR: –
FYE: December 31
Type: Public

TearLab (formerly OccuLogix) can read your tears. The diagnostics company has developed and commercialized the TearLab Osmolarity System a tear collection and analysis system for use at the point of care. The system detects biomarkers that indicate ophthalmic conditions; its first testing product aids in the diagnosis of dry eye disease (DED). After several failed attempts to develop medical therapies for ophthalmic ailments including glaucoma and macular degeneration the company became focused on diagnostic testing; it changed its name to TearLab in 2010.

	Annual Growth	12/10	12/11	12/12	12/13	12/14
Sales ($ mil.)	84.5%	1.7	2.1	4.0	14.6	19.7
Net income ($ mil.)	–	(6.7)	(8.8)	(19.3)	(29.0)	(23.7)
Market value ($ mil.)	4.9%	73.7	37.7	137.9	314.2	89.1
Employees	75.2%	14	19	48	101	132

TECH DATA CORP.
NMS: TECD

5350 Tech Data Drive
Clearwater, FL 33760
Phone: 727 539-7429
Fax: –
Web: www.techdata.com

CEO: Robert M. Dutkowsky
CFO: Charles V. (Chuck) Dannewitz
HR: Lawrence Hamilton
FYE: January 31
Type: Public

Tech Data is 100% committed to IT products distribution. One of the world's largest wholesale distributors of technology products Tech Data provides thousands of different items to more than 115000 resellers in 100-plus countries. Its catalog of products includes computer components (disk drives keyboards and video cards) networking equipment (routers and bridges) peripherals (printers modems and monitors) systems (PCs and servers) and software. Tech Data also provides technical support configuration integration financing electronic data interchange (EDI) and other logistics and product fulfillment services. More than 60% of Tech Data's revenues are generated outside the US.

	Annual Growth	01/11	01/12	01/13	01/14	01/15
Sales ($ mil.)	3.2%	24,376.0	26,488.1	25,358.3	26,821.9	27,670.6
Net income ($ mil.)	(4.9%)	214.2	206.4	176.3	179.9	175.2
Market value ($ mil.)	5.0%	1,753.5	1,940.7	1,903.0	2,015.5	2,134.4
Employees	0.6%	8,700	8,300	9,100	9,100	8,900

TECHE HOLDING CO.
ASE: TSH

1120 Jefferson Terrace
New Iberia, LA 70560
Phone: 337 560-7151
Fax: –
Web: www.teche.com

CEO: –
CFO: –
HR: –
FYE: September 30
Type: Public

Teche Holding is the holding company for Teche Federal Bank which operates some 20 branch offices in the Lafayette metropolitan area of southern Louisiana. Targeting individuals and local business customers the bank offers such traditional retail services as checking and savings accounts NOW accounts and certificates of deposit. Real estate loans make up nearly all of the company's loan portfolio including residential mortgages (about half of all loans) commercial mortgages mobile home loans and land loans.

	Annual Growth	09/09	09/10	09/11	09/12	09/13
Assets ($ mil.)	2.9%	765.1	761.5	793.2	852.0	856.7
Net income ($ mil.)	5.2%	7.1	7.1	7.2	7.3	8.7
Market value ($ mil.)	8.4%	67.8	63.5	60.4	83.0	93.6
Employees	0.5%	317	314	310	323	323

TECHNICA CORPORATION

22970 INDIAN CREEK DR
STERLING, VA 201666739
Phone: 703-662-2000
Fax: –
Web: www.technicacorp.com

CEO: –
CFO: –
HR: –
FYE: December 31
Type: Private

Founded in 1991 Technica provides information technology (IT) consulting services hardware and related software including offerings in voice and data network design installation and performance testing. Technica supplies support for technologies and platforms such as storage area networks and metro optical as well as large systems integration and network security services. The company also offers on-site support and customized training for managers engineers and technicians. Its customers include telecommunications providers government and military agencies health care and educational clients and financial markets.

	Annual Growth	12/05	12/06	12/08*	06/09*	12/12
Sales ($ mil.)	(22.4%)	–	411.8	65.1	27.9	89.7
Net income ($ mil.)	4.1%	–	–	2.2	1.7	2.6
Market value ($ mil.)	–	–	–	–	–	–
Employees	–	–	–	–	–	190

*Fiscal year change

TECHNICAL COMMUNICATIONS CORP.
NAS: TCCO

100 Domino Drive
Concord, MA 01742-2892
Phone: 978 287-5100
Fax: 978 371-1280
Web: www.tccsecure.com

CEO: Carl H Guild Jr
CFO: Michael P Malone
HR: –
FYE: October 03
Type: Public

Technical Communications Corporation also known as TCC helps its customers keep their secrets to themselves. The company makes secure communications equiment that enables users to digitally encrypt and transmit information. It also makes receivers used to decipher the data. TCC's products protect transmissions sent by radios telephones fax machines computer networks the Internet fiber-optic cables and satellite links. The company subcontracts much of its manufacturing and caters largely to government agencies but it also serves financial institutions and other corporations. It derives the bulk of its sales from a very small number of customers including the US Army.

	Annual Growth	09/11	09/12	09/13	09/14*	10/15
Sales ($ mil.)	(16.3%)	12.1	8.1	6.2	6.1	5.9
Net income ($ mil.)	–	2.3	(0.8)	(0.7)	(2.6)	(1.8)
Market value ($ mil.)	(20.8%)	13.5	10.6	12.5	7.9	5.3
Employees	(4.5%)	36	36	36	36	30

*Fiscal year change

TECHNICAL CONSUMER PRODUCTS INC.

325 Campus Dr.
Aurora OH 44202
Phone: 330-995-6111
Fax: 330-995-6188
Web: www.tcpi.com

CEO: Ellis Yan
CFO: Brian Catlett
HR: –
FYE: December 31
Type: Subsidiary

How many people does it take to screw in one of Technical Consumer Products' light bulbs? One and they only have to change the bulb every few years. Technical Consumer Products (TCP) sells energy efficient compact fluorescent light (CFLs) bulbs light emitting diodes (LEDs) high-intensity discharge (HID) lamps and halogen bulbs in the US under the brands TCP DuraBright EcoSave Fresh2 and n:vision. It also offers linear fluorescent bulbs and fixtures exit and emergency lighting CFL fixtures and ballasts to the commercial market under the brands EcoVations and SpringLight. TCP is the US sales arm of Chinese manufacturer TCP International Holdings.

TECHNOLOGY CROSSOVER VENTURES L.P.

528 Ramona St.
Palo Alto CA 94301
Phone: 650-614-8200
Fax: 650-614-8222
Web: www.tcv.com

CEO: Jay Hoag
CFO: –
HR: –
FYE: December 31
Type: Private

Elvis advised to "TCB." IT companies might be advised to "TCV." Technology Crossover Ventures (TCV) makes private equity and venture capital investments in information technology (IT) companies throughout the US. Sectors in which TCV invests include software financial technology communications infrastructure services and the Internet. It usually invests from $20 million to $200 million per transaction and sometimes more with the backing of its limited partners. TCV has nearly $8 billion in assets under management and has invested in more than 160 companies since it was founded in 1995 by general partners Jay Hoag and Rick Kimball.

TECHNOLOGY RESEARCH CORPORATION

5250 140th Ave. North	CEO: G Gary Yetman
Clearwater FL 33760	CFO: J G Cochran
Phone: 727-535-0572	HR: –
Fax: 727-530-4324	FYE: March 31
Web: www.trci.net	Type: Subsidiary

Technology Research Corporation (TRC) doesn't think electrical devices should be shocking. The company makes ground fault protectors portable leakage current interrupters and other electrical safety products that protect people and equipment against electric shock and fires. Its products detect electrical leaks and cut off power to equipment such as copy machines computers and printers. While the military remains an important market for TRC it is focused on building its commercial customer base and has expanded its Fire Shield product line in response to government safety regulations relating to appliance cords. In 2011 TRC was acquired by Coleman Cable in a deal valued at about $51.5 million.

TECHNOLOGY SERVICE CORPORATION

962 WAYNE AVE	CEO: –
SILVER SPRING, MD 209104433	CFO: –
Phone: 301-576-2300	HR: –
Fax: –	FYE: September 30
Web: www.tsc.com	Type: Private

Radar sensor expert Technology Service Corporation (TSC) provides engineering consulting services and specialized products primarily for US government agencies such as the Federal Aviation Administration the Navy and the Department of Defense but also for international civil aviation agencies and major radar system suppliers. Its services encompass research and advanced concept development through integrated logistics support. TSC's products include software for radar siting geographic information services and sensor simulation. Dr. Peter Swerling founded the employee-owned company in 1966.

	Annual Growth	09/05	09/06	09/07	09/08	09/10
Sales ($ mil.)	27.1%	–	–	40.6	75.4	83.3
Net income ($ mil.)	649.1%	–	–	0.0	6.2	6.9
Market value ($ mil.)	–	–	–	–	–	–
Employees	–	–	–	–	–	404

TECHSHOT INC.

7200 Hwy. 150	CEO: –
Greenville IN 47124	CFO: –
Phone: 812-923-9591	HR: –
Fax: 812-923-9598	FYE: December 31
Web: www.techshot.com	Type: Private

Technology research is no shot in the dark for customers of Techshot. The company provides product design engineering and development services specializing in electrical mechanical and software technologies. From feasibility studies to prototype production Techshot helps entrepreneurs manufacturers medical institutions universities and government agencies throughout North America develop products. Formerly known as Space Hardware Optimization Technology (SHOT) the company studied hardware for spaceships and payloads for space shuttle missions. Its work with NASA led to contracts with military institutional and commercial customers. Founded in 1988 Techshot is owned by its officers.

TECHSMITH CORPORATION

2405 WOODLAKE DR	CEO: –
OKEMOS, MI 48864-5910	CFO: –
Phone: 517-333-2100	HR: –
Fax: –	FYE: December 31
Web: www.techsmith.com	Type: Private

TechSmith is a master craftsman when it comes to the screen shot. The company provides screen capture and screen recording software for office professionals. TechSmith's flagship SnagIt software is a screen capture and editing tool that captures images — including animation graphics text and video — then enhances them with special effects and multimedia features. Other products include Camtasia Studio used to produce videos for the Internet and mobile devices; and Morae a market research software. The company sells its software worldwide to corporations educational institutions government agencies and small businesses. TechSmith was founded in 1987 by president William Hamilton and other investors.

	Annual Growth	12/08	12/09	12/10	12/11	12/12
Sales ($ mil.)	14.4%	–	34.4	42.9	45.2	51.4
Net income ($ mil.)	51.8%	–	1.5	3.5	5.5	5.4
Market value ($ mil.)	–	–	–	–	–	–
Employees	–	–	–	–	–	175

TECHTARGET INC

NMS: TTGT

275 Grove Street	CEO: Greg Strakosch
Newton, MA 02466	CFO: Janice Kelliher
Phone: 617 431-9200	HR: Arden Port
Fax: –	FYE: December 31
Web: www.techtarget.com	Type: Public

TechTarget can help you hit the IT professional's bull's-eye. The company operates a network of about 100 websites that focus on information technology topics such as storage security and networking. TechTarget offers original vendor-generated and user-generated content to more than 9 million registered members many of whom are technology buyers. Websites include Whatis.com DesktopReview.com SearchCRM.com and ebizQ.net. TechTarget additionally produces industry events and digital media offerings (e-mail newsletters online white papers webcasts and podcasts) aimed at IT professionals. The company generates most of its revenue through lead-generation advertising campaigns.

	Annual Growth	12/10	12/11	12/12	12/13	12/14
Sales ($ mil.)	2.8%	95.0	105.5	100.0	88.5	106.2
Net income ($ mil.)	–	(1.2)	4.7	4.0	(1.8)	4.1
Market value ($ mil.)	9.4%	256.7	189.0	179.7	222.1	368.1
Employees	4.4%	577	647	661	639	686

TECO ENERGY INC.

NYS: TE

TECO Plaza, 702 N. Franklin Street	CEO: John B. Ramil
Tampa, FL 33602	CFO: Sandra W (Sandy) Callahan
Phone: 813 228-1111	HR: Debi Pridgen
Fax: 813 228-1670	FYE: December 31
Web: www.tecoenergy.com	Type: Public

TECO Energy keeps the energy flowing in west central Florida and New Mexico. The firm's Tampa Electric unit distributes power to more than 706000 customers and has about 4668 MW of generating capacity. The company produces almost all of its electricity from coal. It also distributes power to customers in New Mexico. TECO distributes natural gas in Florida through its Peoples Gas System unit (more than 350000 customers) and in New Mexico through New Mexico Gas Co. (NMGC more than 510000 gas customers). It exited the coal mining business with the sale of TECO Coal in 2015. That year the company agreed to be bought by Emera.

	Annual Growth	12/10	12/11	12/12	12/13	12/14
Sales ($ mil.)	(7.4%)	3,487.9	3,343.4	2,996.6	2,851.3	2,566.4
Net income ($ mil.)	(14.1%)	239.0	272.6	212.7	197.7	130.4
Market value ($ mil.)	3.6%	4,181.2	4,496.0	3,936.9	4,049.7	4,813.1
Employees	1.0%	4,233	4,290	3,900	3,900	4,400

TECOGEN INC

NAS: TGEN

45 First Avenue
Waltham, MA 02451
Phone: 781 622-1120
Fax: –

CEO: John N Hatsopoulos
CFO: Bonnie J Brown
HR: David Pidgeon
FYE: December 31
Type: Public

Tecogen designs and makes natural gas-fueled commercial and industrial cooling and cogeneration systems such as chillers water heaters and other types of cooling refrigeration and co-generation systems. Its product lines include TECOCHILL 25 to 400 ton engine-driven chillers Ilios high-efficiency water heaters and Tecogen co-generation equipment. Tecogen has shipped more than 2000 units throughout the US. The company was founded in the early 1960s and was spun off from Thermo Electron Corp. (a predecessor to Thermo Fisher Scientific) in 1987. Tecogen went public in 2014 after withdrawing a previous offering in 2013.

	Annual Growth	12/10	12/11	12/12	12/13	12/14
Sales ($ mil.)	–	0.0	11.1	15.3	15.8	19.3
Net income ($ mil.)	–	0.0	(1.6)	(1.6)	(3.4)	(3.7)
Market value ($ mil.)	–	0.0	–	–	–	83.0
Employees	7.4%	–	–	65	70	75

TECUMSEH PRODUCTS CO.

NMS: TECU

5683 Hines Drive
Ann Arbor, MI 48108
Phone: 734 585-9500
Fax: 517 423-8760
Web: www.tecumseh.com

CEO: Harold M Karp
CFO: Janice E Stipp
HR: –
FYE: December 31
Type: Public

Named for the legendary Shawnee chief Tecumseh Products makes a line of hermetically sealed compressors and heat pumps for residential and commercial refrigerators and freezers water coolers air conditioners dehumidifiers and vending machines. The company's line of scroll compressor models are suited for demanding commercial refrigeration applications and consist primarily of reciprocating and rotary designs. Tecumseh sells its products to OEMs and aftermarket distributors in more than 100 countries worldwide with 80% of its sales generated outside of the US. It markets its products under brand names that include Celseon L'Unit-© Herm-©tique Masterflux Silensys and Vector.

	Annual Growth	12/09	12/10	12/11	12/12	12/13
Sales ($ mil.)	2.9%	735.9	933.8	864.4	854.7	823.6
Net income ($ mil.)	–	(93.4)	(56.8)	(73.2)	22.6	(37.5)
Market value ($ mil.)	–	–	–	–	–	–
Employees	(0.7%)	7,600	8,600	7,350	7,700	7,400

TED'S MONTANA GRILL INC.

133 Luckie St.
Atlanta GA 30303
Phone: 404-266-1344
Fax: 404-233-6717
Web: www.tedsmontanagrill.com/

CEO: George W McKerrow
CFO: Danielle Clark
HR: Erin Brady
FYE: December 31
Type: Private

You might say this restaurant company is trying to help the Wild West remain wild. Ted's Montana Grill is a chain restaurant operator that combines elements of themed-dining with an ecological ethos. Inspired by saloons of the American West the restaurants specialize in burgers and other homey dishes made from fresh ground bison meat as well as traditional American fare such as beef chicken and seafood items. The chain is also committed to the principles of environmentalism and nature conservation. Ted's Montana Grill has about 45 restaurants in 20 states mostly in the Southeast and in Colorado. Bison rancher and former media mogul Ted Turner started the business with CEO George McKerrow Jr. in 2002.

TEGNA INC

NYS: TGNA

7950 Jones Branch Drive
McLean, VA 22107-0150
Phone: 703 854-7000
Fax: –
Web: www.gannett.com

CEO: Gracia C. Martore
CFO: Victoria D. Harker
HR: Roxanne Horning
FYE: December 28
Type: Public

This company spreads the word through websites and television broadcasts. TEGNA (formerly Gannett) has a large portfolio of media and digital businesses to deliver a wide range of content. Its television and digital businesses make the company one of the largest and most geographically diverse media companies in the US. TEGNA's two top digital properties are automotive-related site Cars.com and job site CareerBuilder. The company's media division includes more than 45 television stations making it the largest independent station group of major network affiliates in the top 25 markets. TEGNA was formed when Gannett spun off its newspaper publishing businesses including USA TODAY.

	Annual Growth	12/10	12/11	12/12	12/13	12/14
Sales ($ mil.)	2.5%	5,438.7	5,240.0	5,353.2	5,161.4	6,008.2
Net income ($ mil.)	15.9%	588.2	458.7	424.3	388.7	1,062.2
Market value ($ mil.)	19.8%	3,498.6	3,072.3	3,992.9	6,625.3	7,201.2
Employees	(1.1%)	32,600	31,000	30,700	31,600	31,250

TEGRANT CORPORATION

1401 Pleasant St.
DeKalb IL 60115
Phone: 800-756-7639
Fax: 815-756-1623
Web: www.tegrant.com

CEO: Ron Leach
CFO: –
HR: Lori Lozeau
FYE: December 31
Type: Subsidiary

Tegrant Corporation delivers the packaging so your goods arrive in tip-top shape. The US maker of custom-molded foam plastic specializes in elegantly engineered protective packaging and energy-efficient components. Tegrant is divided into three business brands: Alloyd Protexic and ThermoSafe. Using custom-molded plastic foam thermoformed plastic corrugated paperboard die-cut foam plastics and wood each produce an array of damage- and temperature-resistant packaging designed for the healthcare consumer electronics major appliance and automotive industries. Formerly known as SCA Packaging North America Tegrant was bought by packaging giant Sonoco Products in 2011.

TEICHERT INC.

3500 American River Dr.
Sacramento CA 95864
Phone: 916-484-3011
Fax: 916-484-6506
Web: www.teichert.com

CEO: Judson T Riggs
CFO: Narendra M Pathipati
HR: –
FYE: March 31
Type: Private

Teichert really does care about each and every grain of sand. The company's materials division produces sand gravel and ready-mixed concrete and supplies it to manufacturers contractors and government entities. In possession of the oldest active contractor's license in the state of California Teichert Construction is involved in building roads bridges parks airports and more. Through its Angelo Utilities division Teichert Construction provides trenching services for underground utility systems needed in residential subdivisions. Established in 1887 the family-owned company primarily operates throughout northern and central California.

TEJON RANCH CO.

NYS: TRC

P.O. Box 1000, Tejon Ranch
Lebec, CA 93243
Phone: 661 248-3000
Fax: –

CEO: Gregory S. Bielli
CFO: Allen E. Lyda
HR: –
FYE: December 31
Type: Public

Home is on the range for Tejon Ranch. Once one of the largest cattle ranches in the US the company hasn't run livestock on its 270000 acres in more than a decade. Instead Tejon Ranch has focused on residential and commercial real estate development on its land which is located 60 miles north of Los Angeles. But the historic ranch which was founded as a Mexican land grant in 1843 hasn't totally sold out. Indeed Tejon Ranch stuck a deal with major environmental groups to conserve about 90% of the vast chunk of open land or about 240000 acres. Beyond real estate development the company is engaged in grape and nut farming in the San Joaquin Valley and the leasing of its land for oil and gas royalties.

	Annual Growth	12/10	12/11	12/12	12/13	12/14
Sales ($ mil.)	9.6%	35.5	63.1	47.1	45.3	51.3
Net income ($ mil.)	7.9%	4.2	15.9	4.4	4.2	5.7
Market value ($ mil.)	1.7%	568.5	505.2	579.5	758.6	608.0
Employees	5.0%	129	145	140	144	157

TEKELEC

NASDAQ: TKLC

5200 Paramount Pkwy.
Morrisville NC 27560
Phone: 919-460-5500
Fax: 919-460-0877
Web: www.tekelec.com

CEO: –
CFO: –
HR: –
FYE: December 31
Type: Private

Tekelec puts calls through. The company's network signaling systems include media gateway controllers and signaling gateways that enable mobile messaging network intelligence and migration to Internet protocol (IP) connectivity. Its performance management and monitoring applications are used to improve network security troubleshoot problems and detect and remedy revenue loss. Tekelec sells directly and through distributors worldwide to telephone network operators and contact centers. AT&T is a key client. In 2012 Tekelec was taken private by a group of investors led by Siris Capital Group for $780 million; other buyers included ComVest Sankaty Advisors and Zelnick-Media.

TEKNI-PLEX INC.

1150 1st Ave. Ste. 500
King of Prussia PA 19406-1334
Phone: 484-690-1520
Fax: 256-722-7440
Web: www.bench.com/viewer/worldwide_site_huntsville

CEO: –
CFO: Robert M Larney
HR: –
FYE: June 30
Type: Private

Tekni-Plex is known for mixing a pinch of complexity into its packaging. The company manufactures packaging industrial materials specialty resins as well as tubing products for the healthcare food and consumer goods industries. Its packaging arm produces egg foam cartons poultry and meat processing trays pharmaceutical blister films and aerosol and dispensing pump components. Its tubing products segment makes garden and irrigation hose pool hose and vinyl medical tubing. Tekni-Plex also churns out polyvinyl chloride (PVC) compounds and recycled polyethylene terephthalate (PET) for industrial applications.

TEKNOR APEX COMPANY

505 CENTRAL AVE
PAWTUCKET, RI 028611900
Phone: 401-725-8000
Fax: –
Web: www.biovinyl.com

CEO: –
CFO: James Morrison
HR: Laurie Meisner
FYE: July 31
Type: Private

The apex of Teknor Apex's business model is to serve its customers by offering a wide-ranging portfolio of chemicals plastic and rubber. The company's business divisions provide chemicals (plasticizers and toll compounding) garden hoses and rubber products (custom mixed and molded rubber compounds). Teknor Apex also manufactures bioplastics color concentrates for plastics (Teknor Color Company) thermoplastic elastomers and vinyl (custom PVC compounds); it also provides specialty compounding (custom thermoplastic compound manufacturing and toll compounding of plastics).

	Annual Growth	07/02	07/03	07/04	07/05	07/14
Sales ($ mil.)	6.3%	–	–	–	574.0	996.8
Net income ($ mil.)	–	–	–	–	0.0	50.3
Market value ($ mil.)	–	–	–	–	–	–
Employees	–	–	–	–	–	2,500

TEKSYSTEMS INC.

7437 RACE RD
HANOVER, MD 210761112
Phone: 410-579-3000
Fax: –
Web: www.teksystems.com

CEO: –
CFO: –
HR: –
FYE: December 31
Type: Private

TEKsystems a subsidiary of staffing giant Allegis provides IT consulting and staffing services from locations in North America and Europe. Considered one of the nation's largest IT staffing firms the company places more than 70000 technical professionals each week who work in a variety of fields including biotechnology telecommunications and construction and engineering. TEKsystems has 100 offices serving more than 6000 clients. In addition the company runs the thingamajob.com website which is an online job board for technical staff. Spinning off of fellow Allegis unit Aerotek TEKsystems was formed in 1994 to focus on the IT needs of clients.

	Annual Growth	12/09	12/10	12/11	12/12	12/13
Sales ($ mil.)	10.5%	–	2,632.5	2,987.2	3,319.2	3,551.3
Net income ($ mil.)	–	–	–	195.0	328.1	0.0
Market value ($ mil.)	–	–	–	–	–	–
Employees	–	–	–	–	–	2,900

TEL FSI INC.

NASDAQ: FSII

3455 Lyman Blvd.
Chaska MN 55318-3052
Phone: 952-448-5440
Fax: 952-448-2825
Web: www.fsi-intl.com

CEO: –
CFO: –
HR: –
FYE: August 31
Type: Public

FSI International stays focused on semiconductor wafers all around the world. The company's surface conditioning equipment performs key cleaning etching and stripping functions that remove contaminants from silicon wafers and prepare them for subsequent production steps. Its equipment is used by electronics manufacturers worldwide such as Intel Samsung Electronics (about one-third of sales) STMicroelectronics and Texas Instruments as well as by other high-tech organizations including Sandia National Laboratories. Customers outside the US account for almost three-quarters of sales. In 2012 Tokyo Electron bought FSI for some $250 million.

TEL INSTRUMENT ELECTRONICS CORP.   ASE: TIK

One Branca Road
East Rutherford, NJ 07073
Phone: 201 933-1600
Fax: –
Web: www.telinst.com

CEO: Jeffrey C O'Hara
CFO: –
HR: –
FYE: March 31
Type: Public

Before airplanes go off into the wild blue yonder attention must be paid to their avionics. Tel-Instrument Electronics manufactures avionics test equipment for the US Army the US Navy and other military and commercial customers. Tel's instruments are used to test navigation and communications equipment installed in aircraft both on the flight line (known as ramp testers) and in the maintenance shop (bench testers). The US government and military avionics customers (such as Boeing) account for more than two-thirds of sales.

	Annual Growth	03/11	03/12	03/13	03/14	03/15
Sales ($ mil.)	7.7%	13.5	16.5	7.8	15.8	18.2
Net income ($ mil.)	–	(0.1)	0.1	(2.8)	0.3	(0.3)
Market value ($ mil.)	(4.2%)	24.8	20.6	11.4	14.4	20.9
Employees	17.2%	36	41	58	64	68

TEL OFFSHORE TRUST   NBB: TELO Z

The Bank of New York Mellon Trust Company, N.A., 919 Congress Avenue
Austin, TX 78701
Phone: 512 236-6599
Fax: –

CEO: –
CFO: –
HR: –
FYE: December 31
Type: Public

TEL Offshore Trust tells it like it is. There is money in oil and gas. The trust is a passive entity formed to distribute revenues received from TEL Offshore Trust Partnership. The partnership has interests in four major properties in the Gulf of Mexico. Chevron the managing general partner operates most of the properties. TEL Offshore Trust's properties have proved reserves of about 137500 barrels of oil and more than 869 million cu. ft. of natural gas. The trust is set to close down when estimated future revenues from partnership properties fall below $2 million.

	Annual Growth	12/10	12/11	12/12	12/13	12/14
Sales ($ mil.)	(57.3%)	0.0	1.5	0.0	1.2	0.0
Net income ($ mil.)	–	–	–	–	–	–
Market value ($ mil.)	(45.9%)	7.0	4.3	3.8	5.7	0.6
Employees	–	–	–	–	–	–

TELCO SYSTEMS INC.

15 Berkshire Rd.
Mansfield MA 02048
Phone: 781-551-0300
Fax: 781-255-2344
Web: www.telco.com

CEO: Itzik Weinstein
CFO: –
HR: –
FYE: December 31
Type: Subsidiary

You can call on Telco Systems. The company's line of EdgeLink integrated voice data and video networking products includes devices for network access and broadband transmission. Telco Systems' transport terminals multiplexers and other network access devices incorporate Ethernet fiber-optic and frame relay technologies to enable service providers to move from traditional circuit switched systems to newer digital packet and cellular networks. A subsidiary of Israel-based networking equipment maker BATM Advanced Communications Telco Systems also distributes BATM products in North America.

TELCORDIA TECHNOLOGIES INC.

1 Telcordia Dr.
Piscataway NJ 08854-4151
Phone: 732-699-2000
Fax: 916-327-0489
Web: www.calottery.com

CEO: Richard Jacowleff
CFO: Jerry Fechter
HR: Linda Graf
FYE: January 31
Type: Subsidiary

Telcordia Technologies wants telecommunications service carriers to call on them for support. The company provides a range of networking and operations software as well as consulting implementation and training services to phone companies worldwide. Its products are used to enable such functions as network design customer care and billing service activation number portability and workforce management. Telcordia's flagship application is known as the Next Generation OSS which is a suite of network management tools covering a variety of functions for network operators. Customers have included Cincinnati Bell and Telenor. In 2012 Ericsson acquired Telcordia for about $1.15 billion.

TELECHECK INC.

5251 Westheimer Ste. 1000
Houston TX 77056
Phone: 713-331-7700
Fax: 713-331-7740
Web: www.telecheck.com

CEO: –
CFO: Harold Winfield
HR: –
FYE: December 31
Type: Subsidiary

Gas in the minivan? Check. Directions to the mall? Check. Shopping list? Check. Checkbook? TeleCheck! The company helps all those merchants process all those checks that all those consumers love to write (or submit electronically). Its services include check acceptance guarantee and verification for transactions that occur at the point of sale over the Internet and over the phone. TeleCheck's clients include financial institutions utilities grocery and big-box stores and other retailers. The company is owned by First Data one of the largest credit-card transaction processors in the US.

TELECOMMUNICATION SYSTEMS INC   NMS: TSYS

275 West Street
Annapolis, MD 21401
Phone: 410 263-7616
Fax: 410 280-4903
Web: www.telecomsys.com

CEO: Maurice B. Tose
CFO: Thomas M. (Tom) Brandt
HR: –
FYE: December 31
Type: Public

TeleCommunication Systems (TCS) keeps businesses and government agencies connected. The company develops software and provides services for wireless telecommunications carriers Internet telephony providers and branches of the US military among other clients. Its hosted applications enable phone companies mainly in the US to deliver 9-1-1 service text messaging location information and other Internet content to wireless phones. The company provides the Defense Department (DoD) with communications systems integration and IT services through its growing government division which represented more than half of the company's revenues in 2013.

	Annual Growth	12/10	12/11	12/12	12/13	12/14
Sales ($ mil.)	(1.9%)	388.8	425.4	487.4	362.3	359.8
Net income ($ mil.)	–	15.9	7.0	(98.0)	(58.6)	(1.7)
Market value ($ mil.)	(9.6%)	279.9	140.9	148.1	139.1	187.0
Employees	(1.9%)	1,205	1,345	1,426	1,286	1,115

TELECT INC.

2111 N. Madson St.
Liberty Lake WA 99019
Phone: 509-926-6000
Fax: 509-926-8915
Web: www.telect.com

CEO: Wayne Williams
CFO: Stan Hilbert
HR: –
FYE: December 31
Type: Private

Telect has the hook-ups that enable hang-ups. The company makes network connectivity and power distribution hardware for telecommunications service providers. Local telephone long-distance and wireless carriers use Telect's mainframe termination units patch bays fuse bays and circuit panels. Telect also sells copper wire and fiber-optic cables. The company works directly through resellers and through agreements with other telecom equipment makers primarily in the US. Distributors include ALLTEL Graybar Sprint and Verizon. Chairman Bill Williams and his wife vice chairman Judi Williams founded Telect in 1982. The Williams and their son CEO Wayne Williams own a controlling stake in the company.

TELEDYNE BENTHOS

49 Edgerton Dr.
North Falmouth MA 02556
Phone: 508-563-1000
Fax: 508-563-6444
Web: www.benthos.com

CEO: –
CFO: Francis E Dunne Jr
HR: –
FYE: September 30
Type: Business Segment

Like its trademark logo — the Benthosaurus — you will find Teledyne Benthos in deep water. The company makes undersea exploration systems for oil and gas companies and oceanographic researchers. Products include underwater modems sensors glass spheres hydrophones and remotely operated vehicles. In addition the company offers contract research and custom engineering design services. Customers include the US government and Sercel. In early 2006 Teledyne Technologies acquired Benthos for about $41 million in cash. The acquisition of Benthos expanded Teledyne's portfolio of underwater acoustic instruments.

TELEDYNE LECROY INC.

NASDAQ: LCRY

700 Chestnut Ridge Rd.
Chestnut Ridge NY 10977-6499
Phone: 845-425-2000
Fax: 845-578-5985
Web: www.lecroy.com

CEO: Thomas H Reslewic
CFO: Sean R O'Connor
HR: –
FYE: June 30
Type: Public

If only Teledyne LeCroy made an instrument to analyze signals exchanged between the sexes. The company (formerly LeCroy) makes high-performance real-time oscilloscopes under the WaveAce WaveExpert WaveJet WaveMaster WavePro WaveRunner and WaveSurfer brand names that capture electronic signals convert them to digital form and perform measurements and analysis. Teledyne LeCroy makes such other products as protocol analyzers arbitrary waveform generators and logic analyzers. It also provides support maintenance and recalibration services. LeCroy was acquired by Teledyne Technologies in a 2012 transaction valued at around $291 million.

TELEDYNE TECHNOLOGIES, INC.

NYS: TDY

1049 Camino Dos Rios
Thousand Oaks, CA 91360-2362
Phone: 805 373-4545
Fax: 805 373-4775
Web: www.teledyne.com

CEO: Robert Mehrabian
CFO: Susan L. (Sue) Main
HR: Annie Musick
FYE: December 28
Type: Public

Offerings by Teledyne Technologies know no boundaries; they are critical to products that work on land in the air and under the sea. The company makes a slew of electronic components and subsystems instruments and communications equipment for both domestic and foreign commercial customers and US government customers. Its lineup ranges from digital imaging and software to data acquisition and communication tools for aircraft monitoring and control devices for environmental marine and industrial projects defense electronics and energy generation storage and propulsion equipment.

	Annual Growth	01/11	01/12*	12/12	12/13	12/14
Sales ($ mil.)	13.3%	1,644.2	1,941.9	2,127.3	2,338.6	2,394.0
Net income ($ mil.)	21.8%	120.5	255.2	164.1	185.0	217.7
Market value ($ mil.)	33.5%	1,611.7	2,010.6	2,333.9	3,388.8	3,834.9
Employees	2.1%	9,200	8,890	9,630	9,600	9,800

*Fiscal year change

TELEFLEX INCORPORATED

NYS: TFX

550 E. Swedesford Rd., Suite 400
Wayne, PA 19087
Phone: 610 225-6800
Fax: –
Web: www.teleflex.com

CEO: Benson F. Smith
CFO: Thomas E. Powell
HR: Cameron B. Hicks
FYE: December 31
Type: Public

Teleflex helps medical professionals manage fluids and oxygen in critical care settings. Teleflex makes surgical instruments medical devices and disposable supplies for hospital procedures especially catheters for all parts of the body. It divides its medical products by use into critical care surgical care and cardiac care. It also makes custom medical instruments which it sells to original equipment manufacturers (OEMs). Although the company primarily distributes its products to hospitals and health care providers (more than 80% of sales) in more than 150 countries the US accounts for more than half of sales. Teleflex manufactures its products in the US the Czech Republic Germany Malaysia and Mexico.

	Annual Growth	12/10	12/11	12/12	12/13	12/14
Sales ($ mil.)	0.5%	1,801.7	1,528.9	1,551.0	1,696.3	1,839.8
Net income ($ mil.)	(1.7%)	201.1	323.3	(190.1)	150.9	187.7
Market value ($ mil.)	20.9%	2,229.8	2,539.8	2,955.0	3,889.5	4,758.0
Employees	(1.6%)	12,500	11,500	11,600	11,400	11,700

TELEFLORA LLC

11444 W. Olympic Blvd. 4th Fl.
Los Angeles CA 90064
Phone: 310-231-9199
Fax: 310-966-3658
Web: www.teleflora.com

CEO: –
CFO: –
HR: –
FYE: December 31
Type: Subsidiary

Teleflora's business is blooming with the help of some of its best buds. Teleflora a subsidiary of Roll International supplies fresh flowers plants and gift items to consumers worldwide through its websites and toll-free number. The floral firm taps into a network of about 18000 florists across the US and Canada as well as another 20000 affiliated florists outside North America. It offers fresh flowers for any occasion as well as plants corporate gifts and fruit and goody baskets some available same day at prices ranging from $29.99 to about $200. Its partner marketing program provides commissions and discounts for affiliates corporate giving and rewards programs. Teleflora was founded in 1934.

TELEMUNDO COMMUNICATIONS GROUP INC.

2290 W. 8th Ave.
Hialeah FL 33010
Phone: 305-884-8200
Fax: 305-889-7980
Web: www.telemundo.com

CEO: Javier Maynulet
CFO: Lynn A Calpeter
HR: –
FYE: December 31
Type: Subsidiary

Telemundo Communications Group is muy popular with Hispanic TV viewers. The company operates the Telemundo Spanish-language broadcast network the #2 Hispanic network the US (behind Univision Communications' flagship network). Offering a mix of general entertainment telenovelas sports and news programming the network reaches more than 94% of US Hispanic viewers in 210 markets through 15 company-owned stations and 48 broadcast affiliates as well as more than 1000 cable TV outlets. In addition to its flagship network Telemundo Communications operates cable channels mun2 ("moon dos") aimed at English-speaking Hispanic viewers and Telemundo Puerto Rico. The company is part of NBCUniversal (NBCU).

TELENAV, INC.

NMS: TNAV

950 De Guigne Drive
Sunnyvale, CA 94085
Phone: 408 245-3800
Fax: –
Web: www.telenav.com

CEO: H. P. Jin
CFO: Michael Strambi
HR: Peg Wynn
FYE: June 30
Type: Public

TeleNav offers a platform and suite of applications that provide mobile navigation and location-based services (LBS) to 34 million users primarily in the US. Flagship product TeleNav GPS Navigator transmits voice and onscreen driving directions to mobile phones and smartphones and is marketed to end users by leading wireless carriers such as Sprint AT&T T-Mobile and U.S. Cellular. The company also offers automotive navigation services to automobile and auto parts manufacturers including Ford and Delphi Automotive Systems. In addition it is expanding into mobile advertising services through its Scout Advertising platform.

	Annual Growth	06/11	06/12	06/13	06/14	06/15
Sales ($ mil.)	(6.6%)	210.5	218.5	191.8	150.3	160.2
Net income ($ mil.)	–	42.6	32.4	13.1	(29.5)	(23.1)
Market value ($ mil.)	(17.9%)	718.7	248.5	212.0	230.7	326.3
Employees	(13.6%)	1,039	901	682	632	579

TELEPHONE & DATA SYSTEMS, INC.

NYS: TDS

30 North LaSalle Street, Suite 4000
Chicago, IL 60602
Phone: 312 630-1900
Fax: 312 630-1908
Web: www.teldta.com

CEO: LeRoy T. (Ted) Carlson
CFO: –
HR: –
FYE: December 31
Type: Public

One of the top US phone companies that's not related to Ma Bell Telephone and Data Systems (TDS) has about 6 million local phone and wireless customers in 36 states. The company's core business unit U.S. Cellular serves about 4.8 million customers in 23 states; key markets are in the central and mid-Atlantic regions. The company also offers fixed-line and broadband Internet services in rural and suburban markets in 36 states through its TDS Telecom subsidiary which provides local service to 1.2 million access lines through more than 110 incumbent local-exchange carriers (ILEC). Data networking and hosted telecom services are provided to business clients through the TDS Business unit.

	Annual Growth	12/10	12/11	12/12	12/13	12/14
Sales ($ mil.)	0.1%	4,986.8	5,180.5	5,345.3	4,901.2	5,009.4
Net income ($ mil.)	–	143.9	200.6	81.9	141.9	(136.4)
Market value ($ mil.)	(5.4%)	3,401.0	2,569.1	2,388.9	2,781.6	2,724.4
Employees	(3.8%)	12,400	12,300	12,100	10,500	10,600

TELEPHONE ELECTRONICS CORPORATION

236 E CAPITOL ST STE 400
JACKSON, MS 392012416
Phone: 601-354-9070
Fax: –
Web: www.tec.com

CEO: –
CFO: Robert J Healea
HR: Brandi F Callison
FYE: December 31
Type: Private

Telephone Electronics Corporation or TEC provides communications services for customers in the South. The privately-owned telecommunications carrier provides wired phone cable TV and Internet services for residential and business customers through subsidiaries such as CommuniGroup. TEC's rural local-exchange service reach include areas of Alabama Louisiana Mississippi and Tennessee. The company also provides long-distance interexchange services. TEC was founded in 1923 with the purchase of local phone company Bay Springs Telephone Company which had about 100 customers tied to its switchboard.

	Annual Growth	12/06	12/07	12/08	12/09	12/13
Sales ($ mil.)	7.0%	–	–	38.8	35.1	54.4
Net income ($ mil.)	(5.3%)	–	–	2.0	2.3	1.6
Market value ($ mil.)	–	–	–	–	–	–
Employees	–	–	–	–	–	250

TELETECH HOLDINGS, INC.

NMS: TTEC

9197 South Peoria Street
Englewood, CO 80112
Phone: 303 397-8100
Fax: –
Web: www.teletech.com

CEO: Kenneth D. Tuchman
CFO: Regina M. Paolillo
HR: –
FYE: December 31
Type: Public

Telephone technique is only the beginning for TeleTech Holdings. A leading global call center operator (behind rival Convergys) TeleTech provides a wide range of business process outsourcing (BPO) services in four areas: customer management direct sales human capital and professional services. The company serves around 150 global clients and maintains a network of some 55 facilities in 24 countries around the world. Customers mainly major global enterprises come from sectors such as automotive communications financial services government health care retail technology and travel and leisure. TeleTech also offers management consulting services.

	Annual Growth	12/10	12/11	12/12	12/13	12/14
Sales ($ mil.)	3.2%	1,094.9	1,179.4	1,163.0	1,193.2	1,241.8
Net income ($ mil.)	9.7%	49.9	74.2	70.0	67.4	72.3
Market value ($ mil.)	3.6%	997.6	784.9	862.5	1,160.0	1,147.4
Employees	0.3%	45,500	42,300	43,000	41,000	46,000

TELETOUCH COMMUNICATIONS, INC.

NBB: TLLE Q

5718 Airport Freeway
Fort Worth, TX 76117
Phone: 800 232-3888
Fax: 817 654-6220
Web: www.teletouch.com

CEO: Robert M McMurrey
CFO: Douglas E Sloan
HR: –
FYE: May 31
Type: Public

Teletouch Communications has its own idea of what it means to "reach out and touch someone." Through its Progressive Concepts Inc. (PCI) subsidiary the company resells mobile voice and data services provided by AT&T Mobility to customers in Texas; it has nearly 80000 consumer and commercial subscribers on its books. PCI also distributes cell phones accessories and car audio and security products through its nearly 20 Hawk Electronics retail locations. Suppliers include Kenwood and and Vertex. The bulk of its stores are located in the Dallas/Fort Worth area but it also has two locations in San Antonio. Chairman Robert McMurrey owns a controlling stake in the company.

	Annual Growth	05/08	05/09	05/10	05/11	05/12
Sales ($ mil.)	(10.9%)	54.5	45.9	52.0	40.4	34.4
Net income ($ mil.)	–	(3.1)	(1.9)	1.6	(2.5)	4.2
Market value ($ mil.)	21.5%	11.2	6.8	14.7	20.5	24.4
Employees	(16.1%)	238	246	202	126	118

TELIGENT INC (NEW)

NMS: TLGT

105 Lincoln Avenue
Buena, NJ 08310
Phone: 856 697-1441
Fax: –
Web: www.igilabs.com

CEO: Jason Grenfell-Gardner
CFO: Jenniffer Collins
HR: –
FYE: December 31
Type: Public

Teligent (formerly IGI) is betting big on small things. It manufactures creams liquids and other topical products for drug and cosmetics companies using its microencapsulation technology. Teligent originally licensed the technology dubbed Novasome from drug firm Novovax. The Novasome process entraps and protects the active ingredients of various skin care products moisturizers shampoos and fragrances allowing for greater stability during storage and a more controlled release when used. The firm is examining further applications of the Novasome technology in food personal care products and pharmaceuticals.

	Annual Growth	12/10	12/11	12/12	12/13	12/14
Sales ($ mil.)	53.4%	6.1	7.8	8.6	18.2	33.7
Net income ($ mil.)	–	(3.4)	(3.0)	(3.9)	(0.1)	5.3
Market value ($ mil.)	51.3%	88.7	60.7	54.9	161.1	464.8
Employees	24.2%	34	36	41	52	81

TELIK INC.

NASDAQ: TELK

3165 Porter Dr.
Palo Alto CA 94304
Phone: 650-845-7700
Fax: 650-845-7800
Web: www.telik.com

CEO: J David Hansen
CFO: Gregory P Hanson
HR: –
FYE: December 31
Type: Public

Go Telik on the mountain: Telik discovers new drugs focusing mainly on treatments for cancer. The company uses its proprietary Target-Related Affinity Profiling (TRAP) technology to identify potential drug compounds by analyzing the way they interact with proteins. Lead drug candidate Telcyta targets chemotherapy-resistant tumors and is undergoing clinical trials for several kinds of cancer including ovarian and non-small cell lung cancers. Another candidate Telintra may treat blood disorders including neutropenia and myelodysplastic syndrome. Telik has a host of other anticancer compounds at earlier stages of development.

TELKONET INC.

NBB: TKOI

20800 Swenson Drive, Suite 175
Waukesha, WI 53186
Phone: 414 223-0473
Fax: –

CEO: Jason L Tienor
CFO: F John Stark
HR: –
FYE: December 31
Type: Public

Telkonet runs its own Internet of things but its things are thermostats and other energy controls for hotels campuses and other properties. The company's SmartEnergy and EcoSmart line of energy efficiency-related systems are used to manage and monitor HVAC consumption. It also provides high-speed Internet access without the high-cost network upgrades through its EthoStream product line which enables computer network and Internet access over electrical lines rather than communications cables. In addition to equipment sales it recognizes recurring support revenue from the 2300 hotels that use its EthoStream broadband Internet systems. All of its product are marketed primarily to the hospitality industry. Customers include InterContinental Marriott and Wyndham.

	Annual Growth	12/10	12/11	12/12	12/13	12/14
Sales ($ mil.)	7.1%	11.3	11.2	12.8	13.9	14.8
Net income ($ mil.)	–	(1.8)	(1.9)	0.4	(4.0)	0.0
Market value ($ mil.)	6.1%	13.8	17.5	16.8	27.5	17.5
Employees	5.7%	80	88	99	98	100

TELLEPSEN BUILDERS LP

777 Benmar Dr. Ste. 400
Houston TX 77060
Phone: 281-447-8100
Fax: 281-447-8177
Web: www.tellepsen.com

CEO: Howard T Tellepsen Jr
CFO: Charles W Sommer
HR: –
FYE: December 31
Type: Private

Tellepsen one of Houston's oldest construction companies works on commercial institutional industrial and pipeline projects in the country's fourth largest city. The company which offers both general contracting and construction management services has built an array of commercial projects: schools health care complexes office buildings parking garages assisted-living communities recreation centers and hotels. Its Tellepsen Industrial division builds refineries processing centers and petrochemical and power plants. Landmark projects include the Coca Cola Bottling Co. the Museum of Fine Arts and Texas Children's Hospital in Houston. Tom Tellepsen founded the family-owned company in 1909.

TELOS CORP. (MD)

NBB: TLSR P

19886 Ashburn Road
Ashburn, VA 20147-2358
Phone: 703 724-3800
Fax: –
Web: www.telos.com

CEO: John B. Wood
CFO: Michele Nakazawa
HR: –
FYE: December 31
Type: Public

Telos is tuned in to the needs of high-tech government. The company provides networking and security products and services primarily to the US Department of Defense and other federal government agencies. Its core secure networking unit offers networking hardware software advanced messaging as well as systems design and support services. Subsidiary Xacta offers automated security software and consulting services. The company also provides identity management software and services through its Telos ID subsidiary. Government clients account for 99% of the company's sales.

	Annual Growth	12/10	12/11	12/12	12/13	12/14
Sales ($ mil.)	(13.3%)	225.8	189.9	226.1	207.4	127.6
Net income ($ mil.)	–	3.0	1.5	7.4	(2.6)	(12.3)
Market value ($ mil.)	(10.5%)	929.8	907.7	664.1	679.6	597.7
Employees	(3.9%)	630	626	560	536	538

TELVISTA INC.

1605 LBJ Freeway Ste. 200
Dallas TX 75234
Phone: 972-919-7800
Fax: 972-919-8145
Web: www.telvista.com

CEO: –
CFO: –
HR: –
FYE: December 31
Type: Private

Say "hasta la vista" to in-house customer care and tech support with a little help from Telvista. Operating contact centers that support both Spanish- and English-speaking customers Telvista offers outsourced customer support to midsized and large companies in such industries as financial services retail technology and travel. Services include customer service sales and tech support via phone and Web. The firm also provides consulting services to improve contact center processes network design and technology utilization. Telvista was founded in 1997 when it opened its first call center in the Dallas area. It also has facilities in Danville Virginia as well as in Tijuana Mexicali and Mexico City.

TELVUE CORPORATION

OTC: TEVE

16000 Horizon Way Ste. 500
Mt. Laurel NJ 08054
Phone: 856-273-8886
Fax: 856-866-7411
Web: www.telvue.com

CEO: Jesse Lerman
CFO: Emmett Hume
HR: –
FYE: December 31
Type: Public

TelVue knows that there is often a price to be paid for spending a lot of time in front of the television. The company's products facilitate the ordering and delivery of pay-per-view programming for cable companies. Its core business is centered around digital video systems (including Princeton-branded video server computers and software) that enable the capture storage editing and playback of broadcast video. TelVue's automatic number identification (ANI) system enables cable and satellite providers to automate telephone orders for programming by subscribers. It also offers services under the WEBUS brand among others that enable the display of programming data over a cable system's access channels.

TEMPLE UNIVERSITY HEALTH SYSTEM INC.

2450 W HUNTING PARK AVE
PHILADELPHIA, PA 191291302
Phone: 215-707-0900
Fax: –
Web: www.temple.edu

CEO: –
CFO: Robert H Lux
HR: –
FYE: June 30
Type: Private

Temple University Health System (TUHS) is a network of academic and community hospitals associated with the Temple University School of Medicine. It provides primary secondary and tertiary care to residents in the Philadelphia County (Pennsylvania) area. The system includes 730-bed Temple University Hospital (a Level 1 trauma center) and a pair of community-based hospitals that provide acute and emergency care as well as the Jeanes Hospital and TUH-Episcopal Hospital (home to a 120-bed behavioral health unit). TUHS supports programs in pediatric and adult cardiology organ transplantation oncology and pulmonary disease. TUHS also includes a community-wide network of primary care physicians.

	Annual Growth	06/08	06/09	06/11	06/12	06/13
Sales ($ mil.)	888.5%	–	0.1	994.2	1,004.9	1,355.9
Net income ($ mil.)	53.9%	–	–	45.4	(48.8)	107.5
Market value ($ mil.)	–	–	–	–	–	–
Employees	–	–	–	–	–	7,573

TEMPLE UNIVERSITY-OF THE COMMONWEALTH SYSTEM OF HIGHER EDUCATION

1801 N BROAD ST
PHILADELPHIA, PA 191226003
Phone: 215-204-1380
Fax: –
Web: www.wrti.org

CEO: –
CFO: Ken Kaiser
HR: –
FYE: June 30
Type: Private

Temple University's owl mascot reflects its start as a night school but the owl's sagacity also points to the school's educational credentials. More than 36000 students are enrolled in Temple's 320 academic programs. Its Health Sciences Center includes Temple University Hospital and schools that teach medicine and dentistry. Part of Pennsylvania's Commonwealth System of Higher Education Temple has nine different campuses in the Philadelphia area as well as in Tokyo and Rome and educational programs in China Greece France Israel and the UK. The system has a student-teacher ratio of about 15:1. Dr. Russell Conwell founded the university in 1884; it was incorporated as Temple University in 1907.

	Annual Growth	06/07	06/08	06/12	06/13	06/14
Sales ($ mil.)	5.0%	–	2,034.0	2,254.8	2,635.5	2,723.9
Net income ($ mil.)	–	–	–	(37.2)	192.1	181.9
Market value ($ mil.)	–	–	–	–	–	–
Employees	–	–	–	–	–	9,061

TEMPUR SEALY INTERNATIONAL, INC.

NYS: TPX

1000 Tempur Way
Lexington, KY 40511
Phone: 800 878-8889
Fax: –
Web: www.tempursealy.com

CEO: Scott L. Thompson
CFO: Barry A. Hytinen
HR: Glen Gilbertson
FYE: December 31
Type: Public

Tempur Sealy International's mattresses are made from material that is out of this world. Formerly Tempur-Pedic the company manufactures premium pressure-relieving temperature-sensitive mattresses pillows and other sleep products made from viscoelastic foam technology developed by NASA during the 1970s to help cushion astronauts during liftoff. Its TEMPUR Sealy Optimum and Stearns & Foster brands are sold in 100-plus countries through three distribution channels: retail (furniture and department stores) direct (online and company-owned stores) and other means (third-party distributors hospitals and medical retailers). Amid declining sales in 2013 Tempur-Pedic bought Sealy to become Tempur Sealy.

	Annual Growth	12/10	12/11	12/12	12/13	12/14
Sales ($ mil.)	28.2%	1,105.4	1,417.9	1,402.9	2,464.3	2,989.8
Net income ($ mil.)	(8.8%)	157.1	219.6	106.8	78.6	108.9
Market value ($ mil.)	8.2%	2,439.7	3,199.1	1,917.7	3,286.2	3,344.0
Employees	47.5%	1,500	1,800	1,950	6,700	7,100

TENASKA INC.

1044 N. 115th St. Ste. 400
Omaha NE 68154-4446
Phone: 402-691-9500
Fax: 402-691-9526
Web: www.tenaska.com

CEO: Jerry K Crouse
CFO: –
HR: –
FYE: December 31
Type: Private

Tenaska is tenacious when it comes to energy. The employee-owned company is a top natural gas marketer in North America selling or managing 2.3 trillion cu. ft. of natural gas a year through Marketing Ventures/Tenaska Marketing Canada (TMV); it is also a leading power producer trading and marketing electricity (including renewable energy). Power marketing unit Tenaska Power Services develops owns or operates eight generating plants with more than 9000 MW of capacity in the US and managed more than 21000 MW of power contracts in 2011. Other operations include fuel supply biofuels development oil and gas exploration and production power transmission and gas transportation contracting.

TENAX THERAPEUTICS INC

NAS: TENX

ONE Copley Parkway, Suite 490
Morrisville, NC 27560
Phone: 919 855-2100
Fax: 919 855-2133
Web: www.oxygenbiotherapeutics.com

CEO: John P Kelley
CFO: Michael B Jebsen
HR: –
FYE: April 30
Type: Public

Oxygen Biotherapeutics prescribes some good ol' O2 for whatever ails you. The development stage biotechnology company develops products that help deliver oxygen to tissues. Its Dermacyte topical cosmetic line is designed to improve the appearance of skin. A concentrate is currently available and the company is developing Dermacyte formulas specifically for acne rosacea sunscreen and other applications. Pipeline products include Oxycyte an IV emulsion created to speed surgical and other healing being tested in Israel and Switzerland and Wundecyte gel and bandages in pre-clinical trials. Oxygen Biotherapeutics was formed through a reverse merger with Synthetic Blood International in 2008.

	Annual Growth	04/11	04/12	04/13	04/14	04/15
Sales ($ mil.)	(37.5%)	0.3	0.4	1.2	0.3	0.0
Net income ($ mil.)	–	(10.4)	(15.7)	(9.4)	(19.5)	(14.1)
Market value ($ mil.)	17.9%	49.8	50.1	7.0	137.2	96.2
Employees	(12.0%)	20	15	12	14	12

TENET HEALTHCARE CORP.

NYS: THC

1445 Ross Avenue, Suite 1400
Dallas, TX 75202
Phone: 469 893-2200
Fax: –
Web: www.tenethealth.com

CEO: Trevor Fetter
CFO: Daniel J. (Dan) Cancelmi
HR: Lisa Whaley
FYE: December 31
Type: Public

Tenet Healthcare is here to spread the doctrine of good health. The for-profit company operates 80 acute care hospitals with more than 20800 beds in 14 US states including California Florida and Texas. They range from small community facilities offering basic care to major hospitals such as the 650-bed Brookwood Medical Center in Birmingham Alabama. In addition to its acute care holdings Tenet also operates specialty hospitals skilled nursing facilities physician practices outpatient centers imaging centers health plans and other health care units that form regional networks around its main hospitals. It also operates Conifer Health Solutions a patient billing and communications company.

	Annual Growth	12/10	12/11	12/12	12/13	12/14
Sales ($ mil.)	15.9%	9,205.0	8,854.0	9,119.0	11,102.0	16,615.0
Net income ($ mil.)	(49.3%)	1,152.0	94.0	133.0	(104.0)	76.0
Market value ($ mil.)	65.9%	658.2	504.7	3,194.5	4,143.8	4,985.0
Employees	17.8%	56,605	57,705	59,164	103,711	108,989

TENGASCO, INC.

ASE: TGC

6021 S. Syracuse Way, Suite 117
Greenwood Village, CO 80111
Phone: 720 420-4460
Fax: –
Web: www.tengasco.com

CEO: Michael J Rugen
CFO: Michael J Rugen
HR: –
FYE: December 31
Type: Public

Tengasco doesn't have the strength of 10 gas companies just yet but it's getting there. The firm is engaged in exploring for producing and transporting oil and natural gas in Kansas (in properties near Hays) and Tennessee (primarily in the Swan Creek Field). Tengasco uses 3-D seismic technology to maximize recovery of its reserves. In 2008 the company reported proved reserves of 900 million cu. ft. of natural gas and 1.3 million barrels of oil. The firm is also involved in natural gas marketing pipeline construction and related energy services. Its Tengasco Pipeline unit manages its pipeline operations. Subsidiary Manufactured Methane Corporation operates a landfill gas project in Tennessee.

	Annual Growth	12/10	12/11	12/12	12/13	12/14
Sales ($ mil.)	1.1%	13.2	17.1	20.6	15.7	13.8
Net income ($ mil.)	–	(1.7)	4.7	(0.1)	2.8	(0.8)
Market value ($ mil.)	(20.1%)	38.5	43.3	36.5	23.7	15.7
Employees	(12.5%)	29	29	25	18	17

TENGION INC.

NASDAQ: TNGN

2900 Potshop Lane Ste. 100
East Norriton PA 19403
Phone: 610-292-8364
Fax: +33-2-28-07-37-11
Web: www.vivalis.com

CEO: –
CFO: –
HR: –
FYE: December 31
Type: Public

Who needs organ donation when Tengion's got organ regeneration. The biotechnology company is focused on developing cell therapies to regenerate human tissue and organs. Its lead candidates are a surgically implanted urinary conduit that uses a patient's own cells to catalyze the regrowth of bladder tissue following bladder removal due to cancer and a Neo-Bladder product designed to help patients suffering from spina bifida and spinal cord injuries. Other product candidates target renal gastrointestinal and vascular diseases. Believing it can fill a niche among current therapies on the bladder market Tengion went public in 2010 through a $26 million IPO to help advance its research and development activities.

TENNANT CO.

NYS: TNC

701 North Lilac Drive, P.O. Box 1452
Minneapolis, MN 55440
Phone: 763 540-1200
Fax: –
Web: www.tennantco.com

CEO: H. Chris Killingstad
CFO: Thomas (Tom) Paulson
HR: –
FYE: December 31
Type: Public

Tennant's tenet is "keep it clean." The company is one of the world's leading manufacturers of industrial floor maintenance equipment. It makes specialty surface coatings and cleaning machines including extractors scrubbers sweepers and vacuums. Parts and supplies are also offered along with maintenance and repair services. Its products feature its ec-H2O technology and clean up surfaces at airports factories offices parking garages stadiums supermarkets warehouses and other high-traffic areas. Brand names include Alfa Tennant Green Machines Nobles and Orbio. Tennant operates in the Americas Asia/Pacific and EMEA (Europe/Middle East/Africa).

	Annual Growth	12/10	12/11	12/12	12/13	12/14
Sales ($ mil.)	5.3%	667.7	754.0	739.0	752.0	822.0
Net income ($ mil.)	9.8%	34.8	32.7	41.6	40.2	50.7
Market value ($ mil.)	17.1%	707.3	715.8	809.3	1,248.7	1,329.0
Employees	2.5%	2,793	2,865	2,816	2,931	3,087

TENNECO INC

NYS: TEN

500 North Field Drive
Lake Forest, IL 60045
Phone: 847 482-5000
Fax: –
Web: www.tenneco.com

CEO: Gregg M. Sherrill
CFO: Kenneth R. (Ken) Trammell
HR: Mike Schneider
FYE: December 31
Type: Public

Tenneco ensures vehicles are riding steady without exhausting a lot of smoke. The auto parts maker designs and distributes ride-control equipment (including shock absorbers struts and suspensions) under the Monroe brand and emissions-control systems (catalytic converters exhaust pipes and mufflers) under the Walker brand. It also makes Clevite elastomer products (bushings mounts and springs) for vibration control in cars and heavy trucks. It supplies both OEMs and aftermarket wholesalers and retailers. Major customers include GM Ford Advance Auto Parts and Uni-Select. Tenneco operates on six continents and is growing its presence in key Asia/Pacific markets.

	Annual Growth	12/10	12/11	12/12	12/13	12/14
Sales ($ mil.)	9.1%	5,937.0	7,205.0	7,363.0	7,964.0	8,420.0
Net income ($ mil.)	55.2%	39.0	157.0	275.0	183.0	226.0
Market value ($ mil.)	8.3%	2,519.4	1,822.8	2,149.1	3,462.6	3,465.1
Employees	7.2%	22,000	24,000	25,000	26,000	29,000

TENNESSEE FARMERS COOPERATIVE

180 Old Nashville Hwy.
LaVergne TN 37086
Phone: 615-793-8011
Fax: 615-287-8859
Web: www.ourcoop.com

CEO: Bart Krisle
CFO: Shannon Huff
HR: –
FYE: July 31
Type: Private - Cooperativ

Talk about multi-tasking. The Tennessee Farmers Cooperative (TFC) keeps the cows fat the bugs away and the tractors running. Through a system of about 60 local co-ops TFC supplies agricultural necessities such as animal-health products feed fertilizer outdoor power equipment seeds and tires to area farmers. Its services include finance credit and risk management. It operates about 150 retail outlets located in more than 80 of Tennessee's 95 counties and five neighboring states. The outlets are open to the public as well as co-op members. TFC was chartered in 1945.

TENNESSEE FOOTBALL INC.

460 Great Circle Rd.
Nashville TN 37228
Phone: 615-565-4000
Fax: 615-565-4105
Web: www.titansonline.com

CEO: Kenneth S Adams Jr
CFO: –
HR: –
FYE: March 31
Type: Private

Interpreting the mythology behind these Titans isn't so hard if you know something about football. Tennessee Football owns and operates the Tennessee Titans professional football team that represents Nashville in the National Football League. A charter member of the American Football League the franchise was founded by Texas oilman Bud Adams as the Houston Oilers in 1959 and joined the NFL in 1970. It moved to the Volunteer State in 1997 originally playing in Memphis before settling in Music City (and changing its name) the following year. Tennessee made its first and only appearance in the Super Bowl at the end of the 1999 season losing to the St. Louis Rams. Adams continues to control the team.

TENNESSEE STATE UNIVERSITY

3500 JOHN A MERRITT BLVD
NASHVILLE, TN 372091561
Phone: 615-963-5000
Fax: –
Web: www.tnstate.edu

CEO: –
CFO: –
HR: –
FYE: June 30
Type: Private

Tennessee State University (TSU) covers its bases in higher learning fields including science and learning. Home to some 9000 students TSU is known for its programs in education nursing biology physical therapy computer engineering agriculture public administration and psychology. The university offers about 45 undergraduate programs and 25 graduate programs through its eight colleges and schools. It also offers doctoral degrees in education philosophy and physical therapy. It has 450 full-time faculty members and a student-to-teacher ratio of 16:1.

	Annual Growth	06/04	06/05	06/08	06/11	06/13
Sales ($ mil.)	52.6%	–	3.7	1.6	105.6	108.0
Net income ($ mil.)	87.3%	–	–	0.4	18.4	10.0
Market value ($ mil.)	–	–	–	–	–	–
Employees	–	–	–	–	–	1,234

TENNESSEE TECHNOLOGICAL UNIVERSITY

1 WILLIAM L JONES DR
COOKEVILLE, TN 385050001
Phone: 931-372-3101
Fax: –
Web: www.tntech.edu

CEO: –
CFO: –
HR: –
FYE: June 30
Type: Private

Tennessee Technological University (TTU or Tennessee Tech) takes on the task of providing academic education and career training services in the Volunteer State. The public university has six college divisions providing more than 60 undergraduate and graduate degrees in the areas of Agriculture and Human Sciences Arts and Sciences Business Education Engineering and Interdisciplinary Studies. it aslo offers The university has some 11500 students enrolled and a faculty of about 400 staff members and has a student-to-faculty ratio of about 22:1.

	Annual Growth	06/09	06/10	06/11	06/12	06/13
Sales ($ mil.)	9.7%	–	65.1	65.1	76.8	86.0
Net income ($ mil.)	(10.1%)	–	–	23.3	5.6	18.8
Market value ($ mil.)	–	–	–	–	–	–
Employees	–	–	–	–	–	1,096

TENNESSEE VALLEY AUTHORITY

NYS: TVE

400 W. Summit Hill Drive
Knoxville, TN 37902
Phone: 865 632-2101
Fax: –
Web: www.tva.gov

CEO: William D. (Bill) Johnson
CFO: John M. Thomas
HR: –
FYE: September 30
Type: Public

Tennessee Valley Authority (TVA) may not be an expert on state attractions like Dollywood and the Grand Ole Opry but it is an authority on power generation. A US government-owned corporation TVA is the largest public power producer in the country. It sells wholesale electricity to more than 150 municipal and cooperative power distributors which serve some 9 million people in Tennessee and parts of Alabama Georgia Kentucky Mississippi North Carolina and Virginia. It also sells power directly to large industries and federal agencies. In addition TVA provides flood control and land management for the Tennessee River system and assists utilities and state and local governments with economic development.

	Annual Growth	09/11	09/12	09/13	09/14	09/15
Sales ($ mil.)	(1.8%)	11,841.0	11,220.0	10,956.0	11,137.0	11,003.0
Net income ($ mil.)	61.8%	162.0	60.0	271.0	469.0	1,111.0
Market value ($ mil.)	–	0.0	0.0	0.0	0.0	0.0
Employees	(4.1%)	12,893	12,762	12,612	11,542	10,918

TEOCO CORPORATION

12150 Monument Dr. Ste. 400
Fairfax VA 22033
Phone: 703-322-9200
Fax: 703-322-9133
Web: www.teoco.com

CEO: Atul Jain
CFO: AVI Goldstein
HR: –
FYE: December 31
Type: Private

TEOCO is a provider of software consulting and audit services that help telecommunications companies and other large enterprises manage their cost expenses and revenue structures. The company's software is used to automate functions related to billing reconciliation by managing and auditing telecom invoices. Its clients have included COLT Cricket Communications ICG Communications and Qwest Communications. TEOCO also runs Respond.com a pay-for-performance directory that enables service professionals to attract new customers. It has offices in India the UK and the US. The employee-owned company was founded in 1994 by CEO Atul Jain and has received funding from TA Associates.

TERADATA CORP (DE)

NYS: TDC

10000 Innovation Drive
Dayton, OH 45342
Phone: 866 548-8348
Fax: –
Web: www.teradata.com

CEO: Michael F. (Mike) Koehler
CFO: Stephen M. (Steve) Scheppmann
HR: –
FYE: December 31
Type: Public

Trillions of bytes of data don't faze Teradata. The company designs and implements enterprise data warehousing systems that store and analyze information about customers financials and operations. Products include its core database software hardware components and applications for managing demand and supply chains marketing performance and risk. It also offers consulting support and training services. Teradata's hardware products are assembled by Flextronics using components supplied by such vendors as NetApp and Intel. It serves some 1200 customers in the financial services government health care manufacturing and transportation industries among others; most of its sales are from the Americas.

	Annual Growth	12/10	12/11	12/12	12/13	12/14
Sales ($ mil.)	9.0%	1,936.0	2,362.0	2,665.0	2,692.0	2,732.0
Net income ($ mil.)	5.1%	301.0	353.0	419.0	377.0	367.0
Market value ($ mil.)	1.5%	6,087.6	7,174.6	9,153.5	6,728.0	6,460.3
Employees	11.7%	7,400	8,600	10,200	10,800	11,500

TERADYNE, INC.

NYS: TER

600 Riverpark Drive
North Reading, MA 01864
Phone: 978 370-2700
Fax: –
Web: www.teradyne.com

CEO: Mark E. Jagiela
CFO: Gregory R. (Greg) Beecher
HR: –
FYE: December 31
Type: Public

Electronics makers concerned about quality and consistency can put their products through the Teradyne tests. The company is a leading supplier of automated test equipment and a maker of systems for testing semiconductors. Teradyne caters to electronics manufacturing services suppliers as well as OEMs who use its test systems to analyze complex electronics used in the computing consumer electronics military/aerospace and telecommunications industries. Customers include Apple government contractors and the US government. Teradyne has operations in Asia Europe and the Americas; but it generates the majority of sales from customers in Asia.

	Annual Growth	12/10	12/11	12/12	12/13	12/14
Sales ($ mil.)	0.6%	1,608.7	1,429.1	1,656.8	1,427.9	1,647.8
Net income ($ mil.)	(32.0%)	379.7	373.8	217.0	164.9	81.3
Market value ($ mil.)	9.0%	3,041.2	2,952.4	3,658.6	3,816.7	4,286.8
Employees	6.8%	3,000	3,200	3,600	3,800	3,900

TEREX ASV

840 Lily Ln.
Grand Rapids MN 55744
Phone: 218-327-3434
Fax: 218-327-9122
Web: asvi.com

CEO: George Ellis
CFO: Thomas R Kages
HR: –
FYE: December 31
Type: Subsidiary

To everything there is a season and Terex ASV (formerly A.S.V. Inc.) has a vehicle for all seasons. The company uses rubber track suspension systems that make its vehicles operable in sand mud swamps snow slippery slopes and rough terrain. Its Posi-Track (PT) Series and ST-50 Tracked Utility Vehicle unveiled in 2008 are used for excavation and brush cutting agriculture fire fighting snow clearance and construction. Remote-controlled PTs are used in military applications to clear unexploded ordnance. Early in 2008 the company was acquired by mining equipment manufacturer Terex in a deal valued at about $488 million.

TEREX CORP.

NYS: TEX

200 Nyala Farm Road
Westport, CT 06880
Phone: 203 222-7170
Fax: 203 222-7976
Web: www.terex.com

CEO: John L. Garrison
CFO: Kevin Bradley
HR: Eileen Mulry
FYE: December 31
Type: Public

Terex is a "T-Rex" when it comes to making a variety of cranes aerial platforms and construction and materials processing equipment. Its construction business makes compaction equipment such as compact track loaders and excavators as well as road building products. Another arm makes aerial lifts from articulating to telescopic booms used in industrial and construction overhead jobs. Terex products are sold in more than 100 countries around the globe to the construction forestry and recycling shipping and utility industries under brands Terex Genie and Powerscreen. In mid-2015 Terex agreed to acquire and merge with Finnish rival Konecranes in an all-stock deal.

	Annual Growth	12/10	12/11	12/12	12/13	12/14
Sales ($ mil.)	13.4%	4,418.2	6,504.6	7,348.4	7,084.0	7,308.9
Net income ($ mil.)	(2.9%)	358.5	45.2	105.8	226.0	319.0
Market value ($ mil.)	(2.6%)	3,271.6	1,424.0	2,962.8	4,425.7	2,938.6
Employees	5.8%	16,300	22,600	21,300	20,500	20,400

TERRA NITROGEN CO., L.P.

NYS: TNH

4 Parkway North, Suite 400
Deerfield, IL 60015
Phone: 847 405-2400
Fax: –
Web: www.cfindustries.com

CEO: W Anthony Will
CFO: Dennis P Kelleher
HR: –
FYE: December 31
Type: Public

Making the earth's soil produce more crops is the long term mission of Terra Nitrogen which manufactures nitrogen fertilizer products. The company operates a plant in Oklahoma that produces ammonia and urea ammonium nitrate (UAN) solutions. Farmers use the company's products to improve both the quantity and the quality of crops. It sells its products to parent company agrochemical giant CF Industries which in turn sells nitrogen products wholesale to dealers distributors and national farm retail chain outlets primarily in the central and Southern Plains and Corn Belt regions of the US. CF Industries has indirect ownership of Terra Nitrogen's general partner and controls the company.

	Annual Growth	12/10	12/11	12/12	12/13	12/14
Sales ($ mil.)	3.5%	564.6	798.9	780.1	736.2	648.3
Net income ($ mil.)	16.4%	201.6	508.0	560.8	502.4	370.0
Market value ($ mil.)	(1.3%)	2,020.1	3,137.7	4,000.4	2,636.5	1,919.0
Employees	–	–	–	–	–	–

TERRACON CONSULTANTS INC.

18001 W 106TH ST STE 300
OLATHE, KS 660616447
Phone: 913-599-6886
Fax: –
Web: www.terracon.com

CEO: David Gaboury
CFO: Roger R. Herting
HR: Robert (Bob) Bergeson
FYE: December 31
Type: Private

Employee-owned Terracon Consultants provides geotechnical environmental construction material evaluation pavement engineering and construction management and facilities engineering services. One of the nation's top design firms the company serves the agriculture energy telecommunications commercial development and transportation sectors as well as government clients. The company has more than 140 offices in some 40 US states. Terracon serves more than 160 clients. It helps its customers comply with new building codes and environmental regulations assess environmental hazards and tackle the problem of aging structures.

	Annual Growth	12/09	12/10	12/11	12/12	12/13
Sales ($ mil.)	9.5%	–	319.7	353.8	380.6	419.4
Net income ($ mil.)	10.1%	–	–	8.8	10.4	10.7
Market value ($ mil.)	–	–	–	–	–	–
Employees	–	–	–	–	–	2,823

TERRACYCLE INC.

121 New York Ave.
Trenton NJ 08638
Phone: 609-393-4252
Fax: 609-393-4259
Web: www.terracycle.net

CEO: Tom Szaky
CFO: Javier Daly
HR: –
FYE: December 31
Type: Private

Dumpster diving has never looked so good. TerraCycle makes upcycled products out of previously non-recyclable trash. The company offers tote bags backpacks and kites made from snack food wrappers; pencils made out of newspaper; and picture frames made from bicycle chains and circuit boards among other products. More than 28 million people around the world collect waste for TerraCycle and ship it to the company free of charge. (Companies such as Kraft and Solo Cup that make packaging and wrappers foot the bill for waste collection.) TerraCycle also offers a line of eco-friendly cleaning products; all of its goods are sold at major retailers such as Target Wal-Mart and Whole Foods.

TERREMARK WORLDWIDE INC.

1 Biscayne Tower 2 S. Biscayne Blvd. Ste. 2800	CEO: –
Miami FL 33131	CFO: –
Phone: 305-961-3200	HR: –
Fax: 305-961-8190	FYE: March 31
Web: www.terremark.com	Type: Subsidiary

Terremark Worldwide isn't afraid to NAP on the job. The company provides colocation exchange point and managed IT infrastructure services from several network access point (NAP) locations. It also leases data center space in Europe and Latin America. Terremark markets to telecom carriers interactive entertainment providers and other businesses. In addition to its commercial customers the company counts agencies of the US federal government among its clients. The company was acquired in 2011 for $1.4 billion by Verizon Communications which is investing in the hosted Web services for corporations offered by Verizon Business.

TERRENO REALTY CORP

NYS: TRNO

101 Montgomery Street, Suite 200	CEO: W. Blake Baird
San Francisco, CA 94104	CFO: Jaime J. Cannon
Phone: 415 655-4580	HR: –
Fax: –	FYE: December 31
Web: www.terreno.com	Type: Public

Terreno Realty has its eyes set on acquiring industrial real estate. The real estate investment trust (REIT) invests in and operates industrial properties in major US coastal markets including Los Angeles San Francisco Bay Area Seattle Miami Northern New Jersey/New York City and Washington DC/Baltimore. The REIT typically invests in warehouse and distribution facilities flex buildings for light manufacturing and research and development and transportation and shipping centers. The company owns more than 125 buildings spanning 9.3 million square feet and two improved land parcels totaling 3.5 acres.

	Annual Growth	12/11	12/12	12/13	12/14	12/15
Sales ($ mil.)	53.0%	17.5	31.2	45.5	68.9	95.9
Net income ($ mil.)	–	(3.7)	4.1	6.6	10.7	14.6
Market value ($ mil.)	10.6%	655.7	668.7	766.6	893.5	979.7
Employees	15.8%	10	13	15	18	18

TERRITORIAL BANCORP INC

NMS: TBNK

1132 Bishop Street, Suite 2200	CEO: Allan S. Kitagawa
Honolulu, HI 96813	CFO: –
Phone: 808 946-1400	HR: –
Fax: –	FYE: December 31
Web: www.territorialsavings.net	Type: Public

Territorial Bancorp serves its customers island-style. It is the financial holding company for Territorial Savings Bank which provides standard products and services such as checking and savings accounts money market accounts CDs IRAs and loans from its nearly 30 branch locations across Hawaii. Its Territorial Financial Services subsidiary sells insurance while LPL Financial offers Mutual funds and annuities. Territorial Savings Bank targets the territorial nature of its customers — one- to four-family residential mortgages account for 95% of its loan portfolio. Multifamily and commercial mortgages and construction and home equity loans round out its lending activities.

	Annual Growth	12/10	12/11	12/12	12/13	12/14
Assets ($ mil.)	4.1%	1,443.4	1,537.6	1,574.6	1,616.9	1,691.9
Net income ($ mil.)	6.3%	11.0	12.8	14.8	14.6	14.1
Market value ($ mil.)	2.0%	197.5	195.9	226.7	230.1	213.8
Employees	1.3%	258	263	277	279	272

TESLA MOTORS INC

NMS: TSLA

3500 Deer Creek Road	CEO: –
Palo Alto, CA 94304	CFO: Jason Wheeler
Phone: 650 681-5000	HR: Mark Lipscomb
Fax: –	FYE: December 31
Web: www.teslamotors.com	Type: Public

Tesla Motors intends to spark the public's passion and eco-conscience for electric vehicles. Founded in 2003 the company designs manufactures and markets high-performance electric cars and powertrain components. Tesla's stylish Roadster is its flagship model which the company continues to upgrade. The fuel-efficient fully electric vehicle recharges its lithium-ion batteries from an outlet and depending on a driver's speed is capable of 245 miles per charge. Tesla's second vehicle the Model S sedan is a four-door five-passenger premium sedan that offers many of the electric powertrain innovations introduced with the Roadster.

	Annual Growth	12/10	12/11	12/12	12/13	12/14
Sales ($ mil.)	128.8%	116.7	204.2	413.3	2,013.5	3,198.4
Net income ($ mil.)	–	(154.3)	(254.4)	(396.2)	(74.0)	(294.0)
Market value ($ mil.)	70.0%	3,347.1	3,589.6	4,257.0	18,907.1	27,954.2
Employees	83.4%	899	1,417	2,964	5,859	10,161

TESORO ALASKA COMPANY

471 W. 36th St.	CEO: –
Anchorage AK 99503	CFO: –
Phone: 907-561-5521	HR: –
Fax: 907-561-5047	FYE: December 31
Web: www.tsocorp.com/tsocorp/productsandservices/re	Type: Business Segment

A pioneer of oil refining in Alaska Tesoro Alaska is a regional oil refinery and refined petroleum products marketing unit of Tesoro Corporation. The unit manages Tesoro Corporation's and Alaska's first oil refinery at Kenai. The 72000 barrels-a-day refinery produces gasoline liquefied petroleum gas heavy oils bunker fuels and liquid asphalt as well as distillates (jet fuel diesel fuel and heating oil). The plant's primary product is jet fuel for Anchorage International Airport located 70 miles from the refinery. A 40000-barrels-per-day pipeline connects the refinery with the airport. The Kenai refinery also supplies gasoline and diesel to about 90 Tesoro-branded retail outlets in Alaska.

TESORO CORPORATION

NYS: TSO

19100 Ridgewood Pkwy	CEO: Gregory J. (Greg) Goff
San Antonio, TX 78259-1828	CFO: Steven M. (Steve) Sterin
Phone: 210 626-6000	HR: –
Fax: –	FYE: December 31
Web: www.tsocorp.com	Type: Public

Once a player in the exploration and production field Tesoro Corporation (formerly Tesoro Petroleum) has been enjoying a more refined existence in recent years as a downstream operator. The independent oil refiner and marketer operates six US refineries — in Alaska California (three) North Dakota Utah and Washington — with a combined capacity of 850000 barrels per day. It produces gasoline jet fuel diesel fuel oil liquid asphalt and other fuel products. Tesoro markets fuel to more than 2200 branded retail gas stations (including 595 company-operated stations under the Tesoro Shell and USA Gasoline brands) primarily in Alaska and the Western US. It owns 36% of Tesoro Logistics LP.

	Annual Growth	12/10	12/11	12/12	12/13	12/14
Sales ($ mil.)	18.5%	20,583.0	30,303.0	32,974.0	37,601.0	40,633.0
Net income ($ mil.)	–	(29.0)	546.0	743.0	412.0	843.0
Market value ($ mil.)	41.5%	2,316.8	2,919.1	5,504.5	7,310.2	9,290.8
Employees	1.4%	5,300	5,400	5,700	7,000	5,600

TESORO LOGISTICS LP

NYS: TLLP

19100 Ridgewood Parkway
San Antonio, TX 78259-1828
Phone: 210 626-6000
Fax: –
Web: www.tesorologistics.com

CEO: Gregory J Goff
CFO: –
HR: Elias Reyna
FYE: December 31
Type: Public

Tesoro Logistics was created to serve its parent. The company a spinoff of oil refiner Tesoro Corporation owns and operates crude oil gathering transportation and storage facilities in the US. Its trucks and 700 miles of Montana and North Dakota pipeline serve Tesoro's Mandan refinery while eight refined product terminals hold petroleum in California Utah Washington Alaska and North Dakota. Tesoro Logistics' primary storage facility in Salt Lake City holds nearly 880000 barrels of crude and refined petroleum. Most of the company's revenue comes from Tesoro and is evenly split between the gathering segment and the transporting and storing segment. It went public in 2011.

	Annual Growth	12/10	12/11	12/12	12/13	12/14
Sales ($ mil.)	125.3%	23.3	80.9	156.8	305.5	600.0
Net income ($ mil.)	–	(20.9)	27.9	56.8	79.7	99.0
Market value ($ mil.)	21.4%	–	2,689.8	3,581.0	4,279.2	4,811.4
Employees	95.6%	–	114	160	470	853

TESSADA & ASSOCIATES INC.

8001 FORBES PL STE 310
SPRINGFIELD, VA 22151-2205
Phone: 703-564-1210
Fax: –
Web: www.mlss.tessada.com

CEO: Deryl W Wright
CFO: –
HR: Phina Pek
FYE: August 31
Type: Private

Tessada & Associates provides a wide variety of business improvement consulting services to government and private sector clients from more than 25 offices throughout the US. Services include facilities management engineering finance and accounting information technology logistics and technical support and security. The company also offers multimedia production and management services helping clients create marketing materials and business presentations. Clients have included the Department of Homeland Security the Department of Agriculture and the Department of Transportation.

	Annual Growth	08/02	08/03	08/04	08/05	08/07
Sales ($ mil.)	(3.4%)	–	–	–	70.0	65.3
Net income ($ mil.)	5.3%	–	–	–	1.8	2.0
Market value ($ mil.)	–	–	–	–	–	–
Employees	–	–	–	–	–	550

TESSCO TECHNOLOGIES, INC.

NMS: TESS

11126 McCormick Road
Hunt Valley, MD 21031
Phone: 410 229-1000
Fax: –
Web: www.tessco.com

CEO: Robert B. (Barney) Barnhill
CFO: Aric M Spitulnik
HR: –
FYE: March 29
Type: Public

TESSCO Technologies distributes communications products from hundreds of manufacturers from Agilent to ZTE. TESSCO sells network systems products (broadband radios bi-directional amplifiers); base station infrastructure equipment (towers and site hardware antennas); installation test and maintenance equipment (tools device repair parts); and mobile devices and accessories. The company also offers training services. TESSCO sells to wireless carriers as well as wireless product resellers and installers manufacturers retailers government agencies and others. While 98% of its sales are in the US the remaining 2% are made in more than 80 countries.

	Annual Growth	03/11*	04/12*	03/13	03/14	03/15
Sales ($ mil.)	(2.4%)	605.2	733.4	752.6	560.1	549.6
Net income ($ mil.)	(3.6%)	10.0	16.4	17.8	16.2	8.6
Market value ($ mil.)	21.3%	95.8	207.8	176.6	286.4	207.4
Employees	(2.6%)	874	843	838	821	786
						*Fiscal year change

TESSERA TECHNOLOGIES INC

NMS: TSRA

3025 Orchard Parkway
San Jose, CA 95134
Phone: 408 321-6000
Fax: 408 321-8257
Web: www.tessera.com

CEO: Thomas A. (Tom) Lacey
CFO: Robert Andersen
HR: –
FYE: December 31
Type: Public

Tessera Technologies would love to be treated like royalty. Though Tessera Intellectual Property Corp. the company licenses its portfolio of patented semiconductor packaging technologies in exchange for royalty payments. More than 70 companies such as Intel Motorola and Samsung use its designs to produce high-performance packages for mobile devices PCs and other electronics. Altogether Tessera has more than 1800 US and foreign patents. In addition it offers custom micro-optics for semiconductor lithography communications medical industrial and other applications. Another 20% of sales come from its DigitalOptics subsidiary which designs and manufactures camera modules for smartphones.

	Annual Growth	12/10	12/11	12/12	12/13	12/14
Sales ($ mil.)	(1.9%)	301.4	254.6	234.0	168.9	278.8
Net income ($ mil.)	31.3%	57.3	(19.3)	(30.2)	(185.6)	170.5
Market value ($ mil.)	12.7%	1,170.4	885.1	869.2	1,041.5	1,889.6
Employees	(19.4%)	480	493	1,085	525	203

TESTAMERICA LABORATORIES INC.

30 Community Dr. Ste. 11
Burlington VT 05403
Phone: 802-660-1990
Fax: 802-660-1919
Web: www.testamericainc.com

CEO: Rachel Brydon Jannetta
CFO: Stuart Stoller
HR: –
FYE: March 31
Type: Private

What's in your water and air? TestAmerica Laboratories can tell you. The company provides chemical physical and biological testing of air drinking water tissue and solid waste. TestAmerica has developed technologies to test air for fire retardants explosives radiation and source emissions. Its affiliates include environmental and geotechnical drilling firm TestAmerica Drilling water sampling equipment and remediation pumping system provider QED Environmental Systems and air quality analysts EMLab P&K) and TestAmerica Air Emissions Corp. (METCO Environmental). The company operates a network of 90 locations (environmental testing laboratories and service centers) in the US.

TETCO INCORPORATED

1100 NE Loop 410 Ste. 900
San Antonio TX 78217-5209
Phone: 210-821-5900
Fax: 210-826-3003
Web: www.tetco.com

CEO: –
CFO: Don Bowden
HR: –
FYE: June 30
Type: Private

TETCO is a Texas-based distributor of gasoline. TETCO was founded by Tom E. Turner (hence the "TETCO" brand) and supplies a network of more than 550 company-owned and dealer-owned gas stations in Texas and six other other states in the South and Southwest. The company supplies unbranded and branded gasoline stations with a range of products. Brands provided include RAM Phillips CITGO Shell Valero Conoco Exxon Texaco Shamrock and Chevron. The family of Tom Turner also own bulk chemical transporter Mission Petroleum Transport fuel distributor United Pump Supply construction firm V.K. Knowlton Construction & Utilities. and San Antonio grocery Green Fields Market.

TETRA TECH, INC.

NMS: TTEK

3475 East Foothill Boulevard
Pasadena, CA 91107
Phone: 626 351-4664
Fax: –
Web: www.tetratech.com

CEO: Dan L. Batrack
CFO: Steven M. Burdick
HR: –
FYE: September 27
Type: Public

Tetra Tech puts technical know-how to work. The environmental management consulting and technical services group focuses on resource management and infrastructure development. Services include environmental engineering restoration groundwater cleanup watershed management information technology and operations and maintenance support. Tetra Tech provides architectural engineering and construction services for public and private facilities and designs and builds water supply systems and other infrastructure systems. The US government is a major customer. Commercial customers include companies in the chemical energy mining and pharmaceutical industries.

	Annual Growth	10/11*	09/12	09/13	09/14	09/15
Sales ($ mil.)	(1.0%)	1,792.3	2,022.1	2,024.8	1,859.9	1,718.7
Net income ($ mil.)	(18.8%)	90.0	104.4	(2.1)	108.3	39.1
Market value ($ mil.)	7.4%	1,112.8	1,559.3	1,542.7	1,496.4	1,479.8
Employees	0.0%	13,000	13,000	14,000	14,000	13,000

*Fiscal year change

TETRA TECHNOLOGIES, INC.

NYS: TTI

24955 Interstate 45 North
The Woodlands, TX 77380
Phone: 281 367-1983
Fax: 281 364-4398
Web: www.tetratec.com

CEO: Stuart M. Brightman
CFO: Elijio V Serrano
HR: –
FYE: December 31
Type: Public

TETRA Technologies is a smooth operator when it comes to discarded oil wells. The company is composed of three divisions: fluids offshore and product enhancement. The fluids unit makes clear brine fluids as well as dry calcium chloride that aid in drilling activities by the oil and gas industry. Its offshore segment decommissions platforms and pipelines and explores for oil and gas. In addition to production testing services for oil and gas operations the product enhancement division also recycles oily residuals a byproduct of refining and exploration.

	Annual Growth	12/10	12/11	12/12	12/13	12/14
Sales ($ mil.)	5.4%	872.7	845.3	880.8	909.4	1,077.6
Net income ($ mil.)	–	(43.7)	5.4	18.8	3.3	(167.6)
Market value ($ mil.)	(13.4%)	945.4	743.9	604.5	984.5	532.1
Employees	6.7%	2,932	3,125	3,648	3,462	3,800

TETRAPHASE PHARMACEUTICALS, INC

NMS: TTPH

480 Arsenal Street, Suite 110
Watertown, MA 02472
Phone: 617 715-3600
Fax: –
Web: www.tphase.com

CEO: Guy Macdonald
CFO: David C Lubner
HR: –
FYE: December 31
Type: Public

Tetraphase Pharmaceuticals knows you have to jump through more than one hoop to have a medication approved for use in the US. The company is developing a powerful antibiotic to treat life-threatening bacterial infections that are resistant to all other antibiotics currently on the market. Its drug candidate eravacycline is a synthetic tetracycline derivative that can be taken orally or intravenously to combat multi-drug resistant bacterial infections which are considered growing threats to public health. Eravacycline is gearing up for Phase III trials. To fund it Tetraphase Pharmaceuticals became a publicly traded comany in early 2013.

	Annual Growth	12/10	12/11	12/12	12/13	12/14
Sales ($ mil.)	–	0.0	0.2	7.6	10.5	9.1
Net income ($ mil.)	–	0.0	(21.6)	(15.1)	(29.6)	(66.7)
Market value ($ mil.)	–	0.0	–	–	416.5	1,223.3
Employees	29.1%	–	–	33	46	55

TEVA PHARMACEUTICALS USA INC.

1090 Horsham Rd.
North Wales PA 19454
Phone: 215-591-3000
Fax: 215-591-8600
Web: www.tevapharm-na.com

CEO: Sigurdur Olafsson
CFO: –
HR: –
FYE: December 31
Type: Subsidiary

When the pharmacist asks you if a generic equivalent is acceptable Teva hopes you'll say "yes." Teva Pharmaceuticals USA the US subsidiary of massive Israeli generic drug maker Teva Pharmaceutical Industries develops manufactures and markets both generic and branded pharmaceuticals. The company is the largest manufacturer of generic drugs in the US; its product roster boasts more than 400 generic equivalents of prescription drugs in a wide variety of therapeutic categories including cardiovascular anti-inflammatory anti-infective oncology central nervous system and dermatological. The company also produces over-the-counter (OTC) drugs and active pharmaceutical ingredients (APIs).

TEXAS A & M RESEARCH FOUNDATION INC

400 HARVEY MTCHL PKWY 3
COLLEGE STATION, TX 778454375
Phone: 979-845-8600
Fax: –
Web: www.iodp.tamu.edu

CEO: –
CFO: Linda Woodman
HR: –
FYE: August 31
Type: Private

Established in 1944 the Texas A&M Research Foundation provides administrative services and support for scientific and technical research primarily within The Texas A&M University System. Its Program Development Department helps university faculty locate and approach potential sponsors and funding opportunities.The organization also provides accounting and financing support as well as grant and contract negotiations. The foundation supports a number of projects and initiatives from the Center for Advancement and Study of Early Texas Art to vaccine research at the university system's college of medicine. It is a private not-for-profit organization.

	Annual Growth	08/10	08/11	08/12	08/13	08/14
Sales ($ mil.)	(15.9%)	–	202.8	195.9	174.2	120.8
Net income ($ mil.)	–	–	–	(2.0)	0.4	(3.5)
Market value ($ mil.)	–	–	–	–	–	–
Employees	–	–	–	–	–	483

TEXAS CAPITAL BANCSHARES INC

NMS: TCBI

2000 McKinney Avenue, Suite 700
Dallas, TX 75201
Phone: 214 932-6600
Fax: –
Web: www.texascapitalbank.com

CEO: George F. Jones
CFO: Peter B. Bartholow
HR: Cara McDaniel
FYE: December 31
Type: Public

Texas Capital Bancshares is the parent company of Texas Capital Bank with more than 10 branches in Austin Dallas Fort Worth Houston and San Antonio. The bank targets high-net-worth individuals and Texas-based businesses with more than $5 million in annual revenue with a focus on the real estate financial services transportation communications petrochemicals and mining sectors. Striving for personalized services for its clients the bank offers deposit accounts Visa credit cards commercial loans and mortgages equipment leasing wealth management and trust services. Its BankDirect division provides online banking services. Founded in 1998 Texas Capital Bancshares has about $11.7 billion in assets.

	Annual Growth	12/10	12/11	12/12	12/13	12/14
Assets ($ mil.)	25.3%	6,446.2	8,137.6	10,540.8	11,714.7	15,899.9
Net income ($ mil.)	38.4%	37.2	76.0	120.7	121.1	136.4
Market value ($ mil.)	26.3%	976.0	1,399.9	2,049.8	2,844.7	2,484.8
Employees	13.1%	699	786	881	1,016	1,142

TEXAS CHILDREN'S HOSPITAL

6621 FANNIN ST
HOUSTON, TX 77030-2399
Phone: 832-824-1000
Fax: –
Web: www.bcm.edu

CEO: Mark Wallace
CFO: –
HR: –
FYE: September 30
Type: Private

Parents in the Lone Star State can rest easy knowing Texas Children's Hospital has the doctors and facilities to diagnose and treat sick children. The hospital is the flagship facility of Texas Children's Hospital Integrated Delivery System. Founded in 1954 the hospital provides full-service medical care for children conducts extensive research and trains pediatric medical professionals. The Houston-area hospital part of the Texas Medical Center complex has clinical facilities for every ailment ranging from psychological troubles to surgery and physical rehabilitation as well as specialized heart cancer and neurological care. It is the primary pediatric training facility for the Baylor College of Medicine.

	Annual Growth	09/04	09/05*	12/05*	09/06	09/09
Sales ($ mil.)	2.7%	–	899.0	856.3	768.1	1,001.2
Net income ($ mil.)	(12.1%)	–	72.4	168.8	104.0	43.2
Market value ($ mil.)	–	–	–	–	–	–
Employees	–	–	–	–	–	6,000

*Fiscal year change

TEXAS CHRISTIAN UNIVERSITY INC

2800 S UNIVERSITY DR
FORT WORTH, TX 761290002
Phone: 817-257-7000
Fax: –
Web: www.tcu.edu

CEO: –
CFO: –
HR: Tracy Thompson
FYE: May 31
Type: Private

Home of the Horned Frogs (the school mascot) Texas Christian University (TCU) offers bachelor's master's and doctorate degrees in more than 200 fields of study. More than 10300 undergraduate and graduate students attend the university's nine colleges and schools the cover fields of study ranging from liberal arts to engineering to business. TCU has about 550 full-time faculty members and a student-to-faculty ratio of 13:1. It also has one of the NCAA's top football programs. TCU is affiliated with the Disciples of Christ a Protestant denomination.

	Annual Growth	05/04	05/05	05/09	05/12	05/13
Sales ($ mil.)	8.0%	–	216.9	263.6	441.6	401.7
Net income ($ mil.)	–	–	–	0.0	(4.1)	270.5
Market value ($ mil.)	–	–	–	–	–	–
Employees	–	–	–	–	–	3,400

TEXAS DEPARTMENT OF TRANSPORTATION

125 E. 11th St.
Austin TX 78701
Phone: 512-463-8585
Fax: 936-437-2123
Web: www.tdcj.state.tx.us

CEO: –
CFO: James M Bass
HR: –
FYE: August 31
Type: Government Agency

Bob Wills saw Miles and Miles of Texas and the Texas Department of Transportation (TxDOT) makes sure that we do too. TxDOT builds and maintains interstate US and state highways as well as farm-to-market roads throughout the state. It also oversees public transportation systems in the state. The aviation division assists local governments manage funds for airport development. In 2009 the agency transferred some its responsibilities including issuing license plates and vehicle titles to the newly created Texas Department of Motor Vehicles. The governor-appointed five-member Texas Transportation Commission oversees TxDOT's work. The agency dates back to the Texas Highway Department created in 1917.

TEXAS GAS TRANSMISSION LLC

3800 Frederica St.
Owensboro KY 42301
Phone: 270-926-8686
Fax: 270-688-5872
Web: www.txgt.com

CEO: –
CFO: –
HR: –
FYE: December 31
Type: Subsidiary

Texas Gas Transmission transmits natural gas from Texas to states in the South and Midwest through the 5900-mile natural gas pipeline system it owns and operates. The pipeline has the capacity to deliver 3.8 billion cu. ft. of gas a day to customers in eight states; major customers include Anadarko Petroleum Louisville Gas and Electric and Memphis Light Gas and Water. Texas Gas uses third-part pipelines to supply gas to off-system markets in the Northeast. The company also owns nine underground gas storage fields in Indiana and Kentucky with a storage capacity of 180 billion cu. ft. of gas. Texas Gas is a subsidiary of Boardwalk Pipeline Partners LP.

TEXAS GUARANTEED STUDENT LOAN CORPORATION

301 SUNDANCE PKWY
ROUND ROCK, TX 786818004
Phone: 512-219-5700
Fax: –
Web: www.tgslc.org

CEO: –
CFO: –
HR: –
FYE: September 30
Type: Private

TG may sound like a college fraternity but it's more about tuition and books than togas and beer. Texas Guaranteed Student Loan Corporation commonly known as TG was formed by the Texas legislature in 1979 to administer the Federal Family Education Loan Program (FFELP) in the Lone Star State. However the FFELP was eliminated in 2010 and private borrowers can no longer originate government-sponsored student loans which are now provided exclusively through the US Department of Education. TG continues to service and provide support for the approximately $26 billion worth of loans in its existing portfolio. TG is a public not-for-profit corporation that receives no state funding.

	Annual Growth	09/03	09/04	09/05	09/08	09/13
Assets ($ mil.)	2.0%	–	459.8	520.3	783.3	551.2
Net income ($ mil.)	–	–	–	60.4	(64.7)	(210.8)
Market value ($ mil.)	–	–	–	–	–	–
Employees	–	–	–	–	–	600

TEXAS HEALTH HARRIS METHODIST HOSPITAL FORT WORTH

1301 PENNSYLVANIA AVE
FORT WORTH, TX 761042122
Phone: 817-250-2000
Fax: –
Web: www.texashealth.org

CEO: –
CFO: –
HR: –
FYE: December 31
Type: Private

Harris Methodist Fort Worth Hospital is the largest and busiest hospital in Fort Worth. It is a private not-for-profit almost 730-bed tertiary care hospital serving the residents of Tarrant County and nearby communities in Texas. Harris Methodist provides both inpatient and outpatient care through its main medical center and on-site health clinics. Specialized services include emergency medicine trauma care orthopedics occupational health women's health oncology and rehabilitation. Its Harris Methodist Heart Center has about 100 beds. The hospital is the flagship facility of the Texas Health Resources hospitals system.

	Annual Growth	12/03	12/04	12/05	12/06	12/13
Sales ($ mil.)	–	–	(1,131.9)	501.3	548.7	713.3
Net income ($ mil.)	0.7%	–	–	56.8	36.8	59.8
Market value ($ mil.)	–	–	–	–	–	–
Employees	–	–	–	–	–	3,500

TEXAS HEALTH RESOURCES INC.

612 E. Lamar Blvd. Ste. 900
Arlington TX 76011
Phone: 817-462-7900
Fax: 817-462-6996
Web: www.texashealth.org

CEO: Barclay Berdan
CFO: Ronald R Long
HR: –
FYE: December 31
Type: Private - Not-for-Pr

Texas Health Resources (THR) is takin' care of the Dallas/Fort Worth and North Texas region. The not-for-profit system includes 24 acute care and short-stay hospitals outpatient and surgical centers and physicians' offices. THR is a partial owner of eight community and specialty hospitals operated as joint ventures with physicians' groups. It also maintains affiliations with imaging diagnostic rehabilitation facilities and home health agencies. THR's network includes more than 5500 doctors and more than 4100 licensed beds. Its Research and Education Institute for Texas Health Resources provides clinical studies management medical device testing and medical training services.

TEXAS HOSPITAL ASSOCIATION

6225 US Hwy. 290 E.
Austin TX 78723
Phone: 512-465-1000
Fax: 512-465-1090
Web: www.thaonline.org

CEO: Daniel Stultz
CFO: Ignacio O Zamarron
HR: Donna Goodman
FYE: August 31
Type: Private - Associatio

The Texas Hospital Association (THA) is like life support to a vital group of institutions. The not-for-profit organization supports more than 460 hospitals and health systems in Texas primarily through lobbying — on both state and federal levels. THA also offers it members education and training and through affiliations with other providers THA offers insurance consulting and software. The association publishes the bi-monthly Texas Hospitals which updates members on issues and trends in the hospital industry; Rural Route a bimonthly for rural and small hospitals; and HOSPAC Notes on the group's Political Action Committee's activities. THA was founded in 1930 by a group of hospital administrators.

TEXAS INDUSTRIES INC.

NYS: TXI

1503 LBJ Freeway, Suite 400
Dallas, TX 75234-6074
Phone: 972 647-6700
Fax: 972 647-3878
Web: www.txi.com

CEO: C Howard Nye
CFO: Anne H Lloyd
HR: Kristin Burk
FYE: May 31
Type: Public

Rock on is more than a catchphrase — it's a way of life for Texas Industries. The construction materials company known as TXI produces cement aggregates and consumer building products including ready-mix concrete and other specialty aggregate products. The company also produces sand gravel crushed limestone well cements shale clay and cement-treated materials used in paving. Products are sold under the Spec Mix Durmax Envirocon Terra Tone and Proset brands. TXI's consumer products division serves construction customers mainly in the southern and southwestern US. Texas Industries has more than 80 manufacturing facilities in Texas California and four other states.

	Annual Growth	05/09	05/10	05/11	05/12	05/13
Sales ($ mil.)	(4.5%)	839.2	621.1	621.8	647.0	697.1
Net income ($ mil.)	–	(17.6)	(38.9)	(64.9)	7.5	24.6
Market value ($ mil.)	20.4%	972.3	1,037.2	1,196.9	914.3	2,040.3
Employees	(0.7%)	2,100	1,930	2,020	1,630	2,040

TEXAS INSTRUMENTS INC.

NMS: TXN

12500 TI Boulevard
Dallas, TX 75243
Phone: 214 479-3773
Fax: –
Web: www.ti.com

CEO: Richard K. (Rich) Templeton
CFO: Kevin P. March
HR: –
FYE: December 31
Type: Public

One of the world's oldest and largest semiconductor makers Texas Instruments (TI) offers more than 100000 products. Its largest segment is analog semiconductors which change real-world signals (such as sound and images) into the digital data streams. Analog product are used to manage power in all electronic devices; TI sells these products to customers in the consumer electronics and industrial markets among others. The company also makes embedded processors which can process data from analog chips and handle specific tasks in electronic devices. TI's other products include digital light processing (DLP) chips used in high-definition projectors custom semiconductors and calculators. It generates most of its sales from the Asia/Pacific region.

	Annual Growth	12/10	12/11	12/12	12/13	12/14
Sales ($ mil.)	(1.7%)	13,966.0	13,735.0	12,825.0	12,205.0	13,045.0
Net income ($ mil.)	(3.3%)	3,228.0	2,236.0	1,759.0	2,162.0	2,821.0
Market value ($ mil.)	13.3%	34,015.4	30,467.3	32,330.3	45,957.4	55,957.9
Employees	2.2%	28,412	34,759	34,151	32,209	31,003

TEXAS LUTHERAN UNIVERSITY

1000 W COURT ST
SEGUIN, TX 781555978
Phone: 830-372-8000
Fax: –
Web: www.tlu.edu

CEO: –
CFO: –
HR: –
FYE: May 31
Type: Private

Texas Lutheran University (TLU) formerly Texas Lutheran College is a private four-year undergraduate university of liberal arts sciences and professional studies. The coeducational school annually enrolls about 1400 students from approximately 23 US states and 8 foreign countries. About two-thirds of its student body resides on campus. TLU offers about 27 majors and more than a dozen pre-professional programs as well as study abroad programs. The institution has 77 full-time faculty members; its student-faculty ratio is 14:1. The college is affiliated with the Evangelical Lutheran Church in America.

	Annual Growth	05/02	05/03	05/05	05/06	05/13
Sales ($ mil.)	–	–	0.0	32.6	31.7	50.9
Net income ($ mil.)	(34.6%)	–	–	26.1	4.3	0.9
Market value ($ mil.)	–	–	–	–	–	–
Employees	–	–	–	–	–	275

TEXAS PACIFIC LAND TRUST

NYS: TPL

1700 Pacific Avenue, Suite 2770
Dallas, TX 75201
Phone: 214 969-5530
Fax: 214 871-7139
Web: www.tpltrust.com

CEO: Roy Thomas
CFO: David M. Peterson
HR: –
FYE: December 31
Type: Public

Texas Pacific Land Trust was created to sell the Texas & Pacific Railway's land after its 1888 bankruptcy and yup they're still workin' on it. The trust began with the railroad's 3.5 million acres; today it is one of the largest private landowners in Texas with around 960000 acres in 20 counties. Texas Pacific Land Trust's sales come from oil and gas royalties (70% of sales) grazing leases easements and land sales. It has a perpetual oil and gas royalty interest under some 470000 acres in West Texas. About 8% of the trust's oil and gas royalties are from leases operated by Chevron U.S.A. Texas Pacific Land Trust uses the revenues from sales and royalties to buy and retire its own shares.

	Annual Growth	12/10	12/11	12/12	12/13	12/14
Sales ($ mil.)	28.8%	20.1	34.3	32.6	44.1	55.2
Net income ($ mil.)	32.4%	11.3	20.6	19.6	27.2	34.8
Market value ($ mil.)	34.1%	303.6	338.6	444.7	832.2	982.0
Employees	0.0%	8	9	9	8	8

TEXAS RANGERS BASEBALL CLUB

1000 Ballpark Way	CEO: –
Arlington TX 76011	CFO: –
Phone: 817-273-5222	HR: –
Fax: 817-273-5174	FYE: December 31
Web: rangers.mlb.com	Type: Business Segment

You might say these Rangers are guided by the Law of the American League West. Texas Rangers Baseball Club is a professional baseball team that represents the Dallas area in Major League Baseball. Founded in 1961 as the second incarnation of the Washington Senators the franchise moved to Texas in 1972. Playing host at Rangers Ballpark in Arlington the Rangers won their first American League pennant in 2010 and their second pennant in 2011. Texas businessman Tom Hicks who had owned the team since 1998 through his Hicks Sports Group Holdings company sold the Rangers in 2010 to a group led by sports lawyer Chuck Greenberg and current team CEO and Hall of Fame pitcher Nolan Ryan.

TEXAS ROADHOUSE INC

NMS: TXRH

6040 Dutchmans Lane, Suite 200	CEO: W. Kent Taylor
Louisville, KY 40205	CFO: Scott M. Colosi
Phone: 502 426-9984	HR: Laura Hoon
Fax: –	FYE: December 30
Web: www.texasroadhouse.com	Type: Public

If people are getting rowdy at this roadhouse it must be because of the steaks ribs or the famous sweet yeast rolls. Texas Roadhouse operates a leading full-service restaurant chain with more than 450 company-owned and franchised locations in 49 states and four countries outside of the US. The Southwest-themed eateries serve a variety of hand-cut steaks ribs chicken pork chops and seafood entrees along with sandwiches chili starters and a variety of side dishes. The company also operates a small number of restaurants under the name Aspen Creek that specialize in hamburgers pasta entrees and pizza.

	Annual Growth	12/10	12/11	12/12	12/13	12/14
Sales ($ mil.)	12.0%	1,005.0	1,109.2	1,263.3	1,422.6	1,582.1
Net income ($ mil.)	10.5%	58.3	64.0	71.2	80.4	87.0
Market value ($ mil.)	18.2%	1,205.3	1,053.5	1,171.2	1,935.7	2,352.1
Employees	7.9%	32,000	33,000	40,000	45,700	43,300

TEXAS SOUTHERN UNIVERSITY

3100 CLEBURNE ST	CEO: –
HOUSTON, TX 770044598	CFO: Jim McShan
Phone: 713-313-7011	HR: Brian Dickens
Fax: –	FYE: August 31
Web: www.tsu.edu	Type: Private

Texas Southern University (TSU) is a historically black public institution. The university located on a 150-acre campus in downtown Houston offers about 40 bachelor's degree programs and more than 30 master's and doctoral degree programs. Its 11 colleges and schools include the Thurgood Marshall School of Law and the Barbara Jordan Mickey Leland School of Public Affairs. (Jordan and Leland are both former US representatives and graduates of TSU.) The university has an enrollment of more than 9500 students and a staff of about 1000 faculty members and support personnel.

	Annual Growth	08/02	08/03	08/11	08/13	08/14
Sales ($ mil.)	3.9%	–	66.0	131.0	112.1	100.8
Net income ($ mil.)	–	–	–	(6.9)	1.1	4.5
Market value ($ mil.)	–	–	–	–	–	–
Employees	–	–	–	–	–	1,000

TEXAS STATE UNIVERSITY

601 UNIVERSITY DR	CEO: –
SAN MARCOS, TX 786664684	CFO: –
Phone: 512-245-2111	HR: –
Fax: –	FYE: August 31
Web: www.careerservices.txstate.edu	Type: Private

Texas State University-San Marcos is saddled up and ready to rope some graduates. The school has about 37000 students pursuing degrees in about 100 undergraduate programs nearly 90 graduate programs and a dozen doctoral programs. Comprising eight colleges as well as a graduate school Texas State is the largest school in the Texas State University system which includes Angelo State University Lamar University Sam Houston State University and Sul Ross State University. It also offers bachelor's and graduate-level courses at a campus in Round Rock.

	Annual Growth	08/10	08/11	08/12	08/13	08/14
Sales ($ mil.)	6.4%	–	313.8	330.5	329.6	377.7
Net income ($ mil.)	95.3%	–	–	19.2	61.5	73.1
Market value ($ mil.)	–	–	–	–	–	–
Employees	–	–	–	–	–	3,156

TEXAS VANGUARD OIL CO.

NBB: TVOC

9811 Anderson Mill Rd., Suite 202	CEO: William G Watson
Austin, TX 78750	CFO: William Watson
Phone: 512 331-6781	HR: –
Fax: –	FYE: December 31
	Type: Public

In the vanguard of companies squeezing oil out of old fields Texas Vanguard Oil explores and develops oil-producing properties in Nebraska New Mexico Oklahoma Texas and Wyoming. The company's growth strategy is to acquire working interests in producing oil and natural gas properties already being operated by other oil and gas firms and to then further develop these assets. In 2008 Texas Vanguard Oil reported proved reserves of 358119 barrels of oil and 2.3 billion cu. ft. of natural gas. A pure exploration and production business the company does not refine or market its own oil and gas. It also engages independent contractors to drill its wells. Chair Linda Watson owns 74% of Texas Vanguard Oil.

	Annual Growth	12/08	12/09	12/10	12/11	12/12
Sales ($ mil.)	(9.3%)	9.7	5.0	6.4	7.2	6.6
Net income ($ mil.)	(38.9%)	2.8	0.2	0.7	1.2	0.4
Market value ($ mil.)	11.0%	9.8	8.9	12.4	13.6	14.9
Employees	0.0%	2	2	2	2	2

TEXON LP

11757 Katy Fwy. Ste. 1400	CEO: Terry Looper
Houston TX 77079-1733	CFO: Leonard Russo
Phone: 281-531-8400	HR: –
Fax: 818-837-7440	FYE: December 31
Web: www.sigue.com	Type: Private

You'd never mistake it for Texaco or Exxon but Texon is also involved in the energy business though at a much more modest level. Texon LP sells natural gas and natural gas liquids (NGLs) to the wholesale market mainly to utilities municipalities and large commercial and industrial customers. Using other companies' pipelines about 50 in all it delivers its products nationwide after buying them from some 400 independent producers. Butane propane and liquefied petroleum gas are among the NGLs that Texon markets and are delivered by truck rail and barge as well as pipeline. The company also offers weather-forecasting services to clients in colder regions of the country. Texon began operations in 1989.

TEXTRON INC.

NYS: TXT

40 Westminster Street
Providence, RI 02903
Phone: 401 421-2800
Fax: –
Web: www.textron.com

CEO: Scott C. Donnelly
CFO: Frank T. Connor
HR: Cheryl H. Johnson
FYE: January 03
Type: Public

Officers corporate and military really take to Textron. The company's E-Z-GO golf carts enrich their golfing jaunts while its Cessna and Beechcraft airplanes and Bell helicopters whisk them around the world. In addition its auto parts keep their cars running and its Financial subsidiary provides loans. Besides golf carts and car parts Textron's industrial segment makes power tools electrical and fiber optic assemblies and turf maintenance equipment. The Textron systems segment sells land and marine systems sensors and unmanned aerial vehicles to the Defense Department. Various US government entities account for about one-third of Textron's sales.

	Annual Growth	01/11*	12/11	12/12	12/13*	01/15
Sales ($ mil.)	7.2%	10,525.0	11,275.0	12,237.0	12,104.0	13,878.0
Net income ($ mil.)	62.5%	86.0	242.0	589.0	498.0	600.0
Market value ($ mil.)	15.6%	6,538.4	5,114.0	6,671.2	10,125.7	11,663.5
Employees	1.5%	32,000	32,000	33,000	32,000	34,000

*Fiscal year change

TEXTURA CORP

NYS: TXTR

1405 Lake Cook Road
Deerfield, IL 60015
Phone: 847 457-6500
Fax: –
Web: www.texturacorp.com

CEO: David C. Habiger
CFO: Jillian Sheehan
HR: –
FYE: December 31
Type: Public

Textura brings tech solutions to one of the most concrete industries — construction. The company's Software-as-a-Service (SaaS) includes tools to facilitate connection and collaboration among commercial construction owners developers general contractors and subcontractors. Its on-demand software covers everything from the bidding process and vendor risk assessment to routing invoices and project documents to billing and documenting subcontractor default. A majority of Textura's revenue comes from customers using its invoicing document-tracking and environmental certification products and monthly subscription fees (collectively "activity-driven revenue"). Formed in 2004 the company went public in 2013.

	Annual Growth	09/10	09/11	09/12	09/13*	12/14
Sales ($ mil.)	79.8%	6.0	10.5	21.7	35.5	63.0
Net income ($ mil.)	–	(15.9)	(18.9)	(15.9)	(36.9)	(24.7)
Market value ($ mil.)	(33.9%)	–	–	–	1,102.3	728.5
Employees	32.6%	–	–	287	385	505

*Fiscal year change

TF FINANCIAL CORP.

NMS: THRD

3 Penns Trail
Newtown, PA 18940
Phone: 215 579-4000
Fax: –
Web: www.thirdfedbank.com

CEO: –
CFO: –
HR: –
FYE: December 31
Type: Public

To Find out what TF Financial does isn't Too tuff. The holding company owns Third Federal Savings Bank which operates about 15 branches in southeastern Pennsylvania's Buck and Philadelphia counties and neighboring Mercer County New Jersey. The bank offers standard deposit products including CDs IRAs and savings checking NOW and money market accounts. It also provides insurance and investment products and services. The bank's lending activities mainly consist of issuing one- to four-family residential mortgages (around half of the company's loan portfolio) multifamily and commercial real estate loans (about a quarter) and construction business and consumer loans.

	Annual Growth	12/08	12/09	12/10	12/11	12/12
Assets ($ mil.)	(0.8%)	733.7	714.1	691.8	681.9	711.8
Net income ($ mil.)	6.2%	4.2	4.5	3.4	3.9	5.4
Market value ($ mil.)	5.4%	54.8	53.8	63.3	64.5	67.6
Employees	(3.9%)	196	191	196	184	167

TFS FINANCIAL CORP

NMS: TFSL

7007 Broadway Avenue
Cleveland, OH 44105
Phone: 216 441-6000
Fax: –
Web: www.thirdfederal.com

CEO: Marc A Stefanski
CFO: David S Huffman
HR: Christine Warfield
FYE: September 30
Type: Public

TFS Financial is the holding company for Third Federal Savings and Loan a thrift with some 45 branches and loan production offices in Ohio and southern Florida. The bank offers such deposit products as checking savings and retirement accounts and CDs. It uses funds from deposits to originate a variety of consumer loans primarily residential mortgages. Third Federal also offers IRAs annuities and mutual funds as well as retirement and college savings plans. TFS subsidiary Third Capital owns stakes in commercial real estate private equity funds and other investments. Mutual holding company Third Federal Savings and Loan Association of Cleveland owns nearly three-quarters of TFS Financial.

	Annual Growth	09/11	09/12	09/13	09/14	09/15
Assets ($ mil.)	3.2%	10,892.9	11,518.1	11,269.3	11,803.2	12,368.9
Net income ($ mil.)	67.0%	9.3	11.5	56.0	65.9	72.6
Market value ($ mil.)	20.7%	2,364.9	2,638.3	3,481.9	4,165.4	5,017.7
Employees	–	–	–	–	–	–

TG THERAPEUTICS INC

NAS: TGTX

3 Columbus Circle, 15th Floor
New York, NY 10019
Phone: 212 554-4484
Fax: 212 554-4531
Web: www.tgtherapeutics.com

CEO: –
CFO: Sean A. Power
HR: –
FYE: December 31
Type: Public

TG Therapeutics is a drug development and commercializing firm that can change hats quickly when necessary. It is currently developing two therapies targeting hematological malignancies: glycoengineered monoclonal antibody TG-1101 (ublituximab) targets a specific epitope on the CD20 antigen found on mature B-lymphocytes while TGR-1202 is an oral P13K delta inhibitor. While its current focus is on cancer drugs TG Therapeutics — like most drug development companies — has acquired developed and spun-off other types of candidates in an effort to build a pipeline of potentially revenue-generating commercial products. Previous candidates included a vitamin B-12 nasal spray and a treatment for involuntary tremors.

	Annual Growth	12/10	12/11	12/12	12/13	12/14
Sales ($ mil.)	182.8%	–	–	0.0	0.2	0.2
Net income ($ mil.)	–	0.6	(0.9)	(18.1)	(20.5)	(55.8)
Market value ($ mil.)	446.1%	0.8	0.9	163.6	175.2	711.7
Employees	68.2%	3	5	6	13	24

THE ADT CORPORATION

NYSE: ADT

1501 Yamato Rd
Boca Raton FL 33431
Phone: 561-988-3600
Fax: 561-988-3601
Web: www.adt.com

CEO: Naren K Gursahaney
CFO: –
HR: Michelle Koran
FYE: September 30
Type: Public

Burglar at your window? ADT wants you to be armed and calm with its alarms. The company provides products and services used for fire protection access control alarm monitoring medical alert system monitoring video surveillance and intrusion detection. It divides its security operations across four disciplines: Residential Security (provides burglar fire carbon dioxide alarms) Small Business (intruder detection and cameras) ADT Pulse (allows users to access and control security systems remotely) and Home Health (emergency response in the case of medical emergencies). ADT was a unit of conglomerate Tyco International until late 2012 when it was spun-off as a publicly traded company.

THE AEROSPACE CORPORATION

2310 E EL SEGUNDO BLVD
EL SEGUNDO, CA 902454609
Phone: 310-336-5000
Fax: –
Web: www.aerospace.org

CEO: Wanda M. Austin
CFO: Ellen M. Beatty
HR: –
FYE: September 30
Type: Private

A not-for-profit company The Aerospace Corporation provides space-related research development and advisory services primarily for US government programs. Its chief sponsor is the US Air Force and its main customers have included the Space and Missile Systems Center of Air Force Space Command and the National Reconnaissance Office. Other clients have included NASA and the National Oceanic and Atmospheric Administration as well as commercial enterprises universities and international organizations. Areas of expertise include launch certification process implementation systems engineering and technology application. The Aerospace Corporation was established in 1960 and operates through about 20 offices.

	Annual Growth	09/10	09/11	09/12	09/13	09/14
Sales ($ mil.)	(2.1%)	–	939.3	903.4	868.6	881.9
Net income ($ mil.)	8.6%	–	–	4.6	0.2	5.4
Market value ($ mil.)	–	–	–	–	–	–
Employees	–	–	–	–	–	3,920

THE AMACORE GROUP INC.

OTC: ACGI

485 N. Keller Rd. Ste. 450
Maitland FL 32751
Phone: 407-805-8900
Fax: 407-805-0045
Web: www.amacoregroup.com

CEO: Jay Shafer
CFO: G Scott Smith
HR: –
FYE: December 31
Type: Public

The Amacore Group wants you to be able to see a smaller optometry bill. Amacore is a provider of non-insurance based discount plans for eyewear and eyecare services including surgery. Amacore Group's products are marketed to individuals families and businesses as well as through the company's affiliations with insurance companies and other membership groups. The company has expanded its discount program offerings to include dental hearing chiropractic and other health services. It also offers traditional health plans through partnerships with insurance providers.

THE AMALGAMATED SUGAR COMPANY LLC

1951 S SATURN WAY STE 100
BOISE, ID 837092924
Phone: 208-658-2243
Fax: –
Web: www.amalgamatedsugar.com

CEO: John McCreedy
CFO: John Landis
HR: –
FYE: December 31
Type: Private

The Amalgamated Sugar Company with roots reaching back to 1915 turns beets into sweets. It's the second-largest US sugar producer processing sugar beets grown on about 180000 acres in Idaho Oregon and Washington. The company manufactures granulated coarse powdered and brown consumer sugar products marketed under the brand White Satin. It also makes products for retail grocery chains under private labels. The sugar company produces beet pulp molasses and other beet by-products for use by food and animal-feed manufacturers. Since 1997 Amalgamated Sugar has been owned by the Snake River Sugar Company a cooperative that comprises sugar beet growers in Idaho Oregon and Washington.

	Annual Growth	12/09	12/10	12/11	12/12	12/13
Sales ($ mil.)	4.2%	–	841.6	886.1	907.9	953.1
Net income ($ mil.)	16.0%	–	–	46.7	14.7	62.8
Market value ($ mil.)	–	–	–	–	–	–
Employees	–	–	–	–	–	1,500

THE AMERICAN AUTOMOBILE ASSOCIATION

1000 AAA Dr.
Heathrow FL 32746
Phone: 407-444-7000
Fax: 407-444-7380
Web: www.aaa.com

CEO: Marshall Doney
CFO: Robert McKee
HR: –
FYE: December 31
Type: Private - Not-for-Pr

This isn't your great-grandfather's American Automobile Association (AAA). The not-for-profit organization is best known for providing emergency roadside assistance to its members. AAA is extending its reach into other areas however such as offering a variety of financial and travel-arrangement services (foreign currency exchange and travelers checks) as well. The organization offers its members credit cards insurance and vehicle financing. AAA operates travel agencies and publishes maps and travel guides to boot. AAA and its affiliated 50-odd auto clubs maintain about 1100 facilities to serve more than 53 million members that span the US and Canada. AAA was founded in 1902.

THE AMERICAN MUSEUM OF NATURAL HISTORY

CENTRAL PARK W AT 79TH ST
NEW YORK, NY 10024
Phone: 212-769-5000
Fax: –
Web: www.amnh.org

CEO: –
CFO: Ellen Gallagher
HR: Dan Scheiner
FYE: June 30
Type: Private

The American Museum of Natural History is one of the world's foremost scientific museums. Its landmark building on New York's Central Park West showcases parts of its immense collections of anthropological and zoological specimens along with meteorites gemstones dinosaur fossils and a butterfly conservatory. The museum which is also home to the Rose Center for Earth and Space and the Hayden Planetarium and a top-flight research library conducts many educational programs offers an IMAX theater and publishes Natural History magazine. The American Museum of Natural History is part of the University of the State of New York. The museum was chartered by the New York legislature in 1869.

	Annual Growth	06/05	06/06	06/07	06/09	06/13
Sales ($ mil.)	–	–	0.0	163.2	135.1	197.3
Net income ($ mil.)	(34.4%)	–	–	100.1	(53.0)	8.0
Market value ($ mil.)	–	–	–	–	–	–
Employees	–	–	–	–	–	1,262

THE ARTHRITIS FOUNDATION INC

1330 W PEACHTREE ST NW # 100
ATLANTA, GA 30309-2922
Phone: 404-872-7100
Fax: –
Web: www.arthritis.org

CEO: Ann M Palmer
CFO: Christopher Corrigan
HR: –
FYE: December 31
Type: Private

Arthritis Foundation (AF) wants the country's aches to go away. The not-for-profit organization funds research advocacy and support services for various kinds of arthritis and related diseases. The foundation has about 45 chapters in 33 states and offers programs and services including aquatic programs information about treatment breakthroughs exercise tips for people with the disease and pain management information. AF raises money through The Arthritis Walk Jingle Bell Walk/Run and Joints in Motion a program that trains participants to run a marathon or hike a tough trail and take part in a fund raising event. The organization was founded in 1948.

	Annual Growth	12/03	12/04	12/05	12/07	12/08
Sales ($ mil.)	(18.3%)	–	122.3	74.8	133.6	54.4
Net income ($ mil.)	(40.8%)	–	7.9	5.8	12.2	1.0
Market value ($ mil.)	–	–	–	–	–	–
Employees	–	–	–	–	–	150

THE ASPEN INSTITUTE

1 DUPONT CIR NW STE 700
WASHINGTON, DC 200361133
Phone: 202-736-5800
Fax: –
Web: www.aspeninstitute.org

CEO: Walter Isaacson
CFO: Dolores Gorgone
HR: –
FYE: December 31
Type: Private

If you're attending one of many seminars at the Aspen Institute you really should have your thinking cap on. The Aspen Institute is an international think tank providing a place to exchange ideas about leadership and contemporary issues. The not-for-profit organization holds seminars programs and conferences emphasizing a nonpartisan and non-ideological setting. Equity in public education ethical leadership practices and global security are among the issues the institute has addressed. It is primarily funded by corporate individual and foundation donations. The Aspen Institute was founded in 1950 by Chicago businessman and philanthropist Walter Paepcke.

	Annual Growth	12/05	12/06	12/07	12/08	12/13
Sales ($ mil.)	5.1%	–	65.8	84.0	73.7	93.2
Net income ($ mil.)	(10.2%)	–	–	21.2	10.2	11.1
Market value ($ mil.)	–	–	–	–	–	–
Employees	–	–	–	–	–	300

THE ASSOCIATED PRESS

450 W 33RD ST FL 16
NEW YORK, NY 100012626
Phone: 212-621-1500
Fax: –
Web: www.ap.org

CEO: Gary Pruitt
CFO: Kenneth Dale
HR: –
FYE: December 31
Type: Private

This just in: The Associated Press (AP) is reporting tonight and every night wherever news is breaking. AP is one of the world's largest news gathering organizations with news bureaus in about 100 countries. It provides news photos graphics and audiovisual services that reach people daily through print radio TV and the Web. It also offers advertising management and distribution services. The not-for-profit cooperative is owned by 1500 US daily newspaper members. A group of New York newspapers founded the AP in 1846 in order to chronicle the US-Mexican War more efficiently. Founding papers include The New York Sun The Journal of Commerce The Courier and Enquirer The New York Herald and The Express.

	Annual Growth	12/09	12/10	12/11	12/12	12/13
Sales ($ mil.)	(1.9%)	–	630.5	627.6	622.2	595.7
Net income ($ mil.)	–	–	–	(193.3)	(25.6)	3.1
Market value ($ mil.)	–	–	–	–	–	–
Employees	–	–	–	–	–	3,533

THE AVEDIS ZILDJIAN COMPANY INC.

22 Longwater Dr.
Norwell MA 02061
Phone: 781-871-2200
Fax: 781-871-9652
Web: www.zildjian.com

CEO: Craigie A Zildjian
CFO: –
HR: –
FYE: December 31
Type: Private

The centuries-old story of Avedis Zildjian is rich in cymbalism. Zildjian the world's #1 maker of cymbals is the oldest family-run firm in the US. In 1623 Turkey Armenian alchemist Avedis created an alloy for making cymbals. (A sultan named him "Zildjian" or cymbalsmith.) The company moved to America in 1929. Traditionally the father passed the secret metallurgical formula on to the eldest son but in 1976 Craigie Zildjian (named CEO in 1999) became the first female family member to be employed there. Zildjian also makes drumsticks and through subsidiary Malletech other percussion instruments. Craigie's uncle Robert owns rival cymbal-maker Sabian which also uses the secret formula.

THE BALTIMORE LIFE INSURANCE COMPANY

10075 Red Run Blvd.
Owings Mills MD 21117-4871
Phone: 410-581-6600
Fax: 410-581-6604
Web: www.baltlife.com

CEO: L John Pearson
CFO: –
HR: Andrea Long
FYE: December 31
Type: Private

Baltimore Life keeps its finger on the pulse of citizens in Baltimore and beyond. The company provides a variety of life insurance products and annuities to some 300000 customers in the US including individuals families and businesses. Products include term universal and whole life policies; retirement immediate and deferred annuities; and illness coverage. Independent and affiliated agents sell the company's policies. Licensed in 49 states and Washington DC the firm operates primarily in Maryland and Pennsylvania. Baltimore Life was founded in 1882 and reorganized to a mutual insurance holding company structure in 2001.

THE BANCORP, INC.

NMS: TBBK

409 Silverside Road
Wilmington, DE 19809
Phone: 302 385-5000
Fax: –
Web: www.thebancorp.com

CEO: Frank M. Mastrangelo
CFO: Paul Frenkiel
HR: –
FYE: December 31
Type: Public

The Bancorp is — what else? — the holding company for The Bancorp Bank which provides financial services in the virtual world. On its home turf of the Philadelphia and Wilmington Delaware metropolitan areas The Bancorp Bank offers deposit lending and related services targeting wealthy individuals and small to midsized businesses it believes are underserved by larger banks in the market. Nationally The Bancorp provides private-label online banking services for some 300 affinity groups issues prepaid debit cards processes merchant credit card transactions and acts as a custodian for health savings accounts (HSAs).

	Annual Growth	12/10	12/11	12/12	12/13	12/14
Assets ($ mil.)	20.1%	2,395.7	3,010.7	3,699.7	4,706.1	4,986.3
Net income ($ mil.)	81.9%	5.2	8.9	16.6	25.1	57.1
Market value ($ mil.)	1.7%	383.5	272.6	413.7	675.4	410.6
Employees	16.4%	373	428	532	624	684

THE BEACON MUTUAL INSURANCE COMPANY

1 Beacon Centre
Warwick RI 02886-1378
Phone: 401-825-2667
Fax: 401-825-2607
Web: www.beaconmutual.com

CEO: –
CFO: Cynthia Lee Lawlor
HR: –
FYE: December 31
Type: Private - Mutual Com

Safety's a beacon in the night (and day) at Beacon Mutual Insurance a provider of workers' compensation employers' liability insurance and claim management services in Rhode Island. It is the state's largest writer of workers' compensation where it has more than 13000 policyholders. The not-for-profit organization operates under statutory duties to provide coverage at the lowest possible cost and to serve as an insurer of last resort. It also offers loss prevention services including workplace and construction safety defensive driving and industrial ergonomics programs. Beacon Mutual Insurance was founded as the State Compensation Insurance Fund in 1990; it began writing policies in 1992.

THE BELT RAILWAY COMPANY OF CHICAGO

6900 S. Central Ave.
Bedford Park IL 60638
Phone: 708-496-4000
Fax: 708-496-2608
Web: www.beltrailway.com

CEO: –
CFO: –
HR: –
FYE: December 31
Type: Joint Venture

Belt Railway of Chicago is a railroad's railroad. Freight trains converge on its Clearing Yards facility to have their cars separated and moved from one rail line to another in order to reach their destinations. To accomplish these tasks the company operates 28 miles of mainline track and 300 miles of switching lines. Belt Railway of Chicago is owned by six of the largest North American railroads: Burlington Northern Santa Fe Canadian National Canadian Pacific CSX Norfolk Southern and Union Pacific. Customers include not only the company's owners but also other railroads that serve the Chicago area which is one of North America's primary rail hubs. Belt Railway of Chicago began operations in 1882.

THE BENECON GROUP INC

147 W AIRPORT RD
LITITZ, PA 175439260
Phone: 717-723-4600
Fax: –
Web: www.benecon.com

CEO: Samuel Lombardo
CFO: Joel E Callihan
HR: –
FYE: December 31
Type: Private

The Benecon Group helps employers create implement and manage benefits programs. Benecon operates through four divisions: Consulting and Actuarial services Broker Services Municipal Insurance and Compliance Services. The Consulting and Actuarial services division helps larger corporate clients design and implement benefits programs while the Municipal Insurance division helps municipalities in central Pennsylvania gain leverage in the benefits markets by creating health insurance cooperatives. Benecon acts as a broker for hundreds of clients including Capital Blue Cross Highmark Blue Shield and- , UnitedHealth; the Compliance division provides advice on regulations and laws related to benefits packages.

	Annual Growth	12/03	12/04	12/05	12/06	12/08
Sales ($ mil.)	15.3%	–	9.7	10.1	12.5	17.1
Net income ($ mil.)	145.0%	–	–	0.0	0.1	0.4
Market value ($ mil.)	–	–	–	–	–	–
Employees	–	–	–	–	–	70

THE BERLIN STEEL CONSTRUCTION COMPANY

76 Depot Rd.
Berlin CT 06037
Phone: 860-828-3531
Fax: 860-828-8581
Web: www.berlinsteel.com

CEO: –
CFO: –
HR: –
FYE: December 31
Type: Private

The Berlin Steel Construction Company had nothing to do with a falling wall but it does know how to erect metal. The specialty contractor fabricates and erects structural steel for all types of buildings as well as staircases handrails and grating. It also erects precast concrete precast garages metal roofs and floor decks and steel joists and girders. In addition to fabrication and site erection Berlin Steel offers project management services. Key projects include a new terminal addition at the Bradley International Airport and structural steel work for a University of Connecticut stadium and a Rhode Island convention center. Berlin Steel serves the New England and Mid-Atlantic regions of the US.

THE BERND GROUP INC

1251 PINEHURST RD STE 101
DUNEDIN, FL 346985428
Phone: 727-733-0122
Fax: –
Web: www.berndgroup.com

CEO: –
CFO: –
HR: –
FYE: December 31
Type: Private

The Bernd Group gets paid to shop for other companies. The supply chain management company distributes computer hardware software and a wide range of industrial and commercial equipment and supplies to companies in the aerospace construction manufacturing and transportation sectors. Customers include Johnson Controls Lockheed Martin Pratt & Whitney Tampa Electric United Technologies and other maintenance repair and operations (MRO) organizations and original equipment manufacturers (OEM). The Bernd Group draws upon a network of more than 18000 vendors and is able to rely on government-based contracts for women-owned companies. President Pilar Ricaurte-Bernd owns the company which she founded in 1989.

	Annual Growth	12/10	12/11	12/12	12/13	12/14
Sales ($ mil.)	(0.6%)	–	55.7	59.3	53.2	54.8
Net income ($ mil.)	(17.1%)	–	–	1.2	0.7	0.8
Market value ($ mil.)	–	–	–	–	–	–
Employees	–	–	–	–	–	69

THE BESSEMER GROUP INCORPORATED

630 5th Ave.
New York NY 10111
Phone: 212-708-9100
Fax: 212-265-5826
Web: www.bessemertrust.com

CEO: Marc D Stern
CFO: –
HR: –
FYE: December 31
Type: Private

Wealth is personal for Bessemer Group. The privately-owned firm manages more than $60 billion in assets for wealthy individuals and families who have at least $10 million to invest. Main subsidiary Bessemer Trust administers portfolios with holdings in domestic and international equities and bonds as well as such alternative assets as hedge funds real estate and private equity funds of funds. The group also provides trust custody tax and estate planning strategic philanthropy and financial advisory services. It also counsels family businesses. The Bessemer Group has some 15 US offices in addition to locations in London and the Cayman Islands.

THE BILTMORE COMPANY

1 LODGE ST
ASHEVILLE, NC 28803
Phone: 828-225-6776
Fax: –
Web: www.biltmore.com

CEO: William A. V. (Bill) Cecil
CFO: Steve Watson
HR: –
FYE: December 31
Type: Private

The Biltmore Company doesn't need to build more. It oversees the Biltmore Estate which includes the 250-room home (the largest privately owned in the US) as well as a hotel a winery restaurants and retail shops and licensing rights for a line of home decor products. (Guests don't stay at the Biltmore House but at the Inn on Biltmore Estate.) Some one million visitors tour the home and grounds each year. The house sits on 8000 acres of land and encompasses four acres of floor space. It has 35 bedrooms some 40 bathrooms 65 fireplaces and three kitchens. The Biltmore is family-owned by descendants of the Vanderbilts and is one of the few National Historic Landmarks that is entirely privately funded.

	Annual Growth	12/02	12/03	12/04	12/06	12/07
Sales ($ mil.)	8.0%	–	57.0	56.8	70.6	77.6
Net income ($ mil.)	(8.3%)	–	–	3.0	2.5	2.3
Market value ($ mil.)	–	–	–	–	–	–
Employees	–	–	–	–	–	1,900

THE BOLER COMPANY

500 Park Blvd. Ste. 1010	CEO: –
Itasca IL 60143	CFO: –
Phone: 630-773-9111	HR: –
Fax: 630-773-9121	FYE: December 31
Web: www.hendrickson-intl.com	Type: Private

This Boler wants the big wheels of the road to ride smoothly in their own lanes. The holding company's main subsidiary Hendrickson makes suspension systems for heavy and medium-duty trucks buses and RVs. A trailer division focuses on air ride suspensions. Auxiliary axle systems and controls are made for heavy-duty trucks and trailers. A stamping division supplies bumpers and components; its spring division makes heavy-duty steel flat-leaf and parabolic taper-leaf springs. Boler sells to heavy-duty truck and trailer OEMs in the US with distribution to countries in Latin America and Europe as well as Australia and Japan. Boler is led by founder and chairman John Boler and his son president and CEO Matthew.

THE BRANCH GROUP INC

442 RUTHERFORD AVE NE	CEO: J William Karbach
ROANOKE, VA 240162116	CFO: Melanie Wheeler
Phone: 540-982-1678	HR: –
Fax: –	FYE: December 31
Web: www.branchgroup.com	Type: Private

It's not going out on a limb to say that The Branch Group has paved a lot of roads and built a lot of structures up and down the Atlantic Seaboard. The company through its subsidiaries provides heavy/highway construction (Branch Highways and E.V. Williams) building construction (Branch & Associates and R.E. Daffan) and mechanical/electrical construction services (G.J. Hopkins). The group has paved roads for highway departments built hospitals schools factories and infrastructure projects. The employee-owned company began in 1963 as Branch & Associates Inc. but traces its roots to 1955 when Billy Branch and C. W. McAlister paired up to provide road and site construction services.

	Annual Growth	12/09	12/10	12/11	12/12	12/13
Sales ($ mil.)	12.7%	–	228.0	238.4	271.2	326.3
Net income ($ mil.)	–	–	–	0.0	0.0	0.0
Market value ($ mil.)	–	–	–	–	–	–
Employees	–	–	–	–	–	800

THE BRIAD GROUP

78 Okner Pkwy.	CEO: Brad Honigfeld
Livingston NJ 07039	CFO: –
Phone: 973-597-6433	HR: Janet Gelman
Fax: 973-597-6422	FYE: December 31
Web: www.briad.com	Type: Private

This hospitality company is thankful for Friday's. The Briad Group is the #1 operator of T.G.I. Friday's restaurants with about 70 locations in six states primarily in Arizona California and New Jersey. Franchised from Carlson Restaurants Worldwide the casual dining restaurants are popular for their appetizers and bar-like atmosphere. Briad Group is also a leading franchisee of Wendy's International (part of Wendy's/Arby's Group) with more than 40 fast food restaurants in New Jersey New York and Pennsylvania. The company also has a small number of Hilton and Marriott hotels and operates one shopping center. Founder and CEO Bradford Honigfeld leads an investment group that owns Briad Group.

THE BRICKMAN GROUP LTD.

18227D Flower Hill Way	CEO: Andrew Kerin
Gaithersburg MD 20879	CFO: –
Phone: 301-987-9200	HR: –
Fax: 240-683-2030	FYE: December 31
Web: www.brickmangroup.com	Type: Private

The Brickman Group offers landscape design and maintenance services for college campuses municipal properties sports facilities and retail establishments. It provides sports turf services such as field design and consulting irrigation mowing and field maintenance for MLB and the Olympic Games. Serving thousands of clients the company has also taken on such special projects as repairing New Orleans City Park's irrigation system after Hurricane Katrina. Founded in 1939 by Theodore Brickman the group has more than 160 branch offices in about 30 US states. Private equity firm Leonard Green & Partners owns a majority shareholding of the company.

THE BROE COMPANIES INC.

252 Clayton St. 4th Fl.	CEO: –
Denver CO 80206	CFO: Tom Mandula
Phone: 303-393-0033	HR: –
Fax: 303-393-0041	FYE: December 31
Web: www.broe.com	Type: Private

Million-dollar investments don't phase this Broe. The secretive Broe Companies invests in a variety of industries in the US and Canada largely funded by profits made in real estate investments. It focuses primarily on hard asset-based investment opportunities as well as distressed businesses. Broe's brotherhood of companies include a short-line railroad owner (OmniTRAX) and a Kentucky coal company (Century Coal). Broe owns interests in some 29 million sq. ft. of commercial industrial and residential real estate in several states and in Canada. Denver property investor Pat Broe controls the company which he founded in 1972.

THE BROOKINGS INSTITUTION

1775 MASSACHUSETTS AVE NW	CEO: –
WASHINGTON, DC 200362103	CFO: –
Phone: 202-797-6000	HR: Anhtuan C Phan
Fax: –	FYE: June 30
Web: www.brookings.edu	Type: Private

The Brookings Institution may know an egghead or two (or 300). The nonpartisan public policy organization is comprised of more than 300 resident and non-resident scholars who research and analyze emerging issues in areas such as economics foreign policy and governance. Its experts perform research; write books papers and articles; testify in front of congressional committees; and participate in public events every year. The non-profit organization which is financed by gifts and grants is named after one of its backers — businessman Robert S. Brookings a well-known civic leader and philanthropist. Founded in 1916 it is the first private organization devoted to analyzing national public policy issues.

	Annual Growth	06/09	06/10	06/11	06/12	06/13
Sales ($ mil.)	14.5%	–	67.1	100.2	130.8	100.6
Net income ($ mil.)	(41.4%)	–	–	11.3	36.8	3.9
Market value ($ mil.)	–	–	–	–	–	–
Employees	–	–	–	–	–	400

THE BROTHER'S BROTHER FOUNDATION

1200 GALVESTON AVE	CEO: –
PITTSBURGH, PA 152331604	CFO: –
Phone: 412-321-3160	HR: –
Fax: –	FYE: December 31
Web: www.brothersbrother.org	Type: Private

He ain't heavy he's my brother's brother. The lyrics aren't quite right but the sentiment is the same. The not-for-profit Brother's Brother Foundation (BBF) provides emergency and nonemergency medical supplies textbooks food shoes and other humanitarian supplies to people in some 120 countries using a combination of gifts from the general public corporations and the US government. BBF is a gift-in-kind charity meaning the bulk of the donations are goods rather than money. The organization was established in 1958 by the renowned anesthesiologist Robert Hingson as Brother's Keeper but later changed its name. Hingson invented the jet inoculation gun used to provide 1000 inoculations per hour.

	Annual Growth	12/09	12/10	12/11	12/12	12/13
Sales ($ mil.)	(3.7%)	–	273.4	242.4	295.9	244.0
Net income ($ mil.)	(11.3%)	–	–	7.3	10.8	5.8
Market value ($ mil.)	–	–	–	–	–	–
Employees	–	–	–	–	–	12

THE BUREAU OF NATIONAL AFFAIRS INC.

1801 S. Bell St.	CEO: –
Arlington VA 22202	CFO: Robert P Ambrosini
Phone: 703-341-3000	HR: –
Fax: 212-290-7362	FYE: December 31
Web: www.thomaspublishing.com	Type: Subsidiary

All you'll find in this bureau is legal and regulatory information. The Bureau of National Affairs (BNA) publishes advisory and research reports books and newsletters for business government and academic professionals. BNA has a staff of 600 reporters editors and legal experts who gather information on topics such as economic health care labor public policy and tax issues. The firm delivers content online and via print and electronic products some available through subscription services such as LexisNexis and Thomson Reuter's Westlaw. Founded in 1929 BNA was incorporated as an employee-owned company in 1946. It is the country's oldest fully employee-owned company. BNA is owned by Bloomberg.

THE BURTON CORPORATION

80 Industrial Pkwy.	CEO: Mike Reesr
Burlington VT 05401	CFO: –
Phone: 802-862-4500	HR: –
Fax: 802-660-3250	FYE: January 31
Web: www.burton.com	Type: Private

The Burton Corporation made snowboards before boardsports became extreme. The company doing business as Burton Snowboards is the world's leading snowboard manufacturer. It also makes a growing lineup of men's women's and youth snowboarding apparel eyewear boots bindings and packs under its namesake as well as the AK Anon and RED brands. The company operates through a network of about 10 retail shops and factory outlets in the US Austria and Japan. It also sells gear through sporting goods stores and online retailers such as Altrec.com and Snow & Rock Sports. Taking to the beach Burton owns surfboard maker Channel Island Surfboards whose goods are available at surf shops worldwide.

THE C.F. SAUER COMPANY

2000 W. Broad St.	CEO: –
Richmond VA 23220	CFO: William F Uhlik
Phone: 804-359-5786	HR: –
Fax: 804-359-2263	FYE: March 31
Web: www.cfsauer.com	Type: Private

For more than a century C.F. Sauer has been adding a little spice to life. In addition to a stable of spices the company produces and wholesales seasonings extracts and flavorings. C.F. Sauer offers an increasing lineup of mixes for baking in a bag microwave steaming grilling and slow cooking. Products are sold under its namesake label as well as the Duke's Bama Spice Hunter Gold Medal and Mrs. Filbert's brands to retail food stores and foodservice operators such as restaurants and concessionaires. C.F. Sauer which operates several plants (including one that makes its packaging) also provides private-label and blending services for food processors. The company has been family-owned since 1887.

THE CADMUS GROUP INC

100 5TH AVE STE 100	CEO: –
WALTHAM, MA 024518703	CFO: Alan V Seferian
Phone: 617-673-7000	HR: –
Fax: –	FYE: April 30
Web: www.cadmusgroup.com	Type: Private

Drinking water protection is one of the areas of sage advice offered by The Cadmus Group. The environmental consulting firm (named after Cadmus the Phoenician prince and renowned wise man who founded the city of Thebes) provides research analytical and technical support services primarily to government agencies. Over time it has established itself as a lead contractor of the US Environmental Protection Agency). Other specialties include air quality energy conservation environmental risk assessment and regulatory support as well as marketing and public education related to environmental programs. Cadmus operates from 10 offices throughout the US.

	Annual Growth	04/10	04/11	04/12	04/13	04/14
Sales ($ mil.)	1.0%	–	66.8	68.8	71.6	68.8
Net income ($ mil.)	(55.1%)	–	–	3.8	4.1	0.8
Market value ($ mil.)	–	–	–	–	–	–
Employees	–	–	–	–	–	350

THE CALIFORNIA ENDOWMENT

1000 N ALAMEDA ST	CEO: –
LOS ANGELES, CA 900121804	CFO: Dan C Deleon
Phone: 213-628-1001	HR: Brytain Ashford
Fax: –	FYE: March 31
Web: www.tcenews.calendow.org	Type: Private

The California Endowment awards grants to health care providers in the Golden State. Funding is directed to not-for-profit organizations particularly those that work with the state's poor and underserved communities as well as studies of the state's health care industry. Its advocacy interests include health care access culturally competent health systems and elimination of health disparities. A private foundation The California Endowment has awarded more than $1.5 billion in grants since it was established in 1996. It has regional offices in Fresno Los Angeles Sacramento San Diego and San Francisco.

	Annual Growth	02/04	02/05	02/09*	03/12	03/13
Sales ($ mil.)	(9.2%)	–	346.0	0.0	207.0	159.7
Net income ($ mil.)	–	–	–	0.0	42.0	(58.6)
Market value ($ mil.)	–	–	–	–	–	–
Employees	–	–	–	–	–	110
						*Fiscal year change

THE CAPITAL GROUP COMPANIES INC.

333 S. Hope St. 53rd Fl.	CEO: Philip De Toledo
Los Angeles CA 90071	CFO: –
Phone: 213-486-9200	HR: Francois Note
Fax: 213-486-9217	FYE: June 30
Web: www.capgroup.com	Type: Private

The Capital Group Companies founded in 1931 has built a business being a steady Eddy for its clients. As a rule the investment firm doesn't advertise or grant many interviews and it prides itself on providing consistent high-level service believing that investment decisions should not be taken lightly. As part of its operations The Capital Group Companies operates Capital Research and Management. The unit manages The American Funds a family of more than 30 mutual funds that ranks among the largest groups of mutual funds by assets in the US. Altogether The Capital Group Companies boasts approximately $1 trillion in assets under management.

THE CARRIAGE HOUSE COMPANIES INC.

196 Newton St.	CEO: Kevin Hunt
Fredonia NY 14063	CFO: –
Phone: 716-673-1000	HR: –
Fax: 716-679-7702	FYE: September 30
Web: www.carriagehousecos.com	Type: Subsidiary

The Carriage House Companies gets a bit carried away when spreading the word about sauces and spreads. The company is one of the largest suppliers of store-brand grocery goods including barbecue sauce jams and jellies peanut butter and table syrup. It also produces private label mayonnaise and salad dressings salsas and sauces. Carriage House products are sold through its sales staff and a broker network to retailers such as Wal-Mart and less so food-service contract and other customers. A subsidiary Beverage Specialties makes the Major Peter's and JERO brand non-alcoholic drink mixes. Carriage House is owned by Ralcorp which counts the subsidiary as part of its Snacks Sauces & Spreads business.

THE CARTER-JONES LUMBER COMPANY

601 TALLMADGE RD	CEO: Neil Sackett
KENT, OH 442407331	CFO: Jeffrey S Donley
Phone: 330-673-6100	HR: –
Fax: –	FYE: December 31
Web: www.carterlumber.com	Type: Private

Carter Lumber has the answer when new home construction has you hollering "timber!" The company owns and operates about 145 lumber and home improvement stores in a dozen states from Michigan to South Carolina. The company caters to both contractors and do-it-yourselfers supplying them with lumber plywood roofing windows doors plumbing and electrical products heating equipment tools siding and other products. The home improvement retailer also owns Carter-Jones Lumber which runs a 17-acre lumberyard and custom millwork facilities in Ohio. The company was founded by Warren E. Carter in 1932 and it continues to be a family-owned business.

	Annual Growth	12/06	12/07	12/08	12/09	12/10
Sales ($ mil.)	–	–	–	(2,083.8)	314.4	334.4
Net income ($ mil.)	–	–	–	0.0	(4.7)	(4.6)
Market value ($ mil.)	–	–	–	–	–	–
Employees	–	–	–	–	–	1,575

THE CATHOLIC UNIVERSITY OF AMERICA

620 MICHIGAN AVE NE	CEO: –
WASHINGTON, DC 200640002	CFO: –
Phone: 202-319-5000	HR: –
Fax: –	FYE: April 30
Web: www.cua.edu	Type: Private

The Catholic University of America (CUA) established in 1887 by US bishops has an enrollment of more than 7000 students from all 50 states and nearly 100 countries. With graduate and undergraduate programs in 13 colleges CUA offers degrees in such fields as architecture and planning arts and sciences engineering music and nursing; it's expanding into business and economics. CUA is the only US university with ecclesiastical faculties granting canonical degrees in canon law philosophy and theology. Some 80% of undergraduates and nearly 60% of graduate students are Catholic. The University's Theological College prepares men for the priesthood serving dioceses nationwide.

	Annual Growth	04/08	04/09	04/13*	06/13*	04/14
Sales ($ mil.)	655.8%	–	0.0	217.4	342.4	222.0
Net income ($ mil.)	57.1%	–	–	18.0	57.5	28.2
Market value ($ mil.)	–	–	–	–	–	–
Employees	–	–	–	–	–	4,239
						*Fiscal year change

THE CENTECH GROUP INC

4600 FAIRFAX DR 400	CEO: –
ARLINGTON, VA 222031553	CFO: Kenneth M Williams
Phone: 703-525-4444	HR: Lawyer Martin
Fax: –	FYE: December 31
Web: www.centechgroup.com	Type: Private

The CENTECH GROUP offers a wide range of information technology services primarily to agencies of the US federal government. The company's areas of expertise include systems engineering security business operations support network services and software development. Among its clients are the Department of Defense the Department of Transportation and the State Department. CENTECH also serves customers in fields that include financial services manufacturing retail and health care. The company's core presence is in Virginia but it operates from offices in four states and serves clients in more than 20 states across the US. CENTECH was founded in 1988 by CEO Fernando Galaviz.

	Annual Growth	12/08	12/09	12/10	12/11	12/12
Sales ($ mil.)	(4.1%)	–	–	152.7	92.4	140.3
Net income ($ mil.)	(3.0%)	–	–	7.2	3.3	6.7
Market value ($ mil.)	–	–	–	–	–	–
Employees	–	–	–	–	–	272

THE CHAIR KING INC

5405 W SAM HOUSTON PKWY N	CEO: –
HOUSTON, TX 770415135	CFO: –
Phone: 713-690-1919	HR: –
Fax: –	FYE: December 31
Web: www.chairking.com	Type: Private

Set atop its throne for the past half century The Chair King has established itself as a leading casual furniture retailer in the state of Texas. The family-run company with about 20 stores in Houston Dallas Austin and San Antonio Texas sells midpriced to high-end indoor (wicker rattan and leather) and outdoor furniture (aluminum cast aluminum wrought iron resin teak wicker) and related accessories. Furniture and bedding account for the majority of company sales. The Chair King founded in 1950 sells well known brands including Garden Classics Berkline and Solaris Designs.

	Annual Growth	12/09	12/10	12/11	12/12	12/13
Sales ($ mil.)	45.1%	–	32.5	34.4	35.5	99.2
Net income ($ mil.)	20.3%	–	–	4.2	5.3	6.0
Market value ($ mil.)	–	–	–	–	–	–
Employees	–	–	–	–	–	110

THE CHARLES MACHINE WORKS INC.

1959 W. Fir Ave.	CEO: Tiffany Sewell-Howard
Perry OK 73077	CFO: Angela Drake
Phone: 580-336-4402	HR: –
Fax: 580-572-3527	FYE: December 31
Web: www.ditchwitch.com	Type: Private

Ditch Witch has cast a spell over the heavy equipment industry since 1949. Captivated by its power and efficiency The Charles Machine Works (CMW) manufactures and sells underground construction equipment and parts bearing the Ditch Witch brand name. Its signature orange lineup features trenchless machines trenchers mini-excavators and plows including tractors backhoes and saws made at the company's 30-acre plant in Oklahoma. CMW also makes a slew of electronic tools: fault locators beacons for ground directional assistance and trailers. Equipment maintenance and repair services are offered too for its roster of construction and utility customers. Founders of CMW the Malzahn family own the company.

THE CHARLOTTE MECKLENBURG HOSPITAL AUTHORITY

1000 Blythe Blvd.	CEO: Michael C Tarwater
Charlotte NC 28203	CFO: Greg A Gombar
Phone: 704-355-2000	HR: –
Fax: 780-466-6126	FYE: December 31
Web: www.zcl.com	Type: Government-owned

The medical facilities under the watchful eye of the Charlotte-Mecklenburg Hospital Authority care for the injured and infirmed. As the largest health care system in the Carolinas the organization operating as Carolinas HealthCare System (CHS) owns or manages more than 30 affiliated hospitals. It also operates long-term care facilities research centers rehabilitation facilities surgery centers home health agencies radiation therapy facilities and other health care operations. Collectively CHS facilities have more than 6400 beds and affiliated physician practices employ more than 1700 doctors. The network's flagship facility is the 875-bed Carolinas Medical Center in Charlotte North Carolina.

THE CHILDREN'S HOSPITAL OF PHILADELPHIA

34th St. & Civic Center Blvd.	CEO: Steven M Altschuler
Philadelphia PA 19104-4399	CFO: Thomas Todorow
Phone: 215 590 1000	HR: –
Fax: 503-614-4601	FYE: June 30
Web: www.normthompson.com	Type: Private - Not-for-Pr

In the City of Brotherly Love sick little boys and girls have a place to get better at the The Children's Hospital of Philadelphia (CHOP). As a leading pediatric hospital CHOP also has one of the largest pediatric research programs in the world. The nation's first hospital devoted exclusively to the care of children it has about 460 beds at its primary facility and is a leader in formal pediatric medical training pediatric emergency medicine and adolescent medicine. In addition to its main hospital facilities CHOP operates a pediatric health care network with owned or affiliated offices clinics and research facilities in Delaware New Jersey and Pennsylvania. The hospital was founded in 1855.

THE CHILDRENS HOSPITAL LOS ANGELES

4650 W SUNSET BLVD	CEO: –
LOS ANGELES, CA 900276062	CFO: Lannie Tonnu
Phone: 323-660-2450	HR: Deann Marshall
Fax: –	FYE: June 30
Web: www.chla.org	Type: Private

Childrens Hospital Los Angeles (CHLA) is dedicated to treating the youngest critical care patients in the region. The about 570-bed hospital specializes in treating seriously ill and injured children from its neonatal intensive care unit to its pediatric organ transplant center. CHLA's pediatric specialists also provide care at its ambulatory care center in Arcadia and through about 40 off-site practice sites. The hospital's pediatric specialties include cancer kidney failure and cystic fibrosis care. CHLA serves more than 107000 children every year. It is one of only 12 children's hospitals in the nation (and the only one in California) ranked in all 10 pediatric specialties by U.S. News & World Report.

	Annual Growth	06/07	06/08	06/09	06/10	06/13
Sales ($ mil.)	8.1%	–	589.6	405.8	564.8	869.7
Net income ($ mil.)	–	–	–	(94.6)	(34.7)	36.2
Market value ($ mil.)	–	–	–	–	–	–
Employees	–	–	–	–	–	3,000

THE CHILDREN'S HOSPITAL CORPORATION

300 LONGWOOD AVE	CEO: –
BOSTON, MA 021155737	CFO: –
Phone: 617-355-6000	HR: Inez Stewart
Fax: –	FYE: September 30
	Type: Private

Children's Hospital Boston is an elder in the world of pediatric care. The 400-bed hospital offers acute health care and specialty services for children from birth to age 21. The medical center is also Harvard Medical School's main teaching hospital for children's health care and it is the world's largest pediatric research center. Its John F. Enders Pediatric Research facility provides research for the treatment of childhood diseases. Specialty services include cardiovascular surgery digestive care neurology oncology ophthalmology orthopedics transplants blood diseases and fetal care. The not-for-profit hospital was founded in 1869.

	Annual Growth	09/02	09/03*	06/05*	09/09	09/13
Sales ($ mil.)	3.1%	–	695.0	4.9	1,348.7	940.0
Net income ($ mil.)	99.3%	–	–	0.6	94.5	157.7
Market value ($ mil.)	–	–	–	–	–	–
Employees	–	–	–	–	–	8,000
						*Fiscal year change

THE CHRISTIAN BROADCASTING NETWORK INC

977 CENTERVILLE TPKE	CEO: –
VIRGINIA BEACH, VA 234631001	CFO: –
Phone: 757-226-3030	HR: Barbara (Barb) Ritter
Fax: –	FYE: March 31
Web: www.cbn.com	Type: Private

Standards & Practices probably won't find much wrong with these TV programs. The Christian Broadcasting Network (CBN) is one of the leading producers of religious television programming in the country offering news and entertainment shows with a spiritual message. Its centerpiece is The 700 Club a daily show featuring a mix of news and commentary interviews feature stories and Christian ministry co-hosted by CBN founder Pat Robertson. The company's programs are syndicated to broadcast and cable TV outlets that reach audiences around the world. CBN generates most of its revenue through ministry donations.

	Annual Growth	03/07	03/08	03/09	03/10	03/11
Sales ($ mil.)	(63.5%)	–	–	2,135.7	283.5	285.3
Net income ($ mil.)	1932.4%	–	–	0.0	8.6	6.8
Market value ($ mil.)	–	–	–	–	–	–
Employees	–	–	–	–	–	941

THE CINCINNATI REDS LLC

100 Main St.	CEO: Robert Castellini
Cincinnati OH 45202	CFO: Doug Healey
Phone: 513-765-7000	HR: –
Fax: 513-765-7048	FYE: October 31
Web: cincinnati.reds.mlb.com	Type: Private

Perhaps being a baseball fan in Cincinnati can color your world view. The Cincinnati Reds LLC owns and operates the Cincinnati Reds professional ball club a storied franchise in Major League Baseball. Founded in 1866 as the Cincinnati Base Ball Club the team gained the nickname the Red Stockings in 1868 and became the first all-professional baseball franchise the next year. The Reds earned four National League pennants during the 1970s and won back-to-back World Series championships in 1975 and 1976 with players such as Pete Rose and Johnny Bench. CEO Robert Castellini heads a group that owns 70% of the team. Former CEO Carl Lindner owns the rest.

THE CITADEL

171 MOULTRIE ST	CEO: –
CHARLESTON, SC 294090002	CFO: Joseph Garcia
Phone: 843-953-5110	HR: –
Fax: –	FYE: June 30
Web: www.citadel.edu	Type: Private

A state-supported military college The Citadel traces its roots back to the 1842 founding of the South Carolina Military Academy. Today's Citadel enrolls about 2000 undergraduate cadets who reside on the campus barracks. Cadets are given military and academic instruction in addition to physical training and a strict disciplinary regime; about a third of all graduates continue on to military careers. The Citadel enrolls another 1250 civilian graduate and undergraduate students who attend evening classes. With a student-to-faculty ratio of 13:1 the institution has schools in business education engineering the humanities and social sciences and science and mathematics.

	Annual Growth	06/10	06/11	06/12	06/13	06/14
Sales ($ mil.)	11.0%	–	67.1	67.7	81.5	91.9
Net income ($ mil.)	156.5%	–	–	2.7	8.7	17.7
Market value ($ mil.)	–	–	–	–	–	–
Employees	–	–	–	–	–	637

THE CLEVELAND CLINIC FOUNDATION

9500 Euclid Ave.	CEO: Delos M Cosgrove
Cleveland OH 44195	CFO: Steven C Glass
Phone: 216-444-2200	HR: –
Fax: 310-327-1999	FYE: December 31
Web: www.clarion.com	Type: Private - Foundation

Cleveland may be home to the Rock and Roll Hall of Fame but you don't have to have the rocking pneumonia or the boogie woogie flu to visit another Cleveland institution: The Cleveland Clinic. The heart of the Cleveland Clinic Foundation the not-for-profit hospital has more than 1300 beds and specializes in cardiac care digestive disease treatment and urological and kidney care along with medical education and research opportunities. The clinic campus includes an international care center children's hospital an outpatient center and several research institutes. The Cleveland Clinic Foundation network also includes about ten hospitals and dozens of health centers in Ohio Florida Nevada and overseas.

THE COBALT GROUP INC.

2200 1st Ave. South Ste. 400	CEO: John Holt
Seattle WA 98134-1408	CFO: Jim Beach
Phone: 206-269-6363	HR: –
Fax: 206-269-6350	FYE: June 30
Web: www.cobaltgroup.com	Type: Subsidiary

The Cobalt Group's websites and services come fully loaded. Cobalt provides Web-based marketing services to auto manufacturers and dealers to help them manage their businesses online. Services include website hosting e-commerce applications Web-based customer relationship management applications social media marketing and best practices training and consulting. The company also provides automotive Internet marketing through its Dealix unit and its IntegraLink division collects automotive data from more than 15000 auto dealerships for manufacturers direct marketing firms and others who work in the automotive industry. In mid-2010 Cobalt was acquired by payroll processing giant ADP for $400 million.

THE COLEMAN COMPANY INC.

3600 N. Hydraulic	CEO: Robert Marcovitch
Wichita KS 67219	CFO: Dan Hogan
Phone: 316-832-2700	HR: –
Fax: 316-832-3060	FYE: December 31
Web: www.coleman.com	Type: Subsidiary

The Coleman Company makes what it takes to be a happy camper. As a leading manufacturer of outdoor recreation gear it produces coolers backpacks tents sleeping bags air mattresses lanterns grills life vests and floats among other items which are sold under the Aerobed Coleman Campingaz Exponent Hodgman Mad Dog Gear Sevylor and Stearns brands. Coleman operates sales offices and distribution facilities worldwide and sells its products mainly through mass merchandisers home centers and other retail stores as well as through its website and a network of about a dozen Coleman Factory Outlet stores. Founded in 1900 Coleman is owned by Jarden Corporation.

THE COLLEGE NETWORK INC

3815 RIVER CROSSING PKWY # 260	CEO: –
INDIANAPOLIS, IN 462407746	CFO: –
Phone: 317-334-7337	HR: Elizabeth Stahl
Fax: –	FYE: December 31
Web: www.collegenetwork.com	Type: Private

The College Network is for students who want all the advantages of a college degree without all of that sitting in classrooms and listening to lectures. The company publishes educational materials that help its customers — typically working adults — gain college credit certificates or degrees from its university partners without attending physical class. Students use the company's online study modules to prepare for college equivalency tests earning up to 82 credit hours. They then enroll in online degree programs through the company's partner schools. Participating schools include Boston University University of Southern California and Angelo State University. The College Network was founded in 1992.

	Annual Growth	12/04	12/05	12/06	12/07	12/08
Sales ($ mil.)	–	–	–	(1,166.4)	102.9	92.8
Net income ($ mil.)	–	–	–	0.0	5.2	(0.1)
Market value ($ mil.)	–	–	–	–	–	–
Employees	–	–	–	–	–	247

THE COLLEGE OF WILLIAM & MARY

261 RICHMOND RD   CEO: –
WILLIAMSBURG, VA 231853534   CFO: –
Phone: 757-221-4000   HR: –
Fax: –   FYE: June 30
Web: www.wm.edu   Type: Private

Not every Tom Dick and Harry gets into The College of William & Mary. The median SAT score for incoming freshmen is about 1345 (out of 1600). The second-oldest college in the US (Harvard is the oldest) William & Mary (W&M) is a "public ivy" university with an enrollment of 8300 undergraduate and graduate students. W&M offers more than 30 undergraduate and 10 graduate programs at schools of arts and sciences business education law and marine sciences. It also conducts research programs. Among its notable alumni are The Daily Show's Jon Stewart and three US presidents: Thomas Jefferson James Monroe and John Tyler.

	Annual Growth	06/02	06/03	06/05	06/06	06/11
Sales ($ mil.)	(4.7%)	–	138.3	166.8	178.4	94.3
Net income ($ mil.)	25.6%	–	–	16.2	(96.4)	63.6
Market value ($ mil.)	–	–	–	–	–	–
Employees	–	–	–	–	–	3,500

THE COLLEGE OF WOOSTER

1189 BEALL AVE   CEO: –
WOOSTER, OH 446912363   CFO: –
Phone: 330-263-2000   HR: Marcia Beasley
Fax: –   FYE: June 30
Web: www.wooster.edu   Type: Private

The College of Wooster is a private college providing undergraduate education in the liberal arts and sciences. It grants Bachelor of Arts (BA) Bachelor of Music (BM) and Bachelor of Music Education (BME) degrees. It offers about 50 majors including English geology film theater dance history biology math neuroscience psychology and computer science as well as pre-law pre-engineering and pre-health programs. The school's unique curriculum includes an independent study requirement in which seniors produce original work in the form of a research project. The College of Wooster enrolls more than 2000 students. The school was founded in 1866 by a group of Ohio Presbyterians.

	Annual Growth	06/06	06/07	06/08	06/10	06/11
Sales ($ mil.)	–	–	–	(994.3)	72.5	76.1
Net income ($ mil.)	9352.3%	–	–	0.0	26.5	26.2
Market value ($ mil.)	–	–	–	–	–	–
Employees	–	–	–	–	–	610

THE COLLEGIATE SCHOOL

103 N MOORELAND RD   CEO: –
RICHMOND, VA 232297170   CFO: –
Phone: 804-740-7077   HR: –
Fax: –   FYE: June 30
Web: www.collegiate-va.org   Type: Private

This school may sound "college like" but it's really meant for Kindergartners through 12th graders. Collegiate School has some 1500 students enrolled in its lower school (grades K through 4th) middle school (grades 5th through 8th) and upper school (grades 9th through 12th). The private school's offerings include multiple foreign languages individual music instruction and community service and travel opportunities. Collegiate was founded in 1915 as Collegiate School for Girls in downtown Richmond Virginia by Helen Baker with help from Mary Carter Anderson. Just 13 years after its founding boys were admitted but just to the Kindergarten. The first group of boys actually graduated in 1963.

	Annual Growth	06/09	06/10	06/11	06/12	06/13
Sales ($ mil.)	18.6%	–	35.2	41.6	42.0	58.6
Net income ($ mil.)	(6.9%)	–	–	12.2	(1.4)	10.6
Market value ($ mil.)	–	–	–	–	–	–
Employees	–	–	–	–	–	–

THE COMMUNITY HOSPITAL GROUP INC

98 JAMES ST STE 400   CEO: John P McGee
EDISON, NJ 088203902   CFO: –
Phone: 732-321-7000   HR: –
Fax: –   FYE: December 31
  Type: Private

JFK Medical Center plays a central role in health care in central New Jersey. The medical center is an acute care facility with some 500 beds and 950 physicians providing emergency surgical trauma and other inpatient services. The hospital includes the JFK New Jersey Neuroscience Institute which treats stroke and other neurological conditions and the JFK Johnson Rehabilitation Institute which treats traumatic injuries. JFK Medical Center also offers diagnostic imaging cancer care senior and hospice care and family practice services. It is also a teaching hospital affiliated with several area universities. The hospital is part of the JFK Health System.

	Annual Growth	12/04	12/05	12/06	12/09	12/10
Sales ($ mil.)	2.4%	–	–	388.4	423.1	427.1
Net income ($ mil.)	–	–	–	0.0	(37.0)	(17.5)
Market value ($ mil.)	–	–	–	–	–	–
Employees	–	–	–	–	–	3,000

THE COMPUTER MERCHANT LTD

95 LONGWATER CIR   CEO: John R Danieli
NORWELL, MA 020611635   CFO: –
Phone: 781-878-1070   HR: –
Fax: –   FYE: December 31
Web: www.tcml.com   Type: Private

The Computer Merchant (TCM) provide customers with information technology assets with a pulse. The company provides IT services such as staffing and consulting primarily to Fortune 1000 companies. It places more than 10000 consultants each year. TCM provides application development infrastructure management help desk and business support and technology deployments. The IT placement firm's clients have included ePresence Unisys and Premier among others. It primarily serves IT service providers large corporations and public sector clients. A preferred vendor for many government contractors TCM was founded in 1980 by CEO and former US Marine John Danieli.

	Annual Growth	12/09	12/10	12/11	12/12	12/13
Sales ($ mil.)	13.0%	–	66.5	80.2	89.5	95.9
Net income ($ mil.)	5.8%	–	–	2.5	3.6	2.8
Market value ($ mil.)	–	–	–	–	–	–
Employees	–	–	–	–	–	1,500

THE CONSERVATION FUND A NONPROFIT CORPORATION

1655 FORT MYER DR # 1300   CEO: –
ARLINGTON, VA 222093113   CFO: –
Phone: 703-525-6300   HR: –
Fax: –   FYE: December 31
Web: www.conservationfund.org   Type: Private

The Conservation Fund was green before green was cool. The nonprofit organization is well known for negotiating deals to protect environmentally sensitive lands. It will typically purchase property financed through a revolving land fund federal and state grants and contributions from various sources and sell it back to local groups to manage. It also invests in small businesses that show a sustainable use of natural resources as well as works with communities and other not-for-profits to plan for growth and conservation. Since its founding in 1985 the Fund and its partners have protected more than 7 million acres of wildlife habitat and watersheds working landscapes and openspaces in all 50 US states.

	Annual Growth	12/04	12/05	12/09	12/12	12/13
Sales ($ mil.)	9.8%	–	68.3	186.7	179.4	144.6
Net income ($ mil.)	(44.4%)	–	–	31.7	41.8	3.0
Market value ($ mil.)	–	–	–	–	–	–
Employees	–	–	–	–	–	95

THE CONTAINER STORE INC.

500 Freeport Pkwy.
Coppell TX 75019
Phone: 972-538-6000
Fax: 972-538-7623
Web: www.containerstore.com

CEO: William A Kip Tindell III
CFO: Natalie Levy
HR: –
FYE: March 31
Type: Private

With its packets pockets and boxes The Container Store has the storage products niche well-contained. Its merchandise ranges from backpacks to recipe holders. The home-organization pioneer operates about 60 stores in more than 20 states mostly in major cities in Texas California Illinois and New York as well as the District of Columbia. It also runs an e-commerce site. The company offers shipping across the US and to Canada as well as same-day delivery in New York City. Stores carry more than 10000 items; the company's Elfa brand of wire shelving (made in Sweden) accounts for a chunk of sales. Founded in 1978 The Container Store is majority owned by private equity firm Leonard Green & Partners.

THE COOPER HEALTH SYSTEM

1 COOPER PLZ
CAMDEN, NJ 081031461
Phone: 856-342-2000
Fax: –
Web: www.cooperhealth.org

CEO: Adrienne Kirby
CFO: Douglas E. Shirley
HR: –
FYE: December 31
Type: Private

The Cooper Health System keeps folks along the Delaware River shoreline feeling fine. The not-for-profit organization includes clinics and hospitals located throughout southern New Jersey and the Delaware Valley including the 600-bed Cooper University Hospital and The Children's Regional Hospital. Cooper University Hospital is a teaching campus for the University of Medicine and Dentistry of New Jersey providing training for medical students nurses residents fellows and health professionals. Its more than 700 physicians operate in about 80 specialties. Founded in 1887 the health care system provides trauma cancer cardiology neuroscience psychiatric and orthopedic specialty centers.

	Annual Growth	12/10	12/11	12/12	12/13	12/14
Sales ($ mil.)	6.8%	–	775.6	823.3	874.9	944.8
Net income ($ mil.)	13.7%	–	–	46.6	0.0	60.3
Market value ($ mil.)	–	–	–	–	–	–
Employees	–	–	–	–	–	4,900

THE COOPER UNION FOR THE ADVANCEMENT OF SCIENCE AND ART

30 COOPER SQ FL 7
NEW YORK, NY 100037120
Phone: 212-353-4150
Fax: –
Web: www.cooper.edu

CEO: –
CFO: –
HR: –
FYE: June 30
Type: Private

The Cooper Union for the Advancement of Science and Art was founded in 1859 by inventor and industrialist Peter Cooper who created the US's first steam train engine and rose from poverty to build a fortune. Cooper's endowment along with subsequent gifts allowed the school to fund a full-tuition scholarship for each of its undergraduate students until Fall 2014 when it implemented a sliding scale tuition. Cooper Union which serves about 1000 students is located in the East Village in downtown New York City. It offers degree programs in art architecture and engineering as well as a wide variety of lectures and continuing education courses for the public.

	Annual Growth	06/07	06/08	06/09	06/10	06/11
Sales ($ mil.)	–	–	–	0.0	47.2	51.8
Net income ($ mil.)	3072.1%	–	–	0.0	(18.3)	16.5
Market value ($ mil.)	–	–	–	–	–	–
Employees	–	–	–	–	–	642

THE CORPORATION OF GONZAGA UNIVERSITY

502 E BOONE AVE
SPOKANE, WA 992581774
Phone: 509-328-4220
Fax: –
Web: www.gonzaga.edu

CEO: –
CFO: –
HR: –
FYE: May 31
Type: Private

Gonzaga University is a private liberal arts institution providing instruction to more than 7800 undergraduate graduate doctoral and law students. The school offers about 75 undergraduate majors two dozen master's degree programs and two leadership study doc at its six colleges and schools. The university offers a juris doctorate degree at its School of Law. The Roman Catholic university is run by the Society of Jesus — the Jesuits — and is named after a sixteenth-century Italian Jesuit Aloysius Gonzaga the patron saint of youth. The university was founded in 1887 as a men's college.

	Annual Growth	05/10	05/11	05/12	05/13	05/14
Sales ($ mil.)	1.3%	–	186.0	194.5	191.1	193.1
Net income ($ mil.)	76.1%	–	–	12.4	56.3	38.6
Market value ($ mil.)	–	–	–	–	–	–
Employees	–	–	–	–	–	650

THE CORPORATION OF HAVERFORD COLLEGE

370 LANCASTER AVE
HAVERFORD, PA 190411336
Phone: 610-896-1000
Fax: –
Web: www.haverford.edu

CEO: –
CFO: –
HR: –
FYE: June 30
Type: Private

Haverford College is one of the nation's top 10 liberal arts colleges according to US News & World Report's 2007 annual ranking. The Quaker-founded college is a private school located 10 miles away from Philadelphia that serves about 1200 students. Among its staff are more than 110 full-time faculty members. Haverford College has a student-faculty ratio of 10:1. The college offers 31 departmental majors. The school boasts such notable alumni as former Time Warner CEO Gerald Levin Time editor-in-chief Norman Pearlstine and humorist Dave Barry.

	Annual Growth	06/09	06/10	06/11	06/13	06/14
Sales ($ mil.)	4.2%	–	76.6	79.3	86.0	90.4
Net income ($ mil.)	2.1%	–	–	51.5	47.0	54.8
Market value ($ mil.)	–	–	–	–	–	–
Employees	–	–	–	–	–	600

THE CORPORATION OF MERCER UNIVERSITY

1400 COLEMAN AVE
MACON, GA 312070001
Phone: 478-301-2700
Fax: –
Web: www.mercer.edu

CEO: –
CFO: –
HR: –
FYE: June 30
Type: Private

Mercer University covers a lot of Georgia with one campus in Macon another in Atlanta and a third in Savannah. The main campus in Macon includes the Walter F. George School of Law (one of the nation's oldest law schools) while The Cecil B. Day Graduate and Professional campus in Atlanta includes schools of theology pharmacy and nursing. Savannah is home to a new four-year M.D. program at the Mercer School of Medicine at Memorial University Medical Center. The university which has a total enrollment of more than 8300 students also has educational centers in Douglas County Henry County and Eastman. Mercer was founded in 1833 by Jesse Mercer a prominent Georgia Baptist.

	Annual Growth	06/08	06/09	06/10	06/11	06/13
Sales ($ mil.)	6.0%	–	235.5	255.6	270.3	297.7
Net income ($ mil.)	165.3%	–	–	0.4	8.0	8.4
Market value ($ mil.)	–	–	–	–	–	–
Employees	–	–	–	–	–	1,658

THE COUNCIL POPULATION INC

1 DAG HAMMARSKJOLD PLZ # 9
NEW YORK, NY 100172220
Phone: 212-339-0500
Fax: –
Web: www.popcouncil.org

CEO: –
CFO: Scott Newman
HR: –
FYE: December 31
Type: Private

The Population Council is a not-for-profit organization that performs biomedical public health and social science research. The organization focuses on areas such as HIV and AIDS; poverty gender and youth; and reproductive health. Specifically it conducts research on sociological topics like gender inequality population trends and sexuality education; it also assists international governments with policy and program development as they pertain to these issues. The Population Council is typically funded by governments foundations individuals and other organizations.

	Annual Growth	12/09	12/10	12/11	12/12	12/13
Sales ($ mil.)	14.0%	–	64.3	64.4	72.6	95.3
Net income ($ mil.)	–	–	–	(23.4)	(4.7)	10.3
Market value ($ mil.)	–	–	–	–	–	–
Employees	–	–	–	–	–	603

THE CRAMER-KRASSELT CO.

225 N. Michigan Ave.
Chicago IL 60601
Phone: 312-616-9600
Fax: 312-616-3839
Web: www.c-k.com

CEO: –
CFO: –
HR: –
FYE: December 31
Type: Private

The Cramer-Krasselt Co. provides its clients with a full range of advertising services including branding digital marketing database marketing public relations and the creative development and placement of television and radio advertisements. Clients include AirTran Airways Corona Crocs Panera Bread and Porsche. The agency has a global reach through its membership in the International Communications Agency Network (iCOM) a partnership of 70 independent advertising and marketing agencies serving clients across more than 50 countries. Cramer-Krasselt was founded in 1898 by Fred "Cody" Cramer and William Krasselt.

THE CULINARY INSTITUTE OF AMERICA

1946 CAMPUS DR
HYDE PARK, NY 125381499
Phone: 845-452-9600
Fax: –
Web: www.ciachef.edu

CEO: –
CFO: –
HR: Richard Mignault
FYE: May 31
Type: Private

At this CIA they work on countertops not counterterrorism. The Culinary Institute of America (CIA) offers bachelor's and associate degrees in Culinary Arts Culinary Science and Baking and Pastry Arts fields of study. It also offers continuing education programs conferences travel programs and e-learning. The independent not-for-profit educational organization enrolls some 2800 students and employs more than 125 chef-instructors and other faculty members at campuses in the US and overseas. Notable graduates include media personalities Anthony Bourdain and Rocco DiSpirito and Steven Ellis founder of Chipotle Mexican Grill.

	Annual Growth	05/10	05/11	05/12	05/13	05/14
Sales ($ mil.)	3.9%	–	129.7	141.4	147.3	145.3
Net income ($ mil.)	38.4%	–	–	11.1	28.7	21.2
Market value ($ mil.)	–	–	–	–	–	–
Employees	–	–	–	–	–	810

THE CW NETWORK LLC

3300 Olive Ave.
Burbank CA 91505
Phone: 818-977-2500
Fax: 818-954-7667
Web: www.cwtv.com

CEO: –
CFO: –
HR: –
FYE: December 31
Type: Joint Venture

This company is out to prove there's room on the small screen for more than just the Big Four. The CW Network operates The CW a national broadcast television network offering primetime programming aimed mostly at the young-adult audience segment. Its top shows include 90210 America's Next Top Model Gossip Girl One Tree Hill Supernatural and The Vampire Diaries. The CW also broadcasts children's programming on Saturday mornings. Local broadcast affiliates including several owned by Tribune Company and CBS Corporation reach about 95% of the country. Launched in 2006 The CW is a 50-50 joint venture between CBS and Time Warner's Warner Bros. Entertainment unit.

THE DANNON COMPANY INC.

100 Hillside Ave.
White Plains NY 10603
Phone: 914-872-8400
Fax: +972-4-654-7788
Web: www.towersemi.com

CEO: Gustavo Valle
CFO: –
HR: –
FYE: December 31
Type: Subsidiary

Yes it is curdled milk with bacteria and with a bit of jam but yogurt by Dannon has risen from health-food obscurity into a supermarket staple. The Dannon Company vies with General Mills maker of dairy label Yoplait for the #1 spot as the best-selling yogurt brand in the US. Dannon supplies a staggering 100-some flavors styles and sizes of yogurts in regular low-fat and nonfat varieties as well as in liquid "drinkable" and smoothie forms. Dannon also makes Danimals yogurt in kid-friendly packaging; and for moms (and Mr. Moms) it launches a slew of flavorful nutritious lines such as Activia a pro-biotic-infused low-fat yogurt for digestion. Dannon is a subsidiary of France's Groupe Danone.

THE DAVID AND LUCILE PACKARD FOUNDATION

300 2ND ST
LOS ALTOS, CA 940223694
Phone: 650-917-7167
Fax: –
Web: www.packard.org

CEO: Carol S Larson
CFO: –
HR: –
FYE: December 31
Type: Private

One of the wealthiest philanthropic organizations in the US The David and Lucile Packard Foundation primarily provides grants to not-for-profit entities. The foundation focuses on operating in three areas: conservation and science; children families and communities; and population. The David and Lucile Packard Foundation boasts approximately $4.6 billion in assets. In 2009 the organization committed $100 million for the expansion of the Lucile Packard Children's Hospital at Stanford. The late David Packard (co-founder of Hewlett-Packard) and his wife the late Lucile Salter Packard created the foundation in 1964. Their children run the organization.

	Annual Growth	12/04	12/05	12/06	12/09	12/10
Sales ($ mil.)	302.5%	–	0.7	809.5	398.2	701.2
Net income ($ mil.)	(8.5%)	–	–	587.9	74.8	412.6
Market value ($ mil.)	–	–	–	–	–	–
Employees	–	–	–	–	–	85

THE DAY & ZIMMERMANN GROUP INC.

1500 Spring Garden St.
Philadelphia PA 19130
Phone: 215-299-8000
Fax: 215-299-8030
Web: www.dayzim.com

CEO: Harold L Yoh III
CFO: Joseph Ritzel
HR: –
FYE: December 31
Type: Private

Day & Zimmermann offers services as distinct as day and night. Its family of companies provides: engineering construction and plant maintenance; staffing; munitions manufacturing and demilitarization; and various government services. A top global contractor Day & Zimmermann provides operations contract support and maintenance services to US and foreign governments as well as commercial customers. Its Day & Zimmermann NPS unit maintains half of nuclear plants in the US. Staffing subsidiary Yoh Services specializes in filling IT engineering and health care positions. Founded in 1901 Day & Zimmermann is owned and managed by the Yoh family which has headed the firm for three generations.

THE DEPOSITORY TRUST & CLEARING CORPORATION

55 Water St. 22nd Fl.
New York NY 10041-0099
Phone: 212-855-1000
Fax: 212-855-8440
Web: www.dtcc.com

CEO: Michael C Bodson
CFO: –
HR: –
FYE: December 31
Type: Private

It's clear that securities trading just wouldn't be the same without The Depository Trust & Clearing Corporation (DTCC). Through subsidiaries the firm provides securities clearing settlement custody and information services. Dealing in equities bonds government and mortgage-backed securities money market instruments and over-the-counter derivatives the company typically processes around 90 million securities transactions each day or more than 20 billion per year. Its depository business provides custody and asset servicing for some $34 trillion worth of securities globally. DTCC is owned by its users which include banks brokerages and NYSE Euronext.

THE DEWBERRY COMPANIES INC.

8401 Arlington Blvd.
Fairfax VA 22031-4666
Phone: 703-849-0100
Fax: 703-849-0118
Web: www.dewberry.com

CEO: Donald E Stone Jr
CFO: –
HR: –
FYE: December 31
Type: Private

Planning design and management services are the fruits of The Dewberry Companies' labor. The company provides architectural and engineering services planning program management and surveying services as well as environmental compliance and security and homeland defense services. Dewberry serves private and public-sector clients. However government customers such as FEMA the Pentagon and the US Department of Labor make up a big portion of business. Dewberry also serves departments of transportation as well as universities real estate developers and other commercial and institutional groups. Dewberry which was founded in 1956 and is owned by the Dewberry family operates from more than 40 offices.

THE DIAL CORPORATION

19001 N. Scottsdale Rd.
Scottsdale AZ 85255-9672
Phone: 480-754-3425
Fax: 303-238-3368
Web: www.globalmedtech.com

CEO: Bradley A Casper
CFO: Jack Tierney
HR: Keith Davis
FYE: December 31
Type: Subsidiary

Don't look for dirt on The Dial Corporation. The company has built a business keeping itself and its customers squeaky clean and smelling as fresh as a daisy. The manufacturer boasts one of the top-selling soaps in the US and counts several leading brands in each of its two core product segments: laundry and home care (with product names Purex Zout 20 Mule Team Combat Soft Scrub and Renuzit) and beauty and personal care (with its Dial soaps bodywashes and hand sanitizers; Tone Coast Dry Idea Soft & Dri and Right Guard). Dial a subsidiary of Henkel KGaA since 2004 is known for its "Aren't You Glad You Use Dial?" slogan which was first used in 1953.

THE DISPATCH PRINTING COMPANY

34 S. 3rd St.
Columbus OH 43215
Phone: 614-461-5000
Fax: 614-461-6087
Web: www.dispatch.com

CEO: Michael J Fiorile
CFO: –
HR: –
FYE: December 31
Type: Private

The Dispatch Printing Company is a leading regional media company anchored by its flagship newspaper The Columbus Dispatch. It also owns a portfolio of almost 20 community papers through subsidiary ThisWeek Community Newspapers and it publishes Columbus Parent a free monthly magazine on parenting. Its Dispatch Media Group owns and operates two TV stations the WBNS radio station the Ohio News Network radio service and a 24-hour cable news channel. Dispatch Printing also has a stake in the Columbus Blue Jackets hockey team. The Columbus Dispatch traces its roots to 1871 when it was first published as The Daily Dispatch. The Wolfe family led by chairman John Wolfe has owned the company since 1905.

THE DOCTORS COMPANY

185 Greenwood Rd.
Napa CA 94558-0900
Phone: 707-226-0100
Fax: 707-226-0111
Web: www.thedoctors.com

CEO: Richard E Anderson
CFO: Eugene M Bullis
HR: –
FYE: December 31
Type: Private

The Doctors Company takes care of its own. The company owned by physicians and operating through nine subsidiaries markets and manages liability insurance for medical malpractice. Representing about 250000 doctors nationwide and 71000 members The Doctors Company is the largest physician and surgeon medical liability carrier in the country. It provides protection and risk management for sole practitioners doctors groups and physicians working in clinics hospitals and managed care organizations. The Doctors Company also oversees DOCPAC a political action committee advocating medical liability reform in nine states as well as at the federal level.

THE DOE RUN RESOURCES CORPORATION

1801 Park 270 Dr. Ste. 300
St. Louis MO 63146
Phone: 314-453-7100
Fax: 314-453-7177
Web: www.doerun.com

CEO: Jerry Lpyatt
CFO: –
HR: Lisa Henn
FYE: October 31
Type: Private

The Doe Run Company assures us that no female deer are harmed in the production of its metal products. The fully integrated company is primarily involved in the entire lead production process from mining to milling to smelting and refining. It is also engaged in the recycling and fabrication of lead and lead products. The company's recycling unit handles about 150000 tons of lead annually. The Doe Run Company has operations in Arizona Missouri and Washington. The company also has an affiliate Doe Run Peru which mines lead and other nonferrous metals in the Andes Mountains region. It's a part of the Renco Group which also owns a stake in military SUV maker AM General among several other businesses.

THE DREES COMPANY

211 GRANDVIEW DR STE 300
FORT MITCHELL, KY 410172790
Phone: 859-578-4200
Fax: –
Web: www.dreeshomes.com

CEO: –
CFO: Mark Williams
HR: Effie McKeehan
FYE: March 31
Type: Private

The Drees Company is a big homebuilder in Cincinnati and one of the nation's top private builders. Drees targets first-time and move-up buyers with homes that are priced from about $100000 to more than $1 million. Drees also builds condominiums townhomes and patio homes. Its homes portfolio ranges from its former Zaring Premier Homes luxury division to the company's more financially accessible and modest Marquis Homes division. Drees is active in Florida Indiana Kentucky Maryland North Carolina Ohio Tennessee Texas Virginia and Washington DC. The family-owned firm was founded in 1928.

	Annual Growth	03/10	03/11	03/12	03/13	03/14
Sales ($ mil.)	8.4%	–	536.2	548.5	585.0	683.8
Net income ($ mil.)	57.4%	–	–	14.5	19.1	35.9
Market value ($ mil.)	–	–	–	–	–	–
Employees	–	–	–	–	–	850

THE DUCHOSSOIS GROUP INC.

845 Larch Ave.
Elmhurst IL 60126
Phone: 630-279-3600
Fax: 919-684-4344
Web: www.duke.edu

CEO: Craig J Duchossois
CFO: –
HR: –
FYE: December 31
Type: Private

The only thing this family of companies has in common is the Duchossois family the third-generation owners of The Duchossois Group Inc. The holding company pronounced "deshy-swa" focuses its investment interests in the consumer products technology and services sectors. The Chamberlain Group a subsidiary is the world's top maker of residential and commercial door openers and a leading maker of access control products. AMX performs systems integration while other companies offer AV equipment Internet-based access control and lighting products. The Duchossois Group also owns an early-stage IT venture capital fund and holds a minority stake in horse racetrack Churchill Downs.

THE DURHAM COMPANY

722 Durham Rd.
Lebanon MO 65536
Phone: 417-532-7121
Fax: 417-532-2366
Web: www.durhamcompany.com

CEO: –
CFO: –
HR: –
FYE: December 31
Type: Private

Employees at The Durham Co. have Thomas Edison to thank for their jobs. For over a half century the company has manufactured electrical hook-ups for investor-owned utilities to rural electric coops and electric municipalities. Its lineup specializes in meter sockets metering enclosures socket-breakers and switch combinations and transformers. Durham enclosures protect breakers and generator transfer switches as well as meter pedestals. For metering relay circuits and instrument circuits Durham also makes an array of test switches. The company's two Missouri plants divide up work; one makes the pad mount product line and the other enclosures and sockets. Durham is owned by the family of George E. Carr.

THE DWYER GROUP INC.

1020 N. University Parks Dr.
Waco TX 76707
Phone: 254-745-2400
Fax: 254-745-2590
Web: www.dwyergroup.com

CEO: Michael Bidwell
CFO: Thomas J Buckley
HR: –
FYE: December 31
Type: Private

The Dwyer Group is made up of seven service franchising businesses whose operations include plumbing electrical repairs carpet cleaning and other home maintenance services. Among the businesses under the Dwyer umbrella are Mr. Rooter (plumbing services) Rainbow International (carpet and upholstery cleaning) Glass Doctor (auto home and commercial glass replacement) and the Grounds Guys. The company has some 1500 franchise owners in the US and about a half dozen other countries plus 35 company-owned Portland Glass glass stores. Established in 1981 by Don Dwyer with the formation of its first company Rainbow International today The Dwyer Group is owned by private equity fund TZP Capital Partners.

THE EDELMAN FINANCIAL GROUP INC.

NASDAQ: EF

JP Morgan Chase Tower 600 Travis Ste. 5800
Houston TX 77002
Phone: 713-224-3100
Fax: 713-224-1101
Web: www.edelmanfinancial.com

CEO: –
CFO: –
HR: –
FYE: December 31
Type: Private

The Edelman Financial Group is a holding company that operates through its subsidiaries and affiliates which provide wealth management services for the mass-affluent market defined as clients with $50000 to $1 million of investable assets. Edelman Financial Group also has units that target high-net-worth clients with more than $1 million to invest. Key subsidiaries include Sanders Morris Harris Edelman Financial Services and Global Financial Services. Edelman Financial Group and its affiliates have more than 65 offices and more than $18 billion of assets under management. In 2012 Edelman was taken private by an affiliate of private equity firm Lee Equity Partners LLC.

THE ENVIRONMENTAL QUALITY COMPANY

36255 Michigan Ave.
Wayne MI 48184
Phone: 734-329-8000
Fax: 734-329-8140
Web: www.eqonline.com

CEO: –
CFO: –
HR: –
FYE: December 31
Type: Private

The Environmental Quality Company known as EQ provides hazardous- and industrial-waste treatment and disposal services. The company also offers facility management cleaning recycling and environmental remediation services. Michigan-based EQ is the largest privately held environmental services business in that state. It also acts as a project manager for the End of Life Vehicle Solutions (ELVS) nationwide mercury switch program which disposes of mercury switches (used in automobiles prior to 2003). EQ operates 28 locations across the US. The company was founded in 1957 by Michael Ferrantino.

THE ESTEE LAUDER COMPANIES INC.

NYSE: EL

767 5th Ave.
New York NY 10153-0023
Phone: 212-572-4200
Fax: 617-476-6150
Web: www.fidelity.com

CEO: Fabrizio Freda
CFO: Tracey T Travis
HR: –
FYE: June 30
Type: Public

The company's Estee and Bobbi are counted among some of the closest friends to women worldwide. Estee Lauder sells cosmetics fragrances and skin care products with brands including upscale Estee Lauder and Clinique as well as professional Bobbi Brown and luxurious Tom Ford beauty and fragrance lines. Its products are sold in upscale department stores specialty retailers online and 670 company-operated single-brand stores and 130 multi-brand stores. Estee Lauder operates a chain of freestanding retail stores (primarily for its M.A.C Origins and Aveda brands). Fabrizio Freda a veteran of Procter & Gamble heads Estee Lauder as CEO.

THE FISHEL COMPANY

1366 DUBLIN RD
COLUMBUS, OH 432151093
Phone: 614-274-8100
Fax: –
Web: www.teamfishel.com

CEO: John E. Phillips
CFO: Paul R. Riewe
HR: –
FYE: December 31
Type: Private

The Fishel Company reels in revenues by laying out lines. The company (also known as Team Fishel) provides engineering construction management and maintenance services for electric and gas utility and communications infrastructure projects. The aerial and underground utility contractor designs and builds distribution networks for telecommunications cable and broadband television gas transmission and distribution and electric utilities throughout the US. It also counts municipalities state and federal agencies universities commercial building owners financial services companies health care providers manufacturers and residential real estate developers among its clients.

	Annual Growth	12/08	12/09	12/11	12/12	12/13
Sales ($ mil.)	17.1%	–	162.9	174.7	281.5	306.3
Net income ($ mil.)	15.5%	–	–	7.9	(2.0)	10.5
Market value ($ mil.)	–	–	–	–	–	–
Employees	–	–	–	–	–	1,400

THE FOOD EMPORIUM INC.

42 W. 39th St. 18th Fl.
New York NY 10018
Phone: 212-915-2202
Fax: 973-625-5130
Web: www.microstrat.com

CEO: –
CFO: –
HR: –
FYE: February 28
Type: Subsidiary

The Food Emporium operates about 15 upscale supermarkets in densely-populated Manhattan and a store in Connecticut. A division of The Great Atlantic & Pacific Tea Company which filed for bankruptcy in 2010 Food Emporium stores are small (8000 to 17000 square feet). The grocery chain also operates an online shopping service (www.thefoodemporium.com) offering pick up and home delivery service to shoppers in 33 ZIP codes in Manhattan where it competes with Internet grocer FreshDirect. Food Emporium offers free delivery with $50 purchases (with some restrictions). The Food Emporium's store count has slipped as its stores in New York State and Connecticut have been converted to other A&P banners.

THE FOX CHASE CANCER CENTER FOUNDATION

333 COTTMAN AVE
PHILADELPHIA, PA 191112434
Phone: 215-728-6900
Fax: –
Web: www.fccc.edu

CEO: Michael Seiden MD PHD
CFO: –
HR: –
FYE: June 30
Type: Private

Fox Chase Cancer Center looks at cancer from all angles. The 100-bed not-for-profit medical center specializes in cancer research detection and treatment. Founded as one of the few US institutions dedicated exclusively to cancer Fox Chase Cancer Center provides diagnostic radiation oncology pathology robotic and laser surgery and other cancer-centric medical services. Its research center supports clinical trials of possible new treatments as well as standard care for cancer patients. Much of its work is focused on cancer prevention and identifying risk levels in populations. Fox Chase Cancer Center is part of the Temple University Health System.

	Annual Growth	06/08	06/09	06/10	06/11	06/12
Sales ($ mil.)	1.7%	–	55.9	49.3	44.1	58.8
Net income ($ mil.)	–	–	–	(7.1)	(9.5)	7.7
Market value ($ mil.)	–	–	–	–	–	–
Employees	–	–	–	–	–	1,900

THE FRANKLIN MINT LLC

801 Springdale Dr. Ste. 200
Exton PA 19341
Phone: 800-843-6468
Fax: 214-887-0998
Web: www.westdale.com

CEO: Robert H Book
CFO: Debbie Listman
HR: –
FYE: December 31
Type: Private

Not to be confused with the US Mint The Franklin Mint was founded in 1964 by Joseph Segal (who later founded QVC) and was known for making coins. Today the company sells die-cast cars and airplanes precision modeling and Harley-Davidson-branded items that are produced under licensing agreements. It also offers hand-painted collectibles such as commemorative dolls (many made to look like living and dead celebrities) as well as jewelry and seasonal giftware. Goods peddled by the collectibles company are distributed to wholesalers and sold online. Stewart and Lynda Resnick owned The Franklin Mint from 1985 to 2006 when the couple sold it to a group led by executives from The Morgan Mint.

THE G W VAN KEPPEL COMPANY

1801 N 9TH ST
KANSAS CITY, KS 661012023
Phone: 913-281-4800
Fax: –
Web: www.vankeppel.com

CEO: –
CFO: –
HR: –
FYE: November 30
Type: Private

If you ask The G. W. Van Keppel Co. being stuck in the middle isn't half bad. The company touts its role as a middle man matching original equipment manufacturers with operators of their heavy duty workhorses. Founded in 1926 it has grown to distribute a slew of construction aggregate and material handling equipment under blue chip brands including Volvo Hyster and Champion Motor Graders. The company also offers repair and maintenance services rental equipment and aftermarket parts for its equipment. G. W. Van Keppel is led by its founder's third generation chairman and president Bill Walker.

	Annual Growth	11/01	11/02	11/04	11/05	11/07
Sales ($ mil.)	9.0%	–	106.2	115.7	139.3	163.3
Net income ($ mil.)	(17.1%)	–	–	2.4	20.6	1.4
Market value ($ mil.)	–	–	–	–	–	–
Employees	–	–	–	–	–	200

THE GAMBRINUS COMPANY

14800 San Pedro Ave.
San Antonio TX 78232-3733
Phone: 210-490-9128
Fax: 210-490-9984
Web: www.gambrinusco.com

CEO: Carlos Alvarez
CFO: James J O'Sullivan
HR: Brad Kohanke
FYE: December 31
Type: Private

Taking its name from the legendary King Gambrinus of Flanders (aka the King of Beer) The Gambrinus Company brews and distributes a fine libation with which to toast — Shiner Beer. Shiner is brewed by Gambrinus' Spoetzl Brewery located in Shiner Texas. The company also owns Portland-based BridgePort Brewery Oregon's oldest microbrewery and Pete's Brewing Company (Pete's Wicked Ale). Gambrinus brews are available throughout the US as well as in Australia New Zealand and Italy. Owner Carlos Alvarez founded Gambrinus in 1986 and serves as its president and CEO.

THE GAP, INC.

NYS: GPS

Two Folsom Street
San Francisco, CA 94105
Phone: 415-427-0100
Fax: –
Web: www.gapinc.com

CEO: –
CFO: Sabrina L. Simmons
HR: Sudarshana Rangachary
FYE: January 31
Type: Public

The ubiquitous clothing retailer Gap has been filling closets with jeans and khakis T-shirts and poplin since the Woodstock era. The firm which operates about 3400 stores worldwide built its iconic casual brand on basics for men women and children but over the years has expanded through the urban chic chain Banana Republic family budgeteer Old Navy online-only retailer Piperlime and Athleta a purveyor of activewear. Other brand extensions include GapBody GapKids and babyGap; each also has its own online incarnation. All Gap clothing is private-label merchandise made exclusively for the company. From the design board to store displays Gap controls all aspects of its trademark casual look.

	Annual Growth	01/11	01/12*	02/13	02/14*	01/15
Sales ($ mil.)	2.9%	14,664.0	14,549.0	15,651.0	16,148.0	16,435.0
Net income ($ mil.)	1.2%	1,204.0	833.0	1,135.0	1,280.0	1,262.0
Market value ($ mil.)	21.0%	8,083.2	7,969.5	13,880.4	16,031.7	17,341.0
Employees	1.3%	134,000	132,000	136,000	137,000	141,000

*Fiscal year change

THE GAVILON GROUP LLC

11 ConAgra Dr.
Omaha NE 68102
Phone: 402-889-4000
Fax: 281-358-2443
Web: www.envirogen.com

CEO: Jim Anderson
CFO: John Neppl
HR: –
FYE: December 31
Type: Private

A gavilon may be one of the world's smaller hawks but The Gavilon Group is a fast-growing operation that keeps a sharp eye on its global network of food and fuel commodities. The company provides storage and handling transport marketing and distribution for grain feed ingredients fertilizer and energy products. Customers include food manufacturers livestock producers fertilizer wholesalers oil refineries and power producers. Spun off by ConAgra Foods in 2008 the company is owned by Gavilon management investment firm General Atlantic and hedge funds Soros Fund Management and Ospraie Management.

THE GENERATION COMPANIES LLC

4208 SIX FORKS RD STE 850
RALEIGH, NC 276095738
Phone: 919-361-9000
Fax: –
Web: www.generationcompanies.com

CEO: –
CFO: J Coupland
HR: –
FYE: December 31
Type: Private

Generation puts out the welcome mat fluffs the pillows and generally invites you to stay. The company develops owns and manages more than 25 extended-stay hotels. Brands in the firm's portfolio include Suburban Extended Stay Hotel Candlewood Suites and Days Inn & Suites; its properties are located in eight states in the US: Arkansas Florida Georgia Kansas North Carolina Tennessee Texas and Virginia. The company is also active in real estate development with some $200 million in real estate assets under management. Generation which has been growing through acquisitions was founded in 1996 by CEO Mark Daley. His father Hugh M. Daley was one of the original Holiday Inn franchisees in 1959.

	Annual Growth	12/08	12/09	12/11	12/12	12/13
Assets ($ mil.)	(46.5%)	–	207.9	4.5	174.6	17.0
Net income ($ mil.)	–	–	–	1.5	0.6	(0.5)
Market value ($ mil.)	–	–	–	–	–	–
Employees	–	–	–	–	–	300

THE GENLYTE GROUP INCORPORATED

3 Burlington Woods
Burlington MA 01803
Phone: 781-418-7900
Fax: 616-772-7348
Web: www.gentex.com

CEO: –
CFO: William G Ferko
HR: Kim Swinnen
FYE: December 31
Type: Subsidiary

The Genlyte Group wants everyone to lighten up. The company which does business as Professional Luminaires North America designs and manufactures a wide range of indoor and outdoor lighting products for commercial and industrial markets. Its incandescent fluorescent emergency high-intensity discharge (HID) and down lighting fixtures and lamps are used in healthcare retail entertainment outdoor hospitality and industrial applications. More than 80% of the company's products are made in its 35 North American facilities and include brand names Canlyte Omega Guth Lightolier and Vari*Lite. The Genlyte Group was purchased by Royal Philips Electronics and picked up its dba in early 2008.

THE GEORGE J FALTER COMPANY

3501 BENSON AVE
BALTIMORE, MD 212271098
Phone: 410-646-3641
Fax: -
Web: www.falterfundraising.com

CEO: Frank H Falter Jr
CFO: -
HR: -
FYE: December 31
Type: Private

The George J. Falter Company is a leading independent wholesale distributor of food and merchandise serving grocery stores convienience stores and other retailers throughout Maryland. It supplies customers with such goods as beverages dry goods and frozen foods as well as health and beauty items tobacco products and other merchandise. In addition George J. Falter distributes candy for fund raising activities. The company has delivery operations as well as a cash & carry outlet in Baltimore. The family-owned business was founded in 1878 as a candy distributor.

	Annual Growth	06/05	06/06	06/07*	12/08	12/09
Sales ($ mil.)	-	-	-	(1,295.1)	181.2	188.4
Net income ($ mil.)	30420.5%	-	-	0.0	0.7	0.6
Market value ($ mil.)	-	-	-	-	-	-
Employees	-	-	-	-	-	130

*Fiscal year change

THE GETTYSBURG HOSPITAL CORPORATION

147 GETTYS ST
GETTYSBURG, PA 173252536
Phone: 717-334-2121
Fax: -
Web: www.wellspan.org

CEO: -
CFO: -
HR: -
FYE: June 30
Type: Private

Gettysburg Hospital serves the here-and-now sick and wounded residents of historic Gettysburg Pennsylvania Adams County and parts of northern Maryland. Specialized services include a maternity center emergency medicine and home health care. The facility is affiliated with nearby York Hospital through the regional WellSpan Health organization. In 2008 Gettysburg Hospital began work on an expansive project to increase ER capacity add new patient floors and build a new maternity center.

	Annual Growth	06/10	06/11	06/12	06/13	06/14
Sales ($ mil.)	1.0%	-	136.6	133.4	141.0	140.6
Net income ($ mil.)	125.6%	-	-	4.9	18.4	25.1
Market value ($ mil.)	-	-	-	-	-	-
Employees	-	-	-	-	-	800

THE GLIK COMPANY

3248 NAMEOKI RD
GRANITE CITY, IL 620405014
Phone: 618-876-1065
Fax: -
Web: www.gliks.com

CEO: -
CFO: -
HR: -
FYE: December 29
Type: Private

Glik's is watching the urban fashion scene closely and working to cater to the crowds. The Glik Company operates about 55 Glik's apparel accessories and shoe stores in small towns in eight Midwestern states (primarily in Illinois Michigan and Minnesota). The stores offer men's and women's products with a hip-hop and sporty flair under national brands such as Roxy DC Shoes Hurley Billabong Burton The North Face Volcom and Silver Jeans. Glik's Grand the company's largest store format features motocross and action sportswear for surfing skating and water sports. Founded in 1897 by Joseph Glik today the family-owned firm is run by president and CEO Jeff Glik his great-grandson.

	Annual Growth	01/10	01/11	01/12*	12/12	12/13
Sales ($ mil.)	8.7%	-	30.7	33.6	35.9	36.2
Net income ($ mil.)	(14.8%)	-	-	1.1	0.9	0.9
Market value ($ mil.)	-	-	-	-	-	-
Employees	-	-	-	-	-	500

*Fiscal year change

THE GLOBE PEQUOT PRESS

246 Goose Ln.
Guilford CT 06437
Phone: 203-458-4500
Fax: 203-458-4603
Web: www.globepequot.com

CEO: -
CFO: -
HR: -
FYE: December 31
Type: Business Segment

Globe Pequot can help you find your way around the world. The Globe Pequot Press is among the top sources for travel books and guides in the US publishing or distributing some 600 titles annually. It also offers books on business cooking literature nature and retirement among other topics. With titles such as "Europe by Rail" and "Cowboy Wisdon" Globe Pequot also handles distribution for other publishers including Thomas Cook Publishing (guidebooks) Stoecklein Publishing (coffee table books) and Woodall's (RV campground directories). In addition it co-publishes travel guides with Bradt Publications of London. Founded in 1947 Globe Pequot became a division of Morris Communications in 1997.

THE GO DADDY GROUP INC.

14455 N. Hayden Rd. Ste. 226
Scottsdale AZ 85260-6947
Phone: 480-505-8800
Fax: 480-505-8844
Web: www.godaddy.com

CEO: Blake Irving
CFO: Scott Wagner
HR: -
FYE: December 31
Type: Private

Go Daddy go! Go Daddy provides individuals and businesses with Internet services such as domain name registration and website hosting along with services and software for functions that include e-mail e-commerce podcasting and website creation. Touting discounted pricing on domain names and hosting services it has become the largest global domain registrar accredited by ICANN (the regulatory body for the public Internet) with some 53 million domain names under management. It targets niche markets such as private domains and reseller programs through affiliates Domains By Proxy and Wild West Domains. In 2011 KKR and Silver Lake became partners in Go Daddy; founder Bob Parsons remains its majority shareholder.

THE GOLDEN 1 CREDIT UNION

8945 Cal Center Dr.
Sacramento CA 95826-3239
Phone: 916-732-2900
Fax: 916-451-8214
Web: www.golden1.com

CEO: Teresa Halleck
CFO: -
HR: -
FYE: December 31
Type: Private - Not-for-Pr

The Golden 1 Credit Union aims to be #1. One of the largest credit unions in California and among the top 10 in the US the member-owned organization serves communities in central and northern parts of the state through 80-plus branches; nearly half of which are in and around Sacramento. The Golden 1 has assets in excess of $7.5 billion and more than 600000 members who are residents of about 35 eligible counties are California state employees or employees of hundreds of select companies or groups. The credit union offers standard products such as checking and savings accounts and credit and check cards. It also provides residential real estate and personal loans as well as investments and insurance.

THE GOLUB CORPORATION

461 NOTT ST
SCHENECTADY, NY 123081812
Phone: 518-355-5000
Fax: –
Web: www.pricechopper.com

CEO: Jerel T. (Jerry) Golub
CFO: John J (Jack) Endres
HR: Margaret Davenport
FYE: April 27
Type: Private

Supermarket operator The Golub Corporation offers tasty come-ons such as table-ready meals gift certificates automatic discount cards and a hotline where cooks answer food-related queries. Golub operates about 135 Price Chopper supermarkets and market 32 stores in six states in the northeastern US (New York is its largest market.) About 80 of the locations have in-store pharmacies and some New York stores provide shopping and delivery service through the Shops4U program. The founding Golub family runs the company and owns about 45% of the regional grocery chain; employees own slightly more than 45%.

	Annual Growth	04/10	04/11	04/12	04/13	04/14
Sales ($ mil.)	0.1%	–	3,459.8	3,627.8	3,484.8	3,472.5
Net income ($ mil.)	(30.0%)	–	–	37.4	24.8	18.3
Market value ($ mil.)	–	–	–	–	–	–
Employees	–	–	–	–	–	21,741

THE GOOD SAMARITAN HOSPITAL OF MD INC

5601 LOCH RAVEN BLVD
BALTIMORE, MD 21239-2945
Phone: 443-444-3780
Fax: –
Web: www.goodsam-md.org

CEO: Jeffrey A Matton
CFO: Deana Stout
HR: –
FYE: June 30
Type: Private

Good Samaritan Hospital of Maryland provides emergency care and promotes good health in the Baltimore area. The 300-bed hospital operating as MedStar Good Samaritan provides acute medical and specialty services including rehabilitation (50-bed ward) transitional care (30-bed sub-acute ward) orthopedics cancer care cardiology dialysis and women's health as well as serving as a community teaching facility. The hospital founded in 1968 also operates nursing and assisted-living facilities for the elderly and it provides educational seminars diagnostic screening and preventative medical care through its Good Health Center. MedStar Good Samaritan of Maryland is part of the MedStar Health system.

	Annual Growth	06/08	06/09	06/10	06/11	06/12
Sales ($ mil.)	0.6%	–	314.5	322.3	331.9	320.0
Net income ($ mil.)	–	–	0.0	10.5	14.0	(1.8)
Market value ($ mil.)	–	–	–	–	–	–
Employees	–	–	–	–	–	2,146

THE GREAT ATLANTIC & PACIFIC TEA COMPANY INC.   PINK SHEETS: GAPT

2 Paragon Dr.
Montvale NJ 07645
Phone: 201-573-9700
Fax: 201-505-3054
Web: www.aptea.com

CEO: Paul Hertz
CFO: Raymond P Silcock
HR: –
FYE: February 28
Type: Private

Once one of the biggest baggers of groceries in the US The Great Atlantic & Pacific Tea Company (A&P) has been reduced to a shrinking portfolio of regional grocery chains. It now runs about 300 supermarkets in New Jersey New York Pennsylvania and three other eastern states. In addition to its mainstay 80-store A&P chain the company operates five banners: Pathmark Waldbaum's Superfresh Food Emporium and Food Basics. A&P acquired its longtime rival in the Northeast Pathmark Stores for about $1.4 billion but the purchase failed to reverse A&P's lagging fortunes. Indeed A&P in 2012 emerged from 15 months in Chapter 11 bankruptcy after a financial restructuring and closing 75 stores.

THE GREEN BAY PACKERS INC.

Lambeau Field Atrium 1265 Lombardi Ave.
Green Bay WI 54304
Phone: 920-569-7500
Fax: 920-569-7301
Web: www.packers.com

CEO: Mark Murphy
CFO: Vicki Vannieuwenhove
HR: –
FYE: March 31
Type: Private - Not-for-Pr

On the frozen tundra of Lambeau Field the Green Bay Packers battle for pride in the National Football League. The not-for-profit corporation owns and operates the storied franchise which was founded in 1919 by Earl "Curly" Lambeau and joined the NFL in 1921. Home to such icons as Bart Starr Ray Nitschke and legendary coach Vince Lombardi Green Bay boasts a record 13 league titles including four Super Bowl victories. The team is also the only community-owned franchise in American professional sports with more than 100000 shareholders. The shares do not increase in value nor pay dividends and can only be sold back to the team.

THE GRIFFIN HOSPITAL INC

130 DIVISION ST
DERBY, CT 064181326
Phone: 203-735-7421
Fax: –
Web: www.griffinhealth.org

CEO: Patrick Charmel
CFO: Mark O'Neill
HR: –
FYE: September 30
Type: Private

Griffin Hospital is a not-for-profit community hospital and subsidiary of Griffin Health Services Corporation. The 160-bed acute-care hospital serves residents in and around Derby Connecticut. Its specialties include cardiac and physical rehabilitation psychiatry and mental health surgical services and centers for childbirth and bladder and bowel control. The hospital is a teaching center affiliated with Yale University's School of Medicine. Griffin Hospital is the flagship hospital of consumer health care organization Planetree which implements a model of patient-centered care that encourages patients to actively participate in their treatment processes.

	Annual Growth	09/07	09/08	09/09	09/12	09/13
Sales ($ mil.)	1.6%	–	118.6	124.7	126.8	128.2
Net income ($ mil.)	–	–	–	0.0	(3.9)	(1.6)
Market value ($ mil.)	–	–	–	–	–	–
Employees	–	–	–	–	–	1,100

THE GYMBOREE CORPORATION

500 Howard St.
San Francisco CA 94105
Phone: 415-278-7000
Fax: 415-278-7100
Web: www.gymboree.com

CEO: Mark Breitbard
CFO: Andrew B North
HR: Kenneth F Meyers
FYE: January 31
Type: Private

Despite being over 30 years old The Gymboree Corp. is still a retail toddler stumbling periodically learning quickly and growing fast. The company sells clothes and accessories for kids in the US Puerto Rico Canada and now Australia at about 635 Gymboree stores that carry colorful fashionable playsuits and rompers for kids up to 12 years old. It also operates some 125 Janie and Jack (better newborn and toddler apparel) and 150-plus Gymboree Outlet stores and corresponding e-commerce sites. Its youngest chain is value-priced Crazy 8. The company also provides parent-child play programs (designed to enhance child development) for newborns to age five. Founded in 1976 Gymboree is owned by Bain Capital.

THE HALLSTAR COMPANY

120 S. Riverside Plaza Ste. 1620
Chicago IL 60606
Phone: 312-554-7400
Fax: 312-554-7499
Web: www.hallstar.com

CEO: John J Paro
CFO: William J Holbrook
HR: –
FYE: September 30
Type: Private

Hey now it's a HallStar! The HallStar Company operates through subsidiaries CPH Solutions and RTD HallStar which make polymer and personal care product additives used to improve the quality of rubber plastics adhesives coatings cosmetics skin care items and other industrial products. It has two US manufacturing facilities and distributes products to customers in the US and abroad. It also holds a joint venture with Scandiflex to market personal care products in Brazil. The company's brands include Paraplex Plasthall Hallcote Quikote Maglite and Marinco. HallStar known as CPH Holding or the C. P. Hall Company until 2007 is owned by members of its executive staff.

THE HARFORD MUTUAL INSURANCE COMPANY

200 N. Main St.
Bel Air MD 21014
Phone: 410-838-4000
Fax: 410-838-8675
Web: www.harfordmutual.com

CEO: Steven D Linkous
CFO: –
HR: –
FYE: December 31
Type: Private - Mutual Com

Harford Mutual provides a variety of commercial property/casualty insurance products to individuals and businesses in a handful of Mid-Atlantic states. Targeting small and mediums sized business owners the company's products include automobile general liability inland marine and workers' compensation insurance as well as multiline commercial and umbrella coverage. Subsidiary Firstline National Insurance Company underwrites special program coverage which is all ceded to Harford Mutual. Harford Mutual and Firstline sell their policies through a network of independent agencies. Harford Mutual was founded as Mutual Fire Insurance Company in 1842.

THE HARVARD DRUG GROUP L.L.C.

31778 Enterprise Dr.
Livonia MI 48150
Phone: 734-743-6000
Fax: 734-743-7000
Web: www.theharvarddruggroup.com

CEO: Kurt Hilzinger
CFO: Steve Bencetic
HR: –
FYE: June 30
Type: Private

Medicines not scholars are what come out of this Harvard. The Harvard Drug Group distributes branded and generic prescription and OTC drugs as well as vitamins and consumer products to more than 15000 independent and chain pharmacies hospitals nursing homes physician practices veterinarians and other purchasing groups. It markets more than 18000 items (primarily generics) through sales representatives and vendor partners in North America and other select global markets. The company is controlled by investment firm Court Square Capital Partners.

THE HEICO COMPANIES L.L.C.

5600 Three First National Plaza
Chicago IL 60602
Phone: 312-419-8220
Fax: 312-419-9417
Web: www.heicocompanies.com

CEO: E A Roskovensky
CFO: L G Wolski
HR: –
FYE: December 31
Type: Private

The Heico Companies specializes in buying distressed companies and turning them around. The firm which typically invests for the long haul has a portfolio of more than 35 companies in North America Europe and Asia active in manufacturing construction and industrial services. Holdings include Davis Wire Canadian steelmaker Ivaco and heavy industrial equipment maker Pettibone. Heico also has interests in other companies in the metals processing construction materials logistics and diversified services industries. Michael Heisley launched Heico in 1979. The privately-owned company holds controlling stakes in each of its operations.

THE HEIL CO.

2030 Hamilton Place Blvd. Ste. 300
Chattanooga TN 37421
Phone: 423-899-9100
Fax: 905-363-0336
Web: www.luxell.com

CEO: –
CFO: Darren Bird
HR: Gail Briggs
FYE: December 31
Type: Subsidiary

It's a heil of a job but someone's gotta do it. The Heil Co. which does business as Heil Environmental makes refuse and recycling collection vehicles. Its vehicles include front rear and side loading refuse collection trucks and recyclers. Heil also offers a line of lifting and recycling products under other brand names including DuaLift (hook lift and cable hoist systems) Bayne (cart trippers and lift systems) and Marathon (waste compaction and recycling systems). Heil sells its products to municipalities and private refuse collection companies in 150 countries through a network of more than 50 distributors. The company is a subsidiary of diversified manufacturer Dover Corporation.

THE HENRY FRANCIS DUPONT WINTERTHUR MUSEUM INC

5105 KENNETT PIKE
WINTERTHUR, DE 197351819
Phone: 302-888-4852
Fax: –
Web: www.winterthur.org

CEO: –
CFO: –
HR: –
FYE: June 30
Type: Private

The Henry Francis du Pont Winterthur Museum offers collections of antiques and Americana a 60-acre naturalistic garden and an 87000-volume library specializing in American culture. Into 2012 the museum showcases The John and Carolyn Grossman Collection of printed paper from the Victorian and Edwardian periods. It also promotes its Enchanted Woods fairy-tale garden aimed at the young and young-at-heart containing sites such as a faerie cottage and a troll bridge. The 979-acre estate is the former home of Henry Francis du Pont a director of chemical maker DuPont from 1915 to 1958. The Winterthur country estate was converted into a museum and opened to the public in 1951.

	Annual Growth	06/08	06/09	06/10	06/11	06/13
Sales ($ mil.)	–	–	(2,109.9)	11.6	28.1	18.1
Net income ($ mil.)	–	–	–	(22.4)	4.7	(4.2)
Market value ($ mil.)	–	–	–	–	–	–
Employees	–	–	–	–	–	160

THE HERB CHAMBERS COMPANIES

259 McGrath Hwy.
Somerville MA 02145
Phone: 617-666-8333
Fax: 617-666-8448
Web: herbchambers.com

CEO: –
CFO: Bruce H Spatz
HR: Jay Gubala
FYE: December 31
Type: Private

Step into the chambers of Herb Chambers Companies and you'll find a wide range of cars. The acquisitive company runs over 50 dealerships throughout Massachusetts and Rhode Island that sell just about everything from pricey new cars by BMW Cadillac Lexus Mercedes-Benz and Porsche to more affordable offerings by Honda Hyundai Scion and Toyota; dealerships also offer Smart cars used cars and even Vespa scooters. All of its vehicles are available online. Herb Chambers also offers parts and service and runs a handful of body shops. Owner and CEO Herb Chambers started his automotive empire with a Cadillac/Oldsmobile dealership in New London Connecticut in 1985.

THE HERITAGE FOUNDATION

214 MSSCHSTTS AVE NE BSMT
WASHINGTON, DC 20002
Phone: 202-546-4400
Fax: –
Web: www.heritage.org

CEO: –
CFO: –
HR: –
FYE: December 31
Type: Private

A conservative public policy think tank The Heritage Foundation offers research and advocacy on topics ranging from agriculture and labor to missile defense religion crime and education. The Heritage Foundation promotes a conservative agenda based on the tenets of free enterprise limited government individual freedom traditional American values and a strong national defense. The foundation is supported mainly by individuals as well as by other foundations and by corporations. Its donors number 410000 and its expense budget has reached $61 million. The late beer magnate Joseph Coors provided seed money for The Heritage Foundation which was founded in 1973.

	Annual Growth	12/05	12/06	12/07	12/08	12/09
Sales ($ mil.)	(52.9%)	–	–	395.7	23.5	87.9
Net income ($ mil.)	47865.5%	–	–	0.0	(37.5)	22.8
Market value ($ mil.)	–	–	–	–	–	–
Employees	–	–	–	–	–	270

THE HIBBERT COMPANY

400 PENNINGTON AVE
TRENTON, NJ 086183105
Phone: 609-392-0478
Fax: –
Web: www.hibbertgroup.com

CEO: Timothy J. (Tim) Moonan
CFO: –
HR: –
FYE: December 31
Type: Private

Hibbert is handy when it comes to marketing. The Hibbert Company doing business as The Hibbert Group offers marketing support services. Its three flagship services consist of the fulfillment and distribution of marketing materials and information; sales and marketing program administration; and database management and direct marketing services. The company serves clients in industries such as pharmaceutical telecommunications finance technology electronics and advertising and marketing. Hibbert has five locations in Delaware Colorado and New Jersey. Tim and Tom Moonan and their family have owned the company since 1936.

	Annual Growth	12/04	12/05	12/06	12/08	12/09
Sales ($ mil.)	(55.1%)	–	–	871.8	78.8	78.8
Net income ($ mil.)	3876.7%	–	–	0.0	3.5	3.5
Market value ($ mil.)	–	–	–	–	–	–
Employees	–	–	–	–	–	446

THE HILLMAN COMPANIES INC.

10590 Hamilton Ave.
Cincinnati OH 45231
Phone: 513-851-4900
Fax: 513-851-4997
Web: www.hillmangroup.com

CEO: –
CFO: Anthony A Vasconcellos
HR: –
FYE: December 31
Type: Private

Nuts bolts screws and other fasteners hold The Hillman Companies together. Operating primarily through wholly owned subsidiary The Hillman Group Inc. the company is one of the largest distributors of fasteners and other hardware products to retail markets in North America. It also distributes key duplication machines engraving systems signs and threaded rod across North America Latin America and Australia. The company purchases products from more than 500 vendors about half of which are non-US suppliers. Its products and value-added merchandising services are mainly sold to major home centers hardware stores and mass merchants.

THE HILLMAN COMPANY

330 Grant St. Ste. 1900
Pittsburgh PA 15219
Phone: 412-281-2620
Fax: 412-338-3520

CEO: Joseph C Manzinger
CFO: –
HR: –
FYE: December 31
Type: Private

Shhh! The Hillman Company is making money. Founded in 1951 the publicity-shy venture capital and investment firm quietly has holdings primarily in real estate as well as in medical technology information technology and other high-tech enterprises. It was an early backer of investment firm Kohlberg Kravis Roberts (KKR). Billionaire philanthropist Henry Hillman (who once told FORTUNE magazine that "a whale is harpooned only when it spouts" when asked why he eschews interviews) stepped down as chairman of The Hillman Company in 2004 but continues to steer the firm's executive committee and charitable activities.

THE HITE COMPANY

3101 BEALE AVE
ALTOONA, PA 166011509
Phone: 814-944-6121
Fax: –
Web: www.hitelighting.com

CEO: R Lee Hite
CFO: Ronald Muffie
HR: –
FYE: December 31
Type: Private

Going from a mill supply house to a 20-plus operation takes a bright idea and The Hite Company has more than a few. It is a wholesale distributor of more than 35000 lighting products and a slew of electrical supplies. The company's lineup includes data and communications equipment industrial automation and motor control devices as well as lamps and professional video and audio equipment. Hite has represented Sylvania for more than 50 years; it also stocks Square D branded products (Schneider Electric) and others by major OEMs. Hite serves electrical contractors builders and residential customers in Pennsylvania New York and West Virginia. Founded in 1949 the company is family owned and operated.

	Annual Growth	12/08	12/09	12/10	12/11	12/12
Sales ($ mil.)	9.7%	–	96.0	96.0	96.0	126.8
Net income ($ mil.)	–	–	–	0.0	0.0	0.0
Market value ($ mil.)	–	–	–	–	–	–
Employees	–	–	–	–	–	230

THE HOWARD UNIVERSITY

2400 6TH ST NW
WASHINGTON, DC 200590002
Phone: 202-806-6100
Fax: –
Web: www.howard.edu

CEO: –
CFO: –
HR: –
FYE: June 30
Type: Private

Howard University is a predominantly African-American university enrolling some 11000 students in Washington DC. The university offers undergraduate graduate and professional degrees in 120 areas including engineering education divinity dentistry law medicine history political science music and social work through its 12 schools and colleges. It has about 1000 full-time faculty members and has a low student-to-teacher ratio of about 8:1. Established in 1867 the school was named after one of its founders General Oliver O. Howard a Civil War hero who was commissioner of the Freedman's Bureau.

	Annual Growth	06/09	06/10	06/11	06/12	06/13
Sales ($ mil.)	(3.6%)	–	941.2	989.0	1,000.0	843.9
Net income ($ mil.)	313.9%	–	–	11.8	(148.9)	202.1
Market value ($ mil.)	–	–	–	–	–	–
Employees	–	–	–	–	–	5,600

THE HUMANE SOCIETY OF THE UNITED STATES

2100 L ST NW STE 500
WASHINGTON, DC 200371595
Phone: 202-452-1100
Fax: –
Web: www.humanesociety.org

CEO: Andrew N. Rowan
CFO: G. Thomas Waite
HR: –
FYE: December 31
Type: Private

The Humane Society of the United States (HSUS) is a watchdog for dogs and all sorts of other domestic animals and wildlife. Founded in 1954 HSUS is the country's largest animal protection organization with 11 million members and constituents. The organization supports the work of local humane societies and implements a variety of investigative educational advocacy and legislative programs to promote animal welfare. Its campaigns have addressed such issues as animal fighting factory farming animal testing the fur trade and hunting practices. Most of HSUS's revenue comes from contributions and grants. An affiliate Humane Society International takes the cause to other countries.

	Annual Growth	12/08	12/09	12/10	12/11	12/13
Sales ($ mil.)	12.8%	–	–	–	133.6	169.9
Net income ($ mil.)	91.8%	–	–	–	5.8	21.3
Market value ($ mil.)	–	–	–	–	–	–
Employees	–	–	–	–	–	440

THE HUNT CORPORATION

6720 N. Scottsdale Rd. Ste. 300
Scottsdale AZ 85253
Phone: 480-368-4700
Fax: 480-368-4747
Web: www.thehuntcorp.com

CEO: –
CFO: –
HR: –
FYE: December 31
Type: Private

The Hunt Corporation doesn't have to prowl around for a good source of revenue. The company was created in 1974 as a holding company for primary subsidiary Hunt Construction Group which is a leading builder of sports facilities in the country. (The company has worked on more than 40 arenas and all-purpose venues for for professional and collegiate sports teams including the Pittsburgh Steelers and St. Louis Cardinals.) The firm provides general contracting design/build construction management and environmental services. Other Hunt Corporation divisions include Hunt Paving Hunt Sports HuntCor and Hunt International. The company has nearly ten offices mainly in the southern and western US.

THE IAMS COMPANY

7250 Poe Ave.
Dayton OH 45414
Phone: 937-898-7387
Fax: 937-264-7264
Web: www.iams.com

CEO: AG Losley
CFO: Brian Robson
HR: –
FYE: June 30
Type: Subsidiary

As Iams tells it Old Mother Hubbard went to the cupboard to fetch her portly pooch a bag of Eukanuba Large Breed Weight Control food. The Iams Company makes Eukanuba and Iams dry and canned versions of premium dog and cat foods and sells them in pet supply stores and veterinarians' offices in more than 70 countries. However North America accounts for the vast majority of the company's sales. Founded by Paul Iams in 1946 Iams also funds research efforts related to animal dermatology geriatrics allergies and nutrition through its Paul F. Iams Technical Center. Former chairman Clayton Mathile acquired the company in 1982 and sold it to consumer products giant Procter & Gamble in 1999.

THE INDEPENDENT FILM CHANNEL LLC

323 6th Ave.
New York NY 10014
Phone: 917-542-6200
Fax: 416-603-7462
Web: www.frontline.ca

CEO: –
CFO: –
HR: –
FYE: December 31
Type: Subsidiary

This media firm depends on no one except consumers looking for entertainment outside the mainstream. The Independent Film Channel operates popular cable networks IFC and Sundance along with movie production and distribution businesses. Its IFC network reaches more than 60 million US homes with a mix of independent movies and original programming aimed at the young male demographic. Reaching more than 40 million homes Sundance offers films and specials for an older audience group. The Independent Film Channel also produces and distributes original movies through IFC Films IFC Productions and joint venture InDigEnt. The company is owned by leading cable television broadcaster AMC Networks.

THE INGALLS MEMORIAL HOSPITAL

1 INGALLS DR
HARVEY, IL 604263558
Phone: 708-333-2300
Fax: –
Web: www.ingallshealthsystem.org

CEO: Kurt Johnson
CFO: Vince Pryor
HR: –
FYE: September 30
Type: Private

Ingalls Memorial Hospital serves Chicago's south suburbs. With more than 560 beds the main hospital offers a variety of acute and tertiary health care services including cancer treatment cardiovascular care orthopedic surgery rehabilitation services neurosurgery women's health and other clinical services. It also includes specialty centers in areas such as sleep therapy and addiction treatment. Ingalls Memorial Hospital also acts as a health system operating outpatient offices and clinics and providing home health and hospice services in the area.

	Annual Growth	09/07	09/08	09/09	09/12	09/13
Sales ($ mil.)	1.4%	–	270.9	267.4	293.3	290.7
Net income ($ mil.)	–	–	–	(15.3)	37.0	34.2
Market value ($ mil.)	–	–	–	–	–	–
Employees	–	–	–	–	–	2,296

THE INLAND REAL ESTATE GROUP OF COMPANIES INC.

2901 Butterfield Rd.	CEO: Daniel L Goodwin
Oak Brook IL 60523	CFO: –
Phone: 630-218-8000	HR: –
Fax: 630-218-4957	FYE: June 30
Web: www.inlandgroup.com	Type: Private

The Inland Real Estate Group lives eats breathes and sleeps real estate. Through a number of affiliated firms the group provides commercial real estate services including property investment portfolio management lending brokerage development and property management/leasing. Through real estate investment trusts (REITs) Inland primarily invests in retail properties. Its portfolio (worth some $26 billion) includes more than 120 million sq. ft. of commercial space throughout the US. Publicly traded Inland Real Estate Corporation invests in properties in the Midwest; private REIT Inland American invest in the US and Canada.

THE INSTITUTE OF ELECTRICAL AND ELECTRONICS ENGINEERS INC

3 Park Ave. 17th Fl.	CEO: –
New York NY 10016-5997	CFO: Thomas Siegert
Phone: 212-419-7900	HR: –
Fax: 212-752-4929	FYE: December 31
Web: www.ieee.org	Type: Private - Associatio

A leading technology-related professional group The Institute of Electrical and Electronics Engineers (IEEE) has almost 416000 members including 100000-plus students in 160 countries. The IEEE provides technical and professional information to members on topics such as aerospace systems biomedical engineering computers consumer electronics electric power and telecommunications. It sponsors more than 1300 annual conferences and publishes a variety of technical literature including journals magazines and conference proceedings. The IEEE was formed in 1964 in a combination of the American Institute of Electrical Engineers (founded in 1884) and the Institute of Radio Engineers (founded in 1912).

THE INTEC GROUP INC.

666 S. Vermont St.	CEO: Steven M Perlman
Palatine IL 60067	CFO: –
Phone: 047 350 0000	HR: –
Fax: 847-358-4391	FYE: September 30
Web: www.intecgrp.com	Type: Private

This company uses a group approach to keep in touch with its core plastic manufacturing identity. The INTEC Group makes precision insert molded and injection-molded thermoplastic parts for the automotive electronics and telecommunication industries. The company's products include antennas and related items custom insert molded parts custom injection-molded parts and single cavity preproduction tools. The INTEC Group has a 60000-sq.-ft. manufacturing facility in the US and additional plants in Mexico and Singapore. The automotive industry accounts for more than 90% of the company's production output.

THE INTERNATIONAL ASSOCIATION OF LIONS CLUBS INCORPORATED

300 W 22ND ST	CEO: –
OAK BROOK, IL 605238815	CFO: –
Phone: 630-468-6881	HR: –
Fax: –	FYE: June 30
Web: www.lionsclubs.org	Type: Private

With a growl of great compassion The International Association of Lions Clubs offers people the opportunity to volunteer in their local areas and global community. Its more than 1 million members are involved in a range of projects from neighborhood initiatives to far-reaching international campaigns. Lions clubs conduct vision and hearing screenings sponsor youth camps build homes for the disabled provide disaster relief and develop international relations. It also promotes educational programs for diabetes and drug awareness. The group has about 45000 branches in more than 200 countries. It was founded in 1917 as a way for business organizations to better their communities and the world.

	Annual Growth	06/07	06/08	06/09	06/12	06/13
Sales ($ mil.)	(12.2%)	–	133.0	0.1	62.0	69.5
Net income ($ mil.)	–	–	–	(0.0)	(11.1)	5.2
Market value ($ mil.)	–	–	–	–	–	–
Employees	–	–	–	–	–	288

THE INTERTECH GROUP INC.

4838 Jenkins Ave.	CEO: Anita G Zucker
North Charleston SC 29405	CFO: –
Phone: 843-744-5174	HR: –
Fax: 843-747-4092	FYE: December 31
Web: www.theintertechgroup.com	Type: Private

The InterTech Group likes to interweave a wide variety of technology-driven manufacturing businesses with other activities such as business services (image marketing financial transaction services) and entertainment. The group a holding company with more than 100 businesses worldwide puts its primary focus on polymer and elastomer plastics and fiber products including industrial protective wear and fabrics used by firefighters and astronauts (through its PBI Performance Products subsidiary). Products include gaskets sealing devices and woven and nonwoven fabrics.

THE IRVINE COMPANY LLC

550 Newport Center Dr.	CEO: –
Newport Beach CA 92660-7011	CFO: Mark Lav
Phone: 949-720-2000	HR: Lenny Pangesa
Fax: 949-720-2218	FYE: June 30
Web: www.irvinecompany.com	Type: Private

At The Irvine Company everything goes according to plan — the master plan. The real estate investment company plans and designs office retail and residential developments in California. It owns some 500 office buildings and 40 retail centers as well as hotels marinas and golf courses. Its Irvine Company Apartment Communities arm manages 115 apartment communities. The star in Irvine's crown Irvine Ranch in Orange County is one of the largest planned communities in the US with some 220000 residents. It covers 93000 acres a drop from its original 120000 acres back in the mid-1800s when James Irvine bought out the debts of Mexican land-grant holders. Billionaire chairman Donald Bren owns the company.

THE JACKSON LABORATORY

600 MAIN ST
BAR HARBOR, ME 046091500
Phone: 207-288-6000
Fax: –
Web: www.library.jax.org

CEO: Edison T. Liu
CFO: Linda Jensen
HR: –
FYE: May 31
Type: Private

The Jackson Laboratory (JAX) was into genetics before genetics was cool. Founded in 1929 the not-for-profit organization is a leading researcher of human diseases their causes and their potential cures. Much of its research into mammalian genetics is focused on mice which share a similar genetic makeup to humans. In addition to its own research in areas such as cancer immunology and metabolic disease the organization maintains colonies of mice and supplies them under the brand name JAX to other laboratories around the globe. Additionally JAX offers educational programs — including internships workshops and predoctoral programs — for both current and future scientists.

	Annual Growth	05/06	05/07	05/08	05/09	05/10
Sales ($ mil.)	–	–	–	(143.1)	166.0	200.3
Net income ($ mil.)	4163.0%	–	–	0.0	(25.0)	29.8
Market value ($ mil.)	–	–	–	–	–	–
Employees	–	–	–	–	–	1,300

THE JAY GROUP INC

700 INDIAN SPRINGS DR
LANCASTER, PA 176011266
Phone: 717-285-6200
Fax: –
Web: www.jaygroup.com

CEO: –
CFO: Craig Robinson
HR: –
FYE: December 31
Type: Private

The Jay Group provides outsourced marketing and fulfillment services to clients such as Reebok iRobot and Pfizer. The company's roster of services includes product fulfillment call center services procurement and packaging services. The Jay Group's fulfillment programs serve business-to-business and business-to-consumer clients providing literature product and catalog fulfillment as well as rebate processing incentive program management and sweepstakes management for sales promotions. The company's contact center services include order processing customer service and help desk support. It was established by J. Freeland Chryst in 1965; his daughter Dana Chryst leads the company as CEO.

	Annual Growth	12/04	12/05	12/06	12/07	12/08
Sales ($ mil.)	2.5%	–	47.5	51.1	47.3	51.2
Net income ($ mil.)	(20.4%)	–	–	2.2	2.2	1.4
Market value ($ mil.)	–	–	–	–	–	–
Employees	–	–	–	–	–	273

THE JIM HENSON COMPANY INC.

1416 N. La Brea Ave.
Hollywood CA 90028
Phone: 323-802-1500
Fax: 323-802-1825
Web: www.henson.com

CEO: Lisa Henson
CFO: Laurie Don
HR: –
FYE: December 31
Type: Private

Puppets are just a few of the creatures to come from this entertainment company. Best known for the creation of such Muppets as Kermit the Frog and Miss Piggy (now owned by The Walt Disney Company) The Jim Henson Company today continues to produce television and film content aimed primarily at children. Its shows include Sid the Science Kid and Pajanimals (both produced for the Public Broadcasting Service). The company is also involved in post-production and special effects services through its TV and film studios and the Jim Henson Creature Shop. In addition it has recording facilities used by commercial recording artists. Jim Henson started the company in 1958; it is run by his son Brian and daughter Lisa.

THE JONES COMPANY

215 Pendleton St.
Waycross GA 31501
Phone: 912-285-4011
Fax: 912-285-0811
Web: www.flashfoods.com

CEO: James C Jones III
CFO: James A Walker Jr
HR: –
FYE: December 31
Type: Private

After more than a half a century The Jones Company has proven it isn't just a flash in the pan. The diversified holding company operates more than 195 Flash Foods convenience stores in Georgia and north Florida. A pair of subsidiaries keep the shelves stocked and gas tanks full. Jones's Fuel South unit supplies the company's service stations with fuel. Its Distribution South unit is a wholesale grocery supplier and provides much of the merchandise sold in the stores. The firm's Jones Company Restaurants subsidiary operates restaurants and Walker-Jones is a family of auto dealerships. Founded in 1952 by J. C. Jones Jr. and his father the company is still owned and run by the Jones family.

THE JONES FINANCIAL COMPANIES L.L.L.P.

12555 Manchester Rd.
Des Peres MO 63131
Phone: 314-515-2000
Fax: 314-515-2622
Web: www.edwardjones.com

CEO: James D Weddle
CFO: Kevin Bastien
HR: Raymond James
FYE: December 31
Type: Private - Partnershi

This isn't your father's broker. Well maybe it is. The Jones Financial Companies is the parent of Edward Jones an investment brokerage network catering to individual investors. Serving some seven million clients the "Wal-Mart of Wall Street" has thousands of offices (mainly in small cities rural communities and suburbs) in all 50 states and Canada. Brokers preach a conservative buy-and-hold approach offering relatively low-risk investment vehicles such as government bonds blue-chip stocks high-quality mutual funds IRAs and annuities as well as insurance. The company also engages in investment banking underwriting and making markets for corporate securities and municipal bonds.

THE JUDGE GROUP INC

300 CONSHOHOCKEN STATE RD # 300
CONSHOHOCKEN, PA 194283801
Phone: 610-667-7700
Fax: –
Web: www.judge.com

CEO: Martin E. Judge
CFO: Robert G. Alessandrini
HR: –
FYE: September 30
Type: Private

If your business requires staffing technology consulting or training services The Judge Group will be predisposed to render a verdict in your favor. The company offers temporary and permanent employee placement services in a wide variety of service and manufacturing sectors but specializes in technology staffing. The company's technology consulting services address such areas as enterprise content management and strategy. It also offers training for IT-related and other professional functions through its Berkeley division. Martin Judge founded the company in 1970.

	Annual Growth	09/07	09/08	09/11	09/12	09/13
Sales ($ mil.)	7.8%	–	188.2	223.0	251.5	274.0
Net income ($ mil.)	(34.4%)	–	–	2.6	2.9	1.1
Market value ($ mil.)	–	–	–	–	–	–
Employees	–	–	–	–	–	570

THE JUILLIARD SCHOOL

60 LINCOLN CENTER PLZ	CEO: –
NEW YORK, NY 100236588	CFO: –
Phone: 212-799-5000	HR: –
Fax: –	FYE: June 30
Web: www.juilliard.edu	Type: Private

The Juilliard School educates some of the top performers from around the world. Students can earn undergraduate and graduate degrees in dance drama and music. The school also has an Evening Division that is geared toward working adults as well as a Pre-College Division that meets on Saturdays between September and May. Primarily a performing arts conservatory the school also enriches the community through outreach and other special programs. Juilliard was founded in 1905 in Greenwich Village and took up residence at Lincoln Center in 1969. Famed alumni include William Hurt Val Kilmer Kevin Kline Laura Linney Winton Marsalis Christopher Reeve Ving Rhames Nadja Salerno-Sonnenberg and Robin Williams.

	Annual Growth	06/04	06/05	06/08	06/09	06/13
Sales ($ mil.)	(65.9%)	–	729,284.6	111.6	35.9	131.8
Net income ($ mil.)	(9.4%)	–	–	35.4	0.0	21.6
Market value ($ mil.)	–	–	–	–	–	–
Employees	–	–	–	–	–	550

THE KANE COMPANY

6500 KANE WAY	CEO: John M. Kane
ELKRIDGE, MD 210756000	CFO: David J Korotkin
Phone: 410-799-3200	HR: –
Fax: –	FYE: December 31
Web: www.kanecompany.com	Type: Private

Many people do business in offices but offices are business for The Kane Company. Through its subsidiaries Kane moves office contents (Office Movers) stores office records (Office Archives) shreds offices records (Office Shredding) and installs office furniture (Office Installers). Another Kane unit offers third-party logistics services including supply chain management and warehousing and distribution; an affiliate provides printing services. Kane which operates from offices in Delaware Maryland New Jersey and Virginia has long relied on federal government agencies in the area as a major source of business. The company was founded in 1969.

	Annual Growth	12/05	12/06	12/07	12/08	12/10
Sales ($ mil.)	(67.4%)	–	–	1,627.5	81.8	56.2
Net income ($ mil.)	2936.3%	–	–	0.0	1.7	1.1
Market value ($ mil.)	–	–	–	–	–	–
Employees	–	–	–	–	–	1,500

THE KANTAR GROUP

501 Kings Hwy. East 4th Fl.	CEO: –
Fairfield CT 06825	CFO: Robert Bowtell
Phone: 203-330-5200	HR: –
Fax: 203-330-5201	FYE: December 31
Web: www.kantargroup.com	Type: Business Segment

The Kantar Group a division of advertising giant WPP Group is one of the world's largest market research organizations. The group offers a wide range of custom and syndicated research services covering such sectors as business-to-business financial services health care and retail. Kantar also encompasses brand consultancies demographics firms and media researchers. It operates across 80 countries through several operating units: Kantar Media Kantar Health Kantar Retail Kantar Japan Kantar Worldpanel and Kantar Operations. Specialist companies include Center Partners Millward Brown Lightspeed Research The Futures Company Added Value Group and TNS Group. The Kantar Group was founded in 1993.

THE KAPLAN THALER GROUP LTD.

Worldwide Plaza 825 8th Ave. 34th Fl.	CEO: Andrew Bruce
New York NY 10019-7498	CFO: –
Phone: 212-474-5000	HR: –
Fax: 212-474-5702	FYE: December 31
Web: www.kaplanthaler.com	Type: Subsidiary

Best known for creating the squawking duck campaign for supplemental insurance firm Aflac The Kaplan Thaler Group is a leading creative advertising agency that not only develops ad campaigns but helps promote those ads in the media. The initiative creates public interest in its campaigns and also scores free media time for its clients. In addition to creative development the firm offers planning and campaign management services as well as branded entertainment development. CEO Linda Kaplan Thaler started the agency in 1997. It is now a subsidiary of Paris-based advertising conglomerate Publicis.

THE KING ARTHUR FLOUR COMPANY INC.

135 Rte. 5 South	CEO: –
Norwich VT 05055	CFO: –
Phone: 802-649-3881	HR: –
Fax: 802-649-3365	FYE: December 31
Web: www.kingarthurflour.com	Type: Private

While other millers are feeling the effect of fewer home bakers The King Arthur Flour Company is doing its best to make its sales rise. King Arthur sells its all-natural flours to retailers bakeries and foodservice companies nationwide. It also sells its flours baking ingredients and equipment at its retail store in Norwich Vermont; through its website; and its catalogs. To drum up confident new customers the company sends baking instructors across the US to teach classes and runs a baking school at its Vermont headquarters. Founded in 1790 King Arthur Flour claims it is the oldest flour company in the US. The company is 100% employee owned.

THE KLEINFELDER GROUP INC

550 W C ST STE 1200	CEO: William Siegel
SAN DIEGO, CA 921013532	CFO: –
Phone: 858-320-2000	HR: Jan Perez
Fax: –	FYE: March 31
Web: www.kleinfelder.com	Type: Private

The Kleinfelder Group isn't afraid to get its hands dirty. Since its start as a materials testing lab in 1961 the company has expanded to become one of the largest engineering consulting and design groups in the US. Kleinfelder's operating subsidiaries offer soils and materials testing geotechnical engineering construction management and environmental services. With about 50 domestic offices and locations in Australia and Guam the group targets the energy transportation water commercial/industrial government and education markets; projects run the gamut from building underground parking garages to establishing wind farms. Jim Kleinfelder who retired in 1993 founded the employee-owned company.

	Annual Growth	03/10	03/11	03/12	03/13	03/14
Sales ($ mil.)	3.0%	–	222.5	216.9	224.2	243.0
Net income ($ mil.)	(43.9%)	–	–	5.3	1.0	1.7
Market value ($ mil.)	–	–	–	–	–	–
Employees	–	–	–	–	–	1,522

THE KOLL COMPANY

4343 Von Karman Ave.
Newport Beach CA 92660
Phone: 949-833-3030
Fax: 949-250-4344
Web: www.koll.com

CEO: Don Koll
CFO: Jim Micell
HR: –
FYE: December 31
Type: Private

The Koll Company knows real estate — commercial real estate to be exact. Founded in 1962 by chairman and CEO Donald Koll as a general construction company Koll quickly grew into a commercial developer of more than 90 million sq. ft. of multi-tenant suburban offices industrial parks and retail centers with a focus on the Western US from Washington to Texas. Its development projects are typically 5 to 50 acres in size while its management portfolio includes more than 6 million sq. ft. of office and light industrial space. Koll acquires and manages these properties for both institutional investors and high-net-worth individuals.

THE LANCASTER GENERAL HOSPITAL

555 N DUKE ST
LANCASTER, PA 176022207
Phone: 717-544-5511
Fax: –
Web: www.lancastergeneralhealth.org

CEO: Thomas E. (Tom) Beeman
CFO: Dennis R. Roemer
HR: Regina Mingle
FYE: June 30
Type: Private

Lancaster General Health (LG Health) is a 690-bed integrated health care delivery system serving residents of Lancaster County Pennsylvania and surrounding areas. Its flagship Lancaster General Hospital (LGH) - opened in 1893 - is known for its cardiology orthopedic and intensive care specialties. A separate Women & Babies hospital cares for those just making it into the world. The not-for-profit system also includes multiple outpatient clinics a rehab hospital home care services and a nursing center and health care college as well as a medical group of more than 300 physicians operating at more than 40 practices throughout the region.

	Annual Growth	06/10	06/11	06/12	06/13	06/14
Sales ($ mil.)	1.2%	–	838.7	852.0	823.0	868.0
Net income ($ mil.)	–	–	–	31.6	(15.4)	(14.0)
Market value ($ mil.)	–	–	–	–	–	–
Employees	–	–	–	–	–	5,000

THE LANE CONSTRUCTION CORPORATION

90 FIELDSTONE CT
CHESHIRE, CT 064101212
Phone: 203-235-3351
Fax: –
Web: www.laneconstruct.com

CEO: Robert E Alger
CFO: James M Ferrell
HR: –
FYE: December 31
Type: Private

Lane likes people to be in the fast lane. For more than a century the heavy civil contractor and its affiliates have been widening paving and constructing lanes for highways bridges runways railroads dams and mass transit systems in the eastern and southern US. The group also produces bituminous and precast concrete and mines aggregates at plants and quarries in the northeastern mid-Atlantic and southern US. Additionally it sells and leases construction equipment. Founded in 1902 Lane Construction has offices in more than 20 states and is owned by descendants of Lane and employees.

	Annual Growth	12/08	12/09	12/11	12/12	12/13
Sales ($ mil.)	6.5%	–	848.3	1,002.4	1,229.9	1,091.1
Net income ($ mil.)	–	–	–	20.4	26.8	(22.8)
Market value ($ mil.)	–	–	–	–	–	–
Employees	–	–	–	–	–	3,500

THE LAYTON COMPANIES INC.

9090 S. Sandy Pkwy.
Sandy UT 84070
Phone: 801-568-9090
Fax: 801-563-4863
Web: www.laytoncompanies.com

CEO: David S Layton
CFO: Dallis Christensen
HR: Utah-Gerald Biesinger
FYE: December 31
Type: Private

The Layton Companies likes to keep its hand in a lot of construction pots. The holding company for Interior Construction Specialists and Layton Construction Company provides engineering and construction services for just about any kind of structure from retail stores to hazardous waste incineration facilities. Founded in 1953 it has completed projects in some 25 states although its primary focus is the West. Interior Construction Specialists provides interior build-outs and remodeling while Layton Construction Company is dedicated to commercial construction. The company sold subsidiary CEntry Constructors & Engineers to Danish firm FLSmidth & Co. in 2008.

THE LEGAL AID SOCIETY

199 WATER ST FRNT 3
NEW YORK, NY 100383526
Phone: 212-577-3346
Fax: –
Web: www.legal-aid.org

CEO: –
CFO: –
HR: Adriene Holder
FYE: June 30
Type: Private

Serving as a law firm for many of New York City's less fortunate residents The Legal Aid Society represents people who could not otherwise afford a lawyer in civil criminal and juvenile rights cases. The society has a staff of some 1100 lawyers. It also draws upon the work of more than 700 investigators social workers and paralegals who combined handle about 300000 individual cases and matters each year. A not-for-profit organization The Legal Aid Society receives government money for its work in criminal and some juvenile matters and it counts on donations to support its efforts in civil cases. The Legal Aid Society was founded in 1876.

	Annual Growth	06/09	06/10	06/11	06/12	06/13
Sales ($ mil.)	8.6%	–	170.0	176.0	189.1	217.8
Net income ($ mil.)	279.1%	–	–	0.6	0.2	8.6
Market value ($ mil.)	–	–	–	–	–	–
Employees	–	–	–	–	–	1,600

THE LINCOLN NATIONAL LIFE INSURANCE COMPANY

1300 S. Clinton St.
Fort Wayne IN 46802
Phone: 260-455-2000
Fax: 208-387-2598
Web: www.syscoidaho.com

CEO: –
CFO: Frederick Crawford
HR: –
FYE: December 31
Type: Subsidiary

Lincoln National Life Insurance is the primary insurance subsidiary of Lincoln National Corporation (which operates as Lincoln Financial Group) — honest. Lincoln National Life Insurance sells term life universal life variable universal life and whole life insurance policies to affluent individuals. It also provides corporate-owned life insurance policies to businesses seeking insurance on their key employees and group insurance products. The company distributes its life insurance policies through Lincoln Financial Distributors and associates of Lincoln Financial Advisors. Founded in 1905 Lincoln National Life Insurance was the first affiliate in the Lincoln Financial Group to bear the Lincoln name.

THE LONG & FOSTER COMPANIES INC.

14501 George Carter Way	CEO: P Wesley Foster Jr
Chantilly VA 20151	CFO: –
Phone: 703-653-8500	HR: –
Fax: 703-591-6978	FYE: December 31
Web: www.longandfoster.com	Type: Private

Longing to find your dream home? Long & Foster will gladly help. The company's flagship subsidiary Long & Foster Real Estate is one of the largest residential real estate brokerages in the Mid-Atlantic with more than 180 offices primarily in the Washington DC/Baltimore area. The brokerage has some 12000 sales agents. Other subsidiaries offer property management commercial brokerage business relocation homeowners insurance title insurance and commercial and residential mortgage financing. Chairman and CEO Wesley Foster co-founded the company which he now owns with partner Henry Long.

THE LOS ANGELES LAKERS INC.

555 N. Nash St.	CEO: Jerry H Buss
El Segundo CA 90245	CFO: –
Phone: 310-426-6000	HR: –
Fax: 310-426-6115	FYE: July 31
Web: www.nba.com/lakers	Type: Private

These Lakers can be found navigating the choppy waters of the National Basketball Association. The Los Angeles Lakers professional basketball franchise is one of the most popular and successful teams in the NBA earning 16 championship titles since joining the league in 1949. The team was founded in 1947 as the Minnesota Lakers of the National Basketball League and moved to California in 1960. Its roster has included such Hall of Fame players as Kareem Abdul-Jabbar Wilt Chamberlain Earvin "Magic" Johnson and Jerry West. The franchise has been controlled by real estate mogul Jerry Buss since 1979; billionaire Philip Anschutz Dr. Soon-Shiong and developer Edward Roski also own minority stakes in the team.

THE LOUIS BERGER GROUP INC.

412 Mt. Kemble Ave.	CEO: –
Morristown NJ 07960-6654	CFO: Luke McKinnon
Phone: 973-407-1000	HR: –
Fax: 973-267-6468	FYE: June 30
Web: www.louisberger.com	Type: Private

The Louis Berger Group provides civil structural mechanical electrical and environmental engineering services for commercial and government projects around the world. It also provides financial services maintenance and management services. Louis Berger has worked on high-profile projects such as the Pennsylvania Turnpike the redevelopment of the World Trade Center site and the renovation of the Lincoln Memorial Reflecting Pool. Louis Berger also has has built highways airports seaports and dams and contributed to cultural and environmental preservation for projects in 140 countries. The privately-held group also has worked on reconstruction projects in Iraq and Afghanistan.

THE LUBRIZOL CORPORATION

29400 Lakeland Blvd.	CEO: James L Hambrick
Wickliffe OH 44092-2298	CFO: Charles P Cooley
Phone: 440-943-4200	HR: –
Fax: 440-943-5337	FYE: December 31
Web: www.lubrizol.com	Type: Subsidiary

Lubrizol is a smooth operator — the company is the world's #1 maker of additives for lubricants and fuels. The manufacturer operates through two business segments: Lubrizol Additives and Lubrizol Advanced Materials. The Lubrizol Additives segment includes engine oil additives that fight sludge buildup viscosity breakdown and component wear; fuel additives designed to control deposits and improve combustion; and additives for paints inks greases metalworking and other markets. Lubrizol's Advanced Materials segment (performance coatings and chemicals) delivers its products to the personal care and rubber and plastics markets.

THE MANISCHEWITZ COMPANY

444 Madison Ave.	CEO: Mark Weinsten
New York NY 10022	CFO: –
Phone: 212-688-4500	HR: Bea Scotti
Fax: 212-888-5025	FYE: March 31
Web: www.rabfoodgroup.com	Type: Private

You might say this company is made from matzo. The Manischewitz Company (formerly R.A.B. Holdings) is a leading producer of packaged kosher foods. Besides its namesake brand of traditional matzo it makes Guiltless Gourmet dips and chips Asian Harvest vegetables and sauces and Tam Tams snack crackers. The company also licenses the Manischewitz name for use with wine and other items. Tracing its heritage to 1888 when Lithuanian immigrant Rabbi Dov Behr (who subsequently added "Manischewitz" to his name) began baking and selling matzo in Cincinnati the company has earned the title as the largest maker of processed kosher food products in the world.

THE MARTIN AGENCY INC.

1 Shockoe Plaza	CEO: Matthew Williams
Richmond VA 23219-4132	CFO: Janet White
Phone: 804-698-8000	HR: –
Fax: 804-698-8001	FYE: December 31
Web: www.martinagency.com	Type: Subsidiary

Those disgruntled cavemen and that anthropomorphic gecko just can't seem to catch a break in today's society. Responsible for those ubiquitous GEICO ads The Martin Agency is a leading full-service advertising firm with offices in Richmond Virginia and in New York. Part of global advertising conglomerate Interpublic Group the agency offers creative development and campaign management services for both national and regional advertisers along with media planning and strategic consulting. It offers services for interactive marketing efforts and direct marketing campaigns. Martin also has a consultancy division which provides corporate communications and media relations services.

THE MARTIN-BROWER COMPANY L.L.C.

9500 W. Bryn Mawr Ave. Ste. 700
Rosemont IL 60018-5218
Phone: 847-227-6500
Fax: 847-671-4725
Web: www.martin-brower.com

CEO: Gregory Nickele
CFO: Joseph Tomczak
HR: –
FYE: December 31
Type: Subsidiary

You can hardly say this food distributor is just clowning around. The Martin-Brower Company is the largest supplier of food and materials to McDonald's restaurants worldwide. The company delivers some 500 million cases of its products to about 17000 Golden Arches locations each year. Martin-Brower supplies such items as frozen refrigerated and dry food and bakery and paper products. In addition to its food-distribution services Martin-Brower provides global logistics management services to other food and beverage suppliers through its MBX Logistics unit. The company is a wholly-owned subsidiary of food and beverage distribution giant Reyes Holdings.

THE MATHWORKS INC.

3 Apple Hill Dr.
Natick MA 01760-2098
Phone: 508-647-7000
Fax: 508-647-7001
Web: www.mathworks.com

CEO: –
CFO: –
HR: –
FYE: December 31
Type: Private

If you haven't heard of MATLAB chances are you aren't a scientist or engineer. The MathWorks provides technical computing software used for data analysis visualization and mathematical computations. Its MATLAB Simulink and Polyspace products are used in such industries as aerospace automotive communications electronics financial services and industrial automation. MathWorks products are also used for teaching and research at more than 5000 universities. The company was co-founded in 1984 by majority owners Jack Little (president) Cleve Moler (chief mathematician) and Steve Bangert.

THE MECHANICS BANK

3170 Hilltop Mall Rd.
Richmond CA 94806
Phone: 510-262-7980
Fax: 510-262-7941
Web: www.mechbank.com

CEO: Kristen Weisser
CFO: –
HR: –
FYE: December 31
Type: Private

The Mechanics Bank operates more than 30 branches serving the San Francisco Bay and greater Sacramento areas of California. It offers standard products such as checking and savings accounts CDs and Visa credit and debit cards. Commercial real estate loans account for more than half of the bank's loan portfolio followed by consumer installment commercial and industrial construction and land development and residential mortgage loans. The bank also offers investment management trust financial planning private banking brokerage and retirement plan administration services. Descendents of founder E.M. Downer control The Mechanics Bank.

THE MEGA LIFE AND HEALTH INSURANCE COMPANY

9151 Boulevard 26
North Richland Hills TX 76180
Phone: 817-255-3100
Fax: 817-255-5394
Web: https://www.megainsurance.com

CEO: Kenneth J Fasola
CFO: K Alec Mahmood
HR: –
FYE: December 31
Type: Subsidiary

The MEGA Life and Health Insurance Company hopes to make big waves in the insurance business. The company primarily offers health insurance plans including traditional PPO and high-deductible policies and related products to small businesses individuals (including the self-employed) and families. In addition the firm offers ancillary dental vision accident and disability coverage. A subsidiary insurance holding company HealthMarkets MEGA is licensed to issue policies in nearly all US states. Its dedicated sales agency markets the company's products through a network of independent and affiliated agents.

THE MELTING POT RESTAURANTS INC.

8810 Twin Lakes Blvd.
Tampa FL 33614
Phone: 813-881-0055
Fax: 813-889-9361
Web: www.meltingpot.com

CEO: Mark Johnston
CFO: Scott Pierce
HR: Connie Troy
FYE: December 31
Type: Private

The Melting Pot Restaurants wants its customers to bubble bubble all their toil and trouble away over a pot of cheesy fondue. The company operates and franchises a chain of more than 140 restaurants in about three dozen states that specialize in themed multi-course fondue meals for couples. Its dipping sauces range from cheeses pestos and teriyakis to flambeed chocolates. Each restaurant also offers an extensive list of wines cognacs and cordials. The first Melting Pot opened in Florida in 1975. Mark and Bob Johnston (brothers) opened the first franchised location in 1979 and bought the chain in 1985.

THE MERCHANTS COMPANY

1100 EDWARDS ST
HATTIESBURG, MS 394015511
Phone: 601-353-2461
Fax: –
Web: www.themerchantscompany.com

CEO: Andrew B. (Andy) Mercier
CFO: Jarrod Gray
HR: June Butler
FYE: September 30
Type: Private

The Merchants Company which does business as Merchants Foodservice is a leading foodservice supplier that serves more than 6000 customers in 10 Southeastern states. From a handful of distribution warehouses in Alabama Georgia Mississippi and South Carolina the company supplies a wide range of food and non-food items to restaurants hospitals schools and other foodservice operations. The company was founded in 1904 as Fain Grocery Co. a wholesale grocery distributor and changed its name to Merchants Company in 1927. It began focusing on foodservice distribution in 1982 and was acquired by family owned holding company Tatum Development in 1988.

	Annual Growth	09/06	09/07	09/08	09/10	09/11
Sales ($ mil.)	–	–	–	(2,033.8)	441.5	489.1
Net income ($ mil.)	2341.1%	–	–	0.0	5.2	2.4
Market value ($ mil.)	–	–	–	–	–	–
Employees	–	–	–	–	–	500

THE METHODIST HOSPITAL

6565 FANNIN ST
HOUSTON, TX 770302707
Phone: 713-790-3311
Fax: –
Web: www.methodisthealth.com

CEO: Marc L. Boom
CFO: Kevin Burns
HR: –
FYE: December 31
Type: Private

Houston Methodist (formerly The Methodist Hospital) owns and operates seven Houston-area medical centers including the flagship location which has more than 800 beds and is known for innovations in urology and neuro-surgery among other specialties. Other hospitals include Houston Methodist West Houston Methodist Sugar Land Houston Methodist San Jacinto Houston Methodist Willowbrook Houston Methodist St. John and Houston Methodist St. Catherine. Together the hospitals have nearly 2000 beds and employ more than 4500 physicians. In addition to hospitals the organization operates emergency care imaging outpatient and rehab centers and manages a physician organization of nearly 400.

	Annual Growth	12/09	12/10	12/11	12/12	12/13
Sales ($ mil.)	7.3%	–	2,115.8	2,284.7	2,331.0	2,616.2
Net income ($ mil.)	160.0%	–	–	101.1	386.6	683.5
Market value ($ mil.)	–	–	–	–	–	–
Employees	–	–	–	–	–	14,000

THE METHODIST HOSPITALS INC

600 GRANT ST
GARY, IN 464026001
Phone: 219-886-4000
Fax: –
Web: www.methodistcms.methodisthospitals.org

CEO: –
CFO: John C Diehl
HR: Alex Horvath
FYE: December 31
Type: Private

The Methodist Hospitals Inc. is a not-for-profit community-based health care system that provides medical care to Indiana residents. More than 580 physicians representing some 60 specialties serve its two campus hospitals which have a combined total of about 640 beds. The system provides care for a range of specialized areas from neurology and neurosurgery oncology and home health and hospice to rehabilitation and orthopedics. The emergency department treats more than 59000 patients a year. The system also provides screenings charitable care and community education programs. The Methodist Hospitals established in 1923 reinvests all of its profits to improve patient care.

	Annual Growth	12/01	12/02	12/03	12/04	12/09
Sales ($ mil.)	1.3%	–	267.1	298.6	310.5	291.9
Net income ($ mil.)	(3.6%)	–	–	7.4	9.9	5.9
Market value ($ mil.)	–	–	–	–	–	–
Employees	–	–	–	–	–	3,260

THE METROHEALTH SYSTEM

2500 METROHEALTH DR
CLEVELAND, OH 441091900
Phone: 216-398-6000
Fax: –
Web: www.metrohealth.org

CEO: Akram Boutros
CFO: Craig Richmond
HR: –
FYE: December 31
Type: Private

Helping Cleveland's metropolitan citizens stay healthy (and healing them when they aren't) is what MetroHealth System is all about. At the center of the system is MetroHealth Medical Center a level I trauma center and acute care hospital that serves as a teaching affiliate for Case Western Reserve University. Services include oncology behavioral health vascular care orthopedics burn care and pediatrics. The system also operates outpatient clinics long-term care facilities a regional rehabilitation clinic a heart and vascular center two skilled nursing centers an outpatient center and a medical helicopter program. MetroHealth is owned by Ohio's Cuyahoga County.

	Annual Growth	12/06	12/07	12/08	12/09	12/13
Sales ($ mil.)	(13.5%)	–	1,942.0	642.3	673.5	813.1
Net income ($ mil.)	–	–	–	(3.8)	58.3	41.8
Market value ($ mil.)	–	–	–	–	–	–
Employees	–	–	–	–	–	6,000

THE METROPOLITAN MUSEUM OF ART

1000 5TH AVE FRNT
NEW YORK, NY 10028-0198
Phone: 212-879-5500
Fax: –
Web: www.metmuseum.org

CEO: –
CFO: –
HR: –
FYE: June 30
Type: Private

You won't find too much about a certain New York baseball team at this Met. One of the world's premier cultural institutions The Metropolitan Museum of Art (also known as "the Met") acquires and exhibits artwork from around the world. Its collection of more than 2 million pieces ranges from the prehistoric era to the present day. In addition to hosting exhibits the Met loans artwork to other museums publishes books and catalogs and develops educational programs. It also displays art online. The City of New York owns the museum's 2 million-sq.-ft. complex which is located on the east side of Central Park; the museum itself owns its art collection. The Met was founded in 1870.

	Annual Growth	06/09	06/10	06/10	06/12	06/13
Sales ($ mil.)	3.7%	–	292.9	470.0	314.2	326.9
Net income ($ mil.)	328.7%	–	3.7	124.7	(193.8)	290.4
Market value ($ mil.)	–	–	–	–	–	–
Employees	–	–	–	–	–	2,372

THE MIDDLE TENNESSEE ELECTRIC MEMBERSHIP CORPORATION

555 NEW SALEM HWY
MURFREESBORO, TN 371293390
Phone: 615-890-9762
Fax: –
Web: www.mtemc.com

CEO: –
CFO: Bernie Steen
HR: Shannon Kaprive
FYE: June 30
Type: Private

Middle Tennessee Electric Membership Corporation's service territory is smack dab in the middle of Tennessee. The utility cooperative distributes electricity to 190750 residential and business customers (member/owners) in four counties (Cannon Rutherford Williamson and Wilson) via more than 10470 miles of power lines connected to 34 electric distribution substations. Middle Tennessee Electric purchases its power supply from the Tennessee Valley Authority. The corporation is Tennessee's largest electric cooperative and the sixth largest in the US.

	Annual Growth	06/09	06/10	06/11	06/12	06/13
Sales ($ mil.)	(0.0%)	–	–	525.1	510.5	524.7
Net income ($ mil.)	(5.9%)	–	–	31.4	19.4	27.8
Market value ($ mil.)	–	–	–	–	–	–
Employees	–	–	–	–	–	375

THE MITRE CORPORATION

202 BURLINGTON RD
BEDFORD, MA 017301420
Phone: 781-271-2000
Fax: –
Web: www.mitre.org

CEO: Alfred Grasso
CFO: Mark W. Kontos
HR: Julie Gravallese
FYE: October 05
Type: Private

Politicians try to engineer a better government but MITRE governs the country's best engineering. A private not-for-profit organization MITRE Corporation provides consulting engineering and technical research services primarily for agencies of the federal government. It employs more than 7000 scientists engineers and other specialists who work at primary research facilities in Massachusetts and Virginia. It also manages serveral federally funded research and development centers serving organizations such as the Department of Defense the Federal Aviation Administration the Internal Revenue Service and the Department of Veterans Affairs. MITRE was founded in 1958 by former MIT researchers.

	Annual Growth	10/04	10/05	10/06	10/07	10/08
Sales ($ mil.)	10.9%	–	–	–	1,113.7	1,234.7
Net income ($ mil.)	(4.6%)	–	–	–	23.4	22.3
Market value ($ mil.)	–	–	–	–	–	–
Employees	–	–	–	–	–	7,000

THE MOSAIC COMPANY
NYSE: MOS

3033 Campus Dr. Ste. E490
Plymouth MN 55441
Phone: 763-577-2700
Fax: 763-559-2860
Web: www.mosaicco.com

CEO: –
CFO: Lawrence W Stranghoener
HR: –
FYE: May 31
Type: Public

Lots of little pieces have joined together to form The Mosaic Company's big picture. The company ranks as one of the world's largest makers of phosphate and potash crop nutrients. Mosaic's potash operations position the company at the top of the industry along with Uralkali and PotashCorp. Mosaic ranks as the second-largest potash fertilizer company in North America (behind PotashCorp). Mosaic's potash mines are located in Canada and the US. The company does about two-thirds of its business outside the US; India and Brazil are its biggest international markets.

THE NATIONAL COLLEGIATE ATHLETIC ASSOCIATION

700 W. Washington St.
Indianapolis IN 46206-6222
Phone: 317-917-6222
Fax: 317-917-6888
Web: www.ncaa.org

CEO: –
CFO: Kathleen McNeely
HR: –
FYE: August 31
Type: Private - Associatio

The National Collegiate Athletic Association (NCAA) supports the intercollegiate sports activities of around 1300 member schools and organizations. A not-for-profit organization the NCAA administers scholarship and grant programs enforces conduct and eligibility rules and works to support and promote the needs of student athletes. The association is known for its lucrative branding and television deals such as those surrounding the popular "March Madness" tournament for Division I men's basketball. Seeking reform of athletics rules and regulations officials from 13 schools formed the Intercollegiate Athletic Association of the United States in 1906. The organization took its current name in 1910.

THE MOTORISTS INSURANCE GROUP

471 E. Broad St. Ste. 200
Columbus OH 43215
Phone: 614-225-8211
Fax: 614-232-1730
Web: www.motoristsgroup.com

CEO: David Kaufman
CFO: Michael L Wiseman
HR: –
FYE: December 31
Type: Private - Mutual Com

Whether you're a driver homeowner or entrepreneur chances are the Motorists Insurance Group has something for you. Through its group of 10 operating companies the firm offers personal and commercial property/casualty and life insurance products primarily in the Midwest but in other areas of the US as well. Its main subsidiaries include Motorists Mutual Insurance (car home and business policies) and Motorists Life Insurance. Motorists Insurance Group is affiliated with several other regional insurers and brokerage groups through management contracts and reinsurance arrangements. Among its affiliates are Motorists Commercial Wilson Mutual Iowa Mutual Insurance and Phenix Mutual Fire Insurance.

THE NATURE CONSERVANCY

4245 N. Fairfax Dr. Ste. 100
Arlington VA 22203-1606
Phone: 703-841-5300
Fax: 703-841-9692
Web: nature.org

CEO: –
CFO: –
HR: –
FYE: June 30
Type: Private - Not-for-Pr

The Nature Conservancy is a nonprofit dedicated to preserving the diversity of Earth's wildlife by saving some 120 million acres of land 5000 miles of rivers and 100 marine areas in every US state and more than 30 countries worldwide. The organization boasts more than 1 million members. The Nature Conservancy originally carried out its mission by simply buying land but it has evolved to incorporate other methods to further its goals. In addition to land acquisition the organization partners with government corporate and private entities to reduce harmful use of natural areas to create conservation-friendly public policy and to increase conservation funding. The Nature Conservancy was founded in 1951.

THE NATIONAL ASSOCIATION FOR THE EXCHANGE OF INDUSTRIAL RESOURCE

560 MCCLURE ST
GALESBURG, IL 614014286
Phone: 309-343-0704
Fax: –
Web: www.naeir.org

CEO: Gary C Smith
CFO: Robert B Gilstrap
HR: Bob Clark
FYE: June 30
Type: Private

The National Association for the Exchange of Industrial Resources (NAEIR) is like a modern day Robin Hood without the stealing or tights. The non-profit organization collects excess inventory from corporations and distributes the merchandise to its members: schools churches and charities. Members pay a fee to join and shipping costs for the items but the goods are free. Donations include office supplies computer software clothing books classroom materials toys and personal care products from donors including Microsoft Kid Brands and General Electric. NAEIR has more than 9500 members and receives donations from some 7500 corporations. Manufacturing executive Norbert Smith founded NAEIR in 1977.

	Annual Growth	06/10	06/11	06/12	06/13	06/14
Sales ($ mil.)	(16.5%)	–	96.4	88.0	86.1	56.1
Net income ($ mil.)	–	–	–	(8.0)	22.5	(12.1)
Market value ($ mil.)	–	–	–	–	–	–
Employees	–	–	–	–	–	80

THE NEW HOME COMPANY INC
NYS: NWHM

85 Enterprise, Suite 450
Aliso Viejo, CA 92656
Phone: 949 382-7800
Fax: –
Web: www.thenewhomecompany.com

CEO: –
CFO: Wayne J. Stelmar
HR: Fabienne Smolinski
FYE: December 31
Type: Public

The New Home Company (TNHC) has been building its business across California since 2009. Founded by a handful of homebuilding executives the developer builds and markets homes throughout the Golden State. TNHC has delivered some 580 homes since its inception via company projects unconsolidated joint ventures and fee building projects. It operates in Northern California's El Dorado Placer and Sacramento counties as well as in Southern California's Orange Ventura and Los Angeles counties. Home range in price from $300000 and $3.2 million and from 800 sq. ft. to 5300 sq. ft. TNHC which serves a variety of clients such as first-time homebuyers and luxury clients filed a $113-million IPO in January 2014.

	Annual Growth	12/10	12/11	12/12	12/13	12/14
Sales ($ mil.)	72.7%	16.8	42.1	55.4	83.2	149.7
Net income ($ mil.)	–	(0.3)	(2.3)	(1.4)	6.7	4.8
Market value ($ mil.)	–	–	–	–	–	238.2
Employees	35.2%	–	–	128	153	234

THE NEW LIBERTY HOSPITAL DISTRICT OF CLAY COUNTY MISSOURI

2525 GLENN HENDREN DR	CEO: –
LIBERTY, MO 640689625	CFO: Erin Parde
Phone: 816-781-7200	HR: Patty Downey
Fax: –	FYE: June 30
Web: www.libertyhospital.org	Type: Private

New Liberty Hospital District which operates as Liberty Hospital hopes to liberate health care patients in northwestern Missouri. The facility is a 250-bed acute care hospital that serves communities located north of Kansas City. Founded in 1974 Liberty Hospital offers general and specialty health care services including trauma care obstetrics cancer care diagnostics surgical services vascular and cardiac medicine (including open-heart surgery) rehabilitation and pediatrics. The not-for-profit medical facility has more than 300 physicians on staff and also operates a skilled nursing facility and offers home health and hospice services.

	Annual Growth	06/02	06/03	06/04	06/05	06/08
Sales ($ mil.)	(47.1%)	–	–	2,010.8	122.9	158.0
Net income ($ mil.)	1690.1%	–	–	0.0	13.8	17.4
Market value ($ mil.)	–	–	–	–	–	–
Employees	–	–	–	–	–	1,700

THE NEW SCHOOL

66 W 12TH ST	CEO: –
NEW YORK, NY 100118871	CFO: –
Phone: 212-229-5600	HR: –
Fax: –	FYE: June 30
Web: www.newschool.edu	Type: Private

When James Lipton asks you what your favorite swear word is you know you've made it. The New School's drama department (formerly called The Actor's Studio) was made famous by the cable show Inside the Actors Studio which features Lipton interviewing movie and television stars. The school offers degrees in theater for playwriting directing and acting and has taught "Method" acting to grads such as Marlon Brando and Robert De Niro. It is also home to Parsons The New School for Design and has schools devoted to general studies liberal arts social research management and urban policy and music. More than 10500 traditional students and 5600 continuing education students are enrolled at The New School.

	Annual Growth	06/10	06/11	06/12	06/13	06/14
Sales ($ mil.)	2.9%	–	305.3	317.0	313.8	332.8
Net income ($ mil.)	–	–	–	(3.6)	11.2	82.4
Market value ($ mil.)	–	–	–	–	–	–
Employees	–	–	–	–	–	855

THE NEW YORK AND PRESBYTERIAN HOSPITAL

525 E 68TH ST	CEO: –
NEW YORK, NY 100654870	CFO: Phyllis R. Lantos
Phone: 212-746-5454	HR: Shaun Smith
Fax: –	FYE: December 31
Web: www.nyp.org	Type: Private

The New York and Presbyterian Hospital is a learned institution: The hospital is affiliated with both the Columbia University College of Physicians & Surgeons and the Weill Cornell Medical College of Cornell University. Known as NewYork-Presbyterian Hospital the organization comprises two major medical centers Columbia University Medical Center and Weill Cornell Medical Center which conduct educational and research programs in partnership with the universities. The two facilities combined have about 2600 beds and offer specialized programs for burns digestive diseases pediatrics women's health and other conditions. NewYork-Presbyterian Hospital is part of the NewYork-Presbyterian Healthcare System.

	Annual Growth	12/02	12/03	12/04	12/06	12/13
Sales ($ mil.)	6.5%	–	–	2,427.2	2,833.5	4,264.5
Net income ($ mil.)	29.9%	–	–	56.5	171.7	595.1
Market value ($ mil.)	–	–	–	–	–	–
Employees	–	–	–	–	–	15,078

THE NEW YORK INDEPENDENT SYSTEM OPERATOR INC

10 KREY BLVD	CEO: Stephen G Whitley
RENSSELAER, NY 121449681	CFO: Mary McGarvey
Phone: 518-356-6000	HR: –
Fax: –	FYE: December 31
Web: www.nyiso.com	Type: Private

Keeping the lights on in Times Square is only part of the job description of the New York Independent System Operator (New York ISO). The company which replaced the New York Power Pool manages and monitors wholesale activities on the state's transmission grid which consists of more than 11000 miles of high-voltage lines. The New York ISO is charged with providing fair access to the state's competitive wholesale power market while ensuring the reliable efficient and safe delivery of power to New York's 19.5 million residents. New York ISO had 37900 MW of generating capacity in 2013. The not-for-profit company is governed by a 10-person board of directors.

	Annual Growth	12/07	12/08	12/09	12/10	12/13
Sales ($ mil.)	–	–	0.0	139.3	149.4	159.8
Net income ($ mil.)	–	–	–	0.0	0.0	0.0
Market value ($ mil.)	–	–	–	–	–	–
Employees	–	–	–	–	–	500

THE NEW YORK OBSERVER LLC

915 Broadway 9th Fl.	CEO: –
New York NY 10010	CFO: Kartos Vos
Phone: 212-755-2400	HR: –
Fax: 212-980-2087	FYE: March 31
Web: www.observer.com	Type: Private

This company's observations help make its paper the talk of the town. Through its eponymous salmon-colored weekly tabloid The New York Observer covers the news and gossip of Gotham's social elite. The paper focuses much of its attention on the high and mighty within the media industry as well as movers and shakers in New York City's real estate business. The company also publishes The Commercial Observer covering the commercial real estate market. In addition to its print publication The New York Observer distributes content online. Former investment banker Arthur Carter started The New York Observer in 1987. The company is now owned by Jared Kushner son of New Jersey developer Charles Kushner.

THE NEWARK GROUP INC.

20 Jackson Dr.	CEO: Frank Papa
Cranford NJ 07016	CFO: –
Phone: 908-276-4000	HR: –
Fax: 908-276-2888	FYE: April 30
Web: www.newarkgroup.com	Type: Private

Newark is proof that one man's trash is another's cash. Through several segments the company collects secondary fibers and produces 100% recycled paperboard and paperboard products. Its Recovery and Recycling segment collects and recovers the recycled raw materials while Paperboard Mills produces more than 500000 tons of recycled paper annually. Its Paperboard Products segment makes roll finishing materials such as cores tubes spools and roll headers and Newark BCI / Graphic Board caters to the coverboard puzzle and game markets. Solidboard Products makes packaging for produce and other food goods. Newark serves the paper and packaging printing recycling and construction industries.

THE NEWTRON GROUP L L C

8183 W EL CAJON DR
BATON ROUGE, LA 708158093
Phone: 225-927-8921
Fax: –
Web: www.thenewtrongroup.com

CEO: Newton B Thomas
CFO: Tami H Misuraca
HR: Jordan Abels
FYE: June 30
Type: Private

Some contractors bomb but The Newtron Group keeps on ticking. Through subsidiaries The Newtron Group offers a variety of industrial electrical and other specialty construction and contracting services nationwide. Services include instrumentation and control systems installation and maintenance; fiber optic installation and testing; industrial pipe and panel fabrication; aviation services; and electrical heat tracing. Newtron serves clients in such industries as refining power generation mining pharmaceuticals and semiconductors. Subsidiaries include electrical contractor Triad Electric and Controls and fiber optics firm Com-Net Services. The Newtron Group has offices in California Louisiana and Texas.

	Annual Growth	06/10	06/11	06/12	06/13	06/14
Sales ($ mil.)	5.6%	–	311.1	296.8	443.1	366.5
Net income ($ mil.)	–	–	–	2.2	0.0	0.0
Market value ($ mil.)	–	–	–	–	–	–
Employees	–	–	–	–	–	2,000

THE NORDAM GROUP INC.

6911 N. Whirlpool Dr.
Tulsa OK 74117
Phone: 918-878-4000
Fax: 918-878-4849
Web: www.nordam.com

CEO: Meredith Siegfried
CFO: –
HR: Michael Williams
FYE: December 31
Type: Private

Trouble getting your engine going? NORDAM one of the world's largest private aerospace companies can give you a lift. The company manufactures overhauls and repairs an array of airframe and engine parts. Its lineup includes bonded-honeycomb and composite parts nacelles (engine housings) and fan/thrust reversers along with interior components. Customers include commercial and business airlines aircraft OEMs US and foreign militaries powerplant manufacturers and aircraft maintenance facility operators. NORDAM was founded in 1969 by Ray Siegfried.

THE NORTH HIGHLAND COMPANY

3333 PIEDMON RD NE STE 10
ATLANTA, GA 303051811
Phone: 404-233-1015
Fax: –
Web: www.northhighland.com

CEO: Dan Reardon
CFO: Kirk Hancock
HR: –
FYE: December 31
Type: Private

The North Highland Company hopes its consulting services help its business clients chart a course toward improved operations. The employee-owned company provides management and technology consulting services through more than 900 professionals working out of 23 offices in 10 US states. Its services cover areas such as business strategy supply chain management marketing and customer service business process improvement and technology management. The company's partners include Big Insight Sourcing Group The Difference and True Bridge Resources.

	Annual Growth	12/02	12/03	12/04	12/05	12/08
Sales ($ mil.)	29.0%	–	47.9	59.5	87.3	170.9
Net income ($ mil.)	(38.8%)	–	–	57.4	2.3	8.0
Market value ($ mil.)	–	–	–	–	–	–
Employees	–	–	–	–	–	2,300

THE NPD GROUP INC.

900 West Shore Rd.
Port Washington NY 11050
Phone: 516-625-0700
Fax: 516-625-2347
Web: www.npd.com

CEO: Tod Johnson
CFO: –
HR: –
FYE: September 30
Type: Private

The NPD Group helps its more than 2000 clients fatten their coffers by giving them the skinny on consumer behavior. A global market research firm the company offers retail sales tracking services partnering with some 900 retailers representing 150000 stores worldwide. It tracks consumer buying behavior through an online panel consisting of nearly 2 million consumers. It offers market insight across numerous industries including apparel consumer electronics foodservice music and software and its DisplaySearch business offers market research analysis specializing in the flat-panel display industry. Controlled by CEO Tod Johnson NPD Group operates through offices in nearly 30 cities around the world.

THE NUTRASWEET COMPANY

222 Merchandise Mart Plaza Ste. 936
Chicago IL 60606
Phone: 312-873-5000
Fax: 312-873-5050
Web: www.nutrasweet.com

CEO: –
CFO: Stephen Gregory
HR: –
FYE: December 31
Type: Private

How sweet are things at The NutraSweet Company? Two hundred times sweeter than sugar its (virtually) no-calorie substitute amply sweetens the company's bottom line. NutraSweet Company is one of the world's largest producers of the artificial sweetener aspartame. It sells its NutraSweet-brand aspartame as an ingredient mostly to manufacturers of food and beverages and less so as a tabletop sweetener to consumers in more than 100 countries worldwide. Since its launch in 1981 NutraSweet's use has grown to enhance more than 5000 food and beverage products. As a sugar substitute it is purchased by millions people worldwide. The company is owned by private investment firm J.W. Childs Associates.

THE OHIO CASUALTY INSURANCE COMPANY

9450 Seward Rd.
Fairfield OH 45014
Phone: 513-603-2400
Fax: 513-603-7900
Web: www.ohiocasualty-ins.com

CEO: –
CFO: –
HR: Ted Heidloff
FYE: December 31
Type: Subsidiary

Ohio Casualty underwrites a variety of commercial property/casualty insurance products including property and general liability equipment breakdown workers' compensation schools and commercial farm policies. The company also offers loss prevention programs to its customers. Ohio Casualty sells its products through independent agents in seven mid-central and eastern states and Washington D.C. Historically half of its customers are contractors or artisans the rest are typically smaller business owners including merchants and service providers. The company is owned by Liberty Mutual.

THE OILGEAR COMPANY

2300 S. 51st St.
Milwaukee WI 53219
Phone: 414-327-1700
Fax: 414-327-0532
Web: www.oilgear.com

CEO: –
CFO: Charles Germain
HR: –
FYE: December 31
Type: Private

A global fluid powerhouse The Oilgear Company (Oilgear) makes hydraulic pumps and other fluid power components (motors valves and fluid meters) electronic controls and systems. Through its Engineered Solutions division the company integrates hydraulic components and electronic controls to ensure they are matched to the appropriate process. Oilgear products are used in the metals machine tool automobile petroleum aerospace chemical plastics lumber rubber and defense industries. It also The company has manufacturing and service facilities in about 15 countries around the globe. Late in 2006 private equity investment firm Mason Wells took Oilgear private at a cost of more than $30 million.

THE OLTMANS CONSTRUCTION CO

10005 MISSION MILL RD
WHITTIER, CA 906011739
Phone: 562-908-9578
Fax: –
Web: www.oltmans.com

CEO: Joseph O. (Joe) Oltmans
CFO: Dan Schlothan
HR: –
FYE: March 31
Type: Private

With projects ranging from the California Speedway to a distribution/warehouse building for TV retail giant HSN Oltmans Construction has done it all. The group offers preconstruction general contracting and design/build project delivery construction management tenant improvements and seismic retrofits among its services for commercial and industrial buildings throughout California Nevada and Arizona. The company also completes its own concrete work. Oltmans is one of the top general contractors in its home state as well as one of the top builders of distribution facilities in the US. The company was founded in 1932 and has been led by three generations of the Oltmans family.

	Annual Growth	03/04	03/05	03/06	03/07	03/08
Sales ($ mil.)	10.4%	–	242.8	317.3	315.5	326.3
Net income ($ mil.)	20.8%	–	–	3.5	4.2	5.1
Market value ($ mil.)	–	–	–	–	–	–
Employees	–	–	–	–	–	409

THE ORCHARD ENTERPRISES INC.

100 Park Ave. 7th Fl.
New York NY 10017
Phone: 212-201-9280
Fax: 212-201-9203
Web: www.theorchard.com

CEO: Bradley Navin
CFO: Nathan Fong
HR: –
FYE: December 31
Type: Private

Music fans looking to pick some tunes online can thank this Orchard. Formerly Digital Music Group The Orchard Enterprises is a leading digital distributor of audio and video recordings serving both digital downloading services and online retailers. The company boasts a catalog of more than 1.3 million music recordings from independent and major labels as well as 4000 titles of video programming. The Orchard supplies digital content to music and video providers such as Apple's iTunes EMusic.com and Netflix and mobile carriers such as Verizon and Vodafone. Dimensional Associates the private equity arm of JDS Capital Management controls the company.

THE PAMPERED CHEF LTD.

1 Pampered Chef Ln.
Addison IL 60101-5630
Phone: 630-261-8900
Fax: 630-261-8522
Web: www.pamperedchef.com

CEO: Tracy Britt Cool
CFO: –
HR: Angel Alvarado
FYE: December 31
Type: Private

Got a hankerin' for crinkle-cut watermelons perfectly wedged apples or artfully zested lemons? Then call The Pampered Chef a direct seller of more than 300 gourmet kitchen gadgets cookware cookbooks and foodstuffs. It boasts about 60000 independent sales reps who hawk their wares at in-home kitchen parties (a la Tupperware) throughout North America Germany and the UK. It's the largest of its kind in the US. Reps demonstrate product use and care and share recipes. As an incentive (a la Mary Kay) reps can ultimately "earn" jewelry and trips. Founded in 1980 by home economist and educator Doris Christopher The Pampered Chef was acquired by Warren Buffett's Berkshire Hathaway in 2002.

THE PARADIES SHOPS LLC

2849 PACES FERRY RD SE # 400
ATLANTA, GA 303396201
Phone: 404-344-7905
Fax: –
Web: www.theparadiesshops.com

CEO: Gregg Paradies
CFO: Kevin Smith
HR: Les Russell
FYE: June 30
Type: Private

For the frequent flyer this is retail paradise. The Paradies Shops operates 550-plus shops in more than 75 airports hotels and aquariums throughout the US and Canada. It serves more than half a billion passengers annually with retail sites that include bookstores gift shops jewelry stores ladies accessory shops newsstands sunglass stores and western stores among others. Paradies Shops is also the exclusive licensee of Brooks Brothers CNBC PGA Tour and the New York Times. The firm operates several hotel properties and the retail program for the Georgia Aquarium in Atlanta. The company was founded by the Paradies family in 1960. In 2010 it sold a majority stake to Freeman Spogli & Co.

	Annual Growth	06/00	06/01	06/02	06/03	06/07
Sales ($ mil.)	10.8%	–	–	223.1	248.0	372.7
Net income ($ mil.)	–	–	–	0.0	0.0	13.7
Market value ($ mil.)	–	–	–	–	–	–
Employees	–	–	–	–	–	4,000

THE PENN MUTUAL LIFE INSURANCE COMPANY

600 Dresher Rd.
Horsham PA 19044
Phone: 215-956-8000
Fax: 215-956-7699
Web: www.pennmutual.com

CEO: Robert E Chappel
CFO: Susan T Deakins
HR: –
FYE: December 31
Type: Private - Mutual Com

Founded in 1847 Penn Mutual Life Insurance offers life insurance annuities and investment products and services. Its core product line consists of life insurance every which way including traditional life insurance products (term life whole and universal life) and a variety of fixed variable and immediate annuities. The company sells its products throughout the US through several channels using both independent and captive agents as well as brokers. Two of its financial services subsidiaries — broker/dealer Hornor Townsend & Kent and Janney Montgomery Scott — also distribute Penn Mutual products.

THE PENNSYLVANIA HOSPITAL OF THE UNIVERSITY OF PENNSYLVANIA HEAL

800 SPRUCE ST	CEO: –
PHILADELPHIA, PA 191076130	CFO: –
Phone: 215-829-3000	HR: Thomas E (Thom) Lawrence
Fax: –	FYE: June 30
Web: www.vet.upenn.edu	Type: Private

Early to bed early to rise may have made Ben Franklin healthy wealthy and wise. But for those not so healthy he (along with Dr. Thomas Bond) found it wise to establish Pennsylvania Hospital the nation's first such medical institution. The hospital is now a part of the University of Pennsylvania Health System (UPHS) and offers a comprehensive range of medical surgical and diagnostic services to the Philadelphia County area. Housing some 520 beds Pennsylvania Hospital offers specialized care in areas such as orthopedics vascular surgery neurosurgery and obstetrics; it is also a leading teaching hospital and a center for clinical research.

	Annual Growth	06/06	06/07	06/08	06/09	06/10
Sales ($ mil.)	7.0%	–	–	–	454.0	485.5
Net income ($ mil.)	–	–	–	–	0.0	27.5
Market value ($ mil.)	–	–	–	–	–	–
Employees	–	–	–	–	–	2,200

THE PENNSYLVANIA LOTTERY

1200 Fulling Mill Rd. Ste. 1	CEO: –
Middletown PA 17057	CFO: –
Phone: 717-702-8000	HR: –
Fax: 717-702-8024	FYE: June 30
Web: www.palottery.state.pa.us	Type: Government-owned

Even if they don't become millionaires senior citizens in Pennsylvania can still benefit from the state lottery. Established in 1971 Pennsylvania Lottery proceeds (more than $18 billion raised since inception) are dedicated to programs geared toward seniors (property-tax relief rent rebates reduced-cost transportation co-pay prescriptions). Proceeds also fund more than 50 Area Agencies on Aging across Pennsylvania. State law mandates that at least 40% of lottery proceeds must be awarded in prizes and about 30% must be used for benefit programs. Games range from the traditional Powerball to daily-wagering game Big 4.

THE PENROD COMPANY

2809 S. Lynnhaven Rd. Ste. 350	CEO: Edward Heidt Jr
Virginia Beach VA 23452	CFO: –
Phone: 757-498-0186	HR: –
Fax: 757-498-1075	FYE: December 31
Web: www.thepenrodcompany.com	Type: Private

Diversified distribution firm The Penrod Company imports and exports forest products for use in the hardwood plywood flooring and furniture industries worldwide. The company also distributes PVC products and metal door hinges and fasteners for use in the residential and commercial construction industries. Penrod operates international subsidiaries: Foresbec in Canada and the UK; Noblebois in France; Penrus in Russia; and St. Raymond Veneers in Canada. Around since 1888 Penrod has supplied materials for some iconic products such as Wurlitzer organs Zenith television cabinets and mahogany interiors for 1965 Cadillac and Buicks. The Penrod Company is owned by CEO Edward Heidt Jr. and President Carl Gade.

THE PERSEUS BOOKS GROUP

387 Park Ave. South	CEO: –
New York NY 10016	CFO: Charles Gallagher
Phone: 212-340-8100	HR: –
Fax: 212-340-8105	FYE: December 31
Web: www.perseusbooksgroup.com	Type: Private

While books from this publishing group don't have wings they do help readers travel great distances. The Perseus Books Group is a large independent publisher made up of about a dozen separate imprints that are Perseus-owned joint ventures or owned by third parties. These include Avalon Travel (travel guides) PublicAffairs (non-fiction) Vanguard Press (fiction and non-fiction) and Westview Press (academic books). Perseus also distributes books from more than 300 smaller presses including Grove/Atlantic and ZAGAT Survey. Its Consortium unit provides marketing and financial services to small independent publishers. The Perseus Books Group was formed in 1996 and is owned by private equity fund Perseus LLC.

THE PEW CHARITABLE TRUSTS

2005 MARKET ST STE 1700	CEO: Rebecca W Rimel
PHILADELPHIA, PA 191037017	CFO: Gina Burkett
Phone: 215-575-9050	HR: –
Fax: –	FYE: June 30
Web: www.pewtrusts.org	Type: Private

Green is the grease The Pew Charitable Trusts uses to help not-for-profits run smoothly. Among the nation's largest private foundations it was established in 1948 in memory of Sun Oil founder Joseph Pew and his wife Mary by four of their children. Seven trusts were created between 1948 and 1979 to promote public health and welfare and to strengthen communities. With more than $5 billion in assets it distributes more than $100 million in grants annually to charitable organizations in culture education environment health and human services public policy and religion. The Pew Trusts has strong ties to Philadelphia and allocates a portion of its grants to programs in that area.

	Annual Growth	06/10	06/11	06/12	06/13	06/14
Sales ($ mil.)	(4.1%)	–	991.0	85.6	588.7	874.7
Net income ($ mil.)	–	–	–	(286.4)	299.5	585.2
Market value ($ mil.)	–	–	–	–	–	–
Employees	–	–	–	–	–	500

THE PHILHARMONIC-SYMPHONY SOCIETY OF NEW YORK INC

10 LINCOLN CENTER PLZ	CEO: Zarin Mehta
NEW YORK, NY 100236912	CFO: David Elliott
Phone: 212-875-5900	HR: –
Fax: –	FYE: August 31
Web: www.nyphil.org	Type: Private

If as in the Chuck Berry song Beethoven were to roll over and tell Tchaikovsky the news that rhythm and blues had supplanted classical music the New York Philharmonic might want to know as well. In addition to the music of Beethoven and Tchaikovsky the orchestra has over the years performed the works of numerous other classical composers along with specially commissioned new music. It presents some 180 concerts annually. The New York Philharmonic's musical director Alan Gilbert is the son of two of the orchestra's violinists and the second-youngest person to hold the position in its history.

	Annual Growth	12/06	12/07	12/08*	08/09	08/10
Sales ($ mil.)	–	–	–	0.0	48.1	60.4
Net income ($ mil.)	–	–	–	0.0	(18.6)	(16.9)
Market value ($ mil.)	–	–	–	–	–	–
Employees	–	–	–	–	–	200

*Fiscal year change

THE PHILLIES

1 Citizens Bank Way	CEO: –
Philadelphia PA 19148	CFO: John N Nickolas
Phone: 215-463-6000	HR: –
Fax: 215-389-3050	FYE: October 31
Web: philadelphia.phillies.mlb.com	Type: Private

Philly Phanatics are a tough breed of baseball fan. The Phillies otherwise known as the Philadelphia Phillies is one of the least successful of the original Major League Baseball franchises posting just seven National League pennants (including back-to-back titles in 2008 and 2009) and two World Series titles since its founding in 1883. The team earned its first championship in 1980 with the help of Hall of Fame players Mike Schmidt and Steve Carlton its second came in 2008. Despite the team's history the Phillies boast a loyal following among Philadelphia baseball fans at Citizens Bank Park. One of six partners chairman Bill Giles owns a controlling interest in the baseball franchise.

THE PICTSWEET COMPANY

10 Pictsweet Dr.	CEO: James I Tankersley
Bells TN 38006	CFO: Brad Strange
Phone: 731-422-7600	HR: –
Fax: 800-561-8810	FYE: February 28
Web: www.pictsweet.com	Type: Private

The Pictsweet Company is a veritable veggie volcano. It grows asparagus corn okra and loads of other vegetables and then quick-freezes them for sale in supermarkets. The firm offers more than 100 products (including stir-fry blends and baby and preseasoned vegetables) in family-sized regular and bulk portions. Pictsweet provides vegetables nationwide under its own name and for retailers' private labels (including Kroger and Wal-Mart's Great Value brands). It also supplies foodservice operators (restaurants and hotels) and institutional customers (such as hospitals and schools); Pictsweet sells its vegetables through military commissaries worldwide.

THE PLAZA GROUP INC.

10375 RICHMOND AVE # 1620	CEO: –
HOUSTON, TX 770424143	CFO: Bob Imm
Phone: 713 266 1050	HR: –
Fax: –	FYE: December 31
Web: www.theplazagrp.com	Type: Private

The Plaza Group (TPG) is an international distributor of petrochemical solvents and chemical intermediates. Established in 1994 TPG is the exclusive marketer of some products from companies such as Shell Oil and Frontier Oil. The company markets to FORTUNE 500 companies major international enterprises direct consumers and chemical distributors. Its products are used in the production of resins coatings and adhesives. TPG partners with global suppliers (like SABIC Innovative Plastics Total Petrochemicals and Alon) in Asia Australia Europe and the Americas. The company is owned by president Randy Velarde.

	Annual Growth	12/09	12/10	12/11	12/12	12/13
Sales ($ mil.)	13.3%	–	198.4	271.6	288.4	288.8
Net income ($ mil.)	(51.8%)	–	–	4.4	3.5	1.0
Market value ($ mil.)	–	–	–	–	–	–
Employees	–	–	–	–	–	18

THE PMI GROUP INC.

NYSE: PMI

3003 Oak Rd.	CEO: L Stephen Smith
Walnut Creek CA 94597-2098	CFO: –
Phone: 925-658-7878	HR: –
Fax: 925-658-6931	FYE: December 31
Web: www.pmigroup.com	Type: Public

If Barbie couldn't afford a full 20% down payment on her Malibu dream home her mortgage lender might have brought in The PMI Group. The company was one of the largest US providers of mortgage insurance which protects lenders in case of borrower default. It also insured the bundles of existing loans known as structured finance products. In addition PMI was the primary investor in the Financial Guaranty Insurance Company which offered financial guaranty insurance on public bonds. The company's international operations provided mortgage insurance and credit enhancement services in Europe. Despite attempts to survive the real estate-market implosion the company filed Chapter 11 bankruptcy protection in 2011.

THE PORT AUTHORITY OF NEW YORK AND NEW JERSEY

225 Park Ave. South	CEO: –
New York NY 10003	CFO: –
Phone: 212-435-7000	HR: –
Fax: 212-435-6670	FYE: December 31
Web: www.panynj.gov	Type: Government Agency

The Port Authority of New York and New Jersey bridges the sometimes troubled waters between the two states and helps with many of the region's other transportation needs. The bistate agency operates and maintains airports tunnels bridges a commuter rail system shipping terminals and other facilities within the 1500-sq.-mi. Port District surrounding New York Harbor including the World Trade Center site in Lower Manhattan. A self-supporting public agency the Port Authority receives no state or local tax money. It relies on tolls fees and rents. Airport operations account for the majority of its revenue. The two governors each appoint six of the 12 members of the agency's board and review its decisions.

THE PRESIDENT AND TRUSTEES OF HAMPDEN-SYDNEY COLLEGE

1 COLLEGE RD	CEO: –
FARMVILLE, VA 23901	CFO: –
Phone: 434-223-6167	HR: –
Fax: –	FYE: June 30
Web: www.hsc.edu	Type: Private

Hampden-Sydney: Where men are men and women are guests. Hampden-Sydney College is a private four-year liberal arts college for men with a student population of more than 1000. The college offers undergraduate degrees in about 30 fields and is affiliated with the Presbyterian Church. Its campus is about 60 miles southwest of Richmond Virginia. Hampden-Sydney College was founded in 1775 and although the school is not co-educational its location places it in an area with 15 colleges and universities including four women's colleges — providing ample opportunities to interact with the opposite sex.

	Annual Growth	06/07	06/08	06/12	06/13	06/14
Sales ($ mil.)	(1.4%)	–	73.0	60.3	59.3	66.9
Net income ($ mil.)	–	–	–	(4.4)	14.1	20.6
Market value ($ mil.)	–	–	–	–	–	–
Employees	–	–	–	–	–	350

THE QUIZNOS MASTER LLC

1001 17th St. Ste. 200	CEO: –
Denver CO 80202	CFO: –
Phone: 720-359-3300	HR: –
Fax: 720-359-3399	FYE: September 30
Web: www.quiznos.com	Type: Private

Quiznos wants to be the toast of the sandwich world. The Quiznos Master operates the #2 sub sandwich chain (behind Subway). Quiznos quick-service restaurants are popular for their made-to-order oven-toasted sandwiches. Patrons can choose from a variety of signature or custom-made subs wraps salads sub sliders and flatbreads. The company has locations in all 50 states and more than 25 countries. Quiznos started getting toasty in 1981 as a single Denver area restaurant. Avenue Capital Group became majority owners in early 2012 after a debt-for-equity deal.

THE RENCO GROUP INC.

1 Rockefeller Plaza 29th Fl.	CEO: Ira Leon Rennert
New York NY 10112	CFO: –
Phone: 212-541-6000	HR: –
Fax: 212-541-6197	FYE: October 31
Web: www.rencogroup.net	Type: Private

Renco Group is a holding company for a diverse group of businesses. Its AM General subsidiary (a joint venture with Ronald Perelman's MacAndrews & Forbes Holdings) makes the HUMVEE an extra-wide all-terrain vehicle used by the military. Other Renco Group companies include Doe Run which is engaged in metals mining smelting recycling and fabrication; Unarco Material Handling which makes pallet racks and systems for warehouses; Inteva Products which manufactures systems for the automotive industry; and US Magnesium the largest primary magnesium producer in North America. Renco Group is owned by billionaire Ira Rennert.

THE READER'S DIGEST ASSOCIATION INC.

750 3rd Ave.	CEO: Bonnie Kintzer
New York NY 10017	CFO: Howard Halligan
Phone: 914-238-1000	HR: –
Fax: 609-261-4853	FYE: December 31
Web: www.pariscorp.com	Type: Private

The Reader's Digest Association (RDA) publishes the undersized general-interest magazine Reader's Digest which boasts 50 editions and is translated into some 20 languages. In addition to publishing its flagship title RDA operates about 80 branded websites. It leverages its extensive consumer database of more than 140 million names to market books (such as Reader's Digest Select Editions how-to guides and cookbooks) special-interest magazines music videos and financial and health products in nearly 80 countries. Suffering from a heavy debt-load amid a down economy RDA filed Chapter 11 for its US businesses which emerged from bankruptcy in 2010. It is owned by RDA Holding Co.

THE RESEARCH FOUNDATION OF STATE UNIVERSITY OF NEW YORK

35 STATE ST	CEO: –
ALBANY, NY 122072826	CFO: Paul Kutey
Phone: 518-434-7000	HR: Paul Kelly
Fax: –	FYE: June 30
	Type: Private

The Research Foundation of State University of New York (The Research Foundation) collects and administers research and education grants from state and federal governments corporations and foundations on behalf of the 24-campus State University of New York known as SUNY. The foundation has formed several affiliated divisions — including Long Island High Technology Incubator and NanoTech Resources — to operate research facilities encourage scientific collaboration and otherwise facilitate research for the university. It facilitates research for studies such as engineering and nanotechnology; physical sciences and medicine; life sciences and medicine; social sciences; and computer and information sciences.

	Annual Growth	06/07	06/08	06/09	06/12	06/13
Sales ($ mil.)	159.5%	–	9.2	985.5	1,114.7	1,079.5
Net income ($ mil.)	–	–	–	(71.5)	13.0	42.5
Market value ($ mil.)	–	–	–	–	–	–
Employees	–	–	–	–	–	8,000

THE REED INSTITUTE

3203 SE WOODSTOCK BLVD	CEO: –
PORTLAND, OR 972028138	CFO: –
Phone: 503-771-1112	HR: –
Fax: –	FYE: June 30
Web: www.academic.reed.edu	Type: Private

Reed College offers bachelor's degrees in nearly 30 fields and a master of arts degree in liberal studies. Its special master's degree allows students to study both liberal arts and the sciences. Each year the school enrolls more than 1400 students who become known as "Reedies." Additionally it boasts an average of 17 students in its conference-style classes and a student-to-faculty ratio of 10 to 1. Reed College which has produced more than 30 Rhodes Scholars also houses a nuclear reactor that is operated primarily by undergraduates. Founded in 1908 Reed College is named for Oregon pioneers Simeon and Amanda Reed.

	Annual Growth	06/10	06/11	06/12	06/13	06/14
Sales ($ mil.)	4.8%	–	124.5	114.0	121.7	143.3
Net income ($ mil.)	221.4%	–	–	5.9	41.9	61.2
Market value ($ mil.)	–	–	–	–	–	–
Employees	–	–	–	–	–	400

THE RICE COMPANIES

334 Chapman St.	CEO: –
Greenfield MA 01301	CFO: –
Phone: 413-772-0227	HR: –
Fax: 413-773-9487	FYE: December 31
Web: www.ricecompanies.com	Type: Private

It's petroleum not rice that is the most popular commodity at Rice Oil and Propane. The company is a regional supplier of heating fuel heating and cooling systems and services to customers in the New England region. In an effort to green up the business its fuel oil includes a vegetable oil blend that it calls BioHeat. It installs and services a variety of oil and propane heating systems as well as central air systems and delivers fuel oil and propane directly to customers. Rice sells Bryant and Daikin air conditioners along with System 2000 Monitor Space and Thermo Pride heaters and furnaces. The company is part of propane and natural gas firm Inergy Holdings.

THE RITZ-CARLTON HOTEL COMPANY L.L.C.

4445 Willard Ave. Ste. 800	CEO: Herve Humler
Chevy Chase MD 20815	CFO: –
Phone: 301-547-4700	HR: Justin Lee
Fax: 301-547-4723	FYE: December 31
Web: www.ritzcarlton.com	Type: Subsidiary

Puttin' on the ritz is second nature to this hotelier. The Ritz-Carlton Hotel Company operates about 100 luxury hotels in some 20 countries offering premium accommodations and amenities for business and leisure travelers. Located in prime destinations its properties are consistently rated among the best in the world. The firm also operates about 15 time-share properties under the Ritz-Carlton Destination Club and Ritz-Carlton Residences brands. Ritz-Carlton was established in 1983 when real estate mogul and former CEO William Johnson acquired the rights to the name made famous by Swiss hotelier Cesar Ritz. Today it is a part of hotel giant Marriott International operating under that company's luxury segment.

THE ROBERT ALLEN GROUP INC.

225 Foxboro Blvd.	CEO: Phil Kowalczyk
Mansfield MA 02035	CFO: Chuck Cioffi
Phone: 800-333-3777	HR: –
Fax: 800-332-8256	FYE: December 31
Web: www.robertallendesign.com	Type: Private

This company's products give designers the tools to get their groove on. The Robert Allen Group is a leading designer and marketer of fabrics and home furnishings under numerous brand names including Robert Allen Robert Allen @ Home Ametex and Beacon Hill. Each line serves a particular price point and market niche. Also the Robert Allen Contract division works to customize fabrics and designs for corporate hospitality and healthcare customers. In 2002 The Robert Allen Group was acquired by family-owned Decor Holdings.

THE ROCKEFELLER UNIVERSITY FACULTY AND STUDENTS CLUB INC

1230 YORK AVE	CEO: –
NEW YORK, NY 100656307	CFO: James H Lapple
Phone: 212-327-8078	HR: –
Fax: –	FYE: June 30
Web: www.rucares.org	Type: Private

Rockefeller University sniffs out solid scientific evidence. The university is a leading US research institution and scientific graduate school providing training in biomedical and physical science fields such as biochemistry structural biology immunology neuroscience and human genetics. The university is centered around 76 research laboratories and a hospital and it runs M.D.-Ph.D. programs in conjunction with the Memorial Sloan-Kettering Cancer Center and the Weill Medical College at Cornell University. Rockefeller University's research is funded by entities such as the National Institutes of Health and the Howard Hughes Medical Institute as well as private gifts and endowments.

	Annual Growth	06/03	06/04	06/05	06/06	06/13
Sales ($ mil.)	1.5%	–	–	413.7	413.7	466.2
Net income ($ mil.)	(6.5%)	–	–	271.1	271.1	159.0
Market value ($ mil.)	–	–	–	–	–	–
Employees	–	–	–	–	–	1,700

THE RUDOLPH/LIBBE COMPANIES INC

6494 LATCHA RD	CEO: –
WALBRIDGE, OH 434659788	CFO: Robert Pruger
Phone: 419-241-5000	HR: –
Fax: –	FYE: December 31
Web: www.rudolphlibbe.com	Type: Private

The corporate model of a conglomerate composed of independent unrelated businesses is not for The Rudolph/Libbe Companies. The group of companies can build or oversee real estate projects (general contractor Rudolph/Libbe Inc.); perform mechanical electrical and structural work (GEM Industrial); and then represent those properties in the market (RLWest Properties). Operating in the Ohio/Michigan corridor the group provides site selection design/build and construction management. Its portfolio includes industrial retail municipal residential educational health care and mixed-use projects. Fritz and Phil Rudolph and their cousin Allan Libbe founded flagship subsidiary Rudolph/Libbe Inc. in 1955.

	Annual Growth	12/09	12/10	12/11	12/12	12/13
Sales ($ mil.)	10.3%	–	237.9	472.2	375.6	319.5
Net income ($ mil.)	(18.9%)	–	–	13.2	13.6	8.7
Market value ($ mil.)	–	–	–	–	–	–
Employees	–	–	–	–	–	600

THE SALVATION ARMY NATIONAL CORPORATION

615 SLATERS LN	CEO: –
ALEXANDRIA, VA 223141112	CFO: Mark Knecht
Phone: 703-684-5500	HR: –
Fax: –	FYE: September 30
Web: www.salvationarmyusa.org	Type: Private

Battling to provide social services The Salvation Army is one of the world's largest faith-based charities with some 3550 officers and 3.3 million volunteers. Its Christian faith-based programs assist alcoholics drug addicts the homeless the elderly prison inmates people in crisis and the jobless through offerings such as community centers housing facilities and rehabilitation centers. The organization also provides disaster-relief services and operates more than 1300 thrift stores. Overall it serves nearly 30 million people and 58 million meals a year. The US organization is a unit of the London-based Salvation Army which oversees activities in more than 100 countries. US operations began in 1880.

	Annual Growth	09/08	09/09	09/10	09/12	09/13
Sales ($ mil.)	229.0%	–	36.8	3.7	42.1	4,315.6
Net income ($ mil.)	1394.9%	–	–	0.4	2.4	1,349.5
Market value ($ mil.)	–	–	–	–	–	–
Employees	–	–	–	–	–	60,000

THE SAVANNAH COLLEGE OF ART AND DESIGN INC

342 BULL ST	CEO: –
SAVANNAH, GA 314014518	CFO: Joseph P Manory
Phone: 912-525-5000	HR: Lesley Hanak
Fax: –	FYE: June 30
Web: www.scad.edu	Type: Private

With more than 11000 students Savannah College of Art and Design (SCAD) is one of the largest art and design schools in the US. It has undergraduate degrees in arts and fine arts as well as master's degrees in a range of subjects. The institution includes nine schools offering courses of study in fields such as architecture interior and graphic design fashion film and television painting dance and art history. The school also offers certificates in digital publishing digital publishing management historic preservation interactive design and typeface design.

	Annual Growth	06/06	06/07	06/08	06/09	06/10
Sales ($ mil.)		–	–	0.0	283.0	314.1
Net income ($ mil.)	32707.6%	–	–	0.0	21.8	10.0
Market value ($ mil.)	–	–	–	–	–	–
Employees	–	–	–	–	–	1,200

THE SAVINGS BANK LIFE INSURANCE COMPANY OF MASSACHUSETTS

1 Linscott Rd.	CEO: Robert K Sheridan
Woburn MA 01801	CFO: James P Loring
Phone: 781-938-3500	HR: –
Fax: 913-469-8824	FYE: December 31
Web: www.ups-scs.com	Type: Private

Is it a bank? Is it an insurer? The Savings Bank Life Insurance Company of Massachusetts (SBLI) is actually an insurer that sells through banks. Originally selling life insurance only through savings banks SBLI now sells a variety of products directly to consumers. Its offerings include term life whole life group life and specialty children's life insurance. While it remains a top writer of life insurance in Massachusetts SBLI has expanded to sell its products in nearly all US states. The company sells its products directly and through independent brokers and agents as well as through banks. It has partnership agreements with several regional banking associations. SBLI was founded in 1907.

THE SCHUMACHER GROUP OF LOUISIANA INC.

200 Corporate Blvd. Ste. 201	CEO: William Schumacher
Lafayette LA 70508	CFO: William D Crays
Phone: 337-354-1332	HR: –
Fax: 337-371-4477	FYE: December 31
Web: schumachergroup.com	Type: Private

When it comes to hospital emergency room management Schumacher Group looks to operate with a helping hand. Offering outsourced staffing and management services to emergency rooms Schumacher Group provides medical professionals such as physicians and emergency room support staff health care managers medical directors and other administrative staff. The company also offers scheduling recruitment support and medical billing and coding services. Schumacher Group operates through a handful of regional offices and serves about 200 hospitals in more than 20 states most of which are located in the southern US. Chairman William C. Schumacher M.D. founded the company in 1994.

THE SCHWAN FOOD COMPANY

115 W. College Dr.	CEO: Dimitrios Smyrnios
Marshall MN 56258	CFO: Robin Galloway
Phone: 507-532-3274	HR: Maryjo Martinson
Fax: 402-342-5568	FYE: December 31
Web: www.scoular.com	Type: Private

Pizza rounds out business at The Schwan Food Company. With well-known retail pizza brands like Tony's Red Baron and Freschetta the company is one of the top frozen pizza makers in the US alongside rival Nestle. But pizza isn't the only product that provides it with dough. Schwan's core business involves a fleet of 5700 Home Service trucks that deliver 350 frozen food products directly to the doorsteps of some 2.5 million customers. Home Service provides entrees breakfasts sandwiches side dishes snacks ice cream and more to homes and by mail order throughout the US mainland. Besides the US market Schwan sells food in Western Europe. The family of the late founder Marvin Schwan owns the company.

THE SCOOTER STORE LTD.

1650 Independence Dr.	CEO: –
New Braunfels TX 78132	CFO: –
Phone: 830-626-5600	HR: –
Fax: 416-620-3666	FYE: December 31
Web: www.parmalat.ca	Type: Private

The SCOOTER Store sells freedom — or at least a motorized scooter or wheelchair — to senior citizens and other persons with physical limitations. The company sells power chairs and outdoor scooters including products made by Pride Mobility and other third parties through a network of retail and distribution facilities in 48 US states and Puerto Rico. It also sells other durable medical equipment (DME) such as wheelchair lifts and home ramps and provides repair services for most major power chair and scooter brands. Doug Harrison and his wife Susanna started The SCOOTER Store in 1991 in response to an increasing elderly population and a fragmented scooter and wheelchair industry.

THE SCOULAR COMPANY

2027 DODGE ST STE 200	CEO: Charles (Chuck) Elsea
OMAHA, NE 681021229	CFO: Richard A. (Rick) Cogdill
Phone: 402-342-3500	HR: –
Fax: –	FYE: May 31
Web: www.scoular.com	Type: Private

The Scoular Company's business is a grind — and that's a good thing. Scoular is best known for buying selling storing handling and transporting agricultural products (mainly grains) worldwide. It deals in the mainstays of farming — corn hay millet rice sorghum soybeans and wheat — and gets them where they need to go. The company transports these products via rail truck barge and seagoing container vessels. Scoular's other divisions offer fishmeal products for farm-animal pet and aquaculture feeds; ingredients for food manufacturers; renewable fuels; and truck freight brokering. It has customers in Asia Africa the Americas and Europe. George Scoular founded the business in Nebraska in 1892.

	Annual Growth	05/10	05/11	05/12	05/13	05/14
Sales ($ mil.)	3.9%	–	203.8	211.3	211.4	228.3
Net income ($ mil.)	3.6%	–	–	27.6	27.3	29.7
Market value ($ mil.)	–	–	–	–	–	–
Employees	–	–	–	–	–	800

THE SCRIPPS RESEARCH INSTITUTE

10550 N TORREY PINES RD	CEO: Peter G Schultz
LA JOLLA, CA 920371000	CFO: Cary E Thomas
Phone: 858-784-1000	HR: –
Fax: –	FYE: September 30
Web: www.scripps.edu	Type: Private

The Scripps Research Institute (TSRI) is a not-for profit organization that performs basic biomedical research in molecular and cellular biology chemistry immunology neuroscience disease and vaccine development. TSRI receives the majority of its funding from federal agencies such as the National Institutes of Health. TRSI opened a second facility in Florida in 2009. Its staff includes more than 2900 scientists and lab technicians and the organization traces its history back to 1924 when philanthropist Ellen Browning Scripps founded Scripps Metabolic Clinic.

	Annual Growth	09/03	09/04	09/05	09/08	09/09
Sales ($ mil.)	2.8%	–	326.5	387.8	464.0	375.5
Net income ($ mil.)	–	–	–	63.4	137.9	(18.8)
Market value ($ mil.)	–	–	–	–	–	–
Employees	–	–	–	–	–	99

THE SEGAL GROUP INC.

333 W. 34th St.
New York NY 10001-2402
Phone: 212-251-5000
Fax: 212-251-5490
Web: www.segalco.com

CEO: Joseph A Locicero
CFO: –
HR: –
FYE: December 31
Type: Private

This Segal guides you through the complexities of HR programs. The Segal Group is an employee-owned actuarial benefits compensation and consulting services firm that primarily does business through subsidiary The Segal Company. Segal focuses on employees in the corporate government and not-for-profit sectors and offers its services to clients throughout North America as well as select overseas markets. Its Sibson Consulting subsidiary offers HR consulting services with expertise in talent and performance management sales force effectiveness and compensation. Its Segal Advisors unit offers investment services. Formed in 1939 the Segal Group operates through more than 20 offices across the US and Canada.

THE SEMINOLE TRIBE OF FLORIDA INC.

6300 Stirling Rd.
Hollywood FL 33024
Phone: 954-966-6300
Fax: 954-967-3477
Web: www.seminoletribe.com

CEO: –
CFO: –
HR: –
FYE: September 30
Type: Private

This tribe knows how to rock. The Seminole Tribe of Florida owns Hard Rock Cafe International which includes a chain of more than 160 Hard Rock Cafes in some 45 countries. In addition to the Hard Rock properties the Seminole Tribe owns two Seminole Hard Rock Hotels & Casinos (in Tampa and Hollywood Florida) as well as a handful of non-Hard Rock casinos also in Florida. The Seminole Tribe also operates a cultural and historical museum adjacent to its gaming facilities in Hollywood as well as various educational programs at six reservations throughout Florida (Big Cypress Brighton Ft. Pierce Hollywood Immokalee and Tampa). The tribe opened the first high stakes bingo hall and casino in the US in 1979.

THE SERVICEMASTER COMPANY

860 Ridge Lake Blvd.
Memphis TN 38120
Phone: 901-597-1400
Fax: 630-663-2001
Web: www.servicemaster.com

CEO: Robert J Gillette
CFO: Alan J M Haughie
HR: –
FYE: December 31
Type: Private

ServiceMaster merrily mows scrubs sprays and trims. A giant in its industry the company serves millions of commercial and residential customers in the US and around the world with housecleaning termite and pest control and landscape maintenance services. Its best-known brands include Terminix TruGreen and Merry Maids. ServiceMaster Clean cleans carpets and flooring for residential and commercial clients. Its AmeriSpec division inspects homes American Home Shield provides home warranty plans and Furniture Medic repairs and restores furniture. ServiceMaster is owned by investment firm Clayton Dubilier & Rice.

THE SHAMROCK COMPANIES INC

24090 DETROIT RD
WESTLAKE, OH 441451513
Phone: 440-899-9510
Fax: –
Web: www.shamrockcompanies.net

CEO: Robert E. (Bob) Troop
CFO: Gary A. Lesjak
HR: –
FYE: December 31
Type: Private

Need a marketing and communications firm that offers a full range of services? It's your lucky day. The Shamrock Companies provides business communications fulfillment information technology e-commerce marketing and creative services packaging print and promotional products. Neil Bennett established the company as Shamrock Forms Inc. in Detroit in 1982. CEO Robert "Bob" Troop who bought the Cleveland division in 1989 expanded the business and changed the company's name to its present form is the company's majority shareowner. The Shamrock Companies operates from about 30 US offices.

	Annual Growth	12/00	12/01	12/02	12/03	12/07
Sales ($ mil.)	8.2%	–	42.7	43.9	51.8	68.4
Net income ($ mil.)	11.3%	–	–	2.5	1.6	4.2
Market value ($ mil.)	–	–	–	–	–	–
Employees	–	–	–	–	–	140

THE SHEPHERD GOOD HOSPITAL INC

700 E MARSHALL AVE
LONGVIEW, TX 756015572
Phone: 903-315-2000
Fax: –
Web: www.gsmc.org

CEO: Edward D Banos
CFO: –
HR: –
FYE: September 30
Type: Private

Leading its citizens toward good health Good Shepherd Health System provides medical and surgical care to patients throughout the Piney Woods region of northeastern Texas. Its flagship facility is Good Shepherd Medical Center in Longview a more than 425-bed regional referral hospital providing specialty care in areas such as trauma cardiology neurology and pulmonology. Good Shepherd also has small inpatient facilities as well as a freestanding outpatient surgery center and several primary care Family Health Centers located throughout its service area. The hospital established in 1935 as the 50-bed Gregg Memorial Hospital is led by CEO Ed Banos.

	Annual Growth	09/10	09/11*	03/12*	09/12	09/13
Sales ($ mil.)	0.5%	–	267.5	24.6	282.8	270.0
Net income ($ mil.)	86.9%	–	–	1.3	(11.7)	2.3
Market value ($ mil.)	–	–	–	–	–	–
Employees	–	–	–	–	–	2,200

*Fiscal year change

THE SMITH & WOLLENSKY RESTAURANT GROUP INC.

120 West 45th St.
New York NY 10036
Phone: 212-789-8100
Fax: 212-302-8032
Web: www.smithandwollensky.com

CEO: –
CFO: –
HR: Kim Dinsmoore
FYE: December 31
Type: Subsidiary

Here are a couple big names in fine dining. The Smith & Wollensky Restaurant Group operates about 10 upscale steakhouses around the country under the iconic Smith & Wollensky name. Based on the original location opened in New York in 1977 the restaurants offer prime grade beef as well as lamb and seafood dishes along with an extensive wine list. Some locations also feature a Wollensky's Grill that serves smaller portioned meals at a lower price. Smith & Wollensky is owned by Project Grill an investment vehicle controlled by restaurateurs Nick Valenti and Joachim Splichial (Patina Restaurant Group).

THE SOUTHERN CONNECTICUT GAS COMPANY

77 Hartland St. 4th Fl.	CEO: Robert M Allessio
East Hartford CT 06108	CFO: –
Phone: 866-268-2887	HR: –
Fax: 860-727-3064	FYE: December 31
Web: www.soconngas.com	Type: Subsidiary

Southern Connecticut Gas brings energy to the Constitution State. Founded in 1847 the subsidiary of New England-based utility UIL Holdings provides natural gas services to 165000 customers in 22 cities and towns in a 560 sq. mi. service area of Fairfield New Haven and Middlesex counties primarily along the shores of Long Island Sound. The company's customer base represents approximately 25% of Connecticut's residents. In 2010 in order to raise capital former parent Iberdrola USA sold the company to UIL Holdings. The sale was part of a $1.3 billion three-utility deal to grow UIL Holdings' market position and give it an entry into gas distribution.

THE SOUTHERN POVERTY LAW CENTER INC

400 WASHINGTON AVE	CEO: –
MONTGOMERY, AL 361044344	CFO: Teenie Hutchison
Phone: 334-956-8200	HR: –
Fax: –	FYE: October 31
Web: www.splcenter.org	Type: Private

Founded in 1971 as a small civil rights law firm the Southern Poverty Law Center (SPLC) is a non-profit organization dedicated to increasing tolerance through education and when or if that fails litigation. The center provides legal services to minorities and the poor while its Intelligence Project monitors hate groups in the US. SPLC's quarterly Intelligence Report is distributed to more than 60000 law enforcement officials. The organization also operates Tolerance.org a collection of online resources for those fighting bigotry in their own communities. SPLC is credited with weakening the financial structure of white supremacist groups the likes of the Ku Klux Klan and Aryan Nation.

	Annual Growth	10/10	10/11	10/12	10/13	10/14
Sales ($ mil.)	80.1%	–	9.3	54.6	76.2	54.4
Net income ($ mil.)	(19.3%)	–	–	18.4	34.7	12.0
Market value ($ mil.)	–	–	–	–	–	–
Employees	–	–	–	–	–	105

THE SPORTSMAN'S GUIDE INC.

411 Farwell Ave. South	CEO: Sylvain Desjonqueres
South St. Paul MN 55075	CFO: Joe Skwira
Phone: 651-451-3030	HR: –
Fax: 651-450-6130	FYE: December 31
Web: www.sportsmansguide.com	Type: Subsidiary

Whether you're tracking closeouts or quail The Sportsman's Guide wants to join the hunt. The catalog and online retailer offers discounted apparel and footwear hunting and fishing gear camping equipment sporting goods automotive accessories and tools among other items for the outdoorsman. In addition to its main catalog The Sportsman's Guide produces specialty catalogs with an extended range of merchandise in the hunting shooting and military surplus categories. It recently added two new brands: BoatingSavings.com and WorkWearSavings.com to its online offering. Founded in 1970 the company is owned by direct marketer Redcats USA itself part of the PPR-owned Redcats Group.

THE SSI GROUP INC.

4721 Morrison Dr.	CEO: Bob E Smith
Mobile AL 36609	CFO: James M Lyons
Phone: 251-345-0000	HR: –
Fax: 251-345-0100	FYE: December 31
Web: www.thessigroup.com	Type: Private

The SSI Group keeps health care operations clicking right along. The company's electronic data interchange (EDI) services and software connect health care providers such as hospitals nursing homes physician groups and surgery centers with more than 800 payers including Medicare/Medicaid and Blue Cross Blue Shield. Its ClickON platform facilitates electronic claims processing document management and imaging hospital and physician billing and payment recovery services. Adventist Health Baystate Health Care New England and Valley Health are among its more than 2200 customers. Founded in 1998 SSI Group has offices in Alabama Colorado Florida and Virginia.

THE STOP & SHOP SUPERMARKET COMPANY

1385 Hancock St.	CEO: Marc E Smith
Quincy MA 02169	CFO: Brian W Hotarek
Phone: 800-453-7467	HR: –
Fax: 708-492-7078	FYE: December 31
Web: home.iaai.com	Type: Subsidiary

A popular stop for shoppers in the Northeast The Stop & Shop Supermarket Company is one of the region's largest supermarket chains with more than 390 outlets in Connecticut Massachusetts New Hampshire New Jersey New York and Rhode Island. The company's Super Stop & Shop superstores offer a wider variety of food and nonfood items than its standard supermarkets including a large number of convenience and specialty departments such as gas stations full-service pharmacies office supplies portrait studios and photo shops. Stop & Shop's owner Ahold USA runs two other East Coast supermarket chains under the Giant banners. Ahold USA is owned by Dutch food giant Royal Ahold.

THE STRIDE RITE CORPORATION

191 Spring St.	CEO: Gregg Ribatt
Lexington MA 02420-9191	CFO: Frank A Caruso
Phone: 617-824-6000	HR: –
Fax: 617-824-6549	FYE: November 30
Web: www.collectivebrands.com/brands/stride-rite	Type: Subsidiary

The pitter-patter of little feet keeps Stride Rite in step. Doing business as Collective Brands Performance + Lifestyle Group the designer and marketer of footwear for children also peddles boots dress shoes sandals and sneakers for adults. Its brand names include Keds Kids Robeez Saucony Sperry Top-Sider Jessica Simpson Kids Tommy Hilfiger Kids and Stride Rite. Its primary business is wholesale to department stores and other retailers but it also sells footwear through some 250 company-owned children's shoe stores a couple company websites leased departments in Macy's stores and 100-plus outlet stores. Collective Brands owner of Payless ShoeSource owns the footwear firm.

THE SUNDT COMPANIES INC

2015 W RIVER RD STE 101	CEO: J Douglas Pruitt
TUCSON, AZ 857041676	CFO: Raymond C Bargull
Phone: 520-750-4600	HR: –
Fax: –	FYE: September 30
Web: www.sundt.com	Type: Private

Sundt has put its stamp on the Southwest. Through Sundt Construction and other subsidiaries The Sundt Companies offers preconstruction construction management general contracting and design/build services for commercial government and industrial clients. Projects include commercial buildings military bases light rails airports and schools. It builds mostly in Arizona Nevada California New Mexico and Texas. Sundt has overseen some notable projects including the development of the top-secret town of Los Alamos New Mexico (where the first atomic bomb was built) and the relocation of the London Bridge to Arizona. Sundt Companies was formed in 1998 as a holding company for various company interests.

	Annual Growth	09/10	09/11	09/12	09/13	09/14
Sales ($ mil.)	–	–	0.0	0.0	897.0	823.8
Net income ($ mil.)	–	–	–	0.0	0.0	0.0
Market value ($ mil.)	–	–	–	–	–	–
Employees	–	–	–	–	–	1,500

THE SUSAN G KOMEN BREAST CANCER FOUNDATION INC

5005 LYNDON B JOHNSON FWY # 250	CEO: Judith A. Salerno
DALLAS, TX 752446100	CFO: Bob Green
Phone: 972-855-1600	HR: –
Fax: –	FYE: March 31
Web: www.komen.org	Type: Private

Susan G. Komen For the Cure is dedicated to fighting breast cancer through education research screening and treatment programs. One of its well known fundraisers is an annual 5-K foot race called the Komen Race for the Cure which is conducted in numerous locations across the US and in other countries. The organization also operates a national help line and a website. Since its founding Komen for the Cure has invested more than $1.7 billion on screening education treatment and psychosocial support programs including more than $800 million to medical research as part of a broad campaign to combat breast cancer.

	Annual Growth	03/04	03/05	03/06	03/07	03/09
Sales ($ mil.)	–	–	–	0.0	307.4	159.2
Net income ($ mil.)	–	–	–	0.0	38.5	3.5
Market value ($ mil.)	–	–	–	–	–	–
Employees	–	–	–	–	–	260

THE SYNERGOS INSTITUTE

51 Madison Ave. 21st Fl.	CEO: –
New York NY 10010	CFO: –
Phone: 212-447-8111	HR: –
Fax: 212-447-8119	FYE: December 31
Web: www.synergos.org	Type: Private

The Synergos Institute is a nonprofit organization that focuses on reducing poverty in the developing world by providing technical assistance to grant-making groups primarily in Africa Asia and Latin America. Each year Synergos helps nearly 200 organizations that work directly with community development tailors giving programs for wealthy families and individuals to channel their funds into poverty-ending work and trains local leaders to help people work together to solve conflict. Synergos was founded in 1987 by Peggy Dulany daughter of bank president David Rockefeller and heir to the Rockefeller Standard Oil fortune.

THE TALBOTS INC.

NYSE: TLB

1 Talbots Dr.	CEO: Michael G Archbold
Hingham MA 02043	CFO: Michael Scarpa
Phone: 781-749-7600	HR: –
Fax: 781-741-4369	FYE: January 31
Web: www.talbots.com	Type: Private

In the trend-driven world of women's fashion The Talbots is a 'head-to-toe' constant. Although it flirted with hipper styles the purveyor of women's apparel shoes and accessories has returned to its hallmark designs in a bid to right its struggling business. Talbots runs about 515 stores in some 45 US states and Canada. The chain specializes in selling mostly private-label classically-styled apparel accessories and shoes to women ages 35 and older. The company founded in 1947 by Rudolf and Nancy Talbot also sells through more than a dozen catalogs and its website. After buyout talks appeared to fail Talbots was taken private by Sycamore Partners for $391 million (including debt) in August 2012.

THE TAYLOR GROUP INC.

650 N. Church Ave.	CEO: –
Louisville MS 39339-2017	CFO: –
Phone: 662-773-3421	HR: –
Fax: 662-773-9143	FYE: December 31
Web: www.taylorbigred.com	Type: Private

Tailor-made for some heavy lifting The Taylor Group led by Taylor Machine Works is a manufacturer of large material handling equipment including gantry cranes marina trucks container handlers log stackers side loaders and industrial pneumatics. The company also known as "Big Red" makes more than 100 models of industrial lift equipment (forklifts) with lift capacities of up to 120000 pounds. Its other divisions include Sudden Service Taylor Environmental Products Taylor Leasing Taylor Power Systems Taylor Rail Group and Temtco Steel. W.A. Taylor Sr. started the company with a "Loggers Dream" in 1927. His family including CEO William Taylor Jr. owns and runs The Taylor Group.

THE TECHS

2400 Second Ave.	CEO: –
Pittsburgh PA 15219	CFO: –
Phone: 412-464-5000	HR: –
Fax: 412-391-0402	FYE: March 31
Web: www.thetechs.com	Type: Subsidiary

Like The Geeks in the computer industry in the world of hot-dipped galvanized steel production The Techs are the smart guys. The company manufactures flat-rolled steel from massive steel coils that are processed through annealing coating surface conditioning and tension leveling technologies. The Techs operate through three facilities: GalvTech MetalTech and NexTech; each runs its own plant for producing galvanized steel in an array of specialized gauges and widths. The Techs cater to a diversity of industries from agriculture to automotive HVAC and consumer appliances. Among many steel applications include grain bins brackets duct work and mail boxes. The company is a subsidiary of Steel Dynamics.

THE THOMAS KINKADE COMPANY

900 Lightpost Way
Morgan Hill CA 95037
Phone: 408-201-5000
Fax: 408-201-5192
Web: www.thomaskinkade.com

CEO: Eric H Halvorson
CFO: Herbert D Montgomery
HR: Rose Capistran
FYE: December 31
Type: Private

Thomas Kinkade's light-infused landscapes are big business. As the sole licenser of Kinkade's paintings The Thomas Kinkade Company oversees the reproduction and sale of photolithographs collectibles and decorative accessories inspired by the works of Kinkade. His name adorns items as diverse as books and furniture and the company boasts partnerships with more than 70 licensees. Paintings and other products are sold in limited and open editions through about 4000 retailers 280 licensed Signature Galleries and 400 Showcase Galleries. The company also operates three company-owned stores and peddles its products online. The Thomas Kinkade Company merged with Media Arts Group in 2004.

THE TIMBERLAND COMPANY

200 Domain Dr.
Stratham NH 03885
Phone: 603-772-9500
Fax: 908-272-9492
Web: www.tofutti.com

CEO: –
CFO: –
HR: –
FYE: December 31
Type: Subsidiary

Even non-hikers can get a kick out of Timberlands. Best known for making men's women's and kids' footwear Timberland manufactures hiking boots boat shoes sandals and dress and outdoor casual footwear. The company also makes apparel (outerwear shirts pants socks) and accessories such as sunglasses watches and belts. Its brands include SmartWool howies IPATH and Timberland. Timberland sells its products through about 230 company-owned stores and through department and athletic shops in Asia Canada Europe Latin America the Middle East and the US. In 2011 uber apparel maker V.F. Corporation purchased the company for more than $2 billion.

THE TOLEDO HOSPITAL

2142 N COVE BLVD
TOLEDO, OH 436063896
Phone: 419-291-4000
Fax: –
Web: www.promedica.org

CEO: Alan Brass
CFO: Cathy Hanley
HR: –
FYE: December 31
Type: Private

One of the region's largest acute-care facilities The Toledo Hospital provides medical care to the residents of northwestern Ohio and southeastern Michigan. Boasting nearly 800 beds the facility offers several specialties and services including the Jobst Vascular Center which provides cardiac and vascular services in conjunction with The University of Michigan. The Toledo Hospital which shares a medical complex with the Toledo Children's Hospital also operates trauma emergency outpatient arthritis sleep disorder and women's health centers. The Toledo Hospital is a member of Toledo-based ProMedica Health System a mission-based not-for-profit healthcare organization formed in 1986.

	Annual Growth	12/03	12/04	12/05	12/08	12/09
Sales ($ mil.)	93.6%	–	23.3	518.4	548.8	635.7
Net income ($ mil.)	(9.3%)	–	–	28.4	33.4	19.2
Market value ($ mil.)	–	–	–	–	–	–
Employees	–	–	–	–	–	5,586

THE TRIZETTO GROUP INC.

6061 S. Willow Dr. Ste. 310
Greenwood Village CO 80111
Phone: 303-495-7000
Fax: 303-495-7001
Web: www.trizetto.com

CEO: Jude Dieterman
CFO: Douglas E Barnett
HR: –
FYE: December 31
Type: Private

The TriZetto Group devotes itself to the companies that pay the doctor's bills. Targeting health plans benefits administrators and other health care payers the company provides software and IT services designed to simplify provider network transaction and business process management. It resells third-party medical billing applications from such vendors as Metavante while its own applications include Web-based payment tools and enterprise software for insurers and benefits administrators. Clients have included BlueCross BlueShield of Tennessee. The company's Gateway EDI subsidiary specializes in revenue cycle management software. TriZetto was founded in 1997 and acquired in 2008 by Apax Partners.

THE TRUMP ORGANIZATION

725 5th Ave.
New York NY 10022-2519
Phone: 212-832-2000
Fax: 212-935-0141
Web: www.trump.com

CEO: –
CFO: –
HR: –
FYE: December 31
Type: Private

The Trump Organization knows all about gilding the lily. Run by flamboyant modern-day King Midas/media czar Donald Trump The Trump Organization owns several pieces of high-end real estate in the Big Apple. Properties include Trump International Hotel & Tower Trump Tower and 40 Wall Street. It also owns and operates hotels resorts residential towers and golf courses in major US markets and abroad. Trump Organization holds a stake in Trump Entertainment Resorts the owner and operator of the Trump Taj Mahal and Trump Plaza casinos in New Jersey's Atlantic City. Together with NBC Trump additionally owns the Miss USA Miss Teen USA and Miss Universe beauty pageants.

THE TRUSTEES OF DAVIDSON COLLEGE

209 RIDGE RD
DAVIDSON, NC 280367886
Phone: 704-894-2000
Fax: –
Web: www.davidson.edu

CEO: –
CFO: –
HR: –
FYE: June 30
Type: Private

The 1850 students at Davidson College account for about a fifth of the population in the small North Carolina town with the same name. Located just north of Charlotte the liberal arts school offers more than 25 majors and 17 minors in areas such as anthropology art economics history and philosophy. It also offers pre-professional programs in medicine law business ministerial and management. Students are bound by a strict honor code that allows self-scheduled unproctored exams and prohibits students from cheating and stealing.

	Annual Growth	06/06	06/07	06/08	06/09	06/10
Sales ($ mil.)	(74.6%)	–	–	1,552.8	97.0	100.3
Net income ($ mil.)	101133.4%	–	–	0.0	(137.1)	71.7
Market value ($ mil.)	–	–	–	–	–	–
Employees	–	–	–	–	–	800

THE TRUSTEES OF GRINNELL COLLEGE

733 BROAD ST
GRINNELL, IA 501122227
Phone: 641-269-3500
Fax: –
Web: www.grinnell.edu

CEO: –
CFO: –
HR: –
FYE: June 30
Type: Private

Ear to ear might be pushing it but the students at Grinnell College have reason to be happy. On its 120-acre campus in rural Grinnell Iowa more than 1600 students choose from courses in some 25 major fields. Programs are centered on social studies science and the humanities at this private four-year liberal arts school. The college has an open curriculum allowing students to design their own academic programs. It also offers general literary studies and has a student-to-teacher ratio of 9:1. The college which was founded in 1846 is named after abolitionist minister Josiah Bushnell Grinnell.

	Annual Growth	06/09	06/10	06/11	06/13	06/14
Sales ($ mil.)	(4.1%)	–	123.8	93.9	99.8	104.6
Net income ($ mil.)	3.5%	–	–	239.3	167.8	265.1
Market value ($ mil.)	–	–	–	–	–	–
Employees	–	–	–	–	–	535

THE TRUSTEES OF MOUNT HOLYOKE COLLEGE

50 COLLEGE ST
SOUTH HADLEY, MA 010751448
Phone: 413-538-2000
Fax: –
Web: www.athletics.mtholyoke.edu

CEO: –
CFO: –
HR: –
FYE: June 30
Type: Private

Mount Holyoke College was the first of the Seven Sisters — the female equivalent of the predominantly male Ivy League. The nation's oldest continuing institution of higher learning for women Mount Holyoke offers nearly 50 departmental and interdisciplinary majors to about 2300 female students. Mount Holyoke is part of the Five College Consortium which also includes Amherst Hampshire Smith and the University of Massachusetts. (Mount Holyoke students can take classes at any of these schools.) Notable alumnae include poet Emily Dickinson and Tony- and Pulitzer Prize-winning playwright Wendy Wasserstein.

	Annual Growth	06/07	06/08	06/09	06/10	06/13
Sales ($ mil.)	–	–	0.0	136.6	156.3	134.4
Net income ($ mil.)	–	–	–	(31.6)	(16.2)	51.8
Market value ($ mil.)	–	–	–	–	–	–
Employees	–	–	–	–	–	1,000

THE TRUSTEES OF THE SMITH COLLEGE

1 CHAPIN WAY
NORTHAMPTON, MA 010636302
Phone: 413-585-2700
Fax: –
Web: www.smith.edu

CEO: –
CFO: –
HR: –
FYE: June 30
Type: Private

Girl Power abounds at Smith. The nation's largest liberal arts college for women Smith College provides 1000 courses in some 50 academic areas including the arts humanities languages sciences and social sciences. It enrolls nearly 2900 undergraduate students and employs about 300 professors. Annually nearly half of Smith juniors study abroad. Founded in 1871 by Sophia Smith (who left funds in her will to create a women's college) and her minister John Greene the school also offers graduate degrees in areas such as education social work and fine arts. Smith's notable alumna include chef Julia Child author and political commentator Molly Ivins and feminist icon Gloria Steinem.

	Annual Growth	12/07	12/08*	06/11	06/12	06/13
Sales ($ mil.)	219.5%	–	0.7	206.7	218.3	219.2
Net income ($ mil.)	(16.4%)	–	–	221.9	(37.6)	155.2
Market value ($ mil.)	–	–	–	–	–	–
Employees	–	–	–	–	–	1,300

*Fiscal year change

THE TRUSTEES OF WHEATON COLLEGE

501 COLLEGE AVE
WHEATON, IL 601875501
Phone: 630-752-5000
Fax: –
Web: www.wheaton.edu

CEO: –
CFO: –
HR: –
FYE: June 30
Type: Private

Wheaton College located in Wheaton Illinois — not to be confused with a school of the same name in Massachusetts — is a interdenominational Christian college. The private school offers dozens of liberal arts programs of study including a Ph.D. in Biblical and Theological Studies to its undergraduate and graduate students. Liberal arts programs include literature music fine arts biology economics and psychology. Wheaton College has about 3000 students and a 12:1 student-teacher ratio. Wheaton College was founded in 1860 and is named after Warren L. Wheaton who donated land to the school.

	Annual Growth	06/09	06/10	06/11	06/12	06/13
Sales ($ mil.)	(6.1%)	–	140.3	139.7	110.3	116.1
Net income ($ mil.)	102.8%	–	–	13.0	(9.4)	53.4
Market value ($ mil.)	–	–	–	–	–	–
Employees	–	–	–	–	–	820

THE UCLA FOUNDATION

10920 WILSHIRE BLVD # 200
LOS ANGELES, CA 90024-6502
Phone: 310-794-3193
Fax: –
Web: www.uclafoundation.org

CEO: –
CFO: –
HR: –
FYE: June 30
Type: Private

Helping to make La-La Land a little more erudite The UCLA Foundation raises manages and disperses funds to help support the tripartite education research and service mission of UCLA. With more than $1 billion in assets the organization funds the aforementioned purposes as well as campus improvements and special programs. About half of the foundation's gifts received are provided by foundations; corporations and alumni each account for some 15% of gifts. The UCLA Progress Fund predecessor of the foundation was established in 1945 by the school's alumni association.

	Annual Growth	06/0-1	06/00	06/09	06/10	06/11
Assets ($ mil.)	8.2%	–	849.2	1,308.6	1,555.2	2,022.7
Net income ($ mil.)	–	–	0.0	(37.0)	157.7	447.5
Market value ($ mil.)	–	–	–	–	–	–
Employees	–	–	–	–	–	317

THE UNION MEMORIAL HOSPITAL

201 E UNIVERSITY PKWY
BALTIMORE, MD 21218-2891
Phone: 410-554-2865
Fax: –
Web: www.unionmemorial.org

CEO: Bradley S Chambers
CFO: –
HR: Holly P Adams
FYE: June 30
Type: Private

Not quite for time immemorial but MedStar Union Memorial Hospital (formerly Union Memorial Hospital) has been caring for patients for a long time (since 1839). The Baltimore-area facility is a specialty acute-care hospital with 250 beds and more than 620 physicians. Areas of clinical research and expertise include cardiac care orthopedics and sports medicine. In addition it offers a range of inpatient and outpatient services including diabetes and endocrine center eye surgery center general surgery oncology and thoracic and vascular surgery. MedStar Union Memorial offers post-graduate programs orthopedic surgery residencies and hand surgery fellowships. The company is a part of MedStar Health.

	Annual Growth	06/07	06/08	06/09	06/11	06/12
Sales ($ mil.)	(0.4%)	–	424.1	438.1	428.0	418.0
Net income ($ mil.)	–	–	28.5	0.0	17.5	(2.1)
Market value ($ mil.)	–	–	–	–	–	–
Employees	–	–	–	–	–	2,400

THE UNITED METHODIST PUBLISHING HOUSE

201 8TH AVE S
NASHVILLE, TN 372033919
Phone: 615-749-6000
Fax: –
Web: www.umph.com

CEO: –
CFO: –
HR: –
FYE: July 31
Type: Private

The United Methodist Publishing House (UMPH) keeps Christian clergy from running out of reading material. Operated by a board of directors selected by the United Methodist Church's jurisdictional conferences and Council of Bishops the company publishes and distributes content for Christian clergy and laity. It develops produces and sells official denominational church school curriculum materials books music software and multimedia resources for homes churches and church offices. Founded in 1789 UMPH is the oldest and largest general agency of the United Methodist Church and it contributes a portion of its annual revenues to the church's clergy pension fund.

	Annual Growth	07/09	07/10	07/11	07/12	07/13
Sales ($ mil.)	(19.7%)	–	88.6	84.3	51.8	45.9
Net income ($ mil.)	–	–	–	6.5	(19.1)	(6.5)
Market value ($ mil.)	–	–	–	–	–	–
Employees	–	–	–	–	–	1,000

THE UNIVERSITY OF ARIZONA MEDICAL CENTER

1501 N CAMPBELL AVE
TUCSON, AZ 857240001
Phone: 520-694-0111
Fax: –
Web: www.umcaz.edu

CEO: Tom Dickson
CFO: Jeff Buehrle
HR: –
FYE: June 30
Type: Private

Banner - University Medicine (formerly The University of Arizona Health Network) heals Arizonans and trains Wildcats. It operates three academic medical centers in Phoenix and Tucson serving as the primary teaching hospital for the University of Arizona (UA) and offering medical treatment research and education services. The not-for-profit center provides cancer cardiology geriatric respiratory transplant and dialysis care as well as general practice and home health services. Specialty services include burn care behavioral health integrative medicine sports medicine and level I trauma care. The network merged with Banner Healthcare in 2015.

	Annual Growth	06/03	06/04	06/05	06/08	06/09
Sales ($ mil.)	(6.5%)	–	–	708.8	512.2	541.5
Net income ($ mil.)	–	–	–	0.0	27.1	0.0
Market value ($ mil.)	–	–	–	–	–	–
Employees	–	–	–	–	–	3,000

THE UNIVERSITY OF CHICAGO MEDICAL CENTER

5841 S MARYLAND AVE MC6098
CHICAGO, IL 606371447
Phone: 773-702-1000
Fax: –
Web: www.uchospitals.edu

CEO: James L Maderd
CFO: James M. Watson
HR: –
FYE: June 30
Type: Private

It may have received its official dedication on Halloween but The University of Chicago Medical Center (UCMC) works hard to make visiting the hospital a little less spooky. UCMC is a complex of facilities located on The University of Chicago campus that include the acute care Bernard A. Mitchell Hospital the Comer Children's Hospital a women's health and maternity facility and an outpatient care center. Established in 1927 (and dedicated on Halloween of that year) the complex includes the affiliated University of Chicago Pritzker School of Medicine and forms the clinical arm of The University of Chicago Division of Biological Sciences. UCMC houses about 550 beds.

	Annual Growth	06/05	06/06	06/07	06/08	06/09
Sales ($ mil.)	14.5%	–	861.9	1,092.0	1,286.3	1,294.9
Net income ($ mil.)	–	–	–	234.8	38.6	(190.1)
Market value ($ mil.)	–	–	–	–	–	–
Employees	–	–	–	–	–	5,000

THE UNIVERSITY OF DAYTON

300 COLLEGE PARK AVE
DAYTON, OH 454690002
Phone: 937-229-1000
Fax: –
Web: www.dining.udayton.edu

CEO: –
CFO: –
HR: Joyce Carter
FYE: June 30
Type: Private

More than 10000 students make the University of Dayton one of the nation's largest Catholic universities and the largest private university in Ohio. The institution offers some 70 majors. Students are recruited on a national basis and from foreign countries. The student population approximates 7300 undergraduate and 3000 graduate students. It has student and faculty ratio of 15:1 and charges tuition and fees of $33400 per annum. Well-known alumni include the late author and columnist Erma Bombeck and Super Bowl-winning NFL coaches Jon Gruden and Chuck Noll.

	Annual Growth	06/10	06/11	06/12	06/13	06/14
Sales ($ mil.)	4.6%	–	402.2	418.9	444.3	460.4
Net income ($ mil.)	–	–	–	(21.2)	96.6	126.1
Market value ($ mil.)	–	–	–	–	–	–
Employees	–	–	–	–	–	4,500

THE UNIVERSITY OF HARTFORD

200 BLOOMFIELD AVE
WEST HARTFORD, CT 061171599
Phone: 860-768-4393
Fax: –
Web: www.admission.hartford.edu

CEO: –
CFO: –
HR: –
FYE: June 30
Type: Private

While its roots date back to 1877 The University of Hartford wasn't officially chartered until 1957 with the merger of the Hartford Art School the Hartt School of Music and Hillyer College. The modern-day university still has a strong arts and music programs and its Museum of American Political Life is home to what has been called the country's largest private collection of political memorabilia. University of Hartford which operates three campuses in West Hartford has about 7000 students enrolled in more than 80 undergraduate and 30 graduate programs including business nursing and engineering.

	Annual Growth	06/10	06/11	06/12	06/13	06/14
Sales ($ mil.)	1.7%	–	165.1	165.6	170.5	173.4
Net income ($ mil.)	–	–	–	(10.5)	21.7	23.2
Market value ($ mil.)	–	–	–	–	–	–
Employees	–	–	–	–	–	950

THE UNIVERSITY OF SOUTH DAKOTA

414 E CLARK ST
VERMILLION, SD 57069-2307
Phone: 605-677-5011
Fax: –
Web: www.usd.edu

CEO: –
CFO: Greg Redlin
HR: –
FYE: June 30
Type: Private

Want to follow in former NBC "Nightly News" anchor Tom Brokaw's footsteps? Head to the University of South Dakota! Along with political science studies (Brokaw's degree) the school offers instruction to more than 10000 undergraduate and graduate students taught by more than 400 faculty members. University of South Dakota students can choose from about 130 undergraduate programs and 65 graduate programs. The university's student-faculty ratio is 17:1. The land-grant school which was founded in 1862 is the home of the only law and medical schools in the state of South Dakota.

	Annual Growth	06/0-1	06/00	06/05	06/06	06/11
Sales ($ mil.)	2.2%	–	92.6	13.4	13.4	117.8
Net income ($ mil.)	25.6%	–	2.3	5.9	5.9	28.4
Market value ($ mil.)	–	–	–	–	–	–
Employees	–	–	–	–	–	1,162

THE UNIVERSITY OF THE SOUTH

735 UNIVERSITY AVE
SEWANEE, TN 373831000
Phone: 931-598-1000
Fax: –
Web: www.sewanee.edu

CEO: –
CFO: –
HR: –
FYE: June 30
Type: Private

With more than two dozen Rhodes Scholars among its alumni The University of the South known as Sewanee is ranked among America's top private liberal arts colleges. Sewanee which serves about 1600 students and boasts a student to faculty ratio of 10:1 offers more than 35 majors including computer science mathematics theology and history. It is also home to a seminary of the Episcopal Church and a School of Letters summer Master's Degree program in English and creative writing. It holds the copyrights to Tennessee Williams' body of work which was left to the school by the playwright. Sewanee traces its roots back to 1857 when Episcopal leaders from 10 southern states met to discuss the formation of the school.

	Annual Growth	06/10	06/11	06/12	06/13	06/14
Sales ($ mil.)	6.6%	–	81.2	81.4	87.0	98.3
Net income ($ mil.)	–	–	–	(1.3)	20.2	53.4
Market value ($ mil.)	–	–	–	–	–	–
Employees	–	–	–	–	–	550

THE UNIVERSITY OF TULSA

800 TUCKER DR
TULSA, OK 741049700
Phone: 918-631-2000
Fax: –
Web: www.utulsa.edu

CEO: –
CFO: –
HR: –
FYE: June 30
Type: Private

If you're "Living on Tulsa Time" and looking for an education then the home of the Golden Hurricanes is the place to be. The University of Tulsa is a private university affiliated with the Presbyterian Church (USA) with an enrollment of about 5000 students. The school offers more than 60 undergraduate and about 35 graduate programs including a dozen doctoral degree programs at colleges of arts and sciences business and engineering and natural sciences. The University of Tulsa was founded in Muskogee in 1882 as the Presbyterian School for Indian Girls and was chartered as Henry Kendall College in 1894. The school moved to Tulsa in 1907 and became The University of Tulsa in 1920.

	Annual Growth	06/09	06/10	06/11	06/12	06/13
Sales ($ mil.)	18.5%	–	163.3	180.1	173.8	271.4
Net income ($ mil.)	(68.9%)	–	–	134.6	(23.3)	13.0
Market value ($ mil.)	–	–	–	–	–	–
Employees	–	–	–	–	–	1,033

THE UPPER DECK COMPANY LLC

5909 Sea Otter Pl.
Carlsbad CA 92010-6621
Phone: 760-929-6500
Fax: 760-929-6548
Web: www.upperdeck.com

CEO: Richard Mc William
CFO: –
HR: –
FYE: November 30
Type: Private

This Upper Deck is open to all sports fans. The company is one of the nation's leading sellers of sports collectibles including trading cards and autographed memorabilia. Upper Deck's products represent basketball football hockey soccer and stock car racing. Its patented Upper Deck Authenticated system combats forgery through a five-step process for ensuring genuine autographs. The company has agreements to produce memorabilia with such sports superstars as Tiger Woods Michael Jordan and LeBron James. Upper Deck was founded in 1988 by CEO and owner Richard McWilliam.

THE URBAN INSTITUTE

2100 M ST NW STE 500
WASHINGTON, DC 200371207
Phone: 202-833-7200
Fax: –
Web: www.urban.org

CEO: –
CFO: Christy Visher
HR: Deborah (Deb) Hoover
FYE: December 31
Type: Private

The Urban Institute is a not-for-profit economic and social policy research organization that oversees research projects in such areas as education health policy employment income and benefits housing and communities population studies poverty and judicial issues. Its Urban Institute Press publishes books and reports addressing social and economic issues from tax policy to prison reform. About three-fourths of the institution's funding comes from the federal government; most of the rest comes from foundations including The Aspen Institute and the California Endowment. The Urban Institute was established as a non-partisan research facility in 1968 by the Johnson Administration.

	Annual Growth	12/08	12/09	12/11	12/12	12/13
Sales ($ mil.)	3.5%	–	67.2	71.8	82.5	77.0
Net income ($ mil.)	–	–	–	(2.8)	17.6	(0.5)
Market value ($ mil.)	–	–	–	–	–	–
Employees	–	–	–	–	–	350

THE VALLEY HOSPITAL INC

223 N VAN DIEN AVE
RIDGEWOOD, NJ 074502736
Phone: 201-447-8000
Fax: –
Web: www.valleyhealth.com

CEO: –
CFO: –
HR: –
FYE: December 31
Type: Private

The Valley Hospital is second to none when it comes to its Same-Day Service program. More than one-third of the company's annual patients experience its longstanding continuum of one-day service; fully half the surgeries performed are same-day. The not-for-profit hospital is a 450-bed facility providing general and emergency services to residents of New Jersey's Bergen County. The hospital belongs to the Valley Health System which also includes subsidiaries Valley Home Care and Valley Health Medical Group and is an affiliate member of NewYork-Presbyterian Healthcare. The Valley Hospital New Jersey's second busiest has more than 800 physicians on its medical staff.

	Annual Growth	12/04	12/05	12/06	12/08	12/09
Sales ($ mil.)	8.8%	–	419.5	446.9	531.4	587.2
Net income ($ mil.)	16.5%	–	–	28.2	33.8	44.5
Market value ($ mil.)	–	–	–	–	–	–
Employees	–	–	–	–	–	2,900

THE VANGUARD GROUP INC.

100 Vanguard Blvd.
Malvern PA 19355
Phone: 610-648-6000
Fax: 952-893-3700
Web: www.rtwi.com

CEO: F William McNabb III
CFO: –
HR: –
FYE: December 31
Type: Private

Vanguard invests both time and money to reach the forefront of the investment community. The Vanguard Group offers individual and institutional investors a comprehensive line of mutual funds and brokerage services. Boasting more than $1.6 trillion of assets under management including $152 billion in exchange-traded fund (ETF) assets the firm is battling rival FMR (best known as Fidelity) for the title of largest retail mutual fund manager worldwide. Vanguard's fund options include approximately 230 stock bond mixed and international offerings as well as variable annuity portfolios; its Vanguard 500 Index Fund is one of the largest in the US. Vanguard was founded in 1975.

THE VONS COMPANIES INC.

618 Michillinda Ave.
Arcadia CA 91007-6300
Phone: 626-821-7000
Fax: 626-821-7933
Web: www.vons.com

CEO: –
CFO: –
HR: –
FYE: December 31
Type: Subsidiary

The Vons Companies shares Southern California's crowded dinner table with some big and hungry rivals. The company has about 280 stores mostly in Southern California which is also home to Ralphs and Food 4 Less (both owned by Kroger) and privately-held Stater Bros. stores. Its stores (also in Nevada) operate under the names Vons (traditional supermarkets) and Pavilions (upscale supermarkets). More than half of its supermarkets offer separate service departments for floral bakery and deli products while some have full-service pharmacies and dry-cleaning departments. The company operates its own facilities for producing milk ice cream and baked goods. Safeway a leading US grocery chain owns Vons.

THE WALDINGER CORPORATION

2601 BELL AVE
DES MOINES, IA 503211189
Phone: 515-284-1911
Fax: –
Web: www.waldinger.com

CEO: Thomas K Koehn
CFO: Brian Worth
HR: –
FYE: December 31
Type: Private

The Waldinger Corporation may actually do most of its work before the walls are even up. The company is an electrical mechanical and sheet metal contractor that primarily serves US customers across the Midwest and Southeast. Through its work in more than 40 states Waldinger designs fabricates installs and maintains HVAC refrigeration electrical plumbing and piping for commercial institutional and industrial clients. Waldinger also operates a division devoted to the food service industry. The company has offices in Iowa Kansas Missouri and Nebraska. Austrian tinsmith Harry Waldinger founded the company as Capital City Tin Shop in 1906.

	Annual Growth	12/09	12/10	12/11	12/12	12/13
Sales ($ mil.)	10.0%	–	155.7	160.3	186.2	207.1
Net income ($ mil.)	–	–	–	0.0	0.0	0.0
Market value ($ mil.)	–	–	–	–	–	–
Employees	–	–	–	–	–	900

THE WALSH GROUP LTD

929 W ADAMS ST
CHICAGO, IL 606073021
Phone: 312-563-5400
Fax: –
Web: www.walshgroup.com

CEO: Matthew M. (Matt) Walsh
CFO: Tim Gerken
HR: Colleen Stack
FYE: December 31
Type: Private

The Walsh Group erects walls halls malls and more. Operating through subsidiaries Walsh Construction and Archer Western Contractors the family-owned group provides design/build general contracting and construction services for industrial public and commercial projects. Walsh provides complete project management services from demolition and planning to general contracting and finance. The company is involved in the construction of bridges highways water treatment facilities airports hotels convention centers correctional facilities and commercial industrial and residential buildings. It also renovates and restores buildings. The company was founded in 1898 by Matthew Myles Walsh.

	Annual Growth	12/06	12/07	12/08	12/09	12/10
Sales ($ mil.)	4.4%	–	–	–	3,316.0	3,462.3
Net income ($ mil.)	(3.0%)	–	–	–	191.9	186.2
Market value ($ mil.)	–	–	–	–	–	–
Employees	–	–	–	–	–	5,000

THE WARMINGTON GROUP

3090 Pullman St. Ste. A
Costa Mesa CA 92626
Phone: 714-557-5511
Fax: 714-641-9337
Web: www.warmingtonhomes.com

CEO: –
CFO: –
HR: –
FYE: December 31
Type: Private

The Warmington Group is fired up on California homebuilding; it's also gambling on residential development in Las Vegas. Warmington has built approximately 30000 residences in Northern and Southern California and Nevada including single-family homes and luxury condominiums and townhomes ranging in price from about $100000 to more than $1 million. The group offers mortgage home financing and loans through affiliate Bayport Mortgage custom interior design services through Chateau Interiors & Design brokerage services for homesellers through Warmington Realty and property management through BayHarbor Management Services. William C. Warmington founded the first Warmington company in 1926.

THE WARRIOR GROUP INC

1624 FALCON DR STE 100
DESOTO, TX 751152543
Phone: 972-228-9955
Fax: –

CEO: Gail Warrior
CFO: Betty Floyd
HR: –
FYE: December 31
Type: Private

The Warrior Group has its work cut out for it literally. A modular construction and construction management services company Warrior Group builds permanent modular buildings — including military dormitories student housing and office buildings — from prefabricated wood and metal components. Its construction management offerings include planning design purchasing engineering and post-construction services. In recent years the company has worked on projects for the Veterans Administration in Marion Illinois; built barracks at Fort Bliss and other military installations; and managed a construction project at the University of North Texas. Warrior Group was founded in 1997 by CEO Gail Warrior-Lawrence.

	Annual Growth	12/05	12/06	12/07	12/08	12/09
Sales ($ mil.)	(70.0%)	–	–	1,375.9	0.3	124.0
Net income ($ mil.)	17217.2%	–	–	0.0	0.1	9.7
Market value ($ mil.)	–	–	–	–	–	–
Employees	–	–	–	–	–	36

THE WASHINGTON AND LEE UNIVERSITY

204 W WASHINGTON ST
LEXINGTON, VA 244502554
Phone: 540-458-8400
Fax: –
Web: www.wlu.edu

CEO: Kenneth P Ruscio
CFO: –
HR: –
FYE: June 30
Type: Private

One of the oldest colleges in the country Washington and Lee University (W&L) was founded in 1749 and is named after George Washington (who bequeathed the school its first major endowment) and Confederate general Robert E. Lee (a former president of the institution). The highly ranked liberal arts school in Lexington Virginia is attended by more than 2300 students who take courses in about 40 major areas including public policy politics international studies physics and biochemistry. The university has more than 200 faculty and a student-to-faculty ratio of 9:1. Former US Supreme Court Justice and W&L alumni Lewis F. Powell donated his personal and professional papers to the university's prestigious law school.

	Annual Growth	06/09	06/10	06/11	06/12	06/13
Sales ($ mil.)	(4.8%)	–	163.3	173.9	254.1	141.1
Net income ($ mil.)	172.5%	–	–	13.6	81.3	100.7
Market value ($ mil.)	–	–	–	–	–	–
Employees	–	–	–	–	–	700

THE WASHINGTON UNIVERSITY

1 BROOKINGS DR	CEO: –
SAINT LOUIS, MO 631304899	CFO: Barbara A. Feiner
Phone: 314-935-8566	HR: –
Fax: –	FYE: June 30
Web: www.wustl.edu	Type: Private

Washington University also known as Washington University in St. Louis (WUSTL) is the gateway to higher education for more than 13000 students. Founded in 1853 the independent university offers 90 bachelor's master's and doctoral degrees and has about 3400 faculty members. It offers approximately 1500 courses in fields such as arts and sciences business design and visual arts engineering law medicine and social work. WUSTL which has multiple campuses in and near the city of St. Louis also offers associate degree and continuing education programs. The affiliated Washington University Medical Center is an acute-care hospital that also provides educational training and research services.

	Annual Growth	06/10	06/11	06/12	06/13	06/14
Sales ($ mil.)	3.3%	–	2,245.6	2,307.9	2,393.1	2,472.1
Net income ($ mil.)	–	–	–	(49.3)	557.6	917.9
Market value ($ mil.)	–	–	–	–	–	–
Employees	–	–	–	–	–	9,600

THE WATERBURY HOSPITAL

64 ROBBINS ST	CEO: –
WATERBURY, CT 067082600	CFO: –
Phone: 203-573-6000	HR: –
Fax: –	FYE: September 30
Web: www.waterburyhospital.org	Type: Private

Where do broken hearts go? Waterbury Hospital hopes it's to its cardiologists. The community teaching hospital serving western Connecticut has been named one of the top hospitals in the nation for cardiac intervention. Of course hearts aren't the only body parts Waterbury Hospital treats; the full-service facility has nearly 370 beds and offers services that include behavioral health care an orthopedic center and an outpatient surgery center. Waterbury Hospital founded in 1890 forms the cornerstone of the Greater Waterbury Health Network which provides a range of outpatient health services from nursing care to hospice imaging and lab services. Prospect Medical Holdings is buying Waterbury Hospital.

	Annual Growth	09/06	09/07	09/08	09/09	09/13
Sales ($ mil.)	(2.7%)	–	–	237.8	251.3	207.7
Net income ($ mil.)	–	–	–	(7.6)	(2.0)	(2.4)
Market value ($ mil.)	–	–	–	–	–	–
Employees	–	–	–	–	–	1,625

THE WEITZ COMPANY LLC

5901 Thornton Ave.	CEO: Len Martling
Des Moines IA 50321	CFO: Donald Blum
Phone: 515-698-4260	HR: –
Fax: 408-434-5351	FYE: December 31
Web: www.intersil.com	Type: Private

It took wits for The Weitz Company to become a top US general building contractor. It provides general contracting construction management and design/build services. Weitz builds everything from office buildings industrial plants senior communities and schools to resort hotels government facilities and malls. The company constructs supermarkets and warehouse/distribution centers through its Hy-Vee/Weitz unit. Weitz and its subsidiaries are active in the US Guam and the Dominican Republic. Founded in 1855 by carpenter Charles H. Weitz the company was run by the Weitz family for four generations before becoming employee-owned in 1995. Egypt's Orascom Construction Industries agreed in 2012 to buy Weitz.

THE WESTERVELT COMPANY

1400 Jack Warner Pkwy. NE	CEO: Michael Case
Tuscaloosa AL 35404	CFO: Gary Bailey
Phone: 205-562-5000	HR: –
Fax: 205-562-5012	FYE: December 31
Web: www.westervelt.com	Type: Private

The Westervelt Company has turned over a new leaf — several actually — since its inception in 1884. A paper and paperboard packaging manufacturer for many years Westervelt now operates several distinct businesses related to land resource management. Besides owning and managing 500000 acres of timberlands the company operates sporting lodges around the world offers wildlife gaming and recreational property management develops master-planned residential communities in Alabama and is involved in creating renewable energy. The company is privately owned by the Westervelt and Warner families.

THE WHITEWAVE FOODS COMPANY

NYSE: WWAV

2711 North Haskell Ave. Ste. 3400	CEO: Gregg L Engles
Dallas TX 75204	CFO: Kelly J Haecker
Phone: 214-303-3400	HR: –
Fax: 412-968-1084	FYE: December 31
Web: www.abarta.com	Type: Public

'Got milk?' WhiteWave Foods has a white mustache alternative. The company is best known for its refrigerated Silk soymilk in the US and Alpro brand soy products in Europe. WhiteWave also produces organic dairy products under the Horizon Organic label and dairy related foods including International Delight coffee creamers and LAND O'LAKES-branded creamers and dairy dessert toppings (licensed from dairy co-op Land O'Lakes). WhiteWave products are sold through natural food and grocery stores as well as mass merchandisers and restaurants and foodservice businesses in the US and Canada and parts of Europe. Founded in 1977 the former division of Dean Foods went public in 2012.

THE WHITING-TURNER CONTRACTING COMPANY

300 E JOPPA RD STE 800	CEO: Timothy J. Regan
BALTIMORE, MD 212863047	CFO: –
Phone: 410-821-1100	HR: –
Fax: –	FYE: December 31
Web: www.whiting-turner.com	Type: Private

Whiting-Turner Contracting provides construction management general contracting and design/build services primarily for large commercial institutional and infrastructure projects conducted across the US. A key player in retail construction the employee-owned company also undertakes such projects as biotech cleanrooms theme parks historical restorations senior living residences educational facilities stadiums and corporate headquarters. Clients past and present include the US military AT&T General Motors and Texas A&M University. Whiting-Turner Contracting operates some 30 locations nationwide.

	Annual Growth	12/08	12/09	12/10	12/11	12/12
Sales ($ mil.)	(3.0%)	–	–	–	3,897.4	3,781.5
Net income ($ mil.)	(1.9%)	–	–	–	57.5	56.4
Market value ($ mil.)	–	–	–	–	–	–
Employees	–	–	–	–	–	1,839

THE WICHITA STATE UNIVERSITY

1845 FAIRMOUNT ST	CEO: –
WICHITA, KS 672600001	CFO: –
Phone: 316-978-3040	HR: –
Fax: –	FYE: June 30
Web: www.hws.wichita.edu	Type: Private

You are still in Kansas if you attend Wichita State University (WSU). The state-supported school enrolls more than 15000 students with more than 89% hailing from Kansas. Along with its main campus WSU provides classes at four additional campuses. The school offers 70 undergraduate degrees in more than 200 subjects. Its Graduate School offers more than 40 master's programs a dozen doctoral degree programs an educational specialist program and more than 20 graduate certificate programs as well as research opportunities. WSU colleges include business education engineering fine arts health professions and liberal arts and sciences. The school was founded in 1895 as a Congregational institution.

	Annual Growth	06/10	06/11	06/12	06/13	06/14
Sales ($ mil.)	(0.7%)	–	182.7	184.9	189.1	178.9
Net income ($ mil.)	(30.2%)	–	–	10.8	16.7	5.2
Market value ($ mil.)	–	–	–	–	–	–
Employees	–	–	–	–	–	3,395

THE WILL-BURT COMPANY

169 S MAIN ST	CEO: Jeffrey Evans
ORRVILLE, OH 446671801	CFO: –
Phone: 330-682-7015	HR: –
Fax: –	FYE: November 13
Web: www.willburt.com	Type: Private

It's a Roger WILCO for Will-Burt Company a manufacturer of roof- and vertical-mounted masts for use in fire and rescue police and security weather military broadcast and cellular applications. The pneumatic and mechanical telescoping masts and accessories elevate lights communication (antennae) and surveillance equipment and cameras. Military masts include vehicle mounted and portable field masts. Will-Burt also designs and develops lighting systems mobile command centers and printed circuit boards. Customers include large companies in the US as well as government and military clients worldwide. Will-Burt an employee-owned company has offices in the US the UK and Singapore.

	Annual Growth	12/06	12/07	12/08	12/09*	11/14
Sales ($ mil.)	5.1%	–	–	–	49.8	63.9
Net income ($ mil.)	0.5%	–	–	–	1.7	1.7
Market value ($ mil.)	–	–	–	–	–	–
Employees	–	–	–	–	–	275

*Fiscal year change

THE WILLAMETTE VALLEY COMPANY

1075 ARROWSMITH ST	CEO: John R Harrison
EUGENE, OR 974029121	CFO: R Larry Deck
Phone: 541-484-9621	HR: –
Fax: –	FYE: December 31
Web: www.wilvaco.com	Type: Private

Willamette Valley makes a wide landscape of synthetic paints primers sealers and adhesives for the wood products industry. It also provides metering dispensing and application equipment. The company's divisions include Canadian Willamette Tapel Willamette (a Chilean coatings subsidiary) Idaho Milling and Grain and Eclectic Products (adhesives spackle and so forth). Willamette Valley has manufacturing operations and subsidiaries throughout the US as well as in Canada and Chile; it also provides services to European and Asian customers.

	Annual Growth	03/09	03/10	03/11*	12/12	12/13
Sales ($ mil.)	–	–	0.0	104.7	126.5	142.1
Net income ($ mil.)	–	–	–	0.0	0.0	0.0
Market value ($ mil.)	–	–	–	–	–	–
Employees	–	–	–	–	–	260

*Fiscal year change

THE WILLIAM AND FLORA HEWLETT FOUNDATION

2121 Sand Hill Rd.	CEO: –
Menlo Park CA 94025	CFO: –
Phone: 650-234-4500	HR: –
Fax: 650-234-4501	FYE: December 31
Web: www.hewlett.org	Type: Private - Foundation

The Hewlett Foundation is dedicated to helping solve the world's social and environmental problems. One of the nation's largest charitable institutions it has more than $6 billion in assets and disbursed more than $425 million million in grants and gifts in 2007. It provides grants in a diverse areas including education reform environmental protection in the West and population growth. The private foundation also promotes the performing arts in the San Francisco Bay Area and has funded conflict resolution and international relations programs in the past. The late Bill Hewlett co-founder of Hewlett-Packard founded the Hewlett Foundation with his wife and eldest son in 1967.

THE WILLIAMS COMPANIES INC.   NYSE: WMB

1 Williams Center	CEO: Alan S Armstrong
Tulsa OK 74172	CFO: Donald R Chappel
Phone: 918-573-2000	HR: –
Fax: 918-573-6714	FYE: December 31
Web: www.williams.com	Type: Public

Williams Companies has several parts but they all add up to the delivery of energy and profits. Williams is primarily engaged in gas marketing and the gathering storing and the processing of natural gas and natural gas liquids (NGLs). It also operates refineries ethanol plants and terminals. The company owns 71% of publicly traded limited master partnership Williams Partners which has gas pipeline operations in the Northwest the Rockies the Gulf Coast and the East. The gas pipeline unit operates three major interstate pipeline companies (Transco Northwest and Gulfstream).

THE WILLS GROUP INC

6355 CRAIN HWY	CEO: –
LA PLATA, MD 206464267	CFO: Jennifer Popescu
Phone: 301-932-3600	HR: –
Fax: –	FYE: September 30
Web: www.willsgroup.com	Type: Private

The Wills Group willingly delivers petroleum products and related products and services to its customer base in southern Maryland and adjacent areas. The family-owned company operates four business subsidiaries: Dash-In Convenience Stores (with 35 locations including 18 franchises); DMO (provider of propane heating oil and HVAC equipment); and Southern Maryland Oil (SMO) and SMO Motor Fuels (distribution of diesel gasoline and kerosene products). More than 90% of SMO's gasoline products are Shell-branded fuels. The Wills Group supplies more than 300 dealer-operated gas stations in Delaware southern Maryland and Washington DC.

	Annual Growth	09/09	09/10	09/11	09/12	09/13
Sales ($ mil.)	6.7%	–	768.7	1,052.9	1,039.5	933.4
Net income ($ mil.)	18.9%	–	–	17.6	15.9	24.9
Market value ($ mil.)	–	–	–	–	–	–
Employees	–	–	–	–	–	280

THE WINTER GROUP OF COMPANIES INC.

191 Peachtree St.
Atlanta GA 30303
Phone: 404-588-3300
Fax: 404-233-5753
Web: www.wintercompanies.com

CEO: S Brent Reid
CFO: Ralph Mumme
HR: –
FYE: December 31
Type: Group

Winter is hot in the Southeast where The Winter Group of Companies does business. The group's general contracting division Winter Construction provides design/build construction and construction management services for projects including health care retail hospitality education religious and multi-family residential buildings. It also oversees industrial projects for municipal chemical and pharmaceutical clients. Winter Environmental offers infrastructure and remediation services for water/wastewater utility and chemical industries. Senior management acquired the majority stakes formerly held by founder and chairman Bob Silverman in early 2009.

THE WISTAR INSTITUTE OF ANATOMY AND BIOLOGY

3601 SPRUCE ST
PHILADELPHIA, PA 191044265
Phone: 215-898-1570
Fax: –
Web: www.wistar.org

CEO: Russel E Kaufman
CFO: –
HR: –
FYE: December 31
Type: Private

When the ailing wish upon a star Wistar might be able to find them a cure. Founded in 1892 The Wistar Institute is a not-for-profit biomedical research institution concentrating on major diseases such as cancer immune-system disorders heart ailments and infectious diseases. The institute operates from about 30 laboratories with research programs targeting genetic molecular and cellular discoveries. The company's research has been used in the development of vaccines pharmaceuticals and biotechnology drugs. Wistar collaborates with educational and governmental partners.

	Annual Growth	12/03	12/04	12/05	12/10	12/11
Sales ($ mil.)	11.3%	–	43.7	45.5	67.1	92.3
Net income ($ mil.)	51.5%	–	–	2.7	10.7	32.3
Market value ($ mil.)	–	–	–	–	–	–
Employees	–	–	–	–	–	350

THE WITKOFF GROUP

220 E. 42nd St.
New York NY 10017
Phone: 212-672-4700
Fax: 212-672-4726
Web: www.witkoff.com

CEO: –
CFO: –
HR: Josata Gonzalez
FYE: December 31
Type: Private

The Witkoff Group performs makeover miracles. Led by real estate lawyer turned developer Steven Witkoff the group buys old office buildings and then refurbishes them; its portfolio includes New York's landmark Woolworth Building. Known for its hands-on management style the company has interests in cleaning construction leasing and property management. The firm owns commercial residential and industrial space as well as land and hotel development interests in such key markets as metropolitan New York City New Jersey Philadelphia Chicago Detroit Hawaii and Dallas.

THE YANKEE CANDLE COMPANY INC.

16 Yankee Candle Way
South Deerfield MA 01373
Phone: 413-665-8306
Fax: 413-665-4815
Web: www.yankeecandle.com

CEO: Hope Margala
CFO: Bruce L Hartman
HR: –
FYE: December 31
Type: Subsidiary

While most Yankees are good at warming their homes the ones at The Yankee Candle Company (YCC) are also good at making their homes smell like Egyptian Cotton or Home Sweet Home. YCC makes and sells candles — known for their burning longevity and strong fragrances — in some 200 fragrances. It also sells candleholders accessories and dinnerware. Its products are sold by some 2900 gift shops nationwide as well as internationally in nearly 50 countries. The company operates about 550 stores in the US mostly in malls and sells online and through catalogs. With roots going back to 1969 YCC has been owned by Madison Dearborn Partners since 2007.

THE YATES COMPANIES INC.

1 Gully Ave.
Philadelphia MS 39350
Phone: 601-656-5411
Fax: 601-656-8958
Web: www.wgyates.com

CEO: –
CFO: Brandon Dunn
HR: Mack Ginn
FYE: December 31
Type: Private

The Yates Companies operates an extended family of construction firms comprising W.G. Yates & Sons Construction (the largest of the group) Yates Electrical Division Mississippi-based JESCO and Tennessee-based Blaine Construction. The group provides a broad range of construction-related services including engineering electrical and mechanical construction millwrighting and steel fabrication. It operates mostly in the Southeast and along the East Coast. Completed projects include casinos sports facilities schools and military facilities. William Yates Jr. co-founded the family-owned company in 1963 with his father the late William Gully Yates. The Yates family continues to lead the company.

THE YORK GROUP INC.

2 NorthShore Center Ste. 100
Pittsburgh PA 15212-5851
Phone: 412-995-1600
Fax: 412-995-1690
Web: www.yorkgrp.com

CEO: –
CFO: –
HR: –
FYE: September 30
Type: Subsidiary

The York Group makes boxes nearly too beautiful to part with. The nation's #2 casket maker (after Hillenbrand's Batesville Casket) produces metal and all-wood caskets memorials and plaques and cremation containers. (Cremation is the industry's growing trend — a third of US deaths are handled this way.) York is staking its vitality on an incentive program designed to boost sales via independent funeral homes. Its caskets and funeral products are sold almost entirely in the US through company-owned and independent distributors. The firm developed the York Merchandising System (YMS) a modular display of casket materials and decorative details. Industry behemoth Matthews International owns York Group.

THE YUCAIPA COMPANIES LLC

9130 W. Sunset Blvd.
Los Angeles CA 90069
Phone: 310-789-7200
Fax: 310-228-2873
Web: www.yucaipaco.com

CEO: –
CFO: –
HR: –
FYE: December 31
Type: Private

Yucaipa has a hungry eye for picking out ripe bargains in different industries but made its name with grocery stores. The investment company which was formed in 1986 forged its reputation as the ultimate grocery shopper executing a series of grocery chain mergers and acquisitions involving such companies as Fred Meyer Ralphs and Jurgensen's that put the company on the supermarket map. It currently owns stakes in about 35 companies including grocery chains A&P and Whole Foods. Yucaipa's chairman billionaire and former grocery store bag boy Ron Burkle is a prominent Democratic activist and fundraiser. He owns a significant stake in the NHL's Pittsburgh Penguins as well.

THE ZIEGLER COMPANIES INC.

PINK SHEETS: ZGCO

200 S. Wacker Dr. Ste. 2000
Chicago IL 60606
Phone: 312-263-0110
Fax: 312-263-4066
Web: www.ziegler.com

CEO: Thomas R Paprocki
CFO: –
HR: –
FYE: December 31
Type: Public

Health and wealth go hand-in-hand for The Ziegler Companies. The firm operating through several subsidiaries offers specialty investment banking and asset management services. Catering mainly to not-for-profit institutions such as health care providers senior living facilities charter schools and churches the company provides financing advisory services and securities underwriting sales and trading. It also serves renewable energy companies. In addition Ziegler offers brokerage financial planning and asset management services including its North Track family of mutual funds to both institutional and individual investors.

THEDACARE INC.

122 E COLLEGE AVE STE 2A
APPLETON, WI 549115741
Phone: 920-735-5560
Fax: –
Web: www.thedacare.org

CEO: Dean Gruner
CFO: Tim Olson
HR: –
FYE: December 31
Type: Private

ThedaCare is a community health system that provides a wide range of health services to residents of nine central Wisconsin counties. It consists of five hospitals including Appleton Medical Center Theda Clark Medical Center New London Family Medical Center Shawano Medical Center and Riverside Medical Center in Waupaca; more than 20 physician locations; and community health and wellness programs. The hospitals provide primary and acute care and offer many specialized diagnostic and medical services including behavioral health care and women's and children's services. ThedaCare also operates long-term care and assisted living facilities and provides occupational health and emergency transport services.

	Annual Growth	12/05	12/06	12/08	12/12	12/13
Sales ($ mil.)	–	–	0.0	3.1	276.5	720.5
Net income ($ mil.)	–	–	–	0.0	(3.1)	129.8
Market value ($ mil.)	–	–	–	–	–	–
Employees	–	–	–	–	–	5,900

THEOREM CLINICAL RESEARCH

630 Allendale Rd.
King of Prussia PA 19406
Phone: 484-679-2400
Fax: 484-679-2410
Web: www.theoremclinical.com/

CEO: –
CFO: –
HR: –
FYE: December 31
Type: Private

Theorem Clinical Research quantifies its clients' medical theories. The company formerly known as Omnicare Clinical Research is a contract research organization (CRO) offering drug development services from Phase I to Phase IV clinical trials to drug and medical device companies worldwide. The CRO has special expertise in the research areas including cardiovascular care dermatology geriatrics infectious disease metabolism oncology and vaccines. Services include patient and investigator recruitment clinical trials management safety monitoring statistical analysis drug packaging medical writing and regulatory review assistance. The company was acquired by equity firm Nautic Partners in 2011.

THERAPEUTICSMD, INC.

ASE: TXMD

6800 Broken Sound Parkway N.W., Third Floor
Boca Raton, FL 33487
Phone: 561 961-1900
Fax: –
Web: www.therapeuticsmd.com

CEO: Robert G. Finizio
CFO: Dan Cartwright
HR: –
FYE: December 31
Type: Public

Moms-to-be should check out TherapeuticsMD. The company makes over-the-counter prenatal vitamins and other supplements under the brand vitaMedMD and prescription-only prenatal vitamins under the brand BocaGreenMD. The vitaMedMD brand also offers skin creams for stretch marks and scars. Its OTC vitamins and creams are sold online through the company's website; its prescription vitamins are first offered as samples at OB/GYN offices and then at pharmacies for the full prescription. Its products are made by Rhode Island-based Lang Pharma Nutrition. In addition TherapeuticsMD is developing prescription-only hormone therapy products for women to alleviate menopause symptoms such as hot flashes.

	Annual Growth	12/10	12/11	12/12	12/13	12/14
Sales ($ mil.)	320.2%	0.0	2.1	3.8	8.8	15.0
Net income ($ mil.)	–	(0.7)	(12.9)	(35.1)	(28.4)	(54.2)
Market value ($ mil.)	246.8%	4.8	234.1	483.9	813.3	694.6
Employees	216.2%	1	51	69	69	100

THERM-O-DISC INCORPORATED

1320 S. Main St.
Mansfield OH 44907
Phone: 419-525-8500
Fax: 419-525-8344
Web: www.tod.com

CEO: Charles C G
CFO: –
HR: –
FYE: September 30
Type: Subsidiary

Some like it hot but in reality most like it moderate. Therm-O-Disc a subsidiary of Emerson Electric keeps indoor temperatures steady with sensor switch and control products for air-conditioning and heating systems home appliances cars and electronics. Products include thermostats toggle and snap-action switches time delay relays and thermal cutoffs. Therm-O-Disc also makes products for various automotive applications (parking brakes sunroof and wiper controls seat heaters and sliding doors). Parts are supplied directly to original equipment manufacturers. Established in 1947 Therm-O-Disc has operations throughout North America and in Asia Mexico the Netherlands South America and the UK.

THERMA-TRU CORP.

1750 Indian Wood Circle	CEO: Carl Hedlund
Maumee OH 43537	CFO: David Haddix
Phone: 419-891-7400	HR: Amanda Nelson
Fax: 419-891-7411	FYE: December 31
Web: www.thermatru.com	Type: Subsidiary

Knock knock Who's there? Therma-Tru. Therma-Tru who? A part of Fortune Brands Home & Security that's who. Therma-Tru manufactures fiberglass and steel exterior doors for residential and light commercial use. The company's patio and entry door systems feature wood-grain that resembles mahogany and oak. Smooth-surfaced fiberglass doors that resemble steel are sold under the Smooth-Star brand. Therma-Tru also offers decorative glass and hinges. Its Tru-Defense doors are built to withstand damaging weather and other harsh conditions. All doors are made with polyurethane foam cores for increased insulation. Therma-Tru products are sold in the US and Canada by distributors lumberyards and home centers.

THERMO FISHER SCIENTIFIC INC

NYS: TMO

81 Wyman Street	CEO: Marc N. Casper
Waltham, MA 02451	CFO: Stephen Williamson
Phone: 781 622-1000	HR: Art Wood
Fax: 781 933-4476	FYE: December 31
Web: www.thermofisher.com	Type: Public

Whether for research analysis discovery or diagnostics Thermo Fisher Scientific gets the laboratory ready to assist mankind. The company makes and distributes analytical instruments equipment and other laboratory supplies — from chromatographs and spectrometers to Erlenmeyer flasks and fume hoods. It also provides specialty diagnostic testing products as well as clinical analytical tools. Thermo Fisher serves more than 40000 customers worldwide in its key markets of health care and diagnostics biotech and pharmaceutical academic research institutions and government and industrial and applied settings including environmental quality and process control.

	Annual Growth	12/10	12/11	12/12	12/13	12/14
Sales ($ mil.)	11.9%	10,788.7	11,725.9	12,509.9	13,090.3	16,889.6
Net income ($ mil.)	16.3%	1,035.6	1,329.9	1,177.9	1,273.3	1,894.4
Market value ($ mil.)	22.7%	22,170.0	18,009.1	25,542.0	44,592.3	50,174.9
Employees	8.2%	37,200	39,300	38,900	50,000	51,000

THERMOENERGY CORP

NBB: TMEN

10 New Bond Street	CEO: –
Worcester, MA 01606	CFO: –
Phone: 508 854-1628	HR: –
Fax: –	FYE: December 31
Web: www.thermoenergy.com	Type: Public

You want clean air and clean water? Then ThermoEnergy Corporation's your guy. The company develops and markets wastewater treatment and clean energy technologies from its base in Little Rock Arkansas. ThermoEnergy licenses three clean water process technologies that serve different purposes along the water treatment assembly line. The company also is the owner of a clean energy technology that converts fossil fuels into electricity without producing air emissions; this process also captures CO_2 in liquid form for alternative uses. ThermoEnergy is contracted to build and operate a 500000 gallon water treatment ammonia recovery plant to serve New York City.

	Annual Growth	12/09	12/10	12/11	12/12	12/13
Sales ($ mil.)	(8.5%)	4.0	2.9	5.6	7.0	2.8
Net income ($ mil.)	–	(13.0)	(9.9)	(17.3)	(7.4)	(1.6)
Market value ($ mil.)	(43.4%)	38.0	35.3	25.1	12.1	3.9
Employees	1.1%	23	25	29	26	24

THERMON GROUP HOLDINGS INC

NYS: THR

100 Thermon Drive	CEO: Rodney L. Bingham
San Marcos, TX 78666	CFO: Jay C. Peterson
Phone: 512 396-5801	HR: –
Fax: –	FYE: March 31
Web: www.thermon.com	Type: Public

Thermon Group's heating products are not merely pipe dreams. Through its subsidiaries Thermon provides specialized cables tubes and control systems used in electric and steam "heat tracing" which involves externally applying heat to industrial-grade pipes tanks and instrumentation. Its core customers include energy chemical and power generation companies that use Thermon's products to maintain temperatures of materials transported or stored in pipes and vessels as well as for freeze protection in harsh environments. The company's customers have included dozens of multinational giants like Exxon Dow ConocoPhillips Procter and Gamble and Kellogg.

	Annual Growth	03/11	03/12	03/13	03/14	03/15
Sales ($ mil.)	8.1%	225.7	270.5	284.0	277.3	308.6
Net income ($ mil.)	–	(14.9)	12.0	27.0	25.8	49.4
Market value ($ mil.)	5.6%	–	656.1	712.5	743.7	772.2
Employees	10.8%	658	755	821	829	991

THESTREET, INC.

NMS: TST

14 Wall Street, 15th Floor	CEO: Elisabeth H. DeMarse
New York, NY 10005	CFO: Eric F. Lundberg
Phone: 212 321-5000	HR: –
Fax: 212 321-5015	FYE: December 31
Web: www.t.st	Type: Public

If you're looking for investment advice you might want to check the word on the street. TheStreet offers financial news tools and analysis as well as community features such as online chats and message boards on both its advertising supported flagship website TheStreet.com and on its subscription-based site RealMoney.com which also features commentary from market experts. Its MainStreet.com site features content related to personal finance topics. Sales come from advertising and subscriber fees. The company also distributes content through syndication deals with sites such as Yahoo! Finance MSN Money and CNN Money and provides equity research and brokerage services to institutional clients.

	Annual Growth	12/10	12/11	12/12	12/13	12/14
Sales ($ mil.)	1.6%	57.2	57.8	50.7	54.5	61.1
Net income ($ mil.)	–	(5.3)	(8.2)	(12.7)	(3.8)	(3.8)
Market value ($ mil.)	(2.8%)	92.7	58.3	58.0	78.5	82.7
Employees	17.6%	291	289	273	276	557

THINGS REMEMBERED INC.

5500 Avion Park Dr.	CEO: Lisa Gavales
Highland Heights OH 44143	CFO: –
Phone: 440-473-2000	HR: –
Fax: 440-473-2018	FYE: December 31
Web: www.thingsremembered.com	Type: Private

Things Remembered is trying hard not to be forgotten. The company primarily sells products such as jewelry leather goods glassware and religious items that can be personalized with engraving or embroidery and given as gifts. The retailer boasts more than 600 mall-based locations in the US across 48 states; it also operates about 160 kiosks. Stores also offer personalization services for items purchased elsewhere. Besides its bricks-and-mortar locations Things Remembered markets products through its catalog and e-commerce site. The company is owned by the Chicago-based private equity firm Madison Dearborn Partners (MDP).

THIRD WAVE TECHNOLOGIES INC.

502 S. Rosa Rd.
Madison WI 53719-1256
Phone: 608-273-8933
Fax: 608-273-8618
Web: www.hologic.com/en/laboratory-solutions/overvi

CEO: Kevin T Conroy
CFO: Maneesh K Arora
HR: Lander R Brown
FYE: December 31
Type: Subsidiary

Third Wave Technologies is riding the biotech breakers. Using its Invader technology Third Wave develops molecular diagnostic tests that detect genetic variations associated with a variety of conditions including cystic fibrosis cardiovascular risk factors and infectious disease. Some tests can determine a patient's likely response to certain drugs making it possible for doctors to avoid prescribing a drug that might cause dangerous side effects. The company also makes products targeted to the women's health market including tests to screen for cervical cancer. Founded in 1993 Third Wave Technologies is a subsidiary of medical device and technologies company Hologic.

THIRTEEN

825 8TH AVE FL 14
NEW YORK, NY 100197435
Phone: 212-560-2000
Fax: –
Web: www.wnet.org

CEO: –
CFO: Robert Clauser
HR: Charlene Shapiro
FYE: June 30
Type: Private

You might say this broadcaster has some public appeal for New Yorkers. Educational Broadcasting Corporation (EBC) operates two public broadcasting stations serving the New York City area. Its flagship Thirteen/WNET the highest-rated public TV station in the US offers a wealth of locally produced content focused on the Big Apple as well as programming supplied by the Public Broadcasting Service (PBS). Thirteen/WNET is also a major producer of shows for PBS that are distributed to other public TV stations. Thirteen/WNET began broadcasting in 1962.

	Annual Growth	06/08	06/09	06/10	06/11	06/12
Sales ($ mil.)	(10.4%)	–	146.1	127.3	105.7	105.2
Net income ($ mil.)	16.3%	–	–	10.0	12.2	13.6
Market value ($ mil.)	–	–	–	–	–	–
Employees	–	–	–	–	–	400

THL CREDIT INC.

NASDAQ: TCRD

100 Federal St. 31st Fl.
Boston MA 02110
Phone: 800-454-4424
Fax: 661-295-0695
Web: https://www.wescoair.com

CEO: Sam W Tillinghast
CFO: Terrence W Olson
HR: –
FYE: December 31
Type: Public

When it comes to its investment strategy THL Credit cares less about industry type and more about investment type. A business development company and closed-end investment fund THL Credit invests in a variety of public and private middle-market companies with annual revenues between $25 million and $500 million. It provides cash for recapitalizations and acquisitions as well as for organic growth initiatives like product expansions. It invests primarily in mezzanine debt and junior capital (a subordinated form of equity); its investments range from $10 million to $50 million per transaction. THL Credit is externally managed by THL Credit Advisors an affiliate of buyout firm Thomas H. Lee Partners.

THOMAS & BETTS CORPORATION

NYSE: TNB

8155 T&B Blvd.
Memphis TN 38125
Phone: 901-252-8000
Fax: 800-816-7810
Web: www.tnb.com

CEO: –
CFO: –
HR: Neva McPruder
FYE: December 31
Type: Public

Thomas & Betts (T&B) bets on its good connections. The company provides electrical connectors HVAC equipment and transmission towers to the commercial construction industrial and utility markets through thousands of distributor locations and wholesalers in North America. Its segments include electrical (electrical connectors enclosures raceways installation tools); HVAC (heaters gas-fired duct furnaces and evaporative cooling products); and steel structures (poles and transmission towers for power companies). Brands include Color-Keyed Elastimold Kindorf Red Dot Reznor and Steel City. In mid-2012 T&B was acquired by power and automation technology powerhouse ABB Ltd.

THOMAS H. LEE PARTNERS L.P.

100 Federal St.
Boston MA 02110
Phone: 617-227-1050
Fax: 617-227-3514
Web: www.thl.com

CEO: –
CFO: Cindy Coslick
HR: –
FYE: December 31
Type: Private

Thomas H. Lee Partners (THL) could be called the teddy bear at the gate. The company uses a mix of debt funds from institutional investors and its own money to buy companies. Unlike the fearsome leveraged buyout outfits of the 1980s THL eschews the axe for the handshake; it builds up its stake works with management then ideally sells the revamped acquisitions or takes them public. The firm has invested some $20 billion since its 1974 founding. It targets companies in the business and information services consumer products financial services health care industrial and media sectors. Major holdings include ARAMARK Clear Channel Dunkin Brands MoneyGram Univision and Warner Chilcott.

THOMAS JEFFERSON SCHOOL OF LAW INC

1155 ISLAND AVE
SAN DIEGO, CA 921017230
Phone: 619-297-9700
Fax: –
Web: www.tjsl.edu

CEO: –
CFO: –
HR: –
FYE: June 30
Type: Private

|If Thomas Jefferson ever wanted to sunbathe between bouts of shaping our nation this would have been the place. Thomas Jefferson School of Law (TJSL) offers a traditional program of legal education leading to the award of master's degrees and Juris Doctor degrees. The private school offers a three year full-time or a four year part-time program. Its campus is located in the historic Old Town section of San Diego. Thomas Jefferson School of Law has about 800 students and was founded in 1969 as the the Western State University College of Law. It achieved independence and accreditation with the American Bar Association in 1996. The school is building a new $40 million downtown campus.

	Annual Growth	06/07	06/08	06/09	06/10	06/13
Sales ($ mil.)	–	–	0.0	29.1	35.5	50.1
Net income ($ mil.)	–	–	–	0.0	3.0	0.9
Market value ($ mil.)	–	–	–	–	–	–
Employees	–	–	–	–	–	120

THOMAS JEFFERSON UNIVERSITY

1020 WALNUT ST STE 1	CEO: Stephen K Klasko
PHILADELPHIA, PA 191075567	CFO: Richard J. Schmid
Phone: 215-955-6000	HR: –
Fax: –	FYE: June 30
	Type: Private

Thomas Jefferson University named after a founding father of diverse interests is itself diversifying the world of medical training. Its Jefferson Medical College boasts departments in surgery and specialized areas including obstetrics neurology and psychiatry. The Graduate Studies department offers programs in public health and biomedical studies. The College of Health Professions has programs in nursing pharmacy bioscience technologies and counseling. Founded as Jefferson Medical College in 1824 it has granted more than 30000 medical degrees. In late 2015 the school agreed to merge with Philadelphia University.

	Annual Growth	06/10	06/11	06/12	06/13	06/14
Sales ($ mil.)	2.8%	–	714.4	731.4	737.8	776.8
Net income ($ mil.)	–	–	–	(38.7)	67.1	131.9
Market value ($ mil.)	–	–	–	–	–	–
Employees	–	–	–	–	–	10,000

THOMAS JEFFERSON UNIVERSITY HOSPITALS INC.

111 S 11TH ST	CEO: –
PHILADELPHIA, PA 191074824	CFO: –
Phone: 215-955-5806	HR: Pamela (Pam) Teufel
Fax: –	FYE: June 30
Web: www.nemours.org	Type: Private

Named after the "Man of the People" Thomas Jefferson University Hospitals serves the people of the Keystone State with a medical staff of more than 1200 and some 950 beds. Part of the Jefferson Health System it provides acute tertiary and specialty medical care. Aside from the main campus it operates through a Center City Campus Methodist Hospital Jefferson Voorhees and Jefferson Hospital for Neuroscience. The hospital also administers cardiac care at the Jefferson Heart Institute which provides everything from minimally invasive surgical procedures to heart transplants. It is also the teaching hospital for Thomas Jefferson University.

	Annual Growth	06/06	06/07	06/08	06/09	06/10
Sales ($ mil.)	781426.9%	–	–	–	0.2	1,250.4
Net income ($ mil.)	–	–	–	–	0.0	49.4
Market value ($ mil.)	–	–	–	–	–	–
Employees	–	–	–	–	–	4,701

THOMAS NELSON INC.

501 Nelson Place	CEO: Mark Schoenwald
Nashville TN 37214	CFO: –
Phone: 615-889-9000	HR: –
Fax: 615-391-5225	FYE: March 31
Web: www.thomasnelson.com	Type: Private

Thomas Nelson is a top commercial publisher of Christian-related materials. The company produces about 10 major Bible translations in the English language and biblical reference products including commentaries help texts and study guides. Thomas Nelson also publishes religious and inspirational titles hosts inspirational conferences (Women of Faith) and produces Christian-oriented and family-focused products for adults and children including books games and audio and video materials. The company can trace its roots back to 1798 when Thomas Nelson began selling Bibles in in a town square in Edinburgh Scotland. Majority-owner Kohlberg & Co. agreed to sell its stake to HarperCollins in 2012.

THOMPSON & KNIGHT LLP

One Arts Plaza 1722 Routh St. Ste. 1500	CEO: Armando Cavanha
Dallas TX 75201	CFO: Diane M Scheffler
Phone: 214-969-1700	HR: –
Fax: 214-969-1751	FYE: December 31
Web: www.tklaw.com	Type: Private - Partnershi

Established in 1887 and headquartered in Dallas Thompson & Knight employs about 330 attorneys working from about a dozen offices. Thompson & Knight provides legal services to publicly owned domestic and international corporations as well as private businesses partnerships and charitable institutions. The firm is known for its expertise in energy finance taxation and business transactions. Subsidiary Thompson & Knight Global Energy Services offers a wide range of services to the energy industry with a focus on procurement and supply chain management.

THOMPSON CREEK METALS COMPANY INC.   NYSE: TC

26 West Dry Creek Cir. Ste. 810	CEO: –
Littleton CO 80120	CFO: –
Phone: 303-761-8801	HR: Chris Gibbs
Fax: 303-761-7420	FYE: December 31
Web: www.thompsoncreekmetals.com	Type: Public

Thompson Creek Metals has branched out from only mining molybdenum at its Thompson Creek site in Idaho to holding a diversified North American portfolio that also includes copper gold and silver assets. The company still obtains most of its sales (97%) from producing molybdenum a metal used to strengthen steel and make it corrosion-resistant. It operates the Thompson Creek mine and mill in Idaho and owns 75% of the Endako mine in British Columbia (Japan's Sojitz owns 25%). Thompson Creek has a metallurgical facility in Pennsylvania and holds exploration assets in British Columbia and in the Yukon and Nunavut territories. It controls about 449 million pounds of molybdenum proved and probable reserves.

THOMPSON HINE LLP

3900 Key Center 127 Public Sq.	CEO: –
Cleveland OH 44114-1291	CFO: Michael Goldberg
Phone: 216-566-5500	HR: –
Fax: 216-566-5800	FYE: December 31
Web: www.thompsonhine.com	Type: Private - Partnershi

Thompson Hine LLP has branched out to Europe but its roots are in the Midwestern US. The law firm is one of Cleveland's largest with more than 400 attorneys. Thompson Hine's clients include financial institutions governments individuals multinational corporations and not-for-profit organizations. The firm practices in such areas as antitrust and trade regulation bankruptcy securities intellectual property litigation product liability and taxation. Clients have included such heavy hitters as Goodyear Verizon Wireless and Exxon Mobil.

THOMPSON HOSPITALITY

1741 BUS CTR DR STE 200
RESTON, VA 20190
Phone: 703-757-5500
Fax: –
Web: www.thompsonhospitality.com

CEO: –
CFO: Ali Azima
HR: Jill Brown
FYE: December 30
Type: Private

A side of diversity please: One of the largest minority-owned companies in the US Thompson Hospitality is a contract foodservice provider to businesses government agencies and educational institutions. The foodservice operator's clients include a number of historically black colleges and universities notably Delaware State and Norfolk State as well as institutions around Washington DC such as Walter Reed Army Hospital. Thompson Hospitality also owns a handful of chain restaurants including Austin Grill. Formed through an alliance with major food provider Compass Group Thompson Hospitality has a presence in more than 45 states and four foreign countries. The two companies still partner on contracts.

	Annual Growth	12/08	12/09	12/10	12/11	12/12
Sales ($ mil.)	3.9%	–	97.2	101.3	109.5	109.0
Net income ($ mil.)	(24.1%)	–	–	10.0	4.6	5.8
Market value ($ mil.)	–	–	–	–	–	–
Employees	–	–	–	–	–	3,000

THOMSON REUTERS (LEGAL) INC.

610 Opperman Dr.
Eagan MN 55123
Phone: 651-687-7000
Fax: 707-523-2046
Web: www.westernfg.com

CEO: –
CFO: –
HR: –
FYE: December 31
Type: Business Segment

Thomson Reuters Legal focuses on the letter of the law. The division of financial information giant Thomson Reuters publishes legal information for law students professionals and consumers. Products are available in print and electronic formats and include law encyclopedias textbooks and study aids; state and federal law books; court opinions; how-to legal guides; and law indexes. The division's flagship online platform is its Westlaw research service which contains databases of legal financial and business news and information. In addition it offers law firm marketing software through its Hubbard One subsidiary and business and practice management applications for law firms through Elite.

THOMSON REUTERS CORPORATION

NYSE: TRI

3 Times Square
New York NY 10036
Phone: 646-223-4000
Fax: 847-205-7551
Web: www.kapstonepaper.com

CEO: James C. (Jim) Smith
CFO: Stephane Bello
HR: –
FYE: December 31
Type: Public

Financial information is king and Thomson Reuters Corporation holds the crown. The company is the market leader in financial data (ahead of rival information provider Bloomberg). Thomson Reuters provides electronic information and services to businesses and professionals worldwide serving the financial services media legal tax and accounting and science markets. Data is primarily offered online and to a lesser extent via CD-ROM and print formats; nearly all revenues come from subscription sales to its plethora of offerings. Thomson Reuters was created in 2008 as the result of the $16 billion cash and stock purchase of news service Reuters by information provider The Thomson Corporation.

THOR INDUSTRIES, INC.

NYS: THO

601 East Beardsley Ave.
Elkhart, IN 46514-3305
Phone: 574 970-7460
Fax: –
Web: www.thorindustries.com

CEO: Robert W. Martin
CFO: Colleen A. Zuhl
HR: Kenneth D. Julian
FYE: July 31
Type: Public

The Norse gods might have laughed at the idea of bedrooms on wheels but that doesn't stop Thor Industries a recreation vehicle builder. Through its subsidiaries the company makes and sells a range of RVs from motor homes to travel trailers as well as related parts. Brands include Airstream and Dutchmen. RV manufacturing plants generally produce vehicles to dealer order; Thor's independent dealers dot the US and Canada catering to private purchasers and municipalities. Thor rolled out in 1980 when Wade Thompson and Peter Orthwein purchased Airstream's business.

	Annual Growth	07/11	07/12	07/13	07/14	07/15
Sales ($ mil.)	9.8%	2,755.5	3,084.7	3,241.8	3,525.5	4,006.8
Net income ($ mil.)	17.0%	106.3	121.7	152.9	179.0	199.4
Market value ($ mil.)	22.6%	1,295.7	1,505.3	2,831.9	2,775.3	2,927.8
Employees	6.1%	8,250	8,800	8,300	9,400	10,450

THORATEC CORP.

NMS: THOR

6035 Stoneridge Drive
Pleasanton, CA 94588
Phone: 925 847-8600
Fax: –
Web: www.thoratec.com

CEO: D Keith Grossman
CFO: Taylor C Harris
HR: Denise Taylor
FYE: December 28
Type: Public

Suffering from a broken heart? Thoratec's there for the rebound. The company a world leader in mechanical circulatory support makes ventricular assist devices (VAD) for patients suffering late-stage heart failure including those awaiting a heart transplant. Thoratec offers external and implantable products that provide circulatory support for both acute and long-term needs. Its products are sold under the HeartMate CentriMag and Thoratec brands. The company works closely with hospitals and cardiac surgery centers primarily in the US and Europe.

	Annual Growth	01/10	01/11*	12/11	12/12	12/13
Sales ($ mil.)	10.4%	373.9	383.0	422.7	491.7	502.8
Net income ($ mil.)	36.9%	28.6	53.2	71.5	56.2	73.3
Market value ($ mil.)	10.3%	1,531.9	1,611.5	1,909.7	2,110.6	2,055.9
Employees	(6.4%)	1,258	714	822	934	1,030
						*Fiscal year change

THORLABS QUANTUM ELECTRONICS INC.

10335 Guilford Rd.
Jessup MD 20794
Phone: 240-456-7100
Fax: 240-456-7200
Web: www.covega.com

CEO: Alex Cable
CFO: Randy Klueger
HR: –
FYE: December 31
Type: Subsidiary

Thorlabs Quantum Electronics (formerly Covega Corporation) makes optical components modules and subsystems used in the telecommunications industrial medical defense and test and measurement industries. Covega's intensity modulators laser diode controllers optical amplifiers and semiconductor lasers are incorporated into equipment such as Internet routers and network test equipment. Its products are sold through distributors including Mitsui and Laser2000. The company was acquired in 2008 by Fremont California-based Gemfire Corporation and again in 2009 by Thorlabs Inc. of Newton New Jersey. Covega was formed in 2003 by the merger of CODEON Corporation and Quantum Photonics.

THRESHOLD PHARMACEUTICALS INC

NAS: THLD

170 Harbor Way, Suite 300	CEO: Harold E. (Barry) Selick
South San Francisco, CA 94080	CFO: –
Phone: 650 474-8200	HR: –
Fax: –	FYE: December 31
Web: www.thresholdpharm.com	Type: Public

By targeting differences in the oxygen levels of normal and diseased cells Threshold Pharmaceuticals hopes to develop drugs that are effective at fighting cancer while preserving healthy tissue. The biotechnology company's most advanced candidate is TH-302 a hypoxia-activated prodrug meaning it begins releasing its cell-killing agents only within the low-oxygen environment common to tumor tissues. TH-302 is in late-stage trials as a treatment for solid tumors and bone marrow cancer; it is co-developing the drug with Merck. The company is also investigating an imaging agent that would identify patients who could most benefit from prodrugs.

	Annual Growth	12/10	12/11	12/12	12/13	12/14
Sales ($ mil.)	519.2%	–	0.1	5.9	12.5	14.7
Net income ($ mil.)	–	(18.7)	(25.7)	(71.1)	(28.4)	(21.6)
Market value ($ mil.)	23.9%	84.9	76.7	264.8	293.7	200.0
Employees	14.1%	36	31	48	53	61

THRUSTMASTER OF TEXAS INC.

6900 THRUSTMASTER DR	CEO: –
HOUSTON, TX 770412682	CFO: Greg Ault
Phone: 713-937-6295	HR: –
Fax: –	FYE: December 31
Web: www.thrustmastertexas.com	Type: Private

Thrustmaster of Texas trades on power but it does not lack finesse. The company manufactures heavy-duty commercial marine propulsion equipment including deck-mounted propulsion units thru-hull azimuthing thrusters retractable thrusters tunnel thrusters and portable dynamic positioning systems. The company's thrusters vary in size power and design with applications that include main propulsion slow-speed maneuvering and dynamic positioning. Thrusters range in power from 35hp to more than 3000hp and find uses in barges cruise ships tugs military vessels offshore platforms and other floating structures. Thrustmaster of Texas serves a global clientele through an international sales network.

	Annual Growth	12/09	12/10	12/11	12/12	12/13
Sales ($ mil.)	8.4%	–	62.9	84.6	87.9	80.1
Net income ($ mil.)	(20.9%)	–	–	7.4	17.0	4.6
Market value ($ mil.)	–	–	–	–	–	–
Employees	–	–	–	–	–	275

THUNDER MOUNTAIN GOLD, INC.

IVX: IHM

11770 W President Dr. STE F	CEO: Eric T Jones
Boise, ID 83713-8986	CFO: Larry Thackery
Phone: 208 658-1037	HR: –
Fax: –	FYE: December 31
Web: www.thundermountaingold.com	Type: Public

Mining company Thunder Mountain Gold is looking for its next project. In 2005 the company sold its real property and mining claims in the Thunder Mountain District of Valley County Idaho to the Trust For Public Land an environmental group that buys land for conservation. No minerals had been produced on Thunder Mountain Gold's Idaho properties since the early 1990s. Currently the company operates no producing mines and owns no mining properties; it is firmly in the exploration stage. In 2007 Thunder Mountain Gold acquired South Mountain Mines. Two years later it agreed to buy Kenai Resources combining to form a new company called Thunder Mountain Resources.

	Annual Growth	12/09	12/10	12/11	12/12	12/13
Sales ($ mil.)	(11.5%)	–	–	–	0.1	0.1
Net income ($ mil.)	–	(0.6)	(1.7)	(0.3)	0.3	0.1
Market value ($ mil.)	(31.7%)	6.9	9.4	3.1	2.8	1.5
Employees	(9.6%)	3	3	3	2	2

TIB FINANCIAL CORP.

NASDAQ: TIBB

599 9th St. North Ste. 101	CEO: R Eugene Taylor
Naples FL 34102	CFO: Christopher G Marshall
Phone: 239-263-3344	HR: –
Fax: 305-451-6241	FYE: December 31
Web: www.capitalbank-us.com	Type: Public

TIB Financial was the holding company for TIB Bank which operated some 30 branches in South Florida until North American Financial Holdings (now Capital Bank Financial) acquired the bank in 2011. After acquiring TIB Bank Capital Bank Financial merged the unit into its own NAFH National Bank (now Capital Bank NA). It also merged Capital Bank a former subsidiary of Capital Bank Corporation into the unit. The company has subsequently made further acquisitions and has plans for more. TIB now serves as the holding company for private bank and trust Naples Capital Advisors and owns a 21% stake in Capital Bank NA. Capital Bank Financial which went public in 2012 plans to acquire TIB Financial.

TIBCO SOFTWARE, INC.

NMS: TIBX

3303 Hillview Avenue	CEO: Murray Rhode
Palo Alto, CA 94304	CFO: Tom Berquist
Phone: 650 846-1000	HR: –
Fax: –	FYE: November 30
Web: www.tibco.com	Type: Public

TIBCO Software develops software that enables customers to integrate manage and monitor enterprise applications and information delivery. The company's software includes tools for coordinating business processes and workflows securely exchanging information with trading partners and managing distributed systems. Its core product line comprises applications for adopting service-oriented architecture (SOA) environments where reusable services are assembled to tackle common tasks such as business process management and application integration. TIBCO's other primary segments center on business optimization and process automation.

	Annual Growth	11/09	11/10	11/11	11/12	11/13
Sales ($ mil.)	14.6%	621.4	754.0	920.2	1,024.6	1,070.0
Net income ($ mil.)	7.8%	62.3	78.1	112.4	122.0	84.0
Market value ($ mil.)	29.5%	1,403.3	3,204.6	4,470.8	4,087.4	3,943.8
Employees	16.4%	2,097	2,540	2,965	3,646	3,856

TICC CAPITAL CORP.

NASDAQ: TICC

8 Sound Shore Dr. Ste. 255	CEO: –
Greenwich CT 06830	CFO: –
Phone: 203-983-5275	HR: –
Fax: 415-904-5635	FYE: December 31
Web: www.ospd.ca.gov	Type: Public

TICC Capital Corp. (formerly Technology Investment Capital Corp.) spends most of its dough on high tech. Through a network of venture capital and private equity funds investment banks accounting and law firms and company relationships TICC invests in small and midsized private technology firms. Target acquisitions are software Internet IT services media telecommunications semiconductor and hardware service providers although the company has flexibility to invest outside the tech sector. Founded in 2003 TICC commands approximately $325 million in total investments and concentrates on target firms with less than $200 million in annual revenues. Its investments range from $5 million to $30 million.

TIDELANDS BANCSHARES INC

NBB: TDBK

875 Lowcountry Blvd.
Mount Pleasant, SC 29464
Phone: 843-388-8433
Fax: –

CEO: Thomas H Lyles
CFO: John D Dalton
HR: Janice Boucher
FYE: December 31
Type: Public

Tidelands Bancshares does its work at the intersection of Southern charm and Coastal cool. The holding company operates Tidelands Bank which has seven branches along the coast of South Carolina. The bank offers traditional retail services and products such as checking and savings accounts money market accounts and commercial and consumer loans. Tidelands Bank grows by opening loan production offices and then when they prove successful converting them into full service locations. The company specializes in services for small businesses and entrepreneurs of which there are plenty in the tourist-laden beachfront locales it calls home. About 75% of its loan activity is in Charleston.

	Annual Growth	12/10	12/11	12/12	12/13	12/14
Assets ($ mil.)	(4.5%)	571.3	534.1	526.7	486.8	475.6
Net income ($ mil.)	–	(15.6)	(9.1)	(3.2)	(1.0)	(0.4)
Market value ($ mil.)	(23.6%)	4.4	0.3	1.3	1.6	1.5
Employees	(2.1%)	85	76	78	80	78

TIDEWATER INC.

NYS: TDW

601 Poydras Street, Suite 1500
New Orleans, LA 70130
Phone: 504-568-1010
Fax: –
Web: www.tdw.com

CEO: Jeffrey M. (Jeff) Platt
CFO: Quinn P. Fanning
HR: –
FYE: March 31
Type: Public

When the tide of offshore energy activity rises Tidewater chooses to chance the wave. The company's fleet of about 300 vessels provides oil and gas exploration field development and production support. Services encompass transporting crews and supplies to offshore platforms towing of and anchor handling for mobile rigs and aiding in offshore construction and seismic operations. Its fleet includes towing-supply and supply vessels deepwater vessels crewboats utility vessels and offshore tugs. In addition to support ships Tidewater owns Quality Shipyards which builds repairs and modifies vessels for its parent and third parties. About 70% of Tidewater's revenues are generated in international waters.

	Annual Growth	03/11	03/12	03/13	03/14	03/15
Sales ($ mil.)	9.1%	1,055.4	1,067.0	1,244.2	1,435.1	1,495.5
Net income ($ mil.)	–	105.6	87.4	150.8	140.3	(65.2)
Market value ($ mil.)	(24.8%)	2,814.7	2,540.5	2,375.0	2,286.6	900.1
Employees	3.2%	7,500	7,650	7,900	8,900	8,500

TIFFANY & CO.

NYS: TIF

727 Fifth Avenue
New York, NY 10022
Phone: 212-755-8000
Fax: 212-605-4465
Web: www.tiffany.com

CEO: Frederic Cumenal
CFO: Ralph J. Nicoletti
HR: Victoria Berger-gro
FYE: January 31
Type: Public

Breakfast at Tiffany & Co. has turned into a bountiful buffet complete with the finest crystal and flatware as well as more ubiquitous fare. While its specialty is fine jewelry the company also puts its name on silverware timepieces china stationery and other luxury items. Many products are packaged in the company's trademarked Tiffany Blue Box. To entice the budget-minded to do more than window shop Tiffany has broadened its merchandise mix to include key chains and other items that sell for much less than the typical Tiffany price tag. The company sells its goods exclusively through nearly 300 Tiffany & Co. stores and boutiques worldwide its website business-to-business accounts and catalogs.

	Annual Growth	01/11	01/12	01/13	01/14	01/15
Sales ($ mil.)	8.3%	3,085.3	3,642.9	3,794.2	4,031.1	4,249.9
Net income ($ mil.)	7.1%	368.4	439.2	416.2	181.4	484.2
Market value ($ mil.)	10.5%	7,517.7	8,251.0	8,503.2	10,758.6	11,204.8
Employees	6.9%	9,200	9,800	9,900	10,600	12,000

TIFFIN MOTOR HOMES INC.

105 2ND ST NW
RED BAY, AL 355823859
Phone: 256-356-8661
Fax: –
Web: www.tiffinmotorhomes.com

CEO: –
CFO: –
HR: Anthony Riley
FYE: February 28
Type: Private

At Tiffin Motorhomes the family that stays together makes recreational vehicles together. The family-owned manufacturer builds a line of luxury recreational vehicles (RVs) including the Allegro Allegro Bus Phaeton and Zephyr models. RVs span 35 to 44 feet in length and offer amenities from washers and dryers to garden tubs to side-by-side refrigerators. Construction pluses feature thick glass windows added storage and reinforced steel crossbracing. Tiffin's vehicles are sold by dealers across the US and Canada. Spotlighting its nameplates the company owns the Allegro Club an organization of local US chapters that promotes race car rallies and RV events. Robert Tiffin founded the company in 1972.

	Annual Growth	02/02	02/03	02/04	02/05	02/07
Sales ($ mil.)	(31.1%)	–	–	1,281.0	286.0	419.6
Net income ($ mil.)	28998.8%	–	–	0.0	(0.5)	24.6
Market value ($ mil.)	–	–	–	–	–	–
Employees	–	–	–	–	–	545

TIFT REGIONAL MEDICAL CENTER FOUNDATION INC.

901 18TH ST E
TIFTON, GA 317943648
Phone: 229-382-7120
Fax: –
Web: www.tiftregional.com

CEO: William T Richardson
CFO: Dennis Crum
HR: –
FYE: September 30
Type: Private

Tift Regional Medical Center (TRMC) helps keep people healthy in the Peach State. The medical center with more than 125 physicians on staff representing some 30 specialties serves residents across a dozen counties in south central Georgia. TRMC offers its patients a wide range of services including cancer treatment cardiology neurology occupational and physical therapy obstetrics and surgical care. The not-for-profit medical center has a capacity of about 190 beds. It also operates an outpatient services clinic Cook Medical Center and Cook Senior Living Center. Tift County Hospital Authority owns and operates TRMC. The hospital is also affiliated with the Emory Healthcare network.

	Annual Growth	09/05	09/06	09/07	09/08	09/09
Sales ($ mil.)	–	–	–	(418.4)	0.6	216.2
Net income ($ mil.)	33890.3%	–	–	0.0	0.3	30.5
Market value ($ mil.)	–	–	–	–	–	–
Employees	–	–	–	–	–	1,400

TIGER X MEDICAL INC.

NBB: CDOM

2934 1/2 Beverly Glen Circle, Suite #203
Los Angeles, CA 90077
Phone: 310-987-7345
Fax: –

CEO: Andrew A Brooks
CFO: Andrew A Brooks
HR: –
FYE: December 31
Type: Public

As an early-stage orthopedic device company Cardo Medical wants to ensure your hips and joints are in check. The company specializes in the development and distribution of reconstructive orthopedic and spinal surgery products. Its product portfolio offers replacement medical devices for hips knees and parts of the spinal column. Cardo Medical has filed more than 25 patent applications for technologies related to the orthopedic field. The company is selling its joint arthroplasty division which includes its hip and knee assets to Arthrex. The publicly traded Cardo is exploring strategic alternatives for its spine division.

	Annual Growth	12/10	12/11	12/12	12/13	12/14
Sales ($ mil.)	228.9%	–	0.0	0.1	0.3	0.4
Net income ($ mil.)	–	(11.5)	9.7	0.3	0.0	0.2
Market value ($ mil.)	22.9%	10.6	16.1	13.4	19.3	24.2
Employees	–	13				

TIGERLOGIC CORP

NBB: TIGR

1532 SW Morrison Street, Suite 200
Portland, OR 97205
Phone: 503 488-6988
Fax: –
Web: www.tigerlogic.com

CEO: Bradley N Timchuk
CFO: Roger Rowe
HR: –
FYE: March 31
Type: Public

TigerLogic (formerly Raining Data) can help you catch data by the tail. The company's ChunkIt! browser-based application enhances and personalizes searches of popular search engines or Web pages. TigerLogic also provides applications that software developers use to construct a variety of software programs and build databases. Its software lets users create compile test and run programs. Customers use TigerLogic's rapid application development software to build programs that can easily be updated. The company also provides maintenance implementation technical support and training services. Through investment firm Astoria Capital Partners former CEO Carlton Baab owns about 60% of the company.

	Annual Growth	03/11	03/12	03/13	03/14	03/15
Sales ($ mil.)	(15.4%)	13.7	13.3	12.8	5.5	7.0
Net income ($ mil.)	–	(3.0)	(3.5)	(2.9)	1.3	(28.7)
Market value ($ mil.)	(45.4%)	139.3	71.2	59.4	43.6	12.4
Employees	(9.5%)	97	86	101	80	65

TIGRENT INC.

OTC: TIGE

1612 E. Cape Coral Pkwy.
Cape Coral FL 33904
Phone: 239-542-0643
Fax: 239-540-6562
Web: www.wincorporate.com

CEO: Anthony C Humpage
CFO: Anne M Donoho
HR: Brenda Kalscheuer
FYE: December 31
Type: Public

Tigrent (formerly Whitney Information Network) wants to help show you the money. The company sells educational materials and provides training courses that teach students strategies for success in real estate investments and financial markets. It offers about 150 educational courses and training programs per month covering dozens of subjects. Its 51%-owned Rich Dad Education subsidiary offers real estate and finance courses based on the writings of Robert Kiyosaki author of the popular Rich Dad Poor Dad series of books. Its other course brand names include Tigrent Learning (formerly Wealth Intelligence Academy) Building Wealth and Teach Me To Trade.

TII NETWORK TECHNOLOGIES INC.

NASDAQ: TIII

141 Rodeo Dr.
Edgewood NY 11717
Phone: 631-789-5000
Fax: 631-789-5063
Web: www.tiinettech.com

CEO: –
CFO: –
HR: Virginia M Hall
FYE: December 31
Type: Private

When lightening strikes Tii products ensure your power stays on. Tii Network Technologies makes overvoltage surge protection devices used by telecommunications companies to protect their equipment during lightning strikes and power surges. Products include the Totel Failsafe brand modular station protectors and In-Line brand broadband coaxial cable protectors. Its Porta Systems line makes copper connectivity and surge protection products. Tii also makes gas tubes custom network interface devices and electronic products used to test the integrity of voice and data lines remotely. In 2012 Tii was acquired by Kelta which had been the contract manufacturer for its products.

TILDEN ASSOCIATES INC.

PINK SHEETS: TLDN

300 Hempstead Tpke. Ste. 110
West Hempstead NY 11552
Phone: 516-746-7911
Fax: 516-746-1288
Web: www.tildencarcare.com

CEO: Christopher Panzeca
CFO: –
HR: –
FYE: December 31
Type: Public

Providing customers with a full line of automotive repairs and services is what drives Tilden Associates. The company franchises about 50 Tilden Your Total Car Care Centers across the country but most shops are located in New York Florida and Colorado. In addition to brake work the stores offer oil changes tune-ups and general automotive repairs. The company's Tilden Equipment Corp. sells shop equipment to franchisees and its real estate subsidiaries hold leases on store sites. The Tilden brand traces its history to a brake shop founded by Sydney G. Tilden in 1923.

TIMBERLAND BANCORP, INC.

NMS: TSBK

624 Simpson Avenue
Hoquiam, WA 98550
Phone: 360 533-4747
Fax: –
Web: www.timberlandbank.com

CEO: Michael R Sand
CFO: Dean J Brydon
HR: –
FYE: September 30
Type: Public

Timberland Bancorp is the holding company for Timberland Savings Bank which operates more than 20 branches in western Washington. The bank targets individuals and regional businesses offering checking savings and money market accounts and CDs. The bank concentrates on real estate lending including commercial and residential mortgages multifamily residential loans and land develoment loans; it also writes business loans and other types of loans. Timberland Savings Bank was founded in 1915 as a savings and loan.

	Annual Growth	09/10	09/11	09/12	09/13	09/14
Assets ($ mil.)	0.1%	742.7	738.2	737.0	745.6	745.6
Net income ($ mil.)	–	(2.3)	1.1	4.6	4.8	5.9
Market value ($ mil.)	27.1%	28.5	28.5	42.3	63.4	74.3
Employees	(2.5%)	283	270	259	267	256

TIMBERLINE RESOURCES CORPORATION

NYSE AMEX: TLR

101 E. Lakeside Ave.
Coeur d?Alene ID 83814
Phone: 208-664-4859
Fax: 208-664-4860
Web: www.timberline-resources.com

CEO: –
CFO: Randal Hardy
HR: –
FYE: September 30
Type: Public

Timberline Resources is hoping that all (or at least some) of what glitters deep in its underground mines is gold. An exploration and development company Timberline Resources conducts underground gold mining operations on two core precious metal properties in Nevada collectively known as South Eureka Property located in the state's Battle Mountain-Eureka gold-producing area. The company also conducts gold mining operations through its Montana-based Butte Highlands Joint Venture in which it owns a 50% interest and is acquiring the rest. In addition to mining Timberline provides contract underground diamond drilling services to third-party mining companies through its Timberline Drilling subsidiary.

TIME INC.

1271 Ave. of the Americas
New York NY 10020-1393
Phone: 212-522-1212
Fax: 212-522-0602
Web: www.timeinc.com

CEO: Joseph A Ripp
CFO: Jeffrey J Bairstow
HR: –
FYE: December 31
Type: Subsidiary

If this company won't give you the Time who will? Time Warner's publishing operations are conducted primarily through Time Inc. a leading consumer magazine publisher with more than 20 US magazines and 45 corresponding websites in its collection. In addition to Time its titles include Entertainment Weekly People Fortune and Sports Illustrated. Subsidiary Essence Communications publishes Essence magazine while IPC Group Limited is the UK's top magazine publisher (Now Look). Time Inc. also manages American Express Publishing Corporation the publishing operations of American Express including the "Travel & Leisure" and "Food & Wine" magazines. Time Inc. accounts for nearly 15% of Time Warner's revenues.

TIMES PUBLISHING COMPANY

490 1st Ave. South
St. Petersburg FL 33701
Phone: 727-893-8111
Fax: 727-893-8675
Web: www.tampabay.com

CEO: Paul Tash
CFO: Jana Jones
HR: –
FYE: December 31
Type: Subsidiary

The times may be a-changing but Times Publishing still prints the "St. Petersburg Times" one of the most respected regional newspapers in the US. Founded in 1884 the "Times" boasts a daily circulation of about 290000 in the Tampa Bay area and plays the role of archrival to "The Tampa Tribune" owned by Media General. Times Publishing also operates local news and information website TampaBay.com and runs fact checking website PolitiFact. Affiliated units include monthly business magazine Florida Trend and community newspaper publisher Tampa Bay Newspapers. Times Publishing is controlled through a holding company by the Poynter Institute a not-for-profit school of journalism in St. Petersburg.

TIME WARNER CABLE INC

NYS: TWC

60 Columbus Circle
New York, NY 10023
Phone: 212 364-8200
Fax: –
Web: www.timewarnercable.com

CEO: Robert D. (Rob) Marcus
CFO: William F. Osbourne
HR: Paul Gilles
FYE: December 31
Type: Public

Time Warner Cable (TWC) makes coaxial quiver. The company is the #2 US cable company after Comcast with operations in more than two dozen states across the country. It serves more than 15.2 million mostly residential customers (about 625000 business customers) with video high-speed data (primarily through ISP brand Road Runner) and voice offerings as well as security and home management. In addition to video voice and data other business services include networking and transport outsourced IT and cloud computing. In April 2015 rival Comcast dropped its $45 billion bid to acquire TWC because of regulatory hurdles. A month after that door closed another opened. TWC accepted a $55 billion offer from Charter Communications.

	Annual Growth	12/11	12/12	12/13	12/14	12/15
Sales ($ mil.)	4.8%	19,675.0	21,386.0	22,120.0	22,812.0	23,697.0
Net income ($ mil.)	2.6%	1,665.0	2,155.0	1,954.0	2,031.0	1,844.0
Market value ($ mil.)	30.7%	18,009.4	27,533.9	38,387.2	43,078.6	52,577.6
Employees	3.9%	48,500	51,000	51,600	55,170	56,600

TIMEX GROUP USA INC.

555 Christian Rd.
Middlebury CT 06762
Phone: 203-346-5000
Fax: 203-346-5139
Web: www.timexgroup.com

CEO: Paolo Marai
CFO: –
HR: –
FYE: December 31
Type: Private

Branching out from its original "takes a licking" designs Timex is strapping on fresh faces so it can tap new markets worldwide. The nation's largest watch manufacturer has expanded its lines from simple low-cost watches to include high-tech tickers capable of paging or downloading computer data. Its sports watches have gone upscale and gadgety with its Expedition and Ironman lines. The company also makes and markets thermostats pedometers and weather instruments. Through a licensing agreement Timex makes watches for Guess? and Versace among others. Founded in 1854 Timex Group is owned by the family of chairman Anette Olsen whose grandfather bought the company in 1942.

TIME WARNER INC

NYS: TWX

One Time Warner Center
New York, NY 10019-8016
Phone: 212 484-8000
Fax: 212 489-6183
Web: www.timewarner.com

CEO: Jeffrey L. (Jeff) Bewkes
CFO: Howard M. Averill
HR: Karen Magee
FYE: December 31
Type: Public

Even among media titans this company is a giant. Time Warner is one of the world's largest media conglomerate behind Walt Disney and News Corporation with operations spanning television and film. Through subsidiary Turner Broadcasting the company runs a portfolio of popular cable TV networks including CNN TBS and TNT. Time Warner also operates pay-TV channels HBO and Cinemax. Its Warner Bros. Entertainment meanwhile includes films studios (Warner Bros. Pictures New Line Cinema) TV production units (Warner Bros. Television Group) and comic book publisher DC Entertainment. In 2014 the company spun off its print publishing operations.

	Annual Growth	12/10	12/11	12/12	12/13	12/14
Sales ($ mil.)	0.4%	26,888.0	28,974.0	28,729.0	29,795.0	27,359.0
Net income ($ mil.)	10.4%	2,578.0	2,886.0	3,019.0	3,691.0	3,827.0
Market value ($ mil.)	27.7%	26,765.4	30,068.5	39,794.6	58,007.0	71,069.4
Employees	(4.7%)	31,000	34,000	34,000	34,000	25,600

TIMIOS NATIONAL CORP

NBB: HOMS

4601 Fairfax Drive, Suite 1200
Arlington, VA 22203
Phone: 703 528-7073
Fax: –
Web: www.timios.com

CEO: Trevor Stoffer
CFO: Michael T Brigante
HR: –
FYE: December 31
Type: Public

Homeland Security Capital stakes its financial security on the nation's security. The investment firm acquires operates and develops companies that offer homeland security services and products. It hopes to capitalize on the highly fragmented nature of the young industry which brings potential customers in the government and private sectors. The company owns Polimnatrix which provides radiation dectection and protection services. Homeland Security Capital entered the mortgage and settlement services industry when it acquired Timios a provider of paperless insurance and escrow services.

	Annual Growth	06/09	06/10	06/11*	12/11	12/12
Sales ($ mil.)	(34.8%)	79.5	97.9	–	9.2	22.0
Net income ($ mil.)	–	(9.5)	1.9	(4.4)	4.2	(2.8)
Market value ($ mil.)	81.7%	0.3	0.1	0.1	0.0	1.8
Employees	(33.1%)	518	476	496	94	155

*Fiscal year change

TIMKEN CO. (THE)
NYS: TKR

4500 Mount Pleasant Street N.W.
North Canton, OH 44720-5450
Phone: 234 262-3000
Fax: –
Web: www.timken.com

CEO: Richard G. Kyle
CFO: Philip D. (Phil) Fracassa
HR: –
FYE: December 31
Type: Public

The Timken Company keeps its bearings straight. The company makes bearings that find their way into products from consumer appliances to railroad cars. Timken also makes bearings helicopter transmission systems rotor-head assemblies turbine engine components gears and housings for civil and military aircraft. Its customers include the makers of cars light and heavy-duty trucks railcars and locomotives and heavy duty industrial vehicles as well as process customers in the energy power transmission and military markets. Timken traces its roots to its founding by carriage maker Henry Timken in 1899.

	Annual Growth	12/10	12/11	12/12	12/13	12/14
Sales ($ mil.)	(6.7%)	4,055.5	5,170.2	4,987.0	4,341.2	3,076.2
Net income ($ mil.)	(11.2%)	274.8	454.3	495.5	262.7	170.8
Market value ($ mil.)	(2.8%)	4,228.5	3,429.4	4,237.3	4,878.7	3,781.1
Employees	(5.2%)	19,839	20,954	19,769	19,052	16,000

TIPTREE FINANCIAL INC
NAS: TIPT

780 Third Avenue, 21st Floor
New York, NY 10017
Phone: 212 446-1400
Fax: –
Web: www.tiptreefinancial.com

CEO: David Adamo
CFO: Julia Wyatt
HR: –
FYE: December 31
Type: Public

Tiptree Financial is interested in health and wealth. The holding company operates through four divisions: insurance and insurance services specialty finance (including corporate consumer and tax-exempt credit) asset management and real estate. Its insurance subsidiaries include the Philadelphia Financial Group of companies. Specialty finance services are conducted through Muni Funding Company of America and Siena Capital Finance while a handful of other subsidiaries provide asset management. Real estate activities include Care Investment Trust a health care REIT that owns a portfolio of senior housing properties. Prior to mid-2013 the company's only operations consisted of Care Investment Trust's real estate portfolio.

	Annual Growth	12/10	12/11	12/12	12/13	12/14
Sales ($ mil.)	94.0%	5.7	14.5	16.0	100.9	80.3
Net income ($ mil.)	–	(2.5)	16.5	(0.5)	16.4	4.6
Market value ($ mil.)	14.3%	197.0	270.4	312.0	305.5	337.0
Employees	251.2%	5	6	4	250	761

TISHMAN HOTEL CORPORATION

666 5th Ave.
New York NY 10103
Phone: 212-399-3600
Fax: 212-957-9791
Web: tishmanhotel.tishman.com

CEO: –
CFO: –
HR: –
FYE: December 31
Type: Private

Hoteliers looking for a place to stay call up Tishman Hotel Corporation. The company develops and owns commercial properties that are leased to hotels and retailers in the US and Puerto Rico. Tishman Hotel has a portfolio of 13 properties including 10 hotels in Chicago Florida (at Disney World) Los Angeles New Mexico New York City and Puerto Rico; and three commercial buildings in New York City. Its hotels are operated by InterContinental Marriott Sheraton and Westin. Tishman Hotel Corporation was created in 2010 when Tishman Realty & Construction split its two divisions after Tishman Construction was sold to engineering firm AECOM and Tishman Realty took over the real estate assets.

TITAN ENERGY WORLDWIDE INC
NBB: TEWI

6321 Bury Drive, Suite 8
Eden Prairie, MN 55346
Phone: 952 960-2371
Fax: –
Web: www.titanenergy.com

CEO: –
CFO: –
HR: –
FYE: December 31
Type: Public

Titan Energy Worldwide provides power in a pinch. The company is a distributor of standby and emergency power equipment and a manufacturer of disaster relief systems. It offers power generators from such manufacturers as Generac Power Systems. It also makes and markets the Sentry 5000 mobile utility system an all-in-one trailer unit that provides electrical power heating and cooling water purification communication and lighting. Titan Energy markets these products to first responders relief agencies defense and homeland security agencies and municipalities. Those that depend on backup power — banks data centers hospitals hotels schools and telcos — are also counted as customers.

	Annual Growth	12/08	12/09	12/10	12/11	12/12
Sales ($ mil.)	20.0%	9.3	10.6	14.0	14.1	19.2
Net income ($ mil.)	–	(1.7)	(2.9)	(3.7)	(3.4)	(1.4)
Market value ($ mil.)	(45.4%)	4.5	31.2	22.2	2.1	0.4
Employees	16.5%	25	49	60	45	46

TITAN INTERNATIONAL INC
NYS: TWI

2701 Spruce Street
Quincy, IL 62301
Phone: 217 228-6011
Fax: 217 228-7499
Web: www.titan-intl.com

CEO: Maurice M. (Morry) Taylor
CFO: John R. Hrudicka
HR: Christy Pieper
FYE: December 31
Type: Public

A colossus of off-roads Titan International makes off-highway steel wheels and tires for the agricultural construction mining and consumer markets. It assembles wheel-tire systems for original equipment manufacturers and aftermarket distributors of tractors cranes combines scrapers all-terrain vehicles golf carts and utility trailers. Other operations include the manufacture and distribution of wheels rims and tires to the military for trucks tanks and personnel carriers as well as boat and trailer wheels for the consumer. Titan sells its products directly to manufactures and through dealers distributors and at its own distribution centers.

	Annual Growth	12/10	12/11	12/12	12/13	12/14
Sales ($ mil.)	21.1%	881.6	1,487.0	1,820.7	2,163.6	1,895.5
Net income ($ mil.)	–	0.4	58.2	95.6	35.2	(80.5)
Market value ($ mil.)	(14.1%)	1,030.3	1,048.0	1,161.4	966.4	571.4
Employees	28.3%	2,400	3,600	6,300	8,500	6,500

TITAN MACHINERY, INC.
NMS: TITN

644 East Beaton Drive
West Fargo, ND 58078-2648
Phone: 701 356-0130
Fax: –
Web: www.titanmachinery.com

CEO: David J. Meyer
CFO: Mark Kalvoda
HR: Jason Anderson
FYE: January 31
Type: Public

For getting the job done Titan Machinery is one titanic dealer. Titan owns one of North America's largest full-service networks that supply construction and agricultural equipment. Its more than 100 dealerships sell and rent new and used machinery and attachments parts as well as service equipment. It represents equipment by CNH's Case IH New Holland Agriculture Case Construction and New Holland Construction. Titan offers excavators seeders tillers and tractors to customers from large-scale farmers to home gardeners. Other products include earthmoving equipment and cranes used for heavy construction and light industrial jobs in commercial or residential building roadwork forestry and mining.

	Annual Growth	01/11	01/12	01/13	01/14	01/15
Sales ($ mil.)	14.8%	1,094.5	1,659.0	2,198.4	2,226.4	1,900.2
Net income ($ mil.)	–	22.3	44.2	42.5	8.9	(32.2)
Market value ($ mil.)	(12.6%)	518.7	529.6	618.8	348.9	302.5
Employees	10.4%	1,874	2,396	2,813	2,823	2,782

TITAN PHARMACEUTICALS INC (DE)　　NAS: TTNP

400 Oyster Point Blvd., Suite 505
South San Francisco, CA 94080
Phone: 650 244-4990
Fax: –
Web: www.titanpharm.com

CEO: Sunil Bhonsle
CFO: –
HR: Robert E Farrll
FYE: December 31
Type: Public

Titan Pharmaceuticals thinks big. The development-stage firm is working on drug treatments for large pharmaceutical markets including central nervous system disorders like chronic pain Parkinson's disease and schizophrenia. On its own the company is developing Probuphine which may treat opioid addiction; Probuphine combines an already-approved chemical compound with Titan's continuous-release drug delivery technology called ProNeura. Titan is working with Vanda Pharmaceuticals on late-stage compound Iloperidone a possible treatment for schizophrenia.

	Annual Growth	12/10	12/11	12/12	12/13	12/14
Sales ($ mil.)	(22.5%)	10.1	4.1	7.1	10.5	3.6
Net income ($ mil.)	–	(6.8)	(15.2)	(15.2)	9.7	(2.4)
Market value ($ mil.)	0.0%	22.2	22.2	22.2	22.2	22.2
Employees	4.3%	11	12	15	13	13

TITAN TECHNOLOGIES INC.　　OTC: TITT

3206 Candelaria Rd. NE
Albuquerque NM 87107
Phone: 505-884-0272
Fax: 505-881-7113
Web: www.titantechnologiesinc.com

CEO: –
CFO: –
HR: –
FYE: July 31
Type: Public

Titan Technologies is not an enterprise of giant primordial gods of Greek mythology but rather a company that is big on recycling tires. The company licenses its technology which uses a proprietary catalyst to reduce tires to carbon black oil and steel to tire-recycling plants. Facilities in South Korea and Taiwan that are no longer operating have used Titan's system; the company is working to find licensees in the US Europe and elsewhere in Asia. Titan also is working with R&D lab Adherent Technologies to develop new ways to recycle electronic scrap (from discarded computers) and waste plastic.

TIVO INC　　NMS: TIVO

2160 Gold Street, P.O. Box 2160
San Jose, CA 95002
Phone: 408 519-9100
Fax: 408 519-5330
Web: www.tivo.com

CEO: Thomas S. (Tom) Rogers
CFO: Naveen Chopra
HR: –
FYE: January 31
Type: Public

Prime time is anytime with TiVo. That's the idea behind TiVo and its digital video recorder (DVR). The DVR (similar to a VCR but using a hard drive instead of videocassette) allows more than 4 million subscribers to record standard- and high-definition TV (broadcast cable or satellite). The company sells DVRs online and through electronics retailers such as Best Buy. In addition to buying a DVR customers pay for TiVo's subscription service which is essentially a high-tech TV listing. TiVo reaches cable and satellite viewers by licensing its technology to DIRECTV Comcast and other service providers worldwide. TiVo is evolving from an "anytime" to an "anywhere" service to stay relevant to mobile viewers.

	Annual Growth	01/11	01/12	01/13	01/14	01/15
Sales ($ mil.)	19.7%	219.6	238.2	303.9	406.3	451.5
Net income ($ mil.)	–	(84.5)	102.2	(5.3)	271.8	30.8
Market value ($ mil.)	2.0%	930.5	998.3	1,283.6	1,192.2	1,006.5
Employees	0.6%	611	631	576	626	625

TIX CORP　　NBB: TIXC

12711 Ventura Blvd., Suite 340
Studio City, CA 91604
Phone: 818 761-1002
Fax: 818 761-1072
Web: www.tixcorp.com

CEO: Mitch Francis
CFO: Steve Handy
HR: –
FYE: December 31
Type: Public

Tix Corporation has got a ticket to ride. Through its Tix4Tonight subsidiary the company sells discounted same-day tickets to Las Vegas shows from about a dozen locations in Las Vegas. Tix4Tonight also includes Tix4Dinner (discounted dinners on the Vegas strip) and Tix4Golf (discounted golf reservations in the Las Vegas area). The company's Exhibit Merchandising sells branded merchandise (souvenir posters memorabilia) related to museum exhibits and theatrical productions. Sales are made in temporary specialty stores set up in conjunction with the touring event.

	Annual Growth	12/10	12/11	12/12	12/13	12/14
Sales ($ mil.)	(7.4%)	30.9	34.5	24.3	22.2	22.7
Net income ($ mil.)	–	(3.0)	0.0	1.4	1.6	4.1
Market value ($ mil.)	3.9%	22.2	33.0	17.0	17.9	25.9
Employees	(13.1%)	204	194	139	134	–

TJX COMPANIES, INC.　　NYS: TJX

770 Cochituate Road
Framingham, MA 01701
Phone: 508 390-1000
Fax: 508 390-2091
Web: www.tjx.com

CEO: Ernie Herrman
CFO: Scott Goldenberg
HR: Kelli McNary
FYE: January 31
Type: Public

Rifling through the racks is an art at TJX stores. The TJX Companies operates nearly 3400 stores worldwide under half a dozen retail brand names including the two largest off-price clothing retailers in the US: T.J. Maxx and Marshalls which operate 2000-plus stores nationwide. T.J. Maxx sells brand-name family apparel accessories shoes domestics giftware and jewelry at discount prices while Marshalls offers similar items plus a broader selection of shoes and menswear through nearly 1000 stores. Its HomeGoods chain of 500-plus US stores focuses exclusively on home furnishings. T.K. Maxx is the company's European retail arm with 400-plus stores in the UK Ireland Germany and Poland.

	Annual Growth	01/11	01/12*	02/13	02/14*	01/15
Sales ($ mil.)	7.3%	21,942.2	23,191.5	25,878.4	27,422.7	29,078.4
Net income ($ mil.)	13.3%	1,343.1	1,496.1	1,906.7	2,137.4	2,215.1
Market value ($ mil.)	8.4%	32,668.6	46,130.5	31,018.4	39,276.3	45,151.3
Employees	4.5%	166,000	168,000	179,000	191,000	198,000

*Fiscal year change

TKS INDUSTRIAL COMPANY

901 Tower Dr. Ste. 250
Troy MI 48098-2817
Phone: 248-786-5000
Fax: 248-786-5001
Web: www.taikisha-group.com/network/usa_and_canada/

CEO: –
CFO: –
HR: –
FYE: March 31
Type: Subsidiary

TKS Industrial designs fabricates and installs paint finishing systems specialized drying ovens industrial ventilation systems and commercial clean rooms for automakers and other manufacturers. The company operates offices and plants in the US in Michigan and Ohio and it has international subsidiaries in Brazil Canada and Mexico. Customers include Toyota Motor Chrysler Ford Motor Honda and General Motors. TKS Industrial established in 1981 is the US subsidiary of Taikisha Ltd. a Japanese supplier of clean room systems electrical and mechanical equipment for buildings and paint finishing systems which was founded in 1913.

TMA RESOURCES INC.

1919 Gallows Rd 4th Fl.
Vienna VA 22182-3964
Phone: 703-564-5200
Fax: 703-564-5201
Web: www.tmaresources.com

CEO: Edi Dor
CFO: –
HR: –
FYE: December 31
Type: Private

TMA Resources wants to be a member of your club. Founded in 1996 the company provides association management and member relationship management software for membership-centered organizations such as trade associations professional societies chambers of commerce and labor unions. TMA Resources offers its TIMSS application for member management either as a licensed software package or a hosted online service. The company's TIMSS e-Business Suite includes transaction processing tools for handling online membership applications product orders meeting registrations subscription orders and other functions. TMA Resources also offers a variety of services including project management training and hosting.

TNEMEC COMPANY INC.

6800 CORPORATE DR
KANSAS CITY, MO 641201372
Phone: 816-483-3400
Fax: –
Web: www.tnemec.com

CEO: Peter Cortelyou
CFO: Steven Eiserer
HR: –
FYE: December 31
Type: Private

Tnemec (prounoced tah-KNEE-mick it is cement spelled backwards) makes more than 100 different paints and coatings that can be used as primers on concrete masonry steel and flooring materials. It also provides waterproofing corrosion prevention (for wastewater facilities) and exterior finishing products. Tnemec serves customers in different markets including architectural industrial manufacturing oilfield services water and wastewater and water storage tanks. Its Chemprobe line specializes in masonry products while the company's StrataShield line focuses on floor and wall coatings.

	Annual Growth	12/09	12/10	12/11	12/12	12/13
Sales ($ mil.)	2.2%	–	115.8	124.8	128.3	123.6
Net income ($ mil.)	11.3%	–	–	4.6	6.1	5.7
Market value ($ mil.)	–	–	–	–	–	–
Employees	–	–	–	–	–	265

TNR TECHNICAL, INC.

NDD: TNRK

301 Central Park Drive
Sanford, FL 32771
Phone: 407-321-3011
Fax: 407-321-3208
Web: www.tnrtechnical.com

CEO: Wayne Thaw
CFO: Anne Provost
HR: –
FYE: June 30
Type: Public

Not long ago batteries were batteries: A AA AAA C D. Now there are nickel cadmium nickel metal hydride lithium and alkaline varieties and TNR Technical assembles and distributes the full gamut of modern batteries for consumer applications. Typical applications include alarms cameras door locks power tools instruments golf carts laptops medical equipment and surveying equipment. TNR sells to the OEM government military leisure and wholesale markets. The company distributes most leading brands including Duracell Energizer Panasonic SANYO and Ultralife. Members of the Thaw family own more than half of the company.

	Annual Growth	06/11	06/12	06/13	06/14	06/15
Sales ($ mil.)	(2.9%)	9.2	9.0	9.2	8.3	8.1
Net income ($ mil.)	2.0%	0.2	0.4	0.3	0.4	0.3
Market value ($ mil.)	(2.9%)	4.5	3.4	2.9	5.1	4.0
Employees	4.3%	23	24	–	–	–

TNS NORTH AMERICA INC.

11 Madison Ave. 12th Fl.
New York NY 10010
Phone: 212-991-6000
Fax: 212-661-0407
Web: www.tns-us.com

CEO: Mike Gettle
CFO: Roel Smits
HR: –
FYE: December 31
Type: Business Segment

TNS North America is certainly in the loop when it comes to consumer behavior. A division of custom market research provider TNS the company is one of the leading providers of panel-based market research in the US. It collects data on consumer behavior brand performance and campaign effectiveness by mail telephone and online surveys. It also conducts qualitative research and measures its clients' relationships with their customers employees distributors and shareholders. In addition to its core consumer research business TNS North America conducts research for the information technology sector as well as the financial services and automotive sectors. It owns more than a dozen offices across the US.

TODD SHIPYARDS CORPORATION

1801 16th Ave. SW
Seattle WA 98134-1089
Phone: 206-623-1635
Fax: 206-442-8505
Web: vigorindustrial.com/companies/vigor_shipyards/

CEO: Frank J Foti
CFO: Lon V Leneve
HR: –
FYE: March 31
Type: Subsidiary

Todd Shipyards helps keep boats afloat. The company operates a handful of Washington-based dry docks through subsidiaries Vigor Shipyards and Everett Shipyard; in the marketplace of private that is non-governmental shipyard owners it is largest in the US Pacific Northwest. Its work focuses on repair (minor jobs to major overhauls) and maintenance of federal government as well as commercial vessels that plow the region's waters. Services include new construction and industrial fabrication for a select group of customers at its shipyards. Contracts with the US Navy Coast Guard and Washington State Ferries represent about 90% of its revenues. Todd was taken over by Vigor Industrial in 2011 for $130 million.

TOFUTTI BRANDS, INC.

ASE: TOF

50 Jackson Drive
Cranford, NJ 07016
Phone: 908-272-2400
Fax: –
Web: www.tofutti.com

CEO: David Mintz
CFO: Steven Kass
HR: –
FYE: December 27
Type: Public

Tofutti Brands makes Tofutti Cuties and Marry Me Bars and while the company may get silly with its brand names don't let that fool you. Its soy-based foods are aimed at lactose-intolerant kosher and health-conscious consumers. Its flagship product Tofutti frozen dessert is sold by the pint and in novelty forms. The company also offers nondairy cheeses and sour cream. Tofutti's products are developed by the company at its own labs but they do no manufacturing of their own. Instead the company contracts with co-packers to furnish its products. Chairman and CEO David Mintz owns about 50% of the firm; the Financial & Investment Management Group owns almost 8%.

	Annual Growth	01/11*	12/11	12/12	12/13	12/14
Sales ($ mil.)	(6.8%)	17.7	15.9	14.3	14.7	14.4
Net income ($ mil.)	–	0.5	0.0	(0.8)	(0.9)	(0.2)
Market value ($ mil.)	39.8%	10.4	8.8	5.9	17.3	28.4
Employees	14.5%	8	10	14	12	12

*Fiscal year change

TOLL BROTHERS INC.

NYS: TOL

250 Gibraltar Road
Horsham, PA 19044
Phone: 215-938-8000
Fax: 215-938-8023
Web: www.tollbrothers.com

CEO: Douglas C Yearley Jr
CFO: Martin P. (Marty) Connor
HR: –
FYE: October 31
Type: Public

Ask not for whom the Tolls build because if you have to ask you probably can't afford it. Toll Brothers builds luxury homes in the US targeting move-up second-home and retired buyers. Its single-family detached houses and condominium apartments sell for an average price of $646000. The company also develops communities for active adults and operates country club communities. Subsidiaries offer related services and products including insurance coverage title and mortgage services and landscaping. Toll Brothers has operations in 50 markets in nearly 20 states. Traditionally a suburban developer Toll Brothers has branched out to high-rise condominiums in urban markets.

	Annual Growth	10/11	10/12	10/13	10/14	10/15
Sales ($ mil.)	29.7%	1,475.9	1,882.8	2,674.3	3,911.6	4,171.2
Net income ($ mil.)	73.8%	39.8	487.1	170.6	340.0	363.2
Market value ($ mil.)	19.8%	3,049.3	5,771.7	5,749.0	5,586.4	6,289.2
Employees	15.2%	2,215	2,396	3,019	3,500	3,900

TOM LANGE COMPANY INC.

755 APPLE ORCHARD RD
SPRINGFIELD, IL 627035914
Phone: 217-786-3300
Fax: –
Web: www.tomlange.com

CEO: Phil Gumpert
CFO: –
HR: –
FYE: August 31
Type: Private

Tom Lange Company wants you to eat your veggies. One of the largest purchasers and distributors of fresh fruits and vegetables in the US Tom Lange supplies its comestibles to clients in the retail wholesale and food service trades. The company also provides third party logistics services specializing in truckload freight movement. The company was founded in 1960 as a three-man operation in St. Louis Missouri Tom Lange has grown to encompass 35 offices in the US and Canada. Produce subsidiaries include Seven Seas M&M Marketing and Seven Seas Fruit.

	Annual Growth	08/07	08/08	08/11	08/12	08/13
Sales ($ mil.)	1.1%	–	407.7	445.8	414.1	431.4
Net income ($ mil.)	(7.1%)	–	–	2.0	0.3	1.7
Market value ($ mil.)	–	–	–	–	–	–
Employees	–	–	–	–	–	110

TOM'S OF MAINE INC.

302 Lafayette Center
Kennebunk ME 04043
Phone: 207-985-2944
Fax: 207-985-2196
Web: www.tomsofmaine.com

CEO: Tom Obrien
CFO: –
HR: –
FYE: June 30
Type: Subsidiary

Tom's of Maine hopes that natural health will lead to corporate wealth. The company has built a business by selling the firm's flagship toothpaste (responsible for more than half of company sales) as well as mouthwash dental floss deodorant soap and shaving cream made from natural ingredients and distributing them in environmentally-friendly packaging. Tom's of Maine gives 10% of its pre-tax profits to charitable organizations and encourages its employees to use 5% of their paid time doing volunteer work. CEO Tom Chappell and his wife Kate Chappell founded the company in 1970. Seeking entry into the specialty toothpaste market Colgate-Palmolive bought Tom's of Maine for about $100 million in 2006.

TOMAX CORPORATION

224 S. 200 West
Salt Lake City UT 84101
Phone: 801-990-0909
Fax: 801-924-3400
Web: www.tomax.com

CEO: Eric Olafson
CFO: –
HR: –
FYE: June 30
Type: Private

Tomax tries to take the ailing out of retailing. The company develops and hosts software that helps retail chains simplify business processes manage marketing channels and reduce IT infrastructure costs. Clients use Tomax's Retail.net suite to manage customer transactions deal with returns streamline workflow processes and forecast staffing needs. The company also provides support and training services. Customers include 24 Hour Fitness Benjamin Moore Kroger Safeway and Trader Joe's. Eric Olafson (president and CEO) and Jaye Olafson (COO) who are husband and wife are the principal shareholders of Tomax. Oracle has a minority equity stake in the company.

TOMMY BAHAMA GROUP INC.

428 Westlake Ave. N. Ste. 388
Seattle WA 98109
Phone: 206-622-8688
Fax: 206-622-4483
Web: www.tommybahama.com

CEO: Terry R Pillow
CFO: Ken Kong
HR: –
FYE: January 31
Type: Subsidiary

Tommy Bahama Group retails the island life. The company designs and markets relaxed sportswear and other items under the Tommy Bahama name. Tommy Bahama's Fishbone pants Cayman Camp shirts and other clothing are sold through specialty stores vacation resorts and about 90 namesake stores as well as through about a dozen tropical-themed Tommy Bahama restaurants in the US. Licensees have extended the Tommy Bahama brand to such items as footwear golf bags luggage handbags eyewear home furnishings and rum. Oxford Industries owns Tommy Bahama Group which was founded in 1992 by marketing director Bob Emfield designer Lucio Dalla Gasperina and former president and CEO Tony Margolis.

TOMPKINS FINANCIAL CORP

ASE: TMP

The Commons, P.O. Box 460
Ithaca, NY 14851
Phone: 888-503-5753
Fax: –
Web: www.tompkinsfinancial.com

CEO: Robert D. (Bob) Davis
CFO: Francis M. Fetsko
HR: Rosemary Hyland
FYE: December 31
Type: Public

Tompkins Financial is the holding company for Tompkins Trust Company The Bank of Castile and Mahopac Bank which offer traditional banking services through some 45 offices in upstate New York. It also owns the 20-branch Pennsylvania-based VIST Bank. Funds from deposit products such as checking savings and money market accounts are mainly used to originate real estate loans and mortgages as well as commercial and consumer loans. Tompkins also offers trust and estate financial and tax planning and investment management services through Tompkins Financial Advisors. Tompkins Insurance Agencies sells property/casualty coverage in central and western New York and Pennsylvania.

	Annual Growth	12/10	12/11	12/12	12/13	12/14
Assets ($ mil.)	12.8%	3,260.3	3,400.2	4,837.2	5,003.0	5,269.6
Net income ($ mil.)	11.4%	33.8	35.4	31.3	50.9	52.0
Market value ($ mil.)	9.0%	580.3	570.7	587.5	761.6	819.5
Employees	7.9%	766	743	939	989	1,037

TOOTSIE ROLL INDUSTRIES INC
NYS: TR

7401 South Cicero Avenue
Chicago, IL 60629
Phone: 773 838-3400
Fax: 773 838-3534
Web: www.tootsie.com

CEO: Ellen R. Gordon
CFO: G. Howard Ember
HR: Peter Lebron
FYE: December 31
Type: Public

Neither taffy nor caramel and certainly not nougat or chocolate Tootsie Roll Industries has its success wrapped in brown-and-white waxed paper. As one of the country's largest candy companies it makes and sells candies including the vaguely chocolate-flavored Tootsie Roll which has been produced with the same formula and name for nearly 120 years. Tootsie Roll Industries also makes such well-known candies as Andes mints Junior Mints Charleston Chew Mason Dots and Sugar Daddy. Its Charms and Tootsie Pops brands make the company one of the largest lollipop producers in the world. Ellen Gordon controls the company's voting power after the 2015 death of her husband former chairman and CEO Melvin Gordon.

	Annual Growth	12/10	12/11	12/12	12/13	12/14
Sales ($ mil.)	1.0%	521.4	532.5	549.9	543.4	543.5
Net income ($ mil.)	4.2%	53.7	43.9	52.0	60.8	63.3
Market value ($ mil.)	1.4%	1,793.2	1,465.1	1,604.4	2,014.1	1,897.1
Employees	(2.4%)	2,200	2,200	2,200	2,000	2,000

TOPCO ASSOCIATES LLC

7711 Gross Point Rd.
Skokie IL 60077
Phone: 847-676-3030
Fax: 847-676-4949
Web: www.topco.com

CEO: Randall J Skoda
CFO: –
HR: –
FYE: December 31
Type: Private - Cooperativ

Topco Associates is a top company in terms of private-label procurement. Topco uses the combined purchasing clout of more than 50 member companies (mostly supermarket operators and foodservice suppliers) nationwide to wring discounts from wholesalers and manufacturers. Topco distributes more than 10000 private-label items including fresh meat and produce dairy and bakery goods and health and beauty aids to retail locations throughout the US. Its brands include Food Club Shurfine and a line of "Top" labels such as Top Crest and Top Care. In addition to procurement Topco helps its members contain costs through financial-services programs and other business services.

TOPPAN PHOTOMASKS INC.

131 Old Settlers Blvd.
Round Rock TX 78664-2211
Phone: 512-310-6500
Fax: 512-255-9627
Web: www.photomask.com

CEO: Michael Hadsell
CFO: Barry F Pomeroy
HR: Vickie Brush
FYE: March 31
Type: Subsidiary

Toppan Photomasks is one of the world's top suppliers of photomasks. Photomasks are customized etched plates of high-purity quartz or glassused by semiconductor manufacturers to transfer circuit patterns onto silicon wafers. The company supplies most major chip makers including Freescale Semiconductor IBM Microelectronics NXP Samsung Electronics STMicroelectronics Texas Instruments and United Microelectronics. It also makes photomasks used to produce other computing products such as flat-panel displays disk-drive heads microelectromechanical products and biochips. Toppan Photomasks became part of the largest photomask supplier in the world when it was acquired by Toppan Printing in 2005.

TOR MINERALS INTERNATIONAL INC
NAS: TORM

722 Burleson Street
Corpus Christi, TX 78402
Phone: 361 883-5591
Fax: –

CEO: Olaf Karasch
CFO: Barbara Russell
HR: –
FYE: December 31
Type: Public

It doesn't make winter outerwear but TOR Minerals International is concerned about good durable coats. The company makes pigments and pigment extenders that are used in paints industrial coatings and plastics. HITOX TOR's primary product is a beige titanium dioxide pigment used to add opacity and durability to paints. Other TOR products include pigment extenders that add strength and weight to end products and pigment fillers with flame-retardant and smoke-suppressant properties. The company's customers include paint and plastics manufacturers. TOR has production facilities in Corpus Christi Texas; the Netherlands; and Malaysia. Chairman Bernard Paulson owns 34% of the company.

	Annual Growth	12/10	12/11	12/12	12/13	12/14
Sales ($ mil.)	10.8%	31.0	41.0	56.7	46.0	46.7
Net income ($ mil.)	–	2.3	3.8	5.0	(1.6)	(0.6)
Market value ($ mil.)	(7.0%)	29.9	47.2	32.6	30.0	22.4
Employees	4.8%	146	156	192	198	176

TORAY PLASTICS (AMERICA) INC.

50 Belver Ave.
North Kingstown RI 02852
Phone: 401-294-4511
Fax: 401-294-2154
Web: www.toraytpa.com

CEO: Richard Schloesser
CFO: David Jose
HR: –
FYE: March 31
Type: Subsidiary

Toray Plastics (America) could sing "foam foam on the range where the polyolefin materials are made" all day. Toray Plastics (America) or TPA makes polyolefin foam that is used for automotive and flooring applications. The company also produces polypropylene (PP) and polyester films for the packaging and industrial markets. The only US producer of both PP and polyester films TPA is a subsidiary of Tokyo-based Toray Industries (a manufacturing conglomerate of synthetic and carbon fibers plastics chemicals and high performance films). TPA was founded in 1985.

TORCH ENERGY ROYALTY TRUST
NBB: TRRU

Rodney Square North, 1100 North Market Street
Wilmington, DE 19890
Phone: 302 636-6016
Fax: –
Web: www.torchroyalty.com

CEO: –
CFO: –
HR: –
FYE: December 31
Type: Public

Investors in Torch Energy Royalty Trust probably won't light an eternal flame in remembrance when the gas is all gone. The trust distributes to shareholders the royalties from natural gas properties and oil wells in which it owns stakes. The trust's gas fields are in Texas Alabama and Louisiana. As a grantor trust Torch Energy does not pay federal income tax; instead the shareholders who receive quarterly royalties are taxed directly but receive tax credits on gas extracted from some of the trust's hard-to-drill properties. Torch Energy Royalty Trust's investors have voted to wind up and liquidate the trust.

	Annual Growth	12/08	12/09	12/10	12/11	12/12
Sales ($ mil.)	(61.5%)	6.4	2.6	3.2	2.7	0.1
Net income ($ mil.)	–	3.2	1.2	2.1	1.3	(1.1)
Market value ($ mil.)	(17.3%)	12.4	40.9	31.2	18.1	5.8
Employees	–	–	–	–	–	–

TORCHMARK CORP.

NYS: TMK

3700 South Stonebridge Drive
McKinney, TX 75070
Phone: 972 569-4000
Fax: –
Web: www.torchmarkcorp.com

CEO: Larry M. Hutchison
CFO: Frank M. Svoboda
HR: –
FYE: December 31
Type: Public

Torchmark aims to be a beacon in the world of insurance. It is the holding company for a family of firms; its member companies specialize in lower-end individual life insurance and supplemental health insurance. Torchmark subsidiaries which include flagship Liberty National Life offer whole and term life insurance supplemental health insurance accidental death insurance Medicare supplements and long-term care health policies for the elderly. Its American Income Life sells life insurance policies to labor union and credit union members in the US Canada and New Zealand. Torchmark sells its products through direct marketing as well as a network of exclusive and independent agents.

	Annual Growth	12/10	12/11	12/12	12/13	12/14
Assets ($ mil.)	5.8%	16,159.8	17,156.4	18,776.9	18,191.7	20,214.7
Net income ($ mil.)	1.2%	517.1	517.9	529.3	528.5	542.9
Market value ($ mil.)	(2.4%)	7,642.6	5,550.9	6,610.2	9,997.8	6,930.0
Employees	(2.5%)	3,291	3,187	3,042	2,890	2,980

TORESCO ENTERPRISES INC.

170 Rte. 22 East
Springfield NJ 07081
Phone: 973-467-2900
Fax: 973-467-1824
Web: www.1800autoland.com

CEO: –
CFO: –
HR: –
FYE: December 31
Type: Private

Auto malls — what a concept! Donald Toresco owner of Toresco Enterprises helped pioneer the idea. The company's Autoland of New Jersey sells new and used Dodge Jeep Scion and Toyota cars trucks and SUVs. The dealership also offers service financing and fleet sales. Visitors to the company's Web site can search inventory build and price a car apply for financing schedule service and order parts. Chairman Toresco founded his company in 1964 as a used car dealership and created the auto mall in 1985. Toresco also has interests in the real estate and insurance industries.

TORO CO. (THE)

NYS: TTC

8111 Lyndale Avenue South
Bloomington, MN 55420
Phone: 952 888-8801
Fax: –
Web: www.thetorocompany.com

CEO: Michael J. (Mike) Hoffman
CFO: Renee J. Peterson
HR: –
FYE: October 31
Type: Public

Need to repair the 13th green after wild rampaging bulls charge through? Call The Toro Company. Toro makes lawn mowers and other tools for professional and residential use. Its professional lineup includes irrigation equipment mowers for commercial projects riding and walk-behind power mowers for fairways and greens trimmers lighting and utility vehicles. Some professional brands are Toro Rain Master Exmark Odyssey and Irritrol. Its residential lines sold to distributors home centers and mass merchants include walk-behind and riding mowers lawn tractors electrical trimmers lighting and snow blowers. Brand names in this segment include Toro Rain Master Irritrol Lawn Genie and Lawn-Boy.

	Annual Growth	10/11	10/12	10/13	10/14	10/15
Sales ($ mil.)	6.1%	1,884.0	1,958.7	2,041.4	2,172.7	2,390.9
Net income ($ mil.)	14.4%	117.7	129.5	154.8	173.9	201.6
Market value ($ mil.)	8.6%	2,953.3	2,307.4	3,221.1	3,373.6	4,113.6
Employees	10.5%	4,618	5,055	5,057	6,134	6,874

TOROTEL, INC.

NBB: TTLO

620 North Lindenwood Drive
Olathe, KS 66062
Phone: 913 747-6111
Fax: –
Web: www.torotelproducts.com

CEO: Dale H Sizemore Jr
CFO: H James Serrone
HR: –
FYE: April 30
Type: Public

Torotel is a military magnet. The company's Torotel Products subsidiary makes more than 32000 magnetic components used to control electrical voltages and currents in aviation missile guidance communication navigational and other systems. Products include transformers inductors chokes and toroidal coils. Subsidiary Electronika designs and sells ballast transformers to the airline industry. Torotel sells its products primarily in the US to commercial customers (including those in the health care oil public safety and financial services industries) but most of the company's sales come from the aerospace and military markets.

	Annual Growth	04/11	04/12	04/13	04/14	04/15
Sales ($ mil.)	5.1%	11.1	10.8	12.0	13.1	13.6
Net income ($ mil.)	(44.1%)	1.2	(0.0)	1.2	0.9	0.1
Market value ($ mil.)	4.5%	3.1	1.6	2.3	4.9	3.7
Employees	1.7%	143	113	121	129	153

TORRANCE MEMORIAL MEDICAL CENTER

3330 LOMITA BLVD
TORRANCE, CA 905055002
Phone: 310-325-9110
Fax: –
Web: www.torrancememorial.org

CEO: Craig Leach
CFO: Bill Larson
HR: Lois Michael
FYE: December 31
Type: Private

Back in 1925 Jared Sydney Torrance founded Torrance Memorial Medical Center in the southern California town that also bears his name. The not-for-profit medical center now includes 400 beds surgical suites clinical and diagnostic labs and specialist centers for cancer metabolic heart and other conditions. It is one of three burn centers in Los Angeles. Torrance Memorial Medical Center reaches beyond its walls and into the community with hospice care and home health care. The hospital also provides nursing residency programs and it offers staffing support services to physicians offices in the area.

	Annual Growth	12/12	12/13*	06/14*	09/14*	12/14
Sales ($ mil.)	2.8%	–	476.2	237.1	362.9	489.6
Net income ($ mil.)	–	–	–	12.7	17.9	27.6
Market value ($ mil.)	–	–	–	–	–	–
Employees	–	–	–	–	–	3,500

*Fiscal year change

TORTOISE CAPITAL RESOURCES CORPORATION

NYSE: TTO

11550 Ash St. Ste. 300
Leawood KS 66211
Phone: 913-981-1020
Fax: 913-981-1021
Web: www.tortoiseadvisors.com/tto.cfm

CEO: David J Schulte
CFO: –
HR: –
FYE: November 30
Type: Public

Slow steady and energy-filled is the way of Tortoise Capital Resources. A closed-end investment management firm Tortoise Capital invests in privately held and public micro-cap energy companies (or companies stock etc. valued between $50 million and $300 million) including midstream and downstream oil and gas companies and coal companies. The firm typically makes equity or debt investments in low-risk established energy companies that will generate steadily increasing returns on its investments over the long term. Tortoise Capital which has more than $90 million in assets under management is managed by Tortoise Capital Advisors a fund manager with five other publicly traded funds under management.

TORTOISE ENERGY CAPITAL CORPORATION

NYSE: TYY

11550 Ash St. Ste. 300
Leawood KS 66211
Phone: 866-362-9331
Fax: 913-981-1021
Web: www.tortoiseadvisors.com/tyy.cfm

CEO: Terry C Matlack
CFO: P Bradley Adams
HR: –
FYE: November 30
Type: Public

Tortoise Energy Capital knows a steady pace of dividends will result in winning investments. The publicly traded closed-end investment management company invests in securities of master limited partnerships (MLPs) in the energy infrastructure sector. It targets midstream oil and gas pipeline companies in the US. Tortoise Energy is managed by Tortoise Capital Advisors which oversees three other publicly traded closed-end funds and two private funds as well as separately managed accounts. Tortoise Energy Capital accounts for about $400 million of Tortoise Capital Advisors' approximately $1.4 billion of assets under management.

TORVEC, INC.

NBB: TOVC

1999 Mt. Read Blvd., Building 3
Rochester, NY 14615
Phone: 585 254-1100
Fax: –
Web: www.torvec.com

CEO: Richard A Kaplan
CFO: Kathleen A Browne
HR: –
FYE: December 31
Type: Public

A development-stage company Torvec hopes to bring its Torvec FTV (full-terrain vehicle) to the markets of developing nations. The FTV has the body of a truck but has tracks similar to those of a tank. The tracks enable the FTV to venture where a mere wheeled vehicle would fear to tread. Several technologies developed by the late Vernon Gleasman and members of his family including an infinitely variable transmission and a steering drive and suspension system for tracked vehicles are being incorporated into the FTV. The company is working with Ford Motor to develop a version of the FTV to be manufactured and distributed in the US initially and then marketed globally.

	Annual Growth	12/10	12/11	12/12	12/13	12/14
Sales ($ mil.)	18.6%	–	0.0	0.1	0.0	0.1
Net income ($ mil.)	–	(3.1)	(3.4)	(3.4)	(2.8)	(2.6)
Market value ($ mil.)	(37.3%)	59.0	37.9	31.5	16.0	9.1
Employees	6.3%	–	10	11	13	12

TOSHIBA AMERICA INC.

1251 Avenue of the Americas Ste. 4110
New York NY 10020
Phone: 212-596-0600
Fax: 212-593-3875
Web: www.toshiba.com

CEO: Hideo Ito
CFO: Takamasa Ikawa
HR: –
FYE: March 31
Type: Subsidiary

Toshiba America Inc. (TAI) is the spitting image of its old man. The holding company a subsidiary of high-tech titan Toshiba handles North American business for its formidable parent. TAI's operating companies market laptops netbooks and PCs; MRIs and other medical imaging systems; semiconductors and hard disk drives; copiers and other office equipment; and a range of consumer electronics products (television sets HD camcorders DVD players). The company also provides grants for science and mathematics education through its not-for-profit organization the Toshiba America Foundation.

TOTAL SYSTEM SERVICES, INC.

NYS: TSS

One TSYS Way, P.O. Box 1755
Columbus, GA 31902
Phone: 706 649-2310
Fax: 706 649-2456
Web: www.tsys.com

CEO: M. Troy Woods
CFO: Paul M. Todd
HR: Mark Andrews
FYE: December 31
Type: Public

Total System Services (TSYS) helps consumers go paperless. The company is one of the largest electronic payment processors in the world serving financial institutions and other companies that issue bank private-label prepaid health care or other types of cards. TSYS' products and services include credit authorization payment processing e-commerce services card issuance and such customer-relations services as fraud monitoring. It also provides merchant services primarily in the US where it serves about 20% of all credit card-accepting merchants. Following the acquisition of NetSpend in 2013 TSYS also issues prepaid and payroll cards to self-bank customers.

	Annual Growth	12/10	12/11	12/12	12/13	12/14
Sales ($ mil.)	9.3%	1,717.6	1,809.0	1,871.0	2,132.4	2,446.9
Net income ($ mil.)	13.6%	193.9	220.6	244.3	244.8	322.9
Market value ($ mil.)	21.9%	2,844.4	3,617.4	3,961.4	6,154.8	6,280.5
Employees	6.2%	7,788	8,200	8,600	9,600	9,900

TOTES ISOTONER CORPORATION

9655 International Blvd.
Cincinnati OH 45246-5658
Phone: 513-682-8200
Fax: 513-682-8602
Web: www.totes-isotoner.com

CEO: –
CFO: Donna Deye
HR: –
FYE: February 28
Type: Private

From head to toe to fingertips totes>Isotoner has the goods to keep its customers dry and comfortable. The company makes and distributes weather gear including umbrellas gloves rubber shoe covers rain hats and raincoats and water-resistant tote bags. It has extended its product line to include slippers and caps through several acquisitions in recent years. It distributes its products through department stores in the US the UK and France. totes>Isotoner also operates a network of more than 100 owned outlet mall-based stores. The company formed by the merger of totes and Isotoner in 1997 is owned by private equity firm MidOcean Partners. MidOcean acquired its majority stake for $288 million.

TOURO COLLEGE & UNIVERSITY SYSTEM

27 33 W 23RD ST
NEW YORK, NY 10010
Phone: 212-463-0400
Fax: –
Web: www.touro.edu

CEO: Bernard J Luskin
CFO: –
HR: –
FYE: June 30
Type: Private

Touro College is a Jewish university (the largest private Jewish-based educational institution in the US) and has sister institutions in France Germany Israel and Russia and branches in California Florida and Nevada. Some 19000 (Jewish and non-Jewish) students are enrolled in its 32 schools on 25 campuses which offer associate bachelor's and master's degrees in business education and law as well as professional degrees in osteopathic medicine pharmacy law and other fields. Touro also oversees the operations of New York Medical College. The institution claims some 75000 alumni.

	Annual Growth	06/07	06/08	06/09	06/10	06/13
Sales ($ mil.)	(30.3%)	–	2,037.4	145.5	277.4	334.2
Net income ($ mil.)	–	–	–	0.0	15.8	42.8
Market value ($ mil.)	–	–	–	–	–	–
Employees	–	–	–	–	–	4,600

TOWER FINANCIAL CORP.

NMS: TOFC

116 East Berry Street
Fort Wayne, IN 46802
Phone: 260 427-7000
Fax: –
Web: www.towerbank.net

CEO: –
CFO: –
HR: –
FYE: December 31
Type: Public

This tower aims to be a power in Indiana. Tower Financial is the holding company for Tower Bank & Trust which was formed in 1999 to fill the void in community banking services left in the wake of the consolidation of local banks into national banking companies. Targeting individuals and small to midsized businesses the bank has some six branches and loan production offices mainly in and around Fort Wayne. It focuses mainly on commercial lending with business mortgages and operating loans making up around three-quarters of its loan portfolio. It also issues residential mortgages and personal loans. Deposit products include checking savings and money market accounts and CDs.

	Annual Growth	12/08	12/09	12/10	12/11	12/12
Assets ($ mil.)	(0.5%)	696.6	680.2	659.9	700.7	684.0
Net income ($ mil.)	32.5%	1.9	(5.6)	3.2	6.6	5.7
Market value ($ mil.)	18.5%	28.6	32.5	35.8	39.3	56.3
Employees	(2.0%)	179	151	156	155	165

TOWER INTERNATIONAL INC

NYS: TOWR

17672 Laurel Park Drive North, Suite 400 E
Livonia, MI 48152
Phone: 248 675-6000
Fax: –
Web: www.towerinternational.com

CEO: Mark Malcolm
CFO: James (Jim) Gouin
HR: Susan (Sue) Talbot
FYE: December 31
Type: Public

Tower International has a tall order to fill; it supplies carmakers worldwide. The company manufactures engineered structural metal components for vehicles such as body chassis and frame structures. It also makes welded assemblies for cars pickups and SUVs and more recently entered the solar energy market as a supplier of stamped mirror-facet panels and welded support structures. Key customers have included noteworthy names like Volkswagen Fiat and Ford Motor. Tower operates through 30 production facilities located throughout the Americas Europe and Asia.

	Annual Growth	12/10	12/11	12/12	12/13	12/14
Sales ($ mil.)	0.9%	1,997.1	2,406.1	2,084.9	2,102.0	2,067.8
Net income ($ mil.)	–	(36.9)	8.1	18.0	(20.3)	21.5
Market value ($ mil.)	9.6%	367.1	222.9	167.1	444.1	530.2
Employees	0.0%	7,800	8,600	9,000	8,700	7,800

TOWERS WATSON & CO.

NYS: TW

901 N. Glebe Road
Arlington, VA 22203
Phone: 703 258-8000
Fax: –
Web: www.towerswatson.com

CEO: John J Haley
CFO: Roger F Millay
HR: –
FYE: June 30
Type: Public

This company is the result of adhering to the axiom keep your friends close and your enemies even closer. Created after the 2010 merger of rivals Towers Perrin and Watson Wyatt Towers Watson is a leading human resources consulting firm providing services related to employee benefits risk and financial services and talent and rewards. The company assists clients (many Fortune 1000 firms) in such matters as controlling health care costs employee retention and negotiating the risks and challenges of mergers and acquisitions. The estimated $4 billion stock merger between Towers Perrin and Watson Wyatt was announced in June 2009 and became effective in January 2010.

	Annual Growth	06/10	06/11	06/12	06/13	06/14
Sales ($ mil.)	9.9%	2,387.8	3,259.5	3,417.7	3,596.8	3,481.9
Net income ($ mil.)	31.4%	120.6	194.4	260.2	318.8	359.3
Market value ($ mil.)	28.0%	2,732.7	4,622.0	4,213.3	5,763.6	7,331.4
Employees	3.8%	12,750	13,100	14,500	14,500	14,800

TOWERSTREAM CORP

NAS: TWER

88 Silva Lane
Middletown, RI 02842
Phone: 401 848-5848
Fax: –
Web: www.towerstream.com

CEO: Jeffrey M Thompson
CFO: Joseph P Hernon
HR: –
FYE: December 31
Type: Public

TowerStream maintains a commanding view of the wireless landscape. The company provides wireless broadband network services to businesses over its network of rooftop and tower-mounted antennas. Its networks can be accessed by customers within a 10-mile radius. The company has about 3600 business customers including retailers educational institutions and banks. Charging a monthly subscription fee TowerStream provides service in a more than a dozen US markets: Boston Chicago Dallas Houston Las Vegas/Reno Los Angeles Miami Nashville New York City Philadelphia San Francisco and Seattle as well Providence Rhode Island.

	Annual Growth	12/10	12/11	12/12	12/13	12/14
Sales ($ mil.)	13.9%	19.6	26.5	32.3	33.4	33.0
Net income ($ mil.)	–	(5.6)	(7.0)	(21.0)	(24.8)	(27.6)
Market value ($ mil.)	(17.8%)	270.6	141.3	216.6	197.3	123.3
Employees	1.5%	132	161	175	159	140

TOWN SPORTS INTERNATIONAL HOLDINGS INC

NMS: CLUB

5 Penn Plaza, 4th Floor
New York, NY 10001
Phone: 212 246-6700
Fax: –
Web: www.mysportsclubs.com

CEO: –
CFO: Carolyn Spatafora
HR: Scott Milford
FYE: December 31
Type: Public

Town Sports International wants to be the apple a day that keeps the doctor away in NYC. The company owns and operates some 160 full-service health clubs about two-thirds of which are in the New York City area under the New York Sports Club banner. The company also has clubs in Boston Philadelphia and Washington D.C. and claims about 510000 members. It offers various membership plans that cater to its members' usage needs. Members designate a specific "home" club they can use at any time and retain an option to upgrade and gain access to multiple clubs within a single region or pay even more to gain access to all clubs in all four regions. Town Sports also has three clubs in Switzerland.

	Annual Growth	12/10	12/11	12/12	12/13	12/14
Sales ($ mil.)	(0.5%)	462.4	466.9	479.0	470.2	453.8
Net income ($ mil.)	–	(0.3)	6.3	12.0	12.3	(69.0)
Market value ($ mil.)	10.0%	98.7	178.8	259.2	359.0	144.7
Employees	(0.3%)	8,100	7,900	7,800	7,800	8,000

TOWNSHIP HIGH SCHOOL DISTRICT 211 FOUNDATION

1750 S ROSELLE RD STE 100
PALATINE, IL 600677302
Phone: 708-359-3300
Fax: –
Web: www.d211.org

CEO: –
CFO: –
HR: –
FYE: June 30
Type: Private

Township High School District 211 is the largest high school district in Illinois with some 12500 students attending its five high schools (grades 9 to 12) — James B. Conant William Fremd Hoffman Estates Palatine and Schaumburg — and two special education academies. The district's student-teacher ratio is nearly 14-to-1 and serves several suburban communities 25 miles northwest of Chicago. The school district started as one school (Palatine High School) in the Palatine-Schaumburg Township area in 1875 with the first graduating class in 1877.

	Annual Growth	06/10	06/11	06/12	06/13	06/14
Sales ($ mil.)	3.8%	–	250.9	257.1	268.3	280.2
Net income ($ mil.)	–	–	–	8.0	19.3	(8.8)
Market value ($ mil.)	–	–	–	–	–	–
Employees	–	–	–	–	–	1,909

TOWNSQUARE MEDIA INC.

2000 Fifth Third Center 511 Walnut St.	CEO: Steven Price
Cincinnati OH 45202	CFO: Stuart Rosenstein
Phone: 513-651-1190	HR: –
Fax: 513-651-1195	FYE: December 31
Web: townsquaremedia.com	Type: Private

You don't have to be in the village commons to hear this local media company. Formerly Regent Communications Townsquare Media is a leading radio broadcasting business with more than 60 stations serving about a dozen markets in 10 states. Operating primarily in smaller markets around the country its portfolio includes stations in such places as El Paso Texas; Flint Michigan; and St. Cloud Minnesota. Townsquare Media's radio stations program a wide variety of formats including adult contemporary music country gospel oldies and rock as well as news sports and talk radio. The company exited bankruptcy in 2010 and is controlled by investment firm Oaktree Capital Management.

TOY QUEST

2228 Barry Ave.	CEO: –
Los Angeles CA 90064	CFO: –
Phone: 310-231-7292	HR: –
Fax: 310-231-7565	FYE: December 31
Web: www.toyquest.com/	Type: Private

When you're on a quest to fill your tot's time Toy Quest can help. Among the world's largest private makers of electronic games and toys the company makes outdoor toys as well as robotic pets such as Tekno the Robotic Puppy. Other products include Planetcare eco-conscious toys Stretch Screamers role-play costume sets and its Banzai Falls line (all the makings of a backyard water park licensed with Six Flags). Toy Quest makes toys under license with Disney Nickelodeon Warner Brothers Sesame Street and Jeep. Toy Quest's products are sold by toy retailers discount stores and online. Founded by Chinese businessman Sampson Chan in 1975 Toy Quest is owned by Chan and president Brian Dubinsky.

TOYOTA MATERIAL HANDLING USA INC.

1 Park Plaza Ste. 1000	CEO: Jeff Rufener
Irvine CA 92623-7419	CFO: –
Phone: 949-474-1135	HR: Phil Wagner
Fax: 949-223-8000	FYE: March 31
Web: www.toyotaforklift.com	Type: Subsidiary

Toyota Material Handling USA (TMHU) doesn't make the kind of forks you can lift to your mouth. A subsidiary of Toyota Industries the #1 selling lift truck supplier in the US manufactures and distributes a full line of forklifts and material handling equipment bearing the Toyota name. In addition to its electric diesel and liquefied propane gas lifts TMHU offers aerial lifts pallet trucks order pickers and accessories such as backup alarms lights and mirrors. TMHU also stands as the sole maker of compressed natural gas powered lift trucks. Of all the TMHU's trucks sold in the US 99% are made in the US at the company's Indiana-based Toyota Industrial Equipment Manufacturing (TIEM) facility.

TOYOTA MOTOR CREDIT CORP.

19001 S. Western Avenue	CEO: –
Torrance, CA 90501	CFO: Chris Ballinger
Phone: 310 468-1310	HR: Julia Wada
Fax: –	FYE: March 31
Web: www.toyotafinancial.com	Type: Public

Toyota Motor Credit (TMCC) is the US financing arm of Toyota Financial Services which is a subsidiary of Toyota Motor Corporation the world's largest carmaker. TMCC provides retail leasing retail and wholesale sales financing and other financial services to Toyota and Lexus dealers and their customers for the purchase of new and used cars and trucks. It offers similar services to Toyota industrial equipment dealers. TMCC which underwrites and services the finance contracts operates three regional customer service centers and some 30 dealer sales and service branches across the US and Puerto Rico.

	Annual Growth	03/11	03/12	03/13	03/14	03/15
Sales ($ mil.)	0.8%	8,843.0	8,146.0	7,988.0	8,099.0	9,142.0
Net income ($ mil.)	(10.3%)	1,853.0	1,486.0	1,331.0	857.0	1,197.0
Market value ($ mil.)	–	–	–	–	–	–
Employees	0.6%	3,170	3,220	3,210	3,210	3,251

TOYOTA MOTOR ENGINEERING & MANUFACTURING NORTH AMERIC

25 Atlantic Ave.	CEO: Osamu Nagata
Erlanger KY 41018	CFO: Charles Brown
Phone: 859-746-4000	HR: –
Fax: 859-746-4190	FYE: March 31
Web: www.toyota.com/about/our_business/engineering_	Type: Subsidiary

Toyota Motor Engineering & Manufacturing North America (TEMA) is the epicenter of Toyota Motor's ever-encroaching dominance in the North American car market. TEMA is responsible for engineering design research and development and manufacturing activities in the US Canada and Mexico. Formerly Toyota Motor Manufacturing North America TEMA develops the upper body portion as well as parts for the adaptation of Toyota vehicles to the North American market. Toyota Research Institute of North America (TRI-NA) conducts automotive research relating to energy and environment. TEMA has 13 manufacturing plants located throughout North America.

TOYOTA MOTOR MANUFACTURING KENTUCKY INC.

1001 Cherry Blossom Way	CEO: –
Georgetown KY 40324	CFO: –
Phone: 502-868-2000	HR: –
Fax: 919-876-3258	FYE: March 31
Web: www.leithcars.com	Type: Subsidiary

Toyota Motor Manufacturing Kentucky (TMMK) is where the land of the rising sun has set on the bluegrass state. TMMK Toyota's largest manufacturing facility outside of Japan makes the Toyota Camry (the #1 choice with American consumers) Avalon and Venza for the North American market. To the red of the sun and the blue of the grass TMMK adds green to the mix with its production of the Camry Hybrid to satisfy the hemisphere's appetite for alternative fueled vehicles. Other products manufactured include 4 cylinder and V6 engines and powertrain components. TMMK which can produce 500000 engines and vehicles per year rolled its first complete car off its assembly line in 1990.

TOYOTA MOTOR NORTH AMERICA INC.

601 Lexington Ave. 49th Fl.
New York NY 10022
Phone: 212-223-0303
Fax: 212-759-7670
Web: www.toyota.com

CEO: Yukitoshi Funo
CFO: –
HR: –
FYE: March 31
Type: Subsidiary

A wholly owned subsidiary of Toyota Motor Corporation Toyota Motor North America is the holding company for all of its parent's North American operations covering sales engineering and manufacturing subsidiaries from offices in New York Miami and Washington DC. It oversees functions related to government and regulatory affairs energy economic research philanthropy advertising corporate communications and investor relations. Through its manufacturing operations Toyota Motor Engineering & Manufacturing North America Toyota builds vehicles and parts at a dozen plus plants in North America. Toyota has invested more than $18 billion in its North American operations which began in 1957.

TOYOTA MOTOR SALES U.S.A. INC.

19001 S. Western Ave.
Torrance CA 90501
Phone: 310-468-4000
Fax: 310-468-7800
Web: www.toyota.com

CEO: Jim Lentz
CFO: Tracey Doi
HR: –
FYE: March 31
Type: Subsidiary

Toyota Motor Sales U.S.A. (TMS) is the US sales distribution and marketing unit for Toyota Motor's Toyota Lexus and Scion brands. A majority of Toyotas sold in the US are also made in the US. Those models include the Avalon Camry Highlander Sequoia Sienna Tacoma Tundra and Venza. TMS is in charge of sales marketing and service of its cars light trucks hybrids and SUVs in 49 states. Sales are conducted through about 1200 dealerships throughout the US. The company's TRD (Toyota Racing Development) U.S.A. division designs and assembles engines and develops chassis and other technology for Toyota-sponsored race cars.

TOYS "R" US INC.

1 Geoffrey Way
Wayne NJ 07470-2030
Phone: 973-617-3500
Fax: 973-617-4006
Web: www.toysrus.com

CEO: David A Brandon
CFO: Michael J Short
HR: Richard Cudrin
FYE: January 31
Type: Private

Kids rule the aisles while parents tag along for the ride at Toys "R" Us. It's one of the world's largest toy retailers but it has lost its top position in the US to retailing behemoth Wal-Mart. Toys "R" Us sells its wares in more than 1650 stores worldwide as well as online. In addition to about 880 US Toys "R" Us and Babies "R" Us stores the retailer operates more than 325 side-by-side stores which sell both toys and juvenile products including infant and toddler apparel furniture and feeding supplies. Privately held by investment companies KKR and Bain Capital and real estate firm Vornado Realty Trust Toys "R" Us filed to go public in 2010 but has yet to list on the New York Stock Exchange.

TPS PARKING MANAGEMENT LLC

200 W. Monroe St.
Chicago IL 60606
Phone: 312-453-1700
Fax: 312-633-1406
Web: www.h2oplus.com

CEO: Kevin J Shrier
CFO: –
HR: –
FYE: December 31
Type: Private

TPS Parking Management doing business as The Parking Spot wants to take you the last bit of the way to the airport. The company operates off-site parking lots near more than 20 major US airports some with multiple locations. Lots have both covered and uncovered areas as well as valet parking. The Parking Spot uses conspicuous black-on-yellow polka-dot vans to shuttle customers to and from the airport terminal. The company takes reservations for parking slots and offers corporate discounts as well as its own version of a frequent flyer program. It was founded by CEO Martin Nesbitt who opened the first lot at Houston's main airport in 1998 and sold in 2011 to Green Courte Partners a private-equity REIT.

TRACFONE WIRELESS INC.

9700 NW 112th Ave.
Miami FL 33178
Phone: 305-640-2000
Fax: 305-640-2070
Web: www.tracfone.com

CEO: Frederick J Pollak
CFO: –
HR: –
FYE: December 31
Type: Subsidiary

With more nearly 19 million active subscribers TracFone is the leading independent reseller of nationwide prepaid wireless telecommunications services. The TracFone product is a pay-as-you-go off-the-shelf mobile phone featuring prepaid airtime with no annual contracts or activation fees. In order to offer service across the US TracFone has agreements with about 30 different wireless carriers nationwide including industry leaders AT&T Mobility and Verizon Wireless. It sells service and phones online as well as nationally through about 80000 retail outlets including Wal-Mart and Walgreen and in Puerto Rico and the US Virgin Islands. TracFone is a subsidiary of Latin America's top wireless carrier America Movil.

TRACK GROUP INC

405 S. Main Street, Suite 700
Salt Lake City, UT 84111
Phone: 801 451-6141
Fax: –
Web: www.trackgrp.com

NBB: TRCK
CEO: –
CFO: John R Merrill
HR: –
FYE: September 30
Type: Public

Thanks in part to SecureAlert you can run but you can not hide. The company (formerly RemoteMDx) develops markets and sells wireless monitoring equipment and services to law enforcement and bail bond agencies. Its primary product is TrackerPAL - tracking devices worn on the ankle to monitor the whereabouts of criminals on parole or probation. Using global positioning system and cellular technology the device features two-way voice communications alarms and Web-based location tracking in real time. The company's SecureAlert Monitoring subsidiary provides monitoring services. The company electronically monitors some 12700 offenders.

	Annual Growth	09/11	09/12	09/13	09/14	09/15
Sales ($ mil.)	3.7%	18.0	19.8	15.6	12.3	20.8
Net income ($ mil.)	–	(9.9)	(17.5)	(17.9)	(8.7)	(5.7)
Market value ($ mil.)	192.2%	1.0	0.3	199.7	150.8	72.9
Employees	(4.1%)	215	139	98	210	182

TRACTOR SUPPLY CO.

NMS: TSCO

5401 Virginia Way
Brentwood, TN 37027
Phone: 615-440-4000
Fax: –
Web: www.tractorsupply.com

CEO: Gregory A. (Greg) Sandfort
CFO: Anthony F. (Tony) Crudele
HR: Samantha Case
FYE: December 27
Type: Public

Farmers and ranchers can gear up for more than just a tractor pull at Tractor Supply Company (TSC). Besides providing agricultural machine parts the farm and ranch supply retailer offers animal feeds fencing power tools riding mowers and work clothing as well as tools for gardening irrigation welding and towing. TSC offers both name-brand merchandise and its own stable of private-label goods. It operates about 1382 stores in some 49 US states under the Tractor Supply Company and Del's Farm Supply banners. Stores are concentrated in rural areas and near large cities to cater to full- and part-time farmers ranchers and contractors. TSC also operates a growing online business.

	Annual Growth	12/10	12/11	12/12	12/13	12/14
Sales ($ mil.)	11.9%	3,638.3	4,232.7	4,664.1	5,164.8	5,711.7
Net income ($ mil.)	21.9%	168.0	222.7	276.5	328.2	370.9
Market value ($ mil.)	12.6%	6,600.9	9,567.2	11,929.3	10,302.3	10,626.9
Employees	9.5%	14,700	16,400	17,300	19,200	21,100

TRACYLOCKE

1999 Bryan St. Ste. 2800
Dallas TX 75201
Phone: 214-969-9000
Fax: 214-259-3550
Web: www.tracylocke.com

CEO: Beth Ann Kaminkow
CFO: –
HR: –
FYE: December 31
Type: Subsidiary

Companies hoping to get a lock on their market might turn to this agency. TracyLocke is an integrated marketing firm offering a full menu of services to highlight brand names. Its capabilities include advertising promotions shopper marketing sports marketing graphic design media planning and buying direct marketing digital strategic planning and production services. Clients have included such heavy hitters as 7-Eleven MasterCard and Pepsi. With five offices across the US TracyLocke operates as part of the Diversified Agency Services division of advertising giant Omnicom Group.

TRADE STREET RESIDENTIAL, INC.

NMS: TSRE

19950 West Country Club Drive
Aventura, NY 33180
Phone: 786-248-5200
Fax: –
Web: www.tradestreetresidential.com

CEO: –
CFO: –
HR: –
FYE: December 31
Type: Public

Trade Street Residential shopped 'til it dropped and is now ready to go home. Formerly Feldman Mall Properties the company changed its business interests in 2012 to move from shopping malls to apartment homes. The real estate investment trust (REIT) owns and operates about 15 apartment complexes in eight states in the Southeast and Texas. (As a REIT it is exempt from paying federal income tax so long as it distributes at least 90% of its income back to shareholders.) Its apartments have an average monthly rent per of $817. In addition the trust has a land portfolio of about 45 acres in Florida and Virginia that it plans to develop into four different properties. The REIT went public in 2013.

	Annual Growth	12/06	12/07	12/11	12/12	12/13
Sales ($ mil.)	(11.0%)	65.3	55.3	9.0	14.5	29.0
Net income ($ mil.)	–	20.2	(16.2)	(3.8)	(8.6)	(16.6)
Market value ($ mil.)	(9.2%)	142.8	42.3	0.7	0.9	72.6
Employees	(8.6%)	207	167	–	–	110

TRADEBEAM INC.

2 Waters Park Dr. Ste. 200
San Mateo CA 94403-1148
Phone: 650-653-4800
Fax: 650-653-4801
Web: www.tradebeam.com

CEO: Edward R Flaherty
CFO: Douglas F Harrison
HR: –
FYE: December 31
Type: Subsidiary

TradeBeam has a special appreciation for the global economy. The company offers a mix of software and hosted services that link clients to global supply and distribution chains. TradeBeam's global trade management software simplifies the navigation of international trading channels to place orders send and receive shipments control imports and exports track inventory and settle bills. The company also offers consulting and implementation services. Its clients include Bank of America Cisco Systems and Neiman Marcus. TradeBeam has received capital investment from Carlyle Venture Partners Enterprise Partners Venture Capital and Sigma Partners. In 2010 the company was acquired by CDC Software.

TRADECARD INC.

75 Maiden Ln. 12th Fl.
New York NY 10038
Phone: 212-405-1800
Fax: 212-405-1801
Web: www.tradecard.com

CEO: –
CFO: –
HR: –
FYE: December 31
Type: Private

This company's more about cloud-based import and export services rather than about a 1952 Topps Mickey Mantle. TradeCard provides domestic and international trade services specializing in financial supply chain management among suppliers buyers and service providers. Its technology and network of trade experts synchronize financial transactions with the global supply chain to help clients automate accounts payable and receivable management purchase order approvals payment decisions chargebacks and settlements. The company also partners with financial institutions to offer automated supply chain funding credit protection export financing and money transfer services.

TRADESTATION GROUP INC.

8050 SW 10th St. Ste. 2000
Plantation FL 33324
Phone: 954-652-7000
Fax: 954-652-7300
Web: www.tradestation.com

CEO: Salomon Sredni
CFO: Edward Codispoti
HR: –
FYE: December 31
Type: Private

TradeStation is a stop on the way to wealth or poverty depending on the skill or luck of the trader. The company offers an electronic trading platform to provide commission-based direct-access online brokerage services. The technology helps traders manage trading systems and automate the execution of orders for equities and futures. Subsidiary TradeStation Technologies offers the TradeStation platform as either a hosted subscription-based service or a licensed software package and it operates an online trading strategy community site. TradeStation Securities is an online brokerage that serves retail and some institutional traders. In 2011 the company was acquired by Japan-based Monex Group for about $400 million.

TRADEWEB MARKETS LLC

Harborside Financial Center 2200 Plaza Five
Jersey City NJ 07311-4993
Phone: 201-536-6500
Fax: 201-915-3160
Web: www.tradeweb.com

CEO: Lee Olesky
CFO: Robert Warshaw
HR: –
FYE: December 31
Type: Subsidiary

Along came a spider sat down beside her and said "Hey wanna buy some treasury notes?" Tradeweb Markets is an electronic securities trading network specializing in bonds stocks derivatives commercial paper money markets and other financial products. It also provides ancillary services such as market data and trade confirmation. The company's electronic marketplace matches more than 45 securities dealers (comprising some of the largest banks and asset managers in the world) with more than 2000 institutional buyers in North America Europe Asia and Australia. Established in 1998 Tradeweb handles an average of some $200 billion worth of fixed-income and derivative trades per day.

TRAILER BRIDGE INC.

NASDAQ: TRBR

10405 New Berlin Rd. East
Jacksonville FL 32226
Phone: 904-751-7100
Fax: 904-751-7444
Web: www.trailerbridge.com

CEO: Chris Dombalis
CFO: –
HR: –
FYE: December 31
Type: Public

Traversing land and sea Trailer Bridge connects the continental US Puerto Rico and the Dominican Republic. The company's oceangoing barges designed to carry shipping containers sail between Jacksonville Florida and the two islands. Southbound shipments which represent about 75% of the freight transported include raw materials consumer goods furniture and vehicles. Trailer Bridge's land-based assets move freight within the US and abroad. Its fleet comprises some 140 tractors 500 dry van trailers and car carriers 3960 high-cube containers and 3150 chassis including two roll-on/roll-off (ro/ro) multiuse barges and two container barges. Trailer Bridge emerged from Chapter 11 proceedings in 2012.

TRAMMELL CROW COMPANY

2001 Ross Ave. Ste. 3400
Dallas TX 75201
Phone: 214-863-4101
Fax: 214-863-3138
Web: www.trammellcrow.com

CEO: Danny Queenan
CFO: Derek R McClain
HR: –
FYE: December 31
Type: Subsidiary

Untrammeled by convention with an unbridled passion for real estate development and acquisition Trammell Crow has cast a wide net over commercial real estate in the US and Canada. A subsidiary of real estate services giant CBRE Trammell Crow's portfolio covers more than 15 major cities and includes some 525 million sq. ft. valued at about $55 billion. The firm serves developers tenants and investors in office industrial retail mixed-use airport multifamily residential and health care facilities. Trammell Crow offers development services to its clients who occupy buildings and investment funding and joint-venture opportunities to its real estate investment clients.

TRAMMELL CROW RESIDENTIAL COMPANY

2001 Bryan St. Ste. 3250
Dallas TX 75201
Phone: 214-922-8400
Fax: 301-459-1069
Web: www.trandes.com

CEO: Kenneth Valach
CFO: Cliff Breining
HR: –
FYE: December 31
Type: Private

Trammell Crow Residential (TCR) builds and maintains quite the nest. It invests in develops builds acquires and manages multifamily residential real estate such as apartments and condominiums. Projects range from upscale to affordable housing. The company which operates through about 20 offices across the US has developed more than 225000 individual units since its founding in the late 1970s. TCR's portfolio includes some 200 properties located in major markets across the country with the heaviest concentrations in Texas the Southeast and the West. Many are are branded Alexan or Wynhaven Communities. The company split from Trammell Crow in 1977 but is still associated with the Crow family empire.

TRAMMO INC.

320 PARK AVE RM 1001
NEW YORK, NY 100226987
Phone: 212-223-3200
Fax: –
Web: www.guide8480.guidechem.com

CEO: Christian Wendel
CFO: Edward G. Weiner
HR: –
FYE: December 31
Type: Private

Fertilizers liquefied petroleum gas (LPG) and petrochemicals are the "ammo" which international trader Trammo (formerly Transammonia) uses in its battle with competitors. The company trades distributes and transports these commodities around the world. Trammo's fertilizer business includes ammonia phosphates and urea. Its Sea-3 subsidiary imports and distributes propane to residential commercial and industrial customers in the northeastern US and Florida. The Trammochem unit trades in petrochemicals specializing in aromatics methanol methyltertiary butyl ether (MTBE) benzene and olefins. Its Trammo Gas trades LPG and propane as well as ethane butane and natural gas in the US.

	Annual Growth	12/09	12/10	12/11	12/12	12/13
Sales ($ mil.)	10.4%	–	8,414.7	11,303.4	12,152.8	11,315.3
Net income ($ mil.)	–	–	–	31.4	35.1	(11.7)
Market value ($ mil.)	–	–	–	–	–	–
Employees	–	–	–	–	–	440

TRANS WORLD CORP.

NBB: TWOC

545 Fifth Avenue, Suite 940
New York, NY 10017
Phone: 212 983-3355
Fax: –
Web: www.transwc.com

CEO: Rami S Ramadan
CFO: Rami S Ramadan
HR: –
FYE: December 31
Type: Public

American-style gambling is a global bread winner for Trans World. The company which focuses on small and midsized casinos and gaming parlors owns and operates four niche casinos that feature slot machines and gaming tables in the Czech Republic. The casinos operate under the name American Chance Casinos and feature themes from different eras of US history (Chicago in the Roaring 1920s Miami Beach in the 1950s New Orleans in the 1920s and the Pacific South Seas). The company also operates a casino in Croatia near a resort city on the coast of the Adriatic Sea. Trans World is in the process of adding hotels to its operations. An investment group led by director Timothy Ewing owns nearly 40% of the company.

	Annual Growth	12/10	12/11	12/12	12/13	12/14
Sales ($ mil.)	3.1%	34.1	38.2	36.0	36.5	38.5
Net income ($ mil.)	11.8%	1.7	3.0	1.8	2.4	2.6
Market value ($ mil.)	6.6%	22.1	26.5	23.4	21.7	28.5
Employees	(5.4%)	627	564	524	479	502

TRANS WORLD ENTERTAINMENT CORP.

NMS: TWMC

38 Corporate Circle
Albany, NY 12203
Phone: 518-452-1242
Fax: –
Web: www.twec.com

CEO: Michael Feurer
CFO: John Anderson
HR: –
FYE: January 31
Type: Public

Just an F.Y.I. but Trans World Entertainment operates F.Y.E. and a handful of other retail ventures. F.Y.E. (aka For Your Entertainment) stores sell CDs DVDs video games software and related products at about 390 locations throughout the US Puerto Rico and the Virgin Islands. Trans World's other bricks-and-mortar operations include about 15 video stores under the Saturday Matinee and Suncoast Motion Pictures banners. Most of the firm's retail outlets are located in shopping malls. Trans World also sells entertainment products via its e-commerce sites (including fye.com secondspin.com and wherehouse.com). Chairman and CEO Bob Higgins founded the company in 1972.

	Annual Growth	01/11	01/12*	02/13	02/14*	01/15
Sales ($ mil.)	(13.9%)	652.4	542.6	458.5	393.7	358.5
Net income ($ mil.)	–	(31.0)	2.2	33.7	8.3	1.8
Market value ($ mil.)	17.3%	57.2	76.2	108.7	123.7	108.4
Employees	(10.6%)	4,700	4,000	3,400	3,200	3,000

*Fiscal year change

TRANS-SYSTEM INC.

7405 S HAYFORD RD
CHENEY, WA 990049633
Phone: 509-623-4001
Fax: –
Web: www.trans-system.com

CEO: James C. (Jim) Williams
CFO: Gary R King
HR: –
FYE: March 31
Type: Private

Freight hauler Trans-System operates through three main units: System Transport (flatbed); TW Transport (refrigerated and dry van); and James J. Williams (bulk commodities). The Trans-System trucking companies operate from some 10 terminals in the western US. Overall the company's fleet consists of about 1000 tractors and 1500 trailers. Trans-System also offers logistics services and runs a driver training school. Chairman and CEO Jim Williams founded the company in 1972 although it got its start when Williams' grandfather began transporting petroleum products throughout northern Idaho and eastern Washington.

	Annual Growth	03/10	03/11	03/12	03/13	03/14
Sales ($ mil.)	4.8%	–	–	191.1	197.7	210.0
Net income ($ mil.)	(13.8%)	–	–	8.8	8.1	6.6
Market value ($ mil.)	–	–	–	–	–	–
Employees	–	–	–	–	–	650

TRANSACT TECHNOLOGIES INC.

NMS: TACT

One Hamden Center, 2319 Whitney Avenue, Suite 3B
Hamden, CT 06518
Phone: 203-859-6000
Fax: –
Web: www.transact-tech.com

CEO: Bart C Shuldman
CFO: Steven (Steve) Demartino
HR: –
FYE: December 31
Type: Public

TransAct Technologies knows how to ink the deal. The company makes thermal inkjet and impact printers under the Epic EPICENTRAL and other brands that record transaction information for point-of-sale (POS) casino and gaming lottery banking food safety and e-commerce transactions. TransAct's printers and terminals produce receipts coupons lottery tickets and other printed records. TransAct also makes document transport mechanisms for ATMs and kiosks and manufactures custom printers for electronics manufacturers and oil and gas exploration companies. TransAct sells its products to OEMs VARs and other distributors as well as directly to end-users. About 75% of sales comes from customers in the US.

	Annual Growth	12/10	12/11	12/12	12/13	12/14
Sales ($ mil.)	(4.3%)	63.2	66.0	68.4	60.1	53.1
Net income ($ mil.)	–	3.9	4.7	3.6	4.9	(2.4)
Market value ($ mil.)	(12.7%)	74.4	57.4	57.0	99.0	43.2
Employees	1.0%	124	134	140	139	129

TRANSAM TRUCKING INC.

15910 S. Hwy. 169
Olathe KS 66062
Phone: 913-782-5300
Fax: 913-324-7047
Web: www.transamtruck.com

CEO: Russ McElliott
CFO: –
HR: –
FYE: December 31
Type: Private

No TransAm Trucking isn't that movie where Burt Reynolds helps haul beer from Texas to Georgia — that was Smokey and the Bandit. TransAm Trucking does haul freight in the South and in most of the rest of the US and the company has carried a little beer in its time along with other products that require temperature-controlled transportation. It operates a fleet of about 1200 tractors and 2400 refrigerated trailers. But no black Pontiac Trans Ams with T-tops. In addition to for-hire transportation TransAm Trucking offers dedicated fleet services in which drivers and equipment are assigned to customers long-term. The company was founded in 1987.

TRANSAMERICA LIFE INSURANCE COMPANY

4333 Edgewood Rd. NE
Cedar Rapids IA 52499
Phone: 319-398-8511
Fax: 319-369-2825
Web: www.transamerica.com

CEO: –
CFO: –
HR: –
FYE: December 31
Type: Subsidiary

Transamerica Life Insurance Company (TLIC) gives its American touch to Dutch insurance giant AEGON's life insurance operations. TLIC which began operations in 1961 is part of the AEGON USA group of companies. The company provides individual and group life insurance and annuities. The company is licensed to provide insurance throughout the US except for New York and Washington DC which are covered by its sister Transamerica Financial Life Insurance Company. Its products are distributed through agents and brokers as well as via direct marketing efforts.

TRANSATLANTIC REINSURANCE COMPANY

80 Pine St.
New York NY 10005
Phone: 212-770-2000
Fax: 212-269-6801
Web: www.transre.com

CEO: Robert F Orlich
CFO: Steven S Skalicky
HR: –
FYE: December 31
Type: Subsidiary

Living up to its name Transatlantic Reinsurance Company provides reinsurance on both sides of the Atlantic and in fact along the Pacific as well. The company offers both treaty (package) and facultative (case by case) reinsurance. Its major lines of business include property catastrophe traditional property/casualty (including auto umbrella and workers' compensation) and specialty casualty (including medical malpractice directors' and officers' liability and accident coverage) reinsurance. Transatlantic Reinsurance and its subsidiaries including Fair American and Trans Re Zurich are the primary operating companies of Transatlantic Holdings which is part of insurance firm Alleghany.

TRANSCAT INC

NMS: TRNS

35 Vantage Point Drive
Rochester, NY 14624
Phone: 585 352-7777
Fax: –
Web: www.transcat.com

CEO: Lee D. Rudow
CFO: John J. Zimmer
HR: –
FYE: March 28
Type: Public

This cat helps you measure up. And calibrate. And test. Transcat distributes test measurement and calibration equipment used in industrial and scientific settings. The company sells products such as multimeters oscilloscopes recorders and temperature devices from a range of instrument manufacturers to customers primarily in North America through its catalog. The company also provides instrument calibration and repair services. Transcat targets customers in the petroleum products and chemical manufacturing industries as well as pharmaceutical and telecommunications companies. Customers have included Dow Chemical Duke Energy DuPont and Exxon Mobil.

	Annual Growth	03/11	03/12	03/13	03/14	03/15
Sales ($ mil.)	7.9%	91.2	110.0	112.3	118.5	123.6
Net income ($ mil.)	9.6%	2.8	3.3	3.7	4.0	4.0
Market value ($ mil.)	4.6%	54.7	89.6	43.5	63.4	65.6
Employees	9.1%	313	338	412	407	443

TRANSCEND SERVICES INC.

NASDAQ: TRCR

1 Glenlake Pkwy. Ste. 1325
Atlanta GA 30328
Phone: 678-808-0600
Fax: 678-808-0601
Web: www.transcendservices.com

CEO: –
CFO: –
HR: –
FYE: December 31
Type: Subsidiary

Transcend Services helps make sense of doctors' gibberish. The medical transcription company uses Internet-based technology to turn doctors' audio patient records into written text. Its home-based medical transcriptionists convert the physicians' recorded notes (made using either Transcend Services' proprietary BeyondTXT technology or the clients' own systems) into text documents. The company counts some 400 hospitals clinics and physician group practices among its customers. It is increasing the use of speech recognition software to automatically convert voice to text after which the documents are edited by transcriptionists. In fact in 2012 Transcend Services was acquired by software firm Nuance Communications.

TRANSCONTINENTAL REALTY INVESTORS, INC.

NYS: TCI

1603 Lyndon B. Johnson Freeway, Suite 300
Dallas, TX 75234
Phone: 469 522-4200
Fax: –

CEO: Daniel J Moos
CFO: Gene S Bertcher
HR: –
FYE: December 31
Type: Public

Transcontinental Realty likes to find diamonds in the rough. The company acquires develops and owns income-producing commercial and residential real estate particularly properties that it believes are undervalued. Its portfolio consists nearly 40 apartment complexes with more than 6000 units in the southern US in addition to about 7.7 million sq.ft. of rentable commercial space including nearly 8 commercial properties. Texas is its largest market by far. Additionally the company has investments in apartment projects under development and more than 4000 acres of undeveloped and partially developed land most of it also in Texas.

	Annual Growth	12/10	12/11	12/12	12/13	12/14
Sales ($ mil.)	(12.6%)	129.9	114.1	77.9	86.2	75.9
Net income ($ mil.)	–	(67.2)	(46.3)	(8.3)	58.5	41.6
Market value ($ mil.)	11.3%	58.5	14.3	37.8	82.3	89.8
Employees	–	–	–	–	–	–

TRANSDIGM GROUP INC

NYS: TDG

1301 East 9th Street, Suite 3000
Cleveland, OH 44114
Phone: 216 706-2960
Web: www.transdigm.com

CEO: W. Nicholas (Nick) Howley
CFO: Terrance M. Paradie
HR: –
FYE: September 30
Type: Public

TransDigm's aviation components transcend any single airframe. Operating through several subsidiaries TransDigm Group makes and distributes a wide range of components for commercial and military aircraft. Subsidiaries include AeroControlex (mechanical controls pumps valves) Adams Rite Aerospace (cockpit security products electromechanical controls interior latches and locks) Marathon Norco Aerospace (batteries connectors) and Champion Aerospace (ignition systems and components). TransDigm estimates that its products are installed on about 95000 transport military and general aviation aircraft.

	Annual Growth	09/11	09/12	09/13	09/14	09/15
Sales ($ mil.)	22.4%	1,206.0	1,700.2	1,924.4	2,372.9	2,707.1
Net income ($ mil.)	27.0%	172.1	325.0	302.8	306.9	447.2
Market value ($ mil.)	27.0%	4,384.5	7,616.3	7,446.1	9,895.8	11,403.2
Employees	21.2%	3,800	5,400	6,100	7,300	8,200

TRANSGENOMIC INC

NAS: TBIO

12325 Emmet Street
Omaha, NE 68164
Phone: 402 452-5400
Fax: –
Web: www.transgenomic.com

CEO: Paul Kinnon
CFO: Paul Kinnon
HR: –
FYE: December 31
Type: Public

Transgenomic travels the uncharted frontiers of the human genome. The company operates through three business divisions. Transgenomic Clinical Laboratories specializes in molecular diagnostics for cardiology neurology mitochondrial disorders and oncology. The Transgenomic Diagnostic Tools unit produces equipment reagents and other consumables for clinical and research applications in molecular testing and cytogenetics. The proprietary WAVE System is used for genetic variation detection in molecular genetic research and molecular diagnostics. Transgenomic Pharmacogenomic Services is a contract research laboratory that supports all phases of pre-clinical and clinical trials for oncology drugs in development.

	Annual Growth	12/10	12/11	12/12	12/13	12/14
Sales ($ mil.)	7.8%	20.0	32.0	31.5	27.5	27.1
Net income ($ mil.)	–	(3.1)	(9.8)	(8.3)	(16.0)	(13.9)
Market value ($ mil.)	37.0%	4.6	4.6	4.9	3.7	16.2
Employees	(1.6%)	162	169	202	171	152

TRANSIT MIX CONCRETE & MATERIALS COMPANY

2525 Stemmons Frwy.
Dallas TX 75207
Phone: 214-631-4420
Fax: 214-589-8171
Web: www.transitmixconcrete.com

CEO: –
CFO: –
HR: –
FYE: December 31
Type: Subsidiary

Transit Mix Concrete & Materials operates about 100 ready-mix concrete plants and portable concrete plants in Arkansas Louisiana and Texas. The company has a fleet of more than 650 mixer trucks to supply its customers in the industrial energy transportation and construction sectors. Through its Trinity Materials subsidiary it has 10 aggregate mining operations in Texas and Louisiana that provide limestone sand and gravel. Trinity Materials also has thre distribution centers. Transit Mix Concrete & Materials was founded in Beaumont Texas in 1939. It is a subsidiary of Trinity Industries.

TRANSITCENTER INC.

1065 AVENUE OF THE AMERIC	CEO: Daniel M Neuburger
NEW YORK, NY 100181878	CFO: Dave Schwartz
Phone: 212-329-2000	HR: -
Fax: -	FYE: December 31
Web: www.transitchek.com	Type: Private

TransitCenter's mission is to get commuters out of their cars and onto a bus ferry train van or cable car. The not-for-profit company is charged with encouraging greater use of public and private transit services to improve mobility reduce traffic help the environment and support the economy. Its website provides transit guides for a dozen US cities including Atlanta and Washington D.C. TransitCenter sold its TransitChek program developed to encourage businesses and their employees to use public transportation through incentives that reduce payroll taxes for employers and allow commuters to pay for daily travel using pretax dollars. It continues to advocate for public transportation.

	Annual Growth	12/04	12/05	12/06	12/07	12/09
Sales ($ mil.)	6.5%	-	17.1	17.9	19.7	22.1
Net income ($ mil.)	-	-	-	(1.8)	0.6	2.7
Market value ($ mil.)	-	-	-	-	-	-
Employees	-	-	-	-	-	74

TRANSMONTAIGNE INC.

1670 Broadway Ste. 3100	CEO: Charles Dunlap
Denver CO 80202	CFO: -
Phone: 303-626-8200	HR: -
Fax: 303-626-8228	FYE: December 31
Web: www.transmontaigne.com	Type: Subsidiary

It is not across the mountain but along the river that TransMontaigne gathers transports stores and markets refined petroleum products chemicals and crude oil. The company operates primarily in the Mississippi River corridor and along the Colonial and Plantation pipelines which run from the Gulf Coast to the eastern US and through the TEPPCO Explorer and other pipeline systems. TransMontaigne operates a supply distribution and marketing network and provides supply management terminal pipeline tug and barge businesses. It controls the general partner of terminaling and storage spinoff TransMontaigne Partners. TransMontaigne is owned by MSCI.

TRANSMONTAIGNE PARTNERS L.P.

NYS: TLP

1670 Broadway, Suite 3100	CEO: Frederick W Boutin
Denver, CO 80202	CFO: -
Phone: 303 626-8200	HR: -
Fax: 303 626-8228	FYE: December 31
Web: www.transmontaignepartners.com	Type: Public

TransMontaigne Partners an affiliate of TransMontaigne Inc. provides integrated terminaling storage and pipeline services for companies that market and distribute refined products and crude oil. TransMontaigne Partners handles light refined products (gasolines heating oils and jet and diesel fuels) heavy refined products (asphalt and residual fuel oils) and crude oil. It operates about 50 terminals (with a storage of capacity of 23.7 million barrels of oil and gas) and other facilities along the Gulf Coast and major rivers in the South and Midwest; it also operates pipelines. Customers include Marathon and a marketing and supply unit of Valero.

	Annual Growth	12/10	12/11	12/12	12/13	12/14
Sales ($ mil.)	(0.1%)	150.9	152.3	156.2	158.9	150.1
Net income ($ mil.)	4.5%	27.2	46.5	38.6	34.7	32.5
Market value ($ mil.)	(3.5%)	599.1	552.8	624.7	699.3	518.5
Employees	(2.5%)	565	587	586	584	510

TRANSNET CORPORATION

OTC: TRNT

45 Columbia Rd.	CEO: -
Somerville NJ 08876-3576	CFO: John J Wilk
Phone: 908-253-0500	HR: -
Fax: 908-253-0601	FYE: June 30
Web: www.transnet.com	Type: Public

TransNet sells and supports computers networking equipment peripherals and software. It provides PCs from Hewlett-Packard IBM and Apple. TransNet also supplies peripherals networking products software and telephony equipment from such manufacturers as Nortel Networks Microsoft 3Com Novell and Cisco. The company's services include network support maintenance systems integration installation and training. Its clients are located primarily in the New York City/New Jersey and Eastern Pennsylvania regions. TransNet's customers have included pharmaceutical giant Schering-Plough.

TRANSPERFECT TRANSLATIONS INTERNATIONAL INC.

3 PARK AVE FL 39	CEO: Phil Shawe
NEW YORK, NY 100165934	CFO: -
Phone: 212-689-5555	HR: Robert (Bob) DeNoia
Fax: -	FYE: December 31
Web: www.transperfect.com.hk	Type: Private

You pick the language or languages and TransPerfect Translations International will aim to get your message through. In addition to translation and interpretation the company offers services such as document management multicultural marketing staffing subtitling and voiceover work. Its network of translators can handle more than 170 languages through offices located in 90 cities spanning six continents. TransPerfect serves a wide array of industries including advertising financial services legal life science technology retail and travel. Clients have include Sony American Airlines and Omnicom. TransPerfect was founded in 1992 by Liz Elting and Phil Shawe.

	Annual Growth	12/03	12/04	12/05	12/06	12/07
Sales ($ mil.)	45.7%	-	-	73.7	79.6	156.5
Net income ($ mil.)	58.5%	-	-	11.5	11.8	29.0
Market value ($ mil.)	-	-	-	-	-	-
Employees	-	-	-	-	-	950

TRANSPLACE INC.

3010 Gaylord Pkwy. Ste. 200	CEO: Thomas K Sanderson
Frisco TX 75034	CFO: Tony Cossentino
Phone: 479-770-7391	HR: -
Fax: 479-770-7844	FYE: December 31
Web: www.transplace.com	Type: Private

When freight moves from one place to another place Transplace wants to be there. A third-party logistics provider Transplace arranges the transportation of its customers' goods via a network of North American trucking companies and railroads. Proprietary software helps the company match shippers' freight with carriers' capacity. Along with its logistics operations Transplace offers supply chain management freight brokerage and consulting services. Customers have included USG Home Depot and AutoZone. Several of the largest US truckload carriers formed Transplace in 2000 by combining their logistics operations. Transplace is owned by private equity investor CI Capital Partners and company executives.

TRANSPORTATION INSIGHT LLC

328 1st Ave. NW
Hickory NC 28601
Phone: 828-485-5000
Fax: 910-482-8083
Web: www.tlc-inc.net

CEO: Chris Baltz
CFO: Reynolds Faulkner
HR: –
FYE: December 31
Type: Private

Transportation Insight can shed some light on why your company's transportation costs are so high. And hopefully find a way to reduce them. The logistics firm provides rate and contract negotiation for parcel less-than-truckload and truckload shipments; routing assistance; invoice processing; supply chain design; and logistics analysis to customers in manufacturing retail service and distribution. It also offers proprietary transportation management software under the names Insight Payer Insight Rater Insight BOL (bill of lading) and Insight Tracker. Transportation Insight works from about 30 offices across the US with a heavy concentration in North Carolina. The company was formed in 2000.

TRANSTECH INDUSTRIES INC.

OTC: TRTI

200 Centennial Ave. Ste. 202
Piscataway NJ 08854
Phone: 732-564-3122
Fax: 732-981-1856
Web: www.transtechindustries.com

CEO: –
CFO: Andrew J Mayer Jr
HR: –
FYE: December 31
Type: Public

Through its subsidiaries Transtech Industries supervises and performs landfill monitoring closure and post-closure procedures and it oversees methane gas recovery operations. The company also generates electricity from methane gas produced at a company-owned landfill site; this business accounts for all of Transtech's revenue from external customers. Transtech's environmental services unit is engaged in closure and remediation of landfill sites formerly operated by other Transtech units. Transtech previously has provided environmental services for third parties and the company hopes to do so again. Members of the family of former company executive Marvin Mahan are the largest shareholders of Transtech.

TRANSTECTOR SYSTEMS INC.

10701 Airport Dr.
Hayden ID 83835
Phone: 208-772-8515
Fax: 208-762-6133
Web: www.transtector.com

CEO: –
CFO: –
HR: –
FYE: July 31
Type: Subsidiary

Transtector Systems makes power surge suppression equipment ranging from plug-in strips for home use to load centers for satellite tracking systems. Primary markets include wireless telecommunications and military and aerospace/space; other applications include industrial automation and control products medical and lighting equipment and manufacturing. Transtector Systems serves such customers as Motorola Raytheon and Varian Medical Systems as well as the US Department of Defense. It provides consulting engineering and training services. The company is part of the Smiths Interconnect division of Smiths Group. Transtector Systems was established in 1967 and was acquired by Smiths in 1998.

TRANZYME INC.

NASDAQ: TZYM

4819 Emperor Blvd. Ste. 400
Durham NC 27703
Phone: 919-313-4760
Fax: 816-421-6677
Web: www.fishnetsecurity.com

CEO: –
CFO: –
HR: –
FYE: December 31
Type: Public

Tranzyme has a gut feeling about its therapies. A drug discovery and development company Tranzyme is developing therapies to treat acute and chronic gastrointestinal (GI) disorders. Its lead candidate ulimorelin is an intravenously-administered treatment for GI motility problems that occur after abdominal surgery. If commercialized the therapy (which is in late clinical stages of development) could be used by hospitals to quickly restore normal intestinal function to patients. The company also has other candidates in earlier stages of development including a mid-stage oral therapy to treat chronic GI motility caused by diabetes. Founded in 1998 Tranzyme went public through a $48 million IPO in 2011.

TRAVEL AND TRANSPORT INC.

2120 S 72ND ST STE 300
OMAHA, NE 681242335
Phone: 402-399-4500
Fax: –
Web: www.travelandtransport.com

CEO: –
CFO: –
HR: James Winterscheid
FYE: December 31
Type: Private

Travel and Transport can get you there and back. The company provides its business clients with travel management solutions such as air hotel vacation packages and meeting planning services. Its corporate travel services include travel policy development vendor negotiation analysis and reporting. Travel and Transport is able to support international travel through its membership in RADIUS a network of 90 US travel agencies with more than 3300 offices worldwide. Travel and Transport also has a travel agent school and works with leisure travelers. The company which was founded in 1946 is 100% owned by its employees.

	Annual Growth	12/09	12/10	12/11	12/12	12/13
Sales ($ mil.)	11.2%	–	–	57.1	70.6	70.6
Net income ($ mil.)	(44.1%)	–	–	3.4	1.1	1.1
Market value ($ mil.)	–	–	–	–	–	–
Employees	–	–	–	–	–	940

TRAVEL MANAGEMENT PARTNERS INC.

3725 National Dr. Ste. 210
Raleigh NC 27612
Phone: 919-782-3810
Fax: 919-782-3595
Web: www.tmptravel.com

CEO: –
CFO: –
HR: Tina Martinuzzi
FYE: December 31
Type: Private

Catering to corporate clients Travel Management Partners (TMP) offers travel services that enable its clients to make commercial air hotel and rental car arrangements. The company sets up on-site and off-site travel offices for clients and operates an online booking system. TMP's proprietary Travel Trakkar travel information reporting system CorpTrip online booking program and CorpProfiles online traveler profiling system support the company's core services. The company operates in 40 states and provides services internationally through an equity ownership stake in travel company GlobalStar Travel. Founded in 1994 TMP is co-owned by president and CEO John Lewis and EVP and COO Wanda Shankle.

TRAVELCENTERS OF AMERICA LLC
NYS: TA

24601 Center Ridge Road, Suite 200
Westlake, OH 44145-5639
Phone: 440 808-9100
Fax: –
Web: www.tatravelcenters.com

CEO: Thomas M. O'Brien
CFO: Andrew J. Rebholz
HR: Bruce Sebera
FYE: December 31
Type: Public

TravelCenters of America (TCA) is in the fuel food and relaxation business for the long haul. The company's network of more than 280 interstate highway travel centers in more than 45 US states and Ontario Canada is one of the largest of its kind in North America. Its TCA and Petro locations provide fuel fast-food and sit-down restaurants (Country Pride Buckhorn Family) convenience stores and lodging. With professional truck drivers as its main customers some outlets also offer "trucker-only" services such as laundry and shower facilities TV rooms and truck repair. TCA leases 184 of its locations from Hospitality Properties Trust (HPT) its largest shareholder.

	Annual Growth	12/10	12/11	12/12	12/13	12/14
Sales ($ mil.)	6.9%	5,962.5	7,888.9	7,995.7	7,944.7	7,778.6
Net income ($ mil.)	–	(65.6)	23.6	32.2	31.6	61.0
Market value ($ mil.)	35.3%	144.5	162.9	180.2	373.4	483.8
Employees	10.1%	15,170	16,000	17,750	20,670	22,330

TRAVELCLICK INC.

7 Times Sq. 38th Fl.
New York NY 10036
Phone: 212-817-4800
Fax: +91-80-4143-6005
Web: centumindia.com/centumelectronics

CEO: Larry Kutscher
CFO: Gary Michel
HR: –
FYE: December 31
Type: Private

TravelCLICK helps hotels navigate the seas of online reservations. The company offers market intelligence and reservations software and services used by hotels to increase revenues and improve profitability. Its iHotelier program is a Web-based central reservation system that lets hotels manage rates and room inventory across multiple channels. Hotelligence360 uses competitive intelligence data to compare revenue and market performance of a customer's hotel against a custom list of competitors. TravelCLICK also offers online marketing and media services. The company has more than 30000 clients — including Accor Banyan Tree and Loews — in 140 countries.

TRAVELERS COMPANIES INC (THE)
NYS: TRV

485 Lexington Avenue
New York, NY 10017
Phone: 917 778-6000
Fax: –
Web: www.travelers.com

CEO: Doreen Spadorcia
CFO: Jay S. Benet
HR: John P. Clifford
FYE: December 31
Type: Public

Running a business is a risk The Travelers Companies will insure. While it does offer personal auto and homeowners insurance the company's largest segment is commercial property/casualty insurance to businesses big and small. It is one of the largest business insurers in the US providing commercial auto property workers' compensation marine and general and financial liability coverage to companies in North America (the largest percentage of business) and the UK. The company also offers surety and fidelity bonds as well as professional and management liability coverage for commercial operations.

	Annual Growth	12/11	12/12	12/13	12/14	12/15
Assets ($ mil.)	(1.1%)	104,602.0	104,938.0	103,812.0	103,078.0	100,184.0
Net income ($ mil.)	24.6%	1,426.0	2,473.0	3,673.0	3,692.0	3,439.0
Market value ($ mil.)	17.5%	17,508.4	21,251.5	26,790.8	31,321.0	33,395.3
Employees	0.2%	30,600	30,500	30,800	30,200	30,900

TRAVELOCITY.COM L.P.

3150 Sabre Dr.
Southlake TX 76092
Phone: 682-605-1000
Fax: +39-06-722-3131
Web: www.cinecitta.com

CEO: –
CFO: John Mills
HR: Cindy N Scovish
FYE: December 31
Type: Subsidiary

Travelocity.com is a high flyer in the world of online travel services. Catering to both leisure and business travelers its Travelocity.com website offers vacation packages and deals from most of the world's airlines hotels and car rental companies. The site has versions in about a dozen languages and handles corporate travel accounts. Travelocity.com also serves customers in Europe through lastminute.com and in the Asia/Pacific region via Zuji. Owned by travel reservation system supplier Sabre Holdings Travelocity.com was formed in 1999 by merging Sabre's Travelocity segment with Preview Travel. Travelocity added Top Secret Hotels shopping and booking to the mobile application in 2011.

TRAVELZOO INC
NMS: TZOO

590 Madison Avenue, 37th Floor
New York, NY 10022
Phone: 212 484-4900
Fax: –
Web: www.travelzoo.com

CEO: Holger Bartel
CFO: Glen Ceremony
HR: Gretchen Johnson
FYE: December 31
Type: Public

Travelzoo keeps the search for travel deals tame. On its websites users find discount offers promotions and related information provided by more than 2000 travel companies. Airlines car rental companies cruise lines hotels and travel agencies pay Travelzoo to publicize fares and promotions on its eponymous website through its newsletters and across its e-mail alert service. Travelzoo also operates SuperSearch a pay-per-click search engine specializing in travel content and Fly.com a search engine that compares flight information. Travelzoo founder Ralph Bartel owns a majority of the company's shares.

	Annual Growth	12/10	12/11	12/12	12/13	12/14
Sales ($ mil.)	5.9%	112.8	148.3	151.2	158.2	142.1
Net income ($ mil.)	5.6%	13.2	3.3	18.2	(5.0)	16.4
Market value ($ mil.)	(25.7%)	609.5	362.1	279.7	314.0	185.9
Employees	14.5%	255	350	417	436	438

TRAYLOR BROS. INC.

835 N CONGRESS AVE
EVANSVILLE, IN 477152484
Phone: 812-477-1542
Fax: –
Web: www.traylor.com

CEO: Thomas W. (Tom) Traylor
CFO: Don C Bartow
HR: –
FYE: December 31
Type: Private

At Traylor Bros. building bridges and tunnels is a family affair. The family-owned heavy/civil construction company also works on dams and ports storm sewers and transmission lines. The company's new mining division focuses on copper gold and coal mine development in North America. Additionally the company offers used and surplus equipment for sale. Traylor Bros operates throughout the US through its heavy/civil underground/tunneling and Traylor Pacific divisions. Traylor Bros.' projects include work for the San Francisco's Bay Area Rapid Transit (BART) system and the I-10 span bridges over Lake Pontchartrain in Louisiana. Civil engineer William Traylor founded Traylor Bros. in Indiana in 1946.

	Annual Growth	12/09	12/10	12/11	12/12	12/13
Sales ($ mil.)	0.0%	–	250.0	0.0	250.0	250.0
Net income ($ mil.)	–	–	–	0.0	0.0	0.0
Market value ($ mil.)	–	–	–	–	–	–
Employees	–	–	–	–	–	500

TRC COMPANIES, INC.
NYS: TRR

21 Griffin Road North
Windsor, CT 06095
Phone: 860 298-9692
Fax: –
Web: www.trcsolutions.com

CEO: Christopher P. (Chris) Vincze
CFO: Thomas W. (Tom) Bennet
HR: –
FYE: June 30
Type: Public

If more people treated the environment with TLC TRC Companies would be less busy. Through its Environmental Energy and Infrastructure segments the firm provides engineering construction and remediation services for commercial industrial and governmental customers. Services include energy efficiency and solid- and hazardous-waste management consulting as well as infrastructure improvements and landfill cleanup. TRC's services also include remediation for brownfield sites discontinued industrial operations operating assets and Superfund sites. It offers an Exit Strategy Program in which it assumes complete responsibility — including liability — for a contaminated site's closure and cleanup.

	Annual Growth	06/11	06/12	06/13	06/14	06/15
Sales ($ mil.)	14.1%	244.7	302.7	325.2	372.9	414.6
Net income ($ mil.)	–	(9.4)	33.6	36.3	12.1	19.4
Market value ($ mil.)	12.9%	190.5	185.3	213.4	189.6	309.4
Employees	12.6%	2,300	2,600	2,800	3,000	3,700

TREATY ENERGY CORP.
NBB: TECO

317 Exchange Place
New Orleans, LA 70130
Phone: 504 301-4475
Fax: –
Web: www.treatyenergy.com

CEO: Chris Tesarski
CFO: –
HR: –
FYE: December 31
Type: Public

Treaty Energy (formerly Alternate Energy) sought to provide alternative methods of fuel and power production but the power of petroleum won out. The company had been involved in hydrogen production and fuel cell development. In 2008 it completed a reverse merger with Treaty Petroleum and changed its focus to oil and gas development. The company focuses on the Permian Basin of West Texas and has more than 2 million barrels of proved reserves. In 2010 it was eyeing exploration prospects in Belize. It also bought Town Oil Company in 2011 to give it about 7800 acres of oil and gas leases in Kansas. In 2011 the company also acquired C&C Petroleum Management with oil and gas properties in Texas.

	Annual Growth	12/08	12/09	12/10	12/11	12/12
Sales ($ mil.)	50.4%	0.0	0.0	0.0	0.1	0.2
Net income ($ mil.)	–	(0.2)	(1.2)	(0.8)	(7.1)	(12.2)
Market value ($ mil.)	25.3%	7.1	14.7	9.5	38.8	17.5
Employees	–	–	–	–	–	–

TRECORA RESOURCES
NYS: TREC

1650 Hwy 6 South, Suite 190
Sugar Land, TX 77478
Phone: 409 385-8300
Fax: –
Web: www.trecora.com

CEO: Simon Upfill-Brown
CFO: Connie J. Cook
HR: –
FYE: December 31
Type: Public

Trecora Resources (formerly Arabian American Development) is an independent refiner in Texas. Through US subsidiary Texas Oil and Chemical Co. II which owns South Hampton Resources it operates a specialty petrochemical product refinery that primarily produces high-purity solvents used in the plastics and foam industries. South Hampton subsidiary Gulf State Pipe Line owns and operates seven pipelines. It owns a minority stake in the Al Masane mineral ore project in Saudi Arabia and 55% of inactive Nevada-based mining company Pioche-Ely Valley Mines.

	Annual Growth	12/10	12/11	12/12	12/13	12/14
Sales ($ mil.)	20.1%	139.1	199.5	222.9	236.2	289.6
Net income ($ mil.)	55.2%	2.7	8.4	11.4	19.5	15.6
Market value ($ mil.)	35.0%	106.0	203.3	199.2	300.9	352.4
Employees	16.9%	145	160	168	166	271

TREDEGAR CORP.
NYS: TG

1100 Boulders Parkway
Richmond, VA 23225
Phone: 804 330-1000
Fax: –
Web: www.tredegar.com

CEO: John D. Gottwald
CFO: Kevin A. O'Leary
HR: –
FYE: December 31
Type: Public

Tredegar's products can be found over under and in-between. The company manufactures primarily a variety of film products and aluminum extrusions. Its film lineup specializes in personal care materials and protective and packaging films such as liners and back sheets used in diapers feminine-hygiene products surgical masks permeable ground covers and cheesecloth. Aluminum extrusions produced by its Bonnell subsidiary are used mainly in building and construction markets. Tredegar's manufacturing facilities are located in the US the Netherlands Hungary China Brazil and India.

	Annual Growth	12/10	12/11	12/12	12/13	12/14
Sales ($ mil.)	6.3%	739.5	800.8	900.3	961.1	945.1
Net income ($ mil.)	8.1%	27.0	24.9	28.3	21.9	36.9
Market value ($ mil.)	3.8%	628.3	720.4	662.1	934.1	729.2
Employees	7.8%	2,000	2,200	2,700	2,700	2,700

TREE TOP INC.

220 E 2ND AVE
SELAH, WA 989421408
Phone: 509-697-7251
Fax: –
Web: www.treetop.org

CEO: –
CFO: Dwaine Brown
HR: Nancy Buck
FYE: July 31
Type: Private

Tree Top has towered over the Pacific Northwest's apple juice market for more than 50 years. The grower-owned cooperative's 1000 members cultivate and harvest thousands of tons of apples and pears each year to make a slew of juicy products. The co-op produces the Tree Top brand of apple and blended fruit juices and applesauce among many offerings for consumers and food service vendors. It also processes dehydrated and frozen fruit products for food makers worldwide through its ingredients unit. Tree Top operates production facilities in Washington Oregon and California and distributes its products through various channels including retailers and brokers in the US and several international markets.

	Annual Growth	07/07	07/08	07/09	07/10	07/13
Sales ($ mil.)	2.7%	–	350.7	359.0	365.0	399.9
Net income ($ mil.)	11.5%	–	–	37.2	27.0	57.6
Market value ($ mil.)	–	–	–	–	–	–
Employees	–	–	–	–	–	1,100

TREEHOUSE FOODS INC
NYS: THS

2021 Spring Road, Suite 600
Oak Brook, IL 60523
Phone: 708 483-1300
Fax: –
Web: www.treehousefoods.com

CEO: Sam K. Reed
CFO: Dennis F. Riordan
HR: –
FYE: December 31
Type: Public

This TreeHouse is has a full canopy. TreeHouse Foods is the nation's #1 manufacturer of non-dairy powdered creamer sold under the Cremora brand and pickles (Farman's Nalley's Peter Piper and Steinfeld). The company also makes private-label soups salad dressings and Mexican sauces drink mixes hot cereals macaroni and cheese skillet dinners and jams. TreeHouse makes private-label products for foodservice distributors and restaurant chains as well as for supermarkets and mass merchandisers — the company's largest market that also buys its own brands. TreeHouse also boasts co-pack business and industrial customers. The company grows through acquisitions.

	Annual Growth	12/10	12/11	12/12	12/13	12/14
Sales ($ mil.)	12.8%	1,817.0	2,050.0	2,182.1	2,293.9	2,946.1
Net income ($ mil.)	(0.3%)	90.9	94.4	88.4	87.0	89.9
Market value ($ mil.)	13.7%	2,179.7	2,789.3	2,224.0	2,940.3	3,649.0
Employees	11.5%	4,000	3,900	4,300	4,786	6,181

TRELLIS EARTH PRODUCTS INC.

9125 S.W. Ridder Rd. Ste. D
Wilsonville OR 97070
Phone: 503-582-1300
Fax: 503-582-1313
Web: www.trellisearth.com

CEO: Michael Senzaki
CFO: –
HR: –
FYE: December 31
Type: Private

Sure you can recycle that disposable plastic cup but you'll earn double points with Mother Nature if it's made from bioplastic. Trellis Earth Products' disposable cups bowls plates trays cutlery and bags are made from bioplastic a material derived from renewable sources such as soybeans corn starch wheat chaff rice hulls or sugarcane. Bioplastic is less expensive and more sustainable than petroleum-based plastic. Its products are sold to more than 500 foodservice customers primarily on the West Coast including Bunzl Distribution USA Costco Food Services of America Kroger Sysco and West Coast Paper. Trellis Earth Products filed a $22 million initial public offering in September 2011.

TREMOR VIDEO INC

NYS: TRMR

1501 Broadway, Suite 801
New York, NY 10036
Phone: 646 723-5300
Fax: –
Web: www.tremorvideo.com

CEO: William Day
CFO: John S Rego
HR: –
FYE: December 31
Type: Public

Tremor Video wants to leave traditional advertising formats shaking in their boots. The company is focused on online video advertising. It doesn't make video ads; its VideoHub platform analyzes them to find the best ad for the best video. For example if someone is about to watch a video for a car then a car ad plays. Its clients' video ads are shown on a network of more than 500 websites (including A&E and Viacom properties) and mobile apps that can be watched from computers mobile devices and connected TVs. Tremor Video counts almost 400 customers mostly auto companies and consumer products makers. Primarily it works for the ad agencies hired by the advertisers. Founded in 2005 Tremor Video went public in mid-2013.

	Annual Growth	12/10	12/11	12/12	12/13	12/14
Sales ($ mil.)	–	0.0	90.3	105.2	131.8	159.5
Net income ($ mil.)	–	0.0	(21.0)	(16.6)	(13.5)	(23.5)
Market value ($ mil.)	–	0.0	–	–	296.4	146.7
Employees	16.7%	–	–	249	291	339

TREX CO INC

NYS: TREX

160 Exeter Drive
Winchester, VA 22603-8605
Phone: 540 542 6300
Fax: –
Web: www.trex.com

CEO: Ronald W Kaplan
CFO: James E. Cline
HR: –
FYE: December 31
Type: Public

Trex Company is all decked out with plenty of places to go. It's the world's largest maker of wood-alternative decking and railing products which are used in the construction of residential and commercial decks rails and trims. Marketed under the Trex name products resemble wood and have the workability of wood but require less long-term maintenance. The Trex Wood-Polymer composite is made of waste wood fibers and reclaimed plastic. Trex serves professional installation contractors and do-it-yourselfers through about 90 wholesale distribution centers which in turn sell to retailers including Home Depot and Lowe's. Trex products are available in more than 5500 locations primarily in the US and Canada.

	Annual Growth	12/10	12/11	12/12	12/13	12/14
Sales ($ mil.)	5.4%	317.7	266.8	307.4	342.5	391.7
Net income ($ mil.)	–	(10.1)	(11.6)	2.7	34.6	41.5
Market value ($ mil.)	15.5%	767.2	733.6	1,192.1	2,546.6	1,363.4
Employees	3.5%	550	550	550	590	630

TRG HOLDINGS LLC

1700 Pennsylvannia Ave. NW Ste. 560
Washington DC 20006
Phone: 202-289-9898
Fax: 770-794-8381
Web: www.ttinc.net

CEO: –
CFO: –
HR: Elizabeth Wilson
FYE: June 30
Type: Holding Company

More than 120 global clients tap into the offerings of The Resource Group (TRG). Specializing in serving companies in the business process outsourcing (BPO) sector TRG provides its clients with equity capital strategic advice custom outsourced services and technology products and services. Its iSky business offers market research analytics and consultation services. TRG has industry knowledge in sectors such as automotive financial services healthcare insurance media and pharmaceuticals. The company has invested in or acquired about 20 BPO businesses since 2002. It has operations in Brazil Pakistan the Philippines Senegal the UK and the US.

TRI POINTE HOMES LLC

NYSE: TPH

19520 Jamboree Rd. Ste. 200
Irvine CA 92612
Phone: 949-478-8600
Fax: 949-478-8601
Web: www.tripointehomes.com

CEO: –
CFO: –
HR: –
FYE: December 31
Type: Private

In a home construction market that's been trying of late Tri Pointe Homes believes it's pointing the way to a successful future. The company designs and constructs single-family homes in urban areas of California singling out communities with growing populations and economies. Tri Pointe was founded in 2009 and the following year it began a partnership with Starwood Capital Group Global to fund land acquisition. There are 13 sites in operation with nearly 700 lots in varying stages of development; home prices range between $300000 and $1.5 million for residences between 1250 and 4300 sq. ft. Tri Pointe Homes went public in early 2013 with an offering worth $232.7 million.

TRI-ARROWS ALUMINUM INC.

9960 Corporate Campus Dr. Ste. 3000
Louisville KY 40223-4048
Phone: 502-566-5700
Fax: 502-566-5740
Web: triaa.com

CEO: Patrick Franc
CFO: David Sourwine
HR: –
FYE: December 31
Type: Private

Tri-Arrows Aluminum aims to make its mark in the North American and Latin American aluminum markets. Formerly known as ARCO Aluminum the aluminum sheet maker is now owned by a Japanese consortium led by Sumitomo. Through Logan Aluminum its 60%-owned joint venture with Novelis Tri-Arrows manufactures aluminum sheet used mainly by the beverage and automotive industries. Logan Aluminum's offerings include automotive sheet building products distributor sheet food and beverage can stock and rigid container sheet. Oil giant BP which acquired ARCO Aluminum as part of its purchase of Atlantic Richfield Company in 2000 sold the company in 2011 for $680 million to the Japanese consortium.

TRI-CITY ELECTRICAL CONTRACTORS INC.

430 WEST DR
ALTAMONTE SPRINGS, FL 327143378
Phone: 407-788-3500
Fax: –
Web: www.tcelectric.com

CEO: –
CFO: Michael A Germana
HR: –
FYE: December 31
Type: Private

Plugged in to the electrical contracting scene Tri-City Electrical Contractors targets Florida's commercial government industrial residential and communications markets. The company designs installs and services electrical systems in apartment buildings courthouses convention centers sports arenas resorts condos single- and multi-family dwellings and more. Once part of now-bankrupt Encompass Services Tri-City Electrical Contractors was repurchased by founder and chairman Buddy Eidel in 2003. Tri-City Electrical Contractors which traces its roots to 1958 operates from its Central Florida headquarters and two divisional offices throughout the Sunshine State.

	Annual Growth	12/09	12/10	12/11	12/12	12/13
Sales ($ mil.)	–	–	0.0	0.0	87.6	126.8
Net income ($ mil.)	–	–	–	0.0	(1.2)	2.7
Market value ($ mil.)	–	–	–	–	–	–
Employees	–	–	–	–	–	504

TRI-UNION SEAFOODS LLC

9330 Scranton Rd. Ste. 500
San Diego CA 92121-3029
Phone: 858-558-9662
Fax: 858-597-4282
Web: www.chickenofthesea.com

CEO: Shue Wing Chan
CFO: –
HR: –
FYE: December 31
Type: Subsidiary

Tri-Union Seafoods tries hard to unite seafood lovers under the Chicken of the Sea and other banners. The company which does business as Chicken of the Sea International makes and markets some of the top brands of canned tuna in the US. Tri-Union cans tuna (Albacore and light) salmon crab shrimp oysters clams sardines and mackerel for sale in North America. The company also offers value-added seafood products such as frozen and shelf-stable pouches (including smoked salmon) and "peel & eat" cups (salmon and tuna). In addition to its own brands Tri-Union also offers product-development and private-label services.

TRI-WEST LTD

12005 PIKE ST
SANTA FE SPRINGS, CA 906706100
Phone: 562-566-1214
Fax: –

CEO: –
CFO: Randy Sims
HR: –
FYE: December 31
Type: Private

Tri-West tends to floor both residential and commercial customers with its broad selection of floor coverings. Founded in 1981 the company distributes floor coverings through about half a dozen warehouse facilities located in the western US and the Hawaiian Islands. In addition Tri-West also serves customers in Texas and Guam. Tri-West offers major manufacturers' products including carpets ceramic and specialty tile hardwood flooring laminate and vinyl flooring and eco-friendly items such as recycled rubber tiles and bamboo flooring. As part of its business the company sells and distributes adhesives and tools from manufacturers such as Armstrong and California-based Taylor Adhesives.

	Annual Growth	12/08	12/09	12/11	12/12	12/13
Sales ($ mil.)	9.8%	–	111.8	117.7	141.9	162.3
Net income ($ mil.)	41.0%	–	–	7.1	10.2	14.2
Market value ($ mil.)	–	–	–	–	–	–
Employees	–	–	–	–	–	325

TRIA BEAUTY INC.

4160 Dublin Blvd. Ste. 200
Dublin CA 94568
Phone: 925-452-2500
Fax: 514-875-0835
Web: www.enerkem.com

CEO: Kevin J Appelbaum
CFO: John J Rangel
HR: –
FYE: December 31
Type: Private

TRIA Beauty helps every woman find her inner esthetician. The company's two medical devices used to zap unwanted hair and clear up acne are designed for at-home use so no more costly trips to the medical spa. Its TRIA Hair Removal Laser is a handheld device that uses laser light to stunt hair growth while its Skin Perfecting Blue Light device treats acne by using blue light therapy to kill underlying bacteria. TRIA Beauty's devices are sold online on television via QVC and infomercials and at high-end retailer Bloomingdale's. A third device the Skin Rejuvenating Laser used to reduce the appearance of facial wrinkles is under development. TRIA Beauty filed and withdrew an initial public offering in 2012.

TRIANGLE CAPITAL CORP

NYS: TCAP

3700 Glenwood Avenue, Suite 530
Raleigh, NC 27612
Phone: 919 719-4770
Fax: –

CEO: E. Ashton Poole
CFO: Steven C. Lilly
HR: –
FYE: December 31
Type: Public

Triangle Capital lends to companies but they must be of a certain shape and size. An internally managed business-development company Triangle provides loans to and invests in lower-middle-market US companies with annual revenues of $20 million-$100 million. The company which likes to partner with its portfolio companies' management prefers to invest in established businesses with stable financial histories. Triangle most often invests in senior and subordinated debt securities and usually takes a equity interest; it contributes between $5 million and $15 million per transaction. The company's portfolio includes some 50 manufacturers business services food services and other types of enterprises.

	Annual Growth	12/10	12/11	12/12	12/13	12/14
Assets ($ mil.)	26.2%	388.0	583.2	794.5	814.9	984.1
Net income ($ mil.)	32.5%	20.1	40.3	57.7	61.5	62.0
Market value ($ mil.)	1.7%	626.1	630.0	839.9	911.1	668.6
Employees	10.1%	17	19	22	25	25

TRIANGLE PETROLEUM CORP

ASE: TPLM

1200 17th Street, Suite 2600
Denver, CO 80202
Phone: 303 260-7125
Fax: 303 260-5080
Web: www.trianglepetroleum.com

CEO: Jonathan Samuels
CFO: Justin J. Bliffen
HR: –
FYE: January 31
Type: Public

Triangle Petroleum has three business - oil and gas exploration and production oilfield services and midstream services. The company holds leasehold interests in about 94000 net acres in the Williston Basin approximately 45000 net acres are located in its core focus area in McKenzie and Williams Counties North Dakota. The assets are mainly unconventional (natural gas produced from shale deposits via hydraulic fracturing). Triangle had proved reserves of 40.3 million barrels of oil equivalent in fiscal 2014. Exploration and production accounted for 46% of the company's 2014 revenues; Oilfield services 54%. Sales of crude oil accounted for about 60% of the company's revenues in fiscal 2014.

	Annual Growth	01/11	01/12	01/13	01/14	01/15
Sales ($ mil.)	471.6%	0.5	8.1	60.7	258.7	573.0
Net income ($ mil.)	–	(20.3)	(23.8)	(13.8)	73.5	93.4
Market value ($ mil.)	(9.4%)	585.6	514.2	472.8	572.1	394.7
Employees	173.8%	10	61	165	332	562

TRIBUNE MEDIA CO.

NYS: TRCO

435 North Michigan Avenue
Chicago, IL 60611
Phone: 212 210-2786
Fax: –
Web: www.tribune.com

CEO: John Batter
CFO: Chandler Bigelow
HR: Melanie Hughes
FYE: December 28
Type: Public

Its roots were in print journalism but the Tribune Media Company (formerly known as Tribune Company) has evolved to embrace virtually every aspect of modern media. Tribune Media currently owns 42 TV stations in about 30 markets cable network WGN America and a stake in the Food Network. In addition Tribune Media owns a number of online media properties Tribune Studios Tribune Digital Ventures WGN-Radio and a significant number of iconic real estate properties and strategic investments. In 2014 Tribune Company spun off its cornerstone newspaper publishing business into a newly formed company called Tribune Publishing Company and changed the name of the TV radio and digital business to Tribune Media.

	Annual Growth	12/05	12/06	12/07	12/13	12/14
Sales ($ mil.)	(11.1%)	5,595.6	5,517.7	5,063.0	1,147.2	1,949.4
Net income ($ mil.)	(1.3%)	534.7	594.0	86.9	241.6	476.7
Market value ($ mil.)	(22.8%)	–	–	–	7,540.5	5,824.4
Employees	(11.3%)	22,400	21,000	19,600	–	7,600

TRICO BANCSHARES (CHICO, CA)

NMS: TCBK

63 Constitution Drive
Chico, CA 95973
Phone: 530 898-0300
Fax: 530 898-0310
Web: www.tcbk.com

CEO: Richard P. Smith
CFO: Thomas J. (Tom) Reddish
HR: –
FYE: December 31
Type: Public

People looking for a community bank in California's Sacramento Valley can try TriCo. TriCo Bancshares is the holding company for Tri Counties Bank which serves customers through some 65 traditional and in-store branches in 23 counties in Northern and Central California. Founded in 1974 Tri Counties Bank provides a variety of deposit services including checking and savings accounts money market accounts and CDs. Most patrons are retail customers and small to midsized businesses. The bank primarily originates real estate mortgages which account for about 65% of its loan portfolio; consumer loans contribute about 25%. TriCo has agreed to acquire rival North Valley Bancorp.

	Annual Growth	12/10	12/11	12/12	12/13	12/14
Assets ($ mil.)	15.6%	2,189.8	2,555.6	2,609.3	2,744.1	3,916.5
Net income ($ mil.)	44.4%	6.0	18.6	19.0	27.4	26.1
Market value ($ mil.)	11.2%	366.8	323.0	380.5	644.4	561.1
Employees	7.7%	749	799	831	794	1,009

TRICO PRODUCTS CORPORATION

3255 W. Hamlin Rd.
Rochester Hills MI 48309
Phone: 240 371 1700
Fax: 248-371-8300
Web: www.tricoproducts.com

CEO: James Wiggins
CFO: Michele Huver
HR: John Bledsoe
FYE: December 31
Type: Private

Onto every car a little rain must fall — that's where Trico Products comes in. One of the leading manufacturers of its kind Trico designs makes and distributes windshield wiper systems and electronics for about two dozen of the world's carmakers as well as wiper blades and accessories for the consumer replacement market. Trico produces millions of wiper products a year including wiper motors wiper arms windshield washer systems and linkages. The company also makes wiper systems for heavy-duty trucks and RVs. Its electronics division makes electronic controls for automotive wiper system rain sensors. Trico is part of a portfolio held by US private equity firm Kohlberg & Company.

TRIDENT SEAFOODS CORPORATION

5303 Shilshole Ave. NW
Seattle WA 98107-4000
Phone: 206-783-3818
Fax: 206-782-7195
Web: www.tridentseafoods.com

CEO: Charles Bundrant
CFO: Phil Bishop
HR: –
FYE: August 31
Type: Private

Something's "supposed" to be fishy at Trident Seafoods. The vertically integrated seafood business hauls in salmon crab and assorted other fin- and shellfish from the icy waters of Alaska and the Pacific Northwest. It then processes and cans or freezes them for retail food and foodservice customers. Trident operates a fleet of some 30 processing boats and trawlers as well as about 20 onshore processing plants in Alaska Washington and Oregon. The company's portfolio includes Trident Louis Kemp and SeaLegs brand of surimi (crab-flavored processed fish). Trident owns Port Chatham Smoked Seafood which smokes salmon and tuna under the Portlock label. The company operates a single retail store in Seattle.

TRIHEALTH INC.

619 Oak St.
Cincinnati OH 45206
Phone: 513-569-5000
Fax: 479-524-3291
Web: www.allencanning.com

CEO: –
CFO: –
HR: –
FYE: December 31
Type: Private - Partnershi

"Try" is not in TriHealth's vocabulary when it comes to providing health care to the trifecta of Cincinnati northern Kentucky and southeastern Indiana. TriHealth operates four acute care and surgery hospitals including Bethesda North Hospital which has 400 beds and provides trauma birthing and heart care services and the 650-bed Good Samaritan Hospital. TriHealth also operates a vast network of outpatient care centers and conducts medical education and research programs. The not-for-profit organization is affiliated with Catholic Health Initiatives. TriHealth was formed in 1995 through the merger of Bethesda North Hospital and Good Samaritan Hospital of Cincinnati.

TRILOGY ENTERPRISES INC.

6011 W. Courtyard Dr.
Austin TX 78730
Phone: 512-874-3100
Fax: 512-874-8900
Web: www.trilogy.com

CEO: Joe Liemandt
CFO: Andrew Price
HR: –
FYE: December 31
Type: Private

Trilogy helps your customers return again and again and again. The company's software helps large corporations manage complex sales and purchasing channels that involve extensive product lines and high transaction volumes. Customers use its software to integrate and manage sales distribution and supplier channels as well as for content management and data integration. In addition the company provides professional services such as consulting and support. Customers have included General Motors Ford Goodyear Nissan and Penn Mutual Life. Founder and CEO Joe Liemandt is the controlling shareholder of the company.

TRILOGY LEASING CO. LLC

2551 Rte. 130
Cranbury NJ 08512-3509
Phone: 609-860-9900
Fax: 609-860-9974
Web: www.trilogyleasing.com

CEO: –
CFO: David Lieberman
HR: –
FYE: December 31
Type: Private

Trilogy Leasing helps companies that need a little technology TLC. Specializing in pre-owned technology equipment the company provides leasing services to businesses in the US and Canada. It offers equipment including personal computers printing and imaging equipment mainframe computers and telecom switches from vendors such as Hewlett-Packard. Trilogy also offers capital equipment such as furniture. In addition to its leasing services the company sells equipment and purchases unwanted inventory. It also offers consulting technical support and equipment liquidation services. Founded in 1999 Trilogy was acquired by Kingsbridge Holdings in 2011.

TRIMAS CORP (NEW)

NMS: TRS

39400 Woodward Avenue, Suite 130
Bloomfield Hills, MI 48304
Phone: 248 631-5450
Fax: 248 631-5455
Web: www.trimascorp.com

CEO: David M. (Dave) Wathen
CFO: Robert J. (Bob) Zalupski
HR: –
FYE: December 31
Type: Public

Whether at work or play TriMas fits the niche. The company makes a diverse mix of products through several segments. Its Cequent division makes trailer hitches towing systems and accessories for cars and RVs as well as agricultural military and industrial vehicles. The Energy division makes seals bolts and gaskets used primarily in the oil and gas industry. TriMas' Packaging segment makes closures and dispensing systems for industrial and consumer packaging for customers in North America and Europe. Aerospace & Defense produces aerospace fasteners and military munitions components including shell casings. Engineered Components manufactures compressed gas pressure cylinders and precision tools.

	Annual Growth	12/10	12/11	12/12	12/13	12/14
Sales ($ mil.)	12.3%	942.7	1,084.0	1,272.9	1,394.9	1,499.1
Net income ($ mil.)	10.9%	45.3	60.4	33.9	75.6	68.5
Market value ($ mil.)	11.2%	926.4	812.8	1,268.2	1,806.2	1,416.8
Employees	15.7%	3,900	4,100	5,500	6,000	7,000

TRIMBLE MOBILE RESOURCE MANAGEMENT

47071 Bayside Pkwy.
Fremont CA 94538
Phone: 510-668-1638
Fax: 510-445-1377
Web: www.trimble.com/mobile_resource_management

CEO: –
CFO: –
HR: –
FYE: December 31
Type: Business Segment

Truckers still ride the lonely highways but Trimble Mobile Resource Management (formerly @Road) makes sure the home office knows exactly where they are. Its mobile resource management (MRM) system includes fleet tracking applications field service management and field asset management. Using GPS technology to fix a vehicle's geographic position the company collects the data at a service center via wireless data transmissions made over the cellular networks of partner telecom companies. Trimble Mobile Resource Management serves customers in the transportation distribution field service telecommunications utilities cable and construction industries. The company is a subsidiary of Trimble Navigation.

TRIMBLE NAVIGATION LTD.

NMS: TRMB

935 Stewart Drive
Sunnyvale, CA 94085
Phone: 408 481-8000
Fax: 408 481-2218
Web: www.trimble.com

CEO: Steven W. Berglund
CFO: Francois Delepine
HR: –
FYE: January 02
Type: Public

Those who fear not knowing their place in the world should Trimble. Trimble Navigation makes systems and software that combine global positioning technology with wireless communications to provide location and position data and make it actionable. Using GPS laser optical and other technologies the company's products target areas such as surveying construction site project management mapping mobile personnel management and mobile and fixed asset management. They are offered to end users such as government entities farmers engineering firms and public safety workers as well as equipment manufacturers (OEMs). About half of sales are made outside the US.

	Annual Growth	12/10	12/11	12/12*	01/14	01/15
Sales ($ mil.)	13.1%	1,293.9	1,644.1	2,040.1	2,288.1	2,395.5
Net income ($ mil.)	15.6%	103.7	150.8	191.1	218.9	214.1
Market value ($ mil.)	(7.6%)	10,348.1	11,247.4	15,186.6	8,959.1	6,973.9
Employees	14.6%	4,166	5,301	6,561	7,086	8,217

*Fiscal year change

TRIMEDYNE, INC.

NBB: TMED

5 Holland #223
Irvine, CA 92618
Phone: 949 951-3800
Fax: 949 855-8206
Web: www.trimedyne.com

CEO: Marvin P Loeb
CFO: D Atchison
HR: Liz Krenik
FYE: September 30
Type: Public

Trimedyne doesn't play tag with lasers but it does use them to help surgeons do their jobs. The company's cold-pulsed lasers and fiber-optic laser energy delivery devices (including needles and fibers) are used in gastrointestinal orthopedic urologic and general surgeries as well as gynecology arthroscopy and ear nose and throat (ENT) procedures. Trimedyne markets its products to hospitals and surgery centers in the US via direct sales and internationally through distributors. The company's Mobile Surgical Technologies unit rents lasers and provides related services to health care facilities on a "fee per use" basis.

	Annual Growth	09/11	09/12	09/13	09/14	09/15
Sales ($ mil.)	(5.4%)	6.7	6.1	6.0	5.5	5.3
Net income ($ mil.)	–	(1.5)	(0.8)	0.3	(0.4)	(0.6)
Market value ($ mil.)	(19.4%)	1.9	1.2	2.9	1.9	0.8
Employees	(7.2%)	62	55	42	52	46

TRIMEGA PURCHASING ASSOCIATION

5600 N RIVER RD STE 700
ROSEMONT, IL 600185165
Phone: 847-699-3330
Fax: –
Web: www.trimega.org

CEO: –
CFO: –
HR: –
FYE: June 30
Type: Private

Smart office products dealers pledge to buy a lotta TriMega. The TriMega Purchasing Association is a product and services buying group made up of 590 independently owned office-supply dealers. TriMega in turn is a member of the larger Business Products Group International (BPGI) which gives TriMega's member dealers even more buying power and helps them compete with nationwide chains such as OfficeMax and Staples. TriMega also supplies its own Value Plus brand of office products. The not-for-profit cooperative was founded in 1987 and serves company's large and small from across the US.

	Annual Growth	03/08	03/09*	06/11*	12/11*	06/13
Sales ($ mil.)	20.4%	–	90.0	280.1	387.9	189.5
Net income ($ mil.)	(3.9%)	–	–	26.1	36.4	24.1
Market value ($ mil.)	–	–	–	–	–	–
Employees	–	–	–	–	–	19

*Fiscal year change

TRIMOL GROUP INC.   OTC: TMOL

1285 Avenue of the Americas 35th Fl.   CEO: Boris Birshtein
New York NY 10019   CFO: Jack Braverman
Phone: 212-554-4394   HR: –
Fax: 212-554-4395   FYE: December 31
                                        Type: Public

Trimol Group has a license for a mechanically rechargeable aluminum-air fuel cell for use in portable consumer electronics but the company isn't actively developing the technology. Its Intercomsoft subsidiary provides technology and consumables for producing secure government identification documents. The technology was developed by Supercom of Israel which broke off its supply agreement with Intercomsoft in early 2005. Intercomsoft continued to provide support services to the Republic of Moldova (traditionally its only customer) but the Republic of Moldova has indicated that it does not intend to renew its supply agreement. Chairman Boris Birshtein owns more than three-quarters of Trimol Group.

TRINITY BROADCASTING NETWORK

2442 Michelle Dr.   CEO: –
Tustin CA 92780   CFO: –
Phone: 714-832-2950   HR: –
Fax: 714-832-7389   FYE: December 31
Web: www.tbn.org   Type: Private

TBN doesn't stand for The Bible Network but much of its source material comes from the good book. Trinity Broadcasting Network (TBN) operates the world's largest Christian TV network reaching nearly 100 million US households through some 7500 cable and more than 400 broadcast affiliates mostly low-powered stations. The network offers mostly original faith programming including its flagship Praise the Lord. It reaches international audiences via approximately 65 satellites. TBN was founded in 1973 by Paul and Jan Crouch who started the network in partnership with Jim and Tammy Faye Bakker broadcasting from a single TV station in Santa Ana California.

TRINITY HEALTH CORPORATION

20555 VICTOR PKWY   CEO: Judith M Persichilli
LIVONIA, MI 48152-7031   CFO: –
Phone: 734-343-1000   HR: –
Fax: –   FYE: June 30
Web: www.trinity-health.org   Type: Private

Hospitals health centers and nursing homes make up Trinity Health. One of the largest Catholic health care systems in the US Trinity Health runs about 50 hospitals (with a total of 6900 beds) 30 long-term care centers (1700 beds) 400 outpatient facilities and numerous home health and hospice agencies. Of the hospitals it owns about 35 and manages another dozen for third parties. Its Trinity Senior Living Communities division operates its nursing homes and senior living facilities. Sponsored by the Catholic Health Ministries Trinity Health has facilities in 10 mostly Midwestern states and its Trinity Health International (THI) unit provides consulting and training to hospitals worldwide.

	Annual Growth	06/07	06/08	06/09	06/10	06/11
Sales ($ mil.)	700.0%	–	1.6	593.8	738.9	814.5
Net income ($ mil.)	–	–	(0.3)	(59.8)	50.6	36.8
Market value ($ mil.)	–	–	–	–	–	–
Employees	–	–	–	–	–	51,100

TRINITY HEALTH SYSTEM

380 SUMMIT AVE   CEO: Fred Brower
STEUBENVILLE, OH 43952-2667   CFO: Elizabeth Allen
Phone: 740-264-8000   HR: –
Fax: –   FYE: December 31
Web: www.trinityhealth.com   Type: Private

Despite its name Trinity Health System serves eastern Ohio through only two facilities: Trinity Medical Center East and Trinity Medical Center West. Combined they have some 470 beds and offer patients emergency and general medical diagnostic and surgical services as well as specialty care in fields including rehabilitation skilled nursing and women's health services. Hospital specialty units also include the Tony Teramana Cancer Center a sleep center and a heart center. Trinity Health's outpatient facilities include an imaging center a school of nursing and community health clinics. The not-for-profit health system is sponsored by Tri-State Health Services and Franciscan Services organizations.

	Annual Growth	12/04	12/05	12/06	12/07	12/09
Sales ($ mil.)	–	–	0.0	153.8	152.9	178.6
Net income ($ mil.)	–	–	0.0	9.0	(0.6)	21.8
Market value ($ mil.)	–	–	–	–	–	–
Employees	–	–	–	–	–	1,646

TRINITY INDUSTRIES, INC.   NYS: TRN

2525 N. Stemmons Freeway   CEO: Timothy R. Wallace
Dallas, TX 75207-2401   CFO: James E Perry
Phone: 214 631-4420   HR: Katherine Collins
Fax: 214 589-8501   FYE: December 31
Web: www.trin.net   Type: Public

If Trinity Industries had a theme song it would be sung by Boxcar Willie. The company manufactures auto carriers box cars gondola cars hopper cars intermodal cars and tank cars — in short railcars for hauling everything from coal to corn syrup. Trinity also leases and manages railcar fleets. Its Inland Barge unit builds barges used to transport coal grain and other commodities. In addition to transportation other Trinity businesses provide products and services to the industrial energy (structural towers for wind turbines metal containers for liquefied petroleum gas and fertilizer) and construction (concrete aggregates highway guardrails) sectors.

	Annual Growth	12/10	12/11	12/12	12/13	12/14
Sales ($ mil.)	29.6%	2,189.1	3,075.1	3,811.9	4,365.3	6,170.0
Net income ($ mil.)	78.1%	67.4	142.2	255.2	375.5	678.2
Market value ($ mil.)	1.3%	4,140.5	4,677.3	5,573.6	8,483.3	4,358.4
Employees	24.0%	9,270	13,390	15,490	18,460	21,950

TRINITY MOTHER FRANCES HEALTH SYSTEM FOUNDATION

800 E DAWSON ST   CEO: Tom Cammack
TYLER, TX 757012036   CFO: William Bellenfant
Phone: 903-531-5057   HR: –
Fax: –   FYE: June 30
Web: www.tmfhs.org   Type: Private

Trinity Mother Frances Health System Foundation (dba Trinity Mother Frances Hospitals and Clinics) has a complicated name but a simple mission: to improve patient health. Consisting of three general hospitals several specialist facilities and a large physicians' group Trinity Mother Frances serves northeastern Texas. Its largest acute-care facility is Mother Frances Hospital-Tyler with more than 400 beds offering comprehensive medical surgical trauma and cardiovascular care. Two smaller hospitals in Jacksonville and Winnsboro provide emergency diagnostic surgery and select specialty services. The Trinity Clinic is a multi-specialty physician group that includes 300 doctors in 36 community clinics.

	Annual Growth	06/08	06/09	06/10	06/13	06/14
Sales ($ mil.)	4.8%	–	562.1	603.4	653.2	711.7
Net income ($ mil.)	16.6%	–	–	19.9	21.5	36.8
Market value ($ mil.)	–	–	–	–	–	–
Employees	–	–	–	–	–	3,551

TRINITY UNIVERSITY

1 TRINITY PL   CEO: Richard Radke
SAN ANTONIO, TX 782127200   CFO: –
Phone: 210-999-7011   HR: –
Fax: –   FYE: May 31
Web: www.web.trinity.edu   Type: Private

Students at Trinity University get an education of the mind body and spirit. Trinity University offers 40-plus undergraduate degree programs in the arts and sciences as well as some 55 interdisciplinary minors. The university also offers master's degree programs in accounting education and health care administration. Trinity University has roughly 2600 undergraduate and graduate students hailing from some 45 states and 70 countries. More than 70% of its first-year students rank among the top 20% of their high school graduating classes. The student/faculty ratio is 9:1. The university was founded by Presbyterians in 1869 in Tehuacana Texas and relocated to San Antonio in 1942.

	Annual Growth	05/09	05/10	05/11	05/12	05/13
Sales ($ mil.)	(9.6%)	–	155.4	179.2	116.1	114.7
Net income ($ mil.)	54.8%	–	–	44.9	(40.8)	107.5
Market value ($ mil.)	–	–	–	–	–	–
Employees	–	–	–	–	–	700

TRIO-TECH INTERNATIONAL   ASE: TRT

16139 Wyandotte Street   CEO: S W Yong
Van Nuys, CA 91406   CFO: Victor H M Ting
Phone: 818 787-7000   HR: Esmeralda Betancourt
Fax: 818 787-9130   FYE: June 30
Web: www.triotech.com   Type: Public

Three's certainly company if the company is Trio-Tech. Performing a trio of functions related to semiconductor manufacturing and testing Trio-Tech International lives up to its name. First the company makes its own chip manufacturing and test equipment; its front- and back-end testing products include temperature-controlled chucks centrifuges leak detectors and burn-in equipment. Second Trio-Tech provides outsourced testing services for chip manufacturers. Third it distributes semiconductor manufacturing and testing equipment made by other companies. Trio-Tech's top customers have included Advanced Micro Devices Freescale Semiconductor and Infineon Technologies.

	Annual Growth	06/11	06/12	06/13	06/14	06/15
Sales ($ mil.)	(1.1%)	35.5	34.2	31.8	36.3	33.9
Net income ($ mil.)	–	(0.7)	(3.1)	(1.0)	0.1	0.5
Market value ($ mil.)	(2.0%)	11.6	5.6	9.8	12.2	10.7
Employees	4.6%	501	392	510	609	599

TRIPADVISOR INC   NMS: TRIP

400 1st Avenue   CEO: Stephen Kaufer
Needham, MA 02464   CFO: Julie M.B. Bradley
Phone: 781 800-5000   HR: –
Fax: –   FYE: December 31
Web: www.tripadvisor.com   Type: Public

Want to crowd source your next trip with advice from millions of fellow travelers? Then turn to TripAdvisor which provides more than 225 million consumer reviews on places from the Yorkshire B&B to the Super 8 and to the Ritz to help travelers plot their journies and make reservations. The global source strives to fine-tune search results to provide information that is free of bias and in a mobile format for smartphone use. TripAdvisor also matches hotels with flights and packages. The company partners with top online travel businesses such as Hotwire Hotels.com and American Airlines and offers some 45 localized versions in France Germany Ireland Italy Spain the UK China and a growing list of other countries. The company was spun off from Expedia in 2011.

	Annual Growth	12/10	12/11	12/12	12/13	12/14
Sales ($ mil.)	26.6%	484.6	637.1	763.0	944.7	1,246.0
Net income ($ mil.)	13.0%	138.8	177.7	194.1	205.4	226.0
Market value ($ mil.)	43.6%	–	3,603.0	5,991.3	11,838.2	10,670.5
Employees	29.3%	1,000	1,250	1,575	2,017	2,793

TRIPADVISOR INC.   NASDAQ: TRIP

141 Needham St.   CEO: –
Newton MA 02464   CFO: Julie MB Bradley
Phone: 617-670-6300   HR: –
Fax: 781-444-1146   FYE: December 31
Web: www.tripadvisor.com   Type: Public

TripAdvisor is primed to give you advice. A subsidiary of online travel services provider Expedia until late 2011 spun off TripAdvisor offers a search engine and directory that matches hotels with flights and packages. The company provides more than 60 million consumer reviews to help travelers plan consumer-savvy trips. The global source strives to fine-tune search results to provide information that is free of bias and in a mobile format for smartphone use. TripAdvisor partners with top online travel businesses such as Hotwire Hotels.com and American Airlines and offers some 30 localized versions in France Germany Ireland Italy Spain the UK China and other countries.

TRIPLE-S MANAGEMENT CORPORATION   NYSE: GTS

1441 F.D. Roosevelt Ave.   CEO: Roberto Garc a-Rodriguez
San Juan PR 00920   CFO: Juan J. Rom ˇn-Jim ©nez
Phone: 787-749-4949   HR: –
Fax: 714-276-9080   FYE: December 31
Web: www.datascension.com   Type: Public

Triple-S Management is the reigning heavyweight when it comes to Puerto Rico's managed health care services. With about 1.7 million members the territory's top health insurance company operates through its Triple-S Salud (TSS) and American Health (AH) subsidiaries under the Blue Cross and Blue Shield names to provide traditional managed care products (HMO and PPO) accident and disability coverage as well as Medicare plans. Its Triple-S Vida subsidiary is Puerto Rico's leading provider of life insurance policies and its Triple-S Propiedad subsidiary offers property/casualty insurance including commercial and individual coverage. Triple-S Management provides for about half of the island's population.

TRIPLEFIN LLC

6000 Creek Rd.   CEO: Gregory T Lalonde
Cincinnati OH 45242   CFO: –
Phone: 513-794-9870   HR: –
Fax: 513-794-0878   FYE: December 31
Web: www.triplefin.com   Type: Private

Triplefin serves companies that just want to focus on the product or service and leave the rest to someone else. The company does everything from taking the order to shipping the product and collecting the bill. It provides order management and fulfillment services customer support product sales and marketing vendor relationship management and financial services. It also offers related IT services including customer relationship management software Web site development and hosting systems integration with vendors and online activity reports. Triplefin which was established in 1981 caters to companies in the consumer products and health care industries.

TRIPPE MANUFACTURING COMPANY

1111 W 35TH ST
CHICAGO, IL 60609-1404
Phone: 773-869-1111
Fax: –
Web: www.tripplite.com

CEO: Elbert Howell
CFO: Charles Lang
HR: –
FYE: December 31
Type: Private

Trippe sells protection from power trips. Doing business as Tripp Lite the company makes over 2500 products used to protect power and connect electronic equipment. Its surge suppressors guard against surges spikes and overvoltages that can damage personal computers and other electronic equipment. Its uninterruptible power supply (UPS) systems provide battery backup power while its inverters are used to power laptops and other products when other power sources are not available. Tripp Lite products also include power strips cables and connectors laptop accessories and power-management software.

	Annual Growth	12/06	12/07	12/08	12/11	12/12
Sales ($ mil.)	–	–	0.0	0.0	300.0	350.0
Net income ($ mil.)	–	–	0.0	0.0	0.0	0.0
Market value ($ mil.)	–	–	–	–	–	–
Employees	–	–	–	–	–	450

TRIQUINT SEMICONDUCTOR, INC.

NMS: TQNT

2300 N.E. Brookwood Parkway
Hillsboro, OR 97124
Phone: 503 615-9000
Fax: 503 615-8900
Web: www.triquint.com

CEO: Robert Bruggeworth
CFO: Steve Buhaly
HR: –
FYE: December 31
Type: Public

TriQuint Semiconductor fills it up with GaAs. TriQuint uses specialized materials — such as gallium arsenide (GaAs) gallium nitride and quartz — instead of silicon as the substrate for its filtering switching and amplification products. Those products are applied in radio frequency (RF) microwave and millimeter-wave settings serving mobile device network and defense and aerospace customers. Major clients have included Foxconn Technology Samsung Electronics and the US government and its contractors. TriQuint also offers contract design and fabrication services. More than three-quarters of its sales come from outside the US.

	Annual Growth	12/08	12/09	12/10	12/11	12/12
Sales ($ mil.)	9.7%	573.4	654.3	878.7	896.1	829.2
Net income ($ mil.)	–	(14.6)	16.2	190.8	48.2	(26.2)
Market value ($ mil.)	8.9%	552.5	963.7	1,877.5	782.2	775.8
Employees	4.3%	2,297	2,393	2,777	2,905	2,723

TRISTATE CAPITAL HOLDINGS, INC.

NMS. TSC

One Oxford Centre, 301 Grant Street, Suite 2700
Pittsburgh, PA 15219
Phone. 412 304-0304
Fax: –

CEO: James F. (Jim) Getz
CFO: Mark L. Sullivan
HR: –
FYE: December 31
Type: Public

TriState Capital Holdings has found its niche right in the middle of the banking industry. The holding company owns TriState Capital Bank a regional business bank that caters to midsized businesses or those annually earning between $5 million and $300 million. TriState Capital also offers private banking services nationally to high-net-worth individuals. Its loan portfolio consists of about 50% commercial loans 30% commercial real estate loans and 20% private banking-personal loans. The bank serves clients from branches in Cleveland; New Jersey; New York City Philadelphia and Pittsburgh. Altogether it has some $2 billion in assets. TriState Capital went public in mid-2013.

	Annual Growth	12/10	12/11	12/12	12/13	12/14
Assets ($ mil.)	15.8%	–	1,833.5	2,073.1	2,290.5	2,846.9
Net income ($ mil.)	1.1%	15.2	7.2	10.7	12.9	15.9
Market value ($ mil.)	(13.7%)	–	–	–	332.8	287.3
Employees	23.7%	–	–	119	129	182

TRIUMPH APPAREL CORP.

PINK SHEETS: TRUA

530 7th Ave. Ste. M1
New York NY 10018
Phone: 212-764-4630
Fax: 913-362-0133
Web: www.laynechristensen.com

CEO: Carol Hockman
CFO: John A Sarto
HR: –
FYE: December 31
Type: Public

Triumph Apparel posts a profit when its customers outfit themselves to bust a move. Formerly known as Danskin the company designs and manufactures girls' and women's dance and active wear (including tights and leotards) and it also offers women's fitness equipment such as toning balls and yoga mats. Triumph sells its products to mass merchandisers (Target Wal-Mart) department stores sporting goods stores and other specialty shops as well as online under the licensed Danskin name. In early 2009 KSL Ventures acquired 55% of the company.

TRIUMPH GROUP INC.

NYS: TGI

899 Cassatt Road, Suite 210
Berwyn, PA 19312
Phone: 610 251-1000
Fax: –
Web: www.triumphgroup.com

CEO: Daniel J. (Dan) Crowley
CFO: Jeffrey L. (Jeff) McRae
HR: Robin Derogatis
FYE: March 31
Type: Public

If it's between nose and tail Triumph Group's got it covered. Triumph's companies design engineer manufacture repair and overhaul a myriad of aerostructures and aircraft components and systems for customers that include commercial general and military original and aftermarket equipment manufacturers. The company has three operating segments including Aerospace Systems; Aftermarket Services (maintenance repair and overhaul); and Aerostructures (makes metallic and composite aerostructures and structural components). It operates through nearly 70 facilities around the world.

	Annual Growth	03/11	03/12	03/13	03/14	03/15
Sales ($ mil.)	7.6%	2,905.3	3,407.9	3,702.7	3,763.3	3,888.7
Net income ($ mil.)	12.3%	149.9	280.9	297.3	206.3	238.7
Market value ($ mil.)	(9.4%)	4,358.2	3,087.4	3,867.9	3,182.1	2,942.6
Employees	5.8%	12,097	12,602	13,900	13,828	15,153

TROUT-BLUE CHELAN-MAGI INC.

8 HOWSER RD
CHELAN, WA 988169590
Phone: 509-682-2591
Fax: –

CEO: Reggie Collins
CFO: Todd Kammers
HR: –
FYE: August 31
Type: Private

Trout-Blue Chelan-Magi has a simpler and more apt name by which it does business — Chelan Fruit. The company is fruit growers' cooperative with some 420 member/growers located in Washington State. The co-op prepares packs and sells its members' apples pears cherries and other stone fruits including peaches apricots nectarines and plums. The fruit is shipped both domestically and internationally. Product marketing is conducted through Chelan Fresh Marketing. The co-op was formed through the 1995 merger of two cooperatives Trout and Blue Chelan; the combined company changed its name again in 2004 with the acquisition of Magi.

	Annual Growth	08/10	08/11	08/12	08/13	08/14
Sales ($ mil.)	4.2%	–	138.3	149.8	180.9	156.3
Net income ($ mil.)	(9.5%)	–	–	5.1	5.1	4.1
Market value ($ mil.)	–	–	–	–	–	–
Employees	–	–	–	–	–	675

TROUX TECHNOLOGIES INC.

8601 FM 2222 Bldg. 3 Ste. 300
Austin TX 78730
Phone: 512-536-6270
Fax: 512-231-8796
Web: www.troux.com

CEO: David Hood
CFO: Paul Baker
HR: –
FYE: December 31
Type: Private

Troux Technologies truly keeps a close eye on IT assets. Troux (pronounced "True") provides software and services for keeping track of information technology (IT) assets within an organization. The company's software helps companies keep their IT strategies in line with business goals anticipate and manage change comply with regulatory policies and cut costs as well as tools that automatically collects and manages data about an organization for IT planning purposes. Troux sells to customers in a variety of industries including biotechnology consumer goods financial services manufacturing and telecommunications as well as to government agencies. Investors include Austin Ventures.

TROVER SOLUTIONS INC.

Trover Plaza 9390 Bunsen Pkwy.
Louisville KY 40220
Phone: 502-214-1340
Fax: 502-214-1350
Web: www.troversolutions.com

CEO: –
CFO: Glen French
HR: –
FYE: December 31
Type: Private

Trover Solutions helps health care payors and property/casualty insurers find missing money. Through HealthcareRecoveries and TransPaC Solutions the firm attempts to recover the value of accident-related health care benefits from third parties (such as auto insurers) on behalf of HMOs health insurers and employee health plans. Trover Solutions' automated recovery process handles everything from initial claim processing to guidance on claim settlement. Its Troveris proprietary software and consulting services help clients build their own internal subrogation departments. The company is owned by ABRY Partners which acquired it from Tailwind Capital Partners in 2011.

TROY UNIVERSITY

600 UNIVERSITY AVE
TROY, AL 360820001
Phone: 334-670-3108
Fax: –
Web: www.troy.edu

CEO: –
CFO: –
HR: –
FYE: September 30
Type: Private

Troy University is not the topic of a Homeric poem but you'd probably find a Helen enrolled there. The school is a public institution comprised of a network of campuses throughout Alabama and worldwide. The network includes 60 campuses in some 7 US states and four other countries. Troy University has a total student enrollment of about 22000 and offers degrees in arts and sciences business communications and fine arts education and health and human services. The school also operates the Confucius Institute to promote understanding of Chinese language and culture.

	Annual Growth	12/04	12/05	12/06*	09/07	09/08
Sales ($ mil.)	–	–	–	(2,023.2)	164.1	156.5
Net income ($ mil.)	35074.6%	–	–	0.0	21.1	29.1
Market value ($ mil.)	–	–	–	–	–	–
Employees	–	–	–	–	–	3,000

*Fiscal year change

TRUE DRINKS HOLDINGS, INC.

NBB: TRUU

18552 MacArthur Blvd., Suite 325
Irvine, CA 92612
Phone: 949 203-3500
Fax: –
Web: www.truedrinks.com

CEO: Lance Leonard
CFO: Daniel Kerker
HR: –
FYE: December 31
Type: Public

True Drinks is focused on providing all-natural healthy alternatives to sodas and other high-calorie beverages. Its flagship product is AquaBall Naturally Flavored Water which is sweetened with all-natural stevia and infused with various vitamins. Marketed directly to children it comes in a variety of fruit flavors and features Disney and Marvel characters on the bottles. True Drinks also makes and markets Bazi All Natural Energy which is designed to boost energy through a combination of 12 vitamins and eight so-called superfruits (such as jujube goji berry and acai). The products are sold primarily through mass-market retailers across the US.

	Annual Growth	12/10	12/11	12/12	12/13	12/14
Sales ($ mil.)	19.9%	2.3	1.3	1.0	2.6	4.7
Net income ($ mil.)	–	(3.4)	(3.9)	(3.1)	(7.1)	(8.1)
Market value ($ mil.)	(1.1%)	9.2	1.0	1.0	10.9	8.8
Employees	2.4%	10	5	8	9	11

TRUE VALUE COMPANY

8600 W BRYN MAWR AVE 100S
CHICAGO, IL 606313505
Phone: 773-695-5000
Fax: –
Web: www.truevalue.com

CEO: John Hartmann
CFO: David A. (Dave) Shadduck
HR: –
FYE: December 28
Type: Private

To survive against home improvement giants such as The Home Depot and Lowe's True Value Co. (TVC) is relying on the true value of service. Formed by the 1997 merger of Cotter & Company and ServiStar Coast to Coast the retailer-owned wholesale hardware cooperative serves some 4400 retail outlets in 58-plus countries. Stores offer home improvement and garden supplies as well as appliances housewares sporting goods and pet food. In addition to the flagship True Value banner members operate under the names of Taylor Rental Grand Rental Station Home & Garden Showplace Induserve Supply and Party Central among others. True Value also manufactures its own brand of paints.

	Annual Growth	01/10	01/11*	12/11	12/12	12/13
Sales ($ mil.)	(11.5%)	–	1,804.0	1,864.8	1,399.1	1,411.5
Net income ($ mil.)	(4.2%)	–	–	60.3	74.9	55.3
Market value ($ mil.)	–	–	–	–	–	–
Employees	–	–	–	–	–	3,000

*Fiscal year change

TRUEBLUE INC

NYS: TBI

1015 A Street
Tacoma, WA 98402
Phone: 253 383-9101
Fax: 253 383-9311
Web: www.trueblue.com

CEO: Steven C. (Steve) Cooper
CFO: Derrek L. Gafford
HR: Kimberly A. Cannon
FYE: December 26
Type: Public

Another day another blue-collar dollar. Staffing firm TrueBlue specializes in providing general laborers on short notice for short-term jobs in fields such as construction hospitality landscaping and transportation. The company offers general labor staffing services from more than 690 branches throughout the US and Canada mostly under the Labor Ready brand. Other units operating through branches include Spartan Staffing (light industrial temporary services) CLP Resources (skilled construction trades) and Centerline Drivers (temporary and dedicated driver placement). TrueBlue mainly serves companies residing in the services construction transportation manufacturing retail and wholesale sectors.

	Annual Growth	12/10	12/11	12/12	12/13	12/14
Sales ($ mil.)	17.3%	1,149.4	1,316.0	1,389.5	1,668.9	2,174.0
Net income ($ mil.)	34.9%	19.8	30.8	33.6	44.9	65.7
Market value ($ mil.)	5.9%	747.1	576.4	645.4	1,076.5	940.7
Employees	17.8%	2,600	2,700	2,900	3,200	5,000

TRUJILLO & SONS INC.

3325 NW 62ND ST
MIAMI, FL 331477533
Phone: 305-633-6482
Fax: –
Web: www.trujilloandsons.com

CEO: –
CFO: –
HR: –
FYE: December 31
Type: Private

Trujillo and Sons is a leading food distributor that supplies foodservice operators and retail grocery stores with dry goods canned foods beverages and a variety of other goods. Most of its products are sold under the Alberto and Don Lucas brands; the company also provides private label packaging services through affiliated companies Trujillo Oil Plant (vegetable and cooking oils) and American Spice Company. Trujillo and Sons serves customers throughout the US and in the Caribbean and South America. The family-owned company was founded in 1966 by Lucas Trujillo Sr.

	Annual Growth	12/04	12/05	12/06	12/08	12/09
Sales ($ mil.)	(37.4%)	–	–	360.9	93.2	88.5
Net income ($ mil.)	237.4%	–	–	0.0	3.7	1.3
Market value ($ mil.)	–	–	–	–	–	–
Employees	–	–	–	–	–	100

TRULAND SYSTEMS CORPORATION

1900 Oracle Way Ste. 700
Reston VA 20190
Phone: 703-464-3000
Fax: 703-796-1718
Web: www.truland.com

CEO: –
CFO: –
HR: –
FYE: December 31
Type: Private

Truland Systems takes current events seriously. The US electrical contractor is a privately-held group made up of about 10 companies that design build test and maintain electrical systems in offices condominiums hospitals hotels sports stadiums and mass transit facilities. Its services focus on building automated systems that increase speed and decrease energy consumption. As a specialty contractor it is hired by general contractors as well as commercial and public facility owners and developers. Clients have included Turner Construction AOL and the US Department of Homeland Security. Founded in 1913 the company is in its second generation of being family run led by CEO Robert Truland.

TRUMAN ARNOLD COMPANIES

701 S ROBISON RD
TEXARKANA, TX 755016747
Phone: 903 794 3035
Fax: –
Web: www.tacenergy.com

CEO: Truman Arnold
CFO: Steve McMillen
HR: –
FYE: September 30
Type: Private

It is not just jibber jabber — this jobber gets the job done by distributing wholesale petroleum across the US. Truman Arnold Companies (TAC) has more than 400 associates with fuel volume of more than 2 billion gallons a year and markets and distributes petroleum products to customers through its TAC Energy subsidiary. Through a partnership it operates two major petroleum terminals one in Arkansas and one in Texas which collectively have more than 1.3 million barrels of capacity. Through its TAC Air unit the company offers fixed-based operations (FBO) including aircraft fueling hangar and ground transportation services through 14 general aviation facilities located across the US.

	Annual Growth	09/10	09/11	09/12	09/13	09/14
Sales ($ mil.)	(4.4%)	–	–	2,471.7	2,172.9	2,259.2
Net income ($ mil.)	3.4%	–	–	11.1	54.4	11.9
Market value ($ mil.)	–	–	–	–	–	–
Employees	–	–	–	–	–	550

TRUMAN MEDICAL CENTER INCORPORATED

2301 HOLMES ST
KANSAS CITY, MO 641082677
Phone: 816-404-1000
Fax: –
Web: www.trumed.org

CEO: –
CFO: Allen (Al) Johnson
HR: –
FYE: June 30
Type: Private

If you're miserable in Missouri Truman Medical Center (TMC) can offer TLC and health care. TMC provides primary and mental health care at two not-for-profit hospitals in the Kansas City (Missouri) area with a combined total of about 540 beds. Its Hospital Hill runs one of the busiest emergency rooms in Kansas City and is known for treatments related to asthma diabetes obstetrics ophthalmology weight management and women's health. TMC Lakewood is a leading academic medical center providing a range of health care services to the greater Kansas City metropolitan area including uninsured patients.

	Annual Growth	06/07	06/08	06/09	06/10	06/13
Sales ($ mil.)	155.5%	–	4.5	424.9	439.2	493.4
Net income ($ mil.)	–	–	–	16.2	5.1	(4.7)
Market value ($ mil.)	–	–	–	–	–	–
Employees	–	–	–	–	–	3,000

TRUMP ENTERTAINMENT RESORTS INC.

15 S. Pennsylvania Ave.
Atlantic City NJ 08401
Phone: 609-449-5866
Fax: 800-824-8329
Web: www.taitroncomponents.com

CEO: Robert F Griffin
CFO: David R Hughes
HR: –
FYE: December 31
Type: Private

Feel like craps? Trump Entertainment Resorts (TER formerly Trump Hotels & Casino Resorts) owns and manages the Trump Plaza and the Trump Taj Mahal casino hotels in Atlantic City New Jersey. The two properties house hotel rooms gaming tables and slot machines. The company also owns the right to use founder and former chairman Donald Trump's name and likeness for gambling promotions. (Unhappy with the actions of the board of directors Trump resigned in 2009.) After spending about a year and a half in Chapter 11 reorganization TER exited bankruptcy in 2010. The company sold its underperforming Trump Marina in 2011.

TRUSTCO BANK CORP. (N.Y.)

NMS: TRST

5 Sarnowski Drive
Glenville, NY 12302
Phone: 518 377-3311
Fax: 518 381-3668
Web: www.trustcobank.com

CEO: Robert J. McCormick
CFO: Michael M. Ozimek
HR: –
FYE: December 31
Type: Public

In Banking They Trust. TrustCo Bank Corp is the holding company for Trustco Bank which boasts more than 140 branches across eastern New York central and western Florida and parts of Vermont Massachusetts and New Jersey. The bank offers personal and business customers a variety of deposit products loans and mortgages and trust and investment services. It primarily originates residential and commercial mortgages which account for more than three-quarters of its loan portfolio. It also writes business construction and installment loans and home equity lines of credit.

	Annual Growth	12/10	12/11	12/12	12/13	12/14
Assets ($ mil.)	4.1%	3,954.8	4,243.6	4,346.6	4,521.5	4,644.4
Net income ($ mil.)	10.8%	29.3	33.1	37.5	39.8	44.2
Market value ($ mil.)	3.4%	601.4	532.1	500.8	681.1	688.7
Employees	(0.0%)	738	726	759	708	737

TRUSTEES OF BOSTON COLLEGE

140 COMMONWEALTH AVE	CEO: –
CHESTNUT HILL, MA 024673800	CFO: –
Phone: 617-552-8000	HR: Leo Sullivan
Fax: –	FYE: May 31
Web: www.bc.edu	Type: Private

Students at Boston College (BC) get both academic excellence and the Red Sox. Located six miles from downtown Boston the university enrolls 14100 full- and part-time students (about a third of whom are graduate students) from every state in the US and 80 other countries. It has a student-teacher ratio of 13:1. BC offers degrees in more than 50 fields of study through its schools and colleges on four campuses. The university also has more than 20 research centers including the Institute for Scientific Research and the Center for International Higher Education. BC is one of the oldest Jesuit Catholic universities in the nation and has the largest Jesuit community in the world.

	Annual Growth	05/10	05/11	05/12	05/13	05/14
Sales ($ mil.)	3.0%	–	643.7	653.7	671.1	702.7
Net income ($ mil.)	–	–	–	(76.5)	270.5	221.2
Market value ($ mil.)	–	–	–	–	–	–
Employees	–	–	–	–	–	2,509

TRUSTEES OF CLARK UNIVERSITY

950 MAIN ST	CEO: –
WORCESTER, MA 016101400	CFO: –
Phone: 508-793-7711	HR: –
Fax: –	FYE: May 31
Web: www.clarku.edu	Type: Private

If you don't want to live in the dark get an education at Clark! Clark University is a private co-educational liberal arts university with an enrollment of more than 2200 undergraduate students and more than 1000 graduate students. It offers about 30 undergraduate majors (psychology is the most popular) and about two dozen master's degree programs. Clark University has 200 full-time faculty members of which 96% hold doctoral or terminal degrees. It has a student/faculty ratio of 10:1. The university offers 17 Varsity sports (NCAA Division III). Clark University has been a pioneer in the academic study of geography; it has awarded more doctorates in the discipline than any other US school.

	Annual Growth	05/10	05/11	05/12	05/13	05/14
Sales ($ mil.)	0.9%	–	101.8	104.9	109.8	104.5
Net income ($ mil.)	–	–	–	(14.4)	57.3	44.6
Market value ($ mil.)	–	–	–	–	–	–
Employees	–	–	–	–	–	600

TRUSTEES OF THE ESTATE OF BERNICE PAUAHI BISHOP

567 S KING ST STE 200	CEO: –
HONOLULU, HI 968133079	CFO: Michael Loo
Phone: 808-523-6200	HR: Winona White
Fax: –	FYE: June 30
Web: www.ksbe.edu	Type: Private

Kamehameha Schools provides an education fit for a king ... or queen. The private charitable trust was founded and endowed by Princess Bernice Pauahi Bishop great granddaughter and last royal descendant of Kamehameha the Great. One of the largest independent schools in the US Kamehameha educates more than 5000 elementary middle school and high school students many of whom board at one of its three Hawaii campuses. In addition it operates some 30 preschools with a total enrollment of about 1500. Kamehameha Schools is also the largest private property owner in the state of Hawaii and uses the proceeds from its real estate operations to support its schools.

	Annual Growth	06/07	06/08	06/09	06/10	06/13
Sales ($ mil.)	308.1%	–	–	1.9	333.8	519.1
Net income ($ mil.)	203.6%	–	–	1.3	(21.9)	109.7
Market value ($ mil.)	–	–	–	–	–	–
Employees	–	–	–	–	–	1,500

TRUSTEES OF TUFTS COLLEGE INC.

169 HOLLAND ST STE 318	CEO: –
SOMERVILLE, MA 021442401	CFO: –
Phone: 617-628-5000	HR: –
Fax: –	FYE: June 30
Web: www.dental.tufts.edu	Type: Private

Tufts University wants to light up the minds of New England scholars. The school offers undergraduate and graduate degrees in areas such as education engineering psychology art English music and medicine. The university enrolls some 11000 students and has 1300 faculty members and it offers classes in 70 fields at three campuses in Massachusetts (Boston Medford/Somerville and Grafton). It also has an international campus in Talloires France. Tufts University's Fletcher School of Law and Diplomacy is the oldest continuous international relations graduate program in the country. The school is also home to New England's only Veterinary School.

	Annual Growth	06/09	06/10	06/11	06/12	06/13
Sales ($ mil.)	0.0%	–	767.8	851.7	769.0	768.9
Net income ($ mil.)	23.6%	–	–	83.7	(100.6)	127.8
Market value ($ mil.)	–	–	–	–	–	–
Employees	–	–	–	–	–	4,100

TRUSTEES OF UNION COLLEGE IN THE TOWN OF SCHENECTADY IN THE STAT

807 UNION ST	CEO: –
SCHENECTADY, NY 12308-3103	CFO: –
Phone: 518-388-6630	HR: –
Fax: –	FYE: June 30
Web: www.union.edu	Type: Private

Union College brings liberal arts and engineering together. Union College is a private liberal arts school that offers courses in the humanities the social sciences the sciences and engineering. Notable alumni include the father of Franklin D. Roosevelt the grandfather of Winston Churchill and former US president Chester A. Arthur (class of 1848). Founded in 1795 with a class of 16 the college is supported by an endowment of more than $270 million.

	Annual Growth	06/07	06/08	06/08	06/11	06/12
Sales ($ mil.)	0.5%	–	156.7	136.1	145.3	159.8
Net income ($ mil.)	(24.5%)	–	32.2	(2.4)	1.2	10.5
Market value ($ mil.)	–	–	–	–	–	–
Employees	–	–	–	–	–	870

TRUSTMARK CORP.

NMS: TRMK

248 East Capitol Street	CEO: Gerard R Host
Jackson, MS 39201	CFO: Louis E. Greer
Phone: 601 208-5111	HR: –
Fax: 601 354-5053	FYE: December 31
Web: www.trustmark.com	Type: Public

Trustmark Corporation is the holding company for Trustmark National Bank which has 208 locations mainly in Mississippi but also in East Texas the Florida panhandle and Tennessee where it also operates its Somerville Bank & Trust subsidiary in the Memphis area. Focusing on individuals and small businesses Trustmark offers a range of financial products and services such as checking and savings accounts certificates of deposit credit cards insurance investments and trust services. The diversified financial services firm has about $11.7 billion in assets.

	Annual Growth	12/10	12/11	12/12	12/13	12/14
Assets ($ mil.)	6.4%	9,553.9	9,727.0	9,828.7	11,790.4	12,250.6
Net income ($ mil.)	5.3%	100.6	106.8	117.3	117.1	123.6
Market value ($ mil.)	(0.3%)	1,676.3	1,639.1	1,515.6	1,811.2	1,656.0
Employees	5.3%	2,490	2,537	2,666	3,110	3,060

TRUSTWAVE HOLDINGS INC.

70 W. Madison St. Ste. 1050
Chicago IL 60602
Phone: 312-873-7500
Fax: 312-443-8028
Web: www.trustwave.com

CEO: Robert J McCullen
CFO: Mark Iserloth
HR: −
FYE: December 31
Type: Private

Because a business can't live on cash alone Trustwave helps credit card merchants and other businesses process secure transactions. The company's TrustKeeper software is a PCI (payment card industry) compliant application that protects merchants against unauthorized access fraud and other security breaches. Its software is sold to companies that process electronic transactions such as American Express Banc of America Merchant Services Chase Paymentech Discover Visa and Wells Fargo among others. These partners in turn offer TrustKeeper subscriptions at credit card merchant locations mainly in the US and Canada. The company also tailors applications for such industries as health care and hospitality.

TSR, INC.

NAS: TSRI

400 Oser Avenue
Hauppauge, NY 11788
Phone: 631 231-0333
Fax: 631 435-1428
Web: www.tsrconsulting.com

CEO: Joseph F Hughes
CFO: −
HR: John Sharkey
FYE: May 31
Type: Public

Prowling for programmers? TSR would like to help. The company provides contract computer programmers and other information technology (IT) personnel mainly to FORTUNE 1000 companies that need to augment their in-house IT staffs. TSR specializes in serving the telecommunications industry; major customers have included purchasing outsourcer ProcureStaff (primarily to fulfill a contract with AT&T) and publishing giant McGraw-Hill. Overall TSR serves more than 80 clients in the northeastern and mid-Atlantic regions of the US. In addition to providing contract personnel TSR offers direct staffing (helping clients find people for permanent placement) and project management services.

	Annual Growth	05/11	05/12	05/13	05/14	05/15
Sales ($ mil.)	9.9%	39.3	45.2	44.9	49.5	57.4
Net income ($ mil.)	(0.6%)	0.2	(0.1)	(0.5)	(0.1)	0.2
Market value ($ mil.)	(4.8%)	9.5	8.3	6.3	6.0	7.8
Employees	11.9%	183	195	229	275	287

TRW AUTOMOTIVE HOLDINGS CORP

NYS: TRW

12001 Tech Center Drive
Livonia, MI 48150
Phone: 734 855-2600
Fax: −
Web: www.trw.com

CEO: Franz Kleiner
CFO: Joseph S Cantie
HR: −
FYE: December 31
Type: Public

TRW Automotive makes cars stop and go around the globe in addition to keeping passengers and pedestrians safe. The company designs and makes systems components and modules primarily for major automakers. Product lines range from chassis systems (brake steering and suspension systems) to safety systems such as airbags seat belts and security and safety electronics (crash and occupant weight sensors). Other products include body controls and engine valves. TRW Automotive has more than 190 facilities in two dozen countries worldwide netting nearly 70% of its sales outside North America.

	Annual Growth	12/09	12/10	12/11	12/12	12/13
Sales ($ mil.)	10.7%	11,614.0	14,383.0	16,244.0	16,444.0	17,435.0
Net income ($ mil.)	104.9%	55.0	834.0	1,157.0	1,008.0	970.0
Market value ($ mil.)	32.9%	2,729.5	6,023.5	3,726.1	6,127.6	8,502.7
Employees	5.3%	63,600	69,800	72,700	75,200	78,200

TSS INC DE

NBB: TSSI

110 E. Old Settlers Road
Round Rock, TX 78664
Phone: 512 310-1000
Fax: −
Web: www.totalsitesolutions.com

CEO: Anthony Angelini
CFO: Kenneth D Schwarz
HR: −
FYE: December 31
Type: Public

Fortress International Group Inc. (FIGI) is a bastion of security. FIGI companies design build and maintain secure temperature-controlled data centers and IT storage facilities for private companies and government agencies. FIGI offers its start-to-finish service by operating through subsidiaries that specialize in a certain function such as IT consulting design construction or engineering. Projects are either built from scratch or upgraded through renovations. While most of its customers are top secret FIGI has worked with Digital Realty Trust and Internap and is cleared to work at Department of Defense and US Army Corps of Engineers properties.

	Annual Growth	12/10	12/11	12/12	12/13	12/14
Sales ($ mil.)	(21.8%)	74.9	36.9	47.7	44.4	28.0
Net income ($ mil.)		0.9	1.8	(4.0)	(2.8)	(2.8)
Market value ($ mil.)	(28.0%)	20.8	13.4	7.3	6.7	5.6
Employees	(4.0%)	114	107	79	104	97

TSI INCORPORATED

500 Cardigan Rd.
Shoreview MN 55126-3996
Phone: 651-490-2811
Fax: 651-490-3824
Web: www.tsi.com

CEO: John J Fauth
CFO: −
HR: −
FYE: March 31
Type: Private

TSI is no stranger to a good test. Founded in 1961 as Thermo-Systems Inc. TSI makes sensors and instruments used in a wide range of environmental safety and quality control applications. The company's products monitor air quality temperature and humidity in working environments; measure pollution conditions; detect gases and analyze gas pressure and temperature; and measure the flow rate of liquids. Wholly-owned subsidiaries include Environmental Systems (products for outdoor environmental monitoring) DICKEY-john (instrumentation for agriculture and public works) and Tekran Instruments (mercury monitoring).The global company has offices in China France Germany India Singapore the UK and the US.

TTI INC.

2441 Northeast Pkwy.
Fort Worth TX 76106-1816
Phone: 817-740-9000
Fax: 817-740-9898
Web: www.ttiinc.com

CEO: Paul Andrews Jr
CFO: Nick M Kypreos
HR: −
FYE: December 31
Type: Subsidiary

TTI is passionate about passives. Each year the company distributes millions of electronic components including passive components (such as resistors and capacitors) interconnects (cables sockets and filter connectors) and discrete components (semiconductors). It sells from suppliers that include AVX KEMET Molex TE Connectivity and Vishay Intertechnology. Customers include manufacturers of military and aerospace equipment computers communications equipment consumer products medical devices instrumentation and industrial products. Founded in 1971 by CEO Paul Andrews TTI is a wholly owned subsidiary of Berkshire Hathaway.

TTM TECHNOLOGIES INC

NMS: TTMI

1665 Scenic Avenue Suite 250
Costa Mesa, CA 92626
Phone: 714 327-3000
Fax: –
Web: www.ttmtech.com

CEO: Kenton K. (Kent) Alder
CFO: Steven W. (Steve) Richards
HR: Jeanette Newman
FYE: December 29
Type: Public

At TTM Technologies it's Time To Market. TTM provides contract printed circuit board (PCB) manufacturing services primarily for the networking communications high-end computing aerospace and defense medical industrial and instrumentation markets as well as to electronics manufacturing service providers that serve those markets. In addition to prototyping TTM offers both quick-turn production — limited quantities delivered in a shortened timeframe — and standard volume production services. Its top OEM customers include Cisco Systems Huawei Apple Ericsson and ZTE. TTM gets almost 60% of its sales from customers outside the US; 28% comes from China.

	Annual Growth	12/10	12/11	12/12	12/13	12/14
Sales ($ mil.)	3.0%	1,179.7	1,428.6	1,348.7	1,368.2	1,325.7
Net income ($ mil.)	(32.7%)	71.5	41.9	(174.6)	21.9	14.7
Market value ($ mil.)	(15.7%)	1,243.5	913.5	765.9	715.9	629.3
Employees	(0.9%)	17,448	16,278	19,934	16,290	16,857

TUCOWS INC

NAS: TCX

96 Mowat Avenue
Toronto, Ontario M6K 3M1
Phone: 416 535-0123
Fax: –
Web: www.tucows.com

CEO: –
CFO: –
HR: –
FYE: December 31
Type: Public

Software and services from Tucows help keep the Internet moving. The company provides wholesale Internet and back-office services to more than 10000 Web hosting companies ISPs and others around the world. Accredited by ICANN Tucows provides registration for such top-level domains as .com .net and .org as well as country-code domains including .ca and .uk. It has more than 10 million domain names under management. In addition to domain services Tucows maintains an online repository of software available for downloading. Its library of freeware and shareware software boasts more than 40000 titles. Tucows also offers online tools to help developers promote and sell their titles.

	Annual Growth	12/10	12/11	12/12	12/13	12/14
Sales ($ mil.)	14.9%	84.6	97.1	114.7	129.9	147.7
Net income ($ mil.)	31.7%	2.1	6.2	4.4	4.2	6.4
Market value ($ mil.)	127.6%	8.2	8.5	16.3	158.6	219.9
Employees	10.7%	150	150	175	200	225

TUCSON ELECTRIC POWER COMPANY

88 East Broadway Boulevard
Tucson, AZ 85701
Phone: 520 571-4000
Fax: –

CEO: –
CFO: Kevin P Larson
HR: Catherine E (Cathy) Ries
FYE: December 31
Type: Public

Avoiding a run-in with a Saguaro cactus in Tucson Arizona is easier when you stick to the paths lit up by Tucson Electric Power (TEP). The utility provides electricity to about 414000 residential commercial and industrial retail customers in Tucson and surrounding areas in southeastern Arizona. With more than 2240 MW of net generating capacity (primarily coal-fired) TEP supplies most of the power it distributes and it also sells energy wholesale to utilities and power marketers in the western US. TEP is a subsidiary of UNS Energy and accounts for the bulk of that company's total revenues.

	Annual Growth	12/10	12/11	12/12	12/13	12/14
Sales ($ mil.)	3.1%	1,125.0	1,156.4	1,161.7	1,196.7	1,269.9
Net income ($ mil.)	(1.1%)	107.0	85.3	65.5	101.3	102.3
Market value ($ mil.)	–	–	–	–	–	–
Employees	1.1%	1,384	1,391	1,392	1,398	1,448

TUESDAY MORNING CORP.

NMS: TUES

6250 LBJ Freeway
Dallas, TX 75240
Phone: 972 387-3562
Fax: –
Web: www.tuesdaymorning.com

CEO: Steven R. (Steve) Becker
CFO: Stephanie Bowman
HR: Sue Elliott
FYE: June 30
Type: Public

Tuesday Morning offers big discounts every day of the week but not every week of the year. The closeout retailer sells discontinued merchandise from name-brand manufacturers at steep discounts. Its merchandise typically includes upscale linens china cookware rugs and collectibles that are not seconds irregulars or factory rejects. Tuesday Morning's 810-plus stores in 41 states operate only during monthly sales events (with the exception of January and July). The retailer keeps costs down by selling from low-rent locations and using seasonal help — only about 22% of its workers are full-time employees. Its customers are primarily women from middle- and upper-income households.

	Annual Growth	06/11	06/12	06/13	06/14	06/15
Sales ($ mil.)	2.5%	821.2	812.8	838.3	864.8	906.4
Net income ($ mil.)	2.0%	9.6	3.9	(56.4)	(10.2)	10.4
Market value ($ mil.)	24.8%	204.9	189.1	457.0	785.3	496.4
Employees	(0.2%)	8,900	8,400	9,756	8,498	8,820

TUFCO TECHNOLOGIES, INC.

NAS: TFCO

P.O. Box 23500
Green Bay, WI 54305
Phone: 920 336-0054
Fax: –
Web: www.tufco.com

CEO: Larry Grabowy
CFO: –
HR: –
FYE: September 30
Type: Public

Tough-sounding Tufco Technologies does business with paper-thin bravado. It operates through two segments: Contract manufacturing its largest custom-converts paper tissue and polyethylene film into such necessaries as cleaning wipes and disposable table cloths. The segment also offers flexographic printing adhesive laminating and custom packaging. The company's business imaging arm operated via subsidiary Hamco Manufacturing and Distributing produces specialty paper rolls (for ATMs and cash registers) standardized and customized guest checks (for restaurants) business forms and other sheeted products. Customers are multinational consumer products businesses and less so business paper distributors.

	Annual Growth	09/09	09/10	09/11	09/12	09/13
Sales ($ mil.)	3.4%	86.8	90.6	109.9	107.0	99.3
Net income ($ mil.)	–	(0.9)	(0.4)	(0.4)	(0.1)	(4.0)
Market value ($ mil.)	14.5%	12.5	14.8	15.9	18.3	21.5
Employees	(3.6%)	306	305	302	293	264

TUFTS ASSOCIATED HEALTH PLANS INC.

705 Mt. Auburn St.
Watertown MA 02472-1508
Phone: 617-972-9400
Fax: 832-355-6182
Web: www.sleh.com

CEO: James Roosevelt Jr
CFO: –
HR: –
FYE: December 31
Type: Private - Not-for-Pr

Getting good health care becomes a little less rough with Tufts. Tufts Associated Health Plans is a leading New England health insurer operating as Tufts Health Plan. The company provides medical coverage to about 1 million members in Massachusetts and (to a lesser degree) Rhode Island. Its products include HMO PPO and point-of-service plans for both employers and individuals as well as Medicare Advantage plans for retirees and managed Medicaid plans for low-income families. With partner CIGNA Tufts also offers a nationwide health network called CareLink for multi-state employers. The company was founded in 1979.

TUMAC LUMBER CO. INC.

805 SW Broadway Ste. 1700   CEO: Bradley McMurchie
Portland OR 97205-3357   CFO: Timothy J Leipzig
Phone: 503-226-6661   HR: –
Fax: 503-273-2652   FYE: December 31
Web: www.tumac.com   Type: Private

Employee-owned Tumac Lumber doesn't just linger around in its own backyard. The company distributes wood and wood products in the US and internationally. The company and its regional subsidiaries sell products such as mouldings hardwoods and softwoods composite products decking and furniture parts to kitchen cabinet companies and furniture manufacturers utility companies pulp mills RV manufacturers and others. Tumac exports lumber (Douglas fir and southern yellow pine) to Europe hardwood logs and lumber to Asia and industrial and construction products to customers in the Caribbean. Paul McCracken and Bill MacPherson established Tumac Lumber in 1959.

TUMBLEWEED INC.

2301 River Rd. Ste. 200   CEO: –
Louisville KY 40206   CFO: Glennon F Mattingly
Phone: 502-893-0323   HR: –
Fax: 502-897-0237   FYE: December 31
Web: www.tumbleweedrestaurants.com   Type: Private

This company brings Tex-Mex flavors to the wild Midwest. Tumbleweed operates and franchises about 60 Tumbleweed Southwest Grill locations in five states primarily Kentucky Ohio and Indiana. The casual-dining locations feature burritos chimichangas and enchiladas as well as mesquite-grilled steaks ribs and chicken. Other menu items include sandwiches burgers and seafood. Most of the restaurants are corporate-run. Founded in 1975 the company was taken private in 2003 by a group led by former CEO Terry Smith and majority investor Gerald Mansbach. It filed for bankruptcy in 2009.

TUMI HOLDINGS INC   NYS: TUMI

1001 Durham Ave.   CEO: Jerome S. Griffith
South Plainfield, NJ 07080   CFO: Michael J. Mardy
Phone: 908-756-4400   HR: –
Fax: –   FYE: December 31
Web: www.tumi.com   Type: Public

Tumi helps the well-heeled get where they're going in style. The high-end designer and manufacturer named after an ancient ceremonial knife makes travel gear (including suitcases and backpacks) and caters to corporate travelers with precious cargo as the company has its own Tumi Tracer tracking system for retrieving lost bags. Tumi which makes Ducati luggage under license also offers laptop covers wallets belts phone chargers and other accessories. Its products are sold in the US and in more than 75 other countries through about 115 of its own retail stores websites and upscale department and specialty stores. A unit of investment firm Doughty Hanson Tumi went public in 2012.

	Annual Growth	12/10	12/11	12/12	12/13	12/14
Sales ($ mil.)	20.2%	252.8	330.0	398.6	467.4	527.2
Net income ($ mil.)	386.0%	0.1	16.6	36.8	54.6	58.0
Market value ($ mil.)	6.7%	–	–	1,415.1	1,530.4	1,610.5
Employees	15.5%	–	963	1,152	1,307	1,484

TUPPERWARE BRANDS CORP   NYS: TUP

14901 South Orange Blossom Trail   CEO: E.V. (Rick) Goings
Orlando, FL 32837   CFO: Michael S. (Mike) Poteshman
Phone: 407-826-5050   HR: Lillian D. Garcia
Fax: –   FYE: December 27
Web: www.tupperwarebrands.com   Type: Public

Tupperware Brands Corporation (TBC) knows that there's more than one way to party. The company makes and sells household products and beauty items. Tupperware parties became synonymous with American suburban life in the 1950s when independent salespeople organized gatherings to sell their plasticware. TBC deploys a salesforce of about 3 million people across some 100 countries. The company also sells its products online. Brands include Armand Dupree Avroy Shlain BeautiControl Fuller NaturCare Nutrimetics Nuvo and of course Tupperware. Its BeautiControl unit sells beauty and skin care products and fragrances in North America Latin America and the Asia/Pacific region.

	Annual Growth	12/10	12/11	12/12	12/13	12/14
Sales ($ mil.)	3.2%	2,300.4	2,585.0	2,583.8	2,671.6	2,606.1
Net income ($ mil.)	(1.3%)	225.6	218.3	193.0	274.2	214.4
Market value ($ mil.)	7.2%	2,395.2	2,780.7	3,113.6	4,715.4	3,163.8
Employees	(0.7%)	13,500	13,600	13,000	13,100	13,100

TURBOCHEF TECHNOLOGIES INC.

4240 International Pkwy. Ste. 105   CEO: Paul P Lehr
Carollton TX 75007   CFO: J Miguel Fernandez De Castro
Phone: 214-379-6000   HR: –
Fax: 214-340-6073   FYE: December 31
Web: www.turbochef.com   Type: Subsidiary

TurboChef Technologies wants to make fast food even faster. The company makes high-speed proprietary ovens that use a microprocessor to distribute heat evenly and offer cooking speeds up to 12 times faster than a conventional oven. The ovens are sold mainly in the US under the TurboChef name primarily to fast-food and traditional restaurants convenience stores and hotels. Major customers include foodservice companies (Subway Starbucks) hotels (Hilton) grocery and convenience stores (Whole Foods 7-Eleven) and movie theaters (Loews) among others. TurboChef speed-cook oven models include the C3 Tornado 2 and High h Batch 2. Commercial foodservice equipment giant Middleby acquired TurboChef in 2009.

TURBODYNE TECHNOLOGIES INC.   OTC: TRBD

36 E. Barnett St.   CEO: –
Ventura CA 93109   CFO: –
Phone: 805-512-9511   HR: –
Fax: 718-260-9017   FYE: December 31
Web: www.cpack.com   Type: Public

Turbodyne Technologies wants to fuel advances in automotive technology. The company has developed engine airflow management products that increase the amount of air an engine receives in order to improve performance and reduce emissions. Its Turbopac electronic supercharger product line was developed for the OEM market. Honeywell Turbodyne's former development partner challenged the companies' agreement and for a time Turbodyne suspended operations because of a lack of money. The two companies have since reached a settlement but Turbodyne suffered recurring losses and ceased operations for several years. Now with fresh financing and management Turbodyne is making another go of it.

TURNER CONSTRUCTION COMPANY

375 Hudson St.
New York NY 10014
Phone: 212-229-6000
Fax: 212-229-6390
Web: www.turnerconstruction.com

CEO: Peter J Davoren
CFO: Karen Gould
HR: –
FYE: December 31
Type: Subsidiary

Turner Construction has been the mastermind for scores of head-turning projects for more than a century. The company that built Madison Square Garden has ranked among the leading general builders in the US since the early 1900s. Turner provides construction and project management services for commercial and multifamily buildings airports and stadiums as well as correctional educational entertainment and manufacturing facilities. The company is also a leader in sustainable or green building practices. Founded in 1902 by Henry Turner the company is the main operating unit of The Turner Corporation which is a subsidiary of German construction group HOCHTIEF.

TUTHILL CORPORATION

8500 S. Madison St.
Burr Ridge IL 60527
Phone: 630-382-4900
Fax: 630-382-4999
Web: www.tuthill.com

CEO: Thomas M Carmazzi
CFO: Jim Ahlborn
HR: –
FYE: December 31
Type: Private

Tuthill makes a mountain of industrial equipment. Specializing in rotating equipment the company manufactures a variety of goods such as pumps meters vacuum systems and blowers for handling both fluids and gases. Key products are marketed under its Fill-Rite Sotera Kinney Vacuum MD Pneumatics and GlobalGear brands. In addition Tuthill operates a plastics division that supplies custom injection-molding services. The company which serves agriculture chemicals construction energy and power and other industries operates 10 locations across the Americas Asia and Europe. In 1892 James Tuthill founded the company which is still owned by his descendants.

TURTLE & HUGHES INC

1900 LOWER RD
LINDEN, NJ 070366586
Phone: 732-574-3600
Fax: –
Web: www.turtle.com

CEO: Jayne Millard
CFO: Christopher Rausch
HR: –
FYE: September 30
Type: Private

Turtle & Hughes' longevity has demonstrated that slow and steady really does win the race when it comes to distributing electrical and industrial equipment. The company's exhaustive lineup is sold through three subsidiaries: Turtle & Hughes Integrated Supply Turtle Data (wire cable and power protection devices) and Turtle Ebay Store. Its customers include industrial and construction companies electrical contractors telecommunications servers utilities and various government agencies. Family-owned the company is led by its fourth generation Jayne Millard its third female CEO. One-third of Turtle & Hughes is employee-owned.

	Annual Growth	09/09	09/10	09/11	09/12	09/13
Sales ($ mil.)	11.8%	–	397.8	452.3	518.0	555.9
Net income ($ mil.)	9.0%	–	–	17.9	23.5	21.3
Market value ($ mil.)	–	–	–	–	–	–
Employees	–	–	–	–	–	450

TUTOR PERINI CORP

NYS: TPC

15901 Olden Street
Sylmar, CA 91342-1093
Phone: 818 362-8391
Fax: –
Web: www.tutorperini.com

CEO: Robert Band
CFO: Gary G. Smalley
HR: Rima McIntire
FYE: December 31
Type: Public

Tutor Perini could teach it peers a thing or two about construction. One of the largest hotel and casino builders in the US Tutor Perini also builds schools health care facilities airports and industrial buildings. The company and its subsidiaries provide pre-construction and design-build services general contracting equipment materials subcontracting and other services. Its civil arm which includes subsidiaries Tutor-Saliba Cherry Hill Construction and Lunda Construction builds and maintains highways bridges and mass transit. Tutor Perini's specialty contracting division offers services such as electrical and mechanical work. All told Tutor Perini has performed work on more than 1500 projects.

	Annual Growth	12/10	12/11	12/12	12/13	12/14
Sales ($ mil.)	8.9%	3,199.2	3,716.3	4,111.5	4,175.7	4,492.3
Net income ($ mil.)	1.1%	103.5	86.1	(265.4)	87.3	107.9
Market value ($ mil.)	3.0%	1,042.1	600.6	666.8	1,280.1	1,171.5
Employees	32.6%	3,538	5,796	11,016	10,206	10,939

TURTLE BEACH CORP

NMS: HEAR

100 Summit Lake Drive, Suite 100
Valhalla, NY 10595
Phone: 914 345-2255
Fax: –
Web: www.parametricsound.com

CEO: Juergen Stark
CFO: John T Hanson
HR: Annette Bucci
FYE: December 31
Type: Public

Using proprietary technology Turtle Beach (formerly Parametric Sound) makes speakers that offer focused and directional sound for an immersive experience. Its current product is the HS-3000 line of speakers for the commercial market including digital kiosks and slot machines. The company is developing its Hypersonic line for the consumer market where it hopes its thin two-speaker system will rival traditional multi-speaker setups used for surround sound and be used in computers video games and mobile devices. Turtle Beach sells its products in North America Asia and Europe to OEMs for inclusion in new and existing products.

	Annual Growth	09/10	09/11	09/12	09/13*	12/14
Sales ($ mil.)	318.5%	0.6	0.1	0.2	0.6	186.2
Net income ($ mil.)	–	(0.9)	(1.5)	(4.5)	(7.7)	(15.5)
Market value ($ mil.)	62.1%	–	31.5	272.8	526.6	134.1
Employees	256.2%	1	3	13	15	161

*Fiscal year change

TUTTLE-CLICK AUTOMOTIVE GROUP

41 Auto Center Dr.
Irvine CA 92618
Phone: 949-598-4800
Fax: 949-830-0980
Web: www.tuttleclick.com

CEO: –
CFO: –
HR: –
FYE: December 31
Type: Private

Despite its connections to the Republican Party Tuttle-Click Automotive Group does sell cars to Democrats. The firm operates a dozen new- and used-car dealerships throughout Orange County California and in Pima County Arizona. The firm's dealerships sell Dodge Ford Hyundai Jeep Lincoln Mazda Mercury Mitsubishi and Nissan branded cars and trucks. The company was founded by Holmes Tuttle in 1946 who sold Ronald Reagan a car and ended up a prominent GOP fundraiser; he even persuaded Reagan to run for governor of California in 1966. Tuttle's son Robert Tuttle co-managed the business with CEO James Click until he was appointed US ambassador to Great Britain in 2005.

TV GUIDE MAGAZINE LLC

11 W 42nd St.
New York NY 10036
Phone: 212-852-7500
Fax: 410-740-2985
Web: www.martekbio.com

CEO: David J Fishman
CFO: Michell Lindquist
HR: –
FYE: December 31
Type: Private

TV Guide Magazine is glued to the tube. The company publishes the weekly TV-focused print publication TV Guide. Formerly an iconic pocket-sized digest the publication was re-formatted to a standard-sized full-color magazine in 2005. TV Guide earns money through subscriptions and advertising and has a circulation of about 2 million readers. TV Guide Magazine is owned by private-equity firm OpenGate Capital which purchased the company from Macrovision Solutions Corporation (later renamed Rovi Corporation) for $1 in 2008. Macrovision loaned OpenGate $9.5 million to finance the magazine. (Other TV Guide holdings including Internet and cable TV assets were sold to movie and TV studio Lionsgate.)

TVAX BIOMEDICAL INC.

8006 Reeder St.
Lenexa KS 66214-1554
Phone: 913-492-2221
Fax: 913-492-2243
Web: www.tvaxbiomedical.com

CEO: –
CFO: Tammie Wahaus
HR: –
FYE: December 31
Type: Private

TVAX may be a clever play on the company's methods but it is completely serious about killing cancer. TVAX Biomedical uses cancer cell vaccination and the introduction of killer T cells to treat cancer. Its TVAX Immunotherapy uses a process of injecting a patient with their own irradiated cancer cells producing a cancer-specific T cell immune response. The company then harvests those cells from the patient's blood turns them into killer T cells and re-injects them. The patient's own immune system does the rest killing the cancer cells and cancer stem cells which are normally resistant to treatment methods. TVAX whose lead candidates attack brain and kidney cancer withdrew its IPO in May 2012.

TW TELECOM INC

NMS: TWTC

10475 Park Meadows Drive
Littleton, CO 80124
Phone: 303 566-1000
Fax: –
Web: www.twtelecom.com

CEO: Larissa L Herda
CFO: Mark A Peters
HR: –
FYE: December 31
Type: Public

tw telecom may opt for lowercase branding but there is nothing diminutive about its ambitions in the US communications industry. Serving 75 metropolitan markets in about 30 states the company provides data networking and Internet access as well as local and long-distance voice services voice over Internet Protocol (VoIP) and other communications services to midsized and large telecom-intensive businesses in such industries as health care finance manufacturing and hospitality. Additionally tw telecom serves local state and federal government organizations and provides wholesale services to other communications carriers and ISPs.

	Annual Growth	12/08	12/09	12/10	12/11	12/12
Sales ($ mil.)	6.1%	1,159.0	1,211.4	1,273.2	1,366.9	1,470.3
Net income ($ mil.)	73.3%	8.5	27.6	271.4	57.9	76.9
Market value ($ mil.)	31.7%	1,282.3	2,596.5	2,581.3	2,934.1	3,856.1
Employees	2.6%	2,844	2,870	2,975	3,051	3,147

TWENTY-FIRST CENTURY FOX INC

NMS: FOXA

1211 Avenue of the Americas
New York, NY 10036
Phone: 212 852-7000
Fax: –
Web: www.21cf.com

CEO: James R. Murdoch
CFO: John P. Nallen
HR: –
FYE: June 30
Type: Public

This media company is crazy like a fox. Twenty-First Century Fox (formerly known as News Corporation) owns and operates a portfolio of cable broadcast film pay television and satellite assets spanning the globe. The company's massive portfolio of cable and broadcasting networks and properties includes FOX FX Fox News Fox Business Network Fox Sports National Geographic Channels Fox Pan America Sports MundoFox STAR and 28 local television stations; film studio Twentieth Century Fox Film; and television production studios Twentieth Century Fox Television and Shine Group.

	Annual Growth	06/11	06/12	06/13	06/14	06/15
Sales ($ mil.)	(3.5%)	33,405.0	33,706.0	27,675.0	31,867.0	28,987.0
Net income ($ mil.)	32.0%	2,739.0	1,179.0	7,097.0	4,514.0	8,306.0
Market value ($ mil.)	16.4%	36,081.3	45,438.0	66,414.1	71,653.0	66,342.7
Employees	(20.4%)	51,000	48,000	25,600	27,000	20,500

TWIN DISC INCORPORATED

NMS: TWIN

1328 Racine Street
Racine, WI 53403
Phone: 262 638-4000
Fax: 262 638-4481
Web: www.twindisc.com

CEO: John H. Batten
CFO: Jeffery S. Knutson
HR: Denise L. Wilcox
FYE: June 30
Type: Public

Twin Disc makes heavy-duty power transmission equipment for the marine and off-highway vehicle markets. Its lineup includes marine transmissions propellers and boat management systems power-shift transmissions hydraulic torque converters and industrial clutches and control systems. Applications for Twin Disc's products include yachts and other pleasure craft and construction and military vehicles. The company also serves the energy and natural resources and industrial markets. Twin Disc markets its products through both a direct sales force and a distributor network; about 60% of its sales are made outside the US.

	Annual Growth	06/11	06/12	06/13	06/14	06/15
Sales ($ mil.)	(3.8%)	310.4	355.9	285.3	263.9	265.8
Net income ($ mil.)	(12.2%)	18.8	26.1	3.9	3.6	11.2
Market value ($ mil.)	(16.7%)	435.3	208.3	267.0	372.4	210.0
Employees	(0.5%)	941	1,029	990	970	921

TWITTER INC

NYS: TWTR

1355 Market Street, Suite 900
San Francisco, CA 94103
Phone: 415 222-9670
Fax: –
Web: www.twitter.com

CEO: Jack Dorsey
CFO: Anthony Noto
HR: –
FYE: December 31
Type: Public

Nearly the whole world is following this company. Twitter operates a free digital service site that blends social networking with the ability to post short messages (or micro-blogs) limited to 140 characters or less commonly known by users as "Tweets." Twitter's service works equally well on personal computers mobile devices and smartphones. The service has become a key communication platform as major events unfold live in real-time around the world. Currently Twitter claims more than 300 million users worldwide. Founded in 2006 Twitter went public in 2013 raising about $1.82 billion in the process.

	Annual Growth	12/10	12/11	12/12	12/13	12/14
Sales ($ mil.)	165.4%	28.3	106.3	316.9	664.9	1,403.0
Net income ($ mil.)	–	(67.3)	(128.3)	(79.4)	(645.3)	(577.8)
Market value ($ mil.)	(43.6%)	–	–	–	40,887.8	23,042.4
Employees	25.8%	–	–	2,300	2,712	3,638

TWO HARBORS INVESTMENT CORP

NYS: TWO

590 Madison Avenue, 36th Floor
New York, NY 10022
Phone: 612 629-2500
Fax: –
Web: www.twoharborsinvestment.com

CEO: Thomas E Siering
CFO: Brad Farrell
HR: –
FYE: December 31
Type: Public

Two Harbors Investment Corp. is ready to double its money. The real estate investment trust (REIT) is managed and advised by (and was founded by) PRCM Advisers a subsidiary of Pine River Capital Management. The trust primarily invests in agency residential mortgage-backed securities (RMBS) with fixed or adjustable interest rates that are backed by government-supported enterprises Fannie Mae Freddie Mac or Ginnie Mae. About a quarter of its mortgage portfolio is made up of non-agency RMBS such as subprime mortgages which carry more risk than federally-backed securities but offer higher yields. Chairman (and Pine River CEO) Brian Taylor controls almost 20% of the trust's stock.

	Annual Growth	12/10	12/11	12/12	12/13	12/14
Sales ($ mil.)	63.5%	47.1	173.0	368.1	846.7	336.4
Net income ($ mil.)	47.0%	35.8	127.4	291.9	579.0	167.1
Market value ($ mil.)	0.6%	3,587.0	3,385.5	4,059.7	3,400.2	3,671.3
Employees	–	–	–	–	–	–

TWO RIVER BANCORP

NMS: TRCB

766 Shrewsbury Avenue
Tinton Falls, NJ 07724
Phone: 732 389-8722
Fax: –
Web: www.tworiverbank.com

CEO: –
CFO: Richard Abrahamian
HR: Nicole Nielsen
FYE: December 31
Type: Public

Community Partners Bancorp is the holding company for Two River Community Bank and The Town Bank (a division of Two River). Through more than a dozen total branches located in eastern New Jersey the two banks offer deposit services like checking and savings accounts as well as a variety of lending services to consumers and small to midsized businesses. The banks' combined loan portfolio consists mainly of commercial real estate loans (about 40%) commercial and industrial loans (25%) and construction loans (20%). Consumer and residential loans make up only about 10% of the portfolio. Two River's branches are located in Middletown while Town Bank's are located in Westfield and Cranford.

	Annual Growth	12/10	12/11	12/12	12/13	12/14
Assets ($ mil.)	5.2%	636.8	674.6	733.9	769.7	781.2
Net income ($ mil.)	13.6%	3.6	4.3	4.8	5.2	6.0
Market value ($ mil.)	15.7%	37.3	37.7	44.4	57.2	66.9
Employees	(2.5%)	156	143	141	143	141

TYCO FIRE & SECURITY LLC

1501 Yamato Rd
Boca Raton FL 33431
Phone: 561-988-7200
Fax: 513-851-2057
Web: www.rumpke.com

CEO: –
CFO: –
HR: –
FYE: September 30
Type: Subsidiary

Tyco Fire & Security takes a global approach to minimizing risk. A subsidiary of Tyco International the company designs sells installs and monitors electronic security systems and services to more than 7 million residential commercial industrial and government customers worldwide. It operates in North America and has a presence in Africa Asia Australia Europe and South America. The company's security systems are primarily marketed under the ADT and Sensormatic brands and are designed to detect intrusion as well as react to hazards such as fire smoke flooding and other environmental conditions.

TYLER TECHNOLOGIES, INC.

NYS: TYL

5101 Tennyson Parkway
Plano, TX 75024
Phone: 972 713-3700
Fax: –
Web: www.tylertech.com

CEO: John S. Marr
CFO: Brian K. Miller
HR: –
FYE: December 31
Type: Public

Tyler Technologies doesn't want local governments tied up in red tape. The company provides software and services intended to help state and local government offices operate more efficiently. Specializing in applications for local governments and public schools Tyler's products include software for accounting and financial management filing court documents electronically tracking and managing court cases and automating appraisals and assessments. Other products include applications that allow citizens to access utility accounts or pay traffic fines online. Tyler complements its software with hosting support and maintenance services. The company counts more than 13000 government and school customers in all 50 states Canada the Caribbean and the UK.

	Annual Growth	12/10	12/11	12/12	12/13	12/14
Sales ($ mil.)	14.3%	288.6	309.4	363.3	416.6	493.1
Net income ($ mil.)	23.8%	25.1	27.6	33.0	39.1	58.9
Market value ($ mil.)	51.5%	694.8	1,007.8	1,621.2	3,418.2	3,662.9
Employees	8.6%	2,054	2,091	2,388	2,573	2,856

TYMCO INC.

225 E. Industrial Blvd.
Waco TX 76705
Phone: 254-799-5546
Fax: 254-799-2722
Web: www.tymco.com

CEO: –
CFO: –
HR: –
FYE: August 31
Type: Private

TYMCO doesn't have to sweep anything under the rug. The company makes regenerative air sweepers used to clean roadways runways and related surfaces. TYMCO's patented regenerative air system is designed to prevent pollutants leaving the vehicle's hopper once they have been swept from the pavement. Some sweeper models can run on alternative fuels such as compressed natural gas or liquefied petroleum gas. TYMCO sells worldwide through dealers. Construction executive B. W. Young founded the company in the late 1960s; it is owned and run by members of his family including sons Kenneth (president) and Gary (VP). TYMCO is an acronym for The Young Manufacturing Company.

TYNDALE HOUSE PUBLISHERS INC.

351 EXECUTIVE DR
CAROL STREAM, IL 601882420
Phone: 630-668-8300
Fax: –
Web: www.tyndale.com

CEO: Mark Taylor
CFO: –
HR: –
FYE: April 30
Type: Private

Christian-focused publisher Tyndale House Publishers publishes fiction nonfiction and children's books as well as bibles. One of its best-selling titles is the novel Left Behind a fictional account of the apocalypse written by Jerry B. Jenkins. The titles success inspired the Left Behind series of novels which has sole some 63 million copies as well as Left Behind comic books music and three movies. Tyndale House was founded in 1962 by Kenneth N. Taylor who wrote The Living Bible in order to translate the old English in the King James Version of the Bible into a more accessible language for his children. Taylor who died in 2005 named the company after 16th Century English translator William Tyndale.

	Annual Growth	04/10	04/11	04/12	04/13	04/14
Sales ($ mil.)	(3.5%)	–	79.3	73.8	70.6	71.2
Net income ($ mil.)	(16.4%)	–	–	4.5	3.2	3.1
Market value ($ mil.)	–	–	–	–	–	–
Employees	–	–	–	–	–	259

TYR SPORT INC.

15391 Springdale Ave.
Huntington Beach CA 92649
Phone: 714-897-0799
Fax: 714-897-6420
Web: www.tyr.com

CEO: Steve Furniss
CFO: –
HR: –
FYE: June 30
Type: Subsidiary

TYR (pronounced tier) Sport wants to ensure that swimmers are well suited for water play and sport. The company designs and makes men's women's and youth swimwear and related gear for professional athletes as well as for recreational use. TYR is named after the Norse god of warriors and athletes. The firm's Aqua Shift technology is said to reduce wave drag by 10% and is worn by such swimmers as double Olympic gold medalist and eight-time world champion Yana Klochkova and Olympic silver medalist and US record holder Erik Vendt. Parent company Swimwear Anywhere is the second-largest branded swimwear manufacturer in North America behind Speedo maker Warnaco Swimwear.

TYSON FOODS, INC.

NYS: TSN

2200 West Don Tyson Parkway
Springdale, AR 72762-6999
Phone: 479 290-4000
Fax: 479 290-7984
Web: www.tyson.com

CEO: Donnie Smith
CFO: Dennis Leatherby
HR: Mary A. Oleksiuk
FYE: October 03
Type: Public

Tyson is more than simply chicken. One of the largest US chicken producers Tyson's Fresh Meats division makes it a giant in the beef and pork sectors as well. The company also offers value-added processed and pre-cooked meats and refrigerated and frozen prepared foods. Its chicken operations are vertically integrated — the company hatches the eggs supplies contract growers with the chicks and feed and brings them back for processing when ready. Tyson's brands include Tyson Jimmy Dean Hillshire Farm Sara Lee Ball Park Wright Aidells and State Fair. Its customers include retail wholesale and food service customers worldwide.

	Annual Growth	10/11*	09/12	09/13	09/14*	10/15
Sales ($ mil.)	6.4%	32,266.0	33,278.0	34,374.0	37,580.0	41,373.0
Net income ($ mil.)	12.9%	750.0	583.0	778.0	864.0	1,220.0
Market value ($ mil.)	26.5%	6,405.8	5,911.4	10,553.4	13,926.1	16,379.9
Employees	(0.4%)	115,000	115,000	115,000	124,000	113,000

*Fiscal year change

TYSON FRESH MEATS INC.

800 Stevens Port Dr.
Dakota Dunes SD 57049
Phone: 605 235 2061
Fax: 605-235-2068
Web: www.tyson.com/corporate/b2b/freshmeats

CEO: –
CFO: –
HR: Craig J Hart
FYE: September 30
Type: Subsidiary

No matter how you slice it steak is the main attraction at Tyson Fresh Meats. A processor of beef and pork Tyson slaughters and sells fresh beef and pork and case-ready ground beef and pork products. Its offerings are sold under brand names including Chairman's Reserve Beef and Supreme Tender Pork to mostly US food retailers foodservice operators and meat processors. Tyson does not raise cattle but has buyers who purchase livestock on the open market. It has swine buyers as well; however it does raise some pigs. Non-edible animal remains are processed and sold to manufacturers of animal feed leather and pharmaceuticals. Tyson Fresh Meats is a subsidiary of chicken and meat producer Tyson Foods.

U G N INC

18410 CROSSING DR STE C
TINLEY PARK, IL 604876209
Phone: 773-437-2400
Fax: –
Web: www.ugnauto.com

CEO: –
CFO: Randy Khalaf
HR: Eric Kerkhoff
FYE: December 31
Type: Private

Buying a Japanese car? Sounds good. Especially if the vehicle has acoustic molding and other sound-dampening acoustic automotive trim products made by UGN. The company produces molding from a variety of materials including cotton fiber and foam for vehicles assembled in North America by US and Japanese auto makers. UGN also makes automotive interior trim and thermal management parts. Its products are used to reduce interior noise and fine tune acoustical signals. The company's clientele has included such heavy hitters as Honda Nissan and Toyota. UGN was established in 1986 and is a joint venture between Autoneum and Nihon Tokushu Toryo (Nittoku).

	Annual Growth	12/04	12/05	12/06	12/07	12/08
Sales ($ mil.)	1.7%	–	213.9	223.1	239.0	225.0
Net income ($ mil.)	(6.6%)	–	–	13.1	0.0	11.4
Market value ($ mil.)	–	–	–	–	–	–
Employees	–	–	–	–	–	1,250

U S CHINA MINING GROUP INC.

NBB: SGZH

15310 Amberly Drive, Suite 250
Tampa, FL 33647
Phone: 813 514-2873
Fax: –
Web: www.uschinamining.com

CEO: Hongwen LI
CFO: Xinyu Peng
HR: –
FYE: December 31
Type: Public

It's a cold coal world for U.S. China Mining Group. The company operates three coal mines in Heilongjiang Province the northeastern-most part of China. Its three mines — Tong Gong Hong Yuan and Sheng Yu — produce almost 1 million tons of coal a year. The group sells its coal to power plants cement factories wholesalers and individuals for home heating. Three customers account for the majority of sales — Heilongjiang QiQiHaEr Huadian Power Plants Co. Ltd. accounted for 60% in 2010; Heilongjiang Beihai Logistics Company and Changchun Rail Transportation Co. Ltd. together accounted for another 30%. Chairman Guoqing Yue owns a third of the company's stock.

	Annual Growth	12/09	12/10	12/11	12/12	12/13
Sales ($ mil.)	(53.6%)	65.0	69.0	54.0	30.9	3.0
Net income ($ mil.)	–	25.1	13.4	15.2	(31.2)	(7.7)
Market value ($ mil.)	(68.5%)	152.9	119.9	20.7	7.2	1.5
Employees	(38.8%)	655	1,017	1,186	91	92

U-SWIRL INC.

NBB: SWRL

265 Turner Dr.
Durango, CO 81303
Phone: 702 586-8700
Fax: –

CEO: Bryan J Merryman
CFO: Jeremy M Kinney
HR: –
FYE: February 28
Type: Public

This company hopes to have customers circling its frozen yogurt shops. U-Swirl (formerly Healthy Fast Food) operates and franchises a small number of U-SWIRL Frozen Yogurt outlets. The chain offers non-fat frozen yogurt treats available with more than 60 different toppings. U-SWIRL locations operate primarily in Nevada. In addition to its yogurt franchising business U-Swirl operates two franchised hamburger outlets under the EVOS banner. Before changing its name to U-Swirl in 2011 Healthy Fast Food acquired the global development rights to the U-SWIRL Frozen Yogurt concept in 2008. U-Swirl plans to build the chain through franchising.

	Annual Growth	12/11	12/12*	02/13	02/14	02/15
Sales ($ mil.)	29.9%	2.6	2.8	0.6	5.5	7.5
Net income ($ mil.)	–	(0.7)	(0.5)	(0.4)	(2.1)	(0.3)
Market value ($ mil.)	7.6%	6.5	4.4	8.1	18.5	8.7
Employees	18.2%	40	80	88	117	78

*Fiscal year change

U. S. SUGAR CORPORATION

111 Ponce de Leon Ave.
Clewiston FL 33440
Phone: 863-983-8121
Fax: 863-983-9827
Web: www.ussugar.com

CEO: Robert H Buker Jr
CFO: Gerard A Bernard
HR: –
FYE: December 31
Type: Private

U.S. Sugar is tangy and sweet. The company is a top US cane sugar maker and citrus grower. It produces up to 700000 tons of sugar a year nearly 8% of the nation's supply. U.S. Sugar farms about 180000 acres of sugarcane in South Florida; it's sold to baked-goods ice-cream and other food manufacturers as well as to food retailers. The company also makes citrus molasses used by distillers and as a feed supplement for cattle. Its subsidiary Southern Gardens Citrus (SGC) is one of the largest suppliers of not-from-concentrate orange juice in the US. SGC farms 16500 acres of orange groves producing more than 100 million gallons of orange juice annually. U.S Sugar was formed in 1931.

U.R.M. STORES INC.

7511 N FREYA ST
SPOKANE, WA 992178043
Phone: 509-467-3619
Fax: –
Web: www.urmstores.com

CEO: –
CFO: Laurie Bigej
HR: Linda Wilson
FYE: August 02
Type: Private

URM Stores is a leading wholesale food distribution cooperative serving more than 160 grocery stores in the Northwest. Its member-owner stores operate under a variety of banners including Family Foods Harvest Foods Super 1 Foods Trading Co. Stores and Yoke's Fresh Market. It also owns the Rosauers Supermarkets chain. In addition to grocery stores URM supplies 1500-plus restaurants hotels and convenience stores; it also offers such services as merchandising store development consulting and technology purchasing. The cooperative was founded in 1921 as United Retail Merchants. The business is privately owned by its members.

	Annual Growth	07/04	07/05	07/06	07/07*	08/08
Sales ($ mil.)	(22.7%)	–	–	1,562.9	859.9	932.8
Net income ($ mil.)	15808.9%	–	–	0.0	7.2	8.8
Market value ($ mil.)	–	–	–	–	–	–
Employees	–	–	–	–	–	2,100

*Fiscal year change

U.S. AUTO PARTS NETWORK INC

NMS: PRTS

16941 Keegan Avenue
Carson, CA 90746
Phone: 310 735-0085
Fax: –
Web: www.usautoparts.net

CEO: Shane Evangelist
CFO: Neil Watanabe
HR: –
FYE: January 03
Type: Public

U.S. Auto Parts Network puts its customers in the fast lane. The company offers about 1.5 million aftermarket auto parts for all makes and models of domestic and foreign cars and trucks. Its inventory includes replacement performance body and engine parts as well as accessories (such as seat covers alarms). U.S. Auto Parts also sells products for motorcycles all-terrain vehicles and RVs. The company generates the bulk of its revenue online; a retail store in Illinois and mail-order catalogs also bring in sales. The company ships parts to about 150 countries. It also distributes a private-label line of mirrors to auto parts stores nationwide and runs a wholesale program for body shops in Southern California.

	Annual Growth	01/11*	12/11	12/12	12/13*	01/15
Sales ($ mil.)	2.0%	262.3	327.1	304.0	254.8	283.5
Net income ($ mil.)	–	(13.9)	(15.1)	(36.0)	(15.6)	(6.9)
Market value ($ mil.)	(28.3%)	282.4	146.9	62.2	84.4	74.6
Employees	(11.6%)	1,612	1,521	1,370	1,032	983

*Fiscal year change

U.S. BANCORP (DE)

NYS: USB

800 Nicollet Mall
Minneapolis, MN 55402
Phone: 651 466-3000
Fax: –
Web: www.usbank.com

CEO: Pamela A. (Pam) Joseph
CFO: Kathleen A. (Kathy) Rogers
HR: Jennie P. Carlson
FYE: December 31
Type: Public

Not quite a bank for the entire US U.S. Bancorp is nonetheless one of the largest bank holding companies in the nation with $403 billion in assets. It owns U.S. Bank (the US' 5th largest commercial bank) and other subsidiaries that provide consumer and commercial loans deposits and credit cards as well as merchant processing mortgage banking trust and investment management brokerage services insurance and corporate payments. The bank has more than 3000 branches and 5000 ATMs in 25 states in the Midwest and West including one of the most extensive networks of branches inside grocery stores. Commercial loans account for roughly 30% of its total loan portfolio; commercial real estate loans 17%.

	Annual Growth	12/10	12/11	12/12	12/13	12/14
Assets ($ mil.)	6.9%	307,786.0	340,122.0	353,855.0	364,021.0	402,529.0
Net income ($ mil.)	15.2%	3,317.0	4,872.0	5,647.0	5,836.0	5,851.0
Market value ($ mil.)	13.6%	48,164.8	48,307.7	57,040.6	72,149.0	80,274.7
Employees	2.5%	60,584	62,529	64,486	65,565	66,750

U.S. CENTRAL FEDERAL CREDIT UNION

9701 Renner Blvd. Ste. 100
Lenexa KS 66219
Phone: 913-227-6000
Fax: 913-227-6250
Web: www.uscentral.coop

CEO: Francis Lee
CFO: –
HR: –
FYE: December 31
Type: Private - Cooperativ

U.S. Central Federal Credit Union is a cooperative "central bank" for a network of about 30 corporate credit unions. These in turn represent approximately 8000 credit unions nationwide. U.S. Central performs a variety of liquidity and cash management functions such as funds transfer settlement services risk management and custody services. Subsidiary CU Investment Solutions provides investment advisory and brokerage services to the corporate credit unions while its majority-owned Corporate Network eCom offers bill payment and technology services to the network and its members. U.S. Central Federal Credit Union was seized and placed in conservatorship by federal regulators in 2009.

U.S. CONCRETE, INC.

NAS: USCR

331 N. Main Street
Euless, TX 76039
Phone: 817 835-4105
Fax: –

CEO: William J. (Bill) Sandbrook
CFO: Joseph C. (Jody) Tusa
HR: –
FYE: December 31
Type: Public

When things get hard U.S. Concrete's products get even harder. The company produces ready-mixed concrete precast concrete and related materials and services for commercial residential and infrastructure construction projects. U.S. Concrete has a fleet of about 940 mixer trucks and about 120 ready-mixed concrete concrete block and 10 aggregate plants. During 2013 the company produced some 5.2 million cu. yd. of concrete and more than 3.5 million tons of aggregates; concrete accounts for about 90% of the company's sales. U.S. Concrete concentrates on major markets such as California New Jersey/New York and Texas.

	Annual Growth	12/10	12/11	12/12	12/13	12/14
Sales ($ mil.)	46.5%	152.9	495.0	531.0	615.0	703.7
Net income ($ mil.)	–	(5.8)	(11.7)	(25.7)	(20.1)	20.6
Market value ($ mil.)	38.8%	107.1	40.5	126.5	316.3	397.7
Employees	2.0%	1,983	1,895	1,854	1,786	2,144

U.S. ENERGY CORP.

NAS: USEG

877 North 8th West
Riverton, WY 82501
Phone: 307 856-9271
Fax: –
Web: www.usnrg.com

CEO: David A. Veltri
CFO: Steven D Richmond
HR: –
FYE: December 31
Type: Public

U.S. Energy (USE) has put its energy in many places including oil and gas exploration and production geothermal energy projects and molybdenum mining. It operates oil and gas wells on the coast of the Gulf of Mexico and in Texas. The company bought a quarter stake in Standard Steam Trust in 2008 giving USE entry into the geothermal energy market. It also is developing a molybdenum mining project in Colorado. U.S. Energy has an agreement with Thompson Creek Metals to fund development of the project. The company had owned almost half of Sutter Gold Mining but sold most of its stake in the gold miner in 2008.

	Annual Growth	12/10	12/11	12/12	12/13	12/14
Sales ($ mil.)	4.5%	27.2	30.1	32.5	33.6	32.4
Net income ($ mil.)	–	(0.8)	(4.8)	(11.2)	(7.4)	(2.1)
Market value ($ mil.)	(29.8%)	170.5	81.6	42.1	105.5	41.5
Employees	(7.4%)	19	19	15	15	14

U.S. FRANCHISE SYSTEMS INC.

13 Corporate Sq. Ste. 250
Atlanta GA 30329
Phone: 404-321-4045
Fax: 404-321-4482
Web: www.usfsi.com

CEO: –
CFO: –
HR: –
FYE: December 31
Type: Subsidiary

Whether you're feeling frugal or longing for luxury U.S. Franchise Systems has a room for you. The company franchises some 400 economy and upper-end hotels in Argentina Canada Honduras Israel Mexico the Philippines and the US. Its brands include Microtel Inn & Suites (limited-service budget hotels) and Hawthorn Suites (upscale extended-stay hotels that offer kitchens exercise facilities and other apartment-like features). Founded in 1995 by former president and CEO Mark Leven U.S. Franchise Systems was acquired by Wyndham Worldwide in 2008.

U.S. GLOBAL INVESTORS, INC.

NAS: GROW

7900 Callaghan Road
San Antonio, TX 78229-1234
Phone: 210 308-1234
Fax: –
Web: www.usfunds.com

CEO: Frank E Holmes
CFO: Lisa C Callicotte
HR: –
FYE: June 30
Type: Public

While it may be a small world financial investment company U.S. Global Investors wants to make it a little greener after all. Primarily serving the U.S. Global Investors Funds and the U.S. Global Accolade Funds the company is a mutual fund manager providing investment advisory transfer agency broker-dealer and mailing services. It offers a family of no-load mutual funds generally geared toward long-term investing. The company also engages in corporate investment activities. U.S. Global Investors had about $724 million in assets under management in 2015.

	Annual Growth	06/11	06/12	06/13	06/14	06/15
Sales ($ mil.)	(31.2%)	41.9	23.9	18.7	11.4	9.4
Net income ($ mil.)	–	7.8	1.5	(0.2)	(1.0)	(4.0)
Market value ($ mil.)	(21.2%)	110.9	67.2	32.5	54.1	42.8
Employees	(16.9%)	88	74	68	52	42

U.S. LEGAL SUPPORT INC.

363 N. Sam Houston Pkwy East Ste. 900
Houston TX 77060-4001
Phone: 713-653-7100
Fax: 713-653-7171
Web: www.uslegalsupport.com

CEO: Charles F Schugart
CFO: Beth Bruce
HR: –
FYE: December 31
Type: Private

This company ensures that everyone in the courtroom gets what they need. U.S. Legal Support offers — surprise surprise — legal support services including court reporting records retrieval and legal personnel placement. The Dine Group its dedicated staffing department places both permanent and temporary legal personnel from paralegals to partners. It staffs attorneys with expertise in such practice areas as antitrust asset management banking bankruptcy real estate securities health care and environmental legislation. U.S. Legal Support operates nationally through its network of more than 35 offices across four US states.

U.S. NEWS & WORLD REPORT L.P.

450 W. 33rd St. 11th Fl.
New York NY 10001
Phone: 212-716-6800
Fax: 212-643-7842
Web: www.usnews.com

CEO: Mortimer B Zuckerman
CFO: –
HR: –
FYE: January 31
Type: Private

This company can report first hand: The news on traditional print journalism in the US is pretty grim. U.S. News & World Report was once the publisher of a print news magazine of the same name; today its content is available online only with special printed issues. USNews.com focuses on topics such as politics and policy education and health. In recent years the company has found more luck in print with its signature America's Best annual series of books that ranks institutions and services such as colleges hospitals and mutual funds. The magazine was founded in 1933 as United States News. Real estate and media tycoon Mort Zuckerman (co-owner of the New York Daily News) has owned the company since 1984.

U.S. PHYSICAL THERAPY, INC.

NYS: USPH

1300 West Sam Houston Parkway South, Suite 300
Houston, TX 77042
Phone: 713 297-7000
Fax: –
Web: www.corporate.usph.com

CEO: Christopher J. (Chris) Reading
CFO: Lawrance W (Larry) McAfee
HR: –
FYE: December 31
Type: Public

U.S. Physical Therapy (USPh) through its subsidiaries lends a hand to injured workers athletes and others in need of some TLC. With more than 500 outpatient clinics in more than 40 states USPh provides physical therapy services for work-related and sports injuries trauma orthopedic conditions osteoarthritis treatment and post-surgical rehabilitation. The clinics operate under a number of local or regional brands including Red River Valley Physical Therapy Pioneer Physical Therapy Bluegrass Physical Therapy and Apex Rehabilitation Center.

	Annual Growth	12/10	12/11	12/12	12/13	12/14
Sales ($ mil.)	9.6%	211.2	237.0	252.1	264.1	305.1
Net income ($ mil.)	7.4%	15.6	21.0	17.9	12.7	20.9
Market value ($ mil.)	20.6%	243.2	241.5	338.0	432.7	515.0
Employees	7.7%	2,338	2,522	2,677	2,805	3,151

U.S. ROBOTICS CORPORATION

1300 E. Woodfield Rd. Ste. 506
Schaumburg IL 60173-5446
Phone: 847-874-2000
Fax: 847-874-2001
Web: www.usr.com

CEO: –
CFO: Kevin Pfau
HR: –
FYE: December 31
Type: Private

U.S. Robotics keeps collecting connections. The company provides internal and external modems card reader/writers hubs adapters and cables for businesses and consumers. It also offers VoIP phones with Skype-compatible technology. The company has designed modems that utilize the V.92 standard a technology that allows faster data transfer than that of standard 56K modems. In addition to dial-up modems U.S. Robotics offers Ethernet modems as well as broadband and DSL routers. Other products include USR Call Director which connects telephone lines with modems Point of Sale units and faxes. U.S. Robotics is owned by Platinum Equity a private equity buyout firm.

U.S. SILICA HOLDINGS INC.

NYSE: SLCA

8490 Progress Dr. Ste. 300
Frederick MD 21701
Phone: 800-345-6170
Fax: 304-258-8295
Web: www.u-s-silica.com

CEO: –
CFO: Donald Merril
HR: –
FYE: December 31
Type: Public

Life's a beach for the sand-sellers at U.S. Silica. The industrial mineral company provides silica and aplite for the glass foundry chemical and construction industries; and fine ground silica and kaolin clay used to make paint plastics and ceramics. Its "frac sand" product — currently its fastest-growing offering — is used by natural gas and oil producers in hydraulic fracturing a process to boost oil and gas production. The company supplies customers in the US and Canada. In addition to its main facility in West Virginia U S. Silica also has a dozen plants in the East. A portfolio holding of private equity firm Golden Gate Capital U.S. Silica filed to go public in 2011.

U.S. TELEPACIFIC CORP.

515 S. Flower St. 47th Fl.
Los Angeles CA 90071
Phone: 213-213-3000
Fax: 213-666-9680
Web: www.telepacific.com

CEO: Richard A Jalkut
CFO: Timothy Medina
HR: –
FYE: December 31
Type: Private

U.S. TelePacific (also known as TelePacific Communications) is a facilities-based competitive local-exchange carrier (CLEC) offering local and long-distance phone service as well as dedicated Internet access private networking data colocation and other data services to business customers primarily in California. The company also provides network services to other carriers on a wholesale basis. It operates from 40 regional offices in areas of California and Nevada including Las Vegas Los Angeles Orange County Sacramento and San Diego. Chairman David Glickman founded TelePacific in 1998. Investors in the company are led by Clarity Partners and Investcorp (which owns more than one quarter).

U.S. VENTURE INC.

425 BETTER WAY
APPLETON, WI 549156192
Phone: 920-739-6101
Fax: –
Web: www.usventure.com

CEO: –
CFO: Jay Walters
HR: Lori Hoersch
FYE: July 31
Type: Private

Smitten with the love of oil distribution the founding Schmidt family owns and operates U.S. Venture (formerly U.S. Oil). The company's U.S. Oil division (formerly U.S. Petroleum Operations) supplies refined oil products to residents in the Midwest and does a lot more. In addition to the wholesale distribution of oil products (its largest revenue generator) the company operates gas stations and installs gas pumps tanks and other petroleum-related equipment. U.S. Venture also provides plumbing and HVAC services (Design Air) collects used waste oil to be processed into burner fuel and has a metal custom manufacturing unit.

	Annual Growth	07/10	07/11	07/12	07/13	07/14
Sales ($ mil.)	23.3%	–	4,847.8	5,906.9	7,346.1	9,088.9
Net income ($ mil.)	(9.8%)	–	–	60.6	47.2	49.3
Market value ($ mil.)	–	–	–	–	–	–
Employees	–	–	–	–	–	1,000

U.S. VISION INC.

1 Harmon Dr. Glen Oaks Industrial Park
Glendora NJ 08029
Phone: 856-228-1000
Fax: 856-228-3339
Web: www.usvision.com

CEO: –
CFO: Carmen J Nepa III
HR: Busayo Ola Ajayi
FYE: January 31
Type: Subsidiary

U.S. Vision sees its future in stores. A subsidiary of Refac Optical Group U.S. Vision has about 700 licensed and company-owned optical centers that operate in major department stores (such as Macy's J. C. Penney) and discount outlets (BJ's Wholesale Club) in the US and Canada. Products include prescription eyewear sunglasses designer frames and contact lenses (contacts are also sold online via jcpenneyoptical.com). U.S. Vision runs its own optical laboratory distribution and lens-grinding facilities to fill orders. In 2011 parent Refac Optical was taken over by private equity firm ACON Investments and members of the management team.

UAB HIGHLANDS HOSPITAL

1201 11th Ave. South
Birmingham AL 35205-3423
Phone: 205-930-7000
Fax: 205-930-7141
Web: www.uabhealth.org/12659

CEO: –
CFO: –
HR: Alan Sconiers
FYE: December 31
Type: Private

UAB Highlands Hospital provides medical services in the Highlands of Alabama. The facility is a general acute-care hospital with nearly 220 licensed beds and 20 operating rooms. Community-based doctors and physicians affiliated with the University of Alabama at Birmingham (UAB) provide many of the hospital's services which include cardiology orthopedics oncology urology and internal medicine. It also operates specialty centers for pain treatment sleep disorders and workplace injury rehabilitation. The medical center is located in downtown Birmingham Alabama near the UAB campus and is part of the UAB Health System.

UBS FINANCIAL SERVICES INC.

1285 Avenue of the Americas
New York NY 10019
Phone: 212-713-2000
Fax: 813-283-7008
Web: www.checkers.com

CEO: Sergio P Ermotti
CFO: Regina A Dolan
HR: –
FYE: December 31
Type: Subsidiary

UBS Financial Services represents the US business of UBS's Wealth Management Americas segment. The broker-dealer offers an array of investment products and services to affluent clients with more than $250000 to invest. Its offerings include banking services stocks bonds mutual funds insurance estate planning philanthropic advice and access to alternative investments such as hedge funds. The company even offers investment services for art lovers and administers employee stock option plans for corporations. UBS Financial Services has a network of some 7000 financial advisors across the US Puerto Rico and Canada. It has more than CHF 709 billion of assets under management.

UC HEALTH

3200 BURNET AVE
CINCINNATI, OH 45229-3019
Phone: 513-585-6000
Fax: –
Web: www.uchealth.com

CEO: James Kingsbury
CFO: –
HR: –
FYE: June 30
Type: Private

UC Health is Cincinnati's scholarly health care provider. The medical provider is a partnership between the University of Cincinnati the 480-bed University of Cincinnati Medical Center and the University of Cincinnati Physicians organization. Additionally UC Health is home to the 160-bed West Chester Hospital (a full-service community hospital) the Drake Center long-term acute care (rehabilitation) hospital the UC Health Surgical Hospital and the Lindner Center of HOPE (mental health services). Specialized services include cancer cardiovascular neuroscience and metabolic disease treatment. The not-for-profit UC Health was formed in 1994.

	Annual Growth	06/07	06/08	06/09	06/10	06/11
Sales ($ mil.)	(10.7%)	–	205.0	102.5	138.5	146.1
Net income ($ mil.)	(37.8%)	–	59.9	0.0	(81.4)	14.4
Market value ($ mil.)	–	–	–	–	–	–
Employees	–	–	–	–	–	13,000

UCARE MINNESOTA

500 Stinson Blvd. NE
Minneapolis MN 55413
Phone: 612-676-6500
Fax: 612-676-6501
Web: www.ucare.org

CEO: –
CFO: Beth Monsrud
HR: Maria A Fonseca
FYE: December 31
Type: Private - Not-for-Pr

I care you care we all care for... Minnesota! UCare Minnesota is one of the largest health plan providers in Minnesota with some 220000 members scattered throughout the Land of 10000 Lakes and in several counties in western Wisconsin. The not-for-profit specializes in health coverage for members of government-funded programs such as Medicare and Medicaid; it also has plans for participants in MinnesotaCare a state-subsidized insurance program for residents unable to afford private health coverage. Some 75000 seniors subscribe to UCare's Medicare products which include a Medicare Advantage plan under the name UCare for Seniors. UCare Minnesota also offers Medicaid plans designed for disabled Minnesotans.

UCI MEDICAL AFFILIATES INC.

PINK SHEETS: UCIA

1818 Henderson St
Columbia SC 29201
Phone: 803-782-4278
Fax: 416-935-3597
Web: www.rogers.com/web/rogers.portal?_nfpb=true&_p

CEO: Dr Michael Stout
CFO: Joseph A Boyle
HR: –
FYE: September 30
Type: Public

UCI Medical Affiliates seeks out doctors looking to avoid paperwork. The company provides practice management services to about 60 freestanding medical clinics mostly in South Carolina. (It has one center in Tennessee.) The clinics operate primarily under the Doctors Care and Progressive Physical Therapy names. UCI provides nonmedical management and administrative services such as planning accounting insurance contracting and billing non-medical staffing and other office services. Its Doctors Care locations are urgent care clinics that handle minor emergencies and provide primary care services. Blue Cross and Blue Shield of South Carolina is the company's principal stockholder.

UCP INC

NYS: UCP

99 Almaden Boulevard, Suite 400
San Jose, CA 95113
Phone: 408 207-9499
Fax: –
Web: www.unioncommunityllc.com

CEO: Dustin L Bogue
CFO: James M. Pirrello
HR: –
FYE: December 31
Type: Public

If you see property as an asset this company might be for you. UCP which stands for Union Community Properties is a residential land developer and homebuilder. It owns more than 5000 single-family lots in Northern California and the Puget Sound area of Washington where it sells developed lots to homebuilders. Homebuilding subsidiary Benchmark Communities has constructed nearly 50 communities in 15-plus cities. Funded by parent PICO the company has capitalized on the real estate bust by purchasing distressed properties in areas it believes exceed the national average for employment opportunities and housing demand. UCP was formed in 2004 purchased in 2008 and went public in 2013.

	Annual Growth	12/11	12/12*	05/13*	12/13	12/14
Sales ($ mil.)	–	0.0	58.1	–	92.7	191.2
Net income ($ mil.)	–	0.0	3.0	–	(1.9)	(5.0)
Market value ($ mil.)	–	0.0	–	–	116.0	83.2
Employees	174.6%	–	–	63	90	173

*Fiscal year change

UDR INC

NYS: UDR

1745 Shea Center Drive, Suite 200
Highlands Ranch, CO 80129
Phone: 720 283-6120
Fax: –
Web: www.udrt.com

CEO: Thomas W. Toomey
CFO: Thomas M (Tom) Herzog
HR: –
FYE: December 31
Type: Public

This company reigns over tenants in multi-family settings. UDR (formerly United Dominion Realty Trust) is a real estate investment trust (REIT) that owns and operates more than 140 multi-family apartment communities with more than 51000 units. Through joint ventures it owns 37 more properties with nearly 10000 units. It holdings are primarily located in fast-growing urban markets on both US coasts; more than half of its income comes from California Washington and metro Washington DC. The acquisitive REIT's strategy is to continue to increase its presence in markets that have strong job growth limited apartment supply and high single-family home prices.

	Annual Growth	12/10	12/11	12/12	12/13	12/14
Sales ($ mil.)	6.1%	646.6	708.7	729.4	758.9	818.0
Net income ($ mil.)	–	(102.9)	20.0	212.2	44.8	154.3
Market value ($ mil.)	7.0%	6,000.3	6,403.4	6,066.6	5,956.9	7,862.6
Employees	(0.8%)	1,632	1,750	1,633	1,681	1,582

UFP TECHNOLOGIES INC.

NAS: UFPT

172 East Main Street
Georgetown, MA 01833-2107
Phone: 978 352-2200
Fax: –
Web: www.ufpt.com

CEO: R. Jeffrey Bailly
CFO: Ronald J. Lataille
HR: –
FYE: December 31
Type: Public

As a maker of polyethylene polyurethane and polystyrene foam products UFP Technologies peddles the primary P's of plastics. Its engineered foam Component Products unit makes car interior parts gaskets and filters carrying cases soundproofing toys beauty products and components for medical diagnostic equipment. Its Packaging unit makes cushion packaging and molded fiber packaging products for automotive computer electronics industrial medical and pharmaceutical manufacturers. UFP uses cross-linked polyethylene foams to laminate fabrics for footwear backpacks and gun holsters. The company also makes recycled paper packaging for computer components medical devices and electronics.

	Annual Growth	12/10	12/11	12/12	12/13	12/14
Sales ($ mil.)	3.6%	120.8	127.2	131.0	139.2	139.3
Net income ($ mil.)	(4.9%)	9.2	10.3	10.9	11.3	7.6
Market value ($ mil.)	19.2%	86.2	104.4	126.7	178.3	173.8
Employees	2.0%	609	617	700	681	658

UGI CORP.

NYS: UGI

460 North Gulph Road
King of Prussia, PA 19406
Phone: 610 337-1000
Fax: –
Web: www.ugicorp.com

CEO: John L. Walsh
CFO: Kirk R. Oliver
HR: Jim Budd
FYE: September 30
Type: Public

UGI (derived from its original name United Gas Improvement) is a leading energy services marketing and distribution company and distributes propane across the US and internationally. The company is led by its 26%-owned propane distributor AmeriGas Partners the largest source of the holding company's sales and a leading US propane marketer. It also has utility operations: Its UGI Utilities subsidiary distributes electricity to 62000 customers and gas to about 617000 customers in Pennsylvania. The company's other operations include energy marketing in the mid-Atlantic region propane distribution in Asia and Europe and electricity generation and energy services.

	Annual Growth	09/11	09/12	09/13	09/14	09/15
Sales ($ mil.)	2.4%	6,091.3	6,519.2	7,194.7	8,277.3	6,691.1
Net income ($ mil.)	4.8%	232.9	199.4	278.1	337.2	281.0
Market value ($ mil.)	7.3%	4,528.6	5,473.3	6,745.6	5,876.7	6,002.6
Employees	8.6%	9,750	9,200	12,800	12,800	13,570

UHY ADVISORS INC.

30 S. Wacker Dr. Ste. 1330
Chicago IL 60606
Phone: 312-578-9600
Fax: 312-346-6500
Web: www.uhyadvisors-us.com

CEO: James B McGuire
CFO: Bill White
HR: –
FYE: December 31
Type: Private

Say "hi" to UHY. UHY Advisors offers tax financial and business consulting services to companies government entities not-for-profit organizations and wealthy individuals. Audit services are provided through the company's alternative practice structure arrangement with independent CPA firm UHY LLP. UHY Advisors and its affiliates also perform litigation valuation risk advisory turnaround and restructuring and wealth management services. The company boasts more than a dozen US offices in nearly 10 states including Illinois New York and Texas. UHY Advisors is an independent member of UHY International a global association of accounting firms.

UIL HOLDING CORP

NYS: UIL

157 Church Street
New Haven, CT 06506
Phone: 203 499-2000
Fax: –
Web: www.uil.com

CEO: James P Torgerson
CFO: Richard J Nicholas
HR: –
FYE: December 31
Type: Public

UIL Holdings parent of electric utility The United Illuminating Company (UI) hopes its well-regulated business will result in regular revenue growth. The public utility distributes electricity to 321000 customers in southwestern Connecticut. Its service area largely urban and suburban includes the principal cities of Bridgeport (population 146000) and New Haven (population 130000) and their surrounding areas. UIL Holdings has teamed up with NRG Energy to operate GenConn Energy LLC a joint venture that focuses on developing new power generation facilities in Connecticut. The company has also diversified through the acquisition of three gas utilities in New England from IBERDROLA USA for $1.3 billion.

	Annual Growth	12/09	12/10	12/11	12/12	12/13
Sales ($ mil.)	15.9%	896.6	997.7	1,570.4	1,486.5	1,618.7
Net income ($ mil.)	20.7%	54.3	54.9	99.7	103.7	115.3
Market value ($ mil.)	8.4%	1,593.6	1,700.3	2,007.4	2,032.4	2,199.2
Employees	15.5%	1,066	1,824	1,868	1,865	1,895

ULLICO INC.

1625 Eye St. NW
Washington DC 20006
Phone: 202-682-0900
Fax: 202-682-7932
Web: www.ullico.com

CEO: Mark Singleton
CFO: David J Barra
HR: –
FYE: December 31
Type: Private

This union is for life. Founded in 1925 by the American Federation of Labor (which became the AFL-CIO) to provide life insurance to union members ULLICO has since grown into an insurance and financial services holding company. The company serves unionized employers individual union members and jointly managed trust funds nationwide through its subsidiaries including Union Labor Life Insurance and ULLICO Investment Advisors. ULLICO offers an array of individual and commercial insurance products including annuities group life and health insurance property & casualty insurance liability coverage for unions and investment services.

ULTA SALON COSMETICS & FRAGRANCE INC.

NMS: ULTA

1000 Remington Blvd., Suite 120
Bolingbrook, IL 60440
Phone: 630 410-4800
Fax: –
Web: www.ulta.com

CEO: Mary N. Dillon
CFO: Scott M. Settersten
HR: –
FYE: January 31
Type: Public

Ulta Salon Cosmetics & Fragrance wants to be every woman's ultimate beauty stop. The company operates more than 700 stores nationwide. About a third of its locations are in Illinois Texas Florida and California. Ulta stocks more than 20000 prestige and mass-market products including cosmetics fragrances skin and hair care products salon styling tools and accessories. Stores offer hair salon services as well as manicures pedicures massages waxing and other beauty treatments. In addition to its brick-and-mortar presence the company markets more than 20000 products and more than 500 brand names through its e-commerce site. Ulta was founded in 1990 by Terry Hanson and Dick George.

	Annual Growth	01/11	01/12*	02/13	02/14*	01/15
Sales ($ mil.)	22.2%	1,454.8	1,776.2	2,220.3	2,670.6	3,241.4
Net income ($ mil.)	37.9%	71.0	120.3	172.5	202.8	257.1
Market value ($ mil.)	37.7%	2,357.5	4,962.1	6,260.5	5,501.2	8,468.4
Employees	17.6%	11,700	14,000	16,100	19,600	22,400

*Fiscal year change

ULTICOM INC.

1020 Briggs Rd.
Mt. Laurel NJ 08054
Phone: 856-787-2700
Fax: 856-866-2033
Web: www.ulticom.com

CEO: Bruce D Swail
CFO: Mark A Kissman
HR: –
FYE: January 31
Type: Private

Ulticom develops signaling software used to connect switching and messaging systems and manage routing and billing information. The company's flagship Signalware software product enables communications providers to offer such services as voice-activated dialing text messaging and Internet call-waiting. It serves telecom equipment manufacturers and communications service providers. Clients have included VeriSign Alcatel-Lucent and Nokia Siemens. It maintains hardware and operating system partnerships with companies such as IBM Oracle and Red Hat. Buyout firm Platinum Equity paid some $90 million to take Ulticom private in 2010 as part of its ongoing pattern of investing in the communications and IT industries.

ULTRA PETROLEUM CORP.

NYSE: UPL

363 N. Sam Houston Pkwy. East Ste. 1200
Houston TX 77060
Phone: 281-876-0120
Fax: 281-876-2831
Web: www.ultrapetroleum.com

CEO: Michael D. Watford
CFO: Garland R. Shaw
HR: –
FYE: December 31
Type: Public

Ultra Petroleum is ultra-keen in its search for petroleum products. The independent exploration and production company recovers natural gas and crude oil from Cretaceous era deposits in the Green River Basin of southwestern Wyoming and from holdings in the Marcellus Shale play in Pennsylvania. Ultra Petroleum owns stakes in 22000 gross developed acres in Wyoming and 28000 gross developed acres in Pennsylvania. In 2010 Ultra Petroleum reported proved reserves of 3.9 trillion cu. ft. of natural gas equivalent and had about 1700 gross and about 840 net productive wells.

ULTIMATE SOFTWARE GROUP, INC.

NMS: ULTI

2000 Ultimate Way
Weston, FL 33326
Phone: 954 331-7000
Fax: –
Web: www.ultimatesoftware.com

CEO: Scott Scherr
CFO: Mitchell K. (Mitch) Dauerman
HR: –
FYE: December 31
Type: Public

The Ultimate Software Group (USG) helps manage a company's ultimate resource: its employees. Customers employ its cloud-based UltiPro software suite to manage hiring human resources compliance benefits enrollment payroll appraisals and time and attendance. Primarily serving clients in the US the company offers UltiPro Enterprise for businesses with more than 1000 employees and UltiPro Workplace for those with fewer than 1000 employees. Communications finance health care retail technology and transportation are the industries it targets. Founded in 1990 USG has more than 19 million people records in its HCM (human capital management) cloud.

	Annual Growth	12/10	12/11	12/12	12/13	12/14
Sales ($ mil.)	22.1%	227.8	269.2	332.3	410.4	505.9
Net income ($ mil.)	113.4%	2.2	4.3	14.6	25.5	44.7
Market value ($ mil.)	31.8%	1,386.3	1,856.3	2,691.3	4,367.7	4,185.1
Employees	20.0%	1,134	1,328	1,614	1,913	2,354

ULTRA STORES INC.

122 S. Michigan Ave. Ste. 800
Chicago IL 60610
Phone: 312-922-3800
Fax: 312-922-3933
Web: www.ultradiamonds.com

CEO: –
CFO: –
HR: –
FYE: January 31
Type: Private

Ultra Stores goes above and beyond to sell fine jewelry for less. It's a leading seller of off-price bridal and diamond and gemstone jewelry as well as watches and gifts. It operates about 100 Ultra Diamonds outlet stores in more than 30 US states as well as licensed jewelry departments in a number of off-price department stores. It also sells jewelry online and buys used jewelry. Founded in 1991 Ultra Stores is owned by jewelry retail giant Signet Jewelers which acquired the company in late 2012 from the Chicago investment firm Crystal Capital.

ULTRA CLEAN HOLDINGS INC

NMS: UCTT

26462 Corporate Avenue
Hayward, CA 94545
Phone: 510 576-4400
Fax: –
Web: www.uct.com

CEO: James P. (Jim) Scholhamer
CFO: Kevin C. (Casey) Eichler
HR: –
FYE: December 26
Type: Public

Ultra Clean Holdings is a pure play in helping computer chip makers keep their manufacturing conditions pristine. The company which does business as Ultra Clean Technology (UCT) designs engineers manufactures and tests customized gas liquid and catalytic steam generation delivery systems used primarily in the production of semiconductors. The company's three biggest customers account for about 76% of revenue. In an effort to reach new markets UCT uses its expertise in the semiconductor industry to develop tools for the flat-panel display medical research and energy industries. By extending its reach the company looks to smooth the effects of the highly cyclical chip industry.

	Annual Growth	12/10	12/11	12/12	12/13	12/14
Sales ($ mil.)	3.8%	443.1	452.6	403.4	444.0	514.0
Net income ($ mil.)	(13.3%)	20.1	23.7	5.2	10.4	11.4
Market value ($ mil.)	0.2%	275.2	180.6	138.4	297.1	277.3
Employees	5.6%	1,241	1,155	1,506	1,622	1,546

ULTRALIFE CORP

NMS: ULBI

2000 Technology Parkway
Newark, NY 14513
Phone: 315 332-7100
Fax: 315 331-7800
Web: www.ultralifecorp.com

CEO: Michael D Popielec
CFO: Philip A Fain
HR: Angie Scanlon
FYE: December 31
Type: Public

Maybe you could sum up Ultralife's business model as PC as in power and communications that is. The company's main business is the design and manufacture of rechargeable and non-rechargeable batteries. Accounting for about a quarter of sales its Communications Systems Division provides such products as amplified speakers and cable assemblies. Ultralife sells its products around the world to OEMs distributors and retailers. The company also sells directly to the US and foreign defense departments. Military sales (both directly and indirectly) account for about 50% of Ultralife's revenues.

	Annual Growth	12/10	12/11	12/12	12/13	12/14
Sales ($ mil.)	(21.9%)	178.6	139.4	101.7	78.8	66.5
Net income ($ mil.)	–	(6.2)	(2.1)	(1.6)	(0.9)	(2.1)
Market value ($ mil.)	(17.0%)	114.6	69.7	56.2	61.6	54.3
Employees	(15.6%)	1,169	975	841	597	594

ULTRATECH INC
NMS: UTEK

3050 Zanker Road
San Jose, CA 95134
Phone: 408 321-8835
Fax: –
Web: www.ultratech.com

CEO: Arthur W. (Art) Zafiropoulo
CFO: Bruce R. Wright
HR: –
FYE: December 31
Type: Public

Ultratech's machines take the ultimate in high-tech baby steps. The company makes step-and-repeat photolithography systems — called steppers — that help manufacturers produce semiconductors thin-film heads for disk drives and micromachined components. Chip makers use the steppers in photolithography a process during which device features are imprinted on semiconductor wafer surfaces through repeated exposures to patterns of light. The company's steppers expose a small section of the wafer then "step" to an adjacent site to repeat the process. Ultratech was founded in 1979.

	Annual Growth	12/10	12/11	12/12	12/13	12/14
Sales ($ mil.)	1.7%	140.6	212.3	234.8	157.3	150.5
Net income ($ mil.)	–	16.8	39.2	47.2	(13.8)	(19.1)
Market value ($ mil.)	(1.7%)	544.6	673.1	1,021.9	794.5	508.5
Employees	3.8%	295	322	353	351	342

ULURU INC
NBB: ULUR

4452 Beltway Drive
Addison, TX 75001
Phone: 214 905-5145
Fax: –
Web: www.uluruinc.com

CEO: Helmut Kerschbaumer
CFO: Terrance K Wallberg
HR: –
FYE: December 31
Type: Public

ULURU named after a giant monolith in Australia is also a specialty pharmaceutical company that develops and commercializes wound care products. Based on its Nanoflex drug delivery technology ULURU has developed marketable products including Altrazeal powder dressing to treat abrasions burns donor sites and surgical wounds and Aphthasol oral paste for canker sores. Using an FDA-approved muco-adhesive thin film technology called OraDisc ULURU is also developing a line of OraDisc disc and strip products that can be applied directly to the mucosal tissue to deliver medication or active ingredients for canker sores oral pain and teeth whitening. It is working with several licensing partners around the world.

	Annual Growth	12/10	12/11	12/12	12/13	12/14
Sales ($ mil.)	(13.7%)	1.6	0.5	0.4	0.4	0.9
Net income ($ mil.)	–	(5.0)	(4.1)	(3.5)	(3.1)	(1.9)
Market value ($ mil.)	66.0%	2.7	5.4	7.1	16.9	20.5
Employees	(6.1%)	9	8	7	7	7

UMB FINANCIAL CORP
NMS: UMBF

1010 Grand Boulevard
Kansas City, MO 64106
Phone: 816 860-7000
Fax: 816 860-7143
Web: www.umb.com

CEO: Dennis L. Triplett
CFO: Brian J. Walker
HR: Lawrence G. (Larry) Smith
FYE: December 31
Type: Public

UMB Financial is the holding company for four UMB-branded commercial banks serving Arizona Colorado Illinois Kansas Nebraska Oklahoma and Missouri. Through some 110 branches the banks offer standard services such as checking and savings accounts credit and debit cards and trust and investment services. Commercial loans account for more than 50% of UMB's loan portfolio. Beyond its banking business it offers insurance brokerage services leasing treasury management health savings accounts and proprietary mutual funds through its more than 20 subsidiaries. Founded in 1913 the bank ranks first in the Kansas City market (based on deposits).

	Annual Growth	12/10	12/11	12/12	12/13	12/14
Assets ($ mil.)	9.0%	12,404.9	13,541.4	14,927.2	16,911.9	17,501.0
Net income ($ mil.)	7.3%	91.0	106.5	122.7	134.0	120.7
Market value ($ mil.)	8.2%	1,886.9	1,696.1	1,995.2	2,926.8	2,590.3
Employees	1.7%	3,355	3,448	3,448	3,498	3,592

UMH PROPERTIES INC
NYS: UMH

Juniper Business Plaza, 3499 Route 9 North, Suite 3-C
Freehold, NJ 07728
Phone: 732 577-9997
Fax: –
Web: www.umh.com

CEO: Samuel A Landy
CFO: Anna T. Chew
HR: –
FYE: December 31
Type: Public

UMH Properties (formerly United Mobile Homes) is a real estate investment trust (REIT) that owns and manages more than 80 manufactured home communities containing approximately 14500 developed lots in New Jersey New York Ohio Pennsylvania and several other states. The company leases home sites to private homeowners on a monthly basis and rents a small number of homes to residents. Communities offer such amenities as swimming pools playgrounds and municipal water and sewer services. The REIT sells and finances manufactured homes through subsidiary UMH Sales and Finance and owns more than 800 acres of land for development. UMH Properties also invests in other REITs.

	Annual Growth	12/10	12/11	12/12	12/13	12/14
Sales ($ mil.)	20.4%	34.0	39.3	46.8	62.2	71.4
Net income ($ mil.)	(10.7%)	6.7	3.7	6.5	5.8	4.2
Market value ($ mil.)	(1.6%)	248.6	226.9	251.8	229.6	232.8
Employees	18.9%	130	150	210	250	260

UMPQUA HOLDINGS CORP
NMS: UMPQ

One SW Columbia Street, Suite 1200
Portland, OR 97258
Phone: 503 727-4100
Fax: –
Web: www.umpquaholdingscorp.com

CEO: Raymond P. (Ray) Davis
CFO: Ronald L. (Ron) Farnsworth
HR: –
FYE: December 31
Type: Public

Umpqua Holdings thinks of itself not so much as a bank but rather a retailer that sells financial products. Consequently many of the company's 395 Umpqua Bank "stores" in northern California northern Nevada Oregon and Washington feature coffee bars and computer cafes. While customers sip Umpqua-branded coffee pay bills online attend a financial seminar catch a poetry reading or check out wares from local merchants staff members pitch deposit accounts mortgages loans life insurance investments and more. Subsidiary Umpqua Investments (formerly Strand Atkinson Williams & York) provides retail brokerage services through more than a dozen locations; most are inside Umpqua Bank branches.

	Annual Growth	12/10	12/11	12/12	12/13	12/14
Assets ($ mil.)	18.0%	11,668.7	11,563.4	11,795.4	11,636.1	22,613.3
Net income ($ mil.)	51.1%	28.3	74.5	101.9	98.4	147.5
Market value ($ mil.)	8.7%	2,681.6	2,727.8	2,595.7	4,213.9	3,744.9
Employees	20.3%	2,185	2,255	2,376	2,490	4,569

UNDER ARMOUR INC
NYS: UA

1020 Hull Street
Baltimore, MD 21230
Phone: 410 454-6428
Fax: –
Web: www.underarmour.com

CEO: Kevin A. Plank
CFO: Lawrence P. (Chip) Molloy
HR: –
FYE: December 31
Type: Public

Under Armour is proving its mettle as an apparel warrior. The maker of performance athletic undies and clothing has risen to the top of the industry pack boasting a big portion of the compression garment market. It is gaining a foothold in footwear too. Under Armour is the official footwear supplier of the NFL and MLB and partners with the NBA. Specializing in sport-specific garments it dresses its consumers from head to toe. Products made from its moisture-wicking and heat-dispersing fabrics keep athletes dry and relatively comfortable during workouts. Under Armour sells its wares online by catalog through its own outlet stores and in more than 25000 retail stores worldwide.

	Annual Growth	12/10	12/11	12/12	12/13	12/14
Sales ($ mil.)	30.5%	1,063.9	1,472.7	1,834.9	2,332.1	3,084.4
Net income ($ mil.)	32.0%	68.5	96.9	128.8	162.3	208.0
Market value ($ mil.)	5.5%	11,730.1	15,355.6	10,380.4	18,673.1	14,523.5
Employees	28.7%	3,900	5,400	5,900	7,800	10,700

UNDERWRITERS LABORATORIES INC.

333 PFINGSTEN RD
NORTHBROOK, IL 600622096
Phone: 847-272-8800
Fax: –
Web: www.ul.com

CEO: Keith E. Williams
CFO: Michael Saltzman
HR: –
FYE: December 31
Type: Private

Products that pass the muster of this company get the UL symbol of approval. Underwriters Laboratories (UL) is one of the world's leading providers of product safety and certification testing services performing more than 90000 evaluations each year. Products that successfully navigate through its stringent tests are registered with the lab and can bear the UL Mark — a widely trusted symbol for product safety and assurance. Nearly 20 billion products from 72000 manufacturers bear the UL Mark each year. UL also offers commercial inspection and regulatory training services as well as consumer safety advice. William Merrill founded the not-for-profit lab in 1894.

	Annual Growth	12/04	12/05	12/06	12/07	12/08
Sales ($ mil.)	(96.5%)	–	–	792,081.9	895.5	994.1
Net income ($ mil.)	–	–	–	0.2	160.5	(23.1)
Market value ($ mil.)	–	–	–	–	–	–
Employees	–	–	–	–	–	10,846

UNICEF

3 United Nations Plaza
New York NY 10017
Phone: 212-326-7000
Fax: 212-887-7465
Web: www.unicef.org

CEO: –
CFO: –
HR: –
FYE: December 31
Type: Private - Not-for-Pr

UNICEF began working to help children around the world when it was created by the United Nations in 1946. The organization strives to protect children's rights and help children who are victims of war poverty disasters and exploitation. UNICEF's focus areas include child survival and development child protection education and gender equality and HIV/AIDS prevention. The group is active in more than 190 countries and has offices in about 125. It boasts representatives from 36 countries that oversee UNICEF as executive board members. Its budget comes from governments and individual contributions and from the sale of products such as greeting cards.

UNICITY INTERNATIONAL INC.

1201 N. 800 East
Orem UT 84097
Phone: 801-226-2600
Fax: 801-226-6232
Web: www.usa.makelifebetter.com

CEO: Stewart Hughes
CFO: –
HR: Krystal Hanson
FYE: December 31
Type: Private

Unicity International prescribes health and wealth. Unicity distributes nutritional supplements and skin care products through a multilevel marketing network of some 350000 independent contractors who sell direct to consumers. Unicity's products include Bios Life branded weight management products and a variety of herbal remedies for allergies anti-aging diabetes digestive problems heart health and stress reduction. Unicity was formed in 2001 when network marketing firms Rexall Showcase International and Enrich International merged. It operates offices in a dozen countries and sells its products in more than 20 countries.

UNICO AMERICAN CORP.

NMS: UNAM

23251 Mulholland Drive
Woodland Hills, CA 91364
Phone: 818 591-9800
Fax: –

CEO: Cary L Cheldin
CFO: Lester A Aaron
HR: –
FYE: December 31
Type: Public

Unico American helps protect California businesses from a variety of afflictions. Its Crusader Insurance subsidiary provides commercial multiperil property/casualty insurance including liability property and workers' compensation. Sister company Unifax Insurance services Crusader's policies. Unico American subsidiaries also act as agents for non-affiliated insurers provide claims-adjusting services and premium financing and market individual and group medical dental life and accidental death coverage. All of its policies are marketed by independent insurance agencies and brokers.

	Annual Growth	12/10	12/11	12/12	12/13	12/14
Assets ($ mil.)	(3.6%)	157.7	150.4	140.0	132.9	136.0
Net income ($ mil.)	(22.4%)	2.3	3.7	2.0	0.6	0.8
Market value ($ mil.)	5.8%	48.8	64.4	67.6	70.8	61.1
Employees	(1.2%)	87	84	81	81	83

UNIFI, INC.

NYS: UFI

7201 West Friendly Avenue
Greensboro, NC 27419-9109
Phone: 336 294-4410
Fax: –
Web: www.unifi.com

CEO: William L. (Bill) Jasper
CFO: Sean D. Goodman
HR: Linda Hakala
FYE: June 28
Type: Public

Unifi has spun more yarns than Mark Twain himself. The company textures dyes and twists multifilament polyester and nylon yarns and allied raw materials. Its polyester yarns are sold to an array of original knitting and weaving manufacturers of apparel goods industrial textiles home furnishings and auto upholstery fabrics. Unifi nylons are marketed for apparel hosiery and sock manufacture. Polyester and nylon partially oriented yarn (POY) which is also purchased from suppliers is often not sold but further treated to create blends offering a variety of performance advantages. Unifi's revenues rely on US customers such as (Hanesbrands and to a degree on markets covered by free trade agreements.

	Annual Growth	06/11	06/12	06/13	06/14	06/15
Sales ($ mil.)	(0.9%)	712.8	705.1	714.0	687.9	687.1
Net income ($ mil.)	13.8%	25.1	11.5	16.6	28.8	42.2
Market value ($ mil.)	29.3%	218.4	215.9	372.2	495.6	611.2
Employees	(1.9%)	2,700	2,600	2,500	2,500	2,500

UNIFIEDONLINE INC

OTC: UOIP

4126 Leonard Drive
Fairfax, VA 22030
Phone: 816 979-1893
Fax: –
Web: www.unifiedonline.net

CEO: Robert M Howe III
CFO: Ellen Sondee
HR: –
FYE: June 30
Type: Public

Oh what a web IceWEB weaves when it works to secure a customer's website. The company generates most of its revenues through its IT Solutions division which provides network security products to local state and federal government agencies. The division specializes in such applications as content filtering e-mail security intrusion detection and network optimization. It implements its products with help from partners including Blue Coat Systems Cisco Systems F5 Networks McAfee and RSA Security. The company also offers data storage products through its INLINE business unit. IceWEB's online services division provides small and midsized businesses with hosted e-mail server and security applications.

	Annual Growth	09/11	09/12	09/13*	06/14	06/15
Sales ($ mil.)	(23.4%)	2.7	2.6	1.0	0.7	0.9
Net income ($ mil.)	–	(4.7)	(6.5)	(7.1)	(4.9)	(1.9)
Market value ($ mil.)	(48.5%)	168.8	83.9	20.9	1.3	11.9
Employees	(26.3%)	–	15	13	9	6

*Fiscal year change

UNIFIRST CORP.

NYS: UNF

68 Jonspin Road
Wilmington, MA 01887
Phone: 978 658-8888
Fax: –
Web: www.unifirst.com

CEO: Ronald D Croatti
CFO: Steven S Sintros
HR: –
FYE: August 29
Type: Public

Think removing lipstick from your collar is tough? Try decontaminating radioactive clothing. As North America's top supplier and servicer of uniforms and work-wear UniFirst designs makes sells or rents launders and delivers work uniforms and protective clothing (shirts pants coveralls coats smocks and aprons) as well as non-garment items (floor mats and mops) to auto service centers restaurants transportation companies and utilities operating nuclear reactors among other customers. About 90% of its revenue comes from its core laundering business. UniFirst produces about 70% of the garments it supplies enabling customization through 240 facilities in North America and Europe. UniFirst also provides first-aid cabinet services and supplies.

	Annual Growth	08/11	08/12	08/13	08/14	08/15
Sales ($ mil.)	6.5%	1,134.1	1,256.3	1,355.5	1,394.9	1,456.6
Net income ($ mil.)	12.9%	76.5	95.0	116.7	119.9	124.3
Market value ($ mil.)	21.9%	985.4	1,310.6	1,927.3	1,948.8	2,173.7
Employees	2.2%	11,000	11,000	11,500	12,000	12,000

UNIGROUP INC.

1 Premier Dr.
Fenton MO 63026
Phone: 636-305-5000
Fax: 636-326-1106
Web: www.unigroupinc.com

CEO: –
CFO: Mark Schroeder
HR: –
FYE: December 31
Type: Private

Moving people's possessions has made UniGroup's family of companies a household name. It transports home and other items in more than 175 countries through subsidiaries United Van Lines and Mayflower Transit and a network of affiliates. Road operations are supported by sister subsidiaries Trans Advantage which sells and leases trucks trailers and moving supplies and Uni-Group Worldwide which coordinates international moves for household and bulk goods. Subsidiary Allegiant Move Management provides relocation management. Clients range from government to corporate entities and private households. UniGroup is owned by its senior executives and agents of United Van Lines and Mayflower Transit.

UNIHEALTH FOUNDATION

800 Wilshire Blvd. Ste. 1300
Los Angeles CA 90017
Phone: 213-630-6500
Fax: 213-630-6509
Web: www.unihealthfoundation.org

CEO: David Carpenter
CFO: Kathleen Salazar
HR: –
FYE: September 30
Type: Private - Foundation

UniHealth Foundation has discovered that charity begins at home. UniHealth Foundation is what is left of what was once one of California's fastest-growing health systems. After spending some 10 years trying to build an integrated health care delivery system the company sold its eight hospitals to Catholic Healthcare West and its CliniShare home health services and ElderMed senior citizens care services to Trinity Care. UniHealth used those assets to begin its second life in 1998 as a grant-making organization with more than $42 million in assets through its Facey Medical Foundation. The foundation focuses on supporting health care education and care for the indigent.

UNILIFE CORP.

NMS: UNIS

250 Cross Farm Lane
York, PA 17406
Phone: 717 384-3400
Fax: –
Web: www.unilife.com

CEO: Alan Shortall
CFO: David C. Hastings
HR: –
FYE: June 30
Type: Public

Needle pricks are never fun but Unilife hopes its medical devices make the practice a little safer and simpler. The company develops and manufactures retractable syringes including the Unifill ready-to-fill syringe which allows pharmaceutical companies to prefill the device with an injectable drug or vaccine and the Unitract 1 mL syringe which is designed for hospital use and for patients who self administer medications like diabetes sufferers. With integrated safety features Unilife's products are designed to help customers comply with needlestick prevention laws that protect health care workers from accidentally acquiring blood-borne diseases such as HIV and hepatitis C.

	Annual Growth	06/11	06/12	06/13	06/14	06/15
Sales ($ mil.)	18.6%	6.7	5.5	2.7	14.7	13.2
Net income ($ mil.)		(40.7)	(52.3)	(63.2)	(57.9)	(90.8)
Market value ($ mil.)	(19.7%)	683.5	446.0	418.3	390.6	283.7
Employees	21.2%	129	128	159	209	278

UNION BANK AND TRUST COMPANY

3643 S 48TH ST
LINCOLN, NE 685064390
Phone: 402-488-0941
Fax: –
Web: www.ubt.com

CEO: Angie Muhliesen
CFO: –
HR: –
FYE: December 31
Type: Private

Union Bank & Trust a subsidiary of financial services holding company Farmers & Merchants Investment operates more than 35 branches throughout Nebraska and in Kansas. As Nebraska's third-largest privately-owned bank it offers traditional deposit and trust services as well as insurance equipment finance and investment management services. Consumer loans account for the largest portion of the bank's portfolio followed by commercial real estate and farmland loans. Union Bank also originates business loans and residential mortgages. Affiliate company Union Investment Advisors manages the Stratus family of mutual funds. Another Farmers & Merchants unit Nelnet Capital offers brokerage services.

	Annual Growth	12/04	12/05	12/06	12/08	12/13
Assets ($ mil.)	9.5%	–	–	1,518.2	2,437.5	2,862.7
Net income ($ mil.)	10.0%	–	–	18.5	16.8	36.0
Market value ($ mil.)	–	–	–	–	–	–
Employees	–	–	–	–	–	800

UNION BANKSHARES CORP (NEW)

NMS: UBSH

1051 East Cary Street, Suite 1200
Richmond, VA 23219
Phone: 804 633-5031
Fax: –
Web: www.bankatunion.com

CEO: G. William (Billy) Beale
CFO: Robert M. (Rob) Gorman
HR: –
FYE: December 31
Type: Public

Union Bankshares (formerly Union First Market Bankshares) is the holding company for Union Bank & Trust which operates approximately 100 branches in central northern and coastal portions of Virginia. The bank offers standard services such as checking and savings accounts credit cards and certificates of deposit. Union Bank & Trust maintains a loan portfolio heavily weighted towards real estate: Commercial real estate loans make up more than 30% while one- to four-family residential mortgages and construction loans account for approximately 15% and 20% respectively. The bank also originates personal and business loans.

	Annual Growth	12/10	12/11	12/12	12/13	12/14
Assets ($ mil.)	17.7%	3,837.2	3,907.1	4,095.9	4,176.6	7,359.2
Net income ($ mil.)	23.1%	22.9	30.4	35.4	34.5	52.6
Market value ($ mil.)	13.0%	667.5	600.2	712.2	1,120.5	1,087.5
Employees	10.0%	1,005	1,045	1,044	1,025	1,471

UNION BANKSHARES, INC. (MORRISVILLE, VT)

NMS: UNB

P.O. Box 667, 20 Lower Main Street	CEO: David S Silverman
Morrisville, VT 05661	CFO: Karyn J Hale
Phone: 802 888-6600	HR: –
Fax: –	FYE: December 31
Web: www.ublocal.com	Type: Public

Union Bankshares is the holding company for Union Bank which serves individuals and small to midsized businesses in northern Vermont through about 15 branches; it opened its first office in New Hampshire in 2006. Founded in 1891 the bank offers standard deposit products such as savings checking money market and NOW accounts as well as certificates of deposit retirement savings programs investment management and trust services. It uses fund from deposits primarily to originate commercial real estate loans (more than 40% of the company's loan portfolio) and residential real estate loans (about 35%). Other loan products include business consumer construction and municipal loans.

	Annual Growth	12/10	12/11	12/12	12/13	12/14
Assets ($ mil.)	8.3%	454.1	552.8	577.3	585.4	624.1
Net income ($ mil.)	8.3%	5.6	5.2	6.8	7.1	7.7
Market value ($ mil.)	6.9%	81.1	84.9	87.1	102.5	105.9
Employees	3.8%	160	161	184	188	186

UNION ELECTRIC COMPANY

1901 Chouteau Ave.	CEO: Michael L Moehn
St. Louis MO 63103	CFO: Martin J Lyons Jr
Phone: 800-552-7583	HR: –
Fax: 314-206-0485	FYE: December 31
Web: www.ameren.com/sites/aue/pages/home.aspx	Type: Subsidiary

Union Electric unites electricity and natural gas services under the Gateway Arch. The utility (a subsidiary of Ameren) operates as Ameren Missouri and serves 1.2 million power customers and 126000 gas customers. The utility's service territory includes 57 Missouri counties; more than half of its customers reside in the St. Louis metropolitan area. The company owns about 3270 miles of natural gas transmission and distribution mains and 33000 of electric distribution lines (and 295 miles of power transmission lines). Ameren Missouri owns or has interests in nine power plants (primarily thermal) with a capacity of almost 10000 MW and it also engages in wholesale power transactions.

UNION HEALTH SERVICE INC

1634 W POLK ST	CEO: –
CHICAGO, IL 606124352	CFO: –
Phone: 312 423 4200	HR: –
Fax: –	FYE: December 31
Web: www.unionhealth.org	Type: Private

Union Health Service brings together doctors and patients in the Chicago area. The company is a not-for-profit health care services provider which supplies health insurance to its members through HMO (health maintenance organization) and medical prepayment plans. Union Health Service also provides primary health care as well as vision laboratory radiology and pharmacy services to its members through about 20 group practice clinics in Aurora Chicago Norridge Oak Park and other area communities. The company was established in 1955.

	Annual Growth	12/03	12/04	12/05	12/09	12/13
Sales ($ mil.)	(21.0%)	–	534.4	40.2	54.6	64.2
Net income ($ mil.)	23.9%	–	–	0.1	1.8	0.4
Market value ($ mil.)	–	–	–	–	–	–
Employees	–	–	–	–	–	250

UNION HOSPITAL INC.

1606 N 7TH ST	CEO: Steven M Holman
TERRE HAUTE, IN 478042780	CFO: Wayne R Hutson
Phone: 812-238-7000	HR: –
Fax: –	FYE: August 31
Web: www.myunionhospital.org	Type: Private

Union Hospital is the flagship facility of the Union Hospital Health Group a health care system that serves communities in western Indiana and eastern Illinois. The not-for-profit hospital has about 320 beds boasts an equal number of physicians and provides general medical and surgical care as well as specialty services in areas such as women's health newborn intensive care unit (Level II) cancer cardiovascular disease and sports medicine. It also offers occupational health and physical rehabilitation as well as medical training programs. Other facilities that comprise the Union system include Union Hospital Clinton physician practices specialty clinics and a home health agency.

	Annual Growth	08/06	08/07	08/08	08/09	08/10
Sales ($ mil.)	–	–	–	(641.0)	408.2	400.4
Net income ($ mil.)	–	–	–	0.0	18.3	(3.3)
Market value ($ mil.)	–	–	–	–	–	–
Employees	–	–	–	–	–	1,960

UNION PACIFIC CORP

NYS: UNP

1400 Douglas Street	CEO: Lance M. Fritz
Omaha, NE 68179	CFO: Robert M. Knight
Phone: 402 544-5000	HR: Sherrye Hutcherson
Fax: –	FYE: December 31
Web: www.up.com	Type: Public

Venerable Union Pacific Railroad (UP) has been chugging down the track since the 19th century. Owned by Union Pacific Corporation (UPC) UP is one of the nation's leading rail carriers operating more than 66000 freight cars and about 8500 locomotives. UP transports automobiles; chemicals; energy (fuel); and industrial agricultural and other bulk freight over a system of some 32000 rail miles in 23 states in the western two-thirds of the US. UPC owns more than 26000 route miles of its rail network; leases and trackage rights which allow it to use other railroads' tracks account for the rest. UP's customers have included automakers General Motors and Toyota as well as retail outlet Lowe's.

	Annual Growth	12/11	12/12	12/13	12/14	12/15
Sales ($ mil.)	2.8%	19,557.0	20,926.0	21,963.0	23,988.0	21,813.0
Net income ($ mil.)	9.7%	3,292.0	3,943.0	4,388.0	5,180.0	4,772.0
Market value ($ mil.)	(7.3%)	89,965.5	106,762.9	142,667.5	101,166.6	66,408.3
Employees	1.4%	44,861	45,928	46,445	47,201	47,457

UNIONBANCAL CORPORATION

400 California St.	CEO: Masashi Oka
San Francisco CA 94104-1302	CFO: John F Woods
Phone: 415-765-2969	HR: –
Fax: 415-765-2220	FYE: December 31
Web: www.unionbank.com	Type: Subsidiary

Whether you're in NorCal SoCal or beyond you can call on UnionBanCal. Its Union Bank subsidiary has more than 400 branches in California Washington Oregon New York and Texas. The bank offers retail banking which provides deposits and loans to consumers and small businesses. Its corporate banking segment provides commercial financing to middle-market and corporate clients with a focus on the energy real estate health care communications and retail sectors. UnionBanCal also provides wealth planning and trust services through HighMark Capital Management. Another subsidiary Cash & Save is a chain of check-cashing stores. UnionBanCal is a subsidiary of Mitsubishi UFJ Financial Group (MUFJ).

UNIPRO FOODSERVICE INC

2500 CUMBRLD PKWY SE 60
ATLANTA, GA 30339
Phone: 770-952-0871
Fax: –
Web: www.uniprofoodservice.com

CEO: Roger Toomey
CFO: –
HR: –
FYE: December 31
Type: Private

UniPro Foodservice knows there's strength in numbers. As the largest US food service cooperative its members include more than 650 independent member companies that provide food and food-related products to more than 800000 food service customers including health care and educational institutions military installations and restaurants. UniPro provides training collective purchasing and marketing materials to all distributors. Its products — which include dry groceries and frozen and refrigerated foods — are sold under the brand names CODE ComSource Nifda and Nugget. Suppliers include Kraft Foods Reynolds Food Packaging Solo Cup Tyson Foods and Unilever Foodsolutions.

	Annual Growth	12/09	12/10	12/11	12/12	12/13
Sales ($ mil.)	23.5%	–	657.5	881.2	987.1	1,238.7
Net income ($ mil.)	–	–	–	0.0	(0.2)	(0.1)
Market value ($ mil.)	–	–	–	–	–	–
Employees	–	–	–	–	–	140

UNIROYAL GLOBAL ENGINEERED PRODUCTS INC

NBB: UNIR

1800 2nd Street, Suite 970
Sarasota, FL 34236
Phone: 941 906-8580
Fax: –

CEO: Edmund C King
CFO: Edmund C King
HR: –
FYE: December 31
Type: Public

Invisa develops and manufactures sensors used to ensure safety and security. The company's SmartGate safety sensors are used in traffic and parking control fence and gate access and industrial automation safety applications. The sensors are meant to keep doors and gates from closing on people or objects. Invisa's InvisaShield technology is designed to detect the presence of intruders in a monitored zone such as the area around a museum exhibit. Customer Magnetic Automation Corp. a manufacturer of barrier gates accounts for nearly 30% of product sales.

	Annual Growth	12/10	12/11	12/12	12/13	12/14
Sales ($ mil.)	493.7%	0.1	0.1	0.0	0.0	98.3
Net income ($ mil.)	–	(0.1)	(0.3)	(0.3)	(0.4)	4.6
Market value ($ mil.)	258.4%	0.2	4.3	3.8	10.0	33.0
Employees	350.0%	1	1	1	1	410

UNISEA INC.

15400 NE 90th St.
Redmond WA 98073-9719
Phone: 425-881-8181
Fax: 425-861-5249
Web: www.unisea.com

CEO: –
CFO: –
HR: Chris Pilasanc
FYE: March 31
Type: Subsidiary

UniSea sticks mainly to one body of water when it trolls for fish. The company produces seafood products from its independent Alaskan fishermen. Unisea offers items such as cod halibut pollock snow and king crab and surimi all of which it markets worldwide. The company owns two automated seafood plants one located in Dutch Harbor Alaska; the other processing facility is in Redmond Washington where Unisea also operates a rental cold-storage facility. UniSea also operates The Grand Aleutian Hotel and the UniSea Inn (both located in Dutch Harbor). UniSea is a wholly-owned subsidiary of Japan-based seafood giant Nippon Suisan Kaisha.

UNISOURCE WORLDWIDE INC.

6600 Governors Lake Pkwy.
Norcross GA 30071
Phone: 770-447-9000
Fax: 770-734-2000
Web: www.unisourceworldwide.com

CEO: Mary A Laschinger
CFO: Stephen J Smith
HR: –
FYE: December 31
Type: Private

This company has a singular mission: Distribute paper to North America. Unisource Worldwide is one of the biggest independent distributors of paper products and related supplies. Operating from 85 distribution centers in the US and Canada it offers commercial printing and business imaging paper and specialty paper products. Its short list includes Xerox ink jet and laser paper and toner cartridges and coated and uncoated commercial printing paper. Unisource also distributes packaging and cleaning supplies and some equipment. The retail stores division PaperPlus provides a similiar paper selection and digital printing services. Unisource is 60% owned by Bain Capital; paper maker Georgia-Pacific owns 40%.

UNISYS CORP.

NYS: UIS

801 Lakeview Drive, Suite 100
Blue Bell, PA 19422
Phone: 215 986-4011
Fax: –
Web: www.unisys.com

CEO: Peter A. Altabef
CFO: Janet B. Haugen
HR: David A. (Dave) Loeser
FYE: December 31
Type: Public

Unisys wants to unite the systems of its customers as smooth functioning IT operations. Among the top global players in the IT consulting business it provides services (about 87% of sales) and technology (13% of sales.) The company's services unit handles outsourcing systems integration and consulting infrastructure services and core maintenance while its technology division develops enterprise-class servers and related operating systems and middleware. Unisys is among the largest government IT contractors serving local state and federal agencies as well as foreign governments. Other key sectors include communications financial services and transportation.

	Annual Growth	12/10	12/11	12/12	12/13	12/14
Sales ($ mil.)	(4.4%)	4,019.6	3,853.8	3,706.4	3,456.5	3,356.4
Net income ($ mil.)	(33.3%)	236.1	134.0	145.6	108.5	46.7
Market value ($ mil.)	3.3%	1,286.7	979.6	859.8	1,668.4	1,465.2
Employees	0.3%	22,900	22,700	22,800	22,800	23,200

UNIT CORP.

NYS: UNT

7130 South Lewis, Suite 1000
Tulsa, OK 74136
Phone: 918 493-7700
Fax: –
Web: www.unitcorp.com

CEO: Larry D. Pinkston
CFO: David T. Merrill
HR: –
FYE: December 31
Type: Public

It's oil for one and one for oil. With a single-minded focus on hydrocarbons Unit conducts onshore drilling of oil and natural gas wells for customers in the Gulf Coast Midcontinent and Rocky Mountain regions of the US. Through Unit Drilling it has a drilling fleet of almost 90 rigs. The company owns stakes in more than 8871 wells. Unit also has upstream and midstream businesses. Unit Petroleum explores for and produces oil and gas in the Anadarko and Arkoma basins of Oklahoma and Texas. In 2014 it reported proved reserves of 179 million barrels of oil equivalent (a 17% increase over the previous year). Its Superior Pipeline subsidiary buys sells gathers processes and treats natural gas.

	Annual Growth	12/10	12/11	12/12	12/13	12/14
Sales ($ mil.)	15.6%	881.8	1,208.4	1,315.1	1,351.9	1,572.9
Net income ($ mil.)	(1.8%)	146.5	195.9	23.2	184.7	136.3
Market value ($ mil.)	(7.5%)	2,305.1	2,301.2	2,234.2	2,560.0	1,691.1
Employees	(0.1%)	1,888	2,674	2,309	2,463	1,880

UNITED AMERICAN HEALTHCARE CORP.

NBB: UAHC

303 East Wacker Drive, Suite 1200
Chicago, IL 60601
Phone: 313 393-4571
Fax: –

CEO: John M Fife
CFO: Robert T Sullivan
HR: –
FYE: December 31
Type: Public

United American Healthcare (UAHC) keeps the pulse of medical device manufacturing services. The company cast its future with the 2010 purchase of California-base Pulse Systems which provides contract manufacturing services to medical device makers. More specifically Pulse Systems provides laser-cutting capabilities and other processing technology for cardiovascular devices. Previously the company operated the UAHC Health Plan of Tennessee a managed care company whose network covered some 900 physicians and 20 hospitals. However when its contract to serve Medicaid recipients in western Tennessee was not renewed in 2009 the company went seeking alternatives.

	Annual Growth	06/10	06/11	06/12	06/13*	12/13
Sales ($ mil.)	(5.4%)	3.8	8.4	6.8	8.5	3.2
Net income ($ mil.)	–	(5.4)	(7.1)	(1.9)	0.5	(0.8)
Market value ($ mil.)	(52.2%)	11.9	2.7	0.2	0.4	1.3
Employees	3.2%	30	27	29	31	33

*Fiscal year change

UNITED AMERICAN INSURANCE COMPANY

3700 S. Stonebridge Dr.
McKinney TX 75070-5934
Phone: 972-529-5085
Fax: 972-569-3653
Web: www.unitedamerican.com

CEO: Vern D Herbel
CFO: –
HR: –
FYE: December 31
Type: Subsidiary

United American Insurance a subsidiary of Torchmark lights the path for Medicare customers. The firm sells supplemental Medicare health insurance policies and Part D drug coverage to seniors across the US. United American also provides limited-benefit individual and group plans for critical medical care. The company began operations in 1947 providing life health and accident insurance to individual customers in Texas. Since then its operations have spread to 49 states the District of Columbia and Canada. In New York State the company operates through a subsidiary First United American Life Insurance Company. United American sells its products through both exclusive branch offices and independent agents.

UNITED ARTISTS CORPORATION

10250 Constellation Blvd.
Los Angeles CA 90067
Phone: 310-449-3000
Fax: 310-449-8857
Web: www.unitedartists.com

CEO: –
CFO: –
HR: –
FYE: December 31
Type: Subsidiary

What do you get when Charlie Chaplin Mary Pickford Douglas Fairbanks and D.W. Griffith get together and form a film company? United Artists (UA). Founded in 1919 by the four Hollywood legends UA is now a unit of Metro-Goldwyn-Mayer (MGM) which acquired the company in 1981. UA is involved in the production sale and acquisition of smaller-budget films. The banner contributes well-known titles to MGM's film library which includes the "Pink Panther" "Rocky" and "James Bond" franchises as well as TV shows such as The Outer Limits and The Fugitive. In 2006 MGM gave control of UA to actor Tom Cruise and his then-business partner Paula Wagner. Wagner left the studio in 2008 in order to return to producing.

UNITED BANCORP, INC. (MARTINS FERRY, OH)

NAS: UBCP

201 South Fourth Street
Martins Ferry, OH 43935-0010
Phone: 740 633-0445
Fax: –
Web: www.unitedbancorp.com

CEO: Scott A Everson
CFO: Randall M Greenwood
HR: –
FYE: December 31
Type: Public

United Bancorp is the holding company of Ohio's Citizens Savings Bank which operates as Citizens Savings Bank and The Community Bank. The bank divisions together operate some 20 branches offering deposit and lending products including savings and checking accounts commercial and residential mortgages and consumer installment loans. Commercial loans and mortgages combined account for about 60% of the company's loan portfolio. In 2008 Citizens Savings Bank acquired the deposits of three failed banking offices from the FDIC.

	Annual Growth	12/10	12/11	12/12	12/13	12/14
Assets ($ mil.)	(1.3%)	423.4	415.6	438.4	389.0	401.8
Net income ($ mil.)	1.0%	2.5	3.1	2.4	2.6	2.7
Market value ($ mil.)	(1.9%)	46.8	45.5	33.7	43.2	43.4
Employees	(6.2%)	191	163	152	151	148

UNITED BANCORP, INC. (TECUMSEH, MI)

OTC: UBMI

2723 South State Street
Ann Arbor, MI 48104
Phone: 517 423-8373
Fax: –
Web: www.ubat.com

CEO: Robert K Chapman
CFO: Randal J Rabe
HR: –
FYE: December 31
Type: Public

Some folks in southeastern Michigan put their trust in United Bancorp the holding company for United Bank & Trust and United Bank & Trust - Washtenaw. Together the banks operate more than 15 branches in Lenawee Washtenaw and Monroe counties. In addition to standard products such as deposits loans and credit cards the company also offers financial planning investments and trust services. Business loans and commercial mortgages make up about 60% of the banks' loan portfolio; residential mortgages personal loans and commercial construction and development loans each account for about 15%. United Bancorp was formed in 1985 but the bank traces its roots to 1860.

	Annual Growth	12/08	12/09	12/10	12/11	12/12
Assets ($ mil.)	2.2%	832.4	909.3	861.7	885.0	907.7
Net income ($ mil.)	–	(0.0)	(8.8)	(3.7)	0.9	4.5
Market value ($ mil.)	(12.1%)	95.9	66.7	44.5	31.8	57.2
Employees	1.0%	274	248	255	282	285

UNITED BANCSHARES INC. (OH)

NMS: UBOH

100 South High Street
Columbus Grove, OH 45830
Phone: 419 659-2141
Fax: –
Web: www.theubank.com

CEO: Brian D Young
CFO: Diana L Engelhardt
HR: –
FYE: December 31
Type: Public

United Bancshares is a blend of checks and (account) balances. The institution is the holding company for The Union Bank Company a community bank serving northwestern Ohio through about a dozen branches. The commercial bank offers such retail services and products as checking and savings accounts NOW and money market accounts IRAs and CDs. It uses funds from deposits to write commercial loans (about half of its lending portfolio) residential mortgages agriculture loans and consumer loans. The Union Bank Company was originally established in 1904.

	Annual Growth	12/10	12/11	12/12	12/13	12/14
Assets ($ mil.)	1.5%	612.6	587.0	572.4	556.2	650.2
Net income ($ mil.)	11.3%	2.8	2.9	4.5	4.6	4.3
Market value ($ mil.)	11.1%	32.0	23.1	32.8	48.2	48.7
Employees	(1.4%)	150	146	138	137	142

UNITED BANK CARD INC.

2202 N IRVING ST
ALLENTOWN, PA 18109-9554
Phone: 800-201-0461
Fax: –
Web: www.harbortouchli.com

CEO: Jared Isaacman
CFO: –
HR: –
FYE: December 31
Type: Private

United Bank Card (UBC) CEO Jared Isaacman knows to give is to receive. UBC a payment and transaction processing company more than doubled its annual profits and set a new standard for the industry when the young innovative Isaacman and his sales team began giving away (rather than selling or leasing) the terminals merchants use to process credit debit EBT government cards and electronic gift and loyalty cards. Today UBC handles accounts for more than 100000 merchants nationwide and processes nearly $10 billion annually. Customers are primarily small to midsized business owners in the e-commerce petroleum lodging mail order supermarket and restaurant industries.

	Annual Growth	12/02	12/03	12/04	12/05	12/10
Sales ($ mil.)	30.3%	–	–	–	19.1	71.8
Net income ($ mil.)	–	–	–	–	0.0	3.5
Market value ($ mil.)	–	–	–	–	–	–
Employees	–	–	–	–	–	195

UNITED BANKSHARES, INC.

NMS: UBSI

300 United Center, 500 Virginia Street, East
Charleston, WV 25301
Phone: 304 424-8716
Fax: –
Web: www.ubsi-inc.com

CEO: Richard M Adams
CFO: W. Mark Tatterson
HR: –
FYE: December 31
Type: Public

United Bankshares (no relation to Ohio's United Bancshares) keeps it together as the holding company for two subsidiaries doing business as United Bank (WV) and United Bank (VA). Combined the banks boast some $12 billion in assets and operate roughly 130 branches that serve West Virginia Virginia and Washington DC as well as nearby portions of Maryland Pennsylvania and Ohio. The branches offer traditional deposit trust and lending services with a focus on residential mortgages and commercial loans. United Bankshares also owns United Brokerage Services which provides investments asset management and financial planning in addition to brokerage services.

	Annual Growth	12/10	12/11	12/12	12/13	12/14
Assets ($ mil.)	14.6%	7,155.7	8,451.5	8,420.0	8,735.3	12,328.8
Net income ($ mil.)	15.9%	71.9	75.6	82.6	85.6	129.9
Market value ($ mil.)	6.4%	2,023.4	1,959.0	1,686.7	2,179.4	2,595.1
Employees	4.1%	1,451	1,619	1,529	1,528	1,703

UNITED BEHAVIORAL HEALTH

425 Market St. 27th Fl.
San Francisco CA 94105-2406
Phone: 415-547-5000
Fax: 415-547-5800
Web: www.unitedbehavioralhealth.com

CEO: Saul Feldman
CFO: Karen Schievelbein
HR: –
FYE: December 31
Type: Subsidiary

United Behavioral Health (UBH) takes on the challenging world of mental health offering employee assistance substance abuse and mental health programs. Its nationwide network of more than 80000 clinicians (including psychiatrists psychologists and therapists) serve more than 43 million people. UBH addresses such issues as alcohol/drug addiction anxiety geriatric care psychotic disorders and child and adolescent concerns. The company operates inpatient outpatient and residential and day treatment programs in more than 3500 facilities. UBH's clients include corporations government entities unions and HMOs. UBH is a subsidiary of UnitedHealth.

UNITED CAPITAL CORP.

NBB: UCAP

9 Park Place
Great Neck, NY 11021
Phone: 516 466-6464
Fax: 516 829-4301
Web: www.unitedcapitalcorp.net

CEO: Attilio F Petrocelli
CFO: Anthony J Miceli
HR: –
FYE: December 31
Type: Public

Making a profit is a capital idea that unites United Capital. The company invests in and manages real estate properties as well as manufactures and sells engineered products using knitted wire. United Capital owns and oversees about 150 retail office hotel and day care properties across the US. Subsidiary Metal Textiles makes knitted wire products and parts for a range of sealing and filtering applications. Under the AFP Transformers brand the company makes transformers for switchgear to motor starters and inverters. The lines are sold to commercial and industrial customers in the automotive electronic aerospace and process and chemical market. CEO Attilio Petrocelli and his wife own 70% of the company.

	Annual Growth	12/09	12/10	12/11	12/12	12/13
Sales ($ mil.)	18.7%	60.1	80.7	90.1	115.8	119.1
Net income ($ mil.)	21.7%	5.7	12.7	17.5	16.7	12.5
Market value ($ mil.)	8.5%	139.4	190.3	125.9	161.0	193.2
Employees	17.3%	390	470	460	630	–

UNITED CEREBRAL PALSY ASSOCIATIONS INC.

1660 L St. NW Ste. 700
Washington DC 20036
Phone: 202-776-0406
Fax: 202-776-0414
Web: www.ucp.org

CEO: Steve Bennett
CFO: –
HR: –
FYE: September 30
Type: Private - Not-for-Pr

United Cerebral Palsy (UCP) fights the good fight. The not-for-profit organization and its affiliates (about 100 chapter throughout North America Australia and Scotland) serve more than 176000 children and adults with cerebral palsy and other disabilities. Cerebral palsy is a group of conditions marked by an inability to fully control muscle movement and coordination caused by poor development or damage to the brain during fetal development birth or infancy. UCP works for the inclusion of the disabled into all facets of life by lobbying Congress providing information and funding research. Direct services include therapy individual and family support employment assistance and technology training.

UNITED CEREBRAL PALSY ASSOCIATIONS OF NEW YORK STATE INC.

330 W 34TH ST FL 15
NEW YORK, NY 100012406
Phone: 212-947-5770
Fax: –
Web: www.cpofnys.org

CEO: Susan Constantino
CFO: –
HR: Jennifer Keane
FYE: June 30
Type: Private

Cerebral Palsy Associations of New York State (CP of NYS) provides health care services for people suffering with cerebral palsy and other developmental disabilities. The organization includes 24 associations that provide day treatment programs community dwelling access and at-home residential support as well as early childhood mental health and transportation services. Serving more than 100000 patients throughout the state it also acts as an advocate for its patients through legislative involvement. CP of NYS was founded in 1946 by parents seeking health and advocacy services for their children. The organization provides services directly to patients.

	Annual Growth	06/05	06/06	06/09	06/10	06/13
Sales ($ mil.)	(24.7%)	–	829.6	105.3	109.1	113.4
Net income ($ mil.)	(45.2%)	–	–	2.0	2.7	0.2
Market value ($ mil.)	–	–	–	–	–	–
Employees	–	–	–	–	–	1,700

UNITED COMMUNITY BANCORP

NASDAQ: UCBA

92 Walnut St.	CEO: Elmer G McLaughlin
Lawrenceburg IN 47025	CFO: Vicki A March
Phone: 812-537-4822	HR: –
Fax: 812-537-5769	FYE: June 30
Web: https://www.bankucb.com	Type: Public

United Community Bancorp is the holding company of United Community Bank a regional bank serving residents and businesses of southeastern Indiana. Through about a dozen branches in Dearborn County the bank offers savings and checking accounts IRAs and CDs as well as loans such as single-family mortgages (the largest segment of its loan portfolio) and commercial and multifamily mortgages. To a lesser extent it originates construction loans business loans and consumer loans.

UNITED COMMUNITY BANKS, INC. (BLAIRSVILLE, GA)

NMS: UCBI

125 Highway 515 East	CEO: Jimmy C. Tallent
Blairsville, GA 30512	CFO: Rex S. Schuette
Phone: 706 781-2265	HR: –
Fax: –	FYE: December 31
Web: www.ucbi.com	Type: Public

United Community Banks is the holding company for United Community Bank (UCB) which provides consumer and business banking products and services through nearly 105 branches across Georgia North Carolina Tennessee and South Carolina. Commercial loans including construction loans and mortgages account for the largest portion of UCB's loan portfolio (more than 50%); residential mortgages make up 30%. The company which boasts roughly $8 billion in assets also has a mortgage lending division and provides insurance through its United Community Insurance Services subsidiary (aka United Community Advisory Services).

	Annual Growth	12/10	12/11	12/12	12/13	12/14
Assets ($ mil.)	0.4%	7,443.2	6,983.4	6,802.3	7,425.4	7,567.0
Net income ($ mil.)	–	(345.6)	(226.7)	33.9	273.1	67.6
Market value ($ mil.)	76.5%	117.5	421.2	568.8	1,069.6	1,141.3
Employees	(3.9%)	1,763	1,706	1,553	1,472	1,506

UNITED COMMUNITY FINANCIAL CORP. (OH)

NMS: UCFC

275 West Federal Street	CEO: –
Youngstown, OH 44503-1203	CFO: Timothy W Esson
Phone: 330 742-0500	HR: Cindy Cerimele
Fax: –	FYE: December 31
Web: www.ucfconline.com	Type: Public

This thrift wants to keep your savings and your loans united. United Community Financial is the holding company for The Home Savings and Loan Company of Youngstown Ohio a community bank with more than 30 full-service branches and about 10 loan production offices in Ohio and western Pennsylvania. Boasting nearly $2 billion in assets the bank offers traditional checking and savings accounts CDs retirement accounts investments and credit cards as well as a variety of loans. Residential mortgages account for over 60% of the company's loan portfolio while commercial and consumer loans split the remainder.

	Annual Growth	12/10	12/11	12/12	12/13	12/14
Assets ($ mil.)	(4.4%)	2,197.3	2,030.7	1,808.4	1,737.9	1,833.6
Net income ($ mil.)	–	(37.3)	0.2	(20.4)	10.0	50.2
Market value ($ mil.)	41.5%	66.0	62.5	142.3	175.8	264.4
Employees	(6.4%)	557	551	490	514	428

UNITED CONCORDIA COMPANIES INC.

4401 Deer Path Rd.	CEO: David L Holmberg
Harrisburg PA 17110	CFO: Daniel J Wright
Phone: 717-260-6800	HR: –
Fax: 717-260-7779	FYE: December 31
Web: www.ucci.com	Type: Subsidiary

Look Ma! I've got dental insurance! United Concordia Companies one of the largest dental insurers in the country provides dental benefits to more than 8 million members in the US and worldwide through corporate government agency and individual accounts. Its Advantage Plus plan includes some 75000 dentists. Through its contract with the US Department of Defense (DOD) the company provides coverage to military personnel and their family members. The company distributes its products through a network of regional sales offices. United Concordia founded in 1971 became an independent operating subsidiary of Highmark in 1992.

UNITED CONTINENTAL HOLDINGS INC

NYS: UAL

233 South Wacker Drive	CEO: Oscar Munoz
Chicago, IL 60606	CFO: Gerald (Gerry) Laderman
Phone: 872 825-4000	HR: Michael P. (Mike) Bonds
Fax: –	FYE: December 31
Web: www.unitedcontinentalholdings.com	Type: Public

United Continental Holdings (UAL) unites cities around the globe through its primary United Air Lines subsidiary. While United Air Lines is its main line the company also has regional operations which are operated under contract by United Express. Combined the company handles an average of roughly 5050 flights a day to more than 370 domestic and international destinations from hubs that include Chicago Denver Houston Los Angeles San Francisco and Washington DC. Like most airlines the company sells the majority of its seat inventory through travel agencies and global distribution systems in addition to its main website.

	Annual Growth	12/10	12/11	12/12	12/13	12/14
Sales ($ mil.)	13.8%	23,229.0	37,110.0	37,152.0	38,279.0	38,901.0
Net income ($ mil.)	45.4%	253.0	840.0	(723.0)	571.0	1,132.0
Market value ($ mil.)	29.5%	8,921.2	7,067.3	8,756.4	14,168.3	25,052.0
Employees	(0.6%)	86,000	8,700	88,000	87,000	84,000

UNITED DAIRYMEN OF ARIZONA

2008 S HARDY DR	CEO: –
TEMPE, AZ 852821211	CFO: –
Phone: 480-966-7211	HR: Jill Romero
Fax: –	FYE: September 30
Web: www.uda.coop	Type: Private

Its name says it all: United Dairymen of Arizona (UDA) is a group of Arizona-based dairy farmers united together to stabilize and strengthen the market for milk products. Supplied by some 90-member producers the cooperative's plant has the capacity to process 10 million pounds of milk per day about 90% of the milk in the state. Products include sweet cream and butter fluid and condensed skim milk and non-fat dry milk among others. Customers include onsite cheese maker Schreiber Foods fluid milk processors and supermarket chains throughout The Grand Canyon State. UDA also makes dried lactose powder for food manufacturers. Started in 1960 the co-op was formed through a merger of two dairy associations.

	Annual Growth	09/07	09/08	09/09	09/10	09/11
Sales ($ mil.)	300.9%	–	–	51.4	612.6	825.8
Net income ($ mil.)	52165.3%	–	–	0.0	12.3	21.3
Market value ($ mil.)	–	–	–	–	–	–
Employees	–	–	–	–	–	190

UNITED ELECTRIC SUPPLY COMPANY INC.

10 BELLECOR DR
NEW CASTLE, DE 197201763
Phone: 800-322-3374
Fax: –
Web: www.unitedelectric.com

CEO: George Vorwick
CFO: Rich Stagliano
HR: –
FYE: December 31
Type: Private

True to its name United Electric Supply distributes electrical parts such as lighting fasteners sensors wire connectors and voice data and fiber-optic products. The employee-owned company carries more than 23000 items from more than 250 manufacturers including Kyocera Panasonic Security and Schneider Electric. It sells to the building and industrial trades government and other markets. United Electric's wide range of services include design value engineering energy audits procurement training inventory management and E-commerce. It also offers value-added services such as next day delivery and Saturday-morning counter hours.

	Annual Growth	12/09	12/10	12/11	12/12	12/13
Sales ($ mil.)	0.9%	–	164.1	185.4	171.2	168.6
Net income ($ mil.)	(21.7%)	–	–	4.8	3.2	2.9
Market value ($ mil.)	–	–	–	–	–	–
Employees	–	–	–	–	–	292

UNITED ENERGY CORP.

OTC: UNRG

600 Meadowlands Pkwy. #20
Secaucus NJ 07094
Phone: 201-842-0288
Fax: 201-842-1307
Web: www.unitedenergycorp.net

CEO: –
CFO: James McKeever
HR: –
FYE: March 31
Type: Public

United Energy is dedicated to creating a more perfect union among environmentally friendly chemicals and customers. Its eco-friendly chemicals serve the oil industry with oil dispersants and protective coatings. Subsidiary Green Globe Industries supplies the US military with environmentally friendly solvents cleaners and paint strippers under the Qualchem brand name. United Energy top sellers are its K-Line chemical products (used in cleaning oil field equipment) and its Green Globe chemical products. Chairman Ronald Wilen owns 14% of the company.

UNITED FARMERS COOPERATIVE

705 E 4TH ST
WINTHROP, MN 553962362
Phone: 507-237-2281
Fax: –
Web: www.ufcmn.com

CEO: Jeff Nielsen
CFO: Lorie Reinarts
HR: Cheri Lebrun
FYE: August 31
Type: Private

United Farmers Cooperative has it all altogether. The agricultural cooperative supplies products and services to its members through 17 locations in eight rural communities across Minnesota. The farmer-owned co-op offers farm supplies such as energy feed seed fertilizer grain milling and blending and farm machinery as well as construction finance insurance and repair services. Originally known as the Cooperative Creamery Association United Farmers Cooperative (UFC) has been helping farmers in central Minnesota since 1915 (the creamery division was sold to Mid America Dairies in 1969).

	Annual Growth	08/03	08/04	08/05	08/06	08/07
Sales ($ mil.)	(59.6%)	–	–	782.4	93.9	127.4
Net income ($ mil.)	13364.0%	–	–	0.0	1.4	2.4
Market value ($ mil.)	–	–	–	–	–	–
Employees	–	–	–	–	–	269

UNITED FINANCIAL BANCORP INC (MD)

NMS: UBNK

95 Elm Street
West Springfield, MA 01089
Phone: 413 787-1700
Fax: –
Web: www.bankatunited.com

CEO: –
CFO: –
HR: –
FYE: December 31
Type: Public

United Financial Bancorp is the holding company for United Bank which operates about 20 branches serving residents and businesses in western Massachusetts. It offers such standard deposit products as CDs and checking money market NOW retirement and savings accounts. Deposits are United Bank's primary source of funds for its lending activities which focus on residential mortgages commercial real estate loans and home equity loans. To a lesser extent the bank provides business construction and consumer loans. Its United Wealth Management Group provides investments and financial planning services.

	Annual Growth	12/08	12/09	12/10	12/11	12/12
Assets ($ mil.)	17.4%	1,263.1	1,541.0	1,584.9	1,623.8	2,402.3
Net income ($ mil.)	(16.0%)	7.3	5.8	10.0	11.2	3.6
Market value ($ mil.)	0.9%	305.1	264.2	307.7	324.2	316.8
Employees	16.7%	223	284	291	292	413

UNITED FIRE GROUP, INC.

NMS: UFCS

118 Second Avenue S.E.
Cedar Rapids, IA 52401
Phone: 319 399-5700
Fax: –
Web: www.unitedfiregroup.com

CEO: Randy A. Ramlo
CFO: Dawn M. Jaffray
HR: Timothy Spain
FYE: December 31
Type: Public

The United Fire Group companies join together to offer a unified range of property/casualty and life insurance products. The group operates through its United Fire & Casualty subsidiary which in turn holds entities that carry a variety of property/casualty offerings including fidelity and surety bonds and fire auto employee liability homeowners and workers' compensation lines. More than 1300 independent agencies in some 45 states sell its property/casualty products to businesses and individuals. The United Life division of United Fire & Casualty sells life annuity and credit life products to individuals and groups through some 950 independent agents in more than 30 states.

	Annual Growth	12/10	12/11	12/12	12/13	12/14
Assets ($ mil.)	6.4%	3,007.4	3,618.9	3,694.7	3,720.7	3,856.7
Net income ($ mil.)	5.6%	47.5	0.0	40.2	76.1	59.1
Market value ($ mil.)	7.4%	558.4	504.9	546.4	717.1	743.8
Employees	10.7%	654	894	909	943	981

UNITED GILSONITE LABORATORIES

1396 JEFFERSON AVE
SCRANTON, PA 185092415
Phone: 570-344-1202
Fax: –
Web: www.ugl.com

CEO: –
CFO: –
HR: –
FYE: December 31
Type: Private

United Gilsonite Laboratories (UGL) prevents leaky roofs and warped decks. The company manufactures paint and wood and masonry finishing products including cement paints caulking compounds wall patching materials and waterproofing products. Its brand names include DRYLOK and ZAR. Founded in 1932 by Gerald Payne UGL has four manufacturing centers in Illinois Mississippi Nevada and Pennsylvania. It sells more than 80 products through 15000 dealers including hardware stores and-, home repair centers paint stores and lumber merchants-, in the US and internationally.

	Annual Growth	12/09	12/10	12/11	12/12	12/13
Sales ($ mil.)	–	–	0.0	0.0	45.0	47.8
Net income ($ mil.)	–	–	–	0.0	(0.1)	1.0
Market value ($ mil.)	–	–	–	–	–	–
Employees	–	–	–	–	–	200

UNITED GUARANTY CORPORATION

230 N. Elm St. 7th Fl.
Greensboro NC 27401
Phone: 336-373-0232
Fax: 336-230-1946
Web: www.ugcorp.com

CEO: Donna Demaio
CFO: Chip Compton
HR: –
FYE: December 31
Type: Subsidiary

United Guaranty is a private mortgage insurer offering mortgage guaranty insurance to lenders for first-lien residential mortgages as well as other contract services to assist mortgage lenders. (Mortgage insurance allows borrowers to purchase a house with a minimal down payment by providing protection to lenders.) The company distributes its products through a broad range of lenders including national and regional lenders credit unions and community banks and state housing finance agencies. A small subsidiary of insurance giant American International Group (AIG) United Guaranty operates primarily in the US but is active in Asia Europe and South America.

UNITED HARDWARE DISTRIBUTING CO

5005 NATHAN LN N
PLYMOUTH, MN 55442-3210
Phone: 763-559-1800
Fax: –
Web: www.unitedhardware.com

CEO: Steven G Draeger
CFO: –
HR: –
FYE: November 30
Type: Private

United Hardware Distributing is in the business of building relationships. The member-owned distributor delivers hammers nails and all the other hardware necessities to dealers in 18 states across the central US. The company is not a franchiser but it does provide retail support education buying markets and consulting services to its members. In addition to providing hardware United Hardware offers expertise in accounting store design pricing marketing purchasing and merchandising. Its client list of about 1200 member stores include Hardware Hank Trustworthy Hardware Golden Rule Lumber Ranch & Pet Supply and other independent retailers.

	Annual Growth	11/08	11/09	11/10	11/11	11/12
Sales ($ mil.)	2.7%	–	180.0	178.9	189.6	195.1
Net income ($ mil.)	(0.9%)	–	3.9	4.0	5.9	3.8
Market value ($ mil.)	–	–	–	–	–	–
Employees	–	–	–	–	–	330

UNITED HEALTH SERVICES HOSPITAL INC.

10-42 MITCHELL AVE
BINGHAMTON, NY 139031617
Phone: 607-762-2200
Fax: –
Web: www.uhs.net

CEO: –
CFO: Kate Knapik
HR: –
FYE: December 31
Type: Private

United Health Services Hospitals (UHS Hospitals) can service injuries from a slip in the snow or a slipped disc to health that's just plain slipping. The organization operates Binghamton General Hospital (about 200 beds) Wilson Medical Center (some 280 beds) and a group of primary and specialty care clinics in upstate New York. Specialty services include cardiology dialysis neurology rehabilitation pediatrics and psychiatry. The Wilson Medical Center serves as a teaching hospital offering residency and fellowship programs. UHS Hospitals is a subsidiary of United Health Services which operates a network of affiliated hospitals clinics long-term care centers and home health agencies in the region.

	Annual Growth	12/09	12/10	12/11	12/12	12/13
Sales ($ mil.)	5.3%	–	442.8	455.9	496.0	516.7
Net income ($ mil.)	23.5%	–	–	18.3	18.6	27.9
Market value ($ mil.)	–	–	–	–	–	–
Employees	–	–	–	–	–	5,000

UNITED INSURANCE HOLDINGS CORP

NAS: UIHC

360 Central Avenue, Suite 900
St. Petersburg, FL 33701
Phone: 727 895-7737
Fax: –

CEO: John L. Forney
CFO: B. Bradford Martz
HR: –
FYE: December 31
Type: Public

United Insurance Holdings insures homeowners in the Sunshine State throughout the seasons even hurricane season. The company underwrites flood fire and homeowners insurance policies in Florida and provides property insurance for automotive service companies. It distributes its products through independent agents. United Insurance was founded in 1999 then underwent a reverse merger in 2008 when it bought the OTC-listed FMG Acquisition Corp. for $95 million ($25 million in cash and 8.75 million shares of stock.) The newly merged company has listed on the NASDAQ exchange.

	Annual Growth	12/10	12/11	12/12	12/13	12/14
Assets ($ mil.)	28.6%	213.6	240.2	313.6	441.2	584.2
Net income ($ mil.)	–	(0.9)	8.1	9.7	20.3	41.0
Market value ($ mil.)	63.1%	64.8	92.0	125.6	294.3	458.9
Employees	27.1%	46	50	68	90	120

UNITED NATIONS FEDERAL CREDIT UNION

Court Square Place 24-01 44th Rd.
Long Island City NY 11101-4605
Phone: 347-686-6000
Fax: 347-686-6400
Web: https://www.unfcu.org

CEO: William F Predmore
CFO: –
HR: Stefanie Smedstad
FYE: December 31
Type: Private - Not-for-Pr

United Nations Federal Credit Union (UNFCU) offers a world of financial products and services to employees of the United Nations and its affiliated agencies. UNFCU's offerings include savings accounts checking accounts money market accounts and credit cards. It also originates mortgages consumer loans automobile loans student loans and other loans. UNFCU provides insurance and investment services as well. The credit union operates about 10 branch and representative offices with locations in Geneva; Nairobi Kenya; New York; Rome; and Vienna Austria. UNFCU has more than 80000 members. It was formed in 1947 by United Nations staffers.

UNITED NATURAL FOODS INC.

NMS: UNFI

313 Iron Horse Way
Providence, RI 02908
Phone: 401 528 8634
Fax: –
Web: www.unfi.com

CEO: Steven L. (Steve) Spinner
CFO: Michael P. Zechmeister
HR: –
FYE: August 01
Type: Public

Distribution is second nature for United Natural Foods Inc. (UNFI). The company is one of the top wholesale distributors of natural organic and specialty foods in the US and Canada. It owns more than 30 distribution centers that supply 85000-plus items to 40000 customers including independently-owned retailers supernatural chain Whole Foods (its #1 customer) and traditional supermarkets. The company offers groceries supplements produce frozen foods and ethnic and kosher food products. UNFI also operates about a dozen natural-products retail stores under the Earth Origins banner and it produces roasted nuts dried fruits and other snack items through subsidiary Woodstock Farms.

	Annual Growth	07/11	07/12*	08/13	08/14	08/15
Sales ($ mil.)	15.9%	4,530.0	5,236.0	6,064.4	6,794.4	8,185.0
Net income ($ mil.)	16.0%	76.7	91.3	107.9	125.5	138.7
Market value ($ mil.)	2.2%	2,091.5	2,736.2	3,021.3	2,941.1	2,280.9
Employees	6.0%	6,900	7,000	7,300	8,700	8,700

*Fiscal year change

UNITED NEGRO COLLEGE FUND INC.

1805 7TH ST NW STE 100
WASHINGTON, DC 200013187
Phone: 703-205-3400
Fax: –
Web: www.uncfsp.org

CEO: –
CFO: –
HR: Manny Diaz
FYE: March 31
Type: Private

A mind is a terrible thing to waste. In this spirit the United Negro College Fund (UNCF) offers financial assistance to students of color from low- to moderate-income families pursuing a higher education. UNCF the oldest and largest higher non-profit education assistance program for African-Americans enables some 60000 students to attend college each year. About 60% of the students are the first in their families to attend college. UNCF also provides operating funds and IT services to historically black colleges and universities such as Bethune-Cookman Morehouse Xavier and Voorhees College.

	Annual Growth	03/07	03/08	03/09	03/10	03/14
Sales ($ mil.)	(2.8%)	–	–	240.5	197.8	208.5
Net income ($ mil.)	(14.9%)	–	–	89.8	51.3	40.1
Market value ($ mil.)	–	–	–	–	–	–
Employees	–	–	–	–	–	257

UNITED ONLINE INC

NMS: UNTD

21255 Burbank Boulevard, Suite 400
Woodland Hills, CA 91367
Phone: 818 287-3000
Fax: –
Web: www.unitedonline.com

CEO: Francis Lobo
CFO: Edward Zinser
HR: –
FYE: December 31
Type: Public

United Online keeps people connected. Through its subsidiaries the company operates subscription-based social networking websites including Memory Lane (historic magazines newsreels sports highlights and yearbook moments) and Classmates and StayFriends. It also operates rewards membership program MyPoints and provides Internet access under the NetZero and Juno Online brands and web hosting through MySite. In late 2013 United Online spun off its largest operation floral retailer FTD. The company was created by the 2001 merger of NetZero and Juno; in subsequent years it moved to diversify its business in light of a decline in dial-up Internet subscribers.

	Annual Growth	12/10	12/11	12/12	12/13	12/14
Sales ($ mil.)	(30.3%)	920.6	897.7	870.9	233.6	217.2
Net income ($ mil.)	–	53.7	51.7	12.5	(82.2)	(5.4)
Market value ($ mil.)	21.9%	94.3	77.7	79.9	196.6	207.9
Employees	(23.7%)	1,606	1,504	1,574	622	545

UNITED PANAM FINANCIAL CORP.

18191 Von Karman Ave. Ste. 300
Irvine CA 92612
Phone: 949-224-1917
Fax: 949-224-1912
Web: www.upfc.com

CEO: James Vagim
CFO: –
HR: –
FYE: December 31
Type: Private

United PanAm Financial flies the choppy skies of nonprime lending. Through subsidiary United Auto Credit Corporation (UACC) the specialty finance firm originates buys and services auto loan contracts for high-risk customers. The company buys contracts from independent and franchised used car dealers. Most borrowers have less-than-perfect credit histories which impairs their ability to secure loans. UACC once heavily localized in California now has more than 15 offices throughout the country — a dramatic decrease from what it had only a few years ago. Chairman Guillermo Bron and investment firm Pine Brook Road bought United PanAm and took it private in 2011.

UNITED PARCEL SERVICE INC

NYS: UPS

55 Glenlake Parkway
N.E. Atlanta, GA 30328
Phone: 404 828-6000
Fax: –
Web: www.ups.com

CEO: David P. Abney
CFO: Richard Peretz
HR: Kevin Foley
FYE: December 31
Type: Public

The ubiquitous Brown is more than chocolate-colored trucks or a plain-vanilla delivery business. United Parcel Service (UPS) is the world's largest package delivery company transporting about 18 million packages and documents per business day throughout the US and to 220-plus countries. Its delivery operations use a fleet of more than 106000 motor vehicles and 600-plus aircraft. In addition to package delivery the company offers services such as logistics and freight forwarding through UPS Supply Chain Solutions and less-than-truckload (LTL) and truckload (TL) freight transportation through UPS Freight.

	Annual Growth	12/10	12/11	12/12	12/13	12/14
Sales ($ mil.)	4.1%	49,545.0	53,105.0	54,127.0	55,438.0	58,232.0
Net income ($ mil.)	(3.4%)	3,488.0	3,804.0	807.0	4,372.0	3,032.0
Market value ($ mil.)	11.2%	65,684.9	66,237.0	66,725.7	95,097.4	100,608.9
Employees	2.1%	400,600	398,000	399,000	395,000	435,000

UNITED PERFORMING ARTS FUND INC.

301 W WSCNSIN AVE STE 600
MILWAUKEE, WI 53202
Phone: 414-273-8723
Fax: –
Web: www.upaf.org

CEO: –
CFO: –
HR: –
FYE: August 31
Type: Private

The United Performing Arts Fund (UPAF) is a not-for-profit organization that does fund raising work for some 40 performing arts groups in greater Milwaukee and southeastern Wisconsin — including symphonies and orchestras ballet and opera companies theater groups dance studios and performing arts schools. Large corporate donations (more than $25000) make up about a third of UPAF's campaign revenues; other categories of giving include individual donations through company campaigns private foundations and special events. The organization was founded in 1966

	Annual Growth	08/10	08/11	08/12	08/13	08/14
Sales ($ mil.)	4.9%	–	11.8	11.2	10.8	13.6
Net income ($ mil.)	121.2%	–	–	0.2	(0.0)	1.2
Market value ($ mil.)	–	–	–	–	–	–
Employees	–	–	–	–	–	21

UNITED PLASTICS GROUP INC.

1420 Kensington Rd. Ste. 209
Oak Brook IL 60523
Phone: 630-706-5500
Fax: 630-706-5510
Web: www.unitedplasticsgroup.com

CEO: –
CFO: –
HR: –
FYE: December 31
Type: Private

From an amorphous blob to a cell phone casing or car dashboard United Plastics Group (UPG) shapes its profits by molding raw plastic into finished products. The company makes plastic products and components utilizing mold building injection molding and micro molding processes. Its divisions are based on the automotive consumer electronics industrial and medical markets. Value-added products include heat transfer decals heat staking pad printing and sonic welding. UPG which operates more than 300 molding machines has about a dozen manufacturing plants in the US China Mexico and the UK.

UNITED REGIONAL HEALTH CARE SYSTEM INC.

1600 11TH ST | CEO: Phyliss Cowling
WICHITA FALLS, TX 763014300 | CFO: –
Phone: 940-764-3211 | HR: –
Fax: – | FYE: December 31
Web: www.unitedregional.org | Type: Private

If you take a fall in Wichita Falls United Regional Health Care System (URHCS) will be there. The health care provider serves the residents of northern Texas through two hospitals that combined have some 500 beds. Specialized services include emergency medicine cardiac care diagnostic imaging surgery obstetrics and pediatrics. The health care system also offers cancer treatment childbirth wound care and sleep diagnostic centers. It is the only comprehensive cardiac care facility and only Level II trauma center in the region. URHCS operates a Care Flight Helicopter to get those traumas to care quicker.

	Annual Growth	12/09	12/10	12/11	12/12	12/13
Sales ($ mil.)	0.6%	–	287.7	289.6	279.1	292.8
Net income ($ mil.)	13.5%	–	–	41.6	41.9	53.6
Market value ($ mil.)	–	–	–	–	–	–
Employees	–	–	–	–	–	1,950

UNITED RENTALS, INC.

NYS: URI

100 First Stamford Place, Suite 700 | CEO: Michael J. Kneeland
Stamford, CT 06902 | CFO: William B. Plummer
Phone: 203 622-3131 | HR: Craig Pintoff
Fax: – | FYE: December 31
Web: www.unitedrentals.com | Type: Public

No cash to buy a bulldozer? No worries — just lease one from United Rentals. The company considers itself the #1 commercial and construction equipment renter in the world serving customers in the commercial infrastructure industrial and residential sectors. It operates through a network of more than 880 locations in the US and Canada and provides about 3300 equipment items — everything from general to heavy construction and industrial equipment to hand tools special-event items (such as aerial towers) power (diesel generators) and HVAC equipment and trench-safety equipment. It also sells new and used equipment as well as rental-related and contractor supplies and parts.

	Annual Growth	12/11	12/12	12/13	12/14	12/15
Sales ($ mil.)	22.2%	2,611.0	4,117.0	4,955.0	5,685.0	5,817.0
Net income ($ mil.)	55.1%	101.0	75.0	387.0	540.0	585.0
Market value ($ mil.)	25.2%	2,712.0	4,177.7	7,154.0	9,362.1	6,657.5
Employees	14.1%	7,500	11,300	11,850	12,500	12,700

UNITED SCAFFOLDING INC.

16073 Airline Hwy. | CEO: –
Baton Rouge LA 70817 | CFO: Kevin Collard
Phone: 225 774 1400 | HR: –
Fax: 225-774-9494 | FYE: December 31
Web: www.unitedscaffold.com | Type: Private

To any one who shudders at the thought of building repairs brace yourself: United Scaffolding sells and rents industrial scaffolding and other equipment to prop up projects along the Gulf Coast. Founded in 1998 the company also offers erection and dismantling engineering and CAD design maintenance turnarounds and safety training. United Scaffolding serves customers in industries from shipyards to pulp and paper mills petrochemical power and a breadth of commercial contractors. In 2007 United Scaffolding was scored by the Brock Group a specialty maintenance contractor. Former parent company Xserv was merged into the Brock Group but United Scaffolding operates under its original name.

UNITED SECURITY BANCSHARES (CA)

NMS: UBFO

2126 Inyo Street | CEO: Dennis R Woods
Fresno, CA 93721 | CFO: Bhavneet Gill
Phone: 559 248-4943 | HR: –
Fax: 559 248-5088 | FYE: December 31
Web: www.unitedsecuritybank.com | Type: Public

United Security Bancshares (unrelated to the Alabama-based corporation of the same name) is the holding company for United Security Bank which operates about 10 branches loan offices and financial services offices in central California's San Joaquin Valley. The bank attracts deposits from area businesses and individuals by offering checking and savings accounts NOW and money market accounts certificates of deposit and IRAs. In 2007 United Security Bancshares bought Legacy Bank which had a single branch in Campbell California. A year later the company purchased ICG Financial and then formed a wealth management consulting and insurance division USB Financial Services.

	Annual Growth	12/10	12/11	12/12	12/13	12/14
Assets ($ mil.)	(0.6%)	678.2	651.3	648.9	635.9	663.2
Net income ($ mil.)	–	(4.4)	(10.8)	6.1	7.3	6.2
Market value ($ mil.)	9.7%	60.4	35.2	41.1	79.0	87.6
Employees	0.0%	132	138	142	138	132

UNITED SECURITY BANCSHARES, INC.

NAS: USBI

131 West Front Street, P.O. Box 249 | CEO: James F House
Thomasville, AL 36784 | CFO: Thomas S Elley
Phone: 334 636-5424 | HR: –
Fax: – | FYE: December 31
Web: www.unitedsecuritybank.com | Type: Public

United Security Bancshares (unrelated to the United Security Bancshares in California) is the holding company for First United Security Bank which has about 20 locations in central and western Alabama and eastern Mississippi. It serves area consumers and businesses offering such standard retail services as savings checking and money market accounts as well as CDs and credit and check cards. Real estate mortgages make up more than 70% of the bank's loan portfolio which also includes business and consumer loans. Bank subsidiary Acceptance Loan Company primarily makes consumer loans through about two dozen offices in Alabama and Mississippi.

	Annual Growth	12/10	12/11	12/12	12/13	12/14
Assets ($ mil.)	(2.2%)	627.0	621.8	567.1	569.8	572.6
Net income ($ mil.)	14.4%	2.1	(9.1)	2.2	3.9	3.5
Market value ($ mil.)	(5.8%)	67.6	25.1	32.3	44.0	53.3
Employees	10.2%	198	297	290	286	292

UNITED SPACE ALLIANCE LLC

600 GEMINI ST | CEO: –
HOUSTON, TX 770582783 | CFO: William R Capol
Phone: 281-212-6200 | HR: Sherri K Lee
Fax: – | FYE: December 31
Web: www.unitedspacealliance.com | Type: Private

United Space Alliance (USA) is a space-race heavyweight; the Houston-based prime contractor has run NASA's 173000 pound Shuttles — Discovery Atlantis and Endeavour. USA a joint venture between Lockheed Martin and Boeing was formed in response to NASA's move to consolidate multiple Space Shuttle contracts under a single entity. It is now wrapping up those contracts. USA has supported mission operations astronaut and flight controller training flight software development Shuttle payload integration and vehicle processing launch and recovery. It also has led training and planning for the International Space Station. USA served the Johnson and Kennedy Space Centers and Marshall Space Flight Center.

	Annual Growth	12/03	12/04	12/05	12/06	12/07
Sales ($ mil.)	(3.2%)	–	–	–	1,920.5	1,859.8
Net income ($ mil.)	14.8%	–	–	–	146.3	168.0
Market value ($ mil.)	–	–	–	–	–	–
Employees	–	–	–	–	–	10,500

UNITED STATES ANTIMONY CORP.

ASE: UAMY

P.O. Box 643
Thompson Falls, MT 59873
Phone: 406 827-3523
Fax: –
Web: www.usantimony.com

CEO: John C Lawrence
CFO: Daniel L Parks
HR: –
FYE: December 31
Type: Public

The products of United States Antimony don't span the alphabet from A to Z but they do include both antimony and zeolite. The company produces antimony oxide which is used as a flame retardant in plastics fiberglass and textiles and as a color fastener in paint. U.S. Antimony buys most of its raw antimony from China and Canada. The company has begun exploratory mining operations on a property in Mexico. U.S. Antimony also processes zeolite which is used in animal feed fertilizer water filtration and other applications.

	Annual Growth	12/10	12/11	12/12	12/13	12/14
Sales ($ mil.)	4.4%	9.1	13.1	12.0	11.0	10.8
Net income ($ mil.)	–	0.8	0.6	(0.6)	(1.6)	(1.6)
Market value ($ mil.)	3.9%	39.6	158.5	116.2	130.1	46.2
Employees	67.6%	27	24	23	80	213

UNITED STATES BASKETBALL LEAGUE INC

OTC: USBL

183 Plains Road, Suite 2
Milford, CT 06461
Phone: 203 877-9508
Fax: –

CEO: –
CFO: Richard C Meisenheimer
HR: –
FYE: February 28
Type: Public

Basketball fans have more hardwood action to enjoy thanks to this enterprise. The United States Basketball League (USBL) operates an association of professional basketball teams that play a 30-game schedule from April through June. The league encompasses a half dozen teams including the Brooklyn Kings the Dodge City Legend and the Kansas Cagerz which compete with 11 players each. The USBL generates revenue mostly through franchise fees and marketing sponsorships. It is intended to be a development league for recent college graduates and international players to showcase their skills for scouts from National Basketball Association teams. The founding Meisenheimer family controls about 90% of the USBL.

	Annual Growth	02/11	02/12	02/13	02/14	02/15
Sales ($ mil.)	–	0.0	0.0	0.0	0.0	0.0
Net income ($ mil.)	–	0.0	(0.3)	(0.2)	(0.1)	0.1
Market value ($ mil.)	–	0.0	0.7	0.5	0.1	1.1
Employees	0.0%	–	–	1	1	1

UNITED STATES BEEF CORPORATION

4923 E 49TH ST
TULSA, OK 741357002
Phone: 918-665-0740
Fax: –
Web: www.usbeefcorp.com

CEO: –
CFO: –
HR: Kim Thompson
FYE: December 31
Type: Private

This company has carved out a sandwich empire in the middle of the country. United States Beef Corporation is the largest franchisee of Arby's fast-food restaurants in the US with more than 280 locations in half a dozen states mostly in Kansas Missouri and Oklahoma. The restaurants franchised from Arby's Restaurant Group (part of Wendy's/Arby's Group) serve the chain's signature roast beef sandwiches and curly fries as well as ham chicken and turkey subs. Bob Davis and his wife Connie opened their first Arby's in 1969 and founded United States Beef in 1974. The Davis family continues to own the company.

	Annual Growth	12/06	12/07	12/08	12/12	12/13
Sales ($ mil.)	0.7%	–	246.1	246.5	246.9	256.5
Net income ($ mil.)	5.5%	–	–	6.1	7.3	7.9
Market value ($ mil.)	–	–	–	–	–	–
Employees	–	–	–	–	–	2,000

UNITED STATES CELLULAR CORP

NYS: USM

8410 West Bryn Mawr
Chicago, IL 60631
Phone: 773 399-8900
Fax: –
Web: www.uscellular.com

CEO: Kenneth R. Meyers
CFO: Steven T. Campbell
HR: –
FYE: December 31
Type: Public

United States Cellular takes calls from sea to shining sea. Doing business as U.S. Cellular the company provides wireless phone service to about 6 million customers in more than two dozen states in the US largely in the Midwest and the South. Its pre- and post-paid products and services — marketed directly through the Internet and from about 400 retail stores — include mobile messaging prepaid calling international long distance mobile Internet and directory assistance. U.S. Cellular service is also sold through contracts with resellers. The company offers phones from HTC LG Electronics BlackBerry and Samsung Electronics.

	Annual Growth	12/10	12/11	12/12	12/13	12/14
Sales ($ mil.)	(1.8%)	4,177.7	4,343.3	4,452.1	3,918.8	3,892.7
Net income ($ mil.)	–	132.3	175.0	111.0	140.0	(42.8)
Market value ($ mil.)	–	–	–	–	–	2,099.5
Employees	(7.5%)	9,000	8,743	8,100	6,700	6,600

UNITED STATES DEPARTMENT OF JUSTICE

950 Pennsylvania Ave. NW
Washington DC 20530-0001
Phone: 202-514-2000
Fax: 202-501-3136
Web: www.cio.gov

CEO: –
CFO: –
HR: –
FYE: September 30
Type: Government Agency

The Department of Justice (DOJ) doesn't make the laws it just enforces them. The DOJ one of 15 federal executive departments is charged with enforcing federal law defending the rights of US citizens and representing the legal interests of the US government. The department covers both civil and criminal areas of federal law and is involved in everything from prosecuting offenders of antitrust laws to investigating organized crime. With the US Attorney General at its helm the DOJ comprises roughly 40 separate components including the FBI ATF US Marshals BOP CRS and US Attorneys. It has an annual budget in excess of $42 billion.

UNITED STATES FUND FOR UNICEF

125 MAIDEN LN FL 11
NEW YORK, NY 100384999
Phone: 212-686-5522
Fax: –
Web: www.unicef.org

CEO: Caryl M Stern
CFO: –
HR: –
FYE: June 30
Type: Private

The US Fund for UNICEF is one of about 40 committees in America that raises money for The United Nations Children's Fund (better known as UNICEF a not-for-profit organization that works for the human rights protection and development of children worldwide through education advocacy and fundraising. Among its dedicated programs are the five-year $100 million fundraising campaign for HIV/AIDS prevention and a campaign to protect mothers and newborns from tetanus. The US Fund for UNICEF derives revenue from public support — through its signature Trick-or-Treat for UNICEF program gifts corporate grants and the sale of greeting cards and educational materials. The organization was founded in 1947.

	Annual Growth	06/10	06/11	06/12	06/13	06/14
Sales ($ mil.)	95.2%	–	–	–	310.9	606.9
Net income ($ mil.)	423.1%	–	–	–	12.9	67.7
Market value ($ mil.)	–	–	–	–	–	–
Employees	–	–	–	–	–	200

UNITED STATES GOLF ASSOCIATION

77 LIBERTY CORNER RD	CEO: –
FAR HILLS, NJ 079312570	CFO: –
Phone: 908-234-2300	HR: –
Fax: –	FYE: November 30
Web: www.usgamuseum.com	Type: Private

Making sure golf stays clear of the rough is par for the course at this organization. The United States Golf Association is the governing body for golf in the US its territories and Mexico. The not-for-profit group writes and interprets the rules of the game provides handicap information offers turf consulting and funds equipment and course maintenance research and testing. It also holds several national championship events including the US Open the US Women's Open and the US Senior Open. The group generates most of its revenue from the sale of broadcast rights to championship tournaments and other matches as well as through membership fees. The USGA was founded in 1894.

	Annual Growth	11/09	11/10	11/11	11/12	11/13
Sales ($ mil.)	6.0%	–	131.6	155.1	147.4	156.6
Net income ($ mil.)	(54.8%)	–	–	33.3	13.7	6.8
Market value ($ mil.)	–	–	–	–	–	–
Employees	–	–	–	–	–	350

UNITED STATES LIME & MINERALS INC.

NMS: USLM

5429 LBJ Freeway, Suite 230	CEO: Timothy W. Byrne
Dallas, TX 75240	CFO: M. Michael Owens
Phone: 972 991-8400	HR: Jaylene Russell
Fax: 972 385-1340	FYE: December 31
Web: www.uslm.com	Type: Public

Don't be crushed there's no tequila; it's not that kind of lime. Instead United States Lime & Minerals operates limestone quarries and lime plants in Arkansas Colorado Oklahoma Louisiana and Texas. It produces high-calcium quicklime and limestone pulverized limestone hydrated lime lime kiln dust and lime slurry used in the construction municipal sanitation aluminum paper glass housing agricultural and environmental sectors. The company has approximately 700 customers primarily in the central US. In addition to its lime operations United States Lime & Minerals also has natural gas interests.

	Annual Growth	12/10	12/11	12/12	12/13	12/14
Sales ($ mil.)	3.1%	132.6	142.6	138.5	133.8	149.8
Net income ($ mil.)	1.8%	18.0	22.2	16.4	14.8	19.4
Market value ($ mil.)	14.7%	235.7	336.3	263.7	342.3	407.7
Employees	1.5%	295	301	294	297	313

UNITED STATES OLYMPIC COMMITTEE INC

27 S TEJON ST	CEO: Scott Blackmun
COLORADO SPRINGS, CO 809031538	CFO: Walter Glover
Phone: 719-632-5551	HR: –
Fax: –	FYE: December 31
Web: www.teamusa.org	Type: Private

Friendship solidarity and fair play are the watchwords for this sports organization. United States Olympic Committee (USOC) is the governing body of the Olympic movement in the US and oversees the organization selection and training of the country's Olympic athletes and teams. The not-for-profit organization operates six training and education centers around the country where athletes prepare for the Olympic Games the Paralympic Games and the Pan American Games. The USOC is funded by corporate sponsorships private contributions and sales of licensed apparel. It also receives money from the International Olympic Committee (IOC). The USOC was formed in 1978.

	Annual Growth	12/06	12/07*	08/08*	12/08	12/13
Sales ($ mil.)	(34.0%)	–	2,033.7	2.9	280.6	168.2
Net income ($ mil.)	–	–	–	0.1	0.0	(27.5)
Market value ($ mil.)	–	–	–	–	–	–
Employees	–	–	–	–	–	400
					*Fiscal year change

UNITED STATES POSTAL SERVICE

475 L'Enfant Plaza SW	CEO: Patrick R Donahoe
Washington DC 20260-2200	CFO: –
Phone: 202-268-2500	HR: –
Fax: 206-342-3000	FYE: September 30
Web: www.vulcan.com	Type: Government Agency

The United States Postal Service (USPS) handles cards letters and packages sent from sea to shining sea. The USPS delivered some 168 billion pieces of mail in fiscal 2011 in the US and its territories and if that's not enough it claims to deliver more than 40% of the world's mail. The independent government agency relies on postage and fees to fund operations. Though it has a monopoly on delivering the mail the USPS faces competition for services such as package delivery. The US president appoints nine of the 11 members of the board who oversee the USPS. The presidential appointees select the postmaster general and together they name the deputy postmaster general; the two also serve on the board.

UNITED STATES SOCCER FEDERATION INC.

1801 S PRAIRIE AVE	CEO: Dan Flynn
CHICAGO, IL 606161319	CFO: –
Phone: 312-808-1300	HR: –
Fax: –	FYE: March 31
Web: www.ussoccer.com	Type: Private

The U.S. Soccer Federation knows how its members like to get their kicks. The organization is the governing body for the sport of soccer (known around the world as football) in the United States. It promotes the game and organizes both recreational and professional competition overseeing such leagues as Major League Soccer United Soccer Leagues and Women's Professional Soccer. U.S. Soccer hosts World Cups and Olympic soccer and runs the National Soccer Training Center. The federation is a member of the F- ©d- ©ration Internationale de Football Association (FIFA) the world soccer governing body. The organization was founded in 1914 as the U.S. Football Association.

	Annual Growth	03/06	03/07	03/09	03/10	03/13
Sales ($ mil.)	(40.6%)	–	1,485.6	45.2	44.3	65.1
Net income ($ mil.)	–	–	–	0.0	0.8	4.3
Market value ($ mil.)	–	–	–	–	–	–
Employees	–	–	–	–	–	92

UNITED STATES STEEL CORP.

NYS: X

600 Grant Street	CEO: Mario Longhi
Pittsburgh PA 15219-2800	CFO: David B. (Dave) Burritt
Phone: 412 433-1121	HR: –
Fax: 412 433-4818	FYE: December 31
Web: www.ussteel.com	Type: Public

Steel crazy after all these years United States Steel (U.S. Steel) is North America's largest integrated steelmaker. The company operates mills throughout the Midwest in the US; in Ontario Canada; and in Slovakia. U.S. Steel makes a wide range of flat-rolled and tubular steel products and its annual production capacity is 24.4 million net tons of raw steel. Its customers are primarily in the automotive appliance construction oil and gas and petrochemical industries. In addition U.S. Steel mines iron ore and procures coke which provide the primary raw materials used in steelmaking. It is also engaged in railroad and barge operations and real estate.

	Annual Growth	12/10	12/11	12/12	12/13	12/14
Sales ($ mil.)	0.2%	17,374.0	19,884.0	19,328.0	17,424.0	17,507.0
Net income ($ mil.)	–	(482.0)	(53.0)	(124.0)	(1,672.0)	102.0
Market value ($ mil.)	(17.7%)	8,509.2	3,854.0	3,473.9	4,296.8	3,894.8
Employees	(14.0%)	42,000	43,000	39,000	38,500	23,000

UNITED STATES TENNIS ASSOCIATION INCORPORATED

70 W. Red Oak Ln.	CEO: –
White Plains NY 10604	CFO: –
Phone: 914-696-7000	HR: –
Fax: 914-696-7019	FYE: December 31
Web: www.usta.com	Type: Private - Not-for-Pr

You might say this sports group makes quite a racquet on the court. The United States Tennis Association (USTA) serves as the governing body for the sport of tennis in the US. It sets the rules of play and develops and promotes the sport at the local and professional levels. USTA also owns and operates the US Open the annual Grand Slam event held at Arthur Ashe Stadium in Flushing Meadows New York. In addition the not-for-profit organization selects players to compete in such tournaments as the Davis Cup the Fed Cup and the Olympics. Founded in 1881 as the United States National Lawn Tennis Association the USTA has grown to more than 700000 members from all age and skill levels.

UNITED SUPERMARKETS L.L.C.

7830 Orlando Ave.	CEO: Robert Taylor
Lubbock TX 79423	CFO: Suzann Kirby
Phone: 806-791-7457	HR: –
Fax: 806-791-7476	FYE: January 31
Web: www.unitedtexas.com	Type: Private

From Muleshoe up to Dalhart and over to Pampa United Supermarkets keeps the Texas Panhandle well fed. The grocer has about 50 supermarkets mostly in rural towns under the United Market Street Amigos and United Express banners. Its stores feature deli floral and bakery shops as well as groceries pharmacies (at most locations) and gas at some locales. Its larger Market Street format stocks more specialty and international foods. United Supermarkets runs its own distribution facility. H. D. Snell founded the firm in Sayre Oklahoma in 1916. He bucked the norms of the day by selling for cash — instead of on credit — at lower prices. United Supermarkets is owned and run by the Snell family.

UNITED SURGICAL PARTNERS INTERNATIONAL INC.

15305 Dallas Pkwy. Ste. 1600	CEO: William H Wilcox
Addison TX 75001	CFO: Jason B Cagle
Phone: 972-713-3500	HR: –
Fax: 972-713-3550	FYE: December 31
Web: www.unitedsurgical.com	Type: Private

United Surgical Partners International (USPI) brings together surgeons from across the US and the UK. The company owns or manages about 200 short-stay ambulatory surgery centers and surgical hospitals in the US and another six medical facilities in the UK. The company creates centers from scratch converts outpatient departments into stand-alone jointly run locations and purchases existing facilities; contract management services are also available. USPI markets its facilities to patients physicians and insurance companies. Health care investment firm Welsh Carson Anderson & Stowe owns USPI.

UNITED TECHNOLOGIES CORP

NYS: UTX

10 Farm Springs Road	CEO: Gregory J. Hayes
Farmington, CT 06032	CFO: Akhil Johri
Phone: 860 728-7000	HR: Kathy Douglas
Fax: 860 728-7028	FYE: December 31
Web: www.utc.com	Type: Public

United Technologies (UTC) has the worldwide industrial expertise to lift you up and cool you down. Its Otis UTC Climate Controls & Security Pratt & Whitney and Sikorsky segments develop technologies systems and services for the aerospace construction and security industries. Climate Controls & Security makes alarms monitoring equipment surveillance and access control systems and fire and hazard detection products. Otis is the world's largest elevator and escalator manufacturing company. Pratt & Whitney makes commercial and military engines while Sikorsky makes helicopters. UTC Aerospace Systems produces engine controls and flight systems for military and commercial clients.

	Annual Growth	12/11	12/12	12/13	12/14	12/15
Sales ($ mil.)	(0.9%)	58,190.0	57,708.0	62,626.0	65,100.0	56,098.0
Net income ($ mil.)	11.2%	4,979.0	5,130.0	5,721.0	6,220.0	7,608.0
Market value ($ mil.)	7.1%	61,274.6	68,752.6	95,403.6	96,409.6	80,539.7
Employees	(0.3%)	199,900	218,000	212,400	211,500	197,200

UNITED THERAPEUTICS CORP

NMS: UTHR

1040 Spring Street	CEO: Martine A. Rothblatt
Silver Spring, MD 20910	CFO: John M. Ferrari
Phone: 301 608-9292	HR: –
Fax: –	FYE: December 31
Web: www.unither.com	Type: Public

United Therapeutics hopes its products will be in vein. Its injectable drug Remodulin treats pulmonary hypertension which affects the blood vessels between the heart and lungs; it also treats cancer and viral illnesses. The product is marketed directly and through distributors in North America Europe and the Asia/Pacific region. Other hypertension treatments include Adcirca Tyvaso and Orenitram. The company's development pipeline includes additional treatments for cardiovascular disease as well as various cancers respiratory conditions and infectious diseases. United Therapeutics has divested its cardiac monitoring division.

	Annual Growth	12/10	12/11	12/12	12/13	12/14
Sales ($ mil.)	20.9%	603.8	743.2	916.1	1,117.0	1,288.5
Net income ($ mil.)	33.9%	105.9	217.9	304.4	174.6	340.1
Market value ($ mil.)	19.6%	2,978.1	2,225.8	2,516.5	5,326.9	6,100.0
Employees	9.2%	520	543	623	706	740

UNITED VAN LINES LLC

One United Dr.	CEO: –
Fenton MO 63026	CFO: –
Phone: 636-343-3900	HR: –
Fax: 636-326-1106	FYE: December 31
Web: www.unitedvanlines.com	Type: Subsidiary

A subsidiary of UniGroup United Van Lines offers moving services to companies and households. The company is one of the largest US movers along with sister company Mayflower Transit and SIRVA's North American Van Lines and Allied Van Lines units. Besides providing moving and relocation services United Van Lines also transports trade show exhibits museum and fine arts items and high-value equipment such as electronics. It works with sister company UniGroup Worldwide UTS to offer international moving services. Overall United Van Lines has a network of more than 1000 agents around the world including some 500 in the US. United Van Lines which traces its roots back to 1928 is owned by its agents.

UNITED WAY WORLDWIDE

701 N FAIRFAX ST LBBY
ALEXANDRIA, VA 223142045
Phone: 703-836-7100
Fax: –
Web: www.unitedway.org

CEO: Brian A Gallagher
CFO: –
HR: –
FYE: December 31
Type: Private

Where there's a will there's a Way. Working to raise money for charitable causes United Way Worldwide unites some 1800 namesake organizations active in about 40 countries and territories. While its specific priorities are set by local entities the global organization tends to focus on helping children achieve their potential promoting financial stability and improving access to health care. Major recipients of its contributions have included the American Cancer Society Big Brothers/Big Sisters Catholic Charities Girl Scouts Boy Scouts and The Salvation Army among other worthy organizations. United Way Worldwide was formed by the merger of United Way of America and United Way International.

	Annual Growth	12/05	12/06	12/08*	09/09*	12/13
Sales ($ mil.)	–	–	(244.8)	1.8	1.8	78.7
Net income ($ mil.)	–	–	–	0.0	(0.1)	(11.2)
Market value ($ mil.)	–	–	–	–	–	–
Employees	–	–	–	–	–	204

*Fiscal year change

UNITED-GUARDIAN, INC.

NMS: UG

230 Marcus Boulevard
Hauppauge, NY 11788
Phone: 631 273-0900
Fax: 631 273-0858
Web: www.u-g.com

CEO: Kenneth H Globus
CFO: Robert S Rubinger
HR: –
FYE: December 31
Type: Public

Through its Guardian Laboratories division United-Guardian makes a variety of cosmetic ingredients personal care products and pharmaceuticals. Its top-selling Lubrajel line is a moisturizer used in cosmetics and as a lubricant for medical catheters. Other cosmetic products include Klensoft surfactants used in shampoos and Unitwix a thickening agent for cosmetic oils and liquids. United-Guardian's main pharmaceutical product is Renacidin Irrigation a prescription drug used to keep urinary catheters clear. In 2007 the company sold the assets of its Eastern Chemical subsidiary which distributed organic and research chemicals dyes reagents and other chemicals.

	Annual Growth	12/10	12/11	12/12	12/13	12/14
Sales ($ mil.)	(0.5%)	13.7	14.3	13.8	15.4	13.4
Net income ($ mil.)	1.6%	3.8	4.7	4.8	5.9	4.1
Market value ($ mil.)	9.1%	64.4	70.1	90.4	129.5	91.1
Employees	0.0%	36	36	36	36	36

UNITEDHEALTH GROUP INC

NYS: UNH

UnitedHealth Group Center, 9900 Bren Road East
Minnetonka, MN 55343
Phone: 952 936-1300
Fax: –
Web: www.unitedhealthgroup.com

CEO: Stephen J. Hemsley
CFO: David S. Wichmann
HR: Christine Anderson
FYE: December 31
Type: Public

UnitedHealth unites its health plans with consumers across the US. As a leading health insurer it offers a variety of plans and services to group and individual customers nationwide. Its UnitedHealthcare health benefits segment manages HMO PPO and POS plans as well as Medicare Medicaid state-funded and supplemental vision and dental options. Together the UnitedHealthcare businesses serve more than 40 million members. In addition UnitedHealth's Optum health services units — OptumHealth OptumInsight and OptumRx — provide wellness and care management programs financial services information technology solutions and pharmacy benefit management (PBM) services to an additional 45 million.

	Annual Growth	12/11	12/12	12/13	12/14	12/15
Sales ($ mil.)	11.4%	101,862.0	110,618.0	122,489.0	130,474.0	157,107.0
Net income ($ mil.)	3.1%	5,142.0	5,526.0	5,625.0	5,619.0	5,813.0
Market value ($ mil.)	23.4%	48,298.0	51,690.7	71,760.9	96,338.8	112,110.9
Employees	19.2%	99,000	133,000	156,000	170,000	200,000

UNITEK GLOBAL SERVICES INC.

NMS: UNTK

1777 Sentry Parkway West, Gwynedd Hall, Suite 302
Blue Bell, PA 19422
Phone: 267 464-1700
Fax: –
Web: www.unitekglobalservices.com

CEO: John Haggerty
CFO: Andrew Herning
HR: –
FYE: December 31
Type: Public

UniTek Global Services has a variety of ways to keep the lines of communications companies open. A provider of outsourced infrastructure services UniTek offers technical engineering and design repair construction and other services to major US satellite cable wired telecom and wireless communications companies. Its services range from residential and commercial installation to design and construction of fiber optic networks. The company operates through offices in Texas Florida California and the northeastern US. It has counted Clearwire T-Mobile and Ericsson as customers. UniTek Global Services was formed in early 2010 when Berliner Communications merged with UniTek Holdings.

	Annual Growth	06/09*	12/09	12/10	12/11	12/12
Sales ($ mil.)	100.3%	54.5	42.9	402.2	432.3	437.6
Net income ($ mil.)	–	(3.4)	(5.5)	(30.6)	(15.6)	(77.7)
Market value ($ mil.)	68.8%	14.1	15.0	184.0	84.9	67.8
Employees	102.7%	432	531	5,000	6,400	3,600

*Fiscal year change

UNITEK INFORMATION SYSTEMS INC.

4670 Auto Mall Pkwy.
Fremont CA 94538
Phone: 510-249-1060
Fax: 510-249-9125
Web: www.unitek.com

CEO: Janis Paulson
CFO: Shiva Jahan
HR: Annie Chow
FYE: December 31
Type: Private

Multiple technologies got you down? Unitek Information Systems offers information technology (IT) consulting training and contracting services. Unitek is an authorized learning partner for both Microsoft and Cisco. It also is a Prometric and Sylvan testing center. Its Unitek Education division offers training for emergency medical technicians and clinical researchers. Unitek also offers courses for professionals who install or sell solar and wind power systems. The Unitek College division offers career training for pharmacy technicians medical assistants and nurses. Founded in 1992 Unitek Information Systems has three California campuses and dozens of IT training locations throughout the US.

UNITIL CORP

NYS: UTL

6 Liberty Lane West
Hampton, NH 03842-1720
Phone: 603 772-0775
Fax: 603 772-4651
Web: www.unitil.com

CEO: Robert G. (Bob) Schoenberger
CFO: Mark H. Collin
HR: –
FYE: December 31
Type: Public

New England electric and gas company Unitil won't be satisfied until it makes all its customers happy. The company serves about 102400 electric customers and 75900 natural gas customers. Unitil Energy Systems provides regulated electric utility services to about 73800 customers in New Hampshire and subsidiary Fitchburg Gas and Electric has some 28605 power and 15615 natural gas customers in Massachusetts. Unitil's utility units provide retail supply services to customers who don't choose to purchase energy from a third-party marketer. Indirect subsidiary Usource provides energy brokerage service to large energy users throughout the Northeast seeking competitive power or natural gas supplies.

	Annual Growth	12/11	12/12	12/13	12/14	12/15
Sales ($ mil.)	4.9%	352.8	353.1	366.9	425.8	426.8
Net income ($ mil.)	12.5%	16.4	18.2	21.6	24.7	26.3
Market value ($ mil.)	6.0%	397.1	362.7	426.6	513.1	502.0
Employees	2.4%	454	467	477	495	500

UNITY BANCORP, INC.
NMS: UNTY

64 Old Highway 22
Clinton, NJ 08809
Phone: 908 730-7630
Fax: –
Web: www.unitybank.com

CEO: –
CFO: Alan J Bedner
HR: Bonnie Steinert
FYE: December 31
Type: Public

Unity Bancorp wants to keep you and your money united. The institution is the holding company for Unity Bank a commercial bank that serves small and midsized businesses as well as individual consumers through nearly 20 offices in north-central New Jersey and eastern Pennsylvania. Unity Bank's deposit products include checking savings money market and NOW accounts and CDs. Lending to businesses is the company's life blood: Commercial loans including Small Business Administration (SBA) and real estate loans account for about 60% of its loan portfolio which is rounded out by residential mortgage and consumer loans.

	Annual Growth	12/10	12/11	12/12	12/13	12/14
Assets ($ mil.)	5.4%	818.4	810.8	819.7	921.1	1,008.8
Net income ($ mil.)	30.1%	2.2	2.5	4.2	5.1	6.4
Market value ($ mil.)	11.8%	50.7	53.7	52.3	64.3	79.1
Employees	1.0%	176	178	172	178	183

UNITY HEALTH PLANS INSURANCE CORPORATION

840 Carolina St.
Sauk City WI 53583
Phone: 608-643-2491
Fax: 608-643-2564
Web: www.unityhealth.com

CEO: Terry Bolz
CFO: –
HR: –
FYE: December 31
Type: Subsidiary

Unity Health Plans Insurance provides health insurance wellness education and disease management services to the residents of some 20 rural counties in southern Wisconsin. The insurer has some 115000 members primarily in Dane County. In addition to its HMO coverage Unity Health Plans offers PPO and point-of-service (POS) plans as well as health savings accounts. Members have access to Unity's network of area hospitals clinics and primary care physicians. The company is a subsidiary of University Health Care which also operates The University of Wisconsin Hospital & Clinics Authority and is part of the larger UW Health organization.

UNIVAR INC.

17425 NE Union Hill Rd.
Redmond WA 98052
Phone: 425-889-3400
Fax: 425-889-4100
Web: www.univar.com

CEO: J Erik Fyrwald
CFO: Carl J Lukach
HR: –
FYE: December 31
Type: Private

With nearly universal coverage Univar distributes a broad range of chemicals. The company is a leading global distributor of specialty chemicals ranking #1 in the US and Canada and #2 in Europe. It operates more than 260 distribution facilities in Asia Europe Latin America and North America with sales offices in Africa and the Middle East. Subsidiaries Univar Europe Univar USA and Univar Canada handle sales marketing and logistics in those key markets. Univar's portfolio includes more than 4500 products and its storage and transportation capabilities further serve customers' chemical needs. Markets include paints and coatings energy food and household and industrial cleaning.

UNIVAR USA

17425 NE Union Hill Rd.
Redmond WA 98052
Phone: 425-889-3400
Fax: 425-889-4100
Web: www.univar.com

CEO: J Erik Fyrwald
CFO: Carl J Lukach
HR: –
FYE: December 31
Type: Business Segment

Univar USA has an unvarying devotion to distributing chemicals across the US. The company a regional unit of global chemical wholesaler heavyweight Univar Inc. distributes hundreds of chemicals including acids alcohols catalysts solvents and flavorings. Its customers include manufacturers in such industries as coating and adhesives building and construction pest control pharmaceuticals food ingredients oil and gas rubber and composites and waste management services. Univar USA ships products made by the likes of BASF Dow Corning Monsanto and Rhodia. It also provides specialty waste management and third-party logistics services.

UNIVERSAL CORP.
NYS: UVV

9201 Forest Hill Avenue
Richmond, VA 23235
Phone: 804 359-9311
Fax: –
Web: www.universalcorp.com

CEO: George C. Freeman
CFO: David C. Moore
HR: Cynthia Futrell
FYE: March 31
Type: Public

Smoking tobacco leaves may be hazardous to your health but selling them has been good for Universal Corporation's wealth. Operating mainly through its flagship subsidiary Universal Leaf Tobacco Company the firm selects buys processes packs stores and ships leaf tobacco to cigarette makers in the US and more than 30 other nations including Belgium China Germany and Russia. Universal also procures and processes dark tobacco used in cigars pipe tobacco and smokeless products. The firm's Universal Leaf subsidiaries are active in Africa Asia Europe South America and the US. Founded in 1918 Universal entered the dehydrated and juiced fruit and vegetable market in 2015 to diversify its business.

	Annual Growth	03/11	03/12	03/13	03/14	03/15
Sales ($ mil.)	(3.1%)	2,571.5	2,446.9	2,461.7	2,542.1	2,271.8
Net income ($ mil.)	(7.5%)	156.6	92.1	132.8	149.0	114.6
Market value ($ mil.)	2.0%	983.7	1,052.8	1,266.1	1,262.7	1,065.5
Employees	0.9%	26,000	26,000	25,000	26,000	27,000

UNIVERSAL DETECTION TECHNOLOGY
NBB: UNDT

340 North Camden Drive, Suite 302
Beverly Hills, CA 90210
Phone: 310 248-3655
Fax: –
Web: www.udetection.com

CEO: Jacques Tizabi
CFO: –
HR: –
FYE: December 31
Type: Public

Universal Detection Technology (UDT) has traded in acid rain for bioterrorism. UDT has leveraged its expertise in air pollution monitoring into products to identify airborne biological and chemical hazards in bioterrorism monitoring systems. Its first product — originally called the Anthrax Smoke Detector and now known as the BSM-2000 — is intended to continuously check the air in public buildings for anthrax spores. The device is an outgrowth of an agreement with NASA's Jet Propulsion Laboratory (JPL) that called for JPL to develop its bacterial spore detection technology for integration into UDT's aerosol monitoring system.

	Annual Growth	12/10	12/11	12/12	12/13	12/14
Sales ($ mil.)	8.8%	0.0	0.2	0.1	0.1	0.0
Net income ($ mil.)	–	(2.2)	(2.6)	(1.6)	(0.4)	(0.1)
Market value ($ mil.)	–	0.0	0.0	0.5	0.1	0.1
Employees	(24.0%)	3	4	4	1	1

UNIVERSAL DISPLAY CORP

NMS: OLED

375 Phillips Boulevard	CEO: Steven V. Abramson
Ewing, NJ 08618	CFO: Sidney D. Rosenblatt
Phone: 609 671-0980	HR: Marilyn Caldwell
Fax: –	FYE: December 31
	Type: Public

Universal Display thinks the world should be flat and lit with its organic light-emitting diode (OLED) technologies and materials. With its own research and through sponsored research agreements with Princeton University the University of Southern California and the University of Michigan the company develops OLED technologies and materials for screens from cell phones to large flat panel displays and solid-state lighting. Based in the US it has facilities around the world.

	Annual Growth	12/10	12/11	12/12	12/13	12/14
Sales ($ mil.)	58.1%	30.5	61.3	83.2	146.6	191.0
Net income ($ mil.)	–	(19.9)	3.2	9.7	74.1	41.9
Market value ($ mil.)	(2.5%)	1,400.8	1,676.9	1,170.9	1,570.4	1,268.3
Employees	14.0%	86	93	117	124	145

UNIVERSAL ELECTRONICS INC.

NMS: UEIC

201 E. Sandpointe Avenue, 8th Floor	CEO: Paul D. Arling
Santa Ana, CA 92707	CFO: Bryan M. Hackworth
Phone: 714 918-9500	HR: Chye H Lim
Fax: –	FYE: December 31
Web: www.uei.com	Type: Public

Universal Electronics can help couch potatoes and TV junkies end multiple remote madness. The company makes One For All-branded universal remote controls with preprogrammed infrared codes allowing them to operate virtually any remote-capable device including TVs DVD players digital video recorders and set-top boxes. Its One For All remotes are sold by retailers worldwide. Universal Electronics also markets audiovisual accessories under the One For All name outside North America and it develops Nevo-branded wireless networking products. The company sells and licenses its technologies to consumer electronics and computer manufacturers and cable companies including DIRECTV its largest customer.

	Annual Growth	12/10	12/11	12/12	12/13	12/14
Sales ($ mil.)	14.1%	331.8	468.6	463.1	529.4	562.3
Net income ($ mil.)	21.2%	15.1	19.9	16.6	23.0	32.5
Market value ($ mil.)	23.0%	451.1	268.3	307.7	606.0	1,034.1
Employees	1.9%	1,843	9,803	1,807	8,505	1,988

UNIVERSAL FOREST PRODUCTS INC.

NMS. UFPI

2801 East Beltline NE.	CEO: Matthew J. Missad
Grand Rapids, MI 49525	CFO: Michael R. Cole
Phone: 616 364-6161	HR: –
Fax: 616 361-7534	FYE: December 27
Web: www.ufpi.com	Type: Public

Universal Forest Products has no trouble separating the trees from the forest. The company is a leading manufacturer and distributor of engineered wood and construction materials which it sells to do-it-yourself retail stores residential and mobile home builders and industrial customers. It also offers composite wood and plastic products. Universal Forest buys its wood from lumber mills and pressure-treats it to make such products as roof trusses wall panels flooring pallets and shipping crates. Founded in 1955 the company operates about 80 facilities in the US Canada and Mexico.

	Annual Growth	12/10	12/11	12/12	12/13	12/14
Sales ($ mil.)	8.9%	1,890.9	1,822.3	2,054.9	2,470.4	2,660.3
Net income ($ mil.)	34.8%	17.4	4.5	23.9	43.1	57.6
Market value ($ mil.)	8.6%	758.6	616.9	755.6	1,039.8	1,055.4
Employees	4.1%	5,100	4,800	5,200	5,500	6,000

UNIVERSAL HEALTH REALTY INCOME TRUST

NYS: UHT

Universal Corporate Center, 367 South Gulph Road	CEO: Alan B. Miller
King of Prussia, PA 19406-0958	CFO: Charles F. Boyle
Phone: 610 265-0688	HR: –
Fax: 610 768-3336	FYE: December 31
Web: www.uhrit.com	Type: Public

Universal Health Realty Income Trust (UHT) is a real estate investment trust (REIT) that primarily invests in healthcare facilities and human services. The REIT owns more than 55 facilities in 16 states including acute care hospitals behavioral healthcare facilities rehabilitation hospitals sub-acute facilities surgery centers childcare centers and medical office buildings. McAllen Medical Center in Texas is UHT's largest facility. Many properties are owned via limited liability companies in which the trust holds an equity interest. UHT's hospitals boast some 1000 beds. Subsidiaries of Universal Health Services lease most of UHT's hospitals and provide their own maintenance and renovation services.

	Annual Growth	12/10	12/11	12/12	12/13	12/14
Sales ($ mil.)	20.0%	28.9	29.5	54.0	54.3	59.8
Net income ($ mil.)	33.3%	16.3	73.8	19.5	13.2	51.6
Market value ($ mil.)	7.1%	485.9	518.7	673.2	532.8	640.1
Employees	–	–	–	–	–	–

UNIVERSAL HEALTH SERVICES, INC.

NYS: UHS

Universal Corporate Center, 367 South Gulph Road	CEO: Alan B. Miller
King of Prussia, PA 19406	CFO: Steve G. Filton
Phone: 610 768-3300	HR: Geraldine Geckle
Fax: –	FYE: December 31
Web: www.uhsinc.com	Type: Public

With dozens of health care facilities in nearly every state Universal Health Services (UHS) isn't quite ubiquitous but it's working on it. One of the nation's largest for-profit hospital operators UHS owns or leases about 25 acute care hospitals with a total of some 5800 beds primarily in rural and suburban communities. It also operates outpatient surgery centers and radiation treatment facilities most of which are located near its acute care hospitals. In addition UHS' behavioral health division operates more than 200 psychiatric and substance abuse hospitals with a combined capacity of more than 20000 beds; its UK-based Cygnet unit operates another 19 facilities. UHS is controlled by founder and CEO Alan Miller.

	Annual Growth	12/10	12/11	12/12	12/13	12/14
Sales ($ mil.)	9.7%	5,568.2	7,500.2	6,961.4	7,283.8	8,065.3
Net income ($ mil.)	24.1%	230.2	398.2	443.4	510.7	545.3
Market value ($ mil.)	26.5%	4,286.3	3,836.1	4,772.9	8,021.7	10,983.2
Employees	1.4%	65,100	65,400	65,100	66,100	68,700

UNIVERSAL INSURANCE HOLDINGS INC

NYS: UVE

1110 W. Commercial Blvd., Suite 100	CEO: Sean P. Downes
Fort Lauderdale, FL 33309	CFO: Frank C Wilcox
Phone: 954 958-1200	HR: –
Fax: –	FYE: December 31
Web: www.universalinsuranceholdings.com	Type: Public

While some companies shy away from insuring homes in hurricane-prone Florida Universal Insurance Holdings is right at home there. Operating through its Universal Property & Casualty Insurance Company and American Platinum Property and Casualty Insurance Company subsidiaries the company underwrites distributes and administers homeowners property and personal liability insurance. The company's additional subsidiaries process claims perform claims adjustments and property inspections provide administrative duties and negotiate reinsurance.

	Annual Growth	12/10	12/11	12/12	12/13	12/14
Assets ($ mil.)	4.4%	766.2	894.0	925.7	920.1	911.8
Net income ($ mil.)	18.5%	37.0	20.1	30.3	59.0	73.0
Market value ($ mil.)	43.2%	170.9	125.7	153.7	508.3	717.8
Employees	7.4%	252	271	279	300	335

UNIVERSAL MANUFACTURING CO

NBB: UFMG

405 Diagonal St.
Algona, IA 50511-0190
Phone: 515 295-3557
Fax: 515 295-5537
Web: www.universalmanf.com

CEO: Donald L Dunn
CFO: –
HR: –
FYE: July 31
Type: Public

Parts are the best part of Universal Manufacturing. The company is a remanufacturer and distributor of automotive parts including fuel pumps engines and master cylinders. Universal Manufacturing sells its remanufactured products wholesale — under the brand name ReTech — to automotive dealers warehouse distributors and parts supply stores in the midwestern US. The firm also distributes remanufactured engines. Although specializing in the car and truck industry it also has facilities for serving the marine railroad aircraft motor sport and industrial engine markets. Universal Manufacturing was founded in 1946.

	Annual Growth	07/07	07/08	07/09	07/13	07/14
Sales ($ mil.)	18.6%	8.4	9.9	10.0	23.1	27.7
Net income ($ mil.)	(10.4%)	3.6	0.3	0.1	0.8	1.7
Market value ($ mil.)	11.1%	5.3	5.1	3.7	6.5	11.1
Employees	–	–	–	–	–	3

UNIVERSAL MUSIC GROUP INC.

1755 Broadway
New York NY 10019
Phone: 212-841-8000
Fax: 212-331-2580
Web: www.umusic.com

CEO: Lucian Grainge
CFO: –
HR: –
FYE: December 31
Type: Subsidiary

For Universal Music Group (UMG) music is a universal language. A subsidiary of Vivendi UMG is the world's largest recording company boasting about 20 record labels including Interscope Geffen A&M Records Island Def Jam Motown Records UMG Nashville and Verve Music Group. Its popular artists include Justin Bieber Mariah Carey Rihanna Sting and Kanye West among many others. Its Universal Music Publishing Group is the world's largest music publishing house with more than a million copyrights under control. UMG owns the largest catalog of recorded music in the world. Its catalog is marketed through Universal Music Enterprises in the US and Universal Strategic Marketing outside of the US.

UNIVERSAL POWER GROUP INC

NBB: UPGI

488 S. Royal Lane
Coppell, TX 75019
Phone: 469 892-1122
Fax: –
Web: www.4components.com

CEO: Ian Colin Edmonds
CFO: –
HR: –
FYE: December 31
Type: Public

Universal Power Group (UPG) gives its customers a charge. The company is a leading distributor of sealed lead-acid batteries to manufacturers and retailers in the US. Other products include lithium and nickel-cadmium batteries portable battery-powered products including jump starters solar power generators and solar panels. UPG also supplies components used in security systems including alarm panels perimeter access controls sirens speakers cable and wire. In addition UPG provides services such as inventory management kitting and packaging and battery recycling. ADT Security Services (16% of sales) Cabelas Protection One and RadioShack are among the company's customers.

	Annual Growth	12/08	12/09	12/10	12/11	12/12
Sales ($ mil.)	(6.0%)	117.9	111.2	107.3	89.3	91.9
Net income ($ mil.)	(40.4%)	1.2	(0.1)	2.9	0.2	0.2
Market value ($ mil.)	(12.0%)	13.0	15.6	18.5	9.6	7.8
Employees	4.7%	90	106	91	116	108

UNIVERSAL SECURITY INSTRUMENTS, INC.

ASE: UUU

11407 Cronhill Drive, Suite A
Owings Mills, MD 21117
Phone: 410 363-3000
Fax: 410 363-2218
Web: www.universalsecurity.com

CEO: –
CFO: James B Huff
HR: Joanne Ebert
FYE: March 31
Type: Public

Where there's smoke there's Universal Security Instruments. The company designs and markets smoke alarms and carbon monoxide alarms as well as other safety products such as outdoor floodlights door chimes and ground fault circuit interrupter (GFCI) units. Universal Security Instruments has warehouse facilities in Maryland and Illinois. Most of its products are sold through retail stores and are designed to be installed by consumers. Products that require professional installation such as smoke alarms for the hearing-impaired are marketed to electrical products distributors by subsidiary USI Electric. The company was founded in 1969.

	Annual Growth	03/11	03/12	03/13	03/14	03/15
Sales ($ mil.)	(7.0%)	13.2	13.3	15.4	12.6	9.9
Net income ($ mil.)	–	0.8	(0.5)	(0.5)	(4.5)	(3.7)
Market value ($ mil.)	(6.6%)	17.5	12.4	10.1	10.3	13.3
Employees	(4.5%)	18	16	17	16	15

UNIVERSAL STAINLESS & ALLOY PRODUCTS, INC.

NMS: USAP

600 Mayer Street
Bridgeville, PA 15017
Phone: 412 257-7600
Fax: –
Web: www.univstainless.com

CEO: Dennis M Oates
CFO: Ross C Wilkin
HR: –
FYE: December 31
Type: Public

At Universal Stainless & Alloy Products even if something isn't totally finished that's OK. The company makes both semi-finished and finished specialty steels including stainless tool and alloyed steels. Universal Stainless' stainless steel products are used in end products made by the automotive aerospace power generation oil and gas and heavy equipment manufacturing and medical industries; its high-temperature steel is produced mainly for the aerospace industry. Before the products get there however Universal Stainless sells them to service centers rerollers OEMs forgers and wire redrawers.

	Annual Growth	12/10	12/11	12/12	12/13	12/14
Sales ($ mil.)	2.1%	189.4	252.6	251.0	180.8	205.6
Net income ($ mil.)	(25.6%)	13.2	18.1	14.6	(4.1)	4.1
Market value ($ mil.)	(5.3%)	221.4	264.4	260.3	255.2	178.0
Employees	8.4%	518	661	724	675	714

UNIVERSAL STUDIOS INC.

100 Universal City Plaza
Universal City CA 91608-1002
Phone: 818-777-1000
Fax: +49-711-2150-269
Web: www.holtzbrinck.com

CEO: –
CFO: Sean Gamble
HR: –
FYE: December 31
Type: Subsidiary

Movies and theme parks are the center of Universal Studios' universe. The company's Universal Pictures produces and distributes mainstream movies (Bridesmaids) while its Focus Features produces smaller films (Hanna). Universal Studios also operates theme parks such as Universal Studios Hollywood and Universal Studios Orlando through Universal Parks & Resorts. Its Universal Studios Home Entertainment unit handles the marketing and distribution of DVDs from its 4000-film library. Universal Studios operates as part of NBCUniversal (NBCU).

UNIVERSAL TAX SYSTEMS INC.

6 Mathis Dr.	CEO: Kevin Robert
Rome GA 30164-2729	CFO: Douglas Winterrose
Phone: 706-625-7757	HR: –
Fax: 706-755-7802	FYE: April 30
Web: www.taxwise.com	Type: Subsidiary

Universal Tax Systems wants to be a universal provider for tax-related software. Founded in 1986 Universal Tax Systems (which does business as Tax-Wise the name of its primary product) makes tax preparation and electronic filing software used by accountants enrolled tax agents bank product providers financial service providers and other professionals. The company's software includes modules for all federal and state tax returns for both businesses and individuals. In 2006 Universal Tax Systems was purchased by CCH a Wolters Kluwer business.

UNIVERSAL TECHNICAL INSTITUTE, INC.   NYS: UTI

16220 North Scottsdale Road, Suite 100	CEO: Kimberly J. (Kim) McWaters
Scottsdale, AZ 85254	CFO: Eugene S. Putnam
Phone: 623 445-9500	HR: –
Fax: –	FYE: September 30
Web: www.uti.edu	Type: Public

Want to make a living working on hot rods? Universal Technical Institute (UTI) offers automotive diesel collision repair motorcycle and marine technician training to 15000 full-time students in the US. The company provides undergraduate degree and certificate programs at about a dozen campuses operating under the UTI Motorcycle Mechanics Institute and Marine Mechanics Institute (MMI) and NASCAR Technical Institute (NTI) banners. It also offers advanced manufacturer-branded training for sponsors such as volkswagen Mercedes-Benz Harley-Davidson and Ford at dedicated training centers. Most undergraduate programs last between 12 and 18 months and tuition ranges from $21000 to $54000.

	Annual Growth	09/11	09/12	09/13	09/14	09/15
Sales ($ mil.)	(5.4%)	451.9	413.6	380.3	378.4	362.7
Net income ($ mil.)	–	27.2	9.0	3.8	2.0	(9.1)
Market value ($ mil.)	(28.7%)	329.3	332.0	293.9	226.6	85.1
Employees	(2.8%)	2,260	2,210	2,150	2,100	2,020

UNIVERSAL TRUCKLOAD SERVICES INC   NMS: UACL

12755 E. Nine Mile Road	CEO: Jeffrey A. (Jeff) Rogers
Warren, MI 48089	CFO: David A. Crittenden
Phone: 586 920-0100	HR: –
Fax: –	FYE: December 31
	Type: Public

Universal Truckload Services (UTSI) hasn't hauled freight beyond its own galaxy but the company does cover the US and parts of Canada (Ontario and Quebec) and Mexico. As an "asset-light" provider of truckload freight transportation the company operates through a network of truck owner-operators rather than employing drivers and investing heavily in equipment. It can call upon a fleet of some 4300 tractors and 6300 trailers including standard dry vans and flatbeds; the majority of its tractors and trailers are owned by others. Its flagship transportation segment transports general commodities such as automotive parts building materials paper food consumer goods furniture steel and other metals.

	Annual Growth	12/10	12/11	12/12	12/13	12/14
Sales ($ mil.)	18.4%	605.9	699.8	1,037.0	1,033.5	1,191.5
Net income ($ mil.)	37.4%	12.7	15.8	47.7	50.6	45.4
Market value ($ mil.)	15.7%	477.6	544.5	547.5	915.2	855.2
Employees	68.4%	714	675	4,701	5,960	5,746

UNIVERSAL WEATHER AND AVIATION INC.

8787 Tallyho Rd.	CEO: Ralph J Vasami
Houston TX 77061-3420	CFO: –
Phone: 713-944-1622	HR: –
Fax: 713-943-4674	FYE: June 30
Web: www.univ-wea.com	Type: Private

You might not need a weatherman to know which way the wind blows but you might very well need the services of Universal Weather and Aviation before you taxi down a runway. Universal Weather and Aviation provides a slew of services including weather briefings international flight planning fueling programs and trip support to the general business aviation community and the airline industry. The company offers necessary planning ground handling support and incidentals for all manner of trips using private airplanes. Chairman C. Gregory Evans and his family own the company which was founded in 1959.

UNIVERSAL WILDE INC.

26 DARTMOUTH ST	CEO: Bill Fitzgerald
WESTWOOD, MA 02090-2301	CFO: Steve Payne
Phone: 781-251-2700	HR: –
Fax: –	FYE: December 31
Web: www.universalwilde.com	Type: Private

Sometimes the world of direct-mail marketing can seem like a jungle but W.A. Wilde can serve as your guide. The company provides tools and services for direct marketing campaigns such as fulfillment mailing print management statement processing and telemarketing. Its offerings can be purchased as a package or a la carte. The company operate through three main units: Wilde Agency a full-service direct-marketing provider; Wilde Interactive which specializes in online campaigns; and L.W. Robbins Associates an agency catering to nonprofit organizations. Family-owned W.A. Wilde traces its roots back to 1868 when William A. Wilde began publishing books.

	Annual Growth	12/08	12/09	12/10	12/11	12/12
Sales ($ mil.)	6.6%	–	–	–	104.2	111.1
Net income ($ mil.)	–	–	–	–	(0.1)	1.3
Market value ($ mil.)	–	–	–	–	–	–
Employees	–	–	–	–	–	560

UNIVERSITY BANCORP INC. (MI)   NBB: UNIB

959 Maiden Lane	CEO: Stephen Lange Ranzini
Ann Arbor, MI 48105	CFO: –
Phone: 734 741-5858	HR: –
Fax: 734 741-5859	FYE: December 31
Web: www.university-bank.com	Type: Public

University Bancorp is the holding company for University Bank. From one branch in Ann Arbor (the home of The University of Michigan) the bank offers standard services such as deposit accounts and loans. It mainly originates residential mortgages with commercial mortgages business loans and consumer loans rounding out its lending activities. Shariah-compliant banking services (banking consistent with Islamic law) are offered through University Islamic Financial which operates within University Bank's office. University Bancorp also owns University Insurance and Investments Services and a majority of Midwest Loan Services which provides mortgage origination and subservicing to credit unions.

	Annual Growth	12/09	12/11	12/12	12/13	12/14
Assets ($ mil.)	(2.1%)	134.4	121.7	132.2	111.2	121.0
Net income ($ mil.)	1.7%	0.7	(0.3)	1.9	1.8	0.8
Market value ($ mil.)	46.2%	4.8	6.7	11.3	17.1	32.1
Employees	–	–	–	–	–	–

UNIVERSITY CORPORATION FOR ATMOSPHERIC RESEARCH

3090 CENTER GREEN DR	CEO: –
BOULDER, CO 803012252	CFO: Kathyrn Schmoll
Phone: 303-497-1000	HR: Bob Roesch
Fax: –	FYE: September 30
Web: www.ucar.edu	Type: Private

The University Corporation for Atmospheric Research (UCAR) is a not-for-profit corporation founded in 1960 to promote research in atmospheric and related environmental sciences. A consortium of more than 100 universities UCAR provides real-time weather data to universities educates weather forecasters and organizes international experiments through its Office of Programs. The organization also maintains radars aircraft and computer models for weather and climate through the National Center for Atmospheric Research (NCAR). UCAR is funded by sponsors such as the National Science Foundation the National Oceanic and Atmospheric Administration and NASA.

	Annual Growth	09/10	09/11	09/12	09/13	09/14
Sales ($ mil.)	(7.3%)	–	269.9	260.5	221.6	214.8
Net income ($ mil.)	(51.7%)	–	–	13.2	8.4	3.1
Market value ($ mil.)	–	–	–	–	–	–
Employees	–	–	–	–	–	1,565

UNIVERSITY FEDERAL CREDIT UNION

3505 Steck Ave.	CEO: –
Austin TX 78757	CFO: Yung Tran
Phone: 512-467-8080	HR: –
Fax: +44-207-749-7890	FYE: December 31
Web: www.asite.com	Type: Private - Not-for-Pr

Founded in 1936 by faculty and staff of the University of Texas at Austin University Federal Credit Union (UFCU) has about a dozen branches in Austin with other locations in the Texas communities of Galveston Cedar Park Lakeway and Round Rock. Serving UT students alumni and employees as well as other residents around Texas' capital city the the member-owned institution provides such financial services as checking and savings accounts IRAs money market accounts home and consumer loans credit and debit cards investments financial planning brokerage and insurance. University Federal has more than 140000 members.

UNIVERSITY HEALTH CARE INC

305 W BROADWAY STE 300	CEO: –
LOUISVILLE, KY 40202-2122	CFO: –
Phone: 502-585-7900	HR: –
Fax: –	FYE: December 31
Web: www.passporthealthplan.com	Type: Private

University Health Care which does business as Passport Health Plan provides managed Medicaid insurance services to 130000 members throughout 16 counties in Kentucky. University Health Care was founded in 1997 by a group of providers that includes University of Louisville Hospital Jewish Hospital and the Louisville/Jefferson County Primary Care Association.

	Annual Growth	12/97	12/98	12/99	12/00	12/09
Sales ($ mil.)	12.9%	–	240.7	284.5	330.1	913.8
Net income ($ mil.)	–	–	(1.4)	5.8	3.8	6.5
Market value ($ mil.)	–	–	–	–	–	–
Employees	–	–	–	–	–	165

UNIVERSITY HEALTH SYSTEM

4502 Medical Dr.	CEO: George B Hernndez Jr
San Antonio TX 78229	CFO: Peggy Demming
Phone: 210-358-4000	HR: –
Fax: 210-358-4763	FYE: December 31
Web: www.universityhealthsystem.com	Type: Private - Not-for-Pr

The hospital system of the Bexar County Hospital District University Health System serves the residents of San Antonio and the surrounding region. Its flagship facility University Hospital has about 500 beds and is the primary teaching facility for The University of Texas Health Science Center at San Antonio. In addition to general medical and surgical care the hospital is a designated Level 1 trauma center. University Health System provides healthcare for families close to its clinic locations including the Robert B. Green Campus Texas Diabetes Institute 13 neighborhood clinics across the community five urgent-care clinics (ExpressMed) and four outpatient renal dialysis centers.

UNIVERSITY HEALTH SYSTEMS OF EASTERN CAROLINA INC.

2100 STANTONSBURG RD	CEO: Janet Mullaney
GREENVILLE, NC 27834-2818	CFO: –
Phone: 252-847-4451	HR: –
Fax: –	FYE: September 30
Web: www.pcmh.com	Type: Private

University Health Systems of Eastern Carolina is an integrated not-for-profit health system that serves residents of eastern North Carolina. Doing business as Vidant Health it operates nine hospitals including eight community hospitals and its tertiary care center Vidant Medical Center with 900 beds and academic affiliation with the Brody School of Medicine at East Carolina University. Vidant Health also operates centers for surgery home health hospice and wellness and engages in community health programs. Its physician group has more than 300 primary and specialty care providers who operate from more than 50 locations.

	Annual Growth	09/08	09/09*	12/10*	09/11	09/13
Sales ($ mil.)	–	–	0.0	318.6	1,304.3	1,601.1
Net income ($ mil.)	–	–	0.0	30.3	68.2	109.6
Market value ($ mil.)	–	–	–	–	–	–
Employees	–	–	–	–	–	8,373

*Fiscal year change

UNIVERSITY HOSPITALS HEALTH SYSTEM INC.

3605 WARRENSVILLE CTR RD	CEO: Thomas S Zenty
SHAKER HEIGHTS, OH 441225203	CFO: Michael Szubski
Phone: 216-844-1000	HR: Jason Elliott
Fax: –	FYE: December 31
Web: www.uhhospitals.org	Type: Private

University Hospitals Health System (UHHS) is on a mission to teach research and administer good health throughout northeastern Ohio. Its flagship facility University Hospitals of Cleveland (UHC) which operates as University Hospitals Case Medical Center (UHCMC) is a more than 1000-bed tertiary care center serving Cleveland and other parts of northeastern Ohio. The teaching hospital which is affiliated with Case Western Reserve University is also home to Rainbow Babies & Children's Hospital Seidman Cancer Center and MacDonald Women's Hospital. the not-for-profit UHHS is also home to community hospitals outpatient health and surgery centers mental health facilities and senior care centers.

	Annual Growth	12/07	12/08	12/09	12/12	12/13
Sales ($ mil.)	5.3%	–	1,800.1	1,938.4	2,266.3	2,326.4
Net income ($ mil.)	22.0%	–	–	110.5	54.3	244.4
Market value ($ mil.)	–	–	–	–	–	–
Employees	–	–	–	–	–	30,000

UNIVERSITY OF COLORADO

4740 WALNUT ST
BOULDER, CO 803012538
Phone: 303-541-1200
Fax: –

CEO: –
CFO: –
HR: Jill Pollock
FYE: June 30
Type: Private

Operating independently from the University of Colorado the University of Colorado Foundation (CU Foundation) engages in not-for-profit fundraising on behalf of the University. It partners with the University to raise manage and invest private support for the University's benefit. The foundation manages more than $125 million annually from nearly 50000 donors; the funds it raises are used to support scholarships research athletics building construction and faculty and staff at the University. The CU Foundation also manages the University's Creating Futures fundraising campaign which aims to raise $1.5 billion.

	Annual Growth	06/07	06/08	06/12	06/13	06/14
Sales ($ mil.)	15.4%	–	134.1	139.8	236.4	317.0
Net income ($ mil.)	2099.3%	–	–	0.4	95.3	186.2
Market value ($ mil.)	–	–	–	–	–	–
Employees	–	–	–	–	–	180

UNIVERSITY OF DETROIT MERCY

4001 W MCNICHOLS RD
DETROIT, MI 482213038
Phone: 313-993-6000
Fax: –
Web: www.udmercy.edu

CEO: –
CFO: –
HR: Netina Anding
FYE: June 30
Type: Private

Perhaps students taking a really tough test wish for mercy at University of Detroit Mercy (UDM). Michigan's largest and most comprehensive Catholic university is sponsored by the Society of Jesus (Jesuits) and the Religious Sisters of Mercy. UDM has an enrollment of about 5100 students at its three campuses (two located in residential northwest Detroit and one in downtown Detroit). UDM has a student-faculty ratio of 13:1. It offers 100 academic programs in fields such as architecture and psychology nursing teacher education and engineering through seven schools and colleges.

	Annual Growth	06/07	06/08	06/10	06/13	06/14
Sales ($ mil.)	3.6%	–	115.7	132.3	143.9	143.3
Net income ($ mil.)	24.0%	–	–	4.3	15.2	10.3
Market value ($ mil.)	–	–	–	–	–	–
Employees	–	–	–	–	–	950

UNIVERSITY OF EVANSVILLE

1800 LINCOLN AVE
EVANSVILLE, IN 477141506
Phone: 812-488-2000
Fax: –
Web: www.evansville.edu

CEO: –
CFO: –
HR: –
FYE: May 31
Type: Private

The University of Evansville affiliated with the United Methodist Church offers more than 80 academic areas of study for undergraduate and graduate students. The university consists of three colleges (College of Arts and Sciences College of Education and Health Sciences College of Engineering and Computer Science) and one school (Schroeder School of Business). It has an annual enrollment of more than 2600 students. Recognized for its study-abroad program the university also has a campus in the UK (Harlaxton College) in addition to its main campus in Indiana's third-largest city. The University of Evansville was founded in 1854 as Moores Hill Male and Female Collegiate Institute.

	Annual Growth	05/10	05/11	05/12	05/13	05/14
Sales ($ mil.)	4.5%	–	68.0	71.8	108.1	77.5
Net income ($ mil.)	–	–	–	(9.9)	49.0	12.7
Market value ($ mil.)	–	–	–	–	–	–
Employees	–	–	–	–	–	500

UNIVERSITY OF GEORGIA

424 E BROAD ST
ATHENS, GA 306021535
Phone: 706-542-2786
Fax: –
Web: www.uga.edu

CEO: –
CFO: –
HR: –
FYE: June 30
Type: Private

Located in the quintessential college town of Athens The University of Georgia (UGA) offers a wide range of degree programs to nearly 35000 students. Forest resources veterinary medicine and law are a few of the school's academic programs. UGA which also runs 170-plus study-abroad and exchange programs administers the prestigious Peabody Awards which honors media achievements and boasts one of the nation's largest map collections. Famous alumni include former US Senator Phil Gramm TV journalist Deborah Norville and former PBS president Pat Mitchell. The University of Georgia was chartered by the State of Georgia in 1785 and graduated its first class in 1804.

	Annual Growth	06/09	06/10	06/11	06/12	06/13
Sales ($ mil.)	7.0%	–	636.3	691.5	776.6	779.4
Net income ($ mil.)	–	–	–	(12.3)	72.0	115.4
Market value ($ mil.)	–	–	–	–	–	–
Employees	–	–	–	–	–	17,800

UNIVERSITY OF KENTUCKY HOSPITAL AUXILIARY INC.

800 ROSE ST
LEXINGTON, KY 40536-0001
Phone: 859-323-5000
Fax: –
Web: www.universityofkentuckyhospital.com

CEO: –
CFO: –
HR: –
FYE: June 30
Type: Private

For the times when there's a physical reason to be carried "back to my old Kentucky home" being lugged to University of Kentucky Chandler Hospital (UK Chandler Hospital) might be a better option. The 500-bed academic hospital is operated by the University of Kentucky Auxiliary. It is located within the University of Kentucky Medical Center complex which includes the specialized medical colleges of the University of Kentucky and their affiliated clinical treatment facilities (organized under the UK HealthCare umbrella). UK Chandler Hospital's services include oncology pediatrics cardiology orthopedics and women's health and it operates eastern Kentucky's only Level I trauma and Level III neonatal ICU units.

	Annual Growth	06/08	06/09	06/10	06/11	06/12
Sales ($ mil.)	9.0%	–	704.9	785.9	797.5	912.8
Net income ($ mil.)	–	–	(47.7)	39.4	41.3	13.1
Market value ($ mil.)	–	–	–	–	–	–
Employees	–	–	–	–	–	2,879

UNIVERSITY OF LA VERNE

1950 3RD ST
LA VERNE, CA 917504401
Phone: 909-593-3511
Fax: –
Web: www.laverne.edu

CEO: –
CFO: Avo Kechichian
HR: Jody Bomba
FYE: June 30
Type: Private

University of La Verne (ULV) offers more than 50 undergraduate degree programs through colleges of arts and sciences business and public management education and organizational leadership and law. It also boasts about 30 graduate and four doctoral programs in education psychology and counseling business leadership public administration health care and gerontology. In addition to the central campus in La Verne California the university operates more than half a dozen regional campuses in California. ULV was founded in 1891 by members of the Church of the Brethren. It has an annual enrollment of more than 7500 undergraduate graduate law continuing education and online students.

	Annual Growth	06/10	06/11	06/12	06/13	06/14
Sales ($ mil.)	(0.4%)	–	151.2	126.0	139.6	149.5
Net income ($ mil.)	42.8%	–	–	11.2	21.0	22.9
Market value ($ mil.)	–	–	–	–	–	–
Employees	–	–	–	–	–	2,200

UNIVERSITY OF MAINE SYSTEM

16 CENTRAL ST
BANGOR, ME 044015106
Phone: 207-973-3300
Fax: –
Web: www.maine.edu

CEO: –
CFO: –
HR: –
FYE: June 30
Type: Private

University of Maine System is composed of seven public universities throughout Maine serving some 40000 students. It also operates eight regional outreach centers as well as distance education programs. The University of Maine System offers nearly 600 majors minors and concentrations; its flagship campus in Orono (UMaine) offers nearly 90 bachelor's degree programs more than 60 master's degree programs and about two dozen doctoral programs. UMaine was established in 1862 as the Maine College of Agriculture and Mechanic Arts; it adopted its current name in 1897. The University of Maine System was created in 1968 by the state legislature.

	Annual Growth	06/04	06/05	06/06	06/12	06/13
Sales ($ mil.)	2.4%	–	381.0	390.4	476.5	460.2
Net income ($ mil.)	(2.8%)	–	–	33.9	38.0	27.9
Market value ($ mil.)	–	–	–	–	–	–
Employees	–	–	–	–	–	5,379

UNIVERSITY OF MARYLAND MEDICAL SYSTEM CORPORATION

22 S GREENE ST
BALTIMORE, MD 212011544
Phone: 410-328-8667
Fax: –
Web: www.umms.org

CEO: Jeffrey A. Rivest
CFO: Henry J. Franey
HR: –
FYE: June 30
Type: Private

The 12 academic specialty and community hospitals of the University of Maryland Medical System (UMMS) dot the map of the state's eastern half on both sides of Chesapeake Bay. UMMS one of the largest employers in the Baltimore area has more than 2300 acute care beds and attends to such specialties as trauma care coma emergence kidney transplants orthopedic rehabilitation stroke intervention and pediatric care. University of Maryland Medical Center the system's teaching hub is one of the oldest academic hospitals in the US. In addition to its hospitals UMMS also includes community clinics to address mental health rehabilitation and primary care. The system was established in 1984.

	Annual Growth	09/09	09/10	09/11*	06/12	06/13
Sales ($ mil.)	–	–	–	0.0	2,504.7	2,571.4
Net income ($ mil.)	–	–	–	0.0	(17.8)	139.4
Market value ($ mil.)	–	–	–	–	–	–
Employees	–	–	–	–	–	12,000

*Fiscal year change

UNIVERSITY OF MISSISSIPPI

113 FALKNER
UNIVERSITY, MS 386779704
Phone: 662-915-7361
Fax: –
Web: www.olemiss.edu

CEO: –
CFO: –
HR: –
FYE: June 30
Type: Private

They call her "Ole Miss" and she really is old: The University of Mississippi was chartered in 1844 as the first public university in the state and opened in 1848. Starting with 80 students the school's enrollment has grown to more than 23000 with most students attending the main Oxford campus. Ole Miss has additional campuses in Southaven (Desoto County) and Tupelo and it operates the University of Mississippi Medical Center in Jackson. The school is home to more than 30 research centers that specialize in business engineering law and other disciplines. Its academic institutes include the Croft Institute for International Studies and the William Winter Institute for Racial Reconciliation.

	Annual Growth	06/07	06/08	06/09	06/10	06/11
Sales ($ mil.)	8.5%	–	–	–	279.0	302.7
Net income ($ mil.)	17.0%	–	–	–	63.6	74.4
Market value ($ mil.)	–	–	–	–	–	–
Employees	–	–	–	–	–	8,700

UNIVERSITY OF MONTANA SYSTEM

32 CAMPUS DR MAIN HALL
MISSOULA, MT 598120001
Phone: 406-243-0211
Fax: –
Web: www.umt.edu

CEO: Shane Giese
CFO: –
HR: –
FYE: June 30
Type: Private

Sometimes referred to as the Harvard of the West The University of Montana's motto is Lux et Veritas (Light and Truth). The Big Sky Country certainly provides plenty of light for the university which is a leading producer of Rhodes Scholars. The University of Montana (UM) is a member of the Montana University System and offers associate's bachelor's master's first-professional and doctoral degrees as well as technical certificates. About 21000 undergraduate and graduate students enroll at UM's four campuses. Founded in 1893 UM also gets high marks for the physical beauty of its campus and nearby wilderness areas.

	Annual Growth	06/07	06/08	06/09	06/12	06/13
Sales ($ mil.)	0.7%	–	251.1	246.6	264.4	259.8
Net income ($ mil.)	–	–	–	27.7	7.4	(8.5)
Market value ($ mil.)	–	–	–	–	–	–
Employees	–	–	–	–	–	2,450

UNIVERSITY OF NORTH CAROLINA HOSPITALS

101 MANNING DR BLDG 2
CHAPEL HILL, NC 275144423
Phone: 919-966-5111
Fax: –
Web: www.dentistry.unc.edu

CEO: –
CFO: Chris Ellington
HR: –
FYE: June 30
Type: Private

University of North Carolina Hospitals (UNCH) is at the heart of the UNC Health Care System (UNC HCS). The medical center provides acute care to the Tar Heel State through North Carolina Memorial Hospital North Carolina Children's Hospital North Carolina Neurosciences Hospital and North Carolina Women's Hospital. Combined the facilities have more than 800 beds. Specialties include cancer treatment at the North Carolina Cancer Hospital organ transplantation cardiac care orthopedics wound management and rehabilitation. Not-for-profit UNC HCS is owned by the state of North Carolina and is affiliated with the UNC-Chapel Hill School of Medicine.

	Annual Growth	06/03	06/04	06/05	06/06	06/07
Sales ($ mil.)	12.7%	–	550.3	614.8	652.6	787.8
Net income ($ mil.)	168.3%	–	–	25.4	36.3	182.9
Market value ($ mil.)	–	–	–	–	–	–
Employees	–	–	–	–	–	6,000

UNIVERSITY OF NORTH DAKOTA

264 CENTENNIAL DR
GRAND FORKS, ND 582026059
Phone: 701-777-2015
Fax: –
Web: www.und.edu

CEO: –
CFO: –
HR: –
FYE: June 30
Type: Private

Way up in the Upper Midwest is the University of North Dakota (UND) the largest and oldest institution of higher learning in the state with an enrollment of approximately 15000 students. It offers undergraduate and graduate programs in close to 225 fields through nine colleges and schools (aerospace sciences arts and sciences business and public administration education and human development engineering and mines law medical and health sciences nursing and a graduate school). The university also has nearly 20 doctoral programs as well as certificate degree programs distance degree programs and a continuing education division. UND was founded in 1883 six years before North Dakota achieved statehood.

	Annual Growth	06/07	06/08	06/09	06/11	06/14
Sales ($ mil.)	1.5%	–	616.4	637.6	278.2	672.4
Net income ($ mil.)	–	–	–	(40.6)	27.3	77.9
Market value ($ mil.)	–	–	–	–	–	–
Employees	–	–	–	–	–	2,756

UNIVERSITY OF PUGET SOUND

1500 N WARNER ST	CEO: –
TACOMA, WA 984160005	CFO: –
Phone: 253-879-3100	HR: –
Fax: –	FYE: June 30
Web: www.pugetsound.edu	Type: Private

The University of Puget Sound is a private liberal arts college located in the Pacific Northwest with an enrollment of some 2600 students and a student-faculty ratio of 12:1. It boasts more than 50 traditional and interdisciplinary programs and about 1200 courses. Based south of Seattle in Tacoma Washington the school offers a wide range of undergraduate degrees as well as graduate degrees in education occupational therapy and physical therapy. Students come from nearly 50 states and 15 countries. Founded in 1888 by the Methodist Church The University of Puget Sound divested its affiliation with the church in 1980. Notable alumni include Verio founder Justin Jaschke and Alaska governor Sean Parnell.

	Annual Growth	06/09	06/10	06/11	06/12	06/13
Sales ($ mil.)	7.0%	–	139.9	147.4	162.4	171.2
Net income ($ mil.)	201.6%	–	–	1.8	10.2	16.5
Market value ($ mil.)	–	–	–	–	–	–
Employees	–	–	–	–	–	850

UNIVERSITY OF REDLANDS

1200 E COLTON AVE	CEO: –
REDLANDS, CA 923743720	CFO: –
Phone: 909-793-2121	HR: Richard Martinez
Fax: –	FYE: June 30
Web: www.redlands.edu	Type: Private

Focused on liberal arts and sciences private University of Redlands consists of a College of Arts and Sciences and a School of Education both located in Southern California's City of Redlands. Its School of Business is located on campus and in regional centers throughout Southern California. The institution offers more than 40 undergraduate majors about a dozen master's degree programs a doctorate in leadership for educational justice and professional credential and certificate programs. With an enrollment of about 2400 students University of Redlands was founded in 1907 on land donated by banker and Baptist layman Karl C. Wells; it maintains an informal relationship with the American Baptist church.

	Annual Growth	06/05	06/06	06/07	06/08	06/10
Sales ($ mil.)	(49.4%)	–	–	1,088.6	136.3	141.2
Net income ($ mil.)	–	–	–	0.0	0.3	(4.8)
Market value ($ mil.)	–	–	–	–	–	–
Employees	–	–	–	–	–	1,017

UNIVERSITY OF RHODE ISLAND

75 LOWER COLLEGE RD	CEO: –
KINGSTON, RI 028811966	CFO: –
Phone: 401-874-1000	HR: –
Fax: –	FYE: June 30
Web: www.uri.edu	Type: Private

The University of Rhode Island (URI) offers more than 80 undergraduate majors specializing in nursing psychology communication studies kinesiology and human development. It also offers master's doctoral and professional degrees from its nine colleges at four campuses across the state. URI's main campus is located in Kingston the W. Alton Jones Campus is in West Greenwich its Graduate School of Oceanography is located on Narragansett Bay and Providence is home to the university's Alan Shawn Feinstein College of Continuing Education. URI which has an enrollment of more than 16500 students was chartered as the state's agricultural school in 1888.

	Annual Growth	06/07	06/08	06/11	06/13	06/14
Sales ($ mil.)	3.9%	–	319.8	392.4	411.0	402.9
Net income ($ mil.)	(6.3%)	–	–	58.4	39.5	48.0
Market value ($ mil.)	–	–	–	–	–	–
Employees	–	–	–	–	–	2,600

UNIVERSITY OF RICHMOND

28 WESTHAMPTON WAY	CEO: –
RICHMOND, VA 231730002	CFO: –
Phone: 804-289-8133	HR: Carl K Sorensen
Fax: –	FYE: June 30
Web: www.richmond.edu	Type: Private

Suffering from arachnophobia? You may want to steer clear of the more than 4300 Spiders who are enrolled at the University of Richmond (UR). UR consists of five schools: Jepson School of Leadership Studies Richmond School of Law Robins School of Business School of Arts and Sciences and School of Continuing Studies. The university offers some 60 undergraduate majors as well as graduate and master's programs in business accounting and law. UR also offers some 75 study-abroad programs in which more than half of its students participate. Founded in 1830 by Virginia Baptists as a seminary for men the school became Richmond College in 1840.

	Annual Growth	06/08	06/09	06/10	06/13	06/14
Sales ($ mil.)	6.1%	–	197.1	210.3	253.7	264.6
Net income ($ mil.)	36.2%	–	–	83.5	185.2	287.4
Market value ($ mil.)	–	–	–	–	–	–
Employees	–	–	–	–	–	1,400

UNIVERSITY OF SAN DIEGO

5998 ALCALA PARK FRNT	CEO: –
SAN DIEGO, CA 921102492	CFO: Terry Kalfayan
Phone: 619-260-4600	HR: –
Fax: –	FYE: June 30
Web: www.sandiego.edu	Type: Private

The University of San Diego (USD) is private college located close to southern California's beaches and the Mexican border. The coeducational Roman Catholic university has an enrollment of more than 7750 full-time students (8350 if you count part-time students as well). USD offers roughly 75 bachelor's master's and doctoral degrees in areas such as arts and sciences business administration education engineering law and nursing. It has a faculty of more than 400 full time staff members. The university also home to the Joan B. Kroc School of Peace Studies established in 2003 by the wife of McDonald's founder Ray Kroc.

	Annual Growth	06/07	06/08	06/09	06/10	06/13
Sales ($ mil.)	(4.4%)	–	–	–	347.2	303.3
Net income ($ mil.)	61.5%	–	–	–	21.5	90.5
Market value ($ mil.)	–	–	–	–	–	–
Employees	–	–	–	–	–	1,600

UNIVERSITY OF SAN FRANCISCO INC

2130 FULTON ST	CEO: Stephen A Privett
SAN FRANCISCO, CA 941171050	CFO: –
Phone: 415-422-5555	HR: –
Fax: –	FYE: May 31
Web: www.cs.usfca.edu	Type: Private

Known for their devotion to education as well as their investment portfolio the Jesuits are evident to all who visit the University of San Francisco (USF). One of 28 Jesuit Catholic colleges and universities in the US the main USF campus sits on 55 acres near Golden Gate Park in San Francisco. The school which was formed in 1855 as St. Ignatius Academy enrolls more than 10000 students. It operates five schools and colleges including the schools of business and management education law and nursing and the colleges of arts and sciences. In addition to its main campus the university operates five satellite sites in Northern and Southern California.

	Annual Growth	05/09	05/10	05/11	05/12	05/13
Sales ($ mil.)	4.0%	–	334.1	380.8	390.4	375.7
Net income ($ mil.)	13.5%	–	–	55.3	36.5	71.3
Market value ($ mil.)	–	–	–	–	–	–
Employees	–	–	–	–	–	1,200

UNIVERSITY OF SCRANTON

800 LINDEN ST
SCRANTON, PA 185104501
Phone: 570-344-6685
Fax: –
Web: www.scranton.edu

CEO: –
CFO: –
HR: –
FYE: May 31
Type: Private

The University of Scranton is a Catholic and Jesuit liberal arts university with a student population of 5900 including more than 600 graduate students. Its schools and colleges include the College of Arts & Sciences Panuska College of Professional Studies and Kania School of Management. It offers programs in areas such as theology music technology athletics nursing and continuing education and has some 300 faculty members. The University of Scranton offers 61 undergraduate and 25 graduate programs. It is overseen by the Society of Jesus (the Jesuits).

	Annual Growth	05/07	05/08	05/09	05/12	05/13
Sales ($ mil.)	3.3%	–	135.1	138.7	212.9	158.7
Net income ($ mil.)	–	–	–	(1.9)	16.3	33.3
Market value ($ mil.)	–	–	–	–	–	–
Employees	–	–	–	–	–	1,050

UNIVERSITY OF SOUTH FLORIDA

4202 E FOWLER AVE
TAMPA, FL 336208000
Phone: 812-974-2001
Fax: –
Web: www.housing.usf.edu

CEO: –
CFO: Nick Trivunovich
HR: Paula N Knaus
FYE: June 30
Type: Private

The University of South Florida (USF) is bullishly educational. The school has some 48000 students at three campuses in Tampa St. Petersburg and Sarasota/Manatee. It offers some 180 undergraduate graduate specialty and doctoral degree programs through more than a dozen colleges including Arts and Sciences Business Education Engineering Marine Science Pharmacy and Public Health. USF also offers graduate certificates continuing education courses and teacher certifications and it is a major research institution among US universities. USF was founded in 1960; its mascot is the bull.

	Annual Growth	06/04	06/05	06/06	06/07	06/09
Sales ($ mil.)	29.3%	–	–	–	533.6	892.0
Net income ($ mil.)	(46.7%)	–	–	–	148.3	42.1
Market value ($ mil.)	–	–	–	–	–	–
Employees	–	–	–	–	–	16,165

UNIVERSITY OF SOUTHERN MISSISSIPPI

118 COLLEGE DR BOX 5005
HATTIESBURG, MS 394060001
Phone: 601-266-4111
Fax: –
Web: www.usm.edu

CEO: Shelby Thames
CFO: –
HR: –
FYE: June 30
Type: Private

You don't have to be a belle to attend Southern Miss but it never hurts. The University of Southern Mississippi (USM or Southern Miss for short) was established by the state legislature in 1910 to educate Mississippi's teachers. The school has grown to boast an enrollment of more than 15000 students with a student-teacher ratio of 17:1. USM offers bachelor's master's doctoral and post-master's degrees through five colleges: College of Arts and Letters College of Business College of Education and Psychology College of Health and College of Science and Technology. Southern Miss also runs an Honors College and engages in extensive research in a range of disciplines including health and technology.

	Annual Growth	06/08	06/09	06/11	06/13	06/14
Sales ($ mil.)	1.4%	–	180.0	193.6	192.2	192.7
Net income ($ mil.)	14.2%	–	–	14.0	17.3	20.8
Market value ($ mil.)	–	–	–	–	–	–
Employees	–	–	–	–	–	4,500

UNIVERSITY OF ST. THOMAS

2115 SUMMIT AVE
SAINT PAUL, MN 551051096
Phone: 651-962-5000
Fax: –
Web: www.stthomas.edu

CEO: –
CFO: –
HR: Amy Petruck
FYE: June 30
Type: Private

Far from any Bahamian beaches or Caribbean hot spots sits The University of St. Thomas (UST). The school is a Catholic university with campuses in Minneapolis and St. Paul Minnesota. It offers about 90 undergraduate and 60 graduate programs in seven academic divisions: education and philosophy arts and sciences business engineering divinity law and social work. The school has an enrollment of about 11000 undergraduate and graduate students with a student-to-teacher ratio of 14:1. UST along with military prep school St. Thomas Academy grew out of St. Thomas Aquinas Seminary which was founded in 1885 by Archbishop John Ireland.

	Annual Growth	06/10	06/11	06/12	06/13	06/14
Sales ($ mil.)	65.0%	–	56.5	239.2	261.0	253.8
Net income ($ mil.)	369.7%	–	–	2.9	69.7	63.0
Market value ($ mil.)	–	–	–	–	–	–
Employees	–	–	–	–	–	1,900

UNIVERSITY OF TENNESSEE

1331 CIRCLE PARK DR
KNOXVILLE, TN 379163801
Phone: 865-974-2303
Fax: –
Web: www.treasurer.tennessee.edu

CEO: –
CFO: –
HR: –
FYE: June 30
Type: Private

Whether you want to learn the art of aviation or get ready for a career in public service the University of Tennessee System (UT) is here to help. The 200-year-old school provides undergraduate graduate and professional academic programs to about 50000 students; programs include business engineering law pharmacy medicine and veterinary medicine. It has a student-teacher ratio of about 16:1. Campuses include the flagship Knoxville location as well as the Health Science Center at Memphis the Space Institute at Tullahoma the statewide Institute for Public Service and the Institute of Agriculture. Other UT System campuses are located in Chattanooga and Martin. UT was founded in 1794 as Blount College.

	Annual Growth	12/07	12/08*	06/11	06/12	06/13
Sales ($ mil.)	287.6%	–	1.3	1,034.3	1,092.9	1,122.9
Net income ($ mil.)	(44.3%)	–	–	296.5	60.5	92.1
Market value ($ mil.)	–	–	–	–	–	–
Employees	–	–	–	–	–	12,000

*Fiscal year change

UNIVERSITY OF THE PACIFIC

3601 PACIFIC AVE
STOCKTON, CA 952110197
Phone: 209-946-2401
Fax: –
Web: www.pacific.edu

CEO: –
CFO: –
HR: –
FYE: June 30
Type: Private

Situated next to the largest body of water on earth the University of the Pacific holds a sizable body of knowledge. The school offers more than 80 undergraduate majors and about 20 graduate programs in such fields as art language biology business computer science engineering history and pharmacy. It offers undergraduate graduate and professional degree programs in nine colleges and enrolls about 7000 students at its main campus in Stockton California the McGeorge School of Law in Sacramento and the Arthur A. Dugoni School of Dentistry in San Francisco. California's first chartered institution of higher education University of the Pacific was founded in 1851.

	Annual Growth	06/09	06/10	06/11	06/12	06/13
Sales ($ mil.)	8.1%	–	354.2	317.1	330.7	447.2
Net income ($ mil.)	83.0%	–	–	43.9	20.8	147.1
Market value ($ mil.)	–	–	–	–	–	–
Employees	–	–	–	–	–	1,500

UNIVERSITY OF WASHINGTON INC

4311 11TH AVE NE STE 600	CEO: –
SEATTLE, WA 981056369	CFO: Barbara Smith
Phone: 206-543-2100	HR: –
Fax: –	FYE: June 30
Web: www.aa.washington.edu	Type: Private

The University of Washington (UW) is Husky indeed with an annual enrollment of more than 54000 students. Founded in 1861 as the Territorial University of Washington UW (pronounced "U-dub" by those on campus) has smaller branches in Tacoma and Bothell in addition to its main campus in downtown Seattle. The university whose mascot is a Husky offers more than 440 undergraduate graduate and professional degree programs through 16 colleges and schools. It also operates four hospitals: University of Washington Medical Center Harborview Medical Center Northwest Hospital and Valley Medical Center.

	Annual Growth	06/08	06/09	06/11	06/12	06/13
Sales ($ mil.)	12.0%	–	2,902.4	3.7	4,258.9	4,563.4
Net income ($ mil.)	2738.7%	–	–	0.5	5.9	424.7
Market value ($ mil.)	–	–	–	–	–	–
Employees	–	–	–	–	–	27,228

UNIVERSITY OF WEST GEORGIA

1601 MAPLE ST	CEO: –
CARROLLTON, GA 301180001	CFO: –
Phone: 678-839-4780	HR: Juanita Hicks
Fax: –	FYE: June 30
Web: www.westga.edu	Type: Private

Go West young men and women and join the approximately 11600 students who attend University of West Georgia (UWG). UWG students major in some 110 areas through the university's schools and colleges (Arts and Sciences Business Education and the Graduate School). UWG also allows select high school students to earn both college and high school credits simultaneously. UWG also offers a full program of distance education via the Internet through its eCore program. The school was founded in 1906 as the Fourth District Agricultural and Mechanical School in Carrollton Georgia. The school became State University of West Georgia in 1996; it dropped "State" from its name in 2005.

	Annual Growth	06/09	06/10	06/11	06/12	06/13
Sales ($ mil.)	1.7%	–	93.6	82.4	95.0	98.5
Net income ($ mil.)	30.3%	–	–	9.6	4.4	16.3
Market value ($ mil.)	–	–	–	–	–	–
Employees	–	–	–	–	–	993

UNIVERSITY OF WISCONSIN FOUNDATION

1848 UNIVERSITY AVE	CEO: Michael M Knetter
MADISON, WI 537264090	CFO: Jennifer Dekrey
Phone: 608-263-4545	HR: –
Fax: –	FYE: December 31
Web: www.uwhealth.org	Type: Private

Because even Badgers need help the University of Wisconsin Foundation raises funds receives gifts and manages assets for The University of Wisconsin-Madison and other donor-designated units of The University of Wisconsin System. (Bucky Badger is the school's mascot.) The foundation supports special programs and projects including professorships fellowships scholarships research efforts and building projects. The not-for-profit organization has received more than $2.4 billion in donations since it was founded in 1945.

	Annual Growth	12/08	12/09	12/10	12/12	12/13
Sales ($ mil.)	8.9%	–	423.6	444.1	434.2	595.6
Net income ($ mil.)	16.1%	–	–	206.8	183.6	323.6
Market value ($ mil.)	–	–	–	–	–	–
Employees	–	–	–	–	–	150

UNIVERSITY OF WISCONSIN MEDICAL FOUNDATION INC.

7974 UW HEALTH CT	CEO: Jeffrey Grossman
MIDDLETON, WI 53562-5531	CFO: Beverly Sears
Phone: 608-821-4223	HR: –
Fax: –	FYE: June 30
Web: www.fammed.wisc.edu	Type: Private

UW Medical Foundation provides administrative services to faculty physicians at the University of Wisconsin School of Medicine and Public Health. The foundation a not-for-profit entity is a physician practice organization that works in cooperation with the UW Hospital and Clinics and other medical offices and clinics throughout the Badger State. The foundation coordinates clinical sites and provides technical and professional staffing services as well as administrative support for legal marketing information technology and logistics functions.

	Annual Growth	06/08	06/09	06/09	06/11	06/12
Sales ($ mil.)	8.1%	–	518.6	571.3	604.8	655.4
Net income ($ mil.)	–	–	(8.4)	22.7	10.6	15.3
Market value ($ mil.)	–	–	–	–	–	–
Employees	–	–	–	–	–	3,200

UNIVERSITY OF WISCONSIN SYSTEM

1220 LINDEN DR	CEO: –
MADISON, WI 537061525	CFO: –
Phone: 608-262-2321	HR: –
Fax: –	FYE: June 30
Web: www.wisconsin.edu	Type: Private

Unfortunately there is no School of Cheese in the University of Wisconsin System (UW System) but across its vast operations there are 13 four-year universities 13 two-year UW Colleges campuses and a statewide extension program that has offices in every Wisconsin county. The UW System is one of the largest public university systems in the US with more than 180000 students and 40000 faculty and staff members. Its top school is UW at Madison which offers more than 400 undergraduate majors master's degree programs and doctoral programs to some 43000 students. The system's other major campus is UW at Milwaukee with about 28000 students. The UW System has a student-teacher ratio of 17:1.

	Annual Growth	06/06	06/07	06/10	06/11	06/13
Sales ($ mil.)	5.7%	–	2,541.5	3,116.5	3,331.7	3,538.6
Net income ($ mil.)	15.2%	–	–	329.0	412.0	503.4
Market value ($ mil.)	–	–	–	–	–	–
Employees	–	–	–	–	–	31,992

UNIVERSITY OF WYOMING

1000 E UNIVERSITY AVE # 3434	CEO: –
LARAMIE, WY 820712001	CFO: –
Phone: 307-766-3264	HR: –
Fax: –	FYE: June 30
Web: www.wwweng.uwyo.edu	Type: Private

For folks who live in Wyoming the University of Wyoming (UW) is it — the only place offering baccalaureate and graduate degrees as well as research and outreach services that stretch across the state. The main campus is in Laramie but the school also has a campus in Casper (offering coordinated education programs with the Casper College) plus regional outreach education centers stationed throughout the state. Founded in 1887 UW has grown to serve more than 13000 students with about 200 programs of study through seven academic colleges as well as numerous schools and institutes. The university has a student-to-faculty ratio of 14:1.

	Annual Growth	06/08	06/09	06/10	06/13	06/14
Sales ($ mil.)	2.0%	–	195.5	195.6	225.3	215.9
Net income ($ mil.)	10.5%	–	–	31.7	117.0	47.2
Market value ($ mil.)	–	–	–	–	–	–
Employees	–	–	–	–	–	7,000

UNIVERSITY SYSTEM OF NEW HAMPSHIRE

25 CONCORD RD
LEE, NH 038616659
Phone: 603-862-1800
Fax: –
Web: www.usnh.edu

CEO: –
CFO: –
HR: –
FYE: June 30
Type: Private

The University of New Hampshire (UNH) is a liberal arts college that serves about 12600 undergraduate and more than 2200 graduate students. The institution offers more than 100 majors and academic programs of study at nine colleges and schools. The student-faculty ratio is 20:1. UNH is the flagship institution of the University System of New Hampshire. In 2007 the university graduated its first international class in Seoul under a program run by its Whittemore School of Business and Economics. Founded in 1866 as the New Hampshire College of Agriculture and the Mechanic Arts UNH is a designated land-grant sea-grant and space-grant chartered school.

	Annual Growth	06/07	06/08	06/12	06/13	06/14
Sales ($ mil.)	3.3%	–	558.1	0.0	800.0	676.9
Net income ($ mil.)	77.8%	–	–	40.8	111.9	129.0
Market value ($ mil.)	–	–	–	–	–	–
Employees	–	–	–	–	–	3,800

UNIVEST CORP. OF PENNSYLVANIA (SOUDERTON)

NMS: UVSP

14 North Main Street
Souderton, PA 18964
Phone: 215 721-2400
Fax: –
Web: www.univest.net

CEO: Jeffrey M Schweitzer
CFO: Michael S Keim
HR: –
FYE: December 31
Type: Public

Univest Corporation of Pennsylvania will keep your money close to its vest. The holding company owns Univest Bank and Trust which serves the southeastern part of the Keystone State though more than 30 traditional and supermarket branches in Bucks and Montgomery counties. The bank provides standard retail and commercial banking services such as checking and savings accounts CDs IRAs and credit cards. Real estate-related loans including residential and commercial mortgages and construction loans account for most of the bank's lending activities; it also offers business personal and municipal loans. Other services include trust and wealth management.

	Annual Growth	12/10	12/11	12/12	12/13	12/14
Assets ($ mil.)	1.2%	2,133.9	2,206.8	2,304.8	2,191.6	2,235.3
Net income ($ mil.)	9.0%	15.8	18.9	20.9	21.2	22.2
Market value ($ mil.)	1.4%	311.0	237.5	277.4	335.5	328.3
Employees	3.7%	551	566	614	612	638

UNIVISION COMMUNICATIONS INC.

605 3rd Ave. 12th Fl.
New York NY 10158
Phone: 212-455-5200
Fax: 212-867-6710
Web: corporate.univision.com

CEO: Randy Falco
CFO: –
HR: –
FYE: December 31
Type: Private

This company's singular vision focuses on Hispanic audiences. Univision Communications is the leading Spanish-language broadcaster in the US with a portfolio of television and radio operations. It runs the top-rated Univision network carried by more than 1400 broadcast and cable affiliates as well as sister networks TeleFutura and Galavision. The company also owns and operates about 60 local broadcast TV stations. Its Univision Radio division boasts about 70 stations. In addition to traditional broadcasting the company distributes content online. Founded in 1961 as Spanish International Network Univision is controlled by a group of private investment firms led by TPG Capital and Thomas H. Lee Partners.

UNMC PHYSICIANS

988101 NEBRASKA MED CTR
OMAHA, NE 681980001
Phone: 402-559-9700
Fax: –
Web: www.unmcphysicians.com

CEO: –
CFO: Troy Wilhelm
HR: –
FYE: June 30
Type: Private

If you're in Nebraska and your doctor suddenly tells you to "Go Big Red!" — don't be shocked he's probably just a member of the not-for-profit UNMC Physicians (formerly University Medical Associates). Many of the more than 500 physicians in the UNMC group practice were trained and now teach at the University of Nebraska Medical Center. Additionally UNMC partners with The Nebraska Medical Center and the Olson Center for Women's Health to share best practices and resources. The physicians who also operate 10 family health clinics in the area provide services in about 50 specialties such as obstetrics cancer care family medicine cardiology and pediatrics.

	Annual Growth	06/09	06/10	06/11	06/12	06/13
Sales ($ mil.)	3.4%	–	203.9	219.0	218.7	225.5
Net income ($ mil.)	14.2%	–	–	5.9	(1.6)	7.7
Market value ($ mil.)	–	–	–	–	–	–
Employees	–	–	–	–	–	1,200

UNS ENERGY CORPORATION

NYSE: UNS

88 E. Broadway Blvd.
Tucson AZ 85701
Phone: 520-571-4000
Fax: 262-638-4481
Web: www.twindisc.com

CEO: David G Hutchens
CFO: Kevin P Larson
HR: Catherine E Ries
FYE: December 31
Type: Public

UNS Energy (formerly UniSource Energy) gets most of its revenues from its energy utilities. Its Tucson Electric Power (TEP) unit generates and distributes electricity to about 404000 customers in southeastern Arizona. The unit has about 2245 MW of generating capacity. Subsidiary UniSource Energy Services (UES) provides electricity (UNS Electric Services) to 91000 customers and natural gas (UNS Gas) to 148000 customers in 30 communities in northern and southern areas of the state. UNS Energy's Millennium Energy Holdings unit invests in unregulated energy and emerging technology companies. In 2012 to make its brand more distinct UniSource Energy changed its name to UNS Energy.

UNUM GROUP

NYS: UNM

1 Fountain Square
Chattanooga, TN 37402
Phone: 423 294-1011
Fax: –
Web: www.unum.com

CEO: Richard P. (Rick) McKenney
CFO: John F. (Jack) McGarry
HR: Debbie Plager
FYE: December 31
Type: Public

Through injury or illness Unum works to keep employees employed. A top disability insurer in the US and the UK it offers short-term and long-term disability insurance as well as life and accidental death and dismemberment insurance to individuals and groups in a workplace benefits setting. Specialty coverage offerings include cancer dental and travel insurance. US subsidiaries include Unum Life Insurance Company of America Provident Life and Accident First Unum Life Colonial Life & Accident Insurance and The Paul Revere Life Insurance Company. It operates as Unum Limited in the UK. Unum's products are sold through field sales agents and independent brokers. In 2014 Unum paid out $6 billion in benefits.

	Annual Growth	12/10	12/11	12/12	12/13	12/14
Assets ($ mil.)	2.2%	57,307.7	60,179.0	62,236.1	59,403.6	62,497.1
Net income ($ mil.)	(17.4%)	886.1	235.4	894.4	858.1	413.4
Market value ($ mil.)	9.5%	6,110.9	5,316.2	5,253.1	8,851.0	8,800.6
Employees	0.0%	9,500	9,400	9,100	9,200	9,500

UNWIRED PLANET, INC.

NMS: UPIP

20 First Street, First Floor
Los Altos, CA 94022
Phone: 650 518-7111
Fax: –
Web: www.unwiredplanet.com

CEO: Boris Teksler
CFO: Dean Witter III
HR: –
FYE: June 30
Type: Public

Unwired Planet comes from a universe where phones work without wires and companies don't need products to make money. The company (formerly Openwave Systems) developed technology behind the wireless application protocol (WAP) standard which allows mobile devices to connect to the Internet. Unwired Planet holds some 2300 US and foreign patents relating to mobile communications smart devices cloud technologies and unified messaging. The company began exploiting its intellectual property portfolio in 2012 when it sold its mediation and messaging product businesses to Marlin Equity Partners.

	Annual Growth	06/11	06/12	06/13	06/14	06/15
Sales ($ mil.)	(58.7%)	155.5	15.1	0.1	36.4	4.5
Net income ($ mil.)	–	(35.2)	14.6	(47.6)	0.4	(41.8)
Market value ($ mil.)	(27.8%)	21.4	21.5	18.2	20.9	5.8
Employees	(58.4%)	536	37	16	15	16

UPMC

200 Lothrop St.
Pittsburgh PA 15213-2582
Phone: 412-647-8762
Fax: 412-692-8468
Web: www.upmc.com

CEO: –
CFO: Robert Be Michiei
HR: –
FYE: June 30
Type: Private - Not-for-Pr

For University of Pittsburgh students and area residents medical care is spelled UPMC. The organization is a leading not-for-profit health care delivery system in western Pennsylvania. UPMC operates about 20 hospitals including campuses in the Pittsburgh area regional and community hospitals and specialty facilities such as Children's Hospital of Pittsburgh and the Magee-Womens Hospital. Combined UPMC has about 4500 inpatient beds. In addition the system provides care through hundreds of physician practices outpatient clinics cancer treatment facilities and rehab centers; it also offers health insurance home health care and long-term care through about 15 senior living facilities.

UPMC ALTOONA

620 HOWARD AVE
ALTOONA, PA 16601-4804
Phone: 814-889-2011
Fax: –
Web: www.altoonaregional.org

CEO: Jerry Murray
CFO: Charles R Zorger
HR: –
FYE: June 30
Type: Private

Altoona Regional Health System moves patients upstream towards better health. Operating in Altoona and surrounding areas in central Pennsylvania the health system's facilities include Altoona Hospital an acute care center with 380 licensed beds that provides specialized care in areas including cardiovascular ailments cancer behavioral health and neurology as well as general emergency trauma birthing and surgery services. Altoona Regional Health System also offers a variety of outpatient care facilities and programs including home health care a primary care physicians' group and laboratory services. The not-for-profit system is governed by a board of community representatives.

	Annual Growth	06/08	06/09*	12/09*	06/10	06/12
Sales ($ mil.)	3.6%	–	436.2	0.9	321.1	485.2
Net income ($ mil.)	–	–	(33.9)	0.0	5.3	36.6
Market value ($ mil.)	–	–	–	–	–	–
Employees	–	–	–	–	–	2,494
						*Fiscal year change

UPROMISE INC.

95 Wells Ave. Ste. 160
Newton MA 02459
Phone: 617-454-6400
Fax: 516-822-0590
Web: www.schonfeld.com

CEO: Thomas Anderson
CFO: Joan M Nevins
HR: –
FYE: December 31
Type: Subsidiary

Upromise doesn't promise to pay for your kid's education — but it might help. By joining Upromise customers receive rebates on purchases from thousands of retailers restaurants grocery stores and companies — ranging from Exxon Mobil (1 cent per gallon) to Bed Bath & Beyond (1% on purchases) — that are credited to a college savings account. Upromise manages about $19 billion in 529 college savings plans (tax-advantaged investment programs for future higher education expenses). Upromise is owned by education financier SLM Corporation (known as Sallie Mae).

UPSON COUNTY HOSPITAL INC.

801 W GORDON ST
THOMASTON, GA 302863426
Phone: 706-647-8111
Fax: –
Web: www.urmc.org

CEO: David L Castleberry
CFO: John Williams
HR: –
FYE: December 31
Type: Private

Upson Regional Medical Center is a 115-bed hospital that serves the communities in and around Thomaston Georgia. In addition to general surgery and acute care the hospital offers specialty services including occupational therapy rehabilitation pediatrics and emergency care. Upson Regional also houses a neonatal special care unit a sleep disorders center and a wound healing center. The medical center has expanded its footprint with new medical offices and dining facilities.

	Annual Growth	12/09	12/10	12/11	12/12	12/13
Sales ($ mil.)	(6.7%)	–	94.3	86.7	71.2	76.7
Net income ($ mil.)	17.6%	–	–	10.8	7.6	14.9
Market value ($ mil.)	–	–	–	–	–	–
Employees	–	–	–	–	–	625

UQM TECHNOLOGIES, INC.

ASE: UQM

4120 Specialty Place
Longmont, CO 80504
Phone: 303 682-4900
Fax: 303 682-4901
Web: www.uqm.com

CEO: Joseph (Joe) Mitchell
CFO: David I Rosenthal
HR: –
FYE: March 31
Type: Public

UQM Technologies is revving up for the electric vehicle wars. The company builds permanent magnet electric motors for hybrid and electric vehicles — and the gears and electronic controls needed to operate them. UQM developed hybrid electric powertrains for GM's Precept concept car and the US Army's Humvee vehicle (made by AM General). UQM has customers in the aerospace industrial medical and telecommunications industries but views the auto industry as having the greatest potential. Denver's Regional Transportation District accounts for 12% of sales while Lippert Components is responsible for 17%; US government agencies and their contractors account for 31%.

	Annual Growth	03/11	03/12	03/13	03/14	03/15
Sales ($ mil.)	(18.3%)	9.0	10.1	7.2	7.0	4.0
Net income ($ mil.)	–	(2.0)	(4.9)	(10.7)	(2.8)	(6.0)
Market value ($ mil.)	(22.1%)	119.2	59.2	29.6	105.6	44.0
Employees	(7.7%)	80	84	67	60	58

URANIUM ENERGY CORP.

NYSE AMEX: UEC

500 N. Shoreline Blvd. #800N	CEO: Amir Adnani
Corpus Christi TX 78471	CFO: Pat Obara
Phone: 361-888-8235	HR: –
Fax: 361-888-5041	FYE: July 31
Web: www.uraniumenergy.com	Type: Public

Maybe one day it will look on Mars but in this lifetime Uranium Energy explores for uranium on our home planet. The uranium production development and exploration company has projects in South Texas including the Palangana and Goliad in-situ recovery projects. The company has bought a Texas database of historical uranium exploration and development and is acquiring promising properties throughout the southwestern US. In 2012 it looked outside the US by acquiring Cue Resources which holds an interest in a uranium exploration property in southeastern Paraguay.

URANIUM RESOURCES INC.

NASDAQ: URRE

405 State Hwy. 121 Bypass Bldg. A Ste. 110	CEO: Christopher M Jones
Lewisville TX 75067	CFO: Jeffrey L Vigil
Phone: 972-219-3330	HR: –
Fax: 972-219-3311	FYE: December 31
Web: www.uraniumresources.com	Type: Public

Mining company Uranium Resources (URI) glows with anticipation when it thinks about the fuel needs of nuclear power plants. The company has been preparing its main uranium assets in South Texas (the Kingsville Dome and Rosita mines and processing plants) for a restart in production. It also has big plans for its exploration and development interests in New Mexico. URI holds 102.1 million pounds of in-place mineralized uranium material. In 2012 the company acquired Neutron Energy in a $38 million deal. The deal adds significantly to the company's New Mexico assets and positions it as one of the US' largest uranium developers. Neutron will operate as a URI subsidiary.

URBAN OUTFITTERS, INC.

NMS: URBN

5000 South Broad Street	CEO: Richard A. Hayne
Philadelphia, PA 19112-1495	CFO: Francis J. (Frank) Conforti
Phone: 215 454-5500	HR: –
Fax: –	FYE: January 31
Web: www.urbanoutfittersinc.com	Type: Public

If you're a metropolitan hipster Urban Outfitters has your outfit. The firm's about 240 namesake stores (mainly in the US but also in Canada and Europe) offer casual clothes accessories housewares and shoes. The retailer courts somewhat older women at more than 200 Anthropologie shops. Urban Outfitters and Anthropologie sell via catalogs and e-commerce sites too. It also operates a bridal brand and garden center stores. The wholesale division makes sells and distributes clothing under the Free People label for more than 100 of its own stores and about 1600 department and specialty stores worldwide including Macy's Nordstrom Bloomingdale's Lord & Taylor and Selfridge's.

	Annual Growth	01/11	01/12	01/13	01/14	01/15
Sales ($ mil.)	9.9%	2,274.1	2,473.8	2,794.9	3,086.6	3,323.1
Net income ($ mil.)	(3.9%)	273.0	185.3	237.3	282.4	232.4
Market value ($ mil.)	0.8%	4,413.6	3,458.3	5,585.5	4,674.6	4,549.3
Employees	10.7%	16,000	17,000	20,600	22,900	24,000

URBAN RETAIL PROPERTIES CO.

900 N. Michigan Ave.	CEO: Craig Delasin
Chicago IL 60611	CFO: Joseph McCarthy
Phone: 312-915-2000	HR: –
Fax: 312-915-3136	FYE: December 31
Web: www.urbanretail.com	Type: Private

Urban Retail Properties has its hands full with a lot of square footage. The third-party management firm oversees more than 40 million sq. ft. of commercial real estate in about 20 states and Washington DC. The company provides a full spectrum of real estate services including leasing marketing accounting and tenant coordination. It also develops properties including shopping malls and mixed-use projects. True to its name Urban Retail Properties' portfolio is primarily retail; however it also manages office buildings and mixed-use projects.

URIGEN PHARMACEUTICALS INC.

OTC: URGP

27 Maiden Lane Suite 595	CEO: William J Garner
San Francisco CA 94108	CFO: Martin E Shmagin
Phone: 415-781-0350	HR: –
Fax: 415-781-0385	FYE: June 30
Web: www.urigen.com	Type: Public

Urigen wants to quell the urgent urge to go go go. Urigen Pharmaceuticals holds a pipeline of investigational drugs focused on urological disorders. The publicly traded company is developing treatments for chronic pelvic pain urethral discomfort and urethritis (inflammation of the urethra). Its main product candidates target painful bladder syndrome in men and women and urinary urgency associated with overactive bladder diagnoses in women. Though the company (which is seeking development partners) doesn't have any products on the market yet it plans to market its products (once approved) in the US through an inside sales force and outside the US through distributors.

UROLOGIX INC.

NBB: ULGX

14405 21st Avenue North	CEO: Gregory J Fluet
Minneapolis, MN 55447	CFO: Scott M Madson
Phone: 763 475-1400	HR: –
Fax: –	FYE: June 30
Web: www.urologix.com	Type: Public

For men whose prostate has them prostrate Urologix has the answer. The company's Targis and CoolWave systems are designed to treat benign prostate hyperplasia or enlargement of the prostate. The systems use Cooled ThermoTherapy a noninvasive catheter-based therapy that applies microwave heat to the diseased areas of the prostate while cooling and protecting urethral tissue. The treatment an alternative to drug therapy does not require anesthesia or surgery and can be administered on an outpatient basis. Urologix markets its products through a direct sales force in the US as well as through international distributors.

	Annual Growth	06/10	06/11	06/12	06/13	06/14
Sales ($ mil.)	(0.9%)	14.8	12.6	17.0	16.6	14.2
Net income ($ mil.)	—	(2.2)	(3.7)	(4.7)	(4.3)	(7.6)
Market value ($ mil.)	(36.2%)	22.4	19.9	16.1	3.5	3.7
Employees	(10.7%)	96	88	94	95	61

UROPLASTY, INC.

NAS: UPI

5420 Feltl Road	CEO: Robert C Kill
Minnetonka, MN 55343	CFO: Brett A Reynolds
Phone: 952 426-6140	HR: Ann Rasmussen
Fax: 952 426-6199	FYE: March 31
Web: www.uroplasty.com	Type: Public

Uroplasty makes implants used primarily to treat urinary incontinence and overactive bladder. Its flagship product is Macroplastique a soft-tissue bulking material for the treatment of urinary incontinence that is injected during a minimally invasive outpatient procedure. Another minimally invasive device the Urgent PC uses electrical pulses to treat overactive bladder symptoms. Uroplasty's I-Stop Mid-Urethral Sling treats female incontinence. The company also sells soft-tissue bulking agents used in plastic surgery vocal cord rehabilitation and treatment of fecal incontinence. Uroplasty markets its products primarily in Europe and the US; it won FDA approval to market Macroplastique in 2006.

	Annual Growth	03/10	03/11	03/12	03/13	03/14
Sales ($ mil.)	20.0%	11.9	13.8	20.6	22.4	24.6
Net income ($ mil.)	–	(3.2)	(4.6)	(4.3)	(3.3)	(5.4)
Market value ($ mil.)	14.9%	45.1	143.1	65.2	53.9	78.6
Employees	16.5%	64	88	108	101	118

URS CORP

NYS: URS

600 Montgomery Street, 26th Floor	CEO: Michael Burke
San Francisco, CA 94111-2728	CFO: –
Phone: 415 774-2700	HR: –
Fax: –	FYE: December 28
Web: www.urs.com	Type: Public

URS Corporation provides a range of engineering construction maintenance and technical services for customers around the world. Through its infrastructure and environment division URS builds manages operates and maintains projects for government agencies and private corporations. Its federal services segment provides management decommissioning and technical support services to agencies including the Department of Defense and the Department of Homeland Security. URS' energy and construction segment provides design management construction maintenance and closure services. Projects include work on power generating facilities transportation networks biotechnology labs and manufacturing plants.

	Annual Growth	01/09	01/10*	12/10	12/11	12/12
Sales ($ mil.)	2.8%	10,086.3	9,249.1	9,177.1	9,545.0	10,972.5
Net income ($ mil.)	12.2%	219.8	269.1	287.9	(465.8)	310.6
Market value ($ mil.)	(2.2%)	3,179.5	3,419.1	3,195.6	2,697.2	2,972.9
Employees	2.6%	50,000	45,000	47,000	46,000	54,000

*Fiscal year change

URSTADT BIDDLE PROPERTIES INC

NYS: UBA

321 Railroad Avenue	CEO: Willing L. Biddle
Greenwich, CT 06830	CFO: John T. Hayes
Phone: 203 863-8200	HR: –
Fax: –	FYE: October 31
Web: www.ubproperties.com	Type: Public

Urstadt Biddle Properties (UBP) provides a retail stomping ground for suburbanites. A self-administered real estate investment trust (REIT) the company invests in and operates commercial real estate primarily neighborhood and community shopping centers in the Northeast. Its target markets include Connecticut's Fairfield County New York's Westchester and Putnam counties and New Jersey's Bergen County. UBP owns a growing portfolio of about 75 properties with approximately 4.9 million square feet of space. Tenants include drugstore chain CVS off-price retailer TJX and the Stop & Shop supermarket chain. The REIT also owns a handful of office properties and bank branches.

	Annual Growth	10/11	10/12	10/13	10/14	10/15
Sales ($ mil.)	6.1%	91.0	91.3	94.2	102.3	115.3
Net income ($ mil.)	11.7%	31.6	28.3	29.8	65.2	49.3
Market value ($ mil.)	3.0%	637.3	676.6	705.1	772.6	718.0
Employees	8.8%	35	39	43	42	49

US 1 INDUSTRIES INC.

OTC: USOO

336 W. US Hwy. 30 Ste. 201	CEO: Michael E Kibler
Valparaiso IN 46385	CFO: Harold E Antonson
Phone: 219-476-1300	HR: –
Fax: 219-476-1385	FYE: December 31
Web: www.uslindustries.com	Type: Public

The US market is the one and only concern for US 1 Industries which partners with its subsidiaries to provide truckload transportation services in the 48 contiguous states. The company owns no trucks; instead it does business through a network of independent sales agents who arrange freight transportation via independent truck owner-operators. About 160 commission-based agents monitor shipments. US 1's contractors transport freight in temperature-controlled trailers and flatbeds as well as in standard dry vans. One of its specialties is the hauling of intermodal shipping containers which can be transported by trucks trains and ships. In 2011 US 1 agreed to be acquired by Trucking Investment Co.

US DAIRY EXPORT COUNCIL

2101 WILSON BLVD STE 400	CEO: Tom Super
ARLINGTON, VA 222013062	CFO: –
Phone: 703-528-3049	HR: –
Fax: –	FYE: December 31
Web: www.usdec.org	Type: Private

Got milk? These guys do. Lots of it. The U.S. Dairy Export Council (USDEC) is a not-for-profit organization designed to increase the volume and value of US-based dairy producers' exported products. The independent membership organization represents the interests of US milk producers dairy cooperatives export traders industry suppliers and proprietary processors. The US dairy industry exports $3.8 billion worth of product each year and USDEC helps its members maintain and hopefully increase that dollar amount through its involvement in global trade issues and building demand for US dairy products. The organization founded in 1995 has offices in 15 countries worldwide.

	Annual Growth	12/06	12/07	12/08	12/09	12/12
Sales ($ mil.)	9.7%	–	–	–	17.4	23.0
Net income ($ mil.)	16.9%	–	–	–	0.2	0.4
Market value ($ mil.)	–	–	–	–	–	–
Employees	–	–	–	–	–	20

US DATAWORKS INC

NBB. UDWK

One Sugar Creek Center Boulevard, 5th Floor	CEO: John Penrod
Sugar Land, TX 77478	CFO: Randall J Frapart
Phone: 281 504-8000	HR: –
Fax: –	FYE: March 31
Web: www.usdataworks.com	Type: Public

US Dataworks keeps bank balances in check. The company provides electronic payment processing and check conversion software that helps banks credit card companies and financial services firms rapidly process financial transactions without having to rely on outsourcers. Its Clearingworks software processes remote and Internet-based automated clearing house (ACH) payments defines rules for processing payments and converts paper checks into payments for high-volume transaction processing. The company's customers have included the Federal Reserve Bank Regulus Group General Electric and Citibank.

	Annual Growth	03/08	03/09	03/10	03/11	03/12
Sales ($ mil.)	3.8%	5.7	8.0	8.5	7.3	6.6
Net income ($ mil.)	–	(11.7)	(2.0)	(0.0)	(0.6)	(0.5)
Market value ($ mil.)	(0.5%)	5.0	7.0	6.4	6.0	4.9
Employees	(1.4%)	36	35	36	32	34

US DEPARTMENT OF AGRICULTURE

1400 Independence Ave. SW	CEO: –
Washington DC 20250	CFO: Patricia E Healy
Phone: 202-720-2791	HR: –
Fax: 630-377-4309	FYE: September 30
Web: www.strategicenhancement.com	Type: Government Agency

If it's on your dinner plate the US Department of Agriculture (USDA) had a hand in getting it there. The USDA oversees matters related to the nation's agricultural industry and food supply. Its main mission is to assist America's farmers and ranchers provide outreach and education to the public and help secure trade agreements to expand agricultural exports. Among its numerous functions it provides training and scientific resources to farmers awards grants monitors food safety operates the Forest Service and aids federal decision-making processes related to agricultural regulations and trade policies.

US DEPARTMENT OF HOMELAND SECURITY

245 Murray Lane SW	CEO: –
Washington DC 20528	CFO: –
Phone: 202-282-8000	HR: –
Fax: 202-447-3543	FYE: September 30
Web: www.dhs.gov	Type: Government Agency

The US Department of Homeland Security exists to keep America safe. Created in the wake of the 9/11 terrorist attacks the department is devoted to keeping the US safe from natural and man-made disaster. Its activities include domestic nuclear detection intelligence coordination and protection of high-level government officials. The department's structure includes agencies for citizenship and immigration services customs and border protection emergency response and recovery (FEMA) and science and technology research. The US Department of Homeland Security has more than 240000 employees and an annual budget of more than $55 billion.

US DEPARTMENT OF STATE

2201 C St. NW	CEO: –
Washington DC 20520	CFO: –
Phone: 202-647-4000	HR: –
Fax: 212-355-5924	FYE: September 30
Web: www.mastersoninstitute.com/	Type: Government Agency

Plainly stated the Department of State represents the interests of the US government around the globe. The agency operates more than 280 US embassies and consulates in more than 160 countries. State's members represent the US to the UN NATO (North American Treaty Organization) UNESCO (United Nations Educational Scientific and Cultural Organization) and the European Union. The department also issues travel warnings to US citizens publishes Congressional testimonies and offers reports on doing business with State and other nations. Its goals include achieving peace and security creating jobs helping developing nations and fostering international cooperation. The Department of State was formed in 1789.

US DEPARTMENT OF THE AIR FORCE

1690 Air Force Pentagon	CEO: –
Washington DC 20330-1690	CFO: –
Phone: 703-695-9664	HR: –
Fax: 703-614-9601	FYE: September 30
Web: www.af.mil	Type: Government Agency

The mission of the US Department of the Air Force is to fly fight and win — in air space and cyberspace. Along with the Army Navy and Marine Corps the US Air Force is a major military branch of the US Department of Defense responsible for defending the US and its interests through aerial space and cyber warfare. The agency includes more than a dozen major commands including the Air Force Reserve and Air National Guard. It also consists of field operating agencies and direct reporting units which are typically assigned to specialized missions. Originally part of the US Army the US Air Force was formed as a separate branch when president Harry S. Truman signed the National Security Act of 1947.

US ECOLOGY, INC.

NMS: ECOL

251 E. Front Street, Suite 400	CEO: Jeffrey R. (Jeff) Feeler
Boise, ID 83702	CFO: Eric L. Gerratt
Phone: 208-331-8400	HR: –
Fax: –	FYE: December 31
Web: www.usecology.com	Type: Public

US Ecology (formerly American Ecology) helps keep a lid on hazardous waste industrial waste and low-level radioactive waste. The company handles hazardous and nonhazardous waste at sites in Texas Michigan Nevada and Idaho and it operates a low-level radioactive waste facility in Washington state. The company does business with private waste companies state and federal agencies and a variety of industries. Customers include nuclear plants steel mills petrochemical facilities and academic and medical institutions. US Ecology retains interests in several non-operating waste-disposal facilities.

	Annual Growth	12/10	12/11	12/12	12/13	12/14
Sales ($ mil.)	43.7%	104.8	154.9	169.1	201.1	447.4
Net income ($ mil.)	32.0%	12.6	18.4	25.7	32.2	38.2
Market value ($ mil.)	23.3%	375.9	406.2	509.2	802.6	867.8
Employees	48.3%	372	387	425	458	1,800

US FOODS INC.

9399 W. Higgins Rd.	CEO: Pietro Satriano
Rosemont IL 60018	CFO: Fareed Khan
Phone: 847-720-8000	HR: Linda Bonfiglio
Fax: 847-720-8099	FYE: December 31
Web: www.usfoods.com	Type: Private

Many restaurant-goers in the US can thank this company for the food on their plates. US Foods (formerly U.S. Foodservice) is the nation's #2 foodservice supplier (with about half the sales of rival SYSCO) distributing food and non-food supplies to more than 250000 customers. The company operates more than 60 distribution facilities that supply thousands of items to restaurants hotels schools health care facilities and institutional foodservice operations. In addition to food items and ingredients US Foods distributes kitchen and cleaning supplies as well as restaurant equipment. Tracing its roots to 1853 the company is jointly owned by private equity firms KKR & Co. and Clayton Dubilier & Rice.

US GEOTHERMAL INC

ASE: HTM

390 E. Parkcenter Blvd., Suite 250
Boise, ID 83706
Phone: 208 424-1027
Fax: 208 424-1030
Web: www.usgeothermal.com

CEO: Dennis Gilles
CFO: Kerry Hawkley
HR: Kerry Hawkey
FYE: December 31
Type: Public

U.S. Geothermal likes things bubbling just under the surface. Operating through its Idaho-based subsidiary Geo-Idaho the company runs geothermal power plants which use heat from beneath the Earth's surface to generate electricity. Its Idaho plant generates 8 MW of power for Idaho Power; the operation is a joint venture with Goldman Sachs which contributed about $34 million to plant construction. The Nevada plant produces about 2.5 MW for Sierra Pacific Power. U.S. Geothermal also has exploration and development-stage properties in Oregon Nevada Idaho and in Guatemala. In addition to power generation the company produces revenue by selling its green energy credits to other power generators (7% of sales).

	Annual Growth	03/11	03/12*	12/12	12/13	12/14
Sales ($ mil.)	111.9%	3.3	5.9	8.6	27.4	31.0
Net income ($ mil.)	–	(4.0)	(6.2)	(1.3)	1.9	11.6
Market value ($ mil.)	(25.2%)	117.7	55.6	38.7	40.6	49.3
Employees	11.9%	35	43	47	47	49

*Fiscal year change

US LABS

2601 Campus Dr.
Irvine CA 92612
Phone: 949-450-0145
Fax: 949-450-0146
Web: www.uslabs.net

CEO: R Judd Jessup
CFO: Steve R Pierce
HR: –
FYE: December 31
Type: Subsidiary

US Labs gives cancer patients an edge in fighting the deadly disease. The esoteric cancer laboratory offers anatomic pathology and hematopathology services as well as other highly advanced gene-based cancer screening and analysis to hospitals and other health care centers insurers drug firms and researchers across the US. To help doctors and patients understand their foe better US Labs offers a variety of test types — including immunohistochemistry flow cytometry and molecular testing - that help doctors diagnose and treat disease effectively and determine what the likely outcome will be. US Labs is a subsidiary of laboratory services giant LabCorp.

US ONCOLOGY INC.

10101 Woodloch Forest
The Woodlands TX 77380
Phone: 281-863-1000
Fax: 847-430-1524
Web: www.culligan.com

CEO: Bruce Broussard
CFO: Michael A Sicuro
HR: –
FYE: December 31
Type: Subsidiary

US Oncology has got the backs (and the back offices) of more than 1000 oncologists across the US. Operating as The US Oncology Network the firm provides management and support services to some 550 oncology practices and radiation treatment centers; it also operates about 80 fully integrated cancer centers. The company's range of management services includes billing recruiting data management purchasing and accounting. It also offers separate drug supply services including purchasing negotiations and distribution for specialty cancer drugs. US Oncology is the primary operating entity of McKesson Specialty Health a division of drug distribution giant McKesson.

US SECURITIES AND EXCHANGE COMMISSION

100 F St. NE
Washington DC 20549
Phone: 202-942-8088
Fax: 202-772-9295
Web: www.sec.gov

CEO: –
CFO: Kenneth Johnson
HR: –
FYE: September 30
Type: Government Agency

The US Securities and Exchange Commission (SEC) is one part law enforcer protecting investors from securities fraud and enforcing securities laws; one part doctor promoting healthy capital markets and contributing to America's economic well-being; and one part rule maker maintaining fair orderly and efficient markets. The agency regulates the sale of securities as well as the people and organizations involved in selling them. It also ensures the disclosure of financial information of public companies via its online EDGAR database and is involved in personal investor education. Established in 1934 the agency is overseen by five presidentially appointed commissioners.

US SILICA HOLDINGS, INC.

NYS: SLCA

8490 Progress Drive, Suite 300
Frederick, MD 21701
Phone: 301 682-0600
Fax: –
Web: www.ussilica.com

CEO: Bryan A. Shinn
CFO: Donald A. Merril
HR: –
FYE: December 31
Type: Public

Life's a beach for the sand-sellers at U.S. Silica. The industrial mineral company provides silica and aplite for the glass foundry chemical and construction industries; and fine ground silica and kaolin clay used to make paint plastics and ceramics. Its "frac sand" product — currently its fastest-growing offering — is used by natural gas and oil producers in hydraulic fracturing a process to boost oil and gas production. U.S. Silica also makes raw materials for solar panels. The company supplies customers in the US and Canada. In addition to its main facility in West Virginia U S Silica also has 15 plants in the East. U.S. Silica went public in 2012 with an offering worth $200 million.

	Annual Growth	12/10	12/11	12/12	12/13	12/14
Sales ($ mil.)	37.5%	245.0	295.6	441.9	546.0	876.7
Net income ($ mil.)	80.7%	11.4	30.3	79.2	75.3	121.5
Market value ($ mil.)	23.9%	–	–	901.8	1,838.6	1,384.8
Employees	12.4%	685	701	785	844	1,092

US SMALL BUSINESS ADMINISTRATION

409 3rd St. SW
Washington DC 20416
Phone: 800-827-5722
Fax: +86-10-6437-4251
Web: www.chinacache.com

CEO: –
CFO: Tom Dumaresq
HR: –
FYE: September 30
Type: Government Agency

The US Small Business Administration (SBA) has the little guy's back. As an independent agency of the federal government it provides services to independently owned for-profit small businesses including those owned by women minorities veterans and disadvantaged people in the US Guam Puerto Rico and the US Virgin Islands. Small businesses are typically defined as having fewer than 500 employees. The agency provides loans and loan guarantees contract opportunities disaster assistance business development counseling and an online library of small business information and resources. The SBA was established in 1953 largely in response to the pressures of the Great Depression and WWII.

US STEM CELL INC

NBB: USRM

13794 NW 4th Street, Suite 212
Sunrise, FL 33325
Phone: 954 835-1500
Fax: 954 845-9976
Web: www.bioheartinc.com

CEO: Mike Tomas
CFO: Mark Borman
HR: Gissela Freeman
FYE: December 31
Type: Public

Broken hearts are no fun but damaged hearts are worse and Bioheart aims to help. The biotech company is focused on the discovery development and commercialization of therapies treating heart damage. Because the heart does not have cells to naturally repair itself Bioheart is exploring the use of cells derived from the patient's own thigh muscle to improve cardiac function after a heart has been damaged by a heart attack. Its lead candidate MyoCell uses precursor muscle cells called myoblasts to strengthen scar tissue with living muscle tissue. The company is also developing a number of proprietary techniques and processes used to obtain and inject MyoCell.

	Annual Growth	12/10	12/11	12/12	12/13	12/14
Sales ($ mil.)	158.0%	0.0	0.0	0.1	0.1	2.1
Net income ($ mil.)	–	(5.2)	(4.7)	(4.0)	(3.1)	(2.3)
Market value ($ mil.)	–	0.5	0.1	0.0	0.0	0.0
Employees	(19.1%)	7	6	3	3	3

USA COMPRESSION PARTNERS LP

NYSE: USAC

100 Congress Ave. Ste. 450
Austin TX 78701
Phone: 512-473-2662
Fax: 408-734-0788
Web: www.ambarella.com

CEO: Eric Long
CFO: –
HR: –
FYE: December 31
Type: Private

When it comes to natural gas USA Compression Partners thinks smaller is better. One of the largest independent gas compression companies in the US USA Compression provides compression services to producers processors gatherers and transporters of natural gas. (Compression involves mechanically compressing gas into a smaller higher-pressure volume to facilitate production and transportation of the gas.) The company which operates primarily through its subsidiaries owns engineers designs and maintains a fleet of compression units that together generate some 632000 horsepower. USA Compression went public in 2013 with an offering worth $198 million.

USA HOCKEY INC.

1775 BOB JOHNSON DR
COLORADO SPRINGS, CO 809064090
Phone: 719-527-3360
Fax: –
Web: www.usahockey.com

CEO: –
CFO: –
HR: –
FYE: August 31
Type: Private

|Whenever a puck is dropped boards banged or empty nets scored on USA Hockey is there. The group serves as the governing body for amateur hockey and works to promote the sport with more than 585000 members (ice and in-line hockey players coaches and officials). An official representative to the United States Olympic Committee and the International Ice Hockey Federation the organization supports development of hockey through its affiliation with more than 30 amateur leagues. It trains Olympians and works with the National Hockey League and the National Collegiate Athletic Association as well as publishing American Hockey Magazine. In-line skaters were included in 1994; the group formed in 1936.

	Annual Growth	08/09	08/10	08/11	08/12	08/13
Sales ($ mil.)	5.2%	–	33.9	34.6	35.4	39.5
Net income ($ mil.)	–	–	–	(0.4)	(0.5)	1.7
Market value ($ mil.)	–	–	–	–	–	–
Employees	–	–	–	–	–	38

USA TECHNOLOGIES INC

NMS: USAT

100 Deerfield Lane, Suite 140
Malvern, PA 19355
Phone: 610 989-0340
Fax: –
Web: www.usatech.com

CEO: Stephen P Herbert
CFO: J Duncan Smith
HR: –
FYE: June 30
Type: Public

Since you can't get much from a vending machine with a quarter these days USA Technologies decided to make them take plastic. Its ePort device attaches onto vending machines and its eSuds works on washing machines and clothes dryers to allow them to accept debit and credit cards. With the Business Express device hotels libraries and universities can run their business centers as self-pay operations; customers simply swipe their cards to use a PC fax machine or copier. USA Technologies also sells energy-saving devices for such "always-on" appliances as vending machines and office equipment. Information from the company's remote devices is transmitted through the company's USALive network.

	Annual Growth	06/11	06/12	06/13	06/14	06/15
Sales ($ mil.)	26.2%	22.9	29.0	35.9	42.3	58.1
Net income ($ mil.)	–	(6.5)	(5.2)	0.9	27.5	(1.1)
Market value ($ mil.)	5.0%	79.4	51.8	62.2	75.4	96.5
Employees	10.0%	45	47	54	61	66

USA TRUCK, INC.

NMS: USAK

3200 Industrial Park Road
Van Buren, AR 72956
Phone: 479 471-2500
Fax: –
Web: www.usa-truck.com

CEO: John R. (Randy) Rogers
CFO: Michael K. Borrows
HR: Donald B Weis
FYE: December 31
Type: Public

Truckload carrier USA Truck moves freight not only in the US but also in Canada and through partners into Mexico. It does most of its business east of the Rocky Mountains. USA Truck has a fleet of more than 2000 tractors and 6200 trailers. It transports general commodities; customers include companies in the consumer goods industrial machinery and equipment paper products rubber and plastics and retail industries. The company provides both medium-haul (800-1200 mile) and regional (500-mile) truckload services along with dedicated contract carriage in which drivers and equipment are assigned to a customer long-term. The company's average length-of-haul is about 550-miles.

	Annual Growth	12/10	12/11	12/12	12/13	12/14
Sales ($ mil.)	7.0%	460.2	519.4	512.4	555.0	602.5
Net income ($ mil.)	–	(3.3)	(10.8)	(17.7)	(9.1)	6.0
Market value ($ mil.)	21.1%	139.3	81.4	36.3	140.9	299.1
Employees	(0.9%)	2,900	3,020	2,990	2,750	2,800

USAA

9800 Fredericksburg Rd.
San Antonio TX 78288
Phone: 210-456-1800
Fax: 206-342-3000
Web: www.vulcan.com

CEO: Josue Robles Jr
CFO: Laura Bishop
HR: –
FYE: December 31
Type: Private - Mutual Com

USAA has a decidedly military bearing. The mutual insurance company serves 8.4 million member customers primarily military personnel military retirees and their families. Its products and services include property/casualty and life insurance banking discount brokerage and investment management. It offers such specialty products as life insurance for soldiers deployed in war zones and financial planning services to invest hazardous duty pay. USAA relies largely on direct marketing to sell its products reaching clients via the telephone and Internet. The company's USAA Alliance Services unit provides discount shopping (floral jewelry and safety items) and travel and delivery services to its members.

USADATA INC.

292 Madison Ave.
New York NY 10017
Phone: 212-679-1411
Fax: 212-679-8507
Web: www.usadata.com

CEO: Ric Murphy
CFO: –
HR: –
FYE: December 31
Type: Private

Want a list of 1000 cat owners in Memphis? How about a list of 500 charity donors in Cleveland? USADATA provides privacy-compliant sales leads and lead generation services for use in creating mailing lists and direct mailing campaigns. USADATA's data is pulled from various sources including catalogs consumer surveys warranty card registration and publications. Serving more than 100000 clients nationwide the company also provides list automation and marketing automation tools through Web portals for clients such as H&R Block Wells Fargo and Allstate.

USANA HEALTH SCIENCES INC

NYS: USNA

3838 West Parkway Blvd.
Salt Lake City, UT 84120
Phone: 801 954-7100
Fax: –

CEO: David A. (Dave) Wentz
CFO: Paul A Jones
HR: Paul Jones
FYE: January 03
Type: Public

Health is a matter of science at USANA Health Sciences. The company makes nutritional personal care and weight management products selling them through a direct-sales network marketing system of more than 250000 independent distributors (or associates). USANA Health Sciences also sells directly to 64000 customers deemed preferred. USANA's associates operate throughout North America as well as the Asia/Pacific region. The company's products portfolio includes nutritional supplements (76% of sales) and foods (12%) sold under the USANA brand and a line of skin and hair care products (9%) marketed under the Sensé label. Chairman Myron Wentz owns more than 50% of the company he founded.

	Annual Growth	01/11*	12/11	12/12	12/13*	01/15
Sales ($ mil.)	11.2%	517.6	581.9	648.7	718.2	790.5
Net income ($ mil.)	13.8%	45.7	50.8	66.4	79.0	76.6
Market value ($ mil.)	23.9%	548.9	383.7	399.2	981.8	1,292.1
Employees	5.3%	1,240	1,290	1,330	1,480	1,527

*Fiscal year change

USDA FOREST SERVICE

1400 Independence Ave. SW
Washington DC 20250-0003
Phone: 202 205 0333
Fax: 202-205-1765
Web: www.fs.fed.us

CEO: –
CFO: –
HR: –
FYE: September 30
Type: Government Agency

Responsible for managing more than 190 million acres of national forests and grasslands the USDA Forest Service is the largest agency of the US Department of Agriculture and has the conflicting mission of both preserving public forest lands and overseeing the commercial harvesting of its timber. The National Forest System consists of 155 national forests and 20 grasslands in 44 states Puerto Rico and the Virgin Islands. Through various programs the agency which began in 1905 provides states and private landowners with technical and financial assistance to promote rural economic development and improve the natural environment of cities and communities.

USF HOLLAND INC.

750 E. 40th St.
Holland MI 49423
Phone: 616-395-5000
Fax: 616-392-3104
Web: www.usfc.com/ltl/home/holland.jsp

CEO: –
CFO: –
HR: –
FYE: December 31
Type: Subsidiary

USF Holland doesn't have time to stop and smell the tulips. Once a subsidiary of USF the company is the largest regional less-than-truckload (LTL) freight hauler operated by YRC Regional Transportation a subsidiary of YRC Worldwide. (LTL carriers consolidate freight from multiple shippers into a single truckload.) USF Holland provides full state regional delivery in about a dozen states and two Canadian provinces (Ontario and Quebec) and direct regional delivery to nine other states. The company provides service to additional regions through its sister company USF Reddaway. USF Holland operates a fleet of some 5400 tractors and 6150 trailers from a network of about 60 terminals.

USFALCON INC.

1 COPLEY PKWY STE 200
MORRISVILLE, NC 27560-9693
Phone: 919-388-3778
Fax: –
Web: www.usfalcon.com

CEO: Peter Von Jess
CFO: Jim Scheuer
HR: –
FYE: September 30
Type: Private

Government contractor USfalcon has been flying high with the big boys — Booz Allen Hamilton CACI and Lockheed Martin — ever since it became a preferred contractor under the Army's S3 (Strategic Services Sourcing) program in 2006. USfalcon assists the Defense Department and other federal agencies with information technology (IT) services in the areas of aerospace national security and intelligence and defense. The company is also awarded contracts through the Navy's SeaPort and works as a subcontractor for IT giants NCI and Leidos. USfalcon operates from seven offices in the US. The veteran-owned small business was taken over by owner Col. Peter von Jess (Ret.) in 2003.

	Annual Growth	09/07	09/08	09/09	09/10	09/11
Sales ($ mil.)	1.1%	–	–	103.1	102.6	105.5
Net income ($ mil.)	(0.1%)	–	–	3.4	3.7	3.4
Market value ($ mil.)	–	–	–	–	–	–
Employees	–	–	–	–	–	140

USG CORP

NYS: USG

550 West Adams Street
Chicago, IL 60661-3676
Phone: 312 436-4000
Fax: –
Web: www.usg.com

CEO: James S. (Jim) Metcalf
CFO: Matthew F. Hilzinger
HR: –
FYE: December 31
Type: Public

Where there's a wall there's likely SHEETROCK. USG the maker of the world's top brand of wallboard is one of the largest building products manufacturers and distributors in the US. The company operates in four divisions. Its gypsum unit which accounts for about half of sales manufactures wallboard gypsum fiberboard and other products for finishing interior walls ceilings and floors under the SHEETROCK DUROCK AND FIBEROCK brands. The ceilings division makes ceiling systems and acoustic tile used mainly in commercial buildings. USG's distribution arm distributes building products through L&W Supply. The company generates roughly 80% of its net sales in the US.

	Annual Growth	12/11	12/12	12/13	12/14	12/15
Sales ($ mil.)	5.7%	3,024.0	3,224.0	3,570.0	3,724.0	3,776.0
Net income ($ mil.)	–	(390.0)	(126.0)	47.0	37.0	991.0
Market value ($ mil.)	24.3%	1,480.0	4,088.9	4,134.0	4,077.2	3,538.3
Employees	0.3%	8,780	8,500	8,900	8,900	8,900

USI HOLDINGS CORPORATION

555 Pleasantville Rd. Ste. 160 S.
Briarcliff Manor NY 10510
Phone: 914-749-8500
Fax: 914-747-6399
Web: www.usi.biz

CEO: Michael J Sicard
CFO: –
HR: –
FYE: December 31
Type: Private

Insurance isn't exactly a product you can store and ship but it still needs distributors and that's where USI Holdings comes in. A major US insurance broker USI Holdings distributes insurance products and provides consulting and administrative services to businesses through 80 offices in some 25 states. It specializes in commercial property/casualty and employee benefits insurance for small and midsized businesses but also dabbles in wealth management and retirement services. The company's USI Consulting and Univers Workplace Benefits units provide benefits-related consulting and administration. Owned by GS Capital Partners USI has agreed to be acquired by private equity firm Onex Corporation.

USPA ACCESSORIES LLC

119 W. 40th St. 3rd Fl.
New York NY 10018
Phone: 212-868-2590
Fax: 212-868-2595
Web: concept1.com

CEO: –
CFO: Neil Goldberg
HR: –
FYE: December 31
Type: Private

USPA Accessories believes that accessories make the man the woman and the child. The company which operates as Concept One boasts a vast portfolio of accessories that includes headwear backpacks gloves and umbrellas among other items. Its products are made through licensing agreements under names Sean John and Levi's Red Tab as well as emblazoned with team names from the NFL MLB NBA and NHL. USPA sells its items through department stores nationwide. The company was founded in 1986 as Drew Pearson Marketing by former Dallas Cowboys wide receiver Drew Pearson. In late 2006 Concept One Accessories purchased Drew Pearson Marketing from Hong Kong's Mainland Headwear Holdings Limited for about $8 million.

USS POSCO INDUSTRIES

900 LOVERIDGE RD
PITTSBURG, CA 945652808
Phone: 800-877-7672
Fax: –
Web: www.ussposco.com

CEO: –
CFO: –
HR: –
FYE: December 31
Type: Private

US and Korean steel manufacturing interests come together in the form of USS-POSCO Industries (UPI) a 50/50 joint venture between United States Steel (US Steel) and POSCO. The company operates a steel plant (formerly owned by US Steel) in Pittsburg Northern California. It manufactures flat-rolled steel sheets in various forms: cold-rolled steel galvanized steel and tinplate. In addition USS-POSCO churns out iron oxide which is used to make hard and soft ferrites. UPI sells its products to more than 150 customers in more than dozen states throughout the western US. End products include office furniture computer cabinets metal studs cans culverts and metal building materials.

	Annual Growth	12/04	12/05	12/06	12/07	12/08
Sales ($ mil.)	11.9%	–	854.5	1,034.7	998.7	1,198.0
Net income ($ mil.)	(10.0%)	–	–	14.7	(40.1)	11.9
Market value ($ mil.)	–	–	–	–	–	–
Employees	–	–	–	–	–	759

UST LLC

6601 West Broad St.
Richmond VA 23230
Phone: 804-274-2200
Fax: 804-484-8231
Web: ussmokeless.com/en/cms/home/default.aspx

CEO: –
CFO: Raymond P Silcock
HR: –
FYE: December 31
Type: Subsidiary

"As American as baseball" could be a phrase coined by UST. Through U.S. Smokeless Tobacco Company (USSTC) UST manufactures and distributes snuff (inhaled) and chewing tobacco products used by a number of tobacco-spitting players. Its lineup includes the #1 and #2 moist premium smokeless tobacco brands Copenhagen and Skoal as well as value-priced brands Red Seal and Husky. With a taste for the grape too its Ste. Michelle Wine Estates unit produces wine; vineyards dot California Oregon and Washington. Brands include Chateau Ste. Michelle Columbia Crest Conn Creek Stag's Leap and Villa Mt. Eden. UST has operated as a subsidiary under its former rival Altria (parent of Philip Morris USA) since 2009.

UTAH MEDICAL PRODUCTS, INC.

NMS: UTMD

7043 South 300 West
Midvale, UT 84047
Phone: 801 566-1200
Fax: 801 566-7305
Web: www.utahmed.com

CEO: –
CFO: –
HR: –
FYE: December 31
Type: Public

Utah Medical Products (UTMD) focuses on expectant moms new moms and newborns. The company designs and makes a variety of medical products used in labor and delivery and in neonatal intensive care as well as products for gynecological and female urinary problems. Products include disposable pressure transducers to monitor blood pressure intrauterine catheters used to monitor pressure in the womb during high-risk births and a device that clamps and cuts the umbilical cord and collects a blood sample from the cord. UTMD which has manufacturing facilities in the US and Ireland sells its products around the world through a domestic sales force and more than 100 international distributors.

	Annual Growth	12/10	12/11	12/12	12/13	12/14
Sales ($ mil.)	13.2%	25.1	37.9	41.6	40.5	41.3
Net income ($ mil.)	17.3%	6.0	7.4	10.2	11.4	11.4
Market value ($ mil.)	22.3%	100.7	101.2	135.1	214.2	225.1
Employees	1.6%	172	187	189	184	183

UTAH STATE UNIVERSITY

2400 OLD MAIN HL
LOGAN, UT 843222400
Phone: 435-797-1064
Fax: –
Web: www.usu.edu

CEO: –
CFO: –
HR: –
FYE: June 30
Type: Private

Utah State University (USU) has more than 40 academic departments at colleges of agriculture arts business education and human services engineering science natural resources and humanities and social sciences. It offers more than 170 bachelor's degree programs and about 140 graduate degree programs. Biology elementary education mechanical and aerospace engineering and business administration are among the university's most popular majors. About 29000 students attend its main campus in northern Utah its three branch campuses or extension facilities located across the state. USU was established in 1888 as an agricultural college.

	Annual Growth	06/10	06/11	06/12	06/13	06/14
Sales ($ mil.)	3.3%	–	328.1	340.3	350.6	362.1
Net income ($ mil.)	0.5%	–	–	68.3	44.5	68.9
Market value ($ mil.)	–	–	–	–	–	–
Employees	–	–	–	–	–	6,000

UTC CLIMATE CONTROLS & SECURITY

9 Farm Springs Rd.	CEO: –
Farmington CT 06034-4065	CFO: –
Phone: 860-284-3000	HR: –
Fax: +82-42-939-5001	FYE: December 31
Web: www.ktng.com	Type: Business Segment

This unit of United Technologies (UTC) has your climate needs under control. UTC Climate Controls & Security provides heating air conditioning and refrigeration systems building controls and automation and fire and security solutions. Its lead heating cooling and refrigeration brand is Carrier while its Automated Logic is a top energy solutions provider. The business supplies fire extinguishers smoke detectors and related equipment under brands such as Chubb and Kidde and security services through GE Security Onity and Lenel units. Customers include government and financial institutions building owners architects and consultants. UTC Climate Controls & Security operates in some 35 countries.

UTG INC

NBB: UTGN

5250 South Sixth Street, P.O. Box 5147	CEO: Jesse T Correll
Springfield, IL 62705	CFO: Theodore C Miller
Phone: 217 241-6300	HR: –
Fax: –	FYE: December 31
Web: www.utgins.com	Type: Public

UTG doesn't feel the need to spell out United Trust Group anymore but it is still a life insurance holding company. Universal Guaranty Life Insurance American Capitol Insurance and other subsidiaries offer individual life insurance as well as third-party administration (TPA) services for other providers. UTG's Roosevelt Equity subsidiary provides investment brokerage services to the company's insurance customers while other subsidiaries handle UTG's real estate investments. Some 20 general agents represent the company's products and focus on retaining and expanding current customer policies. CEO Jesse Correll owns about two-thirds of the company.

	Annual Growth	12/10	12/11	12/12	12/13	12/14
Assets ($ mil.)	(2.4%)	441.6	433.7	441.3	417.1	399.9
Net income ($ mil.)	(2.1%)	7.6	6.3	9.3	3.3	7.0
Market value ($ mil.)	8.7%	37.8	44.5	49.1	47.3	52.8
Employees	(9.5%)	67	67	67	72	45

UTICA COLLEGE

1600 BURRSTONE RD	CEO: –
UTICA, NY 135024092	CFO: –
Phone: 315-792-3111	HR: –
Fax: –	FYE: May 31
Web: www.onlineuticacollege.com	Type: Private

Utica College is a liberal arts college with an enrollment of approximately 2500 full- and part-time students. The private school was founded in 1946 by Syracuse University and became an independent institution in 1995. Utica College offers about 30 undergraduate majors and 15 graduate programs. Its students earn Syracuse baccalaureate degrees for undergrads and Utica College master's and doctorate degrees.

	Annual Growth	05/10	05/11	05/12	05/13	05/14
Sales ($ mil.)	3.6%	–	62.6	67.5	68.2	69.6
Net income ($ mil.)	(33.7%)	–	–	3.0	2.1	1.3
Market value ($ mil.)	–	–	–	–	–	–
Employees	–	–	–	–	–	646

UTILITY TRAILER MANUFACTURING COMPANY

17295 E. Railroad St.	CEO: Paul F Bennett
City of Industry CA 91748	CFO: –
Phone: 626-965-1541	HR: –
Fax: 626-965-2790	FYE: December 31
Web: www.utilitytrailer.com	Type: Private

Utility Trailer Manufacturing likes to play it cool. The company is one of the largest manufacturers of refrigerated trailers (aka reefers) in the US. The company also produces dry freight trailers flatbeds and its branded Tautliners curtain-sided trailers. Its refrigerated trucks include special designs for the whole food distribution and fast-food markets such as trucks with separate chambers for frozen and dry goods. A handful of factories in the US makes its trailers and vans which are distributed through a network of 100 independent dealers dotting North and South America. Two brothers H.C. and E.W. Bennett founded the company in 1914. The privately held company is family operated.

UTZ QUALITY FOODS INC.

900 High St.	CEO: –
Hanover PA 17331	CFO: –
Phone: 717-637-6644	HR: Beverly Carpenter
Fax: 717-633-5102	FYE: March 31
Web: www.utzsnacks.com	Type: Private

Quitting your full-time job to perfect the potato chip may sound like a bad business plan but it worked for Bill Utz in 1921 when he founded Pennsylvania-based Utz Quality Foods. A leader in the snack foods market Utz each week produces more than 1 million pounds of potato chips and 900000 pounds of pretzels. It also makes cheese curls onion rings popcorn and pork rinds as well as sunflower tortilla and corn chips. Utz's snack items are sold throughout the US by national chains including BJ's Wholesale Costco and Wal-Mart. In 2011 Utz acquired Zappe Endeavors which is known for its Zapp's Dirty and California chip brands. Utz is run by third-generation family members.

UWHARRIE CAPITAL CORP.

NBB: UWHR

132 North First Street	CEO: Roger L Dick
Albemarle NC 28001	CFO: R David Beaver III
Phone: 704 983-6181	HR: –
Fax: –	FYE: December 31
Web: www.uwharrie.com	Type: Public

Uwharrie Capital is the multibank holding company for Anson Bank & Trust Bank of Stanly and Cabarrus Bank & Trust which operate a total of about ten branches in west-central North Carolina. Serving consumers and local business customers the banks offer a variety of deposit accounts and credit cards as well as investments insurance asset management and brokerage services offered by other Uwharrie subsidiaries such as insurance agency BOS Agency securities broker-dealer Strategic Alliance mortgage brokerage Gateway Mortgage and Strategic Investment Advisors. The banks mainly write residential and commercial mortgages but also construction business and consumer loans.

	Annual Growth	12/10	12/11	12/12	12/13	12/14
Assets ($ mil.)	(0.8%)	535.4	526.9	545.0	517.3	518.5
Net income ($ mil.)	11.1%	0.7	0.9	0.4	0.5	1.1
Market value ($ mil.)	(2.4%)	25.8	21.3	21.9	20.2	23.4
Employees	(3.2%)	188	188	181	170	165

VAALCO ENERGY, INC.

NYS: EGY

9800 Richmond Avenue, Suite 700
Houston, TX 77042
Phone: 713 623-0801
Fax: 713 623-0982
Web: www.vaalco.com

CEO: Steven P Guidry
CFO: Gregory R Hullinger
HR: –
FYE: December 31
Type: Public

VAALCO Energy valiantly pursues energy opportunities. The small independent is engaged in the acquisition exploration development and production of oil and gas. VAALCO Energy holds high-risk exploration assets in Angola and Gabon through participating in oil company consortia and has exploration assets in Gulf Coast of Texas and Louisiana and in Montana. VAALCO's near-term production strategy is to focus on developing its reserves in Gabon through the exploitation of the Etame Marin block (the Etame Avouma South Tchibala and Ebouri fields). In 2013 the company reported proved reserves of 7.2 million barrels of crude oil (46% developed); and 1.3 million cu ft. of natural gas located in the US).

	Annual Growth	12/10	12/11	12/12	12/13	12/14
Sales ($ mil.)	(1.3%)	134.5	210.4	195.3	169.3	127.7
Net income ($ mil.)	–	37.3	34.1	0.6	43.1	(77.6)
Market value ($ mil.)	(10.7%)	413.9	349.1	500.0	398.2	263.6
Employees	6.2%	89	94	103	111	113

VAIL RESORTS INC.

NYS: MTN

390 Interlocken Crescent
Broomfield, CO 80021
Phone: 303 404-1800
Fax: 303 404-6415
Web: www.vailresorts.com

CEO: Robert A. (Rob) Katz
CFO: Michael Barkin
HR: –
FYE: July 31
Type: Public

Vail Resorts hopes the ski vacation business is all uphill. One of North America's leading ski resort operators Vail Resorts operates four mountain resorts in Colorado (Beaver Creek Breckenridge Mountain Resort Keystone Resort and Vail Mountain) and three in Lake Tahoe on the California/Nevada border (Heavenly Mountain Northstar-at-Tahoe and Kirkwood Mountain Resort). The resorts operate under the company's Mountain segment. Through its Lodging segment the firm owns or manages about 20 resorts in New Mexico Colorado Wyoming and the West Indies; it also operates six golf courses. Vail Resorts also has a Real Estate Development segment that develops real estate in and around the company's resorts.

	Annual Growth	07/11	07/12	07/13	07/14	07/15
Sales ($ mil.)	4.7%	1,167.0	1,024.4	1,120.8	1,254.6	1,399.9
Net income ($ mil.)	35.1%	34.5	16.5	37.7	28.5	114.8
Market value ($ mil.)	24.4%	1,670.5	1,812.5	2,445.7	2,756.8	4,005.2
Employees	3.5%	18,800	20,780	23,800	23,000	21,613

VALCOM INC.

PINK SHEETS: VLCO

429 Rockaway Valley Rd.
Boonton Township NJ 07005
Phone: 727-953-9778
Fax: 202-728-0845
Web: www.judydiamond.com

CEO: Anthony Barrett
CFO: –
HR: –
FYE: September 30
Type: Public

There's value in entertainment. Through its Studio division ValCom leases production facilities and sound stages to major movie studios such as Warner Bros and Universal Studios. The company's Rental division leases out personnel cameras and other production equipment to production companies. Through its TV Stations and Broadcasting unit ValCom owns a small library of TV content and has a 45% stake in ValCom Broadcasting which operates KVPS (Channel 8) an independent TV station in Palm Springs California. ValCom additionally has a Film Production division that has developed and produced TV pilots and feature films such as PCH (Pacific Coast Highway) and the 40 episode TV series AJ's Time Travelers.

VALDOSTA STATE UNIVERSITY

CEO: –
CFO: –
HR: –
FYE: June 30
Type: Private

1500 N PATTERSON ST
VALDOSTA, GA 316980001
Phone: 229-333-5708
Fax: –
Web: www.valdosta.edu

Valdosta State University (VSU) nurtures higher education students as they blossom into professionals. The school a regional university of the University System of Georgia is located in the southern Georgia town of Valdosta which is known for its flower gardens and trails. The school has two campuses less than a mile apart that house six colleges and offer about 60 undergraduate and 40 graduate degree programs as well as doctorates in education and public administration. VSU was founded in 1906 as South Georgia State Normal College. Originally a girls' school the institution became co-educational in 1950. It has some 650 faculty members and a student body of about 12500.

	Annual Growth	06/06	06/07	06/08	06/10	06/11
Sales ($ mil.)	–	–	(739.3)	80.1	92.1	101.5
Net income ($ mil.)	36.0%	–	–	3.6	13.7	9.0
Market value ($ mil.)	–	–	–	–	–	–
Employees	–	–	–	–	–	1,956

VALENCE TECHNOLOGY, INC.

NBB: VLNC Q

12303 Technology Blvd., Suite 950
Austin, TX 78727
Phone: 512 527-2900
Fax: –
Web: www.valence.com

CEO: William J Masuda
CFO: Donald E Gottschalk
HR: –
FYE: March 31
Type: Public

If you charged Valence Technology with battery you'd be right. The company's rechargeable lithium polymer batteries are designed for use in industrial (forklifts) military (robotics) stationary (generators) and transportation-related (cars and boats) electrical power applications. Valence touts its U-Charge lithium iron magnesium phosphate (LiFeMgPO4) energy storage systems as having a longer life and being safer and more stable under extreme conditions than even lithium-ion batteries that use oxide-based cathode materials. In 2012 Valence filed a voluntary petition for a Chapter 11 business reorganization in US Bankruptcy Court. The company expects to complete restructuring in 2012.

	Annual Growth	03/08	03/09	03/10	03/11	03/12
Sales ($ mil.)	20.9%	20.8	26.2	16.1	45.9	44.4
Net income ($ mil.)	–	(19.4)	(21.2)	(23.0)	(12.7)	(12.7)
Market value ($ mil.)	(34.6%)	749.6	362.1	144.5	265.2	137.4
Employees	(8.7%)	490	366	349	433	340

VALERO ENERGY CORP.

NYS: VLO

One Valero Way
San Antonio, TX 78249
Phone: 210 345-2000
Fax: 210 246-2646
Web: www.valero.com

CEO: Joseph W. (Joe) Gorder
CFO: Michael S. (Mike) Ciskowski
HR: –
FYE: December 31
Type: Public

Valero Energy was not only named after a mission (the Mission San Antonio de Valero) it is on a mission to be the largest independent refiner in the US. Valero churns out about 2.9 million barrels per day refining low-cost residual oil and heavy crude into cleaner-burning higher-margin products including low-sulfur diesels. It operates 15 refineries in the US Canada the UK and Aruba. It also has 11 ethanol plants with a combined production capacity of about 1.3 billion gallons per year. Once a more diversified company Valero has exited the retail business in order to focus on its oil refining and ethanol operations.

	Annual Growth	12/10	12/11	12/12	12/13	12/14
Sales ($ mil.)	12.3%	82,233.0	125,987.0	139,250.0	138,074.0	130,844.0
Net income ($ mil.)	83.0%	324.0	2,090.0	2,083.0	2,720.0	3,630.0
Market value ($ mil.)	21.0%	11,890.6	10,826.0	17,547.9	25,920.7	25,457.8
Employees	(16.1%)	20,313	21,942	21,671	10,007	10,065

VALERO ENERGY PARTNERS LP

NYS: VLP

One Valero Way
San Antonio, TX 78249
Phone: 210 345-2000
Fax: –
Web: www.valeroenergypartners.com

CEO: Joseph W Gorder
CFO: Donna M Titzman
HR: –
FYE: December 31
Type: Public

Valero Energy Partners teams up with Valero Energy to bring energy in the form of petroleum products to the world. The company was formed to serve as the transportation and logistics arm of major independent US refiner Valero Energy. It makes money from fees on pipeline transportation and storage of crude oil and refined petroleum along the US Gulf Coast and eastern US. The partnership serves Valero's two plants in Port Arthur and Sunray Texas and one in Memphis. Organized as a limited partnership Valero Energy Partners is exempt from paying corporate income tax as long as it distributes quarterly dividends to shareholders. It went public in 2013.

	Annual Growth	12/10	12/11	12/12	12/13	12/14
Sales ($ mil.)	–	0.0	73.1	86.8	94.5	129.2
Net income ($ mil.)	–	0.0	25.8	42.3	50.2	68.8
Market value ($ mil.)	–	0.0	–	–	2,024.3	2,541.4
Employees	–	–	–	–	–	–

VALHI, INC.

NYS: VHI

5430 LBJ Freeway, Suite 1700
Dallas, TX 75240-2697
Phone: 972 233-1700
Fax: 972 448-1445
Web: www.valhi.net

CEO: Steven L. (Steve) Watson
CFO: Bobby D. O'Brien
HR: –
FYE: December 31
Type: Public

Valhi keeps it interesting by pursuing a variety of things. The company's NL Industries unit operating through subsidiary Kronos is a leading maker of titanium dioxide pigment which is used to whiten and add opacity to fibers paper paint and plastic. Other subsidiaries include CompX (ergonomic computer support systems and office security products) Tremont (titanium metal products for the aerospace and other markets through its stake in Titanium Metals) and Waste Control Specialists (operator of hazardous-waste treatment facilities in Texas). It also has real estate assets.

	Annual Growth	12/10	12/11	12/12	12/13	12/14
Sales ($ mil.)	3.6%	1,651.2	2,141.0	2,157.9	1,951.6	1,904.6
Net income ($ mil.)	1.7%	50.3	217.5	159.8	(98.0)	53.8
Market value ($ mil.)	(26.6%)	7,561.6	20,680.7	4,275.0	6,012.4	2,192.2
Employees	(7.6%)	3,412	2,470	2,555	2,450	2,485

VALLEY FINANCIAL CORP.

NAS: VYFC

36 Church Avenue, S.W.
Roanoke, VA 24011
Phone: 540 342-2265
Fax: –
Web: www.myvalleybank.com

CEO: –
CFO: –
HR: –
FYE: December 31
Type: Public

Down in the valley valley so low ... Valley Financial has a banking business dontcha know? The financial institution is the holding company for Valley Bank which operates about 10 locations in and around Roanoke Virginia. Valley Bank offers traditional banking products and services to individuals and small to midsized businesses in its market area. Deposit products include checking and savings accounts NOW accounts and CDs. Lending operations include residential mortgages business loans construction loans and consumer loans. The bank offers investment and insurance products through subsidiary Valley Wealth Management Services.

	Annual Growth	12/09	12/10	12/11	12/12	12/13
Assets ($ mil.)	3.7%	713.7	767.6	773.5	764.6	825.3
Net income ($ mil.)	–	(5.7)	3.5	5.7	6.5	6.8
Market value ($ mil.)	31.7%	16.8	14.5	23.5	43.3	50.5
Employees	1.3%	136	130	136	139	143

VALLEY HEALTH SYSTEM

1840 AMHERST ST
WINCHESTER, VA 22601-2808
Phone: 540-536-8000
Fax: –
Web: www.valleyhealthlink.com

CEO: Mark H Merrill
CFO: Pete Gallagher
HR: –
FYE: December 31
Type: Private

Valley Health's medical centers can be found in the in the Shenandoah Valley region. The not-for-profit organization operates six hospitals in Virginia and West Virginia that house a combined total of roughly 610 beds. The facilities include the flagship Winchester Medical Center as well as Warren Memorial Hospital Shenandoah Memorial Hospital and a handful of smaller community hospitals. Valley Health also operates outpatient surgery nursing home rehabilitation urgent care and family practice centers and it offers ambulance and home health care services. The system can trace its beginnings back to the opening of Winchester Memorial Hospital in 1903.

	Annual Growth	12/03	12/04	12/05	12/06	12/07
Sales ($ mil.)	–	–	–	(1,286.6)	564.1	612.2
Net income ($ mil.)	43836.8%	–	–	0.0	76.0	52.1
Market value ($ mil.)	–	–	–	–	–	–
Employees	–	–	–	–	–	4,300

VALLEY NATIONAL BANCORP

NYS: VLY

1455 Valley Road
Wayne, NJ 07470
Phone: 973 305-8800
Fax: –
Web: www.valleynationalbank.com

CEO: Gerald H. Lipkin
CFO: Alan D. Eskow
HR: –
FYE: December 31
Type: Public

Valley National Bancorp is high on New Jersey and New York. The holding company owns Valley National Bank which serves commercial and retail clients through more than 200 branches in northern and central New Jersey and in the New York City boroughs of Manhattan Brooklyn and Queens as well as on Long Island. The bank provides standard services like checking and savings accounts loans and mortgages credit cards and trust services. Subsidiaries offer asset management mortgage and auto loan servicing title insurance asset-based lending and property/casualty life and health insurance. Founded as The Passaic Park Trust Company in 1927 Valley National is looking to expand in Florida.

	Annual Growth	12/10	12/11	12/12	12/13	12/14
Assets ($ mil.)	7.4%	14,143.8	14,244.5	16,012.6	16,156.5	18,793.9
Net income ($ mil.)	(3.0%)	131.2	133.7	143.6	132.0	116.2
Market value ($ mil.)	(9.2%)	3,319.2	2,871.2	2,158.6	2,349.0	2,253.8
Employees	1.7%	2,720	2,754	2,910	2,908	2,907

VALMONT INDUSTRIES, INC.

NYS: VMI

One Valmont Plaza
Omaha, NE 68154-5215
Phone: 402 963-1000
Fax: 402 963-1198
Web: www.valmont.com

CEO: Mogens C. Bay
CFO: Mark C. Jaksich
HR: Vanessa K. Brown
FYE: December 27
Type: Public

Valmont Industries has pole position: Its founder Robert Daugherty helped develop the center pivot irrigation pipe that transformed farming. The company has four primary business units: engineered infrastructure products (EIP; metal poles and other structures for lighting traffic and wireless communications industries); irrigation (agricultural irrigation equipment sold under the Valley brand); utilities support structures (steel and concrete poles and other structures used by utilities); and coatings (galvanizing anodizing and powder coating). Other operations include the manufacture of tubular products and industrial fastener distribution.

	Annual Growth	12/10	12/11	12/12	12/13	12/14
Sales ($ mil.)	12.1%	1,975.5	2,661.5	3,029.5	3,304.2	3,123.1
Net income ($ mil.)	18.2%	94.4	228.3	234.1	278.5	184.0
Market value ($ mil.)	10.5%	2,101.4	2,199.8	3,246.7	3,608.5	3,130.2
Employees	5.4%	9,188	9,476	10,543	10,769	11,321

VALPAK DIRECT MARKETING SYSTEMS INC.

8605 Largo Lakes Dr.
Largo FL 33773
Phone: 727-399-3000
Fax: 727-399-3178
Web: www.valpak.com

CEO: –
CFO: Jeff Heinicka
HR: –
FYE: December 31
Type: Subsidiary

Valpak Direct Marketing Systems can pack loads of savings into one little blue envelope. Its well-known package of coupons contains discounts on services ranging from dry cleaning to auto services to home improvement. Formed in 1968 the company has operations with some 180 franchisees in the US Canada and Puerto Rico delivering about 20 billion offers in more than 490 million envelopes a year. Valpak also operates about 10 traditional bricks-and-mortar stores as well as a website Valpak.com that offers the same savings found in its mailers. Valpak is a unit of direct marketer Cox Target Media a subsidiary of Cox Media Group.

VALSPAR CORP.

NYS: VAL

1101 3rd Street South
Minneapolis, MN 55415
Phone: 612 851-7000
Fax: –
Web: www.valsparglobal.com

CEO: Gary E. Hendrickson
CFO: James L. Muehlbauer
HR: Anthony L. Blaine
FYE: October 30
Type: Public

Valspar wants you to put on a coat. The firm makes a variety of coatings and paints for manufacturing automotive and food-packaging companies as well as for consumers. The company's industrial coatings — used by OEMs including building product appliance and furniture makers — include coatings for metal wood plastic and glass. Packaging products include coatings and inks for rigid containers such as food and beverage cans. Its consumer paints include interior and exterior paints primers stains and varnishes sold through mass merchandisers like Wal-Mart and Lowe's. Valspar also makes auto paints and colorants. It is active in Asia the Americas and Europe.

	Annual Growth	10/11	10/12	10/13	10/14	10/15
Sales ($ mil.)	2.7%	3,953.0	4,020.9	4,103.8	4,522.4	4,392.6
Net income ($ mil.)	–	(138.6)	292.5	289.3	345.4	399.5
Market value ($ mil.)	22.6%	2,830.0	4,341.0	5,551.0	6,489.3	6,393.7
Employees	2.6%	10,000	9,800	10,700	10,500	11,100

VALUE CITY FURNITURE INC.

4300 E. 5th Ave.
Columbus OH 43219
Phone: 614-221-9200
Fax: 614-443-9011
Web: www.vcf.com

CEO: –
CFO: –
HR: –
FYE: December 31
Type: Subsidiary

The quest for Value City may not require you to venture outside of your hometown. A leading home furnishings retailer Value City Furniture (VCF) is operated by American Signature and is part of its network of some 125 superstores in 20 US states in the East Midwest and Southeast. The company offers furniture for the bedroom dining room and living room as well as mattresses bedding and other accessories. VCF stores feature furnishings from more than 30 manufacturers and even carry American Signature's private-label furniture and bedding. The retailer also peddles its wares online. Founded in 1948 VCF is owned by holding company Schottenstein Stores.

VALUE DRUG COMPANY

1 GOLFVIEW DR
ALTOONA, PA 166019398
Phone: 814-944-9316
Fax: –
Web: www.valuedrugco.com

CEO: –
CFO: Robert E Tyler
HR: –
FYE: December 31
Type: Private

Value Drug Company sees a great deal of value in keeping independent pharmacies competitive. The company is a purchasing cooperative of hundreds of independent drugstores that provides wholesale pharmaceutical distribution services to its members primarily in the central Pennsylvania area. Its products include pharmaceuticals and non-prescription medications hospital and convalescent equipment health and beauty aids nutritional supplies and other health care-related products. The company works with some of the world's largest pharmaceutical makers. Value Drug was founded in 1934 and incorporated in 1936. The company is led by president Greg Drew a former Rite-Aid executive.

	Annual Growth	12/06	12/07	12/08	12/09	12/13
Sales ($ mil.)	(12.6%)	–	1,599.7	732.1	751.1	715.4
Net income ($ mil.)	41.4%	–	–	0.1	0.1	0.4
Market value ($ mil.)	–	–	–	–	–	–
Employees	–	–	–	–	–	107

VALUE LINE, INC.

NAS: VALU

485 Lexington Avenue
New York, NY 10017-2630
Phone: 212 907-1500
Fax: –
Web: www.valueline.com

CEO: Howard A Brecher
CFO: –
HR: –
FYE: April 30
Type: Public

Value Line's investment-related publications are likely to be found on the bookshelves of the serious investor. Its flagship publication The Value Line Investment Survey features stock reports that incorporate objective analysis financial information and forecasts of stock performance. Its print and electronic products also include Value Line Fund Advisor which offers mutual fund evaluations and rankings and investment analysis software The Value Line Investment Analyzer. The company's electronic products are available via CD-ROM and via the company's website. All total Value Line collects data and provides analysis on some 7000 stocks; 18000 mutual funds; 200000 options; and other securities.

	Annual Growth	04/11	04/12	04/13	04/14	04/15
Sales ($ mil.)	(7.6%)	48.7	36.6	35.8	36.3	35.5
Net income ($ mil.)	(33.7%)	37.8	6.9	6.6	6.8	7.3
Market value ($ mil.)	0.9%	137.2	119.4	91.8	143.0	142.0
Employees	2.7%	175	178	186	196	195

VALUEOPTIONS INC.

240 Corporate Blvd.
Norfolk VA 23502
Phone: 757-459-5100
Fax: 386-418-0342
Web: www.rtix.com

CEO: Heyward R Donigan
CFO: Douglas Thompson
HR: –
FYE: December 31
Type: Subsidiary

If your problem is all in your head ValueOptions may have the answer. A provider of managed health care services the company specializes in management of the behavioral health components of benefit plans administered by government agencies (state and federal) health plans and employers. With a network of some 50000 health care providers ValueOptions oversees mental health and substance abuse benefits for millions of people nationwide. The company's services — offered through its provider network regional service centers and a nurse help line — also include life coaching and health and wellness programs.

VALUERICH INC

NBB: VRCH

1804 N. Dixie Highway, Suite A	CEO: Joseph Visconti
West Palm Beach, FL 33407	CFO: -
Phone: 561 370-3617	HR: -
Fax: -	FYE: December 31
Web: www.ivaluerich.com	Type: Public

The value-add for ValueRich is to create wealth by bringing small-cap companies and investors together. The company's Web-based platform magazine and events are designed to help small-cap companies raise capital go public and attract shareholders. Its iValueRich.com site allows investors to directly connect with companies that are seeking investors.ValueRich also manages and holds regular tradeshows where attendees can highlight their prospects for investment bankers and other potential investors. The company's ValueRich quarterly magazine is distributed free to a select group of executives and investment professionals in the small-cap community. ValueRich was founded in 2003.

	Annual Growth	12/09	12/11	12/12	12/13	12/14
Sales ($ mil.)	43.8%	0.1	0.5	0.5	0.5	0.6
Net income ($ mil.)	-	(0.6)	(0.5)	(0.1)	(0.4)	(0.0)
Market value ($ mil.)	(10.8%)	2.3	0.6	0.2	1.4	1.3
Employees	-	-	-	-	-	-

VAN ARPIN LINES INC

99 JAMES P MURPHY IND HWY	CEO: David Arpin
WEST WARWICK, RI 028932382	CFO: Edward J Braks
Phone: 401-828-8111	HR: -
Fax: -	FYE: December 31
Web: www.arpin.com	Type: Private

From the fairway to the highway and home again Arpin Van Lines provides a wide range of moving services for residential business and government customers which have included the LPGA. The company formerly known as Paul Arpin Van Lines operates through a network of independent agents throughout North America. (The agents handle local moves within assigned geographic territories; Arpin Van Lines coordinates interstate moves.) Arpin Van Lines' fleet includes some 700 trucks. The company which is run by members of the founding Arpin family is a division of Arpin Group which also includes Arpin International Group and Arpin Moving Systems (Canada). The original Arpin moving company was founded in 1900.

	Annual Growth	12/05	12/06	12/07	12/09	12/10
Sales ($ mil.)	-	-	-	(842.7)	105.8	105.7
Net income ($ mil.)	1082.2%	-	-	0.0	1.1	0.4
Market value ($ mil.)	-	-	-	-	-	-
Employees	-	-	-	-	-	250

VAN BUDD LINES INC

24 SCHOOLHOUSE RD	CEO: -
SOMERSET, NJ 088731213	CFO: -
Phone: 732-627-0600	HR: -
Fax: -	FYE: December 31
Web: www.buddvanlines.com	Type: Private

No hothouse flower Budd Van Lines aims to be a hardy perennial of the corporate relocation business. From coast to coast the independent van line company moves the household goods of employees who are relocating at the behest of their employers about 6500 annually. It offers packing and moving services to all 48 contiguous states from branch offices in New Jersey California Wisconsin Georgia Ohio and Texas. Companies that have called upon Budd Van Lines to help employees move include Bristol-Myers Squibb Merck & Co. and PricewaterhouseCoopers. Budd Van Lines was founded in 1975.

	Annual Growth	12/05	12/06	12/07	12/08	12/10
Sales ($ mil.)	-	-	-	(1,131.5)	47.1	47.2
Net income ($ mil.)	3019.9%	-	-	0.0	0.3	1.1
Market value ($ mil.)	-	-	-	-	-	-
Employees	-	-	-	-	-	155

VAN HORN METZ & CO. INC.

201 E ELM ST	CEO: -
CONSHOHOCKEN, PA 194282029	CFO: -
Phone: 610-828-4500	HR: -
Fax: -	FYE: December 31
Web: www.vanhornmetz.com	Type: Private

|Van Horn Metz & Co. (or Van Horn Metz) distributes chemical ingredients such as pigments dyes extenders additives resins lubricants and base stocks. The company's customers include makers of plastic and rubber products inks adhesives and sealants and paints and coatings. Founded in 1950 by Harold Van Horn and Donald Metz the company serves customers throughout the eastern half of the US. Van Horn Metz operates 12 warehouses and six sales offices.

	Annual Growth	12/06	12/07	12/08	12/09	12/10
Sales ($ mil.)	-	-	-	(380.0)	35.5	39.4
Net income ($ mil.)	-	-	-	0.0	0.0	0.0
Market value ($ mil.)	-	-	-	-	-	-
Employees	-	-	-	-	-	24

VANDA PHARMACEUTICALS INC

NMS: VNDA

2200 Pennsylvania Avenue NW, Suite 300 E	CEO: Mihael H. Polymeropoulos
Washington, DC 20037	CFO: James P. Kelly
Phone: 202 734-3400	HR: -
Fax: -	FYE: December 31
Web: www.vandapharma.com	Type: Public

Vanda wants to gain an advantage in the field of neurological medicine. Vanda Pharmaceuticals is a pharmaceutical company that is developing several drugs for disorders of the central nervous system. The company's first commercial drug schizophrenia treatment Fanapt (iloperidone) received FDA approval in 2009. Other drug candidates are treatments for sleep disorders including insomnia and sleep apnea as well as anxiety and depression. Vanda typically licenses development and commercialization rights for its compounds from (and to) companies including Bristol-Myers Squibb Eli Lilly and Novartis.

	Annual Growth	12/10	12/11	12/12	12/13	12/14
Sales ($ mil.)	8.9%	35.7	31.3	32.7	33.9	50.2
Net income ($ mil.)	29.4%	7.2	(9.8)	(27.7)	(20.3)	20.2
Market value ($ mil.)	10.9%	392.5	197.5	153.5	514.8	594.1
Employees	23.0%	28	38	40	53	64

VANGENT INC.

4250 N. Fairfax Dr. Ste. 1200	CEO: -
Arlington VA 22203	CFO: -
Phone: 703-284-5600	HR: -
Fax: 703-284-5628	FYE: December 31
Web: www.vangent.com	Type: Private

While government bureaucracy makes most of us see red Vangent sees dollar signs. The company plans builds and operates technology systems mainly for the US government which account for 90% of sales. Services include network design consulting business process outsourcing and systems integration. Its top clients are the Department of Health and Human Services the Department of Commerce (DoC) and the Department of Education (DoEd). Vangent also serves retail education and banking clients. The company was sold by former owner Veritas Capital to defense contractor General Dynamics for about $960 million in 2011; it was made a part of General Dynamics Information Technology the IT arm of General Dynamics.

VANGUARD NATURAL RESOURCES LLC

NMS: VNR

5847 San Felipe, Suite 3000
Houston, TX 77057
Phone: 832 327-2255
Fax: –
Web: www.vnrllc.com

CEO: Scott W Smith
CFO: Richard A Robert
HR: –
FYE: December 31
Type: Public

Vanguard Natural Resources is at the forefront of oil and natural gas exploration in the Appalachian Basin the Rockies the Permian Basin and South Texas acquiring and developing oil and gas properties in these region. In 2013 Vanguard Natural Resources reported estimated proved reserves of 172.2 million barrels of oil equivalent and an interest in 2551 net and 7277 gross productive wells. The company also owns a 40% working interest in 797118 acres in Appalachia. Vinland Energy Eastern owns the remaining 60% working interest of the acreage. In 2015 the company acquired fellow upstream MLP LRR Energy in a $589 million deal.

	Annual Growth	12/10	12/11	12/12	12/13	12/14
Sales ($ mil.)	70.5%	93.2	319.6	347.2	454.5	788.1
Net income ($ mil.)	30.9%	21.9	62.1	(168.8)	59.5	64.3
Market value ($ mil.)	(15.6%)	2,486.8	2,317.4	2,180.7	2,475.9	1,263.9
Employees	33.0%	83	110	122	172	260

VANS INC.

6550 Katella Ave.
Cypress CA 90630
Phone: 714-889-6100
Fax: 585-343-1097
Web: www.graham-mfg.com

CEO: –
CFO: Scott J Blechman
HR: Carlos Loza
FYE: December 31
Type: Subsidiary

The movie Fast Times at Ridgemont High put Vans sneakers on the map but the company owes its current popularity to the fashion sense of extreme-sports enthusiasts who weren't even born then. Vans designs and sells footwear and apparel for casual wear and for use in activities such as skateboarding snowboarding surfing bicycle motocross (BMX) and motocross. Vans merchandise is sold in the US by national chain stores and in skate surf and specialty shops in North America Europe and Asia. Vans operates about 270 stores in the western US and in Europe. As part of its marketing strategy Vans backs bands through music festivals. The company is owned by V.F. Corporation.

VANTIV INC

NYS: VNTV

8500 Governor's Hill Drive
Symmes Township, OH 45249
Phone: 513 900-5250
Fax: –
Web: www.vantiv.com

CEO: Charles D. Drucker
CFO: Mark L. Heimbouch
HR: Christa Titus
FYE: December 31
Type: Public

You may not know it but every time you swipe your credit card a whole world of transactions takes place in the background. And Vantiv lives to rule that world. Operating through subsidiaries Vantiv is the US's second-largest merchant acquirer; that is a third-party payment processor operating between merchants and customers and their respective banks. The company also handles PIN transactions fraud detection and management and credit card issuing for financials institutions. Vantiv Caters to merchants of all sizes including top retailers grocers pharmacies and restaurants. It also serves small to mid-sized banks and credit unions. Formed in 1970 Vantiv went public in 2012.

	Annual Growth	12/11	12/12	12/13	12/14	12/15
Sales ($ mil.)	18.1%	1,622.4	1,863.2	2,108.1	2,577.2	3,159.9
Net income ($ mil.)	42.1%	36.2	57.6	133.6	125.3	147.9
Market value ($ mil.)	32.4%	–	3,890.6	6,213.2	6,462.8	9,035.0
Employees	7.8%	2,455	2,671	2,791	3,299	3,313

VANTIV INC.

NYSE: VNTV

8500 Governor's Hill Dr.
Symmes Township OH 45249
Phone: 513-900-5250
Fax: 816-464-0510
Web: smithelectric.com

CEO: Charles Drucker
CFO: –
HR: –
FYE: December 31
Type: Public

You may not know it but every time you swipe your credit card a whole world of transactions take place in the background. And Vantiv lives to rule that world. The company which operates through subsidiary Vantiv LLC (formerly Fifth Third Processing Solutions) is a merchant acquirer - a third party payment processor operating between merchants (and their banks) and customers (and their banks). One of the largest merchant acquirers it also handles PIN transactions fraud detection and management and credit card issuing. Catering to small- to mid-size customers Vantiv sells services specific to grocers pharmacies retailers restaurants and others. Formed in 1970 the company went public in 2012.

VARIAN MEDICAL SYSTEMS, INC.

NYS: VAR

3100 Hansen Way
Palo Alto, CA 94304-1038
Phone: 650 493-4000
Fax: –
Web: www.varian.com

CEO: Dow R. Wilson
CFO: Elisha W. Finney
HR: –
FYE: October 02
Type: Public

Varian Medical Systems radiates success in electrotherapeutics. The company develops products related to x-rays and radiation treatment of cancer. It makes and services hardware and software products for treating cancer with radiotherapy stereotactic radiosurgery stereotactic body radiotherapy stereotactic radiosurgery and brachytherapy. The company's oncology unit makes linear accelerators simulators and data management software primarily for cancer radiotherapy. Other cancer treatment offerings include devices for brachytherapy a treatment that protects healthy tissue through the use of radiation implants. Varian's X-ray unit makes imaging subsystems and X-ray-generating tubes.

	Annual Growth	09/11	09/12	09/13	09/14*	10/15
Sales ($ mil.)	4.5%	2,596.7	2,807.0	2,942.9	3,049.8	3,099.1
Net income ($ mil.)	0.8%	398.9	427.0	438.2	403.7	411.5
Market value ($ mil.)	9.6%	5,115.3	5,915.6	7,274.8	7,933.9	7,373.9
Employees	6.4%	5,700	6,100	6,400	6,800	7,300
						*Fiscal year change

VARIAN SEMICONDUCTOR EQUIPMENT ASSOCIATES INC.

NASDAQ: VSEA

35 Dory Rd.
Gloucester MA 01930
Phone: 978-282-2000
Fax: 978-283-6376
Web: www.vsea.com

CEO: Gary E Dickerson
CFO: Robert J Halliday
HR: –
FYE: September 30
Type: Subsidiary

Varian Semiconductor Equipment Associates (VSEA) is the ion king. The company is the world's top designer and manufacturer of ion implantation equipment and systems which beam ions into semiconductor wafers to modify their electrical properties. VSEA has a common equipment platform the VIISta single-wafer system which is designed to cover a complete range of applications such as high-current medium-current and high and ultra high-energy doses of ions. It also offers product upgrades spare parts and technical support. Customers outside North America account for more than 70% of the company's sales. In 2011 Applied Materials acquired VSEA for about $4.2 billion.

VARIETY CHILDREN'S HOSPITAL

3100 SW 62ND AVE
MIAMI, FL 33155-3009
Phone: 305-666-6511
Fax: –
Web: www.mch.com

CEO: Narendra M Kini
CFO: –
HR: –
FYE: December 31
Type: Private

Miami Children's Hospital a not-for-profit medical center boasts some 290 beds and offers more than 40 different health care specialties and subspecialties represented by more than 650 physicians. Some specialties include pediatric emergency care cancer treatment orthopedics and rehabilitation services. The hospital's neonatal unit treats newborns referred from other hospitals. Miami Children's Hospital operates the region's only free-standing pediatric trauma center. The hospital first opened its doors in the 1940s as Miami Tent #33 of Variety Clubs International. Variety Children's Hospital opened in 1950 and became Miami Children's Hospital in 1986.

	Annual Growth	12/04	12/05	12/06	12/07	12/08
Sales ($ mil.)	–	–	–	(819.5)	385.2	381.8
Net income ($ mil.)	76479.7%	–	–	0.0	37.4	269.2
Market value ($ mil.)	–	–	–	–	–	–
Employees	–	–	–	–	–	3,700

VASCO DATA SECURITY INTERNATIONAL INC

NAS: VDSI

1901 South Meyers Road, Suite 210
Oakbrook Terrace, IL 60181
Phone: 630 932-8844
Fax: 630 932-8852
Web: www.vasco.com

CEO: T. Kendall (Ken) Hunt
CFO: Mark S. Hoyt
HR: Arendt Carol
FYE: December 31
Type: Public

VASCO Data Security International holds the key to electronic banking. Its hardware and software lines include authentication platforms security tokens handheld devices and related applications used for authenticating a person's identity on computer networks. The company's products incorporate authentication and digital signature security technologies and can be used to secure intranets extranets and LANs. In addition to banking VASCO's products are used to provide remote workers with secure access to corporate networks; other applications include e-commerce transactions. It counts more than 10000 customers including some 1700 financial institutions such as Citibank BNP-Paribas and HSBC.

	Annual Growth	12/10	12/11	12/12	12/13	12/14
Sales ($ mil.)	16.9%	108.0	168.1	154.0	155.0	201.5
Net income ($ mil.)	32.7%	10.8	18.1	15.6	11.1	33.5
Market value ($ mil.)	36.5%	322.4	258.6	323.6	306.6	1,118.8
Employees	3.4%	325	358	374	396	371

VASCULAR SOLUTIONS INC

NMS: VASC

6464 Sycamore Court North
Minneapolis, MN 55369
Phone: 763 656-4300
Fax: 877 656-4251
Web: www.vasc.com

CEO: Howard C. Root
CFO: James Hennen
HR: –
FYE: December 31
Type: Public

Vascular Solutions helps interventional cardiologists intervene into veins. The company develops manufactures and markets catheters used during treatment of vascular conditions. Its product line includes the Pronto extraction catheter which removes arterial clots and other tools used to get under the skin and into blood vessels. Its hemostat products include the D-Stat a thrombin-infused bandage used to control bleeding following catheterization. It also makes the Vari-Lase a laser system for treating varicose veins. Vascular Solutions markets the devices to interventional cardiologists and radiologists through its own sales team in the US; it uses independent distributors overseas.

	Annual Growth	12/11	12/12	12/13	12/14	12/15
Sales ($ mil.)	13.1%	90.0	98.4	110.5	126.1	147.2
Net income ($ mil.)	1.8%	9.7	9.9	11.1	12.7	10.5
Market value ($ mil.)	32.6%	193.5	274.7	402.5	472.2	597.9
Employees	12.5%	355	377	406	485	568

VASOMEDICAL, INC.

NBB: VASO

180 Linden Avenue
Westbury, NY 11590
Phone: 516 997-4600
Fax: 516 997-2299
Web: www.vasomedical.com

CEO: –
CFO: Michael J Beecher
HR: –
FYE: December 31
Type: Public

Vasomedical's noninvasive treatments for angina and congestive heart failure get patients' blood pumping. The company's main product is the EECP (enhanced external counterpulsation) system which is also approved to treat coronary artery disease and cardiogenic shock. During the company's Medicare-covered treatments cuffs attached to the patient's calves and thighs inflate and deflate in sync with the patient's heartbeat increasing and decreasing aortic blood pressure. After about 35 treatments patients may experience years of symptomatic relief. Vasomedical sells the system to hospitals clinics and other health care providers worldwide through a direct sales force and independent distributors.

	Annual Growth	05/11*	12/11	12/12	12/13	12/14
Sales ($ mil.)	28.8%	16.4	23.5	29.2	32.9	35.0
Net income ($ mil.)	–	(3.9)	5.1	(3.4)	(1.1)	1.1
Market value ($ mil.)	(30.7%)	79.6	34.3	28.5	28.5	26.5
Employees	26.0%	109	175	194	215	218

*Fiscal year change

VASSAR COLLEGE INC

124 RAYMOND AVE BOX 12
POUGHKEEPSIE, NY 126040001
Phone: 845-437-7000
Fax: –
Web: www.admissions.vassar.edu

CEO: –
CFO: –
HR: –
FYE: June 30
Type: Private

A cool nickname and certain heritage aren't enough to assure some students entrance into Vassar College. The highly selective school enrolls some 2400 students annually most of whom graduated in the top 20% of their high school class. It has a student-faculty ratio of 8:1 and a list of alumni that includes standouts in areas from business to philanthropy. Because Vassar has no core curriculum students may concentrate in a single discipline a multidisciplinary program or design an independent major. The only universal requirements for graduation are proficiency in a foreign language a freshman composition class and a quantitative class. Vassar was founded in 1861 as a women's school; it went coed in 1969.

	Annual Growth	06/10	06/11	06/12	06/13	06/14
Sales ($ mil.)	(11.2%)	–	229.5	154.0	175.7	160.6
Net income ($ mil.)	–	–	–	(33.1)	103.1	97.3
Market value ($ mil.)	–	–	–	–	–	–
Employees	–	–	–	–	–	974

VAULT.COM INC.

75 Varick St. 8th Floor
New York NY 10013
Phone: 212-366-4212
Fax: 212-366-6117
Web: www.vault.com

CEO: Eric Ober
CFO: –
HR: –
FYE: December 31
Type: Private

Looking for career gold? You might find it in the Vault.com. The firm provides company and industry information to help job-seekers determine what it's really like inside Merrill Lynch CNN and some 4500 other employers. Vault.com offers information on interviewing pay and corporate culture at various companies. It also publishes 120 digital and print career guidebooks such as Vault Guide to the Top 100 Law Firms and Vault Guide to Biotech. Vault.com additionally offers employee message boards a job listings board and career services such as resume writing. Mark Oldman and brothers Samer and H. S. Hamadeh founded the company in 1997. Today it is owned by private equity firm Veronis Suhler Stevenson.

VBI VACCINES INC

NAS: VBIV

222 Third Street, Suite 2241
Cambridge, MA 02142
Phone: 613 749-4200
Fax: –
Web: www.vbivaccines.com

CEO: Jeff R Baxter
CFO: Egidio Nascimento
HR: –
FYE: December 31
Type: Public

Paulson Capital is a financial services holding company operating through its sole subsidiary Paulson Investment Company. A full-service brokerage Paulson Investment is one of the largest independent brokerage firms in the Pacific Northwest. It acts as an agent for its customers in the purchase and sale of stocks options and debt securities. The company also offers market-making and underwriting services for small and emerging companies. Paulson Investment has more than 40 branches in about a dozen states; most are run by independent contractors. The company has agreed to sell its Paulson Investment retail operations to Tampa-based JHS Capital Advisors.

	Annual Growth	12/09	12/10	12/11	12/12	12/13
Sales ($ mil.)	(8.2%)	15.2	18.1	15.4	7.7	10.8
Net income ($ mil.)	–	(2.4)	(1.2)	(3.1)	(0.4)	(1.5)
Market value ($ mil.)	(9.6%)	1.8	1.3	0.6	0.9	1.2
Employees	(14.2%)	70	65	62	15	38

VCA INC

NMS: WOOF

12401 West Olympic Boulevard
Los Angeles, CA 90064-1022
Phone: 310 571-6500
Fax: –
Web: www.vcaantech.com

CEO: Robert L. (Bob) Antin
CFO: Tomas W. (Tom) Fuller
HR: –
FYE: December 31
Type: Public

At VCA health care doesn't go to the dogs. Dogs — cats and a boatload of other animals — go to it for health services. The company operates the nation's largest chain of animal hospitals — more than 600 in some 41 states and four Canadian provinces. Its hospitals offer basic wellness checkups dental care neutering and spaying vaccinations and specialty surgeries. With about 60 diagnostic laboratories nationwide VCA also tests blood tissue and urine samples for more than 16000 animal hospitals and practices universities and government agencies. Founded in 1986 as Veterinary Centers of America the company has grown over the years through acquisitions of other animal hospitals and veterinary product suppliers.

	Annual Growth	12/10	12/11	12/12	12/13	12/14
Sales ($ mil.)	8.6%	1,381.5	1,485.4	1,699.6	1,803.4	1,918.5
Net income ($ mil.)	5.3%	110.2	95.4	45.6	137.5	135.4
Market value ($ mil.)	20.3%	1,931.6	1,638.0	1,745.8	2,600.9	4,044.8
Employees	5.2%	9,400	9,900	10,500	11,000	11,500

VCG HOLDING CORP.

NASDAQ: VCGH

390 Union Blvd. Ste. 540
Lakewood CO 80228
Phone: 303-934-2424
Fax: 303-922-0746
Web: www.vcgh.com

CEO: Troy H Lowrie
CFO: –
HR: –
FYE: December 31
Type: Private

Patrons with dollar bills might get a little extra entertainment from VCG Holding. The company operates about 20 nightclubs featuring live adult entertainment. In addition to exotic dancers the clubs offer dining and bar services as well as members-only VIP rooms intended for entertaining business clients. Alcohol sales account for more than 40% of its business. Located in about 10 states the clubs operate mainly under the names PT's and The Penthouse Club (through a licensing agreement with FriendFinder Networks the publisher of PENTHOUSE). CEO Troy Lowrie and president and COO Micheal Ocello took the company private in 2010.

VECTOR GROUP LTD

NYS: VGR

4400 Biscayne Boulevard
Miami, FL 33137
Phone: 305 579-8000
Fax: –
Web: www.vectorgroupltd.com

CEO: Howard M. Lorber
CFO: J. Bryant Kirkland
HR: –
FYE: December 31
Type: Public

Vector Group is small potatoes next to Big Tobacco running a distant fourth in the US market. The holding company's Liggett and Vector Tobacco subsidiaries manufacture discount cigarettes under brands including Liggett Select Grand Prix Pyramid and Eve and several private-label brands of cigarettes for other companies including the USA brand. The company manufactures cigarettes in North Carolina and distributes them throughout the US. Vector Group's real estate unit New Valley owns about 70% stake in the New York City broker Douglas Elliman Realty. It's looking to acquire other properties. All of Vector Group's revenue is derived from the sale of discount cigarettes.

	Annual Growth	12/10	12/11	12/12	12/13	12/14
Sales ($ mil.)	10.6%	1,063.3	1,133.4	1,084.5	1,056.2	1,591.3
Net income ($ mil.)	(9.1%)	54.1	75.0	30.6	38.9	37.0
Market value ($ mil.)	5.3%	2,082.3	2,135.2	1,787.8	1,968.1	2,562.0
Employees	20.8%	512	559	587	989	1,090

VECTREN CORP

NYS: VVC

One Vectren Square
Evansville, IN 47708
Phone: 812 491-4000
Fax: 812 491-4149
Web: www.vectren.com

CEO: Carl L. Chapman
CFO: M. Susan Hardwick
HR: Ellis Redd
FYE: December 31
Type: Public

Vectren intends to inundate Indiana and Ohio with energy. Through its utility subsidiaries: Indiana Gas Company (or Vecten North) Southern Indiana Gas and Electric (SIGECO or Vectren South) and Vectren Energy Delivery of Ohio (VEDO) — the company distributes natural gas to more than 1 million business and residential customers in the two states. It also distributes electricity to 143300 customers and almost 1300 MW of primarily coal-fired generating capacity in Indiana. Vectren's other nonregulated businesses include management services and utility infrastructure construction.

	Annual Growth	12/10	12/11	12/12	12/13	12/14
Sales ($ mil.)	5.2%	2,129.5	2,325.2	2,232.8	2,491.2	2,611.7
Net income ($ mil.)	5.7%	133.7	141.6	159.0	136.6	166.9
Market value ($ mil.)	16.2%	2,096.4	2,497.0	2,428.4	2,932.3	3,818.6
Employees	9.7%	3,800	4,500	5,400	5,500	5,500

VEECO INSTRUMENTS INC. (DE)

NMS: VECO

Terminal Drive
Plainview, NY 11803
Phone: 516 677-0200
Fax: –
Web: www.veeco.com

CEO: John R. Peeler
CFO: David D. Glass
HR: Alicia Lazarto
FYE: December 31
Type: Public

Veeco Instruments gives high-tech components the VIP treatment. The company offers precision equipment for manufacturing components such as thin-film magnetic heads photovoltaic solar cells and semiconductor devices. Its deposition etching and lapping and dicing systems are used in the hard-disk drive sensors semiconductor photomask microelectromechanical (MEMS) and coatings industries. The company targets applications in the light-emitting diode (LED) solar and data storage markets. HC SemiTek and Seoul Viosys Co. are among its top customers. Veeco gets around 90% of sales from outside the US.

	Annual Growth	12/10	12/11	12/12	12/13	12/14
Sales ($ mil.)	(19.5%)	933.2	979.1	516.0	331.7	392.9
Net income ($ mil.)		361.8	128.0	30.9	(42.3)	(66.9)
Market value ($ mil.)	(5.1%)	1,733.9	839.5	1,190.2	1,328.2	1,407.8
Employees	(2.9%)	900	917	884	800	800

VEEVA SYSTEMS INC

NYS: VEEV

4280 Hacienda Drive
Pleasanton, CA 94588
Phone: 925 452-6500
Fax: 925 452-6504
Web: www.veeva.com

CEO: Peter P Gassner
CFO: Timothy S Cabral
HR: –
FYE: January 31
Type: Public

Veeva Systems is breathing new life into software for the health care industry. Its cloud-based software and mobile apps are used by pharmaceutical and biotechnology companies to manage critical business functions. Veeva Systems' customer relationship management software uses Salesforce's platform to manage sales and marketing functions. Its Veeva Vault provides content management and collaboration software for quality management in clinical trials and regulatory compliance for new drug submissions. Its software is used in 75 countries and available in more than 25 languages but North America is its largest market. Founded in 2007 Veeva Systems went public in 2013.

	Annual Growth	01/11	01/12	01/13	01/14	01/15
Sales ($ mil.)	81.1%	29.1	61.3	129.5	210.2	313.2
Net income ($ mil.)	79.3%	3.9	4.2	18.8	23.6	40.4
Market value ($ mil.)	(9.5%)	–	–	–	4,166.6	3,769.5
Employees	26.6%	–	–	593	725	951

VELOCITY COMMERCIAL CAPITAL INC.

30699 Russell Ranch Rd. Ste. 295
Westlake Village CA 91362
Phone: 818-532-3700
Fax: 818-575-9005
Web: www.vcc-inc.com

CEO: –
CFO: –
HR: –
FYE: December 31
Type: Private

If you're a small business in need of some new digs Velocity Commercial Capital has a deal for you. The specialty finance company acquires and originates commercial real estate loans up to $3 million for small businesses. Its average loan is less than $400000. It currently holds mortgages for more than 300 properties 30% of which are in California. Its loan portfolio includes multi-family housing retail space mixed-use developments warehouses offices industrial complexes restaurants and mobile home parks. Velocity Commercial Capital does not make construction loans or lend for undeveloped land. The company which filed to go public in 2010 intends to qualify as a real estate investment trust (REIT).

VELOCITY EXPRESS LLC

11104 W. Airport Blvd. Ste. 130
Stafford TX 77477
Phone: 713-346-9100
Fax: +49-611-6029-305
Web: www.sglgroup.com

CEO: Ken Forster
CFO: –
HR: –
FYE: June 30
Type: Private

Fulfilling customers' need for speed Velocity Express specializes in same-day delivery services. The company offers scheduled pickup and delivery distribution logistics (in which customers' shipments are sorted for delivery to multiple locations) and expedited delivery. Customers include retailers office products manufacturers pharmaceutical wholesalers and other merchandise distributors. Velocity Express operates from approximately 80 warehouses and terminal facilities and deliveries are made by independent contractor drivers. In early 2013 Velocity Express was acquired by TransForce a large provider of transportation and logistics services based in Canada.

VENABLE LLP

750 E. Pratt St. Ste. 900
Baltimore MD 21202
Phone: 410-244-7400
Fax: 410-244-7742
Web: www.venable.com

CEO: –
CFO: –
HR: –
FYE: December 31
Type: Private - Partnershi

Law firm Venable serves a wide range of corporate individual institutional and nonprofit clients. The firm has about 500 attorneys. Major practice areas include corporate law and business transactions government and regulatory affairs litigation and dispute resolution and technology and intellectual property. Venable specializes in healthcare and insurance matters. Many of its clients are large corporations with thousands of employees. Companies such as GE Healthcare Lockheed Martin Marriott International Panasonic and Wal-Mart have been clients.

VENAXIS INC

NAS: APPY

1585 South Perry Street
Castle Rock, CO 80104
Phone: 303 794-2000
Fax: –
Web: www.venaxis.com

CEO: Steve T Lundy
CFO: Jeffrey G McGonegal
HR: –
FYE: December 31
Type: Public

Showing up at the ER doubled over with abdominal pain might be the first presentation of appendicitis but AspenBio Pharma wants to offer a more precise diagnostic tool. The biopharmaceutical development company's lead candidate is AppyScore a blood test which measures a biomarker associated with acute appendicitis. If approved it will allow doctors to quickly determine a patient's risk of having the condition. The company is also developing reproductive drugs for animals based on recombinant hormone analogs. Its product candidates include fertility enhancers timed ovulation and the reduction of pregnancy loss in dairy cows.

	Annual Growth	12/10	12/11	12/12	12/13	12/14
Sales ($ mil.)	(18.1%)	0.4	0.2	0.0	0.1	0.2
Net income ($ mil.)	–	(13.3)	(10.2)	(9.2)	(12.1)	(10.4)
Market value ($ mil.)	30.9%	18.7	30.1	79.3	66.3	54.9
Employees	(8.7%)	36	26	27	23	25

VENOCO INC.

NYSE. VQ

370 17th St. Ste. 3900
Denver CO 80202-1370
Phone: 303-626-8300
Fax: 303-626-8315
Web: www.venocoinc.com

CEO: Mark Depuy
CFO: Scott Pinsonnault
HR: –
FYE: December 31
Type: Private

Santa Barbara's pristine beaches and Venoco's oil and gas exploration and production activities make for a volatile mix. Although Venoco has traditionally operated in the environmentally sensitive Santa Barbara Channel it has been expanding its geographic reach and diversifying its operations. It owns interests in more than 790 drilling locations primarily in California's Sacramento Basin and Monterey shale formation. It even has a drilling location in Beverly Hills. In 2011 Venoco reported proved reserves of 95.9 million barrels of oil equivalent (of which 49% was oil). That year the company produced about 6430 barrels of oil equivalent per day.

VENTANA MEDICAL SYSTEMS INC.

1910 E. Innovation Park Dr.
Tucson AZ 85755
Phone: 520-887-2155
Fax: 520-229-4207
Web: www.ventanamed.com

CEO: Christopher M Gleeson
CFO: Lawrence Mehren
HR: –
FYE: December 31
Type: Subsidiary

Ventana Medical Systems wants to be a window into the cause of cancer. The company also known as Roche Tissue Diagnostics is a leading provider of slide staining systems (sold under the names BenchMark NexES and Symphony) used to automate the processing and microscopic analysis of human tissue for the detection and treatment of cancer and infectious diseases. Ventana also sells consumables such as reagents and slides needed to operate the systems. Its products are marketed to hospital pathology and drug discovery labs around the globe. Its tests and equipment are used by many cancer research centers including the Mayo Clinic and Johns Hopkins Hospital. The firm is owned by German drugmaker Roche.

VENTRUS BIOSCIENCES INC.

787 7th Ave. 48th Fl.
New York NY 10019
Phone: 212-554-4300
Fax: 212-554-4314
Web: www.ventrusbio.com

CEO: Derek A Small
CFO: David J Barrett
HR: –
FYE: December 31
Type: Private

Ventrus Biosciences is developing drugs to make it easier for folks to sit and then stay. The pharmaceutical company's product pipeline consists of three topical treatment candidates: an iferanserin ointment for hemorrhoids; a diltiazem cream for pain associated with anal fissures; and a phenylephrine gel for fecal incontinence. Ventrus is optimistic about its development efforts as there are no currently FDA-approved prescription products for the conditions it seeks to treat. Ventrus Biosciences filed to go public in mid-2010 but withdrew the IPO filing later that year.

VENTAS, INC.

NYS: VTR

353 N. Clark Street, Suite 3300
Chicago, IL 60654
Phone: 877 483-6827
Fax: –
Web: www.ventasreit.com

CEO: Debra A. Cafaro
CFO: Robert F. (Bob) Probst
HR: –
FYE: December 31
Type: Public

Ventas puts a roof over many a gray or aching head. A real estate investment trust (REIT) Ventas owns more than 1500 health care properties including senior housing communities skilled nursing facilities hospitals and medical office buildings. The REIT's properties are located throughout the US and Canada. Ventas leases more than a third of its properties to long-term care providers Sunrise Senior Living Brookdale Senior Living and Kindred Healthcare. The company also is a major player in medical office buildings owning or managing nearly 21 million sq. ft. of space. Nearly 50% of Ventas' business comes from rental income while another 50% comes from resident fees and services.

	Annual Growth	12/11	12/12	12/13	12/14	12/15
Sales ($ mil.)	16.8%	1,765.0	2,485.3	2,810.1	3,075.7	3,286.4
Net income ($ mil.)	3.6%	363.3	361.8	454.9	477.2	419.2
Market value ($ mil.)	0.6%	18,432.3	21,638.6	19,151.1	23,972.3	18,866.9
Employees	9.2%	328	439	465	479	466

VENTURA FOODS LLC

40 Pointe Dr.
Brea CA 92821
Phone: 714-257-3700
Fax: 714-257-3702
Web: www.venturafoods.com

CEO: Christopher Furman
CFO: Scott Anthony
HR: –
FYE: March 31
Type: Joint Venture

Ventura Foods is one slick operator. The company makes and distributes branded and private-label vegetable oil-based products including bulk salad oils shortenings margarine butter and butter blends pan coatings mayonnaises dressings and more. It also produces soup and flavor bases and concession items such as popcorn popping oil. Products are sold to foodservice operators such as Sysco and less so other food product manufacturers and retail groceries in the US and abroad. Ventura's core brands are Marie's Dressing Dean's Dip Gold 'n Soft margarine and LouAna oils. The company is a 50-50 joint venture created in 1996 between US agricultural co-op CHS and Japanese trading conglomerate Mitsui & Co.

VENTERA CORPORATION

1881 CAMPUS COMMONS DR # 350
RESTON, VA 201911519
Phone: 703-760-4600
Fax: –
Web: www.ventera.com

CEO: Robert Acosta
CFO: –
HR: –
FYE: December 31
Type: Private

Ventera which likens itself to a bulldog in its marketing materials would like clients to take note of its tenacity as a business rather than looking for a more physical resemblance between its consultants and its mascot. The company provides information technology and management consulting services to clients in both the private and public sectors. It offers application development network design systems integration and project management services among others. Ventera serves the financial services manufacturing telecommunications and retail industries among others. Customers have included the US Department of Agriculture and Sprint Nextel. The company was founded in 1996 by CEO Robert Acosta.

	Annual Growth	12/03	12/04	12/05	12/06	12/07
Sales ($ mil.)	(84.8%)	–	–	1,077.9	30.7	24.8
Net income ($ mil.)	14979.5%	–	–	0.0	(173.4)	1.7
Market value ($ mil.)	–	–	–	–	–	–
Employees	–	–	–	–	–	100

VENTYX INC.

400 Perimeter Center Terrace Ste. 500
Atlanta GA 30346
Phone: 678-830-1000
Fax: 678-830-1010
Web: www.ventyx.com

CEO: Jeff Ray
CFO: Jim Fitzgibbons
HR: –
FYE: December 31
Type: Subsidiary

Ventyx has an energetic customer base. The company provides clients in asset-intensive industries (including energy utilities power generation and telecommunications) with software and services to manage their infrastructure resources workforces and spare parts inventories. Ventyx also provides related applications to manage and automate energy trading energy operations and energy analytics. It serves such clients as nuclear and coal power plants broadband service providers petroleum refiners water treatment plants and oil and mining companies. Customers have included CenterPoint Energy and Peoples Natural Gas. Ventyx is a subsidiary of Swiss electrical engineering firm ABB.

VEOLIA ENVIRONMENTAL SERVICES NORTH AMERICA CORP.

200 E. Randolph Dr. Ste. 7900
Chicago IL 60601
Phone: 312-552-2800
Fax: 212-279-9171

CEO: Jeff Adix
CFO: –
HR: Marty Demeter
FYE: December 31
Type: Subsidiary

Veolia Environmental Services North America brings a French accent to environmental solutions. The company holds the regional operations of the waste management division of French company Veolia Environnement. Veolia Environmental Services North America provides liquid and hazardous waste services and industrial maintenance and cleaning. Its divisions include Veolia ES Technical Solutions (hazardous waste management) Veolia Industrial Services (on-site plant cleaning and maintenance) and Veolia Canadian Operations. In addition its Marine Services industrial services business operates a fleet of ships and provides services to offshore petroleum installations primarily in the Gulf of Mexico.

VERA BRADLEY INC.

NMS: VRA

12420 Stonebridge Road
Roanoke, IN 46783
Phone: 877 708-8372
Fax: –
Web: www.verabradley.com

CEO: Robert Wallstrom
CFO: Kevin J Sierks
HR: –
FYE: January 31
Type: Public

Vera Bradley loves women with lots of baggage. The company designs makes and sells quilted handbags and travel bags as well as accessories such as cosmetic bags curling iron covers and wallets. Its goods are available through 2700 gift and specialty stores and about 100 Vera Bradley full-price stores in 25-plus US states. It also operates about 30 factory outlet shops and an online store. In addition to its core products the company licenses its name for use on Vera Bradley-branded rugs eyewear stationery and home decor items. Founded in 1982 as Vera Bradley Designs by Patricia Miller and Barbara Bradley Baekgaard to provide stylish luggage for women the company went public in 2010.

	Annual Growth	01/11	01/12*	02/13	02/14*	01/15
Sales ($ mil.)	8.6%	366.1	460.8	541.1	536.0	509.0
Net income ($ mil.)	(4.5%)	46.2	57.9	68.9	58.8	38.4
Market value ($ mil.)	(13.4%)	1,356.5	1,375.8	1,033.9	962.6	764.2
Employees	18.4%	1,427	2,078	2,438	2,900	2,800

*Fiscal year change

VERA WANG BRIDAL HOUSE LTD.

225 W. 39th St.
New York NY 10018
Phone: 212-575-6400
Fax: 212-354-2548
Web: www.verawang.com

CEO: Vera W Becker
CFO: –
HR: –
FYE: December 31
Type: Private

A bride needs to budget more for herself if she wants to walk down the aisle in a wedding dress from Vera Wang Bridal House. With gowns reaching $20000 Vera Wang has designed bridal gowns for celebrities the likes of Sharon Stone and Mariah Carey. Vera Wang also designs evening gowns bridesmaid dresses and sportswear and licenses its name for other apparel as well as for china crystal eyewear footwear fragrances jewelry linens silver and more. Vera Wang's products are sold through upscale department stores specialty stores and a pair of company-owned flagship boutiques located in New York City and Los Angeles. Chairman CEO and owner Vera Wang founded the firm in 1990.

VERACYTE INC

NMS: VCYT

7000 Shoreline Court, Suite 250
South San Francisco, CA 94080
Phone: 650 243-6300
Fax: –
Web: www.veracyte.com

CEO: Bonnie Anderson
CFO: Shelly D. Guyer
HR: –
FYE: December 31
Type: Public

Veracyte aims to give patients a verifiable diagnosis with as little discomfort as possible. The company provides molecular cytology tests that use cell samples taken with a needle instead of tissue samples obtained through a biopsy. Its first commercial product Afirma Thyroid FNA is marketed to endocrinologists as a test to diagnose thyroid cancer. (Thyroid diagnostic tests previously required surgery and hormone replacement therapy and still gave uncertain results.) Afirma Thyroid FNA is covered by insurers Aetna Humana Medicare and UnitedHealth. Veracyte even teamed up with Genzyme to market Afirma Thyroid FNA in 40 countries. The company went public in 2013 raising $65 million.

	Annual Growth	12/10	12/11	12/12	12/13	12/14
Sales ($ mil.)	–	0.0	2.6	11.6	21.9	38.2
Net income ($ mil.)	–	0.0	(14.4)	(18.6)	(25.6)	(29.4)
Market value ($ mil.)	–	0.0	–	–	326.6	217.6
Employees	24.9%	–	–	107	115	167

VERAMARK TECHNOLOGIES INC.

OTC: VERA

1565 Jefferson Road Ste. 120
Rochester NY 14623
Phone: 585-381-6000
Fax: 585-383-6800
Web: www.veramark.com

CEO: –
CFO: –
HR: –
FYE: December 31
Type: Public

Veramark Technologies can help all sorts of companies play the "telephone game" and actually keep the information straight. The company's Web-based telecommunications expense management software enables customers to track analyze and allocate telecom-related costs as well as to maintain invoices and manage business process outsourcing. Veramark's installed base of more than 4000 customers includes FORTUNE 500 corporations small and mid-sized businesses and public sector organizations. The company was founded in 1983.

VERASTEM INC.

NASDAQ: VSTM

215 1st St. Ste. 440
Cambridge MA 02142
Phone: 617-252-9300
Fax: +358-20-484-181
Web: www.valmet-automotive.com

CEO: Robert Forrester
CFO: John Green
HR: –
FYE: December 31
Type: Public

Verastem believes the truth behind recurrent tumors lies in cancer stem cells (CSCs) aggressive tumor cells that survive conventional treatment to cause recurrence. Those CSCs are the target of its biopharmaceutical R&D efforts; the company is working to produce small molecule drugs that target the cells while conventional therapy targets the rest of the tumor. Verastem's work rests on a technology licensed from MIT's Whitehead Institute that allows it to create stable CSCs in the lab something not possible in the past. Its leading drug candidate targets a type of breast cancer with a low survival rate. The company is also developing CSC diagnostics. Formed in 2010 Verastem completed an IPO in 2012.

VERICEL CORP

NAS: VCEL

64 Sidney Street
Cambridge, MA 02139
Phone: 800 556-0311
Fax: –
Web: www.vcel.com

CEO: –
CFO: Dominick C Colangelo
HR: –
FYE: December 31
Type: Public

Aastrom Biosciences brings new life to dying tissue. The development-stage company's proprietary tissue repair technology uses a patient's own cells (harvested from bone marrow) to manufacture treatments for a number of chronic diseases. The new cells created through a sterile automated process are then used in tissue regeneration therapies for the donor patient. Aastrom Biosciences' ongoing development activities are primarily focused on applying the technology to cardiovascular applications including cardiomyopathy (weakening of the heart muscle) and critical limb ischemia (severe obstruction of the arteries).

	Annual Growth	12/10	12/11	12/12	12/13	12/14
Sales ($ mil.)	226.6%	0.3	0.0	0.0	0.0	28.8
Net income ($ mil.)	–	(19.1)	(19.7)	(29.5)	(15.6)	(19.9)
Market value ($ mil.)	4.4%	60.9	43.3	30.0	76.8	72.3
Employees	37.0%	54	71	77	40	190

VERIFONE SYSTEMS INC.

NYS: PAY

88 West Plumeria Drive
San Jose, CA 95134
Phone: 408 232-7800
Fax: –
Web: www.verifone.com

CEO: Paul Galant
CFO: Marc E. Rothman
HR: –
FYE: October 31
Type: Public

Don't trust but Verifone would be the twist Verifone might put on the "Trust but Verify" proverb used in arms negotiations. The company is a leading supplier of electronic payment hardware and software for merchant-operated consumer-facing and self-service payment systems. Its products include point-of-sale (POS) software and terminals smart card and check readers receipt printers and Internet commerce software. It also provides installation training and other services. Customers include companies in the hospitality retail and healthcare markets as well as government agencies. VeriFone generates more than 70% of sales outside the US.

	Annual Growth	10/11	10/12	10/13	10/14	10/15
Sales ($ mil.)	11.3%	1,303.9	1,866.0	1,702.2	1,868.9	2,000.5
Net income ($ mil.)	(27.3%)	282.4	65.0	(296.1)	(38.1)	79.1
Market value ($ mil.)	(8.1%)	4,756.4	3,340.0	2,553.4	4,198.6	3,396.3
Employees	8.8%	3,848	4,977	5,699	5,200	5,400

VERINT SYSTEMS, INC

NMS: VRNT

175 Broadhollow Road
Melville, NY 11747
Phone: 631 962-9600
Fax: –
Web: www.verint.com

CEO: Dan Bodner
CFO: Douglas E. (Doug) Robinson
HR: Michelle Meurer
FYE: January 31
Type: Public

Verint Systems helps business take an honest look at structured and unstructured data. The company provides analytic software for capturing and analyzing data from sources such as voice video and text with a focus on unstructured content. Its software and services offered in on-premise and cloud-based versions are used by enterprise customers to improve customer service interactions and operations and by law enforcement and government agencies for combating crime and providing security. Verint customers are in more than 180 countries and include more than 80% of the FORTUNE 100. It has about 50 offices in some 15 countries and generates about half of its sales outside the US.

	Annual Growth	01/11	01/12	01/13	01/14	01/15
Sales ($ mil.)	11.6%	726.8	782.6	839.5	907.3	1,128.4
Net income ($ mil.)	4.9%	25.6	37.0	54.0	53.8	30.9
Market value ($ mil.)	11.6%	2,098.8	1,722.4	2,058.6	2,767.5	3,251.1
Employees	17.7%	2,500	3,200	3,200	3,400	4,800

VERISIGN INC

NMS: VRSN

12061 Bluemont Way
Reston, VA 20190
Phone: 703 948-3200
Fax: –
Web: www.verisign.com

CEO: D. James (Jim) Bidzos
CFO: George E. Kilguss
HR: Ellen Petrocci
FYE: December 31
Type: Public

VeriSign helps companies and consumers connect the dots with the coms and the nets. The company operates two of the world's 13 root nameservers which assign Internet protocol (IP) addresses to devices communicating across the Internet. VeriSign is also the only issuer of the .com and .net domain names that are sold to users by companies such as domain registrars Go Daddy and Register.com. The company also provides network infrastructure services providing hosted cyber intelligence managed domain name systems (DNS) availability and resolution and hosted monitoring and mitigation against the dreaded Distributed Denial of Service (DDoS) attacks. More than 60% of sales are from the US.

	Annual Growth	12/10	12/11	12/12	12/13	12/14
Sales ($ mil.)	10.4%	680.6	772.0	873.6	965.1	1,010.1
Net income ($ mil.)	(19.1%)	831.0	142.9	320.0	544.5	355.3
Market value ($ mil.)	14.9%	3,869.8	4,231.1	4,598.3	7,081.1	6,751.8
Employees	0.3%	1,048	1,009	1,099	1,079	1,061

VERISK ANALYTICS INC

NMS: VRSK

545 Washington Boulevard
Jersey City, NJ 07310-1686
Phone: 201 469-2000
Fax: –
Web: www.verisk.com

CEO: Scott G. Stephenson
CFO: Mark V. Anquillare
HR: Lissette Martinez
FYE: December 31
Type: Public

Insurance is a risky business and Verisk Analytics is in the business of helping to manage that risk. The company compiles data designed to detect fraud and catastrophe and weather risk and predict loss for customers in the US property/casualty insurance health care and mortgage industries. Its Decision Analytics unit provides health care claim payers and mortgage lenders with predictive models loss estimation tools and fraud ID applications. Its Risk Assessment unit runs databases that hold billions of records containing statistical and underwriting data used to price insurance policies and write policy language. Verisk was created by subsidiary Insurance Services Office (ISO) as a means of going public.

	Annual Growth	12/10	12/11	12/12	12/13	12/14
Sales ($ mil.)	11.3%	1,138.3	1,331.8	1,534.3	1,595.7	1,746.7
Net income ($ mil.)	13.3%	242.6	282.8	329.1	348.4	400.0
Market value ($ mil.)	17.1%	5,381.7	6,337.1	8,048.8	10,378.1	10,114.3
Employees	7.6%	4,890	5,401	6,495	7,095	6,550

VERITEQ CORP

NBB: VTEQ

3333 S. Congress Avenue, Suite 401
Delray Beach, FL 33445
Phone: 561 846-7000
Fax: –
Web: www.veriteqcorp.com

CEO: Scott R Silverman
CFO: Michael E Krawitz
HR: –
FYE: December 31
Type: Public

Digital Angel puts a British accent on two-way communication equipment. The company develops emergency identification products for use in global positioning systems and other applications and distributes them in the UK. Digital Angel's conventional radio systems provide such services as site monitoring for construction companies and manufacturers while its trunked radio systems serve the security needs of large customers such as local governments and public utilities. In mid-2012 the company announced a strategic shift toward the development of games and applications for mobile devices. It has several titles in progress.

	Annual Growth	12/10	12/11	12/12	12/13	12/14
Sales ($ mil.)	(74.8%)	37.7	3.7	–	0.0	0.2
Net income ($ mil.)	–	(5.8)	(10.3)	(6.3)	(15.1)	(3.9)
Market value ($ mil.)	–	0.1	0.1	0.0	0.7	0.0
Employees	(47.2%)	167	36	15	13	13

VERIZON COMMUNICATIONS INC   NYS: VZ

1095 Avenue of the Americas	CEO: Lowell C. McAdam
New York, NY 10036	CFO: Francis J. (Fran) Shammo
Phone: 212 395-1000	HR: Lawrence Marcus
Fax: –	FYE: December 31
Web: www.verizon.com	Type: Public

Verizon is the #1 wireless phone service in the US and the #2 US telecom services provider overall (after AT&T). The company's core mobile business Verizon Wireless serves about 137 million total customers. (Verizon Wireless was a joint venture with Vodafone until 2014 when Verizon bought out Vodafone's stake for $130 billion.) Verizon's wireline unit with more than 19 million voice connections (end of 2014) provides local telephone long-distance Internet access and digital TV services to residential and wholesale customers. In addition Verizon offers a wide range of telecom managed network and IT services to commercial and government clients in more than 150 countries. Verizon moved to expand its video and advertising capabilities with the acquisition of AOL.

	Annual Growth	12/10	12/11	12/12	12/13	12/14
Sales ($ mil.)	4.5%	106,565.0	110,875.0	115,846.0	120,550.0	127,079.0
Net income ($ mil.)	39.4%	2,549.0	2,404.0	875.0	11,497.0	9,625.0
Market value ($ mil.)	–	0.0	0.0	0.0	0.0	0.0
Employees	(2.3%)	194,400	193,900	183,400	176,800	177,300

VERMEER MANUFACTURING COMPANY

1210 Vermeer Rd. East	CEO: –
Pella IA 50219	CFO: –
Phone: 641-628-3141	HR: –
Fax: 641-621-7754	FYE: December 31
Web: www.vermeer.com	Type: Private

Vermeer's products have the power to move the earth. The company manufactures a slew of production and farm equipment distributed through a global dealer network. Its line includes hay tools such as balers and rakes tedders and silage wrappers as well as biomass harvesting equipment used in renewable energy. It also offers landscaping products from mowers to cutters and edgers. Vermeer's heavy-duty workhorses include equipment for construction surface mining and organic recycling wood waste processing and tree care. Vermeer sells ground-locating and mapping software for construction use too. Founded by Gary Vermeer in 1948 the company is led by daughter Andringa.

VERMILLION INC.   NASDAQ: VRML

47350 Fremont Blvd.	CEO: Valerie B Palmieri
Fremont CA 94538	CFO: Eric J Schoen
Phone: 510-226-2800	HR: –
Fax: 510-226-2801	FYE: December 31
Web: www.vermillion.com	Type: Public

Vermillion is enabling the next step in biotechnology — deciphering proteins. The company is using a process called translational proteomics to develop diagnostic tests that take multiple protein biomarkers into account thus making the tests more sensitive and test results more specific. Its development efforts target therapeutic areas such as oncology hematology cardiology and women's health. It is working on some tests with Quest Diagnostics (which owns a minority stake in Vermillion) and has additional collaborations with academic and research institutions such as Johns Hopkins and M.D. Anderson. Vermillion emerged from Chapter 11 bankruptcy protection in early 2010.

VERMONT GAS SYSTEMS INC.

85 Swift St.	CEO: Donald J Rendall
South Burlington VT 05403	CFO: –
Phone: 802-863-4511	HR: Donna Leclair
Fax: 802-863-8872	FYE: September 30
Web: www.vermontgas.com	Type: Subsidiary

Vermont Gas Systems pumps gas through the veins of the Vermont mountains and the mains of its towns and cities. A subsidiary of Canadian utility Gaz Metro Vermont Gas Systems distributes natural gas to more than 40000 homes and businesses in the counties of Chittenden and Franklin. Its natural gas is transported through the TransCanada Pipeline which links the gas fields in Alberta Canada to the company's main pipeline at Highgate Vermont on the Canadian border. The company supplies gas to its customers through a more than 650-mile network of underground transmission and distribution lines.

VERONIS SUHLER & ASSOCIATES INC.

Park Avenue Plaza 55 E. 52nd St	CEO: John Veronis
New York NY 10055	CFO: –
Phone: 212-935-4990	HR: –
Fax: 212-381-8168	FYE: December 31
Web: www.vss.com	Type: Private

Just about any kind of news is good news for Veronis Suhler & Associates. The private equity firm (also known as Veronis Suhler Stevenson or VSS) focuses on midsized media communications education information and business services companies often augmenting its holdings with add-on acquisitions. The VSS portfolio includes stakes in trade magazine publisher Access Intelligence media company Advanstar and research and consulting firm Market Strategies. John Veronis founder of "Psychology Today" and John Suhler former head of CBS Publishing founded the company in 1981. Jeffrey Stevenson who joined the company the following year became a name partner in 2001.

VERSAR INC.   ASE: VSR

6850 Versar Center	CEO: Anthony L Otten
Springfield, VA 22151	CFO: Cynthia A Downes
Phone: 703 750-3000	HR: Velma George
Fax: 703 642-6825	FYE: June 26
Web: www.versar.com	Type: Public

Environmental engineering company Versar is well-versed in keeping the homeland clean and secure. The company's infrastructure and management services business which accounts for most of Versar's sales helps clients with six main tasks: compliance with environmental regulations conservation of natural resources construction oversight engineering and design pollution prevention and restoration of contaminated sites. Major customers include the US Department of Defense and the US Environmental Protection Agency. Subsidiary GEOMET Technologies which constitutes Versar's national defense business segment makes biohazard suits for agencies involved in emergency response and counterterrorism efforts.

	Annual Growth	07/11*	06/12	06/13	06/14	06/15
Sales ($ mil.)	3.8%	137.6	119.0	102.6	110.3	159.9
Net income ($ mil.)	(20.1%)	3.4	4.2	2.4	(0.3)	1.4
Market value ($ mil.)	6.6%	30.7	29.5	44.5	33.7	39.7
Employees	0.3%	550	550	450	450	556

*Fiscal year change

VERSO CORP

NBB: VRSZ Q

6775 Lenox Center Court, Suite 400
Memphis, TN 38115-4436
Phone: 901 369-4100
Fax: –
Web: www.versopaper.com

CEO: David J Paterson
CFO: –
HR: –
FYE: December 31
Type: Public

Verso Paper is versatile when it comes to churning out paper products. The company produces coated and supercalendered paper and pulp for publishers commercial printers specialty retail merchandisers and paper merchants throughout North America. It also makes coated groundwood and coated freesheet paper products along with specialty paper offerings. Its products are used for media and marketing purposes from magazines to catalogs brochures annual reports and direct-mail advertising. Verso operates through mills located in Maine and Michigan.

	Annual Growth	12/10	12/11	12/12	12/13	12/14
Sales ($ mil.)	(5.2%)	1,605.3	1,722.5	1,474.6	1,388.9	1,296.6
Net income ($ mil.)	–	(131.1)	(137.1)	(173.8)	(111.2)	(353.0)
Market value ($ mil.)	0.1%	182.4	51.2	57.1	33.4	182.9
Employees	(12.7%)	2,800	2,600	2,200	2,100	1,630

VERST GROUP LOGISTICS INC.

300 SHORLAND DR
WALTON, KY 410949328
Phone: 859-485-1212
Fax: –
Web: www.verstgroup.com

CEO: Paul T Verst
CFO: James Stadtmiller
HR: –
FYE: December 31
Type: Private

Verst wants to be first when it comes to storing its customers' items. A warehousing and distribution specialist Verst Group Logistics maintains over 5 million sq. ft. of warehouse space. The company operates from facilities in the Cincinnati metropolitan area and in northern Kentucky. Verst Group Logistics uses its own trucking fleet to provide freight transportation services through subsidiary Zenith Logistics and a network of carriers to arrange long-distance transportation of customers' freight. It serves customers residing in the food and beverage retail and consumer products paper and automotive industries. William Verst the father of president and CEO Paul Verst founded the company in 1968.

	Annual Growth	12/09	12/10	12/11	12/12	12/13
Sales ($ mil.)	4.0%	–	140.0	143.9	148.8	157.7
Net income ($ mil.)	–	–	–	0.0	0.0	0.0
Market value ($ mil.)	–	–	–	–	–	–
Employees	–	–	–	–	–	1,200

VERTEX PHARMACEUTICALS, INC.

NMS: VRTX

50 Northern Avenue
Boston, MA 02210
Phone: 617 341-6100
Fax: –
Web: www.vrtx.com

CEO: Jeffrey M. (Jeff) Leiden
CFO: Ian F. Smith
HR: Sheila Clark
FYE: December 31
Type: Public

Vertex Pharmaceuticals aims to cure patients with previously incurable diseases. The biotechnology company uses an integrated multidisciplinary approach — employing biophysics computer-based modeling and functional genomics — to speed up the discovery and development of new drugs. Its first commercial product Incivek (telaprevir) for hepatitis C virus (HCV) was launched in 2011 and a second drug for cystic fibrosis Kalydeco was launched in 2012. The company has other drugs in development including additional treatments for HCV and cystic fibrosis as well as epilepsy and rheumatoid arthritis.

	Annual Growth	12/11	12/12	12/13	12/14	12/15
Sales ($ mil.)	(7.5%)	1,410.6	1,527.0	1,212.0	580.4	1,032.3
Net income ($ mil.)	–	29.6	(107.0)	(445.0)	(738.6)	(556.3)
Market value ($ mil.)	39.5%	8,179.8	10,320.3	18,300.6	29,261.3	30,992.8
Employees	(0.6%)	2,000	2,200	1,800	1,830	1,950

VERTICAL COMPUTER SYSTEMS, INC.

NBB: VCSY

101 West Renner Road, Suite 300
Richardson, TX 75082
Phone: 972 437-5200
Fax: –
Web: www.vcsy.com

CEO: Richard S Wade
CFO: –
HR: –
FYE: December 31
Type: Public

Vertical Computer Systems develops Web services development applications and administrative software. The company's SiteFlash software enables Web content management e-commerce and workflow functions. Other Web service-related offerings include ResponseFlash an emergency communications system and the Emily XML scripting language. Its administrative software line includes emPath a Web-based human resources management and payroll application that it offers using the software-as-a-service (SaaS) model. Vertical Computer Systems markets emPath through its NOW Solutions subsidiary.

	Annual Growth	12/10	12/11	12/12	12/13	12/14
Sales ($ mil.)	5.9%	5.9	6.3	5.5	6.1	7.4
Net income ($ mil.)	–	(0.2)	(0.1)	(1.2)	(2.5)	(1.5)
Market value ($ mil.)	(15.5%)	23.5	18.5	24.0	61.1	12.0
Employees	(1.7%)	31	37	33	24	29

VERTICALNET INC.

400 Chester Field Pkwy.
Malvern PA 19355
Phone: 610-240-0600
Fax: 610-240-9470
Web: www.bravosolutionus.com

CEO: –
CFO: –
HR: –
FYE: December 31
Type: Subsidiary

Verticalnet provided strategic sourcing and supply management software. Its suite of enterprise applications allowed companies to interact with their suppliers for product sourcing price negotiation contract management and shipment scheduling. The company's software included tools for sharing product information with customers and managing inventories. Verticalnet also offered spend analysis and supply chain consulting services. The company was acquired by BravoSolution a subsidiary of Italian construction giant Italcementi in 2008. The purchase established a US presence for BravoSolution which previously marketed its supply chain software and services primarily in Europe and Asia.

VERTICALRESPONSE INC.

501 2nd St. Ste. 700
San Francisco CA 94107
Phone: 415-905-6880
Fax: 415-808-2480
Web: www.verticalresponse.com

CEO: Janine Popick
CFO: –
HR: –
FYE: December 31
Type: Private

VerticalResponse wants potential customers responding with a resounding "yes" to your sales pitch. The company provides Web-based direct marketing software and services designed primarily for use by small and midsized businesses. Its products can be used to create and manage e-mail marketing campaigns and online surveys as well as traditional print marketing efforts. Customers have included Brookstone ACT! The Food Guy PetCareRx and Law.com. VerticalResponse also offers services such as consulting support and training. In 2011 it made its first ever acquisition with Roost which offers an online social media marketing management tool. The company was founded by CEO Janine Popick in 2001.

VESCO OIL CORPORATION

16055 W 12 MILE RD
SOUTHFIELD, MI 480762979
Phone: 248-557-0260
Fax: –
Web: www.vesco-oil.com

CEO: Donald R Epstein
CFO: Cheryl R Reitzloff
HR: –
FYE: December 31
Type: Private

Vesco Oil gives motorists a hand in the Upper Hand and elsewhere in the state of Michigan. The company is a wholesale distributor of Valvoline and Exxon Mobil brand lubricants to automotive and industrial customers in Michigan. It also provides environmental services such as bulk and hazardous waste management. Vesco Oil has warehouse and distribution facilities in Detroit Grand Rapids Mancelona and Zilwaukee. It has expanded its warehouse and distribution center in Mancelona to better serve its northern Michigan customers. Vesco Oil is managed by president and CEO Donald Epstein the great-grandson of the company's founder Eugene Epstein.

	Annual Growth	12/06	12/07	12/08	12/09	12/10
Sales ($ mil.)	(73.0%)	–	–	1,486.8	100.8	108.2
Net income ($ mil.)	19257.2%	–	–	0.0	(0.3)	3.3
Market value ($ mil.)	–	–	–	–	–	–
Employees	–	–	–	–	–	210

VESTA CORPORATION

11950 SW Garden Pl.
Portland OR 97223
Phone: 503-790-2500
Fax: 503-790-2525
Web: www.trustvesta.com

CEO: Douglas Fieldhouse
CFO: Sanjay Khare
HR: –
FYE: December 31
Type: Private

Vesta vies for the business of mobile operators financial institutions and online merchants looking to offer electronic payment services online via mobile device or at the retail point of sale. The payment processing firm works as an extension of a client's customer service department handling transactions under the client's brand and bearing liability for fraudulent transactions. Vesta also provides services to banks credit card issuers and others that offer stored value cards and allows consumers to recharge prepaid phone plans. Customers have included AT&T Boost and MasterCard. In addition tho the US Vesta has operations in Ireland and China.

VESTAR CAPITAL PARTNERS INC.

245 Park Ave. 41st Fl.
New York NY 10167
Phone: 212-351-1600
Fax: 212-808-4922
Web: www.vestarcapital.com

CEO: –
CFO: Brondon Spillane
HR: –
FYE: December 31
Type: Private

Vestar Capital Partners is on a quest to invest. Specializing in management buyouts growth capital investments and recapitalizations the firm seeks out established middle-market firms (valued between $250 million and $3 billion) in the consumer products financial services media and communications health care and manufacturing sectors. It typically invests up to $700 million per transaction. An active long-term investor that partners with the management of its portfolio companies the company oversees some $7 billion of committed equity capital on behalf of financial institutions endowments foundations funds of funds and public and private pension plans. It has five offices in the US and Europe.

VETCO GRAY INC.

3010 Briarpark Ave. Ste. 300
Houston TX 77042
Phone: 713-683-2400
Fax: 713-683-2421
Web: www.geoilandgas.com/vetcogray

CEO: –
CFO: Kirk Vincent
HR: Eric Street
FYE: December 31
Type: Subsidiary

Turning onshore and offshore oil and gas activities into onshore profits is the business of Vetco Gray. A unit of GE Oil & Gas the company (which does business as VetcoGray) provides upstream production facilities process systems technology services and products. It maintains modifies and manages technologies for offshore oil and gas production plants. Its products include connectors controls and valves able to withstand harsh environments. Vetco Gray's products and systems can handle a wide range of production challenges from a single well drilling project onshore to multiple well deepwater drilling systems and complex subsea production systems.

VETERANS OF FOREIGN WARS OF THE UNITED STATES

406 W 34TH ST FL 11
KANSAS CITY, MO 641112736
Phone: 816-756-3390
Fax: –
Web: www.vfwca.org

CEO: –
CFO: Jr H Vander Clute
HR: Debra Anderson
FYE: August 31
Type: Private

The Veterans of Foreign Wars of the United States (VFW) serves those who served. The membership organization is an advocacy group for former members of any branch of the US military who have served honorably in conflicts. Services provided by the group include helping veterans secure benefits and entitlements and advocating legislation in support of veterans and their needs. The VFW also provides flag education citizenship classes and other mentoring services to young people. The organization which was chartered by Congress in 1936 serves as a visible reminder of the contributions of all veterans by marching in parades and holding public services on national holidays.

	Annual Growth	08/09	08/10	08/11	08/12	08/13
Sales ($ mil.)	1.9%	–	94.9	101.6	103.8	100.5
Net income ($ mil.)	45.1%	–	–	11.1	4.9	23.4
Market value ($ mil.)	–	–	–	–	–	–
Employees	–	–	–	–	–	185

VF CORP.

NYS: VFC

105 Corporate Center Boulevard
Greensboro, NC 27408
Phone: 336 424-6000
Fax: –
Web: www.vfc.com

CEO: Eric C. Wiseman
CFO: Scott A. Roe
HR: Susan (Sue) Williams
FYE: January 03
Type: Public

V.F. Corporation is the name behind the labels. Among the world's top jeans makers it owns a bevy of denim brands: Lee Riders Wrangler and Rock & Republic. Other holdings include JanSport and Eastpak (backpacks) North Face and Eagle Creek (outdoor gear) Red Kap and Bulwark (work clothes) Nautica (sportswear) lucy (women's athletic apparel) 7 For All Mankind (premium denim casual wear) and Vans (footwear). V.F.'s Majestic label offers licensed MLB NFL and NBA apparel. Direct sales to consumers are rung up through Internet sites and more than 1400 VF-operated retail stores worldwide. About 60% of V.F. products are sold through department and specialty stores mass merchants and discounters.

	Annual Growth	12/10	12/11	12/12	12/13*	01/15
Sales ($ mil.)	9.8%	7,702.6	9,459.2	10,879.9	11,419.6	12,282.2
Net income ($ mil.)	12.9%	571.4	888.1	1,086.0	1,210.1	1,047.5
Market value ($ mil.)	(3.1%)	37,303.9	54,968.9	64,188.8	26,655.5	31,927.7
Employees	4.7%	47,000	58,000	57,000	59,000	59,000

*Fiscal year change

VF OUTDOOR INC.

2701 Harbor Bay Pkwy.
Alameda CA 94502
Phone: 830-626-5200
Fax: 830-626-5310
Web: www.rushenterprises.com

CEO: Steven E Rendle
CFO: –
HR: –
FYE: December 31
Type: Subsidiary

VF Outdoor (doing business as The North Face) wants its customers to take a hike — or take a stab at climbing Mount Everest. A subsidiary of V.F. Corporation The North Face designs distributes and retails its own brand of high-performance outerwear sportswear footwear and outdoor gear (including tents sleeping bags and backpacks). Its Cryptic Flight Series Steep Tech and Summit Series collections feature rugged technical apparel and equipment. The North Face's products are sold through specialty sporting goods stores in North and South America Europe and Asia; more than 300 namesake stores operated by third parties in Europe and Asia; some 60 company-owned European and US outlets; and online.

VI-JON INC.

8515 Page Ave.
St. Louis MO 63114
Phone: 314-427-1000
Fax: 314-427-1010
Web: www.vijon.com

CEO: Jerry Bowe
CFO: –
HR: –
FYE: December 31
Type: Private

Vi-Jon has been keeping it clean for more than a century. The health and beauty care company makes such products as body washes deodorants lotions mouthwashes shampoos and soaps. While it is primarily a private-label manufacturer for national retailer brands Vi-Jon also develops and markets its own brands including Germ-X hand sanitizers and Inspector Hector oral care and hand soap products for children. The company's products are supplied to retailers such as Kroger Target and Walgreens across the US. Vi-Jon was founded as Peroxide Specialty Company in 1908 by John B. Brunner grandfather of chairman John G. Brunner. The family-owned firm was acquired by investment firm Berkshire Partners in 2006.

VIA CHRISTI HEALTH SYSTEM

3720 E. Bayley
Wichita KS 67218
Phone: 316-858-4900
Fax: 316-858-4185
Web: www.via-christi.org

CEO: –
CFO: David Hadley
HR: Mary Heaton
FYE: September 30
Type: Private - Not-for-Pr

How do the sick become well? Via Christi Health of course. Via Christi Health is a Catholic not-for-profit health care system that provides a range of medical services to residents of Kansas and northern Oklahoma through a network of hospitals medical centers and health service organizations. The system's facilities include four hospitals about a dozen senior living communities nearly 20 medical clinics and specialized facilities for behavioral health and rehabilitative care. The system is affiliated with Marian Health System and Ascension Health. Via Christi Health was formed in 1995 when the Sisters of the Sorrowful Mother and the Sisters of St. Joseph of Wichita merged their health care ministries.

VIACOM INC

NMS: VIAB

1515 Broadway
New York, NY 10036
Phone: 212 258-6000
Fax: –
Web: www.viacom.com

CEO: Debra L. Lee
CFO: Wade C. Davis
HR: Wendy Charest
FYE: September 30
Type: Public

Viacom might not be a household name but its famous entertainment brands are welcomed into most living rooms on a daily basis. The company is a leading media conglomerate with an extensive portfolio of cable TV and film production assets. Its MTV Networks unit runs such cable networks as Comedy Central Nickelodeon and the family of MTV channels (MTV MTV2 VH1). Viacom also owns Black Entertainment Television which airs programming on BET BET Gospel and BET Hip Hop. In the film business Viacom operates through Paramount Pictures which includes imprints Paramount Pictures and Paramount Vantage. Chairman Sumner Redstone controls a majority of Viacom through his National Amusements movie theater chain.

	Annual Growth	09/11	09/12	09/13	09/14	09/15
Sales ($ mil.)	(2.9%)	14,914.0	13,887.0	13,794.0	13,783.0	13,268.0
Net income ($ mil.)	(2.6%)	2,136.0	1,981.0	2,395.0	2,391.0	1,922.0
Market value ($ mil.)	2.7%	15,422.4	21,334.2	33,273.2	30,629.8	17,178.0
Employees	(3.4%)	10,580	10,620	10,350	9,900	9,200

VIAD CORP.

NYS: VVI

1850 North Central Avenue, Suite 1900
Phoenix, AZ 85004-4565
Phone: 602 207-1000
Fax: –
Web: www.viad.com

CEO: –
CFO: Ellen M. Ingersoll
HR: Andrea Neal
FYE: December 31
Type: Public

Viad (pronounced VEE-ahd) makes sure convention-goers get to their events. Viad offers convention and event services exhibit design and construction and travel and recreation services. Its event services operations are organized under its Global Experience Specialists (GES) brand which provides convention services to trade associations and exhibitors. It also offers custom exhibit designers for corporations museums trade shows and retail stores. Viad's Travel & Recreation Group operates through its Brewster unit (Canadian accommodations and tour provider) and Glacier Park division (mountain lodge operator). The firm has operations across North America Europe and beyond.

	Annual Growth	12/10	12/11	12/12	12/13	12/14
Sales ($ mil.)	6.0%	844.8	942.4	1,025.2	972.8	1,065.0
Net income ($ mil.)	229.7%	0.4	9.2	5.9	21.6	52.4
Market value ($ mil.)	1.1%	511.8	351.2	545.7	558.2	535.7
Employees	3.3%	3,350	3,510	3,930	3,630	3,810

VIASAT, INC.

NMS: VSAT

6155 El Camino Real
Carlsbad, CA 92009
Phone: 760 476-2200
Fax: –
Web: www.viasat.com

CEO: Mark D. Dankberg
CFO: Shawn Duffy
HR: Melinda Del
FYE: April 03
Type: Public

Live via satellite! It's ViaSat! The company provides digital satellite networking and signal processing equipment for government (its largest customer group) and commercial clients. It makes secure networking products for tactical communications and mobile satellite communications systems designed for military use. For the commercial market ViaSat produces satellite broadband systems for consumer applications as well as antenna systems mobile satellite systems and very small aperture terminal (VSAT) products used in enterprise telecommunications. Consumer satellite Internet services are provided through subsidiary WildBlue Communications.

	Annual Growth	04/11*	03/12	03/13*	04/14	04/15
Sales ($ mil.)	14.6%	802.2	863.6	1,119.7	1,351.5	1,382.5
Net income ($ mil.)	2.8%	36.1	7.5	(41.2)	(9.4)	40.4
Market value ($ mil.)	11.3%	1,867.4	2,299.5	2,310.5	3,112.7	2,861.4
Employees	11.5%	2,200	2,400	2,700	3,100	3,400
						*Fiscal year change

VIASYSTEMS GROUP INC

NMS: VIAS

101 South Hanley Road
St. Louis, MO 63105
Phone: 314 727-2087
Fax: –
Web: www.viasystems.com

CEO: –
CFO: –
HR: –
FYE: December 31
Type: Public

Viasystems thinks its systems are the way to go. The company is a contract manufacturer for printed circuit boards (PCBs) and electro-mechanical (E-M) assemblies. It also offers design prototyping full system assembly testing and supply chain management services. Viasystems' products are used in automotive data networking equipment computer storage equipment flight control systems telecom switching equipment technical instruments in various sectors and wind and solar energy. Its customers total about 800 manufacturers including GE Alcatel-Lucent Continental AG and its largest customer Bosch. Its ten manufacturing facilities include two in the US one in Mexico and seven in China.

	Annual Growth	12/09	12/10	12/11	12/12	12/13
Sales ($ mil.)	23.9%	496.4	929.3	1,057.3	1,159.9	1,171.0
Net income ($ mil.)	–	(54.7)	15.6	30.3	(62.2)	(27.6)
Market value ($ mil.)	(12.1%)	–	418.1	351.2	253.3	284.0
Employees	2.2%	13,783	14,842	14,099	14,128	15,057

VIAVI SOLUTIONS INC

NMS: VIAV

430 North McCarthy Boulevard
Milpitas, CA 95035
Phone: 408 404-3600
Fax: –
Web: www.jdsu.com

CEO: Richard E. (Rick) Belluzzo
CFO: Rex S. Jackson
HR: –
FYE: June 27
Type: Public

Viavi Solutions formerly a part of JDS Uniphase (JDSU) facilitates better communication. The company develops test and measurement instruments and test tools that are used to build and improve communications equipment and broadband networks. Formerly operated as JDSU's Network and Service Enablement unit Viavi develops instruments and software and provides product support that helps customers build and maintain communication equipment and broadband networks. It also provides test products and services for private enterprise networks. The break up of JDSU occurred in August 2015. The former optical security and performance unit of JDSU now operates as Lumentum.

	Annual Growth	07/11*	06/12	06/13	06/14	06/15
Sales ($ mil.)	(1.3%)	1,804.5	1,682.1	1,676.9	1,743.2	1,709.1
Net income ($ mil.)	–	71.6	(55.6)	57.0	(17.8)	(88.1)
Market value ($ mil.)	(8.3%)	3,997.4	2,585.0	3,381.7	2,902.3	2,822.4
Employees	(0.5%)	5,000	4,950	4,900	5,100	4,900

*Fiscal year change

VICAL, INC.

NAS: VICL

10390 Pacific Center Court
San Diego, CA 92121
Phone: 858 646-1100
Fax: 858 646-1150
Web: www.vical.com

CEO: Vijay B Samant
CFO: –
HR: –
FYE: December 31
Type: Public

Vical counts DNA as its main ally in tackling disease. The biopharmaceutical firm researches and develops vaccines based on its DNA delivery technology which uses portions of the genetic code of a pathogen to induce an immune response. Vical has a number of drug candidates in its pipeline that it is developing independently and through corporate and government collaborations. Its pipeline is focused on infectious disease cancer immunotherapies and cardiovascular disease. Vical is developing Allovectin-7 an immunotherapy for metastatic melanoma. It gets most of its revenues from a license agreement for TransVax (designed to prevent reactivation of disease after a transplant) with Astellas Pharma.

	Annual Growth	12/10	12/11	12/12	12/13	12/14
Sales ($ mil.)	15.0%	8.7	30.0	17.5	7.7	15.2
Net income ($ mil.)	–	(30.4)	(7.3)	(22.9)	(31.2)	(16.5)
Market value ($ mil.)	(15.1%)	182.5	398.4	262.9	106.6	94.9
Employees	(12.1%)	114	112	118	67	68

VICOR CORP.

NMS: VICR

25 Frontage Road
Andover, MA 01810
Phone: 978 470-2900
Fax: –
Web: www.vicorpower.com

CEO: Patrizio Vinciarelli
CFO: James A. Simms
HR: Richard (Dick) Zengilowski
FYE: December 31
Type: Public

Vicor makes converters that tame and transfer raw electricity into the stable DC voltages needed to power electronic circuits. The company's zero current and zero voltage switching technologies which allow its converters to operate at high frequencies with relatively little noise are designed to be mounted on a printed circuit board. Customers — including global OEMs and small manufacturers of specialized electronics devices — incorporate the converters into all sorts of electronic equipment ranging from fiber-optic systems to military radar. Vicor derives some 40% of its sales from customers in the US.

	Annual Growth	12/10	12/11	12/12	12/13	12/14
Sales ($ mil.)	(2.6%)	250.7	253.0	218.5	199.2	225.7
Net income ($ mil.)	–	33.3	8.8	(4.1)	(23.6)	(13.9)
Market value ($ mil.)	(7.3%)	634.1	307.8	209.6	518.9	467.9
Employees	(1.3%)	1,070	1,045	1,046	1,002	1,014

VICTOR TECHNOLOGIES GROUP INC.

16052 Swingley Ridge Rd. Ste. 300
Chesterfield MO 63017
Phone: 636-728-3000
Fax: 636-728-3011
Web: www.thermadyne.com

CEO: Martin Quinn
CFO: Jeffrey S Kulka
HR: Sylvette De Jesus
FYE: December 31
Type: Private

Victor Technologies formerly Thermadyne has a hold on men of steel (and other metals). The company makes cutting and welding equipment used in fabricating (cutting joining and reinforcing) metal. Victor sells gas (air and oxy-fuel) torches and related products to OEMs as well as construction and foundry customers in such industries as aerospace oil and gas and shipbuilding. Its lineup includes arc accessories (automatic welding guns) plasma power systems and various welders sold under the Cigweld Victor Stoody Thermal Dynamics and other brands. Victor operates worldwide; the US represents more than 50% of sales. Private equity Irving Place Capital acquired Victor Technologies in 2010.

VICTORIA'S SECRET DIRECT LLC

5 Limited Pkwy. East
Reynoldsburg OH 43068
Phone: 201-802-3000
Fax: 201-782-9601
Web: www.sys-con.com

CEO: –
CFO: –
HR: –
FYE: January 31
Type: Subsidiary

Too busy or shy to shop in person for ladies' unmentionables? Victoria's Secret Direct affords shoppers the luxury privacy and convenience of ordering from home. As the direct sales arm of Victoria's Secret Stores it mails more than 390 million catalogs worldwide annually offering bras and panties sleepwear clothing shoes swimwear beauty products and a look at some of the world's top models. It also operates the website — VictoriasSecret.com — for its bricks-and-mortar sister chain. Both Victoria's Secret Direct (VSD) and Victoria's Secret Stores are owned by Limited Brands.

VICTORIA'S SECRET STORES LLC

4 Limited Pkwy. East	CEO: Lori Greeley
Reynoldsburg OH 43068	CFO: –
Phone: 614-577-7111	HR: –
Fax: 614-577-7844	FYE: January 31
Web: www.victoriassecret.com	Type: Subsidiary

Victoria's Secret Stores is not hush-hush but it is unmentionable(s). The largest subsidiary of Limited Brands (more than 40% of sales) is also North America's #1 specialty retailer of women's intimate apparel operating about 1035 mostly mall-based Victoria's Secret and Victoria's Secret Pink shops throughout the US and Canada. Bras panties hosiery swimwear shoes and more are sold under the Victoria's Secret brand and grouped in collections such as Angels and Very Sexy. Many Victoria's Secret lingerie stores also sell beauty products. The chain's youth-oriented PINK brand targets teens and younger women with less-racy bras and panties as well as sweats and hoodies and beauty products.

VICTORY PACKAGING INC.

3555 Timmons Ln. Ste. 1440	CEO: Benjamin H Samuels
Houston TX 77027	CFO: Leah Borrello
Phone: 713-961-3299	HR: –
Fax: 800-778-7210	FYE: December 31
Web: www.victorypackaging.com	Type: Private

Family-owned Victory Packaging manufactures and distributes corrugated boxes bubble wrap shrink film tape equipment and other packaging materials. It operates through some 50 centers in the US Canada and Mexico. Engineers at Victory Packaging provide customized package services for a diverse group of industries and processes including freight and moving agricultural perishable and just-in-time delivery and inventory management. Customers have included Solo Cup Co. and Graybar Electric as well as AMERCO and Home Fragrance Holdings. Founded by Victor Samuels in 1974 the company is led by his son Benjamin.

VIDEO DISPLAY CORP.

	NBB: VIDE
1868 Tucker Industrial Road	CEO: Ronald D Ordway
Tucker, GA 30084	CFO: Gregory L Osborn
Phone: 770 938-2080	HR: –
Fax: –	FYE: February 28
Web: www.videodisplay.com	Type: Public

Video may have killed the radio star but it's been pretty good to Video Display. The company makes and distributes flat-panel projection and cathode-ray tube (CRT) display systems. Its products — both new and reconditioned — are often customized for specific needs such as space limitations or being ruggedized for adverse environments. They are targeted at niche settings such as military training and simulation displays among other applications. Its data display business (about 10% of sales) focuses on CRTs for uses such as medical monitoring equipment and computer terminals. Its largest customer is the US government primarily the Department of Defense (more than 40% of sales).

	Annual Growth	02/11	02/12	02/13	02/14	02/15
Sales ($ mil.)	(31.7%)	59.0	64.2	49.1	14.4	12.8
Net income ($ mil.)	–	1.1	3.6	0.0	(2.7)	(6.0)
Market value ($ mil.)	(8.5%)	23.0	34.9	22.4	22.9	16.1
Employees	(21.3%)	310	324	285	71	119

VIDEO GAMING TECHNOLOGIES INC

308 MALLORY STATION RD	CEO: Jayme Sevigny
FRANKLIN, TN 37067-8210	CFO: –
Phone: 615-372-1000	HR: Lillian Ray
Fax: –	FYE: December 31
Web: www.vgt.net	Type: Private

It takes more than pencil and paper to make a good video game. Video Gaming Technologies (VGT) is a leading manufacturer of Class II-based gaming machines which mostly include bingo-style platforms found outside the Las Vegas market. The company additionally makes video terminals for skill-based games. It serves primarily the Native American gaming industry and its Live-Call Bingo game is the top-earning bingo based Class II platform for Native American casinos. VGT also serves emerging gaming markets. The company has manufacturing research and development marketing and support services. It does business in Oklahoma Washington Kansas California and Texas. CEO Jon Yarbrough founded VGT in 1991.

	Annual Growth	12/03	12/04	12/05	12/06	12/08
Sales ($ mil.)	(42.8%)	–	–	1,063.5	180.1	199.3
Net income ($ mil.)	28904.0%	–	–	0.0	6.0	24.4
Market value ($ mil.)	–	–	–	–	–	–
Employees	–	–	–	–	–	600

VIDEON CENTRAL INC.

2171 SANDY DR	CEO: –
STATE COLLEGE, PA 168032283	CFO: Paul Brown
Phone: 814-235-1111	HR: –
Fax: –	FYE: June 30
Web: www.videon-central.com	Type: Private

Video Central wants to put high performance video in the center of your world. The consumer electronics maker develops digital audio and video technology components including Blu-Ray and DVD players and 3D systems used in in-flight entertainment centers and home theater systems. It also provides engineering design development integration and testing services to OEMs. Videon's Advanced Technology Group creates Blu-ray Disc and DVD software used for control navigation and playback features. The company manufacturers its products at its facility in Pennsylvania. It was established in 1997 and it is owned by its officers.

	Annual Growth	06/03	06/04	06/06	06/12	06/13
Sales ($ mil.)	13.6%	–	4.3	8.0	14.2	13.6
Net income ($ mil.)	–	–	–	0.3	0.3	(0.1)
Market value ($ mil.)	–	–	–	–	–	–
Employees	–	–	–	–	–	63

VIENNA BEEF LTD.

2501 N. Damen Ave.	CEO: –
Chicago IL 60647	CFO: Richard Steele
Phone: 773-278-7800	HR: –
Fax: 773-278-4759	FYE: April 30
Web: www.viennabeef.com	Type: Private

Don't confuse the products of Vienna Beef (formerly Vienna Sausage Manufacturing) with those soggy little wieners packed in jars. Its beef wieners are the hot dogs Chicago calls its own. The company first unveiled its frankfurters (made from a secret Viennese recipe) at the 1893 World's Fair in Chicago. In addition to sausages and deli meats Vienna Sausage also makes cheesecake on a stick (WunderBar) other desserts (Pie Piper) pickles (Chipico Pickles) soups (Bistro Soups) and kosher foods (King Kold). Vienna Beef's products are available worldwide. The company sells to outside distributors grocery stores restaurants sports and other entertainment venues club stores and hot-dog stands.

VIETNAM VETERANS OF AMERICA INC.

8719 COLESVILLE RD # 100
SILVER SPRING, MD 209103919
Phone: 301-585-4000
Fax: –
Web: www.avva.org

CEO: –
CFO: Joe Sternburg
HR: –
FYE: February 28
Type: Private

Vietnam Veterans of America (VVA) has a Congressional charter to care. The not-for-profit group provides support for Vietnam veterans and their families and is the only such agency sanctioned by the US government. It promotes Vietnam veterans' issues including homelessness and health care — Agent Orange exposure is one key issue — and has about 50000 members and 635 local chapters throughout the US Puerto Rico the Virgin Islands and Guam. VVA seeks to eliminate discrimination toward Vietnam Veterans. It has programs specifically for women and minorities scholarships government benefit assistance and government advocacy. Founded in 1978 VVA is funded completely by private donations.

	Annual Growth	02/08	02/09	02/11	02/12	02/14
Sales ($ mil.)	120.2%	–	0.2	8.5	6.9	9.2
Net income ($ mil.)	(7.1%)	–	–	1.3	(0.5)	1.0
Market value ($ mil.)	–	–	–	–	–	–
Employees	–	–	–	–	–	300

VIEW SYSTEMS, INC.

OTC: VSYM

1550 Caton Center Drive, Suite E
Baltimore, MD 21227
Phone: 410 242-8439
Fax: 410 242-0765
Web: www.viewsystems.com

CEO: Gunther Than
CFO: –
HR: –
FYE: December 31
Type: Public

View Systems keeps a systematic eye out for potential dangers. The company's ViewMaxx digital video system captures and stores closed-circuit television images on computer disks for efficient monitoring. Its View Scan system offers walk-through weapons detectors under the SecureScan brand name. View Systems' wireless video camera system Visual First Responder allows emergency response teams to size up a situation before heading into harm's way. View Systems also offers biometric verification systems that can be integrated with its SecureScan and ViewMaxx products. The company acquired Colorado-based electronics manufacturing company Wytan in 2008.

	Annual Growth	12/10	12/11	12/12	12/13	12/14
Sales ($ mil.)	(15.5%)	0.8	0.4	0.9	0.6	0.4
Net income ($ mil.)	–	(0.5)	(1.8)	(0.9)	(2.0)	(1.3)
Market value ($ mil.)	1.7%	2.9	2.7	8.4	7.0	3.1
Employees	(8.1%)	14	5	5	10	10

VIKING YACHT COMPANY

ON THE BASS RIV RR 9
NEW CRETNA, NJ 08224
Phone: 609 296 6000
Fax: –
Web: www.vikingyachts.com

CEO: Robert T Healey
CFO: Gerard D Straub Sr
HR: –
FYE: July 31
Type: Private

Leif Eriksson's oceangoing Viking explorers could only dream of vessels like those made by the Viking Yacht Company. Viking Yacht can build more than 100 semi-custom fiberglass pleasure boats primarily used for sport fishing. About 90% of each yacht is made in-house. Its line of yachts vary in length from approximately 42 to 92 feet and include convertible and enclosed-bridge convertible vessels open sportfish models and a 52-foot sport yacht. The luxury boats are sold through a network of more than 40 dealers six of which are based outside the US. Founders and brothers Bob and Bill Healey own Viking Yacht Company.

	Annual Growth	07/10	07/11	07/12	07/13	07/14
Sales ($ mil.)	10.9%	–	142.4	143.9	154.1	194.1
Net income ($ mil.)	64.6%	–	–	6.0	10.3	16.3
Market value ($ mil.)	–	–	–	–	–	–
Employees	–	–	–	–	–	775

VILLAGE BANK & TRUST FINANCIAL CORP

NAS: VBFC

13319 Midlothian Turnpike
Midlothian, VA 23113
Phone: 804 897-3900
Fax: –
Web: www.villagebank.com

CEO: William G Foster Jr
CFO: C Harril Whitehurst Jr
HR: –
FYE: December 31
Type: Public

Does it take a village to raise a bank? Village Bank & Trust is the holding company for Village Bank which has about a dozen branches in the suburbs of Richmond Virginia. It offers standard services including deposit accounts loans and credit cards. Deposit funds are used to write loans for consumers and businesses in the area; commercial real estate loans mainly secured by owner-occupied businesses account for about half of the bank's lending portfolio which also includes business construction residential mortgage and consumer loans. In 2008 Village Bank & Trust acquired the three-branch River City Bank in a transaction worth more than $20 million.

	Annual Growth	12/10	12/11	12/12	12/13	12/14
Assets ($ mil.)	(7.5%)	591.8	581.7	510.1	444.2	434.0
Net income ($ mil.)	–	1.4	(11.8)	(10.4)	(4.0)	(1.0)
Market value ($ mil.)	98.1%	0.5	0.4	0.3	0.5	7.7
Employees	(3.7%)	215	203	205	202	185

VILLAGE SUPER MARKET, INC.

NMS: VLGE A

733 Mountain Avenue
Springfield, NJ 07081
Phone: 973 467-2200
Fax: –
Web: www.shoprite.com

CEO: James Sumas
CFO: John L Van Orden
HR: –
FYE: July 25
Type: Public

It may take a village to raise a child but it takes the Sumases to raise and run the Village. Run by the Sumas family since its founding in 1937 Village Super Market operates some 30 ShopRite supermarkets throughout New Jersey northeastern Pennsylvania and Maryland. It is a member of Wakefern Food the largest retailer-owned food cooperative in the US and owner of the ShopRite brand name. The affiliation gives Village Super Market economies of scale in purchasing distribution and advertising. Most outlets are superstores measuring more than 60000 sq. ft. Its Power Alley store format features high-margin fresh and convenience foods such as baked goods sushi and salad bars and take-home hot-meal sections.

	Annual Growth	07/11	07/12	07/13	07/14	07/15
Sales ($ mil.)	5.1%	1,298.9	1,422.2	1,476.5	1,518.6	1,583.8
Net income ($ mil.)	9.9%	21.0	31.4	25.8	5.0	30.6
Market value ($ mil.)	1.3%	380.8	494.7	516.7	337.5	401.1
Employees	4.3%	5,700	5,800	6,050	7,050	6,750

VILLAGEEDOCS INC.

OTC: VEDO

1401 N. Tustin Ave. Ste. 230
Tustin CA 92705
Phone: 714-734-1030
Fax: 714-734-1040
Web: www.villageedocs.com

CEO: K Mason Conner
CFO: Michael A Richard
HR: –
FYE: December 31
Type: Public

VillageEDOCS believes it takes their village of tools to help you solve your business problems. The company provides Software as a Service (SaaS) hosted services that offer outsourced Internet-based broadcast fax transmission services for invoices billing statements and purchase orders through its MessageVision subsidiary. It operates enhanced voice and data communications services through its GoSolutions unit and provides document management and archiving services through subsidiary Questys. VillageEDOCS also provides consulting installation support maintenance and training. The company targets the financial services health care manufacturing and local government markets as a whole.

VILLANOVA UNIVERSITY IN THE STATE OF PENNSYLVANIA

800 E LANCASTER AVE
VILLANOVA, PA 190851603
Phone: 610-519-4500
Fax: –
Web: www.villanova.edu

CEO: –
CFO: –
HR: Ellen Lacorte
FYE: May 31
Type: Private

The oldest and largest Roman Catholic institution of higher learning in Pennsylvania Villanova University offers more than 50 academic undergraduate programs at its six main colleges: Business Engineering Liberal Arts and Sciences Professional Studies and Nursing. The university also has a School of Law and it offers graduate programs in most of its disciplines. Villanova has an enrollment of more than 10730 full and part-time undergraduate and graduate students. It also reports a student-to-faculty ratio of 12:1. Average tuition is $45376 million per year.

	Annual Growth	05/10	05/11	05/12	05/13	05/14
Sales ($ mil.)	3.9%	–	378.7	385.9	401.5	424.7
Net income ($ mil.)	–	–	–	(4.5)	102.0	152.5
Market value ($ mil.)	–	–	–	–	–	–
Employees	–	–	–	–	–	2,022

VINCE HOLDING CORP

NYS: VNCE

500 5th Avenue, 20th Floor
New York, NY 10110
Phone: 212 515-2600
Fax: –
Web: www.vince.com

CEO: Jill Granoff
CFO: Lisa K. Klinger
HR: –
FYE: January 31
Type: Public

If you want to keep up with Kim Kardashian or boast the same look as Beyoncé you need to meet Vince. Upscale apparel company Vince Holding sells its pricey leather and knit clothing outerwear and shoes for women (mostly) in understated tones of gray and black at more than 2100 upscale department stores including Nordstrom Saks Fifth Avenue Neiman Marcus and Bloomingdale's. The company also operates about 30 Vince stores in 10 states and one in Japan. Its target market is affluent style-savvy women between the ages of 18 and 50. The company was formed in 2013 when majority shareholder Sun Capital split up the business of its portfolio company apparel-maker Kellwood.

	Annual Growth	01/11	01/12*	02/13	02/14*	01/15
Sales ($ mil.)	(12.7%)	586.6	662.8	708.0	288.2	340.4
Net income ($ mil.)	–	(104.5)	(147.9)	(107.7)	(27.4)	35.7
Market value ($ mil.)	0.4%	–	–	–	858.4	861.7
Employees	(42.6%)	–	–	1,514	355	498

*Fiscal year change

VIOLIN MEMORY INC

NYS: VMEM

4555 Great America Parkway
Santa Clara, CA 95054
Phone: 650 396-1500
Fax: –
Web: www.vmem.com

CEO: Kevin A. DeNuccio
CFO: Cory J. Sindelar
HR: –
FYE: January 31
Type: Public

Violin Memory plays with more than a dash of flash in orchestrating computer memory. The company designs and sells flash memory arrays and memory cards used in enterprise-level servers that offer more storage than hard disk drives. It pitches its products for use in cloud Big Data analytics and virtualized environments. More than 350 companies use Violin Memory products in markets that include financial services health care Internet government media and entertainment and telecommunications. Its products are sold directly in 30 countries and through resellers such as Dell ePlus and IBM. Violin doesn't manufacture its storage devices; contract manufacturer Flextronics does the heavy lifting.

	Annual Growth	01/11	01/12	01/13	01/14	01/15
Sales ($ mil.)	62.2%	11.4	53.9	73.8	107.7	79.0
Net income ($ mil.)	–	(16.7)	(44.8)	(109.1)	(149.8)	(108.9)
Market value ($ mil.)	1.6%	–	–	–	354.8	360.5
Employees	(14.0%)	–	–	445	437	329

VIRBAC CORPORATION

CEO: –
CFO: Christo White
HR: Roger D Brandt
FYE: December 31
Type: Subsidiary

3200 Meacham Blvd.
Fort Worth TX 76137
Phone: 817-831-5030
Fax: 817-831-8327
Web: www.virbacvet.com

Hairballs and ticks and worms — oh my! Virbac Corporation is an animal health care company that makes pharmaceutical products mainly for companion pets (dogs cats and horses) in the areas of heartworm flea and tick dermatology hormone disorders oral hygiene and antibiotics. It is the North American subsidiary of France's Virbac one of the largest veterinary drugmakers in the world. Among Virbac Corporation's brands are C.E.T. dental products Clintabs antibiotic tablets Epi-Otic ear cleanser Iverhart heartworm preventive Ketochlor and Pyoben shampoos and Preventic tick collars. Products are geared towards veterinarians and pet store retailers in Canada and the US.

VIRCO MANUFACTURING CORP.

NMS: VIRC

2027 Harpers Way
Torrance, CA 90501
Phone: 310 533-0474
Fax: –
Web: www.virco.com

CEO: Gorka Zalbide
CFO: –
HR: –
FYE: January 31
Type: Public

Have childhood memories of metal-legged folding tables upholstered auditorium seats or molded plastic chairs with attached wooden desks designed mostly for right-handers? Thank Virco Mfg. for the memories. The company makes a broad range of furniture and fixtures for the education market including student and teacher desks chairs tables computer furniture mobile pedestals and tables with combined seating for cafeterias A/V equipment and filing and storage cabinets. It also offers seating tables media units and other furniture for hotels government agencies churches and convention centers. Founded in 1950 Virco provides delivery and installation services as well.

	Annual Growth	01/11	01/12	01/13	01/14	01/15
Sales ($ mil.)	(2.4%)	181.0	166.4	158.9	155.9	164.1
Net income ($ mil.)	–	(17.6)	(13.8)	(3.8)	(1.7)	0.8
Market value ($ mil.)	(5.7%)	45.3	26.4	39.7	38.9	35.8
Employees	(10.1%)	1,050	825	760	700	685

VIRGINIA ELECTRIC & POWER CO.

NL:

120 Tredegar Street
Richmond, VA 23219
Phone: 804 819-2000
Fax: –

CEO: Thomas F Farrell
CFO: Mark F McGettrick
HR: –
FYE: December 31
Type: Public

Yes Virginia there is power in the Old Dominion thanks to Dominion Virginia Power. The company (which operates under the Dominion Virginia Power and Dominion North Carolina Power brands) provides regulated electric delivery services to about 2.4 million homes and businesses. Power generation is derived by means of coal gas oil hydro and nuclear plants. The utility's power plants (with 19595 MW of generating capacity) are managed by the Dominion Generation unit of parent Dominion Resources. Control of Virginia Electric and Power's transmission facilities is maintained by PJM Interconnection. Dominion Virginia Power also sells wholesale power to other users.

	Annual Growth	12/10	12/11	12/12	12/13	12/14
Sales ($ mil.)	1.2%	7,219.0	7,246.0	7,226.0	7,295.0	7,579.0
Net income ($ mil.)	0.2%	852.0	822.0	1,050.0	1,138.0	858.0
Market value ($ mil.)	2.2%	28.3	28.6	30.5	30.2	–
Employees	0.0%	6,800	6,800	6,800	6,700	6,800

VIRGINIA WEST UNIVERSITY FOUNDATION INC

1 WATERFRONT PL FL 7
MORGANTOWN, WV 265015978
Phone: 304-293-3708
Fax: –
Web: www.wvuf.org

CEO: Cindi Roth
CFO: Michael Augustine
HR: –
FYE: June 30
Type: Private

The West Virginia University Foundation provides fund raising services and manages the assets of West Virginia University. The Foundation seeks support for faculty programs services equipment and facilities that the state of West Virginia might not be able to fund. The university founded the organization in 1954 as an independent non-profit corporation.

	Annual Growth	06/10	06/11	06/12	06/13	06/14
Assets ($ mil.)	9.8%	–	1,085.8	1,110.4	1,245.5	1,437.4
Net income ($ mil.)	63.4%	–	–	37.5	75.9	100.0
Market value ($ mil.)	–	–	–	–	–	–
Employees	–	–	–	–	–	70

VIRGINIA WEST UNIVERSITY HOSPITALS INC

1 MEDICAL CENTER DR
MORGANTOWN, WV 26506
Phone: 304-598-4000
Fax: –
Web: www.wvuhealthcare.com

CEO: –
CFO: –
HR: Charlotte Bennett
FYE: December 31
Type: Private

West Virginia University Hospitals (WVUH) has West Virginians covered. The health care system's 530-bed main campus includes the Ruby Memorial Hospital the WVU Children's Hospital and the behavioral health Chestnut Ridge Center as well as outpatient care centers. Other services include centers for eye and dental care cancer treatment and family medicine. WVUH's facilities serve as the primary teaching locations for the West Virginia University's health professions schools. Cheat Lake Physicians is the physicians group associated with the health system. WVUH is a member of the West Virginia United Health System.

	Annual Growth	12/04	12/05	12/06	12/12	12/13
Sales ($ mil.)	–	–	0.0	0.0	1,386.7	703.7
Net income ($ mil.)	–	–	–	0.0	96.1	97.2
Market value ($ mil.)	–	–	–	–	–	–
Employees	–	–	–	–	–	6,267

VIRNETX HOLDING CORP

ASE: VHC

308 Dorla Court, Suite 206
Zephyr Cove, NV 89448
Phone: 775 548-1785
Fax: –
Web: www.virnetx.com

CEO: Kendall S. Larsen
CFO: Richard Nance
HR: –
FYE: December 31
Type: Public

VirnetX is involved in a net of legal battles. The company owns more than 80 US technology patents for establishing secure mobile Internet communications over the 4G LTE network but it claims several major tech firms are giving away its patented Internet security software for free. VirnetX bought the core patents from federal IT contractor Leidos in 2006 and has been working to commercialize its mobile communications software branded as GABRIEL Connection Technology as well as a secure domain name registry service. Before the company can convince customers to license its software it must resolve several patent infringement lawsuits against Apple Cisco and Microsoft.

	Annual Growth	12/10	12/11	12/12	12/13	12/14
Sales ($ mil.)	106.9%	0.1	0.0	0.4	2.2	1.2
Net income ($ mil.)	–	41.4	(17.3)	(26.9)	(27.6)	(9.9)
Market value ($ mil.)	(22.0%)	772.2	1,298.4	1,522.5	1,009.3	285.5
Employees	6.2%	11	13	14	15	14

VIRTUA MEMORIAL HOSPITAL BURLINGTON COUNTY INC

175 MADISON AVE
MOUNT HOLLY, NJ 080602099
Phone: 609-267-0700
Fax: –
Web: www.virtua.org

CEO: –
CFO: –
HR: Elizabeth Ferara
FYE: December 31
Type: Private

Virtua Memorial Hospital of Burlington County provides acute care to patients in southern New Jersey and the Philadelphia metropolitan area. Part of the Virtua Health network the hospital has more than 430 beds and is well-known for its women's and children's health services and stroke care. Other specialty programs include a sleep center cardiac rehabilitation diabetes treatment and wound care. Virtua Memorial provides a full range of cancer treatments through its collaboration with Philadelphia's Fox Chase Cancer Center and operates an in-hospital hospice center for terminally ill patients through a partnership with Samaritan Hospice.

	Annual Growth	12/04	12/05	12/06	12/08	12/12
Sales ($ mil.)	–	–	0.0	283.9	328.0	308.2
Net income ($ mil.)	1.0%	–	–	39.1	26.0	41.4
Market value ($ mil.)	–	–	–	–	–	–
Employees	–	–	–	–	–	1,450

VIRTUAL RADIOLOGIC CORPORATION

11995 Singletree Ln. Ste. 500
Eden Prairie MN 55344
Phone: 952-595-1100
Fax: 952-942-3361
Web: www.virtualrad.net

CEO: Jim Burke
CFO: Jeff Harmsen
HR: –
FYE: December 31
Type: Private

Virtual Radiologic diagnoses from a distance. The teleradiology company also known as vRad offers remote diagnostic imaging services interpreting diagnostic scans made by radiology practices throughout the US. It transmits the images and results to more than 2700 health care facilities over a secure broadband network using proprietary workflow management software. Virtual Radiologic operates 24 hours a day 365 days a year and reads images made by a number of modalities including ultrasound nuclear medicine computed tomography (CT) and magnetic resonance imaging (MRI). Virtual Radiologic was taken private by Providence Equity Partners in 2010.

VIRTUALSCOPICS INC

NAS: VSCP

500 Linden Oaks
Rochester, NY 14625
Phone: 585 249-6231
Fax: –
Web: www.virtualscopics.com

CEO: Eric T. Converse
CFO: James Groff
HR: Cheryl Fleming
FYE: December 31
Type: Public

VirtualScopics makes medical imaging analysis tools that help clinical researchers speed up the drug development process. Its patented algorithms let researchers analyze data from computed tomography MRI PET and ultrasound scans with the aim of helping pharmaceutical biotech and medical device companies determine how an investigational drug is working (or not working). The company also hopes its products can be used to develop diagnostic tools to help with disease treatment and surgery. VirtualScopics provides services for many large pharmaceutical companies including GlaxoSmithKline and Johnson & Johnson; its largest customer is Pfizer (which also holds a minority stake).

	Annual Growth	12/10	12/11	12/12	12/13	12/14
Sales ($ mil.)	(6.0%)	13.4	14.3	13.0	11.2	10.5
Net income ($ mil.)	–	(0.6)	0.7	(1.5)	(2.7)	(3.4)
Market value ($ mil.)	10.4%	6.4	2.7	1.7	10.4	9.5
Employees	(14.3%)	176	104	104	81	95

VIRTUS INVESTMENT PARTNERS, INC
NMS: VRTS

100 Pearl St.
Hartford, CT 06103
Phone: 800 248-7971
Fax: –
Web: www.virtus.com

CEO: George R Aylward
CFO: Michael A. (Mike) Angerthal
HR: –
FYE: December 31
Type: Public

Virtus Investment Partners provides investment management services to wealthy individuals corporations pension funds endowments and foundations and insurance companies. With more than $50 billion of assets under management it operates through affiliated advisors including Duff & Phelps Kayne Anderson Rudnick and Newfleet Asset Management as well as outside subadvisors. Virtus markets diverse investment products such as wrap fee programs open- and closed-end funds and managed account services to high-net-worth individuals. It also manages institutional accounts for corporations and other investors. The firm was formed in 1995 through a reverse merger with Duff & Phelps.

	Annual Growth	12/10	12/11	12/12	12/13	12/14
Sales ($ mil.)	32.9%	144.6	204.7	280.1	389.2	450.6
Net income ($ mil.)	78.1%	9.6	145.4	37.8	77.1	97.0
Market value ($ mil.)	39.2%	407.2	682.3	1,085.5	1,795.6	1,530.3
Employees	10.7%	273	299	336	376	410

VIRTUSA CORP
NMS: VRTU

2000 West Park Drive
Westborough, MA 01581
Phone: 508 389-7300
Fax: –
Web: www.virtusa.com

CEO: Kris A. Canekeratne
CFO: Ranjan Kalia
HR: Shakila Banu
FYE: March 31
Type: Public

Virtusa believes that virtually any business can improve its technology. Founded in 1996 the company provides a variety of offshore-based software development and information technology services including software engineering application development application outsourcing maintenance systems integration and legacy system conversion. Virtusa's customers come from industries such as financial services insurance telecommunications and media and healthcare. Its top two customers JPMorgan Chase and insurance giant AIG together account for about 23% of sales.

	Annual Growth	03/11	03/12	03/13	03/14	03/15
Sales ($ mil.)	21.8%	218.0	277.8	333.2	396.9	479.0
Net income ($ mil.)	27.2%	16.2	20.0	28.4	34.4	42.4
Market value ($ mil.)	21.9%	543.1	500.8	689.0	971.7	1,199.9
Employees	31.9%	3,056	5,672	6,911	8,054	9,247

VISA INC
NYS: V

P.O. Box 8999
San Francisco, CA 94128-8999
Phone: 650 432-3200
Fax: –
Web: www.corporate.visa.com

CEO: Charles W. (Charlie) Scharf
CFO: Vasant M. Prabhu
HR: –
FYE: September 30
Type: Public

Paper or plastic? Visa hopes you choose the latter. Visa operates the world's largest consumer payment system (far ahead of rivals MasterCard and American Express) and boasts nearly 2.5 billion credit and other payment cards in circulation across more than 200 countries. As part of its business the company licenses the Visa name to member institutions which issue and market their own Visa products and participate in the VisaNet payment system that provides authorization processing and settlement services. The company also offers debit cards Internet payment systems value-storing smart cards and traveler's checks. Visa's network connects thousands of financial institutions worldwide.

	Annual Growth	09/11	09/12	09/13	09/14	09/15
Sales ($ mil.)	10.9%	9,188.0	10,421.0	11,778.0	12,702.0	13,880.0
Net income ($ mil.)	14.7%	3,650.0	2,144.0	4,980.0	5,438.0	6,328.0
Market value ($ mil.)	–	0.0	0.0	0.0	0.0	0.0
Employees	10.8%	7,500	8,500	9,500	9,500	11,300

VISCOUNT SYSTEMS INC
NBB: VSYS

4585 Tillicum Street
Burnaby, British Columbia V5J 5K9
Phone: 604 327-9446
Fax: –
Web: www.viscount.com

CEO: –
CFO: –
HR: –
FYE: December 31
Type: Public

Lost your keys? This company may help you keep them in your wallet. Viscount Systems provides building access control systems to residential and commercial customers in the US and Canada. Its systems include card readers remote control access gates intercom devices and telephone entry systems. The company's MESH (Multimedia Embedded Security Hub) security product line converges voice data and video. Its Enterphone access control system uses a building's internal phone wiring. Viscount's systems can be found in some 35000 buildings in North America.

	Annual Growth	12/10	12/11	12/12	12/13	12/14
Sales ($ mil.)	1.2%	3.9	3.4	3.6	3.9	4.1
Net income ($ mil.)	–	(1.3)	(2.8)	(2.7)	(2.9)	(0.9)
Market value ($ mil.)	(26.6%)	29.0	7.6	7.6	15.1	8.4
Employees	10.7%	26	26	24	26	39

VISHAY INTERTECHNOLOGY, INC.
NYS: VSH

63 Lancaster Avenue
Malvern, PA 19355-2143
Phone: 610 644-1300
Fax: –
Web: www.vishay.com

CEO: Gerald Paul
CFO: Lori Lipcaman
HR: –
FYE: December 31
Type: Public

Vishay Intertechnology is aggressive when it comes to passives. The company is one of the top makers of passive electronic components such as inductors capacitors and resistors in the world. It is also a leader in the market for discrete semiconductor components including diodes infrared optoelectronic components and MOSFETs (metal-oxide semiconductor field-effect transistors) which function as solid-state switches in power control applications. Vishay's components are used in everything from hybrid cars to spacecraft to wireless phones and laptops. The company operates worldwide and gets most of its sales from customers outside the US.

	Annual Growth	12/10	12/11	12/12	12/13	12/14
Sales ($ mil.)	(2.2%)	2,725.1	2,594.0	2,230.1	2,371.0	2,493.3
Net income ($ mil.)	(24.3%)	359.1	238.8	122.7	123.0	117.6
Market value ($ mil.)	(0.9%)	2,164.6	1,325.6	1,567.4	1,955.2	2,086.5
Employees	0.0%	22,600	20,900	21,600	22,500	22,600

VISHAY PRECISION GROUP INC.
NYS: VPG

3 Great Valley Parkway, Suite 150
Malvern, PA 19355
Phone: 484 321-5300
Fax: 484 321-5301
Web: www.vpgsensors.com

CEO: Ziv Shoshani
CFO: William M. Clancy
HR: –
FYE: December 31
Type: Public

Vishay Precision Group (VPG) likes to weigh in on important measurements and the company takes pleasure in getting foiled. The spinoff of Vishay Intertechnology aggregates a series of acquisitions made by Vishay in weighing modules and systems. VPG also specializes in foil resistors (electronic components that regulate electrical current and voltage) precision sensors strain gauges and other precision measurement equipment employed in process control systems. The company's products are used in industrial applications including military agricultural aerospace medical and construction. European customers account for 40% of sales.

	Annual Growth	12/10	12/11	12/12	12/13	12/14
Sales ($ mil.)	4.9%	207.5	238.1	217.6	240.3	250.8
Net income ($ mil.)	(24.3%)	11.7	10.8	11.7	4.3	3.9
Market value ($ mil.)	(2.3%)	259.1	219.8	181.8	204.8	236.0
Employees	2.5%	2,300	2,350	2,250	2,387	2,536

VISION SERVICE PLAN

3333 Quality Dr.	CEO: James Robinson Lynch
Rancho Cordova CA 95670	CFO: –
Phone: 916-851-5000	HR: –
Fax: 916-851-4858	FYE: December 31
Web: www.vsp.com	Type: Private - Not-for-Pr

With Vision Service Plan (VSP) the bottom line of the eye chart won't read U-O-W-E-B-I-G. The firm is a top managed eye care benefits provider that serves 58 million members in the US Canada and the UK. Its VSP Vision Care programs offer coverage ranging from general plans (eye exams and eyewear) to laser vision correction procedures through a network of about 29000 preferred doctors. Behind the managed care business is VSP's vertically-integrated eye care and eye wear business including frame manufacturing (Marchon Eyewear) optical labs and optical practice management services. Founded in 1955 by a group of optometrists VSP operates as a not-for-profit organization.

VISION SOLUTIONS INC.

15300 Barranca Pkwy.	CEO: Nicolaas Vlok
Irvine CA 92618	CFO: Don Scott
Phone: 949-253-6500	HR: –
Fax: 949-253-6501	FYE: December 31
Web: www.visionsolutions.com	Type: Private

Vision Solutions has a clear picture of what perfect data management should look like. The company provides software used to maintain and manage enterprise data. Designed primarily for IBM Power Systems Microsoft Windows Linux and cloud computing users its software handles disaster recovery systems management enterprise application integration and data archiving. Vision Solution's products are sold worldwide under the Double-Take MIMIX and iTERA brands. The company also offers professional services such as consulting training support installation and maintenance. Founded in 1990 it is a portfolio company of private equity investment firm Thoma Bravo.

VISIONARY INTEGRATION PROFESSIONALS INC.

80 Iron Point Circle Ste. 100	CEO: Jonna A Ward
Folsom CA 95630	CFO: –
Phone: 916-985-9625	HR: –
Fax: 916-985-9632	FYE: December 31
Web: www.vipconsulting.com	Type: Private

Visionary Integration Professionals is an IT VIP. More commonly known as VIP the company offers information technology (IT) services including business intelligence applications development data center and infrastructure consulting technology integration and operations quality management management consulting and program management support. VIP has worked with hundreds of clients across numerous industries as well as supporting a wide swath of federal state and local government entities. Customers have included Boeing Intel IBM and Johnson & Johnson. VIP was founded in 1996 by CEO Jonna Ward. It has offices in the US and India.

VISIONWORKS OF AMERICA INC.

175 E. Houston St.	CEO: David L Holmberg
San Antonio TX 78205	CFO: Jennifer L Taylor
Phone: 210-340-3531	HR: –
Fax: 210-524-6996	FYE: December 31
Web: www.visionworks.com	Type: Subsidiary

Visionworks of America (formerly Eye Care Centers of America) is clearly focused on becoming the top eyewear chain. The company owns or manages more than 550 optical stores in almost 40 states. Its stores — operating under the EyeMasters name and a host of others (including Dr. Bizer's ValuVision EYE DRx Hour Eyes and Vision World) — are being rebranded as Visionworks. The stores sell contact lenses prescription eyewear sunglasses and accessories and offer contacts and eyeglass frames under its own and designer brands as well as one-hour service on-site processing labs and independent optometrists. Founded in 1984 the firm is a subsidiary of HVHC itself a subsidiary of health insurer Highmark.

VISITING NURSE SERVICE OF NEW YORK

107 E. 70th St.	CEO: Mary Ann Christopher
New York NY 10021	CFO: Sameul Heller
Phone: 212-609-6100	HR: –
Fax: 212-794-6610	FYE: December 31
Web: www.vnsny.org	Type: Private - Not-for-Pr

When you're laid up in bed Visiting Nurse Service of New York (VNSNY) can give you something besides your afternoon soap operas to look forward to. VNSNY is one of the largest not-for-profit home health care providers in the US. The company provides a wide range of home health services to some 140000 patients throughout New York City as well as on Long Island. Visitation programs include senior care rehabilitation therapy mental health hospice and pediatrics as well as Medicare/Medicaid programs. The company's 15000 care providers make more than 2 million professional home visits each year.

VISKASE COMPANIES INC.

PINK SHEETS: VKSC

8205 S. Cass Ave. Ste. 115	CEO: Thomas D Davis
Darien IL 60561	CFO: John Plescia
Phone: 630-874-0700	HR: –
Fax: 630-874-0179	FYE: December 31
Web: www.viskase.com	Type: Public

Viskase Companies forces hot dogs sausages and salami to shape up and ship out. The company is one of the world's leading producers of non-edible cellulosic fibrous and plastic casings used to prepare and package processed meat and poultry products. Viskase's casings are sold under brand names such as NOJAX (skinless hot dogs have "no jackets") VISFLEX and VISMAX. It also makes SEALFLEX SILVER heat-shrinkable plastic bags for the meat poultry and deli industries. In the nonfood arena Viskase makes MEMBRA-CEL for use in dialysis. Viskase has production facilities in Brazil Canada France Germany Italy Mexico Poland and the US. More than two-thirds of the company's sales originate outside the US

VISTA GOLD CORP.

NYSE AMEX: VGZ

7961 Shaffer Pkwy. Ste. 5
Littleton CO 80127
Phone: 720-981-1185
Fax: 720-981-1186
Web: www.vistagold.com

CEO: Frederick H Earnest
CFO: John F Engele
HR: –
FYE: December 31
Type: Public

When it views its holdings Vista Gold hopes its prospects for gold are good. Since 2001 the company has acquired five gold projects with the expectation that gold prices would increase. It is developing the Mt. Todd gold project in Australia's Northern Territories and the Concordia gold project in Mexico's Baja California Sur. It also holds a 30% stake in Midas Gold Corp. which has projects in Idaho including the Yellow Pine property once held by Vista. Other holdings by Vista are the Guadalupe de los Reyes gold and silver mining complex in Mexico the Awak Mas gold mine in Indonesia and the Long Valley gold project in California. Vista has proven and probable reserves of 5.4 million ounces of gold.

VISTA HEALTHPLAN OF SOUTH FLORIDA INC.

1340 Concord Terrace
Sunrise FL 33323
Phone: 954-858-3000
Fax: 954-846-0331
Web: www.vistahealthplan.com/

CEO: Joseph R Berding
CFO: Tom Wyss
HR: –
FYE: December 31
Type: Subsidiary

Vista Healthplan of South Florida formerly Foundation Health A Florida Health Plan provides health care plans and related services including PPO HMO point-of-service (POS) Medicaid Medicare and Florida Healthy Kids to about 300000 individuals throughout Florida. It serves its customers through employer group plans state and municipal programs and individual policies. The company which offers both employer group and individual plans provides a network of more than 6500 independent physicians. Vista Healthplan is a subsidiary of Coventry Health Care.

VISTA INTERNATIONAL TECHNOLOGIES INC

NBB: VVIT

4835 Monaco St
Commerce City, CO 80022
Phone: 303 690-8300
Fax: 970 535-4784
Web: www.vvit.us

CEO: Timothy D Ruddy
CFO: Thomas P Pfisterer
HR: –
FYE: December 31
Type: Public

Vista International Technologies sees itself as a potential leader in renewable energy technology on a global scale. The company is working to develop and market its Thermal Gasifier Technology and to build and operate small power plants. Colorado-based Vista has operations in waste-to-energy gassification low-wind-speed generators alternative fuels and energy-saving lighting. Its primary operation is a facility in Texas that converts used tires into fuel. The company is looking for partners to build own and operate small waste-to-energy plants or utilize the company's technology under license. Investor Richard Strain owns just under 50% of Vista while board member Timothy Ruddy owns a 10% stake.

	Annual Growth	12/10	12/11	12/12	12/13	12/14
Sales ($ mil.)	11.0%	0.6	0.5	0.7	0.8	0.9
Net income ($ mil.)	–	(0.9)	(1.1)	(0.4)	(0.8)	(0.3)
Market value ($ mil.)	7.5%	0.6	0.9	1.5	1.7	0.8
Employees	(19.1%)	7	7	3	3	3

VISTEON CORP.

NYS: VC

One Village Center Drive
Van Buren Township, MI 48111
Phone: 734 710-5800
Fax: –
Web: www.visteon.com

CEO: Sachin Lawande
CFO: Jeffrey (Jeff) Stafeil
HR: Keith M Shul
FYE: December 31
Type: Public

Visteon is the visionary-sounding name Ford Motor bestowed on its automotive components unit when it was spun off in 2000. One of the largest auto parts makers in the US the company has evolved to operate two business groups: Climate Control (climate systems powertrain cooling systems); and Electronic Products (audio systems driver control systems infotainment systems powertrain and feature control modules). Ford represents more than 25% of sales; Visteon also provides products and services to aftermarket customers. More than 80% of its sales are made outside the US.

	Annual Growth	12/10	12/11	12/12	12/13	12/14
Sales ($ mil.)	41.2%	1,887.0	8,047.0	6,857.0	7,439.0	7,509.0
Net income ($ mil.)	–	86.0	80.0	100.0	690.0	(295.0)
Market value ($ mil.)	9.5%	3,267.0	2,197.4	2,368.1	3,603.2	4,701.8
Employees	(1.0%)	26,500	26,000	22,000	24,000	25,500

VISTRONIX INC.

1851 Alexander Bell Dr. Ste. 350
Reston VA 20191
Phone: 703-463-2059
Fax: 703-483-2500
Web: www.vistronix.com

CEO: Deepak Hathiramani
CFO: Holly Beveridge Beveridge
HR: –
FYE: December 31
Type: Private

Vistronix keeps on the right side of the information technology (IT) highway. Founded in 1990 the company provides IT consulting services primarily to the government services market in the areas of content management enterprise solutions and grants management. Vistronix's service solutions are divided up into three practice areas or groups: eSolutions Consulting Enterprise Systems Management and Information Management Solutions. The firm's past clients have included the EPA the US Department of Defense and the Bureau of Transportation Statistics.

VITACOST.COM INC

NMS: VITC

5400 Broken Sound Blvd.-N.W., Suite 500
Boca Raton, FL 33487-3521
Phone: 561 982-4180
Fax: –
Web: www.vitacost.com

CEO: Jeffrey J Horowitz
CFO: Brian D Helman
HR: Ellen Finnerty
FYE: December 31
Type: Public

Vitacost.com aims to capitalize on consumer preoccupation with health and wellness. The online retailer offers some 34000 items including dietary supplements from algae to zinc health food and personal and pet care products at discount prices. In addition to 1600-plus name brands such as Atkins and J?SON the company sells Vitacost-label nutritional products supplied by contract manufacturers. Customers shop by in large online. The company has a contact center a third-party center for late-night calls and two distribution hubs in the US. Founded in 1994 Vitacost is almost 20% controlled by Great Hill Equity; Vitacost chairman Michael Kumin and Christopher Gaffney a director are the firm's partners.

	Annual Growth	12/08	12/09	12/10	12/11	12/12
Sales ($ mil.)	23.2%	143.6	191.8	220.7	260.5	330.7
Net income ($ mil.)	–	0.0	5.9	(15.2)	(14.8)	(19.2)
Market value ($ mil.)	(13.4%)	–	349.1	191.0	208.4	227.1
Employees	26.0%	266	292	415	631	671

VITAMIN SHOPPE INC
NYS: VSI

300 Harmon Meadow Blvd.
Secaucus, NJ 07094
Phone: 201 868-5959
Fax: –
Web: www.vitaminshoppe.com

CEO: Colin F. Watts
CFO: Brenda M. Galgano
HR: Teresa Orth
FYE: December 27
Type: Public

Vitamin Shoppe helps vitamin-takers meet their recommended daily requirements. The fast-growing company sells vitamins supplements and minerals as well as herbal homeopathic and sports nutrition and wellness products at more than 600 company-operated The Vitamin Shoppe stores located in some 45 US states the District of Columbia Puerto Rico and Canada. It also sells directly via catalog and the websites VitaminShoppe.com and BodyTech.com. Stores offer about 17500 items including food and beverages and pet products under more than 400 national and private-label brands. Founded in 1977 Vitamin Shoppe entered the Canadian market in 2012.

	Annual Growth	12/10	12/11	12/12	12/13	12/14
Sales ($ mil.)	12.7%	751.5	856.6	950.9	1,087.5	1,213.0
Net income ($ mil.)	20.3%	29.2	44.9	60.8	66.5	61.2
Market value ($ mil.)	8.7%	1,013.8	1,198.3	1,682.1	1,545.7	1,417.4
Employees	11.7%	3,581	3,907	4,247	4,842	5,583

VITAS HEALTHCARE CORPORATION

100 S. Biscayne Blvd. Ste. 1300
Miami FL 33131
Phone: 305-374-4143
Fax: 305-350-6797
Web: www.vitas.com

CEO: Timothy S O'Toole
CFO: David A Wester
HR: –
FYE: December 31
Type: Subsidiary

VITAS Healthcare is a vital provider of hospice services in the US. The firm a subsidiary of Chemed is a top national provider serving patients in more than 15 states and Washington DC. The company provides 50 hospice care programs for terminally ill patients in their homes nursing homes hospitals and at its 36 company-owned inpatient facilities. Its services — provided by teams of nurses doctors aides clergy and social workers — focus on managing pain and symptoms providing personal care helping with financial arrangements handling equipment and medications and offering emotional and spiritual support. The company also provides bereavement services and grief counseling to patients' families.

VITESSE SEMICONDUCTOR CORP.
NMS: VTSS

4721 Calle Carga
Camarillo, CA 93012
Phone: 805 388-3700
Fax: –
Web: www.vitesse.com

CEO: Christopher R Gardner
CFO: Martin S McDermut
HR: –
FYE: September 30
Type: Public

Swiftness and finesse come together in Vitesse Semiconductor's chips. Vitesse (French for "speed") is a leading supplier of high-speed integrated circuits; most of its chips are made with CMOS silicon processes. The company also develops silicon germanium (SiGe) compound semiconductors which are much harder to work with than ordinary silicon (and thus more expensive). But the fancier chips are much faster (electrons travel through the advanced compounds more swiftly) and consume less energy than silicon-based chips of equal size. Vitesse's chips are primarily used in communications gear particularly in networking equipment.

	Annual Growth	09/10	09/11	09/12	09/13	09/14
Sales ($ mil.)	(10.1%)	166.0	141.0	119.5	103.8	108.5
Net income ($ mil.)	–	(20.1)	(14.8)	(1.1)	(22.1)	(18.1)
Market value ($ mil.)	(0.1%)	244.4	199.7	165.2	205.8	243.7
Employees	(6.6%)	467	362	336	331	356

VITRIA TECHNOLOGY INC.

945 Stewart Dr.
Sunnyvale CA 94085
Phone: 408-212-2700
Fax: 408-212-2720
Web: www.vitria.com

CEO: Jomei Chang
CFO: –
HR: Marilyn Reid
FYE: December 31
Type: Private

Vitria develops software used to help businesses gather and analyze vital business data to inform operational decisions (M30) and business process integration applications for mitigating operational delays and managing trading partner communications (BusinessWare). Customers such as AT&T Blue Cross Blue Shield and Reynolds & Reynolds have used its products to track orders across the Web automate fulfillment and graphically model business processes. Vitria targets such industries as financial services health care insurance manufacturing and telecommunications. The company sells directly and through distributors and systems integrators. Vitria was founded in 1994 by CEO JoMei Chang and CTO Dale Skeen.

VITRONICS SOLTEC INC.

2 Marin Way
Stratham NH 03885
Phone: 603-772-7778
Fax: 603-772-7776
Web: www.vitronics-soltec.com

CEO: –
CFO: –
HR: –
FYE: December 31
Type: Subsidiary

In layman's terms Vitronics Soltec makes equipment that joins printed circuit board components together. In industry lingo the company — formed by a merger of two Dover Corporation subsidiaries — produces reflow and wave soldering systems for attaching surface-mounted devices to printed circuit boards. It also makes debridging systems for removing excess soldering materials. Primary customers for the soldering equipment company include OEMs and contract manufacturers whose products incorporate printed circuit boards. Vitronics Soltec was sold by Dover in 2006 to Francisco Partners a private equity buyout firm. Illinois Tool Works (ITW) acquired Vitronics Soltec in 2008.

VIVEVE MEDICAL INC
NRR: VIVM F

150 Commercial Street
Sunnyvale, CA 94086
Phone: 408 530-1900
Fax: –

CEO: Patricia Scheller
CFO: Scott Durbin
HR:
FYE: December 31
Type: Public

PLC Systems guards kidneys against ill effects of dehydration and toxic medicines. Its RenalGuard system marketed in Europe is a fluid balancing device that helps physicians monitor and maintain kidney fluid levels during medical imaging procedures. The company also developed the Heart Laser System a carbon dioxide laser system that performs Transmyocardial Revascularization (or TMR) as an alternative to such conventional therapies as bypass surgery and balloon angioplasty. PLC sold the TMR business to Novadaq in 2011 for $1.6 million to focus on development of RenalGuard for the US market.

	Annual Growth	12/10	12/11	12/12	12/13	12/14
Sales ($ mil.)	(61.0%)	3.9	0.7	1.1	1.3	0.1
Net income ($ mil.)	–	(0.5)	(5.8)	(8.4)	3.5	(6.2)
Market value ($ mil.)	85.6%	0.7	0.7	2.4	0.7	8.3
Employees	3.0%	8	8	8	6	9

VIVID ENTERTAINMENT LLC

3599 Cahuenga Blvd. West
Los Angeles CA 90068
Phone: 323-845-4557
Fax: 323-436-2006
Web: www.vivid.com

CEO: –
CFO: –
HR: –
FYE: December 31
Type: Private

Vivid Entertainment Group one of the world's top adult film producers leaves little to the imagination. Fans of the form know the company best for its Vivid Girls a gaggle of about a dozen porn starlets who include Jenna Jameson Briana Banks and Lanny Barby. Vivid Girls sign exclusive contracts with the company much like in the bygone days of the Hollywood studio system. Vivid sells its titles to the retail and rental markets and directly to consumers through its online mail-order site. Vivid also distributes films to cable and satellite channels and offers Internet subscribers pay-per-view access. Co-CEOs Steven Hirsch David James and Bill Asher own the company that Hirsch and James founded in 1984.

VIVUS, INC.

NMS: VVUS

351 E. Evelyn Avenue
Mountain View, CA 94041
Phone: 650 934-5200
Fax: –
Web: www.vivus.com

CEO: Seth H. Z. Fischer
CFO: Mark K. Oki
HR: –
FYE: December 31
Type: Public

VIVUS is seeking better living through chemistry. The pharmaceutical maker has several therapeutic products in development to treat a variety of conditions including metabolic and sexual health ailments. Its two commercial-stage products obesity drug Qsymia and erectile dysfunction drug Stendra were both approved by the FDA in 2012. VIVUS commercialization strategies include selling its products through direct sales methods or through distribution partnership agreements in the US and abroad. Drug candidates in the company's pipeline include potential treatments for sleep apnea and diabetes.

	Annual Growth	12/10	12/11	12/12	12/13	12/14
Sales ($ mil.)	653.3%	–	–	2.0	81.1	114.2
Net income ($ mil.)	–	(66.1)	(46.1)	(139.9)	(174.5)	(82.6)
Market value ($ mil.)	(25.5%)	971.9	1,011.4	1,392.0	941.9	298.7
Employees	21.6%	43	38	121	98	94

VIZIO INC.

39 TESLA
IRVINE, CA 926184603
Phone: 949-428-2525
Fax: –
Web: www.vizio.com

CEO: William Wang
CFO: Kurt Binder
HR: –
FYE: December 31
Type: Private

VIZIO has done for HDTVs what Dell did for PCs and Southwest Airlines did for air travel: sell them for less. The company sells low-cost flat panel and plasma LCD HDTVs. It competes head-to-head with Japan's Sony and Samsung; its products however are made in China and Taiwan. VIZIO has logged large annual revenue gains by selling quality televisions for hundreds if not thousands of dollars less than its competitors. The company was founded by CEO William Wang in 2002 and initially its TVs were only sold at membership retailers such as Costco Wholesale BJ's Wholesale Club and Sam's Club. Since then it has extended its reach to discount retailers Wal-Mart and Sears. VIZIO entered the PC arena in 2012.

	Annual Growth	12/03	12/04	12/06	12/07	12/08
Sales ($ mil.)	155.8%	–	46.9	671.3	1,929.2	2,006.3
Net income ($ mil.)	181.2%	–	–	1.3	7.6	10.3
Market value ($ mil.)	–	–	–	–	–	–
Employees	–	–	–	–	–	225

VMWARE INC

NYS: VMW

3401 Hillview Avenue
Palo Alto, CA 94304
Phone: 650 427-5000
Fax: –
Web: www.vmware.com

CEO: Patrick (Pat) Gelsinger
CFO: Zane C. Rowe
HR: –
FYE: December 31
Type: Public

VMware makes a virtue of being virtual. The company develops software used to create and manage virtual machines — computer functions spread across multiple systems. Companies use its applications to more efficiently integrate and manage server storage and networking functions to lower the cost of operating their IT systems. VMware also provides an extensive range of consulting technical support training and certification services that accounts for just over half of sales. The company has marketing relationships with top computer hardware vendors including Dell Hewlett-Packard and Cisco. Data storage systems maker EMC holds a controlling stake in VMware.

	Annual Growth	12/10	12/11	12/12	12/13	12/14
Sales ($ mil.)	20.6%	2,857.3	3,767.1	4,605.0	5,207.0	6,035.0
Net income ($ mil.)	25.5%	357.4	723.9	745.7	1,014.0	886.0
Market value ($ mil.)	(1.8%)	38,174.3	35,718.4	40,419.9	38,517.8	35,430.7
Employees	18.9%	9,000	11,000	13,800	14,300	18,000

VOCERA COMMUNICATIONS, INC.

NYS: VCRA

525 Race Street
San Jose, CA 95126
Phone: 408 882-5100
Fax: –
Web: www.vocera.com

CEO: Brent D. Lang
CFO: Justin R. Spencer
HR: –
FYE: December 31
Type: Public

Vocera Communications makes high-tech walkie talkies for hospital employees who have their hands full. Its digital voice communication system works over wireless computer networks and includes a communications badge worn around the neck and server software. The company also offers an optional standard-size phone handset. Its systems support text messaging and can be configured to make and receive telephone calls using smartphones and other mobile devices. Vocera markets its products primarily to health care facilities; it counts more than 875 hospitals as customers and about 200 other customers in hospitality retail and libraries.

	Annual Growth	12/10	12/11	12/12	12/13	12/14
Sales ($ mil.)	13.8%	56.8	79.5	101.0	102.5	95.4
Net income ($ mil.)	–	1.2	(2.5)	2.9	(10.5)	(28.3)
Market value ($ mil.)	(35.6%)	–	–	643.7	400.3	267.2
Employees	8.9%	–	290	343	383	375

VOCOLLECT INC.

703 Rodi Rd.
Pittsburgh PA 15235
Phone: 412-829-8145
Fax: 412-829-0972
Web: www.intermec.com/vocollect/index.aspx

CEO: Joe Pajer
CFO: Steven M Barto
HR: –
FYE: December 31
Type: Business Segment

Vocollect harnesses the power of the human voice. A business unit of Intermec the company designs and installs voice recognition systems that enable factory and warehouse workers to communicate with their databases via headsets and handheld microphones thereby keeping their eyes and hands free to handle physical tasks. Its systems comprise a suite of software tools (VoiceArtrisan VoiceConsole and VoiceApplications among other products) that integrates with warehouse management systems and the Talkman line of wearable computers. Vocollect also provides consulting product implementation training and support services.

VOCUS INC

NMS: VOCS

12051 Indian Creek Court
Beltsville, MD 20705
Phone: 301 459-2590
Fax: –
Web: www.vocus.com

CEO: Peter Granat
CFO: Jack Pearlstein
HR: Chris Castle
FYE: December 31
Type: Public

For this company PR is no hocus-pocus just Vocus. It provides hosted cloud-based software that helps automate a variety of public relations duties including social search and email marketing. It also organizes media contacts and analyzes public relations effectiveness. Its government relations software manages state and federal contacts and offers lobbying analysis tools. Vocus' 120000 users vary from not-for-profits and the government to corporations and public relations professionals. The company also offers a proprietary information database of journalists analysts media outlets and publicity opportunities. Vocus has offices in North America Europe and Asia and offers its tools in seven languages.

	Annual Growth	12/08	12/09	12/10	12/11	12/12
Sales ($ mil.)	21.8%	77.5	84.6	96.8	114.9	170.8
Net income ($ mil.)	–	6.9	(2.0)	(3.7)	(14.6)	(23.6)
Market value ($ mil.)	(1.2%)	358.2	354.1	544.1	434.5	341.9
Employees	28.8%	463	518	687	808	1,273

VOLCANO CORPORATION

NMS: VOLC

3661 Valley Centre Drive, Suite 200
San Diego, CA 92130
Phone: 800 228-4728
Fax: –
Web: www.volcanocorp.com

CEO: R Scott Huennekens
CFO: John T Dahldorf
HR: –
FYE: December 31
Type: Public

Volcano creates its own sound and light show to get your heart's blood flowing. The company develops manufactures and sells medical imaging devices for cardiovascular care and other specialties. Its products include intravascular ultrasound (IVUS) and fractional flow reserve (FFR) consoles and imaging catheters that provide information about the condition of arteries as well as plaque and lesions. Its functional management (FM) consoles and single-use pressure and flow guidewires measure characteristics of blood around plaque in arteries. Volcano sells its products to physicians hospitals and other health care providers worldwide through a direct sales force and distributors.

	Annual Growth	12/08	12/09	12/10	12/11	12/12
Sales ($ mil.)	22.2%	171.5	227.9	294.1	343.5	381.9
Net income ($ mil.)	–	(13.7)	(29.0)	5.2	38.1	8.0
Market value ($ mil.)	12.0%	809.2	937.5	1,473.2	1,283.3	1,273.6
Employees	15.4%	883	969	1,144	1,289	1,565

VOLT INFORMATION SCIENCES, INC.

ASE: VISI

1065 Avenue of Americas
New York, NY 10018
Phone: 212 704 2400
Fax: –
Web: www.volt.com

CEO: Michael D. Dean
CFO: Paul R. Tomkins
HR: –
FYE: November 01
Type: Public

A jolt from Volt can discharge your personnel needs. Volt Information Sciences generates most of its sales by offering temporary and permanent employees to 10000 clients in 55 countries through more than 200 branch and on-site offices throughout Asia Europe and North and South America. Volt's staffing segment also includes businesses that provide project management and consulting services. In addition the company provides telecommunications network engineering and construction services as well as information systems including directory assistance systems.

	Annual Growth	10/11	10/12*	11/13	11/14	11/15
Sales ($ mil.)	(9.6%)	2,238.1	2,246.1	2,090.9	1,710.0	1,496.9
Net income ($ mil.)	–	15.6	(13.6)	(30.9)	(19.0)	(24.6)
Market value ($ mil.)	6.2%	141.2	145.6	178.9	172.2	179.3
Employees	(7.6%)	–	34,700	34,700	32,000	27,400

*Fiscal year change

VOLTARI CORP

NAS: VLTC

601 W. 26th Street, Suite 415
New York, NY 10001
Phone: 212 388-5500
Fax: –
Web: www.voltari.com

CEO: –
CFO: John Breeman
HR: Steve Stulbaum
FYE: December 31
Type: Public

Voltari sees big opportunity in mobile advertising. The company's Voltari Connect software provides customer analytics for mobile sales and marketing campaigns. Consumer brands such as McDonalds Starbucks and Toyota and ad agencies use it to track who looks at a brand's advertisements and when in order to lure them from being passive browsers to active buyers. In 2013 the company merged with Motricity which provided branded content to mobile subscribers until it lost its two top customers AT&T and Verizon. Voltari took the technology behind Motricity to develop Voltari Connect as a digital media and marketing application. Voltari operates from offices in Canada the UK and the US.

	Annual Growth	12/10	12/11	12/12	12/13	12/14
Sales ($ mil.)	(45.0%)	133.4	121.7	90.0	10.3	12.2
Net income ($ mil.)	–	(7.0)	(195.4)	(34.2)	(10.3)	(29.3)
Market value ($ mil.)	(56.7%)	88.5	4.3	2.0	16.3	3.1
Employees	(34.1%)	339	297	152	102	64

VOLUNTEER ENERGY COOPERATIVE

CEO: –

18359 STATE HIGHWAY 58 N
DECATUR, TN 373227825
Phone: 423-334-1020
Fax: –
Web: www.vec.org

CEO: –
CFO: –
HR: –
FYE: June 30
Type: Private

In the strong tradition of volunteering in Tennessee Volunteer Energy Cooperative is voluntarily cooperating with its members to serve their energy needs. The distribution utility serves more than 109000 customers (who also own the cooperative) in 17 central and eastern Tennessee counties. It operates more than 9000 miles of power lines. Volunteer Energy purchases its power supply from the Tennessee Valley Authority. The company also provides metered natural gas and propane service and offers telecommunications (Internet access and long-distance phone) services. In addition Volunteer Energy offers its customer surge protection and security equipment.

	Annual Growth	06/09	06/10	06/11	06/12	06/14
Sales ($ mil.)	4.3%	–	206.5	235.3	228.5	244.3
Net income ($ mil.)	(1.8%)	–	–	13.0	15.6	12.3
Market value ($ mil.)	–	–	–	–	–	–
Employees	–	–	–	–	–	175

VOLUNTEERS OF AMERICA INC.

1660 DUKE ST STE 100
ALEXANDRIA, VA 22314-3427
Phone: 703-341-5000
Fax: –
Web: www.voa.org

CEO: Michael King
CFO: –
HR:
FYE: June 30
Type: Private

There's a volunteer everywhere you look at Volunteers of America a national faith-based organization that provides community-level human services to more than 2.5 million people a year. It works to help abused and neglected children at-risk youth disabled people the homeless people with substance abuse problems the elderly and prisoners and former prisoners. The group operates from about 45 offices across the US and counts some 65000 volunteers in its ranks. It receives government grants as well as support from the public. Volunteers of America was organized in 1896 by Ballington and Maud Booth. Ballington's father William Booth founded the Salvation Army.

	Annual Growth	06/04	06/05	06/06	06/08	06/13
Sales ($ mil.)	–	–	(1,474.8)	29.7	6.4	239.0
Net income ($ mil.)	311.7%	–	0.0	0.9	5.7	13.4
Market value ($ mil.)	–	–	–	–	–	–
Employees	–	–	–	–	–	3,000

VON MAUR INC.

6565 Brady St.	CEO: –
Davenport IA 52806	CFO: Robert L Larsen CPA
Phone: 563-388-2200	HR: Talitha D Bell
Fax: 563-388-2242	FYE: January 31
Web: www.vonmaur.com	Type: Private

Family-owned and -operated Von Maur runs nearly 30 upscale department stores in about a dozen midwestern states offering its customers amenities such as an interest-free credit card free gift wrapping and free shipping within the US. The stores range in size from 42000 to 203000 sq. ft. and offer clothing from brands such as Burberry Kenneth Cole and Tommy Bahama. Distinguishing itself from the rest of the pack the Von Maur chain has avoided advertising and big blowout sales; it even closes up shop on traditional retailer high-dollar days such as the Fourth of July. The von Maur family opened its first store in Davenport Iowa in 1872.

VONAGE HOLDINGS CORP
NYS: VG

23 Main Street	CEO: Alan Masarek
Holmdel, NJ 07733	CFO: David Pearson
Phone: 732 528-2600	HR: –
Fax: –	FYE: December 31
Web: www.vonage.com	Type: Public

Vonage Holdings has helped to ring in a new era of communications. The company's computer telephony service enables customers to turn their high-speed Internet connections into long-distance phone lines for domestic or international calls. A leading provider of broadband Voice-over-Internet Protocol (VoIP) telephony services the company has about 2.4 million subscriber lines in operation. Vonage primarily serves consumers in the US but it also has a number of small business clients and it does business in Canada and the UK. The company markets its services directly and through such retail partners as Wal-Mart and Frys Electronics.

	Annual Growth	12/11	12/12	12/13	12/14	12/15
Sales ($ mil.)	0.7%	870.3	849.1	829.1	869.0	895.1
Net income ($ mil.)	(51.5%)	409.0	36.6	28.3	20.3	22.7
Market value ($ mil.)	23.7%	525.0	507.8	713.6	816.4	1,230.0
Employees	14.8%	1,008	983	1,243	1,400	1,752

VORNADO REALTY TRUST
NYS: VNO

888 Seventh Avenue	CEO: Steven Roth
New York, NY 10019	CFO: Stephen Theriot
Phone: 212 894-7000	HR: –
Fax: –	FYE: December 31
Web: www.vno.com	Type: Public

Vornado Realty Trust is a veritable whirlwind of real estate activity. The company's commercial property holdings total more than 100 million sq. ft. of space primarily in New York City and Washington DC. It also owns the 1700-room Hotel Pennsylvania in Manhattan. The company's retail portfolio consists of about 105 strip shopping centers and single tenant retail assets and six regional malls in the Northeast California and Puerto Rico. Its Merchandise Mart segment owns six showroom properties including Chicago's Merchandise Mart and L.A. Mart; it also produces trade shows. In addition Vornado owns about a third each of New York retail property owner Alexander's and big-box toy giant Toys "R" Us .

	Annual Growth	12/11	12/12	12/13	12/14	12/15
Sales ($ mil.)	(3.8%)	2,915.7	2,766.5	2,760.9	2,635.9	2,502.3
Net income ($ mil.)	3.5%	662.3	617.3	476.0	864.9	760.4
Market value ($ mil.)	6.8%	14,494.0	15,101.2	16,743.7	22,197.4	18,850.1
Employees	(4.0%)	4,823	4,428	4,369	4,503	4,089

VOXEO CORPORATION

189 S. Orange Ave. 10th Fl.	CEO: Robert Ingalls
Orlando FL 32801	CFO: Matthew Hale
Phone: 407-418-1800	HR: –
Fax: 407-264-8530	FYE: December 31
Web: www.voxeo.com	Type: Private

Voxeo gives voice to communications and customer service. The company provides software and services that enable clients to deliver interactive voice response (IVR) and VoIP technology customer self-service applications outbound notifications and unified communications. Its flagship products include CXP a platform for the development and management of multi-channel (voice text web) self-service apps and Prophecy an IVR platform. Voxeo also provides related analytics security and cloud hosting services. It serves some 250000 clients both large and small including DHL Adobe and Swisscom. Key investors include Mayfield Fund and Crosspoint Venture Partners.

VOXWARE INC.

300 American Metro Blvd. Ste. 155	CEO: Keith Phillips
Hamilton NJ 08619	CFO: Roger Maloch
Phone: 609-514-4100	HR: –
Fax: 609-514-4101	FYE: June 30
Web: www.voxware.com	Type: Private

Voxware has a hands-free approach to information management. The company makes speech recognition systems that include voice recognition software a portable computer and a headset microphone. The systems enables workers to enter data by voice keeping their hands and eyes free to pick receive and sort materials; take inventory; and run inspections. Voxware also offers stationary systems for less mobile applications such as mail and package sorting. The company targets distribution centers and warehouses in such markets as consumer goods grocery logistics and retail. Customers have included retailer 7-Eleven vehicle glass repair specialist Belron and U.S. Foodservice.

VOXX INTERNATIONAL CORP
NMS: VOXX

180 Marcus Blvd.	CEO: Patrick M. (Pat) Lavelle
Hauppauge, NY 11788	CFO: Charles M. Stoehr
Phone: 631 231-7750	HR: –
Fax: –	FYE: February 28
Web: www.voxxintl.com	Type: Public

VOXX International Corporation (formerly Audiovox) works to be the one-stop-shop for electronics. It sells consumer electronics for communications mobile and home use and acts as an original equipment manufacturer (OEM) for car makers. Its products include automotive security devices digital picture frames HD TV antennae stereo and speaker systems portable DVD players two-way radios and universal remotes. They are marketed under such names as Acoustic Research Advent Audiovox Code-Alarm Energizer Invision Jensen Mac Audio Schwaiger and Terk. VOXX's distribution network comprises retailers distributors car dealers and other OEMs. Founded by John Shalam in 1960 VOXX went public in 1987.

	Annual Growth	02/11	02/12	02/13	02/14	02/15
Sales ($ mil.)	7.8%	561.7	707.1	835.6	809.7	757.5
Net income ($ mil.)	–	23.0	25.6	22.5	(26.6)	(0.9)
Market value ($ mil.)	1.0%	199.8	308.7	240.1	313.8	207.6
Employees	19.8%	1,020	1,238	2,100	2,100	2,100

VOYAGER ENTERTAINMENT INTERNATIONAL INC.

OTC: VEII

4483 W. Reno Ave.
Las Vegas NV 89118
Phone: 702-221-8070
Fax: 702-221-8059
Web: www.voyager-ent.com

CEO: Richard L Hannigan
CFO: –
HR: –
FYE: December 31
Type: Public

Voyager Entertainment International aims to have the world's tallest observation attractions. Modeled after the Ferris wheel the Voyager attraction will consist of 30 cabs called Orbiters that hold about 20 passengers each and revolve to a height of 600 feet for a view of the surrounding area. Plans are to have Voyager attractions in Las Vegas and Dubai. The company is seeking financing and attempting to acquire proper locations in Las Vegas and Dubai.

VRATSINAS CONSTRUCTION COMPANY

216 LOUISIANA ST
LITTLE ROCK, AR 72201-2706
Phone: 501-376-0017
Fax: –
Web: www.vccusa.com

CEO: Sam K Alley
CFO: –
HR: –
FYE: December 31
Type: Private

Malls and more — office buildings retail shopping centers theater complexes and lodging facilities — are the focus of commercial builder Vratsinas Construction Company (VCC). The company is registered and licensed in all 50 states in the US and builds and renovates large scale commercial buildings such as a hotel and mixed use property for Simon Property Group shopping malls for General Growth Properties and movie theaters for AMC Entertainment. Engineer News-Record ranks the company as one of the top 100 contractors in the US and it operates through offices in Little Rock; Irvine California; Atlanta; Phoenix; and Dallas. Chairman and CEO Gus Vratsinas founded the company in 1987.

	Annual Growth	12/06	12/07	12/07	12/11	12/12
Sales ($ mil.)	(35.2%)	–	663.7	554.6	54.7	75.5
Net income ($ mil.)	–	–	0.0	9.1	0.0	0.0
Market value ($ mil.)	–	–	–	–	–	–
Employees	–	–	–	–	–	300

VRINGO INC

NAS: VRNG

780 3rd Avenue, 12th Floor
New York, NY 10017
Phone: 212 309-7549
Fax: –
Web: www.vringoip.com

CEO: Andrew D Perlman
CFO: Anastasia Nyrkovskaya
HR: –
FYE: December 31
Type: Public

Vringo is brinnggg brinnggg bringing its video ringtones to consumer mobile phones. The upstart company is riding the next wave in mobile ringtone technology beyond just audio clips with video clips that users can upload to their phones. Subscribers of Vringo's service can browse and purchase content from its Web site which houses a library of more than 4000 video ringtones as well as tools to create customize and share them through social media networks. The company reaches subscribers through partnerships with certain mobile carriers in Armenia Malaysia Turkey and the United Arab Emirates with hopes to establish more throughout the world. Vringo filed to go public in January 2010.

	Annual Growth	12/10	12/11	12/12	12/13	12/14
Sales ($ mil.)	61.2%	0.2	0.7	0.4	1.1	1.4
Net income ($ mil.)	–	(9.9)	(7.5)	(20.8)	(52.4)	(109.7)
Market value ($ mil.)	–	–	–	–	–	–
Employees	(20.2%)	32	28	30	18	13

VSB BANCORP INC (NY)

NBB: VSBN

4142 Hylan Boulevard
Staten Island, NY 10308
Phone: 718 979-1100
Fax: –
Web: www.victorystatebank.com

CEO: Raffaele M Branca
CFO: Raffaele M Branca
HR: –
FYE: December 31
Type: Public

To the victor belongs the spoils. VSB Bancorp is the holding company for Victory State Bank which serves New York City's Staten Island from about five offices. It collects deposits from local residents and businesses offering standard products such as checking and savings accounts money market accounts and CDs. Commercial real estate business and construction loans make up almost all of the bank's loan portfolio. Victory State Bank generally does not write residential mortgages. Merton Corn CEO of the bank from its 1997 founding until his 2007 retirement owns approximately 10% of VSB.

	Annual Growth	12/10	12/11	12/12	12/13	12/14
Assets ($ mil.)	4.5%	235.3	241.8	269.7	297.1	281.0
Net income ($ mil.)	(9.3%)	1.9	1.4	1.2	1.1	1.3
Market value ($ mil.)	0.5%	21.3	19.3	18.5	20.1	21.7
Employees	(6.6%)	63	59	55	–	–

VSE CORP.

NMS: VSEC

6348 Walker Lane
Alexandria, VA 22310
Phone: 703 960-4600
Fax: 703 960-2688
Web: www.vsecorp.com

CEO: Maurice A. Gauthier
CFO: Thomas R. (Tom) Loftus
HR: –
FYE: December 31
Type: Public

VSE brings military hand-me-downs back into fashion. The company provides engineering testing and logistics services for the US Army the US Navy and other government agencies on a contract basis. VSE operates through various subsidiaries and divisions that comprise its core federal group segment (engineering logistics communications and management services) and its international group (fleet maintenance and foreign military sales). Other segments include IT energy and management consulting (technical and consulting services for civilian government) and infrastructure (engineering and construction services). VSE generates about half of its revenues from the Department of Defense (DOD).

	Annual Growth	12/10	12/11	12/12	12/13	12/14
Sales ($ mil.)	(16.3%)	866.0	618.6	546.8	471.6	424.1
Net income ($ mil.)	(4.9%)	23.7	20.6	21.3	22.9	19.4
Market value ($ mil.)	18.9%	176.9	130.1	131.3	257.3	353.1
Employees	(13.9%)	2,897	2,516	2,472	1,872	1,589

VSOFT CORPORATION

6455 E JOHNS XING STE 450
DULUTH, GA 300971559
Phone: 770-840-0097
Fax: –
Web: www.vsoftcorp.com

CEO: Murthy Veeraghanta
CFO: –
HR: Devon Hill
FYE: March 31
Type: Private

Turning real checks into virtual checks is money in the bank at VSoft Corporation. Serving primarily financial institutions the company offers check and payment processing software and imaging technologies used to scan and change paper checks into electronic images; the images effectively replace and are processed faster than paper checks. VSoft offers these technologies — teller/branch capture (for financial institution use) and remote capture products (for merchant and financial institution customer use) — to more than 1700 credit unions banks and other financial institutions around the world.

	Annual Growth	03/08	03/09	03/10	03/12	03/13
Sales ($ mil.)	(3.0%)	–	–	17.7	16.4	16.2
Net income ($ mil.)	18.7%	–	–	0.7	0.5	1.2
Market value ($ mil.)	–	–	–	–	–	–
Employees	–	–	–	–	–	85

VU1 CORPORATION

OTC: VUOC

469 7th Avenue Suite 356
New York NY 10018
Phone: 212-359-9503
Fax: 760-476-1355
Web: www.chuaochocolatier.com

CEO: –
CFO: Matthew J Devries
HR: –
FYE: December 31
Type: Public

Vu1 Corporation has a bright idea and it takes the form of a light bulb. Parting ways with existing florescent LED and incandescent light bulb technologies Vu1 (pronounced "view one") is developing a new type of light bulb that it boasts is energy efficient and mercury-free unlike florescent lights which contain trace amounts of the element. Its proprietary technology Electron Stimulated Luminescence or ESL uses cathode ray tube (CRT) technologies to produce light. (CRTs were commonly used in older-style TVs). In 2010 Vu1 received UL certification for its first product a R30 floodlight-style bulb for use in recessed ceiling lighting and subsequently began selling the bulb in the US.

VULCAN INTERNATIONAL CORPORATION

PINK SHEETS: VULC

300 Delaware Ave. Ste. 1704
Wilmington DE 19801
Phone: 302-427-5804
Fax: 202-334-4536
Web: www.washpostco.com

CEO: –
CFO: –
HR: –
FYE: December 31
Type: Public

It would be logical for Star Trek's Mr. Spock to contact Vulcan International for rubber material. The company operates through four subsidiaries one of them Vulcan Corp. manufactures rubber and foam. Its lineup includes rubber sheet stock for US shoemakers (a large customer) flooring for sports centers backing for car mats and various high-density foam products. A property management subsidiary oversees the company's commercial property three office buildings in Cincinnati. Thousands of acres of Michigan timberland are under the watch of Vulcan Timberlands. Vulcan Development manages the company's eclectic asset mix. Chairman Benjamin Gettler and his wife are major corporate stakeholders.

VULCAN MATERIALS CO (HOLDING COMPANY)

NYS: VMC

1200 Urban Center Drive
Birmingham, AL 35242
Phone: 205 298-3000
Fax: 205 298-2963
Web: www.vulcanmaterials.com

CEO: J. Thomas (Tom) Hill
CFO: John R. McPherson
HR: Larry Miller
FYE: December 31
Type: Public

The road to just about everywhere is paved with Vulcan's materials. The company is one of the largest producers of construction aggregates in the US. Vulcan produces and distributes aggregates (crushed stone gravel and sand) asphalt mix calcium and ready-mixed concrete from more than 330 facilities in about 20 states as well as the Bahamas and Mexico. Its aggregates are primarily used to build and maintain infrastructure such as highways bridges railways airports utilities and other public works projects; they're also used in residential commercial and industrial construction. Aggregates account for about 70% of Vulcan's sales.

	Annual Growth	12/10	12/11	12/12	12/13	12/14
Sales ($ mil.)	4.0%	2,558.9	2,564.6	2,567.3	2,770.7	2,994.2
Net income ($ mil.)	–	(96.5)	(70.8)	(52.6)	24.4	204.9
Market value ($ mil.)	10.3%	5,851.4	5,190.5	6,865.8	7,837.9	8,670.2
Employees	(3.9%)	7,749	7,124	6,727	6,902	6,598

VWR FUNDING INC.

100 Matsonford Rd.
Radnor PA 19087
Phone: 610-386-1700
Fax: +44-1932-224-214
Web: www.kbcat.com

CEO: Manuel Brocke-Benz
CFO: Gregory L Cowan
HR: –
FYE: December 31
Type: Private

VWR Funding has all the tools that a lab rat requires. The company through principal operating subsidiary VWR International LLC is a global distributor of scientific and technical laboratory supplies including chemicals glassware instruments protective clothing and production supplies. It also provides technical services on-site storeroom services and lab and furniture design and installation. With operations in roughly 25 countries its primary customers are research labs in North America and Europe within pharmaceutical biotech and chemical companies government agencies and universities and research institutes. VWR Funding is a portfolio company of private equity firm Madison Dearborn Partners.

VYDROTECH INC.

OTC: RNNM

4305 FM 2147 West
Horseshoe Bay TX 78657
Phone: 512-879-6293
Fax: 626-795-8090
Web: www.generalfinance.com

CEO: Don Navarro
CFO: –
HR: –
FYE: December 31
Type: Public

VydroTech (formerly Ronn Motor Company) is seeing green when it comes to automotive design and manufacturing. The company manufactures green-oriented hydrogen injection technology for engines used in both transportation and fixed platforms. Its products are installed in large diesel trucks (18-wheelers) barges tugboats and large land-based diesel generators. They help clients be compliant with government regulations and reduce diesel fuel costs and the amount of harmful gas emissions. In order to reflect its specific product focus the former Ronn Motor Company changed its name to VydroTech in 2012. Its new name stems from the first few letters in the phrase "visionary hydrogen technology."

VYSTAR CORP

NBB: VYST

2480 Briarcliff Rd, #6, Suite 159
Atlanta, GA 30329
Phone: 866 674-5238
Fax: 770 965-0162
Web: www.vytex.com

CEO: William R. Doyle
CFO: –
HR: –
FYE: December 31
Type: Public

Vystar is vying to be a health care star. The company makes Vytex a natural rubber latex product that retains the positive properties of latex (strength comfort availability good barrier) without producing the allergic reaction that plagues about 20% of health care workers and more than 70% of patients. Vytex is used in health care supplies including surgical and exam gloves probe covers catheters tubing and adhesives. Other uses include sponges balloons condoms threads and mattresses. Vystar's goods are made by Revertex Malaysia. In 2012 Vystar entered the sleep disorder market by acquiring Georgia-based SleepHealth. Vystar plans to market its foam bedding products through the company.

	Annual Growth	12/10	12/11	12/12	12/13	12/14
Sales ($ mil.)	(6.8%)	0.9	0.3	0.5	1.3	0.7
Net income ($ mil.)	–	(3.2)	(3.6)	(2.7)	(2.5)	(1.4)
Market value ($ mil.)	(50.1%)	54.8	20.6	13.7	3.4	3.4
Employees	3.9%	6	5	35	25	7

VYSTAR CREDIT UNION

4949 Blanding Blvd.	CEO: Terry R West
Jacksonville FL 32210	CFO: John H Turpish
Phone: 904-777-6000	HR: Gary Slettum
Fax: 904-908-2488	FYE: December 31
Web: www.vystarcu.org	Type: Private - Not-for-Pr

VyStar offers a galaxy of financial services from Northeastern Florida. The credit union boasts more than two dozen locations a handful of high school branches a pair of drive-thru branches and a call center in Jacksonville. It provides traditional retail banking services such as checking and savings accounts CDs credit cards home mortgages and personal loans. Its VyStar Financial Group subsidiary specializes in financial management and investment services for members and non-members alike. Real estate agency VyStar Real Estate Services and VyStar Title Agency are also part of VyStar Financial Group. Membership in VyStar Credit Union is available to all who live or work in one of 17 area counties.

W & T OFFSHORE INC

NYS: WTI

Nine Greenway Plaza, Suite 300	CEO: Tracy W. Krohn
Houston, TX 77046-0908	CFO: John D. (Danny) Gibbons
Phone: 713 626-8525	HR: –
Fax: 713 626-8527	FYE: December 31
Web: www.wtoffshore.com	Type: Public

Offshore exploration suits independent oil and natural gas acquisition exploration and production company W&T Offshore to a T. Focusing on exploiting assets in the Gulf of Mexico in 2013 the company reported proved reserves of 705.9 billion cu. ft. of natural gas equivalent. It holds 1.1 million gross acres in the Gulf of Mexico and has working interests in more than 65 fields. The company hopes to parlay its successful track record in the Gulf to generate capital for more expensive projects in deepwater (water depths in excess of 500 feet) and deep shelf (well depths in excess of 15000 feet) areas of the Gulf of Mexico. Hedging its bets it also holds onshore fields in a handful of Gulf Coast states.

	Annual Growth	12/10	12/11	12/12	12/13	12/14
Sales ($ mil.)	7.7%	705.8	971.0	874.5	984.1	948.7
Net income ($ mil.)	–	117.9	172.8	72.0	51.3	(11.7)
Market value ($ mil.)	(19.9%)	1,356.3	1,609.8	1,216.7	1,214.4	557.1
Employees	2.7%	305	310	337	333	339

W. B. DONER & COMPANY

25900 Northwestern Hwy.	CEO: David Demuth
Southfield MI 48075	CFO: Lawrence A Kempa
Phone: 248-354-9700	HR: –
Fax: 248-827-0880	FYE: February 28
Web: www.doner.com	Type: Private

Doner knows how many licks it takes to get to the center of a Tootsie Roll Pop. W. B. Doner & Company doing business as Doner is one of the largest independent advertising agencies in the US. Responsible for the famous Tootsie Roll Pop owl campaign it provides creative ad development and campaign management services along with media planning and buying. The firm also created iconic campaigns for clients such as Timex ("Takes a licking and keeps on ticking") and Klondike Bar ("What would you do for a Klondike Bar?").

W. E. AUBUCHON CO. INC.

95 AUBUCHON DR	CEO: M Marcus Moran Jr
WESTMINSTER, MA 014731470	CFO: –
Phone: 978-874-0521	HR: –
Fax: –	FYE: December 31
	Type: Private

Old houses in New England get a facelift with assistance from W.E. Aubuchon. The company operates more than 125 hardware stores throughout New England and New York as well as e-commerce site HardwareStore.com and in-store kiosks. Stores stock about 50000 products including appliances plumbing camping gear hardware housewares paint and tools. W.E. Aubuchon carries such name brands as Delta Faucet Honeywell Stanley and Weber. Store services include rug cleaner rentals propane tank filling free assembling and delivery and key cutting among many other services. Founded in 1908 by William Aubuchon a French-Canadian immigrant the company is still owned by the Aubuchon family.

	Annual Growth	12/09	12/10	12/11	12/12	12/13
Sales ($ mil.)	3.1%	–	133.6	140.5	142.7	146.3
Net income ($ mil.)	–	–	–	1.3	2.0	(3.3)
Market value ($ mil.)	–	–	–	–	–	–
Employees	–	–	–	–	–	1,252

W. H. BRAUM INC.

3000 NE 63rd St.	CEO: W Anthony Bostwick
Oklahoma City OK 73121	CFO: Mark A Godwin
Phone: 405-478-1656	HR: –
Fax: 405-475-2460	FYE: December 31
Web: www.braums.com	Type: Private

Ice cream means cold cash for Braum's. W. H. Braum operates a chain of about 280 Braum's Ice Cream and Dairy Stores in Oklahoma Texas and a handful of other states. Popular for its ice cream and other frozen treats the chain also serves breakfast items sandwiches and salads. In addition the stores sell grocery items such as milk cheese and other dairy products along with baked goods. The family-owned company has more than 10000 dairy cows and grows its own cattle feed. Family patriarch Henry Braum started the business in 1933 opening a chain of Peter Pan ice cream stores in Kansas during the 1950s. His son Bill later took over the business sold the stores and started his own retail chain in 1968.

W. K. KELLOGG FOUNDATION

1 MICHIGAN AVE E	CEO: Sterling K Speirn
BATTLE CREEK, MI 490174012	CFO: –
Phone: 269-968-1611	HR: –
Fax: –	FYE: August 31
Web: www.wkkf.org	Type: Private

Charitable grants from W.K. Kellogg Foundation are grrrrrrrrreat! Founded in 1930 by cereal industry pioneer Will Keith Kellogg the foundation provides more than $300 million in grants annually to programs focused on youth and education health food systems and rural development and philanthropy and volunteerism. About two-thirds of its grants go to initiatives in the US (mostly in Michigan Mississippi and New Mexico) although it also serves others through grants in Latin America Mexico the Caribbean Brazil and South Africa. The work of the W.K. Kellogg Foundation is supported by a related trust; together they have assets of more than $9 billion — mainly in Kellogg Company stock.

	Annual Growth	08/08	08/09	08/11	08/12	08/13
Assets ($ mil.)	(0.8%)	–	442.7	465.1	442.3	428.5
Net income ($ mil.)	–	–	–	(13.1)	(106.6)	92.0
Market value ($ mil.)	–	–	–	–	–	–
Employees	–	–	–	–	–	210

W. L. BUTLER CONSTRUCTION INC.

204 FRANKLIN ST
REDWOOD CITY, CA 940631929
Phone: 209-983-4890
Fax: -
Web: www.wlbutler.com

CEO: William L Butler
CFO: -
HR: -
FYE: December 31
Type: Private

W. L. Butler Construction is building up its reputation in the western region. The general contractor caters to customers needing commercial and light industrial construction services in Arizona California Colorado Idaho Montana Nevada and Washington. W. L. Butler Construction also has the capability to complete electrical and HVAC services. Projects include car dealerships retail centers medical offices industrial warehouses corporate headquarters and not-for-profit facilities. Commercial clients include Aetna Life Insurance Cisco Systems Home Depot Target and Walgreen's. W. L. Butler Construction was founded in 1975 by CEO William Butler as a residential remodeling contracting operation.

	Annual Growth	12/06	12/07	12/08	12/09	12/10
Sales ($ mil.)	-	-	-	(553.3)	160.5	129.5
Net income ($ mil.)	862.9%	-	-	0.0	2.6	1.5
Market value ($ mil.)	-	-	-	-	-	-
Employees	-	-	-	-	-	150

W.C. BRADLEY CO.

1017 Front Ave.
Columbus GA 31902
Phone: 706-571-6056
Fax: 706-571-6084
Web: www.wcbradley.com

CEO: Marc R Olivie
CFO: William Yates
HR: -
FYE: December 31
Type: Private

Without the airy outdoors W.C. Bradley would suffocate. The company's Char-Broil division is a leading producers of outdoor barbecue gas and electric grills. In addition W.C. Bradley makes Thermos-brand grills; Lamplight Farms oil lamps Tiki torches and scented candles; and Lew's Martin Quantum Van Staal and Zebco fishing gear. The company's wares are sold to major retailers worldwide including Sears Roebuck Home Depot Kmart and Wal-Mart and through its own Web sites. It also runs a PGA Tour Stop shop in Florida. Founded in 1885 by William C. Bradley the company is run by the family's fourth generation; chairman Steve Butler is the nephew of Bradley's grandson.

W.P. CAREY INC

NYS: WPC

50 Rockefeller Plaza
New York, NY 10020
Phone: 212 492-1100
Fax: -
Web: www.wpcarey.com

CEO: Mark J. DeCesaris
CFO: Hisham A. Kader
HR: -
FYE: December 31
Type: Public

Need help managing your property portfolio? Keep calm and Carey on. W. P. Carey invests in and manages commercial real estate including office distribution retail and industrial facilities. The company owns more than 1000 properties mainly in the US and Europe and manages properties for several non-traded real estate investment trusts (REITs). Its management portfolio totals some $15 billion. W. P. Carey typically acquires properties and then leases them back to the sellers/occupants on a long-term basis. It also provides build-to-suit financing for investors worldwide. W. P. Carey is converting to a REIT a corporate structure that comes with tax benefits and more flexibilty in investing in real estate.

	Annual Growth	12/10	12/11	12/12	12/13	12/14
Sales ($ mil.)	34.9%	273.9	336.4	374.0	489.9	906.2
Net income ($ mil.)	34.2%	74.0	139.1	62.1	98.9	239.8
Market value ($ mil.)	22.3%	3,255.4	4,259.4	5,425.7	6,382.9	7,293.2
Employees	12.5%	170	212	216	251	272

W.S. BADCOCK CORPORATION

205 NW 2ND ST
MULBERRY, FL 338602405
Phone: 863-425-4921
Fax: -
Web: www.badcock.com

CEO: -
CFO: -
HR: Lori Walsh
FYE: June 30
Type: Private

W.S. Badcock furnishes homes down in Dixie and beyond. As one of the largest privately-owned furniture retailers in the US the company sells furniture for every room in the house. It sells its furniture and accessories through more than 300 stores that operate under the banner names Badcock Home Furnishing Centers and Badcock &more. Aside from its e-commerce site Badcock's stores network extends to nearly 10 southeastern states. Stores also carry appliances lawn equipment electronics mattresses rugs bedding lighting wall art and other decorative accessories. The company was founded by Henry S. Badcock in 1904 as a general mercantile store. Today it is in its fourth generation of family management.

	Annual Growth	06/10	06/11	06/12	06/13	06/14
Sales ($ mil.)	6.3%	-	431.3	455.9	463.2	518.6
Net income ($ mil.)	(1.6%)	-	-	12.1	7.0	11.7
Market value ($ mil.)	-	-	-	-	-	-
Employees	-	-	-	-	-	1,000

WABASH COLLEGE

301 W WABASH AVE STE A
CRAWFORDSVILLE, IN 479332484
Phone: 765-361-6100
Fax: -
Web: www.wabash.edu

CEO: -
CFO: Larry Griffith
HR: -
FYE: June 30
Type: Private

Wabash College is a private all-male liberal arts school that confers Bachelor of Arts degrees in 22 majors. Engineering programs are offered in conjunction with Purdue University Washington University in St. Louis and Columbia University. Other programs range from art and biochemistry to Latin and philosophy as well as economics music psychology and religion. With an enrollment of about 900 students Wabash College is an independent and non-sectarian college founded in 1832. The school is one of the few remaining all-male colleges in the US.

	Annual Growth	06/09	06/10	06/11	06/12	06/13
Sales ($ mil.)	(2.4%)	-	68.4	77.4	69.0	63.7
Net income ($ mil.)	-	-	-	18.3	4.8	(0.4)
Market value ($ mil.)	-	-	-	-	-	-
Employees	-	-	-	-	-	225

WABASH NATIONAL CORP.

NYS: WNC

1000 Sagamore Parkway South
Lafayette, IN 47905
Phone: 765 771-5300
Fax: -
Web: www.wabashnational.com

CEO: Richard J. Giromini
CFO: Jeffery L. Taylor
HR: -
FYE: December 31
Type: Public

The teaser trailer for trailer industry giant Great Dane is Wabash National. Wabash is one of North America's top manufacturers of dry freight and refrigerated vans flatbed and drop deck trailers and intermodal equipment. The trailers are marketed under such brands as DuraPlate ArcticLite and RoadRailer via a network of factory-direct sales representatives independent dealers and factory-owned retail outlets. Customers have included Averitt Express FedEx and Swift. The company operates through subsidiaries Transcraft Corporation (flatbed and drop deck trailers) and Wabash National Trailer Centers (retail distributor of trailers and aftermarket parts). Wabash makes most of its sales in the US.

	Annual Growth	12/10	12/11	12/12	12/13	12/14
Sales ($ mil.)	30.6%	640.4	1,187.2	1,461.9	1,635.7	1,863.3
Net income ($ mil.)	-	(141.8)	15.0	105.6	46.5	60.9
Market value ($ mil.)	1.1%	817.6	540.9	618.9	852.1	852.8
Employees	29.7%	1,800	2,600	4,400	4,400	5,100

WACCAMAW BANKSHARES INC.

NASDAQ: WBNK

110 N. J.K. Powell Blvd.
Whiteville NC 28472
Phone: 910-641-0044
Fax: 910-642-2280
Web: www.waccamawbank.com

CEO: –
CFO: –
HR: –
FYE: December 31
Type: Public

Waccamaw Bancshares is the holding company for the Waccamaw Bank which operates about 15 branches in the coastal Carolina region. The bank provides traditional products such as checking and savings accounts and IRAs. It primarily uses funds from deposits to write commercial loans and mortgages including business loans construction loans and land development loans. Hit by an increase in bad loans the company is working with regulators to raise its capital holdings. It is also tightening up its lending practices. In order to raise capital Waccamaw Bankshares is selling 11 branches to First Bancorp.

WACHOVIA PREFERRED FUNDING CORP

NYS: WNA PR

90 South 7th Street, 13th Floor
Minneapolis, MN 55402
Phone: 855 825-1437
Fax: –
Web: www.wellsfargo.com

CEO: Scott C Arves
CFO: Mark J Emmen
HR: –
FYE: December 31
Type: Public

Truckload carrier Transport America delivers the goods on time for manufacturers and retailers in the US and Mexico. Long- and short-haul freight carried by Transport America includes department store merchandise furniture and recreational equipment as well as consumer grocery industrial and paper products. The company operates a fleet of about 1500 tractors and 4400 trailers; its trailer inventory is made up primarily of standard 53-foot dry vans but also includes some refrigerated units. The company also provides third-party logistics services. Owned by investment firm Goldner Hawn Johnson & Morrison Transport America filed to go public in late 2013.

	Annual Growth	12/08	12/09	12/10	12/11	12/12
Assets ($ mil.)	(7.0%)	18,836.9	18,410.1	18,178.1	13,534.4	14,068.8
Net income ($ mil.)	(6.7%)	767.3	867.7	769.4	795.6	581.9
Market value ($ mil.)	7.0%	2,016.0	2,223.0	2,559.0	2,582.0	2,641.0
Employees	(2.4%)	11	11	10	10	10

WACKENHUT SERVICES INCORPORATED

7121 Fairway Dr. Ste. 301
Palm Beach Gardens FL 33418-37
Phone: 561-472-0600
Fax: 561-472-3679
Web: www.wsihq.com

CEO: Paul P Donahue
CFO: Laura Thomas
HR: –
FYE: December 31
Type: Subsidiary

Wackenhut Services Incorporated (WSI) provides safety and security services. Divisions include fire and emergency services facilities management de-mining and ordnance clearance as well as canine weapons remediation training and armed and unarmed security services. The company also operates a Homeland Security division that provides border security information analysis and emergency response for situations involving chemical agents biological warfare and weapons of mass destruction. WSI was founded in 1960; it operates as a subsidiary of G4S Secure Solutions (USA) (formerly the Wackenhut Corp.) itself a subsidiary of UK-based G4S.

WADA FARMS MARKETING GROUP LLC

2155 PROVIDENCE WAY
IDAHO FALLS, ID 834044951
Phone: 208-542-2898
Fax: –
Web: www.wadafarms.com

CEO: –
CFO: –
HR: –
FYE: December 31
Type: Private

The Wada folks have heard absolutely all the Mr. Potato Head jokes known to mankind; still they press resolutely on growing packing and supplying Idaho potatoes all of us meat-and-potatoes folks. And in addition to everyone's favorite starchy tuber Wada Farms Potatoes does the same with sweet potatoes and onions. It also offers value-added items such as Easy-Bakers and Easy-Steamers — potatoes packaged in special plastic that can be cooked right in their packaging. The Idaho company cultivates more than 30000 acres of farmland and operates a 140000-sq.-ft. processing facility. Wada's customers include retail food food wholesaler and foodservice companies throughout the US.

	Annual Growth	12/09	12/10	12/11	12/12	12/13
Sales ($ mil.)	6.3%	–	150.9	201.7	165.8	181.4
Net income ($ mil.)	22.6%	–	–	2.0	1.9	3.1
Market value ($ mil.)	–	–	–	–	–	–
Employees		–	–	–	–	30

WADDELL & REED FINANCIAL, INC.

NYS: WDR

6300 Lamar Avenue
Overland Park, KS 66202
Phone: 913 236-2000
Fax: –
Web: www.waddell.com

CEO: Henry J. (Hank) Herrmann
CFO: Brent K. Bloss
HR: –
FYE: December 31
Type: Public

Waddell & Reed Financial is one of the oldest mutual fund managers in the US. Subsidiaries administer and distribute about 80 mutual funds under the names Waddell & Reed Advisors Funds (the company's longest-running and largest fund complex) Ivy Funds (administered by Ivy Investment Management) and Waddell & Reed InvestEd Portfolios; they also manage accounts for institutional investors and private clients. The firm sells annuities and insurance through agreements with third-party providers. Waddell & Reed has 160-plus registered offices nationwide usually in small cities and rural areas. Founded in 1937 the firm has more than $110 million of assets under management.

	Annual Growth	12/10	12/11	12/12	12/13	12/14
Sales ($ mil.)	11.2%	1,044.9	1,195.2	1,173.8	1,370.4	1,597.8
Net income ($ mil.)	18.9%	157.0	175.5	151.0	250.3	313.3
Market value ($ mil.)	9.0%	2,952.1	2,072.1	2,912.8	5,447.5	4,167.6
Employees	2.6%	1,485	1,616	1,656	1,525	1,648

WAGEWORKS INC

NYS: WAGE

1100 Park Place, 4th Floor
San Mateo, CA 94403
Phone: 650 577-5200
Fax: –
Web: www.wageworks.com

CEO: Joseph L. (Joe) Jackson
CFO: Colm M. Callan
HR: May O'Neal
FYE: December 31
Type: Public

WageWorks wants to make administration of tax-advantaged spending accounts easier. The company helps some 5000 clients — including more than 50% of the Fortune 100 companies — implement and manage flexible spending accounts used for health wellness and dependent care as well as commuting and tuition expenses. The WageWorks SaaS (software as a service) platform also can be used for health savings accounts and other health care reimbursement programs. Its online tools provide real-time visibility into account activity and the ability to work with any combination of insurance carrier or financial institution. Founded in 2000 WageWorks operates through about 10 offices across the US. It went public in 2012.

	Annual Growth	12/10	12/11	12/12	12/13	12/14
Sales ($ mil.)	23.5%	115.0	135.6	177.3	219.3	267.8
Net income ($ mil.)	–	(17.3)	33.3	10.5	21.7	18.2
Market value ($ mil.)	90.5%	–	–	631.5	2,108.9	2,290.9
Employees	21.0%	–	945	1,007	1,200	1,675

WAGNER INDUSTRIES INC.

1201 E 12TH AVE
NORTH KANSAS CITY, MO 641164306
Phone: 816-474-1110
Fax: –
Web: www.wagnerlogistics.com

CEO: John E Wagner Sr
CFO: Kevin Service
HR: –
FYE: December 31
Type: Private

When freight needs to stop between origin and destination Wagner Industries can offer the hospitality of its distribution facilities. The company maintains-, about-, 4-, million sq. ft. of warehouse space largely in the Kansas City metropolitan area but also in several states in the southeastern and western US.-, Overall the company operates-, a dozen distribution centers. In addition to warehousing and distribution Wagner Industries offers packaging and transportation management services. Customers include companies from the consumer products paper and retail industries. Owned by the Wagner family including company president John Wagner Jr. Wagner Industries was founded in 1946.

	Annual Growth	12/04	12/05	12/06	12/07	12/08
Sales ($ mil.)	(8.3%)	–	58.7	51.4	52.0	45.2
Net income ($ mil.)	–	–	–	0.3	40.8	(0.3)
Market value ($ mil.)	–	–	–	–	–	–
Employees	–	–	–	–	–	300

WAKE FOREST UNIVERSITY BAPTIST MEDICAL CENTER

MEDICAL CENTER BLVD
WINSTON SALEM, NC 271570001
Phone: 336-748-8843
Fax: –
Web: www.wakehealth.edu

CEO: Dr John D McConnell
CFO: –
HR: –
FYE: June 30
Type: Private

Wake Forest University Baptist Medical Center (WFUBMC) promotes health in the thick of tobacco country. The not-for-profit system operates Wake Forest University Health Sciences with its School of Medicine Wake Forest University Physicians 16 dialysis centers and Piedmont Triad Research Park. It also operates the North Carolina Baptist Hospital with facilities devoted to geriatrics cancer pediatrics and more. The system has about 20 subsidiary or affiliate hospitals and operates about 120 regional outreach activities from satellite clinics to health fairs. WFUBMC offers rehab skilled nursing and home health services; it also has a unit that coordinates special services for international patients.

	Annual Growth	06/07	06/08	06/09	06/10	06/13
Sales ($ mil.)	–	–	(1,236.5)	0.2	758.4	84.9
Net income ($ mil.)	–	–	–	(0.0)	12.4	74.2
Market value ($ mil.)	–	–	–	–	–	–
Employees	–	–	–	–	–	11,000

WAKEFERN FOOD CORP.

5000 RIVERSIDE DR
KEASBEY, NJ 088321209
Phone: 908-527-3300
Fax: –
Web: www.wakefern.com

CEO: Joseph Colalillo
CFO: Douglas Wille
HR: –
FYE: September 28
Type: Private

Grocery stores getting supplies from this co-op may be on the "Rite" track. Wakefern Food is the largest member-owned wholesale distribution cooperative in the US supplying groceries and other merchandise to more than 250 supermarkets under the ShopRite and The Fresh Grocer banners in New Jersey New York Connecticut Delaware Maryland Pennsylvania and Virginia. It also operates more than 50 PriceRite stores in these states plus Rhode Island and Massachusetts. Beyond supplying its member-owned stores Wakefern distributes products to other supermarkets across the northeastern US and Bermuda. Founded by seven grocers in 1946 the coop now boasts 50 members 70000-plus employees and over $15 billion in annual sales.

	Annual Growth	09/07	09/08*	10/11*	09/12	09/13
Sales ($ mil.)	6.4%	–	8,396.7	10,326.0	11,010.2	11,456.0
Net income ($ mil.)	(87.8%)	–	–	5.0	5.0	0.1
Market value ($ mil.)	–	–	–	–	–	–
Employees	–	–	–	–	–	3,500

*Fiscal year change

WAKEMED

3000 NEW BERN AVE G100
RALEIGH, NC 27610-1231
Phone: 919-350-8000
Fax: –
Web: www.wakemed.org

CEO: Donald R Gintzig
CFO: Michael De Vaughn
HR: –
FYE: September 30
Type: Private

If you wake up in a hospital in Wake County North Carolina you may be at one of WakeMed health system's facilities. WakeMed is a network of medical centers including two hospitals outpatient and emergency clinics rehabilitation facilities skilled nursing centers laboratories physicians' offices and home care service agencies. Its hospitals the WakeMed Raleigh Campus and the WakeMed Cary Hospital include specialty divisions such as heart care stroke trauma critical care diabetes asthma and children's and women's centers. Combined its facilities offer about 870 beds. Founded in 1961 WakeMed also conducts research and medical training programs.

	Annual Growth	09/05	09/06	09/07	09/08	09/09
Sales ($ mil.)	4.6%	–	771.8	780.6	837.0	883.8
Net income ($ mil.)	–	–	77.9	49.3	12.8	0.0
Market value ($ mil.)	–	–	–	–	–	–
Employees	–	–	–	–	–	7,933

WAL-MART STORES, INC.

NYS: WMT

702 S.W. 8th Street
Bentonville, AR 72716
Phone: 479 273-4000
Fax: –
Web: www.walmart.com

CEO: Gregory S. (Greg) Foran
CFO: Michael P. Dastugue
HR: Bill Clark
FYE: January 31
Type: Public

Wal-Mart Stores is an irresistible (or at least unavoidable) retail force that has yet to meet any immovable objects. Bigger than Europe's Carrefour Metro AG and Tesco combined it's the world's #1 retailer with some 2.2 million employees. In the US Wal-Mart operates more than 5160 stores including about 4400 Wal-Mart stores and 650 Sam's Club warehouses and a growing number of smaller format stores. The company's faster growing international division (28% of sales) numbers more than 6100 locations; Wal-Mart is the #1 retailer in Canada and Mexico and has operations in Asia (where it owns a 95% stake in Japanese retailer SEIYU) Africa Europe and Latin America.

	Annual Growth	01/11	01/12	01/13	01/14	01/15
Sales ($ mil.)	3.6%	421,849.0	446,950.0	469,162.0	476,294.0	485,651.0
Net income ($ mil.)	(0.0%)	16,389.0	15,699.0	16,999.0	16,022.0	16,363.0
Market value ($ mil.)	–	0.0	0.0	0.0	0.0	0.0
Employees	1.2%	2,100,000	2,200,000	2,200,000	2,200,000	2,200,000

WALBRIDGE ALDINGER COMPANY

777 Woodward Ave. Ste. 300
Detroit MI 48226
Phone: 313-963-8000
Fax: 313-963-8150
Web: www.walbridge.com

CEO: John Rakolta Jr
CFO: Vincent Deangelis
HR: –
FYE: December 31
Type: Private

The Motor City has been home to Motown Madonna and one Walbridge Aldinger. The US construction company provides construction management design/build and general contracting services for industrial commercial and government facilities. It's a major builder of airports and steel and nonferrous metal plants in the US. Through different divisions it also offers specialty contracting services in the areas of structural concrete equipment installation and facilities management. Although most of its work is done in the US it also has operations and projects in Canada the Middle East and Latin America. Founded in 1916 the business is privately owned and part of The Walbridge Group family of companies.

WALKER & DUNLOP INC

NYS: WD

7501 Wisconsin Avenue, Suite 1200E
Bethesda, MD 20814
Phone: 301 215-5500
Fax: –
Web: www.walkerdunlop.com

CEO: William M. (Willy) Walker
CFO: Stephen P. Theobald
HR: Tia Price
FYE: December 31
Type: Public

When it comes to its commercial real estate loans Walker & Dunlop has the government on its side. The company provides commercial real estate financial services — mainly multifamily loans for apartments health care properties and student housing — to real estate owners and developers across the US. It originates and sells its products (e.g. mortgages supplemental financing construction loans and mezzanine loans) primarily through government-sponsored enterprises (GSEs) like Fannie Mae and Freddie Mac as well as through HUD. To a lesser extent the company originates loans for insurance companies banks and institutional investors.

	Annual Growth	12/10	12/11	12/12	12/13	12/14
Sales ($ mil.)	31.2%	121.8	152.4	256.8	319.0	360.8
Net income ($ mil.)	58.1%	8.2	34.9	33.8	41.5	51.4
Market value ($ mil.)	14.8%	321.1	399.7	530.2	514.6	558.2
Employees	31.2%	157	189	420	402	465

WALKER DIE CASTING INC.

1125 HIGGS RD
LEWISBURG, TN 370914408
Phone: 931-359-6206
Fax: –
Web: www.walkerdiecasting.com

CEO: –
CFO: –
HR: –
FYE: December 31
Type: Private

Walker Die Casting doesn't leave things to chance. The company is a producer of high-pressure aluminum castings for industrial applications. Walker Die Casting provides custom die fabrication services to customers in the automotive appliance lawn and garden marine and power tool industries. Products include parts such as adapter plates brackets oil pans gear cases and housings for transmissions engines axles and flywheels. Walker Die Casting also offers product design finishing testing machining and warehousing services. The company was founded in 1958 by Robert Walker.

	Annual Growth	12/09	12/10	12/11	12/12	12/13
Sales ($ mil.)	0.0%	–	54.9	126.9	54.9	54.9
Net income ($ mil.)	–	–	–	0.0	0.0	0.0
Market value ($ mil.)	–	–	–	–	–	–
Employees	–	–	–	–	–	655

WALKER MAGNETICS GROUP

Rockdale St.
Worcester MA 01606 1921
Phone: 508-853-3232
Fax: 508-852-8649
Web: www.walkermagnet.com

CEO: –
CFO: Debra Krikorian
HR: Allison Picard
FYE: December 31
Type: Private

Polar opposites attract profits at Walker Magnetics Group. The company custom designs and manufactures a vast line of magnetic tools for work-holding material handling and separation applications. From electromagnetic chucks to lifting devices recycling and separation equipment the company caters to just about every industry (textiles to transformers and fishing boats) that uses steel. The company's Canadian operation even built the world's largest (88-ton) suspended electromagnet as certified by the Guinness Book of World Records. Its magnetic conveying systems are widely used by makers of cans and canned goods. Operations reach 190 countries with manufacturing and R&D sites in the US Canada and Europe.

WALSH BROTHERS INCORPORATED

210 COMMERCIAL ST
BOSTON, MA 021091463
Phone: 617-878-4800
Fax: –
Web: www.walshbrothers.com

CEO: –
CFO: –
HR: –
FYE: December 31
Type: Private

This pair of Boston brothers has been building Beantown for more than a century. Walsh Brothers Incorporated a construction management and contracting company has worked on such iconic projects as Boston's Fenway Park and Faneuil Hall. The firm specializes in building cultural educational medical and research facilities throughout New England. It also offers historic renovation services and has refurbished places such as the Boston Symphony Orchestra and New England Conservatory of Music. Clients have included Harvard University Dana-Faber Cancer Institute Amgen Novartis and Proctor & Gamble. Founded in 1901 by brothers James and Thomas Walsh the company is now owned and led by the Walsh family.

	Annual Growth	12/05	12/06	12/07	12/08	12/09
Sales ($ mil.)	3.3%	–	–	383.1	545.8	408.4
Net income ($ mil.)	43001.7%	–	–	0.0	9.2	6.3
Market value ($ mil.)	–	–	–	–	–	–
Employees	–	–	–	–	–	–

WALSWORTH PUBLISHING COMPANY INC.

306 N. Kansas Ave.
Marceline MO 64658-2105
Phone: 660-376-3543
Fax: 660-258-7798
Web: www.walsworthyearbooks.com

CEO: Don O Walsworth
CFO: –
HR: –
FYE: December 31
Type: Private

What's it worth to get your yearbook published? Walsworth Publishing knows. Best known for publishing high school yearbooks Walsworth also provides commercial printing for specialty publications including textbooks cookbooks encyclopedias and travel guides. The company has printing facilities in Missouri and Michigan. Walsworth's additional offerings include Online Design a comprehensive Web-based yearbook creation tool and ClassScene a media-sharing website devoted specifically to school communities. Owned and led by the Walsworth family the company was established in 1937 by three Walsworth brothers (Don Ed and Bill) to print playbills.

WALTER ENERGY, INC.

NBB: WLTG Q

3000 Riverchase Galleria, Suite 1700
Birmingham, AL 35244
Phone: 205 745-2000
Fax: –
Web: www.walterenergy.com

CEO: Walter J Scheller III
CFO: William G Harvey
HR: Kelth M Shull
FYE: December 31
Type: Public

Walter Energy has renewed energy for exploiting natural resources. Its subsidiaries include Jim Walter Resources (coal production) and Walter Coke (foundry and furnace coke). Its primary business is the mining and exporting of hard coking coal for the steel industry through its US Operations segment which accounts for more than 70% of Walter Energy's total sales. The company also develops also produces thermal coal anthracite metallurgical coke and coal bed methane gas (found in coal seams). Formerly a diversified company that included water products homebuilding and financing units Walter Energy has divested itself of all but its natural resources and energy businesses. It declared bankruptcy in 2015.

	Annual Growth	12/10	12/11	12/12	12/13	12/14
Sales ($ mil.)	(3.0%)	1,587.7	2,571.4	2,399.9	1,860.6	1,407.3
Net income ($ mil.)	–	385.8	349.2	(1,060.4)	(359.0)	(470.6)
Market value ($ mil.)	(67.8%)	9,201.7	4,359.0	2,582.6	1,197.0	99.3
Employees	6.3%	2,100	4,200	4,100	3,600	2,680

WALTER INVESTMENT MANAGEMENT CORP

NYS: WAC

3000 Bayport Drive, Suite 1100	CEO: Denmar J. Dixon
Tampa, FL 33607	CFO: Gary L. Tillett
Phone: 813-421-7600	HR: –
Fax: –	FYE: December 31
Web: www.walterinvestment.com	Type: Public

Walter Investment Management does its best to collect from the credit-challenged. The firm owns and services residential mortgages (particularly those of the subprime and nonconforming variety) for itself as well as for government sponsored entities government agencies third-party securitization trusts and other credit owners. Operating through subsidiaries Walter Mortgage Company; Hanover Capital; Marix Servicing; Ditech; and third-party credit servicer Green Tree Walter Investment Management services two million residential loan accounts with unpaid balances of $256 billion making it one of the 10 largest mortgage servicers in the US. The firm also originates residential loans including reverse loans.

	Annual Growth	12/10	12/11	12/12	12/13	12/14
Assets ($ mil.)	77.9%	1,895.5	4,093.6	10,978.2	17,387.5	18,992.0
Net income ($ mil.)	–	37.1	(69.3)	(22.1)	253.5	(110.3)
Market value ($ mil.)	(2.1%)	676.5	773.5	1,622.4	1,333.5	622.6
Employees	109.3%	349	2,600	3,900	6,400	6,700

WALTON ELECTRIC MEMBERSHIP CORPORATION

842 HIGHWAY 78 NW	CEO: D Ronnie Lee
MONROE, GA 306554475	CFO: Marsha L Shumate
Phone: 770-267-2505	HR: –
Fax: –	FYE: December 31
Web: www.waltonemc.com	Type: Private

Good night John-Boy. This Walton family serves more than 118400 residential agricultural commercial and industrial customers in northeastern Georgia. The Walton Electric Membership Corporation (Walton EMC) operates 6840 miles of power lines spanning across all or portions of ten counties (Athens-Clarke Barrow DeKalb Greene Gwinnett Morgan Newton Oconee Rockdale and Walton). Subsidiary Walton EMC Natural Gas competes in the state's deregulated retail gas supply market and has about 64000 customers. Other operations include security systems installation and monitoring appliance sales and rebates and outdoor lighting services.

	Annual Growth	12/06	12/07	12/08	12/09	12/13
Sales ($ mil.)	2.3%	–	212.6	215.8	227.1	243.8
Net income ($ mil.)	–	–	–	17.3	6.2	0.0
Market value ($ mil.)	–	–	–	–	–	–
Employees	–	–	–	–	–	273

WALTON SIGNAGE CORPORATION

3419 E. Commerce	CEO: –
San Antonio TX 78220	CFO: –
Phone: 210-886-0644	HR: –
Fax: +972-3-693-6328	FYE: December 31
Web: www.credit-suisse.com/il	Type: Private

Big stores need big signs. That's where Walton Signage comes in. The commercial signage maker designs and installs storefront streetside and interior signs for major US retailers and leading brands including Old Navy 24 Hour Fitness Verizon and Wells Fargo. Walton Signage's signs are for sale or lease and the company oversees all phases of a project including permitting site surveying sign design manufacturing shipping and installation. Its services also include mass re-branding capable of rolling out hundreds of signs both domestically and abroad under a newly designed corporate identity. Walton Signage was founded in 1980.

WAR MEMORIAL HOSPITAL INC.

1 HEALTHY WAY	CEO: –
BERKELEY SPRINGS, WV 254117463	CFO: Christine Lowman
Phone: 304-258-1234	HR: Helen Miller
Fax: –	FYE: December 31
Web: www.valleyhealthlink.com	Type: Private

|Morgan County War Memorial Hospital provides a wide range of inpatient and outpatient medical services including acute emergency and long-term health services for the residents of Morgan County West Virginia and surrounding areas. The not-for-profit hospital has about 25 beds as well as a 16-bed long-term care unit. War Memorial was founded in 1934 as a treatment center for post-paralysis care.

	Annual Growth	12/09	12/10	12/11	12/12	12/13
Sales ($ mil.)	14.1%	–	14.5	25.4	17.4	21.6
Net income ($ mil.)	(83.1%)	–	–	23.1	(1.2)	0.7
Market value ($ mil.)	–	–	–	–	–	–
Employees	–	–	–	–	–	150

WARBURG PINCUS LLC

450 Lexington Ave.	CEO: –
New York NY 10017	CFO: Timothy J Curt
Phone: 212-878-0600	HR: –
Fax: 212-878-9351	FYE: December 31
Web: www.warburgpincus.com	Type: Private

Infusions of cash from Warburg Pincus keep companies in the pink (and in the black). The partner-owned firm which has stakes in more than 100 companies worldwide participates in venture capital investments growth capital deals leveraged buyouts and recapitalizations. An active investor the company usually holds its stakes for five to seven years. It focuses on a range of industries with prominent holdings in such sectors as health care communications energy media technology financial services and consumer goods. The firm has more than $30 billion in assets under management.

WARD TRUCKING LLC

1436 WARD TRUCKING DR	CEO: –
ALTOONA, PA 166027110	CFO: –
Phone: 814-944-0803	HR: –
Fax: –	FYE: December 31
Web: www.wardtrucking.com	Type: Private

Less-than-truckload (LTL) carrier Ward Trucking operates primarily in the northeastern and mid-Atlantic US. (LTL carriers consolidate freight from multiple shippers into a single truckload.) In addition to its LTL business the company offers full truckload and logistics services through the Ward Transport & Logistics brand name. Ward Trucking operates a fleet of about 450 tractors 60 trucks and 1180 trailers from a network of terminals stretching from New York to Illinois. William W. Ward founded the company in 1931 to haul freight from central Pennsylvania to New York City. Ward Trucking is run by members of the Ward family.

	Annual Growth	12/09	12/10	12/11	12/12	12/13
Sales ($ mil.)	0.6%	–	137.6	150.2	149.5	140.0
Net income ($ mil.)	(57.5%)	–	–	10.9	1.2	2.0
Market value ($ mil.)	–	–	–	–	–	–
Employees	–	–	–	–	–	1,057

WARNER MUSIC GROUP CORP.

75 Rockefeller Plaza
New York NY 10019
Phone: 212-275-2000
Fax: 212-757-3985
Web: www.wmg.com

CEO: Stephen Cooper
CFO: Eric Levin
HR: –
FYE: September 30
Type: Private

These records were made to be listened to not broken. Warner Music Group (WMG) is one of the world's largest recording companies ranking #3 in terms of US market share (behind Universal Music Group and Sony Music Entertainment). It operates through two businesses: Recorded Music and Music Publishing. Its Recorded Music catalog includes best-selling albums The Eagles: Their Greatest Hits 1971-1975 and Led Zeppelin IV. Its Music Publishing business holds more than one million copyrights from some 65000 songwriters. In mid-2011 WMG was acquired by diversified business group Access Industries.

WARRANTECH CORPORATION

2200 Hwy. 121 Ste. 100
Bedford TX 76021
Phone: 817-785-6601
Fax: 800-723-1497
Web: www.warrantech.com

CEO: –
CFO: Steve Knapp
HR: –
FYE: December 31
Type: Subsidiary

So you passed on that extended warranty? Well don't come crying to Warrantech when your computer goes on the fritz. Warrantech provides extended warranty services and service contracts to distributors retailers and manufacturers of such items as automobiles automotive components appliances consumer electronics power tools recreational vehicles heavy machinery office equipment fitness equipment lawn and garden equipment and computers and peripherals. Contracts range in duration from several months to several years and are underwritten by parent company AmTrust Financial Services. Active mainly in the US and Canada Warrantech typically sells more than one million service contracts per year.

WARREN EQUITIES INC.

27 Warren Way
Providence RI 02905
Phone: 401-781-9900
Fax: 401-461-7160
Web: www.warreneq.com

CEO: August Schiesser
CFO: John Dziedzic
HR: –
FYE: May 31
Type: Private

Warren Equities fills car tanks and stomachs in the US Northeast. The holding company sells fuel and groceries from more than 200 XtraMart brand service stations and convenience stores in nine states from Maine to Virginia. Its Warex Terminals unit (which has a network of long term supply arangements with terminals throughout the Northeast) is one of the largest independent distributors of heating oil gasoline and diesel fuel in Connecticut New Jersey New York and Pennsylvania. Drake Petroleum distributes gasoline and diesel in New England. Drake offers petroleum products from a wide range of branded suppliers including BP CITGO Exxon Mobil Gulf Shell Sunoco and Valero.

WARREN RESOURCES INC (MD)

NMS: WRES

1114 Avenue of the Americas
New York, NY 10036
Phone: 720 403-8125
Fax: –
Web: www.warrenresources.com

CEO: James A. Watt
CFO: Frank T. Smith
HR: –
FYE: December 31
Type: Public

Warren Resources believes that its heavy investment in oil and gas is warranted. The independent exploration and production company is focused on waterflood oil recovery programs in tar fields in California's Los Angeles Basin and the development of coalbed methane natural gas properties located in the Washakie Basin in the Greater Green River Basin in southwestern Wyoming. Warren Resources also owns oil and gas properties in New Mexico and Texas. In 2012 the company reported proved reserves of 51.2 billion cu. ft. of natural gas ans 24.9 million barrels of oil.

	Annual Growth	12/10	12/11	12/12	12/13	12/14
Sales ($ mil.)	14.3%	88.3	103.4	121.8	128.8	150.7
Net income ($ mil.)	4.2%	20.4	21.6	15.5	30.4	24.0
Market value ($ mil.)	(22.7%)	365.0	263.3	226.9	253.6	130.0
Employees	11.2%	57	57	67	62	87

WARREN RURAL ELECTRIC COOPERATIVE CORPORATION

951 FAIRVIEW AVE
BOWLING GREEN, KY 421014937
Phone: 270-793-9857
Fax: –
Web: www.wrecc.com

CEO: W Scott Ramsey
CFO: Roxanne Gray
HR: –
FYE: June 30
Type: Private

This Warren needs no commission just a cooperative in order to deliver electric results to the people. Warren Rural Electric Cooperative Corporation (Warren RECC) provides its member customers with electricity security systems and surge suppression equipment as well as with floodlighting and street lighting. It offers propane through non-affiliated Propane Energy Partners. The co-op serves more than 55300 customers in an eight-county service area (Barren Butler Edmonson Grayson Logan Ohio Simpson and Warren counties) in rural south-central Kentucky. Warren RECC is affiliated with the Tennessee Valley Authority and a member of Touchstone Energy a 600-member alliance of electricity co-ops.

	Annual Growth	06/07	06/08	06/09	06/12	06/13
Sales ($ mil.)	3.1%	–	152.2	170.1	171.9	177.3
Net income ($ mil.)	20.6%	–	–	2.2	4.7	4.7
Market value ($ mil.)	–	–	–	–	–	–
Employees	–	–	–	–	–	165

WASHINGTON BANKING CO. (OAK HARBOR, WA)

NMS: WBCO

450 SW Bayshore Drive
Oak Harbor, WA 98277
Phone: 360 679-3121
Fax: –
Web: www.wibank.com

CEO: –
CFO: –
HR:
FYE: December 31
Type: Public

Washington Banking is the holding company for Whidbey Island Bank which serves individuals and businesses through some 30 branches in northwestern Washington. The bank offers standard deposit services such as checking and savings accounts CDs and IRAs. It primarily originates commercial mortgages and consumer and construction loans. To a lesser extent the bank offers one-to four-family residential mortgages and business loans. Whidbey Island Bank sells investment and insurance products through agreements with third-party providers. The bank added about a dozen branches in 2010 from the acquisitions of failed financial institutions City Bank and North County Bank in separate FDIC-assisted transactions.

	Annual Growth	12/08	12/09	12/10	12/11	12/12
Assets ($ mil.)	17.0%	899.6	1,045.9	1,704.5	1,670.6	1,687.7
Net income ($ mil.)	19.2%	8.3	6.2	25.6	16.0	16.8
Market value ($ mil.)	11.9%	134.7	184.9	212.3	184.4	210.9
Employees	16.0%	258	281	448	450	467

WASHINGTON FEDERAL INC.

NMS: WAFD

425 Pike Street
Seattle, WA 98101
Phone: 206 624-7930
Fax: –
Web: www.washingtonfederal.com

CEO: Roy M. Whitehead
CFO: Diane L. Kelleher
HR: Linda S. Brower
FYE: September 30
Type: Public

Washington Federal is the holding company for Washington Federal Savings -which operates about 190 branches in eight western states. The thrift which was founded in 1917 collects deposits from consumers and business by offering standard products such as CDs IRAs and checking savings and money market accounts. With these funds the bank mainly originates single-family residential mortgages which account for nearly three-quarters of its loan portfolio. The bank also writes business consumer construction land and multi-family residential loans. Washington Federal sells life home and auto coverage to individuals and businesses through its First Insurance Agency subsidiary.

	Annual Growth	09/11	09/12	09/13	09/14	09/15
Assets ($ mil.)	2.0%	13,440.7	12,472.9	13,082.9	14,756.0	14,568.3
Net income ($ mil.)	9.6%	111.1	138.2	151.5	157.4	160.3
Market value ($ mil.)	15.6%	1,184.0	1,548.3	1,921.9	1,892.2	2,114.3
Employees	10.8%	1,221	1,260	1,457	1,909	1,838

WASHINGTON HEALTHCARE MARY

2300 FALL HILL AVE # 418
FREDERICKSBURG, VA 224013342
Phone: 540-741-2507
Fax: –
Web: www.marywashingtonhealthcare.com

CEO: Michael P McDermott
CFO: Sean T Barden
HR: –
FYE: March 31
Type: Private

Health care is Mary Washington Healthcare's realm in the Old Dominion State. The medical provider offers a comprehensive range of health services to residents of Fredericksburg and surrounding communities in central Virginia through its not-for-profit regional system of two hospitals and 28 healthcare facilities. The hub of this system is Mary Washington Hospital a 437-bed acute care medical center that provides services including emergency/trauma care and surgical procedures. The health system also includes outpatient care programs and facilities providing primary care and specialty care services for women seniors and children.

	Annual Growth	12/08	12/09	12/10*	03/11	03/12
Sales ($ mil.)	–	–	–	(1,320.3)	174.6	154.9
Net income ($ mil.)	12056.0%	–	–	0.0	6.6	7.0
Market value ($ mil.)	–	–	–	–	–	–
Employees	–	–	–	–	–	4,000

*Fiscal year change

WASHINGTON HOSPITAL CENTER CORPORATION

110 IRVING ST NW
WASHINGTON, DC 20010-3017
Phone: 202-877-7000
Fax: –
Web: www.whcenter.org

CEO: Harrison J Rider III
CFO: –
HR: –
FYE: June 30
Type: Private

Washington Hospital Center may be the official hospital of the Washington Redskins but you don't have to be a professional football player to make use of the facility's services. The hospital at the heart of the MedStar Health system serves about 455000 patients living in and around the nation's capital each year. Washington Hospital Center has approximately 925 beds and includes specialized care centers for cancer cardiovascular conditions and neurosciences. Other services include organ transplantation and a regional burn treatment center as well as emergency air transportation. The hospital also conducts clinical research and offers educational residency and fellowship programs.

	Annual Growth	06/02	06/03	06/04	06/05	06/08
Sales ($ mil.)	5.3%	–	–	–	880.4	1,028.6
Net income ($ mil.)	(13.5%)	–	–	–	22.1	14.3
Market value ($ mil.)	–	–	–	–	–	–
Employees	–	–	–	–	–	5,637

WASHINGTON METROPOLITAN AREA TRANSIT AUTHORITY

600 5th St. NW
Washington DC 20001
Phone: 202-962-1234
Fax: 202-962-1409
Web: www.wmata.com

CEO: –
CFO: Carol Kissal
HR: –
FYE: June 30
Type: Government Agency

Washington Metropolitan Area Transit Authority (WMATA or the Metro) operates the second largest rail transit system (Metrorail) and one of the largest bus networks (Metrobus) in the US. Transporting roughly a third of federal government employees to work and millions of tourists its transit service zone covers Washington DC and neighboring counties and suburbs in Maryland and Virginia. The authority's rail system consists of about 85 stations served by more than 100 miles of track both underground and aboveground. It operates a fleet of about 1400 buses. WMATA also offers MetroAccess paratransit service for eligible people with disabilities.

WASHINGTON NATIONALS BASEBALL CLUB LLC

1500 S. Capitol St. SE
Washington DC 20003-1507
Phone: 202-675-6287
Fax: 202-640-7999
Web: washington.nationals.mlb.com

CEO: Mark Lerner
CFO: Lori Creasy
HR: –
FYE: October 31
Type: Private

This team is hoping to make Washington the capital of baseball. Washington Nationals Baseball Club owns and operates the professional baseball franchise that represents the nation's capital in Major League Baseball. The team was founded in 1968 as the Montreal Expos (the expansion franchise was awarded to Charles Bronfman whose family built the Seagram's distilling business) but struggled for many years to build a fan base in Quebec. MLB which took over the team from Jeffery Loria in 2002 relocated the Expos to Washington DC in 2005. Real estate developer Ted Lerner purchased the team from the league in 2006.

WASHINGTON REAL ESTATE INVESTMENT TRUST

NYS: WRE

1775 Eye Street, NW, Suite 1000
Washington, DC 20006
Phone: 202 774-3200
Fax: –
Web: www.writ.com

CEO: Paul T. McDermott
CFO: Stephen E. Riffee
HR: –
FYE: December 31
Type: Public

Capital-area real estate is writ large on the mission statement of Washington Real Estate Investment Trust (WRIT). The self-administered and self-managed real estate investment trust (REIT) owns and manages commercial real estate in the Mid-Atlantic mainly in the greater Washington/Baltimore corridor. (As a REIT the trust is exempt from paying federal income tax as long as it distributes quarterly dividends to shareholders.) WRIT owns a varied portfolio that includes more than 25 office or medical office buildings about 15 retail centers and about a dozen apartment communities as well as land held for development. Altogether the REIT owns some 7 million sq. ft. of space.

	Annual Growth	12/10	12/11	12/12	12/13	12/14
Sales ($ mil.)	(0.8%)	298.0	289.5	305.0	263.0	288.6
Net income ($ mil.)	31.4%	37.4	104.9	23.7	37.3	111.6
Market value ($ mil.)	(2.8%)	2,101.7	1,854.8	1,773.5	1,584.3	1,875.9
Employees	(11.3%)	293	303	287	263	181

WASHINGTON REGIONAL MEDICAL CENTER

3215 N NORTHHILLS BLVD
FAYETTEVILLE, AR 727034424
Phone: 479-713-1000
Fax: –
Web: www.wregional.com

CEO: William L Bradley
CFO: Dan Eckels
HR: –
FYE: December 31
Type: Private

Washington Regional Medical System (formerly Washington Regional Medical Center) provides acute care services to the people of northwestern Arkansas. The system's main hospital has about 370 beds in Fayetteville and also includes assisted living facilities home health and hospice services and general practice and specialty clinics. Specialty services at the medical center include cardiac and vascular care (Walker Family Heart and Vascular Institute) emergency medicine kidney dialysis women's health services (Johnelle Hunt Women's Center) cancer treatment and rehabilitation.

	Annual Growth	12/01	12/02	12/08	12/09	12/12
Sales ($ mil.)	3.9%	–	139.9	203.4	229.0	205.0
Net income ($ mil.)	370.1%	–	–	0.1	14.2	33.7
Market value ($ mil.)	–	–	–	–	–	–
Employees	–	–	–	–	–	1,600

WASHINGTON SUBURBAN SANITARY COMMISSION

14501 Sweitzer Ln.
Laurel MD 20707
Phone: 301-206-9772
Fax: 301-206-8720
Web: www.wsscwater.com

CEO: –
CFO: –
HR: –
FYE: June 30
Type: Government Agency

Used water in clean safe water out is the job description of the Washington Suburban Sanitary Commission (WSSC). The utility provides water and wastewater services in Maryland's Montgomery and Prince George's counties just outside the nation's capital. WSSC serves 460000 customers representing 1.8 million residents in an area of about 1000 square miles. The agency draws water from the Potomac and Patuxent rivers and maintains three reservoirs. The commission also operates two water filtration plants seven wastewater treatment plants and more than 10000 miles of sewer and water main lines. WSCC was formed in 1818.

WASHINGTON TRUST BANCORP, INC.

NMS: WASH

23 Broad Street
Westerly, RI 02891
Phone: 401 348-1200
Fax: –
Web: www.washtrust.com

CEO: Joseph J. (Joe) MarcAurele
CFO: David V, Devault
HR: Kristen L Disanto
FYE: December 31
Type: Public

Without seeming naive Washington Trust Bancorp can utter Washington and trust in the same breath. The holding company owns The Washington Trust Company one of the oldest and largest banks in Rhode Island and one of the oldest banks in the entire US. Chartered in 1800 the bank boasts over $3.5 billion in assets and operates nearly 20 branches in the state and one in southeastern Connecticut. Washington Trust offers standard services such as deposit accounts CDs and credit cards. The company's commercial mortgages and loans account for more than half of its loan portfolio while residential mortgages and consumer loans make up most of the rest. The bank also offers wealth management services.

	Annual Growth	12/10	12/11	12/12	12/13	12/14
Assets ($ mil.)	5.4%	2,909.5	3,064.1	3,071.9	3,188.9	3,586.9
Net income ($ mil.)	14.1%	24.1	29.7	35.1	36.2	40.8
Market value ($ mil.)	16.4%	366.4	399.6	440.6	623.3	672.9
Employees	2.8%	528	558	592	570	590

WASTE CONNECTIONS, INC.

NYS: WCN

3 Waterway Square Place, Suite 110
The Woodlands, TX 77380
Phone: 832 442-2200
Fax: –
Web: www.wasteconnections.com

CEO: Ronald J. (Ron) Mittelstaedt
CFO: Worthing F. Jackman
HR: –
FYE: December 31
Type: Public

Waste Connections does the dirty work so you don't have to. It provides solid waste collection transfer disposal and recycling services to more than 2 million commercial industrial and residential customers in 32 US states. The integrated solid waste services company does business mainly in smaller markets. Waste Connections owns or operates about 148 solid waste collection operations 69 transfer stations 58 landfills and 35 recycling facilities. It operates 22 liquid exploration and production (E&P) waste injection wells 17 E&P waste treatment facilities and 20 oil recovery facilities. In 2016 Waste Connections agreed to buy Canada-based Progressive Waste for $2.7 billion.

	Annual Growth	12/11	12/12	12/13	12/14	12/15
Sales ($ mil.)	8.9%	1,505.4	1,661.6	1,928.8	2,079.2	2,117.3
Net income ($ mil.)	–	165.2	159.1	195.7	232.5	(95.8)
Market value ($ mil.)	14.2%	4,055.5	4,135.1	5,339.3	5,383.3	6,892.2
Employees	5.2%	5,909	6,606	6,633	6,777	7,227

WASTE CONTROL SPECIALISTS LLC

Three Lincoln Centre 5430 LBJ Freeway Ste. 1700
Dallas TX 75240
Phone: 972-715-9800
Fax: +44-1977-662-450
Web: www.tunstall.co.uk

CEO: Bill Lindquist
CFO: –
HR: –
FYE: December 31
Type: Subsidiary

Everything's bigger in Texas including its capacity to store nuclear waste. Waste Control Specialists (WCS) operates a disposal facility for hazardous toxic and low-level radioactive waste in Andrews County in far West Texas on the border of southeast New Mexico. The 1300-acre site can store up to 1.8 million cu. ft. of class A B and C low-level radioactive waste more than 100 feet underground. It is licensed to accept waste from nuclear power plants in Texas and Vermont and for treatment and storage from commercial and federal generators such as the Dept. of Energy. WCS a subsidiary of Valhi is one of only three private companies in the US licensed to handle nuclear waste.

WASTE MANAGEMENT, INC. (DE)

NYS: WM

1001 Fannin Street, Suite 4000
Houston, TX 77002
Phone: 713 512-6200
Fax: 713 512-6299
Web: www.wm.com

CEO: David P. Steiner
CFO: James C. (Jim) Fish
HR: Tam Barbour
FYE: December 31
Type: Public

Holding company Waste Management tops the heap in the US solid-waste industry. Through subsidiaries the company serves more than 20 million residential industrial municipal and commercial customers in the US and Canada. Waste Management provides waste collection transfer recycling and resource recovery and disposal services. Its sites include about 247 owned or operated landfills (the industry's largest network) 298 transfer stations and around 126 material recovery facilities. Collection services account for more than half of sales.

	Annual Growth	12/10	12/11	12/12	12/13	12/14
Sales ($ mil.)	2.8%	12,515.0	13,378.0	13,649.0	13,983.0	13,996.0
Net income ($ mil.)	8.0%	953.0	961.0	817.0	98.0	1,298.0
Market value ($ mil.)	8.6%	16,906.3	14,998.8	15,471.1	20,574.6	23,532.1
Employees	(1.8%)	42,800	44,300	43,500	42,700	39,800

WASTEQUIP INC.

1901 Roxborough Rd. Ste. 300
Charlotte NC 28211
Phone: 216-292-2554
Fax: 216-292-0625
Web: www.wastequip.com

CEO: –
CFO: Steven Svetik
HR: –
FYE: December 31
Type: Private

Wastequip doesn't talk trash — it takes care of it. Wastequip has been consolidating the waste disposal equipment industry since 1989; it operates more than two dozen waste handling equipment manufacturing plants in North America. The company provides large and small metal containers for on-site waste collection; balers and compactors for waste processing; and containers trailers hoists and other mechanical equipment used to transport solid liquid and hazardous waste. Its brands include Toter Galbreath and Accurate and Cusco. Customers are national and regional solid-waste disposal haulers commercial businesses and public agencies. Private equity firm Centerbridge Partners controls the company.

WASTREN ADVANTAGE INC.

OSU South Centers 1862 Shyville Rd. Ste. 212
Piketon OH 45661
Phone: 740-289-9761
Fax: 740-289-9759
Web: www.wastrenadvantage.com

CEO: Steve Moore
CFO: Thomas Kaupas
HR: –
FYE: December 31
Type: Private

Wastren Advantage's advantage is that it handles the kind of waste that others won't handle. The environmental services company provides radioactive and hazardous waste management including packaging transport and disposal. Wastren Advantage also provides facilities operations and maintenance decontamination and decommissioning pollution prevention site remediation and various environmental engineering services. It manages facilities and cleanups for federal state and local government agencies as well as for private companies. Wastren Advantage also added to its recycling services in 2012 by acquiring Ohio-based Geo-Tech Polymers a plastics recycler.

WATCHGUARD TECHNOLOGIES INC.

505 5th Ave. South Ste. 500
Seattle WA 98104
Phone: 206-613-6600
Fax: 206-521-8342
Web: www.watchguard.com

CEO: Prakash Panjwani
CFO: Richard Barber
HR: –
FYE: December 31
Type: Private

Don't accuse WatchGuard Technologies of falling asleep at its post. The company provides a variety of Internet security software and hardware products including firewalls virtual private network (VPN) appliances and anti-virus applications under the XTM and XCS among others. Its products guard against a variety of digital security threats including hackers viruses and worms. WatchGuard also provides subscription-based managed services to protect computer networks from intruders and provide threat responses software updates and information alerts. It targets small and midsized businesses primarily in the Americas Europe and Asia. The company's strategic partners include Avaya Mitel and Extreme Networks.

WATERFURNACE RENEWABLE ENERGY INC.

PINK SHEETS: WFIFF

9000 Conservation Way
Fort Wayne IN 46809-9794
Phone: 260-479-3925
Fax: 260-747-2828
Web: www.waterfurnace.com

CEO: Tom Huntington
CFO: Fred Andriano
HR: –
FYE: December 31
Type: Public

WaterFurnace Renewable Energy relies on the heat within the earth to energize its products. The company also doing business as WaterFurnace International makes and sells geothermal HVAC systems that utilize heat stored in the ground for residential commercial and institutional applications. Its cooling systems work in reverse extracting heat from indoors. Touting its systems as more efficient safer and more environmentally friendly than HVAC systems that use fossil fuels the company has installed more than 300000 units. Other operations install geothermal loops that heat and cool homes and businesses by circulating pressurized water through hundreds of feet of looped pipe that is buried on-site.

WATERS CORP.

NYS: WAT

34 Maple Street
Milford, MA 01757
Phone: 508 478-2000
Fax: 508 872-1990
Web: www.waters.com

CEO: Christopher J. (Chris) O'Connell
CFO: Eugene G. (Gene) Cassis
HR: Elizabeth B. Rae
FYE: December 31
Type: Public

Waters works with laboratory chemicals much more complex than H_2O. The company named after founder Jim Waters makes high-performance liquid chromatography instruments used by researchers scientists and engineers to separate and identify chemicals. Waters also makes mass spectrometers that help identify chemical compounds. Its products are used for applications including drug development food testing and air and water quality testing. Waters' TA Instruments Division makes thermal analyzers and rheometry instruments used to determine the physical characteristics of polymers and other substances. Customers are in the academic government and industrial sectors; more than 70% of sales are from customers located outside the US.

	Annual Growth	12/10	12/11	12/12	12/13	12/14
Sales ($ mil.)	4.9%	1,643.4	1,851.2	1,843.6	1,904.2	1,989.3
Net income ($ mil.)	3.1%	381.8	433.0	461.4	450.0	431.6
Market value ($ mil.)	9.7%	6,461.4	6,157.0	7,243.8	8,314.7	9,372.3
Employees	3.5%	5,400	5,700	5,900	6,000	6,200

WATKINS AND SHEPARD TRUCKING INC.

6400 US HIGHWAY 10 W
MISSOULA, MT 598089379
Phone: 406-532-6121
Fax: –
Web: www.wksh.com

CEO: Ray Kuntz
CFO: –
HR: –
FYE: December 31
Type: Private

Watkins & Shepard Trucking offers less-than-truckload (LTL) and truckload freight hauling throughout the US from about 20 terminals mainly west of the Rockies. (LTL carriers consolidate cargo from multiple shippers into a single trailer.) The company's fleet consists of about 630 tractors and 1600 trailers. Standard dry vans account for the majority of the company's trailers; Watkins & Shepard also uses flatbed trailers. In addition the company arranges intermodal transportation which involves hauling freight by multiple methods such as road and rail. CEO Ray Kuntz and president Steve Williamson own Watkins & Shepard which was founded in 1974 as Stan Watkins Trucking.

	Annual Growth	12/98	12/99	12/00	12/12	12/13
Sales ($ mil.)	3.8%	–	95.7	102.4	157.9	160.6
Net income ($ mil.)	8.5%	–	–	0.9	3.1	2.5
Market value ($ mil.)	–	–	–	–	–	–
Employees	–	–	–	–	–	950

WATKINS ASSOCIATED INDUSTRIES INC.

1958 Monroe Dr. NE
Atlanta GA 30324
Phone: 404-872-3841
Fax: 404-872-2812
Web: www.watkins.com

CEO: Michael L Watkins
CFO: Michael L Watkins
HR: –
FYE: December 31
Type: Private

Watkins Associated Industries does business over the road on the ground and by the sea. Its trucking businesses include Highway Transport Chemical (liquid chemical transport) Highway Transport Petroleum Highway Transport Logistics Land Span (general cargo) Sunco Carriers (refrigerated cargo) and Watson Truckload Services (regional general cargo). Another unit Tampa Maid Foods sources processes and markets seafood such as shrimp calamari scallops oysters and crab. Its Watkins Retail Group is a shopping center development leasing and management company that was founded in 1977. Bill Watkins founded the family-owned company in 1932 with a $300 pickup truck.

WATONWAN FARM SERVICE INC

233 W CIRO ST
TRUMAN, MN 560882018
Phone: 507-776-1244
Fax: –
Web: www.wfsag.com

CEO: Ed Bosanko
CFO: William Day
HR: –
FYE: July 31
Type: Private

Watonwan Farm Service which does business as WFS helps out its south central Minnesota and north central Iowa member-farmers with complete farm-management services and products. Offering marketing opportunities financial services and farming supplies such as chemicals fertilizers livestock feed petroleum products and seed the agricultural cooperative serves more than 4000 producers from its 22 locations. The primary crops of its members include corn soybean and specialty canning crops; most of its livestock farmers raise hogs and cattle. The co-op was called the Consumers Cooperative Oil Company of St. James when it was founded in 1937.

	Annual Growth	07/10	07/11	07/12	07/13	07/14
Sales ($ mil.)	(4.3%)	–	534.9	592.5	701.2	468.3
Net income ($ mil.)	7.6%	–	–	6.7	7.7	7.7
Market value ($ mil.)	–	–	–	–	–	–
Employees	–	–	–	–	–	255

WATSCO INC.

NYS: WSO

2665 South Bayshore Drive, Suite 901
Miami, FL 33133
Phone: 305 714-4100
Fax: –
Web: www.watsco.com

CEO: Albert H. Nahmad
CFO: Ana M Menendez
HR: –
FYE: December 31
Type: Public

Cooling the Sun Belt keeps Watsco hot. It is one of the largest independent distributors of residential and commercial heating air conditioning and refrigeration equipment and parts and supplies (HVAC/R). Watsco's 570-plus distribution sites span more than 35 states Canada Puerto Rico and Mexico. It also exports to Latin America and the Caribbean. Through subsidiaries Watsco provides installation and repair equipment for its products. Customers number more than 50000 contractors and dealers who install and replace HVAC equipment. Among its key suppliers Carrier (now UTC Climate Controls & Security) represents about half of all Watsco purchases.

	Annual Growth	12/10	12/11	12/12	12/13	12/14
Sales ($ mil.)	8.5%	2,844.6	2,977.8	3,431.7	3,743.3	3,944.5
Net income ($ mil.)	17.0%	80.8	90.5	103.3	127.7	151.4
Market value ($ mil.)	14.1%	2,208.2	2,298.5	2,622.0	3,362.7	3,745.7
Employees	5.7%	4,000	4,300	4,600	4,800	5,000

WATTS WATER TECHNOLOGIES INC

NYS: WTS

815 Chestnut Street
North Andover, MA 01845
Phone: 978 688-1811
Fax: –
Web: www.wattswater.com

CEO: Robert J. (Bob) Pagano
CFO: Todd A. Trapp
HR: –
FYE: December 31
Type: Public

What's Watts got to do with valves? Everything. Watts Water Technologies manufactures a number of valves used to maintain the quality conservation and flow control of water be it in a residential commercial industrial or municipal setting. It also makes water quality products such as backflow preventers and filtration systems water pressure regulators and drainage devices. The lineup is sold under brands Brae FEBCO Flo Safe Orion Powers and Sea Tech. Watts' operations are found in North America Europe and to a lesser extent China. Almost 65% of its sales rely on plumbing heating and mechanical wholesale distributors. Do-it-yourself retail chains and OEMs account for the balance.

	Annual Growth	12/10	12/11	12/12	12/13	12/14
Sales ($ mil.)	4.4%	1,274.6	1,436.6	1,445.6	1,473.5	1,513.7
Net income ($ mil.)	(3.8%)	58.8	66.4	68.4	58.6	50.3
Market value ($ mil.)	14.7%	1,281.8	1,198.4	1,506.0	2,167.4	2,222.4
Employees	3.1%	5,400	5,800	5,900	5,900	6,100

WAUKESHA MEMORIAL HOSPITAL INC.

725 AMERICAN AVE
WAUKESHA, WI 531885099
Phone: 262-544-2011
Fax: –
Web: www.westwoodfitness.org

CEO: –
CFO: Robert W Mlynarek
HR: Peter L Boney
FYE: September 30
Type: Private

Waukesha Memorial Hospital is a 300-bed teaching hospital that provides health care services for Wisconsin's Milwaukee Waukesha and Dane counties. With about 670 physicians representing several specialties and 2700 employees the hospital operates centers for excellence focused on cardiology oncology neurology women's health and orthopedics as well as emergency neonatal and family practice services. Additionally Waukesha Memorial Hospital conducts a physician residency program. Established in 1914 the medical facility is a subsidiary of not-for-profit ProHealth Care a medical network that serves southeastern Wisconsin with acute care and specialty health services.

	Annual Growth	06/05	06/06	06/07*	09/12	09/13
Sales ($ mil.)	7.1%	–	–	277.9	456.0	419.8
Net income ($ mil.)	12.0%	–	–	48.8	53.4	96.2
Market value ($ mil.)	–	–	–	–	–	–
Employees	–	–	–	–	–	2,071

*Fiscal year change

WAUKESHA-PEARCE INDUSTRIES INC.

12320 MAIN ST
HOUSTON, TX 770356206
Phone: 713-723-1050
Fax: –
Web: www.wpi.com

CEO: Al H Bentley
CFO: –
HR: –
FYE: March 31
Type: Private

Waukesha-Pearce Industries (WPI) wants its customers to start their engines. Through its Engine Division the company designs and packages engine-driven equipment such as power generators pumps blowers control panels and switchgear. WPI also offers a slate of heavy construction and mining products including earth movers and demolition equipment made by such OEMs as Komatsu and Gradall Industries through its Construction Machinery Division. As part of its business the company sells used equipment and leases heavy earth-moving equipment. Founded as Portable Rotary Rig Co. in 1924 by Louis M. Pearce Sr. the company is owned and run by the Pearce family.

	Annual Growth	03/02	03/03	03/10	03/11	03/13
Sales ($ mil.)	7.3%	–	183.6	197.8	248.7	369.8
Net income ($ mil.)	86.0%	–	–	1.7	4.7	10.8
Market value ($ mil.)	–	–	–	–	–	–
Employees	–	–	–	–	–	600

WAUSAU PAPER CORP
NYS: WPP

100 Paper Place
Mosinee, WI 54455-9099
Phone: 715 693-4470
Fax: 715 692-2082
Web: www.wausaupaper.com

CEO: –
CFO: –
HR: –
FYE: December 31
Type: Public

With more than 110 years experience Wausau Paper has proficiency in selling paper and tissue products. The company produces Bay West branded towel tissue soap and dispensing products for hotels hospitals schools and office buildings. Other paper brands include DublSoft EcoSoft OptiCore Revolution and Dubl Nature. Its products are primarily sold within the US and Canada. Most of its US customers are regional and national sanitation supply distributors and paper merchants. In 2013 Wausau Paper sold its specialty paper business to Expera Specialty Solutions.

	Annual Growth	12/09	12/10	12/11	12/12	12/13
Sales ($ mil.)	(23.8%)	1,032.1	1,055.7	1,034.6	822.2	348.6
Net income ($ mil.)	–	20.6	36.9	(21.7)	0.7	(97.3)
Market value ($ mil.)	2.2%	573.7	425.8	408.5	428.3	627.1
Employees	(20.9%)	2,300	2,400	2,300	1,900	900

WAVE SYSTEMS CORP
NBB: WAVX Q

480 Pleasant Street
Lee, MA 01238
Phone: 413 243-1600
Fax: 413 243-0045
Web: www.wave.com

CEO: –
CFO: –
HR: –
FYE: December 31
Type: Public

Wave Systems develops software to contend with a very particular sort of crime wave. Designed to work with security chips from such manufacturers as Broadcom and STMicroelectronics the company's digital security applications enable information encryption and identity protection to reduce the risk of data theft or unauthorized network access. Its flagship suite of EMBASSY products is used in devices including PCs made by Dell (the company's largest customer) and computer hard drives from Seagate Technology. Wave's Tel Aviv-based Safend subsidiary (acquired in 2011) provides endpoint data loss protection products and services. Founded in 1988 as Indata Corp. the company became Wave Systems in 1993.

	Annual Growth	12/10	12/11	12/12	12/13	12/14
Sales ($ mil.)	(10.2%)	26.1	36.1	28.8	24.4	17.0
Net income ($ mil.)	–	(4.1)	(10.8)	(34.0)	(20.3)	(12.9)
Market value ($ mil.)	(32.8%)	18.1	10.0	3.3	4.2	3.7
Employees	0.4%	133	249	215	150	135

WAYFAIR LLC

177 Huntington Ave.
Boston MA 02115
Phone: 617-532-6100
Fax: 212-421-6292
Web: www.genesis10.com

CEO: Niraj Shah
CFO: Michael Fleisher
HR: –
FYE: December 31
Type: Private

Online shoppers navigating the Web's vast offering of home goods need only stop at Wayfair (formerly CSN Stores). The company is a leading online retailer of more than 5000 brands of products including cookware home and office furniture and decor lighting strollers and more. Seeking to become the Amazon.com of home goods the e-tailer in 2011 merged some 200 specialty e-commerce sites such as AllModern.com Cookware.com Luggage.com SimplyDesks.com and Strollers.com all under the Wayfair.com brand. Founded in 2002 by CEO Niraj Shah and chairman Steve Conine as a single shopping destination (RacksandStands.com) the company changed its name from CSN Stores to Wayfair in 2011.

WAYLAND BAPTIST UNIVERSITY INC

1900 W 7TH ST
PLAINVIEW, TX 790726998
Phone: 806-291-3440
Fax: –
Web: www.wbu.edu

CEO: –
CFO: James Smith
HR: –
FYE: June 30
Type: Private

You gotta have faith to attend Wayland Baptist University. The private co-educational Baptist institution offers more than 40 undergraduate majors about a dozen pre-professional programs and graduate programs in fields such as business administration Christian ministry counseling education management public administration religion and science. It has an enrollment of approximately 7000 students at some 15 campuses in Alaska Arizona Hawaii New Mexico Oklahoma and Texas as well as Kenya. The university was founded in 1906 by Dr. and Mrs. Henry Wayland and the Staked Plains Baptist Association.

	Annual Growth	06/10	06/11	06/12	06/13	06/14
Sales ($ mil.)	1.3%	–	61.5	66.0	67.0	64.0
Net income ($ mil.)	(45.8%)	–	–	7.5	5.5	2.2
Market value ($ mil.)	–	–	–	–	–	–
Employees						281

WAYNE J. GRIFFIN ELECTRIC INC.

116 HOPPING BROOK RD
HOLLISTON, MA 017461455
Phone: 508-429-8830
Fax: –
Web: www.waynejgriffin.com

CEO: Wayne J. Griffin
CFO: –
HR: –
FYE: December 31
Type: Private

Wayne J. Griffin Electric brings a certain spark to New England and the Southeast. With offices in Massachusetts Georgia North Carolina and Alabama the electrical contractor offers construction and installation services on hospitals hotels industrial and high-tech buildings offices prisons research laboratories retirement communities and schools. The company's service division provides small project management and facility maintenance while its telecom division designs and installs fiber optics fire alarm and security systems as well as systems that control energy use from lighting to heating ventilation and air conditioning (HVAC). Founded in 1978 Wayne J. Griffin Electric is privately held.

	Annual Growth	12/09	12/10	12/11	12/12	12/13
Sales ($ mil.)	0.7%	–	285.2	286.2	286.2	291.2
Net income ($ mil.)	6.0%	–	–	15.6	15.6	17.6
Market value ($ mil.)	–	–	–	–	–	–
Employees	–	–	–	–	–	1,100

WAYNE SAVINGS BANCSHARES INC
NMS: WAYN

151 North Market Street
Wooster, OH 44691
Phone: 330 264-5767
Fax: –

CEO: –
CFO: Myron L Swartzentruber
HR: –
FYE: December 31
Type: Public

Holy bank vaults Batman! Wayne Savings Bancshares is the holding company for Wayne Savings Community Bank which serves individuals and local businesses through about a dozen locations in north-central Ohio. Serving Ashland Holmes Medina Stark and Wayne counties the bank offers checking and savings accounts retirement and education savings accounts certificates of deposit and debit cards. One- to four-family residential mortgages make up more than half of the company's loan portfolio. To a lesser extent the bank writes business commercial mortgage land and consumer loans. It offers investments insurance and brokerage accounts through a agreement with third-party provider Infinex.

	Annual Growth	03/11*	12/11	12/12	12/13	12/14
Assets ($ mil.)	0.8%	407.7	410.1	402.1	410.3	417.7
Net income ($ mil.)	6.2%	2.2	1.3	1.7	2.1	2.6
Market value ($ mil.)	16.1%	24.0	21.8	26.0	30.6	37.6
Employees	(2.9%)	120	124	117	113	110

*Fiscal year change

WAYSIDE TECHNOLOGY GROUP INC

NMS: WSTG

1157 Shrewsbury Avenue
Shrewsbury, NJ 07702
Phone: 732 389-8950
Fax: –
Web: www.waysidetechnology.com

CEO: Simon F. Nynens
CFO: –
HR: –
FYE: December 31
Type: Public

Wayside Technology connects developers with users of IT products. A leading reseller for software developers the firm's TechXtend (formerly Programmer's Paradise) business markets software hardware and services to IT professionals government agencies and educational institutions in the US and Canada. Wayside's Lifeboat Distribution subsidiary provides software to resellers consultants and systems integrators worldwide. (Software accounts for about 95% of the company's sales.) Wayside Technology sells products through its catalogs and e-commerce sites and its suppliers include Quest Software Intel Flexera TechSmith and Vmware among others.

	Annual Growth	12/10	12/11	12/12	12/13	12/14
Sales ($ mil.)	13.3%	206.7	250.2	297.1	300.4	340.8
Net income ($ mil.)	6.8%	4.4	5.5	5.5	6.4	5.8
Market value ($ mil.)	11.2%	55.1	59.7	54.2	66.2	84.2
Employees	5.0%	103	112	120	123	125

WCA WASTE CORPORATION

NASDAQ: WCAA

1 Riverway Ste. 1400
Houston TX 77056
Phone: 713-292-2400
Fax: 713-292-2455
Web: www.wcawaste.com

CEO: William K Caesar
CFO: –
HR: –
FYE: December 31
Type: Private

Some might see a garbage dump but WCA Waste sees a pile of money. The firm provides collection transfer and disposal of nonhazardous solid waste for 441000 commercial industrial and residential customers and 7000 landfill and transfer station customers in the US Southeast and Midwest. It operates some 25 landfills 29 collection businesses and 29 transfer stations and materials recovery facilities. Most sales come from collection and landfill disposal services provided to residential commercial and roll-off (disposal of large waste containers) customers. Macquarie Infrastructure Partners II part of the Macquarie Group through its Cod Intermediate unit bought WCA Waste for $526 million in 2012.

WCI COMMUNITIES INC

NYS: WCIC

24301 Walden Center Drive
Bonita Springs, FL 34134
Phone: 239 947 2600
Fax: –
Web: www.wcicommunities.com

CEO: Reinaldo L. Mesa
CFO: Russell Devendorf
HR: –
FYE: December 31
Type: Public

WCI Communities develops luxury residential communities and homes in Florida. Founded in 1946 it caters primarily to retirement and second-home buyers offering single-family homes vacation homes villas and high-rise condominiums ranging in price from about $150000 to $1.3 million. WCI's 14 master-planned communities typically offer such amenities as golf courses tennis courts dining and entertainment facilities and nature trails. The company also offers architectural and design services as well as financing and title services. Its real estate brokerage Berkshire Hathaway HomeServices boasts 40-plus locations that serve 18 Florida counties. WCI Communities went public in 2013.

	Annual Growth	12/08	12/11	12/12	12/13	12/14
Sales ($ mil.)	(5.1%)	556.1	144.3	241.0	317.3	407.0
Net income ($ mil.)	–	(936.8)	(47.1)	50.8	146.6	21.6
Market value ($ mil.)	2.6%	–	–	–	492.7	505.3
Employees	(12.1%)	1,450	–	–	598	667

WD-40 CO.

NMS: WDFC

1061 Cudahy Place
San Diego, CA 92110
Phone: 619 275-1400
Fax: –
Web: www.wd40company.com

CEO: Garry O Ridge
CFO: Jay W. Rembolt
HR: –
FYE: August 31
Type: Public

Squeaky hinges are the stuff horror movie nightmares — and WD-40's dreams — are made of. The company's WD-40 product used as a lubricant rust preventative and penetrant is a staple in many homes. As well as unsticking locks and loosening rusted bolts the omnipresent blue-and-yellow aerosol can contains the slippery stuff of myth said to combat arthritis and attract fish. Its WD-40 3-IN-ONE Oil and Blue Works lubricants account for most of the company's sales. It also makes household cleaning and deodorizing products under the brands X-14 Carpet Fresh No Vac 1001 and 2000 Flushes and heavy-duty hand cleaners Lava and Solvol. WD-40 contracts with various companies to manufacture its products.

	Annual Growth	08/11	08/12	08/13	08/14	08/15
Sales ($ mil.)	3.0%	336.4	342.8	368.5	383.0	378.2
Net income ($ mil.)	5.3%	36.4	35.5	39.8	43.7	44.8
Market value ($ mil.)	19.4%	594.5	705.3	840.7	992.7	1,210.1
Employees	6.7%	334	347	369	395	433

WEA TRUST

45 Nob Hill Rd.
Madison WI 53713
Phone: 800-279-4000
Fax: 608-276-9119
Web: www.weatrust.com

CEO: Mark Moody
CFO: –
HR: Bob Ceder
FYE: December 31
Type: Private - Not-for-Pr

Bringing the teacher an apple is nice but providing her with good insurance is where WEA Trust makes the grade. The not-for-profit organization serves up health life disability and long-term care insurance for Wisconsin's public school employees through subsidiary WEA Insurance Corporation. Its health offerings include prescription plans diabetes management support and dental policies. It also offers auto and homeowners insurance and promotes health in schools through a variety of public outreach programs. The company insures more than 160000 Wisconsin public school workers and their families along with some other state workers. The Wisconsin Education Association Council founded WEA Trust in 1970.

WEATHER SHIELD MFG INC.

1 Weather Shield Plaza
Medford WI 54451
Phone: 715-748-2100
Fax: 715-748-6999
Web: www.weathershield.com

CEO: –
CFO: –
HR: –
FYE: December 31
Type: Private

To keep bad weather at bay Weather Shield Manufacturing offers impact-resistant windows doors and other related products to homeowners architects and contractors. The company custom builds wood and vinyl windows and entry and patio doors with hurricanes storms and the environment in mind. Its products come in a variety of shapes sizes and finishes and are sold through a network of more than 2000 dealers worldwide with North America as its largest market. Product lines include EnduraShield ProShield and Weather Shield. Founded as Weather Shield Windows & Doors in 1955 the company is owned and managed by the family of founder Edward "Lee" Schield.

WEB.COM GROUP, INC.

NMS: WEB

12808 Gran Bay Parkway, West
Jacksonville, FL 32258
Phone: 904 680-6600
Fax: –
Web: www.web.com

CEO: David L Brown
CFO: Kevin M. Carney
HR: –
FYE: December 31
Type: Public

Web.com Group has everything a growing business needs to create a presence on the Internet. The company provides website building custom design consulting and Web hosting services. Its Register.com business provides domain name registration and its eWorks! XL product offers initial site-design setup and online marketing and technical report services. SmartClicks also offers search engine optimization and local pay-per click advertising services. The company sells to almost 3 million small and midsized US businesses mostly on a subscription basis. In late 2011 Web.com significantly expanded its customer base through the purchase of Network Solutions a website services and domain-names registration firm.

	Annual Growth	12/10	12/11	12/12	12/13	12/14
Sales ($ mil.)	45.8%	120.3	199.2	407.6	492.3	543.9
Net income ($ mil.)	–	(6.5)	(12.3)	(122.2)	(65.7)	(12.5)
Market value ($ mil.)	22.4%	440.3	596.6	771.2	1,656.5	989.5
Employees	16.3%	1,148	1,800	1,900	2,000	2,100

WEBBER OIL COMPANY

700 Main St.
Bangor ME 04401-6800
Phone: 207-942-5505
Fax: 207-941-9597
Web: www.webberenergy.com

CEO: –
CFO: Timothy M Smith
HR: Pamela Kelly
FYE: December 31
Type: Private

Webber Oil (doing business as Webber Energy Fuels) warms up homes on cold New England nights. The company provides home heating oil and propane in Maine and New Hampshire. Webber Oil has 18 heating oil and propane supply locations in Maine and three in New Hampshire. The company which was founded in 1935 by Alburney Webber also rents and installs energy efficient space heaters and hot water heaters and provides other energy-related services. It once owned and operated more than a dozen gas stations and convenience stores in the region but in late 2008 decided to exit that business.

WEBCO INDUSTRIES INC.

NBB: WEBC

9101 West 21st Street
Sand Springs, OK 74063
Phone: 918 241-1000
Fax: 918 245-0306
Web: www.webcoindustries.com

CEO: Dana S. Weber
CFO: Michael P. Howard
HR: –
FYE: July 31
Type: Public

Making carbon steel and stainless steel tubes in Oklahoma and Pennsylvania might not be as exciting as catching a monster "tube" in the waters off Hawaii but Webco Industries knows it's just as competitive. Facing stiff competition from larger tubing suppliers Webco Industries aims to prosper by targeting niche markets in the industries it serves. The company's primary products include mechanical tubing heat exchanger and boiler tubing and stainless steel tube and pipe. Subsidiary Phillips & Johnston makes tubular products from aluminum brass copper and carbon steel. Webco Industries' customers are from the agricultural automotive beverage general instrumentation and refrigeration industries.

	Annual Growth	07/10	07/11	07/12	07/13	07/14
Sales ($ mil.)	7.0%	312.6	465.6	526.8	413.7	409.5
Net income ($ mil.)	(40.7%)	3.3	24.8	14.6	5.8	0.4
Market value ($ mil.)	–	0.0	0.0	0.0	0.0	0.0
Employees	–	–	–	–	–	–

WEBCOR CONSTRUCTION L.P.

951 Mariners Island Blvd. 7th Fl.
San Mateo CA 94404
Phone: 650-349-2727
Fax: 650-524-7399
Web: www.webcor.com

CEO: Jes Pedersen
CFO: Tim Lutz
HR: –
FYE: December 31
Type: Private

The core of Webcor is commercial building in northern California and the Silicon Valley. The company constructs mid- and high-rise office buildings residential and medical facilities hotels and parking structures. Known for its focus on high-tech projects Webcor has worked on headquarters for Oracle and Adobe Systems and a headquarters compound for Industrial Light + Magic and LucasArts Entertainment. The company also provides interior construction and capentry services seismic upgrades concrete construction and consulting services. Webcor which was founded in 1971 is owned by Japanese construction company Obayashi.

WEBER DISTRIBUTION LLC

13530 Rosecrans Ave.
Santa Fe Springs CA 90670
Phone: 562-802-8802
Fax: 562-802-9792
Web: www.weberlogistics.com

CEO: Harry Drajpuch
CFO: –
HR: Sheila Jordan
FYE: December 31
Type: Private

Third-party logistics (3PL) provider Weber Distribution (dba Weber Logistics) arranges the transportation storage and distribution of freight for customers in the chemical food/beverage paper and retail industries including Wal-Mart Target and Spectrum Brands. The company operates about 5 million sq. ft. of warehouse space including more than 1 million sq. ft. of refrigerated space at more than 15 facilities in the Western US. It also operates its own trucking fleet (including about 100 tractors and 200 trailers) and provides a wide range of logistics services. Chairman Nicholas Weber represents the third generation of his family to own and lead the company which was founded in 1924.

WEBMD HEALTH CORP

NMS: WBMD

111 Eighth Avenue
New York, NY 10011
Phone: 212 624-3700
Fax: –
Web: www.webmd.com

CEO: David J. Schlanger
CFO: Peter Anevski
HR: –
FYE: December 31
Type: Public

House calls are a browser click away thanks to this online doctor. WebMD Health Corp. is a leading Web publisher of health information for consumers and health care professionals. Its WebMD.com portal gives consumers information on common health ailments as well as articles and features on staying healthy through diet and exercise. WebMD's Medscape is a Web portal with clinical information for doctors and other health care professionals. All total The WebMD Health Network (including WebMD.com Medscape.com and third-party sites) attracts about 185 million unique users per month. The company also operates private portals for employers and health plans.

	Annual Growth	12/10	12/11	12/12	12/13	12/14
Sales ($ mil.)	2.1%	534.5	558.8	469.9	515.3	580.4
Net income ($ mil.)	(6.1%)	54.1	74.6	(20.3)	15.1	42.1
Market value ($ mil.)	(6.2%)	1,856.2	1,365.1	521.3	1,435.9	1,437.8
Employees	1.1%	1,630	1,700	1,500	1,600	1,700

WEBSTER FINANCIAL CORP (WATERBURY, CONN)   NYS: WBS

145 Bank Street	CEO: James C. (Jim) Smith
Waterbury, CT 06702	CFO: Glenn I. MacInnes
Phone: 203 578-2202	HR: Bernard M. Garrigues
Fax: –	FYE: December 31
Web: www.websterbank.com	Type: Public

Webster Financial is the holding company for Webster Bank which operates about 170 branches in southern New England primarily in Connecticut but also in Massachusetts New York and Rhode Island. The bank provides commercial and retail services such as deposit accounts loans and mortgages and consumer finance as well as government and institutional banking services. It performs asset-based lending through its Webster Business Credit subsidiary and equipment financing through Webster Capital Finance. The company's HSA Bank division offers health savings accounts nationwide. Webster Bank provides brokerage and investment services through an agreement with UVEST a division of LPL Financial.

	Annual Growth	12/10	12/11	12/12	12/13	12/14
Assets ($ mil.)	5.7%	18,038.1	18,714.3	20,146.8	20,853.0	22,533.0
Net income ($ mil.)	28.0%	74.3	151.4	173.7	179.5	199.8
Market value ($ mil.)	13.4%	1,780.5	1,842.9	1,857.3	2,818.1	2,940.1
Employees	(3.0%)	3,123	2,961	2,826	2,744	2,764

WEBSTER UNIVERSITY

470 E LOCKWOOD AVE	CEO: –
SAINT LOUIS, MO 631193194	CFO: –
Phone: 314-968-6900	HR: –
Fax: –	FYE: May 31
Web: www.webster.edu	Type: Private

They have more than dictionaries at this Webster. Webster University is a private school that serves about 22000 undergraduate and graduate students through an international network of more than 100 campuses. Its main campus in St. Louis Missouri has an enrollment of more than 8000 students and 700 faculty and staff members. Other locations span the US and are also present in Europe Asia and other regions; many campuses are on military bases. Alumni include former shuttle commander Eileen Collins actress Marsha Mason and Indonesia's first democratically elected president Susilo Bambang Yudhoyono. Webster University was founded as a small Catholic women's college in 1915.

	Annual Growth	05/09	05/10	05/11	05/12	05/13
Sales ($ mil.)	1.6%	–	199.9	202.6	213.3	209.8
Net income ($ mil.)	3.7%	–	–	21.1	7.4	22.7
Market value ($ mil.)	–	–	–	–	–	–
Employees	–	–	–	–	–	4,500

WEC ENERGY GROUP INC   NYS: WEC

231 West Michigan Street, P.O. Box 1331	CEO: Gale E. Klappa
Milwaukee, WI 53201	CFO: J. Patrick Keyes
Phone: 414 221-2345	HR: Joan M. Shafer
Fax: 414 221-2172	FYE: December 31
Web: www.wisconsinenergy.com	Type: Public

Formerly Wisconsin Energy WEC Energy Group provides electricity and natural gas to nearly 4.5 million customers in four states. One of the largest natural gas distributors in the US the company operates through brands We Energies Wisconsin Public Service People Gas North Shore Gas Michigan Gas Utilities and Minnesota Energy Resources. It serves Wisconsin Illinois Michigan and Minnesota with some 70000 miles of electric distribution lines about 44000 miles of natural gas distribution and transmission lines and 8800 MW of generating capacity. The former Wisconsin Energy acquired Integrys Energy in mid-2015 to create WEC Energy Group.

	Annual Growth	12/10	12/11	12/12	12/13	12/14
Sales ($ mil.)	4.4%	4,202.5	4,486.4	4,246.4	4,519.0	4,997.1
Net income ($ mil.)	6.5%	456.5	526.2	546.3	577.4	588.3
Market value ($ mil.)	(2.7%)	13,274.0	7,884.1	8,310.3	9,322.9	11,893.8
Employees	(1.9%)	4,596	4,595	4,504	4,303	4,248

WEDBUSH SECURITIES INC.

1000 Wilshire Blvd.	CEO: Edward W Wedbush
Los Angeles CA 90017	CFO: Peter Allman-Ward
Phone: 213-688-8000	HR: –
Fax: 213-688-6652	FYE: June 30
Web: www.wedbush.com	Type: Private

Operating from the famed Wilshire Boulevard in L.A. brokerage firm Wedbush Securities offers investment banking and a range of financial services including financial planning sales and trading and clearing services. The firm which targets mid-market growth companies and entrepreneurs in California and the western US also provides research to institutional clients in the consumer products retail health care and other sectors. Its ClientLink service provides clients access to account information and reports via the Internet. Wedbush Securities is affiliated with investment firm Wedbush Capital Partners; both entities are controlled by holding company Wedbush Inc.

WEEDEN & CO. LP

145 Mason St.	CEO: Lance F Lonergan
Greenwich CT 06830	CFO: –
Phone: 203-861-7600	HR: –
Fax: 203-861-7701	FYE: December 31
Web: www.weedenco.com	Type: Private

Weeden & Co. works to weed out information so it can provide clients with institutional equities trading fixed income sales and trading and research services. The firm specializes in difficult-to-execute transactions serving some 1500 institutional clients. Weeden's research division which includes The Leuthold Group produces a variety of analytical reports on equity and fixed-income markets. Research affiliates cover such sectors as technology health care biotechnology and REITs. Brothers Frank and Norman Weeden founded the company in 1922 and the company has been employee-owned (more than 80%) since 1986. It has offices in Boston; Chicago; Greenwich Connecticut; Minneapolis; and San Francisco.

WEEKLEY HOMES L.P.

1111 N. Post Oak Rd.	CEO: David M Weekley
Houston TX 77055	CFO: –
Phone: 713-963-0500	HR: –
Fax: 713-963-0322	FYE: December 31
Web: www.davidweekleyhomes.com	Type: Private

Weekley Homes builds daily. Doing business as David Weekley Homes the company is one of the largest privately-held home builders in the US. It builds single-family detached houses ranging in size from about 1500 to 5000 sq. ft. Prices range from the low $100000s to more than $1 million. The company builds from hundreds of floor plans and offers a variety of custom options and upgrades. David Weekley homes are found in planned communities in more than 15 cities in the West Southeast and Mid-Atlantic. Founded in 1976 by its chairman and owner David Weekley the company has built more than 70000 new homes since its inception.

WEGENER CORP.

NBB: WGNR

11350 Technology Circle
Johns Creek, GA 30097-1502
Phone: 770 623-0096
Fax: 770 623-0698
Web: www.wegener.com

CEO: C Troy Woodbury Jr
CFO: James Traicoff
HR: –
FYE: August 29
Type: Public

Wegener doesn't mind broadcasting its business. The company through its Wegener Communications subsidiary makes transmission and receiving equipment primarily for the broadcast and data communications markets. Its products include digital and analog compression equipment that increases satellite channel capacity cue and control products that enable cable networks to insert local commercials devices that feed data to news and weather services and equipment that transmits background music to businesses. Customers include MUZAK and Roberts Communications.

	Annual Growth	09/10	09/11*	08/12	08/13	08/14
Sales ($ mil.)	(22.8%)	8.9	9.1	7.2	4.5	3.2
Net income ($ mil.)	–	(2.3)	(1.5)	(2.8)	(2.1)	(1.6)
Market value ($ mil.)	(17.6%)	1.3	1.1	0.4	0.2	0.6
Employees	(18.1%)	49	48	35	27	22

*Fiscal year change

WEGMANS FOOD MARKETS INC.

1500 Brooks Ave.
Rochester NY 14624
Phone: 585-328-2550
Fax: 415-772-4011
Web: www.wilbur-ellis.com

CEO: Danny Wegman
CFO: James J Leo
HR: –
FYE: December 31
Type: Private

One name strikes fear in the hearts of supermarket owners in New York New Jersey Pennsylvania Virginia and now Maryland and Massachusetts. Wegmans Food Markets. The regional grocery chain owns about 80 stores but they are hardly typical. Much larger than most supermarkets (up to 140000 sq. ft.) they offer more than 70000 products and house huge in-store cafes cheese shops with some 300 different varieties sub shops and French-style pastry shops. The company is known for its gourmet cooking classes and an extensive employee-training program. Founded in 1916 today Wegmans is one of the largest private companies in the US. The grocery chain is owned and run by the family of founder John Wegman.

WEIGHT WATCHERS INTERNATIONAL, INC.

NYS: WTW

675 Avenue of the Americas, 6th Floor
New York, NY 10010
Phone: 212 589-2700
Fax: –
Web: www.weightwatchersinternational.com

CEO: Ron Boire
CFO: Nicholas P. (Nick) Hotchkin
HR: Melissa Landi
FYE: January 03
Type: Public

Weight Watchers is big in weight loss. It hosts more than 36000 weekly meetings worldwide facilitated by more than 10000 leaders. In the form of a support group per se meetings cover nutrition advice and lifestyle tips to help its 800000 members lose weight and ultimately reach lifetime membership status. Weight Watchers also offers advice and recipes on its website and sells products such as recipe books food activity monitor and vitamins. Its Weight Watchers Magazine has a US readership of 8 million. Jean Nidetch and Al and Felice Lippert started Weight Watchers in 1963; it now holds classes in about 30 countries. European investment firm Artal Luxembourg owns about 52% of Weight Watchers.

	Annual Growth	01/11*	12/11	12/12	12/13*	01/15
Sales ($ mil.)	0.5%	1,452.0	1,819.2	1,826.8	1,724.1	1,479.9
Net income ($ mil.)	(15.6%)	194.2	304.9	257.4	204.7	98.6
Market value ($ mil.)	(12.9%)	2,126.1	3,119.6	2,887.7	1,855.6	1,221.0
Employees	(21.7%)	56,000	56,000	54,000	25,000	21,000

*Fiscal year change

WEIL GOTSHAL & MANGES LLP

767 5th Ave.
New York NY 10153
Phone: 212-310-8000
Fax: 212-310-8007
Web: www.weil.com

CEO: Barry M Wolf
CFO: –
HR: –
FYE: December 31
Type: Private - Partnershi

The seeds of today's Weil Gotshal & Manges may have been planted in New York but over the years the law firm's branches have spread far and wide. Founded in 1931 the firm has more than 1200 lawyers at about 20 offices in the US Europe and the Asia/Pacific region. Weil Gotshal maintains a full range of business-oriented practices which it organizes into five main areas: business finance and restructuring; corporate; litigation and regulatory; tax; and trusts and estates. Clients have included CBS Broadcasting General Electric and HM Capital Partners. Weil Gotshal has served as lead law firm in the clean-up of bankrupt Lehman Brothers whose Chapter 11 filing in 2008 shocked the financial world.

WEINGARTEN REALTY INVESTORS

NYS: WRI

2600 Citadel Plaza Drive, P.O. Box 924133
Houston, TX 77292-4133
Phone: 713 866-6000
Fax: –
Web: www.weingarten.com

CEO: Andrew M. Alexander
CFO: Stephen C. (Steve) Richter
HR: –
FYE: December 31
Type: Public

Weingarten Realty Investors is landlord to some of the nation's largest retailers including Kroger Safeway and The Home Depot. The real estate investment trust (REIT) owns develops manages and leases commercial real estate in some two dozen US states mainly in the South and West. The firm has interests in more than 230 developed income-producing properties and about a dozen projects at various stages of construction and development. Most of Weingarten's properties are community shopping centers anchored by major food retail or discount stores. The company pursues a shopping center-centric strategy.

	Annual Growth	12/10	12/11	12/12	12/13	12/14
Sales ($ mil.)	(1.9%)	554.7	541.6	503.5	497.7	514.4
Net income ($ mil.)	58.0%	46.2	15.6	146.6	220.3	288.0
Market value ($ mil.)	10.1%	2,910.3	2,672.7	3,279.0	3,358.6	4,277.3
Employees	(4.6%)	380	370	345	316	315

WEIRTON MEDICAL CENTER INC.

601 COLLIERS WAY
WEIRTON, WV 260625014
Phone: 304-797-6000
Fax: –
Web: www.weirtonmedical.com

CEO: –
CFO: Robert Frank
HR: Donna Robinson
FYE: June 30
Type: Private

There's nothing weird about Weirton Medical Center. The 240-bed not-for-profit hospital provides a wide range of health services to the tri-state region of West Virginia Ohio and Pennsylvania. Inpatient services include pediatrics obstetrics and other acute care services. Founded in 1953 the hospital also offers clinical and diagnostic care services such as emergency medicine home health care rehabilitation and occupational therapy. Weirton Medical Center has seen a steady decrease in patient volumes in recent years forcing the hospital to enact a number of cost-saving measures including cutting back on some services and laying off employees.

	Annual Growth	06/09	06/10	06/11	06/12	06/13
Sales ($ mil.)	2.3%	–	95.2	95.9	92.1	101.9
Net income ($ mil.)	–	–	–	(1.3)	(10.1)	4.5
Market value ($ mil.)	–	–	–	–	–	–
Employees	–	–	–	–	–	1,000

WEIS MARKETS, INC.

NYS: WMK

1000 S. Second Street, P.O. Box 471
Sunbury, PA 17801-0471
Phone: 570 286-4571
Fax: –
Web: www.weismarkets.com

CEO: Jonathan H. Weis
CFO: Scott F. Frost
HR: Alexander Jarrett
FYE: December 27
Type: Public

The Weis family is wise to the ways of grocery retailing. Weis (pronounced "Wise") Markets runs more than 160 grocery stores (averaging about 49000 sq. ft.) mostly in Pennsylvania but also in Maryland New Jersey New York and West Virginia as well as a single Save-A-Lot discount store in Pennsylvania. (In recent years the company has converted its Mr. Z's Food Mart King's Supermarkets and Cressler's Marketplace stores to the Weis Markets banner to go to market under a unified retail presence.) The founding Weis family controls the company.

	Annual Growth	12/10	12/11	12/12	12/13	12/14
Sales ($ mil.)	1.5%	2,620.4	2,752.5	2,701.4	2,692.6	2,776.7
Net income ($ mil.)	(5.2%)	68.3	75.6	82.5	71.7	55.2
Market value ($ mil.)	4.0%	1,088.6	1,074.3	1,037.5	1,376.1	1,272.8
Employees	0.7%	17,700	17,400	17,400	17,900	18,200

WELCH FOODS INC. A COOPERATIVE

300 BAKER AVE STE 101
CONCORD, MA 017422131
Phone: 978-371-1000
Fax: –
Web: www.welchs.com

CEO: Bradley Irwin
CFO: Michael Perda
HR: –
FYE: August 31
Type: Private

Welch Foods has a taste for the grape. An operating subsidiary of the 1000-plus-farmer owner National Grape Cooperative Welch produces the Welch's brand grape and white grape juices and jellies. Its beverage line includes refrigerated and sparkling juices and cocktails frozen and shelf-stable concentrates and single-serve drinks. Welch supplies fresh grapes as well as preserved offerings (jams and spreads) which are also sold under the BAMA label. The co-op licenses the Welch's name to other manufactures of frozen fruit confections dried fruit and carbonated beverages among many. Its 400-plus products are purchased by grocery retailers and food service operators in the US and 40 other countries.

	Annual Growth	08/10	08/11	08/12	08/13	08/14
Sales ($ mil.)	(1.6%)	–	640.9	649.5	608.5	609.9
Net income ($ mil.)	1.7%	–	–	74.4	65.1	76.9
Market value ($ mil.)	–	–	–	–	–	–
Employees	–	–	–	–	–	1,000

WELLCARE HEALTH PLANS INC

NYS: WCG

8725 Henderson Road, Renaissance One
Tampa, FL 33634
Phone: 813 290-6200
Fax: –
Web: www.wellcare.com

CEO: Kenneth A. (Ken) Burdick
CFO: Andrew L. (Drew) Asher
HR: Michael Wellman
FYE: December 31
Type: Public

WellCare knows that to get well all you need is a little care. WellCare Health Plans provides managed-care administrative services to government-funded health care programs that provide health care benefits via Medicaid Medicare and various State Children's Health Insurance Programs. Services include benefits management and claims processing. WellCare Health Plans administers its Medicaid plans under various brands such as Staywell and HealthEase in Florida; WellCare in Ohio Georgia Kentucky New York and South Carolina; Harmony in Illinois; Missouri Care in Missouri; and 'Ohana in Hawaii. The company's Medicare prescription-drug and Medicare Advantage plans operate primarily under the WellCare brand.

	Annual Growth	12/11	12/12	12/13	12/14	12/15
Sales ($ mil.)	22.8%	6,106.9	7,409.0	9,527.9	12,959.9	13,890.2
Net income ($ mil.)	(18.1%)	264.2	184.7	175.3	63.7	118.6
Market value ($ mil.)	10.5%	2,315.9	2,147.9	3,106.5	3,619.9	3,450.1
Employees	14.7%	3,990	4,460	5,200	6,700	6,900

WELLCO ENTERPRISES INC.

150 Westwood Cir.
Waynesville NC 28786
Phone: 828-456-3545
Fax: 828-456-3547
Web: www.wellco.com

CEO: Lee Ferguson
CFO: –
HR: –
FYE: June 30
Type: Private

Wellco Enterprises keeps in step with US military footwear needs. The company makes rugged footwear primarily for the US military under firm fixed-price contracts. Sales to the military accounts for most of Wellco's sales. The company's boots include general-issue all-leather boots hot-weather (tropical) boots intermediate cold/wet boots desert boots (used in the Persian Gulf War) and antipersonnel mine blast protective boots. The estate of former director James Emerson owned about 57% of Wellco until it was bought by Golden Gate Capital and Integrity Brands in May 2007 and taken private.

WELLINGTON MANAGEMENT COMPANY LLP

75 State St.
Boston MA 02109
Phone: 617-951-5000
Fax: 617-954-6620
Web: www.mfs.com

CEO: Brendan Joseph Swords
CFO: –
HR: –
FYE: December 31
Type: Private - Partnershi

If Napoleon had met this Wellington Waterloo would have taken on a whole new meaning: sound asset management. Wellington Management oversees investments for more than 2000 institutional clients in some 50 countries. It has approximately $620 billion of assets under management. Clients include central banks corporations retirement plans endowments foundations insurance companies and investment funds; the firm's investment minimum is $5 million. Most assets under management are invested in stocks and bonds but alternative investments are also offered. The company has about a dozen offices in the US Europe Asia and Australia. Founded in 1928 Wellington Management is owned by its limited partners.

WELLMONT HEALTH SYSTEM

1905 AMERICAN WAY
KINGSPORT, TN 376605882
Phone: 423-230-8200
Fax: –
Web: www.wellmont.newsroom.meltwaterpress.com

CEO: Margaret (Denny) DeNarvaez
CFO: Alice Pope
HR: –
FYE: June 30
Type: Private

At Wellmont Health System wellness is paramount. Wellmont Health System provides general and advanced medical-surgical care to residents of northeastern Tennessee and southwestern Virginia. The health system consists of about a dozen owned and affiliated hospitals that collectively have more than 1000 licensed beds. One of its facilities is a rehabilitation hospital operated in partnership with HealthSouth. The system's Holston Valley Medical Center features a level I trauma center and a level III neonatal intensive care unit (NICU). Wellmont also operates numerous ancillary facilities including an assisted living center a mental health clinic home health care and hospice agencies and outpatient centers.

	Annual Growth	06/06	06/07	06/08	06/09	06/10
Sales ($ mil.)	(40.8%)	–	–	1,772.0	3.0	622.0
Net income ($ mil.)	4451.4%	–	–	0.0	0.0	33.9
Market value ($ mil.)	–	–	–	–	–	–
Employees	–	–	–	–	–	6,114

WELLS ENTERPRISES INC.

1 Blue Bunny Dr.	CEO: Michael C Wells
Le Mars IA 51031	CFO: –
Phone: 712-546-4000	HR: Brittany Sickels
Fax: 712-548-3011	FYE: December 31
Web: www.wellsenterprisesinc.com	Type: Private

You scream I scream we all scream for Wells Enterprises. The family-owned and operated manufacturer is best known for Blue Bunny brand ice cream and frozen novelties like Bunny Tracks (vanilla ice cream with fudge and peanut butter caramel ribbons and other goodies) and red-white-and-blue Bomb Pop. Wells also makes frozen dairy desserts under license including Cadbury ice cream bars and Yoplait frozen yogurt pints. It sells the lineup through supermarkets discount retailers convenience stores and vending machines nationwide. A foodservice division supplies dairy desserts to restaurants schools and ice cream shops. Wells has a retail presence too through the Blue Bunny Ice Cream Parlor and Museum.

WELLS FARGO ADVISORS LLC

1 N. Jefferson	CEO: –
St. Louis MO 63103	CFO: –
Phone: 314-955-3000	HR: Julie D Joyce
Fax: 847-969-3338	FYE: December 31
Web: www.pliantcorp.com	Type: Subsidiary

The iconic Wells Fargo stagecoach has a few extra stops to make. Wells Fargo Advisors is one of the nation's largest retail brokerages with more than 15000 financial advisors and some $1 trillion in client assets. The company provides advisory services asset management estate and retirement planning brokerage and portfolio monitoring services. Wells Fargo Advisors has around 1300 office locations many within Wells Fargo branches. After buying Wachovia in the largest bank acquisition to date Wells Fargo merged its existing brokerage operations with Wachovia Securities in 2009 and rebranded the firm as Wells Fargo Advisors.

WELLS FINANCIAL CORP

NBB: WEFP

53 First Street, S.W., P.O. Box 310	CEO: James D Moll
Wells, MN 56097	CFO: James Mall
Phone: 507 553-3151	HR: –
Fax: 507 553-6295	FYE: December 31
Web: www.wellsfinancialcorp.com	Type: Public

Wells Financial doesn't want you to get tapped out. It's the holding company for Wells Federal Bank which serves southern Minnesota and northern Iowa through 10 branches and a loan production office. Founded in 1934 the bank offers standard deposit services and credit cards. Mortgages secured by agricultural real estate and one- to four-family residences comprise most of the bank's lending activities; consumer business and construction loans round out its loan portfolio. Bank subsidiary Wells Insurance Agency sells property/casualty life and health insurance and mutual funds and Greater Minnesota Mortgage originates home loans for resale through referrals from other community banks.

	Annual Growth	12/03	12/04	12/12	12/13	12/14
Assets ($ mil.)	1.1%	223.8	239.4	244.2	243.8	251.8
Net income ($ mil.)	(8.7%)	3.5	2.2	1.6	1.2	1.3
Market value ($ mil.)	(0.9%)	22.3	24.1	13.2	16.5	20.1
Employees	–	97	–	–	–	–

WELLS LAMONT CORPORATION

6640 W. Touhy Ave.	CEO: Keith Swain
Niles IL 60714	CFO: Walter Beckman
Phone: 847-647-8200	HR: –
Fax: 800-822-1615	FYE: December 31
Web: www.wellslamont.com	Type: Subsidiary

Let's give a big hand to Wells Lamont. The century-old company established in 1907 is the world's largest glove maker. It manufactures hand coverings including work gloves garden gloves hunting gloves mittens and professional oven mitts. Wells Lamont operates through three business units. Its namesake unit makes gloves for the retail market; Midwest Leather Group operates leather and pigskin tanneries; and Wells Lamont Industry Group makes protective hand coverings for industrial use. Its foreign subsidiaries include Canada's Jomac and Hong Kong's Austins Marmon. It sells its products through such retailers as Wal-Mart Lowe's Sears Callahan's and others. Wells Lamont is owned by The Marmon Group.

WELLSTAR HEALTH SYSTEM INC.

805 SANDY PLAINS RD	CEO: Reynold J Jennings
MARIETTA, GA 30066-6340	CFO: A James Budzinski
Phone: 770-792-7600	HR: –
Fax: –	FYE: June 30
Web: www.wellstar.org	Type: Private

With WellStar in your corner you won't need to wish upon a star for good health and wellness. The not-for-profit WellStar Health System serves four counties in northwest Georgia through five acute care hospitals a physician group and an array of outpatient services. The network's hospitals specialize in cardiac and cancer care diabetes treatments and women's health; together the five hospitals house about 1700 beds. WellStar's physician group operates through some 80 locations with more than 400 providers. The network is also home to hospice and home care programs; Atherton Place an independent living center for senior citizens; and several urgent care facilities.

	Annual Growth	06/06	06/07	06/08	06/09	06/11
Sales ($ mil.)	380.1%	–	–	5.4	397.7	595.7
Net income ($ mil.)	324.7%	–	–	1.8	0.0	136.5
Market value ($ mil.)	–	–	–	–	–	–
Employees	–	–	–	–	–	11,000

WELLTOWER INC

NYS: HCN

4500 Dorr Street	CEO: Thomas J. DeRosa
Toledo, OH 43615	CFO: Scott A. Estes
Phone: 419 247-2800	HR: –
Fax: –	FYE: December 31
Web: www.welltower.com/#investors/governance	Type: Public

Welltower (formerly Health Care REIT) is a real estate investment trust (REIT) that invests in senior living and health care facilities primarily skilled nursing and assisted-living facilities designed for older people needing help with everyday living. The trust also has investments in independent living facilities hospitals medical office buildings and specialty care facilities. Its $22.9 billion portfolio includes more than 1325 properties leased to health care operators in 46 US states Canada and the UK. Additionally the company develops new build-to-suit properties through its HCN Development Services Group subsidiary. It also invests in mortgage loans and provides construction financing for its existing properties.

	Annual Growth	12/10	12/11	12/12	12/13	12/14
Sales ($ mil.)	48.9%	680.5	1,421.2	1,822.1	2,880.6	3,343.5
Net income ($ mil.)	41.2%	128.9	212.7	294.8	138.3	512.3
Market value ($ mil.)	12.3%	15,663.6	17,928.9	20,151.5	17,613.3	24,879.5
Employees	13.6%	263	308	366	404	438

WENDY'S CO (THE)

NMS: WEN

One Dave Thomas Blvd.
Dublin, OH 43017
Phone: 614 764-3100
Fax: –
Web: www.wendys.com

CEO: Emil J. Brolick
CFO: Todd A. Penegor
HR: –
FYE: December 28
Type: Public

The Wendy's Company is the #2 hamburger chain in the US behind #1 McDonald's and just in front of #3 chain Burger King. The Wendy's chain consists of nearly 6515 restaurants in the US and about 27 other countries. Besides burgers and fries the restaurants serve chicken sandwiches wraps and a variety of salads. Instead of milkshakes Wendy's serves its famously thick Frosty. About three-fourths of the company's locations are franchised and it generates most of its sales in the US (around 85%). In 2014 the company was purchased by Global Food Retail Group for about $10 million.

	Annual Growth	01/11	01/12*	12/12	12/13	12/14
Sales ($ mil.)	(15.5%)	3,416.4	2,431.4	2,505.2	2,487.4	2,061.1
Net income ($ mil.)	–	(4.3)	9.9	7.1	45.5	121.4
Market value ($ mil.)	24.5%	1,690.0	1,960.7	1,730.3	3,208.2	3,263.0
Employees	(21.3%)	64,100	42,800	44,000	37,000	31,200

*Fiscal year change

WENDY'S INTERNATIONAL INC.

1 Dave Thomas Blvd.
Dublin OH 43017
Phone: 614-764-3100
Fax: 610-594-3000
Web: www.westpharma.com

CEO: Emil J Brolick
CFO: –
HR: –
FYE: December 31
Type: Subsidiary

Burger lovers lay down their singles for doubles and triples from this company. A leader in the fast food business Wendy's International operates the world's #3 hamburger chain in terms of locations (behind McDonald's and Burger King) with more than 6575 of its Wendy's Old Fashioned Hamburger eateries in the US and about 20 other countries. The Wendy's chain offers made-to-order burgers and fries as well as such alternative menu items as baked potatoes chili and salads. About 1400 of the restaurants are owned by the company while the rest are franchised. Wendy's International is a subsidiary of The Wendy's Company.

WENNER MEDIA LLC

1290 Avenue of the Americas 2nd Fl.
New York NY 10104-0298
Phone: 212-484-1616
Fax: 212-484-3435

CEO: Hugh Scogin
CFO: –
HR: –
FYE: December 31
Type: Private

How does it feel to be a complete unknown? The rock stars that grace the cover of Rolling Stone wouldn't know. Magazine publisher Wenner Media owns "Rolling Stone" its flagship publication that has been covering music and pop culture for more than four decades. The company also publishes men's lifestyle mag "Men's Journal" and gossipy entertainment title "US Weekly". In addition Wenner Media operates its magazines' corresponding websites — RollingStone.com USMagazine.com and MensJournal.com. More than 42 million readers read its magazines each month while 22 million people visit the company's websites. Jann Wenner started "Rolling Stone" in 1967.

WERNER CO.

93 Werner Rd.
Greenville PA 16125
Phone: 724-588-8600
Fax: 724-588-0315
Web: www.wernerladder.com

CEO: William T Allen
CFO: Larry V Friend
HR: –
FYE: December 31
Type: Private

If a man's reach exceeds his grasp perhaps he should buy a Werner. The company is one of the world's top producers of ladders. For the do-it-yourselfer Werner makes extension step attic and platform ladders made of wood fiberglass or aluminum. In addition to traditional ladders Werner manufactures a full line of professional-grade platforms scaffolding stages clotheslines and ladder jacks and accessories. Its brand portfolio includes namesake Werner Knaak Weather Guard Green Bull Keller and Abru in addition to other licensed names. Werner is owned by a group of investment firms including Black Diamond Capital Management Milk Street Investors and Schultze Asset Management.

WERNER ENTERPRISES, INC.

NMS: WERN

14507 Frontier Road, Post Office Box 45308
Omaha, NE 68145-0308
Phone: 402 895-6640
Fax: –
Web: www.werner.com

CEO: Gregory L. Werner
CFO: John J. Steele
HR: Chris Polenx
FYE: December 31
Type: Public

Transportation and logistics is Werner Enterprises' game; hauling truckload shipments — both interstate and intrastate — is its fame. One of the five largest truckload carriers in the US Werner operates more than 7000 tractors and almost 24000 trailers. Its trailer fleet consists of dry vans as well as temperature-controlled vans and flatbeds. Werner's truckload transportation offerings include dedicated contract carriage in which drivers and equipment are assigned to a customer. It also offers freight brokerage intermodal freight transportation and other value-added logistic services as well as freight forwarding.

	Annual Growth	12/10	12/11	12/12	12/13	12/14
Sales ($ mil.)	4.2%	1,815.0	2,002.9	2,036.4	2,029.2	2,139.3
Net income ($ mil.)	5.4%	80.0	102.8	103.0	86.8	98.7
Market value ($ mil.)	8.4%	1,628.1	1,736.1	1,561.1	1,781.5	2,244.0
Employees	2.5%	11,626	11,383	11,580	12,326	12,828

WESBANCO, INC.

NMS: WSBC

1 Bank Plaza
Wheeling, WV 26003
Phone: 304 234-9000
Fax: –
Web: www.wesbanco.com

CEO: Todd F. Clossin
CFO: Robert H. Young
HR: Anthony F. Pietranton
FYE: December 31
Type: Public

WesBanco wants to be the "BesBanco" for its customers. The holding company owns WesBanco Bank which has about 120 branches in West Virginia Ohio and western Pennsylvania. In addition to providing traditional services such as deposits and loans the bank operates a wealth management department with ten offices in West Virginia and Ohio and some $3 billion of assets under management and custody including the company's proprietary WesMark mutual funds. Other units include brokerage firm WesBanco Securities and multiline insurance provider WesBanco Insurance Services.

	Annual Growth	12/10	12/11	12/12	12/13	12/14
Assets ($ mil.)	4.1%	5,361.5	5,536.0	6,078.7	6,144.8	6,296.6
Net income ($ mil.)	18.4%	35.6	43.8	49.5	63.9	70.0
Market value ($ mil.)	16.4%	555.5	570.4	651.0	937.5	1,019.6
Employees	1.3%	1,377	1,368	1,507	1,469	1,448

WESCO AIRCRAFT HOLDINGS INC.

NYS: WAIR

24911 Avenue Stanford
Valencia, CA 91355
Phone: 661 775-7200
Fax: –
Web: www.wescoair.com

CEO: David J. (Dave) Castagnola
CFO: Richard J. (Rick) Weller
HR: Felicia Williams
FYE: September 30
Type: Public

Planes may fly around the world but they can't leave the ground without Wesco Aircraft Holdings. One of the largest logistics and supply chain companies serving the aerospace industry it provides distribution vendor relationship management just-in-time (JIT) delivery quality assurance and kitting. Operating through Wesco Aircraft Hardware and other subsidiaries the company stocks about 525000 different pieces of hardware bearings tools electronic components and machined parts from more than 1200 suppliers. Boeing Airbus and Bombardier are among its largest customers.

	Annual Growth	09/11	09/12	09/13	09/14	09/15
Sales ($ mil.)	20.5%	710.9	776.2	901.6	1,355.9	1,497.6
Net income ($ mil.)	–	75.6	92.2	104.8	102.1	(154.7)
Market value ($ mil.)	2.8%	1,066.1	1,332.4	2,041.5	1,697.2	1,190.0
Employees	27.4%	1,014	1,218	1,354	2,785	2,670

WESCO FINANCIAL LLC

301 E. Colorado Blvd. Ste. 300
Pasadena CA 91101-1901
Phone: 626-585-6700
Fax: 626-449-1455
Web: www.wescofinancial.com

CEO: –
CFO: –
HR: –
FYE: December 31
Type: Subsidiary

Wesco Financial is sort of like Berkshire Hathaway Lite. Charlie Munger Berkshire vice chairman and a confidante of Warren Buffett leads Wesco. And like Berkshire the investment firm provides insurance and reinsurance; in Wesco's case it does so through subsidiaries Wesco-Financial Insurance Company and Kansas Bankers Surety. It also holds shares in some of the same companies as Berkshire like Coca-Cola Kraft Procter & Gamble and Wells Fargo. Other prominent holdings include CORT Business Services and Precision Steel Warehouse which has steel service centers in Chicago and Charlotte North Carolina. In 2011 Berkshire Hathaway acquired the 20% of Wesco that it didn't already own.

WESCO INTERNATIONAL, INC.

NYS: WCC

225 West Station Square Drive, Suite 700
Pittsburgh, PA 15219
Phone: 412 454-2200
Fax: –
Web: www.wesco.com

CEO: John J. Engel
CFO: Kenneth S. Parks
HR: Kimberly G. Windrow
FYE: December 31
Type: Public

When contractors and manufacturers need parts it's WESCO to the rescue. The company distributes electrical products (fuses terminals connectors enclosures circuit breakers transformers switchboards) industrial supplies (tools abrasives filters safety equipment) lighting (lamps fixtures ballasts) wire and conduit materials automation equipment (motors drives logic controllers) and data communication gear (patch panels terminals connectors). WESCO offers more than a million products from some 25000 suppliers with about 100000 customers worldwide. It operates through a dozen subsidiaries. The company generates nearly all of its sales in North America predominantly the US.

	Annual Growth	12/10	12/11	12/12	12/13	12/14
Sales ($ mil.)	11.7%	5,063.9	6,125.7	6,579.3	7,513.3	7,889.6
Net income ($ mil.)	24.3%	115.5	196.3	201.8	276.4	275.9
Market value ($ mil.)	9.6%	2,349.1	2,358.4	3,000.0	4,051.7	3,390.6
Employees	8.4%	6,800	7,100	9,000	9,200	9,400

WESCOM CREDIT UNION

123 S. Marengo Ave.
Pasadena CA 91101
Phone: 626-535-1000
Fax: 925-687-2122

CEO: Darren Williams
CFO: –
HR: –
FYE: December 31
Type: Private - Not-for-Pr

At Wescom you're welcome. Through about 30 branches in Southern California Wescom Credit Union provides checking savings and money market accounts IRAs savings certificates home loans reverse mortgages auto loans and Visa credit cards to approximately 250000 member-owners in seven counties. Its Wescom Financial Services division offers trust investment online trading and financial planning services while Wescom Insurance Services sells auto and home coverage. The credit union's Wescom Resources Group unit develops technology services including online banking statements bill payment and mobile applications for other credit unions.

WESLEYAN UNIVERSITY (INC)

45 WYLLYS AVE
MIDDLETOWN, CT 064593211
Phone: 860-685-2000
Fax: –
Web: www.wesleyan.edu

CEO: –
CFO: –
HR: Patrice T Melley
FYE: June 30
Type: Private

Wesleyan University is a private institution offering liberal arts and sciences education from its 360-acre campus in Middleton Connecticut. Some 3500 undergraduate and graduate students attend the university which has programs in academic areas including American studies film studies and psychology. Notable alumni include television producer Joss Whedon and educational writer Ted Fiske. Founded in 1831 Wesleyan was the first of several US colleges and universities to be named after John Wesley founder of the Methodist church; it ended its formal affiliation with the church in 1937.

	Annual Growth	06/03	06/04	06/05	06/06	06/07
Sales ($ mil.)	4.4%	–	–	–	172.2	179.8
Net income ($ mil.)	(4.9%)	–	–	–	95.0	90.3
Market value ($ mil.)		–	–	–	–	–
Employees	–	–	–	–	–	900

WEST BANCORPORATION, INC.

NMS: WTBA

1601 22nd Street
West Des Moines, IA 50266
Phone: 515 222-2300
Fax: –
Web: www.westbankiowa.com

CEO: David D. (Dave) Nelson
CFO: Douglas R. (Doug) Gulling
HR: –
FYE: December 31
Type: Public

West Bancorporation is the holding company for West Bank which serves individuals and small to midsized businesses through about a dozen branches mainly in the Des Moines and Iowa City Iowa areas. Founded in 1893 the bank offers checking savings and money market accounts CDs Visa credit cards and trust services. The bank's lending activities primarily consist of commercial mortgages; construction land and land development loans; and business loans such as revolving lines of credit inventory and accounts receivable financing equipment financing and capital expenditure loans to borrowers in Iowa.

	Annual Growth	12/10	12/11	12/12	12/13	12/14
Assets ($ mil.)	5.5%	1,305.5	1,269.5	1,448.2	1,442.4	1,615.8
Net income ($ mil.)	10.6%	13.4	15.3	16.0	16.9	20.0
Market value ($ mil.)	21.6%	124.8	153.5	172.7	253.4	272.6
Employees	1.2%	170	190	180	187	178

WEST BEND MUTUAL INSURANCE COMPANY

1900 S. 18th Ave.
West Bend WI 53095
Phone: 262-334-5571
Fax: 262-335-7010
Web: www.westbendmutual.com

CEO: Kevin Steiner
CFO: Dale Kent
HR: –
FYE: December 31
Type: Private - Mutual Com

Homeowners in the Midwest may not worry about hurricanes or tsunamis but mighty storms can be a real concern. As the "Silver Lining" West Bend Mutual helps protect property and other assets for its members in 10 states. The company provides personal and commercial property/casualty insurance including auto homeowners and umbrella coverage. Its National Specialty Insurance (NSI) division offers specialty policies for businesses including child care centers tanning parlors not-for-profit organizations and athletic leagues. Its Argent workers' compensation division specializes in writing large accounts. About 1200 independent agencies represent West Bend Mutual which was founded in 1894.

WEST COAST NOVELTY CORPORATION

2401 MONARCH ST
ALAMEDA, CA 945017513
Phone: 510-748-4248
Fax: –
Web: www.westcoastnovelty.com

CEO: Brian T McCroden
CFO: –
HR: –
FYE: August 31
Type: Private

|West Coast Novelty Corp. founded in the 1920s doesn't make concessions as one of the largest suppliers of licensed sports merchandise in the US. The firm has grown from its beginnings as a souvenir and concession operator to a nationwide distributor of licensed items such as jerseys T-shirts and headwear. West Coast Novelty boasts a vast portfolio of team licenses based on its agreements with the NFL MLB NBA WWF and the Collegiate Licensing Company. To extend its reach into the Eastern and Southern US the company operates a distribution center in Memphis Tennessee to supplement operations at its Alameda California facility.

	Annual Growth	08/06	08/07	08/08	08/09	08/10
Sales ($ mil.)	(86.6%)	–	–	2,104.9	45.0	37.6
Net income ($ mil.)	–	–	–	0.0	(0.5)	(0.0)
Market value ($ mil.)	–	–	–	–	–	–
Employees	–	–	–	–	–	80

WEST CORP.

NMS: WSTC

11808 Miracle Hills Drive
Omaha, NE 68154
Phone: 402 963-1200
Fax: –

CEO: Thomas B. (Tom) Barker
CFO: Jan D. Madsen
HR: Penny Majeski
FYE: December 31
Type: Public

If it's communication services you need why not go West? West Corporation provides technology-driven voice-oriented services through about 45 call centers and automated voice and data centers. It offers inbound and outbound call handling (including 911 support through its Intrado subsidiary) for services such as customer support technical assistance and order processing. It also provides automated and Web-based customer care programs through its West Interactive division and lead management team selling and sales management services through West Business Services. West additionally offers conference call services through its Intercall operations and it is a leading debt collections agency in the US.

	Annual Growth	12/10	12/11	12/12	12/13	12/14
Sales ($ mil.)	(1.8%)	2,388.2	2,491.3	2,638.0	2,685.9	2,218.6
Net income ($ mil.)	27.3%	60.3	127.5	125.5	143.2	158.4
Market value ($ mil.)	28.4%	–	–	–	2,164.3	2,777.9
Employees	(26.6%)	33,400	36,500	35,700	35,100	9,700

WEST MARINE, INC.

NMS: WMAR

500 Westridge Drive
Watsonville, CA 95076-4100
Phone: 831 728-2700
Fax: –
Web: www.westmarine.com

CEO: Matthew (Matt) Hyde
CFO: Jeffrey L. (Jeff) Lasher
HR: –
FYE: January 03
Type: Public

West Marine has the goods to keep your boat shipshape. It is the nation's #1 boating supplies retailer operating through some 300 company-owned stores as well as a port supply wholesale business and direct-to-customer website catalog and call center. Its stores known by the West Marine banner dot 38 US states Canada and Puerto Rico. Five stores are franchised in Turkey. Its direct-to-consumer arm offers about 75000 boating products worldwide. The port supply business provides wholesaling and distribution to commercial government and industrial customers. West Marine's distribution centers are in California and South Carolina. The company was founded by Randolph Repass in 1975 as West Coast Ropes.

	Annual Growth	01/11*	12/11	12/12	12/13*	01/15
Sales ($ mil.)	2.1%	622.8	643.4	675.3	663.2	675.8
Net income ($ mil.)	(38.1%)	13.2	29.7	15.5	7.8	1.9
Market value ($ mil.)	4.3%	258.2	283.8	260.9	345.1	305.0
Employees	(1.9%)	3,927	4,043	3,955	3,783	3,642

*Fiscal year change

WEST PENN ALLEGHENY HEALTH SYSTEM INC.

4800 Friendship Ave.
Pittsburgh PA 15224
Phone: 412-578-5000
Fax: 610-649-1798
Web: www.hajoca.com

CEO: John Paul
CFO: David Samuel
HR: –
FYE: June 30
Type: Private - Not-for-Pr

West Penn Allegheny Health System (WPAHS) makes wellness a priority for Steel Town residents. The health system which operates with some 1600 beds is a network of affiliated hospitals serving the greater Pittsburgh area including Allegheny General Hospital Allegheny Valley Hospital Canonsburg General Hospital The Western Pennsylvania Hospital (West Penn) and the West Penn-Forbes Regional Campus. Among its specialty services are cancer treatment emergency medicine and orthopedics. The system's clinical campuses are affiliated with Drexel University and Temple University. WPAHS handles some 200000 emergency visits each year.

WEST PHARMACEUTICAL SERVICES, INC.

NYS: WST

530 Herman O. West Drive
Exton, PA 19341-0645
Phone: 610 594-2900
Fax: –
Web: www.westpharma.com

CEO: Eric M. Green
CFO: William J. Federici
HR: Brian Stocker
FYE: December 31
Type: Public

West Pharmaceutical Services makes the bits and pieces of health care products that you may not notice but you'd have a hard time doing without. The firm makes drug packaging components and offers other services to pharmaceutical companies. The packaging systems segment manufactures drug packaging disposable medical components and laboratory services products including seals and stoppers for injectable medications and blood collection and prefillable syringe components. The delivery systems division focuses on drug administration items such as advanced injection systems.

	Annual Growth	12/10	12/11	12/12	12/13	12/14
Sales ($ mil.)	6.5%	1,104.7	1,192.3	1,266.4	1,368.4	1,421.4
Net income ($ mil.)	18.1%	65.3	75.5	80.7	112.3	127.1
Market value ($ mil.)	6.6%	2,937.6	2,705.8	3,903.7	3,498.0	3,796.0
Employees	1.5%	6,600	6,300	6,700	6,900	7,000

WEST PUBLISHING CORPORATION

5100 W. Goldleaf Cir. Ste. 100
Los Angeles CA 90056-1271
Phone: 323-642-5200
Fax: 323-642-5400
Web: www.elite.com

CEO: Peter Warwick
CFO: –
HR: –
FYE: December 31
Type: Business Segment

West Publishing (formerly Elite) helps lawyers and other professionals rise above all the paperwork. The software developer provides business and practice management applications for law firms professional services companies and financial services providers. Products include applications for tracking case information managing timekeeping billing accounts payable customer relationships case files and reporting. Other tools automate practice management functions for small and midsized companies outside the legal industry and help them manage their own legal documents. A business segment of media giant Thomson Reuters West Publishing has offices in Asia Australia Europe and North America.

WEST TEXAS GAS INC.

211 N COLORADO ST
MIDLAND, TX 797014607
Phone: 432-682-4349
Fax: –
Web: www.westtexasgas.com

CEO: –
CFO: –
HR: –
FYE: December 31
Type: Private

With a deep understanding the utility of natural gas natural gas utility West Texas Gas distributes more than 25 billion cu. ft. of natural gas propane and other petroleum products to more than 25000 residential commercial agricultural and governmental customers in Texas and Oklahoma Panhandle region. The company the fourth-largest investor-owned public utility in Texas also operates retail gasoline stations and convenience stores and has gas gathering production transmission and marketing operations. West Texas Gas is 100%-owned by CEO J. L. Davis.

	Annual Growth	12/03	12/04	12/05	12/06	12/07
Sales ($ mil.)	12.4%	–	625.7	795.7	745.3	889.3
Net income ($ mil.)	5.3%	–	–	36.4	65.3	40.3
Market value ($ mil.)	–	–	–	–	–	–
Employees	–	–	–	–	–	600

WEST VIRGINIA UNITED HEALTH SYSTEM INC.

1000 TECH DR STE 2320
FAIRMONT, WV 26554
Phone: 304-368-2700
Fax: –

CEO: Christopher Colenda
CFO: –
HR: –
FYE: December 31
Type: Private

West Virginia United Health System (WVUHS) helps residents in the Mountain State stay on top of their health. The system operates United Hospital Center (in Clarksburg) as well as hospitals in the West Virginia University Hospitals (WVUH) system including City Hospital (Martinsburg) Jefferson Memorial Hospital (Ranson) and WVUH's home hospital in Morgantown. In addition WVUHS operates WVUH's Cheat Lake physicians ambulatory center as well as a network of about a dozen primary care clinics located throughout central and northern West Virginia. Combined the system's hospitals and clinics have more than 1000 beds and treat approximately 1.4 million patients annually.

	Annual Growth	12/07	12/08	12/09	12/12	12/13
Sales ($ mil.)	179.1%	–	4.2	4.8	1,386.7	703.7
Net income ($ mil.)	–	–	–	(0.1)	96.1	97.2
Market value ($ mil.)	–	–	–	–	–	–
Employees	–	–	–	–	–	13

WESTAMERICA BANCORPORATION

NMS: WABC

1108 Fifth Avenue
San Rafael, CA 94901
Phone: 707 863-6000
Fax: –
Web: www.westamerica.com

CEO: David L. Payne
CFO: Robert A. Thorson
HR: Pat Kilkenny
FYE: December 31
Type: Public

Annie get your checkbook? Maybe not as wild as Buffalo Bill's West but Westamerica Bancorporation still shoots high with its subsidiary Westamerica Bank. The bank operates almost 100 branches in Northern and Central California. It offers individuals and businesses such standard fare as checking and savings accounts as well as electronic banking trust services and credit cards. It focuses on the banking needs of small businesses; business loans and commercial mortgages together account for more than half of the company's loan portfolio. Westamerica Bank chartered in 1884 also originates construction residential mortgage and consumer loans.

	Annual Growth	12/10	12/11	12/12	12/13	12/14
Assets ($ mil.)	0.5%	4,931.5	5,042.2	4,952.2	4,847.1	5,035.7
Net income ($ mil.)	(10.5%)	94.6	87.9	81.1	67.2	60.6
Market value ($ mil.)	(3.0%)	1,428.1	1,130.2	1,096.5	1,453.6	1,262.0
Employees	(3.7%)	999	961	935	914	858

WESTAR ENERGY INC

NYS: WR

818 South Kansas Avenue
Topeka, KS 66612
Phone: 785 575-6300
Fax: –
Web: www.westarenergy.com

CEO: Mark A. Ruelle
CFO: Anthony D. (Tony) Somma
HR: –
FYE: December 31
Type: Public

Westar Energy wished upon a star and the answer was — "focus on power utility resources." Westar Energy has a generating capacity of about 7200 MW (mostly from fossil-fueled facilities) and serves about 700000 electricity customers in Kansas through its utility subsidiaries. Westar Energy supplies power to retail customers in central and northeastern Kansas and subsidiary Kansas Gas and Electric (KGE) supplies power to retail customers in south-central and southeastern Kansas. The company operates 35100 miles of transmission and distribution lines. It supplies wholesale electric power to more than 30 cities in Kansas and four electric cooperatives that serve rural areas.

	Annual Growth	12/10	12/11	12/12	12/13	12/14
Sales ($ mil.)	6.1%	2,056.2	2,171.0	2,261.5	2,370.7	2,601.7
Net income ($ mil.)	11.3%	203.9	230.2	275.1	292.5	313.3
Market value ($ mil.)	13.1%	3,313.3	3,790.0	3,768.9	4,236.4	5,430.8
Employees	0.0%	2,409	2,424	2,313	2,302	2,411

WESTAT INC.

1600 RESEARCH BLVD
ROCKVILLE, MD 208503129
Phone: 301-251-1500
Fax: –
Web: www.westat.com

CEO: –
CFO: –
HR: Randy Yu
FYE: December 31
Type: Private

Survey the market research business and you'll find Westat among the leaders of the pack. A statistical survey organization the company provides research and consulting services including study design and analysis data collection program evaluation and communications campaign development. It has technical expertise in survey and analytical methods computer systems technology biomedical science and clinical trials. Westat serves US state and local government clients in addition to businesses and foundations. It has offices in six US states as well as international locations around the world. The company was founded in 1963 and is employee-owned.

	Annual Growth	12/09	12/10	12/11	12/12	12/13
Sales ($ mil.)	8.6%	–	455.3	506.5	495.9	582.5
Net income ($ mil.)	(6.9%)	–	–	27.5	28.6	23.8
Market value ($ mil.)	–	–	–	–	–	–
Employees	–	–	–	–	–	2,000

WESTCON GROUP INC.

520 White Plains Rd.
Tarrytown NY 10591-5167
Phone: 914-829-7000
Fax: 914-829-7137
Web: www.westcongroup.com

CEO: Dolph Westerbos
CFO: –
HR: –
FYE: February 28
Type: Subsidiary

The Westcon Group sees more pros than cons in networking equipment. The company distributes networking unified communications and security products to resellers and systems integrators worldwide. It operates through vendor-focused units such as Comstor (Cisco Systems) and ConvergencePoint (Avaya and Polycom). The company's Westcon Security division counts Blue Coat ArcSight RSA Palo Alto Networks and Trend Micro among its suppliers. South Africa-based IT services company Datatec owns Westcon Group which has operations in some 35 countries across six continents.

WESTELL TECHNOLOGIES, INC.

NMS: WSTL

750 North Commons Drive
Aurora, IL 60504
Phone: 630 898-2500
Fax: 630 375-4931
Web: www.westell.com

CEO: J Thomas Gruenwald
CFO: Thomas P Minichiello
HR: –
FYE: March 31
Type: Public

Westell Technologies knows the value of the great outdoors for communication service providers. The company makes outside plant equipment used by telecommunications providers for digital transmission remote monitoring power distribution and other functions that link customer locations with central office facilities. Its products include outdoor passively cooled equipment enclosures mountings and fuse panels. The company also provides services such as design assembly and testing. It generates most of its sales from major US telecommunications service providers.

	Annual Growth	03/11	03/12	03/13	03/14	03/15
Sales ($ mil.)	(18.4%)	190.2	69.7	40.0	102.1	84.1
Net income ($ mil.)	–	67.9	42.0	(44.0)	5.4	(58.0)
Market value ($ mil.)	(21.8%)	212.7	141.6	122.2	224.3	79.6
Employees	(10.7%)	365	136	174	262	232

WESTERN & SOUTHERN FINANCIAL GROUP INC.

400 Broadway
Cincinnati OH 45202
Phone: 513-629-1800
Fax: 513-629-1220
Web: www.westernsouthern.com

CEO: John F Barrett
CFO: Robert L Walker
HR: Beth Brozzart
FYE: December 31
Type: Private

Even if you consider Ohio to be Out West Western & Southern Financial Group wants to be your insurance destination. Through its subsidiaries the company offers a variety of life insurance products and annuities; accident and supplemental health coverage; mutual funds; and other investment management products and services. Western & Southern's financial services include mutual fund administration trust services financial advisory and real estate development; it owns or manages nearly $53 billion in assets. The company is licensed in most states and the District of Columbia. Western & Southern Financial Group was founded in 1888 and is owned by a mutual holding company.

WESTERN ALLIANCE BANCORPORATION

NYS: WAL

One E. Washington Street Suite 1400
Phoenix, AZ 85004
Phone: 602 389-3500
Fax: –
Web: www.westernalliancebancorp.com

CEO: Robert G. Sarver
CFO: Dale M. Gibbons
HR: –
FYE: December 31
Type: Public

The allies behind holding company Western Alliance Bancorporation are Western Alliance Bank (which operates as Alliance Bank of Arizona and First Independent Bank of Nevada) Las Vegas-based Bank of Nevada and Torrey Pines Bank which is active throughout California. Together the banks operate nearly 50 branches. Serving local businesses real estate developers and investors not-for-profit organizations and consumers the banks provide standard deposit products such as checking savings and money market accounts and CDs. Loans to businesses including real estate mortgages commercial and industrial loans and construction and land development loans dominate the banks' lending activities.

	Annual Growth	12/10	12/11	12/12	12/13	12/14
Assets ($ mil.)	14.4%	6,193.9	6,844.5	7,622.6	9,307.1	10,600.5
Net income ($ mil.)	–	(7.2)	31.5	72.8	114.5	148.0
Market value ($ mil.)	39.4%	652.8	552.5	933.9	2,116.2	2,465.6
Employees	5.6%	908	942	982	1,051	1,131

WESTERN AREA POWER ADMINISTRATION

12155 W Alameda Pkwy.
Lakewood CO 80228-8213
Phone: 720-962-7000
Fax: 720-962-7200
Web: www.wapa.gov

CEO: –
CFO: Harrison Pease
HR: –
FYE: September 30
Type: Government-owned

There's power in the West thanks to Western Area Power Administration. One of four power marketing agencies of the US Department of Energy the enterprise operates 57 hydroelectric power plants and one fossil-fueled power generation facility with a combined generating capacity of about 10480 MW. It also manages and maintains more than 17100 miles of transmission lines. Western Area Power Administration sells wholesale power to investor-owned government-owned and cooperative utilities power marketers federal agencies native American tribes and other electricity users (more than 680 direct customers with a total of 11.4 million end users) in 15 western states over a 1.3-million-sq.-mi. service area.

WESTERN CONNECTICUT HEALTH NETWORK INC.

24 Hospital Ave.
Danbury CT 06810
Phone: 203-739-7000
Fax: 734-205-2601
Web: www.foresee.com

CEO: –
CFO: –
HR: –
FYE: June 30
Type: Private - Not-for-Pr

Western Connecticut Health Network is a not-for-profit medical care provider that administers a comprehensive range of health care services to residents of western Connecticut and southeastern New York. At the center of the system is Danbury Hospital a full-service 370-bed 750 doctor community teaching hospital that provides primary emergency surgical and rehabilitative care. Western Connecticut Health Network also operates the 85-bed New Milford Hospital as well as outpatient facilities offering minor emergency diagnostic and primary care. In addition the health network includes an occupational health organization a home health care program and an emergency transportation service.

WESTERN DENTAL SERVICES INC

530 S. Main St.
Orange CA 92868
Phone: 714-480-3000
Fax: 714-480-3001
Web: www.westerndental.com

CEO: Thomas W Erickson
CFO: David Joe
HR: –
FYE: December 31
Type: Private

Need some TLC for your chompers out West? Western Dental can help if you're in Arizona California or Nevada. The company which describes itself as a staff-model dental HMO manages a network of more than 250 Western Dental offices and some 1700 affiliated dentists and 1400 other dental health specialists. Services include general dentistry orthodontics and oral surgery. The company also offers a variety of individual and group HMO plans to some 750000 members. Western Dental also accepts most major private insurance including PPOs and DHMOs. Western Dental's roots go back to 1903 when Dr. Curtis Beauchamp founded the company to provide low-cost dental services.

WESTERN DIGITAL CORP.

NMS: WDC

3355 Michelson Drive, Suite 100
Irvine, CA 92612
Phone: 949 672-7000
Fax: –
Web: www.westerndigital.com

CEO: Stephen D. (Steve) Milligan
CFO: Olivier C. Leonetti
HR: –
FYE: July 03
Type: Public

When it comes to data storage Western Digital has drive and more than a splash of flash. The company is one of the largest independent makers of hard-disk drives (HDDs) which record store and recall volumes of data. It is also active in the fast-growing area of solid-state drives (SSDs) which are faster and lighter than HDDs. Drives for PCs account for most of Western Digital's sales although the company also makes devices used in servers cloud computing data centers and home entertainment products such as set-top boxes and video game consoles. The company sells to manufacturers and through retailers and distributors and generates more than half its sales from the Asia/Pacific region.

	Annual Growth	07/11*	06/12	06/13	06/14*	07/15
Sales ($ mil.)	11.2%	9,526.0	12,478.0	15,351.0	15,130.0	14,572.0
Net income ($ mil.)	19.2%	726.0	1,612.0	980.0	1,617.0	1,465.0
Market value ($ mil.)	80.5%	1,753.8	7,010.4	14,280.7	21,367.0	18,600.1
Employees	4.0%	65,431	103,111	85,777	84,072	76,449

*Fiscal year change

WESTERN EXPRESS HOLDINGS INC.

7135 Centennial Pl.
Nashville TN 37209
Phone: 615-259-9920
Fax: 615-350-9957
Web: www.westernexp.com

CEO: Paul L Weick
CFO: Richard L Prickett
HR: –
FYE: December 31
Type: Private

Pick a point on the compass — Western Express Holdings isn't limited to a single direction when it comes to hauling customers' freight. The company's main subsidiary truckload carrier Western Express will go west but it does most of its business in the eastern and midwestern US concentrating on short to medium-length hauls of between 500 and 1000 miles. The Western Express fleet consists of about 2500 tractors and 4500 trailers including dry vans and flatbeds which haul cargo for a diverse customer base. President and CEO Wayne Wise and his wife Donna Wise own a controlling stake in Western Express Holdings.

WESTERN FAMILY FOODS INC.

6700 SW Sandburg St.
Tigard OR 97223
Phone: 503-639-6300
Fax: 503-684-3469
Web: www.westernfamily.com

CEO: –
CFO: –
HR: –
FYE: April 30
Type: Private

From mayo to mops Western Family Foods supplies private-label products to more than 3500 independent grocery retailers in about two-dozen US states including Alaska and Hawaii. It coordinates with manufacturers and wholesalers to produce more than 6000 products including dry grocery frozen deli household and heath and beauty-care items. The company's flagship brands include Western Family and Shurfine (no relation to competitor Shurfine International which merged with Topco Associates) as well as Better Buy Market Choice and Shur Saving. Established in 1963 Western Family Foods is owned by a consortium that includes Affiliated Foods Associated Food Stores and United Western Grocers.

WESTERN FARMERS ELECTRIC COOPERATIVE

701 NE 7TH ST
ANADARKO, OK 730052297
Phone: 405-247-3351
Fax: –
Web: www.wfec.com

CEO: Gary Roulet
CFO: –
HR: –
FYE: December 31
Type: Private

Power also comes sweeping down the plain in Oklahoma thanks to the Western Farmers Electric Cooperative. Led by its coal- and natural gas-fueled generating plants — three in Anadarko one in Mooreland and one in Hugo (all in Oklahoma) — the generation and transmission co-op produces more than 1845 MW of capacity. It pipes power over 3700 miles of transmission lines to two-thirds of rural Oklahoma and parts of New Mexico. It also operates 264 substations and 59 switch stations. Western Farmers Electric Cooperative which is owned by its member distribution cooperatives supplies 22 distribution co-ops and Altus Air Force base which serve a total of a half million members.

	Annual Growth	12/09	12/10	12/11	12/12	12/13
Sales ($ mil.)	4.9%	–	455.7	462.9	457.2	525.3
Net income ($ mil.)	43.2%	–	–	10.5	13.3	21.5
Market value ($ mil.)	–	–	–	–	–	–
Employees	–	–	–	–	–	378

WESTERN GAS EQUITY PARTNERS LP

NYS: WGP

1201 Lake Robbins Drive
The Woodlands, TX 77380
Phone: 832 636-6000
Fax: 832 636-6001
Web: www.westerngas.com

CEO: Donald R Sinclair
CFO: Benjamin M Fink
HR: –
FYE: December 31
Type: Public

Western Gas Equity Partners LP (WGEP) is taking stock of a fellow energy concern. The entity formed in September 2012 as an investment vehicle for Western Gas Partners LP (WGP). WGEP's sole purpose is to buy a stake in WGP specifically a limited partner interest of almost 45% and a general partner interest of about 2%. As a shareholder of WGP the entity will receive cash distributions at the end of every fiscal quarter from WGP and as a limited partnership WGEP will distribute its profits back to its own shareholders. It will also be exempt from paying federal income taxes. WGEP filed an IPO seeking up to $362.25 million in November 2012 and plans to use the proceeds raised to begin buying shares in WGP.

	Annual Growth	12/10	12/11	12/12	12/13	12/14
Sales ($ mil.)	17.7%	663.3	823.3	849.4	1,053.5	1,273.8
Net income ($ mil.)	36.5%	63.9	75.6	34.0	160.2	221.9
Market value ($ mil.)	41.8%	–	–	6,556.4	8,649.1	13,184.9
Employees	–	–	–	–	–	–

WESTERN GAS PARTNERS LP

NYS: WES

1201 Lake Robbins Drive
The Woodlands, TX 77380
Phone: 832 636-6000
Fax: 832 636-6001
Web: www.westerngas.com

CEO: Donald R Sinclair
CFO: Benjamin M Fink
HR: –
FYE: December 31
Type: Public

Western Gas Partners' style is to gather and go. The company gathers and transports natural gas for its largest customer and parent Anadarko Petroleum and delivers natural gas and natural gas liquids (NGLs) to end-users. It handles gathering processing and throughput of about 2.2 billion cu. ft. of gas a day through eleven natural gas gathering systems seven treating facilities one natural gas liquids pipeline and one interstate pipeline (totaling more than 8820 miles across Wyoming Utah Texas Oklahoma and Kansas). Operating principally under long-term contracts the company gathers natural gas from individual wells after which it is compressed treated and delivered to customers.

	Annual Growth	12/10	12/11	12/12	12/13	12/14
Sales ($ mil.)	27.5%	503.3	664.1	849.4	1,053.5	1,331.6
Net income ($ mil.)	31.5%	126.1	142.9	107.0	275.1	376.5
Market value ($ mil.)	24.6%	4,278.1	5,827.0	6,725.0	8,710.1	10,314.1
Employees	–	–	–	–	–	–

WESTERN MASSACHUSETTS ELECTRIC CO.

NBB: WMAS N

300 Cadwell Drive
Springfield, MA 01104
Phone: 413 785-5871
Fax: –

CEO: Werner J Schweiger
CFO: James J Judge
HR: –
FYE: December 31
Type: Public

Western Massachusetts Electric shines a light on the masses in western Mass. The company provides electric power services to more than 200000 customers in about 60 towns and cities in a 1490-sq.-mi. service area in Massachusetts. Western Massachusetts Electric purchases its electricity from affiliate Select Energy. It is an operating subsidiary of Eversource Energy one of the largest utility companies in New England. The company operates 4200 miles of distribution lines and 415 miles of transmission lines. It also has 45 substations and 35200 transformer locations.

	Annual Growth	12/10	12/11	12/12	12/13	12/14
Sales ($ mil.)	5.7%	395.2	417.3	441.2	472.7	493.4
Net income ($ mil.)	25.8%	23.1	43.1	54.5	60.4	57.8
Market value ($ mil.)	–	–	–	–	–	–
Employees	(3.3%)	354	346	348	308	310

WESTERN PETROLEUM INC.

1521 S. 1500 East
Vernal UT 84078
Phone: 435-789-1832
Fax: 435-789-1832
Web: www.westernpetroleum.net

CEO: –
CFO: Janis Kline
HR: –
FYE: December 31
Type: Private

Western Petroleum Inc. (not to be confused with Minnesota-based Western Petroleum Company) delivers the stuff that keeps big wheels turning. The company transports fuels lubes and industrial oils and provides on-site fueling services to construction sites drill rigs farms mines ski resorts and trucking operations in Colorado Nevada Utah and Wyoming. It also provides contract fleet fueling from 10 terminals mostly in Colorado and Utah. Western Petroleum distributes products from Chevron Conoco Exxon Mobil and Sinclair including kerosene filters methanol solvents and anti-freeze. The company was founded in 1952 and is owned by CEO Perry Taylor and brother Sam Taylor a senior vice president.

WESTERN REFINING INC

NYS: WNR

123 W. Mills Ave., Suite 200
El Paso, TX 79901
Phone: 915 534-1400
Fax: –
Web: www.wnr.com

CEO: Jeff A. Stevens
CFO: Gary R. Dalke
HR: –
FYE: December 31
Type: Public

It's the quality and volumes of its refined products that makes Western Refining a major player in the West. The independent oil refiner operates primarily in the Southwest region of the US although it does have some marketing operations on the East Coast. Western Refining's refineries (one in El Paso one in the Four Corners region of northern New Mexico) have a crude oil refining capacity of 155019 barrels per day. More than 90% of its refined products are made up of light transportation fuels including diesel and gasoline. It owns a wholesale division that complements the refining operations. Western Refining also owns more than 260 convenience stores and gas stations in four Southwestern states.

	Annual Growth	12/10	12/11	12/12	12/13	12/14
Sales ($ mil.)	17.4%	7,965.1	9,071.0	9,503.1	10,086.1	15,153.6
Net income ($ mil.)	–	(17.0)	132.7	398.9	276.0	559.9
Market value ($ mil.)	37.5%	1,017.8	1,278.5	2,711.9	4,079.9	3,634.5
Employees	17.9%	2,950	3,600	3,800	3,800	5,700

WESTERN REFINING LOGISTICS LP

NYS: WNRL

123 W. Mills Avenue, Suite 200
El Paso, TX 79901
Phone: 915 534-1400
Fax: –
Web: www.wnrl.com

CEO: Jeff A Stevens
CFO: Gary R Dalke
HR: –
FYE: December 31
Type: Public

Western Refining Logistics holds the midstream assets of Western Refining. The company owns and operates 300 miles of crude oil pipelines and crude oil storage facilities with a capacity of almost 7 million barrels. Its pipeline and storage facilities serve Western Refining's two refineries in Texas and New Mexico. It also provides asphalt terminalling and processing services for Western Refining's asphalt plants in Arizona New Mexico and Texas. Western Refining formed Western Refining Logistics in 2013 as a limited partnership or an investment vehicle that is exempt from paying federal income tax. The company raised $303 million in its IPO which it will use to pay off Western Refining in exchange for the pipelines and storage facilities.

	Annual Growth	12/10	12/11	12/12	12/13	12/14
Sales ($ mil.)	–	0.0	3.4	3.8	30.8	3,501.9
Net income ($ mil.)	–	0.0	(40.4)	(71.0)	(59.5)	71.8
Market value ($ mil.)	–	0.0	–	–	1,210.5	1,427.2
Employees	–	–	–	–	–	850

WESTERN STATES FIRE PROTECTION COMPANY INC

7026 S TUCSON WAY
CENTENNIAL CO 801123921
Phone: 303-792-0022
Fax: –
Web: www.wsfp.com

CEO: Gene Postma
CFO: –
HR: –
FYE: December 31
Type: Private

Western States Fire Protection (WSFP) is sprinkling its own brand of safety west of the Mississippi. The company a division of APi Group installs water-based fire sprinklers and other fire suppression systems for the commercial residential and industrial markets primarily in the western US. It designs installs and maintains fire protection systems at defense gaming high-tech institutional medical processing and sports facilities. Specific projects include installing systems at the Colorado Convention Center and Microsoft's data storage facility in Washington. WSFP also manufactures fire sprinklers at its own fabrication workshops. The company was founded in 1985.

	Annual Growth	12/09	12/10	12/11	12/12	12/13
Sales ($ mil.)	14.4%	–	150.5	165.7	202.5	225.5
Net income ($ mil.)	26.0%	–	–	12.1	17.3	19.2
Market value ($ mil.)	–	–	–	–	–	–
Employees	–	–	–	–	–	1,429

WESTERN UNION CO.
NYS: WU

12500 East Belford Avenue	CEO: Hikmet Ersek
Englewood, CO 80112	CFO: Rajesh K. Agrawal
Phone: 866 405-5012	HR: Richard L. Williams
Fax: –	FYE: December 31
Web: www.westernunion.com	Type: Public

Western Union's wires don't carry telegrams anymore STOP But they keep on humming with international money transfers STOP The firm has an agent network of about 500000 locations in more than 200 countries worldwide that allows individuals and business customers to transfer money or make payments (in more than 120 currencies) electronically. The pioneering company has taken advantage of technological advances and rolled with the changes since it was founded in 1851. Starting out as a messaging medium it then added the US's first stock ticker helped standardize timekeeping nationally debuted an early charge card and the singing telegram and finally shifted to money transfer services.

	Annual Growth	12/10	12/11	12/12	12/13	12/14
Sales ($ mil.)	1.9%	5,192.7	5,491.4	5,664.8	5,542.0	5,607.2
Net income ($ mil.)	(1.6%)	909.9	1,165.4	1,025.9	798.4	852.4
Market value ($ mil.)	(0.9%)	9,684.3	9,522.6	7,097.6	8,995.9	9,340.1
Employees	9.3%	7,000	8,000	9,000	10,000	10,000

WESTERN WASHINGTON UNIVERSITY

516 HIGH ST	CEO: –
BELLINGHAM, WA 982255996	CFO: –
Phone: 360-650-3000	HR: Michael C Shea
Fax: –	FYE: June 30
Web: www.wwu.edu	Type: Private

If you're in the West and you're looking for a liberal arts education look no further than Western Washington University. The university is located in northwest Washington state and is one of a handful of state-funded four-year institutions of higher education in Washington. The school has an enrollment of about 15000 students; roughly 95% of those are undergraduate students. Western Washington University has a student-teacher ratio of roughly 21:1.The university has students from almost every other state and from three dozen other countries. Western which began as a teachers college accepting its first students in 1899 became a full university in 1977.

	Annual Growth	06/10	06/11	06/12	06/13	06/14
Sales ($ mil.)	6.1%	–	167.9	181.8	196.9	200.6
Net income ($ mil.)	(48.7%)	–	–	14.5	5.5	3.8
Market value ($ mil.)	–	–	–	–	–	–
Employees	–	–	–	–	–	466

WESTFIELD FINANCIAL INC
NMS: WFD

141 Elm Street	CEO: James C Hagan
Westfield, MA 01086	CFO: Leo R Sagan Jr
Phone: 413 568-1911	HR: –
Fax: –	FYE: December 31
Web: www.westfieldbank.com	Type: Public

Westfield Financial is the holding company for Westfield Bank which serves western Massachusetts' Hampden County and surrounding areas from more than 10 branch locations. Founded in 1853 the bank has traditionally been a community-oriented provider of retail deposit accounts and loans but it is placing more emphasis on serving commercial and industrial clients. Commercial real estate loans account for approximately 45% of the company's loan portfolio and business loans are more than 25%. The bank also makes a smaller number of consumer and home equity loans.

	Annual Growth	12/10	12/11	12/12	12/13	12/14
Assets ($ mil.)	1.6%	1,239.5	1,263.3	1,301.5	1,276.8	1,320.1
Net income ($ mil.)	19.7%	3.0	5.9	6.3	6.8	6.2
Market value ($ mil.)	(5.6%)	173.3	137.9	135.5	139.8	137.5
Employees	1.0%	192	198	207	201	200

WESTFIELD GROUP

One Park Circle	CEO: James R Clay
Westfield Center OH 44251	CFO: Robert Krisowaty
Phone: 330-887-0101	HR: –
Fax: 330-887-0840	FYE: December 31
Web: www.westfieldgrp.com/index.jsp	Type: Private

For the Westfield Group farming is in its blood. One of the top agribusiness insurers in the US the company offers commercial and personal property/casualty insurance to customers in about 20 states and surety services to customers in just over 30 states. Westfield Group also offers banking services through Westfield Bancorp (dba Westfield Bank) as well as title and broker services. The firm offers such standard personal lines as auto and homeowners insurance; its niche products include fidelity and surety bonds. The group is represented by more than 1200 independent agents. The privately held Westfield Group is not related to Australian retail property giant Westfield Group.

WESTINGHOUSE AIR BRAKE TECHNOLOGIES CORPORATION
NYSE: WAB

1001 Air Brake Ave.	CEO: Raymond T Betler
Wilmerding PA 15148	CFO: Patrick D Dugan
Phone: 412-825-1000	HR: –
Fax: 412-825-1019	FYE: December 31
Web: www.wabtec.com	Type: Public

More powerful than a speeding locomotive Westinghouse Air Brake Technologies pulls out all the stops. The company (dba Wabtec) manufactures braking equipment and other parts for locomotives freight cars and passenger railcars. Products made by Wabtec's Freight group include air brake systems draft gears hand brakes slack adjusters heat exchanges railroad electronics and monitoring and control equipment. Wabtec's Transit business supplies replacement parts and repair services to operators of passenger transit systems. Major customers include Electro-Motive Diesel General Electric Transportation Union Pacific and CSX Transportation. North America generates almost 70% of sales.

WESTINGHOUSE ELECTRIC COMPANY LLC

4350 Northern Pike	CEO: Danny Roderick
Monroeville PA 15146-2886	CFO: Ichiro Sakamoto
Phone: 412-374-4111	HR: –
Fax: 412-374-3272	FYE: March 31
Web: www.westinghousenuclear.com	Type: Subsidiary

Westinghouse Electric has gone nuclear with nuclear services fuels and power plants. It provides design work and start-up help for new nuclear power plants and makes many of the components. Westinghouse Electric manufactures and supplies the commercial fuel products needed to run the plants and it offers training engineering maintenance and quality management services.The firm also has research and technology operations. Its serves utilities and industrial companies worldwide. Westinghouse Electric which is owned by Japan-based conglomerate Toshiba estimates that almost 50% of nuclear power plants around the world and about 60% of US plants are based on the company's technology.

WESTINGHOUSE LIGHTING CORPORATION

12401 McNulty Rd.
Philadelphia PA 19154-1099
Phone: 215-671-2000
Fax: 215-464-4115
Web: www.westinghouselighting.com

CEO: –
CFO: –
HR: –
FYE: December 31
Type: Private

And George Westinghouse said "Let there be light." Westinghouse Lighting Corporation (WLC) manufactures and distributes more than 5000 electrical and lighting products including light bulbs lighting fixtures and hardware door chimes and wall plates. The Energy Star certified manufacturer also makes ceiling fans for indoor and outdoor use under brands such as Builder and Industrial Plus. Its decorative electrical lineup extends from lighting hardware to glassware. WLC also offers Thomas Kinkade (the world's most collected living artist) branded lighting products. The company's global distribution facilities dot Mexico Germany the UK and Asia catering to residential commercial and industrial markets.

WESTLAKE CHEMICAL CORP

NYS: WLK

2801 Post Oak Boulevard, Suite 600
Houston, TX 77056
Phone: 713 960-9111
Fax: –
Web: www.westlake.com

CEO: Albert Chao
CFO: M. Steven (Steve) Bender
HR: –
FYE: December 31
Type: Public

Money matters and vertically integrated Westlake Chemical turns matter into money. The company produces petrochemicals and plastics such as PVC. Its petrochemicals include ethylene ethyl benzene and styrene which are building blocks in plastics. Its plastics offerings include PVC and polyethylene both of which are common in packaging products and grocery bags. Westlake also produces the chlorine used in PVC as well as caustic soda. Other Westlake operations make PVC products such as pipe (North American Pipe) fencing (Westech Fence) and windows. In 2016 rival Axiall rejected a $1.4 billion buyout from Westlake. The Chao Group owns 69% of Westlake.

	Annual Growth	12/10	12/11	12/12	12/13	12/14
Sales ($ mil.)	8.6%	3,171.8	3,619.8	3,571.0	3,759.5	4,415.4
Net income ($ mil.)	32.3%	221.4	259.0	385.6	610.4	678.5
Market value ($ mil.)	8.9%	5,776.8	5,347.6	10,538.3	16,222.1	8,118.3
Employees	17.3%	1,873	1,811	1,895	2,200	3,550

WESTMINSTER COLLEGE

1840 S 1300 E
SALT LAKE CITY, UT 041053097
Phone: 801-484-7651
Fax: –
Web: www.westminstercollege.edu

CEO: –
CFO: –
HR: –
FYE: June 30
Type: Private

Westminster College is a private liberal arts school that offers more than 70 academic programs including undergraduate bachelor of arts (BA) and bachelor of science (BS) degrees as well as select graduate degrees. Its programs are offered through four schools devoted to arts and sciences business education and nursing and health sciences. The school has an enrollment of approximately 2300 undergraduate students and 800 graduate students and has more than 400 full- and part-time faculty members. Westminster College was founded in 1875 as a preparatory school called the Salt Lake Collegiate Institute. It first offered college classes in 1897 (as Sheldon Jackson College) and adopted its current name in 1902.

	Annual Growth	06/10	06/11	06/12	06/13	06/14
Sales ($ mil.)	(6.8%)	–	95.6	92.2	70.7	77.4
Net income ($ mil.)	240.1%	–	–	0.8	4.0	9.4
Market value ($ mil.)	–	–	–	–	–	–
Employees	–	–	–	–	–	500

WESTMORELAND COAL CO.

NAS: WLB

9540 South Maroon Circle, Suite 200
Englewood, CO 80112
Phone: 855 922-6463
Fax: –
Web: www.westmoreland.com

CEO: Kevin A. Paprzycki
CFO: Jason Veenstra
HR: Loretta Miiller
FYE: December 31
Type: Public

Westmoreland Coal is ready to take its lumps — of coal that is. Through subsidiaries Westmoreland Coal produces about 22 million tons of coal annually from mines in Montana North Dakota Texas and Wyoming. It controls about 486 million tons of proved and probable coal reserves. Most of the company's coal is sold to power producers. Some of Westmoreland Coal's customers maintain power generation facilities adjacent to its mines. In addition to its coal business Westmoreland owns North Carolina's Roanoke Valley (or ROVA) coal-fired power plants which have a capacity of 230 MW and supply power under long-term agreements with Dominion Virginia Power.

	Annual Growth	12/10	12/11	12/12	12/13	12/14
Sales ($ mil.)	21.9%	506.1	501.7	600.4	674.7	1,116.0
Net income ($ mil.)	–	(0.5)	(33.1)	(7.2)	(4.7)	(172.3)
Market value ($ mil.)	29.1%	204.2	218.1	159.7	329.9	568.0
Employees	33.6%	1,081	1,300	1,250	1,370	3,440

WESTMORELAND RESOURCE PARTNERS LP

NYS: WMLP

41 South High Street, Suite 3450
Columbus, OH 43215
Phone: 614 643-0337
Fax: –
Web: www.oxfordresources.com

CEO: Keith E Alessi
CFO: Kevin A Paprzycki
HR: –
FYE: December 31
Type: Public

Oxford Resource Partners strives to get its customers steamed. An operator and acquirer of surface coal mines the company produces steam coal used by power plants and other energy producers to fire steam boilers. It owns and operates about 19 surface mines in the Northern Appalachia region and the Illinois Basin. In 2009 the company which has assets that include more than 91 million tons of proved and probable reserves produced 5.8 million tons of coal. It serves markets in Illinois Indiana Kentucky Ohio Pennsylvania and West Virginia and has counted AEP Duke Energy and East Kentucky Power as major customers. Formed in 2008 Oxford Resource Partners filed an initial public offering (IPO) in 2010.

	Annual Growth	12/09	12/10	12/11	12/12	12/13
Sales ($ mil.)	4.2%	293.8	356.6	400.4	373.5	346.8
Net income ($ mil.)	–	23.5	(7.4)	(13.1)	(26.8)	(24.9)
Market value ($ mil.)	(63.1%)	–	648.3	400.0	117.6	32.7
Employees	(5.9%)	815	836	929	758	638

WESTPOINT HOME INC.

28 E. 28th St. 8th Fl.
New York NY 10016
Phone: 800-533-8229
Fax: 706-645-4396
Web: www.martex.com

CEO: Normand Savaria
CFO: –
HR: –
FYE: December 31
Type: Private

WestPoint Home wants you to cuddle up with everything from flowers to cartoons. The firm makes comforters blankets sheets decorative pillows table covers towels and window coverings which it sells primarily to department stores mass retailers and bed and bath stores. It also supplies hotels and hospitals with its linens. Brand names include Martex Utica Charisma Grand Patrician and Vellux as well as licensed brands such as Ralph Lauren Harley-Davidson IZOD and Rachael Ray. WestPoint Home has roots reaching back some 200 years. Formerly known as WestPoint Stevens it is owned by holding company WestPoint International which is majority owned by corporate raider Carl Icahn's Icahn Enterprises.

WESTSTAR FINANCIAL SERVICES CORPORATION

OTC: WFSC

79 Woodfin Place	CEO: Randall C Hall
Asheville NC 28801	CFO: –
Phone: 828-252-1735	HR: –
Fax: 828-252-1792	FYE: December 31
Web: www.bankofasheville.com	Type: Public

Looking for a destination for your money? Go Weststar young man go Weststar. Weststar Financial Services is the holding company for Bank of Asheville a community bank serving western North Carolina's Buncombe County from about a half-dozen branches. Bank of Asheville provides standard deposit products and services including checking and savings accounts CDs and IRAs. It uses funds from deposits to originate loans — primarily mortgages — as well as construction business a small number of consumer loans. Weststar Financial owns 50% of Asheville Mortgage which provides mortgage brokerage services.

WESTWOOD HOLDINGS GROUP, INC.

NYS: WHG

200 Crescent Court, Suite 1200	CEO: –
Dallas, TX 75201	CFO: Tiffany B. Kice
Phone: 214 756-6900	HR: Leslie Sisk
Fax: –	FYE: December 31
Web: www.westwoodgroup.com	Type: Public

Westwood Ho! Westwood Holdings Group provides investment management services to institutions mutual funds and high-net-worth clients. The asset management company operates through its subsidiaries. Westwood Trust handles trust custody and account management for companies institutions and high-net-worth individuals. Westwood Management is the group's institutional investment management unit overseeing accounts for corporations municipalities and charitable organizations with at least $10 million in investable assets. The firm is also the administrator of the Westwood family of mutual funds WHG Funds. Westwood Holdings Group has about $18.9 billion in assets under management.

	Annual Growth	12/10	12/11	12/12	12/13	12/14
Sales ($ mil.)	19.6%	55.3	68.9	77.5	91.8	113.2
Net income ($ mil.)	24.7%	11.3	14.7	12.1	17.9	27.2
Market value ($ mil.)	11.5%	332.0	303.7	339.8	514.4	513.6
Employees	14.0%	77	80	96	106	130

WET SEAL, INC. (THE)

NMS: WTSL

26972 Burbank	CEO: Edmond Thomas
Foothill Ranch, CA 92610	CFO: Steven Benrubi
Phone: 949 699-3900	HR: –
Fax: –	FYE: February 01
Web: www.wetsealinc.com	Type: Public

Pubescent mall rats are likely to get hooked at The Wet Seal. The company operates about 530 shops across the US and Puerto Rico (down from some 600 stores in 2004) that sell moderate- to value-priced casual clothing and accessories under brand names and private labels. Most of the 475 Wet Seal stores are mall-based and target teenage girls. A contemporary fashion Arden B chain (11% of sales) runs about 55 stores that cater to women age 24 to 34 years old. The Wet Seal also sells apparel through its two banner websites. Amid intense competition from value-priced fast-fashion chains such as Forever 21 and H&M and slumping sales and profits the company is cutting jobs and trimming its store count.

	Annual Growth	01/10	01/11	01/12*	02/13	02/14
Sales ($ mil.)	(1.4%)	560.9	581.2	620.1	580.4	530.1
Net income ($ mil.)	–	93.4	12.6	15.1	(113.2)	(38.4)
Market value ($ mil.)	(8.1%)	283.7	299.0	307.4	234.6	202.4
Employees	4.8%	6,148	6,982	7,283	7,012	7,413

*Fiscal year change

WETHERILL ASSOCIATES INC.

411 Eagleview Blvd. Ste. 100	CEO: –
Exton PA 19341	CFO: Douglas Moul
Phone: 610-495-2200	HR: –
Fax: 800-948-6121	FYE: December 31
Web: www.wai-wetherill.com	Type: Private

Wetherill Associates Inc. (WAI or WAIglobal) is a leading supplier of automotive and heavy duty aftermarket components used primarily in starters and alternators. These components are distributed through independent authorized distributors and company-owned distribution facilities worldwide. WAI also makes a variety of related non-rotating components such as ignition distributors manifold absolute pressure sensors mass airflow sensors and wiper motors. A group dedicated to the teachings of management consultant Richard Wetherill started WAI in 1978 to illustrate his theories. WAI is owned by company chairman Marie Bothe who once served as an assistant to Wetherill and Edith Gripton Wetherill's widow.

WEX INC

NYS: WEX

97 Darling Avenue	CEO: Melissa D. Smith
South Portland, ME 04106	CFO: Steven A. (Steve) Elder
Phone: 207 773-8171	HR: –
Fax: –	FYE: December 31
Web: www.wrightexpress.com	Type: Public

WEX (formerly Wright Express) provides payment processing and information management services to commercial and government vehicle fleets through a network that tracks purchases made on fleet charge cards at more than 190000 fuel and vehicle maintenance facilities throughout the US Canada Australia New Zealand and Europe. The company provides clients with transaction data analysis tools and purchase control capabilities for every vehicle in their fleets. Data collected at the point of sale include expenditures lists of items purchased odometer readings and driver vehicle and vendor identification. WEX serves some 350000 fleets that collectively have a total of approximately 7.7 million vehicles.

	Annual Growth	12/10	12/11	12/12	12/13	12/14
Sales ($ mil.)	20.3%	390.4	553.1	623.2	717.5	817.6
Net income ($ mil.)	23.3%	87.6	133.6	96.9	149.2	202.2
Market value ($ mil.)	21.1%	1,789.3	2,111.3	2,931.7	3,852.0	3,847.7
Employees	22.8%	881	899	1,302	1,431	2,004

WEXFORD HEALTH SOURCES INC.

425 HOLI DR FOST PLZ TWO FOSTER	CEO: –
PITTSBURGH, PA 15220	CFO: Craig Trout
Phone: 888-633-6468	HR: Elaine Gedman
Fax: –	FYE: December 31
Web: www.wexfordhealth.com	Type: Private

Wexford Health Sources provides health care services to inmates doing time in the big house. The company has contracts at more than 100 government-run facilities including county jails state and federal prisons juvenile detention centers substance abuse treatment centers psychiatric hospitals and correctional centers for sex offenders. Wexford Health staffs professionals that perform medical and mental health care dentistry pharmacy services and administration services and serves about 90000 inmates and patients through contracts in five states — Illinois Mississippi Ohio Pennsylvania and West Virginia. Wexford Health was founded in 1992.

	Annual Growth	12/0-1	12/00	12/01	12/05	12/08
Sales ($ mil.)	–	–	–	(1,793.8)	160.6	160.0
Net income ($ mil.)	168.8%	–	–	0.0	6.4	16.6
Market value ($ mil.)	–	–	–	–	–	–
Employees	–	–	–	–	–	1,525

WEYCO GROUP, INC

NMS: WEYS

333 W. Estabrook Boulevard, P.O. Box 1188
Milwaukee, WI 53201
Phone: 414 908-1600
Fax: –
Web: www.weycogroup.com

CEO: Thomas W. (Tom) Florsheim
CFO: John F. Wittkowske
HR: –
FYE: December 31
Type: Public

Weyco Group has him — or at least his feet — covered. The company imports men's footwear including mid-priced leather dress and casual shoes sold under the Florsheim Nunn Bush and Stacy Adams brands. It also offers casual footwear for women and children under the BOGS Rafters and Umi labels. Weyco sells its shoes to more than 10000 shoe clothing and department stores. The company also operates about two dozen Florsheim retail stores in the US and markets shoes online. In addition it licenses the Stacy Adams name for men's clothing and accessories. Founded in 1906 as Weyenberg Shoe Manufacturing the company changed its name to Weyco Group in 1990 and stopped manufacturing shoes in 2003.

	Annual Growth	12/10	12/11	12/12	12/13	12/14
Sales ($ mil.)	8.7%	229.2	271.1	293.5	300.3	320.5
Net income ($ mil.)	8.6%	13.7	15.3	19.0	17.6	19.0
Market value ($ mil.)	4.9%	265.0	265.7	252.8	318.5	321.1
Employees	3.3%	562	621	633	599	640

WEYERHAEUSER CO

NYS: WY

33663 Weyerhaeuser Way South
Federal Way, WA 98063-9777
Phone: 253 924-2345
Fax: –
Web: www.weyerhaeuser.com

CEO: Doyle R. Simons
CFO: Patricia M. Bedient
HR: Clarence Frederick
FYE: December 31
Type: Public

If a tree falls in a Weyerhaeuser forest someone is there to hear it — and he has a chainsaw. The forest products company produces a variety of softwood lumber and other building materials in North America. It also offers cellulose fibers products used to make paper packaging and textiles. The company harvests trees for its products through its timberlands division which owns or controls nearly 7 million acres of forest in the US and Canada. Exports account for more than 30% of the company's sales. Incorporated in 1900 as Weyerhaeuser Timber Co. the company is classified as a real estate investment trust (REIT).

	Annual Growth	12/10	12/11	12/12	12/13	12/14
Sales ($ mil.)	3.1%	6,552.0	6,216.0	7,059.0	8,529.0	7,403.0
Net income ($ mil.)	9.3%	1,281.0	331.0	385.0	563.0	1,826.0
Market value ($ mil.)	17.3%	9,928.3	9,791.9	14,590.9	16,557.7	18,823.4
Employees	(2.6%)	14,250	12,800	13,200	13,700	12,800

WGBH EDUCATIONAL FOUNDATION

1 Guest St.
Boston MA 02135
Phone: 617-300-2000
Fax: 617-300-1026
Web: www.wgbh.org

CEO: Jonathan C Abbott
CFO: –
HR: –
FYE: August 31
Type: Private - Not-for-Pr

Public broadcasting forms the basis of this organization. WGBH Educational Foundation owns and operates the WGBH public TV and radio stations that serve the Boston area. Its television operations include several digital channels (WGBH Create WGBH World) as well as an on-demand service. WGBH is also one of the largest producers of programming for the Public Broadcasting Service including such shows as Antiques Roadshow Arthur Curious George Frontline Masterpiece and Nova. The foundation gets funding from corporate grants and individual contributions as well as from PBS and the Corporation for Public Broadcasting. WGBH first hit the airwaves in 1951.

WGI HEAVY MINERALS INCORPORATED

TORONTO: WG

810 Sherman Ave.
Coeur d'Alene ID 83814
Phone: 208-666-6000
Fax: 208-666-4000
Web: www.wgiheavyminerals.com

CEO: Greg S Emerson
CFO: Persela Reynolds
HR: –
FYE: December 31
Type: Public

OK we get it. They're heavy you're strong. WGI Heavy Minerals produces industrial minerals chiefly garnet but also ilmenite leucoxene rutile and zircon. The company markets these industrial minerals that are sourced primarily from India. It also produces industrial-grade garnet from mining and processing operations in Germany and the US (in Idaho). Subsidiary International Waterjet Parts makes replacement parts for ultra-high pressure waterjet machine tool systems. In 2012 Opta Minerals acquired 94% of WGI and plans to buy the remaining shares.

WGL HOLDINGS, INC.

NYS: WGL

101 Constitution Ave., N.W.
Washington, DC 20080
Phone: 703 750-2000
Fax: –
Web: www.wglholdings.com

CEO: Terry D. McCallister
CFO: Vincent L. Ammann
HR: –
FYE: September 30
Type: Public

Some of the hot air in the US capital is courtesy of WGL Holdings. The holding company's Washington Gas Light utility (Washington Gas) distributes natural gas to more than 1 million customers in Washington DC and adjacent areas of Maryland and Virginia. WGL Holdings' nonregulated operations include Washington Gas Energy Services (WGES) which sells natural gas and electricity to 355000 retail customers in unregulated markets within the utility's service area and beyond. Other operations include HVAC (heating ventilation and air-conditioning) services and natural gas exploration production and storage.

	Annual Growth	09/11	09/12	09/13	09/14	09/15
Sales ($ mil.)	(0.8%)	2,751.5	2,425.3	2,466.1	2,780.9	2,659.8
Net income ($ mil.)	2.9%	118.4	141.1	81.6	107.3	132.6
Market value ($ mil.)	10.2%	1,942.9	2,001.6	2,123.9	2,094.6	2,867.9
Employees	2.5%	1,384	1,362	1,416	1,444	1,529

WHALLEY COMPUTER ASSOCIATES INC.

1 WHALLEY WAY
SOUTHWICK, MA 010779222
Phone: 413-569-4200
Fax: –
Web: www.wca.com

CEO: –
CFO: –
HR: Nicole DeJesus
FYE: December 31
Type: Private

Whalley Computer Associates (WCA) provides information technology products distribution consulting and technical support services primarily in Massachusets. The company sells and distributes computer hardware software and peripherals from such vendors as Hewlett-Packard 3Com and Cisco. Other services include systems integration maintenance network design project management and remote monitoring. WCA's customers come from a variety of industries including manufacturing consumer goods and retail as well as the public sector. The company was founded in 1979 by president John Whalley.

	Annual Growth	12/03	12/04	12/05	12/06	12/07
Sales ($ mil.)	14.9%	–	67.2	73.4	87.8	101.9
Net income ($ mil.)	21.7%	–	–	3.0	3.9	4.5
Market value ($ mil.)	–	–	–	–	–	–
Employees	–	–	–	–	–	104

WHATABURGER RESTAURANTS LP

300 Concord Plaza
San Antonio TX 78216
Phone: 210-476-6000
Fax: 212-354-8113
Web: www.whitecase.com

CEO: Thomas E Dobson
CFO: Julie Gray
HR: –
FYE: September 30
Type: Private

Fans of this chain know they can get quite a burger at the place with the orange and white roof. Whataburger Restaurants is a leading regional hamburger chain with nearly 700 outlets in Texas and about 10 other states in the South and Southwest. The restaurants are open 24 hours a day and serve burgers and fries along with chicken sandwiches salads and a breakfast menu. About 600 of the restaurants are company-owned. Loyal Whataburger fans can also don the company's line of apparel sporting the chain's logo. The late Harmon Dobson founded the family-owned chain in Corpus Christi Texas in 1950 with a single roadside burger stand.

WHEATON COLLEGE

26 E MAIN ST
NORTON, MA 027662322
Phone: 508-286-8200
Fax: –
Web: www.cs.wheatoncollege.edu

CEO: –
CFO: –
HR: Diane Cleary
FYE: June 30
Type: Private

Wheaton College (not to be confused with a school of the same name in Illinois) is a four-year private liberal arts college that enrolls about 1600 undergraduates for study in more than 40 major fields as well as 60 minors. The college boasts a student-faculty radio of 11:1. The most popular courses of study include biology economics English history psychology and sociology. The Wheaton College campus is located 35 miles south of Boston and 15 miles north of Providence. Founded as a seminary for women in 1834 it was chartered as a women's liberal arts college in 1912. Wheaton became coeducational in 1987.

	Annual Growth	06/05	06/06	06/08	06/13	06/14
Sales ($ mil.)	0.7%	–	69.7	102.7	71.0	73.5
Net income ($ mil.)	10.8%	–	–	11.1	15.6	20.5
Market value ($ mil.)	–	–	–	–	–	–
Employees	–	–	–	–	–	545

WHEATON FRANCISCAN SERVICES INC.

26W 171 ROOSEVELT RD
WHEATON, IL 60189
Phone: 414-465-3000
Fax: –
Web: www.wfhealthcare.org

CEO: –
CFO: –
HR: David Smith
FYE: June 30
Type: Private

Wheaton Franciscan Services Inc. (WFSI) is the not-for-profit parent company for more than 100 health care housing and social service organizations in Colorado Illinois Iowa and Wisconsin. Also known as Wheaton Franciscan Healthcare WFSI operates about 15 hospitals including Affinity Health System Rush Oak Park Hospital and United Hospital System with more than 1600 beds total. WFSI also includes long-term care centers home health agencies and physician offices. Its Franciscan Ministries division provides affordable housing units including assisted-living facilities and low-income dwellings. The health system is sponsored by The Franciscan Sisters Daughters of the Sacred Hearts of Jesus and Mary.

	Annual Growth	06/10	06/11	06/12	06/13	06/14
Sales ($ mil.)	0.9%	–	1,710.1	1,723.5	1,763.4	1,754.2
Net income ($ mil.)	–	–	–	(112.6)	177.5	128.7
Market value ($ mil.)	–	–	–	–	–	–
Employees	–	–	–	–	–	18,000

WHEATON VAN LINES INC

8010 CASTLETON RD
INDIANAPOLIS, IN 462502005
Phone: 317-849-7900
Fax: –
Web: www.wheatonworldwide.com

CEO: Mark Kirschner
CFO: –
HR: –
FYE: December 31
Type: Private

Wheaton Van Lines which operates under the Wheaton World Wide Moving and Bekins Van Lines (acquired in 2012) brands provides interstate and international transportation and relocation services for individuals businesses and government agencies. Wheaton also provides relocation services for US military personnel. The company's specialties include transportation of medical equipment computers new furniture store fixtures and Steinway pianos. Wheaton Van Lines operates through a network of about 370 agents in the US. The company is owned by its employees.

	Annual Growth	12/06	12/07	12/08	12/09	12/10
Sales ($ mil.)	(4.6%)	–	104.2	99.3	95.2	90.5
Net income ($ mil.)	(33.7%)	–	–	7.8	7.5	3.4
Market value ($ mil.)	–	–	–	–	–	–
Employees	–	–	–	–	–	725

WHEELER REAL ESTATE INVESTMENT TRUST, INC.

NAS: WHLR

2529 Virginia Beach Blvd., Suite 200
Virginia Beach, VA 23452
Phone: 757 627-9088
Fax: –
Web: www.whlr.us

CEO: Jon S. Wheeler
CFO: Wilkes Graham
HR: –
FYE: December 31
Type: Public

Wheeler Real Estate Investment Trust develops and manages shopping centers and other real estate properties. The REIT owns eight properties including five shopping centers two stand-alone buildings and one office building. Most are in Virginia but the company plans to target the Mid-Atlantic Southeast and Southwest. It will develop and manage strip centers and free-standing retail properties with a specific focus on revamping properties in secondary and tertiary markets. Wheeler Real Estate Investment Trust will be managed by WHLR Management a company owned by company founder chairman and president Jon Wheeler. The REIT was formed in early 2011 and filed to go public later that year.

	Annual Growth	12/10	12/11	12/12	12/13	12/14
Sales ($ mil.)	74.4%	1.9	1.9	2.4	8.7	17.2
Net income ($ mil.)	–	(0.3)	(0.6)	(1.2)	(3.7)	(10.6)
Market value ($ mil.)	(19.9%)	–	–	46.3	32.2	29.7
Employees	152.0%	–	3	–	–	48

WHEELING & LAKE ERIE RAILWAY COMPANY

100 1ST ST SE
BREWSTER, OH 446131202
Phone: 330-767-3401
Fax: –
Web: www.wlerwy.com

CEO: Jane Villard
CFO: Michael D. Mokodean
HR: Donna Manack
FYE: June 30
Type: Private

Wheeling & Lake Erie Railway operates over a network of about 950 miles of track between the Ohio River and Lake Erie passing through parts of Maryland Ohio Pennsylvania and West Virginia. The company's system links the coal fields of West Virginia (Wheeling) with industrial Cleveland and its docks (Lake Erie). In addition to coal the railroad hauls cargo including aggregates iron ore steel products agricultural products plastic resins. Wheeling & Lake Erie Railway owns some 575 miles of track; trackage rights over other railroads account for the rest of the company's network. The railroad traces its roots back to 1871 but took its current form in 1990.

	Annual Growth	06/03	06/04	06/05	06/06	06/14
Sales ($ mil.)	(25.3%)	–	1,860.8	61.6	73.0	100.7
Net income ($ mil.)	12.0%	–	–	6.4	7.7	17.8
Market value ($ mil.)	–	–	–	–	–	–
Employees	–	–	–	–	–	332

WHEELING-NISSHIN INC.

400 PENN ST	CEO: Noboru Onishi
FOLLANSBEE, WV 260371412	CFO: Patstuzo Shiotsuka
Phone: 304-527-2800	HR: –
Fax: –	FYE: December 31
Web: www.nisshin-steel.co.jp	Type: Private

Wheeling-Nisshin a subsidiary of Nisshin Steel produces a variety of hot-dip coated steels such as stainless steel. The company's output includes 400000 tons produced at its aluminizing and galvanizing line facility and 300000 tons produced at its continuous galvanizing line facility. Both of the facilities are located at the company's headquarters site in West Virginia. Its primary customers are in the automotive appliance and construction industries. Wheeling-Nisshin was founded in 1986. It had been a joint venture between Nisshin and US steel producer Wheeling Pitt (now operating as Severstal Wheeling) until the Japanese steel company bought out its partner in early 2008.

	Annual Growth	12/09	12/10	12/11	12/12	12/13
Sales ($ mil.)	(3.4%)	–	434.4	489.3	426.1	391.2
Net income ($ mil.)	(45.3%)	–	–	9.7	6.9	2.9
Market value ($ mil.)	–	–	–	–	–	–
Employees	–	–	–	–	–	175

WHELAN SECURITY CO.

1699 S. Hanley Rd. Ste. 350	CEO: –
St. Louis MO 63144	CFO: –
Phone: 314-644-1974	HR: Dinah Wagner
Fax: 314-644-5524	FYE: December 31
Web: www.whelansecurity.com	Type: Private

Whelan Security Co. helps companies keep their people and perimeters safe. The regional security services contractor and its subsidiary TransNational Security offer uniformed and special events security guards emergency and alarm response personnel vandalism patrol officers and labor dispute specialists. Whelan's security staff is placed at banks government facilities hospitals industrial facilities schools and shopping centers primarily throughout the Central and Mid-Atlantic regions of the US. The firm has branch offices in more than two dozen states. Whelan Security was founded in 1949 by James T. Whelan uncle of current chairman Patrick Twardowski; it is still owned by Twardowski family members.

WHIRLPOOL CORP

	NYS: WHR
2000 North M-63	CEO: Jeff M. Fettig
Denton Harbor, MI 49022-2692	CFO: Larry M. Venturelli
Phone: 269 923-5000	HR: David A (Dave) Binkley
Fax: –	FYE: December 31
Web: www.whirlpoolcorp.com	Type: Public

With brand names recognized by just about anyone who has ever separated dark colors from light Whirlpool is one of the world's top home appliance makers. It specializes in laundry appliances refrigerators and freezers cooking appliances dishwashers and compressors. They're sold under a bevy of brand names including Whirlpool Amana KitchenAid Maytag and Roper. The company markets and distributes these major home appliances in North America Latin America EMEA (Europe the Middle East and Africa) and Asia. It has manufacturing operations in more than a dozen countries. Major customers include retailers Lowe's Home Depot Sears and Best Buy.

	Annual Growth	12/11	12/12	12/13	12/14	12/15
Sales ($ mil.)	2.9%	18,666.0	18,143.0	18,769.0	19,872.0	20,891.0
Net income ($ mil.)	19.0%	390.0	401.0	827.0	650.0	783.0
Market value ($ mil.)	32.6%	3,664.1	7,857.2	12,112.9	14,960.8	11,341.4
Employees	9.2%	68,231	68,000	69,000	100,000	97,000

WHITE CASTLE SYSTEM INC.

555 W. Goodale St.	CEO: Edgar W Ingram III
Columbus OH 43215	CFO: Russell J Meyer
Phone: 614-228-5781	HR: –
Fax: 614-464-0596	FYE: December 31
Web: www.whitecastle.com	Type: Private

The treasure room of this fast food fortress contains Sliders. White Castle System owns and operates more than 400 White Castle hamburger joints known for their little square burgers called Slyders. The meat patty is steamed over a bed of onions rather than grilled and then served on a steamed bun with a single slice of pickle. Patrons typically consume a sack of Slyders at a time. White Castle restaurants can be found in about a dozen mostly Midwestern states. The company also sells frozen Sliders through supermarket chains. The first fast food chain in the US White Castle was founded by Walter Anderson and real estate broker E. W. "Billy" Ingram in 1921. The Ingram family continues to control the company.

WHITE COUNTY MEDICAL CENTER

3214 E RACE AVE	CEO: Ray Montgomery
SEARCY, AR 721434810	CFO: Stuart Hill
Phone: 501-268-6121	HR: Jack Russell
Fax: –	FYE: September 30
Web: www.wcmc.org	Type: Private

If you're sick in Searcy you may want to visit White County Medical Center (WCMC). The organization provides health care to Central Arkansas' residents. It has about 440 licensed inpatient beds on two hospital campuses (WCMC North and WCMC South) as well as a number of outpatient surgery centers primary care clinics and a retirement community called River Oaks Village. The WCMC South campus features an inpatient rehabilitation center that helps patients recover from injury and illness as well as a long-term acute care hospital for patients needing extended general care. In addition WCMC provides home health care services and runs a training program for certified nurse assistants.

	Annual Growth	09/05	09/06	09/08	09/09	09/13
Sales ($ mil.)	(9.8%)	–	365.7	415.4	482.0	178.0
Net income ($ mil.)	14.6%	–	–	8.7	12.0	17.3
Market value ($ mil.)	–	–	–	–	–	–
Employees	–	–	–	–	–	1,010

WHITE FLOWER FARM INC.

167 Litchfield Rd.	CEO: Eliot Wadsworth II
Morris CT 06763	CFO: –
Phone: 800-503-9624	HR: –
Fax: 905-795-0101	FYE: December 31
Web: www.01com.com	Type: Private

White Flower Farms has a lot of colors on its palette. Through catalogs and its Web site White Flower Farm sells a wide range of annuals bulbs houseplants perennials shrubs and vines and vegetables that it grows in its own nursery. The company also offers tools gifts garden accessories and tips for making the garden grow. A retail store at the nursery is open from April to October. The company maintains five acres of display gardens open to the public. White Flower Farm founded in 1950 is owned by CEO Eliot Wadsworth who purchased it from founder William Harris in 1976. Harris and his wife Jane Grant both successful journalists before taking the gardening path founded the nursery.

WHITE MOUNTAINS INSURANCE GROUP LTD.

NYSE: WTM

80 S. Main St.
Hanover NH 03755-2053
Phone: 603-640-2200
Fax: 603-643-4592
Web: www.whitemountains.com

CEO: –
CFO: –
HR: –
FYE: December 31
Type: Public

Incorporated in Bermuda White Mountains Insurance Group enjoys the island's tax-mild climate but slogs out the winters from its corporate headquarters in New Hampshire. The company provides insurance and reinsurance products and services through its US operating office's two main divisions: majority-owned OneBeacon Insurance (specialty and commercial property/casualty policies sold through independent agents in the US) and Sirius Group (domestic and international property/casualty insurance and reinsurance). In 2011 the company sold its Esurance unit (personal auto insurance sold online) to Allstate in a deal worth about $1 billion.

WHITE ROSE INC.

380 Middlesex Ave.
Carteret NJ 07008
Phone: 732-541-5555
Fax: 732-541-3730
Web: www.whiterose.com

CEO: –
CFO: –
HR: –
FYE: December 31
Type: Subsidiary

White Rose delivers little apples and other grocery dairy and frozen food items to the Big Apple. The company is a leading independent wholesale food distributor in the New York City and New Jersey metropolitan areas. White Rose also increasing serves markets in Maryland Pennsylvania and New England. The distributor offers some 21000 products that bear national brands as well as namesake private label White Rose — a household name in New York for more than a century. Its customers include food retailers such as independents and members of co-ops and regional supermarket chains. White Rose is part of distribution co-op Associated Wholesalers.

WHITE RIVER CAPITAL INC.

NYSE AMEX: RVR

1445 Brookville Way Ste. I
Indianapolis IN 46239
Phone: 317-806-2166
Fax: 317-806-2167
Web: www.whiterivercap.com

CEO: John M Eggemeyer
CFO: Martin J Szumski
HR: –
FYE: December 31
Type: Public

White River Capital is a holding company that specializes in auto finance. Subsidiary Coast Credit offers subprime auto financing in more than 20 states. The company acquires the subprime receivables from franchise and independent auto dealers. Another unit Union Acceptance oversees a portfolio of non-prime automobile receivables. In 2005 UAC was bankrupt and stockholders were looking for a way to squeak out value in their investment. The shareholders agreed to exchange UAC for shares of White River. After the swap White River bought the similar yet more successful Coast Credit. The holding-company-hat-trick allowed UAC to carry its business forward even after it declared bankruptcy in 2002.

WHITEGLOVE HEALTH INC.

5300 Bee Cave Rd. Bldg. I Ste. 100
Austin TX 78746
Phone: 512-329-9223
Fax: 512-329-8281
Web: www.whiteglove.com

CEO: Nick Balog
CFO: William J Kerley
HR: –
FYE: December 31
Type: Private

You've heard of doctors making house calls but what about nurses? WhiteGlove House Call provides patients with mobile primary and chronic care including physicals lab work vaccines generic and over-the-counter medications and "well-kits" (i.e. chicken noodle soup and Kleenex) delivered by nurse practitioners. Unlike similar companies WhiteGlove does not file insurance claims. Instead it offers services via membership to employers and the self-insured (often as a benefit of high-deductible plans) as well as through insurance firms like Aetna Humana and UnitedHealth. It operates in major markets in Texas Massachusetts and Arizona. WhiteGlove was founded in 2006.

WHITE RIVER HEALTH SYSTEM INC.

1710 HARRISON ST
BATESVILLE, AR 725017303
Phone: 870-262-1200
Fax: –
Web: www.whiteriverhealthsystem.com

CEO: –
CFO: –
HR: –
FYE: September 30
Type: Private

White River Health System offers health care services to residents of north central Arkansas. The not-for-profit organization operates two hospitals the flagship White River Medical Center and acute care facility Stone County Medical Center which provides health care services to rural communities. Combined the two hospitals have about 225 beds and provide a range of emergency surgical medical and diagnostic services. The system also includes outpatient facilities primary care and specialty physician offices long-term care facilities for the elderly and those unable to live independently.

	Annual Growth	09/07	09/08*	08/09*	09/12	09/13
Sales ($ mil.)	(4.4%)	–	189.8	0.1	148.8	151.6
Net income ($ mil.)	–	–	–	(0.1)	5.4	5.3
Market value ($ mil.)	–	–	–	–	–	–
Employees	–	–	–	–	–	1,500

*Fiscal year change

WHITEHEAD INSTITUTE FOR BIOMEDICAL RESEARCH

9 CAMBRIDGE CTR
CAMBRIDGE, MA 021421479
Phone: 617-258-5000
Fax: –
Web: www.wi.mit.edu

CEO: –
CFO: –
HR: –
FYE: June 30
Type: Private

The Whitehead Institute for Biomedical Research blazes new trails in bioscience. The organization funded by both the public and private sectors investigates such diseases as Parkinson's and cancer and dives into the depths of biology genomics and genetics to gain new understanding about disease and health. The Whitehead Institute contributed to the international effort to map the human genome and is actively researching stem cells. Other achievements include discovering a system for multiplying adult stem cells and creating the first genetically defined human cancer cell. The enterprise draws researchers from nearby MIT (with which it is affiliated in its teaching activities) and from all over the world.

	Annual Growth	06/07	06/08	06/09	06/10	06/13
Sales ($ mil.)	(45.1%)	–	1,441.7	0.0	67.2	71.6
Net income ($ mil.)	–	–	–	0.0	(9.5)	(1.2)
Market value ($ mil.)	–	–	–	–	–	–
Employees	–	–	–	–	–	550

WHITESTONE REIT
NYS: WSR

2600 South Gessner, Suite 500
Houston, TX 77063
Phone: 713 827-9595
Fax: 713 465-8847
Web: www.whitestonereit.com

CEO: James C. Mastandrea
CFO: David K. Holeman
HR: –
FYE: December 31
Type: Public

Whitestone REIT is out to make a name for itself in real estate. The self-managed real estate investment trust owns and operates some 60 retail office and warehouse properties in Texas (Houston is the company's largest market) Illinois and Arizona totaling more than 5 million sq. ft. Whitestone focuses on what it calls community-centered properties or high-visibility properties in established or developing culturally diverse neighborhoods. It recruits retail grocery financial services and other tenants to its Whitestone branded commercial centers. Tenants include Wells Fargo Walgreen and Sports Authority.

	Annual Growth	12/10	12/11	12/12	12/13	12/14
Sales ($ mil.)	23.1%	31.5	34.9	46.6	62.1	72.4
Net income ($ mil.)	61.9%	1.1	1.1	0.1	3.8	7.6
Market value ($ mil.)	0.5%	338.0	271.7	320.8	305.3	345.0
Employees	11.2%	53	62	68	68	81

WHITING PETROLEUM CORP
NYS: WLL

1700 Broadway, Suite 2300
Denver, CO 80290-2300
Phone: 303 837-1661
Fax: –
Web: www.whiting.com

CEO: James J. Volker
CFO: Michael J. Stevens
HR: Heather Duncan
FYE: December 31
Type: Public

Even though it focuses on onshore properties Whiting Petroleum is a fair-sized fish in an ocean full of oil and gas explorers. The company engages in oil and natural gas exploration and production activities mainly in the US Permian Basin and Rocky Mountains regions. In 2014 Whiting reported estimated proved reserves of 780.3 million barrels of oil equivalent (of which 78% was oil). That year Whiting produced 114.5 million barrels of oil equivalent per day. The oil and gas company sells oil and gas production to end users marketers and other purchasers that have access to nearby pipeline facilities.

	Annual Growth	12/10	12/11	12/12	12/13	12/14
Sales ($ mil.)	19.4%	1,516.1	1,899.6	2,173.5	2,828.4	3,085.1
Net income ($ mil.)	(33.8%)	336.7	491.7	414.2	366.1	64.8
Market value ($ mil.)	(27.2%)	19,557.7	7,792.1	7,238.0	10,325.4	5,507.3
Employees	23.0%	561	692	829	958	1,282

WHITMAN COLLEGE

345 BOYER AVE
WALLA WALLA, WA 993622083
Phone: 509-527-5111
Fax: –
Web: www.bookstore.whitman.edu

CEO: –
CFO: –
HR: –
FYE: June 30
Type: Private

Students attending this Walla Walla school hope to get more Bing Bang for their educational buck. Whitman College located in Walla Walla Washington is an independent co-educational non-sectarian undergraduate school. It offers bachelor's degrees in more than 40 liberal arts and sciences areas including education environmental studies biology English music mathematics and religion. Whitman College also offers extensive study abroad programs. It has about 1500 students and a 9:1 student-to-faculty ratio. About two-thirds of Whitman students live on campus.

	Annual Growth	06/10	06/11	06/12	06/13	06/14
Sales ($ mil.)	6.2%	–	68.4	55.0	75.4	81.8
Net income ($ mil.)	–	–	–	(10.9)	56.6	68.7
Market value ($ mil.)	–	–	–	–	–	–
Employees	–	–	–	–	–	399

WHITNEY MUSEUM OF AMERICAN ART

945 MADISON AVE
NEW YORK, NY 100212790
Phone: 212-249-1749
Fax: –
Web: www.whitney.org

CEO: –
CFO: Alice Pratt Burns
HR: –
FYE: June 30
Type: Private

The Whitney Museum of American Art houses some 12000 works of 20th- and 21st-century American art including paintings sculptures drawings photographs and prints by about 2000 artists. It contains the entirety of Edward Hopper's artistic estate as well as pieces by artists such as Georgia O'Keefe Kiki Smith Louise Nevelson and Andy Warhol. The museum also offers public programs including lectures seminars and performances. The museum is housed in a large granite building at the corner of Madison Avenue and 75th Street designed by the Hungarian-born Bauhaus-trained architect Marcel Breuer. Whitney Museum of American Art was founded in 1930 by sculptor and art patron Gertrude Vanderbilt Whitney.

	Annual Growth	06/07	06/08	06/09	06/10	06/13
Sales ($ mil.)	–	–	(1,168.6)	28.1	33.9	91.3
Net income ($ mil.)	–	–	–	0.0	(8.2)	50.8
Market value ($ mil.)	–	–	–	–	–	–
Employees	–	–	–	–	–	167

WHOLE FOODS MARKET, INC.
NMS: WFM

550 Bowie Street
Austin, TX 78703
Phone: 512 477-4455
Fax: 512 477-1069
Web: www.wholefoodsmarket.com

CEO: John P. Mackey
CFO: Glenda J. Flanagan
HR: –
FYE: September 27
Type: Public

With food and other items that are free of pesticides preservatives sweeteners and cruelty Whole Foods Market knows more about guiltless eating and shopping than most retailers. The world's #1 natural foods chain by far — now that it has digested its main rival Wild Oats Markets — the company operates more than 430 stores throughout the US Canada and the UK. The stores emphasize perishable and prepared products which account for about two-thirds of sales. Whole Foods Market offers some 4400 items in four lines of private-label products (such as the premium Whole Foods line). Founded in Austin Texas in 1980 Whole Foods Market pioneered the supermarket concept in natural and organic foods retailing.

	Annual Growth	09/11	09/12	09/13	09/14	09/15
Sales ($ mil.)	11.1%	10,107.8	11,698.8	12,917.0	14,194.0	15,389.0
Net income ($ mil.)	11.8%	342.6	465.6	551.0	579.0	536.0
Market value ($ mil.)	(17.8%)	23,795.0	33,982.9	20,351.3	13,143.1	10,850.8
Employees	9.1%	64,200	72,700	78,400	87,200	90,900

WHYY INC.

150 N 6TH ST
PHILADELPHIA, PA 191061521
Phone: 215-351-1200
Fax: –
Web: www.whyy.org

CEO: –
CFO: –
HR: –
FYE: June 30
Type: Private

WHYY provides the media landscape with a little Fresh Air. The company operates public radio station WHYY 90.9 FM which produces the popular NPR talk show with host Terry Gross. It also runs public television stations WHYY-TV and WDPB-TV. All three serve parts of Pennsylvania Delaware and New Jersey. Its Learning Lab offers multimedia journalism and video production training to WHYY members as well as to teens teachers and seniors. The company-, planted its roots in the 1950s when The Metropolitan Philadelphia Educational Radio and Television Corporation began broadcasting cultural and educational radio programming.-, About 100000 members — along with corporations and government agencies-, — fund WHYY.

	Annual Growth	06/07	06/08	06/09	06/10	06/11
Sales ($ mil.)	(4.1%)	–	30.6	25.7	27.8	27.0
Net income ($ mil.)	–	–	–	(3.9)	1.7	0.3
Market value ($ mil.)	–	–	–	–	–	–
Employees	–	–	–	–	–	160

WIDENER UNIVERSITY

1 UNIVERSITY PL
CHESTER, PA 190135792
Phone: 610-499-4000
Fax: –
Web: www.widener.edu

CEO: –
CFO: Joseph J Baker
HR: Arlene Trapuzzano
FYE: June 30
Type: Private

You probably won't find any narrow-minded students at Widener. A private co-educational liberal arts college Widener University offers a curriculum that emphasizes social awareness and civic engagement. It has an enrollment of some 6500 students and a student-to-faculty ratio of 12:1. The university grants undergraduate and graduate degrees in about 60 different fields; its programs are divided into eight schools and colleges that cover areas including arts and sciences business engineering law hospitality human services and nursing. Widener University has had its current name since 1979 but its roots reach back to a group of 19th century boys' military academies.

	Annual Growth	06/08	06/09	06/10	06/11	06/13
Sales ($ mil.)	(4.3%)	–	184.6	188.5	200.0	155.1
Net income ($ mil.)	19.0%	–	–	5.1	9.9	8.5
Market value ($ mil.)	–	–	–	–	–	–
Employees	–	–	–	–	–	1,021

WIDEPOINT CORP

7926 Jones Branch Drive, Suite 520
McLean, VA 22102
Phone: 703 349-2577
Fax: –
Web: www.widepoint.com

ASE: WYY

CEO: Steve L Komar
CFO: James T McCubbin
HR: –
FYE: December 31
Type: Public

WidePoint stretches to provide a variety of IT services to government and enterprise customers. The company provides wireless telecom management and business process outsourcing (BPO) services. Its cybersecurity segment provides identity management services including identity proofing credential issuing and public key infrastructure. The company also provides more traditional IT services such as architecture and planning integration services and vulnerability testing. WidePoint focuses its operations toward US federal government clients including the Department of Homeland Security (more than a quarter of sales) the TSA (nearly a quarter) the FBI Customs and Border Protection and the Justice department.

	Annual Growth	12/10	12/11	12/12	12/13	12/14
Sales ($ mil.)	1.2%	50.8	41.4	55.8	46.8	53.3
Net income ($ mil.)	–	6.4	0.2	0.8	(1.7)	(8.4)
Market value ($ mil.)	0.7%	109.4	56.2	30.2	133.9	112.7
Employees	26.7%	115	163	227	227	296

WIEDEN + KENNEDY INC.

224 NW 13th Ave.
Portland OR 97209
Phone: 503-937-7000
Fax: 503-937-8000
Web: www.wk.com

CEO: –
CFO: –
HR: –
FYE: December 31
Type: Private

Wieden + Kennedy has made "it" big. The independent advertising agency is best known for the Nike slogan "Just do it." Its roster of high-profile clients also includes Heineken Levi's and Target. Expanding on its traditional advertising services the company launched Wieden + Kennedy Entertainment (WKE) a subsidiary delivering blogs and audio and video content. The agency has international offices in Amsterdam London New Delhi S?o Paulo Shanghai and Tokyo in addition to its US locations in Portland Oregon and New York. Wieden + Kennedy was founded by Dan Wieden and David Kennedy in 1982.

WIKIMEDIA FOUNDATION INC.

149 NEW MONTGOMERY ST # 6
SAN FRANCISCO, CA 941053739
Phone: 415-839-6885
Fax: –
Web: www.wikimediafoundation.org

CEO: –
CFO: V Ronique Kessler
HR: –
FYE: June 30
Type: Private

Want free access to the sum of all human knowledge? Wikimedia Foundation can give it to you. The not-for-profit organization has produced a plethora of free-content wiki projects including one of the most visited sites on the Internet online collaborative encyclopedia Wikipedia (the foundation's first project). The term wiki (a Hawaiian word for "fast") describes a collection of Web pages designed to enable anyone with Internet access to contribute or modify content. Wikimedia has a paid staff of about 30 while hundreds of thousands of volunteers contribute content. The Wikimedia Foundation is funded primarily through donations and grants and was founded by Internet entrepreneur Jimmy Wales in 2003.

	Annual Growth	06/10	06/11	06/12	06/13	06/14
Sales ($ mil.)	28.7%	–	24.8	38.5	48.6	52.8
Net income ($ mil.)	(5.2%)	–	–	9.2	10.3	8.3
Market value ($ mil.)	–	–	–	–	–	–
Employees	–	–	–	–	–	168

WILBERT INC.

2001 Oaks Pkwy.
Belmont NC 28012
Phone: 704-822-1423
Fax: 704-274-3895
Web: www.wilbertinc.com

CEO: –
CFO: –
HR: Pam Walker
FYE: December 31
Type: Holding Company

"Beware of plastics" words of advice in the movie Mean Girls mean business at Wilbert Inc. Wilbert is the holding company of Wilbert Plastic Services and formerly burial vault maker Wilbert Funeral Services. Spun off in 2009 the funeral business (one of the world's largest makers of concrete burial vaults) buys plastic liners from Wilbert. The plastics service one of the largest thermoformers in the US makes components for the automotive agricultural and building and consumer products markets among many through thermoforming and injection-molding which softens a rigid plastic sheet under heat and molds it into finished parts. Wilbert evolved from the L.G. Haase Manufacturing Co. founded in 1893.

WILBUR SMITH ASSOCIATES INC.

1301 GERVAIS ST STE 1600
COLUMBIA, SC 292013361
Phone: 803-758-4500
Fax: –

CEO: M Stevenson Smith
CFO: David S Johnson
HR: –
FYE: December 25
Type: Private

For many cities around the world where there's a Wilbur there's a roadway. Wilbur Smith Associates provides engineering design planning construction and economic consulting services for municipal works and infrastructure jobs including highways bridges railroads waterways airports and public buildings. Wilbur Smith is active throughout the US Europe Central America the UK the Middle East and Asia. Pioneer transportation engineer Wilbur Smith founded the firm in 1952. The company was acquired by Camp Dresser & McKee (CDM) in 2011. The deal helped broaden both firms' service capabilities and geographic reach.

	Annual Growth	12/05	12/06	12/07	12/08	12/09
Sales ($ mil.)	–	–	–	(436.9)	183.4	182.4
Net income ($ mil.)	789.0%	–	–	0.0	3.3	1.3
Market value ($ mil.)	–	–	–	–	–	–
Employees	–	–	–	–	–	1,217

WILBUR-ELLIS COMPANY

345 CALIFORNIA ST FL 27
SAN FRANCISCO, CA 941042644
Phone: 415-772-4000
Fax: –
Web: www.wilbur-ellis.com

CEO: John P. Thacher
CFO: James D. Crawford
HR: –
FYE: December 31
Type: Private

Seed 'em weed 'em and feed 'em could be the motto of San Francisco's Wilbur-Ellis Co. (aka WECO). Through its agribusiness division WECO sells fertilizer herbicides insecticides seed and farm machinery in North America. The Connell Bros. unit exports and distributes food ingredients and specialty chemicals throughout the Pacific Rim. Its feed division serves international customers in the livestock pet food and aquaculture industries. Additionally WECO provides consulting pesticide application and other agriculture-related services. Beyond North America WECO has operations in about 15 countries in the Asia/Pacific Region. WECO was founded in 1921 by Brayton Wilbur Sr. and Floyd Ellis.

	Annual Growth	12/0-1	12/00	12/09	12/10	12/11
Sales ($ mil.)	8.9%	–	1,100.0	0.0	2,342.5	2,812.0
Net income ($ mil.)	–	–	–	0.0	0.0	0.0
Market value ($ mil.)	–	–	–	–	–	–
Employees	–	–	–	–	–	3,200

WILCOHESS LLC

5446 University Pkwy.
Winston-Salem NC 27105
Phone: 336-767-6280
Fax: 336-767-6283
Web: www.wilcousa.com

CEO: –
CFO: Sherry Polowsky
HR: –
FYE: December 31
Type: Joint Venture

WilcoHess owns and operates more than 360 convenience stores and travel plazas as well as about 50 restaurants mostly in North Carolina and Virginia but also in Alabama Georgia Pennsylvania South Carolina and Tennessee. Many locations house quick-serve restaurants (Arby's Dairy Queen Wendy's). The company's travel plazas cater to truckers with fuel programs and rewards programs. The joint venture company was formed in 2001 by partners A.T. Williams Oil Company and Hess Corporation (formerly Amerada Hess) a leading independent oil company along the East Coast. President Steve Williams is the son of the founder of A.T. Williams Oil Co. A. Tab Williams. Jr.

WILDLIFE CONSERVATION SOCIETY

2300 SOUTHERN BLVD
BRONX, NY 101601090
Phone: 718 220 5100
Fax: –
Web: www.wcs.org

CEO: –
CFO: Patricia Calabrese
HR: Herman D Smith
FYE: June 30
Type: Private

From Congo gorillas to humpback whales off the coast of Gabon all life is worth conserving to the Wildlife Conservation Society (WCS). The group founded in 1895 works to protect wildlife and lands throughout the world and to instill in humans a concern about nature. The not-for-profit organization operates New York City's Bronx Zoo New York Aquarium Central Park Zoo Prospect Park Zoo and the Queens Zoo. WCS's environmental education programs are used in US schools as well as those in other nations. The society has ongoing efforts in more than 60 countries to protect endangered species and ecosystems. About a quarter of the funding for its work comes from visitors at its handful of parks.

	Annual Growth	06/04	06/05	06/06	06/09	06/10
Sales ($ mil.)	–	–	–	(2,125.2)	197.3	228.6
Net income ($ mil.)	388.5%	–	–	0.0	0.0	9.3
Market value ($ mil.)	–	–	–	–	–	–
Employees	–	–	–	–	–	4,000

WILEY (JOHN) & SONS INC.

NYS: JW A

111 River Street
Hoboken, NJ 07030
Phone: 201 748-6000
Fax: –
Web: www.wiley.com

CEO: Stephen M. (Steve) Smith
CFO: John A. Kritzmacher
HR: –
FYE: April 30
Type: Public

If there were an Oprah Book Club for science research and education books and journals published by John Wiley & Sons might be frequently featured. The company publishes scientific technical and medical works including journals and reference works such as Current Protocols and Kirk-Othmer Encyclopedia of Chemical Technology. In total it publishes more than 1600 journal titles. It also produces professional and nonfiction trade books and is a publisher of college textbooks. The firm publishes the For Dummies how-to series too. Wiley has publishing marketing and distribution centers in North America Europe Asia and Australia.

	Annual Growth	04/11	04/12	04/13	04/14	04/15
Sales ($ mil.)	1.1%	1,742.6	1,782.7	1,760.8	1,775.2	1,822.4
Net income ($ mil.)	0.7%	171.9	212.7	144.2	160.5	176.9
Market value ($ mil.)	2.8%	2,996.6	2,658.9	2,245.9	3,380.8	3,346.7
Employees	(1.0%)	5,100	5,200	5,400	5,100	4,900

WILHELMINA INTERNATIONAL, INC.

NAS: WHLM

200 Crescent Court, Suite 1400
Dallas, TX 75201
Phone: 214 661-7488
Fax: –

CEO: Alex Vaickus
CFO: –
HR: –
FYE: December 31
Type: Public

Wilhelmina International has a new face. Formerly a billing services and software provider serving the telecommunications industry New Century Equity Holdings reinvented itself as a holding company and in 2009 acquired Wilhelmina International — the company responsible for the iconic modeling agency Wilhelmina Models. The $30 million transaction also included affiliates Wilhelmina Miami Wilhelmina Film & TV and Wilhelmina Artist Management. Upon the deal's closure New Century changed its name to Wilhelmina International reflecting its new primary business focus. The Wilhelmina deal came after more than four years of scouting new investment opportunities.

	Annual Growth	12/10	12/11	12/12	12/13	12/14
Sales ($ mil.)	11.9%	49.0	55.5	56.4	65.9	76.8
Net income ($ mil.)	5.1%	1.0	1.6	1.1	3.4	1.2
Market value ($ mil.)	150.1%	0.9	1.2	0.7	1.8	35.2
Employees	5.3%	78	81	89	92	96

WILLAMETTE UNIVERSITY

900 STATE ST
SALEM, OR 973013930
Phone: 503-370-6728
Fax: –
Web: www.library.willamette.edu

CEO: –
CFO: –
HR: –
FYE: May 31
Type: Private

Willamette University's claim to fame is its status as the first university in the West. About 3000 students are enrolled in the private co-educational liberal arts school that offers undergraduate and graduate degrees. Undergraduate degrees encompass nearly 50 fields — politics biology English psychology and economics are among the most pursued majors — and graduate degrees in business law and education. The university has a student-to-faculty ratio of 10:1. Founded in the early days of the Oregon Territory by missionary Jason Lee as a school for Native American children Willamette University was established in 1842.

	Annual Growth	05/10	05/11	05/12	05/13	05/14
Sales ($ mil.)	3.4%	–	93.7	102.0	104.0	103.6
Net income ($ mil.)	–	–	–	(21.5)	14.8	19.0
Market value ($ mil.)	–	–	–	–	–	–
Employees	–	–	–	–	–	700

WILLAMETTE VALLEY VINEYARD INC.

NAS: WVVI

8800 Enchanted Way, S.E.
Turner, OR 97392
Phone: 503 588-9463
Fax: –
Web: www.wvv.com

CEO: –
CFO: Richard F Goward Jr
HR: James (Jamie) Ellis
FYE: December 31
Type: Public

Willamette Valley Vineyards is a leading producer of premium varietal wines including chardonnay dry riesling and pinot gris along with its flagship pinot noir. In addition to Willamette Valley it also makes wine under the Tualatin Estates and Griffin Creek labels. The winemaker owns leases or contracts almost 800 acres of vineyards and produced about 121000 cases of wine during 2008. Its wines are sold in Oregon through its Bacchus Fine Wines distribution operation and are available elsewhere in the US through other distributors and brokers. Founder and CEO Jim Bernau owns 12% of the company.

	Annual Growth	12/10	12/11	12/12	12/13	12/14
Sales ($ mil.)	(3.4%)	17.4	15.7	12.5	13.3	15.2
Net income ($ mil.)	51.4%	0.4	0.9	1.2	1.4	2.2
Market value ($ mil.)	13.3%	17.1	14.6	18.0	30.6	28.2
Employees	(1.0%)	127	92	112	126	122

WILLBROS GROUP INC (DE)

NYS: WG

4400 Post Oak Parkway, Suite 1000
Houston, TX 77027
Phone: 713 403-8000
Fax: –
Web: www.willbros.com

CEO: Michael J. Fournier
CFO: Van A. Welch
HR: –
FYE: December 31
Type: Public

Willbros Group develops infrastructure worldwide but primarily in North America. A construction and engineering contractor targeting oil gas and power industries the firm specializes in projects in emerging nations. Willbros has completed major pipeline systems oil and gas production plants piers and bridges. Engineering services include design feasibility studies and project management. It also offers specialty services such as dredging and pipeline. Willbros' inventory features a large fleet of company-owned and leased equipment such as camp equipment marine vessels and pipe-laying and transportation equipment. The company also offers utility transmission and distribution services.

	Annual Growth	12/10	12/11	12/12	12/13	12/14
Sales ($ mil.)	14.2%	1,192.4	1,376.4	2,004.2	2,018.8	2,026.7
Net income ($ mil.)	–	(37.0)	(294.0)	(30.2)	(15.9)	(79.8)
Market value ($ mil.)	(10.6%)	497.5	185.9	271.6	477.3	317.7
Employees	2.3%	7,271	8,810	12,054	9,399	7,959

WILLDAN GROUP INC

NMS: WLDN

2401 East Katella Avenue, Suite 300
Anaheim, CA 92806
Phone: 800 424-9144
Fax: –

CEO: Thomas D Brisbin
CFO: Stacy B McLaughlin
HR: Azmi B Ujang
FYE: January 02
Type: Public

Willdan Group can and will do what it takes to meet its customers' engineering needs. The group's subsidiaries provide civil engineering energy efficiency environmental and financial consulting and homeland security services. Clients include federal and local governments school districts public utilities and some private industries. Willdan focuses on small to midsized clients that may fall below the radar of larger competitors. The company's energy efficiency services segment — which serves utilities public agencies not-for-profits and others — accounts for about half of Willdan's revenues.

	Annual Growth	12/10	12/11	12/12	12/13*	01/15
Sales ($ mil.)	6.8%	77.9	107.2	93.4	85.5	108.1
Net income ($ mil.)	28.2%	2.7	1.8	(17.3)	2.6	9.4
Market value ($ mil.)	29.4%	30.5	30.2	17.0	37.5	110.7
Employees	3.4%	540	562	534	534	637

*Fiscal year change

WILLIAM MARSH RICE UNIVERSITY INC

10300 TOWN PARK DR
HOUSTON, TX 770725236
Phone: 713-348-4055
Fax: –
Web: www.rice.edu

CEO: –
CFO: –
HR: –
FYE: June 30
Type: Private

You have to be as wise as an owl to attend Rice University and have really good SAT scores. Often referred to as the "Ivy League of the South" Rice — with mascot "Sammy the Owl" — consistently appears at the top of college academic rankings including those published by U.S. News & World Report. The private university has an enrollment of more than 6000 and about 1100 full-time part-time and adjunct faculty members (giving it a student-teacher ratio of about 6:1). Rice offers programs through eight schools in areas such as engineering computer science economics music and architecture. The university opened in 1912 with funds from the estate of William Marsh Rice.

	Annual Growth	06/10	06/11	06/12	06/13	06/14
Sales ($ mil.)	2.8%	–	551.0	551.0	568.3	599.1
Net income ($ mil.)	–	–	–	(34.0)	460.0	657.6
Market value ($ mil.)	–	–	–	–	–	–
Employees	–	–	–	–	–	2,600

WILLIAM PATERSON UNIVERSITY

300 POMPTON RD
WAYNE, NJ 074702103
Phone: 973-720-2000
Fax: –
Web: www.ww2.wpunj.edu

CEO: –
CFO: –
HR: –
FYE: June 30
Type: Private

William Paterson University has evolved into a fully accredited liberal-arts university. William Paterson which has more than 1000 full-time faculty members enrolls about 11500 undergraduate and graduate students and offers more than offers 45 undergraduate 22 masters one doctoral and three post-baccalaureate certificate programs through five colleges. The university has a 370-acre campus with some 40 major buildings and other facilities including the David and Lorraine Cheng Library which boasts more than 350000 bound volumes. Tuition and fees in 2012 were $11694 for full-time students who were New Jersey residents and $19094 for non-residents. William Paterson is accredited by the Middle States Association of Colleges and Secondary Schools.

	Annual Growth	06/08	06/09	06/12	06/13	06/14
Sales ($ mil.)	369.9%	–	0.1	158.4	157.7	153.2
Net income ($ mil.)	(12.2%)	–	–	8.7	7.1	6.7
Market value ($ mil.)	–	–	–	–	–	–
Employees	–	–	–	–	–	1,300

WILLIAMS & CONNOLLY LLP

725 12th St. NW
Washington DC 20005
Phone: 202-434-5000
Fax: 202-434-5029
Web: www.wc.com

CEO: –
CFO: –
HR: –
FYE: December 31
Type: Private - Partnershi

Washington DC law firm Williams & Connolly has never shied away from representing controversial clients. Founded in 1967 by the late Edward Bennett Williams and the late Paul Connolly the firm sports a client list bulging with familiar names in the legal spotlight. Williams & Connolly has represented President Bill Clinton Iran-Contra defendant Oliver North and Juan Miguel Gonzalez (father of Elian Gonzalez). Specializing in litigation the firm has some 275 attorneys with expertise in such areas as corporate tax and employment law. The firm serves clients across the world from its single office in the nation's capital.

WILLIAMS (CLAYTON) ENERGY, INC.

NYS: CWEI

Six Desta Drive - Suite 6500	CEO: Clayton W. Williams
Midland, TX 79705-5510	CFO: Michael L. Pollard
Phone: 432 682-6324	HR: –
Fax: –	FYE: December 31
Web: www.claytonwilliams.com	Type: Public

Former Texas gubernatorial candidate Clayton Williams once devoted his energy to politics. Now he's devoted to the independent oil and gas firm that he founded. Clayton Williams Energy explores for oil and gas deposits primarily in Louisiana New Mexico and Texas and exploits those resources. In 2012 the company reported estimated proved reserves of 75.4 million barrels of oil equivalent located mainly in the Permian Basin and South Texas. It has 951000 gross undeveloped acres and stakes in more than 3030 gross wells. It also operates gas pipeline and a small natural gas processing infrastructure in Louisiana Mississippi New Mexico and Texas and offers contract drilling services.

	Annual Growth	12/10	12/11	12/12	12/13	12/14
Sales ($ mil.)	9.0%	331.6	426.4	423.1	429.2	468.5
Net income ($ mil.)	4.4%	36.9	93.8	35.1	(24.9)	43.9
Market value ($ mil.)	(6.6%)	1,021.9	923.4	486.8	997.3	776.4
Employees	0.8%	437	505	465	466	451

WILLIAMS CONTROLS INC.

NASDAQ: WMCO

14100 SW 72nd Ave.	CEO: –
Portland OR 97224	CFO: Dennis E Bunday
Phone: 503-684-8600	HR: –
Fax: 503-624-3812	FYE: September 30
Web: www.wmco.com	Type: Public

You want the truck driver behind you on the highway to be able to control his speed and so does Williams Controls. The company's primary business is the manufacture of electronic throttle controls for commercial trucks buses RVs off-highway equipment and military applications. Williams Controls also makes pneumatic throttle controls for diesel heavy-duty vehicles. Most of the company's products are sold directly to heavy-duty truck transit bus and off-road OEMs. However it also sells through a network of independent distributors which sell to smaller OEMs. The company makes more than half of its sales in the US. In late 2012 the company agreed to be acquired by Curtiss-Wright Corporation.

WILLIAMS INTERNATIONAL CO. L.L.C.

2280 E. West Maple Rd.	CEO: –
Walled Lake MI 48390	CFO: –
Phone: 248-624-5200	HR: –
Fax: 248-669-1577	FYE: December 31
Web: www.williams-int.com	Type: Private

Williams International provides jet-powered propulsion. The privately-owned company manufactures general aviation gas turbine engines. Williams' line of powerful efficient gas turbine and turbofan engines are designed for trainer aircraft and private business jets traditionally flown by piston engines. Williams' engines also supply industrial and military small scale craft such as drones used for naval gunnery practice. Its engines propel high profile projects like Tomahawk cruise missiles and subsonic target drones. Guarding its market share the engine builder also offers maintenance and aftermarket parts services.

WILLIAMS PARTNERS L.P.

NYS: WPZ

One Williams Center	CEO: –
Tulsa, OK 74172-0172	CFO: –
Phone: 918 573-2000	HR: –
Fax: –	FYE: December 31
Web: www.williamslp.com	Type: Public

Fractionating natural gas liquids (NGLs) is only a fraction of what Williams Partners does. The company is also engaged in the gathering and processing of natural gas and the storage of NGLs and the operation of three major interstate natural gas pipelines. (These pipelines deliver 14% of the natural gas consumed in the US.) Williams Partners assets include a 3800-mile natural gas gathering system in the San Juan Basin; 60% of Discovery Producer Services and Carbonate Trend (gas gathering systems); and the 9800-mile Transco intestate natural gas pipeline. The Williams Companies has merged its Williams Pipeline Partners (pipelines) unit into Williams Partners (which had focused on midstream operations).

	Annual Growth	12/08	12/09	12/10	12/11	12/12
Sales ($ mil.)	84.1%	637.1	470.2	5,715.0	6,729.0	7,320.0
Net income ($ mil.)	59.3%	191.4	152.5	1,085.0	1,378.0	1,232.0
Market value ($ mil.)	42.1%	4,751.7	12,205.5	18,565.0	23,873.8	19,364.9
Employees	–	–	–	–	–	–

WILLIAMS PARTNERS LP (NEW)

NYS: WPZ

One Williams Center	CEO: Alan S Armstrong
Tulsa, OK 74172-0172	CFO: –
Phone: 918 573-2000	HR: Jay Hawkins
Fax: –	FYE: December 31
Web: www.accessmidstream.com	Type: Public

Williams Partners (formerly Access Midstream Partners) is a midstream gathering company that owns operates develops and acquires natural gas natural gas liquids (NGLs) and oil gathering assets in the US. It gathers about 3.9 billion cu. ft. of natural gas per day via some 5800 miles of gathering and transmission lines. The company also has processing facilities that provide services to thousands of wells. Its assets are located in a dozen states with operations in the Barnett Eagle Ford Haynesville Marcellus Niobrara and Utica shales and several unconventional plays in the Mid-Continent region.

	Annual Growth	12/10	12/11	12/12	12/13	12/14
Sales ($ mil.)	31.6%	459.2	565.9	608.4	1,073.2	1,378.9
Net income ($ mil.)	19.5%	195.2	194.3	178.5	336.0	398.1
Market value ($ mil.)	17.2%	6,348.7	6,399.5	7,401.3	12,485.6	11,960.4
Employees	120.5%	285	445	1,255	1,411	6,742

WILLIAMS SAUSAGE COMPANY INC.

5132 OLD TROY HICKMAN RD	CEO: –
UNION CITY, TN 382617702	CFO: –
Phone: 731-885-5841	HR: –
Fax: –	FYE: March 31
Web: www.williams-sausage.com	Type: Private

Union City Tennessee-headquartered Williams Sausage is a regional meat processor that makes sausage ham and bacon products for both retail and wholesale food customers. Its product lines include several varieties of pork sausage cured hams and smoked bacon. The company also markets microwavable pork biscuit sandwiches and smoked pork sausages. Most of its meat products are sold under the Williams brand but it also markets sausage and bacon under the Ole South label. The family-owned company was founded by Harold Williams in 1958.

	Annual Growth	03/03	03/04	03/05	03/06	03/07
Sales ($ mil.)	–	–	–	(77.8)	49.3	46.6
Net income ($ mil.)	27946.8%	–	–	0.0	6.8	3.1
Market value ($ mil.)	–	–	–	–	–	–
Employees	–	–	–	–	–	250

WILLIAMS SONOMA INC

NYS: WSM

3250 Van Ness Avenue
San Francisco, CA 94109
Phone: 415 421-7900
Fax: 415 434-0881
Web: www.williams-sonomainc.com

CEO: Laura J. Alber
CFO: Julie P. Whalen
HR: Julie Baitinger
FYE: February 01
Type: Public

Epicureans are at home at Williams-Sonoma a leading multichannel retailer of high-end goods for well-appointed kitchens bedrooms and baths. Home products include bath and storage bedding cookware furniture lighting and tableware. The company's retail chains Williams-Sonoma (upscale cookware) West Elm (modern housewares) Rejuvenation (lighting and hardware) Mark and Graham (monogrammed gifts) and Pottery Barn and Pottery Barn Kids (housewares furniture) sell wares through some 601 stores in 44 US states and in Canada and Puerto Rico. In addition Williams-Sonoma distributes half a dozen catalogs and sells merchandise at eight corresponding websites and online bridal and baby registries.

	Annual Growth	01/11	01/12*	02/13	02/14	02/15
Sales ($ mil.)	7.6%	3,504.2	3,720.9	4,042.9	4,387.9	4,698.7
Net income ($ mil.)	11.4%	200.2	236.9	256.7	278.9	308.9
Market value ($ mil.)	24.7%	2,971.8	3,227.2	4,136.9	5,009.9	7,190.5
Employees	(1.1%)	28,000	26,900	26,800	37,200	26,800

*Fiscal year change

WILLIAMS-LABADIE LLC

57 W. Grand Ave. Ste. 800
Chicago IL 60610
Phone: 312-222-5800
Fax: 312-222-2530
Web: www.willab.com

CEO: –
CFO: –
HR: –
FYE: December 31
Type: Subsidiary

You might say this company practices medicinal marketing. Williams-Labadie Advertising is a leading provider of advertising and marketing services to clients in the health care and pharmaceutical industries. The midsized agency offers creative ad development and campaign management services as well as branding and corporate identity services. It also offers services for direct marketing and multimedia communications. Clients have included Abraxis Advanced Medical Optics Oscient Pharmaceuticals and Prometheus Laboratories. Founded by Guy Williams and CEO Peter Labadie in 1990 Williams-Labadie is a unit of Paris-based advertising conglomerate Publicis Groupe.

WILLIS LEASE FINANCE CORP.

NMS: WLFC

773 San Marin Drive, Suite 2215
Novato, CA 94998
Phone: 415 408-4700
Fax: –

CEO: Charles F. Willis
CFO: Bradley Forsyth
HR: –
FYE: December 31
Type: Public

Hey buddy got any spare Pratt & Whitneys? Willis Lease Finance buys and sells aircraft engines that it leases to commercial airlines air cargo carriers and maintenance/repair/overhaul organizations in some 30 countries. Its portfolio includes about 180 aircraft engines and related equipment made by Pratt & Whitney Rolls-Royce CFMI GE Aviation and International Aero. The engine models in the company's portfolio are used on popular Airbus and Boeing aircraft. The Willis Lease portfolio also includes four de Havilland DHC-8 commuter aircraft. Customers include Island Air Alaska Airlines American Airlines and Southwest Airlines. Almost 80% of the company's engines are leased and operated outside the US.

	Annual Growth	12/10	12/11	12/12	12/13	12/14
Sales ($ mil.)	4.1%	148.3	156.7	148.1	158.4	174.3
Net income ($ mil.)	(11.9%)	12.1	14.5	1.5	15.6	7.2
Market value ($ mil.)	13.9%	108.8	99.7	119.4	144.9	182.8
Employees	11.5%	64	74	79	89	99

WILMER CUTLER PICKERING HALE AND DORR LLP

1875 Pennsylvania Ave. NW
Washington DC 20006
Phone: 202-663-6000
Fax: 202-663-6363
Web: www.wilmerhale.com

CEO: –
CFO: –
HR: –
FYE: December 31
Type: Private - Partnershi

Wilmer Cutler Pickering Hale and Dorr known as WilmerHale has more than 1000 lawyers in a dozen cities in the US Europe and Asia. Major practice areas include antitrust and competition; corporate transactions; bankruptcy and financial restructuring; government regulation; intellectual property; securities and government contract litigation; and labor and employment. It has conducted legal work for such business big wigs as Boeing Deutsche Bank Procter & Gamble and Citigroup. WilmerHale was formed in the 2004 merger of Washington DC-based Wilmer Cutler & Pickering and Boston-based Hale and Dorr.

WILSHIRE BANCORP INC

NMS: WIBC

3200 Wilshire Blvd.
Los Angeles, CA 90010
Phone: 213 387-3200
Fax: 213 427-6584
Web: www.wilshirebank.com

CEO: Jae Whan (JW) Yoo
CFO: Gunho (Alex) Ko
HR: Lisa Pai
FYE: December 31
Type: Public

Wilshire Bancorp is the holding company for Wilshire Bank where ethnic minorities are the banking majority. Based in the Koreatown section of Los Angeles the commercial bank boasts $4.2 billion in assets nearly 35 branches and a handful of lending offices mainly across California but also in New Jersey New York and Texas. Wilshire Bank targets small to midsized minority-owned businesses and ethnic groups underserved by many national banking institutions. Beyond standard deposit services (including checking and savings accounts CDs and IRAs) the bank also offers Small Business Administration (SBA) real estate and consumer loans and import/export financing services. Korean-American rival BBCN Bancorp agreed to acquire Wilshire Bancorp for $1 billion in late 2015.

	Annual Growth	12/10	12/11	12/12	12/13	12/14
Assets ($ mil.)	8.8%	2,970.5	2,696.9	2,750.9	3,617.7	4,155.5
Net income ($ mil.)	–	(34.8)	(30.3)	92.3	45.4	59.0
Market value ($ mil.)	7.4%	596.8	284.3	459.8	856.1	793.4
Employees	6.8%	405	382	415	547	527

WILSHIRE ENTERPRISES INC.

PINK SHEETS: WLSE

1 Gateway Center Ste. 1030
Newark NJ 07102
Phone: 201-420-2796
Fax: 201-420-6012
Web: www.wilshireenterprisesinc.com

CEO: S Wilzig Izak
CFO: Francis Elenio
HR: –
FYE: December 31
Type: Public

Wilshire Enterprises invests in and operates commercial real estate and land. It owns a portfolio of more than a dozen multifamily retail and office properties and land tracts in Arizona Florida New Jersey and Texas. The company has shed some of its non-core and other properties and has upgraded other properties. Its land holdings (parcels of land totaling about 20 acres all located in New Jersey) have either been put up for sale or are under contract for sale already. Wilshire Enterprises is seeking sale or merger opportunities. In 2008 it entered an acquisition deal with property investment and redevelopment firm NWJ Companies but the agreement was later terminated.

WILSON ELSER MOSKOWITZ EDELMAN & DICKER LLP

150 E. 42nd St.
New York NY 10017
Phone: 212-490-3000
Fax: 212-490-3038
Web: www.wilsonelser.com

CEO: Hal Stewart
CFO: –
HR: –
FYE: December 31
Type: Private - Partnershi

Law firm Wilson Elser Moskowitz Edelman & Dicker maintains a broad range of practice areas and a considerable geographic scope. Wilson Elser's more than 800 attorneys work out of 20 offices in the US and one in the UK; the firm also maintains affiliations with counterparts in France Germany and Mexico. It has won recognitions for specialties such as lobbying in New York state and professional liability insurance defense; other practice areas include aviation environmental law and intellectual property. Thomas Wilson John Elser Harold Moskowitz Max Edelman and Herbert Dicker founded the firm in 1978.

WILSON SONSINI GOODRICH & ROSATI

650 Page Mill Rd.
Palo Alto CA 94304-1050
Phone: 650-493-9300
Fax: 650-493-6811
Web: www.wsgr.com

CEO: Steven E Bochner
CFO: –
HR: –
FYE: January 31
Type: Private - Partnershi

You might say these lawyers can get downright technical. Wilson Sonsini Goodrich & Rosati (WSGR) is one of the largest law firms in the US specializing in representing high-tech corporations. Its client roster has included several big Silicon Valley names such as Google Cisco Salesforce.com Hewlett-Packard Jive Software Oracle and Bazaarvoice. WSGR has advised hundreds of clients on their IPOs and has been involved in more than 500 merger and acquisition transactions (valued at more than $150 billion) in the last five years. WSGR has litigated hundreds of patent lawsuits over the years. The firm was originally founded in 1961.

WILSON TRUCKING CORPORATION

137 WILSON BLVD
FISHERSVILLE, VA 22939
Phone: 540-949-3200
Fax: –
Web: www.wilsontrucking.com

CEO: C L Wilson
CFO: Michael Herndon
HR: –
FYE: December 31
Type: Private

A less-than-truckload (LTL) carrier Wilson Trucking hauls freight from about 45 terminals in the southeastern and mid-Atlantic US. LTL carriers combine freight from multiple shippers into a single truckload; Wilson Trucking tries to haul freight directly from origin terminal to destination terminal avoiding when possible intermediate stops at terminals to break down and reassemble loads. The company operates a fleet of about 970 tractors and 1800 trailers. Outside its core region Wilson Trucking offers service elsewhere in the US and in parts of Canada through partnerships with other carriers. The company was founded in 1926.

	Annual Growth	12/08	12/09	12/10	12/11	12/12
Sales ($ mil.)	7.1%	–	122.2	125.8	136.8	150.1
Net income ($ mil.)	–	–	–	(2.9)	(1.5)	(6.7)
Market value ($ mil.)	–	–	–	–	–	–
Employees	–	–	–	–	–	1,400

WILSONART INTERNATIONAL HOLDING LLC

2400 Wilson Place
Temple TX 76503
Phone: 254-207-7000
Fax: 254-207-2545
Web: www.wilsonart.com

CEO: Timothy J Obrien
CFO: –
HR: –
FYE: December 31
Type: Private

Countertops and other surfaces are like blank canvases for Wilsonart International. The company manufacturers high pressure laminates and other surfaces used for furniture office and retail space countertops worktops and other uses. Its products are marketed under the Wilsonart Resopal Polyrey Ralph Wilson and Arborite brands. Wilsonart sells its products through a network of company-owned and independent distributors across North America; it also works through independent international distributors. The company was a subsidiary of mega tool supplies maker Illinois Tool Works until 2012 when 51% of its stock was sold to investment firm Clayton Dubilier & Rice.

WILTON BRANDS INC.

2240 W. 75th St.
Woodridge IL 60517
Phone: 630-963-1818
Fax: 630-963-7196
Web: www.wilton.com

CEO: Dan Butler
CFO: Michael Fishoff
HR: –
FYE: July 31
Type: Private

Wilton Brands takes the cake — then shows you how to decorate it. The company's Wilton Enterprises subsidiary founded in 1929 is a leading maker of food crafting products offering cake decorating items and bakeware under the Performance Pans Candy Melts and Cupcakes 'N More brands. It also holds classes in cake decoration and makes teakettles and cookware through its Copco division. Wilton is also home to EK Success Brands which produces scrapbooking supplies and crafting products under the Jolee's Martha Stewart Crafts Paintworks Inkadinkado Dimensions Crafts and K&Company names. Wilton Brands is a subsidiary of Wilton Holdings which is owned by Tower-Brook Capital.

WINCHESTER HEALTHCARE MANAGEMENT INC.

41 Highland Ave.
Winchester MA 01890
Phone: 781-729-9000
Fax: 781-756-2908
Web: www.winchesterhospital.org

CEO: –
CFO: –
HR: –
FYE: September 30
Type: Private - Not-for-Pr

Winchester Healthcare Management provides a variety of health care services to patients in the Boston area. The not-for-profit company owns and operates Winchester Hospital a 230-bed acute care medical center. The hospital is a leading area facility for pediatric and women's health services and it offers specialty services including diagnostics cardiology oncology pulmonary and orthopedic medical care. Winchester Healthcare also operates about 20 community family health and specialty clinics as well as a home care agency. The flagship hospital was founded in 1912.

WINCHESTER MEDICAL CENTER AUXILIARY INC.

190 CAMPUS BLVD STE 220
WINCHESTER, VA 226012872
Phone: 540-536-8000
Fax: –
Web: www.valleyhealthlink.com

CEO: –
CFO: J Craig Lewis
HR: Adrienne McKenna
FYE: December 31
Type: Private

Winchester Medical Center is the flagship facility of Valley Health System a not-for-profit health care organization serving the residents of Virginia's Shenandoah Valley. The full-service general hospital which has more than 400 inpatient beds serves as a regional referral center for the system's smaller community hospitals. It provides medical services across a number of specialties (including neuroscience heart disease and cancer) and offers surgical diagnostic and rehabilitative care. The hospital's campus also features outpatient diagnostic and surgical facilities an adult psychiatric facility and doctors' offices. Winchester Medical Center opened its doors in 1903.

	Annual Growth	12/03	12/04	12/05	12/06	12/07
Sales ($ mil.)	83.9%	–	–	134.2	413.3	453.7
Net income ($ mil.)	40861.4%	–	–	0.0	61.7	48.8
Market value ($ mil.)	–	–	–	–	–	–
Employees	–	–	–	–	–	2,046

WIND RIVER SYSTEMS INC.

500 Wind River Way
Alameda CA 94501-1171
Phone: 510-748-4100
Fax: 510-749-2010
Web: www.windriver.com

CEO: –
CFO: –
HR: –
FYE: January 31
Type: Subsidiary

Wind River Systems' sails are billowing with embedded systems. The company provides software operating systems and development tools for embedded systems (composed of a microprocessor and related software) used in such diverse products as auto braking systems Internet traffic routers jet fighter control panels and traffic signals. Wind River is looking increasingly to set-top boxes mobile phones and other consumer electronics for growth opportunities. The company serves customers in such industries as aerospace automotive IT and health care from offices worldwide. Clients have included Northrop Grumman Huawei and Varian Medical Systems. The company is a subsidiary of Intel.

WINDOW TO THE WORLD COMMUNICATIONS INC.

5400 N SAINT LOUIS AVE
CHICAGO, IL 606254623
Phone: 773-509-1111
Fax: –
Web: www.wttw.com

CEO: Daniel J Schmidt
CFO: –
HR: –
FYE: June 30
Type: Private

|Window To The World Communications (WTTW) broadcasts arts children's current events humanities and science programming via its Chicago television station (WTTW Channel 11 with the nation's largest viewer base) and radio station (98.7 WFMT). The company's programming focuses on events and issues that effect the Chicago metropolitan area and special emphasis is given to cultural and educational topics. WTTW is a nonprofit governed by about 50 trustees representing the greater Chicago community. It is licensed by the FCC as a public TV station and is funded and governed by the community it serves. The station started by Inland Steel chairman Edward Ryerson began broadcasting in 1955.

	Annual Growth	06/08	06/09	06/10	06/12	06/13
Sales ($ mil.)	(3.1%)	–	49.9	45.7	47.9	44.1
Net income ($ mil.)	–	–	–	(7.5)	3.0	(1.1)
Market value ($ mil.)	–	–	–	–	–	–
Employees	–	–	–	–	–	192

WINDSTREAM HOLDINGS INC

NMS: WIN

4001 Rodney Parham Road
Little Rock, AR 72212
Phone: 501 748-7000
Fax: –
Web: www.windstream.com

CEO: Anthony W. (Tony) Thomas
CFO: Bob Gunderman
HR: Don Sain
FYE: December 31
Type: Public

Instead of relying on the prevailing breeze to deliver its services Windstream makes use of more tangible connections such as fiber optics and copper wire. The company provides communications and technology services to business and residential customers in the US through a network of fiber and from 27 data centers. Business services include multi-site networking Internet access cloud computing colocation online backup and other managed services. Along with Internet and voice for its residential customers it also offers video services. Call connection and backhaul services are offered to phone companies and wireless carriers.

	Annual Growth	12/10	12/11	12/12	12/13	12/14
Sales ($ mil.)	11.9%	3,712.0	4,285.7	6,156.3	5,988.1	5,829.5
Net income ($ mil.)	–	310.7	172.3	168.0	241.0	(39.5)
Market value ($ mil.)	(12.3%)	1,400.7	1,179.7	832.0	801.9	828.0
Employees	5.8%	10,086	14,638	13,787	13,434	12,626

WINE.COM INC.

114 Sansome St. 6th Fl.
San Francisco CA 94104
Phone: 415-291-9500
Fax: 415-291-9599
Web: www.wine.com

CEO: Rich Bergsund
CFO: Kenton D Chow
HR: George Garrick
FYE: December 31
Type: Private

Don't know your Cabernet from your Shiraz? Don't worry — Wine.com boasts an online cellar of thousands of wines from around the world and provides in-depth information about wineries and vintages to help you select just the right red white or rose (users can even keep track of orders for future reference in a personalized virtual wine cellar). Besides wine the company sells wine-related accessories including glasses and decanters gift certificates and gift baskets. The company ships non-alcoholic items to all US states and wine only to those without state laws restricting out-of-state sales of wine or alcohol. Wine.com is owned by private investors including Angel Investors and Bear Creek Corporation.

WINGATE PARTNERS

750 N. St. Paul St. Ste. 1200
Dallas TX 75201
Phone: 214-720-1313
Fax: 214-871-8799
Web: www.wingatepartners.com

CEO: –
CFO: –
HR: –
FYE: December 31
Type: Private

Wingate Partners gets by on more than a wing and a prayer rescuing lackluster manufacturing distribution and service businesses. The investment firm founded in 1987 seeks long-term controlling stakes in US-based companies that are underperforming or are in transitional or out-of-favor industries. Targets typically have revenues of $50 million to $250 million and may or may not be profitable at the time of purchase. Wingate often invests between $25 million to $100 million per transaction and avoids financial services media high-tech real estate and certain other businesses. It typically invests in one or two companies a year.

WINLAND ELECTRONICS INC

NBB: WELX

1950 Excel Drive
Mankato, MN 56001
Phone: 507 625-7231
Fax: 507 387-2488
Web: www.winland.com

CEO: –
CFO: Brian D Lawrence
HR: Tami Murphy
FYE: December 31
Type: Public

Winland Electronics has gone from good sleep to loud beeps. Formerly a contract manufacturer of electronics for such products as the Sleep Number bed Winland sold that division in order to focus on its own line of environmental monitoring products including sensors and alarms that check for changes in temperature humidity water leakage and power failure. It also makes a driveway warning system that detects when a vehicle enters a driveway or road. Winland Electronics gets almost all of its sales in the US. The company sold its electronics manufacturing services (EMS) business which made electronic controls and circuit board assemblies to Nortech in early 2011.

	Annual Growth	12/10	12/11	12/12	12/13	12/14
Sales ($ mil.)	3.7%	3.3	3.4	3.7	3.6	3.8
Net income ($ mil.)	–	(3.5)	(0.7)	0.0	(2.6)	0.3
Market value ($ mil.)	2.2%	3.3	1.7	3.0	2.3	3.6
Employees	(17.0%)	7	9	9	4	–

WINMARK CORP

NMS: WINA

605 Highway 169 North, Suite 400
Minneapolis, MN 55441
Phone: 763 520-8500
Fax: –
Web: www.winmarkcorporation.com

CEO: John L. Morgan
CFO: Anthony D. (Tony) Ishaug
HR: –
FYE: December 27
Type: Public

Winmark Corporation loves recycling but it's not collecting cans and paper. Winmark franchises retail chains that buy sell and consign used goods (and some new items) at more than 965 stores. The chains sell sporting goods (Play It Again Sports) children's items (Once Upon A Child) teen apparel (Plato's Closet) women's apparel and accessories (Style Encore) and musical instruments and electronics (Music Go Round). Most operations are in the US but it does have about 70 stores in Canada. In addition the company leases IT equipment to midsized and large businesses through its Winmark Capital unit and it offers financing services to small businesses through its Wirth Business Credit subsidiary.

	Annual Growth	12/10	12/11	12/12	12/13	12/14
Sales ($ mil.)	10.4%	41.2	51.3	51.9	55.7	61.2
Net income ($ mil.)	18.1%	10.3	14.1	12.9	18.2	20.1
Market value ($ mil.)	27.0%	160.7	286.8	287.7	465.3	417.8
Employees	1.9%	100	103	103	109	108

WINN-DIXIE STORES INC.

NASDAQ: WINN

5050 Edgewood Ct.
Jacksonville FL 32254-3699
Phone: 904-783-5000
Fax: 904-370-7224
Web: www.winn-dixie.com

CEO: R Randall Onstead
CFO: Bennett L Nussbaum
HR: –
FYE: June 30
Type: Subsidiary

Winn-Dixie Stores has found — as Jefferson Davis did long ago — that winning Dixie ain't easy. The Deep South supermarket chain operates about 480 combination food and drug stores throughout Alabama Florida Georgia Louisiana and Mississippi under the Winn-Dixie and Winn-Dixie Marketplace banners. Most of Winn-Dixie's supermarkets have pharmacies about 75 house liquor stores and several sell gas. The company's brands include Thrifty Maid Winn & Lovett and Winn-Dixie. Founded in 1925 Winn-Dixie Stores is a subsidiary of BI-LO Holding which merged Winn-Dixie and South Carolina-based BI-LO in 2012 and took them private.

WINNEBAGO INDUSTRIES, INC.

NYS: WGO

P.O. Box 152
Forest City, IA 50436
Phone: 641 585-3535
Fax: 641 585-6966
Web: www.winnebagoind.com

CEO: Michael J. Happe
CFO: Sarah N. Nielsen
HR: –
FYE: August 29
Type: Public

A pioneer in the world of recreational vehicles Winnebago Industries makes products intended to encourage exploration and outdoor escape. Almost all of the company's sales come from its motor homes and towables which are sold via independent dealers throughout the US and Canada under the Winnebago Itasca SunnyBrook and ERA brands. Winnebago Industries also sells RV parts and provides related services; in addition the company produces OEM parts such as extruded aluminum components for other RV manufacturers and for use in commercial vehicles. In mid-2012 Winnebago Industries received a $322 million bid to be bought by private equity firm North Street Capital but deemed the offer untenable.

	Annual Growth	08/11	08/12	08/13	08/14	08/15
Sales ($ mil.)	18.4%	496.4	581.7	803.2	945.2	976.5
Net income ($ mil.)	36.6%	11.8	45.0	32.0	45.1	41.2
Market value ($ mil.)	30.0%	192.4	296.7	600.2	666.5	550.3
Employees	8.0%	2,130	2,380	2,680	2,850	2,900

WINSTON & STRAWN LLP

35 W WACKER DR STE 4200
CHICAGO, IL 60601-1695
Phone: 312-558-5600
Fax: –
Web: www.winstonandstrawn.com

CEO: –
CFO: –
HR: –
FYE: January 31
Type: Private

Over the years Winston & Strawn has developed a reputation for its work in litigation and labor and employment law but the firm's practices encompass a wide range of specialties from antitrust to intellectual property to tax. The firm has around 1000 lawyers in about 15 offices in the US Europe and Asia. Clients have included Abbott Laboratories McDonald's Yahoo Wells Fargo and Philip Morris USA. Winston & Strawn was founded in 1853; since 2000 it has expanded by taking in firms such as New York-based Whitman Breed Abbott & Morgan and San Francisco-based Murphy Sheneman Julian & Rogers.

	Annual Growth	01/07	01/08	01/09	01/11	01/12
Sales ($ mil.)	2.0%	–	697.4	0.0	717.0	754.2
Net income ($ mil.)	3.2%	–	228.1	0.0	238.6	258.3
Market value ($ mil.)	–	–	–	–	–	–
Employees	–	–	–	–	–	1,928

WINTEC INDUSTRIES INC.

675 Sycamore Dr.
Milpitas CA 95035
Phone: 408-856-0500
Fax: 408-856-0501
Web: www.wintecind.com

CEO: David Jeng
CFO: Frank Patchel
HR: –
FYE: December 31
Type: Private

Wintec Industries is trying to rack up big wins in the high-tech world. The company which was founded in 1988 makes computer memory modules for OEMs including customized products for server storage and telecommunications applications. Wintec also provides memory modules and third-party products to resellers and systems integrators. In addition to components the company makes a variety of computer systems servers and peripherals for corporate and government end-users and sells many of its products on its Web site. Wintec also distributes computer hardware and software. It has facilities in China Hong Kong Singapore Taiwan and the US. The company is owned by president Sue Jeng.

WINTER HAVEN HOSPITAL INC.

200 AVENUE F NE
WINTER HAVEN, FL 33881-4193
Phone: 863-293-1121
Fax: –
Web: www.winterhavenhospital.org

CEO: Steve Nierman
CFO: –
HR: –
FYE: September 30
Type: Private

Winter Haven Hospital serves eastern Polk County in central Florida with general medical surgical and emergency care. The health care facility also offers specialty care in areas such as cancer heart disease stroke and a memory clinic for patients suffering from dementia and other memory disorders. The hospital's Regency Medical Center provides maternity and other health care services for women and newborns. Outpatient care is provided through an ambulatory surgery and diagnostic center and several community clinics. Winter Haven Hospital is owned by the local not-for-profit Mid-Florida Medical Services; it was founded in 1926 as a charter hospital.

	Annual Growth	09/08	09/09	09/10	09/11	09/12
Sales ($ mil.)	(3.7%)	–	283.7	279.0	262.9	253.0
Net income ($ mil.)	–	–	(0.2)	0.1	(0.1)	11.7
Market value ($ mil.)	–	–	–	–	–	–
Employees	–	–	–	–	–	1,480

WINTHROP REALTY TRUST

NYS: FUR

7 Bulfinch Place, Suite 500
Boston, MA 02114
Phone: 617 570-4614
Fax: –
Web: www.winthropreit.com

CEO: –
CFO: –
HR: –
FYE: December 31
Type: Public

Winthrop Realty Trust thinks real estate loans can be just as profitable as the real thing. The externally managed real estate investment trust (REIT) invests in property real estate-related collateralized debt and other REITs. Its property portfolio consists of more than a dozen office buildings a handful of retail properties and seven apartment buildings across 15 states totaling 3.5 million square feet. Top commercial tenants include Spectra Energy's Houston headquarters grocer Kroger and e-tailer Football Fanatics' 500000-sq.-ft. distribution center. As a REIT the trust is exempt from paying federal income tax so long as it makes quarterly dividends to shareholders.

	Annual Growth	12/09	12/10	12/11	12/12	12/13
Sales ($ mil.)	13.5%	47.9	55.4	70.1	72.5	79.6
Net income ($ mil.)	–	(84.3)	16.5	10.9	24.6	28.8
Market value ($ mil.)	0.4%	395.3	465.6	370.2	402.2	402.2
Employees	–	–	–	–	–	–

WINTHROP-UNIVERSITY HOSPITAL INC

259 1ST ST
MINEOLA, NY 115013987
Phone: 516-663-0333
Fax: –
Web: www.winthrop.org

CEO: John F. Collins
CFO: –
HR: Stacey Pfeffer
FYE: December 31
Type: Private

From providing it to teaching it Winthrop-University Hospital is focused on health care. The medical center boasts some 590 beds and offers a full range of acute and tertiary health care services. Services include pediatric women's health and cancer care as well as home health services. Winthrop-University Hospital is also a leading provider of cardiovascular surgeries in the region. The hospital is a member of Winthrop-South Nassau University Health System along with sister facility South Nassau Communities Hospital. Winthrop-University Hospital serves as a teaching hospital for the SUNY at Stony Brook School of Medicine.

	Annual Growth	12/04	12/05	12/06	12/07	12/08
Sales ($ mil.)	–	–	0.0	610.6	669.0	725.4
Net income ($ mil.)	–	–	–	15.3	0.2	(134.5)
Market value ($ mil.)	–	–	–	–	–	–
Employees	–	–	–	–	–	6,000

WINTRUST FINANCIAL CORP. (IL)

NMS: WTFC

9700 W. Higgins Road, Suite 800
Rosemont, IL 60018
Phone: 847 939-9000
Fax: 847 615-4091
Web: www.wintrust.com

CEO: Edward J. Wehmer
CFO: David L Stoehr
HR: –
FYE: December 31
Type: Public

Wintrust Financial is a holding company engaged in personal and commercial banking wealth management and specialty lending services primarily in the metropolitan Chicago and Milwaukee areas. With assets of more than $19 billion it operates about 15 subsidiary banks (most bear the name of the community they serve) with more than 120 branches in all. The banks offer traditional deposit services and emphasize business and commercial real estate lending which accounts for about half of the company's loan portfolio. Specifically Wintrust's banks target small business customers. Some of Wintrust's banks also provide niche lending for homeowners associations medical practices franchisees and municipalities.

	Annual Growth	12/10	12/11	12/12	12/13	12/14
Assets ($ mil.)	9.4%	13,980.2	15,893.8	17,519.6	18,097.8	20,010.7
Net income ($ mil.)	24.3%	63.3	77.6	111.2	137.2	151.4
Market value ($ mil.)	9.1%	1,546.0	1,312.9	1,717.7	2,158.6	2,188.6
Employees	7.8%	2,588	2,933	3,269	3,413	3,491

WIRELESS MATRIX USA INC.

TORONTO: WRX

13645 Dulles Technology Dr. Ste. 100
Herndon VA 20171
Phone: 703-262-0500
Fax: 703-262-0380
Web: www.wirelessmatrixcorp.com

CEO: Michael Burdiek
CFO: –
HR: Camryn Macnichol
FYE: April 30
Type: Public

Wireless Matrix doesn't open its customers' eyes with a red pill but rather with mobile resource management software. Its Software-as-a-Service (SaaS) data communications offerings enable businesses in North America to remotely track vehicle fleets and monitor the performance of vehicles and drivers using satellite cellular and Wi-Fi networks. Wireless Matrix's services center around its FleetOutlook GPS-tracking and performance reporting software which ties into mobile communications hardware also sold by the company. It serves clients in the energy telecommunications utilities transportation and other industries in which operations are spread out across large areas. CalAmp is acquiring the company.

WIRELESS TELECOM GROUP, INC.

ASE: WTT

25 Eastmans Road
Parsippany, NJ 07054
Phone: 973 386-9696
Fax: –
Web: www.wtcom.com

CEO: Paul Genova
CFO: Robert Censullo
HR: –
FYE: December 31
Type: Public

In an industry that abhors noise Wireless Telecom Group sure makes a lot of it. The company which markets its products under the brand name Noisecom makes electronic noise generators for wireless telecommunications systems. Its products are used to test whether such systems can receive transmitted information. Its noise emulator products also operate in radar and satellite systems to continually monitor and test receivers or to jam signals. Wireless Telecom's Boonton Electronics subsidiary makes radio-frequency (RF) and microwave test equipment. Its Microlab subsidiary makes high-power passive microwave components. Wireless Telecom Group gets nearly one-third of sales from outside the Americas region.

	Annual Growth	12/10	12/11	12/12	12/13	12/14
Sales ($ mil.)	13.2%	24.6	26.8	29.6	33.8	40.3
Net income ($ mil.)	–	(0.7)	2.4	3.2	3.8	2.4
Market value ($ mil.)	31.7%	17.0	22.6	23.4	41.3	51.1
Employees	5.3%	101	102	108	115	124

WIRTZ BEVERAGE GROUP LLC

680 N. Lakeshore Dr. Ste. 1900
Chicago IL 60611
Phone: 312-943-7000
Fax: 610-370-3495
Web: www.boscovs.com

CEO: –
CFO: –
HR: Brittney Conklin
FYE: June 30
Type: Private

Wirtz Beverage Group does it best on ice. The group owns and operates liquor distributorships and offers a full line of spirits wine and beer in the Midwest. Wirtz Beverage owns the rights to distribute some key Diageo brands such as Crown Royal Johnnie Walker J&B and Tanqueray; it also carries imported and domestic wines including labels from California's Fetzer and France's Baron Philippe de Rothschild Chateau. The company's beers include MillerCoors and Sam Adams from the US and imports the likes of as Corona. The grandson of company founder Arthur Wirtz W. Rockwell (Rocky) is the president of Wirtz Beverage Group.

WIS INTERNATIONAL

9265 Sky Park Ct. Ste. 100
San Diego CA 92123-4375
Phone: 858-565-8111
Fax: 858-492-2751
Web: www.wis.ca

CEO: Jim Rose
CFO: Trey Graham
HR: –
FYE: December 31
Type: Private

WIS International provides inventory management and merchandising services for retailers of all sizes as well as to a range of warehouse service and manufacturing industries. Offerings include physical inventory counting retail price verification and vendor audits. The company operates throughout North America in addition to Central and South America Europe and Asia; overall it has about 220 offices. Customers have included blue chip retailers such as Dollar General Home Depot Publix Super Markets Walgreens and Wal-Mart. Investment firm American Capital owns a controlling stake in WIS International; other shareholders include company executives. The company traces its roots to 1953.

WISDOMTREE INVESTMENTS INC.

NASDAQ: WETF

380 Madison Ave. 21st Fl.
New York NY 10017
Phone: 585-385-0610
Fax: 585-385-0614
Web: www.igius.com

CEO: Jonathan L Steinberg
CFO: Amit Muni
HR: –
FYE: December 31
Type: Public

WisdomTree Investments specializes in exchange-traded funds (ETFs). Through subsidiaries WisdomTree Trust and WisdomTree Asset Management the company manages about 40 index funds that invest in domestic and international securities. It provides an alternative to funds weighted by market capitalization by focusing on fundamentals such as earnings dividends and industry. Serving both individual and institutional investors WisdomTree Investments has nearly $5 billion of assets under management. In 2005 the company reinvented itself with its new name new leaders and a new strategy.

WISE FOODS INC.

228 Raseley St.
Berwick PA 18603-4533
Phone: 570-759-4000
Fax: 919-337-4149
Web: www.overturenetworks.com

CEO: Jolie Weber
CFO: –
HR: Frank Colosimo
FYE: December 31
Type: Private

People who suffer from the munchies would be wise to check out the products portfolio at Wise Foods. Located in Berwick Pennsylvania the company manufactures salty snacks such as its version of Frito-Lay's CHEETOS called cheez doodles (unlike Frito-Lay Wise doesn't use capital letters for the name of this product) and New York Deli potato chips. The regional foods firm also manufactures popcorn pretzels pork rinds tortilla chips and dips and salsa. Its brand names include Bravos Dipsy Doodles Ridgies Wavy Potato Chips Cheez Waffies and Wise. The company's products are sold at retail food and convenience outlets located in the Eastern US.

WITHLACOOCHEE RIVER ELECTRIC COOPERATIVE INC

14651 21ST ST
DADE CITY, FL 335232920
Phone: 352-567-5133
Fax: –
Web: www.wrec.net

CEO: –
CFO: –
HR: Connie Hobbs
FYE: December 31
Type: Private

Withlacoochee River Electric Cooperative keeps the power flowing to the residences and businesses of more than 200360 member-owners in five counties along the central Florida Gulf Coast. The power distribution utility which was originally set up in 1941 receives wholesale generation and transmission services from the Seminole Electric Cooperative. Withlacoochee River Electric a non-profit organization returns any funds remaining at the end of each year to its membership. The cooperative has returned more than $190 million to its member-owners.

	Annual Growth	12/08	12/09	12/11	12/12	12/13
Sales ($ mil.)	578.7%	–	0.2	423.7	421.0	433.3
Net income ($ mil.)	(23.7%)	–	–	28.5	25.7	16.6
Market value ($ mil.)	–	–	–	–	–	–
Employees	–	–	–	–	–	458

WITS BASIN PRECIOUS MINERALS INC.

OTC: WITM

80 S. 8th St. Ste. 900
Minneapolis MN 55402-8773
Phone: 612-349-5277
Fax: 612-395-5276
Web: www.witsbasin.com

CEO: Stephen D King
CFO: Mark D Dacko
HR: –
FYE: December 31
Type: Public

Wits Basin Precious Minerals hopes to use its smarts to find gold in Africa and North America. The company's main mineral property is a gold exploration project in South Africa near the major goldfields of the Witwatersrand Basin. Wits Basin also owns the Bates-Hunter Gold Mine in Colorado and a silver mine in Mexico. In early 2007 the company acquired China Global Mining Resources which owns three minerals properties in China. The next year it sold its rights to 65% of the South African mining project to Communications DVR of Canada in exchange for a two-thirds stake in DVR.

WIZARDS OF THE COAST LLC

1600 Lind Ave. SW Ste. 400
Renton WA 98055
Phone: 425-226-6500
Fax: 425-204-5916
Web: www.wizards.com

CEO: Greg Leeds
CFO: –
HR: –
FYE: December 31
Type: Subsidiary

Wizards of the Coast has built a house of cards. The company a unit of toy behemoth Hasbro is best known for trading card game Magic: The Gathering which is available in several languages. Wizards of the Coast's other offerings include the granddaddy of medieval role-playing games ("Dungeons & Dragons") and various traditional games books and magazines. The company also makes Star Wars games through a license. Through the years Wizards of the Coast's hobby games have earned a cult following with children and teens still playing the firm's games with friends into their adulthood. Former CEO Peter Adkison game designer Richard Garfield and several others founded the company in 1990.

WKI HOLDING COMPANY INC.

5500 N. Pearl St. Ste. 400
Rosemont IL 60018-5303
Phone: 847-233-8600
Fax: 847-678-9424
Web: www.worldkitchen.com

CEO: James A Sharman
CFO: Joseph W McGarr
HR: –
FYE: December 31
Type: Private

WKI Holding has whipped up a kitchen kingpin. The holding company's World Kitchen subsidiary produces many household names in cookware and tableware. Its brand portfolio includes Baker's Secret Chicago Cutlery Corelle CorningWare EKCO Magnalite Olfa Pyrex Revere and Visions. Products are distributed worldwide and sold through mass merchants department stores and specialty retailers as well as through World Kitchen's own factory outlets and e-commerce sites. The company operates manufacturing and distribution centers in the US Canada and the Asia/Pacific region. Originally part of manufacturing giant Corning it adopted the WKI Holding name in 2000.

WM RECYCLE AMERICA LLC

1001 Fannin St. Ste. 4000
Houston TX 77002
Phone: 713-512-6200
Fax: 713-394-2135
Web: www.recycleamerica.com

CEO: –
CFO: –
HR: –
FYE: December 31
Type: Subsidiary

How can you argue with a company whose name embodies environmentalism and patriotism? WM Recycle America provides recycling materials brokerage and container processing services in the US and Canada. Services include materials recovery secondary processing materials marketing (matching up recycled materials producers and purchasers) and recycling audits. The company provides waste recycling operations at nearly 100 recycling plants and provides marketing services for more than 140 locations. The subsidiary which handles 8 million tons of waste per year was formed in 2003 when Waste Management acquired The Peltz Group and combined the two companies' recycling operations.

WM. BOLTHOUSE FARMS INC.

7200 E. Brundage Ln.
Bakersfield CA 93307-3016
Phone: 661-366-7270
Fax: 661-366-9236
Web: www.bolthouse.com

CEO: –
CFO: –
HR: –
FYE: July 31
Type: Business Segment

Eh what's up Doc? What's up is the crop at Bolthouse Farms. The company is one of the country's largest producers of fresh-cut carrots. Bolthouse offers all things carrot including fresh and frozen whole carrots carrot sticks and chips carrot (and other) chilled juices and smoothies and those cute little pre-cut and pre-peeled baby carrots for both retail consumers and foodservice industry customers. Its other products include orange juice passion fruit juice fruit smoothies chai tea Bom Dia acai juice and lemonade. The company also makes a line of Bolthouse Farms-branded salad dressings. Bolthouse Farms is owned by Campbell Soup Co.

WOLFE ENGINEERING INC.

3040 N. 1st St.
San Jose CA 95134
Phone: 408-232-2600
Fax: 408-526-9040
Web: www.wolfe-engr.com

CEO: John P Wolfe
CFO: –
HR: –
FYE: December 31
Type: Private

Seeking to wolf down more market share Wolfe Engineering designs and manufactures equipment for chip makers OEMs and R&D laboratories. The outsourcing company provides comprehensive and integrated engineering consulting manufacturing and assembly services. Products include fluid and gaseous delivery systems and control interfaces for the aerospace biotechnology microelectronics nanotechnology pharmaceutical and semiconductor industries. The company has manufacturing plants in California and Texas and it has opened a design and manufacturing center in Taiwan.

WOLVERINE ADVANCED MATERIALS LLC

5850 Mercury Dr. Ste. 250
Dearborn MI 48126
Phone: 313-749-6100
Fax: 313-749-6150
Web: www.wolverinegasketmaterials.com

CEO: Grant Beard
CFO: Michael Beyer
HR: –
FYE: November 30
Type: Subsidiary

A-Tisket A-Tasket Wolverine's Got-A-Gasket. Wolverine Advanced Materials a business unit of EaglePicher Corporation is a leading developer of gaskets rubber sealants OEM and aftermarket brake shims and sound damping systems for the automotive electronics and other industries. It manufactures high-performance custom-engineered sealing solutions for use in engines fuel systems transmissions automotive A/C industrial compressors and other custom sealing applications. Wolverine has manufacturing and sales offices in Florida Michigan and Virginia and exports to 29 countries around the globe.

WOLVERINE PIPE LINE COMPANY

8075 CREEKSIDE DR STE 210
PORTAGE, MI 490246303
Phone: 269-323-2491
Fax: –
Web: www.wolverinepipeline.com

CEO: –
CFO: –
HR: –
FYE: December 31
Type: Private

Named after a powerful weasel (the mascot of the University of Michigan) Wolverine Pipe Line transports a range of refined petroleum products across the US Midwest. It operates more than 1000 miles of six-inch to 18-inch diameter pipeline which stretches through Illinois Indiana Michigan and Ohio. Wolverine Pipe Line's system also includes 12 pumping stations. The company supplies about 35% of Michigan's refined petroleum products. National pipeline and terminals player Sunoco Logistics Partners' Eastern Pipeline System controls nearly a third of Wolverine Pipe Line.

	Annual Growth	12/09	12/10	12/11	12/12	12/13
Sales ($ mil.)	10.2%	–	63.2	65.1	78.4	84.5
Net income ($ mil.)	40.1%	–	–	15.9	25.2	31.2
Market value ($ mil.)	–	–	–	–	–	–
Employees	–	–	–	–	–	75

WOLVERINE POWER SUPPLY COOPERATIVE INC.

10125 W WATERGATE RD
CADILLAC, MI 496018458
Phone: 231-775-5700
Fax: –
Web: www.wpsci.com

CEO: –
CFO: Janet Kass
HR: Craig S Borton
FYE: December 31
Type: Private

Named after a voracious carnivore Wolverine Power Supply Cooperative makes sure that that voracious consumer of electricity — the American public — gets the power its needs. The non-profit company is an electric generation and transmission utility that provides services to five member distribution cooperatives in Michigan. Wolverine Power Supply Cooperative monitors and operates 1600 miles of bulk transmission lines and owns five power plants that generate 200 megawatts of capacity. It also maintains about 130 distribution substations and 36 transmission stations as well as purchases power (including windpower energy) from other utilities and marketers to distribute to its customers.

	Annual Growth	12/05	12/06	12/07	12/09	12/10
Sales ($ mil.)	21.3%	–	–	164.9	256.2	294.1
Net income ($ mil.)	–	–	–	0.0	13.4	(17.0)
Market value ($ mil.)	–	–	–	–	–	–
Employees	–	–	–	–	–	110

WOLVERINE WORLD WIDE, INC.

NYS. WWW

9341 Courtland Drive N.E.
Rockford, MI 49351
Phone: 616 866-5500
Fax: –
Web: www.wolverineworldwide.com

CEO: Blake W. Krueger
CFO: Michael D. Stornant
HR: –
FYE: January 03
Type: Public

Wolverine World Wide has the shoes to quiet your barking dogs. The company makes Hush Puppies casual shoes and slippers as well as boots sandals and related apparel and accessories. Its boot lines include Merrell (outdoor) Bates (military) HyTest and Wolverine (industrial); footwear is made under the Cushe brand and private labels. Wolverine also boasts several licenses from Caterpillar ("CAT") Harley-Davidson and Patagonia to make branded footwear. It sells worldwide through department and specialty stores independent distributors Internet retailers and more than 440 company-owned retail stores in North America and the UK. Wolverine also maintains more than 60 consumer-direct Internet sites.

	Annual Growth	01/11*	12/11	12/12	12/13*	01/15
Sales ($ mil.)	21.9%	1,248.5	1,409.1	1,640.8	2,691.1	2,761.1
Net income ($ mil.)	6.2%	104.5	123.3	80.7	100.4	133.1
Market value ($ mil.)	(2.3%)	3,246.5	3,629.4	4,091.8	3,401.3	2,956.3
Employees	12.4%	4,139	4,435	8,299	7,274	6,600
					*Fiscal year change	

WOMAN'S HOSPITAL FOUNDATION INC

100 WOMANS WAY
BATON ROUGE, LA 708175100
Phone: 225-927-1300
Fax: –
Web: www.womans.org

CEO: Teri G Fontenot
CFO: Greg Smith
HR: –
FYE: September 30
Type: Private

Woman's Hospital is a 170-bed hospital catering to the needs of women and infants in southern Louisiana. Founded in 1968 the hospital was one of the nation's first women's specialty hospitals. The not-for-profit hospital offers women's health classes as well as other educational resources and delivers about 8500 babies each year. Services include breast care cosmetic surgery general surgery genetics counseling occupational therapy and speech therapy. Woman's Hospital moved to a new 225-acre campus in 2012 to replace its aging facilities. It boasts a five-story hospital building medical office buildings and increased capacity for its inpatient rooms and neonatal intensive care unit.

	Annual Growth	09/09	09/10	09/11	09/12	09/13
Sales ($ mil.)	(0.4%)	–	–	219.1	217.7	217.1
Net income ($ mil.)	–	–	–	46.1	22.5	(12.5)
Market value ($ mil.)	–	–	–	–	–	–
Employees	–	–	–	–	–	1,850

WONDERWARE CORPORATION

26561 Rancho Pkwy. South
Lake Forest CA 92630
Phone: 949-727-3200
Fax: 949-727-3270
Web: www.wonderware.com

CEO: –
CFO: –
HR: –
FYE: March 31
Type: Subsidiary

Ever wonder how manufacturers manage their factory operations? Wonderware an operating unit of London-based Invensys provides industrial automation software used to collect display and manage information from the factory floor in order to optimize production processes. Its products include a graphical interface to display operations data and allow plant operators to control process equipment. The company also offers simulation software that allows plant managers to test new processes and configurations. It serves a wide range of industries including oil and gas pharmaceutical energy manufacturing and chemicals. Clients have included Royal Dutch Shell and Canadian nuclear power company Bruce Power.

WOODFIN OIL COMPANY

8180 Mechanicsville Tpke.
Mechanicsville VA 23111
Phone: 804-730-5000
Fax: 804-730-0861
Web: www.woodfinoil.net

CEO: Jack Woodfin
CFO: Kevin W Walsh
HR: Davis Farran
FYE: December 31
Type: Private

When it comes to heating wood's fine — but kerosene's better. Woodfin Oil provides residential heating oils and kerosene to customers in Richmond Virginia. The company also operates fleet fueling stations and convenience stores and provides air-conditioning plumbing and electrical services. Woodfin Oil manages a heating oil and kerosene supply fleet. It operates 14 Pit Stop Convenience Stores at locations across Virginia. The Woodfin Plumbing unit installs A. O. Smith electric water heaters and In-Sink-Erator food waste disposal equipment. This company also installs fireplace logs for natural gas fireplaces.

WOODMEN OF THE WORLD LIFE INSURANCE SOCIETY

1700 Farnam St.
Omaha NE 68102
Phone: 402-342-1890
Fax: 402-997-7948
Web: www.woodmen.com

CEO: James Mounce
CFO: –
HR: –
FYE: December 31
Type: Insurance Society

Count the rings on Woodmen and you'll get back to 1890. Woodmen of the World Life Insurance Society is a life insurance company formed to benefit the members of Woodmen of the World a fraternal organization with some 750000 members across the US. The company provides its members with traditional life insurance as well as annuities for both individuals and small businesses. It also offers mutual funds variable annuities and 529 college savings accounts through its Woodmen Financial Services subsidiary. Additionally members have access to major medical coverage and disability insurance via marketing agreements with some third-party insurers.

WOODSTOCK HOLDINGS INC

NBB: WSFL

117 Towne Lake Parkway, Suite 200
Woodstock, GA 30188
Phone: 770 516-6996
Fax: 877 431-5727
Web: www.woodstockholdingsinc.com

CEO: –
CFO: Melissa L Whitley
HR: –
FYE: December 31
Type: Public

Woodstock Financial Group offers up financial advice but just don't expect to hear about hippie stock picks. The company formerly Raike Financial Group brokers support services for brokers. Founded in 1995 the company provides licensing clearing IT support education and various administrative services to a network of independent financial planners insurance agents and traditional and discount securities brokers. Woodstock handles a range of investment products including stocks bonds mutual funds annuities and life insurance. Online trading is offered through its Woodstock Discount Brokerage division. Founder and CEO William Raike owns about 80% of the company.

	Annual Growth	12/10	12/11	12/12	12/13	12/14
Sales ($ mil.)	(5.6%)	12.7	13.9	9.6	9.4	10.1
Net income ($ mil.)	(5.4%)	0.3	(0.2)	(0.4)	(0.1)	0.2
Market value ($ mil.)	(8.8%)	1.3	1.9	1.8	0.3	0.9
Employees	(7.9%)	118	111	84	91	85

WOODWARD, INC.

NMS: WWD

1000 East Drake Road
Fort Collins, CO 80525
Phone: 970 482-5811
Fax: –
Web: www.woodward.com

CEO: Thomas A. Gendron
CFO: Robert F. (Bob) Weber
HR: –
FYE: September 30
Type: Public

Woodward likes to remain in control. The company manufactures and services a slew of energy control and optimization systems used in aircraft and vehicles turbine and piston engines and electrical power equipment. Woodward serves OEMs and prime contractors worldwide in commercial and military aerospace power generation and distribution and transportation. These include such noteworthy names as GE Caterpillar Boeing and United Technologies. Woodward's products are primarily made in the US where the company garners more than half of its sales.

	Annual Growth	09/11	09/12	09/13	09/14	09/15
Sales ($ mil.)	4.5%	1,711.7	1,865.6	1,936.0	2,001.2	2,038.3
Net income ($ mil.)	8.2%	132.2	141.6	145.9	165.8	181.5
Market value ($ mil.)	10.4%	1,731.6	2,147.4	2,580.3	3,009.4	2,572.1
Employees	2.7%	6,200	6,600	6,750	6,700	6,900

WOOLRICH INC.

2 MILL ST
WOOLRICH, PA 17779
Phone: 570-769-6464
Fax: –
Web: www.woolrich.com

CEO: –
CFO: William Hill
HR: –
FYE: January 02
Type: Private

Woolrich has branched out beyond woolen textiles. As the US's oldest continuously operating apparel manufacturer and woolen mill the outdoor apparel maker's products include men's and women's sportswear and outerwear woolen fabrics blankets and home furnishings. Woolrich also licenses its name for the sale of furniture and accessories. Its branded products are marketed domestically and internationally. In addition Woolrich supplies woolen yard goods to apparel and home furnishings makers. The firm distributes several million catalogs per year and sells via the Internet. The Rich family founded Woolrich in 1830.

	Annual Growth	12/05	12/06	12/07*	01/09	01/10
Sales ($ mil.)	–	–	–	(1,608.9)	114.4	99.4
Net income ($ mil.)	2152.6%	–	–	0.0	(1.9)	0.8
Market value ($ mil.)	–	–	–	–	–	–
Employees	–	–	–	–	–	200

*Fiscal year change

WORKDAY INC

NYS: WDAY

6230 Stoneridge Mall Road
Pleasanton, CA 94588
Phone: 925 951-9000
Fax: –
Web: www.workday.com

CEO: Aneel Bhusri
CFO: Mark S. Peek
HR: –
FYE: January 31
Type: Public

Workday wants to make every day better for HR and finance professionals. The computer software company makes cloud-based enterprise applications to manage financial and human capital resources. Its products are designed to replace on-site legacy systems with a more collaborative mobile and intuitive interface and a frequently updated product that includes regulatory changes. Major customers including Aviva Flextronics Lenovo Kimberly-Clark TripAdvisor and Service Source use Workday's partner "ecosystem" to manage people payroll time tracking finances procurement and employee expenses in a layout that mimics a typical Internet site.

	Annual Growth	01/11	01/12	01/13	01/14	01/15
Sales ($ mil.)	222.5%	7.3	134.4	273.7	468.9	787.9
Net income ($ mil.)	–	(5.5)	(79.6)	(119.2)	(172.5)	(248.0)
Market value ($ mil.)	22.0%	–	–	10,065.2	16,870.8	14,971.5
Employees	50.7%	–	1,096	1,750	2,600	3,750

WORKSCAPE INC.

123 Felton St.
Marlborough MA 01752
Phone: 508-573-9000
Fax: 508-573-9500
Web: www.workscape.com

CEO: Timothy T Clifford
CFO: Donald R Fitch Jr
HR: –
FYE: December 31
Type: Subsidiary

Workscape is a human resources workhorse. The company provides Web-based software used to automate human resources management and benefits administration functions for large organizations making it possible for employees to access and manage information via the Internet. Its applications and services include online employee benefits administration compensation planning performance management and communications consulting. The company also offers employee support center for benefit- and HR-related questions. Customers have included Avis Budget Group and Raytheon. Workscape has offices in in the US and the UK. Founded in 1999 by CEO Timothy Clifford the company was acquired in 2010 by Automatic Data Processing (ADP).

WORKSTREAM USA INC.

OTC: WSTM

2200 Lucien Way Ste. 201
Maitland FL 32751
Phone: 407-475-5500
Fax: 407-475-5517
Web: www.workstreaminc.com

CEO: David Kennedy
CFO: –
HR: –
FYE: May 31
Type: Public

Workstream puts an oar in the workforce placement and productivity waters to help clients keep their employee ships floating along. The company provides software that automates the hiring process and helps businesses manage human resources operations. Workstream's Software-as-a-Service (SaaS) offerings include recruitment systems for hiring new employees; performance management tools for measuring competencies setting goals and providing feedback; compensation management tools for planning rewards programs; and employee portal applications. The company also offers recruitment research applicant sourcing career transition and outplacement services. Canada accounts for 13% of sales.

WORLD ACCEPTANCE CORP.

NMS: WRLD

108 Frederick Street
Greenville, SC 29607
Phone: 864 298-9800
Fax: –
Web: www.worldacceptance.com

CEO: A. Alexander (Sandy) McLean
CFO: John L. Calmes
HR: Marilyn Messer
FYE: March 31
Type: Public

Who in the world will accept your poor credit? World Acceptance Corp just might. The consumer finance company offers short-term and medium-term loans and credit insurance to individuals with limited access to other credit sources. Borrowers use the loans of $300 to $4000 to meet temporary or unanticipated cash needs such as car repairs and medical bills filling a void left by banks and credit unions which typically don't make loans of less than $5000. Convenience comes at a price: World Acceptance often charges the maximum interest rates and related fees allowed by law. The fast-growing company has more than 1300 offices in 15 states in the US South and Midwest as well as in Mexico.

	Annual Growth	03/11	03/12	03/13	03/14	03/15
Sales ($ mil.)	5.6%	491.4	540.2	583.7	617.6	610.2
Net income ($ mil.)	5.0%	91.2	100.7	104.1	106.6	110.8
Market value ($ mil.)	2.8%	584.8	549.4	770.2	673.5	654.1
Employees	9.0%	3,292	3,435	4,483	4,712	4,643

WORLD AIRWAYS INC.

101 World Dr.
Peachtree City GA 30269
Phone: 770-632-8000
Fax: +34-91-354-2890
Web: www.codere.com

CEO: –
CFO: –
HR: –
FYE: December 31
Type: Subsidiary

Taking to the skies is one foolproof way to see the world... just ask the folks at World Airways. The air carrier provides nonscheduled transportation services for passenger and cargo carriers international freight forwarders the US military and international leisure tour operators. Its fleet consists of more than 20 wide-body MD-11 aircraft and Boeing 747-400 freighters. The air charter operator a subsidiary of Global Aviation Holdings visits more than 120 countries and is the largest commercial carrier of US military personnel. In 2007 World Airways was acquired by Global Aviation which is also the parent of North American Airlines. World Airways was formed in 1948.

WORLD ENERGY SOLUTIONS, INC. (DE)

NAS: XWES

100 Front Street
Worcester, MA 01608
Phone: 508 459-8100
Fax: –
Web: www.worldenergy.com

CEO: Philip V Adams
CFO: James F Parslow
HR: –
FYE: December 31
Type: Public

World Energy Solutions offers its customers some protection from the world of hurt that is rising energy prices. The company offers energy procurement market analysis and risk management services for industrial and commercial customers and government entities in deregulated regions of the US. World Energy Solutions analyzes clients' energy needs and provides savings on electricity and natural gas supply contracts through its online reverse auction platforms; it also manages bill payments and monitors energy usage after the auction process. The company's more than 300 customers include Cargill Energy Marketing Ford Leidos and the US Postal Service.

	Annual Growth	12/08	12/09	12/10	12/11	12/12
Sales ($ mil.)	26.4%	12.4	14.6	18.0	21.1	31.8
Net income ($ mil.)	–	(6.8)	(2.3)	(0.1)	0.5	5.3
Market value ($ mil.)	84.9%	4.5	34.8	33.9	36.1	52.6
Employees	23.0%	55	54	60	82	126

WORLD FINER FOODS INC

1455 BROAD ST STE 4
BLOOMFIELD, NJ 070033039
Phone: 973-338-0300
Fax: –
Web: www.worldfiner.com

CEO: –
CFO: –
HR: Lisa L Accunzo
FYE: December 31
Type: Private

Fine food is quite a find for this company and its customers. World Finer Foods distributes more than 900 specialty food items to US supermarkets and gourmet food stores. Its inventory boasts some 40 brands including Blanchard & Blanchard La Vie Mrs. Leeper's Pasta and Panni. The company also markets its own food products under such names as DaVinci London Pub Pritikin and Reese. Its InterNatural Foods unit represents its natural foods division while its Liberty Richter division distributes domestic and imported gourmet food items. Founded as VIP Foods in 1971 World Finer Foods is a cooperative owned by food distributors Millbrook Distribution (a unit of United Natural Foods) and Kehe Food.

	Annual Growth	12/05	12/06	12/07	12/08	12/10
Sales ($ mil.)	13.2%	–	–	–	126.0	161.4
Net income ($ mil.)	(68.7%)	–	–	–	0.7	0.1
Market value ($ mil.)	–	–	–	–	–	–
Employees	–	–	–	–	–	78

WORLD FUEL SERVICES CORP.

NYS: INT

9800 N.W. 41st Street
Miami, FL 33178
Phone: 305 428-8000
Fax: 305 392-5621
Web: www.wfscorp.com

CEO: Michael J. Kasbar
CFO: Ira M. Birns
HR: Derek Scott
FYE: December 31
Type: Public

You can't fuel all the people all the time but World Fuel Services tries hard to do just that. World Fuel Services provides fuel and services to commercial and corporate aircraft petroleum distributors and ships at more than 8000 locations around the world 24 hours a day. Its aviation fueling business focuses on serving small to midsized air carriers cargo and charter carriers and private aircraft. World Fuel Services also markets fuel and related services to petroleum distributors operating in the land transportation market. All told it has almost 50 offices around the world and does business in more than 200 countries and/or territories.

	Annual Growth	12/10	12/11	12/12	12/13	12/14
Sales ($ mil.)	22.7%	19,131.1	34,622.9	38,945.3	41,561.9	43,386.4
Net income ($ mil.)	10.8%	146.9	194.0	189.3	203.1	221.7
Market value ($ mil.)	6.7%	2,606.5	3,026.0	2,967.6	3,111.1	3,382.8
Employees	28.1%	1,499	1,798	2,490	2,758	4,041

WORLD SURVEILLANCE GROUP INC

NBB: WSGI

State Road 405, Building M6-306A, Room 1400, Kennedy Space CenterCEO: Glenn D Estrella
Merritt Island, FL 32815
Phone: 321 452-3545
Fax: –
Web: www.wsgi.com

CFO: W Jeffrey Sawyers
HR: –
FYE: December 31
Type: Public

Sanswire isn't known for a down-to-earth approach to product development. The company (formerly known as GlobeTel Communications) is developing airship "stratellites" (essentially blimps equipped with wireless gear that float in the stratosphere) to enable its planned wireless broadband network. Other intended uses for Sanswire's unmanned aerial vehicles include security and surveillance (Skysat) and payload transport and delivery (PADD). The company is developing its products in conjunction with Stuttgart Germany-based TAO Technologies GmbH.

	Annual Growth	12/09	12/10	12/11	12/12	12/13
Sales ($ mil.)	95.1%	–	0.3	0.2	1.1	1.9
Net income ($ mil.)	–	(9.4)	(9.8)	(1.1)	(3.4)	(3.4)
Market value ($ mil.)	(39.8%)	48.8	56.2	25.4	8.9	6.4
Employees	15.0%	4	4	5	5	7

WORLD TRAVEL HOLDINGS INC.

100 Fordham Rd. Bldg. C
Wilmington MA 01887
Phone: 617-424-7990
Fax: 617-424-1943
Web: worldtravelholdings.com

CEO: Jeff Tolkin
CFO: Don Graff
HR: –
FYE: December 31
Type: Private

World Travel Holdings (WTH) sells vacations and cruise packages directly to consumers through multiple brands including CruiseOne CruisesOnly Cruise411 Rooms.com Vacation Outlet and Villas of Distinction. It owns licensing agreements with the cruise components of third-party travel companies American Airlines Orbitz priceline.com Delta Air Lines and BJ's Travel. The company has offices in New York Massachusetts Florida and Virginia and a UK subsidiary Cruise 118. WTH was founded in 2005 by brothers and industry veterans Brad and Jeff Tolkin. A year later the fledgling company more than doubled its size when it acquired National Leisure Group a leading vacation package distributor.

WORLD VISION INTERNATIONAL

800 W. Chestnut Ave.
Monrovia CA 91016-3106
Phone: 626-303-8811
Fax: 626-301-7786
Web: www.wvi.org

CEO: Kevin Jenkins
CFO: –
HR: Florencia Curtis
FYE: September 30
Type: Private - Partnershi

World Vision International sees a world where all children are fed sheltered educated valued and loved. The Christian relief organization advocates for children and the poor and the development of families and communities around the globe. Operating in about 100 countries from some 40 offices worldwide it focuses on education health care economic and agricultural development and emergency relief efforts; its donors sponsor more than 3 million children. While the organization prohibits proselytizing 60% of its budget goes to programs that include "domestic ministry." The group receives its contributions mainly from private sources. World Vision was founded in 1950 by the Rev. Bob Pierce.

WORLD WIDE TECHNOLOGY INC.

60 Weldon Pkwy.
St. Louis MO 63043
Phone: 314-569-7000
Fax: 314-569-8300
Web: www.wwt.com

CEO: James P Kavanaugh
CFO: Thomas W Strunk
HR: Tarah Hampton
FYE: December 31
Type: Private

World Wide Technology (WWT) has a broad view of its business. The company primarily provides such IT services as network design and installation systems and application integration and procurement. It also offers a range of Web-based products and services including e-commerce systems development order tracking and catalog management. WWT serves businesses in the automotive retail and telecommunications industries as well as government agencies. Top clients include Dell the State of Missouri and the State of Alaska. WWT was founded in 1990 by chairman David Steward and CEO Jim Kavanaugh.

WORLD WILDLIFE FUND INC.

1250 24TH ST NW FL 2
WASHINGTON, DC 200371193
Phone: 202-293-4800
Fax: –
Web: www.worldwildlife.org

CEO: –
CFO: –
HR: Elaine Bowman
FYE: June 30
Type: Private

A fuzzy-wuzzy with kung fu strength the panda embodies mission of the World Wildlife Fund (WWF). The conservation organization has worked on more than 13000 projects in about 100 countries to save endangered species and natural areas as well as to address threats such as global warming and the exploitation of forests. By 2020 WWF aims to conserve 15 of the world's more ecologically important regions. Its work crosses Africa Asia Latin America North America and Eurasia through national affiliates in about 100 countries. The group publishes data on wildlife wild places and global environmental challenges. Founded in 1961 WWF is joined by 1.1 million members in the US and some 5 million overseas.

	Annual Growth	06/08	06/09	06/11	06/12	06/13
Sales ($ mil.)	10.9%	–	151.6	182.1	208.5	229.2
Net income ($ mil.)	–	–	–	(2.0)	16.9	25.5
Market value ($ mil.)	–	–	–	–	–	–
Employees	–	–	–	–	–	2,500

WORLD WRESTLING ENTERTAINMENT INC

NYS: WWE

1241 East Main Street
Stamford, CT 06902
Phone: 203 352-8600
Fax: –
Web: www.wwe.com

CEO: Vincent K. (Vince) McMahon
CFO: George A Barrios
HR: –
FYE: December 31
Type: Public

The action might be fake but the business of World Wrestling Entertainment (WWE) is very real. The company is a leading producer and promoter of wrestling matches for TV and live audiences with about 250 live events each year including more than 50 international matches. Its main programming includes Monday Night Raw a top US cable program on USA Network; Friday Night SmackDown on Syfy; and WWE NXT on its website. WWE also produces about 12 live pay-per-view programs licenses characters for merchandise and sells videos and DVDs showcasing more than 140 wrestling stars such as Rey Mysterio Triple H and The Undertaker. Two-time WWE world champion Vince McMahon has nearly 90% voting control of the company.

	Annual Growth	12/11	12/12	12/13	12/14	12/15
Sales ($ mil.)	8.0%	483.9	484.0	508.0	542.6	658.8
Net income ($ mil.)	(0.7%)	24.8	31.4	2.8	(30.1)	24.1
Market value ($ mil.)	17.6%	707.4	598.9	1,258.5	936.7	1,354.1
Employees	6.2%	660	721	762	761	840

WORTHINGTON INDUSTRIES, INC.   NYS: WOR

200 Old Wilson Bridge Road	CEO: John P. McConnell
Columbus, OH 43085	CFO: B. Andrew (Andy) Rose
Phone: 614 438-3210	HR: Terrence Dyer
Fax: 614 438-3256	FYE: May 31
Web: www.worthingtonindustries.com	Type: Public

At least when it comes to steel Worthington Industries may be considered a shape-shifter. One of the largest steel processors in the US Worthington Industries shapes and processes flat-rolled steel for industrial customers including automotive appliance and machinery companies. The company also forms flat-rolled steel to exact customer specifications filling a niche not usually served by steelmakers and steel service centers with limited processing capabilities. Worthington's subsidiaries make products such as pressure cylinders metal framing and automotive panels. Through joint ventures the company also makes steel products such as metal ceiling grid systems and laser-welded blanks.

	Annual Growth	05/11	05/12	05/13	05/14	05/15
Sales ($ mil.)	8.5%	2,442.6	2,534.7	2,612.2	3,126.4	3,384.2
Net income ($ mil.)	(9.6%)	115.1	115.6	136.4	151.3	76.8
Market value ($ mil.)	5.7%	1,400.2	1,042.3	2,205.2	2,584.9	1,745.3
Employees	5.7%	8,400	10,500	10,500	10,000	10,500

WOZNIAK INDUSTRIES INC.

2 Mid America Plaza Ste. 706	CEO: Michael Wozniak
Oakbrook Terrace IL 60181-4717	CFO: Michael Powers
Phone: 630-954-3400	HR: –
Fax: 630-954-3605	FYE: December 31
Web: www.wozniakindustries.com	Type: Private

Wozniak Industries forges ahead through the efforts of its three operating units. Its Commercial Forged Products (CFP) division custom manufactures carbon alloy and stainless steel forgings primarily for the automotive market. Companies such as Deere & Co. and Caterpillar use these components to manufacture harvesting and earthmoving equipment. Wozniak's GMP Metal Products unit offers custom stamping fabrication and assembly services to makers of everything from defense equipment to agricultural machinery. Wozniak's Trinity Machined Products division (TMP) serves CFP and GMP with precision milling and turning capabilities. Edward Wozniak founded the family-owned company in 1985.

WPCS INTERNATIONAL INC   NAS: WPCS

521 Railroad Avenue	CEO: Sebastian Giordano
Suisun City, CA 94585	CFO: David Allen
Phone: 707 432-1300	HR: –
Fax: –	FYE: April 30
Web: www.wpcs.com	Type: Public

WPCS International provides the engineering behind communications networks. Through subsidiaries the company designs and installs broadband wireless video security systems and specialty communications systems. Services include product integration fiber-optic cabling project management and technical support. The company also provides engineering services to support wireless networks. Its specialty communication systems division offers support for telematics and telemetry systems as well as networks designed for asset tracking. WPCS serves the enterprise government and education sectors. Clients have included Amtrak the Jacksonville Jaguars and Wake Forest University Baptist Medical Center.

	Annual Growth	04/11	04/12	04/13	04/14	04/15
Sales ($ mil.)	(29.1%)	96.8	92.4	42.3	21.3	24.4
Net income ($ mil.)	–	(36.8)	(20.5)	(6.9)	(11.1)	(8.8)
Market value ($ mil.)	1.9%	2.6	1.1	0.3	1.1	2.8
Employees	(39.5%)	506	456	250	240	68

WPX ENERGY, INC.   NYS: WPX

3500 One Williams Center	CEO: Richard E. (Rick) Muncrief
Tulsa, OK 74172-0172	CFO: J. Kevin Vann
Phone: 855 979-2012	HR: Chris Beck
Fax: –	FYE: December 31
Web: www.wpxenergy.com	Type: Public

WPX Energy looks high and low across the US for hydrocarbon assets. The oil and gas exploration production and marketing company owns producing oil natural gas and natural gas liquids (NGL) properties in the Rocky Mountains North Dakota and Pennsylvania. WPX (a spin off of The Williams Companies) also has operations in Wyoming New Mexico and Colorado. With total proved reserves of 4.4 trillion cu. ft. of gas equivalent in 2014 the company focuses on acquiring and developing large continuous blocks of land to achieve economies of scale.

	Annual Growth	12/10	12/11	12/12	12/13	12/14
Sales ($ mil.)	(3.5%)	4,034.0	3,988.0	3,189.0	2,761.0	3,493.0
Net income ($ mil.)	–	(1,291.0)	(302.0)	(223.0)	(1,185.0)	164.0
Market value ($ mil.)	(11.6%)	–	–	3,031.1	4,151.4	2,369.0
Employees	(2.9%)	–	1,200	1,200	1,200	1,100

WR HAMBRECHT + CO.

Pier 1 Bay 3	CEO: William R Hambrecht
San Francisco CA 94111	CFO: Jonathan Fayman
Phone: 415-551-8600	HR: –
Fax: 415-551-8686	FYE: December 31
Web: www.wrhambrecht.com	Type: Private

Wanna go Dutch on an IPO? Investment banking firm WR Hambrecht uses its OpenIPO Web site to let investors in on initial public offerings via a Dutch auction similar to that used in the sale of US Treasuries. Its OpenBook is an online corporate bond auction and OpenFollowOn provides online auctions of corporate equity follow-ons. The firm also offers trading analysis and research services; it specializes in technology health care/life sciences and consumer/retail. William Hambrecht founded the firm in 1998 after retiring from Hambrecht & Quist which he'd co-founded in 1968. Industry heavyweights such as American Century and Fidelity are among WR Hambrecht's financial backers.

WRIGHT INVESTORS' SERVICE HOLDINGS, INC.   NDD: WISH

177 West Putnam Avenue	CEO: Harvey P Eisen
Greenwich, CT 06830	CFO: Ira J Sobotk
Phone: 914 242-5700	HR: –
Fax: –	FYE: December 31
Web: www.corporateinformation.com	Type: Public

National Patent Development (NPD) is a shell company that holds stakes in plastics molding and precision coatings manufacturer MXL Industries and Endo International which is developing treatments for pain overactive bladder prostate cancer and the early onset of puberty. The scaled-down NPD also owns real estate in Connecticut. In 2010 the company sold its home improvement products wholesaler Five Star Products a core unit that had represented 100% of its 2009 sales to The Merit Group for more than $30 million; NPD netted about $10 million from the deal. Investment management and financial advisory firm The Winthrop Corporation bought NPD in late 2012.

	Annual Growth	12/10	12/11	12/12	12/13	12/14
Sales ($ mil.)	454.9%	–	–	0.2	5.9	5.8
Net income ($ mil.)	–	(3.3)	(2.1)	(5.1)	(6.8)	(2.2)
Market value ($ mil.)	1.4%	29.6	35.0	48.1	37.0	31.3
Employees	91.1%	3	3	39	40	40

WRIGHT MEDICAL GROUP INC.

NMS: WMGI

1023 Cherry Road	CEO: Robert J Palmisano
Memphis, TN 38117	CFO: Lance A Berry
Phone: 901 867-9971	HR: Edward A Steiger
Fax: –	FYE: December 31
Web: www.wmt.com	Type: Public

Wright Medical Group makes replacement parts for humans. The company makes reconstructive implants for the foot ankle hand elbow shoulder and other defective joints. Product lines include the INBONE CLAW and ORTHOLOC systems for feet and ankles MICRONAIL implants to repair wrist fractures. Wright Medical makes an injectable putty for bone defects as well as bone graft and tissue substitute materials such as OSTEOSET pellets used to regenerate bone. The company sold its hip and knee implant business OrthoRecon in 2014. Wright Medical's products are sold in more than 60 countries although the US is its largest market.

	Annual Growth	12/09	12/10	12/11	12/12	12/13
Sales ($ mil.)	(16.0%)	487.5	519.0	512.9	483.8	242.3
Net income ($ mil.)	–	12.1	17.8	(5.1)	5.3	(273.9)
Market value ($ mil.)	12.8%	909.0	745.3	791.9	1,007.4	1,473.9
Employees	(9.2%)	1,320	1,390	1,290	1,400	898

WRIGHT STATE UNIVERSITY

3640 COLONEL GLENN HWY	CEO: –
DAYTON, OH 454350002	CFO: –
Phone: 937-775-3333	HR: Shari Mickey-Boggs
Fax: –	FYE: June 30
Web: www.wright.edu	Type: Private

Wright State University named after aviation pioneers the Wright Brothers has an enrollment of some 18000 students and offers more than 100 undergraduate degrees and about 90 graduate and professional degrees. It consists of eight colleges (including education and human services business engineering and computer science liberal arts nursing and health and science and mathematics) and three schools (graduate studies medicine professional psychology). Wright State has about 900 faculty members. Originally a branch campus of Ohio State University and Miami University Wright State became an independent university in 1967.

	Annual Growth	06/10	06/11	06/12	06/13	06/14
Sales ($ mil.)	(3.7%)	–	263.8	268.0	272.9	235.9
Net income ($ mil.)	–	–	–	(10.7)	0.4	(3.3)
Market value ($ mil.)	–	–	–	–	–	–
Employees	–	–	–	–	–	2,748

WRITERS GUILD OF AMERICA WEST INC.

7000 W 3RD ST	CEO: David Young
LOS ANGELES, CA 900484321	CFO: Don Gor
Phone: 323-951-4000	HR: Christine Sul
Fax: –	FYE: March 31
Web: www.wga.org	Type: Private

The Writers Guild of America west puts the H in Hollywood the T in TV and the N in new media. It's the West Coast version of the Writers Guild of America and-, a labor union-, that-, represents-, more than 7000 writers in the motion picture broadcast cable and new technologies industries. The union which began in 1921-, backs members in contract negotiations and enforcement oversees credits for films and TV shows collects and distributes payments for the reuse of movies and TV shows and conducts educational events.-, It does not-, act as an employment agency-, for writers or recommend them. The WGAw-, also-, maintains-, a registry that covers-, some 55000 written works each year protecting the authors from plagiarism.

	Annual Growth	03/08	03/09	03/10	03/11	03/14
Sales ($ mil.)	–	–	(257.7)	23.9	24.2	27.8
Net income ($ mil.)	22.3%	–	–	2.1	0.2	4.6
Market value ($ mil.)	–	–	–	–	–	–
Employees	–	–	–	–	–	160

WSA GROUP INC.

10311 S. La Cienega Blvd.	CEO: –
Los Angeles CA 90045	CFO: –
Phone: 310-743-3000	HR: –
Fax: 310-743-3005	FYE: December 31
Web: www.wsainc.net	Type: Private

If it moves by air land or sea WSA Group will secure it. The company provides security guard services to corporate and government customers; its offerings include transportation security (passenger and cargo screening for the aviation maritime and railroad industries) corporate security (executive protection and security consulting) and government security (securing courthouses airports government buildings and waterways). WSA Group is approved by the Transportation Security Administration as a vendor for passenger and baggage screening services at US airports.

WSFS FINANCIAL CORP

NMS: WSFS

WSFS Bank Center, 500 Delaware Avenue	CEO: Mark A. Turner
Wilmington, DE 19801	CFO: Rodger Levenson
Phone: 302 792-6000	HR: –
Fax: –	FYE: December 31
Web: www.wsfsbank.com	Type: Public

WSFS isn't a radio station but it is tuned to the banking needs of Delaware. WSFS Financial is the holding company for Wilmington Savings Fund Society (WSFS Bank) a thrift with nearly $5 billion in assets and more than 50 branches mostly in Delaware and Pennsylvania. Founded in 1832 WSFS Bank attracts deposits from individuals and local businesses by offering standard products like checking and savings accounts CDs and IRAs. The bank uses funds primarily to lend to businesses: Commercial loans and mortgages account for about 85% of its loan portfolio. Bank subsidiaries Christiana Trust Cypress Capital Management and WSFS Wealth Investment provide trust and investment advisory services to wealthy clients and institutional investors.

	Annual Growth	12/10	12/11	12/12	12/13	12/14
Assets ($ mil.)	5.3%	3,953.5	4,289.0	4,375.1	4,515.8	4,853.3
Net income ($ mil.)	39.7%	14.1	22.7	31.3	46.9	53.8
Market value ($ mil.)	12.8%	1,338.2	1,014.4	1,191.8	2,187.0	2,168.9
Employees	4.9%	695	767	763	762	841

WSI INDUSTRIES, INC.

NAS: WSCI

213 Chelsea Road	CEO: Benjamin T Rashleger
Monticello, MN 55362	CFO: Paul D Sheely
Phone: 763 295-9202	HR: –
Fax: –	FYE: August 30
Web: www.wsiindustries.com	Type: Public

WSI Industries likes to metal in the affairs of others. The precision contract machining company manufactures metal components. Through the Taurus Numeric Tool division WSI Industries provides contract machining services. Most of the company's revenues are derived from machining work for the aerospace/avionics/military industries and recreational vehicles (all-terrain vehicles and motorcycles) markets. WSI Industries has a plant in Monticello Minnesota. The firm's principal customer ATV maker Polaris Industries represents more than half of the company's sales. National Oilwell Varco accounts for about one-third of sales.

	Annual Growth	08/11	08/12	08/13	08/14	08/15
Sales ($ mil.)	14.6%	25.0	32.5	34.0	42.7	43.0
Net income ($ mil.)	2.6%	0.9	1.5	0.7	1.2	1.0
Market value ($ mil.)	1.3%	15.6	21.0	18.1	22.2	16.4
Employees	4.0%	76	89	85	95	89

WVS FINANCIAL CORP.

NMS: WVFC

9001 Perry Highway
Pittsburgh, PA 15237
Phone: 412-364-1911
Fax: –
Web: www.wvsbank.com

CEO: David J Bursic
CFO: –
HR: –
FYE: June 30
Type: Public

WVS Financial is the holding company for West View Savings Bank which serves Pittsburgh's North Hills suburbs from about a half-dozen offices. The bank which opened in 1908 offers standard deposit products such as checking and savings accounts CDs and IRAs. Its lending activities primarily consist of real estate loans including construction loans and commercial multifamily and single-family mortgages. West View Savings Bank also writes consumer (mainly home equity) and business loans. Interest from investments in securities such as US government agency securities municipal and corporate bonds and mortgage-backed securities account for about half of WVS Financial's revenue.

	Annual Growth	06/11	06/12	06/13	06/14	06/15
Assets ($ mil.)	9.6%	228.9	273.3	287.6	309.9	329.7
Net income ($ mil.)	2.4%	1.2	1.4	1.1	0.9	1.3
Market value ($ mil.)	6.0%	19.0	15.0	23.3	22.2	24.0
Employees	1.1%	44	46	45	44	46

WYCKOFF HEIGHTS MEDICAL CENTER

374 STOCKHOLM ST
BROOKLYN, NY 112374006
Phone: 718-963-7272
Fax: –
Web: www.wyckoffhospital.org

CEO: Dominick Gio
CFO: Wahchung Hsu
HR: –
FYE: December 31
Type: Private

Wyckoff Heights is taking health care to new levels. Serving the New York boroughs of Brooklyn and Queens Wyckoff Heights Medical Center maintains some 350 beds and provides a comprehensive range of specialized services including diagnostics radiology cardiology obstetrics pediatrics surgery and rehabilitative care. The hospital also provides educational services through a partnership with the Weill Medical College of Cornell University and it offers outpatient services through several family health clinics in the area. The not-for-profit medical center is an affiliated member of the New York-Presbyterian Healthcare System but is governed by an independent board of trustees.

	Annual Growth	11/07	11/08*	12/08	12/09	12/12
Sales ($ mil.)	207.5%	–	2.8	233.2	286.2	246.2
Net income ($ mil.)	–	–	–	(33.0)	8.6	4.7
Market value ($ mil.)	–	–	–	–	–	–
Employees	–	–	–	–	–	1,900

*Fiscal year change

WYLE LABORATORIES INC.

1960 E. Grand Ave. Ste. 900
El Segundo CA 90245 5023
Phone: 310-563-6800
Fax: 310-563-6850
Web: www.wyle.com

CEO: George R Melton
CFO: Dana Dorsey
HR: –
FYE: December 31
Type: Private

Wyle Laboratories is wild about the technical expertise it offers. The firm provides engineering testing life cycle management clinical health services operations support and other technical support services to clients in such industries as aerospace life sciences telecommunications and transportation. Besides serving commercial and industrial clients the company is also a large government contractor working with various branches of the Department of Defense and NASA. Founded in 1949 as a testing laboratory Wyle Laboratories operates more than 50 facilities around the country with about 4800 employees. It owns fellow government contractor Wyle Information Systems Group.

WYMAN-GORDON COMPANY

10825 Telge Rd.
Houston TX 77240-0456
Phone: 281-856-9900
Fax: 281-897-2499
Web: www.wyman-gordon.com

CEO: –
CFO: –
HR: –
FYE: March 31
Type: Subsidiary

If a jet engine's operation is a ballet of metallic parts then Wyman-Gordon Company casts many of the dance's leading roles. A subsidiary of Precision Castparts (PCC) the company is one of the largest producers of forgings and castings — the titanium steel nickel alloy and composite parts used in aerospace turbine engines land-based gas turbines and power plants. Its aerospace turbine products include seals shafts and hubs used in jet engines and its structural products include bulkheads tail flaps and similar components for such major OEMs as Lockheed Martin and Boeing. Wyman-Gordon's land-based products include seamless steel pipe shafts and valves for power plant and oil and gas industries.

WYNDHAM VACATION OWNERSHIP

8427 SouthPark Cir.
Orlando FL 32819
Phone: 407-370-5200
Fax: 407-370-5143
Web: www.wyndhamworldwide.com/about/wyndham_vacatio

CEO: –
CFO: –
HR: –
FYE: December 31
Type: Subsidiary

Wyndham Vacation Ownership (WVO) offers vacationers a (time) share of paradise. A top supplier and marketer of timeshare vacation properties worldwide the company operates through two primary consumer brands: Wyndham Vacation Resorts and WorldMark by Wyndham. WVO boasts about 155 vacation ownership resorts in the US Canada Mexico the Caribbean and the South Pacific representing some 20000 individual vacation ownership units and more than 820000 owners of vacation ownership and other real estate interests. It has been expanding its presence in the US. WVO is a subsidiary of Wyndham Worldwide which was spun off from Cendant (now Avis Budget Group) in 2006.

WYNDHAM WORLDWIDE CORP

NYS: WYN

22 Sylvan Way
Parsippany, NJ 07054
Phone: 973-753-6000
Fax: 973-496-8906
Web: www.wyndhamworldwide.com

CEO: Franz S. Hanning
CFO: Thomas G. (Tom) Conforti
HR: Mary R. Falvey
FYE: December 31
Type: Public

This chain promises lodgings wherever the winds may blow you. One of the world's largest hospitality firms Wyndham Worldwide includes a portfolio of some 7700 franchised hotels worldwide through its lodging segment which includes 15 familiar brands such as Days Inn Howard Johnson Ramada and Super 8. Wyndham also operates a vacation exchange and rentals segment which has a relationship with some 100000 vacation exchange and rental properties in about 100 countries. In addition its Wyndham Vacation Ownership operates vacation ownership resorts in North America the Caribbean and the South Pacific. Revenues primarily come from franchise and hotel management fees membership dues and timeshare sales.

	Annual Growth	12/11	12/12	12/13	12/14	12/15
Sales ($ mil.)	6.8%	4,254.0	4,534.0	5,009.0	5,281.0	5,536.0
Net income ($ mil.)	10.1%	417.0	400.0	432.0	529.0	612.0
Market value ($ mil.)	17.7%	4,305.2	6,055.5	8,386.2	9,759.8	8,267.9
Employees	7.9%	27,800	32,500	32,800	34,400	37,700

WYNN RESORTS LTD

NMS: WYNN

3131 Las Vegas Boulevard South
Las Vegas, NV 89109
Phone: 702 770-7555
Fax: –
Web: www.wynnresorts.com

CEO: Stephen A. Wynn
CFO: Stephen L. Cootey
HR: –
FYE: December 31
Type: Public

What happens in Vegas no longer stays in Vegas. It also happens in China. Wynn Resorts the brainchild of gaming mogul and former Mirage Resorts chairman Steve Wynn operates luxury casino resorts in Las Vegas and South China's Macau the only place in China where gambling is legal. The company's Wynn Las Vegas is a $2.4 billion resort and casino built on the site of the former Desert Inn on the Strip. Wynn Resorts operates in China through Wynn Macau Limited. The company has expanded in both markets adding the Encore at Wynn Las Vegas next to the Wynn Las Vegas and the Encore at Wynn Macau adjacent to Wynn Macau.

	Annual Growth	12/10	12/11	12/12	12/13	12/14
Sales ($ mil.)	6.7%	4,184.7	5,269.8	5,154.3	5,620.9	5,433.7
Net income ($ mil.)	46.2%	160.1	613.4	502.0	728.7	731.6
Market value ($ mil.)	9.4%	10,533.5	11,208.0	11,410.9	19,700.5	15,090.1
Employees	0.6%	16,405	16,400	16,000	16,500	16,800

WYOMING MEDICAL CENTER INC.

1233 E 2ND ST
CASPER, WY 826012988
Phone: 307-577-7201
Fax: –
Web: www.wyomingmedicalcenterfoundation.org

CEO: Pam Fulks
CFO: Edmond Renenmas
HR: –
FYE: June 30
Type: Private

Wyoming Medical Center is The Cowboy State's largest medical facility. The hospital founded in 1911 offers those who live in and around Wyoming's Natrona County more than 50 medical specialties thanks to its 150 physicians. The health care services provider boasts nearly 1300 skilled staff members and more than 190 beds. It offers services such as an emergency air transport system trauma care diagnostic services diabetes care center nephrology and surgical care. The facility is a community-owned not-for-profit hospital.that also operates the Heart Center of Wyoming the Wyoming Neuroscience and Spine Institute and a network of about a dozen community clinics throughout Wyoming.

	Annual Growth	06/08	06/09	06/10	06/11	06/13
Sales ($ mil.)	4.1%	–	204.2	236.7	227.9	239.6
Net income ($ mil.)	21.5%	–	–	8.7	14.3	15.6
Market value ($ mil.)	–	–	–	–	–	–
Employees	–	–	–	–	–	1,033

X-RITE INCORPORATED

NASDAQ: XRIT

4300 44th St. SE
Grand Rapids MI 49512
Phone: 616-803-2100
Fax: 616-534-0723
Web: www.x-rite.com

CEO: Thomas J Vacchiano Jr
CFO: Rajesh K Shah
HR: –
FYE: December 31
Type: Public

X-Rite has an eye for color. Its products help manufacturers retailers distributors printers and graphic designers achieve a consistent color appearance. Using spectrophotometers and colorimeters its color measurement products check that fabrics paints and plastics are the correct shade. Its color standards product line uses densitometers to measure optical and photographic density and control color for processing textiles film and inks. Products include paint matching systems for retailers sensitometers for manipulating photographic film exposure and color formulation software for PCs. More than two-thirds of sales come from outside the US. In 2012 Danaher bought X-Rite for about $625 million.

XANODYNE PHARMACEUTICALS INC.

1 Riverfront Place
Newport KY 41071
Phone: 859-371-6383
Fax: 859-371-6391
Web: www.xanodyne.com

CEO: Natasha Giordano
CFO: –
HR: –
FYE: December 31
Type: Private

Xanodyne Pharmaceuticals is out to create a medicinal Xanadu. The company primarily develops and manufactures drugs for pain management. Its commercial offerings include pain treatments Hycet Roxicodone Oramorph SR and Zipsor. In addition the company markets the Duet and Stuart lines of prenatal vitamins. Xanodyne has several other drugs in development including one for mild to moderate pain in late-stage clinical trials. The firm funds its development efforts through sales of its commercial products which are marketed through an internal specialty sales force that targets pain specialists and women's healthcare physicians in the US.

XAP CORPORATION

3534 Hayden Ave.
Culver City CA 90232
Phone: 310-842-9800
Fax: 310-842-9898
Web: www.xap.com

CEO: Eddie Monnier
CFO: –
HR: –
FYE: December 31
Type: Private

XAP Corporation operates XAP.com an online resource for college-bound students. The site offers information and services for high school counselors college recruiting officers and students and their families. It provides students with tools for college planning and the college application process as well as SAT and ACT test preparation services. Offerings for college administrators include online applications and transcripts and prospect management systems. XAP Corporation also helps counselors organize and monitor the status of their students.

XAVIER UNIVERSITY

3800 VICTORY PKWY UNIT 1
CINCINNATI, OH 452071092
Phone: 513-745-3000
Fax: –
Web: www.xavier.edu

CEO: –
CFO: Maribeth Amyor
HR: –
FYE: June 30
Type: Private

Xavier University is a not-for-profit Jesuit Catholic institution that operates from a single campus located in Cincinnati Ohio. The private school which has recently grown its enrollment numbers to about 7000 students offers nearly 90 undergraduate programs and about 20 graduate programs. Xavier University's programs range from arts and sciences to social sciences and business. Boasting small class sizes the university's student-to-faculty ratio is a noteworthy 12:1. Known among sports circles as having a highly respected men's basketball program Xavier University also manages to graduate every member of its men's Musketeers group. Xavier University was founded in 1831.

	Annual Growth	06/10	06/11	06/12	06/13	06/14
Sales ($ mil.)	(0.2%)	–	167.9	166.9	163.5	166.6
Net income ($ mil.)	–	–	–	(22.5)	14.3	37.2
Market value ($ mil.)	–	–	–	–	–	–
Employees	–	–	–	–	–	940

XCEL ENERGY, INC.

NYS: XEL

414 Nicollet Mall
Minneapolis, MN 55401
Phone: 612 330-5500
Fax: –
Web: www.xcelenergy.com

CEO: Benjamin G. S. (Ben) Fowke
CFO: Teresa S. Madden
HR: –
FYE: December 31
Type: Public

Xcel Energy has accelerated its energy engine in utility markets across the US. The utility holding company distributes electricity to 3.5 million customers and natural gas to 1.9 million in eight states through four regulated utilities; Colorado and Minnesota account for most of its customers. Its utilities — Northern States Power (NSP-Minnesota and NSP-Wisconsin) Public Service Company of Colorado and Southwestern Public Service (in New Mexico and Texas) — have the combined capacity of more than 17000 MW of electricity. Xcel owns transmission and distribution lines as well as natural gas assets. It is also a leading wind power provider in the US with wind farms in Colorado Minnesota and Texas.

	Annual Growth	12/10	12/11	12/12	12/13	12/14
Sales ($ mil.)	3.2%	10,310.9	10,654.8	10,128.2	10,914.9	11,686.1
Net income ($ mil.)	7.8%	755.8	841.2	905.2	948.2	1,021.3
Market value ($ mil.)	11.1%	11,910.0	13,978.5	13,508.1	14,130.2	18,165.9
Employees	0.9%	11,290	11,312	11,198	11,581	11,691

XCERRA CORP

NMS: XCRA

825 University Ave.
Norwood, MA 02062
Phone: 781 461-1000
Fax: 408 635-4985
Web: www.xcerra.com

CEO: David G. (Dave) Tacelli
CFO: Mark J. Gallenberger
HR: –
FYE: July 31
Type: Public

Xcerra (formerly LTX-Credence) makes automated test equipment (ATE) used by chip makers to test semiconductors as they're being manufactured and as part of the final package test. The company consolidated its predecessors' product lines into three basic test equipment families — ASL Diamond and X-Series. Top customers include Spirox Atmel and Texas Instruments. Like its competitors Xcerra uses a contractor Jabil Circuit to manufacture its products. Most of its sales come from customers in Asia. The company was created from the 2008 merger of LTX Corp. and rival Credence Systems.

	Annual Growth	07/11	07/12	07/13	07/14	07/15
Sales ($ mil.)	12.4%	249.5	132.1	152.0	330.9	398.0
Net income ($ mil.)	(17.2%)	60.1	(19.9)	(12.1)	0.8	28.2
Market value ($ mil.)	(3.3%)	393.2	320.5	293.2	511.4	343.7
Employees	26.9%	663	639	649	2,059	1,722

XENCOR, INC

NMS: XNCR

111 West Lemon Avenue
Monrovia, CA 91016
Phone: 626 305-5900
Fax: –

CEO: Bassil I. Dahiyat
CFO: –
HR: –
FYE: December 31
Type: Public

Xencor is a biopharmaceutical company developing new types of antibodies to treat autoimmune diseases severe asthma and allergies and cancer. Its XmAb technology platform differs from other antibodies in that it interacts with multiple parts of the immune system not just the target antigens. Xencor is developing three drugs to treat rheumatoid arthritis and lupus severe asthma and allergic diseases and leukemia and non-Hodgkin lymphoma. It also licenses its technology to four major pharmaceutical companies – Boehringer Ingelheim CSL Janssen and Merck. Founded in 1997 Xencor went public in 2013. It raised about $70 million and plans to use the proceeds to further fund clinical development.

	Annual Growth	12/10	12/11	12/12	12/13	12/14
Sales ($ mil.)	–	0.0	6.8	9.5	10.2	9.5
Net income ($ mil.)	–	0.0	(11.2)	(8.6)	(60.3)	(16.4)
Market value ($ mil.)	–	0.0	–	–	287.3	504.2
Employees	12.2%			31	30	39

XENITH BANKSHARES INC

NAS: XBKS

One James Center, 901 E. Cary Street, Suite 1700
Richmond, VA 23219
Phone: 804 433-2200
Fax: –
Web: www.xenithbank.com

CEO: T Gaylon Layfield III
CFO: Thomas W Osgood
HR: –
FYE: December 31
Type: Public

Xenith Bankshares formerly First Bankshares is the holding company of SuffolkFirst Bank a community bank with a handful of offices in southeastern Virginia. The bank targets commercial customers wealthy individuals and investors. It offers traditional products and services including checking and savings accounts CDs debit cards and merchant card processing. Its lending portfolio is primarily made up of real estate loans namely residential and commercial mortgages. Xenith Bankshares was created in late 2009 through the merger of the six-year-old First Bankshares and Xenith Corporation which had originally been established to open a new banking institution. Hampton Roads Bankshares agreed to buy Xenith for $197 million in February 2016.

	Annual Growth	12/10	12/11	12/12	12/13	12/14
Assets ($ mil.)	38.3%	251.2	477.5	563.2	679.9	918.1
Net income ($ mil.)	–	(5.9)	4.4	7.4	2.0	1.3
Market value ($ mil.)	3.9%	71.1	48.2	59.9	76.2	82.8
Employees	10.7%	78	105	104	102	117

XENONICS HOLDINGS INC

NBB: XNNH

3186 Lionshead Avenue
Carlsbad, CA 92010
Phone: 760 477-8900
Fax: –
Web: www.xenonics.com

CEO: Alan P Magerman
CFO: Richard S Kay
HR: –
FYE: September 30
Type: Public

Xenonics Holdings says fiat lux ("Let there be light"). Its NightHunter high-intensity portable lighting products are used worldwide by American military forces and by law enforcement agencies to illuminate dark areas. The SuperVision high-definition night-vision product is aimed at the commercial market and represents a growing portion of the company's sales. Xenonics' products are also used as part of security systems for facilities. Military customers — including the US Air Force US Army US Marine Corps US Navy and military equipment resellers — account for about 90% of the company's sales.

	Annual Growth	09/10	09/11	09/12	09/13	09/14
Sales ($ mil.)	(34.1%)	4.4	7.2	2.2	2.4	0.8
Net income ($ mil.)	–	(1.8)	(0.1)	(2.2)	(1.5)	(2.6)
Market value ($ mil.)	(11.6%)	8.5	9.5	10.0	3.3	5.2
Employees	(12.4%)	17	17	15	10	10

XENOPORT INC

NMS: XNPT

3410 Central Expressway
Santa Clara, CA 95051
Phone: 408 616-7200
Fax: –
Web: www.xenoport.com

CEO: Vincent J. Angotti
CFO: William G. (Bill) Harris
HR: –
FYE: December 31
Type: Public

XenoPort sounds like something straight out of science fiction but there's nothing fictional about XenoPort's job of improving drugs' ability to be absorbed by tissues in the body. The development firm uses genomics to identify transporter proteins. It then designs oral drug molecules to find and ride these transporters through the gastrointestinal tract to their destinations. In 2011 XenoPort received FDA approval for Horizant (gabapentin enacarbil) its first drug which it markets in the US for the treatment of restless legs syndrome (RLS). It first marketed this drug in tandem with GlaxoSmithKline (GSK). In 2012 XenoPort and Astellas Pharma jointly launched gabapentin enacarbil tablets under the name Regnite in Japan.

	Annual Growth	12/10	12/11	12/12	12/13	12/14
Sales ($ mil.)	100.9%	2.9	43.5	21.6	8.0	46.9
Net income ($ mil.)	–	(82.5)	(33.4)	(30.8)	(85.9)	(49.3)
Market value ($ mil.)	0.7%	532.3	238.0	485.4	359.2	547.9
Employees	8.9%	108	112	88	92	152

XERIUM TECHNOLOGIES INC

NYS: XRM

14101 Capital Boulevard
Youngsville, NC 27596
Phone: 919 526-1400
Fax: –
Web: www.xerium.com

CEO: Harold C. Bevis
CFO: Clifford E. Pietrafitta
HR: –
FYE: December 31
Type: Public

Xerium Technologies makes clothing but not the kind that people wear. The company manufactures and supplies clothing and roll covers used on paper-making machinery. Xerium's clothing rolls are used as belts to convey paper through paper-making machines and its roll covers are used on the machines' steel cylinders; both products are consumed during paper production. The company operates about 30 manufacturing facilities in about a dozen countries primarily in North and South America Europe and Asia and nets more than 70% of sales outside North America. Customers have included such big paper and container makers as IP MeadWestvaco RockTenn CP and UPM-Kymmene.

	Annual Growth	12/10	12/11	12/12	12/13	12/14
Sales ($ mil.)	(0.2%)	548.3	587.0	538.7	546.9	542.9
Net income ($ mil.)	–	(73.1)	8.2	(18.0)	4.2	(7.4)
Market value ($ mil.)	(0.3%)	248.2	101.8	47.5	256.6	245.5
Employees	(2.3%)	3,404	3,448	3,279	3,200	3,100

XEROX CORP

NYS: XRX

P.O. Box 4505, 45 Glover Avenue
Norwalk, CT 06856-4505
Phone: 203 968-3000
Fax: –
Web: www.xerox.com

CEO: Ursula M. Burns
CFO: Leslie F. Varon
HR: Mike McQuarrie
FYE: December 31
Type: Public

Xerox has become more than a copier company. So much more that it has been transitioning to become a provider of services for corporations' back offices by providing business process outsourcing (BPO) and document outsourcing (DO). Services include customer service and claims filing infrastructure cloud computing application development managed print services and document and data management. In addition it remains a leading provider of equipment including office printers digital printing systems and multifunction printers and copiers. In January 2016 Xerox announced that it would make the distinction between BPO and DO even starker by splitting them into two independent companies. The split might be final by the end of 2016.

	Annual Growth	12/10	12/11	12/12	12/13	12/14
Sales ($ mil.)	(2.5%)	21,633.0	22,626.0	22,390.0	21,435.0	19,540.0
Net income ($ mil.)	12.5%	606.0	1,295.0	1,195.0	1,159.0	969.0
Market value ($ mil.)	4.7%	12,864.9	8,889.3	7,616.2	13,590.8	15,478.1
Employees	2.0%	136,500	139,650	147,600	143,100	147,500

XETA TECHNOLOGIES INC.

1814 W. Tacoma St.
Broken Arrow OK 74012
Phone: 918-664-8200
Fax: 918-664-6876
Web: www.xeta.com

CEO: Greg Forrest
CFO: Robert Wagner
HR: –
FYE: October 31
Type: Subsidiary

The next time you reach for that phone in the conference room XETA Technologies might be there with you. The company designs distributes and installs phone messaging videoconferencing data networking and contact management systems from such hardware and software vendors as Avaya Mitel Networks Polycom and Hewlett-Packard. It sells communications equipment to the hospitality industry including a line of call accounting products capable of tracking phone usage data. XETA also provides network consulting and installation services and offers managed services for maintenance and upgrades to legacy systems made by bankrupt telecom equipment maker Nortel. XETA was acquired by PAETEC acquired in 2011 for about $61 million.

XFONE INC.

NYSE AMEX: XFN

5307 W. Loop 289
Lubbock TX 79414-1610
Phone: 806-771-5212
Fax: 806-788-3398
Web: www.xfone.com

CEO: –
CFO: –
HR: –
FYE: December 31
Type: Public

Xfone can help you get your lines of communications crossed but in a good way. The company offers a variety of telecommunications services including local long-distance and international phone services as well as broadband Internet access and email service. Other offerings include cellular services and prepaid calling cards; the company also resells equipment (phone systems modems etc.) and sells its various telecom services through resellers which buy access at wholesale rates. Targeting both residential and business customers Xfone operates primarily in the southern US but also offers services in Israel.

XIFIN INC.

3394 Carmel Mountain Rd Ste. 200
San Diego CA 92121
Phone: 858-793-5700
Fax: 858-793-5701
Web: www.xifin.com

CEO: Lale White
CFO: James C Malone
HR: –
FYE: December 31
Type: Private

XIFIN has a formula for the laboratories' financial well-being. Founded in 1997 XIFIN develops financial management software that helps health care providers and laboratories automate their billing systems manage medical claims filing and reduce the costs associated with the complexity and regulatory compliance requirements of medical billing processes. The company which provides its billing software as a hosted Internet-based application aims to help its clients cut down on the considerable costs associated with managing their billing processes.

XILINX, INC.

NMS: XLNX

2100 Logic Drive
San Jose, CA 95124
Phone: 408 559-7778
Fax: –
Web: www.xilinx.com

CEO: Moshe N. Gavrielov
CFO: Jon A. Olson
HR: Nicole Singer
FYE: March 28
Type: Public

Xilinx gives control to the programmer on the ground. The company is a top supplier of field-programmable gate arrays (FPGAs) and complex programmable logic devices (CPLDs). Customers program — and reprogram — these integrated circuits (ICs) to perform specific functions providing greater design flexibility and cutting time to market. Xilinx also offers a broad range of design software and intellectual property used to customize its chips. The company which contracts with third-party manufacturers to produce its chips sells to the automotive aerospace broadcast consumer data processing and wired and wireless communications markets. The company gets almost 70% of its sales outside the US.

	Annual Growth	04/11*	03/12	03/13	03/14	03/15
Sales ($ mil.)	0.1%	2,369.4	2,240.7	2,168.7	2,382.5	2,377.3
Net income ($ mil.)	0.2%	641.9	530.1	487.5	630.4	648.2
Market value ($ mil.)	7.1%	8,305.6	9,424.2	9,860.8	13,909.0	10,932.9
Employees	2.7%	3,099	3,265	3,329	3,500	3,451
						*Fiscal year change

XO GROUP INC

NYS: XOXO

195 Broadway, 25th Floor	CEO: Michael Steib
New York, NY 10007	CFO: Gillian Munson
Phone: 212 219-8555	HR: Gloria Pena
Fax: 212 219-1929	FYE: December 31
Web: www.xogroupinc.com	Type: Public

Here comes the bride surfing online. Where is the groom? He's in a chat room. XO Group (formerly The Knot) is a leading online publisher serving the wedding newlywed and new parent markets. Its TheKnot.com and WeddingChannel.com sites offer wedding-related content on topics from engagement to honeymoon as well as wedding planning tools (budget planner gown finder) chat rooms a directory of local resources and online registry services. Other XO Group websites target newlyweds (TheNest.com) and pregnant women and their partners (TheBump.com). The firm also produces branded video and mobile content and magazines as well as books on lifestyle topics (published by Random House and Chronicle Books).

	Annual Growth	12/10	12/11	12/12	12/13	12/14
Sales ($ mil.)	6.2%	112.9	124.3	129.1	133.8	143.7
Net income ($ mil.)	(40.4%)	3.7	6.0	8.7	5.8	0.5
Market value ($ mil.)	16.5%	263.1	222.1	247.7	395.7	484.9
Employees	1.5%	605	631	677	705	641

XO HOLDINGS INC.

13865 Sunrise Valley Dr.	CEO: Chris Ancell
Herndon VA 20171	CFO: –
Phone: 703-547-2000	HR: –
Fax: 703-547-2881	FYE: December 31
Web: www.xo.com	Type: Private

XO Holdings gets down to the Xs and Os of business telecom services. Through its operational subsidiary XO Communications the company provides telecommunications services to large corporations small and midsized businesses government agencies and other telecom carriers via a network of about 1 million miles of metropolitan fiber. XO Communications offers local and long-distance voice dedicated Internet access private networking data transport and managed services such as Web hosting and bundled voice and data services. The company has customers in about 85 US markets and internationally. Billionaire financier Carl Icahn owns the company through his ACF Industries.

XOMA CORP

NMS: XOMA

2910 Seventh Street	CEO: John Varian
Berkeley, CA 94710	CFO: Thomas Burns
Phone: 510 204-7200	HR: Charles C. Wells
Fax: –	FYE: December 31
Web: www.xoma.com	Type: Public

XOMA Corporation doesn't want to toil in anonymity. Instead the company pairs with larger drug firms to develop and market its products primarily monoclonal antibodies (biotech drugs based on cloned proteins). It's developing lead candidate gevokizumab with French drugmaker Servier. The firm partners on therapeutics for infectious disease inflammatory ailments and autoimmune conditions and receives royalties on drugs developed from licensing its technologies. XOMA has collaborative agreements with pharma companies Takeda Pharmaceutical and Novartis; it also has metabolic and oncology candidates.

	Annual Growth	12/10	12/11	12/12	12/13	12/14
Sales ($ mil.)	(13.5%)	33.6	58.2	33.8	35.5	18.9
Net income ($ mil.)	–	(68.8)	(32.7)	(71.1)	(124.1)	(38.3)
Market value ($ mil.)	(8.5%)	594.5	133.3	278.1	780.0	416.1
Employees	(5.6%)	230	188	166	168	183

XORIANT CORPORATION

1248 REAMWOOD AVE	CEO: –
SUNNYVALE, CA 940892225	CFO: Mahesh Nalavade
Phone: 408-743-4427	HR: Sanjay Arte
Fax: –	FYE: December 31
	Type: Private

Xoriant is not exorbitant about offering IT services. The firm provides outsourced application development engineering and consulting services to technology start-ups such as software developers as well as banks telecommunications companies and health care providers among other businesses. The company specializes in implementing technology to enable cloud Web social networking payment embedded media and mobile applications and services. Other services included testing and technical support. Xoriant's customers have included TIBCO Software.

	Annual Growth	12/09	12/10	12/11	12/12	12/13
Sales ($ mil.)	31.4%	–	40.6	55.8	65.5	92.1
Net income ($ mil.)	91.9%	–	–	2.0	5.5	7.3
Market value ($ mil.)	–	–	–	–	–	–
Employees	–	–	–	–	–	134

XPEDX

6285 Tri-Ridge Blvd.	CEO: –
Loveland OH 45140	CFO: –
Phone: 513-965-2900	HR: –
Fax: +45-4574-8888	FYE: December 31
Web: www.chr-hansen.com	Type: Business Segment

International Paper makes a lot of paper and paper products; xpedx distributes that paper across North America — along with packaging supplies and equipment janitorial products and office furniture. (The company stopped distributing graphic imaging prepress equipment by Agfa Graphics and Ryobi in 2011). Typical customers include commercial printers publishers government agencies manufacturers retailers and creative professionals. The distribution division of International Paper xpedx operates more than 200 distribution centers 120 warehouses and about 130 retail stores in the US Canada and Mexico. It accounts for about a quarter of its parent's sales.

XPLORE TECHNOLOGIES CORP.

NAS: XPLR

14000 Summit Drive, Suite 900	CEO: Philip S. Sassower
Austin, TX 78728	CFO: Tom Wilkinson
Phone: 512 336 7797	HR: –
Fax: –	FYE: March 31
Web: www.xploretech.com	Type: Public

Xplore Technologies ensures that you can take your computer with you no matter what difficult terrain you're exploring. The company manufactures and sells ruggedized tablet PCs and handheld computers. The company primarily targets manufacturers distributors and systems integrators that supply field service personnel factory workers public safety officials military personnel and other customers that require durable mobile computers. Its products incorporate wireless networking technology and can be mounted in vehicles such as carts and forklifts. Xplore was founded in 1996.

	Annual Growth	03/11	03/12	03/13	03/14	03/15
Sales ($ mil.)	24.5%	17.8	27.5	30.5	35.6	42.6
Net income ($ mil.)	–	(6.4)	(0.5)	0.3	(1.8)	0.2
Market value ($ mil.)	204.2%	0.8	0.6	41.8	68.5	68.5
Employees	8.7%	38	40	49	49	53

XPO LOGISTICS, INC.

NYS: XPO

Five Greenwich Office Park	CEO: Bradley S. Jacobs
Greenwich, CT 06831	CFO: John J. Hardig
Phone: 855 976-4636	HR: Angela F Gibbons
Fax: –	FYE: December 31
Web: www.xpologistics.com	Type: Public

XPO Logistics wants your package to be there PDQ. The company specializes in third party logistics (3PL) but doesn't own any ships planes or trucks. Customers' freight is transported throughout the US by independent contractors who give the company's expedited freight forwarding unit access to a fleet of vehicles that includes cargo vans trucks and tractor-trailers. XPO offers domestic and international freight forwarding services as well as truckload freight brokerage service to more than 15000 customers across the US Canada and Mexico. The company has experienced massive revenue growth over the years due to acquisitions.

	Annual Growth	12/10	12/11	12/12	12/13	12/14
Sales ($ mil.)	96.5%	158.0	177.1	278.6	702.3	2,356.6
Net income ($ mil.)	–	4.9	0.8	(20.3)	(48.5)	(63.6)
Market value ($ mil.)	99.9%	198.2	956.2	1,345.6	2,035.4	3,165.0
Employees	169.3%	190	227	892	2,259	10,000

XRS CORP

NAS: XRSC

965 Prairie Center Drive	CEO: John J Coughlan
Eden Prairie, MN 55344	CFO: Michael Weber
Phone: 952 707-5600	HR: –
Fax: 952 894-2463	FYE: September 30
Web: www.xrscorp.com	Type: Public

XRS (formerly Xata) helps companies keep track of their truck fleets. The company's Web-based XRS and Turnpike applications help fleet operators automate driver logs and fuel tax reporting manage vehicle and driver performance track assets and enable two-way messaging. Aimed at the for-hire segment of the transportation sector (as opposed to private fleets) its Mobile-Max Fleet Management System provides similar functionality. XRS markets to customers in the manufacturing distribution and petroleum markets primarily in the US. More than 115000 trucks in North America have a subscription to XRS' products. Customers have included CVS Caremark Harley-Davidson United Rentals Safeway and UPS.

	Annual Growth	09/09	09/10	09/11	09/12	09/13
Sales ($ mil.)	(3.7%)	65.3	70.7	63.0	63.1	56.2
Net income ($ mil.)	–	(2.1)	(1.3)	(2.8)	(10.3)	0.9
Market value ($ mil.)	(0.7%)	31.6	27.3	18.2	6.3	30.7
Employees	(1.6%)	176	200	210	174	165

XTANT MEDICAL HOLDINGS INC

ASE: XTNT

664 Cruiser Lane	CEO: Daniel Goldberger
Belgrade, MT 59714	CFO: John P Gandolfo
Phone: 406 388-0480	HR: –
Fax: 406 388-0422	FYE: December 31
Web: www.bacterin.com	Type: Public

Bacterin International has your back(bone). The company develops manufactures and markets biomedical devices including orthopedic biomaterials used for bone grafts joint surgery and other skeletal reconstructive procedures. Its biologics products include OsteoSponge a bone void filler made of 100% human bone; OsteoLock a stabilization dowel for spinal procedures; and Bac-Fast a dowel with demineralization technology to aid in bone grafting. It also sells sports allografts for ligament repairs and the hMatrix dermal scaffold. Bacterin International was founded in 1998.

	Annual Growth	12/10	12/11	12/12	12/13	12/14
Sales ($ mil.)	23.0%	15.4	30.1	33.0	33.1	35.3
Net income ($ mil.)	–	(19.5)	(3.0)	(7.7)	(12.7)	(10.5)
Market value ($ mil.)	(22.8%)	56.8	19.1	8.3	3.3	20.2
Employees	6.4%	117	184	189	131	150

XTRA CORPORATION

1801 Park 270 Dr. Ste. 400	CEO: William H Franz
St. Louis MO 63146	CFO: Michael J Dreller
Phone: 314-579-9300	HR: –
Fax: 314-542-6496	FYE: December 31
Web: www.xtracorp.com	Type: Subsidiary

To lease or not to lease that is the question XTRA Corporation hopes you will answer affirmatively. Doing business through XTRA Lease the company provides a variety of transportation rental lease and lease/purchase packages. It markets a fleet of over-the-road trailers intermodal "piggyback" trailers and an assortment of intermodal gear. The 100000-plus lineup includes dry vans flat beds temperature-controlled vans as well as domestic containers chassis for container transport and trailer tracking technology. The company caters to railroads shipping lines and trucking companies from offices dotting North America. XTRA is a subsidiary of Berkshire Hathaway.

XTRA LEASE INC.

1801 Park 270 Dr. Ste. 400	CEO: William H Franz
St. Louis MO 63146-4037	CFO: Michael Dreller
Phone: 314-579-9300	HR: –
Fax: 314-579-9138	FYE: December 31
Web: www.xtralease.com	Type: Subsidiary

With a fleet of more than 100000 trailers XTRA Lease is in it for the long haul. The company offers rental lease and lease/purchase packages for over-the-road trailers (including refrigerated storage and flatbed trailers) dry vans and specialty equipment through 80-plus locations throughout North America. The company also offers services including emergency roadside assistance pickup and delivery and registration and licensing. Founded in 1992 after the merger of AJF Leasing and Strick Lease XTRA Lease became a subsidiary of Warren Buffett's Berkshire Hathaway holding company in 2001.

XURA INC

NMS: MESG

200 Quannapowitt Parkway	CEO: Philippe Tartavull
Wakefield, MA 01880	CFO: Jacky Wu
Phone: 781 246-9000	HR: Diane Coffey
Fax: –	FYE: January 31
Web: www.xura.com	Type: Public

Comverse is conversant with communications technology. The company provides communication software and systems that handle messaging billing and accounts call management and data delivery services. It also provides related services such as consulting design implementation interoperability testing maintenance support and training. Its services are sold to more than 450 wireline wireless and cable network providers in more than 125 countries. Top customer Verizon accounts for about 18% of sales. Comverse has offices in about 40 countries and generates most of its revenues in the EMEA (Europe Middle East and Africa) region.

	Annual Growth	01/11	01/12	01/13	01/14	01/15
Sales ($ mil.)	(13.8%)	862.8	771.2	677.8	652.5	477.3
Net income ($ mil.)	–	(90.9)	(15.5)	5.1	18.7	(22.1)
Market value ($ mil.)	(22.8%)	–	–	630.5	786.8	376.1
Employees	(2.7%)	–	2,500	2,500	2,500	2,300

XYLEM INC.

NYS: XYL

1 International Drive
Rye Brook, NY 10573
Phone: 914 323-5700
Fax: 914 323-5800
Web: www.xyleminc.com

CEO: Patrick K. Decker
CFO: Shashank K. Patel
HR: Jennifer Congdon
FYE: December 31
Type: Public

Xylem (formerly ITT Fluid Technology a unit of ITT Corp.) primes the pump for the future of water and other fluids. The company (whose name derives from a Greek term about water and roots) makes fluid-handling and related products for treating and recycling wastewater. It operates in two divisions: Water Infrastructure and Applied Water. Water Infrastructure makes pumps treatment and testing equipment and controls and analytical instruments while Applied Water offers pumps valves heat exchangers controls and dispensing equipment. Xylem's products are sold under about 40 different brands including Flygt and Goulds.

	Annual Growth	12/10	12/11	12/12	12/13	12/14
Sales ($ mil.)	5.2%	3,202.0	3,803.0	3,791.0	3,837.0	3,916.0
Net income ($ mil.)	0.6%	329.0	279.0	297.0	228.0	337.0
Market value ($ mil.)	14.0%	–	4,683.3	4,940.3	6,307.6	6,940.2
Employees	1.7%	11,700	12,500	12,700	12,500	12,500

YADKIN FINANCIAL CORP

NYS: YDKN

3600 Glenwood Avenue, Suite 300
Raleigh, NC 27612
Phone: 919 659-9000
Fax: –

CEO: –
CFO: Jan H. Hollar
HR: Ed Shuford
FYE: December 31
Type: Public

Yadkin Financial Corporation is the holding company for Yadkin Bank (formerly Yadkin Valley Bank and Trust) which serves customers from more than 70 branches across North Carolina and upstate South Carolina. In addition to its standard loans SBA loans and deposit products including checking and savings accounts money market accounts CDs and IRAs Yadkin Bank and its subsidiaries provide mortgage banking investment and insurance services to more than 80000 business and individual customers. Founded in 1968 Yadkin Bank now boasts nearly $1.5 billion in total assets.

	Annual Growth	12/10	12/11	12/12	12/13	12/14
Assets ($ mil.)	16.7%	2,300.6	1,993.2	1,923.4	1,806.0	4,266.3
Net income ($ mil.)	–	(0.0)	(14.4)	(8.7)	18.8	21.7
Market value ($ mil.)	81.5%	57.2	50.9	92.9	538.4	620.9
Employees	9.4%	615	481	481	511	882

YAHOO! INC.

NMS: YHOO

701 First Avenue
Sunnyvale, CA 94089
Phone: 408 349-3300
Fax: –
Web: www.yahoo.com

CEO: Marissa A. Mayer
CFO: Kenneth (Ken) Goldman
HR: Bryan Power
FYE: December 31
Type: Public

Yahoo! wants to spread some cheer to Internet users around the world. Its network of websites offers news entertainment and shopping as well as search results powered by Microsoft's Bing. Yahoo! generates most of its revenue through providing search and display advertising to Web operations in three categories: Communications & Communities (including Yahoo! Mail Yahoo! Groups and Flickr) Search and Marketplaces (Yahoo! Search) and Media (Yahoo! Homepage Yahoo! Finance). Other revenues come from fee-based services such as premium e-mail; royalties licenses and mobile products; and broadband Internet access.

	Annual Growth	12/10	12/11	12/12	12/13	12/14
Sales ($ mil.)	(7.6%)	6,324.7	4,984.2	4,986.6	4,680.4	4,618.1
Net income ($ mil.)	57.2%	1,231.7	1,048.8	3,945.5	1,366.3	7,521.7
Market value ($ mil.)	32.0%	15,579.6	15,111.2	18,643.1	37,885.7	47,319.7
Employees	(2.1%)	13,600	14,100	11,700	12,200	12,500

YAKIMA VALLEY MEMORIAL HOSPITAL ASSOCIATION INC

2811 TIETON DR
YAKIMA, WA 989023761
Phone: 509-249-5129
Fax: –
Web: www.yakimamemorial.org

CEO: Russ Myers
CFO: –
HR: –
FYE: October 31
Type: Private

Whether you're a major yakker or quiet as a mouse Yakima Valley Memorial Hospital serves the health care needs of patients of all types. The health provider's acute-care hospital skilled-nursing facilities and outpatient specialty treatment facilities serve patients in and around Yakima in Washington State. The hospital has about 225 beds and provides a variety of services such as heart care orthopedics pediatrics cancer treatment women's health and mental health care. It also offers sleep and wound care and provides home health and hospice services. The organization is a not-for-profit group governed by a board of directors.

	Annual Growth	10/07	10/08	10/09	10/12	10/13
Sales ($ mil.)	8.1%	–	245.2	276.3	309.8	361.8
Net income ($ mil.)	–	–	–	(18.1)	(6.6)	39.6
Market value ($ mil.)	–	–	–	–	–	–
Employees	–	–	–	–	–	1,150

YALE NEW HAVEN HEALTH SERVICES CORPORATION

789 Howard Ave.
New Haven CT 06519
Phone: 203-688-4608
Fax: 203-688-3774
Web: www.yalenewhavenhealth.org

CEO: –
CFO: –
HR: –
FYE: September 30
Type: Private - Not-for-Pr

Yale New Haven Health Services is a health care haven for residents of Southern Connecticut Southwestern Rhode Island and parts of New York's Westchester County. The company operates Yale-New Haven Hospital Greenwich Hospital and Bridgeport Hospital and has a contract relationship with The Westerly Hospital in Rhode Island (Northeast Medical Group) as well as children's cancer psychiatric care hospitals. In addition Yale New Haven Health Services operates outpatient facilities and provides such managed care services as network contracting as well as disease management programs. The system is affiliated with Yale University's medical school. and has a grand total of about 1600 beds.

YANKEE GROUP RESEARCH INC.

1 Liberty Sq. 7th Fl.
Boston MA 02109-4868
Phone: 617-598-7200
Fax: +61-2-9268-6693
Web: www.burnsphilp.com

CEO: –
CFO: –
HR: –
FYE: December 31
Type: Private

This company's research on the technology market is just dandy. The Yankee Group provides market research and analytical reports focused on information technology topics and helping business leaders keep informed and up-to-date on the latest developments in hardware software and telecommunications (especially smartphones). The company monitors trends in the consumer electronics market and provides decision support tools and consulting services. Yankee Group tracks regional technology trends as well as global trends. Tech research pioneer Howard Anderson started the group in 1970. The company is owned by private equity firm Alta Communications.

YASH TECHNOLOGIES INC

605 17TH AVE
EAST MOLINE, IL 612442045
Phone: 309-755-0433
Fax: –
Web: www.yash.com

CEO: –
CFO: –
HR: –
FYE: December 31
Type: Private

YASH Technologies hashes out all sorts of technological issues. The company provides information technology (IT) services such as consulting systems integration and network design as well as software development and business process outsourcing. It has expertise in business software from leading providers including IBM Microsoft Oracle and SAP. YASH primarily targets corporations in such fields as automotive chemicals education financial services health care manufacturing and retail. The company's customers have included Cox Interactive Hasbro and Winstar Communications. YASH has offices in India Hong Kong Singapore the UK and the US.

	Annual Growth	12/0-1	12/00	12/01	12/06	12/08
Sales ($ mil.)	–	–	0.0	23.0	39.4	79.8
Net income ($ mil.)	–	–	–	0.0	0.5	7.1
Market value ($ mil.)	–	–	–	–	–	–
Employees	–	–	–	–	–	325

YAZAKI NORTH AMERICA INC.

6801 Haggerty Rd.
Canton MI 48187
Phone: 734-983-1000
Fax: 615-443-4619
Web: www.hartmann.com

CEO: Nigel Thompson
CFO: –
HR: –
FYE: December 31
Type: Subsidiary

Your ability to interact with your car's computer system might be predetermined by its YNA. Yazaki North America (YNA) is a leading supplier of wiring harnesses and other vehicle power and data components for the automotive industry. A subsidiary of diversified Japanese manufacturer Yazaki Corporation Yazaki North America also offers passive and active sensors; controls for power distribution terminals and connections; vehicle instrumentation; and products for hybrid and electric vehicles. Yazaki North America began operations in 1966 and has about two dozen facilities throughout North America.

YELLOWBOOK INC.

398 RXR Plaza
Uniondale NY 11556
Phone: 516-730-1900
Fax: 615-329-9627
Web: www.sesac.com

CEO: Mike Pocock
CFO: Jim Haddad
HR: –
FYE: March 31
Type: Subsidiary

Let your fingers do the walking through Yellowbook. Founded in 1930 Yellowbook is one of the country's oldest and largest independent publishers of yellow pages with more than 1000 directories that serve small and medium-sized businesses nationwide. The company has grown through acquisitions and new product launches today offering not just free and paid print advertising in Yellowbook but an array of digital and mobile marketing tools and services for small businesses including custom video ads on Yellowbook.com customer lead tracking hosting and optimization search engine marketing and website design. Yellowbook is part of hibu's US operations.

YELP INC

NYS: YELP

140 New Montgomery Street, 9th Floor
San Francisco, CA 94105
Phone: 415 908-3801
Fax: –
Web: www.yelp.com

CEO: Jeremy Stoppelman
CFO: Robert J. (Rob) Krolik
HR: Jose Martin
FYE: December 31
Type: Public

If yelping doesn't sound like fun you may not be as hip as you think. Yelp offers user-generated reviews and information on local businesses and service providers through its website at Yelp.com and via its mobile app. Its content targets younger urban consumers and covers restaurants bars salons retailers doctors and museums. The site has a social media-friendly interface — users can create and maintain profiles (complete with friend networks and photos) where they can blog on experiences with businesses. Yelp has established a foothold in cities across the US Canada and Europe. The firm was founded in 2004 by former PayPal engineers Jeremy Stoppelman and Russel Simmons. It went public in 2012.

	Annual Growth	12/10	12/11	12/12	12/13	12/14
Sales ($ mil.)	67.7%	47.7	83.3	137.6	233.0	377.5
Net income ($ mil.)	–	(9.6)	(16.7)	(19.1)	(10.1)	36.5
Market value ($ mil.)	70.4%	–	–	1,374.6	5,027.9	3,990.9
Employees	43.5%	–	918	1,387	1,984	2,711

YESHIVA UNIVERSITY

500 W 185TH ST
NEW YORK, NY 100333299
Phone: 212-960-5400
Fax: –
Web: www.yuhsb.org

CEO: –
CFO: Jacob (Jake) Harman
HR: Ilsa Garcia
FYE: June 30
Type: Private

Yeshivas are traditional Jewish schools and Yeshiva University believes strongly in following tradition. The Jewish higher education institution serves more than 7000 undergraduate and graduate students at four campuses in New York City. Subjects taught include liberal arts sciences medicine law business social work and psychology. It also has extensive Jewish studies and education programs including study abroad opportunities. Yeshiva University also known as YU has an undergraduate student-to-teacher ratio of 6:1. Its graduate programs include medicine law psychology and Jewish education.

	Annual Growth	06/08	06/09	06/10	06/11	06/13
Sales ($ mil.)	6.8%	–	541.2	657.4	674.3	704.9
Net income ($ mil.)	–	–	–	(94.8)	(85.7)	(98.1)
Market value ($ mil.)	–	–	–	–	–	–
Employees	–	–	–	–	–	4,500

YORK HOSPITAL

1001 S GEORGE ST
YORK, PA 174033645
Phone: 717-337-4123
Fax: –
Web: www.yorkhospital.edu

CEO: Kevin H Mosser
CFO: Michael F O'Connor
HR: –
FYE: June 30
Type: Private

York Hospital operating as WellSpan York Hospital takes its name from the community whose health it seeks to preserve. Part of WellSpan Health the medical center has about 570 beds and serves residents of York and surrounding area of south-central Pennsylvania. It is a regional leader in cardiovascular and orthopedic care and has programs in other specialty areas including oncology behavioral health and geriatrics. Additionally WellSpan York Hospital operates a Level 1 trauma center offers outpatient surgery emergency home health and diagnostic imaging services. It is also has teaching and research programs. The hospital was founded in 1880.

	Annual Growth	06/10	06/11	06/12	06/13	06/14
Sales ($ mil.)	1.8%	–	807.9	806.0	840.3	853.3
Net income ($ mil.)	122.1%	–	–	27.7	103.5	136.5
Market value ($ mil.)	–	–	–	–	–	–
Employees	–	–	–	–	–	6,200

YORK PENNSYLVANIA HOSPITAL COMPANY LLC

325 S BELMONT ST
YORK, PA 174032608
Phone: 717-843-8623
Fax: –
Web: www.mhyork.org

CEO: Sally J Dixon
CFO: Brent Smith
HR: –
FYE: June 30
Type: Private

Memorial Hospital serves the York County region of southeastern Pennsylvania in the midst of Amish country. The hospital offers emergency critical care diagnostic surgery and rehabilitation services as well as specialty cardiovascular orthopedic and obstetric services. In addition to the 100-bed acute care facility Memorial Hospital operates Greenbriar Medical Center (a diagnostic imaging and rehabilitation center) the Surgical Center of York (outpatient surgery facility) home health and hospice agencies and primary and specialist care clinics. Memorial Hospital is part of the Community Health Systems (CHS) network.

	Annual Growth	06/07	06/08	06/09	06/10	06/12
Sales ($ mil.)	–	–	(1,409.5)	100.7	100.8	102.0
Net income ($ mil.)	–	–	–	0.0	2.1	(5.9)
Market value ($ mil.)	–	–	–	–	–	–
Employees	–	–	–	–	–	900

YORK WATER CO

130 East Market Street
York, PA 17401
Phone: 717 845-3601
Fax: –
Web: www.yorkwater.com

NMS: YORW
CEO: Jeffrey R. Hines
CFO: Kathleen M. Miller
HR: Bruce C. McIntosh
FYE: December 31
Type: Public

The York Water Company goes with the flow as long as its water flows primarily within York County Pennsylvania. The regulated water utility distributes more than 18.6 million gallons of water daily to 39 communities in York County and to seven communities in nearby Adams County. It serves about 63780 residential and business customers in a service territory with a population of 189000. York Water obtains its water primarily from two reservoirs that together hold about 2.2 billion gallons. It gets an additional 12 million gallons of untreated water per day from the Susquehanna River.

	Annual Growth	12/10	12/11	12/12	12/13	12/14
Sales ($ mil.)	4.2%	39.0	40.6	41.4	42.4	45.9
Net income ($ mil.)	6.5%	8.9	9.1	9.3	9.7	11.5
Market value ($ mil.)	7.6%	221.8	226.3	225.4	268.5	297.8
Employees	(0.9%)	110	106	103	105	106

YOUNAN PROPERTIES INC.

21700 Oxnard St. Ste. 800
Woodland Hills CA 91367
Phone: 818-703-9600
Fax: 818-703-5907
Web: www.younanproperties.com

CEO: Zaya S Younan
CFO: –
HR: –
FYE: December 31
Type: Private

With office towers in about a half-dozen cities Younan Properties likely has many stories to tell (and lease). Younan Properties is a holding company that operates through Younan Properties LP a self-administered and self-managed owner and operator of office buildings in the Dallas/Fort Worth area Houston Los Angeles Phoenix and Chicago. Its portfolio includes about 35 Class "A" buildings (modern office buildings less than 10 years old) containing some 6 million sq. ft. of commercial space. Drawn to properties with low occupancy rates the company acquires and manages properties and leases to clients from a variety of industries. Younan withdrew its filing for an initial public offering in early 2012.

YOUNG & RUBICAM INC.

285 Madison Ave.
New York NY 10017
Phone: 212-210-3000
Fax: 212-490-9073
Web: www.yr.com

CEO: Ann Fudge
CFO: Peter Law-Gisiko
HR: –
FYE: December 31
Type: Subsidiary

If you've ever felt the need to "Be a Pepper" you can thank Young & Rubicam Brands (Y&R). As the advertising and media services unit of UK-based WPP Group Y&R has developed memorable commercial spots for many clients including the well-known tag line of Dr Pepper. Y&R operates primarily through its flagship creative ad agency Y&R Advertising but it also offers consulting and marketing services through Wunderman public relations through Burson-Marsteller and Cohn & Wolfe and digital expertise through a partnership with VML. Its Landor unit is a brand-building shop while The Bravo Group is a multicultural advertising agency. Acquired by WPP in 2000 Y&R owns about 185 offices in more than 90 countries.

YOUNG AMERICA CORPORATION

5050 Lincoln Dr. Ste. 450
Edina MN 55346
Phone: 952-467-1100
Fax: 202-833-8069
Web: www.nationaljournal.com

CEO: Christopher Behrens
CFO: –
HR: –
FYE: December 31
Type: Private

Young America is an old hand in engagement marketing. Founded in 1972 as Dile Corporation the company today offers a range of sales promotion and marketing services to help companies understand acquire and retain employees partners and customers. Among its services are incentive loyalty rebate sweepstake and cause marketing programs as well as call center support fulfillment and shipping management print and Web design and reporting and analysis on the effectiveness of consumer promotions. Young America handles marketing programs for many FORTUNE 500 companies including Hewlett-Packard Pepsi-Cola and T-Mobile USA.

YOUNG LIFE

420 N CASCADE AVE
COLORADO SPRINGS, CO 809033352
Phone: 719 301 1000
Fax: –
Web: www.younglife.org

CEO: –
CFO: –
HR: Reid Estes
FYE: September 30
Type: Private

Young Life is focused on promoting Christianity among teenagers in the US and in more than 50 other countries. Founded in 1941 the not-for-profit organization provides activities and support for junior high middle school and high school students located in rural and urban communities. Young Life also operates week-long summer camp programs at about 20 locations throughout North America as well as retreats held throughout the year. The group has grown throughout the years from a single club in Texas to about 600 international Young Life ministries dotting the globe. The organization boasts about 3000 staffers and more than 27000 volunteers.

	Annual Growth	09/10	09/11	09/12	09/13	09/14
Sales ($ mil.)	8.2%	–	245.3	237.8	276.1	311.2
Net income ($ mil.)	1250.7%	–	–	0.2	18.0	31.9
Market value ($ mil.)	–	–	–	–	–	–
Employees	–	–	–	–	–	3,100

YOUNG PECAN COMPANY

1200 Pecan St.
Florence SC 29501
Phone: 843-662-8591
Fax: 843-664-2344
Web: www.youngpecan.com

CEO: –
CFO: –
HR: –
FYE: December 31
Type: Subsidiary

You could say that the Young Pecan Company is a shell company but in a good way. Relieving some 100 million pounds of pecans of their shells every year the company is one of the largest pecan processors in the world. It has state-of-the-art laser shelling operations in Las Cruces New Mexico; Florence South Carolina; and Zaragosa Mexico as well as buying operations and storage facilities in Albany Georgia. Farming no nut orchards of its own Young Pecan purchases pecans from growers located near its plants. It sells its shelled pecan products to mainly domestic and international food manufacturing companies with some distribution in retail food outlets. The company was purchased by the King Ranch in 2006.

YOUNGSTOWN STATE UNIVERSITY INC

1 UNIVERSITY PLZ
YOUNGSTOWN, OH 44555-0002
Phone: 330-941-3000
Fax: –
Web: www.wysu.org

CEO: –
CFO: –
HR: –
FYE: June 30
Type: Private

Youngstown State University (YSU) offers about 100 undergraduate majors more than 30 graduate programs and doctorate programs in education and physical therapy. The university has an enrollment of approximately 14000 students in its six undergraduate colleges (business administration; education; health and human services; fine and performing arts; liberal arts and social sciences; and science technology engineering and mathematics) as well as a school of graduate studies and research. Its tuition is the lowest among Ohio's major public universities. Its athletic teams are known as the Penguins.

	Annual Growth	06/01	06/02	06/05	06/06	06/11
Sales ($ mil.)	(22.0%)	–	1,141.2	92.9	98.5	121.7
Net income ($ mil.)	–	–	0.0	(6.6)	(4.1)	(9.9)
Market value ($ mil.)	–	–	–	–	–	–
Employees	–	–	–	–	–	2,105

YOUR COMMUNITY BANKSHARES INC

NAS: YCB

101 West Spring Street
New Albany, IN 47150
Phone: 812 944-2224
Fax: –
Web: www.yourcommunitybank.com

CEO: James D Rickard
CFO: Paul A Chrisco
HR: –
FYE: December 31
Type: Public

Community Bank Shares of Indiana is the holding company for Your Community Bank and Scott County State Bank. The banks serve customers from about 20 locations in southern Indiana and Louisville Kentucky. Both banks offer deposit products such as checking money market and savings accounts as well as IRAs and CDs. Their lending activities center on commercial mortgages and residential real estate loans (each around 25% of the company's loan portfolio) but also include business construction and consumer (including home equity home improvement and auto) loans and credit cards. Community Bank Shares of Indiana is focused on organic growth within existing markets.

	Annual Growth	12/10	12/11	12/12	12/13	12/14
Assets ($ mil.)	2.6%	801.5	797.4	819.5	846.7	888.7
Net income ($ mil.)	6.6%	7.0	7.4	7.7	8.7	9.0
Market value ($ mil.)	29.6%	33.2	32.4	44.8	67.0	93.8
Employees	1.0%	205	201	202	209	213

YRC WORLDWIDE INC

NMS: YRCW

10990 Roe Avenue
Overland Park, KS 66211
Phone: 913 696-6100
Fax: –
Web: www.yrcw.com

CEO: James L. Welch
CFO: Jamie G. Pierson
HR: Sandra Stocke
FYE: December 31
Type: Public

YRC Worldwide stands for more than Your Regional Carrier. The company has one of the largest less-than-truckload (LTL) networks in North America with local regional national and international capabilities. YRC Worldwide is a holding company that operates through such subsidiaries as YRC Freight and YRC Reimer which transport goods for manufacturing wholesale retail and government customers in the US Canada and certain international markets as well as YRC Regional Transportation which provides regional next-day ground services in the US Canada Mexico and Puerto Rico through subsidiaries New Penn USF Holland and USF Reddaway.

	Annual Growth	12/10	12/11	12/12	12/13	12/14
Sales ($ mil.)	4.0%	4,334.6	4,868.8	4,850.5	4,865.4	5,068.8
Net income ($ mil.)	–	(322.2)	(351.3)	(140.4)	(83.6)	(67.7)
Market value ($ mil.)	56.8%	114.1	305.7	207.0	532.7	689.7
Employees	0.8%	32,000	32,000	32,000	32,000	33,000

YTB INTERNATIONAL INC.

OTC: YTBLA

1901 E. Edwardsville Rd.
Wood River IL 62095
Phone: 618-655-9477
Fax: 618-659-9607
Web: www.ytb.com

CEO: Andrew Cauthen
CFO: Steven Boyd
HR: –
FYE: December 31
Type: Public

YTB International wants its travel business to be your travel business. The company provides an online platform for individuals to set up home-based travel agency businesses. Customers pay monthly fees to have their online travel agencies hosted through YTB's ZamZuu subsidiary. YTB's Travel Network subsidiary processes and handles the transactions derived from additional hosted client websites. The company provides services for home-based travel agents in the US Canada the Bahamas and Bermuda. Reflecting the economy's impact on travel YTB announced plans in 2012 to merge with LTS Nutraceuticals. Before it does YTB has eliminated about a third of its headquarters staff including its president and CEO.

YUM! BRANDS, INC.

NYS: YUM

1441 Gardiner Lane
Louisville, KY 40213
Phone: 502 874-8300
Fax: –
Web: www.yum.com

CEO: Jing-Shyh S. (Sam) Su
CFO: Patrick Grismer
HR: Mary Yamanaka
FYE: December 26
Type: Public

This company puts fast-food yummies in a whole lot of tummies. YUM! Brands is the largest fast-food operator in the world in terms of number of locations with more than 41000 outlets in about 125 countries. (It trails only hamburger giant McDonald's in sales.) The company's flagship chains include #1 chicken fryer KFC (with more than 19400 units) top pizza joint Pizza Hut (more than 15600) and quick-service Mexican leader Taco Bell (more than 6200). YUM! sold the Long John Silver's seafood chain along with several hundred A&W root beer and burger stands to two separate buyers in late 2011. In 2015 YUM! Brands announced it would spin off its Chinese operations into a separately traded public company.

	Annual Growth	12/11	12/12	12/13	12/14	12/15
Sales ($ mil.)	0.9%	12,626.0	13,633.0	13,084.0	13,279.0	13,105.0
Net income ($ mil.)	(0.5%)	1,319.0	1,597.0	1,091.0	1,051.0	1,293.0
Market value ($ mil.)	5.8%	24,784.2	27,182.4	31,025.4	30,718.8	31,080.0
Employees	2.0%	466,000	523,000	539,000	537,000	505,000

YUMA ENERGY INC

ASE: YUMA

1177 West Loop South, Suite 1825
Houston, TX 77027
Phone: 713 968-7000
Fax: –
Web: www.yumaenergyinc.com

CEO: Sam L Banks
CFO: James J Jacobs
HR: –
FYE: December 31
Type: Public

Not as ancient as Egypt's pyramids but quite venerable in its own right Pyramid Oil has been in business for more than a century focusing on the exploration development and production of crude oil and natural gas. The company's major operations and all of its income-producing assets are located in Kern and Santa Barbara counties in Southern California where it owns and operates about 30 oil and gas leases. Pyramid Oil also holds minority stakes in some oil and gas leases in New York Texas and Wyoming. In 2008 Pyramid Oil reported proved reserves of more than 470000 barrels of oil and 330 million cu. ft. of natural gas. Company chairman Michael Herman owns about 36% of Pyramid Oil.

	Annual Growth	12/10	12/11	12/12	12/13	12/14
Sales ($ mil.)	73.0%	4.8	5.7	5.0	5.2	43.3
Net income ($ mil.)	–	0.2	1.1	0.8	0.2	(20.2)
Market value ($ mil.)	(23.0%)	354.0	278.6	277.3	349.2	124.5
Employees	30.8%	14	14	14	13	41

YUMA REGIONAL MEDICAL CENTER INC

2400 S AVENUE A
YUMA, AZ 853647170
Phone: 928-344-2000
Fax: –
Web: www.yumaregional.org

CEO: –
CFO: Tony Struck
HR: Marshall Jones
FYE: September 30
Type: Private

Yuma Regional Medical Center (YRMC) is an acute care hospital that provides medical services for Yuma Arizona and its surrounding communities. The not-for-profit hospital which has more than 400 beds and 300 doctors provides general medical surgical and emergency services as well as 40 specialties through units including a cardiac catheterization lab children's and women's health centers a weight loss department and a cancer treatment center as well as outpatient care divisions. YRMC also offers home health care school health care medical equipment rentals (through First Health Medical Supply) and cardiac and pulmonary rehabilitation services off-site.

	Annual Growth	09/09	09/10	09/11	09/12	09/13
Sales ($ mil.)	(2.8%)	–	317.0	330.5	346.2	291.1
Net income ($ mil.)	66.6%	–	–	4.1	22.9	11.4
Market value ($ mil.)	–	–	–	–	–	–
Employees	–	–	–	–	–	1,600

YUME INC

NYS: YUME

1204 Middlefield Road
Redwood City, CA 94063
Phone: 650 591-9400
Fax: 650 591-9401
Web: www.yume.com

CEO: Jayant Kadambi
CFO: Anthony (Tony) Carvalho
HR: –
FYE: December 31
Type: Public

YuMe is hoping more people like you and me turn to the Internet to watch videos. The company's technology enables video advertisements to display on personal computers smartphones tablets set-top boxes game consoles and Internet-connected TVs. YuMe makes money by selling on a cost-per-click basis and its technology matches the viewer with the most appropriate ad so that an ad for acne cream won't appear on a video targeting an older demographic. Advertising agencies such as Omnicom use YuMe to power digital ads on behalf of some 880 customers including American Express AT&T GlaxoSmithKline Home Depot and McDonald's. The company went public in 2013 raising $46 million in its IPO.

	Annual Growth	12/10	12/11	12/12	12/13	12/14
Sales ($ mil.)	36.1%	51.9	68.6	116.7	151.1	177.8
Net income ($ mil.)	–	(0.4)	(11.1)	6.3	0.3	(8.7)
Market value ($ mil.)	(32.3%)	–	–	–	246.3	166.7
Employees	22.0%	–	–	357	457	531

Z GALLERIE

1855 W 139TH ST
GARDENA, CA 902493013
Phone: 310-630-1200
Fax: –
Web: www.zgallerie.com

CEO: –
CFO: –
HR: Mara Roitman
FYE: December 31
Type: Private

Cain and Abel they're not! Brothers and executives Joe and Mike Zeiden founded Z Gallerie in 1979 using their parents' garage for a warehouse and production facility. Initially Z Gallerie (later joined by sister Carole Malfatti) sold poster art but in the 1980s the trio added home furnishings and accessories to the merchandising mix. Today Z Gallerie stores which span some 10000 sq. ft. on average feature bedding and pillows dinnerware glassware rugs lamps candleholders clocks frames and albums games and gifts. The company's eclectic pieces are sold through its website and about 55 US retail locations in nearly 20 states. Z Gallerie is privately owned.

	Annual Growth	12/09	12/10	12/11	12/12	12/13
Sales ($ mil.)	12.3%	–	–	154.4	176.4	194.8
Net income ($ mil.)	14.2%	–	–	20.6	25.5	26.9
Market value ($ mil.)	–	–	–	–	–	–
Employees	–	–	–	–	–	950

Z-TRIM HOLDINGS, INC

NBB: ZTHO

1011 Campus Drive
Mundelein, IL 60060
Phone: 847 549-6002
Fax: –
Web: www.ztrim.com

CEO: Edward Smith III
CFO: Anthony Saguto
HR: –
FYE: December 31
Type: Public

Z Trim Holdings is trying to cut the fat while at the same time allowing users to chew the fat. Its core product Z Trim developed and licensed by the USDA is a zero-calorie fiber ingredient typically made from corn or oats that is manufactured into gel and powdered form to replace fat gums starches and carbohydrates in foods. Z Trim sells its fat-replacement products as ingredients to food manufacturers and foodservice companies. Founder and former CEO Gregory Halpern owns about 13% of Z Trim Holdings; individual investor Nurieel Akhamzadeh owns 5%.

	Annual Growth	12/10	12/11	12/12	12/13	12/14
Sales ($ mil.)	2.9%	0.9	1.0	1.3	1.4	1.0
Net income ($ mil.)	–	(10.9)	(6.9)	(9.6)	(13.4)	(5.6)
Market value ($ mil.)	(22.7%)	41.7	26.6	69.1	22.3	14.9
Employees	(15.9%)	26	26	19	21	13

ZACKY FARMS LLC

2020 S. East Ave.
Fresno CA 93721
Phone: 559-443-2700
Fax: 559-443-2706
Web: www.zacky.com

CEO: –
CFO: –
HR: –
FYE: December 31
Type: Subsidiary

Zacky Farms really likes to talk turkey. It also likes to raise and process them. The company works at hatching raising and processing turkeys and creating turkey-based deli products (turkey franks turkey bologna turkey ham and yes turkey salami). The vertically integrated firm works from five locations in Southern California producing its own feed and operating a distribution fleet. In addition to products from traditionally raised birds Zacky Farms offers "100% natural" free-range turkey products. It supplies grocery stores and makes items for companies in the foodservice sector. Founded by Russian immigrant Samuel Zacky in 1928 Zacky Farms filed for Chapter 11 bankruptcy protection in fall 2012.

ZAGG INC

NMS: ZAGG

3855 South 500 West, Suite J
Salt Lake City, UT 84115
Phone: 801 263-0699
Fax: –
Web: www.zagg.com

CEO: Randall L. Hales
CFO: Bradley J. Holiday
HR: –
FYE: December 31
Type: Public

ZAGG hopes to stand in the way when a little zig threatens to scratch your iPhone or iPad. Short for "Zealous About Great Gadgets" ZAGG designs makes and sells protective coverings and other products for electronic devices. Its flagship product invisibleSHIELD is a thin scratch-resistant polyurethane film covering that's custom cut to fit invisibly on the screens and displays of Apple iPhones and other smartphones tablets laptops GPS devices and watch faces. ZAGG also offers additional accessories including keyboards headphones for iPods and MP3 players and decorative cases for phones. It sells its products through retailers the likes of Best Buy and Wal-Mart mall kiosks and its own website.

	Annual Growth	12/10	12/11	12/12	12/13	12/14
Sales ($ mil.)	36.1%	76.1	179.1	264.4	219.4	261.6
Net income ($ mil.)	1.2%	10.0	18.2	14.5	4.8	10.5
Market value ($ mil.)	(2.8%)	221.9	205.9	214.3	126.7	197.7
Employees	4.7%	183	261	273	201	220

ZAIS FINANCIAL CORP

NYS: ZFC

Two Bridge Avenue, Suite 322
Red Bank, NJ 07701-1106
Phone: 732 978-7518
Fax: –
Web: www.zaisfinancial.com

CEO: Michael Szymanski
CFO: Donna J Blank
HR: –
FYE: December 31
Type: Public

ZAIS is a REIT that invests in RMBS. As a real estate investment trust ZAIS Financial aims to put its money in residential mortgage-backed securities primarily of the non-agency variety meaning ones that are not issued or guaranteed by such government-sponsored entities as Fannie Mae Freddie Mac and Ginnie Mae. The company also plans to invest in such real estate and financial assets as mortgage servicing rights (MSRs) asset-backed securities (ABS) and commercial mortgage-backed securities (CMBS). Formed in mid-2011 the company went public in early 2013 with an offering worth $120.1 million. It has about $5.4 billion in assets under management.

	Annual Growth	12/10	12/11	12/12	12/13	12/14
Sales ($ mil.)	–	0.0	3.6	9.4	26.4	46.3
Net income ($ mil.)	–	0.0	(5.1)	20.3	7.6	29.9
Market value ($ mil.)	–	0.0	–	–	127.8	137.5
Employees	–	–	–	–	–	216

ZALE CORP.

NYS: ZLC

901 West Walnut Hill Lane
Irving, TX 75038-1003
Phone: 972 580-4000
Fax: –
Web: www.zalecorp.com

CEO: Theo Killion
CFO: Thomas A Haubenstricker
HR: –
FYE: July 31
Type: Public

Zale is multifaceted. One of North America's largest specialty jewelry retailers Zale sells diamond colored stone and gold jewelry (diamond fashion rings semi-precious stones earrings gold chains); watches; and gift items at some 1065 stores and 630 kiosks mostly in malls throughout the US Canada and Puerto Rico. The firm which targets the value-oriented customer has a trio of large chains aimed at different jewelry markets: Gordon's Jewelers flagship chain Zales Jewelers and Piercing Pagoda. Zale also operates about 125 jewelry outlet stores runs more than 200 stores in Canada under the Peoples Jewellers and Mappins Jewellers names sells online and offers jewelry insurance.

	Annual Growth	07/09	07/10	07/11	07/12	07/13
Sales ($ mil.)	1.5%	1,779.7	1,616.3	1,742.6	1,866.9	1,888.0
Net income ($ mil.)	–	(189.5)	(93.7)	(112.3)	(27.3)	10.0
Market value ($ mil.)	11.9%	193.2	57.4	183.1	98.6	302.9
Employees	(4.8%)	14,500	12,800	12,600	12,500	11,900

ZANETT INC.

NASDAQ: ZANE

635 Madison Ave. 15th Fl.
New York NY 10022
Phone: 212-583-0300
Fax: 212-244-3075
Web: www.zanettinc.com

CEO: Claudio M Guazzoni
CFO: Dennis Harkins
HR: –
FYE: December 31
Type: Public

Zanett is in the business of collecting companies. The company selects and acquires IT consulting firms that serve commercial and government clients including FORTUNE 500 and mid-market businesses and government agencies that operate in the defense and homeland security sectors. Services offered include consulting systems integration supply chain management implementation support and network design. Its commercial clients come from a variety of industries such as financial services health care and manufacturing. Founder Claudio Guazzoni and his uncle Bruno Guazzoni own about 24% and 28% of Zanett respectively.

ZAP

NBB: ZAAP

2 West 3rd Street
Santa Rosa, CA 95401
Phone: 707 525-8658
Fax: –
Web: www.zapworld.com

CEO: Charles Schillings
CFO: Michael Ringstad
HR: –
FYE: December 31
Type: Public

ZAP is driving the future. An acronym for "zero air pollution" ZAP provides efficient alternative-energy vehicles and products for corporate and government fleets security and environmentally conscious consumers around the globe. Products include the Xebra Sedan and Truck Zappy 3 and Zapino scooters ZAP Taxi electric bicycles. The company has two primary businesses — ZAP Automotive (alternative energy vehicles) and ZAP Power Systems (personal transporters and ATVs) — to manufacture products that meet the growing demands of eco-friendly consumers.

	Annual Growth	12/10	12/11	12/12	12/13	12/14
Sales ($ mil.)	65.6%	3.8	56.2	50.3	51.5	28.7
Net income ($ mil.)	–	(19.0)	(40.8)	(21.8)	(15.0)	(17.6)
Market value ($ mil.)	(47.5%)	581.4	99.2	36.5	46.1	44.3
Employees	81.6%	37	553	506	405	402

ZAREBA SYSTEMS INC.

13705 26th Ave. North Ste. 102
Minneapolis MN 55441
Phone: 763-551-1125
Fax: 763-509-7450
Web: www.zarebasystemsinc.com

CEO: Dale A Nordquist
CFO: Jeffrey S Mathiesen
HR: –
FYE: June 30
Type: Private

Zareba Systems makes electrical fence and access control systems for animal containment (such as horses and livestock) and humans (for security applications at locations such as airports oil refineries remote utility sites and high value storage sites). The company provides perimeter security products for several prisons. Brands include Blitzer Garden Protector Guard Tower and Pet Controller. Its Zareba Systems Europe subsidiary is a maker of electric fencing for the farming equestrian and defense markets in the UK with products sold under the Rutland Electric Fencing Electric Shepherd and Induced Pulse brands. The company merged with Woodstream Corp. in 2010; Zareba owners received $9.00 per share.

ZAZA ENERGY CORP.

NBB: ZAZA

1301 McKinney St Suite 2800
Houston, TX 77010
Phone: 713 595-1900
Fax: –
Web: www.zazaenergy.com

CEO: –
CFO: Paul F Jansen
HR: Karen Thomas
FYE: December 31
Type: Public

Despite the current economic downturn Toreador Resources is hopeful that a future bull market in oil prices will lift its revenues and its long term prospects. The oil and gas explorer owns royalty and mineral interests in properties located in France (in the Paris Basin Oil Shale) where it has 340000 net acres of primarily undeveloped land. Toreador sells its oil and production to France-based oil giant TOTAL which accounts for 98% of total revenues. Once a global player the company has shifted all its attention to its France. In 2012 the company merged its operations with US oil and gas explorer ZaZa Energy LCC. The expanded company was named ZaZa Energy Corporation.

	Annual Growth	12/10	12/11	12/12	12/13	12/14
Sales ($ mil.)	2.3%	10.5	17.6	205.2	8.9	11.5
Net income ($ mil.)	–	6.5	(2.9)	(106.2)	(67.6)	(8.2)
Market value ($ mil.)	10.9%	–	–	26.9	12.6	33.1
Employees	(36.2%)	–	123	70	29	32

ZEBRA TECHNOLOGIES CORP.

NMS: ZBRA

3 Overlook Point
Lincolnshire, IL 60069
Phone: 847 634-6700
Fax: –
Web: www.zebra.com

CEO: Anders Gustafsson
CFO: Michael C. (Mike) Smiley
HR: –
FYE: December 31
Type: Public

It's a black and white world for Zebra Technologies which makes devices for printing and reading the barcodes affixed to just about anything for sale. The company designs and sells printing devices that print labels plastic cards tickets and receipts. The company also makes equipment to read barcodes with its acquisition of Motorola Solutions in 2014. Its Zebra Location Solutions unit provides asset tags call tags sensors exciters and software — all of which use passive radio-frequency identification (RFID) to help companies track and manage assets. Zebra Technologies serves government customers and many corporate clients in industries ranging from health care to manufacturing to retail.

	Annual Growth	12/10	12/11	12/12	12/13	12/14
Sales ($ mil.)	14.9%	956.8	983.5	996.2	1,038.2	1,670.6
Net income ($ mil.)	(24.9%)	101.8	174.6	122.9	134.4	32.4
Market value ($ mil.)	19.5%	1,962.3	1,848.2	2,030.5	2,793.5	3,998.6
Employees	25.4%	2,750	2,510	2,544	2,583	6,800

ZEE MEDICAL INC.

22 Corporate Park
Irvine CA 92606
Phone: 949-252-9500
Fax: 949-252-9649
Web: www.zeemedical.com

CEO: Stanton J McComb
CFO: –
HR: –
FYE: March 31
Type: Subsidiary

ZEE Medical's familiar green-and-white first aid kits are the working man's medicine cabinet. From aspirin to stretchers ZEE Medical is one of the largest distributors of first aid kits safety products and training services to industrial and commercial enterprises throughout the US and (to a limited degree) in Canada. It uses a van-based delivery system to keep its customers stocked with supplies which can be ordered directly from the company's website and via a direct sales force. The company also offers Internet-based video and on-site training in first aid CPR OSHA compliance and other workplace health and safety issues. ZEE Medical is a subsidiary of health care product distributor McKesson.

ZEELAND COMMUNITY HOSPITAL

8333 FELCH ST STE 202
ZEELAND, MI 494642609
Phone: 616-772-4644
Fax: –
Web: www.spectrumhealth.org

CEO: –
CFO: –
HR: –
FYE: June 30
Type: Private

Zeeland Community Hospital provides acute medical services for the residents of western Michigan. The hospital has nearly 60 beds and provides emergency diagnostic inpatient and outpatient services. Its specialty services include diabetes care orthopedics cardiology pain management rehabilitation and surgery. Zeeland Community Hospital has some 200 physicians on its medical staff which includes its two affiliated physician groups Zeeland Physicians and Georgetown Physicians. Zeeland Community Hospital was founded in 1928 as a 10-bed hospital.

	Annual Growth	09/04	09/05	09/09*	06/12	06/13
Sales ($ mil.)	4.4%	–	36.5	47.8	54.2	51.6
Net income ($ mil.)	14.7%	–	–	1.8	1.7	3.1
Market value ($ mil.)	–	–	–	–	–	–
Employees	–	–	–	–	–	–

*Fiscal year change

ZELTIQ AESTHETICS INC.

NMS: ZLTQ

4698 Willow Road, Suite 100
Pleasanton, CA 94588
Phone: 925 474-2500
Fax: –
Web: www.coolsculpting.com

CEO: Mark J. Foley
CFO: Patrick F. Williams
HR: –
FYE: December 31
Type: Public

ZELTIQ Aesthetics is winning the battle of the bulge. The company's CoolSculpting device offers a non-invasive alternative to liposuction to knock out fat cells. The treatment uses controlled cooling to reduce the temperature of fat cells and melt fat without causing scar tissue or skin damage. ZELTIQ sells the CoolSculpting device and related consumables in the US for use on targeted areas of the torso and thighs but it is also used more freely in about 45 other international markets. The CoolSculpting system is sold to dermatologists plastic surgeons and aesthetic specialists such as medical spas. ZELTIQ was incorporated in 2005 as Juniper Medical Inc. It changed its name in 2007 and went public in 2011.

	Annual Growth	12/10	12/11	12/12	12/13	12/14
Sales ($ mil.)	61.8%	25.5	68.1	76.2	111.6	174.5
Net income ($ mil.)	–	(13.5)	(9.6)	(30.1)	(19.3)	1.5
Market value ($ mil.)	34.9%	–	433.1	176.5	720.9	1,064.0
Employees	28.9%	148	153	209	297	408

ZENITH NATIONAL INSURANCE CORP.

21255 Califa St.
Woodland Hills CA 91367-5021
Phone: 818-713-1000
Fax: 818-710-1860
Web: www.thezenith.com

CEO: Jack D Miller
CFO: Kari L Van Gundy
HR: –
FYE: December 31
Type: Subsidiary

Workers' compensation claims typically mark a low point for employers but Zenith National Insurance aims to get companies back up to their peak. Zenith National is the holding company for Zenith Insurance and ZNAT Insurance which underwrite workers' compensation policies in 45 states and Washington DC. The company also offers agribusiness coverage in California and maintains a portfolio of investments. Approximately 1600 independent agents sell the firm's insurance products. California is its largest market but the company also maintains offices in Alabama Florida Illinois North Carolina Pennsylvania and Texas. Zenith National is a subsidiary of Canada's Fairfax Financial.

ZEP INC
NYS: ZEP

1310 Seaboard Industrial Boulevard
Atlanta, GA 30318-2825
Phone: 404 352-1680
Fax: –
Web: www.zepinc.com

CEO: William E Redmond Jr
CFO: Mark R Bachmann
HR: –
FYE: August 31
Type: Public

Zep hates a mess. A manufacturer of commercial industrial institutional and consumer chemical products it makes such brand lines as Enforcer (fertilizer pest control and drain cleaners) Selig (environmentally friendly hand cleaners and degreasers and equipment used to clean aerospace and automotive parts) and Zep (automotive and janitorial supplies such as hand cleaners degreasers and floor polish). Through its Niagara National unit it provides truck and fleet washing systems and products. The company operates eight manufacturing sites in Europe and North America. It generates more than 80% of sales from the US. Zep began trading publicly in 2007 after a spinoff from former parent Acuity Brands.

	Annual Growth	08/10	08/11	08/12	08/13	08/14
Sales ($ mil.)	5.2%	568.5	646.0	653.5	689.6	696.5
Net income ($ mil.)	(11.2%)	13.5	17.4	21.9	15.2	8.4
Market value ($ mil.)	(2.1%)	387.7	394.8	324.1	315.3	355.7
Employees	(0.5%)	2,350	2,300	2,400	2,400	2,300

ZEVEX INTERNATIONAL INC.

4314 ZEVEX Park Ln.
Salt Lake City UT 84123
Phone: 801-264-1001
Fax: 801-264-1051
Web: www.zevex.com

CEO: David J McNally
CFO: Phillip L McStotts
HR: Karla Soker
FYE: December 31
Type: Subsidiary

For the sick or badly injured ZEVEX offers feeding lifelines. ZEVEX designs manufactures and distributes medical devices. The company's therapeutics unit makes enteral nutrition delivery devices that are used to infuse feeding solutions directly into the stomach or intestines of a patient. ZEVEX also manufactures ultrasonic and optoelectronic sensors fluid management devices and surgical devices and offers contract design and manufacturing services to other medical device companies. ZEVEX was acquired by Moog in 2007 and joined its Medical Devices segment.

ZF GROUP NORTH AMERICAN OPERATIONS INC.

15811 Centennial Dr.
Northville MI 48167
Phone: 734-416-6200
Fax: 734-416-8831
Web: www.zf.com/us

CEO: –
CFO: Hans-Georg Harter
HR: –
FYE: December 31
Type: Subsidiary

ZF Group North American Operations (NAO) is the North American arm of German transmission chassis and driveline manufacturer ZF Friedrichshafen AG. ZF Group NAO which represents about 12% of its parent's annual revenues makes driveline and chassis components for almost anything that rolls — from passenger cars and light trucks to buses heavy-duty trucks and construction and agricultural equipment. Products include axles steering systems suspensions and transmissions. It also specializes in transmissions for rail marine craft and helicopters. Aftermarket parts and service are offered as well. The company has about 17 manufacturing sites in the US and Mexico.

ZHONE TECHNOLOGIES INC
NAS: ZHNE

7195 Oakport Street
Oakland, CA 94621
Phone: 510 777-7000
Fax: –
Web: www.zhone.com

CEO: James D. Norrod
CFO: Kirk Misaka
HR: –
FYE: December 31
Type: Public

Zhone Technologies helps network service providers get into the SLMS zone. The company's all-IP Single Line Multi-Service (SLMS) platform uses existing local-loop infrastructures to deliver broadband services. Telecommunications service providers and wireless and cable operators use SLMS to offer their business and residential subscribers bundled broadband Internet access local and long-distance voice and broadcast video services. Its products are assembled at its plant in Florida using components manufactured in Asia. The company serves some 1000 customers worldwide; about 70% of sales come from outside the US.

	Annual Growth	12/10	12/11	12/12	12/13	12/14
Sales ($ mil.)	(1.7%)	129.0	124.5	115.4	122.2	120.6
Net income ($ mil.)	–	(4.8)	(11.7)	(9.0)	4.3	(4.1)
Market value ($ mil.)	(9.8%)	86.8	28.8	15.4	173.6	57.5
Employees	(5.9%)	353	339	267	283	277

ZIFF DAVIS HOLDINGS INC.

28 E. 28th St.
New York NY 10016-7930
Phone: 212-503-3500
Fax: +972-2-581-5507
Web: www.viryanet.com

CEO: Jason Young
CFO: Neil Glass
HR: –
FYE: December 31
Type: Private

Technophiles in search of reading material have a friend in Ziff Davis. The firm is an online publisher targeting tech enthusiasts. Its flagship PCMag.com website offers technology-related features e-newsletters buying guides and downloads. Other Web brands include ExtremeTech (how-to features) Geek.com (news reviews and an online community) LogicBuy (coupon codes and deals) and BuyerBase (ad targeting platform). The company also offers online consumer events and direct marketing services. Ziff Davis traces its roots to 1927 when William Ziff (a famed WWI flier and author) and Bernard Davis first published Popular Aviation. Today it is owned by former Time executive Vivek Shah and Great Hill Partners.

ZILLIANT INC.

3815 S. Capital of Texas Hwy. Ste. 300
Austin TX 78704
Phone: 512-531-8500
Fax: 512-531-8599
Web: www.zilliant.com

CEO: –
CFO: –
HR: –
FYE: December 31
Type: Private

It's worthwhile to know how much things should or could cost. Zilliant develops software that helps companies price their products and improve profit margins. Combining data analysis with statistical and operations research the company's software automates price setting discounting in-depth price analysis deal management and promotions strategy. Zilliant also offers professional services including change management pricing strategy development and risk planning. It targets clients in a variety of industries including manufacturing advertising transportation and e-commerce. Founded in 1998 Zilliant's investors have included Austin Ventures Trellis Partners SMH and ABS Ventures.

ZILOG INC.

6800 Santa Teresa Blvd.
San Jose CA 95119
Phone: 408-513-1500
Fax: 408-513-1600
Web: www.zilog.com

CEO: Darin G Billerbeck
CFO: Perry J Grace
HR: –
FYE: March 31
Type: Subsidiary

ZiLOG tries to control its own destiny with a portfolio of embedded control chips. The semiconductor company makes a wide variety of integrated circuits including embedded processors and microcontrollers. These chips are used in consumer electronics industrial controls point-of-sale terminals and security systems among other products. ZiLOG has also supplied devices to such communications equipment makers as DISH Network and Samsung Electronics. Other customers have included Emerson Electric Philips Electronics and THOMSON. IXYS Corp. acquired the company for about $62 million in early 2010.

ZIMMER BIOMET HOLDINGS INC

NYS: ZBH

345 East Main Street
Warsaw, IN 46580
Phone: 574 267-6131
Fax: –
Web: www.zimmer.com

CEO: David C. Dvorak
CFO: James T (Jamie) Crines
HR: William (Bill) Fisher
FYE: December 31
Type: Public

Zimmer Biomet (formerly Zimmer) can put the spring back in your step or the zing back in your swing. The company designs and markets orthopedic products including reconstructive implants used in knee or hip replacement surgery shoulder implants that restore function in arthritic joints bone and tissue grafting materials and sports medicine products. It also makes dental implant systems spinal implants to fix aching or injured backs and trauma products (such as plates screws and pins) that help broken bones to heal. Additionally Zimmer Biomet makes surgical products used in orthopedic surgeries including tourniquets and devices for wound cleansing. The firm's products are sold around the globe.

	Annual Growth	12/10	12/11	12/12	12/13	12/14
Sales ($ mil.)	2.6%	4,220.2	4,451.8	4,471.7	4,623.4	4,673.3
Net income ($ mil.)	4.8%	596.9	760.8	755.0	761.0	720.1
Market value ($ mil.)	20.6%	9,109.5	9,065.4	11,312.2	15,814.3	19,247.4
Employees	3.2%	8,800	8,700	9,300	9,500	10,000

ZIMMER GUNSUL FRASCA ARCHITECTS LLP

1223 SW WASHINGTON ST # 200
PORTLAND, OR 972052360
Phone: 503-224-3860
Fax: –
Web: www.zgf.com

CEO: –
CFO: –
HR: –
FYE: December 31
Type: Private

Zimmer Gunsul Frasca may not be a household name but the firm has created homes for businesses and institutions on both coasts. The company which is among the nation's top 10 green design firms provides architectural planning and interior and urban design services for customers through its offices in Los Angeles Portland Seattle New York and Washington D.C. Zimmer Gunsul Frasca (ZGF) works on civic corporate academic health care and research facilities and has designed for such clients as the Environmental Protection Agency Microsoft Iowa State University and The University of Arizona. The firm was established in 1942 by Norman Zimmer.

	Annual Growth	12/06	12/07	12/08	12/09	12/14
Sales ($ mil.)	10.3%	–	65.8	149.0	112.9	130.6
Net income ($ mil.)	(22.3%)	–	–	8.5	39.8	1.9
Market value ($ mil.)	–	–	–	–	–	–
Employees	–	–	–	–	–	458

ZIMMERMAN ADVERTISING LLC

2200 W. Commercial Blvd. Ste. 300
Fort Lauderdale FL 33309
Phone: 954-644-4000
Fax: +44-20-7353-2339
Web: www.eurorscg-riley.co.uk

CEO: Michael Goldberg
CFO: –
HR: –
FYE: December 31
Type: Subsidiary

Marketing products and promoting brands is one and the same for Zimmerman Advertising. One of the largest retail ad firms in the southeastern US Zimmerman offers creative development and branding services to a variety of clients with particular expertise in the automotive retail sector. Its creative philosophy centers on the idea of "brandtailing" the merging of branding strategy and retailing to promote products and services while building brand identity. Founded in 1984 by former "Mr. Florida" Jordan Zimmerman the agency operates through more than 20 offices in 10 states. Zimmerman is a unit of advertising conglomerate Omnicom Group.

ZION OIL AND GAS INC.

NASDAQ: ZN

6510 Abrams Rd. Ste. 300
Dallas TX 75231
Phone: 214-221-4610
Fax: 214-221-6510
Web: www.zionoil.com

CEO: Victor G Carrillo
CFO: Ilan N Sheena
HR: –
FYE: December 31
Type: Public

Zion Oil and Gas is on a mission in Israel. As an oil and gas exploration company Zion has exploration operations primarily on two onshore properties that cover about 162000 acres between Tel-Aviv and Haifa. The company operates through two licenses that were issued by the State of Israel and it owns 100% of the working interest in both licenses. When it eventually discovers oil and gas Zion has stated that it will focus its production operations on helping Israel become a more energy-independent country. The company which was founded in 2000 by chairman John M. Brown went public in 2007.

ZIONS BANCORPORATION

NMS: ZION

One South Main, 15th Floor
Salt Lake City, UT 84133
Phone: 801 844-7637
Fax: –
Web: www.zionsbancorporation.com

CEO: A. Scott (Scott) Anderson
CFO: Paul E. Burdiss
HR: John Tall
FYE: December 31
Type: Public

Multibank holding company Zions Bancorporation operates eight bank subsidiaries with more than 450 branches in 10 western and southwestern states. The banks operate under their own brands and leadership rather than sharing one corporate identity. Its network of banks focuses on commercial and retail banking as well as mortgage and construction lending. The banks provide products and services including deposit accounts home mortgages and home equity lines of credit residential and commercial development loans credit cards and trust and wealth management services. Zions caters to small- to medium-sized businesses by offering Small Business Administration (SBA) loans.

	Annual Growth	12/10	12/11	12/12	12/13	12/14
Assets ($ mil.)	2.9%	51,034.9	53,149.1	55,511.9	56,031.1	57,208.9
Net income ($ mil.)	–	(292.7)	323.8	349.5	263.8	398.5
Market value ($ mil.)	4.2%	4,919.1	3,305.1	4,344.5	6,082.3	5,788.0
Employees	(0.1%)	10,524	10,606	10,368	10,452	10,462

ZIOPHARM ONCOLOGY INC

NAS: ZIOP

One First Avenue, Parris Building 34, Navy Yard Plaza
Boston, MA 02129
Phone: 617 259-1970
Fax: –
Web: www.ziopharm.com

CEO: Laurence J. N. Cooper
CFO: –
HR: –
FYE: December 31
Type: Public

Biopharmaceutical company ZIOPHARM Oncology develops DNA-based drugs for different types of cancer. The company has three cancer drugs currently in various stages of clinical development. Its most promising candidate is palifosfamide (Zymafos) which targets cancers of bone muscle fat and other types of tissues. Others include indibulin (Zybulin which disrupts cancer cell division and migration) and darinaparsin (Zinapar an arsenic-based drug that treats blood and solid cancers). ZIOPHARM's roots go back to 2004 when CEO and co-founder Jonathan J. Lewis started ZIOPHARM Inc.; the next year the company merged with EasyWeb changed its name and went public.

	Annual Growth	12/10	12/11	12/12	12/13	12/14
Sales ($ mil.)	27.2%	–	0.7	0.8	0.8	1.4
Net income ($ mil.)	–	(32.7)	(63.8)	(96.1)	(57.1)	(31.8)
Market value ($ mil.)	2.1%	486.7	460.6	434.5	453.3	529.6
Employees	(4.9%)	33	66	83	43	27

ZIPPO MANUFACTURING COMPANY

33 Barbour St.
Bradford PA 16701
Phone: 814-368-2700
Fax: 604-656-3170
Web: www.premiumbrandsholdings.com

CEO: –
CFO: Richard Roupe
HR: –
FYE: December 31
Type: Private

Antismoking sentiment hasn't been hazardous to the health of Zippo which has found new life in selling its iconic windproof lighters to collectors and fashion-conscious consumers. Zippo's refillable lighters (which come with a lifetime guarantee) are sold in more than 120 countries. Its Ronson unit makes cigarette lighters lighter fluid flints torches and more. Zippo also owns W.R. Case & Sons Cutlery (pocketknives) and makes key holders money clips pocket flashlights tape measures and writing instruments. George Blaisdell founded Zippo in 1932 after watching a friend try to light a cigarette in the wind. His daughters Harriet Wick and Sarah Dorn (and her sons George and Paul Duke) own Zippo.

ZIPREALTY INC

NMS: ZIPR

2000 Powell Street, Suite 300
Emeryville, CA 94608
Phone: 510 735-2600
Fax: –
Web: www.ziprealty.com

CEO: Lanny Baker
CFO: Eric L Mersch
HR: –
FYE: December 31
Type: Public

Whether you're on the go or sitting in the comfort of your home ZipRealty wants to help you close the deal. The residential real estate brokerage firm maintains an online searchable database of homes in some 20 major markets around the US. Buyers are able to streamline their house hunt narrowing searches by location price range and size; sellers can advertise on multiple real estate websites and listing services and post online tours of their homes. In addition to offering personalized tools such as saved searches and automated notifications on its website the company provides mobile access to home listings through a smart phone application.

	Annual Growth	12/08	12/09	12/10	12/11	12/12
Sales ($ mil.)	(9.0%)	107.5	123.1	118.7	85.1	73.8
Net income ($ mil.)	–	(13.3)	(12.9)	(15.6)	(9.7)	(9.7)
Market value ($ mil.)	1.4%	54.8	77.8	53.8	22.8	57.9
Employees	(53.0%)	3,068	3,346	161	126	150

ZIRCON CORPORATION

1580 Dell Ave.
Campbell CA 95008
Phone: 408-963-4550
Fax: 408-963-4597
Web: www.zircon.com

CEO: John Stauss
CFO: –
HR: –
FYE: March 31
Type: Private

Every day's a good day for hanging at Zircon as long as its customers are hanging a picture. Zircon's flagship product the hand-held StudSensor tool finds wall studs electronically and has become one of the world's top selling electronic hand tools. The company's brand names include MetalliScanner Circuit Finder LaserBall 360 and Leak Alert among others. Zircon designs manufactures and markets more than two dozen high-tech hand tools that sense scan level and measure. The company offers two product lines one for do-it-yourselfers and one for building professionals. Most of its products including some private-label tools for retailers are made at its plant in Mexico. Zircon was founded in 1975.

ZIX CORP

NMS: ZIXI

2711 North Haskell Avenue, Suite 2200, LB 36
Dallas, TX 75204-2960
Phone: 214 370-2000
Fax: 214 370-2070
Web: www.zixcorp.com

CEO: David Wagner
CFO: Michael W. English
HR: Lauren Nix
FYE: December 31
Type: Public

Zix wants to nix the idea of unsavory characters reading your e-mail. The company offers secure e-mail encryption data loss prevention and transmission services. Its technology enables users to transmit encrypted e-mail and documents to any address in the world; recipients who are not service subscribers can access the messages through the company's Web-based portal. Zix targets customers in the health care financial services insurance and government sectors and it has an e-mail encryption community with tens of millions of members growing by 110000 members per week. Trademarks and brand names for its products include ZixCorp. ZixGateway ZixDirectory ZixIT Zix-Port and PocketScript.

	Annual Growth	12/10	12/11	12/12	12/13	12/14
Sales ($ mil.)	11.1%	33.1	38.1	43.4	48.1	50.3
Net income ($ mil.)	(43.8%)	41.2	22.6	11.0	10.5	4.1
Market value ($ mil.)	(4.2%)	243.3	160.7	159.0	259.8	205.1
Employees	12.6%	123	127	144	162	198

ZOETIS INC

NYS: ZTS

100 Campus Drive
Florham Park, NJ 07932
Phone: 973 822-7000
Fax: –
Web: www.zoetis.com

CEO: Juan Ram In Alaix
CFO: Paul S. Herendeen
HR: Roxanne Lagano
FYE: December 31
Type: Public

Whether you have cats or cattle Zoetis (formerly Pfizer Animal Health) has something to keep them healthy and happy. The company manufactures and sells veterinary medicines such as parasiticides (for fleas ticks and worms) anti-infectives medicated feed additives vaccines and other pharmaceuticals. Zoetis boasts more than 300 product lines sold in more than 120 countries around the world making it one of the world's largest animal health businesses. In addition to medications and vaccines Zoetis offers diagnostics genetics devices and services such as dairy data management and consulting. Zoetis went public in early 2013 with an offering worth $2.2 billion.

	Annual Growth	12/10	12/11	12/12	12/13	12/14
Sales ($ mil.)	7.5%	3,582.0	4,233.0	4,336.0	4,561.0	4,785.0
Net income ($ mil.)	51.7%	110.0	245.0	436.0	504.0	583.0
Market value ($ mil.)	31.6%	–	–	–	16,388.4	21,572.1
Employees	1.7%	–	9,500	9,300	9,800	10,000

ZOGENIX INC.

NMS: ZGNX

12400 High Bluff Drive, Suite 650
San Diego, CA 92130
Phone: 858 259-1165
Fax: –

CEO: Stephen J. (Steve) Farr
CFO: Ann D. Rhoads
HR: –
FYE: December 31
Type: Public

Zogenix wants to help the pain go away faster. The pharmaceutical company is developing and commercializing central nervous system (CNS) and therapeutic pain medications. Zohydro ER its second marketed product (launched in 2014) is an extended-release oral formulation of hydrocodone without acetaminophen for daily pain management. Other drugs under development include Relday an injectable form of risperidone to treat schizophrenia and bipolar symptoms. Zogenix's first marketed product Sumavel DosePro which combined the company's DosePro needle-free drug delivery technology with migraine drug sumatriptan was sold in 2014.

	Annual Growth	12/10	12/11	12/12	12/13	12/14
Sales ($ mil.)	14.7%	23.4	37.6	44.3	33.0	40.5
Net income ($ mil.)	–	(73.6)	(83.9)	(47.4)	(80.9)	8.6
Market value ($ mil.)	(29.9%)	108.7	42.6	25.5	65.9	26.3
Employees	8.7%	144	161	149	114	201

ZOLL MEDICAL CORPORATION

NASDAQ: ZOLL

269 Mill Rd.
Chelmsford MA 01824-4105
Phone: 978-421-9655
Fax: 978-421-0025
Web: www.zoll.com

CEO: Richard A Packer
CFO: –
HR: –
FYE: September 30
Type: Public

ZOLL Medical knows how to get your heart pounding. The medical equipment firm makes noninvasive cardiac defibrillators and pacing devices used in emergency situations to resuscitate hearts that have stopped beating during sudden cardiac arrest. ZOLL Medical also makes disposable electrodes for use with its products as well as related information technology software. The company's products are used by hospitals paramedics and other emergency medical personnel and are sold through a direct sales force in the US and via representatives and distributors in some 140 countries worldwide. ZOLL Medical manufactures its products at five facilities in the US. Japanese firm Asahi Kasei acquired ZOLL in 2012.

ZOLTEK COMPANIES INC

NMS: ZOLT

3101 McKelvey Road
St. Louis, MO 63044
Phone: 314 291-5110
Fax: –
Web: www.zoltek.com

CEO: Mark Kawamura
CFO: Andrew W Whipple
HR: –
FYE: September 30
Type: Public

Zoltek Companies wants to lighten your load. The advanced materials company makes carbon fibers that can be used in a variety of applications due to their lightweight high-strength conductive and corrosion-resistant properties. Carbon fibers are most common in aircraft brakes but Zoltek has been expanding their use by employing them in composites for wind turbine blades as well as for use by energy and automotive markets. Zoltek has two segments: heat- and flame-resistant acrylic or technical fibers (under the brand Pyron) and carbon fibers (under the brand Panex). Its carbon fibers business accounts for most of its sales. Founder and CEO Zsolt Rumy is Zoltek's largest shareholder with an 18% stake.

	Annual Growth	09/09	09/10	09/11	09/12	09/13
Sales ($ mil.)	0.3%	138.8	128.5	151.7	186.3	140.5
Net income ($ mil.)	–	(4.2)	(6.3)	(3.6)	22.9	5.2
Market value ($ mil.)	12.3%	361.1	334.3	221.1	264.5	574.0
Employees	1.0%	1,136	1,095	1,282	1,380	1,183

ZOOLOGICAL SOCIETY OF SAN DIEGO

2920 ZOO DR
SAN DIEGO, CA 921011646
Phone: 619-231-1515
Fax: –
Web: www.sandiegozoo.org

CEO: –
CFO: Paula S Brock
HR: Lily Hom
FYE: December 31
Type: Private

Talk about animal magnetism! The Zoological Society of San Diego is a not-for-profit organization that operates the 100-acre San Diego Zoo which cares for more than 4000 individual animals as well as a collection of some 3500 species of plants. The Zoological Society also manages the 1800-acre San Diego Zoo Safari Park and the center for Conservation and Research. The zoo entertains all with its daily shows in-park restaurants guided tours and special events. The society also supports conservation education and efforts such as planned travel adventure-tours to exotic destinations in Mexico and Africa. It was founded by Dr. Harry Wegeforth in 1916 and is managed by a 12-member board.

	Annual Growth	01/05	01/06*	12/09	12/10	12/13
Sales ($ mil.)	(8.5%)	–	483.4	173.1	193.5	259.7
Net income ($ mil.)	–	–	–	(15.3)	(6.1)	29.8
Market value ($ mil.)	–	–	–	–	–	–
Employees	–	–	–	–	–	2,300

*Fiscal year change

ZOOM TELEPHONICS, INC.

NBB: ZMTP

207 South Street
Boston, MA 02111
Phone: 617 423-1072
Fax: –
Web: www.zoomtel.com

CEO: Frank B Manning
CFO: Philip Frank
HR: Kerry Smith
FYE: December 31
Type: Public

Even though it offers a variety of communications products Zoom Telephonics' primary mode is modems. Selling under its Hayes and Global Village brands the company specializes in the design and production of hardware used to move data over the Internet including DSL cable and dial-up modems as well as VoIP (Voice over Internet Protocol) and Bluetooth products. It sells its products in the US Europe South America and other markets through retailers like Best Buy Staples and Wal-Mart; it also sells through distributors and to OEMs (original equipment manufacturers). Founded in 1977 Zoom Telephonics was spun off from Zoom Technologies in 2009.

	Annual Growth	12/10	12/11	12/12	12/13	12/14
Sales ($ mil.)	(2.7%)	13.3	12.7	14.7	11.2	11.9
Net income ($ mil.)	(17.8%)	0.3	(0.9)	(0.7)	(1.1)	0.1
Market value ($ mil.)	(8.1%)	2.8	2.0	1.6	0.9	2.0
Employees	(10.3%)	37	31	30	28	24

ZOOTS CORPORATION

45 Industrial Blvd.
Brockton MA 02301
Phone: 508-584-2758
Fax: 508-584-2608
Web: www.zoots.com

CEO: James McManus
CFO: Kyle Gendreau
HR: –
FYE: December 31
Type: Private

Whether its the shirt off your back or the floor beneath your feet Zoots can make it spotless. The company offers laundry and dry cleaning services through about 15 stores in Massachusetts and one in Rhode Island. It also cleans carpet tile furniture and upholstery and provides water damage restoration services (including mildew removal and mold remediation). Zoots offers delivery service to residences and businesses in states where it operates cleaning facilities as well as New Hampshire. Recognized as a green cleaner it doesn't work with perchloroethylene a carcinogen typically used in the process. The firm was founded in 1998 by ex-CEO Todd Krasnow and Tom Stemberg both former Staples executives.

ZUMIEZ INC

NMS: ZUMZ

4001 204th Street S.W.
Lynnwood, WA 98036
Phone: 425 551-1500
Fax: –
Web: www.zumiez.com

CEO: Richard M. Brooks
CFO: Christopher C. Work
HR: –
FYE: January 31
Type: Public

Zumiez's young customers like to zoom. The fast-growing retailer outfits action sports enthusiasts offering apparel footwear accessories and sports equipment for 12- to 24-year-olds who enjoy board sports BMX biking and surfing. It stocks such brands as Billabong Burton Quiksilver Vans and Spy Optic as well as private-label goods. Zumiez operates about 500 mall-based stores across North America and in Europe as well as an online store. Aside from the usual action sports merchandise (hoodies and puffy skater shoes) stores also feature couches video games and sales clerks who really use the gear — all designed to encourage shoppers to chill. Zumiez was founded in 1978 by chairman Thomas Campion.

	Annual Growth	01/11	01/12*	02/13	02/14*	01/15
Sales ($ mil.)	14.1%	478.8	555.9	669.4	724.3	811.6
Net income ($ mil.)	15.6%	24.2	37.4	42.2	45.9	43.2
Market value ($ mil.)	13.7%	656.3	833.4	621.0	633.1	1,097.0
Employees	7.7%	4,840	4,680	5,300	5,600	6,500

*Fiscal year change

ZYGO CORP

NMS: ZIGO

Laurel Brook Road
Middlefield, CT 06455
Phone: 860 347-8506
Fax: –
Web: www.zygo.com

CEO: Frank Hermance
CFO: –
HR: Diana Midolo
FYE: June 30
Type: Public

Zygo knows how to measure precisely what its customers need. The company makes high-precision electro-optical inspection and measurement equipment automation systems and optical components. One of its main products is the interferometer which measures surface shape roughness and other characteristics by means of two light beams ("zygo" is Greek for "pair") used to produce 3D surface profiles for comparing test objects with control samples. Zygo also offers optical design testing certification and assembly services. Its products are used primarily for quality control in the semiconductor and industrial manufacturing markets.

	Annual Growth	06/09	06/10	06/11	06/12	06/13
Sales ($ mil.)	6.5%	116.0	101.3	150.1	166.8	149.4
Net income ($ mil.)	–	(66.1)	(6.3)	19.1	43.0	7.9
Market value ($ mil.)	35.8%	86.4	150.3	245.0	331.0	293.6
Employees	7.1%	484	454	553	609	637

ZYMOGENETICS INC.

1201 Eastlake Ave. East
Seattle WA 98102-3702
Phone: 206-442-6600
Fax: 206-442-6608
Web: www.zymogenetics.com

CEO: –
CFO: –
HR: –
FYE: December 31
Type: Subsidiary

ZymoGenetics has proteins on its plate. The firm culls genomics databases to identify and develop protein-based drugs targeting a variety conditions. Its sole commercial product RECOTHROM (rThrombin) controls bleeding during surgery. Unlike existing forms of thrombin RECOTHROM is derived from recombinant (genetically engineered) proteins instead of animal or human blood which can trigger adverse reactions. ZymoGenetics' research and development pipeline is focused on autoimmune disease oncology and fibrosis treatments. The company is a subsidiary of Bristol-Myers Squibb (BMS).

Hoover's MasterList of U.S. Companies

Indexes

1 Source Consulting Inc. 2
1-800 CONTACTS INC. 2
1-800 Flowers.com, Inc. 2
1105 Media Inc. 2
1mage Software Inc. 2
1st Century Bancshares, Inc. 2
1st Colonial Bancorp Inc 3
1st Constitution Bancorp 3
1st Franklin Financial Corp. 3
1st Source Corp. 3
1st United Bancorp, Inc. 3
1SYNC Inc. 3
21st Century North America Insurance Company 4
24/7 Real Media Inc. 4
30DC Inc 4
360i LLC 4
3D Systems Corp. (DE) 4
3M Co 4
3M Cogent Inc. 5
3M Purification Inc. 5
454 Life Sciences 5
4Licensing Corp 5
5LINX ENTERPRISES INC. 5
7-Eleven Inc. 5
800-JR Cigar Inc. 6
84 Lumber Company 6
8x8 Inc. 6
99 Cents Only Stores 6
A & H Sportswear Co. Inc. 6
A&E Television Networks LLC 6
A&R Logistics Inc. 7
A&W Restaurants Inc. 7
A. B. Boyd Company 7
A. Duie Pyle Inc. 7
A. Eicoff & Company 7
A. Finkl & Sons Company 7
A. P. HUBBARD WHOLESALE LUMBER
    CORPORATION 8
A.C. Moore Arts & Crafts Inc. 8
A.P. Pharma Inc. 8
A.V. THOMAS PRODUCE INC. 8
A2D Technologies 8
AAA COOPER TRANSPORTATION 8
AAC Group Holding Corp. 9
AAMCO Transmissions Inc. 9
AAON, Inc. 9
AAR Corp 9
AARON AND COMPANY INC. 9
Aaron's, Inc. 9
AARP Inc. 10
Aastra Intecom Inc. 10
Abatix Corp. 10
Abaxis, Inc. 10
Abbott Laboratories 10
AbbVie Inc. 10
ABC Appliance Inc. 11
ABC Cable Networks Group 11
ABC Inc. 11
ABDON CALLAIS OFFSHORE LLC 11
Abeona Therapeutics Inc 11
Abercrombie & Fitch Co. 11
ABF Freight System Inc. 12
ABILENE CHRISTIAN UNIVERSITY INC 12
ABINGTON MEMORIAL HOSPITAL INC 12
ABIOMED, Inc. 12
ABM Industries, Inc. 12
ABM Security Services 12
ABP Corporation 13
ABRA Inc. 13
Abraxas Petroleum Corp. 13
ABS Capital Partners L.P. 13
Abt Associates Inc. 13
Acacia Research Corp 13
Acacia Technologies LLC 14
Academy Ltd. 14
ACADEMY OF MOTION PICTURE ARTS &
    SCIENCES 14
Academy of Television Arts & Sciences Inc. 14
Acadia Healthcare Company Inc. 14
Acadia Pharmaceuticals Inc 14
Acadia Realty Trust 15
ACADIAN AMBULANCE SERVICE INC. 15
Accel Partners 15
Accelerate Diagnostics Inc 15

Acceleron Pharma, Inc. 15
AccelPath Inc 15
Accelrys Inc 16
Accentia Biopharmaceuticals Inc 16
Access National Corp 16
ACCESS Systems Americas Inc. 16
Accident Fund Holdings Inc. 16
Acco Brands Corp 16
Accor North America 17
Accredo Health Incorporated 17
Accretive Health, Inc. 17
AccuCode Inc. 17
Accuray Inc (CA) 17
Accuride Corp 17
Accuride International Inc. 18
Accuvant Inc. 18
Ace Hardware Corporation 18
Ace Parking Management Inc. 18
ACE RELOCATION SYSTEMS INC. 18
ACE USA 18
AcelRx Pharmaceuticals Inc 19
Acento Advertising Incorporated 19
Acer America Corporation 19
Aceto Corp 19
ACF Industries LLC 19
ACH Food Companies Inc. 19
Achillion Pharmaceuticals Inc. 20
ACI Worldwide Inc 20
ACMAT Corp. 20
ACME Communications Inc 20
Acme Markets Inc. 20
Acme United Corp. 20
ACNB Corp. 21
ACO Hardware Inc. 21
Acorda Therapeutics Inc 21
Acorn Energy Inc 21
Acosta Inc. 21
Acquity Group L.L.C. 21
ACRE Realty Investors Inc 22
Acsis Inc. 22
ACT Inc. 22
Actavis U.S. 22
Actelis Networks Inc. 22
ACTION FOR BOSTON COMMUNITY
    DEVELOPMENT REAL ESTATE CORP. 22
ACTIONET INC. 23
ACTIONTEC ELECTRONICS INC. 23
Active Day Inc. 23
Active Media Services Inc. 23
Active Power Inc 23
ActiveCare, Inc. 23
ActiveVideo Networks Inc. 24
ActivIdentity Corporation 24
Activision Blizzard, Inc. 24
Actua Corp 24
Actuant Corp. 24
Actuate Corp. 24
ACUATIVE CORPORATION 25
Acuity A Mutual Insurance Company 25
Acuity Brands Inc (Holding Company) 25
Acumen Solutions Inc. 25
Acura Pharmaceuticals, Inc. 25
Acushnet Company 25
Acxiom Corp. 26
ADA-ES Inc. 26
ADAC PLASTICS INC. 26
Adamis Pharmaceuticals Corporation 26
ADAMS FAIRACRE FARMS INC. 26
Adams Golf Inc. 26
Adams Media 27
Adams Resources & Energy, Inc. 27
ADAMS-COLUMBIA ELECTRIC COOPERATIVE 27
ADB Airfield Solutions LLC 27
AdCare Health Systems, Inc. 27
Addus HomeCare Corp 27
ADDvantage Technologies Group, Inc. 28
ADELPHI UNIVERSITY 28
ADENA HEALTH SYSTEM 28
Adeona Pharmaceuticals Inc. 28
Adept Technology Inc. 28
Adexa Inc. 28
Adherex Technologies Inc. 29
Adirondack Park Agency 29
ADM Investor Services Inc. 29

ADM Tronics Unlimited, Inc. 29
Adobe Systems, Inc. 29
ADT Corp 29
Adtran, Inc. 30
Advance America Cash Advance Centers Inc. 30
Advance Auto Parts Inc 30
Advance Display Technologies Inc. 30
Advance Magazine Publishers Inc. 30
Advance Publications Inc. 30
Advanced Analogic Technologies Incorporated 31
Advanced Energy Industries Inc. 31
Advanced Environmental Recycling Technologies Inc
    31
Advanced Health Media LLC 31
Advanced Lighting Technologies Inc. 31
Advanced Micro Devices, Inc. 31
ADVANCED MP TECHNOLOGY INC. 32
Advanced Photonix, Inc. 32
Advanced Proteome Therapeutics Inc. 32
Advanced Technologies Group Ltd. 32
AdvancePierre Foods Inc. 32
AdvanSource Biomaterials Corp 32
Advant-E Corporation 33
Advantage Sales and Marketing LLC 33
Advent International Corporation 33
Advent Software, Inc. 33
Adventist Health System Sunbelt Healthcare
    Corporation 33
Adventist Health System/West 33
ADVENTIST HEALTHCARE INC. 34
ADVENTRX Pharmaceuticals Inc. 34
Adventureland Park 34
Advisory Board Company (The) 34
AdvizeX Technologies LLC 34
ADVOCATE HEALTH AND HOSPITALS
    CORPORATION 34
Advocate Health Care Network 35
AEA Investors LP 35
Aearo Technologies LLC 35
AECOM 35
Aegerion Pharmaceuticals Inc 35
Aegion Corp 35
Aegis Communications Group Inc. 36
AEGON USA LLC 36
Aehr Test Systems 36
Aeolus Pharmaceuticals Inc 36
AEP Industries Inc. 36
Aero Systems Engineering Inc. 36
Aerocentury Corp. 37
Aeroflex Holding Corp. 37
Aerogroup International LLC 37
AeroGrow International, Inc. 37
Aerojet Rocketdyne Holdings Inc 37
Aerojet-General Corporation 37
AEROKOOL AVIATION CORPORATION 38
AERONET INC. 38
Aeropostale Inc 38
AEROTEK INC. 38
AeroVironment, Inc. 38
Aerus LLC 38
AES Corp. 39
AETEA INFORMATION TECHNOLOGY INC. 39
Aetna Inc. 39
Affiliated Computer Services Inc. 39
AFFILIATED FOODS MIDWEST COOPERATIVE INC.
    39
Affiliated Managers Group Inc. 39
Affinia Group Holdings Inc. 40
Affinion Group Holdings Inc 40
Affirmative Insurance Holdings Inc 40
Affymax Inc 40
Affymetrix, Inc. 40
AFLAC Inc. 40
AFRICARE 41
AG Interactive Inc. 41
AG Mortgage Investment Trust Inc 41
Ag Processing Inc. A Cooperative 41
AG&E Holdings Inc 41
Agar Supply Co. Inc. 41
AGC America Inc. 42
AGC Flat Glass North America Inc. 42
AGCO Corp. 42
AGE GROUP LTD. 42
Agent Information Software Inc 42

Agenus Inc 42
AgFirst Farm Credit Bank 43
Agilent Technologies, Inc. 43
Agilysys Inc 43
Agios Pharmaceuticals Inc 43
AGL Resources Inc. 43
AGNES SCOTT COLLEGE INC. 43
Agree Realty Corp. 44
Agri-Mark Inc. 44
AgriBank FCB 44
AGY Holding Corp. 44
AH Belo Corp 44
Ahold U.S.A. Inc. 44
AHS Hillcrest Medical Center LLC 45
AHS Medical Holdings LLC 45
AIMCO Properties L.P. 45
Air Lease Corp 45
Air Methods Corp. 45
Air Products & Chemicals, Inc. 45
Air T Inc 46
Air Transport Services Group, Inc. 46
Air2Web Inc. 46
airBand Communications Holdings Inc. 46
Aircastle Limited 46
Aircraft Service International Inc. 46
Airgas Inc. 47
AirTran Airways Inc. 47
Airvana Inc. 47
AK Steel Holding Corp. 47
AKAL SECURITY INC. 47
Akamai Technologies Inc 47
Akela Pharma Inc. 48
Akers Biosciences Inc. 48
Akibia Inc. 48
Akorn Inc 48
Akron General Medical Center 48
ALABAMA FARMERS COOPERATIVE INC. 48
Alabama Gas Corporation 49
Alabama Power Co. 49
Alacra Inc. 49
Alamo Group, Inc. 49
Alanco Technologies Inc 49
Alaska Air Group, Inc. 49
Alaska Communications Systems Group Inc 50
Alaska Conservation Foundation 50
ALASKA NATIVE TRIBAL HEALTH CONSORTIUM 50
Alaska Pacific Bancshares Inc. 50
Alaska USA Federal Credit Union 50
ALBANY COLLEGE OF PHARMACY AND HEALTH
    SCIENCES 50
Albany International Corp 51
ALBANY MEDICAL CENTER 51
Albany Molecular Research, Inc. 51
Albemarle Corp. 51
ALBERICI CORPORATION 51
Albertson's LLC 51
ALBION COLLEGE 52
ALBRIGHT COLLEGE 52
Alcatel-Lucent USA Inc. 52
ALCO Stores Inc 52
Alcoa, Inc. 52
ALDA Office Properties Inc. 52
Aldagen Inc. 53
ALDRIDGE ELECTRIC INC. 53
Alere Inc. 53
Aleris Corp 53
Aleris Corporation 53
Alex Lee Inc. 53
Alexander & Baldwin Inc. 54
ALEXANDER AND HORNUNG INC. 54
Alexander's, Inc. 54
ALEXANDRIA EXTRUSION COMPANY 54
ALEXANDRIA INOVA HOSPITAL 54
Alexandria Real Estate Equities, Inc. 54
Alexion Pharmaceuticals Inc. 55
Alexza Pharmaceuticals Inc 55
Alfa Corporation 55
ALFRED UNIVERSITY 55
Alico, Inc. 55
Alienware Corporation 55
Align Aerospace LLC 56
Align Technology Inc 56
Alimera Sciences, Inc. 56
ALINABAL HOLDINGS CORPORATION 56

Alion Science and Technology Corporation 56
AlixPartners LLP 56
ALJ Regional Holdings Inc 57
ALL AMERICAN CONTAINERS INC. 57
All American Group Inc. 57
All American Semiconductor LLC 57
ALL POINTS COOPERATIVE 57
All-American SportPark Inc. 57
Alleghany Corp. 58
ALLEGHENY COLLEGE 58
Allegheny Technologies, Inc 58
Allegiant Travel Company 58
ALLEGIS GROUP INC. 58
Allen & Company LLC 58
ALLEN COMMUNICATION LEARNING SERVICES
    INC. 59
Allen Harim Foods LLC 59
ALLEN LUND COMPANY LLC 59
Allen Organ Company 59
Allen Systems Group Inc. 59
Allen-Edmonds Shoe Corporation 59
Allergan, Inc 60
Allete Inc. 60
ALLEY-CASSETTY COMPANIES INC. 60
Alliance Bancorp Inc. of Pennsylvania 60
Alliance Data Systems Corp. 60
Alliance Entertainment LLC 60
Alliance Fiber Optic Products Inc. 61
Alliance Healthcare Services, Inc. 61
Alliance Holdings Group LP 61
Alliance Laundry Holdings LLC 61
ALLIANCE OF PROFESSIONALS & CONSULTANTS
    INC. 61
Alliance One International Inc 61
Alliance Resource Partners LP 62
AllianceBernstein Holding L P 62
Alliant Credit Union 62
Alliant Energy Corp. 62
ALLIANT INTERNATIONAL UNIVERSITY 62
Allianz Life Insurance Company of North America 62
Allied Building Products Corp. 63
Allied Electronics Inc. 63
Allied Healthcare International Inc. 63
Allied Healthcare Product, Inc. 63
ALLIED INTERNATIONAL CORPORATION OF
    VIRGINIA 63
Allied Motion Technologies Inc 63
Allied Resources Inc 64
Allied Systems Holdings Inc. 64
ALLINA HEALTH SYSTEM 64
Allis-Chalmers Energy Inc. 64
Allison Transmission Holdings Inc 64
Allos Therapeutics Inc. 64
Alloy Inc. 65
Allscripts Healthcare Solutions, Inc. 65
Allstate Corp. 65
Allsteel Inc. 65
Ally Commercial Finance LLC 65
Ally Financial Inc 65
ALMA COLLEGE 66
Almost Family Inc 66
Alnylam Pharmaceuticals Inc 66
Aloha Petroleum Ltd. 66
Alon USA Energy Inc 66
Alon USA Partners LP 66
Alorica Inc. 67
Alpha Associates Inc. 67
Alpha Natural Resources Inc 67
Alpha Pro Tech Ltd. 67
alpha-En Corporation 67
Alphabet Inc 67
Alphatec Holdings Inc 68
Alpine Air Express Inc. 68
ALPS Holdings Inc. 68
ALRO STEEL CORPORATION 68
ALSCO INC. 68
Alseres Pharmaceuticals Inc 68
Alston & Bird LLP 69
Alta Bates Summit Medical Center 69
Alta Mesa Holdings LP 69
Altadis U.S.A. Inc. 69
Altair Nanotechnologies Inc 69
ALTARUM INSTITUTE 69
Altec Lansing LLC 70

Altegrity Inc. 70
Altera Corp. 70
Alternet Systems Inc. 70
Alteva 70
Altex Industries, Inc. 70
Alticor Inc. 71
AltiGen Communications Inc 71
Altra Industrial Motion Corp 71
Altria Group Inc 71
Altru Health System 71
ALTUM INCORPORATED 71
Alvarez & Marsal Holdings LLC 72
ALVERNIA UNIVERSITY 72
ALVERNO COLLEGE 72
Aly Energy Services Inc (DE) 72
Alyeska Pipeline Service Company 72
ALZHEIMER"S DISEASE AND RELATED
    DISORDERS ASSOCIATION INC. 72
Am-Mex Products Inc. 73
AMAG Pharmaceuticals, Inc. 73
Amalgamated Life Insurance Company 73
Amarillo Biosciences Inc. 73
Amazon.com Inc. 73
AMB Financial Corp 73
Ambac Financial Group, Inc. 74
Ambassadors Group Inc 74
Ambient Corp. 74
AMC Entertainment Inc. 74
AMC Entertainment Holdings Inc. 74
AMC Networks Inc 74
AMCOL International Corp. 75
AMCON Distributing Company 75
Amedica Corp 75
Amedisys, Inc. 75
Amen Properties Inc 75
AmerAlia Inc. 75
AmeraMex International Inc. 76
AMERCO 76
Ameren Corp. 76
Ameren Illinois Co 76
Ameresco Inc. 76
Ameriana Bancorp 76
AMERICA CHUNG NAM (GROUP) HOLDINGS LLC
    77
America First Credit Union 77
America's Body Company Inc. 77
America's Car-Mart Inc 77
AMERICAN ACADEMY OF PEDIATRICS 77
American Agip Company Inc. 77
American Air Liquide Inc. 78
American Airlines Federal Credit Union 78
American Airlines Group Inc 78
American Apparel, Inc. 78
AMERICAN ARBITRATION ASSOCIATION INC 78
AMERICAN ASSOCIATION FOR THE
    ADVANCEMENT OF SCIENCE 78
American Axle & Manufacturing Holdings Inc 79
AMERICAN BANKERS ASSOCIATION INC 79
AMERICAN BAPTIST HOMES OF THE WEST 79
AMERICAN BAR ASSOCIATION 79
American Biltrite Inc. 79
American Bio Medica Corp. 79
American Buildings Company 80
AMERICAN BUREAU OF SHIPPING INC 80
American Campus Communities Inc 80
American Cannabis Co Inc 80
American Capital Agency Corp 80
American Capital Ltd. 80
American Capital Mortgage Investment Corp. 81
American CareSource Holdings Inc 81
American Chartered Bancorp Inc. 81
AMERICAN CHEMICAL SOCIETY 81
American City Business Journals Inc. 81
AMERICAN CIVIL LIBERTIES UNION FOUNDATION
    INC. 81
American Commerce Solutions Inc 82
American Commercial Lines Inc. 82
American Community Mutual Insurance Company 82
American Crystal Sugar Company 82
American Defense Systems Inc. 82
AMERICAN DENTAL ASSOCIATION 82
American Dental Partners Inc. 83
American DG Energy Inc 83
American Eagle Outfitters, Inc. 83

American Electric Power Company, Inc. 83
American Electric Technologies, Inc. 83
American Equity Investment Life Holding Co 83
American Eurocopter Corporation 84
American Express Co. 84
American Express Publishing Corporation 84
American Family Mutual Insurance Company 84
AMERICAN FEDERATION OF LABOR & CONGRESS
   OF INDUSTRIAL ORGANZATIO 84
AMERICAN FEDERATION OF STATE COUNTY &
   MUNICIPAL EMPLOYEES 84
American Fiber Green Products Inc 85
American Fidelity Assurance Company 85
American Financial Group Inc 85
American Foods Group LLC 85
AMERICAN FRUIT & PRODUCE CORP. 85
American Furniture Manufacturing Inc. 85
AMERICAN FURNITURE WAREHOUSE CO INC 86
American Furukawa Inc. 86
American General Life Insurance Company 86
American Golf Corporation 86
American Heritage Life Insurance Company 86
American HomePatient Inc. 86
AMERICAN HOSPITAL ASSOCIATION 87
American Hotel Register Company 87
American Independence Corp 87
AMERICAN INFRASTRUCTURE INC. 87
AMERICAN INSTITUTE OF ARCHITECTS INC 87
AMERICAN INSTITUTE OF CERTIFIED PUBLIC
   ACCOUNTANTS 87
AMERICAN INSTITUTE OF PHYSICS
   INCORPORATED 88
AMERICAN INSTITUTES FOR RESEARCH IN THE
   BEHAVIORAL SCIENCES 88
American International Industries Inc 88
American Italian Pasta Company 88
American LaFrance LLC 88
American Land Lease Inc. 88
American Learning Corporation 89
American Leather 89
AMERICAN LIBRARY ASSOCIATION 89
American Licorice Company 89
American Life Insurance Company 89
American Locker Group, Inc. 89
AMERICAN MANAGEMENT ASSOCIATION
   INTERNATIONAL 90
American Management Services West LLC 90
American Media Inc. 90
American Medical Alert Corp. 90
AMERICAN MEDICAL ASSOCIATION INC 90
American Medical Response Ambulance Service Inc.
   90
American Medical Systems Holdings Inc. 91
American Midstream Partners LP 91
American National Bankshares, Inc. (Danville, VA) 91
American National Insurance Co. (Galveston, TX) 91
American Natural Energy Corp. 91
American Nutrition Inc. 91
American Oil & Gas Inc. 92
American Pacific Corp. 92
AMERICAN PETROLEUM INSTITUTE INC 92
AMERICAN PLASTIC TOYS INC. 92
American Pop Corn Company 92
American Power Group Corp 92
AMERICAN PSYCHOLOGICAL ASSOCIATION INC.
   93
American Public Education Inc 93
American Railcar Industries Inc 93
American Realty Capital Trust Inc. 93
American Realty Investors, Inc. 93
American Residential Services L.L.C. 93
American Restaurant Group Inc. 94
American River Bankshares 94
American Savings Bank FSB 94
American Science & Engineering Inc 94
American Seafoods Group LLC 94
American Shared Hospital Services 94
American Snuff Company LLC 95
AMERICAN SOCIETY FOR TESTING AND
   MATERIALS 95
AMERICAN SOCIETY FOR THE PREVENTION OF
   CRUELTY TO ANIMALS (INC) 95
American Software Inc 95
American Soil Technologies Inc 95

American Spectrum Realty, Inc. 95
American Standard Energy Corp 96
American States Water Co. 96
American Superconductor Corp. 96
AMERICAN SYSTEMS CORPORATION 96
American Technical Ceramics Corp. 96
AMERICAN TERRAZZO COMPANY LTD. 96
American Tire Distributors Holdings Inc. 97
American Tower Corp (New) 97
AMERICAN TRANSMISSION COMPANY LLC 97
American Trim LLC 97
American TV & Appliance of Madison Inc. 97
AMERICAN UNIVERSITY 97
American Vanguard Corp. 98
American Water Works Co, Inc. 98
American Woodmark Corp. 98
AMERICARES FOUNDATION INC. 98
AMERICA'S HOME PLACE INC. 98
Americo Life Inc. 98
Americold Realty Trust 99
AMERICUS MORTGAGE CORPORATION 99
Ameriflight LLC 99
AmeriGas Partners, L.P. 99
AMERIGROUP Corporation 99
AmeriPath Inc. 99
Ameriprise Financial Inc 100
AmeriQuest Transportation Services Inc. 100
Ameris Bancorp 100
Amerisafe Inc 100
AmeriServ Financial Inc. 100
AmerisourceBergen Corp. 100
Amerisure Mutual Insurance Company 101
Ameritas Mutual Holding Company 101
Ameritrans Capital Corporation 101
Amerityre Corporation 101
Ameron International Corporation 101
AMERY REGIONAL MEDICAL CENTER INC. 101
AMES CONSTRUCTION INC. 102
Ames National Corp. 102
Ames True Temper Inc. 102
AMETEK, Inc. 102
Amexdrug Corp. 102
Amgen Inc 102
Amicus Therapeutics Inc 103
Amkor Technology Inc. 103
AML Communications Inc. 103
AMN Healthcare Services, Inc. 103
Amos Press Inc. 103
Ampacet Corporation 103
Ampco-Pittsburgh Corp. 104
Amphenol Corp. 104
Ampio Pharmaceuticals Inc 104
AmpliPhi Biosciences Corp 104
AmREIT Inc. 104
AMREP Corp. 104
AMRON INTERNATIONAL INC. 105
AMS Health Sciences Inc. 105
Amscan Holdings Inc. 105
Amsted Industries Incorporated 105
AmSurg Corp 105
AMTEC Precision Products Inc. 105
Amtech Systems, Inc. 106
AmTrust Financial Services Inc 106
Amway International Inc. 106
AMX LLC 106
Amy's Kitchen Inc. 106
Amylin Pharmaceuticals Inc. 106
Amyris, Inc. 107
Anacor Pharmaceuticals Inc 107
Anadarko Petroleum Corp 107
ANADIGICS Inc 107
Anadys Pharmaceuticals Inc. 107
Analog Devices, Inc. 107
Analogic Corp 108
Ancestry.com Inc. 108
Anchin Block & Anchin LLP 108
Anchor BanCorp Wisconsin Inc (DE) 108
Anchor Glass Container Corporation 108
Andalay Solar Inc 108
ANDERSEN CONSTRUCTION COMPANY 109
Andersen Corporation 109
ANDERSON AND DUBOSE INC. 109
Anderson Kill & Olick P.C. 109
Anderson Trucking Service Inc. 109

Andersons, Inc. 109
Andrea Electronics Corp. 110
Angelica Corporation 110
ANGELO STATE UNIVERSITY 110
Angels Baseball LP 110
Angie's List Inc. 110
AngioDynamics Inc 110
Angstrom Graphics Inc. 111
Anheuser-Busch Companies Inc. 111
ANI Pharmaceuticals, Inc. 111
Anika Therapeutics Inc. 111
Anixter International Inc 111
ANN & ROBERT H. LURIE CHILDREN'S HOSPITAL
   OF CHICAGO 111
ANN INC 112
Annaly Capital Management Inc 112
ANNE ARUNDEL MEDICAL CENTER INC. 112
Annie's Inc 112
Anomatic Corporation 112
ANR Pipeline Company 112
Anschutz Company 113
Ansen Corporation 113
Ansys Inc. 113
Antares Pharma Inc. 113
Antero Resources Corp 113
Anthelio Healthcare Solutions Inc. 113
Anthem Inc 114
Anthera Pharmaceuticals Inc. 114
Anthony & Sylvan Pools Corporation 114
Anthony Doors Inc. 114
ANTs Software Inc. 114
Anvil International Inc. 114
Anworth Mortgage Asset Corp. 115
ANXeBusiness Corp. 115
AOL Advertising Inc. 115
AOL Inc. 115
Aon Benfield Inc. 115
Aoxing Pharmaceuticals Co., Inc. 115
APAC Customer Services Inc. 116
Apache Corp. 116
Apache Design Solutions Inc. 116
Apartment Investment & Management Co. 116
Apelon Inc. 116
Apex Tool Group LLC 116
API GROUP INC. 117
API Technologies Corp 117
Apogee Enterprises, Inc. 117
Apollo Commercial Real Estate Finance Inc. 117
Apollo Education Group, Inc. 117
Apollo Global Management LLC 117
Apollo Residential Mortgage, Inc. 118
Appalachian Power Co. 118
Appalachian Regional Healthcare Inc. 118
AppLabs Inc. 118
APPLE AMERICAN GROUP LLC 118
Apple Financial Holdings Inc. 118
Apple Inc 119
Appleton Coated LLC 119
Appleton Papers Inc. 119
Appliance Recycling Centers of America 119
APPLIED CARD SYSTEMS INC. 119
Applied Concepts Inc. 119
Applied Discovery Inc. 120
Applied DNA Sciences Inc 120
Applied Energetics Inc 120
Applied Industrial Technologies, Inc. 120
Applied Materials, Inc. 120
Applied Micro Circuits Corp. 120
Applied Minerals Inc 121
Applied Molecular Evolution Inc. 121
Applied Optoelectronics Inc 121
APPLIED RESEARCH ASSOCIATES INC. 121
Applied Systems Inc. 121
Applied Visual Sciences Inc. 121
Appriss Inc. 122
Approach Resources Inc 122
Apptech Corp 122
Apptis Inc. 122
Apptix Inc. 122
Apria Healthcare Group Inc. 122
Apricus Biosciences Inc 123
Apriso Corporation 123
APS Healthcare Inc. 123
Aptalis Pharma Inc. 123

AVX Corp. 165
Aware Inc. (MA) 165
AXA Equitable Life Insurance Company 165
AXA Financial Inc. 165
AXA Rosenberg Investment Managment LLC 165
Axcelis Technologies Inc 165
Axcess International Inc. 166
AXEL JOHNSON INC. 166
Axesstel Inc 166
Axiall Corp 166
Axion International Holdings Inc 166
AXIS CONSTRUCTION CORP. 166
AxoGen Inc 167
AXSUN Technologies Inc. 167
AXT Inc 167
Azure Midstream Partners LP 167
AZUSA PACIFIC UNIVERSITY 167
AZZ Galvanizing Services 167
AZZ Inc 168
B&G Foods Inc 168
B&R Stores Inc. 168
B&W Technical Services Y-12 LLC 168
B. Braun Medical Inc. 168
B. L. Harbert International L.L.C. 168
B/E Aerospace, Inc 169
BAB Inc 169
BABSON COLLEGE 169
BabyCenter L.L.C. 169
Back Yard Burgers Inc. 169
Backus Corporation 169
Bactolac Pharmaceutical Inc. 170
Badger Meter, Inc. 170
Badgerland Meat and Provisions LLC 170
BAE Systems Inc. 170
BAE Systems Norfolk Ship Repair Inc. 170
BAER'S FURNITURE CO. INC. 170
Bain Capital LLC 171
Baird & Warner Holding Company 171
BakeMark USA LLC 171
Baker & Hostetler LLP 171
Baker & McKenzie LLP 171
BAKER BOOK HOUSE COMPANY 171
Baker Botts L.L.P. 172
Baker Boyer Bancorp 172
Baker Capital 172
Baker Commodities Inc. 172
Baker Donelson Bearman Caldwell & Berkowitz PC 172
Baker Hughes Inc. 172
BAKER MICHAEL JR INC 173
Balchem Corp. 173
Baldor Electric Company 173
Baldwin & Lyons, Inc. 173
Baldwin Filters Inc. 173
Baldwin Piano Inc. 173
Baldwin Richardson Foods Co. 174
Baldwin Technology Company Inc. 174
Balkamp Inc. 174
Ball Corp 174
Ball Horticultural Company 174
BALL STATE UNIVERSITY 174
Ballantyne Strong, Inc. 175
Ballard Spahr LLP 175
Bally Technologies Inc 175
Baltic Trading Limited 175
Baltimore Orioles L.P. 175
Baltimore Ravens Limited Partnership 175
Banana Republic LLC 176
Banc of America Merchant Services LLC 176
Banc of California Inc 176
BancFirst Corp. (Oklahoma City, Okla) 176
Bancinsurance Corporation 176
Banco Popular North America Inc. 176
Bancorp of New Jersey, Inc. 177
BancorpSouth Inc. 177
BancTec Inc. 177
BancWest Corporation 177
Band-It-Idex Inc. 177
Bandai America Incorporated 177
Bank Leumi USA 178
Bank Mutual Corp 178
Bank of America Corp. 178
Bank Of Commerce Holdings (CA) 178
Bank of Hawaii Corp 178

Bank of Kentucky Financial Corp. 178
Bank of Marin Bancorp 179
Bank of McKenney (VA) 179
Bank of New York Mellon Corp 179
Bank Of South Carolina Corp. 179
Bank of the Carolinas Corp 179
Bank of the James Financial Group Inc 179
Bank of the Ozarks, Inc. 180
Bank of the West 180
Bank of Virginia 180
Bankers Financial Corporation 180
BankFinancial Corp 180
Bankrate Inc (DE) 180
BankUnited Inc. 181
Banner Corp. 181
BANNER HEALTH 181
Banner Pharmacaps Inc. 181
BAPTIST HEALTH 181
Baptist Health Care 181
BAPTIST HEALTH SOUTH FLORIDA INC. 182
BAPTIST HEALTHCARE SYSTEM INC. 182
BAPTIST HOSPITAL OF MIAMI INC. 182
BAPTIST MEMORIAL HEALTH CARE CORPORATION 182
BAPTIST MEMORIAL HOSPITAL 182
Bar Harbor Bankshares 182
Baran Telecom Inc. 183
Barcelo Crestline Corporation 183
Barclays Bank Delaware 183
Bard (CR) Inc 183
BARD COLLEGE 183
Bare Escentuals Inc. 183
Barkley Inc. 184
Barnes & Noble College Booksellers LLC 184
Barnes & Noble Inc 184
Barnes & Thornburg LLP 184
Barnes Group Inc. 184
Barnes-Jewish Hospital 184
barnesandnoble.com llc 185
Barneys New York Inc. 185
Barnhill Contracting Company 185
Barnwell Industries, Inc. 185
Barracuda Networks Inc 185
Barrett (Bill) Corp 185
Barrett Business Services, Inc. 186
Barry (R.G.) Corp. 186
BARRY UNIVERSITY INC. 186
BARRY-WEHMILLER GROUP INC. 186
BARTON MALOW COMPANY 186
BASF Catalysts LLC 186
Bashas' Inc. 187
Basic American Inc. 187
Basic Energy Services Inc 187
Basin Electric Power Cooperative 187
Basis Technology Corporation 187
Bass Pro Inc. 187
Bassett Furniture Industries, Inc 188
Batesville Tool & Die Inc. 188
Bath & Body Works LLC 188
Bath Iron Works Corporation 188
BATON ROUGE GENERAL MEDICAL CENTER 188
Batson-Cook Company 188
Battalia Winston International 189
BATTELLE MEMORIAL INSTITUTE INC 189
BATTLE CREEK FARMERS COOPERATIVE NON-STOCK 189
BAUER BUILT INC. 189
Bauer Publishing USA 189
Bausch & Lomb Incorporated 189
Baxano Surgical Inc 190
BAXTER COUNTY REGIONAL HOSPITAL INC. 190
Baxter International Inc. 190
Bay Bancorp Inc 190
BAY CITIES PAVING & GRADING INC. 190
BAY MEDICAL CENTER 190
BAY REGIONAL MEDICAL CENTER 191
Bayer Corporation 191
Bayer HealthCare Pharmaceuticals Inc. 191
Baylake Corp. (WI) 191
Baylor Health Care System 191
BAYLOR UNIVERSITY 191
BAYLOR UNIVERSITY MEDICAL CENTER 192
Bayou City Exploration Inc 192
BAYSIDE FUEL OIL DEPOT CORP 192

BAYSTATE HEALTH SYSTEM HEALTH SERVICES INC. 192
BAYSTATE MEDICAL CENTER INC. 192
Bazaarvoice Inc. 192
BB&T Corp. 193
BBDO Worldwide Inc. 193
BBX Capital Corp 193
BCB Bancorp Inc 193
BCT International Inc. 193
BDO USA LLP 193
BDP International Inc. 194
Beacon Capital Partners LLC 194
Beacon Power Corporation 194
Beacon Roofing Supply Inc 194
Bead Industries Inc. 194
Beal Bank s.s.b. 194
BEALL'S INC. 195
Beam Inc 195
Bear State Financial Inc 195
BEARING DISTRIBUTORS INC. 195
Beasley Broadcast Group Inc 195
BeautiControl Inc. 195
Beauty Systems Group LLC 196
BEAVER DAM COMMUNITY HOSPITALS INC. 196
BEAVER STREET FISHERIES INC. 196
Beazer Homes USA, Inc. 196
Bebe Stores Inc 196
Bechtel Group Inc. 196
BECK SUPPLIERS INC. 197
Becton, Dickinson and Co. 197
Bed, Bath & Beyond, Inc. 197
BEEBE MEDICAL CENTER INC. 197
Beech-Nut Nutrition Corporation 197
Behlen Mfg. Co. 197
Behrman Capital L.P. 198
Bekaert Corporation 198
Bekins Holding Corp. 198
Bel Fuse, Inc. 198
BELCAN CORPORATION 198
Belden & Blake Corporation 198
Belden Inc 199
BELFOR USA Group Inc. 199
Belk Inc (DE) 199
Belkin International Inc. 199
Bell Helicopter Textron Inc. 199
Bell Partners Inc. 199
BELOIT COLLEGE 200
BELOIT HEALTH SYSTEM INC. 200
Bemis Co Inc 200
Benchmark Electronics, Inc. 200
BENCO DENTAL SUPPLY CO. 200
Benderson Development Company LLC 200
BENEDICT COLLEGE 201
BENEDICTINE COLLEGE 201
Benedictine Health System 201
Beneficial Life Insurance Company 201
Beneficial Mutual Bancorp Inc 201
BeneFit Cosmetics LLC 201
Benefit Software Inc. 202
BenefitMall Inc. 202
Benihana Inc. 202
Benjamin Moore & Co. 202
Bentley Systems Incorporated 202
BENTLEY UNIVERSITY 202
BEREA COLLEGE 203
BERGELECTRIC CORP. 203
BERGEN REGIONAL MEDICAL CENTER L.P. 203
Berkeley Farms LLC 203
BERKLEE COLLEGE OF MUSIC INC. 203
Berkley (W. R.) Corp. 203
Berkley Insurance Company 204
Berkshire Bancorp Inc (DE) 204
Berkshire Hathaway Inc. 204
Berkshire Health Systems Inc. 204
Berkshire Hills Bancorp, Inc. 204
Berkshire Income Realty Inc 204
Berkshire Partners LLC 205
Berlin Packaging L.L.C. 205
Berlitz Languages Inc. 205
Bernard Chaus Inc. 205
Bernard Hodes Group Inc. 205
BERNATELLO"S PIZZA INC 205
BERNER FOOD & BEVERAGE INC. 206
BERRY COMPANIES INC. 206

Berry Plastics Group Inc 206
Bertucci's Corporation 206
Best Brands Corp. 206
Best Buy Inc 206
Best Friends Pet Care Inc. 207
Best Medical International Inc. 207
BEST WESTERN INTERNATIONAL INC. 207
Best Wings USA Inc. 207
BET Interactive LLC 207
BETH ISRAEL DEACONESS MEDICAL CENTER INC. 207
BETH ISRAEL MEDICAL CENTER 208
BETHUNE-COOKMAN UNIVERSITY INC. 208
Betsey Johnson LLC 208
BFC Financial Corp. 208
BG Medicine Inc 208
BGC Partners, Inc. 208
BHE Environmental Inc. 209
BI-LO Holding LLC 209
BI-RITE RESTAURANT SUPPLY CO. INC. 209
Bidz.com Inc. 209
Big 5 Sporting Goods Corp 209
Big Lots, Inc. 209
Big West Oil LLC 210
Big Y Foods Inc. 210
BIG-D CONSTRUCTION CORP. 210
Biglari Holdings Inc. 210
Bill & Melinda Gates Foundation 210
BILLINGS CLINIC 210
Bimini Capital Management Inc 211
Bind Therapeutics Inc 211
Bingham McCutchen LLP 211
BIO-key International Inc 211
Bio-Rad Laboratories, Inc. 211
Bio-Reference Laboratories, Inc. 211
Bio-Solutions Manufacturing Inc. 212
Bio-Techne Corp 212
BioAmber Inc 212
Bioanalytical Systems, Inc. 212
Biocept, Inc 212
BioCryst Pharmaceuticals, Inc. 212
Biodel Inc. 213
BioDelivery Sciences International Inc 213
BioFuel Energy Corp 213
Biogen Inc 213
BioHorizons Inc. 213
Bioject Medical Technologies Inc. 213
BIOLA UNIVERSITY INC. 214
BioLargo Inc 214
Biolase, Inc 214
Biolife Solutions Inc 214
Biomed Realty Trust Inc 214
Biomerica, Inc. 214
Biomet Inc. 215
BioMimetic Therapeutics Inc. 215
Bion Environmental Technologies, Inc. 215
Biophan Technologies Inc. 215
BioReliance Corporation 215
BioScrip Inc 215
Biospecifics Technologies Corp. 216
Biosynergy, Inc. 216
Biota Pharmaceuticals Inc 216
BioTelemetry, Inc. 216
BioTime Inc 216
Birds Eye Foods LLC 216
Birkenstock USA GP LLC 217
BIRMINGHAM-SOUTHERN COLLEGE INC 217
Birner Dental Management Services, Inc. 217
Biscom Inc. 217
Bison Building Materials Ltd. 217
BISSELL Homecare Inc. 217
Bitco Corporation 218
Bitstream Inc. 218
BJ's Restaurants Inc 218
BJ's Wholesale Club Inc. 218
BJT INC. 218
BKF Capital Group Inc 218
BLACK & VEATCH CORPORATION 219
Black Box Corp. (DE) 219
Black Diamond Inc. 219
Black Entertainment Television LLC 219
Black Hills Corporation 219
Black Hills Power Inc. 219
Black Raven Energy Inc. 220

Blackbaud, Inc. 220
Blackboard Inc. 220
BLACKFOOT TELEPHONE COOPERATIVE INC. 220
Blackhawk Network Holdings Inc 220
BlackRock, Inc. 220
Blackstone Group LP (The) 221
Blackstone Mortgage Trust Inc 221
Blair Corporation 221
BLANCHARD VALLEY FARMERS COOPERATIVE INC. 221
Blank Rome LLP 221
BLARNEY CASTLE OIL CO. 221
BLESSING HOSPITAL 222
BLISH-MIZE CO. 222
Blizzard Entertainment Inc. 222
Block (H & R), Inc. 222
Blockbuster L.L.C. 222
Blonder Tongue Laboratories, Inc. 222
BLOOD SYSTEMS INC. 223
Bloomberg L.P. 223
Bloomin' Brands Inc. 223
Blount International Inc 223
Blucora, Inc. 223
Blue Bird Corporation 223
Blue Care Network of Michigan 224
BLUE CROSS & BLUE SHIELD ASSOCIATION 224
Blue Cross & Blue Shield of Mississippi 224
Blue Cross & Blue Shield of Rhode Island 224
Blue Cross and Blue Shield of Alabama 224
BLUE CROSS AND BLUE SHIELD OF ARIZONA INC. 224
Blue Cross and Blue Shield of Massachusetts Inc. 225
Blue Cross and Blue Shield of Minnesota 225
Blue Cross and Blue Shield of Montana 225
Blue Cross and Blue Shield of North Carolina 225
Blue Cross and Blue Shield of Texas 225
Blue Cross and Blue Shield of Vermont 225
Blue Cross Blue Shield of Georgia Inc 226
Blue Cross Blue Shield of Michigan 226
Blue Cross of California 226
Blue Cross of Idaho Health Service Inc. 226
Blue Dolphin Energy Co. 226
Blue Nile Inc 226
Blue Shield of California Life & Health Insurance Com 227
Blue Sky Studios Inc. 227
BLUE TEE CORP. 227
Blue Valley Ban Corp (KS) 227
BlueArc Corporation 227
bluebird bio Inc 227
BLUEBONNET ELECTRIC COOPERATIVE INC. 228
BlueChoice HealthPlan of South Carolina Inc. 228
BlueCross BlueShield of Tennessee Inc. 228
Blueknight Energy Partners L P 228
BlueLinx Holdings Inc 228
Bluepoint Solutions Inc. 228
BlueStar Energy Services Inc. 229
Bluestem Brands Inc. 229
Blyth, Inc. 229
BMO Financial Corp. 229
BMW of North America LLC 229
BNC Bancorp 229
BNCCORP Inc 230
BNS Holding Inc. 230
BOARD OF TRUSTEES OF COMMUNITY COLLEGE DISTRICT 508 (INC) 230
Boardwalk Pipeline Partners LP 230
Bob Evans Farms, Inc. 230
BOB ROSS BUICK INC. 230
BODDIE-NOELL ENTERPRISES INC. 231
Body Central Corp. 231
Boeing Capital Corp 231
Boeing Co. (The) 231
Boeing Employees' Credit Union 231
Boeing Satellite Systems International Inc. 231
Bofl Holding, Inc. 232
Bogen Communications International Inc. 232
Boingo Wireless Inc 232
Boise Cascade Co. (DE) 232
Bojangles' Restaurants Inc. 232
BOK Financial Corp. 232
Bollinger Shipyards Inc. 233
Bolt Technology Corp. 233
BON SECOURS HEALTH SYSTEM INC 233

Bon-Ton Stores Inc 233
Bonanza Creek Energy, Inc. 233
BONITZ INC. 233
Bonneville Power Administration 234
Bonnier Corporation 234
Books-A-Million, Inc. 234
Bookspan 234
Booz Allen Hamilton Holding Corp. 234
BORGESS MEDICAL CENTER 234
Borghese Inc. 235
BorgWarner Inc 235
Bosch Communications Systems 235
Bosch Security Systems Inc. 235
Boss Holdings Inc. 235
Bosselman Inc. 235
Boston Acoustics Inc. 236
Boston Beer Co., Inc 236
BOSTON MEDICAL CENTER CORPORATION 236
Boston Mutual Life Insurance Company 236
Boston Private Financial Holdings, Inc. 236
Boston Properties, Inc. 236
Boston Red Sox Baseball Club Limited Partnership 237
Boston Restaurant Associates Inc. 237
Boston Scientific Corp. 237
BOSTON SYMPHONY ORCHESTRA INC. 237
BostonCoach 237
Bottomline Technologies (Delaware) Inc 237
Boulder Brands Inc 238
Bovie Medical Corp 238
BOWEN ENGINEERING CORPORATION 238
Bowl America Inc. 238
Bowlin Travel Centers Inc. 238
BOY SCOUTS OF AMERICA 238
Boyd Coffee Company 239
Boyd Gaming Corp. 239
BOYS & GIRLS CLUBS OF AMERICA 239
Bozzuto's Inc. 239
BPZ Resources, Inc. 239
Bradford Soap Works Inc. 239
Bradford White Corporation 240
BRADLEY UNIVERSITY 240
Brady Corp. 240
Brake Parts Inc. 240
BRANCH & ASSOCIATES INC. 240
BRANDEIS UNIVERSITY 240
Brandywine Realty Trust 241
Brant Industries Inc. 241
Brasfield & Gorrie L.L.C. 241
Bravo Brio Restaurant Group Inc 241
Bravo Media LLC 241
BRAZOS ELECTRIC POWER COOPERATIVE INC. 241
BRE Properties, Inc. 242
Breeze-Eastern Corp 242
Breitburn Energy Partners LP 242
BRENTWOOD INDUSTRIES INC. 242
Bridge Bancorp, Inc. (Bridgehampton, NY) 242
Bridge Capital Holdings 242
Bridgeline Digital, Inc. 243
Bridgepoint Education, Inc. 243
BRIDGEPORT HOSPITAL & HEALTHCARE SERVICES INC 243
Bridgestone Americas Inc. 243
Bridgestone Retail Operations LLC 243
Bridgford Foods Corp. 243
Briggs & Stratton Corp. 244
Briggs & Stratton Power Products Group LLC 244
Brigham Exploration Company 244
Bright Horizons Family Solutions Inc. 244
Bright House Networks LLC 244
Brightcove Inc 244
Brightpoint Inc. 245
Brightstar Corp. 245
Brillstein Entertainment Partners LLC 245
Brinker International, Inc. 245
Brinks Co (The) 245
BRISTOL HOSPITAL INCORPORATED 245
Bristol-Myers Squibb Co. 246
Bristow Group Inc 246
Britton & Koontz Capital Corp. 246
Brixmor Property Group Inc 246
Broadcast International Inc 246
Broadcast Music Inc. 246

Broadcom Corp. 247
Broadridge Financial Solutions Inc 247
BroadSoft Inc 247
Broadview Institute Inc 247
Broadview Networks Holdings Inc. 247
BroadVision Inc. 247
Broadway Bancshares Inc. 248
Broadway Financial Corp. (DE) 248
Broadwind Energy, Inc. 248
Broan-NuTone LLC 248
Brocade Communications Systems, Inc. 248
BROCKTON HOSPITAL INC. 248
Broder Bros. Co. 249
Bromley Communications 249
BRONSON HEALTH CARE GROUP INC. 249
BRONSON METHODIST HOSPITAL INC 249
BRONX LEBANON HOSPITAL CENTER (INC) 249
Brookdale Senior Living Inc 249
BROOKHAVEN MEMORIAL HOSPITAL MEDICAL
    CENTER INC. 250
Brookline Bancorp Inc (DE) 250
BROOKLYN ACADEMY OF MUSIC INC 250
BROOKLYN HOSPITAL CENTER 250
BROOKLYN NAVY YARD DEVELOPMENT
    CORPORATION 250
Brookmount Explorations Inc. 250
Brooks Automation Inc 251
BROOKS TROPICALS HOLDING INC. 251
Brookstone Inc. 251
Brother International Corporation 251
BROWN & BIGELOW INC. 251
Brown & Brown, Inc. 251
Brown Brothers Harriman & Co. 252
Brown Jordan International Inc. 252
Brown Printing Company 252
Brown-Forman Corp. 252
Browning Arms Company 252
Broyhill Furniture Industries Inc. 252
BRT Realty Trust 253
Bruce Foods Corporation 253
BRUCE OAKLEY INC. 253
Bruker AXS Inc. 253
Bruker Corp 253
Bruker Daltonics Inc. 253
Bruker Energy & Supercon Technologies Inc. 254
Bruno Independent Living Aids Inc. 254
Brunswick Corp. 254
Bryan Cave LLP 254
BRYAN MEDICAL CENTER 254
Bryce Corporation 254
Bryn Mawr Bank Corp. 255
BRYN MAWR COLLEGE 255
BSB Bancorp Inc. (MD) 255
BSH Home Appliances Corporation 255
BSQUARE Corp 255
BT Conferencing 255
BTU International, Inc. 256
Bubba Gump Shrimp Co. Restaurants Inc. 256
Buckeye Partners, L.P. 256
BUCKEYE POWER INC. 256
Buckhead Life Restaurant Group Inc. 256
Buckle, Inc. (The) 256
BUCKNELL UNIVERSITY 257
Budget Rent A Car System Inc. 257
Buffalo Bills Inc. 257
Buffalo Wild Wings Inc 257
Build-A-Bear Workshop Inc 257
Builders FirstSource Inc. 257
Builders FirstSource-Southeast Group LLC 258
Bulldog Solutions Inc. 258
Bulova Corporation 258
Bulova Technologies Group, Inc 258
Bunge Limited 258
Bunge Milling Inc. 258
Burger King Worldwide Inc. 259
Burgett Inc. 259
BURKHART DENTAL SUPPLY CO. 259
Burlington Northern & Santa Fe Railway Co. (The)
    259
Burlington Northern Santa Fe LLC 259
Burlington Stores Inc 259
Burrell Communications Group LLC 260
Burrill & Company LLC 260
Burroughs & Chapin Company Inc. 260

Burson-Marsteller Inc. 260
Burst Media Corporation 260
BURTON LUMBER & HARDWARE CO. 260
Bush Industries Inc. 261
Bushnell Inc. 261
BUSKEN BAKERY INC. 261
BUSY BEAVER BUILDING CENTERS INC. 261
Butler Manufacturing Company 261
Butler National Corp. 261
Buzzi Unicem USA Inc. 262
BWAY Holding Company 262
BWX Technologies inc 262
BYCOR GENERAL CONTRACTORS INC. 262
C & F Financial Corp. 262
C & K MARKET INC. 262
C&A Industries Inc. 263
C&D Zodiac Inc. 263
C&J Energy Services Inc. 263
C&S Wholesale Grocers Inc. 263
C. B. FLEET COMPANY INCORPORATED 263
C.D. SMITH CONSTRUCTION INC. 263
C.H. Guenther & Son Inc. 264
C.R. ENGLAND INC. 264
CA Inc 264
Cabelas Inc 264
Cable Manufacturing and Assembly Co. Inc. 264
Cable News Network Inc. 264
Cable One Inc. 265
Cablevision Systems Corp. 265
CABLEXPRESS CORPORATION 265
Cabot Corp. 265
Cabot Microelectronics Corp 265
Cabot Oil & Gas Corp. 265
Cache Inc 266
CACI International Inc. 266
Cactus Feeders Inc. 266
Cadence Design Systems Inc 266
CADENCE MCSHANE CONSTRUCTION COMPANY
    LLC 266
Cadence Pharmaceuticals Inc 266
CADIZ Inc 267
Cadus Corporation 267
Cadwalader Wickersham & Taft LLP 267
Caesars Entertainment Corp 267
Cafe Enterprises Inc. 267
CafePress Inc 267
Cahill Gordon & Reindel LLP 268
CAI International Inc 268
Caithness Corporation 268
CAJUN INDUSTRIES LLC 268
Cal Dive International Inc 268
Cal-Maine Foods, Inc. 268
Caladrius Biosciences Inc 269
Calamos Asset Management Inc 269
CalAmp Corp 269
CalAtlantic Group Inc 269
Calavo Growers, Inc. 269
CALCOT LTD. 269
Calendar Holdings LLC 270
Caleres Inc 270
Calgon Carbon Corp. 270
CALIBRE SYSTEMS INC. 270
Calient Networks Inc. 270
California Bank & Trust 270
California Coastal Communities Inc. 271
CALIFORNIA COMMUNITY FOUNDATION 271
California Dairies Inc. 271
California First National Bancorp 271
CALIFORNIA INDEPENDENT SYSTEM OPERATOR
    CORPORATION 271
California Physicians' Service 271
California Pizza Kitchen Inc. 272
California Products Corporation 272
California Public Employees' Retirement System 272
California Steel Industries Inc. 272
California Water Service Group (DE) 272
CALIFORNIA WELLNESS FOUNDATION 272
Caliper Life Sciences Inc. 273
Calix Inc 273
Call Now Inc. 273
Callaway Golf Co. (DE) 273
Callidus Software Inc 273
Callon Petroleum Co. (DE) 273
Calloway's Nursery Inc. 274

Calmare Therapeutics Inc 274
CALNET INC. 274
Calpine Corp 274
CalPortland Company 274
Calumet Specialty Product Partners LP 274
CALVARY HOSPITAL INC. 275
CALVERT COMPANY INC. 275
CALVERT MEMORIAL HOSPITAL OF CALVERT
    COUNTY 275
Calypso Technology Inc. 275
Calypte Biomedical Corporation 275
Cambium Learning Group, Inc. 275
Cambrex Corp 276
Cambridge Bancorp 276
Cambridge Heart Inc. 276
CAMBRIDGE PUBLIC HEALTH COMMISSION 276
Cambridge SoundWorks Inc. 276
Camco Financial Corp 276
Camden National Corp. (ME) 277
Camden Property Trust 277
Camelot Entertainment Group Inc. 277
Cameron International Corp 277
Cameron Mitchell Restaurants LLC 277
CAMPAGNA-TURANO BAKERY INC. 277
Campbell Mithun Inc. 278
Campbell Soup Co. 278
Campbell-Ewald Company 278
Campus Crest Communities Inc 278
Camstar Systems Inc. 278
Can-Cal Resources Ltd. 278
Canaan Management Inc. 279
Canaccord Genuity Inc. 279
Canandaigua National Corp. 279
Cancer Genetics, Inc. 279
Candela Corporation 279
Candlewick Press Inc. 279
Cannondale Bicycle Corporation 280
Canon U.S.A. Inc. 280
Canon Virginia Inc. 280
Cantel Medical Corp 280
Canterbury Park Holding Corp. 280
Cantor Entertainment Technology Inc. 280
Cantor Fitzgerald L.P. 281
Capcom U.S.A. Inc. 281
Cape Bancorp, Inc. 281
CAPE COD HEALTHCARE INC. 281
CAPE COD HOSPITAL 281
CAPE ENVIRONMENTAL MANAGEMENT INC. 281
Capella Education Company 282
Capgemini North America Inc. 282
Capital Bank Corporation 282
Capital Bank Financial Corp 282
Capital BlueCross 282
Capital City Bank Group, Inc. 282
CAPITAL DISTRICT PHYSICIANS' HEALTH PLAN
    INC. 283
CAPITAL HEALTH SYSTEM INC. 283
Capital One Financial Corp 283
Capital Properties, Inc. 283
Capital Senior Living Corp. 283
Capital Southwest Corp. 283
CapitalSource Inc. 284
Capitol Federal Financial Inc 284
Capri Capital Partners LLC 284
Capricor Therapeutics Inc 284
Caprius Inc. 284
CapRock Communications Inc. 284
Capsonic Group LLC 285
Capstone Turbine Corp. 285
Captain D's LLC 285
CAPTECH VENTURES INC. 285
Cara Therapeutics Inc 285
Caraco Pharmaceutical Laboratories Ltd. 285
Carahsoft Technology Corp. 286
Caraustar Recovered Fiber Group Inc. 286
Carbo Ceramics Inc. 286
Carbonite Inc 286
Cardean Learning Group LLC 286
Cardiac Science Corporation 286
Cardica Inc 287
Cardinal Bankshares Corp. 287
Cardinal Financial Corp 287
Cardinal Health Pharmacy Solutions 287
Cardinal Health, Inc. 287

Chesapeake Oilfield Services Inc. 329
Chesapeake Utilities Corp. 329
CHESHIRE OIL COMPANY INC. 329
Cheviot Financial Corp 329
Chevron Corporation 330
Chevron Phillips Chemical Company LP 330
Chevys Restaurants LLC 330
Chicago Airport System 330
Chicago Bears Football Club Inc. 330
Chicago Blackhawk Hockey Team Inc. 330
Chicago Meat Authority Inc. 331
Chicago National League Ball Club Inc. 331
Chicago Rivet & Machine Co. 331
Chicago Transit Authority 331
Chicago White Sox Ltd. 331
CHICKASAW HOLDING COMPANY 331
Chico's FAS Inc 332
Chicopee Bancorp Inc 332
CHIEF INDUSTRIES INC. 332
CHILDFUND INTERNATIONAL USA 332
Children's Health System 332
Children's Health System Inc. 332
Children's Hospital & Medical Center 333
Children's Hospital and Health System 333
Children's Hospital Colorado 333
CHILDREN'S HOSPITAL MEDICAL CENTER 333
Children's Hospital of Orange County 333
Children's Hospital of Pittsburgh of UPMC Health
  System 333
Children's Place, Inc. (The) 334
CHILDRENS HOSPITAL MEDICAL CENTER OF
  AKRON 334
CHILDREN'S MEDICAL CENTER OF DALLAS 334
CHILDREN'S NATIONAL MEDICAL CENTER 334
Childress Klein Properties Inc. 334
CHILTON HOSPITAL 334
Chimera Investment Corp 335
Chimerix Inc. 335
China Education Alliance Inc 335
China Recycling Energy Corp 335
Chindex International Inc 335
Chipotle Mexican Grill Inc 335
CHIPPEWA VALLEY BEAN COMPANY INC. 336
Chiquita Brands International, Inc. 336
Choice Hotels International, Inc. 336
ChoiceOne Financial Services, Inc. 336
Christian Casey LLC 336
CHRISTIAN FOUNDATION FOR CHILDREN AND
  AGING 336
CHRISTIAN HOSPITAL NORTHEAST - NORTHWEST
  337
Christiana Care Health System 337
Christopher & Banks Corp. 337
CHRISTOPHER RANCH LLC 337
CHRISTUS HEALTH 337
CHRISTUS HEALTH CENTRAL LOUISIANA 337
CHRISTUS St. Catherine Hospital 338
CHRISTY SPORTS L.L.C. 338
ChromaDex Corp 338
Chrysler Group LLC 338
CHS Inc 338
Chubb Corp. 338
CHUGACH ALASKA CORPORATION 339
Chugach Electric Association, Inc. 339
Church & Dwight Co., Inc. 339
Church Mutual Insurance Company 339
Church Pension Group Services Corporation 339
Churchill Downs, Inc. 339
Chuy's Holdings Inc 340
ChyronHego Corp 340
CIB Marine Bancshares Inc 340
CIBER, Inc. 340
CIC GROUP INC. 340
Cicero Inc 340
CiCi Enterprises LP 341
Ciena Corp 341
CIFC Corp 341
Cigna Corp 341
CIM Commercial Trust Corp 341
Cimarex Energy Co 341
Cincinnati Bell Inc 342
Cincinnati Bengals Inc. 342
Cincinnati Financial Corp. 342
Cinedigm Corp 342

Cinemark Holdings Inc 342
Ciner Resources LP 342
Cinnabon Inc. 343
Cintas Corporation 343
Circor International Inc 343
Cirrus Design Corporation 343
Cirrus Logic, Inc. 343
CirTran Corp. 343
Cisco Systems, Inc. 344
Cisco WebEx LLC 344
Cision US Inc. 344
CIT Group, Inc. 344
CIT Small Business Lending Corporation 344
Citadel LLC 344
CITATION OIL & GAS CORP. 345
CITGO Petroleum Corporation 345
Citi Trends Inc 345
Citigroup Global Markets Inc. 345
Citigroup Inc 345
CitiMortgage Inc. 345
Citizens & Northern Corp 346
Citizens Bancshares Corp. (GA) 346
Citizens Community Bancorp Inc (MD) 346
CITIZENS ENERGY GROUP 346
Citizens Equity First Credit Union 346
Citizens Financial Corp. (WV) 346
Citizens Financial Group Inc (New) 347
Citizens Financial Services, Inc 347
Citizens First Corp. 347
Citizens Holding Co 347
Citizens Property Insurance Corporation 347
Citizens, Inc. (Austin, TX) 347
Citrix Systems, Inc. 348
CITRUS VALLEY HEALTH PARTNERS INC. 348
CITY HARVEST INC. 348
City Holding Co. 348
City National Corp. (Beverly Hills, CA) 348
City of Houston Texas 348
CITY OF SALINAS 349
City of Seattle - City Light Department 349
City of Tacoma Department of Public Utilities 349
CITY PUBLIC SERVICES OF SAN ANTONIO 349
CITY UTILITIES OF SPRINGFIELD MO 349
CITYSERVICEVALCON LLC 349
Civista Bancshares Inc 350
CKX Inc. 350
CKX Lands Inc 350
CLAFLIN UNIVERSITY 350
Claire's Stores Inc. 350
Clarcor Inc. 350
CLARE ROSE INC. 351
CLAREMONT GRADUATE UNIVERSITY 351
CLAREMONT MCKENNA COLLEGE FOUNDATION
  351
Clarient Inc. 351
Clarion Partners LLC 351
Clark Construction Group LLC 351
Clark Enterprises Inc. 352
CLARK Material Handling Company 352
CLARKSON UNIVERSITY 352
Clarus Therapeutics Inc. 352
Classified Ventures LLC 352
CLAY ELECTRIC COOPERATIVE INC. 352
CLAYCO INC. 353
Clean Diesel Technologies Inc. 353
Clean Energy Fuels Corp 353
Clean Harbors, Inc 353
CLEANNET U.S.A. INC. 353
Clear Channel Communications Inc. 353
Clear Channel Outdoor Holdings Inc 354
CLEARFIELD HOSPITAL 354
Clearfield Inc 354
ClearOne Inc 354
Clearview Hotel Capital LLC 354
Clearwater Paper Corp 354
Cleary Gottlieb Steen & Hamilton LLP 355
CLEARY UNIVERSITY 355
Cleaver-Brooks Inc. 355
Cleco Corp. 355
Clement Pappas & Company Inc. 355
Cleveland BioLabs Inc 355
Cleveland Browns Football Company LLC 356
CLEVELAND CONSTRUCTION INC. 356
Cleveland Indians Baseball Company Inc. 356

Click Commerce Inc. 356
Clicker, Inc. 356
CLIENT NETWORK SERVICES INC. 356
CLIENT SERVICES INC. 357
Cliffs Natural Resources, Inc. 357
Clifton Savings Bancorp Inc 357
CLIFTONLARSONALLEN LLP 357
Clinton Group Inc. 357
Clockwork Home Services Inc. 357
Clopay Corporation 358
Clorox Co (The) 358
Cloud Peak Energy Inc 358
CloudCommerce Inc 358
Clover Technologies Group LLC 358
Clovis Oncology Inc. 358
ClubCorp Holdings Inc 359
Clyde Companies Inc. 359
CME Group Inc 359
CMFG Life Insurance Company 359
CMI Terex Corporation 359
CMS Bancorp Inc 359
CMS Energy Corp 360
CNA Financial Corp. 360
CNA Surety Corporation 360
CNB Corp (MI) 360
CNB Financial Corp. (Clearfield, PA) 360
CNL Financial Group Inc. 360
CNO Financial Group Inc 361
CNX Gas Corporation 361
Coach, Inc. 361
COAST CITRUS DISTRIBUTORS 361
Coast Distribution System 361
COAST ELECTRIC POWER ASSOCIATION 361
Coastal Banking Co Inc 362
COASTAL CAROLINA UNIVERSITY 362
COASTAL PACIFIC FOOD DISTRIBUTORS INC. 362
Coates International, Ltd. 362
Coating Place Inc. 362
Cobalt International Energy L.P. 362
COBB ELECTRIC MEMBERSHIP CORPORATION 363
CoBiz Financial Inc 363
COBORN'S INCORPORATED 363
Cobra Electronics Corp. 363
Coca-Cola Bottling Co. Consolidated 363
Coca-Cola Co (The) 363
Coca-Cola Enterprises Inc 364
CODALE ELECTRIC SUPPLY INC. 364
Codexis Inc 364
Codman & Shurtleff Inc. 364
Codorus Valley Bancorp, Inc. 364
COE COLLEGE 364
Coeur Mining, Inc. 365
Coffee Holding Co Inc 365
Cogent Communications Holdings, Inc. 365
Cogentix Medical Inc 365
Cognex Corp. 365
Cognizant Technology Solutions Corp. 365
Cohen & Steers Inc 366
Cohen Financial L.P. 366
Coherent, Inc. 366
Cohesant Technologies Inc. 366
Cohn & Wolfe 366
Cohu, Inc. 366
COLAVITA USA L.L.C. 367
COLBY COLLEGE 367
Cold Stone Creamery Inc. 367
Coldwater Creek Inc. 367
Cole Haan 367
Coleman Technologies Inc. 367
Colfax Corp 368
Colgate-Palmolive Co. 368
Collabera Inc. 368
Collective Brands Inc. 368
Collectors Universe Inc 368
COLLEGE ENTRANCE EXAMINATION BOARD 368
COLLEGE OF SAINT BENEDICT 369
COLLEGE OF THE HOLY CROSS 369
Collins Industries Inc. 369
Collins Stewart LLC 369
Colonial Financial Services, Inc. 369
Colonial Life & Accident Insurance Company 369
Colonial Pipeline Company 370
Colony Bancorp, Inc. 370
Colony Capital Inc 370

Colony Capital LLC 370
Color Art Integrated Interiors LLC 370
COLORADO COLLEGE 370
Colorado Interstate Gas Co. 371
COLORADO SEMINARY 371
Colorado Springs Utilities 371
COLORADO STATE UNIVERSITY 371
COLQUITT ELECTRIC MEMBERSHIP
    CORPORATION 371
COLSA CORPORATION 371
Colt's Manufacturing Company LLC 372
Columbia Banking System, Inc. 372
COLUMBIA COLLEGE CHICAGO 372
Columbia Gas of Massachusetts 372
Columbia Management Investment Advisers LLC 372
Columbia Pictures 372
Columbia Sportswear Co. 373
Columbia St. Mary's Inc. 373
Columbian Chemicals Company 373
Columbus McKinnon Corp. (NY) 373
Columbus Southern Power Company 373
COMARCO Inc. 373
Combe Incorporated 374
CombiMatrix Corp 374
Comcast Cable Communications LLC 374
Comcast Corp 374
Comcast Spectacor L.P. 374
Comedy Partners 374
Comerica, Inc. 375
COMFORCE Corporation 375
Comfort Systems USA, Inc. 375
Comm-Works Holdings LLC 375
Command Center, Inc. 375
Command Security Corp 375
Commerce Bancshares, Inc. 376
Commerce Group Corp. 376
Commercial Bancshares, Inc. (OH) 376
Commercial Furniture Group Inc. 376
Commercial Metals Co. 376
Commercial National Financial Corp. (PA) 376
Commercial Vehicle Group Inc 377
Commonwealth Edison Company 377
Commonwealth Equity Services LLP 377
COMMONWEALTH HEALTH CORPORATION INC.
    377
Communications Supply Corporation 377
Communications Systems, Inc. 377
Communications Test Design Inc. 378
COMMUNICATIONS WORKERS OF AMERICA AFL-
    CIO CLC 378
COMMUNITY ASPHALT CORP. 378
Community Bancorp. (Derby, VT) 378
Community Bank 378
Community Bank System, Inc. 378
Community Bankers Trust Corp 379
Community Capital Bancshares, Inc. 379
Community Choice Financial Inc 379
Community Financial Corp (The) 379
Community First Bancorporation 379
COMMUNITY HEALTH GROUP 379
COMMUNITY HEALTH NETWORK INC. 380
COMMUNITY HEALTH SYSTEM 380
Community Health Systems, Inc. 380
COMMUNITY HOSPITAL OF ANDERSON AND
    MADISON COUNTY INCORPORATED 380
COMMUNITY HOSPITAL OF THE MONTEREY
    PENINSULA 380
Community Medical Center 380
Community Shores Bank Corp 381
Community Trust Bancorp, Inc. 381
Community West Bancshares 381
CommunityOne Bancorp 381
CommVault Systems Inc 381
COMP-VIEW INC. 381
Companion Life Insurance Company 382
Compass Bancshares Inc. 382
Compass Diversified Holdings 382
Compass Group USA Inc. 382
Compass Minerals International Inc 382
Compellent Technologies Inc. 382
Complete Production Services Inc. 383
Composites One LLC 383
Comprehensive Care Corp. 383
Compressor Systems Inc. 383

ComPsych Corporation 383
CompuCom Systems Inc. 383
Compumed Inc 384
CompuNet Clinical Laboratories LLC 384
Computer Generated Solutions Inc. 384
Computer Programs & Systems Inc 384
Computer Sciences Corp. 384
Computer Task Group, Inc. 384
Computer World Services Corp. 385
CompuWare Corp. 385
CompX International, Inc. 385
comScore Inc 385
Comstock Holding Companies, Inc 385
Comstock Resources, Inc. 385
Comtech Telecommunications Corp. 386
Comtex News Network Inc. 386
Comverge Inc. 386
Con-way Freight Inc. 386
Con-Way Inc 386
ConAgra Foods, Inc. 386
Conair Corporation 387
Concert Pharmaceuticals Inc 387
Concho Resources Inc 387
CONCORD HOSPITAL INC. 387
CONCORD LITHO GROUP 387
Concorde Career Colleges Inc. 387
Concur Technologies Inc 388
Concurrent Computer Corp. 388
Concurrent Technologies Corporation 388
Condor Hospitality Trust Inc 388
Conergy Inc. 388
Congoleum Corporation 388
Conmed Corp. 389
ConnectiCare Inc. 389
CONNECTICUT CHILDREN'S MEDICAL CENTER
    389
CONNECTICUT COLLEGE 389
Connecticut Light & Power Co 389
CONNECTICUT STATE UNIVERSITY SYSTEM 389
Connecticut Water Service, Inc. 390
ConnectOne Bancorp Inc (New) 390
CONNECTRIA CORPORATION 390
Connell Limited Partnership 390
Connextions Inc. 390
CONNEXUS ENERGY 390
CONNOR CO. 391
Conns Inc 391
ConocoPhillips Alaska Inc. 391
Conolog Corp. 391
Conrad Industries, Inc. 391
Conrail Inc. 391
CONSOL Energy Inc 392
Consolidated Communications Holdings Inc 392
Consolidated Container Company LLC 392
Consolidated Edison Co. of New York, Inc. 392
Consolidated Edison Solutions Inc. 392
Consolidated Edison, Inc. 392
CONSOLIDATED PIPE & SUPPLY COMPANY INC.
    393
Consolidated Restaurant Operations Inc. 393
Consolidated-Tomoka Land Co. 393
Consona Corporation 393
Consona CRM Inc. 393
Constant Contact Inc 393
Constar International LLC 394
Constellation Brands Inc 394
Constellation Energy Group Inc. 394
Consumer Portfolio Service, Inc. 394
CONSUMER PRODUCT DISTRIBUTORS INC. 394
Consumers Bancorp, Inc. (Minerva, OH) 394
Consumers Energy Co. 395
CONSUMERS UNION OF UNITED STATES INC 395
Container Store Group, Inc 395
Contango Oil & Gas Co. (DE) 395
CONTI ENTERPRISES INC. 395
Continental Airlines Inc. 395
Continental Building Products Inc 396
Continental Materials Corp. 396
Continental Plastics Co. 396
Continental Resources Inc. 396
Continental Tire the Americas LLC 396
Continucare Corporation 396
CONTRACTORS STEEL COMPANY 397
Contran Corporation 397

Control4 Corp 397
CONVAID PRODUCTS INC. 397
CONVERGENT OUTSOURCING INC. 397
CONVERGINT TECHNOLOGIES LLC 397
Convergys Corp. 398
Conversant Inc 398
Converse Inc. 398
Convio Inc. 398
CONWAY HOSPITAL INC. 398
CONWAY REGIONAL MEDICAL CENTER INC. 398
COOK CHILDREN"S HEALTH CARE SYSTEM 399
Cook Composites and Polymers 399
CookTek LLC 399
Cooley LLP 399
COOPER COMMUNITIES INC. 399
Cooper Companies, Inc. (The) 399
Cooper Lighting LLC 400
Cooper Tire & Rubber Co. 400
Cooper-Standard Holdings, Inc. 400
COOPERATIVE ELEVATOR CO. 400
COOPERATIVE FOR ASSISTANCE AND RELIEF
    EVERYWHERE INC. 400
COOPERATIVE REGIONS OF ORGANIC PRODUCER
    POOLS 400
CoorsTek Inc. 401
Copart, Inc. 401
Coram LLC 401
Corbis Corporation 401
Corcept Therapeutics Inc 401
Cordis Corporation 401
CORE CONSTRUCTION INC. 402
Core Mark Holding Co Inc 402
Core Molding Technologies Inc 402
CoreSite Realty Corp. 402
CoreSource Inc. 402
Corgenix Medical Corp. 402
Corinthian Colleges, Inc. 403
CorMedix Inc 403
Cornerstone Bancorp 403
Cornerstone OnDemand, Inc. 403
Corning, Inc. 403
Corporate Office Properties Trust 403
CORPORATE TRAVEL CONSULTANTS INC 404
CORPORATION FOR PUBLIC BROADCASTING 404
Corrections Corporation of America 404
Corsair Components Inc. 404
CORT Business Services Corporation 404
Cortland Bancorp (OH) 404
CorVel Corp. 405
COSCO FIRE PROTECTION INC. 405
COSI Inc 405
CoSine Communications Inc. 405
Coskata Inc. 405
CosmoCom Inc. 405
Costa Del Mar Sunglasses Inc. 406
CoStar Group, Inc. 406
Costco Wholesale Corp 406
Cottman Transmission Systems LLC. 406
COTTON INCORPORATED 406
Coty, Inc. 406
Cougar Mountain Inc. 407
COUNCIL OF BETTER BUSINESS BUREAUS INC.
    407
COUNCIL ON FOREIGN RELATIONS INC. 407
COUNTERPART INTERNATIONAL INC 407
COUNTRY Mutual Insurance Company Inc. 407
COUNTRY PRIDE COOPERATIVE INC. 407
County Bank Corp.(Lapeer, MI) 408
Courier Corp. 408
Court Square Capital Partners 408
Cousins Properties Inc. 408
Covad Communications Group Inc. 408
Covance Inc. 408
Covanta Energy Corporation 409
Covanta Holding Corp 409
COVENANT HEALTH SYSTEM 409
COVENANT HOUSE 409
COVENANT MEDICAL CENTER INC 409
Covenant Transportation Group Inc 409
Cover-All Technologies, Inc. 410
COVERALL NORTH AMERICA INC. 410
Covisint Corp 410
Cowan Systems LLC 410
Cowen Group Inc 410

Cox Communications Inc. 410
Cox Newspapers LLC 411
CP Kelco 411
CPA2Biz Inc. 411
CPAC Inc. 411
CPG International Inc. 411
CPI Aerostructures, Inc. 411
CPI International Inc. 412
CPS Technologies Corp 412
CR Brands Inc. 412
CRA International Inc 412
Cracker Barrel Old Country Store, Inc. 412
Craft Brew Alliance Inc 412
Craftmade International Inc. 413
Crain Communications Inc 413
Crane & Co. Inc. 413
Crane Co. 413
Cravath Swaine & Moore LLP 413
Crawford & Co. 413
Cray Inc 414
Crayola LLC 414
CREATIVE GROUP INC. 414
Creative Realities Inc 414
Credit Acceptance Corp. (MI) 414
Credit Suisse (USA) Inc 414
Creditors Interchange Receivable Management LLC 415
Creditriskmonitor.com, Inc. 415
CREDO Petroleum Corporation 415
Cree, Inc. 415
CREIGHTON ALEGENT HEALTH 415
CREIGHTON UNIVERSITY 415
Crescent Electric Supply Company 416
Crescent Financial Bancshares Inc. 416
Crescent Real Estate Equities Limited Partnership 416
CREST OPERATIONS LLC 416
Crested Butte LLC 416
Crestwood Midstream Partners LP (New) 416
Crexendo Inc 417
Crider Inc. 417
CRISTA MINISTRIES 417
Critical Care Systems International Inc. 417
CRITTENTON HOSPITAL MEDICAL CENTER 417
Crocs Inc 417
Croghan Bancshares, Inc. 418
CropKing Incorporated 418
Crosby Trucking Service Inc. 418
Croscill Home LLC 418
Crosman Corporation 418
Cross Border Resources Inc. 418
Cross Company 419
Cross Country Healthcare Inc 419
Cross Match Technologies Inc. 419
Cross Timbers Royalty Trust 419
CrossAmerica Partners LP 419
Crossbeam Systems Inc. 419
CROSSLAND CONSTRUCTION COMPANY INC. 420
CROSSMARK Inc. 420
Crossroads Systems Inc 420
Crosstex Energy Inc 420
CROWDER CONSTRUCTION COMPANY INC 420
Crowe Horwath LLP 420
Crowley Maritime Corporation 421
CROWN BATTERY MANUFACTURING COMPANY 421
Crown Crafts, Inc. 421
Crown Gold Corporation 421
Crown Holding Company 421
Crown Holdings Inc 421
Crown Media Holdings Inc 422
CROZER-KEYSTONE HEALTH SYSTEM 422
CRST International Inc. 422
Crucible Industries LLC 422
Crum & Forster Holdings Corp. 422
Cryo-Cell International, Inc. 422
CryoLife, Inc. 423
Crystal Rock Holdings Inc 423
CSG Systems International Inc. 423
CSI Compressco LP 423
CSI LEASING INC. 423
CSK Auto Corporation 423
CSL Behring LLC 424
CSP Inc 424
CSS Industries, Inc. 424

CSSI INC. 424
CST Brands Inc 424
CSU FULLERTON AUXILIARY SERVICES CORPORATION 424
CSX Corp 425
CSX Transportation Inc. 425
CTA Acoustics Inc. 425
CTI BioPharma Corp 425
CTI Group Holdings Inc. 425
CTI Industries Corp 425
CTPartners Executive Search Inc 426
CTS Corp. 426
CTS Valpey Corporation 426
CTSC LLC 426
CubeSmart 426
Cubic Corp 426
Cubic Simulation Systems Inc. 427
Cubist Pharmaceuticals Inc. 427
CUI Global Inc 427
CUIVRE RIVER ELECTRIC COOPERATIVE INC. 427
Cullen/Frost Bankers, Inc. 427
Culp Inc. 427
CULVER FRANCHISING SYSTEM INC. 428
CUMBERLAND COUNTY HOSPITAL SYSTEM INC. 428
Cumberland Farms Inc. 428
Cumberland Packing Corp. 428
Cumberland Pharmaceuticals Inc 428
Cummins Filtration Inc. 428
Cummins, Inc. 429
Cummins-Allison Corp. 429
Cumulus Media Inc. 429
Cunard Line 429
Cupertino Electric Inc. 429
CuraScript Inc. 429
Curis Inc 430
Current USA Inc. 430
CurtCo Media Labs LLC 430
Curtiss-Wright Corp. 430
Cushman & Wakefield Inc. 430
Cushman & Wakefield Sonnenblick-Goldman LLC 430
CUSO FINANCIAL SERVICES L.P. 431
Custom Building Products Inc. 431
Custom Sensors & Technologies Inc. 431
Customers Bancorp Inc 431
CUSTOMINK LLC 431
Cutera Inc 431
Cutter & Buck Inc. 432
CVB Financial Corp. 432
CVD Equipment Corp. 432
Cvent, Inc 432
CVR Energy Inc 432
CVR Partners LP 432
CVR Refining LP 433
CVR Refining, LP 433
CVS Health Corporation 433
Cyalume Technologies Holdings, Inc 433
Cyanotech Corp. 433
CyberDefender Corporation 433
Cybernet Software Systems Inc. 434
Cyberonics, Inc. 434
Cyberoptics Corp. 434
Cyclacel Pharmaceuticals, Inc 434
Cycle Country Accessories Corp. 434
CYIOS Corporation 434
Cynergy Data LLC 435
Cynosure Inc 435
CyOptics Inc. 435
Cypress Bioscience Inc. 435
Cypress Semiconductor Corp. 435
CYS Investments, Inc. 435
CYSTIC FIBROSIS FOUNDATION 436
Cytec Engineered Materials Inc. 436
Cytec Industries, Inc. 436
Cytokinetics Inc 436
Cytori Therapeutics Inc 436
CytoSorbents Corporation 436
CytRx Corp 437
D W W CO. INC. 437
D'Agostino Supermarkets Inc. 437
D. C. TAYLOR CO. 437
D/L COOPERATIVE INC. 437
DAC Technologies Group International Inc. 437

Daegis Inc 438
Daily Journal Corporation 438
Daily News L.P. 438
Dairy Farmers of America Inc. 438
Dairyland Power Cooperative 438
Dais Analytic Corp 438
Daisy Manufacturing Company 439
DAK Americas LLC 439
DAKOTA ELECTRIC ASSOCIATION 439
Dakota Gasification Company 439
DAKOTA SUPPLY GROUP INC. 439
Daktronics Inc. 439
Dale Carnegie & Associates Inc. 440
Dale Jarrett Racing Adventure Inc 440
Dallas Cowboys Football Club Ltd. 440
Dallas/Fort Worth International Airport 440
Dana Holding Corp 440
DANA-FARBER CANCER INSTITUTE INC. 440
Danaher Corp. 441
DANCKER SELLEW & DOUGLAS INC. 441
DANIS BUILDING CONSTRUCTION COMPANY 441
Dantel Inc. 441
DARA BioSciences, Inc. 441
Darcars Automotive Group 441
Darden Restaurants, Inc. 442
Darling Ingredients Inc 442
Dart Transit Company 442
DARTMOUTH-HITCHCOCK CLINIC 442
Dassault Systemes Simulia Corp. 442
Dassault Systemes SolidWorks Corp. 442
Data I/O Corp. 443
Datacolor Inc. 443
Datalink Corp 443
Dataram Corp. 443
DataTrak International Inc. 443
DATAWATCH Corp. 443
DATS TRUCKING INC. 444
Dave & Buster?s Entertainment Inc. 444
Dave's Supermarkets Inc. 444
DAVENPORT UNIVERSITY 444
Davey Tree Expert Co. (The) 444
David E. Harvey Builders Inc. 444
David's Bridal Inc. 445
Davidson Companies 445
Davidson Hotels & Resorts LLC 445
Davis Polk & Wardwell LLP 445
Davis Wright Tremaine LLP 445
Davis-Standard LLC 445
DaVita HealthCare Partners Inc 446
Dawson Geophysical Co (New) 446
Dawson Geophysical Co. 446
DAWSON METAL COMPANY INC. 446
Daxor Corporation 446
DAY KIMBALL HEALTHCARE INC. 446
Day Pitney LLP 447
DAYLIGHT DONUT FLOUR COMPANY LLC 447
Days Inns Worldwide Inc. 447
DayStar Technologies Inc. 447
DC Partners Inc. 447
DCB Financial Corp. 447
DCH Healthcare Authority 448
DCP Midstream Partners LP 448
DCT Industrial Trust Inc 448
DDB Worldwide Communications Group Inc. 448
DDi Corp. 448
DDR Corp. 448
DE PAUL UNIVERSITY 449
DEACON INDUSTRIAL SUPPLY CO. INC. 449
DEACONESS HEALTH SYSTEM INC. 449
DEACONESS HOSPITAL INC 449
DEALERS SUPPLY COMPANY INC. 449
Dealertrack Technologies, Inc. 449
Dean & DeLuca Incorporated 450
Dean Foods Co. 450
Dean Health Plan 450
Debevoise & Plimpton LLP 450
Debt Resolve Inc 450
DeCare Dental LLC 450
DECATUR MEMORIAL HOSPITAL 451
Dechert LLP 451
Decision Diagnostics Corp 451
Decision Resources Inc. 451
DecisionOne Corporation 451
Deckers Outdoor Corp. 451

DECO INC. 452
Deep Down Inc 452
Deere & Co. 452
Deere Credit Services Inc. 452
Defender Security Company 452
Deffenbaugh Industries Inc. 452
Defiance Metal Products Co. 453
DEFOE CORP. 453
DEKALB MEDICAL CENTER INC. 453
Del Frisco's Restaurant Group Inc 453
Del Global Technologies Corp. 453
DEL MONACO SPECIALTY FOODS INC. 453
Del Monte Corporation 454
Del Taco Holdings Inc. 454
Delaware North Companies Inc. 454
DELAWARE STATE UNIVERSITY 454
DELAWARE VALLEY COLLEGE 454
Delcath Systems Inc. 454
Delek Logistics Partners LP 455
Delek US Holdings Inc 455
Delhaize America LLC 455
DELI MANAGEMENT INC. 455
Delmarva Power & Light Co. 455
Deloitte & Touche LLP 455
Deloitte Consulting LLP 456
Deloitte LLP 456
Deloitte Touche Tohmatsu Services Inc. 456
Delphi Financial Group Inc. 456
Delta Air Lines, Inc. (DE) 456
Delta AirElite Business Jets Inc. 456
Delta Apparel Inc. 457
Delta Community Credit Union 457
Delta Dental of California 457
Delta Dental of Rhode Island 457
Delta Dental Plan of Michigan Inc. 457
Delta Mutual Inc. 457
Delta Natural Gas Co., Inc. 458
DELTA REGIONAL MEDICAL CENTER 458
Delta Tau Data Systems Inc. 458
deltathree Inc 458
Deltek Inc. 458
Deltic Timber Corp. 458
Deluxe Corp. 459
Deluxe Entertainment Services Group Inc. 459
Demand Media Inc 459
Demandware Inc 459
Demoulas Super Markets Inc. 459
Denali Incorporated 459
Denbury Resources, Inc. (DE) 460
Dendreon Corp 460
DENISON UNIVERSITY 460
Denmark Bancshares, Inc. 460
Denny's Corp 460
DENSO International America Inc. 460
DENTSPLY International, Inc. 461
Denver Health and Hospital Authority 461
DEPAUW UNIVERSITY 461
Depomed Inc 461
DePuy Inc. 461
DePuy Orthopaedics Inc. 461
Derma Sciences Inc. 462
DESALES UNIVERSITY 462
DESERET GENERATION AND TRANSMISSION CO-
OPERATIVE 462
Desert Schools Federal Credit Union 462
Destination Maternity Corp 462
Destination XL Group Inc 462
Destiny Media Technologies Inc 463
Detector Electronics Corporation 463
Determine Inc 463
Detrex Corp. 463
Detroit Diesel Corporation 463
Detroit Medical Center 463
Detroit Pistons Basketball Company 464
Detroit Tigers Inc. 464
Deublin Company 464
Deutsch Inc. 464
Deutsche Bank Securities Inc. 464
DEVCON CONSTRUCTION INCORPORATED 464
DEVEREUX FOUNDATION 465
Devon Energy Corp. 465
DeVry Education Group Inc 465
Dewey & LeBoeuf LLP 465
Dewey Electronics Corp. 465

DexCom Inc 465
DFB PHARMACEUTICALS INC. 466
DFC Global Corp. 466
DGSE Companies, Inc. 466
DHG Management Company LLC 466
DHI Group Inc 466
DI LLC 466
diaDexus Inc. 467
Dialogic Inc 467
DIALYSIS CLINIC INC. 467
Diamond Discoveries International Corp. 467
Diamond Foods Inc 467
Diamond Hill Investment Group Inc. 467
Diamond Offshore Drilling, Inc. 468
Diamond Resorts Holdings LLC 468
Diamondback Energy Inc. 468
DiamondRock Hospitality Co. 468
dick clark productions inc. 468
Dick's Sporting Goods, Inc 468
DICKINSON COLLEGE 469
Dickinson Financial Corporation II 469
DiCon Fiberoptics Inc. 469
Diebold, Inc. 469
Diedrich Coffee Inc. 469
Dierbergs Markets Inc. 469
Differential Brands Group Inc 470
Digerati Technologies Inc 470
Digi International, Inc. 470
Digi-Key Corporation 470
Digimarc Corp 470
Digirad Corp 470
Digital Ally Inc 471
Digital Cinema Destinations Corp. 471
Digital Envoy Inc. 471
Digital Federal Credit Union 471
Digital Fusion Inc. 471
Digital Power Corp. 471
Digital Realty Trust, Inc. 472
Digital River, Inc. 472
Digital Turbine Inc 472
DigitalGlobe Inc 472
Digitas Inc. 472
Dignity Health 472
DILLARD UNIVERSITY 473
Dillard's Inc. 473
Dillon Companies Inc. 473
Dillon Supply Co. 473
Dime Community Bancshares, Inc 473
DIMENSIONS HEALTH CORPORATION 473
DIMEO CONSTRUCTION COMPANY 474
DineEquity Inc 474
Diodes, Inc. 474
Dionex Corporation 474
Direct Insite Corp 474
Direct Media Millard Inc. 474
DIRECT RELIEF 475
DIRECTV 475
DISABLED AMERICAN VETERANS 475
Discount Drug Mart Inc. 475
Discount Tire Co. Inc. 475
Discover Financial Services 475
Discovery Communications, Inc. 476
Discovery Laboratories, Inc. 476
Dish Network Corp 476
Disney (Walt) Co. (The) 476
Diversey Inc. 476
DIVERSIFIED CHEMICAL TECHNOLOGIES INC.
476
Diversified Restaurant Holdings Inc. 477
DIXIE GAS AND OIL CORPORATION 477
Dixie Group Inc. 477
DLH Holdings Corp 477
DLT SOLUTIONS LLC 477
DMC Operating L.P. 477
DMX Inc. 478
DNB Financial Corp. 478
Do it Best Corp. 478
DoALL Company 478
DOC"S DRUGS LTD. 478
DOCTORS' HOSPITAL INC. 478
DOCTOR'S ASSOCIATES INC. 479
Document Capture Technologies Inc 479
Document Security Systems Inc 479
Doka USA Ltd. 479

Dolan Company (The) 479
Dolby Laboratories Inc 479
Dollar Bank FSB 480
Dollar General Corp 480
Dollar Thrifty Automotive Group Inc. 480
Dollar Tree, Inc. 480
Domain Associates L.L.C. 480
Dominion Homes Inc. 480
Dominion Resources Black Warrior Trust 481
Dominion Resources Inc 481
Dominos Pizza Inc. 481
Don Miguel Mexican Foods Inc. 481
Donahue Schriber Realty Group Inc. 481
Donaldson Co. Inc. 481
Donatos Pizzeria LLC 482
Donegal Group Inc. 482
Donnelley (R.R.) & Sons Co. 482
DOOLEYMACK CONSTRUCTORS INC. 482
Dooney & Bourke Inc. 482
Dopaco Inc. 482
Dorchester Minerals LP 483
Dorel Juvenile Group Inc. 483
Dorman Products Inc 483
Dorsey & Whitney LLP 483
Dot Foods Inc. 483
Dot Hill Systems Corp. 483
Douglas Dynamics, Inc. 484
Douglas Emmett Inc 484
Dover Corp 484
Dover Downs Gaming & Entertainment, Inc. 484
Dover Motorsports, Inc. 484
Dover Saddlery Inc 484
Dow AgroSciences LLC 485
Dow Chemical Co. 485
Dow Jones & Company Inc. 485
DOWLING COLLEGE 485
DOYLESTOWN HOSPITAL HEALTH AND
WELLNESS CENTER INC. 485
DPL Inc. 485
DPR CONSTRUCTION INC. 486
Dr Pepper Snapple Group Inc 486
Drake Beam Morin Inc. 486
DRAKE UNIVERSITY 486
Dreams Inc. 486
DreamWorks Animation SKG Inc 486
DreamWorks Studios 487
Dresser Inc. 487
Dresser-Rand Group Inc. 487
Drew Industries, Inc. 487
DREW UNIVERSITY 487
DREXEL UNIVERSITY 487
Dreyer's Grand Ice Cream Holdings Inc. 488
DRI Corporation 488
Dril-Quip, Inc. 488
Drinker Biddle & Reath LLP 488
Drinks Americas Holdings Ltd. 488
DriveCam Inc. 488
Driver-Harris Company 489
DriveTime Automotive Inc. 489
DRS Technologies Inc. 489
drugstore.com inc. 489
Drummond Company Inc. 489
DS Waters of America Inc. 489
DSC Logistics Inc. 490
DSL.net Inc. 490
DSP Group, Inc. 490
DST Systems Inc. (DE) 490
DSW Inc 490
DTE Electric Company 490
DTE Energy Co. 491
DTJ HOLDINGS INC. 491
DTS Inc 491
Duane Morris LLP 491
Ducommun Inc. 491
Ducommun LaBarge Technologies 491
Dukane Corporation 492
Duke Energy Corp 492
Duke Energy Indiana, Inc. 492
Duke Realty Corp. 492
Dulcich Inc. 492
Dun & Bradstreet Corp (DE) 492
Duncan Energy Partners L.P. 493
DUNCAN EQUIPMENT COMPANY 493
DUNCAN-WILLIAMS INC. 493

Dune Energy, Inc. 493
Dunham's Athleisure Corporation 493
Dunkin' Brands Group Inc. 493
Dunkin' Brands Group, Inc. 494
DuPont Automotive 494
DuPont Fabros Technology Inc 494
DUQUESNE UNIVERSITY OF THE HOLY SPIRIT 494
DURA Automotive Systems LLC 494
DURA COAT PRODUCTS INC. 494
Durata Therapeutics Inc. 495
Durect Corp 495
DUSA Pharmaceuticals Inc. 495
DXP Enterprises, Inc. 495
Dyadic International Inc 495
Dyax Corp 495
Dycom Industries, Inc. 496
Dynacq Healthcare Inc 496
Dynamex Inc. 496
Dynamic Materials Corp. 496
Dynamic Offshore Resources LLC 496
DYNAMIX GROUP INC 496
Dynapac USA Inc. 497
Dynasil Corp of America 497
Dynatronics Corp. 497
Dynavax Technologies Corp 497
DynaVox Inc. 497
DynCorp International Inc. 497
Dynegy Inc (New) 498
Dyneon L.L.C. 498
Dynex Capital, Inc. 498
DynTek Inc. 498
E Z LOADER BOAT TRAILERS INC. 498
E*TRADE Bank 498
E*TRADE Financial Corp. 499
e-Dialog Inc. 499
E-LOAN Inc. 499
E-Z MART STORES INC. 499
E. & J. Gallo Winery 499
E. C. BARTON & COMPANY 499
E. Gluck Corporation 500
e.Digital Corp. 500
E.N.M.R. TELEPHONE COOPERATIVE 500
EA ENGINEERING SCIENCE AND TECHNOLOGY INC. 500
EACO Corp 500
Eagle Bancorp Inc (MD) 500
Eagle Bancorp Montana, Inc. 501
Eagle Bulk Shipping Inc. 501
Eagle Creek Inc. 501
Eagle Materials Inc 501
Eagle Pharmaceuticals, Inc. 501
Eagle Rock Energy Partners LP 501
Earl G. Graves Ltd. 502
EARL L HENDERSON TRUCKING COMPANY 502
EARLHAM COLLEGE 502
Earth Fare Inc. 502
Earth Search Sciences Inc. 502
Earthstone Energy Inc. 502
East Bay Municipal Utility District 503
East Kentucky Power Cooperative Inc. 503
EAST ORANGE GENERAL HOSPITAL INC 503
EAST TENNESSEE CHILDREN'S HOSPITAL ASSOCIATION INC. 503
EAST TENNESSEE STATE UNIVERSITY 503
EAST TEXAS MEDICAL CENTER REGIONAL HEALTHCARE SYST 503
East West Bancorp, Inc 504
EASTER SEALS INC. 504
Eastern American Natural Gas Trust 504
EASTERN BAG AND PAPER COMPANY INCORPORATED 504
Eastern Bank Corporation 504
Eastern Co. 504
Eastern Maine Healthcare Systems 505
EASTERN MICHIGAN UNIVERSITY 505
Eastern Mountain Sports Inc. 505
Eastern Virginia Bankshares, Inc 505
EASTERN VIRGINIA MEDICAL SCHOOL 505
EASTERN WASHINGTON UNIVERSITY INC 505
EastGroup Properties, Inc. 506
Eastman Chemical Co. 506
Eastman Kodak Co. 506
Easton-Bell Sports Inc. 506
EasyLink Services International Corporation 506

Eateries Inc. 506
Eaton Vance Corp 507
EAU Technologies Inc 507
Ebara Technologies Inc. 507
eBay Inc. 507
Ebix Inc 507
EBL&S Development LLC 507
EBSCO Industries Inc. 508
EBY CORPORATION 508
EBY-BROWN COMPANY LLC 508
Echelon Corp. 508
Echo Global Logistics Inc 508
Echo Therapeutics Inc 508
Echopass Corporation 509
EchoStar Corp 509
ECKERD COLLEGE INC. 509
ECKERD YOUTH ALTERNATIVES INC. 509
ECLINICALWORKS LLC 509
Eclipse Inc. 509
Eclipse Resources Corp 510
Ecolab, Inc. 510
Ecology And Environment, Inc. 510
eCom eCom.com Inc. 510
Econolite Control Products Inc. 510
Ecotality Inc 510
Ecova Inc. 511
ECRM Incorporated 511
ECS FEDERAL INC. 511
Edelbrock LLC 511
EDEN FOODS INC. 511
Edgewater Technology Inc 511
Edgewell Personal Care Co 512
Edison International 512
Edison Mission Energy 512
EDP Renewables North America LLC 512
Education Management Corp 512
Education Realty Trust Inc 512
EDUCATIONAL & INSTITUTIONAL COOPERATIVE SERVICE INC. 513
Educational Development Corp. 513
EDUCATIONAL SERVICES OF AMERICA INC. 513
EDUCATIONAL TESTING SERVICE INC 513
Edw. C. Levy Co. 513
Edward Don & Company 513
Edward Rose Building Enterprises 514
Edwards Angell Palmer & Dodge LLP 514
Edwards Lifesciences Corp 514
Edwin Watts Golf LLC 514
EEI HOLDING CORPORATION 514
EF Johnson Technologies Inc. 514
eGain Corp 515
EGPI Firecreek Inc 515
eHealth Inc 515
EIDE BAILLY LLP 515
EILEEN FISHER INC. 515
Einstein Noah Restaurant Group Inc 515
Eisai Inc. 516
EISENHOWER MEDICAL CENTER 516
EISNERAMPER LLP 516
EL DORADO FURNITURE CORP 516
El Paso Corporation 516
El Paso Electric Company 516
El Paso Pipeline Partners LP 517
El Pollo Loco Holdings Inc. 517
Elavon Inc. 517
Eldorado Artesian Springs Inc 517
Elecsys Corp. 517
Election Systems & Software Inc. 517
Electric Boat Corporation 518
Electric Energy Inc. 518
Electric Insurance Company 518
ELECTRIC POWER BOARD OF THE METROPOLITAN GOVERNMENT OF NASHVILLE 518
ELECTRIC POWER RESEARCH INSTITUTE INC. 518
ELECTRIC RELIABILITY COUNCIL OF TEXAS INC. 518
Electro Rent Corp. 519
Electro Scientific Industries, Inc. 519
ELECTRO-MATIC PRODUCTS INC. 519
Electro-Sensors, Inc. 519
Electromed, Inc. 519
Electronic Arts, Inc. 519
Electronic Control Security Inc. 520

Electronic Systems Technology, Inc. 520
Electronics for Imaging, Inc. 520
Elementis Specialties Inc. 520
Elevance Renewable Sciences Inc. 520
Eleven Biotherapeutics Inc 520
Elgin National Industries Inc. 521
Elgin Sweeper Company 521
Elite Pharmaceuticals, Inc. 521
ELIXIR INDUSTRIES 521
Elizabeth Arden Inc. 521
ELKINS CONSTRUCTORS INC. 521
Ellie Mae Inc 522
Ellington Financial LLC 522
Ellington Residential Mortgaging Real Estate Investment Trust 522
ELLIOT HOSPITAL OF THE CITY OF MANCHESTER 522
Ellis (Perry) International Inc 522
ELLIS HOSPITAL 522
ELLSWORTH COOPERATIVE CREAMERY 523
Ellucian Inc. 523
ELMA ELECTRONIC INC. 523
ELMHURST MEMORIAL HOSPITAL INC 523
Elmira Savings Bank (NY) 523
Eloqua Limited 523
Elster American Meter Company LLC 524
Elvis Presley Enterprises Inc. 524
ELWYN 524
ELXSI Corp 524
eMagin Corp 524
Embarcadero Technologies Inc. 524
EmblemHealth Inc. 525
EMBREE CONSTRUCTION GROUP INC. 525
EMBRY-RIDDLE AERONAUTICAL UNIVERSITY INC. 525
EMC Corp. (MA) 525
EMC Insurance Group Inc. 525
Emclaire Financial Corp. 525
EMCOR Group, Inc. 526
EMCORE Corp. 526
EMD Millipore Corporation 526
Emdeon Inc. 526
Emerald Dairy Inc. 526
Emerald Oil, Inc 526
Emerge Energy Services LP 527
Emergent BioSolutions Inc 527
Emergent Capital Inc 527
Emergent Group Inc. 527
Emerging Vision Inc. 527
Emeritus Corp. 527
EMERSON COLLEGE 528
Emerson Electric Co. 528
EMERSON HOSPITAL 528
Emerson Network Power-Embedded Computing Inc. 528
Emerson Radio Corp. 528
EMI Music Publishing 528
Emisphere Technologies Inc. 529
EMJ CORPORATION 529
Emkay Inc. 529
Emmis Communications Corp. 529
Empire District Electric Co. 529
Empire Resorts Inc 529
Empire Resources Inc 530
EMPIRE SOUTHWEST LLC 530
Empire State Realty Trust Inc 530
EMPIRIX INC. 530
Employers Holdings Inc 530
EMPORIA STATE UNIVERSITY 530
Emrise Corp 531
EMS Technologies Inc. 531
Emtec Inc. 531
Emulex Corporation 531
eMusic.com Inc. 531
Enable Holdings Inc. 531
Enable Midstream Partners L.P. 532
Enanta Pharmaceuticals, Inc. 532
Enbridge Energy Management LLC 532
Enbridge Energy Partners, L.P. 532
Encision Inc. 532
Encore Bancshares Inc. 532
Encore Capital Group Inc 533
Encore Energy Partners LP 533
ENCORE NATIONWIDE INC. 533

Encore Wire Corp. 533
Endeavour International Corp 533
Endo Health Solutions Inc 533
Endocyte Inc 534
Endologix Inc. 534
Endurance International Group Holdings Inc 534
Enel Green Power North America Inc. 534
Energen Corp. 534
Energy & Exploration Partners Inc. 534
Energy Alloys L.L.C. 535
Energy and Power Solutions Inc. 535
Energy Brands Inc. 535
Energy Conversion Devices Inc. 535
Energy Focus Inc 535
Energy Future Holdings Corp 535
Energy Recovery Inc 536
Energy Services of America Corp. 536
Energy Transfer Equity L P 536
ENERGYUNITED ELECTRIC MEMBERSHIP
　　CORPORATION 536
EnerJex Resources Inc 536
Enerlabs Inc 536
EnerNOC Inc 537
Enersys 537
EnerVest Ltd. 537
Enesco LLC 537
Enfora Inc. 537
Engility Holdings Inc (New) 537
Engineered Materials Solutions Inc. 538
Englefield Oil Company 538
ENGlobal Corp. 538
enherent Corp. 538
Enigma Inc. 538
Ennis Inc 538
Enova Systems Inc 539
Enphase Energy Inc. 539
EnPro Industries Inc 539
Enservco Corp 539
Ensign Group Inc 539
Ensign-Bickford Industries Inc. 539
EnSync Inc 540
Ent Federal Credit Union 540
ENTECH SALES AND SERVICE INC. 540
Entech Solar Inc. 540
Entegris Inc 540
Entercom Communications Corp 540
Entergy Arkansas, Inc. 541
Entergy Corp. 541
Entergy Gulf States Louisiana LLC 541
Entergy Louisiana LLC (New) 541
Entergy Mississippi, Inc 541
Entergy New Orleans Inc. 541
Entergy Nuclear Inc. 542
EnteroMedics Inc. 542
Enterprise Bancorp, Inc. (MA) 542
ENTERPRISE ELECTRIC LLC 542
Enterprise Financial Services Corp 542
Enterprise Products Partners L.P. 542
Entorian Technologies Inc. 543
Entravision Communications Corp. 543
EntreMed, Inc. 543
Entrepreneur Media Inc. 543
Entropic Communications, Inc. 543
Entrust Inc. 543
Entrx Corporation 544
Envestnet Inc 544
Enviro Voraxial Technology Inc. 544
ENVIRONMENTAL DEFENSE FUND 544
Environmental Tectonics Corp. 544
Envirostar Inc 544
Envision Healthcare Corp 545
Envision Healthcare Holdings Inc 545
Envivio Inc. 545
EnXnet Inc. 545
Enzo Biochem, Inc. 545
Enzon Pharmaceuticals Inc 545
EOG Resources, Inc. 546
EP Energy Corp. 546
Epam Systems, Inc. 546
Epic Systems Corporation 546
Epicore BioNetworks Inc. 546
EPIQ Systems Inc 546
EPITEC INC. 547
Epizyme Inc. 547

EPL Oil & Gas Inc 547
ePlus Inc 547
Epolin Inc. 547
EPR Properties 547
EPSILON SYSTEMS SOLUTIONS INC. 548
Epstein 548
EQT Corp. 548
Equifax, Inc. 548
Equilar Inc. 548
Equinix Inc. 548
Equinox Payments LLC 549
Equistar Chemicals LP 549
Equity Commonwealth 549
Equity Lifestyle Properties Inc 549
Equity Office Management L.L.C. 549
Equity One, Inc. 549
Equity Residential 550
ERA Group Inc 550
ERBA Diagnostics 550
eResearchTechnology Inc. 550
ERHC Energy Inc. 550
Erickson Inc 550
Ericsson Inc. 551
Erie Family Life Insurance Company 551
Erie Indemnity Co. 551
Erin Energy Corp 551
Ernie Ball Inc. 551
eRoom System Technologies Inc 551
Escalade, Inc. 552
Escalera Resources Co 552
Escalon Medical Corp. 552
ESCO Corporation 552
ESCO Technologies, Inc. 552
eScreen Inc. 552
eSilicon Corporation 553
ESL Federal Credit Union 553
Esoterix Inc. 553
Espey Manufacturing & Electronics Corp. 553
ESPN Inc. 553
ESSA Bancorp Inc 553
Essence Communications Inc. 554
Essendant Inc 554
ESSENTIA HEALTH 554
Essex Property Trust, Inc. 554
Essex Rental Corp 554
Essroc Cement Corp. 554
Estee Lauder International Inc. 555
Esterline Technologies Corp 555
ESTES EXPRESS LINES INC. 555
Estwing Manufacturing Company Inc. 555
ET3 LLC 555
Etelos Inc. 555
Ethan Allen Interiors, Inc. 556
Ethicon Endo-Surgery Inc. 556
Ethicon Inc. 556
Etienne Aigner Holdings Inc. 556
ETNA DISTRIBUTORS LLC 556
ETS-Lindgren LP 556
Eureka Financial Corp (MD) 557
Euromarket Designs Inc. 557
Euronet Worldwide Inc. 557
EV Energy Partners LP 557
ev3 Inc. 557
EVANGELICAL COMMUNITY HOSPITAL 557
Evans & Sutherland Computer Corp. 558
Evans Bancorp, Inc. 558
Evapco Inc. 558
Evenflo Company Inc. 558
EVENT NETWORK INC. 558
EverBank Financial Corp 558
Evercore Partners Inc 559
EVERGREEN FS INC 559
EVERGREEN STATE COLLEGE 559
Everi Holdings Inc 559
Eversource Energy 559
EVINE Live Inc 559
Evite LLC 560
Evolution Petroleum Corp 560
Evolving Systems, Inc. 560
Evonik Corporation 560
EWING IRRIGATION PRODUCTS INC. 560
Exa Corp 560
EXACT Sciences Corp. 561
Exact Software North America Inc. 561

Exactech, Inc. 561
ExamWorks Group Inc 561
Exar Corp. 561
Excel Trust Inc. 561
Excellus Health Plan Inc. 562
Exchange Bank 562
Exco Resources Inc. 562
Exel Inc. 562
Exelis Inc. 562
Exelixis Inc 562
Exelon Corp. 563
Exelon Energy Company 563
Exelon Generation Co LLC 563
Exide Technologies 563
ExlService Holdings Inc 563
ExOne Co. (The) 563
Exopack LLC 564
Expedia Inc 564
Expeditors International of Washington, Inc. 564
Experian Information Solutions Inc. 564
EXPERIENCE WORKS INC. 564
Expert Global Solutions Inc. 564
Exponent Inc. 565
Exponential Interactive Inc. 565
Export-Import Bank of the United States 565
Express Scripts Holding Co 565
Express, Inc. 565
ExpressJet Holdings Inc. 565
Extended Stay America Inc 566
Extra Space Storage Inc 566
Extreme Networks Inc 566
EXX INC 566
Exxon Mobil Corp. 566
ExxonMobil Pipeline Company 566
EyeMed Vision Care LLC 567
EZCORP, Inc. 567
F & M Bank Corp. 567
F & S PRODUCE CO INC 567
F&B Manufacturing Company 567
F+W Media Inc. 567
F.A. Wilhelm Construction Company Inc. 568
F.N.B. Corp. 568
F.W. Webb Company 568
F5 Networks, Inc. 568
FAB Universal Corp 568
Facebook, Inc. 568
Facility Solutions Group Inc. 569
Factory Mutual Insurance Company 569
FactSet Research Systems Inc. 569
Fair Isaac Corp 569
Fairchild Fashion Media 569
Fairchild Semiconductor International, Inc. 569
FAIRFIELD MEDICAL CENTER 570
FAIRFIELD UNIVERSITY 570
FAIRLEIGH DICKINSON UNIVERSITY 570
FairPoint Communications Inc 570
FAIRVIEW HEALTH SERVICES 570
Fairway Group Holdings Corp 570
FAITH TECHNOLOGIES INC. 571
Falcon Pharmaceuticals Ltd. 571
FalconStor Software Inc. 571
Fallbrook Technologies Inc. 571
Fallon Group Inc. 571
Family Dollar Stores, Inc. 571
FAMILY EXPRESS CORPORATION 572
FAMILY HEALTH INTERNATIONAL INC 572
Famous Dave's of America Inc. 572
Fandango Inc. 572
Fannie Mae 572
Far East Energy Corp 572
Far East National Bank 573
Fareway Stores Inc. 573
Farm Bureau Property & Casualty Insurance
　　Company 573
Farm Credit Bank of Texas 573
Farm Credit Services of Mid-America ACA 573
Farm Family Casualty Insurance Company 573
FARM SERVICE COOPERATIVE 574
Farmer Bros. Co. 574
Farmers & Merchants Investment Inc. 574
Farmers Capital Bank Corp. 574
FARMERS COOPERATIVE COMPANY 574
FARMERS COOPERATIVE SOCIETY 574
Farmers National Banc Corp. (Canfield,OH) 575

FARMERS TELEPHONE COOPERATIVE INC. 575
FARMINGTON FOODS INC. 575
FARO Technologies Inc. 575
Farrel Corporation 575
FARSTAD OIL INC. 575
Fashion Bug Retail Companies LLC 576
Fastenal Co. 576
Fatburger Corporation 576
FatWire Corporation 576
FaulknerUSA Inc. 576
Fauquier Bankshares, Inc. 576
Faurecia Exhaust Systems Inc. 577
FAYETTE COMMUNITY HOSPITAL INC. 577
Fazoli's Restaurants LLC 577
FBL Financial Group, Inc. 577
FBR & Co. 577
FCCI Mutual Insurance Holding Company 577
FCI CONSTRUCTORS INC. 578
Featherlite Inc. 578
Federal Agricultural Mortgage Corp 578
Federal Aviation Administration 578
Federal Deposit Insurance Corporation 578
Federal Express Corporation 578
Federal Home Loan Bank Boston 579
Federal Home Loan Bank New York 579
Federal Home Loan Bank of Pittsburgh 579
Federal Home Loan Bank Of San Francisco 579
Federal Prison Industries Inc. 579
Federal Realty Investment Trust (MD) 579
Federal Reserve Bank of Atlanta, Dist. No. 6 580
Federal Reserve Bank of Boston, Dist. No. 1 580
Federal Reserve Bank of Chicago, Dist. No. 7 580
Federal Reserve Bank of Cleveland, Dist. No. 4 580
Federal Reserve Bank of Dallas, Dist. No. 11 580
Federal Reserve Bank of Kansas City, Dist. No. 10 580
Federal Reserve Bank of Minneapolis, Dist. No. 9 581
Federal Reserve Bank of New York, Dist. No. 2 581
Federal Reserve Bank of Philadelphia, Dist. No. 3 581
Federal Reserve Bank of Richmond, Dist. No. 5 581
Federal Reserve Bank of San Francisco, Dist. No. 12 581
Federal Reserve Bank of St. Louis, Dist. No. 8 581
Federal Reserve System 582
Federal Screw Works 582
Federal Signal Corp. 582
Federal-Mogul Holdings Corp 582
Federated Insurance Companies 582
Federated Investors Inc (PA) 582
Federated National Holding Co. 583
FedEx Corp 583
FedEx Custom Critical Inc. 583
FedEx Ground Package System Inc. 583
FedEx Office and Print Services Inc. 583
FedFirst Financial Corporation 583
FEED THE CHILDREN INC. 584
FEI Co. 584
FelCor Lodging Trust, Inc. 584
Feld Entertainment Inc. 584
Female Health Co. (The) 584
Fender Musical Instruments Corporation 584
Fentura Financial Inc 585
Fenwick & West LLP 585
Ferguson Enterprises Inc. 585
Ferndale Pharma Group Inc. 585
Ferrellgas Partners, L.P. 585
FERRIS STATE UNIVERSITY 585
Ferro Corp. 586
FFD Financial Corp 586
FFF Enterprises Inc 586
FFW Corp. 586
FHI SERVICES 586
FHM Insurance Company 586
FIBERLINK COMMUNICATIONS CORPORATION 587
FiberMark North America Inc. 587
FiberTower Corporation 587
Fibrocell Science, Inc. 587
Fidelitone Inc. 587
Fidelity & Guaranty Life Insurance Company 587
Fidelity D&D Bancorp, Inc. 588
Fidelity National Financial Inc 588
Fidelity National Information Services Inc 588
Fidelity Southern Corp 588
Fidus Investment Corporation 588
FIELD MUSEUM OF NATURAL HISTORY 588

FieldPoint Petroleum Corp. 589
FIESTA MART INC. 589
Fiesta Restaurant Group, Inc 589
Fifth Street Finance Corp 589
Fifth Third Bancorp (Cincinnati, OH) 589
Fila U.S.A. Inc 589
FileMaker Inc. 590
FileTek Inc. 590
Financial Engines Inc 590
Financial Executives International 590
Financial Guaranty Insurance Company 590
FINANCIAL INDUSTRY REGULATORY AUTHORITY INC. 590
Financial Institutions Inc. 591
FindEx.com Inc. 591
Finisar Corp 591
Finish Line, Inc. (The) 591
Finjan Holdings Inc 591
Finnegan Henderson Farabow Garrett & Dunner LLP 591
Fios Inc. 592
FireEye Inc 592
FIRELANDS REGIONAL HEALTH SYSTEM 592
Fireman's Fund Insurance Company 592
First Acceptance Corp 592
First Advantage Bancorp 592
First American Financial Corp 593
First Aviation Services Inc. 593
First Bancorp 593
First Bancorp (NC) 593
First Bancorp Inc (ME) 593
First Bancorp of Indiana, Inc. 593
First Bancshares Inc 594
First Bancshares Inc. (MO) 594
First Banctrust Corp 594
First Banks, Inc. (MO) 594
First Busey Corp 594
First Business Financial Services, Inc. 594
First Capital Bancorp Inc (VA) 595
First Capital Inc. 595
First Cash Financial Services Inc 595
First Century Bankshares, Inc. 595
First Citizens Bancorporation Inc. 595
First Citizens BancShares, Inc. (NC) 595
First Clover Leaf Financial Corp 596
First Commonwealth Financial Corp. (Indiana, PA) 596
First Commonwealth Inc. 596
First Community Bancshares, Inc. (NV) 596
First Community Corp. (SC) 596
First Connecticut Bancorp Inc. (MD) 596
First Data Corp (New) 597
First Defiance Financial Corp. 597
First Eagle Investment Management LLC 597
FIRST ELECTRIC CO-OPERATIVE CORPORATION 597
First Federal of Northern Michigan Bancorp Inc 597
First Financial Bancorp (OH) 597
First Financial Bankshares, Inc. 598
First Financial Corp. (IN) 598
First Financial Northwest Inc 598
First Financial Service Corp 598
First Franklin Corporation 598
First Hartford Corp 598
First Hawaiian Bank 599
First Horizon National Corp 599
First Independence Corporation 599
First Industrial Realty Trust, Inc. 599
First Internet Bancorp 599
First Interstate BancSystem, Inc. 599
First Keystone Corp. 600
First Marblehead Corp 600
First Mariner Bancorp. 600
First Merchants Corp. 600
First Mid-Illinois Bancshares, Inc. 600
First Midwest Bancorp, Inc. (Naperville, IL) 600
First Mortgage Corporation 601
First National Bank Alaska 601
First National Community Bancorp, Inc. (Dunmore, PA) 601
First National Corp. (Strasburg, VA) 601
First NBC Bank Holding Co. 601
First Niagara Financial Group, Inc. 601
First Niles Financial Inc. 602

First Northern Community Bancorp 602
First of Long Island Corp. 602
First Physicians Capital Group Inc 602
First Potomac Realty Trust 602
First Republic Bank (San Francisco, CA) 602
First Robinson Financial Corp. 603
First Savings Financial Group Inc 603
First Security Group Inc 603
First Solar Inc 603
First South Bancorp Inc (VA) 603
First Tech Federal Credit Union 603
First United Corporation (MD) 604
First West Virginia Bancorp Inc 604
First Wind Holdings Inc. 604
Firstbank Corp. (MI) 604
FirstEnergy Corp. 604
FirstEnergy Solutions Corp. 604
FIRSTFLEET INC. 605
FirstGroup America Inc 605
FIRSTHEALTH OF THE CAROLINAS INC. 605
FirstMerit Corp 605
Fiserv, Inc. 605
Fish & Richardson P.C. 605
Fiskars Brands Inc. 606
Fitch Ratings Inc. 606
Five Below Inc 606
Five Guys Enterprises LLC 606
Five Oaks Investment Corp. 606
Five Prime Therapeutics, Inc 606
FIVE STAR COOPERATIVE 607
Five Star Quality Care Inc 607
Flagstar Bancorp, Inc. 607
Flanders Corporation 607
Flanigan's Enterprises, Inc. 607
Flatbush Federal Bancorp Inc. 607
Flatiron Construction Corp. 608
FleetCor Technologies Inc 608
FleetPride Inc. 608
FLEMING GANNETT INC 608
FLETCHER ALLEN HEALTH CARE INC. 608
FLETCHER MUSIC CENTERS INC. 608
FlexiInternational Software Inc. 609
Flexsteel Industries, Inc. 609
FlightSafety International Inc. 609
FLINT ELECTRIC MEMBERSHIP CORPORATION 609
Flint Telecom Group Inc 609
FLIR Systems, Inc. 609
Florida Crystals Corporation 610
Florida Gaming Corp. 610
FLORIDA HOSPITAL HEARTLAND MEDICAL CENTER 610
FLORIDA HOSPITAL WATERMAN INC 610
Florida Power & Light Co. 610
Florida Power Corp. 610
Florida's Natural Growers 611
FLORSTAR SALES INC. 611
Flotek Industries Inc 611
Flowers Foods, Inc. 611
Flowserve Corp. 611
FLOYD HEALTHCARE MANAGEMENT INC. 611
Fluidigm Corp (DE) 612
Fluor Corp. 612
Flushing Financial Corp. 612
Flying Food Group LLC 612
FMC Corp. 612
FMC Technologies, Inc. 612
FNB Bancorp (CA) 613
FNBH Bancorp, Inc. 613
Focus Features 613
Foilmark Inc. 613
Foley & Lardner LLP 613
Foley Hoag LLP 613
Follett Higher Education Group 614
Fonar Corp. 614
Fontaine Trailer Company Inc. 614
FOOD FOR THE POOR INC. 614
Food Lion LLC 614
Food Technology Service Inc. 614
Foot Locker, Inc. 615
Football Northwest LLC 615
Forbes Energy Services Ltd. 615
Forbes Inc. 615
FORCE 3 INC. 615

Force Protection Inc. 615
Ford Motor Co. (DE) 616
Ford Motor Credit Company LLC 616
FORDHAM UNIVERSITY 616
Foremost Insurance Company 616
FOREST ANTHONY PRODUCTS COMPANY 616
Forest City Enterprises, Inc. 616
Forest Laboratories, Inc. 617
Forest River Inc. 617
FOREST SNAVELY PRODUCTS INC 617
Forestar Group Inc 617
Forever 21 Inc. 617
ForeverGreen Worldwide Corp 617
FORGE INDUSTRIES INC. 618
FormFactor Inc 618
Formica Corporation 618
FORMS & SUPPLY INC. 618
FORREST COUNTY GENERAL HOSPITAL (INC) 618
Forrester Research Inc. 618
Forsythe Technology Inc. 619
Fortegra Financial Corp 619
Fortinet Inc 619
Fortitech Inc. 619
Fortress Investment Group LLC 619
Fortune Brands Home & Security, Inc. 619
Forum Energy Technologies Inc 620
Forward Air Corp 620
Forward Industries, Inc. 620
Fossil Group Inc 620
Foster (L.B.) Co. 620
Foster Dairy Farms of California 620
Foundation Healthcare, Inc 621
Foundation Medicine Inc 621
Four Oaks Fincorp, Inc. 621
Fox & Hound Restaurant Group 621
FOX Broadcasting Company 621
Fox Chase Bancorp, Inc. 621
Fox Factory Holding Corp 622
FOX HEAD INC. 622
FOX News Network LLC 622
Fox Searchlight Pictures Inc. 622
FOXWORTH GALBRAITH LUMBER COMPANY 622
FPB Bancorp Inc. 622
FPIC Insurance Group Inc. 623
Francesca's Holdings Corporation 623
FRANCIS SAINT MEDICAL CENTER 623
FRANCISCAN ALLIANCE INC. 623
Franciscan Health System 623
Franciscan Skemp Healthcare Inc. 623
FRANCISCAN UNIVERSITY OF STEUBENVILLE 624
Frank Consolidated Enterprises Inc. 624
Frank's International Inc. 624
Frankenmuth Mutual Insurance Company 624
FRANKLIN AMERICAN MORTGAGE CO INC 624
FRANKLIN AND MARSHALL COLLEGE 624
FRANKLIN COMMUNITY HEALTH NETWORK 625
Franklin Covey Co 625
Franklin Credit Holding Corporation 625
Franklin Electric Co., Inc. 625
Franklin Electronic Publishers Incorporated 625
Franklin Financial Services Corp 625
FRANKLIN HOSPITAL 626
Franklin Resources, Inc. 626
FRANKLIN SQUARE HOSPITAL CENTER INC. 626
Franklin Street Properties Corp 626
Franklin Wireless Corp 626
FRASER/WHITE INC. 626
FRAZIER INDUSTRIAL COMPANY (INC) 627
Fred Meyer Stores Inc. 627
Fred's Inc. 627
Freddie Mac 627
FREDERICK MEMORIAL HOSPITAL INC. 627
Frederick's of Hollywood Group Inc 627
Frederick's of Hollywood Inc. 628
Freedom Communications Inc. 628
Freedom from Hunger 628
Freedom Group Inc. 628
Freedom Resources Enterprises Inc. 628
FreedomRoads LLC 628
FREEMAN HEALTH SYSTEM 629
FREEPORT REGIONAL HEALTH CARE
   FOUNDATION 629
Freeport-McMoRan Inc 629
Freescale Semiconductor Inc. 629

FREESE AND NICHOLS INC. 629
FreightCar America Inc 629
FREIGHTQUOTE.COM INC. 630
FREMONT AREA MEDICAL CENTER 630
Fremont Bancorporation 630
FREMONT CONTRACT CARRIERS INC. 630
Frequency Electronics Inc 630
Fresh Choice LLC 630
Fresh Enterprises LLC 631
FRESH MARK INC. 631
Fresh Market, Inc. 631
FreshPoint Inc. 631
Fried Frank Harris Shriver & Jacobson LLP 631
Friedman Industries, Inc. 631
Friendfinder Networks Inc 632
Friendly's Ice Cream LLC 632
FRISBIE MEMORIAL HOSPITAL 632
Frisch's Restaurants, Inc. 632
Frito-Lay North America Inc. 632
FROEDTERT MEMORIAL LUTHERAN HOSPITAL
   INC 632
Frontier Airlines Inc. 633
Frontier Communications Corp 633
Frontier Oilfield Services Inc. 633
Frontier Technology LLC 633
FrontRange Solutions Inc. 633
Frost Brown Todd LLC 633
FROZEN SPECIALTIES INC. 634
FRP Holdings Inc 634
Fru-Con Construction Corporation 634
FRUIT GROWERS SUPPLY COMPANY INC 634
Fruit of the Loom Inc. 634
FRUTH INC. 634
Fry's Electronics Inc. 635
Fry's Food and Drug Stores 635
FS Bancorp Inc 635
FTD Companies Inc 635
FTI Consulting Inc. 635
FTS International Inc. 635
FUBU the Collection LLC 636
Fuel Systems Solutions Inc 636
Fuel Tech Inc 636
FuelCell Energy Inc 636
FuelStream, Inc. 636
FUJIFILM Medical Systems USA Inc. 636
FUJIFILM North America Corporation 637
Fujitsu Computer Products of America Inc. 637
Fujitsu Semiconductor America Inc. 637
Fulcrum BioEnergy Inc. 637
Full Circle Capital Corp 637
Full Compass Systems Ltd. 637
Full House Resorts, Inc. 638
Fuller (H.B.) Company 638
FULLER THEOLOGICAL SEMINARY 638
Fullnet Communications Inc 638
Fulton Financial Corp. (PA) 638
Furiex Pharmaceuticals Inc 638
FURMAN FOODS INC. 639
FURMAN UNIVERSITY FOUNDATION INC. 639
Furmanite Corp 639
Fusion Telecommunications International Inc 639
Fusion-io Inc. 639
FusionStorm 639
FusionStorm Global Inc. 640
FutureFuel Corp 640
FX Alliance Inc. 640
FX Energy Inc. 640
FXCM Inc 640
G & J Pepsi-Cola Bottlers Inc. 640
G & K Services, Inc. 641
G&P TRUCKING COMPANY INC. 641
G-I Holdings Inc. 641
G-III Apparel Group Ltd. 641
G. L. Homes of Florida Corporation 641
G. P. & W. Inc. 641
G.S.E. CONSTRUCTION COMPANY INC. 642
G4S Secure Solutions (USA) Inc. 642
Gabriel Brothers Inc. 642
Gage Marketing Group LLC 642
Gaiam Inc 642
GAIN Capital Holdings Inc 642
GAINESVILLE REGIONAL UTILITIES (INC) 643
GAINSCO INC. 643
Galderma Laboratories L.P. 643

Galectin Therapeutics Inc. 643
Galena Biopharma Inc 643
Gallagher (Arthur J.) & Co. 643
GALLAUDET UNIVERSITY 644
GALLERY MODEL HOMES INC. 644
Gallery of History Inc. 644
GALLUP INC. 644
Galpin Motors Inc. 644
GAMCO Investors Inc 644
Game Show Network LLC 645
GameFly Inc. 645
GameStop Corp 645
Gaming Partners International Corp 645
Gander Mountain Company 645
Garan Incorporated 645
GARDEN CITY HOSPITAL 646
Garden Fresh Restaurant Corp. 646
Garden Ridge Corporation 646
Gartner, Inc. 646
Gary Rabine & Sons Inc. 646
Gas Depot Oil Company 646
Gasco Energy Inc. 647
Gate Gourmet Inc. 647
Gates McDonald & Company 647
Gateway Energy Corporation 647
Gateway Health Plan Inc. 647
Gateway Inc. 647
Gateway US Retail Inc. 648
GATX Corp. 648
Gavin de Becker & Associates 648
GC Services Limited Partnership 648
GCT Semiconductor Inc. 648
GE Aviation 648
Geeknet Inc 649
GEHAN HOMES LTD. 649
Gehl Company 649
GEICO Corporation 649
Geisinger Health System Foundation 649
GELBER GROUP LLC 649
Gemma Power Systems 650
Gen-Probe Incorporated 650
GENBAND Inc. 650
GENCO Distribution System Inc. 650
Genco Shipping & Trading Limited 650
Gencor Industries, Inc. 650
GeneLink Inc 651
Genencor International Inc. 651
Genentech Inc. 651
Generac Holdings Inc 651
General Atlantic LLC 651
General Atomics 651
General Atomics Aeronautical Systems Inc. 652
General Bearing Corporation 652
General Cable Corp. (DE) 652
General Casualty Insurance Companies 652
General Cigar Co. Inc. 652
General Communication Inc 652
General Dynamics Corp. 653
General Dynamics Land Systems Inc. 653
General Electric Capital Corporation 653
General Electric Co 653
General Employment Enterprises Inc 653
General Finance Corp 653
General Growth Properties Inc 654
GENERAL HEALTH SYSTEM 654
General Magnaplate Corporation 654
General Maritime Corporation 654
General Microwave Corporation 654
General Mills, Inc. 654
General Moly Inc. 655
General Motors Co. 655
General Motors Financial Company Inc. 655
General Steel Holdings Inc 655
General Supply & Services Inc. 655
Genesco Inc. 655
Genesee & Wyoming Inc. 656
GENESEE VALLEY GROUP HEALTH ASSOCIATION
   656
GENESIS CORP. 656
Genesis Energy L.P. 656
GENESIS HEALTH INC. 656
GENESIS HEALTH SYSTEM 656
Genesis Healthcare Inc 657
Genesis HealthCare LLC 657

GENESIS HEALTHCARE SYSTEM 657
GeneThera Inc. 657
GENICA CORPORATION 657
Genie Energy Ltd. 657
GenMark Diagnostics, Inc. 658
Genocea Biosciences Inc 658
Genomic Health Inc 658
Genoptix Inc. 658
Gentex Corp. 658
Gentherm Inc 658
Gentiva Health Services Inc 659
Genuardi's Family Markets Inc. 659
Genuine Parts Co. 659
GenVec Inc. (DE) 659
Genworth Financial, Inc. (Holding Co) 659
Genworth Mortgage Insurance Corporation 659
Genzyme Corporation 660
Geo Group Inc (The) (New) 660
GeoBio Energy Inc. 660
GeoMet Inc (DE) 660
GeoPetro Resources Co 660
GEORGE E. WARREN CORPORATION 660
George Foreman Enterprises Inc. 661
GEORGETOWN MEMORIAL HOSPITAL 661
Georgia Farm Bureau Mutual Insurance Company 661
Georgia Lottery Corporation 661
Georgia Power Co. 661
GEORGIA SOUTHERN UNIVERSITY 661
GEORGIA TRANSMISSION CORPORATION 662
Georgia-Carolina Bancshares, Inc. 662
Georgia-Pacific LLC 662
Geospace Technologies Corp 662
GERBER CHILDRENSWEAR LLC 662
Gerber Scientific Inc. 662
German American Bancorp Inc 663
Geron Corp. 663
GERRITY'S SUPER MARKET INC. 663
Getty Realty Corp. 663
GETTYSBURG COLLEGE 663
Gevo Inc. 663
GFI Group Inc 664
GGNSC Holdings LLC 664
GHSP Inc. 664
Giant Eagle Inc. 664
Giant Food Inc. 664
Giant Food Stores LLC 664
GIBBS DIE CASTING CORPORATION 665
Gibraltar Industries Inc 665
Gibraltar Packaging Group Inc. 665
Gibson Dunn & Crutcher LLP 665
Gibson Guitar Corp. 665
Giga-tronics Inc. 665
Gigamon Inc 666
GigOptix, Inc. 666
Gilbane Inc. 666
Gilead Sciences, Inc. 666
GILLETTE CHILDREN'S SPECIALTY HEALTHCARE 666
Gillman Companies 666
Gilster-Mary Lee Corporation 667
Ginkgo Residential Trust Inc. 667
GIRL SCOUTS OF THE UNITED STATES OF AMERICA 667
Girling Health Care Inc. 667
GKN Driveline North America Inc. 667
GKN Sinter Metals LLC 667
Glacier Bancorp, Inc. 668
Glacier Water Services Inc. 668
Gladstone Capital Corporation 668
Gladstone Commercial Corp 668
Gladstone Investment Corp 668
Gladstone Land Corp 668
GlassHouse Technologies Inc. 669
Glazer's Wholesale Drug Company Inc. 669
Gleacher & Co, Inc. (DE) 669
Glen Burnie Bancorp 669
GLENDALE ADVENTIST MEDICAL CENTER INC 669
GLENN O. HAWBAKER INC. 669
Glimcher Realty Trust 670
Global Axcess Corp. 670
Global Brass & Copper Holdings Inc 670
Global Brass and Copper Holdings Inc. 670
Global Communication Semiconductors Inc. 670

Global Custom Commerce L.P. 670
Global Diversified Industries Inc. 671
Global Earth Energy Inc. 671
Global Entertainment Corporation 671
Global Geophysical Services Inc 671
Global Healthcare Exchange LLC 671
Global Healthcare REIT Inc 671
Global Imaging Systems Inc. 672
Global Knowledge Training LLC 672
GLOBAL PACIFIC PRODUCE INC. 672
Global Partners LP 672
Global Payments, Inc. 672
Global Power Equipment Group, Inc. 672
Global Telecom & Technology Inc. 673
Global Traffic Network Inc. 673
GlobalFluency 673
GlobalOptions Group Inc. 673
GlobalSCAPE Inc 673
GlobalSpec Inc. 673
Globalstar Inc 674
Globe Specialty Metals Inc 674
GlobeImmune, Inc 674
Globus Medical Inc 674
Glori Energy Inc. 674
Glowpoint Inc 674
Glu Mobile Inc 675
GlycoMimetics Inc 675
GMAC Mortgage LLC 675
GMP Companies Inc. 675
GNC Holdings Inc 675
Godfather's Pizza Inc. 675
GOJO Industries 676
Gold Reserve Inc. 676
Gold Resource Corp 676
Gold Star Chili Inc. 676
Gold's Gym International Inc. 676
GOLD-EAGLE COOPERATIVE 676
Golden Eagle Insurance Corp. 677
Golden Enterprises, Inc. 677
Golden Entertainment Inc 677
Golden Gate Petroleum 677
GOLDEN GRAIN ENERGY LLC 677
Golden Minerals Co 677
Golden State Foods Corp. 678
Goldfield Corp. 678
Goldman Sachs Group, Inc. 678
Golf Galaxy LLC 678
Golfsmith International Holdings Inc. 678
Golub Capital BDC Inc. 678
Gonnella Baking Co. 679
Good Sam Enterprises LLC 679
Good Samaritan Hospital Medical Center 679
Good Source Solutions Inc. 679
Good Technology Inc. 679
Good Times Restaurants Inc. 679
GOOD360 680
Goodby Silverstein & Partners Inc. 680
GOODFELLOW BROS. INC. 680
Goodman Global Inc. 680
Goodman Networks Inc. 680
Goodrich Corporation 680
Goodrich Petroleum Corp. (Holding Co.) 681
GOODWILL INDUSTRIES INTERNATIONAL INC. 681
Goodwin Procter LLP 681
Goody Products Inc. 681
Goodyear Dunlop Tires North America Ltd. 681
Goodyear Tire & Rubber Co. 681
Gordmans Stores Inc 682
Gordon & Rees LLP 682
Gordon Brothers Group LLC 682
GORDON COLLEGE 682
Gordon Food Service Inc. 682
Gorman-Rupp Co. 682
Gosh Enterprises Inc. 683
GOTTLIEB MEMORIAL HOSPITAL 683
Goulds Pumps Incorporated 683
Government Employees Health Association Inc 683
Government Properties Income Trust 683
Goya Foods Inc. 683
GPM INVESTMENTS LLC 684
Grace (WR) & Co 684
GRACELAND FRUIT INC. 684
Graco Inc. 684
Gradall Industries Inc. 684

GRAEBEL COMPANIES INC. 684
Graftech International Ltd. 685
Graham Corp. 685
Graham Holdings Co. 685
Graham Packaging Company L.P. 685
Grainger (W.W.) Inc. 685
Gramercy Property Trust Inc 685
Gran Tierra Energy Inc 686
Grand Aire Inc. 686
Grand Canyon Education Inc 686
Grand Circle LLC 686
GRAND PIANO & FURNITURE CO. 686
GRAND STRAND REGIONAL MEDICAL CENTER LLC 686
GRAND VIEW HOSPITAL 687
Grande Communications Holdings Inc. 687
Grange Mutual Casualty Company 687
Granite Broadcasting Corporation 687
Granite City Food & Brewery Ltd 687
Granite Construction Inc. 687
GRANITE TELECOMMUNICATIONS LLC 688
Graphic Packaging Holding Co 688
Gray Television Inc 688
Graybar Electric Co., Inc. 688
Graycor Inc. 688
Great American Bancorp, Inc. 688
Great American Financial Resources Inc. 689
Great Lakes Aviation Ltd. 689
Great Lakes Cheese Company Inc. 689
Great Lakes Dredge & Dock Corp 689
Great Northern Iron Ore Properties 689
Great Plains Energy, Inc. 689
Great Plains Manufacturing Incorporated 690
Great River Energy 690
Great Southern Bancorp, Inc. 690
Great West Casualty Company 690
Great West Life & Annuity Insurance Co - Insurance Products 690
Great Wolf Resorts Inc. 690
GreatBatch Inc 691
GREATER BALTIMORE MEDICAL CENTER INC. 691
GREATER LAFAYETTE HEALTH SERVICES INC. 691
GREATER WASHINGTON EDUCATIONAL TELECOMMUNICATIONS ASSOCIATION IN 691
Greatwide Logistics Services LLC 691
Green Dot Corp 691
Green Hills Software Inc. 692
Green Mountain Power Corporation 692
Green Plains Inc. 692
Greenberg Traurig P.A. 692
Greenbrier Companies Inc (The) 692
Greene County Bancorp Inc 692
Greene Tweed & Co. Inc. 693
Greenheck Fan Corporation 693
Greenhill & Co Inc 693
GreenHunter Resources, Inc 693
GreenPages Inc. 693
Greenshift Corp 693
GREENSTONE FARM CREDIT SERVICES ACA 694
Greenville Hospital System 694
Greenway Medical Technologies Inc. 694
Greif Inc 694
Grey Global Group Inc. 694
Grey Healthcare Group Inc. 694
GREYHAWK North America LLC 695
Greylock Management Corporation 695
Greystone Logistics Inc. 695
Griffin Industrial Realty Inc 695
Griffith Laboratories Inc. 695
Griffon Corp. 695
Grill Concepts Inc. 696
Grimmway Enterprises Inc. 696
Gristede's Foods Inc. 696
GroceryWorks.com LLC 696
Groen Brothers Aviation Inc 696
GROSSMONT HOSPITAL CORPORATION 696
Grote Industries Inc. 697
Group 1 Automotive, Inc. 697
Group Health Cooperative 697
GROUP O INC. 697
Groupon Inc. 697
GROWMARK INC. 697
GRUNLEY CONSTRUCTION CO. INC. 698
GSE Holding Inc. 698

Hermes Music 739
Herschend Family Entertainment Corporation 739
Hersha Hospitality Trust 739
Hershey Company (The) 739
HERSHEY ENTERTAINMENT & RESORTS
    COMPANY 739
Hertz Global Holdings Inc 740
Heska Corp. 740
Hess Corp 740
Hexcel Corp. 740
Hexion Inc 740
HF Financial Corp. 740
HFB Financial Corp. 741
HFF Inc 741
hhgregg Inc 741
Hi-Shear Technology Corporation 741
HI-Tech Pharmacal Co., Inc. 741
Hibbett Sports Inc 741
HICKMAN WILLIAMS & COMPANY 742
Hickok Inc. 742
Hickory Farms Inc. 742
Hickory Tech Corp. 742
HID Global Corporation 742
HIGH CONCRETE GROUP LLC 742
High Country Bancorp, Inc. 743
HIGH INDUSTRIES INC. 743
High Performance Technologies Inc. 743
HIGH POINT REGIONAL HEALTH SYSTEM 743
HIGH POINT SOLUTIONS INC. 743
HIGH STEEL STRUCTURES LLC 743
Higher One Holdings Inc. 744
HighJump Software Inc. 744
Highlands Bankshares Inc. 744
Highlands Bankshares, Inc. (VA) 744
Highlands Fuel Delivery LLC 744
Highmark BCBSD Inc. 744
Highwoods Properties, Inc. 745
HILAND DAIRY FOODS COMPANY. LLC 745
Hill & Knowlton Inc. 745
HILL COUNTRY MEMORIAL HOSPITAL 745
Hill Holliday Connors Cosmopulos Inc. 745
Hill International Inc 745
Hill Phoenix Inc. 746
HILL PHYSICIANS MEDICAL GROUP INC. 746
Hill-Rom Holdings, Inc. 746
Hillenbrand Inc 746
Hills Bancorporation 746
Hillshire Brands Co 746
Hilltop Holdings, Inc. 747
Hilti Inc. 747
Hilton Worldwide Holdings Inc 747
Hilton Worldwide Inc. 747
HINES INTERESTS LIMITED PARTNERSHIP 747
Hingham Institution for Savings 747
HINSHAW & CULBERTSON LLP 748
Hitachi Global Storage Technologies Inc. 748
Hitachi Metals America Ltd. 748
Hitchiner Manufacturing Co. Inc. 748
HITT CONTRACTING INC. 748
Hittite Microwave Corp 748
HKN Inc 749
HMG/Courtland Properties, Inc. 749
HMI Industries Inc. 749
HMN Financial Inc. 749
HMS Holdings Corp 749
HNI Corp 749
HNTB Corporation 750
HO-CHUNK INC. 750
Hoag Hospital Foundation 750
HOAG MEMORIAL HOSPITAL PRESBYTERIAN 750
HOB Entertainment Inc. 750
HOBART AND WILLIAM SMITH COLLEGES 750
Hoffer Plastics Corporation 751
Holcim (US) Inc. 751
HOLIDAY BUILDERS INC. 751
HOLIDAY WHOLESALE INC. 751
Holland & Hart LLP 751
Holland & Knight LLP 751
HOLLAND COMMUNITY HOSPITAL INC 752
Holley Performance Products Inc. 752
Hollingsworth & Vose Company 752
HOLLINGSWORTH OIL CO. INC. 752
Hollister Incorporated 752
Holly Energy Partners LP 752

Holly Hunt Ltd. 753
HollyFrontier Corp. 753
Hollywood Media Corp 753
HOLMES LUMBER & BUILDING CENTER INC. 753
HOLMES REGIONAL MEDICAL CENTER INC. 753
Hologic, Inc. 753
Holophane 754
HOLY CARITAS FAMILY HOSPITAL INC 754
HOLY CROSS HOSPITAL INC. 754
HOLY SPIRIT HOSPITAL OF THE SISTERS OF
    CHRISTIAN CHARITY 754
Home Bancorp Inc 754
Home BancShares Inc 754
Home City Financial Corp 755
Home Depot Inc 755
Home Federal Bancorp Inc. 755
Home Financial Bancorp 755
Home Instead Inc. 755
Home Loan Financial Corp. 755
Home Meridian International Inc. 756
Home Products International Inc. 756
Home Properties Inc 756
HomeAway, Inc. 756
Homefed Corp. 756
Homeland Stores Inc. 756
HomeStreet Inc 757
Honda Manufacturing of Alabama LLC 757
Honda North America Inc. 757
Honda of America Mfg. Inc. 757
Honeywell Electronic Materials Inc. 757
Honeywell International Inc 757
Honeywell Specialty Materials 758
Honeywell Technology Solutions Inc. 758
Honigman Miller Schwartz and Cohn LLP 758
Hooker Furniture Corp 758
Hooper Holmes Inc 758
HOOSIER ENERGY RURAL ELECTRIC
    COOPERATIVE INC 758
Hooters of America LLC 759
Hoover Precision Products Inc. 759
Hoover's Inc. 759
HopFed Bancorp, Inc. 759
hopTo Inc 759
Horace Mann Educators Corp. 759
Horizon Bancorp (Michigan City, IN) 760
Horizon Bay Management L.L.C 760
Horizon Distributors Inc. 760
Horizon Group Properties Inc. 760
Horizon Health Corporation 760
Horizon Healthcare Services Inc. 760
Horizon Lines Inc 761
Horizon Milling LLC 761
Horizon Pharma Inc 761
Hormel Foods Corp. 761
Hornbeck Offshore Services Inc 761
HORNBLOWER YACHTS INC. 761
Horne International Inc 762
Hornell Brewing Co. Inc. 762
HORRY TELEPHONE COOPERATIVE INC. 762
Horsehead Holding Corp 762
Horton (D.R.) Inc. 762
Horwath International Services Ltd. 762
HOSPICE OF MICHIGAN INC. 763
Hospira Inc 763
HOSPITAL OF CENTRAL CONNECTICUT 763
Hospital Physician Partners Inc. 763
HOSPITAL SERVICE DISTRICT 1 INC 763
HOSPITAL SISTERS HEALTH SYSTEM 763
Hospitality Properties Trust 764
HOSS"S STEAK & SEA HOUSE INC. 764
Host Hotels & Resorts Inc 764
Hostmark Hospitality Group 764
Hotels.com L.P. 764
Houchens Industries Inc. 764
Houghton International Inc. 765
Houghton Mifflin Harcourt Co. 765
Houghton Mifflin Harcourt Publishing Company 765
Houlihan Lokey Inc. 765
Houston American Energy Corp. 765
HOUSTON SAM STATE UNIVERSITY 765
Houston Wire & Cable Co 766
HOVENSA LLC 766
Hovnanian Enterprises, Inc. 766
Howard Hughes Corp 766

Howard Miller Company 766
HP Enterprise Services LLC 766
HP Hood LLC 767
HP Inc 767
HRG Group Inc 767
HSB Group Inc. 767
HSBC USA, Inc. 767
HSN Inc (DE) 767
HTC Global Services Inc. 768
Hub Group, Inc. 768
Hub International Limited 768
Hubbell Inc. 768
Hudson City Bancorp Inc 768
Hudson Global Inc 768
Hudson Group 769
Hudson Pacific Properties Inc 769
Hudson Technologies Inc 769
Hudson Valley Federal Credit Union 769
Hudson Valley Holding Corp. 769
Huffy Corporation 769
Hughes Communications Inc. 770
Hughes Hubbard & Reed LLP 770
Hughes Network Systems LLC 770
HUGHES Telematics Inc. 770
Hugoton Royalty Trust (TX) 770
Huhtamaki Americas Inc. 770
Huhtamaki Inc. 771
Hulu LLC 771
Human Genome Sciences Inc. 771
Human Pheromone Sciences Inc. 771
HUMAN RIGHTS WATCH INC. 771
Humana Inc. 771
HUMAX USA INC. 772
Hunt (J.B.) Transport Services, Inc. 772
Hunter Douglas Inc. 772
Huntington Bancshares, Inc 772
Huntington Hospital 772
Huntington Ingalls Industries Inc. 772
Huntington Ingalls Industries, Inc. 773
Hunton & Williams LLP 773
Huntsman Corp 773
Huntsman International LLC 773
Hurco Companies, Inc. 773
HURLEY MEDICAL CENTER INC. 773
Huron Consulting Group Inc 774
Husch Blackwell LLP 774
Hussmann International Inc. 774
HUSSON UNIVERSITY 774
HUTCHESON MEDICAL CENTER INC. 774
Hutchinson Technology Inc. 774
Huttig Building Products, Inc. 775
HY-VEE INC. 775
Hyatt Hotels Corp 775
Hycroft Mining Corp 775
Hydromer, Inc. 775
Hydron Technologies Inc. 775
Hynix Semiconductor America Inc. 776
Hyperdynamics Corporation 776
Hypertension Diagnostics Inc. 776
Hyster-Yale Materials Handling, Inc. 776
Hytek Microsystems Inc. 776
I.D. Systems, Inc. (DE) 776
I/OMagic Corporation 777
IA Global Inc. 777
IAC/InterActiveCorp 777
iAnywhere Solutions Inc. 777
IASIS Healthcare Corporation 777
IASO Pharma Inc. 777
IBERDROLA RENEWABLES Inc. 778
Iberdrola USA Inc. 778
IBERIABANK Corp 778
IBW Financial Corporation 778
IC Compliance LLC 778
iCAD inc 778
Icagen Inc. 779
Icahn Enterprises LP 779
ICF International Inc 779
ICIMS.COM INC 779
ICL Performance Products LP 779
ICON Capital Corp. 779
ICON Health & Fitness Inc. 780
ICON IDENTITY SOLUTIONS INC. 780
Iconix Brand Group Inc 780
ICONMA L.L.C. 780

Intersections Inc 821
Intersil Corp. 821
Interstate Distributor Co. 821
Interstate National Dealer Services Inc. 821
Interstate Power & Light Co 821
InterSystems Corporation 822
Intertrust Technologies Corporation 822
Interval Leisure Group Inc 822
Intervest Bancshares Corp. 822
InterWest Partners LLC 822
inTEST Corp. 822
Intevac, Inc. 823
INTL FCStone Inc. 823
IntraLinks Holdings Inc 823
Intrawest Resorts Holdings Inc 823
Intrepid Potash Inc 823
Intrexon Corp 823
IntriCon Corp 824
Intrusion Inc 824
INTRUST Financial Corporation 824
Intuit Inc 824
Intuitive Surgical Inc 824
Inuvo Inc 824
Invacare Corp 825
InvenSense, Inc. 825
Invensys Rail Corporation 825
Inventergy Global Inc 825
inVentiv Health Inc. 825
Inventure Foods Inc. 825
Invesco Ltd. 826
Invesco Mortgage Capital Inc. 826
Investment Technology Group Inc. 826
Investors Bancorp Inc (New) 826
Investors Capital Holdings, Ltd. 826
Investors Heritage Capital Corp. 826
Investors Real Estate Trust 827
Investors Title Co. 827
INVISTA B.V. 827
Iomega Corporation 827
ION Geophysical Corp 827
Ionis Pharmaceuticals Inc 827
IOWA HEALTH SYSTEM 828
Iowa Interstate Railroad Ltd. 828
iPass Inc 828
iPayment Inc. 828
IPC Healthcare, Inc. 828
IPC Systems Inc. 828
IPG Photonics Corp 829
Ipreo Holdings LLC 829
Ipswitch Inc 829
iQor US Inc. 829
Irell & Manella LLP 829
IRIDEX Corp. 829
Iridium Communications Inc 830
Iridium Communications Inc. 830
IRIS International Inc. 830
iRobot Corp 830
Iron Mountain Inc (New) 830
IronPlanet Inc. 830
Ironwood Pharmaceuticals Inc. 831
Irvine Sensors Corporation 831
Irving Materials Inc. 831
Isagenix International LLC 831
ISG TECHNOLOGY LLC 831
iSign Solutions Inc 831
Isilon Systems Inc. 832
Isle of Capri Casinos Inc 832
ISO NEW ENGLAND INC. 832
Isola Group Ltd. 832
Isomet Corp. 832
IsoRay, Inc. 832
Israel Discount Bank of New York 833
Isramco, Inc. 833
ISTA Pharmaceuticals Inc. 833
iStar Inc 833
ITA GROUP INC 833
ITC Holdings Corp 833
ITC^DeltaCom Inc. 834
Iteris Inc 834
ITEX Corp. 834
Itron, Inc. 834
ITT Corporation 834
ITT Educational Services, Inc. 834
ITUS Corp 835

IVEY MECHANICAL COMPANY LLC 835
iVillage Inc. 835
iWatt Inc. 835
Ixia 835
IXYS Corp. 835
IXYS Integrated Circuits Division Inc. 836
J M SMITH CORPORATION 836
J&J Snack Foods Corp. 836
J. & W. Seligman & Co. Incorporated 836
J. Crew Group Inc. 836
J. D. STREETT & COMPANY INC. 836
J. F. WHITE CONTRACTING COMPANY 837
J. H. FINDORFF & SON INC. 837
J. L. French Automotive Castings Inc. 837
J. Ray McDermott Inc. 837
J. Walter Thompson Company 837
J.D. ABRAMS L.P. 837
J.D. Power and Associates Inc. 838
J.E. Dunn Construction Group Inc. 838
J.H. Harvey Co. LLC 838
J.M. Huber Corporation 838
J.R. Simplot Company 838
J.W. Childs Associates Limited Partnership 838
Jabil Circuit, Inc. 839
Jack Cooper Transport Co. Inc. 839
Jack Henry & Associates, Inc. 839
Jack in the Box, Inc. 839
Jack Morton Worldwide Inc. 839
JACKSON COUNTY MEMORIAL HOSPITAL
    AUTHORITY 839
JACKSON ELECTRIC MEMBERSHIP CORPORATION
    840
JACKSON ENERGY AUTHORITY 840
Jackson Hewitt Tax Service Inc. 840
JACKSON STATE UNIVERSITY 840
Jacksonville Bancorp Inc (FL) 840
Jacksonville Bancorp Inc. (MD) 840
Jacksonville Jaguars Ltd. 841
JACKSONVILLE UNIVERSITY 841
Jaclyn Inc. 841
JACO OIL COMPANY 841
Jacobs Engineering Group, Inc. 841
Jacobs Entertainment Inc. 841
Jacobs Financial Group Inc 842
JACOBS MALCOLM & BURTT 842
Jacobsen Construction Company Inc. 842
Jacuzzi Brands Corp. 842
Jagged Peak Inc. 842
Jakks Pacific Inc. 842
Jamaica Hospital Medical Center 843
Jamba Inc 843
JAMES MADISON UNIVERSITY INC. 843
James R. Glidewell Dental Ceramics Inc. 843
James River Coal Co 843
Janel Corp 843
Janssen Biotech Inc. 844
Janssen Pharmaceuticals Inc. 844
Janus Capital Group Inc 844
Jarden Corp 844
Jason Incorporated 844
Jason Industries, Inc 844
Jasper Engine Exchange Inc. 845
Javelin Mortgage Investment Corp 845
Javo Beverage Company Inc. 845
Jayco Inc. 845
JDA Software Group Inc. 845
JEA 845
Jefferson Bancshares Inc (TN) 846
JEFFERSON HEALTH SYSTEM INC. 846
JEFFERSON HOMEBUILDERS INC. 846
JEFFERSON HOSPITAL ASSOCIATION INC. 846
JEFFERSON REGIONAL MEDICAL CENTER 846
Jeffersonville Bancorp 846
Jel Sert Co. 847
JELD-WEN Inc. 847
Jelly Belly Candy Company 847
Jenner & Block LLP 847
Jennifer Convertibles Inc. 847
Jenny Craig Inc. 847
Jeppesen Sanderson Inc. 848
JER Investors Trust Inc. 848
JERRY BIGGERS CHEVROLET INC. 848
Jersey Central Power & Light Co. 848
JERSEY CITY MEDICAL CENTER INC 848

Jervis B. Webb Company 848
JetBlue Airways Corp 849
Jewel-Osco 849
Jewett-Cameron Trading Company Ltd. 849
Jewish Hospital & St. Mary's HealthCare 849
JFK HEALTH SYSTEM INC. 849
JG Wentworth Co (The) 849
Jim Palmer Trucking 850
Jim Walter Resources Inc. 850
Jimmy John's Franchise LLC 850
Jive Software Inc 850
JLG Industries Inc. 850
JLM Couture Inc. 850
JM Family Enterprises Inc. 851
JMB Realty Corporation 851
JMP Group LLC 851
Jockey International Inc. 851
John Bean Technologies Corp 851
JOHN BROWN UNIVERSITY 851
JOHN C. LINCOLN HEALTH NETWORK 852
JOHN CARROLL UNIVERSITY (INC) 852
John D. Oil and Gas Company 852
JOHN F KENNEDY CENTER FOR THE
    PERFORMING ARTS 852
John Hancock Financial Services Inc. 852
JOHN HINE PONTIAC 852
John Morrell & Co. 853
John Muir Health 853
JOHN T. MATHER MEMORIAL HOSPITAL OF PORT
    JEFFERSON NEW YORK INC. 853
John Wieland Homes and Neighborhoods Inc. 853
Johns Hopkins Bayview Medical Center 853
JOHNS HOPKINS HEALTH SYS CORP 853
Johns Hopkins Medicine International L.L.C. 854
Johns Manville Corporation 854
Johnson & Johnson 854
Johnson & Johnson Health Care Systems Inc. 854
JOHNSON & WALES UNIVERSITY INC 854
Johnson City Power Board 854
Johnson Controls Inc 855
Johnson Matthey Inc. 855
Johnson Outdoors Inc 855
JOHNSON SUPPLY AND EQUIPMENT
    CORPORATION 855
Johnsonville Sausage LLC 855
JOHNSTON ENTERPRISES INC. 855
Joie de Vivre Hospitality Inc. 856
JOINT COMMISSION ON ACCREDITATION OF
    HEALTHCARE ORGANIZATIONS 856
Jones Day 856
Jones Group Inc 856
Jones International Ltd. 856
Jones Lang LaSalle Inc 856
Jones Soda Co. 857
JORDAN CF INVESTMENTS LLP 857
Jordan Industries Inc. 857
Jordan's Furniture Inc. 857
Jos. A. Bank Clothiers, Inc. 857
Journal Communications Inc 857
Joy Global Inc 858
Joy Mining Machinery 858
JOYCE LESLIE INC. 858
JPI Partners LLC 858
JPMorgan Chase & Co 858
JPS Industries Inc. 858
JTH Holding Inc. 859
JTM Provisions Company Inc. 859
Jujamcyn Theaters LLC 859
JUNIATA COLLEGE 859
Juniata Valley Financial Corp 859
Juniper Group Inc. 859
Juniper Networks Inc 860
Juniper Pharmaceuticals Inc 860
Juno Lighting LLC 860
JUPITER MEDICAL CENTER INC. 860
Just Born Inc. 860
Justin Brands Inc. 860
K&G Men's Company Inc 861
K-Sea Transportation Partners L.P. 861
K-Tron International Inc. 861
K-V Pharmaceutical Company 861
K-VA-T Food Stores Inc. 861
K.V. Mart Co. 861
K12 Inc 862

Kadant Inc 862
KADLEC REGIONAL MEDICAL CENTER 862
Kahala Corp. 862
Kaiser Aluminum Corp. 862
Kaiser Foundation Health Plan of Colorado 862
Kaiser Foundation Health Plan of the Northwest 863
KAISER FOUNDATION HOSPITALS INC 863
Kaiser-Francis Oil Company 863
KALEIDA HEALTH 863
KaloBios Pharmaceuticals Inc. 863
Kaman Aerospace Corporation 863
Kaman Corp. 864
KANA Software Inc. 864
Kane is Able Inc. 864
Kanematsu USA Inc. 864
Kansas City Chiefs Football Club Inc. 864
Kansas City Life Insurance Co. (Kansas City, MO) 864
Kansas City Southern 865
KANSAS ELECTRIC POWER COOPERATIVE INC.
   865
KANSAS STATE UNIVERSITY 865
Kanthal Globar 865
KapStone Paper & Packaging Corp 865
KAR Auction Services Inc. 865
Karsten Manufacturing Corporation 866
Karyopharm Therapeutics Inc 866
kate spade LLC 866
Katun Corporation 866
Katy Industries, Inc. 866
Katz Media Group Inc. 866
Kawneer Company Inc. 867
Kaye Scholer LLP 867
Kaz Inc. 867
KB HOME 867
KBM Group 867
KBR Inc 867
KBS INC. 868
Kearny Financial Corp 868
KECK GRADUATE INSTITUTE 868
KEENAN HOPKINS SCHMIDT AND STOWELL
   CONTRACTORS INC. 868
KeHE Distributors LLC 868
Keithley Instruments Inc. 868
Kelley Drye & Warren LLP 869
Kellogg Co 869
KELLSTROM AEROSPACE LLC 869
Kellwood Company 869
Kelly Services, Inc. 869
Kelly-Moore Paint Company Inc. 869
Kelso & Company 870
KEMET Corp. 870
Kemira Chemicals Inc. 870
Kemper Corp. (DE) 870
Ken's Foods Inc. 870
KENERGY CORP. 870
Kenexa Corporation 871
Kennametal Inc. 871
KENNEDY HEALTH SYSTEM INC. 871
KENNEDY KRIEGER INSTITUTE INC. 871
Kennedy-Wilson Holdings Inc 871
KENNESAW STATE UNIVERSITY 871
Kenneth Cole Productions Inc. 872
Kennywood Entertainment Company Inc. 872
Kensey Nash Corporation 872
KENSINGTON PUBLISHING CORP. 872
KENT COUNTY MEMORIAL HOSPITAL 872
Kent Financial Services Inc. 872
Kentrox Inc. 873
Kentucky First Federal Bancorp 873
KENTUCKY MEDICAL SERVICES FOUNDATION
   INC. 873
Kentucky Power Company 873
Kenwal Steel Corp. 873
KENYON COLLEGE 873
Kerr Drug Inc. 874
Keryx Biopharmaceuticals Inc. 874
KETTERING MEDICAL CENTER 874
KETTERING UNIVERSITY 874
KEUKA COLLEGE 874
Keurig Green Mountain Inc 874
Keurig Incorporated 875
Kewaunee Scientific Corporation 875
KEY CITY FURNITURE COMPANY INC 875
Key Energy Services, Inc. 875

KEY FOOD STORES CO-OPERATIVE INC. 875
Key Plastics L.L.C. 875
Key Technology Inc 876
Key Tronic Corp. 876
KeyCorp 876
Keystone Mercy Health Plan 876
KEYW Holding Corp 876
KFC Corporation 876
Kforce Inc. 877
KGBO HOLDINGS INC 877
Kid Brands, Inc. 877
Kids II Inc. 877
Kiehl's Since 1851 LLC 877
Kiewit Offshore Services Ltd. 877
Killbuck Bancshares, Inc. 878
Kilroy Realty Corp 878
Kimball Electronics Group Inc. 878
Kimball International, Inc. 878
KIMBALL MEDICAL CENTER INC. 878
Kimberly-Clark Corp. 878
Kimco Realty Corp. 879
Kimpton Hotel & Restaurant Group LLC 879
Kinder Morgan Energy Partners, L.P. 879
Kinder Morgan Inc. 879
Kindred Healthcare Inc 879
Kinecta Federal Credit Union 879
Kinetek Inc. 880
Kinetic Concepts Inc. 880
Kinetic Systems Inc. 880
King Kullen Grocery Co. Inc. 880
King Ranch Inc. 880
KING"S COLLEGE 880
Kingold Jewelry Inc 881
Kings Food Markets 881
KINGSBROOK JEWISH MEDICAL CENTER INC 881
Kingstone Companies Inc 881
Kinray Inc. 881
Kinsley Construction Inc. 881
Kintetsu World Express (U.S.A.) Inc. 882
KiOR, Inc. 882
Kips Bay Medical Inc. 882
Kirby Corp. 882
Kirby Inland Marine LP 882
KIRBY RISK CORPORATION 882
Kirkland & Ellis LLP 883
Kirkland's Inc 883
Kissimmee Utility Authority 883
KITCHELL CORPORATION 883
Kite Realty Group Trust 883
Kiwanis International 883
Kiwibox.Com, Inc. 884
KKR & Co. L.P. 884
KKR Financial Holdings LLC 884
KLA-Tencor Corp. 884
Klaussner Furniture Industries Inc. 884
Klein Tools Inc. 884
Kleiner Perkins Caufield & Byers 885
Kmart Corporation 885
KMG Chemicals, Inc. 885
Knape & Vogt Manufacturing Company 885
Knight Transportation Inc. 885
KNIGHTS OF COLUMBUS 885
Knoll Inc 886
KNOUSE FOODS COOPERATIVE INC. 886
Knowles Corp 886
KNOX COUNTY HOSPITAL 886
KOCH ENTERPRISES INC. 886
Koch Foods Incorporated 886
Koch Industries Inc. 887
Kodiak Oil & Gas Corp. 887
Kohl's Corp. 887
Kohlberg Capital Corporation 887
Kohler Co. 887
KOHN PEDERSEN FOX ASSOCIATES PC 887
KOHR BROTHERS INC. 888
Kolbe & Kolbe Millwork Co. Inc. 888
Komatsu America Corp. 888
Kona Grill Inc 888
Kopin Corp. 888
Koppers Holdings Inc 888
Korn/Ferry International (DE) 889
Korn/Ferry International Futurestep Inc. 889
KORTE CONSTRUCTION COMPANY 889
Koss Corp 889

KPH HEALTHCARE SERVICES INC. 889
KPMG L.L.P. 889
KPS Capital Partners LP 890
KQED INC. 890
Kraft Foods Group Inc 890
Kramer Levin Naftalis & Frankel LLP 890
Kraton Performance Polymers Inc 890
Kraton Polymers LLC 890
Kratos Defense & Security Solutions, Inc. 891
Krause Gentle Corp. 891
Kreisler Manufacturing Corp. 891
Krispy Kreme Doughnuts Inc 891
Kroger Co (The) 891
Kroll Background America Inc. 891
Kroll Factual Data Inc. 892
Kroll Inc. 892
Kroll Ontrack Inc. 892
KRONES INC. 892
Kronos Incorporated 892
Kronos Worldwide Inc 892
KRUEGER INTERNATIONAL INC. 893
KSW Inc. 893
Kuni Automotive Group 893
KURT MANUFACTURING COMPANY INC. 893
Kushner Companies 893
Kutak Rock LLP 893
KVH Industries, Inc. 894
KWIK TRIP INC. 894
Kwikset Corporation 894
Kyocera Document Solutions America Inc. 894
Kyocera International Inc. 894
Kyocera Solar Inc. 894
L & S ELECTRIC INC. 895
L Brands, Inc 895
L&L Energy Inc 895
L&W Supply Corporation 895
L-3 Communications Holdings, Inc. 895
L-3 Communications Vertex Aerospace LLC 895
L. & R. DISTRIBUTORS INC. 896
L.A. Darling Company 896
LA FRANCE CORP. 896
La Jolla Pharmaceutical Company 896
La Madeleine of Texas Inc. 896
La-Z-Boy Inc. 896
Laboratory Corporation of America Holdings 897
Lacks Enterprises Inc. 897
Laclede Group Inc 897
LaCrosse Footwear Inc. 897
Ladenburg Thalmann Financial Services, Inc. 897
LADIES PROFESSIONAL GOLF ASSOCIATION 897
LAFAYETTE COLLEGE 898
LAFAYETTE GENERAL MEDICAL CENTER INC 898
Laird Technologies Inc. 898
LAKE AREA CORN PROCESSORS CO-OPERATIVE
   898
LAKE FOREST COLLEGE 898
LAKE HOSPITAL SYSTEM INC. 898
Lake Shore Bancorp Inc 899
Lake Sunapee Bank Group 899
Lakeland Bancorp, Inc. 899
Lakeland Financial Corp. 899
Lakeland Industries, Inc. 899
LAKELAND REGIONAL MEDICAL CENTER INC. 899
Lakeshore Staffing Group Inc. 900
Lakeside Foods Inc. 900
LAKESIDE INDUSTRIES INC. 900
Lam Research Corp 900
Lamar Advertising Co (New) 900
Lancaster Colony Corp. 900
Land O' Lakes Inc 901
Land O'Lakes Purina Feed LLC 901
Landauer, Inc. 901
Landec Corp. 901
Landmark Bancorp Inc 901
Landmark Graphics Corporation 901
Landry's Inc. 902
Landstar System, Inc. 902
Lane Bryant Inc. 902
LANE POWELL PC 902
LANGSTON SNYDER L P 902
LANIER PARKING HOLDINGS INC. 902
Lannett Co., Inc. 903
LANSING BOARD OF WATER AND LIGHT 903
Lantronix Inc. 903

LaPolla Industries Inc 903
Laredo Petroleum Holdings Inc. 903
LARKIN COMMUNITY HOSPITAL INC. 903
Las Vegas Sands Corp 904
Las Vegas Valley Water District 904
LaSalle Hotel Properties 904
LASALLE UNIVERSITY 904
LaserLock Technologies Inc. 904
Latham & Watkins LLP 904
LatinWorks Marketing Inc. 905
Lattice Inc 905
Lattice Semiconductor Corp. 905
LAUREN ENGINEERS & CONSTRUCTORS INC. 905
Lauren Manufacturing Company 905
Laurens County Health Care System 905
LAWRENCE & MEMORIAL HOSPITAL INC. 906
Lawson Products, Inc. 906
Layne Christensen Co. 906
LCA-Vision Inc. 906
LCNB Corp 906
LDI Ltd. LLC 906
LDR Holding Corp 907
LE MOYNE COLLEGE 907
Leap Wireless International Inc 907
LeapFrog Enterprises Inc 907
Lear Corp. 907
Learjet Inc. 907
Learning Tree International Inc 908
Lebhar-Friedman Inc. 908
LEE COUNTY ELECTRIC COOPERATIVE INC. 908
Lee Enterprises, Inc. 908
Lee Hecht Harrison LLC 908
LEE LEWIS CONSTRUCTION INC. 908
LEE UNIVERSITY 909
LEGACY EMANUEL HOSPITAL & HEALTH CENTER 909
LEGACY HEALTH 909
Legacy Partners Inc. 909
Legacy Reserves LP 909
LegacyTexas Financial Group Inc 909
LegalShield 910
LegalZoom.com Inc. 910
Legend Oil & Gas Ltd 910
Legg Mason, Inc. 910
Leggett & Platt, Inc. 910
LEHIGH UNIVERSITY 910
LEHIGH VALLEY HEALTH NETWORK INC. 911
Lehman Trikes USA Inc. 911
Leidos Holdings Inc 911
LeMaitre Vascular Inc 911
LendingTree Inc (New) 911
Lennar Corp. 911
Lennox International Inc 912
LEO A. DALY COMPANY 912
Lescarden, Inc. 912
LESTER E. COX MEDICAL CENTERS 912
Let's Go Publications Inc. 912
Letts Industries Inc. 912
Lettuce Entertain You Enterprises Inc. 913
Leucadia National Corp. 913
Level 3 Communications, Inc. 913
Levenger Company 913
Levi Strauss & Co. 913
LEVINDALE HEBREW GERIATRIC CENTER AND HOSPITAL INC. 913
Leviton Manufacturing Co. Inc. 914
Levy Restaurant Holdings LLC 914
LEWIS & CLARK COLLEGE 914
Lewis Tree Service Inc. 914
Lexar Media Inc. 914
Lexicon Pharmaceuticals, Inc. 914
Lexington Realty Trust 915
LexisNexis Group 915
Lexmark International, Inc. 915
LGI Homes, Inc. 915
LGL Group Inc 915
LHC Group Inc 915
Libbey Inc. 916
Liberty Bancorp Inc (MO) 916
Liberty Diversified International Inc. 916
Liberty Interactive Corp 916
Liberty Mutual Agency Corporation 916
Liberty Mutual Holding Company Inc. 916
LIBERTY ORCHARDS COMPANY INC. 917

Liberty Property Trust 917
Liberty Tax Inc 917
Liberty Travel Inc. 917
LICKING MEMORIAL HEALTH SYSTEMS 917
Liebert Corporation 917
LIFE CARE CENTERS OF AMERICA INC. 918
Life Fitness Inc. 918
Life Partners Holdings Inc 918
Life Quotes Inc. 918
Life Sciences Research Inc. 918
Life-Time Fitness Inc 918
LIFEBRIDGE HEALTH INC. 919
Lifecore Biomedical Inc. 919
Lifelock Inc 919
LifePoint Health Inc 919
LifeQuest World Corporation 919
Lifespan Corporation 919
LifeStore Financial Group 920
Lifetime Brands Inc 920
Lifetime Healthcare Inc. 920
Lifetime Products Inc. 920
LIFEWAY CHRISTIAN RESOURCES OF THE SOUTHERN BAPTIST CONVENTION 920
Lifeway Foods, Inc. 920
Ligand Pharmaceuticals Inc 921
Lightbridge Corp 921
LIGHTHOUSE COMPUTER SERVICES INC. 921
Lighting Science Group Corp 921
LightPath Technologies, Inc. 921
Lightspeed Online Research Inc. 921
Lightspeed Venture Partners 922
LightSquared Inc. 922
Lilly (Eli) & Co. 922
Lime Energy Co 922
Limelight Networks Inc 922
Limoneira Co. 922
Linbeck Group LLC 923
LINC Logistics Company 923
Lincare Holdings Inc. 923
LINCOLN CENTER FOR THE PERFORMING ARTS INC. 923
Lincoln Educational Services Corp 923
Lincoln Electric Holdings, Inc. 923
Lincoln Industries 924
Lincoln National Corp. 924
Lincoln Provision Inc. 924
Lindal Cedar Homes Inc. 924
Lindsay Corp 924
Line 6 Inc. 924
Lineage Power Corporation 925
Linear Technology Corp. 925
LinkedIn Corp 925
LinkShare Corporation 925
Linn Energy LLC 925
LinnCo LLC 925
Lionbridge Technologies Inc. 926
Lions Gate Entertainment Corp. 926
Lippert Components Inc. 926
LIPSCOMB UNIVERSITY 926
LIQUID INVESTMENTS INC. 926
Liquidity Services Inc 926
Liquidmetal Technologies Inc 927
LIRO PROGRAM AND CONSTRUCTION MANAGEMENT P.C. 927
LITEHOUSE INC. 927
Lithia Motors, Inc. 927
Lititz Mutual Insurance Company 927
Litle & Co. LLC 927
Littelfuse, Inc. 928
Little Caesar Enterprises Inc. 928
Little Lady Foods 928
LITTLE SIOUX CORN PROCESSORS LLC 928
Littler Mendelson P.C. 928
Live Nation Entertainment, Inc. 928
Live Ventures Inc 929
LivePerson Inc 929
LiveWorld, Inc. 929
LKQ Corp 929
LMI Aerospace, Inc. 929
LNB Bancorp, Inc. 929
LNR Property LLC 930
Local Corp 930
Local Matters Inc. 930
Locke Lord LLP 930

Lockheed Martin Commercial Space Systems 930
Lodgian Inc. 930
Loeb & Loeb LLP 931
LOEBER MOTORS INC. 931
Loehmann's Holdings Inc. 931
Loews Corp. 931
Logansport Financial Corp. 931
LOGIC Devices Incorporated 931
LOGICALIS INC. 932
LogicQuest Technology Inc 932
LogistiCare Inc. 932
LOGISTICS MANAGEMENT SOLUTIONS L.C. 932
LogMeIn Inc 932
LoJack Corp 932
LONG BEACH MEDICAL CENTER 933
LONG BEACH MEMORIAL MEDICAL CENTER 933
LONG ISLAND UNIVERSITY 933
Long John Silver's LLC 933
Longview Fibre Company 933
LookSmart Ltd. 933
LOOP LLC 934
LoopNet Inc. 934
Lorillard, Inc. 934
Los Angeles County Department of Health Services 934
Los Angeles County Metropolitan Transportation Authority 934
LOS ANGELES DEPARTMENT OF WATER AND POWER 934
Los Angeles Dodgers Inc. 935
LOS ANGELES PHILHARMONIC ASSOCIATION 935
Lotus Development Corporation 935
Louis Vuitton North America Inc. 935
Louisiana Bancorp Inc 935
Louisiana Health Service and Indemnity Company 935
Louisiana-Pacific Corp. 936
Love's Travel Stops & Country Stores Inc. 936
LOW TEMP INDUSTRIES INC. 936
Lowe Enterprises Inc. 936
Lowe's Companies Inc 936
Lowe's Food Stores Inc. 936
Lowenstein Sandler PC 937
Lower Colorado River Authority 937
LOYOLA MARYMOUNT UNIVERSITY INC 937
LOYOLA UNIVERSITY MARYLAND INC. 937
LOYOLA UNIVERSITY NEW ORLEANS INC 937
LPL Financial Holdings Inc. 937
LQ Management LLC 938
LRAD Corp 938
LRI Holdings Inc. 938
LRR Energy, L.P. 938
LSB Financial Corp. 938
LSB Industries, Inc. 938
LSI Corp 939
LSI Industries Inc. 939
LTC Properties, Inc. 939
Luby's, Inc. 939
Lucas Energy Inc 939
Lucasfilm Entertainment Company Ltd. 939
Lucid Inc. 940
LUCKEY FARMERS INC. 940
lululemon athletica inc 940
Lumber Liquidators Holdings Inc 940
Luminescent Systems Incorporated 940
Luminex Corp 940
Lummus Technology Inc. 941
Lumos Networks Corp. 941
Luna Innovations Inc 941
Lund International Inc. 941
Lundbeck Inc. 941
Luster Products Co. 941
LUTHER COLLEGE 942
Lutheran Medical Center 942
Luxottica Retail 942
Luxottica Retail North America Inc. 942
Lydall, Inc. 942
LYNCHBURG COLLEGE 942
Lynden Incorporated 943
LYNTEGAR ELECTRIC COOPERATIVE INC. 943
LynuxWorks Inc. 943
Lyon (William) Homes 943
Lyris, Inc. 943
M & F Bancorp Inc 944

M & F Worldwide Corp. 944
M & H ENTERPRISES INC. 944
M & M MERCHANDISERS INC. 944
M & T Bank Corp 944
M Financial Holdings Incorporated 944
M-I L.L.C. 945
M. B. KAHN CONSTRUCTION CO. INC. 945
M. Shanken Communications Inc. 945
M.D.C. Holdings, Inc. 945
M/A-Com Technology Solutions Holdings Inc. 945
M/I Homes Inc 945
MAC BEATH HARDWOOD COMPANY 946
MACALESTER COLLEGE 946
Macatawa Bank Corp. 946
MacDermid Printing Solutions 946
Mace Security International, Inc. 946
Macerich Co. (The) 946
MACH 1 GLOBAL SERVICES INC. 947
MACHADO/GARCIA-SERRA PUBLICIDAD INC. 947
Mack Cali Realty Corp 947
Mack Trucks Inc. 947
MacKay Life Sciences Inc. 947
Mackinac Financial Corp 947
MacLean-Fogg Company 948
MACOMB OAKLAND REGIONAL CENTER INC 948
Macquarie Infrastructure Corp 948
MacroGenics, Inc 948
Macy's Inc. 948
Madden (Steven) Ltd. 948
Madison Dearborn Partners LLC 949
MADISON ELECTRIC COMPANY 949
MADONNA REHABILITATION HOSPITAL 949
Maersk Inc. 949
MAGEE REHABILITATION HOSPITAL 949
Magellan Health Inc. 949
Magellan Midstream Partners LP 950
Magellan Petroleum Corp. 950
Magma Design Automation Inc. 950
Magna Carta Companies 950
Magna Mirrors 950
MagnaChip Semiconductor Corp 950
MAGNECO/METREL INC. 951
MagneTek, Inc. 951
Magnolia Pictures Inc. 951
Magnum Hunter Resources Corp (DE) 951
Magyar Bancorp Inc 951
Maid-Rite Corporation 951
Maimonides Medical Center 952
MAIN LINE HEALTH INC. 952
MAIN LINE HOSPITALS INC. 952
Main Street America Group Inc. 952
Main Street Capital Corp 952
Maine & Maritimes Corporation 952
Maine Employers' Mutual Insurance Company 953
MAINE MEDICAL CENTER 953
MAINEGENERAL HEALTH 953
MAINEHEALTH 953
MainSource Financial Group Inc 953
Mainstreet Bankshares Inc 953
Majesco Entertainment Co. 954
MAJOR LEAGUE BASEBALL PLAYERS
  ASSOCIATION 954
Major League Soccer L.L.C. 954
MAKE-A-WISH FOUNDATION OF AMERICA 954
Makita U.S.A. Inc. 954
Malvern Bancorp Inc. 954
Mammatech Corporation 955
MANAGEMENT AND TRAINING CORPORATION 955
Mandalay Sports Entertainment LLC 955
Mango Capital Inc. 955
Manhattan Associates, Inc. 955
Manhattan Bridge Capital, Inc. 955
MANHATTAN COLLEGE CORP 956
MANHATTANVILLE COLLEGE 956
Manitex International Inc 956
Manitowoc Co Inc (The) 956
Manitowoc Foodservice Companies Inc. 956
Mannatech Inc 956
Manning & Napier Inc. 957
MannKind Corp 957
ManpowerGroup 957
ManTech International Corp 957
MANUFACTURED HOUSING ENTERPRISES INC.
  957

MapQuest Inc. 957
MAR-JAC POULTRY INC. 958
Marathon Oil Corp. 958
Marathon Petroleum Corp. 958
Marc Glassman Inc. 958
MARCH OF DIMES FOUNDATION 958
Marchex Inc 958
Marchon Eyewear Inc. 959
Marcus & Millichap Real Estate Investment Services
  In 959
Marcus Corp. (The) 959
MARIAN UNIVERSITY INC. 959
Marie Callender Pie Shops Inc. 959
Marin Software Inc. 959
Marina Biotech Inc 960
Marine Products Corp. 960
MarineMax Inc 960
MARIST COLLEGE 960
MARITZ HOLDINGS INC. 960
Maritz Research Inc. 960
Mark IV LLC 961
Markel Corp (Holding Co) 961
MARKET & JOHNSON INC. 961
MARKET AMERICA INC. 961
Market Strategies International 961
MarketAxess Holdings Inc. 961
Marketo Inc 962
MarketTools Inc. 962
MarketWatch Inc. 962
Markwest Energy Partners L.P. 962
Marlabs Incorporated 962
Marlin Business Services Corp 962
MARQUETTE UNIVERSITY 963
Marriott International, Inc. 963
Marriott Vacations Worldwide Corp. 963
Marrone Bio Innovations Inc 963
Mars Incorporated 963
Mars Petcare US Inc. 963
MARS SUPER MARKETS INC 964
Marsh & McLennan Companies Inc. 964
Marsh Supermarkets Inc. 964
Marsh USA Inc. 964
MARSHALL UNIVERSITY 964
MARSHFIELD CLINIC INC. 964
Marten Transport, Ltd. 965
Martha Stewart Living Omnimedia, Inc. 965
MARTIN & BAYLEY INC. 965
Martin Marietta Materials, Inc. 965
Martin Midstream Partners LP 965
Martin's Super Markets Inc. 965
Marubeni America Corporation 966
MARVIN ENGINEERING CO. INC. 966
Mary Kay Holding Corporation 966
Mary Kay Inc. 966
MARYLAND AND VIRGINIA MILK PRODUCERS
  COOPERATIVE ASSOCIATION INC 966
MARYLAND SOUTHERN ELECTRIC COOPERATIVE
  INC 966
MARYMOUNT MANHATTAN COLLEGE 967
Masco Contractor Services LLC 967
Masco Corp. 967
Mascoma Corporation 967
Masergy Communications Inc. 967
Masimo Corp. 967
Mass. Electric Construction Co. 968
MASSACHUSETTS HIGHER EDUCATION
  ASSISTANCE CORPORATION 968
MASSACHUSETTS MEDICAL SOCIETY INC 968
Massachusetts Mutual Life Insurance Company 968
MASSACHUSETTS PORT AUTHORITY 968
MAST Industries Inc. 968
MasTec Inc. (FL) 969
Mastech Holdings Inc 969
Master Lock Company LLC 969
MasterBrand Cabinets Inc. 969
MasterCard Inc 969
Masterplan Inc. 969
Matador Resources Company 970
MATANUSKA TELEPHONE ASSOCIATION
  INCORPORATED 970
Material Sciences Corp. 970
Materion Advanced Materials Technologies and
  Services Inc 970
Materion Corp 970

Matrix Service Co. 970
Matrix Telecom Inc. 971
Matrixx Initiatives Inc. 971
Matson Inc 971
Mattel Inc 971
Mattersight Corp 971
MATTESON-RIDOLFI INC. 971
Matthews International Corp 972
MATTINGLY FOODS INC. 972
Mattress Firm Holding Corp 972
Mattson Technology Inc 972
Maui Land & Pineapple Co., Inc. 972
Maui Wowi Franchising Inc. 972
Maurices Incorporated 973
MAVERICK Technologies LLC 973
Maverick USA Inc. 973
Maxim Crane Works L.P. 973
MAXIM HEALTHCARE SERVICES INC. 973
Maxim Integrated Products, Inc. 973
MAXIMUS Inc. 974
MaxLinear Inc 974
MAXOR NATIONAL PHARMACY SERVICES
  CORPORATION 974
Maxwell Technologies, Inc. 974
Mayer Brown LLP 974
MAYER ELECTRIC SUPPLY COMPANY INC. 974
Mayfield Fund 975
Mayflower Bancorp Inc. 975
Mayo Clinic Jacksonville 975
Mays (J.W.), Inc. 975
MAYVILLE ENGINEERING CO INC 975
Mazak Corporation 975
Mazzio's Corporation 976
MB Financial Inc 976
MBC HOLDINGS INC. 976
MBIA Inc. 976
MBT Financial Corp. 976
MC DONOUGH COUNTY HOSPITAL DISTRICT 976
MC NEESE STATE UNIVERSITY 977
McAfee Inc. 977
McAlister's Corporation 977
McCann Relationship Marketing Inc. 977
McCarter & English LLP 977
MCCARTHY BUILDING COMPANIES INC. 977
McClatchy Co. (The) 978
McCormick & Co., Inc. 978
McCormick & Schmick's Seafood Restaurants Inc.
  978
MCCOY-ROCKFORD INC. 978
MCDANIEL COLLEGE INC 978
McDermott International Inc. 978
McDonald's Corp 979
McEwen Mining Inc. 979
MCG Capital Corp 979
McGladrey LLP 979
McGough Construction Co. Inc. 979
McGrath RentCorp 979
McGraw Hill Financial, Inc. 980
McGuireWoods LLP 980
McKee Foods Corporation 980
McKenna Long & Aldridge LLP 980
McKesson Corp. 980
McKesson Medical-Surgical Inc. 980
McKinstry Co. LLC 981
MCLAREN HEALTH CARE CORPORATION 981
McLaren Performance Technologies Inc. 981
McMaster-Carr Supply Company 981
MCNAUGHTON-MCKAY ELECTRIC CO. 981
McNeil Consumer Pharmaceuticals Co. 981
McNeilus Companies Inc. 982
MCNICHOLS COMPANY 982
MCPHEE ELECTRIC LTD 982
McRae Industries, Inc. 982
McWane Inc. 982
MDU Resources Group Inc. 982
Mead Johnson Nutrition Co 983
Meadowbrook Insurance Group Inc 983
MeadWestvaco Calmar 983
MeadWestvaco Corp. 983
Meals on Wheels Association of America 983
Measurement Specialties, Inc. 983
Mechanical Technology, Inc. 984
Mecklermedia Corp 984
MECO Corporation 984

Meda Pharmaceuticals Inc. 984
Medallion Financial Corp. 984
MedAssets Inc 984
MedCath Corporation 985
MEDecision Inc. 985
Media General Inc (New) 985
Media Sciences International Inc. 985
MEDIA STORM LLC 985
MediaMind Technologies Inc. 985
MediaNet Digital Inc. 986
Medical Action Industries, Inc. 986
Medical Liability Mutual Insurance Company 986
Medical Mutual of Ohio 986
Medical Properties Trust Inc 986
Medical Staffing Network Healthcare LLC 986
Medicine Shoppe International Inc. 987
Medicines Co (The) 987
Medicinova Inc 987
Medicis Pharmaceutical Corporation 987
Medidata Solutions, Inc. 987
Medifast Inc 987
MedImmune L.L.C. 988
Medivation Inc 988
Mediware Information Systems Inc. 988
MEDLER ELECTRIC COMPANY 988
Medline Industries Inc. 988
Mednax, Inc. 988
MedPlus Inc. 989
MEDSEEK INC. 989
MEDSTAR HEALTH INC. 989
MEDSTAR-GEORGETOWN MEDICAL CENTER INC. 989
MedTel Services LLC 989
MEDTOX Scientific Inc. 989
Medtronic Sofamor Danek USA Inc. 990
Medtronic, Inc. 990
Meenan Oil Co. L.P. 990
MeetMe Inc. 990
MegaMex Foods LLC 990
Meggitt (North Hollywood) Inc. 990
Meggitt Aircraft Braking Systems Corporation 991
Meggitt Training Systems Inc. 991
Meggitt-USA Inc. 991
MEI TECHNOLOGIES INC. 991
Meijer Inc. 991
Meineke Car Care Centers Inc. 991
MEMORIAL HEALTH SERVICES CORPORATION 992
Memorial Health System 992
MEMORIAL HEALTH SYSTEM OF EAST TEXAS 992
MEMORIAL HEALTH UNIVERSITY MEDICAL CENTER INC. 992
MEMORIAL HERMANN HEALTHCARE SYSTEM 992
MEMORIAL HOSPITAL 992
Memorial Production Partners LP 993
Memorial Sloan-Kettering Cancer Center 993
Memory Lane Inc. 993
Memphis Light Gas and Water Division 993
Memry Corporation 993
Menard Inc. 993
Menasha Corporation 994
Menasha Packaging Company LLC 994
MENIL FOUNDATION INC. 994
MENLO COLLEGE 994
Menlo Worldwide LLC 994
MENNO TRAVEL SERVICE INC. 994
Mentor Graphics Corp 995
Mentor Worldwide LLC 995
Mera Pharmaceuticals Inc. 995
Mercantile Bancorp Inc. 995
Mercantile Bank Corp. 995
Mercedes-Benz Financial Services USA LLC 995
Mercedes-Benz U.S. International Inc. 996
Mercer Inc. 996
Mercer Insurance Group Inc. 996
Mercer International Inc 996
Merchants Bancshares, Inc. (Burlington, VT) 996
Merck & Co., Inc 996
Mercury General Corp. 997
Mercury Marine 997
Mercury Systems Inc 997
MERCY CHILDREN'S HOSPITAL 997
MERCY COLLEGE 997
MERCY CORPS 997
Mercy Health 998

MERCY HOSPITAL AND MEDICAL CENTER 998
MERCY HOSPITAL SPRINGFIELD 998
MERCY MEDICAL CENTER 998
MERCY MEDICAL CENTER INC. 998
MERCY SHIPS 998
Meredith Corp 999
Merge Healthcare Inc 999
Merial Inc. 999
Meridian Bancorp Inc 999
Meridian Bioscience Inc. 999
Meridian Group International Inc. 999
Merit Medical Systems, Inc. 1000
Meritage Homes Corp 1000
Meritage Hospitality Group Inc 1000
MERITER HEALTH SERVICES INC. 1000
Meritor Inc 1000
MERITUS HEALTH INC. 1000
Merkle Group Inc. 1001
Merkley + Partners Inc. 1001
Merrill Corporation 1001
Merrill Lynch and Co. Inc. 1001
Merrill Lynch Credit Corporation 1001
Merrimack Pharmaceuticals Inc. 1001
Merriman Holdings Inc. 1002
Merry Maids Limited Partnership 1002
Meru Networks Inc. 1002
Merz Pharmaceuticals Inc. 1002
Mesa Laboratories, Inc. 1002
Mesa Royalty Trust 1002
Mesabi Trust 1003
Mesirow Financial Holdings Inc. 1003
MESSER CONSTRUCTION CO. 1003
MESSIAH COLLEGE 1003
Mestek Inc. 1003
Meta Financial Group Inc 1003
Metabolex Inc. 1004
Metabolix Inc 1004
Metal Container Corporation 1004
Metalico Inc 1004
Metavation LLC 1004
Methes Energies International Ltd. 1004
Methode Electronics, Inc. 1005
METHODIST HOSPITAL OF SOUTHERN CALIFORNIA 1005
METHODIST HOSPITALS OF DALLAS INC 1005
METHODIST LE BONHEUR HEALTHCARE 1005
MetLife Inc 1005
MetoKote Corporation 1005
MetricStream Inc. 1006
Metro Bancorp Inc PA 1006
METRO PACKAGING & IMAGING INC 1006
Metro-Goldwyn-Mayer Inc. 1006
Metro-North Commuter Railroad Company 1006
Metrocorp Holdings Inc. 1006
METROPLEX ADVENTIST HOSPITAL INC. 1007
Metropolitan Edison Company 1007
Metropolitan Health Networks Inc. 1007
Metropolitan Opera Association Inc. 1007
Metropolitan Property and Casualty Insurance Company 1007
METROPOLITAN SECURITY SERVICES INC. 1007
Metropolitan Transit Authority of Harris County Texas 1008
Metropolitan Transportation Authority 1008
METROPOLITAN UTILITIES DISTRICT OMAHA NEBRASKA. 1008
Metropolitan Washington Airports Authority 1008
Mettler-Toledo International, Inc. 1008
Metwood Inc 1008
Mexco Energy Corp. 1009
Mexican Restaurants, Inc. 1009
MEYER & WALLIS INC. 1009
MFA Financial, Inc. 1009
MFA INCORPORATED 1009
MFA OIL COMPANY 1009
MFRI Inc. 1010
MGA Entertainment Inc. 1010
MGC Diagnostics Corp 1010
MGE Energy Inc 1010
MGIC Investment Corp. (WI) 1010
MGM Grand Hotel LLC 1010
MGM Resorts International 1011
MGT Capital Investments Inc 1011
MI Windows and Doors Inc. 1011

MIAMI JEWISH HEALTH SYSTEMS INC. 1011
Miami Marlins L.P. 1011
MIAMI UNIVERSITY 1011
MIAMI VALLEY HOSPITAL 1012
Michael Foods Group Inc. 1012
Michaels Stores Inc. 1012
Michelin North America Inc. 1012
Michels Corporation 1012
MICHIGAN MILK PRODUCERS ASSOCIATION 1012
MICHIGAN TECHNOLOGICAL UNIVERSITY 1013
Micrel, Inc. 1013
Micro Imaging Technology Inc. 1013
MicroChip Technology, Inc. 1013
MicroFinancial, Inc. 1013
Microfluidics International Corporation 1013
Micron Technology Inc. 1014
Micronetics Inc. 1014
Micropac Industries, Inc. 1014
Micros Systems, Inc. 1014
Microsemi Corp 1014
Microsoft Corporation 1014
MicroStrategy Inc. 1015
MICROTECHNOLOGIES LLC 1015
Microvision Inc. 1015
Microwave Filter Co., Inc. 1015
Micrus Endovascular Corporation 1015
MID AMERICA CLINICAL LABORATORIES LLC 1015
Mid Penn Bancorp, Inc. 1016
Mid-America Apartment Communities Inc 1016
Mid-Con Energy Partners LP 1016
MidAmerican Energy Holdings Company 1016
Midas Inc. 1016
MidasPlus Inc. 1016
Midcoast Energy Partners LP 1017
Midcontinent Communications Investor LLC 1017
Middle River Aircraft Systems 1017
MIDDLE TENNESSEE STATE UNIVERSITY 1017
Middleburg Financial Corp. 1017
Middleby Corp 1017
Middlefield Banc Corp. 1018
Middlesex Savings Bank 1018
Middlesex Water Co. 1018
Midland Cogeneration Venture Limited Partnership 1018
Midland Financial Co. 1018
Midland Paper Company 1018
Midland States Bancorp Inc. 1019
MidSouth Bancorp, Inc. 1019
Midstates Petroleum Co Inc 1019
MIDWEST ENERGY INC. 1019
Midwest Generation LLC 1019
MidWestOne Financial Group, Inc. 1019
MIKART INC. 1020
Milacron LLC 1020
MILAEGER"S INC. 1020
Milbank Tweed Hadley & McCloy LLP 1020
Milberg LLP 1020
MILES HEALTH CARE INC 1020
Milestone Scientific Inc. 1021
Milford Regional Medical Center Inc. 1021
Millbrook Distribution Services Inc. 1021
Millennial Media Inc 1021
Millennium Pharmaceuticals Inc. 1021
Millennium Prime Inc 1021
Miller (Herman) Inc. 1022
MILLER ELECTRIC COMPANY 1022
MILLER ELECTRIC CONSTRUCTION INC 1022
Miller Energy Resources, Inc. 1022
Miller Industries, (TN) 1022
Miller Publishing Group LLC 1022
MILLER TRANSPORTATION SERVICES INC. 1023
Miller-Valentine Partners Ltd. 1023
MillerCoors LLC 1023
MILLS-PENINSULA HEALTH SERVICES 1023
Millward Brown Inc. 1023
Milwaukee Electric Tool Corporation 1023
Minden Bancorp Inc. 1024
mindSHIFT Technologies Inc. 1024
mindWireless 1024
Miner Enterprises Inc. 1024
Minerals Technologies, Inc. 1024
MINERS INCORPORATED 1024
Mines Management, Inc. 1025
MINISTRY HEALTH CARE INC. 1025

MINITAB INC. 1025
Minn-Dak Farmers Cooperative 1025
Minnesota Twins Baseball Club 1025
Minnesota Vikings Football Club L.L.C. 1025
MINNKOTA POWER COOPERATIVE INC. 1026
Mintz Levin Cohn Ferris Glovsky and Popeo P.C. 1026
MINUTEMAN PRESS INTERNATIONAL INC. 1026
Miramax Film Corp. 1026
Mirapoint Software Inc. 1026
Mirati Therapeutics Inc 1026
MIRENCO Inc. 1027
Misonix, Inc. 1027
Mission Community Bancorp 1027
MISSION HOSPITAL INC. 1027
MISSION PHARMACAL COMPANY 1027
MISSISSIPPI COUNTY ELECTRIC COOPERATIVE
  INC. 1027
Mississippi Power Co. 1028
MISSOURI STATE UNIVERSITY 1028
Mistras Group, Inc. 1028
Mitcham Industries, Inc. 1028
MITCHELL SILBERBERG & KNUPP LLP 1028
Mitek Systems, Inc. 1028
MiTek USA Inc. 1029
Mitsubishi Caterpillar Forklift America Inc. 1029
Mitsubishi Power Systems Americas Inc. 1029
MITY Enterprises Inc. 1029
MKS Instruments, Inc. 1029
mktg, Inc. 1029
MMA Capital Management LLC 1030
MMI Products Inc. 1030
MModal Inc. 1030
MMR GROUP INC. 1030
MMRGlobal Inc 1030
MN Airlines LLC 1030
MNP CORPORATION 1031
Moark LLC 1031
Mobile Area Networks Inc 1031
Mobile Mini, Inc. 1031
MobilePro Corp. 1031
MobiTV Inc. 1031
Mocon Inc. 1032
Model N, Inc 1032
Modern Builders Supply Inc. 1032
MODERN WOODMEN OF AMERICA 1032
Modine Manufacturing Co 1032
Modis Inc. 1032
ModusLink Global Solutions, Inc. 1033
Mohawk Industries, Inc. 1033
Mohegan Tribal Gaming Authority 1033
Molina Healthcare Inc 1033
Moller International Inc. 1033
MOLLOY COLLEGE 1033
Molson Coors Brewing Company 1034
Molycorp Inc. (DE) 1034
Momenta Pharmaceuticals Inc 1034
Momentive Performance Materials Inc. 1034
Monarch Casino & Resort, Inc. 1034
Monarch Cement Co. 1034
Monarch Community Bancorp Inc 1035
Monarch Financial Holdings Inc 1035
Mondelez International Inc 1035
MoneyGram International Inc 1035
MoneyGram Payment Systems Inc. 1035
MONMOUTH MEDICAL CENTER INC. 1035
Monmouth Real Estate Investment Corp 1036
MONMOUTH UNIVERSITY 1036
MONOGRAM FOOD SOLUTIONS LLC 1036
Monolithic Power Systems Inc 1036
Monotype Imaging Holdings Inc 1036
Monro Muffler Brake, Inc. 1036
Monrovia Nursery Company 1037
Monsanto Co. 1037
Monster Beverage Corp (New) 1037
Monster Worldwide Inc 1037
MONTANA STATE UNIVERSITY INC 1037
MontaVista Software Inc. 1037
MONTCLAIR STATE UNIVERSITY 1038
Monumental Sports & Entertainment 1038
Moody's Corp. 1038
Moog, Inc. 1038
Mooney Aerospace Group Ltd. 1038
Moore Medical LLC 1038
MOOREFIELD CONSTRUCTION INC. 1039

MORAVIAN COLLEGE 1039
MoreDirect Inc. 1039
MOREHEAD MEMORIAL HOSPITAL INC 1039
MOREHOUSE COLLEGE (INC.) 1039
Morgan Keegan & Co. Inc. 1039
Morgan Lewis & Bockius LLP 1040
Morgan Properties Trust 1040
Morgan Stanley 1040
Morgan Stanley Smith Barney LLC 1040
Morgan's Foods, Inc. 1040
Morgans Hotel Group Co 1040
Morgenthaler LLP 1041
Morningstar Inc 1041
Moro Corporation 1041
Moroso Performance Products Inc. 1041
MorphoTrust USA Inc. 1041
Morris Business Development Co 1041
Morris Communications Company LLC 1042
MORRIS HOSPITAL 1042
Morris Publishing Group LLC 1042
Morrison & Foerster LLP 1042
MORROW-MEADOWS CORPORATION 1042
MORSE OPERATIONS INC. 1042
Morton Industrial Group Inc. 1043
Morton Salt Inc. 1043
Morton's Restaurant Group Inc. 1043
MOSAIC 1043
Mosaic Co (The) 1043
Moss Adams LLP 1043
MoSys Inc 1044
Motel 6 Operating Partership L.P. 1044
MOTHER MURPHY"S LABORATORIES INC. 1044
Motion Industries Inc. 1044
Motion Picture Association of America 1044
Motiva Enterprises LLC 1044
Motive Inc. 1045
MOTO Franchise Corporation 1045
Motorcar Parts of America Inc 1045
Motorola Mobility Holdings Inc. 1045
Motorola Solutions Inc. 1045
Motorsports Authentics LLC 1045
Mott's LLP 1046
MOUNT CARMEL HEALTH SYSTEM 1046
MOUNT CLEMENS REGIONAL MEDICAL CENTER
  INC. 1046
Mountain Valley Spring Company LLC 1046
Mountaire Corporation 1046
Movado Group, Inc. 1046
Move Inc 1047
Mozilla Foundation 1047
mPhase Technologies Inc. 1047
MPI Research Inc. 1047
MPLX LP 1047
MPW Industrial Services Group Inc. 1047
MRC Global Inc 1048
MRI Interventions Inc 1048
MRIGLOBAL 1048
MRV Communications, Inc. 1048
MSB Financial Corp 1048
MSC Industrial Direct Co., Inc. 1048
MSCI Inc 1049
MSD Capital L.P. 1049
MSG Network Inc 1049
MSGI Technology Solutions Inc. 1049
MSX International Inc. 1049
MTM Technologies Inc. 1049
MTR Gaming Group, Inc. 1050
MTS Medication Technologies Inc. 1050
MTS Systems Corp. 1050
MTV Networks Company 1050
Mueller (Paul) Co. 1050
Mueller Industries, Inc. 1050
Mueller Water Products Inc 1051
Mullen Communications Inc. 1051
MullinTBG 1051
Multek Flexible Circuits Inc. 1051
Multi-Color Corp. 1051
Multi-Fineline Electronix Inc 1051
MULTICARE HEALTH SYSTEM 1052
MultiCell Technologies Inc 1052
Multimedia Games Holding Company, Inc. 1052
MultiPlan Inc. 1052
Munger Tolles & Olson LLP 1052
Munich Reinsurance America Inc. 1052

Municipal Electric Authority of Georgia 1053
Murata Electronics North America Inc. 1053
Murphy Exploration & Production Company - USA
  1053
Murphy Oil Corp 1053
Murphy Oil USA Inc. 1053
Murphy USA Inc 1053
Murphy-Brown LLC 1054
MUSCULAR DYSTROPHY ASSOCIATION INC. 1054
MUSEUM OF FINE ARTS 1054
MUSTANG FUEL CORPORATION 1054
Mustang Tractor & Equipment Company 1054
Mutual of America Life Insurance Company 1054
Mutual of Enumclaw Insurance Company 1055
Mutual of Omaha Insurance Co. (NE) 1055
MutualFirst Financial Inc 1055
Muzak Holdings LLC 1055
MV Oil Trust 1055
MV TRANSPORTATION INC. 1055
MVC Capital Inc. 1056
MVM Inc. 1056
MWH GLOBAL INC. 1056
MWI Veterinary Supply Inc 1056
Myers Industries Inc. 1056
Mylan Inc 1056
Mylan Specialty L.P. 1057
Mymetics Corp 1057
MYR Group Inc 1057
Myrexis Inc. 1057
Myriad Genetics, Inc. 1057
Myriad RBM Inc. 1057
Mzinga Inc. 1058
N-Viro International Corp 1058
Nabors Completion and Production Services Co. 1058
NACCO Industries Inc. 1058
NACCO Materials Handling Group Inc. 1058
Naked Juice Company 1058
Nalco Holding Company 1059
Namasco Corporation 1059
Nano Mask Inc. 1059
Nanometrics, Inc. 1059
Nanophase Technologies Corp. 1059
Nanosphere Inc 1059
NanoString Technologies Inc 1060
Nanosys Inc. 1060
NAPCO Security Technologies, Inc. 1060
Narus Inc. 1060
NASB Financial Inc 1060
NASCAR Media Group 1060
Nasdaq Inc 1061
NASSCO Holdings Incorporated 1061
Nathan's Famous, Inc. 1061
NATIONAL ACADEMY OF RECORDING ARTS &
  SCIENCES INC 1061
National Alliance to End Homelessness Inc. 1061
National American University Holdings Inc. 1061
National Amusements Inc. 1062
National Association for Stock Car Auto Racing Inc.
  1062
NATIONAL ASSOCIATION OF BROADCASTERS 1062
NATIONAL AUDUBON SOCIETY INC. 1062
NATIONAL AUTOMOBILE DEALERS ASSOCIATION
  1062
National Bancshares Corp. (Ohio) 1062
National Bank Holdings Corp 1063
National Bank of Arizona 1063
National Bankshares Inc. (VA) 1063
National Beverage Corp. 1063
NATIONAL CABLE SATELLITE CORP 1063
National Car Rental 1063
National CineMedia Inc 1064
National Cooperative Refinery Association 1064
NATIONAL COUNCIL OF YOUNG MEN"S
  CHRISTIAN ASSOCIATIONS OF THE U 1064
NATIONAL COUNCIL ON AGING INC. 1064
National Dentex Corporation 1064
National Distributing Company Inc. 1064
NATIONAL EDUCATION ASSOCIATION OF THE
  UNITED STATES 1065
National Football League 1065
NATIONAL FOOTBALL LEAGUE PLAYERS
  ASSOCIATION 1065
NATIONAL FROZEN FOODS CORPORATION 1065
National Fuel Gas Co. (NJ) 1065

NATIONAL GRAPE CO-OPERATIVE ASSOCIATION INC. 1065
National Head Start Association 1066
National Health Investors, Inc. 1066
National Healthcare Corp. 1066
National Heritage Academies Inc. 1066
National Holdings Corp 1066
National Indemnity Company 1066
National Information Solutions Cooperative Inc. 1067
National Instruments Corp. 1067
National Interstate Corp 1067
National Life Insurance Company 1067
NATIONAL MULTIPLE SCLEROSIS SOCIETY 1067
National Oilwell Varco Inc 1067
National Penn Bancshares Inc. 1068
National Presto Industries, Inc. 1068
NATIONAL PUBLIC RADIO INC. 1068
National Railroad Passenger Corporation 1068
National Realty & Development Corp. 1068
National Research Corp 1068
National Restaurants Management Inc. 1069
NATIONAL RETAIL FEDERATION INC. 1069
National Retail Properties Inc 1069
National Review Inc. 1069
NATIONAL RIFLE ASSOCIATION OF AMERICA 1069
NATIONAL RURAL ELECTRIC COOPERATIVE ASSOCIATION 1069
National Rural Utilities Cooperative Finance Corp 1070
NATIONAL SAFETY COUNCIL 1070
National Security Group, Inc 1070
National Spinning Company Inc. 1070
National Trust for Historic Preservation in the United St 1070
NATIONAL UNIVERSITY 1070
NATIONAL VAN LINES INC. 1071
National Vision Inc. 1071
National Western Life Insurance Co. (Austin, TX) 1071
NATIONAL WILDLIFE FEDERATION INC 1071
Nationstar Mortgage Holdings Inc 1071
Nationstar Mortgage Holdings Inc. 1071
NATIONWIDE CHILDREN'S HOSPITAL 1072
Nationwide Financial Services Inc. 1072
Nationwide Mutual Insurance Company 1072
Nationwide Recovery Systems Ltd. 1072
NATIVE ENVIRONMENTAL L.L.C. 1072
Natural Alternatives International, Inc. 1072
Natural Gas Services Group Inc 1073
Natural Grocers By Vitamin Cottage Inc 1073
Natural Health Trends Corp. 1073
NATURAL RESOURCES DEFENSE COUNCIL INC. 1073
Natural Resources Partners L.P. 1073
Natural Selection Foods LLC 1073
Naturally Fresh Inc. 1074
Nature's Sunshine Products, Inc. 1074
NatureWorks LLC 1074
Naturipe Farms LLC 1074
Natus Medical Inc. 1074
Naugatuck Valley Financial Corporation 1074
Nautica Apparel Inc. 1075
Nautilus Inc 1075
Navajo Shippers Inc. 1075
NAVARRO RESEARCH AND ENGINEERING INC. 1075
Navidea Biopharmaceuticals, Inc. 1075
Navigant Consulting, Inc. 1075
Navigators Group, Inc. (The) 1076
NaviSite Inc. 1076
Navistar International Corp. 1076
Navitas Energy Inc. 1076
NAVTEQ Corporation 1076
Navy Federal Credit Union 1076
NB&T Financial Group, Inc. 1077
NBCUniversal Media LLC 1077
NBHX TRIM USA CORPORATION 1077
NBT Bancorp, Inc. 1077
NBTY Inc. 1077
NCH CORPORATION 1077
NCH HEALTHCARE SYSTEM INC. 1078
NCI Building Systems, Inc. 1078
NCI Inc 1078

nCircle Network Security Inc. 1078
NCR Corp. 1078
NCS TECHNOLOGIES INC. 1078
Neace Lukens Inc. 1079
Nebraska Book Company Inc. 1079
Nebraska Public Power District 1079
Neenah Foundry Company 1079
Neenah Paper Inc 1079
Neff Rental LLC 1079
Neffs Bancorp Inc. 1080
NEIGHBORHOOD HEALTH PLAN INC 1080
NEIGHBORHOOD REINVESTMENT CORPORATION 1080
Nektar Therapeutics 1080
Nelnet Inc 1080
NEMOURS FOUNDATION 1080
Neogen Corp. 1081
NeoGenomics Inc 1081
NeoMagic Corporation 1081
NeoMedia Technologies, Inc. 1081
NeoPhotonics Corp 1081
Nephros Inc 1081
NES Rentals Holdings Inc. 1082
Ness USA Inc. 1082
Nestle Professional Vitality 1082
Nestle Purina PetCare Company 1082
Nestle Waters North America Inc. 1082
Net Medical Xpress Solutions Inc 1082
NetApp, Inc. 1083
Netezza Corporation 1083
Netflix Inc. 1083
Netgear, Inc. 1083
NetIQ Corporation 1083
Netlist Inc 1083
NetScout Systems Inc 1084
Netsmart Technologies Inc. 1084
NetSol Technologies Inc 1084
Netsuite Inc 1084
Network Engines Inc. 1084
Network Hardware Resale LLC 1084
NETWORK MANAGEMENT RESOURCES INC. 1085
Network Solutions LLC 1085
Networkfleet Inc. 1085
NeuLion Inc. 1085
NEUMANN SYSTEMS GROUP INC. 1085
Neuralstem Inc 1085
Neurocrine Biosciences, Inc. 1086
NeuroMetrix Inc 1086
NeuStar, Inc. 1086
Neutron Energy Inc. 1086
Nevada Gold & Casinos, Inc. 1086
Nevada Power Co. 1086
Nevada State Bank 1087
New Age Electronics Inc. 1087
New Brunswick Scientific Co. Inc. 1087
New CAM Commerce Solutions LLC 1087
New Concept Energy, Inc. 1087
New Edge Networks Inc. 1087
New England Bancshares Inc. 1088
New England Life Insurance Company 1088
New England Motor Freight Inc. 1088
New England Realty Associates L.P. 1088
New Frontier Media Inc. 1088
New Global Telecom Inc. 1088
NEW HAMPSHIRE ELECTRIC COOPERATIVE INC 1089
NEW HANOVER REGIONAL MEDICAL CENTER AUXILIARY INC. 1089
NEW JERSEY INSTITUTE OF TECHNOLOGY (INC) 1089
New Jersey Mining Co. 1089
New Jersey Natural Gas Company 1089
New Jersey Resources Corp 1089
New Jersey Transit Corporation 1090
New Jersey Turnpike Authority 1090
New Media Investment Group Inc 1090
NEW MILFORD HOSPITAL INC. 1090
New Mountain Finance Corp 1090
New Penn Motor Express Inc. 1090
NEW PRIME INC. 1091
New Source Energy Corporation 1091
New Source Energy Partners LP 1091
NEW TANGRAM LLC 1091
New Ulm Telecom Inc 1091

New York & Company Inc 1091
NEW YORK BLOOD CENTER INC. 1092
New York Central Mutual Fire Insurance Company 1092
New York City Health and Hospitals Corporation 1092
New York City Transitional Finance Authority 1092
New York Community Bancorp Inc. 1092
NEW YORK CONVENTION CENTER OPERATING CORPORATION 1092
New York Football Giants Inc. 1093
New York Jets LLC 1093
New York Life Insurance Company 1093
NEW YORK MEDICAL COLLEGE 1093
NEW YORK METHODIST HOSPITAL 1093
New York Mortgage Trust Inc 1093
NEW YORK POWER AUTHORITY 1094
NEW YORK PUBLIC RADIO 1094
New York State and Local Retirement System 1094
NEW YORK STATE CATHOLIC HEALTH PLAN INC 1094
New York State Lottery 1094
New York State Teachers' Retirement System 1094
New York Times Co. 1095
New York Yankees Partnership 1095
NEWARK BETH ISRAEL MEDICAL CENTER INC. 1095
Neways Inc. 1095
NewBridge Bancorp 1095
Newcastle Investment Corp 1095
Newegg Inc. 1096
Newell Rubbermaid, Inc. 1096
NEWESCO INC. 1096
Newfield Exploration Co. 1096
Newgistics Inc. 1096
NewLink Genetics Corp 1096
Newly Weds Foods Inc. 1097
Newmar Corporation 1097
NewMarket Corp 1097
NewMarket Technology Inc. 1097
Newmont Mining Corp. (Holding Co.) 1097
NewPage Group Inc. 1097
Newpark Resources, Inc. 1098
Newport Corp. 1098
News America Marketing FSI LLC 1098
News Corp (New) 1098
NewStar Financial Inc 1098
Newtek Business Services Corp 1098
NEWTON MEMORIAL HOSPITAL INC 1099
Nexsan Corporation 1099
Nexstar Broadcasting Group Inc 1099
NexTec Group 1099
NextEra Energy Inc 1099
NexTrade Holdings Inc. 1099
NFI Industries Inc. 1100
nFinanSe Inc. 1100
NGAS Resources Inc. 1100
NGL Energy Partners LP 1100
NHL ENTERPRISES INC. 1100
NHS HUMAN SERVICES INC. 1100
Niagara Mohawk Power Corporation 1101
NIC Inc. 1101
Nice-Pak Products Inc. 1101
Nicholas Financial Inc. 1101
Nicklos Drilling Company 1101
Nielsen Mobile Inc. 1101
Niemann Foods Inc. 1102
Nightingale-Conant Corporation 1102
NII Holdings Inc. 1102
NIKE Inc 1102
Nimble Storage Inc 1102
Nintendo of America Inc. 1102
NINYO & MOORE GEOTECHNICAL & ENVIRONMENTAL SCIENCES CONSULTANTS 1103
Nippon Express USA Inc. 1103
Niska Gas Storage Partners LLC 1103
NiSource Inc. (Holding Co.) 1103
Nissan Forklift Corporation North America 1103
Nissan North America Inc. 1103
Nixon Peabody LLP 1104
NL Industries, Inc. 1104
NMI Holdings Inc 1104
NN, Inc 1104

Nobel Learning Communities Inc. 1104
Nobility Homes, Inc. 1104
Noble Energy, Inc. 1105
Noble Roman's, Inc. 1105
NOBLIS INC. 1105
NOCO Energy Corp. 1105
Nocopi Technologies, Inc. 1105
Non-Invasive Monitoring Systems Inc. 1105
Nonpareil Corporation 1106
Noodles & Co. 1106
Noranda Aluminum Holding Corp 1106
Nordson Corp. 1106
Nordstrom, Inc. 1106
Norfolk Southern Corp. 1106
Norfolk Southern Railway Company 1107
NORFOLK STATE UNIVERSITY 1107
NORKUS ENTERPRISES INC. 1107
Norse Dairy Systems L.P. 1107
Nortech Systems Inc. 1107
Nortek Inc 1107
NORTH CAROLINA ELECTRIC MEMBERSHIP
    CORPORATION 1108
North Carolina Farm Bureau Mutual Insurance
    Company Inc. 1108
North Castle Partners L.L.C. 1108
North Central Bancshares Inc. 1108
NORTH CENTRAL FARMERS ELEVATOR 1108
NORTH DAKOTA MILL & ELEVATOR ASSOCIATION
    INC 1108
North Dallas Bank & Trust Co. 1109
North European Oil Royalty Trust 1109
NORTH MEMORIAL HEALTH CARE 1109
NORTH MISSISSIPPI HEALTH SERVICES INC. 1109
NORTH MISSISSIPPI MEDICAL CENTER INC. 1109
NORTH PACIFIC PAPER CORPORATION 1109
NORTH PARK UNIVERSITY 1110
NORTH SHORE UNIVERSITY HOSPITAL 1110
North Shore-Long Island Jewish Health System 1110
North Valley Bancorp (Redding, CA) 1110
NORTH WIND INC. 1110
Northeast Bancorp (ME) 1110
Northeast Community Bancorp Inc 1111
NORTHEAST HEALTH SYSTEMS INC. 1111
Northeast Illinois Regional Commuter Railroad
    Corporation 1111
Northeast Indiana Bancorp Inc. 1111
NORTHEASTERN SUPPLY INC. 1111
NORTHERN ARIZONA HEALTHCARE
    CORPORATION 1111
Northern Indiana Public Service Company 1112
Northern Oil & Gas Inc (NV) 1112
Northern States Financial Corp. (Waukegan, IL) 1112
Northern Technologies International Corp. 1112
Northern Tier Energy Inc. 1112
Northern Tier Energy LP 1112
Northern Trust Corp. 1113
NORTHERN VIRGINIA ELECTRIC COOPERATIVE
    1113
Northfield Bancorp Inc. 1113
NorthMarq Capital LLC 1113
Northrim BancCorp Inc 1113
Northrop Grumman Corp 1113
NORTHSHORE UNIVERSITY HEALTHSYSTEM 1114
NORTHSIDE HOSPITAL INC. 1114
Northstar Aerospace Inc. 1114
NORTHSTAR GROUP SERVICES INC. 1114
NorthStar Realty Finance Corp 1114
Northway Financial, Inc. 1114
Northwest Bancorporation, Inc. 1115
Northwest Bancshares Inc. 1115
Northwest Bancshares, Inc. (MD) 1115
Northwest Biotherapeutics Inc 1115
NORTHWEST DAIRY ASSOCIATION 1115
NORTHWEST FARM CREDIT SERVICES ACA 1115
Northwest Indiana Bancorp 1116
Northwest Natural Gas Co. 1116
Northwest Pipe Co. 1116
Northwestern Corp. 1116
NORTHWESTERN MEMORIAL HEALTHCARE 1116
NORTON COMMUNITY HOSPITAL AUXILIARY INC.
    1116
Norton Healthcare Inc. 1117
Norwegian Cruise Line Holdings Ltd. 1117
NORWICH UNIVERSITY 1117

Norwood Financial Corp. 1117
Norwood Promotional Products LLC 1117
Notify Technology Corporation 1117
NOVA SOUTHEASTERN UNIVERSITY INC. 1118
NovaBay Pharmaceuticals Inc 1118
Novartis Pharmaceuticals Corporation 1118
Novatel Wireless Inc. 1118
Novation Companies Inc 1118
Novavax, Inc. 1118
Novelis Inc. 1119
NOVO 1 Inc. 1119
NPC International Inc. 1119
NPS Pharmaceuticals Inc. 1119
NRG Energy Inc 1119
NRG Yield Inc 1119
NRT LLC 1120
NSTAR Electric Co 1120
NTELOS Holdings Corp 1120
NTN Buzztime Inc 1120
NTS Inc 1120
NTS Realty Holdings Ltd Partnership 1120
NTT America Inc. 1121
Nu Horizons Electronics Corp. 1121
NU Skin Enterprises, Inc. 1121
Nuance Communications Inc 1121
Nuclear Solutions Inc. 1121
NuCO2 Inc. 1121
Nucor Corp. 1122
Nucor Steel Tuscaloosa Inc. 1122
NuMobile Inc. 1122
Nuo Therapeutics Inc 1122
NuStar Energy L.P. 1122
NuStar GP Holdings LLC 1122
Nutra Pharma Corp 1123
Nutraceutical International Corp. 1123
NutriSystem Inc 1123
Nutrition 21 LLC 1123
Nutrition Management Services Company 1123
Nutroganics Inc 1123
Nuvasive Inc 1124
Nuveen Investments Inc. 1124
Nuvera Fuel Cells Inc. 1124
Nuvilex Inc. 1124
NV5 Global Inc 1124
NVE Corp 1124
NVIDIA Corp 1125
NVR Inc. 1125
NxStage Medical Inc 1125
NYACK COLLEGE 1125
NYPRO INC. 1125
O P I Products Inc. 1125
O'Charley's Inc. 1126
O'Melveny & Myers LLP 1126
O'Reilly Automotive, Inc. 1126
O'Reilly Media Inc. 1126
O. C. TANNER COMPANY 1126
O. I. Corporation 1126
O.F. Mossberg & Sons Inc. 1127
Oak Management Corporation 1127
Oak Ridge Micro-Energy Inc. 1127
Oak Valley Bancorp 1127
Oak Valley Bancorp (Oakdale, CA) 1127
OAKLAND UNIVERSITY 1127
OAKLEAF Waste Management LLC 1128
Oakley Inc. 1128
Oakridge Energy Inc. 1128
Oakridge Holdings, Inc. 1128
Oaktree Capital Group LLC 1128
OAKWOOD HEALTHCARE INC. 1128
Oasis Petroleum Inc. 1129
OBA Financial Services Inc 1129
OBERLIN COLLEGE 1129
Oberto Sausage Company 1129
Ocata Therapeutics Inc 1129
Occidental Chemical Corporation 1129
OCCIDENTAL COLLEGE 1130
Occidental Oil and Gas Corporation 1130
Occidental Permian Ltd. 1130
Occidental Petroleum Corp 1130
OCEAN BEAUTY SEAFOODS LLC 1130
Ocean Bio-Chem, Inc. 1130
OCEAN DUKE CORPORATION 1131
Ocean Power Technologies Inc 1131
Ocean Shore Holding Co 1131

Oceaneering International, Inc. 1131
OceanFirst Financial Corp 1131
Oceanic Exploration Company 1131
Ocera Therapeutics Inc 1132
Och-Ziff Capital Management Group LLC 1132
OCI Partners LP 1132
Oclaro Inc. 1132
OCLC ONLINE COMPUTER LIBRARY CENTER
    INCORPORATE 1132
Octagon Worldwide Inc. 1132
Oculus Innovative Sciences Inc 1133
Ocwen Financial Corporation 1133
OCZ Technology Group Inc 1133
ODOM CORPORATION 1133
Odwalla Inc. 1133
Odyssey HealthCare Inc. 1133
Odyssey Investment Partners LLC 1134
Odyssey Marine Exploration, Inc. 1134
OEC BUSINESS INTERIORS INC. 1134
Office Depot, Inc. 1134
Official Payments Holdings Inc. 1134
OGE Energy Corp. 1134
Ogilvy & Mather Worldwide Inc. 1135
Ogio International Inc. 1135
Oglethorpe Power Corp 1135
Ohio Edison Co 1135
Ohio Legacy Corp 1135
Ohio National Financial Services Inc. 1135
Ohio Power Company 1136
OHIO STATE UNIVERSITY RESEARCH
    FOUNDATION 1136
Ohio Valley Banc Corp 1136
Ohio Valley Electric Corp. 1136
OHIO VALLEY GENERAL HOSPITAL 1136
OHIO VALLEY MEDICAL CENTER INCORPORATED
    1136
OHIOHEALTH CORPORATION 1137
Oil States International, Inc. 1137
Oil-Dri Corp. of America 1137
Oiltanking Partners LP 1137
OKI Data Americas Inc. 1137
Olan Mills Inc. 1137
Old Dominion Electric Cooperative 1138
Old Dominion Freight Line, Inc. 1138
Old Line Bancshares Inc 1138
Old Mutual (US) Holdings Inc. 1138
Old National Bancorp (Evansville, IN) 1138
Old Navy Inc. 1138
Old Point Financial Corp. 1139
Old Republic International Corp. 1139
Old Second Bancorp., Inc. (Aurora, Ill.) 1139
OLD TIME POTTERY INC. 1139
Old World Industries LLC 1139
Oldcastle Inc. 1139
Oldcastle Materials Inc. 1140
OLE' MEXICAN FOODS INC. 1140
Olin Corp. 1140
OLMSTED MEDICAL CENTER 1140
Olympic Steel Inc. 1140
Olympus Corporation of the Americas 1140
OM Group, Inc. 1141
Omagine Inc. 1141
Omaha Steaks International Inc. 1141
Omega Flex Inc 1141
Omega Healthcare Investors, Inc. 1141
Omega Protein Corp. 1141
Omeros Corp 1142
OMNI CABLE CORPORATION 1142
OMNI Energy Services Corp. 1142
Omni Hotels Corporation 1142
OmniAmerican Bancorp, Inc. 1142
Omnicare Inc. 1143
Omnicell Inc 1143
Omnicom Group, Inc. 1143
OmniComm Systems Inc 1143
OmniSource Corporation 1143
OmniVision Technologies Inc 1143
Omnova Solutions Inc 1143
Omron Scientific Technologies Incorporated 1144
On Assignment, Inc. 1144
ON Semiconductor Corp 1144
ON-SITE FUEL SERVICE INC. 1144
OncoGenex Pharmaceuticals, Inc. 1144
Oncologix Tech Inc 1144

OncoMed Pharmaceuticals Inc. 1145
Onconova Therapeutics Inc 1145
Oncor Electric Delivery Co 1145
Oncothyreon Inc. 1145
ONE Gas, Inc. 1145
One Liberty Properties, Inc. 1145
ONE STOP SYSTEMS INC. 1146
OneBeacon Insurance Group Ltd. 1146
Oneida Ltd. 1146
OneMain Financial Inc. 1146
OneMain Holdings Inc 1146
Oneok Inc. 1146
ONEOK Partners LP 1147
OneSource Information Services Inc. 1147
Onion Inc. 1147
Online Vacation Center Holdings Corp 1147
OnStar LLC 1147
Onstream Media Corp 1147
Onvia Inc 1148
OP-TECH Environmental Services Inc. 1148
OPEN LINK FINANCIAL INC. 1148
Open Solutions Inc. 1148
OpenTable Inc. 1148
OpenTV Corp. 1148
Operating Engineers Funds Inc. 1149
OPERATION SMILE INC. 1149
Opexa Therapeutics Inc 1149
Opko Health Inc 1149
Oplink Communications Inc. 1149
OPNET Technologies Inc. 1149
Opnext Inc. 1150
Oppenheimer Holdings Inc 1150
OppenheimerFunds Inc. 1150
Optical Cable Corp. 1150
OptimumBank Holdings Inc 1150
optionsXpress Holdings Inc. 1150
OptumHealth Inc. 1151
OptumInsight 1151
OptumRx Inc. 1151
Oracle Corp. 1151
Oragenics Inc 1151
ORANGE COUNTY TRANSPORTATION AUTHORITY
    SCHOLARSHIP FOUNDATION IN 1151
OraSure Technologies Inc. 1152
ORBCOMM Inc 1152
Orbit International Corp. 1152
ORBIT/FR, Inc. 1152
Orbital ATK Inc 1152
Orbital Sciences Corp. 1152
Orbitz Worldwide Inc 1153
ORC International Inc. 1153
ORCA BAY SEAFOODS INC. 1153
Orchard Software Corporation 1153
Orchid Cellmark Inc. 1153
Orchid Island Capital, Inc. 1153
Orchids Paper Products Co. (DE) 1154
OREGON HEALTH & SCIENCE UNIVERSITY
    MEDICAL GROUP 1154
OREGON STATE UNIVERSITY 1154
Orexigen Therapeutics, Inc 1154
ORGANICALLY GROWN COMPANY 1154
Organogenesis Inc. 1154
Orgill Inc. 1155
Oriental Financial Group Inc. 1155
Orion Energy Systems Inc 1155
Orion HealthCorp Inc. 1155
Orion Marine Group Inc 1155
Oritani Financial Corp (DE) 1155
ORLANDO HEALTH INC. 1156
Orlando Utilities Commission 1156
Ormat Technologies Inc 1156
Ormet Corporation 1156
Orrick Herrington & Sutcliffe LLP 1156
Orrstown Financial Services, Inc. 1156
Ortho-Clinical Diagnostics Inc. 1157
OrthoLogic Corp. 1157
OrthoSynetics Inc. 1157
Osage Bancshares Inc. 1157
OSBORN & BARR COMMUNICATIONS INC. 1157
OSC SPORTS INC. 1157
OSF HEALTHCARE SYSTEM 1158
OshKosh B'Gosh Inc. 1158
Oshkosh Corp (New) 1158
OSI Group LLC 1158

OSI Pharmaceuticals LLC 1158
OSI Systems, Inc. (DE) 1158
Osiris Therapeutics Inc 1159
OSIsoft LLC 1159
Otelco Inc 1159
OTSUKA AMERICA INC 1159
OTTER PRODUCTS LLC 1159
Otter Tail Corp. 1159
OUR LADY OF LOURDES MEDICAL CENTER INC
    1160
OUR LADY OF LOURDES REGIONAL MEDICAL
    CENTER INC. 1160
OUR LADY OF THE LAKE HOSPITAL INC. 1160
OurPet's Company 1160
Outdoor Resorts of America Inc. 1160
Outerwall Inc 1160
OutStart Inc. 1161
Overhead Door Corporation 1161
OVERLAKE HOSPITAL MEDICAL CENTER 1161
Overland Storage, Inc. 1161
Overseas Shipholding Group Inc (New) 1161
Overstock.com Inc. (DE) 1161
Ovonyx Inc. 1162
Owens & Minor, Inc. 1162
Owens Corning 1162
Owens-Illinois, Inc. 1162
Owensboro Grain Company LLC 1162
OWENSBORO MUNICIPAL UTILITIES ELECTRIC
    LIGHT & POWER SYSTEM 1162
OXBO International Corporation 1163
Oxbow Corporation 1163
Oxford Bioscience Partners L.P. 1163
Oxford Global Resources Inc. 1163
Oxford Health Plans LLC 1163
Oxford Industries, Inc. 1163
Oxford Life Insurance Company 1164
OXFORD UNIVERSITY PRESS INC. 1164
OXiGENE, Inc. 1164
Oxis International Inc. 1164
Oxygen Media LLC 1164
OZARKS ELECTRIC COOPERATIVE CORPORATION
    1164
O'BRIEN & GERE LIMITED 1165
O'NEIL INDUSTRIES INC. 1165
P & F Industries, inc. 1165
P & H Mining Equipment Inc. 1165
P&G-Clairol Inc. 1165
P.A.M. Transportation Services, Inc. 1165
P.F. Chang's China Bistro Inc. 1166
Pabst Brewing Company 1166
Pac-West Telecomm Inc. 1166
PACCAR Inc. 1166
Pace Communications Inc. 1166
PACE UNIVERSITY 1166
Pacer International Inc 1167
Pacific Biosciences of California Inc 1167
PACIFIC BUILDING GROUP 1167
Pacific City Financial Corporation 1167
Pacific Coast Feather Co. 1167
PACIFIC COAST PRODUCERS 1167
Pacific Continental Corp 1168
Pacific Cycle Inc. 1168
Pacific Dental Services Inc. 1168
Pacific Ethanol Inc 1168
Pacific Financial Corp. 1168
PACIFIC HIDE & FUR DEPOT 1168
Pacific Investment Management Company LLC 1169
Pacific Mercantile Bancorp 1169
Pacific Mutual Holding Co. 1169
PACIFIC NATIONAL GROUP 1169
Pacific Northwest National Laboratory 1169
Pacific Office Properties Trust Inc 1169
Pacific Sands Inc 1170
Pacific Sunwear of California, Inc. 1170
Pacific Theatres Corporation 1170
Pacific Webworks, Inc. 1170
PacificHealth Laboratories Inc. 1170
Pacificorp 1170
Pacira Pharmaceuticals Inc. 1171
Packaging Corp of America 1171
Packaging Dynamics Corporation 1171
Pactiv LLC 1171
PacWest Bancorp 1171
Paddock Pool Construction Company 1171

PAETEC Holding Corp. 1172
Page Parkes Corporation 1172
PAGE SOUTHERLAND PAGE L.L.P. 1172
Paid Inc 1172
Pain Therapeutics Inc 1172
Palace Entertainment Holdings LLC 1172
Palace Sports & Entertainment Inc. 1173
Palatin Technologies Inc 1173
Pall Corp. 1173
Palladium Equity Partners LLC 1173
Palmetto Bancshares, Inc. (SC) 1173
PALMETTO HEALTH 1173
PALO ALTO MEDICAL FOUNDATION FOR HEALTH
    CARE RESEARCH AND EDUCAT 1174
Palo Alto Networks, Inc 1174
Palomar Technologies Inc. 1174
Pamida Stores Operating Company LLC 1174
Pan American Goldfields Ltd. 1174
Panasonic Avionics Corporation 1174
Panattoni Development Company Inc. 1175
Panavision Inc. 1175
Panda Energy International Inc. 1175
Panda Restaurant Group Inc. 1175
Pandora Media Inc 1175
Panera Bread Co. 1175
Panhandle Eastern Pipe Line Company LP 1176
Panhandle Oil & Gas Inc 1176
Panini America Inc. 1176
Panther Expedited Services Inc. 1176
Pantry Inc. (The) 1176
Papa John's International, Inc. 1176
PAPER CONVERTING MACHINE COMPANY 1177
PaperWorks Industries Inc. 1177
Pappas Restaurants Inc. 1177
Par Pacific Holdings Inc 1177
Par Pharmaceutical Companies Inc. 1177
Par Technology Corp. 1177
Parade Publications 1178
Paradigm Holdings Inc. 1178
Paradise, Inc. 1178
PARAGON DEVELOPMENT SYSTEMS INC 1178
Paragon Real Estate Equity & Investment Trust 1178
PARAGON SOLUTIONS INC. 1178
Paragon Technologies Inc 1179
Paramount Gold & Silver Corp 1179
Paratek Pharmaceuticals Inc 1179
Paratek Pharmaceuticals Inc. 1179
Parature Inc. 1179
PAREXEL International Corp. 1179
Park Bancorp, Inc. 1180
Park City Group Inc 1180
Park Corporation 1180
Park Electrochemical Corp. 1180
Park National Corp. (Newark, OH) 1180
Park Nicollet Health Services 1180
Park Place Dealerships 1181
Park Sterling Corp 1181
Park-Ohio Holdings Corp. 1181
Parkdale Mills Incorporated 1181
Parke Bancorp Inc 1181
Parker Drilling Co. 1181
Parker Hannifin Corp. 1182
ParkerVision Inc. 1182
Parkland Health & Hospital System 1182
Parkway Properties Inc. 1182
PARKWEST MEDICAL CENTER 1182
Parlux Fragrances LLC 1182
PARRON-HALL CORPORATION 1183
PARSONS ENVIRONMENT & INFRASTRUCTURE
    GROUP INC. 1183
Parsons Infrastructure & Technology Group Inc.
    1183
Parsons Transportation Group Inc. 1183
Partners HealthCare System Inc. 1183
PASADENA HOSPITAL ASSOCIATION 1183
Paschall Truck Lines Inc. 1184
Passur Aerospace, Inc. 1184
Patapsco Bancorp Inc. 1184
Patelco Credit Union 1184
Patheon Inc. 1184
Pathfinder Bancorp, Inc. 1184
Pathfinder Cell Therapy Inc. 1185
PATHFINDER INTERNATIONAL 1185
Pathmark Stores Inc. 1185

Pathology Associates Medical Laboratories 1185
Patient Safety Technologies Inc. 1185
Patrick Cudahy Incorporated 1185
Patrick Industries, Inc. 1186
Patriot Coal Corp 1186
Patriot National Bancorp Inc 1186
Patriot Scientific Corporation 1186
Pattern Energy Group Inc 1186
Patterson Companies Inc 1186
Patterson-UTI Energy Inc. 1187
Paul Hastings Janofsky & Walker LLP 1187
Paul Weiss Rifkind Wharton & Garrison LLP 1187
Pavilion Energy Resources Inc. 1187
PAXTON MEDIA GROUP LLC 1187
Paychex Inc 1187
Payment Alliance International Inc. 1188
Payment Data Systems Inc 1188
Payment Processing Inc. 1188
PayPal Inc. 1188
PBF Energy Inc 1188
PBF Energy Inc. 1188
PC Connection, Inc. 1189
PC Group Inc. 1189
PC-Tel Inc 1189
PCL CONSTRUCTION ENTERPRISES INC 1189
PCM, Inc 1189
PCRE L.L.C 1189
PCS Edventures!.Com Inc 1190
PDB Sports Ltd. 1190
PDC Energy Inc 1190
PDF Solutions Inc. 1190
PDL BioPharma Inc 1190
PDS Gaming Corporation 1190
PDS TECH INC. 1191
Peabody Energy Corp 1191
PEACEHEALTH 1191
Peak Resorts Inc 1191
PEAK Technologies Inc. 1191
PEAK6 Investments L.P. 1191
Peapack-Gladstone Financial Corp. 1192
Pearson Education Inc. 1192
Peavey Electronics Corporation 1192
Pebblebrook Hotel Trust 1192
PECO Energy Company 1192
PECO II Inc. 1192
Pedernales Electric Cooperative Inc. 1193
Pedevco Corp 1193
Pediatric Services of America Inc. 1193
Peerless Insurance Company 1193
Peerless Systems Corp. 1193
Peet's Coffee & Tea Inc. 1193
Pegasus Solutions Inc. 1194
Pegasystems Inc. 1194
Pelican Products Inc. 1194
PEN Inc 1194
PENDLETON GRAIN GROWERS INC. 1194
Pendleton Woolen Mills Inc. 1194
Pendrell Corp. 1195
Penford Corp. 1195
Penguin Computing Inc. 1195
Penn Engineering & Manufacturing Corp. 1195
Penn National Gaming, Inc. 1195
Penn Treaty American Corporation 1195
Penn Virginia Corp 1196
PennantPark Investment Corporation 1196
Penney (J.C.) Co.,Inc. (Holding Co.) 1196
Pennichuck Corporation 1196
PENNONI ASSOCIATES INC. 1196
Penns Woods Bancorp, Inc. (Jersey Shore, PA) 1196
Pennsylvania Higher Education Assistance Agency 1197
Pennsylvania Real Estate Investment Trust 1197
Pennymac Financial Services Inc 1197
Pennymac Mortgage Investment Trust 1197
Pension Benefit Guaranty Corporation 1197
Penske Automotive Group Inc 1197
Penske Motor Group 1198
Penske Truck Leasing Co. L.P. 1198
Pentagon Federal Credit Union 1198
Pentair Ltd. 1198
Pentair Water Pool and Spa Inc. 1198
Penton Media Inc. 1198
People's United Financial, Inc. 1199
Peopleclick Authoria 1199

Peoples Bancorp Inc (Auburn, IN) 1199
Peoples Bancorp of North Carolina Inc 1199
Peoples Bancorp, Inc. (Marietta, OH) 1199
Peoples Educational Holdings, Inc. 1199
Peoples Federal Bancshares, Inc. 1200
Peoples Financial Corp. (Biloxi, MS) 1200
Peoples Financial Services Corp 1200
Pep Boys-Manny, Moe & Jack 1200
Pepco Holdings Inc. 1200
PEPPER CONSTRUCTION GROUP LLC 1200
Pepper Hamilton LLP 1201
Pepsi Bottling Ventures LLC 1201
PEPSI-COLA BOTTLING CO OF CENTRAL VIRGINIA 1201
PepsiCo Inc. 1201
Perceptive Software Inc. 1201
Perceptron, Inc. 1201
Perdue Incorporated 1202
Peregrine Pharmaceuticals Inc. 1202
Peregrine Semiconductor Corporation 1202
PEREZ TRADING COMPANY INC. 1202
Perfection Bakeries Inc. 1202
Perficient Inc. 1202
Performance Food Group Company 1203
Performance Food Group Inc. 1203
Performance Technologies, Inc. 1203
Performant Financial Corp 1203
Perfumania Holdings Inc 1203
Pericom Semiconductor Corp. 1203
PerkinElmer, Inc. 1204
Perkins & Marie Callender's Inc. 1204
Perkins + Will Inc. 1204
Perkins Coie LLP 1204
Perma-Fix Environmental Services, Inc. 1204
Permian Basin Royalty Trust 1204
Pernix Group Inc 1205
Perseon Corp 1205
Pershing LLC 1205
Persian Arts Society Incorporated 1205
Pervasip Corp 1205
PET SUPERMARKET INC. 1205
PETCO Animal Supplies Inc. 1206
Peter Kiewit Sons' Inc. 1206
PETER PAN BUS LINES INC. 1206
Peterson American Corporation 1206
Peterson Power Systems Inc. 1206
PetMed Express Inc 1206
Petro Holdings Inc. 1207
PETRO STAR INC. 1207
PETROCELLI ELECTRIC CO. INC. 1207
Petrohawk Energy Corporation 1207
PETROLEUM MARKETERS INCORPORATED 1207
PETROLEUM TRADERS CORPORATION 1207
PetroLogistics LP 1208
PetroQuest Energy Inc 1208
PetSmart, Inc. 1208
Pettit Oil Company 1208
Pfizer Inc 1208
PFSweb Inc 1208
PG&E Corp. (Holding Co.) 1209
PGT Inc 1209
PH Glatfelter Co 1209
Pharmaceutical Product Development Inc. 1209
Pharmacists Mutual Companies 1209
Pharmacyclics, Inc. 1209
PharmaNet Development Group Inc. 1210
PharmAthene Inc 1210
PharMerica Corp 1210
Pharmos Corporation 1210
PHELPS DUNBAR L.L.P. 1210
PHELPS MEMORIAL HOSPITAL ASSOCIATION 1210
PHH Corp 1211
PHH Mortgage Corp. 1211
PHI Group Inc. 1211
PHI Inc 1211
Phibro Animal Health Corporation 1211
Philadelphia Eagles Limited Partnership 1211
Philadelphia Insurance Companies 1212
PHILADELPHIA UNIVERSITY 1212
PHILADELPHIA WORKFORCE DEVELOPMENT CORPORATION 1212
Philip Morris International Inc 1212
Philips Electronics North America Corporation 1212
Philips Lumileds Lighting Company LLC 1212

Philips Oral Healthcare Inc. 1213
Philips Solid-State Lighting Solutions Inc. 1213
Phillips 66 1213
Phillips 66 Company 1213
Phillips 66 Partners LP 1213
PHILLIPS AND JORDAN INCORPORATED 1213
Phillips de Pury & Company LLC 1214
Phillips-Medisize Corporation 1214
PHOENIX CHILDREN'S HOSPITAL INC. 1214
Phoenix Companies, Inc. (The) 1214
Phoenix Footwear Group, Inc. 1214
Phoenix Technologies Ltd. 1214
Phosphate Holdings Inc. 1215
PhotoMedex, Inc. 1215
Photronics, Inc. 1215
Physical Property Holdings, Inc. 1215
Physicians Formula Holdings Inc. 1215
Physicians Mutual Insurance Company 1215
Physicians Realty Trust 1216
Picerne Investment Corporation 1216
Picis Inc. 1216
PICO Holdings Inc. 1216
Piedmont Natural Gas Co Inc 1216
Piedmont Office Realty Trust Inc 1216
Pier 1 Imports Inc. 1217
Pierce Manufacturing Inc. 1217
Piggly Wiggly Midwest LLC 1217
Pike Corp 1217
PIKEVILLE MEDICAL CENTER INC. 1217
Pilgrims Pride Corp. 1217
Pilkington North America Inc. 1218
Pillar Data Systems Inc. 1218
Pillsbury Winthrop Shaw Pittman LLP 1218
PILOT CORPORATION 1218
Pilot Flying J 1218
PINE GROVE MANUFACTURED HOMES INC. 1218
PineBridge Investments 1219
Pinnacle Bancshares, Inc. 1219
Pinnacle Bankshares Corp 1219
Pinnacle Data Systems Inc. 1219
Pinnacle Entertainment Inc 1219
Pinnacle Financial Partners Inc. 1219
Pinnacle Foods Finance LLC 1220
Pinnacle Foods Inc. 1220
Pinnacle Frames and Accents Inc. 1220
Pinnacle Gas Resources Inc. 1220
PINNACLE HEALTH SYSTEM 1220
Pinnacle West Capital Corp. 1220
Pinnacol Assurance 1221
Pioneer Bankshares Inc. 1221
Pioneer Energy Services Corp 1221
Pioneer Hi-Bred International Inc. 1221
Pioneer Investment Management USA Inc. 1221
Pioneer Natural Resources Co 1221
Pioneer Railcorp 1222
Piper Jaffray Companies 1222
Pismo Coast Village, Inc. 1222
PISTON AUTOMOTIVE L.L.C. 1222
PITCO FOODS 1222
Pitney Bowes Inc 1222
Pitney Bowes Software Inc. 1223
PITT COUNTY MEMORIAL HOSPITAL INCORPORATED 1223
PITT-OHIO EXPRESS LLC 1223
Pittsburgh Steelers Sports Inc. 1223
Pixar Animation Studios Inc. 1223
Pixelworks Inc 1223
Pizza Hut Inc. 1224
PJ United Inc. 1224
PJM INTERCONNECTION LLC 1224
PLACID REFINING COMPANY LLC 1224
Plains All American Pipeline, L.P. 1224
PLAINS COTTON COOPERATIVE ASSOCIATION 1224
Planar Systems Inc. 1225
Planet Hollywood International Inc. 1225
Planet Payment, Inc. 1225
Planet Smoothie Franchises LLC 1225
PlanGraphics Inc. 1225
PLANNED PARENTHOOD FEDERATION OF AMERICA INC. 1225
Plante & Moran PLLC 1226
Plantronics, Inc. 1226
PLANVIEW INC. 1226

Plaskolite Inc. 1226
Plastipak Packaging Inc. 1226
Platinum Energy Solutions Inc. 1226
Platinum Equity LLC 1227
PLATO Learning Inc. 1227
Players Network (The) 1227
PlayNetwork Inc. 1227
Plexus Corp. 1227
Plug Power Inc 1227
Plum Creek Timber Co., Inc. 1228
Plumas Bancorp Inc 1228
PLUMB SUPPLY COMPANY 1228
Pluristem Therapeutics Inc 1228
PLX Technology Inc 1228
PLY Gem Holdings Inc 1228
PM Realty Group L.P. 1229
PMA Companies Inc. 1229
PMC-Sierra Inc. 1229
PMFG, Inc. 1229
PNC Financial Services Group (The) 1229
PNC Real Estate Finance Company 1229
PNM Resources Inc 1230
PNY Technologies Inc. 1230
Poage Bankshares Inc 1230
Pocono Health System 1230
POINT LOMA NAZARENE UNIVERSITY 1230
Point.360 1230
PokerTek Inc 1231
Polaris Industries Inc. 1231
Polaris Venture Management Co. L.L.C. 1231
Polk Audio Inc. 1231
Pollo Operations Inc. 1231
Polycom Inc. 1231
Polymer Group Inc. 1232
PolyOne Corp. 1232
Polypore International Inc 1232
PolyVision Corporation 1232
POMONA COLLEGE 1232
POMP'S TIRE SERVICE INC.. 1232
Pool Corp 1233
Pope Resources LP 1233
Popeyes Louisiana Kitchen Inc 1233
Popular Inc. 1233
POPULATION SERVICES INTERNATIONAL 1233
Populous Inc. 1233
PORT OF HOUSTON AUTHORITY 1234
Port of Los Angeles 1234
Port of Seattle 1234
PORTAGE INC. 1234
Portec Rail Products Inc. 1234
Porter Bancorp Inc 1234
Porter Novelli Inc. 1235
Porter-Cable 1235
Portion Pac Inc. 1235
Portland General Electric Co. 1235
Portola Pharmaceuticals, Inc. 1235
Portsmouth Square, Inc. 1235
PositiveID Corporation 1236
Positron Corp 1236
Post Holdings Inc 1236
Post Properties, Inc. 1236
PostRock Energy Corp 1236
Potbelly Corp 1236
Potlatch Corp 1237
POWELL ELECTRONICS INC. 1237
Powell Industries, Inc. 1237
Powell's Books Inc. 1237
POWER CONSTRUCTION COMPANY LLC 1237
Power Integrations Inc. 1237
PowerBar Inc. 1238
PowerSecure International, Inc. 1238
POWERSOUTH ENERGY COOPERATIVE 1238
PowerSteering Software Inc. 1238
Powertech Uranium Corp. 1238
PowerVerde Inc 1238
Pozen Inc. 1239
PPG Industries, Inc. 1239
PPL Corp 1239
PPL Electric Utilities Corp 1239
PQ Corporation 1239
PR Newswire Association LLC 1239
PRA Group Inc 1240
PRA International 1240
PRAIRIE FARMS DAIRY INC. 1240

PRAIRIE VIEW A & M UNIVERSITY 1240
Pratt Industries (USA) 1240
Praxair, Inc. 1240
Precision Auto Care, Inc. 1241
Precision Castparts Corp. 1241
Precision Optics Corp Inc (MA) 1241
Precyse Solutions LLC 1241
Preferred Apartment Communities Inc. 1241
Preferred Bank (Los Angeles, CA) 1241
Preferred Care Partners Inc. 1242
Preformed Line Products Co. 1242
Premera Blue Cross 1242
PREMIER AG CO-OP INC. 1242
Premier Exhibitions Inc 1242
Premier Financial Bancorp, Inc. 1242
Premiere Global Services Inc 1243
PREMIO INC. 1243
PREMIUM BEERS OF OKLAHOMA L.L.C. 1243
PRESIDENT & TRUSTEES OF BATES COLLEGE
   1243
PRESIDENT & TRUSTEES OF WILLIAMS COLLEGE
   1243
PRESIDENT AND BOARD OF TRUSTEES OF SANTA
   CLARA COLLEGE 1243
PRESIDENT AND FELLOWS OF MIDDLEBURY
   COLLEGE 1244
Presidential Life Corporation 1244
Presidential Realty Corp. 1244
Presidio Inc. 1244
PRESONUS AUDIO ELECTRONICS INC. 1244
Presstek Inc. 1244
Pressure BioSciences Inc 1245
Prestige Brands Holdings Inc 1245
PRESTIGE TRAVEL INC 1245
Pretium Packaging LLC 1245
PRGX Global, Inc. 1245
Priceline Group Inc. (The) 1245
PriceSmart Inc 1246
PricewaterhouseCoopers LLP 1246
PRIDGEON & CLAY INC. 1246
PrimeEnergy Corp. 1246
PrimeVest Financial Services Inc. 1246
PRIMEX INTERNATIONAL TRADING CORP 1246
Primo Water Corp 1247
Primoris Services Corp 1247
PRIMUS BUILDERS INC. 1247
Principal Financial Group, Inc. 1247
Principal Global Investors LLC 1247
PrintingForLess.com Inc. 1247
Printronix Inc. 1248
Priority Health Managed Benefits Inc. 1248
PRISON REHABILITATIVE INDUSTRIES AND
   DIVERSIFIED ENTERPRISES INC 1248
PrivateBancorp, Inc. 1248
PRO Unlimited Inc. 1248
Pro-Dex Inc. (CO) 1248
ProAssurance Corp. 1249
ProBuild Holdings Inc. 1249
Procera Networks Inc 1249
Procter & Gamble Co. 1249
ProcureStaff Ltd. 1249
Procurian Inc. 1249
Procyon Corporation 1250
PRODUCERS RICE MILL INC. 1250
Production Resource Group LLC 1250
PRODUCTION TOOL SUPPLY COMPANY LLC 1250
Professional Diversity Network, Inc. 1250
PROFESSIONAL GOLFERS ASSOCIATION OF
   AMERICA INC 1250
PROFESSIONAL PROJECT SERVICES INC. 1251
Professional Systems Corporation 1251
Progenics Pharmaceuticals, Inc. 1251
Proginet Corporation 1251
Progress Energy Inc. 1251
Progress Software Corp. 1251
Progressive Corp. (OH) 1252
PROHEALTH CARE INC 1252
PROJECT ENHANCEMENT CORP 1252
Project Leadership Associates Inc. 1252
ProLiance Energy LLC 1252
Prologis Inc 1252
Promega Corporation 1253
Prometheus Laboratories Inc. 1253
Prometric Inc. 1253

Promise Technology Inc. 1253
Prommis Solutions LLC 1253
Proofpoint Inc 1253
ProPhase Labs Inc 1254
Prophotonix Ltd. 1254
Pros Holdings Inc 1254
Prosek Partners 1254
ProSight Specialty Insurance Group Inc. 1254
Proskauer Rose LLP 1254
Prospect Capital Corporation 1255
Prospect Medical Holdings Inc. 1255
Prosperity Bancshares Inc. 1255
ProSys Information Systems Inc. 1255
Protalex Inc 1255
Protection One Inc. 1255
Protective Life Corp. 1256
Protective Life Insurance Co 1256
PROTESTANT MEMORIAL MEDICAL CENTER INC.
   1256
Protext Mobility Inc 1256
Proto Labs Inc 1256
Provectus Pharmaceuticals Inc. 1256
Provide Commerce Inc. 1257
Providence & Worcester Railroad Co. 1257
PROVIDENCE COLLEGE 1257
PROVIDENCE HOSPITAL 1257
PROVIDENCE HOSPITAL 1257
Providence Resources Inc. 1257
Providence Service Corp 1258
Provident Community Bancshares, Inc. 1258
Provident Financial Holdings, Inc. 1258
Provident Financial Services Inc 1258
Proxim Wireless Corporation 1258
Prudential Annuities Life Assurance Corp 1258
Prudential Financial, Inc. 1259
Prudential Investment Management Inc. 1259
PRUDENTIAL OVERALL SUPPLY INC. 1259
PRWT SERVICES INC. 1259
PS Business Parks, Inc 1259
PS Energy Group Inc. 1259
PSB Holdings Inc 1260
PSCU INCORPORATED 1260
PSEG Global L.L.C. 1260
PSEG Power LLC 1260
Psychemedics Corp. 1260
PTC Inc 1260
PTC Therapeutics Inc 1261
PUBLIC BROADCASTING SERVICE 1261
PUBLIC COMMUNICATIONS SERVICES INC. 1261
PUBLIC HEALTH SOLUTIONS 1261
Public Service Company of New Hampshire 1261
Public Service Company of Oklahoma 1261
Public Service Electric and Gas Company 1262
Public Service Enterprise Group Inc. 1262
Public Storage 1262
PUBLIC UTILITIES BOARD 1262
Public Utility District No. 1 of Chelan County
   Washington 1262
Public Utility District No. 1 of Clark County 1262
Public Utility District No. 1 of Snohomish County
   Washing 1263
Public Utility District No. 2 of Grant County
   Washington 1263
Publicis & Hal Riney 1263
Publicis Modem 1263
Publishers Clearing House LLC 1263
Publix Super Markets, Inc. 1263
Puerto Rico Electric Power Authority 1264
Puget Energy Inc. 1264
PUGET SOUND BLOOD CENTER & PROGRAM 1264
Pulaski Financial Corp 1264
Pulse Electronics Corp 1264
PULSE Network LLC 1264
PulteGroup, Inc. 1265
Puradyn Filter Technologies Inc 1265
Purdue Pharma L.P. 1265
PURE Bioscience Inc 1265
Pure Cycle Corp. 1265
Purple Communications Inc. 1265
Putnam Investments LLC 1266
PVH Corp 1266
PVR Partners LP 1266
PVS TECHNOLOGIES INC. 1266
PYCO INDUSTRIES INC. 1266

Pzena Investment Management Inc 1266
Q.E.P. Co., Inc. 1267
QAD, Inc. 1267
QC Holdings Inc 1267
QCR Holdings Inc 1267
QEP Resources Inc 1267
Qlik Technologies Inc. 1267
QLogic Corp. 1268
QNB Corp. 1268
Qorvo Inc 1268
QR Energy LP 1268
QST Industries Inc. 1268
QTS Realty Trust Inc 1268
Quad/Graphics, Inc. 1269
Quaker Chemical Corporation 1269
QUAKER VALLEY FOODS INC. 1269
Qualcomm Atheros Inc. 1269
QUALCOMM Flarion Technologies 1269
Qualcomm, Inc. 1269
Quality Dining Inc. 1270
Quality Distribution Inc (FL) 1270
Quality Food Centers Inc. 1270
QUALITY OIL COMPANY LLC 1270
Quality Systems, Inc. 1270
QUALSERV CORPORATION 1270
Qualstar Corp 1271
Qualys, Inc. 1271
Quanex Building Products Corp 1271
Quanta Services, Inc. 1271
Quantum Corp. 1271
Quantum Fuel Systems Technologies Worldwide Inc.
  1271
Quark Pharmaceuticals Inc. 1272
QUEEN OF THE VALLEY MEDICAL CENTER 1272
Queens-Long Island Medical Group P.C. 1272
Quest Diagnostics, Inc. 1272
QUEST MEDIA & SUPPLIES INC. 1272
Quest Software Inc. 1272
Questar Capital Corporation 1273
Questar Corp. 1273
Questar Gas Co. 1273
Questcor Pharmaceuticals Inc 1273
Quick-Med Technologies Inc. 1273
Quicken Loans Inc. 1273
QuickLogic Corp 1274
Quicksilver Production Partners LP 1274
Quicksilver Resources, Inc. 1274
Quidel Corp. 1274
Quiksilver, Inc. 1274
QuikTrip Corporation 1274
Quill Corporation 1275
Quinn Emanuel Urquhart & Sullivan LLP 1275
QUINNIPIAC UNIVERSITY 1275
QuinStreet, Inc. 1275
Quintiles Transnational Holdings Inc 1275
Qumu Corp 1275
Quova Inc. 1276
QVC Inc. 1276
Qvidian Corporation 1276
R&R Products Inc. 1276
R. B. Pamplin Corporation 1276
R. E. MICHEL COMPANY 1276
R. L. JORDAN OIL COMPANY OF NORTH CAROLINA
  INC. 1277
R.J. O'Brien & Associates Inc. 1277
R.S. HUGHES COMPANY INC. 1277
Rabobank N.A. 1277
RaceTrac Petroleum Inc. 1277
Rackspace Hosting Inc 1277
Radian Group, Inc. 1278
Radiant Logistics, Inc. 1278
Radiant Systems Inc. 1278
Radiation Therapy Services Inc. 1278
Radio Flyer Inc. 1278
Radio Frequency Systems Inc. 1278
Radio One Inc 1279
Radisson Hotels & Resorts 1279
RadiSys Corp. 1279
Radius Health Inc. 1279
RadNet Inc 1279
RADY CHILDREN'S HOSPITAL-SAN DIEGO 1279
RAE Systems Inc. 1280
RailAmerica Inc. 1280
Rainmaker Systems Inc. 1280

RAIT Financial Trust 1280
Ralcorp Frozen Bakery Products Inc. 1280
RALEY'S 1280
Rally Software Development Corp. 1281
Ralph Lauren Corp 1281
Rambus Inc. (DE) 1281
Ramco-Gershenson Properties Trust (MD) 1281
Ramtron International Corporation 1281
Ranbaxy Pharmaceuticals Inc. 1281
Rand Logistics Inc 1282
Randa Leather Goods 1282
Randolph-Brooks Federal Credit Union 1282
Random House Inc. 1282
Randstad US L.P. 1282
Range Resources Corp 1282
RAPID CITY REGIONAL HOSPITAL INC. 1283
Rapp Worldwide Inc. 1283
RAPPAHANNOCK ELECTRIC COOPERATIVE 1283
Raptor Networks Technology Inc. 1283
Raptor Pharmaceuticals Corp. 1283
Raritan Americas Inc. 1283
RARITAN BAY MEDICAL CENTER. 1284
RARITAN VALLEY COMMUNITY COLLEGE 1284
Rave Restaurant Group Inc 1284
Raven Industries, Inc. 1284
Rawlings Sporting Goods Company Inc. 1284
RAYBURN COUNTRY ELECTRIC COOPERATIVE INC
  1284
Raycom Media Inc. 1285
Raymond James Financial, Inc. 1285
RAYMOURS FURNITURE COMPANY INC. 1285
Rayonier Inc. 1285
Raytheon Applied Signal Technology Inc. 1285
Raytheon Co. 1285
Raytheon Technical Services Company LLC 1286
RB Rubber Products Inc. 1286
RBC Bearings Inc 1286
RBC Capital Markets LLC 1286
RBC Life Sciences Inc 1286
RBS Global Inc. 1286
RC2 Corporation 1287
RCI Hospitality Holdings Inc 1287
RCM Technologies, Inc. 1287
RCN Telecom Services LLC 1287
RCS Capital Corp 1287
RDO EQUIPMENT CO 1287
RE/MAX International Inc. 1288
ReachLocal Inc. 1288
READING HOSPITAL 1288
Reading International, Inc. 1288
Ready Pac Foods Inc. 1288
Real Goods Solar Inc 1288
Real Mex Restaurants Inc. 1289
RealD Inc. 1289
RealNetworks, Inc. 1289
Realogy Holdings Corp 1289
RealPage Inc 1289
Realty Income Corp. 1289
Recall Corporation 1290
Reckitt Benckiser Inc. 1290
Recology Inc. 1290
RecycleNet Corporation 1290
RED BLOSSOM SALES INC. 1290
Red Gold Inc. 1290
Red Hat Inc 1291
Red Lions Hotels Corp 1291
Red River Computer Co. Inc. 1291
Red Robin Gourmet Burgers Inc 1291
Red Roof Inn 1291
REDNER'S MARKETS INC. 1291
Redpoint Bio Corporation 1292
RedPrairie Corporation 1292
Redwood Trust Inc. 1292
Reebok International Ltd. 1292
Reed & Barton Corporation 1292
Reed's Inc 1292
Refac Optical Group 1293
Regal Beloit Corp 1293
Regal Entertainment Group 1293
Regal Ware Inc. 1293
Regence BlueCross BlueShield of Oregon 1293
Regency Centers Corp. 1293
Regency Energy Partners LP 1294
Regency Enterprises 1294

Regeneron Pharmaceuticals, Inc. 1294
RegeneRX Biopharmaceuticals Inc 1294
REGINA MEDICAL CENTER 1294
Regional Management Corp 1294
Regions Financial Corp 1295
REGIONS HOSPITAL FOUNDATION 1295
Regis Corp. 1295
Regulus Therapeutics Inc 1295
REI SYSTEMS INC. 1295
Reichhold Inc. 1295
Reinsurance Group of America, Inc. 1296
Reis, Inc 1296
Relax the Back Corporation 1296
Reliability Incorporated 1296
Reliance Steel & Aluminum Co. 1296
Reliv' International, Inc. 1296
RELM Wireless Corp. 1297
Remy Cointreau USA Inc. 1297
Remy International Inc. 1297
Renaissance Learning Inc. 1297
Renasant Corp 1297
Renewable Energy Group Inc. 1297
Renewable Energy Group, Inc. 1298
RENFRO CORPORATION 1298
Rennova Health Inc 1298
RENO CONTRACTING INC. 1298
Rent-A-Center Inc. 1298
Rentech, Inc. 1298
Rentrak Corp. 1299
RepairClinic.com Inc. 1299
REPLACEMENT PARTS INC. 1299
REPLACEMENTS LTD. 1299
Repligen Corp. 1299
Repro-Med Systems, Inc. 1299
Repros Therapeutics Inc 1300
Republic Airways Holdings Inc 1300
Republic Bancorp, Inc. (KY) 1300
Republic First Bancorp, Inc. 1300
Republic Mortgage Insurance Company 1300
Republic Services, Inc. 1300
Republic Western Insurance Company 1301
Res-Care Inc. 1301
Research Corporation Technologies Inc. 1301
Research Frontiers Inc. 1301
Research Incorporated 1301
RESEARCH TRIANGLE INSTITUTE INC 1301
Reserve Petroleum Co. 1302
ResMed Inc. 1302
Resolute Forest Products Inc 1302
ResortQuest International Inc. 1302
Resource America, Inc. 1302
Resource Capital Corp 1302
Resources Connection Inc 1303
Restaurant Technologies Inc. 1303
Restoration Hardware Holdings Inc. 1303
Restoration Hardware Holdings, Inc. 1303
RestorGenex Corp 1303
Retail Opportunity Investments Corp 1303
Retail Properties of America, Inc 1304
RetailMeNot, Inc. 1304
Retirement Housing Foundation 1304
Retractable Technologies Inc 1304
Reval Holdings Inc. 1304
Revance Therapeutics Inc 1304
Revett Mining Co Inc 1305
Revlon Inc 1305
Revolution Lighting Technologies Inc 1305
Rewards Network Inc. 1305
REX American Resources Corp 1305
Rex Energy Corp 1305
REX HEALTHCARE INC. 1306
Rexahn Pharmaceuticals Inc. 1306
Rexam Beverage Can Company 1306
Rexel Inc. 1306
Rexford Industrial Realty Inc 1306
Rexnord Corp (New) 1306
Reynolds American Inc 1307
Reynolds Food Packaging 1307
RF Industries Ltd. 1307
RF Micro Devices, Inc. 1307
RF Monolithics, Inc. 1307
RGC Resources, Inc. 1307
RGIS LLC 1308
RHE Hatco Inc. 1308

RHI Entertainment LLC 1308
Rhino Resource Partners LP 1308
RHODE ISLAND SCHOOL OF DESIGN INC 1308
RHODES COLLEGE 1308
Rhythm & Hues Studios Inc. 1309
Rib-X Pharmaceuticals Inc. 1309
Rice Energy Inc 1309
RiceBran Technologies 1309
RICELAND FOODS INC. 1309
RICH PRODUCTS CORPORATION 1309
RICHARD J. CARON FOUNDATION 1310
Richardson Electronics Ltd 1310
Ricoh USA Inc. 1310
Ridge Tool Company 1310
Ridgewood Savings Bank 1310
Rigel Pharmaceuticals Inc 1310
Right Management Inc. 1311
RigNet Inc 1311
RingCentral Inc 1311
RIP GRIFFIN TRUCK SERVICE CENTER INC. 1311
Ripley Entertainment Inc. 1311
Ripplewood Holdings L.L.C. 1311
Risk (George) Industries Inc 1312
Rite Aid Corp. 1312
River Valley Bancorp 1312
Riverbed Technology Inc 1312
RIVERSIDE HEALTHCARE ASSOCIATION INC. 1312
RIVERSIDE HOSPITAL INC. 1312
Riverview Bancorp, Inc. 1313
RIVERVIEW HOSPITAL 1313
Riviera Holdings Corporation 1313
RJF International Corporation 1313
RKA Petroleum Companies Inc. 1313
RLI Corp. 1313
Roadrunner Transportation Services Holdings Inc. 1314
Roadrunner Transportation Systems Inc 1314
Roamware Inc. 1314
Robert Bosch LLC 1314
Robert Bosch Tool Corporation 1314
Robert Half International Inc. 1314
ROBERT MORRIS UNIVERSITY 1315
ROBERT WOOD JOHNSON UNIVERSITY HOSPITAL 1315
ROBERT WOOD JOHNSON UNIVERSITY HOSPITAL AT RAHWAY 1315
ROBERTS DAIRY COMPANY LLC 1315
Robinson (C.H.) Worldwide, Inc. 1315
ROBINSON MEMORIAL HOSPITAL 1315
ROBINSON OIL CORPORATION 1316
Roche Bros. Supermarkets Inc. 1316
ROCHESTER INSTITUTE OF TECHNOLOGY (INC) 1316
Rock Creek Pharmaceuticals Inc 1316
Rock Energy Resources Inc. 1316
Rock of Ages Corporation 1316
Rock-Tenn Co. 1317
Rockefeller Group International Inc. 1317
Rocket Fuel Inc 1317
Rocket Software Inc. 1317
ROCKHURST UNIVERSITY 1317
ROCKVIEW DAIRIES INC. 1317
Rockwell Automation, Inc. 1318
Rockwell Collins, Inc. 1318
Rockwell Medical, Inc 1318
Rockwood Holdings Inc 1318
Rocky Brands Inc 1318
Rocky Mountain Chocolate Factory Inc (DE) 1318
Rodale Inc. 1319
Roehl Transport Inc. 1319
Rofin Sinar Technologies Inc. 1319
Roger Cleveland Golf Company Inc. 1319
Rogers Corp. 1319
Rogue Wave Software Inc. 1319
ROLLINS COLLEGE 1320
Rollins, Inc. 1320
Romacorp Inc. 1320
Ronco Acquisition Corporation 1320
RONILE INC. 1320
ROOFING WHOLESALE CO. INC. 1320
RoomLinx Inc 1321
Rooms To Go 1321
Root Learning Inc. 1321
root9B Technologies Inc 1321

Roper Technologies Inc 1321
Ropes & Gray LLP 1321
Rose Acre Farms Inc. 1322
ROSE INTERNATIONAL INC. 1322
ROSE PAVING CO. 1322
Rose Rock Midstream L P 1322
ROSE"S SOUTHWEST PAPERS INC. 1322
ROSEN HOTELS AND RESORTS INC. 1322
Rosen's Diversified Inc. 1323
Rosendin Electric Inc. 1323
Rosetta Marketing Group LLC 1323
Rosetta Resources, Inc. 1323
Rosetta Stone, Inc. 1323
Ross Stores, Inc. 1323
Ross-Simons of Warwick Inc. 1324
ROTARY INTERNATIONAL 1324
ROTH Capital Partners LLC 1324
ROTH PRODUCE CO. 1324
ROTH STAFFING COMPANIES L.P. 1324
Rothschild North America Inc. 1324
Rothstein Kass & Company P.C. 1325
Round Table Pizza Inc. 1325
Roundy's Inc. 1325
Rouse Properties, Inc. 1325
Rovi Corp. 1325
Rowan Companies Inc. 1325
Rowe Fine Furniture Inc. 1326
Rowland Coffee Roasters Inc. 1326
Royal Appliance Mfg. Co. 1326
Royal Bancshares of Pennsylvania, Inc 1326
Royal Caribbean Cruises Ltd. 1326
Royal Gold, Inc. 1326
Royal Hawaiian Orchards LP 1327
Royale Energy, Inc. 1327
RPC, Inc. 1327
RPM International Inc (DE) 1327
RPX Corp 1327
RSA Security LLC 1327
RSM McGladrey Inc. 1328
RTI International Metals, Inc. 1328
RTI Surgical, Inc. 1328
RTW Inc. 1328
Ruan Transportation Management Systems Inc. 1328
Rubicon Technology Inc 1328
Ruby Tuesday, Inc. 1329
Ruckus Wireless Inc 1329
Rudolph and Sletten Inc. 1329
Rudolph Foods Company Inc. 1329
Rudolph Technologies, Inc. 1329
RUMSEY ELECTRIC COMPANY 1329
Rush Enterprises Inc. 1330
RUSH-COPLEY MEDICAL CENTER INC. 1330
Russ Darrow Group Inc. 1330
Russell Investments 1330
Russell Reynolds Associates Inc. 1330
RUSSELL SIGLER INC. 1330
Ruth's Hospitality Group Inc 1331
RUTHERFORD ELECTRIC MEMBERSHIP CORPORATION 1331
RUTLAND HOSPITAL INC. 1331
RVUE Holdings Inc 1331
RW Stearns Inc. 1331
RYAN BUILDING GROUP INC. 1331
RYAN LLC 1332
Ryder System, Inc. 1332
Ryerson Holding Corp 1332
Ryland Group, Inc. 1332
Ryman Hospitality Properties Inc 1332
S & T Bancorp Inc (Indiana, PA) 1332
S&ME INC 1333
S&W Seed Co. 1333
S. D. Warren Company 1333
S.C. Johnson & Son Inc. 1333
S.P. Richards Company 1333
SA International Inc. 1333
Saatchi & Saatchi North America Inc. 1334
Sabine Royalty Trust 1334
Sabra Health Care REIT Inc 1334
Sabre Industries Inc. 1334
Sacramento Municipal Utility District 1334
SACRED HEART HOSPITAL INC. 1334
SACRED HEART HOSPITAL OF ALLENTOWN 1335
SADDLEBACK MEMORIAL MEDICAL CENTER 1335
Saehan Bancorp 1335

Safe Ride Services Inc. 1335
Safeco Insurance Company of America 1335
Safeguard Scientifics Inc. 1335
Safelite Group Inc. 1336
SafeNet Inc. 1336
Safety Insurance Group, Inc. 1336
Safety-Kleen Inc. 1336
Safeway Inc. 1336
Safeway Insurance Group 1336
Safra National Bank of New York 1337
Saga Communications, Inc. 1337
SAGARSOFT INC. 1337
Sage Instruments Inc. 1337
Sage Software Inc. 1337
Sagent Pharmaceuticals Inc 1337
Saia Inc 1338
SAINT AGNES MEDICAL CENTER 1338
SAINT ALPHONSUS REGIONAL MEDICAL CENTER INC. 1338
SAINT ANSELM COLLEGE 1338
Saint Barnabas Corporation 1338
SAINT EDWARD"S UNIVERSITY INC. 1338
SAINT ELIZABETH MEDICAL CENTER INC. 1339
SAINT ELIZABETH REGIONAL MEDICAL CENTER 1339
SAINT FRANCIS HOSPITAL AND MEDICAL CENTER FOUNDATION INC. 1339
SAINT FRANCIS UNIVERSITY 1339
SAINT JOSEPH'S UNIVERSITY 1339
SAINT LOUIS UNIVERSITY 1339
SAINT MARY"S UNIVERSITY OF MINNESOTA 1340
SAINT TAMMANY PARISH HOSPITAL SERVICE DISTRICT 1 1340
Saint-Gobain Abrasives Inc. 1340
Saint-Gobain Containers Inc. 1340
Sajan Inc. 1340
Saks Fifth Avenue Inc. 1340
Salary.com Inc. 1341
SALEM HOSPITAL 1341
Salem Media Group, Inc. 1341
Salesforce.Com Inc 1341
SALINE MEMORIAL HOSPITAL AUXILIARY 1341
Salisbury Bancorp, Inc. 1341
Salix Pharmaceuticals Ltd 1342
Sally Beauty Holdings Inc 1342
Salon Media Group Inc. 1342
SALT LAKE COMMUNITY COLLEGE 1342
SALVE REGINA UNIVERSITY 1342
Sam Ash Music Corporation 1342
SAM LEVIN INC. 1343
SAM SWOPE AUTO GROUP LLC 1343
Sam's West Inc. 1343
SAMARITAN REGIONAL HEALTH SYSTEM 1343
Sammons Enterprises Inc. 1343
Samson Investment Company 1343
Samsung Electronics America Inc. 1344
Samsung Semiconductor Inc. 1344
Samsung Telecommunications America L.L.C. 1344
Samuels Jewelers 1344
San Diego County Water Authority 1344
San Diego Padres Baseball Club Limited Partnership 1344
SAN DIEGO UNIFIED PORT DISTRICT 1345
San Francisco Bay Area Rapid Transit District 1345
San Francisco Forty Niners Ltd. 1345
SAN FRANCISCO OPERA ASSOCIATION 1345
SAN JOAQUIN REFINING CO. INC. 1345
San Juan Basin Royalty Trust 1345
Sanchez Energy Corp. 1346
Sanchez Production Partners LP 1346
Sanders/Wingo 1346
Sanderson Farms, Inc. 1346
Sandia National Laboratories 1346
SanDisk Corp. 1346
Sandoz Inc. 1347
Sandridge Energy Inc 1347
Sandston Corporation 1347
Sandvik Coromant Company 1347
Sandy Spring Bancorp Inc 1347
Sanfilippo (John B.) & Son, Inc. 1347
Sanford C. Bernstein & Co. LLC 1348
Sanford Health of Northern Minnesota 1348
SANFORD-BURNHAM MEDICAL RESEARCH INSTITUTE 1348

Sangamo BioSciences Inc 1348
Sanmina Corp 1348
Sanofi Pasteur Inc. 1348
Sanofi-Aventis U.S. LLC 1349
SANTA CRUZ SEASIDE COMPANY INC 1349
Santa Fe Financial Corp. 1349
Santa Fe Gold Corp 1349
Santander Consumer USA Holdings Inc 1349
Santander Holdings USA Inc. 1349
SAP America Inc. 1350
Sapient Corp. 1350
SAPP BROS. INC. 1350
SAPP BROS. PETROLEUM INC. 1350
SARAH BUSH LINCOLN HEALTH CENTER 1350
SARAH LAWRENCE COLLEGE 1350
Saratoga Resources Inc 1351
Sarepta Therapeutics Inc 1351
SARGENT ELECTRIC COMPANY 1351
SAS Institute Inc. 1351
SASCO 1351
Satmetrix Systems Inc. 1351
SATTERFIELD AND PONTIKES CONSTRUCTION
    INC. 1352
Saul Centers, Inc. 1352
Savage Companies 1352
SAVE THE CHILDREN FEDERATION INC. 1352
Savi Technology Inc. 1352
Savient Pharmaceuticals Inc 1352
SAVVIS Inc. 1353
SAWNEE ELECTRIC MEMBERSHIP CORPORATION
    1353
Sayers40 Inc. 1353
SB Financial Group Inc 1353
SBA Communications Corp. 1353
SC Fuels 1353
SCA Tissue North America LLC 1354
SCANA Corp 1354
ScanSource, Inc. 1354
Scantron Corporation 1354
Schawk, Inc. 1354
Schein (Henry), Inc. 1354
SCHEWEL FURNITURE COMPANY INCORPORATED
    1355
Schiff Hardin LLP 1355
Schiff Nutrition International Inc. 1355
Schindler Elevator Corporation 1355
Schlotzsky's Ltd. 1355
Schlumberger Limited 1355
Schmitt Industries Inc (OR) 1356
Schmitt Music Company 1356
Schneider National, Inc. 1356
Schnitzer Steel Industries, Inc. 1356
Schnuck Markets Inc. 1356
Scholastic Corp. 1356
School Employees Retirement System of Ohio 1357
SchoolsFirst FCU 1357
Schottenstein Realty Trust Inc. 1357
Schreiber Foods Inc. 1357
Schulman (A.), Inc. 1357
Schulte Roth & Zabel LLP 1357
Schulze and Burch Biscuit Co. 1358
SCHUMACHER ELECTRIC CORPORATION 1358
Schwab (Charles) Corp. 1358
Schweitzer-Mauduit International, Inc. 1358
SciClone Pharmaceuticals, Inc. 1358
Science Applications International Corp (New) 1358
Scientific Industries, Inc. 1359
Scientific Learning Corp. 1359
SCIENTIFIC RESEARCH CORP 1359
Scios Inc. 1359
SciQuest Inc 1359
SCL HEALTH - FRONT RANGE INC. 1359
SCOTT & WHITE HEALTH PLAN 1360
SCOTT & WHITE MEMORIAL HOSPITAL 1360
SCOTT EQUIPMENT COMPANY L.L.C. 1360
Scott's Liquid Gold, Inc. 1360
Scotts Miracle-Gro Co (The) 1360
SCOTTSDALE HEALTHCARE CORP. 1360
Scottsdale Insurance Company 1361
Scripps (E.W.) Co (The) 1361
SCRIPPS COLLEGE 1361
SCRIPPS HEALTH 1361
Scripps Networks Interactive Inc 1361
Sculptz Inc. 1361

SDB TRADE INTERNATIONAL L.P. 1362
SDI Health LLC 1362
SDI Technologies Inc. 1362
Seaboard Corp. 1362
SEABROOK BROTHERS & SONS INC 1362
SeaChange International Inc. 1362
Seacoast Banking Corp. of Florida 1363
SEACOR Holdings Inc 1363
SEALASKA CORPORATION 1363
Sealed Air Corp. 1363
Sears Holdings Corp 1363
Sears Hometown & Outlet Stores Inc 1363
Sears Roebuck and Co. 1364
SEATTLE CHILDREN'S HOSPITAL 1364
Seattle Genetics Inc 1364
SEATTLE UNIVERSITY 1364
SeaWorld Entertainment Inc. 1364
SECURA Insurance Holdings Inc. 1364
SecureWorks Inc. 1365
Securian Financial Group Inc. 1365
SECURITIES INVESTOR PROTECTION
    CORPORATION 1365
Security Benefit Corporation 1365
Security Federal Corp (SC) 1365
SECURITY FINANCE CORPORATION OF
    SPARTANBURG 1365
SECURITY HEALTH PLAN OF WISCONSIN INC.
    1366
Security Land & Development Corp. 1366
Security National Financial Corp. 1366
Security Service Federal Credit Union 1366
SED International Holdings, Inc. 1366
Sedano's Management Inc. 1366
Sedgwick Claims Management Services Inc. 1367
Sedgwick LLP 1367
SEDONA Corporation 1367
See's Candies Inc. 1367
Sefton Resources Inc. 1367
SEGA of America Inc. 1367
Segway Inc. 1368
SEI Investments Co. 1368
Select Bancorp Inc (New) 1368
Select Comfort Corp. 1368
Select Income Real Estate Investment Trust 1368
Select Medical Holdings Corp 1368
Select Portfolio Servicing Inc. 1369
Selective Insurance Group Inc 1369
SEMCO ENERGY Inc. 1369
SemGroup Corp 1369
SEMINOLE ELECTRIC COOPERATIVE INC. 1369
Semler Scientific Inc 1369
Sempra Energy 1370
Semtech Corp. 1370
Seneca Companies Inc. 1370
Seneca Foods Corp. 1370
Senior Housing Properties Trust 1370
Senior Whole Health LLC 1370
Senomyx Inc 1371
Sense Technologies Inc. 1371
Sensient Technologies Corp. 1371
SENTARA HEALTHCARE 1371
SENTARA RMH MEDICAL CENTER 1371
Sentient Flight Group LLC 1371
Sentry Technology Corporation 1372
SEPATON Inc. 1372
Sephora USA Inc. 1372
Sequa Corporation 1372
SEQUACHEE VALLEY ELECTRIC CO-OPERATIVE
    INC 1372
Sequenom Inc 1372
Serco Inc. 1373
SERENA Software Inc. 1373
Serra Automotive Inc. 1373
Serta Inc. 1373
SERVCO PACIFIC INC. 1373
Service Corp. International 1373
ServiceMagic Inc. 1374
ServiceNow Inc 1374
Services Group of America Inc. 1374
ServiceSource International, Inc. 1374
Servigistics Inc. 1374
ServisFirst Bancshares, Inc. 1374
Servotronics, Inc. 1375
SERVPRO INTELLECTUAL PROPERTY INC. 1375

SETON HALL UNIVERSITY 1375
Seton Healthcare Network 1375
Sevcon Inc 1375
SEVEN SEAS TECHNOLOGIES INC. 1375
Seventh Generation Inc. 1376
Severn Bancorp Inc (Annapolis MD) 1376
Severstal North America Inc. 1376
Sevin Rosen Funds 1376
Sevion Therapeutics Inc 1376
SEYFARTH SHAW LLP 1376
SFN Group Inc. 1377
SFX Entertainment, Inc. 1377
SGS North America Inc. 1377
SGT INC. 1377
Shakey's USA Inc. 1377
Shaklee Corporation 1377
SHAMROCK FOODS COMPANY 1378
SHANDS JACKSONVILLE MEDICAL CENTER INC.
    1378
Shands Teaching Hospital and Clinics Inc. 1378
Shaner Hotel Group Limited Partnership 1378
Shapell Industries Inc. 1378
SHARI'S MANAGEMENT CORPORATION 1378
SHARON REGIONAL HEALTH SYSTEM INC. 1379
Sharp Electronics Corporation 1379
SHARP HEALTHCARE 1379
SHARP MEMORIAL HOSPITAL 1379
Sharpe Resources Corporation 1379
Sharps Compliance Corp. 1379
SHAWMUT WOODWORKING & SUPPLY INC. 1380
SHAWNEE MISSION MEDICAL CENTER INC. 1380
Shea Homes Limited Partnership 1380
Shearer's Foods Inc. 1380
Shelco Inc. 1380
Shell Oil Company 1380
Shell Oil Products US 1381
Shenandoah Telecommunications Co. 1381
SHEPHERD CENTER INC. 1381
SHEPHERD ELECTRIC COMPANY INCORPORATED
    1381
Sheppard Mullin Richter & Hampton LLP 1381
SHERIDAN COMMUNITY HOSPITAL
    (OSTEOPATHIC) 1381
Sheridan Healthcare Inc. 1382
Sherwin-Williams Co. 1382
SHI INTERNATIONAL CORP. 1382
Shiloh Industries, Inc. 1382
Shimadzu Scientific Instruments Inc. 1382
Shiner International Inc 1382
Shintech Inc. 1383
Shoe Carnival, Inc. 1383
Shoney's North America Corp. 1383
Shook Hardy & Bacon L.L.P. 1383
Shop 'n Save St. Louis Inc. 1383
Shopping.com Ltd. 1383
Shopzilla Inc. 1384
Shore Bancshares Inc. 1384
SHORE MEMORIAL HOSPITAL 1384
ShoreTel Inc 1384
Shorewood Packaging Corporation 1384
SHPS Inc. 1384
SHRINERS HOSPITALS FOR CHILDREN 1385
Shutterfly Inc 1385
Shutterstock Inc 1385
SI Financial Group Inc (MD) 1385
Sidley Austin LLP 1385
Siebert Financial Corp. 1385
Siemens Industry Inc. 1386
Sierra Bancorp 1386
SIERRA CLUB 1386
Sierra Monitor Corp 1386
Sierra Nevada Corporation 1386
Sierra Pacific Industries 1386
Sierra Pacific Power Co. 1387
SIFCO Industries Inc. 1387
SIGA Technologies Inc 1387
SiGe Semiconductor Inc. 1387
Sigma Designs, Inc. 1387
Sigma-Aldrich Corp. 1387
SigmaTron International Inc. 1388
Signature Bank (New York, NY) 1388
SIGNATURE CONSULTANTS LLC 1388
Signature Eyewear Inc. 1388
Signature Flight Support Corporation 1388

Sika Corporation 1388
Sikorsky Aircraft Corporation 1389
Silgan Containers LLC 1389
Silgan Holdings Inc. 1389
Silgan Plastics LLC 1389
Silicon Graphics International Corp 1389
Silicon Image Inc 1389
Silicon Laboratories Inc 1390
Silver Bay Realty Trust Corp 1390
SILVER CROSS HOSPITAL AND MEDICAL CENTERS 1390
Silver Eagle Distributors L.P. 1390
Silver Lake Technology Management L.L.C. 1390
Silver Spring Networks Inc 1390
Silverleaf Resorts Inc. 1391
Silverstein Properties Inc. 1391
Simmons First National Corp. 1391
Simon Property Group, Inc. 1391
Simon Worldwide Inc. 1391
Simplex Healthcare Inc. 1391
SimplexGrinnell LP 1392
Simplicity Bancorp, Inc 1392
Simpson Housing LLLP 1392
Simpson Investment Company 1392
Simpson Manufacturing Co., Inc. (DE) 1392
Simpson Strong-Tie Company Inc. 1392
Simpson Thacher & Bartlett LLP 1393
Simulations Plus Inc. 1393
SINAI HOSPITAL OF BALTIMORE INC 1393
Sinclair Broadcast Group, Inc. 1393
Sinclair Oil Corporation 1393
Singing Machine Co., Inc. 1393
Sino-Global Shipping America, Ltd. 1394
Sipi Metals Corp. 1394
Sirchie Acquisition Company LLC 1394
Sirius America Insurance Company 1394
Sirius XM Holdings Inc 1394
Sirona Dental Systems Inc 1394
SIRVA Inc. 1395
Sitestar Corporation 1395
Six Flags Entertainment Corp 1395
SJW Corp. 1395
Skadden Arps Slate Meagher & Flom LLP 1395
Skanska USA Building Inc. 1395
Skanska USA Civil 1396
Skechers U S A, Inc. 1396
SKIDMORE COLLEGE 1396
Skinvisible Inc 1396
Skullcandy Inc 1396
Skyline Corp. 1396
SkyMall Inc. 1397
SkyWest Inc. 1397
Skyworks Solutions, Inc. 1397
Skyy Spirits LLC 1397
SL Green Realty Corp. 1397
SL Industries Inc. 1397
Slalom LLC 1398
SLEEPMED INCORPORATED 1398
Sleepy's Inc. 1398
SLM Corp. 1398
SLOAN IMPLEMENT COMPANY INC. 1398
SM Energy Co. 1398
SmallBizPros Inc. 1399
Smart & Final Inc. 1399
SMART Modular Technologies Inc. 1399
SmartFinancial Inc 1399
SmartPros Ltd 1399
SMARTRONIX INC. 1399
SMC Networks Inc. 1400
Smead Manufacturing Company 1400
SMG Indium Resources Ltd 1400
SMG Management Inc 1400
Smile Brands Group Inc. 1400
Smith & Wesson Holding Corp 1400
Smith (A.O.) Corp 1401
Smith Micro Software, Inc. 1401
Smith's Food & Drug Centers Inc. 1401
Smith-Midland Corp. 1401
Smokin Joes Cigars LLC 1401
SMTC Corp. 1401
Smucker (J.M.) Co. 1402
Snap-On, Inc. 1402
SNAPPING SHOALS ELECTRIC TRUST INC. 1402
Snell & Wilmer L.L.P. 1402

Snyder's-Lance Inc. 1402
SOA Software Inc. 1402
SOCIETY OF MANUFACTURING ENGINEERS 1403
Socket Mobile, Inc. 1403
Sodexo Remote Sites Partnership 1403
SOFT COMPUTER CONSULTANTS INC. 1403
SofTech, Inc 1403
SoftSheen/Carson Products 1403
Software & Information Industry Association 1404
Solar Turbines Incorporated 1404
SolarCity Corp 1404
SolarWinds Inc 1404
Solazyme Inc. 1404
Sole Technology Inc. 1404
Solera Capital LLC 1405
Solera Holdings Inc 1405
Soligenix Inc 1405
Solitario Exploration & Royalty Corp 1405
Solitron Devices, Inc. 1405
Solo Cup Company 1405
Solstas Lab Partners LLC 1406
Solutia Inc. 1406
SOMERSET MEDICAL CENTER 1406
SOMERSET TIRE SERVICE INC. 1406
Sonepar Management US Inc. 1406
Sonesta International Hotels Corporation 1406
Sonic Automotive, Inc. 1407
Sonic Corp. 1407
Sonic Foundry, Inc. 1407
Sonics & Materials Inc. 1407
SonicWALL Inc. 1407
Sono-Tek Corp. 1407
Sonoco Products Co. 1408
SonomaWest Holdings Inc. 1408
SonoSite Inc. 1408
Sonus Networks, Inc. 1408
Sony Corporation of America 1408
Sony Pictures Digital Production Inc. 1408
Sony Pictures Entertainment Inc. 1409
Sony Pictures Home Entertainment 1409
Sony Pictures Television 1409
Sony/ATV Music Publishing LLC 1409
Soros Fund Management LLC 1409
Sotera Defense Solutions Inc. 1409
Sotheby's 1410
Sotherly Hotels Inc 1410
Sound Financial Inc. 1410
Souper Salad Inc. 1410
SourceOne Healthcare Technologies Inc. 1410
SOUTH BEND MEDICAL FOUNDATION INC 1410
South Broward Hospital District 1411
South Carolina Electric & Gas Company 1411
South Carolina Public Service Authority 1411
SOUTH CAROLINA STATE PORTS AUTHORITY 1411
SOUTH CENTRAL COMMUNICATIONS CORPORATION 1411
SOUTH DAKOTA STATE UNIVERSITY 1411
SOUTH DAKOTA WHEAT GROWERS ASSOCIATION 1412
South Jersey Gas Co. 1412
South Jersey Industries, Inc. 1412
SOUTH MIAMI HOSPITAL INC. 1412
SOUTH PENINSULA HOSPITALS INC. 1412
South State Corp 1412
SOUTHCO DISTRIBUTING COMPANY 1413
Southcoast Financial Corp 1413
SOUTHCOAST HOSPITALS GROUP INC. 1413
Southcross Energy Partners LP 1413
SOUTHEAST TEXAS INDUSTRIES INC. 1413
Southeastern Bank Financial Corp 1413
Southeastern Freight Lines Inc. 1414
Southeastern Pennsylvania Transportation Authority 1414
Southern Banc Co., Inc. 1414
Southern California Edison Co. 1414
Southern California Gas Co. 1414
Southern California Permanente Medical Group Inc. 1414
Southern California Public Power Authority 1415
SOUTHERN CALIFORNIA REGIONAL RAIL AUTHORITY 1415
Southern Community Financial Corporation 1415
Southern Company (The) 1415
Southern Connecticut Bancorp Inc. 1415

Southern Energy Homes Inc. 1415
Southern First Bancshares, Inc. 1416
SOUTHERN ILLINOIS HEALTHCARE ENTERPRISES INC 1416
SOUTHERN MAINE HEALTH CARE 1416
SOUTHERN METHODIST UNIVERSITY INC 1416
Southern Michigan Bancorp Inc (United States) 1416
SOUTHERN MINNESOTA BEET SUGAR COOPERATIVE 1416
Southern Missouri Bancorp, Inc. 1417
Southern National Bancorp of Virginia Inc 1417
SOUTHERN NEW HAMPSHIRE MEDICAL CENTER 1417
Southern Nuclear Operating Company Inc. 1417
SOUTHERN PIPE & SUPPLY COMPANY INC. 1417
SOUTHERN RESEARCH INSTITUTE INC 1417
Southern Union Company 1418
SouthFirst Bancshares Inc. 1418
SOUTHLAND INDUSTRIES 1418
Southside Bancshares, Inc. 1418
Southwall Technologies Inc. 1418
Southwest Airlines Co 1418
Southwest Bancorp, Inc. (OK) 1419
SOUTHWEST CATHOLIC HEALTH NETWORK CORPORATION 1419
Southwest Gas Corporation 1419
Southwest Georgia Financial Corp. 1419
SOUTHWEST LOUISIANA ELECTRIC MEMBERSHIP CORPORATION 1419
SOUTHWEST RESEARCH INSTITUTE INC 1419
SouthWest Water Company 1420
Southwestern Electric Power Co. 1420
Southwestern Energy Company 1420
SOUTHWESTERN UNIVERSITY 1420
Sovran Self Storage, Inc. 1420
SP Plus Corp 1420
Space Systems/Loral Inc. 1421
Spacelabs Healthcare Inc. 1421
Spacenet Inc. 1421
Span-America Medical Systems, Inc. 1421
Spanish Broadcasting System, Inc. 1421
Spansion Inc 1421
SPAR Group, Inc. 1422
Spark Networks Inc 1422
Sparks Marketing Group Inc. 1422
SPARTA Inc. 1422
Spartan Motors, Inc. 1422
SpartanNash Co. 1422
Sparton Corp. 1423
SPAW GLASS CONSTRUCTION CORPORATION 1423
SPAW GLASS HOLDING L.P. 1423
Speakeasy Inc. 1423
Special Devices Incorporated 1423
Special Diversified Opportunities Inc 1423
Special Metals Corporation 1424
SPECIAL OLYMPICS INC. 1424
Specialty Commerce Corp. 1424
Specialty Products & Insulation Co. 1424
Specialty Vehicle Acquisition Corp. 1424
Spectra Energy Corp 1424
Spectra Energy Partners LP 1425
Spectranetics Corp. (The) 1425
Spectrum Brands Holdings Inc 1425
Spectrum Control Inc. 1425
Spectrum Group International Inc 1425
SPECTRUM HEALTH SYSTEM 1425
Spectrum Pharmaceuticals Inc 1426
Speed Commerce, Inc. 1426
Speedus Corp. 1426
Speedway LLC 1426
Speedway Motorsports, Inc. 1426
SPELMAN COLLEGE 1426
SPF ENERGY INC. 1427
Spherix Inc. 1427
Spiegel Brands Inc. 1427
Spindletop Oil & Gas Co (Tex) 1427
Spire Corp. 1427
Spirit AeroSystems Holdings Inc 1427
Spirit Airlines Inc 1428
Splunk Inc 1428
Spok Holdings Inc 1428
Sport Chalet, Inc. 1428
Sportvision Inc. 1428
SPR Inc. 1428

Sprague Resources LP 1429
Spraylat Corporation 1429
SPRING ARBOR UNIVERSITY 1429
SPRINGFIELD HOSPITAL 1429
Sprouts Farmers Market Inc 1429
SPS Commerce, Inc. 1429
SPX Corp. 1430
SPX Flow Inc 1430
Spy Inc 1430
Spyr Inc 1430
SRAM International Corporation 1430
SRI INTERNATIONAL 1430
SRI/Surgical Express Inc. 1431
SRT COMMUNICATIONS 1431
SS&C Technologies Holdings, Inc. 1431
SSAB Enterprises LLC 1431
SSI (U.S.) Inc. 1431
SSM Health Care Corporation 1431
SSP America Inc. 1432
ST BARNABAS MEDICAL CENTER INC 1432
ST BONAVENTURE UNIVERSITY 1432
ST DAVID ROUND ROCK MEDICAL CENTER 1432
ST FRANCIS HOSPITAL 1432
ST JOHN FISHER COLLEGE 1432
ST JOHNS HOSPITAL SISTERS OF THE THIRD
    ORDER OF ST FRANCIS 1433
ST JOHN'S UNIVERSITY NEW YORK 1433
ST JOSEPH'S COLLEGE NEW YORK 1433
ST JOSEPH''S HOSPITAL 1433
ST JOSEPHS WAYNE HOSPITAL INC 1433
St Jude Medical Inc 1433
ST LAWRENCE UNIVERSITY 1434
ST MARY''S REGIONAL HEALTH CENTER 1434
ST PATRICK HOSPITAL CORPORATION 1434
ST PETER'S MEDICAL CENTER 1434
ST. ALEXIUS MEDICAL CENTER 1434
ST. ANTHONY'S HOSPITAL INC. 1434
ST. ANTHONY'S MEDICAL CENTER 1435
ST. BERNARD HOSPITAL 1435
ST. FRANCIS'' HOSPITAL POUGHKEEPSIE NEW
    YORK 1435
St. Joe Co. (The) 1435
ST. JOHN HEALTH SYSTEM INC. 1435
St. John Knits International Incorporated 1435
ST. JOHN''S COLLEGE 1436
ST. JOSEPH HEALTH SYSTEM 1436
ST. JOSEPH HOSPITAL OF ORANGE 1436
ST. JOSEPH'S HOSPITAL HEALTH CENTER 1436
ST. JUDE CHILDREN'S RESEARCH HOSPITAL INC.
    1436
ST. JUDE HOSPITAL 1436
St. Louis Cardinals L.P. 1437
ST. LUKE'S HEALTH NETWORK INC. 1437
St. Luke's Health System Ltd. 1437
ST. LUKE'S EPISCOPAL-PRESBYTERIAN
    HOSPITALS 1437
ST. LUKE'S HOSPITAL OF DULUTH 1437
ST. MARY'S HEALTH CARE SYSTEM INC. 1437
ST. MARY'S MEDICAL CENTER 1438
ST. NORBERT COLLEGE INC. 1438
ST. OLAF COLLEGE 1438
ST. PETER'S HEALTH PARTNERS 1438
Staar Surgical Co. 1438
STAFF FORCE INC. 1438
Staffmark Holdings Inc. 1439
STAG Industrial Inc. 1439
Stage Stores Inc. 1439
Stamford Health System Inc. 1439
Stamps.com Inc. 1439
Stanadyne Corporation 1439
StanCorp Financial Group Inc 1440
STAND ENERGY CORPORATION 1440
STANDARD ELECTRIC COMPANY 1440
Standard Energy Corporation 1440
Standard Financial Corp (MD) 1440
STANDARD FORWARDING LLC 1440
Standard Microsystems Corporation 1441
Standard Motor Products, Inc. 1441
Standard Register Co. 1441
Standard Steel LLC 1441
Standard Textile Co. Inc. 1441
Standex International Corp. 1441
Stanford Hospital and Clinics 1442
STANION WHOLESALE ELECTRIC CO. INC. 1442

Stanley Black & Decker Inc 1442
Stanley Electric Sales of America Inc. 1442
Stanley Furniture Co., Inc. 1442
Stanley Security Solutions Inc. 1442
STANLEY STEEMER INTERNATIONAL INC. 1443
Stant Manufacturing Inc. 1443
STAPLE COTTON CO-OPERATIVE ASSOCIATION
    1443
Staples Inc 1443
Star Buffet Inc. 1443
Star Gas Partners L.P. 1443
Star Multi Care Services Inc. 1444
STAR OF THE WEST MILLING COMPANY 1444
Star Tribune Media Company LLC 1444
Starbucks Corp. 1444
Starcom MediaVest Group Inc. 1444
Starkey Laboratories Inc. 1444
Starrett (L.S.) Co. 1445
Startek, Inc. 1445
Starwood Hotels & Resorts Worldwide Inc 1445
Starwood Property Trust Inc. 1445
Starz 1445
Starz LLC 1445
State Auto Financial Corp. 1446
State Bank Financial Corp 1446
State Compensation Insurance Fund 1446
State Farm Mutual Automobile Insurance Company
    1446
State of New York Mortgage Agency 1446
State Street Corp. 1446
STATE UNIVERSITY OF IOWA FOUNDATION 1447
Stater Bros. Holdings Inc. 1447
STATIC CONTROL COMPONENTS INC. 1447
Station Casinos LLC 1447
Statoil Marketing & Trading (US) Inc. 1447
STATS LLC 1447
StayinFront Inc. 1448
STC Microwave Systems 1448
Steel Dynamics Inc. 1448
Steel of West Virginia Inc. 1448
Steel Partners Holdings LP 1448
Steel Technologies LLC 1448
Steelcase, Inc. 1449
SteelCloud Inc. 1449
Stefanini TechTeam 1449
Stein Mart, Inc. 1449
STEINER ELECTRIC COMPANY 1449
StemCells Inc 1449
Stemline Therapeutics Inc 1450
Stepan Co. 1450
Stephan Co. (The) 1450
STEPHEN F AUSTIN STATE UNIVERSITY 1450
STEPHEN GOULD CORPORATION 1450
STEPHENSON WHOLESALE COMPANY INC. 1450
Stereotaxis Inc 1451
Stericycle Inc. 1451
Steris Corp. 1451
Sterling Bancorp (DE) 1451
Sterling Chemicals Inc. 1451
Sterling Construction Inc 1451
Sterling Financial Corp. (WA) 1452
Sterling Jewelers Inc. 1452
Sterling Mets LP 1452
STETSON UNIVERSITY INC. 1452
STEVENS INDUSTRIES INC 1452
STEVENS INSTITUTE OF TECHNOLOGY (INC) 1452
STEVENS TRANSPORT INC. 1453
STEVENSON UNIVERSITY INC. 1453
Stew Leonard's LLC 1453
STEWARD HEALTH CARE SYSTEM LLC 1453
Stewardship Financial Corp. 1453
Stewart & Stevenson Inc. 1453
STEWART BUILDERS INC. 1454
Stewart Information Services Corp. 1454
STEWART'S SHOPS CORP. 1454
STG INC. 1454
Stifel Financial Corp. 1454
STILES CORPORATION 1454
Stillwater Mining Co. 1455
Stock Building Supply LLC 1455
Stock Yards Bancorp Inc 1455
Stone Energy Corp. 1455
Stonegate Mortgage Corp 1455
StoneMor Partners L P 1455

Stoneridge Inc. 1456
STORR OFFICE ENVIRONMENTS INC 1456
STR Holdings Inc. 1456
STRACK AND VAN TIL SUPER MARKET INC 1456
Strata Skin Sciences Inc 1456
Strategic Hotels & Resorts, Inc. 1456
Stratosphere Corporation 1457
Strattec Security Corp. 1457
Stratus Properties Inc. 1457
Stratus Technologies International Inc. 1457
Strayer Education, Inc. 1457
Stream Global Services Inc. 1457
Streamline Health Solutions Inc 1458
StreamServe Inc. 1458
STRIKE LLC 1458
Strikeforce Technologies Inc 1458
STRONGWELL CORPORATION 1458
Structural Group Inc. 1458
Stryker Corp. 1459
Stuart C. Irby Company 1459
STUART-DEAN CO. INC. 1459
Studley Inc. 1459
Stuller Inc. 1459
STURDY MEMORIAL HOSPITAL INC. 1459
Sturgis Bancorp Inc 1460
Sturm, Ruger & Co., Inc. 1460
STV Group Incorporated 1460
Sub-Zero Inc. 1460
Subjex Corporation 1460
SUBURBAN HOSPITAL INC 1460
Suburban Propane Partners L.P. 1461
Sucampo Pharmaceuticals Inc 1461
SuccessFactors Inc. 1461
Successories LLC 1461
Suffolk Bancorp 1461
SUFFOLK CONSTRUCTION COMPANY INC. 1461
SUFFOLK COUNTY WATER AUTHORITY INC 1462
SUFFOLK UNIVERSITY 1462
Sugar Cane Growers Cooperative of Florida 1462
Sugar Foods Corporation 1462
Sullivan & Cromwell LLP 1462
SUMMA HEALTH SYSTEM 1462
Summer Infant Inc 1463
Summit Bancshares Inc. 1463
Summit Corporation of America 1463
SUMMIT ELECTRIC SUPPLY CO. INC 1463
Summit Energy Services Inc. 1463
Summit Financial Group Inc 1463
Summit Hotel Properties Inc 1464
Summit Partners L.P. 1464
Summit State Bank 1464
Sun Bancorp Inc. (NJ) 1464
Sun Capital Partners Inc. 1464
Sun Chemical Corporation 1464
SUN COAST RESOURCES INC. 1465
Sun Communities, Inc. 1465
Sun Hydraulics Corp. 1465
SUN ORCHARD FRUIT COMPANY INC. 1465
SUN-MAID GROWERS OF CALIFORNIA 1465
SunAmerica Annuity and Life Assurance Company
    1465
SunAmerica Financial Group Inc. 1466
Sunbelt Beverage Company LLC 1466
Suncoast Schools Federal Credit Union 1466
SunCoke Energy Inc 1466
SunCoke Energy Partners LP 1466
SunEdison Inc 1466
Sunesis Pharmaceuticals Inc 1467
SUNFLOWER ELECTRIC POWER CORPORATION
    1467
SunGard Availability Services LP 1467
SunGard Data Systems Inc. 1467
SunGard Public Sector Inc. 1467
SUNKIST GROWERS INC. 1467
SunLink Health Systems Inc 1468
Sunoco Logistics Partners L.P. 1468
Sunoco LP 1468
Sunovion Pharmaceuticals Inc. 1468
SunPower Corp 1468
Sunquest Information Systems Inc. 1468
Sunrise Medical Inc. 1469
Sunrise Senior Living Inc. 1469
SUNRUN INSTALLATION SERVICES INC. 1469
Sunshine Silver Mines Corporation 1469

Sunstone Hotel Investors Inc. 1469
SUNSWEET GROWERS INC. 1469
Suntron Corporation 1470
SunTrust Banks, Inc. 1470
Sunvalley Solar Inc (NV) 1470
Super 8 Motels Inc. 1470
Super Center Concepts Inc. 1470
Super Micro Computer Inc 1470
Superconductor Technologies Inc 1471
SUPERIOR BULK LOGISTICS INC. 1471
Superior Energy Services, Inc. 1471
Superior Group Inc. 1471
Superior Industries International, Inc. 1471
SUPERIOR OIL COMPANY INC 1471
Superior Uniform Group, Inc. 1472
Supernus Pharmaceuticals Inc 1472
Supertex, Inc. 1472
Supervalu Inc. 1472
support.com, Inc. 1472
Supreme Industries, Inc. 1472
SureWest Communications 1473
Surge Components, Inc. 1473
Surge Global Energy Inc 1473
Surgical Care Affiliates Inc 1473
SurgLine International Inc. 1473
SurModics, Inc. 1473
Surrey Bancorp (NC) 1474
Survey Sampling International LLC 1474
Susquehanna Bancshares, Inc 1474
Susser Holdings Corp 1474
Sussex Bancorp 1474
Sutherland Global Services Inc. 1474
Sutron Corp. 1475
SUTTER WEST BAY HOSPITALS 1475
SVB Financial Group 1475
Swagelok Company 1475
Swank Inc. 1475
SWARTHMORE COLLEGE 1475
SWEDISH HEALTH SERVICES 1476
Swedish Match North America Inc. 1476
Sweetbay Supermarket 1476
SWH Corporation 1476
Swift Energy Company 1476
Swift Transportation Co 1476
SWIMWEAR ANYWHERE INC. 1477
SWINERTON BUILDERS 1477
SWINERTON INCORPORATED 1477
Swisher Hygiene Inc 1477
Swiss Valley Farms Cooperative 1477
SWS Group, Inc. 1477
Sybase Inc. 1478
Sybron Dental Specialties Inc. 1478
Sycamore Entertainment Group Inc. 1478
Sykes Enterprises, Inc. 1478
Sylvan Inc. 1478
Symantec Corp. 1478
Symbion Inc. 1479
Symetra Financial Corp 1479
Symmetry Medical Inc. 1479
SymphonyIRI Group Inc. 1479
Synacor, Inc. 1479
Synageva BioPharma Corp. 1479
Synalloy Corp. 1480
Synapse Group Inc. 1480
Synaptics Inc 1480
SYNARC INC. 1480
Synchronoss Technologies Inc 1480
Synergetics USA Inc 1480
Synergx Systems Inc. 1481
Synergy Pharmaceuticals Inc. 1481
Synergy Resources Corp 1481
Syniverse Holdings Inc. 1481
Synnex Corp 1481
Synopsys Inc 1481
Synovis Life Technologies Inc. 1482
Synovus Financial Corp. 1482
Synovus Mortgage Corp. 1482
Synta Pharmaceuticals Corp 1482
Syntel Inc. 1482
Syntellect Inc. 1482
Synthesis Energy Systems, Inc. 1483
Syntroleum Corp 1483
Synutra International Inc 1483
Synygy Inc. 1483

Sypris Solutions, Inc. 1483
SYRACUSE UNIVERSITY 1483
Sysco Corp. 1484
Sysco Guest Supply LLC 1484
Syska Hennessy Group Inc. 1484
Systemax, Inc. 1484
T Rowe Price Group Inc. 1484
T-3 Energy Services Inc. 1484
T-Mobile US Inc 1485
T. D. Williamson Inc. 1485
T. Marzetti Company 1485
T.J.T., Inc. 1485
T.R. World Gym LLC 1485
TA Associates Inc. 1485
TAB Products Co LLC 1486
Table Trac Inc. 1486
Tableau Software, Inc. 1486
Tachyon Networks Inc. 1486
Taco Bell Corp. 1486
Taco Cabana Inc 1486
Tacoma Power 1487
TACONIC FARMS INC. 1487
Tahoe Resources Inc. 1487
Tailored Brands Inc 1487
Taitron Components Inc. 1487
Take-Two Interactive Software, Inc. 1487
Takeda San Diego Inc. 1488
Tal International Group Inc 1488
TALLAHASSEE MEMORIAL HEALTHCARE INC.
  1488
Tallan Inc. 1488
Tallgrass Energy Partners, LP 1488
Talmer Bancorp Inc 1488
Talon International, Inc. 1489
Talon Therapeutics Inc. 1489
Tamir Biotechnology Inc. 1489
Tampa Electric Company 1489
Tandem Diabetes Care Inc 1489
Tandy Brands Accessories, Inc. 1489
Tandy Leather Factory Inc 1490
Tanger Factory Outlet Centers, Inc. 1490
Tangoe, Inc. 1490
Tanimura & Antle Fresh Foods Inc. 1490
TANNER INDUSTRIES INC. 1490
TAOS HEALTH SYSTEMS INC. 1490
TapImmune Inc. 1491
Targa Resources Corp 1491
Targa Resources Partners LP 1491
Target Corp 1491
TASER International Inc. 1491
TATUNG COMPANY OF AMERICA INC. 1491
TAUBER OIL COMPANY 1492
Taubman Centers, Inc. 1492
TAWA Supermarket Inc. 1492
Taxus Cardium Pharmaceuticals Group Inc 1492
Taylor (Calvin B.) Bankshares, Inc. (MD) 1492
Taylor Capital Group, Inc 1492
Taylor Devices Inc. 1493
Taylor Morrison Home Corp 1493
Taylor Oil Co. Inc. 1493
Taylor Precision Products Inc. 1493
Taylor-Listug Inc. 1493
TaylorMade-adidas Golf 1493
TB Wood's Corporation 1494
TBA Global LLC 1494
TBC Corporation 1494
TBWA Worldwide Inc. 1494
TCF Financial Corp 1494
TCI International, Inc. 1494
TD Ameritrade Holding Corp 1495
Teachers Insurance and Annuity Association - College
  Reti 1495
Team Health Holdings Inc 1495
TEAM INDUSTRIES INC. 1495
Team, Inc. 1495
TearLab Corp. 1495
Tech Data Corp. 1496
Teche Holding Co. 1496
TECHNICA CORPORATION 1496
Technical Communications Corp. 1496
Technical Consumer Products Inc. 1496
Technology Crossover Ventures L.P. 1496
Technology Research Corporation 1497
TECHNOLOGY SERVICE CORPORATION 1497

Techshot Inc. 1497
TECHSMITH CORPORATION 1497
TechTarget Inc 1497
TECO Energy Inc. 1497
Tecogen Inc 1498
Tecumseh Products Co. 1498
Ted's Montana Grill Inc. 1498
Tegna Inc 1498
Tegrant Corporation 1498
Teichert Inc. 1498
Tejon Ranch Co. 1499
Tekelec 1499
Tekni-Plex Inc. 1499
TEKNOR APEX COMPANY 1499
TEKSYSTEMS INC. 1499
TEL FSI Inc. 1499
Tel Instrument Electronics Corp. 1500
TEL Offshore Trust 1500
Telco Systems Inc. 1500
Telcordia Technologies Inc. 1500
TeleCheck Inc. 1500
TeleCommunication Systems Inc 1500
Telect Inc. 1501
Teledyne Benthos 1501
Teledyne LeCroy Inc. 1501
Teledyne Technologies, Inc. 1501
Teleflex Incorporated 1501
Teleflora LLC 1501
Telemundo Communications Group Inc. 1502
Telenav, Inc. 1502
Telephone & Data Systems, Inc. 1502
TELEPHONE ELECTRONICS CORPORATION 1502
TeleTech Holdings, Inc. 1502
Teletouch Communications, Inc. 1502
Teligent Inc (New) 1503
Telik Inc. 1503
Telkonet Inc. 1503
Tellepsen Builders LP 1503
Telos Corp. (MD) 1503
Telvista Inc. 1503
TelVue Corporation 1504
TEMPLE UNIVERSITY HEALTH SYSTEM INC. 1504
TEMPLE UNIVERSITY-OF THE COMMONWEALTH
  SYSTEM OF HIGHER EDUCATION 1504
Tempur Sealy International, Inc. 1504
Tenaska Inc. 1504
Tenax Therapeutics Inc 1504
Tenet Healthcare Corp. 1505
Tengasco, Inc. 1505
Tengion Inc. 1505
Tennant Co. 1505
Tenneco Inc 1505
Tennessee Farmers Cooperative 1505
Tennessee Football Inc. 1506
TENNESSEE STATE UNIVERSITY 1506
TENNESSEE TECHNOLOGICAL UNIVERSITY 1506
Tennessee Valley Authority 1506
TEOCO Corporation 1506
Teradata Corp (DE) 1506
Teradyne, Inc. 1507
Terex ASV 1507
Terex Corp. 1507
Terra Nitrogen Co., L.P. 1507
TERRACON CONSULTANTS INC. 1507
TerraCycle Inc. 1507
Terremark Worldwide Inc. 1508
Terreno Realty Corp 1508
Territorial Bancorp Inc 1508
Tesla Motors Inc 1508
Tesoro Alaska Company 1508
Tesoro Corporation 1508
Tesoro Logistics LP 1509
TESSADA & ASSOCIATES INC. 1509
Tessco Technologies, Inc. 1509
Tessera Technologies Inc 1509
TestAmerica Laboratories Inc. 1509
TETCO Incorporated 1509
Tetra Tech, Inc. 1510
TETRA Technologies, Inc. 1510
Tetraphase Pharmaceuticals, Inc 1510
Teva Pharmaceuticals USA Inc. 1510
TEXAS A & M RESEARCH FOUNDATION INC 1510
Texas Capital Bancshares Inc 1510
TEXAS CHILDREN'S HOSPITAL 1511

The Robert Allen Group Inc. 1549
THE ROCKEFELLER UNIVERSITY FACULTY AND
  STUDENTS CLUB INC 1549
THE RUDOLPH/LIBBE COMPANIES INC 1549
THE SALVATION ARMY NATIONAL CORPORATION
  1549
THE SAVANNAH COLLEGE OF ART AND DESIGN
  INC 1549
The Savings Bank Life Insurance Company of
  Massachusetts 1550
The Schumacher Group of Louisiana Inc. 1550
The Schwan Food Company 1550
The SCOOTER Store Ltd. 1550
THE SCOULAR COMPANY 1550
THE SCRIPPS RESEARCH INSTITUTE 1550
The Segal Group Inc. 1551
The Seminole Tribe of Florida Inc. 1551
The ServiceMaster Company 1551
THE SHAMROCK COMPANIES INC 1551
THE SHEPHERD GOOD HOSPITAL INC 1551
The Smith & Wollensky Restaurant Group Inc. 1551
The Southern Connecticut Gas Company 1552
THE SOUTHERN POVERTY LAW CENTER INC 1552
The Sportsman's Guide Inc. 1552
The SSI Group Inc. 1552
The Stop & Shop Supermarket Company 1552
The Stride Rite Corporation 1552
THE SUNDT COMPANIES INC 1553
THE SUSAN G KOMEN BREAST CANCER
  FOUNDATION INC 1553
The Synergos Institute 1553
The Talbots Inc. 1553
The Taylor Group Inc. 1553
The Techs 1553
The Thomas Kinkade Company 1554
The Timberland Company 1554
THE TOLEDO HOSPITAL 1554
The TriZetto Group Inc. 1554
The Trump Organization 1554
THE TRUSTEES OF DAVIDSON COLLEGE 1554
THE TRUSTEES OF GRINNELL COLLEGE 1555
THE TRUSTEES OF MOUNT HOLYOKE COLLEGE
  1555
THE TRUSTEES OF THE SMITH COLLEGE 1555
THE TRUSTEES OF WHEATON COLLEGE 1555
THE UCLA FOUNDATION 1555
THE UNION MEMORIAL HOSPITAL 1555
THE UNITED METHODIST PUBLISHING HOUSE
  1556
THE UNIVERSITY OF ARIZONA MEDICAL CENTER
  1556
THE UNIVERSITY OF CHICAGO MEDICAL CENTER
  1556
THE UNIVERSITY OF DAYTON 1556
THE UNIVERSITY OF HARTFORD 1556
THE UNIVERSITY OF SOUTH DAKOTA 1556
THE UNIVERSITY OF THE SOUTH 1557
THE UNIVERSITY OF TULSA 1557
The Upper Deck Company LLC 1557
THE URBAN INSTITUTE 1557
THE VALLEY HOSPITAL INC 1557
The Vanguard Group Inc. 1557
The Vons Companies Inc. 1558
THE WALDINGER CORPORATION 1558
THE WALSH GROUP LTD 1558
The Warmington Group 1558
THE WARRIOR GROUP INC 1558
THE WASHINGTON AND LEE UNIVERSITY 1558
THE WASHINGTON UNIVERSITY 1559
THE WATERBURY HOSPITAL 1559
The Weitz Company LLC 1559
The Westervelt Company 1559
The WhiteWave Foods Company 1559
THE WHITING-TURNER CONTRACTING COMPANY
  1559
THE WICHITA STATE UNIVERSITY 1560
THE WILL-BURT COMPANY 1560
THE WILLAMETTE VALLEY COMPANY 1560
The William and Flora Hewlett Foundation 1560
The Williams Companies Inc. 1560
THE WILLS GROUP INC 1560
The Winter Group of Companies Inc. 1561
THE WISTAR INSTITUTE OF ANATOMY AND
  BIOLOGY 1561

The Witkoff Group 1561
The Yankee Candle Company Inc. 1561
The Yates Companies Inc. 1561
The York Group Inc. 1561
The Yucaipa Companies LLC 1562
The Ziegler Companies Inc. 1562
THEDACARE INC. 1562
Theorem Clinical Research 1562
TherapeuticsMD, Inc. 1562
Therm-O-Disc Incorporated 1562
Therma-Tru Corp. 1563
Thermo Fisher Scientific Inc 1563
ThermoEnergy Corp 1563
Thermon Group Holdings Inc 1563
TheStreet, Inc. 1563
Things Remembered Inc. 1563
Third Wave Technologies Inc. 1564
THIRTEEN 1564
THL Credit Inc. 1564
Thomas & Betts Corporation 1564
Thomas H. Lee Partners L.P. 1564
THOMAS JEFFERSON SCHOOL OF LAW INC 1564
THOMAS JEFFERSON UNIVERSITY 1565
THOMAS JEFFERSON UNIVERSITY HOSPITALS
  INC. 1565
Thomas Nelson Inc. 1565
Thompson & Knight LLP 1565
Thompson Creek Metals Company Inc. 1565
Thompson Hine LLP 1565
THOMPSON HOSPITALITY 1566
Thomson Reuters (Legal) Inc. 1566
Thomson Reuters Corporation 1566
Thor Industries, Inc. 1566
Thoratec Corp. 1566
Thorlabs Quantum Electronics Inc. 1566
Threshold Pharmaceuticals Inc 1567
THRUSTMASTER OF TEXAS INC. 1567
Thunder Mountain Gold, Inc. 1567
TIB Financial Corp. 1567
TIBCO Software, Inc. 1567
TICC Capital Corp. 1567
Tidelands Bancshares Inc 1568
Tidewater Inc. 1568
Tiffany & Co. 1568
TIFFIN MOTOR HOMES INC. 1568
TIFT REGIONAL MEDICAL CENTER FOUNDATION
  INC. 1568
Tiger X Medical Inc. 1568
TigerLogic Corp 1569
Tigrent Inc. 1569
Tii Network Technologies Inc. 1569
Tilden Associates Inc. 1569
Timberland Bancorp, Inc. 1569
Timberline Resources Corporation 1569
Time Inc. 1570
Time Warner Cable Inc 1570
Time Warner Inc 1570
Times Publishing Company 1570
Timex Group USA Inc. 1570
Timios National Corp 1570
Timken Co. (The) 1571
Tiptree Financial Inc 1571
Tishman Hotel Corporation 1571
Titan Energy Worldwide Inc 1571
Titan International Inc 1571
Titan Machinery, Inc. 1571
Titan Pharmaceuticals Inc (DE) 1572
Titan Technologies Inc. 1572
TiVo Inc 1572
TIX Corp 1572
TJX Companies, Inc. 1572
TKS Industrial Company 1572
TMA Resources Inc. 1572
TNEMEC COMPANY INC. 1573
TNR Technical, Inc. 1573
TNS North America Inc. 1573
Todd Shipyards Corporation 1573
Tofutti Brands, Inc. 1573
Toll Brothers Inc. 1574
TOM LANGE COMPANY INC. 1574
Tom's of Maine Inc. 1574
Tomax Corporation 1574
Tommy Bahama Group Inc. 1574
Tompkins Financial Corp 1574

Tootsie Roll Industries Inc 1575
Topco Associates LLC 1575
Toppan Photomasks Inc. 1575
TOR Minerals International Inc 1575
Toray Plastics (America) Inc. 1575
Torch Energy Royalty Trust 1575
Torchmark Corp. 1576
Toresco Enterprises Inc. 1576
Toro Co. (The) 1576
Torotel, Inc. 1576
TORRANCE MEMORIAL MEDICAL CENTER 1576
Tortoise Capital Resources Corporation 1576
Tortoise Energy Capital Corporation 1577
Torvec, Inc. 1577
Toshiba America Inc. 1577
Total System Services, Inc. 1577
Totes Isotoner Corporation 1577
TOURO COLLEGE & UNIVERSITY SYSTEM 1577
Tower Financial Corp. 1578
Tower International Inc 1578
Towers Watson & Co. 1578
Towerstream Corp 1578
Town Sports International Holdings Inc 1578
TOWNSHIP HIGH SCHOOL DISTRICT 211
  FOUNDATION 1578
Townsquare Media Inc. 1579
Toy Quest 1579
Toyota Material Handling USA Inc. 1579
Toyota Motor Credit Corp. 1579
Toyota Motor Engineering & Manufacturing North
  Americ 1579
Toyota Motor Manufacturing Kentucky Inc. 1579
Toyota Motor North America Inc. 1580
Toyota Motor Sales U.S.A. Inc. 1580
Toys "R" Us Inc. 1580
TPS Parking Management LLC 1580
TracFone Wireless Inc. 1580
Track Group Inc 1580
Tractor Supply Co. 1581
TracyLocke 1581
Trade Street Residential, Inc. 1581
TradeBeam Inc. 1581
TradeCard Inc. 1581
TradeStation Group Inc. 1581
Tradeweb Markets LLC 1582
Trailer Bridge Inc. 1582
Trammell Crow Company 1582
Trammell Crow Residential Company 1582
TRAMMO INC. 1582
Trans World Corp. 1582
Trans World Entertainment Corp. 1583
TRANS-SYSTEM INC. 1583
TransAct Technologies Inc. 1583
TransAm Trucking Inc. 1583
Transamerica Life Insurance Company 1583
Transatlantic Reinsurance Company 1583
Transcat Inc 1584
Transcend Services Inc. 1584
Transcontinental Realty Investors, Inc. 1584
TransDigm Group Inc 1584
Transgenomic Inc 1584
Transit Mix Concrete & Materials Company 1584
TRANSITCENTER INC. 1585
TransMontaigne Inc. 1585
TransMontaigne Partners L.P. 1585
TransNet Corporation 1585
TRANSPERFECT TRANSLATIONS INTERNATIONAL
  INC. 1585
Transplace Inc. 1585
Transportation Insight LLC 1586
Transtech Industries Inc. 1586
Transtector Systems Inc. 1586
Tranzyme Inc. 1586
TRAVEL AND TRANSPORT INC. 1586
Travel Management Partners Inc. 1586
TravelCenters of America LLC 1587
TravelCLICK Inc. 1587
Travelers Companies Inc (The) 1587
Travelocity.com L.P. 1587
TravelZoo Inc 1587
TRAYLOR BROS. INC. 1587
TRC Companies, Inc. 1588
Treaty Energy Corp. 1588
Trecora Resources 1588

Tredegar Corp. 1588
TREE TOP INC. 1588
TreeHouse Foods Inc 1588
Trellis Earth Products Inc. 1589
Tremor Video Inc 1589
Trex Co Inc 1589
TRG Holdings LLC 1589
TRI Pointe Homes LLC 1589
Tri-Arrows Aluminum Inc. 1589
TRI-CITY ELECTRICAL CONTRACTORS INC. 1590
Tri-Union Seafoods LLC 1590
TRI-WEST LTD 1590
TRIA Beauty Inc. 1590
Triangle Capital Corp 1590
Triangle Petroleum Corp 1590
Tribune Media Co. 1591
TriCo Bancshares (Chico, CA) 1591
Trico Products Corporation 1591
Trident Seafoods Corporation 1591
TriHealth Inc. 1591
Trilogy Enterprises Inc. 1591
Trilogy Leasing Co. LLC 1592
TriMas Corp (New) 1592
Trimble Mobile Resource Management 1592
Trimble Navigation Ltd. 1592
Trimedyne, Inc. 1592
TRIMEGA PURCHASING ASSOCIATION 1592
Trimol Group Inc. 1593
Trinity Broadcasting Network 1593
TRINITY HEALTH CORPORATION 1593
TRINITY HEALTH SYSTEM 1593
Trinity Industries, Inc. 1593
TRINITY MOTHER FRANCES HEALTH SYSTEM
   FOUNDATION 1593
TRINITY UNIVERSITY 1594
Trio-Tech International 1594
Tripadvisor Inc 1594
TripAdvisor Inc. 1594
Triple-S Management Corporation 1594
Triplefin LLC 1594
TRIPPE MANUFACTURING COMPANY 1595
TriQuint Semiconductor, Inc. 1595
TriState Capital Holdings, Inc. 1595
Triumph Apparel Corp. 1595
Triumph Group Inc. 1595
TROUT-BLUE CHELAN-MAGI INC. 1595
Troux Technologies Inc. 1596
Trover Solutions Inc. 1596
TROY UNIVERSITY 1596
True Drinks Holdings, Inc. 1596
TRUE VALUE COMPANY 1596
TrueBlue Inc 1596
TRUJILLO & SONS INC. 1597
Truland Systems Corporation 1597
TRUMAN ARNOLD COMPANIES 1597
TRUMAN MEDICAL CENTER INCORPORATED 1597
Trump Entertainment Resorts Inc. 1597
Trustco Bank Corp. (N.Y.) 1597
TRUSTEES OF BOSTON COLLEGE 1598
TRUSTEES OF CLARK UNIVERSITY 1598
TRUSTEES OF THE ESTATE OF BERNICE PAUAHI
   BISHOP 1598
TRUSTEES OF TUFTS COLLEGE INC. 1598
TRUSTEES OF UNION COLLEGE IN THE TOWN OF
   SCHENECTADY IN THE STAT 1598
Trustmark Corp. 1598
Trustwave Holdings Inc. 1599
TRW Automotive Holdings Corp 1599
TSI Incorporated 1599
TSR, Inc. 1599
TSS Inc DE 1599
TTI Inc. 1599
TTM Technologies Inc 1600
Tucows Inc 1600
Tucson Electric Power Company 1600
Tuesday Morning Corp. 1600
Tufco Technologies, Inc. 1600
Tufts Associated Health Plans Inc. 1600
Tumac Lumber Co. Inc. 1601
Tumbleweed Inc. 1601
Tumi Holdings Inc 1601
Tupperware Brands Corp 1601
TurboChef Technologies Inc. 1601
Turbodyne Technologies Inc. 1601

Turner Construction Company 1602
TURTLE & HUGHES INC 1602
Turtle Beach Corp 1602
Tuthill Corporation 1602
Tutor Perini Corp 1602
Tuttle-Click Automotive Group 1602
TV Guide Magazine LLC 1603
TVAX Biomedical Inc. 1603
TW Telecom Inc 1603
Twenty-First Century Fox Inc 1603
Twin Disc Incorporated 1603
Twitter Inc 1603
Two Harbors Investment Corp 1604
Two River Bancorp 1604
Tyco Fire & Security LLC 1604
Tyler Technologies, Inc. 1604
TYMCO Inc. 1604
TYNDALE HOUSE PUBLISHERS INC. 1604
TYR Sport Inc. 1605
Tyson Foods, Inc. 1605
Tyson Fresh Meats Inc. 1605
U G N INC 1605
U S China Mining Group Inc. 1605
U-Swirl Inc. 1605
U. S. Sugar Corporation 1606
U.R.M. STORES INC. 1606
U.S. Auto Parts Network Inc 1606
U.S. Bancorp (DE) 1606
U.S. Central Federal Credit Union 1606
U.S. Concrete, Inc. 1606
U.S. Energy Corp. 1607
U.S. Franchise Systems Inc. 1607
U.S. Global Investors, Inc. 1607
U.S. Legal Support Inc. 1607
U.S. News & World Report L.P. 1607
U.S. Physical Therapy, Inc. 1607
U.S. Robotics Corporation 1608
U.S. Silica Holdings Inc. 1608
U.S. TelePacific Corp. 1608
U.S. VENTURE INC. 1608
U.S. Vision Inc. 1608
UAB Highlands Hospital 1608
UBS Financial Services Inc. 1609
UC HEALTH 1609
UCare Minnesota 1609
UCI Medical Affiliates Inc. 1609
UCP Inc 1609
UDR Inc 1609
UFP Technologies Inc. 1610
UGI Corp. 1610
UHY Advisors Inc. 1610
UIL Holding Corp 1610
ULLICO Inc. 1610
Ulta Salon Cosmetics & Fragrance Inc. 1610
Ulticom Inc. 1611
Ultimate Software Group, Inc. 1611
Ultra Clean Holdings Inc 1611
Ultra Petroleum Corp. 1611
Ultra Stores Inc. 1611
Ultralife Corp 1611
Ultratech Inc 1612
ULURU Inc 1612
UMB Financial Corp 1612
UMH Properties Inc 1612
Umpqua Holdings Corp 1612
Under Armour Inc 1612
UNDERWRITERS LABORATORIES INC. 1613
UNICEF 1613
Unicity International Inc. 1613
UNICO American Corp. 1613
Unifi, Inc. 1613
UnifiedOnline Inc 1613
Unifirst Corp. 1614
UniGroup Inc. 1614
UniHealth Foundation 1614
Unilife Corp. 1614
UNION BANK AND TRUST COMPANY 1614
Union Bankshares Corp (New) 1614
Union Bankshares, Inc. (Morrisville, VT) 1615
Union Electric Company 1615
UNION HEALTH SERVICE INC 1615
UNION HOSPITAL INC. 1615
Union Pacific Corp 1615
UnionBanCal Corporation 1615

UNIPRO FOODSERVICE INC 1616
Uniroyal Global Engineered Products Inc 1616
UniSea Inc. 1616
Unisource Worldwide Inc. 1616
Unisys Corp. 1616
Unit Corp. 1616
United American Healthcare Corp. 1617
United American Insurance Company 1617
United Artists Corporation 1617
United Bancorp, Inc. (Martins Ferry, OH) 1617
United Bancorp, Inc. (Tecumseh, MI) 1617
United Bancshares Inc. (OH) 1617
UNITED BANK CARD INC. 1618
United Bankshares, Inc. 1618
United Behavioral Health 1618
United Capital Corp. 1618
United Cerebral Palsy Associations Inc. 1618
UNITED CEREBRAL PALSY ASSOCIATIONS OF NEW
   YORK STATE INC. 1618
United Community Bancorp 1619
United Community Banks, Inc. (Blairsville, GA) 1619
United Community Financial Corp. (OH) 1619
United Concordia Companies Inc. 1619
United Continental Holdings Inc 1619
UNITED DAIRYMEN OF ARIZONA 1619
UNITED ELECTRIC SUPPLY COMPANY INC. 1620
United Energy Corp. 1620
UNITED FARMERS COOPERATIVE 1620
United Financial Bancorp Inc (MD) 1620
United Fire Group, Inc. 1620
UNITED GILSONITE LABORATORIES 1620
United Guaranty Corporation 1621
UNITED HARDWARE DISTRIBUTING CO 1621
UNITED HEALTH SERVICES HOSPITAL INC. 1621
United Insurance Holdings Corp 1621
United Nations Federal Credit Union 1621
United Natural Foods Inc. 1621
UNITED NEGRO COLLEGE FUND INC. 1622
United Online Inc 1622
United PanAm Financial Corp. 1622
United Parcel Service Inc 1622
UNITED PERFORMING ARTS FUND INC. 1622
United Plastics Group Inc. 1622
UNITED REGIONAL HEALTH CARE SYSTEM INC.
   1623
United Rentals, Inc. 1623
United Scaffolding Inc. 1623
United Security Bancshares (CA) 1623
United Security Bancshares, Inc. 1623
UNITED SPACE ALLIANCE LLC 1623
United States Antimony Corp. 1624
United States Basketball League Inc 1624
UNITED STATES BEEF CORPORATION 1624
United States Cellular Corp 1624
United States Department of Justice 1624
UNITED STATES FUND FOR UNICEF 1624
UNITED STATES GOLF ASSOCIATION 1625
United States Lime & Minerals Inc. 1625
UNITED STATES OLYMPIC COMMITTEE INC 1625
United States Postal Service 1625
UNITED STATES SOCCER FEDERATION INC. 1625
United States Steel Corp. 1625
United States Tennis Association Incorporated 1626
United Supermarkets L.L.C. 1626
United Surgical Partners International Inc. 1626
United Technologies Corp 1626
United Therapeutics Corp 1626
United Van Lines LLC 1626
UNITED WAY WORLDWIDE 1627
United-Guardian, Inc. 1627
UnitedHealth Group Inc 1627
UniTek Global Services Inc. 1627
Unitek Information Systems Inc. 1627
UNITIL Corp 1627
Unity Bancorp, Inc. 1628
Unity Health Plans Insurance Corporation 1628
Univar Inc. 1628
Univar USA 1628
Universal Corp. 1628
Universal Detection Technology 1628
Universal Display Corp 1629
Universal Electronics Inc. 1629
Universal Forest Products Inc. 1629
Universal Health Realty Income Trust 1629

Universal Health Services, Inc. 1629
Universal Insurance Holdings Inc 1629
Universal Manufacturing Co 1630
Universal Music Group Inc. 1630
Universal Power Group Inc 1630
Universal Security Instruments, Inc. 1630
Universal Stainless & Alloy Products, Inc. 1630
Universal Studios Inc. 1630
Universal Tax Systems Inc. 1631
Universal Technical Institute, Inc. 1631
Universal Truckload Services Inc 1631
Universal Weather and Aviation Inc. 1631
UNIVERSAL WILDE INC. 1631
University Bancorp Inc. (MI) 1631
UNIVERSITY CORPORATION FOR ATMOSPHERIC
    RESEARCH 1632
University Federal Credit Union 1632
UNIVERSITY HEALTH CARE INC 1632
University Health System 1632
UNIVERSITY HEALTH SYSTEMS OF EASTERN
    CAROLINA INC. 1632
UNIVERSITY HOSPITALS HEALTH SYSTEM INC.
    1632
UNIVERSITY OF COLORADO 1633
UNIVERSITY OF DETROIT MERCY 1633
UNIVERSITY OF EVANSVILLE 1633
UNIVERSITY OF GEORGIA 1633
UNIVERSITY OF KENTUCKY HOSPITAL AUXILIARY
    INC. 1633
UNIVERSITY OF LA VERNE 1633
UNIVERSITY OF MAINE SYSTEM 1634
UNIVERSITY OF MARYLAND MEDICAL SYSTEM
    CORPORATION 1634
UNIVERSITY OF MISSISSIPPI 1634
UNIVERSITY OF MONTANA SYSTEM 1634
UNIVERSITY OF NORTH CAROLINA HOSPITALS
    1634
UNIVERSITY OF NORTH DAKOTA 1634
UNIVERSITY OF PUGET SOUND 1635
UNIVERSITY OF REDLANDS 1635
UNIVERSITY OF RHODE ISLAND 1635
UNIVERSITY OF RICHMOND 1635
UNIVERSITY OF SAN DIEGO 1635
UNIVERSITY OF SAN FRANCISCO INC 1635
UNIVERSITY OF SCRANTON 1636
UNIVERSITY OF SOUTH FLORIDA 1636
UNIVERSITY OF SOUTHERN MISSISSIPPI 1636
UNIVERSITY OF ST. THOMAS 1636
UNIVERSITY OF TENNESSEE 1636
UNIVERSITY OF THE PACIFIC 1636
UNIVERSITY OF WASHINGTON INC 1637
UNIVERSITY OF WEST GEORGIA 1637
UNIVERSITY OF WISCONSIN FOUNDATION 1637
UNIVERSITY OF WISCONSIN MEDICAL
    FOUNDATION INC. 1637
UNIVERSITY OF WISCONSIN SYSTEM 1637
UNIVERSITY OF WYOMING 1637
UNIVERSITY SYSTEM OF NEW HAMPSHIRE 1638
Univest Corp. of Pennsylvania (Souderton) 1638
Univision Communications Inc. 1638
UNMC PHYSICIANS 1638
UNS Energy Corporation 1638
Unum Group 1638
Unwired Planet, Inc. 1639
UPMC 1639
UPMC ALTOONA 1639
Upromise Inc. 1639
UPSON COUNTY HOSPITAL INC. 1639
UQM Technologies, Inc. 1639
Uranium Energy Corp. 1640
Uranium Resources Inc. 1640
Urban Outfitters, Inc. 1640
Urban Retail Properties Co. 1640
Urigen Pharmaceuticals Inc. 1640
Urologix Inc. 1640
Uroplasty, Inc. 1641
URS Corp 1641
Urstadt Biddle Properties Inc 1641
US 1 Industries Inc. 1641
US DAIRY EXPORT COUNCIL 1641
US Dataworks Inc 1641
US Department of Agriculture 1642
US Department of Homeland Security 1642
US Department of State 1642

US Department of the Air Force 1642
US Ecology, Inc. 1642
US Foods Inc. 1642
US Geothermal Inc 1643
US Labs 1643
US Oncology Inc. 1643
US Securities and Exchange Commission 1643
US Silica Holdings, Inc. 1643
US Small Business Administration 1643
US Stem Cell Inc 1644
USA Compression Partners LP 1644
USA HOCKEY INC. 1644
USA Technologies Inc 1644
USA Truck, Inc. 1644
USAA 1644
USADATA Inc. 1645
USANA Health Sciences Inc 1645
USDA Forest Service 1645
USF Holland Inc. 1645
USFALCON INC. 1645
USG Corp 1645
USI Holdings Corporation 1646
USPA Accessories LLC 1646
USS POSCO INDUSTRIES 1646
UST LLC 1646
Utah Medical Products, Inc. 1646
UTAH STATE UNIVERSITY 1646
UTC Climate Controls & Security 1647
UTG Inc 1647
UTICA COLLEGE 1647
Utility Trailer Manufacturing Company 1647
Utz Quality Foods Inc. 1647
Uwharrie Capital Corp. 1647
VAALCO Energy, Inc. 1648
Vail Resorts Inc. 1648
ValCom Inc. 1648
VALDOSTA STATE UNIVERSITY 1648
Valence Technology, Inc. 1648
Valero Energy Corp. 1648
Valero Energy Partners LP 1649
Valhi, Inc. 1649
Valley Financial Corp. 1649
VALLEY HEALTH SYSTEM 1649
Valley National Bancorp 1649
Valmont Industries, Inc. 1649
Valpak Direct Marketing Systems Inc. 1650
Valspar Corp. 1650
Value City Furniture Inc. 1650
VALUE DRUG COMPANY 1650
Value Line, Inc. 1650
ValueOptions Inc. 1650
ValueRich Inc 1651
VAN ARPIN LINES INC 1651
VAN BUDD LINES INC 1651
VAN HORN METZ & CO. INC. 1651
Vanda Pharmaceuticals Inc 1651
Vangent Inc. 1651
Vanguard Natural Resources LLC 1652
Vans Inc. 1652
Vantiv Inc 1652
Vantiv Inc. 1652
Varian Medical Systems, Inc. 1652
Varian Semiconductor Equipment Associates Inc.
    1652
VARIETY CHILDREN'S HOSPITAL 1653
VASCO Data Security International Inc 1653
Vascular Solutions Inc 1653
Vasomedical, Inc. 1653
VASSAR COLLEGE INC 1653
Vault.com Inc. 1653
VBI Vaccines Inc 1654
VCA Inc 1654
VCG Holding Corp. 1654
Vector Group Ltd 1654
Vectren Corp 1654
Veeco Instruments Inc. (DE) 1654
Veeva Systems Inc 1655
Velocity Commercial Capital Inc. 1655
Velocity Express LLC 1655
Venable LLP 1655
Venaxis Inc 1655
Venoco Inc. 1655
Ventana Medical Systems Inc. 1656
Ventas, Inc. 1656

VENTERA CORPORATION 1656
Ventrus Biosciences Inc. 1656
Ventura Foods LLC 1656
Ventyx Inc. 1656
Veolia Environmental Services North America Corp.
    1657
Vera Bradley Inc. 1657
Vera Wang Bridal House Ltd. 1657
Veracyte Inc 1657
Veramark Technologies Inc. 1657
Verastem Inc. 1657
Vericel Corp 1658
VeriFone Systems Inc. 1658
Verint Systems, Inc 1658
Verisign Inc 1658
Verisk Analytics Inc 1658
VeriTeQ Corp 1658
Verizon Communications Inc 1659
Vermeer Manufacturing Company 1659
Vermillion Inc. 1659
Vermont Gas Systems Inc. 1659
Veronis Suhler & Associates Inc. 1659
Versar Inc. 1659
Verso Corp 1660
VERST GROUP LOGISTICS INC. 1660
Vertex Pharmaceuticals, Inc. 1660
Vertical Computer Systems, Inc. 1660
Verticalnet Inc. 1660
VerticalResponse Inc. 1660
VESCO OIL CORPORATION 1661
Vesta Corporation 1661
Vestar Capital Partners Inc. 1661
Vetco Gray Inc. 1661
VETERANS OF FOREIGN WARS OF THE UNITED
    STATES 1661
VF Corp. 1661
VF Outdoor Inc. 1662
Vi-Jon Inc. 1662
Via Christi Health System 1662
Viacom Inc 1662
Viad Corp. 1662
ViaSat, Inc. 1662
Viasystems Group Inc 1663
Viavi Solutions Inc 1663
Vical, Inc. 1663
Vicor Corp. 1663
Victor Technologies Group Inc. 1663
Victoria's Secret Direct LLC 1663
Victoria's Secret Stores LLC 1664
Victory Packaging Inc. 1664
Video Display Corp. 1664
VIDEO GAMING TECHNOLOGIES INC 1664
VIDEON CENTRAL INC. 1664
Vienna Beef Ltd. 1664
VIETNAM VETERANS OF AMERICA INC. 1665
View Systems, Inc. 1665
VIKING YACHT COMPANY 1665
Village Bank & Trust Financial Corp 1665
Village Super Market, Inc 1665
VillageEDOCS Inc. 1665
VILLANOVA UNIVERSITY IN THE STATE OF
    PENNSYLVANIA 1666
Vince Holding Corp 1666
Violin Memory Inc 1666
Virbac Corporation 1666
Virco Manufacturing Corp. 1666
Virginia Electric & Power Co. 1666
VIRGINIA WEST UNIVERSITY FOUNDATION INC
    1667
VIRGINIA WEST UNIVERSITY HOSPITALS INC 1667
VirnetX Holding Corp 1667
VIRTUA MEMORIAL HOSPITAL BURLINGTON
    COUNTY INC 1667
Virtual Radiologic Corporation 1667
VirtualScopics Inc 1667
Virtus Investment Partners, Inc 1668
Virtusa Corp 1668
Visa Inc 1668
Viscount Systems Inc 1668
Vishay Intertechnology, Inc. 1668
Vishay Precision Group Inc. 1668
Vision Service Plan 1669
Vision Solutions Inc. 1669
Visionary Integration Professionals Inc. 1669

Visionworks of America Inc. 1669
Visiting Nurse Service of New York 1669
Viskase Companies Inc. 1669
Vista Gold Corp. 1670
Vista Healthplan of South Florida Inc. 1670
Vista International Technologies Inc 1670
Visteon Corp. 1670
Vistronix Inc. 1670
Vitacost.com Inc 1670
Vitamin Shoppe Inc 1671
VITAS Healthcare Corporation 1671
Vitesse Semiconductor Corp. 1671
Vitria Technology Inc. 1671
Vitronics Soltec Inc. 1671
Viveve Medical Inc 1671
Vivid Entertainment LLC 1672
Vivus, Inc. 1672
VIZIO INC. 1672
VMware Inc 1672
Vocera Communications, Inc. 1672
Vocollect Inc. 1672
Vocus Inc 1673
Volcano Corporation 1673
Volt Information Sciences, Inc. 1673
Voltari Corp 1673
VOLUNTEER ENERGY COOPERATIVE 1673
VOLUNTEERS OF AMERICA INC. 1673
Von Maur Inc. 1674
Vonage Holdings Corp 1674
Vornado Realty Trust 1674
Voxeo Corporation 1674
Voxware Inc. 1674
Voxx International Corp 1674
Voyager Entertainment International Inc. 1675
VRATSINAS CONSTRUCTION COMPANY 1675
Vringo Inc 1675
VSB Bancorp Inc (NY) 1675
VSE Corp. 1675
VSOFT CORPORATION 1675
Vu1 Corporation 1676
Vulcan International Corporation 1676
Vulcan Materials Co (Holding Company) 1676
VWR Funding Inc. 1676
VydroTech Inc. 1676
Vystar Corp 1676
VyStar Credit Union 1677
W & T Offshore Inc 1677
W. B. Doner & Company 1677
W. E. AUBUCHON CO. INC. 1677
W. H. Braum Inc. 1677
W. K. KELLOGG FOUNDATION 1677
W. L. BUTLER CONSTRUCTION INC. 1678
W.C. Bradley Co. 1678
W.P. Carey Inc 1678
W.S. BADCOCK CORPORATION 1678
WABASH COLLEGE 1678
Wabash National Corp. 1678
Waccamaw Bankshares Inc. 1679
Wachovia Preferred Funding Corp 1679
Wackenhut Services Incorporated 1679
WADA FARMS MARKETING GROUP LLC 1679
Waddell & Reed Financial, Inc. 1679
WageWorks Inc 1679
WAGNER INDUSTRIES INC. 1680
WAKE FOREST UNIVERSITY BAPTIST MEDICAL
   CENTER 1680
WAKEFERN FOOD CORP. 1680
WAKEMED 1680
Wal-Mart Stores, Inc. 1680
Walbridge Aldinger Company 1680
Walker & Dunlop Inc 1681
WALKER DIE CASTING INC. 1681
Walker Magnetics Group 1681
WALSH BROTHERS INCORPORATED 1681
Walsworth Publishing Company Inc. 1681
Walter Energy, Inc. 1681
Walter Investment Management Corp 1682
WALTON ELECTRIC MEMBERSHIP CORPORATION
   1682
Walton Signage Corporation 1682
WAR MEMORIAL HOSPITAL INC. 1682
Warburg Pincus LLC 1682
WARD TRUCKING LLC 1682
Warner Music Group Corp. 1683

Warrantech Corporation 1683
Warren Equities Inc. 1683
Warren Resources Inc (MD) 1683
WARREN RURAL ELECTRIC COOPERATIVE
   CORPORATION 1683
Washington Banking Co. (Oak Harbor, WA) 1683
Washington Federal Inc. 1684
WASHINGTON HEALTHCARE MARY 1684
WASHINGTON HOSPITAL CENTER CORPORATION
   1684
Washington Metropolitan Area Transit Authority
   1684
Washington Nationals Baseball Club LLC 1684
Washington Real Estate Investment Trust 1684
WASHINGTON REGIONAL MEDICAL CENTER 1685
Washington Suburban Sanitary Commission 1685
Washington Trust Bancorp, Inc. 1685
Waste Connections, Inc. 1685
Waste Control Specialists LLC 1685
Waste Management, Inc. (DE) 1685
Wastequip Inc. 1686
Wastren Advantage Inc. 1686
WatchGuard Technologies Inc. 1686
WaterFurnace Renewable Energy Inc. 1686
Waters Corp. 1686
WATKINS AND SHEPARD TRUCKING INC. 1686
Watkins Associated Industries Inc. 1687
WATONWAN FARM SERVICE INC 1687
Watsco Inc. 1687
Watts Water Technologies Inc 1687
WAUKESHA MEMORIAL HOSPITAL INC. 1687
WAUKESHA-PEARCE INDUSTRIES INC. 1687
Wausau Paper Corp 1688
Wave Systems Corp 1688
Wayfair LLC 1688
WAYLAND BAPTIST UNIVERSITY INC 1688
WAYNE J. GRIFFIN ELECTRIC INC. 1688
Wayne Savings Bancshares Inc 1688
Wayside Technology Group Inc 1689
WCA Waste Corporation 1689
WCI Communities Inc 1689
WD-40 Co. 1689
WEA Trust 1689
Weather Shield Mfg Inc. 1689
Web.Com Group, Inc. 1690
Webber Oil Company 1690
Webco Industries Inc. 1690
Webcor Construction L.P. 1690
Weber Distribution LLC 1690
WebMD Health Corp 1690
Webster Financial Corp (Waterbury, Conn) 1691
WEBSTER UNIVERSITY 1691
WEC Energy Group Inc 1691
Wedbush Securities Inc. 1691
Weeden & Co. LP 1691
Weekley Homes L.P. 1691
Wegener Corp. 1692
Wegmans Food Markets Inc. 1692
Weight Watchers International, Inc. 1692
Weil Gotshal & Manges LLP 1692
Weingarten Realty Investors 1692
WEIRTON MEDICAL CENTER INC. 1692
Weis Markets, Inc. 1693
WELCH FOODS INC. A COOPERATIVE 1693
WellCare Health Plans Inc 1693
Wellco Enterprises Inc. 1693
Wellington Management Company LLP 1693
WELLMONT HEALTH SYSTEM 1693
Wells Enterprises Inc. 1694
Wells Fargo Advisors LLC 1694
Wells Financial Corp 1694
Wells Lamont Corporation 1694
WELLSTAR HEALTH SYSTEM INC. 1694
Welltower Inc 1694
Wendy's Co (The) 1695
Wendy's International Inc. 1695
Wenner Media LLC 1695
Werner Co. 1695
Werner Enterprises, Inc. 1695
WesBanco, Inc. 1695
Wesco Aircraft Holdings Inc. 1696
Wesco Financial LLC 1696
Wesco International, Inc. 1696
Wescom Credit Union 1696

WESLEYAN UNIVERSITY (INC) 1696
West Bancorporation, Inc. 1696
West Bend Mutual Insurance Company 1697
WEST COAST NOVELTY CORPORATION 1697
West Corp. 1697
West Marine, Inc. 1697
West Penn Allegheny Health System Inc. 1697
West Pharmaceutical Services, Inc. 1697
West Publishing Corporation 1698
WEST TEXAS GAS INC. 1698
WEST VIRGINIA UNITED HEALTH SYSTEM INC.
   1698
WestAmerica Bancorporation 1698
Westar Energy Inc 1698
WESTAT INC. 1698
Westcon Group Inc. 1699
Westell Technologies, Inc. 1699
Western & Southern Financial Group Inc. 1699
Western Alliance Bancorporation 1699
Western Area Power Administration 1699
Western Connecticut Health Network Inc. 1699
Western Dental Services Inc 1700
Western Digital Corp. 1700
Western Express Holdings Inc. 1700
Western Family Foods Inc. 1700
WESTERN FARMERS ELECTRIC COOPERATIVE
   1700
Western Gas Equity Partners LP 1700
Western Gas Partners LP 1701
Western Massachusetts Electric Co. 1701
Western Petroleum Inc. 1701
Western Refining Inc 1701
Western Refining Logistics LP 1701
WESTERN STATES FIRE PROTECTION COMPANY
   INC 1701
Western Union Co. 1702
WESTERN WASHINGTON UNIVERSITY 1702
Westfield Financial Inc 1702
Westfield Group 1702
Westinghouse Air Brake Technologies Corporation
   1702
Westinghouse Electric Company LLC 1702
Westinghouse Lighting Corporation 1703
Westlake Chemical Corp 1703
WESTMINSTER COLLEGE 1703
Westmoreland Coal Co. 1703
Westmoreland Resource Partners LP 1703
WestPoint Home Inc. 1703
Weststar Financial Services Corporation 1704
Westwood Holdings Group, Inc. 1704
Wet Seal, Inc. (The) 1704
Wetherill Associates Inc. 1704
Wex Inc 1704
WEXFORD HEALTH SOURCES INC. 1704
Weyco Group, Inc 1705
Weyerhaeuser Co 1705
WGBH Educational Foundation 1705
WGI Heavy Minerals Incorporated 1705
WGL Holdings, Inc. 1705
WHALLEY COMPUTER ASSOCIATES INC. 1705
Whataburger Restaurants LP 1706
WHEATON COLLEGE 1706
WHEATON FRANCISCAN SERVICES INC. 1706
WHEATON VAN LINES INC 1706
Wheeler Real Estate Investment Trust, Inc. 1706
WHEELING & LAKE ERIE RAILWAY COMPANY 1706
WHEELING-NISSHIN INC. 1707
Whelan Security Co. 1707
Whirlpool Corp 1707
White Castle System Inc. 1707
WHITE COUNTY MEDICAL CENTER 1707
White Flower Farm Inc. 1707
White Mountains Insurance Group Ltd. 1708
White River Capital Inc. 1708
WHITE RIVER HEALTH SYSTEM INC. 1708
White Rose Inc. 1708
WhiteGlove Health Inc. 1708
WHITEHEAD INSTITUTE FOR BIOMEDICAL
   RESEARCH 1708
Whitestone REIT 1709
Whiting Petroleum Corp 1709
WHITMAN COLLEGE 1709
WHITNEY MUSEUM OF AMERICAN ART 1709
Whole Foods Market, Inc. 1709

WHYY INC. 1709
WIDENER UNIVERSITY 1710
WidePoint Corp 1710
Wieden + Kennedy Inc. 1710
WIKIMEDIA FOUNDATION INC. 1710
Wilbert Inc. 1710
WILBUR SMITH ASSOCIATES INC. 1710
WILBUR-ELLIS COMPANY 1711
WilcoHess LLC 1711
WILDLIFE CONSERVATION SOCIETY 1711
Wiley (John) & Sons Inc. 1711
Wilhelmina International, Inc. 1711
WILLAMETTE UNIVERSITY 1711
Willamette Valley Vineyard Inc. 1712
Willbros Group Inc (DE) 1712
Willdan Group Inc 1712
WILLIAM MARSH RICE UNIVERSITY INC 1712
WILLIAM PATERSON UNIVERSITY 1712
Williams & Connolly LLP 1712
Williams (Clayton) Energy, Inc. 1713
Williams Controls Inc. 1713
Williams International Co. L.L.C. 1713
Williams Partners L.P. 1713
Williams Partners LP (New) 1713
WILLIAMS SAUSAGE COMPANY INC. 1713
Williams Sonoma Inc 1714
Williams-Labadie LLC 1714
Willis Lease Finance Corp. 1714
Wilmer Cutler Pickering Hale and Dorr LLP 1714
Wilshire Bancorp Inc 1714
Wilshire Enterprises Inc. 1714
Wilson Elser Moskowitz Edelman & Dicker LLP 1715
Wilson Sonsini Goodrich & Rosati 1715
WILSON TRUCKING CORPORATION 1715
Wilsonart International Holding LLC 1715
Wilton Brands Inc. 1715
Winchester Healthcare Management Inc. 1715
WINCHESTER MEDICAL CENTER AUXILIARY INC. 1716
Wind River Systems Inc. 1716
WINDOW TO THE WORLD COMMUNICATIONS INC. 1716
Windstream Holdings Inc 1716
Wine.com Inc. 1716
Wingate Partners 1716
Winland Electronics Inc 1717
Winmark Corp 1717
Winn-Dixie Stores Inc. 1717
Winnebago Industries, Inc. 1717
WINSTON & STRAWN LLP 1717
Wintec Industries Inc. 1717
WINTER HAVEN HOSPITAL INC. 1718
Winthrop Realty Trust 1718
WINTHROP-UNIVERSITY HOSPITAL INC 1718
Wintrust Financial Corp. (IL) 1718
Wireless Matrix USA Inc. 1718
Wireless Telecom Group, Inc. 1718
Wirtz Beverage Group LLC 1719
WIS International 1719
WisdomTree Investments Inc. 1719
Wise Foods Inc. 1719
WITHLACOOCHEE RIVER ELECTRIC COOPERATIVE INC 1719
Wits Basin Precious Minerals Inc. 1719
Wizards of the Coast LLC 1720
WKI Holding Company Inc. 1720
WM Recycle America LLC 1720
Wm. Bolthouse Farms Inc. 1720
Wolfe Engineering Inc. 1720
Wolverine Advanced Materials LLC 1720
WOLVERINE PIPE LINE COMPANY 1721
WOLVERINE POWER SUPPLY COOPERATIVE INC. 1721
Wolverine World Wide, Inc. 1721
WOMAN'S HOSPITAL FOUNDATION INC 1721
Wonderware Corporation 1721
Woodfin Oil Company 1721
Woodmen of the World Life Insurance Society 1722
Woodstock Holdings Inc 1722
Woodward, Inc. 1722
WOOLRICH INC. 1722
Workday Inc 1722
Workscape Inc. 1722
Workstream USA Inc. 1723

World Acceptance Corp. 1723
World Airways Inc. 1723
World Energy Solutions, Inc. (DE) 1723
WORLD FINER FOODS INC 1723
World Fuel Services Corp. 1723
World Surveillance Group Inc 1724
World Travel Holdings Inc. 1724
World Vision International 1724
World Wide Technology Inc. 1724
WORLD WILDLIFE FUND INC. 1724
World Wrestling Entertainment Inc 1724
Worthington Industries, Inc. 1725
Wozniak Industries Inc. 1725
WPCS International Inc 1725
WPX Energy, Inc. 1725
WR Hambrecht + Co. 1725
Wright Investors' Service Holdings, Inc. 1725
Wright Medical Group Inc. 1726
WRIGHT STATE UNIVERSITY 1726
WRITERS GUILD OF AMERICA WEST INC. 1726
WSA Group Inc. 1726
WSFS Financial Corp 1726
WSI Industries, Inc. 1726
WVS Financial Corp. 1727
WYCKOFF HEIGHTS MEDICAL CENTER 1727
Wyle Laboratories Inc. 1727
Wyman-Gordon Company 1727
Wyndham Vacation Ownership 1727
Wyndham Worldwide Corp 1727
Wynn Resorts Ltd 1728
WYOMING MEDICAL CENTER INC. 1728
X-Rite Incorporated 1728
Xanodyne Pharmaceuticals Inc. 1728
XAP Corporation 1728
XAVIER UNIVERSITY 1728
Xcel Energy, Inc. 1729
Xcerra Corp 1729
Xencor, Inc 1729
Xenith Bankshares Inc 1729
Xenonics Holdings Inc 1729
XenoPort Inc 1729
Xerium Technologies Inc 1730
Xerox Corp 1730
XETA Technologies Inc. 1730
Xfone Inc. 1730
XIFIN Inc. 1730
Xilinx, Inc. 1730
XO Group Inc 1731
XO Holdings Inc. 1731
XOMA Corp 1731
XORIANT CORPORATION 1731
xpedx 1731
Xplore Technologies Corp. 1731
XPO Logistics, Inc. 1732
XRS Corp 1732
Xtant Medical Holdings Inc 1732
XTRA Corporation 1732
XTRA Lease Inc. 1732
Xura Inc 1732
Xylem Inc. 1733
Yadkin Financial Corp 1733
Yahoo! Inc. 1733
YAKIMA VALLEY MEMORIAL HOSPITAL ASSOCIATION INC 1733
Yale New Haven Health Services Corporation 1733
Yankee Group Research Inc. 1733
YASH TECHNOLOGIES INC 1734
Yazaki North America Inc. 1734
Yellowbook Inc. 1734
Yelp Inc 1734
YESHIVA UNIVERSITY 1734
YORK HOSPITAL 1734
YORK PENNSYLVANIA HOSPITAL COMPANY LLC 1735
York Water Co 1735
Younan Properties Inc. 1735
Young & Rubicam Inc. 1735
Young America Corporation 1735
YOUNG LIFE 1735
Young Pecan Company 1736
YOUNGSTOWN STATE UNIVERSITY INC 1736
Your Community Bankshares Inc 1736
YRC Worldwide Inc 1736
YTB International Inc. 1736

Yum! Brands, Inc. 1736
Yuma Energy Inc 1737
YUMA REGIONAL MEDICAL CENTER INC 1737
YuMe Inc 1737
Z GALLERIE 1737
Z-Trim Holdings, Inc 1737
Zacky Farms LLC 1737
Zagg Inc 1738
ZAIS Financial Corp 1738
Zale Corp. 1738
Zanett Inc. 1738
ZAP 1738
Zareba Systems Inc. 1738
Zaza Energy Corp. 1739
Zebra Technologies Corp. 1739
ZEE Medical Inc. 1739
ZEELAND COMMUNITY HOSPITAL 1739
ZELTIQ Aesthetics Inc. 1739
Zenith National Insurance Corp. 1739
Zep Inc 1740
ZEVEX International Inc. 1740
ZF Group North American Operations Inc. 1740
Zhone Technologies Inc 1740
Ziff Davis Holdings Inc. 1740
Zilliant Inc. 1740
ZiLOG Inc. 1741
Zimmer Biomet Holdings Inc 1741
ZIMMER GUNSUL FRASCA ARCHITECTS LLP 1741
Zimmerman Advertising LLC 1741
Zion Oil and Gas Inc. 1741
Zions Bancorporation 1741
ZIOPHARM Oncology Inc 1742
Zippo Manufacturing Company 1742
ZipRealty Inc 1742
Zircon Corporation 1742
Zix Corp 1742
Zoetis Inc 1742
Zogenix Inc. 1743
ZOLL Medical Corporation 1743
Zoltek Companies Inc 1743
ZOOLOGICAL SOCIETY OF SAN DIEGO 1743
Zoom Telephonics, Inc. 1743
Zoots Corporation 1743
Zumiez Inc 1744
Zygo Corp 1744
ZymoGenetics Inc. 1744

Index by Headquarters

COLORADO

Aurora
Children's Hospital Colorado 333
GRAEBEL COMPANIES INC. 684

Boulder
AeroGrow International, Inc. 37
Array BioPharma Inc. 135
AURORA DAIRY CORPORATION 156
Boulder Brands Inc 238
Clovis Oncology Inc. 358
Dynamic Materials Corp. 496
Encision Inc. 532
NeoMedia Technologies, Inc. 1081
New Frontier Media Inc. 1088
Rally Software Development Corp. 1281
Rogue Wave Software Inc. 1319
UNIVERSITY CORPORATION FOR ATMOSPHERIC RESEARCH 1632
UNIVERSITY OF COLORADO 1633

Breckenridge
Altex Industries, Inc. 70

Broomfield
ARCA biopharma Inc. 127
Ball Corp 174
Corgenix Medical Corp. 402
Level 3 Communications, Inc. 913
MWH GLOBAL INC. 1056
Noodles & Co. 1106
Vail Resorts Inc. 1648

Castle Rock
Venaxis Inc 1655

Centennial
AccuCode Inc. 17
Advance Display Technologies Inc. 30
Arrow Electronics, Inc. 136
National CineMedia Inc 1064
Penford Corp. 1195
Performance Food Group Inc. 1203
WESTERN STATES FIRE PROTECTION COMPANY INC 1701

Colorado Springs
Century Casinos Inc. 316
COLORADO COLLEGE 370
Colorado Springs Utilities 371
Current USA Inc. 430
Ent Federal Credit Union 540
Gold Resource Corp 676
INTELLIGENT SOFTWARE SOLUTIONS INC. 809
Memorial Health System 992
NEUMANN SYSTEMS GROUP INC. 1085
Ramtron International Corporation 1281
Spectranetics Corp. (The) 1425
UNITED STATES OLYMPIC COMMITTEE INC 1625
USA HOCKEY INC. 1644
YOUNG LIFE 1735

Commerce City
Vista International Technologies Inc 1670

Crestone
Bion Environmental Technologies, Inc. 215

Denver
Accuvant Inc. 18
AIMCO Properties L.P. 45
ALPS Holdings Inc. 68
American Cannabis Co Inc 80
American Midstream Partners LP 91
American Oil & Gas Inc. 92
Anschutz Company 113
Antero Resources Corp 113

Apartment Investment & Management Co. 116
Band-It-Idex Inc. 177
Barrett (Bill) Corp 185
BioFuel Energy Corp 213
Birner Dental Management Services, Inc. 217
Black Raven Energy Inc. 220
Bonanza Creek Energy, Inc. 233
Chipotle Mexican Grill Inc 335
Cimarex Energy Co 341
CoBiz Financial Inc 363
COLORADO SEMINARY 371
Conergy Inc. 388
Coram LLC 401
CoreSite Realty Corp. 402
CREDO Petroleum Corporation 415
DaVita HealthCare Partners Inc 446
DCP Midstream Partners LP 448
DCT Industrial Trust Inc 448
Denver Health and Hospital Authority 461
Emerald Oil, Inc 526
Enservco Corp 539
Escalera Resources Co 552
Frontier Airlines Inc. 633
Gasco Energy Inc. 647
Glowpoint Inc 674
Guaranty Bancorp (DE) 700
Hallador Energy Co 709
HCA-HealthONE LLC 725
Holland & Hart LLP 751
Intrawest Resorts Holdings Inc 823
Intrepid Potash Inc 823
Janus Capital Group Inc 844
Johns Manville Corporation 854
Kaiser Foundation Health Plan of Colorado 862
Kodiak Oil & Gas Corp. 887
Local Matters Inc. 930
M.D.C. Holdings, Inc. 945
Magellan Petroleum Corp. 950
MapQuest Inc. 957
Markwest Energy Partners L.P. 962
Molson Coors Brewing Company 1034
Navajo Shippers Inc. 1075
PCL CONSTRUCTION ENTERPRISES INC 1189
PDC Energy Inc 1190
Pinnacol Assurance 1221
ProBuild Holdings Inc. 1249
QEP Resources Inc 1267
RE/MAX International Inc. 1288
Royal Gold, Inc. 1326
SCL HEALTH - FRONT RANGE INC. 1359
Scott's Liquid Gold, Inc. 1360
Sefton Resources Inc. 1367
Simpson Housing LLLP 1392
SM Energy Co. 1398
Spyr Inc 1430
Sunshine Silver Mines Corporation 1469
Synergy Resources Corp 1481
The Broe Companies Inc. 1518
The Quiznos Master LLC 1548
TransMontaigne Inc. 1585
TransMontaigne Partners L.P. 1585
Triangle Petroleum Corp 1590
Venoco Inc. 1655
Whiting Petroleum Corp 1709

Durango
Rocky Mountain Chocolate Factory Inc (DE) 1318
U-Swirl Inc. 1605

Englewood
Image Software Inc. 2
Air Methods Corp. 45
AMERICAN FURNITURE WAREHOUSE CO INC 86

Ampio Pharmaceuticals Inc 104
Blockbuster L.L.C. 222
CH2M HILL COMPANIES LTD. 320
CSG Systems International Inc. 423
Dish Network Corp 476
EchoStar Corp 509
Evolving Systems, Inc. 560
Gevo Inc. 663
IHS Inc 784
Innospec Inc 801
Jeppesen Sanderson Inc. 848
Jones International Ltd. 856
Liberty Interactive Corp 916
Neutron Energy Inc. 1086
Oceanic Exploration Company 1131
PDB Sports Ltd. 1190
Starz 1445
Starz LLC 1445
TeleTech Holdings, Inc. 1502
Western Union Co. 1702
Westmoreland Coal Co. 1703

Firestone
Flatiron Construction Corp. 608

Fort Collins
Advanced Energy Industries Inc. 31
COLORADO STATE UNIVERSITY 371
OTTER PRODUCTS LLC 1159
Woodward, Inc. 1722

Golden
CoorsTek Inc. 401
Golden Minerals Co 677
Jacobs Entertainment Inc. 841
New Global Telecom Inc. 1088
ServiceMagic Inc. 1374

GRAND JUNCTION
FCI CONSTRUCTORS INC. 578

GREELEY
HENSEL PHELPS CONSTRUCTION CO. 737
Pilgrims Pride Corp. 1217

Greenwood Village
American Medical Response Ambulance Service Inc. 90
Ascent Capital Group, Inc. 140
CIBER, Inc. 340
Envision Healthcare Corp 545
Envision Healthcare Holdings Inc 545
Great West Life & Annuity Insurance Co - Insurance Products 690
Maui Wowi Franchising Inc. 972
Molycorp Inc. (DE) 1034
National Bank Holdings Corp 1063
Newmont Mining Corp. (Holding Co.) 1097
Powertech Uranium Corp. 1238
Red Robin Gourmet Burgers Inc 1291
Startek, Inc. 1445
Tengasco, Inc. 1505
The TriZetto Group Inc. 1554

Highlands Ranch
UDR Inc 1609

LAKEWOOD
CATAMOUNT CONSTRUCTORS INC. 301
CHRISTY SPORTS L.L.C. 338
Einstein Noah Restaurant Group Inc 515
General Moly Inc. 655
Good Times Restaurants Inc. 679
Mesa Laboratories, Inc. 1002
Natural Grocers By Vitamin Cottage Inc 1073
VCG Holding Corp. 1654
Western Area Power Administration 1699

Littleton
ADA-ES Inc. 26
Stillwater Mining Co. 1455
Thompson Creek Metals Company Inc. 1565
TW Telecom Inc 1603
Vista Gold Corp. 1670

Lone Tree
AmerAlia Inc. 75

Longmont
Dot Hill Systems Corp. 483
Sunrise Medical Inc. 1469
UQM Technologies, Inc. 1639

Louisville
Eldorado Artesian Springs Inc 517
Gaiam Inc 642
Global Healthcare Exchange LLC 671
GlobeImmune Inc 674
Real Goods Solar Inc 1288

Loveland
Heska Corp. 740
Kroll Factual Data Inc. 892

Mt. Crested Butte
Crested Butte LLC 416

Niwot
Crocs Inc 417

Salida
High Country Bancorp, Inc. 743

Thornton
Ascent Solar Technologies Inc 140

Watkins
Pure Cycle Corp. 1265

Westminster
Allos Therapeutics Inc. 64
DigitalGlobe Inc 472

Wheat Ridge
GeneThera Inc. 657
Solitario Exploration & Royalty Corp 1405

CONNECTICUT

Ansonia
Farrel Corporation 575

Berlin
Connecticut Light & Power Co 389
The Berlin Steel Construction Company 1517

Bethel
Cannondale Bicycle Corporation 280
Memry Corporation 993

Bloomfield
Cigna Corp 341
Kaman Aerospace Corporation 863
Kaman Corp. 864

Branford
454 Life Sciences 5
CAS Medical Systems Inc 297

BRIDGEPORT
BRIDGEPORT HOSPITAL & HEALTHCARE SERVICES INC 243
People's United Financial, Inc. 1199

Bristol
Barnes Group Inc. 184
BRISTOL HOSPITAL INCORPORATED 245
ESPN Inc. 553

Brookfield
Photronics, Inc. 1215

American Axle & Manufacturing
Holdings Inc 79
Blue Cross Blue Shield of Michigan
226
Caraco Pharmaceutical Laboratories
Ltd. 285
CompuWare Corp. 385
Crain Communications Inc 413
Detroit Diesel Corporation 463
Detroit Medical Center 463
Detroit Tigers Inc. 464
DIVERSIFIED CHEMICAL
TECHNOLOGIES INC. 476
DTE Electric Company 490
DTE Energy Co. 491
General Motors Co. 655
Health Alliance Plan of Michigan 727
HENRY FORD HEALTH SYSTEM 736
Honigman Miller Schwartz and Cohn
LLP 758
HOSPICE OF MICHIGAN INC. 763
Ilitch Holdings Inc. 785
Letts Industries Inc. 912
Little Caesar Enterprises Inc. 928
OnStar LLC 1147
PVS TECHNOLOGIES INC. 1266
Quicken Loans Inc. 1273
UNIVERSITY OF DETROIT MERCY
1633
Walbridge Aldinger Company 1680

EAST LANSING
GREENSTONE FARM CREDIT
SERVICES ACA 694

Eden Prairie
Titan Energy Worldwide Inc 1571

Farmington Hills
ACO Hardware Inc. 21
Amerisure Mutual Insurance Company
101
Edward Rose Building Enterprises
514
ELECTRO-MATIC PRODUCTS INC.
519
Innovation Ventures LLC 801
Jervis B. Webb Company 848
Mercedes-Benz Financial Services USA
LLC 995
Ramco-Gershenson Properties Trust
(MD) 1281
Robert Bosch LLC 1314

Fenton
Fentura Financial Inc 585

Ferndale
Ferndale Pharma Group Inc. 585

Flat Rock
AutoAlliance International Inc. 157

Flint
HealthPlus of Michigan Inc. 729
HURLEY MEDICAL CENTER INC. 773
KETTERING UNIVERSITY 874
MCLAREN HEALTH CARE
CORPORATION 981

Frankenmuth
Frankenmuth Mutual Insurance
Company 624
STAR OF THE WEST MILLING
COMPANY 1444

FRANKFORT
GRACELAND FRUIT INC. 684

Fraser
Continental Plastics Co. 396

GARDEN CITY
GARDEN CITY HOSPITAL 646

Grand Blanc
Serra Automotive Inc. 1373

Grand Haven
GHSP Inc. 664

GRAND RAPIDS
ADAC PLASTICS INC. 26
BISSELL Homecare Inc. 217
CASCADE ENGINEERING INC. 297
DAVENPORT UNIVERSITY 444
ETNA DISTRIBUTORS LLC 556
Gordon Food Service Inc. 682
Independent Bank Corporation (Ionia,
MI) 792
Knape & Vogt Manufacturing
Company 885
Lacks Enterprises Inc. 897
Meijer Inc. 991
Mercantile Bank Corp. 995
Meritage Hospitality Group Inc 1000
National Heritage Academies Inc.
1066
PRIDGEON & CLAY INC. 1246
Priority Health Managed Benefits Inc.
1248
SpartanNash Co. 1422
SPECTRUM HEALTH SYSTEM 1425
Steelcase, Inc. 1449
Universal Forest Products Inc. 1629
X-Rite Incorporated 1728

Grosse Pointe Farms
Saga Communications, Inc. 1337

Holland
Haworth Inc. 722
HOLLAND COMMUNITY HOSPITAL
INC 752
Macatawa Bank Corp. 946
Magna Mirrors 950
USF Holland Inc. 1645

HOUGHTON
MICHIGAN TECHNOLOGICAL
UNIVERSITY 1013

Howell
FNBH Bancorp, Inc. 613

Inkster
Metavation LLC 1004

JACKSON
ALRO STEEL CORPORATION 68
CMS Energy Corp 360
Consumers Energy Co. 395

KALAMAZOO
BORGESS MEDICAL CENTER 234
BRONSON HEALTH CARE GROUP
INC. 249
BRONSON METHODIST HOSPITAL
INC 249
Stryker Corp. 1459

Kentwood
Autocam Corporation 158

Lansing
Accident Fund Holdings Inc. 16
Auto-Owners Insurance Company 157
LANSING BOARD OF WATER AND
LIGHT 903
Neogen Corp. 1081

Lapeer
County Bank Corp.(Lapeer, MI) 408

Livonia
American Community Mutual
Insurance Company 82
CONTRACTORS STEEL COMPANY
397
Market Strategies International 961

McLaren Performance Technologies
Inc. 981
The Harvard Drug Group L.L.C. 1532
Tower International Inc 1578
TRINITY HEALTH CORPORATION
1593
TRW Automotive Holdings Corp 1599

Madison Heights
CTA Acoustics Inc. 425
MCNAUGHTON-MCKAY ELECTRIC
CO. 981

Manistique
Mackinac Financial Corp 947

Mattawan
MPI Research Inc. 1047

Midland
Chemical Financial Corp 327
Dow Chemical Co. 485
Midland Cogeneration Venture
Limited Partnership 1018

Monroe
La-Z-Boy Inc. 896
MBT Financial Corp. 976

MOUNT CLEMENS
MOUNT CLEMENS REGIONAL
MEDICAL CENTER INC. 1046

MOUNT PLEASANT
CENTRAL MICHIGAN UNIVERSITY
314

Muskegon
Community Shores Bank Corp 381
HACKLEY HOSPITAL 708
Horizon Group Properties Inc. 760

NEW YORK
LOGICALIS INC. 932

Northville
Gentherm Inc 658
Hayes Lemmerz International Inc.
723
Key Plastics L.L.C. 875
ZF Group North American Operations
Inc. 1740

Novi
Cooper-Standard Holdings, Inc. 400
ITC Holdings Corp 833
MICHIGAN MILK PRODUCERS
ASSOCIATION 1012

Okemos
Delta Dental Plan of Michigan Inc.
457
TECHSMITH CORPORATION 1497

PIGEON
COOPERATIVE ELEVATOR CO. 400

Plymouth
American Furukawa Inc. 86
Hella Corporate Center USA Inc. 734
Perceptron, Inc. 1201
Plastipak Packaging Inc. 1226
Rofin Sinar Technologies Inc. 1319

Pontiac
ABC Appliance Inc. 11

Port Huron
SEMCO ENERGY Inc. 1369

PORTAGE
WOLVERINE PIPE LINE COMPANY
1721

REDFORD
PISTON AUTOMOTIVE L.L.C. 1222

RIVERVIEW
MATTESON-RIDOLFI INC. 971

Rochester Hills
Energy Conversion Devices Inc. 535
Ovonyx Inc. 1162
Trico Products Corporation 1591

ROCHESTER
OAKLAND UNIVERSITY 1127

Rockford
Wolverine World Wide, Inc. 1721

Romulus
Federal Screw Works 582
RKA Petroleum Companies Inc. 1313

SAGINAW
COVENANT MEDICAL CENTER INC
409
STANDARD ELECTRIC COMPANY
1440

SAINT CLAIR SHORES
ALEXANDER AND HORNUNG INC. 54

SHERIDAN
SHERIDAN COMMUNITY HOSPITAL
(OSTEOPATHIC) 1381

Southfield
AlixPartners LLP 56
Ally Commercial Finance LLC 65
ANXeBusiness Corp. 115
ATWELL LLC 154
BARTON MALOW COMPANY 186
Blue Care Network of Michigan 224
Covisint Corp 410
Credit Acceptance Corp. (MI) 414
DENSO International America Inc.
460
Detrex Corp. 463
Diversified Restaurant Holdings Inc.
477
EPITEC INC. 547
Federal-Mogul Holdings Corp 582
International Automotive Components
Group North America I 815
Lear Corp. 907
Meadowbrook Insurance Group Inc
983
Peterson American Corporation 1206
Plante & Moran PLLC 1226
PROVIDENCE HOSPITAL 1257
Stefanini TechTeam 1449
Sun Communities, Inc. 1465
Superior Industries International, Inc.
1471
VESCO OIL CORPORATION 1661
W. B. Doner & Company 1677

Sparta
ChoiceOne Financial Services, Inc.
336

SPRING ARBOR
SPRING ARBOR UNIVERSITY 1429

Sterling Heights
General Dynamics Land Systems Inc.
653

Sturgis
Sturgis Bancorp Inc 1460

Taylor
Masco Corp. 967

TRAVERSE CITY
CHERRY CENTRAL COOPERATIVE
INC. 328

Troy
DuPont Automotive 494
Flagstar Bancorp, Inc. 607
HTC Global Services Inc. 768
ICONMA L.L.C. 780
Kelly Services, Inc. 869

Marceline
Walsworth Publishing Company Inc. 1681

MARYLAND HEIGHTS
J. D. STREETT & COMPANY INC. 836
SunEdison Inc 1466

Monett
Jack Henry & Associates, Inc. 839

Mountain Grove
First Bancshares Inc. (MO) 594

North Kansas City
Cerner Corp. 319
WAGNER INDUSTRIES INC. 1680

O'Fallon
CitiMortgage Inc. 345
Synergetics USA Inc 1480

Poplar Bluff
Southern Missouri Bancorp, Inc. 1417

SAINT CHARLES
CLIENT SERVICES INC. 357

SAINT JOSEPH
HEARTLAND HEALTH 731
HEARTLAND REGIONAL MEDICAL
CENTER 731

SAINT LOUIS
ALBERICI CORPORATION 51
BARRY-WEHMILLER GROUP INC.
186
CHRISTIAN HOSPITAL NORTHEAST -
NORTHWEST 337
CIC GROUP INC. 340
CONNECTRIA CORPORATION 390
CSI LEASING INC. 423
GUARANTEE ELECTRICAL COMPANY
700
Isle of Capri Casinos Inc 832
KORTE CONSTRUCTION COMPANY
889
LOGISTICS MANAGEMENT
SOLUTIONS L.C. 932
MCCARTHY BUILDING COMPANIES
INC. 977
OSBORN & BARR COMMUNICATIONS
INC. 1157
Perficient Inc. 1202
SAINT LOUIS UNIVERSITY 1339
ST. ANTHONY'S MEDICAL CENTER
1435
THE WASHINGTON UNIVERSITY
1559
WEBSTER UNIVERSITY 1691

SPRINGFIELD
ASSOCIATED ELECTRIC
COOPERATIVE INC. 143
Bass Pro Inc. 187
CITY UTILITIES OF SPRINGFIELD
MO 349
Great Southern Bancorp, Inc. 690
HILAND DAIRY FOODS COMPANY.
LLC 745
LESTER E. COX MEDICAL CENTERS
912
MERCY HOSPITAL SPRINGFIELD
998
MISSOURI STATE UNIVERSITY 1028
Mueller (Paul) Co. 1050
NEW PRIME INC. 1091
O'Reilly Automotive, Inc. 1126

St. Charles
ACF Industries LLC 19
American Railcar Industries Inc 93
LMI Aerospace, Inc. 929

St. Joseph
Chase General Corporation 324

St. Louis
Allied Healthcare Product, Inc. 63
Ameren Corp. 76
Anheuser-Busch Companies Inc. 111
Arch Coal, Inc. 127
Armstrong Energy Inc. 134
Ascension Health 140
Barnes-Jewish Hospital 184
Belden Inc 199
Bryan Cave LLP 254
Build-A-Bear Workshop Inc 257
Bunge Milling Inc. 258
Caleres Inc 270
Cass Information Systems Inc. 299
CCA Global Partners Inc. 305
Centene Corp 311
Centric Group L.L.C. 316
Cequel Communications Holdings I
LLC 318
Color Art Integrated Interiors LLC
370
Ducommun LaBarge Technologies
491
Emerson Electric Co. 528
ESCO Technologies, Inc. 552
Express Scripts Holding Co 565
Federal Reserve Bank of St. Louis,
Dist. No. 8 581
FutureFuel Corp 640
G. P. & W. Inc. 641
Graybar Electric Co., Inc. 688
Harbour Group Industries Inc. 714
Hardee's Food Systems Inc. 715
Huttig Building Products, Inc. 775
ICL Performance Products LP 779
Laclede Group Inc 897
Metal Container Corporation 1004
Monsanto Co. 1037
Nestle Purina PetCare Company 1082
Panera Bread Co. 1175
Patriot Coal Corp 1186
Peabody Energy Corp 1191
Post Holdings Inc 1236
Pulaski Financial Corp 1264
Rawlings Sporting Goods Company
Inc. 1284
Schnuck Markets Inc. 1356
Shop 'n Save St. Louis Inc. 1383
Sigma-Aldrich Corp. 1387
Solutia Inc. 1406
SSM Health Care Corporation 1431
St. Louis Cardinals L.P. 1437
Stereotaxis Inc 1451
Stifel Financial Corp. 1454
The Doe Run Resources Corporation
1527
Union Electric Company 1615
Vi-Jon Inc. 1662
Viasystems Group Inc 1663
Wells Fargo Advisors LLC 1694
Whelan Security Co. 1707
World Wide Technology Inc. 1724
XTRA Corporation 1732
XTRA Lease Inc. 1732
Zoltek Companies Inc 1743

TROY
CUIVRE RIVER ELECTRIC
COOPERATIVE INC. 427

Wildwood
Peak Resorts Inc 1191

MONTANA

Belgrade
Xtant Medical Holdings Inc 1732

BILLINGS
BILLINGS CLINIC 210
First Interstate BancSystem, Inc. 599

BOZEMAN
MONTANA STATE UNIVERSITY INC
1037

Great Falls
Davidson Companies 445
PACIFIC HIDE & FUR DEPOT 1168

Helena
Blue Cross and Blue Shield of Montana
225
Eagle Bancorp Montana, Inc. 501

KALISPELL
CITYSERVICEVALCON LLC 349
Glacier Bancorp, Inc. 668

Lakeside
Earth Search Sciences Inc. 502

Livingston
PrintingForLess.com Inc. 1247

MISSOULA
BLACKFOOT TELEPHONE
COOPERATIVE INC. 220
Jim Palmer Trucking 850
ST PATRICK HOSPITAL
CORPORATION 1434
UNIVERSITY OF MONTANA SYSTEM
1634
WATKINS AND SHEPARD TRUCKING
INC. 1686

Thompson Falls
United States Antimony Corp. 1624

NEBRASKA

BATTLE CREEK
BATTLE CREEK FARMERS
COOPERATIVE NON-STOCK 189

Columbus
Behlen Mfg. Co. 197
Nebraska Public Power District 1079

FREMONT
FREMONT AREA MEDICAL CENTER
630
FREMONT CONTRACT CARRIERS
INC. 630

GOTHENBURG
ALL POINTS COOPERATIVE 57

Grand Island
Bosselman Inc. 235
CHIEF INDUSTRIES INC. 332
Sense Technologies Inc. 1371

Hastings
Gibraltar Packaging Group Inc. 665

Kearney
Baldwin Filters Inc. 173
Buckle, Inc. (The) 256
CASH-WA DISTRIBUTING CO. OF
KEARNEY INC. 299

Kimball
Risk (George) Industries Inc 1312

Las Vegas
Golden Entertainment Inc 677

Lincoln
Ameritas Mutual Holding Company
101
B&R Stores Inc. 168
BRYAN MEDICAL CENTER 254
Farmers & Merchants Investment Inc.
574
Lincoln Industries 924
MADONNA REHABILITATION
HOSPITAL 949

National Research Corp 1068
Nebraska Book Company Inc. 1079
Nelnet Inc 1080
SAINT ELIZABETH REGIONAL
MEDICAL CENTER 1339
UNION BANK AND TRUST COMPANY
1614

Nebraska City
Elster American Meter Company LLC
524

NORFOLK
AFFILIATED FOODS MIDWEST
COOPERATIVE INC. 39
Condor Hospitality Trust Inc 388

Omaha
Ag Processing Inc. A Cooperative 41
AMCON Distributing Company 75
Ballantyne Strong, Inc. 175
Berkshire Hathaway Inc. 204
C&A Industries Inc. 263
Children's Hospital & Medical Center
333
ConAgra Foods, Inc. 386
CREIGHTON ALEGENT HEALTH 415
CREIGHTON UNIVERSITY 415
Election Systems & Software Inc. 517
FindEx.com Inc. 591
Godfather's Pizza Inc. 675
Gordmans Stores Inc 682
Green Plains Inc. 692
H.D.R. INC. 706
HAWKINS CONSTRUCTION
COMPANY 722
Home Instead Inc. 755
Kutak Rock LLP 893
LEO A. DALY COMPANY 912
Lindsay Corp 924
METROPOLITAN UTILITIES
DISTRICT OMAHA NEBRASKA.
1008
MOSAIC 1043
Mutual of Omaha Insurance Co. (NE)
1055
National Indemnity Company 1066
Omaha Steaks International Inc. 1141
Pamida Stores Operating Company
LLC 1174
Peter Kiewit Sons' Inc. 1206
Physicians Mutual Insurance Company
1215
Radisson Hotels & Resorts 1279
ROBERTS DAIRY COMPANY LLC
1315
SAPP BROS. INC. 1350
SAPP BROS. PETROLEUM INC. 1350
TD Ameritrade Holding Corp 1495
Tenaska Inc. 1504
The Gavilon Group LLC 1529
THE SCOULAR COMPANY 1550
Transgenomic Inc 1584
TRAVEL AND TRANSPORT INC. 1586
Union Pacific Corp 1615
UNMC PHYSICIANS 1638
Valmont Industries, Inc. 1649
Werner Enterprises, Inc. 1695
West Corp. 1697
Woodmen of the World Life Insurance
Society 1722

Papillion
Infogroup Inc. 797

Sidney
Cabelas Inc 264

South Sioux City
Great West Casualty Company 690

WINNEBAGO
HO-CHUNK INC. 750

NEVADA

Boulder City
Amerityre Corporation 101

CARSON CITY
CARSON TAHOE REGIONAL
HEALTHCARE 296
Hytek Microsystems Inc. 776

HENDERSON
GLOBAL PACIFIC PRODUCE INC.
672
Spectrum Pharmaceuticals Inc 1426

Incline Village
PDL BioPharma Inc 1190

Las Vegas
All-American SportPark Inc. 57
Allegiant Travel Company 58
American Pacific Corp. 92
Aristocrat Technologies Inc. 132
Bally Technologies Inc 175
Bio-Solutions Manufacturing Inc. 212
Boyd Gaming Corp. 239
Caesars Entertainment Corp 267
Can-Cal Resources Ltd. 278
Cantor Entertainment Technology Inc.
280
Consumer Portfolio Service, Inc. 394
Diamond Resorts Holdings LLC 468
Everi Holdings Inc 559
EXX INC 566
Full House Resorts, Inc. 638
Gallery of History Inc. 644
Gaming Partners International Corp
645
Hard Rock Hotel Holdings LLC 715
Health Plan of Nevada Inc. 728
Herbst Gaming LLC 737
Inova Technology Inc 802
Las Vegas Sands Corp 904
Las Vegas Valley Water District 904
LifeQuest World Corporation 919
Live Ventures Inc 929
M & H ENTERPRISES INC. 944
Methes Energies International Ltd.
1004
MGM Resorts International 1011
Nevada Gold & Casinos, Inc. 1086
Nevada Power Co. 1086
Nevada State Bank 1087
PDS Gaming Corporation 1190
PHI Group Inc. 1211
Pinnacle Entertainment Inc 1219
Players Network (The) 1227
PRESTIGE TRAVEL INC 1245
Riviera Holdings Corporation 1313
Skinvisible Inc 1396
Southwest Gas Corporation 1419
Station Casinos LLC 1447
Stratosphere Corporation 1457
Voyager Entertainment International
Inc. 1675
Wynn Resorts Ltd 1728

North Las Vegas
Archon Corporation 128

Reno
Altair Nanotechnologies Inc 69
AMERCO 76
Crown Gold Corporation 421
Employers Holdings Inc 530
Hycroft Mining Corp 775
Monarch Casino & Resort, Inc. 1034
Nano Mask Inc. 1059
Ormat Technologies Inc 1156
Sierra Pacific Power Co. 1387
Tahoe Resources Inc. 1487

South Las Vegas
MGM Grand Hotel LLC 1010

Sparks
Sierra Nevada Corporation 1386

Winnemucca
Paramount Gold & Silver Corp 1179

Zephyr Cove
VirnetX Holding Corp 1667

NEW HAMPSHIRE

Bedford
Segway Inc. 1368

Berlin
Northway Financial, Inc. 1114

Claremont
Red River Computer Co. Inc. 1291

CONCORD
CONCORD HOSPITAL INC. 387
CONCORD LITHO GROUP 387

Dover
T.R. World Gym LLC 1485

Hampton
UNITIL Corp 1627

Hanover
White Mountains Insurance Group
Ltd. 1708

Hudson
Micronetics Inc. 1014
Presstek Inc. 1244

Keene
C&S Wholesale Grocers Inc. 263
CHESHIRE OIL COMPANY INC. 329
Peerless Insurance Company 1193

LEBANON
DARTMOUTH-HITCHCOCK CLINIC
442
Mascoma Corporation 967

LEE
UNIVERSITY SYSTEM OF NEW
HAMPSHIRE 1638

MANCHESTER
CATHOLIC MEDICAL CENTER 302
ELLIOT HOSPITAL OF THE CITY OF
MANCHESTER 522
Public Service Company of New
Hampshire 1261
SAINT ANSELM COLLEGE 1338

Merrimack
Brookstone Inc. 251
PC Connection, Inc. 1189
Pennichuck Corporation 1196

Milford
Hitchiner Manufacturing Co. Inc. 748

Nashua
GT Advanced Technologies Inc. 699
iCAD inc 778
SOUTHERN NEW HAMPSHIRE
MEDICAL CENTER 1417

Newport
Lake Sunapee Bank Group 899

PEMBROKE
ASSOCIATED GROCERS OF NEW
ENGLAND INC. 143

Peterborough
Eastern Mountain Sports Inc. 505

PLYMOUTH
NEW HAMPSHIRE ELECTRIC
COOPERATIVE INC 1089

Portsmouth
Anvil International Inc. 114
Bottomline Technologies (Delaware)
Inc 237
Highlands Fuel Delivery LLC 744
Sprague Resources LP 1429

Rochester
Albany International Corp 51
FRISBIE MEMORIAL HOSPITAL 632

Salem
Prophotonix Ltd. 1254
Standex International Corp. 1441

Stratham
The Timberland Company 1554
Vitronics Soltec Inc. 1671

NEW JERSEY

ALLENTOWN
UNITED BANK CARD INC. 1618

Atlantic City
Trump Entertainment Resorts Inc.
1597

Basking Ridge
Avaya Inc. 161
Barnes & Noble College Booksellers
LLC 184
Caladrius Biosciences Inc 269
Cellco Partnership 309
Lightspeed Online Research Inc. 921
Mylan Specialty L.P. 1057

Bayonne
BCB Bancorp Inc 193

Bedminster
Cegedim Relationship Management
308
CorMedix Inc 403
GAIN Capital Holdings Inc 642
NPS Pharmaceuticals Inc. 1119
Peapack-Gladstone Financial Corp.
1192
QUALCOMM Flarion Technologies
1269

Berkeley Heights
Authentidate Holding Corp 157
Cyclacel Pharmaceuticals, Inc 434

Berlin
A.C. Moore Arts & Crafts Inc. 8

Bloomfield
Lummus Technology Inc 941
WORLD FINER FOODS INC 1723

Boonton Township
ValCom Inc. 1648

BRANCHBURG
DANCKER SELLEW & DOUGLAS INC.
441
Hydromer, Inc. 775
RARITAN VALLEY COMMUNITY
COLLEGE 1284

Branchville
Selective Insurance Group Inc 1369

BRIDGETON
SEABROOK BROTHERS & SONS INC
1362

Bridgewater
Advanced Health Media LLC 31
Brother International Corporation
251
Cordis Corporation 401
iGate Corp 783
Sanofi-Aventis U.S. LLC 1349

Savient Pharmaceuticals Inc 1352
SOMERSET TIRE SERVICE INC. 1406
Synchronoss Technologies Inc 1480

Buena
Teligent Inc (New) 1503

Burlington
Burlington Stores Inc 259
Franklin Electronic Publishers
Incorporated 625

Camden
Campbell Soup Co. 278
OUR LADY OF LOURDES MEDICAL
CENTER INC 1160
THE COOPER HEALTH SYSTEM
1524

Cape May Court House
Cape Bancorp, Inc. 281

Carneys Point
Clement Pappas & Company Inc. 355

Carteret
White Rose Inc. 1708

Cedar Knolls
Artech Information Systems L.L.C.
137
Emisphere Technologies Inc. 529

Cherry Hill
1st Colonial Bancorp Inc 3
AmeriQuest Transportation Services
Inc. 100
Nuvilex Inc. 1124

Clifton
Clifton Savings Bancorp Inc 357
Electronic Control Security Inc. 520
mPhase Technologies Inc. 1047

Clinton
Unity Bancorp, Inc. 1628

Cranbury
1st Constitution Bancorp 3
Amicus Therapeutics Inc 103
Innophos Holdings Inc 801
Palatin Technologies Inc 1173
Trilogy Leasing Co. LLC 1592

Cranford
Metalico Inc 1004
PARAGON SOLUTIONS INC. 1178
The Newark Group Inc. 1543
Tofutti Brands, Inc. 1573

Dover
Casio America Inc. 299

East Brunswick
K-Sea Transportation Partners L.P.
861

East Hanover
Novartis Pharmaceuticals Corporation
1118

East Millstone
Life Sciences Research Inc. 918

EAST ORANGE
EAST ORANGE GENERAL HOSPITAL
INC 503

East Rutherford
Allied Building Products Corp. 63
Cambrex Corp 276
Hudson Group 769
New York Football Giants Inc. 1093
Tel Instrument Electronics Corp.
1500

Eastampton
Epicore BioNetworks Inc. 546

TAOS
TAOS HEALTH SYSTEMS INC. 1490

NEW YORK

ALBANY
ALBANY COLLEGE OF PHARMACY
AND HEALTH SCIENCES 50
ALBANY MEDICAL CENTER 51
Albany Molecular Research, Inc. 51
CAPITAL DISTRICT PHYSICIANS'
HEALTH PLAN INC. 283
Mechanical Technology, Inc. 984
Momentive Performance Materials Inc.
1034
New York State and Local Retirement
System 1094
New York State Teachers' Retirement
System 1094
ST. PETER'S HEALTH PARTNERS
1438
THE RESEARCH FOUNDATION OF
STATE UNIVERSITY OF NEW YORK
1548
Trans World Entertainment Corp.
1583

ALFRED
ALFRED UNIVERSITY 55

Amherst
Allied Motion Technologies Inc 63
Columbus McKinnon Corp. (NY) 373
Goodyear Dunlop Tires North America
Ltd. 681
International Imaging Materials Inc.
817
Kanthal Globar 865
Mark IV LLC 961

Amityville
HI-Tech Pharmacal Co., Inc. 741
NAPCO Security Technologies, Inc.
1060

Amsterdam
Beech-Nut Nutrition Corporation 197

Ann Arbor
Cephas Holding Corp 317

ANNANDALE ON HUDSON
BARD COLLEGE 183

Ardsley
Acorda Therapeutics Inc 21

Armonk
International Business Machines Corp.
816
Production Resource Group LLC 1250

Aventura
Trade Street Residential, Inc. 1581

BALLSTON SPA
STEWART'S SHOPS CORP. 1454

Batavia
Graham Corp. 685

Bellport
Perfumania Holdings Inc 1203

Bethpage
Cablevision Systems Corp. 265
COMFORCE Corporation 375
King Kullen Grocery Co. Inc. 880

BINGHAMTON
UNITED HEALTH SERVICES
HOSPITAL INC. 1621

Bohemia
Andrea Electronics Corp. 110
Scientific Industries, Inc. 1359

Brentwood
Medical Action Industries, Inc. 986

Briarcliff Manor
USI Holdings Corporation 1646

Bridgehampton
Bridge Bancorp, Inc. (Bridgehampton,
NY) 242

BRONX
BRONX LEBANON HOSPITAL
CENTER (INC) 249
CALVARY HOSPITAL INC. 275
FORDHAM UNIVERSITY 616
Loehmann's Holdings Inc. 931
MANHATTAN COLLEGE CORP 956
New York Yankees Partnership 1095

BRONXVILLE
SARAH LAWRENCE COLLEGE 1350

BRONX
WILDLIFE CONSERVATION SOCIETY
1711

BROOKLYN
BAYSIDE FUEL OIL DEPOT CORP
192
BROOKLYN ACADEMY OF MUSIC INC
250
BROOKLYN HOSPITAL CENTER 250
BROOKLYN NAVY YARD
DEVELOPMENT CORPORATION
250
Cumberland Packing Corp. 428
Dime Community Bancshares, Inc
473
Flatbush Federal Bancorp Inc. 607
KINGSBROOK JEWISH MEDICAL
CENTER INC 881
L. & R. DISTRIBUTORS INC. 896
Lutheran Medical Center 942
Maimonides Medical Center 952
Mays (J.W.), Inc. 975
NEW YORK METHODIST HOSPITAL
1093
ST JOSEPH"S COLLEGE NEW YORK
1433
WYCKOFF HEIGHTS MEDICAL
CENTER 1727

Buffalo
Catholic Health System 302
Cleveland BioLabs Inc 355
Computer Task Group, Inc. 384
Creditors Interchange Receivable
Management LLC 415
Delaware North Companies Inc. 454
First Niagara Financial Group, Inc.
601
Gibraltar Industries Inc 665
Global Earth Energy Inc. 671
KALEIDA HEALTH 863
M & T Bank Corp 944
Materion Advanced Materials
Technologies and Services Inc 970
RICH PRODUCTS CORPORATION
1309
Synacor, Inc. 1479

BURT
SUN ORCHARD FRUIT COMPANY
INC. 1465

Byron
OXBO International Corporation 1163

Camden
International Wire Group Inc. 819

Canandaigua
Canandaigua National Corp. 279

CANTON
ST LAWRENCE UNIVERSITY 1434

Carle Place
1-800 Flowers.com, Inc. 2

Catskill
Greene County Bancorp Inc 692

CAZENOVIA
CAZENOVIA COLLEGE 303

Central Islip
CVD Equipment Corp. 432

Chester
Repro-Med Systems, Inc. 1299

Chestnut Ridge
Teledyne LeCroy Inc. 1501

CLINTON
HAMILTON COLLEGE 710

Corning
Corning, Inc. 403

Deer Park
PC Group Inc. 1189
Surge Components, Inc. 1473

DeWitt
Community Bank System, Inc. 378

DOBBS FERRY
MERCY COLLEGE 997

Dunkirk
Lake Shore Bancorp Inc 899

E. Syracuse
Bright House Networks LLC 244

East Aurora
Astronics Corp. 146
Luminescent Systems Incorporated
940
Moog, Inc. 1038

East Bloomfield
Crosman Corporation 418

East Greenbush
GlobalSpec Inc. 673

EAST PATCHOGUE
BROOKHAVEN MEMORIAL
HOSPITAL MEDICAL CENTER INC.
250

EAST SYRACUSE
D/L COOPERATIVE INC. 437
Microwave Filter Co., Inc. 1015

Edgewood
CPI Aerostructures, Inc. 411
Tii Network Technologies Inc. 1569

Edmeston
New York Central Mutual Fire
Insurance Company 1092

Elma
Servotronics, Inc. 1375

Elmira
Chemung Financial Corp. 327
Elmira Savings Bank (NY) 523
Hardinge Inc. 715

Elmsford
Amscan Holdings Inc. 105
BioScrip Inc 215

Fairport
Bosch Security Systems Inc. 235
Manning & Napier Inc. 957
PAETEC Holding Corp. 1172

Farmingdale
General Microwave Corporation 654
MINUTEMAN PRESS
INTERNATIONAL INC. 1026

Misonix, Inc. 1027
OSI Pharmaceuticals LLC 1158
SWIMWEAR ANYWHERE INC. 1477

Flushing
FlightSafety International Inc. 609
Sterling Mets LP 1452

Fredonia
The Carriage House Companies Inc.
1520

GARDEN CITY
ADELPHI UNIVERSITY 28
Bookspan 234
Lifetime Brands Inc 920
Proginet Corporation 1251
Queens-Long Island Medical Group
P.C. 1272

GENEVA
HOBART AND WILLIAM SMITH
COLLEGES 750

Glen Head
First of Long Island Corp. 602

Glenmont
Farm Family Casualty Insurance
Company 573

Glens Falls
Arrow Financial Corp. 136

Glenville
Trustco Bank Corp. (N.Y.) 1597

GOUVERNEUR
KPH HEALTHCARE SERVICES INC.
889

Great Neck
BRT Realty Trust 253
Manhattan Bridge Capital, Inc. 955
North Shore-Long Island Jewish
Health System 1110
One Liberty Properties, Inc. 1145
United Capital Corp. 1618

Great River
Netsmart Technologies Inc. 1084

GREENVALE
LONG ISLAND UNIVERSITY 933

Hamburg
Evans Bancorp, Inc. 558

Harrison
MGT Capital Investments Inc 1011

HAUPPAUGE
AXIS CONSTRUCTION CORP. 166
Bactolac Pharmaceutical Inc. 170
Dale Carnegie & Associates Inc. 440
Hauppauge Digital, Inc. 721
Orbit International Corp. 1152
Standard Microsystems Corporation
1441
TSR, Inc. 1599
United-Guardian, Inc. 1627
Voxx International Corp 1674

Hawthorne
SmartPros Ltd 1399

Hicksville
Sam Ash Music Corporation 1342
Sleepy's Inc. 1398

Hollywood
Frederick's of Hollywood Group Inc
627

HUDSON
TACONIC FARMS INC. 1487

GOLDSBORO
SOUTHCO DISTRIBUTING COMPANY 1413

GREENSBORO
A. P. HUBBARD WHOLESALE LUMBER CORPORATION 8
Bell Partners Inc. 199
Carolina Bank Holdings Inc 294
CENTER FOR CREATIVE LEADERSHIP INC 311
Cross Company 419
Fresh Market, Inc. 631
International Textile Group, Inc. 819
Lorillard, Inc. 934
Mack Trucks Inc. 947
MARKET AMERICA INC. 961
Merz Pharmaceuticals Inc. 1002
MOTHER MURPHY"S LABORATORIES INC. 1044
NewBridge Bancorp 1095
Pace Communications Inc. 1166
Qorvo Inc 1268
RF Micro Devices, Inc. 1307
Solstas Lab Partners LLC 1406
Tanger Factory Outlet Centers, Inc. 1490
Unifi, Inc. 1613
United Guaranty Corporation 1621
VF Corp. 1661

GREENVILLE
PITT COUNTY MEMORIAL HOSPITAL INCORPORATED 1223
UNIVERSITY HEALTH SYSTEMS OF EASTERN CAROLINA INC. 1632

Hickory
Alex Lee Inc. 53
Dale Jarrett Racing Adventure Inc 440
Transportation Insight LLC 1586

High Point
Banner Pharmacaps Inc. 181
BNC Bancorp 229
Culp Inc. 427
HIGH POINT REGIONAL HEALTH SYSTEM 743
Home Meridian International Inc. 756
Stanley Furniture Co., Inc. 1442

Huntersville
American Tire Distributors Holdings Inc. 97

Lenoir
Broyhill Furniture Industries Inc. 252

Lillington
American Defense Systems Inc. 82

Lincolnton
Carolina Trust Bank 294

Madison
Freedom Group Inc. 628

Maiden
Air T Inc 46

Matthews
CEM Holdings Corporation 310
Family Dollar Stores, Inc. 571
Harris Teeter Inc. 718
PokerTek Inc 1231

MC LEANSVILLE
REPLACEMENTS LTD. 1299

Mocksville
Bank of the Carolinas Corp 179

Mooresville
Lowe's Companies Inc 936

Morrisville
Alliance One International Inc 61

ChannelAdvisor Corp 321
Charles & Colvard Ltd 322
Furiex Pharmaceuticals Inc 638
SciQuest Inc 1359
Tekelec 1499
Tenax Therapeutics Inc 1504
USFALCON INC. 1645

Mount Airy
Insteel Industries, Inc. 805
Pike Corp 1217
RENFRO CORPORATION 1298
Surrey Bancorp (NC) 1474

Mount Gilead
McRae Industries, Inc. 982

Newton
Peoples Bancorp of North Carolina Inc 1199

PINEHURST
FIRSTHEALTH OF THE CAROLINAS INC. 605

RALEIGH
ALLIANCE OF PROFESSIONALS & CONSULTANTS INC. 61
Baxano Surgical Inc 190
BioDelivery Sciences International Inc 213
BJT INC. 218
Capital Bank Corporation 282
Carolina Power & Light Company 294
CARQUEST Corporation 295
Crescent Financial Bancshares Inc. 416
DARA BioSciences, Inc. 441
Dillon Supply Co. 473
First Citizens BancShares, Inc. (NC) 595
Genworth Mortgage Insurance Corporation 659
Headway Corporate Resources Inc. 726
Highwoods Properties, Inc. 745
Inspire Pharmaceuticals Inc. 805
Kent Financial Services Inc. 872
Kerr Drug Inc. 874
Martin Marietta Materials, Inc. 965
NORTH CAROLINA ELECTRIC MEMBERSHIP CORPORATION 1108
North Carolina Farm Bureau Mutual Insurance Company Inc. 1108
Pepsi Bottling Ventures LLC 1201
PRA International 1240
Progress Energy Inc. 1251
Red Hat Inc 1291
REX HEALTHCARE INC. 1306
S&ME INC 1333
Salix Pharmaceuticals Ltd 1342
Stock Building Supply LLC 1455
STORR OFFICE ENVIRONMENTS INC 1456
THE GENERATION COMPANIES LLC 1529
Travel Management Partners Inc. 1586
Triangle Capital Corp 1590
WAKEMED 1680
Yadkin Financial Corp 1733

ROCKY MOUNT
BODDIE-NOELL ENTERPRISES INC. 231

Salisbury
Delhaize America LLC 455
Food Lion LLC 614

Sanford
Pentair Water Pool and Spa Inc. 1198
STATIC CONTROL COMPONENTS INC. 1447

South San Francisco
Catalyst Biosciences Inc 300

Southern Pines
First Bancorp (NC) 593

STATESVILLE
ENERGYUNITED ELECTRIC MEMBERSHIP CORPORATION 536
Kewaunee Scientific Corporation 875

Tarboro
Barnhill Contracting Company 185

Thomasville
Old Dominion Freight Line, Inc. 1138

Wake Forest
PowerSecure International, Inc. 1238

Warsaw
Murphy-Brown LLC 1054

Washington
First South Bancorp Inc (VA) 603
Flanders Corporation 607

Waynesville
Wellco Enterprises Inc. 1693

West Jefferson
LifeStore Financial Group 920

Whiteville
Waccamaw Bankshares Inc. 1679

WILKESBORO
KEY CITY FURNITURE COMPANY INC 875

Wilmington
Cenama Inc. 310
Guilford Mills Inc. 702
NEW HANOVER REGIONAL MEDICAL CENTER AUXILIARY INC. 1089
Pharmaceutical Product Development Inc. 1209

Winston Salem
Hatteras Financial Corp 721
QUALITY OIL COMPANY LLC 1270
WAKE FOREST UNIVERSITY BAPTIST MEDICAL CENTER 1680

Winston-Salem
BB&T Corp. 193
Hanes Companies Inc. 712
HanesBrands Inc 712
Krispy Kreme Doughnuts Inc 891
Lowe's Food Stores Inc. 936
Primo Water Corp 1247
Republic Mortgage Insurance Company 1300
Reynolds American Inc 1307
Southern Community Financial Corporation 1415
WilcoHess LLC 1711

Youngsville
Sirchie Acquisition Company LLC 1394
Xerium Technologies Inc 1730

NORTH DAKOTA

Bismarck
Basin Electric Power Cooperative 187
BNCCORP Inc 230
Dakota Gasification Company 439
MDU Resources Group Inc. 982
ST. ALEXIUS MEDICAL CENTER 1434

FARGO
DAKOTA SUPPLY GROUP INC. 439
EIDE BAILLY LLP 515

RDO EQUIPMENT CO 1287

Grand Forks
Altru Health System 71
MINNKOTA POWER COOPERATIVE INC. 1026
NORTH DAKOTA MILL & ELEVATOR ASSOCIATION INC 1108
UNIVERSITY OF NORTH DAKOTA 1634

MINOT
FARSTAD OIL INC. 575
Investors Real Estate Trust 827
SPF ENERGY INC. 1427
SRT COMMUNICATIONS INC. 1431

Wahpeton
Minn-Dak Farmers Cooperative 1025

West Fargo
Titan Machinery, Inc. 1571

OHIO

Akron
Akron General Medical Center 48
Bekaert Corporation 198
CHILDRENS HOSPITAL MEDICAL CENTER OF AKRON 334
FirstEnergy Corp. 604
FirstEnergy Solutions Corp. 604
FirstMerit Corp 605
GOJO Industries 676
Goodyear Tire & Rubber Co. 681
Jersey Central Power & Light Co. 848
Meggitt Aircraft Braking Systems Corporation 991
Metropolitan Edison Company 1007
Myers Industries Inc. 1056
Ohio Edison Co 1135
SUMMA HEALTH SYSTEM 1462

ARCHBOLD
MBC HOLDINGS INC. 976

ASHLAND
SAMARITAN REGIONAL HEALTH SYSTEM 1343

Aurora
Technical Consumer Products Inc. 1496

Avon Lake
PolyOne Corp. 1232

Batavia
Multi-Color Corp. 1051

Beachwood
Aleris Corporation 53
Cohesant Inc. 366
DDR Corp. 448
Omnova Solutions Inc 1143

Beavercreek
Advant-E Corporation 33

Bedford Heights
Dave's Supermarkets Inc. 444

Berea
Cleveland Browns Football Company LLC 356

BLUE ASH
BELCAN CORPORATION 198
F+W Media Inc. 567

Bolivar
Cable Manufacturing and Assembly Co. Inc. 264

Brewster
Shearer's Foods Inc. 1380

Universal Stainless & Alloy Products, Inc. 1630

Broomall
Alliance Bancorp Inc. of Pennsylvania 60

Bryn Mawr
Aqua America Inc 124
Bryn Mawr Bank Corp. 255
BRYN MAWR COLLEGE 255
MAIN LINE HEALTH INC. 952
MAIN LINE HOSPITALS INC. 952

Camp Hill
Ames True Temper Inc. 102
FLEMING GANNETT INC 608
Harsco Corp. 719
HOLY SPIRIT HOSPITAL OF THE SISTERS OF CHRISTIAN CHARITY 754
Rite Aid Corp. 1312

Canonsburg
Ansys Inc. 113
CENTIMARK CORPORATION 312
CNX Gas Corporation 361
CONSOL Energy Inc 392
Mylan Inc 1056
Rice Energy Inc 1309

Carlisle
Ahold U.S.A. Inc. 44
DICKINSON COLLEGE 469
Giant Food Stores LLC 664

CENTER VALLEY
DESALES UNIVERSITY 462
Olympus Corporation of the Americas 1140

Chambersburg
Franklin Financial Services Corp 625
TB Wood's Corporation 1494

Chesterbrook
AmerisourceBergen Corp. 100
Auxilium Pharmaceuticals Inc 160

Chester
Synygy Inc. 1483
WIDENER UNIVERSITY 1710

CLAIRTON
JEFFERSON REGIONAL MEDICAL CENTER 846

CLEARFIELD
CLEARFIELD HOSPITAL 354
CNB Financial Corp. (Clearfield, PA) 360

Colmar
Dorman Products Inc 483

CONCORDVILLE
LA FRANCE CORP. 896

CONSHOHOCKEN
AMERICAN SOCIETY FOR TESTING AND MATERIALS 95
David's Bridal Inc. 445
Quaker Chemical Corporation 1269
RUMSEY ELECTRIC COMPANY 1329
THE JUDGE GROUP INC 1536
VAN HORN METZ & CO. INC. 1651

Coraopolis
Dick's Sporting Goods, Inc 468
FedEx Ground Package System Inc. 583
ROBERT MORRIS UNIVERSITY 1315

Cynwyd
Royal Bancshares of Pennsylvania, Inc 1326

Danboro
Penn Engineering & Manufacturing Corp. 1195

Danville
Geisinger Health System Foundation 649

DENVER
HIGH CONCRETE GROUP LLC 742

Devon
DecisionOne Corporation 451

Douglassville
STV Group Incorporated 1460

Downingtown
DNB Financial Corp. 478

DOYLESTOWN
DELAWARE VALLEY COLLEGE 454
DOYLESTOWN HOSPITAL HEALTH AND WELLNESS CENTER INC. 485
ProPhase Labs Inc 1254

DUNCANSVILLE
HOSS''S STEAK & SEA HOUSE INC. 764

Dunmore
Fidelity D&D Bancorp, Inc. 588
First National Community Bancorp, Inc. (Dunmore, PA) 601

East Greenville
Knoll Inc 886

East Norriton
Tengion Inc. 1505

East Petersburg
Specialty Products & Insulation Co. 1424

East Stroudsburg
Pocono Health System 1230

Easton
Crayola LLC 414
LAFAYETTE COLLEGE 898
Paragon Technologies Inc 1179

Eighty Four
84 Lumber Company 6

Emlenton
Emclaire Financial Corp. 525

Emmaus
Rodale Inc. 1319

EPHRATA
MENNO TRAVEL SERVICE INC. 994

Erie
Erie Family Life Insurance Company 551
Erie Indemnity Co. 551

Exton
Bentley Systems Incorporated 202
Dopaco Inc. 482
Fibrocell Science, Inc. 587
Innovative Solutions and Support Inc 801
Kensey Nash Corporation 872
Omega Flex Inc 1141
The Franklin Mint LLC 1528
West Pharmaceutical Services, Inc. 1697
Wetherill Associates Inc. 1704

Fairview
Spectrum Control Inc. 1425

Fort Washington
GMAC Mortgage LLC 675

McNeil Consumer Pharmaceuticals Co. 981
NutriSystem Inc 1123

Gettysburg
ACNB Corp. 21
GETTYSBURG COLLEGE 663
THE GETTYSBURG HOSPITAL CORPORATION 1530

Gratz
MI Windows and Doors Inc. 1011

Greenville
Werner Co. 1695

Hanover
Hanover Foods Corporation 713
Utz Quality Foods Inc. 1647

HARLEYSVILLE
DEACON INDUSTRIAL SUPPLY CO. INC. 449
Harleysville Group Inc. 717
Harleysville Savings Financial Corp 717

Harrisburg
Capital BlueCross 282
Hersha Hospitality Trust 739
Metro Bancorp Inc PA 1006
Pennsylvania Higher Education Assistance Agency 1197
PINNACLE HEALTH SYSTEM 1220
United Concordia Companies Inc. 1619

Hatboro
Fox Chase Bancorp, Inc. 621

HAVERFORD
THE CORPORATION OF HAVERFORD COLLEGE 1524

Hershey
Hershey Company (The) 739
HERSHEY ENTERTAINMENT & RESORTS COMPANY 739

Honesdale
Norwood Financial Corp. 1117

Horsham
AAMCO Transmissions Inc. 9
Astea International, Inc. 145
Cottman Transmission Systems LLC. 406
Expert Global Solutions Inc. 564
Janssen Biotech Inc. 844
Mace Security International, Inc. 946
ORBIT/FR, Inc. 1152
PhotoMedex, Inc. 1215
Strata Skin Sciences Inc 1456
The Penn Mutual Life Insurance Company 1545
Toll Brothers Inc. 1574

HUNTINGDON
JUNIATA COLLEGE 859

Indiana
First Commonwealth Financial Corp. (Indiana, PA) 596
S & T Bancorp Inc (Indiana, PA) 1332

Jenkintown
American Realty Capital Trust Inc. 93

Johnstown
AmeriServ Financial Inc. 100
Concurrent Technologies Corporation 388
Crown Holding Company 421

Kennett Square
Exelon Energy Company 563
Exelon Generation Co LLC 563
Genesis Healthcare Inc 657

Genesis HealthCare LLC 657

Kimberton
Nutrition Management Services Company 1123

King of Prussia
AmeriGas Partners, L.P. 99
CSL Behring LLC 424
GSI Commerce Inc. 698
MacKay Life Sciences Inc. 947
Morgan Properties Trust 1040
Nocopi Technologies, Inc. 1105
Procurian Inc. 1249
SEDONA Corporation 1367
Tekni-Plex Inc. 1499
Theorem Clinical Research 1562
UGI Corp. 1610
Universal Health Realty Income Trust 1629
Universal Health Services, Inc. 1629

Kittanning
Sylvan Inc. 1478

Kulpsville
Greene Tweed & Co. Inc. 693

LAFAYETTE HILL
NHS HUMAN SERVICES INC. 1100

Lancaster
Armstrong World Industries Inc 134
Auntie Anne's Inc. 155
FRANKLIN AND MARSHALL COLLEGE 624
Fulton Financial Corp. (PA) 638
HIGH INDUSTRIES INC. 743
HIGH STEEL STRUCTURES LLC 743
THE JAY GROUP INC 1536
THE LANCASTER GENERAL HOSPITAL 1538

Latrobe
Commercial National Financial Corp. (PA) 376

Lawrence
Black Box Corp. (DE) 219

Lebanon
New Penn Motor Express Inc. 1090

Levittown
StoneMor Partners L P 1455

LEWISBURG
BUCKNELL UNIVERSITY 257
EVANGELICAL COMMUNITY HOSPITAL 557

Lititz
Lititz Mutual Insurance Company 927
Susquehanna Bancshares, Inc 1474
THE BENECON GROUP INC 1517

LORETTO
SAINT FRANCIS UNIVERSITY 1339

Macungie
Allen Organ Company 59

Malvern
Acme Markets Inc. 20
BioTelemetry, Inc. 216
Cephalon Inc. 317
CubeSmart 426
Endo Health Solutions Inc 533
Liberty Property Trust 917
PQ Corporation 1239
Ricoh USA Inc. 1310
The Vanguard Group Inc. 1557
USA Technologies Inc 1644
Verticalnet Inc. 1660
Vishay Intertechnology, Inc. 1668
Vishay Precision Group Inc. 1668

SPRINGFIELD

CROZER-KEYSTONE HEALTH SYSTEM 422

State College

Eclipse Resources Corp 510
GLENN O. HAWBAKER INC. 669
MINITAB INC. 1025
Rex Energy Corp 1305
Shaner Hotel Group Limited Partnership 1378
VIDEON CENTRAL INC. 1664

Stroudsburg

ESSA Bancorp Inc 553

Sunbury

Weis Markets, Inc. 1693

SWARTHMORE

SWARTHMORE COLLEGE 1475

Swiftwater

Sanofi Pasteur Inc. 1348

Trevose

Broder Bros. Co. 249
Sculptz Inc. 1361

Valley Forge

CertainTeed Corporation 319

VILLANOVA

DEVEREUX FOUNDATION 465
VILLANOVA UNIVERSITY IN THE STATE OF PENNSYLVANIA 1666

Warren

Blair Corporation 221

Warrendale

Joy Mining Machinery 858

Warren

Northwest Bancshares Inc. 1115
Northwest Bancshares, Inc. (MD) 1115

Warrington

Discovery Laboratories, Inc. 476

Wayne

Escalon Medical Corp. 552
Johnson Matthey Inc. 855
Kenexa Corporation 871
MEDecision Inc. 985
Moro Corporation 1041
Precyse Solutions LLC 1241
Safeguard Scientifics Inc. 1335
SunGard Availability Services LP 1467
SunGard Data Systems Inc. 1467
Teleflex Incorporated 1501

Wellsboro

Citizens & Northern Corp 346

WERNERSVILLE

RICHARD J. CARON FOUNDATION 1310

West Chester

A. Duie Pyle Inc. 7
Communications Test Design Inc. 378
Nobel Learning Communities Inc. 1104
OMNI CABLE CORPORATION 1142
QVC Inc. 1276

West Conshohocken

SMG Management Inc 1400
Superior Group Inc. 1471

West Mifflin

Kennywood Entertainment Company Inc. 872

WILKES BARRE

KING"S COLLEGE 880

Wilkes-Barre

George Foreman Enterprises Inc. 661

Williamsport

Penns Woods Bancorp, Inc. (Jersey Shore, PA) 1196

Willow Grove

Asplundh Tree Expert Co. 142

Wilmerding

Westinghouse Air Brake Technologies Corporation 1702

WOOLRICH

WOOLRICH INC. 1722

WORCESTER

AMERICAN INFRASTRUCTURE INC. 87

Wyomissing

Customers Bancorp Inc 431
Penn National Gaming, Inc. 1195

York

Bon-Ton Stores Inc 233
Codorus Valley Bancorp, Inc. 364
DENTSPLY International, Inc. 461
Graham Packaging Company L.P. 685
Kinsley Construction Inc. 881
PH Glatfelter Co 1209
Unilife Corp. 1614
YORK HOSPITAL 1734
YORK PENNSYLVANIA HOSPITAL COMPANY LLC 1735
York Water Co 1735

Physical Property Holdings, Inc. 1215

PUERTO RICO

San Juan

Oriental Financial Group Inc. 1155
Triple-S Management Corporation 1594

Santurce

Puerto Rico Electric Power Authority 1264

QUEBEC

Montreal

BioAmber Inc 212
Resolute Forest Products Inc 1302

RHODE ISLAND

Cranston

Ross-Simons of Warwick Inc. 1324

East Providence

Capital Properties, Inc. 283

Johnston

Factory Mutual Insurance Company 569

KINGSTON

UNIVERSITY OF RHODE ISLAND 1635

LINCOLN

LIGHTHOUSE COMPUTER SERVICES INC. 921

Middletown

KVH Industries, Inc. 894
Towerstream Corp 1578

NEWPORT

SALVE REGINA UNIVERSITY 1342

North Kingstown

Toray Plastics (America) Inc. 1575

Pawtucket

Hasbro, Inc. 720
TEKNOR APEX COMPANY 1499

Providence

Blue Cross & Blue Shield of Rhode Island 224
CARE NEW ENGLAND HEALTH SYSTEM INC 288
Citizens Financial Group Inc (New) 347
Dassault Systemes Simulia Corp. 442
Delta Dental of Rhode Island 457
DIMEO CONSTRUCTION COMPANY 474
Gilbane Inc. 666
JOHNSON & WALES UNIVERSITY INC 854
Lifespan Corporation 919
Nortek Inc 1107
PROVIDENCE COLLEGE 1257
RHODE ISLAND SCHOOL OF DESIGN INC 1308
Textron Inc. 1514
United Natural Foods Inc. 1621
Warren Equities Inc. 1683

WARWICK

KENT COUNTY MEMORIAL HOSPITAL 872
Metropolitan Property and Casualty Insurance Company 1007
Picerne Investment Corporation 1216
The Beacon Mutual Insurance Company 1516

West Warwick

Astro-Med, Inc. 146
Bradford Soap Works Inc. 239
VAN ARPIN LINES INC 1651

Westerly

Washington Trust Bancorp, Inc. 1685

Woonsocket

CVS Health Corporation 433
MultiCell Technologies Inc 1052
Summer Infant Inc 1463

San Juan

Popular Inc. 1233

Santurce

First Bancorp 593

SHAAN XI PROVINCE

Xi An City

China Recycling Energy Corp 335

SOUTH CAROLINA

Aiken

AGY Holding Corp. 44
Carlisle Tire & Wheel Company 292
Security Federal Corp (SC) 1365

Beaufort

Coastal Banking Co Inc 362

Cayce

SCANA Corp 1354

Charleston

Bank Of South Carolina Corp. 179
Blackbaud, Inc. 220

CAREALLIANCE HEALTH SERVICES 289
Hagemeyer North America Inc. 708
SOUTH CAROLINA STATE PORTS AUTHORITY 1411
THE CITADEL 1522

Clinton

Laurens County Health Care System 905

Columbia

AgFirst Farm Credit Bank 43
BENEDICT COLLEGE 201
BlueChoice HealthPlan of South Carolina Inc. 228
BONITZ INC. 233
Carolina Care Plan Inc. 294
Colonial Life & Accident Insurance Company 369
Companion Life Insurance Company 382
First Citizens Bancorporation Inc. 595
M. B. KAHN CONSTRUCTION CO. INC. 945
PALMETTO HEALTH 1173
South Carolina Electric & Gas Company 1411
South State Corp 1412
UCI Medical Affiliates Inc. 1609
WILBUR SMITH ASSOCIATES INC. 1710

CONWAY

COASTAL CAROLINA UNIVERSITY 362
CONWAY HOSPITAL INC. 398
HORRY TELEPHONE COOPERATIVE INC. 762

Easley

Cornerstone Bancorp 403

Florence

Young Pecan Company 1736

Fort Mill

Continental Tire the Americas LLC 396
Muzak Holdings LLC 1055

Fountain Inn

AVX Corp. 165

GASTON

G&P TRUCKING COMPANY INC. 641

GEORGETOWN

GEORGETOWN MEMORIAL HOSPITAL 661

Greenville

BI-LO Holding LLC 209
Delta Apparel Inc. 457
FURMAN UNIVERSITY FOUNDATION INC. 639
GERBER CHILDRENSWEAR LLC 662
Greenville Hospital System 694
JPS Industries Inc. 858
Michelin North America Inc. 1012
Palmetto Bancshares, Inc. (SC) 1173
Regional Management Corp 1294
ScanSource, Inc. 1354
Southern First Bancshares, Inc. 1416
Span-America Medical Systems, Inc. 1421
World Acceptance Corp. 1723

Greer

Guardian Building Products Distribution Inc. 700

Hartsville

Sonoco Products Co. 1408

WASHINGTON

Aberdeen
Pacific Financial Corp. 1168

Bellevue
Applied Discovery Inc. 120
AudienceScience Inc. 154
Blucora, Inc. 223
BSQUARE Corp 255
Concur Technologies Inc 388
drugstore.com inc. 489
Esterline Technologies Corp 555
Expedia Inc 564
Ignition Partners LLC 783
ITEX Corp. 834
ODOM CORPORATION 1133
Outerwall Inc 1160
OVERLAKE HOSPITAL MEDICAL
    CENTER 1161
PACCAR Inc. 1166
Puget Energy Inc. 1264
Quality Food Centers Inc. 1270
Radiant Logistics, Inc. 1278
Symetra Financial Corp 1479
T-Mobile US Inc 1485

BELLINGHAM
HAGGEN INC. 708
Integral Technologies Inc. 807
WESTERN WASHINGTON
    UNIVERSITY 1702

Bothell
Biolife Solutions Inc 214
Cardiac Science Corporation 286
Helix BioMedix Inc. 734
Marina Biotech Inc 960
OncoGenex Pharmaceuticals, Inc.
    1144
Seattle Genetics Inc 1364
SonoSite Inc. 1408

CASHMERE
LIBERTY ORCHARDS COMPANY INC.
    917

CHELAN
TROUT-BLUE CHELAN-MAGI INC.
    1595

CHENEY
EASTERN WASHINGTON
    UNIVERSITY INC 505
TRANS-SYSTEM INC. 1583

Enumclaw
Mutual of Enumclaw Insurance
    Company 1055

Ephrata
Public Utility District No. 2 of Grant
    County Washington 1263

Everett
Public Utility District No. 1 of
    Snohomish County Washing 1263

Federal Way
Weyerhaeuser Co 1705

Ferndale
Brookmount Explorations Inc. 250

Hoquiam
Pettit Oil Company 1208
Timberland Bancorp, Inc. 1569

Issaquah
Costco Wholesale Corp 406
LAKESIDE INDUSTRIES INC. 900
Spacelabs Healthcare Inc. 1421

Kennewick
Electronic Systems Technology, Inc.
    520

Kent
Oberto Sausage Company 1129

Kirkland
Celebrate Interactive Holdings Inc.
    309
Pendrell Corp. 1195

Liberty Lake
Itron, Inc. 834
Telect Inc. 1501

Longview
Longview Fibre Company 933
NORTH PACIFIC PAPER
    CORPORATION 1109

Lynnwood
Zumiez Inc 1744

Mountlake Terrace
FS Bancorp Inc 635
Premera Blue Cross 1242

Oak Harbor
Washington Banking Co. (Oak Harbor,
    WA) 1683

OLYMPIA
EVERGREEN STATE COLLEGE 559
Heritage Financial Corp. (WA) 738

ORONDO
AUVIL FRUIT COMPANY INC. 159

Poulsbo
Pope Resources LP 1233

Redmond
Data I/O Corp. 443
Microsoft Corporation 1014
Microvision Inc. 1015
Nintendo of America Inc. 1102
PlayNetwork Inc. 1227
UniSea Inc. 1616
Univar Inc. 1628
Univar USA 1628

Renton
Boeing Capital Corp 231
CONVERGENT OUTSOURCING INC.
    397
First Financial Northwest Inc 598
Football Northwest LLC 615
ORCA BAY SEAFOODS INC. 1153
Wizards of the Coast LLC 1720

Richland
IsoRay, Inc. 832
KADLEC REGIONAL MEDICAL
    CENTER 862
Pacific Northwest National Laboratory
    1169

Seattle
Alaska Air Group, Inc. 49
Amazon.com Inc. 73
American Management Services West
    LLC 90
American Seafoods Group LLC 94
Avanade Inc. 161
Bill & Melinda Gates Foundation 210
Blue Nile Inc 226
Cascade Natural Gas Corporation 298
City of Seattle - City Light Department
    349
Corbis Corporation 401
Cray Inc 414
CTI BioPharma Corp 425
Cutter & Buck Inc. 432
Davis Wright Tremaine LLP 445
Dendreon Corp 460
Emeritus Corp. 527
Expeditors International of
    Washington, Inc. 564
F5 Networks, Inc. 568

GeoBio Energy Inc. 660
Group Health Cooperative 697
HomeStreet Inc 757
Impinj Inc. 790
ING DIRECT Investing Inc. 798
Isilon Systems Inc. 832
Jones Soda Co. 857
L&L Energy Inc 895
LANE POWELL PC 902
Lindal Cedar Homes Inc. 924
Lynden Incorporated 943
Marchex Inc 958
McKinstry Co. LLC 981
Memory Lane Inc. 993
Moss Adams LLP 1043
NanoString Technologies Inc 1060
NATIONAL FROZEN FOODS
    CORPORATION 1065
Nordstrom, Inc. 1106
NORTHWEST DAIRY ASSOCIATION
    1115
OCEAN BEAUTY SEAFOODS LLC
    1130
Omeros Corp 1142
Oncothyreon Inc. 1145
Onvia Inc 1148
Pacific Coast Feather Co. 1167
Perkins Coie LLP 1204
Plum Creek Timber Co., Inc. 1228
Port of Seattle 1234
PUGET SOUND BLOOD CENTER &
    PROGRAM 1264
RealNetworks, Inc. 1289
Russell Investments 1330
Safeco Insurance Company of America
    1335
SEATTLE CHILDREN'S HOSPITAL
    1364
SEATTLE UNIVERSITY 1364
Slalom LLC 1398
Sound Financial Inc. 1410
Speakeasy Inc. 1423
Starbucks Corp. 1444
SWEDISH HEALTH SERVICES 1476
Tableau Software, Inc. 1486
TapImmune Inc. 1491
The Cobalt Group Inc. 1522
Todd Shipyards Corporation 1573
Tommy Bahama Group Inc. 1574
Trident Seafoods Corporation 1591
UNIVERSITY OF WASHINGTON INC
    1637
Washington Federal Inc. 1684
WatchGuard Technologies Inc. 1686
ZymoGenetics Inc. 1744

SELAH
TREE TOP INC. 1588

SHORELINE
CRISTA MINISTRIES 417

Snoqualmie
Philips Oral Healthcare Inc. 1213

Spokane Valley
Key Tronic Corp. 876
Revett Mining Co Inc 1305

Spokane
Ambassadors Group Inc 74
Avista Corp. 163
Clearwater Paper Corp 354
E Z LOADER BOAT TRAILERS INC.
    498
Ecova Inc. 511
Gold Reserve Inc. 676
Honeywell Electronic Materials Inc.
    757
Mines Management, Inc. 1025
Northwest Bancorporation, Inc. 1115
NORTHWEST FARM CREDIT
    SERVICES ACA 1115

Pathology Associates Medical
    Laboratories 1185
Potlatch Corp 1237
Red Lions Hotels Corp 1291
Sterling Financial Corp. (WA) 1452
THE CORPORATION OF GONZAGA
    UNIVERSITY 1524
U.R.M. STORES INC. 1606

TACOMA
BURKHART DENTAL SUPPLY CO.
    259
City of Tacoma Department of Public
    Utilities 349
Columbia Banking System, Inc. 372
Franciscan Health System 623
Interstate Distributor Co. 821
MULTICARE HEALTH SYSTEM 1052
Simpson Investment Company 1392
Tacoma Power 1487
TrueBlue Inc 1596
UNIVERSITY OF PUGET SOUND 1635

Tukwila
Boeing Employees' Credit Union 231
Harnish Group Inc. 717

Vancouver
Barrett Business Services, Inc. 186
CALVERT COMPANY INC. 275
Kuni Automotive Group 893
Nautilus Inc 1075
New Edge Networks Inc. 1087
Northwest Pipe Co. 1116
PEACEHEALTH 1191
Public Utility District No. 1 of Clark
    County 1262
Riverview Bancorp, Inc. 1313

Walla Walla
Baker Boyer Bancorp 172
Banner Corp. 181
Key Technology Inc 876
WHITMAN COLLEGE 1709

WENATCHEE
GOODFELLOW BROS. INC. 680
Public Utility District No. 1 of Chelan
    County Washington 1262

YAKIMA
YAKIMA VALLEY MEMORIAL
    HOSPITAL ASSOCIATION INC 1733

WEST VIRGINIA

BERKELEY SPRINGS
WAR MEMORIAL HOSPITAL INC.
    1682

Bluefield
First Century Bankshares, Inc. 595

Charles Town
American Public Education Inc 93

CHARLESTON
CHARLESTON AREA MEDICAL
    CENTER INC. 323
CHARLESTON HOSPITAL INC. 323
City Holding Co. 348
Jacobs Financial Group Inc 842
United Bankshares, Inc. 1618

Chester
MTR Gaming Group, Inc. 1050

Elkins
Citizens Financial Corp. (WV) 346

FAIRMONT
WEST VIRGINIA UNITED HEALTH
    SYSTEM INC. 1698

This Page left intentionally blank